HALSBURY'S
Laws of England

FIFTH EDITION
2010

Volume 61

This is volume 61 of the Fifth Edition of Halsbury's Laws of England, containing the titles INTERNATIONAL RELATIONS LAW, JUDICIAL REVIEW, JURIES and LANDFILL TAX.

The title INTERNATIONAL RELATIONS LAW replaces the Fourth Edition title FOREIGN RELATIONS LAW, contained in volume 18(2) (Reissue). That volume should be retained until remaining material is replaced.

The title JUDICIAL REVIEW replaces Part 4 of the Fourth Edition title ADMINISTRATIVE LAW, contained in volume 1(1) (2001 Reissue). That volume should be retained until remaining material is replaced.

The title JURIES replaces the Fourth Edition title JURIES, contained in volume 26 (2004 Reissue). It also incorporates material relating to juries from the Fourth Edition title CRIMINAL LAW, EVIDENCE AND PROCEDURE, contained in volume 11(3) (2006 Reissue). Both volumes should be retained until remaining material is replaced.

The title LANDFILL TAX replaces Part 18 of the Fourth Edition title PROTECTION OF ENVIRONMENT AND PUBLIC HEALTH, contained in volume 38 (2006 Reissue). That volume should be retained until remaining material is replaced.

For a full list of volumes comprised in a current set of Halsbury's Laws of England please see overleaf.

Fifth Edition volumes:

1 (2008), 2 (2008), 7 (2008), 8 (2010), 11 (2009), 12 (2009), 13 (2009), 14 (2009), 15 (2009), 18 (2009), 39 (2009), 40 (2009), 41 (2009), 48 (2008), 49 (2008), 50 (2008), 52 (2009), 53 (2009), 54 (2008), 61 (2010), 65 (2008), 66 (2009), 67 (2008), 68 (2008), 69 (2009), 72 (2009), 73 (2009), 77 (2010), 78 (2010), 79 (2008), 92 (2010), 93 (2008), 94 (2008), 100 (2009), 101 (2009)

Fourth Edition volumes (bold figures represent reissues):

1(1) (2001 Reissue), **1**(2) (2007 Reissue), 2(2), 2(3), **3**(1) (2005 Reissue), 3(2) (2002 Reissue), **4**(1) (2002 Reissue), **4**(2) (2002 Reissue), 4(3), **5**(1) (2004 Reissue), **5**(3) (2008 Reissue), **5**(4) (2008 Reissue), **7**(3) (2004 Reissue), **7**(4) (2004 Reissue), **8**(1) (2003 Reissue), 8(2), 8(3), 9(1), **9**(2) (2006 Reissue), 10, **11**(1) (2006 Reissue), **11**(2) (2006 Reissue), **11**(3) (2006 Reissue), **11**(4) (2006 Reissue), 12(1), **12**(2) (2007 Reissue), **12**(3) (2007 Reissue), **13** (2007 Reissue), 14, **15**(1) (2006 Reissue), **15**(2) (2006 Reissue), **15**(3) (2007 Reissue), **15**(4) (2007 Reissue), 16(2), 17(2), 18(2), **19**(1) (2007 Reissue), **19**(2) (2007 Reissue), **19**(3) (2007 Reissue), **21** (2004 Reissue), **22** (2006 Reissue), 23(1), 23(2), 24, **25** (2003 Reissue), **26** (2004 Reissue), **27**(1) (2006 Reissue), **27**(2) (2006 Reissue), **27**(3) (2006 Reissue), 28, 29(2), 30(1), 30(2), **31** (2003 Reissue), 34, 35, **36**(1) (2007 Reissue), 36(2), **38** (2006 Reissue), 39(1A), 39(1B), 39(2), **40**(1) (2007 Reissue), **40**(2) (2007 Reissue), **40**(3) (2007 Reissue), **41** (2005 Reissue), 42, 44(1), 44(2), **45**(1) (2005 Reissue), 45(2), 46(1), 46(2), 46(3), **48** (2007 Reissue), **49**(1) (2005 Reissue), **50** (2005 Reissue), 51, 52

Additional Materials: *Shipping and Water (Pollution)* containing vol **43**(2) (Reissue) paras 1135–1369 and vol **49**(3) (2004 Reissue) paras 658–746; *Local Government Finance* containing vol **29**(1) (Reissue) paras 514–618, 624–634; *Trade, Industry and Industrial Relations* containing vol **47** (2001 Reissue) paras 1–4, 601–1000

Fourth and Fifth Edition volumes:

2009 Consolidated Index (A–E), 2009 Consolidated Index (F–O), 2009 Consolidated Index (P–Z), 2010 Consolidated Table of Statutes, 2010 Consolidated Table of Statutory Instruments, etc, 2010 Consolidated Table of Cases (A–L), 2010 Consolidated Table of Cases (M–Z, ECJ Cases)

Updating and ancillary materials:

2010 Annual Cumulative Supplement; Monthly Current Service; Annual Abridgements 1974–2009

March 2010

HALSBURY'S
Laws of England

FIFTH EDITION

LORD MACKAY OF CLASHFERN
Lord High Chancellor of Great Britain
1987–97

Volume 61

2010

 LexisNexis®

Members of the LexisNexis Group worldwide

United Kingdom	LexisNexis, a Division of Reed Elsevier (UK) Ltd, Halsbury House, 35 Chancery Lane, LONDON, WC2A 1EL, and London House, 20–22 East London Street, EDINBURGH, EH7 4BQ
Australia	LexisNexis Butterworths, Chatswood, New South Wales
Austria	LexisNexis Verlag ARD Orac GmbH & Co KG, Vienna
Benelux	LexisNexis Benelux, Amsterdam
Canada	LexisNexis Canada, Markham, Ontario
China	LexisNexis China, Beijing and Shanghai
France	LexisNexis SA, Paris
Germany	LexisNexis Deutschland GmbH Munster
Hong Kong	LexisNexis Hong Kong, Hong Kong
India	LexisNexis India, New Delhi
Italy	Giuffrè Editore, Milan
Japan	LexisNexis Japan, Tokyo
Malaysia	Malayan Law Journal Sdn Bhd, Kuala Lumpur
New Zealand	LexisNexis NZ Ltd, Wellington
Poland	Wydawnictwo Prawnicze LexisNexis Sp, Warsaw
Singapore	LexisNexis Singapore, Singapore
South Africa	LexisNexis Butterworths, Durban
USA	LexisNexis, Dayton, Ohio

FIRST EDITION	*Published in 31 volumes between 1907 and 1917*
SECOND EDITION	*Published in 37 volumes between 1931 and 1942*
THIRD EDITION	*Published in 43 volumes between 1952 and 1964*
FOURTH EDITION	*Published in 56 volumes between 1973 and 1987, with reissues between 1988 and 2008*
FIFTH EDITION	*Commenced in 2008*

A CIP Catalogue record for this book is available from the British Library.

ISBN 13 (complete set, standard binding): 9780406047762

ISBN 13: 9781405736718

ISBN 978-1-4057-3671-8

9 781405 736718

Typeset by Letterpart Ltd, Reigate, Surrey
Printed and bound in Great Britain by CPI William Clowes Beccles NR34 7TL
Visit LexisNexis at www.lexisnexis.co.uk

Editor in Chief

THE RIGHT HONOURABLE

LORD MACKAY OF CLASHFERN

LORD HIGH CHANCELLOR OF GREAT BRITAIN

1987–97

INTERNATIONAL RELATIONS LAW

Contributors

JOANNE FOAKES, MA,
of the Inner Temple, Barrister;
former Legal Counsellor of the Foreign and Commonwealth Office

VAUGHAN LOWE
of Gray's Inn, Barrister;
one of Her Majesty's Counsel;
Chichele Professor of Public International Law and Fellow of All Souls College,
Oxford University

SIMON OLLESON, MA, LLM, Dip Int Law,
of Lincoln's Inn, Barrister

COLIN WARBRICK
Honorary Professor, Birmingham Law School, University of Birmingham

SIR MICHAEL WOOD, KCMG,
of Gray's Inn, Barrister;
Member of the UN International Law Commission

SAMUEL WORDSWORTH, LLM,
of Lincoln's Inn, Barrister;
Visiting Professor, King's College, London

JURIES

Consultant Editor

RICHARD CARD, LLB, LLM, FRSA,
Emeritus Professor of Law, De Montfort University, Leicester

LANDFILL TAX

Consultant Editor

PENNY HAMILTON, LLB, CTA (Fellow), FIIT,
of Gray's Inn, Barrister;
Pump Court Tax Chambers

JUDICIAL REVIEW

General Editors

MICHAEL SUPPERSTONE, MA, BCL,
a Bencher of the Middle Temple;
one of Her Majesty's Counsel;
Deputy High Court Judge;
a Recorder of the Crown Court

CLIVE LEWIS, MA, LLM,
of the Middle Temple, Barrister;
one of Her Majesty's Counsel;
a Recorder of the Crown Court

Contributors

ELISABETH LAING, BA,
of the Middle Temple, Barrister;
one of Her Majesty's Counsel;
a Recorder of the Crown Court

JAMES CORNWELL, MA, MPhil, DPhil, DipLaw,
of the Middle Temple, Barrister

JOANNE CLEMENT, BA, BCL,
of Gray's Inn, Barrister

HOLLY STOUT, MA, DipLaw,
of Lincoln's Inn, Barrister

RACHEL KAMM, BA, DipLaw,
of Lincoln's Inn, Barrister

AMY ROGERS, BA, DipLaw,
of Lincoln's Inn, Barrister

The law stated in this volume is in general that in force on 31 January 2010, although subsequent changes have been included wherever possible.

Any future updating material will be found in the Current Service and annual Cumulative Supplement to Halsbury's Laws of England.

TABLE OF CONTENTS

Volume 61

INTERNATIONAL RELATIONS LAW

HOW TO USE HALSBURY'S LAWS OF ENGLAND

Volumes

Each text volume of Halsbury's Laws of England contains the law on the titles contained in it as at a date stated at the front of the volume (the operative date).

Information contained in Halsbury's Laws of England may be accessed in several ways.

First, by using the tables of contents.

Each volume contains both a general Table of Contents, and a specific Table of Contents for each title contained in it. From these tables you will be directed to the relevant part of the work.

Readers should note that the current arrangement of titles can be found in the Current Service.

Secondly, by using tables of statutes, statutory instruments, cases or other materials.

If you know the name of the Act, statutory instrument or case with which your research is concerned, you should consult the Consolidated Tables of statutes, cases and so on (published as separate volumes) which will direct you to the relevant volume and paragraph. The Consolidated Tables will indicate if the volume referred to is a Fifth Edition volume.

(Each individual text volume also includes tables of those materials used as authority in that volume.)

Thirdly, by using the indexes.

If you are uncertain of the general subject area of your research, you should go to the Consolidated Index (published as separate volumes) for reference to the relevant volume(s) and paragraph(s). The Consolidated Index will indicate if the volume referred to is a Fifth Edition volume.

(Each individual text volume also includes an index to the material contained therein.)

Additional Materials

The reorganisation of the title scheme of Halsbury's Laws for the Fifth Edition means that from time to time Fourth Edition volumes will be *partially* replaced by Fifth Edition volumes.

In certain instances an Additional Materials softbound book will be issued, in which will be reproduced material which has not yet been replaced by a Fifth Edition title. This will enable users to remove specific Fourth Edition volumes from the shelf and save valuable space pending the replacement of that material in the Fifth Edition. These softbound books are supplied to volumes subscribers free of charge. They continue to form part of the set of Halsbury's Laws Fourth Edition Reissue, and will be updated by the Annual Cumulative Supplement and monthly Noter-Up in the usual way.

Updating publications

The text volumes of Halsbury's Laws should be used in conjunction with the annual Cumulative Supplement and the monthly Noter-Up.

The annual Cumulative Supplement

The Supplement gives details of all changes between the operative date of the text volume and the operative date of the Supplement. It is arranged in the same volume, title and paragraph order as the text volumes. Developments affecting particular points of law are noted to the relevant paragraph(s) of the text volumes. As from the commencement of the Fifth Edition, the Supplement will clearly distinguish between Fourth and Fifth Edition titles.

For narrative treatment of material noted in the Cumulative Supplement, go to the Annual Abridgment volume for the relevant year.

Destination Tables

In certain titles in the annual *Cumulative Supplement*, reference is made to Destination Tables showing the destination of consolidated legislation. Those Destination Tables are to be found either at the end of the titles within the annual *Cumulative Supplement*, or in a separate *Destination Tables* booklet provided from time to time with the *Cumulative Supplement*.

The Noter-Up

The Noter-Up is contained in the Current Service Noter-Up booklet, issued monthly and noting changes since the publication of the annual Cumulative Supplement. Also arranged in the same volume, title and paragraph order as the text volumes, the Noter-Up follows the style of the Cumulative Supplement. As from the commencement of the Fifth Edition, the Noter-Up will clearly distinguish between Fourth and Fifth Edition titles.

For narrative treatment of material noted in the Noter-Up, go to the relevant Monthly Review.

REFERENCES AND ABBREVIATIONS

ACT	Australian Capital Territory
A-G	Attorney General
Admin	Administrative Court
Admlty	Admiralty Court
Adv-Gen	Advocate General
affd	affirmed
affg	affirming
Alta	Alberta
App	Appendix
art	article
Aust	Australia
B	Baron
BC	British Columbia
C	Command Paper (of a series published before 1900)
c	chapter number of an Act
CA	Court of Appeal
CAC	Central Arbitration Committee
CA in Ch	Court of Appeal in Chancery
CB	Chief Baron
CCA	Court of Criminal Appeal
CCR	County Court Rules 1981 (SI 1981/1687) as subsequently amended
CCR	Court for Crown Cases Reserved
C-MAC	Courts-Martial Appeal Court
CO	Crown Office
COD	Crown Office Digest
CPR	Civil Procedure Rules 1998 (SI 1998/3132) as subsequently amended (see the Civil Court Practice)
Can	Canada
Cd	Command Paper (of the series published 1900–18)
Cf	compare
Ch	Chancery Division
ch	chapter
cl	clause

Cm	Command Paper (of the series published 1986 to date)
Cmd	Command Paper (of the series published 1919–56)
Cmnd	Command Paper (of the series published 1956–86)
Comm	Commercial Court
Comr	Commissioner
Court Forms (2nd Edn)	Atkin's Encyclopaedia of Court Forms in Civil Proceedings, 2nd Edn. See note 2 post.
Court Funds Rules 1987	Court Funds Rules 1987 (SI 1987/821) as subsequently amended
DC	Divisional Court
DPP	Director of Public Prosecutions
EAT	Employment Appeal Tribunal
EC	European Community
ECJ	Court of Justice of the European Community
EComHR	European Commission of Human Rights
ECSC	European Coal and Steel Community
ECtHR Rules of Court	Rules of Court of the European Court of Human Rights
EEC	European Economic Community
EFTA	European Free Trade Association
EWCA Civ	Official neutral citation for judgments of the Court of Appeal (Civil Division)
EWCA Crim	Official neutral citation for judgments of the Court of Appeal (Criminal Division)
EWHC	Official neutral citation for judgments of the High Court
Edn	Edition
Euratom	European Atomic Energy Community
Ex Ch	Court of Exchequer Chamber
ex p	ex parte
Fam	Family Division
Fed	Federal
Forms & Precedents (5th Edn)	Encyclopaedia of Forms and Precedents other than Court Forms, 5th Edn. See note 2 post.
GLC	Greater London Council
HC	High Court
HC	House of Commons
HK	Hong Kong
HL	House of Lords
IAT	Immigration Appeal Tribunal
ILM	International Legal Materials

INLR	Immigration and Nationality Law Reports
IRC	Inland Revenue Commissioners
Ind	India
Int Rels	International Relations
Ir	Ireland
J	Justice
JA	Judge of Appeal
Kan	Kansas
LA	Lord Advocate
LC	Lord Chancellor
LCC	London County Council
LCJ	Lord Chief Justice
LJ	Lord Justice of Appeal
LoN	League of Nations
MR	Master of the Rolls
Man	Manitoba
n	note
NB	New Brunswick
NI	Northern Ireland
NS	Nova Scotia
NSW	New South Wales
NY	New York
NZ	New Zealand
OHIM	Office for Harmonisation in the Internal Market
OJ	The Official Journal of the European Community published by the Office for Official Publications of the European Community
Ont	Ontario
P	President
PC	Judicial Committee of the Privy Council
PEI	Prince Edward Island
Pat	Patents Court
q	question
QB	Queen's Bench Division
QBD	Queen's Bench Division of the High Court
Qld	Queensland
Que	Quebec
r	rule
RDC	Rural District Council
RPC	Restrictive Practices Court
RSC	Rules of the Supreme Court 1965 (SI 1965/1776) as subsequently amended

reg	regulation
Res	Resolution
revsd	reversed
Rly	Railway
s.	section
SA	South Africa
S Aust	South Australia
SC	Supreme Court
SI	Statutory Instruments published by authority
SR & O	Statutory Rules and Orders published by authority
SR & O Rev 1904	Revised Edition comprising all Public and General Statutory Rules and Orders in force on 31 December 1903
SR & O Rev 1948	Revised Edition comprising all Public and General Statutory Rules and Orders and Statutory Instruments in force on 31 December 1948
SRNI	Statutory Rules of Northern Ireland
STI	Simon's Tax Intelligence (1973–1995); Simon's Weekly Tax Intelligence (1996-current)
Sask	Saskatchewan
Sch	Schedule
Sess	Session
Sing	Singapore
TCC	Technology and Construction Court
TS	Treaty Series
Tanz	Tanzania
Tas	Tasmania
UDC	Urban District Council
UKHL	Official neutral citation for judgments of the House of Lords
UKPC	Official neutral citation for judgments of the Privy Council
UN	United Nations
V-C	Vice-Chancellor
Vict	Victoria
W Aust	Western Australia
Zimb	Zimbabwe

NOTE 1. A general list of the abbreviations of law reports and other sources used in this work can be found at the beginning of the Consolidated Table of Cases.

NOTE 2. Where references are made to other publications, the volume number precedes and the page number follows the name of the publication; eg the reference '12 Forms & Precedents (5th Edn) 44' refers to volume 12 of the Encyclopaedia of Forms and Precedents, page 44.

NOTE 3. An English statute is cited by short title or, where there is no short title, by regnal year and chapter number together with the name by which it is commonly known or a description of its subject matter and date. In the case of a foreign statute, the mode of citation generally follows the style of citation in use in the country concerned with the addition, where necessary, of the name of the country in parentheses.

NOTE 4. A statutory instrument is cited by short title, if any, followed by the year and number, or, if unnumbered, the date.

TABLE OF STATUTES

TABLE OF STATUTORY INSTRUMENTS

TABLE OF CIVIL PROCEDURE

Civil Procedure Rules 1998, SI 1998/3132 (CPR)

Practice Directions supplementing CPR

Protocols

Other Practice Directions

TABLE OF EUROPEAN COMMUNITY LEGISLATION

TABLE OF TREATIES, CONVENTIONS, ETC

W

TABLE OF CASES

PARA

PARA

D

PARA

PARA

PARA

PARA

Decisions of the European Court of Justice are listed below numerically. These decisions
are also included in the preceding alphabetical list.

INTERNATIONAL RELATIONS LAW

1. INTRODUCTION

1.   Scope of international relations law.   International relations law, sometimes called foreign relations law, is that part of English law which governs the international relations of the United Kingdom. It includes what international lawyers refer to as domestic or municipal law, which is to say for these purposes, the law of England and Wales and the provisions of the law of other jurisdictions within the UK which are also relevant to the UK's international relations.

Since public international law is, at least to some extent, part of the law of England[1], or may otherwise fall to be considered in the application of English law, the present title also covers, in outline at least and with selected references to other materials, some areas of public international law that are likely to come before English lawyers and the English courts.

When the English courts are called upon to apply international law, it seems to be well established that they will apply that law faithfully according to its own rules[2].

Certain topics which would otherwise fall within the scope of this title are to be found elsewhere in this work[3].

1   For the relationship between public international law and English law see PARA 12 et seq; and as to the conduct of international relations see PARA 26 et seq.
2   Ie the rules concerning sources (see PARA 2 et seq); and treaties (see PARA 71 et seq).
3   See particularly BRITISH NATIONALITY, IMMIGRATION AND ASYLUM; COMMONWEALTH; EXTRADITION; PRIZE; WAR AND ARMED CONFLICT.

2. PUBLIC INTERNATIONAL LAW

(1) SOURCES OF INTERNATIONAL LAW

(i) Preliminary

2. In general. The International Court of Justice[1], in the exercise of its function to decide such disputes as are submitted to it in accordance with international law, applies the following:

(1) international conventions, whether general or particular, establishing rules expressly recognised by the contesting states[2];

(2) international custom, as evidence of a general practice accepted as law[3];

(3) the general principles of law recognised by civilized nations[4]; and

(4) as subsidiary means for the determination of rules of law, judicial decisions and the teachings of the most highly qualified publicists of the various nations[5].

As such, these are widely accepted as an authoritative statement of the sources of public international law. However, unilateral declarations[6] and decisions of international organisations may be other sources of international law[7]. Although treaties and customary international law provide much of the basis for public international law, in general, there is no hierarchy among the sources[8].

1 As to the International Court of Justice see PARA 499 et seq.
2 See the Statute of the International Court of Justice (San Francisco, 26 June 1945; TS 67 (1946); Cmd 7015) art 38 para 1(a); and PARA 3. As to art 38 see Zimmerman et al *The Statute of the International Court of Justice: A Commentary* (1st Edn, 2006) pp 677–792.
3 See the Statute of the International Court of Justice art 38 para 1(b); and PARA 4.
4 See the Statute of the International Court of Justice art 38 para 1(c); and PARA 5.
5 See the Statute of the International Court of Justice art 38 para 1(d); and PARAS 6, 7.
6 See PARA 8.
7 See PARA 9.
8 See PARA 10 et seq.

(ii) Sources listed in the Statute of the International Court of Justice

3. Treaties. The Statute of the International Court of Justice lists among the sources of public international law 'international conventions, whether general or particular, establishing rules expressly recognised by the contesting states'[1]. 'International conventions' in this context refers to treaties that are in force and binding on the states concerned under international law[2]. The general rule is that a treaty is only binding upon states party to it[3], although the rules laid down in a treaty may, even if the treaty does not enter into force, become part of customary international law[4]. A treaty may also codify existing customary international law, or crystallise an emerging rule of customary international law and in such case the latter is the source of the law[5].

1 See the Statute of the International Court of Justice (San Francisco, 26 June 1945; TS 67 (1946); Cmd 7015) art 38 para 1(a).
2 As to treaties see PARA 71 et seq.
3 See the Vienna Convention on the Law of Treaties (Vienna, 23 May 1969; TS 58 (1980); Cmnd 7964) art 34; and PARA 99.
4 See the Vienna Convention on the Law of Treaties (Vienna, 23 May 1969; TS 58 (1980); Cmnd 7964) art 38; and PARA 99.
5 For further discussion on the relationship between treaties and customary international law see *North Sea Continental Shelf Cases (Federal Republic of Germany/Denmark; Federal Republic of*

Germany/Netherlands) ICJ Reports 1969, 3; *Military and Paramilitary Activities in and against Nicaragua (Nicaragua v United States of America)* ICJ Reports 1986, 14.

4. Customary international law. The Statute of the International Court of Justice lists among the sources of public international law 'international custom, as evidence of a general practice accepted as law'[1]. This refers to customary international law[2]. Customary international law is to be distinguished from mere usage, in that it arises from state practice coupled with a conviction on the part of the states in question that it is required by or is in conformity with international law[3]. State practice takes many forms, and includes what states do, what they say, and what they say about what they do. The practice of an increasing number of states is now published regularly[4]. The English courts will have regard to a wide range of materials in determining rules of customary international law[5].

1   See the Statute of the International Court of Justice (San Francisco, 26 June 1945; TS 67 (1946); Cmd 7015) art 38 para 1(b).
2   Also called 'international customary law', 'international custom', 'custom' and 'general international law', though the last of these terms is used with various meanings. Customary international law may be universal, regional (local) or even bilateral: see *Asylum (Colombia/ Peru)* ICJ Reports 1950, 266; *Right of Passage over Indian Territory (Portugal v India)* ICJ Reports 1960, 6.
3   Thus it is widely accepted that two elements are required for the formation of a rule of customary international law, state practice and *opinio juris sive necessitates (opinio juris)*: see generally the *Lotus Case* PCIJ Ser A No 10 (1927); *North Sea Continental Shelf Cases (Federal Republic of Germany/Denmark; Federal Republic of Germany/Netherlands)* ICJ Reports 1969, 3.
4   For a compilation of British practice, see United Kingdom Materials in International Law published in British Yearbook of International Law (BYIL) from 1978 onwards.
5   See eg *R v Jones (Margaret)* [2006] UKHL 16, [2007] 1 AC 136 at [13]–[19] per Lord Bingham.

5. General principles of law. The Statute of the International Court of justice lists among the sources of public international law 'the general principles of law recognised by civilized nations'[1]. This refers to general principles of law as applied in domestic legal systems, including by domestic courts[2].

1   See the Statute of the International Court of Justice (San Francisco, 26 June 1945; TS 67 (1946); Cmd 7015) art 38 para 1(c).
2   See generally Cheng *General Principles of Law as Applied by International Courts and Tribunals* (1st Edn, 1953 (reissued 2006)).

6. Judicial decisions. The Statute of the International Court of Justice lists judicial decisions as a subsidiary means for the determination of rules of public international law, subject to the condition that a decision of the Court has no binding force except between the parties and in respect of that particular case[1].

1   See the Statute of the International Court of Justice (San Francisco, 26 June 1945; TS 67 (1946); Cmd 7015) arts 38 para 1(d), 59.

7. Writings. The Statute of the International Court of Justice lists 'the teachings of the most highly qualified publicists of the various nations' as a subsidiary means for the determination of rules of public international law[1]. This refers to writings of learned authors on public international law, to which the courts make frequent reference[2]. The product of collective bodies, such as the draft articles with commentaries of the International Law Commission of the United Nations, may be viewed as particularly authoritative, depending on their reception by states[3].

1   See the Statute of the International Court of Justice (San Francisco, 26 June 1945; TS 67 (1946); Cmd 7015) art 38 para 1(d). See also Wood 'Teachings of the Most Highly Qualified Publicists (Art 38(1) ICJ Statute)' *The Max Planck Encyclopaedia of Public International Law*.
2   See eg *R (on the application of Al-Jedda) v Secretary of State for Defence* [2007] UKHL 58, [2008] 3 All ER 28, [2008] 2 WLR 31, at [81]–[82] per Lord Rodger.
3   See eg *Jones v Ministry of the Interior of the Kingdom of Saudi Arabia (Secretary of State for Constitutional Affairs intervening)* [2006] UKHL 26, [2007] 1 AC 270, [2007] 1 All ER 113 at [12] per Lord Bingham; *R (on the application of Al-Jedda) v Secretary of State for Defence* [2006] EWCA Civ 327, [2007] QB 621, [2006] 3 WLR 954 at [66] per Brooke LJ (affd *R (on the application of Al-Jedda) v Secretary of State for Defence* [2007] UKHL 58, [2008] 3 All ER 28, [2008] 2 WLR 31).

(iii) Other Sources

8.   Unilateral declarations.   Under international law, declarations made by way of unilateral acts, concerning legal or factual situations, may have the effect of creating legal obligations. When it is the intention of the state making the declaration that it should become bound according to its terms, that intention confers on the declaration the character of a legal obligation[1].

1   *Nuclear Tests (Australia v France)* ICJ Reports 1974, 253 at 267–268 (paras 43–46); *Nuclear Tests (New Zealand v France)* ICJ Reports 1974, 457 at 472–473 (paras 46–49); *Frontier Dispute (Burkina Faso/Republic of Mali)* ICJ Reports 1986, 554 at 573–574 (paras 39–40); *Armed Activities on the Territory of the Congo (New Application: 2002) (Democratic Republic of the Congo v Rwanda) (Jurisdiction and Admissibility)* ICJ Reports 2006, 6 at 26–29 (paras 45–53). See also the Guiding Principles applicable to unilateral declarations of states capable of creating legal obligations, with commentaries, International Law Commission Report, 58th Session, A/61/10; YILC 2006, vol II(2).

9.   Decisions of international organisations.   Binding decisions of the United Nations Security Council impose obligations on states under international law[1].

1   As to the decisions of the Security Council see PARAS 522, 527. Various means exist for effect to be given to them at the domestic level, in particular the United Nations Act 1946: see PARA 526 et seq.

(2) HIERARCHY IN INTERNATIONAL LAW

10.   Primacy of the Charter of the United Nations.   The Charter of the United Nations[1] provides that in the event of a conflict between the obligations of the members of the United Nations under the Charter and their obligations under any other international agreement, their obligations under the Charter must prevail[2]. Obligations under the Charter include those flowing from binding decisions of the Security Council of the United Nations[3]. The effect the Charter's primacy is to suspend, not terminate, conflicting obligations, and only to the extent of the conflict. It applies to all other obligations including those under human rights treaties and under customary international law, with the possible exception of peremptory norms[4].

1   Ie the Charter of the United Nations (San Francisco 25 June 1945; TS 67 (Cmd 7015)).
2   See the Charter of the United Nations art 103.
3   *Questions of Interpretation and Application of the 1971 Montreal Convention arising from the Aerial Incident at Lockerbie (Libyan Arab Jamahiriya v United Kingdom) (Provisional Measures)* ICJ Reports 1992, 3. The Charter of the United Nations art 103 has been applied in English cases: see eg *R (on the application of Al-Jedda) v Secretary of State for Defence* [2007] UKHL 58, [2008] 3 All ER 28, [2008] 2 WLR 31.
4   The Vienna Convention on the Law of Treaties (Vienna, 23 May 1969; TS 58 (1980); Cmnd 7964) art 30(1) acknowledges the compelling force of art 103: see PARA 92; and *R (on the*

application of Al-Jedda) v Secretary of State for Defence [2006] EWCA Civ 327, [2007] QB 621, [2006] 3 WLR 954 at [72] per Brooke LJ (affd *R (on the application of Al-Jedda) v Secretary of State for Defence* [2007] UKHL 58, [2008] 3 All ER 28, [2008] 2 WLR 31). As to peremptory norms see PARA 11.

11. Peremptory norms and obligations owed to the international community as a whole. A peremptory norm of general international law, sometimes termed 'jus cogens', is accepted and recognised by the international community of states as a whole as a norm from which no derogation is permitted and which can be modified only by a subsequent norm of general international law having the same character[1]. The criteria for identifying peremptory norms are stringent; those that are clearly accepted and recognised include the prohibitions of aggression, genocide, slavery and racial discrimination, crimes against humanity and torture, and the right of self-determination[2].

There are also certain obligations under international law, usually termed 'erga omnes', that a state owes to the international community as a whole[3]. Whilst there is some overlap in the substance of the obligations concerned, the concept of obligations erga omnes is distinct from that of peremptory norms of general international law[4].

1 The International Court of Justice expressly recognised the existence of peremptory norms for the first time in *Armed Activities on the Territory of the Congo (New Application: 2002) (Democratic Republic of the Congo v Rwanda) (Jurisdiction and Admissibility)* ICJ Reports 2006, 6. See also *Application of the Convention on the Prevention and Punishment of the Crime of Genocide (Bosnia and Herzegovina v Serbia and Montenegro)* ICJ Reports, 26 February 2007 (para 147). See also the Vienna Convention on the Law of Treaties (Vienna, 23 May 1969; TS 58 (1980); Cmnd 7964) art 53; and PARA 103.

2 *R (on the application of Al-Jedda) v Secretary of State for Defence* [2006] EWCA Civ 327, [2007] QB 621, [2006] 3 WLR 954 at [66] per Brooke LJ (affd *R (on the application of Al-Jedda) v Secretary of State for Defence* [2007] UKHL 58, [2008] 3 All ER 28, [2008] 2 WLR 31).

3 *Barcelona Traction, Light and Power Co Ltd (Belgium v Spain) (Second Phase)* ICJ Reports 1970, 3 at 32 (paras 33–34). Following the identification by the International Court of Justice of the outlawing of acts of aggression, the prohibition of genocide, and the 'principles and rules concerning the basic rights of the human person, including protection from slavery and racial discrimination' as constituting obligations which are owed to the international community as a whole, are the concern of all states and in relation to which all states have a legal interest in their protection, the International Court of Justice has referred to the concept of obligations erga omnes on a number of other occasions and identified a number of other norms which fall into the category: see *East Timor (Portugal v Australia)* ICJ Reports 1995, 90 at 102 (self-determination of peoples); *Application of the Convention on the Prevention and Punishment of the Crime of Genocide (Bosnia and Herzegovina v Yugoslavia) (Preliminary Objections)* ICJ Reports 1996, 595 at 615–616 (para 31) (prohibition of genocide); *Legal Consequences of the Construction of a Wall in the Occupied Palestinian Territory (Advisory Opinion)* ICJ Reports 2004, 136 at 199 (paras 155–157) (right to self-determination and certain obligations under international humanitarian law); *Armed Activities on the Territory of the Congo (New Application: 2002) (Democratic Republic of the Congo v Rwanda) (Jurisdiction and Admissibility)* ICJ Reports 2006, 6 (paras 64–70) (prohibition of genocide); *Application of the Convention on the Prevention and Punishment of the Crime of Genocide (Bosnia and Herzegovina v Serbia and Montenegro)* ICJ Reports, 26 February 2007 (paras 147, 161 and 185) (prohibition of genocide). Nevertheless, the International Court of Justice has made clear that the fact that an obligation is owed erga omnes does not constitute an exception to the principle that jurisdiction must be based on consent: see eg *East Timor (Portugal v Australia)* ICJ Reports 1995, 90 at 102 (para 29); and *Armed Activities on the Territory of the Congo (New Application: 2002) (Democratic Republic of the Congo v Rwanda) (Jurisdiction and Admissibility)* ICJ Reports 2006, 6 (para 125).

4 See generally Tams *Enforcing Obligations Erga Omnes in International Law* (2005).

3. PUBLIC INTERNATIONAL LAW AND ENGLISH LAW

(1) GENERAL CONSIDERATIONS

12. International law and national legal systems. International law is a legal system distinct from the legal systems of the national states. The relationship between any particular national legal system and international law is a matter regulated by the national law in question, often by the constitutional law of the state concerned. International law requires that a state must comply with its international obligations in good faith[1], which means, among other things, that each state must have the legal means to implement such of its international obligations as require action in national law. In some cases undertaking an international obligation will require a state to modify its domestic law, although, initially, it is for each state to judge what action is required. Where a state accepts that international obligations may be created for it from time to time by organs of international organisations of which it is a member[2], it must be able to give effect to each decision in its domestic law when such action is necessary[3]. A state may not rely on an insufficiency in its domestic law as a justification for failing to comply with an international obligation[4]. However, international law does not, of its own effect, have an impact directly in national law so that, for instance, rules of national law which are incompatible with a state's international obligations will remain valid instruments in national law[5].

1　See the Vienna Convention on the Law of Treaties (Vienna, 23 May 1969; TS 58 (1980); Cmnd 7964) art 26; and Declaration on Principles of International Law concerning Friendly Relations and Co-operation among States in Accordance with the Charter of the United Nations, principle 7, General Assembly Resolution 2625 (XXV) of 24 October 1970.

2　Eg the powers of the Security Council: see the Charter of the United Nations (San Francisco, 26 June 1945; TS 67 (1946); Cmd 7015) art 4(1) Chs V, VII (see PARA 523).

3　Eg in the case of the United Kingdom, the United Nations Act 1946 (see PARA 526).

4　See the Vienna Convention on the Law of Treaties, art 27.

5　The integration of EU law and the national laws of member states is a quite exceptional international law regime.

13. The constitutional context. The informality of the United Kingdom's constitutional arrangements introduces a degree of uncertainty into explaining the relationship between international law and domestic law[1]. The overriding principle of parliamentary sovereignty means that in no case may the express words of a statute be limited by reference to international law[2]. Of almost equal weight is the need for democratic legitimacy for acts of law-making, specifically that the executive has no power to make law or dispense with it by its acts alone[3]. It is a principle which has particular salience for the creation of criminal liability[4]. Given the primary role of the government in making international law, this is a factor of some significance, since the government has the power to bind the state in international law without having the power to secure the implementation of its obligations in domestic law, if that is necessary. Furthermore, the government's powers to conduct international relations[5], including acts which create obligations in international law, are in large part found within the prerogative and may be to a limited extent susceptible to judicial scrutiny[6]. The basic rules which govern the relationship between international law and domestic law should, therefore, be read subject to these considerations.

The basic rules may be stated succinctly. Treaties, being made by the executive alone, have no effect in English law unless, and then only to the extent that, they are implemented by legislation[7]. Customary law, in contrast, is said to be 'part of the law of England', which the courts may rely on without legislative intervention[8]. These practices represent the English law contribution to what has been described as the 'harmonisation' of relations between international law and domestic law, subject to the constitutional powers of national courts[9].

These bald propositions do not, however, give a complete explanation of the relationship between international law and domestic law. First, it is a presumption of statutory interpretation that Parliament does not intend to legislate contrary to the United Kingdom's existing international obligations[10]. There is an equivalent principle that the courts should develop the common law in a way compatible with the United Kingdom's duties in international law[11]. Under neither version is there a presumption or prohibition against the exercise of administrative powers contrary to international law[12]. Where the disposition of a case under other rules of law requires the determination of an issue of international law, the courts will use this 'point of reference' as the basis for considering the relevant international law, without regard to the formal rules set out above. In particular, there is no obstacle to consideration of treaties which have not been implemented in the United Kingdom or, indeed, to which it is not even a party[13]. This power has been extended in recent years by increasing reliance on the supplementary aids to interpretation of treaties set out in the Vienna Convention on the Law of Treaties[14], where the English courts have followed the International Court of Justice in looking at subsequent practice and other relevant international obligations[15].

When the English courts have the power to look at the wider international law context, they make little reference to the formal relationship between the rules of international law and domestic law[16], but frequently refer to the 'subsidiary means' for the determination of rules of international law, judicial decisions, including those of international courts, and academic writing[17].

Finally, in some cases, the English court will not apply international law, even though ostensibly directed to do so by its ordinary rules because of considerations of non-justiciability[18] or the 'foreign act of state' doctrine[19].

1 See Sales and Clement 'International Law in Domestic Courts: The Developing Framework' (2008) 124 LQR 388.
2 *Cheney v Conn (Inspector of Taxes)* [1968] 1 All ER 779, [1968] 1 WLR 242; *R v Asfaw* [2008] UKHL 31, [2008] 1 AC 1061, [2008] 3 All ER 775. In addition, the Executive may exercise its powers without regard to unimplemented international law, even in breach of an obligation (*R (on the application of Corner House Research) v Director of the Serious Fraud Office (BAE Systems plc, interested party)* [2008] UKHL 60, [2009] 1 AC 756, [2008] 4 All ER 927, [2009] Crim LR 47) and the courts do not have a role to secure compliance with unimplemented obligations of the UK (*R v Lyons* [2002] UKHL 44, [2003] 1 AC 976, [2004] 4 All ER 1028 at [40]). See also, however, *R v Horseferry Road Magistrates' Court, ex p Bennett* [1994] 1 AC 42, sub nom *Bennett v Horseferry Road Magistrates' Court* [1993] 3 All ER 138, HL.
3 See *The Parlement Belge* (1879) 4 PD 129, 3 BILC 305 (on appeal (1880) 5 PD 197, 3 BILC 322, CA but without affecting the judgment of Sir Robert Phillimore); and *Rayner (J H) (Mincing Lane) Ltd v Department of Trade and Industry* [1990] 2 AC 418, sub nom *Maclaine Watson & Co Ltd v Department of Trade and Industry* [1989] 3 All ER 523.
4 See *R v Jones* [2006] UKHL 16, [2007] 1 AC 136, [2006] 2 All ER 741 at [59]–[67], although the crucial question of whether or not the UK was obliged by international law to make planning etc a war of aggression a crime was not considered.
5 As to the conduct of international relations see PARA 26 et seq.
6 *Council of Civil Service Trade Unions v Minister for the Civil Service* [1985] AC 374, [1984] 3 All ER 935, HL. As to the royal prerogative see also CONSTITUTIONAL LAW AND HUMAN RIGHTS.

7   As to the implementation of treaties see PARA 18 et seq.
8   See IV Blackstone's Commentaries on the Laws of England, Chapter 5. Such reliance remains
    subject to the discussed constitutional principles: see the text and notes 1–6. See also PARA 16.
9   See O'Connell *International Law* (2nd ed, 1970) pp 51–54. Domestic legislation or rules of the
    common law may coincide with international law, so that no action is required for domestic law
    to be compatible with the state's international obligations: see eg *Masri v Consolidated
    Contractors International Co SAL* [2009] UKHL 43, [2009] 4 All ER 847, [2009] 3 WLR 385
    (the principle of territoriality as a rule of statutory interpretation); *Air India v Wiggins* [1980]
    2 All ER 593, [1980] 1 WLR 815 (principle of territoriality as the basis for criminal liability);
    and *A v Secretary of State for the Home Department* [2004] UKHL 56, [2005] 2 AC 68, [2005]
    3 All ER 169 (prohibition of torture at common law).
10 *R v Secretary of State for the Home Department, ex p Brind* [1991] 1 AC 696, [1990] 1 All ER
    469.
11 See generally *A v Secretary of State for the Home Department* [2004] UKHL 56, [2005] 2 AC
    68, [2005] 3 All ER 169; and *Wainwright v Home Office* [2003] UKHL 53, [2004] 2 AC 406.
12 *R v Secretary of State for the Home Department, ex p Brind* [1991] 1 AC 696, [1990] 1 All ER
    469.
13 Including, for example, the unimplemented provisions of the Charter of the United Nations (San
    Francisco, 26 June 1945; TS 67 (1946); Cmd 7015); see also *Republic of Ecuador v Occidental
    Exploration and Petroleum Co* [2005] EWCA Civ 1116, [2006] QB 432, [2006] 2 All ER 225.
14 Ie the Vienna Convention of the Law of Treaties (Vienna, 23 May 1969; TS 58 (1980);
    Cmnd 7964) art 31: see PARA 95 et seq.
15 See eg *Legal Consequences for States of the Continued Presence of South Africa in Namibia
    (South West Africa) notwithstanding Security Council Resolution 276 (1970) (Advisory
    Opinion)* ICJ Reports 1971, 16 at 22 (para 22); *Oil Platforms (Islamic Republic of Iran v
    United States)* ICJ Reports 2003, 161 at 182–183 (para 42). As to the International Court of
    Justice see PARA 499 et seq. This is a practice which has been relied on extensively in the
    application of the Human Rights Act 1998 (as to which see CONSTITUTIONAL LAW AND HUMAN
    RIGHTS), which gives effect to some of the provisions of the European Convention on Human
    Rights, following the European Court of Human Rights' practice of examining a wide
    international law context when interpreting the Convention: *R (on the application of Al-Skeini)
    v Secretary of State for Defence* [2007] UKHL 26, [2008] 1 AC 153, [2007] 3 All ER 685; *R (on
    the application of Al-Jedda) v Secretary of State for Defence* [2007] UKHL 58, [2008] 1 AC
    332, [2008] 3 All ER 28; *Application 35763/97 Al-Adsani v United Kingdom* (2001) 34 EHRR
    273, ECtHR; *Application 52207/99 Bankovic v Belgium* (2002) 11 BHRC 435, ECtHR.
16 See *R (on the application of Al-Skeini) v Secretary of State for Defence* [2007] UKHL 26, [2008]
    1 AC 153, [2007] 3 All ER 685 at [46]–[49] per Lord Rodger, referring to various international
    legal rules on jurisdiction.
17 See *R (on the application of Al-Skeini) v Secretary of State for Defence* [2007] UKHL 26, [2008]
    1 AC 153, [2007] 3 All ER 685.
18 See PARAS 24, 25.
19 See PARA 23.

14.   Proving international law in the English courts.   International law is
proved by argument before the court as a matter of law, not, as in the case of
foreign law, by the calling of expert evidence, proving the foreign law as a matter
of fact[1]. Recently, the courts have admitted witness statements from Foreign
Office lawyers concerning the condition of international law or the government's
view of the United Kingdom's obligations in international law[2]. The government
has the power under the prerogative and under statute to certify conclusively on
certain matters of fact bearing on the exercise of its powers relating to
international law[3]. Subject to stringent conditions of justiciability and standing,
customary international law may be invoked against the British government[4].
Prize courts apply rules of international law, whether derived from custom or
from treaty directly[5]. Judgments of international courts are admissible either
because legislation so provides[6] or as evidence as to the condition of
international law[7].

1   As to proof of foreign law see CONFLICT OF LAWS vol 8(3) (Reissue) PARA 28 et seq.

2   *Kuwait Airways Corpn v Iraqi Airways Co* [2002] UKHL 19, [2002] 2 AC 883, [2002] 3 All ER
    209 at [114] (referring to a letter from the FCO Legal Adviser about the legal position of the
    government); and *Aziz v Aziz* [2007] EWCA Civ 712, [2008] 2 All ER 501, (where the Foreign
    Office submitted a written statement about international law).
3   The evidence is presented by an 'Executive Certificate' under the hand of the Foreign Secretary:
    see generally PARA 15.
4   *R (on the application of the Campaign for Nuclear Disarmament) v Prime Minister* [2002]
    EWHC 2777 (Admin), (2002) Times, 27 December, [2003] 3 LRC 335 at [36] (justiciability),
    [48] (standing), per Simon Brown LJ; *R (on the application of Al-Haq) v the Secretary of State
    for Foreign and Commonwealth Affairs* [2009] EWHC 1910 (Admin) at [48] (obiter) per Pill LJ
    (doubting whether the applicants had standing), [61] (obiter) per Cranston J (accepting
    standing).
5   *The Zamora* [1916] 2 AC 77, PC; and see *The Maria* (1799) 1 Ch Rob 340; *The Elsebe* (1804)
    5 Ch Rob 173; *The Recovery* (1807) 6 Ch Rob 341; *The Odessa* [1915] P 52 (affd [1916] 1 AC
    145, PC); and PRIZE.
6   See eg the Human Rights Act 1998 s 2(1)(a); and CIVIL PROCEDURE vol 11 (2009) PARA 102.
7   See the Statute of the International Court of Justice (San Francisco, 26 June 1945; TS 67 (1946);
    Cmd 7015) art 38(1); and PARA 509. Judgments of foreign courts may be very useful in
    interpreting harmonisation treaties: *Morris v KLM Royal Dutch Airlines, King v Bristow
    Helicopters Ltd* [2002] UKHL 7, [2002] 2 AC 628, [2002] 2 All ER 565 at [81]; *Corocraft v
    Pan-American Airways Inc* [1969] 1 QB 616 at 655 per Denning LJ, [1969] 1 All ER 82, [1968]
    1 WLR 1273, CA.

15.   'Facts of state'. There is a class of facts, which may be termed 'facts of
state'[1], which consists of matters the determination of which is solely in the
hands of the executive. Examples of 'facts of state' are:

(1)   whether a state of war exists between Her Majesty and another state[2],
      and if so, when it began[3];
(2)   whether a state of war exists between other states[4];
(3)   whether a particular territory is hostile[5], or foreign[6], or within the
      boundaries of a particular state[7];
(4)   whether the Crown claims that a place is within its dominions[8];
(5)   whether British jurisdiction exists in any particular foreign place[9];
(6)   whether an entity claiming to be a foreign state has been recognised as
      such by the Crown[10], and formerly whether and when a particular
      entity was recognised as the government of an independent sovereign
      state[11] and now, the dealings the Crown has with the government of a
      foreign state[12];
(7)   whether an entity is entitled to state immunity[13];
(8)   the status of property which is the subject of claims by a foreign state to
      immunity[14];
(9)   the status of a person claiming immunity from the jurisdiction on the
      ground of his diplomatic status[15]; and
(10) the status of British and allied armed forces[16].

The court will take notice of such facts of state, and for this purpose, in any
case of uncertainty, will seek information from the executive, and the
information received is conclusive[17] except in cases where what is involved is the
construction of some term in a commercial document[18] or an Act of
Parliament[19]. Statute apart, the power of conclusive certification is restricted to
matters of fact.

1   Harrison Moore's Act of State in English Law (1906) pp 33–39.
2   *Esposito v Bowden* (1857) 7 E & B 763 at 793, Ex Ch, per Willes J.
3   *Blackburne v Thompson* (1812) 15 East 81 at 90–91 per Lord Ellenborough CJ; *Driefontein
    Consolidated Gold Mines v Janson, West Rand Central Gold Mines Co v De Rougemont* [1900]
    2 QB 339, 4 BILC 666 (affd sub nom *Janson v Driefontein Consolidated Mines Ltd* [1902] AC
    484, 4 BILC 682, HL). The municipal courts have no power to inquire into the correctness of a

declaration by the Crown that a state of war exists (*Blackburne v Thompson* (1812) 15 East 81) or whether it has ended (*R v Bottrill, ex p Kuechenmeister* [1947] KB 41, [1946] 2 All ER 434, 1 BILC 11, CA).

4 *Kawasaki Kisen Kabushiki Kaisha of Kobe v Bantham Steamship Co Ltd* [1939] 2 KB 544, [1939] 1 All ER 819, CA.

5 *Blackburne v Thompson* (1812) 15 East 81 at 90–91 per Lord Ellenborough CJ; and see *The Manilla* (1808) Edw 1, 2 BILC 7; *The Pelican* (1809) 1 Edw App D iv, 1 BILC 1, PC.

6 *Direct United States Cable Co Ltd v Anglo-American Telegraph Co Ltd* (1877) 2 App Cas 394, 2 BILC 892, PC.

7 *Foster v Globe Venture Syndicate Ltd* [1900] 1 Ch 811, 1 BILC 2; and see *Duff Development Co Ltd v Kelantan Government* [1924] AC 797 at 826–827, 3 BILC 216, HL, per Lord Sumner.

8 *The Fagernes* [1927] P 311, 2 BILC 914, CA.

9 *North Charterland Exploration Co (1910) Ltd v R* [1931] 1 Ch 169; *R v Campbell, ex p Ahmed Hamid Moussa* [1921] 2 KB 473, 4 BILC 524, DC; *Ex p Mwenya* [1960] 1 QB 241 at 280, [1959] 3 All ER 525 at 542, 7 BILC 424, CA. See also the Foreign Jurisdiction Act 1890 s 4; and COMMONWEALTH vol 13 (2009) PARA 708.

10 *Carl Zeiss Stiftung v Rayner and Keeler Ltd* [1967] 1 AC 853, sub nom *Carl Zeiss Stiftung v Rayner and Keeler Ltd (No 2)* [1966] 2 All ER 536, HL; *Gur Corpn v Trust Bank of Africa Ltd* [1987] QB 599, [1986] 3 All ER 449, CA).

11 See e g *The Charkieh* (1873) LR 4 A & E 59, 3 BILC 847; *Mighell v Sultan of Johore* [1894] 1 QB 149, 3 BILC 170, CA; *Carr v Fracis, Times & Co* [1902] AC 176, 2 BILC 823, HL; *Statham v Statham and Gaekwar of Baroda* [1912] P 92, 3 BILC 178; *The Gagara* [1919] P 95, 2 BILC 71, CA; *The Annette, The Dora* [1919] P 105, 2 BILC 76; *The Jupiter* [1924] P 236, 3 BILC 378; *Aksionairnoye Obschestvo AM Luther v James Sagor & Co* [1921] 3 KB 532, 2 BILC 97, CA; *Duff Development Co Ltd v Kelantan Government* [1924] AC 797, 3 BILC 216, HL; *Bank of Ethiopia v National Bank of Egypt and Liguori* [1937] Ch 513, [1937] 3 All ER 8, 2 BILC 146; *Haile Selassie v Cable and Wireless Ltd* [1938] Ch 839, [1938] 3 All ER 384, 3 BILC 165, CA; *Haile Selassie v Cable and Wireless Ltd (No 2)* [1939] Ch 182, [1938] 3 All ER 677, 2 BILC 171, CA; *Banco de Bilbao v Sancha, Banco de Bilbao v Rey* [1938] 2 KB 176, [1938] 2 All ER 253, 2 BILC 152, CA; *Government of the Republic of Spain v SS Arantzazu Mendi* [1939] AC 256, [1939] 1 All ER 719, 2 BILC 198, HL; *Lorentzen v Lydden & Co Ltd* [1942] 2 KB 202, 1 BILC 476; *A/S Tallinna Laevauhisus v Tallinna Shipping Co Ltd* (1946) 79 Ll L Rep 245, 1 BILC 485; *Civil Air Transport Inc v Central Air Transport Corpn* [1953] AC 70, [1952] 2 All ER 733, 7 BILC 523, PC; *Kahan v Pakistan Federation* [1951] 2 KB 1003, 7 BILC 689; *Sultan of Johore v Abubakar Tunku Aris Bendahar* [1952] AC 318, [1952] 1 All ER 1261, 7 BILC 667, PC; *Sayce v Ameer Ruler Sadig Mohammad Abbasi Bahawalpur State* [1952] 2 QB 390, [1952] 2 All ER 64, 7 BILC 662, CA; *Gdynia Ameryka Linie Zeglugowe Spolka Akcyjna v Boguslawski* [1953] AC 11, [1952] 2 All ER 470, 7 BILC 499, HL; *Carl Zeiss Stiftung v Rayner and Keeler Ltd* [1967] 1 AC 853, sub nom *Carl Zeiss Stiftung v Rayner and Keeler Ltd (No 2)* [1966] 2 All ER 536, HL.

12 See *Republic of Somalia v Woodhouse Drake and Carey (Suisse) SA* [1993] QB 54, [1993] 1 All ER 371; *Sierra Leone Telecommunications Co Ltd v Barclays Bank plc* [1998] 2 All ER 821.

13 See the State Immunity Act 1978 s 21; and PARA 245.

14 *The Parlement Belge* (1879) 4 PD 129, 3 BILC 305; revsd (1880) 5 PD 197, 3 BILC 322, CA.

15 *Engelke v Musmann* [1928] AC 433, 6 BILC 129, HL. See now the Diplomatic Privileges Act 1964 s 4; the Consular Relations Act 1968 s 11; the International Organisations Act 1968 s 8; and PARAS 282, 297, 323.

16 *Holdowanski v Holdowanska* [1956] 3 All ER 457, [1956] 3 WLR 935 (revsd sub nom *Taczanowska v Taczanowski* [1957] P 301, [1957] 2 All ER 563, CA); *Preston v Preston* [1963] P 141 (affd [1963] P 411, [1863] 2 All ER 405, CA).

17 *Duff Development Co Ltd v Government of Kelantan* [1924] AC 797, 3 BILC 216, HL; but there is no rule of law compelling the executive to answer a question: *White, Child and Beney Ltd v Eagle Star and British Dominions Insurance Co, White, Child and Beney Ltd v Simmons* (1922) 127 LT 571, 2 BILC 126, CA.

18 *Luigi Monta of Genoa v Cechofracht Co Ltd* [1956] 2 QB 552, [1956] 2 All ER 769, 7 BILC 540 (information not conclusive for purposes of interpreting the word 'government' in a war risks clause); *Reel v Holder* [1981] 3 All ER 321, [1981] 1 WLR 1226, CA (not conclusive as to interpretation of rules of the International Amateur Athletics Association). See also *Spinney's (1948) Ltd v Royal Insurance Co* [1980] 1 Lloyd's Rep 406 (information not sought on whether fighting in Lebanon constituted 'civil war' for the purpose of an insurance contract).

19 *Re Al-Fin Corpn's Patent* [1970] Ch 160, [1969] 3 All ER 396, 9 BILC 1, disapproving *Re Harshaw Chemical Co's Patent* [1965] RPC 97, 8 BILC 1 (meaning of 'foreign state' as used in the Patents Act 1949 s 24(2) (repealed)).

(2) CUSTOMARY INTERNATIONAL LAW AND ENGLISH LAW

16. Customary international law and English law. In numerous cases in the English courts it has been stated that customary international law is incorporated into and forms part of the law of England (the doctrine of incorporation)[1]. In other cases it has been said that international law is only part of English law in so far as the rules of the former system have been accepted by this country and are recognised by the English courts as having been transformed into rules of English law (the doctrine of transformation)[2]. While the English courts have resisted a simple answer to the question of which doctrine is to be preferred[3], the prevailing view appears to be a single rule of the common law allowing the courts to use the rules of customary international law as the basis for their decisions[4]. Each rule of customary international law may be given effect in this way so that the right-holder in international law (usually a state or its organs) may rely on it as a cause of action, a defence or as providing an immunity[5]. Like all rules of the common law, the reception of customary international law is subject to constitutional constraints, and customary international law may not be given effect contrary to the plain words of a statute, nor may it be used as the basis for establishing criminal liability in domestic law[6].

Customary international law does not provide grounds for challenging before the courts the exercise of powers of the British government under the prerogative which remain beyond domestic judicial scrutiny[7]. A remedy sought on the basis of the rule of customary international law must be one which it is within the capacity of the courts to give[8]. The traditional rule has come in for criticism[9]. It will be for the person asserting the rule to prove that it exists as alleged by demonstrating that there is evidence which would satisfy the international law test of custom[10]. The English courts have been troubled by what they perceive as the uncertainty of customary international law[11].

1   This was stated in numerous cases decided between 1737 and 1861: see e g *Barbuit's case* (1737) Cas temp Talb 281, 6 BILC 261; *Triquet v Bath* (1764) 3 Burr 1478, 6 BILC 211; *Heathfield v Chilton* (1767) 4 Burr 2015, 6 BILC 216; *Dolder v Lord Huntingfield* (1805) 11 Ves 283, 2 BILC 1; *Viveash v Becker* (1814) 3 M & S 284, 6 BILC 264; *Wolff v Oxholm* (1817) 6 M & S 92, 1 BILC 201; *Novello v Toogood* (1823) 1 B & C 554, 6 BILC 221; *De Wutz v Hendricks* (1824) 2 Bing 314, 6 BILC 771; *Emperor of Austria v Day and Kossuth* (1861) 3 De GF & J 217, 1 BILC 45. The later case of *R v Keyn* (1876) 2 ExD 63, 2 BILC 701, CCR, is sometimes said to demonstrate the abandonment of the doctrine of incorporation, but the customary rule in the case was permissive: whether or not a coastal state could exercise criminal jurisdiction over the acts of aliens on foreign-flag ships in its territorial sea. There was no provision of English law which allowed the exercise of such a jurisdiction, even if it were a permitted act by international law. There was no jurisdiction at common law and no statutory action having been taken, the courts could not exercise a power which had not been conferred on them in national law. Also, it may have been that the court was uncertain as to whether there was a clear rule of international law permitting a state to exercise jurisdiction over aliens for criminal offences committed in its territorial sea. The effect of the decision was changed by the Territorial Waters Jurisdiction Act 1878 s 3 (see CRIMINAL LAW, EVIDENCE AND PROCEDURE vol 11(3) (2006 Reissue) PARA 1056). It has been noted that while there is 'old and high authority' for the proposition that 'the law of nations to its full extent is part of the law of England and Wales' it is nonetheless difficult 'to accept this proposition in quite the unqualified terms in which it has often been stated': *R v Jones* [2006] UKHL 16, [2007] 1 AC 136, [2006]

2 All ER 741 at [11] per Lord Bingham (concerned with a crime under customary international law). See also O'Keefe 'The Doctrine of Incorporation Revisited' (2008) 79 BYIL 7.

Note also that the language used to describe the relationship between English law and international law is not consistent. When referring to treaties 'incorporation' requires an Act of Parliament giving effect to some or all of the terms of the treaty in national law. Treaties for which there is no incorporating legislation are accordingly referred to as 'unincorporated'. As to the implementation of treaties see generally PARA 18.

2 See e g *West Rand Central Gold Mining Co Ltd v R* [1905] 2 KB 391 at 406, 2 BILC 283, DC, per Lord Alverstone CJ; *Mortensen v Peters* (1906) 8 F 93, Ct of Sess, 3 BILC 754; *Commercial and Estates Co of Egypt v Board of Trade* [1925] 1 KB 271 at 295, CA, per Atkin LJ; *Chung Chi Cheung v R* [1939] AC 160 at 168, [1938] 4 All ER 786 at 790, 3 BILC 96, PC. However, these cases are not unequivocal, and might support the doctrine of incorporation: see Brownlie's Principles of Public International Law (7th Edn) 41–45; and see also *R v Secretary of State for the Home Department, ex p Thakrar* [1974] QB 684, [1974] 2 All ER 261, CA. The ability of an English court to apply a rule of international law directly may be limited by an earlier decision of an English court which points the other way, and the court is bound to apply the earlier decision by the operation of the principle of stare decisis: see *Chung Chi Cheung v R*. As to the relationship between treaties and English law see PARA 17 et seq.

3 See *R v Jones* [2006] UKHL 16, [2007] 1 AC 136, [2006] 2 All ER 741 at [59] per Lord Hoffmann, [100] per Lord Mance, not committing themselves to the same rule in civil and criminal cases; *R (on the application of Al-Haq) v Secretary of State for Foreign and Commonwealth Affairs* [2009] EWHC 1910 (Admin) at [40] per Pill LJ ('The issue of the incorporation of customary international law into domestic law is not susceptible to a simple or general answer').

4 *Trendtex Trading Corpn v Central Bank of Nigeria* [1977] QB 529, [1977] 1 All ER 881, CA. The principle by which a court is bound to follow decisions in former cases applies to this rule but not to individual judgments determining the existence and content of any particular rule of customary international law, matters which are to be determined by reference to the processes of international law. See also *Playa Larga (Owners of Cargo Lately Laden on Board) v I Congreso del Partido (Owners)* [1983] 1 AC 244, sub nom *I Congreso del Partido* [1981] 2 All ER 1064, HL.

5 Foreign states seldom sue in the English court (though see *President of the State of Equatorial Guinea v Royal Bank of Scotland International (Logo Ltd intervening)* [2006] UKPC 7, [2006] 3 LRC 676; and *Mbasogo v Logo Ltd* [2006] EWCA Civ 1370, [2007] QB 846, [2007] 2 WLR 1062) and will often be protected by immunities if they are made defendants. Accordingly, it is immunities under customary law which are most often successfully invoked: see e g *Alcom Ltd v Republic of Colombia* [1984] AC 580, [1984] 2 All ER 6, HL.

6 *R v Jones* [2006] UKHL 16, [2007] 1 AC 136, [2006] 2 All ER 741.

7 *R (on the application of the Campaign for Nuclear Disarmament) v Prime Minister* [2002] EWHC 2777 (Admin), (2002) Times, 27 December, [2003] 3 LRC 335.

8 *R v Keyn (The Franconia)* (1876) 2 ExD 63, 2 BILC 701, CCR, where the court had no authority in English law to exercise a jurisdiction which customary international law permitted nor the power to assume that jurisdiction without Parliamentary intervention. In *R (on the application of Al-Saadoon) v Secretary of State for Defence* [2009] EWCA Civ 7, [2009] 3 WLR 957, [2009] All ER (D) 153 (Jan) at [59] per Laws LJ suggested that a rule of customary international law would have to be a peremptory norm binding on all states to provide a cause of action.

9 *R (on the application of Al-Haq) v Secretary of State for Foreign and Commonwealth Affairs* [2009] EWHC 1910 (Admin) at [60] per Cranston J.

10 It is important that the substance of the rule of customary law demonstrated by the evidence supports the precise claim which the applicant makes: *European Roma Rights Centre v Immigration Officer at Prague Airport (United Nations High Commissioner for Refugees intervening)* [2004] UKHL 55, [2005] 2 AC 1, [2005] 1 All ER 527 at [26]–[28]; and *R (on the application of Al-Saadoon) v Secretary of State for Defence* [2009] EWCA Civ 7, [2009] 3 WLR 957, [2009] All ER (D) 153 (Jan) at [57]–[71] per Laws LJ.

11 *R v Bow Street Metropolitan Stipendiary Magistrate, ex p Pinochet Ugarte (No 3)* [2000] 1 AC 147, sub nom *R v Bow Street Metropolitan Stipendiary Magistrate, ex p Pinochet Ugarte (Amnesty International intervening) (No 3)* [1999] 2 All ER 97, HL.

(3) TREATIES AND ENGLISH LAW

17. Ratification and other treaty processes. The ratification of treaties is a matter for the executive under the prerogative[1], subject to relevant statutory provisions[2]. This power of government extends to modifying and withdrawing from treaties; making reservations to treaties and modifying or withdrawing reservations; making, modifying or withdrawing optional declarations[3]; and deciding on the application of territorial clauses in treaties[4]. As a matter of practice, the government refers treaties which it intends to ratify to Parliament under a procedure known as the 'Ponsonby Rule'[5]. Some treaties are sent to the relevant Select Committee for possible pre-ratification scrutiny but the government does not acknowledge a duty to do this[6]. There is a need for consultation with the devolved authorities if the implementation of a treaty will require legislation within their areas of competence[7].

1 *Blackburn v A-G* [1971] 2 All ER 1380, [1971] 1 WLR 1037 (no power of courts to review the decision to make, or not make, a treaty); *Council of Civil Service Unions v Minister for the Civil Service Council of Civil Service Trade Unions v Minister for the Civil Service* [1985] AC 374, [1984] 3 All ER 935, HL. As to the exercise of the prerogative in relation to the making of treaties see CONSTITUTIONAL LAW AND HUMAN RIGHTS vol 8(2) (Reissue) PARA 801 et seq. As to the rules of international law governing the making of treaties see PARA 71 et seq.
2 Eg the European Parliamentary Elections Act 1978 s 6(1). See also *R v Secretary of State for Foreign and Commonwealth Affairs, ex p Rees-Mogg* [1994] QB 552, [1994] 1 All ER 457, DC.
3 For the announcement by ministerial statement of the modification of the UK's Optional Clause declaration accepting the jurisdiction of the International Court of Justice, see (2004) 75 BYIL 804–805.
4 See eg the Convention for the Protection of Human Rights and Fundamental Freedoms (1950) (Rome, 4 November 1950; TS 71 (1953); Cmd 8969; ETS no 5) art 56; and *R (on the application of Quark Fishing Ltd) v Secretary of State for Foreign and Commonwealth Affairs* [2005] UKHL 57, [2006] 1 AC 529, [2006] 3 All ER 111.
5 See the Foreign and Commonwealth Office explanatory note on the Ponsonby Rule available at the date at this title states the law at www.fco.gov.uk; and CONSTITUTIONAL LAW AND HUMAN RIGHTS vol 8(2) (Reissue) PARA 802.
6 'It is also government practice to send copies of treaties that raise significant human rights issues to the Joint Committee on Human Rights, together with a copy of the Explanatory Memorandum': see the Justice Minister's letter to First Minister of Scotland, 21 November 2008, available at the date at which this volume states the law at www.justice.gov.uk.
7 See the Memorandum of Understanding and Supplementary Agreements between the United Kingdom Government, Scottish Ministers, the Cabinet of the National Assembly for Wales and the Northern Ireland Executive Committee, D1, D4 (December 2001) (Cm 5240), available at the date at which this title states the law at www.justice.gov.uk. The United Kingdom government is responsible for the conduct of the international relations of the UK but the implementation of international agreements may require action by a devolved authority (including legislation) and powers under international agreements may lie with devolved authorities.

18. Implementation of treaties in domestic law. It is a general principle that treaties which are required to have effect in national law must be implemented by legislation[1]. The accepted approach is a 'minimalist' one, providing for the implementation only of those provisions of the treaty which need to be given effect in domestic law. Accordingly, in some cases, Parliament enacts legislation implementing only part of a treaty[2]. Where a series of treaties can be expected to be negotiated on the same topic authority to implement them by delegated legislation is sometimes provided under the primary act[3].

Initially, it is the terms of the implementing statute with which a court will be confronted, and while it is generally said that there must be an ambiguity in the language of the statute before a court may look at the text of the treaty, this may mean no more than that the plain words of a statute will always take priority over a rule of international law. In any event, a court will usually have heard argument about the meaning of the treaty before it reaches a conclusion about the existence of an ambiguity in the statute[4].

The practice with respect to implementing legislation is not uniform. Sometimes, the statute refers to the treaty directly, sometimes specific provisions of the treaty are scheduled to the statute, and sometimes the purport of the treaty may be incorporated in the substance of the statute in language suitable for the English legal context and no indication of the implementing purpose will appear on the face of the legislation. It is for any party who asserts that the statute is designed to implement a treaty provision to demonstrate that this is so[5]. The presumption that Parliament does not intend to legislate contrary to international law takes on a stronger effect here, and the presumption is that Parliament intends to legislate to give effect to the terms of the treaty, and must be interpreted accordingly unless plain words exclude that possibility[6]. The courts must also consider the meaning of the treaty from an international perspective, which requires them to take into account the Vienna Convention on the Law of Treaties, especially its provisions on interpretation[7].

The case law remains unclear on whether the English courts should have regard only to those parts of the treaty directly or implicitly incorporated in the statute (interpreting the statute but taking into account the international origin of the implementing provisions) or if they should try to sit as though they were international court and consider the whole treaty and its context[8]. There are specific standards for the implementation of European Union law[9] and the European Convention on Human Rights[10], but while there are strong obiter dicta about the role of the courts with respect to legislation which implements treaties, there is no general statutory injunction[11].

1　If this were not so, the Crown, by entering into the treaty, would in effect be legislating without the consent of Parliament: *The Parlement Belge* (1879) 4 PD 129, 3 BILC 305. See also *Re Californian Fig Syrup Co's Trade Mark* (1888) 40 ChD 620 at 627, 6 BILC 460 obiter per Stirling J; *Walker v Baird* [1892] AC 491, 6 BILC 465, PC; *A-G for Canada v A-G for Ontario* [1937] AC 326 at 347–348, 6 BILC 330, PC; *Theophile v Solicitor-General* [1950] AC 186, [1950] 1 All ER 405, HL; *Republic of Italy v Hambros Bank Ltd and Gregory* [1950] Ch 314, [1950] 1 All ER 430, 6 BILC 525; *Blackburn v A-G* [1971] 2 All ER 1380 at 1382, [1971] 1 WLR 1037 at 1039, CA; *Pan American Airways Inc v Department of Trade* [1976] 1 Lloyd's Rep 257, CA; *Laker Airways Ltd v Department of Trade* [1977] QB 643, [1977] 2 All ER 182 CA; *JH Rayner (Mincing Lane) Ltd v Department of Trade and Industry* [1990] 2 AC 418, sub nom *Maclaine Watson & Co Ltd v Department of Trade and Industry* [1989] 3 All ER 523, HL; *Philipp Bros v Republic of Sierra Leone and Commission of the European Communities* [1995] 1 Lloyd's Rep 289, CA; *R v Lyons* [2002] UKHL 44, [2003] 1 AC 976, [2004] 4 All ER 1028 at [27] per Lord Hoffmann. With respect to claims against the Crown based upon the provisions of a treaty entered into by the Crown see PARA 389. As to the interpretation of statutes founded upon treaties see PARA 95. For the suggestion that human rights treaties might be treated differently and effect given to an unimplemented human rights treaty, at least against the executive, see *Re McKerr* [2004] UKHL 12, [2004] NI 212, [2004] 2 All ER 409. There are, however, objections to this view: see Sales and Clement 'International Law in Domestic Courts: the Developing Framework' (2008) 124 LQR 398–400. Note that not all treaties require implementation by legislation: see eg the General Treaty for the Renunciation of War as an Instrument of National Policy, 1928 (Paris, 27 August 1928; TS 29 (1929); Cmd 3410); and the Treaty on the Treaty on the Non-Proliferation of Nuclear Weapons (London, Moscow and Washington, 1 July 1968; TS 88 (1970); Cmnd 4474) (see further CONSTITUTIONAL LAW AND HUMAN RIGHTS vol 8(2) (Reissue) PARA 802).

2　See eg the United Nations Act 1946 (and PARA 526); and the Human Rights Act 1998 (and CONSTITUTIONAL LAW AND HUMAN RIGHTS).

3 See eg the Extradition Act 2003 ss 1(1), 69(1); and EXTRADITION. This means that any agreement reached with a foreign state must be compatible with the terms of the primary legislation.

4 See eg *JH Rayner (Mincing Lane) Ltd v Department of Trade and Industry* [1990] 2 AC 418, sub nom *Maclaine Watson & Co Ltd v Department of Trade and Industry* [1989] 3 All ER 523, HL.

5 *Salomon v Customs and Excise Comrs* [1967] 2 QB 116 at 144, [1966] 3 All ER 871 at 876, CA, per Diplock LJ: 'If from extrinsic evidence it is plain that the enactment was intended to fulfil Her Majesty's Government's obligations under a particular convention, it matters not that there is no express reference to the convention in the statute ... The extrinsic evidence of the connection must be cogent.'

6 See STATUTES vol 44(1) (Reissue) PARA 1426.

7 Ie the Vienna Convention on the Law of Treaties (Vienna, 23 May 1969; TS 58 (1980); Cmnd 7964) arts 31–33 (see PARA 95 et seq). The English courts have accepted they may have recourse to the Convention as a statement of customary international law, even though it has not been implemented into domestic law: *Fothergill v Monarch Airlines Ltd* [1981] AC 251 at 282, [1980] 2 All ER 696 at 706, HL per Lord Diplock; *European Roma Rights Centre v Immigration Officer at Prague Airport (United Nations High Commissioner for Refugees intervening)* [2004] UKHL 55, [2005] 2 AC 1, [2005] 1 All ER 527 at [18] per Lord Bingham.

8 The courts have disavowed a wholly national approach to the interpretation of treaty provisions: *Black-Clawson International v Papierwerke Waldhof-Aschaffenburg AG* [1975] AC 591, [1975] 1 All ER 810; *Fothergill v Monarch Airlines* [1981] AC 251 at 290, [1980] 2 All ER 696 at 712 per Lord Scarman; *R v Home Secretary of State for the Home Department ex p Adan* [2001] 2 AC 477, [2001] 1 All ER 593, [2000] All ER (D) 2357. The treaty should be read as a whole: *Fothergill v Monarch Airlines Ltd* [1981] AC 251 at 279, [1980] 2 All ER 696 at 704, HL, per Lord Diplock; *R (on the application of Ullah) v Special Adjudicator* [2004] UKHL 26, [2004] 2 AC 323, [2004] 3 All ER 785. The courts have accepted that the different processes by which legislation and treaties are produced makes reliance on domestic rules of statutory interpretation inappropriate to the interpretation of treaties: *Adan v Secretary of State for the Home Department* [1999] 1 AC 293 at 305, [1998] 2 All ER 453 at 458 per Lord Lloyd. They have been particularly conscious of the purposive approach to interpretation contained in the Vienna Convention, and to the reliance which international courts place on the preparatory work of the treaty and different language versions of the text to resolve ambiguities: *European Roma Rights Centre v Immigration Officer at Prague Airport (United Nations High Commissioner for Refugees intervening)* [2004] UKHL 55, [2005] 2 AC 1, [2005] 1 All ER 527 at [6]; *Belgium (Government of) v Postlethwaite* [1988] AC 924, [1987] 2 All ER 985 (the object of an extradition treaty to facilitate inter-state criminal cooperation); *Fothergill v Monarch Airlines* [1981] AC 251, at 282–283, [1980] 2 All ER 696 at 706–707, HL, per Lord Diplock. For extensive consideration of the preparatory work of the Refugee Convention, see *R v Asfaw* [2008] UKHL 31, [2008] 1 AC 1061, [2008] 3 All ER 775. For criticism that the English courts do not use preparatory work in the way an international judge would, see Gardiner *International Law* (1st Edn, 2003) pp 158–161. For a consideration of treaty texts in languages other than English, see *James Buchanan & Co v Babco Forwarding and Shipping UK Ltd* [1978] AC 141, [1977] 3 All ER 1048, HL; *Fothergill v Monarch Airlines Ltd* [1981] AC 251, [1980] 2 All ER 696. The courts have from time to time taken a wide variety of evidence into account to determine the meaning of implementing language in a statute, including the work of the International Law Commission, decisions of international and national courts, resolutions of the General Assembly and the Handbook of the High Commissioner for Refugees. So long as these materials are used as evidence of the state of international law and not as sources of international law themselves, there can be no objections to this practice: see *R (on the application of Al-Jedda) v Secretary of State for Defence* [2007] UKHL 58, [2008] 1 AC 332, [2008] 3 All ER 28 at [38] per Lord Bingham (subsequent practice of parties to European Convention on Human Rights); *A v Secretary of State for the Home Department (No 2)* [2005] UKHL 71, [2006] 2 AC 221, [2006] 1 All ER 575; *Entico Corpn Ltd v United Nations Educational Scientific and Cultural Association* [2008] EWHC 531 (Comm), [2008] 2 All ER (Comm) 97.

9 See the European Communities Act 1972 ss 2, 3.

10 See the Human Rights Act 1998 s 3(1); and ADMINISTRATIVE LAW vol 1(1) (2001 Reissue) PARA 87.

11 See *The Eschersheim* [1981] AC 920 at 924 per Lord Diplock, stating that the language of an implementing statute should be given the meaning of the treaty, interpreted as an instrument of international law, which it implements if the statute is 'reasonably capable' of bearing that meaning.

19. Unimplemented treaties. Unimplemented treaties (and decisions taken under them) are acts in international law and have no direct consequences in English law. As a general rule it is not the business of the courts to interpret them, or to provide rights or recognise defences based upon them, which is to say that the courts have 'no jurisdiction' with regard to unimplemented treaties[1]. However, the courts may rely on unimplemented treaties, including interpreting them if necessary, to determine rights and duties under other rules of domestic law[2]. The rule of 'no jurisdiction' does not apply where the treaty is relevant to the exercise of a prerogative power which has law-creating effects (essentially, the power of the Crown to extend or reduce the jurisdiction of the state)[3]. Courts may also have regard to unimplemented treaties to determine the limits and contents of public policy[4].

1 *R v Lyons* [2002] UKHL 44, [2003] 1 AC 976, [2002] 4 All ER 1028. Unimplemented treaties are sometimes said to be 'non-justiciable' (although the designation in the text above is to be preferred: PARA 24 note 1): *JH Rayner (Mincing Lane) Ltd v Department of Trade and Industry* [1990] 2 AC 418, sub nom *Maclaine Watson & Co Ltd v Department of Trade and Industry* [1989] 3 All ER 523, HL.
2 *Republic of Ecuador v Occidental Exploration and Production Co* [2005] EWCA Civ 1116, [2006] QB 432, [2006] 2 All ER 225 (where the treaty in questions was one to which the UK was not even a party).
3 *Post Office v Estuary Radio* [1968] 2 QB 740, [1967] 3 All ER 663, CA.
4 See PARA 19.

(4) ADMINISTRATIVE POWERS

20. In general. The exercise of administrative powers under legislation which implements international obligations is subject to the ordinary disciplines of public law, including the obligation to interpret international law correctly where necessary[1]. An administrative decision-maker is not obliged to take into account, and nor is he bound by, the provisions of an unimplemented treaty[2]. It is likely that public law powers are constrained by at least some rules of customary international law[3]. Where the power in question is a prerogative power, the fact that there are international obligations which bear upon it does not alter the non-justiciability of any decision under it, which would be otherwise beyond judicial scrutiny in the absence of legislation[4]. Where a decision-maker legitimately takes into account a question of law, it is a reviewable matter whether or not his understanding of the law is correct. Although this principle has been extended to issues of international law, at least where the European Convention of Human Rights was concerned[5], difficulties may arise if it were to be followed unqualifiedly. Advice on international law is routinely sought by ministers and generally acted upon. If every piece of advice on a matter of international law where an administrative action or power were being considered were subject to judicial review, considerable difficulties for the administration could be anticipated[6]. While considerations of justiciability might reduce the reach of review, many matters of international law, which the government might regard as being within its compass or as being subject to essential confidentiality could be subjected to public scrutiny and, on the existing authorities, a line is not easy to draw[7].

1 Particular statutes may make consideration of international law mandatory: see eg the Diplomatic and Consular Premises Act 1987 ss 1(4), 2(2); and PARAS 270–271. See generally ADMINISTRATIVE LAW.
2 *R v Secretary of State for the Home Department, ex p Brind* [1991] 1 AC 696, [1991] 1 All ER 720, HL; *R (on the application of Hurst) v Northern District of London Coroner* [2007] UKHL

13, [2007] 2 AC 189, [2007] 2 All ER 1025 at [53]–[59] per Lord Brown; *R (on the application of Corner House Research) v Director of Serious Fraud Office (BAE Systems plc, interested party)* [2008] UKHL 60, [2009] 1 AC 756, [2008] 4 All ER 927, [2009] Crim LR 47 (no need to decide whether or not the decision-maker had correctly interpreted the international obligations of the United Kingdom because he had made it clear that his decision would have been the same whatever his conclusion had been because of overriding considerations of national security). As to unimplemented treaties see PARA 19.

3   See *European Roma Rights Centre v Immigration Officer at Prague Airport (United Nations High Comr for Refugees intervening)* [2004] UKHL 55, [2005] 2 AC 1, [2005] 1 All ER 527 at [97]–[103] per Baroness Hale, although the proof of the rule here is rudimentary.

4   *R (on the application of the Campaign for Nuclear Disarmament) v Prime Minister* [2002] EWHC 2777 (Admin), (2002) Times, 27 December, [2003] 3 LRC 335. The domestic act of state doctrine would provide further grounds for excluding the courts: see PARA 22 et seq.

5   *R v Secretary of State for the Home Department, ex p Launder* [1997] 3 All ER 961, [1997] 1 WLR 839. In *R (on the application of Corner House Research) v Director of Serious Fraud Office (BAE Systems plc, interested party)* [2008] UKHL 60, [2009] 1 AC 756, [2008] 4 All ER 927, [2009] Crim LR 47 at [66] Lord Brown suggested that the established jurisprudence of the European Court of Human Rights could reinforce the decision of a domestic court to review a ministerial determination of what the European Convention on Human Rights required.

6   *R (on the application of Corner House Research) v Director of Serious Fraud Office (BAE Systems plc, interested party)* [2008] UKHL 60, [2009] 1 AC 756, [2008] 4 All ER 927, [2009] Crim LR 47 at [65]–[68] per Lord Brown. See also Sales and Clement 'International Law in Domestic Courts: the Developing Framework' 124 LQR 404–407.

7   *R (on the application of the Campaign for Nuclear Disarmament) v Prime Minister* [2002] EWHC 2777 (Admin), (2002) Times, 27 December, [2003] 3 LRC 335 at [15].

21.   Legitimate expectations. There is some scope for reliance on legitimate expectations in the field of foreign affairs but the mere fact that there is an international obligation on the United Kingdom does not give rise to a legitimate expectation that a power will be exercised in accordance with it. In particular, there is no room for arguing that the fact that the state has entered into a treaty which it has not implemented creates a legitimate expectation that public powers will be not be exercised incompatibly with the treaty obligations[1]. A legitimate expectation has been identified in the field of diplomatic protection[2], but it has been suggested that it is unlikely that legitimate expectations having much practical impact could be generated in the field of foreign affairs, and that it might in any event be relatively easy for a government to disavow any which appeared inconvenient[3].

1   Cf *Minister of State for Immigration and Ethnic Affairs v Teoh (Human Rights and Equal Opportunity Commission intervening)* [1995] 3 LRC 1, 183 CLR 273, 128 ALR 353, HC Aus. The English authorities are inconsistent: *R v Secretary of State for the Home Department ex p Ahmed and Patel* [1998] INLR 546; and *R v Uxbridge Magistrates' Court, ex p Adimi* [2001] QB 667, [1999] 4 All ER 520, DC (both following *Minister of State for Immigration and Ethnic Affairs v Teoh*); *Behuli v Secretary of State for the Home Department* [1998] Imm AR 407 (finding no general legitimate expectation).

2   See *R (on the application of Abbasi) v Secretary of State for Foreign and Commonwealth Affairs* [2002] EWCA Civ 1598, (2002) Times, 8 November, [2003] 3 LRC 297.

3   See Sales and Clement 'International Law in Domestic Courts: the Developing Framework' 124 LQR 410–412.

(5) ACTS OF STATE

22.   Introduction. 'Act of state' is not a term of art in English law and, as a description, it is used in more than one way. The 'domestic act of state' is a feature of constitutional law, and is a prerogative act of policy in the field of foreign affairs performed by the Crown[1] in the course of its relationship with another state or its subjects[2]. As an exercise of sovereign power, the courts have no jurisdiction to question the validity of an act of state[3], although the municipal courts may be called upon and have power to decide whether an act is an act of state[4]. An act of state may be pleaded by way of defence by the Crown or its agent in a claim in tort brought by an alien in respect of an allegedly wrongful act committed against him outside the dominions of the Crown[5].

The 'foreign act of state' is in general part of the conflict of laws[6] but, at least as to its exceptions, raises issues of international law[7]. Those questions overlap with matters of justiciability[8].

1   An act of state need not be performed directly by the Sovereign, but may be performed by a subject who has the authority of the Crown: see FOREIGN RELATIONS LAW vol 18(2) (Reissue) PARA 617.

2   Eg making and performance of treaties, the annexation of foreign territory, the seizure of land or goods in right of conquest, declarations of war and of blockade, and the detention of an enemy alien in wartime or his deportation: see FOREIGN RELATIONS LAW vol 18(2) (Reissue) PARA 613. In general there can be no act of state with respect to a British subject: see FOREIGN RELATIONS LAW vol 18(2) (Reissue) PARA 618.

3   Nor can an individual rely upon an act of state in order to found a cause of action: see FOREIGN RELATIONS LAW vol 18(2) (Reissue) PARA 614. As a general rule, since the courts have no jurisdiction over acts of state, they will not enforce duties which the Crown has assumed by virtue of an act of state itself towards individuals, even though they are British subjects: see FOREIGN RELATIONS LAW vol 18(2) (Reissue) PARA 619.

4   See FOREIGN RELATIONS LAW vol 18(2) (Reissue) PARA 616.

5   See FOREIGN RELATIONS LAW vol 18(2) (Reissue) PARA 615.

6   See CONFLICT OF LAWS.

7   See PARA 23

8   See PARAS 24–25.

23.   Acts of foreign states.   There are certain classes of act of a foreign sovereign or government[1] which the English courts will not allow to be questioned before them, in the sense that their validity may not be impugned by an action before those courts. These classes are not clearly defined[2]. The rule is not regarded as required by public international law but as an aspect of the conflict of laws and its application will depend upon the cause of action in which it arises.

Official acts done by a foreign sovereign or state or foreign government recognised as such by Her Majesty[3] or with which the British government has government-to-government dealings cannot be made the basis of responsibility of that sovereign, state or government if those acts are done in the country concerned, whether the act is right or wrong and whether it is according to the country's constitution or not[4].

The English courts will not sit in judgment upon the acts of a sovereign effected by or by virtue of his sovereign capacity abroad[5]. Thus the English courts will not inquire into the validity of acts done by a recognised foreign government or a government with which the British government has government-to-government dealings against its own subjects in respect of property situate at the time of the acts in its own territory[6]. There is some authority for the view that if an act is done against a foreign national in respect of property within the territory of a foreign state in circumstances which amount to a breach of international law the English courts will not give effect to it[7].

No proceedings may be brought in an English court against an individual in respect of any act done by him which was authorised by the sovereign or government of a foreign state within the territory of that state, even though the act may be criminal according to English law[8]. On the other hand, an English court will not entertain proceedings between private litigants which might involve inquiry into whether an act of a foreign state had taken place[9].

1   'Act of State' is not a term of art in English law and, as a description, it is used in more than one way. The 'domestic act of state' is a feature of constitutional law: see PARA 22. The 'foreign act of State' is part of the conflict of laws but, at least as to its exceptions, raises issues of international law, which overlap with matters of justiciability: see PARA 24.

2   *Buttes Gas and Oil Co v Hammer* [1982] AC 888, sub nom *Buttes Gas and Oil Co v Hammer (No 2 and No 3)* [1981] 3 All ER 616, HL. See also *Dubai Bank Ltd v Galadari (No 5)* (1990) Times, 26 June; *Kuwait Airways Corpn v Iraqi Airways Co (No 6)* [1999] CLC 31.

3   As to recognition see PARA 41 et seq.

4   The English courts will not, as a matter of international comity or effectiveness, make a declaration impugning the validity of the laws or constitution of a foreign independent sovereign state, at any rate where that is the object of the action, and in any case ought not to do so: *Buck v A-G* [1965] Ch 745, [1964] 2 All ER 663; affd [1965] Ch 745, [1965] 1 All ER 882, CA. See also *Duke of Brunswick v King of Hanover* (1848) 2 HL Cas 1 at 17, 21, 22, 3 BILC 138 per Lord Cottenham LC, and at 27 per Lord Campbell; cf *Munden v Duke of Brunswick* (1847) 10 QB 656, 3 BILC 148. In so far as an action is begun against a foreign sovereign it will in any event fail as being beyond the jurisdiction of the courts by reason of the defendant's sovereign immunity: see PARA 243.

5   This rule was explained, upon the basis of the rule that an English court will not sit in judgment upon an act of a foreign state or government, in *Aksionairnoye Obschestvo AM Luther v James Sagor & Co* [1921] 3 KB 532 at 548, 2 BILC 97, CA, per Warrington LJ. However, in the same case at 544–545, Bankes LJ did not rely upon this and it is probable that the rule as stated in the text is merely an aspect or application of the rule that the lex situs of property governs questions of title to it: see now *Williams and Humbert Ltd v WH Trademarks (Jersey) Ltd* [1986] AC 368, [1986] 1 All ER 129, HL; *Settebello Ltd v Banco Totta Acores* [1985] 2 All ER 1025, [1985] 1 WLR 1050, CA. If this is so, the rule is not a rule of public international law but a rule of private international law. It seems clear that the English courts will not give effect to decrees of a foreign state affecting property outside its territory and certainly not when such decrees are confiscatory and discriminatory: see eg *Banco de Vizcaya v Don Alfonso de Borbon y Austria* [1935] 1 KB 140; *A-G of New Zealand v Ortiz* [1984] AC 1, [1983] 2 All ER 93, HL. See also *Islamic Republic of Iran v The Barakat Galleries Ltd* [2007] EWCA Civ 1374, [2009] QB 22, [2008] 1 All ER 1177. As to governmental acts affecting property see generally CONFLICT OF LAWS vol 8(3) (Reissue) PARA 422 et seq.

6   *Anglo-Iranian Oil Co Ltd v Jaffrate, The Rose Mary* [1953] 1 WLR 246, Aden SC. However, in *Re Helbert Wagg & Co Ltd* [1956] Ch 323, [1956] 1 All ER 129, 7 BILC 251, Upjohn J preferred to explain this decision on the ground that the Iranian decree in question was contrary to English public policy (see CONFLICT OF LAWS vol 8(3) (Reissue) PARA 358) as being discriminatory. In *Oppenheimer v Cattermole* [1976] AC 249, [1975] 1 All ER 538, HL (distinguished in *Kuwait Airways Corpn v Iraqi Airways Co* [1999] CLC 31), Lord Cross of Chelsea (at 278 and 567) and Lord Salmon (at 281 and 572) were of the opinion (obiter) that legislation enacted by a foreign state which takes away without compensation from a section of its citizen body singled out on racial grounds all their property, and in addition deprives them of their citizenship, is contrary to international law and constitutes so grave an infringement of their human rights that the English courts ought to refuse to recognise it as law at all. It is uncertain whether such an act would be contrary to international law. In *Kuwait Airways Corpn v Iraqi Airways Co* [2002] UKHL 19, [2002] 2 AC 883, [2002] 3 All ER 209 the court found that there was a clear breach of a fundamental principle of international law, an otherwise applicable foreign law was not recognised in England, under a developing head of public policy.

7   *Blad's Case* (1673) 3 Swan 603, PC; *Blad v Bamfield* (1674) 3 Swan 604. If the act was committed within the territory of the foreign state and its authorisation makes it lawful there, then, even if it would have been actionable as a tort if committed in England, the act would not be actionable as such in the English courts by virtue of the rules of English private international law governing liability for torts committed abroad. This appears to be the explanation of *Carr v Fracis, Times & Co* [1902] AC 176, 2 BILC 823, HL; and *Dobree v Napier* (1836) 2 Bing NC 781 may be explained on similar grounds. As to liability in tort for acts done abroad see CONFLICT OF LAWS vol 8(3) (Reissue) PARA 366 et seq.

8   *R v Lesley* (1860) Bell CC 220, 3 BILC 586, CCR, where the conviction of the captain of a British ship for false imprisonment in taking on board and keeping there individuals, under the authority of a foreign government, could not be supported in so far as the acts were done in the waters of the foreign state. However, liability can be imposed for such acts done outside the foreign waters, as for example on a British ship on the high seas: *R v Lesley*. It seems, therefore,

very doubtful whether the rule as stated in the text applies to acts committed within British territory by order of a foreign sovereign or government. There is no direct English authority on the point, but see 1 Hale PC 99. In *The People v McLeod* 1 Hill 377 (USA 1841), the Supreme Court of New York held that the plea of act of state afforded no defence to a British subject who had committed a criminal offence authorised by his own government in the territory of New York State. The governments of this country and of the United States agreed in diplomatic exchanges that the decision was incorrect (39 BFSP 1127, 1131, 1141), but other authorities, including Lord Lyndhurst, agreed with it: see Harrison Moore's Act of State in English Law 122–131. As to state immunity in respect of acts committed by a former foreign head of state see also *R v Bow Street Metropolitan Stipendiary Magistrate, ex p Pinochet Ugarte (No 3)* [2000] 1 AC 147, sub nom *R v Bow Street Metropolitan Stipendiary Magistrate, ex p Pinochet Ugarte (Amnesty International intervening) (No 3)* [1999] 2 All ER 97, HL; PARAS 263, 285; and EXTRADITION.

9   *Buttes Gas and Oil Co v Hammer* [1982] AC 888, sub nom *Buttes Gas and Oil Co v Hammer (No 2 and No 3)* [1981] 3 All ER 616, HL. As to justiciability see PARA 24.

(6) JUSTICIABILITY

24. Justiciability of acts of the United Kingdom government. The terms 'justiciability' and 'non-justiciability' as they apply to acts of the United Kingdom government have not always been used consistently in the case law, and it would sometimes be better to see an issue characterised as justiciability as one of jurisdiction[1]. Confusion arises because the non-statutory powers of government in the area of foreign affairs are found in the prerogative, and as such their exercise is, in general, beyond the jurisdiction of the courts[2]. The legal character of such powers is sometimes also a feature of their substantive character: they are political matters about which there are no legal standards to apply[3]. Where, following the GCHQ case[4], prerogative powers are within the jurisdiction of the courts and there are therefore judicial standards to assess their exercise, their justiciablity may be considered with respect to some foreign affairs powers[5]. So not every decision taken under a particular power is within the jurisdiction of the courts and it is a matter of justiciability to decide if the court might adjudicate on a contested decision. Some powers remain quite outside the jurisdiction of the courts[6], and to the extent that the justification given for this is that there are no judicial standards to apply, it has been argued that international law can supply them[7]. The courts have shown no disposition to accede to this argument[8].

1   It is unhelpful to refer to unimplemented treaties of the UK as being 'non-justiciable' in the English court (see PARA 19), rather it is an absence of jurisdiction which precludes a court from determining an issue of international law which operates only on the international plane: *R v Lyons* [2002] UKHL 44, [2003] 1 AC 976, [2004] 4 All ER 1028 at [27] per Lord Hoffmann; *R (on the application of the Campaign for Nuclear Disarmament) v Prime Minister* [2002] EWHC 2777 (Admin), (2002) Times, 27 December, [2003] 3 LRC 335 at [47].

2   As to the royal prerogative and its exercise see CONSTITUTIONAL LAW AND HUMAN RIGHTS vol 8(2) (Reissue) PARA 367 et seq; and ADMINISTRATIVE LAW vol 1(1) (2001 Reissue) PARA 64.

3   The powers to deploy the troops overseas, or to make treaties, for instance, are wholly a matter of political choice and are 'non-justiciable': *Council of Civil Service Unions v Minister for the Civil Service* [1985] AC 374 at 418, [1984] 3 All ER 935 at 956, HL, per Lord Roskill.

4   *Council of Civil Service Unions v Minister for the Civil Service* [1985] AC 374, [1984] 3 All ER 935.

5   *R (on the application of Abbasi) v Secretary of State for Foreign and Commonwealth Affairs* [2002] EWCA Civ 1598, (2002) Times, 8 November, [2003] 3 LRC 297, where, in the context of diplomatic protection, it was found that there was a minimal duty of consideration of the situation of a British national, but that 'on no view' would it have been appropriate to order the Foreign Secretary to intervene with the United States.

6   See note 3.

7   *R (on the application of the Campaign for Nuclear Disarmament) v Prime Minister* [2002] EWHC 2777 (Admin), (2002) Times, 27 December, [2003] 3 LRC 335 at [47] per Brown LJ.

8   *R (on the application of the Campaign for Nuclear Disarmament) v Prime Minister* [2002] EWHC 2777 (Admin), (2002) Times, 27 December, [2003] 3 LRC 335; *R v Jones* [2006] UKHL 16, [2007] 1 AC 136, [2006] 2 All ER 741 at [30] per Lord Bingham, and at [65]–[66] per Lord Hoffmann; *R (on the application of Gentle) v The Prime Minister* [2008] UKHL 20, [2008] 1 AC 1356, [2008] 3 All ER 1.

25. Justiciability of acts of foreign states. Even if the courts were persuaded to apply international law to matters of high policy[1], there is another form of non-justiciability which would inhibit the exercise of jurisdiction in such cases, and applies as much to acts of foreign states as they do to those of the British government. It has been said that there is doctrine of judicial restraint which requires that the courts do not adjudicate on matters of international law arising in disputes involving foreign states[2]. Later judgments have emphasised that the principle is flexible and is a doctrine of discretionary non-justiciability, rather than jurisdiction[3]. The application of rules of international law to a dispute involving foreign states may be difficult for an English court where the international law is contested between the states, hence the absence of judicial or manageable standards for adjudication[4]. The determination of a dispute may be unacceptable to the states involved, particularly if they would have been entitled to immunity if they had been parties to the action[5]. The availability of alternative avenues to settle the dispute is a factor which weighs against the case being heard by an English court[6].

1   Eg the deployment of troops overseas or to make treaties: see PARA 24.

2   *Buttes Gas and Oil Co v Hammer* [1982] AC 888 at 931–932, sub nom *Buttes Gas and Oil Co v Hammer (No 2 and No 3)* [1981] 3 All ER 616 at 628, HL, per Lord Wilberforce (an action between private parties, so that state immunity could not be raised, but that involved a maritime boundary dispute between two foreign states).

3   *R v Bow Street Magistrate, ex p Pinochet Ugarte* [2000] 1 AC 61 at 104, [1998] 4 All ER 897 at 935, HL; *Kuwait Airways Corpn v Iraqi Airways Co* [2002] UKHL 19, [2002] 2 AC 883, [2002] 3 All ER 209 at [26].

4   *Kuwait Airways Corpn v Iraqi Airways Co* [2002] UKHL 19, [2002] 2 AC 883, [2002] 3 All ER 209; *R (on the application of Al-Haq) v the Secretary of State for Foreign and Commonwealth Affairs* [2009] EWHC 1910 (Admin). The matter is not one of an inherent limitation on the courts as they will take on questions of international law, even where they are contested, if it is necessary to resolve a matter within their jurisdiction in English law: *Republic of Ecuador v Occidental Exploration and Production Co* [2005] EWCA Civ 1116, [2006] QB 432, [2006] 2 All ER 225.

5   *R (on the application of the Campaign for Nuclear Disarmament) v Prime Minister* [2002] EWHC 2777 (Admin), (2002) Times, 27 December, [2003] 3 LRC 335 at [37].

6   *R (on the application of Corner House Research) v Director of Serious Fraud Office (BAE Systems plc, interested party)* [2008] UKHL 60, [2009] 1 AC 756, [2008] 4 All ER 927, [2009] Crim LR 47 at [45].

4. THE CONDUCT OF INTERNATIONAL RELATIONS

26. The Crown. By English law, for external purposes, the Crown represents the community. No person or body save the Queen, by her accredited representatives, can deal with a foreign state so as to acquire rights or incur liabilities on behalf of the community at large[1]. Conforming almost exactly to the classical conception in international law of the head of state[2], invested with the jus omnimodae repraesentionis, the Crown declares war and makes peace[3], makes treaties[4], acquires and cedes territory[5], accords recognition to foreign states and governments[6], appoints as minister for foreign affairs the Secretary of State for Foreign and Commonwealth Affairs[7], sends and receives ambassadors[8], appoints British consular officers and grants exequaturs to foreign consular officers[9]. It is not possible to give an exhaustive list of the functions of the Crown in international relations, as such a list must include all functions of possible international legal relevance, a category which presumably is never closed.

The constitution, while confiding a monopoly of the control and conduct of international relations to the Crown, requires that the Crown's function in this regard, as in all others, is to be exercised only on the advice of the responsible minister or ministers[10] and, in matters to do with the treaty-making power, the war power and the annexation or cession of territory, in concert with Parliament[11].

Whereas, in general, acts of the Crown are required to be done in strict compliance with certain forms from which there is no power to deviate, the principle does not obtain with full force in relation to acts in the sphere of international relations. Thus war may be initiated by proclamation, by an Order in Council for general reprisals, or informally without any declaration[12]. No special formality, either, is requisite to the annexation of territory[13].

In terms of domestic law an act of the Crown in relation to foreign affairs is an act of state, and is not within the courts' power of review[14]. It is a necessary corollary of the Crown's exclusive power in international relations and of the binding quality of an act of state that the declaration by the Crown as to what it has done or not done within its sphere should be accepted by the courts as conclusive. Such declaration usually takes the form of a certificate on behalf of the Secretary of State for Foreign and Commonwealth Affairs or other minister of the Crown concerned[15], but may also be made orally in open court[16].

1 See 2 Anson's Law and Custom of the Constitution (4th Edn) Pt II, 131. As to the illegality of unauthorised dealings with foreign states see *R v Earl of Danby* (1685) 2 Show 335.
2 As to the position, in international law generally and from the point of view of English law, of a foreign head of state see PARA 263 et seq.
3 As to the war power see CONSTITUTIONAL LAW AND HUMAN RIGHTS vol 8(2) (Reissue) PARA 809 et seq; WAR AND ARMED CONFLICT vol 49(1) (2005 Reissue) PARA 406 et seq.
4 See PARA 71 et seq.
5 See PARA 115 et seq.
6 See PARA 41 et seq.
7 As to the Secretary of State for Foreign and Commonwealth Affairs see PARA 29; and CONSTITUTIONAL LAW AND HUMAN RIGHTS vol 8(2) (Reissue) PARA 459 et seq.
8 See PARA 31.
9 See PARA 30.
10 See CONSTITUTIONAL LAW AND HUMAN RIGHTS vol 8(2) (Reissue) PARA 801.
11 See PARAS 71 et seq, 115 et seq, and CONSTITUTIONAL LAW AND HUMAN RIGHTS vol 8(2) (Reissue) PARA 801 et seq.
12 See *The Ionian Ships* (1855) 2 Ecc & Ad 212, 1 BILC 635; 6 British Digest 106–108. See also WAR AND ARMED CONFLICT vol 49(1) (2005 Reissue) PARA 406 et seq.

13 *Re Southern Rhodesia* [1919] AC 211 at 239, 1 BILC 644, PC. As to the principal forms employed in the exercise of the Crown's powers in international relations, ie Order in Council, proclamation, letters patent, other documents (eg instruments of ratification) under the Great Seal and documents under the sign manual, and as to choice of form, see 7 British Digest 19–25. See also CONSTITUTIONAL LAW AND HUMAN RIGHTS vol 8(2) (Reissue) PARA 906 et seq.

14 *Salaman v Secretary of State for India* [1906] 1 KB 613, 1 BILC 594, CA. As to acts of state see PARA 22 et seq.

15 Certification is a fact of state: see PARA 15; and CIVIL PROCEDURE.

16 See the statement as to the limits of territorial waters claimed by the Crown made by the Attorney General in *The Fagernes* [1927] P 311 at 319, 2 BILC 914, CA.

27.   Parliament. In principle, the Crown may exercise the prerogative power to send armed forces into conflict abroad without any Parliamentary discussion or debate, or without Parliamentary consent[1]. In practice, Parliament has very frequently been consulted, or its approbation sought, in cases in which the United Kingdom has become actually involved in war or has resorted to action provocative of war[2].

Equally in practice the treaty-making power of the Crown has to a degree been shared with Parliament, whose co-operation is naturally necessary for the implementation of any treaty calling either for an appropriation of public money or a change in domestic law[3]. The approbation or approval of Parliament is thus sometimes stipulated for in treaties[4], just as their entry into operation may be made dependent on the procuring of legislation[5]. The thesis that the Crown may not fetter its discretion as a member of the legislature by entering, without the concurrence of its partners in the legislative process (the two Houses of Parliament), into any international engagement whatsoever with respect to any matter capable of being legislated upon, although it has been advanced, is not acceptable[6]. Nor is a narrower rule that the Crown may not contract internationally in relation to any matter with respect to which Parliament has already legislated necessarily any more acceptable[7]. In any event the power of the Crown to conclude treaties of peace independently of Parliament has always been conceded[8].

1 See PARA 26; and cf 2 Anson's Law and Custom of the Constitution (4th Edn) Pt II, 136–137. See also CONSTITUTIONAL LAW AND HUMAN RIGHTS vol 8(2) (Reissue) PARA 809 et seq; WAR AND ARMED CONFLICT vol 49(1) (2005 Reissue) PARA 406 et seq. See also the MoJ, MoD and FCO Consultation Paper *The Governance of Britain: War powers and treaties: Limiting Executive powers* (CP26/07), para 35.

2 See the MoJ, MoD and FCO Consultation Paper *The Governance of Britain: War powers and treaties: Limiting Executive powers* (CP26/07), para 35.

3 See the MoJ, MoD and FCO Consultation Paper *The Governance of Britain: War powers and treaties: Limiting Executive powers* (CP26/07), Pt 2.

4 See eg the Treaty of Commerce and Navigation with Portugal (Lisbon, 12 August 1914; TS 6 (1916); Cd 8402), in which additional art 17 stipulated that the treaty would not come into force until the sanction of the British Parliament for art 6 (relating to the imposition of criminal penalties upon the importation and sale as 'Port' or 'Madeira' of wine not produced in Portugal or Madeira) had been obtained.

5 See eg Convention with Prussia for the Mutual Surrender of Criminals (London, 5 March 1864; 54 BFSP 16), which failed to come into operation for lack of statutory approval and was terminated by Protocol (London, 14 May 1872; 62 BFSP 15; C 564).

6 However, no treaty which provides for any increase in the powers of the European Parliament may be ratified by the United Kingdom unless it has been approved by an Act of Parliament: European Parliamentary Elections Act 2002 s 12(1). For this purpose, 'treaty' includes any international agreement, and any protocol or annex to a treaty or international agreement: European Parliamentary Elections Act 2002 s 12(2).

7 See 7 British Digest 52.

8   See generally 7 British Digest 39 et seq. As to whether the Crown's power to conclude treaties of
     peace comprehends power to implement their stipulations domestically see *Walker v Baird*
     [1892] AC 491, 6 BILC 465, PC.

28.   Treaties of cession.   The suggestion that a treaty for the cession of
territory requires the approbation of Parliament may have more substance. The
question in fact is one which goes beyond the scope of the treaty-making power
and involves a consideration of the Crown's power to cede territory whether by
treaty or other means. The limitation, if it exists, applies only in time of peace,
the power of the Crown alone to terminate a war upon any terms whatsoever, by
treaty or otherwise, not being touched upon by the doctrine involved. That
doctrine has been the subject of parliamentary discussion and official
examination on several occasions, the last being, apparently, that of the cession
of Heligoland to Germany in 1890, when statutory indorsement was obtained[1].
This precedent has been followed ever since[2], so that the doctrine would appear
to be established[3]. With a short interval, it has been the practice for the executive
government since 1924 to lay treaties which are subject to ratification before
Parliament before their final conclusion to secure publicity and afford
opportunity for discussion[4]. For more than a century it has been usual to present
treaties to Parliament after conclusion; and the texts so presented are, since
1892, published in the Treaty Series[5].

1   See the Anglo-German Agreement Act 1890 s 1; and see *Damodhar Gordhan v Deoram Kanji*
     (1876) 1 App Cas 332, 2 BILC 604, PC; Forsyth's Cases and Opinions on Constitutional Law
     185; and the survey of practice in 7 British Digest 53–82.
2   See the Anglo-French Convention Act 1904 s 1; the Anglo-Italian Treaty (East African
     Territories) Act 1925; the Straits Settlements and Johore Territorial Waters (Agreement)
     Act 1928; the Dindings Agreement (Approval) Act 1934; and the Anglo-Venezuelan Treaty
     (Island of Patos) Act 1942 s 1.
3   The creation of a new dominion or state, whether or not within the Commonwealth, upon
     territory subject to the sovereignty of the Crown exercised through the government of the
     United Kingdom, and equally the transfer of additional territory to any such dominion or state,
     has similarly been effected by statute. See the Irish Free State (Agreement) Act 1922; the Indian
     Independence Act 1947; the Burma Independence Act 1947; the Ireland Act 1949; the numerous
     later independence Acts; the Cocos Islands Act 1955; and the Christmas Island Act 1958.
4   As to this, the so-called 'Ponsonby rule', see the MoJ, MoD and FCO Consultation Paper *The
     Governance of Britain: War powers and treaties: Limiting Executive powers* (CP26/07),
     para 120 et seq.
5   Treaties and conventions are cited in this title with references to the place where and date when
     they were entered into, and to the appropriate Treaty Series and Command Papers, e g the
     Vienna Convention on Consular Relations (Vienna, 24 April 1963; TS 14 (1973); Cmnd 5219),
     was done at Vienna on 24 April 1963, and the text is to be found in Treaty Series No 14 of 1973
     and in Command Paper No 5219. Upon being presented to Parliament a text may be published
     in the Miscellaneous Series (cited as e g Misc 19 (1975)).

29.   The Secretary of State and other persons who may represent the state.   In
any English enactment, 'Secretary of State' means one of Her Majesty's principal
secretaries of state[1]. The minister of the United Kingdom concerned with
international relations is generally the Secretary of State for Foreign and
Commonwealth Affairs[2]. Under international law other persons may represent
the state in specific fields[3].

1   See the Interpretation Act 1978 s 5, Sch 1. As to the office of Secretary of State see
     CONSTITUTIONAL LAW AND HUMAN RIGHTS vol 8(2) (Reissue) PARA 355.
2   As to the Secretary of State for Foreign and Commonwealth Affairs see CONSTITUTIONAL LAW
     AND HUMAN RIGHTS vol 8(2) (Reissue) PARAS 459–460. Other ministers, such as the Secretary
     of State for the Home Department, may also have some related responsibilities. As to the
     function in relation to the conduct of international relations of organs of the central government

other than the department of the Secretary of State for Foreign and Commonwealth Affairs see 7 British Digest 219–281. As to the Secretary of State for the Home Department see CONSTITUTIONAL LAW AND HUMAN RIGHTS vol 8(2) (Reissue) PARA 466 et seq.

As to the position of the foreign minister of a state in international law generally see the *Arrest Warrant of 11 April 2000 (Democratic Republic of the Congo v Belgium)* ICJ Reports 2002, 3 at 20–25 (paras 51–61); and Watts 'The Legal Position in International Law of Heads of State, Heads of Governments and Foreign Ministers' *Hague Academy of International Law, Receuil des Cours* vol 247 (1994-III).

3   *Armed Activities on the Territory of the Congo (New Application: 2002) (Democratic Republic of the Congo v Rwanda) (Jurisdiction and Admissibility)* ICJ Reports 2006, 6 (paras 45–48).

30. Consular officers. Consular officers are generally members of the Diplomatic Service; there are also non-career or 'honorary' consular officers[1]. Some of a consular officer's duties are derived from statute; others are non-statutory[2]. His statutory duties include the administration of oaths and the performance of any notarial act which a notary public can do within the United Kingdom[3]. He has functions in connection with shipping, seamen and kindred matters[4]; offences on board British aircraft[5]; passports, visas and similar documents[6]; marriages and civil partnerships abroad[7]; births and deaths abroad[8]; and the registration of children and young persons employed abroad[9].

A consular officer may advise and assist British nationals trading in, residing in and visiting his district; this may include the relief and repatriation of distressed British nationals. The fees which may be charged by a consular officer are regulated by Order in Council[10]. The appointment of a consular officer may be given definitive recognition by the foreign government concerned by the issue of an exequatur or other authorisation.

1   In statutes, 'consular officer' means any person, including the head of a consular post, entrusted in that capacity with the exercise of consular functions; 'consular post' means any consulate-general, consulate, vice-consulate or consular agency; and 'head of consular post' means the person charged with the duty of acting in that capacity: Vienna Convention on Consular Relations (Vienna, 24 April 1963; TS 14 (1973); Cmnd 5219) art 1(1) (set out in the Consular Relations Act 1968 s 1, Sch 1); Interpretation Act 1978 s 5, Sch 1. Pro-consuls are not consular officers and are given that title to enable them to perform notarial functions. As to consular functions see the Vienna Convention on Consular Relations art 5: see PARA 290 et seq. As to diplomatic and consular officers acting as notaries see LEGAL PROFESSIONS vol 66 (2009) PARA 1417.
2   See PARA 292.
3   See the Commissioners for Oaths Act 1889 s 6(1) (amended by the Commissioners for Oaths Act 1891 s 2). Every British ambassador, envoy, minister, chargé d'affaires and secretary of an embassy or legation in a foreign country also has these powers. See further CIVIL PROCEDURE. In English statutes, 'United Kingdom' means Great Britain and Northern Ireland (Interpretation Act 1978 s 5, Sch 1); and 'Great Britain' means England, Scotland and Wales (Union with Scotland Act 1706, preamble art I; Interpretation Act 1978 s 22(1), Sch 2 para 5(a)). Neither the Isle of Man nor the Channel Islands are within the United Kingdom. See further CONSTITUTIONAL LAW AND HUMAN RIGHTS.
4   See eg his powers for enforcement in relation to United Kingdom ships under the Merchant Shipping Act 1995 s 257 (see SHIPPING AND MARITIME LAW vol 93 (2008) PARA 47).
5   See eg his functions under the Civil Aviation Act 1982 s 95 in relation to offences on aircraft; and AIR LAW vol 2 (2008) PARA 618.
6   As to passports see BRITISH NATIONALITY, IMMIGRATION AND ASYLUM vol 4(2) (2002 Reissue) PARA 78.
7   See the Foreign Marriage Act 1892; the Foreign Marriage Act 1947; and CONFLICT OF LAWS vol 8(3) (Reissue) PARA 214 et seq. As to the registration of civil partnerships abroad in the presence of a prescribed officer of the Diplomatic Service see the Civil Partnerships Act 2004 s 210, the Civil Partnership (Registration Abroad and Certificates) Order 2005, SI 2005/2761; and MATRIMONIAL AND CIVIL PARTNERSHIP LAW vol 72 (2009) PARAS 145–146.
8   See the Registration of Overseas Births and Deaths Regulations 1982, SI 1982/1123; the Registration (Entries of Overseas Births and Deaths) Order 1982, SI 1982/1526; and REGISTRATION CONCERNING THE INDIVIDUAL vol 39(2) (Reissue) PARA 578 et seq.

9　See the Children and Young Persons Act 1933 ss 25, 26 (both as amended); and CHILDREN AND YOUNG PERSONS vol 5(4) (2008 Reissue) PARA 776 et seq.

10　See the Consular Fees Act 1980 s 1 (amended by the Identity Cards Act 2006 s 36); the Consular Fees Regulations 1981, SI 1981/476 (amended by SI 2000/1017); the Consular Fees Order 2009, SI 2009/700 (amended by SI 2009/1745). See also the Asylum and Immigration (Treatment of Claimants, etc) Act 2004 s 42(3)–(8) (and BRITISH NATIONALITY, IMMIGRATION AND ASYLUM vol 4(2) (2002 Reissue) PARA 6); the Consular Fees Act 1980 (Fees) Order 2000, SI 2000/3353; the Consular Fees Act 1980 (Fees) Order 2002, SI 2002/1618; the Consular Fees Act 1980 (Fees) Order 2005, SI 2005/2112; and the Consular Fees Act 1980 (Fees) (No 2) Order 2005, SI 2005/3198.

31.　Ambassadors and other diplomatic agents. British ambassadors[1] and other diplomatic agents[2] accredited by the Crown in the United Kingdom[3] to other states are a means by which the political relations of the United Kingdom with those states are carried on[4]. In addition to the general duty of diplomatic agents to represent the United Kingdom politically, they are entrusted with certain powers and functions by statute[5].

1　An ambassador is the head of the mission; in certain cases a diplomatic agent of a lower rank, such as a minister, is the head of mission. As to the meaning of 'head of mission' see the Vienna Convention on Diplomatic Relations (Vienna, 18 April 1961; TS 19 (1965); Cmnd 2565) art 1(a). As to the classes of heads of mission see art 14 para 1; and PARA 267.

2　As to the meaning of 'members of the diplomatic staff' see the Vienna Convention on Diplomatic Relations art 1(d); and PARA 269 note 2. As to the meaning of 'diplomatic agent' see art 1(e); and PARA 273 note 1.

3　For the forms of letters of credence, or credentials, used in the United Kingdom see Satow's Diplomatic Practice (6th Edn, 2009) pp 61–62. It is the letter of credence which establishes the right to act in a diplomatic capacity. Generally, the head of mission is considered to have taken up his function in the receiving state when he has presented his credentials to the head of that state: Vienna Convention on Diplomatic Relations art 13 para 1.

4　As to the functions of a diplomatic mission see the Vienna Convention on Diplomatic Relations art 3 para 1; and PARA 266.

5　For the powers in respect of the administration of oaths and notarial acts see the Commissioners for Oaths Act 1889 s 6(1) which is extended with respect to United Kingdom diplomatic representatives in Commonwealth countries by the Consular Relations Act 1968 s 10(3): see further see LEGAL PROFESSIONS vol 66 (2009) PARA 1417; and CIVIL PROCEDURE. As to the performance of marriages in United Kingdom embassies under the Foreign Marriage Acts 1892 to 1947 see CONFLICT OF LAWS vol 8(3) (Reissue) PARA 214 et seq. As to the registration of civil partnerships abroad in the presence of a prescribed officer of the Diplomatic Service, see the Civil Partnerships Act 2004 s 210, the Civil Partnership (Registration Abroad and Certificates) Order 2005, SI 2005/2761; and MATRIMONIAL AND CIVIL PARTNERSHIP LAW vol 72 (2009) PARAS 145–146.

5. SUBJECTS OF INTERNATIONAL LAW

(1) INTERNATIONAL LEGAL PERSONALITY

32. International personality: states. The notion of 'international personality' denotes only that an entity with personality has some rights and duties in international law. The principal category of personality in international law is that of statehood[1]. As a foundational element of the international legal system, statehood originally was a matter of fact but is now well-established to be a matter of law both as to the criteria of statehood and the consequences of being a state[2]. It is also the case that there are a number of circumstances in which the law precludes the acquisition of statehood to entities, otherwise qualified, which have been created by means unlawful in international law or which assert a system of government illegal in international law[3]. States are territorial entities, the governments of which exercise effective control of the population of the territory and which are legally capable of entering into legal relations with other states, that is to say, are independent of any other state[4]. Such states enjoy the status of sovereign equality within the international legal system and are entitled to have their internal independence respected by other states[5]. States are bound by customary international law (in the creation and modification of which they have an equal right to participate) and they may enter into treaty relations with other states and other international persons with treaty-making capacity which create binding obligations for the parties[6].

1   See James Crawford *The Creation of States in International Law* (2nd ed 2006) Ch 2.
2   See James Crawford *The Creation of States in International Law* (2nd ed 2006) pp 40–43.
3   See James Crawford *The Creation of States in International Law* (2nd ed 2006) pp 157–175.
4   See the Pan-American Convention on the Rights and Duties of States (the 'Montevideo Convention') (Montevideo, 26 December 1933; 165 LoNTS 19; 28 AJIL (Supp) 75) art 1.
5   See the Declaration on Principles of International Law concerning Friendly Relations and Co-operation among States in Accordance with the Charter of the United Nations, principle 1, General Assembly Resolution 2625 (XXV) of 24 October 1970.
6   See PARA 56 et seq.

33. Statehood and recognition. The statehood of the earliest states which created the international system was a matter of fact, which those involved accepted of each other[1]. The acquisition of statehood subsequently was sometimes equally a matter of tacit acceptance, where the new states came into existence by a process of peaceful constitutional evolution[2]. However, more generally, and particularly where there was some dispute about the emergence of a new state, as might be the case where there was a forcible secession of part of an established state for example, the status of any entity claiming to be a state might be recognised by other states. Although there is great doctrinal difference about the nature of the recognition decision, the preferred view is that recognition is declaratory of the status of the new state, which must possess the criteria of statehood to be lawfully recognised[3]. In the absence of some specific mechanism for determining statehood in a particular case[4], it is for each state to determine whether or not an entity claiming to be a state satisfies the criteria of statehood. Recognition, then, is not a criterion of statehood but the exercise of an individual discretionary power by a state, indicating that it accepts that the recognised entity satisfies the conditions for statehood and that it intends to deal with the new state according to the rules of international law. If its assessment of the satisfaction of any of the criteria of statehood is without foundation, any dealings with that entity as a state will violate the rights of the existing sovereign[5]. States are not obliged to recognise entities which they regard as being states, nor must they have or maintain diplomatic relations with their governments[6]. Recognition, then, may bind the state in the manner of an estoppel and it is not free to withdraw its recognition unless there is a change in the circumstances which formed the basis for the act of recognition.

The United Kingdom recognises states which satisfy the criteria of statehood. In United Kingdom law, the courts will take judicial notice of the status of established states, but in contested cases statehood is to be proved by evidence[7]. The decisions to recognise states and to establish diplomatic relations and to have other dealings with their governments fall within the foreign affairs prerogative of the Crown[8]. In some cases involving the construction of contracts or other documents of private law, the courts will decide for themselves whether an entity is a 'state' or 'country' for the purposes of the document but these decisions have no implications for the international legal status of the body concerned[9].

1   Cf the doctrine of acquisition of territory by historic title as applied in the *Minquiers and Ecrehos Case (France/United Kingdom)* ICJ Reports 1953, 47. See PARA 118.

2   This is the case notably with states of the Commonwealth which have acquired independence of the UK since the Statute of Westminster 1931: see COMMONWEALTH.

3   See PARA 41.

4   Examples of specific mechanisms are the admission to membership of an international organisation, when a decision about whether an entity is a state will be taken by the organs of the organisation (see eg Charter of the United Nations (San Francisco, 26 June 1945; TS 67 (1946); Cmd 7015) art 4 para 1; and PARA 520) or where the matter falls for determination by an international tribunal (see eg Application 25781/94: *Cyprus v Turkey* (2001) 35 EHRR 731, ECtHR (the status of the 'Turkish Republic of Northern Cyprus')).

5   In these circumstances, recognition is described as 'premature' or 'precipitate': see eg the recognition of Bangladesh by India in December 1971, when the territory of East Pakistan was still under the control of the government of Pakistan. The existing state is protected by the principle of territorial integrity: see the Declaration on Principles of International Law concerning Friendly Relations and Co-operation among States in Accordance with the Charter of the United Nations, principle 6, General Assembly Resolution 2625 (XXV) of 24 October 1970. More recently, Serbia has complained that states which have recognised Kosovo have done so in violation of Serbia's rights: see 476 HC Official Reports (6th series), 22 May 2008, col *518W*.

6   However, it appears that the Democratic People's Republic of Korea was a state from 1953, although it was not recognised by the UK until it was admitted to the UN in 1991. For the dates at which the various successor state to the Socialist Federal Republic of Yugoslavia became states see the Arbitration Commission of the European Conference on Yugoslavia (the 'Badinter Commission'), opinion 8 (1992) 92 ILR 188.

7   Now the presentation of an Executive Certificate from the Foreign Secretary establishes conclusively whether or not HMG recognises the entity as a state: see *Aksionairnoye Obschestvo AM Luther v James Sagor & Co* [1921] 1 KB 456, 2 BILC 85; revsd after recognition [1921] 3 KB 532, [1921] All ER Rep 138, 2 BILC 97, CA. See also *Caglar v Billingham (Inspector of Taxes)* [1996] STC (SCD) 150.

8   See FOREIGN RELATIONS LAW vol 18(2) (Reissue) PARA 606.

9   See PARA 49.

34.   Factors precluding statehood as a matter of international law. In some cases, international law precludes an entity which appears to possess the characteristics of statehood from becoming a state[1]. These instances fall into two overlapping categories: either the criteria of statehood have been established in a way which breaches a fundamental rule of international law[2], or the creation of a new state would be a breach of a fundamental rule of international law[3]. The reason for the disability may be that the rule is a peremptory norm or that the consequence that statehood may not be achieved is part of customary international law[4]. It follows that states may not recognise any such entity as a state. In many cases this obligation results most clearly from a binding decision of the Security Council[5].

1   See generally James Crawford *The Creation of States in International Law* (2nd ed 2006) Ch 3.
2   Eg the forcible exclusion of the existing sovereign: see 'Turkish Republic of Northern Cyprus', HMG MOU (2008) 79 BYIL 622–624; Abkhazia and South Ossetia (2008) 79 BYIL 615–616.
3   Eg the law on self-determination (see the Security Council resolution on Southern Rhodesia: Security Council Resolution 217 of 20 November 1965); or the prohibition of apartheid (see the Security Council resolutions on the South African 'homelands': Security Council Resolutions 402 of 22 December 1976, 417 of 31 October 1977; and see also *Gur Corpn v Trust Bank of Africa Ltd* [1987] QB 599, [1986] 3 All ER 449, CA).
4   As to peremptory norms of international law see PARA 11.
5   In addition to the examples cited in note 3, see the Security Council resolutions on: South Africa's continued presence in South West Africa after the termination of the Mandate (Security Council Resolution 276 of 30 January 1970); the 'Turkish Republic of Northern Cyrpus' (Security Council Resolution 541 of 18 November 1983); and the incorporation of the territory of Kuwait into Iraq (Security Council Resolution 662 of 9 August 1990).

35.   Types of states. It is a central tenet of the internal independence of a state that its constitution and internal organisation are exclusively matters of domestic concern. There is thus no distinction in general international law between, for example, monarchy and republic or democracy and autocracy. However, states may undertake international obligations which have consequences for their domestic political and economic arrangements, particularly by becoming members of certain international organisations which may stipulate conditions for membership[1]. The distinctions drawn in older textbooks between real and personal unions have little relevance today. The difference between unitary and non-unitary states does have some international legal consequences. Although in principle a treaty is binding upon a state with respect to the whole of its territory[2], territorial application clauses of various sorts permitting contracting in or out with respect to constituent parts of a federal entity or with respect to overseas or colonial territories have long been familiar[3].

Various entities which are not states in the sense of international law are nevertheless designated 'states' as constituent parts of the United States, the Commonwealth of Australia, India and the Federal Republic of Germany. This nomenclature has, of course, no effect upon their status, or rather lack of status, in international law but the constituent states of some federal states do have a degree of international capacity and foreign states may be willing to deal with them to a limited extent, for instance, concluding treaties with them or admitting them to international organisations. However, acts or omissions of federal units in violation of the obligations of the federal state will generate international responsibility, regardless of any constitutional infirmity of the federal government to act[4] but some treaties contain 'federal clauses' which take into account problems federal states might have in implementing treaty obligations[5]. Concessions of this sort have been historically significant steps on the road to ultimate independent statehood, particularly in the case of members of the Commonwealth. The grant of original membership of the United Nations to Byelorussia and the Ukraine, which were then merely two of the constituent republics of the Soviet Union, itself also a member, was an anomaly. States may choose to treat entities which do not or only doubtfully satisfy the criteria of statehood as states, so long as doing so does not prejudice the rights of another state, and relations between the two may be governed by international law but these special arrangements have no necessary implications for other states[6].

1 Eg membership of the Council of Europe requires that states respect the rule of law and human rights: see the Statute of the Council of Europe (London, 5 May 1949; TS 51 (1949); Cmd 7778) art 3.

2 See eg the Vienna Convention of the Law of Treaties (Vienna, 23 May 1969; TS 58 (1980); Cmnd 7964) art 29; and PARA 94.

3 See eg the Convention for the Protection of Human Rights and Fundamental Freedoms (Rome, 4 November 1950; TS 71 (1953); Cmd 8969) art 56 para 3.

4 See *LaGrand (Germany v United States of America)* ICJ Reports 2001, 466 at 495 (para 81).

5 See eg the UNESCO Convention for the Protection of the World Cultural and Natural Heritage (Cmnd 9424) (1972) art 34.

6 This may explain the position of the Holy See, which has long been regarded as possessing international personality. The position of the Holy See was to some extent clarified in the Treaty, Concordat and Financial Convention between Italy and the Holy See (the Lateran Treaty) (Rome, 11 February 1929), which created the Vatican state, withdrawn from the territory of Italy and thus constituting a territorial basis for the statehood of the Holy See: see 23 American Journal of International Law (1929) Supp 187. The Holy See, eo nomine, maintains diplomatic relations with some states. The United Kingdom re-established diplomatic relations with the Holy See in 1914, and since 1982 its representative has the rank of ambassador. The Holy See is now represented in the UK by an apostolic nuncio. The Holy See has entered into treaties with other states, including some which have been concluded under the auspices of the United Nations, for example, the Vienna Convention on Diplomatic Relations (Vienna, 18 April 1961; TS 19 (1965); Cmnd 2565).

36.   International organisations. International organisations which have states as members are almost always founded on a constituent treaty, which establishes the purpose of the organisation, the conditions for membership and the organisational structure by which its purposes will be realised[1]. The treaty will govern relations between members and the organisation and it may provide that certain decisions will be binding on the members[2], though, in the main, organisations are restricted to making recommendations to their members. There are many international organisations, some with very wide membership, some with only a few members, and with a wide range of functions, from the great political, economic and social ambitions of the United Nations to the precise functional objectives of, for example, International Maritime Organisation[3]. That they may have an international personality separate from that of their members was confirmed by the International Court of Justice[4]. When they are based on treaty, international organisations have no automatic rights with respect to non-members[5] although, in fact, non-member states seem to be prepared to accept the legal existence of international organisations and deal with them as necessary. International customary law allows certain rights and powers to international organisations, notably the capacity to enter into treaties and otherwise participate in international law-making, to enjoy international immunities and to make international claims and bear international responsibility. Although the terms of an organisation's basic treaty will generally prevail, it is not too much to speak of a 'law of international organisations' in addition to each treaty's particularities[6]. It may require specific legislation to provide for the personality of international organisations in domestic law and to assure the implementation of their rights under international law[7].

1 See PARA 517 et seq.

2 See eg the Charter of the United Nations (San Francisco, 26 June 1945; TS 67 (1946); Cmd 7015) arts 25, 27; and PARA 523.

3 As to the International Maritime Organisation see SHIPPING AND MARITIME LAW vol 93 (2008) PARA 13.

4 See the *Reparation for Injuries Suffered in the Service of the United Nations (Advisory Opinion)* ICJ Reports 1949, 174.

5   However the International Court of Justice was prepared to concede the 'objective' personality of the United Nations: see the *Reparation for Injuries Suffered in the Service of the United Nations (Advisory Opinion)* ICJ Reports 1949, 174 at 185.

6   See PARA 517 et seq.

7   For example, in the UK, see the International Organisations Act 1968; the International Organisations Act 2005; and PARA 307 et seq.

37. Individuals. For many years, there were serious doubts about whether individuals could have international personality. They were treated as 'objects' of international legal rules and the vindication of their interests was in the hands of their national states through the mechanism of diplomatic protection. It was the states which were the subjects of the relevant rules. This position, which still retains its importance[1], has been modified in a number of ways. Principally, this has been through the development of the law of human rights but whether or not an individual has rights under the customary law of human rights is not clear[2]. In the main, an individual depends upon the participation of the state within the jurisdiction of which he finds himself to be a party to an international human rights treaty, which itself provides a mechanism by which the person may takes towards vindicating his rights[3]. Otherwise, it will be necessary for him to rely on the domestic implementation of the international human rights obligations, when his rights will be rights in national law rather than international law[4]. Recently, the International Court of Justice has said that, where states use clear language, they may confer rights on individuals in international law in fields other than human rights, though in the particular case, the protection of those rights at the international level would still depend upon the national state[5]. In addition to rights, individuals have duties in international law, which will impose upon them international criminal liability in the event of their violation. Increasingly, the possibility arises that prosecution for breaches of international criminal law may take place before international criminal tribunals[6]. It is important to appreciate that there is no category of personality of 'individuals' in international law and in each case, it will be necessary to identify the source of the rules of law which provide rights or impose duties on this particular person.

1   See the Articles on Diplomatic Protection, arts 34–50, Report of the International Law Commission, 58th Session (2006), A/61/10, ch IV; and as to diplomatic protection see PARA 385 et seq.

2   See CONSTITUTIONAL LAW AND HUMAN RIGHTS.

3   See e g the Convention for the Protection of Human Rights and Fundamental Freedoms (Rome, 4 November 1950; TS 71 (1953); Cmd 8969) art 34 (individual access to the European Court of Human Rights); and CONSTITUTIONAL LAW AND HUMAN RIGHTS. Participation by individuals in human rights procedures is sometimes by direct complaint to the UN Human Rights Committee under the optional protocol, and is not always by way of a judicial procedure: see the International Covenant on Civil and Political Rights (New York, 16 December 1966; ratified by the United Kingdom 20 May 1976; TS 6 (1977): Cmnd 6702), (First) Optional Protocol.

4   See e g for the UK, the Human Rights Act 1998; and CONSTITUTIONAL LAW AND HUMAN RIGHTS.

5   See *LaGrand (Germany v United States of America)* ICJ Reports 2001, 466 at 494 (para 77).

6   See PARA 421 et seq.

38. Other international persons. The categories of international person are not closed. Developments in the law have established the status of 'peoples' entitled to self-determination[1] and, arguably, to indigenous peoples[2] and minorities[3]. Equally, ad hoc personality, where an entity is treated as having certain rights and duties in international law without falling into the established classes of personality, is not uncommon. Entities like Taiwan, which do not seek independent statehood, may, nonetheless, be dealt with in some respects by some states as having some international rights[4]. In the nature of things, it is impossible to deal comprehensively with these ad hoc legal persons.

1   See the Declaration on the Granting of Independence to Colonial Countries and Peoples, General Assembly Resolution 1514 (XV) of 14 December 1960; and *East Timor (Portugal v Australia)* ICJ Reports 1995, 90 (para 29).
2   See the Declaration on the Rights of Indigenous Peoples, arts 1, 3, General Assembly Resolution 61/295 on 13 September 2007.
3   Human rights instruments protect individual members of minorities rather than minority groups themselves: see the International Covenant on Civil and Political Rights (New York, 16 December 1966; ratified by the United Kingdom 20 May 1976; TS 6 (1977): Cmnd 6702) art 27.
4   Taiwan is a member of several international organisations, including the World Trade Organisation.

(2) STATES AND GOVERNMENTS

(i) Recognition

A. IN GENERAL

39.   Recognition and United Kingdom domestic law.   Recognition of states and governments is the most important use of the recognition power, although the United Kingdom's policy is no longer to recognise governments[1]. In addition to its consequences in international law[2] recognition also has important effects in domestic law; notably that only recognised states and authorities with which the British government has government-to-government dealings may bring actions in UK courts and be entitled to state immunity[3]. Equally, subject to some exceptions, the English courts, when so directed by the English conflict of laws, will take cognisance of the laws and decrees only of recognised states or of authorities with which the British government has government-to-government dealings[4].

1   As to the recognition power in the United Kingdom see PARA 45.
2   See PARA 41 et seq.
3   As to state immunity see PARA 242 et seq.
4   In general, this presents few problems: the status of the foreign state will not be contested and, if it is, that matter would be settled by a certificate from the Foreign and Commonwealth Office saying whether or not the British government had recognised the state: see eg *Gur Corpn v Trust Bank of Africa Ltd* [1987] QB 599, [1986] 3 All ER 449, CA) (Ciskei); and PARAS 15, 43. If the case is concerned with the status of a foreign government, again there will be no difficulties about settled governments. Where the status of a government is contested, evidence, possibly in the form of a certificate from the FCO, may be obtained with the object of establishing whether or not the British government has government-to-government dealings with the foreign authorities: see eg *Aksionairnoye Obschestvo AM Luther v James Sagor & Co* [1921] 3 KB 532, [1921] All ER Rep 138 (Soviet government of USSR); *Republic of Somalia v Woodhouse, Drake and Carey (Suisse) SA, The Mary* [1993] QB 54, [1993] 1 All ER 371 (government of Somalia); and PARAS 15, 45.

40.   The exercise of the recognition power of the United Kingdom.   In English law, recognition of states[1], the institution of diplomatic relations and the establishment of government-to-government dealings[2] are for the Executive in the exercise of the prerogative on foreign affairs[3]. The fact of recognition of statehood and the measure of government-to-government dealings are communicated to the courts by the government by executive certificate[4], conclusively on the matter of recognition of states, of great weight on the assessment of the dealings with a foreign authority[5].

1   For example, the recognition of Kosovo as a state was announced by the Prime Minister on
     18 February 2008: see (2008) 79 BYIL. 604.
2   The government sometimes makes it clear that it does not regard its dealings with a foreign
     entity as amounting to government-to-government activity: see eg (2006) 79 BYIL 618.
3   See FOREIGN RELATIONS LAW vol 18(2) (Reissue) PARA 606.
4   See *Aksionairnoye Obschestvo AM Luther v James Sagor & Co* [1921] 3 KB 532, [1921] All ER
     Rep 138.
5   See *Republic of Somalia v Woodhouse, Drake and Carey (Suisse) SA, The Mary* [1993] QB 54,
     [1993] 1 All ER 371.

41.   Recognition in international law.   Recognition in international law
concerns several different factual situations which call for reactions from states.
These include: (1) the appearance of new states; (2) unconstitutional changes of
governments; (3) territorial changes[1]; and (4) the existence of belligerent parties
to a civil war[2]. The following paragraphs are concerned only with recognition of
new states and how the United Kingdom government deals with new
governments[3].

1   As to recognition of territorial changes see Oppenheim's International Law (9th Edn) pp
     187–197.
2   As to recognition of belligerency and insurgency see Oppenheim's International Law (9th Edn)
     pp 165–169; and *WJ Tatem Ltd v Gamboa* [1939] 1 KB 132, [1938] 2 All ER 135.
3   See PARA 42 et seq.

42.   Methods of recognition.   Recognition of a state can be express or implied.
Express recognition takes place by a formal notification or declaration
announcing the intention of recognition, such as a note addressed to the state
which is to be recognised. Implied recognition takes place by means of an act
which leaves no doubt as to the intention to grant it[1] but which does not refer
expressly to recognition. There are very few acts from which recognition of a
state may be implied, and the formal exchange of diplomatic representatives is
the only unequivocal example[2]. The words of a state denying an intention to
recognise will ordinarily be sufficient to prevent an implication of recognition.
Because bilateral treaties may be entered into with non-state international
persons, recognition of statehood may not necessarily be implied from this kind
of relationship[3]. Nor is recognition necessarily implied from participation with
the unrecognised state in an international conference[4], in the conclusion of a
multilateral treaty to which that state is a party[5], in the retention of diplomatic
representatives in the foreign state for a period after a revolutionary change of
government, or from the admission of the unrecognised state to an international
organisation. However, the United Kingdom accepts that the act of voting for the
admission of a new Member to the UN amounts to recognition of the statehood
of the applicant[6]. Recognition must be distinguished from entering into
diplomatic relations; a state will remain recognised though diplomatic relations
have not been established with it, or have been broken off[7].

1   A formal statement that conduct is not to be taken as amounting to recognition is sometimes
     made, as when the United Kingdom stated that documents concerning the partition of Vietnam
     in 1954 did not involve United Kingdom recognition of North Vietnam: see Vietnam and the
     Geneva Agreements 1956 (London, 30 March to 8 May 1956; Vietnam No 2 (1956);
     Cmd 9763). A similar provision in respect of the government of Taiwan appears in the
     Agreement for the Regulation of the Production and Marketing of Sugar (London, 16 to
     31 October 1953; TS 28 (1956); Cmd 9815). Sometimes the United Kingdom government
     makes it clear that it does not regard its dealings with a foreign entity as
     government-to-government activity from which recognition might be implied: see eg 683 HL
     Official Reports (5th series), 14 June 2006, col 212.

2   In the past, however, the United Kingdom government has received agents representing regimes
     before recognition was accorded. As to reception of agents from the confederate states during
     the American Civil War see 1 Moore's Digest 209; and as to the exchange of agents with the
     Spanish nationalist authorities see 334 HC Official Report (5th series), 4 April 1938, col 4. The
     existence of consular relations does not necessarily imply recognition. The United Kingdom
     government maintained a consul in Taiwan (Formosa) for some years after 1950, although it did
     not recognise the government of the whole of China (which is what it claimed to be) or that
     there was a new state of Taiwan on that island: 695 HC Official Report (5th series), 15 May
     1964, cols 836–837; 696 HC Official Report (5th series), 15 June 1964, col 908. Possibly the
     issue by this country of an exequatur to a consular representative of a foreign state might be
     taken as implying recognition of the government of that state: 1 Oppenheim's International Law
     (9th Edn) p 171.

3   If the agreement is for a limited purpose, recognition will not always be implied. This was the
     case with the Agreement between the governments of Great Britain and Russia for the Exchange
     of Prisoners of War (12 February 1920; 1 Lo N TS 264; Cmd 587). In November 1920, the
     English court was informed that 'His Majesty's government have not recognised the Soviet
     government in any way': *Aksionairnoye Obschestvo AM Luther v James Sagor & Co* [1921]
     1 KB 456, 2 BILC 85.

4   Thus the United Kingdom government did not recognise the government of North Vietnam by
     taking part with it in the conference of 1953–54: see note 1.

5   The United Kingdom and the German Democratic Republic were both parties to the Treaty
     banning Nuclear Weapon Tests in the Atmosphere, in Outer Space and under Water (Moscow,
     5 August 1963; TS 3 (1964); Cmnd 2245), although the United Kingdom did not at that time
     recognise that state, nor did it recognise it as a party to the Treaty. See also PARA 46.

6   In 1991, the United Kingdom supported the admission to the United Nations of the Democratic
     People's Republic of Korea and thereby recognised it: 669 HC Official Report (6th series),
     16 October 1991, col 156W.

7   There were no plans to establish diplomatic relations with the Democratic People's Republic of
     Korea: see note 6.

43.   Recognition of new states. In 1980, the government announced a new
policy on the recognition of governments[1] but at the same time, it confirmed its
policy on the recognition of states[2]. The government continues to recognise new
states in accordance with international doctrine[3] and will do so if the entity has,
and seems likely to continue to have, a clearly defined territory with a
population, a government which is able of itself to exercise effective control of
that territory, and independence in its external relations[4]. Satisfaction of the
'Montevideo criteria' is the minimum condition for recognition but the
government may impose other conditions before it will recognise another state[5].
In some cases where the 'Montevideo criteria' are satisfied, there will be
obligations arising under customary international law or because of UN
resolutions which will preclude recognition or which the government will take
into account in determining its policy[6]. Apart from their consequences in
international relations, recognition decisions may have important effects in
domestic law[7].

1   See PARA 45.

2   See note 4.

3   As to the definition of 'state' see the Pan-American Convention on the Rights and Duties of
     States (the 'Montevideo Convention') (Montevideo, 26 December 1933; 165 LoNTS 19; 28
     AJIL (Supp) 75) art 1 (which is reflected in the statement in note 4). See also 1 Oppenheim's
     International Law (9th Edn) pp 130–134.

4   55 HC Official Reports (6th series), 29 February 1984, written answers, col 226; 102 HC
     Official Reports (6th series), 23 October 1986, written answers, col 997; 105 HC Official
     Reports (6th series), 12 November 1986, col 100; 126 HC Official Reports (6th series),
     3 February 1988, cols 958–959; 169 HC Official Reports (6th series), 19 March 1990, written
     answers, cols 449–450.

5   See the EC Guidelines on the Recognition of New states in Eastern Europe and in the Soviet
     Union, 16 December 1991, 62 BYIL 559, which attached further requirements of a political

nature in order to determine whether European Union member states should recognise such new states. These guidelines appear, however, to be geographically limited.

6   For the cases of Rhodesia (from 1965 to 1980), the Turkish Republic of North Cyprus (since 1983) and the former South African homelands (Bophuthatswana, Transkei, Ciskei and Venda), in all of which United Nations resolutions called upon member states not to recognise these entities, see 1 Oppenheim's International Law (9th Edn) pp 187–190. As to non-recognition by the United Kingdom of the Republic of Ciskei see *Gur Corpn v Trust Bank of Africa Ltd* [1987] QB 599, [1986] 3 All ER 449, CA. As to non-recognition of the Turkish Republic of North Cyprus see *Caglar v Billingham (Inspector of Taxes)* [1996] STC (SCD) 150, Special Commissioners of Inland Revenue; and (2008) 79 BYIL 622–624.

7   See PARA 39.

B. DEALINGS WITH NEW GOVERNMENTS

44. When recognition has been required. The question of a formal act of recognition has not normally arisen unless there has been a change in the head of state or two opposing regimes were each claiming to be the government of a state[1]. Recognition has never been required where the change of government has come about by normal constitutional means. Since 1980 it has been the practice of the United Kingdom not to accord formal recognition, either de jure or de facto, to new governments in a recognised state[2].

1   282 HL Official Report (5th series), 27 April 1967, col *610* (Greece). See also 745 HC Official Report (5th series), 25 April 1967, cols *246–247W* (Sierra Leone).

2   See PARA 45.

45. New governments. In 1980, the United Kingdom government announced that, as a matter of policy, it would no longer accord formal recognition to new governments. It would decide the nature of its dealings with regimes which come to power unconstitutionally in the light of its assessment of whether they are able of themselves to exercise effective control of the territory of the state concerned and seem likely to continue to do so[1]. It will be for others, including the courts, to determine the status of an authority claiming to be the government of a foreign state. The question is whether the authority is a government[2]. If a court concludes that an authority is a government, it seems that it will be treated in English law in the same way as a recognised government once was[3].

The application of this policy is not without its difficulties where there is more than one authority contending to be the government of the same territory[4]. The policy does not preclude a statement by the British government that it does not regard an authority as the legitimate government of a state[5].

1   408 HL Official Reports (5th series), 28 April 1980, cols *1121–1122W*; 983 HC Official Reports (5th series), 25 April 1980, cols *277–279W*; and 985 HC Official Reports (5th series), 23 May 1980, col *385W*. This change of policy and practice may constitute an alteration in form rather than substance and if the nature of the dealings amount to treating the regime as the government of the state, that entails the regime being impliedly recognised as such. As to implied recognition see PARA 42. The United Kingdom government continues formally to recognise new states: see PARA 43.

2   See *Republic of Somalia v Woodhouse, Drake and Carey (Suisse) SA* [1993] QB 54, [1993] 1 All ER 371; *Sierra Leone Telecommunications Co Ltd v Barclays Bank plc* [1998] 2 All ER 821. See also *Gur Corpn v Trust Bank of Africa Ltd* [1987] QB 599, [1986] 3 All ER 449, CA, where the foreign state was itself unrecognised. The Foreign and Commonwealth Office will communicate to the courts information about the authority concerned.

3   This is the implication to be drawn from *Republic of Somalia v Woodhouse, Drake and Carey (Suisse) SA* [1993] QB 54, [1993] 1 All ER 371.

4   See *Sierra Leone Telecommunications Co Ltd v Barclays Bank plc* [1998] 2 All ER 821.

5   See 478 HC Official Report (6th series), 23 June 2008, col *42* (per David Milliband, the Secretary of State for Foreign and Commonwealth Affairs: 'We do not ... recognise the Mugabe government as the legitimate representative of the Zimbabwean people.')

46. States which the United Kingdom government has not recognised and governments with which it has no official dealings. If the United Kingdom government has not recognised a foreign state or has no relations on a government-to-government basis with a foreign government it will generally have no official communication with it[1]. Thus, for example, it will not enter into negotiations with it[2], except for limited purposes; it will not send official delegations to visit it[3], nor invite its members on official visits to the United Kingdom[4]. Passports issued by such a government are not acceptable as valid travel documents for visits to this country[5], and its flag will not be recognised[6]. The accession of such a state to a multilateral agreement is not recognised as having the effect of making the state a party to the convention[7], nor is the signature of its representative of such a convention recognised as a valid signature on behalf of that state[8]. Where the unrecognised state claims to be established on part of the territory of a state recognised by the United Kingdom government, treaties which apply to that state confer no rights on the unrecognised state[9]. However, there may be dealings below the diplomatic level with the authorities of an unrecognised state[10].

1   696 HC Official Report (5th series), 15 June 1964, col 908. A consul in a country whose government is not recognised will have communication with the local authorities only. The United Kingdom government does not regard it as appropriate to accept consular officers appointed by authorities with which it has no dealings: 696 HC Official Report (5th series), 15 June 1964, col 908; 723 HC Official Report (5th series), 2 February 1966, col 253W; and 448 HC Official Report (6th Series), 14 July 2006, col 2135W.
2   690 HC Official Report (5th series), 24 February 1964, written answers, cols 24–25.
3   737 HC Official Report (5th series), 1 December 1966, written answers, col 128.
4   750 HC Official Report (5th series), 19 July 1967, col 2116.
5   690 HC Official Report (5th series), 25 February 1964, cols 399–400; 743 HC Official Report (5th series), 4 April 1967, written answers, cols 18–19; *Fifth Report of the Foreign Affairs Committee* (HC Paper 473 (2006–07)) para 96 n 3.
6   728 HC Official Report (5th series), 9 May 1966, written answers, col 12 (flag of North Korea on postage stamp).
7   See Fourth Supplementary List of Ratifications, Accessions, Withdrawals etc for 1962 (Cmnd 1988) p 2, referring to the Convention for the Unification of Certain Rules relating to International Carriage by Air (Warsaw, 12 October 1929; TS 11 (1933); Cmd 4284).
8   See the Protocol for the Further Prolongation of the International Sugar Agreement of 1958 (London, 1 November 1965; TS 28 (1966); Cmnd 3001).
9   688 HL Official Report (6th series), 8 January 2007, col 18W.
10 The UK government has had informal dealings with the authorities in the Turkish Republic of Northern Cyprus: 462 HC Official Report (6th series), 25 June 2007, col 209W; 694 HL Official Report, 25 July 2007, cols 89–90W; and 673 HL Official Report (5th series) 5 July 2005 cols 591–593. As to the differing nature of relations with authorities of a recognised state and relations with an entity not recognised as a state, see 459 HC Official Report (6th Series), 7 March 2007, col 2002W (Somalia and 'Somaliland').

47. Status of states not recognised by the United Kingdom government or governments with which it has no official dealings. A statement by the government of the United Kingdom that it has 'not recognised' an entity as a state is ambiguous and more information is needed to determine the government's position. It may take the view that the entity is not a state[1], or that the entity does have the characteristics of a state but the government chooses not to recognise it[2]. The government's policy may be because it has not taken a position on the claim[3], or it may be because it regards itself as bound not to recognise the entity (even if it has the characteristics of a state) because of a rule of general international law[4] or a decision of the Security Council[5]. More than one rationale may apply to the same case. Whichever of these positions is taken will have consequences for the application of the rules which apply to entities not recognised by the British government.

A foreign state which the United Kingdom government has not recognised or a government with which the United Kingdom government has no dealings on a government-to-government basis has no locus standi in the English courts. Thus it cannot institute an action in the courts[6], nor can it claim sovereign immunity in respect of an action concerning property in which it claims an interest[7]. The English courts will not give effect to the acts of such a state or government, for example contracts made by it or on its behalf will not be enforced[8]; changes of nationality will not be acknowledged[9]; and legislative and governmental acts, such as decrees affecting property situated within the territory of an unrecognised state or within the territory then being administered by such a government[10], affecting or winding up a company incorporated in that state[11], will be disregarded in any action concerning such property or company[12]. The English courts may restrain the acts of a revolutionary government with which the United Kingdom government has no official dealings in this country in order to protect property of a foreign sovereign[13].

These consequences do not follow if the state and its government are regarded by the United Kingdom government as agents of a state which it recognises as having de jure authority over the territory in question[14].

1   Which is to say that it does not fulfil the criteria of statehood: see eg 327 HC Official Reports (6th series), 19 March 1999, col *1463* (Tibet not independent); and as to the criteria for statehood see PARA 32 et seq.

2   Given the United Kingdom's policy of recognising entities which do satisfy the criteria of statehood, instances like this are rare but not recognising North Korea from 1953 until its admission to the UN in 1991 is an example.

3   442 HC Official Report (6th series), 16 February 2006, col *2287W* (Western Sahara 'status undetermined').

4   This includes respecting the territorial integrity of the existing sovereign: see 450 HC Official Reports (6th series), 24 October 2006, col *1776W* (Somaliland).

5   See eg the Security Council resolutions on the South African 'homelands': Security Council Resolutions 402 of 22 December 1976, 417 of 31 October 1977.

6   *City of Berne v Bank of England* (1804) 9 Ves 347, 2 BILC 1. See also *Dolder v Lord Huntingfield* (1805) 11 Ves 283, 2 BILC 1. The same has been held in the United States in *Russian Socialist Federated Soviet Republic v Cibrario* 235 NY 255 (1923).

7   *The Annette, The Dora* [1919] P 105, 2 BILC 76 (leaving open the possibility that such a government in possession of property might be able to claim immunity). The questions are whether, if such a government be sued eo nomine, the action cannot be maintained, upon the ground that it has no existence in the eyes of the English court, and whether, if it can be so sued, it can claim immunity, appear never to have been raised. The United States courts have upheld a plea of immunity by an unrecognised government: *Wulfsohn v Russian Socialist Federated Soviet Republic* 234 NY 372 (1923). As to state immunity see PARA 242 et seq.

8   *Thompson v Powles* (1828) 2 Sim 194, 2 BILC 20; *Taylor v Barclay* (1828) 2 Sim 213, 2 BILC 28. See also *Jones v Garcia del Rio* (1823) Turn & R 297, 2 BILC 13; *Thomson v Byree* (1828) Times, 31 May, 2 BILC 20; *Thompson v Barclay* (1831) 9 LJOS Ch 215, 2 BILC 32. It seems, however, that, even in the case of a contract with an unrecognised state or government, property acquired under it cannot be recovered if the contract is broken: *Republic of Peru v Dreyfus Bros & Co* (1888) 38 Ch D 348 at 362, 2 BILC 57.

9   *Murray v Parkes* [1942] 2 KB 123, [1942] 1 All ER 558, 4 BILC 480.

10 *Aksionairnoye Obschestvo AM Luther v James Sagor & Co* [1921] 1 KB 456, 2 BILC 85 (revsd after recognition had been granted [1921] 3 KB 532, 2 BILC 97, CA) (see PARA 51); *The Ramava* (1941) 75 ILT 153. It should be noted that whether the law of a foreign state will be applicable in an English court will be decided according to the English conflict of laws, and where the English court is referred to the law of an unrecognised state or an act of a government with which it does not have government-to-government dealings, these rules will apply: see CONFLICT OF LAWS.

11 *Eastern Carrying Insurance Co v National Benefit Life and Property Assurance Co Ltd* (1919) 35 TLR 292, 2 BILC 81; *Carl Zeiss Stiftung v Rayner and Keeler Ltd* [1967] 1 AC 853, sub nom *Carl Zeiss Stiftung v Rayner and Keeler Ltd (No 2)* [1966] 2 All ER 536, HL. In the latter case, however, Lord Wilberforce at 953 and 577 stated that it is an open question whether the English courts must treat all acts of a government with which the United Kingdom government has no dealings on a government-to-government basis as absolutely invalid. See also *Hesperides Hotels Ltd v Aegean Turkish Holidays Ltd* [1978] QB 205 at 218, [1978] 1 All ER 277 at 283, CA, per Lord Denning MR. See also *Caglar v Billingham (Inspector of Taxes)* [1996] STC (SCD) 150 (for court to take cognisance of acts of unrecognised state would be contrary to the foreign policy of the government); cf *Emin v Yeldag (A-G and the Secretary of State for Foreign and Commonwealth Affairs intervening)* [2002] 1 FLR 956, [2001] All ER (D) 501 (Nov) (private acts taking place within the territory of an unrecognised government could be taken account of by English court, though note that the executive intervened on the side of the applicant). As to the position of foreign corporations see now the Foreign Corporations Act 1991; and PARA 48. For a decision of the International Court of Justice to the effect that not all acts of an unrecognised authority should be disregarded see *Legal Consequences for States of the Continued Presence of South Africa in Namibia (South West Africa) notwithstanding Security Council Resolution 276 (1970) (Request for Advisory Opinion)* ICJ Reports 1971, 359.

12 The United States courts have on occasion taken the view that acts of an unrecognised government may be regarded as valid: see *Sokoloff v National City Bank* 623 NY 158 (1920); *Salimoff & Co v Standard Oil Co of New York* 262 NY 220 (1933); *Upright v Mercury Business Machines Co Inc* 213 NYS 2d 417 (1961).

13 *Emperor of Austria v Day and Kossuth* (1861) 3 De GF & J 217, 1 BILC 45, CA.

14 *Carl Zeiss Stiftung v Rayner and Keeler Ltd* [1967] 1 AC 853, sub nom *Carl Zeiss Stiftung v Rayner and Keeler Ltd (No 2)* [1966] 2 All ER 536, HL; *GUR Corpn v Trust Bank of Africa Ltd* [1987] QB 599, [1986] 3 All ER 449, CA.

48.   Foreign corporations.   If, at any time, any question arises whether a body which purports to have, or which appears to have lost, corporate status under the laws of a territory which is not at that time a recognised state[1] should or should not be regarded as having legal personality as a body corporate under English law, then, if it appears that the laws of that territory are at that time applied by a settled court system in that territory, that question and any other material question[2] relating to the body is to be determined, and account is to be taken of those laws, as if that territory were a recognised state[3].

1 A 'recognised state' is a territory which is recognised by the United Kingdom government as a state: Foreign Corporations Act 1991 s 1(2)(a). The laws of a territory which is recognised as a state include the laws of any part of the territory which are acknowledged by the federal or other central government of the territory as a whole: s 1(2)(b). The Foreign Corporations Act 1991 extends to Northern Ireland: s 2(1), (2). As to the meaning of 'United Kingdom' see PARA 30 note 3.

2 A 'material question' is a question, whether as to capacity, constitution or otherwise which, in the case of a body corporate, falls to be determined by reference to the laws of the territory under which the body is incorporated: s 1(2)(c). Any registration or other thing done before the coming into force of s 1 is to be regarded as valid if it would then have been valid had the Foreign Corporations Act 1991 s 1(1), (2) been in force: s 1(3).

3 Foreign Corporations Act 1991 s 1(1). See *R v Minister of Agriculture Fisheries and Food, ex p SP Anastasiou (Pissouri) Ltd* [1994] ECR I-3087, [1995] 1 CMLR 569, ECJ.

49.   Construction of documents.   In cases where it falls to the English court to interpret in a document a term such as 'state' or 'government', used in a statute[1] or commercial agreement[2], regard must be had to the intention of those who framed the document; and the fact that the Crown has not recognised the state or has no official dealings with the government in question may not be conclusive as to the meaning of the document.

1 *Re Al-Fin Corpn's Patent* [1970] Ch 160, [1969] 3 All ER 396, 9 BILC 1, disapproving *Re Harshaw Chemical Co's Patent* [1965] RPC 97, 8 BILC 1 (meaning of 'foreign state' as used in the Patents Act 1949 s 24(2) (repealed)).

2   *Luigi Monta of Genoa v Cechofracht Co Ltd* [1956] 2 QB 552, [1956] 2 All ER 769, 7 BILC 540 (meaning of 'government' in charterparty). See also *Kawasaki Kisen Kabushiki Kaisha of Kobe v Bantham Steamship Co Ltd* [1939] 2 KB 544, [1939] 1 All ER 819, CA (meaning of 'war'); *Reel v Holder* [1981] 3 All ER 321, [1981] 1 WLR 1226, CA (meaning of 'country' in rules of international sporting association).

50. Legal effects of recognition or government-to-government dealings. The recognition of a foreign state or the existence of government-to-government dealings reverses the consequences of non-recognition or the absence of such dealings.[1] A recognised state or a regime with which the government has government-to-government dealings may sue[2], and may claim state immunity if sued, in an English court[3]. Acts of a recognised state or of a regime with which the government has government-to-government dealings are generally recognised as valid and are given effect in accordance with the rules of the conflict of laws[4]. It is sometimes said that courts 'take cognisance' of the acts of a foreign state to distinguish this judicial reaction from the act of recognition which falls within the power of the Executive[5]. Contracts made with and by a foreign recognised regime are valid and enforceable[6], and legislative and executive acts such as decrees affecting property within the state whose territory is administered by a recognised regime[7] and legislation winding up[8] or affecting[9] a company incorporated there will be given effect in the English courts, so long as it conforms to English public policy and unless it is established that the foreign law is a serious violation of a fundamental rule of international law[10]. A recognised regime may claim the public property of the state[11] and the records and state archives deposited in England by a previous regime[12]. Further, the acts of a recognised regime will not be treated as the acts of a usurped authority within the meaning of a general insurance policy, even though the regime has come to power by revolutionary means[13].

1   As to the status of an unrecognised government (which is to say, an authority with which the British government does not have government-to-government dealings), see PARA 47; and as to the distinction between de facto and de jure recognition see PARA 51.

2   As to the right of a foreign state or government to sue in an English court see PARA 262.

3   *The Gagara* [1919] P 95, 2 BILC 71, CA; *Government of the Republic of Spain v SS Arantzazu Mendi* [1939] AC 256, [1939] 1 All ER 719, 2 BILC 198, HL. As to state immunity see PARA 242.

4   For the relevant rules of the conflict of laws see CONFLICT OF LAWS vol 8(3) (Reissue) PARA 139 et seq.

5   See generally O'Connell *International Law* (2nd ed 1970) Ch 6.

6   *Republic of Peru v Peruvian Guano Co* (1887) 36 ChD 489, 2 BILC 273; *Republic of Peru v Dreyfus Bros & Co* (1888) 38 ChD 348, 2 BILC 57.

7   *Aksionairnoye Obschestvo AM Luther v James Sagor & Co* [1921] 3 KB 532, 2 BILC 97, CA; *Princess Paley Olga v Weisz* [1929] 1 KB 718, 2 BILC 136, CA. As to establishing title to property see *In AY Bank Ltd (in liquidation) v Bosnia and Herzegovina* [2006] EWHC 830 (Ch), [2006] 2 All ER (Comm) 463; and *Republic of Croatia v Republic of Serbia* [2009] EWHC 1559 (Ch), [2010] 1 P&CR 64, [2009] All ER (D) 30 (Jul).

8   *Lazard Bros & Co v Midland Bank Ltd* [1933] AC 289, 1 BILC 443, HL.

9   *Carl Zeiss Stiftung v Rayner and Keeler Ltd* [1967] 1 AC 853, sub nom *Carl Zeiss Stiftung v Rayner and Keeler Ltd (No 2)* [1966] 2 All ER 536, HL.

10 As to acts of foreign governments which are contrary to English public policy see CONFLICT OF LAWS vol 8(3) (Reissue) PARA 422. English public policy would not permit the enforcement or recognition of a foreign law which constituted 'a gross violation of established rules of international law of fundamental importance': see *Kuwait Airlines Corpn v Iraqi Airlines Co (No.2)* [2002] UKHL 19, [2002] 2 AC 883, at [29], per Lord Nicholls. See also *Anglo-Iranian Oil Co Ltd v Jaffrate, The Rose Mary* [1953] 1 WLR 246, Aden SC.

11 *Haile Selassie v Cable and Wireless Ltd (No 2)* [1939] Ch 182, [1938] 3 All ER 677, 2 BILC 171. For the distinction in this respect between de facto and de jure governments see PARA 51.

12 *Union of Soviet Socialist Republics v Onou* (1925) 69 Sol Jo 676, 2 BILC 134.

13 *White, Child and Beney Ltd v Eagle Star and British Dominions Insurance Co, White, Child and Beney Ltd v Simmons* (1922) 127 LT 571, 2 BILC 126, CA.

51.   Recognition of de facto and de jure regimes.   A regime which is recognised by the Crown as exercising de facto governmental authority in the territory, or the relevant area of the territory, of a foreign state, will be treated by the English courts on the same footing for most purposes as a government recognised as the de jure government[1] in respect of such territory over which it exercises actual authority since it has full responsibility there[2]. Thus its legislative and executive acts which affect property situated[3] or companies incorporated in that territory[4] will be given effect in the English courts. It is entitled to plead state immunity in respect of an action concerning any property of which it is in possession or control, even in an action commenced by the government recognised de jure[5]. This status and immunity will continue until the de jure government regains control, and a fortiori continues should it never do so[6]. However, as regards property belonging to the state situated outside the territory controlled by the de facto government and claimed by the de jure government, the title of the de jure government will prevail[7]. Should the de jure government regain control and nullify the acts of the de facto government, the acts of the latter will be treated as void[8].

1   In view of the policy of the United Kingdom government not to accord formal recognition to governments, the distinction drawn in this paragraph will rarely arise in practice. However, it may do so if there exist more than one government contending for power in a recognised state and exercising governmental authority over the territory which each controls, as was the case during the Spanish Civil War (1936–39). It would seem to be necessary that the United Kingdom government had government-to-government relations with both authorities for a court to be able to reach the conclusion that both were governments.

2   *Aksionairnoye Obschestvo AM Luther v James Sagor & Co* [1921] 3 KB 532, 2 BILC 97, CA; *White, Child and Beney Ltd v Eagle Star and British Dominions Insurance Co, White, Child and Beney Ltd v Simmons* (1922) 127 LT 571, 2 BILC 126, CA.

3   *Aksionairnoye Obschestvo AM Luther v James Sagor & Co* [1921] 3 KB 532, 2 BILC 97, CA.

4   *Bank of Ethiopia v Bank of Egypt and Liguori* [1937] Ch 513, [1937] 3 All ER 8, 2 BILC 146; *Banco de Bilbao v Sancha, Banco de Bilbao v Rey* [1938] 2 KB 176, [1938] 2 All ER 253, 2 BILC 152, CA.

5   *Government of the Republic of Spain v SS Arantzazu Mendi* [1939] AC 256, [1939] 1 All ER 719, 2 BILC 198, HL. On the relevance of concurrent recognition of the de facto and de jure governments see *The Abodi Mendi* [1939] P 178, sub nom *Spanish Republican Government v Abodi Mendi* [1939] 1 All ER 701, 3 BILC 449, CA; *The Arraiz* (1938) 61 Ll L Rep 39, 3 BILC 422; *The El Neptuno* (1938) 62 Ll L Rep 7, 3 BILC 850. See also PARA 256.

6   See *Civil Air Transport Inc v Central Air Transport Corpn* [1953] AC 70 at 93, [1952] 2 All ER 733 at 744, 7 BILC 523, PC.

7   *Haile Selassie v Cable and Wireless Ltd* [1938] Ch 839, [1938] 3 All ER 384, 3 BILC 165, CA (plea of sovereign immunity by de facto government); *Haile Selassie v Cable and Wireless Ltd (No 2)* [1939] Ch 182, [1938] 3 All ER 677, 2 BILC 171 (earlier decision reversed by the Court of Appeal after recognition of de facto government as de jure sovereign).

8   See *Civil Air Transport Inc v Central Air Transport Corpn* [1953] AC 70 at 93, [1952] 2 All ER 733 at 744, 7 BILC 523, PC.

52.   Retroactivity of recognition.   Upon recognition by the United Kingdom, the government of the newly recognised state has been treated generally as having been the government of the state in question since the date at which it began to exercise actual governmental authority over the territory of that state[1]. Therefore its legislative and executive acts, such as decrees affecting persons and property within the territory of that state[2], and those winding up or affecting companies incorporated there[3], which were enacted during the time between that date and the date at which recognition is accorded, will be given effect by the

English courts. For this purpose the date to which recognition is retroactive is that given by statute or by a statement of the executive if any[4], in the absence of which the question must be decided by the court upon the facts, that is to say, from the date the entity can show that it was a state or from which the foreign government can show that it had government-to-government relations with the United Kingdom government[5]. However, recognition has only operated retroactively to validate the acts of the newly recognised government, and it has not been treated as invalidating the acts of the previously recognised de jure government of the state in respect of persons and property, at any rate where these were not at the relevant time within the territory effectively controlled by the newly recognised government[6]. Retroactivity may still be relevant, although the United Kingdom government no longer accords formal recognition to new governments[7].

1   For the purpose of retroactivity of recognition, English law has not distinguished between de jure and de facto of recognition: see *Aksionairnoye Obschestvo AM Luther v James Sagor & Co* [1921] 3 KB 532, 2 BILC 97, CA.

2   *Aksionairnoye Obschestvo AM Luther v James Sagor & Co* [1921] 3 KB 532, 2 BILC 97, CA (in which the Court of Appeal followed the decisions of the Supreme Court of the United States in *Oetjen v Central Leather Co* 246 US 297 (1918); *Underhill v Hernandez* 168 US 250 (1897); and *Williams v Bruffy* 96 US 176 (1877)). See also *Ricaud v American Metal Co* 246 US 304 (1918); *Princess Paley Olga v Weisz* [1929] 1 KB 718, 2 BILC 136, CA.

3   *Lazard Bros & Co v Midland Bank Ltd* [1933] AC 289, 1 BILC 443, HL. See also *Russian Commercial and Industrial Bank v Comptoir d'Escompte de Mulhouse* [1925] AC 112, 1 BILC 331, HL; *Banque Internationale de Commerce de Petrograd v Goukassow* [1925] AC 150, 2 BILC 355, HL; *Employers' Liability Assurance Corpn v Sedgwick Collins & Co* [1927] AC 95, 1 BILC 365, HL.

4   This may be inferred from *Gdynia Ameryka Linie Zeglugowe Spolka Akcyjna v Boguslawski* [1953] AC 11, [1952] 2 All ER 470, 7 BILC 499, HL; and see *Aksionairnoye Obschestvo AM Luther v James Sagor & Co* [1921] 3 KB 532 at 544, 2 BILC 97, CA, per Bankes LJ; *Lazard Bros & Co v Midland Bank Ltd* [1933] AC 289, 1 BILC 443, HL; *Kolbin & Sons v Kinnear & Co Ltd* 1930 SC 724 (affd 1931 SC 128).

5   See *White, Child and Beney Ltd v Eagle Star and British Dominions Insurance Co, White, Child and Beney Ltd v Simmons* (1922) 127 LT 571, 2 BILC 126, CA.

6   *Gdynia Ameryka Linie Zeglugowe Spolka Akcyjna v Boguslawski* [1953] AC 11, [1952] 2 All ER 470, 7 BILC 499, HL; *Civil Air Transport Inc v Central Air Transport Corpn* [1953] AC 70, [1952] 2 All ER 733, 7 BILC 523, PC.

7   See PARA 51 note 1.

(ii) Succession of States and Governments

A. STATE SUCCESSION

53. In general. The term 'state succession'[1] is employed to describe a great variety of situations involving changes in sovereignty over territory[2]. One possible case is where the whole of the territory of state A becomes absorbed by state B, state A being extinguished. Another is where state B is created out of part of the territory of state A, which continues to survive with diminished territory. But there are many possible intermediate situations, such as that where the territory of state A is divided, wholly or partly, between B and C, where B is created out of the territory of A and C, where part of the territory of a state is placed under an international or quasi-international regime such as a mandate or trusteeship, where a mandated or trust territory becomes a state, and so forth. These various situations, moreover, may be brought about in many different ways, for example by treaty of merger between states, by peaceable constitutional partition of a single state, by revolution and ultimate recognition of the establishment of a new state, or by some species of award or adjudication of a concert of the principal powers. The area and population changing hands, also, may be considerable or it may be virtually insignificant[3]. The disintegration of a state into a number of successor states may require an agreement between them on matters of succession, as well as with other states affected by the changes[4]. Agreements between the entities involved may be of importance in determining how other states view the nature of any changes and the identity of the states which emerge[5]. Not surprisingly, therefore, no rules as to the extinction or transmission of all types of international legal rights and obligations exist or apply in every case of state succession[6].

1   See generally O'Connell's State Succession in Municipal Law and International Law; O'Connell's Law of State Succession (containing an appendix of law officers' opinions on the subject); and 1 Oppenheim's International Law (9th Edn) 208–244.

2   The Convention on Succession of States in respect of Treaties (Vienna, 22 August 1978; Misc 1 (1980); Cmnd 7760) defines 'succession of states' as the replacement of one state by another in the responsibility for the international relations of territory: see art 2 para 1(b) (although note that the United Kingdom is not a party to this convention). As to the difficulties in identifying continuing and successor states see *Application of the Convention on the Prevention and Punishment of the Crime of Genocide (Bosnia and Herzegovina v Yugoslavia) (Preliminary Objections)* ICJ Reports 1996, 595; *Application of the Convention on the Prevention and Punishment of the Crime of Genocide (Bosnia and Herzegovina v Serbia v Montenegro)* ICJ Reports, 26 February 2007; and *Legality of the Use of Force (Serbia and Montenegro v United Kingdom) (Preliminary Objections)* ICJ Reports 2004, 1307.

3   As to attempted classifications of the various types of state succession and the means or modalities by which they may be brought about see especially 7 Verzijl's International Law in Historical Perspective 3–15; First Report of the Special Rapporteurs on Succession in respect of Rights and Duties resulting from Sources other than Treaties, YILC 1968 vol II, 94 at 100–106.

4   See the *Agreement on Succession Issues Between the Five Successor States of the Former Yugoslavia* 41 ILM (2002) 3; considered in *AY Bank Ltd (in liquidation) v Bosnia and Herzegovia* [2006] EWHC 830 (Ch), [2006] 2 All ER (Comm) 463. See also Shaw *International Law* (6th Edn, 2008) pp 962–963.

5   For example, the changes to the Soviet Union in 1991, which the participants regarded as a series of secessions by the new states from the old USSR, which continued as the state of Russia: see 31 ILM (1992) 138, 151.

6   Note the importance of previous territorial arrangements of the colonial powers for states succeeding by way of self-determination because of the doctrine of uti possidetis: see *Frontier Dispute (Burkina Faso/Republic of Mali)* ICJ Reports 1986, 554.

54.   Appurtenant rights and obligations.   A right appurtenant to a particular portion of territory passes with that portion to another sovereign. Thus the air space above the land will pass with the land, and rights and obligations vested in a riparian state will pass with the river bank. Sovereignty over the territorial sea and sovereign rights over the continental shelf will similarly pass with the land territory[1].

1   However, since the delimitation of sea areas always has a subjective element in it, if the pretensions of the predecessor state are either greater or less than those which the successor state itself advances with respect to other areas of the sea, they are not necessarily binding upon the successor state. As to state succession in relation to the territorial sea see 7 Verzijl's International Law in Historical Perspective 326–343; and as to succession to non-sovereign regimes such as protectorates, mandates and trust territories and belligerent occupation see 7 Verzijl's International Law in Historical Perspective 233, 314. As to air space see PARA 197 et seq; as to the territorial sea see PARA 123; and as to the continental shelf see PARA 163 et seq.

55.   Servitudes.   The notion of a right in rem in international law running with the land, though strongly contended for, cannot be said to be wholly established[1]. To a degree the International Court of Justice has acknowledged the possibility of a customary right of passage across territory available against a succession state. But inasmuch as the right in question was held not to be general, being inapplicable to armed forces and the like, it cannot very usefully be described as a servitude[2]. Where jura in re aliena in international law are grounded in treaty the question of their availability against or for the benefit of a succession of an original contracting party is simply one of succession in relation to treaties[3].

1   See generally Vali's Servitudes of International Law (2nd Edn, 1958).
2   *Right of Passage over Indian Territory (Portugal v India)* ICJ Reports 1960, 6. As to the International Court of Justice see PARA 499 et seq.
3   As to state succession in respect of dispositive treaties see PARA 59.

B. TREATY RIGHTS AND OBLIGATIONS

56. In general. According to the principle of the moving treaty frontier, a treaty applies to the whole of the territory of a state, and thus its ambit expands or contracts as the territory of any party expands or contracts. Therefore, a state which loses territory is discharged from treaty obligations[1] and ceases to enjoy treaty rights in respect of any territory which it loses. If the territory is lost to another existing state which is also bound by the treaty towards third states, that territory passes out of the treaty regime of the predecessor state into that of the successor state[2]. The same rule may apply also where a state merges with others to become a new state or a union in which it is the predominant partner[3]. States may make specific provision with new states about the continuation of previous treaty arrangements which apply to the territory of the new state[4].

1   The Vienna Convention on the Law of Treaties (Vienna, 23 May 1969; TS 58 (1980); Cmnd 7964) provides that a state is bound by a treaty in respect of any territory of which it is sovereign: see art 29; and PARA 94. Equally it is not bound by a treaty in respect of territory of which it is no longer sovereign.
2   Rules respecting state succession to treaties were included in the Convention on Succession of States in respect of Treaties (Vienna, 22 August 1978; Misc 1 (1980); Cmnd 7760): see PARAS 58–62. The United Kingdom is not a party. Evidence of clear rules of customary international law is lacking: see 1 Oppenheim's International Law (9th Edn) 236.
3   The matter was much discussed in relation, for example, to the formation of the German Empire out of the state of Prussia and a number of lesser states in 1871. See the International Law Commission's Draft Articles of 1972, art 19, YILC 1972 vol II, 18–35.
4   See eg the Affidavit of the Deputy Legal Adviser, FCO in *R v Foreign and Commonwealth Office, ex p International Transport Federation* (1998) and related materials (Ukraine), UKMIL (1998) 69 BYIL 482–487; FCO statement on succession with respect to Montenegro, UKMIL (2007) 78 BYIL 673, 685.

57. Territorial application clauses. The position of former colonial territories with regard to treaties entered into by their mother state, after their independence, is influenced by the existence in some such treaties of territorial or colonial application clauses[1]. These in effect permit non-metropolitan territorial sub-divisions of states to contract in or contract out of treaties independently of the mother country[2]. Incidentally, therefore, when self-governing dominions of the Crown eventually achieved statehood the question whether they succeeded to United Kingdom treaties did not arise, since they were already parties to them[3]. Similarly, when other British overseas territories were granted independence, the prime question in relation to treaties was often not whether those territories succeeded to the treaties, but whether those treaties already applied to them in their new international capacities by some territorial clause contained in them.

1   For examples of these, and as to the territorial application of treaties generally, see PARA 94.

2   This concession, as a matter of constitutional arrangement, of a degree of delegated authority to contract treaty rights and obligations contributed materially to the progress towards statehood of non-metropolitan British territories.

3   India, which was not then even wholly self-governing, was an original member of the United Nations and a party to the Charter of the United Nations in its own right.

58.   Absence of general succession.   Apart from the matters discussed elsewhere in this title[1], there is no general rule of international law to the effect that, upon a succession of states, the benefit or burden of the treaties of a predecessor state are, by reason of the succession, transferred to the successor state. On the contrary, if a state is extinguished its rights and obligations under such treaties are generally extinguished also. Similarly, although the effect of the creation of a new state out of the territory of an existing state may be to discharge the predecessor state from any obligation under a treaty and equally to deprive it of rights, the successor state cannot ordinarily claim the benefit, or be burdened by the obligations, of a treaty merely by reason of the succession. The rule is rather that a state succession does not of itself produce any succession in relation to treaty rights and obligations since, as regards the other states parties to the treaty, the new state is not a contracting party. A new state thus starts in principle with a clean slate[2]. However, the fact that a treaty is not in force in respect of a successor state does not impair the duty of a state to fulfil any obligation embodied in the treaty to which it would be subject at customary international law and independently of the treaty[3].

1   See PARAS 53 et seq, 59 et seq.

2   The 'clean state' doctrine is implicit in many of the provisions of the Convention on Succession of States in respect of Treaties (Vienna, 22 August 1978; Misc 1 (1980); Cmnd 7760): see PARA 56 note 2. See also McNair's Law of Treaties 605. However, a bilateral treaty may be regarded as in force between the new state and another party if those states expressly so agree or by reason of their conduct they are to be considered as having so agreed: International Law Commission's Draft Articles of 1972, art 19, YILC 1972 vol II, 272. Thus, if a new state claims the benefit under a predecessor's treaty, it is precluded from denying that it succeeds to obligations under it.

3   See the Vienna Convention on Succession of States in respect of Treaties art 5; and cf the Vienna Convention on the Law of Treaties (Vienna, 23 May 1969; TS 58 (1980); Cmnd 7964) art 43, which provides in the same terms for the case where a treaty is invalidated, terminated or suspended: see PARA 106 et seq.

59.   Dispositive treaties.   A treaty delimiting a boundary is binding in favour of and against a successor state[1]. Similarly, obligations and rights established by a treaty and relating to the regime of a boundary are not affected by a succession of states[2]. Further, a succession of states does not as such affect obligations or rights relating to the use of a particular territory or restrictions upon its use, established by a treaty specifically for the benefit of a foreign state and attaching to the territory in question[3], or obligations or rights thus relating to a particular territory established by a treaty specifically for the benefit of a group of states or of all states[4].

1   Convention on Succession of States in respect of Treaties (Vienna, 22 August 1978; Misc 1 (1980); Cmnd 7760) art 11 para 1. A newly independent state is bound by the international boundaries and, if it is emerging by decolonisation, by the internal administrative frontiers of the predecessor colonial power as a matter of general international law: *Frontier Dispute (Burkina Faso/Republic of Mali)* ICJ Reports 1986, 554. The doctrine of uti possidetis which was evolved by the states which belonged to the former Spanish American Empire is, in part, to the same effect. In *Frontier Dispute (Burkina Faso/Republic of Mali)* which was between Burkina Faso and Mali, two states formerly part of French West Africa), rather than holding that uti possidetis was a principle of Spanish American and later of regional law, the

International Court of Justice found it to be a principle of general application. However, in *Land, Island and Maritime Frontier Dispute (El Salvador v Honduras: Nicaragua intervening)* ICJ Reports 1992, 351 (which was between two Spanish-American states, El Salvador and Honduras), a chamber of the International Court of Justice treated uti possidetis simply as applying to former Spanish American colonies and accepted by the contending states; it did not enter into the question of its wider applicability. The principle of uti possidetis was relied upon by the Badinter Commission to determine the units of the former Yugoslavia entitled to self-determination and to establish their boundaries upon them becoming states, including reliance on internal administrative boundaries of the SFRY: see the Arbitration Commission of the European Conference on Yugoslavia (the 'Badinter Commission'), opinions 1, 3 (1992) 92 ILR 162, 170.

2   Vienna Convention on the Succession of States in respect of Treaties art 11 para 2. This would include such obligations as the obligation to proceed to demarcation of frontiers. The parties to *Case concerning the Temple of Preah Vihear (Cambodia v Thailand)* ICJ Reports 1962, 6 do not appear to have disputed this. Boundary disputes have arisen between newly independent states, but not with respect to the question of succession to boundary treaties as such.

3   Vienna Convention on the Succession of States in respect of Treaties art 12 para 1. See also *Free Zones of Upper Savoy and District of Gex Case* PCIJ Ser A No 24 (1930); further hearing PCIJ Ser A/B No 46 at 145 (1932).

4   Vienna Convention on the Succession of States in respect of Treaties art 12 para 2. See also the *Aaland Islands Case* LoNJ 1920 Supp No 3 at 16. This rule might apply to such treaties as those dealing with international canals (see PARA 99 note 7), or rights with respect to border rivers (see *Gabčíkovo-Nagymaros Project (Hungary/Slovakia)* ICJ Reports 1997, 7 at 72).

60.   Multilateral treaties.   With respect to multilateral treaties in force internationally in respect of territory which has become a new state, although that new state may have no direct rights and obligations under such a treaty as part of the treaty regime of its predecessor, it seems that it may have the right of option of becoming a party to the treaty itself if it so wishes[1]. Also, where a multilateral treaty is not yet in force, but the predecessor state has expressed its consent to be bound with reference to the territory in question, the same rule may apply[2]. However, the right of option is not open to the new state where this would be incompatible with the object and purpose of the treaty, nor where the parties to the treaty are limited in number, in which event the consent of all the parties is necessary to the new state becoming a party[3].

1   See the Convention on Succession of States in respect of Treaties (Vienna, 22 August 1978; Misc 1 (1980); Cmnd 7760) art 17 para 1. This, according to the International Law Commission's Report on Succession of States in respect of Treaties (1978) reflects, inter alia, the practice of the Secretary-General of the United Nations with respect to multilateral treaties of which he is the depositary: see the International Law Commission's Draft Articles on Succession of States in respect of Treaties 1972 art 12, Commentary, para (3). The Draft Articles can be found in YILC 1972 vol II, 255.

2   See the Vienna Convention on the Succession of States in respect of Treaties art 18. As to the provisional application of multilateral treaties see art 27. As to treaties establishing an international organisation see art 4. With respect to ratification, acceptance or approval of a treaty signed by the predecessor state see art 19; and as to reservations to multilateral conventions see art 20.

3   See the International Law Commission's Draft Articles on Succession of States in respect of Treaties 1972 art 12 paras 2, 3, 13 paras 2, 3. An example of a treaty whose object and purpose would preclude a new state from the right of option to be a party is one which is geographically limited, or one which requires that the parties be members of a particular organisation, as is the case with the Convention for the Protection of Human Rights and Fundamental Freedoms (Rome, 4 November 1950; TS 71 (1953); Cmd 8969), the parties to which must be members of the Council of Europe. An example where the consent of existing parties is essential is the Treaty of European Union. See further CONSTITUTIONAL LAW AND HUMAN RIGHTS.

61.   Human rights treaties.   There appears to be an emerging principle, based on the objective nature of human rights obligations and the desirability of establishing that the people of an affected territory do not lose the protection which international human rights law affords them[1], that successor states will be bound by the human rights treaty obligations of the predecessor states. Exceptionally, states may make specific agreements providing for the succession of human rights treaties following a change of sovereignty[2].

1   See the Human Rights Committee, General Comment No 26 (A/53/40, Annex VII). For a slightly more nuanced view see I Oppenheim's International Law (9th Edn, 1992) p 222.
2   See eg the Joint Declaration of the Governments of the United Kingdom and the People's Republic of China on the Question of Hong Kong dated 19 December 1984, Annex I, Article XIII (TS 26 (1985); Cmnd 9543) providing for the continuance in force of the provisions of the International Covenant on Civil and Political Rights with respect to [the Special Administrative Region of] Hong Kong.

62.   Newly independent states and devolution agreements.   In cases where a former colonial territory has become independent, several methods of avoiding the lapse of treaty rights and obligations upon independence have been resorted to[1]. New states have sometimes declared unilaterally that they regard themselves as parties to the treaties of their predecessors. Predecessors and successors have entered into agreements, commonly called devolution or inheritance treaties, purporting to indicate which treaties devolve upon succession and which do not[2]. As to the former, it is quite clear that such unilateral declarations are but res inter alios acta from the point of view of third states[3]. As to the latter, such agreements may serve as disclaimers of further responsibility on the part of predecessor states with respect to treaty obligations but will not of themselves discharge that responsibility; this will follow, if at all, rather from the moving treaty frontier rule[4]. Devolution agreements, however, are again res inter alios acta as respects third states and cannot invest successor states with any rights under treaties between those third states and predecessor states[5].

1   Convention on Succession of States in respect of Treaties (Vienna, 22 August 1978; Misc 1 (1980); Cmnd 7760) arts 8, 9.
2   Devolution agreements were entered into by the United Kingdom with some, though not all, colonial territories, upon the latter attaining independence. This was done by means of exchanges of letters with eg Malaysia, 12 September 1957 (Cmnd 346); Ghana, 25 November 1957 (Cmnd 345); Nigeria, 1 October 1960 (Cmnd 1214); Sierra Leone, 5 May 1961 (Cmnd 1464); Jamaica, 7 August 1962 (Cmnd 1918); Trinidad and Tobago, 31 August 1962 (Cmnd 1919); Gambia, 20 June 1966 (Cmnd 3076); and in respect of India and Pakistan (see the Indian Independence (International Arrangements) Order 1947, 147 BFSP 158).
3   Nevertheless such declarations may constitute offers of novation which third states may accept and which they may be construed to have accepted tacitly if they act upon such offers.
4   As to the moving treaty frontier rule see PARA 56.
5   Devolution agreements may, however, serve the purpose ascribed to unilateral declarations: see note 3. There is also the possibility that treaties may be applied provisionally despite succession. However, customary international law appears to have no such rule to this effect.

63.   Concessionary contracts.   Although practice prior to the 1939–45 war suggested that concessionary contracts which related to a particular area sovereignty over which was transferred to another state were binding upon the successor state, the weight of opinion is said now to be against this. The difference of opinion is perhaps immaterial since, if the rule was that there was a successor, it was qualified by the proposition that it was nevertheless competent to the new sovereign to terminate any concession subject to the payment of compensation[1]. And if the rule now is that there is no succession, the concessionaire is nevertheless entitled in theory to compensation when he is deprived of his rights under the concession by territorial transfer or otherwise.

1   See *Mavrommatis Jerusalem Concessions* PCIJ Ser A No 5 (1925); *The Sopron-Koszeg Local Rly Co Case* 2 RIAA 961 (1929); *The Barcs-Pakrac Rly Co Case* (1934) 7 Ann Dig Case

No 190. See also the Report of the Transvaal Concessions Committee 1901 (Cd 623) set up to advise the Colonial Office about concessions granted by the Boer Republics before their annexation in 1900. As to state responsibility in respect of concessions see PARA 474 note 9.

64. Other contractual rights. Although a bare claim to unliquidated damages appears not to be available against a successor state, the case may be different if there is in the claim some element of quasi-contract and both right and obligation may survive[1]. A contractual claim having the character of a vested or acquired right binds the successor state[2].

1 *Lighthouses Arbitration* (1956) 23 Int LR 81 at 83 (claim no 11), at 91 (claim no 4), at 106 (claim no 12). As to claims for unliquidated damages in respect of delictual or tortious liability see *Robert E Brown Case* 6 RIAA 120 (1923); and PARA 65. As to the difficulties of classification involved see 1 O'Connell's International Law (2nd Edn) 387.
2 As to private rights and acquired rights see PARA 68; and as to concessionary contracts see PARA 63.

65. Claims in tort or delict. There is no succession in relation to obligations in respect of claims in tort or delict[1]. Where, however, a claim originating in tort or delict is liquidated, as by an arbitral or judicial decision, the rule may be otherwise[2].

1 *Robert E Brown Case* 6 RIAA 120 (1923); *Hawaiian Claims Case* 6 RIAA 157 (1925). An English court has had occasion to advert to this rule: *West Rand Central Gold Mining Co Ltd v R* [1905] 2 KB 391, 2 BILC 283, DC.
2 The point is not clearly covered by authority, but see *Lighthouses Arbitration* (1956) 23 Int LR 659.

66. Public property. Upon a state succession the successor state succeeds to the public property of the predecessor[1]. In so far as it concerns immovable property within the territory transferred the proposition would appear to do little, if anything, more than reflect the fact that the successor state, in right of its sovereignty, may make what dispositions it wishes with respect to everything within its territorial jurisdiction. The same applies in relation to movables so situate[2]. For the most part the outgoing authorities leave behind them not only immovables, as they must, but also movables constituting public property, and relinquish all claim to assets of this character. But there may be exceptions, such as where the predecessor state seeks to retain a building as an embassy or the like. There may, too, be considerable difficulty in defining public property for the purpose, or the distinction between public and private property may be differently drawn in the laws of predecessor and successor state, or indeed may not exist at all in one or other of them. The matter has been the subject of often very detailed treaty regulation for centuries and has given rise to much litigation[3]. What rules of international law this considerable body of practice can be said to yield, however, is somewhat obscure[4].

1 *Peter Pázmány University Case* PCIJ Ser A/B No 61 at 237 (1933). Rules respecting state succession in respect of public property and other matters were included in the Convention on Succession of States in respect of State Property, Archives and Debts (Vienna; 8 April 1983; 22 ILM (1983) 298). It has not yet entered into force. The United Kingdom has neither signed nor ratified this Convention. For an account of the Convention see 1 Oppenheim's International Law (9th Edn) pp 240–244.
2 Cf the position as to the nationality of individuals and private rights: see PARAS 68–69, 392.
3 When a predecessor state is totally absorbed, its successor may claim public assets situated extraterritorially; in English law this is only so after the conquest has been recognised de jure by the United Kingdom government: see *Haile Selassie v Cable and Wireless Ltd (No 2)* [1939] Ch 182, [1938] 3 All ER 677, 2 BILC 171, CA. As to recognition de facto and de jure see PARA 51.

4   The better view would seem to be that, property being an institution primarily of municipal rather than international law, it is unprofitable to look for some such rule as that public property automatically vests in the successor state: that must depend on the details of the relevant municipal system. In the Vienna Convention on Succession of States in respect of State Property, Archive and Debts 1983 'state property' is defined according to the law of the predecessor state (see art 8). Not all public property need be treated in the same way (see eg the treatment of cultural and military property in the succession states to the SFRY: *Agreement on Succession Issues Between the Five Successor States of the Former Yugoslavia* 41 ILM (2002) 3). On the other hand, it is arguable that there is a rule of international law of a negative sort to the effect that no claim will lie at the suit of a predecessor state if the successor takes steps to appropriate to itself public property. Approached in this way the real question involved may prove to be as to whether the predecessor state ever has any claim of this sort in respect of any species of property. If the answer here is that such a claim, as respects property within the transferred territory, immovable or movable, will lie only in respect of private property of an individual sovereign, then it becomes unnecessary to define public property for this purpose. For an attempt to use the English court in a succession issue to public monies, see *In AY Bank Limited (in liquidation) v Bosnia and Herzegovina* [2006] EWHC 830 (Ch), [2006] 2 All ER (Comm) 463.

     There remains, however, the question as to the position if the predecessor state, in anticipation of the succession, alienates public property. There is some ground for the contention that, where such alienation is attended by circumstances akin to fraud, it ought to be disregarded. Cf *Civil Air Transport Inc v Central Air Transport Corpn* [1953] AC 70, [1952] 2 All ER 733, 7 BILC 523, PC.

67.   Public debts.   Although, for instance, a loan to a state from the International Bank for Reconstruction and Development or from some similar international agency, or from another state directly, may fall into a different category[1], an international loan or international or public debt is commonly contracted according to municipal rather than international law[2]. Although the borrower is a state, the lenders are mostly private persons, and other states are indeed reluctant to exercise the right of protection on their behalf in case of default, the loan having been made in the way of business, which must involve the chance of loss as well as of profit[3]. The lenders' rights are primarily rights under municipal law, normally the law of the borrower state, and they are thus susceptible of change by whatever authority may make and change that law. In consequence, upon a state succession, the position in relation to public debts is not in principle different from that in relation to any other obligation under the law applicable within the territory transferred, and whether or not they survive is exclusively a matter for that law[4]. But though this may be the formal position, in practice provision has frequently been made by treaty for the partition of the public debt of the predecessor state and for the assumption of a proportion of it by the successor state[5]. It is to be doubted, however, whether any coherent principle is to be extracted from this practice[6].

1   See Mann, The Proper Law of Contracts Concluded by International Persons, 35 BYIL (1959) 36 at 38.

2   As to the nature of a loan to a foreign government negotiated in England see *Smith v Weguelin* (1869) LR 8 Eq 198, 3 BILC 486; *Twycross v Dreyfus* (1877) 5 ChD 605, 3 BILC 513, CA. As to the nature of a loan contracted by the United Kingdom government upon a foreign market see *R v International Trustee for Protection of Bondholders AG* [1937] AC 500, [1937] 2 All ER 164, HL.

3   See 2 O'Connell's International Law (2nd Edn) 1080.

4   For a survey of the practice see 1 O'Connell's State Succession in Municipal Law and International Law 373–464. See also the *Ottoman Public Debt Arbitration* 1 RIAA 527 at 573 (1925); *Lighthouses Arbitration* (1956) 23 Int LR 659; *Verein für Schutzgebietsanleihen EV v Conradie NO* [1937] AD 113; and other cases summarised in the Digest of Decisions of National Courts etc YILC 1963 vol II, 95, 137–142, Part A VI (B). As to localised debts see the *Guano Case* 15 RIAA 77 at 330 (1901).

5   See 1 O'Connell's State Succession in Municipal Law and International Law 458–462. See also *West Rand Central Gold Mining Co Ltd v R* [1905] 2 KB 391 at 408, 2 BILC 283, DC, per Lord Alverstone CJ. See also the Convention on Succession of States in respect of State Property, Archives and Debts (Vienna; 8 April 1983; 22 ILM (1983) 298); and PARA 66 note 1.

6   It cannot be said, for instance, that, where the territory of a state is divided, the public debt must also be divided proportionately to the revenues of the several parts, or to their population; and although it is sometimes contended that an odious debt, such as a debt incurred to finance a conflict with the successor state, does not pass to that successor, such a proposition represents only a qualification put on a doubtful and imprecise general rule. According to the Badinter Commission, the general principle is that successor states should consult and reach an agreement on succession questions: see the Arbitration Commission of the European Conference on Yugoslavia (the 'Badinter Commission'), opinions 9, 14 (1992) 92 ILR 203, 96 ILR 729. It has been held that there is 'insufficient evidence to justify a conclusion that a rule as to succession to the property of a dismembered state (however sensible) (see the Vienna Convention on State Succession in respect of Property, Archives and Debts 1983, art 18(1)(b); and 66 note 1) has yet become a sufficiently general or consistent practice among states to qualify as customary international law for the purposes of recognition by English common law': see *Republic of Croatia v Republic of Serbia* [2009] EWHC 1559 (Ch), [2009] All ER (D) 30 (Jul) at [36], per Briggs J.

68.   Private rights. Private rights acquired under existing law do not cease on a change of sovereignty[1]. It is, however, a question exclusively for the municipal legal system concerned whether or not private rights created or recognised by it cease upon a change of sovereignty or on any other event. The doctrine of the survival of acquired or vested rights which is claimed to be established as a rule of international law[2] is in any case qualified by the fact that the successor state may always, in the exercise of its legislative sovereignty, proceed to the abolition of such rights[3] unless inhibited either by treaty[4] or customary law[5].

1   *German Settlers in Poland (Advisory Opinion)* PCIJ Ser B No 6, at 15, 36 (1923); *Certain German Interests in Polish Upper Silesia* PCIJ Ser A No 7 (1926); *Factory at Chorzów* PCIJ Ser A No 17 (1928). In the last two cases, the court was concerned with treaties but applied these with reference to the ordinary customary law.

2   See generally 1 O'Connell's State Succession in Municipal Law and International Law 237 at 269–297, where the practice is set out in great detail.

3   The doctrine of acquired rights, much favoured by American courts (see especially *United States v Percheman* 7 Pet 51 at 86 (USA 1830) per Marshall CJ) has received occasional indorsement in obiter judgments by English courts. See *West Rand Central Gold Mining Co Ltd v R* [1905] 2 KB 391 at 491, 2 BILC 283, DC, per Lord Alverstone CJ: 'As is said in more cases than one, cession of territory does not mean the confiscation of the property of individuals in that territory'. However, the operation of the doctrine is distorted in practice, if not substantively limited, by the doctrine of act of state, which disables the courts for inquiring into annexations of territory made, or cessions taken by the Crown: see *Cook v Sprigg* [1899] AC 572, 2 BILC 279, PC; *Secretary of State for India v Bai Rajbai* (1915) LR 42 Ind App 229, 2 BILC 631, PC; *Salaman v Secretary of State for India* [1906] 1 KB 613, 1 BILC 594, CA; *Amodu Tijani v Secretary, Southern Nigeria* [1921] 2 AC 399, PC; *Secretary of State for India v Sardar Rustam Khan* [1941] AC 356, [1941] 2 All ER 606, 1 BILC 626, PC; *Hoani Te Heuheu Tukino v Aotea District Maori Land Board* [1941] AC 308, [1941] 2 All ER 93, 6 BILC 514, PC; *Oyekan v Adele* [1957] 2 All ER 785, [1957] 1 WLR 876, 7 BILC 572, PC. As to acts of state see PARA 22 et seq.

4   In *German Settlers in Poland (Advisory Opinion)* PCIJ Ser B No 6 at 15, 36 (1923), Poland was bound by the minorities provision contained in the Treaty of Peace with Poland (Versailles, 28 June 1919; TS 8 (1919); Cmd 223) art 7, to secure to all Polish nationals, including the German settlers, civilian rights (interpreted to include proprietary rights) without distinction. Hence the importance of the question whether any rights had been acquired before the territorial transfer and whether they survived that event.

5   Ie notably the duty not to expropriate the property of non-nationals arbitrarily and not for a public purpose: see PARA 473.

69.   Nationality. The frequently repeated proposition that, upon a transfer of territory, at least if the inhabitants are resident or domiciled in the territory concerned, they lose the nationality of the predecessor state and acquire that of the successor state[1] is irreconcilable with the circumstance, for which there is now international judicial authority, that questions of nationality are primarily still questions of municipal rather than international law[2]. Who is or ceases to be a national of a particular state must depend exclusively on the law of that state. It was formerly the rule of English law that a person might become a British subject as a result of the annexation of territory with which he was connected, but precisely what connection was requisite was unclear[3]. It was also accepted that, at common law, upon a cession of territory by the Crown some circumscription of nationality took place[4]; but the details of the matter have been habitually regulated by treaty or proclamation.

1 See the numerous references to writers collected in 1 O'Connell's State Succession in Municipal Law and International Law 499 note 6.

2 *Tunis and Morocco Nationality Decrees Case (Advisory Opinion)* PCIJ Ser B No 4 (1923). See also the International Law Commission's Draft Articles of 1999, paras 47–48 (Nationality of Natural Persons in Relation to a Succession of States), A/54/10; and the Arbitration Commission of the European Conference on Yugoslavia (the 'Badinter Commission'), opinion 2 (1992) 92 ILR 167 at 168–169 (alluding to the possibility that individuals may have the nationality of their choice).

3 In *Calvin's Case* (1608) 7 Co Rep 1a at 5–7, 18, 4 BILC 133, Coke CJ was of the opinion that annexation of territory worked a species of 'denization' or naturalisation, and disagreed with the opinion of Bracton. In *Lyons Corpn v East India Co* (1836) 1 Moo PCC 175 at 286, 2 BILC 483, PC, Lord Brougham interpreted the opinion of Sir Fletcher Norton, Attorney General, dated 27 July 1764 (see Forsyth's Cases and Opinions on Constitutional Law 253), on the status of inhabitants of Quebec to imply 'very distinctly, that the subjects of a conquered or ceded territory, are only to be considered as not being aliens, by virtue of the treaty which gives them the rights of subjects', and held this to be wholly untenable and contrary to authority. However, the opinion was not on the question of the effect of the cession on nationality but on the distinct question as to whether the English law against alien landholding applied in Quebec: *Donegani v Donegani* (1835) 3 Knapp 63 at 72, 2 BILC 470, PC. Furthermore, the matter was in that case regulated by treaty (Treaty of Peace between Great Britain, France and Spain (Paris, 10 February 1763; state Papers 108/123) art IV), and had commonly been so regulated since the Treaty of Peace and Friendship with France (Utrecht, 11 April 1713; state Papers 108/72), although the stipulation of that instrument (see art XIV) is elliptical, providing merely that such of the inhabitants as do not withdraw are to be free to practise the Roman Catholic religion. As to British practice in cases of acquisition of territory without treaty (ie annexation) see 5 British Digest 142–147; Parry's Nationality and Citizenship Laws of the Commonwealth (1st Edn, 1957) 431–435, 659–664.

4 *Re Stepney Election Petition, Isaacson v Durant* (1886) 17 QBD 54, 4 BILC 344, DC (dissolution of union of Crowns; a possibility canvassed but dismissed as 'less than a dream of a shadow, or a shadow of a dream' in *Calvin's Case* (1608) 7 Co Rep 1a at 27, 4 BILC 133). The decision in *Re Stepney Election Petition, Isaacson v Durant*, that the Hanoverians (which category was not sought to be defined) had ceased to be British subjects was based largely on the thesis that double nationality was an impossibility in law, which is misconceived. In *Doe d Thomas v Acklam* (1824) 2 B & C 779, 4 BILC 353, long after the event, the achievement of independence by the United States was held to have effected the expatriation of the inhabitants of the American colonies on a similar line of reasoning that dual status would be an 'inconvenience'. See also *Doe d Stansbury v Arkwright* (1833) 2 Ad & El 182n, 4 BILC 375; *Re Bruce* (1832) 2 Cr & J 436, 4 BILC 368; *Sutton v Sutton* (1830) 1 Russ & M 663, 4 BILC 362.

70. Succession of governments. Where one government succeeds another in the same state, the principle of continuity involves that rights and obligations under international law are unaffected in general[1]. This principle applies no less where the government to which there is a succession was unconstitutional[2], or was suppressed in civil war[3]. The property acquired by one of the political factions in a civil war is attributed to the state and the assets of the defeated may be claimed by the victor, not by title paramount but subject to the liabilities of the defeated faction[4]. Where governmental property is in the United Kingdom at the time of the disappearance of the government it seems that, in the absence of its replacement by another, the property will be held on trust until a successor government is established[5].

1 *Tinoco Arbitration* 1 RIAA 369 (1923). Thus, where two governments are in possession of parts of the territory of a state, each may commit the state as a whole at least with respect to ordinary governmental obligations: *Hopkins Case* 4 RIAA 41 (1926) (postal orders). As to state responsibility for acts of revolutionaries see PARA 349.
2 *Tinoco Arbitration* 1 RIAA 369 (1923); *Republic of Peru v Peruvian Guano Co* (1887) 36 ChD 489, 2 BILC 273; *Republic of Peru v Dreyfus Bros & Co* (1888) 38 ChD 348, 2 BILC 57; and see *Dolder v Bank of England* (1805) 10 Ves 352, 2 BILC 214; *King of the Two Sicilies v Willcox* (1851) 1 Sim NS 301, 2 BILC 230; *Gdynia Ameryka Linie Zeglugowe Spolka Akcyjna v Boguslawski* [1953] AC 11, [1952] 2 All ER 470, 7 BILC 499, HL. Cf *Irish Free State v Guaranty Safe Deposit Co* 222 NYS 182 (1927); *Fogarty v O'Donaghue* [1926] 1 IR 531, 2 BILC 294.
3 *United States of America v McRae* (1867) 3 Ch App 79, 2 BILC 252; *Union of Soviet Socialist Republics v Onou* (1925) 69 Sol Jo 676, 2 BILC 134. As to the position where a territory is temporarily under belligerent occupation see *Gumbes' Case* (1834) 2 Knapp 369, 2 BILC 223.
4 *United States of America v McRae* (1867) 3 Ch App 79, 2 BILC 252; *United States of America v Prioleau* (1865) 2 Hem & M 559, 1 BILC 129.
5 *Republic of Somalia v Woodhouse, Drake and Carey (Suisse) SA, The Mary* [1993] QB 54, [1993] 1 All ER 371.

6. TREATIES AND INTERNATIONAL AGREEMENTS

(1) ENTERING INTO TREATIES

71. Meaning of 'treaty'. The law of treaties is now generally governed by the Vienna Convention on the Law of Treaties[1], which largely reflects customary international law[2], and the following paragraphs are structured around the central provisions of that Convention[3]. For the purposes of the Convention, 'treaty' means an international agreement concluded between states[4] in written form[5] and governed by international law, whether embodied in a single instrument or in two or more related instruments and whatever its particular designation[6]. Except in so far as it excludes agreements between states and international organisations[7], this definition is consistent with United Kingdom law and practice, in which no distinction is made between a treaty expressly so called and an international agreement called by another name[8], and in which an exchange of notes, letters or declarations, consisting of two or more documents, is familiar.

1   Ie the Vienna Convention on the Law of Treaties (Vienna, 23 May 1969; TS 58 (1980); Cmnd 7964). The Convention entered into force on 27 January 1980. See generally I Oppenheim's International Law (9th Edn, 1992) Ch 14; Sinclair's The Vienna Convention on the Law of Treaties (2nd Edn, 1984); Aust *Modern Treaty Law and Practice* (2nd Edn, 2007); Shaw's International Law (6th Edn, 2008) Ch 16.

2   The Vienna Convention on the Law of Treaties does not have retroactive effect: see art 4. However, before it entered into force, the International Court of Justice referred to provisions of the Convention in *Legal Consequences for States of the Continued Presence of South Africa in Namibia (South West Africa) notwithstanding Security Council Resolution 276 (1970) (Request for Advisory Opinion)* ICJ Reports 1971, 359; *Fisheries Jurisdiction (United Kingdom v Iceland) (Jurisdiction of the Court)* ICJ Reports 1973, 3 at 14, 18, 19. Moreover, the International Court of Justice applied provisions of the Convention in interpreting a treaty of 1890, on the basis that they reflected customary international law: *Kasikili/Sedudu Island (Botswana/Namibia)* ICJ Reports 1999, 1045 at 1059 (para 18). See also *Arbitration Regarding the Iron Rhine Railway (Kingdom of Belgium/Kingdom of the Netherlands)*, Award of 24 May 2005, PCA at para 45; and *Gabčíkovo-Nagymaros Project (Hungary/Slovakia)* ICJ Reports 1997, 7 at 38, 62. For an example of the English courts applying the Convention to a treaty concluded prior to the Convention entering into force, on the basis that art 31 of the Convention reflects customary international law, see *European Roma Rights Centre v Immigration Officer at Prague Airport (United Nations High Commissioner for Refugees intervening)* [2004] UKHL 55, [2005] 2 AC 1, [2005] 1 All ER 527 (with respect to the 1951 Refugee Convention). As to the relation of the provisions of the Vienna Convention on the Law of Treaties to customary international law see Aust *Modern Treaty Law and Practice* (2nd Edn, 2007) 12–13.

3   See PARA 72 et seq.

4   As to capacity to enter into treaties see PARA 72. An individual or corporation cannot be a party to a treaty: *Anglo-Iranian Oil Co Case (United Kingdom v Iran) (Preliminary Objections)* ICJ Reports 1952, 93 (concession of 1933 between the company and the government of Persia held not to be a treaty, although the British government had taken part in its negotiation, which was conducted under the auspices of the League of Nations). By contrast, an individual or corporation may have directly enforceable rights under a treaty, for example, a right to bring proceedings under a human rights treaty or a right to arbitrate disputes under an applicable bilateral investment treaty.

5   The written agreement may be informal, for example agreed minutes of a meeting: see *Maritime Delimitation and Territorial Questions between Qatar and Bahrain (Qatar v Bahrain) (Jurisdiction and Admissability)* ICJ Reports 1995, 6. There appears to be no reason why an oral agreement should not be regarded as a treaty if it is made between states: see the 'Ihlen Declaration' by the Norwegian Foreign Minister to the Danish Minister to Norway, which was held to be binding on Norway in the *Legal Status of Eastern Greenland* PCIJ Ser A/B No 53 (1933). However, such an oral agreement would fall outside the scope of the Vienna Convention

on the Law of Treaties (see art 2 para 1(a)), and there would also be difficulties as regards registration of such agreements. As to the registration of treaties see PARA 105.

6   Vienna Convention on the Law of Treaties art 2 para 1(a). As to the particular status of Memoranda of Understanding (MOUs) between states see Aust *Modern Treaty Law and Practice* (2nd Edn, 2007) Ch 3.

7   A treaty can be concluded between a state and another subject of international law, in particular an international organisation, or between international organisations: see PARA 517 et seq. The Vienna Convention on the Law of Treaties does not affect the legal force of such agreements: see art 3. Nor does the Convention affect the legal force of unilateral statements, as to which see PARA 110.

    In 1986, the Convention on the Law of Treaties between States and International Organizations or between International Organizations was concluded in Vienna: see 25 ILM (1986) 543. The substantive provisions of the Convention are similar to those of the Vienna Convention on the Law of Treaties. The United Kingdom has ratified the Convention on the Law of Treaties between States and International Organisations or between International Organisations, but the Convention is not yet in force.

8   Eg Act, agreement, charter, concordat, constitution, convention, covenant, declaration, protocol or statute.

72. Capacity to conclude treaties. Every state possesses capacity to conclude treaties[1]. A treaty made between states may be expressed to be made by heads of state, or on behalf of the states, their governments or, less often, their ministries or state agencies[2]. In the United Kingdom the Crown has, historically, either directly or via the agency of a chartered company, such as the East India Company, entered into innumerable agreements, very often specifically styled 'treaties', with local powers in Asia, Africa and North America[3], although the treaty character of such agreements, in the sense of an agreement governed by international law, has come to be denied[4]. The power to make treaties remains with the Crown notwithstanding the devolution of certain legislative and executive powers to Scotland, Northern Ireland and Wales[5]. On rare occasions, the Crown has entered into agreements with constituent elements of a federal state[6].

International organisations, such as the United Nations, have capacity to conclude such treaties as are within their express or implied powers[7].

1   Vienna Convention on the Law of Treaties (Vienna, 23 May 1969; TS 58 (1980); Cmnd 7964) art 6. 'State' is not defined in the Convention. As to treaty-making power in the United Kingdom see PARA 17 et seq. As to the meaning of 'treaty' see PARA 71.

2   As to representation see PARA 73 et seq.

3   See generally Parry and Hopkins's Index of British Treaties 1101–1968, especially under 'Indian States', 'Malay States'.

4   As to the development of the doctrine of paramountcy and other doctrines to the effect that the Crown's relations with the Princely States were matters of constitutional rather than international law see Panikkar's Relations of Indian States with the Government of India; Lee-Warner The Native States of India; Report of the Indian States Committee (Cmd 3302) (1929).

5   See eg, in respect of Scotland, matters reserved to the Crown pursuant to the Scotland Act 1998 s 30, Sch 5 para 7. The observation and implementation of international obligations is not however a reserved matter.

6   See the Swiss Declaration (Cantons of Valais and Bâle Town) and British Counter-Declaration relative to the Duty on Withdrawal of Private Property (Zürich and London, 31 July 1840; 39 BFSP 1315); Swiss Declaration (Cantons of Soleure and St Gall) and British Counter-Declaration relative to the Duty on Withdrawal of Private Property (Berne and London, 27 January 1841; 39 BFSP 1316).

7   For examples of treaties between the United Kingdom and international organisations see the Headquarters Agreements referred to in PARA 308. As to the capacity of international organisations to conclude treaties see *Reparation for Injuries Suffered in the Service of the United Nations (Advisory Opinion)* ICJ Reports 1949, 174.

73. Representation; full powers. A person is considered as representing a state for the purpose of adopting or authenticating the text of a treaty[1] or for the purpose of expressing the consent of the state to be bound by a treaty, if: (1) he produces appropriate full powers[2]; or (2) it appears from the practice of the states concerned or from other circumstances that their intention was to consider that person as representing the state for such purposes and to dispense with full powers[3].

1 As to the meaning of 'treaty' see PARA 71.

2 Full powers means a document emanating from the competent authority of a state designating a person or persons to represent the state for negotiating, adopting or authenticating the text of a treaty, for expressing the consent of the state to be bound by a treaty, or for accomplishing any other act with respect to a treaty: Vienna Convention on the Law of Treaties (Vienna, 23 May 1969; TS 58 (1980); Cmnd 7964) art 2 para 1(c). The production of full powers is the fundamental safeguard for the representatives of the states concerned of each other's qualifications to represent their states for the purposes of performing the particular act in question: see the final draft of the International Law Commission's Commentary, YILC 1996 vol II, 193.

3 Vienna Convention on the Law of Treaties art 7 para 1. An act relating to the conclusion of a treaty performed by a person who cannot be considered under art 7 as authorised to represent a state for that purpose is without legal effect unless afterwards confirmed by that state: see art 8.

74. Absence of requirement of full powers. In virtue of their functions and without having to produce full powers[1], the following are considered as representing their state: (1) heads of state, heads of government and ministers for foreign affairs, for the purpose of performing all acts relating to the conclusion of a treaty[2]; (2) heads of diplomatic missions, for the purpose of adopting the text of a treaty between the accrediting state and the state to which they are accredited[3]; (3) representatives accredited by states to an international conference or to an international organisation or one of its organs, for the purpose of adopting the text of a treaty in that conference, organisation or organ[4].

The Sovereign, in whom by both international law and the law of the United Kingdom the right of representation resides, may presumably enter into a treaty in person and without any form of authority although it does not appear that the Sovereign has done so since at least the Restoration[5]. The United Kingdom has three types of full power: (a) the Queen's general full powers, which are signed by Her Majesty and empower the Secretary of State for Foreign and Commonwealth Affairs, Ministers of State and Under Secretaries of State to sign any treaty, and the United Kingdom Permanent Representatives to the United Nations and European Union to sign treaties in their respective fields; (b) the Queen's special full powers which are issued for the signing of a specific treaty drawn up between heads of state; and (c) the governmental full powers, which are issued for the signing of specific intergovernmental and interstate treaties[6].

1 As to the meaning of 'full powers' see PARA 73.

2 Vienna Convention on the Law of Treaties (Vienna, 23 May 1969; TS 58 (1980); Cmnd 7964) art 7 para 2(a). An act relating to the conclusion of a treaty performed by a person who cannot be considered under art 7 as authorised to represent a state for that purpose is without legal effect unless afterwards confirmed by that state: see art 8. As to the meaning of 'treaty' see PARA 71.

3 Vienna Convention on the Law of Treaties art 7 para 2(b). See also note 2.

4 Vienna Convention on the Law of Treaties art 7 para 2(c). See also note 2.

5 Even royal marriage treaties, which were more in the nature of family compacts than agreements governed by international law, were not concluded by the Crown in person: Royal Marriage Treaties 1772–1885, Foreign Office Library, 1020 (FO) (partly in manuscript). 'The Honourable

Woodrow Wilson, President of the United States, acting in his own name and by his own perfect authority', signed the Treaty of Peace with Germany (Treaty of Versailles) (Versailles, 28 June 1919; TS 4 (1919); Cmd 153).

6 306 HC Official Report (6th series), 11 February 1998, written answers, col 247. See 69 BYIL (1998) 447.

75. Adoption and authentication of the text of a treaty. The adoption of the text of a treaty[1] takes place by the consent of all the states participating in its drawing up[2]. However, according to the Vienna Convention on the Law of Treaties, the adoption of the text of a treaty at an international conference takes place by the vote of two-thirds of the states present and voting unless by the same majority they decide to apply a different rule[3].

Authentication of a treaty, that is the establishment of its text as authentic and definitive, is effected by such procedure as may be provided for in the text or agreed upon by the states participating in its drawing up[4]; or, failing such procedure, by the signature, signature ad referendum or initialling by the representatives of the states of the text of the treaty or of the final act of a conference incorporating the text[5]. Some other means of authentication may, however, be substituted, for example by incorporation in a resolution of an international organisation[6], or, as in the case of conventions concluded under the auspices of the International Labour Organisation, by two persons only, the President of the International Labour Conference at which the convention is adopted and the Director General of the International Labour Office[7].

In the practice of the United Kingdom, a representative has to be furnished with full powers[8] in order to sign a treaty even for the limited purpose of its authentication[9].

1 Ie the formal act by which the final form and content of the treaty are settled. As to the meaning of 'treaty' see PARA 71.
2 Vienna Convention on the Law of Treaties (Vienna, 23 May 1969; TS 58 (1980); Cmnd 7964) art 9 para 1.
3 Vienna Convention on the Law of Treaties art 9 para 2. In practice, attempts will often be made to reach an agreement on a text by consensus, so, for example, the Third United Nations Conference on the Law of the Sea (1972–1983) proceeded on the basis that 'the Conference should make every effort to reach agreement on substantive matters by way of consensus and there should be no voting on such matters until all efforts at consensus have been exhausted': see the Informal Composite Negotiating Text art 153 para 4 (A/CONF.62/WP.10).
4 Vienna Convention on the Law of Treaties art 10(a).
5 Vienna Convention on the Law of Treaties art 10(b).
6 The Vienna Convention on the Law of Treaties applies to any treaty adopted within an international organisation without prejudice to any relevant rules of the organisation: see art 5.
7 As to authentication of the International Labour Organisation Conventions see the Constitution of the International Labour Organisation (Montreal, 9 September 1946; TS 47 (1948); Cmd 7452) art 19 para 4. As to the International Labour Organisation see PARA 533. Copies of the conventions may be obtained from the Publications Bureau, International Labour Office, 4 rue des Morillons, CH-1211 Geneva 22, Switzerland; or on the website of the International Labour Organisation, accessible on the date at which this title states the law at www.ilo.org.
8 As to the meaning of 'full powers' see PARA 73.
9 7 British Digest 591, citing Jones's Full Powers and Ratification 38.

76. Expressing consent to be bound. The consent of a state to be bound by a treaty[1] may be expressed by signature[2], exchange of instruments[3] constituting a treaty, ratification[4], acceptance, approval or accession[5], or by any other means if so agreed[6].

1 As to the meaning of 'treaty' see PARA 71.
2 As to signature see PARA 77.
3 As to the exchange of instruments see PARA 78.

4   As to ratification see PARA 79.
5   As to accession see PARA 80.
6   Vienna Convention on the Law of Treaties (Vienna, 23 May 1969; TS 58 (1980); Cmnd 7964)
    art 11. The consent of a state to be bound by part of a treaty is (without prejudice to the issue
    of reservations to treaties (see PARA 83)) effective only if the treaty so permits or the other
    contracting states so agree; and the consent of a state to be bound by a treaty which permits a
    choice between differing provisions is effective only if it is made clear to which of the provisions
    the consent relates: see art 17.

77.   Signature.   Signature of the text of a treaty[1] has traditionally served a
more significant purpose than mere authentication[2], as it constituted the first
part of the dual process of signature and ratification, whereby a state becomes
bound by the treaty. At one time subsequent ratification was formally necessary
as a matter of English law to the effectiveness of a signature for this purpose[3].
The modern rule is that the consent of a state to be bound by a treaty is
expressed by the signature of its representative[4] when (1) the treaty provides that
signature has that effect[5]; (2) it is otherwise established that the negotiating
states[6] were agreed that signature should have that effect[7]; or (3) the intention of
the state to give that effect to the signature appears from the full powers of its
representative or was expressed during the negotiation[8]. Although it is not clear
whether, in the absence of any evidence of this kind, the residuary rule is that
ratification is unnecessary or necessary in order that the parties may be bound by
a treaty, the question has little practical importance as treaties generally do
contain express wording on this matter[9].

1   As to the meaning of 'treaty' see PARA 71.
2   As to authentication see PARA 75.
3   *The Eliza Ann* (1813) 1 Dods 244, 6 BILC 345.
4   Vienna Convention on the Law of Treaties (Vienna, 23 May 1969; TS 58 (1980); Cmnd 7964)
    art 12. For these purposes the initialling of a text constitutes a signature of the treaty when it is
    established that the negotiating states so agreed, and the signature ad referendum of a treaty by
    a representative, if confirmed by this state, constitutes a full signature of the treaty: art 12
    para 2.
5   Vienna Convention on the Law of Treaties art 12 para 1(a).
6   'Negotiating state' means a state which took part in the drawing up and adoption of the text of
    the treaty: Vienna Convention on the Law of Treaties art 2 para 1(e).
7   Vienna Convention on the Law of Treaties art 12 para 1(b).
8   Vienna Convention on the Law of Treaties art 12 para 1(c).
9   See Sinclair's The Vienna Convention on the Law of Treaties (2nd Edn, 1984) 39–41; and Aust
    Modern Treaty Law and Practice (2nd Edn, 2007) 96–97 (expressing the view that the issue is
    of no practical importance today as it has long been the practice of states, when they intend a
    treaty to enter into force by a procedure involving more than just signature, to provide evidence
    of that intention, usually by an express provision in the treaty).

78.   Exchange of instruments.   The consent of states to be bound by a treaty[1]
constituted by instruments exchanged between them is expressed by that
exchange when: (1) the instruments provide that their exchange has that effect[2];
or (2) it is otherwise established that those states were agreed that the exchange
of instruments should have that effect[3].

1   As to the meaning of 'treaty' see PARA 71.
2   Vienna Convention on the Law of Treaties (Vienna, 23 May 1969; TS 58 (1980); Cmnd 7964)
    art 13(a).
3   Vienna Convention on the Law of Treaties art 13(b).

79.   Ratification, acceptance or approval.   The consent of a state to be bound
by a treaty[1] is expressed by ratification when: (1) the treaty provides for such
consent to be expressed by means of ratification[2]; (2) it is otherwise established

that the negotiating states[3] were agreed that ratification should be required[4]; (3) the representative of the state has signed the treaty subject to ratification[5]; or (4) the intention of the state to sign the treaty subject to ratification appears from the full powers[6] of its representative or was expressed during the negotiation[7]. A state's consent to be bound by a treaty is expressed by acceptance or approval under conditions similar to those which apply to ratification[8]. Where ratification or the like is required, it is commonly effected by the United Kingdom in the form of an instrument under the Great Seal, but may exceptionally be under a signature of the Secretary of State for Foreign and Commonwealth Affairs[9]. Ratification does not generally have a retroactive effect[10].

1   As to the meaning of 'treaty' see PARA 71.
2   Vienna Convention on the Law of Treaties (Vienna, 23 May 1969: TS 58 (1980); Cmnd 7964) art 14 para 1(a).
3   As to the meaning of 'negotiating state' see PARA 77 note 6.
4   Vienna Convention on the Law of Treaties art 14 para 1(b).
5   Vienna Convention on the Law of Treaties art 14 para 1(c).
6   As to the meaning of 'full powers' see PARA 73.
7   Vienna Convention on the Law of Treaties art 14 para 1(d). As to the question whether ratification is called for when it is not provided for in any of these ways see PARA 77. In the United Kingdom it is the Crown who authorises signature and effects ratification. It should be remembered that ratification (as with acceptance, approval and accession) is an international act whereby a state establishes on the international plane its consent to be bound by a treaty, generally by deposit of an instrument of ratification, to be distinguished from domestic processes that may be required in order to effect ratification.
8   Vienna Convention on the Law of Treaties art 14 para 2. These methods of expressing consent to be bound are increasingly used in modern practice in order chiefly to avoid complication which may arise from the provisions of constitutions of countries such as the United States of America which, while admitting to the making of what are termed executive agreements, which entail the expression of consent to be bound being expressed in an informal fashion, prescribe a formal and often laborious procedure for ratification of treaties expressly so called.
9   For an example of an instrument of ratification in the simplified wording now used see Aust *Modern Treaty Law and Practice* (2nd Edn, 2007) App L. As to the use of the Great Seal see CONSTITUTIONAL LAW AND HUMAN RIGHTS vol 8(2) (Reissue) PARA 909. As to exchange or deposit of instruments of ratification, acceptance, approval or accession see Vienna Convention on the Law of Treaties art 16.
10 As to the date of entry into force of a treaty see Vienna Convention on the Law of Treaties art 24; and PARA 89. The issue of whether a treaty has yet been ratified may be of critical importance in both international and domestic claims. See *Iloilo Claims* 6 RIAA 158 (1925). See also *The Eliza Ann* (1813) 1 Dods 244, 6 BILC 345; *Kotzias v Tyser* [1920] 2 KB 69, 6 BILC 348; *Lloyd v Bowring* (1920) 36 TLR 397, 6 BILC 354. See further *Philippson v Imperial Airways Ltd* [1939] AC 332.

80.   Accession. Where a treaty[1] is already in force between two or more states, another state which wishes to become a party to it may do so by accession. The position is the same when, in the case of a multilateral treaty, a state which has participated in the drawing up of the treaty, but has not signed it before the expiry of the period for signature, wishes to become a party to it. Its consent to be bound by a treaty is expressed by accession when: (1) the treaty provides that such consent may be expressed by that state by means of accession[2]; (2) it is otherwise established that the negotiating states[3] were agreed that such consent may be expressed by that state by means of accession[4]; or (3) all the parties have subsequently agreed that such consent may be expressed by that state by means of accession[5].

1   As to the meaning of 'treaty' see PARA 71.
2   Vienna Convention on the Law of Treaties (Vienna, 23 May 1969; TS 58 (1980); Cmnd 7964) art 15(a).
3   As to the meaning of 'negotiating state' see PARA 77 note 6.

4   Vienna Convention on the Law of Treaties art 15(b).
5   Vienna Convention on the Law of Treaties art 15(c). There is no need for a third state to participate in any process of adoption or authentication of the text, nor for any time to be required by it in which to consider the impact of the treaty upon its relations generally or to amend its laws consistent with the treaty, since this may be done before its accession to the treaty.

81.   Variations on traditional methods of treaty-making. It has become relatively common to adopt variants upon the traditional treaty-making[1] methods of signature[2], signature followed by ratification[3] and accession[4], for the purpose of simplifying or accelerating matters. Thus a text adopted by a conference and authenticated[5] by some simplified device may be 'opened for signature' for all parties, either indefinitely or for a certain time, after which fresh parties will be acceding rather than signatory parties. With the adoption of such variations, signature, ratification and accession tend to become indistinguishable[6].

In this context it is to be observed also that any attempt to categorise the means whereby a state may become party to a treaty can be a source of confusion. The Charter of the United Nations[7], for instance, provides that states other than the original members seeking admission must 'accept the obligations contained in' that instrument, and their admission is subject inter alia to a vote of two-thirds of the members of the United Nations General Assembly present and voting upon a recommendation of the Security Council[8].

1   As to the meaning of 'treaty' see PARA 71.
2   As to signature see PARA 77.
3   As to ratification see PARA 79.
4   As to accession see PARA 80.
5   As to adoption and authentication see PARA 75.
6   In this respect, the consent of a state to be bound by a treaty may be expressed inter alia by any other means if so agreed: see the Vienna Convention on the Law of Treaties (Vienna, 23 May 1969; TS 58 (1980); Cmnd 7964) art 11; and PARA 76.
7   Ie the Charter of the United Nations (San Francisco, 26 June 1945; TS 67 (1946); Cmd 7015).
8   See the Charter of the United Nations arts 4 para 1, 18 para 2; and PARAS 520, 527.

82.   Obligation not to defeat the object and purpose of a treaty prior to its entry into force. A state is obliged to refrain from acts which would defeat the object and purpose of a treaty[1] when (1) it has signed the treaty or has exchanged instruments constituting the treaty subject to ratification, acceptance or approval[2], until it has made its intention clear not to become a party to the treaty[3]; or (2) it has expressed its consent to be bound by the treaty, pending the entry into force of the treaty and provided that such entry into force is not unduly delayed[4].

1   As to the meaning of 'treaty' see PARA 71.
2   As to ratification, acceptance or approval see PARA 79.
3   Vienna Convention on the Law of Treaties (Vienna, 23 May 1969; TS 58 (1980); Cmnd 7964) art 18(1).
4   Vienna Convention on the Law of Treaties art 18(2). See also Aust *Modern Treaty Law and Practice* (2nd Edn, 2007) 116–119.

83.   Reservations. A reservation is a unilateral statement, however phrased or named, made by a state when signing[1], ratifying, accepting, approving[2] or acceding[3] to a treaty[4], whereby it purports to exclude or to modify the legal effect of certain provisions of the treaty in their application to that state[5]. The subject matter of a reservation is commonly a restriction of the obligations of the state making it, but exceptionally it may be a mere variation or even a purported undertaking of something more than the treaty text requires[6]. Where a bilateral treaty is concerned, a reservation is simply the proposal of an amendment of the treaty text. The legality of reservations is only a separate legal issue in the case of multilateral treaties.

1   As to signature see PARA 77.
2   As to ratification, acceptance and approval see PARA 79.
3   As to accession see PARA 80.
4   As to the meaning of 'treaty' see PARA 71.
5   Vienna Convention on the Law of Treaties (Vienna, 23 May 1969; TS 58 (1980); Cmnd 7964) art 2 para 1(d). As to the effect of a reservation that was permissible under the relevant treaty and to which no objection had been taken by the other state concerned see *Legality of Use of Force (Yugoslavia v United States of America) (Provisional Measures)* ICJ Reports 1999, 916 at 924 (where the International Court of Justice found that the reservation had the effect of excluding the relevant provision so far as the two parties were concerned). It is necessary to distinguish between a true reservation and an interpretative declaration, which does not have this effect. For a further distinction between a 'mere' interpretative declaration and a 'qualified interpretative declaration' by which a state seeks to make its acceptance of a treaty provision depend upon acceptance by other states of its interpretation thereof and which is therefore assimilable to a true reservation see *Belilos v Switzerland* (1988) 10 EHRR 446, ECtHR. As to consideration of the effect of an interpretative declaration by the English courts see *Jones v Ministry of the Interior of the Kingdom of Saudi Arabia (Secretary of State for Constitutional Affairs intervening)* [2006] UKHL 26, [2007] 1 AC 270, [2007] 1 All ER 113.
6   See generally I Oppenheim's International Law (9th Edn, 1992) 1240–1248, Shaw's International Law (6th Edn) 913–925; and Aust *Modern Treaty Law and Practice* (2nd Edn, 2007) Ch 8. See also the work of the International Law Commission on Reservations to Treaties including the reports of the Special Rapporteur and the ILC Draft Guidelines which was available at the date at which this volume states the law on www.untreaty.un.org/ilc.

84.   Formulation of reservations.   A state may, when signing[1], ratifying, accepting, approving[2] or acceding[3] to a treaty[4], formulate a reservation[5] unless: (1) the reservation is prohibited by the treaty[6]; (2) the treaty provides that only specified reservations, which do not include the reservation in question, may be made[7]; or (3) in cases not falling under heads (1) or (2) the reservation is incompatible with the object and purpose of the treaty[8].

1   As to signature see PARA 77.
2   As to ratification, acceptance and approval see PARA 79.
3   As to accession see PARA 80.
4   As to the meaning of 'treaty' see PARA 71.
5   As to the meaning of 'reservation' see PARA 83. Although this is not expressly stated in the Vienna Convention on the Law of Treaties (Vienna, 23 May 1969; TS 58 (1980); Cmnd 7964), the regime of reservations is concerned with multilateral as opposed to bilateral treaties: a reservation by one party to a proposed term of the bilateral treaty would necessitate a re-negotiation. The United Kingdom adheres to the view that for a state to seek to attach a reservation to a bilateral treaty as a condition of acceptance of that treaty is in effect to refuse acceptance of the treaty as drafted, and to require a reopening of the negotiations: see (1997) 68 BYIL 482.
6   Vienna Convention on the Law of Treaties art 19(a). See also *Belilos v Switzerland* (1988) 10 EHRR 446, ECtHR. For an example of such a prohibition see the Rome Statute of the International Criminal Court (17.7.98) (UN Doc A/CONF 183/9; 37 ILM (1998) 999) art 120.
7   Vienna Convention on the Law of Treaties art 19(b). For an example of such a provision see the United Nations Convention on the Law of the Sea (Montego Bay, 10 December 1982; TS 81 (1999); Cmnd 4524) art 309; and the Convention on the Continental Shelf (Geneva, 29 April 1958; TS 39 (1964); Cmnd 2422) art 12 para 1.
8   Vienna Convention on the Law of Treaties art 19(c). See *Reservations to the Convention on the Prevention and Punishment of the Crime of Genocide (Advisory Opinion)* ICJ Reports 1951, 15. Where the treaty itself permits reservations, these are, of course, allowed: *Arbitration between the United Kingdom and France on the Delimitation of the Continental Shelf* (Misc 15 (1978); Cmnd 7438); 18 RIAA 3 (1978).

85.   Acceptance of and objections to reservations.   A reservation[1] which is expressly authorised by a treaty[2] does not require any subsequent acceptance[3] by the other contracting states unless the treaty so provides[4]. When it appears from the limited number of negotiating states[5] and the object and purpose of the treaty that the application of the treaty in its entirety between all the parties is an essential condition of the consent of each one to be bound by the treaty, a reservation requires acceptance by all the parties[6]. When a treaty is a constituent instrument of an international organisation, then, unless otherwise provided, a reservation requires the acceptance of the competent organ of that organisation[7].

In cases not falling under any of the conditions noted above, and unless the treaty otherwise provides, (1) acceptance by another contracting state of a reservation constitutes the reserving state a party to the treaty in relation to that other state if or when the treaty is in force for those states[8]; (2) an objection by another state to a reservation does not preclude the entry into force of the treaty as between the objecting and reserving states unless a contrary intention is definitely expressed by the objecting state[9]; and (3) an act expressing a state's consent to be bound by the treaty and containing a reservation is effective as soon as at least one other contracting state has accepted the reservation[10].

Unless the treaty otherwise provides, a reservation is considered to have been accepted by a state if it has raised no objection to the reservation by the end of a period of 12 months after it was notified of it, or by the date on which it expressed its consent to be bound by the treaty, whichever is later[11].

1   As to the meaning of 'reservation' see PARA 83.
2   As to the meaning of 'treaty' see PARA 71.
3   As to acceptance see PARA 79.
4   Vienna Convention on the Law of Treaties (Vienna, 23 May 1969; TS 58 (1980); Cmnd 7964) art 20 para 1.
5   As to the meaning of 'negotiating state' see PARA 77 note 6.
6   Vienna Convention on the Law of Treaties art 20 para 2. A reservation must be formulated in writing and communicated to the other contracting states and other states entitled to become parties to the treaty: art 23 para 1; and see PARA 88. As to when a reservation is deemed to have been accepted see art 20 para 5; and the text to note 11.
7   Vienna Convention on the Law of Treaties art 20 para 3.
8   Vienna Convention on the Law of Treaties art 20 para 4(a).
9   Vienna Convention on the Law of Treaties art 20 para 4(b).
10 Vienna Convention on the Law of Treaties art 20 para 4(c). As to the legal effect of a reservation or an objection to it see art 21; and PARA 86. As to the communication of acceptances of and objections to reservations see art 23; and PARA 88.
11 Vienna Convention on the Law of Treaties art 20 para 5. It follows from art 20 para 4(b) (see the text to note 9) that the onus is on the objecting state to express its objection and, if it wishes to preclude the entry into force of the treaty as between itself and the reserving state, it must make this express.

86.   Legal effect of reservations and objections.   A reservation[1] established with regard to another party to a treaty[2] modifies for the reserving state in its relations with that other party the provisions of the treaty to which the reservation relates to the extent of the reservation, and modifies those provisions to the same extent for that other party in its relations with the reserving state[3]. The reservation does not modify the provisions of the treaty for the other parties to the treaty inter se[4]. When a state objecting to a reservation has not opposed the entry into force of the treaty between itself and the reserving state, the provisions to which the reservation relates do not apply as between the two states to the extent of the reservation[5].

1   As to the meaning of 'reservation' see PARA 83.

2   As to the meaning of 'treaty' see PARA 71.
3   Vienna Convention on the Law of Treaties (Vienna, 23 May 1969; TS 58 (1980); Cmnd 7964)
     art 21 para 1. A reservation therefore operates reciprocally where possible. For example, if in
     respect of a treaty providing for the waiver of port dues in favour of state-owned vessels, state X
     makes a reservation in relation to vessels employed in commerce, Y may levy dues on vessels of
     X of the category described in ports of Y, just as X may do on Y's vessels in X's ports; but if the
     reservation is 'except in the port of N, the capital city of X', this is obviously not capable of
     reciprocal application. It would appear that in order for a reservation to have legal effect as
     provided for in art 21, the procedural requirements of art 23 must be met: see PARA 88.
4   Vienna Convention on the Law of Treaties art 21 para 2.
5   Vienna Convention on the Law of Treaties art 21 para 3. In some cases (as in the example given
     in note 3) this rule must operate to render the reservation as effective as if it had been accepted.
     General international law will fill the gap created by the reservation and objection thereto:
     *Arbitration between the United Kingdom and France on the Delimitation of the Continental
     Shelf* (Misc 15 (1978); Cmnd 7438); 18 RIAA 3 (1978). As to the various unresolved issues in
     relation to the effect of an impermissible reservation, and also reservations to human rights
     treaties, see Shaw's International Law (6th Edn, 2008) 921–924, Aust *Modern Treaty Law and
     Practice* (2nd Edn, 2007) 144–151, and the draft guidelines adopted by the International Law
     Commission in the course of its work on reservations to treaties which were available at the date
     at which this volume states the law at www.untreaty.un.org/ilc.

87.   Withdrawal of reservations and objections.   Unless the treaty[1] otherwise
provides:

(1)   a reservation[2] may be withdrawn at any time and the consent of a state
       which has accepted the reservation is not required for its withdrawal[3];

(2)   an objection to a reservation may be withdrawn at any time[4]

Unless the treaty otherwise provides, or unless it is otherwise agreed, the
withdrawal of a reservation becomes operative in relation to another contracting
state only when notice of it has been received by that state, and the withdrawal
of an objection to a reservation becomes operative only when notice of it has
been received by the state which formulated the reservation[5].

1   As to the meaning of 'treaty' see PARA 71.
2   As to the meaning of 'reservation' see PARA 83.
3   Vienna Convention on the Law of Treaties (Vienna, 23 May 1969; TS 58 (1980); Cmnd 7964)
     art 22 para 1.
4   Vienna Convention on the Law of Treaties art 22 para 2.
5   Vienna Convention on the Law of Treaties art 22 para 3.

88.   Procedure regarding reservations.   A reservation[1], an express acceptance
of a reservation and an objection to a reservation, must be formulated in writing
and communicated to the contracting states and other states entitled to become
parties to the treaty[2]. If formulated when signing[3] the treaty subject to
ratification, acceptance or approval[4], a reservation must be formally confirmed
by the reserving state when expressing its consent to be bound[5] by the treaty[6]. In
such a case the reservation is considered as having been made on the date of its
confirmation[7]. An express acceptance of, or an objection to, a reservation made
previously to confirmation of the reservation does not itself require
confirmation[8]. Finally the withdrawal of a reservation or of an objection to it
must be formulated in writing[9].

1   As to the meaning of 'reservation' see PARA 83.
2   Vienna Convention on the Law of Treaties (Vienna, 23 May 1969; TS 58 (1980); Cmnd 7964)
     art 23 para 1. As to the legal effects of a reservation see PARA 86. It would appear to follow that,
     in order for a reservation to have legal effect as provided for in art 21, the procedural
     requirements of art 23 must be met. As to the expression of consent to be bound by a treaty see
     PARA 76. As to the meaning of 'treaty' see PARA 71.
3   As to signature see PARA 77.

4   As to ratification, acceptance and approval see PARA 79.
5   As to consent to be bound see PARA 76.
6   Vienna Convention on the Law of Treaties art 23 para 2.
7   Vienna Convention on the Law of Treaties art 23 para 2.
8   Vienna Convention on the Law of Treaties art 23 para 3.
9   Vienna Convention on the Law of Treaties art 23 para 4.

(2) APPLICATION OF TREATIES

89.   Entry into force.   A treaty[1] enters into force in such manner and upon such date as it may provide or as the negotiating states[2] may agree[3]. Failing such provision or agreement, a treaty enters into force as soon as consent to be bound[4] by it has been established for all the negotiating states[5]. When the consent of a state to be bound by a treaty is established on a date after the treaty has come into force, the treaty enters into force for that state on that date, unless the treaty otherwise provides[6]. The provisions of a treaty regulating the authentication of its text, the establishment of the consent of states to be bound by the treaty, the manner or date of its entry into force, reservations[7], the functions of the depositary[8] and other matters arising necessarily before the entry into force of the treaty, apply from the time of the adoption of its text[9].

1   As to the meaning of 'treaty' see PARA 71.
2   As to the meaning of 'negotiating state' see PARA 77 note 6.
3   Vienna Convention on the Law of Treaties (Vienna, 23 May 1969; TS 58 (1980); Cmnd 7964) art 24 para 1. See McNair's Law of Treaties 191–205; and Aust *Modern Treaty Law and Practice* (2nd Edn, 2007) 163–177. In the case of modern multilateral treaties it is a frequent practice for the treaty itself to provide that it is to enter into force upon the expiration of a certain period of time after a given number of instruments of ratification or accession have been deposited. For example, the Convention on the Law of Treaties between States and International Organizations or between International Organizations (Vienna, 21 March 1986; Misc 11 (1987); Cm 244; (1986) ILM 543) art 85 para 1 provides that the Convention is to enter into force on the thirtieth day following the date of deposit of the 35th instrument of ratification or accession with the Secretary-General of the United Nations. More exceptionally, entry into force may be dependent on ratification of certain identified states: see the Treaty on the Non-Proliferation of Nuclear Weapons (London, Moscow and Washington, 1 July 1968; TS 88 (1970); Cmnd 4474).
4   As to consent to be bound see PARA 76.
5   Vienna Convention on the Law of Treaties art 24 para 2.
6   Vienna Convention on the Law of Treaties art 24 para 3. This applies to states which accede to a treaty. As to accession see PARA 80.
7   As to the meaning of 'reservation' see PARA 83.
8   As to depositaries see PARA 104.
9   Vienna Convention on the Law of Treaties art 24 para 4. Although these provisions apply, it is difficult to see that they impose any binding obligation. As to adoption see PARA 75.

90.   Provisional application of treaties.   A treaty[1] or part of it may be applied provisionally pending its entry into force, if the treaty itself so provides or if the negotiating states[2] have in some other manner so agreed[3]. Unless the treaty otherwise provides or the negotiating states have otherwise agreed, the provisional application of a treaty or part of a treaty with respect to a state is terminated if that state notifies the other states between which the treaty is being applied provisionally of its intention not to become a party to the treaty[4].

1   As to the meaning of 'treaty' see PARA 71.
2   As to the meaning of 'negotiating state' see PARA 77 note 6.
3   Vienna Convention on the Law of Treaties (Vienna, 23 May 1969; TS 58 (1980); Cmnd 7964) art 25 para 1. By way of practical example, pursuant to the Energy Charter Treaty (Lisbon, December 1994) art 45 (Annex 1 to the Final Act of the European Energy Charter Conference),

each signatory agrees to apply the treaty provisionally pending its entry into force for such signatory (to the extent that such provisional application is not inconsistent with its constitution, laws or regulations). The Russian Federation was a signatory but, on 20 August 2009, officially informed the depository that it did not intend to become a contracting party to the treaty. In accordance with art 45 para 3(a), such notification resulted in Russia's termination of its provisional application of the treaty upon expiration of 60 calendar days.

4   Vienna Convention on the Law of Treaties art 25 para 2.

91.   Performance.   Every treaty[1] in force is binding upon the parties to it and must be performed by them in good faith[2]. A party may not invoke the provisions of its internal law as justification for its failure to perform a treaty[3]. The obligation under a treaty depends upon international law exclusively, and although the implementation of many treaties calls for changes in the internal law of the parties, this is within their contemplation from the outset, and the entry into force of the treaty may be and often is expressly made dependent upon the procurement of the necessary changes in their internal laws[4].

1   As to the meaning of 'treaty' see PARA 71.
2   Vienna Convention on the Law of Treaties (Vienna, 23 May 1969; TS 58 (1980); Cmnd 7964) art 26. This rule (also called pacta sunt servanda) has been described as the fundamental principle of the law of treaties: see the Commentary of the International Law Commission, YILC 1966 II 211. For a practical application of the rule, see *Gabčíkovo-Nagymaros Project (Hungary/Slovakia)* ICJ Reports 1997, 7 at 78–79 (para 142). See also *Rights of Nationals of the United States of America in Morocco (France v United States of America)* ICJ Reports 1952, 176 at 212; *North Atlantic Fisheries Arbitration* 11 RIAA 167 at 188 (1910). For an application of the rule by the English courts, noting that the principle cannot require departure from what has been agreed, see *European Roma Rights Centre v Immigration Officer at Prague Airport (United Nations High Commissioner for Refugees intervening)* [2004] UKHL 55, [2005] 2 AC 1, [2005] 1 All ER 527.
3   Vienna Convention on the Law of Treaties art 27. This proposition is subject to the qualification that a manifest violation of a provision of the internal law of a party regarding competence to conclude treaties may in certain circumstances be invoked by that party: see art 46; and PARA 101. As to the rule that a state may not rely upon the inadequacies of its own law in response to a claim that it has incurred responsibility to another state in international law see PARA 333.
4   As to the relationship between treaties and English law see PARA 17 et seq.

92.   Successive treaties relating to the same subject matter.   It may happen that the same matter is the subject of successive treaties[1], the parties to which may or may not be exactly the same[2]. When a treaty specifies that it is subject to, or that it is not to be considered incompatible with, an earlier or later treaty, the provisions of that other treaty prevail[3]. When all the parties to the earlier treaty are also parties to the later treaty, but the earlier treaty is not terminated or suspended by one later in date[4], the earlier treaty applies only to the extent that its provisions are compatible with those of the later treaty[5]. When the parties to the later treaty do not include all the parties to the earlier one, the same rule applies as between states which are parties to both treaties[6], and as between a state party to both treaties and a state party to only one of the treaties, the treaty to which both are parties governs their mutual rights and obligations[7].

The foregoing rules are subject to the Charter of the United Nations[8] which provides that, in the event of a conflict between the obligations of members of the United Nations under the Charter[9] and their obligations under any other international agreement, their obligations under the Charter prevail[10].

1   As to the meaning of 'treaty' see PARA 71.
2   See Aust *Modern Treaty Law and Practice* (2nd Edn, 2008) Ch 12. The rules set out in the Vienna Convention on the Law of Treaties (Vienna, 23 May 1969; TS 58 (1980); Cmnd 7964) art 30 (see the text and notes 3–10) that regulate this situation are residual in nature and many treaties, in particular multilateral treaties, contain specific provisions regulating their

relationship to other treaty or treaties. Art 30 and the principles it contains have also been considered as part of the work of the International Law Commission under the rubric Fragmentation of international law: difficulties arising from the diversification and expansion of international law: see in particular the Report of the Study Group of 13 April 2006, Report of the International Law Commission, 58th Session, A/CN.4/L.682.

3 Vienna Convention on the Law of Treaties art 30 para 2.

4 As to the potential termination or suspension of treaties where all the parties to the treaty conclude a later treaty relating to the same subject matter see the Vienna Convention on the Law of Treaties art 59; and PARA 106.

5 Vienna Convention on the Law of Treaties art 30 para 3.

6 Vienna Convention on the Law of Treaties art 30 para 4(a).

7 Vienna Convention on the Law of Treaties art 30 para 4(b). See also *Entico Corpn Ltd v United Nations Educational Scientific and Cultural Association* [2008] EWHC 531 (Comm), [2008] 2 All ER (Comm) 97 at [18]. Both art 30 para 4(a) and (b) are without prejudice to art 41 (see PARA 100) or to any question of the termination and suspension of the treaty under art 60 (see PARA 107) or to any question of responsibility which may arise for a state from the conclusion or application of a treaty the provisions of which are incompatible with its obligations towards another state under another treaty: see art 30 para 5.

8 Ie the Charter of the United Nations (San Francisco, 26 June 1945; TS 67 (1946); Cmd 7015).

9 As to the membership of the United Nations see PARA 520.

10 Vienna Convention on the Law of Treaties art 30 para 1; Charter of the United Nations art 103. See the *Questions of Interpretation and Application of the 1971 Montreal Convention arising from the Aerial Incident at Lockerbie (Libyan Arab Jamahiriya v United Kingdom) (Provisional Measures)* ICJ Reports 1992, 3. In *R (on the application of Al-Jedda) v Secretary of State for Defence* [2007] UKHL 58, [2008] 1 AC 332, [2008] 3 All ER 28, the House of Lords considered and applied art 103 of the Charter of the United Nations in the context of conflicting obligations under binding Security Council resolutions and the European Convention of Human Rights. In Joined Cases C-402/05P and C-415/05P *Kadi and Al Barakaat International Foundation (Spain, interveners) v EU Council* [2008] ECR I-6351, [2008] All ER (D) 34 (Sep), ECJ, the European Court of Justice found that it was not a consequence of the principles governing the international legal order under the United Nations (including art 103 of the UN Charter) that any judicial review of the internal lawfulness of a contested EC regulation in the light of fundamental freedoms was excluded by virtue of the fact that that measure was intended to give effect to a resolution of the Security Council adopted under Chapter VII of the Charter.

93. Application of treaties in time. Unless a different intention appears from the treaty[1] or is otherwise established, its provisions do not bind a party in relation to any act or fact which took place or any situation which ceased to exist before the date of entry into force of the treaty with respect to that party[2].

1 As to the meaning of 'treaty' see PARA 71.

2 Vienna Convention on the Law of Treaties (Vienna, 23 May 1969; TS 58 (1980); Cmnd 7964) art 28. See also arts 18, 24 para 4, 25; and PARAS 82, 89, 90. The Convention itself provides that without prejudice to the application of customary international law, the Convention applies only to treaties concluded by states after the entry into force of the Convention with regard to such states: art 4. The principle of non-retroactivity stated in the text is also supported by the *Ambatielos (Greece v United Kingdom) (Preliminary Objection)* ICJ Reports 1952, 28 at 40. In English law the principle is supported by *The Eliza Ann* (1813) 1 Dods 244, 6 BILC 345. A special clause may be expressly given a retroactive application: *Mavrommatis Palestine Concessions* PCIJ Ser A No 2 (1924). See also the Articles on Responsibility of States for Internationally Wrongful Acts ('ARSIWA') arts 13–15, and the Commentary to articles 13–15, International Law Commission Report, 53rd Session, A/56/10, YILC 2001, vol II(2); and PARA 359 et seq. See also Higgins 'Time and the Law: International Perspectives on an Old Problem' in *Themes & Theories: Selected Essays, Speeches, and Writings in International Law* (2009) p 875 et seq.

94. Territorial application. Unless a different intention appears from the treaty[1] or is otherwise established, a treaty is binding upon each party in respect of its entire territory[2]. In the past, because of the constitutional complexities involved in legislating for overseas territories, the United Kingdom has made a practice of procuring the insertion in its treaties of territorial or colonial application clauses, although colonial application clauses are of course no longer used and territorial application clauses are now less common in modern multilateral treaties[3]. There exists also a device whereby a state makes a declaration as to the territorial application of the act of signature[4] or ratification[5]. Since 1967, when expressing consent to be bound by a multilateral treaty the United Kingdom has followed a consistent practice of declaring in writing to the depositary to which, if any, of its overseas territories the treaty will extend.

1 As to the meaning of 'treaty' see PARA 71.
2 Vienna Convention on the Law of Treaties (Vienna, 23 May 1969; TS 58 (1980); Cmnd 7964) art 29. Thus treaties entered into by the United Kingdom apply to overseas territories for which the United Kingdom is internationally responsible in the absence of some indication to the contrary.
3 Such a clause may provide either that the treaty applies to territories for whose international relations the United Kingdom is responsible, if special notice to that effect is given, or, conversely, that such territories are included unless a declaration is made or notice given that the treaty is not to apply to specified territories in the absence of a special acceptance on their behalf. In some cases the United Kingdom has objected to becoming a party to a multilateral convention which did not contain such a clause: see Contemporary Practice of the United Kingdom in the Field of International Law 1962 (II) 237; British Practice in International Law 1963 (II) 144.
4 As to signature see PARA 77.
5 For example, the United Kingdom ratified the Convention on the High Seas (Geneva, 29 April 1958; TS 5 (1963); Cmnd 1929) subject to a declaration that this did not extend to certain specified territories, and ratified the Treaty on the Non-Proliferation of Nuclear Weapons (London, Moscow and Washington, 1 July 1968; TS 88 (1970); Cmnd 4474) in respect of the United Kingdom and other specified territories only. As to modern British practice see Aust *Modern Treaty Law and Practice* (2nd Edn, 2008) 206–208. As to the influence of territorial application clauses on rules regarding state succession to treaties see PARA 57. As to ratification see PARA 79. As to the extra-territorial application of human rights territories see eg Application 52207/99 *Bankovic v Belgium* (2002) 11 BHRC 435, ECtHR; *R (on the application of Al-Skeini) v Secretary of State for Defence* [2007] UKHL 26, [2008] 1 AC 153, [2007] 3 All ER 685.

(3) INTERPRETATION OF TREATIES

95. The general rule. A treaty[1] must be interpreted in good faith in accordance with the ordinary meaning to be given to the terms of the treaty in their context and in the light of its object and purpose[2]. The context comprises[3], in addition to the text, including its preamble and annexes: (1) any agreement relating to the treaty which was made between all the parties in connection with the conclusion of the treaty[4]; and (2) any instrument which was made by one or more parties in connection with the conclusion of the treaty and accepted[5] by the other parties as an instrument related to the treaty[6].

1 As to the meaning of 'treaty' see PARA 71.
2 Vienna Convention on the Law of Treaties (Vienna, 23 May 1969; TS 58 (1980); Cmnd 7964) art 31 para 1; *Factory at Chorzów (Jurisdiction)* PCIJ Ser A No 9 at 24 (1927). See Gardiner *Treaty Interpretation* (2008); I Oppenheim's International Law (9th Edn, 1992) pp 1266–1284; Aust *Modern Treaty Law and Practice* (2nd Edn, 2007) Ch 13. Although the Vienna Convention on the Law of Treaties art 31 para 1 is frequently regarded as the starting point for any exercise in interpretation, the elements of art 31 (see also PARA 96) are not arranged hierarchically, and should be applied in a single combined operation: see the Commentary of the International Law Commission, YILC 1966 vol II, 219–220.
    The most generally favoured basic approach to interpretation is that which has primary regard to the textual meaning of the treaty: see eg the *Polish Postal Service in Danzig Case (Advisory Opinion)* PCIJ Ser B No 11 at 37 (1925); *Competence of the General Assembly for the Admission of a State to the United Nations (Advisory Opinion)* ICJ Reports 1950, 4 at 8.

The primacy of the treaty language, read in context and purposively, is of critical importance: *In re Deep Vein Thrombosis and Air Travel Group Litigation* [2005] UKHL 72, [2006] 1 AC 495, [2006] 1 All ER 786 at [31] per Lord Steyn. For a recent example of the English courts emphasising the importance of the textual approach and rejecting the need to search for the common intention of the parties, save as reflected in the text, see *Czech Republic v European Media Ventures SA* [2007] EWHC 2851 (Comm), [2008] 1 All ER (Comm) 531. As to the principle of effectiveness in the interpretation of treaties and its limitations see the *Interpretation of Peace Treaties with Bulgaria, Hungary and Romania (First Phase) (Advisory Opinion)* ICJ Reports 1950, 65; *Interpretation of Peace Treaties with Bulgaria, Hungary and Romania (Second Phase) (Advisory Opinion)* ICJ Reports 1950, 221; see also *Territorial Dispute (Libyan Arab Jamahiriya v Chad)* ICJ Reports 1994, 6 at 25–26. As to interpretation of treaties in the light of their object and purpose see eg *Oil Platforms (Islamic Republic of Iran v United States of America) (Preliminary Objection)* ICJ Reports 1996, 803 at 813–815; *Military and Paramilitary Activities in and against Nicaragua (Nicaragua v United States of America)* ICJ Reports 1986, 14; *Islam v Secretary of State for the Home Department* [1999] 2 AC 629, [1999] 2 All ER 545, HL. It has been suggested that the reference to the object and purpose of the treaty is a secondary or ancillary process in the application of the general rule on interpretation: Sinclair *The Vienna Convention on the Law of Treaties* (1973) p 130; and see also Aust's Modern Treaty Law and Practice (2nd Edn) 235. Greater weight on object and purpose may be placed so far as concerns the interpretation of human rights treaties such as the European Convention on Human Rights. The case law of the European Court of Human Rights shows that the Court has been willing to imply terms into the Convention when it was judged necessary or plainly right to do so, but the process of implication is to be carried out with caution: *Brown v Stott (Procurator Fiscal, Dunfermline)* [2003] 1 AC 681 at 703, [2003] 2 All ER 97 at 113–114, PC.

It has become increasingly common for the English courts to have to interpret treaties, and to apply the rules established by the Vienna Convention on the Law of Treaties to that effect. As to interpretation by the English courts of treaties incorporated into domestic legislation by virtue of a statute, and the application of the Convention in this context, see eg *Morris v KLM Royal Dutch Airlines, King v Bristow Helicopters Ltd* [2002] UKHL 7, [2002] 2 AC 628, [2002] 2 All ER 565 at [80]–[82]; *Sepet v Secretary of State for the Home Department* [2003] UKHL 15, [2003] 3 All ER 304, [2003] 1 WLR 856 at [6]; *Januzi v Secretary of State for the Home Department* [2006] UKHL 5, [2006] 2 AC 426, [2006] 3 All ER 305 at [4]. As the Vienna Convention on the Law of Treaties art 31 is taken as reflecting customary international law, it may still be applied to treaties that entered into force prior to the convention: see eg *European Roma Rights Centre v Immigration Officer at Prague Airport (United Nations High Commissioner for Refugees intervening)* [2004] UKHL 55, [2005] 2 AC 1, [2005] 1 All ER 527 at [18]–[19]. More generally as to the interpretation by the English courts of statutes which incorporate or are based upon treaties, see eg *Pan-American World Airways Inc v Department of Trade* [1976] 1 Lloyd's Rep 257, 119 Sol Jo 657, CA; *Gatoil International Inc v Arkwright-Boston Manufacturers Mutual Insurance Co* [1985] AC 255, [1985] 1 All ER 129, HL; *Post Office v Estuary Radio Ltd* [1968] 2 QB 740, [1967] 3 All ER 663, CA; *Salomon v Customs and Excise Comrs* [1967] 2 QB 116, [1966] 3 All ER 871, 9 BILC 685, CA; *Monte Ulia (Owners) v Banco (Owners), The Banco* [1971] P 137 at 145, [1971] 1 All ER 524 at 529, CA; *Corocraft Ltd v Pan American Airways Inc* [1969] 1 QB 616, [1969], 1 All ER 82, CA; *Federal Steam Navigation Co Ltd v Department of Trade and Industry* [1974] 2 All ER 97, [1974] 1 WLR 505, HL. As to interpretation of statutes generally see STATUTES.

The general rule remains that English courts have no power to interpret treaties not incorporated by statute into municipal law: see eg *R v Lyons* [2002] UKHL 44, [2003] 1 AC 976, [2002] 4 All ER 1028 at [28] per Lord Hoffman. Exceptionally the court may interpret such a treaty if its provisions have been incorporated into, for example, a contract and may refer to a treaty and its terms as part of the factual background against which a particular issue is to be determined: see *JH Rayner (Mincing Lane) Ltd v Department of Trade and Industry* [1990] 2 AC 418 at 500–501, sub nom *Maclaine Watson & Co Ltd v Department of Trade and Industry* [1989] 3 All ER 523 at 545, HL, per Lord Oliver of Aylmerton; *Littrell v United States of America (No 2)* [1994] 4 All ER 203 at 214–215, [1995] 1 WLR 82 at 93, CA, per Hoffman LJ; *Lonrho Exports Ltd v Export Credits Guarantee Department* [1999] Ch 158, [1996] 4 All ER 673. Similarly, a treaty may fall for interpretation by the English courts where an arbitration award made pursuant to the treaty is challenged within the jurisdiction: see eg *Republic of Ecuador v Occidental Exploration and Production Co* [2005] EWCA Civ 1116, [2006] QB 432, [2006] 2 All ER 225.

3   As an example of consideration of the relevant context by the English courts see *R v Secretary of State for the Home Department, ex p Read* [1989] AC 1014, sub nom *Read v Secretary of State for the Home Department* [1988] 3 All ER 993, HL.
4   Vienna Convention on the Law of Treaties art 31 para 2(a); *Ambatielos (Greece v United Kingdom) (Preliminary Objection)* ICJ Reports 1952, 28 at 44.
5   As to acceptance see PARA 79.
6   Vienna Convention on the Law of Treaties art 31 para 2(b); *Ambatielos (Greece v United Kingdom) (Preliminary Objection)* ICJ Reports 1952, 28 at 44.

96.   Further elements of the general rule.   Together with the context[1], the following must be taken into account: (1) any subsequent agreement between the parties regarding the interpretation of the treaty or the application of its provisions[2]; (2) any subsequent practice in the application of the treaty which establishes the agreement of the parties regarding its interpretation[3]; and (3) any relevant rules of international law applicable in the relations between the parties[4]. A special meaning different from the general or usual meaning is to be given to a term if it is established that the parties to the treaty so intended[5].

1   See PARA 95.
2   Vienna Convention on the Law of Treaties art 31 para 3(a). As to subsequent agreements see generally Gardiner *Treaty Interpretation* (1st Edn, 2008) pp 203–249, Aust's Modern Treaty Law and Practice (2nd Edn, 2008) pp 238–241.
3   Vienna Convention on the Law of Treaties art 31 para 3(b). As to subsequent practice see generally Gardiner *Treaty Interpretation* (1st Edn, 2008) pp 203–249, Aust's Modern Treaty Law and Practice (2nd Edn, 2008) pp 241–243, McNair's Law of Treaties 424–429. See also *R (on the application of Mullen) v Secretary of State for the Home Department* [2004] UKHL 18, [2005] 1 AC 1, [2004] 3 All ER 65.
4   Vienna Convention on the Law of Treaties art 31 para 3(c). See generally Gardiner *Treaty Interpretation* (1st Edn, 2008) pp 250–298. The Vienna Convention on the Law of Treaties art 31 para 3(c) has been the object of considerable scrutiny in recent years (see eg McLachlan 'The Principle of Systemic Integration and Article 31(3)(c) of the Vienna Convention on the Law of Treaties' (2005) 54 ICLQ pp 279–320; and the work of the International Law Commission on Fragmentation of International Law in particular the Report of the Study Group of 13 April 2006, Report of the International Law Commission, 58th Session, A/CN.4/L.682) and was applied to controversial effect in *Oil Platforms (Islamic Republic of Iran v United States of America)* ICJ Reports 2003, 161 (see the Separate Opinion of Judge Higgins at 225, 237). See also Application 35763/97 *Al-Adsani v United Kingdom* (2001) 34 EHRR 273, 12 BHRC 88, ECtHR. As to application in the English courts see *A v Secretary of State for the Home Department* [2005] UKHL 71, [2006] 2 AC 221, [2006] 1 All ER 575 at [29]; and *R (on the application of Al-Jedda) v Secretary of State for Defence* [2007] UKHL 58, [2008] 1 AC 332, [2008] 3 All ER 28 at [36]–[37] (by reference to the jurisprudence of the European Court of Human Rights). See also *Entico Corporation Ltd v United Nations Educational Scientific and Cultural Association, Secretary of State for Foreign and Commonwealth Affairs intervening* [2008] EWHC 531 (Comm), [2008] 2 All ER (Comm) 97. As to the interpretation of constituent treaties by the practice of international organisations see *Competence of the General Assembly for the Admission of a State to the United Nations (Advisory Opinion)* ICJ Reports 1950, 4 at 9; *Constitution of the Maritime Safety Committee of the Inter-Governmental Maritime Consultative Organisation (Advisory Opinion)* ICJ Reports 1960, 150 at 167; *Certain Expenses of the United Nations (Advisory Opinion)* ICJ Reports 1962, 151 at 157; *Legal Consequences for States of the Continued Presence of South Africa in Namibia (South West Africa) notwithstanding Security Council Resolution 276 (1970) (Request for Advisory Opinion)* ICJ Reports 1971, 359.
5   Vienna Convention on the Law of Treaties art 31 para 4. See generally Gardiner *Treaty Interpretation* (1st Edn, 2008) pp 250–298. The burden of proving that a term in a treaty was intended to bear a meaning other than its general or usual meaning is upon the party which alleges it: *Legal Status of Eastern Greenland* PCIJ Ser A/B No 53 (1933) (where Denmark failed to prove that 'Greenland' in administrative and legislative acts bore a meaning other than its usual geographical meaning); *Land, Island and Maritime Frontier Dispute (El Salvador v Honduras: Nicaragua intervening)* ICJ Reports 1992, 351 at 585. The general or usual meaning is that which the term bore at the time the treaty was concluded: *Rights of Nationals of the United States of America in Morocco (France v United States of America)* ICJ Reports 1952,

176; *European Roma Rights Centre v Immigration Officer at Prague Airport (United Nations High Commissioner for Refugees intervening)* [2004] UKHL 55, [2005] 2 AC 1, [2005] 1 All ER 527 at [18]–[19]. For an example of a case where the court referred to the meaning of a given term in customary international law to assist in the interpretation of a treaty term see *R (on the application of Kibris Türk Hava Yollari CTA Holidays) v Secretary of State for Transport (Republic of Cyprus intervening)* [2009] EWHC 1918 (Admin), [2009] All ER (D) 295 (Jul) at [36]–[37].

97. Supplementary means of interpretation. Recourse may be had to supplementary means of interpretation, including the preparatory work[1] of the treaty[2] and the circumstances of its conclusion, in order to confirm the meaning resulting from the application of the general rule[3] or to determine the meaning when the interpretation according to that rule either leaves the meaning ambiguous or obscure or leads to a result which is manifestly absurd or unreasonable[4]. It appears that the use of preparatory work is admissible in such circumstances even as against a party to a treaty which did not itself participate in its negotiation or conclusion, but became a party by subsequent accession[5]. In the interests of uniformity of application of conventions the courts in the United Kingdom can in certain circumstances refer to travaux préparatoires. The following conditions must be fulfilled before such use is made of them: (1) that the material involved is public and accessible[6]; and (2) that the travaux préparatoires clearly point to a definite legislative intention[7].

1 'Preparatory work' is not defined in the Vienna Convention on the Law of Treaties (Vienna, 23 May 1969; TS 58 (1980); Cmnd 7964). In general terms it means the record of the drafting of the treaty and its negotiation; it is very frequently referred to as the travaux préparatoires.

2 As to the meaning of 'treaty' see PARA 71.

3 As to the general rule see the Vienna Convention on the Law of Treaties art 31; and PARAS 95–96. Where the meaning of the text is sufficiently clear there is no need for recourse to such supplementary means of interpretation (see *Competence of the General Assembly for the Admission of a State to the United Nations (Advisory Opinion)* ICJ Reports 1950, 4 at 8), although supplementary means may be used for purposes of confirmation: see eg *Territorial Dispute (Libyan Arab Jamahiriya v Chad)* ICJ Reports 1994, 6; *Maritime Delimitation and Territorial Questions between Qatar and Bahrain (Qatar v Bahrain) (Jurisdiction and Admissability)* ICJ Reports 1995, 6 at 24. See generally Gardiner *Treaty Interpretation* (1st Edn, 2008) pp 306–310, 316–328.

4 Vienna Convention on the Law of Treaties art 32. As to resort to preparatory work in recent cases see eg *Maritime Delimitation and Territorial Questions between Qatar and Bahrain (Qatar v Bahrain) (Jurisdiction and Admissability)* ICJ Reports 1995, 6 at 24 (but cf the Dissenting Opinion of Vice-President Schwebel at 27); *Kasikili/Sedudu Island (Botswana/ Namibia)* ICJ Reports 1999, 1045 at 1074; *Legality of Use of Force (Serbia and Montenegro v Belgium) (Preliminary Objections)* ICJ Reports 2004, 279 at 319; Application 52207/99 *Bankovic v Belgium and Others* [2001] 11 BHRC 435, ECtHR. As to recent application in the English courts see *Effort Shipping Company Limited v Linden Management SA* [1998] AC 605, [1998] 1 All ER 495, HL; *R (on the application of Mullan) v Secretary of State for the Home Department* [2004] UKHL 18, [2005] 1 AC 1, [2004] 3 All ER 65, at [50]–[54]; *Aerotel Ltd v Telco Holdings Ltd* [2006] EWCA Civ 1371, [2007] 1 All ER 225, [2007] RPC 117 at [30]. See also *Black-Clawson International Ltd v Papierwerke Waldhof-Aschaffenburg AG* [1975] AC 591 at 640, [1975] 1 All ER 810 at 838, HL. As to resort to the circumstances of the conclusion of a treaty see *Legality of Use of Force (Serbia and Montenegro v Belgium) (Preliminary Objections)* ICJ Reports 2004, 279 at 319–323 (in conjunction with an analysis of the preparatory works). For further forms of supplementary means of interpretations and interpretative tools see 1 Oppenheim's International Law (9th Edn) pp 1277–1282.

  See generally Gardiner *Treaty Interpretation* (2008) Ch 8, Aust's Modern Treaty Law and Practice (2nd Edn, 2008) pp 244–249.

5 It is submitted that the statement in the text is correct in spite of remarks to the contrary in the *Territorial Jurisdiction of the International Commission of the River Oder Case* PCIJ Ser A No 23 (1929) which, it is thought, does not reflect current international practice: see 1 O'Connell's International Law (2nd Edn) 264; Aust's Modern Treaty Law and Practice (2nd Edn, 2008) pp 247.

6   *Fothergill v Monarch Airlines Ltd* [1981] AC 251, [1980] 2 All ER 696, HL. See *Gatoil International Inc v Arkwright-Boston Manufacturers Mutual Insurance Co* [1985] AC 255, [1985] 1 All ER 129, HL; *Re Deep Vein Thrombosis and Air Travel Group Litigation* [2005] UKHL 72, [2006] 1 AC 495, [2006] 1 All ER 786; *Czech Republic v European Media Ventures* [2007] EWHC 2851 (Comm), [2008] 1 All ER (Comm) 531.

7   *Fothergill v Monarch Airlines Ltd* [1981] AC 251, [1980] 2 All ER 696, HL. See *Gatoil International Inc v Arkwright-Boston Manufacturers Mutual Insurance Co* [1985] AC 255, [1985] 1 All ER 129, HL; *Effort Shipping Co Ltd v Linden Management SA* [1998] AC 605, [1998] 1 All ER 495; *Morris v KLM Royal Dutch Airlines, King v Bristow Helicopters* [2002] UKHL 7, [2002] 2 AC 628, [2002] 2 All ER 565; *R (on the application of Mullen) v Secretary of State for the Home Department* [2004] UKHL 18, [2005] 1 AC 1, [2004] 3 All ER 65 at [50].

98.   Treaties in two or more languages.   When a treaty[1] has been authenticated[2] in two or more languages, the text is equally authoritative in each language, unless the treaty provides or the parties agree that, in case of divergence, a particular text is to prevail[3]. The terms of the treaty are presumed to have the same meaning in each authentic text[4]. Except where a particular text is to prevail as above, when a comparison of the authentic texts discloses a difference of meaning which the general rules as to interpretation[5] do not remove, the meaning which best reconciles the texts, having regard to the object and purpose of the treaty, is to be adopted[6].

1   As to the meaning of 'treaty' see PARA 71.
2   As to authentication see PARA 75.
3   Vienna Convention on the Law of Treaties (Vienna, 23 May 1969; TS 58 (1980); Cmnd 7964) art 33 para 1. See *Fothergill v Monarch Airlines Ltd* [1981] AC 251, [1980] 2 All ER 696, HL (meaning of 'damage' ('avare') in the International Convention for the Unification of Certain Rules Relating to International Carriage by Air (Warsaw, 12 October 1929; TS 11 (1933); Cmd 4284) art 26(2)); cf *R (on the application of the Federation of Tour Operators) v HM Treasury* [2007] EWHC 2062 (Admin), [2008] STC 547, [2007] All ER (D) 18 (Sep), affd [2008] EWCA Civ 752, [2008] STC 2524. See generally Gardiner *Treaty Interpretation* (2008) pp 353–385, Aust's Modern Treaty Law and Practice (2nd Edn, 2008) pp 250–255. A version of the treaty in a language other than one of those in which the text was authenticated is considered an authentic text only if the treaty so provides or the parties so agree: Vienna Convention on the Law of Treaties art 33 para 2. See *Mavrommatis Palestine Concessions* PCIJ Ser A No 2 (1924). For a case concerning the interpretation of a treaty text and its translation incorporated into a statute see *Corocraft Ltd v Pan American Airways Inc* [1969] 1 QB 616, [1969] 1 All ER 82, CA. See also *James Buchanan & Co Ltd v Babco Forwarding and Shipping (UK) Ltd* [1978] AC 141, [1977] 3 All ER 1048, HL.
4   Vienna Convention on the Law of Treaties art 33 para 3. See *Kasikili/Sedudu Island (Botswana/Namibia)* ICJ Reports 1999, 1045 at 1062.
5   For the general rules see the Vienna Convention on the Law of Treaties arts 31, 32; and PARAS 95–97.
6   Vienna Convention on the Law of Treaties art 33 para 4. See *LaGrand (Germany v United States of America)* ICJ Reports 2001, 466 at 501–505; *Border and Transborder Armed Actions (Nicaragua v Honduras) (Jurisdiction and Admissability)* ICJ Reports 1988, 69. See also *Channel Tunnel Group Ltd and France-Manche SA v United Kingdom and France*, Partial Award of 30 January 2007, Arbitral Tribunal, paras 93, 295–302. In *R (on the application of the Federation of Tour Operators) v HM Treasury* [2007] EWHC 2062 (Admin), [2008] STC 547, [2007] All ER (D) 18 (Sep), affd [2008] EWCA Civ 752, [2008] STC 2524, some primacy was given to the English text of the treaty then before the court, not because it was more authentic than the other texts, but because the travaux préparatoires were in English and reference to them necessarily involved reference to the English texts. Furthermore, the court considered that the texts in the other languages were translations of the English text and could not have been intended to change the meaning of the English.

99.   Treaties and third states.   A treaty[1] does not create either obligations or rights for a third state without its consent[2]. However, an obligation arises for a third state from a provision of a treaty if the parties to it intend the provision to be the means of establishing the obligation and the third state expressly accepts[3] that obligation in writing[4]. A right arises for a third state from a provision of a treaty if the parties to the treaty intend the provision to accord that right either to the third state, or to a group of states to which it belongs, or to all states, and the third party assents to it[5]. Its assent is presumed so long as the contrary is not indicated, unless the treaty otherwise provides[6]; and in exercising such a right the third state must comply with the conditions for its exercise provided for in the treaty or established in conformity with the treaty[7].

Nothing in these provisions precludes a rule set forth in a treaty from becoming binding upon a third state as a customary rule of international law, recognised as such[8].

1   As to the meaning of 'treaty' see PARA 71.
2   Vienna Convention on the Law of Treaties (Geneva, 23 May 1969; TS 58 (1980); Cmnd 7964) art 34. 'Third state' means a state not party to the treaty: art 2 para 1(h). This statement of the maxim pacta tertiis nec nocent nec prosunt is also recognised by e g *Free Zones of Upper Savoy and the District of Gex Case* PCIJ Ser A/B No 46 at 147, 148 (1932); *Territorial Jurisdiction of the International Commission of the River Oder Case* PCIJ Ser A No 23 at 19–22 (1929). See also *The Jonge Josias* (1809) Edw 128 at 130–131, 6 BILC 534 obiter per Sir William Scott; *The Marie Glaeser* [1914] P 218. See generally Aust's Modern Treaty Law and Practice (2nd Edn, 2008) pp 256–261; Shaw's International Law (6th Edn, 2008) pp 928–930. As to consent see PARA 76.
3   As to acceptance see PARA 79.
4   Vienna Convention on the Law of Treaties art 35. As to the revocation or modification of obligations or rights of third states see art 37. The provision of art 35 makes clear that it is not the treaty itself but a collateral agreement whereby the third state becomes bound by the obligation. It is subject to an exception whereby an aggressor state may be bound by an obligation in relation to a treaty which may arise for an aggressor state in consequence of measures taken in conformity with the Charter of the United Nations (San Francisco, 26 June 1945; TS 67 (1946); Cmd 7015) with reference to that state's aggression: Vienna Convention on the Law of Treaties art 75. As to measures taken by the United Nations in cases of aggression see PARA 525.
5   Vienna Convention on the Law of Treaties art 36 para 1.
6   Vienna Convention on the Law of Treaties art 36 para 1.
7   Vienna Convention on the Law of Treaties art 36 para 2. As to the revocation or modification of third party rights see art 37. See also the *Free Zones of Upper Savoy and the District of Gex Case* PCIJ Ser A/B No 46 at 147, 148 (1932); *Aaland Islands Case* LoNJ 1920 Supp No 3 at 5.
    For examples of treaties making provisions in favour of third states generally see the Convention respecting the Free Navigation of the Suez Maritime Canal (Constantinople, 29 October 1888; C 5623); Treaty of Peace with Germany (Treaty of Versailles) (Versailles, 28 June 1919; TS 4 (1919); Cmd 153) art 380 (Kiel Canal) (as to which see the *SS 'Wimbledon'* PCIJ Ser A No 1 (1923) at 22 to the effect that the Kiel canal had ceased to be an internal and national navigable waterway and had become an international waterway for the benefit of all nations of the world; i e rights erga omnes had been established by the Treaty of Versailles). As to dispositive treaties and state succession see PARA 59.
8   Vienna Convention on the Law of Treaties art 38. However, a treaty may codify what is existing international law, which is binding upon third states without need for reference to the treaty.

100.   Amendment and modification of treaties. A treaty[1] may be amended by agreement between the parties, and the rules regarding the conclusion and entry into force of treaties laid down in the Vienna Convention on the Law of Treaties[2] apply to such an agreement except in so far as the treaty may otherwise provide[3]. This is the case with both bilateral and multilateral treaties, save that, in the case of multilateral treaties, unless the treaty provides otherwise[4]: (1) any proposal to amend a multilateral treaty as between all the parties must be notified to all the contracting states, each one of which has the right to take part in the decision as to the action to be taken in regard to the proposal and the negotiation and conclusion of any agreement for the amendment of the treaty[5]; (2) every state entitled to become a party to the treaty is also entitled to become a party to the treaty as amended[6]; (3) the amending agreement does not bind any state already a party to the treaty which does not become a party to the amending agreement[7]; and (4) any state which becomes a party to the treaty after the entry into force of the amending agreement is, failing an expression of a different intention by that state, to be considered as a party to the treaty as amended and to be considered as a party to the unamended treaty in relation to any party to the treaty not bound by the amending agreement[8].

Two or more of the parties to a multilateral treaty may conclude an agreement to modify the treaty as between themselves alone if (a) the possibility of such a modification is provided for in the treaty[9]; or (b) the modification in question is not prohibited by the treaty and does not affect the enjoyment by the other parties of their rights under the treaty or the performance of their obligations, and does not relate to a provision, derogation from which is incompatible with the effective execution of the object and purpose of the treaty as a whole[10].

1   As to the meaning of 'treaty' see PARA 71.
2   Ie the Vienna Convention on the Law of Treaties (Vienna, 23 May 1969; TS 58 (1980); Cmnd 7964).
3   Vienna Convention on the Law of Treaties art 39. See generally Aust's Modern Treaty Law and Practice (2nd Edn, 2008) p 262, with particular reference to the practical importance of amendments to treaties and examples of differing mechanisms for amendment established by specific multilateral treaties; and Shaw's International Law (6th Edn, 2008) pp 930–932.
4   See the Vienna Convention on the Law of Treaties art 40 para 1. It should be noted that the amendment provided for is by way of agreement, ie the formalities of a further treaty are not necessarily required.
5   Vienna Convention on the Law of Treaties art 40 para 2.
6   Vienna Convention on the Law of Treaties art 40 para 3.
7   Vienna Convention on the Law of Treaties art 40 para 4. In this case the provisions of art 30 para 4(b) (see PARA 92) apply: see art 40 para 4.
8   Vienna Convention on the Law of Treaties art 40 para 5.
9   Vienna Convention on the Law of Treaties art 41 para 1(a). In a case falling under para 1(a), unless the treaty otherwise provides, the parties in question must notify the other parties of their intention to conclude the agreement and the modification to the treaty for which it provides: art 41 para 2.
10 Vienna Convention on the Law of Treaties art 41 para 1(b).

(4) INVALIDITY OF TREATIES

101.   Invalidity: lack of competence to conclude treaties. A state may not invoke the fact that its consent to be bound[1] by a treaty[2] has been expressed in violation of a provision of its internal law regarding competence to conclude treaties as invalidating its consent unless that violation was manifest[3] and concerned a rule of its internal law of fundamental importance[4]. If the authority of a representative to express the consent of a state to be bound by a particular treaty has been made subject to a specific restriction, his omission to observe that restriction may not be invoked as invalidating the consent expressed by him unless the restriction was notified to the other negotiating states[5] prior to his expressing such consent[6].

1   As to consent to be bound see PARA 76.
2   As to the meaning of 'treaty' see PARA 71.
3   A violation is manifest if it would be objectively evident to any state conducting itself in the matter in accordance with normal practice and in good faith: Vienna Convention on the Law of Treaties (Vienna, 23 May 1969; TS 58 (1980); Cmnd 7964) art 46 para 2.
4   Vienna Convention on the Law of Treaties art 46 para 1. As to the procedure in such cases see art 65; and PARA 109. As to the separability of treaty provisions in certain circumstances see art 44. As to the loss of a right to invoke a ground for invalidating a treaty by reason of waiver

or acquiescence see art 45. As to the consequences of invalidity see arts 43, 69. The provisions of a void legal treaty have no force. See generally 1 Oppenheim's International Law (9th Edn) pp 1284–1295; Aust's Modern Treaty Law and Practice (2nd Edn, 2008) Ch 17.

Arguments based on alleged unconstitutionality of treaties were rejected in the *Maritime Delimitation and Territorial Questions between Qatar and Bahrain (Qatar v Bahrain) (Jurisdiction and Admissability)* ICJ Reports 1994, 112 at 121–122; *Application of the Convention on the Prevention and Punishment of the Crime of Genocide (Bosnia and Herzegovina v Yugoslavia) (Preliminary Objections)* ICJ Reports 1996, 595 at 621–622. A limitation of a head of state's capacity is not manifest unless at least properly publicised; there is no general legal obligation for states to keep themselves informed of legislative and constitutional developments in other states which are or may become important for the international relations of these states: *Land and Maritime Boundary between Cameroon and Nigeria (Cameroon v Nigeria: Equatorial Guinea Intervening)* ICJ Reports 2002, 303 at 430. The rule stated in the text appears to mean that a state cannot invoke its internal law unless its agent acted in open and notorious excess of his authority. The case contemplated therefore appears to be unlikely to arise in practice. See also *Legal Status of Eastern Greenland* PCIJ Ser A/B No 53 (1933); *British Claims in the Spanish Zone of Morocco* 2 RIAA 615 at 724 (1925). In neither of these cases did the tribunal pay any regard to the point. As to the rule precluding a state from invoking the provisions of its internal law as justification for its failure to perform a treaty see the Vienna Convention on the Law of Treaties art 27; and PARA 91.

5   As to the meaning of 'negotiating states' see PARA 77 note 6.
6   Vienna Convention on the Law of Treaties art 47. This seems to be a largely theoretical case.

102.   Invalidity: error, fraud and corruption. A state may invoke an error in a treaty[1] as invalidating its consent to be bound[2] by the treaty if the error relates to a fact or situation which was assumed by that state to exist at the time when the treaty was concluded and formed an essential basis of its consent to be bound by the treaty[3]. If a state has been induced to conclude a treaty by the fraudulent conduct of another negotiating state[4], the state may invoke the fraud as invalidating its consent to be bound by the treaty[5]. Likewise, if the expression of a state's consent to be bound by a treaty has been procured through the corruption of its representative directly or indirectly by another negotiating state, the state may invoke such corruption as invalidating its consent to be bound by the treaty[6].

1   As to the meaning of 'treaty' see PARA 71.
2   As to consent to be bound see PARA 76.
3   Vienna Convention on the Law of Treaties (Vienna, 23 May 1969; TS 58 (1980); Cmnd 7964) art 48 para 1. The error cannot be invoked if the state in question contributed by its own conduct to the error or if the circumstances were such as to put the state on notice of a possible error (art 48 para 2), and an error relating only to the wording of the text of a treaty does not affect its validity (art 48 para 3). As to the corrections of errors see art 79. An error in a map annexed to a boundary treaty was invoked in the *Case concerning the Temple of Preah Vihear (Cambodia v Thailand)* ICJ Reports 1962, 6, but without success. See generally, as to error, fraud and corruption, Aust's Modern Treaty Law and Practice (2nd Edn, 2008) pp 315–317; Shaw's International Law (6th Edn) pp 941–944. As to the procedure in such cases see Vienna Convention on the Law of Treaties art 65; and PARA 109. As to the separability of treaty provisions in certain circumstances see art 44. As to the loss of a right to invoke a ground for invalidating a treaty by reason of waiver or acquiescence see art 45. As to the consequences of invalidity see arts 43, 69.
4   As to the meaning of 'negotiating state' see PARA 77 note 6.
5   Vienna Convention on the Law of Treaties art 49. As to separability of treaty provisions see art 44(4). As to the meaning of 'fraud' see YILC 1966 vol II, 244.
6   Vienna Convention on the Law of Treaties art 50. As to separability of treaty provisions see art 44(4). As to the meaning of 'corruption' see YILC 1966 vol II, 245.

103.   Invalidity: coercion, threat or use of force, and conflict with a peremptory norm. The expression of a state's consent to be bound[1] by a treaty[2] which has been procured by the coercion of its representative through acts or threats directed against him is without any legal effect[3]. Further, a treaty is void if its conclusion has been procured by the threat or use of force in violation of the principles of international law embodied in the Charter of the United Nations[4]. A treaty is also void if, at the time of its conclusion, it conflicts with a peremptory norm of general international law, which is to say a norm accepted and recognised by the international community of states as a whole as a norm from which no derogation is permitted and which can be modified only by a subsequent norm of general international law having the same character[5].

1   As to consent to be bound see PARA 76.

2   As to the meaning of 'treaty' see PARA 71. As to the consequences of invalidity see the Vienna Convention on the Law of Treaties (Vienna, 23 May 1969; TS 58 (1980); Cmnd 7964) art 69.

3   Vienna Convention on the Law of Treaties (Vienna, 23 May 1969; TS 58 (1980); Cmnd 7964) art 51. For the case of Dr Hacha, President of Czechoslovakia, against whom threats were used by Nazis on 15 March 1939 see McNair's Law of Treaties 208. For the consequences of invalidity see the Vienna Convention on the Law of Treaties arts 43, 69. The provisions of a treaty which is void under art 51 are not separable, and the whole treaty is therefore void in its entirety: art 44 para 5. See generally, 1 Oppenheim's International Law (9th Edn) pp 1294–1295; Aust's Modern Treaty Law and Practice (2nd Edn, 2008) pp 317–323.

4   See the Vienna Convention on the Law of Treaties art 52. The principle of international law referred to is embodied in the Charter of the United Nations (San Francisco, 26 June 1945; TS 67 (1946); Cmd 7015) art 2 para 4, which sets out the modern customary international law on the use of force. Unquestionably treaties of peace concluded before the era of the Covenant of the League of Nations (Versailles, 28 June 1919; TS 4 (1919); Cmd 153) and the International Treaty for the Renunciation of War as an Instrument of National Policy (The Kellogg-Briand Pact) (Paris, 27 August 1928; TS 29 (1929); Cmd 3410) were and are valid. Further, the Vienna Convention on the Law of Treaties art 52 does not apply to the threat or use of lawful force. A plea that an agreement was procured by the use of unlawful force was rejected in the *Fisheries Jurisdiction (United Kingdom v Iceland) (Jurisdiction of the Court)* ICJ Reports 1973, 3 at 14.
    The provisions of a treaty which is void under art 52 are not separable, and the whole treaty is therefore void in its entirety: art 44 para 5.

5   Vienna Convention on the Law of Treaties art 53. Further, if a new peremptory norm of general international law (jus cogens) emerges, any existing treaty which is in conflict with that norm becomes void and terminates: see art 64. Mere emergence of new requirements of international law for the protection of the environment, short of a new peremptory norm of environmental law, does not preclude performance of a treaty: *Gabčíkovo-Nagymaros Project (Hungary/Slovakia) (Order of 5 February 1997)* ICJ Reports 1997, 3. For procedures in relation to the settlement of disputes concerning the application or interpretation of Vienna Convention on the Law of Treaties arts 53 and 64, see art 66(a). As to the consequences of invalidity see art 71. The concept of jus cogens was referred to by the International Court of Justice in eg *Armed Activities on the Territory of the Congo (New Application: 2002) (Democratic Republic of the Congo v Rwanda) (Jurisdiction and Admissibility)* ICJ Reports 2006, 6 at 32, 52 (paras 64, 125), and has become well established, not least in terms of application by the English courts (see *R v Bow Street Metropolitan Stipendiary Magistrate, ex p Pinochet Ugarte (No 3)* [2000] 1 AC 147 at 197–199, sub nom *R v Bow Street Metropolitan Stipendiary Magistrate, ex p Pinochet Ugarte (Amnesty International intervening) (No 3)* [1999] 2 All ER 97 at 107–109, HL; *A v Secretary of State for the Home Department (No 2)* [2005] UKHL 71, [2006] 2 AC 221, [2006] 1 All ER 575 at [33]; *Jones v Ministry of the Interior of the Kingdom of Saudi Arabia (Secretary of State for Constitutional Affairs intervening)* [2006] UKHL 26, [2007] 1 AC 270, [2007] 1 All ER 113 at [42]–[44] per Lord Hoffman). See also Application 35763/97 *Al-Adsani v United Kingdom* (2001) 34 EHRR 273, 12 BHRC 88, ECtHR. However, there are no clearly established criteria for identifying which norms of international law have a peremptory character, and there is controversy as to which norms do qualify and as to their precise effect. Those peremptory norms that are clearly accepted and recognised include the prohibitions of aggression, genocide, slavery and racial discrimination, crimes against humanity and torture, and the right to self-determination: see Articles on Responsibility of States for Internationally Wrongful Acts ('ARSIWA') art 26 and the Commentary to Article 26, para 5, Report of the International Law Commission, 53rd Session (2001), YILC 2001, vol II(2) (referred to in *R (on the application of Al Jedda) v Secretary of State for Defence* [2006] EWCA Civ 327, [2007] QB 621, [2006] 3 WLR 954 at [66]); and PARA 362.

(5) DEPOSIT AND REGISTRATION OF TREATIES

104. Depositaries. It is usual in modern multilateral treaties to designate one or more states, or the chief executive officer of an international organisation, such as the Secretary-General of the United Nations, as the depositary[1]. The designation of the depositary of a treaty[2] may be made by the negotiating states[3], either in the treaty itself or in some other manner[4]. The functions of the depositary of a treaty are international in character and the depositary is under an obligation to act impartially in their performance; in particular, the fact that a treaty has not entered into force between certain of the parties or that a difference has appeared between a state and a depositary with regard to the performance of the latter's functions does not affect that obligation[5].

The functions of a depositary, unless otherwise provided in the treaty or agreed by the contracting states, comprise in particular:

(1)   keeping custody of the original text of the treaty and of any full powers delivered to the depositary[6];

(2)   preparing certified copies of the original text and preparing any further text of the treaty in such additional languages as may be required by the treaty and transmitting them to the parties and to the states entitled to become parties to the treaty[7];

(3)   receiving any signatures to the treaty and receiving and keeping custody of any instruments, notifications and communications relating to it[8];

(4)   examining whether the signature or any instrument, notification or communication relating to the treaty is in due and proper form and, if need be, bringing the matter to the attention of the state in question[9];

(5)   informing the parties and the states entitled to become parties to the treaty of acts, notifications and communications relating to the treaty[10];

(6)   informing the states entitled to become parties to the treaty when the number of signatures or of instruments of ratification, acceptance, approval or accession required for the entry into force of the treaty has been received or deposited[11];

(7)   registering the treaty with the Secretariat of the United Nations[12];

(8)   performing other specified functions[13].

In the event of any difference appearing between a state and the depositary as to the performance of the latter's functions, the depositary must bring the question to the attention of the signatory states and the contracting states or, where appropriate, of the competent organ of the international organisation concerned[14].

1   The depositary may be one or more states, an international organisation or the chief administrative officer of the organisation: Vienna Convention on the Law of Treaties (Vienna, 23 May 1969; TS 58 (1980); Cmnd 7964) art 76 para 1.
2   As to the meaning of 'treaty' see PARA 71.
3   As to the meaning of 'negotiating state' see PARA 77 note 6.
4   Vienna Convention on the Law of Treaties art 76 para 1.
5   Vienna Convention on the Law of Treaties art 76 para 2.
6   Vienna Convention on the Law of Treaties art 77 para 1(a).
7   Vienna Convention on the Law of Treaties art 77 para 1(b).
8   Vienna Convention on the Law of Treaties art 77 para 1(c).
9   Vienna Convention on the Law of Treaties art 77 para 1(d).
10   Vienna Convention on the Law of Treaties art 77 para 1(e).
11   Vienna Convention on the Law of Treaties art 77 para 1(f).
12   Vienna Convention on the Law of Treaties art 77 para 1(g). As to the registration of treaties see PARA 105.

13   Vienna Convention on the Law of Treaties art 77 para 1(h).

14   Vienna Convention on the Law of Treaties art 77 para 2.

105.   Registration of treaties. The Charter of the United Nations[1] provides that every treaty[2] and every international agreement entered into by any member of the United Nations must be registered with the secretariat and published by it[3], and that no party to any treaty or agreement not so registered may invoke it before any organ of the United Nations[4].

1   Ie the Charter of the United Nations (San Francisco, 26 June 1945; TS 67 (1946); Cmd 7015).

2   As to treaties see PARA 71.

3   Charter of the United Nations art 102 para 1. See generally Cadell, 'Treaties, Registration and Publication', *Max Planck Encyclopaedia of Public International Law*; and Aust *Modern Treaty Law and Practice* (2nd Edn, 2007) Ch 19.

4   Charter of the United Nations art 102 para 2. See also the Vienna Convention on the Law of Treaties (Vienna, 23 May 1969; TS 58 (1980); Cmnd 7964) art 80. The organs of the United Nations include the International Court of Justice (Charter of the United Nations art 7). As to the International Court of Justice see PARA 499 et seq. In *Maritime Delimitation and Territorial Questions between Qatar and Bahrain (Qatar v Bahrain) (Jurisdiction and Admissability)* ICJ Reports 1994, 112 the ICJ observed that an international agreement or treaty that has not been registered with the Secretariat of the United Nations may not, according to the provisions of article 102 of the Charter of the United Nations, be invoked by the parties before any organ of the United Nations, but also found that non-registration, or late registration, does not have any consequence for the actual validity of an agreement, which remains no less binding upon the parties, and it further took full account in its reasoning of a double exchange of letters that both parties agreed constituted an international agreement, although that agreement had not been registered. In the Covenant of the League of Nations (Versailles, 28 June 1919; TS 4 (1919); Cmd 153) art 18 stipulated that no treaty should be binding until registered. The Permanent Court of International Justice, however, did not regard unregistered treaties as not being in force: *Mavrommatis Palestine Concessions* PCIJ Ser A No 2 (1924); *Polish Postal Service in Danzig Case* PCIJ Ser B No 11 (1925).

(6) TERMINATION OF TREATIES

106.   Termination in accordance with the treaty or by consent. The termination of a treaty[1] or the withdrawal of a party may take place in conformity with the provisions of the treaty[2] or, at any time, by consent of all the parties after consultation with the other contracting states[3]. Thus, a treaty concluded for a certain time will terminate when that period expires; equally, if there is a clause permitting a party to denounce the treaty or to withdraw from it, denunciation or withdrawal in accordance with that clause will produce a termination of the treaty obligations for the party concerned. If there is no such clause, a treaty is not subject to denunciation or withdrawal unless: (1) it is established that the parties intended to admit the possibility of denunciation or withdrawal[4]; or (2) a right of denunciation or withdrawal may be implied by the nature of the treaty[5].

1   Termination of a treaty denotes that it ceases altogether to be binding. As to suspension of the operation of a treaty see the Vienna Convention on the Law of Treaties (Vienna, 23 May 1969; TS 58 (1980); Cmnd 7964) arts 57, 58; and as to the consequences of suspension see art 72.

    The termination of a treaty does not affect any right, obligation or legal situation of the parties created through the execution of the treaty prior to its termination: see art 70(1)(b). As to the consequences of termination generally see art 70. It follows from the binding nature of a treaty that it is not subject to unilateral denunciation except in the cases discussed in the following paragraphs: see PARAS 107–110. See generally 1 Oppenheim's International Law (9th Edn) pp 1296–1311; also Aust's Modern Treaty Law and Practice (2nd Edn, 2008) pp 277–311. As to the meaning of 'treaty' see PARA 71.

2   Vienna Convention on the Law of Treaties art 54(a). The Convention also contains a rule that, unless it otherwise provides, a multilateral treaty does not terminate by reason only of the fact that the number of the parties falls below the number necessary for its entry into force: see art 55.

3   Vienna Convention on the Law of Treaties art 54(b). A subsequent agreement may also impliedly terminate an earlier treaty. The Convention contains a rule that a treaty is considered as terminated if all the parties to it conclude a later treaty relating to the same subject matter and (1) it appears from the later treaty or is otherwise established that the parties intended the matter to be governed by that treaty; or (2) the provisions of the later treaty are so far incompatible with those of the earlier one that the two treaties are not capable of being applied at the same time: see art 59 para 1. Mutual non-compliance with a treaty as opposed to mutual consent to its termination does not terminate the treaty: *Gabčíkovo-Nagymaros Project (Hungary/Slovakia)* ICJ Reports 1997, 7 at 68.

4   Vienna Convention on the Law of Treaties art 56 para 1(a).

5   Vienna Convention on the Law of Treaties art 56 para 1(b). By way of a practical application of art 56 para 1 see the UN Human Rights Committee ('HRC'), CCPR General Comment No 26: *Continuity of Obligations*, 8 December 1997, CCPR/C/21/Rev 1/Add 8/Rev 1, concluding that the drafters of the Covenant deliberately intended to exclude the possibility of denunciation, and that the Covenant is not the type of treaty which, by its nature, implies a right of denunciation. A party must give not less than 12 months' notice of its intention to denounce or withdraw from a treaty under these provisions: art 56 para 2. As to the requirement of a reasonable time for withdrawal from or termination of treaties that contain no provision regarding the duration of their validity see *Interpretation of the Agreement of 25 March 1951 between the World Health Organisation and Egypt (Advisory Opinion)* ICJ Reports 1980, 73 at 96; and *Military and Paramilitary Activities in and against Nicaragua (Nicaragua v United States of America) (Jurisdiction and Admissibility)* ICJ Reports 1984, 392 at 420. The United Kingdom denounced numerous anti-slave trade treaties after the 1914–18 war, the mischief aimed at having long been removed. It may be suggested that in the case of very ancient treaties, certain provisions might be terminated through having become meaningless. For a discussion of obsolescence in relation to treaties see *Nuclear Tests (Australia v France)* ICJ Reports 1974, 253 at 337 (Joint Dissenting Opinion of Judges Onyeama, Dillard, Jiménez de Arechaga and Sir Humphrey Waldock). See also the Commentary of the International Law Commission, YILC 1966, vol II, 237 ('while 'obsolescence' or 'desuetude' may be a factual cause of the termination of a treaty, the legal basis of such termination, when it occurs, is the consent of the parties to abandon the treaty, which is to be implied from their conduct in relation to the treaty').

107.   Breach of treaty. A material breach of a bilateral treaty[1] by one of the parties entitles the other to invoke the breach as a ground for terminating the treaty[2]. A material breach of a multilateral treaty by one of the parties has more complex consequences with regard to a party's option to terminate[3]. Thus breach of a treaty does not automatically terminate it. A material breach of a treaty[4] consists in: (1) an unsanctioned repudiation of the treaty[5]; or (2) the violation of a provision essential to the accomplishment of the object or purpose of the treaty[6]. These rules do not apply to provisions relating to the protection of the human person contained in treaties of a humanitarian character, in particular to provisions prohibiting any form of reprisals against persons protected by such treaties[7].

1   As to the meaning of 'treaty' see PARA 71.

2   See the Vienna Convention on the Law of Treaties (Vienna, 23 May 1969; TS 58 (1980); Cmnd 7964) art 60 para 1. Such a breach also permits the innocent party to suspend the operation of the treaty in whole or in part: art 60 para 1. As to the customary nature of the principles set out in arts 60–62 of the Convention see *Gabčíkovo-Nagymaros Project (Hungary/ Slovakia)* ICJ Reports 1997, 7 at 38. The provisions of the Vienna Convention on the Law of Treaties art 60 paras 1–3 are without prejudice to any provision in the treaty applicable in the event of a breach: see art 60 para 4.

3   As to the elaborate rules regarding the consequences of a material breach of a multilateral treaty by one of the parties to it see the Vienna Convention on the Law of Treaties art 60 para 2. See also note 2.

4   Ie for the purposes of the Vienna Convention on the Law of Treaties.

5   Vienna Convention on the Law of Treaties art 60 para 3(a). For these purposes unsanctioned implies unsanctioned by the present Convention. See also note 2.

6   Vienna Convention on the Law of Treaties art 60 para 3(b). See also note 2. See *Legal Consequences for States of the Continued Presence of South Africa in Namibia (South West Africa) notwithstanding Security Council Resolution 276 (1970) (Advisory Opinion)* ICJ Reports 1971, 16 at 47 in respect of South African violations of the Mandate for South West Africa and the consequent termination of the Mandate by the United Nations General Assembly. Support for the distinction between material and non-material breaches is to be found in the *Tacna-Arica Arbitration* 2 RIAA 921 (1925). The material breach must be of the treaty itself. Violation of the provisions of other treaties or rules of general international law does not constitute a ground for termination of the treaty: *Gabčíkovo-Nagymaros Project (Hungary/ Slovakia)* ICJ Reports 1997, 7 at 65. As to a premature termination in circumstances where the breach in question had not yet occurred: *Gabčíkovo-Nagymaros Project (Hungary/Slovakia)* ICJ Reports 1997, 7 at 66.

7   Vienna Convention on the Law of Treaties art 60 para 5. The types of treaty covered by art 60 para 5 are exemplified by the Geneva Red Cross Conventions: see WAR AND ARMED CONFLICT vol 49(1) (2005 Reissue) PARA 421. Further, a state may lose the right to terminate a treaty because of a material breach by another party if it has expressly agreed that the treaty remains in force or continues in operation, or has acquiesced in its maintenance in force or its operation: see the Vienna Convention on the Law of Treaties art 45.

108.   Supervening impossibility and fundamental change of circumstances. A party may invoke the impossibility of performing a treaty[1] as a ground for terminating or withdrawing from it if the impossibility results from the permanent disappearance or destruction of an object indispensable for the execution of the treaty[2]. This ground may not be invoked by a party as a ground for terminating, withdrawing from or suspending the operation of a treaty if the impossibility is the result of a breach by that party either under the treaty or of any other international obligation owed to any other party to the treaty[3].

A fundamental change of circumstances which has occurred with regard to those existing at the time of the conclusion of a treaty, and which was not foreseen by the parties, may not be invoked as a ground for terminating or withdrawing from the treaty unless: (1) the existence of those circumstances constituted an essential basis of the consent of the parties to be bound by the treaty[4]; and (2) the effect of the change is radically to transform the extent of obligations still to be performed under the treaty[5]. A fundamental change of circumstances may not be invoked as a ground for terminating or withdrawing from a treaty: (a) if the treaty establishes a boundary[6]; or (b) if the fundamental change is the result of a breach by the party invoking it either of an obligation under the treaty or of any other international obligation owed to any other party to the treaty[7].

1   As to the meaning of 'treaty' see PARA 71.

2   Vienna Convention on the Law of Treaties (Vienna, 23 May 1969; TS 58 (1980); Cmnd 7964) art 61 para 1. If the impossibility is temporary, it may be invoked only as a ground for suspending the operation of the treaty: art 61 para 1. Examples might be the submergence of an island, the drying up of a river or the destruction of a dam or hydro-electric installation indispensable for the execution of a treaty: see YILC 1966 vol II, 256. A state of necessity is not a ground for termination, though the treaty may be ineffective so long as the state of necessity continues to exist: *Gabčíkovo-Nagymaros Project (Hungary/Slovakia)* ICJ Reports 1997, 7 at 63; and the Articles on Responsibility of States for Internationally Wrongful Acts ('ARSIWA') arts 25, 27, Report of the International Law Commission, 53rd Session (2001), YILC 2001, vol II(2); and PARAS 362, 368. With respect to force majeure and distress, which are to be distinguished from situations of impossibility, see ARSIWA arts 23–24, 27 (and PARAS 362, 366–367); and *Rainbow Warrior Arbitration* (1990) 82 Int LR 499. For a recent application of the Vienna Convention on the Law of Treatiesart 61 para 1 in the English courts see *R (on the application of Kibris Türk Hava Yollari CTA Holidays) v Secretary of State for Transport*

(Republic of Cyprus intervening) [2009] EWHC 1918 (Admin), [2009] All ER (D) 295 (Jul) at [59]–[62]. As to defences to liability see PARA 362.

3   Vienna Convention on the Law of Treaties art 61 para 2.

4   Vienna Convention on the Law of Treaties art 62 para 1(a). As to consent to be bound see PARA 76.

5   Vienna Convention on the Law of Treaties art 62 para 1(b). A fundamental change of circumstances may also be invoked as a ground for suspending the operation of a treaty: art 62 para 3. The plea that an unforeseen and fundamental change of circumstances (known in customary international law as rebus sic stantibus) has had the effect of terminating a treaty obligation has never been successfully advanced before an international tribunal, so that the precise operation of the plea remains uncertain. The doctrine was invoked in *Tunis and Morocco Nationality Decrees (Advisory Opinion)* PCIJ Ser B No 4, at 29 (1923), but the court did not find it necessary to pronounce upon it. In the *Free Zones of Upper Savoy and the District of Gex Case* PCIJ Ser A/B No 46 (1932) the argument failed on the facts, although the court appeared to acknowledge the doctrine. In the *Fisheries Jurisdiction (United Kingdom v Iceland) (Jurisdiction of the Court)* ICJ Reports 1973, 3 at 17, 18; and in the *Case concerning the Gabčíkovo-Nagymaros Project (Hungary/Slovakia) Judgment* ICJ Reports 1997, 7, the court referred to the Vienna Convention on the Law of Treaties art 62 stating that it represented customary international law, but held that no fundamental change had been established. See in particular the *Gabčíkovo-Nagymaros Project (Hungary/Slovakia)* ICJ Reports 1997, 7 at 65 where the International Court of Justice emphasised that the stability of treaty relations requires that the plea of fundamental change of circumstances be applied only in exceptional cases. See also Case C-162/96 *Racke (A) GmbH & Co v Hauptzollamt Mainz* [1998] ECR I-3655, [1998] 3 CMLR 219.

The Convention contains the rule that the severance of diplomatic or consular relations between parties to a treaty does not affect the legal relations established between them by a treaty except in so far as the existence of diplomatic or consular relations is indispensable for the application of the treaty: see art 63. The Convention also provides that if a new peremptory norm of general international law emerges, any existing treaty which is in conflict with that norm becomes void and terminates: see art 64. See also arts 53, 71; and PARA 105.

6   Vienna Convention on the Law of Treaties art 62 para 2(a).

7   Vienna Convention on the Law of Treaties art 62 para 2(b). A state may not invoke this ground for terminating, withdrawing from or suspending a treaty if it has expressly agreed that the treaty remains in force or continues in operation, or acquiesces in the maintenance in force of the treaty or its operation: see art 45.

109.   Procedure in respect of invalidity, termination, withdrawal or suspension.

A state which invokes[1] either a defect in its consent to be bound[2] by a treaty[3] or a ground for impeaching the validity of a treaty[4], terminating it[5], withdrawing from it or suspending its operation must notify the other parties of its claim, and indicate in the notification the measure proposed to be taken with respect to the treaty and the reasons therefore[6]. Except in cases of special urgency the period of notice thereof must be at least three months, upon which the proposed measure may be implemented provided no objection to it has been raised[7]. Should another party to the treaty raise an objection, the parties must seek a solution through peaceful means[8].

1   Ie under the provisions of the Vienna Convention on the Law of Treaties (Vienna, 23 May 1969; TS 58 (1980); Cmnd 7964).

2   As to consent to be bound see PARA 76.

3   As to the meaning of 'treaty' see PARA 71.

4   As to the invalidity of treaties see PARA 101 et seq.

5   As to the termination of treaties see PARA 106 et seq.

6   Vienna Convention on the Law of Treaties art 65 para 1. Without prejudice to art 45 (see PARA 101 note 4) the fact that a state has not previously made the notification so prescribed does not prevent it from making such notification in answer to another party claiming performance of the treaty or alleging its violation: art 65 para 5. As to the instruments for declaring invalid, terminating, withdrawing from or suspending the operation of a treaty see art 67. Nothing in art 65 paras 1–3 affects the rights or obligations of the parties concerned under any provisions in force binding the parties with regard to the settlement of disputes: see art 65 para 4.

7   Vienna Convention on the Law of Treaties art 65 para 2. Customary international law requires 'reasonable notice': *Interpretation of the Agreement of 25 March 1951 between the World Health Organisation and Egypt (Advisory Opinion)* ICJ Reports 1980, 73 at 96. See also *Military and Paramilitary Activities in and against Nicaragua (Nicaragua v United States of America) (Jurisdiction and Admissibility)* ICJ Reports 1984, 392 at 420. As to proportionate counter-measures against a party which is in breach of a treaty see *Air Services Arbitration* (1978) 54 Int LR 306; and *Gabčíkovo-Nagymaros Project (Hungary/Slovakia)* ICJ Reports 1997, 7 at 66. See also the Articles on Responsibility of States for Internationally Wrongful Acts ('ARSIWA') art 22, Report of the International Law Commission, 53rd Session (2001), YILC 2001, vol II(2).

8   Vienna Convention on the Law of Treaties art 65 para 3 (which refers to the Charter of the United Nations (San Francisco, 26 June 1945; TS 67 (1946); Cmd 7015) art 33). If, under art 65 para 3, no solution is reached within 12 months of the objection being raised, provision is made for judicial settlement, arbitration and conciliation: see art 66.

110.   Legal effects of unilateral acts.

A unilateral statement or promise made by a state, which the state intends to be binding on itself, though it does not constitute a treaty, will impose a legal obligation upon it[1]. International law has no requirement of consideration[2].

1   *Legal Status of Eastern Greenland* PCIJ Ser A/B No 53 (1933); *Nuclear Tests (Australia v France)* ICJ Reports 1974, 253 at 267. See, however, *Frontier Dispute (Burkina Faso/Republic of Mali)* ICJ Reports 1986, 554 at 573–574, emphasising that all depends on the intention of the State in question. See generally 1 Oppenheim's International Law (9th Edn) pp 1187–1196.

2   As to consideration generally see CONTRACT vol 9(1) (Reissue) PARA 727 et seq.

7. TERRITORY

111. Nature and extent of title to territory. Territory is a central component of the state, and its protection a vital aid to stability in international relations. A state must be able to demonstrate title to its territory, which in practice means that it has a better claim than any other state[1]. Where title is established, the state enjoys protection of its rights by the principle of territorial integrity[2] and of its right to act according to its own decisions within its territory by the principle of non-intervention[3]. Title to territory may not be changed by resort to the use of armed force[4].

Territory is not simply a two-dimensional land area: states with coastlines have a band of territorial waters over which they enjoy sovereignty[5], and states have sovereignty over the airspace over the whole of their territory up to the limit of outer space[6].

1 As to disputes about title see PARA 114.
2 The Charter of the United Nations (San Francisco, 26 June 1945; TS 67 (1946); Cmd 7015) forbids the use or threat of force against the territorial integrity of any state: see art 2 para 4.
3 Ie 'the rights of every sovereign state to conduct its affairs without outside interference': see *Military and Paramilitary Activities in and against Nicaragua (Nicaragua v United States of America)* ICJ Reports 1986, 14 at 106. See also *Corfu Channel (United Kingdom v Albania)* ICJ Reports 1949, 4 at 35. The International Court of Justice (the 'ICJ') has recognised the principle of non-intervention as part of customary international law: see *Military and Paramilitary Activities in and against Nicaragua (Nicaragua v United States of America)* ICJ Reports 1986, 14. See also *Armed Activities on the Territory of the Congo (Democratic Republic of Congo v Uganda)* ICJ Reports, 19 December 2005 (paras 161–165).
4 See PARA 113 et seq.
5 See PARA 123 et seq.
6 See PARA 207 et seq.

112. The territory of the United Kingdom. The territory of the United Kingdom as an international personality[1] consists of England, Wales, Scotland, Northern Ireland[2], the British Islands[3] and the British overseas territories[4].

There are no territorial disputes with other states about title to the territory of the United Kingdom itself[5] or the British Islands, but dispute remains over the titles to the Falklands Islands[6] and Gibraltar[7].

1 As to international personality see PARA 32.
2 See the Northern Ireland Act 1998 s 1(1); and CONSTITUTIONAL LAW AND HUMAN RIGHTS.
3 The United Kingdom, the Isle of Man and the Channel Islands together make up the British Islands: see COMMONWEALTH vol 13 (2009) PARAS 790, 799.
4 See generally COMMONWEALTH vol 13 (2009) PARA 801 et seq. All the British overseas territories are regarded as non-self-governing territories by the UN but the UK takes the view that they all should be removed from UN supervision because of the modernisation of the relationships between the UK and each overseas territory.
5 As to the possession of the Island of Rockall see PARA 115 note 3. There are, however, disputes over certain sea areas adjacent to the United Kingdom: see PARA 114.
6 For a recent statement regarding the dispute with Argentina over title to the Falklands Islands see the FCO letter to the Foreign Affairs Committee: *Foreign Affairs Committee, Written Evidence, Miscellaneous Matters* (HC Paper 1329 (2006)) no 12.
7 As to the dispute with Spain over title to Gibraltar see 450 HC Official Report (5th Series), 17 October 2006 cols 47–48WS; and the 'Cordoba Ministerial Trilateral Forum Communiqué'. See also COMMONWEALTH vol 13 (2009) PARA 859.

113. Acquisition and disposal of territory. In the exercise of the foreign affairs prerogative, the government may acquire and dispose of territory and may fix the frontiers of British territory[1]. As a matter of practice, when title to territory is surrendered, it is done so pursuant to an Act of Parliament[2]. When independence has been granted to British colonial territories, it has been accompanied by an Act of Parliament[3].

1   See generally CONSTITUTIONAL LAW AND HUMAN RIGHTS vol 8(2) (Reissue) PARA 3.
2   A practice that commenced with surrender of Heligoland to Germany: see the Anglo-German Agreement Act 1890; and PARA 28.
3   See eg the Zimbabwe Act 1979 (and COMMONWEALTH vol 13 (2009) PARA 734).

114.   Disputes about territorial title.   In determining disputes between states about title to territory, two principles must be borne in mind.

(1)   The critical date. In many territorial disputes, there will be time by which the dispute between the contending states has crystallised and the dispute must be resolved according to the facts and law established to that time. The typical example is where there has been an agreement between states which purports to settle the question of title. This principle is intended to prevent the parties seeking to improve their legal positions by actions after the critical date[1].

(2)   The intertemporal law. In assessing the legal value to be attached to facts relating to title to territory, account must be taken of the state of international law as it was at the time the facts occurred[2]. However, in interpreting treaties which bear on matters of title, it may be necessary to take into account international law as it is at the time of interpretation, especially with respect to legal (sometimes called 'generic') terms, the understanding of which may have changed over time[3].

1   *Island of Palmas Case* 2 RIAA 829 (1928).
2   *Island of Palmas Case* 2 RIAA 829 (1928).
3   *Aegean Sea Continental Shelf (Greece v Turkey)* ICJ Reports 1978, 3. As to the interpretation of treaties see PARA 95 et seq.

115.   Acquisition by occupation.   Land territory which is unoccupied may become part of a state through occupation[1]. In order to acquire title to territory it is not enough that the state's agents have discovered the territory[2]. Discovery and a formal declaration of possession may constitute a root of title[3], but such title must be perfected by acts of effective occupation[4]. A state must continuously and peaceably administer the territory[5]. The extent of the authority which must be asserted and the area over which administration is exercised depend upon the circumstances, and in particular the physical characteristics, of the territory in question[6]. It is clear that while there is little or no unoccupied territory today, occupation as a mode of acquisition remains an historically important source of present title[7]. Sovereignty may be lost by abandonment, namely by failure to exercise state authority over the territory in question with the intention to abandon it[8].

1   Title can only be acquired by occupation over territory which is res nullius; it cannot therefore be acquired thus over sea areas, since the high seas are not res nullius but res communis (ie belonging to all states). However, rights in sea areas may be acquired by a state in other ways than by occupation, eg by prescription: see PARA 118. As to the status of the high seas generally see PARA 147 et seq; and as to the status of Antarctica see PARA 218. For a discussion of the modes of acquisition of territory generally see Jennings's Acquisition of Territory in International Law.
2   *Island of Palmas Case* 2 RIAA 829 (1928). The independent activity of private individuals is of little value in this connection unless it can be shown that they have acted in pursuance of a licence or some other authority received from their governments or that in some other way their

governments have asserted jurisdiction through them: *Fisheries (United Kingdom v Norway)* ICJ
Reports 1951, 116 at 184 per Judge McNair. See, however, PARA 118 note 2.

3   Possession of the island of Rockall was taken in the name of Her Majesty on 18 September 1955
    in pursuance of a Royal Warrant dated 14 September 1955, addressed to the captain of Her
    Majesty's ship Vidal: see the Island of Rockall Act 1972 s 1, which provided for the
    incorporation of the island into that part of the United Kingdom known as Scotland and for it to
    form part of the District of Harris in the County of Inverness, the law of Scotland applying
    accordingly.

4   *Island of Palmas Case* 2 RIAA 829 (1928). See also PARA 119.

5   *Island of Palmas Case* 2 RIAA 829 (1928).

6   *Island of Palmas Case* 2 RIAA 829 (1928); *Clipperton Island Case* 2 RIAA 1105 (1931) (remote
    guano island); *Legal Status of Eastern Greenland* PCIJ Ser A/B No 53 (1933) (sparse population
    along the coast and a vast unpopulated hinterland). In most cases there have been two
    competing claims and the tribunal has been satisfied with very little in the way of exercise of
    sovereign rights provided that the other state could not make out a superior claim: *Legal Status
    of Eastern Greenland* at 46.

7   *Western Sahara (Advisory Opinion)* ICJ Reports 1975, 12 at 80 (by the 1880s at the latest
    territory inhabited by tribes or peoples having a social and political organisation was not
    regarded as terra nullius).

8   *Clipperton Island Case* 2 RIAA 1105 at 1110–1111 (1931).

116.   Acquisition by accretion. Title to territory may be acquired by accretion,
namely by addition to its existing territory by reason of natural changes, as
where an island arises within the internal or territorial sea[1] of a state[2] or where
the bed of a river forming the boundary between states shifts imperceptibly by
land which has left one bank of the river being added to the other[3].

1   As to the territorial sea see PARA 123 et seq.

2   *The Anna* (1805) 5 Ch Rob 373, 2 BILC 694; *Secretary of State for India v Chelikani Rama Rao*
    (1916) LR 43 Ind App 192, 2 BILC 841, PC.

3   Thus it may have the effect of causing the boundary to alter. Accretion is distinguished from
    avulsion, the term given to the case where a river suddenly and violently changes its course, in
    which case the boundary retains its original line: see *Chamizal Arbitration* 11 RIAA 316 (1910).

117.   Acquisition by cession. Title to territory may be acquired by cession,
namely by the peaceful transfer by one state to another of sovereignty over the
territory, usually by treaty, or by way of gift, purchase or exchange. A treaty of
cession is followed by the handing over of the territory, or tradition[1]. Cession
depends upon the agreement of the states concerned[2]. Formerly, conquest
followed by annexation with or without a treaty of cession gave good title to
territory[3]. In that this is a consequence of the use of force by one state against
another, it cannot now be considered as a legal method of acquisition of title to
territory[4].

1   It is controversial, however, whether the transfer of sovereignty takes place at the time of
    effective transfer of authority to the transferee state (ie at the time of tradition) or whether this
    occurs when the treaty enters into force. If the latter is the case, the transferee state would be
    able lawfully to alienate the territory to a third state without itself taking actual possession of it:
    see 1 Oppenheim's International Law (9th Edn) 683. Traditio was not regarded as essential in
    Award between Colombia and Venezuela 1 RIAA 223 (1922). See also the Joint Declaration of
    the Governments of the United Kingdom and the People's Republic of China on the Question of
    Hong Kong dated 19 December 1984 (TS No 26 (1985); Cmnd 9543) (and COMMONWEALTH
    vol 13 (2009) PARA 727), by which, inter alia, the United Kingdom ceded the territory of Hong
    Kong to the People's Republic of China.

2   Cf secession or the creation of new states. There is no right of secession in international law and
    even acts of effective secession may not create new states because of their impact on the
    application of the principle of self-determination to the territory eg the claim to statehood of
    Somaliland (see 443 HC Official Reports (5th series), 8 May 2006, col 1568W; and 450 HC
    Official Reports (5th Series), 24 October 2006, col 1777W). In the case of secession, the

acquisition of title depends upon achieving effective independence by the seceding entity; and in the case of independence, the acquisition of title depends on the unilateral act of the state granting independence.

3   This is true of treaties of peace, e g at the end of the 1914–18 war. The conqueror, however, only acquired sovereignty over the territory of the conquered state if he intended to do so. Thus in 1945 the United Nations expressly disclaimed the intention of annexing Germany: see Jennings 'Government in Commission' 23 BYIL 112.

4   The use or threat of force is forbidden under international law: see the Charter of the United Nations (San Francisco, 26 June 1945; TS 67 (1946); Cmd 7015) art 2 para 4; and the Declaration on Principles of International Law concerning Friendly Relations and Co-operation among States in Accordance with the Charter of the United Nations, principle 1, General Assembly Resolution 2625 (XXV) of 24 October 1970. See also the Articles on Responsibility of States for Internationally Wrongful Acts ('ARSIWA') arts 40, 41 (in particular art 41(2)), International Law Commission Report, 53rd Session, A/56/10, YILC 2001, vol II(2); and PARA 382. In 1967 the Security Council of the United Nations passed a resolution on the Middle East calling for a withdrawal of Israel from occupied territories and emphasising the inadmissibility of the acquisition of territory by war: Security Council Resolution 242 (XXII) of 2 November 1967. See also Security Council Resolution 662 of 9 August 1990 (incorporation of the territory of Kuwait into Iraq).

    Under the law of the Charter of the United Nations, it appears that neither the sovereign dispossessed by force nor other states may lawfully recognise the title of the aggressor: Declaration on Principles of International Law concerning Friendly Relations and Co-operation among States in Accordance with the Charter of the United Nations, principle 1, General Assembly Resolution 2625 (XXV) of 24 October 1970. Peace treaties imposed by force are void: see the Vienna Convention on the Law of Treaties (Vienna, 23 May 1969; TS 58 (1980); Cmnd 7964) art 52; and PARA 105. The principle of non-acquisition applies whether or not a state originally resorted to force lawfully. A state using force to take control of the territory of another state becomes the belligerent occupant of territory, its powers limited by international law: see WAR AND ARMED CONFLICT vol 49(1) (2005 Reissue) PARA 573; and the UK Ministry of Defence *Manual of the Law of Armed Conflict* (2004) Ch 10. Providing that a certain degree of control is acquired by the occupant, it may also be subject to duties under human rights treaties: see WAR AND ARMED CONFLICT vol 49(1) (2005 Reissue) PARA 573.

118.   Acquisition by prescription. Prescription[1] denotes the acquisition of title to territory by means of de facto exercise of state authority in the mistaken belief that it is part of the territory of the state which is prescribing for it[2]. The exercise of authority must be undisturbed and not protested against by the state against which it is exercised[3]. It is possible to acquire rights in the high seas by prescription[4].

The period of time which must elapse before title is acquired by prescription is not fixed by international law, although it seems clear that the running of some time is necessary[5].

1   Prescription in this sense is acquisitive prescription as opposed to extinctive prescription which may result in the barring of state claims by lapse of time: see PARA 93. It is distinguishable from occupation (see PARA 115) by reason of its being concerned with territory which is not res nullius. However, in some cases (e g *Island of Palmas Case* 2 RIAA 829 (1928); and *Legal Status of Eastern Greenland* PCIJ Ser A/B No 53 (1933)) it is not clear whether they were decided upon the basis of occupation or of prescription. See also *Western Sahara (Advisory Opinion)* ICJ Reports 1975, 12. In *Kasikili/Sedudu Island (Botswana/Namibia)* ICJ Reports 1999, 1045 at 1103 (para 94), although the ICJ found the claim to title to an island on the basis of acquisitive prescription not made out, the parties agreed on the characteristics of it as a means of obtaining title.

2   When two states claim title to the same territory which was not res nullius, then, as is the case with occupation, the case will be decided upon the relative strengths of the evidence of the exercise of state authority such as local administration, legislation, registration or the holding of inquests: see the *Minquiers and Ecrehos Case (France/United Kingdom)* ICJ Reports 1953, 47 (acquisition by historic title). Any acts of non-state actors must be undertaken 'a titre de souverain' (i e consistent with sovereignty) in order to go towards establishing title by acquisitive prescription: *Kasikili/Sedudu Island (Botswana/Namibia)* ICJ Reports 1999, 1045 at 1105 (para 98). Cf *Dispute regarding Navigational and Related Rights (Costa Rica v Nicaragua)* ICJ

Reports, 13 July 2009, where the Court held that Nicaragua was bound by a right of subsistence fishing established by the practices of the local population, to which Nicaragua had not objected.

3 *Island of Palmas Case* 2 RIAA 829 (1928) at 868 (absence of protests by Spain against Dutch acts). As to acquiescence and recognition in respect of the acquisition of territory see also *Legal Status of Eastern Greenland* PCIJ Ser A/B No 53 (1933); *Case concerning the Temple of Preah Vihear (Cambodia v Thailand)* ICJ Reports 1962, 6. See also PARA 119.

4 Eg as in the case of historic bays: see PARA 131.

5 Under the British Guiana-Venezuela Boundary Arbitration Agreement 1899 adverse holding or prescription during a period of 50 years was to make a good title: see 92 BFSP 160.

119.   Effective control.   Consolidating title gained by occupation[1], gaining title by prescription[2] and demonstrating title where the original title is obscure[3] have overlapping characteristics. A state is required to show its effective control over the area, the kind and degree of effectiveness ('effectivites') being dependent upon the nature of the territory and its geographical location. What is more, there is an obligation on states to maintain their title by demonstrating continuing acts of governmental authority with respect to the title. Where title is contested between two states, it will often be the case that the one which shows the greater degree of activity will be the one to be entitled to sovereignty over the territory, however little that might be[4]. The activities, evidence of which will contribute to establishing title, are the exercise of sovereign functions with respect to the contested area and people present there[5].

1 See PARA 115.

2 See PARA 118.

3 For an example of obscurity of original title, see *Territorial and Maritime Dispute between Nicaragua and Honduras in the Caribbean Sea (Nicaragua v Honduras)* ICJ Reports, 8 October 2007.

4 *Minquiers and Ecrehos Case (France/United Kingdom)* ICJ Reports 1953, 47.

5 *Island of Palmas Case* 2 RIAA 829 at 840 (1928); *Eritrea–Yemen Arbitration (First Stage: Territorial Sovereignty and Scope of Dispute)* (9 October 1998) (1998) 12 RIAA 209, (2001) 40 ILM 900; but see *Territorial and Maritime Dispute between Nicaragua and Honduras in the Caribbean Sea (Nicaragua v Honduras)* ICJ Reports, 8 October 2007.

120.   Acquisition by creation of new states.   When states agree to create a new state from the territory of one or more of them[1], the new state's title to its territory is derived from the legal act which created it[2]. This is also true of cases where colonial territories become independent from the mother country and acquire title by the act of independence[3].

1 Examples include the creation of Belgium in 1839, and the creation by agreement of the states of the Czech Republic and Slovakia on the territory of what had been Czechoslovakia in 1993. It is necessary that the previous title be clear and that the previous sovereign consents to the creation of the new state.

2 This case is distinguishable from cession, since there is no state to which the territory is transferred, and from secession, which requires a voluntary act on the part of the entity which has become the new state. As to cession and secession see PARA 117.

3 As to state succession in respect of boundaries and the doctrine of uti possidetis see PARA 59. As to the Acts granting independence in the case of former British colonial territories see COMMONWEALTH vol 13 (2009) PARA 720.

8. LAW OF THE SEA

(1) INTERNAL WATERS AND THE TERRITORIAL SEA

121.   Internal waters.   Internal or national waters are those areas of water, including parts of the sea, which are under the full sovereignty of the territorial state. They consist of all the waters that lie landward of the baselines from which the territorial sea[1] is delimited[2], and include inland waters, ports, and certain estuaries and bays[3]. Internal waters differ from territorial waters in that there exists in territorial waters, but not in internal waters, a right of innocent passage for foreign vessels[4]. Foreign warships require specific permission to enter internal waters. While maritime ports are in practice ordinarily open to foreign merchant vessels, there is no general legal right for foreign ships to enter them, and entry to them is conditional upon compliance with conditions determined by the territorial state[5]. Exceptionally, ships in distress have a general right to enter maritime ports in order to save the lives of those on board; but it is probable that no such right is exercisable in order to save the ship or its cargo[6].

1   As to baselines see PARA 125 et seq. As to the territorial sea see PARA 123 et seq.

2   See the United Nations Convention on the Law of the Sea (Montego Bay, 10 December 1982; TS 81 (1999); Cmnd 4524) art 8; and PARA 125 et seq. The United Kingdom became a party on 24 August 1997: see the London Gazette 29 August 1997. The Convention supersedes the Convention on the Territorial Sea and the Contiguous Zone (Geneva, 29 April 1958; TS 3 (1965); Cmnd 2511). The latter remains in force between the United Kingdom and other states which are parties to it but not to the United Nations Convention. As to the delimitation of the territorial sea see PARAS 125–126.

3   See the United Nations Convention on the Law of the Sea art 8. Special provisions apply to certain archipelagic states: see Part IV of the Convention. The United Kingdom is not an archipelagic state for these purposes.

4   As to the right of innocent passage see PARA 134 et seq; but see the United Nations Convention on the Law of the Sea art 8 para 2, which provides that where the establishment of straight baselines encloses as internal waters areas of the sea which had previously been part of the territorial sea or of the high seas, the right of innocent passage exists in those waters.

5   See 432 HL Official Report (5th series) 29 June 1982, col 156 per Lord Lyell; (1982) 53 BYIL 468–469. See, however, the Convention and Statute on the International Regime of Maritime Ports (Geneva, 9 December 1923; TS 24 (1925); Cmd 2419), to which the United Kingdom is a party, which provides for national treatment on a reciprocal basis for the merchant ships of each other state in ports (art 2), and includes reservations concerning immigration (art 12), quarantine (art 17) and belligerency (art 18). The regime of navigation in internal waters may be prescribed by the local state, which may reserve to itself cabotage or coastal trade and the right to reserve the exploitation of internal waters to itself and its nationals: see generally *Saudi Arabia v Arabian American Oil Co (Aramco) Arbitration* (1958) 27 Int LR 117. Access to ports may be guaranteed by bilateral treaties. See eg the Treaty of Commerce, Establishment and Navigation between the United Kingdom and Iran (Teheran, 11 March 1959; Iran 1 (1959); Cmnd 698). See also the Convention on Facilitation of International Maritime Traffic (London, 9 April 1965; TS 46 (1967); Cmnd 3299.

6   See *ACT Shipping (PTE) Ltd v Minister for the Marine* [1995] 3 IR 406.

122.   Jurisdiction in internal waters.   The territorial state has jurisdiction over foreign merchant vessels[1] in its internal waters and over crimes committed on board such vessels. It may arrest persons on board foreign ships in internal waters[2]. In practice, jurisdiction is not exercised unless the consequences of the crime extend to the territorial state or the crime is serious or the assistance of the local authorities is sought by the master of the ship or by the flag state[3]. United Kingdom courts may by Order in Council be barred from entertaining without the consent of the flag state proceedings in respect of crimes on board foreign ships, unless the crime is committed by or against a British national or is punishable by more than five years imprisonment or falls within certain categories designated in the Order[4].

Foreign vessels which enter ports in distress are exempt from penalties to which they would have been liable had they entered voluntarily, but have no general immunity from the jurisdiction of the territorial state[5]. The jurisdiction of the territorial state is concurrent with that of the flag state of the vessel[6].

Under United Kingdom law, a member of the crew of a ship belonging to a state designated for the purpose by Order in Council[7] who is detained in custody on board for a disciplinary offence is not to be deemed to be unlawfully detained unless (1) his detention is unlawful under the laws of that state or the conditions of detention are inhumane or unjustifiably severe[8]; or (2) there is reasonable cause for believing that his life or liberty will be endangered for reasons of race, nationality, political opinion or religion in any country to which the ship is likely to go[9].

1 For the position of foreign warships and public ships, which enjoy immunity from the jurisdiction, see *The Schooner Exchange v McFaddon* 7 *Cranch* 116, US SC (1812). The immunity may be waived: *Chung Chi Cheung v R* [1939] AC 160, [1938] 4 All ER 786, 3 BILC 96, PC.

2 *R v Garrett, ex p Sharf* [1917] 2 KB 99, 5 BILC 95, CA (arrest on Danish ship for offences against the Defence of the Realm Acts). In certain cases proceedings for offences committed on board a foreign vessel by the master or a member of the crew may not be commenced without the request or consent of the consul of the flag state: see the Consular Relations Act 1968 s 5; PARA 303; and CRIMINAL LAW, EVIDENCE AND PROCEDURE vol 11(3) (2006 Reissue) PARA 1054. Extradition law extends on board, so British police may arrest a person on board a foreign ship which is in a British port for extradition to a third state: *Case of Eisler* (1949) 26 BYIL 468. As to civil jurisdiction and the application of the local law to transactions and events on board see CONFLICT OF LAWS vol 8(3) (Reissue) PARA 372.

3 Cf United Nations Convention on the Law of the Sea (Montego Bay, 10 December 1982; TS 81 (1999); Cmnd 4524) art 27 for a similar rule applicable as a matter of law to foreign ships in the territorial sea.

4 See the Consular Relations Act 1968 s 5; and PARA 303.

5 See *Cashin v Canada* [1935] Ex C R 103. As to the meaning of 'distress' see *ACT Shipping (PTE) Ltd v Minister for the Marine* [1995] 3 IR 406.

6 *R v Anderson* (1868) LR 1 CCR 161, 3 BILC 40. As to the jurisdiction of English courts over crimes committed on British merchant ships in foreign waters see CRIMINAL LAW, EVIDENCE AND PROCEDURE vol 11(3) (2006 Reissue) PARA 1057.

7 For Orders in Council designating states for this purpose see PARA 303 note 6.

8 Consular Relations Act 1968 s 6(a).

9 Consular Relations Act 1968 s 6(b).

123. The territorial sea. The United Kingdom is a party to the United Nations Convention on the Law of the Sea[1]. Part II of this Convention, which reflects the rules of customary international law[2], stipulates that the sovereignty of a state extends beyond its land territory and its internal waters to an adjacent belt of sea, described as the territorial sea[3]. The sovereignty of the coastal state extends to the air space over the territorial sea as well as to its bed and subsoil[4].

1 United Nations Convention on the Law of the Sea (Montego Bay, 10 December 1982; TS 81 (1999); Cmnd 4524) Pt II (arts 2–33) contains provisions concerning the territorial sea.

2 For the view that the territorial sea is an inseparable appurtenance of land territory see *Grisbadarna Arbitration, Permanent Court of Arbitration* 11 RIAA 147 (1909).

3 United Nations Convention on the Law of the Sea art 2 para 1. The sovereignty of the coastal state is exercised subject to the rules set out in the Convention (eg the right of innocent passage: see PARA 133 et seq) and other rules of international law (eg sovereign and diplomatic immunity: see PARAS 243, 266): art 2 para 3.

4 See the United Nations Convention on the Law of the Sea art 2 para 2.

124. Breadth of territorial sea. A state may establish the breadth of its territorial sea[1] up to a limit not exceeding 12 nautical miles from its baselines[2]. The territorial sea of the United Kingdom extends up to 12 nautical miles[3], measured from the baselines established by Order in Council, unless otherwise provided[4]. Her Majesty may, for the purpose of implementing any international agreement or otherwise, by Order in Council provide that any part of the territorial sea adjacent to the United Kingdom is to extend to such other line as may be specified in the Order[5].

1   As to the territorial sea see PARA 123 et seq.
2   United Nations Convention on the Law of the Sea (Montego Bay, 10 December 1982; TS 81 (1999); Cmnd 4524) art 3. As to baselines see PARA 125 et seq. Roadsteads normally used for the loading, unloading and anchoring of ships and which would be otherwise situated wholly or partly outside the outer limit of the territorial sea are included in the territorial sea: art 12. They must be demarcated and indicated on charts, to which due publicity must be given: art 6.
3   Territorial Sea Act 1987 s 1(1)(a). For the purposes of s 1, 'nautical miles' means international nautical miles of 1852 metres: s 1(7). Subject to the provisions of the Territorial Sea Act 1987, any enactment or instrument which (whether passed or made before or after 1 October 1987) contains a reference (however worded) to the territorial sea adjacent to, or to any part of, the United Kingdom is to be construed in accordance with s 1 and with any provision made, or having effect as if made, under s 1: s 1(5). Without prejudice to the Territorial Sea Act 1987 s 1(5) (see PARA 124), in relation to a reference to the baselines from which the breadth of the territorial sea adjacent to the United Kingdom is measured, nothing in s 1(5) requires any reference in any enactment or instrument to a specified distance to be construed as a reference to a distance equal to the breadth of that territorial sea: s 1(6). As to the statutory meaning of 'United Kingdom' see PARA 30 note 3.
4   See the Territorial Sea Act 1987 s 1; PARAS 125–126; and WATER AND WATERWAYS vol 100 (2009) PARA 31.
5   See the Territorial Sea Act 1987 s 1(2); and WATER AND WATERWAYS vol 100 (2009) PARA 31.

125. Baselines for delimitation. According to the United Nations Convention on the Law of the Sea, the outer limit of the territorial sea[1] is the line every point of which is at a distance from the nearest point of the baseline equal to the breadth of the territorial sea[2]. The normal baseline for measuring the breadth of the territorial sea is the low-water mark along the coast, as marked on large scale charts officially recognised by the coastal state[3]. For the purpose of delimiting the territorial sea the outermost permanent harbour works which form an integral part of a harbour system are regarded as forming part of the coast[4].

The baselines from which the breadth of the territorial sea of the United Kingdom is measured are established by Her Majesty by Order in Council[5].

1   As to the territorial sea see PARA 123 et seq.
2   United Nations Convention on the Law of the Sea (Montego Bay, 10 December 1982; TS 81 (1999); Cmnd 4524) art 4. For the methods of constructing baselines and measuring the outer limit of the territorial sea, see United Nations, Office of Legal Affairs *Handbook on the Delimitation of Maritime Boundaries* (2000) and Office for Ocean Affairs and the Law of the Sea, United Nations *Baselines: An Examination of the Relevant Provisions of the United Nations Convention on the Law of the Sea* (1989).
3   United Nations Convention on the Law of the Sea art 5. As to Admiralty charts as evidence in proceedings in the English courts see *Office v Estuary Radio Ltd* [1968] 2 QB 740, [1967] 3 All ER 663, 9 BILC 187, CA. As to departures from the normal rule see PARA 126.
4   United Nations Convention on the Law of the Sea art 11. Offshore installations and artificial islands are not permanent harbour works: art 11.
5   Territorial Sea Act 1987 s 1(1)(b). In any legal proceedings, a certificate issued by or under the authority of the Secretary of State stating the location of any baseline established under s 1(1) is conclusive of what is stated in the certificate: s 1(3). As to the Secretary of State see PARA 29.
      As to the limits see the Territorial Waters Order in Council 1964, dated 25 September 1964 (amended by SI 1998/2564). See also the Territorial Sea (Limits) Order 1989, SI 1989/482. As from 1 October 1987, the Territorial Waters Order in Council 1964 and the Territorial Waters

(Amendment) Order in Council 1979 have effect for all purposes as if they were Orders in Council made by virtue of the Territorial Sea Act 1987 s 1(1)(b): s 1(4). These Orders were initially made by virtue of the royal prerogative on 25 September 1964 and on 23 May 1979 and were not issued in the SI series. The Fishery Limits Act 1976 refers to the baselines from which the territorial sea is measured but without expressly defining them: see s 1(1); and AGRICULTURE AND FISHERIES. As to the meaning of 'United Kingdom' see PARA 30 note 3. As to the baselines drawn around the United Kingdom coast see United Kingdom Hydrographic Office *The Territorial Sea Limits of the United Kingdom* (2006).

126. Straight baselines. The normal low-water baseline may be departed from in localities where the coastline is deeply indented or cut into, or where there is a fringe of islands along the coast in its immediate vicinity. In such a case, a straight baseline may be drawn by joining appropriate points on the coast[1]. This has been done in respect of parts of the coast of Scotland[2]. The drawing of such baselines must not depart to any appreciable extent from the general direction of the coast[3], and the sea areas lying behind the baselines must be sufficiently closely linked to the land domain to be subject to the regime of the internal waters[4]. In applying the technique of straight baselines, account may be taken in determining particular baselines of economic interests peculiar to the region concerned, the reality and the importance of which are clearly evidenced by long usage[5]. The system may not be applied in such a manner as to cut off from the high seas the territorial sea[6] or an exclusive economic zone of another state[7], and the coastal state must indicate straight baselines on charts to which due publicity must be given[8]. Waters on the landward side of the baseline form part of the internal waters of the coastal state[9].

1   United Nations Convention on the Law of the Sea (Montego Bay, 10 December 1982; TS 81 (1999); Cmnd 4524) art 7 para 1. For low-tide elevations such as drying rocks and sandbanks see PARA 128.
2   The method of drawing straight baselines has been adopted in the United Kingdom with respect to the area between Cape Wrath and the Mull of Kintyre: see the Territorial Waters Order in Council, dated 25 September 1964, art 3(1), Schedule and the Territorial Waters (Amendment) Order in Council 1979, dated 23 May 1979 (substituted by SI 1998/2564).
3   United Nations Convention on the Law of the Sea art 7 para 3.
4   United Nations Convention on the Law of the Sea art 7 para 3. As to internal waters see PARA 121.
5   United Nations Convention on the Law of the Sea art 7 para 5.
6   As to the territorial sea see PARA 123 et seq.
7   United Nations Convention on the Law of the Sea art 7 para 6. As to the exclusive economic zone see PARA 154.
8   See the United Nations Convention on the Law of the Sea art 16.
9   United Nations Convention on the Law of the Sea art 8 para 1. As to internal waters see PARA 121. As to the effect of the drawing of straight baselines on the right of innocent passage see art 8 para 2; and PARA 133.

127. Islands and rocks. The United Nations Convention on the Law of the Sea lays down a regime for islands[1]. An island is a naturally formed area of land, surrounded by water, which is above water at high tide[2]. An island's territorial sea[3], contiguous zone[4], exclusive economic zone[5] and continental shelf[6] are determined in the same way as those of other land territory[7]. Rocks which cannot sustain human habitation or economic life of their own are entitled to their own territorial sea and contiguous zone but not to an exclusive economic zone, exclusive fishery zone, or continental shelf[8].

1   United Nations Convention on the Law of the Sea (Montego Bay, 10 December 1982; TS 81 (1999); Cmnd 4524) Pt VIII (art 121).
2   United Nations Convention on the Law of the Sea art 121 para 1.
3   As to the territorial sea see PARA 123 et seq.

4   As to the contiguous zone see PARA 153.
5   As to the exclusive economic zone see PARA 154.
6   As to the continental shelf see PARA 163.
7   United Nations Convention on the Law of the Sea art 121 para 2.
8   United Nations Convention on the Law of the Sea art 121 para 3. In *Maritime Delimitation in the Area between Greenland and Jan Mayen (Denmark v Norway)* ICJ Reports 1993, 38, a conciliation commission rejected the argument that Jan Mayen island was a rock under this provision. The United Kingdom appeared formerly to regard Rockall, an uninhabited rock to the west of the Hebrides, not as a rock but rather as an island, since it claimed an exclusive fishery zone around it: see the Island of Rockall Act 1972 s 1; and PARA 115. See also 924 HC Official Report (6th series) 24 January 1977, written answers col 384. However in 1997 that claim seems to have been abandoned: see 298 HC Official Report (6th series) 22 July 1997, written answers col 911. See further 298 HC Official Report (6th series) 21 July 1997, written answers col 397; the Fishery Limits Order 1997, SI 1997/1750; and AGRICULTURE AND FISHERIES vol 1(2) (2007 Reissue) PARA 961.

128.   Low-tide elevations. A low-tide elevation is a naturally formed area of land which is surrounded by and above water at low tide but submerged at high tide[1]. Where a low-tide elevation, such as a drying rock or sandbank, is situated wholly or partly at a distance not exceeding the breadth of the territorial sea[2] from the mainland or an island, the low-water line on that elevation may be used as the baseline from which the breadth of the territorial sea is measured[3]. Where a low-tide elevation is wholly situated at a distance exceeding the breadth of the territorial sea from the mainland or an island, it has no territorial sea of its own[4]. Baselines may not, however, be drawn to and from low-tide elevations unless lighthouses or similar installations which are permanently above sea level have been built on them or unless such drawing has received general international recognition[5].

1   United Nations Convention on the Law of the Sea (Montego Bay, 10 December 1982; TS 81 (1999); Cmnd 4524) art 13 para 1. The definition in the Territorial Waters Order in Council, dated 25 September 1964, art 5(1) is slightly different, and defines a low-tide elevation as a naturally formed area of drying land surrounded by water which is below water at mean high water spring tides. Such low-tide elevations are to be treated as islands: art 2(2); and see *R v Kent Justices, ex p Lye* [1967] 2 QB 153, [1967] 1 All ER 560, 9 BILC 147, DC (structure erected on a sandbank).
2   As to the territorial sea see PARA 123 et seq.
3   United Nations Convention on the Law of the Sea art 13 para 1.
4   United Nations Convention on the Law of the Sea art 13 para 2. See also *Fisheries (United Kingdom v Norway)* ICJ Reports 1951, 116. As to the breadth of the territorial sea see PARA 124; and as to islands see PARA 127.
5   United Nations Convention on the Law of the Sea art 7 para 4.

129.   Bays. A baseline may be drawn across a bay[1], leaving the waters on the landward side of the line as internal waters[2] of the coastal state and providing the baseline for the delimitation of the territorial sea[3]. For this purpose, in respect of bays the coast of which belongs to a single state[4], a bay is a well-marked indentation of the land whose penetration into the land is in such proportion to the width of its mouth as to contain landlocked waters and constitute more than a curvature of the coast[5]. An indentation is only to be regarded as a bay if its area is as large as, or larger than, that of the semi-circle whose diameter is a line drawn across the mouth of that indentation[6]. The area of an indentation is that which lies between the low-water mark around its shore and a line joining the low-water mark of its natural entrance points[7]. Where, because of the presence of islands[8], an indentation has more than one mouth, the area of semi-circle may be calculated as if drawn on a line as long as the sum total of the lengths of the lines across the different mouths[9]. Islands within an indentation are included as if they formed part of its water area[10].

These principles have been applied to the coastline of the United Kingdom[11].

1   As to baselines see PARAS 125–126. The term 'bay' includes gulfs and estuaries: see *Post Office v Estuary Radio Ltd* [1968] 2 QB 740, [1967] 3 All ER 663, 9 BILC 187, CA (Thames Estuary); and see the United Nations Convention on the Law of the Sea (Montego Bay, 10 December 1982; TS 81 (1999); Cmnd 4524) art 10. If a river flows directly into the sea, the baseline is a straight line across the mouth of the river between points on the low-water line of its banks: art 9.

2   As to internal waters see PARA 121.

3   As to the territorial sea see PARA 123 et seq.

4   United Nations Convention on the Law of the Sea art 10 para 1.

5   United Nations Convention on the Law of the Sea art 10 para 2; Territorial Waters Order in Council, dated 25 September 1964, art 5(1).

6   United Nations Convention on the Law of the Sea art 10 para 2; Territorial Waters Order in Council, dated 25 September 1964, art 5(1). See eg *Post Office v Estuary Radio Ltd* [1968] 2 QB 740, [1967] 3 All ER 663, 9 BILC 187, CA.

7   United Nations Convention on the Law of the Sea art 10 para 3; Territorial Waters Order in Council, dated 25 September 1964, art 5(1). As to the natural entrance points in the Thames Estuary see *Post Office v Estuary Radio Ltd* [1968] 2 QB 740, [1967] 3 All ER 663, 9 BILC 187, CA.

8   As to islands see PARA 127.

9   United Nations Convention on the Law of the Sea art 10 para 3; Territorial Waters Order in Council, dated 25 September 1964, art 5(1).

10 United Nations Convention on the Law of the Sea art 10 para 3.

11 The Orders in Council set out the principles but do not specify which indentations are to count as juridical bays. As to the baselines drawn around the United Kingdom coast see United Kingdom Hydrographic Office *The Territorial Sea Limits of the United Kingdom* (2006). See also the Explanatory Note to the Territorial Waters Order in Council, dated 25 September 1964.

130.   Closing limits of bays.   If the distance between the low-water marks at the natural entrance points of a bay does not exceed 24 nautical miles, a closing line may be drawn between those two low-water marks[1]. Where the distance between the low-water marks at the natural entrance exceeds 24 miles, a straight baseline may be drawn within the bay so as to enclose the maximum area of water that is possible with a line of that length[2]. In principle, where the boundary line between two or more countries reaches the coast at a point in an indentation that would, under this definition, be recognised as a bay, the waters are not internal waters: the baseline would be drawn along the low-water mark inside the bay and the territorial sea[3] drawn accordingly[4].

1   United Nations Convention on the Law of the Sea (Montego Bay, 10 December 1982; TS 81 (1999); Cmnd 4524) art 10 para 4; Territorial Waters Order in Council, dated 25 September 1964, art 4. Art 10 of the United Nations Convention on the Law of the Sea does not apply where the system of straight baselines (as to which see PARA 126) is applied, or in the case of 'historic bays' (ie bays claimed as internal waters on the basis of long usage establishing an historic title) art 10 para 6. As to historic title see PARA 118.

2   United Nations Convention on the Law of the Sea art 10 para 5; Territorial Waters Order in Council, dated 25 September 1964, art 4. In the United Kingdom, at common law the definition was given as whether a man could see from headland to headland (see *Fitzherbert's Coronae* 399, 8 Edw 2; Coke 4th Inst, c xxii, 140, as to the performance by a coroner of his office); or that arm or branch of the sea which lies within the fauces terrae where a man may reasonably discern between shore and shore, which is, or at least may be, within the body of a county (see Hale's de Jure Maris, c 4). See also *Direct United States Cable Co Ltd v Anglo-American Telegraph Co Ltd* (1877) 2 App Cas 394, 2 BILC 892, PC. In *R v Cunningham* (1859) Bell CC 72, 2 BILC 885, CCR, a point in the Bristol Channel, ten miles from the coast of Somerset, was held to be within the body of the county of Glamorgan; cf *The Fagernes* [1927] P 311, 2 BILC 914, CA, where the Crown disclaimed dominion over a place further down the Channel.

3   As to the territorial sea see PARA 123 et seq.

4   The point is, however, not free from doubt. The provisions of the United Nations Convention on
     the Law of the Sea are limited to bays whose coast is within one state: see art 10 para 1; and
     PARA 129. The bay may form the internal waters of the coastal states jointly as in the case of the
     Gulf of Fonseca, jointly claimed by Honduras, Nicaragua and El Salvador: see the decision of
     the Central American Court of Justice on 9 March 1917, 1 Hackworth's Digest 702–705; *Land,
     Island and Maritime Frontier Dispute (El Salvador v Honduras: Nicaragua intervening)* ICJ
     Reports 1992, 351. Conversely, a 'border' bay may be claimed in its entirety by one of the
     bordering states. The United Kingdom claims that the waters of Lough Foyle, for example, fall
     within the United Kingdom: see 12 HC Official Reports (6th series), 11 November 1981,
     written answers col 82.

131.   Historic bays.   A bay may become a part of internal waters by general
acquiescence, even though the length of the closing line exceeds the limits
permitted by the general law. Such bays are known as historic bays[1]. In the case
of historic bays, the territorial waters are measured from a baseline passing
across the bay at the place recognised as forming the limit of the national
territory[2].

1   United Kingdom reply to the Questionnaire of the League of Nations 1930, League of Nations
     Doc C74, M39, 1929 V, Question IV (b). The provisions of the United Nations Convention on
     the Law of the Sea (Montego Bay, 10 December 1982; TS 81 (1999); Cmnd 4524) do not apply
     to such bays: art 10 para 6.
2   For a list of bays which have been claimed as historic bays see the United Nations *Historic Bays:
     Memorandum by the Secretariat of the United Nations* (UN Doc: A/CONF.13/1) 30 September
     1957, which includes the Bristol Channel. See further the United Nations *Secretariat paper,
     Juridical Regime of Historic Waters, including Historic Bays*, (UN Doc: A/CN.4/143) 9 March
     1962. The closing rule adopted in the United Nations Convention on the Law of the Sea art 10
     reduces the importance of historic bays.

132.   Territorial sea boundary; opposite and adjacent states.   Failing
agreement to the contrary, where the coasts of two states are opposite or
adjacent to each other, neither is entitled to extend its territorial sea[1] beyond the
median line every point of which is equidistant from the nearest points on the
baselines[2] from which the breadth of the territorial sea of each state is
measured[3].

1   As to the territorial sea see PARA 123 et seq.
2   As to baselines see PARAS 125–126.
3   United Nations Convention on the Law of the Sea (Montego Bay, 10 December 1982; TS 81
     (1999); Cmnd 4524) art 15. This does not apply where for reasons of historic title or special
     circumstances a different line is justifiable: art 15. As to the marking of the line on large scale
     charts see art 15. As to the delimitation of their territorial seas in the Straits of Dover between
     the United Kingdom and France see the Agreement between the Government of the United
     Kingdom of Great Britain and Northern Ireland and the Government of the French Republic
     relating to the Delimitation of the Territorial Sea in the Straits of Dover (Paris, 2 November
     1988; TS 26 (1989); Cm 733); and see PARA 141. There is no agreed boundary between the
     territorial seas of the United Kingdom and of Ireland.

133.   Innocent passage.   Customary international law recognises a right of
innocent passage through the territorial sea[1] for vessels of states other than the
coastal state. This is a feature which distinguishes the territorial sea from internal
or national waters[2]. The United Nations Convention on the Law of the Sea
provides that ships of all states, whether coastal or not, enjoy the right of
innocent passage through the territorial sea[3].

'Passage' means navigation through the territorial sea for the purpose of
traversing the territorial sea without entering internal waters, or of proceeding to
internal waters from the high seas and of making for the high seas from internal
waters[4]. It includes stopping and anchoring in so far as these are incidental to

ordinary navigation or are rendered necessary by force majeure or distress or to render assistance to persons, ships or aircraft in danger or distress[5].

Passage is innocent so long as it is not prejudicial to the peace, good order or security of the coastal state, and provided it takes place in accordance with international law[6]. Passage is prejudicial to those interests in this context if a foreign ship engages in the territorial sea in any of the following activities: (1) a threat or use of force against the sovereignty, territorial integrity or political independence of the coastal state or in any other manner in violation of the principles of international law embodied in the United Nations Charter[7]; (2) any exercise or practice with weapons[8]; (3) any act aimed at collecting information to the prejudice of the defence or security of the coastal state[9]; (4) any act of propaganda aimed at affecting the defence or security of the coastal state[10]; (5) launching, landing or taking on board of an aircraft[11]; (6) launching, landing or taking on board of any military device[12]; (7) loading or unloading a commodity, currency or person contrary to the customs, fiscal, immigration or sanitary laws of the coastal state[13]; (8) an act of wilful and serious pollution[14]; (9) fishing[15]; (10) carrying out research or survey activities[16]; (11) an act aimed at interfering with any systems of communication or any other facilities or installations of the coastal state[17]; and (12) any other activity which does not have a direct bearing on passage[18]. There are indications that this list of activities provides an exhaustive set of criteria for determining the innocence of passage[19].

Submarines must navigate on the surface and show their flags[20]. There is no right of innocent passage for aircraft.

1   As to the territorial sea see PARA 123 et seq.
2   See, however, the United Nations Convention on the Law of the Sea (Montego Bay, 10 December 1982; TS 81 (1999); Cmnd 4524) art 8 para 2, which provides that where, by reason of the coastal state's adoption of the straight baseline method for the delimitation of its waters, areas of the sea which were previously territorial waters or high seas have now become part of its internal waters, the right of innocent passage continues to exist in that area of the internal waters.
3   United Nations Convention on the Law of the Sea art 17 para 1. The Convention contains articles dealing with innocent passage generally: see Pt II Section 3 (arts 17–31). Part II Section 3(A) (arts 17–26) applies to all ships including government ships whether operated commercially or not (arts 21, 22 para 1). Part II Section 3(B) (arts 27–28) applies to merchant ships and to government ships operated commercially (art 27). Part II Section 3(C) (arts 29–32) applies to warships and other government ships operated for non-commercial purposes.
4   United Nations Convention on the Law of the Sea art 18 para 1. Voyages of vessels engaged in the coasting trade or cabotage are not included in this definition. Passage for other purposes is not innocent passage, and the ship is completely subject to the authority of the coastal state.
5   United Nations Convention on the Law of the Sea art 18 para 2. Stopping for other reasons may, however, not be illegal.
6   United Nations Convention on the Law of the Sea art 19 para 1. The intention appears to be that the innocence or otherwise of the passage is to be tested by the manner in which it is carried out. It may also be tested by the object of the passage: see *Corfu Channel (United Kingdom v Albania)* ICJ Reports 1949, 4.
7   United Nations Convention on the Law of the Sea art 19 para 2(a). For the Charter of the United Nations (San Francisco, 26 June 1945, see TS 67 (1946); Cmd 7015).
8   United Nations Convention on the Law of the Sea art 19 para 2(b).
9   United Nations Convention on the Law of the Sea art 19 para 2(c).
10 United Nations Convention on the Law of the Sea art 19 para 2(d).
11 United Nations Convention on the Law of the Sea art 19 para 2(e).
12 United Nations Convention on the Law of the Sea art 19 para 2(f).
13 United Nations Convention on the Law of the Sea art 19 para 2(g).
14 United Nations Convention on the Law of the Sea art 19 para 2(h).
15 United Nations Convention on the Law of the Sea art 19 para 2(i).
16 United Nations Convention on the Law of the Sea art 19 para 2(j).
17 United Nations Convention on the Law of the Sea art 19 para 2(k).

18 United Nations Convention on the Law of the Sea art 19 para 2(l).
19 See the USA-USSR Joint Statement on the Uniform Interpretation of Rules of International Law
    Governing Innocent Passage (Jackson Hole, Wyoming, 23 September 1989) 14 (UN) Law of the
    Sea Bulletin 13.
20 United Nations Convention on the Law of the Sea art 20.

134.   Laws and regulations of coastal states in relation to innocent passage.
The United Nations Convention on the Law of the Sea specifically provides that
the coastal state may adopt laws and regulations[1] relating to innocent passage[2] in
respect of all or any of the following: (1) safety of navigation and the regulation
of maritime traffic[3]; (2) protection of navigational and other aids and facilities[4];
(3) protection of cables and pipelines[5]; (4) conservation of the living resources of
the sea[6]; (5) prevention of infringement of its fisheries laws and regulations[7]; (6)
preservation of its environment and prevention, reduction and control of
pollution thereof[8]; (7) marine scientific research and hydrographic surveys[9]; and
(8) prevention of infringement of its customs, fiscal, immigration or sanitary laws
and regulations[10]. The laws and regulations must not apply to the design,
construction, manning or equipment of foreign ships unless they give effect to
generally accepted international rules or standards[11]. The sovereignty of a
coastal state over its territorial sea[12] would, in any event, entitle the coastal state
to adopt any laws and regulations that are consistent with the right of innocent
passage and with the provisions of the Convention.

1   Due publicity must be given to any laws and regulations: United Nations Convention on the
    Law of the Sea (Montego Bay, 10 December 1982; TS 81 (1999); Cmnd 4524) art 21 para 3.
2   As to the meaning of 'innocent passage' see PARA 133. As to the laws and regulations on the
    coastal state in relation to transit passage see PARA 144.
3   United Nations Convention on the Law of the Sea art 21 para 1(a). Article 22 enables the
    coastal state to require foreign ships to use such sea lanes and traffic separation schemes as it
    may designate or prescribe. Foreign ships must comply with all such laws and regulations and
    all generally accepted international regulations relating to the prevention of collisions at sea:
    art 21 para 4.
4   United Nations Convention on the Law of the Sea art 21 para 1(b).
5   United Nations Convention on the Law of the Sea art 21 para 1(c).
6   United Nations Convention on the Law of the Sea art 21 para 1(d).
7   United Nations Convention on the Law of the Sea art 21 para 1(e).
8   United Nations Convention on the Law of the Sea art 21 para 1(f). Nuclear-powered ships and
    ships carrying nuclear or other inherently dangerous or noxious substances must carry
    documents and observe special precautionary measures established for them by international
    agreements: art 23.
9   United Nations Convention on the Law of the Sea art 21 para 1(g).
10 United Nations Convention on the Law of the Sea art 21 para 1(h).
11 United Nations Convention on the Law of the Sea art 21 para 2. Measures adopted by the
    International Maritime Organization are the main source of such rules and standards.
12 As to the sovereignty of a coastal state over its territorial sea see PARA 136 et seq.

135.   Duties of the coastal states in relation to innocent passage.   The coastal
state must not hamper innocent passage[1] through its territorial sea. In applying
the United Nations Convention on the Law of the Sea[2] or any laws or
regulations it has adopted in conformity with it, the coastal state must not
impose requirements on foreign ships which have the practical effect of denying
or impairing the right of innocent passage or which discriminate in form or in
fact against the ships of any state or ships carrying cargoes to, from or on behalf
of any state[3]. It must give appropriate publicity to any danger to navigation of
which it has knowledge within its territorial sea[4].

1   As to the meaning of 'innocent passage' see PARA 133.

2   Ie the United Nations Convention on the Law of the Sea (Montego Bay, 10 December 1982; TS 81 (1999); Cmnd 4524).
3   United Nations Convention on the Law of the Sea art 24 para 1. In this, as in all other matters, the UN Security Council may order states to act contrary to the Convention and to prevent the passage of certain ships, e g in order to implement UN sanctions: as to the powers and functions of the Security Council see PARA 523.
4   United Nations Convention on the Law of the Sea art 24 para 2. As to the territorial sea see PARA 123 et seq.

136. Rights of protection of the coastal state. The coastal state may take the necessary steps in its territorial sea[1] to prevent passage which is not innocent[2]; and with respect to ships proceeding to its internal waters it may take any steps to prevent a breach of the conditions to which admission to those waters is subject[3]. The coastal state, without discrimination among foreign ships, may temporarily suspend the right of innocent passage in specified areas of its territorial sea if that is essential for the protection of its security, including the conduct of weapons exercises[4].

1   As to the territorial sea see PARA 123 et seq.
2   United Nations Convention on the Law of the Sea (Montego Bay, 10 December 1982; TS 81 (1999); Cmnd 4524) art 25 para 1. As to innocent passage see PARA 133.
3   United Nations Convention on the Law of the Sea art 25 para 2.
4   United Nations Convention on the Law of the Sea art 25 para 3. Thus a permanent prohibition over part of or all, or a temporary prohibition over all, the territorial sea would not be warranted by this provision. Nonetheless, some states have permanently closed areas in front of military ports. Such suspension as is permitted only takes effect after being duly published: art 25 para 3. There being no provision for independent assessment, it may be presumed that the coastal state is in fact the sole judge of its security requirements.

137. Charges on foreign ships. No charge may be levied upon foreign ships by reason only of their passage through the territorial sea[1]. Charges may only be levied for services rendered to ships passing through the territorial sea, and on a non-discriminatory basis[2].

1   United Nations Convention on the Law of the Sea (Montego Bay, 10 December 1982; TS 81 (1999); Cmnd 4524) art 26 para 1.
2   See the United Nations Convention on the Law of the Sea art 26 para 2. As to the territorial sea see PARA 123 et seq.

138. Criminal jurisdiction over foreign ships. The criminal jurisdiction of the coastal state should not be exercised on board a foreign ship passing through the territorial[1] sea to arrest any person or conduct any investigation in connection with a crime committed on board a ship during its passage through the territorial sea unless: (1) the consequences of the crime extend to the coastal state; (2) the crime is of a kind to disturb the peace of the country or the good order of the territorial sea; (3) the captain or the consul of the country whose flag the ship flies has requested the assistance of the local authorities; or (4) it is necessary for the suppression of the illicit traffic in narcotic drugs or psychotropic substances[2]. This does not affect the right of the coastal state to arrest or carry out an investigation on board a foreign ship passing through the territorial sea after leaving internal waters[3]. On the other hand, as a general rule the coastal state may not take any steps on board a foreign ship passing through the territorial waters to arrest any person or to conduct any investigation in connection with any crime committed before the ship entered the territorial waters if the ship is only passing through the territorial waters without entering internal waters[4].

1   As to the territorial sea see PARA 123 et seq.

2   United Nations Convention on the Law of the Sea (Montego Bay, 10 December 1982: TS 81
     (1999); Cmnd 4524) art 27 para 1. The use of the word 'should' in this article is deliberate; it
     thus appears that the formulation is not of a rule of law but of comity: cf art 27 para 5 (see the
     text and note 4). A foreign ship is a merchant ship or a government ship operated for
     commercial purposes. Warships and persons on them enjoy immunity from the jurisdiction of
     the coastal state: see art 32; and *Chung Chi Cheung v R* [1939] AC 160, [1938] 4 All ER 786,
     3 BILC 96, PC, where, however, the immunity was waived. See also *Pianka v R* [1979] AC 107,
     [1977] 3 WLR 859, PC. The rules stated in the text are only concerned with the exercise of
     jurisdiction over or on board the ship itself, and do not affect the right of the coastal state to
     exercise its criminal jurisdiction over persons who were on board the ship at the time of the
     offence but who later come into the custody of the coastal state by means other than the
     stopping of the ship: see the Territorial Waters Jurisdiction Act 1878; but see also the Consular
     Relations Act 1968 ss 1(2), 5; PARA 303.
3   United Nations Convention on the Law of the Sea art 27 para 2. Whenever the coastal state
     does exercise its jurisdiction over or on board a ship under this provision or art 27 para 1 (see
     the text and note 2), it must, if the captain requests, notify a diplomatic agent or consular officer
     of the flag state and facilitate contact between them before taking any steps, although, in case of
     emergency, this may be done while the steps are being taken: art 27 para 3. In making an arrest,
     the authorities must pay due regard to the interests of navigation: art 27 para 4.
4   United Nations Convention on the Law of the Sea art 27 para 5. The crime would not be one
     which falls within heads (1)–(4) in the text. However, art 27 para 5 provides that the coastal
     state 'may not' take any steps, whereas art 27 para 1 provides that it 'should not': see the text
     and note 2. The rule here stated does not affect the situation where, while in territorial waters,
     the ship is at anchor not incidentally to navigation and therefore outside the right of innocent
     passage. Such ships are fully subject to the jurisdiction of the coastal state.

139.   Civil jurisdiction over merchant ships.   The coastal state should[1] not stop
or divert a foreign ship passing through the territorial sea[2] for the purpose of
exercising civil jurisdiction in relation to persons on board the ship[3]. It may not[4]
levy execution nor arrest the ship for the purpose of any civil proceedings, save
only in respect of obligations or liabilities of the ship itself assumed or incurred
in the course of, or for the purpose of, its voyage through the waters of the
coastal state[5], unless the vessel is either lying in the territorial sea or passing
through it after leaving internal waters[6].

1   As to the significance of the word 'should' see PARA 138 note 2.
2   As to the territorial sea see PARA 123 et seq.
3   United Nations Convention on the Law of the Sea (Montego Bay, 10 December 1982; TS 81
     (1999); Cmnd 4524) art 28 para 1. As to torts committed on board ships in territorial waters see
     CONFLICT OF LAWS vol 8(3) (Reissue) PARA 372.
4   See PARA 138 note 4.
5   United Nations Convention on the Law of the Sea art 28 para 2.
6   United Nations Convention on the Law of the Sea art 28 para 3.

140.   Passage of warships.   If any warship[1] does not comply with the
regulations of the coastal state concerning passage through the territorial sea[2]
and disregards any request for compliance made to it, the coastal state may
require the warship to leave its territorial sea[3]. The United Kingdom considers
that the right of innocent passage extends to warships, and that their entry into
the territorial sea cannot be made subject to the prior notification or the
authorisation of the coastal state[4].

1   For the purposes of the United Nations Convention on the Law of the Sea (Montego Bay,
     10 December 1982; TS 81 (1999); Cmnd 4524) 'warship' means a ship belonging to the armed
     forces of a state bearing the external marks distinguishing such ships of its nationality, under the
     command of an officer duly commissioned by the government of the state and whose name
     appears in the appropriate service list or its equivalent, and manned by a crew which is under
     regular armed forces discipline: art 29. See also UK Ministry of Defence *The Manual of the Law
     of Armed Conflict* (2004) para 13.5.
2   As to the territorial sea see PARA 123 et seq.

3   United Nations Convention on the Law of the Sea art 30. This provision is needed because
     warships and other government ships operated non-commercially are generally immune from
     the jurisdiction of the coastal state: see art 32; and PARA 138 note 2. The flag state bears
     international responsibility for damage to the coastal state resulting from non-compliance by
     such ships with laws and regulations of the coastal state concerning passage (see PARA 134) or
     the provisions of the Convention or other rules of international law: art 31.
4   See 388 HL Official Report (6th series), 1 February 1978, written answers cols *846–847*; and
     the Notice issued by the UK Hydrographic Office on 1 January 2002, (2001) 72 BYIL 634, at
     639. The articles of the United Nations Convention on the Law of the Sea concerning the right
     of innocent passage are stated therein to be applicable to 'all ships': United Nations Convention
     on the Law of the Sea Pt II Section 3(A) (arts 17–26). Submarines and other underwater vehicles
     are required to navigate on the surface in the territorial sea and to show their flags: art 20.

141.   Passage through straits used for international navigation. Under the
United Nations Convention on the Law of the Sea[1] there exists, in straits which
are used for international navigation[2] between one part of the high seas[3] or an
exclusive economic zone[4] and another part of the high seas or an exclusive
economic zone, a right of transit passage[5] for all ships and aircraft both military
and commercial, which must not be impeded[6].

However, where the strait is formed by an island of a state bordering the state
and the mainland, transit passage does not apply therein if there exists seaward
of the island a route through the high seas[7] or through an exclusive economic
zone[8] of similar convenience with respect to navigational and hydrographical
characteristics[9]. The right of innocent passage[10] applies to such straits excluded
from the regime of transit passage[11]. Innocent passage also applies in straits used
for international navigation between a part of the high seas or an exclusive
economic zone and the territorial sea of a foreign state[12]. The coastal state may
not suspend innocent passage through such straits[13].

Although high seas routes or routes through exclusive economic zones in
straits wider than 24 nautical miles are excluded from the regime of transit
passage, the freedoms of navigation and of overflight exist in such routes[14].

The extent to which the Convention's provisions extend beyond customary
international law rights of passage through straits is controversial[15].

1   See the United Nations Convention on the Law of the Sea (Montego Bay, 10 December 1982;
     TS 81 (1999); Cmnd 4524) Pt III (arts 34–45).
2   The term 'international navigation' is taken from the judgment of the International Court of
     Justice in *Corfu Channel (United Kingdom v Albania)* ICJ Reports 1949, 4.
3   As to the high seas see the United Nations Convention on the Law of the Sea Pt VII; and PARA
     147 et seq.
4   As to the exclusive economic zone see the United Nations Convention on the Law of the Sea
     Pt V (arts 55–75); and PARA 154.
5   As to the meaning of 'transit passage' see PARA 143. The provisions on transit passage are more
     favourable to ships of non-coastal states than is the right of innocent passage: see PARAS
     133–140. They were a concession to the major shipping states in return for their acceptance of
     a 12-mile limit for the territorial sea, which resulted in some straits, part of which had
     previously been high seas (see Pt VII (arts 86–120, especially arts 87, 90), falling within the
     territorial sea of one or more coastal states. As to the territorial sea see Pt II (arts 2–33) of the
     Convention, and PARA 123 et seq. As to the breadth of the territorial sea see art 3; and PARA
     124.
6   United Nations Convention on the Law of the Sea art 38 para 1.
7   United Nations Convention on the Law of the Sea art 38 para 1. As to the high seas see PARA
     147 et seq.
8   As to the exclusive economic zone see PARA 154.
9   United Nations Convention on the Law of the Sea art 38 para 1.
10   As to innocent passage see PARAS 133–140.
11   United Nations Convention on the Law of the Sea art 45 para 1(a). The Pentland Firth south of
     Orkney, and the passage between the Scilly Isles and Cornwall, for example, fall into this
     category.

12   United Nations Convention on the Law of the Sea art 45 para 1(b).

13   United Nations Convention on the Law of the Sea art 45 para 2.

14   United Nations Convention on the Law of the Sea art 36. As to the freedom of the high seas see PARA 147 et seq.

15   Before it became a party to the United Nations Convention on the Law of the Sea, the United Kingdom already regarded the right of transit passage as part of customary international law. Straits in which it accords transit passage are the Straits of Dover (which since 1987 fall within the territorial seas of the United Kingdom and France), the North Channel, and the passage between Shetland and Orkney: 804 HL Official Report (5th series), 5 February 1987, col 382. The 'right of unimpeded transit passage' through the Straits of Dover was confirmed by the Agreement between the Government of the United Kingdom of Great Britain and Northern Ireland and the Government of the French Republic relating to the Delimitation of the Territorial Sea in the Straits of Dover (Paris, 2 November 1988; TS 26 (1989); Cm 733).

142.   Legal status of waters. A right of transit passage[1] does not otherwise affect the legal status of the waters of the straits through which it exists, or the exercise by the coastal states of their sovereignty or jurisdiction over the waters of such straits and the corresponding air space, seabed and subsoil[2]. Nor does it affect the legal regime in straits in which passage is regulated in whole or in part by long-standing international conventions in force specifically relating to them[3].

1   As to the meaning of 'transit passage' see PARA 143.

2   United Nations Convention on the Law of the Sea (Montego Bay, 10 December 1982; Misc 11 (1983); Cmnd 8491) art 34 para 1. The sovereignty or jurisdiction of the coastal state is exercised subject to Pt II (arts 2–33) and to other rules of international law: art 34 para 2.

3   United Nations Convention on the Law of the Sea art 35(c). The Turkish straits, governed by the Convention regarding the Regime of the Straits (of the Dardanelles) (Montreux, 20 July 1936; TS 30 (1937); Cmd 5551) (the 'Montreux Convention') to which the United Kingdom is a party, is an example.

143.   Meaning of 'transit passage'. 'Transit passage' means the exercise in accordance with Part III of the United Nations Convention on the Law of the Sea of freedom of navigation and overflight solely for the purpose of continuous and expeditious transit of the strait, refraining from the threat or use of force in violation of international law, and refraining from any activities other than those incident to their normal modes of continuous and expeditious transit unless rendered necessary by force majeure or distress[1]. The requirement of continuous and expeditious transit does not preclude passage through the strait for the purpose of entering, leaving or returning from a coastal state subject to the conditions of entry to that state[2]. Transit passage differs from innocent passage inter alia in having no criterion of innocence and in including a right of overflight[3].

1   United Nations Convention on the Law of the Sea (Montego Bay, 10 December 1982; TS 81 (1999); Cmnd 4524) art 38 para 2.

2   See the United Nations Convention on the Law of the Sea art 38 para 2.

3   The right of coastal states to make laws and regulations for ships in transit passage is also restricted, as to which see the United Nations Convention on the Law of the Sea arts 41 and 42; and PARA 144. Some states consider that the reference to 'normal modes of continuous and expeditious transit' indicates that submarines may exercise the right while submerged.

144.   Laws and regulations of coastal states in relation to transit passage. The right of states to legislate for ships in transit passage[1] is constrained by the duty not to deny, hamper or impair the right of transit passage[2]. Coastal states may adopt non-discriminatory[3] laws and regulations relating to transit passage in respect of all or any of the following: (1) the safety of navigation and the regulation of maritime traffic, as provided[4] in the United Nations Convention on the Law of the Sea[5]; (2) the prevention, reduction and control of pollution by giving effect to applicable international regulations regarding the discharge of oil, oily waters and other noxious substances in the strait[6]; (3) the prevention of fishing by fishing vessels, including the stowing of fishing gear[7]; and (4) the loading of any commodity, currency or person in contravention of their customs, fiscal, immigration laws and regulations[8].

The laws and regulations referred to must not be discriminatory[9], and must be given due publicity[10]. Foreign ships must comply with them[11]. The flag state of a ship or the state of registry of an aircraft which is entitled to sovereign immunity bears international responsibility for any loss or damage to the coastal state resulting from non-compliance with such laws and regulations by that ship or aircraft[12].

1 As to the meaning of 'transit passage' see PARA 143. As to the laws and regulations of the coastal state in relation to innocent passage see PARA 134.
2 See the United Nations Convention on the Law of the Sea (Montego Bay, 10 December 1982; TS 81 (1999); Cmnd 4524) art 42 para 2.
3 See the United Nations Convention on the Law of the Sea art 42 para 2. Coastal states may establish sea lanes and traffic separation schemes in straits where necessary to promote the safe passage of ships, after referring them to the competent international organisation (which is the International Maritime Organization): see art 41.
4 Ie as provided by the United National Convention on the Law of the Sea art 41.
5 United Nations Convention on the Law of the Sea art 42 para 1(a).
6 United Nations Convention on the Law of the Sea art 42 para 1(b). The reference to 'international regulations' precludes the adoption of regulations at variance with applicable regulations framed by bodies such as the International Maritime Organization.
7 United Nations Convention on the Law of the Sea art 42 para 1(c).
8 United Nations Convention on the Law of the Sea art 42 para 1(d).
9 United Nations Convention on the Law of the Sea art 42 para 2.
10 United Nations Convention on the Law of the Sea art 42 para 3.
11 United Nations Convention on the Law of the Sea art 42 para 4.
12 United Nations Convention on the Law of the Sea art 42 para 5.

145. Duties of states bordering straits in relation to transit passage. States bordering straits must not hamper transit passage[1]. They must give appropriate publicity to any danger to navigation or overflight within or over the strait of which they have knowledge[2]. They may not suspend transit passage[3].

1 United Nations Convention on the Law of the Sea (Montego Bay, 10 December 1982; TS 81 (1999); Cmnd 4524) article 44. As to the meaning of 'transit passage' see PARA 143.
2 United Nations Convention on the Law of the Sea art 44. The duty arises because the waters of the strait are by definition a part of the territorial sea of the coastal state, in respect of which the responsibility to notify known dangers subsists: see PARA 135.
3 United Nations Convention on the Law of the Sea art 44. Contrast the right temporarily to suspend innocent passage through parts of the territorial sea that do not constitute straits: art 25 para 2; and PARA 136.

146. Duties of ships and aircraft. Ships and aircraft exercising the right of transit passage must: (1) proceed without delay through or over the strait[1]; (2) refrain from any threat or use of force against the sovereignty, territorial integrity or political independence of the states bordering the strait or in any other manner inconsistent with the principles of international law embodied in the Charter of the United Nations[2]; (3) refrain from activities other than those incident to their normal modes of continuous and expeditious transit[3] unless rendered necessary by force majeure or distress[4]; and (4) comply with relevant provisions of Part II of the United Nations Convention on the Law of the Sea[5]. Ships must comply with generally accepted international regulations[6], procedures and practices for safety at sea including the International Regulations for

Preventing Collisions at Sea[7] and with international regulations, procedures and practices for the prevention, reduction and control of pollution from ships[8]. Civil aircraft must observe the Rules of the Air established by the International Civil Aviation Organisation[9] and monitor radio frequencies, including the appropriate international distress frequency[10]. Ships may not carry out research or survey activities without prior authorisation of the coastal states[11].

1   United Nations Convention on the Law of the Sea (Montego Bay, 10 December 1982; TS 81 (1999); Cmnd 4524) art 39 para 1(a).
2   United Nations Convention on the Law of the Sea art 39 para 1(b). The Charter referred to is the Charter of the United Nations (San Francisco, 26 June 1945; TS 67 (1946); Cmd 7015). The Charter obligations include a duty to refrain from any threat or use of force against the sovereignty, territorial integrity or political independence of any state, whether or not bordering the strait.
3   The reference to 'normal modes of continuous and expeditious transit' is widely understood to acknowledge the right of submarines to exercise the right of transit passage while submerged, in contrast to the right of innocent passage which must be exercised on the surface: see PARA 133.
4   United Nations Convention on the Law of the Sea art 39 para 1(c).
5   United Nations Convention on the Law of the Sea art 39 para 1(d). The provisions referred to in the text are Pt II (arts 2–33) concerning the territorial sea, as to which see PARA 123 et seq above.
6   The reference to 'generally accepted international regulations' is understood to refer to measures adopted by the competent international agencies, notably the International Maritime Organization.
7   Ie the Convention on the International Regulations for Preventing Collisions at Sea (London, 20 October 1972; TS 77 (1977); Cmnd 6962): see SHIPPING AND MARITIME LAW vol 94 (2008) PARA 715 et seq.
8   United Nations Convention on the Law of the Sea art 39 para 2. For the relevant measures regarding pollution from ships see Pt XII (arts 192–237); and PARA 193.
9   As to the International Civil Aviation Organisation see AIR LAW vol 2 (2008) PARA 20 et seq. As to the domestic Rules of the Air see AIR LAW vol 2 (2008) PARA 357.
10 United Nations Convention on the Law of the Sea art 39 para 3.
11 See the United Nations Convention on the Law of the Sea art 40.

(2) THE HIGH SEAS

(i) In general

147. Freedom of the high seas. In the United Nations Convention on the Law of the Sea[1], the term 'high seas' denotes all parts of the sea not included in the exclusive economic zone, the territorial sea or internal waters of a state or in the archipelagic waters of an archipelagic state[2]. The high seas are res communis and open to all states, whether coastal or land-locked[3], so that no state may validly purport to subject any part of the high seas to its sovereignty[4]. They are reserved for peaceful purposes[5]. Freedom of the high seas comprises, inter alia, both for coastal and land-locked states: (1) freedom of navigation[6]; (2) freedom of overflight[7]; (3) freedom to lay submarine cables and pipelines[8]; (4) freedom to construct artificial islands and other permitted installations[9]; (5) freedom of fishing[10]; and (6) freedom of scientific research[11]. These freedoms must be exercised subject to the conditions laid down in the Convention and by other rules of international law[12] and with due regard to the interests of other states in their exercise of the freedom of the high seas[13].

1   United Nations Convention on the Law of the Sea (Montego Bay, 10 December 1982; TS 81 (1999); Cmnd 4524). Pt VII (arts 86–115) contains provisions relating to the high seas. The United Kingdom became a party to the Convention on 24 August 1997: see the London Gazette, 29 August 1997. The Convention supersedes the Convention on the High Contiguous Zone

(Geneva, 29 April 1958; TS 5 (1963); Cmnd 1929). The latter remains in force between the United Kingdom and other states which are parties to it but not to the United Nations Convention on the Law of the Sea.

2   United Nations Convention on the Law of the Sea art 86. As to the exclusive economic zone see Pt V (arts 55–75); and PARA 154. As to the territorial sea and contiguous zone see Pt II (arts 2–33); and PARAS 123 et seq, 153. As to archipelagic states see Pt IV (arts 46–54) of the Convention.

3   United Nations Convention on the Law of the Sea art 87.

4   United Nations Convention on the Law of the Sea art 89.

5   United Nations Convention on the Law of the Sea art 88.

6   United Nations Convention on the Law of the Sea art 87 para 1(a).

7   United Nations Convention on the Law of the Sea art 87 para 1(b).

8   United Nations Convention on the Law of the Sea art 87 para 1(c). This is subject to the provisions in Pt VI (arts 56–85) concerning the continental shelf (see PARA 163 et seq).

9   United Nations Convention on the Law of the Sea art 87 para 1(d). This is also subject to the provisions in Pt VI concerning the continental shelf (see PARA 163 et seq).

10 United Nations Convention on the Law of the Sea art 87 para 1(e). This is subject to the provisions of Pt VII Section 2 (arts 116–120) concerning the conservation and management of the living resources of the high seas (PARA 190 et seq).

11 United Nations Convention on the Law of the Sea art 87 para 1(f). This is subject to the provisions of Pt VI concerning the continental shelf (see PARA 163 et seq) and Pt XIII (arts 238–269) concerning marine scientific research: see PARA 194.

12 United Nations Convention on the Law of the Sea art 87 para 1.

13 United Nations Convention on the Law of the Sea art 87 para 2.

148.   Freedom of navigation and jurisdiction over foreign ships on the high seas. The high seas are open to navigation by ships of all states whether coastal or land-locked[1]. No state may interfere with the ships of other states or exercise jurisdiction over them[2] in time of peace[3] except within the contiguous zone[4], under the doctrine of hot pursuit[5], and in the exercise of self-defence[6]. A warship which encounters a foreign merchant ship on the high seas is not justified in boarding it without the consent of the state whose flag the ship is flying[7], except where the act of interference derives from powers conferred by treaty[8], unless there is reasonable ground for suspecting that the ship is engaged in piracy[9], the slave trade[10], or unauthorised broadcasting[11], or that, despite the appearance of the flag that it is flying or its refusal to fly any flag[12], the ship is without nationality[13] or is, in reality, of the same nationality as the warship[14]. In such cases the warship has the right to verify the ship's right to fly its flag[15].

1   See the United Nations Convention on the Law of the Sea (Montego Bay, 10 December 1982; TS 81 (1999); Cmnd 4524) art 90.

2   *Lotus Case* PCIJ Ser A No 10 (1927). See also *Le Louis* (1817) 2 Dods 210 at 243, 3 BILC 691 per Lord Stowell; *The Costa Rica Packet Case* (1897) 5 Moore Int Arb 4948; *The Jessie, The Thomas F Bayard and The Pescawha* 6 RIAA 57 (1921).

3   As to the exercise of jurisdiction or control over foreign ships in time of armed conflict, see UK Ministry of Defence *Manual on the Law of Armed Conflict* (2005) Ch 13; and WAR AND ARMED CONFLICT.

4   As to the contiguous zone see the United Nations Convention on the Law of the Sea art 133; and PARA 153.

5   As to hot pursuit see the United Nations Convention on the Law of the Sea art 111; and PARA 161.

6   See eg *The Virginius Case* (1874) 76 Parliamentary Papers 299, 391, where Great Britain recognised a capture on the high seas as an exercise of self-defence. The UK adopted a similar position with respect to visit and search on the high seas during the 1980–1988 Iran-Iraq war: see 127 HC official Reports (6th series), 15 February 1988, cols *424–425*. As to self-defence generally see WAR AND ARMED CONFLICT vol 49(1) (2005 Reissue) PARA 403 et seq.

7   It is not clear whether such consent may be given by the master of the ship or must be given by the governmental authorities of the flag state.

8   Including a treaty other than the United Nations Convention on the Law of the Sea itself: United Nations Convention on the Law of the Sea art 110 para 1.

9 United Nations Convention on the Law of the Sea art 110 para 1(a). As to piracy see arts 101–107; and PARA 155 et seq.

10 United Nations Convention on the Law of the Sea art 110 para 1(b). As to the slave trade see art 99; and CONSTITUTIONAL LAW AND HUMAN RIGHTS vol 8(2) (Reissue) PARA 125.

11 United Nations Convention on the Law of the Sea art 110 para 1(c). As to unauthorised broadcasting see art 109; PARA 196; and TELECOMMUNICATIONS AND BROADCASTING vol 45(1) (2005 Reissue) PARA 582 et seq.

12 A warship may interfere with a merchant vessel which is flying a flag of no state: *Naim Molvan (Owners of Motor Vessel Asya) v A-G for Palestine* [1948] AC 351, 1 BILC 674, PC.

13 United Nations Convention on the Law of the Sea art 110 para 1(d).

14 United Nations Convention on the Law of the Sea art 110 para 1(e).

15 United Nations Convention on the Law of the Sea art 110 para 2. It may send a boat under the command of an officer to the suspected ship, and if suspicion remains after the ship's documents have been checked, it may proceed to a further examination on board ship, which must be carried out with all possible consideration: art 110 para 2. If the suspicions prove to be unfounded and the ship boarded has not committed any act justifying them, it must be compensated for any loss or damage that may have been sustained: art 110 para 3. These provisions (ie art 110 paras 1–3) apply mutatis mutandis to military aircraft (art 110 para 4) and to any other duly authorised ships or aircraft clearly marked and identifiable as being on government service (art 110 para 5).

149.   Status of ships. A ship may sail under the flag of one state only and may not change its flag during a voyage or while in a port of call, unless there is a real transfer of ownership or change of registry[1]. A ship which sails under the flags of two or more states, using them as flags of convenience, may not claim the nationality of any of those flag states against another state and may be treated as a ship with no nationality[2].

1 United Nations Convention on the Law of the Sea (Montego Bay, 10 December 1982; TS 81 (1999); Cmnd 4524) art 92 para 1.

2 United Nations Convention on the Law of the Sea art 92 para 2. This provision and that referred to in note 1 do not prejudice the question of ships employed on the official service of the United Nations, its specialised agencies or the International Atomic Energy Agency (as to which see PARA 533) flying the flag of the organisation. As to the nationality of ships see PARA 395. See also PARA 396. As to the exercise of jurisdiction over ships with no nationality see PARA 148 note 12.

150.   Penal jurisdiction over ships on the high seas in matters of collision etc. Save in exceptional cases expressly provided for in international treaties or in the United Nations Convention on the Law of the Sea[1], a ship on the high seas is subject to the exclusive jurisdiction of its flag state[2]. In the event of a collision or other incident of navigation[3] concerning a ship on the high seas which involves the responsibility of the master or of any other person in the service of the ship, no penal or disciplinary proceedings may be instituted against such persons except before the judicial or administrative authorities either of the flag state or the state of which that person is a national[4]. Only the authorities of the flag state may order the arrest or detention of the ship, even for purposes of investigation[5].

1 United Nations Convention on the Law of the Sea (Montego Bay, 10 December 1982; TS 81 (1999); Cmnd 4524).

2 United Nations Convention on the Law of the Sea art 97 para 1. See also art 110, and PARA 148. As to jurisdiction over offences committed on board British ships on the high seas see CRIMINAL LAW, EVIDENCE AND PROCEDURE vol 11(2) (2006 Reissue) PARA 625. See also PARA 144.

3 Eg damage to a pipeline or submarine telegraph cable: see the United Nations Convention on the Law of the Sea art 113; and PARA 169.

4 United Nations Convention on the Law of the Sea art 97 para 1. This effectively negatives the decision of the Permanent Court of International Justice in *Lotus Case* PCIJ Ser A No 10 (1927). See, to the same effect, the International Convention for the Unification of Certain Rules

relating to Penal Jurisdiction in Matters of Collisions or other Incidents of Navigation (Brussels, 10 May 1952; TS 47 (1960); Cmnd 1128). In disciplinary matters only the state which has issued a master's certificate of competence or licence is competent to withdraw the certificate even if the holder is the national of another state: United Nations Convention on the Law of the Sea art 97 para 2. For the duties in respect of dangers to life at sea see art 98.

5   United Nations Convention on the Law of the Sea art 97 para 3.

151.   Jurisdiction over warships.   Warships on the high seas have complete immunity from the jurisdiction of any state other than the flag state[1], as do ships owned or operated by a state and used only on government non-commercial service[2].

1   United Nations Convention on the Law of the Sea (Montego Bay, 10 December 1982; TS 81 (1999); Cmnd 4524) art 95.
2   United Nations Convention on the Law of the Sea art 96.

152.   Obligations of states in respect of the high seas.   The freedom of the high seas must be exercised by all states with due regard for the interests of other states in their exercise of the freedom of the high seas[1].

Every state must adopt effective measures to prevent and punish the transport of slaves in vessels flying its flag and the unlawful use of its flag for that purpose[2]. It must co-operate to the fullest possible extent in the repression of piracy[3]. Every state must effectively exercise its jurisdiction and control in administrative, technical and social matters over ships under its flag[4], and must maintain a register of ships and assume jurisdiction under its internal law over such ships, and their masters, officers and crew in such matters[5].

Every state must take such measures as are necessary to ensure safety at sea with regard, inter alia, to: (1) the construction, equipment and seaworthiness of ships; (2) the manning of ships, labour conditions and the training of crews; and (3) the use of signals, the maintenance of communications and the prevention of collisions[6]. These measures must be taken in the light of generally accepted international regulations, procedures and practices and a state must take necessary steps to secure their observance[7].

A state which has clear grounds to believe that proper jurisdiction and control with respect to a ship have not been exercised may report the facts to the flag state which must investigate the matter and, if appropriate, take any action necessary remedy the situation[8]. A flag state must cause an inquiry to be held by or before a suitably qualified person or persons into every marine casualty or incident of navigation on the high seas causing loss of life or serious injury to nationals of another state or serious damage to ships or installations of another state or to the marine environment[9]. The flag state and the other state must co-operate in the conduct of such inquiry[10].

1   United Nations Convention on the Law of the Sea (Montego Bay, 10 December 1982; TS 81 (1999); Cmnd 4524) art 87 para 2.
2   United Nations Convention on the Law of the Sea art 99. See also art 110 para 1(b). As to slavery and the slave trade see CONSTITUTIONAL LAW AND HUMAN RIGHTS vol 8(2) (Reissue) PARA 125.
3   United Nations Convention on the Law of the Sea art 100. See also art 110 para 1(a). As to piracy see PARA 155 et seq.
4   United Nations Convention on the Law of the Sea art 94 para 1.
5   United Nations Convention on the Law of the Sea art 94 para 2.
6   United Nations Convention on the Law of the Sea art 94 para 3. See also art 94 para 4.
7   United Nations Convention on the Law of the Sea art 94 para 5.
8   United Nations Convention on the Law of the Sea art 94 para 6.

9   United Nations Convention on the Law of the Sea art 94 para 7. As to shipping inquiries see
    SHIPPING AND MARITIME LAW.
10 United Nations Convention on the Law of the Sea art 94 para 7.

153. Contiguous zone. In a zone contiguous to its territorial sea a coastal
state may exercise the control necessary (1) to prevent infringement of its
customs, fiscal, immigration or sanitary laws and regulations within its territory
or territorial sea; and (2) to punish infringement of those laws and regulations
committed within its territory or territorial sea[1]. A coastal state may also
presume that the removal from the seabed of the contiguous zone of objects of
an archaeological or historical nature would result in an infringement of those
laws and regulations[2]. A contiguous zone may not extend beyond 24 nautical
miles from the baseline from which the breadth of the territorial sea is
measured[3].

1   United Nations Convention on the Law of the Sea (Montego Bay, 10 December 1982; TS 81
    (1999); Cmnd 4524) art 33 para 1. The zone remains part of, and subject to the local regime of,
    the high seas or (if an exclusive economic zone is claimed) the exclusive economic zone; and the
    establishment of a contiguous zone does not confer jurisdiction of the coastal state for any
    purposes other than those stated in arts 33 and 303. There is no provision for the establishment
    of contiguous zones for purposes of security, nor does art 33 confer exclusive fishing rights. The
    United Kingdom does not claim a contiguous zone. As to fishery zones and the United Kingdom
    fishery limits see AGRICULTURE AND FISHERIES vol 1(2) (2007 Reissue) PARA 961.
2   See the United Nations Convention on the Law of the Sea art 303. The United Kingdom
    legislation on underwater archaeology is confined in its application to the territorial sea: see the
    Protection of Wrecks Act 1973; the National Heritage Act 2002; and NATIONAL CULTURAL
    HERITAGE vol 77 (2010) PARA 1064 et seq. As to the territorial sea see PARA 123.
3   United Nations Convention on the Law of the Sea art 33 para 2. As to the method of measuring
    the territorial sea see PARA 123 et seq. Unlike the Convention on the Territorial Sea and the
    Contiguous Zone (Geneva, 29 April 1958; TS 3 (1965); Cmnd 2511) art 24 para 3, the United
    Nations Convention on the Law of the Sea contains no provision regarding the boundary
    between the contiguous zones of opposite or adjacent state.

154. Exclusive economic zones and exclusive fishery zones. The United
Nations Convention on the Law of the Sea[1] provides for the establishment by
coastal states of an exclusive economic zone[2], whose legal status is sui generis,
being neither territorial sea[3] nor high seas[4]. The inner limit of the exclusive
economic zone is the outer limit of the territorial sea[5] and its outer limit is 200
nautical miles from the baselines from which the territorial sea is measured[6].

The delimitation of the exclusive economic zone between states with opposite
or adjacent coasts is to be effected by agreement in order to achieve an equitable
solution[7].

The rights and duties of the coastal state in respect of its exclusive economic
zone include sovereign rights for the purpose of exploring, exploiting, conserving
and managing the natural resources, whether living or non-living, of the waters
superjacent to the sea bed and of the sea bed and its subsoil[8]; and jurisdiction
with respect to: (1) the establishment and use of artificial islands, installations
and structures[9]; (2) marine scientific research[10]; and (3) the protection and
preservation of the marine environment[11]. In exercising its rights and performing
its duties under the United Nations Convention on the Law of the Sea in the
exclusive economic zone, the coastal state must have due regard to the rights and
duties of other states and must act in a manner compatible with the
Convention[12]. The coastal state's rights and limitations thereon are specifically
regulated[13], in particular as concerns (a) the exclusive right to construct and
regulate the construction of artificial islands, installations and structures and
safety zones round them[14]; (b) the conservation and utilisation of the living

resources, including the determination of the allowable catch[15]; (c) rights relating to 'straddling' stocks[16] and highly migratory species[17]; and (d) rights relating to marine mammals[18], anadromous stocks[19] and catadromous species[20].

In the exclusive economic zone, states other than the coastal states enjoy, in so far as they are compatible with the provisions of the Convention concerning the exclusive economic zone, the freedoms they enjoy in the high seas[21], in particular, the rights of navigation and overflight, the right to lay submarine cables and pipelines, and other internationally lawful uses of the sea related to these freedoms[22]. In exercising their rights and performing their duties under the United Nations Convention on the Law of the Sea, such states must have due regard to the rights and duties of coastal states and comply with the regulations of those states[23]. Specific provision is made for the rights of land-locked and geographically disadvantaged states[24], and for the restriction of the transfer of rights[25].

Conflicts between the interests of the coastal state and those of any other state in cases where the United Nations Convention on the Law of the Sea does not attribute rights or jurisdiction to the coastal state or to other states should be resolved on the basis of equity and in the light of all the relevant circumstances, taking into account the respective importance of the interests involved to the parties as well as to the international community as a whole[26].

Some states, including the United Kingdom, have not claimed an exclusive economic zone but have asserted some (though not all) of the legal competences associated with an exclusive economic zone, typically by establishing a 200 nautical mile exclusive fishery zone[27].

1   Ie the United Nations Convention on the Law of the Sea (Montego Bay, 10 December 1982; TS 81 (1999); Cmnd 4524) Pt V (arts 55–75). In the exclusive economic zone, unlike the continental shelf, the coastal state has jurisdiction over the resources both of the seabed and of the superjacent waters, and in addition jurisdiction in respect of pollution, scientific research and the establishment of installations etc.

2   There is no exclusive economic zone established as such in the waters around the United Kingdom (although the United Kingdom proclaimed a 200 nautical mile zone around South Georgia and the South Sandwich Islands in 1993 (see the United Kingdom and Northern Ireland Proclamation (Maritime Zone) No 1 of 1993) and a 200 nautical mile exclusive economic zone around Pitcairn, Henderson, Ducie and Oeno Islands in 1997 (see the United Kingdom Proclamation establishing an Exclusive Economic Zone (Pitcairn, Henderson, Ducie and Oeno Islands) No 1 of 1997). In the waters around the United Kingdom, the United Kingdom and the European Union (which has legal competence in fisheries matters, as to which see AGRICULTURE AND FISHERIES vol 1(2) (2007 Reissue) PARA 796; and Case C-459/03 *Commission of the European Communities v Ireland* [2006] ECR I-4635, [2006] All ER (EC) 1013, [2006] All ER (D) 14 (Jun), ECJ) claim a 200-mile exclusive fishery zone. In addition, the United Kingdom asserts jurisdiction over matters of marine pollution in waters over designated areas of the United Kingdom continental shelf (as to which see PARA 172) and within United Kingdom fishery limits (as to which see AGRICULTURE AND FISHERIES vol 1(2) (2007 Reissue) PARA 961): see the Food and Environment Protection Act 1985; and SHIPPING AND NAVIGATION.

3   As to the territorial sea see PARA 123 et seq.

4   As to the high seas see PARA 147 et seq.

5   Ie 12 nautical miles: PARA 124.

6   United Nations Convention on the Law of the Sea art 57. The outer limit of the exclusive economic zone must be shown on charts to which due publicity is given: see the United Nations Convention on the Law of the Sea art 75. As to baselines see PARAS 125–126.

7   United Nations Convention on the Law of the Sea art 74(1). The position concerning the delimitation of the exclusive economic zone is essentially the same as that concerning the delimitation of the continental shelf, as to which see PARA 163.

8   United Nations Convention on the Law of the Sea art 56 para 1(a). By virtue of this provision the rights of a coastal state over its exclusive economic zone duplicate its rights over its continental shelf in so far as the continental shelf lies within 200 nautical miles of the baseline. As to the continental shelf see PARA 163 et seq.

9   United Nations Convention on the Law of the Sea art 56 para 1(b)(i). The coastal state's jurisdiction in this regard is exclusive. As to artificial islands, installations and structures on the continental shelf see PARA 170.

10   United Nations Convention on the Law of the Sea art 56 para 1(b)(ii). As to marine scientific research see Pt XIII (arts 238–265); and PARA 194.

11   United Nations Convention on the Law of the Sea art 56 para 1(b)(iii). As to protection of the marine environment see Pt XII (arts 192–237); and PARA 193.

12   United Nations Convention on the Law of the Sea art 56 para 2. The rights contained in art 56 with respect to the seabed and subsoil must be exercised in accordance with Pt VI (arts 76–85) (as to which see PARA 163 et seq): art 56 para 3.

13   See the United Nations Convention on the Law of the Sea arts 60–71.

14   See the United Nations Convention on the Law of the Sea art 60.

15   See the United Nations Convention on the Law of the Sea arts 61, 62.

16   See the United Nations Convention on the Law of the Sea art 63. See also the Agreement for the Implementation of the Provisions of the United Nations Convention on the Law of the Sea Relating to the Conservation and Management of Straddling Fish Stocks and Highly Migratory Fish Stocks (New York, 4 August 1995; Misc 12 (1995); Cm 3125; 2167 UNTS 88).

17   United Nations Convention on the Law of the Sea art 64. See also the Agreement for the Implementation of the Provisions of the United Nations Convention on the Law of the Sea Relating to the Conservation and Management of Straddling Fish Stocks and Highly Migratory Fish Stocks. The provisions of the United Nations Convention on the Law of the Sea Pt V (arts 55–75) do not apply to sedentary species, which are governed by the provisions on the resources of the continental shelf (as to which see PARA 163): art 68.

18   United Nations Convention on the Law of the Sea art 65.

19   United Nations Convention on the Law of the Sea art 66.

20   United Nations Convention on the Law of the Sea art 67.

21   United Nations Convention on the Law of the Sea art 87; and see PARA 147.

22   United Nations Convention on the Law of the Sea art 58 para 1. As to the right to lay submarine cables and pipelines see PARA 169. The provisions of the United Nations Convention on the Law of the Sea Pt VII (arts 86–115) apply to the exclusive economic zone in so far as they are not incompatible with Pt V: art 58 para 2.

23   United Nations Convention on the Law of the Sea art 58 para 3. As to enforcement of the laws and regulations of the coastal state see art 73.

24   United Nations Convention on the Law of the Sea arts 69, 70. However, arts 69, 70 do not apply to a coastal state whose economy is overwhelmingly dependent on the exploitation of the living resources of its exclusive economic zone: art 71.

25   See the United Nations Convention on the Law of the Sea art 72.

26   United Nations Convention on the Law of the Sea art 59.

27   See note 2.

(ii) Piracy

155. Piracy in international law. By customary international law, a pirate is subject to universal jurisdiction[1]: any state that seizes a pirate may try him for an offence under its own municipal law. A pirate ship or aircraft may be stopped by the ships or aircraft of other states, and a pirate ship may be boarded on the high seas by the warship of any state[2].

1   For the principles of international jurisdiction over criminal offences and offenders generally see PARAS 143–233.

2   Suspicion that a ship is a pirate ship is one of the exceptional cases in which a warship is justified in exercising the right of visit over a foreign merchant vessel on the high seas: see the United Nations Convention on the Law of the Sea (Montego Bay, 10 December 1982; TS 81 (1999); Cmnd 4524) art 110 para 1(a); and PARA 148.

156. Meaning of 'piracy'. Piracy in international law (piracy jure gentium) is defined by the United Nations Convention on the Law of the Sea[1], and this definition forms part of United Kingdom domestic law[2]. According to the Convention, piracy consists of the following acts:

     (1)   any illegal acts of violence or detention, or any act of depredation[3],

committed for private ends[4] by the crew or the passengers of a private ship or a private aircraft, and directed (a) on the high seas, against another[5] ship or aircraft, or against persons or property on board such ship or aircraft; or (b) against a ship, aircraft, persons or property in a place outside the jurisdiction of any state[6];

(2)   any act of voluntary participation in the operation of a ship or of an aircraft with knowledge of facts making it a pirate ship or aircraft[7]; or

(3)   any act of inciting or intentionally facilitating an act described in head (1) or head (2) above[8].

The acts described in heads (1), (2) and (3) above, if committed by a warship, government ship or government aircraft whose crew has mutinied and taken control of the ship or aircraft, are assimilated to acts committed by a private ship or aircraft[9]. A ship or aircraft is considered a pirate ship or aircraft if it is intended by the persons in dominant control to be used for any of the acts which constitute piracy[10]. The same applies if the ship or aircraft has been used to commit any such act, so long as it remains under the control of the persons guilty of that act[11].

1   United Nations Convention on the Law of the Sea (Montego Bay, 10 December 1982; TS 81 (1999); Cmnd 4524) arts 101–103.

2   For the purposes of any proceedings before a court in the United Kingdom in respect of piracy, the United Nations Convention on the Law of the Sea arts 101–103, which are set out in the Merchant Shipping and Maritime Security Act 1997 s 26, Sch 5, are to be treated as part of the law of nations: s 26(1); and see SHIPPING AND MARITIME LAW vol 94 (2008) PARA 1249. As to the jurisdiction of the English courts see PARA 159. English courts have in the past attempted definitions of piracy jure gentium. References to some cases in which this has been done appear in the following paragraphs, but they must now be read in the light of the Merchant Shipping and Maritime Security Act 1997.

3   This may include a frustrated attempt to commit a piratical robbery: *Re Piracy Jure Gentium* [1934] AC 586, 3 BILC 836, PC disapproving the charge to the grand jury in *R v Dawson* (1696) 13 State Tr 451 at 454 in so far as it suggested that actual robbery was essential. In *A-G for Colony of Hong Kong v Kwok-a-Sing* (1873) LR 5 PC 179 at 199–200, 3 BILC 812 it was said that piracy is merely robbery on the high seas.

4   The term 'private ends' is not defined. It appears to embrace acts done without authorisation from the government of any state: *Re Piracy Jure Gentium* [1934] AC 586 at 599–600, 3 BILC 836, PC. As to the position of insurgents see *Re Piracy Jure Gentium* at 595; *The Magellan Pirates* (1853) 1 Ecc & Ad 81, 3 BILC 796; *Republic of Bolivia v Indemnity Mutual Marine Assurance Co Ltd* [1909] 1 KB 785, 3 BILC 825, CA.

5   It appears that at least two vessels must be involved and consequently, whatever the earlier position, under the definition in the United Nations Convention on the Law of the Sea art 101(a) when upon the high seas, acts done solely upon a single vessel and against the authority of that ship or persons or property on board is not now piracy in international law. As to the earlier position see *Re Piracy Jure Gentium* [1934] AC 586, PC; *A-G for Colony of Hong Kong v Kwok-a-Sing* (1873) LR 5 PC 179, 37 JP 772. Consequently the hijacking of a vessel by members of its crew or passengers may not constitute piracy. However the Convention for the Suppression of Unlawful Acts Against the Safety of Maritime Navigation (Rome, 10 March 1988; TS 64 (1995); Cm 2947) is prospectively amended by the Protocol of 2005 to the Convention for the Suppression of Unlawful Acts against the Safety of Maritime Navigation, 14 October 2005 to make provision for action against a wider range of offences, including the hijacking of ships.

6   United Nations Convention on the Law of the Sea art 101(a). By 'place outside the jurisdiction of any state' the International Law Commission (whose draft proposals formed the basis of the Convention) had chiefly in mind acts committed by persons connected with a ship or aircraft on an island constituting terra nullius or on the shores of an unoccupied territory: see YILC 1956 vol II, 282, Commentary para (3). Some states consider that Antarctica is a place outside the jurisdiction of any state: as to Antarctica see PARA 218. From the definition of 'piracy' in the United Nations Convention on the Law of the Sea art 101 it seems to follow that piracy connotes only acts committed upon or over the high seas or a place outside the jurisdiction of any state. Thus, whatever the position may be under municipal law, piracy in international law

does not include theft of a tug tied to a wharf (see *Britannia Shipping Corpn v Globe and Rutgers Fire Insurance* Co 244 NYS 720 at 723 (1930)) or of a ship in a river (see *Republic of Bolivia v Indemnity Mutual Marine Assurance Co Ltd* [1909] 1 KB 785 at 799, 3 BILC 825, CA), nor does it include any act done in territorial waters (cf *Cameron v HM Advocate* 1971 SLT 333 at 335–336 per Lord Walker). It has been held that if the initial act of depredation takes place in internal waters the subsequent cruising on the high seas by the actors in such circumstances as to give them the character of hostes humani generis is piracy: see *The Magellan Pirates* (1853) 1 Ecc & Ad 81, 3 BILC 796; *The Serhassan Pirates* (1845) 2 Wm Rob 354, 3 BILC 778.

7   United Nations Convention on the Law of the Sea art 101(b).
8   United Nations Convention on the Law of the Sea art 101(c).
9   United Nations Convention on the Law of the Sea art 102. Otherwise, if committed by a properly commissioned warship, such acts cannot amount to piracy, though the acts of the ship might give rise to the international responsibility of the flag state to other states: see *The Magellan Pirates* (1853) 1 Ecc & Ad 81, 3 BILC 796.
10 United Nations Convention on the Law of the Sea art 103.
11 United Nations Convention on the Law of the Sea art 103.

157. Rights and obligations of states. All states are under an obligation to co-operate in the repression of piracy[1]. Any state may seize a pirate ship or aircraft or a ship taken by piracy and under the control of pirates and arrest the persons and seize the property on board[2]. The courts of the state which carried out the seizure may decide upon the penalties to be imposed, and may also determine the action to be taken with regard to the ships, aircraft or property, subject to the rights of third parties acting in good faith[3]. A seizure on account of piracy may only be carried out by warships or military aircraft, or other ships or aircraft clearly marked and identifiable as being on government service and authorised to that effect[4]. If a seizure on suspicion of piracy is made without adequate grounds, the state making the seizure is liable to the state whose nationality is possessed by the ship or aircraft for any loss or damage caused by the seizure[5].

1   United Nations Convention on the Law of the Sea (Montego Bay, 10 December 1982; TS 81 (1999); Cmnd 4524) art 100. As to the meaning of 'piracy' see PARA 156.
2   United Nations Convention on the Law of the Sea art 105.
3   United Nations Convention on the Law of the Sea art 105. See the explanation offered in the *Lotus Case* PCIJ Ser A No 10 at 70 (1927) per Moore J. For rights in property taken possession of from pirates by British ships see the Piracy Act 1850 s 5.
4   United Nations Convention on the Law of the Sea art 107.
5   United Nations Convention on the Law of the Sea art 106.

158. Nationality of pirate ships and aircraft. A ship or aircraft which has become a pirate ship or aircraft does not for that reason alone lose its nationality. The retention or loss of nationality is determined by the law of the state from which such nationality was derived[1].

1   United Nations Convention on the Law of the Sea (Montego Bay, 10 December 1982; TS 81 (1999); Cmnd 4524) art 104. As to the nationality of ships see PARA 395; and SHIPPING AND NAVIGATION.

159. Jurisdiction of English courts. The English courts[1] have jurisdiction to try all cases of piracy jure gentium in whatever part of the high seas and upon whosesoever's property it may be committed, and whether the accused are British subjects or the subjects of any foreign state with whom Her Majesty is at amity[2].

If the act of depredation was committed, even without the Queen's commission, upon a subject of a state at enmity with Her Majesty, this does not amount to piracy; but it is piracy for a person who holds her commission to despoil those with whom his commission does not authorise him to fight, if they are at amity with Her Majesty[3].

The place where the alleged piracy was committed must be within the jurisdiction of the Admiral[4], although the ordinary rule that an indictment will not lie in an English court for an offence committed at sea beyond the limits of the territorial waters on board a foreign vessel by a foreigner does not apply to such a case[5].

1   Jurisdiction is vested in the Crown Court: see the Senior Courts Act 1981 s 46(2). The Senior Courts Act 1981 was previously known as the Supreme Court Act 1981 and was renamed by the Constitutional Reform Act 2005 s 59(5), Sch 11 Pt 1 as from 1 October 2009: see the Constitutional Reform Act 2005 (Commencement No 11) Order 2009, SI 2009/1604; and COURTS.

2   1 Hawk PC c 20, s 1; *R v Dawson* (1696) 13 State Tr 451 at 455. For the purposes of any proceedings in respect of piracy the United Nations Convention on the Law of the Sea (Montego Bay, 10 December 1982; TS 81 (1999); Cmnd 4524) arts 101–103 (see PARA 156) are to be treated as part of the law of nations. Any court in the United Kingdom having jurisdiction in respect of piracy committed on the high seas has jurisdiction in respect of piracy committed by or against an aircraft, wherever that piracy is committed: Aviation Security Act 1982 s 5(1). See also AIR LAW vol 2 (2008) PARA 623; CRIMINAL LAW, EVIDENCE AND PROCEDURE vol 11(3) (2006 Reissue) PARAS 1057–1058; and note 4.

3   4 Co Inst 154; Charge of Sir Leoline Jenkins (see 1 Life of Sir Leoline Jenkins xciv); see *Re Tivnan* (1864) 5 B & S 645, 5 BILC 407.

4   3 Co Inst 113; 1 Hawk PC c 20, s 15; *R v Allen* (1837) 1 Mood CC 494, 3 BILC 573, CCR; *R v Anderson* (1868) LR 1 CCR 161 at 169, 3 BILC 40; *R v Carr and Wilson* (1882) 10 QBD 76, 3 BILC 593, CCR.

5   *R v Keyn* (1876) 2 ExD 63, 2 BILC 701, CCR; *R v Anderson* at 169. For the extent of Admiralty jurisdiction see CRIMINAL LAW, EVIDENCE AND PROCEDURE; SHIPPING AND MARITIME LAW vol 93 (2008) PARA 79 et seq.

160. Punishment. Whoever with intent to commit, or at the time of or immediately before or after committing, the crime of piracy in respect of any ship, assaults with intent to murder any person on board the ship, or who stabs, cuts or wounds any such person, or unlawfully does any act whereby the life of such person may be endangered, must on conviction be sentenced to imprisonment for life[1].

1   Piracy Act 1837 s 2 (amended by the Statute Law Revision (No 2) Act 1888; Criminal Law Act 1967 s 10(2), Sch 3 Pt III; Crime and Disorder Act 1998 s 36(5)). As to the condemnation of property captured from pirates and the restitution to owners see the Piracy Act 1850 s 5; and see SHIPPING AND MARITIME LAW vol 93 (2008) PARA 139.

(iii) Hot Pursuit

161. Hot pursuit. The United Nations Convention on the Law of the Sea stipulates certain conditions that must be fulfilled if hot pursuit is to be lawful[1]. The hot pursuit of a foreign ship on the high seas may be undertaken when the competent authorities of the coastal state have good reason to believe that the ship has violated the laws and regulations of that state[2]. The right arises whenever the ship or its authorities could have been apprehended in the territorial sea wherein the ship has subjected itself to the local jurisdiction[3].

Pursuit must be commenced when the foreign ship, or one of its boats, is within the internal waters[4], the territorial waters[5] or the contiguous zone[6] of the pursuing state[7]. The ship itself need not be in the territorial sea or the contiguous zone, provided that, if it is not, one of its boats or other craft working as a team and using the ship pursued as a mother ship is within those areas[8]. Nor is it necessary that at the time when the foreign ship within the territorial sea or contiguous zone receives the order to stop, the ship giving the order is itself within those areas; it may be upon the high seas outside those limits[9]. Hot pursuit is only deemed to begin when the pursuing ship has satisfied itself by such practicable means as are available as to the whereabouts of the vessel pursued and may only be commenced after a visual or auditory signal to stop has been given at a distance which enables it to be seen or heard by the foreign ship[10].

The right of hot pursuit may be exercised by warships or military aircraft[11]. Where the pursuit is effected by an aircraft, in addition to the requirements previously stated, the aircraft giving the order to stop must itself actively pursue the ship until a ship or aircraft of the coastal state, summoned by the aircraft, arrives to take over the pursuit. The ship pursued must be ordered to stop and be pursued either by the aircraft which sighted it, or by other aircraft or ships which continue pursuit without interruption; arrest on the high seas is not justified sufficiently by the fact that the ship was sighted as an offender by the aircraft[12].

These requirements are express and cumulative[13]. Courts in certain jurisdictions have, however, taken a flexible view, upholding the validity of arrests in circumstances where some of the conditions have not been met[14]. The right ceases[15] as soon as the ship pursued enters the territorial sea of its own state or of a third state[16]. Where a ship has been stopped or arrested on the high seas in circumstances which do not justify its pursuit, it must be compensated for any loss or damage that may have been sustained[17]. The pursuing state may use necessary and reasonable force in order to board, search, seize and bring into port the suspected vessel, and if sinking should occur incidentally, it might be blameless[18]. If fire is opened, there must first be a shot across the bow; there must be no greater danger to life than necessary, and a warship of the flag of the vessel pursued may protect it against excessive use of force[19].

1   See the United Nations Convention on the Law of the Sea (Montego Bay, 10 December 1982; TS 81 (1999); Cmnd 4524) art 111. Hot pursuit is not defined in the United Nations Convention on the Law of the Sea but is understood to mean the continuous pursuit of a foreign ship by military vessels or aircraft of a coastal state, beginning in waters under the jurisdiction of the coastal state and ending in the arrest of the pursued ship on the high seas.

2   United Nations Convention on the Law of the Sea art 111 para 1. See also *The 'I'm Alone'* 3 RIAA 1609 (1935); *The M/V 'Saiga' (No 2) (Saint Vincent and the Grenadines v Guinea)* ITLOS Reports 1999, 10, 120 ILR 143.

3   *R v The North* (1905) 11 Ex CR 141. Hot pursuit may also be exercised in case of violations of laws in the contiguous zone or continental shelf or exclusive economic zone: see note 6.

4   As to internal waters see PARA 121. Pursuit may also be commenced when in archipelagic waters. As to the internal waters of archipelagic states see the United Nations Convention on the Law of the Sea art 50.

5   As to territorial waters see PARA 123.

6   As to the contiguous zone see PARA 153. If the vessel is in the contiguous zone pursuit may only be undertaken if there has been a violation of a right for the protection of which the zone was established: United Nations Convention on the Law of the Sea art 111 para 1. Thus, it is limited in such case to the pursuit of ships which have violated laws adopted by the coastal state concerning customs, fiscal, immigration or sanitary matters or the protection of objects of an archaeological and historical nature found at sea of the coastal state: see PARA 153; United Nations Convention on the Law of the Sea arts 33, 303. Hot pursuit applies mutatis mutandis to violations in the exclusive economic zone or on the continental shelf, including safety zones around continental shelf installations, of the laws and regulations of the coastal state applicable thereto: art 111 para 2. As to the exclusive economic zone see PARA 154. As to the continental shelf see PARA 163 et seq.

7   United Nations Convention on the Law of the Sea art 111 para 1. As to the doctrine of constructive presence see PARA 162.

8   United Nations Convention on the Law of the Sea art 111 para 4. Canadian courts have adopted a wide interpretation of the concept of the 'mother ship': see *R v Sunila and Soleyman* (1986) 28 DLR (4th) 450, (1987) 78 NSR (2d) 24.

9   United Nations Convention on the Law of the Sea art 111 para 1.

10 United Nations Convention on the Law of the Sea art 111 para 4. On a strict interpretation of the United Nations Convention on the Law of the Sea a signal by radio would not suffice. But see *R v Mills* (1995, unreported), Croydon Crown Court, W Gilmore, *Hot Pursuit: The Case of R v Mills and Others* (1995) 44 ICLQ 949.

11 United Nations Convention on the Law of the Sea art 111 para 5. It may also be exercised by other ships or aircraft clearly marked and identifiable as being on government service and authorised to that effect: art 111 para 5. This would include police vessels or customs or coastguard ships. The ship or aircraft which finally effects the arrest need not be the same as the one which began it, provided it is in fact a continuation of the pursuit: c f art 111 para 6(b). The release of a ship arrested in the jurisdiction of a state and escorted to a port of that state for the purposes of an inquiry cannot be claimed solely on the ground that the ship, in the course of its voyage, was escorted across a portion of the exclusive economic zone or the high seas, if the circumstances rendered this necessary: art 111 para 7.

12 United Nations Convention on the Law of the Sea art 111 para 6(b).

13 *The M/V 'Saiga' (No 2)* (*Saint Vincent and the Grenadines v Guinea*) ITLOS Reports 1999, 10, 120 ILR 143.

14 See *R v Sunila and Soleyman* (1986) 28 DLR (4th) 450, (1987) 78 NSR (2d) 24; *United States v Postal et al* 589 F 2d 862 (USA 5th Cir 1979), certificate denied 444 US 832 (1979); *R v Mills* (1995, unreported), Croydon Crown Court, W Gilmore *Hot Pursuit: The Case of R v Mills and Others* (1995) 44 ICLQ 949. But see *R v Charrington* (1999, unreported), Bristol Crown Court, W Gilmore *Drug Trafficking at Sea: The Case of R v Charrington and Others* (2000) 49 ICLQ 477.

15 Ie the right terminates; it is not merely suspended so as to permit resumption of pursuit if the ship re-emerges on the high seas.

16 United Nations Convention on the Law of the Sea art 111 para 3. Pursuit continued in the territorial sea of another state would engage the international responsibility of the pursuing state: *The Itata* (1892) Moore Int Arb 3067.

17 United Nations Convention on the Law of the Sea art 111 para 8.

18 See *The 'I'm Alone'* 3 RIAA 1609 at 1615 (1935) where the sinking was, however, held to have been unjustified.

19 *The Red Crusader* (1962) 35 Int LR 485 (Anglo-Danish Commission of Inquiry).

162.   Constructive presence.   A ship may be arrested on the high seas if at the time of arrest it is engaged in illegal action within the territorial sea or on land[1]. The distinction between constructive presence and hot pursuit[2] is that under the former doctrine an offending vessel outside the jurisdiction of the coastal state is treated as being within the jurisdiction of that state for the purpose of determining whether an offence has been committed, whereas the latter permits the arrest of ships outside the jurisdiction of the coastal state in respect of offences committed within the jurisdiction of that state.

1   Eg where the vessel is outside the territorial sea, but is carrying on fishing in it by means of its boats (*The Araunah* (1888) Moore Int Arb 824) or where it is using its boats in order to smuggle goods on shore (*The Grace and Ruby* 283 F 475 (USA 1922)). See *R v Sunila and Soleyman* (1986) 28 DLR (4th) 450, (1987) 78 NSR (2d) 24.

2   As to hot pursuit see PARA 161.

(iv)   The Continental Shelf

163.   The continental shelf.   Under the United Nations Convention on the Law of the Sea[1], the coastal state exercises sovereign rights[2] over the continental shelf for the purpose of exploring it and exploiting its natural resources[3]. Thus, the coastal state does not possess territorial sovereignty over the continental shelf, but only certain sovereign rights for limited purposes[4]. These rights are exclusive in the sense that if the coastal state does not itself explore the continental shelf and exploit its resources no one may undertake such activities or make a claim to the shelf without the coastal state's express consent[5]. The rights of the coastal state over the continental shelf do not depend upon occupation, effective or notional, or upon any express proclamation[6], and do not affect the legal status of the superjacent waters as high seas, or that of the air space above those waters[7].

1   Ie under the United Nations Convention on the Law of the Sea, (Montego Bay, 10 December 1982; TS 81 (1999); Cmnd 4524) Pt VI (arts 76–85). The origin of the legal doctrine of the continental shelf is generally traced to the proclamation by the United States of 1945, known as the Truman Proclamation. For the text of the proclamation see 4 Whiteman's Digest 756. In *North Sea Continental Shelf Cases (Federal Republic of Germany/Denmark; Federal Republic of Germany/Netherlands)* ICJ Reports 1969, 3, the International Court of Justice was of the opinion that the doctrine of the continental shelf was part of customary international law and that the Convention on the Continental Shelf (Geneva, 29 April 1958; TS 39 (1964); Cmnd 2422) arts 1–3 were declaratory of it. The United Nations Convention on the Law of the Sea supersedes the Convention on the Continental Shelf. The latter remains in force between the United Kingdom and other states which are parties to it but not to the United Nations Convention on the Law of the Sea.
2   As to the exercise of these rights in the United Kingdom see the Continental Shelf Act 1964; and PARA 172.
3   United Nations Convention on the Law of the Sea art 77 para 1.
4   The Truman Proclamation claimed the continental shelf as 'appertaining to the United States, subject to its jurisdiction and control'.
5   United Nations Convention on the Law of the Sea art 77 para 2. The coastal state has the exclusive right to authorise and regulate drilling on the continental shelf: art 81. As to payments and contributions by the coastal state in respect of exploitation beyond 200 nautical miles see art 82.
6   United Nations Convention on the Law of the Sea art 77 para 3. See also *North Sea Continental Shelf Cases (Federal Republic of Germany/Denmark; Federal Republic of Germany/ Netherlands)* ICJ Reports 1969, 3 at 31.
7   United Nations Convention on the Law of the Sea art 78 para 1.

164. Meaning of 'continental shelf'. The continental shelf of a coastal state comprises the sea bed and subsoil of the submarine areas that extend beyond its territorial sea throughout the natural prolongation of its land territory to the outer edge of the continental margin, or to a distance of 200 nautical miles from the baselines from which the breadth of the territorial sea is measured where the outer edge of the continental margin does not extend up to that distance[1].

The continental margin comprises the submerged prolongation of the land mass of the coastal state, and consists of the sea bed and subsoil of the shelf, the slope and the rise, but does not include the deep ocean floor with its oceanic ridges or the subsoil thereof[2].

1   United Nations Convention on the Law of the Sea (Montego Bay, 10 December 1982; TS 81 (1999); Cmnd 4524) art 76 para 1. The continental shelf is thus a legal, and not a geological, concept. As to the baselines from which the territorial sea is measured see arts 5–14; and PARAS 125–126. As to the determination of the outer limits of the continental shelf see PARA 166.
2   United Nations Convention on the Law of the Sea art 76 para 3. Whenever a given submarine area does not constitute a natural extension of the land territory of a coastal state, even though it is nearer to it than to the territory of another state, it cannot be regarded as appertaining to it, at any rate in the face of a competing claim by a state of whose land territory it is to be regarded as a natural extension: *North Sea Continental Shelf Cases (Federal Republic of Germany/ Denmark; Federal Republic of Germany/Netherlands)* ICJ Reports 1969, 3 at 31.

165. Natural resources. The natural resources of the continental shelf[1] consist of the mineral and other non-living resources of the sea bed and subsoil together with living organisms belonging to sedentary species, which, at the harvestable stage, are either immobile on or under the sea bed or unable to move except in constant physical contact with the sea bed or the subsoil[2].

1   As to the meaning of 'continental shelf' see PARA 164.
2   United Nations Convention on the Law of the Sea (Montego Bay, 10 December 1982; TS 81 (1999); Cmnd 4524) Pt VI (arts 76–85) art 77 para 4. The importance of the distinction between sedentary and non-sedentary species is greatly reduced by the fact that the Convention establishes the exclusive rights of the coastal state over all living resources (and other economic resources) within its 200 nautical mile exclusive economic zone: see PARA 154 et seq.

166.   Outer limit.   The coastal state must establish the outer edge of its continental margin[1] wherever it extends beyond 200 nautical miles from the baselines by either[2] (1) a line delineated by reference to the outermost fixed points at each of which the thickness of sedimentary rocks is at least 1 per cent of the shortest distance from such point to the foot of the continental slope[3]; or (2) a line delineated by reference to fixed points not more than 60 nautical miles from the foot of the continental slope[4]. The fixed points either must not exceed 350 nautical miles from the baselines[5] or not exceed 100 nautical miles from the 2,500 metre isobath, which is a line connecting the depth of 2,500 metres[6]. Where the continental shelf extends beyond 200 nautical miles from the baselines, it must be delineated by straight lines not exceeding 60 nautical miles length, connecting fixed points, defined by co-ordinates of latitude and longitude[7]. States parties to the United Nations Convention on the Law of the Sea are obliged to submit information on the outer limits of the continental shelf to the Commission on the Limits of the Continental Shelf, and limits established by the state on the basis of the Commission's consequent recommendations are final and binding[8].

1   As to the continental margin see the United Nations Convention on the Law of the Sea (Montego Bay, 10 December 1982; TS 81 (1999); Cmnd 4524) art 76 para 3; and see PARA 164.
2   United Nations Convention on the Law of the Sea art 76 para 4(a). As to the baselines from which the territorial sea is measured see arts 5–14; and PARAS 125–126.
3   United Nations Convention on the Law of the Sea art 76 para 4(a)(i). In the absence of evidence to the contrary, the foot of the continental slope is determined as the point of maximum change in the gradient at its base: see art 76 para 4(b).
4   United Nations Convention on the Law of the Sea art 76 para 4(a)(ii).
5   As to the baselines see note 2.
6   United Nations Convention on the Law of the Sea art 76 para 5. Special provision is made for submarine ridges: see art 76 para 6.
7   United Nations Convention on the Law of the Sea art 76 para 7. As to the procedure for the establishment of the outer limit of the continental shelf and to publicity see art 76 paras 8, 9.
8   See the United Nations Convention on the Law of the Sea art 76 para 8. The United Kingdom has made a number of notifications in relation to different areas of the continental shelf adjacent to British coasts: see the Submissions, through the Secretary-General of the United Nations, to the Commission on the Limits of the Continental Shelf, pursuant to article 76, paragraph 8, of the United Nations Convention on the Law of the Sea of 10 December 1982. While compliance with Commission recommendations is sufficient to make a continental shelf limit final and binding as between states parties to the Convention it is doubtful, given the inherent rights of the coastal state over the continental shelf (as to which see the United Nations Convention on the Law of the Sea art 77 and PARA 163), whether such compliance is a necessary condition for the establishment of a final and binding limit.

167.   State boundaries.   Delimitation of the continental shelf between states with opposite or adjacent coast must be effected by them by agreement on the basis of international law in order to achieve an equitable solution[1]. Where there is already an agreement between the states concerned, questions of delimitation must be determined in accordance with its provisions[2].

1   United Nations Convention on the Law of the Sea (Montego Bay, 10 December 1982; TS 81 (1999); Cmnd 4524) art 83. This provision replaces the Convention on the Continental Shelf (Geneva, 29 April 1958 to 31 October; TS 39 (1964); Cmnd 2422) art 6 of which provided that

the boundary was to be determined by agreement between the states concerned, failing which and in the absence of special circumstances, the boundary would be the median line or line of equidistance. The notion of an 'equitable result' has been examined in detail in several cases concerning maritime delimitation brought before the International Court of Justice or international arbitral tribunals: see eg *Maritime Delimitation in the Black Sea (Romania v Ukraine)* ICJ Reports 2009, 132; and *Continental Shelf (Lybian Arab Jamahiriya/Malta)* ICJ Reports 1985, 13. Decisions are greatly influenced by the particular coastal configurations in each case, and the jurisprudence is not easy to summarise. In broad terms, the general approach involves three stages: (1) the construction of a strictly geometrical provisional equidistance line, drawn from the nearest points on the two coasts; (2) the adjustment of that provisional line to take account of any factors (eg, concave coastlines or small offshore islands) that distort the effects of equidistance and tend to produce an inequitable result; and (3) checking that the resulting line does not lead to an inequitable result by reason of any marked disproportion between the ratio of the respective coastal lengths of the states and the ratio between the relevant maritime area attributed to each of them: see *Maritime Delimitation in the Black Sea (Romania v Ukraine)* ICJ Reports 2009, 132.

2   Agreements on the delimitation of the continental shelf concluded by the United Kingdom and its neighbouring states are published in the UK Treaty Series and have been notified to the UN Department (DOALOS): for example the Agreement between the Government of the United Kingdom of Great Britain and Northern Ireland and the Government of the Kingdom of Belgium relating to the delimitation of the continental shelf between the two countries (Brussels, 29 May 1991; TS 20 (1994); Cm 1735); the Agreement between the Government of the United Kingdom of Great Britain and Northern Ireland and the Government of the Kingdom of Denmark relating to the delimitation of the continental shelf between the two countries, (London, 3 March 1966; TS 35 (1967); Cmd 2973); the Agreement between the Government of the French Republic and the Government of the United Kingdom of Great Britain and Northern Ireland relating to the completion of the delimitation of the continental shelf in the southern North Sea (London, 23 July 1991; TS 46 (1992); Cm 1979); the Agreement between the Government of the Kingdom of the Netherlands and the Government of the United Kingdom of Great Britain and Northern Ireland relating to the delimitation of the continental shelf under the North Sea between the two countries (London, 6 October 1965; TS 23 (1967); Cmd 3253); and the Agreement between the Government of the United Kingdom of Great Britain and Northern Ireland and the Government of the Kingdom of Norway relating to the delimitation of the continental shelf between the two countries (London, 10 March 1965; TS 71 (1965); Cmnd 2757).

168.   Submarine cables and pipelines on the continental shelf. All states are entitled to lay submarine cables and pipelines on the continental shelf[1]. Subject to its right to take reasonable measures for the exploration of the continental shelf, the exploitation of its natural resources, and the prevention, reduction and control of pollution from pipelines, the coastal state may not impede the laying or maintenance of submarine cables or pipelines on the continental shelf[2]. The delineation of the course of such cables and pipelines across the continental shelf is subject to the consent of the coastal state[3].

1   United Nations Convention on the Law of the Sea (Montego Bay, 10 December 1982; TS 81 (1999); Cmnd 4524) art 79 para 1. The state laying cables or pipelines must pay due regard to those already in position: art 79 para 5. As to submarine cables, pipelines and installations beyond the continental shelf see art 112; and PARA 169. The Continental Shelf Act 1964 s 8 extends the provisions of the Submarine Telegraph Act 1885 to the continental shelf: see TELECOMMUNICATIONS AND BROADCASTING vol 45(1) (2005 Reissue) PARA 200 et seq.
2   United Nations Convention on the Law of the Sea art 79 para 2. The right is confined to cables and pipelines traversing the continental shelf. A coastal state may establish conditions for cables and pipelines that (1) enter its territory or territorial sea; or (2) are used in connection with the exploration of its continental shelf or the exploitation of its resources or the operation of offshore islands, installations and structures within its jurisdiction: art 79 para 4.
3   United Nations Convention on the Law of the Sea art 79 para 3.

169.   Submarine cables and pipelines on the bed of the high seas. All states may lay submarine cables and pipelines on the bed of the high seas beyond the continental shelf[1]. Every state must legislate so as to make the breaking or injury by a ship flying its flag, or by a person subject to its jurisdiction[2], of a submarine cable, wilfully or through culpable negligence, so as to impede telegraphic or telephonic communications, or the breaking or injury of a pipeline or high voltage power cable, a punishable offence[3]. Every state must legislate so as to ensure that persons subject to its jurisdiction who, being owners of a cable or pipeline, in laying or repairing it, cause a break in or injury to another cable or pipeline, bear the cost of the repairs[4]. Every state must legislate to ensure that owners of a cable or pipeline indemnify owners of ships who can prove that they have sacrificed an anchor, net or other fishing gear to avoid injuring a cable or pipeline, provided the owner of the ship has taken all reasonable precautionary measures beforehand[5].

1   United Nations Convention on the Law of the Sea (Montego Bay, 10 December 1982; TS 81 (1999); Cmnd 4524) art 112 para 1. The state laying cables or pipelines must pay due regard to those already in position: art 79 para 5 (applied by art 112 para 2). As to submarine cables, pipelines and installations on the continental shelf see art 79; and PARA 168.

2   Under the Convention for the Protection of Submarine Cables (Paris, 14 March 1884; 75 BFSP 356; C 5910) art 10 a state is authorised to board vessels of other parties to the Convention on suspicion of interfering with submarine cables. This Convention was implemented in England by the Submarine Telegraph Act 1885 s 2: see TELECOMMUNICATIONS AND BROADCASTING vol 45(1) (2005 Reissue) PARA 200 et seq.

3   United Nations Convention on the Law of the Sea art 113. This does not apply to any break or injury caused by persons acting with the legitimate object of saving their own lives or ships, after having taken all necessary precautions: art 113. For the UK legislation see the Submarine Telegraph Act 1885 s 3; the Continental Shelf Act 1964 s 8; and TELECOMMUNICATIONS AND BROADCASTING vol 45(1) (2005 Reissue) PARA 200.

4   United Nations Convention on the Law of the Sea art 114. For the UK legislation see the Submarine Telegraph Act 1885 s 2; the Continental Shelf Act 1964 s 8; and TELECOMMUNICATIONS AND BROADCASTING vol 45(1) (2005 Reissue) PARA 200.

5   United Nations Convention on the Law of the Sea art 115. For the UK legislation see the Submarine Telegraph Act 1885 s 2; the Continental Shelf Act 1964 s 8; and TELECOMMUNICATIONS AND BROADCASTING vol 45(1) (2005 Reissue) PARA 200.

170.   Artificial islands, installations and structures.   On its continental shelf[1], the coastal state has the exclusive right to construct and to authorise and regulate the construction, operation and use of: (1) artificial islands[2]; (2) installations and structures for the purpose of exploring and exploiting, conserving and managing the natural resources and other economic purposes[3]; and (3) installations and structures which may interfere with the exercise of the rights of the coastal state[4]. The coastal state has exclusive jurisdiction over them, including jurisdiction with regard to customs, fiscal, health, safety and immigration laws and regulations[5]. Due notice must be given of their construction, and permanent means for giving warning of their presence must be maintained[6]. The coastal state may, where necessary, establish reasonable safety zones[7] of a breadth to be established by the state but not, generally, exceeding a distance of 500 metres around them[8] which must be respected by all ships[9]. Artificial islands, installations and structures and the safety zones around them may not be established where interference may be caused to the use of recognised sea lanes essential to international navigation[10]. Artificial islands, installations and structures do not possess the status of islands[11] and accordingly do not generate territorial seas or other maritime zones.

Any installations or structures which are abandoned or disused must be removed, having due regard to fishing, the protection of the marine environment and the rights and duties of other states, to ensure safety of navigation[12]. Appropriate publicity must be given to the depth, position and dimensions of any installations or structures not entirely removed[13].

1   As to the continental shelf see PARA 163. As to artificial islands, installations and structures in
    the exclusive economic zone see PARA 154.
2   United Nations Convention on the Law of the Sea (Montego Bay, 10 December 1982; TS 81
    (1999); Cmnd 4524) arts 60 para 1(a), 80.
3   United Nations Convention on the Law of the Sea arts 60 para 1(b), 80.
4   United Nations Convention on the Law of the Sea arts 60 para 1(c), 80.
5   United Nations Convention on the Law of the Sea arts 60 para 2, 80. The United Nations
    Convention on the Law of the Sea does not define the term 'artificial island', 'installation' or
    'structure'.
6   United Nations Convention on the Law of the Sea arts 60 para 3, 80.
7   United Nations Convention on the Law of the Sea arts 60 para 4, 80.
8   United Nations Convention on the Law of the Sea arts 60 para 5, 80. Wider zones may be
    established in accordance with generally accepted international standards or as recommended by
    the competent international organisation, which is the International Maritime Organization.
9   United Nations Convention on the Law of the Sea arts 60 para 6, 80.
10 United Nations Convention on the Law of the Sea arts 60 para 7, 80.
11 United Nations Convention on the Law of the Sea arts 60 para 8, 80. They have no territorial
    sea of their own, and their presence does not affect the delimitation of the territorial sea, the
    exclusive economic zone or the continental shelf: arts 60 para 8, 80. As to the territorial sea and
    its delimitation see PARAS 123–126. As to the delimitation of the exclusive economic zone see
    PARA 154. As to the delimitation of the continental shelf see PARA 167.
12 United Nations Convention on the Law of the Sea arts 60 para 3, 80. The International
    Maritime Organization published Guidelines and Standards for the Removal of Offshore
    Installations and Structures on the Continental Shelf and in the Exclusive Economic Zone
    (Resolution A.672(16)) adopted on 19 October 1989.
13 United Nations Convention on the Law of the Sea arts 60 para 3, 80.

171.   Tunnelling. The coastal state has the right to exploit the subsoil of the
continental shelf by tunnelling[1].

1   See the United Nations Convention on the Law of the Sea (Montego Bay, 10 December 1982;
    TS 81 (1999); Cmnd 4524) art 85. The provisions of the United Nations Convention on the
    Law of the Sea are stipulated to be without prejudice to the right of a coastal state to exploit the
    subsoil of the sea bed irrespective of the depth of water above the subsoil, but this provision is
    a redundant survival of the legal regime established in the Convention on the Continental Shelf
    (Geneva, 29 April 1958; TS 39 (1964); Cmnd 2422) art 1 of which defined the continental shelf
    by a formula referring to the depth of the superjacent waters.

172.   United Kingdom legislation. The Continental Shelf Act 1964 provides
that any rights exercisable by the United Kingdom outside territorial waters[1]
with respect to the sea bed and subsoil and their natural resources, except in so
far as they are exercisable in relation to coal, are vested in the Crown[2]. The
Secretary of State, on behalf of Her Majesty, may grant licences to search and
bore for and get petroleum[3]. The rights to exploit coal are vested in the Coal
Authority[4]. The foregoing provisions relate to the continental shelf: the
exploitation of hard mineral resources[5] of the high seas beyond the continental
shelf is regulated by the Deep Sea Mining (Temporary Provisions) Act 1981[6].
The Crown may designate the areas within which rights of exploitation are to be
exercised[7].

1   As to the territorial waters of the United Kingdom see PARA 124. As to the meaning of 'United
    Kingdom' see PARA 30 note 3.
2   See the Continental Shelf Act 1964 s 1(1); and FUEL AND ENERGY vol 19(3) (2007 Reissue) PARA
    1636.
3   See the Petroleum Act 1998 s 3(1); and FUEL AND ENERGY vol 19(3) (2007 Reissue) PARA 1639.
    As to the Secretary of State see PARA 29.
4   See the Coal Industry Act 1994 s 8(1)(a); and MINES, MINERALS AND QUARRIES vol 31 (2003
    Reissue) PARAS 67–69.
5   As to the meaning of 'hard mineral resources' see PARA 175 note 4.
6   See PARA 174.

7   See the Continental Shelf Act 1964 s 1(7); and FUEL AND ENERGY vol 19(3) (2007 Reissue) PARA
    1636.

(v) The Deep Sea Bed

173.   The deep sea bed. The United Nations Convention on the Law of the
Sea[1] prescribes a regime for the exploration of the deep sea bed, which is the
seabed and ocean floor and subsoil thereof beyond the limits of national
jurisdiction and is known as the 'Area'[2]. The Area and its resources[3] are the
common heritage of mankind[4]. States may not claim or exercise sovereignty or
sovereign rights over any part of the Area or its resources, nor may any state or
natural or juridical person appropriate any part of it[5]. No such claim or exercise
of sovereignty or sovereign rights or appropriation will be recognised[6]. All rights
in the resources of the Area are vested in mankind as a whole, on whose behalf
the International Seabed Authority acts[7]. These resources may not be alienated[8].
The minerals[9] recovered, however, may only be alienated in accordance with the
Convention and the rules, regulations and procedures of the Authority[10]. No
state or natural or juridical person may claim, acquire or exercise rights with
respect to the minerals recovered from the Area except in accordance with the
Convention[11].

Nothing in the Convention nor rights granted or exercised under it affects the
legal status of the waters superjacent to the Area or that of the air space above
those waters[12]. Conduct of states in the Area must be in accordance with the
Convention, the principles embodied in the Charter of the United Nations[13] and
other rules of international law in the interests of maintaining peace and security
and promoting international co-operation and mutual understanding[14]. States
and international organisations are responsible for ensuring that activities in the
Area comply with the Convention[15] and states may be liable for damage[16].
Activity in the Area must be carried out for the benefit of mankind as a whole[17]
and the Area may only be used for peaceful purposes[18].

A complex legal regime was established in Part XI of the Convention to
implement these principles and to provide a legal framework for the development
of the Area. Provision was made for safeguarding the rights and legitimate
interests of coastal states[19], marine scientific research[20], transfer of technology[21],
protection of the marine environment[22] and human life[23], the accommodation of
activities in the Area and in the marine environment[24], participation of
developing states in the Area[25] and the preservation of archaeological and
historical objects[26]. Provision was made for the settlement of disputes[27].

The above regime was extensively modified by the 1994 Agreement Relating
to the Implementation of Part XI of the United Nations Convention on the Law
of the Sea[28]. The 1994 Agreement is designed to be consistent with a provisional
regime established for deep seabed mining by a number of states including the
United Kingdom, the United States of America (which is not a party to the
United Nations Convention on the Law of the Sea), and practically all other
states whose nationals might wish to engage in deep seabed mining in the
foreseeable future[29]. This provisional regime (sometimes known as the
'reciprocating states regime') is based upon the principle of the reciprocal
recognition of licences issued by a participating state for deep seabed mining in
defined concession areas. The regime is implemented in the United Kingdom by
the Deep Sea Mining (Temporary Provisions) Act 1981[30].

1   Ie the United Nations Convention on the Law of the Sea (Montego Bay, 10 December 1982;
    TS 81 (1999); Cmnd 4524) Pt XI Sections 1, 2 (arts 133–149).

2 United Nations Convention on the Law of the Sea art 1 para 1. The Area thus consists of the seabed beyond the limits of the legal continental shelves appertaining to coastal states, as to which see PARA 163 et seq.

3 Ie all solid, liquid or gaseous mineral resources in situ in the Area at or beneath the sea bed, including polymetallic nodules: United Nations Convention on the Law of the Sea art 133(a).

4 United Nations Convention on the Law of the Sea art 136.

5 United Nations Convention on the Law of the Sea art 137 para 1.

6 United Nations Convention on the Law of the Sea art 137 para 1.

7 United Nations Convention on the Law of the Sea art 137 para 2. As to the International Seabed Authority see SHIPPING AND MARITIME LAW vol 93 (2008) PARA 12.

8 United Nations Convention on the Law of the Sea art 137 para 2.

9 Ie resources when recovered from the Area: United Nations Convention on the Law of the Sea art 133(b).

10 United Nations Convention on the Law of the Sea art 137 para 2.

11 United Nations Convention on the Law of the Sea art 137 para 3.

12 United Nations Convention on the Law of the Sea art 135. The superjacent waters are high seas.

13 Charter of the United Nations (San Francisco, 26 June 1945; TS 67 (1946); Cmd 7015).

14 See the United Nations Convention on the Law of the Sea art 138.

15 See the United Nations Convention on the Law of the Sea art 139 para 1.

16 See the United Nations Convention on the Law of the Sea art 139 para 2.

17 United Nations Convention on the Law of the Sea art 140.

18 United Nations Convention on the Law of the Sea art 141.

19 See the United Nations Convention on the Law of the Sea art 142.

20 See the United Nations Convention on the Law of the Sea art 143.

21 See the United Nations Convention on the Law of the Sea art 144.

22 See the United Nations Convention on the Law of the Sea art 145.

23 See the United Nations Convention on the Law of the Sea art 146.

24 See the United Nations Convention on the Law of the Sea art 147.

25 See the United Nations Convention on the Law of the Sea art 148.

26 See the United Nations Convention on the Law of the Sea art 149.

27 See PARA 490 et seq.

28 Agreement Relating to the Implementation of Part XI of the United Nations Convention on the Law of the Sea of 10 December 1982 (New York, 28 July 1994; UKTS 82 (1999), Cm 4525). There is no practical possibility of the original regime in Part XI of the United Nations Convention on the Law of the Sea being implemented.

29 See the Agreement Concerning Interim Arrangements Relating to Polymetallic Nodules of the Deep Sea Bed (Washington, 2 September 1982; TS 46 (1982); Cmnd 8685); Provisional Understanding on Deep Sea Matters (Geneva, 3 August 1984; TS 24 (1985); Cmnd 9536).

30 As to the Deep Sea Mining (Temporary Provisions) Act 1981 see PARA 174 et seq.

174. Deep sea mining. Before the conclusion of the United Nations Convention of the Law of the Sea[1], several states enacted legislation and entered into international agreements for the avoidance of conflicts over deep sea mining areas[2]. In 1981, the United Kingdom enacted the Deep Sea Mining (Temporary Provisions) Act 1981 to make provision for deep sea mining operations[3]. If it appears to the Secretary of State that an international agreement on the law of the sea which has been adopted by a United Nations Conference on the law of the sea is to be given effect within the United Kingdom, the Secretary of State may by order provide for the repeal of the Deep Sea Mining (Temporary Provisions) Act 1981[4].

1 Ie the United Nations Convention on the Law of the Sea (New York, 10 December 1982; TS 81 (1999); Cmnd 4524).

2 Eg the Agreement Concerning Interim Arrangements Relating to Polymetallic Nodules of the Deep Sea Bed (Washington, 2 September 1982; TS 46 (1982); Cmnd 8685); Provisional Understanding on Deep Sea Matters (Geneva, 3 August 1984; TS 24 (1985); Cmnd 9536).

3 Deep Sea Mining (Temporary Provisions) Act 1981 preamble, s 18(1). The Act applies to Northern Ireland: s 18(7). Her Majesty may by Order in Council direct that any of the provisions of the Act are to extend, with such modifications (if any) as may be specified in the order, to the Channel Islands, the Isle of Man or any colony: s 18(6). In exercise of this power the following orders have been made: Deep Sea Mining (Temporary Provisions) Act 1981

(Guernsey) Order 1997, SI 1997/2978; Deep Sea Mining (Temporary Provisions) Act 1981 (Jersey) Order 1997, SI 1997/2979; Deep Sea Mining (Temporary Provisions) Act 1981 (Isle of Man) Order 2000, SI 2000/1112.

4   Deep Sea Mining (Temporary Provisions) Act 1981 s 18(3). The order may contain such incidental, supplementary and transitional provisions as the Secretary of State thinks fit: s 18(5). At the date at which this volume states the law, no such order had been made. As to the Secretary of State see PARA 29.

175. Prohibition of unlicensed deep sea mining.

Exploration[1] or exploitation[2] of any part of the deep sea bed[3] for hard mineral resources[4] without a licence is prohibited[5] and any person who does so is guilty of an offence[6]. This applies to any person who is a United Kingdom national[7], a Scottish firm or a body incorporated under the law of any part of the United Kingdom, and is resident in any part of the United Kingdom[8]. In any proceedings, a certificate issued by the Secretary of State certifying that sovereign rights are not exercisable in relation to any part of the sea bed by the United Kingdom or by any other sovereign power will be conclusive as to that fact[9]. Her Majesty may by Order in Council extend the application of the prohibition of unlicensed deep sea mining[10].

1   'Exploration', in relation to the hard mineral resources (see note 4) of any part of the deep sea bed (see note 3), means the investigation of that part of the deep sea bed for the purpose of ascertaining whether or not the hard mineral resources of that part of the deep sea bed can be commercially exploited: Deep Sea Mining (Temporary Provisions) Act 1981 s 17.

2   'Exploitation' means commercial exploitation: Deep Sea Mining (Temporary Provisions) Act 1981 s 17.

3   'Deep sea bed' means that part of the bed of the high seas in respect of which sovereign rights in relation to the natural resources of the sea bed are neither exercisable by the United Kingdom nor recognised by Her Majesty's Government in the United Kingdom as being exercisable by another sovereign power or, in a case where disputed claims are made by more than one sovereign power, by one or other of those sovereign powers: Deep Sea Mining (Temporary Provisions) Act 1981 ss 1(6), 17. As to the meaning of 'United Kingdom' see PARA 30 note 3.

4   'Hard mineral resources' means deposits of nodules containing (in quantities greater than trace) at least one of the following elements: manganese, nickel, cobalt, copper, phosphorus and molybdenum: Deep Sea Mining (Temporary Provisions) Act 1981 ss 1(6), 17. As to minerals in general see MINES, MINERALS AND QUARRIES vol 31 (2003 Reissue) PARA 12.

5   Deep Sea Mining (Temporary Provisions) Act 1981 s 1(1), (2).

6   Deep Sea Mining (Temporary Provisions) Act 1981 s 1(3). A person guilty of such an offence is liable, on conviction on indictment, to a fine; or, on summary conviction, to a fine not exceeding the statutory maximum: s 1(3)(a), (b). As to the supplementary provisions relating to offences under the Deep Sea Mining (Temporary Provisions) Act 1981 see PARA 187. As to the statutory maximum see SENTENCING AND DISPOSITION OF OFFENDERS vol 92 (2010) PARA 140.

7   'United Kingdom national' means: (1) a British citizen, a British overseas territories citizen, a British National (Overseas) or a British Overseas citizen; (2) a person who under the British Nationality Act 1981 is a British subject; or (3) a British protected person within the meaning of the British Nationality Act 1981: Deep Sea Mining (Temporary Provisions) Act 1981 s 1(6) (amended by the British Overseas Territories Act 2002 s 2(3); and SI 1986/948).

8   Deep Sea Mining (Temporary Provisions) Act 1981 s 1(4) (amended by the British Nationality Act 1981 s 52(6), Sch 7).

9   Deep Sea Mining (Temporary Provisions) Act 1981 s 1(7). Any document purporting to be such a certificate will be received in evidence and will, unless the contrary is proved, be deemed to be such a certificate: s 1(7).

10 Deep Sea Mining (Temporary Provisions) Act 1981 s 1(5). Her Majesty may extend the application to all United Kingdom nationals, Scottish firms and bodies incorporated under the law of any part of the United Kingdom who are resident outside the United Kingdom, or to such nationals, firms and bodies who are resident in any country specified in the order: s 1(5)(a) (amended by the British Nationality Act 1981 s 52(6)). Her Majesty may also extend the application to bodies incorporated under the law of any of the Channel Islands, the Isle of Man, or any colony: Deep Sea Mining (Temporary Provisions) Act 1981 s 1(5)(b) (amended by the Statute Law (Repeals) Act 1995).

176. Exploration and exploitation licences. The Secretary of State may, on payment of such a fee[1] as may with the consent of the Treasury be prescribed[2], grant to such persons as he thinks fit licences for the exploration[3] or exploitation[4] of the deep sea bed[5] for hard mineral resources[6], and in determining whether to grant a licence in any case he is to have regard to any relevant factors including, in particular, the desirability of keeping an area or areas of the deep sea bed free from deep sea bed mining operations[7] so as to provide an area or areas for comparison with licensed areas[8] in assessing the effects of such operations[9]. An exploration or an exploitation licence is granted for such period as the Secretary of State thinks fit and contains such terms and conditions as he thinks fit and, in particular, but without prejudice to the generality of the foregoing, a licence may include terms and conditions[10]: (1) relating to the safety, health or welfare of persons employed in the licensed operations[11] or in the ancillary operations[12]; (2) relating to the processing or other treatment of any hard mineral resources won in pursuance of the licence which is carried out by or on behalf of the licensee[13] on any ship[14]; (3) relating to the disposal of any waste material resulting from such processing or other treatment[15]; (4) requiring plans, returns, accounts or other records with respect to any matter connected with any licensed area or licensed operations or ancillary operations to be furnished to the Secretary of State[16]; (5) requiring samples of any hard mineral resources discovered or won in any licensed area, or assays of such samples, to be furnished to the Secretary of State[17]; (6) requiring any exploration or exploitation of the hard mineral resources of the licensed area to be diligently carried out[18]; (7) requiring the payment to the Secretary of State of such sums as may with the consent of the Treasury be prescribed at such times as may be prescribed[19]; and (8) permitting the transfer of the licence in prescribed cases or with the written consent of the Secretary of State[20]. Where the Secretary of State has granted an exploration licence he must not grant an exploitation licence in respect of any part of the licensed area otherwise than to the licensee except with the licensee's written consent[21].

1   As to the fee payable for the grant of an exploration licence see the Deep Sea Mining (Exploration Licences) (Applications) Regulations 1982, SI 1982/58, reg 3. As to the additional fees payable see the Deep Sea Mining (Exploration Licences) Regulations 1984, SI 1984/1230, reg 5. As to the Secretary of State see PARA 29.

2   'Prescribed' means prescribed by regulations under the Deep Sea Mining (Temporary Provisions) Act 1981 s 12: s 17.

3   As to the meaning of 'exploration' see PARA 175 note 1. 'Exploration licence' means a licence authorising the licensee (see note 13) to explore for the hard mineral resources (see note 6) of such part of the deep sea bed (see note 5) as may be specified in the licence: Deep Sea Mining (Temporary Provisions) Act 1981 ss 2(1), 17. An exploration licence may not be granted in respect of any period before 1 July 1981: s 2(4).

4   As to the meaning of 'exploitation' see PARA 175 note 2. 'Exploitation licence' means a licence authorising the licensee to exploit the hard mineral resources of such part of the deep sea bed as may be specified in the licence: Deep Sea Mining (Temporary Provisions) Act 1981 ss 2(1), 17. An exploitation licence may not be granted in respect of any period before 1 January 1988: s 2(4).

5   As to the meaning of 'deep sea bed' see PARA 175 note 3.

6   As to the meaning of 'hard mineral resources' see PARA 175 note 4.

7   'Deep sea bed mining operations' means any exploration or exploitation of the hard mineral resources of the deep sea bed: Deep Sea Mining (Temporary Provisions) Act 1981 s 17.

8   'Licensed area' means any part of the deep sea bed in respect of which there is in force an exploration or exploitation licence: Deep Sea Mining (Temporary Provisions) Act 1981 s 17.

9   Deep Sea Mining (Temporary Provisions) Act 1981 s 2(2).

10 Deep Sea Mining (Temporary Provisions) Act 1981 s 2(3).

11 'Licensed operations' means any activities which the licensee may carry on by virtue of his licence: Deep Sea Mining (Temporary Provisions) Act 1981 s 17.

12 Deep Sea Mining (Temporary Provisions) Act 1981 s 2(3)(a). 'Ancillary operations', in relation to any licensed operations, means any activity carried on by or on behalf of the licensee which is ancillary to the licensed operations (including the processing and transportation of any substances recovered): s 17.

13 'Licensee' means the holder of an exploration or exploitation licence: Deep Sea Mining (Temporary Provisions) Act 1981 s 17.

14 Deep Sea Mining (Temporary Provisions) Act 1981 s 2(3)(b).

15 Deep Sea Mining (Temporary Provisions) Act 1981 s 2(3)(c).

16 Deep Sea Mining (Temporary Provisions) Act 1981 s 2(3)(d).

17 Deep Sea Mining (Temporary Provisions) Act 1981 s 2(3)(e).

18 Deep Sea Mining (Temporary Provisions) Act 1981 s 2(3)(f).

19 Deep Sea Mining (Temporary Provisions) Act 1981 s 2(3)(g).

20 Deep Sea Mining (Temporary Provisions) Act 1981 s 2(3)(h).

21 Deep Sea Mining (Temporary Provisions) Act 1981 s 2(5).

177. Licences granted by reciprocating countries. Where, in the opinion of Her Majesty, the law of any country contains provisions similar in their aims and effects to the provisions of the Deep Sea Mining (Temporary Provisions) Act 1981, Her Majesty may by Order in Council designate that country as a reciprocating country[1]. Where a person holds a licence or other authorisation issued and for the time being in force under the law of a reciprocating country for the exploration[2] or exploitation[3] of the hard mineral resources[4] of any area of the deep sea bed[5] specified in that authorisation[6] the Secretary of State must not grant an exploration or exploitation licence in respect of any part of the authorised area[7] and if the relevant provision[8] applies to that person, he must not be prohibited from engaging in the exploration or, as the case may be, exploitation of the hard mineral resources of the authorised area[9]. It is the duty of the licensee[10] to exercise his rights under the licence with reasonable regard to the interests of other persons in their exercise of the freedom of the high seas[11].

1 Deep Sea Mining (Temporary Provisions) Act 1981 s 3(1). In exercise of this power the following order was made: Deep Sea Mining (Reciprocating Countries) Order 1985, SI 1985/2000. 'Reciprocating country' means a country designated as such by an order under the Deep Sea Mining (Temporary Provisions) Act 1981 s 3: s 17.

2 As to the meaning of 'exploration' see PARA 175 note 1. As to the meaning of 'exploration licence' see PARA 176 note 3.

3 As to the meaning of 'exploitation' see PARA 175 note 1. As to the meaning of 'exploitation licence' see PARA 176 note 4.

4 As to the meaning of 'hard mineral resources' see PARA 175 note 4.

5 As to the meaning of 'deep sea bed' see PARA 175 note 3.

6 Deep Sea Mining (Temporary Provisions) Act 1981 s 3(2). Any reference to a reciprocal authorisation in the Deep Sea Mining (Temporary Provisions) Act 1981 is a reference to an authorisation within s 3(2): ss 3(3), 17. For the purposes of any proceedings, a reciprocal authorisation may be proved by the production of a copy of the authorisation certified to be a true copy by an official of the government or other body which issued the authorisation, and any document purporting to be such a copy is to be received in evidence and will, unless the contrary is proved, be deemed to be such an authorisation: s 3(4).

7 Deep Sea Mining (Temporary Provisions) Act 1981 s 3(2)(a). As to the Secretary of State see PARA 29.

8 Ie the Deep Sea Mining (Temporary Provisions) Act 1981 s 1: see PARA 175.

9 Deep Sea Mining (Temporary Provisions) Act 1981 s 3(2)(b). References in s 3(2)(b) to any person who holds a reciprocal authorisation include references to his agents or employees acting in their capacity as such: s 3(3).

10 As to the meaning of 'licensee' see PARA 176 note 13.

11 Deep Sea Mining (Temporary Provisions) Act 1981 s 7.

178. Prevention of interference with licensed operations. A person to whom the prohibition of unlicensed deep sea mining[1] applies must not intentionally interfere with any operations carried on in pursuance of an exploration[2] or exploitation licence[3] or a reciprocal authorisation[4]. Any person who contravenes this provision is guilty of an offence[5].

1   Ie the prohibition in the Deep Sea Mining (Temporary Provisions) Act 1981 s 1: see PARA 175.
2   As to the meaning of 'exploration licence' see PARA 176 note 3.
3   As to the meaning of 'exploitation licence' see PARA 176 note 4.
4   Deep Sea Mining (Temporary Provisions) Act 1981 s 4(1). As to the meaning of 'reciprocal authorisation' see PARA 177 note 6.
5   Deep Sea Mining (Temporary Provisions) Act 1981 s 4(2). A person guilty of such an offence is liable, on conviction on indictment, to a fine; or, on summary conviction, to a fine not exceeding the statutory maximum: s 4(2)(a), (b). As to the statutory maximum see SENTENCING AND DISPOSITION OF OFFENDERS vol 92 (2010) PARA 140. As to the supplementary provisions relating to offences under the Deep Sea Mining (Temporary Provisions) Act 1981 see PARA 187.

179. Protection of the marine environment. In determining whether to grant an exploration[1] or exploitation licence[2] the Secretary of State must have regard to the need to protect (so far as reasonably practicable) marine creatures, plants and other organisms and their habitat from any harmful effects which might result from any activities to be authorised by the licence[3]. The Secretary of State must consider any representations made to him concerning such effects[4].

1   As to the meaning of 'exploration licence' see PARA 176 note 3.
2   As to the meaning of 'exploitation licence' see PARA 176 note 4.
3   Deep Sea Mining (Temporary Provisions) Act 1981 s 5(1). Without prejudice to s 2(3) (see PARA 176), any exploration or exploitation licence granted by the Secretary of State must contain such terms and conditions as he considers necessary or expedient to avoid or minimise any such harmful effects: s 5(2). As to the Secretary of State see PARA 29.
4   Deep Sea Mining (Temporary Provisions) Act 1981 s 5(1).

180. Variation and revocation of licences. The Secretary of State[1] may vary or revoke any exploration[2] or exploitation licence[3] where the variation or revocation is in his opinion required (1) to ensure the safety, health or welfare of persons engaged in any of the licensed operations[4] or ancillary operations[5]; or (2) to protect any marine creatures, plants or other organisms or their habitat[6]; or (3) in pursuance of foreign discriminatory action[7]; or (4) to avoid a conflict with any obligation of the United Kingdom arising out of any international agreement in force for the United Kingdom[8]. The Secretary of State may vary or revoke any exploration or exploitation licence in any case, with the consent of the licensee[9]. The Secretary of State may revoke an exploration or exploitation licence in any case where a term or condition of the licence or any regulation made under the Deep Sea Mining (Temporary Provisions) Act 1981 has not been complied with[10].

1   As to the Secretary of State see PARA 29.
2   As to the meaning of 'exploration licence' see PARA 176 note 3.
3   As to the meaning of 'exploitation licence' see PARA 176 note 4.
4   As to the meaning of 'licensed operation' see PARA 176 note 11.
5   Deep Sea Mining (Temporary Provisions) Act 1981 s 6(1)(a)(i). As to the meaning of 'ancillary operations' see PARA 176 note 12.
6   Deep Sea Mining (Temporary Provisions) Act 1981 s 6(1)(a)(ii).
7   Deep Sea Mining (Temporary Provisions) Act 1981 s 6(1)(a)(iii). As to foreign discriminatory action see PARA 181.
8   Deep Sea Mining (Temporary Provisions) Act 1981 s 6(1)(a)(iv). As to the meaning of 'United Kingdom' see PARA 30 note 3.
9   Deep Sea Mining (Temporary Provisions) Act 1981 s 6(1)(b). As to the meaning of 'licensee' see PARA 176 note 13.
10   Deep Sea Mining (Temporary Provisions) Act 1981 s 6(2).

181. Foreign discriminatory action. Where any ship[1] which is registered in a country of which the government[2], in the opinion of the Secretary of State, has adopted or is proposing to adopt discriminatory measures or practices prohibiting or otherwise restricting the use, in connection with any deep sea bed mining operations[3], of ships registered in the United Kingdom[4], the Secretary of State may include in any exploration[5] or exploitation licence[6], either on granting the licence or by a subsequent variation, such terms and conditions as he considers expedient for prohibiting or otherwise restricting the use in connection with the licensed operations[7] or any ancillary operations[8] of any ship[9].

1 'Ship' includes every description of vessel used in navigation: Deep Sea Mining (Temporary Provisions) Act 1981 s 17.
2 Or an agency or authority of the government: Deep Sea Mining (Temporary Provisions) Act 1981 s 8(1). In s 8, references to an agency or authority of a government include references to any undertaking appearing to the Secretary of State to be, or to be acting on behalf of, an undertaking which is in effect owned or controlled (directly or indirectly) by a state other than the United Kingdom: s 8(4). As to the Secretary of State see PARA 29. As to the meaning of 'United Kingdom' see PARA 30 note 3.
3 As to the meaning of 'deep sea bed mining operations' see PARA 176 note 7.
4 Deep Sea Mining (Temporary Provisions) Act 1981 s 8(1). The Secretary of State may by order extend s 8 to ships which are registered in any country of which the government (or any agency or authority of the government), in his opinion, has adopted or is proposing to adopt discriminatory measures or practices prohibiting or otherwise restricting the use in connection with any deep sea bed mining operations of ships registered in the Channel Islands, the Isle of Man or any colony.
5 As to the meaning of 'exploration licence' see PARA 176 note 3.
6 As to the meaning of 'exploitation licence' see PARA 176 note 4.
7 As to the meaning of 'licensed operation' see PARA 176 note 11.
8 As to the meaning of 'ancillary operations' see PARA 176 note 12.
9 Deep Sea Mining (Temporary Provisions) Act 1981 s 8(2). This provision does not prejudice the Secretary of State's ability to include the terms and conditions listed under s 2(3): s 8(2).

182. The deep sea mining levy. The holder of an exploitation licence[1] must, at the prescribed[2] times, pay to the Secretary of State[3]: (1) an amount equal to 3.75 per cent of the value of the hard mineral resources[4] recovered in pursuance of the licence during any prescribed period; or (2) if the value of the hard mineral resources so recovered cannot be ascertained under head (1) above, 0.75 per cent of the value of any manganese, nickel, cobalt, copper, phosphorus or molybdenum[5], or any compound containing any of the elements, found in those hard mineral resources[6]. If any hard mineral resources recovered by the licensee during any prescribed period contain less than the amount[7] prescribed in relation to that period of any of the elements or any compound containing any of the elements, the licensee is not liable to make any payment in respect of that element or compound[8]. A licensee may elect, in writing and at the prescribed times, in respect of any element or compound specified in the election to defer payment until the element or compound is separated from any other matter with which it was recovered or, if earlier, until he disposes of the hard mineral resources containing that element or compound[9].

1 As to the meaning of 'exploitation licence' see PARA 176 note 4.
2 As to the meaning of 'prescribed' see PARA 176 note 2.
3 As to the Secretary of State see PARA 29.
4 As to the meaning of 'hard mineral resources' see PARA 175 note 4.
5 These are known collectively as 'the elements': Deep Sea Mining (Temporary Provisions) Act 1981 s 9(1).
6 Deep Sea Mining (Temporary Provisions) Act 1981 s 9(1). The value of any hard mineral resources, element or compound is, for the purposes of s 9(1), determined in accordance with such rules as may be prescribed: s 9(2). Where a licensee fails at the prescribed time to pay to the

Secretary of State any amount which he is required by s 9(1) to pay at that time, the amount will, as from that time, carry interest at the relevant rate until payment: s 9(5).

As to the meaning of 'licensee' see PARA 176 note 13. For the purposes of s 9, 'relevant rate' means such rate as the Secretary of State may with the consent of the Treasury prescribe: s 9(5). As to the Treasury see CONSTITUTIONAL LAW AND HUMAN RIGHTS vol 8(2) (Reissue) PARAS 512–517.

7   Ie by weight or proportion or otherwise: Deep Sea Mining (Temporary Provisions) Act 1981 s 9(3).
8   Deep Sea Mining (Temporary Provisions) Act 1981 s 9(3).
9   Deep Sea Mining (Temporary Provisions) Act 1981 s 9(4). Where any payment has been deferred under s 9(4) and becomes due, the amount due is to be calculated in accordance with s 9(1)–(3), and, for the purposes of s 9(5), that amount is to be deemed to have become due on the date when it would have been due had the election not been made: s 9(6).

183. The deep sea mining fund. A fund is to be established under the control and management of the Treasury[1] called the Deep Sea Mining Fund, into which any sums paid to the Secretary of State[2] under the Deep Sea Mining (Temporary Provisions) Act 1981[3] are to be paid[4]. The Treasury must prepare accounts of the fund[5]. If an international organisation for the deep sea bed[6] is established in pursuance of an international agreement on the law of the sea which has been adopted by a United Nations Conference on the Law of the Sea and has entered into force for the United Kingdom, the Secretary of State may by order designate that organisation as the relevant international organisation for the purposes of this provision[7].

1   As to the Treasury see CONSTITUTIONAL LAW AND HUMAN RIGHTS vol 8(2) (Reissue) PARAS 512–517.
2   As to the Secretary of State see PARA 29.
3   Ie under the Deep Sea Mining (Temporary Provisions) Act 1981 s 9: see PARA 182.
4   Deep Sea Mining (Temporary Provisions) Act 1981 s 10(1).
5   Deep Sea Mining (Temporary Provisions) Act 1981 s 10(2). The Treasury must send the accounts to the Comptroller and Auditor General not later than the end of the month of November following the financial year to which the accounts relate; and the Comptroller and Auditor General must examine and certify every such account and must lay copies of the accounts, together with his report on them, before Parliament: s 10(2). This provision will not have effect until the first payment into the fund is made: s 10(3). As to the Comptroller and Auditor General see CONSTITUTIONAL LAW AND HUMAN RIGHTS vol 8(2) (Reissue) PARA 724 et seq.
     For these purposes, 'financial year' means a period of 12 months ending on 31 March except that the Secretary of State may direct that: (1) the first financial year for the fund is to be of such period not exceeding two years and ending on 31 March as he may specify in the direction; and (2) where an order under s 10(7) is made (see note 7), the last financial year will be of such period not exceeding 12 months as he may specify in the direction; and, where a direction is given under head (1) above, s 10(2) will apply in relation to the accounts for that last financial year with the substitution for the reference to the end of the month of November of a reference to the end of the eighth month following the end of that year: s 10(4).
6   As to the International Seabed Authority see SHIPPING AND MARITIME LAW vol 93 (2008) PARA 12. As to the meaning of 'deep sea bed' see PARA 175 note 3.
7   Deep Sea Mining (Temporary Provisions) Act 1981 s 10(5). An order designating an international organisation as the relevant international organisation for the purposes of s 10 may also make provision for the payment to that organisation of any sums for the time being standing to the credit of the fund: s 10(6). At the date at which this volume states the law, no such order had been made.
     If within ten years of the coming into force of s 10 no organisation has been designated as the relevant international organisation, the Secretary of State may by order made with the approval of the Treasury provide for the winding up of the Fund and the payment into the Consolidated Fund of any sums standing to its credit, and for the repeal of s 9: s 10(7). At the date at which this volume states the law no such order had been made.
     Until such time as an international organisation is so designated, any money in the Fund may from time to time be paid over to the National Debt Commissioners and invested by them, in accordance with such directions as may be given by the Treasury, in any such manner as may be

specified by an order of the Treasury for the time being in force under the National Savings Bank Act 1971 s 22(1) (repealed): Deep Sea Mining (Temporary Provisions) Act 1981 s 10(9). As to investment deposits with the National Savings Bank see the Finance Act 1980 s 120; and FINANCIAL SERVICES AND INSTITUTIONS vol 49 (2008) PARA 812.

184. Inspectors. The Secretary of State[1] may appoint as inspectors to discharge such functions as may be prescribed[2] and generally to assist him in the execution of the Deep Sea Mining (Temporary Provisions) Act 1981 such persons appearing to him to be qualified for the purpose as he considers appropriate from time to time[3].

1 As to the Secretary of State see PARA 29.
2 As to the meaning of 'prescribed' see PARA 176 note 2.
3 Deep Sea Mining (Temporary Provisions) Act 1981 s 11(1). The Secretary of State may make to or in respect of any inspector appointed under s 11(1) such payments by way of remuneration or otherwise as the Secretary of State may determine with the approval of the Minister for the Civil Service: s 11(2). As to the Minister for the Civil Service see CONSTITUTIONAL LAW AND HUMAN RIGHTS vol 8(2) (Reissue) PARAS 427, 550.

185. Regulations and orders. The Secretary of State[1] may make regulations prescribing anything required or authorised to be prescribed under the Deep Sea Mining (Temporary Provisions) Act 1981 and generally for carrying the Act into effect[2].

1 As to the Secretary of State see PARA 29.
2 Deep Sea Mining (Temporary Provisions) Act 1981 s 12(1). Regulations under s 12(1) may make different provision for different cases or classes of cases and may exclude the operation of any provision of the regulations in specified cases; and must be made by statutory instrument subject to annulment in pursuance of a resolution of either House of Parliament: s 12(2). Without prejudice to the generality of the foregoing, regulations may be made with respect to any of the matters mentioned in the Schedule: s 12(1).
    Any power of the Secretary of State to make an order under the Deep Sea Mining (Temporary Provisions) Act 1981 is to be exercisable by statutory instrument: s 12(3). The following orders have been made under s 12: the Deep Sea Mining (Exploration Licences) (Applications) Regulations 1982, SI 1982/58; and the Deep Sea Mining (Exploration Licences) Regulations 1984, SI 1984/1230.

186. Disclosure of information. A person must not disclose any information which he has received in pursuance of the Deep Sea Mining (Temporary Provisions) Act 1981 and which relates to any other person except: (1) with the written consent of that other person[1]; or (2) to the Treasury, the Commissioners of Customs and Excise or the Secretary of State[2]; or (3) with a view to the institution of or otherwise for the purposes of any criminal proceedings under this Act or regulations made under this Act[3]; or (4) in accordance with regulations made under this Act[4]; or (5) to the government of a reciprocating country or an agency of such a government or to any international organisation designated as the relevant international organisation for the purposes of the Deep Sea Fund Mining Fund[5]. Any person who discloses any information in contravention this provision is to be guilty of an offence[6].

1 Deep Sea Mining (Temporary Provisions) Act 1981 s 13(1)(a).
2 Deep Sea Mining (Temporary Provisions) Act 1981 s 13(1)(b). As to the Treasury see CONSTITUTIONAL LAW AND HUMAN RIGHTS vol 8(2) (Reissue) PARAS 512–517. As to the Commissioners of Customs and Excise see CUSTOMS AND EXCISE vol 12(2) (2007 Reissue) PARA 905 et seq. As to the Secretary of State see PARA 29.
3 Deep Sea Mining (Temporary Provisions) Act 1981 s 13(1)(c).
4 Deep Sea Mining (Temporary Provisions) Act 1981 s 13(1)(d).
5 Deep Sea Mining (Temporary Provisions) Act 1981 s 13(1)(e). As to the Deep Sea Mining Fund see PARA 183.

6   Deep Sea Mining (Temporary Provisions) Act 1981 s 13(2). Any person guilty of such an offence
     is liable, on conviction on indictment, to imprisonment for a term not exceeding two years or to
     a fine or to both (s 13(2)(a)) or, on summary conviction, to a fine not exceeding the statutory
     maximum (s 13(2)(b)). As to the statutory maximum see SENTENCING AND DISPOSITION OF
     OFFENDERS vol 92 (2010) PARA 140. As to the supplementary provisions relating to offences
     under the Deep Sea Mining (Temporary Provisions) Act 1981 see PARA 187.

187.   Supplementary provisions relating to offences.   Proceedings for an
offence under the Deep Sea Mining (Temporary Provisions) Act 1981 or under
regulations made under the Act may be taken, and the offence may for incidental
purposes be treated as having been committed, in any place in the United
Kingdom[1]. A person may be guilty of an offence under regulations made under
the Deep Sea Mining (Temporary Provisions) Act 1981 whether or not he is a
British citizen, a British overseas territories citizen, a British National (Overseas)
or a British Overseas citizen or, in the case of a body corporate, it is incorporated
under the law of any part of the United Kingdom[2]. Where an offence has been
committed by a body corporate and is proved to have been committed with the
consent or connivance of, or to be attributable to any neglect on the part of, a
director[3], manager, secretary or other similar officer of the body corporate or any
person who was purporting to act in any such capacity, he as well as the body
corporate is guilty of that offence and is liable to be proceeded against and
punished accordingly[4]. In any proceedings for an offence of failing to comply
with any provision of the Deep Sea Mining (Temporary Provisions) Act 1981 or
of regulations made under the Act, it is a defence to prove that the accused used
all due diligence to comply with that provision[5].

1   Deep Sea Mining (Temporary Provisions) Act 1981 s 14(1). Proceedings for such an offence are
     not to be instituted in England and Wales or Northern Ireland except: (1) in the case of
     proceedings in England and Wales, by or with the consent of the Director of Public Prosecutions;
     or (2) in the case of proceedings in Northern Ireland, by or with the consent of the Director of
     Public Prosecutions for Northern Ireland; or (3) in any case, by the Secretary of State or a person
     authorised by him in that behalf: s 14(2). As to the meaning of 'United Kingdom' see PARA 30
     note 3. As to the Director of Public Prosecutions see CRIMINAL LAW, EVIDENCE AND PROCEDURE
     vol 11(3) (2006 Reissue) PARAS 1066, 1079 et seq. As to the Secretary of State see PARA 29.
2   Deep Sea Mining (Temporary Provisions) Act 1981 s 14(3) (amended by the British Overseas
     Territories Act 2002 s 2(3); and SI 1986/948).
3   For these purposes, 'director', in relation to a body corporate which (1) is established by or
     under any enactment for the purpose of carrying on under public ownership any industry or
     part of an industry or undertaking; and (2) is a body whose affairs are managed by its members,
     means a member of the body corporate: Deep Sea Mining (Temporary Provisions) Act 1981
     s 14(4).
4   Deep Sea Mining (Temporary Provisions) Act 1981 s 14(4).
5   Deep Sea Mining (Temporary Provisions) Act 1981 s 14(5).

188.   Civil liability for breach of statutory duty.   Breach of a duty imposed on
any person by a provision of certain regulations made in pursuance of the Deep
Sea Mining (Temporary Provisions) Act 1981[1] is actionable so far, and only so
far, as the breach causes personal injury[2]. A defence to a charge which is
available by virtue of the supplementary provisions relating to offences under the
Deep Sea Mining (Temporary Provisions) Act 1981[3] or by virtue of regulations
made under that Act is not a defence in any civil proceedings[4].

1   Ie regulations which state that the Deep Sea Mining (Temporary Provisions) Act 1981 s 15(1)
     applies to such a breach: see s 15(1).
2   Deep Sea Mining (Temporary Provisions) Act 1981 s 15(1). References in the Fatal Accidents
     Act 1976 s 1 to a wrongful act, neglect or default, include references to any such breach which
     is so actionable: Deep Sea Mining (Temporary Provisions) Act 1981 s 15(1). As to the Fatal
     Accidents Act 1976 see NEGLIGENCE vol 78 (2010) PARA 25 et seq. 'Personal injury' includes any

disease, any impairment of a person's physical or mental condition and any fatal injury: s 15(4). Nothing in s 15(1) is to prejudice any action which lies apart from these provisions: s 15(2).
3   Ie the Deep Sea Mining (Temporary Provisions) Act 1981 s 14(5): see PARA 187.
4   Deep Sea Mining (Temporary Provisions) Act 1981 s 15(3).

189. Disapplication of Part II of the Food and Environment Protection Act 1985. Nothing in Part II of the Food and Environment Protection Act 1985[1] applies in relation to anything done in pursuance of an exploration[2] or exploitation[3] licence or a reciprocal authorisation[4].

1   Ie the Food and Environment Protection Act 1985 Pt II (ss 5–15): see SHIPPING AND NAVIGATION vol 43(2) (Reissue) PARA 1310.
2   As to the meaning of 'exploration licence' see PARA 176 note 3.
3   As to the meaning of 'exploitation licence' see PARA 176 note 4.
4   Deep Sea Mining (Temporary Provisions) Act 1981 s 16 (amended by the Food and Environment Act 1985 s 15). As to the meaning of 'reciprocal authorisation' see PARA 177 note 6.

(vi) Conservation and Management of the Living Resources of the High Seas

190. Right to fish on the high seas. All states have the right for their nationals to engage in fishing on the high seas[1], subject to[2]: (1) their treaty obligations[3]; (2) the rights and duties, as well as the interests, of coastal states provided for in provisions respecting the exclusive economic zone[4]; and (3) the provisions of the United Nations Convention on the Law of the Sea relating to the conservation and management of the living resources of the high seas[5].

1   As to the freedom of the 'high seas' see PARA 147 et seq.
2   United Nations Convention on the Law of the Sea (Montego Bay, 10 December 1982, TS 81 (1999); Cmnd 4524) art 116.
3   United Nations Convention on the Law of the Sea art 116(a). As to multilateral and bilateral treaties to which the United Kingdom is a party see PARA 192 et seq.
4   United Nations Convention on the Law of the Sea art 116(b). The provisions referred to in the text are, inter alia, arts 63 para 2, 64–67; see PARA 154. As to the exclusive economic zone see PARA 154.
5   United Nations Convention on the Law of the Sea art 116(c). The provisions referred to in the text are contained in Pt VII s 2 (arts 116–120).

191. Duties of states. All states have the duty to take, or to co-operate with other states in taking, such measures for their respective nationals as may be necessary for the conservation of the living resources of the high seas[1]. States must co-operate in the conservation and management of such resources[2]. In determining the allowable catch and establishing other conservation measures, states are to take measures which are designed, on the best scientific evidence available, to maintain or restore populations of harvested species at levels which can produce the maximum sustainable yield as qualified by relevant environmental and economic factors[3], and take into consideration the effects on species associated with or dependent upon the harvested species[4]. States must also ensure that conservation measures and their implementation do not discriminate in form or fact against the fishermen of any state[5].

1   United Nations Convention on the Law of the Sea (Montego Bay, 10 December 1982; Misc 11 (1983) Cmnd 8941) art 117.
2   United Nations Convention on the Law of the Sea art 118.
3   United Nations Convention on the Law of the Sea art 119 para 1(a). As to the exchange of available scientific information, relevant statistics and other data see art 119 para 2.
4   United Nations Convention on the Law of the Sea art 119 para 1(b).
5   United Nations Convention on the Law of the Sea art 119 para 3.

192.   International fisheries agreements.   As a matter of European Union law, the United Kingdom has transferred competence to the European Union (EU) with regard to the conservation and management of living marine resources. Hence, in this field, it is for the EU to adopt the relevant rules and regulations (which the United Kingdom and other member states enforce), and it is within the competence of the EU to enter into external undertakings with third states or competent organisations[1]. With regard to fisheries, for a certain number of matters that are not directly related to the conservation and management of sea fishing resources, for example research and technological development and development cooperation, competence is shared between the EU and its member states[2]. Although the European Union is more active in relation to fisheries[3], the United Kingdom remains a party to certain international agreements concerning the living resources of the seas, such as the International Convention for the Regulation of Whaling[4].

1   See the Declaration concerning the Competence of the European Community with regard to matters Governed by the United Nations Convention on the Law of the Sea of 10 December and the Agreement of 28 July 1994 relating to the Implementation of Part XI of the Convention (Declaration made pursuant to article 5(1) of Annex IX to the Convention and to article 4(4) of the Agreement); and the Declarations concerning the Agreement for the Implementation of the Provisions of the United Nations Convention on the Law of the Sea of 10 December 1982 relating to the Conservation and Management of Straddling Fish Stocks and Highly Migratory Fish Stocks.

2   See the Declaration concerning the Competence of the European Community with regard to matters Governed by the United Nations Convention on the Law of the Sea of 10 December and the Agreement of 28 July 1994 relating to the Implementation of Part XI of the Convention (Declaration made pursuant to article 5(1) of Annex IX to the Convention and to article 4(4) of the Agreement); and the Declarations concerning the Agreement for the Implementation of the Provisions of the United Nations Convention on the Law of the Sea of 10 December 1982 relating to the Conservation and Management of Straddling Fish Stocks and Highly Migratory Fish Stocks.

3   See eg the North East Atlantic Fisheries Commission established under Council Decision 81/608 (OJ L227, 12/08/1981, p 22) concerning the conclusion of the Convention on Future Multilateral Cooperation in the North-East Atlantic Fisheries (see art 3(1)) and Council Decision 2009/550 (OJ L184, 16.7.2009, p 12–15) on the approval of amendments to the Convention on future multilateral cooperation in the North-East Atlantic Fisheries allowing for the establishment of dispute settlement procedures, the extension of the scope of the Convention and a review of the objectives of the Convention.

4   Ie the International Convention for the Regulation of Whaling (Washington, 2 December 1946; TS 5 (1949); Cmd 7604). This Convention, which replaces earlier agreements, has frequently been amended. As to whaling see AGRICULTURE AND FISHERIES.

193.   Protection and preservation of the marine environment.   The United Nations Convention on the Law of the Sea[1] makes provision for the protection and preservation of the marine environment[2]. States are obliged to protect and preserve the marine environment[3]. They have the sovereign right to exploit their natural resources pursuant to their environmental policies and in accordance with their duty to protect the marine environment[4]. States must take, individually or jointly as appropriate, all measures to prevent, reduce and control pollution of the marine environment[5]. They must so act as not to transfer, directly or indirectly, damage or hazards from one area to another or transform one type of pollution into another[6], and must take all measures necessary to prevent, reduce and control pollution from the use of technologies or the introduction of alien or new species to a part of the marine environment which may cause significant and harmful changes thereto[7]. Provision is made for global and regional co-operation[8], technical assistance and preferential treatment for developing states[9] and monitoring and environmental assessment[10]. States are under the duty to establish international rules and national legislation to prevent, reduce and control pollution of the marine environment[11]. These must cover pollution: (1) from land based sources[12]; (2) from sea bed activities subject to national jurisdiction[13]; (3) from activities in the Area[14]; (4) by dumping[15]; (5) from vessels[16]; and (6) from or through the atmosphere[17]. Provision is also made for the enforcement of laws and regulations[18]. In particular, flag states must ensure compliance[19] and port states and coastal states may also do so[20]. There are provisions concerned with ice-covered areas[21], state responsibility and liability[22] and sovereign immunity[23].

These provisions[24] are without prejudice to the specific obligations assumed by states under special conventions and agreements concluded previously which relate to the protection and preservation of the marine environment and to agreements which may be concluded in furtherance of the general principles set forth in the United Nations Convention on the Law of the Sea[25].

1　Ie the United Nations Convention on the Law of the Sea (Montego Bay, 10 December 1982; TS 81 (1999); Cmnd 4524).
2　See the United Nations Convention on the Law of the Sea Pt XII (arts 192–237).
3　United Nations Convention on the Law of the Sea art 192.
4　United Nations Convention on the Law of the Sea art 193.
5　United Nations Convention on the Law of the Sea art 194.
6　United Nations Convention on the Law of the Sea art 195.
7　United Nations Convention on the Law of the Sea art 196.
8　United Nations Convention on the Law of the Sea Pt XII Section 2 (arts 197–201).
9　United Nations Convention on the Law of the Sea Pt XII Section 3 (arts 202–203).
10　United Nations Convention on the Law of the Sea Pt XII Section 4 (arts 204–206).
11　United Nations Convention on the Law of the Sea Pt XII Section 5 (arts 207–212).
12　United Nations Convention on the Law of the Sea art 207.
13　United Nations Convention on the Law of the Sea art 208.
14　United Nations Convention on the Law of the Sea art 209. As to 'the Area' see PARA 173.
15　United Nations Convention on the Law of the Sea art 210.
16　United Nations Convention on the Law of the Sea art 211.
17　United Nations Convention on the Law of the Sea art 212.
18　United Nations Convention on the Law of the Sea Pt XII Section 6 (arts 213–222).
19　United Nations Convention on the Law of the Sea art 217.
20　United Nations Convention on the Law of the Sea arts 218, 220. As to measures by port states regarding the seaworthiness of vessels see art 219. As to measures to avoid pollution from maritime casualties see art 221. Provision is made for safeguards where the port or coastal state takes enforcement action under arts 218–220: see Pt XII Section 7 (arts 223–233).
21　United Nations Convention on the Law of the Sea art 234.
22　United Nations Convention on the Law of the Sea art 235.
23　United Nations Convention on the Law of the Sea art 236.
24　Ie the provisions contained in the United Nations Convention on the Law of the Sea Pt XII: see the text and notes 1–23.
25　United Nations Convention on the Law of the Sea art 237 para 1. Many international agreements relating to the protection and preservation of the marine environment have been concluded; and many of them are frequently updated. Among the more important of the agreements to which the United Kingdom is a party are the following: Convention Relating to Intervention on the High Seas in Cases of Oil Pollution Casualties (Brussels, 29 November 1969; TS 77 (1975); Cmnd 6056); the International Convention for the Prevention of Pollution from Ships (MARPOL) (London, 2 November 1973), as amended by the Protocol (London, 1 June 1978) (1340 UNTS 61), and the Convention for the Protection of the Marine Environment of the North-East Atlantic, 1992 (Paris, 22 September 1992; TS 14 (1999); Cm 4278). For further provisions relating to the prevention of pollution from ships see SHIPPING AND NAVIGATION vol 43(2) (Reissue) PARA 1135 et seq.

194. Marine scientific research. The United Nations Convention on the Law of the Sea[1] makes provision for the conduct of marine scientific research[2]. All states, irrespective of their geographical location, and competent international organisations, have the right to conduct such research[3] and to promote and facilitate its development and conduct[4], which must be carried out exclusively for peaceful purposes[5]. Marine research activities may not constitute the legal basis for any claims to any part of the marine environment or its resources[6]. States and competent international organisations are to promote international co-operation in marine scientific research[7], create favourable conditions[8] and publish and disseminate information and knowledge[9]. Marine scientific research in the territorial sea[10], in the exclusive economic zone and on the continental shelf is subject to the consent of the coastal state[11]. States must endeavour to adopt reasonable rules, regulations and procedures to promote and facilitate marine scientific research conducted in accordance with the Convention[12]. All states and competent international organisations have the right to conduct research on the deep sea bed[13] and in the water[14] column beyond the exclusive economic zone[15]. Provision is made regarding scientific research installations or equipment and their status[16], for the responsibility and liability of states and competent international organisations[17] and for the settlement of disputes[18]. The Convention also provides for the development and transfer of marine technology[19].

1 Ie the United Nations Convention on the Law of the Sea (Montego Bay, 10 December 1982; TS 81 (1999); Cmnd 4524).
2 See United Nations Convention on the Law of the Sea Pt XIII (arts 238–265). As to the freedom to conduct scientific research and the high seas see PARA 147.
3 United Nations Convention on the Law of the Sea art 238.
4 United Nations Convention on the Law of the Sea art 239.
5 United Nations Convention on the Law of the Sea art 240(a). For the other general principles for the conduct of marine scientific research see art 240(b)–(d).
6 United Nations Convention on the Law of the Sea art 241.
7 United Nations Convention on the Law of the Sea art 242 para 1.
8 United Nations Convention on the Law of the Sea art 243.
9 United Nations Convention on the Law of the Sea art 244.
10 United Nations Convention on the Law of the Sea art 245. As to the territorial sea see PARA 123 et seq.
11 United Nations Convention on the Law of the Sea art 246. As to the exclusive economic zone see PARA 154. As to the continental shelf see PARA 163 et seq. States and competent international organisations which intend to undertake marine scientific research in the exclusive economic zone or on the continental shelf are bound to provide information to the coastal state: art 248. They also have the duty to comply with certain conditions: art 249. Communications concerning the marine scientific projects must be made through official channels, unless otherwise agreed: art 250. Under certain circumstances a coastal state has the right to require the suspension of any marine scientific research activities in progress: art 253. Neighbouring land-locked and geographically disadvantaged states are given the opportunity to participate in proposed marine scientific research: art 254.
12 United Nations Convention on the Law of the Sea art 255.
13 United Nations Convention on the Law of the Sea art 256. As to the deep sea bed see PARA 173.
14 Ie in the waters of the high seas.
15 United Nations Convention on the Law of the Sea art 257.
16 United Nations Convention on the Law of the Sea Pt XIII Section 4 (arts 258–262).
17 United Nations Convention on the Law of the Sea art 263.
18 United Nations Convention on the Law of the Sea Pt XIII Section 6 (arts 264, 265). As to settlement of disputes see PARA 514.
19 United Nations Convention on the Law of the Sea Pt XIV (arts 266–278).

(3) DRUG TRAFFICKING

195. Narcotic drugs and psychotropic substances. States must co-operate in the suppression of the illicit traffic in narcotic drugs and psychotropic substances by ships on the high seas contrary to international conventions[1]. A state which reasonably believes that a ship flying its flag is engaged in such illicit traffic may request the co-operation of other states to suppress it[2].

1   United Nations Convention on the Law of the Sea (Montego Bay, 10 December 1982; TS 81 (1999); Cmnd 4524) art 108 para 1. The Convention against Illicit Traffic in Narcotic Drugs and Psychotropic Substances (Vienna, 20 December 1988; Misc 14 (1989); Cm 804) art 17 deals with the illicit traffic in drugs by sea and confers powers to board, search and inspect ships by states other than the flag state.
2   United Nations Convention on the Law of the Sea art 108 para 2.

(4) BROADCASTING

196.   Broadcasting at sea; pirate radio.   States must co-operate in the suppression of unauthorised broadcasting from the high seas[1]. A person engaged in unauthorised broadcasting may be prosecuted before the courts of: (1) the flag state; (2) the state of registry of the installation; (3) the state of which the person is a national; (4) any state where the transmissions can be received; or (5) any state where authorised radio communication is suffering interference[2]. On the high seas, any such state may arrest any person or ship engaged in unauthorised broadcasting and seize the broadcasting apparatus[3].

1   United Nations Convention on the Law of the Sea (Montego Bay, 10 December 1982; TS 81 (1999); Cmnd 4524) art 109 para 1. For the purposes of the Convention, 'unauthorised broadcasting' means the transmission of sound radio or television broadcasts from a ship or installation on the high seas intended for reception by the general public contrary to international regulations, but excluding the transmission of distress calls: art 109 para 2. As to the high seas see PARA 147 et seq. As to the domestic legislation see TELECOMMUNICATIONS AND BROADCASTING vol 45(1) (2005 Reissue) PARA 582.
2   United Nations Convention on the Law of the Sea art 109 para 3.
3   United Nations Convention on the Law of the Sea art 109 para 4. An arrest or seizure must be in conformity with art 110: art 109 para 4; and see PARA 148.

9. AIR SPACE, OUTER SPACE, AND ANTARCTICA

(1) AIR SPACE

(i) In general

197. Sovereignty in air space. The sovereignty of a state extends to the air space above its land territory and its territorial sea[1]. Thus, in the absence of a treaty limiting its sovereignty in this regard, a state is free to permit or to forbid the flight of foreign aircraft through its air space[2].

1　This principle is part of customary international law and is recognised in major international conventions, notably the International Convention for the Regulation of Aerial Navigation (Paris, 13 October 1919; TS (1922); Cmd 1609), which was superseded by the Convention on International Civil Aviation (Chicago Convention) (Chicago, 7 December 1944; TS 8 (1953); Cmd 8742), to which the United Kingdom is a party and which recognises that every state has complete and exclusive sovereignty over the air space above its territory (art 1), which is deemed to be the land areas and territorial waters adjacent to it under the sovereignty, suzerainty, protection or mandate of the state (art 2). The United Nations Convention on the Law of the Sea (Montego Bay, 10 December 1982; TS 81 (1999); Cmnd 4524) also provides that the sovereignty of a coastal state extends to the air space over the territorial sea (art 2(2)). As to the Chicago Convention see AIR LAW vol 2 (2008) PARA 2 et seq. There is no definition in international law of the upper limit of air space, and there is no right of innocent passage through the air space above the territorial sea akin to that through the territorial sea itself. As to the territorial sea see PARA 123 et seq. As to innocent passage see PARA 133. As for transit passage through straits used for international navigation see PARA 143.
2　The leading treaty which restricts the exercise of these sovereign rights is the Chicago Convention: see AIR LAW vol 2 (2008) PARA 2 et seq.

198. Jurisdiction in international law over offences on aircraft. Jurisdiction in international law over offences against aircraft is exercised on general principles[1]. The state of registration of the aircraft and the state of the nationality of the offender thus have jurisdiction. The United Kingdom is a party to three international conventions dealing with offences on or against aircraft, namely the Tokyo Convention[2], the Hague Convention[3] and the Montreal Convention[4].

1　See PARA 219 et seq.
2　Ie the Convention on Offences and Certain Other Acts Committed on Board Aircraft (Tokyo Convention) (Tokyo, 14 September 1963; TS 126 (1969); Cmnd 4230), which entered into force on 4 December 1969. See PARA 199 et seq; and AIR LAW vol 2 (2008) PARA 13.
3　Ie the Convention for the Suppression of Unlawful Seizure of Aircraft (Hague Convention) (The Hague, 16 December 1970; TS 39 (1972); Cmnd 4956), which entered into force on 14 October 1971. See PARAS 783–784; and AIR LAW vol 2 (2008) PARA 14.
4　Ie the Convention for the Suppression of Unlawful Acts against the Safety of Civil Aviation (Montreal Convention) (Montreal, 23 September 1971; TS 10 (1974); Cmnd 5524), which entered into force generally on 24 January 1973 and as respects the United Kingdom on 24 November 1974. See PARAS 205–206; and AIR LAW vol 2 (2008) PARA 15.

(ii) The Tokyo Convention

199. Application of the Tokyo Convention. The Tokyo Convention[1] applies in respect of offences against penal law and acts which, whether or not they are offences, may jeopardise the safety of aircraft or persons or property in them or which jeopardise good order and discipline on board[2]. The Convention applies in respect of any offences committed or acts done by a person on board any aircraft registered in a contracting state while the aircraft is in flight, or on the surface of the high seas or of any other area outside the territory of any state[3]. It does not apply to aircraft used in military, customs or police services[4].

1　Ie the Convention on Offences and Certain Other Acts Committed on Board Aircraft (Tokyo Convention) (Tokyo, 14 September 1963; TS 126 (1969); Cmnd 4230).

2　Convention on Offences and Certain Other Acts Committed on Board Aircraft art 1 para 1. For the law enacted in the United Kingdom see the Civil Aviation Act 1982; and AIR LAW vol 2 (2008) PARA 13.

3　Convention on Offences and Certain Other Acts Committed on Board Aircraft art 1 para 2. This is subject to exceptions in Ch III (arts 5–10) relating to powers of the aircraft commander. An aircraft is considered to be 'in flight' from the moment when power is applied for the purpose of take-off until the moment when the landing run ends: art 1 para 3. Cf PARA 203.

4　Convention on Offences and Certain Other Acts Committed on Board Aircraft art 1 para 4.

200.　Jurisdiction over offenders.　The state of registration is competent to exercise jurisdiction over offences and acts committed on board the aircraft[1]. Each contracting state must take such measures as may be necessary to establish its jurisdiction as the state of registration over offences committed on board[2]. Criminal jurisdiction exercised over an offender in accordance with national law is specifically not excluded[3].

1　Convention on Offences and Certain Other Acts Committed on Board Aircraft (Tokyo Convention) (Tokyo, 14 September 1963; TS 126 (1969); Cmnd 4230) art 3 para 1. Offences committed on board an aircraft registered in a contracting state are to be treated for purposes of extradition as if they had been committed not only in the place where they have occurred but also in the territory of the state of registration: art 16 para 1. As to the jurisdiction over offenders under the Hague Convention see PARA 204. As to the jurisdiction over offenders under the Montreal Convention see PARA 206.

2　Convention on Offences and Certain Other Acts Committed on Board Aircraft art 3 para 2.

3　Convention on Offences and Certain Other Acts Committed on Board Aircraft art 3 para 3.

201.　Interference with aircraft in flight.　A state which is not the state of registration may not interfere with an aircraft in flight[1] in order to exercise its criminal jurisdiction over an offence committed on board[2] except where: (1) the offence has its effect on the territory of such state[3]; (2) it has been committed by or against a national or permanent resident of such state[4]; (3) the offence is against the security of such state[5]; (4) it consists of a breach of any rules or regulations relating to the flight or manoeuvre of aircraft in force in such state[6]; and (5) the exercise of jurisdiction is necessary to ensure the observance of any obligation of such state under a multilateral international agreement[7].

1　As to the meaning of 'in flight' see PARA 199 note 3.

2　Convention on Offences and Certain Other Acts Committed on Board Aircraft (Tokyo Convention) (Tokyo, 14 September 1963; TS 126 (1969); Cmnd 4230) art 4. In taking any measures for investigation or arrest or in otherwise exercising jurisdiction in connection with any offence, states must pay due regard to the safety and other interests of air navigation and so act as to avoid unnecessary delay of the aircraft passengers, crew or cargo: art 17.

3　Convention on Offences and Certain Other Acts Committed on Board Aircraft art 4(a).

4　Convention on Offences and Certain Other Acts Committed on Board Aircraft art 4(b).

5　Convention on Offences and Certain Other Acts Committed on Board Aircraft art 4(c).

6　Convention on Offences and Certain Other Acts Committed on Board Aircraft art 4(d).

7　Convention on Offences and Certain Other Acts Committed on Board Aircraft art 4(e).

202.　Restoration of aircraft.　When a person on board has unlawfully committed by force or threat of force an act, seizure or other wrongful exercise of control of an aircraft in flight[1], or where such act is about to be committed, states must take all appropriate measures to restore control of the aircraft to its lawful commander or to preserve his control of it[2]. In such cases the passengers and crew must be permitted to continue their journey as soon as practicable and the aircraft and cargo must be returned to the persons lawfully entitled to possession[3].

1   As to the meaning of 'in flight' see PARA 199 note 3.
2   Convention on Offences and Certain Other Acts Committed on Board Aircraft (Tokyo Convention) (Tokyo, 14 September 1963; TS 126 (1969); Cmnd 4230) art 11 para 1.
3   Convention on Offences and Certain Other Acts Committed on Board Aircraft art 11 para 2. As to the restoration of aircraft see PARAS 204 note 10, 206.

(iii) The Hague Convention

203. Application of the Hague Convention. The Hague Convention[1], which is concerned with hijacking of aircraft, provides that any person who on board an aircraft in flight[2] unlawfully, by force, threat of force or any other form of intimidation, seizes or exercises control of that aircraft or attempts to do so, or is an accomplice of a person who performs or attempts to perform any such act, commits an offence[3]. The contracting states undertake to make the offence punishable by severe penalties[4]. It does not apply to aircraft used in military, customs or police services[5].

1   Ie the Convention for the Suppression of Unlawful Seizure of Aircraft (Hague Convention) (The Hague, 16 December 1970; TS 39 (1972); Cmnd 4956). The Convention is implemented into the law of the United Kingdom by the Aviation Security Act 1982: see AIR LAW vol 2 (2008) PARA 14.
2   An aircraft is deemed to be 'in flight' at any time from the moment when all its external doors are closed following embarkation until the moment when any such door is opened for disembarkation; and, in case of a forced landing, the flight is deemed to continue until the competent authorities take over the responsibility for the aircraft and for persons and property on board: Convention for the Suppression of Unlawful Seizure of Aircraft art 3 para 1. Cf PARA 205 note 2.
3   Convention for the Suppression of Unlawful Seizure of Aircraft art 1. The Convention only applies if the place of take-off or the place of actual landing of the aircraft is situated outside the territory of the state of registration, although it is immaterial whether the aircraft is engaged in an international or domestic flight: art 3 para 3 (but see art 3 para 4 for an exception). Articles 6–8, 10 (which concern criminal jurisdiction over the offender and extradition) apply whatever the place of actual landing, if the offender is found in the territory of a state other than the state of registration: art 3 para 5.
4   Convention for the Suppression of Unlawful Seizure of Aircraft art 2.
5   Convention for the Suppression of Unlawful Seizure of Aircraft art 3 para 2.

204. Jurisdiction over offenders. A contracting state must take the measures necessary to establish its jurisdiction over the offence when: (1) it is committed on board an aircraft registered in that state[1]; (2) the aircraft lands on its territory with the alleged offender on board[2]; or (3) the offence is committed on board an aircraft leased without crew to a lessee who has his principal place of business or, if none, his permanent residence in that state[3]; and (4) the offender is present in its territory and it does not extradite[4] him to one of the states mentioned in heads (1) to (3) above[5]. The state where he is present must take the offender into custody and make a preliminary inquiry[6]. It must inform the state of registration and of the offender's nationality and the state mentioned in head (3) above and any other interested state, and indicate whether it intends to exercise jurisdiction[7]. If it does not extradite the offender it must submit the case to its competent authorities for prosecution[8]. The Hague Convention provides for assistance in criminal proceedings[9] and for making reports to the International Civil Aviation Organisation[10]. Criminal jurisdiction exercised over an offender in accordance with national law is specifically not excluded[11].

1 Convention for the Suppression of Unlawful Seizure of Aircraft (Hague Convention) (The Hague, 16 December 1970; TS 39 (1972); Cmnd 4956) art 4 para 1(a). As to the jurisdiction of the state of registration in cases of joint operating organisations or international agencies see art 5.

2 Convention for the Suppression of Unlawful Seizure of Aircraft art 4 para 1(b).

3 Convention for the Suppression of Unlawful Seizure of Aircraft art 4 para 1(c).

4 Convention for the Suppression of Unlawful Seizure of Aircraft art 8 creates an obligation to make hijacking an extraditable offence. As to extradition generally see EXTRADITION.

5 Convention for the Suppression of Unlawful Seizure of Aircraft art 4 para 2.

6 Convention for the Suppression of Unlawful Seizure of Aircraft art 6 paras 1, 2.

7 Convention for the Suppression of Unlawful Seizure of Aircraft art 6 para 4.

8 Convention for the Suppression of Unlawful Seizure of Aircraft art 7. This obligation is without any exception whatsoever and applies whether or not the offence was committed within its territory: art 7.

9 Convention for the Suppression of Unlawful Seizure of Aircraft art 10 para 1.

10 Convention for the Suppression of Unlawful Seizure of Aircraft art 11. The Convention contains provisions with respect to the restoration of aircraft: see art 9. As to the restoration of aircraft see PARAS 202 note 3, 206. As to the International Civil Aviation Organisation see AIR LAW vol 2 (2008) PARA 20 et seq.

11 Convention for the Suppression of Unlawful Seizure of Aircraft art 4 para 3.

(iv) The Montreal Convention

205. Application of the Montreal Convention. The Convention for the Suppression of Unlawful Acts Against the Safety of Civil Aviation[1] provides that a person commits an offence if he unlawfully and intentionally: (1) performs an act of violence against a person on board an aircraft in flight[2] if that act is likely to endanger its safety[3]; (2) destroys an aircraft in service or damages it so as to render it incapable of flight or so as to endanger its safety in flight[4]; (3) places, or causes to be placed, on such an aircraft any device or substance which is likely to destroy it or damage it[5]; (4) destroys or damages air navigation facilities or interferes with their operation so as to endanger the safety of an aircraft in flight[6]; (5) communicates information knowing it to be false, thereby endangering the safety of an aircraft in flight[7]; (6) using any device, substance, or weapon performs an act of violence against an airport serving international civil aviation which causes or is likely to cause serious injury or death, or destroys or seriously damages the facilities of an airport serving international civil aviation or aircraft not in service located thereon or disrupts the services of the airport, if such an act endangers or is likely to endanger safety at that airport[8]. An offence is also committed by anyone who attempts to commit any of these offences or is an accomplice of a person who commits or attempts to commit such an offence[9]. The contracting states undertake to make these offences punishable by severe penalties[10]. The Convention does not apply to aircraft used in military, customs or police services[11].

1 Ie the Convention for the Suppression of Unlawful Acts Against the Safety of Civil Aviation (Montreal Convention) (Montreal, 23 September 1971; TS 10 (1974); Cmnd 5524). The Convention is implemented into the law of the United Kingdom by the Aviation Security Act 1982: see AIR LAW vol 2 (2008) PARA 15.

2 An aircraft is deemed to be 'in flight' at any time from the moment when all its external doors are closed following embarkation until the moment when any such door is opened for disembarkation; and, in case of a forced landing, the flight is deemed to continue until the competent authorities take over the responsibility for the aircraft and for persons and property on board: Convention for the Suppression of Unlawful Acts Against the Safety of Civil Aviation art 2(a). Cf PARA 203 note 3. Additionally, an aircraft is deemed to be in service from the beginning of the pre-flight preparation by ground personnel or by the crew for a specific flight until 24 hours after any landing; and the period of service in any event extends for the entire period during which the aircraft is in flight: art 2(b).

3 Convention for the Suppression of Unlawful Acts Against the Safety of Civil Aviation art 1(a).
4 Convention for the Suppression of Unlawful Acts Against the Safety of Civil Aviation art 1(b).
5 Convention for the Suppression of Unlawful Acts Against the Safety of Civil Aviation art 1(c).
6 Convention for the Suppression of Unlawful Acts Against the Safety of Civil Aviation art 1(d).
7 Convention for the Suppression of Unlawful Acts Against the Safety of Civil Aviation art 1(e).
8 Convention for the Suppression of Unlawful Acts Against the Safety of Civil Aviation art 1 para 1 (added by Protocol (Montreal, 24 February 1988; TS 20 (1991); Cm 1470)).
9 Convention for the Suppression of Unlawful Acts Against the Safety of Civil Aviation art 1 para 2.
10 Convention for the Suppression of Unlawful Acts Against the Safety of Civil Aviation art 3.
11 Convention for the Suppression of Unlawful Acts Against the Safety of Civil Aviation art 4 para 1. For further restrictions see art 4 paras 2–6.

206. Jurisdiction over offenders. The Montreal Convention[1] contains provisions similar, mutatis mutandis, to the Hague Convention[2] as regards jurisdiction over offenders, extradition, assistance in criminal proceedings and reports to the International Civil Aviation Organisation[3]. There is a similar obligation in regard to the restoration of aircraft[4]. The contracting states are under an obligation, in accordance with international and national law, to take all practicable measures for the purpose of preventing the offences created by the Montreal Convention[5].

1 Ie the Convention for the Suppression of Unlawful Acts against the Safety of Civil Aviation (Montreal Convention) (Montreal, 23 September 1971; TS 10 (1974); Cmnd 5524).
2 Ie the Convention for the Suppression of Unlawful Seizure of Aircraft (Hague Convention) (The Hague, 16 December 1970; TS 39 (1972); Cmnd 4956).
3 See the Convention for the Suppression of Unlawful Acts Against the Safety of Civil Aviation arts 5–9, 11–13. Cf the provisions set out in PARA 204.
4 Convention for the Suppression of Unlawful Acts Against the Safety of Civil Aviation art 10 para 2. Cf PARA 204.
5 Convention for the Suppression of Unlawful Acts Against the Safety of Civil Aviation art 10 para 1.

(2) OUTER SPACE

207. International law in outer space. The General Assembly of the United Nations has accepted the principle that international law, including the Charter of the United Nations[1], applies to outer space and celestial bodies[2]. The United Kingdom is a party to the Outer Space Treaty[3], to the Agreement on the Rescue of Astronauts, the Return of Astronauts and the Return of Objects launched into Outer Space[4], the Convention on International Liability for Damage caused by Space Objects[5], and the Convention on Registration of Objects launched into Outer Space[6]. There is also an Agreement governing Activities of States on the Moon and other Celestial Bodies[7].

1 See the Charter of the United Nations (San Francisco, 26 June 1945; TS 67 (1946); Cmd 7015).
2 General Assembly Resolution 1721 (XVI) of 20 December 1961.
3 See the Treaty on Principles governing the Activities of States in the Exploration and Use of Outer Space including the Moon and other Celestial Bodies (London, Moscow and Washington, 27 January 1967; TS 10 (1968); Cmnd 3519). See PARA 208.
4 See the Agreement on the Rescue of Astronauts, the Return of Astronauts and the Return of Objects launched into Outer Space (London, Moscow and Washington, 22 April 1968; TS 56 (1969); Cmnd 3997).
5 See the Convention on International Liability for Damage caused by Space Objects (London, Moscow and Washington, 29 March 1972; TS 16 (1974); Cmnd 5551).
6 See the Convention on Registration of Objects launched into Outer Space (New York, 14 January 1975; TS 70 (1978); Cmnd 7271).

7   See the Agreement governing Activities of States on the Moon and other Celestial Bodies 1979.
     The Agreement can be found in 18 ILM (1979) 1434. See further 1 Oppenheim's International
     Law (9th Edn) 836–838.

208.   The Outer Space Treaty.   Under the provisions of the Outer Space
Treaty[1], the exploration and use of outer space is to be carried out for the benefit
and in the interests of all countries[2]. Outer space is free for exploration and use
by all states on a basis of equality and in accordance with international law;
there is freedom of access to all areas of celestial bodies, and freedom of scientific
research; and states must facilitate co-operation in scientific investigation[3]. Outer
space, including the moon and other celestial bodies, is not subject to national
appropriation by claim of sovereignty, by means of use, occupation or by any
other means[4].

1   Ie the Treaty on Principles governing the Activities of States in the Exploration and Use of Outer
     Space including the Moon and other Celestial Bodies (London, Moscow and Washington,
     27 January 1967; TS 10 (1968); Cmnd 3519).
2   Treaty on Principles governing the Activities of States in the Exploration and Use of Outer Space
     including the Moon and other Celestial Bodies art I.
3   Treaty on Principles governing the Activities of States in the Exploration and Use of Outer Space
     including the Moon and other Celestial Bodies art I. See also art II.
4   Treaty on Principles governing the Activities of States in the Exploration and Use of Outer Space
     including the Moon and other Celestial Bodies art III. There is no definition in international law
     of the lower limit of outer space.

209.   Demilitarisation.   The states parties to the Outer Space Treaty[1]
undertake not to place in orbit round the earth any nuclear weapons or weapons
of mass destruction, install them on celestial bodies or otherwise station them in
outer space[2]. The moon and other celestial bodies must be used exclusively for
peaceful purposes; military bases, installations and fortifications testing military
manoeuvres thereon are forbidden[3].

1   Ie the Treaty on Principles governing the Activities of States in the Exploration and Use of Outer
     Space including the Moon and other Celestial Bodies (London, Moscow and Washington,
     27 January 1967; TS 10 (1968); Cmnd 3519).
2   Treaty on Principles governing the Activities of States in the Exploration and Use of Outer Space
     including the Moon and other Celestial Bodies art IV. For provisions for observation and
     inspection see arts X-XII. See also General Assembly Resolution 1884 (XVIII) of 17 October
     1963. Nuclear testing in outer space is forbidden by the Treaty banning Nuclear Weapon Tests
     in the Atmosphere, in Outer Space and under Water (Moscow, 5th August 1963; TS 3 (1964);
     Cmnd 2245) art I para 1(a).
3   Treaty on Principles governing the Activities of States in the Exploration and Use of Outer Space
     including the Moon and other Celestial Bodies art IV.

210.   State responsibility.   International responsibility for activities in outer
space is borne by states parties to the Outer Space Treaty[1] whether these are
carried out by governmental agencies or non-governmental entities[2]. The
activities of non-governmental entities require authorisation and supervision by
their state[3]. When activities are carried out by international organisations,
responsibility for compliance with the Treaty is borne by the international
organisation and the states parties to the Treaty participating in such
organisation[4]. A state which launches or procures the launching of an object into
outer space, and each state from whose territory or facilities an object is
launched, is internationally liable for damage to another state or to its natural or
juridical persons on earth, in the air space or in outer space[5].

1   Ie the Treaty on Principles governing the Activities of States in the Exploration and Use of Outer
     Space including the Moon and other Celestial Bodies (London, Moscow and Washington,
     27 January 1967; TS 10 (1968); Cmnd 3519).

2   Treaty on Principles governing the Activities of States in the Exploration and Use of Outer Space including the Moon and other Celestial Bodies art VI.

3   Treaty on Principles governing the Activities of States in the Exploration and Use of Outer Space including the Moon and other Celestial Bodies art VI.

4   Treaty on Principles governing the Activities of States in the Exploration and Use of Outer Space including the Moon and other Celestial Bodies art VI. See also arts IX, X, XIII.

5   Treaty on Principles governing the Activities of States in the Exploration and Use of Outer Space including the Moon and other Celestial Bodies art VII (supplemented by the Convention on International Liability for Damage caused by Space Objects (London, Moscow and Washington, 29 March 1972; TS 16 (1974); Cmnd 5551), which imposes strict liability to pay compensation for damage caused by a space object to something on the surface of the earth or to aircraft in flight (art II), and liability on the basis of fault in other cases (art III).

211. Enforcement of United Kingdom's international obligations. The Outer Space Act 1986[1] confers licensing powers on the Secretary of State to secure compliance with international obligations of the United Kingdom[2] with respect to the launching or procuring the launching of a space object[3], operating a space object[4] and any other activity carried on[5] in outer space[6].

1   The Outer Space Act 1986 came into force on 31 July 1989: see s 15(1); and the Outer Space Act 1986 (Commencement) Order 1989, SI 1989/1097. The Act extends to England and Wales, Scotland and Northern Ireland: Outer Space Act 1986 s 15(5). The Act also extends to bodies incorporated under the law of the Bailiwicks of Guernsey and Jersey, to the Isle of Man, Gibraltar, Cayman Islands and Bermuda, subject, in each case, to specified exceptions and modifications: see ss 2(3), 15(6); and the Outer Space Act 1986 (Guernsey) Order 1990, SI 1990/248; the Outer Space Act 1986 (Isle of Man) Order 1990, SI 1990/596; the Outer Space Act 1986 (Jersey) Order 1990, SI 1990/597; the Outer Space Act 1986 (Gibraltar) Order 1990, SI 1996/1916; the Outer Space Act 1986 (Cayman Islands) Order 1998, SI 1998/2563; and the Outer Space Act 1986 (Bermuda) Order 2006, SI 2006/2959.

2   As to the international obligations see PARA 207. As to the Secretary of State see PARA 29.

3   Outer Space Act 1986 s 1(a). 'Space object' includes component parts of a space object, its launch vehicle and the component parts of that: s 13(1).

4   Outer Space Act 1986 s 1(b).

5   A person carries on an activity if he causes it to occur or is responsible for its continuing: Outer Space Act 1986 s 13(2).

6   Outer Space Act 1986 s 1(c). 'Outer space' includes the moon and other celestial bodies: s 13(1).

212. Licensing of activities. A person[1] must not carry on any activity[2] unless a licence has been granted by the Secretary of State[3], except where the person is acting as employee or agent of another[4] or in the case of activities in respect of which arrangements have been made between the United Kingdom and another country to secure compliance with its international obligations[5]. If it appears to the Secretary of State that an unlicensed activity is being carried on, the Secretary of State may give such directions as are necessary to secure compliance with the United Kingdom's international obligations[6].

The Secretary of State may grant a licence if he thinks fit[7], but he must not grant a licence unless he is satisfied that the activity to be authorised: (1) will not jeopardise public health or safety of persons or property[8]; (2) will be consistent with the United Kingdom's international obligations[9]; and (3) will not impair the United Kingdom's national security[10]. The Secretary of State may make regulations as to the form and procedure of applications and to prescribe fees in connection with them[11].

A licence must describe the authorised activities and is granted for such period and subject to such conditions as the Secretary of State thinks fit[12]. A licence may in particular contain conditions with regard to the supervision and conduct of activities, insurance against liability in respect of damage suffered by third parties, disposal of the payload on the termination of operations and termination of the licence on the occurrence of a specified event[13]. If it appears to the Secretary of State that an activity is being carried on in contravention of the conditions of the licence, the Secretary of State may give such directions as are necessary to secure compliance with the conditions of the licence[14].

A licence may be transferred with the written consent of the Secretary of State and in other such cases as may be prescribed[15]. The Secretary of State may revoke, vary or suspend a licence with the consent of the licensee where it appears to the Secretary of State that a condition or regulation has not been complied with[16] or that it is necessary to make the revocation, variation or suspension of the licence in the interests of public health or national security or to comply with any international obligation of the United Kingdom[17].

1 Ie a United Kingdom national, Scottish firm or a body incorporated in the United Kingdom: Outer Space Act 1986 s 2(1). 'United Kingdom national' means an individual who is: (1) a British citizen, a British overseas territories citizen, a British National (Overseas) or a British Overseas citizen; (2) a person who under the British Nationality Act 1981 is a British subject; or (3) a British protected person within the meaning of the British Nationality Act 1981: Outer Space Act 1986 s 2(2) (amended by virtue of the British Overseas Territories Act 2002 s 1(2)). As to British nationality see BRITISH NATIONALITY, IMMIGRATION AND ASYLUM.

2 Ie an activity to which the Outer Space Act 1986 applies: see PARA 211.

3 Outer Space Act 1986 s 3(1). As to the Secretary of State see PARA 29.

4 Outer Space Act 1986 s 3(2) (a).

5 Outer Space Act 1986 s 3(2) (b). The Secretary of State may also by order except other persons or activities if he is satisfied that the requirement of a licence is not necessary to secure compliance with the United Kingdom's international obligations: s 3(3).

6 Outer Space Act 1986 s 8(1). He may, in particular, give such directions as appear to him necessary to secure the cessation of the activity or the disposal of any space object: s 8(2). The Secretary of State may apply for an injunction to secure compliance with a direction: see s 8(3). Where an unlicensed activity is being carried on or a direction has not been complied with, a justice of the peace may issue a warrant authorising a named person to take direct action to secure compliance with the United Kingdom's international obligations: see s 9.

7 Outer Space Act 1986 s 4(1).

8 Outer Space Act 1986 s 4(2)(a).

9 Outer Space Act 1986 s 4(2)(b).

10 Outer Space Act 1986 s 4(2)(c).

11 See the Outer Space Act 1986 s 4(3); and the Outer Space Act 1986 (Fees) Regulations 1989, SI 1989/1306 (amended by SI 1993/406; SI 1998/2032). The Secretary of State may make regulations prescribing anything required or authorised to be prescribed under the Outer Space Act 1986, and generally for carrying the Act into effect: s 11(1). Such regulations must be made by statutory instrument: see s 11(2).

12 Outer Space Act 1986 s 5(1).

13 See the Outer Space Act 1986 s 5(2).

14 Outer Space Act 1986 s 8(1). As to enforcement of directions and warrants issued by a justice of the peace authorising direct action see ss 8, 9.

15 Outer Space Act 1986 s 6(1).

16 Outer Space Act 1986 s 6(2)(a).

17 Outer Space Act 1986 s 6(2)(b). The suspension, revocation or expiry of a licence does not affect the obligations of the licensee under the conditions of the licence: s 6(3).

213. Offences. It is an offence to: (1) carry on an unlicensed activity[1]; (2) make knowingly or recklessly a statement which is false in a material particular, for the purpose of obtaining a licence[2]; (3) fail to comply with the conditions of the licence[3]; (4) fail to comply with a direction[4]; (5) intentionally obstruct a person in the exercise of the powers conferred by a warrant authorising direct action[5]; (6) fail to comply with any regulations[6]. A person[7] committing such an offence is liable on conviction on indictment to a fine and on summary conviction to a fine not exceeding the statutory maximum[8]. It is a defence (except in relation to heads (2) and (5) above) for the accused to show that he used all due diligence and took all reasonable precautions to avoid commission of the offence[9].

Where it is proved that an offence committed by a body corporate was committed with the consent or connivance of, or is attributable to neglect by, a director[10], secretary or other similar officer of that body corporate, or a person purporting to act in any such capacity, he as well as the body corporate is guilty of the offence and liable to be proceeded against and punished accordingly[11].

1   Outer Space Act 1986 s 12(1)(a). An unlicensed activity is an activity carried on in contravention of s 3 (the licensing requirement): see PARA 212.
2   Outer Space Act 1986 s 12(1)(b).
3   Outer Space Act 1986 s 12(1)(c).
4   Outer Space Act 1986 s 12(1)(d). The direction referred to in the text is a direction under s 8: see PARA 212.
5   Outer Space Act 1986 s 12(1)(e). As to warrants authorising direct action see s 9.
6   Outer Space Act 1986 s 12(1)(f).
7   Persons against whom criminal proceedings may be brought are not restricted to persons in the Outer Space Act 1986 s 2 (see PARA 212): s 12(7). As to persons to whom this Act does not apply in respect of activities carried on outside the United Kingdom see s 12(6). Proceedings for an offence committed outside the United Kingdom may be taken and the offence may for incidental purposes be treated as having been committed in any place in the United Kingdom: s 12(4). As to the meaning of 'United Kingdom' see PARA 30 note 3.
8   Outer Space Act 1986 s 12(2). As to the statutory maximum see SENTENCING AND DISPOSITION OF OFFENDERS vol 92 (2010) PARA 140.
9   Outer Space Act 1986 s 12(5).
10 'Director', in relation to a body corporate whose affairs are managed by the members, means a member of the body corporate: Outer Space Act 1986 s 12(3).
11 Outer Space Act 1986 s 12(3).

214.   Register of space objects.   The Secretary of State must maintain a register of space objects[1] containing such particulars of space objects as the Secretary of State considers appropriate to comply with the United Kingdom's international obligations[2]. Any person may inspect a copy of the register on payment of the appropriate fee[3].

1   Outer Space Act 1986 s 7(1). As to the meaning of 'space object' see PARA 211 note 3. As to the Secretary of State see PARA 29.
2   Outer Space Act 1986 s 7(2).
3   Outer Space Act 1986 s 7(3).

215.   Obligation to indemnify the government against claims.   A person[1] must indemnify the United Kingdom government against any claims brought against the government in respect of damage or loss[2] arising out of activities carried on by him[3].

1   As to the persons to whom the Outer Space Act 1986 applies see PARA 212 note 1. Section 10 does not apply to a person acting as employee or agent of another: s 10(2)(a).
2   The Outer Space Act 1986 s 10 does not apply to damage or loss resulting from anything done on the instructions of the Secretary of State: s 10(2)(b). As to the Secretary of State see PARA 29.
3   Outer Space Act 1986 s 10(1).

216.   Astronauts.   States must render astronauts who land on the territory of a state, or on the high seas, all possible assistance in the event of accident, distress or emergency; and the astronauts must be safely and promptly returned to the state of registry of their space vehicle[1]. In carrying out their activities, astronauts must assist astronauts of other states; and states must make public any phenomena they discover in outer space which could be a danger to astronauts[2].

1 Treaty on Principles governing the Activities of States in the Exploration and Use of Outer Space including the Moon and other Celestial Bodies (London, Moscow and Washington, 27 January 1967; TS 10 (1968); Cmnd 3519) art v This is supplemented by the Agreement on the Rescue of Astronauts, the Return of Astronauts and the Return of Objects launched into Outer Space (London, Moscow and Washington, 22 April 1968; TS 56 (1969); Cmnd 3997).

2 Treaty on Principles governing the Activities of States in the Exploration and Use of Outer Space including the Moon and other Celestial Bodies art V.

217. Jurisdiction over space objects. A state on whose registry an object launched into outer space is carried retains jurisdiction and control over it and over any of its personnel while in outer space or on a celestial body[1]. Ownership of such objects is not affected by their presence in those places or by their return to earth, and, if found beyond the limits of the state of registration, they must be returned to that state[2].

1 Treaty on Principles governing the Activities of States in the Exploration and Use of Outer Space including the Moon and other Celestial Bodies (London, Moscow and Washington, 27 January 1967; TS 10 (1968); Cmnd 3519) art VIII. See the Agreement on the Rescue of Astronauts, the Return of Astronauts and the Return of Objects launched into Outer Space (London, Moscow and Washington, 22 April 1968; TS 56 (1969); Cmnd 3997).

2 See note 1.

(3) ANTARCTICA

218. The Antarctic Treaty. Certain states (including the United Kingdom[1]) have laid claim to sovereignty over various sectors of the continent of Antarctica. Some of these claims have been recognised by some other states; others have not[2].

The United Kingdom is a party to the Antarctic Treaty[3] and the Protocol on Environmental Protection to the Antarctic Treaty[4] and has implemented their provisions in the Antarctic Act 1994[5]. The United Kingdom is also a party to the Convention on the Conservation of Antarctic Marine Living Resources[6], which is implemented by EC Regulations[7].

No acts or activities taking place in Antarctica, while the Antarctic Treaty is in force, are to constitute a basis for asserting, supporting or denying a claim to sovereignty or for creating any rights of sovereignty; no new claim may be asserted while the treaty is in force[8], and existing rights are preserved[9]. Antarctica is to be used for peaceful purposes only, and any measures of a military nature are prohibited[10]. There is provision for a system of inspection by the appointment of observers[11]. Observers are subject only to the jurisdiction of their own states in respect of acts or omissions while they are in Antarctica for the purpose of exercising their functions[12]. The states parties to the Treaty are to agree on measures by way of recommendations adopted at consultation meetings[13].

1 Examples of British claims include the Letters Patent dated 21 July 1908 and 28 March 1917, concerning the Falkland Islands Dependencies. See generally Waldock, Disputed Sovereignty in the Falkland Islands Dependencies, 25 BYIL 311. The British Antarctic Territory is now a British overseas territory constituted by the British Antarctic Territory Order 1989, SI 1989/842: see COMMONWEALTH vol 13 (2009) PARA 855.

2 In 1955 the United Kingdom instituted proceedings against Argentina and Chile before the International Court of Justice in respect of claims to overlapping sectors of Antarctica. Failing any acceptance by the respondent states of the jurisdiction of the court, the applications were removed from the court's list in 1956: see *Antarctica Cases (United Kingdom v Argentina)* ICJ Reports 1956, 12; and *(United Kingdom v Chile)* ICJ Reports 1956, 15.

3 Antarctic Treaty (Washington, 1 December 1959; TS 97 (1961); Cmnd 1535). The Treaty entered into force on 23 June 1961. As to the treaty's duration see art XII.

4   Ie the Protocol on Environmental Protection to the Antarctic Treaty (Madrid, 4 October 1991; TS 6 (1999); Cm 4256).

5   See ANIMALS vol 2 (2008) PARAS 990–993.

6   Ie the Convention on the Conservation of Antarctic Marine Living Resources (Canberra, 7 May 1980; TS 48 (1982); Cmnd 8714).

7   See EC Council Decision 1981/691 (OJ L252, 5.9.1981, pp 26–35) on the conclusion of the Convention on the conservation of Antarctic marine living resources; EC Council Regulation 1035/2001 (OJ L145, 31.5.2001, pp 1–9) establishing a catch documentation scheme for Dissostichus spp; EC Council Regulation 600/2004 (OJ L97, 1.4.2004, p 1–15) laying down certain technical measures applicable to fishing activities in the area covered by the Convention on the conservation of Antarctic marine living resources; and EC Council Regulation 601/2004 (OJ L97, 1.4.2004, pp 16–29) laying down certain control measures applicable to fishing activities in the area covered by the Convention on the conservation of Antarctic marine living resources.

8   Antarctic Treaty art IV para 2.

9   Antarctic Treaty art IV para 1.

10 Antarctic Treaty art I. This includes the establishment of military bases and fortifications, manoeuvres and the testing of weapons (art I para 1), but does not preclude the use of military personnel or equipment for scientific and other peaceful purposes (art I para 2).

11 Antarctic Treaty art VII.

12 Antarctic Treaty art VIII. See also COMMONWEALTH.

13 Antarctic Treaty art IX.

10. JURISDICTION

(1) GENERAL PRINCIPLES

219. Jurisdiction in international law. The jurisdiction of a state in international law denotes the competence of the state to govern persons and property by its domestic law. It includes: (1) competence to prescribe rules of conduct[1]; (2) competence to enforce those rules of conduct by executive action[2]; and (3) competence to try individuals and hear causes of action by judicial means[3]. The rules of international law concerning jurisdiction are not concerned with the substantive municipal law of a state, which is usually a matter of its domestic jurisdiction. The international law on jurisdiction generally confers powers on a state to act, although states are increasingly bound by international law to exercise their powers in particular ways, generally by the enactment of appropriate national laws. Some jurisdictional powers may be exclusive to one state; others may be exercised concurrently with the jurisdiction of other states[4]. Although the basic principles of the law on jurisdiction are established by customary international law, there is increasing action under treaty, sometimes specific to particular crimes or categories of crimes, most notably in counter-terrorism treaties[5]. Human rights law has an impact on the exercise of states' jurisdiction[6]. Whilst jurisdiction may be concerned with civil matters or criminal matters, only criminal matters are discussed in the following paragraphs[7].

1 See PARA 221 et seq.
2 For example, investigation and the detention of suspects and defendants: see PARA 230.
3 See PARAS 221, 232 et seq. For a discussion of the international rules of jurisdiction generally see the *Lotus Case* PCIJ Ser A No 10 (1927).

4 Prescriptive jurisdiction is concurrent, so that where a national of one state indulges in conduct in another state and the act is contrary to the law of both states then both states have jurisdiction. A particular example is where a national of one state commits an offence on board a merchant vessel of another state, at a time when that vessel is in a port of a third state. All three states may have prescriptive jurisdiction over the conduct. As to jurisdiction over offences committed on merchant ships see PARAS 138, 150. Concurrency of judicial jurisdiction (eg where one state seeks the extradition of a defendant from a state where he might also be put on trial) is becoming increasingly common: see *R (on the application of Bermingham) v Director of the Serious Fraud Office* [2006] EWHC 200 (Admin), [2007] QB 727, [2006] 3 All ER 239. See also the Attorney-General's Guidance for Handling Criminal Cases with Concurrent Jurisdiction between the United Kingdom and the United States, 18 January 2007; and *R (on the application of Ahsan) v DPP* [2008] EWHC 666 (Admin), [2008] All ER (D) 149 (Apr) at [14]–[42].
5 As to International Criminal Law see PARA 421 et seq.
6 This is mainly with regard to procedural standards of fair criminal trial: see CONSTITUTIONAL LAW AND HUMAN RIGHTS vol 8(2) (Reissue) PARA 134 et seq. There is some effect on substantive jurisdiction, negatively in restricting certain exercises of prescriptive criminal jurisdiction (see eg *Dudgeon v United Kingdom* A/45 (1981) 4 EHRR 149, ECtHR) and in permitting exceptions to the non-retrospectivity principle of criminal law, where the conduct constituted a crime according to international law at the time of its commission, even if it did not in domestic law (see the Convention for the Protection of Human Rights and Fundamental Freedoms (1950) (Rome, 4 November 1950; TS 71 (1953); Cmd 8969; ETS no 5) art 7; and the International Criminal Courts Act 2001 s 65A (not yet in force) (see PARAS 454–455)).

7 Regulatory law accompanied by coercive sanctions is 'criminal' in this sense, although there may be some differences about the reach of regulatory jurisdiction compared to 'pure' criminal law. As to jurisdiction in civil matters see CIVIL PROCEDURE; CONFLICT OF LAWS vol 8(3) (Reissue) PARAS 34, 62 et seq. See also the British government's intervention in *Sosa v Alvarez-Machin* 124 S Ct 2739, reproduced in (2004) BYIL 770, expressing concerns about extensive extraterritorial civil jurisdiction.

220. English law and international law. The exercise of jurisdictional powers will ordinarily be through acts of and under national legislation[1] The examples given here are mainly from English law (which includes the common law as an exercise of prescriptive jurisdiction) but it should not be understood that the discretions exercised by the English authorities in all cases go to the maximum of what international law would permit[2]. Until recently, the United Kingdom has been cautious about exercising extraterritorial, prescriptive criminal jurisdiction[3]. The pre-eminence of the territorial principle is as much a reflection of the principles of the common law and pragmatic matters such as the availability of evidence as it is of a conscious adoption of international law[4].

1 From the perspective of national law, there must be a legal basis for the criminal conduct, for executive action taken in pursuance of the investigation and prosecution of crime and for the jurisdiction of a court before which any trial takes place. From the point of view of international law, all these actions must be taken under laws which conform to the limits of jurisdiction which international law provides.
2 Now, the courts no longer claim a right to create new crimes at common law (see *Knuller (Publishing, Printing and Promotions) Ltd v DPP* [1973] AC 435, [1972] 2 All ER 898, HL) and crimes at common law are purely territorial, so that considerations of international legality of prescriptive jurisdiction are unlikely to arise; see, however, PARA 224.
3 For instance, the United Kingdom has made only limited use of the nationality principle as a basis for criminal jurisdiction: see PARA 225.
4 See *Air India v Wiggins* [1980] 2 All ER 593, [1980] 1 WLR 815, HL.

221. Jurisdiction to prescribe conduct. State practice discloses the existence of five principles upon which claims to prescribe rules of conduct[1] are based and on which the United Kingdom has from time to time relied[2]. These are: (1) the territorial principle, on the basis of which a state criminalises conduct which takes place within its territory (which may include quasi-territorial areas such as ships, aircraft of spacecraft)[3]; (2) the nationality or active personality principle, on the basis of which a state criminalises the conduct of its nationals outside its territory[4]; (3) the protective principle, on the basis of which a state criminalises conduct occurring outside its territory which seriously affects any important national interest[5]; (4) the passive nationality or passive personality principle, on the basis of which a state criminalises conduct outside its territory of which its national is the victim[6]; and (5) the universal principle, on the basis of which a state criminalises conduct wherever it takes place, regardless of the nationality of the person whose conduct it is or the nationality of the victim[7].

1 'Conduct' includes acts and omissions. 'Conduct' constituting a crime may occur in more than one state and some 'conduct' may be regarded as continuing from one state to another: *Treacy v DPP* [1971] AC 537, 55 Cr App Rep 113, HL.
2 As to enforcement and judicial jurisdiction see PARA 230.
3 See PARAS 222–223.
4 See PARA 225.
5 See PARA 226.
6 See PARA 228.
7 See PARA 227; and the Harvard Research, Draft Convention on Jurisdiction with respect to Crime (1935), Introductory Comment, 29 American Journal of International Law Supp 435 at 439. This document does not, however, accept that the passive personality principle is a rule of international law: see at 578–579.

222. Territorial principle. A state has jurisdiction on the territorial principle to criminalise conduct which occurs within its territory[1]. The power to regulate conduct occurring in its territory, both in terms of the substantive rules which apply and to identify the persons bound by those rules is a fundamental characteristic of the state[2]. A state may exercise jurisdiction on the basis of the territorial principle by making criminal conduct only part of which occurs within its territory and it may regard continuing conduct, which may occur in more than one state, as occurring in its territory for the purpose of exercising jurisdiction on the territorial principle[3].

For this purpose, the territory of a state generally includes its land territory, its internal or national waters, its territorial waters and the air space above those areas and its quasi-territorial regimes, such as ships, aircraft, and space vehicles[4].

While there are few limits on the exercise of a state's substantive territorial prescriptive jurisdiction, its powers to investigate, try and punish infractions of those rules are subject to rules of law with respect to immunity from the jurisdiction of a state enjoyed by other states and their instrumentalities, diplomatic agents, consular agents, international organisations and others[5].

1   There are few, if any rules of customary international law which limit the substantive power of the state to make conduct in its territory criminal, although it is sometimes suggested that a state does not have the right to conscript aliens on its territory into its armed forces and to make non-compliance criminal: see *Polites v Commonwealth* (1945) 70 CLR 60, Aust HC. Human rights treaties may forbid the criminalisation of certain conduct within a state's territory: see *Dudgeon v United Kingdom* A 45 (1981), 4 EHRR 149, ECtHR. A 'crime' in this context means an act or omission which is made an offence by the domestic law of the state assuming jurisdiction. For a statement that a state has exclusive competence with regard to its own territory see *Island of Palmas Case* 2 RIAA 829 at 838–839 (1928). For statements of this principle as a general principle of English law see *R v Page* [1954] 1 QB 170 at 175, [1953] 2 All ER 1355 at 1356, 7 BILC 895, C-MAC, per Goddard CJ; *Cox v Army Council* [1963] AC 48 at 67, [1962] 1 All ER 880 at 882, 8 BILC 377, HL, per Viscount Simonds.
2   See PARA 32.
3   See PARA 223.
4   As to land territory see PARA 111; and CRIMINAL LAW, EVIDENCE AND PROCEDURE vol 11(3) (2006 Reissue) PARA 1055. As to internal or national waters see PARA 121; and CRIMINAL LAW, EVIDENCE AND PROCEDURE vol 11(3) (2006 Reissue) PARA 1056. As to territorial waters see PARA 123; and CRIMINAL LAW, EVIDENCE AND PROCEDURE vol 11(3) (2006 Reissue) PARA 1057. As to air space and crimes committed aboard aircraft see PARA 197 et seq; and AIR LAW vol 2 (2008) PARA 620 et seq; and CRIMINAL LAW, EVIDENCE AND PROCEDURE vol 11(3) (2006 Reissue) PARA 1058.
5   As to immunities of states and sovereigns see PARA 243 et seq; as to diplomatic immunity see PARA 265 et seq; as to consular immunity see PARA 290 et seq; and as to the immunity of international organisations and of persons connected with them see PARA 307 et seq. Immunities do not imply exceptions to the prescriptive jurisdiction of the forum state but rather to its executive and judicial jurisdiction to investigate and prosecute certain persons for conduct in its territory or elsewhere which the forum state has made criminal.

223. Extensions of the territorial principle. Under what is known as the subjective territorial principle, a state has jurisdiction to criminalise conduct which takes place in its own territory even when the consequence of that conduct takes place outside its territory, it being understood that 'consequence' here means a part of the offence and not merely some non-criminal effect within the state[1]. Under what is known as the objective territorial principle, a state has jurisdiction to criminalise conduct which takes place outside its territory if the consequence of that conduct takes place within its own territory[2]. The criminal law of England and Wales has not adopted either principle consistently, although examples can be found relying on each[3]. The objective territorial principle only applies if what are the consequences of the act are an essential or constituent element of the crime which is alleged to have been committed and, as such, the so-called 'effects' principle has no foundation as an aspect of the territorial principle[4].

1 Eg if a person in France discharges a gun, killing another in Germany, France has jurisdiction. For examples in English law see *Treacy v DPP* [1971] AC 537 at 546, [1971] 1 All ER 110, 9 BILC 212, HL; and CRIMINAL LAW, EVIDENCE AND PROCEDURE vol 11(3) (2006 Reissue) PARA 1059.

2 In the example given in note 1, Germany would also have jurisdiction. In the *Lotus Case* PCIJ Ser A No 10 (1927), a French officer on board a French vessel on the high seas was accused in a Turkish court of negligent navigation which caused a collision with a Turkish vessel, persons on which were killed. The Permanent Court of International Justice held that Turkey had jurisdiction, since the constituent element of the offence resulting from the officer's conduct took place on Turkish territory. This was based on the hypothesis that the Turkish ship was Turkish territory. On this point the case was partly overruled by the United Nations Convention on the Law of the Sea (Montego bay, 10 December 1982; TS 81 (1999); Cmnd 4524) art 97, which reserves the exercise of judicial penal jurisdiction 'for collision or any other incident of navigation' to the flag state: see PARA 150. This does not, however, affect the objective territorial principle as stated in the text. See also the Convention on Offences and certain other Acts committed on Board Aircraft (Tokyo Convention) (Tokyo, 14 September 1963; TS 126 (1969); Cmnd 4230) art 4(a); and PARA 201. For examples in municipal law see *Fermanagh County Council v Farrendon* [1923] 2 IR 180; *R v Baxter* [1972] 1 QB 1, [1971] 2 All ER 359, CA; *Secretary of State for Trade v Markus* [1976] AC 35, [1975] 1 All ER 958, HL. Extradition cases bear out the principle: see especially *R v Nillins* (1884) 53 LJMC 157, 5 BILC 446, DC; *R v Godfrey* [1923] 1 KB 24, 5 BILC 507; *Office of the King's Prosecutor, Brussels v Cando Armas* [2005] UKHL 67, [2006] 2 AC 1, [2006] 1 All ER 647 at [40] per Lord Hope (with regard to conduct and double criminality in extradition). For examples of United States law see *Adams v The People* 1 Comst 173 (USA 1848); *Ford v United States* 273 US 593 (1927).

3 See CRIMINAL LAW, EVIDENCE AND PROCEDURE vol 11(3) (2006 Reissue) PARA 1059.

4 The usual source of the effects doctrine is the judgment in *United States v Aluminum Co of America* 148 F 2d 416 (1945) at 443, although the full consequences of that judgment have been modified by *Timberlane Lumber v Bank of America* 549 F 2d 597 (1976) and *Mannington Mills v Congoleum Corpn* 595 F 2d 1287 (1979). See Jennings 'Extraterritorial Jurisdiction and the United States Anti-Trust Laws' 33 BYIL 146 at 159–160. The United Kingdom government has emphasised the need for some part of the offence to have taken place in the territory of the state assuming jurisdiction: Aide-Memoire of HM Government to the Commission of the European Communities, 20 October 1969, British Practice in International Law 1967, 58. Although this was written in connection with anti-trust proceedings and not criminal proceedings, the statements made therein are equally applicable to both.

224. Territorial jurisdiction and participation; attempts and conspiracy. The extensions of the territorial principle[1] apply also to participation in or attempts to commit a crime which take place in one state, the substantive crime being committed or being intended to be committed in another. The state in which the participation or attempt occurred, and the state in which its consequence occurred, both have jurisdiction[2]. A state has jurisdiction over a person accused of conspiracy to commit a crime if: (1) the formation of the conspiracy takes place within the territory of that state even though things are done in pursuance of the conspiracy outside its territory[3]; or (2) if the formation of the conspiracy takes place outside its territory and it is a conspiracy to commit a crime within the territory[4].

1 See PARA 223.

2 See *DPP v Stonehouse* [1978] AC 55, [1977] 2 All ER 909, HL.

3 Aide-memoire of HM Government to the Commission of the European Communities, 20 October 1969, British Practice in International Law 1967, 58; but see PARA 810 note 5. It has been held that in such cases a conspiracy in England to commit a crime abroad is indictable only if the conduct constituting that crime would be an offence by English law: *Board of Trade v Owen* [1957] AC 602, [1957] 1 All ER 411, 7 BILC 622, HL; *R v Cox* [1968] 1 All ER 410, [1968] 1 WLR 88, 9 BILC 207, CA; *R v Governor of Brixton Prison, ex p Rush* [1969] 1 All ER 316, [1969] 1 WLR 165, 9 BILC 544, DC. As to conspiracy to commit offences abroad see now also the Criminal Law Act 1977 s 1A (added by the Criminal Justice (Terrorism and Conspiracy) Act 1998 s 5(1)); the Sexual Offences (Conspiracy and Incitement) Act 1996 s 2; and CRIMINAL LAW, EVIDENCE AND PROCEDURE vol 11(1) (2006 Reissue) PARA 243.

4   As to conspiracies formed abroad to commit offences in England see *DPP v Doot* [1973] AC
807, [1973] 1 All ER 940, HL; *Somchai Liangsiriprasert v Government of the United States of
America* [1991] 1 AC 225, [1990] 2 All ER 866, PC; *R v Sansom* [1991] 2 QB 130, [1991]
2 All ER 145, CA; *R v Latif and Shahzad* [1996] 1 All ER 353, [1996] 1 WLR 104, HL; *R (on
the application of Al-Fawwaz) v Governor of Brixton Prison* [2001] UKHL 69, [2002] 1 AC
556, sub nom *Re Al-Fawwaz* [2002] 1 All ER 545. See also the Criminal Justice Act 1993 Pt I
(ss 1–6); and CRIMINAL LAW, EVIDENCE AND PROCEDURE vol 11(1) (2006 Reissue) PARA 362.

225.   Nationality or active personality principle. A state has jurisdiction to
make criminal conduct by its nationals when that conduct occurs outside its
territory[1]. This principle extends also to crimes committed by certain classes of
aliens, who are for this purpose assimilated to nationals[2]. Jurisdiction should
only be exercised by the state of the offender's nationality if it does not cause an
interference with the legitimate affairs of other states or cause the national to act
in a manner contrary to the law of the state in which he finds himself[3]. There is
an increasing tendency to criminalise some extra-territorial conduct of those
resident in the United Kingdom[4].

1   Eg the Offences against the Person Acts 1861 s 9 gives jurisdiction over murder or manslaughter
committed by a British subject while abroad; the Merchant Shipping Act 1995 s 281 gives
jurisdiction over offences committed by British passengers on a foreign ship (see *R v Kelly*
[1982] AC 665, [1981] 2 All ER 1098, HL); and the Anti-terrorism, Crime and Security
Act 2001 s 109 gives jurisdiction over bribery and corruption committed outside the United
Kingdom). See generally CRIMINAL LAW, EVIDENCE AND PROCEDURE vol 11(3) (2006 Reissue)
PARA 1061.
      By virtue of the fact that the person who is prosecuted is a national of the state assuming
jurisdiction over him, his prosecution and punishment cannot in general give rise to any breach
of international law.

2   This includes persons who are holders of public offices in the state (see the Criminal Justice
Act 1948 s 31) or who are members of its armed forces (Armed Forces Act 2006 s 42(1)). See
also the Intelligence Services Act 1994 s 7(1) which removes liability for crimes committed
overseas if done on the authorisation of the Secretary of State for intelligence purposes.
      Foreign members of the crew of a state's merchant vessels enjoy the protection of the state
and, as a corollary, are assimilated to its nationals for the purpose of criminal jurisdiction: see
the Merchant Shipping Act 1995 ss 281, 282; and SHIPPING AND MARITIME LAW vol 94 (2008)
PARA 1105. By English law aliens who owe allegiance to the Crown are also assimilated to
nationals for certain purposes, such as the law of treason, and are thus liable to prosecution for
offences abroad: *Joyce v DPP* [1946] AC 347, [1946] 1 All ER 186, 3 BILC 51, HL. See
generally CRIMINAL LAW, EVIDENCE AND PROCEDURE vol 11(3) (2006 Reissue) PARA 1062.

3   Aide-memoire of HM Government to the Commission of the European Communities,
20 October 1969, British Practice in International Law 1967, 58. See also 1 Oppenheim's
International Law (9th Edn) 462–465. Most states have placed restrictions upon their reliance
on the nationality principle, for instance by imposing a requirement of double criminality (see
the Sexual Offences Act 2003 s 72(1); and CRIMINAL LAW, EVIDENCE AND PROCEDURE vol 11(1)
(2006 Reissue) PARA 243). See also Harvard Research, 29 American Journal of International
Law Supp 519–539. Crime is strictly territorial at common law. Since early times, however,
statutes have made certain types of conduct abroad criminal, and have provided for their
prosecution in England: see CRIMINAL LAW, EVIDENCE AND PROCEDURE vol 11(3) (2006
Reissue) PARA 1060 et seq. In *R v Azzopardi* (1843) 2 Mood CC 288, 3 BILC 574, CCR, the
question was asked by Cresswell J whether a killing of a person in a foreign country which did
not constitute homicide by the laws of that country would amount to an offence under what is
now the Offences against the Person Act 1861 s 9. The question remained unanswered. Any
conflict between the territorial and nationality principles might be avoided if the plea of
autrefois acquit or autrefois convict were available in respect of acts committed abroad: see
CRIMINAL LAW, EVIDENCE AND PROCEDURE vol 11(3) (2006 Reissue) PARA 1064.

4   See the Slave Trade Act 1824, the War Crimes Act 1991, the Sexual Offences Act 2003 and the
International Criminal Court Act 2001 ss 51, 67A (see PARA 454) (s 67A not yet in force), which
make residence in the United Kingdom as well as nationality a test for jurisdiction in relation to
certain acts done abroad.

226. Protective principle. Under the protective principle a state has jurisdiction to criminalise extra-territorial conduct, regardless of the nationality of the offender, where that conduct is against the security[1], territorial integrity or political independence of the state[2]. This principle includes jurisdiction over crimes which consist of the falsification, counterfeiting or uttering of falsified copies or counterfeits of the seals, currency, stamps, passports or public documents issued by the state or under its authority[3].

1   An example is to be found in the Convention on Offences and certain other Acts committed on Board Aircraft (Tokyo Convention) (Tokyo, 14 September 1963; TS 126 (1969); Cmnd 4230) art 4(c) (see PARA 201).

2   British practice does not in general adopt this principle, but it is possible to explain upon this ground the type of case exemplified by *Joyce v DPP* [1946] AC 347, [1946] 1 All ER 186, 3 BILC 51, 1 IIL. See also *Naim Molvan (Owner of Motor Vessel Asya) v A-G for Palestine* [1948] AC 351, 1 BILC 674, PC (abetment of illegal immigration by acts on the high seas). Certain offences related to terrorism which are not referable to treaty obligations might also be explained by the protective principle: eg the Terrorism Act 2006 s 8 (see CRIMINAL LAW, EVIDENCE AND PROCEDURE vol 11(1) (2006 Reissue) PARA 440).

3   Harvard Research, 29 American Journal of International Law Supp 561. The Harvard Research proposed that jurisdiction might not be exercised where the alleged offence was done under cover of a liberty guaranteed by the local law of the state where it was done (although where the conduct poses a threat to a serious security interest of a foreign state, such protection might involve the responsibility of the local state): Harvard Research, 29 American Journal of International Law Supp 543, 557.

227. Universal principle. In certain cases a state has jurisdiction to criminalise conduct by an alien outside its territory, regardless of the nationality of the victim or of any impact which the conduct may have on a security interest of the state. The implication is that any state may exercise prescriptive jurisdiction over the conduct. At customary international law, piracy is such an offence[1]. Crimes committed outside the jurisdiction of any state[2] may fall within this principle. Universal jurisdiction may be exercised only with respect to conduct which constitutes a crime against international law[3]. War crimes which are crimes under international law are triable by the courts of any state[4]. For the purpose of national jurisdiction other activities which are prohibited by international conventions are sometimes regarded as universal crimes[5].

1   As to piracy see PARA 155 et seq.

2   Eg crimes committed on ships or floating objects which have no international character. In *R v Waina and Swatoa* (1874) 2 NSWLR 403, it was held that a British ship's long-boat was not a British ship for jurisdictional purposes. A few states have provisions in their penal legislation with respect to crimes committed in a place not subject to the authority of any state, but usually only if these are committed by their own nationals: Harvard Research, 29 American Journal of International Law Supp 588–592. As to Antarctica and jurisdiction over offences committed there see PARA 218; and ANIMALS vol 2 (2008) PARAS 990–993.

3   Crimes against international law arise under customary international law: see PARA 421 et seq. States may have obligations under treaties to create crimes in their domestic law equivalent to international crimes, to which prescriptive jurisdictional obligations may attach. For example the Convention on the Prevention and Punishment of the Crime of Genocide (Paris, 9 December 1948; TS 58 (1970); Cmnd 4421). art VI requires only that parties make genocide an offence when it occurs within their territory. There is no treaty obligation to make genocide a crime of universal jurisdiction though states may make it an extraterritorial offence under customary international law: see *Application of the Convention on the Prevention and Punishment of the Crime of Genocide (Bosnia and Herzegovina v Serbia and Montenegro)* ICJ Reports, 26 February 2007. As to the Genocide Convention see PARA 429.

    As to the relation between crimes under customary international law and the law of England and Wales see *R v Jones* [2006] UKHL 16, [2007] 1 AC 136 at [28] per Lord Bingham.

4   See the UK Ministry of Defence *The Manual of the Law of Armed Conflict* (2004) paras 16.20–16.30.3. See also United Nations War Crimes Commission, 15 War Crimes Rep 26

(1949). British military courts have jurisdiction over war crimes committed not only by members of enemy armed forces but also by enemy civilians and certain other categories of persons of any nationality. As to jurisdiction over grave breaches of the Geneva Red Cross Conventions see PARA 426 et seq; and WAR AND ARMED CONFLICT vol 49(1) (2005 Reissue) PARA 421 et seq. However, these are examples of punishment of breaches of international law rather than of acts which are not in themselves breaches of international law which states are free to punish.

5   Eg torture, and slavery and the slave trade: see CONSTITUTIONAL LAW AND HUMAN RIGHTS vol 8(2) (Reissue) PARAS 124, 125. As to the International Criminal Court see PARA 437 et seq.

228.   Passive nationality or passive personality principle.   It is sometimes contended that a state has jurisdiction to make extra-territorial conduct of aliens an offence where the victim of the offence was a national of the legislating state under the passive personality principle[1]. This principle has not secured general acceptance[2], but it is gaining ground as a basis for the exercise of jurisdiction, particularly where the victims are targeted because of their nationality[3].

1   Turkey attempted to justify its assumption of jurisdiction on this basis in the *Lotus Case* PCIJ Ser A No 10 (1927) (see PARA 223 note 2). It was not, however, adopted as the ground for the decision of the Permanent Court of International Justice. The principle was relied on in *A-G of the Government of Israel v Eichmann* (1961) 36 Int L R 5, though since the victims were killed before Israel was a state, it was on the basis that they were Jews.

2   The principle was rejected by some of the dissenting judges in the *Lotus Case* PCIJ Ser A No 10 (1927). The United States argued against the existence of this principle in a dispute with Mexico in *Cutting's Case*, Foreign Relations of the United States (1887) 751; Foreign Relations of the United States (1888) vol II, 1114, 1180; 2 Moore's Digest 228 at 235, 242. See, however, the Convention on Offences and certain other Acts committed on Board Aircraft (Tokyo Convention) (Tokyo, 14 September 1963; TS 126 (1969); Cmnd 4230) art 4(b) (see PARA 201).

3   The passive personality principle 'meets with relatively little opposition, at least so far as a particular category of offences are concerned': *Arrest Warrant of 11 April 2000 (Democratic Republic of the Congo v Belgium)* ICJ Reports 2002, 3 at 77 (para 47) (Joint Separate Opinion of Judges Higgins, Kooijmans and Buergenthal). See also the United States Anti-terrorism and Effective Death Penalty Act 1996, Pub L No 104–132.

229.   Extraterritorial application of trade laws and economic sanctions.   The courts of the United States have asserted the right to extend the application of United States domestic anti-trust laws[1] to the conduct of foreign corporations which has taken place outside the United States but which is alleged to have affected the trade of the United States[2]. In so far as this assumption of jurisdiction involves extraterritorial enforcement of such laws, directly or indirectly, the English courts would not recognise it[3]. The United Kingdom government has stated that the territorial and nationality principles[4] are exhaustive bases of jurisdiction in such cases, and that it does not regard the territorial principle as warranting the application of domestic anti-trust laws to conduct taking place entirely outside the territory of the state concerned[5].

1   See, in particular, the Antitrust Act 1890, 26 Stat 209 (United States) (Sherman Act); and the Anti-Trust Act 1914, 38 Stat 730 (United States) (Clayton Act). The considerations which apply to the extraterritorial application of anti-trust measures by the US apply mutatis mutandis to extraterritorial measures for other regulatory purposes: see, in regard to trading relations with Cuba, the Cuban Liberty and Democratic Solidarity (Libertad) Act 1996 110 Stat 785 (United States) (Helms-Burton Act) (trading relations with Cuba); Iran, Libya (terrorism sanctions).

2   In earlier United States decisions, the application of these laws was limited to agreements made abroad in pursuance of which some act was done in the United States, and was not extended to affect conduct which took place entirely outside that country: *American Banana Co v United Fruit Co* 213 US 347 at 356 (1909); see also eg *United States of America v American Tobacco Co* 221 US 106 (1911). These cases were concerned also with transactions involving American companies. In 1944 the United States courts expanded their jurisdiction to such cases where acts were done entirely outside the United States, but were intended to affect and did

affect trade with that country (see *United States of America v Aluminum Co of America* 148 F 2d 416 (1945)), and also to cases where no intention necessarily existed (*United States of America v General Electric Co* 115 F Supp 835 (1953)). In the last-mentioned case, however, the orders made against the foreign companies contained a 'savings clause', as they did in *United States of America v Imperial Chemical Industries Ltd* 105 F Supp 215 (1952). See also *British Nylon Spinners Ltd v Imperial Chemical Industries Ltd* [1953] Ch 19, [1952] 2 All ER 780, 7 BILC 599, CA; and PARA 231 note 2. However, no such clauses were found in *United States of America v Holophane Co Inc* 119 F Supp 114 (1954) or in *United States of America v Watchmakers of Switzerland Information Center Inc* 113 F Supp 40 (re-argument denied 134 F Supp 710 (1955), 22 Int LR 168). See, however, *Vanity Fair Mills Inc v T Eaton Co Ltd* 352 US 871 (1956), 23 Int LR 134. In *Timberlane Lumber Co v Bank of America* 549 F 2d 597 (1976) and *Mannington Mills Inc v Congoleum Corpn* 595 F 2d 1287 (1979), United States courts adopted a 'balancing of interests' test (ie weighing the interests of the United States in having its laws applied against the interests of the other state or states involved). However, in subsequent cases, eg *Laker Airways Ltd v Sabena Belgian World Airlines* 731 F 2d 909 (1984), this test was not applied. See also *Hartford Fire Insurance Co v California* 113 S Ct 2891 (1993) (allegation that London insurance companies acting in the United Kingdom had violated the Sherman Act in refusing to grant reinsurance to United States businesses otherwise than on terms agreed among themselves; defendants argued their conduct was lawful in the United Kingdom and in accordance with United Kingdom law concerning regulation of the insurance market; United States Supreme Court held balance came down in favour of exercising extraterritorial jurisdiction).

Attempts to apply United States anti-trust laws to activities of foreign (including United Kingdom) airlines were the subject of an order made under the Protection of Trading Interests Act 1980: see the Protection of Trading Interests (US Antitrust Measures) Order 1983, SI 1983/900; and PARA 235 note 3.

3   *British Nylon Spinners Ltd v Imperial Chemical Industries Ltd* [1953] Ch 19, [1952] 2 All ER 780, 7 BILC 599, CA. As to indirect enforcement see PARA 231.

4   As to the territorial and nationality principles see PARAS 222–225. These are the bases for criminal offences in the United Kingdom (including the conduct of companies incorporated in the UK) when it implements Security Council decisions imposing sanctions on a particular territory by Orders made under the United Nations Act 1946, eg Al-Qaeda and Taliban (UN Measures) Order 2002, SI 2002/111; Somalia (United Nations Sanctions) Order 2002, SI 2002/2628.

5   Aide-Memoire of HM Government to the Commission of the European Communities, 20 October 1969, British Practice in International Law 1967, 58. The European Court of Justice has seemingly upheld the application of principles similar to those adopted in the United States cases referred to in note 2: see Case 48/69 *Imperial Chemical Industries Ltd v EC Commission* [1972] ECR 619, [1972] CMLR 557, ECJ; Case 22/71 *Beguelin Import Co v GL Import Export SA* [1971] ECR 949, [1972] CMLR 81. However, in Cases 89, 104, 114, 116, 117, 125–9/85A *Åhlström Osakeyhtiö v EC Commission (The Woodpulp Cases)* [1988] ECR 5193, [1988] 4 CMLR 901, ECJ, the same court appears to have adopted the objective territorial principle (see PARA 223) (Commission had jurisdiction to impose fines in respect of pricing agreement concluded outside the EEC by non-EEC companies but implemented within the EEC. The exercise of prescriptive jurisdiction was regarded as territorial, regarding the whole of a corporate group as being a single person for the purposes of criminalising its conduct, the acts of subsidiaries within the EEC being attributable to their foreign controlling companies).

230.   Enforcement jurisdiction. The enforcement jurisdiction of a state comprises, inter alia, its powers to investigate crime, to examine witnesses and gather evidence, to question and detain suspects, to initiate prosecutions and to execute any punishment awarded by a court after a criminal trial. Executive jurisdiction of a state is strictly territorial in the sense that a state may not exercise its powers or authority in the territory or jurisdictional area of another state except by virtue of a permissive rule derived from international custom or from a treaty or convention[1]. Thus a state is not entitled to use physical force in the territory of another state to assert its alleged rights[2]. Nor is it entitled to exert peaceable measures on the territory of any other state by way of enforcement of its national laws, civil or criminal, without the consent of that other state, by way for example of service of documents, police or tax investigations, or by the performing of notarial acts[3].

1   *Lotus Case* PCIJ Ser A No 10 at 18 (1927). For an example of provisions of a convention giving the right to a state to exercise jurisdiction over foreign vessels on the high seas see the United Nations Convention on the Law of the Sea (Montego Bay, 10 December 1982; TS 81 (1999); Cmnd 4524) art 110; and PARA 148. For further examples of powers of extra-territorial enforcement jurisdiction see the Agreement regarding the Status of Forces of Parties to the North Atlantic Treaty (London, 19 June 1951; TS 3 (1955); Cmd 9363) arts VII paras 1(a), 2(a), 10(a) (and PARA 325); and the Protocol between the United Kingdom of Great Britain and Northern Ireland and the French Republic concerning Frontier Controls and Policing, Co-operation in Criminal Justice, Public Safety and Mutual Assistance relating to the Channel Fixed Link (Sangatte; 25 November 1991; TS 70 (1993); Cm 2366), and an Additional Protocol thereto (Brussels, 29 May 2000; TS 33 (2002); Cm 5586) (and POLICE vol 36(1) (2007 Reissue) PARA 130).

2   States have extensive networks of bilateral and multilateral arrangements to obtain custody of suspects overseas (see EXTRADITION) and evidence etc (CRIMINAL LAW, EVIDENCE AND PROCEDURE). As to seizure of persons outside the United Kingdom in violation of international law see PARA 233.

3   In English law a subpoena cannot be issued if the addressee is resident outside the United Kingdom, except to enforce a revenue claim against a British subject: *A-G v Prosser* [1938] 2 KB 531, [1938] 3 All ER 32, CA. As to service of documents abroad see also the Convention on Service Abroad of Judicial and Extrajudicial Documents in Civil or Commercial Matters (The Hague, 15 November 1965; TS 50 (1969); Cmnd 3986). As to the taking of evidence in England for use in foreign tribunals see the Evidence (Proceedings in Other Jurisdictions) Act 1975; and CIVIL PROCEDURE vol 11 (2009) PARA 1055 et seq. The performance of notarial acts by consuls is frequently permitted under consular conventions: see the Vienna Convention on Consular Relations (Vienna, 24 April 1963; TS 14 (1973); Cmnd 5219) art 5 (set out in the Consular Relations Act 1968, s 1, Sch 1); and PARA 30. See also PARA 290 et seq. As to forced marriage protection orders which require or forbid conduct outside England and Wales but exclude extra-territorial enforcement see the Family Law Act 1996 Pt 4A; and MATRIMONIAL AND CIVIL PARTNERSHIP LAW vol 73 (2009) PARA 723 et seq.

231. Indirect enforcement. A state may not enforce its own laws or obedience to them in the territory of a foreign state by indirect means, such as by ordering an alien over whom it has personal jurisdiction to do or to refrain from doing an act in the foreign state, without the consent of that foreign state. This prohibition applies to measures taken by way of economic sanctions and intended to operate extraterritorially over persons and property[1]. It also applies to the issuing of injunctions or decrees of specific performance or orders having like effect[2], and to orders to produce documents situated in the foreign state[3], if obedience to such orders would be unlawful in the foreign state[4].

1   Examples include:
    (1)   the 'freezing' by the United States of Iranian assets held outside the United States by foreign, including United Kingdom, subsidiaries of United States companies (see 18 ILM (1979) 1549), which English courts refused to accept as effective over Iranian assets held in branches of United States banks in England: *Libyan Arab Foreign Bank v Bankers Trust Co* [1989] QB 728, [1989] 3 All ER 252; *Libyan Arab Foreign Bank v Manufacturers Hanover Trust Co (No 2)* [1989] 1 Lloyd's Rep 608;
    (2)   United States Re-export Control Regulations directed at trade with the Soviet Union, which were the subject of the Protection of Trading Interests (US Re-export Control) Order 1982, SI 1982/885 (see PARA 235);
    (3)   the United States Cuban Democracy Act 1992, which prohibited the granting of licences under the United States Assets Control Regulations for certain transactions between United States owned or controlled firms in the United Kingdom and Cuba, which was the subject of a démarche from the European Communities (see 63 BYIL (1992), 725) and of the Protection of Trading Interests (US Cuban Assets Control Regulations) Order 1992, SI 1992/2449, made under the Protection of Trading Interests Act 1980 s 1(1) (see PARA 235);

(4)   the United States Cuban Liberty and Democratic Solidarity Act 1996, by which nationals of third states (eg the United Kingdom) dealing with United States property expropriated by Cuba or using or taking its benefit can be sued before the United States courts and barred from entry into the United States, which was the subject of a protest from the European Union: see 35 ILM (1996) 397;

(5)   the United States Iran and Libya Sanctions Act 1996, which was intended to impose sanctions on persons or entities participating in the development of the petroleum resources of Iran or Libya.

The legislation referred to in heads (4) and (5) was the subject of an order made under the Protection of Trading Interests Act 1980: see the Extraterritorial United States Legislation (Sanctions against Cuba, Iran and Libya) (Protection of Trading Interests) Order 1996, SI 1996/3171; and PARA 236. This order was a consequence of EC Council Regulation 2271/96 (OJ L309, 29.11.1996, 1) 39, which was issued so as to afford protection to member states against extraterritorial legislation. Subsequently, the European Union and the United States concluded a memorandum of understanding: see the Memorandum of Understanding concerning the United States Helms-Burton Act and the United States Iran and Libya Sanctions Act (11 April 1997) 36 ILM (1997) 529, by which, inter alia, the United States agreed to continue its suspension of the operation of part of the Helms-Burton Act, announced by the President on 3 January 1997 (see 36 ILM (1997) 216) during the remainder of the President's term of office (ie until January 2001).

2   In certain anti-trust cases, the courts of the United States have ordered foreign corporations over whom they had assumed jurisdiction by reason of their doing business or allegedly doing business in that country, to make their conduct in foreign countries conform to United States law: see *United States of America v Imperial Chemical Industries Ltd* 105 F Supp 215 (1952). In subsequent proceedings, the English courts restrained the defendant company from complying with the American order: see *British Nylon Spinners Ltd v Imperial Chemical Industries Ltd* [1953] Ch 19, [1952] 2 All ER 780, 7 BILC 593, 599, CA. See also *United States of America v General Electric Co* 115 F Supp 835 (1953), which drew a diplomatic protest from the Netherlands government. As to when a corporation is held to be doing business in the United States by reason of the activities of associated companies see *United States of America v Watchmakers of Switzerland Information Center Inc* 133 F Supp 40; re-argument denied 134 F Supp 710 (1955), 22 Int LR 168. The United Kingdom government has stated its opinion that a state only has personal jurisdiction over a foreign corporation if that corporation carries on business or resides within its territory, and that for this purpose a corporation also carries on business or resides there through an agent if the agent has legal powers to enter into contracts on behalf of the corporation. A corporation does not carry on business within a state merely because its subsidiary does so, unless the subsidiary is an agent in the sense explained. The distinct legal personalities of the parent and subsidiary companies must be respected: see Aide-Memoire of HM Government to the Commission of the European Communities, 20 October 1969, British Practice in International Law 1967, 58. In the case in connection with which this statement was made, the European Court rejected a similar argument, however, on the basis that the subsidiary companies in question enjoyed no real autonomy in the matter: Case 48/69 *Imperial Chemical Industries Ltd v EC Commission* [1972] ECR 619, [1972] CMLR 557, ECJ.

3   The United States courts have ruled that whenever they have obtained jurisdiction over a party personally, it is possible to order the production of documents in his possession wherever the documents may be situated, provided their production is not contrary to their lex situs: *Re Investigation of World Arrangements with relation to the Production, Transporting, Refining and Distribution of Petroleum* 13 FRD 280 (1952), 19 Int LR 197. In that case, however, service of a subpoena for the production of documents upon the company concerned was set aside on the ground that the company was indistinguishable from the United Kingdom government and therefore entitled to sovereign immunity. For the letters to the company from the Minister of Fuel and Power and the Secretary of State for Foreign Affairs, forbidding the disclosure of the documents without the authority of the government, see the reports cited. The basis in English law for these instructions is unclear. In 1960 the United States Federal Maritime Commission made demands upon foreign shipping companies to produce documents relating to their activities, and objections to compliance where the documents were not in the United States were overruled: *Montship Lines Ltd v Federal Maritime Board* 295 F 2d 147 (1961). As to the views of the United Kingdom government on that case and the declarations made by 11 states, including the United Kingdom, see Lauterpacht's Contemporary Practice of the United Kingdom in the Field of International Law 1962 (I), 15–18; British Practice in International law 1963 (I), 13–14; British Practice in International Law 1964 (I), 36–37, 1964, (II), 146–157; British Practice in International Law 1965 (I), 30–31.

4   Clauses were inserted in some orders made by United States courts upon foreign corporations which had the effect of relieving them from compliance if their compliance would be unlawful under the law of a foreign state. See the cases cited in note 2. The extraterritorial application and enforcement of United States trade laws was met by 'blocking' legislation of other states. By the Shipping Contracts and Commercial Documents Act 1964 ss 1, 2 (both now repealed), the relevant Minister of the Crown was empowered to forbid the production to a foreign court or tribunal of documents in the United Kingdom in circumstances in which it appeared to him that the foreign court was asserting jurisdiction which by international law properly appertains to the United Kingdom: see SHIPPING AND NAVIGATION. The Shipping Contracts and Commercial Documents Act 1964 was repealed and greater protection against exorbitant exercise of jurisdiction is now accorded by the Protection of Trading Interests Act 1980: see PARA 235. As to the need for such legislation see 973 HC Official Report (5th series), 15 November 1979, cols 1533–1546.

    In 1991 an Agreement Regarding the Application of Competition Laws was reached between the European Commission and the United States, which provided for notification and co-ordination of such activities. However, the European Court of Justice held that it was ultra vires the Commission: Case C–327/91 *France v EC Commissio* [1994] ECR-I 3641, [1994] 5 CMLR 517, ECJ. The Agreement Regarding the Application of Competition Laws was reintroduced with rectification in EC Council and EC Commission Decision 95/45 (OJ L51, 8.3.1995, p 13). The Agreement Regarding the Application of Competition Laws does not deal with private actions in the United States courts.

232.   The exercise of judicial jurisdiction. Judicial jurisdiction is ordinarily dependent upon the presence of the defendant in the territory of the prosecuting state following his arrest within that territory. There may be circumstances where a court is able to proceed in the absence of the defendant, as trials in absentia are not, per se, contrary to international law. Human rights law, however, imposes some limitations on a state's power so to proceed[1]. Where the forum law requires the presence of the defendant, obtaining custody over him if he is not in the territory may depend upon the existence of extradition arrangements with the state where, for the time being, he is[2]. National legislation may allow for ad hoc transfer of a defendant to a foreign state for trial[3]. Informal transfers may be possible, and do not conflict with international law or human rights law[4], but national law and the human rights obligations of the custody state may make an informal transfer difficult to achieve lawfully[5].

1   See *Colozza v Italy* A 89 (1985), 7 EHRR 516, ECtHR; and Application 56581/00 *Sejdovic v Italy*, Judgment of 1 March 2006, ECtHR (Grand Chamber).

2   There is no obligation in customary international law on one state to transfer to another state a person wanted for trial there, and extradition arrangements are generally dependent upon treaties between the states involved: see generally EXTRADITION vol 17(2) (Reissue) PARA 1120 et seq.

3   See the Extradition Act 2003 ss 193, 194; and EXTRADITION vol 17(2) (Reissue) PARAS 1536, 1537. See also *Brown v Government of Rwanda* [2009] EWHC 770 (Admin), [2009] All ER (D) 98 (Apr).

4   *Ocalan v Turkey* (2005) 41 EHRR 985, [2005] ECHR 46221/99 at [87], [89].

5   *R v Horseferry Road Magistrates' Court ex p Bennett* [1994] 1 AC 42, sub nom *Bennett v Horseferry Road Magistrates' Court* [1993] 3 All ER 138, HL; *R v Mullen* [2000] QB 520, [1999] 2 Cr App Rep 143, CA.

233.   The seizure of persons in violation of international law. States may resort to the seizure of a suspect in the territory of another state, although such action without the consent of the local state is unlawful in international law and engages the responsibility of the intervening state[1]. However, it appears that obtaining custody in this way does not inevitably make any subsequent exercise of judicial jurisdiction unlawful[2].

    An individual does not derive rights of which he can claim benefit from the breach of sovereignty of another state[3]. However, the English court has allowed that the trial of an individual who has been returned to this country in oppressive circumstances involving UK officials may amount to an abuse of process, such that, in the court's discretion, the trial should not be permitted to proceed[4]. It has been suggested that where the officials have acted in breach of international law, this is a significant factor in persuading the court to exercise its discretion against proceeding with a trial[5].

1   Eg, after the abduction of Eichmann from Argentina by agents of the state of Israel, Argentina requested on 15 June 1960 reparation in the form of the return of Eichmann and the punishment of those who had violated Argentine territory: see United Nations Doc S/4336. The Security Council of the United Nations resolved on 24 June 1960 that Israel should make appropriate reparation: see United Nations Doc S/4349. On 3 August 1960 the two states agreed to regard the incident as closed. See generally Fawcett 38 BYIL 181. Other examples include the abduction of Salomon from Switzerland by Nazi agents in 1936 and his subsequent return, and of Argoud from Germany by French agents in 1963. See also *Colunje Case* 6 RIAA 342 (1933). The seizing state may be under an obligation to return the person to the state from which he was abducted: see *Lawler's Case* 1 McNair's International Law Opinions 78; *Martin's Case* 1 McNair's International Law Opinions 79. For opinions to the effect that foreign authorities may not convey through British waters vessels or persons who have committed no wrong against British law, and that the British government could demand their release see Martin's Case at 80, 82. See also *Savarkar Case* Scott's Hague Reports 516 (1916).

2   This is true of English law (*Ex p Scott* (1829) 9 B & C 446, 3 BILC 1; *R v Officer Commanding Depot Battalion RASC Colchester, ex p Elliott* [1949] 1 All ER 373, 3 BILC 10), and of Scottish law (*Sinclair v Lord Advocate* (1890) 17 R (Ct of Sess) 38, 3 BILC 5). The same has been held in the United States (*Ker v Illinois* 119 US 436 (1886); *Ex p Lopez* 6 F Supp 342 (1934); and see *United States of America v Alvarez-Machain* 119 L Ed 2d 441 (1992)) and in the courts of Palestine (*Afouneh v A-G* (1941–42) 10 Ann Dig 327, Case no 97) and Israel (*A-G for the Government of Israel v Eichmann* (1961) 36 Int LR 5; cf the French case of *Re Jolis* (1933–34) 7 Ann Dig 191, Case no 77). In *Corfu Channel (United Kingdom v Albania)* ICJ Reports 1949, 4 the International Court of Justice admitted evidence which had been obtained by acts of the Royal Navy which the court had held to have been a violation of Albanian sovereignty.

3   Although the European Court of Human Rights has suggested that extraterritorial action by a party to the European Convention on Human Rights to seize an individual without the consent of the local state would breach art 5(1) (see *Ocalan v Turkey* [2005] ECHR 46221/99, 18 BHRC 293 at para 85; *Stocke v Germany* [1991] ECHR 11755/85, 13 EHRR 839 at para 167) it does not follow that human rights law protects an individual from trial in these circumstances, except, perhaps, where his abduction has involved a breach of his right not to be tortured or subjected to inhuman or degrading treatment (see *Bozano v Italy* (Application No 9991/82) (1984) 39 DR 147 (this decision might not stand after *Ocalan v Turkey*)).

4   *R v Horseferry Road Magistrates' Court ex p Bennett* [1994] 1 AC 42, sub nom *Bennett v Horseferry Road Magistrates' Court* [1993] 3 All ER 138, HL; *R v Mullen* [2000] QB 520, [1999] 2 Cr App Rep 143, CA.

5   *R v Horseferry Road Magistrates' Court ex p Bennett* [1994] 1 AC 42, sub nom *Bennett v Horseferry Road Magistrates' Court* [1993] 3 All ER 138, HL (although there was no breach of international law in that case). See also *R v Plymouth Justices, ex p Driver* [1986] QB 95, [1985] 2 All ER 681, DC; *R v Latif* [1996] 1 All ER 353, [1996] 1 WLR 104, HL; and *Re Schmidt* [1995] 1 AC 339, sub nom *Schmidt v Federal Government of Germany* [1994] 3 All ER 65, HL.

(2) PROTECTION OF TRADING INTERESTS

234. The Protection of Trading Interests Act 1980. The Protection of Trading Interests Act 1980 provides protection from requirements, prohibitions or judgments imposed or given under the laws of countries outside the United Kingdom and affecting the trading or other interests of persons in the United Kingdom[1].

1   Protection of Trading Interests Act 1980 preamble, s 8(1). See PARA 235 et seq. The Act extends to Northern Ireland: s 8(7). Her Majesty may by Order in Council direct that the Act extends with such exceptions, adaptations and modifications, if any, as may be specified in the order to

any territory outside the United Kingdom, being a territory for the international relations of which Her Majesty's government in the United Kingdom are responsible: s 8(8). The Protection of Trading Interests Act 1980 applies with modifications to Guernsey (see the Protection of Trading Interests Act 1980 (Guernsey) Order 1983, SI 1983/1703), the Isle of Man (see the Protection of Trading Interests Act 1980 (Isle of Man) Order 1983, SI 1983/1704) and Jersey (see the Protection of Trading Interests Act 1980 (Jersey) Order 1983, SI 1983/607). As to the meaning of 'United Kingdom' see PARA 30 note 3.

235.   Overseas measures affecting United Kingdom trading interests.   The Protection of Trading Interests Act 1980 provides protection from measures that have been or are proposed to be taken by or under the law of any overseas country for regulating or controlling international trade, which, in so far as they apply or would apply to things done or to be done outside the territorial jurisdiction of that country by persons carrying on business in the United Kingdom, are damaging or threaten to damage the trading interests[1] of the United Kingdom[2]. In such circumstances, the Secretary of State may by order direct that these provisions are to apply to those measures either generally or in their application to such cases as may be specified in the order[3].

The Secretary of State may by order make provision for requiring, or enabling the Secretary of State to require, a person in the United Kingdom who carries on business there to give notice to the Secretary of State of any requirement or prohibition imposed or threatened to be imposed on that person pursuant to any measures in so far as these provisions apply[4] to them[5]. The Secretary of State may also give such a person such directions for prohibiting compliance with any such requirement or prohibition as he considers appropriate for avoiding damage to the trading interests[6] of the United Kingdom[7].

Any person who without reasonable excuse fails to comply with any requirement to give notice, or knowingly contravenes directions given, is guilty of an offence[8].

1   'Trade' includes any activity carried on in the course of a business of any description, and 'trading interests' is to be construed accordingly: Protection of Trading Interests Act 1980 s 1(6).

2   See the Protection of Trading Interests Act 1980 s 1(1), (3). Section 1(1), (3) (see the text and notes 3–8) are disapplied to the extent that EC Council Regulation 2271/96 (OJ L309, 22.11.96, p 1) (protecting against the effects of the extraterritorial application of legislation adopted by a third country) applies; and it is an offence to breach art 2 or art 5: Extraterritorial US Legislation (Sanctions against Cuba, Iran and Libya (Protection of Trading Interests) Order 1996, SI 1996/3171, art 3(1). As to the meaning of 'United Kingdom' see PARA 30 note 3.

3   Protection of Trading Interests Act 1980 s 1(1). The power of the Secretary of State to make such an order is exercisable by statutory instrument subject to annulment in pursuance of a resolution of either House of Parliament: s 1(4). In exercise of this power the Secretary of State has made the following orders: the Protection of Trading Interests (US Re-export Control) Order 1982, SI 1982/885; the Protection of Trading Interests (US Antitrust Measures) Order 1983, SI 1983/900; and the Protection of Trading Interests (US Cuban Assets Control Regulations) Order 1992, SI 1992/2449. The effect of the Protection of Trading Interests (US Antitrust Measures) Order 1983, SI 1983/900, was judicially considered in *British Airways Board v Laker Airways Ltd* [1985] AC 58, [1984] 3 All ER 39, HL.

4   Ie by virtue of an order under the Protection of Trading Interests Act 1980 s 1(1): s 1(2).

5   Protection of Trading Interests Act 1980 s 1(2).

6   See note 1.

7   Protection of Trading Interests Act 1980 s 1(3). See also note 2. Such directions may be either general or special and may prohibit compliance either absolutely or in such cases or subject to such conditions as to consent or otherwise as may be specified: s 1(5). General directions are to be published in such manner as appears to the Secretary of State to be appropriate: s 1(5).

8   Protection of Trading Interests Act 1980 s 3(1). A person guilty of such an offence is liable on conviction on indictment to a fine or on summary conviction to a fine not exceeding the statutory maximum: s 3(1). As to the statutory maximum see SENTENCING AND DISPOSITION OF OFFENDERS vol 92 (2010) PARA 140. Proceedings may only be instituted by the Secretary of

State, or with the consent of the Attorney General: s 3(3). Proceedings may be taken before the appropriate United Kingdom court having jurisdiction in the place where that person is for the time being: s 3(4). A person who is not a citizen of the United Kingdom and Colonies nor a body corporate incorporated in the United Kingdom is not guilty of an offence under s 3(1) by reason of any action taken outside the United Kingdom in contravention of directions under s 1(3): s 3(2).

236. Documents and information required by overseas courts and authorities.
If it appears to him that either:

(1) a requirement has been or may be imposed[1] on a person or persons in the United Kingdom to produce to any court, tribunal or authority of an overseas country[2] any commercial document[3] which is not within the territorial jurisdiction of that country or to furnish any commercial information[4] to any such court, tribunal or authority[5]; or

(2) any such authority has imposed or may impose a requirement[6] on a person or persons in the United Kingdom to publish such document or information[7],

the Secretary of State may give directions[8] for prohibiting compliance with the requirement, if it appears to him that the requirement is inadmissible[9].

Any person who knowingly contravenes any such directions[10] is guilty of an offence[11].

1 The making of a request or demand is to be treated as the imposition of a requirement if it is made in circumstances in which a requirement to the same effect could be or could have been imposed; and (1) any request or demand for the supply of a document or information which, pursuant to the requirement of any court, tribunal or authority of an overseas country, is addressed to a person in the United Kingdom; or (2) any requirement imposed by such a court, tribunal or authority to produce or furnish any document or information to a person specified in the requirement, is to be treated as a requirement to produce or furnish that document or information to that court, tribunal or authority: Protection of Trading Interests Act 1980 s 2(5). Section 2 is disapplied to the extent that EC Council Regulation 2271/96 (OJ 309, 22.11.96, p 1) (protecting against the effects of the extraterritorial application of legislation adopted by a third country) applies: Extraterritorial US Legislation (Sanctions against Cuba, Iran and Libya) (Protection of Trading Interests) Order 1996, SI 1996/3171, art 3(1). As to the meaning of 'United Kingdom' see PARA 30 note 3.

2 References to the law or a court, tribunal or authority of an overseas country include, in the case of a federal state, references to the law or a court, tribunal or authority of any constituent part of that country: Protection of Trading Interests Act 1980 s 8(3). 'Overseas country' means any country or territory outside the United Kingdom other than one for whose international relations Her Majesty's government in the United Kingdom are responsible: s 8(2).

3 'Commercial document' and 'commercial information' mean a document or information relating to a business of any description; and 'document' includes any record or device by means of which material is recorded or stored: Protection of Trading Interests Act 1980 s 2(6).

4 See note 3.

5 Protection of Trading Interests Act 1980 s 2(1)(a).

6 See note 1.

7 Protection of Trading Interests Act 1980 s 2(1)(b).

8 Directions may be either general or special and may prohibit compliance with any requirement either absolutely or in such cases or subject to specified conditions as to consent or otherwise as may be specified in the directions: Protection of Trading Interests Act 1980 s 2(4). General directions are to be published in such manner as appears appropriate to the Secretary of State: s 2(4).

9 Protection of Trading Interests Act 1980 s 2(1). A requirement is inadmissible if it infringes the jurisdiction of the United Kingdom or is otherwise prejudicial to the sovereignty of the United Kingdom (s 2(2)(a)), or if compliance with it would be prejudicial to the security of the United Kingdom or to the United Kingdom government's relations with any other country (s 2(2)(b)).
  A requirement under s 2(1)(a) (see head (1) in the text) is also inadmissible if it is made otherwise than for the purposes of civil or criminal proceedings which have been instituted in the overseas country (s 2(3)(a)) or if it requires a person to state what documents relevant to any

such proceedings are or have been in his possession, custody or power or to produce for the purposes of any such proceedings any documents other than particular documents specified in the requirement (s 2(3)(b)).

10	Ie directions under the Protection of Trading Interests Act 1980 s 2(1).

11	Protection of Trading Interests Act 1980 s 3(1). A person guilty of such an offence is liable on conviction on indictment to a fine or on summary conviction to a fine not exceeding the statutory maximum: s 3(1). As to the statutory maximum see SENTENCING AND DISPOSITION OF OFFENDERS vol 92 (2010) PARA 140. No proceedings for such an offence are to be instituted in England, Wales or Northern Ireland except by the Secretary of State or with the consent of the Attorney General or, as the case may be, the Attorney General for Northern Ireland: s 3(3). Proceedings may be taken before the appropriate United Kingdom court having jurisdiction in the place where that person is for the time being: s 3(4). A person who is neither a citizen of the United Kingdom and Colonies nor a body corporate incorporated in the United Kingdom is not guilty of an offence under s 3(1) by reason of anything done or omitted outside the United Kingdom in contravention of directions under s 2(1): s 3(2).

237. Requests for evidence for proceedings in other jurisdictions. A United Kingdom court may not make an order under the Evidence (Proceedings in Other Jurisdictions) Act 1975[1] for giving effect to a request issued by or on behalf of a court or tribunal of an overseas country[2] if it is shown that the request infringes the jurisdiction of the United Kingdom or is otherwise prejudicial to the sovereignty of the United Kingdom[3]. A certificate signed by or on behalf of the Secretary of State to that effect is conclusive evidence that it infringes that jurisdiction or is so prejudicial[4].

1	Ie under the Evidence (Proceedings in Other Jurisdictions) Act 1975 s 2: see CIVIL PROCEDURE vol 11 (2009) PARA 1058.
2	As to references to courts and overseas tribunals see PARA 236 note 2.
3	Protection of Trading Interests Act 1980 s 4. As to the meaning of 'United Kingdom' see PARA 30 note 3.
4	Protection of Trading Interests Act 1980 s 4.

238. Restriction on enforcement of certain overseas judgments. A judgment for multiple damages[1], a judgment based on a provision or rule of law specified or described in an order[2], and a judgment on a claim for contribution[3] in respect of damages awarded by either of the aforementioned judgments[4] may not be registered under Part II of the Administration of Justice Act 1920[5] or Part I of the Foreign Judgments (Reciprocal Enforcement) Act 1933[6], and no United Kingdom court may entertain proceedings at common law for the recovery of any sum payable under such a judgment[7].

1	Ie a judgment for an amount arrived at by doubling, trebling or otherwise multiplying a sum assessed as compensation for loss or damage sustained by the person in whose favour the judgment is given: Protection of Trading Interests Act 1980 s 5(2)(a), (3). This applies to a judgment given before 20 March 1980 as well as to a judgment given on or after that date but s 5 does not affect any judgment which has been registered before that date under the Administration of Justice Act 1920 Pt II (ss 9–14) or the Foreign Judgments (Reciprocal Enforcement) Act 1933 Pt I (ss 1–7), or in respect of which such proceedings have been finally determined before that date: Protection of Trading Interests Act 1980 s 5(6). Note that the fact that part of a judgment is for multiple damages does not make the remainder of that judgment unenforceable: see *Lucasfilm Ltd v Ainsworth* [2008] EWHC 1878 (Ch), [2009] IP & T 401; and *Lewis v Eliades* [2003] EWCA Civ 1758, [2004] 1 All ER 1196, [2004] 1 All ER (Comm) 545, [2004] 1 WLR 692.
2	Ie an order made by the Secretary of State in respect of any provision or rule of law which appears to him to be concerned with the prohibition or regulation of agreements, arrangements or practices designed to restrain, distort or restrict competition in the carrying on of business of any description or to be otherwise concerned with the promotion of such competition: Protection of Trading Interests Act 1980 s 5(2)(b), (4). The power of the Secretary of State to make such an order is exercisable by statutory instrument subject to annulment in pursuance of

a resolution of either House of Parliament: s 5(5). In exercise of this power, the Protection of Trading Interests (Australian Trade Practices) Order 1988, SI 1988/569, was made.

3 References to a claim for, or entitlement to, contribution are references to a claim or entitlement based on an enactment or rule of law: Protection of Trading Interests Act 1980 s 8(4).

4 Protection of Trading Interests Act 1980 s 5(2)(c).

5 Ie the Administration of Justice Act 1920 Pt II (ss 9–14): see CONFLICT OF LAWS vol 8(3) (Reissue) PARA 166 et seq.

6 Ie the Foreign Judgments (Reciprocal Enforcement) Act 1933 Pt I (ss 1–7): see CONFLICT OF LAWS vol 8(3) (Reissue) PARA 171 et seq.

7 Protection of Trading Interests Act 1980 s 5(1). The provisions of the Foreign Judgments (Reciprocal Enforcement) Act 1933 may, however, be applied by order. As to the meaning of 'United Kingdom' see PARA 30 note 3.

239. Recovery of awards for multiple damages. Where a court of an overseas country has given a judgment for multiple damages[1] on or after 20 March 1980[2] against a qualifying defendant[3] and an amount on account of the damages has been paid[4] by the qualifying defendant either to the party in whose favour the judgment was given[5] or to another party who is entitled as against the qualifying defendant to contribution[6] in respect of damages[7], the qualifying defendant is entitled to recover from the party in whose favour judgment was given so much of that amount as exceeds the part attributable to compensation[8]. A United Kingdom court may entertain proceedings brought by a person claiming to be so entitled notwithstanding that the person against whom the proceedings are brought is not within the jurisdiction[9].

A qualifying defendant is also entitled to recover when an order is made by a tribunal or authority of an overseas country which would, if that tribunal or authority were a court, be a judgment for multiple damages[10].

If it appears that the law of an overseas country provides or will provide for the enforcement in that country of judgments given under the above provisions relating to the recovery of multiple awards[11], an Order in Council may be made providing for the enforcement in the United Kingdom of judgments of any description specified in the order which are given under any provision of the law of that country relating to the recovery of sums paid or obtained pursuant to a judgment for multiple damages[12], whether or not that provision corresponds to the above provisions[13].

1 Ie within the meaning of the Protection of Trading Interests Act 1980 s 5(3) (see PARA 238): s 6(1). Section 6 is disapplied to the extent that EC Council Regulation 2271/96 (OJ L309, 22.11.96, p 1) (protecting against the effects of the extraterritorial application of legislation adopted by a third country) applies; and it is an offence to breach art 2 or art 5: Extraterritorial US Legislation (Sanctions against Cuba, Iran and Libya) (Protection of Trading Interests) Order 1996, SI 1996/3171, art 3(2).

2 Protection of Trading Interests Act 1980 s 6(8).

3 'Qualifying defendant' means (1) a citizen of the United Kingdom and Colonies; (2) a body corporate incorporated in the United Kingdom or in a territory outside the United Kingdom for whose international relations the United Kingdom government is responsible; or (3) a person carrying on business in the United Kingdom: Protection of Trading Interests Act 1980 s 6(1). As to the meaning of 'United Kingdom' see PARA 30 note 3.

4 This includes an amount obtained by execution against the qualifying defendant's property or against the property of a company which directly or indirectly is wholly owned by him: Protection of Trading Interests Act 1980 s 6(6).

5 Or to any person in whom the rights of any such party have become vested by succession or assignment or otherwise: Protection of Trading Interests Act 1980 s 6(6).

6 This includes such a party's successors and assignees: Protection of Trading Interests Act 1980 s 6(6). As to references to 'contribution' see PARA 238 note 3.

7 Protection of Trading Interests Act 1980 s 6(1).

8 Protection of Trading Interests Act 1980 s 6(2). That part is taken to be such part as bears the same proportion to the whole of it as the sum assessed by the court that gave the judgment as

compensation for the loss or damage sustained by the party in whose favour the judgment was given bears to the whole of the damages awarded to that party: s 6(2). However, this does not apply where the qualifying defendant is an individual who was ordinarily resident in the overseas country at the time when the proceedings in which the judgment was given were instituted or a body corporate which had its principal place of business there at that time: s 6(3). Further, s 6(2) does not apply where the qualifying defendant carried on business in the overseas country and the proceedings in which the judgment was given were concerned with activities exclusively carried on in that country: s 6(4).

9   Protection of Trading Interests Act 1980 s 6(5).

10   Protection of Trading Interests Act 1980 s 6(7).

11   Ie under the Protection of Trading Interests Act 1980 s 6: see the text and notes 1–10.

12   See PARA 238 note 1.

13   Protection of Trading Interests Act 1980 s 7(1) (amended by the Civil Jurisdiction and Judgments Act 1982 s 38(1), (2)). As to the orders made see the Reciprocal Enforcement of Foreign Judgments (Australia) Order 1994, SI 1994/1901.

   Such an Order in Council may, as respects judgments to which it relates, make different provision for different descriptions of judgment and impose conditions or restrictions on the enforcement of judgments of any description: Protection of Trading Interests Act 1980 s 7(1A) (added by the Civil Jurisdiction and Judgments Act 1982 s 38(1), (3)). An order under the Protection of Trading Interests Act 1980 s 7 may apply, with or without modification, any of the provisions of the Foreign Judgments (Reciprocal Enforcement) Act 1933: Protection of Trading Interests Act 1980 s 7(2). See CONFLICT OF LAWS.

(3) FOREIGN JURISDICTION

240.   Jurisdiction over British subjects abroad. In certain foreign countries[1], and also in British protectorates[2], the Crown has in the past acquired jurisdiction[3] over British subjects, and in some cases over foreigners, by treaty, capitulation, grant, usage, sufferance and other lawful means[4]; and where a foreign country is not subject to any government from whom the Crown might obtain jurisdiction in any of these ways, jurisdiction has been conferred upon the Crown by statute over British subjects for the time being resident in or resorting to that country[5].

The jurisdiction so acquired or to be acquired in any foreign country may be held, exercised and enjoyed by the Crown in the same and as ample a manner as if acquired by the cession or conquest of territory[6], and every act and thing done in pursuance of it is to be as valid as if it had been done according to the local law then in force in that foreign country[7].

If, in any proceeding, civil or criminal, in a court in Her Majesty's dominions or held under the authority of Her Majesty, any question arises as to the existence or extent of any jurisdiction of Her Majesty in a foreign country, a Secretary of State must, on the application of the court, send to the court within a reasonable time his decision on the question[8].

1   'Foreign country' means any country or place out of Her Majesty's dominions (Foreign Jurisdiction Act 1890 s 16), and in this context includes trust territories which were formerly administered under mandate of the League of Nations. The area within which this jurisdiction is exercised has probably now disappeared.

2   As to British protectorates and trust territories generally, and the jurisdiction there exercised by the Crown, see COMMONWEALTH.

3   'Jurisdiction' includes power: Foreign Jurisdiction Act 1890 s 16. The view that the protecting state cannot exercise jurisdiction over subjects of third states within the protectorate or protected state without the consent of that state seems to have been abandoned after 1890. It is implicit in the wording of s 1 that the United Kingdom may exercise such jurisdiction generally over foreigners in such territories: see the text to note 6; and the Report of the Law Officers of the Crown, 14 February 1895, 1 McNair's International Law Opinions 54. As to the meaning of 'United Kingdom' see PARA 30 note 3.

4   These are the modes of acquisition recited in the preamble to the Foreign Jurisdiction Act 1890.

5   Foreign Jurisdiction Act 1890 s 2. Note that the jurisdiction conferred is confined to British subjects. Section 2 would not, it seems, afford a valid argument by a foreigner in support of a plea of want of jurisdiction in a protectorate court, since foreign nations themselves have claimed and exercised jurisdiction over foreigners in their protectorates: see Hall's Foreign Jurisdiction 221 et seq.

6   Foreign Jurisdiction Act 1890 s 1. As to jurisdiction in ceded and conquered colonies see COMMONWEALTH vol 13 (2009) PARAS 803, 808. As to suspension of the royal prerogative while letters patent were in force and the rule that the Crown has no prerogative right to legislate in settlements see *Sammut v Strickland* [1938] AC 678, [1938] 3 All ER 693, 2 BILC 648, PC.

7   Foreign Jurisdiction Act 1890 s 3.

8   Foreign Jurisdiction Act 1890 s 4(1). The Secretary of State's decision is, for the purposes of the proceeding, final: s 4(1). The court must send to the Secretary of State, in a document under the seal of the court, or signed by a judge of the court, questions framed so as properly to raise the question, and sufficient answers to those questions are to be returned by the Secretary of State to the court, and those answers are conclusive evidence of the matters contained: s 4(2). As to the power to send a person charged with an offence cognisable in one of Her Majesty's courts in a foreign country for trial to a British possession see s 6. As to execution of sentences see s 7. For the power of deportation of a British court in a foreign country see s 8. For the power to extend, by Order in Council, specified Acts to foreign countries in which the Crown has jurisdiction see s 5, Sch 1; and COMMONWEALTH vol 13 (2009) PARA 871.

241.   Consular and other courts in foreign countries.

The jurisdiction vested in the Crown[1] was exercised by means of courts established in foreign countries by Order in Council under statutory powers[2]. Such courts had in some cases permanent judges and assistant judges[3], or were held by consuls-general, consuls or vice-consuls, according to the provisions of the various orders in force. In some cases an appellate jurisdiction was vested either in the court of some adjacent colony or in a supreme court specially constituted for some particular foreign territory, and in others the appeal lay direct to the Sovereign in Council. In some cases the laws obtaining in other portions of the Commonwealth were made applicable[4].

1   See PARA 240.

2   These are conferred by the Foreign Jurisdiction Act 1890. Every Order in Council made in pursuance of the Foreign Jurisdiction Act 1890 is to be laid before both Houses of Parliament: s 11.

3   See eg the Bahrain Order 1959, SI 1959/1035 (spent).

4   Eg certain laws of India and the United Kingdom were made applicable in Bahrain: see the Bahrain Order 1959, SI 1959/1035 (spent).

11. JURISDICTIONAL IMMUNITIES

(1) STATE IMMUNITY

242.   State immunity under international law. The law on state immunity is derived from rules of international law which limit the rights of the courts of one state to exercise authority over other states and their officials[1]. The rules stem from the basic principle of the sovereign equality of states and are designed to ensure that international relations can be properly and effectively conducted[2]. Their significance as a part of the international legal order has long been recognised by domestic courts[3] and has also been acknowledged by international courts and tribunals, including the European Court of Human Rights[4]. In 1972, the United Kingdom signed the European Convention on State Immunity[5]. More recently, the United Nations Convention on Jurisdictional Immunities of States and Their Property[6] was adopted by the UN General Assembly[7].

1   State immunity is not a self-imposed restriction on the jurisdiction of the courts but a limitation imposed from without: *Holland v Lampen-Wolfe* [2000] 3 All ER 833 at 847–848, [2000] 1 WLR 1573 at 1588, HL. See also *Jones v Ministry of the Interior of the Kingdom of Saudi Arabia* [2006] UKHL 26, [2007] 1 AC 270, [2007] 1 All ER 113 at [101].

2   1 *Oppenheim's International Law* (9th Edn, 1992) Vol 1 pp 341–343; Lady Fox *The Law of State Immunity* (2nd Edn, 2008) pp 57–59.

3   See eg *Le Parlement Belge* (1880) 5 PD 197, CA; *The Schooner Exchange v Mcfaddon* 7 Cranch 116, US SC (1812); *R v Bow Street Metropolitan Stipendiary Magistrate, ex p Pinochet Ugarte (No 3) (Amnesty International intervening)* [2000] 1 AC 147 at 201, 268–269 [1999] 2 All ER 97 at 110, 169–170.

4   *Al Adsani v United Kingdom* (ECHR Application 35753/97) (2002) 34 EHRR 273, 123 ILR 23; *Fogarty v United Kingdom* (ECHR Application 37112/97) (2001) 34 EHRR 302, 123 ILR 53; *McElhinney v Ireland and United Kingdom* (ECHR Application 31253/96) (2002) 34 EHRR 323, 123 ILR 73; *Kalogeropolou v Greece and Germany* (ECHR Application 0059021/00), 129 ILR 537.

5   Basle 16 May 1972; TS 74 (1979); Cmnd 7742. The United Kingdom ratified this Convention and the International Convention for the Unification of Certain Rules Concerning the Immunity of State-owned Ships (Brussels 10 April 1926, with Protocol, Brussels 24 May 1934; TS 15 (1980); Cmnd 7800) after the enactment of the State Immunity Act 1978. The Convention has not achieved wide acceptance and has been ratified by only eight states: Austria (10 July 1975); Belgium (27 October 1975); Cyprus (10 March 1976); Germany (15 may 1990); Luxembourg (11 December 1986); the Netherlands (21 February 1985); Switzerland (6 July 1982) and the United Kingdom (3 July 1979). All except the UK have also ratified the Additional Protocol which came into force on 22 May 1985. For the history and structure of the Convention see Sir Iain Sinclair 'The European Convention on State Immunity' ICLQ 22 (1973) 254; and Lady Fox *The Law of State Immunity*, (2nd Edn, 2008) pp 187–193.

6   United Nations Convention on Jurisdictional Immunities of States and Their Property (New York, 2 December 2004). The Convention is not yet in force, although 28 states, including the United Kingdom have signed it and the courts have already drawn upon its provisions in seeking to clarify the rules on state immunity: see *Jones v Ministry of the Interior of the Kingdom of Saudi Arabia* [2006] UKHL 26, [2007] 1 AC 270, [2007] 1 All ER 113; *Koo Golden East Mongolia v Bank of Nova Scotia* [2007] EWCA Civ 1443, [2008] QB 717, [2008] 2 All ER (Comm) 314; *AIG Capital Partners Inc v Republic of Kazakhstan (National Bank of Kasakhstan intervening)* [2005] EWHC 2239 (Comm) at [80], [2006] 1 All ER 284 at [80], [2006] 1 All ER (Comm) 1 at [80].

7   United Nations General Assembly Resolution 59/38 of 16 December 2004.

243.   State immunity at common law. At common law, a foreign sovereign state and its head of state were entitled to claim immunity from the jurisdiction of the English courts in any action in which it was directly or indirectly impleaded. No distinction was drawn between actions which arose from the foreign state's official acts (acta jure imperii) and those which arose from its commercial activities (acta jure gestionis), as was the case under the law of many other states[1]. In 1972, the United Kingdom signed the European Convention on State Immunity[2], which draws this distinction and confers immunity on the foreign state in respect of the former but not the latter, class of actions. Beginning in 1976, the English courts adhered to the distinction[3] and in the State Immunity Act 1978, which, subject to exceptions, replaces the rules of common law, the distinction between the two classes of case is drawn. However, in certain situations the Act does not apply[4] and another statute or the common law governs the immunity of the foreign states[5].

1 See eg *Thai-Europe Tapioca Service Ltd v Government of Pakistan* [1975] 3 All ER 961, [1975] 1 WLR 1485, CA.
2 See PARA 242 note 5.
3 See *Philippine Admiral (Owners) v Wallem Shipping (Hong Kong) Ltd* [1977] AC 373, [1976] 1 All ER 78, PC; *Trendtex Trading Corpn v Central Bank of Nigeria* [1977] QB 529, [1977] 1 All ER 881, CA; *Playa Larga (Owners of Cargo Lately Laden on Board) v I Congreso del Partido (Owners)* [1983] 1 AC 244, sub nom *I Congreso del Partido* [1981] 2 All ER 1064, HL.
4 As to matters excluded from the operation of the State Immunity Act 1978 Pt I (ss 1–17) see s 16; and PARAS 259, 324.
5 'In the absence of statutory enactment, it is the common law including the incorporated rules of customary international law, which identifies and defines the extent of sovereign immunity': *Littrell v United States of America (No 2)* [1994] 4 All ER 203 at 210–211, [1995] 1 WLR 82 at 89, CA, per Rose LJ. See also *Holland v Lampen-Wolfe* [2000] 3 All ER 833, [2000] 1 WLR 1573, HL (affg [1999] 1 WLR 188, CA); and *Re AY Bank Ltd (in liquidation) v Bosnia and Herzegovina* [2006] EWHC 830 (Ch), [2006] 2 All ER (Comm) 463. For an illustration of the common law approach see the cases cited in note 3.

(2) STATE IMMUNITY UNDER THE STATE IMMUNITY ACT 1978

244. State immunity. A state[1] is immune from the jurisdiction of the United Kingdom courts[2], except as otherwise provided[3]. A court must give effect to the immunity conferred even though the state does not appear[4] in the proceedings in question[5].

1 As to the meaning of 'state' see PARA 245.
2 'Court' includes any tribunal or body exercising judicial functions and a reference to the courts or law of the United Kingdom includes the courts or law of any part of the United Kingdom: State Immunity Act 1978 s 22(1). As to the meaning of 'United Kingdom' see PARA 30 note 3.
3 State Immunity Act 1978 s 1(1). See *Re P (Children Act: Diplomatic Immunity)* [1998] 1 FLR 624 (diplomatic agent and family ordered home by the United States government, his employer; claim against him subject to state immunity). For the exceptions from immunity see PARA 246 et seq. As to matters excluded from the scope of the State Immunity Act 1978, including criminal proceedings, see PARA 259.
4 References to entry of appearance, and judgment in default of appearance, include references to any corresponding procedures: State Immunity Act 1978 s 22(2). In proceedings in the United Kingdom, 'entry of appearance', in proceedings to which the CPR apply, has been replaced by acknowledgment of service. As to acknowledgment of service see CPR Pt 10. As to judgment in default of acknowledgment of service see CPR Pt 12. As to the proceedings to which the CPR do not apply see CPR 2.1. See further CIVIL PROCEDURE.
5 State Immunity Act 1978 s 1(2). See also *United Arab Emirates v Abdelghafar* [1995] ICR 65, [1995] IRLR 243; *Aziz v Bethnal Green City Challenge Co Ltd* [2000] IRLR 111, CA; *Caramba-Coker v Military Affairs Office of the Embassy of Kuwait* [2003] All ER (D) 186 (Apr), EAT.

245. Meaning of 'state'. The immunities and privileges conferred by the State Immunity Act 1978[1] apply to any foreign or Commonwealth state other than the United Kingdom[2]. A state includes (1) the sovereign or other head of that state in his public capacity; (2) the government of that state; and (3) any department of that government, but not an entity (a 'separate entity')[3] which is distinct from the executive organs of the government of the state and capable of suing or being sued[4].

A certificate by or on behalf of the Secretary of State[5] is conclusive evidence on any question whether any country is a state, whether any territory is a constituent territory of a federal state for those purposes, or as to the person or persons to be regarded for those purposes as the head or government of a state[6].

The State Immunity Act 1978 does not expressly provide for cases where an action is brought against the servants or agents of a foreign state, but there is authority that, in such cases, a state is entitled to claim immunity for its servants or agents as it could if it were sued itself[7]. A foreign state's entitlement to immunity cannot, therefore, be circumvented by suing its servants or agents[8].

1   Ie conferred by the State Immunity Act 1978 Pt I (ss 1–17).

2   State Immunity Act 1978 s 14(1). As to the meaning of 'United Kingdom' see PARA 30 note 3.

3   A separate entity is immune from United Kingdom jurisdiction only if (1) the proceedings relate to anything done by it in the exercise of sovereign authority; and (2) the circumstances are such that a state (or, in the case of proceedings to which the State Immunity Act 1978 s 10 applies, a state which is not a party to the Brussels Convention (see PARA 254)) would have been so immune: State Immunity Act 1978 s 14(2). Where the provisions of Pt I do not apply to a constituent territory by virtue of an order under s 14(5) (see note 4), s 14(2) applies to it as if it were a separate entity: s 14(6). See also *Kuwait Airways Corpn v Iraqi Airways Co* [1995] 3 All ER 694, [1995] 1 WLR 1147, HL (in determining whether 'separate entity' has acted in the exercise of sovereign authority all the relevant circumstances must be taken into consideration. State-owned aircraft company not entitled to state immunity where acts not of a governmental nature, even though performed on direction of state); *Grovit v De Nederlandsche Bank; Thorncroft v De Nederlandsche Bank* [2005] EWHC 2944 (QB), [2006] 1 All ER (Comm) 397, [2006] 1 WLR 3323 (central bank of the Netherlands capable of being separate entity); and *Pocket Kings Ltd v Safenames Ltd* [2009] EWHC 2529 (Ch), [2009] All ER (D) 205 (Oct).

4   State Immunity Act 1978 s 14(1). Part I may be extended to any constituent territory specified by order: s 14(5). See the State Immunity (Federal States) Order 1979, SI 1979/457; and the State Immunity (Federal States) Order 1993, SI 1993/2809.

   The State Immunity Act 1978 may be extended to any British overseas territory: s 23(7) (amended by virtue of the British Overseas Territories Act 2002 s 1(2)). 'British overseas territory' means (1) any of the Channel Islands; (2) the Isle of Man; (3) any colony other than one for whose external relations a country other than the United Kingdom is responsible; or (4) any country or territory outside Her Majesty's dominions in which Her Majesty has jurisdiction in right of the government of the United Kingdom: State Immunity Act 1978 s 22(4) (amended by virtue of the British Overseas Territories Act 2002 s 1(2)). See the State Immunity (Overseas Territories) Order 1979, SI 1979/458; the State Immunity (Guernsey) Order 1980, SI 1980/871; the State Immunity (Isle of Man) Order 1981, SI 1981/1112; and the State Immunity (Jersey) Order 1985, SI 1985/1642.

   The European Union is not entitled to foreign sovereign immunity: *J H Rayner (Mincing Lane) Ltd v Department of Trade and Industry* [1989] 1 Ch 72 at 196–203, sub nom *Maclaine Watson & Co Ltd v Department of Trade and Industry* [1988] 3 All ER 257 at 316–320, CA.

5   As to the Secretary of State see PARA 29.

6   State Immunity Act 1978 s 21(a).

7   *Jones v Ministry of the Interior of the Kingdom of Saudi Arabia* [2006] UKHL 26 at [10], [2007] 1 AC 270 at [10], [2007] 1 All ER 113 at [10]. The term 'government' as it appears in the State Immunity Act 1978 s 14(1) must be given a broad meaning and would include police functions as part of governmental activity: *Propend Finance Property Ltd v Sing* (1997) 111 ILR 611 at 669, Times 2 May, CA. A state's entitlement to immunity for the acts of its servants and agents does not require that they should have been acting in accordance with their instructions or authority. A state may claim immunity on behalf of such persons for any act for which it is, in international law responsible, save where an established exception applies: see *Jones v Ministry of the Interior of the Kingdom of Saudi Arabia* above at [12] and [74]–[78].

8   See note 7.

246. Submission to jurisdiction. A state[1] is not immune from proceedings in respect of which it has submitted[2] to the jurisdiction of the United Kingdom courts[3]. A state may submit after the dispute giving rise to the proceedings has arisen or by a prior written agreement[4].

A state is deemed to have submitted if (1) it has instituted the proceedings; or (2) it has intervened or taken any step in the proceedings[5]. However, head (2) above does not apply to: (a) intervention or any step taken for the purpose only of claiming immunity or asserting an interest in property in circumstances such that the state would have been entitled to immunity if the proceedings had been brought against it[6]; or (b) any step taken by the state in ignorance of facts entitling it to immunity if those facts could not reasonably have been ascertained and immunity is claimed as soon as reasonably practicable[7].

1   As to the meaning of 'state' see PARA 245.

2   The head of a state's diplomatic mission in the United Kingdom, or the person performing his functions, is deemed to have authority to submit on behalf of the state in respect of any proceedings; any person who has entered into a contract on behalf of and with the authority of a state is deemed to have authority to submit on its behalf to proceedings arising out of the contract: State Immunity Act 1978 s 2(7). As to the meaning of 'United Kingdom' see PARA 30 note 3. The State Immunity Act 1978 requires an express submission to the jurisdiction of the courts. A failure to challenge an award made without jurisdiction would not in itself amount to an agreement in writing to submit the dispute to arbitration. However, where such submission has occurred it will remove a state's immunity in proceedings brought before the English courts for leave to enforce such an award whether the award was made in the United Kingdom or abroad. See *Svenska Petroleum Exploration AB v Government of the Republic of Lithuania* [2006] EWCA Civ 1529, [2007] QB 886, [2007] 1 All ER (Comm) 909 (affg [2005] EWHC 2437 (Comm) 1529, [2006] 1 All ER (Comm) 731); *Donegal International Ltd v Rebpublic of Zambia* [2007] EWHC 197 (Comm), [2007] 1 Lloyd's Rep 397, [2007] All ER (D) 184 (Feb) (written submissions to the jurisdiction with regard to a compromise agreement amounted to waiver of immunity).

3   State Immunity Act 1978 s 2(1). As to the meaning of 'court' see PARA 244 note 2.

4   State Immunity Act 1978 s 2(2). However, a provision in any agreement that it is to be governed by the law of the United Kingdom is not to be regarded as a submission: s 2(2). 'Agreement' includes a treaty, convention or other international agreement: s 17(2). See also *Ahmed v Government of the Kingdom of Saudi Arabia* [1996] 2 All ER 248, [1996] ICR 25, CA (letter from state's solicitor to state's military attaché did not constitute prior written agreement between state and dismissed employee).

    A submission in respect of any proceedings extends to any appeal but not to any counterclaim unless it arises out of the same legal relationship or facts as the claim: State Immunity Act 1978 s 2(6).

5   State Immunity Act 1978 s 2(3)(a), (b). See eg *London Branch of the Nigerian Universities Commission v Bastians* [1995] ICR 358, EAT (requirements of the Industrial Tribunals (Rules of Procedure) Regulations 1985, SI 1985/16, reg 3(1) (repealed: see now the Employment Tribunals (Constitution and Rules of Procedure) Regulations 2004, SI 2004/1861, reg 16(1), Sch 1 r 4) were not satisfied where a foreign state returned an uncompleted, undated and unsigned notice of appearance with an accompanying note, through the Foreign Office); *Arab Republic of Egypt v Gamal-Eldin* [1996] 2 All ER 237, [1996] ICR 13, EAT (no steps taken in proceedings where person who was not authorised to submit to jurisdiction on state's behalf wrote to industrial tribunal stating complainant's nationality). A member of a diplomatic mission or solicitors instructed by such a mission cannot take a step under the State Immunity Act 1978 s 2(3)(b) without the authority of the head of the mission or the person for the time being performing his functions: *Republic of Yemen v Aziz* [2005] EWCA Civ 745, [2005] ICR 1391, [2005] All ER (D) 188 (Jun).

6   State Immunity Act 1978 s 2(4). See *Caramba-Coker v Military Affairs Office of the Embassy of Kuwait* [2003] All ER (D) 186 (Apr), EAT (no submission to the jurisdiction will occur if the state disputing jurisdiction takes part in the proceedings solely for the purpose of securing a favourable finding on facts on which the question of jurisdiction depends).

7   State Immunity Act 1978 s 2(5).

247. Commercial transactions and contracts to be performed in the United Kingdom. A state[1] is not immune from proceedings relating to: (1) a commercial transaction[2] entered into by the state[3]; or (2) an obligation of the state which by virtue of a contract (whether a commercial transaction or not) falls to be performed wholly or partly in the United Kingdom[4], unless the parties to the dispute are states or have otherwise agreed in writing[5].

The provisions described above do not apply to certain Admiralty proceedings[6].

1   As to the meaning of 'state' see PARA 245.
2   'Commercial transaction' means (1) any contract for the supply of goods or services; (2) any loan or other transaction for the provision of finance and any guarantee or indemnity in respect of any such transaction or of any other financial obligation; and (3) any other transaction or activity (whether of a commercial, industrial, financial, professional or other similar character) into which a state enters or in which it engages otherwise than in the exercise of sovereign authority: State Immunity Act 1978 s 3(3). However, s 3(1) (see the text and notes 3–4) does not apply to a contract of employment between a state and an individual: s 3(3). In Pt I (ss 1–17), 'commercial purposes' means purposes of such transactions or activities as are mentioned in s 3(3): s 17(1).
      See also *Planmount Ltd v Republic of Zaire* [1981] 1 All ER 1110, [1980] 2 Lloyd's Rep 393 (defence of sovereign immunity not available in action on contract for repair of ambassadorial residence); *Alcom Ltd v Republic of Colombia* [1984] AC 580, [1984] 2 All ER 6, HL (United Kingdom bank account maintained by embassy for daily running expenses of mission immune from proceedings enforcing embassy's judgment debt); *Koo Golden East Mongolia v Bank of Nova Scotia* [2007] EWCA Civ 1443, [2008] QB 717, [2008] 2 All ER (Comm) 314 (central bank regarded as 'separate entity' and enjoys same immunity from enforcement measures as the state itself).
3   State Immunity Act 1978 s 3(1)(a). See *Sabah Shipyard (Pakistan) Ltd v Islamic Republic of Pakistan* [2002] EWCA Civ 1643, [2003] 2 Lloyd's Rep 571 (clause requiring state to submit to jurisdiction of English court construed under ordinary principles of construction for commercial contracts).
4   State Immunity Act 1978 s 3(1)(b). This does not apply if the contract (not being a commercial transaction) was made in the territory of the state concerned and the obligation in question is governed by its administrative law: s 3(2).
      For these purposes, and the purposes of ss 4–8 (see PARAS 248–252), the territory of the United Kingdom is deemed to include any British overseas territory in respect of which the United Kingdom is a party to the European Convention on State Immunity (Basle, 16 May 1972; TS 74 (1979); Cmnd 7742): State Immunity Act 1978 ss 17(3), 22(3) (s 17(3) amended by virtue of the British Overseas Territories Act 2002 s 1(2)). Further, in the State Immunity Act 1978 ss 3(1), 4(1), 5, 16(2), references to the United Kingdom include reference to its territorial waters and any area designated under the Continental Shelf Act 1964 s 1(7) (see PARA 172): State Immunity Act 1978 s 17(4). As to the general statutory meaning of 'United Kingdom' see PARA 30 note 3. As to the meaning of 'British overseas territory' see PARA 245 note 4.
      A certificate by or on behalf of the Secretary of State is conclusive evidence on any question whether a state is a party to the European Convention on State Immunity, whether it has made a declaration under art 24, or as to the territories in respect of which the United Kingdom or any other state is a party: State Immunity Act 1978 s 21(c). As to the Secretary of State see PARA 29.
5   State Immunity Act 1978 s 3(2).
6   See the State Immunity Act 1978 s 10(6); and PARA 254 note 1.

248. Contracts of employment. A state[1] is not immune from proceedings relating to a contract of employment[2] between the state and an individual where the contract was made in the United Kingdom[3] or the work is to be wholly or partly performed there[4].

Subject to exceptions[5], this does not apply if: (1) when the proceedings are brought, the individual is a national of the state concerned[6]; or (2) when the contract was made the individual was neither a national of the United Kingdom[7] nor habitually resident there[8]; or (3) the parties to the contract have otherwise agreed in writing[9]. Further, the provisions described above do not apply to proceedings concerning the employment of the members of a diplomatic mission[10] or the members of a consular post[11].

The provisions described above do not apply to certain Admiralty proceedings[12].

1 As to the meaning of 'state' see PARA 245.
2 'Proceedings relating to a contract of employment' include proceedings between the parties to a contract of employment in respect of any statutory rights or duties to which they are entitled or subject as employer or employee: State Immunity Act 1978 s 4(6). See also *Sengupta v Republic of India* [1983] ICR 221, (1982) 126 Sol Jo 855, EAT.
3 As to the meaning of 'United Kingdom' for these purposes see PARA 247 note 4. As to the statutory meaning of 'United Kingdom' generally see PARA 30 note 3.
4 State Immunity Act 1978 s 4(1).
5 Where the work is for an office, agency or establishment maintained by the state in the United Kingdom for commercial purposes, heads (1) and (2) in the text do not exclude the application of the State Immunity Act 1978 s 4 unless the individual was habitually resident in that state when the contract was made: s 4(3). Head (3) in the text does not exclude the application of s 4 where the law of the United Kingdom requires the proceedings to be brought before a United Kingdom court: s 4(4). As to the meaning of 'court' see PARA 244 note 2. As to the meaning of 'commercial purposes' see PARA 247 note 2. See also *Arab Republic of Egypt v Gamal-Eldin* [1996] 2 All ER 237, [1996] ICR 13, EAT (state's medical office used to provide medical guidance, advice and expert care, not established for commercial purposes).
6 State Immunity Act 1978 s 4(2)(a).
7 'National of the United Kingdom' means a British citizen, a British overseas territories citizen, a British National (Overseas), a British Overseas citizen, a British subject or a British protected person: State Immunity Act 1978 s 4(5) (amended by the British Nationality Act 1981 s 52(6), Sch 7; the British Overseas Territories Act 2002 s 2(3); and SI 1986/948).
8 State Immunity Act 1978 s 4(2)(b). See *Arab Republic of Egypt v Gamal-Eldin* [1996] 2 All ER 237, [1996] ICR 13, EAT.
9 State Immunity Act 1978 s 4(2)(c).
10 Ie a mission within the meaning of the Diplomatic Privileges Act 1964 (see PARA 265 et seq). See also *Sengupta v Republic of India* [1983] ICR 221, EAT; *Ahmed v Government of the Kingdom of Saudi Arabia* [1996] 2 All ER 248, [1996] ICR 25, CA (a secretary employed in the administrative and technical services of a foreign embassy was a 'member of a mission' even though she was a British national who had been recruited in the United Kingdom); *Republic of Yemen v Aziz* [2005] EWCA Civ 745, [2005] ICR 1391, [2005] All ER (D) 188 (Jun); *Caramba-Coker v Military Affairs Office of the Embassy of Kuwait* [2003] All ER (D) 186 (Apr), EAT.
11 State Immunity Act 1978 s 16(1)(a). As to consular posts see PARA 290 et seq.
12 See the State Immunity Act 1978 s 10(6); and PARA 254 note 1.

249. Personal injuries and damage to property. A state[1] is not immune from proceedings in respect of (1) death or personal injury; or (2) damage to or loss of tangible property, caused by an act or omission in the United Kingdom[2].

There is no express requirement for the act or omission to be of a commercial or private law nature[3] provided it occurs within the United Kingdom. Where the alleged act or omission occurs abroad, however, the exception will not apply and the general immunity from jurisdiction in the State Immunity Act 1978[4] will apply so as to confer immunity upon the foreign state even though the acts alleged contravene the international prohibition against torture[5].

1 As to the meaning of 'state' see PARA 245.
2 State Immunity Act 1978 s 5. As to the meaning of 'United Kingdom' for these purposes see PARA 247 note 4. As to the statutory meaning of 'United Kingdom' generally see PARA 30 note 3.
   These provisions do not apply to certain Admiralty proceedings: see s 10(6); and PARA 254 note 1.
3 See *Letelier v Chile*, USA 488 F Supp 665 (1980), 63 ILR 378 (US Court rejected claim that torts exception in US Foreign Sovereign Immunities legislation referred only to private acts and

held that it could apply to political assassination). Cf the position under common law: see *Holland v Lampen-Wolfe* [2000] 3 All ER 833, [2000] 1 WLR 1573, HL.

4   Ie under the State Immunity Act 1978 s 1; see PARA 244.

5   *Al Adsani v Government of Kuwait* (1996) Times, 29 March, CA; *Jones v Ministry of the Interior of the Kingdom of Saudi Arabia (Secretary of State for Constitutional Affairs intervening)* [2006] UKHL 26, [2007] 1 AC 270, [2007] 1 All ER 113.

250.   Property.   A state[1] is not immune from proceedings relating to (1) any interest of the state in, or its possession or use of, immovable property in the United Kingdom[2]; or (2) any obligation of the state arising out of its interest in, or its possession or use of, any such property[3]. Neither is a state immune as respects proceedings relating to any interest of the state in moveable or immovable property, being an interest arising by way of succession, gift or bona vacantia[4].

The fact that a state has or claims an interest in any property does not preclude any court[5] from exercising in respect of it any jurisdiction relating to the estates of deceased persons or persons of unsound mind, insolvency, the winding up of companies or the administration of trusts[6].

In specified circumstances[7], a court may entertain proceedings against a person other than a state notwithstanding that the proceedings relate to property which is in the possession or control of a state, or in which a state claims an interest[8].

1   As to the meaning of 'state' see PARA 245.

2   State Immunity Act 1978 s 6(1)(a). As to the meaning of 'United Kingdom' for these purposes see PARA 247 note 4. As to the statutory meaning of 'United Kingdom' generally see PARA 30 note 3. Section 6(1) does not apply to proceedings concerning a state's title to or its possession of property used for the purposes of a diplomatic mission: s 16(1)(b). As to diplomatic missions see PARA 265 et seq. See *Intpro Properties (UK) Ltd v Sauvel* [1983] QB 1019, [1983] 2 All ER 495, CA (private residence of diplomat (not head of mission) not included within the State Immunity Act 1978 s 16(1)(b) exclusion. Proceedings for breach of covenant not to be construed as 'proceedings concerning title or possession').

3   State Immunity Act 1978 s 6(1)(b).

4   State Immunity Act 1978 s 6(2). As to bona vacantia see CROWN PROPERTY vol 12(1) (Reissue) PARA 235 et seq.

5   As to the meaning of 'court' see PARA 244 note 2.

6   State Immunity Act 1978 s 6(3). Thus a foreign state which is a creditor of an insolvent company cannot claim its debts in priority to other creditors: *Re Rafidain Bank* [1992] BCLC 301, [1992] BCC 376.

7   Ie (1) if the state would not have been immune had the proceedings been brought against it; or (2) in a case within the State Immunity Act 1978 s 6(1)(b) (see head (2) in the text), if the claim is neither admitted nor supported by prima facie evidence: s 6(4).

8   State Immunity Act 1978 s 6(4).

251.   Patents, trade-marks, etc.   A state[1] is not immune from proceedings relating to (1) any patent, trade-mark, design or plant breeders' rights belonging to the state and registered or protected in the United Kingdom[2], or for which the state has applied in the United Kingdom[3]; (2) an alleged infringement by the state in the United Kingdom of any patent, trade-mark, design, plant breeders' rights or copyright[4]; or (3) the right to use a trade or business name in the United Kingdom[5].

1   As to the meaning of 'state' see PARA 245.

2   As to the meaning of 'United Kingdom' for these purposes see PARA 247 note 4. As to the statutory meaning of 'United Kingdom' generally see PARA 30 note 3.

3   State Immunity Act 1978 s 7(a).

4 State Immunity Act 1978 s 7(b). See *J H Rayner (Mincing Lane)Ltd v Department of Trade and Industry* [1987] BCLC 667, Staughton J; *Gerber Products Co v Gerber Foods International Ltd* [2002] EWHC 428 (Ch), [2002] All ER (D) 264 (Mar).
5 State Immunity Act 1978 s 7(c).

252. Membership of bodies corporate etc. A state[1] is not immune from proceedings[2] relating to its membership of a body corporate, an unincorporated body or a partnership which (1) has members other than states[3]; and (2) is incorporated or constituted under the law of the United Kingdom or is controlled from or has its principal place of business in the United Kingdom[4].

However, this does not apply if contrary provision has been made by a written agreement between the parties to a dispute or by the constitution or other instrument establishing or regulating the body or partnership in question[5].

1 As to the meaning of 'state' see PARA 245.
2 Ie proceedings between the state and the body or its other members or between the state and the other partners: State Immunity Act 1978 s 8(1).
3 State Immunity Act 1978 s 8(1)(a).
4 State Immunity Act 1978 s 8(1)(b). As to the meaning of 'United Kingdom' for these purposes see PARA 247 note 4. As to the statutory meaning of 'United Kingdom' generally see PARA 30 note 3.
5 State Immunity Act 1978 s 8(2).

253. Arbitrations. Where a state[1] has agreed in writing to submit a dispute which has arisen, or may arise to arbitration, it is not immune from proceedings in the United Kingdom[2] courts[3] which relate to the arbitration[4]. However, this is subject to any contrary provision in the arbitration agreement and does not apply to any arbitration agreement between states[5].

1 As to the meaning of 'state' see PARA 245.
2 As to the statutory meaning of 'United Kingdom' see PARA 30 note 3.
3 As to the meaning of 'court' see PARA 244 note 2.
4 State Immunity Act 1978 s 9(1). See *Svenska v Petroleum Exploration AB v Government of the Republic of Lithuania* [2006] EWCA Civ 1529, [2007] QB 886, [2007] 1 All ER (Comm) 909 (if, on the overall construction of the transaction, the state is held to be bound by a written arbitration agreement, that will be sufficient to find that it had agreed in writing to refer the dispute to arbitration within the terms of the State Immunity Act 1978 s 9). There is no basis for construing s 9 as excluding proceedings relating to the enforcement of a foreign arbitral award: *Svenska v Petroleum Exploration AB v Government of the Republic of Lithuania*.
5 State Immunity Act 1978 s 9(2).

254. Ships used for commercial purposes. In the case of Admiralty proceedings and proceedings on any claim which could be made the subject of Admiralty proceedings[1], a state[2] is not immune from (1) an action in rem against a ship[3] belonging to that state[4]; or (2) an action in personam for enforcing a claim in connection with such a ship, if, when the cause of action arose, the ship was in use or intended for use for commercial purposes[5].

A state is not immune from (a) an action in rem against a cargo belonging to that state if both the cargo and ship carrying it were, when the cause of action arose, in use or intended for use for commercial purposes[6]; or (b) an action in personam for enforcing a claim in connection with such a cargo if the ship carrying it was then in use or intended for use for commercial purposes[7].

1 State Immunity Act 1978 s 10(1). As to Admiralty proceedings see SHIPPING AND MARITIME LAW. Sections 3–5 (see PARAS 247–249) do not apply to proceedings specified in s 10(1), if the state in question is a party to the Brussels Convention and the claim relates to the operation of a ship owned or operated by that state, the carriage of cargo or passengers on such a ship or the carriage of cargo owned by that state on any other ship: s 10(6). The Brussels Convention is the

International Convention for the Unification of Certain Rules concerning the Immunity of State-owned Ships (Brussels, 10 April 1926, with Protocol, Brussels 24 May 1934; TS 15 (1980); Cmnd 7800): State Immunity Act 1978 s 17(1). A certificate by or on behalf of the Secretary of State is conclusive evidence on any question whether a state is a party to the Brussels Convention: State Immunity Act 1978 s 21(b). As to the Secretary of State see PARA 29.

2 As to the meaning of 'state' see PARA 245.

3 'Ship' includes hovercraft: State Immunity Act 1978 s 17(1). See also note 4.

4 State Immunity Act 1978 s 10(2)(a). Where an action in rem is brought against a ship belonging to a state for enforcing a claim in connection with another ship belonging to that state, s 10(2)(a) does not apply to the first ship unless both ships were in use or intended for use for commercial purposes when the cause of action relating to the other ship arose: s 10(3). As to the meaning of 'commercial purposes' see PARA 247 note 2.

   References to a ship or cargo belonging to a state include a ship or cargo in its possession or control or in which it claims an interest, and subject to s 10(4) (see the text and notes 6–7) s 10(2) applies to property other than a ship as it applies to a ship: s 10(5).

5 State Immunity Act 1978 s 10(2)(b).

6 State Immunity Act 1978 s 10(4)(a).

7 State Immunity Act 1978 s 10(4)(b).

255. Value added tax, customs duties etc. A state[1] is not immune from proceedings relating to its liability for (1) value added tax, any duty of customs or excise or any agricultural levy; or (2) rates in respect of premises occupied by it for commercial purposes[2].

Other than in these respects, the provisions of Part I of the State Immunity Act 1978[3] do not apply to proceedings in respect of taxation[4].

1 As to the meaning of 'state' see PARA 245.

2 State Immunity Act 1978 s 11. As to the meaning of 'commercial purposes' see PARA 247 note 2.

3 Ie the State Immunity Act 1978 Pt I (ss 1–17).

4 See PARA 259. See also *R v IRC, ex p Camacq Corpn* [1990] 1 All ER 173, [1990] 1 WLR 191, CA (proceedings relating to any tax not mentioned in the State Immunity Act 1978 s 11 are wholly outside the scope of Act, and the position rests on the common law).

256. Service of documents. Any writ[1] or other document required to be served for instituting proceedings against a state[2] must be served by being transmitted through the Foreign and Commonwealth Office to the state's ministry of foreign affairs and service is deemed to have been effected when the writ or document is received at that ministry[3].

Any time for acknowledging service[4] (whether prescribed by rules of court or otherwise) begins to run two months after the date on which the writ or document is received at the ministry[5]. No judgment in default of acknowledgment of service[6] may be given against a state except on proof that the provisions regarding service[7] have been complied with and that the time for acknowledging service[8] has expired[9].

A copy of any judgment given against a state in default of acknowledgment of service must be transmitted through the Foreign and Commonwealth Office to the state's ministry of foreign affairs; and any time for applying to have the judgment set aside (whether prescribed by rules of court or otherwise)[10] begins to run two months after the date on which the copy of the judgment is received at the ministry[11].

A certificate by, or on behalf of, the Secretary of State, is conclusive evidence on any question whether, and if so when, a document has been served or received as mentioned above[12].

The provisions described above are not to be construed as applying to proceedings against a state by way of counterclaim or to an action in rem[13].

1   Proceedings in the High Court or county court to which the CPR apply are now generally begun by claim form: see CPR Pt 7; and CIVIL PROCEDURE vol 11 (2009) PARA 116 et seq. As to the proceedings to which the CPR do not apply see CPR 2.1; and COURTS vol 10 (Reissue) PARA 575.

2   Proceedings against the constituent territories of a federal state are included: State Immunity Act 1978 s 14(5). As to the meaning of 'state' see PARA 245.

3   State Immunity Act 1978 s 12(1). A state which appears in proceedings cannot afterwards object that s 12(1) has not been complied with: s 12(3).

     Section 12(1) does not prevent the service of a writ or other document in any manner which the state has agreed and s 12(2), (4) (see the text and notes 5, 9) does not apply to service in such a manner: s 12(6). Where s 12(6) applies and the state has agreed to a method of service other than through the Foreign and Commonwealth Office, the claim may be served either by the method agreed or in accordance with CPR 6.44: CPR 6.44(7).

     The State Immunity Act 1978 s 12(1) must not be construed as affecting any rules of court whereby leave is required for the service of process outside the jurisdiction: s 12(7). As to service of a claim form out of the jurisdiction where leave of the court is required see CPR 6.36. Where a claimant wishes to serve a claim form on a state, he must lodge in Central Office a request for service to be arranged by the Foreign and Commonwealth Office, a copy of the notice and, if the official language of the state is not English, a translation: see CPR 6.27, 6.28. Every such request for service must contain an undertaking by the person making the request (1) to be responsible for all expenses incurred by the Foreign and Commonwealth Office or foreign judicial authority; and (2) to pay those expenses to the Foreign and Commonwealth Office or foreign judicial authority on being informed of the amount: CPR 6.29.

4   As to acknowledgement of service see CPR Pt 10; and CIVIL PROCEDURE vol 11 (2009) PARA 184.

5   State Immunity Act 1978 s 12(2).

6   See CPR Pt 12; and CIVIL PROCEDURE vol 11 (2009) PARA 506 et seq.

7   Ie as contained in the State Immunity Act 1978 s 12(1): see the text and note 3. See also *Westminster City Council v Government of the Islamic Republic of Iran* [1986] 3 All ER 284, [1986] 1 WLR 979.

8   Ie as extended by the State Immunity Act 1978 s 12(2): see the text and note 5.

9   State Immunity Act 1978 s 12(4).

10 As to setting aside default judgments see CPR Pt 13; and CIVIL PROCEDURE vol 11 (2009) PARA 516.

11 State Immunity Act 1978 s 12(5). Where judgment has been obtained against a state in default of acknowledgment of service, it does not take effect until two months after service on the state of (1) a copy of the judgment; and (2) a copy of the evidence in support of the application for permission to enter default judgment (unless the evidence has already been served on the state): CPR 40.10.

12 State Immunity Act 1978 s 21(d). As to the Secretary of State see PARA 29.

13 State Immunity Act 1978 s 12(7).

257.   Other procedural privileges.   No penalty by way of committal or fine may be imposed in respect of any failure or refusal by or on behalf of a state[1] to disclose or produce any document or other information for the purposes of proceedings to which it is a party[2].

Relief may not be given against a state by way of injunction or order for specific performance or for the recovery of land or other property[3]. The property of a state may not be subject to any process for the enforcement of a judgment or arbitration award or, in an action in rem, for its arrest, detention or sale[4]. However, this does not prevent the giving of any relief or the issue of any process with the written consent[5] of the state concerned and any such consent (which may be contained in a prior agreement[6]) may be expressed so as to apply to a limited extent or generally[7].

The provisions described above[8] apply to a separate entity[9] (not being a state's central bank or other monetary authority) which submits to the jurisdiction in respect of proceedings in the case of which it is entitled to immunity[10].

1   As to the meaning of 'state' see PARA 245.
2   State Immunity Act 1978 s 13(1).

3   State Immunity Act 1978 s 13(2)(a).
4   State Immunity Act 1978 s 13(2)(b). This does not prevent the issue of any process in respect of property used or intended for use for commercial purposes, but if s 10 does not apply (see PARA 254), s 13(2)(b) applies to property of a state party to the European Convention on State Immunity (ie the European Convention on State Immunity (Basle 16 May 1972; TS 74 (1979); Cmnd 7742)) only if (1) the process is for enforcing a judgment which is final within the meaning of the State Immunity Act 1978 s 18(1)(b) (see PARA 260 note 2) and the state has made a declaration under the European Convention on State Immunity art 24; or (2) the process is for enforcing an arbitration award: State Immunity Act 1978 s 13(4). See also note 5.
     As to the meaning of 'commercial purposes' see PARA 247 note 2. Property of a state's central bank or other monetary authority must not be regarded for the purposes of the State Immunity Act 1978 s 13(4) as in use or intended for use for commercial purposes; and where any such bank or authority is a separate entity s 13(1)–(3) apply to it as if references to a state were references to the bank or authority: s 14(4). 'Property of a state's central bank or other monetary authority' means any asset in which the central bank has some kind of 'property' interest, which asset is allocated to or held in the name of a central bank, irrespective of the capacity in which the central bank holds it, or the purpose for which the property is held: *AIG Capital Partners Inc v Republic of Kazakhstan (National Bank of Kasakhstan intervening)* [2005] EWHC 2239 (Comm), [2006] 1 All ER 284, [2006] 1 All ER (Comm) 1 (cash and securities held abroad by third parties on behalf of central bank fell within the State Immunity Act 1978 s 4(4)). See also *Alcom Ltd v Republic of Colombia* [1984] AC 580 at 602, [1984] 2 All ER 6 at 11, HL, per Lord Diplock; and *AIC Ltd v Federal Republic of Nigeria* [2003] EWHC 1357 (QB) at [47], [2003] All ER (D) 190 (Jun). See further note 5.
5   The head of a state's diplomatic mission in the United Kingdom or the person performing his functions is deemed to have authority to give any such consent on behalf of the state: State Immunity Act 1978 s 13(5). For the purposes of s 13(4) (see note 4), the certificate of such person that any property is not used or intended for use by or on behalf of the state for commercial purposes is sufficient evidence of that fact unless the contrary is proved: s 13(5). As to the statutory meaning of 'United Kingdom' see PARA 30 note 3.
6   As to the meaning of 'agreement' see PARA 246 note 4.
7   State Immunity Act 1978 s 13(3). A provision merely submitting to the jurisdiction of the courts is not to be regarded as a consent: s 13(3).
8   Ie the State Immunity Act 1978 s 13(1)–(3).
9   As to the meaning of 'separate entity' see PARA 245.
10   See the State Immunity Act 1978 s 14(3). Where the provisions of Pt I (ss 1–17) do not apply to a constituent territory by virtue of an order under s 14(5) (see PARA 245 note 4), s 14(2) applies to it as if it were a separate entity: s 14(6).

258.   Restriction and extension of immunities.   If it appears that the immunities and privileges conferred on any state[1] (1) exceed those accorded by the law of that state in relation to the United Kingdom[2]; or (2) are less than those required by any treaty, convention or other international agreement to which that state and the United Kingdom are parties, provision may be made by Order in Council[3] restricting or extending those immunities and privileges to such extent as appears appropriate[4].

1   Ie conferred by the State Immunity Act 1978 ss 1–13. As to the meaning of 'state' see PARA 245.
2   As to the statutory meaning of 'United Kingdom' see PARA 30 note 3.
3   Any statutory instrument containing such an order is subject to annulment in pursuance of a resolution of either House of Parliament: State Immunity Act 1978 s 15(2).
4   State Immunity Act 1978 s 15(1). At the date at which this volume states the law, no Order in Council was in force under this provision extending or restricting immunities and privileges conferred on any state. See the State Immunity (Merchant Shipping) (Revocation) Order 1999, SI 1999/668, which revoked the State Immunity (Merchant Shipping) Order 1997, SI 1997/2591.

259.   Excluded matters.   Part I of the State Immunity Act 1978[1] does not affect any immunity or privilege conferred by the Diplomatic Privileges Act 1964 or the Consular Relations Act 1968[2]. Nor does it apply to: (1) proceedings relating to anything done by or in relation to the armed forces of a state[3] while present in the United Kingdom[4]; (2) proceedings to which a specified provision of the Nuclear Installations Act 1965 applies[5]; (3) criminal proceedings[6]; or (4) proceedings relating to taxation[7].

1 Ie the State Immunity Act 1978 Pt I (ss 1–17).
2 State Immunity Act 1978 s 16(1). Certain proceedings relating to interests in property are also excluded from the application of the State Immunity Act 1978: see s 16(1)(a), (b); and PARAS 248, 250.
3 As to the meaning of 'state' see PARA 245.
4 State Immunity Act 1978 s 16(2). In particular Pt I takes effect subject to the Visiting Forces Act 1952: see PARAS 324–326; and ARMED FORCES. As to the meaning of 'United Kingdom' for these purposes see PARA 247 note 4. As to the statutory meaning of 'United Kingdom' generally see PARA 30 note 3.
5 State Immunity Act 1978 s 16(3). The provision referred to is the Nuclear Installations Act 1965 s 17(6): see FUEL AND ENERGY vol 19(3) (2007 Reissue) PARA 1507.
6 State Immunity Act 1978 s 16(4). As to the immunity from criminal proceedings afforded to diplomatic staff see PARA 274.
7 State Immunity Act 1978 s 16(5) (which excepts those proceedings mentioned in s 11; see PARA 255).

260. Recognition of judgments against the United Kingdom. Subject to exceptions[1], certain judgments[2] given against the United Kingdom by a court in another state party to the European Convention on State Immunity[3] must be recognised in any court in the United Kingdom as conclusive between the parties thereto in all proceedings founded on the same cause of action and may be relied on by way of defence or counterclaim in such proceedings[4].

However, recognition need not be accorded in the case of a judgment if: (1) to do so would be manifestly contrary to public policy or if any party to the proceedings in which the judgment was given had no adequate opportunity to present his case[5]; or (2) the judgment was given without provisions regarding service[6] being complied with and the United Kingdom had not entered an appearance or applied to have the judgment set aside[7].

Recognition of a judgment may also be refused:

(a) if proceedings between the same parties, based on the same facts and having the same purpose: (i) are pending before a court in the United Kingdom and were the first to be instituted; or (ii) are pending before a court in another state party to the Convention, were the first to be instituted and may result in a judgment to which the requirement for recognition will apply[8];

(b) if the result of the judgment is inconsistent with the result of another judgment given in proceedings between the same parties and (i) the other judgment is by a court in the United Kingdom and either those proceedings were the first to be instituted or the judgment of that court was given before the first-mentioned judgment became final[9]; or (ii) the other judgment is by a court in another state party to the Convention and the requirement for recognition has already become applicable to it[10];

(c) where the judgment was given against the United Kingdom in proceedings in respect of which the United Kingdom was not entitled to immunity by virtue of a provision corresponding to certain provisions exempting immunity in relation to immovable property[11], if the court that gave the judgment (i) would not have had jurisdiction in the matter if it had applied rules of jurisdiction corresponding to those applicable to such matters in the United Kingdom; or (ii) applied a law other than that indicated by the United Kingdom rules of private international law and would have reached a different conclusion if it had applied the law so indicated[12].

1 See the text and notes 5–12.
2 Ie a judgment (1) given in proceedings in which the United Kingdom was not entitled to immunity under provisions corresponding to the State Immunity Act 1978 ss 2–11 (see PARA 246 et seq); and (2) which is final, ie which is not or is no longer subject to appeal, or, if given in default of appearance, liable to be set aside: s 18(1)(a), (b). As to the meaning of 'appearance' see PARA 244 note 4. As to the statutory meaning of 'United Kingdom' see PARA 30 note 3.
3 State Immunity Act 1978 s 18(1). References to a court in a state party to the European Convention on State Immunity (Basle, 16 May 1972; TS 74 (1979); Cmnd 7742) include a court in any territory in respect of which it is a party: State Immunity Act 1978 s 18(4). As to the meaning of 'court' see PARA 244 note 2.
4 State Immunity Act 1978 s 18(2). This also has effect in relation to any settlement entered into by the United Kingdom before a court in another state party to the European Convention on State Immunity which the law of that state treats as equivalent to a judgment: State Immunity Act 1978 s 18(3). As to counterclaim generally see CIVIL PROCEDURE vol 11 (2009) PARA 618 et seq.
5 State Immunity Act 1978 s 19(1)(a).
6 Ie provisions corresponding to the State Immunity Act 1978 s 12 (see PARA 256).
7 State Immunity Act 1978 s 19(1)(b).
8 State Immunity Act 1978 s 19(2)(a). In this provision, and in the text and note 10, references to a court in the United Kingdom include references to a court in any British overseas territory in respect of which the United Kingdom is a party to the European Convention on State Immunity; and references to a court in another state party to the Convention include references to a court in any territory in respect of which it is a party: State Immunity Act 1978 s 19(4) (amended by the British Overseas Territories Act 2002 s 1(2)).
9 Ie final within the meaning of the State Immunity Act 1978 s 18(1)(b) (see note 2).
10 State Immunity Act 1978 s 19(2)(b).
11 Ie corresponding to the State Immunity Act 1978 s 6(2): see PARA 250.
12 State Immunity Act 1978 s 19(3).

261. Recognition and enforcement in the United Kingdom of foreign judgments against foreign states. A judgment[1] given by a court of an overseas country against a state[2] other than the United Kingdom or the state to which that court belongs must be recognised and enforced in the United Kingdom[3] if, and only if: (1) it would be so recognised and enforced if it had not been given against a state[4]; (2) the court would have had jurisdiction in the matter if it had applied rules corresponding to those applicable to such matters in the United Kingdom in accordance with the State Immunity Act 1978[5]. Certain provisions of the State Immunity Act 1978 as to service of process and procedural privileges[6] apply to proceedings for the recognition or enforcement in the United Kingdom of a judgment given by a court of an overseas country (whether or not that judgment is within the provisions described above) as they apply to other proceedings[7].

1 Ie any judgment or order (by whatever name called) given or made by a court in any civil proceedings: Civil Jurisdiction and Judgments Act 1982 s 50.
2 'A judgment given against a state' includes references to judgments of any of the following descriptions given in relation to a state: (1) judgments against the government, or a department of the government, of the state, but not judgments against an entity which is distinct from the executive organs; (2) judgments against the sovereign or head of state in his public capacity; (3) judgments against any such separate entity as is mentioned in head (1) given in proceedings relating to anything done by it in the exercise of the sovereign authority of the state: Civil Jurisdiction and Judgments Act 1982 s 31(2). A 'state', in the case of a federal state, includes any of its constituent territories: s 31(5).
3 Civil Jurisdiction and Judgments Act 1982 s 31(1). This does not affect recognition or enforcement in the United Kingdom of a judgment to which the Foreign Judgments (Reciprocal Enforcement) Act 1933 Pt I (ss 1–7) applies by virtue of the Carriage of Goods by Road

Act 1965 s 4, the Nuclear Installations Act 1965 s 17(4), the Merchant Shipping Act 1995 s 166(4) or the Railways (Convention and International Carriage By Rail)Regulations 2005, SI 2005/2092): Civil Jurisdiction and Judgments Act 1982 s 31(3) (amended by the International Transport Conventions Act 1983 s 11(2); the Merchant Shipping Act 1995 s 314(2), Sch 13 para 66(a); Statute Law Repeals Act 2004; and SI 2005/2092). As to the statutory meaning of 'United Kingdom' see PARA 30 note 3.

4   Civil Jurisdiction and Judgments Act 1982 s 31(1)(a).

5   Civil Jurisdiction and Judgments Act 1982 s 31(1)(b). See the State Immunity Act 1978 ss 2–11; and PARA 246 et seq. See also *NML Capital Ltd v Republic of Argentina* [2010] EWCA Civ 41, 2010 All ER (D) 57 (Feb).

6   Ie the Civil Jurisdiction and Judgments Act 1982 ss 12, 13, 14(3), (4): see PARAS 256–257.

7   Civil Jurisdiction and Judgments Act 1982 s 31(4).

(3) THE FOREIGN STATE AS CLAIMANT

262.   Foreign state as claimant.   A foreign sovereign or state may be a claimant in proceedings in the English courts[1]. A foreign state need not sue in the name of the personal head of state[2]. When a foreign state sues in an English court it must comply with the procedural rules of the court[3]. Thus the foreign state may be required to furnish security for costs[4], and it must make disclosure[5].

1   *Hullett and Widder v King of Spain* (1828) 2 Bli NS 31 at 53, 1 BILC 97, HL, applying *King of Spain v Pountes* (1618) Roll Abr, Court de Admiraltie (E3), 1 BILC 106n; *Emperor of Austria v Day and Kossuth* (1861) 3 De GF & J 217 at 238, 253, 1 BILC 45, CA. In *Barclay v Russell* (1797) 3 Ves 424 at 431, 2 BILC 207, Lord Loughborough had expressed doubts upon the point. For examples of actions instituted by foreign sovereigns see *King of Greece v Wright* (1837) 6 Dowl 12, 1 BILC 123; *Emperor of Brazil v Robinson* (1837) 6 Ad & El 801, 1 BILC 127; *King of the Two Sicilies v Willcox* (1851) 1 Sim NS 301, 2 BILC 230; *King of the Hellenes v Brostrom* (1923) 16 LI L Rep 167 at 192, 2 BILC 128. However, the court will not determine a claim that amounts to the performance of an act of a sovereign character: *Mbasogo,President of the State of Equatorial Guinea v Logo Ltd* [2006] EWCA Civ 1370, [2007] QB 846, [2007] 2 WLR 1062 (tort claims made by a state were not justiciable in the English courts as they amounted to a claim for losses sustained in the exercise of a sovereign power to prevent an attempted coup). As to the position of unrecognised states see PARA 47. As to counterclaims against a claimant state see the State Immunity Act 1978 s 2(3)(a), (b); and PARA 243 et seq.

2   *United States of America v Prioleau* (1865) 35 LJ Ch 7, 1 BILC 129; *Prioleau v United States of America and Johnson* (1866) LR 2 Eq 659, 1 BILC 134; *United States of America v Wagner* (1867) 2 Ch App 582, 1 BILC 146 (revsg (1867) LR 3 Eq 724, 1 BILC 140); *Yzquierdo v Clydebank Engineering and Shipbuilding Co Ltd* [1902] AC 524, 1 BILC 183, HL (revsg (1901) 4 F (Ct of Sess) 319, 1 BILC 171). The envoy of a foreign state, however, does not represent his sovereign for the purpose of suing in his own name in respect of that sovereign's property: *Baron Penedo v Johnson* (1873) 29 LT 452, 1 BILC 157. See also *Republic of Liberia v Imperial Bank Ltd and Chinery* (1871) 25 LT 866, 1 BILC 153. In an action in respect of property alleged to belong to a foreign government, that government must be made a party to the action: *Schneider v Lizardi* (1845) 9 Beav 461, 6 BILC 775.

3   *King of Spain v Hullett and Widder* (1833) 7 Bli NS 359 at 393, 1 BILC 111.

4   *King of Greece v Wright* (1837) 6 Dowl 12, 1 BILC 123; *Emperor of Brazil v Robinson* (1837) 5 Dowl 522, 1 BILC 127, distinguishing *Duke of Montellano v Christin* (1816) 5 M & S 503, 6 BILC 4, where security for costs against an ambassador who was not about to leave the jurisdiction was not ordered. See also *Republic of Costa Rica v Erlanger* (1876) 3 ChD 62, 1 BILC 167, CA.

5   *Rothschild v Queen of Portugal* (1839) 3 Y & C Ex 594, 1 BILC 128; *Prioleau v United States of America and Johnson* (1866) LR 2 Eq 659, 1 BILC 134; *United States of America v Wagner* (1867) 2 Ch App 582, 1 BILC 146, CA; *Republic of Costa Rica v Erlanger* (1874) LR 19 Eq 33, 1 BILC 159; *Republic of Peru v Weguelin* (1875) LR 20 Eq 140, 1 BILC 158; *South African Republic v Compagnie Franco-Belge du Chemin de Fer du Nord* [1898] 1 Ch 190, 3 BILC 536 (other proceedings [1897] 2 Ch 487, 3 BILC 531, CA). A defendant to an action brought by a foreign sovereign or state is entitled to an affidavit of documents: *Republic of Liberia v Imperial Bank* (1873) LR 16 Eq 179, 1 BILC 155; on appeal sub nom *Republic of Liberia v Roye* (1876) 1 App Cas 139, HL.

(4) HEADS OF STATE, HEADS OF GOVERNMENT, FOREIGN MINISTERS AND OTHER HIGH OFFICIALS

263. Privileges and immunities of heads of state etc. Subject to any necessary modifications, the Diplomatic Privileges Act 1964[1] applies to (1) a sovereign or other head of state[2]; (2) members of his family forming part of his household[3]; and (3) his private servants[4] as it applies to the head of a diplomatic mission, members of his family forming part of his household and his private servants[5].

The position of a former head of state is, therefore, broadly comparable to that of a former head of a diplomatic mission as respects immunity for acts done while he was head of state in the exercise of his functions as such[6]. In addition to the personal inviolability enjoyed by a sovereign or other head of state, the authorities of the receiving state are obliged to treat him with due respect and take all appropriate steps to prevent any attack on his person, freedom or dignity[7]. Under rules of customary international law, holders of other high-ranking offices such as a head of government or a Minister for Foreign Affairs who, like a head of state, are recognised as representatives of the state solely by virtue of their office, enjoy similar immunities from jurisdiction[8]. In recent years, the courts have accepted that a Minister of Defence and a Minister of Commerce (including international trade) are entitled to immunity from criminal jurisdiction by virtue of their office[9].

1   As to the Diplomatic Privileges Act 1964 generally see PARAS 265–289. As to the limits of immunity from civil proceedings under that Act see PARA 274.

2   State Immunity Act 1978 s 20(1)(a). This applies to the sovereign or other head of any state on whom immunities and privileges are conferred by Pt I (ss 1–17) (see s 14(1); and PARA 245); and is without prejudice to the application of Pt I to any such sovereign or head of state in his public capacity: s 20(5). Part I (see PARA 244 et seq) does not affect any immunity or privilege conferred by the Diplomatic Privileges Act 1964: State Immunity Act 1978 s 16(1). A head of state, therefore, who does not enjoy immunity under the State Immunity Act 1978 may nevertheless enjoy the same immunity as a diplomatic agent under the Diplomatic Privileges Act 1964: *Bank of Credit and Commerce International (Overseas) Ltd (in liquidation) v Price Waterhouse* [1997]4 All ER 108. The effect of these provisions is, inter alia, that immunity from criminal proceedings is conferred on heads of state in accordance with the Diplomatic Privileges Act 1964. See *R v Bow Street Metropolitan Stipendiary Magistrate, ex p Pinochet Ugarte (No 3)* [2000] 1 AC 147, sub nom *R v Bow Street Metropolitan Stipendiary Magistrate, ex p Pinochet Ugarte (Amnesty International intervening) (No 3)* [1999] 2 All ER 97, HL. See also *Re Mugabe* (7 January 2004, unreported), Bow Street Magistrates' Court (judgment reproduced in Warbrick 'Immunity and International Crimes in English Law' (2004) 53 ICLQ 769). As to certificates of the Secretary of State as to who is a head of state see PARA 245. As to the Secretary of State see PARA 29.

3   State Immunity Act 1978 s 20(1)(b). The immunities and privileges conferred by s 20(1)(a) are not subject to the restrictions by reference to nationality or residence contained in the Diplomatic Privileges Act 1964 Sch 1 arts 37 para 1, 38 (see PARAS 274–279); State Immunity Act 1978 s 20(2).

4   State Immunity Act 1978 s 20(1)(c). This provision reflects the view that, under customary international law, persons forming part of a head of state's retinue, accompanying him during his stay abroad, are entitled to the same privileges and immunities as the head of state himself. However, the retinue of a head of state may include persons whose status and functions go beyond those of private servants: see Oppenheim's International Law (9th Edn, 1992) Vol 1 p 1039. Section 20(1) (which applies only to heads of state, their families and private servants) may not, therefore, wholly cover those who accompany a head of state on visits abroad.

5   State Immunity Act 1978 s 20(1). See PARA 273 et seq. Subject to a contrary Direction by a Secretary of State, a person on whom immunities and privileges are conferred by s 20(1) is entitled to the exemption conferred by the Immigration Act 1971 s 8(3) (see PARA 273): State Immunity Act 1978 s 20(3). Except as respects value added tax and customs and excise duty, s 20 does not affect any question whether a person is exempt from or immune as respects proceedings relating to taxation: s 20(4).

6   See *R v Bow Street Metropolitan Stipendiary Magistrate, ex p Pinochet Ugarte (No 3)* [2000]
    1 AC 147, sub nom *R v Bow Street Metropolitan Stipendiary Magistrate, ex p Pinochet Ugarte
    (Amnesty International intervening) (No 3)* [1999] 2 All ER 97, HL. See also Satow's
    Diplomatic Practice (6th Edn, 2009) p 183.
7   Diplomatic Privileges Act 1964 Sch 1 art 29. See *Aziz v Aziz (Sultan of Brunei intervening)*
    [2007] EWCA Civ 712, [2008] 2 All ER 501, [2007] NLJR 1047 (application by ruling head of
    state to redact and anonymise references to himself and matters relating to a former marriage, in
    proceedings between his former wife and a third party, dismissed); Satow's Diplomatic Practice
    (6th Edn, 2009) p 183. See also *Harb v His Majesty King Fahd Bin Abdul Aziz* [2005] EWCA
    Civ 632, [2005] 2 FCR 342, [2005] 2 FLR 1108 (no breach of the Diplomatic Privileges
    Act 1964 Sch 1 art 29 by hearing of immunity issue in open court where sovereign challenge to
    maintenance application to be heard in private).
8   See *Arrest Warrant of 11 April 2000 (Democratic Republic of the Congo v Belgium)* ICJ
    Reports 2002, 3 (where the International Court of Justice upheld the personal immunity of an
    incumbent Minister for Foreign Affairs). For a detailed discussion of how the law has evolved
    see Watts 'The Legal Position in International Law of Heads of State, Heads of Governments
    and Foreign Ministers' *Hague Academy of International Law, Receuil des Cours* vol 247
    (1994-III) pp 100–108. See also 1 Oppenheim's International Law (9th Edn, 1992) p 1033.
9   See *Re Mofaz* (12 February 2004), Bow Street Magistrates' Court, (2004) 128 ILR 713; *Re Bo
    Xilai* (8 November 2005), Bow Street Magistrates' Court, (2005) 128 ILR 713. See also the
    decision of Westminster Magistrate's Court, 29 September 2009 (unreported), upholding
    immunity from prosecution of Israeli Defence Minister Ehud Barak. The International Court of
    Justice (the 'ICJ') has itself noted that the conduct of government business with foreign states is
    no longer confined to Foreign Ministers and that 'with increasing frequency in modern
    international relations other persons representing a State in specific fields may be authorized by
    that State to bind it': see *Armed Activities on the Territory of the Congo (New Application:
    2002) (Democratic Republic of the Congo v Rwanda) (Jurisdiction and Admissibility)* ICJ
    Reports 2006, 6 (para 47).

(5) SPECIAL MISSIONS

264.   Immunity of persons on special missions. International law does not lay
down any clear rules as to the precise extent of the privileges and immunities to
which persons on a special mission are entitled. It is, however, acknowledged
that such missions do have a public, official character and that the members of
such missions should, therefore, be entitled to special treatment[1]. The English
courts have accordingly recognised that a representative of a foreign state on
special mission may enjoy personal inviolability and immunity from jurisdiction
comparable to that of a diplomatic agent[2]. Where there is a special agreement
governing the terms of a special mission, recourse should be had to that
agreement in order to determine the extent of the immunities conferred[3]. A
Convention on Special Missions was adopted by the United Nations General
Assembly in 1969[4]. It has not been widely ratified and there are conflicting views
as to the extent to which it reflects existing customary international law. Unlike a
permanent diplomatic mission within the terms of the Vienna Convention on
Diplomatic Relations[5], a special mission is a temporary ad hoc mission
representing a state which is sent to another state for the purpose of dealing with
it on specific questions or performing a specific task. Such a mission must have
the consent of the receiving state[6].

1   1 Oppenheim's International Law (9th Edn, 1992) pp 1125–1126. See also YILC 1967 vol II,
    358.
2   *Re Bo Xilai*, 8 November 2005, Bow Street Magistrates' Court, 128 ILR 709, 713. See also
    Tabatabai case (Germany) (1983–86) 80 ILR 389; *Chong Boon Kim v Kim Yong Shik* (1964) 58
    AJIL186; and *Kilroy v Windsor, Prince of Wales (USA)* (1978) ILR 81 at 605.
3   See *Fenton Textile Association v Krassin et al* (1921) 38 TLR 259, CA.
4   The UN Convention on Special Missions was adopted together with an Optional Protocol to the
    Convention on Special Missions concerning the Compulsory Settlement of Disputes (New York;

8 December 1969, Misc 3 (1970); Cmnd 4300). The Convention came into force in June 1985. Both Convention and Protocol have been signed by the United Kingdom but not ratified. See also Satow's Diplomatic Practice (6th Edn, 2009) pp 188–193.

5   Convention on Diplomatic Relations (Vienna, 18 April 1961; TS 19 (1965); Cmnd 2565). See also PARA 265.

6   See UN Convention on Special Missions, arts 1(a), 2.

(6) DIPLOMATIC PRIVILEGES AND IMMUNITIES

265.   The Vienna Convention on Diplomatic Relations. The United Kingdom is a party to the Vienna Convention on Diplomatic Relations[1]. Certain provisions of the Convention form part of the law of England by virtue of the Diplomatic Privileges Act 1964[2]. The Act applies to all diplomatic missions whether or not the sending state is a party to the Convention. It applies to all foreign and Commonwealth missions in the United Kingdom, but does not apply to consular officers or Commonwealth representatives of comparable status[3], nor to international organisations and persons connected with them[4]. The Act also applies to sovereigns and other heads of state[5].

1   Ie the Convention on Diplomatic Relations (Vienna, 18 April 1961; TS 19 (1965); Cmnd 2565). The Convention was adopted at the United Nations Conference on Diplomatic Intercourse and Immunities. It is not clear how far it was intended to be declaratory of customary international law. See 1 Oppenheim's International Law (9th Edn, 1992) pp 1070–1071. The conference also adopted an Optional Protocol concerning the Acquisition of Nationality (Vienna, 18 April 1961; Misc 6 (1961); Cmnd 1368), to which the United Kingdom is not a party; and an Optional Protocol concerning the Compulsory Settlement of Disputes (Vienna, 18 April 1961; TS 19 (1965); Cmnd 2565), to which the United Kingdom is a party. In 1969 the General Assembly adopted a Convention on Special Missions with an Optional Protocol concerning the Compulsory Settlement of Disputes (United Nations General Assembly, 8 December 1969; Misc 3 (1970); Cmnd 4300), which have been signed but not ratified by the United Kingdom (see PARA 264). As to the imperative nature in international law of the principles of diplomatic and consular immunity see *United States Diplomatic and Consular Staff in Teheran (United States of America v Iran) (Provisional Measures)* ICJ Reports 1979, 7 at 19–20; *United States Diplomatic and Consular Staff in Teheran (United States of America v Iran)* ICJ Reports 1980, 3 at 42. As to the continued application of the Convention, notwithstanding the existence of a state of armed conflict between the states concerned see *Armed Activities on the Territory of the Congo (Democratic Republic of the Congo v Uganda)* ICJ Reports, 19 December 2005.

2   Diplomatic Privileges Act 1964 s 2(1), Sch 1. The provisions of the Vienna Convention on Diplomatic Relations there set out are arts 1, 22–24, 27–40, 45.

3   As to consular agents see the Consular Relations Act 1968; and PARA 290 et seq.

4   As to international organisations see the International Organisations Act 1968; and PARA 307 et seq.

5   See the State Immunity Act 1978 s 20; and PARA 263.

266.   In general. Those articles of the Vienna Convention on Diplomatic Relations[1] which are not included in the Diplomatic Privileges Act 1964[2] do not give rise to rights and duties directly enforceable in the domestic courts of the United Kingdom. According to these articles, the functions of a diplomatic mission consist inter alia in representing the sending state, protecting its interests and those of its nationals, negotiating with the receiving state, ascertaining conditions there and promoting friendly relations[3]. There are provisions concerning the appointment and accrediting of the head of the mission[4] and its staff, and the size of the mission[5], the declaring of a member persona non grata[6], the time at which the head of mission is considered to have taken up his functions[7] and the termination of those functions[8].

1   Ie the Convention on Diplomatic Relations (Vienna, 18 April 1961; TS 19 (1965); Cmnd 2565).

2   See the Diplomatic Privileges Act 1964 Sch 1; and PARA 265 note 2.

3   Vienna Convention on Diplomatic Relations art 3 para 1. A diplomatic mission may perform consular functions (see PARA 292): art 3 para 2.

    See *Propend Finance Property Ltd v Sing* (1997) 111 ILR 611, Times 2 May, CA (where court took a broad view of diplomatic functions to include police liaison functions). See also *Re P (Diplomatic Immunity; Jurisdiction)* [1998] 1 FLR 1026, CA.

4   'Head of the mission' means the person charged by the sending state with the duty of acting in that capacity: Vienna Convention on Diplomatic Relations art 1(a).

5   Vienna Convention on Diplomatic Relations arts 4–8, 10, 11. Without the prior express consent of the receiving state, the sending state may not establish an office forming part of the mission in localities other than those in which the mission itself is established: art 12.

6   Vienna Convention on Diplomatic Relations art 9.

7   Vienna Convention on Diplomatic Relations art 13.

8   Vienna Convention on Diplomatic Relations art 43. The receiving state must facilitate the departure of persons enjoying privileges and immunities, other than its own nationals, even in case of armed conflict: art 44. There are provisions concerning the representation of states in the case of breach of diplomatic relations (art 45) and for the temporary protection of interests of third states (art 46).

267. Classes of heads of mission. The classes of heads of mission[1] established by the Vienna Convention on Diplomatic Relations[2] are (1) ambassadors or nuncios[3] accredited to heads of state and other heads of mission of equivalent rank; (2) envoys, ministers and internuncios[4] accredited to heads of state; and (3) chargés d'affaires accredited to ministers of foreign affairs[5]. Heads of mission enjoy precedence in their respective classes in order of the date and time of taking up their function[6].

1   As to the meaning of 'head of the mission' see PARA 266 note 4.

2   Ie the Convention on Diplomatic Relations (Vienna, 18 April 1961; TS 19 (1965); Cmnd 2565). As to the provisions of the Convention given force of law in the United Kingdom see PARA 265 note 2.

3   'Ambassador' or 'nuncio' includes a High Commissioner accredited from one Commonwealth country to another. 'Nuncio' is the title given to a diplomatic representative of the Holy See having equivalent rank to an ambassador.

4   'Internuncio' is the title given to a diplomatic representative of the Holy See having equivalent rank to an envoy or minister.

5   Vienna Convention on Diplomatic Relations art 14 para 1. The only differentiation between these classes is concerned with precedence and etiquette: see art 14 para 2. The class to which heads of mission are to be assigned is as agreed between the sending and receiving states: art 15. As to the different classes of members of a mission for the purposes of privileges and immunities see PARAS 279–281.

6   Vienna Convention on Diplomatic Relations art 16 para 1. In practice this is upon presentation or receipt of credentials to or by the receiving state (art 15 para 1), although this provision is without prejudice to the practice of a receiving state regarding the precedence of the representative of the Holy See (art 16 para 3). Procedure for the reception of the heads of mission must be uniform in respect of members of the same class: art 18. The precedence of members of the staff of a mission must be notified by the head of the mission to the minister for foreign affairs: art 17. As to the performance of the functions of a head of mission who is absent or unable to act see art 19.

268. Archives, correspondence, fees and charges. The archives and documents of the mission are inviolable at any time and wherever they may be[1], and the United Kingdom must permit and protect free communication on the part of the mission for all official purposes[2]. The official correspondence of the mission is inviolable[3]: the diplomatic bag may not be opened or detained[4], and the diplomatic courier must be protected in the United Kingdom in the performance of his functions[5]. He enjoys personal inviolability and is not liable to any form of arrest or detention[6]. The fees and charges levied by the diplomatic mission in the course of its official duties are exempt from all duties and taxes[7].

1   Diplomatic Privileges Act 1964 s 2(1), Sch 1 art 24. The embassy's internal documents are
    protected in an action for defamation by the defence of absolute privilege: *Fayed v Al-Tajir*
    [1988] QB 712, [1987] 2 All ER 396, CA. See also BYIL 58 (1987) pp 438–447. As to the
    meaning of 'inviolability' see *Shearson Lehman Brothers Inc v Maclaine Watson & Co Ltd
    (No 2)* [1988] 1 All ER 116, [1988] 1 WLR 16, HL (affinity assumed between immunity
    accorded to documents of an international organisation and that accorded to those of a
    diplomatic mission). See also PARA 309 note 4.
2   Diplomatic Privileges Act 1964 Sch 1 art 27 para 1. In communicating with the government and
    other missions of the sending state, the mission may employ all appropriate means including
    diplomatic couriers and messages in code and cipher, but the mission may only install and use a
    wireless transmitter with the consent of the United Kingdom: Sch 1 art 27 para 1. Third states
    must accord to official correspondence and other official communications in transit, including
    code or cipher messages, the same freedom and protection as is accorded by the United
    Kingdom: Sch 1 art 40 para 3. The same is true in the case of official communications whose
    presence in United Kingdom territory is due to force majeure: see Sch 1 art 40 para 4. As to the
    statutory meaning of 'United Kingdom' see PARA 30 note 3.
3   Diplomatic Privileges Act 1964 Sch 1 art 27 para 2. 'Official correspondence' means all
    correspondence relating to the mission and its functions: Sch 1 art 27 para 2.
4   Diplomatic Privileges Act 1964 Sch 1 art 27 para 3. The packages constituting the diplomatic
    bag must bear visible external marks of their character and must contain only diplomatic
    correspondence or articles intended for diplomatic use: Sch 1 art 27 para 4. A diplomatic bag
    may be entrusted to the captain of a commercial aircraft, from whom a member of a mission
    may receive possession of the bag at its destination directly and freely: see Sch 1 art 27 para 7.
    The captain of such an aircraft is not, however, a diplomatic courier: Sch 1 art 27 para 7.
5   Diplomatic Privileges Act 1964 Sch 1 art 27 para 5. He must also be provided with an official
    document indicating his status and the number of packages constituting the diplomatic bag:
    Sch 1 art 27 para 5. The sending state or the diplomatic mission may designate a courier ad hoc,
    in which case Sch 1 art 27 para 5 applies to him except that the immunities cease to apply when
    he has delivered to the assignee the diplomatic bag in his charge: Sch 1 art 27 para 6. The United
    Kingdom must accord inviolability to diplomatic bags in transit as well as to couriers: see Sch 1
    art 40 para 3. The same is true in the case of diplomatic couriers who have been granted a
    passport visa, if such visa was necessary, and official communications and diplomatic bags
    whose presence in United Kingdom territory is due to force majeure: see Sch 1 art 40 para 4.
6   Diplomatic Privileges Act 1964 Sch 1 art 27 para 5.
7   Diplomatic Privileges Act 1964 Sch 1 art 28.

269.   The mission's premises. The premises of the diplomatic mission[1] are
inviolable and may not be entered by the agents of the United Kingdom except
with the consent of the head of the mission[2]. The United Kingdom is under a
special duty to take all appropriate steps to protect them against any intrusion or
damage and to prevent any disturbance of the peace of the mission or
impairment of its dignity[3]. The premises, their furnishings and other property
and the mission's means of transport are immune from search, requisition,
attachment or execution[4]. Embassy bank accounts which fund diplomatic
activities in the receiving state are not held on mission premises and are,
therefore, not directly covered by inviolability but the courts have established
that such accounts cannot be made subject to attachment or execution[5]. The
sending state and the head of mission are exempt from all national, regional or
municipal dues and taxes in respect of the mission's premises, whether owned or
leased, other than such as represent payment for specific services rendered[6].

Under the Vienna Convention on Diplomatic Relations the receiving state
must either facilitate the acquisition on its territory by the sending state of
premises necessary for the mission or assist the mission to obtain
accommodation in any other way[7]; and where necessary it must assist a mission
in obtaining suitable accommodation for its members[8]. The sending state must
not use the mission's premises in any manner incompatible with the functions[9] of
the mission as laid down in the Convention, or by other rules of international
law or by any special agreement between that state and the receiving state[10].

1   'Premises of the mission' means the buildings or parts of buildings and the land ancillary to
    them, irrespective of ownership, used for the purposes of the mission, including the residence of
    the head of the mission: Diplomatic Privileges Act 1964 s 2(1), Sch 1 art 1(i). The express
    reference to the residence of the head of mission has been held to exclude the residences of other
    members of the mission from the scope of such 'premises': see *Intpro Properties (UK) Ltd v
    Sauvel* [1983] QB 1019, [1983] 2 All ER 495. As to the meaning of 'head of the mission' see
    PARA 266 note 4. The mission has the right to display the sending state's flag and emblem on the
    premises: Convention on Diplomatic Relations (Vienna, 18 April 1961; TS 19 (1965);
    Cmnd 2565) art 20. Diplomatic immunity of a mission's premises applies only to premises
    currently in use; it is irrelevant that they were used for the mission's purposes in the past:
    Westminster City Council v Government of the Islamic Republic of Iran [1986] 3 All ER 284,
    [1986] 1 WLR 979. As to the acquisition and loss by land of diplomatic status see the
    Diplomatic and Consular Premises Act 1987; and PARA 270. As to the protection of diplomatic
    premises if diplomatic relations have been broken off or the mission in question is recalled see
    the Diplomatic Privileges Act 1964 Sch 1 art 45; and PARA 272. As to the provisions of the
    Vienna Convention on Diplomatic Relations given force of law in the United Kingdom see PARA
    265 note 2.

2   Diplomatic Privileges Act 1964 Sch 1 art 22 para 1. As to the statutory meaning of 'United
    Kingdom' see PARA 30 note 3. In 1896, Sun Yat Sen, who was then a political refugee, was
    found to be held hostage in the Chinese Legation in London. The court refused to issue a writ of
    habeas corpus: see McNair *International Law Opinions* (Oxford, 1956) Vol 1 p 85. The
    Diplomatic Privileges Act 1964 Sch 1 art 22 para 1 does not mean that the premises are
    extraterritorial in the sense that they form part of the territory of the sending state: see *Radwan
    v Radwan* [1973] Fam 24, [1972] 3 All ER 967 (where it was held that a divorce obtained in a
    foreign consulate in London was not an overseas divorce within the Recognition of Divorces
    and Legal Separations Act 1971 s 2 (repealed)). As to the recognition of foreign divorces see
    CONFLICT OF LAWS vol 8(3) (Reissue) PARA 254 et seq. See also *Rio Tinto Zinc Corpn v
    Westinghouse Electric Corpn* [1978] AC 547, [1978] 1 All ER 434 (where the court held that
    witnesses, attending before a US judge hearing evidence in the US Embassy in London, had not
    thereby become subject to the jurisdiction of the US courts). As to the consular post see PARA
    293.
       Inviolability may also be claimed for the private residences of the members of the diplomatic
    and of the administrative and technical staff of the mission: see the Diplomatic Privileges
    Act 1964 Sch 1 arts 30 para 1, 37 para 2; and PARAS 273, 280. 'Members of the diplomatic
    staff' means members of the staff of the mission having diplomatic rank; and 'members of the
    administrative and technical staff' means the members of the staff of the mission employed in
    the administrative and technical service of the mission: Sch 1 art 1(d), (f). Schedule 1 has effect
    as if references to the members of the administrative and technical staff of a mission included
    references to persons designated as auxiliary personnel for an inspection carried out under the
    Stockholm Document and performing administrative and technical services: Arms Control and
    Disarmament (Privileges and Immunities) Act 1988 s 1(1)(b). As to the Stockholm document,
    and the extension of privileges in connection therewith, see PARA 273 note 1.

3   Diplomatic Privileges Act 1964 Sch 1 art 22 para 2. For a discussion of the receiving state's duty
    to protect mission premises see *Minister for Foreign Affairs and Trade v Magno* (1992-3)
    112 ALR 529, (1992) 101 ILR 202. See also *Aziz v Aziz (Sultan of Brunei intervening)* [2007]
    EWCA Civ 712, [2008] 2 All ER 501, [2007] NLJR 1047. For the purposes of the rule that
    conspiracy to commit trespass is an indictable offence if committed in the public domain, a
    foreign embassy or High Commission is part of the public domain: *Kamara v DPP* [1974] AC
    104, [1973] 2 All ER 1242, HL.

4   Diplomatic Privileges Act 1964 Sch 1 art 22 para 3. The same appears to apply to the service of
    a writ within the diplomatic premises. Personal service of legal process within the premises or at
    the door is prohibited: see *Adams v DPP, Judge for District No 16, Her Majesty's Secretary of
    State for Home Affairs, Ireland* [2001] 1 IR 47, [2001] 2 ILRM 401 (Irish court held that service
    of proceedings on British Ambassador to Ireland was illegal under art 22 of the Vienna
    Convention on Diplomatic Relations). It is also generally accepted that service by post on
    inviolable premises is a breach of such inviolability and therefore ineffective: see Denza
    Diplomatic Law: Commentary on the Vienna Convention on Diplomatic Relations (3rd Edn,
    2008) pp 151-153. As to the requirement that proceedings against a state must be transmitted
    through the diplomatic channel to the Ministry of Foreign Affairs of the defendant state see the
    State Immunity Act 1978 s 12(1); and PARA 256.

5   See *Alcom Ltd v Republic of Colombia* [1984] AC 580, [1984] 2 All ER 6; and *Liberian Eastern
    Timber Corpn v Government of Liberia* ICSID Case No ARB/83/2, (1992) 89 ILR 360.

6　Diplomatic Privileges Act 1964 Sch 1 art 23 para 1. This exemption does not apply to such dues and taxes payable under the law of the United Kingdom by persons contracting with the sending state or the head of mission (eg rates payable by a lessor of premises leased by the sending state for use as premises of the mission): Sch 1 art 23 para 2. See also PARA 275 text to note 7.

7　Vienna Convention on Diplomatic Relations art 21 para 1. This includes the residence of the head of the mission: see note 1.

8　Vienna Convention on Diplomatic Relations art 21 para 2.

9　For the functions of a diplomatic mission see the Vienna Convention on Diplomatic Relations art 3; and PARA 266.

10　Vienna Convention on Diplomatic Relations art 41 para 3.

270.　Acquisition and loss by land of diplomatic or consular status.　Where a state desires that land[1] should be diplomatic or consular premises[2], it must apply to the Secretary of State[3] for his consent to the land being such premises[4]. Unless he has given such consent[5], land is in no case to be regarded as a state's diplomatic or consular premises for the purposes of any enactment or rule of law[6]. If a state ceases to use land for the purposes of its mission or exclusively for the purposes of a consular post, or if the Secretary of State withdraws his consent[7], the land ceases to be diplomatic or consular premises for the purposes of all enactments and rules of law[8]. If a state intends to cease using land as premises of its mission or as consular premises, it must give the Secretary of State notice of that intention, specifying the date on which it intends to cease so using them[9].

In any proceedings a certificate issued by or under the authority of the Secretary of State stating any fact relevant to the question whether or not land was at any time diplomatic or consular premises is conclusive of that fact[10].

1　'Land' includes buildings and other structures, land covered with water and any estate, interest, easement, servitude or right in or over land: Diplomatic and Consular Premises Act 1987 s 5 (amended by the Land Registration Act 2002 Sch 11 para 21(2)).

2　'Diplomatic premises' means premises of the mission of a state: Diplomatic and Consular Premises Act 1987 s 5. 'Consular premises' has the meaning given by the definitions in the Convention on Consular Relations (Vienna, 24 April 1963; TS 14 (1973); Cmnd 5219) art 1 para 1(a), (j), as it has effect in the United Kingdom by virtue of the Consular Relations Act 1968 s 1, Sch 1 (see PARA 290 et seq): Diplomatic and Consular Premises Act 1987 s 5.

3　As to the Secretary of State see PARA 29.

4　Diplomatic and Consular Premises Act 1987 s 1(1). A state need not make such an application in relation to land if the Secretary of State accepted it as diplomatic or consular premises immediately before 1 January 1988: ss 1(2), 9(2); Diplomatic and Consular Premises Act 1987 (Commencement No 2) Order 1987, SI 1987/2248.

5　Or unless he has accepted the land as diplomatic or consular premises under the Diplomatic and Consular Premises Act 1987 s 1(2) (see note 4): see s 1(3).

6　Diplomatic and Consular Premises Act 1987 s 1(3).

7　Or his acceptance under the Diplomatic and Consular Premises Act 1987 s 1(2) (see note 4).

8　Diplomatic and Consular Premises Act 1987 s 1(3). The Secretary of State may only give or withdraw consent or withdraw acceptance if he is satisfied that to do so is permissible under international law: s 1(4). In determining whether to do so he must have regard to all material considerations, and in particular, but without prejudice to the generality of this requirement: (1) to the safety of the public; (2) to national security; and (3) to town and country planning: s 1(5).

9　Diplomatic and Consular Premises Act 1987 s 1(6). 'Premises of the mission' has the meaning given by the Convention on Diplomatic Relations (Vienna, 18 April 1961; TS 19 (1965); Cmnd 2565) art 1(i), as it has effect in the United Kingdom by virtue of the Diplomatic Privileges Act 1964 s 2, Sch 1 (see PARA 269 note 1): Diplomatic and Consular Premises Act 1987 s 5.

10　Diplomatic and Consular Premises Act 1987 s 1(7).

271.　Vesting of former diplomatic or consular premises in the Secretary of State.　In the case of former diplomatic or consular premises[1], the Secretary of State may by order[2] provide that the following provisions are to apply to the land in question³. He may by deed poll vest in himself such estate or interest in the land as appears to him to be appropriate⁴.

Where circumstances have arisen in consequence of which the power to make an order is exercisable, but the Secretary of State serves on the owner of the land in relation to which it has become exercisable notice that he does not intend to exercise the power in relation to that land, it ceases to be exercisable in relation to it in consequence of those circumstances⁵. If the Secretary of State has exercised the power to make an order in relation to land, but serves on the owner notice that he does not intend to execute a deed poll as described above relating to the land, the power to vest ceases to be exercisable⁶.

Where an estate or interest in land has vested in the Secretary of State under the provisions described above, it is his duty to sell it as soon as it is reasonably practicable to do so, taking all reasonable steps to ensure that the price is the best that can reasonably be obtained⁷. He must apply the purchase money firstly in payment of expenses properly incurred by him as incidental to the sale or any attempted sale⁸; secondly in discharge of prior incumbrances to which the sale is not made subject or in the making of any required⁹ payments to mortgagees¹⁰; thirdly in payment of expenses relating to the land reasonably incurred by him on repairs or security¹¹; fourthly in discharge of such liabilities to pay rates or sums in lieu of rates on the land or on any other land as the Secretary of State thinks fit¹²; and fifthly in discharge of such judgment debts arising out of matters relating to the land or to any other land as he thinks fit¹³. He must pay any residue to the person divested of the estate or interest¹⁴.

1   Ie where (1) the Secretary of State formerly accepted land as diplomatic or consular premises but did not accept it as such premises immediately before 1 January 1988 (ie the date of the coming into force of the Diplomatic and Consular Premises Act 1987 s 2: Diplomatic and Consular Premises Act 1987 (Commencement No 2) Order 1987, SI 1987/2248); or (2) land has ceased to be diplomatic or consular premises after the coming into force of the Diplomatic and Consular Premises Act 1987 s 2 but not less than 12 months before the exercise of the power conferred on the Secretary of State by s 2: s 2(1)(a), (b). As to the meanings of 'diplomatic premises' and 'consular premises' see PARA 270 note 2. As to the Secretary of State see PARA 29.

2   Such an order must be made by statutory instrument, and a statutory instrument containing any such order is subject to annulment in pursuance of a resolution of either House of Parliament: Diplomatic and Consular Premises Act 1987 s 2(4). At the date at which this volume states the law, the Diplomatic and Consular Premises (Cambodia) Order 1988, SI 1988/30, had been made under this provision.

3   Diplomatic and Consular Premises Act 1987 s 2(1). He may only exercise this power if he is satisfied that to do so is permissible under international law: s 2(2). In determining whether to exercise it he must have regard to all material considerations, and in particular, but without prejudice to the generality of this requirement, to any of the considerations mentioned in s 1(5) (see PARA 270 note 8) that appears to him to be relevant: s 2(3). See *R v Secretary of State for Foreign and Commonwealth Affairs, ex p Samuel* (1989) 83 ILR 232, CA. See also associated proceedings in *Westminster City Council v Tomlin* [1990] 1 All ER 920, [1989] 1 WLR 1287.

4   Diplomatic and Consular Premises Act 1987 s 2(5). Such a deed poll may also comprise any portion of a building in which the former diplomatic or consular premises are situated: s 2(6).

     In a case falling within s 2(1)(a) (see head (1) in note 1), the Secretary of State might only exercise the power conferred by s 2(1) before the end of the period of two months beginning with the 1 January 1988: see s 2(8). However, the power continues to be exercisable after the end of that period if within that period he (1) certified that he reserves the right to exercise it; and (2) unless he considers it inappropriate or impracticable to do so, serves a copy of the certificate on the owner of any estate or interest in the land: s 2(9).

     A deed poll has effect to vest in the Secretary of State the benefit of any covenant touching and concerning the land to which the deed relates but not annexed to it if, immediately before the vesting of the estate to which the deed relates, the covenant was enforceable by the person divested of that estate: s 4, Sch 1 para 3. Where a term of years has vested in the Secretary of State, and assignment of the term is absolutely prohibited, the prohibition must be treated, in relation to an assignment on sale, as if it were a provision to the effect that the term may not be assigned without the consent of the landlord and that such consent is not to be unreasonably withheld: Sch 1 para 4.

    Further provision is made for the machinery to give effect, in terms of land law, to the transactions under s 2: see Sch 1 para 5 (registered land), Sch 1 paras 6, 7 (unregistered land), Sch 1 para 8 (production of title).

5   Diplomatic and Consular Premises Act 1987 s 2(10).
6   Diplomatic and Consular Premises Act 1987 s 2(11).
7   Diplomatic and Consular Premises Act 1987 s 3(1).
8   Diplomatic and Consular Premises Act 1987 s 3(2)(a).
9   Ie required by the Diplomatic and Consular Premises Act 1987 Sch 1: s 3(2)(b).
10   Diplomatic and Consular Premises Act 1987 s 3(2)(b). 'Mortgage' includes a charge or lien for securing money or money's worth; and 'mortgagees' falls to be construed accordingly: s 5.
11   Diplomatic and Consular Premises Act 1987 s 3(2)(c).
12   Diplomatic and Consular Premises Act 1987 s 3(2)(d).
13   Diplomatic and Consular Premises Act 1987 s 3(2)(e).
14   Diplomatic and Consular Premises Act 1987 s 3(2). Where a state was divested but there is no person with whom Her Majesty's government of the United Kingdom has dealings as the government of that state, the Secretary of State must hold the residue until there is such a person and then pay it: s 3(3). A sum so held must be placed in a bank account bearing interest at such rate as the Treasury may approve: s 3(4). As to the statutory meaning of 'United Kingdom' see PARA 30 note 3. As to the Treasury see CONSTITUTIONAL LAW AND HUMAN RIGHTS vol 8(2) (Reissue) PARAS 512–517.

272.   Status of diplomatic premises if relations broken off or mission recalled.

If diplomatic relations are broken off between two states, or if a mission is permanently or temporarily recalled, the following provisions apply[1]. The United Kingdom must, even in case of armed conflict, respect and protect the premises of the mission, together with its property and archives[2]. The sending state may entrust the custody of the premises of the mission, together with its property and archives, to a third state acceptable to the United Kingdom[3]. The sending state may also entrust the protection of its interests and those of its nationals to a third state acceptable to the United Kingdom[4].

1   Diplomatic Privileges Act 1964 s 2(1), Sch 1 art 45 (added by the Diplomatic and Consular Premises Act 1987 s 6, Sch 2 para 1).
2   Diplomatic Privileges Act 1964 Sch 1 art 45(a) (as added: see note 1). As to the statutory meaning of 'United Kingdom' see PARA 30 note 3.
3   Diplomatic and Consular Premises Act 1987 Sch 1 art 45(b) (as added: see note 1).
4   Diplomatic and Consular Premises Act 1987 Sch 1 art 45(c) (as added: see note 1).

273.   Personal privileges and immunities of diplomatic agents.

The person of a diplomatic agent[1] is inviolable[2]. He is not liable to any form of arrest or detention, and the United Kingdom must treat him with due respect and take all appropriate steps to prevent any attack on his person, freedom or dignity[3]. His private residence enjoys the same inviolability and protection as the premises of the mission[4]. His papers, correspondence and property likewise enjoy inviolability[5]. Members of a diplomatic mission are not subject to restrictions upon immigration of persons who are not British citizens[6].

1   'Diplomatic agent' means the head of the mission or a member of the diplomatic staff: Diplomatic Privileges Act 1964 s 2(1), Sch 1 art 1(e). As to the meaning of 'head of the mission' see PARA 266 note 4; and as to the meaning of 'member of the diplomatic staff' see PARA 269 note 2. References to 'diplomatic agent' also include:
    (1)   references to any person designated by the government of the People's Republic of China as a member of the Joint Liaison Group set up under the Joint Declaration of the Government of the United Kingdom and the Government of the People's Republic of China on the Question of Hong Kong which was signed in Peking on 19 December 1984 para 5 (Hong Kong Act 1985 ss 1(2), 2(2), Schedule para 4);

(2)   any person designated by a state other than the United Kingdom as an observer or inspector under the Stockholm Document (ie the document dated 19 September 1986 and concluded at the Stockholm Conference on confidence and security building measures and disarmament in Europe) (Arms Control and Disarmament (Privileges and Immunities) Act 1988 s 1(1)(a), (4)).

As to the statutory meaning of 'United Kingdom' see PARA 30 note 3.

Her Majesty may by Order in Council confer such privileges and immunities (not exceeding those conferred by the Diplomatic Privileges Act 1964) as appear to Her Majesty to be required for giving effect to any provision of an international agreement or arrangement superseding the Stockholm Document or otherwise making provision for furthering arms control or disarmament; but no such order may be made unless a draft of it has been laid before and approved by a resolution of each House of Parliament: Arms Control and Disarmament (Privileges and Immunities) Act 1988 s 1(2). For orders under this provision see the Treaty on the Elimination of Intermediate-Range and Shorter-Range Missiles (Inspections) (Privileges and Immunities) Order 1988, SI 1988/792; the Treaty on Open Skies (Privileges and Immunities) Order 1993, SI 1993/1246; the Treaty on Open Skies (Privileges and Immunities) (Overseas Territories) Order 1993, SI 1993/1247; and the Treaty on Open Skies (Privileges and Immunities) (Guernsey) Order 1993, SI 1993/2669; the Vienna Document 1999 (Privileges and Immunities) Order 2003, SI 2003/2621.

If in any proceedings any question arises whether or not any person is entitled to any privilege or immunity by virtue of the Arms Control and Disarmament (Privileges and Immunities) Act 1988, a certificate issued by or under the authority of the Secretary of State stating any fact relating to that question is conclusive evidence of that fact: s 1(3). As to the Secretary of State see PARA 29.

The Arms Control and Disarmament (Privileges and Immunities) Act 1988 may be extended to the Channel Islands, the Isle of Man, or any colony: see s 2(3). See the Arms Control and Disarmament Act 1988 (Guernsey) Order 1993, SI 1993/2666; and the Arms Control and Disarmament (Privileges and Immunities) Act 1988 (Overseas Territories) Order 1992, SI 1992/1298, extending the Act, subject to modifications, to the following: Anguilla; Bermuda; British Antarctic Territory; British Indian Ocean Territory; Cayman Islands; Falkland Islands; Gibraltar; Hong Kong; Montserrat; Pitcairn, Henderson, Ducie and Oeno Islands; St Helena and Dependencies; South Georgia and the South Sandwich Islands; Sovereign Base Areas of Akrotiri and Dhekelia; Turks and Caicos Islands; Virgin Islands.

The members of inspection teams and observers under the Chemical Weapons Act 1996 enjoy the same privileges and immunities as are enjoyed by diplomatic agents in accordance with the Diplomatic Privileges Act 1964 Sch 1 arts 29, 30 paras 1, 2, 31 paras 1–3, 34: Chemical Weapons Act 1996 s 27 (see WAR AND ARMED CONFLICT vol 49(1) (2005 Reissue) PARA 490). Similar (but not identical) provision is made by the Arms Control and Disarmament (Inspections) Act 1991 s 5 (see WAR AND ARMED CONFLICT vol 49(1) (2005 Reissue) PARA 503), the Nuclear Explosions (Prohibition and Inspections) Act 1998 s 8 (not in force at the date at which this volume states the law), and the Landmines Act 1998 s 15 (see WAR AND ARMED CONFLICT vol 49(1) (2005 Reissue) PARA 500).

2   Diplomatic Privileges Act 1964 Sch 1 art 29. Such inviolability precludes personal service of legal process on a diplomat: see *Adams v DPP, Judge for District No 16, Her Majesty's Secretary of State for Home Affairs, Ireland* [2001] 1 IR 47, [2001] 2 ILRM 401 (Irish court held service of process on British Ambassador to Ireland contravened his personal inviolability under art 29 as well as the inviolability of the premises, and was therefore ineffective).

In 1974 the United Nations adopted a Convention on the Prevention and Punishment of Crimes against Internationally Protected Persons, including Diplomatic Agents (New York, 14 December 1973; TS 3 (1980); Cmnd 7765), which provides for punishment for attacks and threats of attacks on certain persons, including heads of states, representatives or international organisations and members of their families and households. Its provisions were implemented by the Internationally Protected Persons Act 1978: see CRIMINAL LAW, EVIDENCE AND PROCEDURE vol 11(1) (2006 Reissue) PARA 477. As to immunity from criminal and civil jurisdiction see the Diplomatic Privileges Act 1964 Sch 1 art 31; and PARA 274.

3   Diplomatic Privileges Act 1964 Sch 1 art 29. See *Aziz v Aziz (Sultan of Brunei intervening)* [2007] EWCA Civ 712, [2008] 2 All ER 501, [2007] NLJR 1047.

4   Diplomatic Privileges Act 1964 Sch 1 art 30 para 1. As to the premises of the mission see PARA 269; and *Agbor v Metropolitan Police Comr* [1969] 2 All ER 707, [1969] 1 WLR 703, CA (private residence temporarily vacated: court held flat no longer residence of a diplomatic agent and therefore executive had no right to evict subsequent occupiers who claimed to be there as of right); *Re B (Care Proceedings: Diplomatic Immunity)* [2002] EWHC 1751 (Fam), [2003] Fam 16, [2003]1 FLR 241 (where court considered issue of whether proper to continue interim

care order in respect of a child of a member of the administrative and technical staff of a diplomatic mission, given that the father and his private residence were inviolable, so that order may not be capable of enforcement). See also Denza *Diplomatic Law: Commentary on the Vienna Convention on Diplomatic Relations* (3rd Edn, 2008) pp 271–274.

5   Diplomatic Privileges Act 1964 Sch 1 art 30 para 2. With respect to property, this provision is subject to the exception relating to execution: see Sch 1 art 31 para 3; and PARA 274.

6   See the Immigration Act 1971 s 8(3) (amended by the British Nationality Act 1981 s 39(6); and the Immigration Act 1988 s 4). This applies to all members of a mission or persons who are members of the family forming part of the household of such a member, or a person otherwise entitled to like immunity: Immigration Act 1971 s 8(3) (as so amended). For the purposes of s 8(3), a member of a mission other than a diplomatic agent is not to count as a member of a mission unless (1) he was resident outside the United Kingdom, and was not in the United Kingdom, when he was offered a post as such a member; and (2) he has not ceased to be such a member after having taken up the post: s 8(3A) (added by the Immigration Act 1988 s 4; and substituted by the Immigration and Asylum Act 1999 s 6).

274.   Immunity from jurisdiction.   A diplomatic agent enjoys immunity from the criminal jurisdiction of the courts of the United Kingdom[1]. He also enjoys immunity from the civil and administrative jurisdiction except in the following cases[2]:

(1)   a real action relating to his private immovable property in the territory of the United Kingdom, unless he holds it on behalf of the sending state for the purposes of the mission[3];

(2)   an action relating to succession in which he is involved as executor, administrator, heir or legatee as a private person and not on behalf of the sending state[4]; and

(3)   an action relating to any professional or commercial activity which he may exercise in the United Kingdom outside his official functions[5].

Except in these cases, no measures of execution may be taken in respect of him, and then only if the measures can be taken without infringing the inviolability of his person or of his residence[6]. He is not obliged to give evidence as a witness[7]. Except and in so far as additional immunities may be conferred on them by Order in Council, diplomatic agents who are citizens of the United Kingdom and Colonies, or permanently resident in the United Kingdom, only enjoy immunity in respect of official acts performed in the exercise of their functions[8].

The immunity of a diplomatic agent from the jurisdiction of the United Kingdom does not exempt him from the jurisdiction of the sending state[9].

1   Diplomatic Privileges Act 1964 s 2(1), Sch 1 art 31 para 1. As to the meaning of 'diplomatic agent' see PARA 273 note 1. He is, however, under a duty to respect United Kingdom laws and regulations and to abstain from interfering in its internal affairs: Convention on Diplomatic Relations (Vienna, 18 April 1961; TS 19 (1965); Cmnd 2565) art 41 para 1. For an official Memorandum of Diplomatic Privileges and Immunities in the United Kingdom see British Practice in International Law (1966) 126. For an extension of the immunities conferred by these provisions see the Acts and orders noted in PARA 273 note 1. As to the provisions of the Vienna Convention on Diplomatic Relations given force of law in the United Kingdom see PARA 265 text and note 2. As to the statutory meaning of 'United Kingdom' see PARA 30 note 3.

2   Diplomatic Privileges Act 1964 Sch 1 art 31 para 1. A person becoming entitled to immunity after an action has begun is entitled to a stay of proceedings: *Ghosh v D'Rozario* [1963] 1 QB 106, [1962] 2 All ER 640, CA. Immunity does not import exemption from legal liability, but only from jurisdiction: *Dickinson v Del Solar* [1930] 1 KB 376, 6 BILC 142. See also *Shaw v Shaw* [1979] Fam 62, [1979] 3 All ER 1 (loss of diplomatic immunity before summons heard removed jurisdictional bar to the hearing).

3   Diplomatic Privileges Act 1964 Sch 1 art 31 para 1(a); and see *Intpro Properties (UK) Ltd v Sauvel* [1983] QB 1019, [1983] 2 All ER 495, CA (the fact that premises were used as a private residence by a diplomat and for social entertaining was not sufficient to satisfy test of their being 'used for the purposes of a diplomatic mission').

4   Diplomatic Privileges Act 1964 Sch 1 art 31 para 1(b).
5   Diplomatic Privileges Act 1964 Sch 1 art 31 para 1(c). See *Propend Finance Property Ltd v Sing* (1997) 111 ILR 611 at 659–661, Times 2 May, CA. See also and Denza *Diplomatic Law: Commentary on the Vienna Convention on Diplomatic Relations* (3rd Edn, 2008) pp 306–308. A diplomatic agent in the receiving state must not practise any professional or commercial activity for personal profit: Vienna Convention on Diplomatic Relations art 42.
6   Diplomatic Privileges Act 1964 Sch 1 art 31 para 3.
7   Diplomatic Privileges Act 1964 Sch 1 art 31 para 2.
8   Diplomatic Privileges Act 1964 ss 2(6), 6, Sch 1 art 38 para 1. Citizenship of the United Kingdom and Colonies (ie the territories comprising the United Kingdom and Colonies on 1 January 1949) no longer exists, having been replaced by new categories of citizenship: see BRITISH NATIONALITY, IMMIGRATION AND ASYLUM vol 4(2) (2002 Reissue) PARA 16 et seq. A person who is a member of the mission (or is a private servant of such a member) of any of the countries mentioned below who is also a British national is entitled to such privileges and immunities as he would have been entitled to were he not a citizen of the United Kingdom and Colonies: Antigua and Barbuda; Australia; The Bahamas; Bangladesh; Barbados; Belize; Botswana; Brunei; Cameroon; Canada; Republic of Cyprus; Dominica; Fiji; The Gambia; Ghana; Grenada; Guyana; India; Republic of Ireland; Jamaica; Kenya; Kiribati; Lesotho; Malawi; Malaysia; Maldives; Malta; Mauritius; Mozambique; Namibia; Nauru; New Zealand; Nigeria; Pakistan; Papua New Guinea; St Christopher and Nevis; St Lucia; St Vincent and the Grenadines; Seychelles; Sierra Leone; Singapore; Solomon Islands; South Africa; Sri Lanka; Swaziland; Tanzania; Tonga; Trinidad and Tobago; Tuvalu; Uganda; Vanuatu; Western Samoa; Zambia; Zimbabwe: Diplomatic Privileges (British Nationals) Order 1999, SI 1999/670, art 2(2), Sch 1. 'British national' means a person who under the British Nationality Act 1981 and the British Nationality (Falkland Islands) Act 1983 is a British citizen, a British overseas territories citizen or a British Overseas citizen or who under the Hong Kong (British Nationality) Order 1986, SI 1986/948, is a British National (Overseas) (see generally BRITISH NATIONALITY, IMMIGRATION AND ASYLUM): Diplomatic Privileges (British Nationals) Order 1999, SI 1999/670, art 2(3) (amended by virtue of the British Overseas Territories Act 2002 s 2(3)).

    For provisions relating to members of missions other than diplomatic agents see PARA 279 et seq. Jurisdiction must be exercised over those persons in such a manner as not to interfere unduly with the performance of the functions of the mission: Diplomatic Privileges Act 1964 Sch 1 art 38 para 2.
9   Diplomatic Privileges Act 1964 Sch 1 art 31 para 4.

275.   Exemption from taxes.   A diplomatic agent[1] is exempt from all dues and taxes, personal and real, national, regional or municipal, except:

(1)   indirect taxes of a kind which are normally incorporated in the price of goods or services[2];

(2)   dues and taxes on private immovable property situated in the territory of the United Kingdom, unless he holds it on behalf of the sending state for the purposes of the mission[3];

(3)   estate, succession or inheritance duties[4];

(4)   dues and taxes on private income having its source in the United Kingdom and capital taxes on investments made in commercial undertakings in the United Kingdom[5];

(5)   charges levied for specific services rendered[6]; and

(6)   registration, court or record fees, mortgage dues and stamp duty, with respect to immovable property[7].

The exemption does not normally apply to persons who are nationals of or permanently resident in the United Kingdom[8].

1   As to the meaning of 'diplomatic agent' see PARA 273 note 1. For extension of the immunities conferred by these provisions see the Acts and orders noted in PARA 273 note 1.
2   Diplomatic Privileges Act 1964 s 2(1), Sch 1 art 34(a).
3   Diplomatic Privileges Act 1964 Sch 1 art 34(b). As to the statutory meaning of 'United Kingdom' see PARA 30 note 3.
4   Diplomatic Privileges Act 1964 Sch 1 art 34(c). This is subject to Sch 1 art 39 para 4: see PARA 286.

5 Diplomatic Privileges Act 1964 Sch 1 art 34(d).

6 Diplomatic Privileges Act 1964 Sch 1 art 34(e).

7 Diplomatic Privileges Act 1964 Sch 1 art 34(f). This is subject to Sch 1 art 23: see PARA 269. Although the Convention on Diplomatic Relations (Vienna, 18 April 1961; TS 19 (1965); Cmnd 2565) art 34, as reproduced in the Diplomatic Privileges Act 1964 Sch 1, refers to stamp duty with respect to immovable property such duty has now largely been replaced by stamp duty land tax in English law: see STAMP DUTIES AND STAMP DUTY RESERVE TAX. HMRC guidance indicates the view that the relief afforded to stamp duty for diplomatic premises is applicable to stamp duty land tax see HMRC Stamp Duty Land Tax Manual para 20500, accessible on the date at which this volume states the law at www.hmrc.gov.uk.

8 Diplomatic Privileges Act 1964 ss 2(6), 6, Sch 1 art 38 para 1. See PARA 274.

276. Exemption from social security provisions. A diplomatic agent[1] is exempt from the social security provisions in force in the United Kingdom with respect to services rendered for the sending state[2]. This also applies to private servants[3] in the sole employ of a diplomatic agent on condition that they are not citizens of the United Kingdom and Colonies or permanently resident in the United Kingdom and that they are covered by the social security provisions which may be in force in the sending state or a third state[4]. This does not preclude voluntary participation in the social security system of the United Kingdom by either of these classes of person[5].

Nothing in the provisions described above affects bilateral or multilateral agreements concerning social security already concluded or to be concluded in the future[6].

1 As to the meaning of 'diplomatic agent' see PARA 273 note 1.

2 Diplomatic Privileges Act 1964 s 2(1), Sch 1 art 33 para 1. The exemption is deemed to except the services concerned from any class of employment which is insurable employment or in respect of which contributions are required to be paid under enactments relating to social security (see SOCIAL SECURITY AND PENSIONS) or any enactment relating to Northern Ireland, but not so as to render any person liable to pay any contribution which he would not be required to pay if those services were not so excepted: see s 2(4) (amended, and prospectively amended, by the Social Security Act 1973 ss 100, 101, Sch 27 para 24; and the Social Security (Consequential Provisions) Act 1975 ss 1(2), 5, Sch 1 Pt I). The exemption does not normally apply to persons who are nationals of the United Kingdom and Colonies or permanently resident in the United Kingdom: see PARA 274 text and note 8. As to the statutory meaning of 'United Kingdom' see PARA 30 note 3. As to the expression 'United Kingdom and Colonies' see PARA 274 note 8.

3 'Private servant' means a person who is in the domestic service of a member of the mission and who is not an employee of the sending state: Diplomatic Privileges Act 1964 Sch 1 art 1(h). 'Members of the mission' means the head of the mission (see PARA 266 note 4) and the members of the staff of the mission; and 'members of the staff of the mission' means the members of the diplomatic staff and of the administrative and technical staff (see 269 note 2) and the members of the service staff of the mission: Sch 1 art 1(b), (c). 'Members of the service staff' means the members of the staff of the mission in the domestic service of the mission (Sch 1 art 1(g)); and it includes persons designated as auxiliary personnel by a state other than the United Kingdom performing domestic service (Arms Control and Disarmament (Privileges and Immunities) Act 1988 s 1(1)(b)). As to the Stockholm document, and the extension of privileges in connection therewith, see PARA 273 note 1.

4 Diplomatic Privileges Act 1964 Sch 1 art 33 para 2. A diplomatic agent who employs persons to whom the exemption does not apply must observe the obligations which the social security provisions impose upon employers: Sch 1 art 33 para 3.

5 See the Diplomatic Privileges Act 1964 Sch 1 art 33 para 4.

6 Diplomatic Privileges Act 1964 Sch 1 art 33 para 5.

277. Exemption from services. Diplomatic agents[1] are exempted from all personal services, from any public service of any kind whatsoever, and from military obligations such as those connected with requisitioning, military contributions and billeting[2]. The exemption does not normally apply to persons who are nationals of the United Kingdom and Colonies or who are permanently resident in the United Kingdom[3].

1   As to the meaning of 'diplomatic agent' see PARA 273 note 1.
2   Diplomatic Privileges Act 1964 s 2(1), Sch 1 art 35.
3   See PARA 274 text and note 8. As to the expression 'United Kingdom and Colonies' see PARA 274 note 8.

278. Importation of articles. The Crown permits entry of and grants exemption from all customs duties[1], taxes and related charges other than charges for storage, cartage and similar services, on articles for the official use of the mission and articles for the personal use of a diplomatic agent[2] or members of his family forming part of his household, including articles intended for his establishment[3]. The personal baggage of a diplomatic agent is exempt from inspection unless there are serious grounds for presuming that it contains articles not covered by the exemptions mentioned, or articles the import or export of which is prohibited or is controlled by quarantine regulations[4]. This exemption does not normally apply to persons who are nationals of the United Kingdom and Colonies or who are permanently resident in the United Kingdom[5].

1   The reference to customs duties must be construed as including a reference to excise duties chargeable on goods imported into the United Kingdom (see generally CUSTOMS AND EXCISE), and to value added tax charged in accordance with the Value Added Tax Act 1994 s 10 or s 15 (acquisitions from other member states and importations from outside the European Union) (see VALUE ADDED TAX vol 49(1) (2005 Reissue) PARAS 19, 113): Diplomatic Privileges Act 1964 s 2(5A) (added by the Customs and Excise Management Act 1979 s 177(1), Sch 4 para 3; and amended by the Finance (No 2) Act 1992 s 14, Sch 3 para 87; and the Value Added Tax Act 1994 s 100(1), Sch 14 para 1). As to the relief from customs and excise duties for persons enjoying privileges and immunities under the Diplomatic Privileges Act 1964 see the Customs and Excise Duties (General Reliefs) Act 1979 ss 13A–13C; and CUSTOMS AND EXCISE vol 12(3) (2007 Reissue) PARAS 887, 894. As to the statutory meaning of 'United Kingdom' see PARA 30 note 3.
2   As to the meaning of 'diplomatic agent' see PARA 273 note 1.
3   Diplomatic Privileges Act 1964 s 2(1), Sch 1 art 36 para 1. Articles for the official use of the mission include inspection equipment relating to the treaty on the elimination of intermediate and shorter-range missiles made between the United States and the Soviet Union; articles for the personal use of a diplomatic agent include those of inspectors and aircrew in the United Kingdom in connection with their official functions: Treaty on the Elimination of Intermediate-Range and Shorter-Range Missiles (Inspections) (Privileges and Immunities) Order 1988, SI 1988/792, arts 2, 4. The members of inspection teams and observers under the Chemical Weapons Act 1996 enjoy the same privileges as are enjoyed by diplomatic agents in accordance with the Diplomatic Privileges Act 1964 Sch 1 art 36 para 1(b), except in relation to articles the importing or exporting of which is prohibited by law or controlled by the enactments relating to quarantine: see the Chemical Weapons Act 1996 s 27; and WAR AND ARMED CONFLICT vol 49(1) (2005 Reissue) PARA 490. A similar extension (subject to the same restriction) is made for the members of inspection teams and observers under the Nuclear Explosions (Prohibition and Inspections) Act 1998: Nuclear Explosions (Prohibition and Inspections) Act 1998 s 8 (not in force at the date at which this volume states the law).
4   Diplomatic Privileges Act 1964 Sch 1 art 36 para 2. Such inspection must be conducted in the presence of the diplomatic agent or his authorised representative: Sch 1 art 36 para 2.
5   See PARA 274 text and note 8. As to the expression 'United Kingdom and Colonies' see PARA 274 note 8.

279. Privileges of diplomatic agent's family. The members of the family of a diplomatic agent forming part of his household enjoy the privileges and immunities of a diplomatic agent[1]. This does not apply, however, in the case of citizens of the United Kingdom and Colonies[2].

1 Diplomatic Privileges Act 1964 s 2(1), Sch 1 art 37 para 1. The privileges and immunities referred to are those set out in Sch 1 arts 29–36: see PARA 273 et seq. As to the meaning of 'diplomatic agent' see PARA 273 note 1. As to waiver of these privileges and immunities see PARA 283. As to the meaning of the term 'members of the family of a diplomatic agent forming part of his household' see Denza *Diplomatic Law: Commentary on the Vienna Convention on Diplomatic Relations* (3rd Edn, 2008) pp 391–396.
2 See PARA 274 text and note 8. As to the expression 'United Kingdom and Colonies' see PARA 274 note 8.

280. Privileges of the administrative and technical staff. Members of the administrative and technical staff[1] of the mission, together with members of their families forming part of their respective households, who are not citizens of the United Kingdom and Colonies or permanently resident in the United Kingdom, enjoy all the privileges and immunities of a diplomatic agent[2] with the exception of those relating to the inspection of baggage[3]. The immunity from civil and administrative jurisdiction is confined to acts performed in the course of their duties[4]. The privilege relating to importation of articles[5] is confined to those imported at the time of first installation[6].

1 As to the meaning of 'members of the administrative and technical staff' see PARA 269 note 2.
2 The privileges and immunities referred to are those set out in the Diplomatic Privileges Act 1964 s 2(1), Sch 1 arts 29–35, 36(1): see PARA 273 et seq. As to the meaning of 'diplomatic agent' see PARA 273 note 1. As to the statutory meaning of 'United Kingdom' see PARA 30 note 3. As to the expression 'United Kingdom and Colonies' see PARA 274 note 8.
3 Diplomatic Privileges Act 1964 Sch 1 art 37 para 2. As to the baggage exception see Sch 1 art 36 para 2; and PARA 278. As to waiver of these privileges and immunities see PARA 283.
4 Diplomatic Privileges Act 1964 Sch 1 art 37 para 2. As to this immunity see Sch 1 para 31 art 1; and PARA 274. See also *Re B (Care Proceedings: Diplomatic Immunity)* [2002] EWHC 1751 (Fam), [2003] Fam 16, [2003]1 FLR 241 (acts leading to imposition of interim care order in respect of child of member of the administrative and technical staff of a diplomatic mission were acts performed outside the course of father's diplomatic duties). Where the immunity of a diplomatic agent was removed by this provision upon his being classified as a member of the administrative and technical staff, an existing action against him which had been stayed could be continued: *Empson v Smith* [1966] 1 QB 426, [1965] 2 All ER 881, CA.
5 See the Diplomatic Privileges Act 1964 Sch 1 art 36 para 1; and PARA 278.
6 Diplomatic Privileges Act 1964 Sch 1 art 37 para 2.

281. Privileges of the service staff. Members of the service staff[1] of the mission who are not citizens of the United Kingdom and Colonies or permanently resident in the United Kingdom enjoy immunity in respect of acts performed in the course of their duties, exemption from dues and taxes on the emoluments they receive by reason of their employment and exemption from social security provisions[2].

Private servants[3] of members of the mission, unless they are citizens of the United Kingdom and Colonies or permanently resident in the United Kingdom, are exempt from dues and taxes on the emoluments they receive by reason of their employment[4]. In other respects they may enjoy such privileges and immunities only as specified by Order in Council[5]. However, jurisdiction must be exercised in such a manner as not to interfere unduly with the performance of the functions of the mission[6].

1 As to the meaning of 'members of the service staff' see PARA 276 note 3.
2 Diplomatic Privileges Act 1964 s 2(1), Sch 1 art 37 para 3. As to the exemption in respect of social security provisions see PARA 276. As to waiver of these privileges and immunities see PARA 283. As to the statutory meaning of 'United Kingdom' see PARA 30 note 3. As to the expression 'United Kingdom and Colonies' see PARA 274 note 8.
3 As to the meaning of 'private servant' see PARA 276 note 3.

4   Diplomatic Privileges Act 1964 Sch 1 art 37 para 4. As to waiver of these privileges and immunities see PARA 283.
5   Diplomatic Privileges Act 1964 ss 2(6), 6, Sch 1 art 37 para 4. See the Diplomatic Privileges (British Nationals) Order 1999, SI 1999/670; and PARA 274.
6   Diplomatic Privileges Act 1964 Sch 1 art 37 para 4.

282.   Official information as to status.   If in any proceedings any question arises whether or not any person is entitled to any privilege or immunity under the Diplomatic Privileges Act 1964, a certificate issued by or under the authority of the Secretary of State[1] stating any fact relating to that question is conclusive evidence of that fact[2].

1   As to the Secretary of State see PARA 29.
2   Diplomatic Privileges Act 1964 s 4.

283.   Waiver of privilege.   The privileges and immunities of diplomatic agents and their families and of the administrative, technical and service staff and private servants[1] may be waived by the sending state[2]. A waiver by the head of the mission or any person for the time being performing his functions is deemed to be a waiver by that state[3]. Waiver must always be express[4]. Accordingly, even if a person entitled to immunity has entered an appearance or pleaded otherwise than to the jurisdiction, he may at a later stage prove that his government has not consented to a waiver of his immunity[5]. Waiver in respect of civil or administrative proceedings is not to be held to imply waiver in respect of execution, for which a separate waiver is necessary[6]. In such a case, judgment may be given against the defendant but not enforced until a reasonable time after the termination of his mission[7].

1   Ie persons enjoying immunity under the Diplomatic Privileges Act 1964 s 2(1), Sch 1 art 37: see PARAS 885–887. As to the meaning of 'diplomatic agent' see PARA 273 note 1; As to the meaning of 'members of the administrative and technical staff' see PARA 269 note 2. As to the meaning of 'private servants' see PARA 276 note 3.
2   Diplomatic Privileges Act 1964 Sch 1 art 32 para 1. See *Fayed v Al-Tajir* [1988] QB 712, [1987] 2 All ER 396, CA (the defendant's defence filed in proceedings brought against him not an appropriate vehicle for waiver of immunity by his state).
3   Diplomatic Privileges Act 1964 s 2(3). This provision embraces the case where the head of mission waives his own privilege, not merely that of a subordinate member of the staff of the mission. As to the meaning of 'head of the mission' see PARA 266 note 4.
4   Diplomatic Privileges Act 1964 Sch 1 art 32 para 2. See *A Company Ltd v Republic of X* [1990] 2 Lloyd's Rep 520 at 524 per Saville J; *Propend Finance Pty Ltd v Sing* (1997) 111 Int LR 611, CA (undertaking given to the court not an express waiver).
5   *Republic of Bolivia Exploration Syndicate Ltd* [1914] 1 Ch 139 at 156, 6 BILC 39; and see *R v Madan* [1961] 2 QB 1, [1961] 1 All ER 588, CCA (criminal prosecution).
6   Diplomatic Privileges Act 1964 Sch 1 art 32 para 4.
7   *Re Suarez, Suarez v Suarez* [1918] 1 Ch 176, 6 BILC 64, CA.

284.   Waiver by institution of proceedings.   Institution of proceedings by a diplomatic agent or member of his family or the staff of the mission precludes him from invoking immunity from the jurisdiction in respect of a counterclaim directly connected with the principal claim[1]. If such a person brings an action the court may order him to give security for costs[2].

1   Diplomatic Privileges Act 1964 s 2(1), Sch 1 art 32 para 3. The agent may, however, invoke immunity in respect of a counterclaim not directly connected with the principal claim: *High Comr for India v Ghosh* [1960] 1 QB 134, [1959] 3 All ER 659, CA. As to the meaning of 'diplomatic agent' see PARA 273 note 1.
2   See *Emperor of Brazil v Robinson* (1837) 6 Ad & El 801, 1 BILC 127 (head of state). Cf, however, *Duke of Montellano v Christin* (1816) 5 M & S 503, 6 BILC 4.

285. Duration of privileges and immunities. A person entitled to privileges and immunities enjoys them from the moment he enters the United Kingdom in proceeding to take up his post or, if he is already there, from the moment when his appointment is notified[1] to the department of the Secretary of State[2]. When his functions have come to an end the privileges and immunities normally cease when he leaves the United Kingdom, or on expiry of a reasonable period in which to do so, but subsist until that time even in case of armed conflict; with respect to acts performed by such a person in the exercise of his functions as a member of the mission, immunity continues[3].

1   If the person was not already in this country he enjoys privileges and immunities from the moment of entry, and this does not depend on notification; if he was already in this country, he enjoys privileges and immunities from the time of notification, and this does not depend on his acceptance by the Secretary of State: *R v Secretary of State for the Home Department, ex p Bagga* [1991] 1 QB 485, [1991] 1 All ER 777, CA (doubting dictum in *R v Governor of Pentonville Prison, ex p Teja* [1971] 2 QB 274, [1971] 2 All ER 11, DC; and disagreeing with *R v Lambeth Justices, ex p Yusufu* [1985] Crim LR 510). As to the Secretary of State see PARA 29. As to the statutory meaning of 'United Kingdom' see PARA 30 note 3.

2   Diplomatic Privileges Act 1964 s 2(1), (2), Sch 1 art 39 para 1. He can claim immunity if he only becomes entitled to it after service of the claim form: *Ghosh v D'Rozario* [1963] 1 QB 106, [1962] 2 All ER 640, CA. The running of a period of limitation is suspended during such time as immunity subsists: *Musurus Bey v Gadban* [1894] 2 QB 352, 6 BILC 32, CA.

3   Diplomatic Privileges Act 1964 Sch 1 art 39 para 2. See also *Re P (Children Act: Diplomatic Privilege)* [1998] 1 FLR 624 (removing children from the jurisdiction at the end of a diplomaticing not an act within the exercise of diplomatic functions). Cf *Zoernsch v Waldock* [1964] 2 All ER 256, [1964] 1 WLR 675, CA. A former head of state is in a comparable position: see the State Immunity Act 1978 s 20(1); *R v Bow Street Metropolitan Stipendiary Magistrate, ex p Pinochet Ugarte (No 3)* [2000] 1 AC 147, sub nom *R v Bow Street Metropolitan Stipendiary Magistrate, ex p Pinochet Ugarte (Amnesty International intervening) (No 3)* [1999] 2 All ER 97, HL; and PARA 263.

286. Death. In the case of the death of a member of the mission[1], his family continue to enjoy privileges and immunities until the expiry of a reasonable time in which to leave the United Kingdom[2]. In the event of the death of a member of a mission who is not a citizen of the United Kingdom and Colonies[3] or not permanently resident in the United Kingdom, or of a member of his family forming part of his household, withdrawal from the country of his movable property, except any acquired here and whose export is prohibited at the time of his death, is permitted[4]. Accordingly, inheritance tax is not levied on movable property the presence of which in the United Kingdom was due solely to the deceased's presence as a member of the mission or as a member of the family of a member of the mission[5].

1   As to the meaning of 'members of the mission' see PARA 276 note 3.

2   Diplomatic Privileges Act 1964 s 2(1), Sch 1 art 39 para 3. A coroner is precluded from investigating the death of a person who, if alive, would have been entitled to diplomatic immunity unless the privilege is waived: see CORONERS vol 9(2) (2006 Reissue) PARA 958. As to the statutory meaning of 'United Kingdom' see PARA 30 note 3.

3   As to the expression 'United Kingdom and Colonies' see PARA 274 note 8.

4   Diplomatic Privileges Act 1964 Sch 1 art 39 para 4.

5   See the Diplomatic Privileges Act 1964 Sch 1 art 39 para 4; and INHERITANCE TAXATION vol 24 (Reissue) PARA 610.

287. Diplomatic agents accredited to third states. If a diplomatic agent[1] passes through or is in the United Kingdom while proceeding to take up or to return to his post, or when returning to his own country, he is accorded inviolability and such other immunities as may be required to ensure his transit or return[2]. The same applies to any members of his family enjoying privileges or immunities who are accompanying him, or travelling separately to join him or return to their own country[3]. In such circumstances the United Kingdom is under an obligation not to hinder the passage of members of the administrative and technical or service staff[4] of a mission and of members of their families[5]. These obligations apply to such persons whose presence in the United Kingdom is due to force majeure[6].

1   As to the meaning of 'diplomatic agent' see PARA 273 note 1.

2   Diplomatic Privileges Act 1964 s 2(1), Sch 1 art 40 para 1. See Satow's Diplomatic Practice (6th Edn, 2009) pp 169–174. There is no requirement that the diplomatic agent or his family be in transit between his country and the country to which he is accredited: *R v Guildhall Magistrates' Court, ex p Jarrett-Thorpe* (1977) Times, 6 October, DC. As to the statutory meaning of 'United Kingdom' see PARA 30 note 3.

3   Diplomatic Privileges Act 1964 Sch 1 art 40 para 1.

4   As to the meaning of 'members of the administrative and technical staff' see PARA 269 note 2; and as to the meaning of 'members of the service staff' see PARA 276 note 3.

5   Diplomatic Privileges Act 1964 Sch 1 art 40 para 2. As to communications and diplomatic couriers see Sch 1 art 40 para 3; and PARA 268 notes 2, 5.

6   Diplomatic Privileges Act 1964 Sch 1 art 40 para 4. The Act does not deal with other diplomatic agents present in the United Kingdom otherwise than in transit or because of force majeure, on which conflicting views were expressed in *New Chile Gold Mining Co v Blanco* (1888) 4 TLR 346, 6 BILC 236, DC, which was decided upon another point. See also *R v Governor of Pentonville Prison, ex p Teja* [1971] 2 QB 274, [1971] 2 All ER 11, DC, where an economic adviser to Costa Rica on a special mission, carrying a diplomatic passport and credentials, was held not to have diplomatic immunity.

288.   Reciprocal withdrawal of privileges. If the privileges and immunities accorded to a mission of Her Majesty in the territory of any state, or to persons connected with that mission, are less than those conferred under the law of the United Kingdom[1] on the mission of that state or upon persons connected with it, the latter may be withdrawn by Order in Council[2].

1   Ie under the Diplomatic Privileges Act 1964 (see s 3(1)); and the Diplomatic and other Privileges Act 1971 (see s 1(3)). As to the statutory meaning of 'United Kingdom' see PARA 30 note 3.

2   Diplomatic Privileges Act 1964 s 3(1). Any such Order in Council must be disregarded for the purposes of the British Nationality Act 1981 s 50(4) (see BRITISH NATIONALITY, IMMIGRATION AND ASYLUM vol 4(2) (2002 Reissue) PARA 26): Diplomatic Privileges Act 1964 s 3(2) (substituted by the British Nationality Act 1981 s 52(6), Sch 7). At the date at which this volume states the law no such orders were in force.

289.   Reciprocal extension of privileges. Where any special agreement or arrangement between the government of any state and the government of the United Kingdom was in force on 1 October 1964[1] providing for more extended immunities than are conferred by the Diplomatic Privileges Act 1964, such arrangements continue after that date for so long as the agreement or arrangement continues in force[2].

1   Ie the date of commencement of the Diplomatic Privileges Act 1964: see s 8(3); and the Diplomatic Privileges Act 1964 (Commencement) Order 1964, SI 1964/1400. As to the statutory meaning of 'United Kingdom' see PARA 30 note 3.

2   See the Diplomatic Privileges Act 1964 s 7(1) (amended by the Customs and Excise Management Act 1979 s 177(1), Sch 4 para 12). Publication of such agreements or arrangements is to be made in the London, Edinburgh and Belfast Gazettes: Diplomatic Privileges Act 1964 s 7(2). See the London Gazettes of 1 October 1964, and 1 March 1965; and British Practice in International Law 1964 (II) 225.

(7) CONSULAR PRIVILEGES AND IMMUNITIES

290. The Vienna Convention on Consular Relations. The United Kingdom is a party to the Vienna Convention on Consular Relations[1], certain provisions of which[2] form part of the law of the United Kingdom by virtue of the Consular Relations Act 1968[3]. The Act applies to every consular post in the United Kingdom, whether or not the sending state is a party to the Convention. It does not apply to diplomatic posts or diplomatic agents[4], nor to international organisations and persons connected with them[5].

1 Ie the Convention on Consular Relations (Vienna, 24 April 1963; TS 14 (1973); Cmnd 5219). The Convention was adopted at the United Nations Conference on Consular Relations, which also adopted an Optional Protocol concerning the Compulsory Settlement of Disputes, to which the United Kingdom is a party, and an Optional Protocol concerning Acquisition of Nationality, to which it is not a party. The Convention codified customary international law: *United States Diplomatic and Consular Staff in Teheran (United States of America v Iran) (Provisional Measures)* ICJ Reports 1979, 7 at 19–20; *United States Diplomatic and Consular Staff in Teheran (United States of America v Iran)* ICJ Reports 1980, 3 at 42.
   The United Kingdom has not signed the European Convention on Consular Functions of 1967 (Paris, 11 December 1967; European TS No 61).
2 Ie the Vienna Convention on Consular Relations arts 1, 5, 15, 17, 31 (paras 1, 2, 3, 4), 32, 33, 35, 39, 41, 43–45, 48–54, 55 (paras 2, 3), 57, 58, 59, 60–62, 66, 67, 70 (paras 1, 2, 4), 71.
3 Consular Relations Act 1968 s 1(1), Sch 1. Sections 7–11 came into operation upon receiving the royal assent on 10 April 1968 (s 16(3)), and the remainder on 1 January 1971 (Consular Relations Act 1968 (Commencement) Order 1970, SI 1970/1684). As to the statutory meaning of 'United Kingdom' see PARA 30 note 3.
4 As to diplomatic agents see the Diplomatic Privileges Act 1964; and PARA 265 et seq.
5 As to international organisations see the International Organisations Act 1968; and PARA 307 et seq.

291. In general. Those articles of the Vienna Convention on Consular Relations[1] which are not included in the Consular Relations Act 1968[2] do not give rise to rights and duties directly enforceable in the domestic courts of the United Kingdom. They include provisions respecting the establishment of consular relations[3] and consular posts[4] and the exercise of consular functions[5]. Heads of consular posts are divided into four classes: (1) consuls-general; (2) consuls; (3) vice-consuls; and (4) consular agents[6]. The convention also contains provisions regarding precedence of consular posts[7], the appointment of members of consular staffs[8], the size of consular staffs[9], precedence between members of the staff[10], their nationality[11], persons who are declared persona non grata[12] and notification of appointments, arrivals and departures[13].

1 Ie the Convention on Consular Relations (Vienna, 24 April 1963; TS 14 (1973); Cmnd 5219).
2 For the articles of the Vienna Convention on Consular Relations which are included in the Consular Relations Act 1968 see PARA 290 note 2.
3 See the Vienna Convention on Consular Relations art 2.
4 See the Vienna Convention on Consular Relations art 4. As to the meaning of 'consular post' see PARA 292 note 4.
5 See the Vienna Convention on Consular Relations arts 5–8. As to consular functions see PARA 292.
6 Vienna Convention on Consular Relations art 9. As to the meaning of 'head of consular post' see PARA 292 note 4.
7 See the Vienna Convention on Consular Relations art 16.
8 See the Vienna Convention on Consular Relations arts 18, 19. 'Members of the consular staff' means consular officer, other than the head of a consular post, consular employees and members of the service staff: art 1 para 1(h). As to the meaning of 'consular officer' see PARA 292 note 5. As to the meanings of 'consular employee' and 'member of the service staff' see PARA 295 note 1.
9 See the Vienna Convention on Consular Relations art 20.

10 See the Vienna Convention on Consular Relations art 21.
11 See the Vienna Convention on Consular Relations art 22.
12 See the Vienna Convention on Consular Relations art 23.
13 See the Vienna Convention on Consular Relations art 24.

292. Functions. Unlike diplomatic agents, consular agents do not represent states in all their international relations and they are not accredited to the receiving state[1]. A consul renders in the territory of the receiving state only non-political and technical services for the sending state and its nationals and nationals of the receiving state. The Vienna Convention on Consular Relations lists a great variety of functions, the principal ones being:

(1)   the protection and promotion of trade;

(2)   the assistance to vessels and aircraft and their crews and aid in the inspection of ships in accordance with local health and sanitary laws;

(3)   the provision of services to nationals of the sending state, as by assisting in the protection of their rights and interests; and

(4)   the performance of various administrative and notarial functions for nationals of both the sending state and the receiving state including the issue of passports, visas and travel documents[2].

The Convention makes provisions regarding the termination of the consular function[3]. Further provisions are made regarding the temporary exercise of the functions of the head of a consular post[4], the performance of diplomatic acts by consular officers[5] where the sending state has no diplomatic mission or facilities[6], for the exercise of consular functions by diplomatic missions[7], and for the representation of states at intergovernmental organisations by their consular officers[8].

1   Appointment of a consular agent is usually effected by a commission or similar instrument and recognition of his authority by the receiving state by means of an exequatur. For the provisions of the Convention on Consular Relations (Vienna, 24 April 1963; TS 14 (1973); Cmnd 5219) concerning these matters see arts 10–14; and as to the appointment of the same person by two or more states see art 18.

2   See the Vienna Convention on Consular Relations art 5. The list of functions contained in the Convention is enacted into the law of the United Kingdom by the Consular Relations Act 1968 s 1(1), Sch 1 art 5. As to functions in relation to the administration of estates of deceased persons, and to shipping and aircraft see PARA 303. As to the statutory meaning of 'United Kingdom' see PARA 30 note 3.

3   See the Vienna Convention on Consular Relations arts 25, 26.

4   Consular Relations Act 1968 Sch 1 art 15. 'Head of a consular post' means the person charged with the duty of acting in that capacity: Sch 1 art 1 para 1(c). 'Consular post' means any consulate-general, consulate, vice-consulate or consular agency; and 'consular district' means the area assigned to a consular post for the exercise of consular functions: Sch 1 art 1 para 1(a), (b).

5   'Consular officer' means any person, including the head of a consular post, entrusted in that capacity with the exercise of consular functions: Consular Relations Act 1968 Sch 1 art 1(d). Consular officers are of two categories: career consular officers and honorary consular officers: Sch 1 art 1 para 2.

6   If a sending state has no diplomatic mission in the United Kingdom, and is not represented by a diplomatic mission of a third state, a consular officer may, with the consent of the United Kingdom, and without affecting his consular status, be authorised to perform diplomatic acts. The performance of such acts by a consular officer does not confer upon him any right to claim diplomatic privileges and immunities: Consular Relations Act 1968 Sch 1 art 17.

7   See the Consular Relations Act 1968 Sch 1 art 70 para 1. The names of members of a diplomatic mission assigned to the consular section or otherwise charged with the exercise of the consular functions of the mission must be notified to the Secretary of State: see Sch 1 art 70 para 2. The privileges and immunities of those persons continue to be governed by the provisions of the Diplomatic Privileges Act 1964 (see PARA 265 et seq): Consular Relations Act 1968 s 1(10), Sch 1 art 70 para 4. As to the Secretary of State see PARA 29.

8   A consular officer may, after notification addressed to the United Kingdom, act as representative of the sending state to any intergovernmental organisation; when so acting, he is entitled to enjoy any privileges and immunities accorded to such a representative by customary international law or by international agreements; however, in respect of the performance by him or any consular function, he is not entitled to any greater immunity from jurisdiction than that to which a consular officer is generally entitled: see Consular Relations Act 1968 Sch 1 art 17 para 2.

293.   The consular post.   Consular premises[1] are inviolable to the extent that the authorities of the United Kingdom[2] must not enter that part of them which is used exclusively for the purpose of the work of the consular post, except with the consent of the head of the consular post[3] or his designee or the head of the diplomatic mission of the sending state[4]. The premises, their furnishings, the property of the consular post and its means of transport are exempt from any form of requisition for purposes of national defence or public utility[5]. Consular premises and the residence of the career head of the consular post[6] of which the sending state is the owner or lessee are exempt from taxes and dues other than those representing payment for services rendered[7]. Consular archives[8] and documents, wherever they may be, and official correspondence[9] are inviolable[10]. The consular post may levy such fees and charges as are provided for consular acts by United Kingdom law[11], and sums collected in this form are exempt from all dues and taxes[12].

1   'Consular premises' means the buildings or parts of buildings and the land ancillary to them, irrespective of ownership, used exclusively for the purposes of the consular post: Consular Relations Act 1968 s 1(1), Sch 1 art 1 para 1(j). As to the meaning of 'consular post' see PARA 292 note 4. The United Kingdom is under an obligation to facilitate and assist in the acquisition of consular premises and accommodation for members of the consular post (see PARA 295 note 1): Convention on Consular Relations (Vienna, 24 April 1963; TS 14 (1973); Cmnd 5219) art 30. The national flag and coat of arms may be displayed: art 29. The premises must not be used in a manner incompatible with the exercise of diplomatic functions: Consular Relations Act 1968 Sch 1 art 55 para 2. As to protection of consular premises and archives in exceptional circumstances see Sch 1 art 27; and PARA 294. As to the acquisition and loss by land of consular status see the Diplomatic and Consular Premises Act 1987 s 1; and PARA 270. As to consular functions see PARA 292. The consular post does not form part of the territory of the sending state: see *Radwan v Radwan* [1973] Fam 24, [1972] 3 All ER 967; and PARA 269 note 2.

2   'Authorities of the United Kingdom' is to be construed as including any constable and any person exercising a power of entry to any premises under any enactment: Consular Relations Act 1968 s 1(2). As to the statutory meaning of 'United Kingdom' see PARA 30 note 3.

3   As to the meaning of 'head of consular post' see PARA 292 note 4.

4   Consular Relations Act 1968 Sch 1 art 31 paras 1, 2. The consent may be assumed in case of fire or other disaster requiring prompt protective action: Sch 1 art 31 para 1. The United Kingdom is under a special duty to take all appropriate steps to protect the consular premises against any intrusion or damage and to prevent any disturbance of the peace of the consular post or impairment of its dignity: Sch 1 art 31 para 3 (added by the Diplomatic and Consular Premises Act 1987 s 6, Sch 2 para 5). See also PARA 269 note 3.

5   Consular Relations Act 1987 Sch 1 art 31 para 4. If, however, expropriation is necessary for such purposes, all possible steps must be taken to avoid impeding the performance of consular functions, and prompt and adequate compensation must be paid to the sending state: Sch 1 art 31 para 4.

6   See PARA 292 note 5.

7   Consular Relations Act 1968 Sch 1 art 32 para 1. The exemption does not apply to such dues and taxes if they are payable by the person who contracted with the state or with a person acting on its behalf: Sch 1 art 32 para 2.

8   'Consular archives' includes all the papers, documents, correspondence, books, films, tapes and registers of the consular post, together with ciphers and codes, the card indexes and articles of furniture intended for their protection or safekeeping: Consular Relations Act 1968 Sch 1 art 1 para 1(k).

9   'Official correspondence' means all correspondence relating to the consular post and its functions: Consular Relations Act 1968 Sch 1 art 35 para 2.

10 Consular Relations Act 1968 Sch 1 arts 33, 35 para 2. As to freedom of communication see PARA 295.
11 Consular Relations Act 1968 Sch 1 art 39 para 1.
12 Consular Relations Act 1968 Sch 1 art 39 para 2.

294. Protection of consular premises and archives and of the interests of the sending state in exceptional circumstances. In the event of the severance of consular relations between two states[1]:

(1)   the receiving state must, even in case of armed conflict, respect and protect the consular premises[2], together with the property of the consular post[3] and the consular archives[4];

(2)   the sending state may entrust the custody of the consular premises, together with the property contained therein and the consular archives, to a third state acceptable to the receiving state[5];

(3)   the sending state may entrust the protection of its interests and those of its nationals to a third state acceptable to the receiving state[6].

In the event of the temporary or permanent closure of a consular post, head (1) above applies[7]. In addition, if the sending state, although not represented in the receiving state by a diplomatic mission, has another consular post in the territory of that state, that consular post may be entrusted with the custody of the premises of the consular post which has been closed, together with the property contained therein and the consular archives, and, with the consent of the receiving state, with the exercise of consular functions in the district of that consular post[8]. However, if the sending state has no diplomatic mission and no other consular post in the receiving state, heads (2) and (3) above apply in addition to head (1)[9].

1 Consular Relations Act 1968 s 1(1), Sch 1 art 27 para 1 (Sch 1 art 27 added by the Diplomatic and Consular Premises Act 1987 s 6, Sch 2 para 4).
2 As to the meaning of 'consular premises' see PARA 293 note 1.
3 As to the meaning of 'consular post' see PARA 292 note 4.
4 Consular Relations Act 1968 Sch 1 art 27 para 1(a) (as added: see note 1). As to the meaning of 'consular archives' see PARA 293 note 8.
5 Consular Relations Act 1968 Sch 1 art 27 para 1(b) (as added: see note 1).
6 Consular Relations Act 1968 Sch 1 art 27 para 1(c) (as added: see note 1).
7 Consular Relations Act 1968 Sch 1 art 27 para 2 (as added: see note 1).
8 Consular Relations Act 1968 Sch 1 art 27 para 2(a) (as added: see note 1).
9 Consular Relations Act 1968 Sch 1 art 27 para 2(b) (as added: see note 1).

295. Freedom of movement and communication. Members of a consular post[1] are to be guaranteed freedom of movement and travel[2]. The United Kingdom must also protect the freedom of communication on the part of the consular post for all official purposes[3]. Freedom of communication includes the right to use diplomatic or consular couriers[4], and diplomatic or consular bags[5], and to send coded messages[6]. In the performance of their functions, consular couriers must be protected by the United Kingdom: they enjoy personal inviolability and are not liable to any form of arrest or detention[7].

Consular bags may not be opened or detained unless the authorities of the United Kingdom have serious reason to believe that they are being used for other than official purposes[8].

1 'Members of the consular post' means consular officers, consular employees and members of the service staff: Consular Relations Act 1968 s 1(1), Sch 1 art 1 para 1(g). 'Consular employee' means any person employed in the administrative or technical service of a consular post; and 'member of the service staff' means any person employed in the domestic service of a consular

post: Sch 1 art 1 para 1(e), (f). As to the meaning of 'consular officer' see PARA 292 note 5. As to the meaning of 'consular post' see PARA 292 note 4.

2	Convention on Consular Relations (Vienna, 24 April 1963; TS 14 (1973); Cmnd 5219) art 34. This is expressed to be subject to the laws of the receiving state concerning security zones. As to the Convention see generally PARA 290 note 1. As to the provisions of the Convention given force of law in the United Kingdom see PARA 290 text and note 2.

3	Consular Relations Act 1968 Sch 1 art 35 para 1. The Vienna Convention on Consular Relations art 36 further requires protection of the freedom to communicate with and visit nationals of the sending state who are in prison or otherwise detained. As to the statutory meaning of 'United Kingdom' see PARA 30 note 3.

4	The consular courier must be provided with an official document indicating his status and the number of packages constituting the consular bag; except with the consent of the United Kingdom, he must be neither a national of the United Kingdom, nor, unless he is a national of the sending state, a permanent resident of the United Kingdom: Consular Relations Act 1968 Sch 1 art 35 para 5. Consular couriers may be designated ad hoc: Sch 1 art 35 para 6. See further note 7.

5	The packages constituting the consular bag must bear visible external marks of their character and may contain only official correspondence and documents or articles intended exclusively for official use: Consular Relations Act 1968 Sch 1 art 35 para 4. As to the meaning of 'official correspondence' see PARA 293 note 9. A consular bag may be entrusted to the captain of a ship or of a commercial aircraft scheduled to land at an authorised port of entry, from whom a member of the consular post may receive possession of the bag directly and freely: see Sch 1 art 35 para 7. The captain of such an aircraft is not, however, a consular courier: Sch 1 art 35 para 7.

6	See the Consular Relations Act 1968 Sch 1 art 35 para 1. A wireless transmitter may only be installed with the consent of the United Kingdom: Sch 1 art 35 para 1.

7	Consular Relations Act 1968 Sch 1 art 35 para 5. Where a consular courier is designated ad hoc, Sch 1 art 35 para 5 also applies except that the immunities therein mentioned cease to apply when such a courier has delivered to the consignee the consular bag in his charge: Sch 1 art 35 para 6.

8	See the Consular Relations Act 1968 Sch 1 art 35 para 3. Cf the provisions relating to the diplomatic bag set out in PARA 268. If a request by the authorities (see PARA 293 note 2) that the consular bag be opened is refused, the bag must be returned to its place of origin: Sch 1 art 35 para 3.

**296.	Privileges and immunities of consular officers.** Consular officers[1] are not liable to arrest or detention pending trial except in case of a grave crime[2] and pursuant to a decision of the competent judicial authority[3]. In any other case they may not be committed to prison or be restricted in their personal freedom save in execution of a judicial decision of final effect[4].

Consular officers and employees[5] are not amenable to the jurisdiction of the United Kingdom courts in respect of acts performed in the exercise of their functions[6], except in respect of a civil action (1) arising out of a contract concluded by a consular officer or a consular employee in which he did not contract expressly or impliedly as an agent of the sending state[7]; or (2) by a third party arising from an accident caused by a motor vehicle, vessel or aircraft[8]. The members of the consular post[9] may be called upon to give evidence[10], although they may refuse to give evidence concerning matters connected with the exercise of their functions[11], or to produce official documents and correspondence, and may also decline to give evidence as expert witnesses with regard to the law of their sending state[12].

The sending state may waive any of the privileges and immunities described above[13] provided the waiver is express, but initiation of proceedings by a consular officer precludes him from invoking immunity in respect of any counterclaim directly connected with the principal claim[14].

1   As to the meaning of 'consular officer' see PARA 292 note 5. The State Immunity Act 1978 Pt I (ss 1–17) (see PARA 244 et seq) does not affect any immunity or privilege conferred by the Consular Relations Act 1968: State Immunity Act 1978 s 16(1). These provisions apply to career consular officers: see PARA 297.

2   'Grave crime' means any offence punishable on first conviction with imprisonment for at least five years: Consular Relations Act 1968 s 1(2).

3   Consular Relations Act 1968 s 1(1), Sch 1 art 41 para 1. Consular officers must be treated with due respect and appropriate measures must be taken to prevent any attack on their person, freedom or dignity: Convention on Consular Relations (Vienna, 24 April 1963; TS 14 (1973); Cmnd 5219) art 40. See *Aziz v Aziz (Sultan of Brunei intervening)* [2007] EWCA Civ 712, [2008] 2 All ER 501, [2007] NLJR 1047; and PARA 273 note 3. As to notification in case of arrest, detention or prosecution see art 42. As to the provisions of the Convention given force of law in the United Kingdom see PARA 290 text and note 2.

4   Consular Relations Act 1968 Sch 1 art 41 para 2.

5   As to the meaning of 'consular employee' see PARA 295 note 1.

6   Consular Relations Act 1968 Sch 1 art 43 para 1. As to consular functions see PARA 292.

7   Consular Relations Act 1968 Sch 1 art 43 para 2(a).

8   Consular Relations Act 1968 Sch 1 art 43 para 2(b). Consular officers must comply with the laws of the receiving state concerning insurance against third party risks: Vienna Convention on Consular Relations art 56.

9   As to the meaning of 'members of the consular post' see PARA 295 note 1.

10   Consular Relations Act 1968 Sch 1 art 44 para 1. A consular employee or member of the service staff may not refuse to give evidence except in the case referred to in the text to note 12; and if a consular officer declines to give evidence, no coercive measure or penalty may be applied to him: Sch 1 art 44 para 1. The authority requiring the officer's evidence must avoid interference with his functions and may, when possible, take evidence at his residence or consular post or accept a written statement: Sch 1 art 44 para 2. As to the meaning of 'member of the service staff' see PARA 295 note 1.

11   The references to matters connected with the exercise of the functions of members of a consular post must be construed as references to matters connected with the exercise of consular functions by consular officers or consular employees: Consular Relations Act 1968 s 1(4).

12   Consular Relations Act 1968 Sch 1 art 44 para 3.

13   Ie in the Consular Relations Act 1968 Sch 1 arts 41, 43, 44.

14   Consular Relations Act 1968 Sch 1 art 45 paras 1–3. The waiver of immunity from jurisdiction for the purposes of civil or administrative proceedings does not imply the waiver of immunity from the measures of execution resulting from the judicial decision; in respect of such measures, a separate waiver is necessary: Sch 1 art 45 para 4. For the purposes of Sch 1 art 45, and of Sch 1 art 45 as applied by Sch 1 art 58, a waiver is deemed to have been expressed by a state if it had been expressed by the head, or any person for the time being performing the functions of head, of the diplomatic mission of that state or, if there is no such mission, of the consular post concerned: s 1(5).

297. Persons entitled to privileges, immunities and exemptions. Specified facilities, privileges and exemptions[1] apply generally in the case of consular posts headed by career consular officers[2]. They are not accorded to consular employees or members of the service staff who carry on a private gainful occupation in the United Kingdom or members of their families[3].

In the case of posts headed by honorary consular officers, only certain facilities, privileges and immunities are accorded[4]; these include exemption from taxation generally of consular premises[5], inviolability of consular archives and documents[6], exemption from customs duties[7], taxation[8] and liability to service[9]. Consular officers who are nationals of or permanently resident in the United Kingdom enjoy only immunity from jurisdiction and personal inviolability in respect of official acts performed in the exercise of their functions, and from the giving of evidence of matters connected therewith[10]. Other members of the consular post and their families and private staff[11] who are such nationals or permanent residents enjoy only such facilities, privileges and immunities as the United Kingdom specially grants to them[12].

If in any proceedings any question arises whether or not any person is entitled to any privilege or immunity under the Consular Relations Act 1968, a certificate issued by or under the authority of the Secretary of State stating any fact relating to that question is conclusive evidence of that fact[13].

1 Ie those specified in the Consular Relations Act 1968 s 1(1), Sch 1 Ch II Section II (arts 41–57): s 1(9), Sch 1 art 1 para 2. See PARAS 296, 298–300.

2 Consular Relations Act 1968 Sch 1 art 1 para 2. As to career consular officers see PARA 292 note 5.

3 Consular Relations Act 1968 Sch 1 art 57 para 2. As to the meanings of 'consular employee' and 'member of the service staff' see PARA 295 note 1. As to the statutory meaning of 'United Kingdom' see PARA 30 note 3.

4 See the Consular Relations Act 1968 Sch 1 art 58. As to honorary consular officers see PARA 292 note 5. As to protection of the consular premises of a consular post headed by an honorary consular officer see Sch 1 art 59 (added by the Diplomatic and Consular Premises Act 1987 s 6, Sch 2 para 6); and PARA 296 note 14. See also Satow's Diplomatic Practice (6th Edn, 2009) p 272.

5 Consular Relations Act 1968 Sch 1 art 60. As to the meaning of 'consular premises' see PARA 293 note 1.

6 Consular Relations Act 1968 Sch 1 art 61. As to the meaning of 'consular archives' see PARA 293 note 8.

7 Consular Relations Act 1968 Sch 1 art 62. See also s 8(1) (amended by the Diplomatic and other Privileges Act 1971 s 4(2)(b); the Customs and Excise Management Act 1979 s 177(1), Sch 4 para 12, Table Pt I; and the Finance (No 2) Act 1992 s 14, Sch 3 para 89). The reference to customs duties must be construed as including references to excise duties chargeable on goods imported into the United Kingdom and to value added tax charged in accordance with the Value Added Tax Act 1994 s 10 or s 15 (acquisitions from other member states and importations from outside the European Union) (see VALUE ADDED TAX vol 49(1) (2005 Reissue) PARAS 19, 113): Consular Relations Act 1968 s 1(8A) (added by the Customs and Excise Management Act 1979 Sch 4 para 6; the Finance (No 2) Act 1992 Sch 3 para 89; and the Value Added Tax Act 1994 s 100(1), Sch 14 para 3).

8 Consular Relations Act 1968 Sch 1 art 66.

9 Consular Relations Act 1968 Sch 1 art 67.

10 Consular Relations Act 1968 s 1(2), Sch 1 art 44 para 3 (see PARA 296) art 71 para 1.

11 'Member of private staff' means a person who is employed exclusively in the private service of a member of the consular post: Consular Relations Act 1968 Sch 1 art 1 para 1(i). As to the meaning of 'consular post' see PARA 295 note 1.

12 Consular Relations Act 1968 Sch 1 arts 1 para 3, 71 para 2. These additional privileges and immunities are such as may be specified by Order in Council: ss 1(11), 14. At the date at which this volume states the law no such order had been made.

13 Consular Relations Act 1968 s 11. As to the Secretary of State see PARA 29.

298. Exemptions. Members of the consular post[1], members of their families forming part of their households and, members of the private staff[2] in their sole employ, are exempt from social security provisions[3]. However, this does not preclude voluntary participation in the social security system of the United Kingdom, where such participation is permitted by the United Kingdom[4].

Consular officers[5] and employees[6] and members of their families forming part of their households are exempt from all dues and taxes, apart from certain indirect taxes[7]. Members of the service staff[8] are exempt from dues and taxes on the wages they receive for their services[9]. Various articles for official and personal use of the consular post[10] and consular officers and members of their families are exempt from customs duties and inspection[11]. The estates of a member of a consular post and his family are not liable to inheritance tax in respect of certain movable property[12]. Members of the consular post and their families are exempt from personal services, public service and military obligations[13].

The Treasury may authorise the Secretary of State or the Commissioners of Customs and Excise to make, if he or they think fit, arrangements for securing the refund of duty[14] (whether of customs or excise) paid on imported hydrocarbon oil[15] or value added tax paid on the importation or acquisition from another member state of such oil which is (1) bought in the United Kingdom; and (2) used for a purpose that, had it been imported for that use, exemption from duty would have been required to be granted by Order in Council[16] by virtue of the provisions referred to above in relation to exemption from duty[17].

1 As to the meaning of 'members of the consular post' see PARA 295 note 1.

2 As to the meaning of 'member of the private staff' see PARA 297 note 11. This exemption applies to members of the private staff in sole employ provided they are not nationals of, or permanently resident in, the United Kingdom and Colonies, and provided they are covered by social security provisions in the sending state or a third state: Consular Relations Act 1968 s 1(1), Sch 1 art 48 para 2. Members of the consular post who employ persons to whom this exemption does not apply must observe the obligations which the social security provisions of the United Kingdom imposes upon employers: Sch 1 art 48 para 3. As to the statutory meaning of 'United Kingdom' see PARA 30 note 3.

3 Consular Relations Act 1968 Sch 1 art 48 para 1. This provision does not affect any agreement between the United Kingdom and any other state made before 1 January 1971 (the date of commencement of the Act: see PARA 290 note 3), and does not prevent agreements being made after that date: s 1(7). The exemption granted by Sch 1 art 48 with respect to any services is deemed to except those services from any class of employment in respect of which contributions or premiums are payable under the enactments relating to social security (see SOCIAL SECURITY AND PENSIONS), including enactments in force in Northern Ireland, but not so as to render any person liable to any contribution or premium which he would not be required to pay if those services were not so excepted: s 1(6) (amended by the Social Security Act 1973 ss 100, 101, Sch 27 para 78; and the Social Security (Consequential Provisions) Act 1975 ss 1(2), 5, Sch 1 Pt I).

4 Consular Relations Act 1968 Sch 1 art 48 para 4. See further SOCIAL SECURITY AND PENSIONS vol 44(2) (Reissue) PARA 470.

5 As to the meaning of 'consular officer' see PARA 292 note 5.

6 As to the meaning of 'consular employee' see PARA 295 note 1.

7 See the Consular Relations Act 1968 Sch 1 art 49 para 1. The exceptions are: (1) indirect taxes of a kind which are normally incorporated in the price of goods or services; (2) dues and taxes on private immovable property situated in the territory of the United Kingdom (subject to Sch 1 art 32 (see PARA 293)); (3) estate, succession or inheritance duties, and duties on transfers (subject to art 51(b) (see the text and note 12)); (4) dues and taxes on private income having its source in the United Kingdom and capital taxes on investments made in commercial undertakings in the United Kingdom; (5) charges levied for specific services rendered; and (6) registration, court or record fees, mortgage dues and stamp duties (subject to art 32 (see PARA 293)): Sch 1 art 49 para 1(a)–(f).

Members of the consular post who employ persons whose wages or salaries are not exempt from income tax in the United Kingdom must observe the obligations which United Kingdom law imposes upon employers concerning the levying of income tax: Sch 1 art 49 para 3.

8 As to the meaning of 'members of the service staff' see PARA 295 note 1.

9 Consular Relations Act 1968 Sch 1 art 49 para 2. See also Sch 1 art 49 para 3; and note 7.

10 As to the meaning of 'consular post' see PARA 292 note 4.

11 See the Consular Relations Act 1968 s 1(8), Sch 1 art 50 para 1. Consular employees enjoy these privileges and exemptions in respect of articles imported at the time of first installation: Sch 1 art 50 para 2. Personal baggage is exempt from inspection, unless there is serious reason to believe that it contains articles other than those permitted by Sch 1 art 50 para 1, or articles the import or export of which is prohibited by the United Kingdom or which are subject to its quarantine laws; such inspection must be carried out in the presence of the consular officer or member of his family concerned: see Sch 1 para 50 art 3. As to the relief from customs and excise duties for persons enjoying privileges and immunities under the Consular Relations Act 1968 see the Customs and Excise Duties (General Reliefs) Act 1979 ss 13A–13C; and CUSTOMS AND EXCISE vol 12(3) (2007 Reissue) PARAS 887, 894.

12 See the Consular Relations Act 1968 s 1(8), Sch 1 art 51; and INHERITANCE TAXATION vol 24 (Reissue) PARA 610.

13 See the Consular Relations Act 1968 Sch 1 art 52.

14 Any such arrangements may impose conditions subject to which any refund is to be made: Consular Relations Act 1968 s 8(2). Any amount refunded under such arrangements must be defrayed (1) if the arrangements are made by the Secretary of State, out of moneys provided by Parliament; and (2) if the arrangements are made by Commissioners for Her Majesty's Revenue and Customs, out of the moneys standing to the credit of the general account of the Commissioners of Customs and Excise: s 8(3) (amended by virtue of the Commissioners for Revenue and Customs Act 2005 s 50). As to the Secretary of State see PARA 29. As to the Treasury see CONSTITUTIONAL LAW AND HUMAN RIGHTS vol 8(2) (Reissue) PARAS 512–517. As to the Commissioners for Her Majesty's Revenue and Customs see CUSTOMS AND EXCISE vol 12(3) (2007 Reissue) PARA 900 et seq.

15 Ie hydrocarbon oil within the meaning of the Hydrocarbon Oil Duties Act 1979: see CUSTOMS AND EXCISE vol 12(2) (2007 Reissue) PARA 510.

16 Ie by Order in Council under the Consular Relations Act 1968 s 3(1): see PARA 301. This also extends to an order under s 12 (see PARA 302): s 12(1) (substituted by the Diplomatic and other Privileges Act 1971 s 4(1), Schedule).

17 Consular Relations Act 1968 s 8(1) (amended by the Diplomatic and other Privileges Act 1971 s 4(2)(b); the Customs and Excise Management Act 1979 s 177(1), Sch 4 para 12, Table Pt I; and the Finance (No 2) Act 1992 s 14, Sch 3 para 89).

299. Duration of privileges and immunities. A member of a consular post[1] enjoys his privileges and immunities from the moment he enters the United Kingdom on proceeding to take up his post or, if already there, from the moment he enters on his duties[2]. They end when he leaves the country or on the expiry of a reasonable period in which to do so, but they subsist until then even in case of an armed conflict[3]. With respect to acts performed by a consular officer[4] in the exercise of his functions, immunity from jurisdiction continues to subsist without limitation of time[5].

1 As to the meaning of 'members of the consular post' see PARA 295 note 1.

2 Consular Relations Act 1968 s 1(1), Sch 1 art 53 para 1. Members of his family forming part of his household and members of his private staff enjoy their immunities from the date on which the member of the enjoys them, or from when they enter the United Kingdom, or from the date when they become a member of the family or private staff, whichever is the latest: Sch 1 art 53 para 2. As to the statutory meaning of 'United Kingdom' see PARA 30 note 3.

3 Consular Relations Act 1968 Sch 1 art 53 para 3. The privileges and immunities of the family and staff of a consular officer come to an end when they cease to belong to the household or staff, but if such member intends to leave the United Kingdom within a reasonable period the privileges subsist until departure: Sch 1 art 53 para 3. If a consular officer dies, the members of his family forming part of his household continue to enjoy the privileges and immunities until they leave the United Kingdom or, if it occurs sooner, until a reasonable period of time enabling them to do so expires: Sch 1 art 53 para 5.

4 As to the meaning of 'consular officer' see PARA 292 note 5.

5 Consular Relations Act 1968 Sch 1 art 53 para 4. As to the functions of a consular officer see PARA 292.

300. Persons passing through the United Kingdom. Consular officers[1] passing through the United Kingdom on their way between the sending state and their posts are entitled to such immunities as may be required to ensure their transit or return[2]. These obligations also extend towards such persons, correspondence and official communications, couriers and consular bags in transit or whose presence in the United Kingdom is due to force majeure[3].

1 As to the meaning of 'consular officer' see PARA 292 note 5.

2 See the Consular Relations Act 1968 s 1(1), Sch 1 art 54 para 1. Similar provisions apply to members of the family of consular officers forming part of his household (whether travelling with him or travelling separately to join him), other members of the consular post and their families and official correspondence and communications: see Sch 1 art 54 paras 2, 3. As to the statutory meaning of 'United Kingdom' see PARA 30 note 3.

3 See the Consular Relations Act 1968 s 1(8), Sch 1 art 54 para 4.

301. Reciprocal withdrawal and extension of privileges. Where the privileges and immunities contained in the Consular Relations Act 1968 are greater than those accorded to a consular post[1] of the United Kingdom in a territory of any state or to persons connected with such consular post, they may be withdrawn by Order in Council[2]. Where, by any agreement made between the United Kingdom and any other state, additional or reduced privileges and immunities relative to those accorded by the Act are provided for, effect may be given to such agreement by Order in Council[3].

1   As to the meaning of 'consular post' see PARA 30 note 1.
2   See the Consular Relations Act 1968 ss 2, 14. At the date at which this volume states the law no such orders had been made. As to the statutory meaning of 'United Kingdom' see PARA 30 note 3.
3   See the Consular Relations Act 1968 ss 3, 14. Such agreements are envisaged by the Convention on Consular Relations (Vienna, 24 April 1963; TS 14 (1973); Cmnd 5219) art 73. The following Orders in Council have been made giving effect to such agreements: the Consular Relations (Privileges and Immunities) (Republic of Austria) Order 1970, SI 1970/1921; the Consular Relations (Privileges and Immunities) (Kingdom of Belgium) Order 1970, SI 1970/1922; the Consular Relations (Privileges and Immunities) (People's Republic of Bulgaria) Order 1970, SI 1970/1923; the Consular Relations (Privileges and Immunities) (People's Republic of China) Order 1984, SI 1984/1978; the Consular Relations (Privileges and Immunities) (Kingdom of Denmark) Order 1970, SI 1970/1924; the Consular Relations (Privileges and Immunities) (French Republic) Order 1970, SI 1970/1925; the Consular Relations (Privileges and Immunities) (Federal Republic of Germany) Order 1970, SI 1970/1926; the Consular Relations (Privileges and Immunities) (Kingdom of Greece) Order 1970, SI 1970/1927; the Consular Relations (Privileges and Immunities) (Italian Republic) Order 1970, SI 1970/1928; the Consular Relations (Privileges and Immunities) (Japan) Order 1970, SI 1970/1929; the Consular Relations (Privileges and Immunities) (United States of Mexico) Order 1970, SI 1970/1930; the Consular Relations (Privileges and Immunities) (Kingdom of the Netherlands) Order 1970, SI 1970/1931; the Consular Relations (Privileges and Immunities) (Kingdom of Norway) Order 1970, SI 1970/1932; the Consular Relations (Privileges and Immunities) (Socialist Republic of Romania) Order 1970, SI 1970/1934; the Consular Relations (Privileges and Immunities) (Spanish State) Order 1970, SI 1970/1935; the Consular Relations (Privileges and Immunities) (Kingdom of Sweden) Order 1970, SI 1970/1936; the Consular Relations (Privileges and Immunities) (United States of America) Order 1970, SI 1970/1937; the Consular Relations (Privileges and Immunities) (Union of Soviet Socialist Republics) Order 1970, SI 1970/1938; the Consular Relations (Privileges and Immunities) (Socialist Federal Republic of Yugoslavia) Order 1970, SI 1970/1939; the Consular Relations (Privileges and Immunities) (Polish People's Republic) Order 1978, SI 1978/1028; and the Consular Relations (Privileges and Immunities) (People's Republic of China) Order 1984, SI 1984/1978.

302. Representatives of members of the Commonwealth and the Republic of Ireland. In relation to certain Commonwealth representatives, Her Majesty may provide by Order in Council for conferring all or any of the privileges and immunities[1] which are conferred or may be conferred on consular posts and persons connected with consular posts[2].

The Commonwealth representatives concerned are persons in the service of the government of any country within the Commonwealth who hold offices appearing to Her Majesty to involve the performance of duties substantially corresponding to those which, in the case of a foreign sovereign power, would be performed by a consular officer[3], and any person for the time being recognised by the United Kingdom government as the chief representative in the United Kingdom of a state or province of a country within the Commonwealth[4].

These provisions have effect in relation to persons in the service of the government of the Republic of Ireland as they have effect in relation to persons in the service of the government of a country within the Commonwealth[5].

1   See PARAS 295–299.
2   Consular Relations Act 1968 s 12(1) (s 12 substituted by the Diplomatic and other Privileges
    Act 1971 s 4, Schedule). The privileges and immunities which may be conferred include those
    which in other cases may, if an agreement so requires, be conferred by virtue of the Consular
    Relations Act 1968 Sch 2: s 12(3) (as so substituted). See the Commonwealth Countries and
    Republic of Ireland (Immunities and Privileges) Order 1985, SI 1985/1983 (amended by
    SI 2005/246; SI 2006/309; SI 2009/1741). As to the Commonwealth see COMMONWEALTH
    vol 13 (2009) PARA 701.
3   Consular Relations Act 1968 s 12(2)(a) (as substituted: see note 2).
4   Consular Relations Act 1968 s 12(2)(b) (as substituted: see note 2). As to the statutory meaning
    of 'United Kingdom' see PARA 30 note 3.
5   Consular Relations Act 1968 s 12(4) (as substituted: see note 2). See also PARA 298 note 16.

303.   Consuls' powers in relation to property, ships and aircraft. Certain
powers relating to the administration of the estates and property of deceased
persons may be conferred upon consular officers of foreign states with which
consular conventions have been concluded by the Crown[1]. If a national of a state
to which the Consular Conventions Act 1949 has been applied by Order in
Council is entitled to a grant of probate or administration in respect of property
in England or Wales and the court is satisfied, on application by a consular
officer of that state, that the person in question is not resident in England or
Wales and has not by attorney applied for a grant, the court must make a grant
to that officer[2]. Such a grant of administration is made to the consular officer by
his official title and the powers and duties conferred on him as administrator are
vested in his successor without further grant[3].

Similarly, where such a national is entitled to money or property as a result of
another person's death and the national is not resident in England or Wales, the
consular officer may receive the money or property as though he were authorised
by power of attorney[4].

A consular officer is not, however, entitled to any immunity or privilege in
respect of any act done by virtue of the powers conferred on him in this regard or
in respect of any document for the time being in his possession which relates to
it[5].

A consular officer of a foreign state also has certain powers in respect of ships
and aircraft if the appropriate statutory powers have been applied by Order in
Council to that state. Such an Order in Council, which may specify the
circumstances in which ships and aircraft are to be treated as belonging to the
state concerned[6], may (1) exclude or limit the jurisdiction of a United Kingdom
court to hear proceedings relating to the remuneration or contract of service of
the master or commander or a crew member of a ship or aircraft of that state
except where a consular officer of that state has been notified and has not
objected to the invoking of the jurisdiction[7]; and (2) secure that where an offence
is alleged to have been committed on board a ship belonging to that state by the
master or a crew member, proceedings for the offence will not be entertained by
a United Kingdom court otherwise than at the request or with the consent of a
consular officer of that state unless certain conditions[8] are satisfied[9].

1   See the Consular Conventions Act 1949 s 1. Her Majesty may by Order in Council direct that
    ss 1, 2 are to apply to any foreign state specified in the Order, being a state with which a
    consular convention providing for such matters has been concluded: Consular Conventions
    Act 1949 s 6(1) (amended by the Consular Relations Act 1968 s 16(3), (4)). Any such Order in
    Council may be revoked by a subsequent order: Consular Conventions Act 1949 s 6(2). Any
    such Order in Council must be laid before Parliament after being made: s 6(3).
        The following Orders in Council have been made under these provisions, in consequence of
    consular conventions made with the states in question: the Consular Conventions (Kingdom of
    Norway) Order in Council 1951, SI 1951/1165; the Consular Conventions (Kingdom of

Sweden) Order 1952, SI 1952/1218; the Consular Conventions (United States of America) Order 1952, SI 1952/1416; the Consular Conventions (Kingdom of Greece) Order 1953, SI 1953/1454; the Consular Conventions (French Republic) Order 1953, SI 1953/1455; the Consular Conventions (United States of Mexico) Order 1955, SI 1955/425; the Consular Conventions (Federal Republic of Germany) Order 1957, SI 1957/2052; the Consular Conventions (Italian Republic) Order 1957, SI 1957/2053; the Consular Conventions (Kingdom of Denmark) Order 1963, SI 1963/370; the Consular Conventions (Spanish State) Order 1963, SI 1963/614; the Consular Conventions (Republic of Austria) Order 1963, SI 1963/1927; the Consular Conventions (Kingdom of Belgium) Order 1964, SI 1964/1399; the Consular Conventions (Japan) Order 1965, SI 1965/1714; the Consular Conventions (Socialist Federal Republic of Yugoslavia) Order 1966, SI 1966/443; the Consular Conventions (Union of Soviet Socialist Republics) Order 1968, SI 1968/1378; the Consular Conventions (People's Republic of Bulgaria) Order 1968, SI 1968/1861; the Consular Conventions (Polish People's Republic) Order 1971, SI 1971/1238; the Consular Conventions (Hungarian People's Republic) Order 1971, SI 1971/1845; the Consular Conventions (Mongolian People's Republic) Order 1976, SI 1976/1150; the Consular Conventions (Czechoslovak Socialist Republic) Order 1976, SI 1976/1216; the Consular Conventions (Arab Republic of Egypt) Order 1986, SI 1986/216.

In addition, orders in respect of the following states, made under the Domicile Act 1861 s 4 (repealed), continue in force by virtue of the Consular Conventions Act 1949 s 8: the Administration of Estates by Consular Officers (Finland) Order in Council 1939, SR & O 1939/1452; the Administration of Estates by Consular Officers (Thailand) Order in Council 1939, SR & O 1939/1457; and the Administration of Estates by Consular Officers (Turkey) Order in Council 1939, SR & O 1939/1458.

2   Consular Conventions Act 1949 s 1(1). The grant may be postponed in appropriate circumstances: s 1(1) proviso. Notwithstanding anything in the Senior Courts Act 1981 s 114(1) (see EXECUTORS AND ADMINISTRATORS vol 17(2) (Reissue) PARA 161), administration of an estate may in any case be granted to a consular officer alone under the Consular Conventions Act 1949 s 1; the Senior Courts Act 1981 s 114(2) does not apply in such a case: Consular Conventions Act 1949 s 1(4) (amended by virtue of the Senior Courts Act 1981 s 152(1), Sch 5).

3   See the Consular Conventions Act 1949 s 1(3) (amended by the Administration of Estates Act 1971 s 12, Sch 2). This provision does not affect any limitation in the grant or any power of the court to revoke the grant: Consular Conventions Act 1949 s 1(3) proviso.

4   See the Consular Conventions Act 1949 s 1(2). No one may pay or deliver to the consular officer if he knows any other person in England has been expressly authorised to receive the property or money on behalf of the national: s 1(2) proviso.

5   Consular Conventions Act 1949 s 3.

6   Consular Relations Act 1968 s 16(2). The following Orders in Council have been made partly under s 16(2): the Republic of Austria (Consular Relations (Merchant Shipping) (Republic of Austria) Order 1970, SI 1970/1903; the Consular Relations (Merchant Shipping) (Kingdom of Belgium) Order 1970, SI 1970/1904; the Consular Relations (Merchant Shipping) (Kingdom of Denmark) Order 1970, SI 1970/1905; the Consular Relations (Merchant Shipping) (French Republic) Order 1970, SI 1970/1906; the Consular Relations (Merchant Shipping) (Federal Republic of Germany) Order 1970, SI 1970/1907; the Consular Relations (Merchant Shipping) (Kingdom of Greece) Order 1970, SI 1970/1908; the Consular Relations (Merchant Shipping) (Italian Republic) Order 1970, SI 1970/1909; the Consular Relations (Merchant Shipping) (Japan) Order 1970, SI 1970/1910; the Consular Relations (Merchant Shipping) (United States of Mexico) Order 1970, SI 1970/1911; the Consular Relations (Merchant Shipping) (Kingdom of Norway) Order 1970, SI 1970/1912; the Consular Relations (Merchant Shipping) (Spanish State) Order 1970, SI 1970/1913; the Consular Relations (Merchant Shipping) (Kingdom of Sweden) Order 1970, SI 1970/1914; the Consular Relations (Merchant Shipping) (United States of America) Order 1970, SI 1970/1915; the Consular Relations (Merchant Shipping) (Socialist Federal Republic of Yugoslavia) Order 1970, SI 1970/1917; the Consular Relations (Merchant Shipping and Civil Aviation) (People's Republic of Bulgaria) Order 1970, SI 1970/1918; the Consular Relations (Merchant Shipping and Civil Aviation) (Socialist Republic of Romania) Order 1970, SI 1970/1920; the Consular Relations (Merchant Shipping and Civil Aviation) (Hungarian People's Republic) Order 1970, SI 1971/1846; the Consular Relations (Merchant Shipping and Civil Aviation) (Czechoslovak Socialist Republic) Order 1976, SI 1976/768; the Consular Relations (Merchant Shipping and Civil Aviation) (German Democratic Republic) Order 1976, SI 1976/1152; the Consular Relations (Merchant Shipping and Civil Aviation) (Polish People's Republic) Order 1978, SI 1978/275; the Consular Relations (Merchant Shipping and Civil Aviation (Arab Republic of Egypt) Order 1986 SI 1986/217.

The orders in respect of Austria, Belgium, Czechoslovakia, Denmark, German Democratic Republic, German Federal Republic, Hungary, Italy, Japan, Spain, and Yugoslavia are also made under the Consular Relations Act 1968 ss 4–6 (see the text and notes 7–9); the orders in respect of Greece, Mexico, Norway and Sweden are also made under ss 4, 6; the orders in respect of Bulgaria, Egypt, Poland and Romania are also made under s 4; and the orders in respect of France and the United States of America are also made under s 6.

7 Consular Relations Act 1968 s 4. For orders made under this provision see note 6. As to the statutory meaning of 'United Kingdom' see PARA 30 note 3.

8 Ie (1) the offence is alleged to have been committed by or against a citizen of the United Kingdom and Colonies or is otherwise a national of the receiving state or against a person other than the master or a crew member; or (2) the offence involves the tranquillity or safety of a port, or the law relating to safety of life at sea, public health, oil pollution, wireless telegraphy, immigration or customs, or is of any other description specified in the order; or (3) the offence is a grave crime: Consular Relations Act 1968 s 5(1)(a)–(c). 'National of the receiving state' means (a) a British citizen, a British overseas territories citizen, a British National (Overseas) or a British Overseas Citizen; or (b) a person who under the British Nationality Act 1981 is a British subject; or (c) a British protected person, within the meaning of that Act (see generally BRITISH NATIONALITY, IMMIGRATION AND ASYLUM): Consular Relations Act 1968 s 1(2) (definition amended by the British Nationality Act 1981 s 52(6), Sch 7; the British Overseas Territories Act 2002 s 2(3); and SI 1986/948). As to the meaning of 'grave crime' see PARA 296 note 2. 'The law relating to customs', to the extent that it here refers to duties, refers to the law relating to duties (whether customs or excise) chargeable on goods imported into the United Kingdom: s 5(1A) (added by the Customs and Excise Management Act 1979 s 177(1), Sch 4 para 7). As to the expression 'United Kingdom and Colonies' see PARA 274 note 8.

9 Consular Relations Act 1968 s 5(1). For orders made under this provision see note 6. An offence affecting a person's property is deemed to have been committed against him: s 5(2). A document purporting to be signed by or on behalf of a consular officer and stating that he has requested or consented to the institution of proceedings is sufficient proof of that fact unless the contrary is proved: s 5(3).

(8) INSTITUTIONS OF THE EUROPEAN UNION

304. Privileges and immunities afforded to European institutions. The European Union (EU) and the European Atomic Energy Community (EAEC) enjoy in the territories of the member states such privileges and immunities as are necessary for the performance of their tasks, subject to conditions[1]. These privileges extend also to the European Investment Bank and the European Central Bank[2].

The premises and buildings of the EU are inviolable. They are exempt from search, requisition, confiscation and expropriation. EU property and assets may not be the subject of any administrative or legal measure of constraint without the authorisation of the European Court of Justice[3]. The EU's archives are inviolable[4].

The EU, its assets, revenues and other property are exempt from all direct taxes. The governments of the member states must, wherever possible, take the appropriate measures to remit or refund the amount of indirect taxes or sales taxes included in the price of movable or immovable property, where the EU makes, for its official use, substantial purchases the price of which includes taxes of this kind. These provisions must not be applied, however, so as to have the effect of distorting competition within the EU[5].

The EU is exempt from all customs duties, prohibitions and restrictions on imports and exports in respect of articles intended for its official use; articles so imported must not be disposed of, whether or not in return for payment, in the territory of the country into which they have been imported, except under conditions approved by the government of that country. The EU is also exempt from any customs duties and any prohibitions and restrictions on imports and exports in respect of its publications[6].

For their official communications and the transmission of all their documents, the institutions of the EU enjoy in the territory of each member state the treatment accorded by that state to diplomatic missions. Official correspondence and other official communications of the institutions of the EU are not subject to censorship[7].

The member state in whose territory the EU has its seat must accord the customary diplomatic immunities and privileges to missions of third countries accredited to the EU[8].

1 Treaty on the Functioning of the European Union art 343 (formerly art 291 of the Treaty Establishing the European Community (Rome, 25 March 1957; TS 1 (1973); Cmnd 5179), which was renamed and renumbered by the Treaty of Lisbon Amending the Treaty on European Union and the Treaty Establishing the European Community (Lisbon, 13 December 2007; ECS 13 (2007); Cm 7294) (OJ C306, 17.12.2007, p 1); see the consolidated text of the EU Treaties (OJ C115, 9.5.2008, p 194). See also Protocol (No 2) Amending the Treaty Establishing the European Atomic Energy Community (which is annexed to the Treaty of Lisbon, which entered into force on 1 December 2009). The European Union (Amendment) Act 2008 enables the United Kingdom to ratify the treaty. The details of the privileges and immunities are set out in the Protocol on the Privileges and Immunities of the European Union (Brussels, 8 April 1965; TS 1 (1973); Cmnd 5179) (as amended by Protocol (No 1) to the Lisbon Treaty). The institutions of the European Union are required to co-operate with the responsible authorities of the member states for the purpose of applying the Protocol: art 18. See Case C-2/88 *JJ Zwartveld* [1990] ECR-I 3365, [1990] 3 CMLR 457, ECJ.

   The European Union is not entitled to foreign sovereign immunity: *J H Rayner (Mincing Lane) Ltd v Department of Trade and Industry* [1989] Ch 72 at 196–203, sub nom *Maclaine Watson & Co Ltd v Department of Trade and Industry* [1988] 3 All ER 257 at 316–320, CA.

   The Protocol on the Privileges and Immunities of the European Union may be applied to other designated organisations, eg the European Office for Harmonisation in the Internal Market (see EC Council Regulation 40/94 (OJ L11, 14 January 1994, p 1) art 113); and the Community Plant Variety Office (see EC Council Regulation 2100/94 (OJ L227, 1 September 1994, p 1)).

2 See the Treaty on the Functioning of the European Union art 343 (formerly art 291: see note 1); and the Protocol on the Privileges and Immunities of the European Union arts 21, 22 (art 22 substituted by the Amsterdam Treaty (OJ C340) art 9 para 5; both articles later renumbered by Protocol (No 1) to the Lisbon Treaty: see note 1). The privileges also extended to the European Monetary Institute. As to the liquidation of the European Monetary Institute see the Protocol on the Statute of the European Monetary Institute art 23. For these purposes, references to the European Union should be read as including references to the European Investment Bank and the European Central Bank.

   The European Investment Bank and the European Central Bank are additionally exempt from any form of taxation or imposition of a like nature on the occasion of any increase in their capital and from the various formalities which may be connected therewith in the state where they have their seats; similarly, their dissolution or liquidation will not give rise to any imposition; the activities of the Banks and their organs carried on in performance of their functions are not subject to any turnover tax: see the Protocol on the Privileges and Immunities of the European Union arts 21, 21 (as so substituted and renumbered).

3 Protocol on the Privileges and Immunities of the European Union art 1. As to applications under art 1 see Case 1/87 *Universe Tankship Co Inc v EC Commission* [1987] ECR 2807, ECJ.

4 Protocol on the Privileges and Immunities of the European Union art 2.

5 Protocol on the Privileges and Immunities of the European Union art 3. No exemption may be granted in respect of taxes and dues which amount merely to charges for public utility services: art 3. See Case C-437/04 *EC Commission v Belgium* [2008] STC 1563 (failure by the Commission to obtain exemption from landlord of a leased building for direct taxation meant that the Commission, as tenants, were liable to pay tax according to terms of lease).

6 Protocol on the Privileges and Immunities of the European Union art 4.

7 Protocol on the Privileges and Immunities of the European Union art 5 (renumbered by Protocol (No 1) to the Lisbon Treaty: see note 1).

8 Protocol on the Privileges and Immunities of the European Union art 16 (renumbered by Protocol (No 1) to the Lisbon Treaty: see note 1).

305. Members of the European Parliament. No administrative or other restriction may be imposed on the free movement of members of the European Parliament travelling to or from the place of meeting of that Parliament[1].

Members of the European Parliament, in respect of customs and exchange control, must be accorded (1) by their own government, the same facilities as those accorded to senior officials travelling abroad on temporary official missions; (2) by the governments of other member states, the same facilities as those accorded to representatives of foreign governments on temporary official missions[2].

Members of the European Parliament are not subject to any form of inquiry, detention or legal proceedings in respect of opinions expressed or votes cast by them in the performance of their duties[3].

During the sessions of the European Parliament, its members enjoy: (a) in the territory of their own state, the immunities accorded to members of their parliament; and (b) in the territory of any other member state, immunity from any measure of detention and from legal proceedings[4]. This immunity likewise applies to members while they are travelling to and from the place of meeting of the European Parliament[5]. However, immunity cannot be claimed when a member is found in the act of committing an offence; and the European Parliament is not prevented from exercising its right to waive the immunity of one of its members[6].

1 Protocol on the Privileges and Immunities of the European Union (Brussels, 8 April 1965; TS 1 (1973); Cmnd 5179 II) art 7 first para (arts 7, 8, 9 amended by the Single European Act 1986 art 3(1); and renumbered by Protocol (No 1) to the Lisbon Treaty: see PARA 304 note 1).

2 Protocol on the Privileges and Immunities of the European Union art 7 second para (as amended and renumbered: see note 1).

3 Protocol on the Privileges and Immunities of the European Union art 8 (as amended and renumbered: see note 1).

4 Protocol on the Privileges and Immunities of the European Union art 9 first para (as amended and renumbered: see note 1). As to when the European Parliament is in session for these purposes see Case 149/85 *Wybot v Faure* [1986] ECR 2391, [1987] 1 CMLR 819, ECJ.

5 Protocol on the Privileges and Immunities of the European Union art 9 second para (as amended and renumbered: see note 1).

6 Protocol on the Privileges and Immunities of the European Union art 9 third para (as amended and renumbered: see note 1).

306. Representatives, officials and servants. Representatives of member states taking part in the work of the institutions of the European Union (EU), their advisers and technical experts, in the performance of their duties and during their travel to and from the place of meeting, enjoy the customary privileges, immunities and facilities[1].

In the territory of each member state and whatever their nationality, officials and other servants of the EU:

(1) subject to the provisions of the European law relating, on the one hand, to the rules on the liability of officials and other servants towards the EU and, on the other hand, to the jurisdiction of the Court of Justice in disputes between the EU and its officials and other servants, are immune from legal proceedings in respect of acts performed by them in their official capacity, including their words spoken or written[2];

(2)   together with their spouses and dependent members of their families, are not subject to immigration restrictions or to formalities for the registration of aliens[3];

(3)   in respect of currency or exchange regulations, must be accorded the same facilities as are customarily accorded to officials of international organisations[4];

(4)   enjoy the right to import free of duty their furniture and effects at the time of first taking up their post in the country concerned, and the right to re-export free of duty their furniture and effects, on termination of their duties in that country, subject in either case to the conditions considered to be necessary by the government of the country in which this right is exercised[5];

(5)   have the right to import free of duty a motor car for their personal use, acquired either in the country of their last residence or in the country of which they are nationals on the terms ruling in the home market in that country, and to re-export it free of duty, subject in either case to the conditions considered to be necessary by the government of the country concerned[6].

Officials and other servants of the EU are liable to a tax for the benefit of the EU on salaries, wages and emoluments paid to them by the EU, but are exempt from national taxes on salaries, wages and emoluments paid by the EU[7].

Privileges, immunities and facilities must be accorded to officials and other servants of the EU solely in the interests of the EU. Accordingly, each institution of the EU is required to waive the immunity accorded to an official or other servant wherever that institution considers that the waiver of such immunity is not contrary to the interests of the EU[8].

The majority of the provisions described above[9] apply to members of the Commission of the European Union[10], and to the judges, advocates-general, registrar and assistant rapporteurs of the Court of Justice of the European Union[11].

1   Protocol on the Privileges and Immunities of the European Union (Brussels, 8 April 1965; TS 1 (1973); Cmnd 5179) art 10 first para (articles renumbered by Protocol (No 1) to the Lisbon Treaty: see PARA 304 note 1). This also applies to members of the advisory bodies of the EU: art 10 second para (as so renumbered). The terms 'representative' and 'customary privileges, immunities and facilities' are not defined. Cf, however, PARA 317 for the privileges and immunities accorded to representatives of international organisations; and PARA 292 text and note 8 for the immunities afforded to consular officers. As to the application of these provisions to the financial institutions of the EU see PARA 304 note 2. As to the inadmissibility of an action by an individual regarding the interpretation and application of the Protocol see Case 1/82 *D v Luxembourg* [1982] ECR 3709, ECJ.

2   Protocol on the Privileges and Immunities of the European Union art 11(a) (as renumbered: see note 1). They continue to enjoy this immunity after ceasing to hold office: art 11(a) (as so renumbered). The persons to whom arts 11–13 apply are to be determined by the EC Parliament and Council and their details communicated to the governments of member states: art 15 (as so renumbered).

3   Protocol on the Privileges and Immunities of the European Union art 11(b) (as renumbered: see note 1). See also art 15; and note 2.

4   Protocol on the Privileges and Immunities of the European Union art 11(c) (as renumbered: see note 1). See also art 15; and note 2. As to international organisations see PARA 307.

5   Protocol on the Privileges and Immunities of the European Union art 11(d) (as renumbered: see note 1). See also art 15; and note 2.

6   Protocol on the Privileges and Immunities of the European Union art 11(d). See also art 15; and note 2.

7   Protocol on the Privileges and Immunities of the European Union art 12 (as renumbered: see note 1). See also Case 85/86 *EC Commission v Board of Governors of the European Investment*

Bank [1986] ECR 2215, [1989] 1 CMLR 103, ECJ; Case C-333/88 *Tither v IRC* [1990] ECR I-1133, [1990] 2 CMLR 779, ECJ. As to the place deemed to be the country of domicile for tax purposes, and the exemption of movable property from tax and duties, see also the Protocol on the Privileges and Immunities of the European Union art 13 (as renumbered: see note 1). See also art 15; and note 2.

8   Protocol on the Privileges and Immunities of the European Union art 17 (as renumbered: see note 1).

9   Ie the Protocol on the Privileges and Immunities of the European Union arts 11–14, 17: see the text and notes 2–8.

10 Protocol on the Privileges and Immunities of the European Union art 19 (as renumbered: see note 1).

11 Protocol on the Privileges and Immunities of the European Union art 20 (as renumbered: see note 1), which is expressed to be without prejudice to the immunity from suit enjoyed by the judges and advocates-general under the Statute of the Court of Justice of the European Union.

(9) INTERNATIONAL ORGANISATIONS

307.   Conventions respecting status, immunities and privileges of international organisations. The United Kingdom is a party to numerous international arrangements providing for the legal status, privileges and immunities of international organisations and persons connected with them[1]. The Charter of the United Nations stipulates that the organisation is to enjoy in the territory of each of the member states such privileges and immunities as are necessary for the fulfilment of its purposes, and that representatives of member states and officials of the organisation are similarly to enjoy such immunities as are necessary for the independent exercise of their functions[2]. In 1946 the General Assembly adopted a Convention on the Privileges and Immunities of the United Nations[3], which provides for immunity from jurisdiction, inviolability of premises and archives, currency and fiscal privileges, freedom of communications, and privileges and immunities of the organisation's personnel. In 1947 the General Assembly likewise approved a Convention on the Privileges and Immunities of the Specialised Agencies of the United Nations[4], which is on similar lines. Among other agreements respecting international organisations of which the United Kingdom is a member, under which recognition of the status of the organisation and its privileges and the immunities of its personnel are stipulated[5], are those concerning the Council of Europe[6], the European Court of Human Rights[7], the North Atlantic Treaty Organisation[8] and the European Union and its organs[9].

1   As to the privileges and immunities of international organisations see PARA 309.

2   Charter of the United Nations (San Francisco, 26 June 1945; TS 67 (1946); Cmd 7015) art 105 paras 1, 2. See also Statute of the International Court of Justice (San Francisco, 26 June 1945; TS 67 (1946); Cmd 7015) art 19, which provides that members of the court, when engaged on its business, enjoy diplomatic privileges and immunities; and see art 32 para 8, which provides that salaries of judges and officials of the court are to be immune from taxation.

3   Ie the Convention on the Privileges and Immunities of the United Nations (London, 13 February 1946; TS 10 (1950); Cmd 7891). It is for the Secretary-General to determine whether a particular expert on mission is entitled to immunity under the Convention: *Difference relating to Immunity from Legal Process of a Special Rapporteur of the Commission on Human Rights (Request for Advisory Opinion)* ICJ Reports 1998, 423.

4   Ie the Convention on the Privileges and Immunities of the Specialised Agencies of the United Nations (adopted 21 November 1947; TS 69 (1959); Cmnd 855). As to the specialised agencies see PARA 533. The Convention applies with modifications and variations to all the specialised agencies.

5   In addition to the organisations referred to in notes 6–9 see those referred to in PARA 311.

6   General Agreement on Privileges and Immunities of the Council of Europe (Paris, 2 September 1949; TS 34 (1953); Cmd 8852). See also the First Protocol to the General Agreement on Privileges and Immunities of the Council of Europe (Strasbourg, 6 November 1952; TS 17

(1957); Cmnd 84); and the Fifth Protocol to the General Agreement on Privileges and Immunities of the Council of Europe (Strasbourg, 18 June 1990; TS 96 (1990); Cm 1764).

7   Second Protocol to the General Agreement on Privileges and Immunities of the Council of Europe (Paris, 15 December 1956; TS 50 (1958); Cmnd 579) (Commission of Human Rights); Fourth Protocol to the General Agreement on Privileges and Immunities of the Council of Europe (Paris, 16 December 1961; TS 58 (1971); Cmnd 4739) (European Court of Human Rights).

8   See the Agreement on the Status of the North Atlantic Treaty Organisation, National Representatives and International Staff (Ottawa, 20 September 1951; TS 11 (1955); Cmd 9383).

9   Protocol on the Privileges and Immunities of the European Union (Brussels, 8 April 1965; TS 1 (1973); Cmnd 5179): see PARA 304 et seq.

308.   Headquarters agreements. The United Kingdom has entered into headquarters agreements with certain international organisations which have their headquarters in the United Kingdom. These agreements confer privileges and immunities upon the premises and archives and the personnel attached to the organisation, and secure exemption from direct taxation and customs duties and freedom of communication. The organisations are the International Maritime Organisation[1], the International Grains Council (formerly the International Wheat Council)[2], the International Sugar Organisation[3], the International Coffee Organisation[4], the International Cocoa Organisation[5], the International Whaling Commission[6], the European Centre for Medium-Range Weather Forecasts[7], the International Lead and Zinc Study Group[8], CAB International (formerly the Commonwealth Agricultural Bureau)[9], the North-East Atlantic Fisheries Commission[10], the International Rubber Study Group[11], the International Oil Pollution Compensation Fund[12], the International Maritime Satellite Organisation[13], the Commonwealth Foundation[14], the Commonwealth Telecommunication Organisation[15], the North Atlantic Salmon Conservation Organisation[16], the European Bank for Reconstruction and Development[17], the International Oil Pollution Compensation Fund 1992[18], the International Mobile Satellite Organisation[19], and INTELSAT[20].

1   Agreement between the Government of the United Kingdom and the Inter-Governmental Maritime Consultative Organisation (now International Maritime Organisation) regarding the Headquarters of the Organisation (London, 29 November 1968; TS 18 (1969); Cmnd 3964); amended by Exchange of Notes (London, 28 October to 1 November 1971; TS 25 (1972); Cmnd 4917); by Exchange of Notes (London, 13 to 25 February 1974; TS 133 (1975); Cmnd 6340); by Exchange of Notes (London, 20 January 1982; TS 30 (1982); Cmnd 8623); by Exchange of Notes (London, 19 August to 23 October 1997; TS 17 (2000); Cm 4634); and by Exchange of Notes (4 and 23 January 2002; TS 03 (2002); Cm 5473).

2   Headquarters Agreement between the Government of the United Kingdom and the International Wheat Council (London, 28 November 1968; TS 14 (1969); Cmnd 3882); amended by Exchange of Notes (London, 13 February to 13 March 1974; TS 138 (1975); Cmnd 6281); and by Exchange of Notes (London, 22 October to 10 November 1997; TS 16 (2000); Cm 4633).

3   Headquarters Agreement between the Government of the United Kingdom and the International Sugar Organisation (London, 29 May 1969; TS 88 (1969); Cmnd 4127); amended by Exchange of Notes (London, 18 to 30 January 1974; TS 141 (1975); Cmnd 6287); and by Exchange of Notes (London, 10 July to 15 August 1997; TS 19 (2000); Cm 4636).

4   Headquarters Agreement between the Government of the United Kingdom and the International Coffee Organisation (London, 28 May 1969; TS 86 (1969); Cmnd 4120); amended by Exchange of Notes (London, 2 to 15 May 1974; TS 147 (1975); Cmnd 6294); and by Exchange of Notes (London, 10 to 28 July 1997; TS 14 (2000); Cm 4628).

5   Headquarters Agreement between the Government of the United Kingdom and the International Cocoa Organisation (London, 26 March 1975; TS 94 (1975); Cmnd 6095); amended by Exchange of Notes (London, 10 to 21 July 1997; Cm 4628).

6   Headquarters Agreement between the Government of the United Kingdom and the International Whaling Commission (London, 21 August 1975; TS 108 (1975); Cmnd 6278); amended by Exchange of Notes (London/Cambridge, August 1981; TS 75 (1981); Cmnd 8387); and by Exchange of Notes (London, 10 July to 19 August 1997; TS 20 (2000); Cm 4637).

7   Headquarters Agreement between the government of the United Kingdom and the European
     Centre for Medium-Range Weather Forecasts (London, 1 March 1977; TS 49 (1977);
     Cmnd 6842); amended by Exchange of Notes (London, 11 to 28 July 1997; TS 33 (2000);
     Cm 4654).
8   Headquarters agreement between the government of the United Kingdom and the International
     Lead and Zinc Study Group (London, 21 December 1978; TS 42 (1979); Cmnd 7538); amended
     by Exchange of Notes (London, 10 to 28 July 1997; TS 36 (2000); Cm 4659).
9   Headquarters Agreement between the Government of the United Kingdom and the
     Commonwealth Agricultural Bureau (London, August 1982; TS 49 (1982); Cmnd 8715)
     amended by Exchange of Notes (London, 11 to 18 July 1997; TS 35 (2000); Cm 4650).
10   Headquarters Agreement between the Government of the United Kingdom and the North-East
     Atlantic Fisheries Commission (London, February 1999; TS 9 (1999); Cm 4265).
11   Headquarters Agreement between the Government of the United Kingdom and the International
     Rubber Study Group (London, 14 February 1978; TS 51 (1978); Cmnd 7211); amended by
     Exchange of Notes (London, 24 July to 13 August 1997; TS 18 (2000); Cm 4635).
12   Headquarters Agreement between the Government of the United Kingdom and the International
     Oil Pollution Compensation Fund (London, 27 July 1979; TS 80 (1979); Cmnd 7692); amended
     by Exchange of Notes (London, 1 to 8 December 1997; TS 22 (2000); Cm 4639).
13   Headquarters Agreement between the Government of the United Kingdom and the International
     Maritime Satellite Organisation (London, 25 February 1980; TS 44 (1980); Cmnd 7917).
14   Headquarters Agreement between the Government of the United Kingdom and the
     Commonwealth Foundation (London, 14 February 1983; TS 22 (1983); Cmnd 8862); amended
     by Exchange of Notes (London, 10 July to 5 August 1997; Cm 4223).
15   Headquarters Agreement between the Government of the United Kingdom and the
     Commonwealth Telecommunication Organisation (London, 30 March 1983; TS 36 (1983);
     Cmnd 8956); amended by Exchange of Notes (London, 7 to 12 November 1997; TS 15 (2000);
     Cm 4632).
16   Headquarters Agreement between the Government of the United Kingdom and the North
     Atlantic Salmon Conservation Organisation (London, 26 April 1985; TS 18 (1986);
     Cmnd 9752); amended by Exchange of Notes (London, 20 December 2000 and 4 January 2001;
     TS 5 (2001); Cm 5093).
17   Headquarters Agreement between the Government of the United Kingdom and the European
     Bank for Reconstruction and Development (London, 15 April 1991; TS 45 (1991); Cm 1615).
18   Headquarters Agreement between the Government of the United Kingdom and the International
     Oil Pollution Compensation Fund 1992 (London, 30 May 1996; TS 78 (1996); Cm 3354);
     amended by Exchange of Notes (London, 1 to 8 December 1997; TS 22 (2000); Cm 4223).
19   Headquarters Agreement between the Government of the United Kingdom and the International
     Mobile Satellite Organisation (London, 15 April 1999; TS 73 (1999); Cm 4511).
20   See the Exchange of Notes amending the Headquarters Agreement between the Government of
     the United Kingdom and INTELSAT (Washington, 18 September and 7 October 1997; TS 34
     (2000); Cm 4655).

309.   General privileges and immunities of international organisations. Where
an organisation is declared by Order in Council to be one of which the United
Kingdom or its government and one or more foreign sovereign powers[1], are
members, then, to the extent specified by Order in Council, the legal capacities of
a body corporate and certain immunities and privileges may be conferred on
such an organisation[2]. The immunities and privileges which may be conferred
are:

(1)   immunity from suit and legal process[3];

(2)   the like inviolability of official archives and premises of the organisation
       as are accorded under the Vienna Convention on Diplomatic Relations
       to a diplomatic mission[4];

(3)   exemption or relief from taxes, other than duties (whether customs or
       excise) and taxes on the importation of goods[5], and the same relief as in
       accordance with the Vienna Convention on Diplomatic Relations is
       accorded in respect of the premises of a diplomatic mission[6];

(4)   exemption from duties (whether customs or excise) and taxes on the
       importation of goods imported for the official use of the organisation in

the United Kingdom, and on publications of the organisation imported by it or on its behalf, subject to compliance with such conditions as may be prescribed for the protection of the revenue by the Commissioners for Her Majesty's Revenue and Customs[7];

(5) exemptions from prohibitions and restrictions on importation or exportation in the case of goods imported or exported by the organisation for its official use and on publications of the organisation[8];

(6) relief under arrangements made with the Secretary of State or the Commissioners for Her Majesty's Revenue and Customs by way of refund of duty (whether customs or excise) or value added tax paid on hydrocarbon oil[9] imported and used for official purposes[10]; and

(7) relief under arrangements made by the Secretary of State by way of refund of car tax paid on any vehicles and value added tax paid on the supply of any goods or services which are used for the official purposes of the organisation[11].

Limited exemptions from taxes are given in respect of securities issued by certain designated organisations of which the United Kingdom or any of the European Communities (including the European Investment Bank) is a member[12].

An international organisation and its officers have no sovereign or diplomatic immunity unless these are conferred by a legislative instrument[13]. However, a United Kingdom court has no jurisdiction to make an order for the winding up of an international organisation[14], and an application for the appointment of a receiver of an international organisation is not justiciable[15].

Priority must be given to telecommunications to and from the Secretary-General of the United Nations, the heads of principal organs of the United Nations and the International Court of Justice[16].

1   See the International Organisations Act 1968 s 1(1)(a), (b) (s 1(1)(b) substituted by the International Organisations Act 1981 s 1(1), so as to remove the previous exclusion of Commonwealth states). If at any time, the Organisation for Security and Co-operation in Europe (the 'OSCE') is not, for the purpose of the International Organisations Act 1968 s 1, an organisation of which the United Kingdom, or Her Majesty's Government in the United Kingdom, and at least one other sovereign power, or the government of such a power are members, it is to be treated for those purposes as such an organisation: International Organisations Act 2005 s 4(1). Any agreement or formal understanding between the United Kingdom, or Her Majesty's Government in the United Kingdom and any other sovereign power or the government of such a power relating to the OSCE is to be treated for the purposes of the International Organisations Act 1968 s 1(5) and s 1(6)(a) (see PARAS 321–322) as an agreement between the United Kingdom and the OSCE: International Organisations Act 2005 s 4(1). The International Tribunal for the Law of the Sea (see PARAS 311, 497) is to be treated for the purposes of the International Organisations Act 1968 s 1 as an organisation of which the United Kingdom, or Her Majesty's government in the United Kingdom, and at least one other sovereign power, or the government of such a power, are members: International Organisations Act 2005 s 8. As to the statutory meaning of 'United Kingdom' see PARA 30 note 3.

2   International Organisations Act 1968 s 1(1), (2)(a) (s 1(1) as amended: see note 1). Orders in Council must be laid in draft before Parliament and approved by a resolution of each House: see s 10(1), (2). They may be revoked or varied by other orders: s 10(3). Orders made under the International Organisations (Immunities and Privileges) Act 1950 (repealed) remain in force: International Organisations Act 1968 s 12(5); and see s 12(6).

3   International Organisations Act 1968 s 1(2)(b), Sch 1 para 1.

4   International Organisations Act 1968 s 11(1), Sch 1 para 2. See the articles of the Convention on Diplomatic Relations (Vienna, 18 April 1961; TS 19 (1965); Cmnd 2565) (which are contained in the Diplomatic Privileges Act 1964 Sch 1: see PARA 265 note 2). As to the extent of inviolability of official archives see *Shearson Lehman Bros v Maclaine Watson & Co Ltd (No 2)* [1988] 1 All ER 116, [1988] 1 WLR 16, HL.

5   International Organisations Act 1968 Sch 1 para 3(1) (amended by the Customs and Excise Management Act 1979 s 177(1), Sch 4 para 12 Table Pt I).

6   International Organisations Act 1968 Sch 1 para 3(2). See the Vienna Convention on Diplomatic Relations art 23; the Diplomatic Privileges Act 1964 Sch 1; and PARA 269.

7   International Organisations Act 1968 Sch 1 para 4 (amended by the Customs and Excise Management Act 1979 Sch 4 para 12 Table Pt I); Revenue and Customs Act 2005 s 50. See CUSTOMS AND EXCISE vol 12(3) (2007 Reissue) PARA 900.

8   See the International Organisations Act 1968 Sch 1 para 5.

9   Ie hydrocarbon oil within the meaning of the Hydrocarbon Oil Duties Act 1979: see CUSTOMS AND EXCISE vol 12(23) (2007 Reissue) PARA 509 et seq.

10 International Organisations Act 1968 Sch 1 para 6 (amended by the Customs and Excise Management Act 1979 Sch 4 para 12 Table Pt I). This is subject to compliance with such conditions as may be imposed: International Organisations Act 1968 Sch 1 para 6 (as so amended).

11 International Organisations Act 1968 Sch 1 para 7 (amended by the Finance Act 1972 s 55(5), (7)). Any amount refunded under any arrangements must, if the arrangements were made by the Secretary of State, be made out of money provided by Parliament; or, if they were made by the Commissioners for Her Majesty's Revenue and Customs, be made out of money standing to the credit of the general account of the Commissioners: International Organisations Act 1968 s 9 (amended by the Finance Act 1972 s 55(5)); Revenue and Customs Act 2005 s 50. As to the relief from customs and excise duties for persons enjoying privileges and immunities under the International Organisations Act 1968 see the Customs and Excise Duties (General Reliefs) Act 1979 ss 13A–13C; and CUSTOMS AND EXCISE vol 12(3) (2007 Reissue) PARAS 887, 894. As to the Secretary of State see PARA 29.

12 See PARA 310.

13 *Standard Chartered Bank Ltd v International Tin Council* [1986] 3 All ER 257, [1987] 1 WLR 641.

14 *Re International Tin Council* [1987] Ch 419 (a petition for winding up would also have attracted immunity under the relevant Order in Council made under the International Organisations Act 1968).

15 *JH Rayner (Mincing Lane) Ltd v Department of Trade and Industry* [1990] 2 AC 418, sub nom *Maclaine Watson & Co Ltd v Department of Trade and Industry* [1989] 3 All ER 523, HL. As to an order for discovery of assets in aid of execution see *Maclaine Watson & Co Ltd v International Tin Council (No 2)* [1989] Ch 286, sub nom *Maclaine Watson & Co Ltd v Department of Trade and Industry* [1988] 3 All ER 257, CA.

16 International Organisations Act 1968 s 7. This is so far as necessary for giving effect to the International Telecommunication Convention (Montreux, 12 November 1965; TS 41 (1967); Cmd 3383): see the International Organisations Act 1968 s 7.

310.   Tax exemptions for certain international organisations. Where the United Kingdom or the European Union is a member of an international organisation, and the agreement under which it became a member provides for exemption from tax, in relation to the organisation, of the kind described below, the Treasury may, by order made by statutory instrument, designate that organisation for the purpose[1]. Where an organisation has been so designated, the provisions apply in relation to that organisation, with the exception of any which may be excluded by the designation order[2].

Any security issued by the organisation must be taken, for the purposes of inheritance tax[3], to be situated outside the United Kingdom[4]. No stamp duty is chargeable[5] on the issue of any instrument by the organisation or on the transfer of the stock constituted by, or transferable by means of, any instrument issued by the organisation[6]. No stamp duty reserve tax is chargeable[7] in respect of the issue of securities by the organisation[8].

Similar provision is made in relation to exemption from income tax[9], and tax on chargeable gains[10].

Orders made or having effect under the provisions described above have been made designating the following bodies: (1) the Asian Development Bank[11]; (2) the African Development Bank[12]; (3) the European Economic Community, the

European Coal and Steel Community, the European Atomic Energy Community and the European Investment Bank[13]; and (4) the European Bank for Reconstruction and Development[14].

1   Finance Act 1984 s 126(1). The Treasury may designate any of the Communities or the European Investment Bank for these purposes: s 126(4) (added by the Finance Act 1985 s 96(1)). As to the Treasury see CONSTITUTIONAL LAW AND HUMAN RIGHTS vol 8(2) (Reissue) PARAS 512–517. As to the statutory meaning of 'United Kingdom' see PARA 30 note 3.
2   Finance Act 1984 s 126(2).
3   As to inheritance tax generally see INHERITANCE TAXATION.
4   Finance Act 1984 s 126(3)(b) (amended by the Taxation of Chargeable Gains Act 1992 s 290, Sch 12).
5   Ie under the Finance Act 1999 Sch 15: see STAMP DUTIES AND STAMP DUTY RESERVE TAX.
6   Finance Act 1984 s 126(3)(c) (amended by the Finance Act 1999 s 113(3), Sch 16 para 4). In so far as it is applied by a designation under the Finance Act 1984 s 126(4) (see note 1), s 126(3)(c) is modified: see s 126(5) (added by the Finance Act 1985 s 96(1); and amended by the Finance Act 1999 Sch 16 para 4). The Finance Act 1984 s 126(3)(c), (5) are prospectively repealed by the Finance Act 1990 s 132, Sch 19 Pt VI as from the abolition day appointed under s 111.
7   Ie under the Finance Act 1986 s 93 (depositary receipts) or s 96 (clearance services). See STAMP DUTIES AND STAMP DUTY RESERVE TAX.
8   Finance Act 1984 s 126(3)(d) (added by the Finance Act 1990 s 114).
9   See the Income Tax (Trading and Other Income) Act 2005 s 774; and INCOME TAXATION vol 23(2) (Reissue) PARA 1233.
10 See the Taxation of Chargeable Gains Act 1992 s 265; and CAPITAL GAINS TAXATION vol 5(1) (2004 Reissue) PARA 286.
11 International Organisations (Tax Exempt Securities) Order 1984, SI 1984/1215.
12 International Organisations (Tax Exempt Securities) (No 2) Order 1984, SI 1984/1634.
13 European Communities (Tax Exempt Securities) Order 1985, SI 1985/1172.
14 International Organisations (Tax Exempt Securities) Order 1991, SI 1991/1202.

311.   Organisations with privileges and immunities, and status of body corporate.   Certain privileges and immunities and the legal capacities of a body corporate[1] have been conferred upon the following organisations by Order in Council made or having effect under the International Organisations Act 1968[2]: the Advisory Centre on WTO Law[3], the African Development Bank[4], the African Development Fund[5], the Asian Development Bank[6], the Caribbean Development Bank[7], the Central Treaty Organisation[8], the Commission for Technical Co-operation in Africa South of the Sahara[9], the Common Fund for Commodities[10], the Commonwealth Agricultural Bureaux[11], the Commonwealth Foundation[12], the Commonwealth Telecommunications Organisation[13], the Council of Europe[14], the Customs Co-operation Council[15], the European Centre for Medium-range Weather Forecasts[16], the European Bank for Reconstruction and Development[17], the European Molecular Biology Laboratory[18], the European Organisation for Astronomical Research in the Southern Hemisphere[19], the European Organisation for the Exploitation of Meteorological Satellites (EUMETSTAT)[20], the European Organisation for Nuclear Research[21], the European Organisation for the Safety of Air Navigation (Eurocontrol)[22], the European Patent Organisation[23], the European Police College[24], the European Police Office (EUROPOL)[25], the European Space Agency[26], the European Telecommunications Satellite Organisation (EUTELSAT)[27], the Inter-American Development Bank[28], the International Atomic Energy Agency[29], the International Cocoa Organisation[30], the International Coffee Organisation[31], the International Court of Justice[32], the International Fund for Agricultural Development[33], the International Fund for Ireland[34], the International Grains Council and the Food Aid Committee[35], the International Jute Organisation[36], the International Lead and Zinc Study Group[37], the International Maritime

Organisation[38], the International Mobile Satellite Organisation[39], the International Monetary Fund[40], the International Natural Rubber Organisation[41], the International Oil Pollution Compensation Fund[42], the International Oil Pollution Compensation Fund 1992[43], the International Organisation for Migration[44], the International Rubber Study Group[45], the International Sea-Bed Authority[46], the International Sugar Organisation[47], the International Telecommunications Satellite Organisation (INTELSAT)[48], the International Tin Council[49], the International Trust Fund for Tuvalu[50], the International Tribunal for the Law of the Sea[51], the International Whaling Commission[52], the North Atlantic Treaty Organisation[53], the Organisation for Economic Co-operation and Development[54], the OECD Financial Support Fund[55], the Organisation for Joint Armament Co-operation[56], the Organisation for the Prohibition of Chemical Weapons[57], the Oslo Commission and the Paris Commission[58], the OSPAR Commission[59], the Preparatory Commission for the Comprehensive Nuclear-Test-Ban Treaty Organisation[60], the South-East Asia Treaty Organisation[61], the United Nations[62], the Western European Union[63], and the World Trade Organisation[64].

Immunities, privileges and capacity have also been conferred on the following specialised agencies of the United Nations: the Food and Agriculture Organisation, the International Civil Aviation Organisation, the International Labour Organisation, the International Telecommunication Union, the United Nations Educational, Scientific and Cultural Organisation, the Universal Postal Union, the World Health Organisation, the World Meteorological Organisation, and the World Intellectual Property Organisation[65]. Immunities and privileges have also been conferred on the Military Staff of the European Union (EUMS)[66].

1 See PARA 309.
2 Ie made or having effect under the International Organisations Act 1968 s 1: see PARA 309. For provisions conferring comparable immunities under other legislation see PARA 313.
3 Advisory Centre on WTO Law (Immunities and Privileges) Order 2001, SI 2001/1868.
4 African Development Bank (Immunities and Privileges) Order 1983, SI 1983/142 (amended by SI 1999/2034).
5 African Development Fund (Immunities and Privileges) Order 1973, SI 1973/958 (amended by SI 1975/1209; SI 1999/2034).
6 Asian Development Bank (Immunities and Privileges) Order 1974, SI 1974/1251 (amended by SI 1975/1209; SI 1999/2034).
7 Caribbean Development Bank (Immunities and Privileges) Order 1972, SI 1972/113 (amended by SI 1975/1209; SI 1999/2034).
8 Central Treaty Organisation (Immunities and Privileges) Order 1974, SI 1974/1252 (amended by SI 1975/1209).
9 International Organisations (Immunities and Privileges of the Commission for Technical Co-operation in Africa South of the Sahara) Order 1955, SI 1955/1208.
10 Common Fund for Commodities (Immunities and Privileges) Order 1981, SI 1981/1802.
11 Commonwealth Agricultural Bureaux (Immunities and Privileges) Order 1982, SI 1982/1071 (amended by SI 1999/2034).
12 Commonwealth Foundation (Immunities and Privileges) Order 1983, SI 1983/143 (amended by SI 1999/2034).
13 Commonwealth Telecommunications Organisation (Immunities and Privileges) Order 1983, SI 1983/144 (amended by SI 1999/2034).
14 Council of Europe (Immunities and Privileges) Order 1960, SI 1960/442.
15 Customs Co-operation Council (Immunities and Privileges) Order 1974, SI 1974/1253 (amended by SI 1975/1209; SI 2006/1075).
16 European Centre for Medium-range Weather Forecasts (Immunities and Privileges) Order 1975, SI 1975/158 (amended by SI 1975/1209; SI 1976/216; SI 1981/1109; SI 1999/2034).
17 European Bank for Reconstruction and Development (Immunities and Privileges) Order 1991, SI 1991/757 (amended by SI 1999/2034). See also the Bretton Woods Agreements Order in Council 1946, SR & O 1946/36 (amended by SI 1974/1261; SI 1976/221; SI 1977/825),

conferring immunities and privileges on the International Bank for Reconstruction and Development and the International Monetary Fund: see PARA 313.

18 European Molecular Biology Laboratory (Immunities and Privileges) Order 1994, SI 1994/1890 (amended by SI 1999/2034).

19 European Organization for Astronomical Research in the Southern Hemisphere (Immunities and Privileges) Order 2009, SI 2009/1748.

20 EUMETSAT (Immunities and Privileges) Order 1988, SI 1988/1298 (amended by SI 1999/2034).

21 European Organisation for Nuclear Research (Privileges and Immunities) Order 2006, SI 2006/1922.

22 Eurocontrol (Immunities and Privileges) Order 1970, SI 1970/1940 (amended by SI 1975/1209; SI 1980/1076; SI 1984/127; SI 1999/2034). See also PARA 313.

23 European Patent Organisation (Immunities and Privileges) Order 1978, SI 1978/179 (amended by SI 1980/1096; SI 1999/2034).

24 European Police College (Immunities and Privileges) Order 2004, SI 2004/3334.

25 European Communities (Immunities and Privileges of the European Police Office) Order 1997, SI 1997/2973 (amended by SI 2004/3330); and prospectively replacing the European Police Office (Legal Capacities) Order 1996, SI 1996/3157 (see PARA 312 note 10).

26 European Space Agency (Immunities and Privileges) Order 1978, SI 1978/1105 (amended by SI 1980/1096; SI 1999/2034).

27 EUTELSAT (Immunities and Privileges) Order 1988, SI 1988/1299 (amended by SI 1999/2034; SI 2001/963).

28 Inter-American Development Bank (Immunities and Privileges) Order 1976, SI 1976/222 (amended by SI 1980/1096; SI 1984/1981; SI 1999/2034).

29 International Atomic Energy Agency (Immunities and Privileges) Order 1974, SI 1974/1256 (amended by SI 1975/1209; SI 2006/1075).

30 International Cocoa Organisation (Immunities and Privileges) Order 1975, SI 1975/411 (amended by SI 1975/1209; SI 1999/2034).

31 International Coffee Organisation (Immunities and Privileges) Order 1969, SI 1969/733 (amended by SI 1975/1209; SI 1999/2034).

32 United Nations and International Court of Justice (Immunities and Privileges) Order 1974, SI 1974/1261 (amended SI 1975/1209; SI 2002/1828; SI 2006/1075).

33 International Fund for Agricultural Development (Immunities and Privileges) Order 1977, SI 1977/824 (amended by SI 1980/1096).

34 International Fund for Ireland (Immunities and Privileges) Order 1986, SI 1986/2017.

35 International Wheat Council (Immunities and Privileges) Order 1968, SI 1968/1863 (amended by SI 1975/1209; SI 1999/2034).

36 International Jute Organisation (Immunities and Privileges) Order 1983, SI 1983/1111.

37 International Lead and Zinc Study Group (Immunities and Privileges) Order 1978, SI 1978/1893 (amended by SI 1984/1982; SI 1999/2034).

38 International Maritime Organisation (Immunities and Privileges) Order 2002, SI 2002/1826.

39 International Mobile Satellite Organisation (Immunities and Privileges) Order 1999, SI 1999/1125.

40 International Monetary Fund (Immunities and Privileges) Order 1977, SI 1977/825. See also the Bretton Woods Agreements Order in Council 1946, SR & O 1946/36 (amended by SI 1974/1261; SI 1976/221; SI 1977/825), conferring immunities and privileges on the International Bank for Reconstruction and Development and the International Monetary Fund.

41 International Natural Rubber Organisation (Immunities and Privileges) Order 1981, SI 1981/1804.

42 International Oil Pollution Compensation Fund (Immunities and Privileges) Order 1979, SI 1979/912 (amended by SI 1999/2034).

43 International Oil Pollution Compensation Fund 1992 (Immunities and Privileges) Order 1996, SI 1996/1295 (amended by SI 1999/2034).

44 International Organisation for Migration (Immunities and Privileges) Order 2008, SI 2008/3124

45 International Rubber Study Group (Immunities and Privileges) Order 1978, SI 1978/181 (amended by SI 1980/1096; SI 1999/2034).

46 International Sea-Bed Authority (Immunities and Privileges) Order 2000, SI 2000/1815 (amended by SI 2006/1075).

47 International Sugar Organisation (Immunities and Privileges) Order 1969, SI 1969/734 (amended by SI 1975/1209; SI 1999/2034). The International Organisations Act 1968 continues to apply to the International Sugar Organisation even if Her Majesty should cease to be a member of it: International Sugar Organisation Act 1973 s 1. The International Sugar Organisation (Immunities and Privileges) Order 1969, SI 1969/734, thus continues in force.

48 INTELSAT (Immunities and Privileges) Order 1979, SI 1979/911 (amended by SI 1999/2032).
49 International Tin Council (Immunities and Privileges) Order 1972, SI 1972/120 (amended by SI 1975/1209).
50 International Trust Fund for Tuvalu (Immunities and Privileges) Order 1988, SI 1988/245.
51 International Tribunal for the Law of the Sea (Immunities and Privileges) Order 2005, SI 2005/2047. The International Tribunal for the Law of the Sea (see PARA 497) is to be treated for the purposes of the International Organisations Act 1968 s 1 as an organisation of which the United Kingdom, or Her Majesty's Government in the United Kingdom, and at least one other sovereign power, or the government of such a power, are members: see the International Organisations Act 2005 s 8; and PARA 309.
52 International Whaling Commission (Immunities and Privileges) Order 1975, SI 1975/1210 (amended by SI 1999/2034).
53 North Atlantic Treaty Organisation (Immunities and Privileges) Order 1974, SI 1974/1257 (amended by SI 1975/1209).
54 Organisation for Economic Co-operation and Development (Immunities and Privileges) Order 1974, SI 1974/1258 (amended by SI 1975/1209; SI 2006/1075).
55 OECD Financial Support Fund (Immunities and Privileges) Order 1976, SI 1976/224 (amended by SI 1980/1096).
56 Organisation for Joint Armament Co-operation (Immunities and Privileges) Order 2000, SI 2000/1105.
57 Organisation for the Prohibition of Chemical Weapons (Immunities and Privileges) Order 2001, SI 2001/3921 (amended by SI 2006/1075).
58 Oslo and Paris Commissions (Immunities and Privileges) Order 1979, SI 1979/914 (amended by SI 1999/2034).
59 OSPAR Commission (Immunities and Privileges) Order 1997, SI 1997/2975.
60 Preparatory Commission for the Comprehensive Nuclear-Test-Ban Treaty Organisation (Immunities and Privileges) Order 2004, SI 2004/1282 (amended by SI 2006/1075).
61 South-East Asia Treaty Organisation (Immunities and Privileges) Order 1974, SI 1974/1259 (amended by SI 1975/1209).
62 United Nations and International Court of Justice (Immunities and Privileges) Order 1974, SI 1974/1261 (amended by SI 1975/1209; SI 2002/1828; SI 2006/1075). Notwithstanding the entry into force for the United Kingdom of the constitution of the United Nations Industrial Development Organisation (UNIDO), the provisions of the United Nations and International Court of Justice (Immunities and Privileges) Order 1974, SI 1974/1261, continue to apply to UNIDO, its officers and representatives of members: United Nations Industrial Development Organisation (Immunities and Privileges) Order 1982, SI 1982/1074.
63 Western European Union (Immunities and Privileges) Order 1960, SI 1960/444.
64 World Trade Organisation (Immunities and Privileges) Order 1995, SI 1995/266 (amended by SI 2006/1075).
65 Specialised Agencies of the United Nations (Immunities and Privileges) Order 1974, SI 1974/1260 (amended by SI 1975/1209; SI 1985/451; SI 1985/753; SI 2002/1827; SI 2006/1075); Specialised Agencies of the United Nations (Immunities and Privileges of UNESCO) Order 2001, SI 2001/2650. See also *Entico Corpn v UNESCO* [2008] EWHC 532 (Comm), [2008] 2 All ER (Comm) 97, [2008] All ER (D) 255 (Mar) (no contravention of Art 6(1) European Convention on Human Rights where specialised agency enjoys immunity from suit).
66 European Union Military Staff (Immunities and Privileges) Order 2009, SI 2009/887.

312. Legal capacities of bodies corporate. The legal capacities of a body corporate (but no privileges or immunities)[1] have been conferred[2] upon the Agency for International Trade Information and Co-operation[3], the Commission for the Conservation of Antarctic Marine Living Resources[4], the European Organisation for Nuclear Research[5], the International Copper Study Group[6], the International Hydrographic Organisation[7], the International Tropical Timber Organisation[8], the International Union for the Protection of New Varieties of Plants[9], and the European Police Office (EUROPOL)[10].

1 For the organisations on which both legal capacity and privileges and immunities have been conferred see PARA 311.
2 Ie under the International Organisations Act 1968 s 1: see PARA 309.

3 Agency for International Trade Information and Co-operation (Legal Capacities) Order 2004, SI 2004/3332.
4 Commission for the Conservation of Antarctic Marine Living Resources (Immunities and Privileges) Order 1981, SI 1981/1108.
5 European Organisation for Nuclear Research (Immunities and Privileges) Order 1972, SI 1972/115; European Organisation for Nuclear Research (Immunities and Privileges) Order 2006, SI 2006/1922. See PARA 311 note 21.
6 International Copper Study Group (Legal Capacities) Order 1999, SI 1999/2033.
7 International Hydrographic Organisation (Immunities and Privileges) Order 1972, SI 1972/119.
8 International Tropical Timber Organisation (Legal Capacities) Order 1984, SI 1984/1152.
9 International Union for the Protection of New Varieties of Plants (Legal Capacities) Order 1985, SI 1985/446.
10 European Police Office (Legal Capacities) Order 1996, SI 1996/3157 (revoked and replaced, as from a day to be appointed, by the European Communities (Immunities and Privileges of the European Police Office) Order 1997, SI 1997/2973 (amended by SI 2004/3330) (see PARA 311 note 25)). At the date at which this volume states the law no such day had been appointed.

313. Further provisions for immunities and privileges. The European Organisation for the Safety of Air Navigation (Eurocontrol)[1] has the legal capacity of a body corporate and is entitled to inviolability of official archives and premises and to relief from rates and taxes[2].

The Commonwealth Telecommunications Bureau has the legal capacity of a body corporate[3].

Provision may be made by Order in Council with regard to the status of the International Bank for Reconstruction and Development, the International Finance Corporation and the International Development Association, and their governors, directors, alternates, officers and employees[4].

Provision may be made by Order in Council with regard to the status of the International Monetary Fund and its governors, directors, alternates, officers and employees[5].

Legal status, privileges and immunities are also conferred on: the Multilateral Investment Guarantee Agency (and its governors, directors, alternates, president and staff)[6]; the Independent Commission for the Location of Victims' Remains[7] (and its members)[8]; the Independent International Commission on Decommissioning[9] (and its members)[10]; the Commonwealth Secretariat (and its officers and servants and their families)[11]; the North-East Atlantic Fisheries Commission[12]; the European School[13]; the North Atlantic Salmon Conservation Organisation[14]; the Joint European Torus[15]; and the International Criminal Court (and certain specified categories of individuals connected with it)[16].

1 The organisation was established under the Convention relating to Co-operation for the Safety of Air Navigation (Eurocontrol) (Brussels, 13 December 1960; TS 39 (1963); Cmnd 2114); and see the Additional Protocol of 6 July 1970 (Cmnd 4499). See also AIR LAW vol 2 (2008) PARA 23.
2 See the Civil Aviation Act 1982 s 24, Sch 4 para 1 (amended by the Civil Aviation (Eurocontrol) Act 1983 s 2). See also the Eurocontrol (Immunities and Privileges) Order 1970, SI 1970/1940 (amended by SI 1975/1209; SI 1980/1076; SI 1984/127; SI 1999/2034); and PARA 311 note 22.
3 Commonwealth Telecommunications Act 1968 s 1.
4 See the International Development Act 2002 s 12.
5 See the International Monetary Fund Act 1979 s 5(1), (3). The Bretton Woods Agreements Order in Council 1946, SR & O 1946/36 (amended by SI 1974/1261; SI 1976/221; SI 1977/825) has effect partly under these provisions: International Monetary Fund Act 1979 s 6(2). As to the power to extend the provisions by Order in Council beyond the United Kingdom see s 5(2). See also PARA 311 note 40.
6 See the Multilateral Investment Guarantee Agency Act 1988 ss 1(2), 3, Schedule arts 1, 44, 45, 46(a), 47, 48(i), 50. These provisions are extended to Anguilla, British Virgin Islands, Cayman Islands, Falkland Islands, Gibraltar, Hong Kong, Montserrat, Pitcairn, Henderson, Ducie and

Oeno Islands, St Helena, Turks and Caicos Islands: Multilateral Investment Guarantee Agency (Overseas Territories) Order 1988, SI 1988/791 (amended by SI 1988/1300).

7 See generally the Northern Ireland (Location of Victims' Remains) Act 1999 s 2.

8 See the Northern Ireland (Location of Victims' Remains) Act 1999 (Immunities and Privileges) Order 1999, SI 1999/1437, made under the Northern Ireland (Location of Victims' Remains) Act 1999 s 2(1).

9 See generally the Northern Ireland Arms Decommissioning Act 1997; and CONSTITUTIONAL LAW AND HUMAN RIGHTS.

10 See the Northern Ireland Arms Decommissioning Act 1997 (Immunities and Privileges) Order 1997, SI 1997/2231, made under the Northern Ireland Arms Decommissioning Act 1997 s 7(2).

11 See the Commonwealth Secretariat Act 1966 s 1, Schedule; and COMMONWEALTH vol 13 (2009) PARA 723. There is no contravention of the European Convention on Human Rights art 6(1) where the Commonwealth Secretariat enjoys immunity from suit: *Jananygam v Commonwealth Secretariat* [2007] All ER (D) 193 (Mar), EAT. The Convention for the Protection of Human Rights and Fundamental Freedoms (Rome, 4 November 1950; TS 71 (1953); Cmd 8969) (commonly referred to as the 'European Convention on Human Rights') is set out in the Human Rights Act 1998 Sch 1: see CONSTITUTIONAL LAW AND HUMAN RIGHTS vol 8(2) (Reissue) PARA 122 et seq.

12 European Communities (Immunities and Privileges of the North-East Atlantic Fisheries Commission) Order 1999, SI 1999/278.

13 European Communities (Privileges of the European School) Order 1990, SI 1990/237 (amended by SI 2001/3674).

14 European Communities (Immunities and Privileges of the North Atlantic Salmon Conservation Organisation) Order 1985, SI 1985/1773 (amended by SI 2001/3673).

15 European Communities (Privileges of the Joint European Torus) Order 1978, SI 1978/1033 (amended by SI 1980/1096).

16 See the International Criminal Court Act 2001 Sch 1 para 1 (amended by the International Organisations Act 2005 ss 6, 11); the International Criminal Court (Immunities and Privileges) (No 1) Order 2006, SI 2006/1907; and the International Criminal Court (Immunities and Privileges) (No 2) Order 2006, SI 2006/1908.

314. International judicial proceedings. An Order in Council may confer such privileges, immunities and facilities as may be required to give effect to any agreement to which the United Kingdom[1] or its government is or will be party, or to any resolution of the General Assembly of the United Nations[2], upon:

(1)   judges or members of any international tribunal[3] or persons exercising or performing or appointed to exercise or perform any jurisdiction or functions of such a tribunal[4];

(2)   registrars or other officers of any such tribunal[5];

(3)   parties to proceedings before such a tribunal[6];

(4)   the agents, advisers and advocates of parties[7]; and

(5)   witnesses and assessors[8].

Orders have been made in respect of the European Court of Human Rights[9], the International Court of Justice[10], the tribunal established by the Convention on the Establishment of a Security Control in the Field of Nuclear Energy[11], arbitration proceedings relating to INTELSAT[12], the European Committee for the Prevention of Torture and Inhuman or Degrading Treatment or Punishment[13], and the International Tribunal for the Law of the Sea[14].

1 As to the statutory meaning of 'United Kingdom' see PARA 30 note 3.

2 International Organisations Act 1968 s 5(1). Section 5 applies to members of the family of a judge of the European Court of Human Rights as it applies to a judge of that court: s 7.

3 'International tribunal' means any court (including the International Court of Justice), tribunal, commission or body which in pursuance of any such agreement or resolution exercises jurisdiction or performs judicial functions or is appointed to do so: International Organisations Act 1968 s 5(5).

4 International Organisations Act 1968 s 5(2)(a).

5 International Organisations Act 1968 s 5(2)(b).

6   International Organisations Act 1968 s 5(2)(c). 'Proceedings' means any communication made to the tribunal, with a view to its being acted upon by the tribunal, and whether or not it is made through a person who may receive it in accordance with the practice of the tribunal: s 5(3).

7   International Organisations Act 1968 s 5(2)(d). 'Parties' includes persons acting in the proceedings as next friend, guardian or other representative of a party and any other person allowed by the practice of the tribunal to participate by way of advising or assisting: s 5(4). Any person making a communication to the tribunal within s 5(3) is deemed to be a party to the proceedings: s 5(3).

8   International Organisations Act 1968 s 5(2)(e).

9   See the European Commission and Court of Human Rights (Immunities and Privileges) Order 1970, SI 1970/1941 (amended by SI 1990/2290); European Court of Human Rights (Immunities and Privileges) Order 2000, SI 2000/1817 (amended by SI 2005/3425; SI 2006/1075). See CONSTITUTIONAL LAW AND HUMAN RIGHTS.

10 See the United Nations and International Court of Justice (Immunities and Privileges) Order 1974, SI 1974/1261 (amended by SI 1975/1209; SI 2002/1828; SI 2006/1075). As to the International Court of Justice see PARA 499 et seq.

11 See the Organisation for Economic Co-operation and Development (Immunities and Privileges) Order 1974, SI 1974/1258 (amended by SI 1975/1209; SI 2006/1075).

12 See the INTELSAT (Immunities and Privileges) Order 1979, SI 1979/911 (amended by SI 1999/2032).

13 See the European Committee for the Prevention of Torture and Inhuman or Degrading Treatment or Punishment (Immunities and Privileges) Order 1988, SI 1988/926.

14 International Tribunal for the Law of the Sea (Immunities and Privileges) Order 1996, SI 1996/272 (revoked and replaced, as from a day to be appointed, by the International Tribunal for the Law of the Sea (Immunities and Privileges) Order 2005, SI 2005/2047): see PARA 311. At the date at which this volume states the law no such day had been appointed.

315.   Organisations of which the United Kingdom is not a member.   Where an organisation of which two or more sovereign powers[1] or governments are members, but of which the United Kingdom[2] is not a member, maintains or proposes to maintain an establishment in the United Kingdom, then, for the purpose of giving effect to any agreement between the United Kingdom or its government and such organisation, the legal capacities of a body corporate may be conferred by Order in Council[3] and the organisation may be entitled, to the extent specified in the order, to such exemptions or relief from taxes on income and capital gains as is accorded to a foreign sovereign power[4].

Such an order made with respect to an international commodity organisation[5] may: (1) confer certain privileges and immunities[6] in respect of the organisation[7]; (2) confer certain other privileges and immunities[8] on persons of any specified class[9]; (3) provide that the official papers of such persons are inviolable[10]; and (4) confer certain privileges and immunities[11] on officers and servants of the organisation[12].

Further, an Order in Council made under the provisions described above may confer certain privileges and immunities on representatives to conferences in the United Kingdom convened by an international organisation[13].

An international organisation created by a treaty to which the United Kingdom is not a party cannot be recognised by the courts without the intervention of Parliament, but it will be recognised by the courts if it is created also as a corporate body under the law of a foreign state[14]. However, any questions as to the meaning, effect and operation of the constitution of the organisation must be determined by the treaty and international law, not by the domestic law of the state[15].

1   'Sovereign powers' here includes Commonwealth states: see PARA 309 note 1.

2   As to the statutory meaning of 'United Kingdom' see PARA 30 note 3.

3   At the date at which this volume states the law no such order had been made.

4   International Organisations Act 1968 s 4 (amended by the European Communities Act 1972 s 4, Sch 3; and the International Organisations Act 1981 ss 1(2), 6(4), Schedule).

5   'International commodity organisation' means any such organisation as is mentioned in the International Organisations Act 1968 s 4 which appears to Her Majesty to satisfy each of the following conditions: (1) that the members of the organisation are states or the governments of states in which a particular commodity is produced or consumed; (2) that the exports or imports of that commodity from or to those states account (when taken together) for a significant volume of the total exports or imports of that commodity throughout the world; and (3) that the purpose or principal purpose of the organisation is to regulate trade in that commodity (whether as an import or an export or both) or to promote or study that trade, or to promote research into that commodity or its uses or further development: s 4A(1) (s 4A added by the International Organisations Act 1981 s 2). 'Commodity' means any produce of agriculture, forestry or fisheries or any mineral, either in its natural state or having undergone only such processes as are necessary or customary to prepare the produce or mineral for the international market: International Organisations Act 1968 s 4A(5) (as so added).

6   Ie those set out in the International Organisations Act 1968 Sch 1 paras 2, 3, 4, 6, 7 (see PARA 309).

7   International Organisations Act 1968 s 4A(2)(a) (as added: see note 5).

8   Ie those set out in the International Organisations Act 1968 Sch 1 paras 11, 14 (see PARAS 317, 319). An Order in Council under s 4 in respect of an international commodity organisation may to such extent as may be specified in the order confer on persons of any such class as may be specified in the order, being persons who are or are to be representatives (whether of governments or not) at any conference which the organisation may convene in the United Kingdom, the privileges and immunities set out in Sch 1 paras 11, 14, and provide that the official papers of such persons are inviolable: s 5A(1)(a), (b) (s 5A added by the International Organisations Act 1981 s 3). See further the International Organisations Act 1968 s 5A(2), (3) (as so added).

9   International Organisations Act 1968 s 4A(2)(b) (as added: see note 5). The classes of persons referred to are: (1) persons who (whether they represent governments or not) are representatives to the organisation or representatives on, or members of, any organ, committee or other subordinate body of the organisation (including any sub-committee or other subordinate body of a subordinate body of the organisation); or (2) persons who are members of the staff of any such representative and who are recognised by the United Kingdom government as holding a rank equivalent to that of a diplomatic agent: s 4A(3) (as so added). An Order in Council may not confer on any person of such class as is mentioned in head (1) or head (2) of this note any immunity in respect of a civil action arising out of an accident caused by a motor vehicle or other means of transport belonging to or driven by such a person, or in respect of a traffic offence involving such a vehicle and committed by such a person: s 4A(4) (as so added).

10 International Organisations Act 1968 s 4A(2)(c) (as added: see note 5).

11 Ie those set out in the International Organisations Act 1968 Sch 1 paras 13, 15, 16 (see PARAS 317, 319).

12 International Organisations Act 1968 s 4A(2)(d) (as added: see note 5).

13 See the International Organisations Act 1968 s 5A; and PARA 317.

14 *Arab Monetary Fund v Hashim (No 3)* [1991] 2 AC 114, [1991] 1 All ER 871, HL.

15 *Westland Helicopters Ltd v Arab Organisation for Industrialisation* [1995] QB 282, [1995] 2 All ER 387.

316.   Bodies established under Treaty on European Union.   Her Majesty may by Order in Council make any one or more of the following provisions in respect of a specified[1] body[2]:

(1)   confer on the body the legal capacities of a body corporate[3];

(2)   provide that the body must, to such extent as is specified, have such specified privileges and immunities as, having regard to the obligations referred to[4], it is in the opinion of Her Majesty in Council appropriate for the body to have[5];

(3)   confer on specified classes of persons[6], to such extent as is specified, such specified privileges and immunities as, having regard to those obligations, it is in the opinion of her Majesty in Council appropriate to confer on them[7].

1 'Specified' means specified in the Order in Council: International Organisations Act 1968 s 4B(4) (s 4B added by the International Organisations Act 2005 s 5).
2 Ie any body established under the Treaty on European Union (Maastricht, 7 February 1992; Cmnd 1934) Title V or Title VI as amended from time to time (International Organisations Act 1968 s 4B(1)(a) (as added: see note 1)) and in relation to which the United Kingdom, or Her Majesty's government in the United Kingdom, has obligations by virtue of any agreement to which the United Kingdom, or her Majesty's government in the United Kingdom, is a party, whether made with another sovereign power or the government of such a power or not (s 4B(1)(b) (as so added)).
3 International Organisations Act 1968 s 4B(2)(a) (as added: see note 1).
4 Ie referred to in the International Organisations Act 1968 s 4B(1)(b): see note 2.
5 International Organisations Act 1968 s 4B(2)(b) (as added: see note 1).
6 Ie the body's officers or staff, other persons connected with the body, and members of their families who form part of their households: International Organisations Act 1968 s 4B(3) (as added: see note 1).
7 International Organisations Act 1968 s 4B(2)(c) (as added: see note 1).

317. Representatives, members of subordinate bodies, high officers, experts and persons on missions. Representatives of international organisations and other persons may have conferred on them by Order in Council to the extent specified by the order certain privileges and immunities[1].

The classes of persons on whom these privileges and immunities may be conferred are: (1) persons who (whether they represent governments or not) are representatives to an organisation specified by Order in Council to be one of which the United Kingdom[2] or its government and one or more foreign powers[3] or governments are members, or representatives on, or members of, any organ, committee or other subordinate body of the organisation, including any sub-committee or other subordinate body of a subordinate body of the organisation[4]; (2) holders of high offices, specified by Order in Council, in the organisation[5]; (3) persons employed by or serving under the organisation as experts or as persons engaged on missions for the organisation[6]; (4) representatives, specified by Order in Council, of a foreign sovereign power or government at a conference held in the United Kingdom attended by representatives of the United Kingdom or its government and one or more foreign sovereign powers or governments[7]; (5) persons of any such class as may be specified by Order in Council, being persons who are or are to be representatives (whether of governments or not) at any conference which a specified organisation may convene in the United Kingdom[8].

The privileges and immunities are:
(a) the same immunity from suit and legal process, the same inviolability of residence, and the same exemption or relief from taxes and rates, other than duties (whether of customs or excise) and taxes on the importation of goods, as are accorded to the head of a diplomatic mission[9];
(b) the same exemption or relief from being liable to pay anything in respect of council tax, as is accorded to the head of a diplomatic mission[10];
(c) the same exemption from duties (whether of customs or excise) and taxes on the importation of certain articles for personal use as is accorded to a diplomatic agent[11];
(d) the same exemption and privileges in respect of personal baggage as are accorded to a diplomatic agent[12];
(e) relief under arrangements by way of refund of duty (whether of customs or excise) or value added tax paid on the importation of hydrocarbon oil[13] subject to compliance with conditions[14];
(f) exemptions whereby services rendered are deemed to be excepted from

any class of employment in respect of which contributions are payable under the social security legislation[15];

(g)   the same inviolability of official premises as is accorded in respect of the premises of a diplomatic mission[16].

1   See the International Organisations Act 1968 s 1(2)(c), (3), Sch 1 Pt II. For Orders in Council made under s 1 see PARA 311.
2   As to the statutory meaning of 'United Kingdom' see PARA 30 note 3.
3   'Foreign powers' here includes Commonwealth states: see PARA 309 note 1.
4   International Organisations Act 1968 s 1(1), (2)(c), (3)(a) (s 1(1) amended by the International Organisations Act 1981 s 1(1)).
5   See the International Organisations Act 1968 s 1(3)(b).
6   International Organisations Act 1968 s 1(3)(c).
7   See the International Organisations Act 1968 s 6(1)–(3) (s 6(1), (2) amended by the International Organisations Act 1981 s 1(3)). The CSCE Information Forum (Immunities and Privileges) Order 1989, SI 1989/480, the G8 Gleneagles (Immunities and Privileges) Order 2005, SI 2005/1456, and the London Summit (Immunities and Privileges) Order 2009, SI 2009/222, were made under this provision.
8   International Organisations Act 1968 s 5A(1)(a)(i) (s 5A added by the International Organisations Act 1981 s 3). See further the International Organisations Act 1968 s 5A(2), (3) (as so added).
9   International Organisations Act 1968 s 1(2)(c), Sch 1 paras 8, 9 (Sch 1 para 9 amended by the Customs and Excise Management Act 1979 s 177(1), Sch 4 para 12 Table Pt I). Customs duties include excise duties chargeable on goods imported into the United Kingdom: see PARA 278 note 1. See also PARA 267 et seq.
10 International Organisations Act 1968 Sch 1 para 9B (added by Local Government and Housing Act 1989 s 194(1), Sch 11 para 14; and amended by the Local Government Finance Act 1992 s 117(1), Sch 13 para 28).
11 International Organisations Act 1968 Sch 1 para 10 (amended by the Customs and Excise Management Act 1979 Sch 4 para 12 Table Pt I; and the International Organisations Act 1981s 5(2)). This exemption is accorded under the Convention on Diplomatic Relations (Vienna, 18 April 1961; TS 19 (1965); Cmnd 2565) art 36 para 1 (see the Diplomatic Privileges Act 1964 Sch 1; and PARA 278).
12 International Organisations Act 1968 Sch 1 para 11. This exemption is accorded under the Vienna Convention on Diplomatic Relations art 36 para 2 (see the Diplomatic Privileges Act 1964 Sch 1; and PARA 278).
13 Ie hydrocarbon oil within the meaning of the Hydrocarbon Oil Duties Act 1979: see CUSTOMS AND EXCISE vol 12(2) (2007 Reissue) PARA 510.
14 International Organisations Act 1968 Sch 1 para 12 (amended by the Customs and Excise Management Act 1979 Sch 4 para 12 Table Pt I).
15 See the International Organisations Act 1968 Sch 1 para 13 (amended by the Social Security Act 1973 s 100, Sch 27 para 80; and the Social Security (Consequential Provisions) Act 1975 ss 1(2), 5, Sch 1).
16 International Organisations Act 1968 Sch 1 para 9A (added by the International Organisations Act 1981 s 5(1)).

318.   Officers holding rank equivalent to that of diplomatic agent.   Where an Order in Council is made in respect of an organisation which is a specialised agency of the United Nations having its headquarters or principal office in the United Kingdom, then, for the purpose of giving effect to any agreement between the United Kingdom or its government and that organisation, the following exemptions, privileges and reliefs may be conferred to the extent specified in the order on officers of the organisation who are recognised as holding a rank equivalent to that of diplomatic agent[1].

The exemptions, privileges and reliefs are the same as those accorded a diplomatic agent in respect of: (1) income tax, capital gains tax, rates and council tax; and (2) customs duties and taxes on the importation of certain articles for personal use, personal baggage, relief, under arrangements by way of refund of customs or excise duty paid on or value added tax paid on the importation of hydrocarbon oil, subject to compliance with conditions, and exemption from vehicle excise duty[2].

Where an Order in Council is made specifying an organisation to be an organisation of which the United Kingdom or its government and one or more foreign powers or governments are members for the purpose of giving effect to an agreement between the United Kingdom or its government and the organisation, members of the staff of the organisation recognised as holding a rank equivalent to that of diplomatic agent may by order have conferred on them in the event of death exemptions from inheritance tax in respect of certain moveable property[3].

A member of the official staff of a representative who is recognised as holding a rank equivalent to that of diplomatic agent may in certain circumstances be entitled to the same privileges and immunities as the representative[4].

1 International Organisations Act 1968 s 2(1). As to the statutory meaning of 'United Kingdom' see PARA 30 note 2.

2 International Organisations Act 1968 s 2(2) (amended by the Diplomatic and other Privileges Act 1971 s 3; the Local Government Finance Act 1988 s 137, Sch 12 Pt III para 40; the Local Government Finance Act 1992 s 117(1), Sch 13 para 27; and the Vehicle Excise and Registration Act 1994 s 65, Sch 5 Pt I). The exemptions in head (1) in the text are those accorded by the Convention on Diplomatic Relations (Vienna, 18 April 1961; TS 19 (1965); Cmnd 2565) arts 34, 36: see PARAS 275, 278. As to the exemptions mentioned in head (2) in the text see the International Organisations Act 1968 s 1(2), Sch 1 paras 10–12; and PARA 317.

3 International Organisations Act 1968 s 1(5)(b), Sch 1 para 24 (amended by the Taxation of Chargeable Gains Act 1992 s 290(3), Sch 12). For orders made under the International Organisations Act 1968 s 1 conferring immunities and privileges see PARA 311.

4 See the International Organisations Act 1968 Sch 1 para 20.

319. Officers and servants of classes specified by Order in Council. Officers and servants belonging to a class specified by Order in Council of an organisation specified by Order in Council to be one of which the United Kingdom or its government and one or more foreign powers or governments are members may have conferred on them by Order in Council, to the extent specified by the order, the following privileges and immunities[1]:

(1) immunity from suit and legal process in respect of things done or omitted to be done in performance of official duties[2];

(2) exemption from income tax in respect of emoluments received as an officer or servant[3];

(3) the same exemption from duties (whether of customs or excise) and taxes on articles which were imported at or about the time when the officer or servant first entered the United Kingdom for his personal use or that of members of his family forming part of his household, including articles intended for his establishment, or which were in his ownership or possession or that of such a member of his family, or which he or such a member of his family was under contract to purchase, immediately before he entered, and the same privilege as to the importation of such articles, as is accorded to a diplomatic agent[4];

(4) exemption from duties (whether of customs or excise) and taxes on the importation of a motor vehicle to replace one imported under the previous exemption[5];

(5) the same exemption and privileges in respect of personal baggage as is accorded to a diplomatic agent[6].

1   International Organisations Act 1968 s 1(2)(c), (d). The privileges and immunities referred to
    are those mentioned in Sch 1 Pt III. A European Union national working in another member
    state as employee of an international organisation and enjoying a right of entry, residence and
    work derived from the privileges and immunities of that organisation does not thereby lose his
    status as a Community worker: Cases 389–390/87 *Echternach v Minister van Onderwijs En
    Wetenschappen* [1989] ECR 723, [1990] 2 CMLR 305, ECJ. As to the statutory meaning of
    'United Kingdom' see PARA 30 note 3.
2   International Organisations Act 1968 Sch 1 para 14.
3   International Organisations Act 1968 Sch 1 para 15.
4   International Organisations Act 1968 Sch 1 para 16 (amended by the Customs and Excise
    Management Act 1979 s 177(1), Sch 4 para 12 Table Pt I; and the International Organisations
    Act 1981 s 5(3)). These exemptions are conferred on diplomatic agents by the Convention on
    Diplomatic Relations (Vienna, 18 April 1961; TS 19 (1965); Cmnd 2565) art 36 para 1: see the
    Diplomatic Privileges Act 1964 Sch 1; and PARA 278.
5   International Organisations Act 1968 Sch 1 para 17 (amended by the Customs and Excise
    Management Act 1979 Sch 4 para 12 Table Pt I).
6   International Organisations Act 1968 Sch 1 para 18. See the Vienna Convention on Diplomatic
    Relations art 36 para 2; the Diplomatic Privileges Act 1964 Sch 1; and PARA 278.
        Where an order is made for the purpose of giving effect to an agreement additional
    exemptions relating to social security may be conferred on the officers and servants and
    members of their family forming part of their households: International Organisations Act 1968
    s 1(5)(a). See Sch 1 para 13; and PARA 317. For Orders in Council made under s 1 and
    conferring privileges and immunities see PARA 311.

320.   Official staffs of representatives.   Where an Order in Council has been
made, except in so far as the order otherwise provides, official staffs of
representatives[1] have the following privileges and immunities[2].

A member of the official staff[3] who is recognised as holding a rank equivalent
to that of a diplomatic agent is entitled to the same privileges and immunities as
the representative he accompanies[4].

A member of the official staff who is employed in the administrative or
technical service is entitled to certain of the same privileges and immunities[5] as
the representative he accompanies[6], but is not entitled to immunity from any civil
proceedings in respect of any cause of action arising otherwise than in the course
of his official duties[7]. He is entitled to exemptions relating to customs and excise
duties and taxes[8] as if he were the holder of a high office specified by order[9].

A member of the official staff who is employed in the domestic service is
entitled to immunity from suit and legal process in respect of things done or
omitted to be done in the course of the performance of official duties, certain
exemptions from social security contributions[10], and, to the same extent as the
representative he accompanies, exemption from taxes on his emoluments[11].

1   'Representative' means a person who is such a representative to the organisation specified in the
    relevant order, or such a representative on, or member of, an organ, committee or other
    subordinate body of that organisation as is mentioned in the International Organisations
    Act 1968 s 1(3)(a): Sch 1 para 19(a). In relation to members of the official staffs of persons who
    are representatives at international conferences, 'representative' means a person of a class
    specified by order under s 6: see s 6(3).
2   International Organisations Act 1968 ss 1(4), 6(3).
3   'Member of the official staff' means a person who accompanies a representative as part of his
    official staff in his capacity as a representative: International Organisations Act 1968 Sch 1
    para 19(b).
4   International Organisations Act 1968 Sch 1 para 20. The privileges and immunities referred to
    are those set out in Sch 1 Pt II (paras 8–13), to the extent specified by the relevant order: see
    PARA 317.
5   Ie those set out in the International Organisations Act 1968 Sch 1 paras 9, 13 to the extent
    specified by the relevant order: see PARA 317.
6   International Organisations Act 1968 Sch 1 para 21(1).
7   International Organisations Act 1968 Sch 1 para 21(2).

8   Ie the exemptions in the International Organisations Act 1968 Sch 1 para 16: see PARA 319.
9   International Organisations Act 1968 Sch 1 para 21(3).
10 Ie the exemptions in the International Organisations Act 1968 Sch 1 para 13: see PARA 317.
11 International Organisations Act 1968 Sch 1 para 22.

321.   Representatives' families.   Where an Order in Council has been made, then, except in so far as the order otherwise provides, members of the families of representatives[1] have the following privileges and immunities[2]. Persons who are members of the family of and form part of the household of a representative, a high officer specified by order and, with certain exceptions, members of the official staff employed in the administrative or technical service are entitled to the same privileges as the representative, high officer or member of the official staff[3].

Certain exemptions and privileges which may be conferred on officers or members of staff holding a rank equivalent to that of diplomatic agent may also be conferred on members of their family who form part of their household[4].

1   As to the meaning of 'representative' see PARA 320 note 1.
2   International Organisations Act 1968 s 1(4).
3   International Organisations Act 1968 s 1(4), Sch 1 para 23. As to the privileges and immunities see Sch 1 Pt I (paras 8–13); and PARA 317.
4   International Organisations Act 1968 ss 1(5)(b)(ii), 2(3). See also s 1(5)(a).

322.   Conditions of grant of immunities.   An Order in Council must be so framed as to secure:

(1)   that there are not conferred on any persons any immunities or privileges greater in extent than those which at the time of the making of the order are required to be conferred on that person in order to give effect to any agreement to which the United Kingdom or the United Kingdom government is then a party, whether made with any other sovereign power or government or with one or more organisations in that behalf[1]; and

(2)   that no immunity or privilege is in general conferred on any person as the representative of the United Kingdom or of the United Kingdom government or as a member of the staff of such a representative[2].

1   International Organisations Act 1968 s 1(6)(a) (amended by the International Organisations Act 1981 s 1(1)). Notwithstanding the International Organisations Act 1968 s 6(1)(a), where any agreement to which the United Kingdom or Her Majesty's government in the United Kingdom is a party requires the conferral of any privileges and immunities on the spouse of any individual, Her Majesty may, by Order in Council, confer the same privileges and immunities on the civil partner of that individual: s 1(7) (added by SI 2005/3542). As to the general power to make Orders in Council under the International Organisations Act 1968 s 1 see PARA 309. As to the statutory meaning of 'United Kingdom' see PARA 30 note 3.
2   International Organisations Act 1968 s 1(6)(b). However, an Order in Council may confer immunities on representatives of the United Kingdom to the Assembly of the Western European Union or to the Consultative Assembly of the Council of Europe (see PARAS 518, 534): International Organisations Act 1981 s 4.

323.   Official information as to status.   If in any proceedings a question arises whether a person is or is not entitled to any privilege or immunity, a certificate issued by or under the authority of the Secretary of State stating any fact relating to that question is conclusive evidence of that fact[1].

1   International Organisations Act 1968 s 8; and see *Zoernsch v Waldock* [1964] 2 All ER 256, [1964] 1 WLR 675, 8 BILC 837, CA. As to the Secretary of State see PARA 29.

(10) ARMED FORCES

324. Foreign armed forces. Where a state grants a right of passage through its territory to a foreign armed force, it thereby waives its jurisdiction over the force and its members and permits their conduct to be regulated by the disciplinary bodies of the force[1]. It is not clear whether, at customary international law, a foreign armed force and its members who are stationed in, as opposed to passing through, the territory of a foreign state are entitled to immunity from the jurisdiction of the state in which they are stationed, and if so, to what extent[2]. The view of the United Kingdom government is that such a force is not immune from the local jurisdiction, even when the force is stationed in the United Kingdom during hostilities against a common enemy[3]. In relation to foreign armed forces stationed in the United Kingdom, the matter is regulated to a large extent by a NATO agreement[4]. The state to which the armed force belongs is entitled to such immunity as it enjoys at common law[5].

1   *Schooner Exchange v McFaddon* 7 Cranch 116 at 140 (1812), US SC, obiter per Marshall CJ. It has been held that in such cases the state to which the force belongs is responsible for damage caused by and violations of the local law by members of the force: *Republic of Panama v Schwartzfiger* (1925) 4 Ann Dig Case no 114, Panama SC.

2   It has sometimes been supposed that the United States Supreme Court equated sojourn with passage in *Coleman v Tennessee* 97 US 509 (1878) and in *Dow v Johnson* 100 US 158 (1879). However, these cases concerned forces which were in effect forces in occupation of hostile territory. The supremacy of the law of the receiving state was affirmed by the same court in *Wilson v Girard* 354 US 524 (1957). The view that the foreign armed force enjoys absolute immunity from the local law was rejected in Canada: see *Reference Re Exemption of United States Forces from Canadian Criminal Law* [1943] 4 DLR 11. The courts of Australia have asserted that the law of the receiving state applies to visiting forces: *Wright v Cantrell* (1943) 44 SR (NSW) 45 (officer in charge of unit of United States army not entitled to immunity in respect of civil action); *Chow Hung Ching v R* (1949) 77 CLR 449, Aust HC (exclusive jurisdiction of the authorities of a visiting force limited to administrative control and discipline). Possibly all that international law requires is that internal disciplinary organisation should not be interfered with. See Barton 'Foreign Armed Forces: Immunity from Supervisory Jurisdiction' 26 BYIL 380; Barton 'Foreign Armed Forces: Immunity from Criminal Jurisdiction' 27 BYIL 186; Barton 'Foreign Armed Forces: Qualified Jurisdictional Immunity' 31 BYIL 341.

3   This was the view taken in 1942 with respect to the stationing of United States forces in the United Kingdom: see 8 Whiteman's Digest 386, 388. See also the United States of America (Visiting Forces) Act 1942. With respect to areas of territory leased to another state for the purpose of the stationing there of armed forces on permanent bases see the Agreement relating to the Bases Leased to the United States of America (London, 27 March 1941; TS 2 (1941); Cmd 6259); amended by Exchanges of Notes (Washington, 18 January and 22 February 1946; TS 63 (1946); Cmd 7000; and Washington, 19 July and 1 August 1950; TS 65 (1950); Cmd 8076); and see *Hans v R* [1955] AC 378, 7 BILC 884, PC.

4   Ie the Agreement regarding the Status of Forces of Parties to the North Atlantic Treaty (London, 19 June 1951; TS 3 (1955); Cmd 9363), known as the NATO Status of Forces Agreement: see PARA 325. But note also the agreement between the member states of the European Union concerning the status of military and civilian staff seconded to the institutions of the EU: see the EU Status of Forces Agreement (EU SOFA) (Brussels, 17 November 2003; EC 2 (2009); Cm 7572); and Satow's Diplomatic Practice (6th Edn, 2009) pp 313–314.

5   Ie to immunity in respect of governmental acts and activities only: see PARA 243. The State Immunity Act 1978 Pt I (ss 1–7: see PARA 244 et seq) does not apply to actions against foreign states in respect of their armed forces: see s 16(2); and PARA 259. Nor does the Visiting Forces Act 1952 (see PARA 325) apply: see *Littrell v United States of America* [1994] 4 All ER 203, [1995] 1 WLR 82, CA (state immune: treatment of member of its armed forces in its own military hospital is a governmental activity); *Holland v Lampen-Wolfe* [2000] 3 All ER 833, [2000] 1 WLR 1573, HL; affg [1999] 1 WLR 188, CA (state immune: provision of education for members of a state's own armed forces is a governmental activity).

325.   The NATO Status of Forces Agreement and Visiting Forces Act 1952.
The jurisdictional competence of the authorities of a visiting force (the 'sending
state') and of the state on whose territory the force is stationed (the 'receiving
state') are regulated by what is known as the NATO Status of Forces
Agreement[1]. The Visiting Forces Act 1952 was enacted in order that the United
Kingdom could become a party to the Agreement[2]. In general the military
authorities of the sending state may exercise criminal and disciplinary
jurisdiction within the receiving state over all persons subject to the military law
of the sending state and committing offences against that law[3]. This jurisdiction
is exclusive in respect of offences which are punishable only by the law of the
sending state and not by the law of the receiving state[4]. The receiving state may
punish any breach of its own law by members of the visiting force and their
dependants[5]. This jurisdiction is exclusive with respect to offences punishable
only by the law of the receiving state and not by the law of the sending state[6].
Where there exists concurrent jurisdiction in both states, the military authorities
of the sending state have the primary right to exercise jurisdiction over a member
of the force or a civilian component in relation to offences committed solely
against the property or security of that state or against the person or property of
another member of the force or civilian component or a dependant, and offences
arising out of any act or omission done in the performance of official duty[7]. The
receiving state has the primary right to exercise jurisdiction in any other case[8].
Either state may waive its jurisdiction, and the state with the primary right may
request the other state to do so[9].

1   Ie the Agreement regarding the Status of Forces of Parties to the North Atlantic Treaty (London,
    19 June 1951; TS 3 (1955); Cmd 9363) (amended by the Protocol on the Status of International
    Military Headquarters set up pursuant to the North Atlantic Treaty (Paris, 28 August 1952;
    TS 81 (1965); Cmnd 2777); and the Agreement Supplementary to the Agreement of 1951
    (Bonn, 3 August 1959; TS 74 (1963); Cmnd 2192)).
2   See the Visiting Forces Act 1952 ss 1–14; and ARMED FORCES. The Act is not confined (as is the
    Agreement) to members of the armed forces of countries which are members of the North
    Atlantic Treaty Organisation. See also the International Headquarters and Defence Organisation
    Act 1964; and PARA 326. As to the statutory meaning of 'United Kingdom' see PARA 30 note 3.
3   Agreement regarding the Status of Forces of Parties to the North Atlantic Treaty art VII
    para 1(a). See also Fleck *The Handbook of the Law of Visiting Forces* (2001) p 108.
4   Agreement regarding the Status of Forces of Parties to the North Atlantic Treaty art VII
    para 2(a).
5   Agreement regarding the Status of Forces of Parties to the North Atlantic Treaty art VII
    para 1(b).
6   Agreement regarding the Status of Forces of Parties to the North Atlantic Treaty art VII
    para 2(b).
7   Agreement regarding the Status of Forces of Parties to the North Atlantic Treaty art VII
    para 3(a). As to the meaning of 'security' see art VII para 2(c).
8   Agreement regarding the Status of Forces of Parties to the North Atlantic Treaty art VII
    para 3(b). The military authorities of the sending state may not exercise authority over nationals
    of the receiving state or persons ordinarily resident there unless they are members of the forces
    of the sending state: art VII para 4.
9   Agreement regarding the Status of Forces of Parties to the North Atlantic Treaty art VII
    para 3(c). Provision is also made for mutual assistance, and for custody and sentencing of
    offenders (art VII paras 5–7), for the avoidance of double jeopardy (art VII para 8), and for
    securing a fair trial (art VII para 9).

326.   International headquarters and defence organisations.   Where, in
pursuance of any arrangement for common defence to which the United
Kingdom[1] government is for the time being a party, any international
headquarters or defence organisation has been or is about to be set up, an Order
in Council may be made designating the headquarters or organisation and

conferring upon it the legal capacity of a body corporate and, to the extent specified, immunity from legal process and the like privileges as respects the inviolability of official archives as are accorded to an envoy of a foreign power accredited to the United Kingdom[2].

1   As to the statutory meaning of 'United Kingdom' see PARA 30 note 3.
2   International Headquarters and Defence Organisations Act 1964 s 1. See the International Headquarters and Defence Organisations (Designation and Privileges) Order 1965, SI 1965/1535 (amended by SI 1987/927; SI 1994/1642; SI 1999/1735; SI 2009/704). As to the inviolability of diplomatic archives see PARA 268. See further ARMED FORCES.

12. INTERNATIONAL RESPONSIBILITY

(1) INTRODUCTION

327. In general. The concern of the law of international responsibility is to identify and set out the conditions which must be fulfilled in order for responsibility to arise, as well as to regulate the content and implementation of that responsibility[1]. Historically, the law of international responsibility developed principally in relation to the international responsibility of states, and for this reason reference has often been made merely to the law of state responsibility. However, with the recognition of the international legal personality of other actors, in particular international organisations and that such actors may be the possessors of rights and owe obligations under international law[2], it has been recognised that there exists a wider law of international responsibility encompassing the responsibility of international organisations. However, given the relative paucity of practice in relation to the responsibility of international organisations, in many aspects the rules proposed have been developed on the basis of an analogy with the parallel rules under the law of state responsibility.

1   As to the notion of internationally wrongful acts see PARA 336 et seq; as to the content of international responsibility see PARA 373.
2   See *Reparation for Injuries Suffered in the Service of the United Nations (Advisory Opinion)* ICJ Reports 1949, 174 at 179; and *Difference Relating to Immunity from Legal Process of a Special Rapporteur of the Commission on Human Rights (Advisory Opinion)* ICJ Reports 1999, 62 at 88. See also PARA 355 et seq.

328. The work of the International Law Commission in the field of international responsibility. The modern law of international responsibility has to a very large extent been shaped by the work of the International Law Commission ('ILC')[1], in particular its long-running examination of the topic of state responsibility, as well as its work on diplomatic protection, responsibility of international organisations and liability for acts not prohibited by international law. The topic of state responsibility was included in the original plan of work for the ILC. A complete set of draft Articles was eventually adopted on first reading by the International Law Commission in 1996[2]. The process of second reading was finally completed in 2001, resulting in the adoption by the ILC of the draft Articles on the Responsibility of States for Internationally Wrongful Acts[3]. Upon consideration by the General Assembly in 2001, the draft Articles were commended to the attention of states and the General Assembly annexed them to its resolution; they thereby became the Articles on Responsibility of States for International Wrongful Acts[4]. The General Assembly deferred consideration of what further action, if any, to take in relation to the Articles, including whether to convene an international diplomatic conference to conclude a multilateral treaty based on the Articles, until 2004 when the Articles were once again commended to the attention of states and further consideration was deferred until 2007[5]. In 2007 consideration of the question was again deferred until 2010[6].

A sub-topic of the law of state responsibility, concerning the specific rules relating to the institution of diplomatic protection, has also been the subject of study by the ILC[7]. In 2006 the ILC adopted the draft Articles on Diplomatic Protection on second reading, together with accompanying Commentaries[8], and the General Assembly took note of the draft and invited governments to submit their comments[9]. In 2007 the General Assembly commended the Articles on Diplomatic Protection to the attention of governments, and it was decided that the question of what action to take, including whether to conclude a multilateral convention on the basis of the Articles on Diplomatic Protection, would be examined by a working group in 2010[10].

Following completion of its work on state responsibility, the ILC turned its attention to the topic of international responsibility of international organisations, provisionally adopting draft Articles on Responsibility of International Organization on first reading in 2009[11].

The ILC has also studied the topic of international liability for injurious consequences arising out of acts not prohibited by international law[12]. Its work has in particular focused on questions resulting from transboundary environmental harm resulting from lawful but potentially hazardous activities and it adopted draft Articles on Prevention of Transboundary Harm from Hazardous Activities, together with accompanying Commentaries in 2001[13], and draft Principles on the Allocation of Loss in the Case of Transboundary Harm Arising out of Hazardous Activities, together with accompanying Commentaries in 2006[14]. The extent to which either draft represents a codification of customary international law, rather than progressive development, is far from clear[15].

1 The International Law Commission is a subsidiary body of the General Assembly of the United Nations; it was established and its statute (since amended) was adopted by United Nations General Assembly Resolution 174 (II) of 21 November 1947. The Commission has as its object the promotion of the progressive development of international law and its codification: see the Statute of the International Law Commission art 1 para 1; and the Charter of the United Nations (San Francisco 25 June 1945; TS 67 (Cmd 7015)) art 13 para 1. For these purposes, 'progressive development' is understood as meaning the preparation of conventions on subjects which have not yet been regulated by international law or in relation to which the law has not yet been sufficiently developed in the practice of states, while 'codification' is understood to mean the more precise formulation and systematization of rules of international law in fields where there already has been extensive state practice, precedent and doctrine: see the Statute of the International Law Commission art 15; and see further arts 16–24. Despite the division between the two approaches envisaged by the Statute of the ILC, as a matter of practice, most topics examined by the Commission involve elements of codification coupled with some measure of progressive development.

2 See the Report of the International Law Commission, 48th Session, A/51/10, YILC 1996, vol II(2), pp 58–65.

3 For the Articles on Responsibility of States for Internationally Wrongful Acts ('ARSIWA') and accompanying Commentaries see the Report of the International Law Commission, 53rd Session (2001), YILC 2001, vol II(2), pp 26–30. ARSIWA and the ILC's accompanying Commentaries are also reproduced in Crawford *The International Law Commission's Articles on State Responsibility* (2002).

4 See United Nations General Assembly Resolution 56/83 of 12 December 2001.

5 See United Nations General Assembly Resolution 59/35 of 2 December 2004. For discussion of the positions taken by states during the debate in 2004, see Crawford and Olleson 'The Continuing Debate on a UN Convention on State Responsibility' (2005) 54 ICLQ 959.

6 See United Nations General Assembly Resolution 62/61, of 6 December 2007.

7 As to the law of diplomatic protection see PARA 383 et seq.

8 See the Report of the International Law Commission, 58th Session (2006), A/61/10, ch IV.

9 See United Nations General Assembly Resolution 61/35 of 4 December 2006. For government comments thereon see the Report of the Secretary-General A/62/118 (2007).

10 See United Nations General Assembly Resolution 62/67 of 6 December 2007.

11 For the draft Articles on Responsibility of International Organizations ('DARIO') and accompanying draft Commentaries see the Report of the International Law Commission, 61st Session (2009), A/64/10, ch IV. Although dealing principally with questions of the responsibility of international organisations, DARIO also deal with a number of questions relating to the responsibility of states in connection with the activities of international organisations: see draft art 1(2); and see also draft arts 57–62.

12 As to the distinction between international responsibility for internationally wrongful acts and international liability for lawful acts see PARA 334.

13 See the Report of the International Law Commission, 53rd Session (2001), YILC 2001, vol II(2), pp 146–148. For the action of the General Assembly in relation to the draft Articles on prevention see United Nations General Assembly Resolutions 56/82 of 12 December 2001, and 62/68 of 6 December 2007 by which the Articles on prevention, the text of which was annexed to the resolution, were commended to the attention of governments without prejudice as to any future action.

14 See the Report of the International Law Commission, 58th Session (2006), A/61/10, ch v For the action of the General Assembly in relation to the draft Principles on allocation of loss see United Nations General Assembly Resolution 61/36 of 4 December 2006 by which the Principles, the text of which was annexed to the resolution, were commended to the attention of governments without prejudice as to any future action. See also General Assembly Resolution 62/68 of 6 December 2007.

15 As to the distinction between codification and progressive development in the work of the ILC see note 1.

329. Objective responsibility and responsibility as the corollary of an internationally wrongful act. The commission of an internationally wrongful act engages the responsibility under international law of the state or international organisation responsible for the act or omission and entails secondary obligations, including in particular the obligation to make reparation for any damage caused[1]. In this sense, international responsibility is objective, in that the various secondary obligations which form the content of international responsibility come into being merely upon the occurrence of an internationally wrongful act[2]. Although traditionally international responsibility was seen as the corollary of the breach of a right, resulting primarily in the obligation of the responsible state to make reparation to the state whose right was infringed[3], the evolution of international law, in particular the growth of multilateral treaty obligations and the recognition of obligations giving effect to community interests (including the category of peremptory norms, and the parallel notion of obligations erga omnes) has resulted in a profound modification of this traditional position[4]. It appears that states may be entitled to invoke the secondary obligations constituting the objective international responsibility of the responsible state resulting from the breach of certain obligations even if they are not directly affected by the breach of the obligation in question[5]. Accordingly, it is probably now more correct to state that international responsibility is the corollary of an internationally wrongful act, that is to say, the breach of an international obligation, rather than that of the breach of a right.

1 As to internationally wrongful acts see PARA 336 et seq; and as to the obligation to make reparation see PARA 374.

2 As to the content of international responsibility and secondary obligations see PARA 373 et seq.

3 See eg *British Claims in the Spanish Zone of Morocco* 2 RIAA 615 at 641 (1925); *Factory at Chorzów (Jurisdiction)* PCIJ Ser A No 9 at 21 (1927); *Factory at Chorzów* PCIJ Ser A No 17 at 29 (1928); *Reparation for Injuries Suffered in the Service of the United Nations (Advisory Opinion)* ICJ Reports 1949, 174 at 184; *Corfu Channel (United Kingdom v Albania)* ICJ Reports 1949, 4 at 23.

4 As to peremptory norms and obligations erga omnes see PARA 11.

5 Ie the invocation by a state or international organisation of the responsibility of a responsible state or international organisation where either the obligation in question is owed to a group of states or international organisations and is established for the protection of a collective interest of the group, or the obligation in question is owed to the international community as a whole (ie it is an obligation erga omnes): see the Articles on Responsibility of States for Internationally Wrongful Acts ('ARSIWA') art 48, Report of the International Law Commission, 53rd Session (2001), YILC 2001, vol II(2); and the draft Articles on Responsibility of International Organizations ('DARIO') draft art 48, Report of the International Law Commission, 61st

Session (2009), A/64/10, ch IV. The International Law Commission in adopting ARSIWA art 48 expressly disavowed the restrictive approach taken by the International Court of Justice in relation to standing in *South West Africa Cases (Ethiopia v South Africa; Liberia v South Africa) (Second Phase)* ICJ Reports 1966, 6: see ARSIWA, Commentary to Article 48, para (7).

330. Distinction between primary and secondary rules. In discussing the law of international responsibility, a distinction is often drawn between the primary rules of international law, which lay down the substantive obligations of states or other international actors, and the secondary rules which make up the law of international responsibility[1]. The law of international responsibility consists of the secondary rules which govern: (1) the circumstances in which conduct is to be regarded as attributable to a state or international organisation so as to be capable of giving rise to its international responsibility[2]; (2) when an international obligation has been breached by a state or international organisation, including questions of the extension in time of an internationally wrongful act[3]; (3) the circumstances which may be relied upon by way of defence or justification in relation to conduct for which a state or international organisation would otherwise incur international responsibility[4]; (4) the legal consequences which constitute international responsibility and which arise as a result of an internationally wrongful act[5]; and (5) the procedural or substantive preconditions for a state or international organisation to invoke the international responsibility of another state or international organisation for its internationally wrongful acts, as well as the circumstances in which the right to invoke responsibility may be lost[6].

1 The validity of the distinction between primary and secondary rules underlies the entire approach of the International Law Commission's Articles on Responsibility of States for Internationally Wrongful Acts ('ARSIWA'): see eg Commentary to Article 1, paras (1)–(3), Report of the International Law Commission, 53rd Session (2001), YILC 2001, vol II(2).

2 As to attribution see PARA 337 et seq.

3 As to breach of an international obligation for the purposes of international responsibility see PARA 359 et seq.

4 As to circumstances precluding wrongfulness see PARA 362 et seq.

5 As to the content of international responsibility see PARA 373 et seq.

6 As to invocation of responsibility by a state or international organisation which is injured by the internationally wrongful act see ARSIWA art 42; and the draft Articles on Responsibility of International Organizations ('DARIO') draft art 42, Report of the International Law Commission, 61st Session (2009), A/64/10, ch IV. As to the conditions in which responsibility may be invoked by a state other than an injured state, or an international organisation other than an injured international organisation, see PARA 329 note 5. In invoking responsibility, a state or international organisation is required to give notice of its claim to the state or international organisation responsible; the notice of claim may specify both the conduct necessary to cease the internationally wrongful act, if it is continuing, as well as the form which the reparation claimed should take: see ARSIWA art 43; and DARIO draft art 43. Responsibility may not be invoked to the extent to which any claim is not brought in accordance with any applicable rule relating to nationality of claims, nor to the extent that any rule requiring exhaustion of local remedies is applicable and has not been complied with: see ARSIWA art 44; and DARIO draft art 44. As to the rules relating to nationality of claims for the purposes of claims brought by way of diplomatic protection see PARA 391 et seq; as to the requirement of exhaustion of local remedies in the context of diplomatic protection see PARA 405 et seq. The right to invoke responsibility may be lost either because it has been validly waived by the injured state or international organisation, or because the injured state or international organisation, is, by reason of its conduct, to be held to have validly acquiesced in the lapse of the claim: see ARSIWA art 45; and DARIO draft art 45; and see also *Russian Indemnity Case* 11 RIAA 421 (1912); *Certain Phosphate Lands in Nauru (Nauru v Australia) (Preliminary Objections)* ICJ Reports 1992, 240; *Avena and Other Mexican Nationals (Mexico v United States of America)* ICJ Reports 2004, 12 at 37–38 (paras 43–44); and *Armed Activities on the Territory of the Congo (Democratic Republic of the Congo v Uganda)* ICJ Reports, 19 December 2005 (paras 292–295).

331.   The absence of any general requirement of fault or of damage.   As a matter of the general law of international responsibility, the existence of an international wrongful act is ascertained objectively and there is no general requirement of fault, in the sense of either negligence or an intention to harm on the part of the state or its agent[1]. Nevertheless, by way of exception to that general principle and in application of the principle of lex specialis[2], a particular primary rule of international law may require improper motives or a particular mental state in order for the act of which complaint is made in order to breach the obligation in question[3]. Similarly, proof that individuals whose conduct is attributable to the state and who are alleged to have committed the acts in question held the necessary specific intent to destroy, in whole or in part, a national, ethnical, racial or religious group as such is required before the state itself will incur responsibility for genocide[4].

Although in the past it was suggested that in order for international responsibility to arise it was necessary that an internationally wrongful act should cause some injury or damage, as a consequence of the consolidation of the objective nature of international responsibility it is now settled that there is no such general requirement[5]. Nevertheless, through application of the lex specialis principle and by way of derogation from the general secondary rules, a particular primary rule may require the occurrence of some injury or damage either to a state or to one of its nationals before there is a breach of the obligation in question[6].

1   See eg *Neer Case* 4 RIAA 60 at 61, 62 (1926); *Roberts Case* 4 RIAA 77 at 80 (1926); *Caire* 5 RIAA 516 (1929). In determining whether international responsibility has been incurred, international tribunals have not in general inquired into the state of mind of the individual agent who caused the harm complained of, and states have been held liable for damage suffered as a result of errors of judgment in good faith on the part of states' agents: see PARA 337 et seq. In certain cases states have been held liable for omissions to prevent the occurrence of certain events which caused damage to another state by reason of a lack of due diligence on the part of the state caused by negligence of its agents, but such negligence is not a necessary condition of liability in such cases; this may occur because of a failure in the structure of the administration of the state or the insufficiency of the legal powers of the government of the state under its domestic law, which disables it from acting with the due diligence required of international law: see the *Alabama Arbitration* (1871) 61 BFSP 40. In *Corfu Channel (United Kingdom v Albania)* ICJ Reports 1949, 4 the International Court did not hold Albania liable to the United Kingdom for damage to British warships on the basis of any principle of fault or risk or absolute liability, but because Albania, which must have had knowledge of the existence of mines in its territorial sea, was in breach of its international obligations in not warning third states of the danger.

2   As to the lex specialis principle see PARA 332.

3   This is required, for example, in certain cases of denial of justice: see PARA 464.

4   See the Convention on the Prevention and Punishment of the Crime of Genocide (Paris, 9 December 1948; TS58 (1970); Cmnd 4421) art II; and PARA 429. See also *Application of the Convention on the Prevention and Punishment of the Crime of Genocide (Bosnia and Herzegovina v Serbia and Montenegro)* ICJ Reports, 26 February 2007.

5   As to the objective nature of international responsibility see note 1.

6   As to the lex specialis principle see PARA 332.

332.   The lex specialis principle.   The customary rules of international responsibility are residual, default rules which apply in relation to the ascertainment of the existence of an internationally wrongful act as well as its consequences[1]. To the extent that the relevant primary rule in question provides by way of lex specialis for different rules as to what acts are attributable to an international actor, when an internationally wrongful act has taken place, or the consequences of international responsibility consequent upon an internationally wrongful act, any such rules will apply to the exclusion of the customary rules of international responsibility[2].

1   See generally PARA 327 et seq.
2   See the Articles on Responsibility of States for Internationally Wrongful Acts ('ARSIWA') art 55, Report of the International Law Commission, 53rd Session (2001), YILC 2001, vol II(2); and the draft Articles on Responsibility of International Organizations ('DARIO') draft art 63, Report of the International Law Commission, 61st Session (2009), A/64/10, ch IV. See also the *Application of the Convention on the Prevention and Punishment of the Crime of Genocide (Bosnia and Herzegovina v Serbia and Montenegro)* ICJ Reports, 26 February 2007 (para 401) (where the International Court of Justice rejected an argument that, due to the particular nature of the crime of genocide, the applicable rules of attribution were different from those under the general customary international law of state responsibility, and observed that 'the rules for attributing alleged internationally wrongful conduct to a state do not vary with the nature of the wrongful act in question in the absence of a clearly expressed lex specialis').

333.   Relationship between the international law of responsibility and municipal law.   The responsibility of a state in international law must be distinguished from any responsibility which it may bear as a matter of its own municipal law. From the viewpoint of international law, the content of municipal law is generally treated as a question of fact[1]. A number of consequences follow from that principle which are relevant for the purposes of the law of international responsibility: whether or not any particular conduct is internationally wrongful is governed by international law[2], and accordingly a state cannot attempt to avoid international responsibility by invoking the provisions of its own municipal law, in particular by relying on the fact that an act was lawful (or unlawful) as a matter of municipal law[3]. Nor can it avoid responsibility by relying on the absence of rules in its municipal law, the existence of which might have led to the injury being avoided[4], nor can it rely on the federal nature of its internal structure so as to justify non-compliance with its obligations[5]. That principle applies not only as regards compliance with the substantive obligations under the primary rules of international law, but also in relation to compliance with the secondary obligations of reparation and cessation arising as a matter of the international law of responsibility[6]. A state cannot seek to contest the entry into force of international obligations by reference to municipal law constraints which it failed to observe[7]. Further, a state cannot subsequently seek to overturn a finding of international responsibility by obtaining a judgment in its national courts which changes the basis on which that international finding of responsibility was made[8]. Nor can a state rely on its own error in the characterisation of an administrative act as a matter of domestic law in order to argue that domestic remedies were in fact available to an individual and should have been exhausted[9]. By contrast, if a particular person or entity is regarded as an organ of the state as a matter of domestic law, the state cannot argue to the contrary for the purposes of denying that the conduct of the organ is attributable to it for the purposes of determining whether it has committed an internationally wrongful act[10]. A breach of municipal law, or of a contract governed by domestic law, does not ipso facto result in a breach of international law, although in certain circumstances this may be the case[11].

1   See *Certain German Interests in Polish Upper Silesia* PCIJ Ser A No 7 at 19 (1926).
2   See the Articles on Responsibility of States for Internationally Wrongful Acts ('ARSIWA') art 3, Report of the International Law Commission, 53rd Session (2001), YILC 2001, vol II(2). The International Law Commission has taken the view that it is not necessary to reiterate the principle in the context of the responsibility of international organisations: see the draft Articles

on Responsibility of International Organizations ('DARIO') draft Commentary to draft article 4, paragraph (4), Report of the International Law Commission, 61st Session (2009), A/64/10, ch IV.

3 This principle was recognised by the Permanent Court of International Justice in the *SS 'Wimbledon'* PCIJ Ser A No 1 at 29, 30 (1923); *Greco-Bulgarian Communities* PCIJ Ser B No 17 at 32 (1930); *Free Zones of Upper Savoy and District of Gex Case* PCIJ Ser A No 24 at 12 (1930); and PCIJ Ser A/B No 46 at 96 (1932); and *Treatment of Polish Nationals and Other Persons of Polish Origin or Speech in the Danzig Territory* PCIJ Ser A/B No 44 at 24 (1932). See also *Acquisition of Polish Nationality* PCIJ Ser B No 7 at 26 (1923). For recognition of the principle by the International Court of Justice, see e g *Reparation for Injuries Suffered in the Service of the United Nations (Advisory Opinion)* ICJ Reports 1949, 174 at 180. Cf the specific parallel rule in the law of treaties prohibiting reliance on domestic law to justify non-performance of obligations arising under a treaty: see the Vienna Convention on the Law of Treaties (Vienna, 23 May 1969; TS 58 (1980); Cmnd 7964) art 27; and para 91.

4 *Jurisdiction of the Courts of Danzig* PCIJ Ser B No 15 at 26–27 (1928); *Exchange of Greek and Turkish Populations* PCIJ Ser B No 10 at 19–22 (1925). In other cases the principle has been implicitly recognised and has been stated by judges in separate and dissenting judgments: see e g the *Application of the Convention of 1902 Governing the Guardianship of Infants (Netherlands v Sweden)* ICJ Reports 1958, 55 at 67, 74, 83, 125, 126, 128, 129, 137, 138, 140. Arbitral decisions make the same point, especially the *Alabama Arbitration* (1871) 61 BFSP 40; and see also *Norwegian Shipowners Case* 1 RIAA 307 (1922); *Tinoco Arbitration* 1 RIAA 369 at 386 (1923); *Pinson* 5 RIAA 327 at 393 (1928); *Shufeldt* 2 RIAA 1079 (1930).

5 The *'Montijo'* (1875) Moore Int Arb 1421; *Pellat* 5 RIAA 534 at 536 (1929). See also *Garrido and Baigorria v Argentina (Reparations and Costs)* (1998) Inter-Am Ct HR (Ser C) No 39 para 38; *The Right to Information on Consular Assistance in the Framework of the Guarantees of the Due Process of Law (Advisory Opinion OC-16/99)* (1999) Inter-Am Ct HR (Ser A) No 16.

6 See ARSIWA art 32; and the cases cited in note 5. Cf the parallel rule relating to international organisations pursuant to which an international organisation cannot rely on its own internal rules as justification for a failure to comply with the secondary obligations under the law of international responsibility: see DARIO draft art 31.

7 See *Free Zones of Upper Savoy and the District of Gex Case* PCIJ Ser A/B No 46 at 96, 167, 170 (1932); *Legal Status of Eastern Greenland* PCIJ Ser A/B No 53 at 22, 91–92 (1933). In relation to the law of treaties, see Vienna Convention on the Law of Treaties (Vienna, 23 May 1969; TS 58 (1980); Cmnd 7964) arts 27, 46; and paras 91, 101.

8 *Factory at Chorzów* PCIJ Ser A No 17, at 33 (1928).

9 *Ahmadou Sadio Diallo (Republic of Guinea v Democratic Republic of the Congo) (Preliminary Objections)* ICJ Reports, 24 May 2007 (para 46). As to the requirement of exhaustion of domestic remedies as a precondition to the presentation of a claim by way of diplomatic protection see PARA 405 et seq.

10 See e g ARSIWA art 4(2), and Commentary to Article 4, para (11). See also the *Application of the Convention on the Prevention and Punishment of the Crime of Genocide (Bosnia and Herzegovina v Serbia and Montenegro)* ICJ Reports, 26 February 2007 (para 386).

11 *Elettronica Sicula SpA (ELSI) (United States of America v Italy)* ICJ Reports 1989, 15 at 74 (para 124); *Compañía de Aguas del Aconquija SA and Vivendi Universal v Argentine Republic* ICSID Case No ARB/97/3, Decision on Annulment of 3 July 2002, at paras 95–97 (referring to ARSIWA art 3, and Commentary to Article 3, paras (4) and (7)). See also UN Human Rights Committee's General Comment No 31: Nature of the General Legal Obligation Imposed on States Parties to the Covenant, para 4 (CCPR/C/21/Rev 1/Add 13), 26 May 2004. As to so-called 'umbrella' clauses in investment protection treaties see e g *SGS Société Générale de Surveillance SA v Islamic Republic of Pakistan* ICSID Case No ARB/01/13, Decision on Objections to Jurisdiction of 6 August 2003; *SGS Société Générale de Surveillance SA v Republic of the Philippines* ICSID Case No ARB/02/6, Decision on Objections to Jurisdiction of 29 January 2004; and *Noble Ventures, Inc v Romania* ICSID Case No ARB/01/11, Award of 12 October 2005.

334. International responsibility and international liability for lawful acts.

International responsibility arises upon the commission of an internationally wrongful act; responsibility is thus the corollary of the breach of an international obligation[1]. As such international responsibility is to be distinguished from what has come to be referred to as liability for acts not prohibited by international law[2]. The precise scope of the latter category is not entirely clear; a number of the leading cases often relied upon to justify the existence of liability as a separate category may be analysed as in fact concerning breach of an international obligation (and thus concerning questions of international responsibility properly so-called), or as concerning the quantification of damage where liability was not in fact disputed[3].

1 See PARA 329.

2 For discussion of the International Law Commission's work on the topic of international liability for injurious consequences arising out of acts not prohibited by international law see PARA 328. In general on the distinction between state responsibility and liability, see further Boyle 'State Responsibility and International Liability for Injurious Consequences of Acts Not Prohibited by International Law: A Necessary Distinction?' (1990) 39 ICLQ 1.

3 See eg *Corfu Channel (United Kingdom v Albania)* ICJ Reports 1949, 4; *Trail Smelter* 3 RIAA 1905 (1935/1941). In addition, reference has been made to the provisions of international conventions which provide for strict liability for damage caused as the result of activities in particular spheres: see eg the Convention on International Liability for Damage caused by Space Objects (London, Moscow and Washington, 29 March 1972; TS 16 (1974); Cmnd 5551); and PARA 207 (although the duty imposed upon individuals under the Convention is not so strict). Under the provisions of several conventions strict liability is to be imposed, not upon the states parties themselves, but by those states upon persons within their jurisdictions and subject to their domestic laws: see eg the Convention on Third Party Liability in the Field of Nuclear Energy (Paris, 29 July 1960; TS 69 (1968); Cmnd 3755). See also the Nuclear Installations Act 1965; and FUEL AND ENERGY vol 19(3) (2007 Reissue) PARA 1487 et seq. There is also a Vienna Convention on Civil Liability for Nuclear Damage (Vienna, 21 May 1963), which the United Kingdom has signed but not ratified: see FUEL AND ENERGY vol 19(3) (2007 Reissue) PARA 1487; however, the United Kingdom has enacted legislation giving effect to the Convention: see FUEL AND ENERGY vol 19(3) (2007 Reissue) PARA 1347. As to the imposition of strict liability upon individuals see also the International Convention on Civil Liability for Oil Pollution Damage (Brussels, 29 November 1970); the Merchant Shipping Act 1995; and SHIPPING AND NAVIGATION vol 43(2) (Reissue) PARA 1135 et seq. The United Kingdom is not a party to the Convention on the Liability of Operators of Nuclear Ships (Brussels, 25 May 1962; 57 American Journal of International Law 268) (not in force) which provides for liability of the operators of nuclear ships in case of accidents, whether the operator is a private entity or the state itself.

335. **Doctrine of abuse of rights.** According to the doctrine of abuse of rights, a state may incur responsibility under international law for an improperly motivated exercise of a right whose exercise would otherwise be lawful. However, the existence, scope and conditions for application of the principle are not clearly established[1].

1 Reference has been made to the principle in cases where it was argued that a right had been exercised in order to cause damage without there being any advantage to the state entitled to exercise the right: *Certain German Interests in Polish Upper Silesia* PCIJ Ser A No 7 at 30 (1926); *Free Zones of Upper Savoy and District of Gex Case* PCIJ Ser A No 24 at 12 (1930); PCIJ Ser A/B No 46 at 96, 167 (1932). In each of those decisions, although implicitly recognising the existence of the principle, the Permanent Court held that an abuse of rights could not be presumed and had not been shown to exist on the facts of the case. The decision most frequently cited in this connection is arguably irrelevant, since it was based upon the absence of any right to carry out the activity in question and the injury was in any event held to be unlawful: see *Trail Smelter* 3 RIAA 1907 at 1965 (1935) (no state has the right to use or permit the use of its territory in such a manner as to cause injury by fumes in or to the territory of another).

(2) THE INTERNATIONALLY WRONGFUL ACT AS THE SOURCE OF INTERNATIONAL RESPONSIBILITY

(i) Introduction

336. Elements of an internationally wrongful act. The modern law of international responsibility, both of states and of international organisations, is based upon the concept of the 'internationally wrongful act'[1]. An internationally wrongful act consists of conduct which is both attributable to a state or international organisation and which is inconsistent with what is required of that state or international organisation by one or more of the international obligations binding upon it[2]. The bases on which conduct may be attributed to a state or to an international organisation are different, reflecting their different structural and functional characteristics[3]. The conduct constituting an internationally wrongful act may consist of either action or omission[4].

In addition to the two positive conditions, namely that there should be conduct which is attributable and that that conduct should be in breach of an international obligation, it is also necessary that there should not exist any circumstance which precludes the wrongfulness of the conduct in question[5]. Further in certain specific circumstances, a state or international organisation may engage its international responsibility as the result of its involvement or complicity in the internationally wrongful act of another state or international organisation[6].

1   As to international responsibility as the corollary of an internationally wrongful act see PARA 329.
2   See the Articles on Responsibility of States for Internationally Wrongful Acts ('ARSIWA') art 2, Report of the International Law Commission, 53rd Session (2001), YILC 2001, vol II(2); and the draft Articles on Responsibility of International Organizations ('DARIO') draft art 4, Report of the International Law Commission, 61st Session (2009), A/64/10, ch IV. For statements by the International Court of Justice in this sense see *United States Diplomatic and Consular Staff in Teheran (United States of America v Iran)* ICJ Reports 1980, 3 at 29 (para 56); *Application of the Convention on the Prevention and Punishment of the Crime of Genocide (Bosnia and Herzegovina v Serbia and Montenegro)* ICJ Reports, 26 February 2007 (paras 385–386).
    As to the requirement of attributability of conduct see ARSIWA art 2(a); and see generally Commentary to Article 2, paras (5)–(6), and Introductory Commentary to Part One, Chapter II. See also the *Application of the Convention on the Prevention and Punishment of the Crime of Genocide (Bosnia and Herzegovina v Serbia and Montenegro)* ICJ Reports, 26 February 2007 (paras 379, 385) and PARA 337 et seq. For the equivalent position in relation to international organisations see DARIO art 4(a); and PARA 355 et seq. As to the requirement of breach of an international obligation see ARSIWA art 2(b); and see generally Commentary to Article 2, paras (7)–(8). For the equivalent position in relation to international organisations see DARIO art 4(b). See further PARA 359 et seq.
3   As to attribution of conduct to states see PARA 337 et seq; as to attribution of conduct to international organisations see PARA 355 et seq.
4   See ARSIWA art 2; Commentary to Article 2, para (4); and DARIO draft art 4.
5   See PARA 362 et seq.
6   See PARA 369 et seq.

(ii) Attribution of Conduct

A. ATTRIBUTION OF CONDUCT TO STATES

337. In general. The bases on which conduct may be attributed to a state for the purposes of state responsibility are relatively settled. The rules relating to attribution as codified in the International Law Commission's Articles on

Responsibility of States for Internationally Wrongful Acts[1] apply solely for the purposes of determining whether a state has committed an internationally wrongful act[2], and are not as such applicable for the purpose of determining whether conduct is attributable to the state for any other purpose[3]. International law provides for particular rules governing attribution in other specific circumstances, for instance those governing which organs of a state are able to bind it in undertaking international treaty obligations[4]. Nevertheless, the rules of attribution which apply in order to determine whether conduct is attributable to the state for the purposes of the law of state responsibility may be of assistance in ascertaining which organs, entities and individuals enjoy sovereign immunity before the courts[5].

It is generally accepted that for the purposes of state responsibility, conduct may be attributed to a state on the following bases:

(1) where it is conduct of an organ of the state, whether de jure or de facto[6];

(2) where it is conduct of persons or entities who are not formally organs of the state, but which nevertheless exercise elements of its governmental authority[7];

(3) where it is conduct of an organ of another state which has been placed at the disposal of the state[8];

(4) where it is conduct of persons or entities acting on the instructions or under the direction or control of the state[9];

(5) exceptionally where it is conduct of an insurgent or other movement which succeeds in becoming the government of a state, or succeeds in establishing a new state on the territory of a pre-existing state[10];

(6) where it is conduct of persons or groups who are exercising elements of governmental authority in the absence or default of the official authorities[11]; and

(7) where the state acknowledges or adopts the particular conduct as its own[12].

Apart from the specific recognised bases of attribution, in general a state will not incur responsibility for the conduct of private individuals. However, it may nevertheless incur responsibility for its own failures or omissions in preventing or failing to punish the actions of such private individuals[13].

---

1 See the Articles on Responsibility of States for Internationally Wrongful Acts ('ARSIWA'), Report of the International Law Commission, 53rd Session (2001), YILC 2001, vol II(2)(5).

2 See PARA 336.

3 Although the rules of attribution for such other purposes may have the same or very similar content: see eg *Request for Interpretation of the Judgment of 31 March 2004 in the Case concerning Avena and Other Mexican Nationals (Mexico v United States of America) (Mexico v United States of America) (Provisional Measures)* ICJ Reports, 16 July 2008 (paras 55–56); and see the Joint Dissenting Opinion of Judges Owada, Tomka and Keith (paras 15–17); the Dissenting Opinion of Judge Buergenthal (paras 13, 23); and the Dissenting Opinion of Judge Skotnikov (paras 2–5).

4 See the Vienna Convention on the Law of Treaties (Vienna, 23 May 1969; TS 58 (1980); Cmnd 7964) arts 7, 8, 46 and 47; and PARAS 73–74, 101.

5 See *Jones v Ministry of Interior of Saudi Arabia; Mitchell v Al-Dali* [2006] UKHL 26, [2007] 1 AC 270, at [10]–[13] per Lord Bingham, and at [74]–[78] per Lord Hoffman (referring to ARSIWA arts 4, 7, 8, and passages from the accompanying Commentaries).

6 See PARAS 338–344.

7 See PARA 345.

8 See PARA 347.

9 See PARA 348.

10 See PARA 349.

11 See PARA 350.
12 See PARA 351.
13 See PARAS 352–354.

338. Acts of organs: general considerations. The primary basis of attribution for the purposes of the law of state responsibility is that the conduct of any organ of the state is considered to be an act of the state and thus to be attributable to it under international law[1]. For these purposes, the notion of 'organ' covers all of the individual or collective entities which go to make up the organisation of the state and act on its behalf[2]. It is irrelevant whether the organ in question exercises legislative, executive, judicial or other functions[3]. Further, the position the organ in question holds within the organisation of the state, whether of the central government or a territorial governmental entity is irrelevant[4]. Conduct of an organ is attributable whether or not the conduct in question was ultra vires or otherwise illegal under the domestic law of the state in question[5].

1 See the Articles on Responsibility of States for Internationally Wrongful Acts ('ARSIWA') art 4(1), Report of the International Law Commission, 53rd Session (2001), YILC 2001, vol II(2). Article 4 has been endorsed by the International Court of Justice as reflecting customary international law: see *Armed Activities on the Territory of the Congo (Democratic Republic of the Congo v Uganda)* ICJ Reports, 19 December 2005 (para 160); and *Application of the Convention on the Prevention and Punishment of the Crime of Genocide (Bosnia and Herzegovina v Serbia and Montenegro)* ICJ Reports, 26 February 2007 (para 385). For endorsement of an earlier version of the provision which became ARSIWA, art 4 see *Difference Relating to Immunity from Legal Process of a Special Rapporteur of the Commission on Human Rights (Advisory Opinion)* ICJ Reports 1999, 62, at 87 (para 62). See also *LaGrand (Germany v United States of America) (Provisional Measures)* ICJ Reports 1999, 9 at 16 (para 28).
2 *Application of the Convention on the Prevention and Punishment of the Crime of Genocide (Bosnia and Herzegovina v Serbia and Montenegro)* ICJ Reports, 26 February 2007 (para 388). An organ also includes any person or entity which has that status in accordance with the internal law of the state: ARSIWA art 4(2).
3 See ARSIWA art 4(1).
4 See ARSIWA art 4(1).
5 See PARA 339.

339. Acts of organs: municipal and federal entities. A state incurs responsibility for the acts and omissions of its municipal and regional officials, courts and legislatures, whatever position the organ holds in the organisation of the state and whatever its character as an organ of the central government or of a territorial unit of the state[1]. A state having a federal structure incurs responsibility for the acts and omissions of its component entities if the federal state has the sole authority to represent the state internationally[2].

1 *Pieri Dominique & Co* 10 RIAA 139 at 156 (1905); *Heirs of the Duc de Guise* 13 RIAA 150 at 161 (1951–53).
2 See eg *LaGrand (Germany v United States of America) (Provisional Measures)* ICJ Reports 1999, 9 at 16 (para 28). For older cases, see eg *Montijo* (1875) Moore Int Arb 1421; *De Brissot and Others* (1885) Moore Int Arb, 2967, at 2970–2971; *The 'William Yeaton'* (1885) Moore Int Arb 2944 at 2967; *Davy* 9 RIAA 467 (1903); *Pieri Dominique & Co* 10 RIAA 139 at 156 (1905); *Janes Case* 4 RIAA 82 at 86 (1926); *Swinney Case* 4 RIAA 98 (1926); *Quintanilla* 4 RIAA 101 (1926); *Youmans Case* 4 RIAA 110 (1926); *Mallén Case* 4 RIAA 173 (1927); *Venable* 4 RIAA 219 at 230 (1927); *Tribolet Case* 4 RIAA 598 (1930); *Pellat* 5 RIAA 534 (1929); see also the case of lynching of Italian nationals at issue in *Italians at New Orleans* (1891) 6 Moore's Digest 837. The rule is based upon the principle that a state cannot rely upon its own municipal law, including constitutional law, in order to avoid its international responsibility: see PARA 333. Since 1875 the only cases in which it has been denied appear to be *Tunstall*, Foreign Relations of the United States 1885, 450, and *The 'William Yeaton'*.

In *Avena and Other Mexican Nationals (Mexico v United States of America)* ICJ Reports 2004, 12 the United States did not contest that it was responsible for the acts of the relevant law enforcement authorities and agencies of the federal sub-units in question. In *Request for Interpretation of the Judgment of 31 March 2004 in the Case concerning Avena and Other Mexican Nationals (Mexico v United States of America) (Mexico v United States of America) (Provisional Measures)* ICJ Reports, 16 July 2008 (para 77), the Court noted the express recognition by the United States that it was responsible under international law for the actions of its political subdivisions, including federal, state and local officials.

In addition, a state may also be responsible for events which take place in a dependent state which it represents internationally, although such relationships are now relatively rare: see eg *British Claims in the Spanish Zone of Morocco* 2 RIAA 615 (1925) (protected state); *Mavrommatis Palestine Concessions* PCIJ Ser A No 2 (1924) (mandated territory); *Studer* 6 RIAA 149 (1925) (protectorate).

340. Acts of organs: the executive. In accordance with the general principle of attribution of the acts of organs, a state may incur international responsibility for acts of the executive and executive officers[1]. For this purpose no distinction is drawn between the acts of superior and inferior state authorities and officials[2]. Thus, the conduct of a very wide range of officials has been held to be attributable and as capable of giving rise to the responsibility of states: this is the case for example of conduct of various types of law enforcement officials[3], members of the armed forces[4], a railway superintendent[5], a receiver or administrator of property[6] and a mayor[7]. In the case of individuals who constitute organs of the state, conduct is only attributable when the individual is in fact acting in that capacity[8].

1 See generally *El Triunfo* 15 RIAA 455 at 477 (1902).

2 See the Articles on Responsibility of States for Internationally Wrongful Acts ('ARSIWA') art 4(1), and Commentary to Article 4, para (7), Report of the International Law Commission, 53rd Session (2001), YILC 2001, vol II(2). Historically, a distinction was drawn by some writers between superior and inferior authorities, on the basis that responsibility could be incurred only by acts of superior officials; in relation to the acts of inferior officials, the state would only be responsible for a failure to punish the officer: see Harvard Research Draft Convention, art 7 (23 American Journal of International Law Supp 133 at 165–167); Borchard, *Diplomatic Protection of Citizens Abroad*, at 189, 190. In most of the cases referred to in support of this view the claim failed because the alien had not exhausted local remedies: see eg *Bensley* (1850) Moore Int Arb 3016; *Slocum* (1876) Moore Int Arb 3140; *Leichardt* (1868) Moore Int Arb 3133. The approach was expressly rejected in *Moses* (1871) Moore Int Arb 3127 at 3129; *Roper Case* 4 RIAA 145 (1927); *Massey Case* 4 RIAA 155 (1927); *Way* 4 RIAA 391 at 400 (1928); *Baldwin* 6 RIAA 328 (1933); *Currie* 14 RIAA 21 at 24 (1954); *Dispute concerning the interpretation of Article 79 of the Italian Peace Treaty* 13 RIAA 389 at 431–432 (1955); and *Mossé* 13 RIAA 486 at 492–493 (1953). As to the irrelevance of the position of the official or authority in the organisation of the state see PARA 339.

3 Eg police officers (*Maal Case* 10 RIAA 730 (1903); see also *Roper Case* 4 RIAA 145 (1927); *Brown, Sanders and Small* 4 RIAA 149 (1927); *Mallén Case* 4 RIAA 173 (1927); *Way* 4 RIAA 391 (1928); *Pugh* 3 RIAA 1439 (1933); *Richeson* 6 RIAA 325 (1933); *Mossé* 13 RIAA 486 at 492 (1953); *Menghi* 13 RIAA 801 (1958)); a deputy sheriff (*Quintanilla* 4 RIAA 101 (1926)); a jailhouse keeper (*Massey Case* 4 RIAA 155 (1927)); and customs officers (*Compagnie Générale des Asphaltes de France* 9 RIAA 389 (1903); *Pieri Dominique & Co* 10 RIAA 139 (1905); *Coquitlam* 6 RIAA 45 (1920); *The Jessie, The Thomas F Bayard and The Pescawha* 6 RIAA 57 (1921); *The 'Wanderer'* 6 RIAA 68 (1921); *The 'Kate'* 6 RIAA 77 (1921); *The 'Favourite'* 6 RIAA 82 (1921); *Union Bridge Co* 6 RIAA 138 (1924); *Koch* 4 RIAA 408 (1928)).

4 See *Jeannotat* (1875) Moore Int Arb 3673; *British Claims in the Spanish Zone of Morocco* 2 RIAA 615 (1925); *Swinney Case* 4 RIAA 98 (1926); *Falcón* 4 RIAA 104 (1926); *Youmans Case* 4 RIAA 110 (1926); *Connelly* 4 RIAA 117 (1926); *García and Garza Case* 4 RIAA 119 (1926); *Munroe* 4 RIAA 538 (1929); *Caire* 5 RIAA 516 at 516 (1929); *Ruiz* 6 RIAA 345 (1933); *Díaz* 6 RIAA 341 (1933). See also *Chevreau* 2 RIAA 1113 (1931); *Responsibility of Germany for Damage Caused to Portuguese Colonies ('Naulilaa')* 2 RIAA 1011 (1928); *Eis* 30 ILR 116 (1959); *The 'Rainbow Warrior' (ruling of the Secretary-General)* 19 RIAA 199 (1986), 26 ILM 1346; *Rainbow Warrior (New Zealand/France)* 20 RIAA 215 (1990). The conduct of auxiliaries

is also attributable: *Stephens Case* 4 RIAA 265 (1927); and *The 'Zafiro'* 6 RIAA 160 (1925). As to acts of soldiers unaccompanied by an officer see *Solis* 4 RIAA 358 at 362–363 (1928); *Kling* 4 RIAA 575 at 578–581 (1930). As a matter of customary international law, a state party to an armed conflict is responsible for all actions of the members of its armed forces during that conflict: as to war crimes see PARA 431.

5 *Venable* 4 RIAA 219 (1927).

6 See *Currie* 14 RIAA 21 at 24 (1954); *Société Verdol* 13 RIAA 9 (1949); *Ousset* 13 RIAA 252 (1954).

7 *Elettronica Sicula SpA (ELSI) (United States of America v Italy)* ICJ Reports 1989, 15. Cf *Sancheti v City of London* [2008] EWCA Civ 1283, [2009] 1 Lloyd's Rep 117, [2008] All ER (D) 204 (Nov) (held that although the acts of the Corporation of London may be attributable to the United Kingdom as a matter of international law for the purposes of a claim by a foreign investor for breach of a bilateral investment treaty, this did not mean that an action before the English courts by the Corporation of London to recover rent against the investor had to be stayed as in breach of the arbitration agreement contained in the treaty; the Corporation of London was not party to the arbitration agreement, which was with the United Kingdom, and was therefore not bound by it).

8 In relation to the attributability of ultra vires acts see PARA 346; for the non-attributability of private acts of officials see PARA 352.

341. Acts of organs: members of the armed forces during armed conflict. The acts of members of the armed forces of a state will normally be attributable to it as conduct of an organ of the state[1]. Further, it appears that as a matter of customary international law, during an armed conflict a state party to the conflict is responsible for all acts of persons forming part of its armed forces[2].

1 See PARA 340.

2 See *Armed Activities on the Territory of the Congo (Democratic Republic of the Congo v Uganda)* ICJ Reports, 19 December 2005 (paras 213–214, 243); cf the Dissenting Opinion of Judge ad hoc Kateka ICJ Reports 2005, 361 at 377–378 (para 54).

342. Acts of organs: the legislature. The acts of the legislature of a state, including the adoption of legislation which is inconsistent with the state's international obligations, are attributable to it under international law and may give rise to its international responsibility[1]. In accordance with the general principle of attribution of the acts of all organs of the state, for these purposes it is irrelevant whether the legislature is the central legislature or that of a territorial sub-unit[2]. It is not clear to what extent the actions of individual members of a legislature (whether federal or provincial) may be attributable to the state[3]. Whether or not the mere enactment or maintenance of legislation will, without more, give rise to the international responsibility of the state in question depends on the substance and content of the primary obligation in question: for instance, the potential applicability of legislation to an individual (even if not applied in practice), or a high probability that legislation will be applied to his situation in the future, may result in a breach of the state's international human rights obligations[4]. By contrast, in the case of a claim brought by a state by way of diplomatic protection on behalf of one of its nationals, it may be necessary to establish that the alien has in fact suffered damage as a result of the application of the legislation in question: for instance, the adoption of a law which renders property of a foreign national liable to expropriation will not normally constitute a breach of international law and it is only when the legislation is in fact applied to the individual and there is interference with the individual's property that an international claim for expropriation will arise[5]. On the other hand, the acts or omissions of the legislature may produce liability without more: for instance where an obligation arising under a treaty requires that a particular result be achieved by legislation or particular terms of the treaty are to be incorporated into domestic law and this is not done, or where on a reasonable construction of a treaty, the domestic legislation in question constitutes a clear breach of the treaty[6].

1   See e g *El Triunfo* 15 RIAA 455 at 477 (1902); *Certain German Interests in Polish Upper Silesia* PCIJ Ser A No 7 at 19 (1926). The question whether a state should be held responsible for, inter alia, acts committed by its legislature was considered in: *German Settlers in Poland (Advisory Opinion)* PCIJ Ser B No 6 at 35–36 (1923); *Treatment of Polish Nationals and Other Persons of Polish Origin or Speech in the Danzig Territory* PCIJ Ser A/B No 44 at 4, 24–25 (1932); *Phosphates in Morocco* PCIJ Ser A/B No 74 at 10, 25–26 (1938); *Rights of Nationals of the United States of America in Morocco (France v United States of America)* ICJ Reports 1952, 176; *Monetary Gold Removed from Rome in 1943 (Italy v France, United Kingdom and United States of America) (Jurisdiction)* ICJ Reports 1954, 19; *Application of the Convention of 1902 Governing the Guardianship of Infants (Netherlands v Sweden)* ICJ Reports 1958, 55. See also *Norwegian Shipowners Case* 1 RIAA 307 (1922); *Tinoco Arbitration* 1 RIAA 369 at 375 (1923); *Shufeldt* 2 RIAA 1079 at 1083 (1930).

2   See PARA 339.

3   See *Compañía de Aguas del Aconquija SA and Vivendi Universal v Argentine Republic* ('*Vivendi II*') ICSID Case No ARB/97/3, Award of 20 August 2007, at para 7.4.44 (although the respondent state expressly accepted that it was responsible for acts of the legislature in the exercise of its governmental authority, it denied that it was responsible for the acts of individual members of the opposition, and the Tribunal abstained from expressing a view as to whether the acts of individual members of a legislature were attributable to the state).

4   See, for example, the approach of the European Court of Human Rights to the question of whether an individual can claim to be the victim of a violation of Convention rights as the result of legislation which has not in fact been applied to him: see eg *Klass v Federal Republic of Germany* A 28 (1978) 2 EHRR 214, ECtHR; *Marckx v Belgium* A 31 (1979) 2 EHRR 330, ECtHR; *Dudgeon v United Kingdom* A 45 (1981) 4 EHRR 149, ECtHR; *Johnston v Ireland* A 112 (1986) 9 EHRR 203, ECtHR; *Norris v Ireland* A 142 (1988) 13 EHRR 186, ECtHR; *Modinos v Cyprus* A 259 (1993) 16 EHRR 485, ECtHR; *Burden v United Kingdom* [2008] STC 1305, ECtHR.

5   *Mariposa Development Co* 6 RIAA 338 (1933). As to diplomatic protection see PARA 385 et seq.

6   For the Panama Canal Tolls controversy in 1913 between Great Britain and the United States see McNair's Law of Treaties 547–550; 6 Hackworth's Digest 59. See also *Phosphates in Morocco* PCIJ Ser A/B No 74 (1938).

343. Acts of organs: courts and the judiciary. A state may incur responsibility in international law by reason of the acts of its courts and the judiciary[1]. This is particularly the case in relation to a claim of denial of justice in breach of customary international law brought by a state by way of diplomatic protection of a national, but responsibility may also arise by reason of acts of the courts or judiciary in other circumstances[2]. Although the judiciary may be independent of interference by the executive, it nevertheless constitutes, for the purposes of international law, an organ of the state such that its acts are attributable to the state[3].

1   See eg: *Lotus Case* PCIJ Ser A No 10 (1927); *Jurisdiction of the Courts of Danzig* PCIJ Ser B No 15 (1928); *Phosphates in Morocco* PCIJ Ser A/B No 74 (1938); *Ambatielos (Greece v United Kingdom)* ICJ Reports 1953, 10; *Difference Relating to Immunity from Legal Process of a Special Rapporteur of the Commission on Human Rights (Advisory Opinion)* ICJ Reports 1999, 62 at 87 (para 62).

2   As to denial of justice see PARA 464.

3   To the extent that earlier decisions (eg *Croft* (1856) 50 BFSP 1288; *Yuille Shortridge* 2 Lapradelle and Politis, Recueil des Arbitrages Internationaux 78 (1861)) suggest otherwise, they must now be regarded as incorrect on this point.

344. Acts of organs: de facto organs. Persons, groups of persons or entities may be equated with state organs even if that status does not follow from the internal law of the state provided that in fact the person, group of persons or entity acts in 'complete dependence' on the state, of which in reality they are ultimately merely the instrument[1]. However, attribution to a state on this basis is exceptional, in so far as it requires a particularly high degree of control[2]. Where such a great degree of control is found to exist, it is appropriate to look beyond legal status alone, in order to grasp the reality of the relationship between the person taking action, and the state to which he is so closely attached as to appear to be nothing more than its agent[3]. Attribution of conduct to a state on the basis that the person, group of persons or entity carrying out the conduct is a de facto organ is to be distinguished from attribution of persons or entities which are not organs of the state but whose conduct is nevertheless attributable on the basis that they act under the state's direction and control[4]. In the case of de facto organs, once the requisite high degree of dependence is proved, all conduct of the de facto organ performed in such capacity is attributable to the state for the purposes of international responsibility[5]. By contrast, in the case of attribution on the basis of instructions, direction or control by a state it is necessary to demonstrate that the conduct complained of was carried out under the 'effective control' of the state[6].

1　*Application of the Convention on the Prevention and Punishment of the Crime of Genocide (Bosnia and Herzegovina v Serbia and Montenegro)* ICJ Reports, 26 February 2007 (paras 391, 397); and see *Military and Paramilitary Activities in and against Nicaragua (Nicaragua v United States of America)* ICJ Reports 1986, 14 at 62–63 (paras 109–110).

2　*Application of the Convention on the Prevention and Punishment of the Crime of Genocide (Bosnia and Herzegovina v Serbia and Montenegro)* ICJ Reports, 26 February 2007 (para 393). The justification for this exceptional approach is that any other solution would allow states to escape their international responsibility by choosing to act through persons or entities whose supposed independence would be purely fictitious: *Application of the Convention on the Prevention and Punishment of the Crime of Genocide (Bosnia and Herzegovina v Serbia and Montenegro)* ICJ Reports, 26 February 2007 (para 391); and see the Dissenting Opinion of Judge ad hoc Mahiou (para 103).

3　*Application of the Convention on the Prevention and Punishment of the Crime of Genocide (Bosnia and Herzegovina v Serbia and Montenegro)* ICJ Reports, 26 February 2007 (para 392).

4　*Application of the Convention on the Prevention and Punishment of the Crime of Genocide (Bosnia and Herzegovina v Serbia and Montenegro)* ICJ Reports, 26 February 2007 (paras 384, 397). As to attribution on the basis of direction and control see PARA 348.

5　*Application of the Convention on the Prevention and Punishment of the Crime of Genocide (Bosnia and Herzegovina v Serbia and Montenegro)* ICJ Reports, 26 February 2007 (para 397).

6　*Application of the Convention on the Prevention and Punishment of the Crime of Genocide (Bosnia and Herzegovina v Serbia and Montenegro)* ICJ Reports, 26 February 2007 (para 400).

345.　Acts of persons or entities exercising elements of governmental authority. The conduct of a person or entity which is not an organ of the state but which is empowered under the state's domestic law to exercise elements of governmental authority is attributable to the state provided that the person or entity was acting in that capacity in committing the conduct in question[1]. Attribution of conduct on this basis extends to the conduct of parastatal entities which are empowered to exercise elements of governmental authority in place of state organs, and state corporations which have been privatised but which retain certain governmental or regulatory functions[2]. As with the acts of organs, conduct of a person or entity exercising elements of governmental authority is attributable even if the particular conduct carried out in exercise of governmental authority was ultra vires or otherwise illegal under the domestic law of the state[3].

1　See Articles on Responsibility of States for Internationally Wrongful Acts ('ARSIWA') art 5, Report of the International Law Commission, 53rd Session (2001), YILC 2001, vol II(2). See also *Armed Activities on the Territory of the Congo (Democratic Republic of the Congo v Uganda)* ICJ Reports, 19 December 2005 (para 160) (where ARSIWA art 5 was cited with apparent approval); *Noble Ventures, Inc v Romania* ICSID Case No ARB/01/11, Award of 12 October 2005, at paras 69–80; and *Application of the Convention on the Prevention and Punishment of the Crime of Genocide (Bosnia and Herzegovina v Serbia and Montenegro)* ICJ Reports, 26 February 2007 (para 414). See also *Compañía de Aguas del Aconquija SA and Vivendi Universal v Argentine Republic ('Vivendi II')* ICSID Case No ARB/97/3, Award of 20 August 2007, at para 7.4.44 (actions of an Ombudsman).

2   ARSIWA, Commentary to Article 5, para (1). As to what is to be understood as constituting governmental authority for these purposes see the Commentary to Article 5, para (6).

3   See PARA 346.

346.   Ultra vires acts of organs and persons or entities exercising elements of governmental authority.   A state may incur international responsibility for the act or omission of an organ or a person or entity exercising elements of governmental authority even if the conduct was outside the scope of the actual authority of the organ or official, and even if the act was committed in violation of the state's domestic law[1]. Responsibility may arise within the scope of apparent authority, as for example when it is an act of the type which an official is engaged to perform[2]. It may also arise if the act is beyond the scope of the official's apparent authority but is made possible by means put at his disposal by the state, provided the alien could not have avoided the injury[3]. It is immaterial that the act was done maliciously and with a private motive, or that it was done mistakenly[4]. It may be, however, that exceptionally the state will not incur responsibility if the official's lack of authority to do the act was so blatant that the alien could not in good faith have relied upon it[5]. It appears that all acts of the armed forces of a state during an armed conflict are attributable to it, whether or not they are ultra vires or in contravention of orders[6].

1   See the Articles on Responsibility of States for Internationally Wrongful Acts ('ARSIWA') art 7, Report of the International Law Commission, 53rd Session (2001), YILC 2001, vol II(2). See also *Jones v Ministry of the Interior of the Kingdom of Saudi Arabia; Mitchell v Al-Dali* [2006] UKHL 26, [2007] 1 AC 270, [2007] 1 All ER 113 at [12] per Lord Bingham, at [77] per Lord Hoffman, referring to ARSIWA art 7 in support of the conclusion that alleged acts of torture by officials, even if ultra vires, were nevertheless attributable to the state for the purposes of the application of the rules of immunity before the English courts. A state is not, however, responsible for an act of its organ or official while that organ or official is acting on behalf of another state: see PARA 347.

     In at least two older cases, responsibility of states for ultra vires acts was denied: see *Tunstall* Foreign Relations of the United States (1885) 450 (shooting by a deputy sheriff); *The 'William Yeaton'* (1885) Moore Int Arb 2944 at 2946, 2947 (obiter). However, the principle of responsibility for ultra vires acts was adopted at the Hague Codification Conference 1930 draft art 8(2) (Acts of the Conference, vol IV, League of Nations Publication 1930, V, 17 at 236–237).

2   *Union Bridge Co* 6 RIAA 138 (1924). See also *Maal Case* 10 RIAA 730 (1903); *Compagnie Générale de Asphaltes de France* 9 RIAA 389 (1903); *Venable* 4 RIAA 219 (1927) (police); *Coquitlam* 6 RIAA 45 (1920); *The Jessie, The Thomas F Bayard and The Pescawha* 6 RIAA 57 (1921); *The 'Wanderer'* 6 RIAA 68 (1921); *The 'Kate'* 6 RIAA 77 (1921); *The 'Favourite'* 6 RIAA 82 (1921) (customs officials); *Roberts Case* 4 RIAA 77 (1926); *Turner* 4 RIAA 278 (1927); *Knotts* 4 RIAA 537 (1929); *Chazen* 4 RIAA 564 (1930) (illegal arrests and detentions for longer than the prescribed period under the local law). In *Peabody & Co* 4 RIAA 477 (1929), Mexico was held responsible for the imposition of taxes under an invalid law. See also generally *Military and Paramilitary Activities in and against Nicaragua (Nicaragua v United States of America)* ICJ Reports 1986, 14.

3   See eg *Magee* 65 BFSP 875 (1874) (flogging of British vice-consul by local military commander and his troops); *Avalos Tariff* Moore Int Arb 2868 (1868); *Youmans Case* 4 RIAA 110 (1926); *Connelly* 4 RIAA 117 (1926); *Munroe* 4 RIAA 538 (1929) (cases arising out of attacks by mobs on aliens; soldiers who were sent to suppress the riot joined the mob). In the *Mallén Case* 4 RIAA 173 (1927), Mexico was held responsible for one of two attacks, clearly illegal, by a

deputy constable against an alien to whom he had shown his badge of office in order to assert his authority (at 176–177). For a personally motivated issue of a void arrest warrant by a judicial authority see *Way* 4 RIAA 391 (1928).

4 For examples of acts done maliciously and from motives of personal revenge see many of the cases cited in the preceding note, especially the *Mallén Case* 4 RIAA 173 at 174–175 (1927); and *Way* 4 RIAA 391 (1928). For an example of acts done by mistake see *Union Bridge Co* 6 RIAA 138 (1924).

5 *Tinoco Arbitration* 1 RIAA 369 at 375, 394 (1923); see also Hague Codification Conference draft art 8(2), proviso.

6 See PARA 341.

347. Conduct of organs placed at the disposal of a state by another state. The conduct of an organ placed at the disposal of a state by another state is considered an act of the former state under international law if the organ is acting in the exercise of elements of the governmental authority of the state at whose disposal it is placed[1]. In such circumstances, although remaining an organ of the 'lending' state, the conduct is to be attributable solely to the state at the disposal of which the organ in question has been placed. For these purposes, the organ must be acting with the consent, under the authority of and for the purposes of the receiving state and not only must the organ be appointed to perform functions appertaining to the state at whose disposal it is placed, but in performing the functions entrusted to it by the beneficiary state, the organ must also act in conjunction with the machinery of that state and under its exclusive direction and control, rather than on instructions from the sending state[2].

1 Articles on Responsibility of States for Internationally Wrongful Acts ('ARSIWA') art 6, Report of the International Law Commission, 53rd Session (2001), YILC 2001, vol II(2). See also *Chevreau* 2 RIAA 1113 (1931) (acts of British Consul temporarily placed in charge of a French consulate not attributable to Great Britain); *Drozd and Janousek v France and Spain* A 240 (1992) 14 EHRR 745, ECtHR (conduct of French and Spanish judges sitting as judges of the courts of Andorra not attributable to France and Spain); and *Xhavara v Italy and Albania* (Application 39473/98) (11 January 2001, unreported), ECtHR (international cooperation between Italy and Albania in relation to immigration control not sufficient as such to render acts of an Italian warship attributable to Albania). See also the observations of the International Court of Justice in *Application of the Convention on the Prevention and Punishment of the Crime of Genocide (Bosnia and Herzegovina v Serbia and Montenegro)* ICJ Reports, 26 February 2007 (para 389, and cf para 414). As to the parallel situation in which organs of a state or an international organisation are placed at the disposal of an international organisation, and the question of apportionment of responsibility between them, see PARA 357.

2 See ARSIWA Commentary to Article 6, para (2). See also *R (on the application of Al-Saadoon and Mufhdi) v Secretary of State for Defence* [2008] EWHC 3098 (Admin), [2008] All ER (D) 246 (Dec) at [80] (affd on other grounds [2009] EWCA Civ 7, [2010] 1 All ER 271, [2009] 3 WLR 957) where it was held that ARSIWA art 6 deals with a limited situation in which the organ in question is acting under the exclusive direction and control of the state at the disposal of which it was placed.

348. Persons or bodies acting upon instructions or under the direction and control of the state. The conduct of a person, group of persons, or entity which does not constitute an organ of a state may nevertheless be attributable to that state if and to the extent that they or it in fact acted upon the instructions or under the direction and control of the state in carrying out the conduct in question[1]. For these purposes, at least in relation to the conduct of armed groups, it is necessary to demonstrate that the particular conduct was in fact directed and controlled by the state[2]. What is relevant is that the state had 'effective control' over the operation in question; for the purposes of state responsibility it is not sufficient that the state merely had 'overall control' of the person, group of persons or entity[3]. Given their separate legal personality, the conduct of state-owned companies or other corporate entities established by the state, whether or not by legislation, will not normally be attributable to the state merely on the basis of partial or total state-ownership[4]. Although in the absence of any evidence of direction or control, the conduct of a state-owned corporation will not in general be attributable to the state, the situation may be different where it can be shown that the state was in fact using its ownership or powers of control over a corporation to achieve a particular result[5] or that a corporation was exercising public powers[6].

1   See the Articles on Responsibility of States for Internationally Wrongful Acts ('ARSIWA') art 8, and the Commentary to art 8, Report of the International Law Commission, 53rd Session (2001), YILC 2001, vol II(2). See also *Military and Paramilitary Activities in and against Nicaragua (Nicaragua v United States of America)* ICJ Reports 1986, 14 at 63–65 (paras 113–116); *Armed Activities on the Territory of the Congo (Democratic Republic of the Congo v Uganda)* ICJ Reports, 19 December 2005 (paras 155–160); *Application of the Convention on the Prevention and Punishment of the Crime of Genocide (Bosnia and Herzegovina v Serbia and Montenegro)* ICJ Reports, 26 February 2007 (paras 396–412).

2   See ARSIWA art 8, and Commentary to Article 8, paras (4)–(5).

3   As to the requirement of 'effective control' see *Military and Paramilitary Activities in and against Nicaragua (Nicaragua v United States of America)* ICJ Reports 1986, 14 at 64–65 (para 115). In *Prosecutor v Tadić*, Case No IT-94-1-A, 38 ILM 1518 at 1541 (1999) (para 117), the Appeals Chamber of the International Criminal Tribunal for the former Yugoslavia ('ICTY') had proposed an alternative test of 'overall control' and had disapproved the approach of the International Court of Justice ('ICJ') in *Military and Paramilitary Activities in and against Nicaragua (Nicaragua v United States of America)* even though the issue before it was not one of state responsibility but of whether the armed conflict in question was to be characterised as international or non-international. The International Law Commission ('ILC') preferred the approach of the ICJ: see ARSIWA art 8, and Commentary to Article 8, paras (4)–(5). In *Application of the Convention on the Prevention and Punishment of the Crime of Genocide (Bosnia and Herzegovina v Serbia and Montenegro)* ICJ Reports, 26 February 2007, at paras 398, 401–407 the ICJ endorsed ARSIWA art 8 as representing customary international law and reaffirmed the test of 'effective control' as set out in *Military and Paramilitary Activities in and against Nicaragua (Nicaragua v United States of America)* and in the process strongly criticised the decision in *Prosecutor v Tadić*. Direction and control must be established to have existed in respect of each operation in which the alleged violations occurred, and not merely generally in respect of the overall actions taken by the persons or groups of persons having committed the violations: see *Application of the Convention on the Prevention and Punishment of the Crime of Genocide* at para 400. For the Court's explanation of the distinction compared to attribution on the basis that a person, group of persons or entity constitutes a de facto organ of the state (as to which see PARA 344) see *Application of the Convention on the Prevention and Punishment of the Crime of Genocide* at para 400.

4   See eg *Schering Corpn v Islamic Republic of Iran* 5 Iran-US CTR 361 (1984); *Otis Elevator Co v Islamic Republic of Iran* 14 Iran-US CTR 283 (1987); and *Eastman Kodak Co v Government of Iran* 17 Iran-US CTR 153 (1987).

5   Cf *Foremost Tehran Inc v Government of the Islamic Republic of Iran* 10 Iran-US CTR 228 (1986); *American Bell International Inc v Islamic Republic of Iran* 12 Iran-US CTR 170 (1986); *SEDCO Inc v National Iranian Oil Co* 15 Iran-US CTR 23 (1987); *International Technical Products Corpn v Government of the Islamic Republic of Iran* 9 Iran-US CTR 206 (1985); and *Flexi-Van Leasing Inc v The Government of the Islamic Republic of Iran* 12 Iran-US CTR 335 (1986). See also *Consorzio Groupement LESI-DIPENTA v People's Democratic Republic of Algeria* ICSID Case No ARB/03/8, Award of 10 January 2005; *LESI, SpA and Astaldi, SpA v People's Democratic Republic of Algeria* ICSID Case No ARB/05/3, Decision of 12 July 2006; and *EnCana Corpn v Republic of Ecuador*, LCIA Case No UN3481, Award of 3 February 2006, at para 154.

6   See eg *Phillips Petroleum Co Iran v Islamic Republic of Iran* 21 Iran-US CTR 79 (1989); and *Petrolane Inc v Government of the Islamic Republic of Iran* 27 Iran-US CTR 64 (1991).

349.   Revolutions, civil wars and insurrectional or other movements. Where an insurrectional movement succeeds in displacing the legitimate government and becomes the new government of a state, the state is responsible retroactively for its acts dating back to their time as insurgents[1]. It will also be responsible for acts of the former legitimate government[2]. Similarly, where an insurrectional or other movement succeeds in establishing a new state in part of the territory of a pre-existing state, the movement's conduct is considered to be an act of the new state[3]. Apart from those specific circumstances, a state does not as such incur international responsibility for the conduct of revolutionaries or insurgents[4]. Responsibility will only be incurred if the legitimate authorities failed to exercise due diligence in the use of the forces at their disposal so as to prevent damage being inflicted by the rebels or insurgents[5].

1 See the Articles on Responsibility of States for Internationally Wrongful Acts ('ARSIWA') art 10(1), Report of the International Law Commission, 53rd Session (2001), YILC 2001, vol II(2). See also *French Co of Venezuelan Railroads* 10 RIAA 285 (1903); *Kummerow* 10 RIAA 369 (1903); *Dix* 9 RIAA 119 (1903); *Pinson* 5 RIAA 327 (1928).
2 See ARSIWA art 10(3). See also *French Co of Venezuelan Railroads* 10 RIAA 285 (1903).
3 ARSIWA art 10(2).
4 As to the non-attributability of the conduct of private persons see PARAS 353–354.
5 This has been held in many arbitral awards: eg *Sambiaggio* 10 RIAA 499 (1903); *Volkmar* 9 RIAA 317 (1903); *Aroa Mines Ltd* 9 RIAA 402 (1903); *Kummerow* 10 RIAA 369 (1903); *Henriquez* 10 RIAA 713 (1903); *Home (Frontier and Foreign) Missionary Society* 6 RIAA 42 (1920); *British Claims in the Spanish Zone of Morocco* 2 RIAA 615 at 642, 730 (1925); *Solis* 4 RIAA 358 (1928); *Russell* 4 RIAA 805 (1931). See also *Socony Vacuum Oil Co* (1954) 21 Int LR 55. The principle was acknowledged by the replies of states to the League of Nations Questionnaire for the Hague Codification Conference 1930: see 2 McNair's International Law Opinions 244, 245. A revolution does not as such entitle investors to compensation: *Starrett Housing Corpn v Islamic Republic of Iran* 4 Iran-US CTR 122 (1983). Iran was held to be not as such responsible for the initial stages of the attacks by militants on US diplomatic and consular premises in Iran and on their occupants, but rather to be in breach of its international obligations to take steps to protect those premises from attack: *United States Diplomatic and Consular Staff in Teheran (United States of America v Iran)* ICJ Reports 1980, 3.

350. Conduct carried out in the absence or default of the official authorities. Exceptionally, the conduct of a person or group of persons not constituting an organ of the state may be attributed to that state where the person or group of persons is in fact exercising elements of the governmental authority in the absence or default of the official authorities and in circumstances such as to call for the exercise of those elements of authority[1]. The action of private persons in such circumstances is attributable on the basis that they are in fact exercising elements of governmental authority in circumstances in which such an exercise is objectively called for due to the partial or total absence of the properly constituted authorities[2]. Such a situation is to be distinguished from that where there exists a de facto government, the acts of which are to be regarded as constituting acts of an organ of the state[3].

1 See the Articles on Responsibility of States for Internationally Wrongful Acts ('ARSIWA') art 9, Report of the International Law Commission, 53rd Session (2001), YILC 2001, vol II(2) art 9. See also eg *Yeager v Islamic Republic of Iran* 17 Iran-US CTR 92 at 104 (para 43) (1987) (actions of revolutionary guards in the immediate aftermath of the Iranian revolution).
2 See ARSIWA, Commentary to Article 9, para (6).
3 See *Tinoco Arbitration* 1 RIAA 369 at 381–382 (1923). See PARA 338.

351. Conduct acknowledged and adopted by the state as its own. It appears that conduct, including conduct of private persons or individuals, which would not otherwise be attributable to the state may nevertheless be held to be attributable if and to the extent that the state has subsequently acknowledged and adopted the conduct as its own[1]. In this regard, it would appear that a mere expression of approval or endorsement of the actions of private individuals is unlikely to be sufficient in order to justify attribution of that conduct; what is necessary is that the state endorses the conduct and in some sense makes it its own[2].

1   See Articles on Responsibility of States for Internationally Wrongful Acts ('ARSIWA') art 11, Report of the International Law Commission, 53rd Session (2001), YILC 2001, vol II(2); and *United States Diplomatic and Consular Staff in Teheran (United States of America v Iran)* ICJ Reports 1980, 3 at 35 (para 74). See also Case No IT-94–2-PT *Prosecutor v Dragan Nikolić ('Sušica Camp'), Decision on Defence Motion Challenging the Exercise of Jurisdiction by the Tribunal,* 9 October 2002 (ARSIWA art 11 referred to by way of analogy in relation to the question of whether the acts of private individuals in detaining and delivering an individual to the NATO-led Stabilization Force in Bosnia and Herzegovina (SFOR), which then rendered him to the International Criminal Tribunal for Yugoslavia for trial, were to be attributed to SFOR); *Application of the Convention on the Prevention and Punishment of the Crime of Genocide (Bosnia and Herzegovina v Serbia and Montenegro)* ICJ Reports, 26 February 2007 (para 414) (where the International Court of Justice made passing reference to ARSIWA art 11); and *Certain Questions of Mutual Assistance in Criminal Matters (Djibouti v France)* ICJ Reports, 4 June 2008 (para 196). As to acts of private individuals see PARA 353.
2   See ARSIWA, Commentary to Article 11, para (6).

352.   Non-attributable acts: private acts of officials.   A state will not as such incur international responsibility for the act of an official if, when the official in question commits that act, he was not exercising any of his official powers or functions and where there is no ostensible relationship between his acts and his official position[1]. However, the state may nevertheless be responsible if it has failed to exercise due diligence to prevent the injury[2], or if it fails to punish the culprit or otherwise acquiesces in his act[3]. In such circumstances, responsibility arises as a result of the state's own default in failing to act, rather than due to attribution of the act of the official as such.

1   *Bensley* (1850) Moore Int Arb 3016 at 3018; *Putnam Case* 4 RIAA 151 (1927); *Mallén Case* 4 RIAA 173 (1927) (first attack); *Morton* 4 RIAA 428 (1929) (murder by off-duty and drunken army colonel); *Gordon* 4 RIAA 586 (1930).
2   *The 'Zafiro'* 6 RIAA 160 (1925). See also *Jeannaud* (1880) Moore Int Arb 3000.
3   *Montano* (1863) Moore Int Arb 1630.

353.   Non-attributable acts: acts of private individuals.   Acts of private individuals within a state, whether directly committed against a foreign state or its representatives or against the persons or property of individual aliens, do not in themselves engage the responsibility of the territorial state under international law[1]. However, the territorial state may incur liability to the extent that it fails to comply with an obligation incumbent upon it requiring it to exercise due diligence to prevent the injury in question, or to take adequate steps to arrest and punish the offender or to provide redress to the alien or to the foreign state[2]. In such a case the state is responsible for its own actions or omissions in failing to comply with the relevant obligation, and not because of any complicity in the acts of the private individual or individuals in question[3].

1   *British Claims in the Spanish Zone of Morocco* 2 RIAA 615 (1925); *Kennedy Case* 4 RIAA 194 (1927); *Venable* 4 RIAA 219 (1927).
2   See eg *Noyes* 6 RIAA 308 at 311 (1933); *British Claims in the Spanish Zone of Morocco* 2 RIAA 615 at 707 (1925); *Ziat* 2 RIAA 729 (1924); *Neer Case* 4 RIAA 60 (1926); *Galvan Case* 4 RIAA 273 (1927); *Sevey Case* 4 RIAA 474 (1929); *Ermerins* 4 RIAA 476 (1929); *Janes Case* 4 RIAA 82 (1926); *Youmans Case* 4 RIAA 110 (1926); *United States Diplomatic and Consular Staff in Teheran (United States of America v Iran)* ICJ Reports 1980, 3. There may also exist a duty of inquiry and explanation: see *Corfu Channel (United Kingdom v Albania)* ICJ Reports 1949, 4 at 18. In relation to the specific rules applicable to the treatment of aliens and their property see PARA 462 et seq.

3   The notion that the state is impliedly an accomplice in the acts of individuals who have injured aliens or foreign states if it fails to prevent the injury or afford redress was adopted in several cases: see eg *Cotesworth and Powell* (1875) Moore Int Arb 2050 at 2083; *Poggioli* 10 RIAA 669 (1903). However, it was subsequently rejected: see, in particular, *Janes Case* 4 RIAA 82 at 87 (1926).

354.   Mob violence.   The principles relating to the acts of a private individual[1] apply whether the private persons act individually or in a group as in the case of mob violence or riot. The state is not an insurer of lives and property[2]. However, it may incur responsibility if its agents acted in connivance with the mob or if it has failed to comply with an obligation of due diligence in preventing the act or punishing the offenders[3], or where the mob or rioters have been prompted, encouraged or charged to carry out an operation on behalf of the state[4].

1   See PARA 353.
2   *Home (Frontier and Foreign) Missionary Society* 6 RIAA 42 at 44 (1920); *Walker* 5 RIAA 135 (1931).
3   *British Claims in the Spanish Zone of Morocco* 2 RIAA 615 at 642 (1925). See also *Youmans Case* 4 RIAA 110 (1926); *Mead Case* 4 RIAA 653 (1930); *Pinson* 5 RIAA 327 (1928); *Noyes* 6 RIAA 308 (1933). See also *Sarropoulos v Bulgarian State* (1927–28) 4 Ann Dig 263 Case No 173. Evidence that the rioters have directed their attacks against persons of a particular nationality may result more readily in a finding of responsibility of the state than in other cases.
4   *The 'Zafiro'* 6 RIAA 160 (1925); *Stephens Case* 4 RIAA 265 (1927); *Lehigh Valley Railroad Co* 8 RIAA 84 (1940). The distinction between persons acting as agents of the state and as its mere supporters was drawn in *United States Diplomatic and Consular Staff in Teheran (United States of America v Iran)* ICJ Reports 1980, 3; see also *Yeager v Islamic Republic of Iran* 17 Iran-US CTR 92 (1987); *Short v Islamic Republic of Iran* 16 Iran-US CTR 76 (1987).

B.   ATTRIBUTION OF CONDUCT TO INTERNATIONAL ORGANISATIONS

355.   In general.   The principal basis of attribution of conduct to an international organisation is that it constitutes the conduct of an organ or agent of the organisation carried out in the performance of the functions of that organ or agent[1]. In addition, an international organisation may incur responsibility as the result of the conduct of organs or agents of another international organisation or of a state which have been placed at its disposal, if and to the extent that it exercises effective control over the conduct in question[2]. Finally, an international organisation may incur responsibility if and to the extent that it acknowledges or adopts particular conduct as its own[3].

1   See PARA 356.
2   See PARA 357.
3   See PARA 358.

356.   Conduct of organs and agents of international organisations.   The conduct of an organ or agent of an international organisation in the performance of the functions of that organ or agent is attributable to the international organisation whatever position the organ or agent holds in respect of the organisation[1]. The rules of the organisation are applicable to determine the functions of its organs and agents[2]. In relation to the category of 'agents', whether or not an individual has any official status and whether or not he or she is permanently employed is not relevant; what is important is whether the individual has been charged by an organ of the international organisation with carrying out or helping to carry out one of the functions of the organisation[3]. Although the distinction between organs and agents is probably of little relevance given that the key factor is whether or not the actor was carrying out functions on behalf of the international organisation, if a person or entity is characterised as an organ by the internal rules of the organisation, action carried out in that capacity is in principle attributable to the organisation[4]. The acts of an organ or agent are only attributable when the organ or agent is acting in the performance of the functions entrusted to that organ or agent; acts carried out in a private capacity are not attributable[5].

However, the conduct of an organ or agent of an international organisation acting in that capacity will be attributable even if the conduct exceeds the authority of the organ or agent or exceeds instructions[6].

1   Draft Articles on Responsibility of International Organizations ('DARIO') draft art 5(1), Report of the International Law Commission, 61st Session (2009), A/64/10, ch IV.

2   DARIO draft art 5(2). By virtue of its rules, an international organisation establishes which functions are entrusted to each organ or agent: see the draft Commentary to draft Article 5, para (8). 'Rules of the organisation' for these purposes means, in particular, the constituent instruments, decisions, resolutions and other acts of the organisation adopted in accordance with those instruments, and established practice of the organisation: draft art 2(b). See further the draft Commentary to draft Article 2, para (14).

3   In other words whether the individual is one of the persons through which the organisation acts: see, in relation to the United Nations, *Reparation for Injuries Suffered in the Service of the United Nations (Advisory Opinion)* ICJ Reports 1949, 174 at 177. See also *Applicability of Article VI, Section 22 of the Convention on the Privileges and Immunities of the United Nations* ICJ Reports 1989, 177 at 194 (paras 47, 48) (where the International Court of Justice noted that the UN has increasingly frequently entrusted missions to persons not having the status of UN officials, and that the question of whether such persons enjoy privileges and immunities depends not on their administrative position but upon the nature of their mission); and *Difference Relating to Immunity from Legal Process of a Special Rapporteur of the Commission on Human Rights (Advisory Opinion)* ICJ Reports 1999, 62 at 88–89 (para 66) (noting that although agents of the UN may enjoy immunity from legal process for acts carried out in their official capacity, the corollary is that the UN may be required to bear responsibility for damage caused arising from such acts). It would appear that similar rules apply to other international organisations, although in every case special attention will normally need to be paid to the specific characteristics and functions of the international organisation in question: see DARIO, draft Commentary to draft Article 5, para (4).

4   See DARIO, draft Commentary to draft Article 5, para (5).

5   See DARIO, draft Commentary to draft Article 5, para (6).

6   See DARIO draft art 7. See also *Legality of the Use by a State of Nuclear Weapons in Armed Conflicts (Advisory Opinion)* ICJ Reports 1996, 66 at 78 (para 25) (where the International Court of Justice observed that, unlike states, international organisations do not possess general competence and that they are governed by the 'principle of speciality', according to which they are invested by the states which create them with powers, the limits of which are a function of the common interests the promotion of which those states entrust to them); *Certain Expenses of the United Nations (Advisory Opinion)* ICJ Reports 1962, 151 at 168; and *Difference Relating to Immunity from Legal Process of a Special Rapporteur of the Commission on Human Rights (Advisory Opinion)* ICJ Reports 1999, 62 at 89 (para 66). As to the UN's responsibility for the off-duty acts of members of peacekeeping forces see DARIO, draft Commentary to draft Article 7, para (9).

357.   Organs or agents placed at the disposal of an international organisation by a state or another international organisation.   The conduct of the organ of a state or the organ or agent of an international organisation placed at the disposal of another international organisation may be attributable to that latter organisation if that organisation exercises effective control over the conduct in question[1].

Where the organ of a state or the organ or agent of one international organisation is placed fully at the disposal of an international organisation on the basis of a full secondment, the general rule of attribution of conduct to international organisations will apply given that the organ or agent will constitute an organ or agent of the international organisation to which it has been seconded[2]. However, situations may arise in which the organ or agent placed at the disposal of the international organisation to some extent remains the organ or agent of the lending state or international organisation[3]. Although questions of division of responsibility may be dealt with by agreement, it will still often be necessary to ascertain to which entity particular conduct of the lent organ or agent is to be attributed. It appears that the determining factor is one of factual control over the specific conduct in question and that in order for conduct to be attributable to the international organisation at the disposal of which the organ or agent has been placed, it is necessary that it should have had effective control over that conduct[4].

1   See the Draft Articles on Responsibility of International Organizations ('DARIO') draft art 6, Report of the International Law Commission, 61st Session (2009), A/64/10, ch IV.

2   DARIO, draft Commentary to draft Article 6 para (1). As to the general basis of attribution to international organisations see PARA 327.

3   This occurs often in the field of United Nations peacekeeping operations for example, given that the contributing state normally retains powers of discipline as well as criminal jurisdiction over the members of the national contingent: see DARIO, draft Commentary to draft Article 6 para (2).

4   DARIO, draft Commentary to draft Article 6 para (3), (6)–(8). Cf the decision of the European Court of Human Rights in _Behrami v France and Saramati v France_ (2007) 22 BHRC 477, ECtHR in which reference was made to an earlier draft of DARIO draft art 6, but the Court considered that the relevant factor in assessing whether the actions of troops placed at the disposal of the United Nations or whose actions were authorised by the United Nations could be attributed to the United Nations was whether the Security Council retained ultimate authority and control, rather than where the operational control over the troops reposed. See also _Kasumaj v Greece_ Decision on Admissibility of Application 6974/05 (5 July 2007, unreported), ECtHR; _Gajić v Germany_ Decision on Admissibility of Application 31446/02 (28 August 2008, unreported), ECtHR; _Berić v Bosnia and Herzegovina_, Decision on Admissibility of Applications 36357/04, 36360/04, 38346/04, 41705/04, 45190/04, 45578/04, 45579/04, 45580/04, 91/05, 97/05, 100/05, 101/05, 1121/05, 1123/05, 1125/05, 1129/05, 1132/05, 1133/05, 1169/05, 1172/05, 1175/05, 1177/05, 1180/05, 1185/05, 20793/05 and 25496/05 (16 October 2007), ECtHR. The International Law Commission ('ILC') has expressed doubts about the approach of the European Court of Human Rights in those decisions and its application of the ILC's own previous work: see DARIO, draft Commentary to draft Article 6, paras (9)–(10). By contrast, the judgments of the majority in _R (on the application of Al-Jedda) v Secretary of State for Defence_ [2007] UKHL 58, [2008] 1 AC 332, which likewise referred to an early version of DARIO draft art 6, concluded that the actions of British troops present in Iraq pursuant to authorisation by Security Council resolution could not be said to be subject to the effective command and control of the United Nations and the actions of British troops in detaining the applicant were not therefore attributable to the United Nations.

358.   Conduct acknowledged and adopted by an international organisation as its own.   As is the position with states[1], it would appear that conduct which would not otherwise be attributable may be attributed to an international organisation to the extent that it acknowledges and adopts that conduct as its own[2].

1   As to attribution to states on the basis of acknowledgment and adoption see PARA 351.

2   See the Draft Articles on Responsibility of International Organizations ('DARIO') draft art 8, Report of the International Law Commission, 61st Session (2009), A/64/10, ch IV. Draft Article 8 is closely modelled upon Articles on Responsibility of States for Internationally Wrongful Acts ('ARSIWA') art 8, Report of the International Law Commission, 53rd Session (2001), YILC 2001, vol II(2): see Commentary to DARIO draft art 8 para (2). See also Case No IT-94-2-PT _Prosecutor v Dragan Nikolić ('Sušica Camp'), Decision on Defence Motion Challenging the Exercise of Jurisdiction by the Tribunal_, 9 October 2002.

(iii) Breach of an International Obligation

359. In general. For the purposes of state responsibility there is a breach of an international obligation[1] where conduct attributable to the state or international organisation[2] is not in conformity with what is required of it by the international obligation in question[3]. The international obligation in question must be in force and binding for the state or international organisation before it can be breached[4]. The origin of the obligation or its character is irrelevant; breach of an international obligation may occur from conduct inconsistent with an obligation under customary international law, an obligation pursuant to a treaty or an obligation arising from a unilateral act[5].

1   As to breach of an international obligation as an element of an internationally wrongful act see PARA 336.
2   As to the attribution of conduct see PARA 337 et seq.
3   See the Articles on Responsibility of States for Internationally Wrongful Acts ('ARSIWA') art 12, Report of the International Law Commission, 53rd Session (2001), YILC 2001, vol II(2); and the draft Articles on Responsibility of International Organizations ('DARIO') draft art 9(1), Report of the International Law Commission, 61st Session (2009), A/64/10, ch IV. See also the various formulations used by the International Court of Justice: eg *United States Diplomatic and Consular Staff in Teheran (United States of America v Iran)* ICJ Reports 1980, 3 at 29 (para 56); *Elettronica Sicula SpA (ELSI) (United States of America v Italy)* ICJ Reports 1989, 15 at 50 (para 70); *Gabčíkovo-Nagymaros Project (Hungary/Slovakia)* ICJ Reports 1997, 7 at 46 (para 57); *Legal Consequences of the Construction of a Wall in the Occupied Palestinian Territory (Advisory Opinion)* ICJ Reports 2004, 136 at 193–194 (para 137); *Avena and Other Mexican Nationals (Mexico v United States of America)* ICJ Reports 2004, 12 at 58 (para 115); *Application of the Convention on the Prevention and Punishment of the Crime of Genocide (Bosnia and Herzegovina v Serbia and Montenegro)* ICJ Reports, 26 February 2007 (paras 383, 385). In the case of an international organisation, the breach may be of an international obligation arising under the rules of the organisation: DARIO draft art 9(2).
        Quite apart from the consequences as a matter of the law of state responsibility, the material breach of a treaty by a state party may provide a basis on which other state parties may either terminate the treaty or suspend its operation in whole or in part: see the Vienna Convention on the Law of Treaties (Vienna, 23 May 1969; TS 58 (1980); Cmnd 7964) art 60; and PARA 107.
4   See ARSIWA art 13; and DARIO draft art 10. This is an application of the principle of the inter-temporal law in accordance with which 'a juridical fact must be appreciated in the light of the law contemporary with it, and not of the law in force at the time when a dispute in regard to it arises or falls to be settled': see *Island of Palmas Case* 2 RIAA 829 at 845 (1928). See also Application 59532/00 *Blečić v Croatia* Judgment of 8 March 2006, ECtHR (Grand Chamber). For the presumption of non-retroactivity of obligations under the law of treaties, see the Vienna Convention on the Law of Treaties (Vienna, 23 May 1969; TS 58 (1980); Cmnd 7964) art 28; and PARA 93.
5   See eg *Gabčíkovo-Nagymaros Project (Hungary/Slovakia)* ICJ Reports 1997, 7 at 38 (para 47); *Rainbow Warrior (New Zealand/France)* 20 RIAA 215 at 251 (1990). See ARSIWA art 12; and DARIO draft art 9 which make clear that the question of whether or not there is a breach of an international obligation turns solely on whether the conduct in question is in conformity with what is required by the obligation regardless of its origin and character.

360. Extension in time of the breach of an international obligation. The breach of an international obligation not having a continuing character[1] occurs at the moment the relevant conduct is performed, even if its effects continue[2]. A breach having a continuing character extends over the whole period in which the conduct in question continues and remains not in conformity with what is required by the international obligation in question[3]. Whether or not an internationally wrongful act is of a continuing nature is relevant to, inter alia, the incidence of the secondary obligation of cessation[4]. It may also be relevant to the jurisdiction ratione temporis of international courts and tribunals[5].

1   As to the important distinction between a breach having a continuing character and those which do not see generally the Articles on Responsibility of States for Internationally Wrongful Acts

('ARSIWA') Commentary to Article 14 paras (4), (5), Report of the International Law Commission, 53rd Session (2001), YILC 2001, vol II(2). The mere fact that the consequences of an internationally wrongful act extend for some considerable period of time (for instance, the pain and suffering resulting from an act of torture, or the economic effects of an act of expropriation) does not render such breaches of a continuing character: Commentary to Article 14 para (6).

2   ARSIWA art 14(1); draft Articles on Responsibility of International Organizations ('DARIO') draft art 11(1), Report of the International Law Commission, 61st Session (2009), A/64/10, ch IV.

3   ARSIWA art 14(2); DARIO draft art 11(2). The breach of an international obligation requiring a state to prevent a given event occurs when the event occurs and extends over the entire period during which the event continues and remains not in conformity with the obligation: ARSIWA art 14(3); and DARIO draft art 11(3). Nevertheless, certain obligations of prevention are breached instantaneously when the given event occurs and do not result in a continuing breach: see eg ARSIWA Commentary to Article 14 para (14). See also the observations of the International Court of Justice in *Application of the Convention on the Prevention and Punishment of the Crime of Genocide (Bosnia and Herzegovina v Serbia and Montenegro)* ICJ Reports, 26 February 2007 (para 431) in the course of which the court endorsed ARSIWA art 14(3) as representing a general rule of the law of state responsibility.

4   See PARA 381.

5   See eg *Blake v Guatemala (Preliminary Objections)* (1996) Inter-Am Ct HR (Ser C) No 27 at para 40; and *(Merits)* (1998) Inter-Am Ct HR (Ser C) No 36 at para 67 (forced disappearance); *Loizidou v Turkey (Preliminary Objections)* (1995) A 310, ECtHR; and *(Merits)* ECHR Reports 1996–VI (interference with right to property); *Cyprus v Turkey* ECHR Reports 2001–IV (forced disappearance); *Ilaşcu v Russia and Moldova* ECHR Reports 2004–VII (prolonged deprivation of liberty).

361.   Composite internationally wrongful acts.   The breach of some international obligations may occur only through the combination of a series of acts or omissions which, taken singly, do not breach the obligation in question, but in the aggregate, are internationally wrongful[1]. In such cases a breach occurs upon the occurrence of the particular action or omission which, taken with the other actions or omissions, is sufficient to constitute the internationally wrongful act[2]. A breach consisting of such a composite act is of a continuing character[3] and extends over the entire period starting with the first of the actions or omissions in the series and lasts for as long as these actions or omissions are repeated and remain not in conformity with the international obligation in question[4].

1   Examples include the prohibitions of genocide, apartheid and crimes against humanity, the prohibition of systematic acts of racial discrimination, and systematic acts of discrimination prohibited by a trade agreement: Articles on Responsibility of States for Internationally Wrongful Acts ('ARSIWA') Commentary to Article 15, para (2), Report of the International Law Commission, 53rd Session (2001), YILC 2001, vol II(2).

2   See the ARSIWA art 15(1); and the draft Articles on Responsibility of International Organizations ('DARIO') draft art 12(1), Report of the International Law Commission, 61st Session (2009), A/64/10, ch IV.

3   As to breaches of a continuing character see PARA 360.

4   ARSIWA art 15(2); DARIO draft art 12(2).

(iv) Circumstances Precluding Wrongfulness

362.   Circumstances precluding wrongfulness.   The modern law of international responsibility recognises a category of defences or justifications called 'circumstances precluding wrongfulness'[1] which are separate from and parallel to the rules of the law of treaties which govern the termination and suspension of treaties or obligations arising under treaties[2]. Where a situation constituting a circumstance precluding wrongfulness is established, it precludes the wrongfulness of conduct only for so long as the situation in question persists and is without prejudice to the resumption of the performance of the obligation or obligations in question if and to the extent that the circumstance precluding wrongfulness in question no longer exists[3]. Despite the successful invocation of a circumstance precluding wrongfulness in some circumstances the state or international organisation to which the act in question is attributable may nevertheless be required to pay compensation to those injured[4]. The generally recognised circumstances in which the wrongfulness of an act may be precluded are:

(1)   where the other state has validly consented to the commission of the act in question[5];

(2)   where the act constitutes a lawful measure of self-defence[6];

(3)   where the act in question constitutes a valid countermeasure[7];

(4)   where the act in question occurs as the result of force majeure[8];

(5)   where the author of the act in question was in a situation of distress and had no other means of saving his life or the lives of persons entrusted to his care[9]; and

(6)   where there exists a state of necessity[10].

A general limitation on the invocation of circumstances precluding wrongfulness as a defence to an internationally wrongful act is that they have no effect to the extent that the conduct in question involves a breach of an obligation deriving from a peremptory norm of general international law (jus cogens)[11]. Nevertheless, valid consent may constitute a good defence in relation to, inter alia, an allegation that a state has breached the prohibition of the use of force[12].

1   See the Articles on Responsibility of States for Internationally Wrongful Acts ('ARSIWA'), Pt 1, Ch V, Report of the International Law Commission, 53rd Session (2001), YILC 2001, vol II(2); and the draft Articles on Responsibility of International Organizations ('DARIO') Pt 1, Ch V, Report of the International Law Commission, 61st Session (2009), A/64/10, ch IV. The question of whether the successful invocation of a circumstance precluding wrongfulness precludes the internationally wrongful character of the act itself, or whether it merely has the effect of precluding the responsibility of the invoking state in relation to an act which is nevertheless internationally wrongful remains unresolved, although the International Law Commission ('ILC') has taken the view that the former is correct: see further *CMS Gas Transmission Co v Argentine Republic* ICSID Case No ARB/01/8, Decision on Annulment of 25 September 2007, at paras 132–134.

2   See eg *Rainbow Warrior (New Zealand/France)* 20 RIAA 215 at 251–252 (1990); *Gabčíkovo-Nagymaros Project (Hungary/Slovakia)* ICJ Reports 1997, 7 at 38–39 (paras 47–48).

3   See ARSIWA art 27(a); DARIO art 26(a). See also *Gabčíkovo-Nagymaros Project (Hungary/ Slovakia)* ICJ Reports 1997, 7 at 63 (para 101).

4   See ARSIWA art 27(b); DARIO art 26(b). See also *Gabčíkovo-Nagymaros Project (Hungary/ Slovakia)* ICJ Reports 1997, 7 at 39 (para 48) (not disputed that establishment of the existence of a state of necessity would not have precluded an obligation to pay compensation). Whether or not compensation is due depends on the primary obligation in question: see ARSIWA Commentary to Article 27, paras (4)–(6). There was consideration of the question of whether compensation is payable as a matter of customary international law in circumstances in which reliance is placed on a circumstance precluding wrongfulness in some of the cases concerning Argentina's assertions of the existence of a state of necessity arising out of the Argentine financial crisis: see eg *CMS Gas Transmission Co v Argentine Republic* ICSID Case No ARB/01/8, Award of 12 May 2005; and Decision on Annulment of 25 September 2007; *LG&E Energy Corpn, LG & E Capital Corpn, and LG & E International Inc v Argentine Republic* ICSID Case No ARB/02/1, Decision on Liability of 3 October 2006; *Enron Creditors Recovery Corpn (formerly Enron Corpn) and Ponderosa Assets LP v Argentine Republic* ICSID Case No ARB/01/3, Award of 22 May 2007; *Sempra Energy International v Argentine Republic* ICSID Case No ARB/02/16, Award of 28 September 2007; *BG Group plc v Republic of Argentina*

Final Award of 24 December 2007, UNCITRAL; *Continental Casualty Co v Argentine Republic* ICSID Case No ARB/03/9, Award of 5 September 2008; *National Grid plc v Republic of Argentina* Award of 3 November 2008, UNCITRAL.

5 As to consent see PARA 363.
6 As to self-defence see PARA 364.
7 As to countermeasures see PARA 365.
8 As to force majeure see PARA 366.
9 As to distress see PARA 367.
10 As to necessity see PARA 368.
11 See ARSIWA art 26; DARIO draft art 25. As a consequence, a state may not validly consent to, for instance, a violation of the jus cogens prohibitions of genocide or of torture: see ARSIWA Commentary to Article 26, para (6). As to the concept of jus cogens see PARA 11.
12 See ARSIWA Commentary to Article 26, para (6). Further to the extent that the military forces of a state are present on the territory of another pursuant to consent validly granted by the latter state, there is no internationally wrongful act: see eg *Armed Activities on the Territory of the Congo (Democratic Republic of Congo v Uganda)* ICJ Reports, 19 December 2005. See further PARA 363.

363.   Consent.   The wrongfulness of conduct which would otherwise constitute a breach of international obligations owed to a state or international organisation is precluded to the extent that that state or international organisation has given its valid consent to the conduct in question[1]. Consent will normally need to be clearly expressed and is not to be presumed[2]. The wrongfulness of an act will be precluded only to the extent that it is within the limits of any consent validly given[3]. In relation to an ongoing situation, for instance where consent has been given by a state to the presence and activities of troops of another state on its territory, the consent may be withdrawn so long as the fact of the withdrawal is communicated in a sufficiently unambiguous fashion[4]. Consent as a circumstance precluding wrongfulness operates only bilaterally, such that to the extent that a particular obligation is owed to more than one state or international organisation, consent by one of the actors to which the obligation is owed does not preclude wrongfulness as against the others[5].

1 See the Articles on Responsibility of States for Internationally Wrongful Acts ('ARSIWA') art 20, Report of the International Law Commission, 53rd Session (2001), YILC 2001, vol II(2); and the draft Articles on Responsibility of International Organizations ('DARIO') draft art 19, Report of the International Law Commission, 61st Session (2009), A/64/10, ch IV. For consent to be valid it must have been given by a person having the appropriate authority to do so and must not be affected by coercion or other vitiating factors: see generally ARSIWA Commentary to Article 20, paras (4)–(6). In relation to certain situations international law lays down specific primary rules as to who is able to provide consent: see eg the Convention on Diplomatic Relations (Vienna, 18 April 1961; TS 19 (1965); Cmnd 2565) 1961 art 22(1). Whether or not a person has sufficient authority to provide consent may depend on the act in question: see eg *Savarkar* 11 RIAA 243 at 253–255 (1911) (the arrest of an individual by British agents on French territory did not violate France's sovereignty as implicit consent had been given to the actions of the British agents as a result of assistance in the capture provided by a French gendarme). Wrongfulness may not in general be precluded when the breached obligation arises under a peremptory norm: see PARA 362.
2 See *Armed Activities on the Territory of the Congo (Democratic Republic of the Congo v Uganda)* ICJ Reports, 19 December 2005 (paras 101, 104); and ARSIWA Commentary to Article 20, para (6).
3 See eg ARSIWA Commentary to Article 20, paras (1), (9); and see *Armed Activities on the Territory of the Congo (Democratic Republic of the Congo v Uganda)* ICJ Reports, 19 December 2005 (para 52).
4 *Armed Activities on the Territory of the Congo (Democratic Republic of the Congo v Uganda)* ICJ Reports, 19 December 2005 (para 106).
5 See eg *Customs Régime between Germany and Austria* PCIJ Ser A/B No 41 at 37, 46, 49 (1931); ARSIWA Commentary to Article 20, para (9).

**364.	Self-defence.** The wrongfulness of an act which would otherwise be inconsistent with the international obligations of a state or international organisation is precluded to the extent the act in question constitutes a lawful measure of self-defence taken in conformity with the Charter of the United Nations[1]. The categories of obligations in relation to which wrongfulness may be precluded are not limited to the prohibition of the use of force. Nevertheless, the wrongfulness of the breach of certain obligations which either are expressly envisaged as applying to armed conflict or which are expressed to be absolute in all circumstances may not be precluded on the basis that the action in question was taken by way of self-defence[2].

1	See the Articles on Responsibility of States for Internationally Wrongful Acts ('ARSIWA') art 21, Report of the International Law Commission, 53rd Session (2001), YILC 2001, vol II(2); and draft Articles on Responsibility of International Organizations ('DARIO') draft art 20, Report of the International Law Commission, 61st Session (2009), A/64/10, ch IV (although draft art 20 contains no reference to the Charter of the United Nations, and refers instead to self-defence under international law). See also *Legality of the Threat or Use of Nuclear Weapons (Advisory Opinion)* ICJ Reports 1996, 226 at 244, 263 (paras 38, 96); *Legal Consequences of the Construction of a Wall in the Occupied Palestinian Territory (Advisory Opinion)* ICJ Reports 2004, 136 at 194 (paras 138–139); *Armed Activities on the Territory of the Congo (Democratic Republic of Congo v Uganda)* ICJ Reports, 19 December 2005. Cf *Oil Platforms (Islamic Republic of Iran v United States of America)* ICJ Reports 2003, 161 (the question of whether action could be said to fall within an exception to the substantive obligations under a bilateral treaty in relation to situations involving the 'essential security interests' of the states involved was to be determined in the light of the law relating to the use of force, including the rules relating to self-defence, under the Charter and customary international law).

2	For instance, the rules of international humanitarian law, in particular those contained in the four 1949 Geneva Conventions and Additional Protocol I, adopted in 1977 (as to which see WAR AND ARMED CONFLICT vol 49(1) (2005 Reissue) PARA 421): see e g *Legality of the Threat or Use of Nuclear Weapons (Advisory Opinion)* ICJ Reports 1996, 226 at 242, 257 (paras 30, 79) where the International Court of Justice referred to the fundamental rules of international humanitarian law as constituting 'intransgressible principles of international customary law'; and to obligations of 'total restraint' as regards rules of environmental law. A number of international human rights treaties enumerate obligations which are non-derogable under any circumstances, including in time of armed conflict: as to the relationship between international humanitarian law and international human rights law in this regard see *Legality of the Threat or Use of Nuclear Weapons (Advisory Opinion)* ICJ Reports 1996, 226 at 240 (para 25); and *Legal Consequences of the Construction of a Wall in the Occupied Palestinian Territory (Advisory Opinion)* ICJ Reports 2004, 136 at 177–178 (paras 105–106).

**365.	Countermeasures.** The wrongfulness of an act of a state or an international organisation which is not in conformity with what is required of it by an international obligation is precluded if and to the extent that it constitutes a lawful countermeasure[1]. The adoption of countermeasures is to be distinguished from the termination or suspension of a treaty by reason of a material breach thereof[2]. The adoption of countermeasures is subject to stringent conditions: countermeasures may only be adopted against a state or international organisation which is responsible for an internationally wrongful act in order to induce it to comply with the secondary obligations which arise as the result of the commission of an internationally wrongful act[3]. Countermeasures are limited to the non-performance for the time being of international obligations owed towards the responsible state or international organisation[4] and must, so far as possible, be adopted in such a way as to permit the resumption of performance of the obligation in question[5]. Countermeasures must be terminated as soon as the responsible state has complied with the secondary obligations arising from its internationally wrongful act[6].

Certain obligations may not be affected by way of countermeasures; this is the case with the prohibition of the threat or use of force, obligations for the protection of fundamental human rights, obligations of a humanitarian character prohibiting reprisals and other obligations arising under peremptory norms of general international law[7]. Similarly, even when adopting countermeasures, a state or international organisation is not relieved from complying with any applicable obligations relating to the peaceful settlement of disputes which apply in the relations between it and the responsible state or international organisation[8]. A state taking countermeasures is not relieved from its obligations relating to the inviolability of diplomatic or consular agents, premises, archives or documents[9].

The countermeasures open to a state in reaction to a breach of its international obligations are not unlimited, and any countermeasures adopted must be proportionate, in the sense that the measure adopted must be commensurate with the injury suffered, taking into account the gravity of the internationally wrongful act and the rights in question[10].

The adoption of a valid countermeasure is subject to various procedural conditions: prior to adopting countermeasures, it is normally necessary to first call upon the responsible state or international organisation to fulfil the secondary obligations of cessation and reparation which arise as a result of the commission of an internationally wrongful act[11]. In addition, it appears that there is a requirement that notification of the decision to adopt countermeasures must be given, and an offer to negotiate prior to the actual adoption of the countermeasures be made[12]. It has also been proposed that, given that the underlying purpose of countermeasures is to ensure compliance with the secondary obligations of international responsibility, they may not be taken, or if taken must be suspended immediately, if the underlying internationally wrongful act has ceased and the dispute is pending before a court or tribunal which has the power to take decisions binding on the parties[13].

If a measure consisting of suspension of performance of an obligation constitutes a valid countermeasure, wrongfulness is only precluded as against the target which committed the prior internationally wrongful act and not as against any other entity to which an obligation affected by the countermeasure is owed[14].

1 See the Articles on Responsibility of States for Internationally Wrongful Acts ('ARSIWA') arts 22, Report of the International Law Commission, 53rd Session (2001), YILC 2001, vol II(2); and the draft Articles on Responsibility of International Organizations ('DARIO') draft art 21, Report of the International Law Commission, 61st Session (2009), A/64/10, ch IV. The extent to which a state which is not directly injured or affected by a breach of an international obligation may take countermeasures is a question of some controversy and it is not clear to what extent such states may legitimately adopt measures otherwise inconsistent with their international obligations in order to ensure compliance with the secondary obligations of cessation and reparation. For the International Law Commission's ('ILC') position see ARSIWA art 54; DARIO draft art 56. Wrongfulness may not be precluded when the breached obligation arises under a peremptory norm: see PARA 368.

2 As to which see the Vienna Convention on the Law of Treaties (Vienna, 23 May 1969; TS 58 (1980); Cmnd 7964) art 60; and PARA 107.

3 ARSIWA art 49(1); DARIO draft art 50(1). As to the secondary obligations which constitute the content of international responsibility see PARA 373 et seq.

4 ARSIWA art 49(2); DARIO draft art 50(2).

5 ARSIWA art 49(3); DARIO draft art 50(3).

6 See ARSIWA art 53; DARIO draft art 55.

7 ARSIWA art 50(1)(a)–(d); DARIO draft art 52(1)(a)–(d). In relation to countermeasures against international organisations, the ILC has proposed that the member states of an international

organisation may not take countermeasures against that organisation unless the adoption of the countermeasures are not inconsistent with the rules of the organisation and no available means are otherwise available for inducing compliance with the secondary obligations of the international organisation: see DARIO draft art 51.

8   ARSIWA art 50(2)(a); see also DARIO draft art 52(2)(a). See also *United States Diplomatic and Consular Staff in Teheran (United States of America v Iran)* ICJ Reports 1980, 3 at 28 (para 53).

9   See ARSIWA art 50(2)(b). See also *United States Diplomatic and Consular Staff in Teheran (United States of America v Iran)* ICJ Reports 1980, 3 at 38, 40 (paras 83, 86) (the possible remedies for dealing with illicit activities of members of diplomatic and consular missions are expressly laid down in diplomatic law such that that body of law constitutes a self-contained regime and the adoption of countermeasures consisting of the suspension of the rules relating to inviolability of diplomatic and consular representatives is never permissible). As to diplomatic and consular privileges and immunities see PARA 265 et seq. The ILC has suggested that a similar limitation upon countermeasures exists in relation to obligations relating to inviolability of agents of a responsible international organisation and the premises, archives and documents of the organisation: DARIO draft art 52(2)(b).

10   See ARSIWA art 51; DARIO draft art 53. See also *Air Services Agreement (USA v France)* 18 RIAA 417 (1978); and *Gabčíkovo-Nagymaros Project (Hungary/Slovakia)* ICJ Reports 1997, 7 at 56 (paras 85, 87)

11   See ARSIWA art 52(1)(a); DARIO draft art 54(1)(a). See also *Gabčíkovo-Nagymaros Project (Hungary/Slovakia)* ICJ Reports 1997, 7 at 56 (para 84). As to the content of international responsibilty see PARA 373 et seq.

12   See ARSIWA art 52(1)(b); DARIO draft art 54(1)(b). See also *Air Services Agreement (USA v France)* (1978) 18 RIAA 417 at 444 (paras 85–87). Notwithstanding this restriction, the injured state or international organisation may take such urgent countermeasures as are necessary to preserve its rights: ARSIWA art 52(2); DARIO draft art 54(2).

13   See ARSIWA art 52(3). The requirement does not apply to the extent that the responsible entity fails to implement the dispute resolution procedures in good faith: art 52(4). As to the proposed position in relation to countermeasures against international organisations see DARIO draft Article 54(3), (4).

14   See ARSIWA Commentary to Article 22, paras (4), (5). In the specific field of investment protection, there exist conflicting decisions as to whether the adoption of a countermeasure by a host state in reaction to a prior breach of its international obligations by the state of nationality of an investor is in principle capable of precluding the wrongfulness of that measure as against the investor to the extent that it is inconsistent with the substantive obligations of protection owed by the host state to the investor: see *Archer Daniels Midland Co and Tate & Lyle Ingredients Americas, Inc v United Mexican States* ICSID Case No ARB(AF)/04/5, Award of 21 November 2007; and *Corn Products International, Inc v United Mexican States* ICSID Case No ARB(AF)/04/1, Decision on Liability of 15 January 2008 (both of which relate to claims brought by investors under NAFTA).

366.   Force majeure.   The wrongfulness of what would otherwise constitute an internationally wrongful act because it was not in conformity with what is required by an international obligation may be precluded to the extent that the inability to comply with the international obligation in question was the result of force majeure, that is to say, as the result of the occurrence of an irresistible force or of an unforeseen event, beyond the control of the state or international organisation, making it materially impossible in the circumstances to perform the obligation in question[1]. The occurrence in question must make performance impossible: it is not sufficient that it merely made performance of the obligation in question more difficult or onerous[2].

Force majeure is to be distinguished from situations of distress by the involuntary nature, or lack of free choice, in the conduct inconsistent with an international obligation[3]. Force majeure may not be relied upon to preclude the wrongfulness of an act if the occurrence constituting force majeure is due, either alone or in combination with other factors, to the conduct of the state or international organisation invoking it[4], nor if there has been an assumption of the risk of the event in question occurring by the state seeking to rely upon it[5].

1   Articles on Responsibility of States for Internationally Wrongful Acts ('ARSIWA') art 23, Report of the International Law Commission, 53rd Session (2001), YILC 2001, vol II(2); draft Articles on Responsibility of International Organizations ('DARIO') draft art 22, Report of the International Law Commission, 61st Session (2009), A/64/10, ch IV. As to the extent to which force majeure may permit termination of a treaty see the Vienna Convention on the Law of Treaties (Vienna, 23 May 1969; TS 58 (1980); Cmnd 7964) art 61; and PARA 108. As to force majeure in relation to ships involved in innocent passage see the United Nations Convention on the Law of the Sea (Montego Bay, 10 December 1982; TS 81 (1999); Cmnd 4524) art 18; and PARA 133. The existence of the principle of force majeure has been recognised by the Permanent Court of International Justice: see eg *Serbian Loans* PCIJ Ser A No 20, 39–40 (1929); and *Brazilian Loans* PCIJ Ser A No 21, 120 (1929) (although no force majeure was found on the facts). See also *Russian Indemnity Case* 11 RIAA 421 at 443 (1912); and *Lighthouses* 12 RIAA 155, at 219–220 (1956) (the restitution of lighthouses which had been requisitioned was denied on the basis that they had been destroyed by enemy action); and *Rainbow Warrior (New Zealand/France)* 20 RIAA 215 (1990). For recognition of force majeure as a matter of European Community law see Case 145/85 *Denkavit Belgie NV v Belgium* [1987] ECR 565, [1988] 2 CMLR 679, ECJ. As to force majeure as a matter of English law see CONTRACT vol 9(1) (Reissue) PARA 906.

2   *Rainbow Warrior (New Zealand/France)* 20 RIAA 215 at 252–253 (1990). Accordingly, the category of force majeure does not encompass situations of political or economic crisis if their effects are only to make performance more difficult: see ARSIWA Commentary to Article 23, para (3); and *Enron Creditors Recovery Corpn (formerly Enron Corpn) and Ponderosa Assets, LP v Argentine Republic* ICSID Case No ARB/01/3, Award of 22 May 2007, at para 217; *Sempra Energy International v Argentine Republic* ICSID Case No ARB/02/16, Award of 28 September 2007, at para 246; cf however, *Autopista Concesionada de Venezuela CA v Bolivarian Republic of Venezuela* ICSID Case No ARB/00/5, Award of 23 September 2003, at paras 120–125.

3   ARSIWA Commentary to Article 23, para (1). As to distress see PARA 367.

4   ARSIWA art 23(2)(a); DARIO draft art 22(2)(a). See also *Libyan Arab Foreign Investment Co v Republic of Burundi* (1994) 96 ILR 279 at 318 (para 55); *Gould Marketing, Inc v Ministry of National Defense of Iran* 3 Iran-US CTR 147 at 153 (1983); cf *Autopista Concesionada de Venezuela CA v Bolivarian Republic of Venezuela* ICSID Case No ARB/00/5, Award of 23 September 2003, at para 128.

5   ARSIWA art 23(2)(b); DARIO draft art 22(2)(b).

367. Distress. The wrongfulness of conduct which is not in conformity with the international obligations of a state or international organisation is precluded to the extent that the author of the act in question had no other reasonable way, in a situation of distress, of saving either his own life or the lives of others entrusted to his care[1]. In contrast to a situation of force majeure, the individual author of the conduct which is attributable to the state or international organisation in question and is inconsistent with its obligations has some freedom of choice and is not acting involuntarily, even if the choices available are effectively limited[2]. Distress is most often invoked in relation to ships and aircraft which violate maritime boundaries, although it is not so limited[3].

Distress may not be relied upon where the situation is one which is due, either alone or in combination with other factors, to the conduct of the state or international organisation which seeks to invoke it[4]. Further, distress may not be relied upon to the extent that the act in question is likely to create a comparable or greater peril than that which it is sought to avoid[5].

1   Articles on Responsibility of States for Internationally Wrongful Acts ('ARSIWA') art 24, Report of the International Law Commission, 53rd Session (2001), YILC 2001, vol II(2); draft Articles on Responsibility of International Organizations ('DARIO') draft art 23, Report of the International Law Commission, 61st Session (2009), A/64/10, ch IV. For an example of embodiment of the principle in a treaty relating to the law of the sea, see United Nations Convention on the Law of the Sea (Montego Bay, 10 December 1982; TS 81 (1999); Cmnd 4524) arts 18 para 2, 39 para 1(c), 98 and 109 para 2 (see PARAS 133, 146, 150, 196).

2   See ARSIWA, Commentary to Article 24 para (1). As to force majeure see PARA 366.

3   See eg *Rainbow Warrior (New Zealand/France)* 20 RIAA 215 (1990) (distress was invoked on
    the basis of medical emergencies and was held in the particular circumstances partially to
    preclude the wrongfulness of the act).
4   ARSIWA art 24(2)(b); DARIO draft art 23(2)(b).
5   ARSIWA art 24(2)(a); DARIO draft art 23(2)(a).

368.   Necessity. The wrongfulness of conduct that would otherwise constitute
a breach by a state or international organisation of one or more of its
international obligations may be precluded to the extent that the state or
international organisation can establish that the conduct in question was taken
in response to a state of necessity[1].

A state may not invoke a state of necessity unless the act in question is the
only way[2] for it to safeguard an essential interest[3] against a grave and imminent
peril[4]. An international organisation may not invoke a state of necessity unless
the act in question is the only way for the organisation to safeguard against a
grave and imminent peril an essential interest of the international community as
a whole when the organisation has, in accordance with international law, the
function to protect that interest[5]. Neither a state nor an international
organisation may invoke a state of necessity unless the act in question does not
seriously impair an essential interest of the state or states to which the obligation
is owed, or of the international community as a whole[6]. Further, necessity may
not be invoked where the primary international obligation in question excludes
the possibility of invoking necessity[7], nor where the state or international
organisation invoking necessity has contributed to the situation[8]. The defence of
necessity is exceptional such that the conditions noted above must be
cumulatively satisfied, and the state or international organisation involved is not
the sole judge of whether the conditions in question are fulfilled[9].

The extent to which the results of a financial crisis may be relied upon as
giving rise to a state of necessity such as to preclude the wrongfulness of acts
adopted to combat the crisis is not entirely clear[10].

1   The International Court of Justice has stated that the existence of a state of necessity is
    recognised by customary international law as a ground for precluding the wrongfulness of an act
    not in conformity with an international obligation: *Gabčíkovo-Nagymaros Project (Hungary/
    Slovakia)* ICJ Reports 1997, 7 at 40 (para 51); *Legal Consequences of the Construction of a
    Wall in the Occupied Palestinian Territory (Advisory Opinion)* ICJ Reports 2004, 136 at
    194–195 (para 140). See also *R (Corner House Research and Campaign Against Arms Trade) v
    Director of the Serious Fraud Office* [2008] EWHC 714 (Admin), [2009] 1 AC 756 (revsd on
    other grounds [2008] UKHL 60; [2009] 1 AC 756).

2   See eg *Legal Consequences of the Construction of a Wall in the Occupied Palestinian Territory
    (Advisory Opinion)* ICJ Reports 2004, 136 at 195 (para 140). See also the cases on the
    Argentine financial crisis in note 10.

3   A state's essential interests do not solely concern matters implicating its very existence, and an
    essential interest may be constituted by concerns in relation to the natural environment: see
    Gabčíkovo-Nagymaros Project (Hungary/Slovakia) ICJ Reports 1997, 7 at 41 (para 53).

4   Articles on Responsibility of States for Internationally Wrongful Acts ('ARSIWA') art 25(1)(a),
    Report of the International Law Commission, 53rd Session (2001), YILC 2001, vol II(2). As to
    the requirement that the peril be grave and imminent, the mere apprehension of a possible peril
    is insufficient, and the requirement of imminence is synonymous with immediacy or proximity
    and goes far beyond the concept of 'possibility'; however, that does not exclude the possibility
    that a peril appearing in the long term might be held to be 'imminent' as soon as it is established
    that its realization, however far off in the future it might be, is certain and inevitable: see
    Gabčíkovo-Nagymaros Project (Hungary/Slovakia) ICJ Reports 1997, 7 at 42 (para 54).

5   Draft Articles on Responsibility of International Organizations ('DARIO') draft art 24(1)(a),
    Report of the International Law Commission, 61st Session (2009), A/64/10, ch IV.

6   ARSIWA art 25(1)(b); DARIO draft art 24(1)(b).

7   ARSIWA art 25(2)(a); DARIO draft art 24(2)(a). The International Court of Justice has raised, but not answered, the question: see *Legal Consequences of the Construction of a Wall in the Occupied Palestinian Territory (Advisory Opinion)* ICJ Reports 2004, 136 at 194–195 (para 140).

8   ARSIWA art 25(2)(b); DARIO draft art 24(2)(b). See also *Gabčíkovo-Nagymaros Project (Hungary/Slovakia)* ICJ Reports 1997, 7 at 45–46 (para 57).

9   *Gabčíkovo-Nagymaros Project (Hungary/Slovakia)* ICJ Reports 1997, 7 at 40 (para 51).

10   See the various decisions arising out of the Argentine financial crisis (although the reasoning as to the customary international law defence of necessity in a number of those decisions is obscured by considerations relating to the operation of provisions contained in the applicable bilateral investment treaties which dealt with situations of emergency or exceptions to their application based on considerations of security): *CMS Gas Transmission Co v Argentine Republic* ICSID Case No ARB/01/8, Award of 12 May 2005; and Decision on Annulment of 25 September 2007; *LG & E Energy Corpn, LG & E Capital Corpn, and LG & E International Inc v Argentine Republic* ICSID Case No ARB/02/1, Decision on Liability of 3 October 2006; *Enron Creditors Recovery Corpn (formerly Enron Corpn) and Ponderosa Assets LP v Argentine Republic* ICSID Case No ARB/01/3, Award of 22 May 2007; *Sempra Energy International v Argentine Republic* ICSID Case No ARB/02/16, Award of 28 September 2007; *BG Group plc v Republic of Argentina* Final Award of 24 December 2007, UNCITRAL; *Continental Casualty Co v Argentine Republic* ICSID Case No ARB/03/9, Award of 5 September 2008; *National Grid plc v Republic of Argentina* Award of 3 November 2008, UNCITRAL. One Tribunal queried, without expressing any view, whether the customary international law state of necessity could be invoked in order to preclude the wrongfulness of acts taken against an investor, rather than against another state: *BG Group plc v Republic of Argentina*, at para 408.

(v) Ancillary Responsibility in connection with the Act of another State or International Organisation

369. In general. Quite apart from the direct breach of its own obligations, a state or international organisation may incur responsibility as the result of its actions in connection with the internationally wrongful act of another state or international organisation[1]. Responsibility may arise due to the fact that the state or international organisation provides aid or assistance in relation to a breach by another state or international organisation of its own international obligations, because it directs and controls another state or international organisation in the breach of its international obligations[2], or because it exerts coercion over another state or international organisation so as to force it to breach its own international obligations[3]. In addition, it has been suggested that, in certain specific circumstances, the member states of an international organisation may incur responsibility as the result of conduct of the international organisation[4].

1   See PARA 370.

2   See PARA 371.

3   See PARA 372.

4   For the International Law Commission's proposals in this regard, see the draft Articles on Responsibility of International Organizations ('DARIO') draft arts 17, 60, 61, Report of the International Law Commission, 61st Session (2009), A/64/10, ch IV. Where a member state of an international organisation attempts to avoid compliance with its own international obligations by taking advantage of the fact that the international organisation has competence in relation to the subject matter of that obligation it is proposed that it should be irrelevant whether the conduct in question is internationally wrongful for the international organisation: see draft art 60. The rule proposed in draft art 61 deals with situations in which a member state is to be regarded as responsible for an internationally wrongful act of the international organisation of which it is a member on the basis that either it has accepted responsibility for the act in question, or it has led the injured party to rely on its responsibility it is proposed that the responsibility of the member state should be presumed to be subsidiary to that of the international organisation: draft art 61. It is also proposed that the responsibility of an international organisation which is a member of another international organisation should arise under similar conditions as for member states under draft arts 60 and 61: draft art 17.

**370.		Aid and assistance in the breach by a state or international organisation of its international obligations.** A state which aids or assists another state in the breach of an international obligation may thereby incur its own responsibility[1]. A state which provides aid or assistance is responsible for its own internationally wrongful act, consisting in the provision of the aid and assistance which assists the other state to breach its international obligation; it is not responsible, as such, for the act of the assisted state[2].

It is necessary that the state providing the aid or assistance should have knowledge of the circumstances giving rise to the breach of its international obligations by the aided or assisted state[3]. Further, the aid or assistance must be provided with a view to facilitating the commission of the internationally wrongful act by the other state, and must in fact do so, although it appears that there is no requirement that the aid or assistance should have been essential to the performance of the internationally wrongful act and it will be sufficient if the aid or assistance contributed significantly to the internationally wrongful act of the other state[4]. Finally, it appears that, in order for the responsibility of the state providing aid or assistance to arise, it is necessary that the internationally wrongful act in relation to which aid or assistance is provided must be such that it would have been wrongful if committed by the state providing the aid or assistance[5].

It seems that analogous rules apply in relation to the situation in which a state aids or assists an international organisation in breaching its international obligations[6], as well as to that in which an international organisation aids or assists another international organisation or a state in breaching its international obligations[7].

1	See the Articles on Responsibility of States for Internationally Wrongful Acts ('ARSIWA') art 16, Report of the International Law Commission, 53rd Session (2001), YILC 2001, vol II(2). The International Court of Justice has affirmed that that provision represents customary international law: *Application of the Convention on the Prevention and Punishment of the Crime of Genocide (Bosnia and Herzegovina v Serbia and Montenegro)* ICJ Reports, 26 February 2007 (para 420) (the court observed that the notion of 'complicity in genocide' was not different in substance from that aid or assistance provided by a state in relation to the internationally wrongful act of another state under ARSIWA art 16).

2	See ARSIWA Commentary to Article 16, para (10).

3	See ARSIWA art 16(a); and Commentary to Article 16, para (4). See also the approach of the International Court of Justice in *Application of the Convention on the Prevention and Punishment of the Crime of Genocide (Bosnia and Herzegovina v Serbia and Montenegro)* ICJ Reports, 26 February 2007 (paras 421, 432).

4	See ARSIWA, Commentary to Article 16, para (5).

5	See ARSIWA art 16(b); and Commentary to Article 16, para (6). In the field of treaty obligations, that requirement would appear to follow from the principle of the relative effect of treaties: see the Vienna Convention on the Law of Treaties (Vienna, 23 May 1969; TS 58 (1980); Cmnd 7964) arts 34, 35; and PARA 99.

6	Draft Articles on Responsibility of International Organizations ('DARIO') draft art 57, Report of the International Law Commission, 61st Session (2009), A/64/10, ch IV.

7	DARIO draft art 13.

**371.		Direction and control over the breach by a state or international organisation of its international obligations.** A state may incur international responsibility to the extent that it exercises direction or control over another state in the commission of an internationally wrongful act by that latter state[1]. In such circumstances each of the states involved incurs its own responsibility[2].

Historically, situations in which one state had power to direct and control another state in the commission of an internationally wrongful act arose principally in the context of relations of dependency such as suzerainty or a protectorate[3]. In modern practice, such situations have arisen in particular in the context of belligerent occupation[4], although it is possible that one state may have the power to direct and control the conduct of another in a specific sector by virtue of treaty[5].

The dominant state must actually direct and control[6] the conduct of the dependent state which breaches its international obligations, it is not sufficient that the dominant state may merely have the power to exercise direction and control over another state in some field, or that it may have the power to interfere in matters of administration internal to a dependent state, if it did not in fact do so[7]. It appears that it is also necessary that the dominant state should direct and control the commission of the wrongful act with knowledge of the circumstances, and that the internationally wrongful act of the dependent state must be such that it would be internationally wrongful if committed by the dominant state[8].

Rules analogous to those noted above appear to apply to situations in which a state directs or controls an international organisation in breaching its international obligations[9], and where an international organisation directs or controls either another international organisation or a state in breaching its international obligations[10].

1   See Articles on Responsibility of States for Internationally Wrongful Acts ('ARSIWA') art 17, Report of the International Law Commission, 53rd Session (2001), YILC 2001, vol II(2). See also *Robert E Brown Case* 6 RIAA 120 (1923); and *Heirs of the Duc de Guise* 13 RIAA 150 (1953).

2   Exceptionally the dependent state may be able to rely on a circumstance precluding wrongfulness, for instance, force majeure: see ARSIWA, Commentary to Article 17, para (9). As to force majeure see PARA 366.

3   See eg *Robert E Brown Case* 6 RIAA 120 (1923); *British Claims in the Spanish Zone of Morocco* 2 RIAA 615 (1925); *Rights of Nationals of the United States of America in Morocco (France v United States of America)* ICJ Reports 1952, 176; and see also ARSIWA, Commentary to Article 17, paras (2), (3). To the extent that a dependent territory or the constituent units of a federal state do not have separate legal personality and are not considered to be states under international law, their situation falls to be governed by the normal rules of state responsibility, such that their conduct is to be attributed to the state upon which they are dependent or of which they form part: see ARSIWA, Commentary to Article 17, para (4). As to the attribution of the acts of constituent entities of a federal state see PARA 339.

4   See eg *Heirs of the Duc de Guise* 13 RIAA 150 (1953).

5   See ARSIWA, Commentary to Article 17, para (5).

6   'Direct' requires more than mere incitement or suggestion, rather there must be actual direction of an operative kind; 'control' refers to cases of domination over the commission of wrongful conduct and not simply the exercise of oversight, still less of influence or concern: ARSIWA, Commentary to Article 17, para (7).

7   See ARSIWA, Commentary to Article 17, para (6); and *Heirs of the Duc de Guise* 13 RIAA 150 at 161 (1953) (where it was held despite the fact of Allied occupation and administrative control of Sicily at the relevant time, Italy could not avoid international responsibility arising from the requisition of the property of a foreign national since there had been no interference by the commander of the Allied Forces or of any of the Allied Authorities which had resulted in the relevant decrees issued by the Region of Sicily); and *Robert E Brown Case* 6 RIAA 120 at 130,131 (1923) (where it was held that the suzerainty exercised by Great Britain over the South African Republic was not sufficient to make it responsible for all acts of the legislature, executive and judiciary of the South African Republic, and that Great Britain had not in fact interfered in the internal administration of the South African Republic).

8   ARSIWA art 17(a), (b).

9   Draft Articles on Responsibility of International Organizations ('DARIO') draft art 58, Report of the International Law Commission, 61st Session (2009), A/64/10, ch IV.

10 DARIO draft art 14. It is also proposed that an international organisation should incur responsibility where it adopts a decision binding a member state or another international organisation to commit an act that would be internationally wrongful if committed by the international organisation adopting the decision and which would circumvent its international

obligations, or where it authorises or recommends a member state or international organisation to take such action and such action is in fact taken as a result of the authorisation or recommendation: see draft art 16(1). In this regard, it is suggested that it is irrelevant whether or not the act in question is internationally wrongful for the member state or international organisation which actually commits the act: see draft art 16(3).

372.   Coercion resulting in the breach by a state or international organisation of its international obligations.   A state which coerces another state to commit an internationally wrongful act will incur international responsibility for the act if, but for the coercion, the act in question would have been an internationally wrongful act of the coerced state and the coercing state applies the coercion with knowledge of the circumstances of the act[1]. It appears that the coercion will normally have to amount to force majeure for the coerced state, such that its will is forced, giving it no effective choice other than to comply with the wishes of the coercing state[2]. In this regard, it is not sufficient that compliance with the obligation in question is made more difficult or onerous, or that assistance or direction is provided[3]. Coercion for these purposes is not limited to unlawful coercion, but may extend to serious economic pressure[4]. Given the equation of coercion with force majeure, the coerced state will often be able to successfully invoke a circumstance precluding wrongfulness in order to avoid its own responsibility[5].

Rules analogous to those noted above appear to apply to situations in which an international organisation coerces a state or another international organisation[6].

1   Articles on Responsibility of States for Internationally Wrongful Acts ('ARSIWA') art 18, Report of the International Law Commission, 53rd Session (2001), YILC 2001, vol II(2). Practice in this regard is rare, although see *Standard Oil Co (Romano-Americana)* (1925/1928) 5 Hackworth's Digest 702–705; and see also ARSIWA, Commentary to Article 18, para (7). As to coercion as a factor vitiating consent in the law of treaties see PARA 103.
2   See ARSIWA, Commentary to Article 18, para (2).
3   See ARSIWA, Commentary to Article 18, para (2). As to force majeure as a circumstance precluding wrongfulness see PARA 366; as to the possible responsibility of a state which aids or assists another state in the commission of an internationally wrongful act see PARA 370; as to the possible responsibility of a state which directs or controls another state in the commission of an internationally wrongful act see PARA 371.
4   See ARSIWA, Commentary to Article 18, para (3)
5   See ARSIWA, Commentary to Article 18, para (4).
6   Draft Articles on Responsibility of International Organizations ('DARIO') draft art 15, Report of the International Law Commission, 61st Session (2009), A/64/10, ch IV.

(3) THE CONTENT OF INTERNATIONAL RESPONSIBILITY

373.   In general.   Every internationally wrongful act of a state or international organisation entails the international responsibility of that state or international organisation[1]. Accordingly, the international responsibility of a state or international organisation arises as the result of the breach of an international obligation by conduct which is attributable to the state or international organisation[2].

The content of international responsibility consists of a number of legal consequences which occur upon the commission of an internationally wrongful act[3]. The principal consequence is the coming into existence of new obligations, sometimes referred to as secondary obligations, for the responsible state or international organisation[4]. In this regard, the most important obligation incumbent upon the responsible state or international organisation is that requiring it to make reparation in an adequate form for the breach of the international obligation[5]. In addition, obligations arise for the responsible state or international organisation to cease the internationally wrongful act if it is of a continuing character, and, if appropriate, to provide appropriate assurances and guarantees of non-repetition[6]. Exceptionally, as the result of certain serious breaches of obligations deriving from peremptory norms of international law, obligations may arise for actors other than the state or international organisation responsible for the internationally wrongful act[7]. Depending upon the character and content of the obligation breached, the secondary obligations in question may be owed to one or more states, one or more international organisations, or to the international community as a whole[8]. Further, it appears that the beneficiary of the obligation to make reparation may be an entity other than a state or an international organisation[9]. The coming into existence of these secondary obligations does not affect the continuing obligation to perform the underlying primary obligation which has been breached[10].

1　Articles on Responsibility of States for Internationally Wrongful Acts ('ARSIWA') art 1, Report of the International Law Commission, 53rd Session (2001), YILC 2001, vol II(2); draft Articles on Responsibility of International Organizations ('DARIO') draft art 3, Report of the International Law Commission, 61st Session (2009), A/64/10, ch IV.

2　As to attribution see PARA 337 et seq; as to breach of an international obligation see PARA 359 et seq.

3　See ARSIWA art 28; DARIO art 27. See also eg *Legal Consequences of the Construction of a Wall in the Occupied Palestinian Territory (Advisory Opinion)* ICJ Reports 2004, 136 at 195–197 (paras 143–148); *Armed Activities on the Territory of the Congo (Democratic Republic of the Congo v Uganda)* ICJ Reports, 19 December 2005 (para 251); *Avena and Other Mexican Nationals (Mexico v United States of America)* ICJ Reports 2004, 12 at 58 (para 115). As to the objective nature of international responsibility see PARA 329.

4　The distinction between the primary obligation breached and the secondary obligations arising as a consequence is to be distinguished from the distinction sometimes drawn between primary (substantive) rules of international law and the secondary rules of the law of international responsibility, as to which see PARA 330.

5　*Factory at Chorzów (Jurisdiction)* PCIJ Ser A No 9 at 21 (1927); and *Factory at Chorzów* PCIJ Ser A No 17 at 47 (1928). As to the obligation to make reparation see PARA 374 et seq.

6　See PARA 381.

7　See PARA 382.

8　See ARSIWA art 33(1); DARIO draft art 32(1). As to the possibility of a plurality of injured states or international organisations see ARSIWA art 46; and DARIO draft art 46.

9　See ARSIWA art 33(2); DARIO draft art 32(2). As to the possibility that a state or international organisation which is not injured by an internationally wrongful act may invoke the responsibility of the responsible state or international organisation and claim performance of the obligation of reparation on behalf of the injured state or international organisation or any other beneficiary of the obligation breached see ARSIWA art 48(2)(b); and DARIO draft art 48(4)(b). As to the possibility that such states may also require cessation and, if appropriate, the provision of assurances and guarantees of non-repetition see ARSIWA art 48(2)(a); and DARIO draft art 48(4)(b).

10　See ARSIWA art 29; DARIO art 28. See also *Legal Consequences of the Construction of a Wall in the Occupied Palestinian Territory (Advisory Opinion)* ICJ Reports 2004, 136 at 197 (para 150).

374. The obligation to make reparation. It is a fundamental principle of international law that the breach of an international obligation involves an obligation to make reparation in an adequate form[1]. The obligation upon the responsible state is to make full reparation for the injury caused by the internationally wrongful act; reparation must, so far as possible, wipe out the consequences of the breach of obligation and re-establish the situation which would, in all probability, have existed if the internationally wrongful act had not been committed[2]. For these purposes, injury includes any damage, whether material or moral, caused by the internationally wrongful act[3].

Reparation may take various forms, consisting of one or more of restitution, the payment of compensation or the provision of satisfaction, either singly or in combination[4].

1　See *Factory at Chorzów (Jurisdiction)* PCIJ Ser A No 9 at 21 (1927); *(Merits)* PCIJ Ser A No 17 at 47 (1928). See also *Gabčíkovo-Nagymaros Project (Hungary/Slovakia)* ICJ Reports 1997, 7 at 81 (para 152); *Arrest Warrant of 11 April 2000 (Democratic Republic of the Congo v Belgium)* ICJ Reports 2002, 3 at 31–32 (para 76); *Avena and Other Mexican Nationals (Mexico v United States of America)* ICJ Reports 2004, 12 at 59 (para 119); *Legal Consequences of the Construction of a Wall in the Occupied Palestinian Territory (Advisory Opinion)* ICJ Reports 2004, 136 at 198 (para 152); *Armed Activities on the Territory of the Congo (Democratic Republic of the Congo v Uganda)* ICJ Reports, 19 December 2005 (para 259); *Application of the Convention on the Prevention and Punishment of the Crime of Genocide (Bosnia and Herzegovina v Serbia and Montenegro)* ICJ Reports, 26 February 2007 (para 460). See also the Articles on Responsibility of States for Internationally Wrongful Acts ('ARSIWA') art 31(1), Report of the International Law Commission, 53rd Session (2001), YILC 2001, vol II(2); draft Articles on Responsibility of International Organizations ('DARIO') draft art 30(1), Report of the International Law Commission, 61st Session (2009), A/64/10, ch IV. See also the Statute of the International Court of Justice (San Francisco, 26 June 1945; TS 67 (1946); Cmd 7015) art 36(2)(d) (the Optional Clause) which includes 'the nature or extent of the reparation to be made for the breach of an international obligation' among the matters in relation to which states may accept the compulsory jurisdiction of the court to resolve disputes. Where the jurisdiction of the International Court of Justice derives from a specific treaty provision, a dispute regarding the appropriate remedies for violation of one of the provisions of the treaty is a dispute that arises out of its interpretation or application and accordingly falls within the court's jurisdiction; as such where jurisdiction exists over a dispute on a particular matter, no separate basis for jurisdiction is required by the court to consider the remedies a party has requested for the breach of the obligation: see eg *Factory at Chorzów (Jurisdiction)* PCIJ Ser A No 9 at 22 (1927); *LaGrand (Germany v United States of America)* ICJ Reports 2001, 466 at 485 (para 48).

2　*Factory at Chorzów* PCIJ Ser A No 17 at 47 (1928); *Martini Case* 2 RIAA 975 at 1002 (1930); *Arrest Warrant of 11 April 2000 (Democratic Republic of the Congo v Belgium)* ICJ Reports 2002, 3 at 31–32 (paras 76–77); *Armed Activities on the Territory of the Congo (Democratic Republic of the Congo v Uganda)* ICJ Reports, 19 December 2005 (para 259); *Application of the Convention on the Prevention and Punishment of the Crime of Genocide (Bosnia and Herzegovina v Serbia and Montenegro)* ICJ Reports, 26 February 2007 (para 460) (referring to art 31 ARSIWA).

3　See ARSIWA art 31(2); DARIO draft art 30(2).

4　See ARSIWA art 34; DARIO draft art 33. As to restitution see PARA 375; as to compensation see PARA 376 et seq; as to satisfaction see PARA 380.

375.　Restitution.　Given that the underlying purpose of the obligation of reparation is to re-establish, so far as possible, the situation which would have existed if the wrongful act or omission had not occurred[1], restitution in kind (restitutio in integrum) constitutes the primary form of reparation[2]. The obligation to make restitution does not apply to the extent that restitution is materially impossible[3], or to the extent that provision of restitution would involve a burden out of all proportion to the benefit deriving from restitution instead of compensation[4].

Where restitution is not materially possible, the obligation to make reparation may be limited to an obligation to pay compensation or provide satisfaction[5]. Even where restitution may in theory be possible, a claimant state may claim monetary compensation in its place[6].

As a matter of the law of England, the secondary obligation of restitution incumbent on the United Kingdom as a matter of the customary international law of state responsibility as the result of the breach of an obligation under a treaty may not be relied upon in order to enforce indirectly that treaty obligation[7].

1   See PARA 374.

2   For instance, the release of a person unlawfully detained (see eg *United States Diplomatic and Consular Staff in Teheran (United States of America v Iran)* ICJ Reports 1980, 3 at 44–45 (para 95)); the repeal or rescission of a legal or executive measure or a judgment (*Martini Case* 2 RIAA 975 at 1002 (1930); *Arrest Warrant of 11 April 2000 (Democratic Republic of the Congo v Belgium)* ICJ Reports 2002, 3 at 32–34 (paras 76–78)); the refund of customs duties or taxes which were levied unlawfully (*Compagnie Générale des Asphaltes de France* 9 RIAA 389 (1903); *Palmarejo and Mexican Gold Fields Ltd* 5 RIAA 298 at 302 (1931)); or the allocation of premises for use as a foreign embassy or consulate (*British Claims in the Spanish Zone of Morocco* 2 RIAA 615 at 726 (1925)). Territorial disputes may be settled by restitution of territory: see *Case concerning the Temple of Preah Vihear (Cambodia v Thailand)* ICJ Reports 1962, 6 (where the court also held that Thailand should return certain objects removed from the temple); and *Legal Consequences of the Construction of a Wall in the Occupied Palestinian Territory (Advisory Opinion)* ICJ Reports 2004, 136 at 198 (paras 152–153) (held that Israel was obliged to return the 'land, orchards, olive groves and other immovable property' seized from natural or legal persons in order to construct the wall in breach of international law).

3   Articles on Responsibility of States for Internationally Wrongful Acts ('ARSIWA') art 35(a), Report of the International Law Commission, 53rd Session (2001), YILC 2001, vol II(2); draft Articles on Responsibility of International Organizations ('DARIO') draft art 34(a), Report of the International Law Commission, 61st Session (2009), A/64/10, ch IV. Restitution may be impossible for material reasons (eg where a ship which has been unlawfully seized has subsequently been sunk), for legal reasons (eg where a state has, in the exercise of its sovereign powers, put an end to a contract or a licence, or any other foreign investor's entitlement, specific performance must be deemed legally impossible: see *Occidental Petroleum Corpn and Occidental Petroleum and Exploration Co v Republic of Ecuador* ICSID Case No ARB/06/11, Decision on Provisional Measures of 17 August 2007, at paras 75–81; *Government of Kuwait v American Independent Oil Co (Aminoil)* (1982) 66 ILR 519 at 533). The incidence of the rights of third parties may also lead to a conclusion that restitution is impossible: see eg *Forests of Central Rhodope* 3 RIAA 1406 at 1432 (1933) (although in that case there were a number of other factors which in combination formed the basis for the conclusion that restitution was not possible). Where the jurisdiction of an arbitral tribunal is based on a compromise, the particular terms thereof may give the tribunal discretion to decide on the most appropriate form of reparation, and it may either grant pecuniary compensation or leave the choice of which of the means of reparation should be provided to the respondent state: see eg *Walter Fletcher Smith* 2 RIAA 913 at 918 (1929); *Forests of Central Rhodope* 3 RIAA 1406 at 1432 (1933); *Junghans* 3 RIAA 1845 at 1850 (1939).

4   ARSIWA art 35(b); DARIO draft art 34(b).

5   See eg *Gabčíkovo-Nagymaros Project (Hungary/Slovakia)* ICJ Reports 1997, 7 at 81 (para 152); *Application of the Convention on the Prevention and Punishment of the Crime of Genocide (Bosnia and Herzegovina v Serbia and Montenegro)* 26 February 2007, para 460. As to compensation see PARA 376 et seq; as to satisfaction see PARA 380.

6   See *Factory at Chorzów* PCIJ Ser A No 17 at 47 (1928). See also ARSIWA art 43(2)(b); DARIO draft art 43(2)(b).

7   See *R v Lyons* [2002] UKHL 44, [2003] 1 AC 976, [2002] 4 All ER 1028, at [36]–[41].

376. Compensation. Reparation for breach of an international obligation may consist of a pecuniary payment, normally referred to as compensation[1]. The claimant state may choose to claim compensation instead of restitution, and may be required to do so to the extent that restitution is materially impossible[2]. The requirement that reparation be full presupposes the payment of such a sum as would put the claimant so far as possible in a financial position identical to that in which he would have been placed had restitution been made[3]. The value of compensation must therefore be calculated as at the date of the award or judgment and not as at the date of the unlawful act[4]. Arbitral tribunals have rejected claims for punitive or exemplary damages inspired by disapproval of an unlawful act and as a measure of deterrence[5].

1   *Factory at Chorzów* PCIJ Ser A No 17 at 27 (1928); *The 'Lusitania'* 7 RIAA 32 at 34 (1923). In
    some of the older cases, this form of reparation is referred to as 'indemnity'. For detailed
    consideration of the principles applicable to calculation of compensation, see Articles on
    Responsibility of States for Internationally Wrongful Acts ('ARSIWA') Commentary to
    Article 36, Report of the International Law Commission, 53rd Session (2001), YILC 2001,
    vol II(2).
2   As to restitution see PARA 375.
3   See PARA 374.
4   In *Factory at Chorzów* PCIJ Ser A No 17 (1928), the court distinguished between a lawful
    taking of property, for which the compensation would be computed on the basis of the market
    value of the property at the date of the dispossession and interest to the date of payment, and an
    unlawful taking, as in that case where the taking amounted to a violation of a treaty, in which
    the compensation should be based on the value of the property including any increase in value
    since the time of the taking and loss of profits. As to loss of profits see PARA 377. If an object is
    destroyed, the replacement cost is the basis for computation of compensation: *British Claims in
    the Spanish Zone of Morocco* 2 RIAA 615 at 735 (1925). As to compensation for expropriation
    of property see PARA 473.
5   *The 'Lusitania'* 7 RIAA 32 at 39, 43 (1923); *Responsibility of Germany to Portugal (Cysne)* 2
    RIAA 1035 at 1077 (1930); *Trail Smelter* 3 RIAA 1905 at 1932, 1954 (1935/1941); *Torrey* 9
    RIAA 225 (1903); *The 'Carthage'* 11 RIAA 457 (1913); *The 'Manouba'* 11 RIAA 471 (1913);
    Vélasquez Rodríguez v Honduras (Reparations and Costs) (1989) Inter-Am Ct HR (Ser C) No 7.
    Cf *The 'I'm Alone'* 3 RIAA 1609 (1935), in which payment of a sum of $25,000 was ordered by
    way of reparation for the violation of the flag on the high seas; however, the report was of a
    conciliation and advisory board and not an arbitral award. In some older cases involving
    personal injury to nationals, small amounts were awarded to the claimant government by way
    of sanction as part of the measure of damages; this seems to have been done in most cases in
    order to persuade the delinquent government to improve its system of justice: see the *Putnam
    Case* 4 RIAA 151 (1927); *Massey Case* 4 RIAA 155 (1927); *Kennedy Case* 4 RIAA 194 (1927);
    Venable 4 RIAA 219 (1927); *Mecham Case* 4 RIAA 440 (1929); *Richeson* 6 RIAA 325 (1933).
    Penal damages based on the theory of implied state complicity have been rejected: *Janes Case* 4
    RIAA 82 (1926). Cf the award of a substantial sum for 'moral damage' in *Desert Line Projects
    LLC v Republic of Yemen* ICSID Case No ARB/05/17, Award of 6 February 2008, at
    paras 289–290.

377. Compensation for loss of profits.

In view of the principle that compensation for breach of an international obligation requires that the claimant be placed in a financial position identical with that in which he would have been had restitution been made[1], loss of expected profits constitutes part of the compensation required[2]. In cases of repudiation of state contracts, a distinction has often been drawn between actual losses and expenses (damnum emergens) and loss of profits (lucrum cessans)[3]. Both have been allowed[4], provided, in the case of loss of profits, that they are not too remote or speculative, and that they were earnings which could have been possible in the ordinary course of events[5].

1   See PARAS 374–375.
2   *Factory at Chorzów* PCIJ Ser A No 17 at 53 (1928); see also *Cape Horn Pigeon* 9 RIAA 63
    (1902); *Norwegian Shipowners Case* 1 RIAA 307 at 338 (1922); *The 'Kate'* 6 RIAA 77 at 81
    (1921); *Thomas E Bayard* 6 RIAA 154 (1925).
3   *Delagoa Bay Railway Co* (1893) Moore Int Arb 1865; *May* 15 RIAA 47 at 71 (1900); *Shufeldt*
    2 RIAA 1079 at 1099 (1930); *Walter Fletcher Smith* 2 RIAA 913 (1929).
4   *Oliva* 10 RIAA 600 (1903); *Rudloff Case* 9 RIAA 244 (1903); *Tattler* 6 RIAA 48 (1920);
    Sonora Land and Timber Co 5 RIAA 263 (1931); *Factory at Chorzów* PCIJ Ser A No 17 at 57
    (1928); SS *'Wimbledon'* PCIJ Ser A No 1 at 32 (1923).
5   *Cape Horn Pigeon* 9 RIAA 63 (1902); *British Claims in the Spanish Zone of Morocco* 2 RIAA
    615 at 658 (1925); *Shufeldt* 2 RIAA 1079 (1930); *Phillips Petroleum Co v Islamic Republic of
    Iran* 21 Iran-US CTR 79 (1989).

378. Causation and remoteness of damage.

Given that the obligation to make reparation of the state or international organisation responsible for the breach of an international obligation is to efface all the consequences of the unlawful act, the obligation to make reparation extends so as cover all those consequences which flow from the breach of the obligation and are proximate consequences of it[1]. Losses which are the consequence only of an unexpected concatenation of circumstances are excluded[2]. The conduct of the victim as contributing to his losses may be taken into account[3].

1 *Administrative Decision No II (United States v Germany)* 7 RIAA 23 at 29, 30 (1923); *Administrative Decision No VII (United States v Germany)* 7 RIAA 330 (1926); *China Navigation Co Ltd* 6 RIAA 64 (1921). See also *Application of the Convention on the Prevention and Punishment of the Crime of Genocide (Bosnia and Herzegovina v Serbia and Montenegro)* ICJ Reports, 26 February 2007 (para 462) (in which the International Court of Justice framed the test in terms of whether there was a 'sufficiently direct and certain causal nexus' between the internationally wrongful act and the injury suffered, and concluded that the requisite causal nexus between the violation of the obligation to prevent genocide and the damage resulting from the commission of genocide by third parties had not been established).

2 See eg *Responsibility of Germany for Damage to Portuguese Colonies ('Naulilaa')* 2 RIAA 1011 at 1031 (1928); *British Claims in the Spanish Zone of Morocco* 2 RIAA 615 at 658 (1925); *Provident Mutual Life Insurance Co* 7 RIAA 91 at 112, 113 (1924); *Garland Steamship Corpn* 7 RIAA 73 (1924).

3 *Responsibility of Germany to Portugal (Cysne)* 2 RIAA 1035 at 1076 (1930); *Dix* 9 RIAA 119 (1903); *Roberts* 9 RIAA 204 (1903). Generally, in the determination of reparation, account is to be taken of any contribution to the injury suffered by any wilful or negligent action or omission on the part of the injured state or international organisation, or of any individual or entity in relation to which reparation is sought: see Articles on Responsibility of States for Internationally Wrongful Acts ('ARSIWA') art 39, Report of the International Law Commission, 53rd Session (2001), YILC 2001, vol II(2); draft Articles on Responsibility of International Organizations ('DARIO') draft art 38, Report of the International Law Commission, 61st Session (2009), A/64/10, ch IV.

379. Interest. Given the overall aim of reparation of wiping out all the consequences of an internationally wrongful act, the payment of interest may constitute a proper element in the award of compensation, given that it makes good the loss of the claimant of the use of the principal sum during the period in which the principal sum has been withheld[1]. Generally, interest runs from the date when the principal sum should have been paid until the date the obligation to pay is fulfilled[2]. In cases where property has been taken and destroyed, if no allowance for loss of profits is made, interest will normally run from the date of the taking[3]. In cases of personal injuries, where a lump sum is awarded for all damage sustained, or in the case of liquidated debts, interest runs only from the date of the award[4]. The rate of interest is not fixed[5], but should be set so as to compensate for the actual loss suffered[6]. In general claims for compound interest have been rejected[7], although in exceptional circumstances an award for compound interest may be appropriate in order to ensure full reparation[8].

1 See the Articles on Responsibility of States for Internationally Wrongful Acts ('ARSIWA') art 38(1), Report of the International Law Commission, 53rd Session (2001), YILC 2001, vol II(2); draft Articles on Responsibility of International Organizations ('DARIO') draft art 37(1), Report of the International Law Commission, 61st Session (2009), A/64/10, ch IV. See also *Illinois Central Railroad Co* 4 RIAA 134 (1926); *Administrative Decision No III (United States v Germany)* 7 RIAA 64 at 66 (1923); *Islamic Republic of Iran v United States of America (Case A-19)* 16 Iran-US CTR 285 at 289–290 (1987). Interest should be specifically requested and the claim for interest should be included with the principal claim: *Friede* 26 ILR 352 (1956). If interest is not requested, a tribunal may not be able to award it: see eg *Postal Claim* 9 RIAA 328 (1903).

2 See ARSIWA art 38(2); DARIO draft art 37(2)

3 *British Claims in the Spanish Zone of Morocco* 2 RIAA 615 at 657, 697, 735 (1925); *Bethune Case* 6 RIAA 32 (1914); *Administrative Decision No III (United States v Germany)* 7 RIAA 64 (1923); *National Paper and Type Co* 4 RIAA 327 (1928); *Cook* 4 RIAA 661 (1930); *Shufeldt* 2 RIAA 1079 at 1101 (1930). Where the wrong is a refusal to pay, it is committed at the time of the refusal, and interest begins to run at that date: *Stevenson* 9 RIAA 494 at 510 (1903).

4   *SS 'Wimbledon'* PCIJ Ser A No 1 at 32 (1923); *Administrative Decision No III (United States v Germany)* 7 RIAA 64 (1923); *Trail Smelter* 3 RIAA 1905 at 1933 (1935/1941). However, in some claims involving personal injuries, claims for interest have been disallowed altogether: *De Sabla Case* 6 RIAA 358 (1933); *Faulkner Case* 4 RIAA 67 (1926).

5   In *SS 'Wimbledon'* PCIJ Ser A No 1 (1923), the Permanent Court of International Justice took into account the financial situation of the world and the conditions prevailing for public loans and awarded 6%. In *British Claims in the Spanish Zone of Morocco* 2 RIAA 615 at 650 (1925), interest at 7% was awarded as the rate prevailing in Morocco; the same rate was awarded in *Pinson* 5 RIAA 327 (1928) as the rate prevailing in Mexico.

6   See ARSIWA art 38(1); DARIO draft art 37(1); and *Norwegian Shipowners Case* 1 RIAA 307 (1922). A contractual rate of interest may also be awarded; see e g *Zohrer* 6 RIAA 272 (1928).

7   See e g *British Claims in the Spanish Zone of Morocco* 2 RIAA 615 at 650 (1925); *French Claims against Peru* 1 RIAA 215 at 220 (1920); *Norwegian Shipowners Case* 1 RIAA 307 at 341 (1922); *RJ Reynolds Tobacco Co v Government of the Islamic Republic of Iran* 7 Iran-US CTR 181 at 191–192 (1984).

8   See ARSIWA Commentary to Article 38, paras (8), (9); and see *Compania del Desarrollo de Santa Elena, SA v Republic of Costa Rica* ICSID Case No ARB/96/1, Award of 17 February 2000, 5 ICSID Reports 157 at paras 103–105.

380.   Satisfaction. The responsible state or international organisation is under an obligation to provide satisfaction for the injury caused by its internationally wrongful act to the extent that that injury cannot be made good by restitution or compensation[1]. Satisfaction may take the form of an acknowledgment of the breach, an expression of regret, a formal apology or any other appropriate modality[2]. Where a dispute involving questions of international responsibility has resulted in litigation, a judicial declaration that there has been a breach of international law may constitute satisfaction for the injured party[3]. In some cases the court or tribunal may make a declaration of legal rights[4].

1   Articles on Responsibility of States for Internationally Wrongful Acts ('ARSIWA') art 37(1), Report of the International Law Commission, 53rd Session (2001), YILC 2001, vol II(2); draft Articles on Responsibility of International Organizations ('DARIO') draft art 36(1), Report of the International Law Commission, 61st Session (2009), A/64/10, ch IV.

2   ARSIWA art 37(2); DARIO draft art 36(2). However, it appears that there are some limits upon the forms of satisfaction which may be demanded, in so far as satisfaction may not be out of proportion to the injury or take a form humiliating to the responsible state or international organisation: ARSIWA art 37(3); DARIO draft art 36(3).

3   See e g *The 'Carthage'* 11 RIAA 457 (1913); *The 'Manouba'* 11 RIAA 471 (1913); *Corfu Channel (United Kingdom v Albania)* ICJ Reports 1949, 4 at 35, 113, 114; *Arrest Warrant of 11 April 2000 (Democratic Republic of the Congo v Belgium)* ICJ Reports 2002, 3 at 31 (para 75); *Application of the Convention on the Prevention and Punishment of the Crime of Genocide (Bosnia and Herzegovina v Serbia and Montenegro)* ICJ Reports, 26 February 2007 (para 463); *Certain Questions of Mutual Assistance in Criminal Matters (Djibouti v France)* ICJ Reports, 4 June 2008 (paras 203–205).

4   See e g *Mavrommatis Jerusalem Concessions* PCIJ Ser A No 5 at 44, 51 (1925).

381.   Cessation and assurances and guarantees of non-repetition. In the case of a breach of a continuing character[1], quite apart from the continued duty to comply with the underlying primary obligation breached[2], there arises an obligation incumbent upon the responsible state to cease the continuing wrongful conduct[3]. In addition, in an appropriate case, the responsible state may be under an obligation to provide assurances and guarantees of non-repetition[4].

1   As to breaches of continuing character see PARA 360.

2   See the Articles on Responsibility of States for Internationally Wrongful Acts ('ARSIWA') art 29, Report of the International Law Commission, 53rd Session (2001), YILC 2001, vol II(2); draft Articles on Responsibility of International Organizations ('DARIO') draft art 28, Report of the International Law Commission, 61st Session (2009), A/64/10, ch IV.

3   ARSIWA art 30(a); DARIO draft art 29(a). See *Haya de la Torre (Colombia/Peru)* ICJ Reports 1951, 71 at 82; *United States Diplomatic and Consular Staff in Teheran (United States of*

America v Iran) ICJ Reports 1980, 3 at 44 (para 95); *Military and Paramilitary Activities in and against Nicaragua (Nicaragua v United States of America)* ICJ Reports 1986, 14 at 149 (para 292(12)); *Legal Consequences of the Construction of a Wall in the Occupied Palestinian Territory (Advisory Opinion)* ICJ Reports 2004, 136 at 197 (para 150); *Avena and Other Mexican Nationals (Mexico v United States of America)* ICJ Reports 2004, 12 at 68 (para 148) (request for an order requiring cessation refused on the basis that the breach was not of a continuing character); and *Armed Activities on the Territory of the Congo (Democratic Republic of the Congo v Uganda)* ICJ Reports, 19 December 2005 (para 254).

4   ARSIWA art 30(b); DARIO draft art 29(b). See *LaGrand (Germany v United States of America)* ICJ Reports 2001, 466 at 512–513 (para 124); and *Avena and Other Mexican Nationals (Mexico v United States of America)* ICJ Reports 2004, 12 at 68–69 (paras 149–150) (in both of which the International Court of Justice declined to make orders requiring the provision of assurances or the giving of guarantees of non-repetition on the basis that the commitments expressed by the respondent state as to steps to be taken in the future to avoid further breaches had to be regarded as meeting the requests). See also *Request for Interpretation of the Judgment of 31 March 2004 in the Case Concerning Avena and Other Mexican Nationals (Mexico v United States of America) (Mexico v United States of America)* ICJ Reports, 19 January 2009 (paras 58–60); *Land and Maritime Boundary between Cameroon and Nigeria (Cameroon v Nigeria: Equatorial Guinea Intervening)* ICJ Reports 2002, 303 at 452 (para 318) (while recognising that a request to require the respondent state to give assurances and guarantees of non-repetition was undoubtedly admissible, the International Court of Justice declined to make such an order on the basis that its judgment had defined the boundary and it was not possible to envisage a situation in which either party would not respect the territorial integrity of the other); and *Armed Activities on the Territory of the Congo (Democratic Republic of the Congo v Uganda)* ICJ Reports, 19 December 2005 (paras 256–257).

382.   Obligations arising for third states as the result of serious breaches of obligations arising under peremptory norms of general international law.

It appears that in relation to certain breaches of international law, obligations may arise for all other third states or international organisations[1]. In this regard, it would appear that the relevant category is that of serious breaches of obligations arising under peremptory norms of general international law (jus cogens)[2]. In relation to such breaches, at least in certain circumstances, third states and international organisations may be under an obligation to cooperate to bring the breach to an end through lawful means, not to recognise as lawful any situation created by a such a breach, nor to render any aid or assistance in maintaining that situation[3].

1   See the Articles on Responsibility of States for Internationally Wrongful Acts ('ARSIWA') arts 40, 41, Report of the International Law Commission, 53rd Session (2001), YILC 2001, vol II(2); draft Articles on Responsibility of International Organizations ('DARIO') draft arts 40, 41, Report of the International Law Commission, 61st Session (2009), A/64/10, ch IV. See also *Legal Consequences for States of the Continued Presence of South Africa in Namibia (South West Africa) notwithstanding Security Council Resolution 276 (1970) (Advisory Opinion)* ICJ Reports 1971, 16; *Legal Consequences of the Construction of a Wall in the Occupied Palestinian Territory (Advisory Opinion)* ICJ Reports 2004, 136 at 197 (para 148).

2   ARSIWA art 40, 41; DARIO drafts arts 40 and 41. See also ARSIWA, Commentary to Article 40, paras (4)–(6). In *Legal Consequences of the Construction of a Wall in the Occupied Palestinian Territory (Advisory Opinion)* ICJ Reports 2004, 136 at 199–200 (paras 155–159), the International Court of Justice appeared to attach the consequences for third states and international organisations to the erga omnes character of the obligations in question, rather than to the fact that they constitute peremptory norms (jus cogens), although the relevant passages of the court's advisory opinion are far from clear in this regard. According to the approach taken by the International Law Commission ('ILC') in order to attract the additional consequences a breach of an obligation arising under a peremptory norm must be serious, and will be serious if it involves a 'gross or systematic failure' to comply with the obligation in question: ARSIWA, Commentary to Article 40, para (7). As to peremptory norms of international law (jus cogens) and obligations erga omnes see PARA 11.

3   ARSIWA art 41; DARIO draft art 41. The existence of such obligations for third states and international organisations is relatively well established in relation to illegal territorial situations

(for instance, the unlawful annexation of territory, or the unlawful denial of self-determination to the population of a territory: see eg *Legal Consequences for States of the Continued Presence of South Africa in Namibia (South West Africa) notwithstanding Security Council Resolution 276 (1970) (Advisory Opinion)* ICJ Reports 1971, 16; and *Legal Consequences of the Construction of a Wall in the Occupied Palestinian Territory (Advisory Opinion)* ICJ Reports 2004, 136 at 200 (paras 159, 160). However, whether or not such obligations arise as a matter of customary international law in relation to other serious breaches of obligations arising under peremptory norms of general international law (jus cogens) is far from clear. For English decisions in this regard see *R (on the application of Mohamed) v Secretary of State for Foreign and Commonwealth Affairs* [2008] EWHC 2048 (Admin), [2009] 1 WLR 2579, [2008] All ER (D) 123 (Aug) at [170]–[183] (the jus cogens prohibition of torture did not entail any obligation for the government to disclose documents which could help prove that an individual had been subjected to torture); *R (on the application of Al Rawi and others) v Secretary of State for Foreign and Commonwealth Affairs and Secretary of State for the Home Department* [2006] EWHC 972 (Admin), [2006] NLJR 797, (2006) Times, 19 May at [69]–[70] (affd on other grounds [2006] EWCA Civ 1279, [2008] QB 289, [2007] 2 WLR 1219); *R (on the application of Al-Haq) v Secretary of State for Foreign and Commonwealth Affairs* [2009] EWHC 1910 (Admin) at [57]; and cf *A v Secretary of State for the Home Department (No 2)* [2005] UKHL 71, [2006] 2 AC 221, [2006] 1 All ER 575 at [34].

13. DIPLOMATIC PROTECTION AND CONSULAR ASSISTANCE

(1) IN GENERAL

383.   Introduction. A distinction is to be drawn between, on the one hand, the exercise of diplomatic protection by a state[1] and, on the other, the provision of measures of consular assistance[2]. Both types of action fall within the much broader category of action which may be taken by states on the international plane in reaction to the actions of other states, which includes also the making of diplomatic representations or demarches[3].

1   As to diplomatic protection see PARAS 385–411.
2   As to the actions which states have the right to take by way of consular assistance see PARAS 412–420.
3   As to the distinctions between the types of action see PARA 384.

384.   Distinction between diplomatic protection, consular assistance and other forms of action by states on the international plane. In its strict sense, diplomatic protection refers to the invocation by one state of the international responsibility of another state arising as a result of an alleged violation of international law committed by the other state in relation to persons, whether natural or legal, having the nationality of the invoking state[1]. Diplomatic protection may be exercised either by diplomatic action, including the direct presentation of a claim by the national state of the injured person to the responsible state, or by other means of peaceful settlement of disputes, including, where jurisdiction exists, the bringing of a claim before an international court or tribunal. Consular assistance encompasses those actions which a state has a right to take under international law in relation to its nationals within the territory of another state, including in particular certain specific rights in relation to nationals who have been arrested or otherwise detained[2]. Such actions by way of consular assistance are normally carried out by the consular officers of the state of nationality, present in the other state for that purpose[3]. Given that they involve the invocation of the responsibility of another state in relation to injury caused to a national, measures taken by way of diplomatic protection are by their nature essentially remedial and are aimed at ensuring the implementation of the secondary obligations of the international law of responsibility arising upon the commission of an internationally wrongful act[4]. By contrast, measures taken by way of consular assistance will often not envisage a situation of breach of international law at all, in particular in so far as they relate to the mere provision of assistance to nationals of the state, and in any case are largely preventive and aimed at preventing a national of a state from being subjected to an internationally wrongful act[5]. The exercise of diplomatic protection and the taking of action by way of consular assistance form part of the far wider category of actions which it is open to a state to take on the international plane in relation to the actions of other states, which includes the making of diplomatic representations or demarches. That category covers a spectrum of possible action which includes, for instance, an expression of concern as to whether particular actions of another state are consistent with its obligations under international law, a call for an inquiry into particular events in another state, or an informal call for compliance by the other state with its international obligations. In addition, a state may formally invoke the responsibility of the other state, whether specifically by way of diplomatic protection in relation to the treatment of a national, or more generally in relation to the breach by the other state of any other obligation owed to the invoking state[6]. However, such diplomatic representations or demarches do not necessarily involve any allegation of internationally wrongful conduct on the part of the other state or the invocation of its international responsibility; for instance, given the absence of any clear prohibition of the imposition of the death penalty as a matter of general international law, this will often be the case in relation to pleas for clemency. Diplomatic representations or demarches may be made in relation to the treatment of any individual alleged to be in breach of international law, including in relation to the treatment of individuals who are not nationals of the state making the representation and even as regards the treatment of nationals of the state to which the representations are made. To the extent that such diplomatic representations and demarches do not constitute the exercise of diplomatic protection in relation to an injury caused to a national, the specific rules of the law of diplomatic protection as to nationality and exhaustion of local remedies are not applicable and there is no need to comply with them[7]. In international practice and usage the exact dividing lines between the exercise of diplomatic protection and other diplomatic representations or demarches, as well as those between those measures and actions taken by way of consular assistance, are far from clear[8], and a similar imprecision in the use of the terms is apparent in some decisions of the English courts[9].

1   As to diplomatic protection see PARAS 385–411. As to the nature of diplomatic protection under international law see PARA 386; and as to the requirement of nationality see PARA 391.

2   As to consular assistance see PARA 412 et seq.

3   As to consular officers see PARA 30. Nevertheless, particular actions constituting consular assistance may in certain cases be undertaken by the state's diplomatic personnel: c f Convention on Consular Relations (Vienna, 24 April 1963; 596 UNTS 262; TS 14 (1973); Cmnd 5219) art 70.

4   See the Articles on Diplomatic Protection ('ADP'), Commentary to Article 1, para (9), Report of the International Law Commission ('ILC'), 58th Session (2006), A/61/10, ch IV. As to state responsibility and the notion of an internationally wrongful act see PARA 327 et seq.

5   See ADP, Commentary to Article 1, para (9).

6   As to the distinction between direct claims and claims made by way of diplomatic protection see PARA 387.

7   As to the requirement of nationality in claims by way of diplomatic protection see PARA 391 et seq; and as to the requirement to exhaust local remedies in claims by way of diplomatic protection see PARA 405 et seq. As to the possibility that a state may invoke the responsibility of the state responsible for breaches of certain obligations even if one of its nationals or the state itself is not directly injured thereby see *Barcelona Traction, Light and Power Co Ltd (Belgium v Spain) (Second Phase)* ICJ Reports 1970, 3 at 33 (para 32) (obligations erga omnes). See also the Articles on Responsibility of States for Internationally Wrongful Acts ('ARSIWA') art 48, Report of the International Law Commission, 53rd Session, A/56/10, YILC 2001, vol II(2); and PARAS 329, 373.

8   See e g Warbrick 'Diplomatic Representations and Diplomatic Protection' (2002) 51 ICLQ 723; Künzli 'Exercising Diplomatic Protection: The Fine Line Between Litigation, Demarches and Consular Assistance' (2006) 66 ZaöRV 321.

9   See e g the use of the terms in *R (on the application of Abbasi) v Secretary of State for Foreign and Commonwealth Affairs* [2002] EWCA Civ 1598, [2002] All ER (D) 70 (Nov); and *R (on the application of Al-Rawi) v Secretary of State for Foreign and Commonwealth Affairs (United Nations High Commissioner for Refugees intervening)* [2006] EWCA Civ 1279, [2008] QB 289, [2006] All ER (D) 138 (Oct).

(2) DIPLOMATIC PROTECTION

(i) Introduction

385. General considerations. Diplomatic protection consists of the invocation by a state, through diplomatic action or other means of peaceful settlement, of the responsibility of another state for an injury caused by an internationally wrongful act of that state to a natural or legal person that is a national of the former state with a view to the implementation of such responsibility[1]. As such it is a specific sub-category of the general international law of state responsibility, relating specifically to the invocation of the responsibility of a state as a consequence of breaches of international law committed in relation to the nationals of another state. As a result, except in the case of contrary agreement between the states in question[2], the general rules of state responsibility apply in relation to claims made by way of diplomatic protection as concerns questions such as attribution of conduct to the allegedly responsible state[3], whether or not an international obligation has been breached[4], and the content and implementation of the international responsibility which arises as a result of the internationally wrongful conduct which is attributable to the responsible state, including, in particular, the obligation to make reparation[5]. Nevertheless, claims made by way of diplomatic protection are subject to specific rules which are left by the general law of state responsibility to the more specific rules of diplomatic protection[6]. These specific rules relate to the nationality of the persons, corporations, ships and aircraft in relation to which a state may invoke the responsibility of the responsible state and the related rules concerning the nationality of claims[7]; and the requirement of exhaustion of local remedies as a precondition for the presentation or admissibility of an international claim by way of diplomatic protection[8].

1   See eg the Articles on Diplomatic Protection ('ADP') art 1, Report of the International Law Commission ('ILC'), 58th Session (2006), A/61/10, ch IV. The International Court of Justice has confirmed that that definition reflects customary international law: *Ahmadou Sadio Diallo (Republic of Guinea v Democratic Republic of the Congo) (Preliminary Objections)* ICJ Reports, 24 May 2007 (para 39). As to state responsibility and the invocation of responsibility see PARA 327 et seq.
2   As to the principle of lex specialis in the law of state responsibility see PARA 332.
3   See PARA 337 et seq.
4   See PARA 359 et seq.
5   See PARA 374. As to the content of international responsibility see PARA 373 et seq.
6   The ILC dealt with diplomatic protection as a topic distinct from the general law of state responsibility, although the inter-relationship of the two areas of law is expressly recognised in the ILC Articles on Responsibility of States for Internationally Wrongful Acts ('ARSIWA'), International Law Commission Report, 53rd Session, A/56/10, YILC 2001, vol II(2). See eg ARSIWA art 44, which deals with the admissibility of claims and provides that the responsibility of a state may not be invoked if the claim is not bought in accordance with any applicable rule relating to the nationality of claims (see the text and note 7), or the claim is one to which the rule of exhaustion of local remedies applies and any effective and available local remedy has not been exhausted (see the text and note 8); and PARA 330.
7   As to nationality and nationality of claims see PARA 391 et seq.
8   As to exhaustion of local remedies see PARA 405.

386. Nature of diplomatic protection. In the classic formulation, in bringing an international claim by way of diplomatic protection on behalf of one its nationals, a state was to be treated as in reality asserting its own rights, namely the right to ensure, in the person of its subjects, respect for the rules of international law[1]. Strong vestiges of that traditional approach remain in the modern law of diplomatic protection, in particular in the general rule that only the national state of an injured person may bring a claim by way of diplomatic protection on his, her or its behalf[2]. Historically, the exercise of diplomatic protection arose principally in the context of violations of international standards as to the treatment of aliens and their property under customary international law[3]. However, as a result of the development of the rights recognised as belonging to individuals under international law, the scope of the obligations which may be the subject of a claim in the nature of diplomatic protection has expanded so that diplomatic protection is no longer so limited[4]. The exercise of diplomatic protection may thus also concern the invocation of responsibility arising from a breach of obligations under the international law of human rights (whether arising under customary international law or deriving from multilateral human rights instruments)[5], under other multilateral treaties (for instance, in relation to violations of specific obligations in the field of consular relations)[6], or under bilateral treaties (including bilateral investment treaties)[7]. In parallel, it has been recognised that at least some of the international obligations the breach of which may be the subject of a claim by way of diplomatic protection may be owed directly to individuals and confer rights on them under international law, irrespective of whether those individuals rights are to be characterised as constituting human rights[8].

1   *Mavrommatis Palestine Concessions* PCIJ Ser A No 2 at 12 (1924); *Panevezys-Saldutiskis Railway (Estonia v Lithuania)* PCIJ Ser A/B No 76 at 16 (1939).
2   As to the requirements relating to nationality see PARA 391 et seq.
3   As to the rules of customary international law relating to treatment of aliens and their property see PARA 462 et seq.
4   See *Ahmadou Sadio Diallo (Republic of Guinea v Democratic Republic of the Congo) (Preliminary Objections)* ICJ Reports, 24 May 2007 (para 39).
5   See eg *Armed Activities on the Territory of the Congo (Democratic Republic of the Congo v Uganda)* ICJ Reports, 19 December 2005. Many international human rights instruments provide for specific mechanisms by which inter-state complaints may be made, whether or not the victims are nationals of an applicant state: see eg the Convention for the Protection of Human Rights and Fundamental Freedoms (Rome, 4 November 1950; TS 71 (1953); Cmd 8969) (the 'European Convention on Human Rights') art 33 (as amended by Protocol 11); claims brought under such mechanisms are not in the nature of diplomatic protection, although there may exist parallel requirements relating to the exhaustion of local remedies (see eg the European Convention on Human Rights art 35 (as amended by Protocol 11)). In that regard, the European Court of Human Rights has held that the conventional rule requiring exhaustion of local remedies contained in the European Convention on Human Rights art 35 does not apply to inter-state applications brought under art 33 in so far as the applicant state does not bring a claim in relation to violations of the rights of particular individuals but rather alleges a breach of the substantive provisions of the Convention as the result of the legislation or administrative practices of the defendant state: see eg *Ireland v United Kingdom* A 25 (1978) 2 EHRR 25, ECtHR.
6   See eg *LaGrand (Germany v United States of America)* ICJ Reports 2001, 466; *Avena and Other Mexican Nationals (Mexico v United States of America)* ICJ Reports 2004, 12.
7   However, claims brought on behalf of an investor for breach of a bilateral investment treaty are rare; diplomatic action on behalf of an investor may be excluded to the extent that the host state and the state of the investor are parties to the Convention on the Settlement of Investment Disputes between States and Nationals of Other States (Washington, 18 March 1965; TS 25 (1967) Cmnd 3255) (the 'ICSID Convention') and the investor and the host state have consented to submit or have submitted the dispute to ICSID arbitration: see art 27. In addition, claims may be made by way of diplomatic protection on behalf of nationals in relation to breach of obligations under other bilateral treaties (eg older bilateral treaties of Friendship, Commerce and Navigation): see eg *Elettronica Sicula SpA (ELSI) (United States of America v Italy)* ICJ Reports 1989, 15. In such cases, the applicability of the specific rules relating to claims by way of diplomatic protection as concerns exhaustion of local remedies depends on whether the essential nature of the claim is direct injury to the state, or whether the state is in reality asserting a claim for injury to its national: see PARA 387.

8   *LaGrand (Germany v United States of America)* ICJ Reports 2001, 466 at 493–494
     (paras 76–77); *Avena and Other Mexican Nationals (Mexico v United States of America)* ICJ
     Reports 2004, 12 (para 40). As to the right (at issue in both cases) of arrested or otherwise
     detained individuals to be notified of their consular rights under the Vienna Convention on
     Consular Relations (Vienna, 24 April 1963; TS 14 (1973); Cmnd 5219) see PARA 415.

**387.   Distinction between claims by way of diplomatic protection and claims
for direct injury to the state.** Although on the traditional approach the exercise
of diplomatic protection was classically justified on the basis that the state, in
taking up the claim of its national, was asserting its own rights[1], international
judicial practice nevertheless evidences the existence of a distinction between
claims made by way of diplomatic protection and claims by a state concerning
direct injury caused to it by a breach of international law. In this respect it is
necessary to have regard to the nature of the claim as a whole and whether the
essential nature of the claim is such that it is brought preponderantly in relation
to an injury to a national[2]. Certain specific types of claim, despite the fact that
they relate to actions taken in relation to nationals, are nevertheless not regarded
as being brought by way of diplomatic protection but rather as constituting
direct claims by the state[3]. The restrictive rules of diplomatic protection, in
particular the rule requiring exhaustion of local remedies, are not applicable to
such direct actions[4]. In certain cases, a claim brought by a state may
appropriately be characterised as concerning the violation of both the individual
rights of a national as well as obligations owed to the state and therefore as
constituting both a claim by way of diplomatic protection and a claim for direct
injury[5]. In such cases, due to the interdependence of the rights of the state and
the rights of individuals, the requirement of exhaustion of local remedies may
not need to be complied with[6].

1   As to the nature of diplomatic protection see PARA 386.
2   See eg *Interhandel (Switzerland v United States of America) (Preliminary Objections)* ICJ
     Reports 1959, 6 at 28–29; *Elettronica Sicula SpA (ELSI) (United States of America v Italy)* ICJ
     Reports 1989, 15 at 43 (paras 51–52). See also the Articles on Diplomatic Protection ('ADP')
     art 14(3), Commentary to Article 14, paras (9)–(10), Report of the International Law
     Commission ('ILC'), 58th Session (2006), A/61/10, ch IV. The ILC has taken the view that local
     remedies must be exhausted in all cases where an international claim, or request for a
     declaratory judgment related to the claim, is brought preponderantly on the basis of an injury to
     a national. There appears to be no rule that remedies do not need to be exhausted where a state
     requests only a declaratory judgment of an international tribunal as to whether a treaty or
     convention is applicable; what is important is whether the essential nature of the claim is one
     brought by way of diplomatic protection on behalf of a national: see *Interhandel (Switzerland v
     United States of America) (Preliminary Objections)* ICJ Reports 1959, 6 at 29, where the
     non-exhaustion of domestic remedies rule was held to apply even to the alternative claim
     seeking merely declaratory remedies. See also *Elettronica Sicula SpA (ELSI) (United States of
     America v Italy)* ICJ Reports 1989, 15 at 42–43 (para 51), where the chamber of the court
     rejected an argument that the rule did not apply in so far as the applicant state sought a merely
     declaratory judgment; cf, however, *Certain German Interests in Polish Upper Silesia* PCIJ Ser A
     No 7 at 33–34 (1926) (where, however, the remedy in question was before another international
     tribunal); *Swiss Confederation v German Federal Republic (No 1)* (1958) 25 Int LR 33 at 42–50
     (Arbitral Tribunal for Agreement on German External Debts).
3   This is particularly the case as concerns injury caused to individuals performing representative
     functions on behalf of the state, in particular diplomatic and consular agents: see eg *United
     States Diplomatic and Consular Staff in Teheran (United States of America v Iran)* ICJ Reports
     1980, 3 (the claims of the claimant included a claim for reparation brought both in its own right
     and by way of diplomatic protection of its nationals; the respondent state did not participate in
     the proceedings and no objection on the basis of failure to exhaust local remedies was made,
     and the court did not advert to the question). A claim based on the violation of the immunity
     from criminal proceedings before the courts of another state enjoyed by the incumbent foreign
     minister of a state was not a claim in the nature of diplomatic protection as the claimant state

was not seeking to protect the rights of its national, but was rather bringing a claim for a direct violation of its own rights: *Arrest Warrant of 11 April 2000 (Democratic Republic of the Congo v Belgium)* ICJ Reports 2002, 3 at 17 (para 40). See also *Armed Activities on the Territory of the Congo (Democratic Republic of the Congo v Uganda)* ICJ Reports, 19 December 2005 (paras 330–331) (counterclaims based on breach of the Vienna Convention on Diplomatic Relations (Vienna, 18 April 1961; TS 19 (1965); Cmnd 2565) due to mistreatment of diplomats of the respondent state and violations of the inviolability of its embassy were held not to be claims in the nature of diplomatic protection as they sought reparation for the direct injury to the respondent itself).

4   For examples of claims made by states which were held to be in the nature of diplomatic protection see eg *Interhandel (Switzerland v United States of America) (Preliminary Objections)* ICJ Reports 1959, 6 at 28–29; *Elettronica Sicula SpA (ELSI) (United States of America v Italy)* ICJ Reports 1989, 15 at 43 (paras 51–52) (alleged violation of a bilateral treaty of Friendship Commerce and Navigation); *Armed Activities on the Territory of the Congo (Democratic Republic of the Congo v Uganda)* ICJ Reports, 19 December 2005 (para 333) (counterclaim in relation to mistreatment of nationals of the respondent state not having diplomatic status). See also *LaGrand (Germany v United States of America)* ICJ Reports 2001, 466; *Avena and Other Mexican Nationals (Mexico v United States of America)* ICJ Reports 2004, 12 (claims of violation of the obligations of notification under the Vienna Convention on Consular Relations (Vienna, 24 April 1963; TS 14 (1973); Cmnd 5219) and rights of individuals arising thereunder in part in the nature of claims by way of diplomatic protection and in part a claim of direct injury).

5   See eg *Avena and Other Mexican Nationals (Mexico v United States of America)* ICJ Reports 2004, 12.

6   *LaGrand (Germany v United States of America)* ICJ Reports 2001, 466; *Avena and Other Mexican Nationals (Mexico v United States of America)* ICJ Reports 2004, 12.

388.   Discretion of the executive as to whether and how to exercise diplomatic protection. As a consequence of the classical understanding of diplomatic protection as constituting the assertion by a state of an infringement of its own right[1], as a matter of international law the national state of an individual may exercise diplomatic protection by whatever means and to whatever extent it thinks fit, and should the natural or legal person on whose behalf the state is acting consider that his or its rights are not adequately protected, he or it has no remedy in international law[2]. As a matter of international law, the state is the sole judge of whether its protection will be granted, to what extent it is granted and when it will cease, and in this regard has an absolute discretion which may be determined by considerations of a political or other nature unrelated to the particular case[3]. As a consequence, a state is free to waive a claim by way of diplomatic protection[4], or to settle or compromise it on whatever terms it sees fit[5]. Nevertheless, although a national has no right to compel the exercise of diplomatic protection as a matter of international law, there is no rule of international law prohibiting the domestic law of the state in question providing such redress[6]. As a matter of the law of England, the exercise of discretion on the part of the executive as to whether to exercise diplomatic protection in respect of a national, or more generally to make other diplomatic representations on his behalf, is not non-justiciable merely on the basis that it concerns an element of the royal prerogative in the field of international relations, and, at least in theory, such decisions are subject to judicial review[7]. However, given its subject matter, the scope of any such review is likely to be extremely restricted; although the courts will not in general interfere with the policy decision as to whether or not to take particular action on behalf of any particular national, a national may have a legitimate expectation that, at the least, consideration will be given by the executive as to whether or not to make diplomatic representations on his behalf or to exercise diplomatic protection[8].

1   See PARA 386.

2   *Barcelona Traction, Light and Power Co Ltd (Belgium v Spain) (Second Phase)* ICJ Reports 1970, 3 at 44 (para 78).

3   *Barcelona Traction, Light and Power Co Ltd (Belgium v Spain) (Second Phase)* ICJ Reports 1970, 3 at 44 (para 79).

4   This follows from the fact that a state is pursuing its own claim. It appears that a national cannot as such waive the claim of the state himself: see the discussion of the Calvo clause in PARAS 408–410. However, see *Tattler* 6 RIAA 48 (1920).

5   *Administrative Decision No V (United States v Germany)* 7 RIAA 119 at 152 (1924).

6   See *Barcelona Traction, Light and Power Co Ltd (Belgium v Spain) (Second Phase)* ICJ Reports 1970, 3 at 44 (para 78). Cf, however, the Articles on Diplomatic Protection ('ADP') art 19(a), Commentary to Article 19, paras (2)–(3), Report of the International Law Commission ('ILC'), 58th Session (2006), A/61/10, ch IV.

7   *R (on the application of Abbasi) v Secretary of State for Foreign and Commonwealth Affairs* [2002] EWCA Civ 1598, [2002] All ER (D) 70 (Nov). For similar decisions from other jurisdictions see e g *Mohamed v President of the Republic of South Africa* 2001 (3) SA 893; but c f *Kaunda v President of the Republic of South Africa* [2004] ZACC 5, SA Const Ct; *Khadr v Canada (Minister of Foreign Affairs)* 2004 FC 1145, Can FC; *Hicks v Ruddock* [2007] FCA 299, Aust FC. For further discussion see Vermeer-Künzli 'Restricting Discretion: Judicial Review of Diplomatic Protection' (2006) 75 Nordic Journal of International Law 279.

8   *R (on the application of Abbasi) v Secretary of State for Foreign and Commonwealth Affairs* [2002] EWCA Civ 1598 at [104], [2002] All ER (D) 70 (Nov) at [104].

389.   Distribution of compensation obtained by diplomatic protection. As a further consequence of the classical understanding of diplomatic protection that, in asserting a claim by way of diplomatic protection on behalf of one of its nationals, a state is bringing a claim for an infringement of its own rights[1], as a matter of international law there is probably no obligation requiring a state which has successfully obtained compensation in respect of damage done to one of its nationals to pay that compensation to the injured person[2]. As a matter of the law of England, even where the executive has called for individuals to submit details of any damage suffered by reason of violation of international law, moneys received in settlement of such international claims are not received by the Crown as agent or trustee for the British nationals to which the international claim related, nor as money had and received to their use[3]. Exceptionally however, the Crown may expressly constitute itself agent or trustee of the money for the national[4]. When, by agreement with another state, the Crown has received payment from that other state on account of a wrong done to a British national, the national has no legally enforceable right to such money in the hands of the Crown[5]. In recent times, where compensation has been obtained from foreign governments, it has generally been the practice for the Crown to distribute the compensation through the Foreign Compensation Commission[6].

1   As to the nature of diplomatic protection see PARA 386.

2   See e g *Finnish Shipowners* 3 RIAA 1479 at 1485 (1934); c f *Administrative Decision No V (United States v Germany)* 7 RIAA 119 at 152 (1924). See also *Civilian War Claimants Association v R* [1932] AC 14, HL; *Lonrho Exports Ltd v Export Credits Guarantee Department* [1999] Ch 158, [1996] 4 All ER 673. Cf however, the Articles on Diplomatic Protection ('ADP') art 19, Commentary to Article 19, paras (5)–(8), Report of the International Law Commission ('ILC'), 58th Session (2006), A/61/10, ch IV.

3   *Civilian War Claimants Association v R* [1932] AC 14, HL.

4   See *Rustomjee v R* (1876) 2 QBD 69 at 74, CA, obiter per Coleridge CJ; *Civilian War Claimants Association v R* [1932] AC 14 at 26–27, HL, obiter per Lord Atkin. However, no such intention on the part of the Crown can be implied from the terms of the agreement with the foreign government.

5   *Rustomjee v R* (1876) 2 QBD 69, CA; *Civilian War Claimants Association v R* [1932] AC 14, HL; *Lonrho Exports Ltd v Export Credits Guarantee Department* [1999] Ch 158, [1996] 4 All ER 673. This follows from the rule that the individual cannot rely on an act of state as a cause of action. As to acts of state see PARA 22 et seq.

6 The Commission was established under the Foreign Compensation Act 1950 s 1. As to the Commission's constitution and powers see CONSTITUTIONAL LAW AND HUMAN RIGHTS vol 8(2) (Reissue) PARA 803 et seq. It appears that if the distribution of compensation has been regulated by statute, the claimant may only recover it by following the statutory procedure: see *Baron de Bode v R* (1851) 3 HL Cas 449. The Foreign Compensation Act 1950 did not curtail the prerogative powers of the Crown. In most cases where the Crown has received compensation under global agreements with foreign governments, the Commission has been entrusted with the task of distribution. However, between 1960 and 1962 the Foreign Office decided some 430 pre-war claims of British subjects against Japan and distributed the money itself: see Lillich *International Claims: Post War British Practice* 6, note 36.

390. Conditions for the exercise of diplomatic protection. In light of the fact that diplomatic protection constitutes a specific form of state responsibility, before presenting an international claim by way of diplomatic protection based upon another state's responsibility in respect of treatment of individuals, it is generally necessary for the government of the injured state to consider the following questions: (1) whether the claim complies with the applicable rules relating to the nationality of claims[1]; (2) whether the rule which requires any available and effective local remedies to be exhausted is applicable to the claim and, if so, whether any relevant remedies have in fact been exhausted[2]; (3) whether the conduct causing the injury is attributable to the respondent state[3]; (4) whether that conduct fell below the level of treatment of aliens which is required by customary international law, or whether it violated some other international obligation binding the allegedly responsible state in relation to the treatment of individuals[4]; (5) whether the claim has been extinguished by lapse of time or otherwise waived[5]. The issues of nationality and of exhaustion of local remedies relate specifically to the exercise of diplomatic protection and are the main concern of the law of diplomatic protection[6].

1 As to nationality and the rules relating to continuous nationality of claims see PARA 391 et seq. See also the International Law Commission ('ILC') Articles on Responsibility of States for Internationally Wrongful Acts ('ARSIWA') art 44, International Law Commission Report, 53rd Session, A/56/10, YILC 2001, vol II(2); and PARA 330.
2 As to the requirement of exhaustion of local remedies see PARAS 405–411. See also ARSIWA art 44; and PARA 330.
3 As to attribution for the purposes of state responsibility see PARA 337 et seq.
4 As to the substantive rules relating to treatment of aliens and their property see PARA 462. As to the categories of rules of international law which may be the subject of a claim in the nature of diplomatic protection see PARA 386.
5 As to acquiescence and waiver of claims generally in the law of state responsibility see PARA 330; and as to the freedom of a state to waive a claim by way of diplomatic protection involving injury to one of its nationals see PARA 388.
6 See PARAS 391–411.

(ii) Nationality and Nationality of Claims

A. IN GENERAL

391. General considerations. A general precondition for the presentation of an international claim made by way of diplomatic protection is that the natural or legal person injured by the act of the responsible state should have the nationality of the claimant state[1]. Further, that nationality should normally have been maintained from the date of injury up to the date of presentation of the claim[2].

1 See the Articles on Diplomatic Protection ('ADP') art 3, Report of the International Law Commission ('ILC'), 58th Session (2006), A/61/10, ch IV. See also *Ahmadou Sadio Diallo*

(Republic of Guinea v Democratic Republic of the Congo) (Preliminary Objections) ICJ Reports, 24 May 2007 (paras 40, 61); *Armed Activities on the Territory of the Congo (Democratic Republic of the Congo v Uganda)* ICJ Reports, 19 December 2005 (para 333). The ILC has suggested, expressly by way of progressive development, that an exception to the requirement of nationality as regards individuals should exist by which a state may exercise diplomatic protection on behalf of a stateless person or a refugee lawfully and habitually resident at the date of injury and at the date of the claim; however, even under the proposed rule no action by way of diplomatic protection can be taken against the state of nationality of the refugee: see ADP art 8. It has been held that the proposed rule, at least in so far as it relates to refugees habitually resident in a state, does not represent customary international law: see *R (on the application of Al-Rawi) v Secretary of State for Foreign and Commonwealth Affairs (United Nations High Commissioner for Refugees intervening)* [2006] EWCA Civ 1279, [2008] QB 289, [2006] All ER (D) 138 (Oct). As to the ability of the flag state of a ship to bring a claim on behalf of non-nationals who are members of a ship's crew (although this is probably not a true case of diplomatic protection) see PARA 403. As to nationality of individuals see PARA 392; and as to nationality of corporations see PARA 394. As to nationality of claims see PARA 398 et seq.

2   See PARA 399.

B. NATIONALITY

392. Nationality of individuals. Nationality, which denotes the quality of political membership of a particular state, is governed primarily by municipal law; in the present state of international law, and subject to any relevant treaty obligations entered into by a state, questions of the nationality of individuals are in principle within its sole jurisdiction[1]. There is a growing body of treaty provisions, binding on the states party to them, relating to questions of nationality of individuals[2]. Although the Universal Declaration of Human Rights[3] asserts that everyone has a right to a nationality[4] that proposition arguably does not reflect customary international law[5]. There exists a rough harmony between national laws relating to nationality which obviates the necessity for international regulation[6].

1   *Tunis and Morocco Nationality Decrees (Advisory Opinion)* PCIJ Ser B No 4 at 23 (1923); International Convention on Certain Questions Relating to the Conflict of Nationality Laws (The Hague, 12 April 1930; TS 33 (1937); Cmd 5553) art 3. See also the European Convention on Nationality (Strasbourg, 6 November 1997; ETS 166; 2135 UNTS 189) art 3 (although the United Kingdom is not party). The principle extends to the term employed to describe nationality, which in many systems of domestic law, including that of the United Kingdom, is called citizenship: see the British Nationality Act 1981; and BRITISH NATIONALITY, IMMIGRATION AND ASYLUM vol 4(2) (2002 Reissue) PARA 5 et seq. Although questions of nationality are in principle for each state to determine, an international court or tribunal may nevertheless have to make findings as to the nationality of an individual applying the rules of domestic law, as well as determine the extent to which the nationality of an individual validly conferred by the domestic law of a state should be recognised and given effect as a matter of international law: see e g *Nottebohm (Liechtenstein v Guatemala) (Second Phase)* ICJ Reports 1955, 4. See also *Soufraki v United Arab Emirates* ICSID Case No ARB/02/7, Decision on Jurisdiction of 7 July 2004, Decision of the ad hoc Committee on the Application for Annulment of 5 June 2007; *Siag and Vecchi v Arab Republic of Egypt* ICSID Case No ARB/05/15, Decision on Jurisdiction of 11 April 2007, Award of 1 June 2009 (both of the latter two cases decided under bilateral investment treaties).

2   See e g the International Convention on Certain Questions Relating to the Conflict of Nationality Laws; the Protocol Relating to a Certain Case of Statelessness (The Hague, 12 April 1930; TS 31 (1937); Cmd 5552); the International Protocol Relating to Military Obligations in Certain Cases of Double Nationality (The Hague, 12 April 1930; TS 22 (1937); Cmd 5460); and the European Convention on the Reduction of Cases of Multiple Nationality and Military Obligations in Cases of Multiple Nationality (Strasbourg, 6 May 1963; TS 88 (1971); Cmnd 4802) and the various Protocols thereto. See also the Convention on the Nationality of Married Women (New York, 20 February 1957; TS 59 (1958); Cmnd 601); and the Convention on the Reduction of Statelessness (New York, 30 August 1961; Misc 27 (1962); Cmnd 1825). See further the International Law Commission ('ILC') Draft Articles on Nationality of Natural

Persons in relation to the Succession of States, YILC 1999, vol II(2) Ch IV paras 44–45; and in relation to the ILC Draft Articles see United Nations General Assembly Resolution 54/112 of 9 December 1999, General Assembly Resolution 55/153 of 12 December 2000, General Assembly Resolution 59/34 of 2 December 2004, and General Assembly Resolution 63/118 of 11 December 2008. By Resolution 54/112, the General Assembly took note of the ILC Draft Articles, which were annexed to the Resolution, and invited governments to take them into account as appropriate. By Resolution 55/153, the General Assembly reiterated its invitation to governments to take into account, as appropriate, the provisions of the ILC Draft Articles in dealing with issues of nationality of natural persons in relation to the succession of states; and it further encouraged the elaboration, at the regional or sub-regional level, of legal instruments regulating questions of nationality of natural persons in relation to the succession of states, with a view, in particular, to preventing the occurrence of statelessness as a result of a succession of states.

The member states of the Council of Europe have elaborated the Convention on the Avoidance of Statelessness in relation to State Succession (Strasbourg, 19 May 2006; CETS 200). The Convention entered into force for those states party to it on 1 May 2009; the United Kingdom is not a party.

3   Ie the Universal Declaration of Human Rights (Paris, 10 December 1948; UN 2 (1949); Cmd 7662). As to human rights and freedoms see CONSTITUTIONAL LAW AND HUMAN RIGHTS vol 8(2) (Reissue) PARA 101 et seq.

4   Universal Declaration of Human Rights art 18(1). Similar provisions are contained in some international human rights treaties: see eg the American Convention on Human Rights 1969 (San José, Costa Rica; 22 November 1969; (1970) 9 ILM 673) art 20. The right to acquire a nationality contained in the International Covenant of Civil and Political Rights (New York, 16 December 1966; TS 6 (1977); Cmnd 6702) is expressly limited to children: art 24(3); and see also the Convention on the Rights of the Child (20 November 1989; TS 44 (1992); Cm 1976) arts 7, 8. As to the prohibition of racial discrimination in relation to questions of nationality see the International Convention on the Elimination of All Forms of Racial Discrimination (New York, 7 March 1966; TS 77 (1966); Cmnd 4108) art 5(d)(iii) (although cf art 1(3)). As to the prohibition of discrimination on the basis of sex in relation to questions of nationality see the Convention on the Elimination of All Forms of Discrimination against Women (New York, 1979; 1239 UNTS 13) art 9(1); as to the obligation to ensure that neither marriage to an alien nor change of nationality by the husband during marriage will automatically change the nationality of the wife, render her stateless or force upon her the nationality of the husband see art 9(1); and as to the obligation to grant women rights equal to men with respect to the nationality of their children see art 9(2).

5   The proposition contained in the Universal Declaration of Human Rights art 15(2), to the effect that no one may (in conformity with international law) be arbitrarily deprived of his nationality or be denied the right to change nationality, probably also does not represent customary international law, although some writers have urged that there must be some limit to the apparently absolute discretion of states in the matter of nationality, and in particular that the doctrine of abuse of rights does or should apply. A similar provision is contained in the American Convention on Human Rights art 20(3).

6   See Parry's Nationality and Citizenship Laws of the Commonwealth 8–27.

393.   Multiple nationality and citizenship.   One result of the virtually complete liberty of action of states in relation to nationality is that an individual may possess the nationality of more than one state under their respective laws. Although occasional judicial pronouncements may be found to the effect that the common law, or English law, does not countenance multiple nationality[1], such statements are misconceived and it is clear that the phenomenon must have been perfectly familiar not only to administrative authorities but also to the courts for some centuries[2]. To the extent that the voluntary acquisition of another nationality or citizenship does not result in the loss of British citizenship[3], the present law of the United Kingdom may be seen as favouring rather than discouraging multiple nationality. Customary international law does not differentiate in any way between the power and jurisdiction of a state over nationals who hold only its nationality and those who are also nationals of another state, although particular provision as to the treatment of dual nationals may be provided for by treaty[4]. Special rules apply as to the extent to which a claim by way of diplomatic protection can be brought on behalf of a dual national against a state of which he is also a national[5].

1   *Fasbender v A-G, Kramer v A-G* [1922] 2 Ch 850 at 878, CA, per Younger LJ; cf *Kramer v A-G* [1923] AC 528, HL. Compare *Zedtwitz v Sutherland* 26 F 2d 525 at 527 (US Dist CA, DC 1928) per Martin CJ.

2   See eg *Proceedings against Macdonald* (1747) 18 State Tr 857, which disproves the suggestion of Lord Coleridge CJ in *Re Stepney Election Petition, Isaacson v Durant* (1886) 17 QBD 54 at 63, that it cannot be the law that a man 'rightfully and legally in the allegiance of one sovereign could be also rightfully and legally treated as a traitor by another'. See also *Drummond's Case* (1834) 2 Knapp 295, PC.

3   The rule according to which a British citizen who voluntarily acquired another nationality lost British citizenship, originally contained in the Naturalization Act 1870 s 6 and perpetuated by the British Nationality and Status of Aliens Act 1914 (subsequently the Status of Aliens Act 1914) s 13, lapsed with the repeal of those provisions by the British Nationality Act 1948. However, the Secretary of State has power to deprive a person of British citizenship on the ground that it would be conducive to the public good under the British Nationality Act 1981 s 40(2): see BRITISH NATIONALITY, IMMIGRATION AND ASYLUM vol 4(2) (2002 Reissue) PARAS 42–43. Pursuant to s 40(4) such an order may not be made if the Secretary of State is satisfied that the order would make a person stateless (see eg *Al Jedda v Secretary of State for the Home Department* [2008] UKSIAC 66/2008, SIAC); as a consequence, the power of deprivation is normally only applicable to British nationals who also hold the nationality of another state.

4   See eg the International Protocol Relating to Military Obligations in Certain Cases of Double Nationality (The Hague, 12 April 1930; TS 22 (1937); Cmd 5460). Article 1 provides that, where a person with multiple nationalities habitually resides in one of the countries whose nationality he possesses and is in fact most closely connected with that country, he is to be exempt from all military obligations in the other country or countries; however, exemption from military service may result in the loss of nationality. Article 2 provides that, where a dual or multiple national of one of the state parties is entitled under its law to renounce or decline the nationality of that state, he is exempt from carrying out military service for that state during his minority. See also the European Convention on the Reduction of Cases of Multiple Nationality and Military Obligations in Cases of Multiple Nationality (Strasbourg, 6 May 1963; TS 88 (1971); Cmnd 4802) and the various Protocols thereto.

5   See PARA 401.

394.   Nationality of corporations.   Corporations are essentially a creation of municipal law, and as such, international law has to recognise the institutions created by the municipal law of states in an area which remains essentially within their domestic jurisdiction[1]. Accordingly, whenever questions arise as to the rights of corporate entities and their shareholders as to which international law lays down no specific rules, it is necessary for international law to have regard to the relevant rules of municipal law[2]. Although international law contains no rules of its own relating to the creation, management and dissolution of corporations, nevertheless it governs which state is to be regarded as the national state of a corporation for the purposes of identifying which state may exercise diplomatic protection on its behalf in relation to an injury inflicted upon it by another state in violation of international law[3]. As a matter of English law, unlike other systems[4], the attribution of nationality to a body corporate is unnecessary, whether in relation to jurisdiction, taxation or for any other purpose. The rules relating to trading with an enemy provide no exception, although the 'commercial domicile' test of enemy character, by which incorporation in an enemy state creates an irrefutable presumption[5], is sometimes referred to as one of national character[6]. The United Kingdom has entered into numerous treaties stipulating reciprocal recognition of entities incorporated under the laws of the contracting states[7], but these provisions are strictly superfluous from the point of view of English law, since it is well established that a foreign-incorporated corporation may sue and be sued in the courts[8]. These provisions, furthermore, imply no necessary acceptance of the view that the nationality of a corporation is determined exclusively or at all by the place of incorporation. Other treaty provisions referring explicitly to 'nationals' of this or that state have upon occasion fallen to be considered by the courts in relation to their application to corporations, and it has been held that although the term 'nationality' can only be used in regard to corporate bodies 'by a figure of speech', nevertheless it must necessarily be only too plain that a corporate body, which owes its very existence to the laws of a particular country and which has its principal place of business in that particular country, must be treated as a national of that country[9].

1   *Barcelona Traction, Light and Power Co Ltd (Belgium v Spain) (Second Phase)* ICJ Reports 1970, 3 at 33 (para 38).
2   *Barcelona Traction, Light and Power Co Ltd (Belgium v Spain) (Second Phase)* ICJ Reports 1970, 3 at 33–34 (para 38); *Ahmadou Sadio Diallo (Republic of Guinea v Democratic Republic of the Congo) (Preliminary Objections)* ICJ Reports, 24 May 2007 (para 61) (international law has regard to municipal law in relation to whether a corporation possesses independent and distinct legal personality).
3   See the Articles on Diplomatic Protection ('ADP') Commentary to Article 9, para (3), Report of the International Law Commission ('ILC'), 58th Session (2006), A/61/10, ch IV. As to which state is to be regarded as constituting the state of nationality of a corporation for the purposes of diplomatic protection see PARA 402.
4   For an authoritative discussion of the development of the notion of nationality or quasi-nationality of corporations in other legal systems see the Report of the Sub-Committee of the League of Nations Committee of Experts for the Progressive Codification of International Law 1927, 22 American Journal of International Law, Official Documents, 172. See also Parry's Nationality and Citizenship Laws of the Commonwealth 133–142.
5   McNair and Watts *Legal Effects of War* (4th Edn) 102, 236. There is apparently only obiter judicial authority for this rule: see *Janson v Driefontein Consolidated Mines Ltd* [1902] AC 484 at 490, HL, per Lord Halsbury LC, at 497 per Lord Macnaghten, at 498 per Lord Davey, at 501 per Lord Brampton, and at 505 per Lord Lindley. For the proposition that bare incorporation in an enemy state fixes a company with enemy character see *Daimler Co Ltd v Continental Tyre and Rubber Co (Great Britain) Ltd* [1916] 2 AC 307 at 342, HL, per Lord Parker; and WAR AND ARMED CONFLICT vol 49(1) (2005 Reissue) PARA 575. See also the Trading with the Enemy Act 1939 s 2(1)(d); and WAR AND ARMED CONFLICT vol 49(1) (2005 Reissue) PARA 577.
6   See McNair 'National Character and Status of Corporations' (1923–1924) 4 BYIL 44. In so far as the general test of enemy character is territorial (ie commercial domicile) rather than personal, the usage is justifiable.
7   See eg 'Companies and Associations', Handbook of Commercial Treaties (4th Edn) 1103–1104.
8   As to actions by or against foreign companies see COMPANIES vol 15 (2009) PARA 1837 et seq. See also *Arab Monetary Fund v Hashim (No 3)* [1991] 2 AC 114, [1991] 1 All ER 871, HL, where it was held that recognition should be given to the right to sue and be sued in the English courts of an international organisation created by a group of foreign states and which had been recognised as a corporate body having separate legal personality under the laws of one of those foreign states which was recognised by the United Kingdom.
9   *Bohemian Union Bank v Administrator of Austrian Property* [1927] 2 Ch 175 at 180, 195 per Clauson J with reference to the expression 'Nationality of an Allied or Associated Power' in the Treaty of St Germain (Treaty for the Protection of Minorities) (St Germain, 10 September 1919; TS 20 (1919); Cmd 223) art 249(b). See also *Assicurazioni Generali v Selim Cotran* [1932] AC 268, PC, decided with reference to a similar expression in the Treaty of Peace with Turkey (Treaty of Lausanne) (Lausanne, 24 July 1923; TS 16 (1923); Cmd 1929). Bilateral investment treaties normally define the classes of legal persons which qualify as investors and therefore enjoy substantive protection under the treaty by reference to their place of incorporation, although other requirements may also be stipulated; under the provisions of some bilateral investment treaties, the class of protected investors may include corporations incorporated in any state (including the host state), but which are controlled by natural or legal persons of the investor state.

395. Nationality of ships. International law lays down no general rules concerning which ship is to be treated as belonging to which state, but leaves the rules in this regard to municipal law[1]. However, pursuant to international convention, every state must fix the conditions for the grant of its nationality to ships, for the registration of ships in its territory and for the right to fly its flag[2]. A ship must have the nationality of the state whose flag it is entitled to fly[3]. There must exist a genuine link between the state and the ship[4]. Each state must issue to ships to which it has granted the right to fly its flag documents to that effect[5].

1 See Rienow *The Test of the Nationality of a Merchant Vessel, Comparative Study of National Laws Governing the Right to Fly a Merchant Flag* (UN 1955). See also *Muscat Dhows Arbitration* 11 RIAA 83 (1905). This is perhaps a reflection of the general rule as regards the grant of nationality to individuals: see PARA 392.

2 For the conditions governing the granting of nationality and the registration of British merchant ships see the Merchant Shipping Act 1995 Pts I, II (ss 1–23); and SHIPPING AND MARITIME LAW vol 93 (2008) PARA 245 et seq.

3 United Nations Convention on the Law of the Sea (Montego Bay, 10 December 1982; TS 81 (1999); Cmnd 4524) art 91(1). The Convention on Fishing and Conservation of the Living Resources of the High Seas (Geneva, 29 April 1958; TS 39 (1966); Cmnd 3028) art 14 defines 'nationals' as ships having the nationality of the state concerned irrespective of the nationalities of the crew members. A ship without nationality lacks a state to protect it, although it is not outside the application of domestic laws: see *Naim Molvan (Owner of Motor Vessel Asya) v A-G for Palestine* [1948] AC 351, PC. As to the nationality of pirate ships see PARA 158.

4 United Nations Convention on the Law of the Sea art 91(1). The requirement of a 'genuine link' is founded upon the judgment of the International Court of Justice in *Nottebohm (Liechtenstein v Guatemala) (Second Phase)* ICJ Reports 1955, 4. It appears to be directed against ships using so called 'flags of convenience', such as those flown by ships registered in Panama, Liberia and Honduras (as to which see Boczek's Flags of Convenience): see also PARA 396. However, the court disregarded any requirement of a genuine link in relation to the question whether such states were ship-owning states and in ascertaining the extent of the tonnage sailing under their flags for the purpose of determining whether the Maritime Safety Committee of the Inter-Governmental Maritime Consultative Organisation was properly constituted, treating the matter as solely one concerning the constituent instrument creating that organisation: see *Constitution of the Maritime Safety Committee of the Inter-Governmental Maritime Consultative Organisation (Advisory Opinion)* ICJ Reports 1960, 150.

5 United Nations Convention on the Law of the Sea art 91(2). As to the duties of the flag state with respect to its ships see the United Nations Convention on the Law of the Sea art 94; and PARA 152.

396. Changes of flag; ships sailing under two or more flags. A ship may sail under the flag of one state only and, save in exceptional cases expressly provided for in the United Nations Convention on the Law of the Sea[1] or other international treaties, is subject to its exclusive jurisdiction on the high seas[2]. A ship may not change its flag during a voyage or while in a port of call, save in the case of a real transfer of ownership or change of registry[3]. A ship which sails under the flags of two or more states, using them according to convenience, may not claim any of the nationalities in question with respect to any other state, and may be assimilated to a ship without nationality[4].

1 Ie the United Nations Convention on the Law of the Sea (Montego Bay, 10 December 1982; TS 81 (1999); Cmnd 4524).

2 United Nations Convention on the Law of the Sea art 92(1). Under some multilateral conventions, a state may also be positively required to establish its jurisdiction over particular offences committed on board a ship flying its flag: see eg the International Convention for the Suppression of Terrorist Bombings (New York, 15 December 1997) art 6(1)(b); and the International Convention for the Suppression of Acts of Nuclear Terrorism (New York, 13 April 2005; Misc 9 (2007); Cm 7301) art 9(1)(b). See further PARA 138. As to the circumstances in which a state other than the flag state may assume jurisdiction over a ship on the high seas see PARA 148.

3 United Nations Convention on the Law of the Sea art 92(1).

4 United Nations Convention on the Law of the Sea art 92(2). As to ships without nationality see PARA 395 note 3. The provisions of art 91 (see PARA 395) and art 92 of the United Nations Convention on the Law of the Sea are without prejudice to the question of ships employed on the official service of the United Nations, its specialised agencies or the International Atomic Energy Authority flying the flag of the organisation: art 93.

397. Nationality of aircraft. Pursuant to the Convention on International Civil Aviation[1] an aircraft has the nationality of the state in which it is registered[2]. It may not be registered in more than one state, although registration may be changed from one state to another[3]. Registration and transfer of registration of aircraft in any contracting state must take place in accordance with that state's regulations and laws[4].

1 Ie the Convention on International Civil Aviation (Chicago, 7 December 1944; TS 8 (1953); Cmd 8742). As to the Chicago Convention see AIR LAW vol 2 (2008) PARA 2 et seq.
2 Convention on International Civil Aviation art 17.
3 Convention on International Civil Aviation art 18. For further consideration of these provisions and of the relevant law of the United Kingdom see AIR LAW vol 2 (2008) PARA 358. The state of registration has jurisdiction over offences on board: Convention on Offences and Certain Other Acts Committed on Board Aircraft (Tokyo, 14 September 1963; TS 126 (1969); Cmnd 4230) art 3(1); see PARAS 199–202. It may also be positively required by treaty to establish its jurisdiction over particular offences committed on board an aircraft registered under its laws: see eg the International Convention for the Suppression of Terrorist Bombings (New York, 15 December 1997) art 6(1)(b); and the International Convention for the Suppression of Acts of Nuclear Terrorism (New York, 13 April 2005; Misc 9 (2007); Cm 7301) art 9(1)(b). With respect to joint operating organisations see the Convention on International Civil Aviation arts 77–79; Resolutions of the Council of the International Civil Aviation Organisation; 9 Whiteman's Digest 383–390.
4 Convention on International Civil Aviation art 19.

C. NATIONALITY OF CLAIMS

398. Nationality of claims: the general rule. In order to be able to take up by way of diplomatic protection a claim which arises out of an injury committed in relation to an individual person or corporation, a state must normally be in a position to demonstrate that the injured person or corporation possesses its nationality[1]. This rule is one of the consequences of the historical conception of diplomatic protection, namely that, in presenting an international claim which arises from an injury to an individual, the state is asserting its own rights and is claiming for an injury to itself, suffered through the injured person[2]. In order for a state to take up a claim, a legal right of the injured person must have been infringed by the respondent state; it is insufficient that a mere interest which is unprotected by law has been affected[3]. It appears that diplomatic protection cannot be exercised on behalf of stateless individuals[4].

1 See eg *Armed Activities on the Territory of the Congo (Democratic Republic of the Congo v Uganda)* ICJ Reports, 19 December 2005 (para 333) (individuals); *Ahmadou Sadio Diallo (Republic of Guinea v Democratic Republic of the Congo) (Preliminary Objections)* ICJ Reports, 24 May 2007 (para 40) (individuals), (para 61) (corporations). For older decisions holding that states are not permitted to take up claims of persons other than their own nationals see *Orazio de Attellis* (1839) Moore Int Arb 3333; *Administrative Decision No V (United States v Germany)* 7 RIAA 119 at 141 (1924). Exceptionally, a state may be able to bring a claim on behalf of a protected person: *British Claims in the Spanish Zone of Morocco* 2 RIAA 615 at 647 (1925). Further, it appears that a state may be able to bring a claim on behalf of a non-national seaman serving on a ship flying its flag, although such a claim probably does not constitute diplomatic protection as such: see PARA 403. In general the United Kingdom government will not take up a claim unless the claimant is a United Kingdom national: Foreign and Commonwealth Office, Rules Applying to International Claims 1985 r 1, and comment para (b) (reproduced in 37 ICLQ 1006 (1988)). This term includes persons who fall into one of the

following categories under the British Nationality Act 1981 (or one of the corresponding categories under earlier legislation): (1) British citizens; (2) British overseas territories citizens; (3) British overseas citizens; (4) British subjects under Pt IV (ss 30–35); and (5) British protected persons. See further BRITISH NATIONALITY, IMMIGRATION AND ASYLUM vol 4(2) (2002 Reissue) PARA 5 et seq. The term also includes companies incorporated under the law of the United Kingdom or of any territory for which the United Kingdom is internationally responsible. As to the nationality of individuals in international law see PARA 392. As to the nationality of corporations in international law see PARA 394. As to claims on behalf of corporations and their members see PARA 402. Under some treaties in the field of international human rights law, a state may be entitled to complain of a breach committed in relation to any person, including a person not having its nationality: see eg the Convention for the Protection of Human Rights and Fundamental Freedoms (Rome, 4 November 1950; TS 71 (1953); Cmd 8969) (the 'European Convention on Human Rights') art 33 (as amended by Protocol 11). See CONSTITUTIONAL LAW AND HUMAN RIGHTS vol 8(2) (Reissue) PARA 172.

2   *Mavrommatis Palestine Concessions* PCIJ Ser A No 2 (1924); *Panevezys-Saldutiskis Railway (Estonia v Lithuania)* PCIJ Ser A/B No 76 (1939); *Barcelona Traction, Light and Power Co Ltd (Belgium v Spain) (Second Phase)* ICJ Reports 1970, 3 at 46. See also *Factory at Chorzów* PCIJ Ser A No 17 (1928); *Reparation for Injuries Suffered in the Service of the United Nations (Advisory Opinion)* ICJ Reports 1949, 174. As to the nature of diplomatic protection see PARA 386.

3   *Factory at Chorzów* PCIJ Ser A No 17 (1928); *Interhandel (Switzerland v United States of America) (Preliminary Objections)* ICJ Reports 1959, 6 at 27; *Barcelona Traction, Light and Power Co Ltd (Belgium v Spain) (Second Phase)* ICJ Reports 1970, 3 at 36 (para 46). Accordingly, a state cannot bring a claim where an internationally wrongful act has affected the interests of one of its nationals as a shareholder of a corporation, rather than actually affecting that national's rights. As to the extent to which claims may be brought on behalf of shareholders see PARA 402. Further, it has been held that a creditor has no legal interest arising directly out of an injury to his debtor: *McNear* 4 RIAA 373 (1928); *British Claims in the Spanish Zone of Morocco* 2 RIAA 615 at 730 (1925); *Forests of Central Rhodope* 3 RIAA 1405 at 1425 (1933); *Dickson Car Wheel Co* 4 RIAA 669 at 679 (1931); *Barcelona Traction, Light and Power Co Ltd (Belgium v Spain) (Second Phase)* ICJ Reports 1970, 3 at 35 (para 44). With respect to mortgages see *Tlahualilo* Foreign Relations of the United States (1913) 931; 5 Hackworth's Digest 848. As to insurance claims see 1 O'Connell's International Law (2nd Edn) 1050.

4   See *Dickson Car Wheel Co* 4 RIAA 669 at 678 (1931). However, to the extent that this decision suggests that a state does not commit an internationally wrongful act in inflicting an injury upon a stateless person and that no state is entitled to intervene on his behalf, it has clearly been overtaken by the evolution in international law, in particular the emergence of international human rights law.
     The International Law Commission ('ILC') has proposed, expressly de lege ferenda, that, by way of exception to the normal requirement of nationality, a state should be able to exercise diplomatic protection in relation to stateless persons and refugees who were lawfully and habitually resident at the date of injury and at the date of the claim: see the Articles on Diplomatic Protection ('ADP') art 8, Report of the International Law Commission ('ILC'), 58th Session (2006), A/61/10, ch IV; and PARA 391 note 1. However, it has been held that the proposed rule does not represent customary international law: see *R (on the application of Al-Rawi) v Secretary of State for Foreign and Commonwealth Affairs (United Nations High Commissioner for Refugees intervening)* [2006] EWCA Civ 1279, [2008] QB 289, [2006] All ER (D) 138 (Oct).

399.   Continuous nationality.   In general, and in the absence of any express treaty stipulation to the contrary, in order for a state to take up a claim arising out of an injury to an individual or corporation, that individual or corporation must have possessed the nationality of that state at the time of the injury[1] and continuously thereafter up to the date of the presentation of the claim[2]. Thus a claim may not normally be presented where the injured person has changed his nationality since the date of the injury[3], or where the claim has changed its nationality, as where the injured national has died and his heirs do not possess the same nationality or, if they do, possess also the nationality of the state responsible for the injury[4]. The same may be the case when the injured person has assigned his rights to a national of another state[5]. It has been suggested that a state may not continue to exercise diplomatic protection in respect of a natural or legal person who acquires the nationality of the state against which the claim is brought after the date of the official presentation of the claim[6].

1   *Panevezys-Saldutiskis Railway (Estonia v Lithuania)* PCIJ Ser A/B No 76 at 16–17 (1939); *Forests of Central Rhodope* 3 RIAA 1405 at 1421 (1933); *Corvaià* 10 RIAA 609 (1903); *Gleadell* 5 RIAA 44 at 49 (1929); Rules Applying to International Claims 1985 r I, and comment (reproduced in 37 ICLQ 1006 (1988)). As to the practice of the Foreign Claims Settlement Commission see Lillich *International Claims: Post War British Practice* 24–31.
     The International Law Commission ('ILC') has proposed that a claim may be made by a state in relation to an individual who is a national at the date of the presentation of the claim but was not a national at the date of the injury, provided that the individual either had the nationality of a predecessor state at the date of the injury and as a result of the law of state succession had acquired the nationality of the new state, or had lost the previous nationality and acquired, for a reason unrelated to the bringing of the claim, the nationality of the claiming state in a manner not inconsistent with international law: see the Articles on Diplomatic Protection ('ADP') art 5(2), Report of the International Law Commission ('ILC'), 58th Session (2006), A/61/10, ch IV. Even in such circumstances, however, diplomatic protection may not be exercised by the new state of nationality against a former state of nationality for an injury caused when the individual was a national of the former state of nationality but not of the new state of nationality: see ADP art 5(3).

2   This is the approach taken in ADP art 5(1) (natural persons) and art 10(1) (corporations), which require continuous nationality from the date of injury up to the date of presentation of the claim. However, the ILC has made clear that, given the lack of clarity of state practice as to the requirement of continuous nationality for the period between injury and presentation and claim, this is a progressive development of the law; the requirement of continuity of nationality between injury and claim is included expressly on the basis that there exists a rebuttable presumption of continuity if nationality is proved to have existed at both the date of injury and the date of presentation of the claim: see ADP, Commentary to Article 5, para (2), Commentary to Article 10, para (2). It is also the position taken by the United Kingdom, which likewise takes the position that in practice it is normally sufficient to prove nationality at the date of injury and at the date of presentation of the claim: see the Rules Applying to International Claims 1985 r I and comment (reproduced in 37 ICLQ 1006 (1988)). Some international decisions have taken a different approach as to the precise date up to which the victim of the violation is required to possess the nationality of the claimant state: in *The Loewen Group, Inc and Raymond L Loewen v United States of America* ICSID Case No ARB(AF)/98/3, Award of 26 June, (2003) 7 ICSID Reports 442, an arbitral tribunal, in relation to a claim of violation of the North American Free Trade Agreement brought by a corporation which had changed its nationality to that of the respondent state after commencing its claim but prior to the making of the final award, took the view that, under the customary international law of diplomatic protection, nationality had to be continuous not only up to the date of presentation but also up to the time of the resolution of the claim. The ILC has expressly declined to follow the reasoning of that decision as to the date to which nationality has to be continuous, although it accepted that the result was correct in so far as the claimant had subsequently acquired the nationality of the respondent state: see ADP art 5(4), Commentary to Article 5, para (5) (individuals). See also art 10(2) (corporations). Where a corporation was a national at the date of injury but has subsequently ceased to exist under the law of the state of incorporation, the ILC has suggested that that state should nevertheless remain entitled to exercise diplomatic protection on its behalf: see art 10(3).

3   Where the claimant has become or ceases to be a United Kingdom national after the date of the injury, the United Kingdom government may, in an appropriate case, take up his claim in concert with the government of the country of his former or subsequent nationality: Rules Applying to International Claims 1985 r II. Cf the proposal contained in ADP art 5(2) (see note 1); in any case, it is clear that a state may not exercise diplomatic protection on behalf of an individual who acquires its nationality subsequent to the date of an injury if the individual was a national of the responsible state at the time of the injury (see art 5(3); and note 1).

4   See eg *Stevenson* 9 RIAA 494 at 502–506 (1903); *Maninat* 10 RIAA 55 at 76 (1905); *Massiani* 10 RIAA 159 at 183 (1905); *Miliani* 10 RIAA 584 at 591 (1904); *Giacopini* 10 RIAA 594 at 596 (1903); *Poggioli* 10 RIAA 669 at 679 (1903). The ADP, although recognising the impermissibility of a claim where the heirs of the injured person have the nationality of the allegedly responsible state, do not attempt to lay down any rules in relation to the issue of

whether a claim may be brought by the state of nationality of the injured person who has died where the heirs have the nationality of a third state: see ADP, Commentary to Article 5, para (14). In the practice of the United Kingdom government, where the claimant has died since the date of the injury to him or his property, his personal representatives may seek to obtain relief or compensation for the injury on behalf of his estate. Such a claim is not to be confused with a claim by a dependant of a deceased person for damages for his death: Rules Applying to International Claims 1985 r XI. Where the personal representatives are of a different nationality from that of the original claimant, the rules would probably be applied as if it were a case of a single claimant who had changed his national status: r XI and comment.

5   This would seem to follow from the principle. However, the right of a state was not regarded as defeated by reason of an assignment in *Administrative Decision No V (United States v Germany)* 7 RIAA 119 at 150 (1924). See also *Landreau* 1 RIAA 347 (1922); *Alsop* 11 RIAA 349 (1911) (assignment to creditors).

6   See ADP arts 5(4), 10(2). The ADP thus reflect the outcome, if not the reasoning, of the decision of the arbitral tribunal in *The Loewen Group, Inc and Raymond L Loewen v United States of America* ICSID Case No ARB(AF)/98/3, Award of 26 June, (2003) 7 ICSID Reports 442: see note 2.

400.   The genuine link. It has been held that a state cannot present an international claim on account of an injury to one of its nationals against another state unless the individual in question also has a genuine link or substantial connection with the claimant state[1]. However, that requirement is probably too broadly stated and merely entails that a claimant state cannot present the claim if, although not possessing the nationality of the respondent state, its national in fact has closer links or connections with the latter state than with the former[2].

1   *Nottebohm (Liechtenstein v Guatemala) (Second Phase)* ICJ Reports 1955, 4. As to the requirement of a genuine link see also United Nations Convention on the Law of the Sea (Montego Bay, 10 December 1982; TS 81 (1999); Cmnd 4524) art 91(1); and PARA 395. It is not clear whether this applies in the case of a person who has the nationality of the claimant state at birth or in cases of individuals who have that nationality by descent, or whether it only applies (as in *Nottebohm (Liechtenstein v Guatemala) (Second Phase)* ICJ Reports 1955, 4) to persons who have acquired the nationality of the claimant state by naturalisation. Further, it is not clear whether the genuine link principle applies to protection of corporations: see PARA 402. See also *Barcelona Traction, Light and Power Co Ltd (Belgium v Spain) (Second Phase)* ICJ Reports 1970, 3 at 42–45, and the separate declarations and opinions at 52, 80–84.

2   This appears to have been the view taken by the Italian-United States Conciliation Commission in *Flegenheimer* 14 RIAA 327 (1958). See also *Barcelona Traction, Light and Power Co Ltd (Belgium v Spain) (Second Phase)* ICJ Reports 1970, 3 at 81. In *Nottebohm (Liechtenstein v Guatemala) (Second Phase)* ICJ Reports 1955, 4, the International Court of Justice merely held that the Liechtenstein nationality acquired by the individual in replacement of his previous German nationality was not in the circumstances of the case opposable to Guatemala, whose nationality he did not possess but with whom he had considerable connections in respect of his domicile and property at the time of the injury complained of. The International Law Commission ('ILC') has likewise taken the view that there is no general requirement of an 'effective' or 'genuine' link with the state exercising diplomatic protection, and interpreted the decision in *Nottebohm (Liechtenstein v Guatemala) (Second Phase)* as limited to its particular facts: see the Articles on Diplomatic Protection ('ADP') Commentary to Article 4, para (5) (individuals), Commentary to Article 9, para (3) (corporations), Report of the International Law Commission ('ILC'), 58th Session (2006), A/61/10, ch IV.

401.   Claims on behalf of individuals having multiple nationality. In relation to persons who possess more than one nationality[1], although at one time it was thought that the state of one of those nationalities could not in general present a claim arising out of an injury to such a person arising out of acts attributable to the state of his other nationality and that rule was embodied in a multilateral treaty provision[2], the general rule appears to be that a claim can be brought against another state of nationality if the claimant state is the state of dominant nationality at both the time of injury and the date of presentation of the claim[3]. Where a person having multiple nationality is injured by the acts of a state of which he is not a national, it appears that any of the states of which he is a national may present a claim, or they may do so jointly, and there is no rule that only the state of dominant nationality (that is, that with which he has the closest links) or a state with which he had genuine links may bring a claim[4]. When injury has been caused to a national of a state who subsequently dies and whose claim passes to his heirs, some of whom have the nationality of the state which committed the injury, the compensation recoverable from that state will normally have to be scaled down appropriately[5].

1　See PARA 393.

2　See the International Convention on Certain Questions Relating to the Conflict of Nationality Laws (The Hague, 12 April 1930; TS 33 (1937); Cmd 5553) art 4.

3　This is the approach adopted in the Articles on Diplomatic Protection ('ADP') art 7, Report of the International Law Commission ('ILC'), 58th Session (2006), A/61/10, ch IV. The ADP art 7 takes the view that a state of nationality of an individual may not exercise diplomatic protection against another state of which he has nationality unless the nationality of the claimant state is predominant, both at the date of injury and at the date of presentation of the claim. See also *Carnevaro Case* 11 RIAA 397 (1912); *Mergé* 14 RIAA 236 (1955); and the other cases referred to in ADP, Commentary to Article 7, para (3). The dominant nationality principle has also been applied by the Iran-US Claims Tribunal so as to allow claims by dual nationals: *Esphahanian v Bank Tejarat* 2 Iran-US CTR 157 at 166 (1983); *Case No A/18* 5 Iran-US CTR 251 (1984); *Golpira v Government of the Islamic Republic of Iran* 2 Iran-US CTR 174 (1983), 72 ILR 493. The United Kingdom government will not normally take up the claim of a dual national as a United Kingdom national if the respondent state is the state of his second nationality; it may do so, however, if in the circumstances which gave rise to the injury the respondent state has treated the claimant as a United Kingdom national: Rules Applying to International Claims 1985, r III (reproduced in 37 ICLQ 1006 (1988)). See also 5 British Digest 382–384; British Practice in International Law 1964 (I) 60. For the practice of the Foreign Compensation Commission see Lillich *International Claims: Post War British Practice* 32–34.

4　See ADP art 6; and the cases cited in the Commentary to Article 6. See in particular *Salem Case* 2 RIAA 1161 (1932); *Flegenheimer* 14 RIAA 327 (1958); *Dallal v Iran* (1983) 3 Iran-US CTR 23. In *Barcelona Traction, Light and Power Co Ltd (Belgium v Spain) (Second Phase)* ICJ Reports 1970, 3 at 50, the International Court of Justice did not exclude the possibility of concurrent claims being made on behalf of persons having dual nationality, although it was thought that in such a case the lack of a genuine link with one of the states might be set up by the respondent state against the right of the former state to present the claim. As to the postulated requirement of a genuine link see PARA 400. See also the International Convention on Certain Questions relating to the Conflict of Nationality Laws art 5. In this type of case, the United Kingdom government may take up the claim alone, but will usually prefer to do so jointly with the other government entitled to do so: Rules Applying to International Claims 1985 r III.

5　See PARA 399.

402.　Claims for injuries to corporations and shareholders. As a general rule, under international law, a state may take up by way of diplomatic protection a claim which arises out of an injury committed against a corporation or other juridical person which possesses its nationality[1]. For the purposes of diplomatic protection, what is important from the point of view of international law is whether a corporation is granted separate legal personality independent of its members, which implies that it has been granted rights over its own property, which it alone is capable of protecting[2]; as a result, only the state of nationality of a corporation may exercise diplomatic protection on its behalf when its rights are injured by an internationally wrongful act of another state[3]. As concerns the question of whether a corporation has separate legal personality, international law has regard to the rules of municipal law[4]. Traditionally international law regarded the right to exercise diplomatic protection of a company as appertaining to the state under the laws of which it was incorporated and in whose territory it had its registered offices; however, some states have only been willing to exercise diplomatic protection where the seat or management or centre of control was also located in its territory, or where a majority of the shares in the corporation were owned by nationals, such as to provide a genuine connection or genuine link with that state[5]. In that regard, it would appear that there is no clear settled rule which is generally accepted requiring a 'genuine connection' between the corporation and the state[6]. Accordingly, the state of incorporation will normally constitute the state of nationality of a corporation for the purposes of the exercise of diplomatic protection[7], although there may exist some additional requirement that there be a 'close and permanent connection' with the state purporting to exercise diplomatic protection[8]. It has been proposed that although the national state entitled to exercise diplomatic protection on behalf of a company is normally the state in which the company is incorporated, by way of exception, where the corporation is controlled by nationals of another state or states and has no substantial business activities in the state of incorporation and the seat of management and the financial control of the corporation are both located in another state, that state should be regarded as the state of nationality[9]. In the practice of the United Kingdom the requirement as to nationality is taken to mean a corporation which is created and regulated under the law of the United Kingdom or any territory for which it is internationally responsible[10]. In general a state may not take up a claim arising out of an injury to a foreign corporation, nor may it do so on behalf of the members or shareholders of any such corporation who happen to possess its nationality[11]. It is not clear whether a state may present a claim on behalf of a foreign corporation, or members or shareholders having its own nationality, when the corporation suffered the injury at the hands of the state of which it is a national[12]. In either event, however, a state may take up a claim for an injury to its nationals who are members of a foreign corporation when that injury was inflicted not upon the corporation itself, but against the members directly[13].

1   *Barcelona Traction, Light and Power Co Ltd (Belgium v Spain) (Second Phase)* ICJ Reports 1970, 3 at 42 (para 70), 48 (para 93); *Ahmadou Sadio Diallo (Republic of Guinea v Democratic Republic of the Congo) (Preliminary Objections)* ICJ Reports, 24 May 2007 (para 61). As to the nationality of corporations see PARA 394.

2   *Ahmadou Sadio Diallo (Republic of Guinea v Democratic Republic of the Congo) (Preliminary Objections)* ICJ Reports, 24 May 2007 (para 61). As to separate legal personality of companies see further COMPANIES vol 14 (2009) PARA 120 et seq.

3   *Ahmadou Sadio Diallo (Republic of Guinea v Democratic Republic of the Congo) (Preliminary Objections)* ICJ Reports, 24 May 2007 (para 61). Rules similar to those applicable to corporations would appear to apply, mutatis mutandis, to other legal persons: see the Articles on Diplomatic Protection ('ADP') art 13, Report of the International Law Commission ('ILC'), 58th Session (2006), A/61/10, ch IV.

4   *Ahmadou Sadio Diallo (Republic of Guinea v Democratic Republic of the Congo) (Preliminary Objections)* ICJ Reports, 24 May 2007 (para 61).

5   *Barcelona Traction, Light and Power Co Ltd (Belgium v Spain) (Second Phase)* ICJ Reports 1970, 3 at 42 (para 70). In this case the International Court of Justice did not have to take a firm position in this regard given the very strong links of the company in question with Canada and that it had not been disputed by any of the states involved that Canada was the national state: *Barcelona Traction, Light and Power Co Ltd (Belgium v Spain) (Second Phase)* ICJ Reports 1970, 3 at 42–45. As to the requirement of a 'genuine link' in relation to nationality of individuals see PARA 400. As to state practice requiring some connection other than mere incorporation see Beckett, 17 Transactions of the Grotius Society 175 at 177 note (f); White's Nationalisation of Foreign Property 62–63. It has been argued that there is little if any evidence that a state may present an international claim on behalf of a corporation on the mere ground that it is incorporated under its laws: Parry's Nationality and Citizenship Laws of the

Commonwealth 139. For the British practice, which appears to bear this out, see 5 British Digest 503–573 (especially the Report of the Inter-Departmental Committee dated 29 April 1913 set out at 527–535). In British practice, each case has been dealt with in the light of its own facts: see *Enrique Cortes & Co* (1896) 5 British Digest 514 (where the United Kingdom government refused to take up the claim); *Santa Clara Estates Co Ltd* (1903) 5 British Digest 518, 9 RIAA 455 (1903) (where the claim was taken up and subsequently allowed). In determining whether to exercise its right of protection, the United Kingdom government may consider whether the company has in fact a real and substantial connection with the United Kingdom: Rules Applying to International Claims 1985 r IV, and comment (reproduced in 37 ICLQ 1006 (1988)). For the practice of the United States see 5 Hackworth's Digest 839. In *The 'I'm Alone'* 3 RIAA 1609 (1935), although a breach of international law was found, no damages were awarded in respect of injury to a company whose members were almost all nationals of the respondent state.

6   *Barcelona Traction, Light and Power Co Ltd (Belgium v Spain) (Second Phase)* ICJ Reports 1970, 3 at 42 (para 70); and see also the separate declarations and opinions at 52, 80–84.

7   See ADP art 9; and see also Commentary to Article 9, para (3), which observes that as a matter of most systems of domestic law, a corporation incorporated under the law of the state must have its registered office within that state.

8   *Barcelona Traction, Light and Power Co Ltd (Belgium v Spain) (Second Phase)* ICJ Reports 1970, 3 at 42 (para 71).

9   ADP art 9. The Commentary makes clear that it is envisaged that where the seat of management and financial control of the corporation are located in different states, the national state remains the state of incorporation: ADP, Commentary to Article 9, para (6).

10   Rules Applying to International Claims 1985 r IV. See also r I para (b).

11   *Barcelona Traction, Light and Power Co Ltd (Belgium v Spain) (Second Phase)* ICJ Reports 1970, 3 (claim by Belgium on behalf of Belgian members of a Canadian company allegedly injured by Spain). When a United Kingdom national has an interest as a shareholder or otherwise in a company incorporated in another state, and that company is injured by the acts of a third state, the United Kingdom government will normally take up his claim only in concert with the government of the state in which the company is incorporated. Exceptionally, as for example, where the company is defunct, there may be independent intervention: Rules Applying to International Claims 1985 r V. However, a right to exercise diplomatic protection in such circumstances is not clear as a matter of customary international law. In *Barcelona Traction, Light and Power Co Ltd (Belgium v Spain) (Second Phase)* ICJ Reports 1970, 3 at 41 (para 66), the International Court of Justice stated that the term 'practically defunct' lacks all legal precision. The court suggested that two types of special circumstances might justify 'lifting the veil' of incorporation: (1) cases of enemy property in war; and (2) specific agreements on nationalisation of property (although the court appeared to regard these as sui generis). See also *Standard Oil Co (Romano-Americana)* 5 Hackworth's Digest 840. In *Elettronica Sicula SpA (ELSI) (United States of America v Italy)* ICJ Reports 1989, 15, the United States brought a claim before the International Court of Justice for injuries to the Italian subsidiaries of an American company without objection from either Italy or the Chamber of the Court; however, the claim was brought on the basis of violation of the provisions of a bilateral treaty.

12   In *Delagoa Bay Railway Co* (1893) 5 British Digest 535, such a claim was successfully presented by the governments of Great Britain and the United States, but for the purposes of the arbitration, which was only concerned with the assessment of compensation, the government of the respondent state, Portugal, had conceded the locus standi of the former states. See also Correspondence with the Mexican government regarding the Expropriation of Oil Properties in Mexico (Cmd 5758) (1938) (concerning the Mexican Eagle Oil Company). The United Kingdom government has stated that where a United Kingdom national has an interest as a shareholder or otherwise in a company incorporated in another state, and of which it is therefore a national, and that state injures the company, the United Kingdom government may intervene to protect the interests of that United Kingdom national: Rules Relating to International Claims 1985 r VI. Where the capital in a foreign company is owned in various proportions by nationals of several states, including the United Kingdom, it is unusual for the United Kingdom government to make representations unless the states whose nationals hold the bulk of the capital will support them in making representations: comment to r VI. Although the practice of the Foreign Compensation Commission has been to allow such claims (Lillich *International Claims: Post War British Practice* 42), that practice depends upon the compensation agreements and the orders made under the Foreign Compensation Acts (see CONSTITUTIONAL LAW AND HUMAN RIGHTS vol 8(2) (Reissue) PARA 803 et seq). The United States government declined to intervene in *Antioquia* (1866) 6 Moore's Digest 644, although it obtained compensation in *El Triunfo* 15 RIAA 455 at 464 (1902). However, this may be a case

of direct interference with the members' rights: see note 13. The claimant state succeeded also on this point in *British Claims in the Spanish Zone of Morocco* RIAA 615 at 729 (1925), *Shufeldt* 2 RIAA 1079 (1930), and *Alsop* 11 RIAA 349 (1911), although the first two of these were arguably partnerships and the third was decided not by an arbitrator but by an amiable compositeur. Claims on behalf of members of foreign corporations injured by the state of incorporation were denied in *Brewer, Moller & Co* 10 RIAA 433 (1903); *Baasch and Römer* 10 RIAA 723 (1903); and *Henriquez* 10 RIAA 713 at 727 (1903). The International Court of Justice in *Barcelona Traction, Light and Power Co Ltd (Belgium v Spain) (Second Phase)* ICJ Reports 1970, 3 at 48 (para 92) expressed no settled view one way or another, and stated only that the situation of a state of nationality of shareholders bringing a claim against the state of incorporation of a company had no application to the facts of the case before the court 'whatever the validity of this theory may be'. Judges Fitzmaurice (at 72–74), Tanaka (at 134) and Jessup (at 191–193) were in favour of permitting the state of the nationality of the members to take up their claim in such a situation; Judges Morelli (at 240), Padilla Nervo (at 257–259) and Ammoun (at 318) were against. The ILC has proposed that the state of nationality of shareholders in a corporation should not be able to exercise diplomatic protection in respect of those shareholders in relation to an injury to the corporation unless either the corporation has ceased to exist according to the law of the state of incorporation for a reason unrelated to the injury (see ADP art 11(a)), or the corporation, at the date of the injury, had the nationality of the state allegedly responsible for causing the injury and incorporation in that state was required as a precondition for doing business there (see art 11(b)). In *Ahmadou Sadio Diallo (Republic of Guinea v Democratic Republic of the Congo) (Preliminary Objections)* ICJ Reports, 24 May 2007, the applicant state claimed exceptionally to be able to exercise diplomatic protection on behalf of its national who was a shareholder in corporations incorporated under the law of the respondent state 'by way of substitution'; the court held that no such exception permitting the exercise of diplomatic protection existed as matter of customary international law (para 89), but did not find it necessary to express any view as to whether there existed a narrower exception reflecting the second hypothesis proposed by ADP art 11(b) such that diplomatic protection might be exercised by the state of nationality of a shareholder if the corporation in which the shares were held was incorporated in the state alleged to have caused the injury and incorporation had been required as a precondition of it doing business there; it held that, on the facts, the corporations did not fall within the scope of any such protection: *Ahmadou Sadio Diallo (Republic of Guinea v Democratic Republic of the Congo) (Preliminary Objections)* ICJ Reports, 24 May 2007 (paras 91–93).

13 *Barcelona Traction, Light and Power Co Ltd (Belgium v Spain) (Second Phase)* ICJ Reports 1970, 3 at 36. According to the court, the separate rights of the shareholders include the right to any declared dividend, the right to attend and vote at meetings and the right to share in the residual assets of the corporation on liquidation. See also *Baasch and Römer* 10 RIAA 723 (1903) (claims allowed in respect of Dutch interests in Venezuelan companies injured by Venezuela when the companies were extinguished); *Kunhardt & Co* 9 RIAA 171 (1903). The possibility of a claim in relation to direct injury to the rights of a national who was a shareholder in a company was also expressly recognised by the International Court of Justice in *Ahmadou Sadio Diallo (Republic of Guinea v Democratic Republic of the Congo) (Preliminary Objections)* ICJ Reports, 24 May 2007, in the context of its examination of the admissibility of that part of the claim alleging infringement of the rights of the individual national of the applicant state who was a shareholder of a corporation incorporated under the law of the respondent state. The court emphasised that, in so far as such a claim seeks to engage the responsibility of another state for an injury caused to a national by an internationally wrongful act committed by that state, it is no more than the exercise of diplomatic protection on behalf of that national; in such circumstances, the conduct amounting to an internationally wrongful act is the violation by the respondent state of the shareholder's direct rights in relation to the corporation; the court stressed that such a claim was not to be regarded as an exception to the general legal regime of diplomatic protection for natural or legal persons under customary international law (para 64). The court left the question of what rights of the shareholder in the corporation might have been affected by the actions of the respondent state for the merits phase (para 66).

403.   Claims on behalf of the crews of ships. It would seem that, by way of exception to the general requirement of nationality[1], the state of nationality or flag state of a ship[2] may seek redress on behalf of crew members of the ship, irrespective of their nationality, when they have been injured in connection with an injury to the vessel resulting from an internationally wrongful act[3]. This possibility is without prejudice to the right of the state of nationality of the crew members to exercise diplomatic protection on their behalf[4].

1　As to the nationality requirement see PARA 391 et seq.

2　As to nationality of ships see PARAS 395–396.

3　See *The M/V 'Saiga' (No 2) (Saint Vincent and the Grenadines v Guinea)* ITLOS Reports 1999, 10, 120 ILR 143. For earlier decisions see e g *McCready* (1868) III Moore Int Arb 2536; and *The 'I'm Alone'* 3 RIAA 1609 (1935) (a decision of a conciliation commission). See also *Reparation for Injuries Suffered in the Service of the United Nations* ICJ Reports 1949, 174 at 202–203 (Dissenting Opinion of Judge Hackworth), and 206–207 (Dissenting Opinion of Judge Badawi Pasha); and Watts 'The Protection of Alien Seamen' (1958) 7 ICLQ 691. The International Law Commission has endorsed the existence of the exception: see the Articles on Diplomatic Protection ('ADP') art 18, Report of the International Law Commission ('ILC'), 58th Session (2006), A/61/10, ch IV. The ILC has taken the position that although the possibility for the state of nationality of a ship (flag state) to claim redress on behalf of crew members of the ship does not as such constitute diplomatic protection given the lack of any bond of nationality between the foreign crew-members and the state of nationality of the ship, there is a very close resemblance: see ADP, Commentary to Article 18, para (1).

4　See ADP art 18.

404.　Claims presented by international organisations by way of functional protection.　Where an individual is injured in the course of service with an international organisation, the right to present a claim by way of functional protection which is possessed by that organisation is parallel to the right to do so which is possessed by his state of nationality[1].

1　*Reparation for Injuries Suffered in the Service of the United Nations (Advisory Opinion)* ICJ Reports 1949, 174 at 185.

(iii) Exhaustion of Local Remedies

405.　Exhaustion of local remedies.　As a general rule, a state may not take up the claim of one of its nationals against another state by way of diplomatic protection until such time as the injured person has exhausted all effective and available local remedies[1]. For these purposes, local remedies include all the legal remedies which are open to the injured person before the judicial or administrative courts or other bodies in the state alleged to have caused the injury[2]. Unless they constitute an essential prerequisite for the admissibility of subsequent contentious proceedings, administrative remedies are only relevant for the purposes of the local remedies rule if they are aimed at vindicating a right and not at obtaining a favour[3]. There is normally no requirement to pursue a remedy which consists of making a request to the executive to exercise powers which are purely discretionary or by way of grace[4]. The claimant must pursue his action by way of appeal up to the highest tribunal[5], and must employ all the procedural steps which are essential to the vindication of his rights of action[6]. The individual must have raised before the domestic authorities the arguments which form the essence of the claim brought before the international forum[7]. As regards the distribution of the burden of proof, it is incumbent on the applicant to prove that local remedies were indeed exhausted or to establish that exceptional circumstances relieved the allegedly injured person whom the applicant seeks to protect of the obligation to exhaust available local remedies[8]. By contrast, it is for the respondent to show that there were effective remedies available in its domestic legal system that were not exhausted[9]. In deciding whether local remedies have been exhausted, the allegations of fact and law advanced in the claim are normally assumed to be correct[10].

1　*Panevezys-Saldutiskis Railway (Estonia v Lithuania)* PCIJ Ser A/B No 76 (1939); *Interhandel (Switzerland v United States of America) (Preliminary Objections)* ICJ Reports 1959, 6 (in particular at 27, 83, 88 where the rationale of the rule is explained). See also the International Law Commission ('ILC') Articles on Responsibility of States for Internationally Wrongful Acts ('ARSIWA') art 44, International Law Commission Report, 53rd Session, A/56/10, YILC 2001, vol II(2); and PARA 330. See further the Articles on Diplomatic Protection ('ADP') art 14, Report of the International Law Commission ('ILC'), 58th Session (2006), A/61/10, ch IV.

　　The rule has been described as being 'a well-established rule of customary international law': *Interhandel (Switzerland v United States of America) (Preliminary Objections)* ICJ Reports 1959, 6 at 27. See also *Elettronica Sicula SpA (ELSI) (United States of America v Italy)* ICJ Reports 1989, 15 at 42 ('an important principle of customary international law'); *Ahmadou Sadio Diallo (Republic of Guinea v Democratic Republic of the Congo) (Preliminary Objections)* ICJ Reports, 24 May 2007 (para 44). See generally Amerasinghe *Local Remedies in International Law* (2004, 2nd Edn).

　　The United Kingdom government will not normally take over and formally espouse the claim of a United Kingdom national unless all the legal remedies available to him have been exhausted: Rules Applying to International Claims 1985 r VII (reproduced in 37 ICLQ 1006 (1988)). Many international claims have been rejected by arbitral tribunals on this ground: see Borchard's Diplomatic Protection of Citizens Abroad 819 n 1.

　　The rule is also incorporated as a condition of the admissibility of individual applications under the Convention for the Protection of Human Rights and Fundamental Freedoms (Rome, 4 November 1950; TS 71 (1953); Cmd 8969) (the 'European Convention on Human Rights') art 35(1) (as amended by Protocol 11), as well as constituting a precondition for the right of individual petition under other international instruments for the protection of human rights (see CONSTITUTIONAL LAW AND HUMAN RIGHTS vol 8(2) (Reissue) PARA 173 et seq).

　　As to the nationality of claims rule see PARA 398 et seq.

2　Cf ADP art 14(2).

3　*Ahmadou Sadio Diallo (Republic of Guinea v Democratic Republic of the Congo) (Preliminary Objections)* ICJ Reports, 24 May 2007 (para 47).

4　*Finnish Shipowners* 3 RIAA 1479 (1934). Accordingly, there is normally no requirement to make a request for clemency: cf *Avena and Other Mexican Nationals (Mexico v United States of America)* ICJ Reports 2004, 12 at 63–66 (paras 135–143).

5　*Electricity Co of Sofia and Bulgaria* PCIJ Ser A/B No 77 (1939). This does not apply where an appeal would be incapable of providing effective redress: see PARA 407. An application to a court for a re-opening of the case is a remedy for the purpose of the rule: *Interhandel (Switzerland v United States of America) (Preliminary Objections)* ICJ Reports 1959, 6 (certiorari to United States Supreme Court). In *Salem Case* 2 RIAA 1161 (1932) it was held that a litigant need not resort to an extraordinary remedy by way of appeal to a court outside the regular legal system.

6　*Ambatielos Claim* 12 RIAA 83 (1956) where it was held that it is the whole system of legal protection as provided by municipal law which must have been put to the test before a state can prosecute the claim at the international level. The plaintiff had failed to call a witness at first instance, and the Court of Appeal had refused him leave to call the witness later. It was held that he had failed to exhaust the remedies available, since he had rendered an appeal futile. See also *Electricity Co of Sofia and Bulgaria* PCIJ Ser A/B No 77 (1939).

7　The requirement that the individual should have raised the essence of the complaint was endorsed by the ILC: see ADP art 14; and Commentary to Article 14, para (6). This is in preference to the stricter test enunciated in some earlier decisions to the effect that all contentions of fact and propositions of law relied upon in the international proceedings had to have been investigated and adjudicated upon by the municipal courts (see eg *Finnish Shipowners* 3 RIAA 1479 at 1502 (1934); *SS Lisman* 3 RIAA 1767 at 1790 (1937)).

8　*Elettronica Sicula SpA (ELSI) (United States of America v Italy)* ICJ Reports 1989, 15 at 43–44 (para 53); *Ahmadou Sadio Diallo (Republic of Guinea v Democratic Republic of the Congo) (Preliminary Objections)* ICJ Reports, 24 May 2007 (para 44).

9　*Elettronica Sicula SpA (ELSI) (United States of America v Italy)* ICJ Reports 1989, 15 at 46 (para 59).

10　*Ambatielos Claim* 12 RIAA 83 (1956).

406.　Cases to which the rule is not applicable.　The exhaustion of local remedies rule[1] has no application in cases where the essential basis of the claim by a state is one of direct injury to it caused by the acts of another state, and not a claim relating to treatment of its national[2]. It has also been suggested that where an injury is caused to a national of the claimant state, the rule does not apply unless there is some voluntary link between the national and the defendant state[3]. The rule may be waived or modified by agreement[4].

1   As to the exhaustion of local remedies rule see PARA 405.
2   As to the distinction between claims for direct injury and claims by way of diplomatic protection see PARA 387. To the extent that a particular claim may be regarded as being both a direct claim and a claim by way of diplomatic protection, it may not be necessary to exhaust local remedies: see e g *Avena and Other Mexican Nationals (Mexico v United States of America)* ICJ Reports 2004, 12 at 36 (para 40).
3   Eg this was argued by Israel in *Aerial Incident of 27 July 1955 (Israel v Bulgaria) (Preliminary Objections)* ICJ Reports 1959, 127 at 531–532. The court did not deal with the point. If this is so, the rule would not apply in cases such as an injury to an alien present in a state through force majeure, or the sinking of a merchant ship by a warship on the high seas.
    The International Law Commission ('ILC') has suggested that there is a requirement that there should be some 'relevant connection' between the injured person and the state alleged to be responsible at the date of the injury, on the basis that in the absence of such a link it would be unreasonable, unfair or cause great hardship to require exhaustion, albeit that it expressly recognised that there is no judicial authority or state practice which provides clear guidance on the existence of such a requirement: see the Articles on Diplomatic Protection ('ADP') art 15(c), Commentary to Article 15, paras (7)–(10), Report of the International Law Commission ('ILC'), 58th Session (2006), A/61/10, ch IV.
4   The rule has been excluded or modified in various international treaties providing for mechanisms for the settlement of particular claims: e g it was excluded in the Convention for the Settlement of British Pecuniary Claims in Mexico Arising from Loss or Damage from Revolutionary Acts (Mexico City, 19 November 1926; TS 11 (1928); Cmd 3085) art 6, 5 RIAA 7, and modified in the Agreement between Great Britain and the United States of America for the Settlement of Certain Pecuniary Claims (Washington, 18 August 1910; TS 11 (1912); Cd 6201) (see *Robert E Brown Case* 6 RIAA 120 at 129 (1923)). The treaty must clearly be to this effect and the rule should not be held to have been dispensed with tacitly: *Elettronica Sicula SpA (ELSI) (United States of America v Italy)* ICJ Reports 1989, 15 at 42 (para 50). See also ADP art 15(e). See further PARA 411.

407.   Cases in which there is no requirement to exhaust local remedies.   The exhaustion of local remedies rule[1] cannot apply if there are no reasonably available local remedies to exhaust, and does not apply if any available remedies provide no reasonable possibility of effective redress[2]. This may be so where the courts are completely under the control of the government which has caused the injury[3]; where there is an undue delay in hearing the case[4]; where the case is likely to result in the application of a uniform line of decisions, or of clearly applicable legislation[5]; where the result would not prevent further damages or a repetition of the injury in relation to which complaint is made[6]; where the courts have no jurisdiction under domestic law to hear the case[7], for instance where there can be no action against the government[8]; where the remedy would not afford adequate or appropriate reparation[9]; or where the state has taken measures to prevent access to the tribunals in question[10]. It has also been proposed that there should be a residual exception such that there is no requirement to exhaust local remedies where the injured person is 'manifestly precluded' from pursuing such remedies[11], although normally an injured person is not excused from attempting to exhaust local remedies merely through lack of means[12].

1   As to the exhaustion of local remedies rule see PARA 405.
2   Cf the Articles on Diplomatic Protection ('ADP') art 15(a), Report of the International Law Commission ('ILC'), 58th Session (2006), A/61/10, ch IV. The ILC preferred the formulation that there is no requirement to exhaust local remedies where there is 'no reasonably available local remedies to provide effective redress, or the local remedies provide no reasonable possibility of such redress'; in doing so, it considered and rejected alternative formulations that the local remedies should not be 'obviously futile' or 'offer no reasonable prospect of success',

although those alternative formulations both find some support in the authorities: see ADP art 15(a), Commentary to Article 15, paras (2)–(4). See also the ILC Articles on Responsibility of States for Internationally Wrongful Acts ('ARSIWA') art 44 (which refers to 'available and effective' remedies), International Law Commission Report, 53rd Session, A/56/10, YILC 2001, vol II(2); and PARA 330.

As to the 'obvious futility' test see *Finnish Shipowners* 3 RIAA 1479 (1934), where it was held that it must be possible to demonstrate on the basis of clear evidence that resort to the remedies would not produce a decision in favour of the foreign national. It has been suggested that if the remedy is not obviously futile, however contingent or theoretical it may be, an effort should be made to exhaust it: see eg *Certain Norwegian Loans (France v Norway) (Preliminary Objections)* ICJ Reports 1957, 9 at 39 per Judge Lauterpacht. As to non-existence of remedies see eg *Ahmadou Sadio Diallo (Republic of Guinea v Democratic Republic of the Congo) (Preliminary Objections)* ICJ Reports, 24 May 2007 (para 47). In the United Kingdom government's view, failure to exhaust the local remedies is no bar to a claim if it is clearly established that in the circumstances of the case an appeal to a higher municipal tribunal would have had no effect, nor is a claimant in another state required to exhaust justice in that state where there is no justice to exhaust: Rules Applying to International Claims 1985 r VII, comment (reproduced in 37 ICLQ 1006 (1988)). Further, the United Kingdom government may intervene on the claimant's behalf to secure redress of injustice: Rules Applying to International Claims 1985 r VIII.

3   *Robert E Brown Case* 6 RIAA 120 (1923). The same has been held to be the case where the courts have been appointed by the legislature which has annulled the rights of the foreign national: *Tinoco Arbitration* 1 RIAA 369 at 375, 387 (1923).

4   See *El Oro Mining and Rly Co Ltd* 5 RIAA 191 (1931) (nine years' delay); *Administration of the Prince Von Pless* PCIJ Ser A/B No 52 (1933). All the circumstances must be taken into account: see *Interhandel (Switzerland v United States of America) (Preliminary Objections)* ICJ Reports 1959, 6 (ten years from institution of the action; remedies held not to have been exhausted). See also ADP art 15(b), which clarifies that the undue delay must be attributable to the state.

5   See eg *Finnish Shipowners* 3 RIAA 1479 at 1495 (1934); *Panevezys-Saldutiskis Railway (Estonia v Lithuania)* PCIJ Ser A/B No 76 at 18 (1939).

6   *De Sabla Case* 6 RIAA 358 (1933).

7   *Finnish Shipowners Case* 3 RIAA 1479 (1934) (appeal only on point of law, not on facts). The case must be a clear one: see *Panevezys-Saldutiskis Railway (Estonia v Lithuania)* PCIJ Ser A/B No 76 (1939); *Certain Norwegian Loans (Preliminary Objections) (France v Norway)* ICJ Reports 1957, 9 at 39; *Interhandel (Switzerland v United States of America) (Preliminary Objections)* ICJ Reports 1959, 6 at 27–28.

8   *Forests of Central Rhodope* 3 RIAA 1406 at 1420 (1953). However, although this case suggests that remedies need not be exhausted if the government itself has caused the injury complained of, this is only true if the local law does not permit proceedings against the government. As to the position of the United Kingdom see the Crown Proceedings Act 1947; and CROWN PROCEEDINGS AND CROWN PRACTICE vol 12(1) (Reissue) PARA 110 et seq. Where a government may be sued in its own courts for violation of rights under international law the action must be pressed to a conclusion: *Interhandel (Switzerland v United States of America) (Preliminary Objections)* ICJ Reports 1959, 6 at 27.

9   There is no obligation to have recourse to courts which cannot award compensation: see eg *Finnish Shipowners* 3 RIAA 1479 at 1479 (1934).

10 *Factory at Chorzów (Jurisdiction)* PCIJ Rep Ser A No 9 at 25–31 (1927).

11 See ADP art 15(d). As to the narrow scope of the proposed exception see ADP, Commentary to Article 15, para (11).

12 Cf the discussion in *The Loewen Group, Inc and Raymond L Loewen v United States of America* ICSID Case No ARB(AF)/98/3, Award of 26 June, (2003) 7 ICSID Reports 442 in relation to a requirement under the applicable law of the posting of an appeal bond as a condition for an appeal.

408.   Calvo clauses.   The insertion of a 'Calvo clause'[1] in a contract between a state[2] and an alien is intended to have as its effect: (1) that all disputes concerning the contract, its interpretation and performance are to be decided solely by the courts of that state, whose law is the applicable law of the contract[3]; and (2) that the alien makes a complete or partial surrender of his rights as well as those of his state under international law, and waives the possibility of protection by his own state[4].

1   The 'Calvo clause' is named after Carlos Calvo, the Argentine jurist who propounded it in 1868.

2   In order to have effect, it is necessary that the clause must emanate from the central government and not from a subordinate authority: *MacNeill* 5 RIAA 135 (1931).

3   As to the applicable law see CONFLICT OF LAWS vol 8(3) (Reissue) PARA 349 et seq.

4   For an analysis of various terms of clauses in contracts which have been considered by international arbitral tribunals see Lipstein 'The Place of the Calvo Clause in International Law' 22 BYIL 130.

409.   Effect of Calvo clauses.   In so far as a Calvo clause[1] provides for submission of disputes to the local courts, it appears to do no more than to state the requirement of exhaustion of local remedies[2] and is therefore unnecessary, but in so far as it imports a submission to the local law it may be effective[3]. In so far as the clause purports to be a waiver of the rights of the alien and of the right of his state to make a claim on his behalf by way of diplomatic protection, it appears to be invalid[4]. In any case, a Calvo clause may be of no relevance if an international claim is not based upon the contract in which it is contained[5].

1   As to Calvo clauses see PARA 408.

2   As to the rule regarding the exhaustion of local remedies see PARA 405.

3   See eg *North American Dredging Co of Texas* 4 RIAA 26 at 29 (1926). As to the applicable law see CONFLICT OF LAWS vol 8(3) (Reissue) PARA 349 et seq.

4   *Martini* 10 RIAA 644 (1903); *Woodruff* 9 RIAA 213 (1905); *Tinoco Arbitration* 1 RIAA 369 at 384 et seq (1923); *International Fisheries* 4 RIAA 691 (1931). See also the Reply of the United Kingdom Government to the League of Nations Preparatory Commission for the Hague Codification Conference 1930 Bases of Discussion vol III, 134. As to the principle that when a state brings an international claim it is claiming for an injury to itself see PARA 387. For the view that, although municipal law states what the rights of the alien are, international law decides whether they are violated see *Orinoco Steamship Co* 9 RIAA 180 (1903); *Woodruff* 9 RIAA 213 (1905); *North and South American Construction Co* (1892) Moore Int Arb 2318. Cf *Turnbull* 9 RIAA 261 at 304 (1904).

5   Eg if the claim is for damage to property during a civil disturbance or for acts of expropriation by the government: *Selwyn* 9 RIAA 380 (1903).

410.   Calvo clause by legislation.   Any rule that an alien is bound by a renunciation clause[1] does not apply if the clause is not contained in an agreement to which he is a party, but purports to be imposed by legislation. Although such legislation forms part of the law of contract, it does not preclude an international claim[2].

1   Ie such as a Calvo clause. As to Calvo clauses see PARA 408.

2   *North American Dredging Co of Texas* 4 RIAA 26 (1926). In 1921 the United Kingdom government stated, in connection with Ecuadorian legislation of 1921, that 'the circumstances in which they are entitled to afford diplomatic protection are not affected in any way by foreign domestic legislation': 114 BFSP 734n.

411.   Waiver of application of local remedies rule by treaty.   The agreement nominating an arbitral tribunal may be framed so as to subject claims to its jurisdiction even though local remedies have not been exhausted[1]. In such a case, the tribunal will have jurisdiction and claims will be not be inadmissible merely on the basis that local remedies have not been exhausted[2]. If, however, the parties have agreed to the settlement of any dispute arising out of a contract by the local courts of the contracting state, the tribunal is not able to decide such a dispute until the alien has exhausted the domestic remedies, although other claimants are not bound to do so[3].

1   For examples see PARA 406 note 4. As to the exhaustion of local remedies see PARA 405.
2   *Martini* 10 RIAA 644 (1903). Where the tribunal is given power to decide claims on an equitable basis, thus dispensing with technical rules of international law, a Calvo clause may not be relied on, as such, by way of defence: *Pinson* 5 RIAA 327 (1928). As to Calvo clauses see PARA 408.
3   In such case the claimant may not ignore the local remedies, since to do so would place the state inequitably in a worse position than the claimant: *Rudloff Case* 9 RIAA 244 (1903). See also *French Co of Venezuela Railroads* 10 RIAA 285 at 335 (1903); *Martini* 10 RIAA 644 (1903); *Selwyn* 9 RIAA 380 (1903); *American Electric and Manufacturing Co* 9 RIAA 145 (1904); *North American Dredging Co of Texas* 4 RIAA 26 (1926).

(3) CONSULAR ACCESS AND ASSISTANCE

412. In general. The rules of international law relating to consular access and assistance are of relevance both in relation to the situation of foreign nationals within the United Kingdom, as well as regards the provision of consular access and assistance by the United Kingdom to British nationals abroad[1].

1   The principal instrument is the Vienna Convention on Consular Relations (Vienna, 24 April 1963; TS 14 (1973); Cmnd 5219). As to the Vienna Convention, and its incorporation into English law by the Consular Relations Act 1968, see PARA 290. In addition, the United Kingdom has entered into various bilateral agreements relating to consular matters: see PARA 416 note 2. See also the Treaty on the Functioning of the European Union (Rome, 25 March 1957; TS 1 (1973); Cmnd 5179) art 20(c), which envisages that any citizen of the European Union present in the territory of a third country in which his state of nationality is not represented, is to be entitled to protection by the consular or diplomatic authorities of any member state of the Union on the same conditions as the nationals of that member state (the Treaty was formerly known as the Treaty Establishing the European Community; it has been renamed and its provisions renumbered: see PARA 304 note 1). As to consular protection by the authorities of member states see Decision of the Representatives of the Governments of the Member States meeting within the Council of 19 December 1995 regarding protection for citizens of the European Union by diplomatic and consular representations 95/553/EC (*OJ L314, 28.12.1995, p 73);* cf in this regard the Vienna Convention on Consular Relations art 8, which provides that a state may exercise consular functions on behalf of another state provided that the state in which the functions are to be performed has been notified and does not object. The EC Treaty art 20 envisages that international negotiations will be required to secure such protection. See also the Green Paper on Diplomatic and Consular Protection of Union Citizens in Third Countries (COM (2006) 712). As to the distinction between consular assistance, the exercise of diplomatic protection and other action (including diplomatic representations or demarches) on the international plane see PARA 384. As to the meaning of 'British national' for these purposes see PARA 420.

413. General considerations. Under the Vienna Convention on Consular Relations[1], the functions of the consular officers[2] of a sending state present in the receiving state are defined as including the protection in the receiving state, within the limits permitted by international law, of the interests of the sending state and of its nationals, both individuals and bodies corporate[3], and helping and assisting nationals, both individuals and bodies corporate, of the sending state[4]. With a view to facilitating the exercise of consular functions relating to nationals of the sending state[5], a receiving state is under general obligations relating to access and communication between the consular officers of the sending state and its nationals, as well as certain specific obligations in relation to the provision of information, notification and communication in circumstances in which nationals of the sending state are arrested or otherwise detained[6].

1   Ie the Vienna Convention on Consular Relations (Vienna, 24 April 1963; TS 14 (1973); Cmnd 5219).
2   As to the meaning of 'consular officer' see PARA 30 note 1.

3   Vienna Convention on Consular Relations art 5(a). Article 5 forms part of English law, by virtue
    of the Consular Relations Act 1968 s 1, Sch 1: see PARA 419.
4   Vienna Convention on Consular Relations art 5(e).
5   See the Vienna Convention on Consular Relations art 36(1). Article 36 is not among the
    provisions of the Convention which have been given the force of law in the United Kingdom by
    the Consular Relations Act 1968 s 1, Sch 1: see PARA 419.
6   See the Vienna Convention on Consular Relations art 36(1)(a)–(c); and PARAS 414–418. All of
    those rights must be exercised in conformity with the laws and regulations of the receiving state,
    provided that those laws and regulations must enable full effect to be given to the purposes for
    which the rights are intended: see art 36(2). See note 5.
        In addition, the Convention imposes a number of other obligations requiring the provision of
    notice in certain other circumstances concerning the nationals, ships or aircraft of other states
    parties. Where a national of another state party dies within the receiving state, the receiving
    state is under an obligation to inform the consular post of the state of nationality for the district
    in which the death occurred without delay: see art 37(a). A receiving state is under an obligation
    to provide information to the relevant consular post where the appointment of a guardian or
    trustee appears to be in the interests of a minor or other person lacking full capacity who is a
    national of another state, although the provision of such information is expressly stipulated to
    be without prejudice to the operation of the laws and regulations concerning such appointments:
    see art 37(b). See also art 5(h), which defines consular functions as including safeguarding,
    within the limits imposed by the laws and regulations of the receiving state, the interests of
    minors and other persons lacking full capacity who are nationals of the sending state,
    particularly where any guardianship or trusteeship is required with respect to such persons.
    Where a vessel having the nationality of one state party to the Convention is wrecked or runs
    aground in the territorial sea or internal waters of another state party, or an aircraft registered in
    one state party suffers an accident on the territory of another state party, the state in which the
    incident occurs is under an obligation to inform without delay the consular post nearest to the
    scene of the occurrence: see art 37(c). In all of these cases, the obligations are limited to
    circumstances in which the relevant information is available: see art 37. Article 37 is not among
    the provisions of the Convention which have been given the force of law in the United Kingdom
    by the Consular Relations Act 1968 s 1, Sch 1 (see PARA 419), and no other legislation has been
    adopted giving effect to the obligations in question. As to the meaning of 'consular post' see
    PARA 30 note 1.

**414.   Freedom of communication and access between foreign nationals and
consular authorities.**   The consular officers[1] of any state party to the Vienna
Convention on Consular Relations[2] have the freedom to communicate with their
nationals and to have access to them, and nationals of the sending state have the
same freedom with respect to communication with and access to the consular
officers of their state of nationality[3].

1   As to the meaning of 'consular officer' see PARA 30 note 1.
2   Ie the Vienna Convention on Consular Relations (Vienna, 24 April 1963; TS 14 (1973);
    Cmnd 5219).
3   Vienna Convention on Consular Relations art 36(1)(a).

415.   Notification of consular rights to detained foreign nationals.   A national
of a state party to the Vienna Convention on Consular Relations[1] who has been
arrested or detained has a right to be informed by the competent authorities
without delay of the right to request that the consular post of his state of
nationality be informed and of his right to send communications to the consular
post[2]. The requirement that the detained individual be informed of his rights
'without delay' does not require provision of the relevant information
immediately upon arrest and prior to any interrogation; nevertheless, the
obligation to inform the individual of his rights arises at such time as it is realised
that the detainee is a foreign national, or once there are grounds to think that the
individual is probably a foreign national[3]. It is no defence to argue that it was
assumed that the individual would prefer that the consular authorities of his state
of nationality should not be informed of his arrest[4]. In this regard, the

Convention not only imposes an obligation owed to the state of nationality of the detained individual, breach of which constitutes a direct violation of the rights of that state[5], but also creates an individual right under international law for the detained individual, which can be enforced on his behalf by the state of nationality by way of diplomatic protection[6]. Further, depending on the circumstances, a breach of the obligation to provide information as to his consular rights to a detained national of a state party to the Convention may result in a violation of other rights under the Convention of the state of nationality relating to detained nationals[7].

1 Ie the Vienna Convention on Consular Relations (Vienna, 24 April 1963; TS 14 (1973); Cmnd 5219).
2 See the Vienna Convention on Consular Relations art 36(1)(b). As to the meaning of 'consular post' see PARA 30 note 1.
3 *Avena and Other Mexican Nationals (Mexico v United States of America)* ICJ Reports 2004, 12 at 43 (para 63), 48–49 (paras 83–88).
4 *Avena and Other Mexican Nationals (Mexico v United States of America)* ICJ Reports 2004, 12 at 46 (para 76).
5 *Avena and Other Mexican Nationals (Mexico v United States of America)* ICJ Reports 2004, 12 at 35–36 (para 40).
6 *LaGrand (Germany v United States of America)* ICJ Reports 2001, 466 at 494 (para 77); *Avena and Other Mexican Nationals (Mexico v United States of America)* ICJ Reports 2004, 12 at 35–36 (para 40). As to the nature of diplomatic protection see PARA 386. Given the dual character of the violation as involving a breach of the rights of both the national state and of the individual, it has been held that there is no obligation to exhaust local remedies before bringing a claim: *Avena and Other Mexican Nationals (Mexico v United States of America)* ICJ Reports 2004, 12 at 36 (para 40). The International Court of Justice has not felt it necessary to decide whether the right to notification constitutes a human right of the detained individual: *LaGrand (Germany v United States of America)* ICJ Reports 2001, 466 at 494 (para 78); and see *Avena and Other Mexican Nationals (Mexico v United States of America)* ICJ Reports 2004, 12 at 61 (para 124); cf the decision of the Inter-American Court of Human Rights in *The Right to Information on Consular Assistance in the Framework of the Guarantees of the Due Process of Law* (Advisory Opinion OC-16/99) I-ACtHR Ser A No 16 (1999) (the decision that the right constituted a human right was reached in the context of the American Convention on Human Rights 1969 (San José, Costa Rica; 22 November 1969; (1970) 9 ILM 673) art 64(1), which gives the Inter-American Court jurisdiction to give advisory opinions concerning the interpretation of the American Convention 'or of other treaties concerning the protection of human rights in the American states').
7 See *LaGrand (Germany v United States of America)* ICJ Reports 2001, 466 at 492 (para 74); cf *Avena and Other Mexican Nationals (Mexico v United States of America)* ICJ Reports 2004, 12 at 52–53 (paras 99–105).

416. Notification of detention of foreign nationals to consular post of state of nationality. If a national of any state party to the Vienna Convention on Consular Relations[1] is arrested, or is committed to prison or to custody pending trial, or is detained in any other manner, the competent authorities must at his request inform, without delay, that state's consular post for the relevant consular district[2].

1 Ie the Vienna Convention on Consular Relations (Vienna, 24 April 1963; TS 14 (1973); Cmnd 5219).
2 See the Vienna Convention on Consular Relations art 36(1)(b). As to the meaning of 'consular post' see PARA 30 note 1. As to the right under the Convention of the detained person to be notified in this regard see PARA 415. In addition to the obligations contained in the Convention, the United Kingdom has entered into a number of bilateral agreements relating to consular matters which require notification to the appropriate High Commission, embassy or consulate as soon as is practicable when one of the nationals of the other state is arrested, and without any prior request by the detainee. The Police and Criminal Evidence Act 1984 Code of Practice C Annex F (see CRIMINAL LAW, EVIDENCE AND PROCEDURE vol 11(2) (2006 Reissue) PARA 954) lists the countries with which such agreements had been concluded, as follows: Armenia,

Austria, Azerbaijan, Belarus, Belgium, Bosnia-Herzegovina, Bulgaria, China, Croatia, Cuba, Czech Republic, Denmark, Egypt, France, Georgia, German Federal Republic, Greece, Hungary, Italy, Japan, Kazakhstan, Macedonia, Mexico, Moldova, Mongolia, Norway, Poland, Romania, Russia, Slovak Republic, Slovenia, Spain, Sweden, Tajikistan, Turkmenistan, Ukraine, USA, Uzbekistan, and Yugoslavia; but note that, in relation to nationals of China arrested or detained in the United Kingdom, the police are required to inform Chinese consular officials of arrest or detention only in the Manchester consular district (comprising Derbyshire, Durham, Greater Manchester, Lancashire, Merseyside, North, South and West Yorkshire, and Tyne and Wear) (see Whormersley 'The United Kingdom-China Consular Agreement' (1985) 34 ICLQ 621).

417. Communication of detained foreign nationals with consular post of state of nationality. In addition to the general right of communication between foreign nationals and the consular officers[1] of their state of nationality[2], any communication by a foreign national of a state party to the Vienna Convention on Consular Relations[3] who is arrested or otherwise detained, which is addressed to the consular post[4] of his state of nationality, must be forwarded without delay by the competent authorities[5].

1   As to the meaning of 'consular officer' see PARA 30 note 1.
2   See PARA 414.
3   Ie the Vienna Convention on Consular Relations (Vienna, 24 April 1963; TS 14 (1973); Cmnd 5219).
4   As to the meaning of 'consular post' see PARA 30 note 1.
5   See the Vienna Convention on Consular Relations art 36(1)(b). As to the right under the Convention of the detained person to be notified in this regard see PARA 415.

418. Rights of consular access and assistance in relation to detained persons. Under the Vienna Convention on Consular Relations[1], the consular officers[2] of a state party have a right to visit a national who is in prison, custody or detention, to converse and correspond with him, and to arrange for his legal representation[3]. In addition, the consular officers of a state party to the Convention have a right to visit any national who is in prison, custody or detention pursuant to a judgment[4]. However, a consular officer must refrain from taking action on behalf of a national who is in prison, custody or detention if the national expressly opposes such action[5].

1   Ie the Vienna Convention on Consular Relations (Vienna, 24 April 1963; TS 14 (1973); Cmnd 5219).
2   As to the meaning of 'consular officer' see PARA 30 note 1.
3   See the Vienna Convention on Consular Relations art 36(1)(c).
4   See the Vienna Convention on Consular Relations art 36(1)(b).
5   See the Vienna Convention on Consular Relations art 36(1)(b).

419. Implementation in the United Kingdom of international obligations relating to consular access and assistance. Although some provisions of the Vienna Convention on Consular Relations[1] have been incorporated and given the force of law in the United Kingdom by the Consular Relations Act 1968[2], the provisions of the Convention relating to consular access and assistance in relation to detained nationals and the rights of a detained foreign national to information as to his consular rights are not among those provisions[3]. However, some of those obligations are implemented through the relevant Codes of Practice adopted under the Police and Criminal Evidence Act 1984[4], although they are not limited in their application to nationals of states parties to the Convention and apply to all foreign nationals[5]. The Codes of Practice recognise the right of a detained foreign national to communicate with the relevant consular authorities of his state of nationality[6]. A detained foreign national must be informed as soon as practicable of that right and of the right to request that the consular authorities be informed of his whereabouts and the grounds for his detention[7]. Any such request must be acted upon as soon as is practicable[8]. The Codes of Practice also recognise the right of the consular authorities to visit a detained foreign national and to meet with him out of the hearing of a police officer, as well as, if required, to arrange for his legal representation[9]. Compliance with consular obligations in relation to foreign nationals may not be delayed, even if other rights of the detainee, including those relating to notification to a responsible adult or member of family and access to a solicitor, are delayed[10]. Provision is also made in the Codes of Practice for compliance with those bilateral consular conventions which require immediate notification to the consular authorities of the state of nationality upon arrest, irrespective of a request by the national[11]. However, if the detainee is a political refugee or seeks political asylum, notification of arrest and access to information about the detainee is not to be provided to consular officers except at the express request of the detainee[12].

1 Ie the Vienna Convention on Consular Relations (Vienna, 24 April 1963; TS 14 (1973); Cmnd 5219).
2 See the Consular Relations Act 1968 s 1(1), Sch 1 (amended by the Diplomatic and Consular Premises Act 1987 Sch 2), giving force of law in the United Kingdom to the Vienna Convention on Consular Relations arts 1, 5, 15, 17, 27, 31–33, 35, 39, 41, 43–45, 48–55, 57, 58 (in part), 59–62, 66, 67 and 70–71. See further PARA 290.
3 As to the provisions relating to consular access and assistance in relation to detained nationals, and information as to consular rights, see the Vienna Convention on Consular Relations art 36; and PARAS 413–418. Article 37, relating to the other specific obligations of notification, is also not among the provisions incorporated into United Kingdom law: see PARA 413 note 6.
4 See Code C: Code of Practice for the Detention, Treatment and Questioning of Persons by Police Officers; and CRIMINAL LAW, EVIDENCE AND PROCEDURE vol 11(2) (2006 Reissue) PARA 908 et seq. See also Code H: Code of Practice in connection with the Detention, Treatment and Questioning by Police Officers of Persons under Section 41 of, and Schedule 8 to, the Terrorism Act 2000; and CRIMINAL LAW, EVIDENCE AND PROCEDURE vol 11(1) (2006 Reissue) PARA 421 et seq. See in particular CRIMINAL LAW, EVIDENCE AND PROCEDURE vol 11(2) (2006 Reissue) PARA 954.
5 Code C para 7.1; Code H para 7.1.
6 Code C para 7.1; Code H para 7.1. See also PARAS 413–414, 416–417.
7 Code C para 7.1; Code H para 7.1. See also PARA 415.
8 Code C para 7.1; Code H para 7.1.
9 Code C para 7.3; Code H para 7.3. See also PARA 418.
10 See Code C Guidance note 7A, Annex B; and Code H Guidance note 7A, Annex B.
11 Code C para 7.2; Code H para 7.2. For the list of states in question see Code C Annex F; Code H Annex F; and PARA 416 note 2.
12 Code C para 7.4; Code H para 7.4.

420. Consular access and assistance in relation to United Kingdom nationals abroad. Under the Vienna Convention on Consular Relations[1], the United Kingdom enjoys the various rights of communication, access and notification in relation to British nationals abroad (including those detained)[2]. The Foreign and Commonwealth Office from time to time publishes guidance on the consular assistance it will provide to British nationals abroad[3]. For these purposes, a British national is a British citizen, a British overseas territories citizen, a British overseas citizen, a British national (overseas), a British subject, or a British protected person[4]. As a matter of policy, financial assistance may exceptionally be provided to British nationals who are the victims of terrorist attacks abroad, or other major catastrophes[5].

The subject matter of a decision relating to the conduct of international relations is subject to only limited judicial review by the courts[6]. It has been held that a refusal to seek to effect consular visits, to provide other consular assistance, or to make diplomatic representations in relation to a non-British national lawfully resident in the United Kingdom does not constitute discrimination under the Race Relations Act 1976[7], or a discriminatory interference with the right to family life of such an individual or his close family under the Human Rights Act 1998[8].

1 Ie the Vienna Convention on Consular Relations (Vienna, 24 April 1963; TS 14 (1973); Cmnd 5219).

2 See PARAS 413–418.

3 See Foreign and Commonwealth Office *Support for British Nationals Abroad: A Guide* (2009).

4 Foreign and Commonwealth Office *Support for British Nationals Abroad: A Guide* (2009) pp 7, 28 (Appendix). As to British citizens, British overseas territories citizens, British overseas citizens, British nationals (overseas), British subjects, and British protected persons see PARA 398 note 1; and see further BRITISH NATIONALITY, IMMIGRATION AND ASYLUM vol 4(2) (2002 Reissue) PARA 5 et seq. No consular assistance is provided to British nationals (overseas) of Chinese ethnic origin in China, or in the Hong Kong and Macao Special Administrative Regions given that the Chinese authorities consider British nationals (overseas) of Chinese ethnic origin to be Chinese nationals. In relation to dual nationals in third countries, consular assistance will normally be provided if the individual was travelling on a British passport; assistance will not normally be provided in the other state of nationality, although an exception may be made if there is an exceptional humanitarian reason for doing so: Foreign and Commonwealth Office *Support for British Nationals Abroad: A Guide* (2009) p 7. In relation to protection of citizens of the European Union by the consular or diplomatic authorities of other member states in third states where the member state of which they are a national is not represented see the Treaty on the Functioning of the European Union (Rome, 25 March 1957; TS 1 (1973); Cmnd 5179) art 20; and PARA 412 note 1.

5 As to the written ministerial statement relating to exceptional assistance measures for victims of terrorist incidents overseas see 476 HC Official Report (6th series), 2 June 2008, cols 40–41. See also Foreign and Commonwealth Office *Support for British Nationals Abroad: A Guide* (2009) p 24.

6 *R (on the application of Abbasi) v Secretary of State for Foreign and Commonwealth Affairs* [2002] EWCA Civ 1598, [2002] All ER (D) 70 (Nov) (diplomatic representations on behalf of a British national). See also PARA 388.

7 *R (on the application of Al-Rawi) v Secretary of State for Foreign and Commonwealth Affairs (United Nations High Commissioner for Refugees intervening)* [2006] EWCA Civ 1279, [2008] QB 289, [2006] All ER (D) 138 (Oct) at [65]–[83], [87]. As to the requirement of nationality for the purposes of the exercise of diplomatic protection see PARA 391 et seq.

8 *R (on the application of Al-Rawi) v Secretary of State for Foreign and Commonwealth Affairs (United Nations High Commissioner for Refugees intervening)* [2006] EWCA Civ 1279, [2008] QB 289, [2006] All ER (D) 138 (Oct) at [84]–[87] (the court reasoned that, the Articles on Diplomatic Protection ('ADP') art 8, Report of the International Law Commission ('ILC'), 58th Session (2006), A/61/10, ch IV being lex ferenda, there is no generally accepted rule as a matter of international law which grants a state the right to provide consular assistance or to make diplomatic representations in relation to non-nationals habitually resident and having refugee status: see at [115]–[119]).

14. INTERNATIONAL CRIMINAL LAW

(1) IN GENERAL

421. Introduction. 'International Criminal Law' is not a term of art but a description of conduct made criminal in international law, in national law because of an international obligation or, sometimes, both[1]. It is not restricted to identifying conduct which is or must be made criminal but deals inter alia with jurisdiction over crime[2], and co-operation with other states with regard to obtaining custody of suspects, their trial and sentencing[3]. International criminal law also covers the creation and powers of international criminal tribunals, with which states have obligations of co-operation different from those they owe to other states[4].

The various sources of international criminal law may contain specific standards of fair trial or may rely indirectly on the international obligations and national laws of individual states[5]. There has been some development of substantive international criminal law in recent years and a considerable expansion in international tribunals which have a criminal jurisdiction[6]. Combined with the national implementation of crimes against international law, itself based on extended jurisdictional claims[7], these changes are part of a project to deny impunity to those responsible for the commission of crimes against international law.

1   Crimes created in national law because of an international obligation which correspond with crimes against international law, such as genocide, are to be distinguished from 'transnational crimes' created in national law because of a treaty obligation to do so, such as those directed against terrorism, although the two categories have much in common: see PARA 427.

2   See PARA 425.

3   See PARA 436.

4   See PARA 436.

5   As to the sources of international criminal law see PARA 423.

6   This process effectively began with the establishment of the International Criminal Tribunal for the Former Yugoslavia in 1993 (see the Statute of the International Tribunal for the Prosecution of Persons Responsible for Serious Violations of International Humanitarian Law Committed in the Territory of the Former Yugoslavia since 1991, UN Doc S/25704 at 36, annex (1993) and S/25704/Add 1 (1993), adopted by Security Council on 25 May 1993, UN Doc S/RES/827 (1993)) and has continued, inter alia, with the establishment of the International Criminal Tribunal for Rwanda (see the Statute of the International Criminal Tribunal for the Prosecution of Persons Responsible for Genocide and Other Serious Violations of International Humanitarian Law Committed in the Territory of Rwanda and Rwandan Citizens Responsible for Genocide and Other Such Violations Committed in the Territory of Neighbouring States, between 1 January 1994 and 31 December 1994, adopted by the Security Council on 8 November 1994, UN Doc S/RES/955 (1994)), and the International Criminal Court (see the Rome Statute of the International Criminal Court (17.7.98) (UN Doc A/CONF 183/9; 37 ILM (1998) 999); and PARA 437).

7   Notably claims of universal or quasi-universal jurisdiction over the conduct constituting crimes against international law: see PARA 425.

422. International crimes. In an early codification of international criminal law[1], the Charter of the International Military Tribunal at Nuremberg listed three crimes within the jurisdiction of the tribunal which have had continuing significance in the development of international criminal law[2]: crimes against peace[3]; war crimes[4]; and crimes against humanity[5]. It remains a matter of contention as to which of these offences were actually established as international crimes by customary law by the time of the commencement of World War II, although it is widely accepted that these crimes had attained customary law status by 1950[6].

The United Nations Security Council accepted that grave breaches of the Geneva Conventions, violations of the laws and customs of war, genocide and crimes against humanity were international crimes by customary law by 1993[7]. It has also been suggested that torture was established as a crime in international law before the UN Torture Convention of 1984[8].

The Statute of the International Criminal Court (the 'ICC') contains a list of four international crimes, some set out in great detail, not every item of which is confirmed by customary international law: aggression (which has yet to be defined and is to be distinguished from the Nuremburg crime of planning etc a war of aggression); genocide; war crimes; and crimes against humanity[9]. Together, these are frequently referred to as the 'core' international crimes and it is suggested that they are surrounded by similar regimes of obligations of jurisdiction, investigation, trial and co-operation[10].

1   It is sometimes suggested that piracy was the first crime against international law but, although there is an international definition, it is better to see piracy as conduct which states may proscribe and punish in their national laws without any restrictions as to jurisdiction: see PARA 155 et seq.

2   See the Charter of the International Military Tribunal (London, 8 August 1945; TS 27 (1946); Cmd 6903) art 6. It is to be noticed that genocide was not, eo nomine, among the offences within the jurisdiction of the International Military Tribunal: as to genocide see PARA 429.

3   Namely, planning, preparation, initiation or waging of a war of aggression, or a war in violation of international treaties, agreements or assurances, or participation in a common plan or conspiracy for the accomplishment of any of the foregoing: see the Charter of the International Military Tribunal, art 6(a).

4   Namely, violations of the laws or customs of war, including, but not limited to, murder, ill-treatment or deportation to slave labour or for any other purpose of civilian population of or in occupied territory, murder or ill-treatment of prisoners of war or persons on the seas, killing of hostages, plunder of public or private property, wanton destruction of cities, towns or villages, or devastation not justified by military necessity: the Charter of the International Military Tribunal, art 6(b).

5   Namely, murder, extermination, enslavement, deportation, and other inhumane acts committed against any civilian population, before or during the war; or persecutions on political, racial or religious grounds in execution of or in connection with any crime within the jurisdiction of the tribunal, whether or not in violation of the domestic law of the country where perpetrated: the Charter of the International Military Tribunal, art 6(c).

6   See the Principles of International Law Recognized in the Charter of the Nüremberg Tribunal and in the Judgment of the Tribunal 1950 International Law Commission (the 'ILC'), A/1316 (1950), principle VI. See also *Reservations to the Convention on the Prevention and Punishment of the Crime of Genocide (Advisory Opinion)* ICJ Reports 1951, 15 at 23; and *R v Jones; Ayliffe v DPP; Swain v DPP* [2006] UKHL 16, [2007] 1 AC 136 at [19] per Lord Bingham (planning etc a war of aggression).

7   See the Statute of the International Tribunal for the Prosecution of Persons Responsible for Serious Violations of International Humanitarian Law Committed in the Territory of the Former Yugoslavia since 1991 ('ICTY'), UN Doc S/25704 at 36, annex (1993) and S/25704/Add 1 (1993), adopted by Security Council on 25 May 1993, UN Doc S/RES/827 (1993) arts 2–5; Statute of the International Criminal Tribunal for the Prosecution of Persons Responsible for Genocide and Other Serious Violations of International Humanitarian Law Committed in the Territory of Rwanda and Rwandan Citizens Responsible for Genocide and Other Such Violations Committed in the Territory of Neighbouring States, between 1 January 1994 and 31 December 1994 ('ICTR'), adopted by the Security Council on 8 November 1994, UN Doc S/RES/955 (1994) arts 2–4 (note that there are some differences in the ways the crimes are defined). See also the Report of the Secretary-General pursuant to paragraph 2 of Security Council Resolution 808 of 22 February 1993; and *Prosecutor v Tadic* Case No IT-94-1-AR72 (Decision on the Defence Motion for Interlocutory Appeal on Jurisdiction, 2 October 1995), ICTY (Appeals Chamber).

8   See *R v Bow Street Metropolitan Stipendiary Magistrate, ex p Pinochet Ugarte (No 3) (Amnesty International intervening)* [2000] 1 AC 147, [1999] 2 All ER 97; and *A v Secretary of State for the Home Department (No 2)* [2005] UKHL 71, [2006] 2 AC 221, [2006] 1 All ER 575 at [33]. Similar claims are made about slavery but the evidence is less specific. See PARAS 433–434. The UN Torture Convention 1984 means the Convention against Torture and other Cruel, Inhuman or Degrading Treatment or Punishment (New York, 4 February 1985; Misc 12 (1985); Cmnd 9593).

9   See the Rome Statute of the International Criminal Court (17.7.98) (UN Doc A/CONF 183/9; 37 ILM (1998) 999) arts 5–8; and PARAS 429–431. There are, in addition, 'Elements of Crimes' to assist the ICC in the interpretation and application of arts 6–8: art 9(1). For procedural matters relating to the Elements of Crimes see art 9. The text of the Elements of Crimes was adopted by the assembly of states parties on 22 September 2002 (see the UN Doc PCNICC/2000/1/Add 2 (2000)), and is set out in the International Criminal Court Act 2001 (Elements of Crimes) (No 2) Regulations 2004, SI 2004/3239, Sch.

10 See PARA 428 et seq. These obligations, or variants on them, are sometimes included in treaties which refer to the international criminal nature of the conduct constituting the particular crimes in the treaty: see e g the Convention on the Prevention and Punishment of the Crime of Genocide (Paris, 9 December 1948; TS 58 (1970); Cmnd 4421).

423. Sources of international criminal law. International criminal law is found in treaties and customary international law, and is closely related to the international law of human rights[1]. The United Nations Security Council has exercised its powers[2] to take action in the sphere of international criminal law[3]. It is important to emphasise that only the parties to treaties dealing with international criminal law are bound by their provisions[4].

Because it is envisaged that some trials of those accused of conduct amounting to crimes under international law will be held before national courts, the accurate implementation of international law into national law is essential if the impunity of those suspected of crimes against international law is to be diminished[5]. Conduct made criminal in national law might already be criminal in international law, and under those circumstances there is no objection from the perspective of the principle of legality to making the conduct criminal retrospectively[6].

It is essential that where a state exercises extraterritorial prescriptive jurisdiction over conduct constituting an international crime that it does so compatibly with international law[7].

1   As to human rights law see CONSTITUTIONAL LAW AND HUMAN RIGHTS vol 8(2) (Reissue) PARA 101 et seq.

2   Including those under the Charter of the United Nations (San Francisco, 26 June 1945; TS 67 (1946); Cmd 7015) Ch VII. The Security Council also has powers under the Rome Statute of the International Criminal Court (17.7.98) (UN Doc A/CONF 183/9; 37 ILM (1998) 999) arts 13(b), 16.

3   It has, for example, established the International Criminal Tribunal for the Former Yugoslavia ('ICTY') (see the Statute of the International Tribunal for the Prosecution of Persons Responsible for Serious Violations of International Humanitarian Law Committed in the Territory of the Former Yugoslavia since 1991, UN Doc S/25704 at 36, annex (1993) and S/25704/Add.1 (1993), adopted by Security Council on 25 May 1993, UN Doc S/RES/827 (1993)) and the International Criminal Tribunal for Rwanda ('ICTR') (see the Statute of the International Criminal Tribunal for the Prosecution of Persons Responsible for Genocide and Other Serious Violations of International Humanitarian Law Committed in the Territory of Rwanda and Rwandan Citizens Responsible for Genocide and Other Such Violations Committed in the Territory of Neighbouring States, between 1 January 1994 and 31 December 1994, adopted by the Security Council on 8 November 1994, UN Doc S/RES/955 (1994)); and referred matters to the International Criminal Court (see e g UN Doc S/RES/1593 (2005) (Darfur)).

4   As to treaties and treaty obligations see PARA 71 et seq.

5   As to the implementation of international law into United Kingdom law see e g the Geneva Conventions Act 1957 (see WAR AND ARMED CONFLICT); the International Criminal Courts

Act 2001 (see PARA 437 et seq); the Criminal Justice Act 1988 ss 134–138 (see CRIMINAL LAW, EVIDENCE AND PROCEDURE vol 11(1) (2006 Reissue) PARA 160); and the War Crimes Act 1991 (WAR AND ARMED CONFLICT vol 49(1) (2005 Reissue) PARA 465).

6 See the Convention for the Protection of Human Rights and Fundamental Freedoms (1950) (Rome, 4 November 1950; TS 71 (1953); Cmd 8969; ETS no 5) art 7(1) (and CONSTITUTIONAL LAW AND HUMAN RIGHTS vol 8(2) (Reissue) PARA 148); and *Kononov v Latvia* (2008) 25 BHRC 317, [2008] ECHR 36376/04 (the case has been referred to the Grand Chamber).

7 *Jorgic v Germany* (2007) 47 EHRR 207, 25 BHRC 287, [2007] ECHR 74613/01.

424. The nature of substantive international criminal law. States do not have criminal liability in customary international law nor are they made potentially criminally responsible by treaties requiring action to create crimes in national law[1]. Criminal liability is ordinarily confined to individuals, though there is no reason in principle why other legal persons should not be made criminally liable by international law[2]. In international law, the fact that a person was acting in an official capacity is not a barrier to his liability[3], though in some special cases official status is a bar to liability for crimes created in domestic law[4]. Criminal liability may arise not only from direct commission of the forbidden conduct but by reason of ordering, failing to prevent or failing to punish the forbidden conduct of others[5].

The question of immunities and international criminal law is complex but it is clear that treaties may exclude, expressly or impliedly, immunities of one kind or another[6]. Binding decisions of the United Nations Security Council will take priority over immunities, whether they depend upon treaties or customary international law[7].

1 'Crimes against international law are committed by men, not by abstract entities, and only by punishing individuals who commit such crimes can the provisions of international law be enforced': see the Judgment of the International Military Tribunal for the Trial of the Major War Criminals (1946; Misc 12 (1946); Cmd 6964) at p 41. The International Law Commission (the 'ILC') did not include any notion of state criminal responsibility in its Articles on Responsibility of States for Internationally Wrongful Acts ('ARSIWA'): see the International Law Commission Report, 53rd Session, A/56/10; YILC 2001, vol II(2), pp 26–30; and PARA 328 et seq.

2 See eg the Charter of the International Military Tribunal (London, 8 August 1945; TS 27 (1946); Cmd 6903) art 9.

3 See eg the Charter of the International Military Tribunal, art 9; Statute of the International Tribunal for the Prosecution of Persons Responsible for Serious Violations of International Humanitarian Law Committed in the Territory of the Former Yugoslavia since 1991 ('ICTY'), UN Doc S/25704 at 36, annex (1993) and S/25704/Add 1 (1993), adopted by Security Council on 25 May 1993, UN Doc S/RES/827 (1993) art 7(2); Rome Statute of the International Criminal Court (the 'ICC') (17.7.98) (UN Doc A/CONF 183/9; 37 ILM (1998) 999) art 27(1).

4 See eg the International Convention for the Suppression of Terrorist Bombings (New York, 15 December 1997; TS 57 (2001); Cm 5347) art 19(2).

5 See eg the Statute of the ICC art 28; and the International Criminal Court Act 2001 s 65 (as to which see PARA 458).

6 As to immunities see PARA 242 et seq.

7 See *Prosecutor v Milosevic (Decision on Preliminary Motions)* Case No IT-99-37-PT (8 November 2001) ICTY. See also the International Criminal Court (Darfur) Order 2009, SI 2009/699, which precludes any state or diplomatic immunity from preventing proceedings under the International Criminal Court Act 2001 arising as a result of the reference to the ICC by the Security Council of the situation in Darfur; and PARA 446.

425. International crimes and jurisdiction. Although some crimes against international law arise by reason of customary international law[1], the jurisdiction of international tribunals to try persons accused under international law depends on treaty or a decision of the United Nations Security Council[2]. There are various aspects to the jurisdiction of international tribunals:

(1)   substantive jurisdiction; meaning the offences which fall within the tribunal's competence[3];

(2)   personal jurisdiction; meaning the persons who may be brought before the tribunal[4];

(3)   temporal jurisdiction; meaning the time at which the conduct constituting the crime occurred[5]; and

(4)   locational jurisdiction; meaning the place where the conduct constituting the crime occurred[6].

It is sometimes said that states have universal jurisdiction over international crimes under customary international law, although the United Kingdom has been notably cautious on this issue[7]. It is far from clear whether or not the exercise of this kind of jurisdiction is dependent upon the presence of the defendant in the territory or on the willingness or capacity of the territorial state to exercise jurisdiction itself, which is to say that while a state may have universal jurisdiction to criminalise conduct in the abstract, the exercise of that jurisdiction against a particular defendant may be subject to further conditions, beyond mere custody of the defendant[8]. Universal jurisdiction is, like other heads of jurisdiction, facilitative, but there may be duties to exercise jurisdiction[9] or to take alternative measures under treaty[10].

1   See generally PARA 422.

2   Jurisdiction over any particular international crime and jurisdiction to try any particular defendant depends upon the terms of the treaty or Security Council resolution establishing the tribunal.

3   See Statute of the International Tribunal for the Prosecution of Persons Responsible for Serious Violations of International Humanitarian Law Committed in the Territory of the Former Yugoslavia since 1991 ('ICTY'), UN Doc S/25704 at 36, annex (1993) and S/25704/Add.1 (1993), adopted by Security Council on 25 May 1993, UN Doc S/RES/827 (1993) art 2–5; Statute of the International Criminal Tribunal for the Prosecution of Persons Responsible for Genocide and Other Serious Violations of International Humanitarian Law Committed in the Territory of Rwanda and Rwandan Citizens Responsible for Genocide and Other Such Violations Committed in the Territory of Neighbouring States, between 1 January 1994 and 31 December 1994 ('ICTR'), adopted by the Security Council on 8 November 1994, UN Doc S/RES/955 (1994)) art 2–4; Rome Statute of the International Criminal Court (the 'ICC') (17.7.98) (UN Doc A/CONF 183/9; 37 ILM (1998) 999) arts 5–9.

4   See the Statute of the ICTY art 6; the Statute of the ICTR art 5; and the Statute of the ICC arts 12(2), 25(1), 26.

5   See the Statute of the ICTY art 1; the Statute of the ICTR art 1; and the Statute of the ICC art 24.

6   See the Statute of the ICTY art 1; the Statute of the ICTR art 1 (partly combined with a nationality criterion); and the Statute of the ICC art 12(2) (supplemented by a nationality criterion).

8   See the United Kingdom's statement in General Assembly Sixth Committee, October 2009, UN Doc GA/L/3372. See also, more generally, Reydams *Universal Jurisdiction: International and Municipal Legal Perspectives* (2004).

9   See eg the Convention on the Prevention and Punishment of the Crime of Genocide (Paris, 9 December 1948; TS 58 (1970); Cmnd 4421) art 1; and *Application of the Convention on the Prevention and Punishment of the Crime of Genocide (Bosnia and Herzegovina v Serbia and Montenegro)* ICJ Reports, 26 February 2007 (paras 428–450).

10   This is often expressed as the principle aut judicare, aut dedere (to judge, or, strictly, to submit for prosecution, or to hand over). The United Kingdom takes the view that this is an obligation which arises only by treaty: see (2007) BYIL 888–889.

426. International crimes and United Kingdom law. Crimes under customary international law or treaties are not crimes in English law without implementing legislation to make them so[1]. There is universal jurisdiction for grave breaches of the Geneva Conventions[2], and for torture[3]. For the offences of genocide, war crimes and crimes against humanity[4], jurisdiction is territorial or where conduct abroad is that of a United Kingdom national or resident or a person under United Kingdom service jurisdiction[5]. The implementing legislation frequently makes other provisions, such as providing for extraterritorial jurisdiction.

Other things being equal, the general part of the criminal law and the law of criminal procedure will apply to the investigation and prosecution of the domestic crime which mirrors the international crime[6]. However, legislation may make offence-specific provisions, where domestic law differs from the international law which surrounds the international crime[7]. Where conduct constituting an international crime is made criminal in national law, it will be so only from the date of the statute regardless of the date from which the conduct might have been criminal in international law, except where the statute provides to the contrary[8].

1   *R v Jones; Ayliffe v DPP; Swain v DPP* [2006] UKHL 16, [2007] 1 AC 136. Piracy may be an exception, although the definition of piracy in the United Nations Convention on the Law of the Sea has been introduced into national law 'for the avoidance of doubt': see the Merchant Shipping and Maritime Security Act 1997 s 26(1); and PARA 156.

2   See PARA 432; the Geneva Conventions Act 1957 s 1(1); and WAR AND ARMED CONFLICT vol 49(1) (2005 Reissue) PARA 424.

3   See the Criminal Justice Act 1988 s 134(1); and CRIMINAL LAW, EVIDENCE AND PROCEDURE vol 11(1) (2006 Reissue) PARA 160. See also *R v Zardad* [2007] EWCA Crim 279, [2007] All ER (D) 90 (Feb) (conviction of an Afghan national for acts of torture and hostage-taking in Afghanistan).

4   Ie under the Rome Statute of the International Criminal Court (17.7.98) (UN Doc A/CONF 183/9; 37 ILM (1998) 999) arts 6–8 (see PARA 422).

5   See the International Criminal Court Act 2001 s 51; and PARA 454.

6   See eg the International Criminal Court Act 2001 s 56(1); and PARA 454.

7   See eg the International Criminal Court Act 2001 ss 65, 66; and PARAS 457–458.

8   See eg the War Crimes Act 1991 s 1(1)(a) (and WAR AND ARMED CONFLICT vol 49(1) (2005 Reissue) PARA 465); and the International Criminal Court Act 2001 ss 65A–65B (not yet in force) (see PARAS 454–455). There is no objection under human rights law to the retrospective criminalisation in national law of conduct earlier made criminal in international law: see the International Covenant on Civil and Political Rights (New York, 16 December 1966; ratified by the United Kingdom 20 May 1976; TS 6 (1977): Cmnd 6702) art 15(2); and the Convention for the Protection of Human Rights and Fundamental Freedoms (1950) (Rome, 4 November 1950; TS 71 (1953); Cmd 8969; ETS no 5) art 7; and CONSTITUTIONAL LAW AND HUMAN RIGHTS vol 8(2) (Reissue) PARA 148.

427. Transnational criminal law. Transnational criminal law differs from international criminal law in that the conduct which is made criminal is criminal only in national law. The principal category is a series of suppression conventions in the field of counter-terrorism[1], the central international obligation of which is to make certain identified conduct an offence in national law[2], and with no equivalent international crime springing from the same conduct. An exception to this general rule is the crime of torture, and the United Nations Torture Convention belongs to the class of transnational criminal law treaties[3].

The feature common to all of the suppression conventions is the obligation to make defined conduct criminal in a state's national law, punishable by penalties appropriate to the seriousness of the crimes[4]. In various ways the transnational criminal law treaties both require and allow that crimes thus created carry extraterritorial jurisdiction, although they do not explicitly require or permit universal jurisdiction[5]. The United Kingdom makes all of these offences of universal or quasi-universal jurisdiction[6]. There is ordinarily a requirement that elements of the crime or the context in which it is committed have a transnational character[7]. These crimes are also accompanied by criminal assistance obligations, supported by an aut judicare, aut dedere obligation[8].

Since this obligation may arise from the mere presence of a suspect in their territories, states which impose a locational double criminality requirement in extradition need to have universal jurisdiction over the crimes so that they would be able to extradite a person to a requesting state which wanted him for an extraterritorial (by its own law) offence[9]. It is far from clear that an exercise of universal jurisdiction by a state on the basis of a transnational criminal treaty would be good against an objecting non-party over one of its nationals[10]. There are extensive obligations about extradition and mutual assistance in each of the conventions[11]. Criminal assistance obligations are discharged under the ordinary law of the requested state, so that nationality obstacles to return or political offence exceptions to return or the provision of mutual assistance still apply (subject to any specific obligation to the contrary in a particular treaty or to any supplementary treaty arrangements which states have made)[12]. With certain exceptions[13], persons facing removal from the territory of a state would be entitled to any human rights non-refoulement obligation of the requested state[14].

The offences are offences in national law and trials therefore take place under national criminal law and procedure[15]. Because these laws are not unified, there is the possibility that a trial in one jurisdiction would lead to an acquittal, and a conviction in another. The Conventions have dispute-settlement provisions which may ultimately lead to a dispute being submitted to the International Court of Justice[16], and while some have provisions for supervision of states' obligation by international organisations, there are no routine mechanisms with binding authority to establish authoritative meaning.

The great bulk of transnational criminal law treaties are counter-terrorism arrangements but the same patterns occur for treaties against drug-trafficking, organized crime[17], money-laundering[18] and corruption[19].

Participation is by no means universal, although recent years have seen an increasing number of ratifications of the counter-terrorism treaties under the prompting of the Security Council[20].

1   Among the treaties of this kind to which the UK is a party are: (1) the Convention for the Suppression of Unlawful Seizure of Aircraft (The Hague, 16 December 1970; Misc 5 (1971); Cmnd 4577) (the 'Hague Convention') (implemented by the Aviation Security Act 1982) (see AIR LAW vol 2 (2008) PARAS 14, 624 et seq); (2) the Convention for the Suppression of Unlawful Acts against the Safety of Civil Aviation (Montreal, 23 September 1971; Misc 26 (1971); Cmnd 4822) (the 'Montreal Convention') (implemented by the Aviation Security Act 1982) (see AIR LAW vol 2 (2008) PARAS 15, 622 et seq); (3) the International Convention against the Taking of Hostages (New York, 18 December 1979; TS 81 (1983); Cmnd 9100) (the 'Hostages Convention') (implemented by the Taking of Hostages Act 1982) (see CRIMINAL LAW, EVIDENCE AND PROCEDURE vol 11(1) (2006 Reissue) PARA 468); (4) the Convention on the Prevention and Punishment of Crimes against Internationally Protected Persons, including Diplomatic Agents (New York, 14 December 1973; TS 3 (1980); Cmnd 7765) (the 'Attacks on Diplomats Convention') (implemented by the Internationally Protected Persons Act 1978) (see CRIMINAL LAW, EVIDENCE AND PROCEDURE vol 11(1) (2006 Reissue) PARA 477); (5) the Convention on the Safety of United Nations and Associated Personnel (New York, 9 December 1994, TS 92 (2000); Cm 4803) (the 'Safety of UN Personnel Convention') (implemented by the United Nations Personnel Act 1997) (see PARA 532); (6) the Convention on Physical Protection of Nuclear Material (Vienna and New York from 3 March 1980; Misc 27 (1980); Cmnd 8112) (the 'Nuclear Material Convention') (implemented by the Nuclear Material (Offences) Act 1983) (see FUEL AND ENERGY vol 19(3) (2007 Reissue) PARAS 1350, 1583); (7) the Convention for the Suppression of Unlawful Acts against the Safety of Maritime Navigation (Rome, 10 March 1988; TS 64 (1995); Cm 2947) (the 'Safety of Maritime Navigation Convention'); and the Protocol for the Suppression of Unlawful Acts against the Safety of Fixed Platforms located on the Continental Shelf, supplementary to the Rome Convention (Rome, 10 March 1988; TS 64 (1995); Cm 2947) (implemented by the Aviation and Maritime Security Act 1990) (see SHIPPING AND MARITIME LAW vol 94 (2008) PARA 1210 et seq); (8) the International Convention for the Suppression of Terrorist Bombings (New York, 15 December 1997; TS 57 (2001); Cm 5347)

(the 'Terrorist Bombings Convention') and the International Convention for the Suppression of the Financing of Terrorism (New York, 10 January 2000; TS 28 (2002); Cm 4663) (the 'Terrorist Financing Convention') (implemented by the Terrorism Act 2000); (9) the Convention against Illicit Traffic in Narcotic Drugs and Psychotropic Substances (Vienna, 20 December 1988; Misc 14 (1989); Cm 804) (the 'Vienna Convention') (implemented by the Criminal Justice (International Cooperation) Act 1990).

See generally Boister 'Transnational Criminal Law?' (2003) 14(5) European Journal of International Law 953. It should be noted that there is no international crime of 'terrorism'.

2   An exception is the Terrorist Financing Convention, which is directed against financial support for conduct made criminal as a result of obligations under other suppression conventions.

3   Ie the Convention against Torture and other Cruel, Inhuman or Degrading Treatment or Punishment (New York, 4 February 1985; Misc 12 (1985); Cmnd 9593) (implemented by the Criminal Justice Act 1988 s 134); see PARA 433. Slavery is sometimes said to be a crime against international law but has no settled definition, and there is a crime of slavery in English law, which relies on an international human rights standard to define the conduct criminal in English law: see PARA 434.

4   The offence creating provisions are: (1) the Hague Convention arts 1–3; (2) the Montreal Convention arts 1–4; (3) the Hostages Convention arts 1, 2; (4) the Attacks on Diplomats Convention arts 1, 2; (5) the Safety of UN Personnel Convention arts 1, 9; (6) the Nuclear Material Convention arts 1, 7; (7) the Safety of Maritime Navigation Convention arts 1–3; and Protocol, art 2; (8) the Terrorist Bombings Convention arts 1–3, and the Terrorist Financing Convention arts 1, 2; (9) the Vienna Convention arts 1, 2.

5   See eg (1) the Hague Convention art 4(1) (offence on aircraft registered in its territory; offence on aircraft which lands in its territory; where offence on aircraft leased without crew to a lessee with principal place of business in its territory or, if there is no such place, where the lessee is a permanent resident of the state); (2) the Montreal Convention art 5 (offence committed in state's territory; offence committed on or against an aircraft registered in its territory; when aircraft lands in its territory with offender still on board; where offence on aircraft leased without crew to a lessee with principal place of business in its territory or, if there is no such place, where the lessee is a permanent resident of the state); (3) the Hostages Convention art 5 (offence committed in its territory or on board a ship or aircraft registered in the state; offence committed by any of its nationals; where the offence is committed to compel the state to do or to abstain from doing any act; where the hostage is a national of the state, if the state deems it appropriate); (4) the Attacks on Diplomats Convention art 3 (where the offence is committed in its territory on board a ship or aircraft registered in its territory; when the offender its national; where the internationally protected person enjoys his status by virtue of functions he performs for the state); (5) the Safety of UN Personnel Convention art 10 (where the offence is committed on the state's territory or on board a ship or aircraft registered in its territory; when the offender is a national of the state; and may establish jurisdiction if the offence is committed by a stateless person, habitually resident in the state or a national of the state is the victim or where there is an attempt to compel the state to do or to abstain from doing any act); (6) the Nuclear Material Convention art 8 (where the offence is committed in the state's territory or on board a ship or aircraft registered in its territory; the offender is a national of the state); (7) the Safety of Maritime Navigation Convention art 6 (where offence committed against a ship flying the flag of the state; where the offence is committed within the territory of the state; where the offence is committed by a national of the state; and may establish jurisdiction where the offence is committed by a stateless person who is a habitually resident in the state, where a national of the state is seized, threatened, injured or killed, or the offence is committed to compel the state to do or abstain from doing any act); and Protocol, art 3 (where offence committed against or on board a fixed platform on the state's continental shelf; where the offence is committed by a national of the state; and may establish jurisdiction where the offence is committed by a stateless person habitually resident in the state, a national of the state is seized, threatened injured of killed, or the offence is committed to compel the state to do or to abstain from doing any act); (8) the Terrorist Bombings Convention art 6 (where the offence is committed on the territory of the state; where the offence is committed on board a ship or aircraft registered in the state; where the offence is committed by a national of the state; and it may establish jurisdiction where the offence is committed against a national of the state, where the offence is committed against a government facility abroad, including an embassy or other diplomatic or consular premises, the offence is committed by a stateless person habitually resident in the state, the offence is committed to compel a state to do or to abstain from doing any act or the offence is committed on board an aircraft operated by the government of the state), and the Terrorist Financing Convention art 7 (offence committed in the territory of the state; offence committed on board a ship or aircraft registered in the state; offence committed by a national of the state; and may

establish jurisdiction where the financing offence was directed towards carrying out an offence on the territory or against a national of the state, where the financing offence was directed towards carrying out an offence against a state or government facility abroad, where the financing offence was directed to an offence aimed to compel the state to do or to abstain from doing any act, where it was committed by a stateless person habitually resident in the state or where the offence was committed on an aircraft operated by the government of a state); (9) the Vienna Convention art 4 (offence committed on its territory; offence committed on a ship or aircraft registered in its territory; and may establish jurisdiction where the offence was committed by its national or a person habitually resident in its territory, where the offence was committed on a vessel over which a state was taking action under art 17 or where offence outside its territory was a preparatory or participatory offence with respect to an offence established under the Convention).

6   See eg Aviation Security Act 1982 s 1(1) (and AIR LAW vol 2 (2008) PARA 624); Aviation Security Act 1982 s 2(3) (and AIR LAW vol 2 (2008) PARA 628); Taking of Hostages Act 1982 s 1(1) (and CRIMINAL LAW, EVIDENCE AND PROCEDURE vol 11(1) (2006 Reissue) PARA 468); Internationally Protected Persons Act 1978 s 1(1) (and CRIMINAL LAW, EVIDENCE AND PROCEDURE vol 11(1) (2006 Reissue) PARA 477); Nuclear Materials (Offences) Act 1983 ss 1–4 (and FUEL AND ENERGY vol 19(3) (2007 Reissue) PARA 1583); Aviation and Maritime Security Act 1990 ss 36–43 (and SHIPPING AND MARITIME LAW vol 94 (2008) PARA 1210); Terrorism Act 2000 ss 62, 63 (and CRIMINAL LAW, EVIDENCE AND PROCEDURE vol 11(1) (2006 Reissue) PARAS 470–471); and Criminal Justice (International Cooperation) Act 1990 s 21 (and CRIMINAL LAW, EVIDENCE AND PROCEDURE vol 11(3) (2006 Reissue) PARA 1056). As to universal jurisdiction see PARA 227.

7   So that, for example, a purely domestic aircraft hijacking would not fall within the terms of the Hague Convention (see art 3(3)), whereas an attack on a foreign diplomat within a state's territory would be within the ambit of the Attacks on Diplomats Convention (see art 1(1)).

8   See eg (1) the Hague Convention art 7; (2) the Montreal Convention art 7; (3) the Hostages Convention art 8; (4) the Attacks on Diplomats Convention art 7; (5) the Safety of UN Personnel Convention art 14; (6) the Nuclear Material Convention art 10; (7) the Safety of Maritime Navigation Convention art 10; (8) the Terrorist Bombings Convention art 8, and the Terrorist Financing Convention art 10; (9) the Vienna Convention art 6(9).

9   This explains the UK practice of legislating on the basis of universal jurisdiction: see note 7.

10 In *R v Bow Street Metropolitan Stipendiary Magistrate, ex p Pinochet Ugarte (No 3)* [1999] UKHL 17, [2000] 1 AC 147, sub nom *R v Bow Street Metropolitan Stipendiary Magistrate, ex p Pinochet Ugarte (Amnesty International intervening) (No 3)* [1999] 2 All ER 97, HL, the majority attached importance to the date the Torture Convention (see note 3) had come into force for the states involved (UK, Spain, Chile) before applying the terms of the Criminal Justice Act 1988 (which give effect to the Torture Convention in UK law).

11 See, in general, EXTRADITION.

12 See eg the Terrorist Bombing Convention art 11, and the Terrorist Financing Convention art 14 (which exclude offences under the Conventions as being regarded as political offences for the purposes of extradition).

13 See the Hostages Convention art 9 (allowing for a refusal to extradite where there is a risk of discriminatory treatment in the requesting state); and the Terrorist Bombing Convention art 14, and Terrorist Financing Convention art 17 (guaranteeing fair treatment to persons being dealt with under the Conventions including enjoyment of all rights and guarantees in conformity with the law of the state in the territory of which that person is present and applicable provisions of international law, including international human rights law).

14 See the Convention for the Protection of Human Rights and Fundamental Freedoms (Rome, 4 November 1950; TS 71 (1953); Cmd 8969) art 3 (and CONSTITUTIONAL LAW AND HUMAN RIGHTS vol 8(2) (Reissue) PARA 124); *Soering v United Kingdom* A 161 (1989), 11 EHRR 439, ECtHR; Application 37201/06 *Saadi v Italy* (2008) 24 BHRC 123, ECtHR; *Brown v Government of Rwanda* [2009] EWHC 770 (Admin), [2009] All ER (D) 98 (Apr).

15 See eg *R v Abdul-Hussain* [1998] EWCA Crim 3528, [1999] Crim LR 570.

16 See eg *Questions of Interpretation and Application of the 1971 Montreal Convention arising from the Aerial Incident at Lockerbie (Libyan Arab Jamahiriya v United Kingdom) (Provisional Measures)* ICJ Reports 1992, 3.

17 See the United Nations Convention against Transnational Organized Crime (New York, 15 November 2000; TS 12 (2006); Cm 6852); Protocol to Prevent, Suppress and Punish Trafficking in Persons, Especially Women and Children, supplementing the United Nations Convention against Transnational Organized Crime (New York, 15 November 2000; TS 17 (2006); Cm 6881); Protocol against the Smuggling of Migrants by Land, Sea and Air,

supplementing the United Nations Convention against Transnational Organized Crime (New York 15 November 2000; TS 16 (2006); Cm 6880).

18　See the **United Nations Convention against Transnational Organized Crime (TS 2006, No 12, Cm 6852).**

19　**See the** Criminal Law Convention on Corruption (Strasbourg, 27 Jan 1999; TS 27 (2006); Cm 6958); and the Additional Protocol to the Criminal Law Convention on Corruption (Strasbourg, 15 May 2003).

20　See eg Security Council Resolution 1373 of 28 September 2001.

428.　Aggression.　Although it is a crime within the jurisdiction of the International Criminal Court (the 'ICC') there is no definition of the crime of aggression in the Statute of the ICC[1]. Until the term has been defined, there will no definition available for implementation by United Kingdom legislation[2]. It is very unlikely indeed that any other source for a definition of a crime of aggression would be used by Parliament for the purpose of domestic law.

1　See the Rome Statute of the International Criminal Court (17.7.98) (UN Doc A/CONF 183/9; 37 ILM (1998) 999) art 5(2). The ICC exercises jurisdiction over the crime of aggression once a provision is adopted defining the crime and setting out the conditions under which it may exercise jurisdiction over it: see arts 121, 123. The United Kingdom would not in any event be obliged to accept and implement any definition of a crime of aggression ultimately agreed upon: see art 121(5).

2　Crimes under customary international law, including the crime of planning, preparing or waging a war of aggression, are not crimes in English law unless implemented by legislation: *R v Jones; Ayliffe v DPP; Swain v DPP* [2006] UKHL 16, [2007] 1 AC 136.

429.　Genocide.　Genocide is defined in the United Nations Convention on the Prevention and Punishment of the Crime of Genocide[1] as meaning any of the following acts committed with intent to destroy, in whole or in part[2], a national, ethnical, racial or religious group[3]:

(1)　killing members of the group[4];

(2)　causing serious bodily or mental harm to members of the group[5];

(3)　deliberately inflicting on the group conditions of life calculated to bring about its physical destruction in whole or in part[6];

(4)　imposing measures intended to prevent births within the group[7];

(5)　forcibly transferring children of the group to another group[8].

This definition is incorporated into the Statutes of the International Criminal Tribunals for Yugoslavia ('ICTY') and Rwanda ('ICTR')[9], into the Statute of the International Criminal Court (the 'ICC')[10] and, via the latter, into English law[11]. Genocide is a crime under customary international law and may have been so since as early as 1951[12], although it may not be prosecuted in English law solely on that account[13].

The limited definition and specific intent required make genocide a very particular crime, and not all attacks against groups, however serious, will amount to it[14]. Genocide does not cover attacks against political groups, and it is clear that the definition was not intended to encompass the destruction of the elements of a group's cultural identification, ultimately by assimilation ('cultural genocide')[15].

The specific requirement of intent to destroy in whole or in part means that actions designed to remove large groups of people from a territory ('ethnic cleansing') or acts committed during a conflict which have serious collateral effects on groups will not in themselves amount to genocide[16]. Moreover, the specific intent needs to be shown for everyone accused of genocide, whether as the designer of a policy or as an individual taking part in the execution of a genocidal enterprise. This means that genocide may be committed not only by those who conceive or order the execution of a plan of genocide but by those, however low down or even outside the chain of command, provided that they act with the requisite genocidal intent[17]. These strict rules reflect the perception that genocide is an exceptional crime. However, if genocidal intent cannot be proved, conduct which would satisfy the actus reus of genocide is likely to involve liability for crimes against humanity or war crimes[18].

The Convention on the Prevention and Punishment of the Crime of Genocide states that genocide, whether committed in time of peace or war, is a crime under international law, which the contracting parties must undertake to prevent and punish[19]. The following acts are punishable: (a) genocide; (b) conspiracy to commit genocide; (c) direct and public incitement to commit genocide; (d) attempt to commit genocide; (e) complicity in genocide[20].

1   Ie the Convention on the Prevention and Punishment of the Crime of Genocide (Paris, 9 December 1948; TS 58 (1970); Cmnd 4421). The Convention was adopted by the United Nations General Assembly on 9 December 1948, and is derived from the concept of crimes against humanity contained in the Charter of the International Military Tribunal (London, 8 August 1945; TS 27 (1946); Cmd 6903) which sat at Nuremberg. The General Assembly declared in General Assembly Resolution 96 (I) of 11 December 1946 that genocide is a crime under international law. The Convention on the Prevention and Punishment of the Crime of Genocide entered into force on 12 January 1951 and for the United Kingdom on 30 January 1970. The principles underlying the Convention are such as are recognised by civilised nations as binding upon states, even without any conventional obligation: *Reservations to the Convention on the Prevention and Punishment of the Crime of Genocide (Advisory Opinion)* ICJ Reports 1951, 15 at 21. See also *A-G for the Government of Israel v Eichmann* (1961) 36 Int LR 5.

2   It is accepted that the 'part' must be substantial, and if not wholly a question of numbers or proportion, then such that the destruction of the part would have an impact on the group as a whole or that its members were of such prominence within the whole group that their preservation was essential to the survival of the group itself: *Application of the Convention on the Prevention and Punishment of the Crime of Genocide (Bosnia and Herzegovina v Serbia and Montenegro)* ICJ Reports, 26 February 2007 (para 198); *Prosecutor v Krstic* Case no IT-98-33-A (judgment, 19 April 2004), ICTY (Appeals Chamber), para 12. The International Court of Justice ('ICJ') concluded that there had been a genocide at Srebrenica, where a 'substantial part' of the group of Bosnian Muslims had been killed with the intention of destroying the group as such: *Application of the Convention on the Prevention and Punishment of the Crime of Genocide (Bosnia and Herzegovina v Serbia and Montenegro)* ICJ Reports, 26 February 2007 (para 296). The ICJ was not persuaded that there had been other genocides in Bosnia: *Application of the Convention on the Prevention and Punishment of the Crime of Genocide (Bosnia and Herzegovina v Serbia and Montenegro* at para 376.

3   These terms have no objective definitions and clearly overlap: see *Prosecutor v Krstic* Case no IT-98-33-T (judgment, 2 August 2001), ICTY (Trial Chamber I), paras 555–556; and *Prosecutor v Akayesu* Case no ICTR-96-4-T (judgment, 2 September 1998), paras 512–515, 702. Even on this restricted basis, the identification of any particular group (and establishing that any particular person is a member of it) is not without its difficulties: see *Application of the Convention on the Prevention and Punishment of the Crime of Genocide (Bosnia and Herzegovina v Serbia and Montenegro)* ICJ Reports, 26 February 2007 (paras 192–196) (negative definition of the group attacked at Srebrenicia as 'non-Serbs' rejected by the ICTY; identified as 'Bosnian Muslims', not any particular segment of that group). The international tribunals have approached the matter by objectively assessing whether the group falls within one or more of these prescribed heads, combined with an assessment of the perpetrators' subjective perceptions: *Prosecutor v Laurent Semanza* Case no ICTR-97-20-T (judgment, 15 May 2003), para 317.

4   See the Convention on the Prevention and Punishment of the Crime of Genocide art II. Given the nature of genocide and the general requirements as to mens rea, killing here means causing deaths intentionally (though in addition, the specific genocidal intent must be shown): see generally the Rome Statute of the International Criminal Court (17.7.98) (UN Doc A/CONF 183/9; 37 ILM (1998) 999) art 30. The fact that genocidal intention is not shown does not mean that a defendant may not be responsible in other ways: see *Prosecutor v Krstic* Case no IT-98-33-A (judgment, 19 April 2004), ICTY (Appeals Chamber) (defendant found guilty of

aiding and abetting genocide, while lacking the genocidal intention of a principal). Command responsibility (eg for failing to act to prevent a genocide or punish its perpetrators) may arise in the absence of a genocidal intent on the part of the commander but he would be responsible for genocide: see generally the Statute of the ICC art 28.

5 See the Convention on the Prevention and Punishment of the Crime of Genocide art II. This may include acts of torture, rape, sexual violence or inhuman or degrading treatment: Elements of Crimes art 6(b) para 1 fn 3. As to the Elements of Crimes see PARA 422 note 9. The notion of 'serious' harm does not lend itself to an objective standard but it is a common feature of international standards of ill-treatment, though usually taking into account the characteristics of the victim: see eg *Menesheva v Russia* (2006) 44 EHRR 1162, [2006] ECHR 59261/00. For genocide, the characteristics of the group must be taken into account, although some of the conduct contemplated by this provision is so severe that it would cause the forbidden consequences to any group of people: *A-G for the Government of Israel v Eichmann* (1961) 36 Int LR 5.

6 See the Convention on the Prevention and Punishment of the Crime of Genocide art II. Examples of such conditions include the deliberate deprivation of resources indispensable for survival, such as food or medical services or systematic expulsion from homes: Elements of Crimes art 6(c), para 4 fn 4. As to the Elements of Crimes see PARA 422 note 9. Where 'ethnic cleansing' is the policy being pursued, it is necessary to show that the destruction of the group was intended, not merely its removal from a particular territory by the imposition on it of severe conditions: *Application of the Convention on the Prevention and Punishment of the Crime of Genocide (Bosnia and Herzegovina v Serbia and Montenegro)* ICJ Reports, 26 February 2007 (para 190), citing *Prosecutor v Stakic* Case No IT-97–24-T (judgment, 21 July 2003), ICTY (Trial Chamber), para 519.

7 See the Convention on the Prevention and Punishment of the Crime of Genocide art II. The actions contemplated here clearly include enforced sterilisation and prohibitions upon procreation but they may go further, depending upon certain cultural traditions of a particular group, for instance where rape would exclude women from normal child-bearing. The prohibited sexual conducts which form part of crimes against humanity are a good guide here; in each case, of course, the actus reus would have to be accompanied by the requisite genocidal intent: see PARA 430.

8 See the Convention on the Prevention and Punishment of the Crime of Genocide art II. Children are persons under the age of 18 years: Elements of Crimes art 6(e) para 6. The transfer must take place from their group to another: art 6(e) para 4. Forcibly is not restricted to physical force, and to include threat of force or coercion, such as that caused by fear of violence, duress, detention, psychological oppression or abuse of power against such person or persons or another person, or by taking advantage of a coercive environment: Elements of Crimes, art 6(e), para 1 fn 5. As to the Elements of Crimes see PARA 422 note 9.

9 Statute of the International Tribunal for the Prosecution of Persons Responsible for Serious Violations of International Humanitarian Law Committed in the Territory of the Former Yugoslavia since 1991, UN Doc S/25704 at 36, annex (1993) and S/25704/Add.1 (1993), adopted by Security Council on 25 May 1993, UN Doc S/RES/827 (1993) art 4; Statute of the International Criminal Tribunal for the Prosecution of Persons Responsible for Genocide and Other Serious Violations of International Humanitarian Law Committed in the Territory of Rwanda and Rwandan Citizens Responsible for Genocide and Other Such Violations Committed in the Territory of Neighbouring States, between 1 January 1994 and 31 December 1994, adopted by the Security Council on 8 November 1994, UN Doc S/RES/955 (1994) art 2.

10 Statute of the ICC art 6.

11 See the International Criminal Court Act 2001 s 50, Sch 8; and PARA 454.

12 See the *Reservations to the Convention on the Prevention and Punishment of the Crime of Genocide (Advisory Opinion)* ICJ Reports 1951, 15 at 23.

13 *R v Jones; Ayliffe v DPP; Swain v DPP* [2006] UKHL 16, [2007] 1 AC 136. See also, therefore, the International Criminal Court Act 2001 ss 51(2)(b) (and PARA 454), 67A (not yet in force) (and PARA 454).

14 See the International Commission of Inquiry on Violations of International Humanitarian Law and Human Rights Law in Darfur UN Doc S/2005/60.

15 *Prosecutor v Krstic* Case no IT-98–33-T (judgment, 2 August 2001), ICTY (Trial Chamber I), para 580; and Case no IT-98–33-A (judgment, 19 April 2004), ICTY (Appeals Chamber), para 25.

16 It is crucial to emphasise the importance of the special intent required for genocide for it is this which gives conduct the special opprobrium which distinguishes genocide from other atrocious behaviour: see eg *Application of the Convention on the Prevention and Punishment of the Crime of Genocide (Bosnia and Herzegovina v Serbia and Montenegro)* ICJ Reports,

26 February 2007 (para 190). 'Destroy' designates physical or biological elimination: *Prosecutor v Krstic* Case no IT-98–33-A (judgment, 19 April 2004), ICTY (Appeals Chamber), para 25.

17 However, knowledge of the required specific intention on the part of others may involve the liability of such persons as accomplices to the principal offenders where other actus reus are present.

18 See e g *Prosecutor v Kupreskic et al* Case no IT-95–16-T (judgment, 14 January 2000), ICTY (Trial Chamber II), para 751 (severe violations of human rights of a population with the object of expelling them the crime against humanity of persecution rather than genocide). See also PARA 430.

19 Convention on the Prevention and Punishment of the Crime of Genocide, art I. The violation of duties under the Convention engages state responsibility rather than individual international criminal responsibility: *Application of the Convention on the Prevention and Punishment of the Crime of Genocide (Bosnia and Herzegovina v Serbia and Montenegro)* ICJ Reports, 26 February 2007 (paras 425–466). The duty to prevent and punish genocide is a peremptory norm of international law and imposes obligations erga omnes: *Armed Activities on the Territory of the Congo (New Application: 2002) (Democratic Republic of the Congo v Rwanda) (Jurisdiction and Admissibility)* ICJ Reports 2006, 6 (para 64); *Barcelona Traction, Light and Power Co Ltd (Belgium v Spain) (Second Phase)* ICJ Reports 1970, 3 at 32. As to international responsibility see PARA 327 et seq. As to peremptory norms and obligations erga omnes see PARA 11.

20 Convention on the Prevention and Punishment of the Crime of Genocide, art III. Note that this article was not mentioned in the Statute of the ICC art 6, and consequently not enacted in the International Criminal Court Act 2001.

430. Crimes against humanity. Crimes against humanity were within the jurisdiction of the International Military Tribunal at Nuremberg[1] and were, in a slightly different form, included in the International Law Commission's ('ILC') statement of the Nuremberg Principles[2]. The United Nations Security Council accepted that crimes against humanity were crimes by customary international law in 1993[3], and again in different terms, the Security Council provided for the jurisdiction of the International Criminal Tribunal for Rwanda ('ICTR') over crimes against humanity[4].

A more elaborate statement of crimes against humanity is contained in the Statute of the International Criminal Court (the 'ICC')[5] and it is this which has been implemented into English law[6]. For these purposes a crime against humanity means any of the following acts when committed as part of a widespread or systematic attack[7] directed against any civilian population[8], with knowledge of the attack[9]:

(1)　murder[10];

(2)　extermination[11];

(3)　enslavement[12];

(4)　deportation or forcible transfer of population[13];

(5)　imprisonment or other severe deprivation of liberty in violation of fundamental rules of international law[14];

(6)　torture[15];

(7)　rape, sexual slavery, enforced prostitution, forced pregnancy, enforced sterilisation, or any other form of sexual violence of comparable gravity[16];

(8)　persecution against any identifiable group or collectivity on political, racial, national, ethnic, cultural, religious, gender, or other grounds that are universally recognised as impermissible under international law, in connection with any act referred to in this paragraph or any crime within the jurisdiction of the Court[17];

(9)　enforced disappearance of persons[18];

(10)　the crime of apartheid[19];

(11) other inhumane acts of a similar character intentionally causing great suffering, or serious injury to body or to mental or physical health[20].

In general terms, crimes against humanity may be committed by an official against his own nationals[21] and they may be committed whether or not in the context of an international or internal armed conflict[22]. There must be some element of contextual scale to the attack although individual or relatively limited numbers of acts committed as part of and with knowledge of such an attack may be crimes against humanity[23]. There must be an attack directed at a civilian population, pursuant to or in furtherance of a state or organisational policy to commit such an attack, to distinguish crimes against humanity from high levels of ordinary crime[24]. With the exception of the crime of persecution there is no requirement in general that crimes against humanity be committed on discriminatory grounds; in particular, it is not necessary to show that an individual defendant was acting with a discriminatory intent[25].

1 Although with the significant limitation that they were committed in execution of or in connection with other crimes within the jurisdiction of the Tribunal: see the Charter of the International Military Tribunal (London, 8 August 1945; TS 27 (1946); Cmd 6903) art 6(c). As to the International Military Tribunal at Nuremburg see PARA 422.

2 See International Law Commission, A/1316 (1950): Nuremberg Principles, principle VI.

3 Ie when the Council conferred jurisdiction on the International Tribunal for the Former Yugoslavia ('ICTY'): see the Statute of the International Tribunal for the Prosecution of Persons Responsible for Serious Violations of International Humanitarian Law Committed in the Territory of the Former Yugoslavia since 1991, UN Doc S/25704 at 36, annex (1993) and S/25704/Add.1 (1993), adopted by Security Council on 25 May 1993, UN Doc S/RES/827 (1993) art 5. This resolution granted the tribunal power to prosecute persons responsible for the following crimes when committed in armed conflict, whether international or internal in character, and directed against any civilian population: (1) murder; (2) extermination; (3) enslavement; (4) deportation; (5) imprisonment; (6) torture; (7) rape; (8) persecutions on political, racial and religious grounds; (9) other inhumane acts: see art 5. Crimes against humanity are complex and it could be doubted whether any purely customary law definition would satisfy the principle of legality.

4 The International Tribunal for Rwanda ('ICTR') had the power to prosecute persons responsible for the following crimes when committed as part of a widespread or systematic attack against any civilian population on national, political, ethnic, racial or religious grounds: (1) murder; (2) extermination; (3) enslavement; (4) deportation; (5) imprisonment; (6) torture; (7) rape; (8) persecutions on political, racial and religious grounds; (9) other inhumane acts: see the Statute of the International Criminal Tribunal for the Prosecution of Persons Responsible for Genocide and Other Serious Violations of International Humanitarian Law Committed in the Territory of Rwanda and Rwandan Citizens Responsible for Genocide and Other Such Violations Committed in the Territory of Neighbouring States, between 1 January 1994 and 31 December 1994, adopted by the Security Council on 8 November 1994, UN Doc S/RES/955 (1994) art 3.

5 Ie the Rome Statute of the International Criminal Court (17.7.98) (UN Doc A/CONF 183/9; 37 ILM (1998) 999).

6 See the International Criminal Court Act 2001 s 50; Sch 8; and PARA 454.

7 While 'widespread' or 'systematic' are alternative requirements, the element of an 'attack', suggests that there may be some overlap between them.

8 'Attack directed against any civilian population' means a course of conduct involving the multiple commission of acts which constitute a crime against humanity (see the text and notes 10–20) against any civilian population, pursuant to or in furtherance of a state or organisational policy to commit such attack: Statute of the ICC art 7(2)(a). 'Civilian' is to distinguish the population from widespread or systematic attacks against military targets, which are governed by international humanitarian law. Attacks on civilian population may also constitute war crimes, however: see art 8(2)(b)(i), (e)(i); and PARA 431.

9 Statute of the ICC art 7(1).

10 Statute of the ICC art 7(1)(a). The required mental element may exclude circumstances in which death results but where the defendant intends only to cause grievous bodily harm, making 'killing' a narrower concept than murder under English law: see art 30.

11 Statute of the ICC art 7(1)(b). 'Extermination' includes the intentional infliction of conditions of life, inter alia the deprivation of access to food and medicine, calculated to bring about the

destruction of part of a population: art 7(2)(b). Extermination is killing, including by inflicting conditions of life calculated to bring about the destruction of part of a population, which is part of the mass killing of members of a civilian population: see the Elements of Crimes art 7(1)(b). As to the Elements of Crimes see PARA 422 note 9. Extermination need not be accompanied by the specific intention required for genocide and covers cases where the targeted group is not one of the four required for genocide: see PARA 429.

12 Statute of the ICC art 7(1)(c). 'Enslavement' means the exercise of any or all of the powers attaching to the right of ownership over a person and includes the exercise of such power in the course of trafficking in persons, in particular women and children: art 7(2)(c). This is not restricted to reducing persons to chattel slavery but includes similar deprivations of liberty: see Elements of Crimes art 7(1)(c) para 1. It is anticipated that international law definitions of slavery and slavery like practices will be relied upon by the ICC but enslavement may not be so restricted: see the Supplementary Convention on the Abolition of Slavery, the Slave Trade and Institutions and Practices Similar to Slavery (7 September 1956; UN TS vol 266 p 3); and the Elements of Crimes art 7(1)(c) para 1 fn 11.

13 Statute of the ICC art 7(1)(d). 'Deportation or forcible transfer of population' means forced displacement of the persons concerned by expulsion or other coercive acts from the area in which they are lawfully present, without grounds permitted under international law: art 7(2)(d). This crime covers 'ethnic cleansing' (deportation if across an international boundary, forcible transfer if from one area to another within a state); the removals must be without grounds permitted by international law by expulsion or other coercive acts: see generally Elements of Crimes art 7(1)(d) paras 1, 2. Flight by a population to escape persecution would fall within the notions of deportation or forcible transfer, whereas voluntary flight to avoid, say, becoming involved in conflicts areas, would not.

14 Statute of the ICC art 7(1)(e). The prohibited conduct is not restricted to confinement in prison and severe deprivation may cover conditions and length of time: see the Elements of Crimes art 7(1)(e) para 1. Deprivation in breach of international law includes the absence or non-application of procedural safeguards to protect against arbitrary confinement.

15 Statute of the ICC art 7(1)(f). 'Torture' means the intentional infliction of severe pain or suffering, whether physical or mental, upon a person in the custody or under the control of the accused; except that torture does not include pain or suffering arising only from, inherent in, or incidental to lawful sanctions: art 7(2)(e). The Statute of the ICC does not adopt in its entirety the definition of torture in the United Nations Convention against Torture (see PARA 433) in that it does not require that the ill-treatment be inflicted for any identified purpose, nor does it restrict torture to acts of or done under the authority or direction of officials, requiring instead that the victims be under the custody or control of the perpetrator: see Elements of Crimes art 7(1)(f) fn 14. Rape may amount to torture and, where the circumstances justify it an allegation of rape should be treated as such. See generally the Convention Against Torture and Other Cruel, Inhuman or Degrading Treatment or Punishment, art 1, General Assembly Resolution 39/46 of 10 December 1984.

16 Statute of the ICC art 7(1)(g). 'Forced pregnancy' means the unlawful confinement of a woman forcibly made pregnant, with the intent of affecting the ethnic composition of any population or carrying out other grave violations of international law. This definition shall not in any way be interpreted as affecting national laws relating to pregnancy: art 7(2)(f). Rape, which is gender-neutral, is where the perpetrator has invaded the body of a person by conduct resulting in penetration, however slight, of any part of the body of the victim or of the perpetrator with a sexual organ or of the anal or genital opening of the victim with any object of any other part of the body: Elements of Crimes art 7(1)(g)-1 para 1. There is no mention of any purpose associated with the infliction of severe pain or suffering in the statute or in the Elements of Crimes. The penetration must be committed by force or the threat of force or where the perpetrator takes advantage of a coercive environment or the penetration was of a person incapable of giving consent: see the Elements of Crimes art 7(1)(g)-1 para 2. See also *Prosecutor v Kunarac et al* Case No IT-96–23-A, (judgment, 12 June 2002), ICTY (Appeals Chamber), para 129. For rules of evidence specific to cases involving sexual violence see the ICC Rules of Procedure and Evidence (2002), ICC-ASP/1/3, rr 70–71. Sexual slavery requires that the victim be kept in conditions which would satisfy 'enslavement' under the Statute of the ICC art 7(1)(c) (see the text and note 12) and the defendant caused the victim to engage in one or more acts of a sexual nature: Elements of Crimes art 7(1)(g)-2 para 1. Enforced prostitution involves coercion in the same terms as described above for rape where the victim is caused to engage in acts of a sexual nature where the perpetrator or another persons obtained or expected to obtain a financial or other advantage in exchange for the sexual activity: art 7(1)(g)-3 para 2. The definition does not affect national laws relating to pregnancy (meaning those covering abortion): Statute of the ICC art 7(2)(f). The crime of enforced sterilisation is the deprivation of biological

reproductive capacity neither justified by medical treatment nor carried out with the victim's consent: see the Elements of Crimes art 7(1)(g)-5 paras 1, 2. The omnibus offence of other sexual violence of comparable gravity relies on the definition of coercion for rape to cause acts of sexual nature comparable to those specifically condemned, a term which must be interpreted carefully to avoid complaints of vagueness: see generally art 7(1)(g)-6.

17 Statute of the ICC art 7(1)(h). 'Persecution' means the intentional and severe deprivation of fundamental rights contrary to international law by reason of the identity of the group or collectivity: art 7(2)(g). 'Persecution' has close affinities with genocide, save that there is no requirement to show genocidal intent: as to which see PARA 429. See also *Prosecutor v Kupreskic et al* Case no IT-95–16-T (judgment, 14 January 2000), ICTY (Trial Chamber II), para 580. The objection is that the condition appears to return to something like the limitation in the Nuremberg Charter but there can be no legal objection to conferring on the Tribunal a narrower jurisdiction than customary law might have permitted. Persecution includes destruction of property, where the property attacked was chosen on discriminatory grounds: *Prosecutor v Blaskic* Case No IT-95–14-T (judgment, 3 March 2000), ICTY (Trial Chamber), para 233.

18 Statute of the ICC art 7(1)(i). 'Enforced disappearance of persons' means the arrest, detention or abduction of persons by, or with the authorization, support or acquiescence of, a state or a political organisation, followed by a refusal to acknowledge that deprivation of freedom or to give information on the fate or whereabouts of those persons, with the intention of removing them from the protection of the law for a prolonged period of time: art 7(2)(i). The definition of the crime of enforced disappearance is taken from United Nations General Assembly Resolution 47/133 of 18 December 1992, and is itself further incorporated in the International Convention for the Protection of All Persons from Enforced Disappearance 2006 (General Assembly Resolution 61/177 of 20 December 2006; 14 IHRR 582 (2007)) (not yet in force; and the United Kingdom is not a signatory). It is a complex crime involving the arrest, detention or abduction of a person and the refusal to acknowledge that this has happened or to give information about the person's whereabouts, and it must have been carried out by or with the authorisation, support or acquiescence of a state or political organisation: see the Elements of Crimes art 7(1)(i) paras 1–5. The perpetrator must have intended to remove the person from the protection of the law for a prolonged period of time: art 7(1)(i) para 6. It is likely that more than one person would have been responsible for different element of the crime but involvement in one of them with the requisite knowledge and intention is sufficient: art 7(1)(i) para 8. International human rights law establishes that enforced disappearance violates the rights of the family and close friends of the persons 'disappeared' but the crimes committed against them are more likely to have been torture or inhuman treatment: *Kurt v Turkey* [1998] ECHR 24276/94, 5 BHRC 1.

19 Statute of the ICC art 7(1)(j). 'The crime of apartheid' means inhumane acts of a character similar to those referred to in para 1 (see the text and notes 10–20), committed in the context of an institutionalized regime of systematic oppression and domination by one racial group over any other racial group or groups and committed with the intention of maintaining that regime: art 7(2)(h). The definition of the crime of apartheid is a modification of the definition provided in the International Convention for the Suppression and Punishment of the Crime of Apartheid (New York, 30 November 1973), which was directed at the system in South Africa.

20 Statute of the ICC art 7(1)(k). While all definitions of crimes against humanity have a residual clause to cover other serious ill-treatment beyond that specifically prohibited, the principle of legality requires that there be a close identity between any conduct falling within this head and the other heads of prohibited conduct: see the Elements of Crimes art 7(1)(k) para 2. While the defendant must be aware of the factual nature of his conduct which gives it its inhumane character, he does not need to have made a subjective assessment of it those terms: see art 7(1)(k) para 3. The experiences of the ICTY and ICTR have demonstrated the importance of the residual clause, even though the catalogue of prohibited conduct in the Statute of the ICC has been extended to take into account some of the practices which came before those tribunals.

21 This was the great innovation of the Charter of the International Military Tribunal (London, 8 August 1945; TS 27 (1946); Cmd 6903) and makes it possible to treat grave violations of human rights by state officials against their own populations as crimes against international law.

22 Previous definitions which stipulate a link between crimes against humanity and armed conflict are regarded as jurisdictional limitations on the wider notion of crimes against humanity in customary international law: *Prosecutor v Tadic* Case No IT-94–1-A (judgment, 15 July 1999) ICTY (Appeals Chamber), paras 282–288.

23 *Prosecutor v Kunarac et al* Case No IT-96–23-A, (judgment, 12 June 2002), ICTY (Appeals Chamber), para 96; *Prosecutor v Tadic* Case No IT-94–1-A (judgment, 15 July 1999) ICTY (Appeals Chamber), para 248.

24 It has been suggested that the requirement of state policy or encouragement of the attack goes beyond what customary international law requires by excluding acquiescence of officials in the acts of private individuals from the ambit of crimes against humanity, A Cassese, 'Crimes against Humanity' in A Cassese et al, I *The Rome Statute of the International Criminal Court: A Commentary* (2002).

25 See *Prosecutor v Akayesu* ICTR 96–1-A (judgment, 1 June 2001) (Appeals Chamber), paras 461–469.

431. International standards for war crimes. The International Military Tribunal at Nuremberg held that breaches of some treaty-based provisions of the law of war, which were not explicitly made criminal offences by the treaties themselves, were criminal by customary international law[1]. The Geneva Conventions 1949, established a category of 'grave breaches' of their provisions, which engage individual criminal responsibility[2], and which may be committed only in an international armed conflict[3]. States are obliged to make grave breaches crimes within their national law, with universal jurisdiction, and to seek out those accused of grave breaches and bring them to trial or extradite them[4]. Additional Protocol I, which was added to the Geneva Conventions 1949 in 1977, added to the list of grave breaches[5].

War crimes, both 'grave breaches' and breaches of the laws and customs of war[6], are part of the jurisdiction of the International Criminal Tribunal for Yugoslavia ('ICTY')[7]. The conflicts in Yugoslavia were international and internal, and although there are some standards applicable to internal armed conflicts in the Geneva Conventions 1949 and Additional Protocol II (which applies specifically to internal armed conflicts), violation of these provisions is not specifically made criminal[8]. The conflict in Rwanda was a wholly internal armed conflict and the jurisdiction of the International Criminal Tribunal for Rwanda ('ICTR') includes crimes committed in the internal armed conflict[9]. Perhaps partly because of this provision the ICTY has held that some conduct in internal armed conflicts is criminal by customary international law and fell within the tribunal's jurisdiction[10]. These developments reflect a view that the criminal law applicable to international armed conflicts and that which applies to internal armed conflicts are converging. However, it appears that there has not been a complete assimilation of the two bodies of law.

War crimes[11] are defined in the Statute of the International Criminal Court (the 'ICC')[12] as:

(1)   grave breaches of the Geneva Conventions 1949[13];

(2)   other serious violations of the laws and customs applicable in international armed conflict, within the established framework of international law[14];

(3)   in the case of an armed conflict not of an international character, serious violations of certain acts committed against persons taking no active part in the hostilities, including members of armed forces who have laid down their arms and those placed hors de combat by sickness, wounds, detention or any other cause[15];

(4)   other serious violations of the laws and customs applicable in armed conflicts not of an international character, within the established framework of international law[16].

Head (3) applies to armed conflicts not of an international character and thus does not apply to situations of internal disturbances and tensions, such as riots, isolated and sporadic acts of violence or other acts of a similar nature[17]. Head (4) applies to armed conflicts not of an international character and thus does not apply to situations of internal disturbances and tensions, such as riots, isolated and sporadic acts of violence or other acts of a similar nature; it applies to armed conflicts that take place in the territory of a state when there is protracted armed conflict between governmental authorities and organised armed groups or between such groups[18].

1   See the Judgment of the International Military Tribunal for the Trial of the Major War Criminals (1946; Misc 12 (1946); Cmd 6964) at pp 64–65. War Crimes came within the jurisdiction of the tribunal and were defined as violations of the laws or customs of war, including, but not be limited to, murder, ill-treatment or deportation to slave labour or for any other purpose of civilian population of or in occupied territory, murder or ill-treatment of prisoners of war or persons on the seas, killing of hostages, plunder of public or private property, wanton destruction of cities, towns or villages, or devastation not justified by military necessity: see the Charter of the International Military Tribunal (London, 8 August 1945; TS 27 (1946); Cmd 6903) art 6(b). As to the International Military Tribunal at Nuremburg see PARA 422.

2   See the Geneva Conventions 1949: (1) the Geneva Convention for the Amelioration of the Condition of the Wounded and Sick in Armed Forces in the Field (Geneva, 12 August 1949; TS 39 (1958); Cmnd 550) art 50; (2) the Geneva Convention for the Amelioration of the Condition of the Wounded, Sick and Shipwrecked Members of the Armed Forces at Sea (Geneva, 12 August 1949; TS 39 (1958); Cmnd 550) art 51; (3) the Geneva Convention relative to the Treatment of Prisoners of War (Geneva, 12 August 1949; TS 39 (1958); Cmnd 550) art 130; and (4) the Geneva Convention relative to the Protection of Civilian Persons in Time of War (Geneva, 12 August 1949, TS 39 (1958); Cmnd 550) art 147. As to grave breaches see also WAR AND ARMED CONFLICT vol 49(1) (2005 Reissue) PARA 424.

3   See the Geneva Conventions 1949 (see note 2), common art 2.

4   See the Geneva Conventions 1949 (see note 2): (1) art 49; (2) art 50; (3) art 129; and (4) art 146.

5   See the Protocol, additional to the Geneva Conventions of 12 August 1949, relating to the Protection of Victims of International Armed Conflicts done on 10 June 1977 (Geneva, 12 December 1977; Misc 19 (1977); Cmnd 6927) ('Protocol I') arts 11, 85. Wars of national liberation are within the concept of 'international armed conflict': see art 1(4).

6   ICTY has the power to prosecute persons committing or ordering to be committed grave breaches of the Geneva Conventions of 12 August 1949, namely the following acts against persons or property protected under the provisions of the relevant Geneva Convention: (1) wilful killing; (2) torture or inhuman treatment, including biological experiments; (3) wilfully causing great suffering or serious injury to body or health; (4) extensive destruction and appropriation of property, not justified by military necessity and carried out unlawfully and wantonly; (5) compelling a prisoner of war or a civilian to serve in the forces of a hostile power; (6) wilfully depriving a prisoner of war or a civilian of the rights of fair and regular trial; (7) unlawful deportation or transfer or unlawful confinement of a civilian; (8) taking civilians as hostages: see the Statute of the International Tribunal for the Prosecution of Persons Responsible for Serious Violations of International Humanitarian Law Committed in the Territory of the Former Yugoslavia since 1991 ('ICTY'), UN Doc S/25704 at 36, annex (1993) and S/25704/Add 1 (1993), adopted by Security Council on 25 May 1993, UN Doc S/RES/827 (1993) art 2.

    ICTY also has the power to prosecute persons violating the laws or customs of war, including, but not be limited to: (a) employment of poisonous weapons or other weapons calculated to cause unnecessary suffering; (b) wanton destruction of cities, towns or villages, or devastation not justified by military necessity; (c) attack, or bombardment, by whatever means, of undefended towns, villages, dwellings, or buildings; (d) seizure of, destruction or wilful damage done to institutions dedicated to religion, charity and education, the arts and sciences, historic monuments and works of art and science; (e) plunder of public or private property: art 3.

7   See PARA 423 note 3.

8   See the Geneva Conventions 1949 (see note 2), common art 3; Protocol Additional to the Geneva Conventions of 12 August 1949 and relating to the Protection of Victims of Non-International Armed Conflict done on 10 June 1977 (Geneva, 12 December 1977; Misc 19 (1977); Cmnd 6927) ('Protocol II').

9   ICTR has the power to prosecute persons committing or ordering to be committed serious violations of Article 3 common to the Geneva Conventions of 12 August 1949 for the Protection of War Victims, and of Additional Protocol II thereto of 8 June 1977, including, but not be limited to: (1) violence to life, health and physical or mental well-being of persons, in particular murder as well as cruel treatment such as torture, mutilation or any form of corporal

punishment; (2) collective punishments; (3) taking of hostages; (4) acts of terrorism; (5) outrages upon personal dignity, in particular humiliating and degrading treatment, rape, enforced prostitution and any form of indecent assault; (6) pillage; (7) the passing of sentences and the carrying out of executions without previous judgment pronounced by a regularly constituted court, affording all the judicial guarantees which are recognised as indispensable by civilised peoples; (8) threats to commit any of the foregoing acts: Statute of the International Criminal Tribunal for the Prosecution of Persons Responsible for Genocide and Other Serious Violations of International Humanitarian Law Committed in the Territory of Rwanda and Rwandan Citizens Responsible for Genocide and Other Such Violations Committed in the Territory of Neighbouring States, between 1 January 1994 and 31 December 1994 ('ICTR'), adopted by the Security Council on 8 November 1994, UN Doc S/RES/955 (1994) art 4. As to ICTR see PARA 423 note 3.

10 See *Prosecutor v Tadic* Case No 11-94-1-AR72 (Decision on the Defence Motion for. Interlocutory Appeal on Jurisdiction, 2 October 1995), ICTY (Appeals Chamber), paras 126–130. Note *Prosecutor v Kanyabashi* Case No ICTR-96-15-T (Decision on the Defence Motion of Jurisdiction, 18 June 1997), ICTR (Trial Chamber), para 8.

11 As to war crimes see WAR AND ARMED CONFLICT vol 49(1) (2005 Reissue) PARA 463 et seq.

12 Ie the Rome Statute of the International Criminal Court (17.7.98) (UN Doc A/CONF 183/9; 37 ILM (1998) 999).

13 Namely, any of the following acts against persons or property protected under the provisions of the relevant Geneva Convention: (1) wilful killing; (2) torture or inhuman treatment, including biological experiments; (3) wilfully causing great suffering, or serious injury to body or health; (4) extensive destruction and appropriation of property, not justified by military necessity and carried out unlawfully and wantonly; (5) compelling a prisoner of war or other protected person to serve in the forces of a hostile power; (6) wilfully depriving a prisoner of war or other protected person of the rights of fair and regular trial; (7) unlawful deportation or transfer or unlawful confinement; (8) taking of hostages: Statute of the ICC art 8(2)(a).

14 Namely, any of the following acts: (1) intentionally directing attacks against the civilian population as such or against individual civilians not taking direct part in hostilities; (2) intentionally directing attacks against civilian objects, that is, objects which are not military objectives; (3) intentionally directing attacks against personnel, installations, material, units or vehicles involved in a humanitarian assistance or peacekeeping mission in accordance with the United Nations Charter, as long as they are entitled to the protection given to civilians or civilian objects under the international law of armed conflict; (4) intentionally launching an attack in the knowledge that such attack will cause incidental loss of life or injury to civilians or damage to civilian objects or widespread, long-term and severe damage to the natural environment which would be clearly excessive in relation to the concrete and direct overall military advantage anticipated; (5) attacking or bombarding, by whatever means, towns, villages, dwellings or buildings which are undefended and which are not military objectives; (6) killing or wounding a combatant who, having laid down his arms or having no longer means of defence, has surrendered at discretion; (7) making improper use of a flag of truce, or of the flag or of the military insignia and uniform of the enemy or of the United Nations, as well as of the distinctive emblems of the Geneva Conventions, resulting in death or serious personal injury; (8) the transfer, directly or indirectly, by the occupying power of parts of its own civilian population into the territory it occupies, or the deportation or transfer of all or parts of the population of the occupied territory within or outside this territory; (9) intentionally directing attacks against buildings dedicated to religion, education, art, science or charitable purposes, historic monuments, hospitals and places where the sick and wounded are collected, provided they are not military objectives; (10) subjecting persons who are in the power of an adverse party to physical mutilation or to medical or scientific experiments of any kind which are neither justified by the medical, dental or hospital treatment of the person concerned nor carried out in his or her interest, and which cause death to or seriously endanger the health of such person or persons; (11) killing or wounding treacherously individuals belonging to the hostile nation or army; (12) declaring that no quarter will be given; (13) destroying or seizing the enemy's property unless such destruction or seizure be imperatively demanded by the necessities of war; (14) declaring abolished, suspended or inadmissible in a court of law the rights and actions of the nationals of the hostile party; (15) compelling the nationals of the hostile party to take part in the operations of war directed against their own country, even if they were in the belligerent's service before the commencement of the war; (16) pillaging a town or place, even when taken by assault; (17) employing poison or poisoned weapons; (18) employing asphyxiating, poisonous or other gases, and all analogous liquids, materials or devices; (19) employing bullets which expand or flatten easily in the human body, such as bullets with a hard envelope which does not entirely cover the core or is pierced with incisions; (20) employing weapons, projectiles and

material and methods of warfare which are of a nature to cause superfluous injury or unnecessary suffering or which are inherently indiscriminate in violation of the international law of armed conflict, provided that such weapons, projectiles and material and methods of warfare are the subject of a comprehensive prohibition; (21) committing outrages on personal dignity, in particular humiliating and degrading treatment; (22) committing rape, sexual slavery, enforced prostitution, forced pregnancy, enforced sterilisation, or any other form of sexual violence also constituting a grave breach of the Geneva Conventions; (23) utilising the presence of a civilian or other protected person to render certain points, areas or military forces immune from military operations; (24) intentionally directing attacks against buildings, material, medical units and transport, and personnel using the distinctive emblems of the Geneva Conventions in conformity with international law; (25) intentionally using starvation of civilians as a method of warfare by depriving them of objects indispensable to their survival, including wilfully impeding relief supplies as provided for under the Geneva Conventions; (26) conscripting or enlisting children under the age of 15 years into the national armed forces or using them to participate actively in hostilities: Statute of the ICC art 8(2)(b). Note that art 8(2)(b)(20) has not been enacted in the International Criminal Court Act 2001; as to which see PARA 437 et seq.

15 Namely, any of the following acts: (1) violence to life and person, in particular murder of all kinds, mutilation, cruel treatment and torture; (2) committing outrages on personal dignity, in particular humiliating and degrading treatment; (3) taking of hostages; (4) the passing of sentences and the carrying out of executions without previous judgment pronounced by a regularly constituted court, affording all judicial guarantees which are generally recognised as indispensable: Statute of the ICC art 8(2)(c).

16 Namely, any of the following acts: (1) intentionally directing attacks against the civilian population as such or against individual civilians not taking direct part in hostilities; (2) intentionally directing attacks against buildings, material, medical units and transport, and personnel using the distinctive emblems of the Geneva Conventions in conformity with international law; (3) intentionally directing attacks against personnel, installations, material, units or vehicles involved in a humanitarian assistance or peacekeeping mission in accordance with the United Nations Charter, as long as they are entitled to the protection given to civilians or civilian objects under the international law of armed conflict; (4) intentionally directing attacks against buildings dedicated to religion, education, art, science or charitable purposes, historic monuments, hospitals and places where the sick and wounded are collected, provided they are not military objectives; (5) pillaging a town or place, even when taken by assault; (6) committing rape, sexual slavery, enforced prostitution, forced pregnancy, enforced sterilisation, and any other form of sexual violence also constituting a serious violation of the Geneva Conventions; (7) conscripting or enlisting children under the age of 15 years into armed forces or groups or using them to participate actively in hostilities; (8) ordering the displacement of the civilian population for reasons related to the conflict, unless the security of the civilians involved or imperative military reasons so demand; (9) killing or wounding treacherously a combatant adversary; (10) declaring that no quarter will be given; (11) subjecting persons who are in the power of another party to the conflict to physical mutilation or to medical or scientific experiments of any kind which are neither justified by the medical, dental or hospital treatment of the person concerned nor carried out in his or her interest, and which cause death to or seriously endanger the health of such person or persons; (12) destroying or seizing the property of an adversary unless such destruction or seizure be imperatively demanded by the necessities of the conflict: Statute of the ICC art 8(2)(e).

17 Statute of the ICC art 8(2)(d). Nothing in art 8(2)(c), (d) affects the responsibility of a government to maintain or re-establish law and order in the state or to defend the unity and territorial integrity of the state, by all legitimate means: art 8(3). Note that art 8(3) has not been enacted in the International Criminal Court Act 2001; as to which see PARA 437 et seq.

18 Statute of the ICC art 8(2)(f).

432. War crimes, United Kingdom jurisdiction and the temporal element. The International Criminal Courts Act 2001 is the principal basis for the exercise of criminal jurisdiction in the United Kingdom over international crimes, and the substantive definitions of war crimes are taken directly from the Statute of the International Court of Justice (the 'ICC')[1] and accordingly cover conduct in international and internal armed conflicts[2].

Grave breaches of the Geneva Conventions 1949, and of Additional Protocol I are offences of universal jurisdiction in English law[3]. This fact remains important for two reasons, each deriving from the claim of universal jurisdiction over grave breaches offences[4]. The first is that the Geneva Conventions 1949 are widely ratified and apply to many more states than are parties to the Statute of the ICC, so that very few states could object to the exercise of extraterritorial jurisdiction by the United Kingdom courts over acts of their nationals. The second is that the Statute of the ICC and the International Criminal Court Act 2001 do not rely on universal jurisdiction but on jurisdiction based on territory or nationality (and, in the case of the International Criminal Court Act 2001, on residence)[5]. Therefore, the possibility remains that there may be an individual, a national of a party to the Statute of the ICC, who is in the United Kingdom but suspected of war crimes on the territory of a third state. Whether to be able to exercise jurisdiction in the United Kingdom or to be able to extradite such a person to a third state, it is necessary that the United Kingdom has universal jurisdiction over the offence, which, for war crimes, it could find under the Geneva Conventions Act 1957.

The War Crimes Act 1991 provides for a particular jurisdiction in the United Kingdom courts in cases of homicide committed during the period beginning with 1st September 1939 and ending with 5th June 1945 in a place which at the time was part of Germany or under German occupation, regardless of the nationality of the defendant at the time of the offence, where the conduct constituted also a violation of the laws and customs of war[6]. Only one conviction has been obtained under this legislation but it creates a jurisdiction in the courts to try those accused of conduct amounting a crime under international law which would not be available otherwise[7].

Criminality in customary international law is not a basis for founding a criminal offence in English law[8], so the possibility of a prosecution for war crimes will depend upon the enactment of a statute making the international offences in English law. In the ordinary way, the offences would operate from the date of the coming into force of the statute, although provision may be made to give them retrospective effect[9].

1	Ie the Rome Statute of the International Criminal Court (17.7.98) (UN Doc A/CONF 183/9; 37 ILM (1998) 999); and see PARA 437
2	See the International Criminal Court Act 2001 ss 50, 51; and PARA 454.
3	See the Geneva Conventions Act 1957 s 1; and WAR AND ARMED CONFLICT vol 49(1) (2005 Reissue) PARA 424. As to the Geneva Conventions 1949 see PARA 431 note 2. As to the Additional Protocol see PARA 431 note 5.
4	As to universal jurisdiction see PARA 227.
5	See the International Criminal Court Act 2001 ss 51, 67; and PARA 454. The International Criminal Court Act 2001 provides in addition extraterritorial jurisdiction over the acts of those subject to UK service jurisdiction: see s 67(3); and PARA 454.
6	See the War Crimes Act 1991 s 1(1); and WAR AND ARMED CONFLICT vol 49(1) (2005 Reissue) PARA 465.
7	See *R v Sawoniuk* [2000] 2 Cr App Rep 220, [2000] All ER (D) 154, CA.
8	See *R v Jones; Ayliffe v DPP; Swain v DPP* [2006] UKHL 16, [2007] 1 AC 136.
9	See the International Criminal Court Act 2009 s 65A (not yet in force); and PARAS 454–455, 458.

433. Torture. Torture is an international crime under customary international law, although its exact lineaments are elusive[1]. Torture simpliciter is not a crime within the jurisdiction of any international tribunal but, in the appropriate contexts, it may be prosecuted as a crime against humanity or as a war crime[2].

The United Kingdom is a party to the UN Convention against Torture and other Cruel, Inhuman or Degrading Treatment or Punishment 1984[3], and has implemented that Convention in domestic law[4]. For these purposes torture is defined as severe pain or suffering inflicted on another by or at the instigation of or with the consent or acquiescence of a public official or a person acting in an official capacity[5]. Torture in this sense was not a crime in English law until the implementing statute came into force and it is possible that the extraterritorial jurisdiction provisions may be limited to United Kingdom nationals and nationals of states party to the Convention[6].

It is a defence for a person charged with the offence of torture in the United Kingdom to prove that he had lawful authority, justification or excuse[7]. The Convention contains an aut judicare aut derere obligation[8]. There is a specific non-refoulement obligation with respect to those accused of torture who themselves face a risk of torture if returned to a particular jurisdiction[9]. Torture being an offence which may be committed only by officials or under the direction of officials is an offence for which immunity ratione materiae may not be claimed in English law[10], although immunity ratio personae may be[11].

1   *R v Bow Street Metropolitan Stipendiary Magistrate, ex p Pinochet Ugarte (No 3)* [2000] 1 AC 147 at 198, sub nom *R v Bow Street Metropolitan Stipendiary Magistrate, ex p Pinochet Ugarte (Amnesty International intervening) (No 3)* [1999] 2 All ER 97 at 108, HL per Lord Browne-Wilkinson: 'I have no doubt that long before the Torture Convention of 1984, torture was an international crime in the highest sense'. In *A v Secretary of State for the Home Department (No 2)* [2005] UKHL 71, [2006] 2 AC 221, [2006] 1 All ER 575 it was held that torture was prohibited at common law but there is no crime of that name and no extraterritorial jurisdiction over crimes, such as grievous bodily harm, which might cover conduct otherwise understood to be torture.

2   See eg the Rome Statute of the International Criminal Court (17.7.98) (UN Doc A/CONF 183/9; 37 ILM (1998) 999, arts 7(1)(f) (crimes against humanity; see PARA 430), 8(2)(a)(ii), 8(2)(c)(i) (war crimes; see PARA 431).

3   Ie the Convention against Torture and other Cruel, Inhuman or Degrading Treatment or Punishment (New York, 4 February 1985; Misc 12 (1985); Cmnd 9593) (the 'Torture Convention'). There is an optional protocol to the Convention (to which the UK is not a party) which gives jurisdiction to the Committee on Torture established under the Convention to hear individual applications: see UN General Assembly Resolution 57/199 of 18 December 2002. See generally Nowak and McArthur *The United Nations Convention against Torture: a Commentary* (2008).

4   Ie under the Criminal Justice Act 1988 ss 134–138: see CRIMINAL LAW, EVIDENCE AND PROCEDURE vol 11(1) (2006 Reissue) PARA 160. The Convention is concerned with more than the criminalisation and prosecution of torture but the UK has given effect to the criminalisation provisions of the Convention.

5   See the Torture Convention art 1(1); Criminal Justice Act 1988 s 134(1); and CRIMINAL LAW, EVIDENCE AND PROCEDURE vol 11(1) (2006 Reissue) PARA 160.

6   The UK government has made torture an offence of universal jurisdiction: see the Criminal Justice Act 1988 s 134; and CRIMINAL LAW, EVIDENCE AND PROCEDURE vol 11(1) (2006 Reissue) PARA 160. See also *R v Zardad* [2007] EWCA Crim 279, [2007] All ER (D) 90 (Feb) (conviction of an Afghan national for acts of torture and hostage-taking in Afghanistan). The Torture Convention itself requires only that states must take jurisdiction over acts within their territory and acts of its nationals and allows jurisdiction where a national of the state has been a victim of torture abroad: see art 5(1).

7   See the Torture Convention art 1(1); the Criminal Justice Act 1988 s 134(5); and CRIMINAL LAW, EVIDENCE AND PROCEDURE vol 11(1) (2006 Reissue) PARA 160. Note also the Secretary of State's power to authorise acts of intelligence officers outside the UK which would otherwise be offences in UK law: see the Intelligence Services Act 1994 s 7(1); and CONSTITUTIONAL LAW AND HUMAN RIGHTS vol 8(2) (Reissue) PARA 474.

8   States are required to prosecute or extradite torturers in their custody: see the Torture Convention art 5. In order that the UK has the option to prosecute or to satisfy double criminality requirements for extradition in all cases, it is necessary that torture be a crime of universal jurisdiction in UK law: see the text and note 6.

9   See the Torture Convention art 3. This obligation overlaps with the obligation under the European Convention for the Protection of Human Rights and Fundamental Freedoms (1950) (Rome, 4 November 1950; TS 71 (1953); Cmd 8969; ETS no 5) art 3: see CONSTITUTIONAL LAW AND HUMAN RIGHTS vol 8(2) (Reissue) PARA 124.

10 *R v Bow Street Metropolitan Stipendiary Magistrate, ex p Pinochet Ugarte (No 3)* [2000] 1 AC 147, sub nom *R v Bow Street Metropolitan Stipendiary Magistrate, ex p Pinochet Ugarte (Amnesty International intervening) (No 3)* [1999] 2 All ER 97, HL.

11 A serving head of state was granted immunity ratione personae against the issue of an arrest warrant on an accusation of torture: see *Re Mugabe* (7 January 2004, unreported), Bow Street Magistrates' Court, judgment reproduced in Warbrick 'Immunity and International Crimes in English Law' (2004) 53 ICLQ 769.

434.   Slavery.   Slavery and the slave trade are probably crimes under customary international law, although their exact identification is difficult and any definition narrow compared with the widespread manifestations of exploitation which fall short of slavery and which are covered by the term 'servitude'[1]. The obligation on a state not to engage in or make possible slavery is an obligation erga omnes[2], and there is no specific treaty obligation which requires states to make slavery a crime or which specifically acknowledges the international criminality of slavery.

Slavery is prohibited by human rights treaties and the forbidden practices are extended to cover servitude and, with certain qualifications, forced or compulsory labour[3]. The European Convention on Human Rights contains an implied positive obligation on states to criminalise slavery and servitude but this obligation extends only where the victims are within the territory or the jurisdiction of party states[4].

'Enslavement' may, in the appropriate context, amount to a crime against humanity[5]. As from a day to be appointed 'slavery' is a crime in English law, drawing its definition from international human rights law, although with no extraterritorial extension at all[6].

1 'Slavery' is understood as 'chattel slavery' in which one person exercises rights of property over the person of another. Exploitation without ownership is 'servitude'.

2 See *Barcelona Traction, Light and Power Co Ltd (Belgium v Spain) (Second Phase)* ICJ Reports 1970, 3 at 32; and PARA 11. The rule prohibiting slavery is a rule of ius cogens: see the Articles on Responsibility of States for Internationally Wrongful Acts ('ARSIWA'), Pt 1, Ch V, International Law Commission Report, 53rd Session, A/56/10, YILC 2001, vol II(2) art 26, and the Commentary to Article 26 para (5); and PARA 362.

3 See the International Covenant on Civil and Political Rights (New York, 16 December 1966; ratified by the United Kingdom 20 May 1976; TS 6 (1977): Cmnd 6702) art 8.

4 See the European Convention for the Protection of Human Rights and Fundamental Freedoms (1950) (Rome, 4 November 1950; TS 71 (1953); Cmd 8969; ETS no 5) art 4: and CONSTITUTIONAL LAW AND HUMAN RIGHTS vol 8(2) (Reissue) PARA 125.

5 See the Rome Statute of the International Criminal Court (17.7.98) (UN Doc A/CONF 183/9; 37 ILM (1998) 999, arts 7(1)(c) (crimes against humanity; see PARA 430).

6 See the Coroners and Justice Act 2009 s 71 (not yet in force).

435.   Immunities and international criminal law.   Specifically or by implication, it is established that immunities in international law ratione materiae may not be relied on before international criminal tribunals[1]. Where the tribunal is established by a United Nations Security Council resolution, this applies to all members of the United Nations[2]. Where the tribunal is established by treaty, the non-application of any immunity is limited to officials of parties to the treaty[3].

It remains unresolved whether or not a person entitled to immunity ratione personae would be entitled to benefit from that immunity before an international tribunal. For a Security Council tribunal it seems that the immunity will be inapplicable[4]. For a tribunal based on treaty, the terms of the treaty will determine the question[5]. Where the treaty does not clearly resolve the matter, the implication should be drawn that nationals of parties to the treaty may not rely on the immunity but that nationals of non-parties might do so[6].

Before national courts, two situations arise: a national prosecution or extradition proceedings to another state, and the transfer of the defendant requested by an international tribunal. Generally, in a national trial or extradition proceedings, immunities apply in the ordinary way so that no proceedings would be lawful against those entitled to a personal or material immunity[7]. However, treaty obligations may limit the effect of immunities[8]. It has been argued that material immunity will not protect a person charged with any crime against international law (in the same way as it does not before an international tribunal) but there is no English authority to this effect. Where an international tribunal seeks the transfer of a defendant, there will be no immunity of any kind if the tribunal is established by the Security Council[9]. If the tribunal is established by treaty, the terms of the treaty will determine the matter for parties to the treaty. Persons claiming immunity by reason of a connection with a non-party will be entitled to rely on their immunity[10].

1   For immunities in international law see PARA 242 et seq. See *Prosecutor v Blaskic* Case No IT-95-14-A (judgment, 29 July 2004), ICTY (Appeals Chamber), para 78. Uncertainties arise because of the broad language in *Arrest Warrant of 11 April 2000 (Democratic Republic of the Congo v Belgium)* ICJ Reports 2002, 3 at 23, 25 (paras 56, 61).

2   As to the primacy of the Charter of the United Nations see the Charter of the United Nations (San Francisco 25 June 1945; TS 67 (Cmd 7015) art 103; and PARA 10. In the event of a conflict between the obligations of members of the United Nations under the present Charter and their obligations under any other international agreement, the present Charter prevails: see PARA 10.

3   Rome Statute of the International Criminal Court (17.7.98) (UN Doc A/CONF 183/9; 37 ILM (1998) 999) art 98(1).

4   See the Charter of the United Nations art 103; and PARA 10. See also *Prosecutor v Milosevic (Decision on Preliminary Motions)* Case No IT-99-37-PT (8 November 2001) ICTY. See also note 9.

5   See eg the Rome Statute of the International Criminal Court (17.7.98) (UN Doc A/CONF 183/9; 37 ILM (1998) 999) art 27(2).

6   But for the contrary conclusion see *Prosecutor v Charles Taylor (Decision on Immunity from Jurisdiction)* SCSL-2003-01-I-059, Special Court of Sierra Leone (Appeals Chamber).

7   *R v Bow Street Metropolitan Stipendiary Magistrate, ex p Pinochet Ugarte (No 3) (Amnesty International intervening)* [2000] 1 AC 147, [1999] 2 All ER 97, [1999] 2 WLR 827 per Lord Millett; and see (dealing with Mugabe as a serving President, and Mofaz, as a serving Defence Minister), Warbrick 'Immunity and International Crimes in English Law' (2004) 53 ICLQ 769.

8   *R v Bow Street Metropolitan Stipendiary Magistrate, ex p Pinochet Ugarte (No 3) (Amnesty International intervening)* [2000] 1 AC 147, [1999] 2 All ER 97, [1999] 2 WLR 827 (the judgments rely on the International Convention against Torture and other Cruel, Inhuman or Degrading Treatment or Punishment 1984 to find that there was no immunity ratione materiae for an ex-Head of State, such that the denial of immunity applied only to conduct after the Convention was in force for the states involved).

9   *Prosecutor v Milosevic (Decision on Preliminary Motions)* Case No IT-99-37-PT (8 November 2001) ICTY; *Prosecutor v Kambanda* Case No ICTR-97-23-S (judgment, 4 September 1998).

10   See eg the International Criminal Court Act 2001 s 23; and PARA 446. See also International Criminal Court (Darfur) Order, SI 699/2009, precluding any state or diplomatic immunity from preventing proceedings under the International Criminal Court 2001 arising as a result of the reference to the ICC by the Security Council of the situation in Darfur by Security Council Resolution 1593 of 31 March 2005.

436.   Co-operation.   States have different co-operation obligations towards other states, and towards international tribunals.

Co-operation with other states may involve the extradition of persons for trial in another state or various forms of mutual assistance. Prima facie, the United Kingdom will rely on its ordinary extradition processes to secure the return of a person wanted by another state to face charges of having committed crimes against international law[1]. Crimes within the jurisdiction of the International Criminal Court (the 'ICC') are on the European Framework List for the purposes of extradition in the United Kingdom[2], and the double criminality rule does not apply for requests for international offences[3]. Crimes against international law are extradition crimes[4]. Where there is no extradition treaty or arrangement between the United Kingdom and the requesting state, the government may agree special extradition arrangements with that state[5]. The ordinary bars to extradition[6] apply to requests for international crimes[7]. The defendant will be able to resist extradition if he can show that his removal would give rise to substantial evidence of a real risk of a violation of a fundamental right under the European Convention on Human Rights[8].

Co-operation with international tribunals depends upon the legal basis for the creation of the tribunal and the particulars of the instruments establishing each tribunal, which may include specific provisions of a tribunal's rules as well as its constitutive instrument. Discharge of obligations of co-operation with international tribunals requires legislation, and regulations have been made to ensure co-operation with the international tribunals in the former Yugoslavia ('ICTY') and Rwanda ('ICTR')[9]. Established under the United Nations Charter, the powers of these tribunals take priority over any other international obligations of the members of the United Nations and apply to all members of the United Nations[10]. While not disallowing proceedings in national courts against defendants on charges which fall within their jurisdiction these tribunals have 'primacy' over domestic proceedings, which means that the tribunal may require that national proceedings be terminated and the defendant transferred[11].

Co-operation with the International Criminal Court (the 'ICC') is governed by the terms of its statute[12] and the necessary powers are conferred by the International Criminal Court Act 2001[13]. The obligations of parties to the statute are less peremptory than those under the statutes of the tribunals for Yugoslavia and Rwanda, and the ICC operates under the principle of 'complementarity', which is to say that a case will be inadmissible before the ICC unless it can be shown that a state is unable or unwilling to proceed with an investigation and prosecution[14].

The United Kingdom has additionally accepted obligation with regard to the Special Court for Sierra Leone[15].

1　See generally EXTRADITION.

2　See the Extradition Act 2003 Sch 2.

3　See the Extradition Act 2003 s 196; and EXTRADITION vol 17(2) (Reissue) PARA 1163.

4　For the purposes of category 2 territories: see the Extradition Act 2003 s 137(5), (6); and EXTRADITION vol 17(2) (Reissue) PARA 1451. As to the meaning of 'category 2 territory' see EXTRADITION vol 17(2) (Reissue) PARA 1447.

5　See the Extradition Act 2003 s 194; and EXTRADITION vol 17(2) (Reissue) PARA 1163. As to the memorandum of understanding with Rwanda for the return of defendants to face genocide charges see *Brown v Government of Rwanda* [2009] EWHC 770 (Admin), [2009] All ER (D) 98 (Apr), at [4].

6　Ie in the Extradition Act 2003 ss 11–21, 79–87; see EXTRADITION.

7　See the Extradition Act 2003 s 11; and EXTRADITION vol 17(2) (Reissue) PARA 1412.

8　See *Soering v United Kingdom* (1989) 11 EHRR 439 at para 88; and *Brown v Government of Rwanda* [2009] EWHC 770 (Admin), [2009] All ER (D) 98 (Apr), at [119]–[121] (where the principle was confirmed even in the face of requests for persons to face charges of genocide). The European Convention on Human Rights means the Convention for the Protection of Human Rights and Fundamental Freedoms (1950) (Rome, 4 November 1950; TS 71 (1953); Cmd 8969; ETS no 5): see CONSTITUTIONAL LAW AND HUMAN RIGHTS vol 8(2) (Reissue) PARA 122.

9	See the United Nations (International Tribunal) (Former Yugoslavia) Order 1996, SI 1996/716; the United Nations (International Tribunal) (Rwanda) Order 1996, SI 1996/1296; and EXTRADITION vol 17(2) (Reissue) PARA 1163. See also the International Criminal Court Act 2001 s 77.

10	Ie established under Chapter VII of the Charter of the United Nations: see the Statute of the ICTY, preamble; and the Statute of the ICTR, preamble. As to the Charter see PARA 10.

11	As to ICTY see the Statute of the International Tribunal for the Prosecution of Persons Responsible for Serious Violations of International Humanitarian Law Committed in the Territory of the Former Yugoslavia since 1991, UN Doc S/25704 at 36, annex (1993) and S/25704/Add.1 (1993), adopted by Security Council on 25 May 1993, UN Doc S/RES/827 (1993) art 9(2); and the United Nations (International Tribunal) (Former Yugoslavia) Order 1996, SI 1996/716, art 14. As to ICTR see Statute of the International Criminal Tribunal for the Prosecution of Persons Responsible for Genocide and Other Serious Violations of International Humanitarian Law Committed in the Territory of Rwanda and Rwandan Citizens Responsible for Genocide and Other Such Violations Committed in the Territory of Neighbouring States, between 1 January 1994 and 31 December 1994, adopted by the Security Council on 8 November 1994, UN Doc S/RES/955 (1994) art 8(2); and United Nations (International Tribunal) (Rwanda) Order 1996, SI 1996/1296, art 14. Tharcisse Muvunyi, the only person wanted by either Tribunal who was found within the United Kingdom, agreed to his transfer to the Rwanda Tribunal: see generally *Prosecutor v Muvunyi* Case No ICTR-2000-55.

12	See the Rome Statute of the International Criminal Court (17.7.98) (UN Doc A/CONF 183/9; 37 ILM (1998) 999), Pt 9: International Cooperation and Judicial Assistance; and art 59.

13	See the International Criminal Court Act 2001, Pts 2, 3 and 4; and PARA 437 et seq.

14	The ICC determines that a case is inadmissible where: (1) the case is being investigated or prosecuted by a state which has jurisdiction over it, unless the state is unwilling or unable genuinely to carry out the investigation or prosecution; (2) the case has been investigated by a state which has jurisdiction over it and the state has decided not to prosecute the person concerned, unless the decision resulted from the unwillingness or inability of the state genuinely to prosecute; (3) the person concerned has already been tried for conduct which is the subject of the complaint, and a trial by the ICC is not permitted; (4) the case is not of sufficient gravity to justify further action by the ICC: Statute of the ICC art 17(1). In order to determine unwillingness in a particular case, the ICC must consider, having regard to the principles of due process recognised by international law, whether one or more of the following exist, as applicable: (a) the proceedings were or are being undertaken or the national decision was made for the purpose of shielding the person concerned from criminal responsibility for crimes within the jurisdiction of the court; (b) there has been an unjustified delay in the proceedings which in the circumstances is inconsistent with an intent to bring the person concerned to justice; (c) the proceedings were not or are not being conducted independently or impartially, and they were or are being conducted in a manner which, in the circumstances, is inconsistent with an intent to bring the person concerned to justice: art 17(2).

	In order to determine inability in a particular case, the court must consider whether, due to a total or substantial collapse or unavailability of its national judicial system, the state is unable to obtain the accused or the necessary evidence and testimony or otherwise unable to carry out its proceedings: art 17(3).

	The International Criminal Court Act 2001 adopts the definition of the offences for the purposes of national law in the same terms as the statute, takes the same jurisdictional basis as apply to the ICC and has modified the general part of English criminal law where it differs significantly to bring it into line with the provisions of the ICC Statute (see PARA 437 et seq). Investigations and prosecutions under national law should, therefore, satisfy the Statute of the ICC's standard of complementarity and allow the pre-emption of cases with a UK element from being admissible before the ICC.

15	Her Majesty may by Order in Council make in relation to the Special Court for Sierra Leone provision having effect in England and Wales, and corresponding to that made in relation to the ICC by the International Criminal Court Act 2001 ss 42–48 (see PARA 450 et seq) (enforcement of sentences of imprisonment), with any necessary modifications: the International Criminal Court Act 2001 s 77A(1) (added by the International Tribunals (Sierra Leone) Act 2007 s 1. The International Tribunals (Sierra Leone) (Application of Provisions) Order 2007, SI 2007/2140, have been so made. The United Kingdom government's obligation is, in particular, to take into custody Charles Taylor, the ex-President of Liberia, if he be convicted by the Special Court for Sierra Leone.

(2) CO-OPERATION WITH THE INTERNATIONAL CRIMINAL COURT

(i) Introduction

437. The International Criminal Court. The International Criminal Court (the 'ICC') has international jurisdiction over persons with respect to: (1) genocide; (2) crimes against humanity; (3) war crimes; and (4) crimes of aggression[1]. The court's proceedings are governed by the ICC Statute, which has been given effect in the United Kingdom[2].

1 See the Rome Statute of the International Criminal Court (17.7.98) (UN Doc A/CONF 183/9; 37 ILM (1998), 999) (the 'ICC Statute') art 5(1). See also EXTRADITION vol 17(2) (Reissue) PARA 1164.
2 The International Criminal Court Act 2001 gives effect to the ICC Statute, as to which see PARA 437 et seq. As to the International Criminal Court Act 2001 see PARAS 438–458. See also WAR AND ARMED CONFLICT vol 49(1) (2005 Reissue) PARA 463. As to the meaning of 'United Kingdom' see PARA 30 note 3.
     By virtue of the International Criminal Court Act 2001 Sch 1 para 1 (amended by the International Organisations Act 2005 ss 6, 9, Schedule) and the International Criminal Court (Immunities and Privileges) (No 1) Order 2006, SI 2006/1907, the legal capacities of a body corporate are conferred on the International Criminal Court, and privileges and immunities are conferred on its judges, the prosecutor, the deputy prosecutors, the registrar, the deputy registrar, the staff of the office of the prosecutor, the staff of the registry, counsel, experts, witnesses and certain other persons.
     Provision is made for the International Criminal Court Act 2001 to be extended to any of the Channel Islands, the Isle of Man or any colony: see s 79(3). Certain provisions have been extended, with modifications, to the Isle of Man: see the International Criminal Court Act 2001 (Isle of Man) Order 2004, SI 2004/714. Certain provisions have been extended, with adaptations and modifications, to the following overseas territories: Anguilla; Bermuda; Cayman Islands; Falkland Islands; Montserrat; Pitcairn, Henderson, Ducie and Oeno Islands; St Helena and its Dependencies; Sovereign Base Areas of Akrotiri and Dhekelia; Turks and Caicos Islands; Virgin Islands: see the International Criminal Court Act 2001 (Overseas Territories) Order 2009, SI 2009/1738.

(ii) Arrest and Surrender of Persons

438. Procedure on request for arrest and delivery up. Where the Secretary of State[1] receives a request from the International Criminal Court (the 'ICC')[2] for the arrest and surrender of a person alleged to have committed an ICC crime[3], or to have been convicted by the ICC, he must transmit the request and the documents accompanying it to an appropriate judicial officer[4]. If the request is accompanied by a warrant of arrest and the appropriate judicial officer is satisfied that the warrant appears to have been issued by the ICC[5], he must indorse the warrant for execution in the United Kingdom[6]. If in the case of a person convicted by the ICC the request is not accompanied by a warrant of arrest, but is accompanied by: (1) a copy of the judgment of conviction; (2) information to demonstrate that the person sought is the one referred to in the judgment of conviction; and (3) where the person sought has been sentenced, a copy of the sentence imposed and a statement of any time already served and the time remaining to be served, the officer must issue a warrant for the arrest of the person to whom the request relates[7]. A person arrested under such a warrant must be brought before a competent court[8] as soon as is practicable[9].

Where the Secretary of State receives from the ICC a request for the provisional arrest of a person alleged to have committed an ICC crime or to have been convicted by the ICC and it appears to the Secretary of State that application for a provisional warrant should be made, he must transmit the request to a constable and direct the constable to apply for a provisional warrant for the arrest of that person; and, on an application by a constable stating on oath that he has reason to believe that a request has been made on grounds of urgency by the ICC for the arrest of a person and that the person is in, or on his way to, the United Kingdom, an appropriate judicial officer must issue a provisional warrant for the arrest of that person[10]. On issuing a provisional warrant the appropriate judicial officer must notify the Secretary of State that he has done so[11].

A person arrested under a provisional warrant must be brought before a competent court as soon as is practicable[12]. If a warrant[13] is produced to the court in respect of that person, the court must proceed as if he had been arrested under that warrant[14]. If no such warrant is produced, the court must remand him pending the production of such a warrant[15]. If at any time when the person is so remanded there is produced to the court a warrant in respect of him, the court must terminate the period of remand[16]; and he is to be treated as if arrested under that warrant, if he was remanded in custody, at the time the warrant was produced to the court, or, if he was remanded on bail, when he surrenders to his bail[17]. If no such warrant is produced to the court before the end of the period of the remand, including any extension of that period, the court must discharge him[18].

Where the ICC informs the Secretary of State that a person arrested[19] is no longer required to be surrendered, the Secretary of State must notify an appropriate judicial officer of that fact; and that officer must, on receipt of the notification, make an order for that person's discharge[20].

1   As to the Secretary of State see PARA 29.

2   As to the International Criminal Court see PARA 437.

3   'ICC crime' means a crime (other than the crime of aggression) over which the ICC has jurisdiction in accordance with the Rome Statute of the International Criminal Court (17.7.98) (UN Doc A/CONF 183/9; 37 ILM (1998), 999) (the 'ICC Statute'): International Criminal Court Act 2001 s 1(1). As to the ICC Statute see PARA 422 et seq.

4   International Criminal Court Act 2001 s 2(1). 'Appropriate judicial officer' means a district judge (magistrates' courts) designated for the purposes of the International Criminal Court Act 2001 by the Lord Chief Justice after consulting the Lord Chancellor: s 26(1) (amended by the Courts Act 2003 Sch 8 para 404, Sch 10; and the Constitutional Reform Act 2005 Sch 4 Pt 1 para 299). The Lord Chief Justice may nominate a judicial office holder (as defined in the Constitutional Reform Act 2005 s 109(4)) to exercise his functions under the International Criminal Court Act 2001 s 26: s 26(2) (added by the Constitutional Reform Act 2005 Sch 4 Pt 1 para 299).

5   As to proof of orders, judgments, warrants or requests of the ICC see the International Criminal Court Act 2001 Sch 1 para 5.

6   International Criminal Court Act 2001 s 2(3). For the purposes of any enactment or rule of law relating to warrants of arrest, a 'section 2 warrant' indorsed or issued in any part of the United Kingdom, or a provisional warrant issued in any part of the United Kingdom, must be treated as if it were a warrant for the arrest of a person for an offence committed in that part of the United Kingdom: s 14(1). Any such warrant may be executed in any part of the United Kingdom, and may be so executed by any person to whom it is directed or by any constable: s 14(2). A person arrested under any such warrant is to be deemed to continue in legal custody until he is brought before a competent court: s 14(3). A 'section 2 warrant' is a warrant indorsed or issued under the International Criminal Court Act 2001 s 2 (see the text and notes 4–6): s 2(5). As to the meaning of 'United Kingdom' see PARA 30 note 3.

    The copy of a warrant issued by the ICC that is transmitted to the Secretary of State is to be treated as if it were the original warrant (see s 25(1)), and faxed documents are to be treated as if they were the originals and may accordingly be received in evidence (see s 25(2)). Where the

ICC amends a warrant of arrest, the provisions of Pt 2 (ss 2–26) apply to the amended warrant as if it were a new warrant although this does not affect the validity of anything done in reliance on the old warrant: s 25(3).

7 International Criminal Court Act 2001 s 2(4).

8 'Competent court' means a court consisting of an appropriate judicial officer: International Criminal Court Act 2001 s 26(1).

9 International Criminal Court Act 2001 s 5(1). As to proceedings for a delivery order under s 5 see PARA 439.

10 International Criminal Court Act 2001 s 3(1), (2). For the purposes of Pt 2, a warrant issued under s 3 is referred to as a 'provisional warrant': s 3(5).

11 International Criminal Court Act 2001 s 3(4).

12 International Criminal Court Act 2001 s 4(1).

13 Ie a 'section 2 warrant'.

14 International Criminal Court Act 2001 s 4(2).

15 International Criminal Court Act 2001 s 4(3). A person may be remanded at any time pending the production of a 'section 2 warrant' in respect of him for a period of 18 days; and the total period for which a person may be so remanded is 60 days: see the International Criminal Court Act 2001 s 4(4); and the International Criminal Court (Remand Time) Order 2008, SI 2008/3135.

16 International Criminal Court Act 2001 s 4(5)(a).

17 International Criminal Court Act 2001 s 4(5)(b).

18 International Criminal Court Act 2001 s 4(6). The fact that a person has been discharged under s 4 does not prevent his subsequent arrest under a 'section 2 warrant': s 4(7).

19 Ie under the International Criminal Court Act 2001 Pt 2.

20 International Criminal Court Act 2001 s 20(1).

439. Delivery order. If, in relation to a person arrested under a warrant[1] and brought before a competent court[2], the court is satisfied that the warrant is a warrant of the International Criminal Court (the 'ICC')[3] and has been duly indorsed[4], or has been duly issued[5], and that the person brought before the court is the person named or described in the warrant, the court must make a delivery order[6]. In the case of a person alleged to have committed an ICC crime[7], the competent court may adjourn the proceedings pending the outcome of any challenge before the ICC to the admissibility of the case or to the jurisdiction of the ICC[8].

In deciding whether to make a delivery order the court is not concerned to inquire whether any warrant issued by the ICC was duly issued, or, in the case of a person alleged to have committed an ICC crime, whether there is evidence to justify his trial for the offence he is alleged to have committed[9]. Whether or not it makes a delivery order, the competent court may of its own motion, and must on the application of the person arrested, determine whether that person was lawfully arrested in pursuance of the warrant, and whether his rights have been respected[10]. If the court determines that the person has not been lawfully arrested in pursuance of the warrant, or that the person's rights have not been respected, it must make a declaration to that effect, but may not grant any other relief[11].

The court has the like powers, as nearly as may be, including power to adjourn the case and meanwhile to remand the person whose surrender is sought, as if the proceedings were the summary trial of an information against that person[12]. If the court adjourns the proceedings, it must on doing so remand the person whose surrender is sought[13].

Where a competent court makes a delivery order in respect of a person, the court must: (1) commit the person to custody or on bail to await the Secretary of State's directions as to the execution of the order[14]; (2) inform the person of his rights to a review of the delivery order[15] in ordinary terms and in a language which appears to the court to be one which he fully understands and speaks[16]; and (3) notify the Secretary of State of its decision[17].

A delivery order is sufficient authority for any person acting in accordance with the directions of the Secretary of State to receive the person to whom the order relates, keep him in custody and convey him to the place where he is to be delivered up into the custody of the ICC or, as the case may be, the state of enforcement, in accordance with arrangements made by the Secretary of State[18]. A person in respect of whom a delivery order is in force is deemed to be in legal custody at any time when, being in the United Kingdom or on board a British ship[19], a British aircraft[20] or a British hovercraft[21], he is being taken under the order to or from any place or is being kept in custody pending his delivery up under the order[22]. If a person in respect of whom a delivery order is in force escapes or is unlawfully at large, he may be arrested without warrant by a constable and taken to any place where or to which he is required to be or to be taken[23].

If the person in respect of whom a delivery order has been made is not delivered up under the order within 40 days after it was made, an application may be made, by him or on his behalf, for his discharge[24]. On such an application, the court must order the person's discharge unless reasonable cause is shown for the delay[25].

1 Ie under a 'section 2 warrant': see PARA 438. As to the meaning of 'section 2 warrant' see PARA 438 note 6.
2 As to the meaning of 'competent court' see PARA 438 note 8.
3 As to the International Criminal Court see PARA 437.
4 Ie under the International Criminal Court Act 2001 s 2(3): see PARA 438.
5 Ie under the international Criminal Court Act 2001 s 2(4): see PARA 438.
6 See the International Criminal Court Act 2001 s 5(1), (2). A 'delivery order' is an order that the person be delivered up into the custody of the ICC or, if the ICC so directs in the case of a person convicted by the ICC, into the custody of the state of enforcement, in accordance with arrangements made by the Secretary of State: s 5(3). As to the Secretary of State see PARA 29.
   As to the procedure where the court refuses to make a delivery order see s 8; and PARA 442.
7 As to the meaning of 'ICC crime' see PARA 438 note 3.
8 International Criminal Court Act 2001 s 5(4).
9 International Criminal Court Act 2001 s 5(5).
10 International Criminal Court Act 2001 s 5(6). In making such a determination the court must apply the principles which would be applied on an application for judicial review: s 5(7). As to judicial review see JUDICIAL REVIEW.
11 International Criminal Court Act 2001 s 5(8). The court must notify the Secretary of State of any such declaration and the Secretary of State must transmit that notification to the ICC: s 5(9).
12 International Criminal Court Act 2001 s 6(1), (2)(a). The proceedings are criminal proceedings for the purposes of the Access to Justice Act 1999 Pt I (ss 1–26) (advice, assistance and representation: see LEGAL AID): International Criminal Court Act 2001 s 6(1), (2)(c). The Prosecution of Offences Act 1985 s 16(1)(c) (defence costs on dismissal of proceedings: see CRIMINAL LAW, EVIDENCE AND PROCEDURE vol 11(4) (2006 Reissue) PARA 2059) applies, reading the reference to the dismissal of the information as a reference to the discharge of the person arrested: International Criminal Court Act 2001 s 6(1), (2)(d).
13 International Criminal Court Act 2001 s 6(1), (2)(b).
14 International Criminal Court Act 2001 s 11(1)(a). The person must be committed to prison or to the custody of a constable: s 11(2). A court which commits a person to custody under this provision may subsequently grant bail: s 11(3).
15 Ie under the International Criminal Court Act 2001 s 12: see PARA 443.
16 International Criminal Court Act 2001 s 11(1)(b).
17 International Criminal Court Act 2001 s 11(1)(c).
18 International Criminal Court Act 2001 s 15(1). A person authorised for the purposes of a delivery order to take the person to whom the order relates to or from any place, or to keep him in custody, has all the powers, authority, protection and privileges: (1) if he is in the United Kingdom, of a constable in that part of the United Kingdom; or (2) if he is outside the United Kingdom, of a constable in the part of the United Kingdom to or from which the other person is to be taken: s 15(3). As to the meaning of 'United Kingdom' see PARA 30 note 3.

19 'British ship' means a British ship within the meaning of the Merchant Shipping Act 1995 (see SHIPPING AND MARITIME LAW vol 93 (2008) PARA 230) or one of Her Majesty's ships: International Criminal Court Act 2001 s 76(1). References in s 76(1) to Her Majesty's aircraft, hovercraft or ships are to the aircraft, hovercraft or, as the case may be, ships which belong to, or are exclusively employed in the service of, Her Majesty in right of the government of the United Kingdom: s 76(2).

20 'British aircraft' means a British-controlled aircraft within the meaning of the Civil Aviation Act 1982 s 92 (application of criminal law to aircraft: see AIR LAW vol 2 (2008) PARA 619), or one of Her Majesty's aircraft: International Criminal Court Act 2001 s 76(1). See note 19.

21 'British hovercraft' means a British-controlled hovercraft within the meaning of the Civil Aviation Act 1982 s 92 as applied in relation to hovercraft by virtue of provision made under the Hovercraft Act 1968, or one of Her Majesty's hovercraft: International Criminal Court Act 2001 s 76(1). See note 19.

22 International Criminal Court Act 2001 s 15(2).

23 International Criminal Court Act 2001 s 15(4). 'Constable', for these purposes, means a person who is a constable in any part of the United Kingdom, and, in relation to any place, a person who, at that place, has, under any enactment (including s 15(3): see note 18), the powers of a constable in any part of the United Kingdom: s 15(5).

24 International Criminal Court Act 2001 s 19(1). The application must be made to the High Court: s 19(2).

25 International Criminal Court Act 2001 s 19(3).

440. Consent to surrender. A person arrested following a request from the International Criminal Court (the 'ICC')[1] may consent to being delivered up into the custody of the ICC or, in the case of a person convicted by the ICC, of the state of enforcement[2]. Such a consent is referred to as a 'consent to surrender'[3].

Consent to surrender may be given by the person himself or, in circumstances in which it is inappropriate for the person to act for himself by reason of his physical or mental condition or his youth, by an appropriate person acting on his behalf[4]. Consent to surrender must be given in writing in the prescribed form[5] or a form to the like effect[6], and must be signed in the presence of a justice of the peace[7].

Where consent to surrender has been given: (1) a competent court[8] before which the person is brought must forthwith make a delivery order[9]; and (2) the person is taken to have waived his rights to a review of the delivery order[10]. Notice that consent to surrender has been given must be given: (a) if the person is in custody, to the prison governor, constable or other person in whose custody he is[11]; or (b) if the person is on bail, to the officer in charge of the police station at which he is required to surrender to custody[12].

1 Ie a person arrested under the International Criminal Court Act 2001 Pt 2 (ss 2–26). As to the power of arrest see PARA 438. As to the International Criminal Court see PARA 437.

2 International Criminal Court Act 2001 s 7(1).

3 International Criminal Court Act 2001 s 7(1).

4 International Criminal Court Act 2001 s 7(2).

5 'Prescribed form' means that prescribed by Criminal Procedure Rules: International Criminal Court Act 2001 s 7(3) (amended by the Courts Act 2003 Sch 8 para 403). As to the Criminal Procedure Rules see CRIMINAL LAW, EVIDENCE AND PROCEDURE.

6 International Criminal Court Act 2001 s 7(3)(a).

7 International Criminal Court Act 2001 s 7(3)(b).

8 As to the meaning of 'competent court' see PARA 438 note 8.

9 International Criminal Court Act 2001 s 7(4)(a). As to the meaning of 'delivery order' see PARA 439 note 6; and as to delivery orders generally see PARA 439.

10 International Criminal Court Act 2001 s 7(4)(b). As to the right to review of a delivery order see s 12; and PARA 443.

11 International Criminal Court Act 2001 s 7(5)(a).

12 International Criminal Court Act 2001 s 7(5)(b). For the purposes of s 7(5)(b), notice is to be treated as given if it is sent by registered post, or recorded delivery, addressed to the officer mentioned: s 7(6).

441.   Delivery up of a person subject to other proceedings. Provision is made for cases where the Secretary of State[1] receives a request from the International Criminal Court (the 'ICC')[2] for the arrest and surrender, or provisional arrest, of a person: (1) against whom criminal proceedings are pending or in progress before a national court[3], or who has been dealt with in such proceedings; (2) against whom extradition proceedings are pending or in progress in the United Kingdom, or in respect of whom a warrant or order has been made in such proceedings; or (3) against whom proceedings are pending or in progress in the United Kingdom for a delivery order[4], or against whom a delivery order has been made in such proceedings[5].

Where the Secretary of State receives a request from the ICC for the arrest and surrender, or provisional arrest, of a person, and criminal proceedings[6] against that person are pending or in progress before a court in England and Wales, the Secretary of State must inform the court of the request[7]. The court must, if necessary, adjourn the proceedings before it, for such period or periods as it thinks fit, so as to enable proceedings to be taken to determine whether a delivery order should be made[8]. If a delivery order is made and the criminal proceedings are still pending or in progress, the Secretary of State must consult the ICC before giving directions for the execution of the order, and may direct that the criminal proceedings are to be discontinued[9]. Where the Secretary of State directs that criminal proceedings are to be discontinued, the court before which the proceedings are pending or in progress must order their discontinuance, and make any other order necessary to enable the delivery order to be executed, including any necessary order as to the custody of the person concerned[10]. The discontinuance under these provisions of criminal proceedings in respect of an offence does not prevent the institution of fresh proceedings in respect of the offence[11]. Corresponding provision is made in relation to proceedings before a service court[12] and in relation to extradition proceedings[13], and similar provision is also made to deal with the situation where other delivery proceedings are pending or in progress[14].

Where a person who is a prisoner[15] is delivered up into the custody of the ICC, or into the custody of a state where he is to undergo imprisonment under a sentence of the ICC, he continues to be liable to complete any term of imprisonment or detention to which he had been sentenced by a national court[16], but any time during which he is in the custody of the ICC or of another state is to be counted towards the completion of that term[17]. Where a court orders the discharge of a person who is a prisoner, the discharge is without prejudice to the liability of the prisoner to complete any term of imprisonment or detention to which he has been sentenced by a national court[18]; accordingly, a prisoner to whom such an order relates and whose sentence has not expired must be transferred in custody to the place where he is liable to be detained under the sentence to which he is subject[19]. Where a delivery order is made in respect of a person who is a prisoner, the order may include provision: (a) authorising the return of the prisoner into the custody of the Secretary of State in accordance with arrangements made by the Secretary of State with the ICC or, in the case of a prisoner taken to a place where he is to undergo imprisonment under a sentence of the ICC, in accordance with arrangements made by the Secretary of State with the state where that place is situated; and (b) for his transfer in custody to the place where he is liable to be detained under the sentence of the national court to which he is subject[20].

1   As to the Secretary of State see PARA 29.

2   As to the International Criminal Court see PARA 437.

3   'National court' means a court in the United Kingdom or a service court; and 'service court' means the Court Martial, the Service Civilian Court, the Court Martial Appeal Court, or the Supreme Court on an appeal brought from the Court Martial Appeal Court: International Criminal Court Act 2001 s 75 (amended by the Armed Forces Act 2006 Sch 16 para 190). As to the meaning of 'United Kingdom' see PARA 30 note 3.

4   Ie under the United Nations (International Tribunal) (Former Yugoslavia) Order 1996, SI 1996/716, or the United Nations (International Tribunal) (Rwanda) Order 1996, SI 1996/1296. As to the meaning of 'delivery order' see PARA 439 note 6; and as to delivery orders generally see PARA 439.

5   International Criminal Court Act 2001 s 24.

6   For these purposes, 'criminal proceedings' means proceedings before a national court: (1) for dealing with an individual accused of an offence; (2) for dealing with an individual convicted of an offence; or (3) on an appeal from any such proceedings: International Criminal Court Act 2001 Sch 2 para 1.

7   International Criminal Court Act 2001 Sch 2 para 2(1).

8   International Criminal Court Act 2001 Sch 2 para 2(2). As to the procedure for delivery up of arrested persons see PARA 439.

9   International Criminal Court Act 2001 Sch 2 para 2(3). Where a court makes a delivery order in respect of a person in respect of whom an order (other than a sentence of imprisonment or detention) has been made in criminal proceedings before a national court, the court may make any order necessary to enable the delivery order to be executed, and may in particular suspend or revoke an order: Sch 2 para 6.

10 International Criminal Court Act 2001 Sch 2 para 2(4).

11 International Criminal Court Act 2001 Sch 2 para 2(5).

12 See the International Criminal Court Act 2001 Sch 2 para 4.

13 See the International Criminal Court Act 2001 Sch 2 para 8 (amended by the Extradition Act 2003 Sch 3 paras 1, 13); and the International Criminal Court Act 2001 Sch 2 para 10 (amended by the Extradition Act 2003 Sch 3 paras 1, 13, Sch 4). For these purposes, 'extradition proceedings' means proceedings before a court or judge in the United Kingdom under the Extradition Act 2003: International Criminal Court Act 2001 Sch 2 para 7 (amended by the Extradition Act 2003 Sch 3 paras 1, 13).

14 See the International Criminal Court Act 2001 Sch 2 paras 12, 14. 'Other delivery proceedings' means proceedings before a court in the United Kingdom for a delivery order under the United Nations (International Tribunal) (Former Yugoslavia) Order 1996, SI 1996/716, or the United Nations (International Tribunal) (Rwanda) Order 1996, SI 1996/1296: see the International Criminal Court Act 2001 Sch 2 para 11.

15 For these purposes, 'prisoner' means a person serving a sentence in a prison or other institution to which the Prison Act 1952 applies, or a person serving a sentence of service detention (within the meaning of the Armed Forces Act 2006: see ARMED FORCES) or imprisonment imposed by a service court: International Criminal Court Act 2001 Sch 2 para 5(5) (amended by the Armed Forces Act 2006 Sch 16 para 191).

16 International Criminal Court Act 2001 Sch 2 para 5(1).

17 International Criminal Court Act 2001 Sch 2 para 5(1).

18 International Criminal Court Act 2001 Sch 2 para 5(2).

19 International Criminal Court Act 2001 Sch 2 para 5(2).

20 International Criminal Court Act 2001 Sch 2 para 5(3).

442.   Procedure where court refuses delivery order. If a competent court[1] refuses to make a delivery order[2], it must make an order remanding the person arrested, and notify the Secretary of State[3] of its decision and of the grounds for it[4]. If the court is informed without delay that an appeal is to be brought[5], the order remanding the person arrested continues to have effect[6]. If the court is not so informed, it must discharge the person arrested[7].

If a competent court refuses to make a delivery order, the Secretary of State may appeal against the decision to the High Court[8]. If the High Court allows the appeal it may make a delivery order, or remit the case to the competent court to make a delivery order in accordance with the decision of the High Court[9]. If the High Court dismisses the appeal, the Secretary of State may, with the permission of the High Court or the Supreme Court, appeal to the Supreme Court[10]. The Supreme Court may exercise any of the powers conferred[11] on the High Court[12].

1   As to the meaning of 'competent court' see PARA 438 note 8.

2   As to the meaning of 'delivery order' see PARA 439 note 6; and as to delivery orders generally see PARA 439.

3   As to the Secretary of State see PARA 29.

4   International Criminal Court Act 2001 s 8(1).

5   Ie under the International Criminal Court Act 2001 s 9 (see the text and notes 8–12) or s 10 (appeals in Scotland).

6   International Criminal Court Act 2001 s 8(2). The order ceases to have effect if the High Court dismisses the appeal and the Secretary of State does not without delay apply for permission to appeal to the Supreme Court or inform the High Court that he intends to apply for such permission: s 9(6) (amended by the Constitutional Reform Act 2005 Sch 9 para 75). Subject to that, any such order has effect so long as the case is pending: International Criminal Court Act 2001 s 9(6). For this purpose, a case is pending (unless proceedings are discontinued) until, disregarding any power of a court to allow a step to be taken out of time, there is no step that the Secretary of State can take: s 9(6).

7   International Criminal Court Act 2001 s 8(3).

8   International Criminal Court Act 2001 s 9(1). No permission is required for such an appeal, which must be by way of re-hearing: s 9(1).

9   International Criminal Court Act 2001 s 9(2). Where a delivery order is made by the High Court or by the Supreme Court (see the text and notes 11–12), the provisions of s 11(1)(a), (c), (2), (3) (procedure where court makes a delivery order: see PARA 439) apply in relation to that court as they apply to a competent court which makes a delivery order: s 9(5) (amended by the Constitutional Reform Act 2005 Sch 9 para 75).

10 International Criminal Court Act 2001 s 9(3) (amended by the Constitutional Reform Act 2005 Sch 9 para 75). In relation to a decision of the High Court on an appeal under these provisions, the Administration of Justice Act 1960 s 1 (appeals to the Supreme Court: see COURTS vol 10 (Reissue) PARA 362) applies with the omission of so much of s 1(2) as restricts the grant of leave to appeal: International Criminal Court Act 2001 s 9(3) (as so amended).

11 Ie by the International Criminal Court Act 2001 s 9(2): see the text and note 8.

12 International Criminal Court Act 2001 s 9(4) (amended by the Constitutional Reform Act 2005 Sch 9 para 75). See note 9.

443.   Right to review of delivery order.   The Secretary of State[1] must not give directions for the execution of a delivery order[2] until after the end of the period of 15 days beginning with the date on which the order is made[3]. If before the end of that period an application for habeas corpus[4] is made by the person in respect of whom the delivery order is made, or on his behalf, directions for the execution of the order must not be given while proceedings on the application are still pending[5]. On such an application for habeas corpus, the court must set aside the delivery order and order the person's discharge if it is not satisfied of certain matters[6].

A person in respect of whom a delivery order has been made may waive his right to review of the order[7]. Waiver of the right to review may be made by the person himself or, in circumstances in which it is inappropriate for the person to act for himself by reason of his physical or mental condition or his youth, by an appropriate person acting on his behalf[8]. Waiver of the right to review must be made in writing in the prescribed form[9] or a form to the like effect[10], and must be signed in the presence of a justice of the peace[11].

Where a person has waived his right to review of the delivery order no application for habeas corpus as mentioned above may be made, and the order must be taken for all purposes to be validly made[12]. Notice that a person has waived his right to review must be given: (1) if the person is in custody, to the prison governor, constable or other person in whose custody he is[13]; or (2) if the person is on bail, to the officer in charge of the police station at which he is required to surrender to custody[14].

1 As to the Secretary of State see PARA 29.
2 As to the meaning of 'delivery order' see PARA 439 note 6; and as to delivery orders generally see PARA 439.
3 International Criminal Court Act 2001 s 12(1). This does not apply if the person in respect of whom the order is made waives his rights under s 12 (see s 13; and the text and notes 7–14), or is taken to have done so (see s 7(4)(b); and PARA 440): s 12(1).
4 As to habeas corpus see ADMINISTRATIVE LAW vol 1(1) (2001 Reissue) PARA 207 et seq.
5 International Criminal Court Act 2001 s 12(2). Proceedings on any such application must be treated as pending until they are discontinued or there is no further possibility of an appeal; and, for this purpose, any power of a court to allow an appeal out of time is to be disregarded: s 12(3).
6 International Criminal Court Act 2001 s 12(4)(a). The matters referred to in the text are those mentioned in s 5(2) (see PARA 439): s 12(4)(a). The provisions of s 5(4)–(9) apply (with the necessary modifications) in relation to the court to which the application is made as they apply to the court that made the delivery order: see s 12(4)(b).
7 International Criminal Court Act 2001 s 13(1).
8 International Criminal Court Act 2001 s 13(2).
9 'Prescribed form' means that prescribed by Criminal Procedure Rules: International Criminal Court Act 2001 s 13(3) (amended by the Courts Act 2003 Sch 8 para 403). As to the Criminal Procedure Rules see CRIMINAL LAW, EVIDENCE AND PROCEDURE.
10 International Criminal Court Act 2001 s 13(3)(a).
11 International Criminal Court Act 2001 s 13(3)(b).
12 International Criminal Court Act 2001 s 13(4).
13 International Criminal Court Act 2001 s 13(5)(a).
14 International Criminal Court Act 2001 s 13(5)(b). For the purposes of s 13(5)(b), notice is to be treated as given if it is sent by registered post, or recorded delivery, addressed to the officer mentioned: s 13(6).

444. Bail and custody. Where a court has power to remand a person[1], it may: (1) remand him in custody, that is, commit him for the period of the remand to prison or to the custody of a constable[2]; or (2) if an application for bail is made to the court, remand him on bail, that is, direct him to surrender himself into the custody of the officer in charge of a specified police station at the time appointed for him to do so[3]. A court is not authorised[4] to grant bail to a person who is serving a sentence of imprisonment or detention to which he has been sentenced by a national court, or who is in custody awaiting trial or sentence by a national court[5].

Where a person is granted bail by a competent court[6] but the court is unable to release the person because no surety or suitable surety is available, and the court fixes the amount in which the surety is to be bound with a view to the recognisance of the surety being entered into subsequently, the court must in the meantime commit the person to the custody of a constable[7]. During the period between the surrender to custody of a person granted bail and the end of the period of remand he must be treated as committed to the custody of the constable to whom he surrenders[8]; and where it appears to that officer that the end of the period of remand will be unexpectedly delayed, he must grant the person bail subject to a duty to surrender himself into the custody of the officer in charge of the specified police station[9] at the time appointed for him to do so[10].

Where an application for bail is made[11]: (a) the court must notify the Secretary of State[12] of the application[13]; (b) the Secretary of State must consult with the International Criminal Court (the 'ICC')[14]; and (c) bail must not be granted without full consideration of any recommendations made by the ICC[15]. In considering any such application the court must consider: (i) whether, given the gravity of the offence or offences the person concerned is alleged to have committed or, as the case may be, of which he has been convicted by the ICC, there are urgent and exceptional circumstances justifying release on bail[16]; and (ii) whether any necessary measures have been or will be taken to secure that the person will surrender to custody in accordance with the terms of his bail[17].

1 Ie under the International Criminal Court Act 2001 Pt 2 (ss 2–26).
2 International Criminal Court Act 2001 s 16(1)(a).
3 International Criminal Court Act 2001 s 16(1)(b). The time appointed for a person to surrender to custody must be a time appointed by the officer in charge of the specified police station and notified in writing to the person remanded, and must not be more than 24 hours before the time at which it appears to that officer that the period of remand is likely to end: s 16(3). The provisions of the Bail Act 1976 apply to proceedings under the International Criminal Court Act 2001 Pt 2 as to proceedings against a fugitive offender: s 16(2).
4 Ie by anything in the International Criminal Court Act 2001 Pt 2.
5 International Criminal Court Act 2001 s 16(5).
6 As to the meaning of 'competent court' see PARA 438 note 8.
7 International Criminal Court Act 2001 s 17(1), (2).
8 International Criminal Court Act 2001 s 17(1), (3).
9 Ie the police station specified by the competent court under the International Criminal Court Act 2001 s 16(1)(b) (see the text and note 3): see s 17(6).
10 International Criminal Court Act 2001 s 17(1), (4). The time is to be appointed by the officer in charge of the specified police station and notified in writing to the person remanded, and must not be more than 24 hours before the time at which it appears to that officer that the period of remand is likely to end: s 17(4).
      If a person required to surrender to custody in accordance with s 17(4) fails to do so: (1) the court by which he was remanded may issue a warrant for his arrest (s 17(5)(a)); (2) the provisions of s 14 (effect of warrant of arrest: see PARA 438) apply in relation to the warrant (s 17(5)(b)); and (3) on his arrest the person must be brought before the court which must reconsider the question of bail (s 17(5)(c)).
11 Ie in proceedings under the International Criminal Court Act 2001 Pt 2 (ss 2–26).
12 As to the Secretary of State see PARA 29.
13 International Criminal Court Act 2001 s 18(1)(a).
14 International Criminal Court Act 2001 s 18(1)(b). As to the International Criminal Court see PARA 437.
15 International Criminal Court Act 2001 s 18(1)(c).
16 International Criminal Court Act 2001 s 18(3)(a).
17 International Criminal Court Act 2001 s 18(3)(b).

445. Request for transit and unscheduled landing. Where the Secretary of State[1] receives a request from the International Criminal Court (the 'ICC')[2] for transit of a person being surrendered by another state and the Secretary of State accedes to the request: (1) the request is to be treated as if it were a request for that person's arrest and surrender[3]; (2) the warrant accompanying the request is to be deemed to have been indorsed[4]; and (3) the person to whom the request relates is to be treated on arrival in the United Kingdom[5] as if he had been arrested under that warrant[6]. A person in transit under these provisions must not be granted bail[7].

If a person being surrendered by another state makes an unscheduled landing in the United Kingdom, he may be arrested by any constable and must be brought before a competent court[8] as soon as is practicable[9]. The court must remand him in custody pending: (a) receipt by the Secretary of State of a request from the ICC for his transit[10]; and (b) the Secretary of State's decision whether to accede to the request[11]. If no such request is received by the Secretary of State before the end of the period of 96 hours beginning with the time of the arrested person's unscheduled landing, the Secretary of State must forthwith notify the court of that fact[12]; and the court must, on receipt of the notification, discharge the arrested person[13]. If the Secretary of State receives such a request before the end of that period, he must notify the court without delay of his decision whether to accede to the request[14]. If the Secretary of State notifies the court that he has decided to accede to the request, the court must, on receipt of the notification, terminate the period of remand[15]. If the Secretary of State notifies the court that he has decided not to accede to the request, the court must, on receipt of the notification, discharge the arrested person[16].

1 As to the Secretary of State see PARA 29.
2 As to the International Criminal Court see PARA 437.
3 International Criminal Court Act 2001 s 21(1), (2)(a). As to requests for arrest and surrender see PARA 438.
   In relation to a case where s 21 applies: (1) the reference in s 5(2)(a)(i) (see PARA 439) to the warrant having been duly endorsed under s 2(3) (see PARA 438) is to be read as a reference to the Secretary of State having acceded to the request for transit; and (2) the provisions of s 12(1) (right to review of delivery order: period for making application: see PARA 443) have effect as if the reference to 15 days (the period during which directions to execute delivery order are not to be given) were a reference to two days: s 21(3).
4 International Criminal Court Act 2001 s 21(1), (2)(b). As to indorsement of warrants see s 2(3); and PARA 438.
5 As to the meaning of 'United Kingdom' see PARA 30 note 3.
6 International Criminal Court Act 2001 s 21(1), (2)(c).
7 International Criminal Court Act 2001 s 21(4). As to the grant of bail see PARA 444.
8 As to the meaning of 'competent court' see PARA 438 note 8.
9 International Criminal Court Act 2001 s 22(1).
10 International Criminal Court Act 2001 s 22(2)(a).
11 International Criminal Court Act 2001 s 22(2)(b).
12 International Criminal Court Act 2001 s 22(3)(a).
13 International Criminal Court Act 2001 s 22(3)(b).
14 International Criminal Court Act 2001 s 22(4).
15 International Criminal Court Act 2001 s 22(5)(a). The provisions of s 21 (see the text and notes 1–7) apply, with the substitution for the reference in s 21(2)(c) (see head (3) in the text) to the time of arrival in the United Kingdom of a reference to the time of notification to the court: s 22(5)(b).
16 International Criminal Court Act 2001 s 22(6).

446. State or diplomatic immunity. Any state or diplomatic immunity[1] attaching to a person by reason of a connection with a state party to the ICC Statute[2] does not prevent proceedings under Part 2 of the International Criminal Court Act 2001[3] in relation to that person[4]. Where state or diplomatic immunity attaches to a person by reason of a connection with a state other than a state party to the ICC Statute, and waiver of that immunity is obtained by the International Criminal Court (the 'ICC')[5] in relation to a request for that person's surrender, the waiver is to be treated as extending to the proceedings under Part 2 of the International Criminal Court Act 2001 in connection with that request[6].

A certificate by the Secretary of State[7] that a state is or is not a party to the ICC Statute, or that there has been a waiver as mentioned above, is conclusive evidence of that fact for the purposes of Part 2 of the International Criminal Court Act 2001[8].

The Secretary of State may in any particular case, after consultation with the ICC and the state concerned, direct that proceedings (or further proceedings), which but for these provisions would be prevented by state or diplomatic immunity attaching to a person, are not to be taken against that person[9].

Provision is made to enable immunity to be overridden in relation to a referral made by the United Nations Security Council[10] to the ICC[11].

1 'State or diplomatic immunity' means any privilege or immunity attaching to a person, by reason of the status of that person or another as head of state, or as representative, official or

agent of a state, under: (1) the Diplomatic Privileges Act 1964, the Consular Relations Act 1968, the International Organisations Act 1968 or the State Immunity Act 1978; (2) any other legislative provision made for the purpose of implementing an international obligation; or (3) any rule of law derived from customary international law: International Criminal Court Act 2001 s 23(6).

2   Ie the Rome Statute of the International Criminal Court (17.7.98) (UN Doc A/CONF 183/9; 37 ILM (1998), 999). As to the ICC Statute see PARA 422 et seq.
3   Ie the International Criminal Court Act 2001 Pt 2 (ss 2–26).
4   International Criminal Court Act 2001 s 23(1).
5   As to the International Criminal Court see PARA 437.
6   International Criminal Court Act 2001 s 23(2).
7   As to the Secretary of State see PARA 29.
8   International Criminal Court Act 2001 s 23(3).
9   International Criminal Court Act 2001 s 23(4).
10 As to the Security Council see PARAS 522–525.
11 See the International Criminal Court Act 2001 s 23(5). See also the International Criminal Court (Darfur) Order 2009, SI 2009/699.

(iii) Investigations

447.   Questioning of persons, obtaining evidence and service of process. Powers are conferred[1] on the Secretary of State[2] which are exercisable for the purpose of providing assistance to the International Criminal Court (the 'ICC')[3] in relation to investigations or prosecutions where an investigation has been initiated by the ICC, and the investigation and any proceedings arising out of it have not been concluded[4].

Where the Secretary of State receives a request from the ICC for assistance in questioning a person being investigated or prosecuted, the person concerned must not be questioned in pursuance of the request unless he has been informed of his rights[5], and he consents to be interviewed[6].

Where the Secretary of State receives a request from the ICC for assistance in the taking or production of evidence[7], the Secretary of State may nominate a court[8] to receive the evidence to which the request relates[9]. If in order to comply with the request it is necessary for the evidence received by the court to be verified in any manner, the notice nominating the court must specify the nature of the verification required[10]. In proceedings before a nominated court a person must not be compelled to give evidence or produce anything that he could not be compelled to give or produce in criminal proceedings in the part of the United Kingdom[11] in which the nominated court has jurisdiction[12]. The court may direct that the public be excluded from the court, if it thinks it necessary in order to protect: (1) victims and witnesses, or a person alleged to have committed an ICC crime[13]; or (2) confidential or sensitive information[14]. The court must ensure that a register is kept of the proceedings that indicates in particular: (a) which persons with an interest in the proceedings were present; (b) which of those persons were represented and by whom; and (c) whether any of those persons was denied the opportunity of cross-examining a witness as to any part of his testimony[15]. A copy of the register of the proceedings must be sent to the Secretary of State for transmission to the ICC[16]. No order for costs may be made[17].

Where the Secretary of State receives a summons or other document from the ICC together with a request for it to be served on a person[18], he may direct the chief officer of police for the area in which the person appears to be to cause the document to be personally served on him[19]. If the document is so served, the chief officer of police must forthwith inform the Secretary of State when and how it was served[20], and if it does not prove possible to serve the document, the chief officer of police must forthwith inform the Secretary of State of that fact and of the reason for it[21].

1 Ie by the International Criminal Court Act 2001 Pt 3 (ss 27–41). Nothing in Pt 3 is to be read as preventing the provision of assistance to the ICC otherwise than under Pt 3: s 27(3).
2 As to the Secretary of State see PARA 29.
3 As to the International Criminal Court see PARA 437.
4 International Criminal Court Act 2001 s 27(1). Where facsimile transmission is used for the making of a request by the ICC for assistance or the transmission of any supporting documents, or for the transmission of any document in consequence of such a request, Pt 3 applies as if the documents so sent were the originals of the documents so transmitted, and any such document may accordingly be received in evidence: see s 27(2).
  Any evidence or other material obtained under Pt 3 by a person other than the Secretary of State, together with any requisite verification, must be sent to the Secretary of State for transmission to the ICC: s 41(1). Where any evidence or other material is to be transmitted to the ICC:
  (1)   if the material consists of a document, the original or a copy must be transmitted; and
  (2)   if the material consists of any other article, the article itself or a photograph or other description of it must be transmitted,
  as may be necessary to comply with the request of the ICC: s 41(2).
5 The text refers to rights under the Rome Statute of the International Criminal Court (17.7.98) (UN Doc A/CONF 183/9; 37 ILM (1998), 999) (the 'ICC Statute') art 55. As to the provisions of art 55 see the International Criminal Court Act 2001 s 28(3), Sch 3. As to the ICC Statute see PARA 422 et seq.
6 International Criminal Court Act 2001 s 28(1), (2). For these purposes, consent may be given by the person himself or, in circumstances in which it is inappropriate for the person to act for himself by reason of his physical or mental condition or his youth, by an appropriate person acting on his behalf: s 28(4). Such consent may be given orally or in writing, but if given orally it must be recorded in writing as soon as is reasonably practicable: s 28(5).
7 For these purposes, 'evidence' includes documents and other articles: International Criminal Court Act 2001 s 29(1).
8 The nominated court has the same powers with respect to securing the attendance of witnesses and the production of documents or other articles as it has for the purpose of other proceedings before the court, and may take evidence on oath: International Criminal Court Act 2001 s 29(3).
9 International Criminal Court Act 2001 s 29(1), (2).
10 International Criminal Court Act 2001 s 29(5).
11 As to the meaning of 'United Kingdom' see PARA 30 note 3.
12 International Criminal Court Act 2001 s 29(4).
13 As to the meaning of 'ICC crime' see PARA 438 note 3.
14 See the International Criminal Court Act 2001 s 30(1), (2).
15 International Criminal Court Act 2001 s 30(1), (3). The register must not be open to inspection except as authorised by the Secretary of State or with the leave of the court: s 30(4).
16 International Criminal Court Act 2001 s 30(5).
17 International Criminal Court Act 2001 s 29(6).
18 International Criminal Court Act 2001 s 31(1).
19 International Criminal Court Act 2001 s 31(2).
20 International Criminal Court Act 2001 s 31(3).
21 International Criminal Court Act 2001 s 31(4).

448.   Transfer of prisoners. Where the Secretary of State[1] receives a request from the International Criminal Court (the 'ICC')[2] for the temporary transfer of a prisoner[3] to the ICC for purposes of identification or for obtaining testimony or other assistance, he may issue a warrant (a 'transfer warrant') requiring the prisoner to be delivered up, in accordance with arrangements made by the Secretary of State with the ICC, into the custody of the ICC[4]. A transfer warrant must not be issued unless the prisoner consents to the transfer, but consent may not be withdrawn after the issue of the warrant[5].

1 As to the Secretary of State see PARA 29.

2 As to the International Criminal Court see PARA 437.
3 'Prisoner' means: (1) a person serving a sentence in a prison to which the Prison Act 1952 applies; (2) a person serving a sentence of service detention (within the meaning of the Armed Forces Act 2006: see ARMED FORCES) or imprisonment imposed by a service court (as to the meaning of which see PARA 441 note 3); (3) a person detained in custody otherwise than in pursuance of a sentence, including in particular a person in custody awaiting trial or sentence, a person committed to prison for contempt or for default in paying a fine, a person in custody in connection with proceedings to which the International Criminal Court Act 2001 Sch 2 Pt 2 or Sch 2 Pt 3 (see PARA 441) applies; (4) a person detained under any provision of the Immigration Act 1971 or the Nationality, Immigration and Asylum Act 2002: International Criminal Court Act 2001 s 32(6) (amended by the Armed Forces Act 2006 Sch 16 para 188; and by SI 2003/1016).
4 International Criminal Court Act 2001 s 32(1), (3). Section 15 (see PARA 439), s 24 and Sch 2 (see PARA 441) apply in relation to a transfer warrant under s 32 as they apply in relation to a delivery order: s 32(5). As to the meaning of 'delivery order' see PARA 439 note 6; and as to delivery orders generally see PARA 439.
   For the purposes of the Immigration Acts (within the meaning given by the Nationality, Immigration and Asylum Act 2002 s 158: see BRITISH NATIONALITY, IMMIGRATION AND ASYLUM), a person detained under any provision of the Immigration Act 1971 or the Nationality, Immigration and Asylum Act 2002 is not to be regarded as having left the United Kingdom at any time when a transfer warrant is in force in respect of him (including any time when he is in the custody of the ICC): International Criminal Court Act 2001 s 32(7) (amended by SI 2003/1016). As to the meaning of 'United Kingdom' see PARA 30 note 3.
5 International Criminal Court Act 2001 s 32(4).

449. Powers of entry, search and seizure and other powers. Where the Secretary of State[1] receives from the International Criminal Court (the 'ICC')[2] a request for assistance which appears to him to require the exercise of any of the powers of entry, search and seizure conferred by Part 2 of the Police and Criminal Evidence Act 1984[3], he may direct a constable to apply for a warrant or order, which is to apply in relation to an ICC crime[4] as it applies to an indictable offence[5].

Provision is made with respect to the taking of fingerprints or a non-intimate sample[6] in response to a request from the ICC for assistance in obtaining evidence as to the identity of a person[7]. Where the Secretary of State receives such a request from the ICC, he may nominate a court to supervise the taking of the person's fingerprints or a non-intimate sample, or both[8]. He may only do so, however, if he is satisfied that other means of identification have been tried and have proved inconclusive, and he has notified the ICC of that fact and the ICC has signified that it wishes to proceed with the request[9].

A coroner has power to order an exhumation in connection with proceedings before the ICC in respect of an ICC crime[10].

Where the Secretary of State receives a request from the ICC for assistance in ascertaining whether a person has benefited from an ICC crime, or in identifying the extent or whereabouts of property derived directly or indirectly from an ICC crime, the Secretary of State may direct a constable[11] to apply for a production or access order or for a search warrant[12]. Where the Secretary of State receives a request from the ICC for assistance in the freezing or seizure of proceeds, property and assets or instrumentalities of crime for the purpose of eventual forfeiture, he may authorise a person to act on behalf of the ICC for the purposes of applying for a freezing order, and direct that person to apply for such an order[13].

Where the Secretary of State receives a request from the ICC for the provision of records and documents relating to the evidence given in any proceedings in respect of conduct that would constitute an ICC crime, or the results of any investigation of such conduct with a view to such proceedings, he must take such steps as appear to him to be appropriate to obtain the records and documents requested, and on their being produced to him he must transmit them to the ICC[14].

Nothing in these provisions requires or authorises the production of documents, or the disclosure of information, which is prejudicial to the security of the United Kingdom[15].

If in order to comply with a request of the ICC it is necessary for any evidence or other material to be verified in any manner, the Secretary of State may give directions as to the nature of the verification required[16].

1   As to the Secretary of State see PARA 29.
2   As to the International Criminal Court see PARA 437.
3   Ie the Police and Criminal Evidence Act 1984 Pt 2 (ss 8–23): see CRIMINAL LAW, EVIDENCE AND PROCEDURE vol 11(2) (2006 Reissue) PARA 869 et seq.
4   As to the meaning of 'ICC crime' see PARA 438 note 3.
5   International Criminal Court Act 2001 s 33(1), (2) (s 33(2) amended by the Serious Organised Crime and Police Act 2005 Sch 7 para 49). As to the meaning of 'indictable offence' see CRIMINAL LAW, EVIDENCE AND PROCEDURE vol 11(3) (2006 Reissue) PARA 1102.
6   For these purposes, 'fingerprints' and 'non-intimate sample' have the meanings given by the Police and Criminal Evidence Act 1984 s 65 (see CRIMINAL LAW, EVIDENCE AND PROCEDURE vol 11(2) (2006 Reissue) PARAS 1021, 1027): International Criminal Court Act 2001 s 34(2).
7   See the International Criminal Court Act 2001 s 34(1), Sch 4.
8   International Criminal Court Act 2001 Sch 4 para 1(1). Fingerprints and samples so taken must be destroyed in the same way as if they had been taken under the Police and Criminal Evidence Act 1984: see the International Criminal Court Act 2001 Sch 4 para 8.
9   International Criminal Court Act 2001 s 34(1), Sch 4 para 1(2).
10 See the International Criminal Court Act 2001 s 35 (prospectively amended by the Coroners and Justice Act 2009 Sch 21 para 45).
11 For these purposes, 'constable' includes a person commissioned by the Commissioners for Her Majesty's Revenue and Customs: International Criminal Court Act 2001 Sch 5 para 11 (amended by virtue of the Commissioners for Revenue and Customs Act 2005 s 50(1)).
12 International Criminal Court Act 2001 s 37(1). As to production or access orders see Sch 5 Pt 1; as to the issuing of search warrants see Sch 5 Pt 2; and as to supplementary provisions see Sch 5 Pt 3.
13 International Criminal Court Act 2001 s 38. As to freezing orders see Sch 6.
14 International Criminal Court Act 2001 s 36(1), (2).
15 International Criminal Court Act 2001 s 39(1). As to the meaning of 'United Kingdom' see PARA 30 note 3. For these purposes, a certificate signed by or on behalf of the Secretary of State to the effect that it would be prejudicial to the security of the United Kingdom for specified documents to be produced, or for specified information to be disclosed, is conclusive evidence of that fact: s 39(2).
16 International Criminal Court Act 2001 s 40.

(iv) Enforcement of Sentences and Orders

450. Detention in pursuance of an International Criminal Court sentence. Where the United Kingdom[1] is designated by the International Criminal Court (the 'ICC')[2] as the state in which a person (the 'prisoner') is to serve a sentence of imprisonment imposed by the ICC, and the Secretary of State[3] informs the ICC that the designation is accepted, he must issue a warrant authorising the bringing of the prisoner to the jurisdiction, the detention of the prisoner there in accordance with the sentence of the ICC, and the taking of the prisoner to a specified place where he is to be detained[4]. A prisoner subject to such a warrant authorising his detention is to be treated[5] as if he were subject to a sentence of imprisonment imposed in exercise of its criminal jurisdiction by a court in the part of the United Kingdom in which he is to be detained[6].

Where a person who completes a term of imprisonment imposed by the ICC is still subject to a domestic sentence[7] of imprisonment, whether imposed before or during his imprisonment in pursuance of the sentence of the ICC, and has been transferred[8] to another part of the United Kingdom, he is to be treated as if he had been transferred[9] from the part of the United Kingdom in which the domestic sentence was imposed, on a restricted transfer subject to such conditions as Secretary of State may consider appropriate[10].

1 As to the meaning of 'United Kingdom' see PARA 30 note 3.
2 As to the International Criminal Court see PARA 437.
3 As to the Secretary of State see PARA 29.
4 International Criminal Court Act 2001 s 42(1), (3). Any reference to a person being detained in a part of the United Kingdom is to his being subject to a warrant authorising his detention there: s 48(1).The provisions of the warrant may be varied by the Secretary of State, and must be so varied to give effect to any variation of the ICC's sentence: s 42(3). As to enforcement of sentences imposed by the International Criminal Court see the Agreement between the government of the United Kingdom of Great Britain and Northern Ireland and the International Criminal Court on the enforcement of sentences imposed by the International Criminal Court (London, 8 November 2007; TS 1 (2008); Cm 7306).
5 Ie for all purposes, subject to the International Criminal Court Act 2001 s 42(5) and Sch 7. Section 42(5) provides that the Repatriation of Prisoners Act 1984 (see PRISONS vol 36(2) (Reissue) PARA 555 et seq) and the Crime (Sentences) Act 1997 Sch 1 (transfers of prisoners within the British Islands: see PRISONS vol 36(2) (Reissue) PARA 548 et seq) do not apply to a person detained in pursuance of a sentence of the ICC; as to transfer of such a person within the United Kingdom see the International Criminal Court Act 2001 ss 44, 45; and PARA 451. The operation of certain other statutory provisions is excluded in relation to a person detained in pursuance of a sentence of the ICC: see s 42(6), Sch 7 (Sch 7 amended by the Criminal Justice Act 2003 Sch 32 para 139; the Criminal Justice and Immigration Act 2008 s 22(7); SI 2001/2565; SI 2008/1241).
6 International Criminal Court Act 2001 s 42(4).
7 'Domestic sentence' means a sentence imposed by a court in the United Kingdom: International Criminal Court Act 2001 s 46(2).
8 Ie under the International Criminal Court Act 2001 ss 44, 45: see note 5.
9 Ie by order under the Crime (Sentences) Act 1997 Sch 1: see PRISONS vol 36(2) (Reissue) PARA 548 et seq.
10 International Criminal Court Act 2001 s 46(1).

451.   Temporary return or transfer of custody to another state, or another part of the United Kingdom.   Where the Secretary of State[1] receives a request from the International Criminal Court (the 'ICC')[2] for the temporary return of a prisoner to the custody of the ICC for the purposes of any proceedings, or for the transfer of the prisoner to the custody of another state in pursuance of a change in designation of state of enforcement, he must: (1) issue a warrant authorising the prisoner's temporary return or transfer in accordance with the request; (2) make the necessary arrangements with the ICC or, as the case may be, the other state; and (3) give such directions as to the custody, surrender and, where appropriate, return of the prisoner as appear to him appropriate to give effect to the arrangements[3]. Where the prisoner is temporarily returned to the custody of the ICC, the warrant authorising his detention in any part of the United Kingdom[4] continues to have effect so as to apply to him again on his return[5].

The Secretary of State may make an order, subject to such conditions (if any) as he may impose from time to time, for the transfer of the prisoner to another part of the United Kingdom to serve the whole or part of the remainder of the ICC sentence there[6]. If such an order is made the warrant authorising the prisoner's detention in the part of the United Kingdom from which he is transferred continues to have effect, and has effect as if it were a warrant authorising his detention in the part of the United Kingdom to which he is transferred[7].

Where it appears to the Secretary of State that the prisoner should be transferred to another part of the United Kingdom for the purpose of attending criminal proceedings against him there, or that the attendance of the prisoner at a place in another part of the United Kingdom is desirable in the interests of justice, or for the purposes of any public inquiry[8], he may, subject to such conditions (if any) as he thinks fit to impose[9], make an order for the transfer of the prisoner to that part of the United Kingdom[10]. Where such an order is made the warrant authorising the prisoner's detention in the part of the United Kingdom from which he is transferred continues to have effect, and he must be returned to that part of the United Kingdom when the purposes for which the order is made are fulfilled[11].

1   As to the Secretary of State see PARA 29.
2   As to the International Criminal Court see PARA 437.
3   International Criminal Court Act 2001 s 43(1), (3).
4   As to the meaning of 'United Kingdom' see PARA 30 note 3.
5   International Criminal Court Act 2001 s 43(4).
6   International Criminal Court Act 2001 s 44(1), (3). No such order may be made for the transfer of the prisoner to Scotland without the agreement of the Scottish Ministers, or for the transfer of the prisoner from Scotland without the agreement of the Secretary of State: s 44(2).
7   International Criminal Court Act 2001 s 44(4). A prisoner transferred under s 44 is treated for all purposes, subject as mentioned in s 42(4) (see PARA 450), as if he were serving a sentence of imprisonment imposed in exercise of its criminal jurisdiction by a court in the part of the United Kingdom to which he is transferred: s 44(5).
8   International Criminal Court Act 2001 s 45(1).
9   International Criminal Court Act 2001 s 45(4). Any such conditions may be varied or removed at any time: s 45(4).
10   International Criminal Court Act 2001 s 45(2). No such order may be made for the transfer of the prisoner to Scotland without the agreement of the Scottish Ministers, or for the transfer of the prisoner from Scotland without the agreement of the Secretary of State: s 45(3).
11   International Criminal Court Act 2001 s 45(5).

452. Custody of prisoner in transit. Where a prisoner is subject to a warrant[1], but is not in legal custody under the Prison Act 1952, the prisoner is deemed to be in the legal custody of the Secretary of State[2] at any time when, being in the United Kingdom[3] or on board a British ship[4], a British aircraft[5] or a British hovercraft[6], he is being taken to or from any place or is being kept in custody[7]. The Secretary of State may, from time to time, designate a person as a person who is for the time being authorised to take the prisoner to or from any place or to keep the prisoner in custody[8]. A person so authorised has all the powers, authority, protection and privileges of a constable in the part of the United Kingdom in which that person is for the time being, or, if he is outside the United Kingdom, of a constable in the part of the United Kingdom to or from which the prisoner is to be taken[9]. If the prisoner escapes or is unlawfully at large, he may be arrested without warrant by a constable[10] and taken to any place to which he may be taken under the original warrant[11].

1   Ie under any provision of the International Criminal Court Act 2001 Pt 4 (ss 42–49).
2   As to the Secretary of State see PARA 29.
3   As to the meaning of 'United Kingdom' see PARA 30 note 3.
4   As to the meaning of 'British ship' see PARA 439 note 19.
5   As to the meaning of 'British aircraft' see PARA 439 note 20.
6   As to the meaning of 'British hovercraft' see PARA 439 note 21.
7   International Criminal Court Act 2001 s 47(1), (2).
8   International Criminal Court Act 2001 s 47(3).
9   International Criminal Court Act 2001 s 47(4).
10   For the purposes of the International Criminal Court Act 2001 s 47(5), 'constable', in relation to any part of the United Kingdom, means: (1) a person who is a constable in that or any other

part of the United Kingdom; or (2) a person who, at the place in question, has under any enactment (including s 47(4): see the text and note 9) the powers of a constable in that or any other part of the United Kingdom: s 47(5). The 'original warrant' is the warrant referred to in s 47(1) (see the text and notes 1–7).

11 International Criminal Court Act 2001 s 47(5).

453. Power to make provision for enforcement of orders relating to fines, forfeitures and reparations. The Secretary of State[1] may make provision by regulations for the enforcement of: (1) fines or forfeitures ordered by the International Criminal Court (the 'ICC')[2]; and (2) orders by the ICC against convicted persons specifying reparations to, or in respect of, victims[3].

The regulations may authorise the Secretary of State: (a) to appoint a person to act on behalf of the ICC for the purposes of enforcing the order[4]; and (b) to give such directions to the appointed person as appear to him necessary[5].

The regulations must provide for the registration of the order by a court as a precondition of enforcement[6]. An order must not be so registered unless the court is satisfied that the order is in force and not subject to appeal[7]. If the order has been partly complied with, the court must register the order for enforcement only so far as it has not been complied with[8].

The regulations may provide that:

(i)   for the purposes of enforcement, an order so registered has the same force and effect;

(ii)   the same powers are exercisable in relation to its enforcement; and

(iii) proceedings for its enforcement may be taken in the same way,

as if the order were an order of an English court[9].

A court must not exercise its powers of enforcement under the regulations in relation to any property unless it is satisfied: (A) that a reasonable opportunity has been given for persons holding any interest in the property to make representations to the court[10]; and (B) that the exercise of the powers will not prejudice the rights of bona fide third parties[11].

The regulations may provide that the reasonable costs of and incidental to the registration and enforcement of an order are to be recoverable as if they were sums recoverable under the order[12].

1 As to the Secretary of State see PARA 29.
2 As to the International Criminal Court see PARA 437.
3 International Criminal Court Act 2001 s 49(1). As to the regulations that have been made see the International Criminal Court Act 2001 (Enforcement of Fines, Forfeiture and Reparation Orders) Regulations 2001, SI 2001/2379 (amended by SI 2002/822). Rules provide that an application to the High Court to register an order of the ICC for enforcement, or to vary or set aside the registration of an order, may be made to a judge or a master of the Queen's Bench Division: CPR Sch 1 RSC Ord 115 r 38(1). CPR Sch 1 RSC Ord 115 rr 13, 15–20 apply, with such modifications as are necessary and subject to the provisions of any regulations made under the International Criminal Court Act 2001 s 49, to the registration for enforcement of an order of the ICC as they apply to the registration of an external confiscation order: CPR Sch 1 RSC Ord 115 r 38(2). 'Order of the ICC' means a fine or forfeiture ordered by the ICC, or an order by the ICC against a person convicted by the ICC specifying a reparation to, or in respect of, a victim: CPR Sch 1 RSC Ord 115 r 37.
4 International Criminal Court Act 2001 s 49(2)(a).
5 International Criminal Court Act 2001 s 49(2)(b).
6 International Criminal Court Act 2001 s 49(3).
7 International Criminal Court Act 2001 s 49(3).
8 International Criminal Court Act 2001 s 49(3).
9 See the International Criminal Court Act 2001 s 49(4). The regulations may for that purpose apply all or any of the provisions (including provisions of subordinate legislation) relating to enforcement of orders of a court of a country or territory outside the United Kingdom: s 49(4). As to the meaning of 'United Kingdom' see PARA 30 note 3.

10 International Criminal Court Act 2001 s 49(5)(a).
11 International Criminal Court Act 2001 s 49(5)(b).
12 International Criminal Court Act 2001 s 49(6).

(v) Offences under Domestic Law

454. Genocide, crimes against humanity and war crimes. It is an offence[1] against the law of England and Wales for a person to commit genocide[2], a crime against humanity[3], or a war crime[4]. This applies to acts[5] committed: (1) in England or Wales; or (2) outside the United Kingdom[6] by a United Kingdom national[7], a United Kingdom resident[8] or a person subject to UK service jurisdiction[9]. Proceedings for a substantive offence[10] may be brought against a person in England or Wales who commits acts outside the United Kingdom at a time when he is not a United Kingdom national, a United Kingdom resident or a person subject to United Kingdom service jurisdiction and who subsequently becomes resident in the United Kingdom, if he is resident in the United Kingdom at the time the proceedings are brought, and the acts in respect of which the proceedings are brought would have constituted that offence if they had been committed in that part of the United Kingdom[11]. A person is regarded as committing an act or crime mentioned above only if the material elements are committed with intent and knowledge[12].

In interpreting and applying the definitions of 'genocide', 'crime against humanity' and 'war crime' the court must take into account any relevant Elements of Crimes[13], and any relevant judgment or decision of the International Criminal Court (the 'ICC')[14]. Account may also be taken of any other relevant international jurisprudence[15]. Furthermore the definitions of 'genocide', 'crime against humanity' and 'war crime' are to be construed subject to and in accordance with any relevant reservation or declaration made by the United Kingdom when ratifying any treaty or agreement relevant to the interpretation of those definitions[16].

As from a day to be appointed the provisions noted above[17] apply to acts committed on or after 1 January 1991[18].

1 In determining whether an offence under the International Criminal Court Act 2001 Pt 5 (ss 50–70) has been committed the court must apply the principles of the law of England and Wales: s 56(1). Nothing in Pt 5 may be read as restricting the operation of any enactment or rule of law relating to the extra-territorial application of offences (including offences under Pt 5), or offences ancillary to offences under Pt 5 (wherever committed): s 56(2). Provision is also made for the protection of victims and witnesses: see s 57.
2 'Genocide' means an act of genocide as defined in the Statute of the ICC art 6 (see PARA 429): International Criminal Court Act 2001 s 50(1).
3 'Crime against humanity' means a crime against humanity as defined in the Statute of the ICC art 7 (see PARA 430): International Criminal Court Act 2001 s 50(1).
4 International Criminal Court Act 2001 s 51(1). 'War crime' means a war crime as defined in the Statute of the ICC art 8.2 (see PARA 431): International Criminal Court Act 2001 s 50(1).
5 For the purposes of the International Criminal Court Act 2001 Pt 5 (ss 50–70), 'act' includes an omission, except where the context otherwise requires; and references to conduct have a corresponding meaning: s 69.
6 As to the meaning of 'United Kingdom' see PARA 30 note 3.
7 For the purposes of the International Criminal Court Act 2001 Pt 5, 'United Kingdom national' means an individual who is a British citizen; a British overseas territories citizen; a British national (overseas); a British overseas citizen; a person who under the British Nationality Act 1981 is a British subject; or a British protected person within the meaning of that Act: International Criminal Court Act 2001 s 67(1) (amended by the Overseas Territories Act 2002 s 2(3)). See further BRITISH NATIONALITY, IMMIGRATION AND ASYLUM vol 4(2) (2002 Reissue) PARA 5 et seq.

8　'United Kingdom resident' means a person who is resident in the United Kingdom: International Criminal Court Act 2001 s 67(2). As from a day to be appointed the following individuals are, to the extent that it would not otherwise be the case, to be treated for the purposes of Pt 5 (ss 50–70) as being resident in the United Kingdom: (1) an individual who has indefinite leave to remain in the United Kingdom; (2) any other individual who has made an application for such leave (whether or not it has been determined) and who is in the United Kingdom; (3) an individual who has leave to enter or remain in the United Kingdom for the purposes of work or study and who is in the United Kingdom; (4) an individual who has made an asylum claim, or a human rights claim, which has been granted; (5) any other individual who has made an asylum claim or human rights claim (whether or not the claim has been determined) and who is in the United Kingdom; (6) an individual named in an application for indefinite leave to remain, an asylum claim or a human rights claim as a dependant of the individual making the application or claim if: (a) the application or claim has been granted; or (b) the named individual is in the United Kingdom (whether or not the application or claim has been determined); (7) an individual who would be liable to removal or deportation from the United Kingdom but cannot be removed or deported because of the Human Rights Act 1998 s 6 (see CONSTITUTIONAL LAW AND HUMAN RIGHTS) or for practical reasons; (8) an individual (a) against whom a decision to make a deportation order under the Immigration Act 1971 s 5(1) by virtue of s 3(5)(a) (deportation conducive to the public good) (see BRITISH NATIONALITY, IMMIGRATION AND ASYLUM vol 4(2) (2002 Reissue) PARA 160) has been made; (b) who has appealed against the decision to make the order (whether or not the appeal has been determined); and (c) who is in the United Kingdom; (9) an individual who is an illegal entrant within the meaning of the Immigration Act 1971 s 33(1) (see BRITISH NATIONALITY, IMMIGRATION AND ASYLUM vol 4(2) (2002 Reissue) PARA 118) or who is liable to removal under the Immigration and Asylum Act 1999 s 10 (see BRITISH NATIONALITY, IMMIGRATION AND ASYLUM vol 4(2) (2002 Reissue) PARA 154); (10) an individual who is detained in lawful custody in the United Kingdom: International Criminal Court Act 2001 s 67A(1) (s 67A prospectively added by the Coroners and Justice Act 2009 s 70(1), (4). At the date at which this volume states the law no such day had been appointed under s 182(5)). When determining for the purposes of the International Criminal Court Act 2001 Pt 5 whether any other individual is resident in the United Kingdom regard is to be had to all relevant considerations including: (i) the periods during which the individual has been or intends to be in the United Kingdom; (ii) the purposes for which the individual is, has been or intends to be in the United Kingdom; (iii) whether the individual has family or other connections to the United Kingdom and the nature of those connections; and (iv) whether the individual has an interest in residential property located in the United Kingdom: s 67A(2) (as so prospectively added). Section 67A applies in relation to any offence under Pt 5 (whether committed before or after the coming into force of this section): s 67A(4) (as so prospectively added).

　　For the Purposes of s 67A, the following definitions apply. 'Asylum claim' means a claim that it would be contrary to the United Kingdom's obligations under the Refugee Convention for the claimant to be removed from, or required to leave, the United Kingdom, or a claim that the claimant would face a real risk of serious harm if removed from the United Kingdom: s 67A(3) (as so prospectively amended). 'Convention rights' means the rights identified as Convention rights by the Human Rights Act 1998 s 1 (see CONSTITUTIONAL LAW AND HUMAN RIGHTS): International Criminal Court Act 2001 s 67A(3) (as so prospectively amended). 'Detained in lawful custody' means: (A) detained in pursuance of a sentence of imprisonment, detention or custody for life or a detention and training order; (B) remanded in or committed to custody by an order of a court; (C) detained pursuant to an order under the Colonial Prisoners Removal Act 1884 s 2 (see COMMONWEALTH vol 13 (2009) PARA 849) or a warrant under the Repatriation of Prisoners Act 1984 ss 1, 4A (see PRISONS vol 36(2) (Reissue) PARA 555 et seq); (D) detained under the Mental Health Act 1983 Pt 3 (see CRIMINAL LAW, EVIDENCE AND PROCEDURE vol 11(4) (2006 Reissue) PARA 1694 et seq) or by virtue of an order under the Criminal Procedure (Insanity) Act 1964 s 5 (see CRIMINAL LAW, EVIDENCE AND PROCEDURE vol 11(3) (2006 Reissue) PARA 1265) or the Criminal Appeal Act 1968 ss 6, 14 (see CRIMINAL LAW, EVIDENCE AND PROCEDURE vol 11(4) (2006 Reissue) PARAS 1883, 1889): International Criminal Court Act 2001 s 67A(3) (as so prospectively amended). 'Human rights claim' means a claim that to remove the claimant from, or to require the claimant to leave, the United Kingdom would be unlawful under the Human Rights Act 1998 s 6 (public authority not to act contrary to Convention) as being incompatible with the person's Convention rights: International Criminal Court Act 2001 s 67A(3) (as so prospectively amended). 'Refugee Convention' means the Convention relating to the Status of Refugees done at Geneva on 28 July 1951 and the Protocol to the Convention (Geneva, 28 July 1951; TS 39 (1954); Cmd 9171) and Protocol (New York, 31 January 1967; TS 15 (1969); Cmnd 3906): International Criminal Court

Act 2001 s 67A(3) (as so prospectively amended). 'Serious harm' has the meaning given by article 15 of Council Directive 2004/83/EC on minimum standards for the qualification and status of third country nationals or stateless persons as refugees or as persons who otherwise need international protection and the content of the protection granted: International Criminal Court Act 2001 s 67A(3) (as so prospectively amended). A reference to having leave to enter or remain in the United Kingdom is to be construed in accordance with the Immigration Act 1971 (see BRITISH NATIONALITY, IMMIGRATION AND ASYLUM): International Criminal Court Act 2001 s 67A(3) (as so prospectively amended).

9   International Criminal Court Act 2001 s 51(2). 'Person subject to UK service jurisdiction' means a person subject to service law, or a civilian subject to service discipline, within the meaning of the Armed Forces Act 2006 (see ARMED FORCES): International Criminal Court Act 2001 s 67(3) (amended by the Armed Forces Act 2006 Sch 16 para 189).

10   For these purposes, 'substantive offence' means an offence other than an ancillary offence: International Criminal Court Act 2001 s 68(4). As to the meaning of 'ancillary offence' see PARA 455 note 5.

11   International Criminal Court Act 2001 s 68(1), (2). Nothing in s 68 is to be read as restricting the operation of any other provision of Pt 5: s 68(5).

12   International Criminal Court Act 2001 s 66(1), (2). This applies unless it is otherwise provided: see s 66(2).
    For these purposes, a person has intent: (1) in relation to conduct, where he means to engage in the conduct; and (2) in relation to a consequence, where he means to cause the consequence or is aware that it will occur in the ordinary course of events: s 66(3)(a). 'Knowledge' means awareness that a circumstance exists or a consequence will occur in the ordinary course of events: s 66(3)(b).
    In interpreting and applying the provisions of s 66, the court must take into account any relevant judgment or decision of the ICC: s 66(4). Account may also be taken of any other relevant international jurisprudence: s 66(4).

13   See the International Criminal Court Act 2001 s 50(2). As to the Elements of Crimes see s 50(3); and the International Criminal Court Act 2001 (Elements of Crimes) (No 2) Regulations 2004, SI 2004/3239.

14   International Criminal Court Act 2001 s 50(5). As to the International Criminal Court see PARA 437.

15   International Criminal Court Act 2001 s 50(5).

16   International Criminal Court Act 2001 s 50(4). Her Majesty may by Order in Council: (1) certify that a reservation or declaration has been made and the terms in which it was made; (2) if any such reservation or declaration is withdrawn (in whole or part), certify that fact and revoke or amend any Order in Council containing the terms of that reservation or declaration: see s 50(4). As to the order that has been made see the International Criminal Court Act 2001 (Reservations and Declarations) Order 2001, SI 2001/2559.

17   Ie the International Criminal Court Act 2001 s 51.

18   International Criminal Court Act 2001 s 65A(1) (s 65A prospectively added by the Coroners and Justice Act 2009 s 70(1), (3). At the date at which this volume states the law no day had been appointed under s 182(5) bringing this section into force). The International Criminal Court Act 2001 s 51 does not apply to a crime against humanity (see PARA 430), or a war crime within the Statute of the ICC art 8.2(b) or (e) (see PARA 431), committed by a person before 1 September 2001 (ie the date on which s 51 came into force) unless, at the time the act constituting that crime was committed, the act amounted in the circumstances to a criminal offence under international law: s 65A(2) (as so prospectively added).

455.   Ancillary offences.   It is an offence against the law of England and Wales for a person to engage in conduct[1] ancillary to an act that if committed in England or Wales would constitute an offence of genocide[2], crime against humanity[3] or war crime[4], or would constitute an ancillary offence[5], but which, being committed or intended to be committed outside England and Wales, does not constitute such an offence[6]. These provisions apply where the conduct in question consists of or includes an act committed: (1) in England or Wales; or (2) outside the United Kingdom[7] by a United Kingdom national[8], a United Kingdom resident[9] or a person subject to UK service jurisdiction[10].

Proceedings for an ancillary offence may be brought against a person in England and Wales if he is resident in the United Kingdom at the time the proceedings are brought, and the acts in respect of which the proceedings are brought would have constituted that offence if they had been committed in that part of the United Kingdom[11].

1   As to the meaning of 'conduct' 454 note 5.
2   As to the meaning of 'genocide' see PARA 429.
3   As to the meaning of 'crime against humanity' see PARA 430.
4   As to the meaning of 'war crime' see PARA 431.
5   The International Criminal Court Act 2001 s 55 (amended by the Serious Crime Act 2007 Sch 6 para 61(2), Sch 7 para 49, Sch 14) provides that, for the purposes of Pt 5 (ss 50–70), references to an 'ancillary offence' are to:
    (1)   aiding, abetting, counselling or procuring the commission of an offence (ie conduct that in relation to an indictable offence would be punishable under the Accessories and Abettors Act 1861 s 8: see CRIMINAL LAW, EVIDENCE AND PROCEDURE vol 11(1) (2006 Reissue) PARAS 49–51);
    (2)   inciting a person to commit an offence;
    (3)   attempting or conspiring to commit an offence; and for these purposes the reference to an attempt is to conduct amounting to an offence under the Criminal Attempts Act 1981 s 1 (see CRIMINAL LAW, EVIDENCE AND PROCEDURE vol 11(1) (2006 Reissue) PARA 79), and the reference to conspiracy is to conduct amounting to an offence under the Criminal Law Act 1977 s 1 (see CRIMINAL LAW, EVIDENCE AND PROCEDURE vol 11(1) (2006 Reissue) PARA 67); or
    (4)   assisting an offender or concealing the commission of an offence; and for these purposes the reference to assisting an offender is to conduct that in relation to a relevant offence would amount to an offence under the Criminal Law Act 1967 s 4(1) (see CRIMINAL LAW, EVIDENCE AND PROCEDURE vol 11(1) (2006 Reissue) PARA 58), and the reference to concealing an offence is to conduct that in relation to a relevant offence would amount to an offence under s 5(1) (see CRIMINAL LAW, EVIDENCE AND PROCEDURE vol 11(2) (2006 Reissue) PARA 734).
    Note that references to the common law offence of incitement have effect as references to the statutory offence under the Serious Crime Act 2007 (see CRIMINAL LAW, EVIDENCE AND PROCEDURE): see Sch 6 para 42.
6   See the International Criminal Court Act 2001 s 52(1), (2), (3). As from a day to be appointed s 52 applies to conduct in which a person engaged on or after 1 January 1991, and references to an offence include an act or conduct which would not constitute an offence under the law of England and Wales but for this section: s 65A(3) (s 65A prospectively added by the Coroners and Justice Act 2009 s 70(1), (3). At the date at which this volume states the law no such day had been appointed under s 182(5)). As from a day to be appointed any enactment or rule of law relating to an offence ancillary to a relevant Pt 5 offence applies to conduct in which a person engaged on or after 1 January 1991, and applies even if the act or conduct constituting the relevant Pt 5 offence would not constitute such an offence but for this section: s 65A(5) (as so prospectively added). But s 52, and any enactment or rule of law relating to an offence ancillary to a relevant Pt 5 offence, do not apply to conduct in which the person engaged before 1 September 2001, or conduct in which the person engaged on or after that date which was ancillary to an act or conduct which: (1) was committed or engaged in before that date, and (2) would not constitute a relevant Pt 5 offence, or fall within section 52(2), but for this section, unless, at the time the person engaged in the conduct, it amounted in the circumstances to a criminal offence under international law: s 65A(6) (as so prospectively added). For these purposes a 'relevant Pt 5 offence' means an offence under ss 51, 52 or an offence ancillary to such an offence: s 65A(9) (as so prospectively added).
7   As to the meaning of 'United Kingdom' see PARA 30 note 3.
8   As to the meaning of 'United Kingdom national' see PARA 454 note 7.
9   As to the meaning of 'United Kingdom resident' see PARA 454 note 8.
10   International Criminal Court Act 2001 s 52(4). As to the meaning of 'person subject to United Kingdom service jurisdiction' see PARA 454 note 9.
11   See the International Criminal Court Act 2001 s 68(3).

456. Trial and punishment of offences of genocide, crimes against humanity and war crimes, and ancillary offences. Offences of genocide, crimes against humanity and war crimes[1] and ancillary offences[2] are triable only on indictment[3]. Proceedings must not be instituted except by or with the consent of the Attorney General[4]. If the offence is not committed in England or Wales proceedings may be taken, and the offence is for incidental purposes treated as having been committed, in any place in England or Wales[5].

A person convicted of an offence involving murder[6], or an offence ancillary to an offence involving murder, must be dealt with as for an offence of murder or, as the case may be, the corresponding ancillary offence in relation to murder[7]. In any other case, a person convicted of an offence mentioned above is liable to imprisonment for a term not exceeding 30 years[8].

1   Ie offences under s 51: see PARA 454. As to the meaning of 'genocide' see PARA 429; as to the meaning of 'crime against humanity' see PARA 430; and as to the meaning of 'war crime' see PARA 431.

2   Ie offences under the International Criminal Court Act 2001 s 52 (see PARA 455), and offences ancillary to offences under s 51 or s 52.

3   International Criminal Court Act 2001 s 53(1), (2).

4   International Criminal Court Act 2001 s 53(3).

5   International Criminal Court Act 2001 s 53(4).

6   For these purposes, 'murder' means the killing of a person in such circumstances as would, if committed in England or Wales, constitute murder: International Criminal Court Act 2001 s 53(5).

7   International Criminal Court Act 2001 s 53(5). As from a day to be appointed s 53(5), (6) (see the text and note 8) are subject to s 65B (see note 8): s 53(7) (prospectively added by the Coroners and Justice Act 2009 s 70(1), (2)). At the date at which this volume states the law no such day had been appointed.

8   International Criminal Court Act 2001 s 53(6). As from a day to be appointed in the case of a pre-existing E&W offence committed before 1 September 2001, in '30 years' is to be read as '14 years': s 65B(1) (prospectively added by the Coroners and Justice Act 2009 s 70(1), (3). At the date at which this volume states the law no such day had been appointed under s 182(5)). In the case of an offence of the kind mentioned in the International Criminal Court Act 2001 s 55(1)(d) (see PARA 455) which is ancillary to a pre-existing E&W offence committed before 1 September 2001, nothing in s 53(5) and (6) disapplies the penalties provided for in the Criminal Law Act 1967 ss 4, 5 (see CRIMINAL LAW, EVIDENCE AND PROCEDURE vol 11(1) (2006 Reissue) PARAS 58, 734): s 65B(2) (as so prospectively added). For these purposes 'pre-existing E&W offence' means: (1) an offence under the International Criminal Court Act 2001 s 51 (see PARA 454) on account of an act constituting genocide, if at the time the act was committed it also amounted to an offence under the Genocide Act 1969 s 1; (2) an offence under section 51 on account of an act constituting a war crime, if at the time the act was committed it also amounted to an offence under the Geneva Conventions Act 1957 s 1 (grave breaches of the Conventions); (3) an offence of a kind mentioned in s 55(1)(a) to (c) (see PARA 455) which is ancillary to an offence within para (1) or (2) above: s 65B(5) (as so prospectively added).

457. Offences in relation to the International Criminal Court. The International Criminal Court (the 'ICC')[1] has jurisdiction over the following offences against its administration of justice when committed intentionally: (1) giving false testimony when under an obligation to tell the truth; (2) presenting evidence that the party knows is false or forged; (3) corruptly influencing a witness, obstructing or interfering with the attendance or testimony of a witness, retaliating against a witness for giving testimony or destroying, tampering with or interfering with the collection of evidence; (4) impeding, intimidating or corruptly influencing an official of the ICC for the purpose of forcing or persuading the official not to perform, or to perform improperly, his duties; (5) retaliating against an official of the ICC on account of duties performed by that or another official; (6) soliciting or accepting a bribe as an official of the ICC in connection with his official duties[2].

A person intentionally committing any of the above acts may be dealt with as for the corresponding domestic offence committed in relation to a superior court in England and Wales[3]. In interpreting and applying the relevant provisions, the court must take into account any relevant judgment or decision of the ICC, and account may also be taken of any other relevant international jurisprudence[4].

These provisions and, so far as may be necessary for the purposes of these provisions, the enactments and rules of law relating to the corresponding domestic offences apply to acts committed: (a) in England or Wales; or (b) outside the United Kingdom[5] by a United Kingdom national[6], a United Kingdom resident[7] or a person subject to UK service jurisdiction[8]. If an offence under these provisions, or an offence ancillary to such an offence, is not committed in England or Wales, proceedings may be taken, and the offence is for incidental purposes to be treated as having been committed, in any place in England or Wales[9].

Proceedings for an offence under these provisions, or for an offence ancillary to such an offence, must not be instituted except by or with the consent of the Attorney General[10].

A person is regarded as committing an act or crime mentioned above only if the material elements are committed with intent and knowledge[11].

1   As to the International Criminal Court see PARA 437.
2   See the International Criminal Court Act 2001 s 54(7), Sch 9 (which sets out the Rome Statute of the International Criminal Court (17.7.98) (UN Doc A/CONF 183/9; 37 ILM (1998), 999) (the 'ICC Statute') art 70.1). As to the ICC Statute see PARA 422 et seq.
3   International Criminal Court Act 2001 s 54(1). The corresponding domestic offences are: (1) in relation to head (1) in the text, an offence against the Perjury Act 1911 s 1(1) (see CRIMINAL LAW, EVIDENCE AND PROCEDURE vol 11(2) (2006 Reissue) PARA 712); (2) in relation to head (3) in the text, an offence against the Criminal Justice and Public Order Act 1994 s 51 (see CRIMINAL LAW, EVIDENCE AND PROCEDURE vol 11(2) (2006 Reissue) PARA 726) or at common law; (3) in relation to head (2), (4), (5) or (6) in the text, an offence at common law: International Criminal Court Act 2001 s 54(3).
4   International Criminal Court Act 2001 s 54(2).
5   As to the meaning of 'United Kingdom' see PARA 30 note 3.
6   As to the meaning of 'United Kingdom national' see PARA 454 note 7.
7   As to the meaning of 'United Kingdom resident' see PARA 454 note 8.
8   International Criminal Court Act 2001 s 54(4). As to the meaning of 'person subject to United Kingdom service jurisdiction' see PARA 454 note 9.
9   International Criminal Court Act 2001 s 54(6).
10 International Criminal Court Act 2001 s 54(5).
11 International Criminal Court Act 2001 s 66(1), (2). This applies unless it is otherwise provided: see s 66(2).
     For these purposes, a person has intent: (1) in relation to conduct, where he means to engage in the conduct; and (2) in relation to a consequence, where he means to cause the consequence or is aware that it will occur in the ordinary course of events: s 66(3)(a). 'Knowledge' means awareness that a circumstance exists or a consequence will occur in the ordinary course of events: s 66(3)(b).
     In interpreting and applying the provisions of s 66, the court must take into account any relevant judgment or decision of the ICC: s 66(4). Account may also be taken of any other relevant international jurisprudence: s 66(4).

458. Responsibility of commanders and other superiors.   A military commander, or a person effectively acting as a military commander, is responsible for offences[1] committed by forces under his effective command and control, or (as the case may be) his effective authority and control, as a result of his failure to exercise control properly over such forces where: (1) he either knew, or owing to the circumstances at the time, should have known that the forces were committing or about to commit such offences; and (2) he failed to take all necessary and reasonable measures within his power to prevent or repress their commission or to submit the matter to the competent authorities for investigation and prosecution[2].

With respect to superior and subordinate relationships not described above, a superior is responsible for offences committed by subordinates under his effective authority and control, as a result of his failure to exercise control properly over such subordinates, where: (a) he either knew, or consciously disregarded information which clearly indicated, that the subordinates were committing or about to commit such offences; (b) the offences concerned activities that were within his effective responsibility and control; and (c) he failed to take all necessary and reasonable measures within his power to prevent or repress their commission or to submit the matter to the competent authorities for investigation and prosecution[3].

A person responsible under these provisions for an offence is regarded as aiding, abetting, counselling or procuring the commission of the offence[4].

In interpreting and applying these provisions the court must take into account any relevant judgment or decision of the International Criminal Court (the 'ICC')[5], and account may also be taken of any other relevant international jurisprudence[6].

Nothing in these provisions is to be read as restricting or excluding any other liability of the commander or superior, or the liability of persons other than the commander or superior[7].

1   Ie offences under the International Criminal Court Act 2001 Pt 5 (ss 50–70), and offences ancillary to such offences: s 65(1). As from a day to be appointed, in so far as it has effect in relation to relevant Pt 5 offences s 65 applies to failures to exercise control of the kind mentioned in s 65(2) or (3) which occurred on or after 1 January 1991, and applies even if the act or conduct constituting the relevant Part 5 offence would not constitute such an offence but for this section: s 65A(8) (prospectively added by the Coroners and Justice Act 2009 s 70(1), (3). At the date at which this volume states the law no such day had been appointed under s 182(5)). But the International Criminal Court Act 2001 s 65, so far as it has effect in relation to relevant Pt 5 offences, does not apply to a failure to exercise control of the kind mentioned in s 65(2) or (3) which occurred before 1 September 2001 unless, at the time the failure occurred, it amounted in the circumstances to a criminal offence under international law: s 65A(9) (as so prospectively added).
2   International Criminal Court Act 2001 s 65(2).
3   International Criminal Court Act 2001 s 65(3).
4   International Criminal Court Act 2001 s 65(4).
5   International Criminal Court Act 2001 s 65(5). As to the International Criminal Court see PARA 437.
6   International Criminal Court Act 2001 s 65(5).
7   International Criminal Court Act 2001 s 65(6).

15. INTERNATIONAL ECONOMIC AND TRADE LAW; ALIENS

(1) INTERNATIONAL FINANCIAL AND TRADE ORGANISATIONS

459. International financial organisations. The United Kingdom is a member of a number of international financial and economic institutions which are specialised agencies of the United Nations[1]. The United Kingdom is also party to agreements establishing international development banks[2], including the Asian Development Bank[3].

1　As to the financial and economic specialised agencies of the United Nations see PARA 533. As to European financial and economic co-operation see FINANCIAL SERVICES AND INSTITUTIONS vol 49 (2008) PARA 1396.

2　As to international development banks see FINANCIAL SERVICES AND INSTITUTIONS vol 49 (2008) PARA 1391 et seq.

3　As to the Asian Development Bank see FINANCIAL SERVICES AND INSTITUTIONS vol 49 (2008) PARA 1389 et seq.

460. General Agreement on Tariffs and Trade. After the 1939–45 war, international conventions and agreements, to which the United Kingdom is a party, were concluded on subjects which include customs duties[1]. In 1947 the General Agreement on Tariffs and Trade was concluded at Geneva, and has since been revised from time to time[2].

1　As to customs duties see CUSTOMS AND EXCISE vol 12(2) (2007 Reissue) PARA 1 et seq.

2　See the General Agreement on Tariffs and Trade (Geneva, 30 October 1947; 55–61 UN TS; Cmd 7258); Supplementary Agreement between Great Britain and the United States of America (Geneva, 30 October 1947; TS 87 (1947); Cmd 7276). The most recent agreement is that of 1994 (GATT 1994). The GATT 1994 agreement can be found annexed to the Agreement establishing the World Trade Organisation: see the Agreement establishing the World Trade Organisation (Marrakesh, 15 April 1994; TS 57 (1996) Cm 3277) Annex 1A. As to the World Trade Organisation see PARA 461.

461. World Trade Organisation. The World Trade Organisation was established in 1994[1] to facilitate the implementation, administration and operation of the General Agreement on Tariffs and Trade[2] and of multilateral trading agreements[3]. The World Trade Organisation has legal personality, and is accorded by each of its members such legal capacity as may be necessary for the exercise of its functions[4] and such privileges and immunities as are necessary for the exercise of its functions[5]. It is not a specialised agency of the United Nations[6]. However, the World Trade Organisation is required to co-operate, as appropriate, with the International Monetary Fund[7] and the International Bank for Reconstruction and Development[8]. The World Trade Organisation may enter into arrangements for consultation and co-operation with other international organisations[9].

The World Trade Organisation consists of: (1) the Ministerial Conference (with representatives of all members meeting at least once every two years)[10]; (2) the General Council (composed of representatives of all members)[11], which also convenes to discharge the responsibilities of the Dispute Settlement Body[12] and the Trade Policy Review Body[13]; (3) the Councils for Trade in Goods, Trade in Services and Trade-Related Aspects of Intellectual Property Rights[14]; and (4) Committees on Trade and Development, Balance-of-Payments Restrictions and the Budget, Finance and Administration[15]. At meetings of the Ministerial Conference and the General Council each member of the World Trade Organisation has one vote[16]. There is a Director General and a Secretariat[17].

1   Agreement establishing the World Trade Organisation (Marrakesh, 15 April 1994; TS 57 (1996) Cm 3277). The Agreement entered into force on 1 January 1995. The European Union is a member, its individual member states are not. At meetings of World Trade Organisation organs, the European Union has the number of votes equal to the number of member states: art IX para 1. As to membership of the World Trade Organisation see arts XI (original membership), XII (accession).
2   Ie the General Agreement on Tariffs and Trade (Geneva, 30 October 1947; 55–61 UN TS; Cmd 7258). As to the General Agreement on Tariffs and Trade see PARA 460.
3   See the Agreement establishing the World Trade Organisation art III.
4   Agreement establishing the World Trade Organisation art VIII para 1.
5   Agreement establishing the World Trade Organisation art VIII para 2. As to privileges and immunities of World Trade Organisation officials and representatives see art VIII paras 3, 4. As to immunities and privileges of international organisations, including the World Trade Organisation, see PARA 309.
6   As to specialised agencies of the United Nations see PARA 533.
7   As to the International Monetary Fund see FINANCIAL SERVICES AND INSTITUTIONS vol 49 (2008) PARA 1391.
8   Agreement establishing the World Trade Organisation art III para 5. As to the International Bank for Reconstruction and Development see PARA 533.
9   Agreement establishing the World Trade Organisation art V.
10 See the Agreement establishing the World Trade Organisation art IV para 1.
11 See the Agreement establishing the World Trade Organisation art IV para 2.
12 See the Agreement establishing the World Trade Organisation art IV para 3.
13 See the Agreement establishing the World Trade Organisation art IV para 4.
14 See the Agreement establishing the World Trade Organisation art IV para 5. These councils may establish subsidiary bodies: art IV para 6.
15 See the Agreement establishing the World Trade Organisation art IV para 7.
16 Agreement establishing the World Trade Organisation art IX para 1. Except as otherwise provided, where a decision cannot be arrived at by consensus, the matter will be decided by voting: art IX para 1. Decisions of the Ministerial Conference and the General Council must be taken by a majority of the votes cast, unless otherwise provided in the Agreement establishing the World Trade Organisation or in the relevant multilateral trade agreement: art IV para 1. Decisions by the General Council when convened as a Dispute Settlement Body must be taken by consensus: see art IX para 1 note 3. The Dispute Settlement Body is deemed to have decided by consensus a matter submitted for its consideration, if no member present at the meeting of the Dispute Settlement Body when the decision is taken objects to the proposed decision: Annex 2 art 2 para 4 note 1.
17 See the Agreement establishing the World Trade Organisation art VI.

(2) TREATMENT OF ALIENS GENERALLY

462.   Admission of aliens.   In customary international law a state is free to refuse the admission of aliens[1] to its territory[2], or to attach whatever conditions it pleases to their entry[3]. This discretion may be limited by treaty[4]. It is usual, when admitting an alien, to require the production of a passport, or in some cases a visa[5].

1   As to aliens in English law see BRITISH NATIONALITY, IMMIGRATION AND ASYLUM vol 4(2) (2002 Reissue) PARA 13.
2   As to statehood and territory see PARA 32 et seq.
3   See 1 Oppenheim's International Law (9th Edn) pp 897–900; *A-G for Canada v Cain* [1906] AC 542 at 546. For the present law of the United Kingdom with respect to immigration see BRITISH NATIONALITY, IMMIGRATION AND ASYLUM.
4   See eg the Treaty on the Functioning of the European Union (Rome, 25 March 1957; TS 1 (1973); Cmnd 5179) providing at art 45 for free movement of workers within the European Community, and at art 49 for the prohibition of restrictions on the freedom of establishment of nationals of a member state in the territory of another member state. The Treaty was formerly

known as the Treaty Establishing the European Community; it has been renamed and its provisions renumbered: see PARA 304 note 1. See also the European Convention on Establishment (Paris, 13 December 1955; TS 1 (1971); Cmnd 4573), which provides that each of the states parties must facilitate the entry into its territory by nationals of other states parties for the purpose of temporary visits and permit those persons to travel freely within its territory, except where this would be contrary to public order, national security, public health or morality: art 1. Further, subject to economic and social conditions, each contracting state must facilitate the prolonged or permanent residence of such persons in its territory: art 2. For an example of a bilateral treaty see the Treaty of Commerce, Establishment and Navigation with Japan (London, 14 November 1962; TS 53 (1963); Cmnd 2085) under which each state grants most favoured nation treatment in this respect to nationals of the other. As to bilateral investment treaties see PARA 481 et seq.

5   As to passports see BRITISH NATIONALITY, IMMIGRATION AND ASYLUM vol 4(2) (2002 Reissue) PARA 78. The United Kingdom has concluded numerous agreements with other states for the mutual abolition of visas.

463.   International minimum standard.   As a general rule, if a state chooses to admit an alien[1] into its territory it must conform in its treatment of him to the international minimum standard[2]. The precise content of the standard is a matter for debate. According to the formulation most frequently referred to, to breach the standard the conduct in question would have to amount to an outrage, to bad faith, to wilful neglect of duty or to an insufficiency of governmental action so far short of international standards that every reasonable and impartial man would readily recognise its insufficiency[3]. However, it is commonly recognised that the standard has evolved since this formulation[4]. It has also been held that although the application of the standard may vary from case to case, it requires that the state should accord treatment which measures up to the ordinary standards of civilisation[5]. Although an alien must take the foreign country as he finds it and is thus liable to suffer the political vicissitudes of life in that country and to share to that extent the fortunes of its citizens[6], equality of treatment of the alien with that state's citizens does not conform with the international minimum standard if the state treats its own nationals in a manner which falls below the standard of civilisation[7]. This international standard applies in respect of fundamental human rights, such as the right to life and integrity of persons[8], and not to political rights, in respect of which an alien can only expect equality of treatment, or even less than equality, with that accorded to the state's own nationals[9]. It also comprises protection against denials of justice[10].

1   See PARA 462. As to aliens in English law see BRITISH NATIONALITY, IMMIGRATION AND ASYLUM vol 4(2) (2002 Reissue) PARA 13.

2   See 1 Oppenheim's International Law (9th Edn) pp 897–900.

3   *Neer Case* 4 RIAA 60 at 61, 62 (1926). See also the *Chapman Case* 4 RIAA 632 (1930). In the context of the protection of foreign investors, see generally Dolzer and Schreuer *Principles of International Investment Law* (1st Edn, 2008) pp 11–17. There is an ongoing debate as to whether the fair and equitable treatment standard that is frequently contained in bilateral investment treaties comprises anything more than the international minimum standard: see PARA 483.

4   See eg *Mondev International Ltd v United States of America* ICSID Case No ARB (AF)/99/2, Award of 11 October 2002, 42 ILM 85, 6 ICSID Rep 192 (2004) para 125; *ADF v United States of America* ICSID Case No ARB(AF)/00/1, Award of 9 January 2003, 6 ICSID Rep 470 (2004) para 179.

5   *Roberts Case* 4 RIAA 77 (1926); *Hopkins Case* 4 RIAA 41 (1926). The state must at least use the means at its disposal to look after an alien and deal with him in accordance with natural justice: *Chattin Case* 4 RIAA 282 (1927). The justification for the manner of treatment of an alien may depend to some extent upon the conditions existing at the time and the resources available to the state: *Janes Case* 4 RIAA 82 (1926). The standard has been held to comprise a due diligence obligation to accord protection and security to the property of an alien: see eg *Asian Agricultural Products Ltd (AAPL) v Sri Lanka* ICSID Case No ARB/87/3, Award of

27 June 1990, 30 ILM (1991) 577, 4 ICSID Rep 245 (1997); *Noble Ventures Inc v Romania* ICSID Case No ARB/01/11, Award of 12 October 2005, para 164.

6   *Starrett Housing Corpn v Iran* 4 Iran-US CTR 122 (1983); and *Bayindir Insaat Turizm Ticaret Ve Sanayi AS v Republic of Pakistan* ICSID Case No ARB/03/29, Award of 27 August 2009 (in the context of protections under a bilateral investment treaty). See also *Rosa Gelbtrunk Case* Foreign Relations of the United States (1902) 876 at 877–878; *British Claims in the Spanish Zone of Morocco* 2 RIAA 615 at 644 (1925). A resident alien owes a local allegiance to the state of his residence sufficient to convict him of treason: see *De Jager v A-G of Natal* [1907] AC 326, 5 BILC 74, PC; *Joyce v DPP* [1946] AC 347, HL. In English law, the plea of act of state is not available to the Crown by way of defence to a claim in tort by a foreign friendly person: *Johnstone v Pedlar* [1921] 2 AC 262, HL. As to acts of state see PARA 22 et seq.

7   This was stated in the *Roberts Case* 4 RIAA 77 (1926); *Hopkins Case* 4 RIAA 41 (1926). The sufficiency of national treatment was held to be the rule of international law in some early decisions: *Canevaro Case* 11 RIAA 397 (1912); *Cadenhead Case* 6 RIAA 40 (1914); *Standard Oil Co Case* 2 RIAA 781 at 794 (1926). However, the Permanent Court of International Justice stated that a measure of treatment of aliens which is prohibited by international law does not become legitimate merely by virtue of its being meted out to nationals: *Certain German Interests in Polish Upper Silesia* PCIJ Ser A No 7 at 33 (1926). This is consistent with the well-established principle that a state cannot rely on its own internal law to defeat an international law obligation.

8   It is probable that the international minimum standard demands that a state should accord to aliens the fundamental personal rights and freedoms contained in international instruments respecting human rights: see CONSTITUTIONAL LAW AND HUMAN RIGHTS vol 8(2) (Reissue) PARA 101 et seq. See also the United Nations General Assembly Declaration on the Human Rights of Individuals who are not Nationals of the Country in which they Live: General Assembly Resolution 144 (XL) GAOR 40 Sess Supp 53, p 252. The wanton killing of an alien (*Youmans Case* 4 RIAA 110 (1926)), false imprisonment and ill-treatment in prison (*Roberts Case* 4 RIAA 77 (1926)), or the looting and damaging of property (The *'Zafiro'* 6 RIAA 160 (1925)) have been held to amount to violation of the international minimum standard. See also the developing jurisprudence in relation to art 1105 of the North Atlantic Free Trade Agreement ('NAFTA') (available at the date at which this volume states the law on the NAFTA Secretariat website at www.nafta-sec-alena.org) which (as officially interpreted by the NAFTA Free Trade Commission) provides for the treatment required by the customary international law minimum standard of treatment of aliens.

9   As to political and property rights see PARAS 471–472.

10 As to denial of justice see PARA 464.

464.   Denial of justice.   Denial of justice refers to a failure by the courts of a state to ensure fundamental fairness in the administration of justice[1], such as fundamental breaches of due process[2]. The failure may equally be by administrative bodies of a state that are engaged in the administration of justice[3]. A denial of justice engages the international responsibility of a state, but only where there has been a failure to exhaust local remedies[4].

1   This has been termed 'procedural denial of justice' (see O'Connell's International Law (2nd Edn) 947), although denial of justice may now be regarded as always procedural in nature: see Paulsson *Denial of Justice in International Law* (1st Edn, 2005) pp 7, 98. See also Fitzmaurice 'The Meaning of the term Denial of Justice' 13 BYIL 93. The threshold is a high one for claimants to meet: see eg *Mondev International Ltd v United States of America* ICSID Case No ARB (AF)/99/2, Award of 11 October 2002, 42 ILM 85, 6 ICSID Rep 192 (2004), where the tribunal considered that 'the question is whether, at an international level and having regard to generally accepted standards of the administration of justice, a tribunal can conclude in the light of all the facts that the impugned decision was clearly improper and discreditable'. See also *Loewen Group Inc and Raymond L Loewen v United States of America* ICSID Case No ARB (AF)/98/3, Award of 26 June 2003, 42 ILM (2003) 811, 7 ICSID Rep 442 (2005). The term 'denial of justice' was at one stage used in a way that was interchangeable with 'state responsibility' in general, but this is no longer common practice.

2   See eg *Loewen Group Inc and Raymond L Loewen v United States of America* ICSID Case No ARB (AF)/98/3, Award of 26 June 2003, 42 ILM (2003) 811, 7 ICSID Rep 442 (2005), where the tribunal found that by any standards the trial of the claimants in the courts of Mississippi had been a disgrace and that by any standards the trial judge had failed to afford due process. The tribunal nonetheless dismissed the claim on jurisdictional grounds. See also Paulsson *Denial*

of Justice in International Law (1st Edn, 2005) pp 180–206 (also considering discrimination, corruption, arbitrariness, retroactive applications of laws, gross incompetence and pretence of form).

3   See Paulsson *Denial of Justice in International Law* (1st Edn, 2005) pp 44–53; Fitzmaurice 'The Meaning of the term Denial of Justice' 13 BYIL 93 at 94. See also *Waste Management Inc v United Mexican States* ICSID Case No ARB(AF)/00/3, Award of April 30, 2004, 43 ILM (2004) 967 para 98 (considering conduct of the state in breach of the international minimum standard (as reflected in art 1105 of the North Atlantic Free Trade Agreement ('NAFTA') (available at the date at which this volume states the law on the NAFTA Secretariat website at www.nafta-sec-alena.org)) that involves a lack of due process leading to an outcome which offends judicial propriety; e g manifest failure of natural justice in judicial proceedings or a complete lack of transparency and candour in an administrative process).

4   An alien who has been injured by a denial of justice must exhaust any remedies which may be available in superior courts: see PARA 405. This follows where the claim is brought on the basis of diplomatic protection, but also as a necessary element of the international wrong i e as a substantive as well as a procedural requirement: see *Loewen Group Inc and Raymond L Loewen v United States of America* ICSID Case No ARB (AF)/98/3, Award of 26 June 2003, 42 ILM (2003) 811, 7 ICSID Rep 442 (2005) paras 150–156 (the purpose of the requirement that a decision of a lower court must be challenged through the judicial process is to afford the state the opportunity of redressing through its legal system the inchoate breach of international law occasioned by the lower court decision). See also Paulsson *Denial of Justice in International Law* (1st Edn, 2005) pp 100–130.

465.   Refusal of access to courts; delay.   A state commits a denial of justice if an alien is refused access to the courts[1] for the protection and enforcement of his rights[2]. The same is true if it is established that there has been an unconscionable delay on the part of the courts[3], or where the court which is theoretically open to aliens never meets or, if convened, reaches no decision[4]. Application of rules of domestic law permitting non-disclosure of documents is not a denial of justice[5].

1   As to the meaning of 'denial of justice' see PARA 464. As to aliens in English law see BRITISH NATIONALITY, IMMIGRATION AND ASYLUM vol 4(2) (2002 Reissue) PARA 13. See also PARA 462 et seq.

2   *Ambatielos Claim* 12 RIAA 83 (1956). See also *Ruden & Co Case* (1869) Moore Int Arb 1653 (refusal to entertain a claim because the government had forbidden judgment to be pronounced against the state treasury); *Tagliaferro Case* 10 RIAA 592 (1903). This also includes a refusal to allow delivery of copies of documents which are essential to the case: *Ballistini Case* 10 RIAA 18 (1903). See also Paulsson *Denial of Justice in International Law* (1st Edn, 2005) pp 134–146. Note that where a claim cannot be brought because the defendant benefits from sovereign immunity, there is no breach of art 6 of the Convention for the Protection of Human Rights and Fundamental Freedoms (Rome, 4 November 1950; TS 71 (1953); Cmd 8969) (commonly referred to as the 'European Convention on Human Rights'): see *Jones v Ministry of the Interior of the Kingdom of Saudi Arabia (Secretary of State for Constitutional Affairs intervening)* [2006] UKHL 26, [2007] 1 AC 270, [2007] 1 All ER 113; and *Al-Adsani v United Kingdom* (2001) 34 EHRR 273, ECtHR. In *Jones v Ministry of the Interior of the Kingdom of Saudi Arabia* both Lord Bingham (at [14]) and Lord Hoffman (at [64]) expressed doubts as to whether art 6 of the European Convention on Human Rights was engaged (c f the conclusion of the majority in *Al-Adsani v United Kingdom*) on the basis that a state cannot be said to deny access to a court if it has no access to give. The provisions of the European Convention on Human Rights are set out in the Human Rights Act 1998 Sch 1: see CONSTITUTIONAL LAW AND HUMAN RIGHTS vol 8(2) (Reissue) PARA 123 et seq.

3   *Fabiani Case* (1896) Moore Int Arb 4877. See also the *Cotesworth and Powell Case* (1875) Moore Int Arb 2050 (refusal by a judicial authority to exercise its functions, to give a decision on the request submitted to it and also wrongful delay in giving judgment); *Medina Case* (1860) Moore Int Arb 2315; *Orinoco Steamship Co* 9 RIAA 180 (1903); *Rudloff Case* 9 RIAA 244 (1903); *Bullis Case* 9 RIAA 231 (1903); *Interoceanic Rly of Mexico Case* 5 RIAA 178 (1931); *El Oro Mining and Rly Co Ltd* 5 RIAA 191 (1931). States have been held liable for delays in respect of investigation of charges against aliens: *Jones Case* (1880) Moore Int Arb 3253 (alien acquitted after process lasting three years). See also the *Chattin Case* 4 RIAA 282 (1927); *Parrish Case* 4 RIAA 314 (1927); *Dyches Case* 4 RIAA 458 (1929). Everything depends, however, on the circumstances, including the complexity of the case. A state was held not liable

in, for example, the *White Case* (1864) Moore Int Arb 4967 (nine months' delay in trial of alien); *McCurdy Case* 4 RIAA 418 (1929). See also Paulsson *Denial of Justice in International Law* (1st Edn, 2005) pp 177–178.

4   *Fabiani Case* (1896) Moore Int Arb 4877 (where the court also encouraged a debtor's unjustified delay). For a refusal to recognise the locus standi of the claimant see the *Venable* 4 RIAA 219 (1927). See also Paulsson *Denial of Justice in International Law* (1st Edn, 2005) pp 176–177. As to illegitimate assertions of jurisdiction, governmental interference and manipulation of the composition of courts see Paulsson *Denial of Justice in International Law* (1st Edn, 2005) pp 157–164, 178–179.

5   *Ambatielos Claim* 12 RIAA 83 (1956). In *RB (Algeria) v Secretary of State for the Home Department* [2009] UKHL 10, [2009] 4 All ER 1045, [2009] 2 WLR 512 at [265] Lord Mance noted that there appeared to be a considerable resemblance between the concept of flagrant unfairness adopted by the European Court of Human Rights and the concept of denial of justice in public international law generally.

466. Erroneous and unjust decisions. A state is not responsible merely because a decision given in its courts[1] in a case brought by or against an alien[2] is erroneous in terms of its own municipal law[3]. It may, however, incur responsibility if the decision is so erroneous that no properly constituted court could honestly have arrived at such a decision, or where it is due to corruption or pressure of the executive or legislative organs of the state[4]; discrimination against foreigners[5]; procedure so faulty as to exclude all reasonable possibility of a just decision[6]; or the conduct of proceedings being such that a judgment pronounced and executed is in open violation of the law or otherwise manifestly iniquitous[7]. There is a presumption in favour of the due exercise of the judicial process[8].

1   As to the position of administrative bodies of a state that are engaged in the administration of justice see PARA 464.

2   See PARA 462 et seq. As to aliens in English law see BRITISH NATIONALITY, IMMIGRATION AND ASYLUM vol 4(2) (2002 Reissue) PARA 13.

3   See *Azinian v United Mexican States* ICSID Case No ARB(AF)/97/2, Award of 1 November 1999, 39 ILM (2000) 537, 5 ICSID Rep 269 (2002) at paras 97–100. See also Paulsson *Denial of Justice in International Law* (1st Edn, 2005) pp 73–81; Fitzmaurice 'The Meaning of the Term Denial of Justice' (1932) 13 BYIL 93 at 111. See the Reply of the United Kingdom government to the Questionnaire of the League of Nations Preparatory Commission for the Hague Codification Conference 1930, League of Nations Doc C, 75, M 69, 1929 V, 44 at 49; *Martini Case* 2 RIAA 975 at 987 (1930). See *Putnam Case* 4 RIAA 151 at 153 (1927); *Cotesworth and Powell Case* (1875) Moore Int Arb 2050 at 2083; *Garcìa and Garza Case* 4 RIAA 119 at 123, 126 (1926); *Gordon* 4 RIAA 586 at 590 (1930); *Salem Case* 2 RIAA 1161 at 1202 (1932); *Denham Case* 6 RIAA 312 (1933). A mere difference in procedure between different legal systems does not give rise to a denial of justice per se.

4   *Fabiani Case* (1896) Moore Int Arb 4877 at 4882, 4901; *Robert E Brown Case* 6 RIAA 120 (1923) (obstructions on the part of the executive, legislature and judiciary). An unjust judgment raises a strong presumption of dishonesty on the part of the court. It may even afford conclusive evidence, if the injustice is sufficiently flagrant, so that the judgment is of a kind which no honest or competent court could possibly have given: see Fitzmaurice, 'The Meaning of the Term Denial of Justice', (1932) 13 BYIL 93 at 112–113; and Paulsson *Denial of Justice in International Law* (1st Edn, 2005) pp 89, 98. As to corruption or pressure of the executive or legislative organs of the state see Paulsson *Denial of Justice in International Law* (1st Edn, 2005) pp 157–167, 195–196.

5   *Loewen Group Inc and Raymond L Loewen v United States of America* ICSID Case No ARB (AF)/98/3, Award of 26 June 2003, 42 ILM (2003) 811, 7 ICSID Rep 442 (2005) at para 135; *Salem Case* 2 RIAA 1161 at 1202 (1932).

6   *Loewen Group Inc and Raymond L Loewen v United States of America* ICSID Case No ARB (AF)/98/3, Award of 26 June 2003, 42 ILM (2003) 811, 7 ICSID Rep 442 (2005) at paras 53, 119–137. See also Paulsson *Denial of Justice in International Law* (1st Edn, 2005) pp 180–192. See the Reply of the United Kingdom Government to the Questionnaire of the League of Nations Preparatory Commission for the Hague Codification Conference 1930 point 5. This includes the use of menaces or threats and secrecy. As to the trial of the Metropolitan-Vickers Co Employees in Moscow in 1933 see Correspondence etc, Parliamentary Paper Russia No 12 (Cmd 4286, 4290) (1933). It also includes refusal to hear evidence on

behalf of the accused in a criminal trial (*Chattin Case* 4 RIAA 282 (1927)); failure to inform an alien of a charge against him (*Way* 4 RIAA 391 (1928); *Faulkner Case* 4 RIAA 67 (1926)); refusal to summon eye witnesses (*Morton* 4 RIAA 428 (1929)); and probably refusal to allow legal assistance and the services of an interpreter (cf the Convention for the Protection of Human Rights and Fundamental Freedoms (Rome, 4 November 1950; TS 71 (1953); Cmd 8969) art 6 which expressly provides for these: see CONSTITUTIONAL LAW AND HUMAN RIGHTS vol 8(2) (Reissue) PARA 134).

7   See the *Cotesworth and Powell Case* (1875) Moore Int Arb 2050 at 2083; *Driggs Case* (1885) Moore Int Arb 3125 (criminal trial of an alien). Punishment in contravention of the provisions of the local law amounts to a denial of justice: *Rogé Case* 10 RIAA 13 (1903). See also the *Ballistini Case* 10 RIAA 18 (1903). Trial by an illegally constituted court is a denial of justice: *Davy Case* 9 RIAA 467 (1903). The final interpretation of a state's own laws must, as a general rule, be a matter for its own courts: *Garcia and Garza Case* 4 RIAA 119 (1926); see *Serbian Loans* PCIJ Ser A No 20, ar 46–47 (1929); and *Brazilian Loans* PCIJ Ser A No 21, at 120 (1929). However, the international tribunal may overrule the local courts and disregard the decision if the latter has clearly misinterpreted the local law: *De Sabla Case* 6 RIAA 358 (1933); *Solomon Case* 6 RIAA 370 (1933).

     For the right of an accused alien to communicate with the consul of his own state see art 36(1) of the Convention on Consular Relations (Vienna, 24 April 1963; TS 14 (1973); Cmnd 5219); and *Avena and Other Mexican Nationals (Mexico v United States of America)* ICJ Reports 2004, 12.

8   *Interoceanic Rly of Mexico Case* 5 RIAA 178 (1931).

467.   Refusal to execute judgment.   A refusal or other unjustified failure to execute a judgment favourable to an alien in a civil case may constitute a denial of justice[1]. This may arise from the alien's inability to recover damages from the defendant by reason of an amnesty granted him by the state[2].

1   *Interoceanic Rly of Mexico Case* 5 RIAA 178 (1931); *Montano Case* (1863) Moore Int Arb 1630; *Bethune Case* 6 RIAA 32 (1914) (court clerk embezzled the funds which the court had ordered to be paid to the claimant); *Fabiani Case* (1896) Moore Int Arb 4877 at 4899; and see Paulsson *Denial of Justice in International Law* (1st Edn, 2005) pp 168–170. See also Application 58263/00 *Timofeyev v Russia* [2003] ECHR 58263/00 at 40 (concerning art 6 of the Convention for the Protection of Human Rights and Fundamental Freedoms (Rome, 4 November 1950; TS 71 (1953); Cmd 8969). As to the meaning of 'denial of justice' see PARA 464. As to aliens in English law see BRITISH NATIONALITY, IMMIGRATION AND ASYLUM vol 4(2) (2002 Reissue) PARA 13.

2   *Cotesworth and Powell Case* (1875) Moore Int Arb 2050 at 2085; *Montijo Case* (1875) Moore Int Arb 1421 at 1438. However, see also *Pringle (Santa Isabel Claims) ((USA) v United Mexican States)* 4 RIAA 783 (1926). As to aliens in English law see BRITISH NATIONALITY, IMMIGRATION AND ASYLUM vol 4(2) (2002 Reissue) PARA 13. See also PARA 462 et seq.

468.   Internationally erroneous decisions.   As a matter of rules on attribution, the conduct of any state organ is to be considered an act of that state under international law, including where the organ exercises judicial functions[1]. A state incurs responsibility if a decision of its courts is inconsistent with a treaty obligation of the state[2], its international competence[3] or an international award binding on the state[4]. This is, however, a separate matter to denial of justice[5].

1   Articles on Responsibility of States for Internationally Wrongful Acts ('ARSIWA') art 4(1), Report of the International Law Commission, 53rd Session (2001), YILC 2001, vol II(2); and PARA 338. See also *Difference Relating to Immunity from Legal Process of a Special Rapporteur of the Commission on Human Rights (Advisory Opinion)* ICJ Reports 1999, 62 at 87 (para 62).

2   Eg when proceedings in a court conflict with the provisions of a treaty calling for the dispensing of particular treatment to an alien: *Van Bokkelen Case* (1888) Moore Int Arb 1807; *Yuille Shortridge Case* 2 Lapradelle and Politis, Recueil des Arbitrages Internationaux 78 (1861).

3   This would include an assumption of jurisdiction in a case in which a court has no jurisdiction over an alien by international law: *Costa Rica Packet Case* (1895) 89 BFSP 1181 (arrest and trial of British captain for offence allegedly in Dutch waters; proved that the act took place on the high seas); *Lotus Case* PCIJ Ser A No 10 (1927) (where this was assumed). If there is a wrongful assumption of jurisdiction the fact that it was taken in error may be no defence: *Coquitlam* 6 RIAA 45 (1920).

4   See eg *Request for Interpretation of the Judgment of 31 March 2004 in the Case concerning Avena and Other Mexican Nationals (Mexico v United States of America) (Mexico v United States of America)* ICJ Reports, 19 January 2009 (paras 44, 52–53), where the failure of the Texan courts to give effect to the International Court's provisional measures order of 16 July 2008 led to a breach of international law by the United States. See also *Martini Case* 2 RIAA 975 (1930) (dealing with a judgment contrary to an earlier award of 1905 (see 10 RIAA 644)); *Saipem SpA v People's Republic of Bangladesh* ICSID Case No ARB/05/7, Award of 30 June 2009 (failure to enforce an arbitral award).

5   See eg Paulsson *Denial of Justice in International Law* (1st Edn, 2005) pp 84–85.

469. Failure to punish offences. A state may incur international responsibility as a matter of customary international law[1] if it fails to take reasonable steps to apprehend[2], prosecute[3] and punish[4] offences against aliens[5]. In such a case the state is responsible for its own wrong, committed by its own agents, and not because of complicity in the wrong committed by the culprit[6].

1   Liability may also be established pursuant to treaty, in particular by reference to the investigative duty under arts 2 and 3 of the Convention for the Protection of Human Rights and Fundamental Freedoms (Rome, 4 November 1950; TS 71 (1953); Cmd 8969): see CONSTITUTIONAL LAW AND HUMAN RIGHTS vol 8(2) (Reissue) PARA 122 et seq).

2   If reasonable efforts have been made to apprehend or prosecute the culprit, the state is not liable: see the *Sevey Case* 4 RIAA 474 (1929) (delay of four hours in arriving on the scene of the crime); *Costello Case* 4 RIAA 496 (1929) (insufficient evidence given to authorities); *Willis Case* 4 RIAA 544 (1929); *Sturtevant Case* 4 RIAA 665 (1930). But it will be liable if its failure to do so after some time is unexplained: see the *Massey Case* 4 RIAA 155 (1927); *Richards Case* 4 RIAA 275 (1927); *Kling* 4 RIAA 575 (1930); *Austin Case* 4 RIAA 623 (1930). It will be liable if there have been only dilatory measures in tracking down the culprit or investigating a criminal offence: *Janes Case* 4 RIAA 82 (1926); *Neer Case* 4 RIAA 60 (1926); *Youmans Case* 4 RIAA 110 (1926); *Massey Case*; *Roper Case* 4 RIAA 145 (1927); *Boyd Case* 4 RIAA 380 (1928); *Canahl Case* 4 RIAA 389 (1928); *Corcoran Case* 4 RIAA 470 (1929); *Almaguer Case* 4 RIAA 523 (1929); *Tribolet Case* 4 RIAA 598 (1930); *Gorham Case* 4 RIAA 640 (1930).

3   An inordinate lapse of time before the culprit is brought to trial or negligence, laxity or undue delay in his prosecution may engage the state's responsibility: see *Janes Case* 4 RIAA 82 (1926); *Swinney Case* 4 RIAA 98 (1926); *Roper Case* 4 RIAA 145 (1927); *Stephens Case* 4 RIAA 265 (1927); *Galvan Case* 4 RIAA 273 (1927); *Richards Case* 4 RIAA 275 (1927); *Chase Case* 4 RIAA 337 (1928); *Mecham Case* 4 RIAA 440 (1929); *Munroe* 4 RIAA 538 (1929). An eight months' delay in criminal proceedings did not impose liability: see the *McCurdy Case* 4 RIAA 418 (1929). Merely to arrest the culprit does not exonerate the state: *Swinney Case* 4 RIAA 98 (1926); *Gorham Case* 4 RIAA 640 (1930); *East Case* 4 RIAA 646 (1930); *Mead Case* 4 RIAA 653 (1930); *Chase Case* (1846) Moore Int Arb 3336. Nor is it sufficient that the culprit is convicted of an offence other than that committed against the alien: *Connolly Case* 4 RIAA 387 (1928). However, the state is not responsible solely because the culprit is prosecuted and properly found not guilty: *Willis Case* 4 RIAA 544 (1929); *Gordon* 4 RIAA 586 (1930).

4   The state may be liable for inadequate punishment of the culprit (*Kennedy Case* 4 RIAA 194 (1927); *Morton* 4 RIAA 428 (1929); *Sewell Case* 4 RIAA 626 (1930); *Gust Adams Case* 6 RIAA 321 (1933)) or if it fails to give effect to a sentence awarded (*Mallén Case* 4 RIAA 173 (1927)). However, commutation of a death sentence has been held not to engage state responsibility: *Putnam Case* 4 RIAA 151 (1927); *Sewell Case* 4 RIAA 626 (1930). Reversal of the sentence of a court-martial on proper grounds has been held not to render the state liable: *García and Garza Case* 4 RIAA 119 (1926). An amnesty to a common criminal may give rise to responsibility: *West Case* 4 RIAA 270 (1927); *Denham Case* 6 RIAA 312 (1933). However, a general amnesty may not do so where the amnesty is concerned with the pacification of a country. For the distinction in such cases between crimes of a political nature and common crimes see the *Buena Tierra Mining Co Ltd Case* 5 RIAA 247 (1931); *Pringle (Santa Isabel) Case* 4 RIAA 783 (1926).

5   As to aliens in English law see BRITISH NATIONALITY, IMMIGRATION AND ASYLUM vol 4(2) (2002 Reissue) PARA 13.

6   *Janes Case* 4 RIAA 82 (1926).

470. Equality of aliens and nationals. In some respects, international law requires only that a state should accord the same treatment to aliens[1] as it does to its own nationals[2]. Thus, a state has the right to require that an alien should pay taxes and local rates[3], undertake jury service if it is asked of him[4], be subject to billeting of troops and to belligerent military requisitions in time of national emergency[5], and serve in the police and the militia[6]. It appears, however, that an alien cannot be compelled to serve in the armed forces[7], unless he is admitted into the state with a view to permanent residence or eventual naturalisation[8].

1 See PARA 462 et seq. As to aliens in English law see BRITISH NATIONALITY, IMMIGRATION AND ASYLUM vol 4(2) (2002 Reissue) PARA 13.

2 By the European Convention on Establishment (Paris, 13 December 1955; TS 1 (1971); Cmnd 4573), the member states of the Council of Europe guaranteed common treatment of the nationals of each of them with respect to admission and expulsion and with regard to the enjoyment of civil rights, protection of property, social security benefits and taxation and, subject to certain exceptions, the same economic rights as those enjoyed by nationals. Similar benefits are guaranteed as between themselves by the member states of the European Union under the Treaty on the Functioning of the European Union (Rome, 25 March 1957; TS 1 (1973); Cmnd 5179). The Treaty was formerly known as the Treaty Establishing the European Community; it has been renamed and its provisions renumbered: see PARA 304 note 1.

3 *Cook Case* 4 RIAA 593 at 595 (1930). The right to tax may be modified by rules of international law regarding confiscation of property: see PARA 473. The mere fact that a person is an alien is irrelevant to his tax liability under United Kingdom law: see generally INCOME TAXATION. The United Kingdom has entered into several agreements with other states for the avoidance of double taxation.

4 Report of the Law Officers of the Crown, 12 May 1873, 6 British Digest 367.

5 See 6 British Digest 398–401. As to taxation for military purposes see 6 British Digest 402–405.

6 See the Reports of the Law Officers of the Crown, 6 British Digest 368–372.

7 *Polites v The Commonwealth* (1945) 70 CLR 60 at 70, Aust HC, per Latham CJ. The court, however, held that it was bound to apply an Australian statute which imposed such liability upon aliens. See 6 British Digest 372–394. See also Brownlie *Principles of Public International Law* (7th Edn, 2008) p 521. During the 1939–45 War alien nationals of allied powers were conscripted into HM armed forces under the Allied Powers (War Service) Act 1942 (repealed), although this was done with the consent of the allied powers themselves. As to national service see CONSTITUTIONAL LAW AND HUMAN RIGHTS vol 8(2) (Reissue) PARA 27.

Great Britain has in the past entered into treaties with other states containing stipulations for reciprocal exemption of nationals from military service obligations: 6 British Digest 394–398. See the International Protocol relating to Military Obligations in Certain Cases of Double Nationality (The Hague, 12 April 1930; TS 22 (1937); Cmd 5460) amended by Protocol (Strasbourg 24 November 1977; TS 108 (1979); Cmnd 7756) and the Convention on Reduction of Cases of Multiple Nationality and Military Obligations in Cases of Multiple Nationality (Strasbourg, 6 May 1963; TS 88 (1971); Cmnd 4802) Chs II, III and IV. Chapter II deals with military obligations.

8 For example, the law of the United States of America requires that an alien who is admitted for permanent residence may be obliged to serve in the armed forces of the state (see the Universal Military Training Service Act 1951 (United States)), and that an alien who claims exemption from military service is thereafter permanently ineligible for citizenship (see Immigration and Nationality Act 1952 (United States)). The United Kingdom government has stated that it cannot object to the requirement of military service thus imposed upon immigrant British subjects into the United States in the absence of discrimination upon the basis of their nationality: 725 HC Official Report (5th series), 28 February 1966, col 899.

471. Treatment of aliens less favourable than national treatment. As a matter of customary international law a state may impose restrictions upon the exercise of certain rights by aliens[1] whom it has admitted into its territory[2]. Thus, it may impose restrictions upon the participation by aliens in political or public life[3], ownership of property by aliens[4] or upon their taking employment[5].

1 See PARA 462 et seq. As to aliens in English law see BRITISH NATIONALITY, IMMIGRATION AND ASYLUM vol 4(2) (2002 Reissue) PARA 13.

2 For the practice of the United Kingdom in this respect generally see 6 British Digest 254–269. As to territory see PARA 111 et seq.

3 An alien may be denied the right to vote or membership in the legislature. Under the law of the United Kingdom an alien cannot vote in a parliamentary election (see the Representation of the

People Act 1983 s 1(1) (substituted by the Representation of the People Act 2000 s 1(1))) or sit in the House of Commons (Act of Settlement 1700 s 3 (modified by the Electoral Administration Act 2006 s 18)): see ELECTIONS AND REFERENDUMS vol 15(3) (2007 Reissue) PARAS 110, 231). Nationals of member states of the European Union may vote in elections to local government authorities in the United Kingdom: see the Representation of the People Act 1983 s 2(1) (substituted by the Representation of the People Act 2000 s 1(1)). Nationals of member states of the European Union may also vote in the United Kingdom in the elections for the Parliament of the European Union: European Parliamentary Elections Act 2002 s 8(5)); and see CONSTITUTIONAL LAW AND HUMAN RIGHTS vol 8(2) (Reissue) PARA 118.

4   If, however, an alien is permitted to own property, he may only be deprived of it in accordance with the rules of international law governing the expropriation of alien property: see PARA 473.

5   Under the law of the United Kingdom an alien may not hold any office of profit under the Crown (see the Act of Settlement 1700 s 3), but he may hold civil employment if this is outside the United Kingdom, or if a responsible minister certifies that a suitably qualified British subject is not available for the post in question or that the alien has exceptional qualifications: see the Aliens' Employment Act 1955 s 1 (amended by SI 1991/1221; SI 2007/617). Note that nothing in the Act of Settlement s 3 invalidates (1) any appointment, whether made before or after the passing of the Courts Act 2003 (ie 20 November 2003), of a justice of the peace; or (2) any act done by virtue of such an appointment: s 42.

Certain persons with alien parents may be refused employment under the Crown: see the Aliens' Restriction (Amendment) Act 1919 s 6; the Aliens' Employment Act 1955 s 1; and see BRITISH NATIONALITY, IMMIGRATION AND ASYLUM vol 4(2) (2002 Reissue) PARA 13.

An alien may not be a member of the regular forces or any of Her Majesty's forces raised under the law of a British overseas territory, but regulations may be made so as to provide for this restriction not to apply to an alien who satisfies prescribed conditions: see the Armed Forces Act 2006 s 340. In exercise of this power, the Armed Forces (Aliens) Regulations 2009, SI 2009/835, have been made which specify that the restriction in the Armed Forces Act 2006 s 340(1) does not apply to a citizen or national of Nepal who serves, or has for not less than five years served, in the Brigade of Gurkhas: see ARMED FORCES.

As to discrimination on the basis of nationality see DISCRIMINATION vol 13 (2007 Reissue) PARA 441.

472.   Expulsion of aliens.   As a matter of customary international law, a state may expel an alien[1] from its territory[2] at its discretion[3]. However, this discretion is not absolute: a state must not abuse its right by acting arbitrarily in taking a decision to expel an alien, and an international tribunal may require reasons to be given for the expulsion of an alien and may pronounce upon their adequacy[4]. The manner of expulsion may engage the international responsibility of the expelling state to that of the alien's nationality. In particular, the expulsion should be consistent with the domestic law of the expelling state[5] and be carried out with the minimum of inconvenience and indignity to the alien[6]. The right to expel aliens may be limited by treaty[7]. An alien should not be deported except to the country of which he is a national[8].

1   See PARA 462 et seq. As to aliens in English law see BRITISH NATIONALITY, IMMIGRATION AND ASYLUM vol 4(2) (2002 Reissue) PARA 13.

2   As to territory see PARA 111 et seq.

3   See 1 Oppenheim's International Law (9th Edn) 940–945. The general right to expel aliens was recognised in the *Boffolo Case* 10 RIAA 528 at 537 (1903). See also *A-G for Canada v Cain* [1906] AC 542 at 546, PC. The right to expel aliens is recognised by the United Kingdom government: see 460 HC Official Report (5th series), 19 January 1949, cols *154–155*; 682 HC Official Report (5th series), 1 August 1963, written answers, col *164*; 725 HC Official Report (5th series), 8 March 1966, col *1880*. As to the present law of the United Kingdom on the deportation of non-British citizens see BRITISH NATIONALITY, IMMIGRATION AND ASYLUM vol 4(2) (2002 Reissue) PARA 160. As to extradition generally see EXTRADITION. There are limitations on deportation and extradition: see eg *Soering v United Kingdom* (1989) 11 EHRR 439, ECtHR; *Chahal v United Kingdom* (1996) 23 EHRR 413, ECtHR (extradition or deportation might result in individual suffering inhuman or degrading treatment contrary to art 3 of the Convention for the Protection of Human Rights and Fundamental Freedoms (Rome, 4 November 1950; TS 71 (1953); Cmd 8969) (commonly referred to as the 'European

Convention on Human Rights')); and *R (on the application of Ullah) v Special Adjudicator* [2004] UKHL 26, [2004] 2 AC 323, [2004] 3 All ER 785 (successful reliance on articles other than art 3 of the European Convention on Human Rights as a ground for resisting extradition or expulsion demand the presentation of a very strong case). The expulsion of persons who, by long residence, have acquired prima facie the effective nationality of the host state is not a matter of discretion, since the issue of nationality places the right to expel in question: see Brownlie *Principles of Public International Law* (7th Edn, 2008) p 521.

4   See 1 Oppenheim's International Law (9th Edn) 940–945. See also *Boffolo Case* 10 RIAA 528 (1903); *Chase Case* (1846) Moore Int Arb 3336; *Costa's Case* (1868) Moore Int Arb 3724. An alien may be 'constructively' expelled, ie although no law, regulation or directive forces him to leave, his continued presence in the state is made impossible because of conditions brought about by wrongful acts of the state: *Rankin v Islamic Republic of Iran* 17 Iran-US CTR 135 (1987); *Yeager v Islamic Republic of Iran* 17 Iran-US CTR 92 (1987); *International Technical Products and ITP Export Corpn v Islamic Republic of Iran* 9 Iran-US CTR 18 (1986). See *Short v Islamic Republic of Iran* 16 Iran-US CTR 76 (1987).

5   *Boffolo Case* 10 RIAA 528 (1903) (where it was also held that in time of peace an alien should only be expelled in the interests of public order or for reasons of state security). See also the International Covenant on Civil and Political Rights 1966, 16 December 1966 (UN TS vol 999, p 171) art 13. It appears that in time of war a state has the right to expel all enemy aliens from its territory: see 1 Oppenheim's International Law (9th Edn) 941. Under the Convention relative to the Protection of Civilian Persons in Time of War (Geneva Red Cross Convention) (Geneva, 12 August 1949; TS 39 (1958); Cmnd 550), the right of civilians to depart from the territory of an enemy state on the outbreak of war is stipulated for in art 35 (set out in the Geneva Conventions Act 1957 Sch 4: see WAR AND ARMED CONFLICT). As to the meaning of 'state' see PARA 39 et seq.

6   The state must act reasonably in the manner in which it effects an expulsion: see 1 Oppenheim's International Law (9th Edn) 940, 945–948. See also *Maal Case* 10 RIAA 730 (1903); *Ben Tillett's Case* (1898) 6 British Digest 124 at 147; *Attellis Case* (1839) Moore Int Arb 3333; *Dillon Case* 4 RIAA 368 (1928). See British Practice in International Law 1966, 111–115.

7   See eg the European Convention on Establishment (Paris, 13 December 1955; TS 1 (1971); Cmnd 4573); Treaty on the Functioning of the European Union (Rome, 25 March 1957; TS 1 (1973); Cmnd 5179) arts 49–55 (formerly arts 52–58 of the Treaty Establishing the European Economic Community, which was renamed and renumbered by the Treaty of Lisbon Amending the Treaty Establishing the European Union and the Treaty Establishing the European Community (Lisbon, 13 December 2007, ECS 13 (2007); Cm 7294)). See also the International Covenant on Civil and Political Rights 1966 art 13, and the limitations imposed by virtue of the European Convention of Human Rights (eg the right not to be subjected to torture or to inhuman or degrading treatment or punishment: see art 3; and note 3). As to the meaning of 'treaty' see PARA 71.

8   Reply of the United Kingdom Government to League of Nations Questionnaire for the Hague Codification Conference 1930; League of Nations Official Journal (1934) 373. It is not the practice to deport stateless aliens from the United Kingdom.

473.   Expropriation of aliens' property. It is now generally accepted that, subject to any international engagements to the contrary[1], expropriation[2] of the property of aliens[3] is not in itself contrary to international law, provided that certain conditions are met[4]. The debate has focused on the nature of these conditions. It is now generally considered that expropriation will not be contrary to international law[5], provided: (1) it is for some bona fide public purpose[6]; (2) it is not discriminatory[7]; and (3) it is accompanied by compensation[8].

1   As to bilateral investment treaties see PARAS 481–487. The engagement could also be contained in a contract with the state that is governed by international law.

2   As to the nature of expropriation see PARA 474.

3   See PARA 462 et seq. As to aliens in English law see BRITISH NATIONALITY, IMMIGRATION AND ASYLUM vol 4(2) (2002 Reissue) PARA 13.

4   See 1 Oppenheim's International Law (9th Edn) pp 918–922 (the expropriation must not be arbitrary); Shaw's International Law (6th Edn, 2008) pp 828–829. See also General Assembly Resolution 1803 (XVII) of 14 December 1962 concerning Permanent Sovereignty over Natural Resources art 4; Resolution 2158 (XXI) of 25 November 1966; Draft OECD Convention on Protection of Foreign Investment 1967 (the Draft Convention can be found in 7 ILM (1968)

241, 248); Harvard Draft Convention on International Responsibility of States for Injuries to Aliens 1961 art 10 (the Draft Convention can be found in 55 American Journal of International Law 553). See also American Law Institute, Restatement (Third) of the Foreign Relations Law of the United States (1987) para 712; *Taking of Property*, UNCTAD Series on issues in international investment agreements (2000) pp 11–17 (also referring to a requirement of due process); and *International Investment Agreements: Key Issues Vol I*, UNCTAD Series on issues in international investment agreements (2004) p 235. See also *International Investment Law: A Changing Landscape*, OECD (2005) pp 45–48. In *Methanex Corpn v United States* 44 ILM (2005) 1343 a tribunal constituted under Ch 11 of the North Atlantic Free Trade Agreement ('NAFTA') found that as a matter of general international law, a non-discriminatory regulation for a public purpose which is enacted in accordance with due process and which affects a foreign investor or investment is not deemed expropriatory and compensable unless specific commitments had been given by the regulating government to the then putative foreign investor contemplating investment that the government would refrain from such regulation. However, see the controversial approach adopted in General Assembly Resolution 3281 (XXIX) 12 December 1974 (Charter of Economic Rights and Duties of States) art 2.

5   Differing types of expropriation have been distinguished as follows: (1) expropriation for certain public purposes (eg exercise of police power and defence measures in wartime is lawful even if no compensation is payable); (2) expropriation of particular items of property is unlawful unless there is payment of effective compensation; (3) nationalisation, (ie expropriation of a major industry or resource) is unlawful only if there is no provision for compensation payable on a basis compatible with the economic objectives of the nationalisation and the viability of the economy as a whole: see Brownlie *Principles of Public International Law* (7th Edn, 2008) p 538.

6   As to public purpose see PARA 475.

7   As to discrimination see PARA 476.

8   As to compensation see PARA 478.

474. The nature of expropriatory conduct. At its most straightforward expropriation consists of an outright deprivation of the owner's title to property, but expropriation may take many forms and action that falls short of a direct taking of the assets in question by the state may still constitute expropriation[1]. For example expropriation may be constituted by depriving the owner of the use of property[2], or excessive use of national legislation to deprive the owner of the fruits of his property (as in the use of tax or exchange laws[3]), or by a government taking successive measures which result in the foreign company being rendered incapable of managing its property[4]. One relevant factor will be whether the acts of the given state are in conflict with undertakings and assurances given in good faith to aliens as an inducement to their making the investments affected by the action[5]. While there has been limited analysis as to the types of property that may be subject to expropriation as a matter of customary international law, it is now well established that property is not confined to immoveable or tangible assets or assets such as shares, but also extends to rights under a contract[6].

1   See 1 Oppenheim's International Law (9th Edn) pp 916–918; Shaw's International Law (6th Edn, 2008) pp 830–832; OECD's International Investment Law, A Changing Landscape (2005) pp 45–48. See generally Judge Higgins 'The Taking of Property by the State: Recent Developments in International Law' Recueil des Cours (1982), vol 176, issue III.

2   See the Harvard Draft Convention on International Responsibility of States for Injuries to Aliens 1961 art 3 (55 American Journal of International Law 548); cited in *Pope & Talbot v Government of Canada* 122 Int LR 293 at 336; Whiteman's Damages in International Law 1387. See also the Note of the United Kingdom government to that of Indonesia respecting British owned Commercial Properties, British Practice in International Law 1964, 194, 195.

3   As to use of tax laws see 704 HC Official Report (5th series), 22 December 1964, col 1036 (Burma company taxation); as to exchange laws see 262 HL Official Report (5th series), 9 December 1964, cols 91–92.

4   See *Starrett Housing Corpn v Islamic Republic of Iran* 4 Iran-US CTR 122 (1983), 154, where the tribunal found that it is recognised in international law that measures taken by a state can interfere with property rights to such an extent that these rights are rendered so useless that they must be deemed to have been expropriated, even though the state does not purport to have

expropriated them and the legal title to the property remains with the original owner. See also *Tippetts v TAMS-AFFA Consulting Engineers of Iran*, Award of 22 June 1984, 6 Iran-US CTR 219 at 225. However, see the *Elettronica Sicula SpA (ELSI) (United States of America v Italy)* ICJ Reports 1989, 15; *Sedco Inc v National Iranian Oil Co* 10 Iran-US CTR 180 (1986).

5 See *Revere Copper & Brass v OPIC* (1978) 56 Int LR 257 at 271.

6 See *Libyan American Oil Co (LIAMCO) v Government of the Libyan Arab Republic* (1977) 62 Int LR 140 at 189. See also the Harvard Draft Convention on International Responsibility of States for Injuries to Aliens 1961 art 10(7) (55 American Journal of International Law 548); Judge Higgins 'The Taking of Property by the State: Recent Developments in International Law' Recueil des Cours (1982), vol 176, issue III. As to expropriation of concessionary contracts see e g *Rudloff Case* 9 RIAA 244 at 250 (1903); *Saudi-Arabia v Arabian American Oil Co (Aramco) Arbitration* (1958) 27 Int LR 117 at 204; *Arbitration between Valentine Petroleum and Chemical Corpn and Agency for International Development* (1967) 44 Int LR 79 at 87; *Starrett Housing Corpn v Islamic Republic of Iran* 4 Iran-US CTR 122 (1983); *Amoco International Finance Corpn v Islamic Republic of Iran* 15 Iran-US CTR 189 (1987).

475. Public purpose. The expropriation[1] must be motivated in good faith by some social or economic public purpose involving the use of the property which is expropriated[2]. Taking property for the purpose of exerting pressure in a political dispute[3], or in order to hand it over to another individual or company would therefore be unlawful[4].

1 See PARA 473 et seq.

2 *Certain German Interests in Polish Upper Silesia* PCIJ Ser A No 7 at 22 (1926); *Norwegian Shipowners Case* 1 RIAA 307 (1922). See also Shaw's International Law (6th Edn, 2008) pp 833–834. As to cases involving an environmental context see *Compañía Del Desarrollo de Santa Elena SA v Republic of Costa Rica* ICSID Case No ARB/96/1, 39 ILM (2000) 1317; and *Methanex Corpn v United States* 44 ILM (2005) 1343, 1456 para 7 (part IV/D of the award). As to the peaceful enjoyment of possessions see the Protocol to the European Convention for the Protection of Human Rights and Fundamental Freedoms (Paris, 20 March 1952; TS 46 (1954); Cmd 9221) art 1; and see CONSTITUTIONAL LAW AND HUMAN RIGHTS vol 8(2) (Reissue) PARA 165. For cases where tribunals have accepted a clear case of a genuine public need see *British Claims in the Spanish Zone of Morocco* 2 RIAA 615 at 665, 679, 680 (1925); *Portuguese Religious Properties Case* 1 RIAA 7 (1920); *Application 511/59, Gudmundsson v Iceland* 3 Yearbook HR 394 at 422; *Amoco International Finance Corpn v Islamic Republic of Iran* 15 Iran-US CTR 189 (1987).

3 For the position of the Netherlands regarding Indonesian expropriation of Dutch properties see 8 Whiteman's Digest 1048–1053. For Indonesian measures against British properties see British Practice in International Law 1964, 194–200. The Cuban nationalisations of American property in 1960 were for avowedly political purposes: see 8 Whiteman's Digest 1042–1047. The Cuban decrees were disregarded as being not for a public purpose and as discriminatory and confiscatory in *Banco Nacional de Cuba v Sabbatino* 307 F 2d 845 (USA Cir 1962); revsd by the Supreme Court by reliance on the 'act of state' doctrine 376 US 398 (1964); re-affd by the Court of Appeals, after an amendment to the Foreign Assistance Act 1961 (United States) in relation to the discriminatory and political nature of the decrees, sub nom *Banco Nacional de Cuba v Farr* 272 F Supp 836 (USA 1965). As to acts of state see PARA 22 et seq.

In 1971 Libya seized the property of British Petroleum Ltd for an avowedly political purpose, and the United Kingdom government protested on 23 December 1971. The dispute was settled by agreement between the company and Libya in December 1974. For the award of the arbitrator in that case see *BP Exploration Co (Libya) Ltd v Government of the Libyan Arab Republic* (1973) 53 Int LR 297 (damages awarded). See also *Texaco Overseas Petroleum Co and California Asiatic Oil Co v Government of the Libyan Arab Republic* (1977) 53 Int LR 389; *Libyan American Oil Co (LIAMCO) v Government of the Libyan Arab Republic* (1977) 62 Int LR 140 at 194 (stating that the public utility principle is not a necessary requisite for the legality of a nationalisation, although it was relevant to the question of whether there had been discrimination).

4 *Walter Fletcher Smith* 2 RIAA 913 (1929).

476. Discrimination. The expropriation[1] of alien[2] property must not be such as to discriminate against the property or its owners[3].

1 See PARA 473 et seq.

2   See PARA 462 et seq. As to aliens in English law see BRITISH NATIONALITY, IMMIGRATION AND
     ASYLUM vol 4(2) (2002 Reissue) PARA 13.
3   *Norwegian Shipowners Case* 1 RIAA 307 at 339 (1922); *British Claims in the Spanish Zone of
     Morocco* 2 RIAA 615 at 647 (1925); *Standard Oil Co Case* 2 RIAA 781 (1926). See the
     Indonesian, Cuban and Libyan nationalisations referred to in PARA 475 note 3. In arbitrations
     which arose out of Libyan nationalisations between British and American oil companies, the
     principle of non-discrimination was confirmed. In *BP Exploration Co (Libya) Ltd v
     Government of the Libyan Arab Republic* (1973) 53 Int LR 297 and *Libyan American Oil Co
     (LIAMCO) v Government of the Libyan Arab Republic* (1977) 62 Int LR 140, the Libyan
     measures were held to be discriminatory. In *Texaco Overseas Petroleum Co and California
     Asiatic Oil Co v Government of the Libyan Arab Republic* (1977) 53 Int LR 389, the measures
     in question were held to be non-discriminatory. The Iran-US Claims Tribunal held that certain
     Iranian measures were non-discriminatory in *Amoco International Finance Corpn v Islamic
     Republic of Iran* 15 Iran-US CTR 189 (1987). See also *Kuwait v American Independent Oil Co*
     (1982) 66 ILR 519, 584. The absence of discrimination is only one factor which may render an
     expropriation lawful; eg a measure prohibited by an international agreement cannot become
     lawful simply because it is applied by the state also to its own nationals: *Certain German
     Interests in Polish Upper Silesia* PCIJ Ser A No 7 at 32 (1926); *Peter Pázmány University Case*
     PCIJ Ser A/B No 61 at 39 (1933).

477.   Treaty obligations.   Expropriation[1] contrary to a treaty[2] obligation
engages state responsibility[3].

1   See PARA 473 et seq.
2   As to the meaning of 'treaty' see PARA 71.
3   Most expropriation claims are now brought pursuant to the provisions in bilateral investment
     treaties (as to which see PARAS 481–487). See also *Factory at Chorzów* PCIJ Ser A No 17 at 46
     (1928). General Assembly Resolution 1803 (XVII) 14 December 1962 provides that foreign
     investment agreements entered into by or between states must be observed in good faith.

478.   Compensation.   Even if an expropriation[1] fulfils the conditions of public
purpose[2] and non-discrimination[3], it is still unlawful if there is a failure to
provide for compensation[4]. One formula commonly used is that the
compensation must be prompt, adequate and effective[5], although according to a
different school of thought the applicable standard is one of 'appropriate
compensation'[6]. A claimant may, in any event, agree to accept less than full
compensation[7].

1   See PARA 473 et seq.
2   See PARA 475.
3   See PARA 476.
4   The general entitlement to compensation has been a subject of controversy but is now largely
     accepted, although there may be exceptions, eg where expropriation follows from a legitimate
     exercise of police power: see Brownlie's Principles of Public International Law (7th Edn, 2008)
     pp 533–536. See also generally Ripinsky and Williams *Damages in International Investment
     Law* (1st Edn, 2008).
5   This is the so-called Hull formula: see the note of Secretary of State Cordell Hull to the
     Government of Mexico dated 21 July 1938, 3 Hackworth's Digest 662. This is reflected in the
     wording of many bilateral investment treaties. See also *Santa Elena v Costa Rica* 39 ILM 1317
     at para 71, and the *Norwegian Shipowners Case* 1 RIAA 307 at 338, 340 (1922) referring to the
     right of the claimants to receive immediate and full compensation. According to the Articles on
     Responsibility of States for Internationally Wrongful Acts ('ARSIWA') art 31(1), Report of the
     International Law Commission, 53rd Session (2001), YILC 2001, vol II(2) (see PARA 374), the
     general obligation on a responsible state is to make full reparation for the injury caused by the
     internationally wrongful act. See also art 35 and the Commentary thereto (see PARA 375)
     dealing with the obligation to pay compensation.
6   See General Assembly Resolution 1803 (XVII) 14 December 1962, which requires that in taking
     property on grounds of public utility, the owner must be paid appropriate compensation in
     accordance with the rules in force in the state taking such measures, and in accordance with
     international law. See also General Assembly Resolution 3281 (XXIX) 12 December 1974
     (Charter of Economic Rights and Duties of States) art 2(c), which provides only that the state

taking property should pay appropriate compensation taking into account its relevant laws and regulations and all circumstances that the state considers pertinent. The United Kingdom voted against the adoption of art 2.

In *Texaco Overseas Petroleum Co and California Asiatic Oil Co v Government of the Libyan Arab Republic* (1977) 53 Int LR 389, the arbitrator held that because the capital exporting states had voted against or had abstained from voting upon art 2 (and in some cases General Assembly Resolution 3281 (XXIX) as a whole) that article did not represent customary international law. Some tribunals have applied the 'appropriate compensation' principle contained in General Assembly Resolution 1803 (XVII): *Kuwait v American Independent Oil Co* 21 ILM (1982) 976. The Iran-US Claims Tribunal also applied the 'appropriate compensation' principle in several cases: see e g *Amoco International Finance Corpn v Islamic Republic of Iran* 15 Iran-US CTR 189 (1987).

It is to be noted that the World Bank Guidelines on the Treatment of Foreign Direct Investment 31 ILM (1992) 1366, 1382 equate appropriate compensation with compensation that is adequate, effective and prompt.

7 This has occurred in the case of several post-war global settlements between the United States government and those of foreign states.

(3) INVESTMENT PROTECTION AND DISPUTE SETTLEMENT

479. Differing sources of investment protection. A foreign investor investing in another state may benefit from specific protections in the form of legislation protecting foreign investments in the host state, protections established by bilateral or multilateral investment treaties[1], or protections established by the terms of a given concession or investment contract with the host state or a state entity. The foreign investor investing in another state benefits from certain protections established as a matter of customary international law[2], but these may be of limited benefit unless the foreign investor has a forum before which international claims can be brought[3].

1 As to the most important substantive protections commonly established by bilateral or multilateral investment treaties see PARAS 481–487.
2 See PARA 480. As to substantive protections of particular importance to investors that are established by customary international law see PARAS 463 et seq, 473–478.
3 The foreign investor may be of the view that he will not be accorded an impartial hearing in the courts of the host state. As to the difficulties that may be encountered in establishing an inter-state claim based on the exercise of diplomatic protection by the state of the investor see PARAS 386–387. Investment claims brought on the basis of diplomatic protection are now very rare.

480. Substantive protections accorded to foreign investors as a matter of customary international law. As a matter of customary international law, the investment of a foreign investor will be protected by application of the international minimum standard[1] and the prohibition of expropriation by the host state save where this is (1) for some bona fide public purpose; (2) not discriminatory; and (3) accompanied by compensation[2].

1 See PARA 463.
2 See PARAS 473–478.

481. Substantive protections accorded to foreign investors as a matter of treaty law. The United Kingdom is party to various bilateral investment treaties (which are termed Investment Promotion and Protection Agreements or 'IPPA's)[1]. There are also multilateral treaties in force that contain important investment protections[2]. Bilateral investment treaties typically contain guarantees that the state will accord to qualifying investors and/or their investments[3] full protection and security[4], fair and equitable treatment[5], national[6] and most favoured nation treatment[7], and typically contain a prohibition of expropriation[8] (unless in compliance with certain stated criteria), and a guarantee of the free transfer in relation to returns and the capital of the investment[9]. Bilateral investment treaties are important to investors not just for the substantive protections they contain but also because they commonly (but not invariably) contain an offer to refer disputes with investors to international arbitration and thus provide an impartial forum for the settlement of disputes[10].

It has also been said that, by virtue of the very large number of bilateral investment treaties concluded, the substantive protections in such treaties impact on the content of customary international law[11]. There is no system of binding precedent either as a matter of the Convention on the Settlement of Investment Disputes between States and Nationals of Other States (the 'ICSID Convention')[12] or so far as concerns other investment treaty arbitrations. It follows that different treaty tribunals may interpret substantively similar treaty provisions to different effect. This happens not infrequently in practice, and the law is currently unsettled regarding many of the provisions typically found in bilateral investment treaties[13]. However, the precise wording of the substantive protections varies from treaty to treaty, and it will be for each given arbitral tribunal to interpret the wording before it[14].

1   See eg the Agreement between the United Kingdom of Great Britain and Northern Ireland and Bosnia and Herzegovina for the Promotion and Protection of Investments (Blackpool, 2 October 2002; TS 37 (2003); Cm 5973). The text of all the UK IPPAs is available on the Foreign Office website (see www.fco.gov.uk). Other bilateral investment treaties are available on the United Nations Conference on Trade and Development website (see www.unctad.org). See also Dolzer and Schreuer *Principles of International Investment Law* (1st Edn, 2008) p 17. As to damages in investment treaty claims see generally Ripinsky and Williams *Damages in International Investment Law* (1st Edn, 2008).

2   See eg the Energy Charter Treaty and Energy Charter Protocol on Energy Efficiency and Related Environmental Aspects (Lisbon, 17 December 1994; TS 78 (2000); Cm 4761) (to which the United Kingdom is a party along with all other EU states and various other states). The United Kingdom instrument of ratification was deposited on 16 December 1997 and the Treaty and Protocol entered into force for the United Kingdom on 16 April 1998. See also the North Atlantic Free Trade Agreement ('NAFTA') to which Canada, Mexico and the United States of America are parties.

3   Bilateral investment treaties invariably contain definitions for qualifying investors and investments that will have to be met in each case. In part for this reason, jurisdictional objections are very common in bilateral investment treaty cases. For a consideration of the principles and jurisprudence relevant to jurisdictional issues see eg Dolzer and Schreuer *Principles of International Investment Law* (1st Edn, 2008) pp 46–65; Douglas *The International Law of Investment Claims* (1st Edn, 2009); McLachlan, Shore and Weiniger *International Investment Arbitration* (1st Edn, 2007) Chs 4–6.

4   See PARA 482.

5   See PARA 483. As is fairly common in bilateral treaties, UK IPPAs (including the latest UK model IPPA) contain a provision by which each state agrees to observe any obligation it may have entered into with regard to investments of nationals or companies of the other state (a so-called 'umbrella clause'): see PARA 483 text and note 6.

6   See PARA 484.

7   See PARA 485.

8   See PARA 486.

9   See PARA 487.

10   As to jurisdictional objections see note 3. As to the different nature of the direct right of action by the investor against the state, as compared to the exercise of a right of diplomatic protection by the state of the investor, see Douglas 'The Hybrid Foundations of Investment Treaty Arbitration' [2003] BYIL 151 cited in *Republic of Ecuador v Occidental Petroleum and Production Co* [2005] EWCA Civ 1116, [2006] QB 432, [2006] 2 All ER 225. In that case the court held, in the context of the justiciability of a challenge under the Arbitration Act 1996 to the award of a treaty tribunal, that the bilateral investment treaty involved a deliberate attempt

to ensure for private investors the benefits and protection of consensual arbitration, which was an aim to which national courts should aspire to give effect. The court also concluded (obiter) that the arbitration agreement created when the investor accepted the offer to arbitrate would itself be governed by international law. This finding has been applied in *ETI Euro Telecom International NV v Republic of Bolivia* [2008] EWCA Civ 880, [2009] 2 All ER (Comm) 37, [2009] 1 WLR 665; and *Sancheti v City of London* [2008] EWCA Civ 1283, [2009] 1 Lloyd's Rep 117, [2008] All ER (D) 204 (Nov). It has always been central to the position of the United Kingdom, and indeed of other states, in the business of concluding IPPAs that an agreement without effective provisions for the settlement of disputes between an investor and the host state is not worth having: see Denza and Brooks 'Investment Protections Treaties: United Kingdom Experience' 36 ICLQ 908 at 923.

11 See eg *Mondev International Ltd v United States of America* ICSID Case No ARB (AF)/99/2, Award of 11 October 2002, 42 ILM 85, 6 ICSID Rep 192 (2004).

12 See eg *Bayindir Insaat Turizm Ticaret Ve Sanayi AS v Republic of Pakistan* ICSID Case No ARB/03/29, Award of 27 August 2009 at para 145. However, tribunals will pay regard to previous decisions and will follow these if they find the reasoning persuasive. As to the Convention on the Settlement of Investment Disputes between States and Nationals of Other States (Washington, 18 March 1965; Cmnd 3255) see PARA 488 note 1.

13 Eg as to the fair and equitable treatment standard and most favoured nation treatment: see PARAS 483, 485.

14 Ie in accordance with arts 31, 32 of the Vienna Convention on the Law of Treaties (Vienna, 23 May 1969; TS 58 (1980); Cmnd 7964): see PARAS 95–97.

482. Full protection and security. Bilateral investment treaties (including UK Investment Promotion and Protection Agreements or 'IPPA's[1]) commonly provide that investors are at all times to enjoy full protection and security in the territory of the host state[2]. This has generally been interpreted as protecting the investor against failures by the state to protect the physical integrity of the investor's property, either in relation to damage caused by state officials or by the actions of others where the state has failed to exercise due diligence[3]. The standard has on occasion been interpreted as going beyond physical security to regulatory security, and some bilateral investment treaties contain wording that suggests that both physical and other forms of security are intended to be provided[4]. In such cases the provision may overlap to some degree with the fair and equitable treatment standard[5].

1 See PARA 481 note 1.

2 This is the formulation commonly used in UK IPPAs and other bilateral investment treaties, but the precise wording varies and this may impact on the correct interpretation of the provision. The provision has its origins in bilateral treaties of friendship, commerce and navigation (FCN treaties) and customary international law. See generally McLachlan, Shore and Weiniger *International Investment Arbitration* (1st Edn, 2007) pp 247–250, Reinisch (ed) *Standards of Investment Protection* (1st Edn, 2008) pp 131–150.

3 See *Asian Agricultural Products Ltd (AAPL) v Sri Lanka* ICSID Case No ARB/87/3, Award of 27 June 1990, 30 ILM (1991) 577, 4 ICSID Rep 245 (1997); *Noble Ventures Inc v Romania* ICSID Case No ARB/01/11, Award of 12 October 2005, at para 164.

4 See eg the treaty under consideration in *Siemens AG v Argentine Republic* ICSID Case No ARB/02/8, Award of 6 February 2007, which made express reference to legal security. For a broader interpretation of the full protection and security standard see *Compañía de Aguas del Aconquija SA and Vivendi Universal SA v Argentine Republic* ICSID Case No ARB/97/3, Award of 20 August 2007.

5 See PARA 483.

483. The fair and equitable treatment standard. Most bilateral investment treaties (including UK Investment Promotion and Protection Agreements or 'IPPA's[1]) provide that investors must at all times be accorded fair and equitable treatment in the territory of the host state[2]. There is considerable uncertainty as to the precise content of the fair and equitable treatment standard and there is an ongoing debate as to whether the standard accords to investors any protection beyond the minimum standard applicable as a matter of customary international law[3]. It has been held that the minimum standard of treatment of fair and equitable treatment is infringed by conduct attributable to the state and is harmful to the claimant if the conduct is arbitrary, grossly unfair, unjust or idiosyncratic, or is discriminatory and exposes the claimant to sectional or racial prejudice, or involves a lack of due process leading to an outcome which offends judicial propriety (as might be the case with a manifest failure of natural justice in judicial proceedings or a complete lack of transparency and candour in an administrative process)[4]. A simple breach of contract by the state is not generally considered to amount to a breach of the fair and equitable treatment standard, although the position is likely to be different where the state commits the breach in exercise of its sovereign power[5]. Certain bilateral investment treaties, including many UK IPPAs, contain a provision by which each state agrees to observe any obligation it may have entered into with regard to investments of nationals or companies of the other state (a so-called 'umbrella clause')[6].

1   See PARA 481 note 1.
2   See generally McLachlan, Shore and Weiniger *International Investment Arbitration* (1st Edn, 2007) pp 226–247; Reinisch (ed) *Standards of Investment Protection* (1st Edn, 2008) pp 111–130. The precise wording of the standard may vary from treaty to treaty.
3   See eg the consideration of this topic in OECD, International Investment Law: A Changing Landscape (2005) Ch 3.
4   See *Waste Management Inc v United Mexican States* ICSID Case No ARB(AF)/00/3, Award of 30 April 2004, 43 ILM (2004) 967 para 98. This is in the context of a consideration of prior cases on fair and equitable treatment under art 1105 of the North Atlantic Free Trade Agreement ('NAFTA') (available at the date at which this volume states the law on the NAFTA Secretariat website at www.nafta-sec-alena.org), which has been authoritatively interpreted as confined to the international minimum standard. However, this is a frequently cited case outside the NAFTA context. The *Waste Management Inc v United Mexican States* award also states that in applying the standard it is relevant that the treatment is in breach of representations made by the host state which were reasonably relied on by the claimant. This is consistent with other cases in which considerable attention has been paid to the investor's legitimate or investment-backed expectations. For a consideration of the contents of the fair and equitable treatment standard in the context of the UK-Tanzania IPPA see *Biwater Gauff (Tanzania) Ltd v United Republic of Tanzania* ICSID Case No ARB/05/22, Award of 24 July 2008 at paras 588–603.
     As to the definition of arbitrariness see *Elettronic Sicula SPA (ELSI) (United States v Italy)* (1989) ICJ Reports 15, 76 (considered by the tribunal in *Mondev International Ltd v United States of America* ICSID Case No ARB (AF)/99/2, Award of 11 October 2002, 42 ILM 85, 6 ICSID Rep 192 (2004) at para 127).
     As to protection from a denial of justice which is part of the fair and equitable treatment standard see PARAS 464–469. In deciding whether there has been a breach of the fair and equitable treatment standard, it may be relevant that the investor knew that there was a politically unstable climate in the host state at the time of investing: see eg *Bayindir Insaat Turizm Ticaret Ve Sanayi AS v Republic of Pakistan* ICSID Case No ARB/03/29, Award of 27 August 2009 at para 193. See also *S D Myers v Canada*, Partial Award of 14 November 2000, in a NAFTA arbitration under the UNCITRAL arbitration rules, at para 263, referring to the high measure of deference that international law generally extends to the right of domestic authorities to regulate matters within their own borders.
5   See eg *Bayindir Insaat Turizm Ticaret Ve Sanayi AS v Republic of Pakistan* ICSID Case No ARB/03/29, Award of 27 August 2009 at para 180. The availability of an agreed forum for the resolution of a contractual dispute may also have an impact on the question of whether the standard has been breached: see *Waste Management Inc v United Mexican States* ICSID Case No ARB(AF)/00/3, Award of 30 April 2004, 43 ILM (2004) 967 at para 116.
6   The meaning and effect of the umbrella clause is far from settled. The precise wording of the umbrella clause may of course vary from treaty to treaty, and this may account for some of the differing interpretations in the jurisprudence. For a survey of the recent jurisprudence see Dolzer and Schreuer *Principles of International Investment Law* (1st Edn, 2008) pp 153–162. See also 'Interpretation of the Umbrella Clause in Investment Agreements' OECD Finance & Investment/ Insurance & Pensions, Vol 2008 No 2 (March 2008) pp 106–141.

484. National treatment. Bilateral investment treaties (including UK Investment Promotion and Protection Agreements or 'IPPA's[1]) commonly provide that investors and investments must be accorded treatment no less favourable than that which is accorded to investors or investments of nationals of the host state[2]. This provision is generally seen as directed against measures that distinguish on the basis of nationality[3]. It appears that a claimant need not establish discriminatory intent; discriminatory effect will suffice[4].

1 See PARA 481 note 1.
2 See generally McLachlan, Shore and Weiniger *International Investment Arbitration* (1st Edn, 2007) 251–254; Reinisch (ed) *Standards of Investment Protection* (1st Edn, 2008) pp 29–58. The precise wording of the standard varies from treaty to treaty.
3 See eg *Consortium RFCC v Morocco* ICSID Case No ARB/00/06, Award of 22 December 2003, 20 ICSID Rev FILJ 391 (2005) para 75; *Noble Ventures Inc v Romania* ICSID Case No ARB/01/11, Award of 12 October 2005 at para 180.
4 See eg *Feldman v United Mexican States* ICSID Case No ARB(AF)/99/01, Award of 16 December 2002, 42 ILM (2003) 625, 7 ICSID Rep 341 (2005) at paras 181–184. It is to be noted that many of the cases concerning national treatment have been brought by reference to art 1102 of the North Atlantic Free Trade Agreement ('NAFTA') (available at the date at which this volume states the law on the NAFTA Secretariat website at www.nafta-sec-alena.org) which contains an express requirement that the foreign investor/investment and the investor/investment of the host state be in 'like circumstances'.

485. Most favoured nation treatment. Bilateral investment treaties (including UK Investment Promotion and Protection Agreements or 'IPPA's[1]) commonly provide that investors and investments must be accorded treatment no less favourable than that which is accorded to investors or investments of any third state[2]. The precise wording of such provisions varies and may be critical to the scope and extent of the most favoured nation ('MFN') treatment[3]. It is generally considered that as one aspect of MFN treatment an investor will be entitled to benefit from any more favourable substantive protections offered by the host state to investors of other nationalities in other bilateral investment treaties[4]. There is considerable debate as to whether an investor is also entitled to use the MFN provision to benefit from more favourable dispute settlement provisions in another bilateral investment treaty, whether in respect of more favourable notice or negotiation periods or an actual offer to arbitrate[5]. The wording of the given treaty may make this express[6].

1 See PARA 481 note 1.
2 See generally the OECD's International Investment Law, A Changing Landscape (2005) Ch 4. See also Reinisch (ed) *Standards of Investment Protection* (1st Edn, 2008) pp 59–86. The topic of MFN provisions is also under consideration by the International Law Commission.
3 See eg *RosInvest v Russian Federation* Award on Jurisdiction, October 2007, at paras 128–130 (concerning the UK-USSR IPPA of 6 April 1989: see the Agreement between the Government of the United Kingdom of Great Britain and Northern Ireland and the Government of the Union of Soviet Socialist Republics for the Promotion and Reciprocal Protection of Investments (London, 6 April 1989; TS 3 (1992); Cm 1791)). The scope of the provision in question was found to turn on the question of whether most favoured nation treatment was accorded to investors (in which case there would be entitlement to benefit from an arbitration offer in a different bilateral investment treaty) or whether it was accorded to investments (in which case there would be no such entitlement).
4 See eg *Bayindir Insaat Turizm Ticaret Ve Sanayi AS v Republic of Pakistan* ICSID Case No ARB/03/29, Award of 27 August 2009 at paras 157–160. It will nonetheless be necessary in each case to ascertain the intentions of the treaty parties as this appears from the MFN provision, particularly when a contrary intention may also appear from the omissions of a given substantive provision from the treaty in question. In addition, the question of whether a given substantive protection in another treaty is ejusdem generis is one that will have to be answered in every case: see Arbitration Award No 24/2007 *Renta 4 SVSA et al v Russian Federation*, 20 March 2009, SCC, and the jurisprudence of the International Court of Justice considered

there. It should also be noted that bilateral investment treaties (including UK IPPAs) frequently contain express exceptions to most favoured nation treatment, eg in respect of a preference or privilege resulting from being a national of a state party to a given customs, economic or monetary union or a given international taxation agreement. The existence or otherwise of such exceptions may be a factor in determining the intended scope of the MFN provision.

5   The law on this point is far from settled. The debate stems from the decision in *Maffezini v Spain* ICSID Case No ARB/97/7, Decision on Objections to Jurisdiction, 25 January 2000, 5 ICSID Rep 396 (2002), where the tribunal held that the claimant was entitled to rely on another bilateral investment treaty that did not contain a requirement to resort to the host state's domestic courts for 18 months before the institution of arbitration. This decision has been followed in one line of later cases. For example, it has been held that an investor was entitled to benefit from a more extensive offer to arbitrate in a different bilateral investment treaty even though the offer in the first treaty was expressly limited: see *RosInvest v Russian Federation* Award on Jurisdiction, October 2007. A different conclusion was reached in *Plama Consortium Ltd v Republic of Bulgaria* ICSID Case No ARB/03/24, Decision on Jurisdiction of 8 February 2005, 20 ICSID Rev FILJ 262 (2005), 44 ILM (2005) 721. For a consideration of the issues see Arbitration Award No 24/2007 *Renta 4 SVSA et al v Russian Federation*, 20 March 2009, SCC. For differing views in the doctrine compare Douglas *The International Law of Investment Claims* (1st Edn, 2009) pp 344–362 and Dolzer and Schreuer *Principles of International Investment Law* (1st Edn, 2008) pp 253–257.

6   Eg the more recent UK IPPAS confirm (for the avoidance of doubt) that most favoured nation treatment applies to listed arts of the IPPA (including the dispute settlement provision).

486.   Expropriation as a treaty standard.   Almost all bilateral investment treaties (including UK Investment Promotion and Protection Agreements or 'IPPA's[1]) contain a prohibition against expropriation[2]. Such provisions typically prohibit expropriation or measures having effect equivalent to expropriation except where the expropriation is for a public purpose, is not discriminatory and is accompanied by prompt adequate and effective compensation[3]. In order for the conduct of the state to constitute an expropriation the interference with the investor's rights must be such as substantially to deprive the investor of the economic value, use or enjoyment of its investment[4]. The effect of the expropriatory conduct is often considered to be the critical factor, as opposed to the expropriatory intent (or otherwise) of the state[5]. However, general regulatory measures of a state (that is measures that are non-discriminatory, made for a public purpose and enacted with due process) may not be expropriatory in nature and hence will not attract compensation[6]. It is well established that contractual rights may be the subject of an expropriation[7]. However, the mere non-compliance by a government with contractual obligations is not the same thing as, or equivalent to, an expropriation[8].

1   See PARA 481 note 1.

2   See generally the OECD's International Investment Law, A Changing Landscape (2005) Ch 2. See also Reinisch (ed) *Standards of Investment Protection* (1st Edn, 2008) pp 151–204. As to the relevant principles from previous North Atlantic Free Trade Agreement ('NAFTA') cases and customary international law see *Fireman's Fund Insurance Co v Mexico*, ICSID Case No ARB(AF)/02/1, Award of 17 July 2006, para 176.

3   The precise wording of such provisions varies. Article 5(1) of the 2008 UK model IPPA provides: 'Investments of nationals or companies of either Contracting Party shall not be nationalised, expropriated or subjected to measures having effect equivalent to nationalisation or expropriation (hereinafter referred to as 'expropriation') in the territory of the other Contracting Party except for a public purpose related to the internal needs of that Party on a non-discriminatory basis and against prompt, adequate and effective compensation. Such compensation shall amount to the genuine value of the investment expropriated immediately before the expropriation or before the impending expropriation became public knowledge, whichever is the earlier, shall include interest at a normal commercial rate until the date of payment, shall be made without delay, be effectively realizable and be freely transferable. The national or company affected shall have a right, under the law of the Contracting Party making the expropriation, to prompt review, by a judicial or other independent authority of that Party,

of his or its case and of the valuation of his or its investment in accordance with the principles set out in this paragraph.' This wording has changed little since the expropriation provision of the first UK IPPAs, as to which the intention of the drafters was not to go beyond what was thought to represent customary international law: see Denza and Brooks 'Investment Protections Treaties: United Kingdom Experience' 36 ICLQ 908, at 911–912. As to the customary international law in relation to expropriation see PARAS 473–478. As to compensation for breach of an expropriation provision in the treaty context see Ripinsky and Williams *Damages in International Investment Law* (1st Edn, 2008).

4   See *Telenor Mobile Communications AS v Hungary*, ICSID Case No ARB/04/15, Award of 13 September 2006. Various different formulations have been employed, including whether the conduct of the state has effectively neutralised the enjoyment of the property in question (see *Ronald S Lauder v Czech Republic*, UNCITRAL award of 3 September 2001, 9 ICSID Rep 66) or (at its most broad) has the effect of depriving the owner, in whole or in significant part, of the use or reasonably to be expected economic benefit of property (see *Metalclad Corpn v Mexico*, Award of 30 August 2000, 40 ILM (2001) 36 para 103).

5   See eg *Metalclad Corpn v Mexico*, Award of 30 August 2000, 40 ILM (2001) 36 para 111. See also Dolzer and Schreuer *Principles of International Investment Law* (1st Edn, 2008) pp 101–104.

6   See eg *Methanex Corpn v United States*, Award of 8 March 2005, 44 ILM (2005) 1343 at pt IV/D para 7; *Saluka Investments BV v Czech Republic* Partial Award of 17 March 2006, Arbitral Tribunal, para 262. The proportionality of the measure may also be a factor: see Dolzer and Schreuer *Principles of International Investment Law* (1st Edn, 2008) pp 109–112.

7   This follows from customary international law: see eg *Libyan American Oil Co (LIAMCO) v Libya* 62 Int Law Rep 140 at 189. See also Dolzer and Schreuer *Principles of International Investment Law* (1st Edn, 2008) pp 115–118.

8   See *Waste Management Inc v United Mexican States* ICSID Case No ARB(AF)/00/3, Award of 30 April 2004, 43 ILM (2004) 967 para 175 (where the tribunal concluded that it was necessary to show an effective repudiation of the right, unredressed by any remedies available to the claimant, which has the effect of preventing its exercise entirely or to a substantial extent). Labelling is, however, no substitute for analysis. The words 'confiscatory', 'destroy contractual rights as an asset', or 'repudiation' may serve as a way to describe breaches which are to be treated as extraordinary, and therefore as acts of expropriation, but they do not indicate on what basis the critical distinction between expropriation and an ordinary breach of contract is to be made. The egregiousness of any breach is in the eye of the beholder, and that is not satisfactory for present purposes: see *Azinian v United Mexican States* ICSID Case No ARB(AF)/97/2, Award of 1 November 1999, 39 ILM (2000) 537, 5 ICSID Rep 269 (2002) at para 90.

487.   Freedom of transfer.   Bilateral investment treaties (including UK Investment Promotion and Protection Agreements or 'IPPA's[1]) generally contain some form of guarantee to investors in relation to the transfer of their investments and returns in a freely convertible currency[2]. Such guarantees are often subject to expressly stated exceptions[3].

1   See PARA 481 note 1.
2   The wording in recent UK IPPAs is as follows. 'Each contracting party shall in respect of investments guarantee to nationals or companies of the other contracting party the unrestricted transfer of their investments and returns. Transfers shall be effected without delay in the convertible currency in which the capital was originally invested or in any other convertible currency agreed by the investor and the contracting party concerned. Unless otherwise agreed by the investor transfers shall be made at the rate of exchange applicable on the date of transfer pursuant to the exchange regulations in force': see eg Agreement between the United Kingdom of Great Britain and Northern Ireland and Bosnia and Herzegovina for the Promotion and Protection of Investments (Blackpool, 2 October 2002; TS 37 (2003); Cm 5973) art 6.
3   See Dolzer and Schreuer *Principles of International Investment Law* (1st Edn, 2008) pp 191 194; Reinisch (ed) *Standards of Investment Protection* (1st Edn, 2008) pp 205–243. As to the good faith imposition of such restrictions see *Re Helbert Wagg & Co Ltd* [1956] Ch 323 at 352, [1956] 1 All ER 129 at 142.

488.   Settlement of investment disputes; arbitration under the 1965 ICSID Convention.   The International Centre for Settlement of Investment Disputes ('ICSID') is an autonomous international institution established under the

Convention on the Settlement of Investment Disputes between States and Nationals of Other States (the 'ICSID Convention')[1]. The primary purpose of the ICSID is to provide facilities for conciliation and arbitration of international investment disputes, and many bilateral investment treaties (including UK Investment Promotion and Protection Agreements or 'IPPA's[2]) contain some form of consent to arbitration under the ICSID Convention. In order for the investor to bring a claim under the ICSID Convention, the jurisdictional requirements of the Convention[3] must be satisfied (in addition to the jurisdictional requirements of the given bilateral investment treaty or other source of consent), including that there be a legal dispute arising directly out of an investment, between a contracting state (or any constituent subdivision or agency of a contracting state designated to the ICSID by that state) and a national of another contracting state, which the parties to the dispute consent in writing to submit to the ICSID[4]. Consent of the parties to arbitration under the Convention is, unless otherwise stated[5], deemed consent to such arbitration to the exclusion of any other remedy[6]. Arbitration under the ICSID Convention is conducted pursuant to the ICSID Arbitration Rules[7]. The Arbitration Act 1996 does not apply to proceedings under the ICSID Convention (with certain exceptions)[8]. Each ICSID contracting state must recognise an award rendered pursuant to the ICSID Convention as binding and enforce the pecuniary obligations imposed by that award within its territories as if it were a final judgment of a court in that state[9]. There is, however, no derogation from the law in force in any contracting state relating to immunity of that state or of any foreign state from execution[10].

1   Ie the Convention on the Settlement of Investment Disputes between States and Nationals of Other States (Washington, 18 March 1965; Cmnd 3255), referred to as the 'Convention on the Settlement of Investment Disputes' or the 'ICSID Convention'. The Convention is set out in the Arbitration (International Investment Disputes) Act 1966: see s 1(1), Schedule; and ARBITRATION vol 2 (2008) PARA 1294. As to the ICSID see further ARBITRATION vol 2 (2008) PARAS 1295–1297. See also Schreuer's ICSID Convention: A Commentary (2nd Edn, 2009).

2   See PARA 481 note 1.

3   Ie under the Convention on the Settlement of Investment Disputes between States and Nationals of Other States (Washington, 18 March 1965; Cmnd 3255) art 25.

4   See the Arbitration (International Investment Disputes) Act 1966 Schedule art 25. This also provides that when the parties have given their consent, no party may withdraw its consent unilaterally. See further ARBITRATION vol 2 (2008) PARA 1296. See also Schreuer's ICSID Convention: A Commentary (2nd Edn, 2009) pp 71–347.

5   Such a statement might be contained in a given investment contract. For an overview of the relevant jurisprudence see Schreuer's ICSID Convention: A Commentary (2nd Edn, 2009) pp 348–413.

6   See the Arbitration (International Investment Disputes) Act 1966 Schedule art 26. See also *ETI Euro Telecom International NV v Republic of Bolivia* [2008] EWCA Civ 880, [2009] 2 All ER (Comm) 37, [2009] 1 WLR 665, where the claimant had commenced ICSID proceedings under a bilateral investment treaty between the Netherlands and Bolivia, and had obtained an attachment order in New York in aid of the ICSID arbitration. The appeal was dismissed on various grounds, including state immunity, but also that arts 26 and 47 of the ICSID Convention and r 39(6) of the ICSID Arbitration Rules taken together meant that the parties had agreed not to seek interim measures before a national court. Article 47 of the ICSID Convention provides: 'Except as the parties otherwise agree, the tribunal may, if it considers that the circumstances so require, recommend any provisional measures which should be taken to preserve the respective rights of either party' (see the Arbitration (International Investment Disputes) Act 1966 Schedule art 47). Rule 39(6) of the ICSID Arbitration Rules provides: 'Nothing in this rule prevents the parties, provided that they have so stipulated in the agreement recording their consent, from requesting any judicial or other authority to order provisional measures, prior to or after the institution of the proceeding, for the preservation of their respective rights and interests'.

7   The Rules of Procedure for Arbitration Proceedings (the 'ICSID Arbitration Rules') are available at the ICSID website: see http://icsid.worldbank.org.

8   The Arbitration Act 1996 does not apply to proceedings pursuant to the ICSID Convention, but
    this does not affect the Arbitration Act 1996 s 9 (stay of legal proceedings in respect of matter
    subject to arbitration): see the Arbitration (International Investment Disputes) Act 1966 s 3(2)
    (s 3 substituted by the Arbitration Act 1996 Sch 3 para 24). For an example of the application
    of the Arbitration Act 1996 s 9 in the context of a bilateral investment treaty claim (albeit not
    an ICSID claim) see *Sancheti v City of London* [2008] EWCA Civ 1283, [2009] 1 Lloyd's Rep
    117, (2008) Times, 1 December.
        The Lord Chancellor may by order direct that any of the provisions contained in the
    Arbitration Act 1996 ss 36, 38–44 (provisions concerning the conduct of arbitral proceedings
    etc) are to apply to such proceedings pursuant to the ICSID Convention as are specified in the
    order with or without any modifications or exceptions specified in the order: see the Arbitration
    (International Investment Disputes) Act 1966 s 3(1), (3) (as so substituted). At the date at which
    this volume states the law, no such order had been made. See also *ETI Euro Telecom
    International NV v Republic of Bolivia* [2008] EWCA Civ 880, [2009] 2 All ER (Comm) 37,
    [2009] 1 WLR 665.
9   See the Arbitration (International Investment Disputes) Act 1966 ss 1(2), 2(1) (giving effect to
    art 54 of the ICSID Convention); and ARBITRATION vol 2 (2008) PARAS 1295–1297.
10 See the Arbitration (International Investment Disputes) Act 1966 Schedule art 55. See also *AIG
    Capital Partners Inc v Republic of Kazakhstan* [2005] EWHC 2239 (Comm), [2006] 1 All ER
    284, [2006] 1 WLR 1420, where the investor sought unsuccessfully to enforce an ICSID award
    through a third party debt and charging order against assets of the National Bank of
    Kazakhstan held by a private bank in London. The attempt to enforce failed as the court found
    that the assets belonged to the host state's central bank which benefited from immunity pursuant
    to the State Immunity Act 1978 s 14(4).

489.   Settlement of investment disputes; other common forms of arbitration.
Many bilateral investment treaties (including UK Investment Promotion and
Protection Agreements or 'IPPA's[1]) provide to the investor a choice of arbitral
procedure which may include arbitration pursuant to the Convention on the
Settlement of Investment Disputes between States and Nationals of Other States
(the 'ICSID Convention')[2], arbitration pursuant to the Rules of Arbitration of
the International Chamber of Commerce ('ICC') or the Arbitration Rules of the
Arbitration Institute of the Stockholm Chamber of Commerce, arbitration by an
ad hoc tribunal to be appointed by a special agreement or established under the
Arbitration Rules of the United Nations Commission on International Trade
Law (the UNCITRAL Arbitration Rules)[3]. The conduct of such arbitration will
be pursuant to the applicable arbitration rules and (except in the case of
arbitration pursuant to the ICSID Convention) the law of the seat or place of
arbitration[4]. Where the seat or place of the arbitration is in England, Wales or
Northern Ireland, the Arbitration Act 1996 will apply[5], and the arbitral award
may be challenged before the English courts[6]. The dispute settlement provision
of the bilateral investment treaty may also provide dispute resolution in the
courts of the host state as an alternative to arbitration[7].

1   See PARA 481 note 1.
2   Ie the Convention on the Settlement of Investment Disputes between States and Nationals of
    Other States (Washington, 18 March 1965; Cmnd 3255): see PARA 488 note 1.
3   See eg the Agreement Between the Government of the United Kingdom of Great Britain and
    Northern Ireland and the Government of the Republic of India for the Promotion and
    Protection of Investments (London, 14 March 1994; TS 27 (1995); Cm 2797) considered in
    Sancheti v City of London [2008] EWCA Civ 1283, [2009] 1 Lloyd's Rep 117, (2008) Times,
    1 December.
4   As to the seat of arbitration as a matter of English law see ARBITRATION vol 2 (2008) PARA
    1212.
5   See ARBITRATION vol 2 (2008) PARA 1209.
6   See eg *Ecuador v Occidental Exploration and Production Co* [2005] EWCA Civ 1116, [2006]
    QB 432, [2006] 2 All ER 225, where, in the context of an investment treaty award made in
    London pursuant to the UNCITRAL Arbitration Rules, the court rejected the claim that a
    challenge to such an award under the Arbitration Act 1996 s 67 is non-justiciable. In particular,

the court rejected the contention that the challenge would require it to enforce or interpret the terms of an unincorporated treaty (cf *JH Rayner (Mincing Lane) Ltd v Department of Trade and Industry* [1990] 2 AC 418, sub nom *Maclaine Watson & Co Ltd v Department of Trade and Industry* [1989] 3 All ER 523, HL). The court also considered that the fact that the states party to the treaty deliberately chose to provide for a mechanism for dispute resolution which invoked consensual arbitration, with its domestic legal connotations, should make the English court hesitate before subjecting such arbitration proceedings to special principles of judicial restraint developed in relation to international transactions (cf *Buttes Gas and Oil Co v Hammer* [1982] AC 888, sub nom *Buttes Gas and Oil Co v Hammer (No 2 and No 3)* [1981] 3 All ER 616, HL) or treaties lacking any foundation or incorporation into domestic law. As to non-justiciability see PARA 24 et seq.

7   For a recent consideration of such a provision and the impact on a potential treaty claim where an investor does refer the dispute to the local courts see *Pantechniki SA Contractors & Engineers v Republic of Albania* ICSID Case No ARB/07/21, Award of 30 July 2009.

16. SETTLEMENT OF INTERNATIONAL DISPUTES

(1) METHODS OF SETTLEMENT

490.   In general. Members of the United Nations[1] must settle their international disputes by peaceful means[2]. The parties to any dispute whose continuance is likely to endanger the maintenance of international peace and security must seek a solution by non-judicial means (negotiation, inquiry, mediation, conciliation)[3], by adjudication (arbitration, judicial settlement)[4], or by resort to regional agencies or arrangements or other means of their own choice[5]. As a matter of European Union Law the United Kingdom, as a Member of the European Union, may be bound to take certain disputes with other member states to the European Court of Justice rather than to any other international tribunal[6].

1   As to the United Nations see PARA 519 et seq.
2   Charter of the United Nations (San Francisco, 26 June 1945; TS 67 (1946); Cmd 7015) art 2 para 3.
3   See PARA 491.
4   See PARA 491.
5   Charter of the United Nations art 33 para 1. Should the Security Council deem it necessary, it must call upon the parties to settle their dispute by such means: art 33 para 2. The General Assembly has repeated and expanded upon the wording of art 33 para 1: Declaration on Principles of International Law concerning Friendly Relations and Co-operation among States in Accordance with the Charter of the United Nations, General Assembly Resolution 2625 (XXV) of 24 October 1970. The General Assembly amplified it in the Manila Declaration on the Peaceful Settlement of Disputes between States, General Assembly Resolution 37/10, 15 November 1982. As to the Security Council see PARAS 523 et seq. As to the General Assembly see PARA 527 et seq.
6   See Case C-459/03 EC *Commission v Ireland* [2006] ECR I-4635, [20067] All ER (EC) 1013, ECJ.

(2) NON-JUDICIAL SETTLEMENT

491.   Negotiation, inquiry, conciliation, mediation, 'good offices'. Non-judicial methods of settlement of international disputes refer to procedures involving the exchange of views between the parties to the dispute, either with (in the case of inquiry, mediation, conciliation, and 'good offices') or without (in the case of negotiation) the involvement of a third party (whether a third state or states, a disinterested individual, or an organ of the United Nations[1] or of another international organisation). In an inquiry the third party establishes the precise facts underlying a dispute; in a mediation the third party facilitates negotiations between the parties; the term 'good offices', often used interchangeably with 'mediation', signifies the encouragement and facilitation of negotiations directly between the parties; in conciliation the third party encourages and facilitates negotiations and may itself propose possible bases of a settlement. In practice, in each of these procedures the degree of participation of the third party may vary, and the different types of non-judicial settlement are not watertight categories. They are brought together under the same heading because a settlement reached by these methods need not be based upon the legal rights and duties of the parties.

The chief method by which governments settle international disputes, whether arising in respect of governmental interests or in respect of the treatment of the state's nationals, is by direct negotiation between the governments of the states concerned[2]. In some circumstances states may be obliged by treaty[3] to seek a solution to their disagreements by negotiation[4], often as a preliminary step before resort to other means of settlement[5]. There is, however, no general requirement in international law to exhaust negotiations before a dispute is taken to an international tribunal[6].

The other methods of non-judicial settlement appear in various major international treaties, again usually as a preliminary step before resort to other (mostly adjudicatory) means[7]. The United Nations as well as its subsidiary bodies and other international organisations have adopted model rules on conciliation and other methods of non-judicial dispute settlement[8]. Arrangements for all non-judicial methods of dispute settlement can be made ad hoc[9].

1   The General Assembly and the Security Council of the United Nations may recommend the use of good offices or mediation by a member state or an agency or to offer their own: Charter of the United Nations arts (San Francisco, 26 June 1945; TS 67 (1946); Cmd 7015) 14, 36, 37 para 2.

2   *Mavrommatis Palestine Concessions* PCIJ Ser A No 2 at 13 (1924).

3   As to the meaning of 'treaty' see PARA 71.

4   Negotiation is one of the methods of peaceful settlement of disputes enumerated in the Charter of the United Nations art 33 para 1: see PARA 490 et seq.

     The obligation to negotiate does not include an obligation to reach agreement: *Railway Traffic between Lithuania and Poland (Railway Sector Landwarów-Kaisiadorys) Case* PCIJ Ser A/B No 42, 108 at 116 (1931). However, in the *Legality of the Threat or Use of Nuclear Weapons (Advisory Opinion)* ICJ Reports 1996, 226 at 263 reference was made to the 'obligation of states to pursue negotiations for nuclear disarmament and bring them to a successful completion'.

5   Eg see the Treaty Concerning the Establishment of the Republic of Cyprus (Nicosia, 16 August 1960; TS 4 (1961); Cmnd 1252) art 10; the United Nations Convention on the Law of the Sea (Montego Bay, 10 December 1982; TS 81 (1999); Cmnd 4524) art 283 para 1; the World Trade Organisation Agreement (Marrakesh, 15 April 1994; TS 57 (1996) Cm 3277), Annex 2 establishing the Understanding on Rules and Procedures Governing the Settlement of Disputes art 3 para 7, art 4.

6   *Land and Maritime Boundary between Cameroon and Nigeria (Cameroon v Nigeria) (Preliminary Objections)* ICJ Reports 1998, 275. An obligation to enter into negotiations cannot delay legal proceedings if one party refuses to negotiate: *United States Diplomatic and Consular Staff in Teheran (United States of America v Iran)* ICJ Reports 1980, 3.

7   Eg see the Charter of the United Nations art 33 para 1; the United Nations Convention on the Law of the Sea art 284; the World Trade Organisation Agreement Annex 2 establishing the Understanding on Rules and Procedures Governing the Settlement of Disputes arts 5 and 24 para 2.

8   See eg the United Nations Model Rules for the Conciliation of Disputes between States 30 ILM (1991) 229; adopted as General Assembly Resolution 50/50 of 11 December 1995; the Permanent Court of Arbitration *Optional Conciliation Rules* (1996); the Permanent Court of Arbitration *Optional Rules for Fact-finding Commissions of Inquiry* (1997); the Permanent Court of Arbitration *Optional Rules for Conciliation of Disputes Relating to Natural Resources and/or the Environment* (2002); the United Nations Commission on International Trade Law (UNCITRAL) Conciliation Rules (1980) adopted as General Assembly Resolution 35/52 of 4 December 1980; the UNCITRAL Model Law on International Commercial Conciliation with Guide to Enactment and Use (2002); and the International Chamber of Commerce Alternative Dispute Resolution Rules (1 July 2001).

9   For an instance where ad hoc provision for inquiry was made see the Exchange of Notes between Great Britain and Denmark establishing a Commission of Enquiry to investigate certain Incidents affecting the British trawler 'Red Crusader' (London, 15 November 1961; TS 118 (1961); Cmnd 1575); for an account of the report, which contained opinions on law as well as fact, see Contemporary Practice of the United Kingdom in the Field of International Law 1962 (I) 50–53.

(3) ADJUDICATION

(i) Arbitration

492. In general. Arbitration denotes the determination of a difference between states or between a state and a non-state entity by a legal decision of a tribunal consisting of one or more arbitrators that is established by the parties for the specific purpose of resolving a particular dispute[1] or class of disputes, and is thus not a permanent tribunal such as the International Court of Justice[2]. The tribunal consists of persons selected by the parties[3]. The award is generally binding upon the parties, and, unless the parties stipulate otherwise, is based upon rules of international law.

1 Arbitral tribunals have frequently been created to deal with particular boundary disputes, and with disputes concerning the treatment of foreign investors.

2 Arbitration is a method mentioned in the Charter of the United Nations (San Francisco, 26 June 1945; TS 67 (1946); Cmd 7015) art 33 para 1 (see PARA 490). For examples of multilateral conventions providing for arbitration see: the Convention for the Pacific Settlement of International Disputes (The Hague, 18 October 1907; TS 6 (1971); Cmnd 4575) art 37; the European Convention for the Peaceful Settlement of Disputes (Strasbourg, 29 April 1957; TS 10 (1961); Cmnd 1298); and the Convention on the Settlement of Investment Disputes between States and Nationals of other States 1965 (Washington, 18 March 1965; TS 25 (1967); Cmnd 3255). As to the International Court of Justice see PARA 499 et seq. As to the meaning of 'treaty' see PARA 71.

3 For the right of states parties to a case before the International Court of Justice to select ad hoc judges to sit with the permanent judges see the Statute of the International Court of Justice (San Francisco, 26 June 1945; TS 67 (1946); Cmd 7015) art 31 paras 2–6; and PARA 500.

493. Ad hoc arbitration. Parties to a particular dispute may at any time agree to refer the dispute to arbitration. The parties retain control over the establishment of the arbitral tribunal and the appointment of its members, its terms of reference, its rules of procedure, the applicable law[1], and the legal effect of the award to be rendered, including whether it will be subject to interpretation, revision, appeal, or nullification. This will be stipulated in the arbitration agreement or *compromis*, which creates the tribunal and limits its jurisdiction. In case the parties have not provided for an eventuality, the tribunal will decide under its competence to determine its own jurisdiction. This competence includes the power to interpret any provision in the *compromis*[2].

There are 'model' or 'optional' rules that parties can incorporate in their *compromis*, so as to avoid having to draw up a full set of provisions regarding the tribunal's establishment, rules of procedure, and the like. Prominent among these are the various Optional Rules devised by the Permanent Court of Arbitration[3], while the International Law Commission has also devised Model Rules of Arbitral Procedure[4].

1 If no applicable law is specified, international law will be applicable in inter-state disputes: *Norwegian Shipowners Claims* 2 RIAA 309 at 331 (1922); *The Matter of the Diverted Cargoes Arbitration (Greece v Great Britain)* (1955) 22 Int LR 820 at 824. See also the Convention for the Pacific Settlement of International Disputes 1907 art 37. For power to decide ex aequo et bono see the European Convention for the Peaceful Settlement of Disputes (Strasbourg, 29 April 1957; TS 10 (1961); Cmnd 1298) art 30.

2 *The Betsey* (1802) 4 Moore Int Arb 81 at 85 per Lord Loughborough; Convention for the Pacific Settlement of International Disputes (The Hague, 29 July 1889; TS 9 (1901); Cd 798) art 48; Convention for the Pacific Settlement of International Disputes (The Hague, 18 October 1907; TS 6 (1971); Cmnd 4575) art 73. See also the *Nottebohm (Liechtenstein v Guatemala) (Preliminary Objection)* ICJ Reports 1953, 111 at 119.

3 See the Permanent Court of Arbitration *Optional Rules for Arbitrating Disputes between Two States* (1992); the Permanent Court of Arbitration *Optional Rules for Arbitrating Disputes*

between Two Parties of which Only One is A State (1993); the Permanent Court of Arbitration *Optional Rules for Arbitration involving International Organizations and States* (1996); the Permanent Court of Arbitration *Optional Rules for Arbitration between International Organizations and Private Parties* (1996); the Permanent Court of Arbitration *Optional Rules for Arbitration of Disputes Relating to Natural Resources and/or the Environment* (2001). As to the Permanent Court of Arbitration see PARA 495.

4   See the United Nations *Yearbook of the International Law Commission* Vol II (1958). States may also choose to utilise model rules drawn up primarily for the purposes of commercial arbitration, such as the United Nations Commission on International Trade Law arbitration rules (recommended in General Assembly Resolution 31/98 of 15 December 1976) or the rules of one of the national arbitration centres such as the London Court of International Arbitration or the Stockholm Chamber of Commerce.

494.   Institutional arbitration.   'Institutional arbitration' or 'administered arbitration' refers to the settlement of disputes by arbitration procedures administered by a standing international body, such as the Permanent Court of Arbitration[1], and the International Centre for the Settlement of Investment Disputes[2]. The standing body does not itself decide the dispute: it acts as the secretariat for arbitral tribunals established on an ad hoc basis under its auspices.

1   As to the Permanent Court of Arbitration see PARA 495.
2   As to the International Centre for the Settlement of Investment Disputes see PARA 496.

495.   Permanent Court of Arbitration.   The Permanent Court of Arbitration (the 'PCA') was established in 1899 as a facility through which states parties to the Hague Conventions of 1899 and 1907 may establish ad hoc arbitral tribunals to hear particular cases[1]. The only permanent organ of the PCA, which is based in The Hague, is the International Bureau, which functions as a registry for the tribunals thus established[2].

1   See the Convention for the Pacific Settlement of International Disputes (The Hague, 29 July 1899; TS 9 (1901); Cd 798) art 20 et seq; and the Convention for the Pacific Settlement of International Disputes (The Hague, 18 October 1907; TS 6 (1971); Cmnd 4575). The latter convention contains detailed rules governing the arbitration procedure (arts 51–85) and rules for arbitration by summary procedure (arts 86–90).

2   See the Convention for the Pacific Settlement of International Disputes (The Hague, 18 October 1907; TS 6 (1971); Cmnd 4575) art 43.

496.   International Centre for the Settlement of Investment Disputes.   The Washington Convention on the Settlement of Investment Disputes between States and Nationals of Other States[1] established the International Centre for Settlement of Investment Disputes ('ICSID') for the purpose of providing for conciliation and arbitration of investment disputes between Contracting States and nationals of other Contracting States in accordance with the provisions of the Convention[2]. The ICSID has an Administrative Council and a Secretariat as its permanent organs, located at the World Bank headquarters in Washington DC[3].

ICSID jurisdiction is limited to disputes arising 'directly out of an investment' between a contracting state and a national of another contracting state, when the parties to the dispute have agreed in writing to refer the dispute to the Centre[4]. Many bilateral investment protection treaties and investment agreements include provisions for the arbitration of disputes under the auspices of ICSID[5]. Further, certain multilateral treaties such as the North American Free Trade Agreement[6] and the Energy Charter Treaty[7] provide for ICSID arbitration of disputes arising under them, activated simply by initiation of proceedings by the investor[8].

ICSID maintains a list ('Panel') of arbitrators and conciliators, nominated by the contracting states and by the Chairman of its Administrative Council, who is also the President of the World Bank[9]. ICSID Tribunals operate under rules laid down by ICSID[10]. Any party to the proceedings has the power to order provisional measures[11].

ICSID awards are binding on the parties to the dispute, and are not subject to any appeal or other remedy not provided for by ICSID convention[12]. An award may be annulled on the grounds that the tribunal was improperly constituted, that it manifestly exceeded its powers, that there was corruption on the part of a member of the tribunal, that there was a serious departure from a fundamental rule of procedure, or that no reasons were stated for the award[13]. Awards under ICSID Convention are enforceable in all contracting states as if they are final judgments of the state's own courts[14], but they remain subject to the laws of the state concerning sovereign immunity[15].

1   Ie the Convention on the Settlement of Investment Disputes between States and Nationals of Other States 1965 (Washington, 18 March 1965; TS 25 (1967); Cmnd 3255). The Convention is set out in the Schedule to the Arbitration (International *Investment Disputes*) Act 1966: see s 1; and ARBITRATION vol 2 (2008) PARA 1294 et seq.
2   See the Convention on the Settlement of Investment Disputes between States and Nationals of Other States art 1; and ARBITRATION vol 2 (2008) PARA 1295.
3   See the Convention on the Settlement of Investment Disputes between States and Nationals of Other States arts 2–3; and ARBITRATION vol 2 (2008) PARA 1295.
4   See the Convention on the Settlement of Investment Disputes between States and Nationals of Other States art 25; and ARBITRATION vol 2 (2008) PARA 1296.
5   See eg *Asian Agricultural Products Ltd v Democratic Socialist Republic of Sri Lanka*, ICSID Case No ARB/87/3, Award of 27 June 1990, 4 ICSID Rep 246, 30 ILM (1991) 557, based on the 1980 Treaty between the UK and Sri Lanka, where the recourse by AAPL was enough to immediately establish ICSID jurisdiction. Other UK treaties may require that a certain period of negotiation or pursuit of local remedies be exhausted without leading to resolution of the dispute before recourse to ICSID can be made.
6   North American Free Trade Agreement (17 December 1992; US Government Printing Office 1992).
7   Energy Charter Treaty (Lisbon, 17 December 1994; Misc 6 (1995); Cm 2952).
8   See the North American Free Trade Agreement art 1120; and the Energy Charter Treaty.
9   See the Convention on the Settlement of Investment Disputes between States and Nationals of Other States arts 3, 5, 13. States are not confined to the names on the lists in their choice of arbitrators and conciliators.
10 See the ICSID Rules of Procedure for Arbitration Proceedings.
11 See the ICSID Rules of Procedure for Arbitration Proceedings r 39(1).
12 See the Convention on the Settlement of Investment Disputes between States and Nationals of Other States art 53.
13 See the Convention on the Settlement of Investment Disputes between States and Nationals of Other States art 52.
14 See the Convention on the Settlement of Investment Disputes between States and Nationals of Other States art 54. See also the Arbitration (International *Investment Disputes*) Act 1966 ss 1, 2; and ARBITRATION vol 2 (2008) PARA 1294 et seq.
15 See the Convention on the Settlement of Investment Disputes between States and Nationals of Other States art 55. As to immunity from jurisdiction see PARA 274.

497. Arbitration under the United Nations Convention on the Law of the Sea. The United Nations Convention on the Law of the Sea[1] establishes a system for the compulsory resolution of certain categories of dispute concerning the interpretation and application of the Convention[2]. States may make declarations[3] choosing one or more of the following procedures for the settlement of disputes[4]: (1) the International Tribunal for the Law of the Sea[5]; (2) the International Court of Justice[6]; (3) an arbitral tribunal[7]; or (4) a special arbitral tribunal[8].

A state party to a dispute that is not covered by a declaration in force will be deemed to have accepted arbitration in accordance with the arbitration provisions of the Convention[9]. If the parties to a dispute have accepted the same procedure for the settlement of the dispute, it may only be submitted to that procedure, unless the parties otherwise agree[10]. If the parties to a dispute have not accepted the same procedure for the settlement of the dispute, it may be submitted only to arbitration in accordance with the arbitration provisions of the Convention[11], unless the parties otherwise agree[12].

1 Ie the United Nations Convention on the Law of the Sea (Montego Bay, 10 December 1982; TS 81 (1999); Cmnd 4524).

2 See the United Nations Convention on the Law of the Sea Pt XV (arts 279–299) and in particular art 286. For excluded categories of dispute see arts 297–298.

3 Declarations of such choices must be deposited with the Secretary-General of the United Nations: see the United Nations Convention on the Law of the Sea art 287 para 8.

4 United Nations Convention on the Law of the Sea art 287. A state may select different procedures for different categories of case.

5 United Nations Convention on the Law of the Sea art 287 para 1(a). The International Tribunal for the Law of the Sea is established under Annex VI of the Convention: see PARA 514.

6 United Nations Convention on the Law of the Sea art 287 para 1(b). As to the International Court of Justice see PARA 499 et seq.

7 United Nations Convention on the Law of the Sea art 287 para 1(c). An arbitral tribunal mentioned in the text is one constituted in accordance with Annex VII of the Convention. Unless the parties otherwise agree, the following provisions apply to the constitution of an arbitral tribunal for the purpose of proceedings under Annex VII of the Convention: Annex VII art 3. The arbitral tribunal consists of five members, one chosen by each of the parties and the other three by the parties jointly: Annex VII art 3(a)–(d). A list of persons nominated by states who might act as arbitrators is maintained, but parties need not choose arbitrators from that list: see Annex VII art 2, 3. At the date at which this volume states the law the list, which includes persons available for the conciliation of disputes, is available on the United Nations website. Unless the parties to the dispute otherwise agree, the arbitral tribunal is to determine its own procedure, assuring to each party a full opportunity to be heard and to present its case: see Annex VII art 5. The award of the tribunal is final, unless the parties to the dispute have agreed in advance to an appellate procedure: see Annex VII art 11. The award of the arbitral tribunal must be confined to the subject-matter of the dispute and state the reasons on which it is based: see Annex VII art 10.

8 United Nations Convention on the Law of the Sea art 287 para 1(d). A special arbitral tribunal mentioned in the text is one constituted in accordance with Annex VIII of the Convention. Annex VII arts 4–13 (see note 7) apply mutatis mutandis to the special arbitration proceedings in accordance with Annex VIII: Annex VIII art 4. Annex VIII special arbitral tribunals are competent with respect to disputes concerning: (1) fisheries; (2) protection and preservation of the marine environment; (3) marine scientific research; or (4) navigation, including pollution from vessels and by dumping: see Annex VIII art 1. A list of experts is maintained in respect of heads (1) to (4) above: Annex VIII art 2. The states party to the Convention are entitled to nominate two experts in each field: Annex VIII art 2 para 3. A special arbitral tribunal consists of five members: Annex VIII art 3(a). Each party to the dispute may appoint two members, preferably from the appropriate list: Annex VIII art 3(b), (c). One member appointed by each party may be its national: Annex VIII art 3(b), (c). The parties to the dispute are to appoint by agreement the president of the special arbitral tribunal, chosen preferably from the appropriate list: Annex VIII art 3(d). The president must be a national of a third state, unless the parties otherwise agree: Annex VIII art 3(d). The special arbitral tribunals may be used by the parties to a dispute, if they so agree, to carry out an inquiry and establish the facts giving rise to the dispute: Annex VIII art 5 para 1. If all the parties to the dispute so request, the special arbitral tribunal may formulate recommendations which, without having the force of a decision, will only constitute the basis for a review by the parties of the questions giving rise to the dispute: Annex VIII art 5 para 3.

9 United Nations Convention on the Law of the Sea art 287 para 3. The arbitration provisions mentioned in the text are those set out in Annex VII to the Convention (see PARA 497).

10 United Nations Convention on the Law of the Sea art 287 para 4.

11 Ie in accordance with the United National Convention on the Law of the Sea Annex VII (see PARA 497).

12 United Nations Convention on the Law of the Sea art 287 para 5.

498.   World Trade Organisation Panels. The World Trade Organisation ('WTO')[1] system of dispute settlement is contained in the Dispute Settlement Understanding[2]. The system is administered by the WTO Dispute Settlement Body[3], which has the power to establish panels for hearing disputes, to adopt reports from panels and from the Appellate Body[4], to maintain surveillance of implementation of rulings and recommendations, and to authorise suspension of trade concessions and other WTO obligations[5]. Upon notification by one party to a dispute concerning agreements or commitments made in the WTO, the other party or parties must join in consultations[6]. Good offices[7], conciliation[8] and mediation[9] are offered to assist the parties in reaching a solution[10]. Should the dispute not be resolved it must be submitted, if the complainant requests, to a panel to be established by the Dispute Settlement Body unless the latter resolves by consensus not to do so[11].

A panel consists of three members proposed to the parties by the WTO Secretariat[12]. If there is no agreement on panellists within 20 days after the date of the establishment of a panel, at the request of either party, the Director General[13], in consultation with the Chairman of the relevant Council[14] or Committee[15], will determine the composition of the panel by appointing the panellists whom the Director General considers most appropriate in accordance with any relevant special or additional rules or procedures of the covered agreement or covered agreements which are at issue in the dispute, after consulting with the parties to the dispute[16]. The terms of reference of the panel may be drawn up by the chairman of the Disputes Settlement Body in consultation with the parties[17]. Panel reports are automatically adopted by the Dispute Settlement Body unless a party to the dispute appeals against the report or the Disputes Settlement Body decides by consensus not to adopt it[18]. A party to a dispute may appeal to the Appellate Body against a final panel report[19] but only on a point of law covered in the panel report and the legal interpretation developed by the panel[20].

Unless otherwise agreed by the parties to the dispute, the period from the date of establishment of the panel by the Dispute Settlement Body until the date the Dispute Settlement Body considers the panel report for adoption must as a general rule not exceed nine months where the panel report is not appealed[21]. The member states involved must explain their intentions regarding compliance with recommendations contained in the panel report[22]. The Dispute Settlement Body keeps compliance under surveillance[23]. If a member state fails to comply with recommendations, the complainant state may request the authority of the Dispute Settlement Body to suspend the application to the defaulting member of concessions or other obligations[24]. If that member objects to the level of suspension authorised, the matter must be referred to arbitration[25]. The decision of the arbitrator is final[26].

1   As to the World Trade Organisation see PARA 461.

2   Ie the World Trade Organisation Agreement (Marrakesh, 15 April 1994; TS 57 (1996); Cm 3277) Annex 2 establishing the Understanding on Rules and Procedures governing the Settlement of Disputes. Authoritative interpretation of the World Trade Organisation Agreement and of the associated agreements is vested in the World Trade Organisation Ministerial Conference and General Council: see the World Trade Organisation Agreement art IX para 2.

3   See the World Trade Organisation Agreement Annex 2 establishing the Understanding on Rules and Procedures governing the Settlement of Disputes art 2 para 1. The General Council of the World Trade Organisation acts as the Dispute Settlement Body: World Trade Organisation Agreement art IV para 3; and see PARA 461.

4   As to the Appellate Body see PARA 515.

5   World Trade Organisation Agreement Annex 2 establishing the Understanding on Rules and Procedures governing the Settlement of Disputes art 2 para 1.

6   See the World Trade Organisation Agreement Annex 2 establishing the Understanding on Rules and Procedures governing the Settlement of Disputes art 4.

7   As to good offices see PARA 491.

8   As to conciliation see PARA 491.

9   As to mediation see PARA 491.

10 See the World Trade Organisation Agreement Annex 2 establishing the Understanding on Rules and Procedures governing the Settlement of Disputes art 5.

11 See the World Trade Organisation Agreement Annex 2 establishing the Understanding on Rules and Procedures governing the Settlement of Disputes art 6 para 1.

12 World Trade Organisation Agreement Annex 2 establishing the Understanding on Rules and Procedures governing the Settlement of Disputes art 8 para 5. This holds true unless the parties to a dispute agree, within ten days from the establishment of the panel, to a panel composed of five panellists: art 8 para 5. As to the composition of panels see art 8 para 1. Panellists sit in their individual capacity: art 8 para 9. As to procedures for multiple complainants see art 9. As to the interests of third parties see art 10. As to the World Trade Organisation Secretariat see PARA 461.

13 As to the Director General see PARA 461.

14 As to the General Council see PARA 461.

15 As to the Committees see PARA 461.

16 World Trade Organisation Agreement Annex 2 establishing the Understanding on Rules and Procedures governing the Settlement of Disputes art 8 para 7.

17 See the World Trade Organisation Agreement Annex 2 establishing the Understanding on Rules and Procedures governing the Settlement of Disputes art 7. As to the function of panels see art 11. As to their procedures see art 12, Appendix 3.

18 World Trade Organisation Agreement Annex 2 establishing the Understanding on Rules and Procedures governing the Settlement of Disputes art 16. As to confidentiality see art 14. As to the interim review stage see art 15.

19 Only parties to the dispute, not third parties, may appeal a panel report: World Trade Organisation Agreement Annex 2 establishing the Understanding on Rules and Procedures governing the Settlement of Disputes art 17 para 4. Third parties who have notified the Dispute Settlement Body of a substantial interest in the matter pursuant to art 10 para 2 may make submissions to, and be heard by, the Appellate Body: art 17 para 4.

20 See the World Trade Organisation Agreement Annex 2 establishing the Understanding on Rules and Procedures governing the Settlement of Disputes art 17 para 6.

21 See the World Trade Organisation Agreement Annex 2 establishing the Understanding on Rules and Procedures governing the Settlement of Disputes art 20.

22 See the World Trade Organisation Agreement Annex 2 establishing the Understanding on Rules and Procedures governing the Settlement of Disputes art 21 para 3.

23 See the World Trade Organisation Agreement Annex 2 establishing the Understanding on Rules and Procedures governing the Settlement of Disputes art 21.

24 See the World Trade Organisation Agreement Annex 2 establishing the Understanding on Rules and Procedures governing the Settlement of Disputes art 22 para 2.

25 See the World Trade Organisation Agreement Annex 2 establishing the Understanding on Rules and Procedures governing the Settlement of Disputes art 22 para 6.

26 See the World Trade Organisation Agreement Annex 2 establishing the Understanding on Rules and Procedures governing the Settlement of Disputes art 22 para 7.

(ii) Permanent International Courts and Tribunals

A. THE INTERNATIONAL COURT OF JUSTICE

499.   Organisation. The International Court of Justice, which is the principal judicial organ of the United Nations[1], consists of 15 judges, no two of whom may be nationals of the same state[2]. They are elected for periods of nine years[3] by the General Assembly and the Security Council proceeding independently of each other[4] from a list of persons nominated by the national groups in the Permanent Court of Arbitration[5]. The President and Vice-President are elected for three years by the court[6], as are the Registrar and other necessary officers[7]. Members of the court, when engaged upon its business, enjoy diplomatic privileges and immunities[8].

1   Statute of the International Court of Justice (San Francisco, 26 June 1945; TS 67 (1946); Cmd 7015) art 1; Charter of the United Nations (San Francisco, 26 June 1945; TS 67 (1946); Cmd 7015) art 92. The Statute of the International Court of Justice forms an integral part of the charter and is annexed thereto: art 92.
2   Statute of the International Court of Justice art 3 para 1. Otherwise they are elected regardless of nationality, although all main forms of civilization and the principal legal systems of the world must be represented: see arts 2, 9. Their qualification must be either that they are persons who possess the qualifications required in their respective countries for appointment to the highest judicial office or are jurisconsults of recognised competence in international law: art 2. As to ad hoc judges see PARA 500.
3   Statute of the International Court of Justice art 13 para 1. Judges are eligible for re-election: art 13 para 1. As to resignation see art 13 para 4. As to dismissal see art 18. Restrictions are imposed upon the judges' exercise of professional, administrative or political functions and activities: see art 16. No member of the court may act as agent, counsel or advocate in any case (art 17 para 1), or participate in the decision of any case in which he has so previously acted or has acted as a member of a tribunal or in any other capacity (art 17 para 2).
4   Statute of the International Court of Justice art 8.
5   See the Statute of the International Court of Justice arts 5–7. As to the Permanent Court of Arbitration see PARA 495. As to the elections see arts 10–13. As to the filling of vacancies see arts 14, 15.
6   Statute of the International Court of Justice art 21 para 1. They may be re-elected: art 21 para 1. The President must reside at the seat of the court (art 22 para 2), which is at The Hague (art 22 para 1), although the court may sit and exercise its functions elsewhere (art 22 para 1).
7   Statute of the International Court of Justice art 21 para 2. The Registrar must also reside at The Hague: art 22.
8   Statute of the International Court of Justice art 19. For United Kingdom law as to the privileges and immunities of persons connected with the court see PARA 314.

500.   Sittings; ad hoc judges. The full court must sit[1], unless it forms a chamber for any case or class of cases[2]. A quorum is nine judges[3]. Judges of the nationality of the parties to the case retain their right to sit[4]. In a case in which the court includes a judge of the nationality of one of the parties, any other party may choose a person to sit as judge[5]; if there is no judge of the nationality of either party, each may appoint one[6]. The court lays down its own rules of procedure and practice directions[7].

1   Statute of the International Court of Justice (San Francisco, 26 June 1945; TS 67 (1946); Cmd 7015) art 25 para 1. As to dispensation of judges from sitting see art 25 para 2. As to the Statute of the International Court of Justice see PARA 499 note 1.
2   As to chambers see PARA 501.
3   Statute of the International Court of Justice art 25 para 3. As to the abstention or disqualification of a judge from sitting in a particular case see art 24.
4   Statute of the International Court of Justice art 31 para 1.
5   Statute of the International Court of Justice art 31 para 2.
6   Statute of the International Court of Justice art 31 para 3.
7   Statute of the International Court of Justice art 30 para 1. The Court may provide in its rules for assessors to sit: art 30 para 2. The Rules of Court in force at the date at which this volume states the law are those adopted on 14 April 1978, which are available at the date this volume states the law at www.icj-cij.org.

501.   Chambers. The International Court of Justice[1] may form one or more chambers for dealing with particular categories of cases[2] and may at any time form a chamber for dealing with a particular case[3]. The number of judges to constitute such a chamber is determined by the court with the approval of the parties[4]. The court forms annually a chamber composed of five judges to hear and determine cases by summary procedure[5]. A judgment of a chamber is considered a judgment of the court[6].

1   As to the International Court of Justice see PARA 499.
2   Statute of the International Court of Justice (San Francisco, 26 June 1945; TS 67 (1946); Cmd 7015) art 26 para 1. As to the Statute of the International Court of Justice see PARA 499 note 1.
3   Statute of the International Court of Justice art 26 para 2.
4   Statute of the International Court of Justice art 26 para 2. Chambers were requested by the parties in the Case concerning the *Delimitation of the Maritime Boundary in the Gulf of Maine Area (Canada/United States of America)* ICJ Reports 1984, 246; *Frontier Dispute (Burkina Faso/Republic of Mali)* ICJ Reports 1986, 554; *Elettronica Sicula SpA (ELSI) (United States of America v Italy)* ICJ Reports 1989, 15; *Land, Island and Maritime Frontier Dispute (El Salvador/Honduras) (Constitution of a Chamber)* ICJ Reports 1987, 10. A chamber is subject to the court only with regard to its composition, and once it is constituted it is for all purposes the court itself: *Land, Island and Maritime Frontier Dispute (El Salvador/Honduras) (Application for Permission to Intervene)* ICJ Reports 1990, 92. It is unclear whether the court is obliged to create a chamber under the Statute of the International Court of Justice art 26 para 2 if the parties request it to do so.
5   See the Statute of the International Court of Justice art 29.
6   Statute of the International Court of Justice art 27.

502.   Access to the court.   Only states may be parties to contentious proceedings before the International Court of Justice[1]. The Court is open to all states parties to its statute[2]; and the Security Council of the United Nations may lay down conditions under which other states may have access to the court[3].

1   See the Statute of the International Court of Justice (San Francisco, 26 June 1945; TS 67 (1946); Cmd 7015) art 34 para 1. For the cases in which international organisations may be informed of proceedings and asked for information see art 34 paras 2, 3. Bodies, such as the UN General Assembly and Security Council, authorised by or in accordance with the UN Charter may request Advisory Opinions from the Court: see art 65; and see PARA 512. As to the International Court of Justice see PARA 499. As to the Statute of the International Court of Justice see PARA 499 note 1.
2   Statute of the International Court of Justice art 35 para 1. All states members of the United Nations are automatically parties to the statute. States not members may become parties under the Charter of the United Nations (San Francisco, 26 June 1945; TS 67 (1946); Cmd 7015) art 93 para 2.
3   Statute of the International Court of Justice art 35 para 2. Such states may not be placed on a footing of inequality with respect to other parties: art 35 para 2. For conditions of access for such states see Security Council Resolution 9 (1946) 15 October 1946.

503.   Jurisdiction.   The jurisdiction of the International Court of Justice[1] derives from the consent of the parties[2]. It comprises all cases which the parties agree to refer to it[3], and all matters specially provided for in the Charter of the United Nations[4] or in treaties[5] or conventions[6] in force[7]. Disputes as to jurisdiction are settled by decision of the court[8].

1   As to the International Court of Justice see PARA 499.
2   See eg the *Anglo-Iranian Oil Co Case (United Kingdom v Iran) (Preliminary Objections)* ICJ Reports 1952, 93; *Monetary Gold Removed from Rome in 1943 (Italy v France, United Kingdom and United States of America) (Jurisdiction)* ICJ Reports 1954, 19.
3   The parties may refer a dispute to the court by specific agreement (*compromis*). An example is the *Minquiers and Ecrehos Case (France/United Kingdom)* ICJ Reports 1953, 47. As to what amounts to an agreement see *Aegean Sea Continental Shelf (Greece v Turkey) (Interim Protection)* ICJ Reports 1976, 3. The Court also has jurisdiction when a party makes a unilateral reference of a dispute to the court, which the other party expressly or impliedly accepts. As to this see generally *Right of Minorities in Upper Silesia (Minority Schools) (Preliminary Objection)* PCIJ Ser A No 15 (1928); *Corfu Channel (United Kingdom v Albania) (Preliminary Objection)* ICJ Reports 1948, 15; and cf *Certain Questions of Mutual Assistance*

in Criminal Matters (Djibouti v France) ICJ Reports, 4 June 2008 (para 39 et seq). The maintaining of an objection to the jurisdiction by the respondent state does not amount to consent: *Anglo-Iranian Oil Co Case (United Kingdom v Iran) (Preliminary Objections)* ICJ Reports 1952, 93. As to how under such an agreement the court may be seised of a case see *Maritime Delimitation and Territorial Questions between Qatar and Bahrain (Qatar v Bahrain) (Jurisdiction and Admissability)* ICJ Reports 1994, 112; *Maritime Delimitation and Territorial Questions between Qatar and Bahrain (Qatar v Bahrain) (Jurisdiction and Admissability)* ICJ Reports 1995, 6.

4 Charter of the United Nations (San Francisco, 26 June 1945; TS 67 (1946); Cmd 7015). There appear to be no matters specifically provided for. The only provision to which these words could refer is art 36 para 3, which enables the Security Council to recommend to the parties in dispute recourse to the court: see *Corfu Channel (United Kingdom v Albania) (Preliminary Objection)* ICJ Reports 1948, 15 at 31.

5 As to the meaning of 'treaty' see PARA 71.

6 This is effected by means of a compromissory clause in a multilateral or bilateral treaty. There are many of these. For a list of such treaties see the current Yearbook of the International Court of Justice, and the ICJ's website (available at the date at which this volume states the law at www.icj-cij.org). Where a treaty or convention in force provides for reference of a matter to the Permanent Court of International Justice, then, as between the parties to the Statute of the International Court of Justice (San Francisco, 26 June 1945; TS 67 (1946); Cmd 7015), the matter must now be referred to that latter court: see *Barcelona Traction, Light and Power Co Ltd (Belgium v Spain) (Preliminary Objection)* ICJ Reports 1964, 6. An example of a case in which jurisdiction was founded on a compromissory clause is the *Avena and Other Mexican Nationals (Mexico v United States of America)* ICJ Reports 2004, 12.

7 Statute of the International Court of Justice (San Francisco, 26 June 1945; TS 67 (1946); Cmd 7015) art 36 para 1. As to the Statute of the International Court of Justice see PARA 499 note 1. Note that as a matter of European Union Law the United Kingdom may be obliged to adjudicate certain categories of dispute with any other member state only before the European Court of Justice: see Case C-459/03 *EC Commission v Ireland* [2006] ECR I-4635, [20067] All ER (EC) 1013, ECJ.

8 Statute of the International Court of Justice art 36 para 6. See *Nottebohm (Liechtenstein v Guatemala) (Preliminary Objection)* ICJ Reports 1953, 111 at 119.

504. The optional clause.

According to the so-called 'optional clause', a state may at any time declare that it recognises as compulsory, ipso facto and without special agreement, in relation to any other state accepting the same obligation, the jurisdiction of the International Court of Justice[1] in all legal disputes concerning[2]: (1) the interpretation of a treaty[3]; (2) any question of international law[4]; (3) the existence of any fact which, if established, would constitute a breach of an international obligation[5]; or (4) the nature or extent of the reparation to be made for the breach of an international obligation[6]. A declaration is a unilateral act of the state which makes it, but it creates a series of bilateral relationships with other states which also make declarations[7].

1 As to the International Court of Justice see PARA 499.

2 Statute of the International Court of Justice (San Francisco, 26 June 1945; TS 67 (1946); Cmd 7015) art 36 para 2. Declarations must be deposited with the Secretary-General of the United Nations who must transmit copies to the parties to the Statute and to the Registrar of the Court: art 36 para 4. For a list of declarations made under the Statute of the International Court of Justice art 36 para 2 see the current Yearbook of the International Court of Justice, and the ICJ's website (available at the date at which this volume states the law at www.icj-cij.org). Declarations made under the corresponding provision of the Statute of the Permanent Court of International Justice must now be treated as acceptances of the compulsory jurisdiction of the International Court of Justice: Statute of the International Court of Justice art 36 para 5. However, this is subject to the respondent state having been a party to the Statute of the ICJ in 1945: *Aerial Incident of 27 July 1955 (Israel v Bulgaria) (Preliminary Objections)* ICJ Reports 1959, 127; cf *Case concerning the Temple of Preah Vihear (Cambodia v Thailand) (Preliminary Objections)* ICJ Reports 1961, 17.

3 Statute of the International Court of Justice art 36 para 2(a). As to the meaning of 'treaty' see PARA 71.

4 Statute of the International Court of Justice art 36 para 2(b).

5   Statute of the International Court of Justice art 36 para 2(c).

6   Statute of the International Court of Justice art 36 para 2(d).

7   So, once state A has filed a declaration with the United Nations Secretary-General, state B cannot, unless it has reserved the right to do so, withdraw its declaration so as to deprive the court of jurisdiction over a case between A and B of which it is already seised: *Right of Passage over Indian Territory (Portugal v India) (Preliminary Objection)* ICJ Reports 1957, 125; *Nuclear Tests (Australia v France)* ICJ Reports 1974, 253; *Nuclear Tests (New Zealand v France)* ICJ Reports 1974, 457; *Military and Paramilitary Activities in and against Nicaragua (Nicaragua v United States of America) (Jurisdiction and Admissibility)* ICJ Reports 1984, 392.

505. Optional clause reservations. Declarations accepting the compulsory jurisdiction of the International Court of Justice[1] may be made unconditionally or on condition of reciprocity or for a certain time[2]. Many declarations have, however, contained other types of reservation[3]. Examples of these are: (1) reservations of matters which, by international law, are within the domestic jurisdiction of the state[4]; (2) reservations of disputes which arose before a certain date and out of facts which existed before that date[5]; and (3) reservations of disputes in regard to which the parties have agreed or will agree to have recourse to some other method of settlement[6]. On a basis of reciprocity the declarations of the parties to a case may be read together, thus permitting the respondent state to rely on a reservation or condition to be found not in its own declaration but in the declaration of the applicant state alone[7].

1   As to the International Court of Justice see PARA 499.

2   Statute of the International Court of Justice (San Francisco, 26 June 1945; TS 67 (1946); Cmd 7015) art 36 para 3. 'A certain time' may, for example, be a period of ten years or until notice to withdraw. However, once the court is seised of a dispute, the subsequent termination of a declaration by a party does not deprive the court of jurisdiction: *Nottebohm (Liechtenstein v Guatemala) (Preliminary Objection)* ICJ Reports 1953, 111. As to the Statute of the International Court of Justice see PARA 499 note 1.

3   The United Kingdom Declaration concerning the Optional Clause of the Statute of the International Court of Justice (New York, 5 July 2004; TS 50 (2004); Cm 6454) gives the court jurisdiction over disputes arising after 1 January 1974 with regard to subsequent situations or facts other than: (1) where the United Kingdom has agreed with the other party or parties to a dispute to settle by some other method of peaceful settlement; (2) a dispute with a country which is or has been a Member of the Commonwealth; or (3) a dispute with a party which has only accepted the compulsory jurisdiction in relation to or for the purposes of that dispute or where the acceptance of compulsory jurisdiction by the other party was deposited less than 12 months prior to the filing of the application before the court. The declaration is made on condition of reciprocity and is subject to the right to terminate on notice. The right to add to, amend or withdraw any reservation is preserved: see Letter No 2. States are free to make such reservations though they are not expressly permitted by the Statute of the International Court of Justice: *Military and Paramilitary Activities in and against Nicaragua (Nicaragua v United States of America) (Jurisdiction and Admissibility)* ICJ Reports 1984, 392.

4   This is strictly unnecessary, for a plea that a matter is within the domestic jurisdiction would be available under general international law. The United States of America (in its declaration of 1946), and other states, have made 'automatic' reservations of the type reserving from the jurisdiction of the court disputes with regard to matters which are essentially within the domestic jurisdiction of the United States as determined by the United States. This would appear to be incompatible with the Statute of the International Court of Justice, and more particularly art 36 para 6. The court itself has avoided determining the question when it has been raised: see the *Certain Norwegian Loans (France v Norway) (Preliminary Objections)* ICJ Reports 1957, 9; *Interhandel (Switzerland v United States of America) (Preliminary Objections)* ICJ Reports 1959, 6. Some judges have expressed the view that such a reservation is illegal and vitiates the declaration as a whole: see Judge Lauterpacht in the *Certain Norwegian Loans (France v Norway) (Preliminary Objections)* at 42 et seq; *Interhandel (Switzerland v United States of America) (Preliminary Objections)* at 97 et seq.

5   For the interpretation of this type of reservation see *Phosphates in Morocco* PCIJ Ser A/B No 74 (1938); *Electricity Co of Sofia and Bulgaria* PCIJ Ser A/B No 77 (1939); *Right of Passage over Indian Territory (Portugal v India) (Preliminary Objection)* ICJ Reports 1957, 125. For the

United Kingdom reservation see the United Kingdom Declaration concerning the Optional Clause of the Statute of the International Court of Justice (note 3).

6 See the *Certain Phosphate Lands in Nauru (Nauru v Australia) (Preliminary Objections)* ICJ Reports 1992, 240; *Arbitral Award of 31 July 1989 (Guinea-Bissau v Senegal)* ICJ Reports 1991, 53.

7 *Electricity Co of Sofia and Bulgaria* PCIJ Ser A/B No 77 (1939); *Certain Norwegian Loans (France v Norway) (Preliminary Objections)* ICJ Reports 1957, 9. There are, however, limitations upon this: see *Right of Passage over Indian Territory (Portugal v India) (Preliminary Objection)* ICJ Reports 1957, 125 at 143, 147; *Interhandel (Switzerland v United States of America) (Preliminary Objections)* ICJ Reports 1959, 6.

506. Withdrawal, termination or variation of a declaration under optional clause. A state may withdraw or terminate its declaration under the optional clause if it has reserved the right to do so[1]. If a period of notice is specified in the declaration, its withdrawal will be valid if notice is given within that period[2]. If it has not reserved the right to do so, a state may withdraw its declaration if it gives notice of a reasonable length of time[3]. A state cannot, by withdrawing a declaration after the International Court of Justice[4] has been seised of a case, deprive the court of jurisdiction to hear it. Nor is the court, once seised of a case, deprived of jurisdiction by termination of the declaration by lapse of time[5].

A state may, if it has reserved the right to do so, vary its declaration by adding new or cancelling existing reservations[6]. If it has not reserved the right to do so, it may not vary its declaration[7].

1 The United Kingdom has reserved the right to do so: see PARA 505 note 3.
2 *Military and Paramilitary Activities in and against Nicaragua (Nicaragua v United States of America) (Jurisdiction and Admissibility)* ICJ Reports 1984, 392 at 418.
3 *Military and Paramilitary Activities in and against Nicaragua (Nicaragua v United States of America) (Jurisdiction and Admissibility)* ICJ Reports 1984, 392 at 420. The court said that this was by way of analogy with the Law of Treaties. The Vienna Convention on the Law of Treaties (Vienna, 23 May 1969; TS 58 (1980); Cmnd 7964) art 56 para 2 requires 12 months' notice of termination. However, for limitations on the treaty analogy see the *Fisheries Jurisdiction (Spain v Canada)* ICJ Reports 1998, 127. As to the meaning of 'treaty' see PARA 71.
4 As to the International Court of Justice see PARA 499.
5 *Nottebohm (Liechtenstein v Guatemala) (Preliminary Objection)* ICJ Reports 1953, 111.
6 *Right of Passage over Indian Territory (Portugal v India) (Preliminary Objection)* ICJ Reports 1957, 125. However, the court stated that such a variation could not deprive it of jurisdiction over a case of which it had already been seised.
7 *Military and Paramilitary Activities in and against Nicaragua (Nicaragua v United States of America) (Jurisdiction and Admissibility)* ICJ Reports 1984, 392.

507. Admissibility. The International Court of Justice[1] will not entertain a claim which is inadmissible[2]. Non-compliance with the nationality of claims rule[3] or the rule requiring exhaustion of local remedies[4] renders a claim inadmissible. The court will not deal with a case which is hypothetical and lacking in real purpose[5], or has ceased to have any purpose[6]. The claimant state must have a sufficient legal interest of its own in the case[7], otherwise it lacks standing to bring the case before the court[8]. The court will decline to hear the case if a legal interest of a state which is not a party thereto would form the very subject matter of its decision[9]. The court has no power to determine the jurisdiction of another tribunal, such as an arbitrator[10].

1 As to the International Court of Justice see PARA 499.
2 Admissibility must be distinguished from jurisdiction. Lack of jurisdiction means that the court cannot hear a particular case at all; a claim which is inadmissible may become admissible, as for example, by exhaustion of local remedies: see the *Interhandel (Switzerland v United States of America) (Preliminary Objections)* ICJ Reports 1959, 6.
3 As to the nationality of claims see PARA 398 et seq.

4   As to exhaustion of local remedies see PARA 405 et seq.

5   *Northern Cameroons (Cameroon v United Kingdom) (Preliminary Objection)* ICJ Reports 1963, 15 which was distinguished in *Certain Phosphate Lands in Nauru (Nauru v Australia) (Preliminary Objections)* ICJ Reports 1992, 240.

6   *Nuclear Tests (Australia v France)* ICJ Reports 1974, 253; *Nuclear Tests (New Zealand v France)* ICJ Reports 1974, 457. The conclusion of an agreement between the parties to the case to establish a modus vivendi while the court is hearing the case does not, however, prevent the court from continuing to hear it since an actual dispute still exists: *Fisheries Jurisdiction (United Kingdom v Iceland)* ICJ Reports 1974, 3.

7   *South West Africa Cases (Ethiopia v South Africa; Liberia v South Africa) (Second Phase)* ICJ Reports 1966, 6.

8   *Barcelona Traction, Light and Power Co Ltd (Belgium v Spain) (Second Phase)* ICJ Reports 1970, 3.

9   *Monetary Gold Removed from Rome in 1943 (Italy v France, United Kingdom and United States of America) (Jurisdiction)* ICJ Reports 1954, 19; *East Timor (Portugal v Australia)* ICJ Reports 1995, 90. See also *Certain Phosphate Lands in Nauru (Nauru v Australia) (Preliminary Objections)* ICJ Reports 1992, 240; *Land and Maritime Boundary between Cameroon and Nigeria (Cameroon v Nigeria) (Preliminary Objections)* ICJ Reports 1998, 275. For the application of this principle to requests for advisory opinions see PARA 512. As to intervention by a third state see PARA 508.

10   *Interpretation of Peace Treaties with Bulgaria, Hungary and Romania (First Phase) (Advisory Opinion)* ICJ Reports 1950, 65 at 71. This rule reflects the principle of equality of international tribunals. The court may, however, investigate the meaning of a treaty in order to determine whether the parties are under an obligation to refer a particular dispute to arbitration: *Ambatielos (Greece v United Kingdom) (Preliminary Objection)* ICJ Reports 1952, 28 at 39; *Ambatielos (Greece v United Kingdom)* ICJ Reports 1953, 10. As to the meaning of 'treaty' see PARA 71.

508.   Intervention.   A state has a right to intervene in a case in which it is not a party whenever the construction of a convention to which it is a party is involved; and if it does intervene the construction given by the judgment is binding on it[1]. The International Court of Justice[2] may permit a state to intervene in a case in which the state considers that it has an interest of a legal nature which may be affected by the decision in the case[3]. The intervening state does not become a party to the case, but only acquires the right to be heard[4].

1   See the Statute of the International Court of Justice (San Francisco, 26 June 1945; TS 67 (1946); Cmd 7015) art 63. The conditions were fulfilled in the *Haya de la Torre (Colombia/Peru)* ICJ Reports 1951, 71, but not in *Military and Paramilitary Activities in and against Nicaragua (Nicaragua v United States of America) (Declaration of Intervention)* ICJ Reports 1984, 215. As to the Statute of the International Court of Justice see PARA 499 note 1.

2   As to the International Court of Justice see PARA 499.

3   Statute of the International Court of Justice art 62. The applicant state must show that it has an interest of a legal nature and that it could be affected by the decision in the case, the precise object of its intervention and any basis of jurisdiction between it and the parties: see Rules of Court (adopted 14 April 1978) art 81 para 2. The Rules of Court are contained in Acts and Documents concerning the Organisation of the Court No 2: see PARA 500 note 7. Intervention was permitted in eg the *SS 'Wimbledon'* PCIJ Ser A No 1 (1923); *Land, Island and Maritime Frontier Dispute (El Salvador/Honduras) (Application for Permission to Intervene)* ICJ Reports 1990, 92; *Land and Maritime Boundary between Cameroon and Nigeria (Cameroon v Nigeria) (Application by Equatorial Guinea for Permission to Intervene)* ICJ Reports 1999, 1029. Permission was refused in eg *Nuclear Tests (Australia v France) (Application by Fiji to Intervene)* ICJ Reports 1973, 320 (case has become moot; see PARA 507 note 6); *Continental Shelf (Tunisia/Libyan Arab Jamahiriya) (Application for Permission to Intervene)* ICJ Reports 1981, 3; *Continental Shelf (Libyan Arab Jamahiriya/Malta) (Application for Permission to Intervene)* ICJ Reports 1984, 3; and *Sovereignty over Pulau Ligatan and Pulau Sipadan (Indonesia/Malaysia) (Application to Intervene)* ICJ Reports 2001, 575.

4   *Military and Paramilitary Activities in and against Nicaragua (Nicaragua v United States of America) (Declaration of Intervention)* ICJ Reports 1984, 215. The court does not need to have jurisdiction to determine cases brought between the states which are parties to the case and the intervening state: *Land, Island and Maritime Frontier Dispute (El Salvador/Honduras)*

(Application for Permission to Intervene) ICJ Reports 1990, 92; *Land and Maritime Boundary between Cameroon and Nigeria (Cameroon v Nigeria) (Application by Equatorial Guinea for Permission to Intervene)* ICJ Reports 1999, 1029. As to the jurisdiction of the court see PARAS 503–506. Should the third state's legal interest be the very subject matter of the decision in the case, then the case itself is inadmissible under the principle stated in the *Monetary Gold Removed from Rome in 1943 (Italy v France, United Kingdom and United States of America) (Jurisdiction)* ICJ Reports 1954, 19: see PARA 507.

509. Law applicable. The International Court of Justice[1], whose function is to decide in accordance with international law such disputes as are submitted to it, must apply: (1) international conventions, whether general or particular, establishing rules expressly recognised by the contesting states; (2) international custom, as evidence of a general practice accepted as law; (3) the general principles of law recognised by civilised nations; and (4) judicial decisions and the teaching of the most highly qualified publicists of the various nations, as subsidiary means for the determination of rules of law[2]. This does not prejudice the court's power to decide a case ex aequo et bono, if the parties agree to it[3].

1   As to the International Court of Justice see PARA 499.
2   Statute of the International Court of Justice (San Francisco, 26 June 1945; TS 67 (1946); Cmd 7015) art 38 para 1. The reference to judicial decisions is subject to art 59, according to which the court's decision has no binding force except between the parties and in respect of that particular case, thus excluding any doctrine of stare decisis. The parties to the case may not, therefore, agree that the court is to decide the case in accordance with rules created by themselves for the purpose of the decision nor, save for art 38 para 2, may they require the court not to apply rules of international law. As to arbitration see PARA 492 et seq. For a discussion of the provisions of art 38 para 1, in the context of sources of international law, see PARA 2. As to the Statute of the International Court of Justice see PARA 499 note 1.
3   Statute of the International Court of Justice art 38 para 2. There have not been any cases in which the parties have agreed to this.

510. Provisional measures. The International Court of Justice[1] has the power to indicate, if it considers that circumstances so require, any provisional measures which must be taken to preserve the respective rights of the parties[2]. These measures may be indicated without prejudice to the question of whether the court has the jurisdiction to hear the case on its merits, provided that some instrument prima facie confers jurisdiction on the court[3]. The court has discretion whether or not to indicate provisional measures[4]. The rights which it is sought to protect by such measures must be those which are the subject matter of the proceedings before the court[5]. Provisional measures are binding upon the states to which they are addressed[6].

1   As to the International Court of Justice see PARA 499.
2   The Statute of the International Court of Justice (San Francisco, 26 June 1945; TS 67 (1946); Cmd 7015) art 41 para 1 provides that the Court may 'indicate' measures which 'ought to be taken', but the Court has interpreted an order of provisional measures as imposing binding international obligations upon the addressees: *LaGrand (Germany v United States of America)* ICJ Reports 2001, 466 at 501–506; see also note 6. Pending the final decision, notice of the measures suggested must forthwith be given to the parties and to the United Nations Security Council: art 41 para 2. As to the Statute of the International Court of Justice see PARA 499 note 1.
3   *Interhandel (Switzerland v United States of America) (Interim Protection)* ICJ Reports 1957, 105 at 118–119 per Sir Herch Lauterpacht; *Fisheries Jurisdiction (United Kingdom v Iceland) (Interim Protection)* ICJ Reports 1972, 12; *Nuclear Tests (Australia v France) (Interim Protection)* ICJ Reports 1973, 99; *Border and Transborder Armed Actions (Nicaragua v Honduras) (Jurisdiction and Admissibility)* ICJ Reports 1988, 69. See *Arbitral Award of 31 July 1989 (Guinea-Bissau v Senegal) (Provisional Measures)* ICJ Reports 1990, 64; *Passage through the Great Belt (Finland v Denmark) (Provisional Measures)* ICJ Reports 1991, 41; *Application of the Convention on the Prevention and Punishment of the Crime of Genocide (Bosnia and*

Herzegovina v Yugoslavia) (Provisional Measures) ICJ Reports 1993, 3; *Request for an Examination of the Situation in Accordance with Paragraph 63 of the Court's Judgment of 20 December 1974 in the Nuclear Tests (New Zealand v France) Case* ICJ Reports 1995, 288; *Land and Maritime Boundary between Cameroon and Nigeria (Cameroon v Nigeria) (Provisional Measures)* ICJ Reports 1996, 13; *Vienna Convention on Consular Relations (Paraguay v United States of America)* ICJ Reports 1998, 248; *LaGrand (Germany v United States of America) (Provisional Measures)* ICJ Reports 1999, 9; *Request for Interpretation of the Judgment of 31 March 2004 in the Case concerning Avena and Other Mexican Nationals (Mexico v United States Of America)* ICJ Reports, 19 January 2009.

4   Cases in which provisional measures were indicated include: the *Anglo-Iranian Oil Co Case (United Kingdom v Iran) (Preliminary Objections)* ICJ Reports 1952, 93; *Nuclear Tests (Australia v France) (Interim Protection)* ICJ Reports 1973, 99; *Military and Paramilitary Activities in and against Nicaragua (Nicaragua v United States of America) (Provisional Measures)* ICJ Reports 1984, 169; *United States Diplomatic and Consular Staff in Teheran (United States of America v Iran) (Provisional Measures)* ICJ Reports 1979, 7; *Application of the Convention on the Prevention and Punishment of the Crime of Genocide (Bosnia and Herzegovina v Yugoslavia) (Provisional Measures)* ICJ Reports 1993, 3; *Land and Maritime Boundary between Cameroon and Nigeria (Cameroon v Nigeria) (Provisional Measures)* ICJ Reports 1996, 13; *Vienna Convention on Consular Relations (Paraguay v United States of America) (Provisional Measures)* ICJ Reports 1998, 248; *LaGrand (Germany v United States of America) (Provisional Measures)* ICJ Reports 1999, 9; *Request for Interpretation of the Judgment of 31 March 2004 in the Case concerning Avena and Other Mexican Nationals (Mexico v United States Of America)* ICJ Reports, 19 January 2009.

The court declined to indicate such measures in eg the *Aegean Sea Continental Shelf (Greece v Turkey) (Interim Protection)* ICJ Reports 1976, 3 (Greece's rights could not be affected nor would it suffer irreparable prejudice by Turkey's activities); *Passage through the Great Belt (Finland v Denmark) (Provisional Measures)* ICJ Reports 1991, 41 (the matter was not urgent); *Questions of Interpretation and Application of the 1971 Montreal Convention arising from the Aerial Incident at Lockerbie (Libyan Arab Jamahiriya v United Kingdom) (Provisional Measures)* ICJ Reports 1992, 3 at 15 (Security Council Resolutions prevailed over the rights of Libya under the Convention and an indication of provisional measures might impair the rights of the United Kingdom and the United States under those resolutions); *Legality of the Use of Force (Yugoslavia v Belgium) (Provisional Measures)* ICJ Reports 1999, 124.

5   *Arbitral Award of 31 July 1989 (Guinea Bissau v Senegal) (Provisional Measures)* ICJ Reports 1990, 64 (the rights must not merely be those which would be affected by the outcome of the proceedings). See *Application of the Convention on the Prevention and Punishment of the Crime of Genocide (Bosnia and Herzegovina v Yugoslavia) (Provisional Measures)* ICJ Reports 1993, 3.

6   See the *Request for Interpretation of the Judgment of 31 March 2004 in the Case concerning Avena and Other Mexican Nationals (Mexico v United States of America)* ICJ Reports, 19 January 2009.

511. Judgments. Upon the completion of the presentation of a case[1], the International Court of Justice[2] retires to consider its judgments[3]. All questions are decided by a majority of the judges present[4], and in the event of equality of votes the President or presiding judge has a casting vote[5]. The judgment, which must state the reasons upon which it is based[6], must contain the names of the judges who took part in it[7]. Separate and dissenting judgments are permitted[8].

Any dispute as to the meaning or scope of a judgment must be construed by the Court at the request of any party[9]. The Court may give a declaratory judgment[10]. The court's judgment is final and without appeal[11]. Its decision has no binding force except between the parties and in respect of the particular case[12].

1   Statute of the International Court of Justice (San Francisco, 26 June 1945; TS 67 (1946); Cmd 7015) art 54 para 1. As to the Statute of the International Court of Justice see PARA 499 note 1.

2   As to the International Court of Justice see PARA 499.

3   Statute of the International Court of Justice art 54 para 2. The deliberations are in private and remain secret: art 54 para 3. As to the court's practice considering its judgment see the

Resolution concerning the Internal Judicial Practice of the Court made under Rules of Court art 33. The Resolution can be found in Acts and Documents concerning the Organization of the Court No 6. As to the Rules of Court see PARA 500 note 7.

4   Statute of the International Court of Justice art 55 para 1.

5   Statute of the International Court of Justice art 55 para 2. The President used his casting vote in the *Lotus Case* PCIJ Ser A No 10 (1927) and in the *South West Africa Cases (Ethiopia v South Africa; Liberia v South Africa) (Second Phase)* ICJ Reports 1966, 6. As to the President of the International Court of Justice see PARA 499.

6   Statute of the International Court of Justice art 56 para 1.

7   Statute of the International Court of Justice art 56 para 2. It must be signed by the President and Registrar, and must be read in open court: art 58.

8   See the Statute of the International Court of Justice art 57.

9   Statute of the International Court of Justice art 60. See the *Asylum (Colombia/Peru)* ICJ Reports 1950, 266; *Request for Interpretation of the Judgment of 31 March 2004 in the Case concerning Avena and Other Mexican Nationals (Mexico v United States Of America)* ICJ Reports, 19 January 2009.

10 See the *Factory at Chorzów (Interpretation)* PCIJ Ser A No 13 at 20 (1927); *Corfu Channel (United Kingdom v Albania)* ICJ Reports 1949, 4 at 34.

11 Statute of the International Court of Justice art 60. As to revision of a judgment see art 61; and e g *Continental Shelf (Tunisia/Libyan Arab Jamahiriya)* ICJ Reports 1985, 192; *Application for Revision of the Judgment of 11 July 1996 in the Case Concerning the Application of the Convention on the Prevention and Punishment of the Crime of Genocide (Yugoslavia v Bosnia and Herzegovina)* ICJ Reports 2003, 7; *Application for Revision of the Judgment of 11 September 1992 in the Case concerning the Land, Island and Maritime Frontier Dispute (El Salvador/Honduras: Nicaragua intervening) (El Salvador v Honduras)* ICJ 2003, 392.

12 Statute of the International Court of Justice art 59. See *Certain German Interests in Polish Upper Silesia* PCIJ Ser A No 7 (1926). As to the obligation of a state member of the United Nations to comply with a decision, see the Charter of the United Nations (San Francisco, 26 June 1945; TS 67 (1946); Cmd 7015) art 94.

512.   Advisory opinions. The International Court of Justice[1] may give an advisory opinion upon any legal question[2] at the request of a body authorised to do so[3] by or in accordance with the Charter of the United Nations[4]. Other organs and specialised agencies may be authorised by the General Assembly to ask for an opinion on a legal question arising out of their activities[5]. The uses of advisory opinions are to assist the political organs of the United Nations to settle disputes and to provide guidance on points of law in connection with the functioning of those organs and specialised agencies.

In proceedings on requests for advisory opinions the court is guided by the provisions of the Statute of the International Court of Justice applicable in contentious cases between states to the extent to which it recognises them to be applicable[6]. The Court must give notice of a request for an advisory opinion to all states entitled to appear before it[7], and to international organisations which it considers as likely to be able to furnish information on the matter[8]. Because there are no parties to the case, an advisory opinion technically has no binding force as res judicata; but it is nonetheless entitled to respect as a considered opinion on a question of law, given by the International Court of Justice after hearing argument and after deliberating.

1   As to the International Court of Justice see PARA 499.

2   Provided the question relates to a legal issue it is immaterial that it affects a political issue. See e g the *Certain Expenses of the United Nations (Advisory Opinion)* ICJ Reports 1962, 151 at 155; *Legal Consequences of the Construction of a Wall in the Occupied Palestinian Territory (Advisory Opinion)* ICJ Reports 2004, 136.

3   Ie the General Assembly and the Security Council of the United Nations: Charter of the United Nations (San Francisco, 26 June 1945; TS 67 (1946); Cmd 7015) art 96 para 1.

4   Statute of the International Court of Justice (San Francisco, 26 June 1945; TS 67 (1946); Cmd 7015) art 65 para 1. As to the Statute of the International Court of Justice see PARA 499 note 1.

5   Charter of the United Nations art 96 para 2. The Economic and Social Council and the
     Trusteeship Council have been so authorised. The following specialised agencies have been
     authorised: Inter-Governmental Maritime Consultative Organisation; International Bank for
     Reconstruction and Development; International Civil Aviation Organisation; International
     Labour Organisation; International Monetary Fund; International Telecommunication Union;
     International Trade Organisation; United Nations Educational, Scientific and Cultural
     Organisation; World Health Organisation. An advisory opinion was given to the Economic and
     Social Council: see *Difference relating to Immunity from Legal Process of a Special Rapporteur
     of the Commission on Human Rights (Request for Advisory Opinion)* ICJ 1998, 423. It was
     refused to the World Health Organisation in *Legality of the Threat or Use of Nuclear Weapons
     (Advisory Opinion)* ICJ Reports 1996, 66 on the ground that the question did not arise out of
     its activities. An Opinion was, however, given to the General Assembly on the same question:
     Legality of the Threat or Use of Nuclear Weapons (Advisory Opinion) ICJ Reports 1996, 226.
     As to the specialised agencies of the United Nations see PARA 533. As to the Economic and
     Social Council see PARA 529.

6   Statute of the International Court of Justice art 68. The International Court of Justice must,
     above all, consider whether the request relates to a legal question pending between two or more
     states: Rules of Court (adopted 14 April 1978) art 102 para 2. The Rules of Court are contained
     in Acts and Documents concerning the Organisation of the Court No 2: see PARA 500 note 7. If
     it does, the court may decline to give an opinion when this would be tantamount to deciding an
     issue between them in the absence of one of them from the proceedings: *Eastern Carelia Case*
     PCIJ Ser B No 5 (1923). However, see the *Interpretation of Peace Treaties with Bulgaria,
     Hungary and Romania (Second Phase) (Advisory Opinion)* ICJ Reports 1950, 221; *Western
     Sahara (Advisory Opinion)* ICJ Reports 1975, 12; *Legal Consequences of the Construction of a
     Wall in the Occupied Palestinian Territory (Advisory Opinion)* ICJ Reports 2004, 136.
        See also the Statute of the International Court of Justice art 89, which, by reference to art 31,
     gives the Court the right to allow a party to appoint an ad hoc judge in such a case. The court
     allowed the appointment of an ad hoc judge in the *Western Sahara (Advisory Opinion)* ICJ
     Reports 1975, 12, but not in *Legal Consequences for States of the Continued Presence of South
     Africa in Namibia (South West Africa) notwithstanding Security Council Resolution 276 (1970)
     (Request for Advisory Opinion)* ICJ Reports 1971, 359. As to ad hoc judges see PARA 500.

7   Statute of the International Court of Justice art 66 para 1.

8   Statute of the International Court of Justice art 66 para 2. States and organisations may make
     both written and oral observations: art 66 para 3.

                    B. OTHER PERMANENT INTERNATIONAL COURTS AND TRIBUNALS

513.   European Court of Human Rights. The European Court of Human
Rights, which has its seat in Strasbourg, was established under the European
Convention on Human Rights[1]. Each contracting state, of which there are
currently 47, nominates three persons of whom one is elected by the
parliamentary Assembly of the Council of Europe[2]. Judges sit in an individual
capacity[3], in committees of three judges, in Chambers of seven judges, and in
Grand Chambers of seventeen judges, depending upon the nature of the case and
question before them[4]. The court has jurisdiction in respect of cases alleging
violations of rights protected by the European Convention on Human Rights
that are brought against a state party either by another state party[5] or, more
commonly, by an individual applicant[6]. Cases are admissible only after all
domestic remedies have been exhausted, according to the generally recognised
rules of international law, and within a period of six months from the date on
which the final decision was taken[7]. A state party has a right to intervene in cases
in which its nationals are applicants[8]; and in the interests of the proper
administration of justice the President of the Court may invite any other state
party to intervene orally or in writing[9]. Judgments of the court are final and
binding[10], and states undertake to comply with the judgment in any case to
which they are parties[11]. The court may also give advisory opinions on the

interpretation of the European Convention on Human Rights and its Protocols, at the request of the Committee of Ministers of the Council of Europe[12].

1 See the Convention for the Protection of Human Rights and Fundamental Freedoms (Rome, 4 November 1950; TS 71 (1953); Cmd 8969) art 19. See further CONSTITUTIONAL LAW AND HUMAN RIGHTS vol 8(2) (Reissue) PARA 179 et seq.

2 See the Convention for the Protection of Human Rights and Fundamental Freedoms art 22. See also CONSTITUTIONAL LAW AND HUMAN RIGHTS.

3 See the Convention for the Protection of Human Rights and Fundamental Freedoms art 21. See also CONSTITUTIONAL LAW AND HUMAN RIGHTS.

4 See the Convention for the Protection of Human Rights and Fundamental Freedoms arts 27–31. See also CONSTITUTIONAL LAW AND HUMAN RIGHTS.

5 See the Convention for the Protection of Human Rights and Fundamental Freedoms art 33. See also CONSTITUTIONAL LAW AND HUMAN RIGHTS.

6 See the Convention for the Protection of Human Rights and Fundamental Freedoms art 34. See also CONSTITUTIONAL LAW AND HUMAN RIGHTS.

7 See the Convention for the Protection of Human Rights and Fundamental Freedoms art 35. See also CONSTITUTIONAL LAW AND HUMAN RIGHTS.

8 See the Convention for the Protection of Human Rights and Fundamental Freedoms art 36. See also CONSTITUTIONAL LAW AND HUMAN RIGHTS.

9 See the Convention for the Protection of Human Rights and Fundamental Freedoms art 36. See also CONSTITUTIONAL LAW AND HUMAN RIGHTS.

10 See the Convention for the Protection of Human Rights and Fundamental Freedoms art 44. See also CONSTITUTIONAL LAW AND HUMAN RIGHTS.

11 See the Convention for the Protection of Human Rights and Fundamental Freedoms art 46. See also CONSTITUTIONAL LAW AND HUMAN RIGHTS.

12 See the Convention for the Protection of Human Rights and Fundamental Freedoms art 47. See also CONSTITUTIONAL LAW AND HUMAN RIGHTS.

514. The International Tribunal for the Law of the Sea. A state may choose the International Tribunal for the Law of the Sea[1] as a means for the settlement of disputes concerning the United Nations Convention on the Law of the Sea[2]. The Tribunal consists of 21 independent members elected from among persons enjoying the highest reputation for fairness and integrity and of recognised competence in the field of the law of the sea[3]. The members of the Tribunal are elected by secret ballot[4] for nine years and may be re-elected[5]. All available members of the Tribunal must sit, and a quorum of 11 elected members is required to constitute the Tribunal[6]. The Tribunal may, however, form a chamber of three or more of its members for particular categories of disputes[7]; and it must form a chamber at the request of the parties for dealing with a particular dispute[8]. With a view to the speedy dispatch of business, the Tribunal must form annually a chamber composed of five of its elected members which may hear and determine disputes by summary procedure[9]. It must establish a Seabed Disputes Chamber[10] consisting of 11 members[11], which itself must establish an ad hoc chamber of three members at the request of any party to a dispute falling within the jurisdiction of the Seabed Disputes Chamber[12].

The Tribunal has the power to issue orders for provisional measures in respect of cases submitted to an arbitral tribunal constituted under the Convention on the Law of the Sea, in the period prior to the constitution of the arbitral tribunal[13].

1 The International Tribunal for the Law of the Sea was established by the United Nations Convention on the Law of the Sea (Montego Bay, 10 December 1982; TS 81 (1999); Cmnd 4524) Annex VI. The Tribunal sits in Hamburg: see Annex VI art 1 para 2.

2 See the United Nations Convention on the Law of the Sea art 287 para 1(a).

3 United Nations Convention on the Law of the Sea Annex VI art 2 para 1. In the Tribunal as a whole the representation of the principal legal systems of the world and equitable geographical distribution is to be assured: Annex VI art 2 para 2. No two members of the Tribunal may be

nationals of the same state: Annex VI art 3 para 1. There are to be no fewer than three members from each geographical group as established by the General Assembly of the United Nations: Annex VI art 3 para 2. When engaged on the business of the tribunal, its members enjoy diplomatic privileges and immunities: Annex VI art 10; and see PARA 267. As to diplomatic privileges and immunities in general see PARA 265 et seq.

4   United Nations Convention on the Law of the Sea Annex VI art 4 para 4. As to elections and nominations see Annex VI art 4.

5   United Nations Convention on the Law of the Sea Annex VI art 5 para 1. As to terms of office see Annex VI art 5. The Tribunal elects its President and Vice-President for three years: Annex VI art 12 para 1.

6   United Nations Convention on the Law of the Sea Annex VI art 13 para 1. The competence and jurisdiction of the Tribunal are provided for in Annex VI arts 20–23. The procedure of the Tribunal is provided for in Annex VI arts 24–34.

7   United Nations Convention on the Law of the Sea Annex VI art 15 para 1.

8   United Nations Convention on the Law of the Sea Annex VI art 15 para 2. The composition of such a chamber is determined by the tribunal with the approval of the parties: Annex VI art 15 para 2.

9   United Nations Convention on the Law of the Sea Annex VI art 15 para 3.

10   United Nations Convention on the Law of the Sea Annex VI art 14. The composition of the Seabed Disputes Chamber, access, the applicable law and the enforcement of its decisions are provided for in Annex VI arts 35–40.

11   United Nations Convention on the Law of the Sea Annex VI art 35 para 1.

12   United Nations Convention on the Law of the Sea Annex VI art 36 para 1. As to the jurisdiction of the Seabed Disputes Chamber see arts 186–188.

13   See the United Nations Convention on the Law of the Sea art 290(4).

515.   The World Trade Organisation Appellate Body. The Appellate Body consists of seven persons appointed by the World Trade Organisation Dispute Settlement Body, and it sits in divisions of three persons, selected by rotation[1]. It may uphold, modify or reverse the panel's legal findings[2]. An Appellate Body report must automatically be adopted by the Dispute Settlement Body and unconditionally accepted by the parties to the dispute unless the Dispute Settlement Body decides by consensus not to adopt the Appellate Body report within 30 days following its circulation to the members[3].

It appears that the exhaustion of local remedies rule does not apply to such procedures[4]. Arbitration is permitted as an alternative means of dispute settlement[5].

Unless otherwise agreed to by the parties to the dispute, the period from the date of establishment of the panel by the Dispute Settlement Body until the date the Dispute Settlement Body considers the appellate report for adoption must as a general rule not exceed 12 months where the report is appealed[6]. The member states involved must explain their intentions regarding compliance with recommendations contained in the Appellate Body report[7]. The Dispute Settlement Body keeps compliance under surveillance[8]. If a member state fails to comply with recommendations, the complainant state may request the authority of the Dispute Settlement Body to suspend the application to the defaulting member of concessions or other obligations[9]. If that member objects to the level of suspension authorised, the matter must be referred to arbitration[10]. The decision of the arbitrator is final[11].

1   See the World Trade Organisation Agreement (Marrakesh, 15 April 1994; TS 57 (1996) Cm 3277), Annex 2 establishing the Understanding on Rules and Procedures Governing the Settlement of Disputes art 17 para 1. The Understanding applies to 'covered agreements' (ie agreements listed in Appendix 1 to the understanding): see art 1 para 1. The Dispute Settlement Body appoints persons to serve on the Appellate Body for a four-year term, and each person may be re-appointed once: art 17 para 2. The Appellate Body must comprise persons of recognised authority, with demonstrated expertise in law, international trade and the subject matter of the covered agreements generally: art 17 para 3. They must be unaffiliated with any

government: art 17 para 3. The Appellate Body membership must be broadly representative of the membership of the World Trade Organisation: art 17 para 3. Proceedings of the Appellate Body are confidential (see art 17 para 10), as are communications with the Panel or the Appellate Body (see art 18). As to the Dispute Settlement Body see PARA 498.

2   World Trade Organisation Agreement Annex 2 establishing the Understanding on Rules and Procedures governing the Settlement of Disputes art 17 para 13.

3   World Trade Organisation Agreement Annex 2 establishing the Understanding on Rules and Procedures governing the Settlement of Disputes art 17 para 14.

4   As to exhaustion of local remedies see PARA 405 et seq.

5   See the World Trade Organisation Agreement Annex 2 establishing the Understanding on Rules and Procedures governing the Settlement of Disputes art 25.

6   World Trade Organisation Agreement Annex 2 establishing the Understanding on Rules and Procedures governing the Settlement of Disputes art 20.

7   World Trade Organisation Agreement Annex 2 establishing the Understanding on Rules and Procedures governing the Settlement of Disputes art 21 para 3.

8   World Trade Organisation Agreement Annex 2 establishing the Understanding on Rules and Procedures governing the Settlement of Disputes art 21.

9   See the World Trade Organisation Agreement Annex 2 establishing the Understanding on Rules and Procedures governing the Settlement of Disputes art 22 para 2.

10   See the World Trade Organisation Agreement Annex 2 establishing the Understanding on Rules and Procedures governing the Settlement of Disputes art 22 para 6.

11   See the World Trade Organisation Agreement Annex 2 establishing with Understanding on Rules and Procedures governing the Settlement of Disputes art 22 para 7.

516.   Other permanent international tribunals.   Permanent international tribunals have been established to hear various other types of case, including criminal cases[1] and appeals against cases determined by sports tribunals[2], among others[3].

1   See eg the Rome Statute of the International Criminal Court (Rome, 17 July 1998; TS No 35 (2002) Cm 5590); the International Criminal Court Act 2001; and PARA 437. There are also ad hoc international criminal tribunals for the former Yugoslavia and Rwanda established by the UN Security Council: see Security Council Resolutions 808 (1993) 22 February 1993 and 827 (1993) 25 May 1993, and 955 (1994) 8 November 1994 respectively; as well as a number of 'hybrid' or 'internationalised' criminal courts usually established by agreement between the United Nations and the interested state.

2   Eg the Court of Arbitration for Sport.

3   See generally the website of the Project on International Courts and Tribunals.

17. INTERNATIONAL ORGANISATIONS

(1) IN GENERAL

517. Law of international organisations. This part of this title is concerned with international intergovernmental organisations, almost always established by treaty, whose membership consists of states and sometimes other entities. It does not deal with international non-governmental organisations (NGOs).

The powers and functions of each international organisation are set out in its constituent instrument, and are specific to each organisation[1]. While each international organisation is unique, with its own constituent instrument and other rules (sometimes referred to as the 'internal law' of the organisation), there are certain common issues that arise and reference may therefore be made to a 'law of international organisations' (or, as it is sometimes called, 'international institutional law' or even 'common law of international organisations')[2].

Certain aspects of the law of international organisations are covered elsewhere in this title[3].

1   See *Legality of the Use by a State of Nuclear Weapons in Armed Conflict (Advisory Opinion)* ICJ Reports 1996, 66. The constitutions of international organisations have various names, such as agreement, constitution, charter, covenant, etc; a common way of referring to them is as the 'constituent instrument' of the organisation concerned. As to the meaning of 'international organisation' see the International Law Commission ('ILC') Draft Articles on the Responsibility of International Organizations ('DARIO') art 2(a), International Law Commission Report, 61st Session (2009), A/64/10, ch IV.

2   See Satow's Diplomatic Practice (6th Edn, 2009); Bowett's Law of International Institutions (6th Edn, 2009); Amerasinghe *Principles of the Institutional Law of International Organizations* (2nd Edn, 2005); Schermers and Blokker *International Institutional Law* (4th Edn, 2004). For a qualified reference to the notion of a common law of international organisations see *de Merode v World Bank* WBAT Reports [1981], Decision No 1,p 13.

3   As to treaties see PARA 71 et seq. As to the international legal personality of international organisations see PARA 36. As to the privileges and immunities of international organisations see PARA 307 et seq. As to the responsibility of international organisations see PARA 327 et seq.

518. International and European organisations generally. The United Kingdom is a member of various international and European organisations, such as the United Nations[1], the North Atlantic Treaty Organisation[2], the Organisation for Economic Co-operation and Development[3], the Council of Europe[4], and the European Union[5].

1   As to the United Nations see PARAS 519–533.

2   The North Atlantic Treaty Organisation developed from the Brussels Treaty Organisation created by the Treaty of Economic, Social and Cultural Collaboration and Collective Self-Defence (Brussels, 17 March 1948; TS 1 (1949); Cmd 7599). The North Atlantic Treaty was signed at Washington on 4 April 1949 (TS 56 (1949); Cmd 7789). The following countries are members of the North Atlantic Treaty Organisation: Albania; Belgium; Bulgaria; Canada; Croatia; Czech Republic; Denmark; Estonia; France; Germany; Greece; Hungary; Iceland; Italy; Latvia; Lithuania; Luxembourg; Netherlands; Norway; Poland; Portugal; Romania; Slovakia; Slovenia; Spain; Turkey; United Kingdom; United States.

3   The Organisation for Economic Co-operation and Development developed from the Organisation for European Economic Co-operation, which was created in 1948 to administer aid under the Marshall Plan for the reconstruction of Europe after the 1939–45 war: see the Convention for European Economic Co-operation (Paris, 16 April 1948; TS 59 (1949); Cmd 7796). The Organisation for Economic Co-operation and Development is a reconstitution of Organisation for European Economic Co-operation by the Convention on the Organisation for Economic Co-operation and Development (Paris, 14 December 1960; TS 21 (1962); Cmnd 1646). The following countries are members of the Organisation for Economic Co-operation and Development: Australia; Austria; Belgium; Canada; Czech Republic;

Denmark; Finland; France; Germany; Greece; Hungary; Iceland; Ireland; Italy; Japan; Republic of Korea; Luxembourg; Mexico; The Netherlands; New Zealand; Norway; Poland; Portugal; Slovak Republic; Spain; Sweden; Switzerland; Turkey; United Kingdom; United States. There is provision for co-operation between the European Union and the Organisation for Economic Co-operation and Development: see the Treaty on the Functioning of the European Union (Rome, 25 March 1957; TS 1 (1973); Cmnd 5179) art 220. The Treaty was formerly known as the Treaty Establishing the European Community; it has been renamed and its provisions renumbered: see PARA 304 note 1.

4　As to the Council of Europe see PARA 534. The Council of Europe is a separate organisation from the European Union (see the text and note 5).

5　Since the Treaty of Lisbon Amending the Treaty Establishing the European Union and the Treaty Establishing the European Community (Lisbon, 13 December 2007, ECS 13 (2007); Cm 7294) (the 'Lisbon Treaty') came into force on 1 December 2009, all references to the Communities or the Community are replaced by references to the European Union (EU): see the European Union (Amendment) Act 2008. As a member of the European Union, the United Kingdom is represented on both the European Council and the Council of the European Union. The European Council consists of the heads of state or government of the member states of the European Union, and is distinct from the Council of the European Union which consists of national ministers.

(2) THE UNITED NATIONS

519.　In general.　The Charter of the United Nations[1] was signed at San Francisco on 26 June 1945, and entered into force on 24 October 1945[2]. It has been amended on three occasions[3].

1　Ie the Charter of the United Nations (San Francisco, 26 June 1945; TS 67 (1946); Cmd 7015).

2　As to the United Nations see Satow's Diplomatic Practice (6th Edn, 2009); Simma *The Charter of the United Nations: A Commentary* (2nd Edn, 2002).

3　The amendments, adopted in 1963, 1965 and 1971 came into force in 1965, 1968 and 1973 respectively. Their effect was to enlarge the Security Council (see PARA 522) and the Economic and Social Council (see PARA 529), as well as to amend the procedure for reviewing and amending the Charter. As to the procedure for reviewing and amending the Charter of the United Nations see Ch XVIII (arts 108–109) (as subsequently amended).

520.　Membership.　The membership of the United Nations comprises: (1) those states which participated in the United Nations Conference at San Francisco in 1945 or, having previously signed the Declaration by United Nations of 1 January 1942, signed and ratified the Charter of the United Nations[1]; and (2) all other peace-loving states which accept the obligations contained in the Charter and, in the judgment of the organisation, are willing and able to carry out these obligations[2].

1　Ie in accordance with the provisions of the Charter of the United Nations (San Francisco, 26 June 1945; TS 67 (1946); Cmd 7015) art 110: art 3.

2　Charter of the United Nations art 4 para 1. Admission is effected by the General Assembly upon the recommendation of the Security Council: art 4 para 2. For the criteria upon which admission should be based see *Competence of the General Assembly for the Admission of a State to the United Nations (Advisory Opinion)* ICJ Reports 1950, 4. Provision is made for the suspension and expulsion of member states by the General Assembly on the recommendation of the Security Council: Charter of the United Nations arts 5, 6. There is no provision for withdrawal. As to the General Assembly see PARA 527 et seq. As to the Security Council see PARA 522 et seq.

521.　Principal organs.　The principal organs of the United Nations are the General Assembly[1], the Security Council[2], the Economic and Social Council[3], the Trusteeship Council[4], the International Court of Justice[5] and the Secretariat[6].

1　As to the General Assembly see PARA 527 et seq.

2　As to the Security Council see PARA 522 et seq.

3　As to the Economic and Social Council see PARA 529.

4   As to the Trusteeship Council see PARA 530.
5   As to the International Court of Justice see PARA 499 et seq.
6   Charter of the United Nations (San Francisco, 26 June 1945; TS 67 (1946); Cmd 7015) art 7
    para 1. As to the Secretariat see PARA 531.
        Subsidiary organs may be established in accordance with the Charter: art 7 para 2. The
    General Assembly and the Security Council have the power to establish subsidiary organs:
    arts 22, 29.

522.   Security Council: composition and decision-making.   The Security
Council consists of 15 members, namely the five permanent members (China,
France, the Russian Federation, the United Kingdom and the United States) and
ten other members elected by the General Assembly[1]. Each member has one
representative[2], and one vote[3]. Decisions are taken on procedural matters by an
affirmative vote of nine members[4]. On all other matters decisions must be taken
by an affirmative vote of nine members, including the concurring votes of the
permanent members[5].

1   Charter of the United Nations (San Francisco, 26 June 1945; TS 67 (1946); Cmd 7015) art 23
    para 1 (art 23 amended: 17 December 1963; TS 2 (1966); Cmnd 2900); and see General
    Assembly Resolution 1991 (XVIII) of 17 December 1963, Resolution A para 3. In electing the
    non-permanent members, the General Assembly must pay due regard, in the first instance, to the
    contribution of members to the maintenance of international peace and security and to the other
    purposes of the organisation, and also to equitable geographical distribution: see the Charter of
    the United Nations art 23(1). The non-permanent members are elected for two years: see art 23
    para 2 (as so amended). As to the purposes of the United Nations see art 1. As to the General
    Assembly see PARA 527 et seq.
2   Charter of the United Nations art 23 para 3.
3   Charter of the United Nations art 27 para 1.
4   Charter of the United Nations art 27 para 2 (as amended: 17 December 1963; TS 2 (1966);
    Cmnd 2900). There is no definition of 'procedural matters'. Under the Rules of Procedure, the
    President of the Council may rule that a matter is procedural. As to the procedure of the Council
    see the Charter of the United Nations arts 28–32.
5   Charter of the United Nations art 27 para 3 (as amended: 17 December 1963; TS 2 (1966);
    Cmnd 2900). If a permanent member votes against on a non-procedural matter, which secures
    nine votes, that is a 'veto'. The practice of the Security Council has been to regard the abstention
    of a permanent member as not preventing decision and absence of such a member as having the
    same effect, as when the Union of Soviet Socialist Republics was absent in the Korean crisis of
    1950. This practice was found to be lawful by the International Court of Justice: see *Legal
    Consequences for States of the Continued Presence of South Africa in Namibia (South West
    Africa) notwithstanding Security Council Resolution 276 (1970) (Advisory Opinion)* ICJ
    Reports 1971, 16.

523.   Security Council: functions and powers.   The Security Council[1] has
primary responsibility for the maintenance of international peace and security[2].
The members of the United Nations agree that, in carrying out its duties in this
respect, the Security Council acts on their behalf[3]. They agree to accept and carry
out the Security Council's decisions[4] in accordance with the Charter of the
United Nations[5]. In the event of a conflict between obligations under the Charter
and obligations under any other international agreement, obligations under the
Charter prevail[6]. For this purpose obligations under the Charter include
obligations imposed by decisions of the Security Council[7].

1   As to composition etc of the Security Council see PARA 522.
2   Charter of the United Nations (San Francisco, 26 June 1945; TS 67 (1946); Cmd 7015) art 24
    para 1.
3   See the Charter of the United Nations art 24 para 1. For the Security Council's powers in this
    respect see art 24 para 2; Ch VI (arts 33–38); Ch VII (arts 39–51); Ch XII (arts 75–85).
4   A decision is binding in law upon the member states, but a recommendation is not. The Security
    Council may make decisions under Ch VII (see PARA 525) and may make recommendations
    under Ch VI (see PARA 524).

5   Charter of the United Nations art 25.
6   Charter of the United Nations art 103.
7   See *Questions of Interpretation and Application of the 1971 Montreal Convention arising from the Aerial Incident at Lockerbie (Libyan Arab Jamahiriya v United Kingdom) (Provisional Measures)* ICJ Reports 1992, 3; *R (on the application of Al-Jedda) v Secretary of State for Defence* [2007] UKHL 58, [2008] 1 AC 332, [2008] 3 All ER 28.

524.   Security Council: peaceful settlement of disputes.   The Security Council[1] may use various means to assist in the pacific settlement of disputes likely to endanger the maintenance of international peace and security[2]. It may investigate any dispute or situation in order to determine whether its continuance is likely to endanger the maintenance of international peace and security[3]. The General Assembly[4], the Secretary-General[5] and member states[6] may submit disputes or situations of such character to the attention of the Security Council, and non-member states may submit disputes affecting them[7]. Member states are under a duty to refer such disputes to which they are party to the Council if they cannot settle them by other means[8].

Once seised of a dispute, the Security Council must invite the parties to participate in the discussion of it, without a right to vote[9]. In addition to calling upon the states to settle their dispute by traditional means[10], the Security Council may recommend a particular means of settlement[11] and, where the dispute involves international peace and security, may recommend the terms of settlement[12]. The Security Council may refer the dispute to an existing organ, for example the General Assembly[13].

1   As to the composition etc of the Security Council see PARA 522.
2   Charter of the United Nations (San Francisco, 26 June 1945; TS 67 (1946); Cmd 7015) art 33 para 1. See Ch VI (arts 33–38). These are supplementary to negotiation, inquiry, mediation, conciliation, arbitration, judicial settlement, resort to regional agencies or arrangements or other peaceful means, which the parties must first employ for the solution of a dispute: see art 33 para 1; and PARA 490. The Security Council may call upon them to do so: art 33 para 2.
3   Charter of the United Nations art 34.
4   As to the General Assembly's powers see the Charter of the United Nations arts 11, 12. As to the General Assembly see PARA 527 et seq.
5   As to the Secretary-General's powers see the Charter of the United Nations art 99.
6   As to the powers of member states see the Charter of the United Nations art 35 para 1. As to membership of the United Nations see PARA 520.
7   Charter of the United Nations art 35 para 2. In submitting such a dispute, non-member states must accept in advance, for the purposes of the dispute, the obligations of pacific settlement provided in the Charter of the United Nations: art 35 para 2.
8   Charter of the United Nations art 37 para 1.
9   Charter of the United Nations art 32. Any state whose interests are deemed to be affected may be invited to participate in the discussion of any question: art 31.
10   See the Charter of the United Nations art 33 para 2.
11   Charter of the United Nations art 36 para 1. The Security Council should take into consideration that, as a general rule, legal disputes should be referred by the parties to the International Court of Justice (the 'ICJ'): art 36 para 3. This was recommended in *Corfu Channel (United Kingdom v Albania) (Preliminary Objection)* ICJ Reports 1948, 15. The majority of the ICJ held that this did not of itself confer jurisdiction upon the court in respect of the dispute. As to the International Court of Justice see PARA 499 et seq.
12   Charter of the United Nations art 37 para 2. If the dispute is not of this nature, the Security Council could only act with the consent of the parties: art 38.
13   See the Charter of the United Nations art 12 para 1.

525.   Security Council: enforcement action.   Where the Security Council[1] determines the existence of a threat to the peace, breach of the peace or act of aggression[2], it may adopt one of several courses of action[3]. It may: (1) call upon the parties to comply with such provisional measures as it deems to be appropriate[4]; (2) decide upon, and call upon member states[5] to apply, measures (often referred to as 'sanctions')[6], which may include interruption of economic relations and means of communication and the severance of diplomatic relations[7]; or (3) take such action by the use of armed forces as may be necessary to maintain or restore international peace and security[8]. Member states must join in giving mutual assistance in carrying out measures decided on by the Security Council[9].

1   As to the composition of the Security Council see PARA 522.
2   Ie under the Charter of the United Nations (San Francisco, 26 June 1945; TS 67 (1946); Cmd 7015) art 39. For the definition of 'aggression' adopted by the United Nations General Assembly see General Assembly Resolution 3314 (XXIX) of 14 December 1974. As to the General Assembly see PARA 527 et seq.
3   See the Charter of the United Nations Ch VII (arts 39–51).
4   Charter of the United Nations art 40. An example of such a measure might be a cease-fire.
5   As to membership of the United Nations see PARA 520.
6   Ie measures not involving the use of armed force pursuant to the Charter of the United Nations art 41.
7   Charter of the United Nations art 41. The Security Council first imposed measures under art 41 in respect of Southern Rhodesia: see Security Council Resolution 221 (1966), 9 April; Security Council Resolution 232 (1966), 16 December; Security Council Resolution 253 (1968), 29 May. It has subsequently decided upon measures under the Charter of the United Nations art 41 on many occasions. These have included the imposition of general trade sanctions; arms embargoes; targeted sanctions against individuals, including persons associated with particular regimes or associated with particular terrorist groups; the establishment of ad hoc international criminal tribunals; the requirement to hand over certain individuals for trial; the reference of a situation to the International Criminal Court; and other measures in connection with that court. As to the International Criminal Court see PARA 437 et seq.
8   Charter of the United Nations art 42. Article 43 envisages the conclusion of special agreements for the provision of armed forces with member states, and only in respect of such agreements are member states legally obliged to comply with an order for the supply of armed forces. However, the absence of such agreements does not invalidate measures taken under art 43 with the voluntary co-operation of member states: *Certain Expenses of the United Nations (Advisory Opinion)* ICJ Reports 1962, 151 at 166, 171–172, 177.
9   Charter of the United Nations art 49.

526. Application of Security Council measures by the United Kingdom. Her Majesty may make such provision by Order in Council as appears necessary or expedient for enabling the effective application of any measures which the United Kingdom[1] government is called upon to apply[2] by the Security Council of the United Nations[3].

1·   As to the statutory meaning of 'United Kingdom' see PARA 30 note 3.
2   Ie under the Charter of the United Nations (San Francisco, 26 June 1945; TS 67 (1946); Cmd 7015) art 41 (measures not involving the use of force): see PARA 525.
3   See the United Nations Act 1946 s 1(1). As to the provisions made in the United Kingdom under this power see CONSTITUTIONAL LAW AND HUMAN RIGHTS vol 8(2) (Reissue) PARA 808. See *A v HM Treasury* [2010] UKSC 2, [2010] All ER (D) 179 (Jan). As to the composition of the Security Council see PARA 522.

527. General Assembly: composition and decision-making. The General Assembly consists of all the members of the United Nations[1]. Each member of the General Assembly has one vote[2]. Voting on important questions[3] is by a two-thirds majority of the members present and voting[4]. Decisions on other questions are made by a simple majority of the members present and voting[5].

1   Charter of the United Nations (San Francisco, 26 June 1945; TS 67 (1946); Cmd 7015) art 9 para 1. As to membership to the United Nations see PARA 520.
2   Charter of the United Nations art 18 para 1. For the voting rights of members in arrears with their contributions to the organisation see art 19.

3   'Important questions' include recommendations respecting the maintenance of international peace and security; the election of new members of the principal organs; the admission of new members; the suspension and expulsion of members; questions relating to the operation of the trusteeship system; and budgetary questions: Charter of the United Nations art 18 para 2.
4   Charter of the United Nations art 18 para 2.
5   Charter of the United Nations art 18 para 3. These include the determination of additional categories of questions to be decided by a two-thirds majority: art 18 para 3.

528.   General Assembly: functions and powers. The General Assembly[1] may discuss any matters within the scope of the Charter of the United Nations[2] or relating to the powers and functions of any United Nations organs and may make recommendations to the member states[3] or the Security Council[4] on such questions or matters[5]. It may discuss any question relating to the maintenance of international peace and security[6]. Such questions may be brought before the General Assembly by any member state and non-member state, or by the Security Council; and the General Assembly may make recommendations with regard to any such question[7]. Further, the General Assembly may make recommendations with regard to the peaceful adjustment of any situation, regardless of origin, which it deems likely to impair general welfare among nations[8]. The General Assembly's powers in these respects are limited in that it may not make any recommendation with regard to a dispute or situation in respect of which the Security Council is exercising the functions assigned to it unless the Security Council so requests[9], and any question upon which action is necessary must be referred to the Security Council[10].

The General Assembly also has various other functions[11], including the power to consider and approve the organisation's budget[12] and to apportion the organisation's expenses among the members[13].

1   As to the General Assembly see PARA 527 et seq.
2   Ie the Charter of the United Nations (San Francisco, 26 June 1945; TS 67 (1946); Cmd 7015).
3   As to membership of the United Nations see PARA 520.
4   As to the Security Council see PARA 522 et seq.
5   Charter of the United Nations art 10.
6   See the Charter of the United Nations art 11 para 2.
7   Charter of the United Nations art 11 para 2. See also art 11 para 1.
8   Charter of the United Nations art 14.
9   Charter of the United Nations art 12 para 1. See *Legal Consequences of the Construction of a Wall in the Occupied Palestinian Territory (Advisory Opinion)* ICJ Reports 2004, 136.
10 Charter of the United Nations art 11 para 2.
11 See the Charter of the United Nations arts 13, 15, 16.
12 Charter of the United Nations art 17 para 1.
13 Charter of the United Nations art 17 para 2. As to the organisation's expenses in connection with peace-keeping operations authorised by the General Assembly and the Security Council see *Certain Expenses of the United Nations (Advisory Opinion)* ICJ Reports 1962, 151.
    The General Assembly also has powers in relation to the financial and budgetary affairs of the organisation's specialised agencies: see the Charter of the United Nations art 17 para 3.

529.   Economic and Social Council. The Economic and Social Council of the United Nations consists of 54 members elected for a term of three years[1]. Each member has one representative[2] and one vote[3]. Decisions are taken by a majority of the members present and voting[4]. The Council's principal functions lie in the field of international economic and social co-operation[5], in particular in respect of the activities of the specialised agencies[6]. The Council's competence is limited to discussion and the making of reports, and it is placed under the overall authority of the General Assembly[7].

1   Charter of the United Nations (San Francisco, 26 June 1945; TS 67 (1946); Cmd 7015) art 61 (substituted 20 December 1971; TS 130 (1973); Cmnd 5511).
2   Charter of the United Nations art 61 para 4 (as substituted: see note 1).
3   Charter of the United Nations art 67 para 1.
4   Charter of the United Nations art 67 para 2.
5   As to the objects of the United Nations in this field and the duties of member states, together with the general relationship of the United Nations with the specialised agencies, see the Charter of the United Nations Ch IX (arts 55–60).
6   For the functions and powers of the Council see the Charter of the United Nations arts 62–66. As to the specialised agencies see PARA 533.
7   As to the General Assembly see PARA 527 et seq.

530.   Trusteeship Council. The Trusteeship Council suspended its operation in 1 November 1994, having completed its task under the Charter of the United Nations[1] with the independence of the last trust territory[2] on 1 October 1994.

1   Ie the Charter of the United Nations (San Francisco, 26 June 1945; TS 67 (1946); Cmd 7015) Chs XII, XIII (arts 75–91).
2   Ie Palau.

531.   Secretariat. The United Nations Secretariat consists of a Secretary-General and such staff as the organisation may require[1]. The Secretary-General is appointed by the General Assembly on the recommendation of the Security Council[2]. He is the chief administrative officer of the United Nations[3] and acts in this capacity at all meetings of the other principal organs[4]. He may bring to the attention of the Security Council any matter which in his opinion may threaten the maintenance of international peace and security[5]. The Secretary-General and staff are international officials responsible only to the organisation[6]. Employment disputes between staff members and the United Nations are dealt with internally[7]; the organisation has immunity from the jurisdiction of national courts in this as in other respects[8].

1   Charter of the United Nations (San Francisco, 26 June 1945; TS 67 (1946); Cmd 7015) art 97. The staff are appointed by the Secretary-General under regulations established by the General Assembly: art 101 para 1. As to the General Assembly see PARA 527 et seq.
2   Charter of the United Nations art 97. There is no fixed term of office. As to the Security Council see PARA 522 et seq.
3   Charter of the United Nations art 97.
4   Charter of the United Nations art 98. As to the principal organs see PARA 521. This does not apply to the International Court of Justice. As to the International Court of Justice see PARA 499 et seq.
5   Charter of the United Nations art 99.
6   Charter of the United Nations art 100 para 1.
7   Since 1 July 2009, this has involved a two-tier judicial system (consisting of a United Nations Dispute Tribunal and a United Nations Appeal Tribunal): see General Assembly Resolution 62/228 of 6 February 2008.
8   See PARA 307 et seq.

532.   Protection of United Nations personnel. If a person does outside the United Kingdom[1] any act[2] to or in relation to a United Nations worker[3] which, if he had done it in any part of the United Kingdom, would have made him guilty in that part of the United Kingdom of an offence of a specified description, he is guilty in that part of the United Kingdom of that offence[4]. The offences in question are: (1) murder, manslaughter, culpable homicide, rape, assault causing injury, kidnapping, abduction and false imprisonment[5]; (2) an offence under certain provisions of the Offences Against the Person Act 1861[6]; or (3) an offence under the Explosive Substances Act 1883[7].

If a person does outside the United Kingdom any act, in connection with an attack on relevant premises[8] or on a vehicle[9] ordinarily used by a United Nations worker which is made when a United Nations worker is on or in the premises or vehicle, which, if he had done it in any part of the United Kingdom, would have made him guilty of certain offences[10], he will in that part of the United Kingdom be guilty of an offence[11].

A person in the United Kingdom or elsewhere is guilty of an offence[12] if, in order to compel a person to do or abstain from doing any act, he: (a) makes to a person a threat that any person will do an act which is an offence of a specified kind[13]; and (b) intends that the person to whom he makes the threat will fear that it will be carried out[14].

A person is guilty of an offence under or by virtue of the above provisions[15] regardless of his nationality[16]; and, for the purposes of those provisions, it is immaterial whether or not a person knows that another person is a United Nations worker[17]. Provision is made as to the institution of proceedings[18]. The provisions may be extended by Order in Council to any of the Channel Islands, the Isle of Man or any colony[19].

1   As to the statutory meaning of 'United Kingdom' see PARA 30 note 3.

2   For the purposes of the United Nations Personnel Act 1997, 'act' includes omission: s 8.

3   For the purposes of the United Nations Personnel Act 1997, a person is a United Nations worker in relation to an alleged offence if at the time of the alleged offence: (1) he is engaged or deployed by the Secretary-General of the United Nations as a member of the military, police or civilian component of a United Nations operation; (2) he is, in his capacity as an official or expert on mission of the United Nations, a specialised agency of the United Nations or the International Atomic Energy Agency, present in an area where a United Nations operation is being conducted; (3) he is assigned, with the agreement of an organ of the United Nations, by the government of any state or by an international governmental organisation to carry out activities in support of the fulfilment of the mandate of a United Nations operation; (4) he is engaged by the Secretary-General, a specialised agency or the International Atomic Energy Agency to carry out such activities; or (5) he is deployed by a humanitarian non-governmental organisation or agency under an agreement with the Secretary-General, with a specialised agency or with the International Atomic Energy Agency to carry out such activities: ss 4(1), 8. As to the Secretary-General see PARA 531. 'Specialised agency' has the meaning assigned to it by the Charter of the United Nations (San Francisco, 26 June 1945; TS 67 (1946); Cmd 7015) art 57 (see PARA 533): United Nations Personnel Act 1997 s 4(4).

'United Nations operation' means an operation which: (a) is established, in accordance with the Charter of the United Nations, by an organ of the United Nations; (b) is conducted under the authority and control of the United Nations; and (c) has as its purpose the maintenance or restoration of international peace and security or has, for the purposes of the Convention on the Safety of United Nations and Associated Personnel adopted by the General Assembly of the United Nations on 9 December 1994 (New York, 9 December 1994, TS 92 (2000); Cm 4803), been declared by the Security Council or the General Assembly of the United Nations to be an operation where there exists an exceptional risk to the safety of the participating personnel: United Nations Personnel Act 1997 s 4(2), (4). It does not include any operation which is authorised by the Security Council as an enforcement action under the Charter of the United Nations Ch VII (arts 39–51) (see PARA 525), and in which United Nations workers are engaged as combatants against organised armed forces, and to which the law of international armed conflict applies: United Nations Personnel Act 1997 s 4(3). As to the Security Council see PARA 522 et seq. As to the General Assembly see PARA 527 et seq. As from a day to be appointed, instead of referring to the maintenance or restoration of international peace and security, head (c) is to refer to the purposes of maintaining or restoring international peace and security, delivering humanitarian, political or development assistance in peace building, and delivering emergency humanitarian assistance; and the definition of 'United Nations operation' will also not include any operation in respect of which a declaration is made in accordance with art II(3) of the Optional Protocol to the Convention adopted by the General Assembly of the United Nations on 8 December 2005 (New York, 8 December 2005; Misc 12 (2009); Cm 7733) (opt-out for operation to deliver emergency humanitarian assistance in response to natural disaster): see the United Nations Personnel Act 1997 s 4(2), (2A), (3A), (4) (s 4(2), (4) prospectively amended, and s 4(2A), (3A) prospectively added, by the Geneva Conventions and United Nations Personnel (Protocols) Act 2009 s 2). At the date at which this volume states the law, no such day had been appointed.

If, in any proceedings, a question arises as to whether a person is or was a United Nations worker, or whether an operation is or was a United Nations operation, a certificate issued by or under the authority of the Secretary of State and stating any fact relating to the question is conclusive evidence of that fact: United Nations Personnel Act 1997 s 4(5).

4 United Nations Personnel Act 1997 s 1(1).

5 United Nations Personnel Act 1997 s 1(2)(a).

6 United Nations Personnel Act 1997 s 1(2)(b). The offences referred to in the text are those under the Offences Against the Person Act 1861 s 18, s 20, s 21, s 22, s 23, s 24, s 28, s 29, s 30 or s 47 (see CRIMINAL LAW, EVIDENCE AND PROCEDURE): see the United Nations Personnel Act 1997 s 1(2)(b).

7 United Nations Personnel Act 1997 s 1(2)(c). The offence referred to in the text is that under the Explosive Substances Act 1883 s 2 (see EXPLOSIVES): see the United Nations Personnel Act 1997 s 1(2)(c).

8 'Relevant premises' means premises at which a United Nations worker resides or is staying or which a United Nations worker uses for the purpose of carrying out his functions as such a worker: United Nations Personnel Act 1997 s 2(3).

9 'Vehicle' includes any means of conveyance: United Nations Personnel Act 1997 s 2(3).

10 The offences referred to are: (1) an offence under the Explosive Substances Act 1883 s 2 (see EXPLOSIVES); (2) an offence under the Criminal Damage Act 1971 s 1 (see CRIMINAL LAW, EVIDENCE AND PROCEDURE); (3) an offence under the Criminal Damage (Northern Ireland) Order 1977, SI 1977/426 (NI 1) art 3; and (4) wilful fire-raising: see the United Nations Personnel Act 1997 s 2(2).

11 United Nations Personnel Act 1997 s 2(1).

12 United Nations Personnel Act 1997 s 3(1).

13 The specified offence is an offence mentioned in the United Nations Personnel Act 1997 s 1(2) (see heads (1)–(3) in the text) against a United Nations worker, or an offence mentioned in s 2(2) (see note 10) in connection with such attack as is mentioned in s 2(1) (see the text and notes 8–11): see s 3(2).

14 United Nations Personnel Act 1997 s 3(2). A person guilty of an offence under s 3 is liable on conviction on indictment to imprisonment for a term not exceeding ten years, and not exceeding the term of imprisonment to which a person would be liable for the offence constituted by doing the act threatened at the place where the conviction occurs and at the time of the offence to which the conviction relates: s 3(3).

15 Ie the United Nations Personnel Act 1997 ss 1–3: see the text and notes 1–14.

16 United Nations Personnel Act 1997 s 5(3).

17 United Nations Personnel Act 1997 s 5(4).

18 Proceedings for an offence which (disregarding the provisions of the Internationally Protected Persons Act 1978, the Suppression of Terrorism Act 1978, the Nuclear Materials (Offences) Act 1983 and the Terrorism Act 2000) would not be an offence apart from the United Nations Personnel Act 1997 s 1, s 2 or s 3 (see the text and notes 1–14) must not be begun except by or with the consent of the Attorney General: s 5(1) (amended by the Crime (International Co-operation) Act 2003 Sch 5 paras 66, 67).

19 United Nations Personnel Act 1997 s 9(2). The following orders have been made: the United Nations Personnel (Guernsey) Order 1998, SI 1998/1075; the United Nations Personnel (Jersey) Order 1998, SI 1998/1267; and the United Nations Personnel (Isle of Man) Order 1998, SI 1998/1509.

(3) THE SPECIALISED AGENCIES

533. Specialised agencies of the United Nations. The specialised agencies of the United Nations are not part of the United Nations, being separate international organisations with their own legal personalities, but they nevertheless are bought into relationship with the United Nations[1]. The United Kingdom is a member of most of the specialised agencies. The specialised financial agencies of the United Nations to which the United Kingdom belongs are: (1) the International Bank for Reconstruction and Development[2]; (2) the International Development Association[3]; (3) the International Finance

Corporation[4]; (4) the Multilateral Investment Guarantee Agency[5]; and (5) the
International Monetary Fund[6]. In addition the United Kingdom belongs to the
following specialised agencies of the United Nations: (a) the Food and
Agriculture Organisation of the United Nations[7]; (b) the International Maritime
Organisation[8]; (c) the International Civil Aviation Organisation[9]; (d) the
International Labour Organisation[10]; (e) the International Telecommunication
Union[11]; (f) the United Nations Educational, Scientific and Cultural
Organisation[12]; (g) the Universal Postal Union[13]; (h) the World Health
Organisation[14]; (i) the World Meteorological Organisation[15]; (j) the World
Intellectual Property Organisation[16]; (k) the International Fund for Agricultural
Development[17]; and (l) the United Nations Industrial Development
Organisation[18].

The International Atomic Energy Agency, though not a specialised agency,
stands in a similar relationship to the United Nations[19].

1   See the Charter of the United Nations (San Francisco, 26 June 1945; TS 67 (1946); Cmd 7015)
    arts 57, 63. See Satow's Diplomatic Practice (6th Edn, 2009). The United Nations makes
    recommendations for the co-ordination of the policies and activities of the specialised agencies:
    see the Charter of the United Nations art 58. As to the responsibility for the discharge of these
    functions of the United Nations by the General Assembly, and under the General Assembly by
    the Economic and Social Council see art 60 and Ch X (arts 61–72). As to the privileges and
    immunities of the specialised agencies see the Convention on the Privileges and Immunities of
    the Specialised Agencies of the United Nations (21 November 1947; TS 69 (1959); Cmnd 855).
    As to the General Assembly see PARA 527 et seq. As to the Economic and Social Council see
    PARA 529.

2   The International Bank for Reconstruction and Development was created at the Bretton Woods
    Conference in 1944. As to its constitution see the Articles of Agreement of the International
    Bank for Reconstruction and Development (Washington, 27 December 1945; TS 21 (1946);
    Cmd 6885). See further FINANCIAL SERVICES AND INSTITUTIONS vol 49 (2008) PARAS
    1391–1392.

3   The International Development Association was created in 1960 as an affiliate of the
    International Bank for Reconstruction and Development and, for operational purposes, is at one
    with that agency. As to its constitution see the Articles of Agreement of the International
    Development Organisation (Washington, 29 January 1960; TS 1 (1961); Cmnd 1244). See
    further FINANCIAL SERVICES AND INSTITUTIONS vol 49 (2008) PARAS 1391–1392.

4   The International Finance Corporation was created in 1955. It is an affiliate of the International
    Bank for Reconstruction and Development. As to its constitution see the Articles of Agreement
    of the International Finance Corporation (Washington, 25 May 1955; TS 37 (1961);
    Cmnd 1377). See further FINANCIAL SERVICES AND INSTITUTIONS vol 49 (2008) PARAS
    1391–1392.

5   The Multilateral Investment Guarantee Agency was created in 1985. As to its constitution see
    the Convention Establishing the Multilateral Investment Guarantee Agency (Seoul, 11 October
    1985; TS 47 (1989); Cm 812). See also the Multilateral Investment Guarantee Agency Act 1988.

6   The International Monetary Fund was created at the Bretton Woods Conference in 1944. The
    constitution of the International Monetary Fund can be found in the Articles of Agreement of
    the International Monetary Fund (Washington, 27 December 1945; TS 21 (1946); Cmd 6885).
    See the International Monetary Fund Act 1979; and FINANCIAL SERVICES AND INSTITUTIONS
    vol 49 (2008) PARA 1391. As to European financial and economic co-operation see FINANCIAL
    SERVICES AND INSTITUTIONS vol 49 (2008) PARA 1396 et seq.

7   The Food and Agriculture Organisation of the United Nations was founded in 1945 to replace
    the International Institute of Agriculture. As to its constitution see the Constitution of the Food
    and Agriculture Organisation of the United Nations (Quebec, 16 October 1945; TS 47 (1946);
    Cmd 6955).

8   The International Maritime Organisation (formerly the Inter-Governmental Maritime
    Consultative Organisation) was founded in 1948 but did not come into existence until 1957. As
    to its constitution see the Convention for the Establishment of the Inter-Governmental Maritime
    Consultative Organisation (Geneva, 6 March 1948; TS 54 (1958); Cmnd 589). See also
    SHIPPING AND MARITIME LAW vol 93 (2008) PARA 13. As to the relevant headquarters agreement
    with the United Kingdom see PARA 308 note 1.

9   The International Civil Aviation Organisation was founded in 1944. Its constitution is part of the Convention on International Civil Aviation (Chicago, 7 December 1944; TS 8 (1955); Cmd 8742). As to the Chicago Convention see AIR LAW vol 2 (2008) PARA 2 et seq.

10   The constitution of the International Labour Organisation was originally annexed to the Treaty of Peace with Germany (the 'Treaty of Versailles') (Versailles, 28 June 1919; TS 4 (1919); Cmd 153). It was amended by the Constitution of the International Labour Organisation Instrument of Amendment 1946 (Montreal, 9 October 1946; TS 47 (1948); Cmd 7452), to which the revised constitution is annexed, and was amended further by instruments (Geneva, 25 June 1953; TS 59 (1961); Cmnd 1428; Geneva, 22 June 1962; TS 9 (1964); Cmnd 2259; Geneva, 22 June 1972; TS 110 (1975); Cmnd 6207).

11   The International Telecommunication Union was founded in 1932. As to its constitution see the International Telecommunications Convention (Madrid, 9 December 1932; 151 LNTS 5) which was radically revised by the International Telecommunication Convention (Montreux, 12 November 1965; TS 41 (1967); Cmnd 3383), by the International Telecommunication Convention (Malaga, 25 October 1973; TS 104 (1975); Cmnd 6219), and by the International Telecommunication Convention 1982 (Nairobi, 6 November 1982; TS 33 (1985); Cmnd 9557). See also TELECOMMUNICATIONS AND BROADCASTING vol 45(1) (2005 Reissue) PARA 71.

12   The United Nations Educational, Scientific and Cultural Organisation was founded in 1945. As to its constitution see the Constitution of the United Nations Educational, Scientific and Cultural Organisation (London, 16 November 1945; TS 36 (1961); Cmnd 1376). As to educational, scientific and cultural institutions generally see EDUCATION; NATIONAL CULTURAL HERITAGE.

13   The Universal Postal Union was originally founded in 1874, but its present constitution is found in the Constitution of the Universal Postal Union (Vienna, 10 July 1964; TS 70 (1966); Cmnd 3141). See also the Additional Protocol (Tokyo, 14 November 1969; TS 72 (1973); Cmnd 5358); the Universal Postal Convention (Tokyo, 14 November 1969; TS 73 (1973); Cmnd 5357); the Universal Postal Convention (Lausanne, 5 July 1974; TS 57 (1976); Cmnd 6538); the Second Additional Protocol (Lausanne, 5 July 1974; TS 56 (1976); Cmnd 6539); and the Third Additional Protocol (TS 81 (1991); Cm 1748). See further POST OFFICE vol 36(2) (Reissue) PARA 11.

14   The World Health Organisation was founded in 1946 and assumed the functions of the International Office of Public Health. As to its constitution see the Constitution of the World Health Organisation (New York, 22 July 1946; TS 43 (1948); Cmd 7458).

15   The World Meteorological Organisation was founded in 1947. As to its constitution see the Convention of the World Meteorological Organisation (Washington, 11 October 1947; TS 36 (1950); Cmd 7989).

16   The World Intellectual Property Organisation was established in 1967. As to its constitution see the Convention establishing the World Intellectual Property Organisation (WIPO) (Stockholm, 14 July 1967 to 13 January 1968; TS 52 (1970); Cmnd 4408).

17   The International Fund for Agricultural Development was established in 1977. As to its constitution see the Agreement Establishing the International Fund for Agricultural Development (Rome, 13 June 1976; TS 41 (1978); Cmnd 7195).

18   The United Nations Industrial Development Organisation was established by the General Assembly of the United Nations in 1966. It became a specialised agency in 1985 with the entry into force of the Constitution of the United Nations Industrial Development Organisation (Vienna, 8 April 1979).

19   The International Atomic Energy Agency was founded in 1956. As to its constitution see the Statute of the International Atomic Energy Agency (New York, 26 October 1956; TS 19 (1958); Cmnd 450). See further FUEL AND ENERGY vol 19(3) (2007 Reissue) PARA 1354.

(4) THE COUNCIL OF EUROPE

534–600. The Council of Europe. The Council of Europe was created in 1949[1] in order to achieve a greater unity between its members for the purpose of safeguarding and realising the ideals and principles which are their common heritage and facilitating their economic and social progress[2]. This is pursued by discussion of questions of common concern and by agreements and common action in economic, social, cultural, scientific, legal and administrative matters, and in the maintenance and further realisation of human rights and fundamental freedoms[3]. The main organs are: (1) the Committee of Ministers, consisting of the respective ministers for foreign affairs of the members states or their alternates or deputies[4], which is charged, among other matters, with supervising the execution of the judgments of the European Court of Human Rights[5]; and (2) the Parliamentary Assembly whose members are appointed by the legislatures of the member states[6], and whose function is deliberative[7]. Both these organs are to be served by the Secretariat of the Council[8]. The Council has been active in the formulation of conventions, agreements and protocols[9]. Among these are the conventions relating to human rights[10] and state immunity[11], and the European Social Charter[12].

1　See the Statute of the Council of Europe (London, 5 May 1949; TS 51 (1949); Cmd 7778). The following countries are members of the Council of the European Union: Albania; Andorra; Armenia; Austria; Azerbaijan; Belgium; Bosnia and Herzegovina; Bulgaria; Croatia; Cyprus; Czech Republic; Denmark; Estonia; Finland; France; Georgia; Germany; Greece; Hungary; Iceland; Ireland; Italy; Latvia; Liechtenstein; Lithuania; Luxembourg; Malta; Moldova; Monaco; Montenegro; Netherlands; Norway; Poland; Portugal; Romania; Russian Federation; San Marino; Serbia; Slovak Republic; Slovenia; Spain; Sweden; Switzerland; the former Yugoslav Republic of Macedonia; Turkey; Ukraine; United Kingdom. There is provision for co-operation between the European Union and the Council of Europe: see the Treaty on the Functioning of the European Union (Rome, 25 March 1957; TS 1 (1973); Cmnd 5179) art 220. The Treaty was formerly known as the Treaty Establishing the European Community; it has been renamed and its provisions renumbered: see PARA 304 note 1.

2　Statute of the Council of Europe art 1 para (a). Matters relating to the national defence do not fall within the scope of the Council of Europe: art 1 para (d).

3　Statute of the Council of Europe art 1 para (b).

4　See the Statute of the Council of Europe art 14. As to the Committee of Ministers see Ch IV (arts 13–21).

5　See the Convention for the Protection of Human Rights and Fundamental Freedoms (Rome, 4 November 1950; TS 71 (1953); Cmd 8969) art 46 (as amended by Protocol 11); and CONSTITUTIONAL LAW AND HUMAN RIGHTS vol 8(2) (Reissue) PARA 180.

6　See the Statute of the Council of Europe art 25 para (a). The Assembly consists of representatives from each member state, each member state being represented by a number in proportion to its population. The United Kingdom is entitled to 18 representatives: see art 26.

7　See the Statute of the Council of Europe art 22. As to the Assembly see Ch V (arts 22–35).

8　Statute of the Council of Europe art 10. As to the Secretariat see Ch VI (arts 36, 37).

9　There are more than 200 of these published in the European Treaty Series (ETS Nos 1 to 193) and Council of Europe Treaty Series (CETS No 194 et seq).

10　Ie the Convention for the Protection of Human Rights and Fundamental Freedoms: see CONSTITUTIONAL LAW AND HUMAN RIGHTS vol 8(2) (Reissue) PARA 122 et seq.

11　Ie the European Convention on State Immunity (Basle, 16 May 1972; Misc 31 (1972); Cmnd 5081): see PARA 242.

12　Ie the European Social Charter (Turin, 18 October 1961; TS 38 (1965); Cmnd 2643).

JUDICIAL REVIEW

1. THE AMBIT OF JUDICIAL REVIEW

(1) INTRODUCTION

601. General principles. The courts have an inherent jurisdiction to review the exercise by public bodies or officers of statutory powers impinging on legally recognised interests[1]. Powers must be exercised fairly[2], and must not be exceeded[3] or abused[4]. Moreover, the repository of a statutory power or duty will be required genuinely to discharge its functions when the occasion for their performance has arisen[5].

The superior courts have a somewhat similar inherent jurisdiction over inferior courts and tribunals. If such a body has exceeded or acted without jurisdiction[6], or has failed to act fairly or in accordance with the rules of natural justice[7], or if it has committed an error of law in reaching a decision[8], its decision may be set aside. Alternatively, a tribunal may be prohibited from violating the conditions precedent to a valid adjudication before it has made a final determination[9]. A tribunal wrongfully refusing to carry out its duty to hear and determine a matter within its jurisdiction may be ordered to act according to law[10].

The courts also have an inherent jurisdiction to review those exercises of Crown prerogative which are justiciable. The Crown prerogative must be exercised fairly and the prerogative must not be exceeded or abused[11].

1   See ADMINISTRATIVE LAW vol 1(1) (2001 Reissue) PARA 19.
2   See PARAS 648–649.
3   See ADMINISTRATIVE LAW vol 1(1) (2001 Reissue) PARAS 19–25.
4   See PARAS 617–624.
5   See ADMINISTRATIVE LAW vol 1(1) (2001 Reissue) PARAS 27–33. See also PARA 689.
6   See PARAS 610–616.
7   See PARA 629 et seq.
8   See PARAS 612, 616.
9   See PARA 693 et seq. In the subsequent text the word 'tribunal' is to be read as including inferior courts where appropriate.
10   See PARA 703 et seq.
11   See PARAS 607–608.

602. The nature of judicial review. Judicial review[1] is the process by which the High Court exercises its supervisory jurisdiction over the proceedings and decisions of inferior courts, tribunals and other bodies or persons who carry out quasi-judicial functions or who are charged with the performance of public acts and duties[2]. This jurisdiction was originally derived from the common law, and was exercised[3] by the issue of the prerogative writs of mandamus, certiorari and prohibition[4], but it is now conferred and regulated by statute and rules of court[5].

Judicial review is concerned with reviewing not the merits of the decision in respect of which the application for judicial review is made, but with ensuring that the bodies exercising public functions observe the substantive principles of public law and that the decision-making process itself is lawful[6]. It is thus different from an ordinary appeal[7]. The purpose of the remedy of judicial review is to ensure that the individual is given fair treatment by the authority to which he has been subjected: it is no part of that purpose to substitute the opinion of the judiciary or of individual judges for that of the authority constituted by law to decide the matters in question[8]. Unless that restriction on the power of the court is observed, the court will, under the guise of preventing the abuse of power, be itself guilty of usurping power[9]. That is so whether or not there is a right of appeal against the decision on the merits. The duty of the court is to confine itself to the question of legality[10]. Its concern is with whether a decision-making authority exceeded its powers, committed an error of law, committed a breach of the rules of natural justice[11], reached a decision which no reasonable tribunal could have reached[12] or abused its powers[13]. The grounds upon which administrative action is subject to control by judicial review have been conveniently classified as threefold[14]. The first ground is 'illegality': the decision-maker must understand correctly the law that regulates his decision-making power and must give effect to it. The second is 'irrationality', namely *Wednesbury* unreasonableness[15]. The third is 'procedural impropriety'[16]. What procedure will satisfy the public law requirement of procedural propriety depends upon the subject matter of the decision, the executive functions of the decision-maker (if the decision is not that of an administrative tribunal) and the particular circumstances in which the decision came to be made[17]. Even where facts are 'jurisdictional', the court's investigation of them is of a supervisory character and not by way of appeal[18].

On an application for judicial review the court has power to grant a quashing order (formerly known as an order of certiorari), a prohibiting order (formerly known as an order of prohibition) or a mandatory order (formerly known as an order of mandamus)[19]. In addition, the court has power, in specified circumstances, to grant a declaration or an injunction[20], or to award damages[21]. Where the claimant seeks an injunction or a declaration in addition to a mandatory, prohibiting or quashing order, he must use the judicial review procedure[22].

Judicial review also applies to enable the court to grant an injunction restraining a person from acting in an office in which he is not entitled to act[23].

1 The procedure for claims for judicial review under CPR Pt 54 applies with appropriate modifications to both civil and criminal causes and matters. For detailed consideration of judicial review see PARA 687 et seq; and for the procedure see PARA 659 et seq. As to the CPR see PARA 659.

2 'Judicial review ... provides the means by which judicial control of administrative action is exercised': *Council of Civil Service Unions v Minister for the Civil Service* [1985] AC 374 at 408, [1984] 3 All ER 935 at 949, HL, per Lord Diplock. It does not, however, extend to matters which merely constitute maladministration, whether in central or local government or in the National Health Service. These are matters for the Parliamentary Ombudsman (also known as the Parliamentary Commissioner for Administration) (see ADMINISTRATIVE LAW vol 1(1) (2001 Reissue) PARAS 41–45), a commissioner for local administration (also known as the Local Government Ombudsman) (see ADMINISTRATIVE LAW vol 1(1) (2001 Reissue) PARAS 46–49) or the Health Service Commissioners (see ADMINISTRATIVE LAW vol 1(1) (2001 Reissue) PARA 54). See also *Re Fletcher's Application* [1970] 2 All ER 527n, CA; *R v Local Comr for Administration for the North and East Area of England, ex p Bradford Metropolitan City Council* [1979] QB 287, [1979] 2 All ER 881, CA; and *R v Local Comr for Administration for the South, the West, the West Midlands, Leicestershire, Lincolnshire and Cambridgeshire, ex p Eastleigh Borough Council* [1988] QB 855, [1988] 3 All ER 151, CA (judicial review of findings in a report of the local commissioner; the fact that Parliament had not created a right of appeal against the findings in a local commissioner's report, and the public law character of the commissioner's office and powers, founded the right of a local authority to relief by way of judicial review: per Lord Donaldson MR at 866 and 157–158); *R v Local Comr for Administration in North and North East England, ex p Liverpool City Council* [2001] 1 All ER 462, [2000] LGR 571, CA; *R (on the application of Turpin) v Comr for Local Administration* [2001] EWHC Admin 503, [2003] LGR 133. As to judicial review of the Health Service Commissioner see *R (on the application of Redmond) v Health Service Comr* [2005] EWCA Civ 1578, [2006] 3 All ER 543, [2006] 1 WLR 1229 (Commissioner exceeded her statutory jurisdiction in investigating complaint); *R (on the application of Attwood) v Health Service Comr* [2008] EWHC 2315 (Admin), [2009] 1 All ER 415; *R (on the application of Kay) v Health Service Comr* [2009] EWCA Civ 732.

Decisions of the Parliamentary Ombudsman are amenable to judicial review: see *R v Parliamentary Comr for Administration, ex p Dyer* [1994] 1 All ER 375, [1994] 1 WLR 621, DC; *R v Parliamentary Comr for Administration, ex p Balchin* [1998] 1 PLR 1, [1997] JPL 917; *R v Parliamentary Comr for Administration, ex p Balchin (No 2)* (1999) 79 P & CR 157, [1999] EGCS 78; *R (on the application of Balchin) v Parliamentary Comr for Administration (No 3)* [2002] EWHC 1876 (Admin), [2002] All ER (D) 449 (Jul).

By contrast, decisions of the Parliamentary Commissioner for Standards (see PARLIAMENT vol 78 (2010) PARA 1073) are not amenable to judicial review because his activities relate to what happens in Parliament and to the activities of those engaged within Parliament. Responsibility for his supervision rests with the Committee on Standards and Privileges of the House, not the courts. For the court to review the decisions of the Parliamentary Commissioner for Standards would abrogate the principle that the activities of Parliament are not a suitable subject for judicial review: *R v Parliamentary Comr for Standards, ex p Al Fayed* [1998] 1 All ER 93, [1998] 1 WLR 669, CA (challenge to the Commissioner's decision that a member of Parliament alleged to have received a corrupt payment had no case to answer).

The Upper Tribunal has been held to be equivalent to the High Court so that it is not amenable to judicial review when acting within the ambit of its statutory remit; but would be amenable if acting outside that remit: see *R (on the application of Cart) v Upper Tribunal* [2009] EWHC 3052 (Admin) at para [94] per Laws LJ.

3   It was exercised before 1875 by the Court of Queen's Bench, and later by the Queen's Bench Divisional Court. See COURTS.

4   These prerogative writs subsequently became prerogative orders, which could be employed in the same way as the writs had been employed: see the Administration of Justice (Miscellaneous Provisions) Act 1938 s 7 (repealed). References in any enactments to the old writs are to be read as references to the corresponding modern orders: see the Senior Courts Act 1981 s 29(5) (substituted by SI 2004/1033). The prerogative orders of certiorari, mandamus and prohibition are now known as quashing orders, mandatory orders and prohibiting orders respectively: see PARA 687. The Senior Courts Act 1981 was previously known as the Supreme Court Act 1981 and was renamed by the Constitutional Reform Act 2005 s 59(5), Sch 11 Pt 1 as from 1 October 2009: see the Constitutional Reform Act 2005 (Commencement No 11) Order 2009, SI 2009/1604; and COURTS.

5   See the Senior Courts Act 1981 s 31; CPR Pt 54; and the text and notes 19–23. The two sets of provisions lie in juxtaposition to each other and to a considerable extent employ the same wording. Where there is a difference or inconsistency, the statute prevails: see *Hartmont v Foster* (1881) 8 QBD 82 at 85–86, CA, per Lindley LJ. The statute and the rules have created a uniform, flexible and comprehensive code of procedure, eliminating procedural technicalities and differences as to the remedies which the applicant may claim: see *R v IRC, ex p National Federation of Self-Employed and Small Businesses Ltd* [1980] QB 407 at 429, [1980] 2 All ER 378 at 396, CA, per Ackner LJ; on appeal sub nom *IRC v National Federation of Self Employed and Small Businesses* [1982] AC 617 at 638, [1981] 2 All ER 93 at 102, HL, per Lord Diplock; and see *Caswell v Dairy Produce Quota Tribunal for England and Wales* [1990] 2 AC 738, [1990] 2 All ER 434, HL.

6   *Chief Constable of the North Wales Police v Evans* [1982] 3 All ER 141 at 154, [1982] 1 WLR 1155 at 1173, HL, per Lord Brightman ('Judicial review, as the words imply, is not an appeal from a decision, but a review of the manner in which the decision was made' (per Lord Brightman at 155 and 1174)). See also *R v Panel on Take-overs and Mergers, ex p Datafin plc* [1987] QB 815 at 842, [1987] 1 All ER 564 at 580, CA, per Sir John Donaldson MR ('an application for judicial review is not an appeal'); *Lonrho plc v Secretary of State for Trade and Industry* [1989] 2 All ER 609 at 617, [1989] 1 WLR 525 at 535, HL, per Lord Keith of Kinkel ('Judicial review is a protection and not a weapon'); *R v Secretary of State for the Home Department, ex p Brind* [1991] 1 AC 696, sub nom *Brind v Secretary of State for the Home Department* [1991] 1 All ER 720, HL; *R v Secretary of State for the Home Department, ex p Launder* [1997] 3 All ER 961 at 978, [1997] 1 WLR 839 at 857, HL, per Lord Hope of Craighead ('The function of the court in the exercise of its supervisory jurisdiction is that of review. This is not an appeal against the Secretary of State's decision on the facts'); *R (on the application of Malik) v Manchester Crown Court* [2008] EWHC 1362 (Admin), [2008] 4 All ER 403.

7   When hearing an appeal the court is concerned with the merits of the decision under appeal. In *Re Amin* [1983] 2 AC 818 at 829, [1983] 2 All ER 864 at 868, HL, Lord Fraser of Tullybelton observed that: 'Judicial review is concerned not with the merits of a decision but with the manner in which the decision was made ... Judicial review is entirely different from an ordinary appeal. It is made effective by the court quashing an administrative decision without substituting its own decision, and is to be contrasted with an appeal where the appellate tribunal substitutes

its own decision on the merits for that of the administrative officer'. In *R v Crown Court at Carlisle, ex p Marcus-Moore* (1981) Times, 26 October, DC, Donaldson LJ said that judicial review was capable of being extended to meet changing circumstances, but not to the extent that it became something different from review by developing an appellate nature. See also *R v Secretary of State for the Home Department, ex p Brind* [1991] 1 AC 696 at 765, sub nom *Brind v Secretary of State for the Home Department* [1991] 1 All ER 720 at 737, HL, per Lord Lowry ('judicial review of administrative action is a supervisory and not an appellate jurisdiction'; the court 'is not sitting on appeal but satisfying itself as to whether the decision-maker has acted within the bounds of his discretion'). The courts invented the remedy of judicial review not to provide an appeal but to ensure that the decision-maker did not exceed or abuse his powers: *R v Independent Television Commission, ex p TSW Broadcasting Ltd* [1996] EMLR 291, (1992) Times, 30 March, HL.

8   *Chief Constable of the North Wales Police v Evans* [1982] 3 All ER 141 at 143, [1982] 1 WLR 1155 at 1160, HL, per Lord Hailsham of St Marylebone LC. In *R v Panel on Take-overs and Mergers, ex p Guinness plc* [1989] 1 All ER 509 at 526, [1989] 2 WLR 863 at 885, CA, Lord Donaldson of Lymington MR referred to the judicial review jurisdiction as being a supervisory or 'longstop' jurisdiction; see also *WM (Democratic Republic of Congo) v Secretary of State for the Home Department* [2006] EWCA Civ 1495, [2007] Imm AR 337 at [16] per Buxton LJ.

9   *Chief Constable of the North Wales Police v Evans* [1982] 3 All ER 141 at 154, [1982] 1 WLR 1155 at 1173, HL, per Lord Brightman; *Lonrho plc v Secretary of State for Trade and Industry* [1989] 2 All ER 609 at 617, [1989] 1 WLR 525 at 535, HL, per Lord Keith of Kinkel; *R v Secretary of State for the Home Department, ex p Brind* [1991] 1 AC 696 at 757–758, sub nom *Brind v Secretary of State for the Home Department* [1991] 1 All ER 720 at 731, HL, per Lord Ackner. See also *Ridge v Baldwin* [1964] AC 40 at 96, [1963] 2 All ER 66 at 91, HL, per Lord Evershed.

10 But judicial review is not to be used as a means for obtaining a decision on a question of law in advance of the hearing: *R v Crown Court at Reading, ex p Hutchinson* [1988] QB 384 at 396, [1988] 1 All ER 333 at 340, DC, per Lloyd LJ.

11 In *Council of Civil Service Unions v Minister for the Civil Service* [1985] AC 374 at 414, [1984] 3 All ER 935 at 954, HL, Lord Roskill observed that the use of the phrase 'principles of natural justice' 'is no doubt hallowed by time and much judicial repetition, but it is a phrase often widely misunderstood and therefore as often misused. That phrase perhaps might now be allowed to find a permanent resting-place and be better replaced by speaking of a duty to act fairly. But that latter phrase must not in its turn be misunderstood or misused. It is not for the courts to determine whether a particular policy or particular decisions taken in fulfilment of that policy are fair. They are only concerned with the manner in which those decisions have been taken and the extent of the duty to act fairly will vary greatly from case to case as, indeed, the decided cases since 1950 consistently show. Many features will come into play including the nature of the decision and the relationship of those involved on either side before the decision was taken'.

12 *Associated Provincial Picture Houses Ltd v Wednesbury Corpn* [1948] 1 KB 223 at 229, [1947] 2 All ER 680 at 683, CA, per Lord Greene MR. See note 15; and PARA 649.

13 *Re Preston* [1985] AC 835 at 862, [1985] 2 All ER 327 at 337, HL, per Lord Templeman; *R v IRC, ex p Unilever plc* [1996] STC 681, 68 TC 205, CA. As to judicial review proceedings as an abuse of process see *Land Securities PLC v Fladgate Fielder (a firm)* [2009] EWCA Civ 1402, [2009] All ER (D) 187 (Dec).

14 *Council of Civil Service Unions v Minister for the Civil Service* [1985] AC 374 at 410, [1984] 3 All ER 935 at 950–951, HL, per Lord Diplock ('That is not to say that further developments on a case by case basis may not in course of time add further grounds'). The threefold classification is 'a valuable and already 'classical', but certainly not exhaustive analysis of the grounds upon which the courts will embark on the judicial review of administrative power exercised by a public officer': *Nottinghamshire County Council v Secretary of State for the Environment* [1986] AC 240 at 249, [1986] 1 All ER 199 at 203, HL, per Lord Scarman. One development to which Lord Diplock himself referred specifically (at 410 and 950) was the possible recognition of the principle of proportionality. See *R v Barnsley Metropolitan Borough Council, ex p Hook* [1976] 3 All ER 452, [1976] 1 WLR 1052, CA. See also *R v Panel on Take-overs and Mergers, ex p Datafin plc* [1987] QB 815 at 842, [1987] 1 All ER 564 at 580, CA, per Sir John Donaldson MR; and generally PARA 618. Proportionality is not at present a separate ground for judicial review: see *R v Secretary of State for the Home Department, ex p Brind* [1991] 1 AC 696 at 766, sub nom *Brind v Secretary of State for the Home Department* [1991] 1 All ER 720 at 738, HL, per Lord Lowry. It was held in *R v Secretary of State for the Home Department, ex p Brind* at 763 and 735 per Lord Ackner that there was no

basis upon which the doctrine of proportionality developed by the European courts could be followed by English courts unless and until the Convention for the Protection of Human Rights and Fundamental Freedoms (Rome, 4 November 1950; TS 71 (1953) Cmd 8969) was incorporated into English law. In *R v Secretary of State for the Environment and Secretary of State for Wales, ex p National and Local Association of Government Officers* (1992) 5 Admin LR 785, CA, Neill LJ held that it was not open to any court below the House of Lords to depart from the traditional *Wednesbury* basis for reviewing the exercise of ministerial discretion. His Lordship recognised, however, that it was possible that proportionality would develop as a separate ground for intervention in the review of decisions taken at a lower level than government level (see at 800–801).

The Convention for the Protection of Human Rights and Fundamental Freedoms (1950) has now largely been incorporated into English law by the Human Rights Act 1998: see PARA 651; and CONSTITUTIONAL LAW AND HUMAN RIGHTS vol 8(2) (Reissue) PARA 101 et seq. Section 2(1) requires courts when applying the Convention for the Protection of Human Rights and Fundamental Freedoms (1950) to have regard to the jurisprudence of the European Court of Justice. The principle of proportionality is well established in the jurisprudence of that court. Accordingly English courts have to apply the principle of proportionality in cases which, by reason of the Human Rights Act 1998, raise questions falling within the ambit of the Convention. See also *R (on the application of Alconbury Developments Ltd) v Secretary of State for the Environment, Transport and the Regions* [2001] UKHL 23, [2003] 2 AC 295, [2001] 2 All ER 929 at [51] per Lord Slynn of Hadley.

In *R v Panel on Take-overs and Mergers, ex p Guinness plc* [1989] 1 All ER 509 at 512–513, [1989] 2 WLR 863 at 869, CA, Lord Donaldson of Lymington MR observed that 'in the context of a body [such as the Take-over Panel] whose constitution, functions and powers are sui generis, the court should review the panel's acts and omissions more in the round than might otherwise be the case and, whilst basing its decision on familiar concepts, should eschew any formal categorisation'. The court should 'consider whether something has gone wrong of a nature and degree which require [its] intervention' (at 527 and 886 per Lord Donaldson of Lymington MR and at 538–539 and 901 per Woolf LJ).

15 *Associated Provincial Picture Houses Ltd v Wednesbury Corpn* [1948] 1 KB 223, [1947] 2 All ER 680, CA. The concept of irrationality may vary according to the circumstances of the case. In *R v Ministry of Defence, ex p Smith* [1996] QB 517, [1996] 1 All ER 257, CA (challenge to the policy of the Ministry of Defence that homosexuality is incompatible with service in the armed forces) the Court of Appeal approved the following formulation of the law: 'The court may not interfere with the exercise of administrative discretion on substantive grounds save where the court is satisfied that the decision is unreasonable in the sense that it is beyond the range of responses open to a reasonable decision-maker. But in judging whether the decision-maker has exceeded this margin of appreciation the human rights context is important. The more substantial the interference with human rights, the more the court will require by way of justification before it is satisfied that the decision is reasonable in the sense outlined above' (see at 554 and 263 per Lord Bingham MR, at 563 and 271 per Henry LJ and at 564 and 272 per Thorpe LJ).

The Court of Appeal applied the same formulation in *R v Lord Saville of Newdigate, Sir Edward Somers, ex p A* [1999] 4 All ER 860, [2000] 1 WLR 1855, CA (challenge to the decision of the tribunal sitting as the Bloody Sunday Inquiry regarding anonymity of witnesses). The court held that where fundamental human rights are involved the options available to a reasonable decision-maker are curtailed. It would be unreasonable to contravene such human rights unless there were significant countervailing considerations. The courts would anxiously scrutinise the strength of the countervailing circumstances and the degree of the interference with human rights. See also *R v Secretary of State for the Home Department, ex p Turgut* [2001] 1 All ER 719, [2000] Imm AR 306, CA (in a case where an applicant challenged the Secretary of State's refusal to grant him exceptional leave to remain in the United Kingdom on the basis that he was not at risk of ill-treatment if returned to Turkey, the court would subject that decision to rigorous examination by considering the factual material itself; the application would succeed only if the applicant could show that the material compelled a different conclusion); *R (on the application of Yogathas) v Secretary of State for the Home Department* [2002] UKHL 36, [2003] 1 AC 920, [2002] 4 All ER 800 at [9] per Lord Bingham of Cornhill.

16 Lord Diplock described the third head as 'procedural impropriety' rather than failure to observe basic rules of natural justice or failure to act with procedural fairness towards the person who will be affected by the decision 'because susceptibility to judicial review under this head covers also failure by an administrative tribunal to observe procedural rules that are expressly laid down in the legislative instrument by which its jurisdiction is conferred, even where such failure

does not involve any denial of natural justice': *Council of Civil Service Unions v Minister for the Civil Service* [1985] AC 374 at 411, [1984] 3 All ER 935 at 951, HL.

17 *Council of Civil Service Unions v Minister for the Civil Service* [1985] AC 374 at 411, [1984] 3 All ER 935 at 951, HL, per Lord Diplock.

18 *Khawaja v Secretary of State for the Home Department* [1984] AC 74 at 105, [1983] 1 All ER 765 at 777, HL, per Lord Wilberforce (on an application for judicial review of an immigration officer's order detaining any person in the United Kingdom as an 'illegal entrant' under the Immigration Act 1971 s 33(1) (see BRITISH NATIONALITY, IMMIGRATION AND ASYLUM vol 4(2) (2002 Reissue) PARA 151) it was the court's duty to inquire whether there had been sufficient evidence to justify the immigration officer's belief that the entry had been illegal). Also see *R v Secretary of State for the Home Department, ex p Herbage (No 2)* [1987] QB 1077 at 1088–1089, [1987] 1 All ER 324 at 332, CA, per May LJ. But in *Puhlhofer v Hillingdon London Borough Council* [1986] AC 484, [1986] 1 All ER 467, HL (judicial review of housing authority's decision under homeless persons legislation refused), Lord Brightman said at 518 and 474: 'Where the existence or non-existence of a fact is left to the judgment and discretion of a public body and that fact involves a broad spectrum ranging from the obvious to the debatable to the just conceivable, it is the duty of the court to leave the decision of that fact to the public body to whom Parliament has entrusted the decision-making power save in a case where it is obvious that the public body, consciously or unconsciously, are acting perversely'. But see *R v Tower Hamlets London Borough Council, ex p Monaf* (1988) 86 LGR 709, (1988) 20 HLR 529, CA (where the council failed to carry out the necessary balancing exercise required by the Housing Act 1985 s 60(4) (repealed: see now the Housing Act 1996 s 177(2)) (see HOUSING vol 22 (2006 Reissue) PARA 278), the court intervened). See also *R v Crown Court at Knightsbridge, ex p Quinlan* [1989] COD 287, (1988) Times, 13 December (to mount an attack on a finding of fact which had been the basis of a judgment in the Crown Court by means of judicial review was an abuse of the process of the court).

19 Senior Courts Act 1981 s 31(1)(a) (amended by SI 2004/1033); CPR 54.2. The High Court has jurisdiction to make mandatory, prohibiting and quashing orders in those classes of case in which, immediately before 1 May 2004, it had jurisdiction to make orders of mandamus, prohibition and certiorari respectively: Senior Courts Act 1981 s 29(1A) (added by SI 2004/1033). Every such order will be final, subject to any right of appeal: Senior Courts Act 1981 s 29(2). In relation to the jurisdiction of the Crown Court, other than its jurisdiction in matters relating to trial on indictment, the High Court has the same jurisdiction to make mandatory, prohibiting or quashing orders as it has in relation to the jurisdiction of an inferior court: s 29(3) (amended by SI 2004/1033).

20 See the Senior Courts Act 1981 s 31(1)(b); CPR 54.3; and PARA 716.

21 See the Senior Courts Act 1981 s 31(4) (substituted by SI 2004/1033); CPR 54.3(2); and PARAS 687, 691.

22 Senior Courts Act 1981 s 31(1); CPR 54.3.

23 Senior Courts Act 1981 ss 30, 31(1)(c); CPR 54.2(d).

603.   Judicial review and human rights.   In addition to seeking review of an administrative act on the grounds of illegality, procedural impropriety and irrationality[1], a claimant in a judicial review matter may challenge the act of a public authority on the grounds that the act is incompatible with the Convention for the Protection of Human Rights and Fundamental Freedoms[2]. The court also has power to declare that primary legislation is incompatible with Convention rights[3].

1 See PARA 602.

2 Ie the Convention for the Protection of Human Rights and Fundamental Freedoms (Rome, 4 November 1950; TS 71 (1953) Cmd 8969). See further PARA 650 et seq; and CONSTITUTIONAL LAW AND HUMAN RIGHTS vol 8(2) (Reissue) PARA 101 et seq.

3 See the Human Rights Act 1998 s 4; and PARA 650.

(2) PERSONS AGAINST WHOM JUDICIAL REVIEW MAY LIE

604. The test for determining whether a body may be amenable to judicial review. There is no single test for determining whether a body will be amenable to judicial review[1]. The source of the body's power is a significant factor[2]. If the source of the body's power is statute or subordinate legislation it will usually be amenable to judicial review. Decisions of bodies whose authority is derived solely from contract or from the consent of the parties will usually not be amenable to judicial review. In between these extremes it is helpful to look not only at the source of the power but also at the nature of the power[3]. The principal distinction that appears from the cases is between a domestic or private tribunal on the one hand and a body of persons who are under some public duty or exercising some public function on the other[4]. If the duty is a public duty or the function a public function, then the body in question will be subject to public law[5]. 'Possibly the only essential elements' giving rise to the exercise of the supervisory jurisdiction of the court are 'what can be described as a public element, which can take many different forms, and the exclusion from the jurisdiction of bodies whose sole source of power is a consensual submission to its jurisdiction'[6]. A 'public element' suggests a governmental or quasi-governmental element[7]. A public element is not to be equated with the interest of the public[8]. A body which, although not established through the exercise of governmental power, is integrated into a system of statutory or public regulation, will be amenable to judicial review[9]. Factors which indicate that the body is so integrated include whether the body is supported indirectly by a periphery of statutory powers and penalties[10]. A governmental element may also be said to exist where, if the body did not exist, the government would intervene to create a body to carry out the same functions[11]. By contrast, if the nature of the functions are not such as to generate any governmental interest, the body will not be amenable to judicial review[12]. If the source of power is contractual, as in the case of private arbitration, then the arbitrator is not subject to judicial review[13]. Thus judicial review is not the appropriate procedure to challenge the decisions of private or domestic tribunals or any body whose jurisdiction derives from contract or from the consensual submission of the parties[14]. Where a disciplinary body has no statutory powers, its jurisdiction must be based on contract. Thus members of trade unions[15], business associations and social clubs who have contractual rights based on contracts of membership, should in appropriate cases seek the private law remedies of declaration and injunction and not the remedy of judicial review.

Where legislation permits a public body to enter into arrangements with a private sector body, whereby the private sector body undertakes responsibility for performing the public body's functions, the private body is not amenable to judicial review. This is so even if the public body would have been amenable to judicial review if it had performed the functions itself[16]. However, where a private sector body has 'stepped into the shoes' of a public body, the position is different. When the private sector body has succeeded the public body such that the public body no longer has any role in relation to the function, that private sector body will often be amenable to judicial review[17].

The position in relation to students in universities and colleges is more complex. A small number of universities have been created or recognised by statute, and are amenable to judicial review[18]. The majority of older universities, and the Oxford and Cambridge colleges, are chartered bodies. Students in non-chartered universities have both a contract with the university and are able to seek judicial review to ensure that the university acts in accordance with its own rules and regulations[19]. It is likely that a similar conclusion would be reached in relation to chartered universities[20]. New universities are statutory bodies with public law functions and are amenable to judicial review[21]. The courts will normally require students to use the complaints machinery set up under Part 2 of the Higher Education Act 2004[22] before seeking judicial review of decisions of higher education institutions[23].

The role of the visitor in relation to the Inns of Court remains amenable to judicial review[24].

Thus a body may be amenable to judicial review by reason either of the source from which it derives its power[25] or because it discharges public duties or performs public functions. However, not every act of such a body is of a type which is suitable for judicial review. It is also necessary to consider the nature of the decision of which complaint is made. The crucial consideration will be whether there is a sufficient public law element to a particular decision. That will involve consideration both of the nature of the decision and whether the decision was made under a statutory power.

Where the disciplinary appeal procedure set up by the British Broadcasting Corporation depended purely on the contract of employment between the applicant and the British Broadcasting Corporation, it was a procedure of purely private or domestic character[26]. Private employment is clearly outside the realms of judicial review. Employment by a public body does not per se inject any element of public law[27]; nor does the fact that an employee is in a 'higher grade' or is an 'officer'. This only makes it more likely that there will be special statutory restrictions upon dismissal, or other underpinning of his employment[28]. It will be this underpinning and not the seniority which injects the element of public law[29]. The allegation that a health authority had dismissed an employee in breach of contract raised no issue of public law[30]. It was otherwise where the employment was one which was the subject of a code of discipline deriving its authority from statute[31].

Where a body exercises contractual powers which are in part regulated by statute, the matter depends on the extent of the statutory intervention. There must be some form of statutory, rather than contractual, restriction of a body's common law powers before judicial review is available[32].

Although a local authority's powers in general are derived from statute, not all its activities raise public law issues[33]. Where statutory provisions expressly or impliedly impose restrictions on the exercise of contractual power by a public body, judicial review will be available to determine whether a contract violates those statutory restrictions[34]. Public law principles apply when a local authority is performing a statutory function, which may include exercise of contractual powers by a local authority[35].

However, the process by which a public body determines how to award a contract following a tendering exercise will not ordinarily be subject to judicial review. Judicial review will be available if there is a specific statutory requirement that the tendering exercise be carried out in a particular way, or where there has been bad faith, or corruption or the contract was awarded pursuant to an unlawful policy[36].

Formerly decisions which were characterised as managerial were regarded as not being susceptible to judicial review. Thus at one time it was thought that a prison governor's powers of discipline were managerial, in the sense that they were intimately connected with his functions of day to day administration and for that reason not susceptible to review[37]. These powers were contrasted with the 'judicial functions' of the board of visitors, whose powers were susceptible to judicial review[38]. However, from 1988 onwards, it has been recognised that the court has jurisdiction to entertain an application for judicial review of a prison governor's disciplinary award[39]. It has also been held that a decision whether or not to prosecute a person suspected of a crime is also susceptible to judicial review, albeit on limited grounds[40]. As a general proposition, where any person or body exercises a power conferred by statute which affects the rights or legitimate expectations of citizens and is of a kind which the law requires to be exercised in accordance with the rules of natural justice, the court has jurisdiction to review the exercise of that power[41].

Judicial review is designed to prevent the excess and abuse of power by public authorities[42]. In most cases the powers of public authorities are conferred by statute. It is therefore with statutory powers that judicial review is primarily concerned. However, public bodies are not immune from judicial review merely because they act in pursuance of a power derived from a common law, or prerogative[43], rather than a statutory source[44]. Thus, the decisions of the Criminal Injuries Compensation Board[45] were subject to judicial review if they were not in accordance with the rules for the board's determination of the claims, even though the scheme was wholly non-statutory[46]. It is well established that a quashing order[47] is not limited to bodies performing judicial functions[48]. The decisions of immigration officers have been quashed on the basis that they have misinterpreted the immigration rules[49]. A minister acting under prerogative power might, depending on its subject matter, be under the same duty to act fairly as in the case of action under a statutory power[50]; if so, the minister's decision may be subject to judicial review. Judicial review may also extend to guidance circulars of a purely advisory nature issued by a department of state without any statutory authority[51].

In general terms, '[for] a decision to be susceptible to judicial review the decision-maker must be empowered by public law (and not merely, as in arbitration, by agreement between private parties) to make decisions that, if validly made, will lead to administrative action or abstention from action by an authority endowed by law with executive powers', and that decision must affect the private rights of some person or deprive another of some benefit which he had been allowed to enjoy, and expected to enjoy in the future or which he has a legitimate expectation of acquiring or enjoying[52].

1   See *R v Panel on Take-overs and Mergers, ex p Datafin plc* [1987] QB 815 at 838, [1987] 1 All ER 564 at 577, CA, per Donaldson MR, and at 848 and 584 per Lloyd LJ; *R v Disciplinary Committee of the Jockey Club, ex p Massingberd-Mundy* [1993] 2 All ER 207 at 218, DC, per Neill LJ and at 221 per Roch J; *R v Insurance Ombudsman Bureau, ex p Aegon Life Assurance Ltd* [1994] COD 426, (1994) Times, 7 January, DC; *R (on the application of Tucker) v Director General of the National Crime Squad* [2003] EWCA Civ 57, [2003] ICR 599, [2003] IRLR 439 at [13] per Scott Baker LJ; *R (on the application of Beer (t/a Hammer Trout Farm)) v Hampshire Farmers Market Ltd* [2003] EWCA Civ 1056, [2004] 1 WLR 233.

2   Ie whether the power is derived from statute or prerogative: *R v Panel on Take-overs and Mergers, ex p Datafin plc* [1987] QB 815 at 847, [1987] 1 All ER 564 at 583, CA, per Lloyd LJ; *Council of Civil Service Unions v Minister for the Civil Service* [1985] AC 374 at 409, [1984] 3 All ER 935 at 950, HL, per Lord Diplock.

3   *R v Panel on Take-overs and Mergers, ex p Datafin plc* [1987] QB 815 at 847, [1987] 1 All ER 564 at 583, CA, per Lloyd LJ.

4   *R v Panel on Take-overs and Mergers, ex p Datafin plc* [1987] QB 815 at 847, [1987] 1 All ER 564 at 583, CA; *R v Criminal Injuries Compensation Board, ex p Lain* [1967] 2 QB 864 at 882,

[1967] 2 All ER 770 at 778, DC, per Lord Parker CJ; *R v British Broadcasting Corpn, ex p Lavelle* [1983] 1 All ER 241 at 249, [1983] 1 WLR 23 at 31 per Woolf J; *R v Disciplinary Committee of the Jockey Club, ex p Aga Khan* [1993] 2 All ER 853 at 866–867, [1993] 1 WLR 909 at 923–924, CA, per Sir Thomas Bingham MR, at 929–930 and 872–873 per Farquharson LJ, and at 931 and 873 per Hoffmann LJ (and see *R v Disciplinary Committee of the Jockey Club, ex p Massingberd-Mundy* [1993] 2 All ER 207, DC; and *R v Jockey Club, ex p RAM Racecourses Ltd* [1993] 2 All ER 225, [1990] COD 346, DC); *R (Mullins) v Appeal Board of the Jockey Club and the Jockey Club* [2005] EWHC 2197 (Admin), (2005) Times, 24 October; *R v Football Association Ltd, ex p Football League Ltd* [1993] 2 All ER 833 at 848–849, [1992] COD 52 at 53 per Rose J.

    CPR Pt 54 defines a claim for judicial review as a claim to review the lawfulness of, inter alia, 'a decision, action or failure to act in relation to the exercise of a public function': see CPR 54.1(2); and PARA 662 note 9.

5   *R v Panel on Take-overs and Mergers, ex p Datafin plc* [1987] QB 815 at 848, [1987] 1 All ER 564 at 584, CA, per Lloyd LJ; *R v Criminal Injuries Compensation Board, ex p Lain* [1967] 2 QB 864 at 882, [1967] 2 All ER 770 at 778, DC, per Lord Parker CJ.

6   *R v Panel on Take-overs and Mergers, ex p Datafin plc* [1987] QB 815 at 838, [1987] 1 All ER 564 at 577, CA, per Sir John Donaldson MR.

7   An example from the cases is the Panel on Take-overs and Mergers, which has no statutory, prerogative or common law powers and is not in contractual relationship with the financial market or with those who deal in the market. However, the Panel operates as an integral part of the government framework for the non-statutory regulation of financial activity in the City; it is supported indirectly by a periphery of statutory powers and is under a duty in exercising what amount to public law powers to act judicially: *R v Panel on Take-overs and Mergers, ex p Datafin plc* [1987] QB 815 at 825, 835, 838–839, [1987] 1 All ER 564 at 566, 574, 576–577, CA, per Donaldson MR, and at 846–847, 848–849, 852 and 582–583, 584–585, 587 per Lloyd LJ; *R v Panel on Take-overs and Mergers, ex p Guinness plc* [1989] 1 All ER 509 at 511, [1989] 2 WLR 863 at 867, CA, per Lord Donaldson of Lymington MR. See also *R v Advertising Standards Authority Ltd, ex p Insurance Service plc* (1989) 2 Admin LR 77, DC (decisions of the Advertising Standards Authority are susceptible to judicial review); and *Czarnikow v Roth, Schmidt & Co* [1922] 2 KB 478 at 488, CA, per Scrutton LJ (concerning the Council of the Refined Sugar Association, a self-regulatory body for the sugar trade): 'There must be no Alsatia in England where the King's writ does not run'. The Infertility Services Ethical Committee of a hospital, although an informal and non-statutory body, may be subject to judicial review in appropriate cases, eg where its advice is illegal or discriminatory: *R v Ethical Committee of St Mary's Hospital (Manchester), ex p H (or Harriott)* [1988] 1 FLR 512, [1988] Fam Law 165. See also *Mercury Energy Ltd v Electricity Corpn of New Zealand Ltd* [1994] 1 WLR 521, 138 Sol Jo LB 61, PC (a state enterprise established under statute in New Zealand is amenable to judicial review). For an analogy drawn from European law consider the concept of the emanation of the state: see eg *Foster v British Gas plc* [1991] 2 AC 306, [1991] 2 All ER 705, HL.

8   *R v East Berkshire Health Authority, ex p Walsh* [1985] QB 152 at 164, [1984] 3 All ER 425 at 430, CA, per Donaldson MR; *R v Chief Rabbi of the United Hebrew Congregations of Great Britain and the Commonwealth, ex p Wachmann* [1993] 2 All ER 249 at 254, [1992] 1 WLR 1036 at 1041 per Simon Brown J.

9   *R v Disciplinary Committee of the Jockey Club, ex p Aga Khan* [1993] 2 All ER 853 at 864, [1993] 1 WLR 909 at 921, CA, per Sir Thomas Bingham MR and at 931–932 and 874 per Hoffmann LJ. See eg *R (on the application of Siborurema) v Office of the Independent Adjudicator* [2007] EWCA Civ 1365, [2008] ELR 209 (decisions of the Office of the Independent Adjudicator are subject to judicial review, partly as a result of the statutory context in which the scheme operates and the nature of the functions performed); *R (on the application of the British Board of Film Classification) v Video Appeals Committee* [2008] EWHC 203 (Admin), [2008] 1 WLR 1658.

10 *R v Panel on Take-overs and Mergers, ex p Datafin plc* [1987] QB 815 at 835, 838–839, [1987] 1 All ER 564 at 574, 576–577, CA, per Donaldson MR, and at 846–847, 848–849, 852 and 582–583, 584–585, 587 per Lloyd LJ. See also *R v Committee of Lloyd's, ex p Postgate* (1983) Times, 12 January (powers exercised by the Committee of Lloyd's); and *R v Committee of Lloyd's, ex p Moran* (1983) Times, 24 June. The primary difficulty in discerning a public case from a private case on the basis of the type of body (whether it be prerogative, statutory or contractual) is the complexity of a highly developed mixed economy society where organisations cannot readily be stereotyped as exclusively public or private. It would appear from *R v Panel on Take-overs and Mergers, ex p Datafin plc* that the functions of a body, and not merely its origin, may warrant judicial review of a decision of the body. See *Bank of Scotland, Petitioner*

(1988) Times, 21 November (although the relationship between the Investment Management Regulatory Organisation Ltd (IMRO) and its members was contractual in nature, IMRO performed public and administrative functions as an integral part of the scheme of self-regulation of the financial services industry set up by the Financial Services Act 1986; accordingly its acts and decisions were amenable to judicial review). See also the following cases involving challenges to other financial regulatory bodies: *R v Financial Intermediaries Managers and Brokers Regulatory Association, ex p Cochrane* [1990] COD 33, [1991] BCLC 106; *R v Life Assurance and Unit Trust Regulatory Organisation Ltd, ex p Ross* [1993] QB 17, [1993] 1 All ER 545, CA.

11 *R v Advertising Standards Authority Ltd, ex p Insurance Service plc* (1989) 2 Admin LR 77 at 86, DC, per Glidewell LJ; *R v Chief Rabbi of the United Hebrew Congregations of Great Britain and the Commonwealth, ex p Wachmann* [1993] 2 All ER 249 at 254, [1992] 1 WLR 1036 at 1041 per Simon Brown J; *R v Football Association Ltd, ex p Football League Ltd* [1993] 2 All ER 833 at 848, [1992] COD 52 at 53 per Rose J; *R v Disciplinary Committee of the Jockey Club, ex p Aga Khan* [1993] 2 All ER 853 at 874, [1993] 1 WLR 909 at 932, CA, per Hoffmann LJ; *R (Mullins) v Appeal Board of the Jockey Club and the Jockey Club* [2005] EWHC 2197 (Admin), (2005) Times, 24 October.

12 See, for example, the following cases in which it has been held that religious authorities are not subject to judicial review: *R v Chief Rabbi of the United Hebrew Congregations of Great Britain and the Commonwealth, ex p Wachmann* [1993] 2 All ER 249, [1992] 1 WLR 1036; *R v Imam of Bury Park Jame Masjid Luton, ex p Sulaiman Ali* [1994] COD 142, (1994) Times, 20 May, CA; *R v London Beth Din (Court of the Chief Rabbi), ex p Bloom* [1998] COD 131. See also *R (on the application of West) v Lloyds of London* [2004] EWCA Civ 506, [2004] 3 All ER 251 (Lloyd's is not governmental); *R (on the application of Moreton) v Medical Defence Union Ltd* [2006] EWHC 1948 (Admin), [2006] NLJR 1253, [2006] All ER (D) 370 (Jul).

13 *R v Panel on Take-overs and Mergers, ex p Datafin plc* [1987] QB 815 at 847, [1987] 1 All ER 564 at 583, CA, per Lloyd LJ; *R v National Joint Council for the Craft of Dental Technicians (Disputes Committee), ex p Neate* [1953] 1 QB 704, [1953] 1 All ER 327.

14 *R v Criminal Injuries Compensation Board, ex p Lain* [1967] 2 QB 864 at 882, [1967] 2 All ER 770 at 778, DC, per Lord Parker CJ. But see *R v General Medical Council, ex p Gee* [1986] 1 WLR 1247 at 1252, CA, per Lloyd LJ; affd sub nom *Gee v General Medical Council* [1987] 2 All ER 193, [1987] 1 WLR 564, HL. Domestic bodies may have as much power as statutory bodies: see *Breen v Amalgamated Engineering Union* [1971] 2 QB 175 at 190, [1971] 1 All ER 1148 at 1154, CA, per Lord Denning MR. In this context see *Finnigan v New Zealand Rugby Football Union* [1985] 2 NZLR 159, NZ CA (decision of the New Zealand Rugby Football Union to send a team to tour South Africa; although technically a private and voluntary sporting association the Rugby Union was in a position of major national importance; the plaintiffs, who were members of local clubs, were held to have standing to challenge the decision as they were linked to the Rugby Union by a chain of contracts). Decisions of the Jockey Club are not amenable to judicial review because, inter alia, the basis of the Club's jurisdiction is the contractual relationship between the Club and those agreeing to be bound by the Rules of Racing: *R v Disciplinary Committee of the Jockey Club, ex p Aga Khan* [1993] 2 All ER 853, [1993] 1 WLR 909, CA. See also *R v Disciplinary Committee of the Jockey Club, ex p Massingberd-Mundy* [1993] 2 All ER 207, DC; *R v Jockey Club, ex p RAM Racecourses Ltd* [1993] 2 All ER 225, [1990] COD 346, DC; *R (Mullins) v Appeal Board of the Jockey Club and the Jockey Club* [2005] EWHC 2197 (Admin), (2005) Times, 24 October. The Football Association is not amenable to judicial review, in particular not at the instigation of the Football League with whom it was in a contractual relationship: *R v Football Association Ltd, ex p Football League Ltd* [1993] 2 All ER 833, [1992] COD 52. Lloyd's of London is not amenable to judicial review: see *R v Lloyd's of London, ex p Briggs* [1993] 1 Lloyd's Rep 176, DC; *R (on the application of West) v Lloyd's of London* [2004] EWCA Civ 506, [2004] 2 All ER (Comm) 1, [2004] 3 All ER 251. Nor are decisions of the Association of British Travel Agents subject to judicial review: see *R (on the application of Sunspell Ltd) v Association of British Travel Agents* [2000] All ER (D) 1368. See also *R (on the application of Moreton) v Medical Defence Union* [2006] EWHC 1948 (Admin), [2006] NLJR 1253, [2006] All ER (D) 370 (Jul) (rights of members of medical defence union were derived from the union's association and from company law, not public law).

15 It may be that unless the decision of a club or trade union is so perverse as to be described properly as a 'mere caprice' the failure to take account of matters that were relevant or the decision to take into account matters that were irrelevant is not the proper scope of a review by the courts: *Hamlet v General Municipal Boilermakers and Allied Trades Union* [1987] 1 All ER

631 at 634, [1987] 1 WLR 449 at 452–453 per Harman J. See also *IRC v National Federation of Self-Employed and Small Businesses Ltd* [1982] AC 617 at 639, [1981] 2 All ER 93 at 103, HL, per Lord Diplock.

16 *R v Servite Houses, ex p Goldsmith* [2001] LGR 55, 33 HLR 369; *R (on the application of Heather) v The Leonard Cheshire Foundation* [2001] EWHC Admin 429, [2001] All ER (D) 156 (Jun). Both these cases concerned the duty of the local authority to provide residential accommodation for the disabled and the elderly. The local authority had the power to enter into contractual arrangements with private sector bodies to provide that accommodation. In both cases, the private sector body decided to close the home in question. The court held that the private sector bodies were not subject to judicial review as there was no statutory underpinning to the private body's functions and the relationship between the public authority and the private body was purely contractual.

17 *R (on the application of Beer (t/a Hammer Trout Farm) v Hampshire Farmers Market Ltd* [2003] EWCA Civ 1056, [2004] 1 WLR 233 (company responsible for farmers markets amenable to judicial review even though its functions were not woven into a system of governmental control, because it was performing a public function and had stepped into the shoes of the local authority which had previously run the farmers markets); *R (on the application of Birmingham and Solihull Taxi Association) v Birmingham International Airport Ltd* [2009] EWHC 1913 (Admin), [2009] All ER (D) 275 (Jul).

18 Eg the Universities of Oxford and Cambridge (as opposed to the individual colleges which were created by royal charter) and the University of London. Such universities are amenable to judicial review: see *R (on the application of Persaud) v University of Cambridge* [2001] EWCA Civ 534, [2001] ELR 480; *R (on the application of Galligan) v Chancellor, Masters and Scholars of the University of Oxford* [2001] EWHC Admin 965, [2002] ELR 494.

19 *Clark v University of Lincolnshire and Humberside* [2000] 3 All ER 752, [2000] 1 WLR 1988.

20 Formerly, chartered institutions had a visitor whose jurisdiction was exclusive and ousted that of the courts: see *Thomas v University of Bradford* [1987] AC 795 at 824, [1987] 1 All ER 834 at 849, HL, per Lord Griffiths and at 828 and 852 per Lord Ackner; and *R v Judicial Committee of the Privy Council, ex p Vijayatunga* [1988] QB 322 at 332–333, sub nom *R v University of London, ex p Vijayatunga* [1987] 3 All ER 204 at 212, DC, per Kerr LJ (affd sub nom *R v HM the Queen in Council, ex p Vijayatunga* [1990] 2 QB 444, sub nom *R v University of London, ex p Vijayatunga* [1989] 2 All ER 843, CA). Where a visitor makes a decision which it is within his power to make (in the sense that he had power under the regulating documents to enter into the adjudication) his decision is not amenable to judicial review on the ground of error of fact or law in his decision. However, judicial review does lie where the visitor does not have power to adjudicate in the dispute in question or where he abuses his power or where he acts in breach of natural justice: *R v Lord President of the Privy Council, ex p Page* [1993] AC 682, sub nom *Page v Hull University Visitor* [1993] 1 All ER 97, HL.

The jurisdiction of the visitor in relation to student complaints has now been abolished by the Higher Education Act 2004 Pt 2 (ss 11–21) and the above cases are of historical interest only (save for residual areas where the visitor may be involved). The scheme under the Higher Education Act 2004 Pt 2 is operated by the Office of the Independent Adjudicator, which is subject to judicial review: see *R (on the application of Siborurema) v Office of the Independent Adjudicator* [2007] EWCA Civ 1365, [2008] ELR 209. See further EDUCATION vol 15(2) (2006 Reissue) PARA 1039 et seq.

21 *Clark v University of Lincolnshire and Humberside* [2000] 3 All ER 752, [2000] 1 WLR 1988. Students also have a contract of membership with the university and may bring claims in appropriate cases by way of a claim for breach of contract. See also the text and note 23.

22 Ie the Higher Education Act 2004 Pt 2 (ss 11–21): see EDUCATION vol 15(2) (2006 Reissue) PARA 1039 et seq.

23 See *R (on the application of Carnell) v Regent's Park College* [2008] EWHC 739 (Admin), [2008] ELR 268; *R (Peng Hu Shi) v King's College London* [2008] EWHC 857 (Admin), [2008] ELR 414.

24 The fact that such visitors are High Court judges does not preclude review on the grounds identified in *R v Lord President of the Privy Council, ex p Page* [1993] AC 682, sub nom *Page v Hull University Visitor* [1993] 1 All ER 97, HL: *R v Visitors to Inns of Court, ex p Calder* [1994] QB 1, [1993] 2 All ER 876, CA. The visitors hear appeals from the disciplinary tribunal which adjudicates on allegations of professional misconduct by barristers and appeals from examiners. The scope of judicial review is restricted in respect of these visitorial decisions in the same way as visitors of chartered colleges and universities: see the text and notes 18–23.

25 *R v Panel on Take-overs and Mergers, ex p Datafin plc* [1987] QB 815 at 847, [1987] 1 All ER 564 at 583, CA, per Lloyd LJ; *R v Electricity Comrs, ex p London Electricity Joint*

Committee Co (1920) Ltd [1924] 1 KB 171 at 205, CA, per Atkin LJ; *R v Local Government Board* (1882) 10 QBD 309 at 321, CA, per Brett LJ.

26 *R v British Broadcasting Corpn, ex p Lavelle* [1983] 1 All ER 241 at 249, [1983] 1 WLR 23 at 31 per Woolf J. 'An application for judicial review has not and should not be extended to a pure employment situation. Nor does it, in my view, make any difference that what is sought to be attacked is a decision of a domestic tribunal, such as the series of disciplinary tribunals provided for by the BBC': *R v British Broadcasting Corpn, ex p Lavelle* at 249 and 30 per Woolf J; approved in *Law v National Greyhound Racing Club Ltd* [1983] 3 All ER 300, [1983] 1 WLR 1302, CA ('this is a claim against a body of persons whose status is essentially that of a domestic, as opposed to a public, tribunal, albeit one whose decisions may be of public concern': see at 307–308 and 1312 per Slade LJ); *R v Disciplinary Committee of the Jockey Club, ex p Aga Khan* [1993] 2 All ER 853, [1993] 1 WLR 909, CA (and see *R v Disciplinary Committee of the Jockey Club, ex p Massingberd-Mundy* [1993] 2 All ER 207, DC; and *R v Jockey Club, ex p RAM Racecourses Ltd* [1993] 2 All ER 225, [1990] COD 346, DC); *R v Football Association Ltd, ex p Football League Ltd* [1993] 2 All ER 833, [1992] COD 52. See also *R v Office, ex p Byrne* [1975] ICR 221, DC (Post Office employee alleging dismissal in breach of terms of employment).

27 *R v East Berkshire Health Authority, ex p Walsh* [1985] QB 152 at 164, [1984] 3 All ER 425 at 430, CA, per Sir John Donaldson MR. See also *McClaren v Home Office* [1990] ICR 824, [1990] IRLR 338, CA (prison officer with no individual contract of employment); *R v Lord Chancellor's Department, ex p Nangle* [1992] 1 All ER 897, [1991] ICR 743, DC (where there was a contract of employment between the parties there was no scope for judicial review; however, even if there had been no such contract, there was no remedy in public law arising out of disciplinary proceedings; such proceedings were of a purely domestic nature and without a sufficient element of public law; *R v Civil Service Appeal Board, ex p Bruce* [1988] 3 All ER 686, [1988] ICR 649, DC, not followed). See also *R v Lambeth London Borough Council, ex p Thompson* [1996] COD 217, Independent, 30 October.

28 *Malloch v Aberdeen Corpn* [1971] 2 All ER 1278, [1971] 1 WLR 1578, HL. The Civil Service Appeal Board, a body established pursuant to Order in Council, is amenable to judicial review: see *R v Civil Service Appeal Board, ex p Bruce* [1988] 3 All ER 686, [1988] ICR 649, DC (affd [1989] 2 All ER 907, [1989] ICR 171, CA); *R v Civil Service Appeal Board, ex p Cunningham* [1991] 4 All ER 310, [1992] ICR 816, CA.

29 *R v East Berkshire Health Authority, ex p Walsh* [1985] QB 152 at 164–165, [1984] 3 All ER 425 at 430–431, CA, per Sir John Donaldson MR; *Malloch v Aberdeen Corpn* [1971] 2 All ER 1278 at 1282–1283, [1971] 1 WLR 1578 at 1582, HL, per Lord Reid. See also *R v Secretary of State for the Home Department, ex p Benwell* [1985] QB 554 at 573, [1984] 3 All ER 854 at 867 per Hodgson J; *R v Trent Regional Health Authority, ex p Jones* (1986) Times, 19 June (decision of a health authority not to appoint to the post of consultant orthopaedic surgeon a candidate recommended by the advisory appointment committee not susceptible to judicial review); *R v Brent London Borough Council, ex p Assegai* (1987) 151 LG Rev 891 (dismissal of school governor); *R v Derbyshire County Council, ex p Noble* [1989] COD 285, (1988) Times, 21 November, DC (deputy police surgeon); *R v Salford Health Authority, ex p Janaway* [1989] AC 537, [1988] 2 WLR 442, CA; affd on different grounds sub nom *Janaway v Salford Area Health Authority* [1989] AC 537, [1988] 3 All ER 1079, HL (secretary).

30 *R v East Berkshire Health Authority, ex p Walsh* [1985] QB 152 at 164, [1984] 3 All ER 425 at 430, CA (senior nursing officer at a National Health Service Hospital). This was the case even though the authority was required by statute to contract on such terms as were negotiated by a statutory negotiating body and approved by a government minister. Had the allegation been that the negotiated terms had not in fact been included in the employee's contract of employment the case would have raised public law issues (per Sir John Donaldson MR at 165 and 431). See also *R v Hertfordshire County Council v National Union of Public Employees* [1985] IRLR 258; *R v Post Office, ex p Byrne* [1975] ICR 221.

31 *R v Secretary of State for the Home Department, ex p Benwell* [1985] QB 554, [1984] 3 All ER 854 (applicant appointed by the Home Secretary to the prison service as a person holding the office of constable). Hodgson J pointed out two distinguishing features between *R v East Berkshire Health Authority, ex p Walsh* [1985] QB 152, [1984] 3 All ER 425, CA, and the present case. First, Benwell was subject to the code of discipline by virtue of his appointment as a prison officer and not by the incorporation of the disciplinary code in his contract of employment. 'In (the present case) ... in making a disciplinary award of dismissal, the Home Office ... was performing the duties imposed upon it as part of the statutory terms under which it exercises its power' (*R v Secretary of State for the Home Department, ex p Benwell* at 574 and 868). Secondly, unlike Walsh, because of his status as a constable Benwell had no private law rights that could be enforced in civil proceedings. He could not resort to an industrial tribunal

under the Employment Protection (Consolidation) Act 1978 (now the Employment Rights Act 1996): see *Home Office v Robinson* [1982] ICR 31, [1981] IRLR 524, EAT. See also *Chief Constable of the North Wales Police v Evans* [1982] 3 All ER 141, [1982] 1 WLR 1155, HL (probationary constable); *King v University of Saskatchewan* (1969) 6 DLR (3d) 120. The Disciplinary Committee of the Medical Council and the Disciplinary Committee of the Law Society have statutory powers but in practice their decisions in the past have been reviewed by actions for injunctions and declarations; but now see *Gee v General Medical Council* [1987] 2 All ER 193, [1987] 1 WLR 564, HL; *Colman v General Medical Council* [1989] 1 Med LR 23, (1988) Times, 14 December; and *R v Pharmaceutical Society of Great Britain, ex p Sokoh* (1986) Times, 4 December.

32   Analysis of the cases suggests that there must be a strong statutory underpinning to the terms of employment: *R v East Berkshire Health Authority, ex p Walsh* [1985] QB 152, [1984] 3 All ER 425, CA (no judicial review of dismissal of senior nursing officer employed by the health authority merely because conditions of employment governed by a statutory instrument); and see *R v Secretary of State for the Home Office, ex p Benwell* [1985] QB 554, [1984] 3 All ER 854 (judicial review of dismissal of prison officer where employment was the subject of a code of discipline deriving its authority from statute); *R v Hertfordshire County Council, ex p National Union of Public Employees* [1985] IRLR 258, CA.
  There was nothing in the employment of the applicant in *R v East Berkshire Health Authority, ex p Walsh* which took his case out of the ordinary master and servant category. The cases of *Ridge v Baldwin* [1964] AC 40, [1963] 2 All ER 66, HL, *Vine v National Dock Labour Board* [1957] AC 488, [1956] 3 All ER 939, HL, and *Malloch v Aberdeen Corpn* [1971] 2 All ER 1278, [1971] 1 WLR 1578, HL, where the courts had accorded the appellants a special status, were distinguished on the basis that there was in all three cases a special statutory provision bearing directly on the right of the public authority to dismiss: *R v East Berkshire Health Authority, ex p Walsh* at 162–164 and 429–430 per Sir John Donaldson MR. In any event the consequences of the status were an additional set of procedural safeguards, which may be matters for the protection of which ordinary proceedings rather than judicial review are appropriate: see *R v East Berkshire Health Authority, ex p Walsh*. See also *R v Trent Regional Health Authority, ex p Jones* (1986) Times, 19 June (consultant surgeon).

33   For example, a local authority's decision not to sell land was not amenable to judicial review because that decision lacked any statutory underpinning: *R v Leeds City Council, ex p Cobleigh* [1997] COD 69; *R (on the application of Pepper) v Bolsover District Council* [2001] LGR 43, [2000] EGCS 107. But see *R (on the application of Ise Lodge Amenity Committee) v Kettering Borough Council* [2002] EWHC 1132 (Admin), [2002] All ER (D) 525 (May).

34   *Mass Energy Ltd v Birmingham City Council* [1994] Env LR 298.

35   *R (on the application of Molinaro) v Kensington and Chelsea Royal London Borough Council* [2001] EWHC Admin 896, [2002] LGR 336; *R (on the application of Birmingham and Solihull Taxi Association) v Birmingham International Airport Ltd* [2009] EWHC 1913 (Admin), [2009] All ER (D) 275 (Jul).

36   *R v Lord Chancellor, ex p Hibbet and Saunders (a firm)* [1993] COD 326, (1993) Times, 12 March; *R v Great Western Trains Co Ltd, ex p Frederick* [1998] COD 239; *Mercury Energy Ltd v Electricity Corpn of New Zealand Ltd* [1994] 1 WLR 521; *R (on the application of Cookson and Clegg) v Ministry of Defence* [2005] EWCA Civ 811, [2005] All ER (D) 83 (Jun); *R (on the application of Gamesa Energy UK Ltd) v National Assembly for Wales* [2006] EWHC 2167 (Admin), [2006] All ER (D) 26 (Aug); *R (on the application of Menai Collect Ltd) v Department for Constitutional Affairs* [2006] EWHC 727 (Admin), [2006] All ER (D) 101 (Apr).

37   *R v Deputy Governor of Camphill Prison, ex p King* [1985] QB 735, [1984] 3 All ER 897, CA.

38   *R v Board of Visitors of Hull Prison, ex p St Germain* [1978] QB 678, [1978] 2 All ER 198, DC (on appeal [1979] QB 425, [1979] 1 All ER 701, CA); *R v Board of Visitors of Dartmoor Prison, ex p Smith* [1987] QB 106, [1986] 2 All ER 651, CA. See also *R v Secretary of State for the Home Department, ex p McAvoy* [1984] 3 All ER 417, [1984] 1 WLR 1408.

39   *Leech v Deputy Governor of Parkhurst Prison* [1988] AC 533 at 583, [1988] 1 All ER 485 at 512, HL, per Lord Oliver of Aylmerton ('the susceptibility of a decision to the supervision of the courts must depend, in the ultimate analysis, upon the nature and consequences of the decision and not upon the personality or individual circumstances of the person called upon to make the decision').

40   See *R v Metropolitan Police Comr, ex p Blackburn* [1968] 2 QB 118, [1968] 1 All ER 763, CA; *Selvarajan v Race Relations Board* [1976] 1 All ER 12, sub nom *R v Race Relations Board, ex p Selvarajan* [1975] 1 WLR 1686 (decision of Board not to pursue complainant's allegations of discrimination); *Raymond v A-G* [1982] QB 839, [1982] 2 All ER 487, CA; *R v Police Complaints Board, ex p Madden* [1983] 2 All ER 353, [1983] 1 WLR 447; *R v General Council*

of the Bar, ex p Percival [1991] 1 QB 212 at 234, [1990] 3 All ER 137 at 152, DC, per Watkins LJ (decision of Bar Council to prefer a lesser charge against a barrister); *R v DPP, ex p Langlands-Pearse* [1991] COD 92; *R v Chief Constable of the Kent County Constabulary, ex p L* [1993] 1 All ER 756, [1991] Crim LR 841, DC (decision of the Director of Public Prosecutions to discontinue a prosecution of a juvenile was amenable to judicial review only where it could be shown that the decision was clearly contrary to a settled policy; a decision to discontinue a prosecution of an adult is unlikely to be available); *R v DPP, ex p Manning* [2001] QB 330, [2000] 3 WLR 463, DC (power to review to be sparingly exercised because Parliament has entrusted the decision whether to prosecute to an independent, professional service); *R (on the application of Da Silva) v DPP* [2006] EWHC 3204 (Admin), [2007] NLJR 31, [2006] All ER (D) 215 (Dec); *R (on the application of B) v DPP (Equality and Human Rights Commission intervening)* [2009] EWHC 106 (Admin), [2009] 1 WLR 2072, [2009] 1 Cr App Rep 580.

41 *Leech v Deputy Governor of Parkhurst Prison* [1988] AC 533 at 561, [1988] 1 All ER 485 at 496, HL, per Lord Bridge of Harwich; *R v British Coal Corpn, ex p Vardy* [1993] ICR 720 at 751, [1993] IRLR 104 at 116, DC, per Glidewell LJ (decision to close coal pits amenable to review because such decisions governed by a statutory machinery; decision in *R v National Coal Board, ex p National Union of Mineworkers* [1986] ICR 791 doubted).

42 See PARA 602.

43 There are conflicting theories concerning the definition of the 'prerogative'. A narrow view explained by Bl Com (1.239) is that the 'prerogative' is a non-statutory power invested in the Crown, but appertaining to no-one else. A looser sense of the term which appears to have most judicial support at present is that the prerogative is any action of the Executive without the power of statute (see *R v Criminal Injuries Compensation Board, ex p Lain* [1967] 2 QB 864, [1967] 2 All ER 770, DC; *Laker Airways Ltd v Department of Trade* [1977] QB 643, [1977] 2 All ER 182, CA; *Council of Civil Service Unions v Minister for the Civil Service* [1985] AC 374, [1984] 3 All ER 935, HL). However, in *R v Panel on Take-overs and Mergers, ex p Datafin plc* [1987] QB 815 at 848, [1987] 1 All ER 564 at 584, CA, Lloyd LJ noted that there has been 'a certain imprecision' in the use of the term 'prerogative'. He was of the view that strictly the term 'prerogative' should be confined to those powers which are unique to the Crown. In *R v Broadcasting Complaints Commission, ex p Owen* [1985] QB 1153 at 1172–1173, [1985] 2 All ER 522 at 530, DC, the Divisional Court expressly left open the question of whether in appropriate circumstances judicial review would lie against the British Broadcasting Corporation, which was established by royal charter (see TELECOMMUNICATIONS AND BROADCASTING vol 45(1) (2005 Reissue) PARA 306 et seq).

44 *Council of Civil Service Unions v Minister for the Civil Service* [1985] AC 374 at 407, [1984] 3 All ER 935 at 948, HL, per Lord Scarman, at 410 and 950 per Lord Diplock and at 417 and 956 per Lord Roskill. See also *R (on the application of Bancoult) v Secretary of State for Foreign and Commonwealth Affairs* [2008] UKHL 61, [2009] 1 AC 453, [2008] 4 All ER 1055.

45 The board was established under the royal prerogative for the purpose of awarding compensation to victims of criminal injuries out of money voted by Parliament. The board has now been replaced by a statutory scheme established by the Home Secretary pursuant to powers conferred by the Criminal Injuries Compensation Act 1995. See further CRIMINAL LAW, EVIDENCE AND PROCEDURE vol 11(4) (2006 Reissue) PARA 2033 et seq.

46 *R v Criminal Injuries Compensation Board, ex p Lain* [1967] 2 QB 864, [1967] 2 All ER 770, DC; *R v Criminal Injuries Compensation Board, ex p Schofield* [1971] 2 All ER 1101, [1971] 1 WLR 926, DC; *R v Criminal Injuries Compensation Board, ex p Lawton* [1972] 3 All ER 582, [1972] 1 WLR 1589, DC; *R v Criminal Injuries Compensation Board, ex p Ince* [1973] 3 All ER 808, [1973] 1 WLR 1334, CA; *R v Criminal Injuries Compensation Board, ex p Tong* [1977] 1 All ER 171, [1976] 1 WLR 1237, CA; *R v Criminal Injuries Compensation Board, ex p Clowes* [1977] 3 All ER 854, [1977] 1 WLR 1353, DC; *R v Criminal Injuries Compensation Board, ex p RJC (an infant)* (1978) 122 Sol Jo 95; *R v Criminal Injuries Compensation Board, ex p Thompstone* [1984] 3 All ER 572, [1984] 1 WLR 1234, CA; *R v Criminal Injuries Compensation Board, ex p Webb* [1987] QB 74, [1986] 2 All ER 478, CA; *R v Criminal Injuries Compensation Board, ex p A* [1999] 2 AC 330 at 342, [1999] 2 WLR 974 at 979, HL, per Lord Slynn of Hadley. For the statutory framework which enables the Home Secretary to establish a scheme for providing compensation to the victims of crime see the Criminal Injuries Compensation Act 1995; and CRIMINAL LAW, EVIDENCE AND PROCEDURE vol 11(4) (2006 Reissue) PARA 2033 et seq. The Criminal Injuries Compensation Authority, established under the Criminal Injuries Compensation Act 1995, is amenable to judicial review: see *R v Criminal Injuries Compensation Authority, ex p Leatherland* (2000) Times, 12 October.

47 As to quashing orders see PARA 693 et seq.

48 *Council of Civil Service Unions v Minister for the Civil Service* [1985] AC 374 at 400, [1984] 3 All ER 935 at 943, HL, per Lord Fraser of Tullybelton; *R v Secretary of State for the Home*

Department, ex p Hosenball [1977] 3 All ER 452 at 459, [1977] 1 WLR 766 at 781, CA, per Lord Denning MR: 'if the body concerned, whether it be a minister or advisers, has acted unfairly, then the courts can review their proceedings so as to ensure, as far as may be, that justice is done'.

49 *R v Chief Immigration Officer, Gatwick Airport, ex p Kharrazi* [1980] 3 All ER 373, [1980] 1 WLR 1396, CA. The Immigration Rules are made under the Immigration Act 1971 and require the approval of both Houses of Parliament, but are not statutory instruments: see BRITISH NATIONALITY, IMMIGRATION AND ASYLUM vol 4(2) (2002 Reissue) PARA 83.

50 *Council of Civil Service Unions v Minister for the Civil Service* [1985] AC 374, [1984] 3 All ER 935, HL. The mechanism on which the Minister for the Civil Service relied to alter the terms and conditions of service at Government Communications Headquarters ('GCHQ') was an 'instruction' issued by her under the Civil Service Order in Council of 1982 art 4: the Order in Council was not issued under powers conferred by any Act of Parliament. Like the previous Orders in Council on the same subject it was issued by the Sovereign by virtue of her prerogative, but of course on the advice of the government of the day (per Lord Fraser of Tullybelton at 397 and 941). However, the evidence established that the minister had considered, with reason, that prior consultation about her instruction would have involved a risk of precipitating disruption at GCHQ and revealing vulnerable areas of operation, and, accordingly, she had shown that her decision had in fact been based on considerations of national security that outweighed the applicant's legitimate expectation of prior consultation (per Lord Fraser at 403 and 944; per Lord Scarman at 407 and 948; per Lord Diplock at 412–413 and 952; per Lord Roskill at 423 and 960; per Lord Brightman at 424 and 960). See also *R v Secretary of State for the Home Department, ex p Ruddock* [1987] 2 All ER 518 at 526–527, [1987] 1 WLR 1482 at 1491–1492 per Taylor J (prerogative power to issue warrants to monitor telephone calls subject to judicial review; the court would not abdicate its judicial function merely because the Secretary of State maintained a policy of silence on the issue of interceptions in the interests of national security: cogent evidence of potential damage to national security flowing from the trial of the issue would have to be adduced to justify any modification to the court's normal procedure).

51 See eg *Gillick v West Norfolk and Wisbech Area Health Authority* [1986] AC 112 at 163, [1985] 3 All ER 402 at 405, HL, obiter per Lord Fraser of Tullybelton, and at 178 and 416 obiter per Lord Scarman. The Department of Health and Social Security issued to area health authorities a memorandum of guidance on family planning services which contained a section dealing with contraceptive advice and treatment for young people. As a general rule such advice cannot be the subject of judicial review. However in certain circumstances the court would not refuse jurisdiction. Lord Bridge of Harwich said (at 193 and 427): 'We must now say that if a government department, in a field of administration in which it exercises responsibility, promulgates in a public document, albeit non-statutory in form, advice which is erroneous in law, then the court, in proceedings in appropriate form commenced by an applicant or plaintiff who possesses the necessary locus standi, has jurisdiction to correct the error of law by an appropriate declaration'. See also *Royal College of Nursing of the United Kingdom v Department of Health and Social Security* [1981] AC 800, [1981] 1 All ER 545, HL; *R v Worthing Borough Council and Secretary of State for Environment, ex p Burch* (1983) 50 P & CR 53, [1984] JPL 261 (misconstruction of a ministerial circular relating to appropriate development of a site held reviewable by certiorari); and *Asiedu v Secretary of State for the Home Department* [1988] Imm AR 186 at 188–189, CA, per Woolf LJ (judicial review will rarely be available in relation to letters written by the Secretary of State in response to investigations initiated as a result of the intention of Members of Parliament: this is purely an extra-statutory function performed by the Secretary of State). See also *R v Secretary of State for the Home Department, ex p Urmaza* [1996] COD 479 at 484, (1996) Times, 23 July per Sedley J (judicial review of the Home Secretary's internal policy). See further PARA 607.

52 *Council of Civil Service Unions v Minister for the Civil Service* [1985] AC 374 at 408–409, [1984] 3 All ER 935 at 949, HL, per Lord Diplock; *R v Gaming Board for Great Britain, ex p Benaim and Khaida* [1970] 2 QB 417, [1970] 2 All ER 528, CA.

605. The test for determining whether a body is a public authority for the purposes of the Human Rights Act 1998. It is unlawful for a public authority to act in a way which is incompatible with certain rights derived from the Convention for the Protection of Human Rights and Fundamental Freedoms[1]. A public authority does not act unlawfully[2] if, as a result of primary legislation, the public authority was required to act in a way which was incompatible with a person's Convention rights[3].

A 'public authority' includes a court or tribunal[4], and any person certain of whose functions are functions of a public nature[5]. In relation to a particular act, a person is not a public authority[6] if the nature of the act is private[7].

Public authorities for the purpose of the Human Rights Act 1998 include standard or 'core' public authorities which must always comply with a person's Convention rights. These are bodies whose nature is governmental, such as government departments, local authorities, the police and the armed forces[8]. Hybrid bodies or 'functional' public authorities must comply with a person's Convention rights when exercising their public functions, but do not have to comply with the Convention in respect of acts which are private in nature. There is no test of universal application to determine whether functions are public. Factors to be taken into account include the extent to which in carrying out the relevant function the body is publicly funded, or is exercising statutory powers, or is taking the place of central government or local authorities, or is providing a public service[9]. The fact that the function is regulated by statute is unlikely to be sufficient to render it a public function[10]. The fact that a function is performed by a private company, under contract to a local authority, is an indication that the function is not public, at least in the absence of strong countervailing factors. The fact that the function is amenable to judicial review is an indication as to whether or not the function is a public function for the purposes of the Human Rights Act 1998, but is not determinative[11]. The courts have held that a private care home is not exercising a public function when terminating the placement of local authority placed residents, whereas a registered social landlord is exercising a public function when taking steps to terminate a tenancy for social housing[12].

Even if a body is a hybrid public authority, it will not be subject to Convention principles if the challenged act is a private act. It has been suggested that the termination of a tenancy or a licence agreement is necessarily a private act because it originates from the exercise of contractual rights[13]. However, the Court of Appeal has held that the act of a registered social landlord in terminating a tenancy is not a private act as it is inextricably linked to the provision of social housing as part of the registered social landlord's public function[14]. The source of the power is a relevant factor in determining whether the act in question is private or not, but this is not decisive, as the nature of the activities in issue in the case are also important. The Court of Appeal further held that the act of termination of the tenancy was so bound up with the provision of social housing, that once the latter was seen as the exercise of a public function, then acts which are necessarily involved in the regulation of the function were also held to be public acts[15].

If a body is exercising a public function for the purposes of the Human Rights Act 1998, judicial review will be available against that body in respect of that function to ensure that it acted in accordance with Convention rights. It will normally also be a public body for the purposes of judicial review.

1 Human Rights Act 1998 s 6(1). The text refers to the Convention for the Protection of Human Rights and Fundamental Freedoms (Rome, 4 November 1950; TS 71 (1953) Cmd 8969). See further PARAS 603, 650, 651; and CONSTITUTIONAL LAW AND HUMAN RIGHTS vol 8(2) (Reissue) PARA 101 et seq.
2 Ie for the purposes of the Human Rights Act 1998 s 6.
3 See the Human Rights Act 1998 s 6(2); and *R (on the application of Bono) v Harlow District Council* [2002] EWHC 423 (Admin), [2002] 1 WLR 2475.
4 Human Rights Act 1998 s 6(3)(a).
5 Human Rights Act 1998 s 6(3)(b). Neither House of Parliament nor a person exercising functions in connection with proceedings in Parliament is a public authority: s 6(3).
6 Ie by virtue of the Human Rights Act 1998 s 6(3)(b): see the text and note 5.

7　Human Rights Act 1998 s 6(5).

8　*Aston Cantlow and Wilmcote with Billesley Parochial Church Council v Wallbank* [2003] UKHL 37, [2004] 1 AC 546, [2003] 3 All ER 1213 at [7] per Lord Nicholls of Birkenhead and at [35] per Lord Hope of Craighead. Such bodies possess special powers, are democratically accountable, receive public funding in whole or in part, are under an obligation to act only in the public interest, and have a statutory constitution. A core public authority is incapable of having Convention rights of its own.

9　*Aston Cantlow and Wilmcote with Billesley Parochial Church Council v Wallbank* [2003] UKHL 37, [2004] 1 AC 546, [2003] 3 All ER 1213 at [11]–[12] per Lord Nicholls of Birkenhead. A hybrid public authority is not disabled from having Convention rights of its own.

10　Ie for the purposes of the Human Rights Act 1990 s 6(3)(b): see the text and note 5.

11　*YL v Birmingham City Council* [2007] UKHL 27, [2008] 1 AC 95, [2007] 3 All ER 957.

12　See *YL v Birmingham City Council* [2007] UKHL 27, [2008] 1 AC 95, [2007] 3 All ER 957; *R (on the application of Weaver) v London and Quadrant Housing Trust* [2009] EWCA Civ 587, [2009] 25 EG 137 (CS). The actual decision in *YL v Birmingham City Council* has now been reversed by the Health and Social Care Act 2008 s 145 (see SOCIAL SERVICES AND COMMUNITY CARE vol 44(2) (Reissue) PARAS 1029, 1033), but the reasoning of the majority of the House of Lords is still binding. A head teacher and governors are a public authority for the purposes of the Human Rights Act 1998 (*Ali v Head Teacher and Governors of Lord Grey School* [2006] UKHL 14, [2006] 2 AC 363, [2006] 2 All ER 457); an independent contractor running an immigration detention centre is a hybrid public authority (*R (on the application of D) v Secretary of State for the Home Department* [2006] EWHC 980 (Admin), 150 Sol Jo LB 743, [2006] All ER (D) 300 (May)); utilities companies have been found to be public authorities (see *Marcic v Thames Water Utilities Ltd* [2002] EWCA Civ 64, [2002] QB 929, [2002] 2 All ER 55; *Dobson v Thames Water Utilities Ltd* [2009] EWCA Civ 28, [2009] 3 All ER 319); managers of a psychiatric hospital are a hybrid public authority (*R (on the application of A) v Partnerships in Care Ltd* [2002] EWHC 529 (Admin), [2002] 1 WLR 2610). The RSPCA is not a public authority (see *RSPCA v A-G* [2001] 3 All ER 530, [2002] 1 WLR 448); nor is Lloyd's of London (*R (on the application of West) v Lloyd's of London* [2004] EWCA Civ 506, [2004] 2 All ER (Comm) 1, [2004] 3 All ER 251); nor is Network Rail (*Cameron v Network Rail Infrastructure Ltd* [2006] EWHC 1133 (QB), [2007] 3 All ER 241, [2007] 1 WLR 163).

13　*YL v Birmingham City Council* [2007] UKHL 27, [2008] 1 AC 95, [2007] 3 All ER 957. See also *Aston Cantlow and Wilmcote with Billesley Parochial Church Council v Wallbank* [2003] UKHL 37, [2004] 1 AC 546, [2003] 3 All ER 1213 where it was held that the act of enforcing liability by the parish council was a private act, akin to the enforcement of a restrictive covenant.

14　*R (on the application of Weaver) v London and Quadrant Housing Trust* [2009] EWCA Civ 587, [2009] 4 All ER 865 at [102], [2009] 25 EG 137 (CS) at [102] per Lawrence Collins LJ.

15　*R (on the application of Weaver) v London and Quadrant Housing Trust* [2009] EWCA Civ 587, [2009] 4 All ER 865, [2009] 25 EG 137 (CS).

606. Non-statutory tribunals. Judicial review of determinations by non-statutory tribunals discharging functions of a public nature is based on the same principles as review of determinations by statutory tribunals[1]. Judicial review will not lie in respect of the proceedings of private non-statutory tribunals, such as private arbitrators or the committees of clubs and other voluntary associations[2]. The jurisdiction of the courts extends to determining whether a non-statutory tribunal has acted within its powers, fairly and in good faith[3], and in accordance with natural justice[4]. The courts' power to determine the proper legal interpretation of the rules of a voluntary association cannot be ousted by the rules themselves[5].

1　*R v Criminal Injuries Compensation Board, ex p Lain* [1967] 2 QB 864, [1967] 2 All ER 770, DC; *R v Criminal Injuries Compensation Board, ex p Schofield* [1971] 2 All ER 1011, [1971] 1 WLR 926, DC; *R v Criminal Injuries Compensation Board, ex p Lawton* [1972] 3 All ER 582, [1972] 1 WLR 1589, DC; *R v Criminal Injuries Compensation Board, ex p Ince* [1973] 3 All ER 808, [1973] 1 WLR 1334, CA; *R v Criminal Injuries Compensation Board, ex p Tong* [1977] 1 All ER 171, [1976] 1 WLR 1237, CA; *R v Criminal Injuries Compensation Board, ex p Clowes* [1977] 3 All ER 854, [1977] 1 WLR 1353; *R v Criminal Injuries Compensation Board, ex p RJC (an infant)* (1978) 122 Sol Jo 95, DC; *R v Criminal Injuries Compensation Board, ex p Thompstone* [1984] 3 All ER 572, [1984] 1 WLR 1234, DC; *R v*

Criminal Injuries Compensation Board, ex p Webb [1987] QB 74, [1986] 2 All ER 478, CA; *R v Criminal Injuries Compensation Board, ex p P* [1995] 1 All ER 870, [1995] 1 WLR 845, CA; *R v Criminal Injuries Compensation Board, ex p A* [1999] 2 AC 330, [1999] 2 WLR 974, HL. The Criminal Injuries Compensation Board has been replaced by a scheme established by the Home Secretary under the Criminal Injuries Compensation Act 1995: see PARA 604 note 45. See also *R v Civil Service Appeal Board, ex p Cunningham* [1991] 4 All ER 310, [1992] ICR 816, CA; *R v Panel on Take-overs and Mergers, ex p Datafin plc* [1987] QB 815, [1987] 1 All ER 564, CA.

2   See, by way of example of the refusal to permit judicial review of the decision of a club, *R v Disciplinary Committee of the Jockey Club, ex p Aga Khan* [1993] 2 All ER 853, [1993] 1 WLR 909, CA. As to the test for determining whether a body may be amenable to judicial review see PARA 604. The opportunity for redress, however, has been considerably enlarged in the case of members of trade unions who are unreasonably expelled or excluded or who are subject to unjustifiable disciplinary action: see the Trade Union and Labour Relations (Consolidation) Act 1992 s 64 (complaints are presented to employment tribunals in the first instance, with an appeal on a point of law to the Employment Appeal Tribunal): see EMPLOYMENT vol 40 (2009) PARA 980.

3   See eg *Breen v Amalgamated Engineering Union* [1971] 2 QB 175, [1971] 1 All ER 1148, CA; *Shotton v Hammond* (1976) 120 Sol Jo 780.

4   As to the scope of the duty to observe natural justice see PARAS 629–630.

5   See PARA 630 note 28.

(3) DECISIONS IN RESPECT OF WHICH JUDICIAL REVIEW MAY LIE

607. A justiciable issue. The subject matter of a judicial review is generally a decision made by some person[1]. To qualify as a subject for judicial review such a decision must have consequences which affect some person or persons other than the decision-maker, although it may affect him too[2].

The courts will not accord protection to an interest not regarded as being entitled to legal recognition. Thus, they will not pronounce upon the merits of a dispute between parties on a question of professional ethics[3], or award a declaration as to an issue that is academic, hypothetical, premature or dead[4], or make any order in relation to a matter excluded from their jurisdiction[5].

The validity of an Act of Parliament will not be questioned by the courts[6] except where the Act is inconsistent with European Union law[7] or by way of a declaration given pursuant to the Human Rights Act 1998 that the Act of Parliament is incompatible with the Convention for the Protection of Human Rights and Fundamental Freedoms[8]; nor will the exercise by Parliament of any right of veto it may have in relation to the promulgation of subordinate legislation be subject to review[9].

Many Crown prerogative powers will not be reviewed by the courts on the grounds that they are not justiciable[10], such as the prerogative of entering into treaties[11], the defence of the realm, the prerogative of mercy[12], the granting of honours, the dissolution of Parliament and the appointment of ministers. Matters of national security and the defence of the realm are non-justiciable, provided that there is some evidence that national security is at stake[13]. Similarly, the courts will not review the exercise of the Attorney-General's discretion in deciding whether to bring relator proceedings[14].

Ordinary management powers of government departments and public bodies may not be amenable to judicial review because the exercise of such powers lacks a sufficient public law element or because the exercise of the power lacks any statutory underpinning[15].

1   The issuing of guidance in the form of a circular by a government department may be the subject of judicial review: eg *Royal College of Nursing of the United Kingdom v Department of Health*

and Social Security [1981] AC 800, [1981] 1 All ER 545, HL; *Gillick v West Norfolk and Wisbech Area Health Authority* [1986] AC 112, [1985] 3 All ER 402, HL; *R v Secretary of State for the Environment, ex p Greenwich London Borough Council* [1989] COD 530, (1989) Times, 17 May, DC; cf *R v London Waste Regulation Authority, ex p Specialist Waste Management Ltd* (1988) Times, 1 November. See also *R (on the application of BAPIO Action Ltd) v Secretary of State for the Home Department* [2008] UKHL 27, [2008] 1 AC 1003, [2009] 1 All ER 93; *R (on the application of Axon) v Secretary of State for Health* [2006] EWHC 37 (Admin), [2006] QB 539, [2006] 2 WLR 1130 (guidance on giving contraceptive advice to young persons without informing their parents); *R (on the application of Burke) v General Medical Council* [2005] EWCA Civ 1003, [2006] QB 273, [2005] 3 WLR 1132; *R (on the application of Eisai Ltd) v National Institute for Health and Clinical Excellence* [2008] EWCA Civ 438, 101 BMLR 26 (challenge to guidance issued by the National Institute on the cost-effectiveness of new drug).

A policy adopted by a public authority may also be the subject of judicial review: see eg *S v Secretary of State for the Home Department* [2006] EWCA Civ 1157, (2006) Times, 9 October, [2006] All ER (D) 30 (Aug) (policy relating to temporary admission); *R (on the application of Daly) v Secretary of State for the Home Department* [2001] UKHL 26, [2001] 2 AC 532, [2001] 3 All ER 433 (policy of searching prisoners' correspondence); *R (on the application of the Howard League for Penal Reform) v Secretary of State for the Home Department* [2002] EWHC 2497 (Admin), [2003] 1 FLR 484, [2003] Fam Law 149; *R v Secretary of State for the Home Department, ex p Urmaza* [1996] COD 479, (1996) Times, 23 July (policy adopted by the Home Secretary); *A-G (ex rel Tilley) v Wandsworth London Borough Council* [1981] 1 All ER 1162, [1981] 1 WLR 854, CA; *R v Oxford, ex p Levey* (1985) Times, 18 December; *Re Findlay* [1985] AC 318, sub nom *Findlay v Secretary of State for the Home Department* [1984] 3 All ER 801, HL; *R v Secretary of State for the Home Department, ex p Handscomb* (1987) 86 Cr App Rep 59, DC; *R v Secretary of State for the Home Department, ex p Benson* (1988) Independent, 16 November; (1988) Times, 21 November, DC; *R v General Medical Council, ex p Colman* (1988) Independent, 29 November, DC (challenge to guidelines issued by the General Medical Council to doctors regarding the dissemination of information about their services); and see *R v Worthing Borough Council and Secretary of State for the Environment, ex p Burch* (1983) 50 P & CR 53 (judicial review of opinion given by Secretary of State as to how he would have dealt with an appeal relating to an application for planning permission); *R v Agricultural Dwelling-House Advisory Committee for Bedfordshire, Cambridgeshire and Northamptonshire* (1986) 19 HLR 367 (advice which was likely to be acted upon could be reviewed prior to action being taken); *R v Ethical Committee of St Mary's Hospital (Manchester), ex p H (or Harriott)* [1988] 1 FLR 512, [1988] Fam Law 165 (advice from informal ethical committee might in some cases be subject to review); *Wellcome Foundation Ltd v Secretary of State for Social Services* [1988] 2 All ER 684, [1988] 1 WLR 635, HL (indication from the Secretary of State as to the matters he would take into account in deciding whether to grant licences to other persons in the future subjected to review).

Only in the most exceptional circumstances will a court review a decision made by another body in the course of a hearing before that hearing is concluded: *R v Association of Futures Brokers and Dealers Ltd, ex p Mordens Ltd* (1990) 3 Admin LR 254. The courts generally require claimants to wait until the decision-making process has been completed before seeing judicial review but, in exceptional circumstances, the court may grant judicial review in respect of matters occurring during the decision-making process: see eg *Gee v General Medical Council* [1987] 2 All ER 193, [1987] 1 WLR 564, HL; *Futures Brokers and Dealers Ltd, ex p Mordens Ltd* (1990) 3 Admin LR 254 (especially at 263).

2   *Council of Civil Service Unions v Minister for the Civil Service* [1985] AC 374 at 408, [1984] 3 All ER 935 at 949, HL, per Lord Diplock.

3   *Cox v Green* [1966] Ch 216, [1966] 1 All ER 268. Where a public authority issues guidance on a matter of professional ethics, that guidance may be reviewed and quashed if it gives advice which is wrong in relation to a clearly defined issue of law; but where any proposition of law is interwoven with questions of social and ethical controversy, the court will exercise its discretion with restraint: *Gillick v West Norfolk and Wisbech Area Health Authority* [1986] AC 112 at 194, [1985] 3 All ER 402 at 427, HL, per Lord Bridge of Harwich and at 206 and 436 per Lord Templeman.

4   The court has a discretion to adjudicate on academic questions. However, even in the public law area that discretion should be exercised with caution and only if there is good reason in the public interest to do so: *R v Secretary of State for the Home Department, ex p Salem* [1999] 1 AC 450, [1999] 2 All ER 42, HL, in which the House of Lords declined to exercise its discretion on the basis that the unusual facts of the case did not provide a good basis for deciding a question of principle. Cf *R v Secretary of State for the Home Department, ex p Adan*

[1999] 4 All ER 774 at 781–782, [1999] 3 WLR 1274 at 1282–1283, CA, per Lord Woolf MR, where the Court of Appeal did adjudicate on an academic question on the grounds that there was a point of importance which arose in numerous other cases and which it was in the public interest to determine. In *Abdi v Secretary of State for the Home Department* [1996] 1 All ER 641, sub nom *R v Secretary of State for the Home Department, ex p Abdi* [1996] 1 WLR 298, HL, the House of Lords addressed an academic issue which it described as 'a question of fundamental importance and a very difficult case' (see at 645 and 302 per Lord Slynn of Hadley). See also *R v DPP, ex p Merton London Borough Council (No 2)* [1999] COD 358, DC; *Mellstrom v Garner* [1970] 2 All ER 9, [1970] 1 WLR 603, CA; *R (on the application of Ullah) v Special Adjudicator* [2004] UKHL 26, [2004] 2 AC 323, [2004] 3 All ER 785 at [5] per Lord Bingham of Cornhill; and see PARA 719.

The House of Lords has indicated very firmly that it is inappropriate to consider hypothetical questions. In the case of a hypothetical issue there is no decision which can properly be made the subject of an application for judicial review. Any conclusion reached by the court is necessarily obiter and therefore does not establish a precedent: *R (on the application of Rusbridger) v A-G* [2003] UKHL 38, [2004] 1 AC 357, [2003] 3 All ER 784; *Wynne v Secretary of State for the Home Department* [1993] 1 All ER 574, sub nom *R v Secretary of State for the Home Department, ex p Wynne* [1993] 1 WLR 115, HL.

5   See PARA 655.

6   *Cheney v Conn* [1968] 1 All ER 779 at 782, [1968] 1 WLR 242 at 247 per Ungoed-Thomas J; *British Railways Board v Pickin* [1974] AC 765, [1974] 1 All ER 609, HL (the validity of a private Act of Parliament will not be questioned by the courts even where fraud on the part of the promoters is alleged); *Manuel v A-G* [1983] Ch 77 at 86, [1982] 3 All ER 786 at 793 per Sir Robert Megarry V-C (the point was not addressed in the Court of Appeal: [1983] Ch 77, [1982] 3 All ER 822, CA).

7   See eg *R v Secretary of State for Employment, ex p Equal Opportunities Commission* [1995] 1 AC 1, sub nom *Equal Opportunities Commission v Secretary of State for Employment* [1994] 1 All ER 910, HL. See *R v Secretary of State for Transport, ex p Factortame Ltd (No 2)* [1991] 1 AC 603, sub nom *Factortame Ltd v Secretary of State for Transport (No 2)* [1991] 1 All ER 70.

8   Ie the Convention for the Protection of Human Rights and Fundamental Freedoms (Rome, 4 November 1950; TS 71 (1953) Cmd 8969). The Human Rights Act 1998 s 4(2) empowers the higher courts to declare primary legislation incompatible with the Convention. However, such a declaration does not affect the validity, continuing operation or enforcement of any incompatible primary legislation, whether passed before or after the coming into force of the Human Rights Act 1998 on 2 October 2000: see s 3; and CONSTITUTIONAL LAW AND HUMAN RIGHTS.

9   *R v HM Treasury, ex p Smedley* [1985] QB 657 at 672, [1985] 1 All ER 589 at 597, CA, per Slade LJ. The validity of the subordinate legislation itself may be questioned in the courts: see PARA 609.

10   See generally *Council of Civil Service Unions v Minister for the Civil Service* [1985] AC 374 at 418, [1984] 3 All ER 935 at 956, HL, per Lord Roskill. As to judicial review of the Crown prerogative see PARA 608.

11   *Blackburn v A-G* [1971] 2 All ER 1380, [1971] 1 WLR 1037, CA; *Ex p Molyneaux* [1986] 1 WLR 331; *JH Rayner (Mincing Lane) Ltd v Department of Trade and Industry* [1990] 2 AC 418 at 476, sub nom *Maclaine Watson & Co Ltd v Department of Trade and Industry* [1989] 3 All ER 523 at 526, HL, per Lord Templeman and at 499 and 544 per Lord Oliver of Aylmerton; *R v Secretary of State for Foreign and Commonwealth Affairs, ex p Rees-Mogg* [1994] QB 552, [1994] 1 All ER 457, CA (the court had no jurisdiction to consider the decision of the United Kingdom to ratify the Treaty Establishing the European Community (Rome, 25 March 1957; TS 1 (1973); Cmnd 5179)); *R (on the application of Wheeler) v Office of the Prime Minister* [2008] EWHC 1409 (Admin), [2008] All ER (D) 333 (Jun) (the court doubted that the question of whether two treaties, the Constitutional Treaty and the Treaty of Lisbon, both concerned with reforms to the European Union, were materially similar was a justiciable issue for the courts to determine, as such a question depended on matters of political judgment and perspective).

12   *Hanratty v Lord Butler of Saffron Walden* (1971) 115 Sol Jo 386, CA; *Lewis v A-G of Jamaica* [2001] 2 AC 50, [2000] 3 WLR 1785; *R (on the application of Page) v Secretary of State for Justice* [2007] EWHC 2026 (Admin). In *R v Secretary of State for the Home Department, ex p Bentley* [1994] QB 349, [1993] 4 All ER 442, DC, the court accepted that it was probably right to say that the formulation of criteria for the exercise of the prerogative of mercy by the grant of a free pardon was entirely a matter of policy and not justiciable. However, the Secretary of State's decision was capable of review on the grounds that he had failed to recognise that the

prerogative of mercy was capable of being exercised in many different circumstances over a wide range and had therefore failed to consider the form of pardon which might be appropriate. Thus the court did not review the exercise of the prerogative. Rather it reviewed the decision of the Secretary of State on the basis that he had failed to appreciate the full extent of his powers. See also *R (on the application of Shields) v Secretary of State for Justice* [2008] EWHC 3102 (Admin), [2009] 3 All ER 265, [2009] 3 WLR 765.

13 *Council of Civil Service Unions v Minister for the Civil Service* [1985] AC 374, [1984] 3 All ER 935, HL; *The Zamora* [1916] 2 AC 77, PC; *Chandler v DPP* [1964] AC 763, [1962] 3 All ER 142, HL; *R v Secretary of State for the Home Department, ex p Ruddock* [1987] 2 All ER 518, [1987] 1 WLR 1482; *R v Director of Government Communications Headquarters, ex p Hodges* [1988] COD 123, (1988) Times, 26 July, DC; and see *R v Secretary of State for the Home Department, ex p Hosenball* [1977] 3 All ER 452, [1977] 1 WLR 766, CA. Cf *A-G v Observer Ltd* [1990] 1 AC 109, sub nom *A-G v Guardian Newspapers Ltd (No 2)* [1988] 3 All ER 545, HL (a case in which the court found that a threat to national security from publication of material already published elsewhere in the world had not been made out on the evidence before it). See also *R v Jones* [2006] UKHL 16, [2007] 1 AC 136, [2006] 2 All ER 741; *R (on the application of the Campaign for Nuclear Disarmament) v Prime Minister* [2002] EWHC 2777 (Admin), [2003] 3 LRC 335 (the Divisional Court could not consider whether it would be a breach of international law for the United Kingdom to engage in military action in Iraq without a further United Nations resolution); *R (on the application of Marchiori) v Environment Agency* [2001] EWCA Civ 03, [2002] All ER (D) 220 (Jan) (courts will not review the merits of the possession of nuclear weapons).

14 *Gouriet v Union of Office Workers* [1978] AC 435, [1977] 3 All ER 70, HL; *Mohit v DPP of Mauritius* [2006] UKPC 20, [2006] 1 WLR 3343. As to the Attorney-General see CONSTITUTIONAL LAW AND HUMAN RIGHTS vol 8(2) (Reissue) PARA 529.

15 *Leech v Deputy Governor of Parkhurst Prison* [1988] AC 533, [1988] 1 All ER 485, HL (extent of judicial review of prison governor's decisions); *R v Lord Chancellor, ex p Hibbit and Saunders (a firm)* [1993] COD 326, (1993) Times, 12 March, DC (no challenge to the process by which the Lord Chancellor considered tenders for court reporting services; the process of entering into commercial contracts lacked a public law element (in the absence of any challenge to the policy decision to seek tenders or allegation of bad faith or malice) and the exercise of the function was not pursuant to any statutory power); cf *R v British Coal Corpn, ex p Vardy* [1993] ICR 720 at 751, [1993] IRLR 104 at 116, DC, per Glidewell LJ (decision to close coal pits amenable to review because such decisions governed by a statutory machinery; decision in *R v National Coal Board, ex p National Union of Mineworkers* [1986] ICR 791 in which it had been held that the decision to close pits was purely managerial and so not subject to judicial review doubted). See also *R (on the application of Tucker) v Director General of the National Crime Squad* [2003] EWCA Civ 57, [2003] ICR 599, [2003] IRLR 439 (decision to terminate secondment of police officer to the national crime squad a purely managerial decision lacking the necessary public law element to make the decision amenable to judicial review). See further PARAS 604, 617–623.

608. Judicial review of the Crown prerogative. The courts will review the exercise of the Crown's prerogative powers to the extent that such powers are justiciable[1]. The exercise of the prerogative may be reviewed on grounds similar to those on which the exercise of statutory powers is reviewed, namely for illegality[2], irrationality[3] or procedural impropriety[4]. However, many prerogative powers are not justiciable and so are not subject to judicial review[5].

Whether the exercise of a prerogative power can be challenged depends upon the subject matter of the prerogative power which is exercised[6]. If the subject matter in respect of which the prerogative power is exercised is a matter upon which the court can adjudicate then the exercise of that power is subject to review in accordance with the principles developed in respect of the review of statutory powers[7]. It is a question for determination on a case by case basis whether or not a particular prerogative power is amenable to review. This will depend on whether the courts are qualified to deal with the subject matter or whether the decision involves such questions of policy that the court is ill-equipped to do so[8]. Prerogative powers such as those relating to the defence of the realm, and conduct by the government of foreign policy and relations with other states (including the making of treaties) are not subject to judicial review[9]. Prerogative powers relating to the formulation of the criteria for the exercise of the prerogative of mercy by the grant of a free pardon, the grant of honours, the dissolution of Parliament and the appointment of ministers are probably not susceptible to judicial review because their nature and subject matter are such as not to be amenable to the judicial process[10]. The court may also define the extent of the prerogative having regard to the extent to which statute curtails the ambit of prerogative power[11].

1   *Council of Civil Service Unions v Minister for the Civil Service* [1985] AC 374 at 407, [1984] 3 All ER 935 at 948, HL, per Lord Scarman, at 409–411 and 950–951 per Lord Diplock and at 417–418 and 955–956 per Lord Roskill (all obiter); *R v Criminal Injuries Compensation Board, ex p Lain* [1967] 2 QB 864, [1967] 2 All ER 770, DC; *R v Civil Service Appeal Board, ex p Bruce* [1988] 3 All ER 686, [1988] ICR 649, DC; *R v Secretary of State for Foreign and Commonwealth Affairs, ex p Everett* [1989] QB 811, [1989] 1 All ER 655, CA (review of the prerogative in relation to the issuing of passports; cf *Secretary of State for the Home Department v Lakdawalla* [1970] Imm AR 26). See also *Chandler v DPP* [1964] AC 763 at 809–810, [1962] 3 All ER 142 at 157–158, HL, per Lord Devlin; and *Laker Airways Ltd v Department of Trade* [1977] QB 643 at 705–706, [1977] 2 All ER 182 at 192, CA, per Lord Denning MR (a minority view on this point and an approach criticised as far too wide in *Council of Civil Service Unions v Minister for the Civil Service* at 416 and 955 per Lord Roskill); cf *R v Panel on Take-overs and Mergers, ex p Datafin plc* [1987] QB 815, [1987] 1 All ER 564, CA (the nature of a power, rather than its source alone, may in some cases determine its reviewability by the courts); *Gillick v West Norfolk and Wisbech Area Health Authority* [1986] AC 112 at 192–194, [1985] 3 All ER 402 at 426–427, HL, per Lord Bridge of Harwich, and at 206 and 436 per Lord Templeman (the courts may review the correctness of guidance given by a public authority even where that guidance is not issued in the performance of a statutory discretion), but see at 163 and 405 per Lord Fraser of Tullybelton, and at 177, 181 and 415, 418 per Lord Scarman; *R v Norfolk County Council, ex p M* [1989] QB 619, [1989] 2 All ER 359 (review of entry in child abuse register established without statutory authority pursuant to Department of Health and Social Security circulars); *R v Secretary of State for the Environment, ex p Greenwich London Borough Council* [1989] COD 530, (1989) Times, 17 May, DC (dissemination of information by government department not pursuant to any specific statutory authority); *R v Criminal Injuries Compensation Board, ex p P* [1995] 1 All ER 870 at 880, [1995] 1 WLR 845 at 855, CA, per Neill LJ ('if a question arises as to the legality of any action taken by the Executive the court as a general rule has jurisdiction to entertain the question, unless the court's powers in this regard have been removed or restricted by Parliament'); *R v Secretary of State for the Home Department, ex p Bentley* [1994] QB 349, [1993] 4 All ER 442, DC (criteria for the exercise of the prerogative of mercy not amenable to judicial review, but the court could review the refusal to grant mercy on the basis that the minister had failed to appreciate the full extent of his powers); *R v Ministry of Defence, ex p Smith* [1996] QB 517 at 539, [1995] 4 All ER 427 at 446, DC, per Simon Brown LJ (challenge to the Ministry of Defence's policy excluding homosexuals from the armed forces; 'only the rarest cases will today be ruled strictly beyond the court's purview—only cases involving national security properly so called and where in addition the courts really do lack the expertise or material to form a judgment on the point at issue'). See also *R (on the application of Abbasi) v Secretary of State for Foreign and Commonwealth Affairs* [2002] EWCA Civ 1598, [2003] 3 LRC 297.
     It is well established that the courts will determine whether a prerogative exists (*Prohibitions del Roy* (1607) 12 Co Rep 63; *Proclamations' Case* (1611) 12 Co Rep 74; *A-G v De Keyser's Royal Hotel Ltd* [1920] AC 508, HL); or whether statute has circumscribed the exercise of the prerogative (see *R v Secretary of State for the Home Department, ex p Fire Brigades Union* [1995] 2 AC 513, [1995] 2 All ER 244, HL). See further CONSTITUTIONAL LAW AND HUMAN RIGHTS vol 8(2) (Reissue) PARA 7. As to justiciability see PARA 607.
2   *Council of Civil Service Unions v Minister for the Civil Service* [1985] AC 374 at 411, [1984] 3 All ER 935 at 951, HL, per Lord Diplock, at 414, 417 and 953–954, 955–956 per Lord Roskill (as, for example, where the authority purports to exercise a power which in law it does not possess) and at 407 and 948 per Lord Scarman; *R (on the application of Bancoult) v Secretary of State for Foreign and Commonwealth Affairs* [2008] UKHL 61, [2009] 1 AC 453, [2008] 4 All ER 1055. See eg *Proclamations' Case* (1611) 12 Co Rep 74; *Re Lord Bishop of Natal* (1864) 3 Moo PCC NS 115; *A-G v De Keyser's Royal Hotel Ltd* [1920] AC 508, HL; *Burmah Oil Co (Burma Trading) Ltd v Lord Advocate* [1965] AC 75, [1964] 2 All ER 348, HL;

Universities of Oxford and Cambridge v Eyre and Spottiswoode Ltd [1964] Ch 736, [1963] 3 All ER 289. See also PARA 612; and CONSTITUTIONAL LAW AND HUMAN RIGHTS vol 8(2) (Reissue) PARA 6.

3   Ie on the basis of the principles in *Associated Provincial Picture Houses Ltd v Wednesbury Corpn* [1948] 1 KB 223, [1947] 2 All ER 680, CA. See *Council of Civil Service Unions v Minister for the Civil Service* [1985] AC 374 at 410–412, [1984] 3 All ER 935 at 951–952, HL, per Lord Diplock (although the scope for judicial review of an exercise of the prerogative on this ground is limited: see at 412 and 952), at 414, 417 and 953, 955–956 per Lord Roskill and at 407 and 948 per Lord Scarman. See PARAS 617–624.

4   Also referred to as breach of the principles of natural justice. See note 3. See also *R v Secretary of State for Foreign and Commonwealth Affairs, ex p Everett* [1989] QB 811, [1989] 1 All ER 655, CA; and PARA 625 et seq.

5   See PARA 607.

6   *Council of Civil Service Unions v Minister for the Civil Service* [1985] AC 374 at 418, [1984] 3 All ER 935 at 956, HL, per Lord Roskill; *R (on the application of Abbasi) v Secretary of State for Foreign and Commonwealth Affairs* [2002] EWCA Civ 1598, [2003] 3 LRC 297 at [85] per Lord Phillips MR giving the judgment of the court; *R (on the application of Bancoult) v Secretary of State for Foreign and Commonwealth Affairs* [2008] UKHL 61, [2009] 1 AC 453, [2008] 4 All ER 1055.

7   *Council of Civil Service Unions v Minister for the Civil Service* [1985] AC 374 at 407, [1984] 3 All ER 935 at 948, HL, per Lord Scarman; *R (on the application of Bancoult) v Secretary of State for Foreign and Commonwealth Affairs* [2008] UKHL 61, [2009] 1 AC 453, [2008] 4 All ER 1055.

8   *R v Secretary of State for the Home Department, ex p Bentley* [1994] QB 349 at 363, DC, per Watkins LJ.

9   *Council of Civil Service Unions v Minister for the Civil Service* [1985] AC 374 at 418, [1984] 3 All ER 935 at 956, HL, per Lord Roskill. The power to make treaties is not amenable to challenge in an English court: *Blackburn v A-G* [1971] 2 All ER 1380, [1971] 1 WLR 1037, CA; *Ex p Molyneaux* [1986] 1 WLR 331; *JH Rayner (Mincing Lane) Ltd v Department of Trade and Industry* [1990] 2 AC 418 at 476, sub nom *Maclaine Watson & Co Ltd v Department of Trade and Industry* [1989] 2 All ER 523 at 526, HL, per Lord Templeman and at 499 and 544 per Lord Oliver of Aylmerton; *R v Secretary of State for Foreign and Commonwealth Affairs, ex p Rees-Mogg* [1994] QB 552, [1994] 1 All ER 457, DC (the court had no jurisdiction to consider the decision of the United Kingdom to ratify the Treaty Establishing the European Community (Rome, 25 March 1957; TS 1 (1973); Cmnd 5179)); *R (on the application of Wheeler) v Office of the Prime Minister* [2008] EWHC 1409 (Admin), [2008] All ER (D) 333 (Jun) (the court doubted that the question of whether two treaties, the Constitutional Treaty and the Treaty of Lisbon, both concerned with reforms to the European Union, were materially similar was a justiciable issue for the courts to determine, as such a question depended on matters of political judgment and perspective).

See also *R (on the application of the Campaign for Nuclear Disarmament) v Prime Minister* [2002] EWHC 2777 (Admin), [2003] 3 LRC 335 (the Divisional Court could not consider whether it would be a breach of international law for the United Kingdom to engage in military action in Iraq without a further United Nations resolution) and *R (on the application of Al-Rawi) v Secretary of State for Foreign and Commonwealth Affairs* [2006] EWCA Civ 1279, [2008] QB 289, [2007] 2 WLR 1219; *R (on the application of Marchiori) v Environment Agency* [2001] EWCA Civ 3, [2002] All ER (D) 220 (Jan) (courts will not review the merits of the possession of nuclear weapons); *R v Jones* [2006] UKHL 16, [2007] 1 AC 136, [2006] 2 All ER 741. But see *R (on the application of Abbasi) v Secretary of State for Foreign and Commonwealth Affairs* [2002] EWCA Civ 1598, [2003] 3 LRC 297, where the court held that judicial review is available to ensure that a person's legitimate expectation that the government would at least consider whether to make representations to a foreign state if that state was apparently violating his human rights; while recognising that the decision whether to make such representations and whether any foreign policy considerations outweighed the interests of the government were ultimately matters for the Secretary of State).

See also *R v Director of Government Communications Headquarters, ex p Hodges* (1988) Times, 26 July, DC (the question whether an individual's positive vetting clearance should be removed was a matter to be decided with reference to national security interests and as such was not a matter the courts were entitled to look into). See *Ex p Molyneaux* [1986] 1 WLR 331 at 336 per Taylor J (establishment of inter-governmental conference concerned with Northern Ireland and relations between the two parts of Ireland by an agreement which was akin to a treaty and, accordingly, it was not the function of the court to inquire into the exercise of the prerogative in either entering into or implementing the agreement). But see the decision of the Supreme Court of Canada in *Operation Dismantle et al v R* (1985) 18 DLR (4th) 481, SC Canada.

10 In *R v Secretary of State for the Home Department, ex p Bentley* [1994] QB 349, [1993] 4 All ER 442, DC, the court accepted that it was probably right to say that the formulation of criteria for the exercise of the prerogative of mercy by the grant of a free pardon was entirely a matter of policy and not justiciable. However, the Secretary of State's decision was capable of review on the grounds that he had failed to recognise that the prerogative of mercy was capable of being exercised in many different circumstances over a wide range and had therefore failed to consider the form of pardon which might be appropriate. Thus the court did not review the exercise of the prerogative. Rather it reviewed the decision of the Secretary of State on the basis that he had failed to appreciate the full extent of his powers.

  See also *R (on the application of Page) v Secretary of State for Justice* [2007] EWHC 2026 (Admin); *R (on the application of Shields) v Secretary of State for Justice* [2008] EWHC 3102 (Admin), [2009] 3 All ER 265, [2009] 3 WLR 765.

  However, the refusal to issue a passport is amenable to judicial review: *R v Secretary of State for Foreign and Commonwealth Affairs, ex p Everett* [1989] QB 811, [1989] 1 All ER 655, [1989] 2 WLR 224, CA. So too is the prerogative power to regulate the civil service: see *Council of Civil Service Unions v Minister for the Civil Service* [1985] AC 374, [1984] 3 All ER 935, HL.

11 *A-G v De Keyser's Royal Hotel Ltd* [1920] AC 508, HL; *R v Secretary of State for the Home Department, ex p Fire Brigades Union* [1995] 2 AC 513 at 552, 554, [1995] 2 All ER 244 at 254, 255, HL, per Lord Browne-Wilkinson. In the latter case, Parliament had enacted a new scheme for criminal injuries compensation which the Secretary of State was empowered to bring into effect. Lord Browne-Wilkinson held that in those circumstances the Secretary of State could not lawfully use the prerogative to introduce a scheme different to that approved by Parliament. Such action was an abuse of the prerogative power.

609.   Challenges to delegated legislation and byelaws. There can be no challenge in the courts to an Act of Parliament[1] otherwise than by an application alleging that the Act is inconsistent with European Union law[2] or seeking a declaration that the Act is incompatible with the Convention for the Protection of Human Rights and Fundamental Freedoms[3]. However, delegated legislation[4] and byelaws[5] may be attacked, either directly[6] or collaterally[7]. The grounds of challenge may be that the making of the instrument in question was not intra vires the relevant enabling power[8]; or that the correct procedure for making it was not followed[9]; or that it is repugnant to the enabling legislation[10] or to the general law[11]; or that it is bad for uncertainty[12]. It may also be alleged that the discretion involved in making the relevant statutory instrument or byelaw was abused, for example because the authority allowed its discretion to be fettered[13], or on grounds of unreasonableness[14]. But the fact that delegated legislation has been approved by Parliament means that the court will be reluctant to strike it down on this ground[15]. Where the court has a discretion as to whether to grant relief[16], it has been suggested that, whereas an administrative act performed in excess or abuse of power will normally be struck down[17], a statutory instrument ought only to be quashed where special circumstances make it desirable to do so[18]. However, the courts have recently taken a different approach and held that delegated legislation does not have a specially protected position[19]. It may be possible to sever the invalid portion of a statutory instrument or byelaw and thereby uphold the remainder[20].

1 See eg *British Railways Board v Pickin* [1974] AC 765, [1974] 1 All ER 609, HL; and STATUTES vol 44(1) (Reissue) PARA 1256. In *R (on the application of Jackson) v A-G* [2005] UKHL 56, [2006] 1 AC 262, [2005] 4 All ER 1253, the House of Lords rejected the suggestion that legislation enacted in accordance with the Parliament Act 1911 was a form of delegated legislation and amenable to judicial review. Rather, the House of Lords held that such Acts are primary legislation and the courts cannot hold such Acts of Parliament to be invalid.

2 For a case in which a declaration was granted that an Act was incompatible with European Community law see *R v Secretary of State for Employment, ex p Equal Opportunities Commission* [1995] 1 AC 1, sub nom *Equal Opportunities Commission v Secretary of State for Employment* [1994] 1 All ER 910, HL. However, there is no power to grant an injunction (whether interim or final) declaring that an Act of Parliament is not the law until some unspecified future date: see *R v Secretary of State for Transport, ex p Factortame Ltd* [1990] 2 AC 85, sub nom *Factortame Ltd v Secretary of State for Transport* [1989] 2 All ER 692, HL. See also *Re M* [1994] 1 AC 377, sub nom *M v Home Office* [1993] 3 All ER 537, HL.

3 Ie the Convention for the Protection of Human Rights and Fundamental Freedoms (Rome, 4 November 1950; TS 71 (1953) Cmd 8969). The power to grant a declaration that primary legislation is incompatible with the Convention is contained in the Human Rights Act 1998 s 4. Only the higher courts are empowered to grant such a declaration: see s 4. The grant of the declaration does not affect the validity, continuing operation or enforcement of the legislation whether passed before or after the coming into force of the Human Rights Act 1998 on 2 October 2000: see s 3(2)(b). See further CONSTITUTIONAL LAW AND HUMAN RIGHTS.

4 As to delegated legislation generally see STATUTES vol 44(1) (Reissue) PARA 1428.

5 As to byelaws generally see CORPORATIONS vol 9(2) (2006 Reissue) PARA 1187; LOCAL GOVERNMENT vol 69 (2009) PARA 553.

6 There is a presumption of regularity (*omnia praesumuntur rite esse acta*), and the burden of proof is therefore upon the party seeking to challenge the instrument: *McEldowney v Forde* [1971] AC 632, [1969] 2 All ER 1039, HL; *Corfield v Bugg* (1987) Independent, 14 January, DC; *Boddington v British Transport Police* [1999] 2 AC 143 at 155, 162, [1998] 2 All ER 203 at 210, 217, HL, per Lord Irvine of Lairg LC. The Human Rights Act 1998 empowers the higher courts to declare that subordinate legislation is incompatible with the Convention for the Protection of Human Rights and Fundamental Freedoms (1950): see the Human Rights Act 1998 s 4(4). However, subordinate legislation which is intra vires the primary legislation pursuant to which it is made remains enforceable even where it is declared to be incompatible with the Convention: see the Human Rights Act 1998 s 3(2)(c). See further CONSTITUTIONAL LAW AND HUMAN RIGHTS.

7 For the jurisdiction of magistrates to rule on the validity of a byelaw see *Boddington v British Transport Police* [1999] 2 AC 143, [1998] 2 All ER 203, HL, and the explanation therein of the decisions in *R v Crown Court at Reading, ex p Hutchinson* [1988] QB 384, [1988] 1 All ER 333, DC; and *Quietlynn Ltd v Portsmouth City Council* [1988] QB 114, [1987] 2 All ER 1040, DC.

8 See eg *R v Secretary of State for the Home Department, ex p Leech* [1994] QB 198, [1993] 4 All ER 539, CA (Prison Rules 1964, SI 1964/388 (now revoked)); *R v Secretary of State for the Home Department, ex p Saleem* [2000] 4 All ER 814, [2001] 1 WLR 443, CA (Asylum Appeals (Procedure) Rules 1996, SI 1996/2070 (now revoked)); *Hotel and Catering Industry Training Board v Automobile Proprietary Ltd* [1969] 2 All ER 582, [1969] 1 WLR 697, HL; *R v Customs and Excise Comrs, ex p Hedges & Butler Ltd* [1986] 2 All ER 164, DC. The modern practice is to apply the maxim *ut res magis valeat quam pereat* and to seek a benevolent construction which will bring the instrument within the enabling power: *Cinnamond v British Airports Authority* [1980] 2 All ER 368 at 373–374, [1980] 1 WLR 582 at 589, CA, per Lord Denning MR; *Lewis v Dyfed County Council* (1978) 77 LGR 339 at 346, CA. It is not clear to what extent there can be implied into a statute the power to make delegated legislation: contrast *Wansbeck District Council v Charlton* (1981) 79 LGR 523, CA (reference in Act to form of notice implies power in Secretary of State to prescribe form) with dicta of the House of Lords in *A-G for Northern Ireland's Reference (No 1 of 1975)* [1977] AC 105 at 142–143, [1976] 2 All ER 937 at 951, HL, per Viscount Dilhorne and at 150 and 957 per Lord Simon of Glaisdale (but cf Lord Diplock at 131 and 942). Where subordinate legislation is validly made by a statutory authority, it continues in force notwithstanding any change in the identity of that authority: *Wiseman v Canterbury Bye-Products Co Ltd* [1983] 2 AC 685 at 693, [1983] 3 WLR 116 at 122, PC.

9 This might result from, for example, a failure to consult (*Agricultural, Horticultural and Forestry Industry Training Board v Aylesbury Mushrooms Ltd* [1972] 1 All ER 280, [1972] 1 WLR 190; *R v Secretary of State for Social Services, ex p Association of Metropolitan Authorities* [1986] 1 All ER 164, [1986] 1 WLR 1), or from a failure to lay before Parliament as required (see ADMINISTRATIVE LAW vol 1(1) (2001 Reissue) PARA 35), or from a failure to comply with requirements as to publication (see STATUTES vol 44(1) (Reissue) PARA 1248 et seq). See also *R (on the application of C) v Secretary of State for Justice* [2008] EWCA Civ 882, [2009] QB 657, [2009] 2 WLR 1039, where a statutory instrument was quashed because of a failure to produce a race equality impact assessment prior to laying the statutory instrument before Parliament.

Where a statutory instrument incorporates another document by reference, that document does not form part of the instrument so as to fall within any requirement that it should be laid before Parliament, and any controls over this practice are a matter for Parliament itself and not the courts: *R v Secretary of State for Social Services, ex p Camden London Borough Council* [1987] 2 All ER 560, [1987] 1 WLR 819, CA; see also *Corfield v Bugg* (1987) Independent, 14 January, DC. As to the meaning of 'laying' see *R v Immigration Appeal Tribunal, ex p Joyles* [1972] 3 All ER 213, [1972] 1 WLR 1390, DC. In *Burnley Borough Council v England* (1978) 77 LGR 227 the court appears to have accepted in principle (whilst rejecting on the facts) the argument that a byelaw requiring the minister's approval could be challenged if that approval had resulted from mistake or misrepresentation.

10 See *Utah Construction & Engineering Pty Ltd v Pataky* [1966] AC 629, [1965] 3 All ER 650, PC; *Daymond v South West Water Authority* [1976] AC 609, [1976] 1 All ER 39, HL.

11 See eg *Powell v May* [1946] KB 330, [1946] 1 All ER 444, DC; *Mixnam's Properties Ltd v Chertsey UDC* [1964] 1 QB 214 at 238, [1963] 2 All ER 787 at 799, CA (affd [1965] AC 735, [1964] 2 All ER 627, HL); *Re Grosvenor Hotel, London (No 2)* [1965] Ch 1210 at 1243, [1964] 3 All ER 354 at 360, CA, per Lord Denning MR (cf *Comfort Hotels Ltd v Wembley Stadium Ltd* [1988] 3 All ER 53, [1988] 1 WLR 872); *Ward v James* [1966] 1 QB 273, [1965] 1 All ER 568, CA. Where there is a general power to make regulations dealing with a particular matter, there will not be implied a qualification that they should follow existing general principles to be found in the law dealing with that subject: *Milford Haven Conservancy Board v IRC* [1976] 3 All ER 263, 74 LGR 449, CA (assessment of rateable value). However, delegated legislation may not deprive a person of fundamental constitutional rights, such as the right of access to the court, unless made pursuant to primary legislation which specifically provides for the abrogation of that right: *R v Lord Chancellor, ex p Witham* [1998] QB 575, [1997] 2 All ER 779, DC; cf *R v Lord Chancellor, ex p Lightfoot* [2000] QB 597, [1999] 4 All ER 583, CA; *R v Secretary of State for the Home Department, ex p Saleem* [2000] 4 All ER 814, CA. Inconsistency with European Union law may also provide a ground of challenge in certain cases: see Case 63/83 *R v Kirk* [1985] 1 All ER 453, [1984] ECR 2689, ECJ; *Brown v Secretary of State for Scotland* [1988] 2 CMLR 836, Ct of Sess; *R v Secretary of State for Employment, ex p Equal Opportunities Commission* [1995] 1 AC 1, sub nom *Equal Opportunities Commission v Secretary of State for Employment* [1994] 1 All ER 910, HL (primary legislation). Incompatibility with the Convention for the Protection of Human Rights and Fundamental Freedoms (1950) also provides a basis for challenge in the form of a declaration of incompatibility: see the text and note 3.

12 See eg *Nash v Finlay* (1901) 85 LT 682; *Staden v Tarjanyi* (1980) 78 LGR 614 at 623, DC (person engaging in otherwise lawful pursuit entitled to know with reasonable certainty whether breaking law); see also *McEldowney v Forde* [1971] AC 632, [1969] 2 All ER 1039, HL. But a successful challenge on this ground will be unusual: *Staden v Tarjanyi* at 624 per Woolf J; and see *R v Secretary of State for Trade and Industry, ex p Kynaston Ford* (1985) 4 Tr L 150. Cf *R v Barnet London Borough Council, ex p Johnson* (1989) 88 LGR 73, (1989) Times, 26 April, DC.

13 See ADMINISTRATIVE LAW vol 1(1) (2001 Reissue) PARA 32; cf *Customs and Excise Comrs v Cure & Deeley Ltd* [1962] 1 QB 340, [1961] 3 All ER 641 (unlawful delegation).

14 *Kruse v Johnson* [1898] 2 QB 91, DC, referring to byelaws partial and unequal in their operation between different classes; or manifestly unjust; or disclosing bad faith; or involving oppressive or gratuitous interference with the rights of those subject to them. But this does not prevent the authority from balancing the rights of one class of persons against another: *Staden v Tarjanyi* (1980) 78 LGR 614, DC. The test to be applied is the normal *Wednesbury* test of reasonableness (see *Associated Provincial Picture Houses Ltd v Wednesbury Corpn* [1948] 1 KB 223, [1947] 2 All ER 680, CA; and PARA 617): *Belfast Corpn v Daly* [1963] NI 78 at 89; *Burnley Borough Council v England* (1978) 77 LGR 227. The better view is that this head of review is applicable to delegated legislation generally as well as to byelaws: *Mixnam's Properties Ltd v Chertsey UDC* [1964] 1 QB 214 at 237, [1963] 2 All ER 787 at 799, CA (affd [1965] AC 735, [1964] 2 All ER 627, HL); *Rajput v Immigration Appeal Tribunal* [1989] Imm AR 350, Independent, 8 February, CA; cf *Taylor v Brighton Borough Council* [1947] KB 736, [1947] 1 All ER 864, CA; *Fawcett Properties Ltd v Buckinghamshire County Council* [1961] AC 636 at 679, [1960] 3 All ER 503 at 518, HL, per Lord Denning.

15 *Sparks v Edward Ash Ltd* [1943] 1 KB 223, [1943] 1 All ER 1, CA; *McEldowney v Forde* [1971] AC 632, [1969] 2 All ER 1039, HL; *Nottinghamshire County Council v Secretary of State for the Environment* [1986] AC 240, [1986] 1 All ER 199, HL; see also *DPP v Hutchinson and Smith* [1989] QB 583, [1989] 1 All ER 1060, DC. But the mere fact of parliamentary approval does not confer immunity from challenge: *Hoffman-La Roche & Co AG v Secretary of State for Trade and Industry* [1975] AC 295, [1974] 2 All ER 1128, HL; *R v HM Treasury, ex p Smedley* [1985] QB 657, [1985] 1 All ER 589, CA.

16 That is, in granting a declaration or injunction or in allowing any of the prerogative orders. See PARA 687 et seq.

17 *Grunwick Processing Laboratories Ltd v Advisory, Conciliation and Arbitration Service* [1978] AC 655 at 695, [1978] 1 All ER 338 at 364, HL, per Lord Diplock.

18 *R v Secretary of State for Social Services, ex p Association of Metropolitan Authorities* [1986] 1 All ER 164 at 175–176, [1986] 1 WLR 1 at 14–16 per Webster J. A declaration may be preferable to striking down the regulations: see *R v Secretary of State for Social Services, ex p Association of Metropolitan Authorities* [1986] 1 All ER 164, [1986] 1 WLR 1. If regulations are struck down as being ultra vires, this cannot result in the revival of the predecessor regulations: *R v Immigration Appeal Tribunal, ex p Ruhul Amin* [1987] 3 All ER 705 at 713, [1987] 1 WLR 1538 at 1549, CA, per Slade LJ.

19 *R (on the application of C) v Secretary of State for Justice* [2008] EWCA Civ 882, [2009] QB 657 at [41]–[42], [2009] 2 WLR 1039 at [41]–[42] per Buxton LJ ('the imperative that public life should be conducted lawfully suggests that it is more important to correct unlawful legislation ... than it is to correct a single decision that affects only a limited range of people').

20 *DPP v Hutchinson* [1990] 2 AC 783, [1990] 2 All ER 836, HL. See e g *Strickland v Hayes* [1896] 1 QB 290, DC; *Thomas v A-G of Trinidad and Tobago* [1982] AC 113, [1981] 3 WLR 601, PC; *R v Secretary of State for Transport, ex p GLC* [1986] QB 556, [1985] 3 All ER 300; c f *Port Swettenham Authority v TW Wu and Co (M) Sdn Bhd* [1979] AC 580 at 592, [1978] 3 All ER 337 at 342, PC. The question is whether or not the valid portion is inextricably interconnected with the valid: *Dunkley v Evans* [1981] 3 All ER 285, [1981] 1 WLR 1522, DC. The strict 'blue pencil' approach applied to questions of severability in private law is not appropriate here: *Thames Water Authority v Elmbridge Borough Council* [1983] QB 570, [1983] 1 All ER 836, CA; *R v Secretary of State for Transport, ex p GLC; DPP v Hutchinson and Smith* [1989] QB 583, [1989] 1 All ER 1060, DC (conviction upheld where clear that maker of byelaw would have given effect to statutory limitation if had been aware of it, and that byelaw would still have caught present defendants). As to severability generally see ADMINISTRATIVE LAW vol 1(1) (2001 Reissue) PARA 25.

2. SUBSTANTIVE GROUNDS FOR JUDICIAL REVIEW

(1) ULTRA VIRES AND ILLEGALITY

610. Jurisdiction and vires in general. The courts will intervene to ensure that the powers of public decision-making bodies[1] are exercised lawfully[2]. Such a body will not act lawfully if it acts ultra vires[3] or outside the limits of its jurisdiction. The term 'jurisdiction' has been used by the courts in different senses[4]. A body will lack jurisdiction in the narrow sense[5] if it has no power to adjudicate upon the dispute, or to make the kind of decision or order, in question; it will lack jurisdiction in the wide sense[6] if, having power to adjudicate upon the dispute, it abuses its power[7], acts in a manner which is procedurally irregular[8], or, in a *Wednesbury*[9] sense, unreasonable[10], or commits any other error of law[11]. In certain exceptional cases, the distinction between errors of law which go to jurisdiction in the narrow sense and other errors of law remains important[12].

A body which acts without jurisdiction in the narrow or wide sense may also be described as acting outside its powers or ultra vires. If a body arrives at a decision which is within its jurisdiction in the narrow sense, and does not commit any of the errors which go to jurisdiction in the wide sense, the court will not quash its decision on an application for judicial review even if it considers the decision to be wrong[13].

There is a presumption that the acts of public bodies, such as orders, decisions and byelaws, are lawful and valid until declared otherwise by the court[14]. Although some acts or measures may be described as being 'void ab initio' or as 'nullities'[15], the modern view is that it is for the court to determine both whether an act is unlawful and what the consequences of that finding of unlawfulness should be[16].

1   Ie such as inferior courts, administrative tribunals and bodies exercising statutory powers or otherwise carrying out public functions: see PARA 604.

2   This is the fundamental principle of judicial review: *R v Lord President of the Privy Council, ex p Page* [1993] AC 682 at 701, HL, per Lord Browne-Wilkinson; *R v Visitors to the Inns of Court, ex p Calder* [1994] QB 1 at 37, CA, per Sir Donald Nicholls V-C.

3   Ultra vires means outside the powers. It is a concept borrowed by public law from company law in the 19th century (see *R (on the application of Bancoult) v Secretary of State for Foreign and Commonwealth Affairs* [2007] EWCA Civ 498 at [59], [2008] QB 365 at [59], [2007] 3 WLR 768 at [59] per Sedley LJ, overruled on other grounds [2008] UKHL 61, [2009] 1 AC 453, [2008] 4 All ER 1055). In company law powers are spelt out in articles of association and acts can be measured against them. The doctrine of ultra vires has been described as the juristic or constitutional basis for judicial review. In the case of bodies exercising statutory powers, the underlying principle is that the powers may only be exercised in the way in which Parliament intended, and it is presumed that Parliament must have intended those powers to be exercised lawfully. Any legislation, act or decision may be described as ultra vires if it is incompatible with the limits imposed by a superior element of the law, for example primary legislation may be ultra vires EC legislation, subordinate legislation may be ultra vires primary legislation and decisions made by public bodies may be ultra vires any of the superior forms of law. See generally: *R v Lord President of the Privy Council, ex p Page* [1993] AC 682 at 701, sub nom *Page v Hull University Visitor* [1993] 1 All ER 97 at 107, HL, per Lord Browne-Wilkinson; *Anisminic Ltd v Foreign Compensation Commission* [1969] 2 AC 147 at 171, [1969] 1 All ER 208 at 214, HL, per Lord Reid; *O'Reilly v Mackman* [1983] 2 AC 237 at 278, [1982] 3 All ER 1124 at 1128, HL, per Lord Diplock; *R v Secretary of State for the Home Department, ex p Brind* [1991] 1 AC 696 at 755, sub nom *Brind v Secretary of State for the Home Department* [1991] 1 All ER 720 at 729, HL, per Lord Ackner; *Hazell v Hammersmith and Fulham London Borough Council* [1992] 2 AC 1 at 22, 29, [1991] 1 All ER 545 at 548, 554, HL, per Lord Templeman; *Boddington v British Transport Police* [1999] 2 AC 143 at 164, [1998] 2 All ER 203 at 218, HL, per Lord Browne-Wilkinson, and at 171 and 225 per

Lord Steyn; *R v Secretary of State for Social Security, ex p Joint Council for the Welfare of Immigrants* [1996] 4 All ER 385, [1997] 1 WLR 275 at 293, CA, per Waite LJ. It is often said that 'ultra vires' is the unifying theme in public law and that all grounds of review are ultimately concerned with vires: see eg *R v Lord President of the Privy Council, ex p Page* [1993] AC 682 at 701, sub nom *Page v Hull University Visitor* [1993] 1 All ER 97 at 107, HL, per Lord Browne-Wilkinson; *R v Wicks* [1998] AC 92 at 105, [1997] 2 All ER 801 at 804–805, HL, per Lord Nicholls of Birkenhead; *Credit Suisse v Allerdale Borough Council* [1997] QB 306 at 352, [1996] 4 All ER 129 at 167, CA, per Hobhouse LJ; and *Boddington v British Transport Police* [1999] 2 AC 143 at 164, [1998] 2 All ER 203 at 218 per Lord Browne-Wilkinson, and at 171–172 and 225 per Lord Steyn.

4   See *In Re McC (A Minor)* [1985] AC 528 at 536, sub nom *McC v Mullan* [1984] 3 All ER 908 at 912, HL (NI), per Lord Bridge (few words in common usage in the law have been used with so many different shades of meaning in different contexts or have so freely acquired new meanings); and *R v Bedwellty Justices, ex p Williams* [1997] AC 225 at 232, sub nom *Williams v Bedwellty Justices* [1996] 3 All ER 737 at 742, HL, per Lord Cooke of Thorndon.

5   *Anisminic Ltd v Foreign Compensation Commission* [1969] 2 AC 147 at 171, [1969] 1 All ER 208 at 214, HL, per Lord Reid (the term 'jurisdiction' should only be used in the narrow sense of power to enter upon the inquiry in question); *R v Lord President of the Privy Council, ex p Page* [1993] AC 682 at 701, sub nom *Page v Hull University Visitor* [1993] 1 All ER 97 at 107, HL, per Lord Browne-Wilkinson; *R v Secretary of State for the Home Department, ex p Malhi* [1991] 1 QB 194 at 207–208, [1990] 2 WLR 932 at 939–940, CA, per Mustill LJ (narrow and wide sense of the term 'power'); *R (on the application of Strickson) v Preston County Court* [2007] EWCA Civ 1132 at [26], [2008] All ER (D) 269 (Feb) at [26] per Laws LJ (the narrower pre-*Anisminic* sense of jurisdiction refers to the decision-maker's right to embark upon the question in hand at all, ie what might be called the condition precedent for its having any jurisdiction in the matter). See also PARA 611.

6   See the examples of errors given in *Anisminic Ltd v Foreign Compensation Commission* [1969] 2 AC 147 at 171, [1969] 1 All ER 208 at 214, HL, per Lord Reid.

7   Eg by acting in bad faith (see PARA 621) or for an improper purpose (see PARA 622).

8   See PARA 625 et seq.

9   See *Associated Provincial Picture Houses Ltd v Wednesbury Corpn* [1948] 1 KB 223, [1947] 2 All ER 680, CA.

10   See PARA 617.

11   Eg by asking itself the wrong question, or failing to take into account relevant, or taking into account irrelevant, considerations: see further PARA 623. In the past, a distinction was drawn between errors of law within jurisdiction, errors of law which went to jurisdiction, and errors of law on the face of the record: see eg *R v Governor of Brixton Prison, ex p Armah* [1968] AC 192 at 234, HL, per Lord Reid (if a magistrate or any other tribunal has jurisdiction to decide a particular issue, and there is no irregularity in the procedure, he does not destroy his jurisdiction by reaching a wrong decision; if he has jurisdiction to make a right decision, he has jurisdiction to make a wrong decision); and *R v Northumberland Compensation Appeal Tribunal, ex p Shaw* [1952] 1 KB 338, [1952] 1 All ER 122, CA. However, there is now a general (but rebuttable) presumption that no public decision-making body has jurisdiction to commit an error of law and the old law that held that only errors of law on the face of the record were amenable to judicial review has been rendered obsolete: see *Anisminic Ltd v Foreign Compensation Commission* [1969] 2 AC 147 at 174, [1969] 1 All ER 208 at 216, HL, per Lord Reid; *In re Racal Communications Ltd* [1981] AC 374 at 383, [1980] 2 All ER 634 at 638, HL, per Lord Diplock (the break-through made by *Anisminic Ltd v Foreign Compensation Commission* was that, as respects administrative tribunals and authorities, the old distinction between errors of law that went to jurisdiction and errors of law that did not, was for practical purposes abolished); *R v Lord President of the Privy Council, ex p Page* [1993] AC 682 at 696, 701–702, sub nom *Page v Hull University Visitor* [1993] 1 All ER 97 at 103, 107–108, HL, per Lord Browne-Wilkinson, at 693 and 100 per Lord Griffiths and at 706 and 111 per Lord Slynn of Hadley; *R v Bedwellty Justices, ex p Williams* [1997] AC 225 at 233, sub nom *Williams v Bedwellty Justices* [1996] 3 All ER 737 at 743, HL, per Lord Cooke of Thorndon; *Boddington v British Transport Police* [1999] 2 AC 143 at 154, [1998] 2 All ER 203 at 209, HL, per Lord Irvine of Lairg LC. See further PARAS 612, 616.

12   The exceptional cases are: (1) visitors to universities and other institutions applying non-domestic law (ie internal statutes or regulations) whose decisions have been held at common law to be final and conclusive and not reviewable by the courts; and (2) inferior courts of law in respect of which Parliament has provided that their decisions are to be final and conclusive. On an application for judicial review the court will quash the decisions of these bodies only on the ground that they have acted without jurisdiction in the narrow sense, abused

their power, or acted in breach of natural justice: see *R v Lord President of the Privy Council, ex p Page* [1993] AC 682 at 703–704, sub nom *Page v Hull University Visitor* [1993] 1 All ER 97 at 109, HL, per Lord Browne Wilkinson; *R v Bedwellty Justices, ex p Williams* [1997] AC 225 at 233, sub nom *Williams v Bedwellty Justices* [1996] 3 All ER 737 at 743, HL, per Lord Cooke of Thorndon; *Re Racal Communications Ltd* [1981] AC 374 at 383, [1980] 2 All ER 634 at 638, HL, per Lord Diplock (where Parliament conferred exclusive jurisdiction on inferior courts, no review for error of law within jurisdiction). For cases on visitors see: *R v Lord President of the Privy Council, ex p Page*; *R (on the application of Ferguson) v Visitor, University of Leicester* [2003] EWCA Civ 1082, [2003] ELR 562; *R v Visitors to the Inns of Court, ex p Calder* [1994] QB 1, [1993] 2 All ER 876, CA; *R v Committee of the Lords of the Judicial Committee of the Privy Council acting for the Visitor of the University of London, ex p Vijayatunga* [1988] QB 322, sub nom *R v University of London, ex p Vijayatunga* [1987] 3 All ER 204, DC; *R v Visitors to the Inns of Court, ex p Calder* [1994] QB 1, [1993] 2 All ER 876, CA. Compare also the approach to tribunals and persons fulfilling similar roles to visitors in other spheres, see eg *R (on the application of Siborurema) v Office of the Independent Adjudicator* [2007] EWCA Civ 1365, [2008] ELR 209 (Office of the Independent Adjudicator (OIA) that replaced the university visitor system amenable to judicial review; court cautioned against applying the old rules on visitors to the OIA, but nevertheless found that OIA has a broad discretion as to how it conducts its business and that a similar limited level of review would be appropriate), applied in *R (on the application of Arratoon) v Office of the Independent Adjudicator for Higher Education* [2008] EWHC 3125 (Admin), [2009] ELR 186; *R v Edmundsbury and Ipswich Diocese Chancellor, ex p White* [1948] 1 KB 195 at 219–220, [1947] 2 All ER 170 at 180, CA, per Evershed LJ (diocesan chancellor amenable to review only in narrow sense); *R v Chief Rabbi of the United Hebrew Congregations of Great Britain and the Commonwealth, ex p Wachmann* [1993] 2 All ER 249 at 254, [1992] 1 WLR 1036 at 1042 per Simon Brown J; *R v Charity Comrs for England and Wales, ex p Baldwin* (2001) 33 HLR 538. For cases on inferior courts or tribunals stipulated by Parliament to have final jurisdiction in respect of certain matters, see: *R v Wells Street Stipendiary Magistrate, ex p Seillon* [1978] 3 All ER 257, [1978] 1 WLR 1002, DC (High Court has no power to intervene in the conduct of committal proceedings by magistrates' court until magistrates have reached a determination that is reviewable); *R v Surrey Coroner, ex p Campbell* [1982] QB 661, [1982] 2 All ER 545, DC (where Parliament had provided for High Court review of coroner's decisions in only particular circumstances, the High Court's power to intervene in cases not provided for by Parliament limited to intervention on the 'narrow' jurisdictional sense); *R v Registrar of Companies, ex p Central Bank of India* [1986] QB 1114, [1986] 1 All ER 105, CA (limitations in Companies Act 1985 prevented review by High Court other than on 'narrow' jurisdictional grounds); *R v Preston Supplementary Benefits Appeal Tribunal, ex p Moore* [1975] 2 All ER 807, [1975] 1 WLR 624, CA. As to ouster clauses generally see MAGISTRATES vol 29(2) (Reissue) PARA 884.

13 See eg *Anisminic Ltd v Foreign Compensation Commission* [1969] 2 AC 147 at 171, [1969] 1 All ER 208 at 214, HL, per Lord Reid, explaining his dictum in *Armah v Government of Ghana* [1968] AC 192 at 234, [1966] 3 All ER 177 at 187, HL, that if a tribunal has jurisdiction to go right it has jurisdiction to go wrong, but providing always that it does not err in law. As to the distinction between appeal and review see PARA 602.

14 See eg *Smith v East Elloe RDC* [1956] AC 736 at 770, [1956] 1 All ER 855 at 872, HL, per Lord Radcliffe; *Boddington v British Transport Police* [1999] 2 AC 143 at 155, [1998] 2 All ER 203 at 210, HL, per Lord Irvine of Lairg LC; *Crédit Suisse v Allerdale Borough Council* [1997] QB 306 at 337–338, [1996] 4 All ER 129 at 153–154, CA, per Neill LJ; *R v Restormel Borough Council, ex p Corbett* [2001] EWCA Civ 330 at [15], [2001] 1 PLR 108 at [15] per Schiemann LJ. This presumption is sometimes expressed in terms of a decision being 'voidable'.

15 See eg *Anisminic Ltd v Foreign Compensation Commission* [1969] 2 AC 147 at 171, [1969] 1 All ER 208 at 234, HL, per Lord Pearce (strictly no need to quash a decision found to be in excess of jurisdiction because it is a nullity); *Boddington v British Transport Police* [1999] 2 AC 143 at 154–155, [1998] 2 All ER 203 at 209–210, HL, per Lord Irvine of Lairg LC, and at 164–165 and 219–220 per Lord Slynn of Hadley, overruling *Bugg v DPP* [1993] QB 473, [1993] 2 All ER 815.

16 See *London and Clydeside Estates Ltd v Aberdeen District Council* [1979] 3 All ER 876 at 883, [1980] 1 WLR 182 at 189–190, HL, per Lord Hailsham of St Marylebone LC (there is a spectrum of illegality and it is for the court to determine what the consequences of illegality should be); *Chief Constable of the North Wales Police v Evans* [1982] 3 All ER 141 at 145, [1982] 1 WLR 1155 at 1163, HL, per Lord Hailsham of St Marylebone LC (referring to the difficulty in applying the language of 'void' and 'voidable' to administrative decisions which give rise to practical and legal consequences which cannot be reversed); *R v Secretary of State for the*

Home Department, ex p Malhi [1991] 1 QB 194 at 208, [1990] 2 All ER 357 at 363–364, CA, per Mustill LJ (noting that with the current rapid development of the law of judicial review the distinction between 'void' and 'voidable' is now in some fields becoming obsolete); *Main v Swansea City Council* (1985) 49 P & CR 26, CA; *Calvin v Carr* [1980] AC 574, [1979] 2 All ER 440, PC (observing that a decision made contrary to natural justice is void, but that until it is so declared by a competent body or court, it may have some effect, or existence, in law); *R v Secretary of State for Social Services, ex p Association of Metropolitan Authorities* [1986] 1 All ER 164, [1986] 1 WLR 1 (statutory instrument declared to be ultra vires but court declined to quash it so that further acts done in reliance on it were not invalidated). See also ADMINISTRATIVE LAW vol 1(1) (2001 Reissue) PARA 26.

611. Jurisdictional defects. An inferior court, administrative tribunal or other public decision-making body will also lack jurisdiction and act ultra vires in the narrow sense[1] where it has no power to adjudicate upon the dispute or to make the kind of decision or order in question[2]. A public body will lack jurisdiction or vires in this sense where it is improperly constituted[3], or the proceedings have been improperly constituted[4], or authority to decide has been delegated to it unlawfully[5]. A public body purporting to exercise statutory powers will also act without such jurisdiction or vires where its act or decision lies outside the ambit of the enabling power[6] by reason of the parties[7], the subject matter[8], or the geographical area in which the subject matter arose[9]. Where the exercise of statutory powers is subject to the existence of a fact or fulfilment of a condition, the exercise of those powers in the absence of that fact[10] or without fulfilment of that condition[11] will be without jurisdiction and ultra vires. A body may by taking a valid decision exhaust its powers such that any further decision on the same matter will be made without jurisdiction or vires[12].

Save where Parliament has otherwise provided, a tribunal of limited statutory jurisdiction cannot acquire jurisdiction to determine a matter by consent of the parties[13]. Nor can it decline to adjudicate in respect of a matter on which it is bound to adjudicate[14].

1 See PARA 610.
2 *Anisminic Ltd v Foreign Compensation Commission* [1969] 2 AC 147 at 171, [1969] 1 All ER 208 at 213–214, HL, per Lord Reid; *R v Lord President of the Privy Council, ex p Page* [1993] AC 682, sub nom *Page v Hull University Visitor* [1993] 1 All ER 97, HL. The distinction between acting without jurisdiction in the narrow sense and acting without jurisdiction in the wide sense is no longer determinative of whether judicial review is available, save in exceptional cases: see PARA 610 note 11.
3 See eg *George v Chambers* (1843) 11 M & W 149; *R (Dobbyn) v Belfast Justices* [1917] 2 IR 297; *R (Department of Agriculture) v Londonderry City Justices, R (Meehan) v Hardy* [1917] 2 IR 283; *R v Inner London Quarter Sessions, ex p D'Souza* [1970] 1 All ER 481, [1970] 1 WLR 376, DC; *Robinson v DPP* [1991] RTR 315, [1992] COD 235, DC (magistrates had no power to set aside convictions because not properly constituted); *R v Secretary of State for Education, ex p Prior* [1994] ICR 877, [1994] ELR 231 (committee's decision to dismiss teacher ultra vires because not properly constituted); *R v Tower Hamlets London Borough Council, ex p Khalique* [1994] 2 FCR 1074, 26 HLR 517 (decision taken by unauthorised officer or unauthorised group of councillors quashed as 'the product of a usurpation of power'); *R v Secretary of State for Health v Wagstaff, R v Secretary of State for Health, ex p Associated Newspapers Ltd* (2000) 56 BMLR 199; *Baldock v Webster* [2004] EWCA Civ 1869, [2006] QB 315, [2005] 3 All ER 655 (recorder hearing High Court matter not knowing that he was not authorised to do so).
4 Eg magistrates proceeding without information duly laid or complaint duly made: *R v Manchester Stipendiary Magistrate, ex p Hill* [1983] 1 AC 328 at 342, sub nom *Hill v Anderton* [1982] 2 All ER 963 at 971, HL, per Lord Roskill (laying of information in a criminal case and making of complaint in a civil case is the foundation of magistrates' jurisdiction). See further MAGISTRATES vol 29(2) (Reissue) PARA 681. See also *R v Paddington and St Marylebone Rent Tribunal, ex p Bell London and Provincial Properties Ltd* [1949] 1 KB 666, [1949] 1 All ER 720 (rent tribunal's adjudication quashed because initiating reference invalid); and cf *R v Barnet and Camden Rent Tribunal, ex p Frey Investments Ltd* [1972] 2 QB 342, [1972] 1 All ER 1185, CA (where the references were held to be valid).

5   See *Caudle v Seymour* (1841) 1 QB 889 (magistrate convicting on depositions taken by his clerk
     in his absence); *Barnard v National Dock Labour Board* [1953] 2 QB 18, [1953] 1 All ER
     1113, CA (board had no jurisdiction to delegate, port manager had no jurisdiction to
     adjudicate, both purported to do so); *Vine v National Dock Labour Board* [1957] AC 488,
     [1956] 3 All ER 939, HL (action taken by a delegated authority when there was no power to
     delegate goes to the root of the jurisdiction); *R v Secretary of State for the Environment,
     ex p Hillingdon London Borough Council* [1986] 1 All ER 810, [1986] 1 WLR 192; affd [1986]
     2 All ER 273n, [1986] 1 WLR 807n, CA (single member of authority not a committee for the
     purposes of delegation); *R v Secretary of State for Education, ex p Prior* [1994] ICR 877, [1994]
     ELR 231 (decision to dismiss ultra vires because improperly delegated to staff committee); *R (on
     the application of Queen Mary University of London) v Higher Education Funding Council for
     England* [2008] EWHC 1472 (Admin), [2008] ELR 540 at [39] per Burnett J (decision taken by
     person not authorised to do so under scheme of delegation); though cf *R (on the application of
     Varma) v HRH The Duke of Kent* [2004] EWHC 1705 (Admin), [2004] ELR 616 (university
     visitor could appoint a competent person to advise him provided he did not delegate the decision
     to him). See further ADMINISTRATIVE LAW vol 1(1) (2001 Reissue) PARA 31.
6   See ADMINISTRATIVE LAW vol 1(1) (2001 Reissue) PARAS 20–22.
7   See e g *Marshalsea Case* (1613) 10 Co Rep 68b; *Turly v Panton* (1975) 29 P & CR 397, 236 EG
     197, DC (reference to rent tribunal by only one of four joint tenants invalid); *R v Broadcasting
     Complaints Commission, ex p British Broadcasting Corpn* (1994) 6 Admin LR 714 (no
     jurisdiction to hear complaints unless made by 'affected' person); *R v Broadcasting Complaints
     Commission, ex p British Broadcasting Corpn* (1995) 7 Admin LR 575; and see *R v Secretary of
     State for Health, ex p Barratt* [1994] COD 406, (1994) 21 BMLR 54 (erroneous decision that
     jurisdiction to entertain appeal by father purporting to act on behalf of non-consenting daughter
     who had reached 18).
8   See e g *A-G v Fulham Corpn* [1921] 1 Ch 440 (power to establish washhouses does not include
     power to establish a municipal laundry); *Crédit Suisse v Allerdale Borough Council* [1997] QB
     306, [1996] 4 All ER 129, CA (power to provide 'recreational facilities' does not include power
     to provide time-share accommodation). See also *Polley v Fordham (No 2)* (1904) 68 JP 504, DC
     (offence as charged no longer cognizable); *R v Milk Marketing Board, ex p Brook* (1992) 6
     Admin LR 369 (no jurisdiction to determine complaint which in substance amounted to
     complaint of criminal offence); *R v Prosthetists and Orthotists Board, ex p Lewis* [2000] All ER
     (D) 2346 (disciplinary committee had jurisdiction to consider alleged misconduct committed
     before claimant registered with board); *Chen v Government of Romania* [2007] EWHC 520
     (Admin), [2008] 1 All ER 851 at [62]–[63], [2009] 1 WLR 257 at [62]–[63] (acting beyond the
     question which had been remitted when the statute did not permit the judge to do so). As to
     errors of fact see PARA 624.
9   Eg in the case of magistrates and coroners whose jurisdiction is subject to territorial limitation:
     see e g *Houlden v Smith* (1850) 14 QB 841; *Re McC (A Minor)* [1985] AC 528 at 546, sub nom
     McC v Mullan [1984] 3 All ER 908 at 920, HL, per Lord Bridge. See also *R v East Sussex
     Coroner, ex p Healy* [1989] 1 All ER 30, [1988] 1 WLR 1194, DC. As to coroners see generally
     CORONERS; and as to magistrates see generally MAGISTRATES.
10   See PARA 624.
11   See e g *Re McC (A Minor)* [1985] AC 528, sub nom *McC v Mullan* [1984] 3 All ER 908, HL
     (magistrates making order without first informing juvenile defendant of right to legal aid were
     acting 'without jurisdiction or in excess of jurisdiction' within the meaning of the Magistrates
     Courts (NI) Act 1964 s 15); *R v Cockshott* [1898] 1 QB 582; *R v Kettering Justices,
     ex p Patmore* [1968] 3 All ER 167, [1968] 1 WLR 1436, DC (failure to comply with mandatory
     statutory requirement to inform defendant of right to elect trial by jury); *R v Liskerrett Justices,
     ex p Child* [1972] RTR 141, DC (failure to allow an adjournment before sentencing); *R v
     Manchester City Magistrates Court, ex p Davies* [1989] QB 631 at 637–638, [1989] 1 All ER 90
     at 94–95, CA, per O'Connor LJ and at 642 and 98 per Neill LJ (inquiry into reason for failure
     to pay rates a statutory condition precedent to the imposition of a sentence of imprisonment);
     Robinson v DPP [1991] RTR 315, [1992] COD 235, DC (power to set aside conviction only
     exercisable within 28 days, decision to set aside after that time without jurisdiction and void);
     R v Mid-Warwickshire Licensing Justices, ex p Patel [1994] COD 251 (magistrates had no
     power to grant licence where they failed to inquire whether errors in notice had misled anyone);
     Robbins v Secretary of State for the Environment [1989] 1 All ER 878, [1989] 1 WLR 201, HL
     (condition precedent to serving compulsory purchase order that acquiring authority serve
     repairs notice); *R v Managers of South Western Hospital, ex p M* [1993] QB 683, [1994]
     1 All ER 161 (authority to detain patient under the Mental Health Act 1983 s 3 only if statutory
     preconditions in s 11(4) fulfilled); *R v Secretary of State for Education and Employment,
     ex p National Union of Teachers* (2000) Times, 8 August, [2000] All ER (D) 991 (decision to

amend teachers' terms of employment not using prescribed statutory routes invalid). As to the distinction between mandatory and directory requirements see ADMINISTRATIVE LAW vol 1(1) (2001 Reissue) PARA 24.

12 Such a body may be described as functus officio. See eg *R v Fulham, Hammersmith and Kensington Rent Tribunal, ex p Gormly* [1952] 1 KB 179, [1951] 2 All ER 1030, DC (no jurisdiction to entertain further application for rent reduction); *R v Parliamentary Commissioner for Administration, ex p Dyer* [1994] 1 All ER 375, [1994] 1 WLR 621 (having reported to MP in question, no jurisdiction to reopen complaint); *R v Dorset Police Authority, ex p Vaughan* [1995] COD 153 (no power to reconsider decision which regulations stated was 'final'); *Aparau v Iceland Frozen Foods plc* [2000] 1 All ER 228, [2000] ICR 341, CA (tribunal exhausted its jurisdiction on making dispositive determination in the case, subject only to the limited power of review prescribed in the governing regulations); and cf *Terry v East Sussex Coroner* [2001] EWCA Civ 1094, [2002] QB 312, [2002] 2 All ER 141 (issuing of coroner's certificate that inquest not necessary did not exhaust his powers to hold an inquest if new evidence was presented).

13 *Essex County Council v Essex Incorporated Congregational Church Union* [1963] AC 808, [1963] 1 All ER 326, HL; *Secretary of State for Employment v Globe Elastic Thread Co Ltd* [1980] AC 506, [1979] 2 All ER 1077, HL; *R v Northern and Yorkshire Regional Health Authority, ex p Trivedi* [1995] 1 WLR 961 at 973–974 per Auld J.

14 It is for the court to determine the limits of an inferior tribunal or public authority's jurisdiction: see eg *R v Shoreditch Assessment Committee, ex p Morgan* [1910] 2 KB 859 at 880, CA, per Farwell LJ. See also PARA 615.

612. Errors of law. There is a general presumption that a public decision-making body[1] has no jurisdiction or power to commit an error of law; thus where a body errs in law in reaching a decision or making an order, the court may quash that decision or order[2]. The error of law must be relevant, that is to say it must be an error in the actual making of the decision which affects the decision itself[3]. Even if the error of law is relevant, the court may exercise its discretion not to quash where the decision would have been no different had the error not been committed[4]. Where a notice, order or other instrument made by a public body is unlawful only in part, the whole instrument will be invalid unless the unlawful part can be severed[5].

In certain exceptional cases, the presumption that there is no power or jurisdiction to commit an error of law may be rebutted[6], in which case the court will not quash for an error of law made within jurisdiction in the narrow sense[7]. The previous law which drew a distinction between errors of law on the face of the record and other errors of law is now obsolete[8].

A public body will err in law if it acts in breach of fundamental human rights[9]; misinterprets a statute, or any other legal document, or a rule of common law[10]; frustrates the purpose of a statute or otherwise acts for an improper purpose[11]; takes a decision on the basis of secondary legislation, or any other act or order, which is itself ultra vires[12]; takes legally irrelevant considerations into account, or fails to take relevant considerations into account[13]; admits inadmissible evidence[14], rejects admissible and relevant evidence[15], or takes a decision on no evidence[16] or on the basis of a material mistake of fact[17]; misdirects itself as to the burden of proof[18]; fails to follow the proper procedure required by law[19]; fetters its discretion[20] or improperly delegates the decision[21]; fails to fulfil an express or implied duty to give reasons[22]; acts arbitrarily[23] or discriminately[24]; or otherwise abuses its power[25].

1 See ADMINISTRATIVE LAW vol 1(1) (2001 Reissue) PARA 6.

2 *Anisminic Ltd v Foreign Compensation Commission* [1969] 2 AC 147, [1969] 1 All ER 208, HL. Any error of law is correctable, not just those errors apparent on the face of the record: see *R (on the application of Q) v Secretary of State for the Home Department* [2003] EWCA Civ 364, [2004] QB 36, [2003] 2 All ER 905 at [112] per Lord Phillips of Worth Matravers giving the judgment of the court. See PARA 610.

3   See *R v Lord President of the Privy Council, ex p Page* [1993] AC 682 at 702, sub nom *Page v Hull University Visitor* [1993] 1 All ER 97 at 107–108, HL, per Lord Browne-Wilkinson (need for an error in the making of the decision which affected the decision itself), applied in *R v Governor of Brixton Prison, ex p Levin* [1997] AC 741, [1997] 3 All ER 289, HL; *Sivarajah v General Medical Council* [1964] 1 All ER 504 at 507, [1964] 1 WLR 112 at 117, PC (error of law will not invalidate decision unless of sufficient significance), followed in *McEniff v General Dental Council* [1980] 1 All ER 461, [1980] 1 WLR 328, PC; *Pearlman v Keepers and Governors of Harrow School* [1979] QB 56 at 70, [1979] 1 All ER 365 at 371–372, CA, per Lord Denning MR; *Robbins v Secretary of State for the Environment* [1989] 1 All ER 878 at 885, 886, [1989] 1 WLR 201 at 212, 214, HL, per Lord Bridge of Harwich (inclusion of unlawful items in repairs notice did not render notice invalid and Secretary of State had not relied on the unlawful items in reaching decision about compliance with the notice); *R v Boundary Commission for England, ex p Foot* [1983] QB 600, [1983] 1 All ER 1099, CA (no sufficient grounds for thinking that the misdirection affected the ultimate conclusion in any way); *R v Investors Compensation Scheme Ltd, ex p Bowden* [1996] AC 261 at 281, [1995] 3 All ER 605 at 612, HL, per Lord Lloyd (reason for decision irrelevant in law but subsidiary and so made no difference to the decision); *Doughty v General Dental Council* [1988] AC 164 at 171, [1987] 3 All ER 843 at 846, PC (misdirection in law did not invalidate decision because neither caused prejudice nor miscarriage of justice).

4   Relief in judicial review proceedings is at the discretion of the court: *R v Greater Manchester Coroner, ex p Tal* [1985] QB 67 at 83, [1984] 3 All ER 240 at 249, CA, per Goff LJ. Where an error of law has occurred, a high degree of certainty that the decision would have been the same despite the error is required before the court will refuse relief: see *Kalra v Secretary of State for the Environment* (1995) 72 P & CR 423, [1996] 1 PLR 37, CA (question for the court is whether it can 'safely' be said that the inspector would 'inevitably' have reached the same decision if she had correctly directed herself in law); *R v Vale of Glamorgan Borough Council and Associated British Ports, ex p James* [1996] Env LR 102 at 115–116 per Popplewell J (whether decision would 'inevitably' have been the same despite the misdirection). See also *R v Wolverhampton Coroner, ex p McCurbin* [1990] 2 All ER 759 at 767, [1990] 1 WLR 719 at 730, CA, per Woolf LJ (need to be 'confident' that the outcome would not have been different but for the error before relief will be refused); *R v Criminal Injuries Compensation Board, ex p Aston* [1994] COD 500, [1994] PIQR P460 (decision technically flawed but on the facts the Board acting lawfully could have reached no other result); *R v HM Coroner for Western District of East Sussex, ex p Homberg* [1994] COD 279, (1994) 19 BMLR 11, DC (misdirection by coroner but jury could not have reached different verdict); *M v Secretary of State for the Home Department* [1996] 1 All ER 870 at 875, [1996] 1 WLR 507 at 512, CA, per Butler Sloss LJ and at 880 and 517 per Ward LJ (tribunal applied erroneous proposition of law but entitled to come to conclusion on evidence and not perverse); *R v Inner South London Coroner, ex p Douglas-Williams* [1999] 1 All ER 344 at 347, CA, per Woolf MR (coroner's decision will only be quashed where in interests of justice; not in interests of justice to quash where misdirection would not have affected outcome).

5   In general, severance is possible only where deletion of the unlawful part does not substantially alter the purpose or effect of the instrument: see ADMINISTRATIVE LAW vol 1(1) (2001 Reissue) PARA 25.

6   See PARA 610 note 12.

7   See PARA 610.

8   This is the effect of the decision in *Anisminic Ltd v Foreign Compensation Commission* [1969] 2 AC 147, [1969] 1 All ER 208, HL: see *Re Racal Communications Ltd* [1981] AC 374 at 383, [1980] 2 All ER 634 at 638–639, HL, per Lord Diplock (the breakthrough made by *Anisminic Ltd v Foreign Compensation Commission* was that, as respects administrative tribunals and authorities, the old distinction between errors of law that went to jurisdiction and errors of law that did not, was for practical purposes abolished); *O'Reilly v Mackman* [1983] 2 AC 237 at 278, [1982] 3 All ER 1124 at 1129, HL, per Lord Diplock; *R v Lord President of the Privy Council, ex p Page* [1993] AC 682 at 696, 701–702, sub nom *Page v Hull University Visitor* [1993] 1 All ER 97 at 102, 107–108, HL, per Lord Browne-Wilkinson, at 693 and 100 per Lord Griffiths, and at 706 and 111 per Lord Slynn of Hadley; *R v Bedwellty Justices, ex p Williams* [1997] AC 225 at 233, sub nom *Williams v Bedwellty Justices* [1996] 3 All ER 737 at 744, HL, per Lord Cooke of Thorndon; *Boddington v British Transport Police* [1999] 2 AC 143 at 154, [1998] 2 All ER 203 at 209, HL, per Lord Irvine of Lairg LC.

9   Ie whether rights at common law (see *R v Secretary of State for the Home Department, ex p Pierson* [1998] AC 539 at 575, [1997] 3 All ER 577 at 592, HL, per Lord Browne-Wilkinson; *R v Governor of Frankland Prison, ex p Russell* [2000] 1 WLR 2027) or under the Convention for the Protection of Human Rights and Fundamental Freedoms

(Rome, 4 November 1950; TS 71 (1953) Cmd 8969), as incorporated into domestic legislation by the Human Rights Act 1998 (see *R v Secretary of State for the Home Department, ex p Simms* [2000] 2 AC 115 at 130, [1999] 3 All ER 400 at 411, HL, per Lord Steyn; and *R (on the application of Q) v Secretary of State for the Home Department* [2003] EWCA Civ 364, [2004] QB 36, [2003] 2 All ER 905 at [112] per Lord Phillips of Worth Matravers giving the judgment of the court). Compare *R v Secretary of State for Social Security, ex p Joint Council for the Welfare of Immigrants* [1996] 4 All ER 385, [1997] 1 WLR 275, CA (regulations made under one statute ultra vires because cut down statutory rights under another statute). See further PARA 651.

10 See eg *Ashbridge Investments Ltd v Minister of Housing and Local Government* [1965] 3 All ER 371 at 373–374, [1965] 1 WLR 1320 at 1326, CA, per Lord Denning MR (statute accorded decision to minister, but court can interfere on ground that the minister has gone outside the powers of the enabling statute or that any requirement of the statute has not been complied with). See also *Padfield v Minister of Agriculture, Fisheries and Food* [1968] AC 997 at 1030, [1968] 1 All ER 694 at 699, HL, per Lord Reid; *Brutus v Cozens* [1973] AC 854 at 861, [1972] 2 All ER 1297 at 1299, HL, per Lord Reid; *Shah v Barnet London Borough Council* [1983] 2 AC 309 at 341, [1983] 1 All ER 226 at 233–234, HL, per Lord Scarman; *Nottinghamshire County Council v Secretary of State for the Environment* [1986] AC 240 at 250–251, [1986] 1 All ER 199 at 204, HL, per Lord Scarman; *R v Secretary of State for the Environment ex p, Hammersmith and Fulham London Borough Council* [1991] 1 AC 521, sub nom *Hammersmith and Fulham London Borough Council v Secretary of State for the Environment* [1990] 3 All ER 589, HL; *T v Immigration Officer* [1996] AC 742, sub nom *T v Secretary of State for the Home Department* [1996] 2 All ER 865, HL. Cf *R (on the application of the British Board of Film Classification) v Video Appeals Committee* [2008] EWHC 203 (Admin), [2008] 1 WLR 1658 (committee wrongly taking into account comments of minister in Parliament when interpreting the relevant statute).

11 See PARAS 621–622.

12 See *Chief Adjudication Officer v Foster* [1993] AC 754 at 762, [1993] 1 All ER 705 at 709, HL, per Lord Bridge of Harwich; *R v Middleton, Bromley and Bexley Justices, ex p Collins* [1970] 1 QB 216, [1969] 3 All ER 800, DC (second conviction based on erroneous supposition that earlier conviction was valid), though note that there is an important exception to this proposition in the 'second actor theory' espoused in *Boddington v British Transport Police* [1999] 2 AC 143 at 172, [1998] 2 All ER 203 at 226, HL, per Lord Steyn. For examples of cases in which public bodies acting in reliance on ultra vires acts or measures are held not themselves to have acted ultra vires see: *Percy v Hall* [1997] QB 924 at 947–948, [1996] 4 All ER 523 at 541, CA, per Simon Brown LJ (arrest under byelaws valid on their face at the time but subsequently found to be unlawful; arrest nonetheless lawful); *R v Central London County Court, ex p London* [1999] QB 1260, [1999] 3 All ER 991, CA (hospital manager's admission of patient pursuant to unlawful County Court orders was lawful); *R v Governor of Brockhill Prison, ex p Evans (No 2)* [2001] 2 AC 19, [2000] 4 All ER 15, HL (imprisonment pursuant to conviction lawful even if conviction subsequently overturned on appeal). Note that careful analysis is required in order to determine whether the decision-maker is truly a 'second actor' or not: see *D v Home Office* [2005] EWCA Civ 38, [2006] 1 All ER 183, [2006] 1 WLR 1003.

13 See PARA 623.

14 As to the effect of inadmissible evidence on committal proceedings see *R v Bedwellty Justices, ex p Williams* [1997] AC 225, sub nom *Williams v Bedwellty Justices* [1996] 3 All ER 737, HL (court should quash where committal so influenced by inadmissible evidence as to amount to an irregularity having substantial adverse consequences for the defendant; court should be slow to quash where evidence admissible but insufficient). See also *Neill v North Antrim Magistrates' Court* [1992] 4 All ER 846, [1992] 1 WLR 1220, HL; *R v Governor of Brixton Prison, ex p Levin* [1997] AC 741, [1997] 3 All ER 289, HL (error in failing to exercise discretion to exclude evidence in extradition proceedings but this was immaterial).

15 See eg *R v Industrial Injuries Comr, ex p Ward* [1965] 2 QB 112, [1964] 3 All ER 907, DC; *R v Registered Homes Tribunal, ex p Hertfordshire County Council* (1996) 95 LGR 76, 32 BMLR 101.

16 See PARA 613.

17 See PARA 624.

18 *Rowing v Minister of Pensions* [1946] 1 All ER 664; *R (Hanna) v Ministry of Health and Local Government* [1966] NI 52 at 61; *R v HM Coroner for City of London, ex p Barber* [1975] 3 All ER 538, [1975] 1 WLR 1310, DC; *R v South Glamorgan Health Authority, ex p Phillips* (1986) Times, 21 November; *R v West London Coroner, ex p Gray* [1988] QB 467, [1987]

2 All ER 129, DC; *Cranford Hall Parking Ltd v Secretary of State for the Environment* [1989] JPL 169, [1991] 1 EGLR 283; *R v Bradford Magistrates' Court, ex p Lockley* (1995) Times, 17 February, DC.

19 See PARA 625 et seq.

20 See PARAS 615 note 10, 620.

21 See ADMINISTRATIVE LAW vol 1(1) (2001 Reissue) PARA 31.

22 As to the duty to give reasons see PARA 629; and ADMINISTRATIVE LAW vol 1(1) (2001 Reissue) PARA 24. The giving of reasons facilitates the detection of errors of law by the courts (see *In re Racal Communications Ltd* [1981] AC 374 at 383, [1980] 2 All ER 634 at 638, HL, per Lord Diplock). It will often be from an authority's reasons that an error of law may be inferred: see e g *Secretary of State for Education and Science v Tameside Metropolitan Borough Council* [1977] AC 1014 at 1065, [1976] 3 All ER 665 at 695–696, HL, per Lord Diplock (scrutiny of reasons revealing misdirection or irrelevancy); and *R v DPP, ex p Jones* [2000] IRLR 373, [2000] Crim LR 858 (although DPP reciting correct test, read as a whole reasons indicating had applied a different test). A failure to give reasons may permit the court to infer that the decision was reached by reason of an error of law: *Padfield v Minister of Agriculture, Fisheries and Food* [1968] AC 997 at 1053–1054, [1968] 1 All ER 694 at 715, HL, per Lord Pearce and at 1061 and 719 per Lord Upjohn (where all prima facie reasons point in one direction absence of reasons for taking contrary course enables the court to infer that minister had no good reason for taking that course); *Mountview Court Properties Ltd v Devlin* (1970) 21 P & CR 689, DC; *Crake v Supplementary Benefits Commission* [1982] 1 All ER 498; *R (on the application of Quark Fishing Ltd) v Secretary of State for Foreign and Commonwealth Affairs* [2002] EWCA Civ 1409, [2002] All ER (D) 450 (Oct) (where conflicting reasons given, court not prepared to assume that decision taken on rational grounds); *R (on the application of Farrakhan) v Secretary of State for the Home Department* [2002] EWCA Civ 606 at [7], [2002] QB 1391 at [7], [2002] 4 All ER 289 at [7] per Lord Phillips of Worth Matravers MR giving the judgment of the court; *Lonrho plc v Secretary of State for Trade and Industry* [1989] 2 All ER 609 at 620, sub nom *R v Secretary of State for Trade and Industry, ex p Lonrho plc* [1989] 1 WLR 525 at 539–540, HL, per Lord Keith of Kinkel (absence of reasons may give rise to presumption that none exist); though c f *R v IRC, ex p TC Coombs & Co* [1991] 2 AC 283 at 300, 302, sub nom *TC Coombs & Co (a firm) v IRC* [1991] 3 All ER 623 at 636–637, HL, per Lord Lowry (if there is an obvious explanation for the lack of reasons no inference will be drawn).

23 See e g *R (on the application of Limbu) v Secretary of State for the Home Department* [2008] EWHC 2261 (Admin), [2008] HRLR 48 (transparency, clarity and avoidance of arbitrary results were aspects of the principle of legality; entry clearance arrangements for Gurkhas arbitrary and unlawful); *R (on the application of S) v Secretary of State for the Home Department* [2007] EWCA Civ 546 at [52], [2007] All ER (D) 193 (Jun) at [52] (arbitrary deferral of older asylum cases unlawful); *R v Ministry of Agriculture, Fisheries and Food, ex p Hamble (Offshore) Fisheries Ltd* [1995] 2 All ER 714 at 722 per Sedley J; *R v Ministry of Agriculture, Fisheries and Food, ex p First City Trading Ltd* [1997] 1 CMLR 250.

24 Although mere inconsistency is not a sufficient basis for review of an act or decision of a public authority (see *R v Special Adjudicator, ex p Kandasamy* [1994] Imm AR 333), like cases must be treated alike unless there is a justification for the difference in treatment: see *Matadeen v Pointu* [1999] 1 AC 98, [1998] 3 WLR 18, PC, cited with approval in *A v Secretary of State for the Home Department* [2004] UKHL 56, [2005] 2 AC 68, [2005] 3 All ER 169 at [46] per Lord Bingham of Cornhill; *R (on the application of G) v Barnet London Borough Council* [2003] UKHL 57 at [46], [2004] 2 AC 208 at [46], [2004] 1 All ER 97 at [46] per Lord Nicholls of Birkenhead; *R (on the application of Zeqiri) v Secretary of State for the Home Department* [2002] UKHL 3 at [56], [2002] INLR 291 at [56] per Lord Hoffmann; *Gurung v Ministry of Defence* [2002] EWHC 2463 (Admin) at [35]–[39], [2002] All ER (D) 409 (Nov) at [35]–[39] per McCombe J; *R (Association of British Civilian Internees: Far East Region) v Secretary of State for Defence* [2003] EWCA Civ 473 at [86], [2003] QB 1397 at [86] per Dyson LJ; *R (on the application of Kelsall) v Secretary of State for the Environment, Food and Rural Affairs* [2003] EWHC 459 (Admin) at [63], [2003] All ER (D) 186 (Mar) at [63] per Stanley Burnton J; *R (on the application of Middlebrook Mushrooms Ltd) v Agricultural Wages Board of England and Wales* [2004] EWHC 1447 (Admin) at [74], [2004] All ER (D) 183 (Jun) at [74] per Stanley Burnton J; *Ghaidan v Godin-Mendoza* [2004] UKHL 30 at [132], [2004] 2 AC 557 at [132], sub nom *Ghaidan v Mendoza* [2004] 3 All ER 411 at [132] per Baroness Hale. Similarly, unlike cases must normally be treated differently unless there is justification for treating them the same: see *Matadeen v Pointu* [1999] 1 AC 98, [1998] 3 WLR 18, PC, cited with approval in *A v Secretary of State for the Home Department* [2004] UKHL 56 at [46], [2005] 2 AC 68 at [46], [2005] 3 All ER 169 at [46] per Lord Bingham of Cornhill; *R (on the application of Kaur) v Ealing London Borough Council* [2008] EWHC 2062 (Admin) at [52], [2008] All ER (D) 08

(Oct) at [52] per Moses LJ; *R v Tower Hamlets London Borough Council, ex p Uddin* (2000) 32 HLR 391 at 403 (housing transfer points scheme irrational because failing to distinguish between households with markedly different needs). It is an open question as to whether the principle of equality is a free-standing principle or an aspect of *Wednesbury* reasonableness (see PARA 617): see *R (Association of British Civilian Internees: Far East Region) v Secretary of State for Defence* at [85]–[86] per Dyson LJ.

25 *R v North and East Devon Health Authority, ex p Coughlan* [2000] 3 All ER 850, [2000] 2 WLR 622, CA (abuse of power can be said to be but another name for acting contrary to law); *R v Department for Education and Employment, ex p Begbie* [2000] 1 WLR 1115 at 1129, [2000] ELR 445 at [76], CA, per Laws LJ (abuse of power is the root concept which governs and conditions the general principles of public law); *Nottinghamshire County Council v Secretary of State for the Environment* [1986] AC 240 at 249, [1986] 1 All ER 199 at 203, HL, per Lord Scarman (power may be abused in a variety of ways). See further PARA 617 et seq.

613. The distinction between law and fact. The distinction between what will be treated as a question of law and what will be treated as a question of fact is one of importance. In general, where a body makes an error of law in reaching a decision, it will act without jurisdiction or power, and the court may quash that decision on an application for judicial review[1]. By contrast the court will generally not intervene on the ground that a body has reached an erroneous finding of fact unless the finding is manifestly unreasonable[2] or a mistake has been made as to an established and material fact that gives rise to unfairness[3] or the finding of fact was otherwise reached through an error of law[4] or is a precedent fact[5].

There is often difficulty in deciding whether a question should be classified as one of law or as one of fact (or fact and degree)[6]. Determination of the primary facts is not a matter of law, but to make a finding unsupported by any evidence is an error of law[7]. Drawing inferences from the facts as found, and in particular determining whether the primary or secondary facts fall within the ambit of a statutory description, are potentially classifiable as questions of law, as questions of fact, or as questions of mixed law and fact[8]. The method of classification may be important, for judicial review of findings of law may entail an independent determination of the matter already decided, whereas a review of findings of fact is likely to be more limited. It has been said that if the question is one which only a trained lawyer can be expected to decide correctly, there is a presumption that it will be categorised as one of law[9]. Otherwise the question is usually treated as one of mixed law and fact, so that the range of meanings that can reasonably be ascribed to a statutory expression is a question of law[10]; but whether the facts as found fall within the ambit of that expression will be held to be a question of fact[11], on which the decision of the competent authority will not be disturbed unless it is perverse (or is such that no reasonable authority properly instructed in the law could have arrived at it), or is erroneous because a wrong legal approach has been adopted[12].

A court will generally be reluctant to disturb the findings of a tribunal with specialised knowledge of technical subject matter, irrespective of whether these findings be classified as law or fact[13].

1 See PARA 612.
2 See PARAS 624, 617.
3 See PARA 624.
4 Eg by taking irrelevant matters into consideration or ignoring relevant matters: see PARAS 612, 623.
5 See e g *R (on the application of M) v Lambeth London Borough Council* [2009] UKSC 8, [2009] 1 WLR 2557, [2009] 3 FCR 607; and PARA 624.
6 For examples of errors of law see PARA 612. The term 'question of degree' is normally used to denote a finding, inference or conclusion on which reasonable persons might come to divergent

conclusions because of a lack of clear-cut precision in the standards to be applied: see _Ransom v Higgs_ [1974] 3 All ER 949 at 970–971, [1974] 1 WLR 1594 at 1618, HL, per Lord Simon of Glaisdale. Questions of fact and degree are for the decision-maker to determine, subject only to _Wednesbury_ review (see PARA 617): see _R v Monopolies and Mergers Commission, ex p Argyll Group plc_ [1986] 2 All ER 257, [1986] 1 WLR 763, CA; _R (on the application of Cherwell District Council) v First Secretary of State_ [2004] EWCA Civ 1420 at [50], [57], [2005] 1 WLR 1128 at [50], [57] per Chadwick LJ; _R v Yorkshire Regional Health Authority, ex p Suri_ (1995) Times, 5 December, (1995) 30 BMLR 78, CA. Examples of questions of degree include: whether operations constitute a 'material change' in the use of land for which planning permission is required (_Bendles Motors Ltd v Bristol Corpn_ [1963] 1 All ER 578, [1963] 1 WLR 247, DC); whether a proposed relocation of pharmacist's premises was a 'minor relocation' (_R v Yorkshire Regional Health Authority, ex p Suri_); whether the circumstances of a claimant for housing benefit are 'exceptional' (_R v Maidstone Borough Council, ex p Bunce_ (1994) 27 HLR 375, (1994) Times, 30 June); whether education is 'suitable' (_R v East Sussex County Council, ex p Tandy_ [1998] AC 714 at 745–746, [1998] 2 All ER 769 at 774, HL, per Lord Browne-Wilkinson; _R v Family Health Services Appeal Authority, ex p Tesco Stores_ (1999) 11 Admin LR 1007 at 1012–1013, (1999) Times, 25 August per Kay J). See also note 11. Generally the meaning of ordinary English words is a question of fact, while the proper construction of a statute is a question of law: see _Moyna v Secretary of State for Work and Pensions_ [2003] UKHL 44 at [24]–[27], [2003] 1 WLR 1929 at [24]–[27], [2003] 4 All ER 162 at [24]–[27] per Lord Hoffmann; applied in _R (on the application of Cherwell District Council) v First Secretary of State_ [2004] EWCA Civ 1420 at [57], [2005] 1 WLR 1128 at [57] per Chadwick LJ; and _Pabari v Secretary of State for Work and Pensions_ [2004] EWCA Civ 1480 at [32], [2005] 1 All ER 287 at [32] per Holman J.

7 See PARA 624.

8 See _In re Racal Communications Ltd_ [1981] AC 374 at 383, [1980] 2 All ER 634 at 638, HL, per Lord Diplock (inter-relationship between fact and law). As to the extent to which the court will interfere with the drawing of inferences see: _British Launderers' Research Association v Hendon Borough Rating Authority_ [1949] 1 KB 434, 462 at 471–472, [1949] 1 All ER 21 at 25–26, CA, per Lord Denning MR (determination of primary facts essentially a question of fact for the tribunal of fact; inferences drawn from primary facts may be questions of fact if they can as well be drawn by a layman as by a lawyer; if, however, they properly require to be determined by a trained lawyer, then they are questions of law). See also _R v Rowe, ex p Mainwaring_ [1992] 4 All ER 821 at 828–829, [1992] 1 WLR 1059 at 1066–1068, CA, per Farquharson LJ; _B v Secretary of State for the Home Department_ [2000] Imm AR 478 at p 484, CA.

9 _British Launderers' Research Association v Hendon Borough Rating Authority_ [1949] 1 KB 434, 462 at 471–472, [1949] 1 All ER 21 at 25–26, CA, per Lord Denning MR; _Morren v Swinton and Pendlebury Borough Council_ [1965] 2 All ER 349, [1965] 1 WLR 576, DC (distinguished in _Global Plant Ltd v Secretary of State for Health and Social Security_ [1972] 1 QB 139, [1971] 3 All ER 385); _Hoveringham Gravels Ltd v Secretary of State for the Environment_ [1975] QB 754 at 763–764, [1975] 2 All ER 931 at 936–937, CA, per Lord Denning MR (question of causation requires trained lawyer; see also _R v Criminal Injuries Compensation Board, ex p Ince_ [1973] 3 All ER 808 at 812–813, [1973] 1 WLR 1334 at 1341, CA, per Lord Denning MR; cf _Stapley v Gypsum Mines Ltd_ [1953] AC 663, [1953] 2 All ER 478, HL).

10 See _South Yorkshire Transport Ltd v Monopolies and Mergers Commission_ [1993] 1 All ER 289, sub nom _R v Monopolies and Mergers Commission, ex p South Yorkshire Transport Ltd_ [1993] 1 WLR 23, HL (range of meanings which fall within the concept of 'substantial'); _Edwards (Inspector of Taxes) v Bairstow_ [1956] AC 14, [1955] 3 All ER 48, HL (concept of an adventure in the nature of 'trade' for the purpose of income taxation); _R v Poplar Coroner, ex p Thomas_ [1993] QB 610 at 630, [1993] 2 All ER 381 at 388, CA, per Simon Brown LJ (although statute using ordinary word of English language application of the statute was not a pure question of fact); _R v Gloucestershire County Council, ex p Barry_ [1997] AC 584, [1997] 2 All ER 1, HL ('necessary' and 'needs' are expressions admitting a range of meanings). See also the cases cited in note 11.

11 _R (on the application of Cherwell District Council) v First Secretary of State_ [2004] EWCA Civ 1420 at [50], [2005] 1 WLR 1128 at [50] per Chadwick LJ (whether development of Crown land by private contractor could constitute Crown development was a matter of law; if so, whether this development properly did so was a question of fact); _South Yorkshire Transport Ltd v Monopolies and Mergers Commission_ [1993] 1 All ER 289 at 298, sub nom _R v Monopolies and Mergers Commission, ex p South Yorkshire Transport Ltd_ [1993] 1 WLR 23 at 32, HL, per Lord Mustill (once court has ruled out as a matter of law certain meanings of a statutory word such as 'substantial' what remains will be a question of fact for the public body

to determine in each case, subject to *Wednesbury* review (see PARA 617)). See also *Edwards (Inspector of Taxes) v Bairstow* [1956] AC 14, [1955] 3 All ER 48, HL; *Global Plant Ltd v Secretary of State for Health and Social Security* [1972] 1 QB 139, [1971] 3 All ER 385, DC; *Bardrick v Haycock* (1976) 31 P & CR 420, CA (application of the word 'building': relevant factors in construing matter as one of fact for the county court judge were that Parliament had used an ordinary English word with no precise meaning and the county court judge was in a better position than the appeal court to appreciate local conditions); *South Oxfordshire District Council v Secretary of State for the Environment* (1985) 52 P & CR 1 (whether development would result in a 'building'); *R v Secretary of State for the Environment, ex p Powis* [1981] 1 All ER 788, [1981] 1 WLR 584, CA (material change in use of land; the material on which a decision-maker is entitled to rely as evidence depends on the statutory context); *Hollier v Plysu Ltd* [1983] IRLR 260, CA (extent of contributory fault of employee who is unfairly dismissed); *Martin v Glynwed Distribution Ltd* [1983] ICR 511, sub nom *Martin v MBS Fastings (Glynwed) Distribution Ltd* [1983] IRLR 198, CA (appellate tribunal must not treat findings of fact as findings of mixed law and fact in order to intervene in a factual conclusion reached by a first-tier tribunal; factual conclusions can only be overturned if irrational); *O'Kelly v Trusthouse Forte plc* [1984] QB 90, [1983] 3 All ER 456, CA (whether persons 'employees' a question of law, but involved questions of fact and degree that were for the employment tribunal to determine); *Nancollas v Insurance Officer* [1985] 1 All ER 833, CA (injury arising in course of employment); *Hancock v Secretary of State for the Environment* (1986) 55 P & CR 216 (use of building for agriculture); *Mallinson v Secretary of State for Social Security* [1994] 2 All ER 295 at 304–305, [1994] 1 WLR 630 at 638–639, HL, per Lord Woolf (question whether acts are 'attention' or 'supervision' one of law; question whether they are 'frequent' one of fact); *R v Broadcasting Complaints Commission, ex p Granada TV Ltd* [1995] EMLR 163, (1994) Times, 16 December, CA; *R v Broadcasting Standards Commission, ex p BBC* [2001] QB 885, [2000] 3 All ER 989, CA (provided 'privacy' interpreted by the Commission in a way wide enough to protect rights under the Convention for the Protection of Human Rights and Fundamental Freedoms (Rome, 4 November 1950; TS 71 (1953) Cmd 8969) art 8, what amounted to an unwarranted interference with privacy in any particular case was a matter for the Broadcasting Complaints Commission); *R v Radio Authority, ex p Guardian Media Group plc* [1995] 2 All ER 139, [1995] 1 WLR 334 (whether one company controlled by another is for radio authority to determine); *R v South Hams District Council, ex p Gibb* [1995] QB 158, [1994] 4 All ER 1012, CA (once local authority applied the right test, question whether someone gipsy was one of fact); see also *R v Gloucestershire County Council, ex p Dutton* [1992] COD 1, (1991) 24 HLR 246 (question whether someone was gipsy was one of fact); *R v East Sussex County Council, ex p Tandy* [1998] AC 714, [1998] 2 All ER 769, HL (whether education 'suitable'); *R v Radio Authority, ex p Bull* [1998] QB 294, [1997] 2 All ER 561, CA (what constituted a 'political object' within meaning of the Broadcasting Act 1990 was a question of fact for the authority, provided it adopted the right approach in law).

12 See PARA 612. See also *R (on the application of Goodman) v Lewisham London Borough Council* [2003] EWCA Civ 140 at [8], [2003] Env LR 644 at [8] per Buxton LJ (determining the meaning of the legislation is a question of law for the court to decide for itself without deference to the decision-maker, whereas the decision-maker's application of the law to the facts is normally subject to review only on *Wednesbury* grounds (see PARA 617)); *Edwards (Inspector of Taxes) v Bairstow* [1956] AC 14 at 36, [1955] 3 All ER 48 at 57, HL, per Lord Radcliffe; *Bracegirdle v Oxley* [1947] KB 349, [1947] 1 All ER 126, DC; *Bendles Motors Ltd v Bristol Corpn* [1963] 1 All ER 578, [1963] 1 WLR 247, DC; *Global Plant Ltd v Secretary of State for Social Services* [1972] 1 QB 139, [1971] 3 All ER 385; *Firstcross Ltd v Teasdale* (1982) 47 P & CR 228; *Re Islam* [1983] 1 AC 688, [1981] 3 All ER 901, HL; *Burton v Gilbert* [1984] RTR 162, DC; *R v Horsham Justices, ex p Richards* [1985] 2 All ER 1114, [1985] 1 WLR 986, DC.

13 See *AH (Sudan) v Secretary of State for the Home Department* [2007] UKHL 49 at [30], [2008] 1 AC 678 at [30], [2008] 4 All ER 190 at [30], HL, per Baroness Hale of Richmond (decisions of expert tribunals should normally be respected unless it is quite clear they have misdirected themselves in law). The courts have also acknowledged the special expertise of a number of decision-making bodies: see *R v Industrial Injuries Comr, ex p Amalgamated Engineering Union (No 2)* [1966] 2 QB 31, [1966] 1 All ER 97, CA; *R v Preston Supplementary Benefits Appeal Tribunal, ex p Moore* [1975] 2 All ER 807, [1975] 1 WLR 624, CA; *R (on the application of Great North Eastern Railway Ltd) v Office of Rail Regulation* [2006] EWHC 1942 (Admin) at [39], [2006] All ER (D) 414 (Jul) at [39] per Sullivan J; *R (on the application of Campaign to End All Animal Experiments) v Secretary of State for the Home Department* [2008] EWCA Civ 417 at [1], [2008] All ER (D) 319 (Apr) at [1] per May LJ (on question of scientific judgment of Chief Inspector); *Napp Pharmaceutical Holdings Ltd v Director General of Fair Trading* [2002]

EWCA Civ 796 at [34], [2002] 4 All ER 376 at [34] per Buxton LJ; *R (on the application of Kwik-fit (GB) Ltd) v Central Arbitration Committee* [2002] EWCA Civ 512 at [2], [2002] ICR 1212 at [2], [2002] IRLR 395 at [2] per Buxton LJ; *R v Parole Board, ex p Watson* [1996] 2 All ER 641, [1996] 1 WLR 906, CA; *Presho v Insurance Officer* [1984] AC 310 at 318, [1984] 1 All ER 97 at 101–102, HL, per Lord Brandon of Oakbrook; *R v Social Fund Inspector, ex p Ali* [1993] COD 263, (1994) 6 Admin LR 205; *Re Preston* [1985] AC 835 at 864, sub nom *Preston v IRC* [1985] 2 All ER 327 at 339, HL, per Lord Templeman; *W v Lancashire County Council (Education Appeal Committee)* [1994] 3 FCR 1, [1994] ELR 530, CA. Particular deference will be paid to the educated predictions for the future of expert decision-makers: see *R v Director General of Telecommunications, ex p Cellcom Ltd* [1999] COD 105, [1998] All ER (D) 635. The courts may intervene, however, in order to provide guidance where tribunals reach contradictory decisions: *R v National Insurance Comr, ex p Michael* [1977] 2 All ER 420, [1977] 1 WLR 109, CA; *R v National Insurance Comr, ex p Stratton* [1979] QB 361 at 369, [1979] 2 All ER 278 at 282, CA, per Lord Denning MR; *H v East Sussex County Council* [2009] EWCA Civ 249, [2009] ELR 161 (special educational needs tribunal).

614. Jurisdiction ousted by claim of title or right. In some cases the inferior tribunal, having jurisdiction to enter upon an inquiry and having rightly entered upon it, becomes incapacitated to proceed because some fact appears which ousts its jurisdiction. Thus, it is an established principle of the common law that the jurisdiction of magistrates is ousted by a bona fide claim of title on the part of a defendant[1]. If the claim of right put forward is of a character unknown to the law, it will not oust the jurisdiction of the magistrates although it is made bona fide[2]. If, however, the claim is known to the law and is supported by some show of reason, it will oust their jurisdiction, if the assertion is made bona fide[3]; and, even if the claim of right is not put forward at the first available opportunity, a quashing order[4] may still be granted[5]. Whether a claim of right is put forward bona fide or not is a question for the lower court to decide in the first instance[6].

Where the jurisdiction of magistrates is expressly ousted by statute, in cases where the defendant has acted on 'a fair and reasonable supposition' that he had a right, the common law restriction in favour of bona fide claims of right is superseded; and the magistrates may properly proceed with the case, even though the defendant's claim was bona fide, if they find that the claim was not based upon a fair and reasonable supposition[7].

Even although a claim of title is put forward bona fide by the defendant, if the claim is necessarily involved in the very question which the magistrates have to decide, their jurisdiction is not ousted and a quashing order will not be granted[8]. Although the court below must decide in the first instance whether its jurisdiction is ousted by a claim put forward by the defendant, this question, being collateral to the merits, may be inquired into on an application for a quashing order[9], and the decision of the magistrates may be quashed, at any rate, if there was no evidence proper to be considered by the magistrates in support of it[10].

1   *R v Pearson* (1870) LR 5 QB 237; *R (Kennedy) v Cork County Justices* [1913] 2 IR 391. As to claims of right see also MAGISTRATES. As to claim of right in relation to game rights see ANIMALS vol 2 (2008) PARA 763 et seq; and in relation to fishing rights see AGRICULTURE AND FISHERIES vol 1(2) (2007 Reissue) PARA 789 et seq. The common law principle is excluded by the Criminal Damage Act 1971, which empowers magistrates to determine disputes of title to property when trying offences under that Act or any other offences of destroying or damaging property: s 7(2).
2   *Hudson v MacRae* (1863) 4 B & S 585; *Hargreaves v Diddams* (1875) LR 10 QB 582; *Foulger v Steadman* (1872) LR 8 QB 65; *Watkins v Major* (1875) LR 10 CP 662; *R v Tyrone County Justices* [1917] 2 IR 96.
3   *Cornwell v Sanders* (1862) 3 B & S 206.
4   As to quashing orders see PARA 693 et seq.
5   *R v Taunton St Mary Inhabitants* (1815) 3 M & S 465.

6 *Thompson v Ingham* (1850) 14 QB 710 at 718; *R v Cridland* (1857) 7 E & B 853. See also *R v Wrottesley and Gordon* (1830) 1 B & Ad 648; *R v Colling* (1852) 17 QB 816.

7 *White v Feast* (1872) LR 7 QB 353; *R v Musset* (1872) 26 LT 429.

8 *R v Bradley* (1894) 70 LT 379, DC (where the offence was under highways legislation for the erection of a fence on a highway, and the defendant contended that the land on which the fence was erected was his land, and therefore that a question of title arose, and the court held that that was part of the very question for the justices to decide). See also *R v Ogden, ex p Long Ashton RDC* [1963] 1 All ER 574, [1963] 1 WLR 274, DC (where mandamus was issued to magistrates who had erroneously declined to determine whether the accused was guilty of wilfully obstructing the highway once he had made a bona fide claim of title). See further PARA 710. Orders of mandamus are now known as mandatory orders: see PARA 687 note 3. As to mandatory orders see PARA 703 et seq.

9 *Thompson v Ingham* (1850) 14 QB 710 at 718; *Pease v Chaytor* (1863) 3 B & S 620 at 641; *R v Nunneley* (1858) EB & E 852. See, however, *Anima v Ahyeye* [1956] AC 404, PC, where in the particular statutory context, jurisdiction was ousted only if the prescribed circumstances became apparent to the tribunal itself or were made apparent to the tribunal before the end of the case.

10 *R v Stimpson* (1863) 4 B & S 301; *R v Nunneley* (1858) EB & E 852; *Usher v Luxmore* (1889) 62 LT 110, DC; *Cornwell v Sanders* (1862) 3 B & S 206; and see *Anon* (1830) 1 B & Ad 382, DC.

615. Declining jurisdiction. A mandatory order[1] will issue to an inferior tribunal or other decision-maker[2] which wrongfully refuses to hear and determine a matter within its jurisdiction or the scope of its powers[3]. The tribunal or other body may have declined jurisdiction by incorrectly determining that it has no power to proceed to entertain a matter on its merits[4]; it will not be deemed to have declined jurisdiction merely by coming to a wrong decision on the merits of the case[5]. Refusal of jurisdiction may also be conveyed indirectly by conduct, as where a tribunal or other decision-maker fails to address itself to the question before it and answers a different question[6], or has acted under the dictation of another body[7], or has wrongfully delegated its powers to another body[8], or has rejected relevant evidence on the ground that it has no power to inquire into the matter which that evidence was intended to prove[9], or has dismissed an application on the basis of a fixed rule of policy not to entertain applications of that character, irrespective of the individual merits of the case[10], or has postponed or adjourned a hearing on improper grounds or for an unreasonably long period, so that its conduct is tantamount to a refusal to exercise the jurisdiction or discretion vested in it[11].

1 As to mandatory orders see PARA 703 et seq.

2 See *R v Visitors for the Inns of Court, ex p Calder* [1994] QB 1 at 40, [1993] 2 All ER 876 at 903, CA, per Nicholls V-C.

3 As to jurisdiction and powers generally see PARA 610. See also PARA 708 et seq.

4 Common examples occur in cases concerning magistrates and other inferior courts. Thus in *Re Harrington* [1984] AC 743, sub nom *Harrington v Roots* [1984] 2 All ER 474, HL, magistrates dismissed charges without hearing prosecution evidence and then refused an application to 'reopen' the matter on the ground that the 'double jeopardy' rule meant that the accused could not be tried having once been acquitted. The House of Lords held: (1) that the original decision to dismiss the charges was a nullity because the magistrates had acted outwith their jurisdiction in declining to hear the prosecution case; and (2) accordingly, the 'double jeopardy' rule did not apply and the proceedings could be re-opened. See also *R v County of London Quarter Sessions, ex p Downes* [1954] 1 QB 1, [1953] 2 All ER 750, DC; *R v Norfolk Quarter Sessions, ex p Brunson* [1953] 1 QB 503, [1953] 1 All ER 346, DC; *R v Value Added Tax Tribunal, ex p Happer* [1982] 1 WLR 1261, [1982] STC 700; *R v Oxford Justices, ex p D* [1987] QB 199, [1986] 3 All ER 129; *R v Nottingham County Court, ex p Byers* [1985] 1 All ER 735, [1985] 1 WLR 403; *R v Corby Juvenile Court, ex p M* [1987] 1 All ER 992, [1987] 1 WLR 55; *R v Calder Justices, ex p Kennedy* (1992) 156 JP 716, (1992) Times, 18 February, DC; *R v Nottingham Justices, ex p Taylor* [1992] QB 557, [1991] 4 All ER 860, DC; *R v Bromley Magistrates' Court, ex p Smith* [1995] 4 All ER 146, [1995] 1 WLR 944; *R v Liverpool City Justices, ex p DPP* [1993] QB 233, [1992] 3 All ER 249, DC; *Re Wilson* [1985] AC 750, [1985]

2 All ER 97, HL. Compare also *Beecham Group plc v Gist-Brocades NV* [1986] 1 WLR 51, sub nom *Allen & Hanburys Ltd v Generics (UK) Ltd* [1986] RPC 203, HL (Comptroller-General of Patents, Designs and Trade Marks wrongly refusing to entertain licence application before expiry of previously granted licence); *R v Gaming Licensing Committee of North Hertfordshire, ex p Gala Leisure Ltd* [1996] COD 312, (1985) Times, 5 April (committee wrongly refusing to hear licensing application on basis premises not yet built); *R (on the application of Gashi) v Chief Adjudicator* [2001] EWHC Admin 916 at [19]–[21], [2001] 39 LS Gaz R 38 at [19]–[21] per Wilkie J (provision of incompetent interpreter at hearing before adjudicator capable of being a procedural error within the chief adjudicator's statutory jurisdiction and therefore he was wrong to refuse to hear appeal).

5   As to the distinction between matters which go to jurisdiction and those which do not see PARA 624.

6   See eg *Board of Education v Rice* [1911] AC 179, HL; *R v Manchester Legal Aid Committee, ex p RA Brand & Co Ltd* [1952] 2 QB 413, [1952] 1 All ER 480; *R v Wells Street Metropolitan Stipendiary Magistrate, ex p Westminster City Council* [1986] 3 All ER 4, [1986] 1 WLR 1046, DC. Such a failure may also be described as an error of law: see PARA 612.

7   See ADMINISTRATIVE LAW vol 1(1) (2001 Reissue) PARA 30.

8   This follows from the rule against sub-delegation of judicial or discretionary power: see ADMINISTRATIVE LAW vol 1(1) (2001 Reissue) PARA 31.

9   *R v Marsham* [1892] 1 QB 371, CA; *R v Wells Street Metropolitan Stipendiary Magistrate, ex p Westminster City Council* [1986] 3 All ER 4, [1986] 1 WLR 1046, DC; *R v Oxford City Justices, ex p Berry* [1988] QB 507, [1987] 1 All ER 1244, DC; and see *R v Kensington and Chelsea Rent Tribunal, ex p MacFarlane* (1975) 29 P & CR 13, DC (refusal to hear party to the proceedings). See also PARA 612.

10 See *R v Port of London Authority, ex p Kynoch Ltd* [1919] 1 KB 176, CA (although on the facts it was held there was no refusal to exercise discretion in that case); *R v Police Complaints Board, ex p Maddon* [1983] 2 All ER 353, [1983] 1 WLR 447 (board unlawfully fettering its discretion by reference to decisions of the Director of Public Prosecutions); *R v Hampshire County Council, ex p W* [1994] ELR 460, (1994) Times, 9 June (council's refusal even to consider paying for a private school for W unlawful). This is an aspect of fettering of discretion: see PARA 620.

11 *R v Evans* (1890) 54 JP 471, DC (distinguished in *R v Southampton Justices, ex p Lebern* (1907) 96 LT 697, DC); *R v Central Professional Committee for Opticians, ex p Brown* [1949] 2 All ER 519 at 522, DC; *R v Secretary of State for the Home Department, ex p Phansopkar* [1976] QB 606, [1975] 3 All ER 497, CA; *R v Rent Officer for Camden, ex p Ebiri* [1981] 1 All ER 950, [1981] 1 WLR 881, DC; *R v Secretary of State for Wales, ex p South Glamorgan County Council* [1988] COD 104, (1988) Times, 25 June; cf *Engineers' and Managers' Association v Advisory, Conciliation and Arbitration Service and United Kingdom Association of Professional Engineers* [1980] 1 All ER 896, [1980] 1 WLR 302, HL (deferment reasonable in the circumstances but indefinite delay would be abdication of power); *R v Secretary of State for the Home Department, ex p Rofathullah* [1989] QB 219, sub nom *R v Secretary of State for the Home Department, ex p Ullah* [1987] 1 All ER 1025; *R v St Albans Magistrates' Court, ex p Read* (1993) 6 Admin LR 201, [1994] 1 FCR 50; *R v Secretary of State for the Home Department, ex p Fire Brigades Union* [1995] 2 AC 513, [1995] 2 All ER 244, HL (unlawful decision not to bring statute into force); *R v Customs and Excise Comrs, ex p Kay & Co Ltd* [1996] STC 1500 (unlawful to defer statutory duty to repay VAT).

616. Error on the face of the record. A distinction used to be drawn between errors of law within jurisdiction, errors of law which go to jurisdiction and errors of law on the face of the record. The distinction between errors of law on the face of the record and other errors of law has now been rendered obsolete[1]. A distinction between errors of law within jurisdiction and errors of law which go to jurisdiction may still be drawn in certain exceptional cases[2]. The old law on error on the face of the record is as follows.

Where upon the face of the proceedings themselves it appears that the determination of an inferior tribunal is wrong in law, a quashing order[3] will be granted[4]. Thus, it will be granted where a charge laid before magistrates, as stated in the information, does not constitute an offence punishable by the magistrates[5], or where it does not amount in law to the offence of which the accused is convicted[6], or where an order is made which is unauthorised by the finding of the magistrates[7], or is materially defective in form[8]. Most of these cases are to be regarded as usurpations of jurisdiction[9]; but it is settled that a quashing order will also be granted to quash a determination for error of law on the face of the record although the error does not go to jurisdiction[10]. The meaning of the record for this purpose has not been authoritatively determined[11], but it may be taken to include the decision itself, such reasons, if any, as are given for the decision[12], and any other material or instrument identified therein with a sufficient degree of particularity for it to be construed as forming part of the record[13]. The record cannot usually be supplemented by affidavit or other evidence designed to disclose a latent error of law[14]. A quashing order will not issue to quash a decision for error of fact unless the error goes to jurisdiction[15] but, if a tribunal sets out in its order the evidence adduced before it and the conclusions drawn from the evidence, the court may quash the decision for patent error of law[16] if there is no evidence proper to be considered in support of a material point[17], or if the order discloses on its face that the tribunal has perpetrated an error of law in the process of drawing inferences or conclusions from the facts as found[18].

A statutory provision to the effect that the determination of a tribunal is to be final does not protect it from review for error of law on the face of the record[19] or for any other relevant ground[20], and, subject to limited exceptions[21], a provision in an Act passed before 1 August 1958 that an order or determination is not to be called into question in any court, or any provision in such an act which by similar words excludes any of the powers of the High Court, is equally ineffective to bar review[22].

1   This the effect of the decision in *Anisminic Ltd v Foreign Compensation Commission* [1969] 2 AC 147, [1969] 1 All ER 208, HL. See further PARA 610 note 11.

2   See PARA 610 note 11.

3   As to quashing orders see PARA 693 et seq.

4   *R v Nat Bell Liquors Ltd* [1922] 2 AC 128 at 155–156, PC; *R v Northumberland Compensation Appeal Tribunal, ex p Shaw* [1952] 1 KB 338, [1952] 1 All ER 122, CA. See also *Walsall Overseers of the Poor v London and North Western Rly Co* (1878) 4 App Cas 30, HL.

5   *R v Cridland* (1857) 7 E & B 853 (four accused ordered to be imprisoned for one month, until the costs and charges of conveying all four to gaol should be paid).

6   *R v Bolton* (1841) 1 QB 66 at 72 per Lord Denman CJ.

7   *R v Tomlinson* (1872) LR 8 QB 12; *R v Kay* (1873) LR 8 QB 324 (bastardy orders given retroactive effect); *R v London Justices, ex p Saunders* (1895) 64 LJMC 273, DC (imprisonment with hard labour ordered in default of distress for non-payment of fine; no power to inflict hard labour); *R v Willesden Justices, ex p Utley* [1948] 1 KB 397, [1947] 2 All ER 838, DC (fine imposed in excess of statutory maximum); *R v Highgate Justices, ex p Petrou* [1954] 1 All ER 406, [1954] 1 WLR 485, DC (fine imposed under guise of order for costs).

8   *R v Darlington Corpn Juvenile Court, ex p West Hartlepool Corpn* [1957] 1 All ER 398, [1957] 1 WLR 363, DC (order committing child to care of local authority failed to state that consent of the local authority had been obtained).

9   Cf PARAS 610–613.

10 *R v Northumberland Compensation Appeal Tribunal, ex p Shaw* [1952] 1 KB 338, [1952] 1 All ER 122, CA, not following observations as to the scope of certiorari by members of the Court of Appeal in *Racecourse Betting Control Board v Secretary for Air* [1944] Ch 114, [1944] 1 All ER 60, CA. See also *R v Medical Appeal Tribunal, ex p Gilmore* [1957] 1 QB 574, sub nom *Re Gilmore's Application* [1957] 1 All ER 796, CA. The error must cause injustice: *R v Crown Court at Knightsbridge, ex p Marcrest Properties Ltd* [1983] 1 All ER 1148, [1983] 1 WLR 300, CA; *R v Chief Registrar of Friendly Societies, ex p New Cross Building Society* [1984] QB 227 at 260–261, [1984] 2 All ER 27 at 42–43, CA, per Griffiths LJ.

11 The question was left open by the majority of their Lordships in *Baldwin and Francis Ltd v Patents Appeal Tribunal* [1959] AC 663, [1959] 2 All ER 433, HL, but Lord Denning's view (at 688–690, 444–455), that it included not only the decision of the tribunal but other documents appearing therefrom to be the basis of the decision, including the patent specifications and the original decision of the superintending examiner, was adopted by the Divisional Court in *R v*

Patents Appeal Tribunal, ex p Swift & Co [1962] 2 QB 647, [1962] 1 All ER 610, DC. In *R v Northumberland Compensation Appeal Tribunal, ex p Shaw* [1952] 1 KB 338 at 352, [1952] 1 All ER 122 at 130, CA, Denning LJ said that the record had to include at least the document initiating the proceedings, the pleadings, if any, and the adjudication. Any such definition must, however, be subject to statutory prescriptions as to the form of a determination. In any event, the record for this purpose is not necessarily to be identified with the formal record of a court of record. Quaere how far the record is to be defined by reference to authorities on the meaning of the face of an award for the purposes of arbitration law: see eg *Giacomo Costa Fu Andrea v British Italian Trading Co Ltd* [1963] 1 QB 201, [1962] 2 All ER 53, CA.

    The trend in later cases is towards a generous definition of the record: see *R v Supplementary Benefits Commission, ex p Singer* [1973] 2 All ER 931, [1973] 1 WLR 713, DC (informal letter sent after decision giving reasons therefore); *R v Preston Supplementary Benefits Appeal Tribunal, ex p Moore* [1975] 2 All ER 807 at 810, [1975] 1 WLR 624 at 628, CA, per Lord Denning MR (all the documents in the case); *R v Crown Court at Knightsbridge, ex p The Aspinall Curzon Ltd* (1982) Times, 16 December (court may look at evidence before the tribunal; but this is open to doubt, as the error would not appear on the face of the record); and see note 12.

12   In *R v Chertsey Justices, ex p Franks* [1961] 2 QB 152, [1961] 1 All ER 825, DC (oral reasons given by magistrates for their decision were held to be part of the record, and since they disclosed an erroneous legal approach that order was quashed); *R v Crown Court at Knightsbridge, ex p International Sporting Club (London) Ltd* [1982] QB 304, [1981] 3 All ER 417, DC (transcript of oral judgment part of the record; cf *R v Newington Licensing Justices* [1948] 1 KB 681 at 686, [1948] 1 All ER 346 at 348, DC). Under the Tribunals and Inquiries Act 1992 s 10(1), (6), an oral statement of reasons for decisions given by tribunals specified in Sch 1 or by ministers notifying a decision following a statutory inquiry (s 16(1)) or where a person could have required the holding of such an inquiry, are to be taken to be incorporated in the record. Normally, in the absence of a statutory requirement to that effect, there is no duty to give reasons for decisions: see eg *R v Gaming Board for Great Britain, ex p Benaim and Khaida* [1970] 2 QB 417, [1970] 2 All ER 528, CA. As to whether failure to give reasons or adequate reasons is in itself an error of law where a statute imposes such a duty, the authorities are in conflict: see PARA 613. If the reasons given (whether or not they form part of the record) show that legally irrelevant considerations have been taken into account, there is a jurisdictional defect and a quashing order will issue: *Anisminic Ltd v Foreign Compensation Commission* [1969] 2 AC 147, [1969] 1 All ER 208, HL, overruling *Davies v Price* [1958] 1 All ER 671, [1958] 1 WLR 434, CA, on this point.

13   See notes 11–12; *R v Medical Appeal Tribunal, ex p Gilmore* [1957] 1 QB 574, sub nom *Re Gilmore's Application* [1957] 1 All ER 796, CA (specialist's report, an extract of which was embodied in the record, became part of the decision); *IRC v Hood Barrs* (1961) 39 TC 683, HL (question whether directives as to ascertainment of loss issued by General Commissioners of Income Tax were to be treated as part of the record on appeal, left undecided).

    It seems that an order may also issue to quash a determination for an error of law not disclosed by the record but admitted by the respondent to the court or possibly where the parties agree to treat such an error as if it were incorporated in the record (*R v Northumberland Compensation Appeal Tribunal, ex p Shaw* [1952] 1 KB 338 at 353–354, [1952] 1 All ER 122 at 131–132, CA, per Denning LJ; *R v Southampton Justices, ex p Green* [1976] QB 11 at 22, [1975] 2 All ER 1073 at 1080, CA, per Browne LJ); but it is doubtful whether the court has any inherent jurisdiction to order the completion of the record save where the content of the record is prescribed by statute: *R v Southampton Justices, ex p Corker* (1976) 120 Sol Jo 214 (although justices may give reasons for their decision by affidavit, they cannot be forced to do so); cf *R v Northumberland Compensation Appeal Tribunal, ex p Shaw* at 352, 130 per Denning LJ; *R v Medical Appeal Tribunal, ex p Gilmore* at 582–583 and 800–801 per Denning LJ, citing *Williams v Lord Bagot* (1824) 4 Dow & Ry KB 315; *R v Warnford* (1825) 5 Dow & Ry KB 489.

14   *R v Nat Bell Liquors Ltd* [1922] 2 AC 128 at 155–156, PC; *R v Bolton* (1841) 1 QB 66; *R v Agricultural Land Tribunal (South Eastern Area), ex p Bracey* [1960] 2 All ER 518, [1960] 1 WLR 911, DC; *Re Allen and Matthews' Arbitration* [1971] 2 QB 518, [1971] 2 All ER 1259. But affidavits from justices giving the reasons for their decisions may be treated as part of the record: *R v Southampton Justices, ex p Green* [1976] QB 11 at 22, [1975] 2 All ER 1073 at 1080, CA, per Browne LJ; cf the second paragraph of note 11. See also *R v Crown Court at Knightsbridge, ex p The Aspinall Curzon Ltd* (1982) Times, 16 December; and note 11.

15   *R v Bolton* (1841) 1 QB 66; *R v Cambridgeshire Justices* (1835) 4 Ad & El 111; *Tarry v Newman* (1846) 15 M & W 645 at 653; *Colonial Bank of Australasia Ltd v Willan* (1874) LR 5 PC 417; *Ex p McVittie* (1914) 78 JP Jo 340; *R (Redmond) v Jellett* [1919] 2 IR 79;

R (Romney) v Lupton [1919] 2 IR 131; *R (Rooney) v Local Government Board* [1920] 2 IR 347, CA; *R v Murphy* [1921] 2 IR 190; *R v Nat Bell Liquors Ltd* [1922] 2 AC 128, PC; *R (Limerick Corpn) v Local Government Board* [1922] 2 IR 76, CA; *R (Armagh County Council) v Local Government Board* (1922) 56 ILT 98; *R v Markham, ex p Marsh* [1923] WN 112, DC; *R v Criminal Injuries Compensation Board, ex p Staten* [1972] 1 All ER 1034, [1972] 1 WLR 569, DC.

16 As to the meaning of 'error of law' see PARA 613.

17 *R v Smith* (1800) 8 Term Rep 588; *R v Birmingham Compensation Appeal Tribunal of Ministry of Labour and National Service, ex p Road Haulage Executive* [1952] 2 All ER 100n, DC; *Armah v Government of Ghana* [1968] AC 192 at 233–234, [1966] 3 All ER 177 at 186–187, HL, per Lord Reid; *R v Criminal Injuries Compensation Board, ex p Staten* [1972] 1 All ER 1034, [1972] 1 WLR 569, DC.

18 See *R v Crown Court at Knightsbridge, ex p Marcrest Properties Ltd* [1983] 1 All ER 1148, [1983] 1 WLR 300, CA; and PARA 613.

19 *R v Medical Appeal Tribunal, ex p Gilmore* [1957] 1 QB 574, sub nom *Re Gilmore's Application* [1957] 1 All ER 796, CA.

20 These include want of jurisdiction, breach of the rules of natural justice, fraud or perjury. See PARAS 610–614, 648 et seq.

21 The exceptions are: (1) any order or determination of a court of law; and (2) where an Act makes special provision for application to the High Court within a time limited by the Act: see the Tribunals and Inquiries Act 1992 s 12(3).

22 Tribunals and Inquiries Act 1992 s 12(1), reproducing the terms of the Tribunals and Inquiries Act 1958 s 11(1) (repealed). 1 August 1958 was the date of the passing of this earlier Act. General exclusionary formulae, including formulae expressly taking away the right to a quashing order, not covered by the terms of these Acts are effective to bar review by a quashing order for error of law on the face of the record: see eg *Ex p Hopwood* (1850) 15 QB 121; *Re Shropshire Justices, ex p Blewitt* (1866) 14 LT 598 (where the record showed that there was no evidence in support of the convictions of the accused, so that the convictions were erroneous in law); *Anisminic Ltd v Foreign Compensation Commission* [1969] 2 AC 147, [1969] 1 All ER 208, HL; see also *South East Asia Fire Bricks Sdn Bhd v Non-Metallic Mineral Products Manufacturing Employees Union* [1981] AC 363, [1980] 2 All ER 689, PC. This does not apply in respect of other grounds for review by a quashing order: see *Anisminic Ltd v Foreign Compensation Commission*; and PARA 614; and ADMINISTRATIVE LAW vol 1(1) (2001 Reissue) PARA 21.

(2) ABUSE OF POWER

(i) Irrationality

617. Manifest unreasonableness. A decision of a tribunal or other body exercising a statutory discretion will be quashed for 'irrationality'[1], or as is often said, for '*Wednesbury* unreasonableness'[2]. As grounds of review, bad faith and improper purpose[3], consideration of irrelevant considerations and disregard for relevant considerations[4] and manifest unreasonableness[5] run into one another[6]. However, it is well established as a distinct ground of review that a decision which is so perverse that no reasonable body, properly directing itself as to the law to be applied, could have reached such a decision, will be quashed[7].

Ordinarily the circumstances in which the courts will intervene to quash decisions on this ground are very limited[8]. The courts will not quash a decision merely because they disagree with it or consider that it was founded on a grave error of judgment[9], or because the material upon which the decision-maker could have formed the view he did was limited[10]. However, the standard of reasonableness varies with the subject matter of an act or decision[11]. The court will quash an act or decision which interferes with fundamental human rights for unreasonableness if there is no substantial objective justification for the interference[12]. By contrast, the exercise of discretionary powers involving a large element of policy will generally only be quashed on the basis of manifest unreasonableness in exceptional cases[13].

In addition to administrative acts and decisions, byelaws may be held to be void for manifest unreasonableness[14].

Generally where a statute provides that one body or person may substitute its own determination for that of another body where that body is 'proposing to act unreasonably', such a provision will be construed as applying only where the latter body is proposing to act unreasonably in the *Wednesbury*[15] sense[16].

1   See *Council of Civil Service Unions v Minister for the Civil Service* [1985] AC 374 at 410, [1984] 3 All ER 935 at 950–951, HL, per Lord Diplock and at 415 and 954 per Lord Roskill; *Wheeler v Leicester City Council* [1985] AC 1054 at 1078, [1985] 2 All ER 1106 at 1111, HL, per Lord Roskill; *R v Secretary of State for the Home Department, ex p Brind* [1991] 1 AC 696 at 757, sub nom *Brind v Secretary of State for the Home Department* [1991] 1 All ER 720 at 731, HL, per Lord Ackner.

2   *Associated Provincial Picture Houses Ltd v Wednesbury Corpn* [1948] 1 KB 223 at 229, [1947] 2 All ER 680 at 682–683, CA, per Lord Greene MR; and see *George v Devon County Council* [1988] 3 All ER 1002 at 1008, [1988] 3 WLR 1386 at 1393–1394, HL, per Lord Keith of Kinkel. See also note 1.

3   See PARA 622.

4   See PARA 623.

5   Various terms are used in the authorities, e g absurdity, perversity or irrationality.

6   See *Associated Provincial Picture Houses Ltd v Wednesbury Corpn* [1948] 1 KB 223 at 229, [1947] 2 All ER 680 at 682–683, CA, per Lord Greene MR; *Kruse v Johnson* [1898] 2 QB 91, DC, per Lord Russell of Killowen CJ; *Re City of Plymouth City Centre Declaratory Order 1942, Robinson v Minister of Town and Country Planning* [1947] KB 702 at 724, [1947] 1 All ER 851 at 863, CA, per Somervell LJ; *R v Governor of Pentonville Prison, ex p Osman* [1989] 3 All ER 701 at 722, [1990] 1 WLR 277 at 301, DC, per Lloyd LJ; *R v Secretary of State for the Environment, ex p Hammersmith and Fulham London Borough Council* [1991] 1 AC 521 at 562, sub nom *Hammersmith and Fulham London Borough Council v Secretary of State for the Environment* [1990] 3 All ER 589 at 615, HL, per Lord Donaldson but c f at 597 and 637 per Lord Bridge of Harwich; *R v Secretary of State for the Home Department, ex p Oladehinde* [1991] 1 AC 254 at 280, [1990] 2 All ER 367 at 380, CA, per Lord Donaldson MR (judicial review jurisdiction not a series of separate boxes but a rich tapestry of many strands which cross, re-cross and blend to produce justice); *Boddington v British Transport Police* [1999] 2 AC 143 at 152, [1998] 2 All ER 203 at 208, HL, per Lord Irvine of Lairg LC and at 170 and 224 per Lord Steyn; *R (on the application of Bancoult) v Secretary of State for Foreign & Commonwealth Affairs* [2007] EWCA Civ 498 at [60], [2008] QB 365 at [60] per Sedley LJ (abuse of power the root concept into which other grounds of judicial review merge); overruled on other grounds [2008] UKHL 61, [2009] 1 AC 453, [2008] 4 All ER 1055. That reasonable conduct was implicit in the exercise of statutory powers in good faith was asserted by Lord Macnaghten in *Westminster Corpn v London and North Western Rly Co* [1905] AC 426 at 430, HL, but the distinctiveness of the concepts of good faith and reasonableness is often clear cut: see *R v Roberts, ex p Scurr* [1924] 2 KB 695 at 719, CA, per Scrutton LJ; and *R v Secretary of State for the Environment, ex p Greenwich London Borough Council* [1989] COD 530, (1989) Times, 17 May, DC. Bad faith must also be particularised and proved to a stricter standard than 'mere' unreasonableness: see further PARA 621.

7   There are many statements to this effect and different formulations of this test: see eg *Short v Poole Corpn* [1926] Ch 66 at 90–91, CA, per Warrington LJ (giving the example of a red-haired teacher, dismissed because she had red hair); *Associated Provincial Picture Houses Ltd v Wednesbury Corpn* [1948] 1 KB 223 at 229, [1947] 2 All ER 680 at 682–683, CA, per Lord Greene MR; *Secretary of State for Education and Science v Tameside Metropolitan Borough Council* [1977] AC 1014, [1976] 3 All ER 665, CA and HL; *Bromley London Borough Council v GLC* [1983] 1 AC 768 at 821, [1982] 1 All ER 129 at 159, HL, per Lord Diplock; *Council of Civil Service Unions v Minister for the Civil Service* [1985] AC 374 at 410, [1984] 3 All ER 935 at 951, HL, per Lord Diplock; *Wheeler v Leicester City Council* [1985] AC 1054 at 1064, [1985] 2 All ER 151 at 158, CA, per Browne Wilkinson LJ; *Puhlhofer v Hillingdon London Borough Council* [1986] AC 484 at 518, [1986] 1 All ER 467 at 474, HL, per Lord Brightman; *Nottinghamshire County Council v Secretary of State for the Environment* [1986] AC 240 at 247, [1986] 1 All ER 199 at 202, HL, per Lord Scarman; *Champion v Chief*

Constable of the Gwent Constabulary [1990] 1 All ER 116 at 124, [1990] 1 WLR 1 at 12, HL, per Lord Ackner (dissenting); *R v Secretary of State for the Home Department, ex p Brind* [1991] 1 AC 696 at 757, sub nom *Brind v Secretary of State for the Home Department* [1991] 1 All ER 720 at 731, HL, per Lord Ackner; *R v Secretary of State for Defence, ex p Smith* [1996] QB 517 at 556, [1996] 1 All ER 257 at 265, CA, per Sir Thomas Bingham MR; *R v Chief Constable of Sussex, ex p International Trader's Ferry Ltd* [1999] 2 AC 418, [1999] 1 All ER 129, HL; *R (on the application of Mahmood) v Secretary of State for the Home Department* [2001] 1 WLR 840, [2001] 2 FCR 63, CA; *R (on the application of Isiko) v Secretary of State for the Home Department* [2001] 1 FCR 633, [2001] 1 FLR 930, CA.

8   As to the concept of reasonableness see *Council of Civil Service Unions v Minister for the Civil Service* [1985] AC 374 at 410, [1984] 3 All ER 935 at 950–951, HL, per Lord Diplock (decision *Wednesbury* unreasonable where it is so outrageous in its defiance of logic or of accepted moral standards that no sensible person who had applied his mind to the question to be decided could have arrived at it); applied in *AA (Uganda) v Secretary of State for the Home Department* [2008] EWCA Civ 579, [2008] All ER (D) 300 (May) at [41] per Buxton LJ; *Boddington v British Transport Police* [1999] 2 AC 143 at 175, [1998] 2 All ER 203 at 229, HL, per Lord Steyn (question is whether the decision was within the range of reasonable decisions open to a decision-maker); *R v Chief Constable of Sussex, ex p International Trader's Ferry Ltd* [1999] 2 AC 418 at 452, [1999] 1 All ER 129 at 157, HL, per Lord Cooke of Thorndon (question is whether the decision in question was one which a reasonable authority could reach); *Re W (an infant)* [1971] AC 682 at 695–700, [1971] 2 All ER 49 at 52–56, HL, per Lord Hailsham of St Marylebone LC (two persons can reasonably come to opposite conclusions on the same set of facts; not every mistaken exercise of judgment is unreasonable); approved in *Secretary of State for Education and Science v Tameside Metropolitan Borough Council* [1977] AC 1014 at 1070, [1976] 3 All ER 665 at 700, HL, per Lord Salmon. The test is an objective one: see *R v Department for Education and Employment, ex p Begbie* [2000] 1 WLR 1115 at 1130, [2000] ELR 445 at [78], CA, per Laws LJ; *Secretary of State for Education and Science v Tameside Metropolitan Borough Council* at 1054 and 687 per Viscount Dilhorne. See also the cases cited in notes 1, 7.

9   The underlying principle is that the court exercises a supervisory and not an appellate jurisdiction and accordingly will not substitute its view for that of the body charged by Parliament with exercising a discretion. See eg *Chief Constable of the North Wales Police v Evans* [1982] 3 All ER 141 at 143, [1982] 1 WLR 1155 at 1160, HL, per Lord Hailsham of St Marylebone LC; *Lonrho plc v Secretary of State for Trade and Industry* [1989] 2 All ER 609, sub nom *R v Secretary of State for Trade and Industry, ex p Lonrho plc* [1989] 1 WLR 525, HL; *R v IRC, ex p Unilever plc* [1996] STC 681 at 695, CA, per Simon Brown LJ, cited with approval in *R (Association of British Civilian Internees: Far East Region) v Secretary of State for Defence* [2003] EWCA Civ 473 at [86], [2003] QB 1397 at [86] per Dyson LJ; *WM (Democratic Republic of Congo) v Secretary of State for the Home Department* [2006] EWCA Civ 1495 at [16], [2007] Imm AR 337 at [16] per Buxton LJ (wrong for court to take the short cut of deciding the issue for itself, even if well placed to do so). The court is especially reluctant to interfere where the decision taken has a high political content: see note 13. The position is otherwise, though, where fundamental rights are involved: see PARA 619.

10   See eg *R v Bournemouth Borough Council, ex p Thompson* (1985) 83 LGR 662; and PARA 613 note 6. However, a decision will be quashed if there was no basis on which the decision-maker could properly have taken it or if the basis was insufficient: see PARA 613 note 6.

11   See eg *R v Department for Education and Employment, ex p Begbie* [2000] 1 WLR 1115 at 1130, [2000] ELR 445 at [78], CA, per Laws LJ (reasonableness is a spectrum not a single point; review will be more or less intrusive according to the nature and gravity of what is at stake). See also PARA 619.

12   The more substantial the interference, the greater the justification required: see eg *Brown v Stott* [2003] 1 AC 681 at 720, [2001] 2 All ER 97 at 130, PC; *R v Secretary of State for the Home Department, ex p Brind* [1991] 1 AC 696, sub nom *Brind v Secretary of State for the Home Department* [1991] 1 All ER 720, HL; *R v Secretary of State for Defence, ex p Smith* [1996] QB 517 at 554, [1996] 1 All ER 257 at 263, CA, per Lord Bingham MR; *R v Secretary of State for the Home Department, ex p Launder* [1997] 3 All ER 961 at 988, [1997] 1 WLR 839 at 866, HL, per Lord Hope of Craighead; *R v Lord Saville, ex p A* [1999] 4 All ER 860 at 872, [2000] 1 WLR 1855 at 1867, CA, per Lord Woolf MR; *R (on the application of Mahmood) v Secretary of State for the Home Department* [2001] 1 WLR 840, [2001] 2 FCR 63, CA. Note that the court may quash a decision or act which is incompatible with human rights protected by the Convention for the Protection of Human Rights and Fundamental Freedoms (Rome, 4 November 1950; TS 71 (1953) Cmd 8969) for unlawfulness: see the Human Rights Act 1998 s 6(1); and PARA 651.

13   At one time it was thought that most Crown prerogative powers fell into this category: see *Council of Civil Service Unions v Minister for the Civil Service* [1985] AC 374 at 411, [1984] 3 All ER 935 at 951, HL, per Lord Diplock; *Re McFarland* [2004] UKHL 17 at [41], [2004] 1 WLR 1289 at [41] per Lord Scott of Foscote; and c f *R v Criminal Injuries Compensation Board, ex p* [1995] 1 All ER 870, [1995] 1 WLR 845, CA (non-statutory functions will rarely be interfered with). However, the position is now that the exercise of prerogative powers will be subject to the review of the courts in the same way as any other executive act: see *R (on the allocation of Bancoult) v Secretary of State for Foreign and Commonwealth Affairs* [2008] UKHL 61 at [35], [2009] 1 AC 453 at [35], [2008] 4 All ER 1055 at [35] per Lord Hoffmann. Nonetheless, the courts will still exercise caution where judgments as to political, social and economic policy are involved. Indeed, in some cases it is said that the 'political' content of a policy is such that it can only be impugned on 'grounds of irrationality short of bad faith, improper motive or manifest absurdity': *Nottinghamshire County Council v Secretary of State for the Environment* [1986] AC 240 at 247, [1986] 1 All ER 199 at 202, HL, per Lord Scarman; *R v Secretary of State for the Environment, ex p Hammersmith and Fulham London Borough Council* [1991] 1 AC 521 at 596–597, sub nom *Hammersmith and Fulham London Borough Council v Secretary of State for the Environment* [1990] 3 All ER 589 at 635–636, HL, per Lord Bridge of Harwich. For examples of such policy cases see: *R v Lambeth London Borough, ex p G* [1994] ELR 207 at 213 per Potts J (education policy); *R v Secretary of State for the Home Department, ex p Launder* [1997] 3 All ER 961 at 985, [1997] 1 WLR 839 at 854, HL, per Lord Hope (extradition policy); *Clark v University of Lincolnshire and Humberside* [2000] 3 All ER 752, [2000] 1 WLR 1988 (issues of academic or pastoral judgment); *Puhlhofer v Hillingdon London Borough Council* [1986] AC 484 at 518, [1986] 1 All ER 467 at 474, HL, per Lord Brightman (questions of housing allocation); *R v Secretary of State for Education and Science, ex p Malik* [1994] ELR 121 (school closure); *R (on the application of Gurung) v Secretary of State for Defence* [2008] EWHC 1496 (Admin) at [55], [2008] All ER (D) 15 (Jul) at [55] (Gurkha pensions compensation scheme); *R (on the application of the Countryside Alliance) v A-G* [2007] UKHL 52, [2008] 1 AC 719, [2008] 2 All ER 95 (hunting policy). Decisions of independent prosecuting or enforcement authorities will rarely be interfered with: see *R v Chief Constable of the Kent County Constabulary, ex p L (a minor)* [1993] 1 All ER 756 at 770 per Watkins LJ, applied in *R (on the application of F) v Crown Prosecution Service* [2003] EWHC 3266 (Admin) at [79], 168 JP 93 at [79]; *R v Customs and Excise Comrs, ex p International Federation for Animal Welfare* [1998] Env LR D3, CA; *R (on the application of Corner House Research) v Director of the Serious Fraud Office)* [2008] UKHL 60 at [30], [2009] 1 AC 756 at [30], [2008] 4 All ER 927 at [30] per Lord Bingham of Cornhill, though c f *R v Director General of Water Services, ex p Oldham Metropolitan Borough Council* (1998) 96 LGR 396, 31 HLR 224 (Director General under a duty to take enforcement action in the circumstances). Caution will also be exercised where questions of allocation of resources or economic policy are concerned: see *R v Chief Constable of Sussex, ex p International Trader's Ferry Ltd* [1999] 2 AC 418 at 430, [1999] 1 All ER 129 at 136–137, HL, per Lord Slynn of Hadley (police resources); *R v Lord Chancellor, ex p Maxwell* [1996] 4 All ER 751 at 758–759, [1997] 1 WLR 104 at 109, DC, per Henry LJ (judicial resources); *R v Brent and Harrow Health Authority, ex p Harrow London Borough Council* [1997] ELR 187, (1996) 95 LGR 741 (health authority resources); *R v Secretary of State for Trade and Industry, ex p Isle of Wight Council* [2000] COD 245, [2000] All ER (D) 504 (national economic policy); *R v Secretary of State for the Environment, ex p Hammersmith & Fulham London Borough Council* at 593 and 632–633 per Lord Bridge of Harwich; *R (on the application of T) v Secretary of State for the Home Department* [2003] EWCA Civ 1285 at [11], [2004] HLR 254 at [11] per Kennedy LJ; *R (on the application of Mabanaft Ltd) v Secretary of State for Trade and Industry* [2008] EWHC 1052 (Admin) at [72], [2008] All ER (D) 178 (May) at [72] (EC oil stocks duties) (affd on appeal [2009] EWCA Civ 224, [2009] Eu LR 799); *R (British American Tobacco) v Secretary of State for Health* [2004] EWHC 2493 (Admin) at [27], [2004] All ER (D) 91 (Nov) at [27] per Beatson J (protection of public health); though c f *R (on the application of James) v Secretary of State for Justice* [2009] UKHL 22, [2009] 4 All ER 255, [2009] 2 WLR 1149 (unlawful not to fund adequate offending behaviour courses in prisons) and *R (on the application of Otley) v Barking and Dagenham NHS Primary Care Trust* [2007] EWHC 1927 (Admin), 98 BMLR 182 (unreasonable to refuse cancer drug). Similar caution is exercised in respect of areas of 'difficult value judgments': see eg *R v Southwark London Borough Council, ex p Cordwell* (1994) 27 HLR 594, CA. Where the allegation is that the policy in question interferes with human rights, even an ex gratia policy may be examined in the same way as a less 'political' decision: see *R (on the application of Elias) v Secretary of State for Defence* [2006] EWCA Civ 1293, [2006] 1 WLR 3213, [2006] IRLR 934. See further PARA 619.

14 *Boddington v British Transport Police* [1999] 2 AC 143, [1998] 2 All ER 203, HL; *Kruse v Johnson* [1898] 2 QB 91 at 99–100, DC, per Lord Russell of Killowen CJ. Local authority byelaws are, however, to be benevolently construed and they have seldom been pronounced invalid for unreasonableness per se, though see *Repton School Governors v Repton RDC* [1918] 2 KB 133, CA; *Anderson v Alnwick District Council* [1993] 3 All ER 613, [1993] 1 WLR 1156, DC; cf *R v Parking Adjudicator for London, ex p Bexley London Borough Council* [1998] COD 116, [1998] RTR 128 (parking byelaw quashed for *Wednesbury* unreasonableness); and LOCAL GOVERNMENT vol 69 (2009) PARA 553 et seq. As to the approach of the courts to measures approved by Parliament see PARA 619 note 9. See also PARA 612; and ADMINISTRATIVE LAW vol 1(1) (2001 Reissue) PARA 31.

15 *Associated Provincial Picture Houses Ltd v Wednesbury Corpn* [1948] 1 KB 223, [1947] 2 All ER 680, CA.

16 See *Secretary of State for Education and Science v Tameside Metropolitan Borough Council* [1977] AC 1014, [1976] 3 All ER 665, HL; cf *R v Hampshire County Council, ex p W* [1994] ELR 460, (1994) Times, 9 June (in determining whether request for educational assessment 'unreasonable' local authority must apply an objective factual test and not the *Wednesbury* test); followed in *R v Devon County Council, ex p S* [1995] COD 268.

(ii) Proportionality

618. The principle of proportionality. The principle of proportionality requires that there be a reasonable relationship between the objective which is sought to be achieved and the means used to achieve that end[1]. The principle of proportionality will be applied by the court when reviewing action or legislation for compatibility with the Convention for the Protection of Human Rights and Fundamental Freedoms[2] or European Union law[3]. The courts will also quash punishments imposed by administrative bodies or inferior courts which are wholly out of proportion to the relevant misconduct[4]. It remains an open question whether proportionality is a free-standing ground of review in domestic law[5]. However, the courts will often consider a lack of proportionality an indication or aspect of *Wednesbury*[6] unreasonableness[7]. Although normally in judicial review proceedings the court will not substitute its own view for that of the decision-maker[8], where the proportionality principle applies, the court will assess for itself whether the right balance has been struck[9].

1 The objective itself must be legitimate, in the sense that it must be an aim which is expressly or impliedly authorised by the enabling legislation (see further PARAS 621–622), or, in a case where the Convention for the Protection of Human Rights and Fundamental Freedoms (Rome, 4 November 1950; TS 71 (1953) Cmd 8969) or European Union law is applicable, by the Convention or other relevant European legislation. A measure will not be proportionate unless it is necessary to achieve the relevant objective: see *B v Secretary of State for the Home Department* [2000] All ER (D) 684 at [17], CA, per Sedley LJ (measure which interferes with rights under the Convention for the Protection of Human Rights and Fundamental Freedoms (1950) must be appropriate and necessary to its legitimate aim). The court will ask whether: (1) the legislative objective is sufficiently important to justify limiting a fundamental right; (2) the measures designed to meet the legislative objective are rationally connected to it; and (3) the means used to impair the right or freedom are no more than is necessary to accomplish the objective: *De Freitas v Permanent Secretary of Ministry of Agriculture, Fisheries, Lands and Housing* [1999] 1 AC 69 at 80, [1998] 3 WLR 675 at 684, PC, applied in *R (on the application of Daly) v Secretary of State for the Home Department* [2001] UKHL 26, [2001] 2 AC 532, [2001] 3 All ER 433; *R v A* [2001] UKHL 25, [2002] 1 AC 45, [2001] 3 All ER 1; *R (on the application of Pretty) v DPP* [2001] UKHL 61, [2002] 1 AC 800; *A-G v Scotcher* [2005] UKHL 36, [2005] 3 All ER 1, [2005] 1 WLR 1867. In *Huang v Secretary of State for the Home Department* [2007] UKHL 11 at [19], [2007] 2 AC 167 at [19], [2007] 4 All ER 15 at [19] per Lord Bingham of Cornhill, the House of Lords added to the template in *De Freitas v Permanent Secretary of Ministry of Agriculture, Fisheries, Lands and Housing* the overriding requirement that a balance should be struck between the interests of society and the individual or group. There is no need, however, for the public authority to adopt the least intrusive measure provided an appropriate balance has been struck: see *R (on the application of Corner House Research) v*

Director of the Serious Fraud Office [2008] UKHL 60 at [38], [2009] 1 AC 756 at [38], [2008] 4 All ER 927 at [38] per Lord Bingham of Cornhill; *Pascoe v First Secretary of State* [2006] EWHC 2356 (Admin) at [75], [2006] 4 All ER 1240 at [75] per Forbes J; *Smith v Secretary of State for Trade and Industry* [2007] EWHC 1013 (Admin), [2008] 1 WLR 394. See further the cases cited in notes 2–3.

The principle of proportionality is included in recommendation No R(80)2 of the Committee of Ministers of the Council of Europe, adopted on 11 March 1980, concerning the exercise of discretionary powers by administrative authorities.

2   *AG's Reference (No 2 of 2001)* [2003] UKHL 68 at [120], [2004] 2 AC 72 at [120], [2004] 1 All ER 1049 at [120] per Lord Hobhouse of Woodborough; *R (on the application of Alconbury Developments Ltd) v Secretary of State for the Environment, Transport and the Regions* [2001] UKHL 23 at [51], [2003] 2 AC 295 at [51], [2001] 2 All ER 929 at [51] per Lord Slynn of Hadley; *R (on the application of Daly) v Secretary of State for the Home Department* [2001] UKHL 26 at [27], [2001] 2 AC 532 at [27], [2001] 3 All ER 433 at [27] per Lord Steyn; *R v DPP, ex p Kebeline* [1999] 4 All ER 801 at 844, [1999] 3 WLR 972 at 994, HL, per Lord Hope of Craighead; *A-G v Guardian Newspapers Ltd* [1999] EMLR 904, DC; *R v Secretary of State for the Home Department, ex p Turgut* [2001] 1 All ER 719, [2000] Imm AR 306, CA; *B v Secretary of State for the Home Department* [2000] Imm AR 478, CA; *R (on the application of Mahmood) v Secretary of State for the Home Department* [2001] 1 WLR 840, [2001] 2 FCR 63, CA; *R (on the application of Isiko) v Secretary of State for the Home Department* [2001] 1 FCR 633, [2001] 1 FLR 930, CA.

For the approach of the court to decisions which interfered with human rights prior to the incorporation of the Convention for the Protection of Human Rights and Fundamental Freedoms (1950) by the Human Rights Act 1998 see *R v Secretary of State for the Home Department, ex p Smith* [1996] QB 517, [1996] 1 All ER 257, CA; approved in *R v Lord Saville of Newdigate, ex p A* [1999] 4 All ER 860, [2000] 1 WLR 1855, CA. See also PARA 651.

For the test of proportionality applied in relation to Convention rights see eg *Handyside v United Kingdom* (1976) 1 EHRR 737 at para 49, ECtHR; *Ashingdane v United Kingdom* (1985) 7 EHRR 528 at para 57, ECtHR (limitation on right of access to the court must pursue a legitimate aim and there must be a reasonable relationship of proportionality between the means employed and the aim sought to be achieved); *A-G v Observer Ltd* [1990] 1 AC 109, sub nom *A-G v Guardian Newspapers Ltd (No 2)* [1988] 3 All ER 545, HL (interference with freedom of expression should be no more than is proportionate to the legitimate aim pursued); *Brown v Stott* [2003] 1 AC 681 at 720, [2001] 2 All ER 97 at 130, PC (the principle that there must be a fair balance between the general interest of the community and the personal rights of the individual); *Ghaidan v Godin-Mendoza* [2004] UKHL 30 at [18], [2004] 2 AC 557 at [18], sub nom *Ghaidan v Mendoza* [2004] 3 All ER 411 at [18] per Lord Nicholls of Birkenhead (discrimination against same-sex partners regarding inheritance of tenancies had no legitimate aim); *A v Secretary of State for the Home Department* [2004] UKHL 56, [2005] 2 AC 68, [2005] 3 All ER 169 (detention of non-nationals without trial was not rationally connected with any security objective because nationals posed a similar threat). See further CONSTITUTIONAL LAW AND HUMAN RIGHTS vol 8(2) (Reissue) PARA 103.

3   See *R v Secretary of State for the Environment, ex p Oldham Metropolitan Borough Council* [1998] ICR 367, (1996) 96 LGR 287. As to its application see eg *Internationale Handelsgesellschaft v Einfuhr Und Vorratstelle für Getreide und Futtermittel* (Case 11/70) [1970] ECR 1125; (Case C-331/88) *R v Minister for Agriculture, Fisheries and Food, ex p Fedesa* [1990] ECR I-4023 at 4063 para 13; *R v Intervention Board for Agricultural Produce, ex p ED & F Man (Sugar) Ltd* (Case 181/184) [1986] 2 All ER 115, ECJ and DC; *Johnston v Chief Constable of the Royal Ulster Constabulary* (Case 222/84) [1987] ICR 83 at 104–105; *Milk Marketing Board v Cricket St Thomas Estate* [1991] 3 CMLR 123; *R v Chief Constable of Sussex, ex p International Trader's Ferry Ltd* [1999] 2 AC 418, [1999] 1 All ER 129, HL; *R v Secretary of State for Health, ex p Eastside Cheese Co* [1999] COD 321, 55 BMLR 38, CA; *R v Secretary of State for Employment, ex p Seymour-Smith* [1999] 2 AC 554, [1999] ECR I-623, ECJ.

4   *R v Northumberland Compensation Appeal Tribunal, ex p Shaw* [1952] 1 KB 338, [1952] 1 All ER 122, CA, (excessive fine); *R v Barnsley Metropolitan Borough Council, ex p Hook* [1976] 3 All ER 452, [1976] 1 WLR 1052, CA (excessive punishment for trivial misconduct); *R v Crown Court at Lewes, ex p Castle* (1979) 70 Cr App Rep 278, DC (order of costs against prosecution without proper basis); *R v Crown Court at St Albans, ex p Cinnamond* [1981] QB 480, [1981] 1 All ER 802, DC ('harsh and oppressive' punishment quashed on principles analogous to *Wednesbury* principles; followed in *R v Tottenham Justices, ex p Dwarkados Joshi* [1982] 2 All ER 507, [1982] 1 WLR 631, DC (excessive costs order); and in *Universal Salvage Ltd and Robinson v Boothby* [1984] RTR 289, DC (excessive penalty); cf *R v Crown*

Court at Croydon, ex p Miller (1986) 85 Cr App Rep 152, DC); *R v Secretary of State for the Home Department, ex p Benwell* [1984] ICR 723 at 736 per Hodgson J (excessive penalty); *R v Nottingham Magistrates' Court, ex p Fohmann* (1986) 84 Cr App Rep 316, DC (excessive costs order); *R v Secretary of State for the Home Department, ex p Herbage (No 2)* [1987] QB 1077 at 1095, [1987] 1 All ER 324 at 337, CA, per Purchas LJ (reference to Bill of Rights (1688) against cruel and unusual punishments); *Shah v Statutory Committee of the Pharmaceutical Society of Great Britain* (27 April 1988, unreported), QBD; *R v Eastbourne Magistrates' Court, ex p Hall* [1993] COD 140 (committal harsh and oppressive and lacking in proportionality); *R v Crown Court at Truro, ex p Warren* [1993] COD 294, DC (harsh and oppressive); *R v Warley Justices, ex p Harrison* [1994] COD 340 (whether harsh, oppressive and lacking in proportionality); *R v Maidstone Crown Court, ex p Lever* [1995] 2 All ER 35, [1995] 1 WLR 928, CA; *R v Secretary of State for the Home Department, ex p Hindley* [2000] QB 152 at 177, [1999] 2 WLR 1253 at 1273, CA, per Lord Woolf MR (whether tariff fixed by Secretary of State unreasonable and disproportionate); *Dad v General Dental Council* [2000] 1 WLR 1538 at 1543, PC (professional conduct committee required to balance the nature and gravity of the offences and their bearing on the appellant's fitness to practise against the need for the imposition of the penalty and its consequences and should have considered alternative penalties); *R v Governors of B School, ex p W* [2001] EWCA Civ 1199, [2001] LGR 561, CA (pupil had right to return to school, therefore, in dealing with threat of industrial action, governors had to take the course that interfered least with the right of the pupil whilst also safeguarding the interests of others at the school); *R v London (North) Industrial Tribunal, ex p Associated Newspapers Ltd* [1998] ICR 1212, [1998] IRLR 569 (reporting restrictions should extend no further than necessary). As to judicial review of penalties imposed without reason see PARAS 621–622.

5   *Somerville v Scottish Ministers* [2007] UKHL 44 at [55]–[56], [2007] 1 WLR 2734 at [55]–[56] per Lord Hope of Craighead, [82] per Lord Scott of Foscote, [147] per Lord Roger of Earlsferry and at [198] per Lord Mance.

6   *Associated Provincial Picture Houses Ltd v Wednesbury Corpn* [1948] 1 KB 223, [1947] 2 All ER 680, CA. See also PARA 617.

7   *R v Secretary of State for the Home Department, ex p Brind* [1991] 1 AC 696 at 762, sub nom *Brind v Secretary of State for the Home Department* [1991] 1 All ER 720 at 735, HL, per Lord Ackner; *R v Brent London Borough Council, ex p Assegai* (1987) Times, 18 June; *R v General Medical Council, ex p Colman* [1990] 1 All ER 489, CA; *R v Secretary of State for Health, ex p United States Tobacco International Inc* [1992] QB 353, [1992] 1 All ER 212, DC; *R v Secretary of State for the Home Department, ex p Cox* [1992] COD 72, (1991) 5 Admin LR 17 at 27 per Popplewell J; *R v Ramsgate Magistrates' Court and Thanet District Council, ex p Haddow* (1992) 5 Admin LR 359 at 363, (1992) 157 JP 545 at 548, DC, per Tucker J.

      As to the difference between the *Wednesbury* test and proportionality see *R v Secretary of State for the Home Department, ex p Brind* at 762 and 735 per Lord Ackner (*Wednesbury* test a different and more severe test than proportionality); *R v Governors of St Gregory's RC Aided High School, ex p M* [1995] ELR 290 at 301 (decision would be same if proportionality test applied); *R v Ministry of Agriculture, Fisheries and Food, ex p First City Trading Ltd* [1997] 1 CMLR 250 at 278–279, (1996) Times, 20 December per Laws J; *R v Chief Constable of Sussex, ex p International Trader's Ferry Ltd* [1999] 2 AC 418 at 439, [1999] 1 All ER 129 at 145, HL, per Lord Slynn of Hadley and at 452 and 157 per Lord Cooke of Thorndon (difference in tests less than has been suggested; same result in that case whichever test applied); *R v Secretary of State for Health, ex p Eastside Cheese Co* [1999] COD 321, 55 BMLR 38, CA (test of proportionality more demanding than that of *Wednesbury* unreasonableness); *R v Secretary of State for the Home Department, ex p Al-Fayed* [2001] Imm AR 134, [2000] All ER (D) 1056, CA (very few cases where a disproportionate decision would not also be irrational and vice versa); *R (Association of British Civilian Internees: Far East Region) v Secretary of State for Defence* [2003] EWCA Civ 473 at [40], [2003] QB 1397 at [40] per Dyson LJ, giving the judgment of the court (requirements of proportionality and *Wednesbury* the same).

8   See PARA 617 note 9.

9   See *R (on the application of Daly) v Secretary of State for the Home Department* [2001] UKHL 26 at [27], [2001] 2 AC 532 at [27], [2001] 3 All ER 433 at [27] per Lord Steyn; *R (on the application of Baiai) v Secretary of State for the Home Department* [2008] UKHL 53 at [25], [2009] 1 AC 287 at [25], [2008] 3 All ER 1094 at [25] per Lord Bingham of Cornhill; *A v Secretary of State for the Home Department* [2004] UKHL 56 at [40], [2005] 2 AC 68 at [40], [2005] 3 All ER 169 at [40] per Lord Bingham of Cornhill; *R (on the application of Begum) v Headteacher and Governors of Denbigh High School* [2006] UKHL 15 at [30], [2007] 1 AC 100 at [30], [2006] 2 All ER 487 at [30] per Lord Bingham of Cornhill.

619. The intensity of review. Where a body is endowed by statute with a discretionary power, the court will not quash any exercise of that power which is lawful and reasonable simply because the court disagrees with the decision taken[1]. The court will review the exercise of a discretionary power to ensure that it was lawful and reasonable, according to the principles set out above[2]. The intensity of scrutiny will vary according to the subject matter[3] and statutory context.

Where the exercise of a discretionary power is liable to interfere with fundamental human rights, the courts will examine the decision-maker's actions more rigorously than where such interests are not directly affected by the action taken[4]. The court will decide for itself whether, as a matter of law, a fundamental human right has been breached[5]. Scrutiny of administrative action may be less intense where the exercise of a discretion involves considerations of policy[6] or allocation of resources[7], national security[8], where statutory powers are required to be exercised in emergencies[9], or where they are subject to political controls[10].

1   See *Associated Provincial Picture Houses Ltd v Wednesbury Corpn* [1948] 1 KB 223, [1947] 2 All ER 680, CA; and PARA 617.

2   See PARAS 610–617.

3   See eg *R v Secretary of State for Education and Employment, ex p Begbie* [2000] 1 WLR 1115 at 1130, [2000] ELR 445 at [78], CA, per Laws LJ (reasonableness is a spectrum not a single point; review will be more or less intrusive according to the nature and gravity of what is at stake); *R (on the application of Daly) v Secretary of State for the Home Department* [2001] UKHL 26 at [27]–[28], [2001] 2 AC 532 at [27]–[28], [2001] 3 All ER 433 at [27]–[28] per Lord Steyn and at [32] per Lord Cooke of Thorndon; *R (on the application of Javed) v Secretary of State for the Home Department* [2001] EWCA Civ 789 at [49], [2002] QB 129 at [49] per Lord Phillips of Worth Matravers MR, giving the judgment of the court (extent to which exercise of statutory power open to review on rationality grounds depends on the nature and purpose of the statutory provision); *Sheffield City Council v Smart* [2002] EWCA Civ 04 at [42], [2002] LGR 467 at [42] per Laws LJ (intensity of review varies with the subject matter). See also *R v Secretary of State for Defence, ex p Smith* [1996] QB 517, [1996] 1 All ER 257, CA; *R (on the application of Mahmood) v Secretary of State for the Home Department* [2001] 1 WLR 840, [2001] 2 FCR 63, CA.

4   This is often called 'anxious scrutiny' or 'close scrutiny'. It is a principle that applies both at common law (see eg *Bugdaycay v Secretary of State for the Home Department* [1987] AC 514, [1987] 1 All ER 940, HL; *R v Secretary of State for the Home Department, ex p Brind* [1991] 1 AC 696 at 757, sub nom *Brind v Secretary of State for the Home Department* [1991] 1 All ER 720 at 731, HL, per Lord Ackner; *R (on the application of D) v Secretary of State for Health* [2006] EWCA Civ 989, [2006] All ER (D) 268 (Jul) at [26]–[31] per Laws LJ) and under the Human Rights Act 1998 (see eg *R (on the application of Daly) v Secretary of State for the Home Department* [2001] UKHL 26 at [26]–[27], [2001] 2 AC 532 at [26]–[27], [2001] 3 All ER 433 at [26]–[27] per Lord Steyn; *R (on the application of Yogathas) v Secretary of State for the Home Department* [2002] UKHL 36 at [9], [2003] 1 AC 920 at [9], [2002] 4 All ER 800 at [9] per Lord Bingham of Cornhill; *R (on the application of Razgar) v Secretary of State for the Home Department* [2004] UKHL 27 at [16], [2004] 3 All ER 821 at [16], [2004] 2 AC 368 at [16] per Lord Bingham of Cornhill; *R v Secretary of State for the Home Department, ex p Turgut* [2001] 1 All ER 719, [2000] Imm AR 306, CA; *WM (Democratic Republic of Congo) v Secretary of State for the Home Department* [2006] EWCA Civ 1495 at [10], [2007] Imm AR 337 at [10] per Buxton LJ). Even when reviewing decisions which interfere with human rights, the intensity of the court's review will vary according to factors such as the nature of the right in issue, the importance of the right for the individual and the nature of the activities involved: see *R v DPP, ex p Kebeline* [1999] 4 All ER 801 at 843–844, [1999] 3 WLR 972 at 993–994, HL, per Lord Hope of Craighead; *R v Ministry of Agriculture, Fisheries and Food, ex p Astonquest Ltd* [1999] All ER (D) 1488, CA; *R (on the application of ProLife Alliance) v British Broadcasting Corpn* [2003] UKHL 23 at [138], [2004] 1 AC 185 at [138], [2003] 2 All ER 977 at [138] per Lord Walker of Gestingthorpe; *A v Secretary of State for the Home Department* [2004] UKHL 56 at [29], [2005] 2 AC 68 at [29], [2005] 3 All ER 169 at [29], [39] per Lord Bingham of Cornhill and at [80] per Lord Nicholls of Birkenhead; *Tweed v Parades Commission for Northern Ireland* [2006] UKHL 53 at [36], [2007] 1 AC 650 at [36], [2007] 2 All ER 273 at [36] per Lord Carswell; *Council of Civil Service Unions v United Kingdom*

(1987) 10 EHRR 269, EComHR; and cf *R (on the application of Wright) v Secretary of State for Health* [2009] UKHL 3 at [23], [2009] 1 AC 739 at [23], [2009] 2 All ER 129 at [23] per Baroness Hale of Richmond (nature of review required by the Convention for the Protection of Human Rights and Fundamental Freedoms (Rome, 4 November 1950; TS 71 (1953) Cmd 8969) art 6 varies according to the right at issue). The intensity of the court's review may also be described in terms of the level of deference accorded to the decision-maker. The European Court of Human Rights uses the term 'margin of appreciation' which includes an element of international deference to domestic authorities. The domestic courts, however, being in a better position to assess local needs and conditions, in principle apply a slightly stricter standard, but still allow the domestic public authority a 'discretionary area of judgment' within which the court will not interfere: see *R v DPP, ex p Kebeline* at 843–844 and 993–994, HL, per Lord Hope of Craighead; *Huang v Secretary of State for the Home Department* [2005] EWCA Civ 105, [2006] QB 1, [2005] 3 All ER 435 (reversed on appeal but not on this point [2007] UKHL 11, [2007] 2 AC 167, [2007] 4 All ER 15, though cf Lord Bingham at [14] on the unhelpfulness of considering the case in terms of 'deference'); *Sheffield City Council v Smart* [2002] EWCA Civ 04 at [42], [2002] LGR 467 at [42] per Laws LJ; *Brown v Stott* [2003] 1 AC 681 at 703, 710–711, [2001] 2 All ER 97 at 114, 121, PC; *International Transport Roth GmbH v Secretary of State for the Home Department* [2002] EWCA Civ 158 at [81], [2003] QB 728 at [81] per Laws LJ. For the application of the difference between 'margin of appreciation' and 'discretionary area of judgment' in practice see *Re G (Adoption: Unmarried Couple,* sub nom Re P (adoption: unmarried couple) [2008] 2 FCR 366, [2008] UKHL 38, [2009] 1 AC 173 sub nom *Re P (adoption: unmarried couple)* [2008] 2 FCR 366 (House of Lords found violation of Human Rights Act 1998 even though European Court of Human Rights would have accepted that the decision fell within the 'margin of appreciation'); *A v Secretary of State for the Home Department* [2004] UKHL 56 at [131], [2005] 2 AC 68 at [131], [2005] 3 All ER 169 at [131] per Lord Hope of Craighead and at [176] per Lord Rodger of Earlsferry (deference of European Court of Human Rights to national authorities in matters of national security presupposes that the national courts will police the limits more strictly); *Montgomery v HM Advocate* [2003] 1 AC 641, [2001] 2 WLR 779, PC.

5   *R (on the application of Baiai) v Secretary of State for the Home Department* [2008] UKHL 53 at [25], [2009] 1 AC 287 at [25], [2008] 3 All ER 1094 at [25] per Lord Bingham of Cornhill; *A v Secretary of State for the Home Department* [2004] UKHL 56 at [40], [2005] 2 AC 68 at [40], [2005] 3 All ER 169 at [40] per Lord Bingham of Cornhill; *B v Secretary of State for the Home Department* [2000] 2 CMLR 1086, [2000] All ER (D) 684; *Huang v Secretary of State for the Home Department* [2007] UKHL 11, [2007] 2 AC 167, [2007] 4 All ER 15 (immigration judge needs to decide proportionality for himself when reviewing Secretary of State's decision); *R (on the application of Daly) v Secretary of State for the Home Department* [2001] UKHL 26 at [23], [2001] 2 AC 532 at [23] per Lord Bingham of Cornhill; *Wilson v First County Trust Ltd* [2003] UKHL 40 at [116], [2004] 1 AC 816 at [116], [2003] 4 All ER 97 at [116] per Lord Hope of Craighead and at [141] per Lord Hobhouse of Woodborough (whether legislation compatible a matter for the court). Note that the normal position in judicial review is that the court will not substitute its view for that of the decision-maker: see PARA 617 note 9. The same is true in cases where reliance is placed on fundamental human rights where what is at issue is a matter of social policy rather than the rights of an individual: see *R (on the application of Carson) v Secretary of State for Work and Pensions* [2005] UKHL 37 at [17], [2006] 1 AC 173 at [17], [2005] 4 All ER 545 at [17] per Lord Hoffmann; *R (British America Tobacco) v Secretary of State for Health R (British American Tobacco) v Secretary of State for Health* [2004] EWHC 2493 (Admin) at [27], [2004] All ER (D) 91 (Nov) at [27] per Beatson J; and see further note 4.

6   See PARA 617 note 13.

7   See PARA 617 note 13.

8   At one time the courts regarded decisions involving national security issues to be reviewable only on 'narrow' ultra vires grounds (see PARA 610) or on grounds of bad faith: *R v Secretary of State for the Home Department, ex p Cheblak* [1991] 2 All ER 319 at 330, 334, [1991] 1 WLR 890 at 902, 907, CA, per Lord Donaldson MR (decisions on national security are the exclusive responsibility of the executive and can only be impugned if the executive acted otherwise than in good faith or outside limitations imposed on it by statute); *R v Secretary of State for Defence, ex p Smith* [1996] QB 517 at 556, [1996] 1 All ER 257 at 264, CA, per Sir Thomas Bingham. The modern view is that the courts will intervene in appropriate cases involving national security issues, but will give great weight to the views of the executive on such matters: see *Secretary of State for the Home Department v Rehman* [2001] UKHL 47, [2003] 1 AC 153, [2002] 1 All ER 122 at [31] per Lord Steyn and at [53]–[54] per Lord Hoffmann; *A v Secretary of State for the Home Department* [2004] UKHL 56, [2005] 2 AC 68, [2005] 3 All ER 169

(whether terror threat constituted a public emergency was a matter on which great weight should be given to the views of the Government). Where what is at issue is a fundamental human right, such as the right to liberty, the courts will scrutinise closely any claim that national security justifies the act or measure in question: see *A v Secretary of State for the Home Department*.

9   *Pickwell v Camden London Borough Council* [1983] QB 962 at 989, [1983] 1 All ER 602 at 620, DC, per Forbes J (decision taken in an emergency must not be scrutinised as closely as one taken not under such pressure); *Langley v Liverpool City Council* [2005] EWCA Civ 1173 at [76], [2006] 2 All ER 202 at [76] per Thorpe LJ (urgent state intervention in family life); *Secretary of State for Employment v Associated Society of Locomotive Engineers and Firemen (No 2)* [1972] 2 QB 455 at 493, [1972] 2 All ER 949 at 967–968, CA, per Lord Denning MR; *A v Secretary of State for the Home Department* [2004] UKHL 56, [2005] 2 AC 68, [2005] 3 All ER 169; though cf *R v Secretary of State for the Home Department, ex p Moon* (1995) 8 Admin LR 477; and *R (on the application of Amvac Chemical UK Ltd) v Secretary of State for the Environment, Food and Rural Affairs* [2001] EWHC Admin 1011, [2001] All ER (D) 10 (Dec) (urgency not justifying unfairness). See also ADMINISTRATIVE LAW vol 1(1) (2001 Reissue) PARA 21.

10   Primary legislation is not reviewable save on grounds that it is incompatible with rights protected by the Human Rights Act 1998 or with provisions of European Union law: see *R (on the application of the Countryside Alliance) v A-G* [2007] UKHL 52 at [134], [2008] 1 AC 719 at [134], [2008] 2 All ER 95 at [134] per Lord Brown of Eaton-under-Heywood. However, secondary legislation and other measures are reviewable, even if they have been subject to approval by one or both Houses of Parliament, though the courts will normally exercise greater restraint when considering such cases: *Nottinghamshire County Council v Secretary of State for the Environment* [1986] AC 240, [1986] 1 All ER 199, HL; *Re M* [1994] 1 AC 377 at 413, sub nom *M v Home Office* [1993] 3 All ER 537 at 556, HL, per Lord Woolf (caution where measure approved by the House of Commons); *Lonrho plc v Secretary of State for Trade and Industry* [1989] 2 All ER 609 at 617, sub nom *R v Secretary of State for Trade and Industry, ex p Lonrho plc* [1989] 1 WLR 525 at 536, HL, per Lord Keith of Kinkel (where report laid before Parliament, courts must be careful not to invade the political field and substitute their own judgment for that of the minister). See also *R v Secretary of State for the Environment ex p, Hammersmith and Fulham London Borough Council* [1991] 1 AC 521 at 597–598, sub nom *Hammersmith and Fulham London Borough Council v Secretary of State for the Environment* [1990] 3 All ER 589 at 636, HL, per Lord Bridge of Harwich; *Chief Adjudication Officer v Foster* [1993] AC 754 at 765, [1993] 1 All ER 705 at 711, HL, per Lord Bridge of Harwich; *Sparks v Edward Ash Ltd* [1943] 1 KB 223, [1943] 1 All ER 1, CA; *McEldowney v Forde* [1971] AC 632, [1969] 2 All ER 1039, HL; *Glanville v Secretary of State for Social Services* (1979) 130 NLJ 46, CA; *R v Secretary of State for Social Security, ex p Joint Council for the Welfare of Immigrants* [1996] 4 All ER 385, [1997] 1 WLR 275, CA. However, cf *R (on the application of Javed) v Secretary of State for the Home Department* [2001] EWCA Civ 789 at [51], [2002] QB 129 at [51] per Lord Phillips of Worth Matravers MR, giving the judgment of the court (there is no principle of law that circumscribes the extent to which the court can review an order that has been approved by both Houses of Parliament under the affirmative resolution procedure). See also *MB (Somalia) v Entry Clearance Officer* [2008] EWCA Civ 102, [2008] Fam Law 383 (court willing to consider whether provision of immigration rules that had been subject to the negative resolution procedure was irrational); *Gurung v Ministry of Defence* [2002] EWHC 2463 (Admin), [2002] All ER (D) 409 (Nov) (whether pension arrangements for former Gurkha soldiers rational, though court should exercise caution before intervening in such an area); and *R (on the application of Limbu) v Secretary of State for the Home Department* [2008] EWHC 2261 (Admin), [2008] NLJR 1414, [2008] All ER (D) 122 (Sep) (discretionary arrangements approved by Parliament for admitting former Gurkha soldiers to the United Kingdom were irrational). See also ADMINISTRATIVE LAW vol 1(1) (2001 Reissue) PARA 31.

(iii)   Fettering of Discretion

620.   Fettering of discretion. Where a public body has discretion in exercising its public functions, it must not fetter that discretion by adopting an over-rigid policy[1]. There is a balance to be struck between certainty, rigidity and individual consideration[2]. It is generally lawful, and can be desirable, for a public body to have a policy which allows for exceptions[3], so long as there is genuine flexibility in practice⁴. In limited circumstances, even a policy without exceptions may be lawful⁵. A policy must not take into account irrelevant considerations⁶ or exceed the statutory purpose⁷. A policy can in some circumstances create a legitimate expectation⁸.

1   See *British Oxygen Co Ltd v Board of Trade* [1971] AC 610, [1970] 3 All ER 165, HL. See also *R v Secretary of State for the Home Department, ex p Venables* [1998] AC 407, [1997] 3 All ER 97, HL.

2   See *R v Minister of Agriculture, Fisheries and Food, ex p Hamble (Offshore) Fisheries Ltd* [1995] 2 All ER 714 at 722 per Sedley J (overruled in part, on a different issue, by *R v Secretary of State for the Home Department, ex p Hargreaves* [1997] 1 All ER 397, [1997] 1 WLR 906, CA).

3   A policy can be 'an essential element in securing the coherent and consistent performance of administrative functions': *R (on the application of Alconbury Developments Ltd) v Secretary of State for the Environment, Transport and the Regions* [2001] UKHL 23 at [143], [2003] 2 AC 295 at [143], [2001] 2 All ER 929 at [143] per Lord Clyde.
    For examples of lawful policies which allowed for exceptions see *R v Torquay Licensing Justices ex p Brockman* [1951] 2 KB 784, [1951] 2 All ER 656; *Re Findlay* [1985] AC 318, [1984] 3 All ER 801, HL; *R v Law Society, ex p Reigate Projects Ltd* [1992] 3 All ER 232, [1993] 1 WLR 1531; *R v Governors of Bishop Challoner Roman Catholic Comprehensive Girls' School, ex p Choudhury and Purkayastha* [1992] 2 AC 182, [1992] 3 WLR 99, HL (school allocation policy); *Secretary of State for the Home Department v Hastrup* [1996] Imm AR 616 (lawful policy stating that immigration history was seldom relevant).
    For examples of unlawful policies which did not allow for exceptions see: *Kilmarnock Magistrates v Secretary of State for Scotland* 1961 SC 350, Ct of Sess; *R v Barnsley Supplementary Benefits Appeal Tribunal, ex p Atkinson* [1977] 3 All ER 1031, [1977] 1 WLR 917, CA (unlawful policy assumed every student had parental contribution); *A-G (ex rel Tilley) v Wandsworth London Borough Council* [1981] 1 All ER 1162, [1981] 1 WLR 854, CA (unlawful policy of never helping intentionally homeless families to find alternative accommodation); *R v Secretary of State for the Environment, ex p Halton Borough Council* (1983) 82 LGR 662 (unlawful policy of disallowing all local objections to allocation of land for particular purpose); *R v Home Secretary, ex p Bennett* (1986) Times, 18 August, CA (over-rigid criteria for approval of police rent allowance); *R v Tower Hamlets London Borough Council, ex p Khalique* [1994] 2 FCR 1074, 26 HLR 517 (over-rigid policy of suspending from housing list for rent arrears); *R v Bexley London Borough Council, ex p Jones* [1995] ELR 42, [1994] COD 393; *R v Secretary of State for the Home Department, ex p Venables* [1998] AC 407, [1997] 3 All ER 97, HL; *R v Westminster City Council, ex p Hussain* (1999) 31 HLR 645 (unlawful blanket policy of suspending from the housing register); *Gunn-Russo v Nugent Care Society* [2001] EWHC Admin 566, [2002] 1 FLR 1; *R (on the application of Kilby) v Basildon District Council* [2007] EWCA Civ 479, [2007] 22 EG 161 (CS) (the policy was unlawful because it abrogated the statutory purpose and considering it as fettering of discretion would produce the same result).

4   See *Smith v Inner London Education Authority* [1978] 1 All ER 411, 142 JP 136, CA (local authority had in fact considered objections); *R v Secretary of State for the Environment, ex p Brent London Borough Council* [1982] QB 593, [1983] 3 All ER 321 (unlawful policy because the minister would not meet the representatives to consider any representations); *R v Lambeth London Borough Council, ex p Njomo* (1996) 28 HLR 737, [1996] COD 299 (local authority, in practice, treated stated categories of exceptions as exhaustive); *R v Southwark London Borough Council, ex p Melak* (1996) 29 HLR 223 (policy was not unlawful per se but had been applied inflexibly); *R v Secretary of State for Education and Employment, ex p* [2000] ELR 300 (departmental policy had been applied too strictly); *R v Legal Aid Board, ex p Duncan* [2000] COD 159, [2000] All ER (D) 189 (policy was lawful so long as the Board responded rapidly to weaknesses); *R (on the application of P) v Secretary of State for the Home Department* [2001] EWCA Civ 1151, [2001] 1 WLR 2002, [2001] 3 FCR 416 (legitimate policy of separating female prisoners from their children at 18 months, but only if it was applied flexibly); *Lindsay v Customs and Excise Comrs* [2002] EWCA Civ 267, [2002] 3 All ER 118, [2002] 1 WLR 1766 (a policy which did not distinguish between commercial and domestic use could not be condemned where each case was considered on its own facts); *R (on the application of Stephenson) v Stockton on Tees Borough Council* [2005] EWCA Civ 960, [2006] LGR 135, [2005] 3 FCR 248 (lawful policy, but the local authority had failed to consider whether this case fell within the exception); *R (on the application of Rogers) v Swindon NHS Primary Care Trust* [2006] EWCA Civ 392, [2006] 1 WLR 2649, 89 BMLR 211 (for a policy to be lawful, the

decision-maker had to be able to envisage the exceptional circumstances in which the normal policy would not be applied); *R (on the application of Elias) v Secretary of State for Defence* [2006] EWCA Civ 1293, [2006] 1 WLR 3213, [2006] IRLR 934 (until a scheme made under a rule-making power was amended, it was lawful not to consider ex gratia payments outside that scheme).

5   See eg *R v Warwickshire County Council, ex p Williams* [1995] ELR 326, [1995] COD 182 (Secretary of State entitled to have a policy that excluded students who could obtain a loan from access to a grant); *R v Secretary of State for the Home Department, ex p Zulfikar* [1996] COD 256, (1995) Times, 26 July (blanket policy of strip searching prison visitors was lawful); *R (on the application of S) v Chief Constable of South Yorkshire* [2004] UKHL 39, [2004] 4 All ER 193, [2004] 1 WLR 2196 (unrealistic and impractical to consider each case individually).

6   See eg *R v North Yorkshire County Council, ex p Hargreaves* (1997) 96 LGR 39, [1997] COD 390 (policy was unlawful because it excluded consideration of means, which was a relevant factor). As to relevant and irrelevant considerations see PARA 623.

7   See PARA 610 et seq.

8   See PARA 649 note 8.

(iv) Improper Purpose

621. Bad faith. The exercise of a discretion by a public body in bad faith is unlawful and will be quashed by the court[1]. A decision is taken in bad faith if it is taken dishonestly or maliciously[2] although the courts have also equated bad faith with any deliberate improper purpose[3]. A decision or order, though itself taken or made in good faith, will be quashed by the court if procured by fraud[4]. In very exceptional circumstances a narrow definition of the statutory grounds for challenging an administrative act may be effective to exclude fraud or bad faith as a ground of challenge[5]; but it is well established that in general legislative formulae purporting to exclude judicial review of a tribunal's proceedings altogether do not operate to exclude challenges founded on fraud[6]. Fraud or bad faith must be expressly pleaded by the party alleging it[7].

There are situations where tortious liability may be incurred in respect of acts done in bad faith although no liability would arise were the same acts to be done in good faith[8].

1   There are numerous dicta to this effect: see eg *Associated Provincial Picture Houses Ltd v Wednesbury Corpn* [1948] 1 KB 223 at 229, [1947] 2 All ER 680 at 682, CA, per Lord Greene MR (bad faith and dishonesty stand by themselves as grounds of review); *Biddulph v St George's, Hanover Square, Vestry* (1863) 33 LJ Ch 411 at 417, CA, per Turner LJ; *Westminster Corpn v London & North Western Rly Co* [1905] AC 426 at 430, HL, per Lord Macnaghten; *Board of Education v Rice* [1911] AC 179 at 182, HL, per Lord Loreburn LC; *Short v Poole Corpn* [1926] Ch 66 at 88, CA, per Sir Ernest Pollock MR; *Roberts v Hopwood* [1925] AC 578 at 589, HL, per Lord Buckmaster, at 603 per Lord Sumner, and at 616–617 per Lord Wrenbury; *Carltona Ltd v Works Comrs* [1943] 2 All ER 560 at 563–564, CA, per Lord Greene MR; *Demetriades v Glasgow Corpn* [1951] 1 All ER 457 at 463, HL, per Lord Reid; *Anisminic v Foreign Compensation Commission* [1969] 2 AC 147 at 171, [1969] 1 All ER 208 at 213, HL, per Lord Reid; *British Oxygen Co Ltd v Minister of Technology* [1971] AC 610 at 624, [1970] 3 All ER 165 at 170, HL, per Lord Reid; *Nottinghamshire County Council v Secretary of State for the Environment* [1986] AC 240 at 247, 250–251, [1986] 1 All ER 199 at 202, 204, HL, per Lord Scarman; *R v Commission for Racial Equality, ex p Hillingdon London Borough Council* [1982] QB 276, [1981] 3 WLR 520, CA (Parliament can never be taken to have authorised the exercise of a statutory power in bad faith); *R v Secretary of State for the Environment, ex p Hammersmith and Fulham London Borough Council* [1991] 1 AC 521 at 596, sub nom *Hammersmith and Fulham London Borough Council v Secretary of State for the Environment* [1990] 3 All ER 589 at 636, HL, per Lord Bridge of Harwich; *R v Secretary of State for the Home Department, ex p Cheblak* [1991] 2 All ER 319 at 334, [1991] 1 WLR 890 at 907, CA, per Lord Donaldson MR; *R v Secretary of State for the Home Department, ex p Fire Brigades Union* [1995] 2 AC 513 at 563, [1995] 2 All ER 244 at 264, HL, per Lord Mustill (good faith an indispensable element of any exercise of a statutory discretion).

Subordinate legislation must be enacted in good faith: *Kruse v Johnson* [1898] 2 QB 91, DC; *Re Toohey* (1980) 38 ALR 439; cf *British Railways Board v Pickin* [1974] AC 765, [1974] 1 All ER 609, HL (the court may not impugn an Act of Parliament on the ground that it was procured by fraud).

2 *Western Fish Products Ltd v Penwith District Council* (1978) 77 LGR 185 at 195, CA, per Megaw LJ (bad faith should not be alleged in the absence of dishonesty or malice); *Cannock Chase District Council v Kelly* [1978] 1 All ER 152 at 156, [1978] 1 WLR 1 at 6, CA, per Megaw LJ; *R v Port Talbot Borough Council, ex p Jones* [1988] 2 All ER 207 at 214 per Nolan J; *R v Greenwich London Borough Council, ex p Lovelace* [1991] 3 All ER 511, [1991] 1 WLR 506, CA (duty not to act maliciously or vindictively).

Examples of bad faith in this sense are rare and have remained mainly in the region of hypothetical cases: *Smith v East Elloe RDC* [1956] AC 736 at 770, [1956] 1 All ER 855 at 872, HL, per Lord Somervell; *Nakkuda Ali v MF De S Jayaratne* [1951] AC 66 at 77, PC. See, however, *R v Derbyshire County Council, ex p Times Supplements Ltd* (1990) 3 Admin LR 241 at 250, 253, (1990) Times, 19 July, DC, per Watkins LJ (decision of local authority to withdraw advertising from newspaper unlawful because activated by vindictiveness); and *Watkins v Secretary of State for the Home Department* [2006] UKHL 17, [2006] 2 AC 395, [2006] 2 All ER 353 (opening of a prisoner's legally privileged correspondence in bad faith).

For examples of deliberate or reckless use of powers for illegal purposes see *R v Liverpool City Council, ex p Ferguson* (1985) Times, 20 November, DC; *Smith v Skinner* [1986] RVR 45 at 79, DC, per Glidewell LJ (reckless indifference to the lawfulness of actions taken), and at 86 per Caulfield J (deliberate disregard of known statutory duties); affd sub nom *Lloyd v McMahon* [1987] AC 625, [1987] 1 All ER 1118, HL. See also *Derwent Holdings Ltd v Liverpool City Council* [2008] EWHC 3023 (Admin), [2008] All ER (D) 132 (Dec).

3 See eg *Biddulph v St George's, Hanover Square, Vestry* (1863) 33 LJ Ch 411 at 417, CA, per Turner LJ; *Westminster Corpn v London and North Western Rly Co* [1905] AC 426, HL (and see [1904] 1 Ch 759 at 767, CA, per Vaughan Williams LJ); *Denman & Co Ltd v Westminster Corpn* [1906] 1 Ch 464 at 476 per Buckley J; *Roberts v Hopwood* [1925] AC 578 at 603, HL, per Lord Sumner; and see PARA 622. More recently, the courts have tended to refer to bad faith and improper motives as distinct grounds of review: see eg *R v IRC, ex p Unilever plc* [1996] STC 681 at 693, 68 TC 205 at 231, CA, per Simon Brown LJ; *Nottinghamshire County Council v Secretary of State for the Environment* [1986] AC 240, [1986] 1 All ER 199, HL; *R v Derbyshire County Council, ex p Times Supplements Ltd* (1991) 3 Admin LR 241, (1990) Times, 19 July, DC.

4 See eg *Al-Mehdawi v Secretary of State for the Home Department* [1990] 1 AC 876 at 895–896, [1989] 3 All ER 843 at 847–848, HL, per Lord Bridge of Harwich (fraud unravels everything); *R v Leyland Justices, ex p Hawthorn* [1979] QB 283, [1979] 1 All ER 209, DC; *R v Blundeston Prison Board of Visitors, ex p Fox-Taylor* [1982] 1 All ER 646, [1982] Crim LR 119; *R v Bolton Justices, ex p Scally* [1991] 1 QB 537, [1991] 2 All ER 619, DC (innocent conduct of police in contaminating evidence analogous to fraud, collusion and perjury).

5 See *Smith v East Elloe RDC* [1956] AC 736, [1956] 1 All ER 855, HL, where the relevant statutory provision (the Acquisition of Land (Authorisation Procedure) Act 1946 Sch 1 para 15 (repealed)) enabled compulsory purchase orders to be challenged within six weeks on the ground that they were 'not empowered to be granted'. These words were interpreted, obiter, by Lord Morton of Henryton (at 754–756, 862–863), by Lord Reid (at 763–764, 867) and by Lord Somervell of Harrow (at 772, 873), as referring only to orders that were ultra vires in the narrow sense (see PARA 610) and as not covering a challenge to the validity of the order on the ground that it had been made or procured in bad faith. The House of Lords held (Lords Reid and Somervell dissenting) that the wording of Sch 1 para 16, precluding any challenge 'in any legal proceedings whatsoever' after the expiry of six weeks following the confirmation of the order, was effective thereafter to bar a challenge based on fraud. See, however, the observations on this decision in *Anisminic Ltd v Foreign Compensation Commission* [1969] 2 AC 147, [1969] 1 All ER 208, HL. *Smith v East Elloe RDC* was followed in *R v Secretary of State for the Environment, ex p Ostler* [1977] QB 122, [1976] 3 All ER 90, CA and *Derwent Holdings Ltd v Liverpool City Council* [2008] EWHC 3023 (Admin), [2008] All ER (D) 132 (Dec). See further PARA 655.

6 *Colonial Bank of Australasia Ltd v Willan* (1874) LR 5 PC 417. See also ADMINISTRATIVE LAW vol 1(1) (2001 Reissue) PARA 21.

A public body's decision that is not otherwise amenable to judicial review due to its commercial decision, will nevertheless be so amenable if there is an allegation of fraud, corruption or bad faith: *R (on the application of Menai Collect Ltd) v Department for*

Constitutional Affairs [2006] EWHC 727 (Admin), [2006] All ER (D) 101 (Apr); *R (on the application of Gamesa Energy UK Ltd) v National Assembly for Wales* [2006] EWHC 2167 (Admin), [2006] All ER (D) 26 (Aug).

7   See eg *Demetriades v Glasgow Corpn* [1951] 1 All ER 457 at 460–461, HL, per Lord MacDermot and at 463 per Lord Reid; *Cannock Chase District Council v Kelly* [1978] 1 All ER 152, [1978] 1 WLR 1, CA, per Megaw LJ; *Sevenoaks District Council v Emmott* (1979) 78 LGR 346 at 350, CA, per Megaw LJ; *Mercury Energy Ltd v Electricity Corpn of New Zealand* [1994] 1 WLR 521, 138 Sol Jo LB 61, PC. See further MISREPRESENTATION AND FRAUD vol 31 (2003 Reissue) PARA 789 et seq.

8   In particular, in the exercise of functions analogous to the judicial see ADMINISTRATIVE LAW vol 1(1) (2001 Reissue) PARAS 204–205.

622.   Improper purpose.   The exercise of a discretionary power for a purpose alien to that for which it was granted is unlawful[1], regardless of whether or not that alien purpose is in the public interest[2]. If the purposes for which the power can legitimately be exercised are specified by statute and those purposes are construed as being exhaustive, an exercise of that power in order to achieve a different and collateral object will be pronounced invalid[3]. The fact that the relationship between the subject matter of the power and the prescribed purposes for which it may lawfully be exercised is expressed to be ascertained to the satisfaction of the competent authority does not necessarily preclude the court from deciding independently whether those purposes have indeed been pursued[4]. If the permitted purposes are left unspecified, or are not exhaustively specified, by statute, it lies with the court to determine what, if any, are the implied restrictions on the purposes for which the power is exercisable[5]; statutory powers are not to be employed so as to defeat the spirit of the Act conferring them[6]. An exercise of a statutory power which would undermine the operation of provisions in the statute for consultation or appeal will conflict with the objects of the Act[7]. The use of statutory powers to impose penalties in respect of conduct of which the decision-maker does not approve will be quashed where that is not a legitimate purpose[8], as will the improper use of a power to obtain financial benefits[9], or the use of a power for illegitimate political purposes[10]. In some contexts the motives or purposes animating those performing an act or making a decision may be immaterial, provided that the object for which the power was conferred has been substantially fulfilled and that the repository of the power was acting in good faith[11].

Where a power is exercised for purposes partly authorised and partly unauthorised by law, the court generally adopts one of two approaches. It may ascertain the dominant[12] or true[13] purpose for which a power is exercised, and if that purpose is permitted, the exercise will be lawful even though some secondary or incidental advantage may be gained for a purpose which is outside the authority's powers[14]. Alternatively, it will ascertain whether the decision to exercise the power was significantly influenced by the existence of the unauthorised purpose, and if it was, quash the exercise of the power on the ground that it was exercised having regard to an irrelevant consideration[15].

Where a prima facie case of misuse of power has been made out, it is open to a court to draw the inference that unauthorised purposes have been pursued if the competent authority fails to adduce any grounds supporting the validity of its conduct[16].

1   *Padfield v Minister of Agriculture, Fisheries and Food* [1968] AC 997, [1968] 1 All ER 694, HL; *Smith v East Elloe RDC* [1956] AC 736 at 767, [1956] 1 All ER 855 at 870, HL, per Lord Radcliffe; *R v Secretary of State for the Home Department, ex p Brind* [1991] 1 AC 696 at 756, sub nom *Brind v Secretary of State for the Home Department* [1991] 1 All ER 720 at

730, HL, per Lord Ackner; *Crédit Suisse v Allerdale London Borough Council* [1997] QB 306 at 333–334, [1996] 4 All ER 129 at 150–151, CA, per Neill LJ.

2   *Stewart v Perth and Kinross Council* [2004] UKHL 16, 2004 SLT 383.

3   See eg *Galloway v London Corpn* (1866) LR 1 HL 34 at 43; *Birmingham and Midland Motor Omnibus Co Ltd v Worcestershire County Council* [1967] 1 All ER 544 at 549, [1967] 1 WLR 409 at 416, CA, per Lord Denning MR (traffic diverted for unauthorised purpose); *Laker Airways Ltd v Department of Trade* [1977] QB 643, [1977] 2 All ER 182, CA (guidance issued by minister under statute had to be consistent with the express general objectives in that statute); *Bromley London Borough Council v GLC* [1983] 1 AC 768, [1982] 1 All ER 129, HL (fare structure for public transport in London had to promote the statutory purpose of organising an 'economic' service); *Freight Transport Association Ltd v London Boroughs Transport Committee* [1991] 3 All ER 915, sub nom *London Boroughs Transport Committee v Freight Transport Association Ltd* [1991] 1 WLR 828, HL (order regulating heavy goods traffic intended and effective to carry out policy of the statute); *South Lakeland District Council v Secretary of State for the Environment* [1992] 2 AC 141, [1992] 1 All ER 573, HL (development permitted where it would preserve or enhance conservation area); *Crédit Suisse v Allerdale Borough Council* [1997] QB 306, [1996] 4 All ER 129, CA (scheme could not be used for purpose of circumventing statutory restrictions on borrowing); *R v Wilson, ex p Williamson* [1996] COD 42 (power to detain mental health patient could not be used except for period specified); *R v Southwark Crown Court, ex p Bowles* [1998] AC 641, [1998] 2 All ER 193, HL (production order could only be obtained for the purpose of assisting recovery of proceeds of criminal conduct and not for the purpose of investigating criminal offence); *St Georges Healthcare NHS Trust v S* [1999] Fam 26, [1998] 3 All ER 673, CA (power to detain mental health patient misused); *R v Secretary of State for the Environment, Transport and the Regions, ex p Spath Holme Ltd* [2001] 2 AC 349, [2001] 1 All ER 195, HL (it is not legitimate to confine a statute by reference to the parliamentary record, unless there is genuine ambiguity satisfying the test in *Pepper (Inspector of Taxes) v Hart* [1993] AC 593, [1993] 1 All ER 42, HL).

There are several decisions in which a purported exercise of compulsory purchase powers has been held to be invalid because an unauthorised purpose (eg resale at a profit) had been pursued: see *Gard v City of London Sewers Comrs* (1885) 28 ChD 486, CA; *Lynch v London Sewers Comrs* (1886) 32 ChD 72, CA; *Donaldson v South Shields Corpn* (1899) 68 LJ Ch 162, CA; *Fernley v Limehouse Board of Works* (1899) 68 LJ Ch 344; *Sydney Municipal Council v Campbell* [1925] AC 338, PC; *Grice v Dudley Corpn* [1958] Ch 329, [1957] 2 All ER 673; *London and Westcliff Properties Ltd v Minister of Housing and Local Government* [1961] 1 All ER 610, [1961] 1 WLR 519; *Webb v Minister of Housing and Local Government* [1965] 2 All ER 193, [1965] 1 WLR 755, CA. The last two cases show that ministerial confirmation of an order tainted with invalidity does not protect it. See also COMPULSORY ACQUISITION OF LAND vol 18 (2009) PARAs 526, 850. For cases in which teachers dismissible on educational grounds were held to have been invalidly dismissed for reasons of economy see *Hanson v Radcliffe UDC* [1922] 2 Ch 490, CA; *Sadler v Sheffield Corpn* [1924] 1 Ch 483.

4   *Customs and Excise Comrs v Cure and Deeley Ltd* [1962] 1 QB 340, [1961] 3 All ER 641 (commissioners, although empowered to make regulations for any matter for which provision appeared to them necessary for giving effect to purposes of Act, held not entitled to constitute themselves sole judges of taxpayer's liability); although cf *B Marsh (Wholesale) Ltd v Customs and Excise Comrs* [1970] 2 QB 206, [1970] 1 All ER 990. In wartime and post-war emergency cases the courts have refused even to consider the adequacy of the grounds on which the competent authority was satisfied that a regulation or order was necessary or expedient for the defence of the realm and the maintenance of essential supplies and services: see *R v Comptroller-General of Patents, ex p Bayer Products Ltd* [1941] 2 KB 306, [1941] 2 All ER 677, CA; *Progressive Supply Co Ltd v Dalton* [1943] Ch 54, [1943] 2 All ER 646; *Carltona Ltd v Works Comrs* [1943] 2 All ER 560, CA; *Point of Ayr Collieries Ltd v Lloyd-George* [1943] 2 All ER 546, CA; *Underhill v Ministry of Food* [1950] 1 All ER 591; and see *Demetriades v Glasgow Corpn* [1951] 1 All ER 457, HL (land requisitioning). For an intermediate position, namely that the exercise of power must be reasonably capable of being related to an authorised purpose, see *A-G for Canada v Hallet and Carey Ltd* [1952] AC 427 at 450, PC; *Ross-Clunis v Papadopoullos* [1958] 2 All ER 23 at 32, [1958] 1 WLR 546 at 559, PC; *R v Secretary of State for Foreign Affairs, ex p World Development Movement Ltd* [1995] 1 All ER 611, [1995] 1 WLR 386, DC; *R v National Rivers Authority, ex p Haughey* (1996) 8 Admin LR 567, (1996) Times, 21 May (authority not entitled to use licensing powers as means for enforcing its argument in separate dispute); *UK Waste Management Ltd v West Lancashire District Council* [1997] RTR 201, (1996) Times, 5 April (unlawful to make experimental traffic order where purpose to ban heavy goods vehicles from road). Cf *R v Secretary of State for Employment, ex p National Association of Colliery Overmen, Deputies and Shotfirers* [1994] COD 218, DC

(power to make regulations 'designed to maintain or improve health and safety'; 'designed' means suited in the opinion of the regulation maker).

5   See e g *Padfield v Minister of Agriculture, Fisheries and Food* [1968] AC 997, [1968] 1 All ER 694, HL (power vested in minister, if he 'so directs', to appoint a committee to inquire into complaints by milk producers, did not confer unfettered discretion, but had to be exercised in conformity with the implied purposes of the Act). See also *R v Lord Leigh, Re Kinchant* [1897] 1 QB 132, CA; *R v Paddington and St Marylebone Rent Tribunal, ex p Bell London and Provincial Properties Ltd* [1949] 1 KB 666, [1949] 1 All ER 720, DC, as explained in *R v Barnet and Camden Rent Tribunal, ex p Frey Investments Ltd* [1972] 2 QB 342, [1972] 1 All ER 1185, CA; *Lambeth London Borough Council v Secretary of State for Social Services* (1980) 79 LGR 61 (use of reserve emergency powers over long period); *Derby City Council v Secretary of State for the Environment* (1982) 81 LGR 134; *R v Tower Hamlets London Borough Council, ex p Chetnik Developments Ltd* [1988] AC 858, sub nom *Tower Hamlets London Borough Council v Chetnik Developments Ltd* [1988] 1 All ER 961, HL; *R v Walsall Justices, ex p W* [1990] 1 QB 253, [1989] 3 All ER 460, DC (decision to adjourn trial until new law comes into force improper exercise of discretion); *R v Secretary of State for the Environment, ex p Haringey London Borough Council* [1994] COD 518, 92 LGR 538, CA (no express limitation on power to issue directions but must be issued in accordance with purpose as stated in long title of Act); *R v Crown Court at Maidstone, ex p Clark* [1995] 3 All ER 513, [1995] 1 WLR 831, DC; *R v Crown Court at Maidstone, ex p Hollstein* [1995] 3 All ER 503 at 511, 159 JP 73 at 84, DC, per McCowan LJ (power to arraign not to be used as mechanism for denying right to bail where custody time limit expired); *R v Coventry City Council, ex p Phoenix Aviation* [1995] 3 All ER 37, 7 Admin LR 597, DC (to close harbour to those who had a right to use it was exercise of discretion for improper purpose); *Hamilton v Naviede* [1995] 2 AC 75, [1994] 3 All ER 814, HL (discretion under Insolvency Rules improperly exercised to seek to prevent use of transcripts in criminal proceedings); *R v Secretary of State for Education and Employment, ex p Begbie* [2000] 1 WLR 1115 at 1132, [2000] ELR 445 at [87]–[93], CA, per Sedley LJ (discretion to provide funds for assisted places); *R v Secretary of State for the Home Department, ex p Fire Brigades Union* [1995] 2 AC 513 at 551, 554, [1995] 2 All ER 244 at 253, 256, HL, per Lord Browne-Wilkinson; *R v Secretary of State for the Environment, Transport and the Regions, ex p Spath Holme Ltd* [2001] 2 AC 349, [2001] 1 All ER 195, HL; *S v Secretary of State for the Home Department* [2006] EWCA Civ 1157, (2006) Times, 9 October, [2006] All ER (D) 30 (Aug) (use of temporary admission as an alternative to discretionary leave for hijackers was unlawful where that purpose had not been sanctioned by Parliament and the Secretary of State had had sufficient time to obtain parliamentary authority).

The imposition of planning restrictions for reasons other than the regulation of land use is generally invalid: see *Tesco Stores Ltd v Secretary of State for the Environment* [1995] 2 All ER 636 at 648–649, [1995] 1 WLR 759 at 771–772, HL, per Lord Hoffmann (planning conditions must fairly and reasonably relate to permitted development and cannot be used for ulterior object even if that object desirable in the public interest). See also *Pyx Granite Co Ltd v Ministry of Housing and Local Government* [1958] 1 QB 554 at 572, [1958] 1 All ER 625 at 633, CA, per Lord Denning; *R v Hillingdon London Borough Council, ex p Royco Homes Ltd* [1974] QB 720, [1974] 2 All ER 643, DC; *Newbury District Council v Secretary of State for the Environment* [1981] AC 578, [1980] 1 All ER 731, HL; *Grampian Regional Council v City of Aberdeen District Council* (1983) 47 P & CR 633, [1994] JPL 590, HL; *R v South Northamptonshire District Council, ex p Crest Homes plc* [1994] PLR 47, 93 LGR 205, CA; *R v Westminster City Council, ex p Monahan* [1990] 1 QB 87 at 121, [1989] 2 All ER 74 at 103, CA, per Nicholls LJ. However, the wording of a grant of power may be wide enough to validate a refusal of planning permission prompted by a desire to avoid payment of compensation to a developer if a decision to impose restrictions were to be taken under another Act: see *Westminster Bank Ltd v Minister of Housing and Local Government* [1971] AC 508, [1970] 1 All ER 734, HL. See also HIGHWAYS, STREETS AND BRIDGES vol 21 (2004 Reissue) PARAS 491, 494; TOWN AND COUNTRY PLANNING vol 46(1) (Reissue) PARA 485.

6   See, in particular, *Padfield v Minister of Agriculture, Fisheries and Food* [1968] AC 997, [1968] 1 All ER 694, HL; *R v Tower Hamlets London Borough Council, ex p Chetnik Developments Ltd* [1988] AC 858, sub nom *Tower Hamlets London Borough Council v Chetnik Developments Ltd* [1988] 1 All ER 961, HL; *R v Governors of Haberdasher's Aske's Hatcham Schools, ex p Inner London Education Authority* [1989] COD 435, (1989) Times, 7 March, CA (affd sub nom *Brunyate v Inner London Education Authority* [1989] 2 All ER 417, sub nom *Inner London Education Authority v Brunyate* [1989] 1 WLR 542, HL); *R v Lambeth London Borough Council, ex p Ghous* [1993] COD 302 (policy on discretionary educational grants unlawful because it thwarted provisions in Education Acts on parental

choice); cf *R v Southwark London Borough Council, ex p Udu* [1996] ELR 390, (1995) 8 Admin LR 25, (1995) Times, 30 October, CA; *R v Warwickshire County Council, ex p Williams* [1995] COD 182, [1995] ELR 326 (policies on educational grants did not thwart purpose of Education Acts); *R v Secretary of State for the Home Department, ex p Fire Brigades Union* [1995] 2 AC 513, [1995] 2 All ER 244, HL (Secretary of State cannot rely on events procured by himself as ground for not exercising discretion to bring statute into force).

7 See *Padfield v Minister of Agriculture, Fisheries and Food* [1968] AC 997, [1968] 1 All ER 694, HL (improper failure to refer matter to committee of investigation); *Kent County Council v Kingsway Investments (Kent) Ltd* [1971] AC 72, [1970] 1 All ER 70, HL; *Westminster City Council v Great Portland Estates plc* [1985] AC 661, sub nom *Great Portland Estates plc v Westminster City Council* [1984] 3 All ER 744, HL (the detail in a development plan should not be left to be filled in by non-statutory guidelines; such a course would prevent debate concerning such detail at a public inquiry); *R v Worthing Borough Council, ex p Burch* (1983) 50 P & CR 53; *R v Burnham Primary and Secondary Committee, ex p Professional Association of Teachers* (1985) Times, 30 March (exclusion of association from consultation would frustrate the policy of the statute); *R v Secretary of State for Transport, ex p Gwent County Council* [1988] QB 429, [1987] 1 All ER 161, CA (inspector may not use his discretionary powers to regulate the procedure of an inquiry to frustrate the objects of that inquiry); cf *Lonrho plc v Secretary of State for Trade and Industry* [1989] 2 All ER 609, sub nom *R v Secretary of State for Trade and Industry, ex p Lonrho plc* [1989] 1 WLR 525, HL; *Good v Epping Forest District Council* [1994] 2 All ER 156, [1994] 1 WLR 376, CA.

8 *Weymouth Corpn v Cook* (1973) 71 LGR 458, DC; *Congreve v Home Office* [1976] QB 629 at 651, [1976] 1 All ER 697 at 709, CA, per Lord Denning MR (television licence should not be revoked where the licensee has done nothing wrong); *Wheeler v Leicester City Council* [1985] AC 1054 at 1080, [1985] 2 All ER 1106 at 1113, HL, per Lord Templeman (punishment where no wrong done); *R v Ealing London Borough Council, ex p Times Newspapers Ltd* (1986) 85 LGR 316, [1987] IRLR 129, DC; *R v Lewisham London Borough Council, ex p Shell UK Ltd* [1988] 1 All ER 938, DC; *R v Barnet London Borough Council, ex p Johnson* (1989) 88 LGR 73, DC (disciplinary regulations promulgated by local authority outside statutory objects). Cf *Asher v Secretary of State for the Environment* [1974] Ch 208, [1974] 2 All ER 156, CA (a case in which the purpose of instituting a procedure which could result in penalties was legitimate); *R v Newham London Borough Council, ex p Haggerty* (1986) 85 LGR 48; *R v Waltham Forest London Borough Council, ex p Baxter* [1988] QB 419, [1987] 3 All ER 671, CA; *R v Derbyshire County Council, ex p Times Supplements Ltd* (1990) 3 Admin LR 241, (1990) Times, 19 July, DC (ban on advertising motivated by desire to punish newspaper); *R v Greenwich London Borough Council, ex p Lovelace* [1991] 3 All ER 511, [1991] 1 WLR 506, CA (unlawful to punish councillor for way in which he cast vote); *R v Secretary of State for the Environment, ex p Haringey London Borough Council* [1994] COD 518, 92 LGR 538, CA (no evidence Secretary of State motivated by desire to punish council); *R v Hendon Justices, ex p DPP* [1994] QB 167, [1993] 1 All ER 411, DC (power to dismiss information not to be used to punish shortcomings of prosecution). See also *Roncarelli v Duplessis* (1959) 16 DLR (2d) 689, SC Can.

9 *Congreve v Home Office* [1976] QB 629, [1976] 1 All ER 697, CA; *R v Secretary of State for the Environment, ex p Leicester City Council* (1987) 55 P & CR 364; *R v Wirral Metropolitan Borough Council, ex p Milstead* [1989] RVR 66, 87 LGR 611, DC; *Crédit Suisse v Allerdale Borough Council* [1997] QB 306, [1996] 4 All ER 129, CA; and see note 3.

10 *R v Secretary of State for the Environment, ex p GLC* (1983) Times, 2 December; *Pickwell v Camden London Borough Council* [1983] QB 962 at 1004, [1983] 1 All ER 602 at 628, DC, per Ormrod LJ; *R v GLC, ex p Westminster City Council* (1984) Times, 27 December; *R v Hackney London Borough Council, ex p Fleming* (1985) 85 LGR 626n; *Wheeler v Leicester City Council* [1985] AC 1054, [1985] 2 All ER 1106, HL; *R v Ealing London Borough Council, ex p Times Newspapers Ltd* (1986) 85 LGR 316, DC; *Smith v Skinner* [1986] RVR 45, DC (deliberate failure to set rate for political reasons (affd sub nom *Lloyd v McMahon* [1987] AC 625, [1987] 1 All ER 1118, CA and HL)); *R v Lewisham London Borough Council, ex p Shell UK Ltd* [1988] 1 All ER 938, DC; *R v Port Talbot Borough Council, ex p Jones* [1988] 2 All ER 207; *Brunyate v Inner London Education Authority* [1989] 2 All ER 417 sub nom *Inner London Education Authority v Brunyate* [1989] 1 WLR 542, HL; cf *R v Warwickshire County Council, ex p Dill-Russell* [1991] COD 24, (1990) 3 Admin LR 1, DC (decision to remove school governors in order to maintain party political balance lawful); *R v Greenwich London Borough Council, ex p Lovelace* [1991] 3 All ER 511, [1991] 1 WLR 506, CA; *R v Secretary of State for the Environment, ex p Haringey London Borough Council* [1994] COD 518 at 519, 92 LGR 538 at 546–547, CA, per Ralph Gibson LJ (not improper to publicise lawful decision for political purposes); *R v Leeds City Council, ex p Cobleigh* [1997] COD 69 (local authority

not acting for improper political purpose when putting forward views of people it represents); *R v Local Comr for Administration in North and North East England, ex p Liverpool City Council* [2001] 1 All ER 462, [2000] LGR 571, CA (political influence on determination of planning application was decisive); *Porter v Magill* [2001] UKHL 67, [2002] 2 AC 357, [2002] 1 All ER 465 (use of power to sell council houses for electoral advantage was deliberate, blatant and dishonest abuse of public power). See also ADMINISTRATIVE LAW vol 1(1) (2001 Reissue) PARA 32.

11 See *Re Walker's Decision* [1944] 1 KB 644 at 649–650, [1944] 1 All ER 614 at 615, CA, per Du Parcq LJ (only material question for district auditor was whether payments by local authority to employees were 'reasonable' in amount); and see dictum of Lord Sumner in *Roberts v Hopwood* [1925] AC 578 at 604, HL, to like effect; but it seems that the local authority would have to determine the matter in good faith for its decision to be fully immune from challenge: *Roberts v Hopwood* at 589 per Lord Buckmaster, at 603–604 per Lord Sumner, and at 617–618 per Lord Carson. See also *Pickwell v Camden London Borough Council* [1983] QB 962 at 999–1000, [1983] 1 All ER 602 at 625, DC, per Ormrod LJ. Sed quaere whether these observations are consistent with the emphasis which is placed on the decision-making process rather than the decision itself: see eg *Chief Constable of the North Wales Police v Evans* [1982] 3 All ER 141 at 154, [1982] 1 WLR 1155 at 1173, HL, per Lord Brightman; *Re Amin* [1983] 2 AC 818 at 829, [1983] 2 All ER 864 at 868, HL, per Lord Fraser of Tullybelton; *Council of Civil Service Unions v Minister for the Civil Service* [1985] AC 374 at 414, [1984] 3 All ER 935 at 953, HL, per Lord Roskill.

12 *R v Southwark Crown Court, ex p Bowles* [1998] AC 641, [1998] 2 All ER 193, HL; *Earl Fitzwilliam's Wentworth Estate Co v Minister of Town and Country Planning* [1951] 2 KB 284 at 307, [1951] 1 All ER 982 at 996, CA, per Denning LJ. See also *Webb v Minister of Housing and Local Government* [1965] 2 All ER 193 at 207, [1965] 1 WLR 755 at 778, CA, per Danckwerts LJ; *Grieve v Douglas-Home* 1965 SC 315, Ct of Sess; *R v Immigration Appeals Adjudicator, ex p Perween Khan* [1972] 3 All ER 297, [1972] 1 WLR 1058, DC; *Waters v Secretary of State for the Environment* (1977) 33 P & CR 410; *R v Merseyside County Council, ex p Great Universal Stores Ltd* (1982) 80 LGR 639 at 658; and see *Westminster City Council v Great Portland Estates plc* [1985] AC 661 at 669–671, HL, per Lord Scarman (it is unclear which test is applied; cf at 669 'irrelevant factor').

13 See *R v Governor of Brixton Prison, ex p Soblen* [1963] 2 QB 243, [1963] 3 All ER 641, CA (deportation of alien had practical effect of extraditing him for non-extraditable offence; order nevertheless valid, as there was evidence that the Home Secretary had genuinely deemed the deportation to be conducive to the public good; the decision would have been different had the deportation order been shown to be a mere sham).

14 *R v Governor of Brixton Prison, ex p Soblen* [1963] 2 QB 243, [1962] 3 All ER 641, CA; *Westminster Corpn v London and North Western Rly Co* [1905] AC 426, HL; *R v Brighton Corpn, ex p Shoosmith* (1907) 96 LT 762, CA; and see *R v Secretary of State for Foreign Affairs, ex p World Development Movement Ltd* [1995] 1 All ER 611 at 626–627, [1995] 1 WLR 386 at 401–402, DC, per Rose LJ (once there is a legitimate purpose within the meaning of the statute, the Secretary of State may take into account political and economic considerations); *R (on the application of Richards) v Pembrokeshire County Council* [2004] EWCA Civ 1000, [2005] LGR 105 (where the purpose is improper, the decision is unlawful even if a collateral consequence is that a statutory purpose is achieved).

A version of the predominant purpose test may be appropriate to determine the purpose of a multi-member body, such as a local council: see *R v LCC, ex p London and Provincial Electric Theatres Ltd* [1915] 2 KB 466 at 490–491, CA, per Pickford LJ; *R v Barnet and Camden Rent Tribunal, ex p Frey Investments Ltd* [1972] 2 QB 342 at 351, [1971] 3 All ER 759 at 765–766, DC, per Lord Widgery CJ (affd without reference to this point [1972] 2 QB 342, [1972] 1 All ER 1185, CA); and see *Smith v Skinner* [1986] RVR 45 at 52, 77, DC, per Glidewell LJ (a council's resolutions are evidence of the attitude of those members who voted for them and of its intentions as a body) (affd without reference to this point sub nom *Lloyd v McMahon* [1987] AC 625, [1987] 1 All ER 1118, CA and HL); *R v Greenwich London Borough Council, ex p Lovelace* [1990] 1 All ER 353, [1990] 1 WLR 18, DC; cf ADMINISTRATIVE LAW vol 1(1) (2001 Reissue) PARA 32. See also *Smith v Hayle Town Council* (1978) 77 LGR 52, [1978] ICR 996, CA; *Maund v Penwith District Council* [1984] ICR 143, [1984] IRLR 24, CA; *Jones v Swansea City Council* [1990] 3 All ER 737, [1990] 1 WLR 1453, HL (proving motive behind council resolution for purpose of establishing misfeasance in public office). There is a presumption that all members of a council in taking a collective decision have taken account of material in documents put before them: *R v Bristol City Council, ex p Pearce* (1984) 83 LGR 711 at 719 per Glidewell J.

15 See PARA 623. See also *Sadler v Sheffield Corpn* [1924] 1 Ch 483 at 504–505 per Lawrence J. In *Hanks v Minister of Housing and Local Government* [1963] 1 QB 999 at 1018–1020, [1963] 1 All ER 47 at 54–55 (a compulsory purchase case) Megaw J considered purpose and relevance as tests of validity and preferred to ask whether the making of the order had been significantly affected by legally irrelevant considerations. The latter approach has been adopted and applied in recent cases: *R v Rochdale Metropolitan Borough Council, ex p Cromer Ring Mill Ltd* [1982] 3 All ER 761, [1982] RVR 113; *R v Broadcasting Complaints Commission, ex p Owen* [1985] QB 1153, [1985] 2 All ER 522, DC (challenge failed because had the commission not had regard to the irrelevant consideration the result would have been the same: see PARA 623 note 34); *R v Inner London Education Authority, ex p Westminster City Council* [1986] 1 All ER 19, [1986] 1 WLR 28; *R v Lewisham London Borough Council, ex p Shell UK Ltd* [1988] 1 All ER 938, DC (decision will be quashed where the illegitimate purpose exerted a substantial influence on the relevant decision), followed in *R v Greenwich London Borough Council, ex p Lovelace* [1991] 3 All ER 511, [1991] 1 WLR 506, CA; *R v GLC, ex p Westminster City Council* (1984) Times, 27 December; cf *R v Exeter City Council, ex p JL Thomas & Co Ltd* [1991] 1 QB 471, [1990] 1 All ER 413; *R (on the application of Unison) v First Secretary of State* [2006] EWHC 2373 (Admin), [2007] LGR 188, [2006] IRLR 926 (applying *R v Broadcasting Complaints Commission, ex p Owen*).

The material time at which the decision-maker's purpose is to be assessed is the time at which the decision is taken: *Varsari v Secretary of State for the Environment* (1980) 40 P & CR 354.

16 See, in particular, dicta in *Padfield v Minister of Agriculture, Fisheries and Food* [1968] AC 997 at 1032–1033, [1968] 1 All ER 694 at 701, HL, per Lord Reid, at 1049 and 712 per Lord Hodson, at 1053–1054 and 715 per Lord Pearce, and at 1061–1062 and 719 per Lord Upjohn; distinguished in *Secretary of State for Employment v Associated Society of Locomotive Engineers and Firemen (No 2)* [1972] 2 QB 455, [1972] 2 All ER 949, CA; and in *Lonrho plc v Secretary of State for Trade and Industry* [1989] 2 All ER 609, sub nom *R v Secretary of State for Trade and Industry, ex p Lonrho* [1989] 1 WLR 525, HL. See also *R v Governor of Brixton Prison, ex p Soblen* [1963] 2 QB 243 at 302, [1962] 3 All ER 641 at 661, CA, per Lord Denning MR, and at 307–308 and 664 per Donovan LJ; and see *Marquess of Clanricarde v Congested Districts Board for Ireland* (1914) 79 JP 481, HL, where, however, the challenge to a compulsory purchase order failed; *Minister of National Revenue v Wrights' Canadian Ropes Ltd* [1947] AC 109, PC (the court will not assume from a minister's silence that he had good reasons for action); *Coleen Properties Ltd v Minister of Housing and Local Government* [1971] 1 All ER 1049, [1971] 1 WLR 433, CA; *Elliott v Southwark London Borough Council* [1976] 2 All ER 781, [1976] 1 WLR 499, CA (court declined to infer that council had failed to take account of relevant matters from inadequate reasons given for its action); *R v Secretary of State for Transport, ex p Cumbria County Council* [1983] RTR 129 at 135, CA; *R v Secretary of State for the Environment, ex p Halton Borough Council* (1983) 82 LGR 662 at 668; *R v Secretary of State for the Environment, ex p Manchester City Council* (1986) 53 P & CR 369 (decision not prima facie unreasonable, so no inference of improper purpose was drawn from the absence of reasons; affd sub nom *Manchester City Council v Secretary of State for the Environment* (1987) 54 P & CR 212, CA); *R v Secretary of State for Social Services, ex p Connolly* [1986] 1 All ER 998, [1986] 1 WLR 421, CA (no adverse inference drawn from failure to give reasons where the decision-maker was exempt from the duty to give reasons in the Tribunals and Inquiries Act 1971 s 12; cf *R v Lancashire County Council, ex p Huddleston* [1986] 2 All ER 941 at 945, CA, per Sir John Donaldson MR: reasons should be given in the interests of high standards of public administration); *R v Secretary of State for the Home Department, ex p Handscomb* (1987) 86 Cr App Rep 59, DC; *Lonrho plc v Secretary of State for Trade and Industry* (no adverse inference to be drawn from failure to give reasons if decision did not appear unreasonable); *R v Secretary of State for the Home Department, ex p Adams* [1995] All ER (EC) 177 at 185, [1995] 3 CMLR 476, DC, per Steyn LJ (where no duty to give reasons for exclusion order because decision taken on national security grounds, the court cannot draw inference of improper purpose from absence of material).

Inadequacy or lack of reasons may support an inference that a tribunal has made an error of law in making its decision: *Mountview Court Properties Ltd v Devlin* (1970) 21 P & CR 689, DC; *Pepys v London Transport Executive* [1975] 1 All ER 748, [1975] 1 WLR 234, CA; *Crake v Supplementary Benefits Commission* [1982] 1 All ER 498; *R (on the application of Kelsall) v Secretary of State for the Environment, Food and Rural Affairs* [2003] EWHC 459 (Admin), (2003) Times, 27 March, [2003] All ER (D) 186 (Mar) (deficiencies in reasons can give substance to argument that decision was unlawful).

623.   Relevant and irrelevant considerations.   A discretionary power must be exercised for proper purposes which are consistent with the conferring statute[1]. The exercise of such a power will be quashed where, on a proper construction of the relevant statute, the decision-maker has failed to take account of relevant considerations or has taken into account irrelevant considerations[2]. In some statutes, some or all of the relevant considerations may be express[3]; where the statute is silent or the express considerations are not exhaustive, the courts will determine whether any particular consideration is relevant or irrelevant to the exercise of the discretion by reference to the implied objects of the statute[4].

In practice the scope of judicial review will vary according to the context. If a very wide range of considerations needs to be taken into account by a minister determining whether to take certain discretionary action on grounds of national policy, the courts will seldom interfere at the instance of a person claiming to be aggrieved by the action taken unless the act has been vitiated by lack of jurisdiction or power in the narrow sense[5], or non-compliance with procedural requirements, bad faith, or the bona fide pursuit of an unauthorised purpose where the ambit of the power is adequately defined with reference to purpose[6]. Abstention from judicial intervention is all the more likely where a power conferred on a minister or other public authority is expressed to be exercisable when that authority is satisfied that it is requisite[7], or satisfied that it is expedient in the national or public interest[8], that a particular course of action be adopted[9]. Due regard, moreover, will be paid to the undesirability of setting narrow limits to the exercise of wide discretionary powers vested in local authorities[10].

However, in many contexts, including those involving a wide discretionary element, the courts will identify the relevant considerations germane to the exercise of a statutory power, and will quash such exercise if those considerations are ignored[11] or if irrelevant considerations are taken into account[12]. Thus a magistrate or tribunal taking irrelevant factors into account or failing to have regard to relevant factors will be held to have failed to hear and determine the matter according to law[13], or to have declined jurisdiction[14] or to have exceeded jurisdiction[15]. A licensing body, empowered to attach such conditions as it thinks fit to the grant of a licence or permit, can lawfully attach only conditions that fairly and reasonably relate to the grant[16]. Similarly, the immigration authorities must have regard to relevant factors and ignore irrelevant factors in the exercise of their statutory powers[17], as must a police constable exercising a power of arrest[18].

What is or is not a relevant consideration in any case will depend on the statutory context. A public authority must have regard to matters material to its statutory obligation not to act in a way which is incompatible with human rights[19]. The cost of exercising a discretion may be relevant, depending on the statutory context[20]. The courts will also require local authorities to have regard to an implied fiduciary duty owed to ratepayers in respect of the funds at the authorities' disposal[21]. Fairness to persons affected by administrative action or personal hardship which may be caused thereby will also often be relevant considerations to be taken into account[22]. In some contexts a decision-maker should have regard to the general public interest[23], while in others it may be inappropriate to do so[24]. Where policy guidelines have been promulgated regarding the exercise of a discretion such guidelines will be a relevant factor which should be taken into account by the decision-maker[25]. A decision-maker will generally not be required to have regard to treaty obligations which are not part of domestic law when exercising a statutory power[26].

The weight to be given to a relevant consideration is a matter for the decision-maker[27]; but in certain limited circumstances a decision may be quashed owing to insufficient or excessive weight given to a particular factor[28]. If the decision-maker asks himself the wrong question, his error may lead him to take account of irrelevant matters or to disregard relevant matters so that his decision will be quashed[29]. Similarly, if a body fails to give an affected party a hearing before exercising a discretion, contrary to the rules of natural justice or an obligation to consult that party, it may fail to take account of relevant material which could have been put forward by that party[30]. A body empowered to exercise a discretion is under a duty to take reasonable steps to acquaint itself with matters relevant to its decision, but the extent of its obligation to make inquiries and consider alternative courses of action will vary according to context[31]. Government ministers taking decisions will be assumed to be aware of all relevant information available to their departments[32]. In some circumstances, a failure by one body to take account of relevant considerations may not invalidate the action taken, where that action has been confirmed on an appeal to another body which has taken all relevant matters into consideration[33].

The exercise of a discretion will not be quashed for failure to have regard to a relevant matter or for taking account of an irrelevant matter where the court is satisfied that the relevant decision would have been the same had there been no error in the decision-making process[34].

1 See PARAS 621–622.

2 See generally *Associated Provincial Picture Houses Ltd v Wednesbury Corpn* [1948] 1 KB 223 at 229, [1947] 2 All ER 680 at 682–683, CA, per Lord Greene MR; *R (on the application of Alconbury Developments Ltd) v Secretary of State for the Environment, Transport and the Regions* [2001] UKHL 23, [2003] 2 AC 295, [2001] 2 All ER 929; *Re Duffy* [2008] UKHL 4, [2008] NI 152.

3 See eg the statutory duties to have regard to equality matters: *R (on the application of Chavda) v Harrow London Borough Council* [2007] EWHC 3064 (Admin), [2008] LGR 657 (disability equality); *R (on the application of Baker) v Secretary of State for Communities and Local Government* [2008] EWCA Civ 141, [2008] 2 P & CR 119, [2008] LGR 239 (race equality); *R (on the application of Brown) v Secretary of State for Work and Pensions* [2008] EWHC 3158 (Admin), [2008] All ER (D) 208 (Dec); *R (on the application of Isaacs) v Secretary of State for Communities and Local Government* [2009] EWHC 557 (Admin), [2009] All ER (D) 265 (Oct); *R (on the application of Brooke) v Secretary of State for Justice* [2009] EWHC 1396 (Admin), [2009] All ER (D) 272 (Oct); *R (on the application of Sanders) v Harlow District Council* [2009] EWHC 559 (Admin), [2009] All ER (D) 86 (Mar) (requirement to have due regard, not regard). See also eg the Education Act 1980 ss 6(2) and (5) (repealed) (local authorities required to consider education preferences of parents both inside and outside the borough); the Town and Country Planning Act 1990 s 70 (see TOWN AND COUNTRY PLANNING vol 46(1) (Reissue) PARA 484); the Food and Environment Protection Act 1985 s 8 (see SHIPPING AND NAVIGATION vol 43(2) (Reissue) PARAS 1316–1319). See also *R v Secretary of State for the Environment, ex p Lancashire County Council* [1994] 4 All ER 165, 93 LGR 29; *R v Sunderland City Council, ex p Redezeus Ltd* (1994) 27 HLR 477, (1994) 92 LGR 105; *R v Licensing Authority of the Department of Health, ex p Scotia Pharmaceuticals Ltd* (Case C-440/93) (1995) 34 BMLR 171, ECJ; *R v Oadby and Wigston Borough Council, ex p Dickman* [1996] COD 233, (1995) 28 HLR 806.

Where a decision-maker is required by statute to take account of a matter, it is not necessarily perverse to consider it but to give it no weight: *Swords v Secretary of State for Communities and Local Government* [2007] EWCA Civ 795, [2007] LGR 757.

4 See PARA 621. The question of whether something is a relevant consideration is one of law, but the weight to be given to any relevant consideration is a matter for the decision-maker, with which the court will only interfere on the grounds of *Wednesbury* irrationality (see PARA 617): *Tesco Stores v Secretary of State for the Environment* [1995] 1 WLR 759 at 780, HL, per Lord Hoffmann; and see note 23. In some contexts, there may be considerations which the decision-maker may, but need not, take into account: see *Hillbank Properties Ltd v Hackney London Borough Council* [1978] QB 998, [1978] 3 All ER 343, CA; *R v Hillingdon Health*

Authority, ex p Goodwin [1984] ICR 800 (referring to CREEDNZ Inc v Governor-General [1981] 1 NZLR 172 at 182 per Cooke J, NZ CA); Re Findlay [1985] AC 318 at 333–334, [1984] 3 All ER 801 at 827, HL, per Lord Scarman; R v Secretary of State for Transport, ex p Richmond-upon-Thames London Borough Council [1994] 1 All ER 577, [1994] 1 WLR 74; R v Somerset County Council, ex p Fewings [1995] 3 All ER 20 at 31–32, [1995] 1 WLR 1037 at 1049–1050, CA, per Simon Brown LJ (dissenting but not on this point); R (on the application of Adlard) v Secretary of State for Environment, Transport and the Regions [2002] EWCA Civ 735, [2002] 1 WLR 2515; R (on the application of Greenpeace) v Secretary of State for Environment, Food and Rural Affairs [2005] EWCA Civ 1656, [2005] All ER (D) 365 (Oct); R (on the application of Al Rawi) v Secretary of State for Foreign and Commonwealth Affairs [2006] EWCA Civ 1279, [2008] QB 289. A decision will not be quashed simply because there has been 'a failure to take into account a consideration which the decision-maker is not obliged by the law or the facts to take into account, even if he may properly do so': R (on the application of Corner House Research) v Director of the Serious Fraud Office [2008] UKHL 60 at [40], [2009] 1 AC 756 at [40], [2008] 4 All ER 927 at [40] per Lord Bingham of Cornhill. Where a matter is clearly of fundamental importance in deciding whether to exercise a discretion, the decision-maker will be bound to consider that matter: R v Hillingdon Health Authority, ex p Goodwin; R (on the application of Coghlan) v Chief Constable of Greater Manchester Police [2004] EWHC 2801 (Admin), [2005] 2 All ER 890; R (on the application of Ireneschild) v Lambeth London Borough Council [2007] EWCA Civ 234, [2007] LGR 619.

5   See PARA 612.

6   See R v Secretary of State for the Environment, ex p Hammersmith and Fulham London Borough Council [1991] 1 AC 521, sub nom Hammersmith and Fulham London Borough Council v Secretary of State for the Environment [1990] 3 All ER 589, HL (setting reduced budgets for local authorities); R v Leman Street Police Station Inspector, ex p Venicoff [1920] 3 KB 72, DC; Schmidt v Secretary of State for Home Affairs [1969] 2 Ch 149, [1969] 1 All ER 904, CA (regulation of aliens); McEldowney v Forde [1971] AC 632, [1969] 2 All ER 1039, HL (minister empowered to make regulations for preservation of the peace and maintenance of order); Franklin v Minister of Town and Country Planning [1948] AC 87, [1947] 2 All ER 289, HL (designation of area as site of new town); Essex County Council v Ministry of Housing and Local Government (1967) 66 LGR 23, 18 P & CR 531 (location of third London airport); B Johnson & Co (Builders) Ltd v Minister of Health [1947] 2 All ER 395, CA (confirmation of compulsory purchase order); Lonrho plc v Secretary of State for Trade and Industry [1989] 2 All ER 609, sub nom R v Secretary of State for Trade and Industry, ex p Lonrho plc [1989] 1 WLR 525, HL (whether commercial activity in public interest); R v Secretary of State for the Environment, ex p Greenpeace Ltd [1994] 4 All ER 352, 3 CMLR 737; R v Secretary of State for the Home Department, ex p Cheblak [1991] 2 All ER 319, [1991] 1 WLR 890, CA (decision involving national security); R v Secretary of State for Trade and Industry, ex p Isle of Wight Council [2000] COD 245 (whether area should be designated assisted area for grant purposes); cf R v Secretary of State for Foreign Affairs, ex p World Development Movement Ltd [1995] 1 All ER 611, [1995] 1 WLR 386, DC (provision of overseas aid; Secretary of State entitled to take into account political and economic considerations but provision outside purpose of Act); and see the cases cited in PARA 622 note 3. The proposition in the text is not necessarily confined to situations where issues of national policy call for decision; there are others where the discretion of the competent authority is virtually unfettered: see eg Re Fletcher's Application [1970] 2 All ER 527n, CA (absolute discretion of Parliamentary Commissioner for Administration whether to investigate a complaint); Gallagher v Post Office [1970] 3 All ER 712 (absolute discretion of Office in deciding which organisation it is to consult for prescribed purposes); Re Watch House, Boswinger (1967) 66 LGR 6, sub nom Re Lamplugh (1967) 19 P & CR 125 (local planning authority's direction to remove a building not reviewable for unreasonableness); A-G (ex rel Rivers-Moore) v Portsmouth City Council (1978) 76 LGR 643 at 651 per Walton J (council's decision to refuse to declare a rehabilitation area not reviewable for unreasonableness). See further PARA 619; and ADMINISTRATIVE LAW vol 1(1) (2001 Reissue) PARAS 21, 66.

7   Re City of Plymouth (City Centre) Declaratory Order 1946, Robinson v Minister of Town and Country Planning [1947] KB 702, [1947] 1 All ER 851, CA; B Marsh (Wholesale) Ltd v Customs and Excise Comrs [1970] 2 QB 206, [1970] 1 All ER 990; cf ADMINISTRATIVE LAW vol 1(1) (2001 Reissue) PARA 21.

8   R v Secretary of State for the Home Department, ex p Cheblak [1991] 2 All ER 319, [1991] 1 WLR 890 (court may only impugn decision where Secretary of State deems something to be conducive to the public good on the ground of bad faith); Re Beck and Pollitzer's Application,

Re Requisitioned Land and War Works Act 1945 [1948] 2 KB 339; *Land Realisation Co Ltd v Postmaster-General* [1950] Ch 435, [1950] 1 All ER 1062; cf ADMINISTRATIVE LAW vol 1(1) (2001 Reissue) PARA 21.

9 See also the cases cited in PARAS 621–622; and the qualification that if prima facie grounds are shown for believing that the competent authority could not genuinely have been so satisfied, a court may now infer, in the absence of an adequate answer, that the conditions necessary for a valid exercise of the power were not present. As to the reluctance of the courts to hold their supervisory jurisdiction in respect of matters of law and fact to be ousted by a subjectively worded formula see ADMINISTRATIVE LAW vol 1(1) (2001 Reissue) PARA 21.

10 See eg *Kruse v Johnson* [1898] 2 QB 91, DC; *Associated Provincial Picture Houses Ltd v Wednesbury Corpn* [1948] 1 KB 223, [1947] 2 All ER 680, CA; *R v Brighton Corpn, ex p Thomas Tilling Ltd* (1916) 85 LJKB 1552 at 1555, DC. Where a local authority has exercised a broad discretionary power not impinging directly on individual rights, the courts may be reluctant to intervene at the instance of a person claiming to be aggrieved on the ground that the authority has taken irrelevant matters into account or has disregarded relevant matters, unless that authority had acted capriciously or in bad faith: *R v Barnet and Camden Rent Tribunal, ex p Frey Investments Ltd* [1972] 2 QB 342, [1972] 1 All ER 1185, CA (where the validity of a reference of 22 contracts of letting by the local authority to the rent tribunal under the Rent Act 1968 s 72 (repealed) was unsuccessfully challenged); *Associated Provincial Picture Houses Ltd v Wednesbury Corpn* and *R v Paddington and St Marylebone Rent Tribunal, ex p Bell London and Provincial Properties Ltd* [1949] 1 KB 666, [1949] 1 All ER 720, DC, distinguished. In *R v Barnet and Camden Rent Tribunal, ex p Frey Investments Ltd* it was held that the fact that most of the tenants did not wish their agreements to be referred to the tribunal did not affect the validity of the local authority's decision, which had been based on a careful consideration of the circumstances of each case. Since the court did not find that the local authority had been swayed by irrelevant factors or had disregarded relevant factors in coming to its decision, observations by members of the court as to the tests of legality to be applied in such a situation were strictly obiter; the decision was followed in *Asher v Secretary of State for the Environment* [1974] Ch 208, [1974] 2 All ER 156, CA. See also *Re Hurle-Hobbs' Decision* [1944] 1 All ER 249, DC; on appeal [1944] 2 All ER 261, CA.

11 *Re Findlay* [1985] AC 318, [1984] 3 All ER 801, HL (approving *CREEDNZ Inc v Governor-General* [1981] 1 NZLR 172, NZ CA). For recent examples see *R (on the application of Mersey Care Trust) v Mental Health Review Tribunal* [2004] EWHC 1749 (Admin), [2005] 2 All ER 820, [2005] 1 WLR 2469; *R (on the application of T) v Enfield London Borough Council* [2004] EWHC 2297 (Admin), [2005] 3 FCR 55; *R (on the application of McCarthy) v Basildon District Council* [2008] EWHC 987 (Admin), [2008] All ER (D) 118 (May); *R (on the application of Assura Pharmacy Ltd) v National Health Service Litigation Authority (Family Health Services Appeal Unit)* [2008] EWHC 289 (Admin), [2008] All ER (D) 304 (Feb).

12 See eg *R (on the application of Campbell) v General Medical Council* [2005] EWCA Civ 250, [2005] 2 All ER 970; *R (on the application of Stace) v Milton Keynes Magistrates' Court* [2006] EWHC 1049 (Admin), 171 JP 1.

13 See *R v De Rutzen* (1875) 1 QBD 55, DC; *R v Bowman* [1898] 1 QB 663, DC; *R v Cotham* [1898] 1 QB 802, DC (where decisions of licensing justices were based on irrelevant grounds); and see *R v Southampton Justices, ex p Green* [1976] QB 11, [1975] 2 All ER 1073, CA; *R v Horseferry Road Stipendiary Magistrate, ex p Pearson* [1976] 2 All ER 264, [1976] 1 WLR 511, DC; *R v Tottenham Justices, ex p Dwarkados Joshi* [1982] 2 All ER 507, [1982] 1 WLR 631, DC; *R v Inner London Crown Court, ex p Springall* (1986) 85 Cr App Rep 214, DC; *R v Newcastle-upon-Tyne Justices, ex p Skinner* [1987] 1 All ER 349, [1987] 1 WLR 312, DC. The principles upon which the Court of Appeal will review on appeal the exercise of a judicial discretion by a judge are not identical with the principles in *Associated Provincial Picture Houses Ltd v Wednesbury Corpn* [1948] 1 KB 223, [1947] 2 All ER 680, CA: see *G v G (Minors: Custody Appeal)* [1985] 2 All ER 225, [1985] 1 WLR 647, HL.

14 See *R v Adamson* (1875) 1 QBD 201 (refusal to issue summons on grounds that could not lawfully be taken into account, equated with declining jurisdiction). See further PARAS 615, 708.

15 See *Anisminic Ltd v Foreign Compensation Commission* [1969] 2 AC 147, [1969] 1 All ER 208, HL; and PARA 612.

16 See *Tesco Stores Ltd v Secretary of State for the Environment* [1995] 2 All ER 636, [1995] 1 WLR 759, HL; *Pyx Granite Co Ltd v Ministry of Housing and Local Government* [1958] 1 QB 554 at 572, [1958] 1 All ER 625 at 633, CA, per Lord Denning (conditions annexed to grant of planning permission); revsd on another point [1960] AC 260, [1959] 3 All ER 1, HL; *Fawcett Properties Ltd v Buckingham County Council* [1961] AC 636, [1960] 3 All ER 503, HL.

17 See eg *R v Immigration Appeal Tribunal, ex p Bastiampillai* [1983] 2 All ER 844; *R v Immigration Appeal Tribunal, ex p Bakhtaur Singh* [1986] 1 WLR 910, HL. For the approach of the court in cases involving interference with human rights in the immigration context see eg *R (on the application of Mahmood) v Secretary of State for the Home Department* [2001] 1 WLR 840, [2001] 2 FCR 63, CA; note 19; and PARA 651.

18 *Holgate-Mohammed v Duke* [1984] AC 437, [1984] 1 All ER 1054, HL.

19 The duty arises under the Human Rights Act 1998 s 6(1), which incorporates parts of the Convention for the Protection of Human Rights and Fundamental Freedoms (Rome, 4 November 1950; TS 71 (1953) Cmd 8969) into domestic law: see PARA 651. For the general approach of the court when reviewing decisions which are alleged to infringe human rights see PARA 651. For the law on human rights generally see CONSTITUTIONAL LAW AND HUMAN RIGHTS vol 8(2) (Reissue) PARA 101 et seq. Where a decision touches convention rights, the decision-maker must consider whether the right has been violated: *R v Secretary of State for the Home Department, ex p Quaquah* [2000] INLR 196, [1999] All ER (D) 1437. See also *R (on the application of Fuller) v Chief Constable of Dorset Police* [2001] EWHC Admin 1057, [2003] QB 480, [2002] 3 All ER 57; *R (on the application of Goldsmith) v Wandsworth London Borough Council* [2004] EWCA Civ 1170, 148 Sol Jo LB 1065, [2004] All ER (D) 154 (Aug).

Prior to the coming into force of the Human Rights Act 1998 on 2 October 2000, the rights protected by the Convention for the Protection of Human Rights and Fundamental Freedoms (1950) were relevant to the exercise of discretion by a public authority, but an act or decision incompatible with those rights was not necessarily unlawful: see generally *R v Secretary of State for the Home Department, ex p Brind* [1991] 1 AC 696, sub nom *Brind v Secretary of State for the Home Department* [1991] 1 All ER 720, HL; *R v Ministry of Defence, ex p Smith* [1996] QB 517 at 554, [1996] 1 All ER 257 at 263, CA, per Lord Bingham MR; *R v DPP, ex p Kebeline* [2000] 2 AC 326, [1999] 4 All ER 801, HL. See also PARA 651.

20 *R v Gloucestershire County Council, ex p Barry* [1997] AC 584, [1997] 2 All ER 1, HL (resources relevant consideration to what constitute 'needs' of a disabled person); *Harris v Sheffield United Football Club Ltd* [1988] QB 77, [1987] 2 All ER 838, CA; *R v Cambridge Health Authority, ex p B* [1995] 2 All ER 129, [1995] 1 WLR 898, CA; *R v Gloucestershire County Council, ex p Mahfood* (1995) 8 Admin LR 180, sub nom *R v Islington London Borough Council, ex p McMillan* (1995) 30 BMLR 20, DC; *R v Sefton Metropolitan Borough Council, ex p Help the Aged* [1997] 4 All ER 532, [1997] 3 FCR 573, CA; *B v Special Educational Needs Tribunal* [1998] 3 FCR 231, [1999] LGR 144, CA; *R v Chief Constable of Sussex, ex p International Trader's Ferry Ltd* [1999] 2 AC 418, [1999] 1 All ER 129, HL (resources relevant to Chief Constable's determination of how to keep the peace and enforce the law); *R v North and East Devon Health Authority, ex p Coughlan* [2001] QB 213, [2000] 3 All ER 850, CA (resources relevant to duty to provide health services); *R (on the application of G) v Barnet London Borough Council* [2003] UKHL 57, [2004] 2 AC 208, [2004] 1 All ER 97; *R (on the application of Calgin) v Enfield London Borough Council* [2005] EWHC 1716 (Admin), [2006] 1 All ER 112, [2006] 1 FCR 58; *Crofton v National Health Service Litigation Authority* [2007] EWCA Civ 71, [2007] LGR 507.

Costs may also be relevant in the planning context: see *Tesco Stores Ltd v Secretary of State for the Environment* [1995] 2 All ER 636, [1995] 1 WLR 759, HL; *Dowty Boulton Paul Ltd v Wolverhampton Corpn (No 2)* [1976] Ch 13, [1973] 2 All ER 491, CA, per Buckley LJ; *Eckersley v Secretary of State for the Environment* (1977) 76 LGR 245, (1977) 34 P & CR 124, CA; *Sovmots Investments Ltd v Secretary of State for the Environment* [1977] QB 411, [1976] 3 All ER 720, CA; *R v Brent London Borough Council, ex p Gunning* (1985) 84 LGR 168. But the cost of development of a site will be an irrelevant consideration in relation to the decision whether to grant planning permission in all but exceptional cases: *J Murphy & Sons Ltd v Secretary of State for the Environment* [1973] 2 All ER 26, [1973] 1 WLR 560; *Niarchos (London) Ltd v Secretary of State for the Environment* (1977) 76 LGR 480, 35 P & CR 259; *Walters v Secretary of State for Wales* (1978) 77 LGR 529; *Brighton Borough Council v Secretary of State for the Environment* (1978) 39 P & CR 46; *Sosmo Trust Ltd v Secretary of State for the Environment* [1983] JPL 806; *R v Westminster City Council, ex p Monahan* [1990] 1 QB 87, [1989] 2 All ER 74, CA (it is unreal and contrary to common sense to exclude consideration of financial constraints on the economic viability of a development in a planning decision). See also TOWN AND COUNTRY PLANNING vol 46(1) (Reissue) PARA 485.

In other cases, costs will not be a relevant consideration and the court will quash a decision taken with regard to them: see eg *R v Secretary of State for the Environment, ex p Kingston-upon-Hull* [1996] Env LR 248, (1996) Times, 31 January (cost not relevant to establishing estuarine boundary); *R v Birmingham City Council, ex p Mohammed* [1998]

3 All ER 788, [1999] 1 WLR 33 (cost not relevant to disabled facilities grant); *R v East Sussex County Council, ex p Tandy* [1998] AC 714, [1998] 2 All ER 769, HL (resources not relevant consideration to what constitutes 'suitable education'; *R v Gloucestershire County Council, ex p Barry* distinguished); *R (on the application of Conville) v Richmond upon Thames London Borough Council* [2006] EWCA Civ 718, [2006] 4 All ER 917, [2006] 1 WLR 2808 (distinguishing *R (on the application of G) v Barnet London Borough Council* [2003] UKHL 57, [2004] 2 AC 208, [2004] 1 All ER 97).

21 *Roberts v Hopwood* [1925] AC 578, HL; *Prescott v Birmingham Corpn* [1955] Ch 210, [1954] 3 All ER 698, CA; *Taylor v Munrow* [1960] 1 All ER 455, [1960] 1 WLR 151, DC; *Luby v Newcastle-under-Lyme Corpn* [1964] 2 QB 64, [1964] 1 All ER 84 (on appeal [1965] 1 QB 214, [1964] 3 All ER 169, CA); *R v Merseyside County Council, ex p Great Universal Stores Ltd* (1982) 80 LGR 639; *Bromley London Borough Council v GLC* [1983] 1 AC 768, [1982] 1 All ER 129, HL; *Pickwell v Camden London Borough Council* [1983] QB 962 at 987, [1983] 1 All ER 602 at 618, DC, per Forbes J; *R v London Transport Executive, ex p GLC* [1983] QB 484, [1983] 2 All ER 262, DC; *R v Greenwich London Borough Council, ex p Cedar Transport Group Ltd* [1983] RA 173, DC; *Smith v Skinner* [1986] RVR 45 at 75, DC, per Glidewell LJ and at 86 per Russell J; affd without reference to this point sub nom *Lloyd v McMahon* [1987] AC 625, [1987] 1 All ER 1118, CA and HL; *R v Secretary of State for the Environment, ex p Manchester City Council* (1986) 53 P & CR 369 (no breach of the fiduciary duty where local authority compelled to take action by central government); affd without reference to this point sub nom *Manchester City Council v Secretary of State for the Environment* (1987) 54 P & CR 212, CA. As to local authorities generally see LOCAL GOVERNMENT vol 69 (2009) PARA 22 et seq. Cf *R v Manchester City Council, ex p King* [1991] COD 422, 89 LGR 696, DC (unlawful to base fees on market rate not administrative costs); *R v Camden London Borough Council, ex p Cran* (1995) 94 LGR 8, sub nom *Cran v Camden London Borough Council* [1995] RTR 346 (surplus funds generated by parking scheme irrelevant consideration).

22 See *Laker Airways Ltd v Department of Trade* [1977] QB 643 at 707, [1977] 2 All ER 182 at 194, CA, per Lord Denning MR (in a minority judgment); *New Forest District Council v Secretary of State for the Environment and Clarke* [1984] JPL 178; *Tameside Metropolitan District Council v Secretary of State for the Environment* [1984] JPL 180; *Ynys Mon Isle of Anglesey Borough Council v Secretary of State for Wales and Parry Bros (Builders) Co Ltd* [1984] JPL 646; *Westminster City Council v Great Portland Estates plc* [1985] AC 661 at 670, sub nom *Great Portland Estates plc v Westminster City Council* [1984] 3 All ER 744 at 750, HL, per Lord Scarman; *Nash v Secretary of State for the Environment* (1985) 52 P & CR 261, [1986] JPL 128, CA; *R v Port Talbot Borough Council, ex p Jones* [1988] 2 All ER 207 at 214 per Nolan J; *Essex County Council v Secretary of State* [1989] JPL 187; *Vasiliou v Secretary of State for Transport* [1991] 2 All ER 77, [1991] JPL 858, CA; *R v Lincolnshire County Council and Wealden District Council, ex p Atkinson* [1995] EGCS 145, 8 Admin LR 529. See also PARAS 648, 649, 636.

23 See *Rother Valley Rly Co Ltd v Minister of Transport* [1971] Ch 515, [1970] 3 All ER 805, CA; *Stringer v Minister of Housing and Local Government* [1971] 1 All ER 65 at 72, [1970] 1 WLR 1281 at 1289 per Cooke J; *Bradford City Metropolitan Council v Secretary of State for the Environment* (1986) 53 P & CR 55, CA; *R v Monopolies and Mergers Commission, ex p Elders IXL Ltd* [1987] 1 All ER 451, [1987] 1 WLR 1221; *R v DPP, ex p Duckenfield* [1999] 2 All ER 873, 11 Admin LR 611, DC.

The Secretary of State may have regard to considerations of a public nature when taking decisions about the tariff of prisoners subject to life sentences: see *R v Secretary of State for the Home Department, ex p Doody* [1994] 1 AC 531 at 559, sub nom *Doody v Secretary of State for the Home Department* [1993] 3 All ER 92 at 105, HL, per Lord Mustill. He may not, however, have regard to 'public clamour' about an individual prisoner: *R v Secretary of State for the Home Department, ex p Venables* [1998] AC 407, [1997] 3 All ER 97, HL; *R v Secretary of State for the Home Department, ex p Pierson* [1998] AC 539, [1997] 3 All ER 577, HL; *R v Secretary of State for the Home Department, ex p Stafford* [1999] 2 AC 38, [1998] 4 All ER 7, HL.

For the relevance of moral or ethical considerations to decisions by local authorities see *R v Somerset County Council, ex p Fewings* [1995] 3 All ER 20, [1995] 1 WLR 1037, CA (moral objections to deer hunting); *R v Newcastle-upon-Tyne City Council, ex p Christian Institute* [2001] LGR 165, [2000] All ER (D) 1188 (view that sex shops should not be allowed to exist irrelevant to licensing decision).

24 See *R v Secretary of State for the Environment, ex p Ostler* [1977] QB 122 at 135, [1976] 3 All ER 90 at 95, CA, obiter per Lord Denning MR (in making a judicial decision a tribunal considers the rights of the parties without regard to the public interest, but in an administrative

decision the public interest plays an important part); and see *Bushell v Secretary of State for the Environment* [1981] AC 75 at 102, [1980] 2 All ER 608 at 617–618, HL, per Lord Diplock; and the cases cited in note 23.

25 In some statutory contexts there is an express requirement that regard should be had to particular guidelines: see eg the Town and Country Planning Act 1990 s 70 (development plan) (see TOWN AND COUNTRY PLANNING vol 46(1) (Reissue) PARAS 484, 486) (considered in *Tesco Stores Ltd v Secretary of State for the Environment* [1995] 2 All ER 636, [1995] 1 WLR 759, HL). See also *R (on the application of Khatun) v Newham London Borough Council* [2004] EWCA Civ 55, [2005] QB 37; *Prospect v Ministry of Defence* [2008] EWHC 2056 (Admin), [2008] All ER (D) 139 (Aug). Statutory guidance should be given great weight: *R (on the application of Munjaz) v Mersey Care NHS Trust* [2005] UKHL 58, [2006] 2 AC 148, [2006] 4 All ER 736.

Where there is no such express provision regard should still be had to relevant policy guidelines in exercising a statutory discretion: *Bristol District Council v Clark* [1975] 3 All ER 976 at 982, [1975] 1 WLR 1443 at 1451, CA, per Scarman LJ; *JA Pye (Oxford) Estates Ltd v West Oxfordshire District Council* (1982) 47 P & CR 125 (but a draft circular setting out guidelines will not be a relevant consideration; see also *Westminster City Council v Secretary of State for the Environment and City Commercial Real Estates Investments Ltd* [1984] JPL 27); *R v Secretary of State for the Home Department, ex p Khan* [1985] 1 All ER 40 at 52, [1984] 1 WLR 1337 at 1352, CA, per Dunn LJ (guidance letter indicated the relevant considerations); *Gransden & Co Ltd v Secretary of State for the Environment* (1985) 54 P & CR 86 (affd (1986) 54 P & CR 361, CA); *Newham London Borough v Secretary of State for the Environment* (1986) 53 P & CR 98; and see *Surrey Heath Borough Council v Secretary of State for the Environment* (1986) 53 P & CR 428 (misinterpretation of central government circular); *R v Secretary of State for the Home Department, ex p Lancashire Police Authority* [1992] COD 161, (1991) Times, 19 November (circulars issued by Police Negotiating Board); *R v Plymouth City Council, ex p Plymouth and South Devon Co-operative Society Ltd* [1993] 2 EGLR 206, 67 P & CR 78, CA; *Iye v Secretary of State for the Home Department* [1994] Imm AR 63; *R v Wandsworth London Borough Council, ex p Hawthorne* [1995] 2 All ER 331, [1994] 1 WLR 1442; *R v Southwark London Borough Council, ex p Cordwell* (1994) 27 HLR 594, CA; *R (on the application of Coghlan) v Chief Constable of Greater Manchester Police* [2004] EWHC 2801 (Admin), [2005] 2 All ER 890.

The policy guidelines must be construed properly by the decision-maker, otherwise he will be held not to have had regard to them: *Gransden & Co Ltd v Secretary of State for the Environment* at 94 per Woolf J (affd (1986) 54 P & CR 361, CA); *Wycombe District Council v Secretary of State for the Environment* (1987) 57 P & CR 177; *Fitchett (Contractors) Ltd v Secretary of State for the Environment* (1988) 56 P & CR 380; *Cranford Hall Parking Ltd v Secretary of State for the Environment* [1991] 1 EGLR 283, [1989] JPL 169; cf *Waverley Borough Council v Secretary of State for the Environment* (1986) 55 P & CR 111 (Secretary of State construed policy correctly); *G v Legal Services Commission* [2004] EWHC 276 (Admin), [2004] All ER (D) 182 (Feb); *R (on the application of the Heath and Hampstead Society) v Vlachos* [2008] EWCA Civ 193, [2008] 3 All ER 80; *R (on the application of Shashwar) v Secretary of State for the Home Department* [2008] EWHC 2069 (Admin), [2008] All ER (D) 11 (Oct). See also *Niarchos (London) Ltd v Secretary of State for the Environment* (1977) 76 LGR 480 at 485 per Sir Douglas Franks QC; *Manchester City Council v Secretary of State for the Environment* [1988] JPL 774.

However, if the policy or guidelines seek to promote a purpose outside the statute or call attention to factors which are not relevant, a decision-maker will err in having regard to them: *R v Birmingham Licensing Planning Committee, ex p Kennedy* [1972] 2 QB 140, sub nom *Kennedy v Birmingham Licensing Planning Committee* [1972] 2 All ER 305, CA; *A-G (ex rel Tilley) v Wandsworth London Borough Council* [1981] 1 All ER 1162, [1981] 1 WLR 854, CA; *Gransden & Co Ltd v Secretary of State for the Environment* (a policy statement cannot transform a relevant consideration into an irrelevant consideration; see also *R v Westminster City Council, ex p James Monaham* [1989] 2 All ER 74, [1988] JPL 557); *R v Cumbria Family Practitioner Committee, ex p Boots the Chemists Ltd* (1988) Times, 25 November, DC. It is also improper for a body to have regard to guidelines which are not addressed to it: *Westminster Renslade Ltd v Secretary of State for the Environment* (1983) 48 P & CR 255.

26 *Rayner (JH) (Mincing Lane) Ltd v Department of Trade and Industry* [1990] 2 AC 418, sub nom *Maclaine Watson & Co Ltd v Department of Trade and Industry* [1989] 3 All ER 523, HL; *Pan-American World Airways Inc v Department of Trade* [1976] 1 Lloyd's Rep 257, CA; *R v Chief Immigration Officer, Heathrow Airport, ex p Salamat Bibi* [1976] 3 All ER 843, [1976] 1 WLR 979, CA (doubting observations to the contrary in *R v Secretary of State for the Home Department, ex p Bhajan Singh* [1976] QB 198, [1975] 2 All ER 1081, CA); *R v Secretary of*

State for the Home Department, ex p Kirkwood [1984] 2 All ER 390, [1984] 1 WLR 913; *R v Immigration Appeal Tribunal, ex p Alsawaf* (1987) Times, 29 August, DC; and see *Bugdaycay v Secretary of State for the Home Department* [1987] AC 514 at 524–525, [1987] 1 All ER 940 at 947, HL, per Lord Bridge of Harwich; *R v Secretary of State for the Home Department, ex p Brind* [1991] 1 AC 696, sub nom *Brind v Secretary of State for the Home Department* [1991] 1 All ER 720, HL. Note, however, that the Convention for the Protection of Human Rights and Fundamental Freedoms (1950) has now been incorporated into domestic law by the Human Rights Act 1998: see note 19. Where a decision-maker says that he took into account international law, the decision will be flawed if he misdirected himself in respect of it: *R v Secretary of State for the Home Department, ex p Launder* [1997] 3 All ER 961, [1997] 1 WLR 839, HL; *R (on the application of Corner House Research) v Director of the Serious Fraud Office* [2008] UKHL 60, [2009] 1 AC 756, [2008] 4 All ER 927.

27 There are many statements to this effect: see *Tesco Stores Ltd v Secretary of State for the Environment* [1995] 2 All ER 636 at 657, [1995] 1 WLR 759 at 780, HL, per Lord Hoffmann; *Brookdene Investments Ltd v Minister of Housing and Local Government* (1970) 21 P & CR 545 at 550 per Fisher J; *Elliott v Southwark London Borough Council* [1976] 2 All ER 781 at 788, [1976] 1 WLR 499 at 507, CA, per James LJ; *Seddon Properties Ltd and James Crosbie & Sons Ltd v Secretary of State for the Environment and Macclesfield Borough Council* (1978) 42 P & CR 26n at 28 per Forbes J; *Pickwell v Camden London Borough Council* [1983] QB 962 at 990, [1983] 1 All ER 602 at 621, DC, per Forbes J; *R v Devon and Cornwall Police Authority, ex p Willis* (1984) 82 LGR 369 at 373 per Taylor J; *Ynys Mon Isle of Anglesey Borough Council v Secretary of State for Wales* [1984] JPL 646 per Woolf J; *R v Lancashire County Council, ex p Huddleston* [1986] 2 All ER 941 at 946, CA, per Parker LJ; *ELS Wholesale (Wolverhampton) Ltd v Secretary of State for the Environment* (1987) 56 P & CR 69 at 81, DC, per May LJ (weight to be given to evidence a matter for the tribunal); *Wycombe District Council v Secretary of State for the Environment* (1987) 57 P & CR 177 at 180 per Graham Eyre QC (assessment of the relevance and weight to be accorded to a policy statement is a matter for the deciding authority alone); *R v Secretary of State for Education and Science, ex p Avon County Council (No 2)* [1990] COD 349, 88 LGR 737n, CA; *London Residuary Body v Lambeth London Borough Council* [1990] 2 All ER 309, [1990] 1 WLR 744, HL; *R v Somerset County Council, ex p Fewings* [1995] 3 All ER 20, [1995] 1 WLR 1037, CA; *R v Secretary of State for Foreign Affairs, ex p World Development Movement Ltd* [1995] 1 All ER 611, [1995] 1 WLR 386, DC; *R v Southwark London Borough Council, ex p Cordwell* [1993] COD 479 at 481, 26 HLR 107 at 124 per Auld J; *R v Mid-Hertfordshire Justices, ex p Cox* (1995) 8 Admin LR 409, (1995) 160 JP 507; *Tsao v Secretary of State for the Environment* (1995) 28 HLR 259, [1995] EGCS 123; *R v Gloucestershire County Council, ex p Barry* [1997] AC 584, [1997] 2 All ER 1, HL (weight to be given to cost of providing services to be assessed by actual resources available); *R v DPP, ex p Duckenfield* [1999] 2 All ER 873, 11 Admin LR 611, DC; *R v Video Appeals Committee of the British Board of Film Classification, ex p British Board of Film Classification* [2000] EMLR 850, (2000) Times, 7 June; *R (on the application of Bulger) v Secretary of State for the Home Department* [2001] EWHC 119, [2001] 3 All ER 449; *R (on the application of Manchester City Council) v Secretary of State for the Environment, Food and Rural Affairs* [2007] EWHC 3167 (Admin), [2007] All ER (D) 236 (Dec); *R (on the application of Staff Side of the Police Negotiating Board) v Secretary of State for the Home Department* [2008] EWHC 1173 (Admin), [2008] All ER (D) 101 (Jun). See also PARA 613.

It is not necessarily irrational for a relevant consideration to be considered but given no weight: *Swords v Secretary of State for Communities and Local Government* [2007] EWCA Civ 795, [2007] LGR 757. However, a court is not precluded from finding a decision to be void for unreasonableness simply because there are factors on both sides; if the factors in favour of a particular decision are overwhelming, then a decision the other way may be quashed: *West Glamorgan County Council v Rafferty* [1987] 1 All ER 1005, [1987] 1 WLR 457, CA.

The court may intervene more readily where it considers that a decision-maker has accorded the wrong weight to a relevant consideration in cases where the decision interferes with fundamental human rights: see *R (on the application of Samaroo) v Secretary of State for the Home Department* [2001] EWCA Civ 1139, [2001] 34 LS Gaz R 40; and PARA 651.

28 This will occur where the decision-maker has misdirected himself in law as to the onus of proof in a matter before him (see PARA 613; and *Steinberg v Secretary of State for the Environment* (1988) 58 P & CR 453); or where in a certain context particular weight is required to be attached to one factor: see *Sagnata Investments Ltd v Norwich Corpn* [1971] 2 QB 614, [1971] 2 All ER 1441, CA; *Secretary of State for Education and Science v Tameside Metropolitan Borough Council* [1977] AC 1014 at 1048, [1976] 3 All ER 665 at 682–683, HL, per Lord Wilberforce; *Lothbury Investment Corpn Ltd v IRC* [1981] Ch 47, [1979] 3 All ER 860; *South Oxfordshire District Council v Secretary of State for the Environment* [1981] 1 All ER

954, [1981] 1 WLR 1092 (probable misdirection as to the relevant question led to excessive weight being given to one factor (see also note 29)); *R v Manchester City Council, ex p Fulford* (1982) 81 LGR 292, DC; *R v Brent London Borough Council, ex p Gunning* (1985) 84 LGR 168 (inadequate consideration of cost of closure of school, a matter fundamental to the decision taken); *R v Hertfordshire County Council, ex p Cheung* (1986) Times, 4 April, CA, per Sir John Donaldson MR (a cardinal principle of good public administration that persons in a similar position should be treated similarly); *West Glamorgan County Council v Rafferty* [1987] 1 All ER 1005, [1988] JPL 169, CA (breach of duty by the decision-maker an important factor); *R v Secretary of State for the Home Department, ex p Benson* [1989] COD 329, (1988) Times, 21 November, DC, per Lloyd LJ (if a relevant matter was so minor that it should have been disregarded, the court will quash a decision which took it into account); *R v Immigration Appeal Tribunal, ex p Shameen Wali* [1989] Imm AR 86 (excessive weight given to one factor because of misdirection as to relevant question (see also note 29)); *R v Inner London Crown Court, ex p Barnes* [1996] COD 17, (1995) Times, 7 August, DC (weight to be given to interests of young person); *R v Secretary of State for the Home Department, ex p Zulfikar* [1996] COD 256, (1995) Times, 26 July; *R v City of Westminster Housing Benefit Review Board, ex p Mehanne* [2001] UKHL 11, [2001] 2 All ER 690, [2001] 1 WLR 539; *R (on the application of Manchester City Council) v Secretary of State for the Environment, Food and Rural Affairs* [2007] EWHC 3167 (Admin), [2007] All ER (D) 236 (Dec). As to the wider powers of the Court of Appeal to overturn on appeal an exercise of discretion by a judge at first instance if excessive or insufficient weight is given to particular matters see *G v G (Minors: Custody Appeal)* [1985] 2 All ER 225, [1985] 1 WLR 647, HL.

29 See eg *Harwich Harbour Conservancy Board v Secretary of State for the Environment* [1975] 1 Lloyd's Rep 334, CA; *North Surrey Water Co v Secretary of State for the Environment* (1976) 34 P & CR 140; *Niarchos (London) Ltd v Secretary of State for the Environment* (1977) 76 LGR 480; *Secretary of State for Education and Science v Tameside Metropolitan Borough Council* [1977] AC 1014 at 1052, [1976] 3 All ER 665 at 685–686, HL, per Lord Wilberforce, at 1065 and 695–696 per Lord Diplock, and at 1072 and 701 per Lord Salmon; *R v Chief Immigration Officer, Gatwick Airport, ex p Kharrazi* [1980] 3 All ER 373, [1980] 1 WLR 1396, CA; *Federated Estates v Secretary of State for the Environment* [1983] JPL 812 (misconstruction of structure plan); *R v IRC, ex p Harrow London Borough Council* [1983] STC 246; *Re West Anstey Common, North Devon* [1985] Ch 329, [1985] 1 All ER 618, CA; *Newham London Borough v Secretary of State for the Environment* (1986) 53 P & CR 98; *Surrey Heath Borough Council v Secretary of State for the Environment* (1986) 53 P & CR 428; *R v South East Hampshire Family Proceedings Court, ex p D* [1994] 2 All ER 445, [1994] 1 WLR 611.

30 See *R v Secretary of State for Transport, ex p GLC* [1986] QB 556, [1985] 3 All ER 300; *R v Secretary of State for the Environment, ex p Fielder Estates (Canvey) Ltd* (1988) 57 P & CR 424, [1989] JPL 39; *Geha v Secretary of State for the Environment* [1994] COD 359, (1993) 68 P & CR 139, CA. A failure to comply with the rules of natural justice will usually of itself render a decision invalid: see PARA 629 et seq.

31 *Secretary of State for Education and Science v Tameside Metropolitan Borough Council* [1977] AC 1014 at 1065, [1976] 3 All ER 665 at 696, HL, per Lord Diplock; *Prest v Secretary of State for Wales* (1982) 81 LGR 193, CA; *R v Barnes Borough Council, ex p Conlan* [1938] 3 All ER 226, DC (councillor's duty to keep himself reasonably informed; approved in *Birmingham City District Council v O* [1983] 1 AC 578 at 593, [1983] 1 All ER 497 at 504–505, HL, per Lord Brightman; and see *R v Hackney London Borough Council, ex p Gamper* [1985] 3 All ER 275, [1985] 1 WLR 1229; *R v Sheffield City Council, ex p Chadwick* (1985) 84 LGR 563; *R v Eden District Council, ex p Moffat* (1988) Times, 24 November, CA (see also PARA 627)); *Associated Provincial Picture Houses Ltd v Wednesbury Corpn* [1948] 1 KB 223 at 229, [1947] 2 All ER 680 at 682–683, CA, per Lord Greene MR; *Van Boeckel v Customs and Excise Comrs* [1981] 2 All ER 505 at 511 per Woolf J (it is desirable as a matter of good administrative practice that reasonable investigations should be carried out); *Edwin H Bradley & Sons Ltd v Secretary of State for the Environment* (1982) 47 P & CR 374 at 391–392 obiter per Glidewell J (a policy in a structure plan could be quashed if there was some clearly material factor on which the Secretary of State had no information); *R v Birmingham Juvenile Court, ex p G (Minors)* [1990] 2 QB 573, [1989] 3 All ER 336, CA; *R v Secretary of State for the Environment, ex p Fielder Estates (Canvey) Ltd* (1988) 57 P & CR 424, [1989] JPL 39; *R v Secretary of State for the Home Department, ex p Gaima* (1988) Independent, 7 December, CA; *R v Secretary of State for the Home Department, ex p Yemoh* [1988] Imm AR 595 (Secretary of State failed to make adequate investigation into medical condition of immigrant who claimed he had been tortured); and see *R v Panel on Take-overs and Mergers, ex p Guinness plc* [1990] 1 QB 146, [1989] 1 All ER 509, CA (reasonable for Take-over Panel to refuse adjournment to obtain

further evidence); *R v Camden London Borough Council, ex p Adair* (1996) 29 HLR 236, (1996) Times, 30 April; *R v Wolverhampton Metropolitan Borough Council, ex p Dunne* (1996) 29 HLR 745, (1997) Times, 2 January, DC (duty to investigate humanitarian issues before requiring travellers to leave land; in this context see also *Buckley v United Kingdom* (1996) 23 EHRR 101, ECtHR; and *Shropshire County Council v Wynne* (1997) 96 LGR 689, (1997) Times, 22 July, DC); *R v Barnet London Borough Council, ex p Babalola* (1995) 28 HLR 196; *R v Brent London Borough Council, ex p Baruwa* (1995) 28 HLR 361; *R v Camden London Borough Council, ex p H* [1996] ELR 360, (1996) Times, 15 August, CA; *R v Lincolnshire County Council and Wealden District Council, ex p Atkinson* (1995) 8 Admin LR 529, [1995] EGCS 145; *R v Criminal Injuries Compensation Board, ex p Milton* [1996] COD 264, [1997] PIQR P74 (Board under no duty to make inquiries or seek evidence of its own initiative); *R v Secretary of State for Education, ex p London Borough of Southwark* [1995] ELR 308 at 323, [1994] COD 298 at 299 per Laws J; *R v HM Coroner for Coventry, ex p O'Reilly* [1996] COD 268, 35 BMLR 48, DC; *R v Secretary of State for the Home Department, ex p Venables* [1998] AC 407, [1997] 3 All ER 97, HL (duty of Secretary of State to obtain information relevant to setting tariff of prisoners); *R v Advertising Standards Authority Ltd, ex p Mathias Rath BV* (2001) Times, 10 January) (duty to consider new evidence). See also *R v Secretary of State for Transport, ex p Philippine Airways Ltd* (1984) Times, 17 October, CA, per Lawton LJ (the Secretary of State should not have relied on clearly incomplete figures); *R v Hertfordshire County Council, ex p B* (1986) Times, 19 August (reliance on unsubstantiated allegations without testing them by putting them to the person affected was in breach of natural justice); see further PARA 629 et seq. Under some statutes there may be an express duty of inquiry imposed (see eg *Palmer v Peabody Trust* [1975] QB 604, [1974] 3 All ER 355, DC; *Re West Anstey Common, North Devon* [1985] Ch 329, [1985] 1 All ER 618, CA), or a body may be expressly relieved of any duty of inquiry (*R v Immigration Appeal Tribunal, ex p Hassanin* [1987] 1 All ER 74 at 77, [1986] 1 WLR 1448 at 1453, CA, per Dillon LJ); *R (on the application of National Association of Health Stores) v Secretary of State for Health* [2005] EWCA Civ 154, (2005) Times, 9 March, [2005] All ER (D) 324 (Feb) (minister was not required to know the qualifications of the Medicines Commission's representative, who had given a view which the minister had ignored).

A statute may provide machinery for investigations into relevant matters to be carried out, such as by an inquiry. As to the purpose of an inquiry see *Bushell v Secretary of State for the Environment* [1981] AC 75 at 94, [1980] 2 All ER 608 at 612, HL, per Lord Diplock, and at 1071 and 621 per Viscount Dilhorne; *Prest v Secretary of State for Wales* at 212–213 per Fox LJ; *R v Secretary of State for Transport, ex p Gwent County Council* [1988] QB 429, [1987] 1 All ER 161, CA. Where such machinery is provided by the statute, the decision-making body may only decide not to make use of it where it is satisfied on reasonable grounds that it can properly and fairly weigh the views of objectors to a scheme without giving them an opportunity of putting those views forward at an inquiry: *Binney and Anscomb v Secretary of State for the Environment* [1984] JPL 871 (where there are many objectors, an inquiry will be necessary); see also PARA 629 et seq; cf *Shorman v Secretary of State for the Environment* [1977] JPL 98 (reasonable not to hold inquiry where few objectors); *Bushell v Secretary of State for the Environment* at 103 and 618 per Lord Diplock, at 110 and 623–624 per Viscount Dilhorne, and at 123–124 and 633 per Lord Lane; *R v Secretary of State for Transport, ex p GLC* (1985) Times, 31 October, CA; *R v Secretary of State for the Environment, ex p GLC* [1986] JPL 32.

However, a decision-maker will only be required to make such inquiries as are reasonable in the circumstances; thus there is no obligation to inquire into matters which do not fairly and reasonably relate to the relevant discretion: *Lovelock v Minister of Transport* (1980) 78 LGR 576, CA. An inspector or the minister is not under a duty to inquire into matters which are not put to him at an inquiry: *Rhodes v Minister of Housing and Local Government* [1963] 1 All ER 300, [1963] 1 WLR 208; *Chris Fashionware (West End) Ltd v Secretary of State for the Environment* [1980] JPL 678; *Glover v Secretary of State for the Environment* [1981] JPL 110; *Ynystawe, Ynyforgan and Glais Gypsy Site Action Group v Secretary of State for Wales and West Glamorgan County Council* [1981] JPL 874 (Secretary of State not bound to seek alternative sites, but if evidence as to alternative sites is given he is bound to consider and evaluate that); *Finlay v Secretary of State for the Environment and Islington London Borough of Council* [1983] JPL 802 at 813 per Forbes J; *Hewlett v Secretary of State and Brentwood District Council* [1983] JPL 105; *Federated Estates Ltd v Secretary of State for the Environment* [1983] JPL 812; *Mason v Secretary of State for the Environment* [1984] JPL 332 at 334 per David Widdicombe QC; *R v Secretary of State for the Environment, ex p Melton Borough Council* (1985) 52 P & CR 318; *Fuller v Secretary of State for the Environment* (1987) 56 P & CR 84; *Ricketts and Fletcher v Secretary of State for the Environment* [1988] JPL 768 at

773 per Graham Eyre QC; *Garbutt & Sons Ltd v Secretary of State for the Environment* (1988) 57 P & CR 284 (planning authority's duty to consider only the application for planning permission which is made); and see TOWN AND COUNTRY PLANNING vol 46(2) (Reissue) PARA 651 et seq. See also *Van Boeckel v Customs and Excise Comrs* [1981] 2 All ER 505 (commissioners to assess tax due to the best of their judgment; required to consider fairly all matters put before them by the taxpayer, but not required to make further investigations so long as they had some material on which they could reasonably base their assessment); *Hotter v Spackman* (1984) 54 TC 774, CA (general commissioners did not err in law by failing to take account of matters not before them); *Tandridge District Council v Secretary of State for the Environment and Nutley Print (Reigate) Ltd* [1983] JPL 667 (it is for the Secretary of State to decide if there is sufficient information before him to determine a matter, subject to review on the principles in *Associated Provincial Picture Houses Ltd v Wednesbury Corpn*); *Green v Secretaries of State for the Environment and for Transport* [1985] JPL 119 (no requirement to seek further evidence on a matter which was not relevant or determining); *R v Vincent and the Department of Transport, ex p Turner* [1987] JPL 511 (whether further inquiries necessary is a matter for the discretion of the decision-maker, and he may take account of the relevancy of the matters to be inquired into and the likely cost and delay in exercising that discretion); *R v Immigration Appeal Tribunal, ex p Martinez-Tobon* [1987] Imm AR 536 (no duty to inquire into veracity of a hearsay statement which was not challenged in the proceedings and was not taken into account in reaching the decision); *R v Westminster City Council, ex p James Monahan* [1988] JPL 557 at 561 per Webster J (doubting whether planning committee bound to make inquiries into alternative proposals in granting planning permission) (affd [1990] 1 QB 87, [1989] COD 241, CA); *R v Secretary of State for the Environment, ex p Kent* (1988) 57 P & CR 431, [1988] JPL 706 (no general duty on Secretary of State to seek out objectors); *R v Secretary of State for the Home Department, ex p Gaima* (1988) Independent, 7 December, CA; *Duggan v Chief Adjudication Officer* (1988) Times, 19 December, CA; *R v Nottinghamshire County Council, ex p Costello* (1989) Times, 14 February (in considering whether to quash a decision for inadequacy of inquiries the court had to establish what material was before the court; the decision could only then be quashed if no reasonable council, possessed of that material, could suppose that the inquiries made were sufficient); *R v Sedgemoor District Council ex p McCarthy* (1996) 28 HLR 607.

A decision to reopen an inquiry where such further inquiry would serve no useful purpose may itself be quashed: *R v Secretary of State for the Environment, ex p Fielder Estates (Canvey) Ltd* (1988) 57 P & CR 424, [1989] JPL 39.

32 *Secretary of State for Education and Science v Tameside Metropolitan Borough Council* [1977] AC 1014, [1976] 3 All ER 665, HL; *Hollis v Secretary of State for the Environment* (1982) 47 P & CR 351; and see *R v Bristol City Council, ex p Pearce* (1984) 83 LGR 711 at 719 per Glidewell J (there is a presumption that documents put before council members have been taken into account by them); *R v Basildon District Council, ex p Martin Grant Homes Ltd* (1986) 53 P & CR 397 (all knowledge available to council to be imputed to its planning committee; sed quaere). A licensing authority may have regard to information provided to it in confidence by third parties in carrying out its statutory duties: *Re Smith Kline & French Laboratories Ltd* [1990] 1 AC 64, sub nom *Smith Kline & French Laboratories Ltd v Licensing Authority* [1989] 1 All ER 578, HL.

33 This is so where the appeal is a decision de novo, as in *Stringer v Minister of Housing and Local Government* [1971] 1 All ER 65, [1970] 1 WLR 1281; see also *Calvin v Carr* [1980] AC 574, [1979] 2 All ER 440, PC (deficiency of natural justice cured on appeal); and PARA 629 et seq. In such cases, the appellate decision-maker must have regard to all relevant considerations which have come to his attention up to the date of his decision: *Price Bros (Rode Heath) Ltd v Department of the Environment* (1978) 38 P & CR 579; *Bradwell Industrial Aggregates v Secretary of State for the Environment* [1981] JPL 276; *JA Pye (Oxford) Estates Ltd v West Oxfordshire District Council* (1982) 47 P & CR 125; *Prest v Secretary of State for Wales* (1982) 81 LGR 193, CA; cf *R v Immigration Appeal Tribunal, ex p Hassanin* [1987] 1 All ER 74, [1986] 1 WLR 1448, CA.

34 *Hanks v Minister of Housing and Local Government* [1963] 1 QB 999, [1963] 1 All ER 47; *Chichester District Council v Secretary of State for the Environment and Hall Aggregates (South Coast) Ltd* [1981] JPL 591; *R v Hammersmith and Fulham London Borough Council, ex p People Before Profit Ltd* (1981) 45 P & CR 364; *Meadows v Secretary of State for the Environment and Gloucester City Council* [1983] JPL 538; *R v Chief Registrar of Friendly Societies, ex p New Cross Building Society* [1984] QB 227 at 273, [1984] 2 All ER 27 at 51, CA, per Slade LJ; *R v Broadcasting Complaints Commission, ex p Owen* [1985] QB 1153, [1985] 2 All ER 522, DC; *Gransden & Co Ltd v Secretary of State for the Environment* (1985) 54 P & CR 86 at 94 per Woolf J (affd (1986) 54 P & CR 361, CA); *Dudley Bowers*

Amusements Enterprises Ltd v Secretary of State for the Environment (1986) 52 P & CR 365; *R v Secretary of State for Social Services, ex p Wellcome Foundation Ltd* [1987] 2 All ER 1025, [1987] 1 WLR 1166, CA (affd on other grounds sub nom *Wellcome Foundation Ltd v Secretary of State for Social Services* [1988] 2 All ER 684, [1988] 1 WLR 635, HL); *Simplex GE (Holdings) Ltd v Secretary of State for the Environment* (1988) 57 P & CR 306, CA; *R v Wolverhampton Coroner, ex p McCurbin* [1990] 2 All ER 759, [1990] 1 WLR 719, CA; *Bolton Metropolitan Borough Council v Secretary of State for the Environment* [1991] JPL 241, (1990) 61 P & CR 343; *R v Thurrock Borough Council, ex p Tesco Stores Ltd* [1993] 3 PLR 114, [1994] JPL 328; *Kwaku Boateng Kwapong v Secretary of State for the Home Department* [1994] Imm AR 207, CA; *R v Crown Court at Teeside, ex p Amanda Bullock* [1996] COD 6, DC; *R v Wandsworth London Borough Council, ex p Onwudiwe* [1994] COD 229; *R v Swansea City Council, ex p Elitestone Ltd* [1993] 2 PLR 65, 66 P & CR 422, CA; *Crédit Suisse v Allerdale Borough Council* [1995] 1 Lloyd's Rep 315, (1994) 159 LG Rev 549; *R v Secretary of State for the Home Department, ex p Yiadom* [1998] COD 298, (1998) Times, 1 May, CA; *Ali v Kirklees Metropolitan Council* [2001] EWCA Civ 582, [2001] LGR 448; *R (on the application of Mount Cook Land Ltd) v Westminster City Council* [2003] EWCA Civ 1346, [2004] 2 P & CR 405; *R (on the application of Hampson) v Wigan Metropolitan Borough Council* [2005] EWHC 1656 (Admin), [2005] All ER (D) 383 (Jul); *R (on the application of Assura Pharmacy Ltd) v National Health Service Litigation Authority (Family Health Services Appeal Unit)* [2008] EWHC 289 (Admin), [2008] All ER (D) 304 (Feb). For a wider doctrine of doubtful validity see PARA 622.

(v) Material Error of Fact

624. Errors of fact. In exercising their functions, public bodies[1] evaluate evidence and reach conclusions of fact. The court will not ordinarily interfere with the evaluation of evidence[2] or conclusions of fact reached by a public body properly directing itself in law[3]. The exercise of statutory powers on the basis of a mistaken view of the relevant facts will, however, be quashed where there was no evidence, or no sufficient evidence, available to the decision-maker on which, properly directing himself as to the law, he could reasonably have formed that view[4]. The court may also intervene where a body has reached a decision which is based on a material mistake as to an established fact[5]. Although the general rule is that a judicial review is determined on the basis of the material that was before the decision-maker[6], where it is alleged that there has been a mistake of fact fresh evidence may be admitted[7].

The court adopts a different approach where the existence of a state of affairs is a statutory precondition to the jurisdiction[8] of a public body. Where the existence of such a state of affairs is put in issue, the decision-maker must determine that issue[9], but his determination is subject to review by the court. In each case, the extent to which the court will intervene depends on the proper construction of the governing statutory provision[10]. In some cases the jurisdiction of the decision-maker has been held to depend on the existence, objectively determined, of a particular fact or facts[11]. Such facts may be described as jurisdictional or precedent facts[12]. The court will itself determine whether a jurisdictional fact exists and intervene if its conclusion differs from that of the decision-maker[13]. In doing so, the court may admit evidence on the issue[14]. In other cases the statute will provide that a body is to have power or jurisdiction where it 'is satisfied' of certain matters, or where certain facts 'appear' to that body. In that case the court will generally only intervene if the body's finding that the necessary facts existed was not one which a reasonable person, properly directed as to the question to be determined, could have come to[15], or if the body is not in fact satisfied as to the relevant matters[16]. Where the determination of the jurisdictional fact is not in terms expressed to be a question for the subjective consideration of the relevant body, the courts may still construe the statutory provision as requiring only that the body should be subjectively satisfied as to the existence of any jurisdictional fact[17].

1   As to the bodies who are amenable to judicial review see PARAS 604–606.

2   See e g *Adan v Newham London Borough Council* [2001] EWCA Civ 1916 at [35]–[36] and [41], [2002] 1 All ER 931 at [35]–[36] and [41], [2002] 1 WLR 2120 at [35]–[36] and [41] per Brooke LJ (court of supervisory jurisdiction does not, without more, have the power to substitute its own view of the primary facts for the view reasonably adopted by the body to whom the fact-finding power has been entrusted); *R v Criminal Injuries Compensation Board, ex p A* [1999] 2 AC 330 at 343, [1992] 2 WLR 974 at 980, HL, per Lord Slynn of Hadley (board entitled to evaluate evidence and accept one side rather than another; application for judicial review is not an appeal on fact); *R (on the application of Malik) v Manchester Crown Court* [2008] EWHC 1362 (Admin) at [31], [2008] 4 All ER 403 at [31] per Dyson LJ, giving the judgment of the court (judicial review is not an appeal); *Puhlhofer v Hillingdon London Borough Council* [1986] AC 484 at 518, [1986] 1 All ER 467 at 474, HL, per Lord Brightman (duty of the court to leave decisions as to facts to the decision-making body to whom Parliament has entrusted that power), approved as still relevant in *R (on the application of Ireneschild) v Lambeth London Borough Council* [2007] EWCA Civ 234 at [44], [2007] LGR 619 at [44] per Hallett LJ, but cf *Edwards (Inspector of Taxes) v Bairstow* [1956] AC 14 at 38–39, [1955] 3 All ER 48 at 59, HL, per Lord Radcliffe (court's duty is only to accord a 'decent respect' to the tribunal; if it has reached an unreasonable conclusion, the court must so hold). See also *Secretary of State for Education and Science v Tameside Metropolitan Borough Council* [1977] AC 1014 at 1047, [1976] 3 All ER 665 at 681–682, HL, per Lord Wilberforce (evaluation of facts for Secretary of State alone); *R v Nat Bell Liquors Ltd* [1922] 2 AC 128 at 144, PC, per Lord Sumner; *Collis Radio Ltd v Secretary of State for the Environment* (1975) 73 LGR 211 at 215, 29 P & CR 390 at 394, DC, per Lord Widgery CJ; *Hilliard v Secretary of State for the Environment* (1978) 37 P & CR 129 at 139, CA, per Shaw LJ; *R v Devon and Cornwall Police Authority, ex p Willis* (1984) 82 LGR 369 at 373, (1984) Times, 24 January per Taylor J; *ELS Wholesale (Wolverhampton) Ltd v Secretary of State for the Environment* (1987) 56 P & CR 69 at 81, (1987) Times, 19 May, DC, per May LJ; *Nesbitt v United Kingdom Central Council for Nursing, Midwifery and Health Visiting* [1993] COD 395, DC (it is for disciplinary committee to assess misconduct); *R v Parole Board, ex p Watson* [1996] 2 All ER 641, [1996] 1 WLR 906, CA (not for court to interfere with findings of specialist tribunal on material before it); *R v Secretary of State for the Home Department, ex p Canbolat* [1998] 1 All ER 161, [1997] 1 WLR 1569, CA (it is for the Secretary of State to evaluate material showing that deportation of applicant contrary to international law); *Rae v Criminal Injuries Compensation Board* 1997 SLT 291; *R v Bow Street Magistrates' Court, ex p Proulx* [2001] 1 All ER 57, [2000] COD 454, DC.

    The general rule is that the question of what weight to attribute to a particular factor (if any) is a matter for the primary decision-maker: see e g *Tesco Stores Ltd v Secretary of State for the Environment* [1995] 2 All ER 636 at 642, [1995] 1 WLR 759 at 764, HL, per Lord Keith of Kinkel and at 657 and 784 per Lord Hoffmann; *City of Edinburgh Council v Secretary of State for Scotland* [1998] 1 All ER 174, [1997] 1 WLR 1447, HL. However, where a decision-maker has unreasonably attributed no or insufficient weight to a particular issue the courts will intervene: see e g *R (on the application of von Brandenburg) v East London and The City Mental Health NHS Trust* [2001] EWCA Civ 239 at [41], [2002] QB 235 at [41] per Sedley LJ (affd [2003] UKHL 58, [2004] 2 AC 280, [2004] 1 All ER 400); *R v Secretary of State for the Home Department, ex p Yousaf* [2000] 3 All ER 649 at [51] per Sedley LJ; *R (on the application of BT3G Ltd) v Secretary of State for Trade and Industry* [2001] EuLR 325 at [187] per Silber J. Similarly where the decision-maker has unreasonably attributed too much weight to a particular issue the courts will intervene: see e g *R v Waltham Forest London Borough Council, ex p Baxter* [1988] QB 419 at 427–428, [1987] 3 All ER 671 at 677, CA, per Stocker LJ; *R v South Gloucestershire Housing Benefit Review Board, ex p Dadds* (1996) 29 HLR 700; *R v Local Comr for Administration in North and North East England, ex p Liverpool City Council* [2001] 1 All ER 462 at [36], [2000] LGR 571 at [36], CA, per Henry LJ (allowing party political considerations to be decisive). For examples of cases in which the courts have been willing to examine the strength of the evidence see e g *Tormes Property Co Ltd v Landau* [1971] 1 QB 261, [1970] 3 All ER 653, DC (rents for similar properties in the area may be the best evidence to establish a fair rent; and see *Mason v Skilling* [1974] 3 All ER 977 at 978–979, [1974] 1 WLR 1437 at 1439, HL, per Lord Reid; *London Rent Assessment Committee v St George's Court Ltd* (1984) 48 P & CR 230, 16 HLR 90, CA); *Emma Hotels Ltd v Secretary of State for the Environment* (1980) 41 P & CR 255, 258 EG 64, DC; *Forkhurst v Secretary of State for the Environment* [1982] JPL 448, 46 P & CR 89; *R v Secretary of State for the Home*

Department, ex p Dinesh [1987] Imm AR 131, (1986) Times, 11 December (insufficient regard to the fact that applicant was innumerate and illiterate); *DPP v Singh* [1988] RTR 209, DC. Where cases involve fundamental rights, however, it is always for the court to assess for itself the balance to be struck between the rights of the individual and the justification advanced for interfering with that right: see PARA 619 note 5.

3 See eg *Begum v Tower Hamlets London Borough Council* [2003] UKHL 5 at [99], [2003] 2 AC 430 at [99], [2003] 1 All ER 731 at [99] per Lord Millett. The principle behind this approach is that judicial review is concerned with the legality and not the merits of a decision; accordingly the court will not examine the evidence with a view to forming its own view about the substantial merits of the case: see PARA 617 note 9. However, the position is otherwise where fundamental rights are involved: see PARA 619. As to errors of law see PARA 612.

4 *O'Reilly v Mackman* [1983] 2 AC 237 at 282, [1982] 3 All ER 1124 at 1131, HL, per Lord Diplock; *Cocks v Thanet District Council* [1983] 2 AC 286 at 292, [1982] 3 All ER 1135 at 1137, HL, per Lord Bridge of Harwich; *R (on the application of Beresford) v Sunderland City Council* [2003] UKHL 60, [2004] 1 AC 889, [2004] 1 All ER 160 (conclusion unsupported by evidence); *Office of Fair Trading v IBA Healthcare Ltd* [2004] EWCA Civ 142 at [93], [2004] 4 All ER 1103 at [93] per Carnwath LJ; *R v Bedwellty Justices, ex p Williams* [1997] AC 225, sub nom *Williams v Bedwellty Justices* [1996] 3 All ER 737, HL (in absence of inadmissible evidence no evidential basis for conviction); *Ashbridge Investments Ltd v Minister of Housing and Local Government* [1965] 3 All ER 371 at 373–374, [1965] 1 WLR 1320 at 1326–1327, CA, per Lord Denning MR; *Mahon v Air New Zealand* [1984] AC 808 at 820, [1984] 3 All ER 201 at 209–210, PC (principle of natural justice that decision must be based on evidence of some probative value); *Abdi v Secretary of State for the Home Department* [1996] 1 All ER 641 at 658, sub nom *R v Secretary of State for the Home Department, ex p Abdi* [1996] 1 WLR 298 at 315, HL, per Lord Lloyd (statement of opinion of Secretary of State that Spain a safe country sufficient evidence of that issue) cf at 651 and 308 per Lord Slynn of Hadley and at 644 and 301 per Lord Mustill (opinion of Secretary of State not itself evidence, accordingly no evidence before special adjudicators); *Secretary of State for Education and Science v Tameside Metropolitan Borough Council* [1977] AC 1014 at 1047, [1976] 3 All ER 665 at 681–682, HL, per Lord Wilberforce (and see at 1062 and 693 per Viscount Dilhorne and at 1072 and 701 per Lord Salmon: no evidence on which, applying the correct test, the Secretary of State could have reached the conclusion he did). See also *Faridian v General Medical Council* [1971] AC 995, [1971] 1 All ER 144, PC; *Armah v Government of Ghana* [1968] AC 192 at 234, HL, per Lord Reid; *Maradana Mosque Board of Trustees v Mahmud* [1967] 1 AC 13, [1966] 1 All ER 545, PC.

The court will also intervene where, although there is some evidence to support a finding, it is insufficient: see eg *Stefan v General Medical Council* [2002] UKPC 10 at [6], [2002] All ER (D) 96 (Mar) at [6]; *Office of Fair Trading v IBA Healthcare Ltd* [2004] EWCA Civ 142 at [93], [2004] 4 All ER 1103 at [93] per Carnwath LJ; *R v Sefton Metropolitan Borough Council, ex p Cunningham* (1991) 23 HLR 534 at 541 per Hutchinson J (decision taken on the basis of inadequate evidence); *Reid v Secretary of State for Scotland* [1999] 2 AC 512 at 541, [1999] 1 All ER 481 at 506, HL, per Lord Clyde (error of law where there is an absence of evidence or sufficient evidence to support decision); *R v West London Coroner, ex p Gray* [1988] QB 467 at 479–480, [1987] 2 All ER 129 at 139 per Watkins LJ (jury verdict at inquest cannot stand if based on no or wholly insufficient evidence); *Mahon v Air New Zealand* [1984] AC 808 at 820, [1984] 3 All ER 201 at 209–210, PC; *A-G v Ryan* [1980] AC 718, [1980] 2 WLR 143, PC. This ground of review is closely linked to that of *Wednesbury* or manifest unreasonableness: see further PARA 617.

A decision reached on the basis of findings of fact supported only by fraudulent evidence or evidence which should not have been adduced will be quashed: *R v Bedwellty Justices, ex p Williams*. See further PARAS 612, 621.

Most of the cases in which the 'no evidence' rule has been applied are concerned with the application of the law to the primary facts. Where the decision-maker has made secondary findings based on primary facts (eg as to credibility), the test is whether the primary facts found justify the secondary finding: see *Furniss (Inspector of Taxes) v Dawson* [1984] AC 474 at 527–528, [1984] 1 All ER 530 at 543, HL, per Lord Brightman. The more serious the secondary fact, the more cogent must be the primary facts on which it is based: see *R (on the application of Higham) v University of Plymouth* [2005] EWHC 1492 (Admin) at [32], [2005] ELR 547 at [32] per Stanley Burnton J.

Note that there are dicta in some cases suggesting that the court may not interfere on the ground of total absence of evidence: see eg *Germany v Sotiriadis* [1975] AC 1 at 29–30, [1974] 1 All ER 692 at 705, HL, per Lord Diplock; but see the explanation for such dicta in *R v Bedwellty Justices, ex p Williams* at 234–235 and 744–755 per Lord Cooke of Thorndon.

5   This principle applies both where there has been a misunderstanding as to the evidence before the decision-maker and where the decision-maker has reached his decision on an incorrect factual basis through ignorance of the existence of evidence on that matter. The requirements are: (1) that there must have been a mistake as to an existing fact, including a mistake as to the availability of evidence on a particular matter; (2) the fact or evidence must have been 'established', in the sense that it was uncontentious and objectively verifiable; (3) the appellant, or his advisers, must not have been responsible for the mistake; (4) the mistake must have played a material (not necessarily decisive) part in the decision-maker's reasoning: see *E v Secretary of State for the Home Department* [2004] EWCA Civ 49 at [66], [2004] QB 1044 at [66] per Carnwath LJ, giving the judgment of the court, though cf *Montes v Secretary of State for the Home Department* [2004] EWCA Civ 404 at [21], [2004] Imm AR 250 at [21] per Dyson LJ (the principle in *E v Secretary of State for the Home Department* is 'closely and carefully circumscribed'). See also *Secretary of State for Education and Science v Tameside Metropolitan Borough Council* [1977] AC 1014 at 1047, [1976] 3 All ER 665 at 681–682, HL, per Lord Wilberforce, and at 1031 and 675 per Lord Scarman (review for misunderstanding or ignorance of an established and relevant fact or taking into account a mistake of fact); *R (on the application of Alconbury Developments Ltd) v Secretary of State for the Environment Transport and the Regions* [2001] UKHL 23 at [53], [2003] 2 AC 295 at [53], [2001] 2 All ER 929 at [53] per Lord Slynn of Hadley, at [61]–[62] per Lord Nolan and at [169] per Lord Clyde; *Begum v Tower Hamlets London Borough Council* [2003] UKHL 5 at [7], [2003] 2 AC 430 at [7], [2003] 1 All ER 731 at [7] per Lord Bingham of Cornhill; *Secretary of State for Employment v ASLEF (No 2)* [1972] 2 QB 455 at 493, [1972] 2 All ER 949 at 967–968, CA, per Lord Denning MR; *Laker Airways Ltd v Department of Trade* [1977] QB 643 at 706, [1977] 2 All ER 182 at 193, CA, per Lord Denning MR; *Hollis v Secretary of State for the Environment* (1982) 47 P & CR 351, 265 EG 476 (error of fact on matter where correct information available to the department); *R v Secretary of State for the Environment, ex p Norwich City Council* [1982] QB 808 at 824–825, sub nom *Norwich City Council v Secretary of State for the Environment* [1982] 1 All ER 737 at 745, CA, per Lord Denning MR (decision will be reviewed if minister misdirects himself in fact or in law); *Jagendorf v Secretary of State for the Environment* [1987] JPL 771 (Parliament could not have intended to empower the Secretary of State to decide matter on a materially incorrect factual basis); *R v Secretary of State for the Home Department, ex p Malhi* [1991] 1 QB 194, [1990] 2 All ER 357, CA.
    If a body discovers that it has acted on the basis of a mistake of fact, it may be under a duty to reconsider its decision where the decision is not irrevocable: see *R (on the application of Touche) v Inner London North Coroner* [2001] EWCA Civ 383 at [36], [2001] QB 1206 at [36] per Simon Brown LJ (although decision was originally correct, coroner should have changed his mind on information subsequently brought to his attention); *Rootkin v Kent County Council* [1981] 2 All ER 227, [1981] 1 WLR 1186, CA; *R v Newham London Borough Council, ex p Begum* (1996) 28 HLR 646 (error of fact not a sufficient basis to quash but there was a duty to reconsider in the light of it).
    Note that this ground of review is closely related to review for taking into account irrelevant factors: see eg *Simplex GE (Holdings) Ltd v Secretary of State for the Environment* (1988) 57 P & CR 306, [1988] JPL 809, CA (minister's mistake of fact amounted to taking into account an irrelevant factor); and see further PARA 623. Where this ground of review is based on a 'misunderstanding' of a fact it is closely related to manifest unreasonableness: see eg *R v Housing Benefit Review Board of the London Borough of Sutton, ex p Keegan* (1995) 27 HLR 92; and PARA 617.

6   See eg *R v Derbyshire County Council, ex p Noble* [1990] ICR 808 at 813, [1990] 1 RLR 332 at 333, CA, per Woolf LJ. This is because the general principle is that the review of the decision is to be undertaken from the decision-maker's point of view on the basis of the evidence available to him at the time: see eg *R v Secretary of State for Education and Science, ex p Malik* [1994] ELR 121 at 129 per Rose J. The court generally regards judicial review as being an inappropriate forum for resolving factual disputes: see eg *Tweed v Parades Commission for Northern Ireland* [2006] UKHL 53, [2007] 1 AC 650 at [2], [2007] 2 All ER 273 at [2] per Lord Bingham of Cornhill; *R v Horsham District Council, ex p Wenman* [1994] 4 All ER 681, [1995] 1 WLR 680; and *St Helens Borough Council v Manchester Primary Care Trust* [2008] EWCA Civ 931, [2009] PIQR P69, [2008] All ER (D) 58 (Aug) at [13] per May LJ. However, the court will not shut out evidence that is relevant to the issues (see eg *R v Secretary of State for the Home Department, ex p Turgut* [2001] 1 All ER 719 at 735, [2000] Imm AR 306, CA, per Schiemann LJ) and will admit evidence that was not before the decision-maker for a variety of reasons, including as to the appropriateness of relief sought (eg *R (on the application of Malik) v Manchester Crown Court* [2008] EWHC 1362 (Admin) at [32], [2008] 4 All ER 403 at [32] per Dyson LJ, giving the judgment of the court), and as to misconduct or bias or procedural

unfairness in the decision-making process (see *R v Secretary of State for the Environment, ex p Powis* [1981] 1 All ER 788, [1981] 1 WLR 584, CA). In cases involving fundamental rights the court will normally determine the matter on the basis of the facts as known to the court at the time of the hearing rather than on the basis of the facts as they were at the time the decision was taken: see eg *R v Secretary of State for the Home Department, ex p Launder* [1997] 3 All ER 961 at 981, [1997] 1 WLR 839 at 860–861, HL, per Lord Hope of Craighead; *R (on the application of Limbuela) v Secretary of State for the Home Department* [2004] EWCA Civ 540 at [113], [2004] QB 1440 at [113], [2005] 3 All ER 29 at [113] per Carnwath LJ; *R (on the application of Middlebrook Mushrooms Ltd) v Agricultural Wages Board of England and Wales* [2004] EWHC 1447 (Admin) at [84], [2004] All ER (D) 183 (Jun) at [84] per Stanley Burnton J (when court required to determine the proportionality of a measure it should have all relevant evidence before, including expert evidence not available to the decision-maker at the time); *Wilson v First County Trust Ltd* [2003] UKHL 40 at [141]–[142], [2004] 1 AC 816 at [141]–[142], [2003] 4 All ER 97 at [141]–[142] per Lord Hobhouse of Woodborough.

7 See *E v Secretary of State for the Home Department* [2004] EWCA Civ 49 at [68], [2004] QB 1044 at [68] per Carnwath LJ, giving the judgment of the court; *R v Criminal Injuries Compensation Board, ex p A* [1999] 2 AC 330 at 344–345, [1992] 2 WLR 974 at 981, HL, per Lord Slynn of Hadley; *R v Haringey London Borough Council, ex p Norton* (1998) 1 CCLR 168 at 180 per Mr Henderson QC, sitting as a deputy judge of the Queen's Bench division.

8 As to the meaning of 'jurisdiction' see PARA 610.

9 *Bunbury v Fuller* (1853) 9 Exch 111; *R v London, etc Rent Tribunal, ex p Honig* [1951] 1 KB 641 at 646, [1951] 1 All ER 195 at 197, DC, per Lord Goddard CJ; *R v Fulham, Hammersmith and Kensington Rent Tribunal, ex p Zerek* [1951] 2 KB 1 at 10, [1951] 1 All ER 482 at 488, DC, per Devlin J; *Goldsack v Shore* [1950] 1 KB 708 at 715, [1950] 1 All ER 276 at 279, CA, per Evershed MR; *R v Croydon and South West London Rent Tribunal, ex p Ryzewska* [1977] QB 876, [1977] 1 All ER 312, DC; *R v Kensington and Chelsea Royal London Borough Rent Officer, ex p Noel* [1978] QB 1, [1977] 1 All ER 356, DC; *R v Rent Officer for Camden, ex p Ebiri* [1981] 1 All ER 950, [1981] 1 WLR 881, DC. It may be proper for the relevant body to hold a preliminary hearing to inquire into the jurisdictional issue: *Potts v IRC* (1982) 56 TC 25 at 35, [1982] STC 611 at 619–620 per Watton J.

10 See generally *R (on the application of Lim) v Secretary of State for the Home Department* [2007] EWCA Civ 773 at [17]–[22], [2007] All ER (D) 402 (Jul) at [17]–[22] per Sedley LJ.

11 Modern examples of this approach are rare. They are generally only found in cases concerning the liberty of the subject: see *Khawaja v Secretary of State for the Home Department* [1984] AC 74, [1983] 1 All ER 765, HL (detention of person only permitted if he was in fact an illegal immigrant; the court will review the material on which the immigration officer formed his conclusion regarding the jurisdictional fact and will form its own view on that material); overruling *Zamir v Secretary of State for the Home Department* [1980] AC 930, [1980] 2 All ER 768, HL, but distinguished in *Bugdaycay v Secretary of State for the Home Department* [1987] AC 514, [1987] 1 All ER 940, HL. *Khawaja v Secretary of State for the Home Department* was applied in *Tan Te Lam v Superintendent of Tai A Chau Detention Centre* [1997] AC 97, [1996] 4 All ER 256, [2006] 1 WLR 1003, PC, and *D v Home Office* [2005] EWCA Civ 38, [2006] 1 All ER 183; and cf *R (on the application of Lim) v Secretary of State for the Home Department* [2007] EWCA Civ 773 at [17]–[22], [2007] All ER (D) 402 (Jul) at [17]–[22] per Sedley LJ for the flexible approach that the court will take depending on the nature of the precedent fact in question; see also *R v Secretary of State for the Environment, ex p Tower Hamlets London Borough Council* [1993] QB 632 at 642, [1993] 3 All ER 439 at 446, CA, per Stuart-Smith LJ (question whether someone an illegal entrant matter of objective fact for court to determine); *Islington London Borough Council v Camp* [2004] LGR 58 at 67 per Richards J (whether councillor 'disqualified' a precedent fact); *R (on the application of Lim) v Secretary of State for the Home Department* [2006] EWHC 3004 (Admin) at [22], [2006] All ER (D) 410 (Nov) at [22] per Lloyd Jones J (breach of condition on leave to remain a precedent fact), though cf *R (on the application of Queen Mary University of London) v Higher Education Funding Council for England* [2008] EWHC 1472 (Admin) at [22], [2008] ELR 540 at [22] per Burnett J (whether breach of grant conditions not precedent fact); *R (on the application of M) v Lambeth London Borough Council* [2008] EWHC 1364 (Admin), [2008] 2 FLR 1026 at [146] per Bennett J; *R (on the application of M) v Lambeth London Borough Council* [2009] UKSC 8, [2009] 1 WLR 2557, [2009] 3 FCR 607 (whether asylum seeker 'a child' was a precedent fact).

For other older illustrations of issues held to be jurisdictional see: *Bunbury v Fuller* (1853) 9 Exch 111; *Re Bailey, Re Collier* (1854) 3 E & B 607; *Re Baker* (1857) 2 H & N 219; *Milward v Caffin* (1779) 2 Wm Bl 1330; *Cornwell v Sanders* (1862) 3 B & S 206; *Liverpool United Gas-Light Co v The Overseers of the Poor of Everton* (1871) LR 6 CP 414; *Stanhope v Thorsby*

(1866) LR 1 CP 423; *R v Manchester Justices* [1899] 1 QB 571, DC (but see *R v Woodhouse* [1906] 2 KB 501, CA); *R v Bradford* [1908] 1 KB 365, DC; *R v Norfolk Justices, ex p Wayland Union* [1909] 1 KB 463 at 469, DC, per Lord Alverstone CJ; *R (Greenaway) v Armagh Justices* [1924] 2 IR 55, CA; *Eshugbayi Eleko v Government of Nigeria* [1931] AC 662 at 669, PC; *R (Magee) v Down Justices* [1935] NI 51; *White and Collins v Minister of Health* [1939] 2 KB 838, sub nom *Re Rippon (Highfield) Housing Order, 1938, Applications of White and Collins* [1939 3 All ER 548, CA; *R v Lewes Justices, ex p Trustees of Plumpton and District Club* [1960] 2 All ER 476, [1960] 1 WLR 700, DC. It is not always easy to understand the principles upon which the court has classified a matter as jurisdictional rather than going to the merits.

There are many examples of cases involving rent tribunals where facts have been held to be jurisdictional: see eg *R v Fulham, Hammersmith and Kensington Rent Tribunal, ex p Philippe* [1950] 2 All ER 211, 48 LGR 544, DC; *R v Barnet (and Area) Rent Tribunal, ex p Millman* [1950] 2 KB 506, [1950] 2 All ER 216, DC (this could be regarded as an error of law: see PARA 612); *R v Blackpool Rent Tribunal, ex p Ashton* [1948] 2 KB 277, [1948] 1 All ER 900, DC; *R v Paddington and St Marylebone Rent Tribunal, ex p Haines* [1962] 1 QB 388, [1961] 3 All ER 1047, DC; *R v West London Rent Tribunal, ex p Napper* [1967] 1 QB 169, [1965] 3 All ER 734, DC; cf *R v Kensington and Chelsea Royal London Borough Rent Officer, ex p Noel* [1978] QB 1, [1977] 1 All ER 356, DC (court would only review rent officer's decision on the existence of jurisdictional fact to determine whether it was a decision to which no reasonable person could have come, or was reached after a misdirection on a point of law).

There are also cases where the question whether a jurisdictional fact is established is a question of mixed fact and law: see PARA 613.

12 This is the modern terminology used by the courts: see eg *R v Oldham Metropolitan Borough Council, ex p Garlick* [1993] AC 509 at 520, [1993] 2 All ER 65 at 72, HL, per Lord Griffiths (a 'precedent fact going to jurisdiction'). See also *Anisminic Ltd v Foreign Compensation Commission* [1969] 2 AC 147 at 242, [1969] 1 All ER 208 at 244, HL, per Lord Wilberforce; *Khawaja v Secretary of State for the Home Department* [1984] AC 74 at 101, [1983] 1 All ER 765 at 774–775, HL, per Lord Wilberforce; *South Yorkshire Transport Ltd v Monopolies and Mergers Commission* [1993] 1 All ER 289, sub nom *R v Monopolies and Mergers Commission, ex p South Yorkshire Transport Ltd* [1993] 1 WLR 23, HL ('jurisdictional precondition').

In older cases, such facts have also been described as collateral to the merits: see eg *R v Fulham, Hammersmith and Kensington Rent Tribunal, ex p Zerek* [1951] 2 KB 1, [1951] 1 All ER 482, DC; and the cases cited in note 15.

13 See *R (on the application of M) v Lambeth London Borough Council* [2009] UKSC 8, [2009] 1 WLR 2557, [2009] 3 FCR 607; *R (on the application of Lim) v Secretary of State for the Home Department* [2007] EWCA Civ 773 at [19], [2007] All ER (D) 402 (Jul) at [19] per Sedley LJ; *Khawaja v Secretary of State for the Home Department* [1984] AC 74, [1983] 1 All ER 765, HL; applied in *R (on the application of Ullah) v Secretary of State for the Home Department* [2003] EWCA Civ 1366 at [28], [2003] All ER (D) 179 (Oct) at [28] per Potter LJ. See also *R (Maiden Outdoor Advertising Ltd) v Lambeth London Borough Council* [2003] EWHC 1224 (Admin) at [35], [2003] JPL 820 at [35] per Collins J; *R (on the application of P) v Haringey London Borough Council* [2008] EWHC 2357 (Admin) at [43], [2009] ELR 49 at [43] per Collins J (for court to determine whether valid notice of appeal given); *R v Shoreditch Assessment Committee ex p Morgan* [1910] 2 KB 859 at 880, CA, per Farwell LJ; cited with approval in *Anisminic Ltd v Foreign Compensation Commission* [1969] 2 AC 147 at 197, [1969] 1 All ER 208 at 235, HL, per Lord Pearce, and at 208–209 and 245 per Lord Wilberforce; *White and Collins v Minister of Health* [1939] 2 KB 838, sub nom *Re Rippon (Highfield) Housing Order, 1938, Applications of White and Collins* [1939] 3 All ER 548, CA (for court to determine whether land part of a park); *South Yorkshire Transport Ltd v Monopolies and Mergers Commission* [1993] 1 All ER 289 at 298, sub nom *R v Monopolies and Mergers Commission, ex p South Yorkshire Transport Ltd* [1993] 1 WLR 23 at 32, HL, per Lord Mustill; *R v Oldham Metropolitan Borough Council, ex p Garlick* [1993] AC 509 at 520, [1993] 2 All ER 65 at 72, HL, per Lord Griffiths (question whether fact is a precedent fact to be decided by the court). See also the cases cited in note 11.

14 See eg *R v Bolton* (1841) 1 QB 66; *Eshugbayi Eleko v Government of Nigeria* [1931] AC 662 at 675, PC; *R v West Sussex Quarter Sessions, ex p Albert and Maud Johnson Trust Ltd* [1974] QB 24 at 40–42, [1973] 3 All ER 289 at 299–301, CA, per Lawton LJ; *R v Secretary of State for the Environment, ex p Powis* [1981] 1 All ER 788, [1981] 1 WLR 584, CA; *R (Maiden Outdoor Advertising Ltd) v Lambeth London Borough Council* [2003] EWHC 1224 (Admin) at [36]–[37], [2003] JPL 820 at [36]–[37] per Collins J. See also *R (on the application of Beckett) v Secretary of State for the Home Department* [2008] EWHC 2002 (Admin) at [3], [2008] All ER (D) 106 (Aug) at [3] per Ouseley J (court taking unusual step of hearing oral evidence on judicial review in order to determine precedent fact) and *R (on the application of*

Lim) v Secretary of State for the Home Department [2006] EWHC 3004 (Admin) at [47], [2006] All ER (D) 410 (Nov) at [47] per Lloyd Jones J (cross-examination appropriate for precedent fact) (rvsd on other grounds [2007] EWCA Civ 773, [2007] All ER (D) 402 (Jul)), though c f *R v City of Westminster ex p Moozary-Oraky* (1993) 26 HLR 213. Evidence on a question of precedent fact is not subject to the ordinary rules of evidence in court and may include hearsay evidence: *R v Secretary of State for the Home Department, ex p Rahman* [1998] QB 136 at 166, [1997] 1 All ER 769 at 806, CA, per Hutchison LJ. As to hearsay evidence see CIVIL PROCEDURE vol 11 (2009) PARA 806 et seq.

Generally the court is reluctant to hear evidence on an application for judicial review: see note 6.

15 See *R v Income Tax Special Purposes Comrs* (1888) 21 QBD 313 at 319, CA, per Lord Esher MR (the legislature may entrust the tribunal or body with jurisdiction to determine whether the preliminary state of facts exists); *R v Bloomsbury Income Tax Comrs* [1915] 3 KB 768, DC; *R v Swansea Income Tax Comrs, ex p English Crown Spelter Co* [1925] 2 KB 250, DC; *R v Ludlow, ex p Barnsley Corpn* [1947] KB 634, [1947] 1 All ER 880, DC; *Secretary of State for Employment v Associated Society of Locomotive Engineers and Firemen (No 2)* [1972] 2 QB 455, [1972] 2 All ER 949, CA; *De Falco v Crawley Borough Council* [1980] QB 460, [1980] 1 All ER 913, CA (whether applicants for housing 'intentionally homeless'); *Cocks v Thanet District Council* [1983] 2 AC 286 at 292, [1982] 3 All ER 1135 at 1137, HL, per Lord Bridge of Harwich (intentionally homeless); *O'Reilly v Mackman* [1983] 2 AC 237 at 282, [1982] 3 All ER 1124 at 1131, HL, obiter per Lord Diplock (the same principles applicable to tribunals and to other statutory bodies); *R v Chief Registrar of Friendly Societies, ex p New Cross Building Society* [1984] QB 227 at 273, [1984] 2 All ER 27 at 51, CA, per Slade LJ (subjective language does not exclude the application of the principles in *Associated Provincial Picture Houses Ltd v Wednesbury Corpn* [1948] 1 KB 223, [1947] 2 All ER 680, CA (see PARA 617) where a crucial finding of fact is clearly wrong); *R v Secretary of State for Social Services, ex p Official Custodian of Charities* (1984) Times, 28 February, CA (the Secretary of State could not properly have found that the preconditions for the exercise of his statutory powers were satisfied); *R v Gloucester City Council, ex p Miles* (1985) 83 LGR 607, [1985] FLR 1043, CA (intentionally homeless); *Puhlhofer v Hillingdon London Borough Council* [1986] AC 484 at 518, [1986] 1 All ER 467 at 474, HL, per Lord Brightman (where the existence or otherwise of a fact is left to the judgment of a local authority, the court will only intervene if its finding is perverse); followed in *Davies v Secretary of State for the Environment* [1989] JPL 601, (1989) Times, 15 May); *R v Brent London Borough Council, ex p Awua* [1996] AC 55, sub nom *Awua v Brent London Borough Council* [1995] 3 All ER 493, HL (intentionally homeless).

In certain cases, a higher standard of review than reasonableness may be applied to the exercise of subjectively worded powers: see *R v Secretary of State for the Home Department, ex p Cheblak* [1991] 2 All ER 319, [1991] 1 WLR 890, CA (Secretary of State may deport where he 'deems' it conducive to the public good; court will only review on grounds of bad faith).

As to review on grounds of manifest unreasonableness generally see PARA 617.

16 See e g *Hillingdon London Borough Council v Commission for Racial Equality* [1982] AC 779, [1982] 3 WLR 159, HL; *Re Prestige Group plc* [1984] 1 WLR 335, [1984] ICR 483, HL.

17 In such a case the court will interfere only if the decision that the fact exists is one which no reasonable decision-maker, properly directing himself in law, could have reached (as in the case of subjectively worded statutory provisions: see note 15). There are numerous examples of this approach, see: *Dowty Boulton Paul Ltd v Wolverhampton Corpn (No 2)* [1976] Ch 13, [1973] 2 All ER 491, CA (local authority better able to judge whether land required for particular purpose than the court); *R v Kensington and Chelsea Royal London Borough Rent Officer, ex p Noel* [1978] QB 1, [1977] 1 All ER 356, DC (although c f the cases cited in note 11); *R v Camden London Borough Council, ex p Rowton (Camden Town) Ltd* (1983) 82 LGR 614, (1983) 10 HLR 28 (local authority could reasonably conclude on a proper view of the law that a hostel was a 'house'); *Bugdaycay v Secretary of State for the Home Department* [1987] AC 514, [1987] 1 All ER 940, HL; *Ali v Secretary of State for the Home Department* [1988] Imm AR 274, Independent, 19 January, CA; *R v Oldham Metropolitan Borough Council, ex p Garlick* [1993] AC 509, [1993] 2 All ER 65, HL (for local authority to determine whether applicant had capacity to make application); *R v Secretary of State for the Environment, ex p Haringey London Borough Council* [1994] COD 518, 92 LGR 538, CA (for Secretary of State to determine whether authority acted in breach of statutory conditions); *R v Secretary of State for Employment, ex p National Association of Colliery Overmen, Deputies and Shotfirers* [1994] COD 218, DC (whether statutory language subjective or not, generally decision-maker is responsible for fact finding necessary for the exercise of power); *R v Radio Authority, ex p Guardian Media Group plc* [1995] 2 All ER 139 at 150, [1995] 1 WLR 334 at 344 per

Schieman J (for radio authority to determine whether one company controlled by another); *R v South Hams District Council, ex p Gibb* [1995] QB 158, [1994] 4 All ER 1012, CA (whether applicant a gipsy was a question for local authority); *Re S (Minors)* [1995] ELR 98 at 105, CA, per Butler-Sloss LJ (for local authority to decide whether a school is suitable); *R v Secretary of State for the Home Department, ex p Onibiyo* [1996] QB 768 at 785, [1996] 2 All ER 901 at 912, CA, per Sir Thomas Bingham MR; *Ravichandranm v Secretary of State for the Home Department* [1996] Imm AR 97, CA (for Secretary of State to determine whether fresh claim made for asylum); *R v Southwark London Borough Council, ex p Ryder* (1996) 28 HLR 56 (question whether person might reasonably be expected to reside with homeless person one of fact for local authority); *R v Secretary of State for the Home Department, ex p Canbolat* [1998] 1 All ER 161, [1997] 1 WLR 1569, CA (for Secretary of State to determine whether deportation would be contrary to international law); *R v Gloucestershire County Council, ex p Barry* [1997] AC 584, [1997] 2 All ER 1, HL (for local authority to set eligibility criteria by which needs of disabled person to be assessed); *R v Family Health Services Appeal Authority, ex p Tesco Stores Ltd* [1999] COD 503, 11 Admin LR 1007.

In cases where there is scope for legitimate disagreement as to whether a fact falls within a statutory description, the court will determine the ambit of the statutory description and interfere only if the fact is not one which falls within that ambit: *South Yorkshire Transport Ltd v Monopolies and Mergers Commission* [1993] 1 All ER 289, sub nom *R v Monopolies and Mergers Commission, ex p South Yorkshire Transport Ltd* [1993] 1 WLR 23, HL (whether area a 'substantial part' of the United Kingdom); and see eg *R v Radio Authority, ex p Bull* [1998] QB 294, [1997] 2 All ER 561; *R v Broadcasting Standards Commission, ex p British Broadcasting Corpn* [2000] 3 All ER 989 at 991, [2000] 3 WLR 1327 at 1329, CA, per Lord Woolf MR (whether a broadcast constitutes an 'infringement of privacy'). See further PARA 613.

A comparable result was achieved in earlier case law by holding that a matter determined, correctly or incorrectly, by a decision-maker went to the merits and was not collateral or a preliminary issue: see *Brittain v Kinnaird* (1819) 1 Brod & Bing 432; *Cave v Mountain* (1840) 1 Man & G 257 at 262 per Tindal CJ; *R v Bolton* (1841) 1 QB 66 at 74 per Lord Denman CJ; *R v St Olave's District Board* (1857) 8 E & B 529; *Ex p Smith* (1890) 7 TLR 42, DC; *R (Martin) v Mahony* [1910] 2 IR 695; *R v Cheshire Justices, ex p Heaver* (1912) 108 LT 374, DC; *R v Lincolnshire Justices, ex p Brett* [1926] 2 KB 192, CA; *R v Minister of Health* [1939] 1 KB 232, [1938] 4 All ER 32, CA; *Tithe Redemption Commission v Wynne* [1943] KB 756, [1943] 2 All ER 370, CA; *R v Weston-super-Mare Justices, ex p Barkers (Contractors) Ltd* [1944] 1 All ER 747, DC; *R v Minister of Transport, ex p WH Beech-Allen Ltd* (1963) 62 LGR 76, DC; *Punton v Ministry of Pensions and National Insurance (No 2)* [1964] 1 All ER 448, [1964] 1 WLR 226, CA. See also the review of the authorities by Browne J in *Anisminic Ltd v Foreign Compensation Commission* [1969] 2 AC 223n at 241–244.

(3) PROCEDURAL FAIRNESS

(i) Overview

625. Overview. Procedural fairness, or the duty to act fairly, are the terms now generally used to describe the range of procedural standards which are applied to the administrative decision-making process[1]. They encompass both specific statutory requirements as to consultation, notice or hearings, and the requirements of natural justice derived from common law. Both must now be considered in light of the requirements of the Human Rights Act 1998, and in particular the provision of the Convention for the Protection of Human Rights and Fundamental Freedoms dealing with the right to a fair trial[2], which is incorporated into English law[3].

It is now impossible to regard these 'process rights' as 'mere' procedures. In each situation the requirements of procedural fairness exist in order to have a direct impact on the quality of the decision-making process. Although the link between process and substance may be seen most clearly in developments in the law relating to legitimate expectations[4], it arises in all cases where procedural rights exist. The concept of fairness is necessarily a flexible one, and the requirements which it imposes will differ depending on the circumstances which prevail[5].

1 See eg *O'Reilly v Mackman* [1983] 2 AC 237 at 275, [1982] 3 All ER 1124 at 1226–1227, HL, per Lord Diplock. As to the application and scope of the duty to act fairly see PARA 630.

2 Ie the Convention for the Protection of Human Rights and Fundamental Freedoms (Rome, 4 November 1950; TS 71 (1953) Cmd 8969) art 6: see CONSTITUTIONAL LAW AND HUMAN RIGHTS vol 8(2) (Reissue) PARA 134 et seq. As to the application of art 6 to civil proceedings see PARA 653. Certain provisions of the Convention for the Protection of Human Rights and Fundamental Freedoms (1950) have been incorporated into English law by the Human Rights Act 1998: see CONSTITUTIONAL LAW AND HUMAN RIGHTS vol 8(2) (Reissue) PARA 122 et seq.

3 Although to a large extent it is arguable that the requirements of the Convention for the Protection of Human Rights and Fundamental Freedoms (1950) art 6 are already present through the development of the rules on natural justice, this cannot be assumed in all situations. All previous case law in relation to procedural fairness must, following the coming into force of the Human Rights Act 1998, now be read subject to the requirements of the Convention for the Protection of Human Rights and Fundamental Freedoms (1950) art 6 where that provision applies.

4 See *R v North and East Devon Health Authority, ex p Coughlan* [2001] QB 213, [2000] 3 All ER 850. As to legitimate expectations see PARA 649.

5 In *R v Secretary of State for the Home Department, ex p Doody* [1994] 1 AC 531 at 560, sub nom *Doody v Secretary of State for the Home Department* [1993] 3 All ER 92 at 106, HL, per Lord Mustill, the duty to act fairly was described as an 'intuitive judgment' having regard to all the material circumstances of the situation.

(ii) Mandatory and Directory Requirements under Statute

626.   Mandatory and directory requirements.   Historically the legal consequence of non-compliance with procedural or formal requirements has been regarded as wholly or partly dependent upon the answer to the question whether the requirement is to be classified as mandatory or directory, but a variety of different meanings have been attached to this distinction[1]. Where a statute provides a mandatory procedure it must be followed. The suggestion that requirements which are not mandatory are merely permissive or an indication of what is desirable[2] is probably not correct[3]. However, it appears that where a provision is construed as merely directory, substantial compliance will suffice[4]. Further, a party complaining of breach of a directory requirement must show some prejudice[5], whereas this is not a precondition of relief where the requirement is held to be mandatory[6]. Older authorities tended to assume that an act done or decision reached in breach of a mandatory requirement was a nullity and void ab initio, so that it was as if it had never existed[7], whereas an act done in breach of a merely directory provision was merely voidable and therefore effective until set aside. However, it is now clear that even where an act is void for failure to comply with a mandatory provision, that act may nonetheless have an existence until set aside and cannot usually be safely disregarded[8]. Further, the court always retains a discretion, even in the case of mandatory requirements, as to whether one of the prerogative orders is appropriate or a declaration or injunction should be granted[9]. In this context, to describe an act or decision as void for breach of a mandatory requirement or voidable for breach of a directory requirement appears to mean only that different considerations may govern the court's exercise of the discretion[10].

In classifying a provision as mandatory or directory, the court must look to its purpose and its relationship with the scheme, subject matter and objective of the statute in which it appears[11], and must attempt to assess the importance attached to it by Parliament[12]. It is broadly true that such provisions will more readily be held to be directory if they relate to the performance of a statutory duty, especially if serious public inconvenience would result from holding them to be mandatory, rather than to the exercise of a power on individual interests[13], and that the more severe the potential impact of the exercise of a power on individual interests, the greater is the likelihood of procedural or formal provisions being held to be mandatory[14]. If, in the opinion of the court, a procedural code laid down by a statute is intended to be exhaustive and strictly enforced, its provisions will be regarded as mandatory[15], but even a mandatory procedural requirement may be held to be susceptible of waiver by a person having an interest in securing strict compliance[16]. Under some statutes non-compliance with procedural requirements accompanying the exercise of a statutory power directly affecting individual rights is expressly declared to have no vitiating effect unless a person aggrieved is substantially prejudiced thereby[17]. Among requirements likely to be held to be mandatory are provisions as to the composition of the repository of the power[18], and obligations to consult[19], to give notice so as to enable representations to be made[20], to conduct an inquiry or to consider objections[21], to give reasons for a decision[22], and to give proper notice of rights of appeal[23]. Whether provisions as to the time for taking prescribed steps are to be considered mandatory or directory will depend upon the context[24]. Unauthorised sub-delegation of power[25], and breach of the rules of natural justice where they are applicable[26], will normally invalidate any action taken[27].

The distinction between mandatory and directory requirements is now less frequently used by the courts[28].

1   In practical terms, the best approach to determining where the distinction between 'mandatory' and 'directory' is to be drawn is one of construction. The primary issue is, therefore, whether, having regard to the scope and purpose of the legislation in which the provision appears, the failure to satisfy the provision is sufficiently serious so as to invalidate the whole decision-making process: see *Secretary of State for the Home Department v Ravichandran; R v Secretary of State for the Home Department, ex p Jeyeanthan* (1999) 11 Admin LR 824, [2000] 1 WLR 354; *R v Soneji* [2005] UKHL 49, [2006] 1 AC 340, [2005] 4 All ER 321; *R v Clarke* [2008] UKHL 8, [2008] 2 All ER 665, [2008] 1 WLR 338. Other significant cases include *Howard v Bodington* (1877) 2 PD 203, HL; *Montreal Street Rly Co v Normandin* [1917] AC 170, PC (applied by the Privy Council in *DPP of the Virgin Islands v Penn* [2008] UKPC 29, [2009] 2 LRC 90); *Francis Jackson Developments v Hall* [1951] 2 KB 488, [1951] 2 All ER 74, CA (distinguished by *R v Folkestone and Area Rent Tribunal, ex p Sharkey* [1952] 1 KB 54, [1951] 2 All ER 921; and *R v Paddington and St Marylebone Rent Tribunal, ex p Haines* [1962] 1 QB 388, [1961] 3 All ER 1047, DC); *R v Devon and Cornwall Rent Tribunal, ex p West* (1974) 29 P & CR 316 (applying *Francis Jackson Developments v Hall*); *Coney v Choyce* [1975] 1 All ER 979, [1975] 1 WLR 422; *London and Clydeside Estates Ltd v Aberdeen District Council* [1979] 3 All ER 876, [1980] 1 WLR 182, HL; *R v Birmingham City Council, ex p Quietlynn Ltd* (1985) 83 LGR 461 (on appeal sub nom *R v Peterborough City Council, ex p Quietlynn Ltd* (1986) 85 LGR 249, CA and disapproved in part by *Quietlynn Ltd v Plymouth City Council* [1988] QB 114, [1987] 2 All ER 1040); *R v Tower Hamlets London Borough Council, ex p Tower Hamlets Combined Traders Association* [1994] COD 325 (for a comprehensive review of the distinction, see *R (on the application of West End Street Traders' Association) v Westminster City Council* [2004] EWHC 1167 (Admin), [2005] LGR 143); *Nina TH Wang v IRC* [1995] 1 All ER 367, [1994] 1 WLR 1286, PC. See further STATUTES vol 44(1) (Reissue) PARA 1238.

2   See eg *Howard v Secretary of State for the Environment* [1975] QB 235, (1974) 27 P & CR 131, CA (directory requirements only 'informative'); *Re St Cuthbert's, Doveridge* [1983] 1 WLR 845, Const Ct (provisions were 'permissive').

3   Parliament expects to be obeyed down to the minutest detail: *London and Clydeside Estates Ltd v Aberdeen District Council* [1979] 3 All ER 876 at 883, [1980] 1 WLR 182 at 189, HL, per Lord Hailsham of St Marylebone LC. See also *Re T (A Minor)* [1986] Fam 160, [1986] 1 All ER 817, CA; although cf *O'Reilly v Mackman* [1983] 2 AC 237 at 276, [1982] 3 All ER 1124 at 1127, HL, obiter per Lord Diplock (discretion in body not to comply with directory requirement

if it is of opinion that exceptional circumstances justify departure). Sometimes the true construction of a provision may be that it merely permits a particular procedure to be followed when administratively convenient: see *Hadley v Hancox* (1986) 85 LGR 402, DC. Even if the act or decision is not quashed or held altogether invalid, account may be taken of the failure in the exercise of a discretion (*Re T (A Minor)*); or some penalty may be imposed on the person or body in breach (*Montreal Street Rly Co v Normandin* [1917] AC 170, PC); or there may be an order that the defect should be made good (*Howard v Secretary of State for the Environment* [1974] 1 All ER 644 at 650, 27 P & CR 131 at 138, CA, per Roskill LJ; *R v Croydon Justices, ex p Lefore Holdings Ltd* [1981] 1 All ER 520, [1980] 1 WLR 1465, CA).

4   *Coney v Choyce* [1975] 1 All ER 979, [1975] 1 WLR 422; *Grunwick Processing Laboratories Ltd v Advisory, Conciliation and Arbitration Service* [1978] AC 655, [1978] 1 All ER 338, HL; *R v Croydon Justices, ex p Lefore Holdings Ltd* [1981] 1 All ER 520, [1980] 1 WLR 1465, CA; *Re T (A Minor)* [1986] Fam 160, [1986] 1 All ER 817, CA; *Dodd v British Telecommunications plc* [1988] ICR 116, [1988] IRLR 16, EAT. See also *R v Secretary of State for the Environment, ex p Leicester City Council* [1985] RVR 31. However, a breach which is wholly trivial or de minimis will be disregarded even if the provision is mandatory: *Noble v Inner London Education Authority* (1985) 82 LGR 291, CA; *R v Birmingham City Council, ex p Quietlynn Ltd* (1985) 83 LGR 461; on appeal sub nom *R v Peterborough City Council, ex p Quietlynn Ltd*(1986) 85 LGR 249, CA (the statutory purpose must still be amply fulfilled). See also *R v Dacorum Gaming Licensing Committee, ex p EMI Cinemas and Leisure Ltd* [1971] 3 All ER 666, DC (distinguished by *R v Leicester Gaming Licensing Committee, ex p Shine* [1971] 3 All ER 1082, [1971] 1 WLR 1648, CA).

5   See eg *R v Liverpool City Council, ex p Liverpool Taxi Fleet Operators' Association* [1975] 1 All ER 379 at 384, [1975] 1 WLR 701 at 706, DC, per Lord Widgery CJ; but cf *London and Clydesdale Estates Ltd v Aberdeen District Council* [1979] 3 All ER 876 at 887, [1980] 1 WLR 182 at 195, HL, per Lord Fraser of Tullybelton. See also *R (on the application of Richardson) v North Yorkshire County Council* [2003] EWCA Civ 1860, [2004] 2 All ER 31, [2004] 1 WLR 1920 (non-compliance could be remedied); *R (on the application of Wembley Field Ltd) v Chancerygate Group Ltd* [2005] EWHC 2978 (Admin), [2006] Env LR 34 (grant of planning permission survived despite failure to comply with the regulations, because there had been substantial compliance and no prejudice).

6   *London and Clydeside Estates Ltd v Aberdeen District Council* [1979] 3 All ER 876, [1980] 1 WLR 182, HL; *R v Board of Visitors of Dartmoor Prison, ex p Smith* [1987] QB 106, [1986] 2 All ER 651, CA; *R v Birmingham City Council, ex p Quietlynn Ltd* (1985) 83 LGR 461; on appeal sub nom *R v Peterborough City Council, ex p Quietlynn Ltd* (1986) 85 LGR 249, CA; and see *Noble v Inner London Education Authority* (1983) 82 LGR 291, CA. Cf *R v Manchester City Council, ex p Fulford* (1982) 81 LGR 292, DC; *R v Secretary of State for Transport, ex p Gwent County Council* [1988] QB 429, [1987] 1 All ER 161, CA.

7   *Bodington v Howard* (1877) 2 PD 203, PC; *R v Liverpool City Council, ex p Liverpool Taxi Fleet Operators' Association* [1975] 1 All ER 379, [1975] 1 WLR 701, DC; *Noble v Inner London Education Authority* (1983) 82 LGR 291, CA. See also *West Ham Corpn v Charles Benabo & Sons* [1934] 2 KB 253; *Graddage v Haringey London Borough Council* [1975] 1 All ER 224, [1975] 1 WLR 241 (no need to pay any attention to demand bad on its face, i e manifestly not complying with statutory requirements or in terms so utterly extravagant that anyone acquainted with the facts would unhesitatingly say that there must be a mistake somewhere).

8   *London and Clydeside Estates Ltd v Aberdeen District Council* [1979] 3 All ER 876, [1980] 1 WLR 182, HL; *Co-operative Retail Services Ltd v Taff-Ely Borough Council* (1979) 39 P & CR 223, CA (on appeal sub nom *A-G (HM) (ex rel Co-operative Retail Services Ltd) v Taff-Ely Borough Council* (1981) 42 P & CR 1); *Main v Swansea City Council* (1984) 49 P & CR 26, CA (distinguished by *R (on the application of Pridmore) v Salisbury District Council* [2004] EWHC 2511 (Admin), [2005] 1 P & CR 551, where the purpose of the legislation had come close to being undermined). See also *Calvin v Carr* [1980] AC 574, [1979] 2 All ER 440, PC; and the cases cited in PARA 645 note 11. But a defect may still be so gross that it is as if there was no act or decision at all: *London and Clydeside Estates Ltd v Aberdeen District Council* at 883 and 189 per Lord Hailsham of St Marylebone LC (spectrum of possibilities from outrageously and flagrantly ignoring fundamental obligation to nugatory or trivial defects). Also, the structure of the relevant statute may be such that the relevant step must be taken as a condition precedent to the valid occurrence of further acts and decisions: *R v Pontypool Gaming Licensing Committee, ex p Risca Cinemas Ltd* [1970] 3 All ER 241, [1970] 1 WLR 1299, DC; *Steeples v Derbyshire County Council* [1984] 3 All ER 468, [1985] 1 WLR

256 (where entry of notice in register is moment from which time begins to run, on expiry of which power arises); *R v Lambeth London Borough Council, ex p Sharp* (1984) 50 P & CR 284 (affd (1986) 55 P & CR 232, CA).

Where a document such as an enforcement notice (see TOWN AND COUNTRY PLANNING vol 46(2) (Reissue) PARA 561 et seq) is served on a person, it need not contain any particular form of words or mirror the language of the relevant statute (*Eldon Garages Ltd v Kingston-upon-Hull Corpn* [1974] 1 All ER 358, [1974] 1 WLR 276; cf *R v Newcastle-upon-Tyne Gaming Licensing Committee, ex p White Hart Enterprises Ltd* [1977] 3 All ER 961, [1977] 1 WLR 1135, CA); but it must tell that person fairly what he has done wrong and what he must do to remedy it (*Miller-Mead v Minister of Housing and Local Government* [1963] 2 QB 196, [1963] 1 All ER 459, CA; *Metallic Protectives Ltd v Secretary of State for the Environment* [1976] JPL 166, DC). Thus an ambiguity which cannot be resolved is fatal (*Payne v National Assembly for Wales* [2006] EWHC 597 (Admin), [2007] 1 P & CR 93), and in assessing the validity of the notice the court must have regard not to technical nuances, but rather to what the persons affected by the notice can reasonably be expected to know: *Dudley Bowers Amusements Enterprises Ltd v Secretary of State for the Environment* (1986) 52 P & CR 365; *Bracken v East Hertfordshire District Council* [2000] COD 366, [2000] All ER (D) 579.

A similar test may be applied in assessing whether there has been sufficient compliance in a particular case where not every breach will lead to invalidity: *Coney v Choyce* [1975] 1 All ER 979, [1975] 1 WLR 422 (public notice must at least enable minister to carry out statutory duty to consider proposals in light of any objections from public); *R v Secretary of State for Transport, ex p Gwent County Council* [1988] QB 429, [1987] 1 All ER 161, CA (for minister to have no power to make order, necessary that inquiry procedure so flawed or inspector's report so inadequate that unable to perform obligation to consider inquiry and report before making order).

9 *Coney v Choyce* [1975] 1 All ER 979, [1975] 1 WLR 422; *London and Clydeside Estates Ltd v Aberdeen District Council* [1979] 3 All ER 876, [1980] 1 WLR 182, HL; *Steeples v Derbyshire County Council* [1984] 3 All ER 468 at 480–481, [1985] 1 WLR 256 at 271–272 per Webster J; *R v St Edmundsbury Borough Council, ex p Investors in Industry Commercial Properties Ltd* [1985] 3 All ER 234, [1985] 1 WLR 1168; *R v Birmingham City Council, ex p Quietlynn Ltd* (1985) 83 LGR 461 (on appeal sub nom *R v Peterborough City Council, ex p Quietlynn Ltd* (1986) 85 LGR 249, CA); *R v Secretary of State for Social Services, ex p Association of Metropolitan Authorities* [1986] 1 All ER 164 at 168–169, [1986] 1 WLR 1 at 6 per Webster J; *R v Greenwich London Borough Council, ex p Patel* (1985) 84 LGR 241, CA; *R (on the application of Aldergate Projects Ltd) v Nottinghamshire County Council* [2008] EWHC 2881 (Admin), [2009] JPL 939. As to the prerogative orders see PARA 688 et seq. As to declarations and injunctions see PARA 716 et seq.

10 Breach of a mandatory requirement goes to jurisdiction (see *Main v Swansea City Council* (1984) 49 P & CR 26, CA) and, where a statutory authority has acted ultra vires, any person who would be affected by the act if it were valid (see *Durayappah v Fernando* [1967] 2 AC 337, [1967] 2 All ER 152, PC) may be entitled as a matter of right to have it set aside or declared void, subject to factors such as laches, acquiescence or possibly the complainant having himself acted unlawfully: *Grunwick Processing Laboratories Ltd v Advisory, Conciliation and Arbitration Service* [1978] AC 655 at 695, [1978] 1 All ER 338 at 364, HL, per Lord Diplock; and see *Co-operative Retail Services Ltd v Taff-Ely Borough Council* (1979) 39 P & CR 223, CA; cf *R v Secretary of State for Social Services, ex p Association of Metropolitan Authorities* [1986] 1 All ER 164, [1986] 1 WLR 1. However, this clear-cut position has been doubted even in respect of mandatory requirements and it is now generally accepted that the courts have discretion: *R (on the application of Grierson) v Office of Communications* [2005] EWHC 1899 (Admin), [2005] EMLR 868, [2005] 35 LS Gaz R 41.

In the case of non-mandatory requirements it will be necessary to look broadly at the position, and especially at what prejudice the complainant has suffered in the light of a concrete state of facts and a continuing chain of events: *R v Devon and Cornwall Rent Tribunal, ex p West* (1974) 29 P & CR 316 at 320–321, DC, per Lord Widgery CJ; *R v Birmingham City Council, ex p Quietlynn Ltd* (1985) 83 LGR 461 (on appeal sub nom *R v Peterborough City Council, ex p Quietlynn Ltd* (1986) 85 LGR 249, CA); *R v Secretary of State for Education and Science, ex p Threapleton* [1988] COD 102, (1988) Times, 2 June, DC. Other factors are the nature and extent of the departure from the proper procedure, the lapse of time since the breach, and the effect upon third parties or the public generally of quashing the act or decision: *Coney v Choyce* [1975] 1 All ER 979, [1975] 1 WLR 422; *Main v Swansea City Council*.

11 *Coney v Choyce* [1975] 1 All ER 979, [1975] 1 WLR 422; *Grunwick Processing Laboratories Ltd v Advisory, Conciliation and Arbitration Service* [1978] AC 655, [1978]

1 All ER 338, HL. The question is whether Parliament can fairly be taken to have intended total invalidity: *Nina TH Wang v IRC* [1995] 1 All ER 367 at 377, [1994] 1 WLR 1286 at 1296, PC; *Charles v Judicial and Legal Services Commission* [2002] UKPC 34, [2003] 2 LRC 422; *R v Soneji* [2005] UKHL 49, [2006] 1 AC 340, [2005] 4 All ER 321; *Joachim v A-G* [2007] UKPC 6, [2007] All ER (D) 191 (Jan); *Seal v Chief Constable of South Wales Police* [2007] UKHL 31, [2007] 4 All ER 177, [2007] 1 WLR 1910; *DPP of the Virgin Islands v Penn* [2008] UKPC 29, [2009] 2 LRC 90; *Club Cruise Entertainment and Travelling Services Europe BV v Department for Transport (The Van Gogh)* [2008] EWHC 2794 (Comm), [2009] 1 All ER (Comm) 955; *JJB Sports plc v Telford and Wrekin Borough Council* [2008] EWHC 2870 (Admin), [2009] RA 33; *JN (Cameroon) v Secretary of State for the Home Department* [2009] EWCA Civ 307. See also the cases referred to in note 1.

12 One guide to this may be the language used; the word 'shall' is prima facie mandatory, but may often be construed as merely directory: *Grunwick Processing Laboratories Ltd v Advisory, Conciliation and Arbitration Service* [1978] AC 655 at 698, [1978] 1 All ER 338 at 366–367, HL, per Lord Salmon. See also *Noble v Inner London Education Authority* (1983) 82 LGR 291, CA; *R v Lambeth London Borough Council, ex p Sharp* (1984) 50 P & CR 284 (affd (1986) 55 P & CR 232, CA); *R v Registrar General, ex p Smith* [1991] 2 QB 393, [1991] 2 All ER 88, CA. Conversely, the word 'may' indicates a power and not a duty: *R v HM Inspector of Taxes, ex p Lansing Bagnall Ltd* [1986] STC 453, CA. Another indicator is whether the requirement represents a matter of substance or only of machinery: *Grunwick Processing Laboratories Ltd v Advisory, Conciliation and Arbitration Service* [1978] AC 655 at 690–691, [1978] 1 All ER 338 at 360–361, HL, per Lord Diplock; *Howard v Secretary of State for the Environment* [1975] QB 235, (1974) 27 P & CR 131, CA; *Steeples v Derbyshire County Council* [1984] 3 All ER 468 at 490–491, [1985] 1 WLR 256 at 284–285 per Webster J. It has been suggested that where a particular procedure or time-limit is not laid down in the primary legislation, then a statutory instrument may only make such a requirement directory: *Francis Jackson Developments Ltd v Hall* [1951] 2 KB 488, [1951] 2 All ER 74, CA; *R v Devon and Cornwall Rent Tribunal, ex p West* (1974) 29 P & CR 316, DC; but cf *London and Clydeside Estates Ltd v Aberdeen District Council* [1979] 3 All ER 876 at 887, [1980] 1 WLR 182 at 194, HL, per Lord Fraser of Tullybelton.

13 *Montreal Street Rly Co v Normandin* [1917] AC 170 at 175, PC; *Cullimore v Lyme Regis Corpn* [1962] 1 QB 718, [1961] 3 All ER 1008 (distinguished by *Nina TH Wang v IRC* [1995] 1 All ER 367, [1994] 1 WLR 1286, PC); *R v Lambeth London Borough Council, ex p Sharp* (1984) 50 P & CR 284; affd (1986) 55 P & CR 232, CA. As to taking account of third party interests, especially those of persons who will not easily be able to tell whether there has been compliance or not, see *Co-operative Retail Services Ltd v Taff-Ely Borough Council* (1979) 39 P & CR 223, CA; *Re T (A Minor)* [1986] Fam 160, [1986] 1 All ER 817, CA.

14 *Patchett v Leathem* (1948) 65 TLR 69; *Grunwick Processing Laboratories Ltd v Advisory, Conciliation and Arbitration Service* [1978] AC 655, [1978] 1 All ER 338, HL; *O'Reilly v Mackman* [1983] 2 AC 237, [1982] 3 All ER 1124, HL; *Noble v Inner London Education Authority* (1983) 82 LGR 291, CA; *R v Birmingham City Council, ex p Quietlynn Ltd* (1985) 83 LGR 461 at 479 per Forbes J (on appeal sub nom *R v Peterborough City Council, ex p Quietlynn Ltd* (1986) 85 LGR 249, CA).

15 *R v Pontypool Gaming Licensing Committee, ex p Risca Cinemas Ltd* [1970] 3 All ER 241, [1970] 1 WLR 1299, DC; *R v Leicester Gaming Licensing Committee, ex p Shine* [1971] 3 All ER 1082, [1971] 1 WLR 1648, CA; *Guest v Alpine Soft Drinks Ltd* [1982] ICR 110, EAT. Where there may be real room for doubt about whether a particular requirement has been complied with, then in the interests of certainty it is less likely to be held mandatory: see eg *R v St Edmundsbury Borough Council, ex p Investors in Industry Commercial Properties Ltd* [1985] 3 All ER 234, [1985] 1 WLR 1168; *Re T (A Minor)* [1986] Fam 160, [1986] 1 All ER 817, CA (giving example of adoption agency's obligation to give such advice as it considers necessary). Conversely, it may only be by holding a provision to be mandatory that certainty can be achieved: see eg *Epping Forest District Council v Essex Rendering Ltd* [1983] 1 All ER 359, [1983] 1 WLR 158, HL (local authority consent to carrying on offensive trades to be in writing).

16 *Kammins Ballrooms Co Ltd v Zenith Investments (Torquay) Ltd* [1971] AC 850, [1970] 2 All ER 871, HL; *Re St Cuthbert's, Doveridge* [1983] 1 WLR 845, Const Ct; *Cottrell v King* [2004] EWHC 397 (Ch), [2004] 2 BCLC 413.

17 See eg the Town and Country Planning Act 1990 s 288(1); and TOWN AND COUNTRY PLANNING vol 46(1) (Reissue) PARA 47. Similar wording appears in a number of statutes dealing, in particular, with powers of compulsory acquisition: see eg the Acquisition of Land Act 1981 s 23; and COMPULSORY ACQUISITION OF LAND vol 18 (2009) PARA 612. The meaning of 'substantial' prejudice is not clear: see eg *de Rothschild v Wing RDC* [1967] 1 All ER 597,

[1967] 1 WLR 470, CA; and contrast *Rayner v Stepney Corpn* [1911] 2 Ch 312 with *Re Bowman, South Shields (Thames Street) Clearance Order 1931* [1932] 2 KB 621. See also *Allen v Bagshot RDC* (1970) 69 LGR 33. But see *Gordonsdale Investments Ltd v Secretary of State for the Environment* (1971) 70 LGR 158, CA, for an illustration of the meaning of 'substantial prejudice; and see *Wilson v Secretary of State for the Environment* [1974] 1 All ER 428, [1973] 1 WLR 1083; *Hibernian Property Co Ltd v Secretary of State for the Environment* (1973) 27 P & CR 197; *North Surrey Water Co v Secretary of State for the Environment* (1976) 34 P & CR 140. Where the statute is silent on the point there is no general legal principle to the same effect, although see *Nina TH Wang v IRC* [1995] 1 All ER 367, [1994] 1 WLR 1286, PC. As to persons aggrieved see PARA 664.

18 See e g *R v Inner London Quarter Sessions, ex p D'Souza* [1970] 1 All ER 481, [1970] 1 WLR 376, DC. If the deciding body is improperly constituted its decision will normally be set aside, but if it decides by counting votes on either side, the votes of disqualified participants may simply be disallowed: see *Re Wolverhampton Borough Council's Aldermanic Election* [1962] 2 QB 460, [1961] 3 All ER 446, DC; c f *Noble v Inner London Education Authority* (1983) 82 LGR 291, CA.

19 *Agricultural, Horticultural and Forestry Industry Training Board v Aylesbury Mushrooms Ltd* [1972] 1 All ER 280, [1972] 1 WLR 190; *May v Beattie* [1927] 2 KB 353, DC; *R v Minister of Transport, ex p Skylark Motor Coach Co Ltd* (1931) 47 TLR 325, DC; *R v Manchester City Council, ex p Fulford* (1982) 81 LGR 292, DC; *R v Secretary of State for Social Services, ex p Association of Metropolitan Authorities* [1986] 1 All ER 164 at 168–169, [1986] 1 WLR 1 at 6 per Webster J; *R v Secretary of State for Transport, ex p GLC* [1986] QB 556 at 588, [1985] 3 All ER 300 at 320 per McNeill J; *Swords v Secretary of State for Communities and Local Government* [2007] EWCA Civ 795, [2007] LGR 757; *R (on the application of Edwards) v Environment Agency* [2008] UKHL 22, [2009] 1 All ER 57, [2008] 1 WLR 1587. However, see also *Secretary of State for the Home Department v E* [2007] UKHL 47, [2008] 1 AC 499, [2008] 1 All ER 699, where a failure to consult did not invalidate a control order.

20 *Bradbury v Enfield London Borough Council* [1967] 3 All ER 434, [1967] 1 WLR 1311, CA; *R v Lambeth London Borough Council, ex p Sharp* (1984) 50 P & CR 284 (affd (1986) 55 P & CR 232, CA); *R v Board of Visitors of Long Lartin Prison, ex p Cunninham* (17 May 1988, unreported), DC.

21 *Franklin v Minister of Town and Country Planning* [1948] AC 87 at 102–103, [1947] 2 All ER 289 at 296, HL, per Lord Thankerton.

22 Nevertheless, breach of a statutory duty to give reasons for a decision, though enforceable by way of mandatory order does not necessarily render the decision in question a nullity (see *Brayhead (Ascot) Ltd v Berkshire County Council* [1964] 2 QB 303, [1964] 1 All ER 149, DC) or even, of itself, constitute an error of law (*Mountview Court Properties Ltd v Devlin* (1970) 21 P & CR 689, DC); but c f *Re Poyser and Mills' Arbitration* [1964] 2 QB 467, [1963] 1 All ER 612 (substantially inadequate reasons constituted error of law); and see *Givaudan & Co Ltd v Minister of Housing and Local Government* [1966] 3 All ER 696, [1967] 1 WLR 250 (unintelligible reasons given by minister for dismissing planning appeal; held to be failure to comply with the relevant statutory requirements; decision quashed). See further PARAS 644, 646.

23 *London and Clydeside Estates Ltd v Aberdeen District Council* [1979] 3 All ER 876, [1980] 1 WLR 182, HL; *Rayner v Stepney Corpn* [1911] 2 Ch 312; *Agricultural, Horticultural and Forestry Industry Training Board v Kent* [1970] 2 QB 19, [1970] 1 All ER 304, CA. Conversely, a requirement as to the content of a notice of appeal or similar document will not normally be held mandatory so as to deny a party access to the seat of justice: *Howard v Secretary of State for the Environment* [1975] QB 235, (1974) 27 P & CR 131, CA; *Seldun Transport Services Ltd v Baker* [1978] ICR 1035, EAT; *R v Croydon Justices, ex p Lefore Holdings Ltd* [1981] 1 All ER 520, [1980] 1 WLR 1465; *Robinson v Whittle* [1980] 3 All ER 459, [1980] 1 WLR 1476, DC; *Burns International Security Services (UK) Ltd v Butt* [1983] ICR 547, EAT; *Dodd v British Telecommunications plc* [1988] ICR 116, [1988] IRLR 16, EAT; *Grimmer v KLM Cityhopper UK* [2005] IRLR 596, [2005] All ER (D) 218 (May), EAT. See also *R (on the application of Actis SA) v Secretary of State for Communities and Local Government* [2007] EWHC 2417 (Admin), [2007] All ER (D) 30 (Nov), where notice had not been given as required under EU Directive.

24 Contrast *James v Minister of Housing and Local Government* [1965] 3 All ER 602, [1966] 1 WLR 135, CA (revsd on other grounds [1968] AC 409, [1966] 3 All ER 964, HL); *R v Inspector of Taxes, ex p Clarke* [1971] 2 QB 640, [1971] 3 All ER 394, DC (affd [1974] QB 220, [1972] 1 All ER 545, CA); *London and Clydeside Estates Ltd v Aberdeen District Council* [1979] 3 All ER 876 at 894, [1980] 1 WLR 182 at 203, HL, per Lord Keith of Kinkel; *Parsons v FW Woolworth & Co Ltd* [1980] 3 All ER 456, [1980] 1 WLR 1472, DC; *R v Governor of Spring Hill Prison, ex p Sohi* [1988] 1 All ER 424, [1988] 1 WLR 596, DC (time conditions

directory); *Cullimore v Lyme Regis Corpn* [1962] 1 QB 718, [1961] 3 All ER 1008; *R v Pontypool Gaming Licensing Committee, ex p Risca Cinemas Ltd* [1970] 3 All ER 241, [1970] 1 WLR 1299, DC; *Howard v Secretary of State for the Environment* [1974] 1 All ER 644 at 647–648, 27 P & CR 131 at 135–136, CA, per Lord Denning MR (time conditions mandatory). More recently, the Privy Council upheld a failure to observe time limits where the delays were in good faith and were not lengthy: *Charles v Judicial and Legal Services Commission* [2002] UKPC 34, [2003] 2 LRC 422. See also *R (on the application of Rutter) v General Teaching Council for England* [2008] EWHC 133 (Admin) (even where the excuses for delay were threadbare, the delay did not invalidate a decision where the rules in question included scope for flexibility). Where the Civil Procedure Rules included a time limit for appealing an extradition decision with no power to extend time, a late appeal was not valid: *Mucelli v Government of Albania* [2009] UKHL 2, [2009] 3 All ER 1035, [2009] 1 WLR 276 (this decision was found in *Mitchell v Nursing and Midwifery Council* [2009] EWHC 1045 (Admin), [2009] All ER (D) 29 (Jun) to have overruled *Hume v Nursing and Midwifery Council* [2007] CSIH 53, 2007 SC 644).

25 As to sub-delegation of powers see ADMINISTRATIVE LAW vol 1(1) (2001 Reissue) PARA 31.

26 As to natural justice and the application and scope of the duty to act fairly see PARAS 629–630.

27 *O'Reilly v Mackman* [1983] 2 AC 237 at 276, [1982] 3 All ER 1124 at 1127, HL, per Lord Diplock; and see PARA 645. Cf *R v Monopolies and Mergers Commission, ex p Argyll Group plc* [1986] 2 All ER 257, [1986] 1 WLR 763, CA (unauthorised delegation; relief refused as matter of discretion).

28 The distinction has been said to have outlived its usefulness (*R v Soneji* [2005] UKHL 49 at [23], [2006] 1 AC 340 at [23], [2005] 4 All ER 321 at [23] per Lord Steyn) and as being opaque (*Sumukan Ltd v Commonwealth Secretariat* [2007] EWCA Civ 1148 at [42], [2008] 2 All ER (Comm) 175 at [42] per Sedley LJ). The modern starting point is the speech of Lord Steyn in *R v Soneji* at [14] et seq: *JJB Sports plc v Telford and Wrekin Borough Council* [2008] EWHC 2870 (Admin), [2009] RA 33.

(iii) Consultation and Written Representations

627. Consultation. A duty to consult before reaching a decision or exercising a function may be imposed by statute or may arise because of a legitimate expectation possessed by a potential consultee[1]. Legislation has over the years imposed a variety of obligations to consult, or to take similar steps[2]. It may impose a duty to ascertain the views of specific persons[3], or to give public notice of proposals and to consider any representations received[4]. Where consultees are specified by legislation, others will not normally be able to argue that they should also have been consulted[5]. Legislation may give the decision-maker some discretion as to whom he should consult[6]. In such a case, the court will not interfere with the choice of consultee unless it was based on a misinterpretation of the relevant provision, was made in bad faith or was one which no reasonable decision-maker could have made[7]. Sometimes consultation may take place through a representative organisation[8]. A duty to consult may be a continuing one[9] but it will not normally arise until there are in existence proposals sufficiently well formulated for sensible consultation about them to take place[10]. A statutory (or similar) requirement to consult will normally be construed as a mandatory one[11].

Consultation is a word which is in general use and its meaning is well understood[12]. The decision-maker must consult with an open mind[13], but he is not bound by the views expressed to him[14], nor is he normally obliged to enter into a dialogue with those who express them[15]. Those consulted must be provided with sufficient information to enable them to express their views[16], and they must be allowed sufficient time in which to do so[17].

1 An analogous duty to hear a person before making a decision which directly affects his interests (see PARA 630) may be implied either as a matter of fairness or as part of the duty to take into account relevant considerations: see *R v Secretary of State for Transport, ex p GLC* [1986] QB

556, [1985] 3 All ER 300. For examples of a legitimate expectation of consultation see *Council of Civil Service Unions v Minister for the Civil Service* [1985] AC 374, [1984] 3 All ER 935, HL; *R v Brent London Borough Council, ex p Gunning* (1985) 84 LGR 168; *R v Rochdale Metropolitan Council, ex p Schemet* (1992) 91 LGR 425, [1993] 1 FCR 306; cf *R v Secretary of State for the Environment, ex p GLC* [1985] JPL 543. As to legitimate expectation generally see PARA 649. The court may be reluctant to superimpose a wider duty to consult arising out of legitimate expectation where the relevant statute already provides for consultation in particular circumstances: *R v Hammersmith and Fulham London Borough Council, ex p Beddowes* [1987] QB 1050 at 1069, [1987] 1 All ER 369 at 382, CA, per Fox LJ. But this does not prevent a duty to consult arising from a distinct legal obligation: *R v British Coal Corpn, ex p Vardy* [1993] ICR 720, [1993] IRLR 104, DC. The scope and nature of the obligation to consult may vary according to whether it arises from statute or from legitimate expectation: *R v Sutton London Borough Council, ex p Hamlet* (26 March 1986, unreported); *R v Gwent County Council, ex p Bryant* [1988] COD 19; cf *R v Brent London Borough Council, ex p Gunning*.

Where there is no legitimate expectation of consultation, the courts have been reluctant to find an implied statutory duty to consult: see eg *Wood v Ealing London Borough Council* [1967] Ch 364, [1966] 3 All ER 514; *Bates v Lord Hailsham of St Marylebone* [1972] 3 All ER 1019 at 1024, [1972] 1 WLR 1373 at 1378 per Megarry J (doubts were expressed about this decision in *R (on the application of BAPIO Action Ltd) v Secretary of State for the Home Department* [2007] EWCA Civ 1139, [2007] All ER (D) 172 (Nov), but it is suggested that it is correct); *R v Sheffield City Council, ex p Mansfield* (1978) 37 P & CR 1, DC; *Re Findlay* [1985] AC 318 at 333–334, [1984] 3 All ER 801 at 827, HL, per Lord Scarman (not unreasonable in the circumstances not to exercise statutory power of consultation); cf *R v Secretary of State for Transport, ex p GLC* [1986] QB 556, [1985] 3 All ER 300 (in that case, perhaps exceptionally, the court held that the financial consequences of the impugned decision were such that fairness required that the applicant be given an opportunity to make representations). But in *R (on the application of BAPIO Action Ltd) v Secretary of State for the Home Department*, the court refused to find an implied legislative obligation to consult in the light of the sheer variety of express legislative obligations to consult in a range of different statutes. Further, in *R (on the application of Hillingdon London Borough Council) v Lord Chancellor* [2008] EWHC 2683 (Admin) at [38]–[45], [2009] LGR 554 at [38]–[45], the court held that an express statutory obligation to consult particular persons was 'fatal' to an implied obligation to consult others. When the function at issue is a legislative or quasi-legislative one, and Parliament has laid down an express procedure which does not include consultation, no implied obligation to consult can arise (absent a distinct legitimate expectation): see *R (on the application of BAPIO Action Ltd) v Secretary of State for the Home Department* at [58] per Maurice Kay LJ and at [63]–[65] per Rimer LJ.

The statutory context will be carefully construed by the court in order to see whether an obligation to consult has been imposed, and if so, what steps it requires; in some contexts consultation may proceed in stages: *R (on the application of Breckland District Council) v Boundary Committee* [2009] EWCA Civ 239, [2009] LGR 589.

2   See eg the following list appended to the judgment of the Court of Appeal in *R (on the application of BAPIO Action Ltd) v Secretary of State for the Home Department* [2007] EWCA Civ 1139, [2007] All ER (D) 172 (Nov).

    (1)   Repealed legislation: Local Government Act 1933 s 112; Local Government Act 1933 ss 270(1), 285; National Insurance Act 1946 s 77; National Insurance (Industrial Injuries) Act 1946 s 61(1), (2); Fire Services Act 1947 s 26(6); Police Pensions Act 1947 s 1(1); National Assistance Act 1948 s 6; Local Government Act 1958 ss 27, 41; Teachers' Superannuation Act 1967 s 15(6).

    (2)   Legislation which is still in force: Farm and Garden Chemicals Act 1967 s 1; Industrial Organisation and Development Act 1947 ss 1, 9; Local Authorities (Land) Act 1963 s 9; Local Government (Financial Provisions) Act 1963 s 12; Medicines Act 1968 ss 58(6), 78, 79(3); Public Health Act 1961 s 82(4); Public Libraries and Museums Act 1964 s 3(4); Recorded Delivery Service Act 1962 s 1(4); Trades Descriptions Act 1968 s 38(3)(a); Transport Act 1968 s 101(6).

    (3)   Introduction of duty to consult by subsequent amendment: Agriculture Act 1967 s 13; Census Act 1920 s 3; Cereals Marketing Act 1965 s 16; Trade Descriptions Act 1968 s 38(2A).

3   See eg the Employment Protection Act 1975 s 14(1) (repealed).

4   A general duty to engage in a 'notice and comment' procedure in respect of delegated legislation was contained in the Rules Publication Act 1893 s 1, but was repealed by the Statutory Instruments Act 1946 s 12(1). There may be other levels of duty to take account of the views of interested parties: see eg *R v Secretary of State for the Environment, ex p Brent London*

Borough Council [1982] QB 593 at 643–644, [1983] 3 All ER 321 at 355, DC, per Ackner LJ (having consulted earlier in decision-making process, no duty on minister to take positive steps to hear further representations, but obliged to listen to interested parties with new representations to make). Note that in *R (on the application of Hillingdon London Borough Council) v Lord Chancellor* [2008] EWHC 2683 (Admin) at [41], [2009] LGR 554 at [41], Dyson LJ left open whether, in the light of later cases (*Nottinghamshire County Council v Secretary of State for the Environment* [1986] AC 240, [1986] 1 All ER 199, HL; *Re Westminster City Council* [1986] AC 668, [1986] 2 All ER 278, HL; *R (on the application of BAPIO Action Ltd) v Secretary of State for the Home Department* [2007] EWCA Civ 1139, [2007] All ER (D) 172 (Nov); *R (on the application of Bhatt Murphy (a firm)) v Independent Assessor* [2008] EWCA Civ 755, [2008] All ER (D) 127 (Jul)), the decision in *R v Secretary of State for the Environment, ex p Brent London Borough Council* was still good law. A statutory duty to consult implies a process more organised than the informal acquisition of information by an authority: cf *R v Sheffield City Council, ex p Mansfield* (1978) 37 P & CR 1, DC; but contrast *Re the Union of the Benefices of Whippingham and East Cowes, St James* [1954] AC 245, [1954] 2 All ER 22, PC.

5   See eg *Bates v Lord Hailsham of St Marylebone* [1972] 3 All ER 1019, [1972] 1 WLR 1373; *R (on the application of Hillingdon London Borough Council v Lord Chancellor* [2008] EWHC 2683 (Admin), [2009] LGR 554. Similarly where the statute prescribes particular occasions for consultation: *Re Findlay* [1985] AC 318, [1984] 3 All ER 801, HL. Where a statute also confers a power to consult, a failure to consult will only be unlawful if it is unreasonable in the circumstances: *Re Findlay*. See also PARA 630 notes 6–8.

6   Eg by the use of words such as 'such other bodies as appear to [the minister] to be representative of the interests concerned' (Building Act 1984 s 14(3)); or 'any organisation appearing to [the Post Office] to be appropriate' (Post Office Act 1969 ss 6, 43, 88, Sch 1 para 11(1) (repealed)). See also note 2.

7   *Gallagher v Post Office* [1970] 3 All ER 712; *Agricultural, Horticultural and Forestry Industry Training Board v Aylesbury Mushrooms Ltd* [1972] 1 All ER 280, [1972] 1 WLR 190; *R v Sheffield City Council, ex p Mansfield* (1978) 37 P & CR 1, DC. See also *R v Hammersmith and Fulham London Borough Council, ex p Beddowes* [1987] QB 1050 at 1068, [1987] 1 All ER 369 at 382, CA, per Fox LJ; *R v British Coal Corpn, ex p Union of Democratic Mineworkers* [1988] ICR 36, DC; *National Coal Board v National Union of Mineworkers* [1986] ICR 736, [1986] IRLR 439. Such a discretion is like any other discretion governed by public law: see eg *R v Post Office, ex p Association of Scientific, Technical and Managerial Staff* [1981] 1 All ER 139, [1981] ICR 76, CA; *R v British Coal Corpn, ex p Union of Democratic Mineworkers*. In reviewing the exercise of the discretion the court will consider the purpose for which the duty to consult appears to have been imposed: *Gallagher v Post Office*. The court will look carefully at the language of the relevant provision in order to ascertain the scope of any duty to consult: *Grunwick Processing Laboratories Ltd v Advisory, Conciliation and Arbitration Service* [1978] AC 655, [1978] 1 All ER 338, HL. See also *R v Secretary of State for the Environment, ex p Dudley Metropolitan Borough Council* [1990] JPL 683, DC (duty to consider whether local authority ought to be heard).

The authority may also have some discretion as to the scope of the consultation: *National Employers Life Assurance Co Ltd v Advisory, Conciliation and Arbitration Service* [1979] ICR 620, [1979] IRLR 282 (ACAS not obliged to ascertain workers' opinions on matters it reasonably considered irrelevant); and see *Rollo v Minister of Town and Country Planning* [1948] 1 All ER 13, CA. However, the question whether there has been proper consultation is ultimately for the court, and is not whether a reasonable body could have regarded the consultation as sufficient: *Re NUPE and COHSE's Application* [1989] IRLR 202.

8   See eg *Council of Civil Service Unions v Minister for the Civil Service* [1985] AC 374, [1984] 3 All ER 935, HL, where it was clearly assumed that the prima facie obligation to consult could have been discharged by consulting the employees' trades unions because that was the nature of the previous practice of consultation.

9   *Re Westminster City Council* [1986] AC 668, [1986] 2 All ER 278, HL (major change in circumstances required fresh consultation); *National Coal Board v National Union of Mineworkers* [1986] ICR 736, [1986] IRLR 439. As to changes in the form of the proposals following consultation see also *Legg v Inner London Education Authority* [1972] 3 All ER 177, [1972] 1 WLR 1245; *Bates v Lord Hailsham of St Marylebone* [1972] 3 All ER 1019, [1972] 1 WLR 1373; *R v Brent London Borough Council, ex p Gunning* (1985) 84 LGR 168; *R v Hammersmith and Fulham London Borough Council, ex p Beddowes* [1987] QB 1050, [1987] 1 All ER 369, CA. Consultation may be a continuous process so that in considering the effect of one meeting it may be necessary to consider the background of earlier ones: *Fletcher v Minister of Town and Country Planning* [1947] 2 All ER 496.

10 *Short v Tower Hamlets London Borough Council* (1985) 18 HLR 171, CA; cf *R v Hammersmith and Fulham London Borough Council, ex p Beddowes* [1987] QB 1050 at 1068, [1987] 1 All ER 369 at 382, CA, per Fox LJ.

11 Eg *R v Manchester City Council, ex p Fulford* (1982) 81 LGR 292, DC; *R v Secretary of State for Social Services, ex p Association of Metropolitan Authorities* [1986] 1 All ER 164, [1986] 1 WLR 1; *R v British Railways Board, ex p Bradford Metropolitan City Council* (1987) Times, 8 December, CA (irrelevant whether proposals would cause significant hardship). See also *Grunwick Processing Laboratories Ltd v Advisory, Conciliation and Arbitration Service* [1978] AC 655, [1978] 1 All ER 338, HL; *R v Secretary of State for Wales, ex p South Glamorgan County Council* [1988] COD 104 (technical defects did not deprive minister of jurisdiction); and see *R v Governors of Small Heath School, ex p Birmingham City Council* (1989) Times, 31 May, DC; *Re NUPE and COHSE's Application* [1989] IRLR 202. An extremely strict approach to the question of whether a failed attempt to consult a necessary party was fatal was taken in *Agricultural, Horticultural and Forestry Industry Training Board v Aylesbury Mushrooms Ltd* [1972] 1 All ER 280, [1972] 1 WLR 190; cf *Fletcher v Minister of Town and Country Planning* [1947] 2 All ER 496 (minister could not be expected to inquire into whether those attending the meeting on behalf of consultee local authorities had the authority to express the views which they did). An authority is not precluded from reaching a decision if the consultee has no views or is unwilling to express them: *Port Louis Corpn v A-G of Mauritius* [1965] AC 1111, [1965] 3 WLR 67, PC; cf *R v North East Thames Regional Health Authority, ex p de Groot* (1988) Times, 16 April.

As to the discretion whether to hold a public inquiry see *R v Secretary of State for the Environment, ex p Binney* (1983) Times, 8 October; cf *R v Secretary of State for Transport, ex p GLC* (1985) Times, 31 October, CA. See also *R v Secretary of State for the Environment, ex p Fielder Estates (Canvey) Ltd* (1988) 57 P & CR 424; *R v Secretary of State for the Environment, ex p Dudley Metropolitan Borough Council* [1990] JPL 683, DC; *R (on the application of Smith) v North Eastern Derbyshire Primary Care Trust* [2006] EWCA Civ 1291, [2006] 1 WLR 3315.

A failure to comply with an obligation to consult will lead to the quashing of a decision unless the decision inevitably would have been the same: see *R (on the application of Smith) v North Eastern Derbyshire Primary Care Trust* at [10] per May LJ, using a synthesis of *R v Chief Constable of the Thames Valley Police, ex p Cotton* [1990] IRLR 344 at 352 per Bingham LJ, *Simplex GE (Holdings) Ltd v Secretary of State for the Environment* [1988] JPL 809, 57 P & CR 306, CA, and *Secretary of State for the Environment, ex p Brent London Borough Council* [1982] QB 593 at 646, [1983] 3 All ER 321 at 356, DC, per Ackner LJ.

12 *Fletcher v Minister of Town and Country Planning* [1947] 2 All ER 496 at 500 per Morris J. The usual requirements are said to be as formulated by Mr Sedley QC, as he then was, in argument, in *R v Brent London Borough Council, ex p Gunning* (1985) 84 LGR 168 at 189, and adopted by Hodgson J in his judgment. They have been approved on many occasions since; for example in *R (on the application of Wainwright) v Richmond upon Thames London Borough Council* [2001] EWCA Civ 2062 at [9], [2001] All ER (D) 422 (Dec) at [9] per Clark LJ. They are: 'First, that the consultation must be at a time when proposals are still at a formative stage. Second, that the proposer must give sufficient reasons for any proposal to permit of intelligent consideration and response. Third, that adequate time must be given for consideration and response, and finally, fourth that the product of consultation must be conscientiously taken into account in finalising any statutory proposals'.

The nature and object of consultation must be related to the circumstances which call for it: *Port Louis Corpn v A-G of Mauritius* [1965] AC 1111, [1965] 3 WLR 67, PC. However, the essence of the concept is that the decision-maker supplies the consultees with sufficient information to enable them to tender advice, and gives them sufficient opportunity to tender that advice: *Rollo v Minister of Town and Country Planning* [1948] 1 All ER 13, CA; *R v Secretary of State for Social Services, ex p AMA* [1986] 1 All ER 164, [1986] 1 WLR 1 (distinguished in *Desmond v Bromley London Borough Council* (1995) 28 HLR 518); *R v Gwent County Council, ex p Bryant* [1988] COD 19; *R v Lambeth London Borough Council, ex p N* [1996] ELR 299; *R v Secretary of State for Trade and Industry, ex p UNISON* [1996] ICR 1003, [1996] IRLR 438. See also *Re the Union of the Benefices of Whippingham and East Cowes, St James* [1954] AC 245, [1954] 2 All ER 22, PC; *R (on the application of Breckland District Council) v Boundary Committee* [2009] EWCA Civ 239, [2009] LGR 589.

13 *Rollo v Minister of Town and Country Planning* [1947] 2 All ER 488; affd [1948] 1 All ER 13, CA. See also *R v Brighton Rent Officers, ex p Elliott* (1975) 29 P & CR 456, DC. But it is not wrong for the authority to have formed a provisional view (which may indeed be necessary before there can be proposals upon which to consult): *R v Hillingdon Health Authority, ex p Goodwin* [1984] ICR 800; *Nichol v Gateshead Metropolitan Borough Council* (1988)

87 LGR 435, CA. See also *R v Secretary of State for the Environment, ex p Brent London Borough Council* [1982] QB 593 at 643, [1983] 3 All ER 321 at 355, DC, per Ackner LJ (listening with mind 'ajar'); and c f *R v City of London Corpn, ex p Allan* (1980) 79 LGR 223 (not wrong in principle to take account of draft local plan and determine planning applications pending outcome of inquiry into plan).

14 This would be an unlawful fettering of discretion; c f *H Lavender & Son v Minister of Housing and Local Government* [1970] 3 All ER 871, [1970] 1 WLR 1231; and see PARA 620. See also *Harvey v Strathclyde Regional Council* 1989 SLT 612, HL (duty to take account of parents' wishes; no presumption of breach where decision at variance with those wishes). But a failure to pay any heed to the views expressed in consultation might be impugned on the ground of failure to take account of relevant considerations: see PARA 623. See also *R v Waltham Forest London Borough Council, ex p Baxter* [1988] RVR 6 (affd [1988] QB 419, [1987] 3 All ER 671, CA); *R (on the application of Island Farm Development Ltd) v Bridgend County Borough Council* [2006] EWHC 2189 (Admin), [2007] LGR 60; *R (on the application of Lewis) v Persimmon Homes Teeside Ltd* [2008] EWCA Civ 746, sub nom *R (on the application of Lewis) v Redcar and Cleveland Borough Council* [2009] 1 WLR 83 (weight to be given to party political considerations).

15 Cf *Port Louis Corpn v A-G of Mauritius* [1965] AC 1111, [1965] 3 WLR 67, PC (person being consulted not entitled to demand assurances about solutions to problems foreseen with proposals); *Elphick v Church Comrs* [1974] AC 562, [1974] 2 WLR 756, PC; *R v Islington London Borough Council, ex p East* [1996] ELR 74 (no duty to consult further where proposals altered as a result of responses to consultation exercise); *R v Secretary of State for Wales, ex p Williams* [1996] COD 127, [1997] ELR 100 (no duty to extend consultation period).

16 *Rollo v Minister of Town and Country Planning* [1948] 1 All ER 13, CA; *Port Louis Corpn v A-G of Mauritius* [1965] AC 1111, [1965] 3 WLR 67, PC; *R v Brent London Borough Council, ex p Gunning* (1985) 84 LGR 168; *R v Secretary of State for Social Services, ex p Association of Metropolitan Authorities* [1986] 1 All ER 164, [1986] 1 WLR 1 (not necessary to provide ample information, but at least enough to enable the purpose of the consultation to be fulfilled); *Re NUPE and COHSE's Application* [1989] IRLR 202. See also *Legg v Inner London Education Authority* [1972] 3 All ER 177, [1972] 1 WLR 1245; *R v Secretary of State for the Environment, ex p Hammersmith and Fulham London Borough Council* (1985) Times, 18 May; *R v Tunbridge Wells Health Authority, ex p Goodridge* (1988) Times, 21 May; and c f *Powley v Advisory, Conciliation and Arbitration Service* [1978] ICR 123, [1977] IRLR 190; *Elphick v Church Comrs* [1974] AC 562, [1974] 2 WLR 756, PC (not necessary to cite detailed arguments in support of scheme proposed). But c f *R (on the application of Eisai Ltd) v National Institute for Health and Clinical Excellence* [2008] EWCA Civ 438, 101 BMLR 26 (NICE's failure when consulting on its guidance to provide Eisai Ltd with a fully executable version of its economic model led to the quashing of the guidance).

17 See e g *R v Brent London Borough Council, ex p Gunning* (1985) 84 LGR 168; *Transport and General Workers' Union v Ledbury Preserves (1928) Ltd* [1986] ICR 855, [1985] IRLR 412, EAT. The scale, complexity and importance of the subject matter are factors in assessing how much time is required: see e g *R v Brent London Borough Council, ex p Gunning*; *Lee v Secretary of State for Education and Science* (1967) 66 LGR 211. The court will make allowances where decisions are required to be taken urgently, and will assess the time allowed by reference to the facts as they appeared to the authority at the time: *R v Secretary of State for Social Services, ex p Association of Metropolitan Authorities* [1986] 1 All ER 164, [1986] 1 WLR 1. See also *R v Tunbridge Wells Health Authority, ex p Goodridge* (1988) Times, 21 May. It has been held that no degree of urgency can absolve the authority from the obligation to consult at all: *R v Secretary of State for Social Services, ex p Association of Metropolitan Authorities*; but that was a case about a statutory duty rather than a legitimate expectation of consultation; c f *R v Powys County Council, ex p Horner* [1989] Fam Law 320. An authority cannot rely upon urgency caused by its own earlier procedural errors: *Lee v Secretary of State for Education and Science*. If the original time-limit set is very short, the authority may be unreasonable if it refuses a request for an extension: *Port Louis Corpn v A-G of Mauritius* [1965] AC 1111, [1965] 3 WLR 67, PC. Cf *Trent Strategic Health Authority v Jain* [2009] UKHL 4, [2009] 1 AC 853, [2009] 1 All ER 957.

   If a statutory timetable is complied with, it is not for the court to say that too little time has been allowed: *R v Lambeth London Borough Council, ex p Sharp* (1984) 50 P & CR 284 at 298 per Croom-Johnson LJ.

628. Written representations. A statutory duty to consult is usually interpreted by the courts as obliging an authority to give consultees an opportunity to submit written representations. Moreover, in some situations a right to submit written representations has also been regarded as sufficient to satisfy requirements of procedural fairness where there is a common law entitlement to be heard[1]. Examples have included first applications for licences[2], some issues relating to prisoners[3], and some matters concerning grievances over which the courts do not have jurisdiction[4]. The decisions of the courts show, however, that a decision-maker should always consider whether the case can be dealt with fairly on the basis of written representations alone. There is no universal test for deciding when written representations, rather than an oral hearing, will suffice. In practice, where this line is drawn will depend on the circumstances in which the decision is taken, the nature of the interest at stake, and the nature of the decision to be taken[5].

1   *Local Government Board v Arlidge* [1915] AC 120, HL (appeal to local government board from decision of local authority; appellant, who had appeared at public local inquiry, not entitled to disclosure of report made to the board by inspector at inquiry, or to present oral argument to the board; opportunity to appear at inquiry and thereafter to make written representations to board sufficient). However, if an inspector relies on matters not canvassed at an inquiry, he must give the parties an opportunity to comment and adduce evidence before reaching his conclusions: *Fairmount Investments Ltd v Secretary of State for the Environment* [1976] 2 All ER 865, [1976] 1 WLR 1255, HL; *Edward Ware New Homes Ltd v Secretary of State for the Local Government, Transport and the Regions* [2003] EWCA Civ 566, 147 Sol Jo LB 509; *Kavanagh v Chief Constable of Devon and Cornwall* [1974] QB 624 (decision of Crown Court on an administrative appeal deriving from the former administrative jurisdiction of quarter sessions may be based on the same material as influenced the primary decision-maker, including hearsay evidence). As to natural justice see PARA 629 et seq.
2   *R v Huntingdon District Council, ex p Cowan* [1984] 1 All ER 58, [1984] 1 WLR 501 (an oral hearing is not necessary in every case, provided the applicant is given the gist of relevant objections so that he has the opportunity to deal with them).
3   *R v Secretary of State for the Home Department, ex p Doody* [1994] 1 AC 531, sub nom *Doody v Secretary of State for the Home Department* [1993] 3 All ER 92, HL; *R v Secretary of State for the Home Department, ex p McCartney* [1994] COD 528, CA; *R v Secretary of State for the Home Department, ex p Duggan* [1994] 3 All ER 277; *R (on the application of Lord) v Secretary of State for the Home Department* [2003] EWHC 2073 (Admin).
4   *R v Army Board of the Defence Council, ex p Anderson* [1992] QB 169, [1991] 3 All ER 375, DC (investigation by army board of a complaint of racial discrimination by a soldier; board acted unlawfully, among other things, by adopting a general rule that an oral hearing was never necessary); *R v Department of Health, ex p Gandhi* [1991] 4 All ER 547, [1991] 1 WLR 1053, DC (oral hearing and disclosure may be necessary to deal fairly with complaint of racial discrimination); *R (on the application of Hammond) v Secretary of State for the Home Department* [2005] UKHL 69, [2006] 1 AC 603, [2006] 1 All ER 219; *R (on the application of Smith) v Parole Board* [2005] UKHL 1, [2005] 1 All ER 755, [2005] 1 WLR 350; cf *R (on the application of Ewing) v Department for Constitutional Affairs* [2006] EWHC 504 (Admin), [2006] 2 All ER 993 (civil restraint order).
5   See *Lloyd v McMahon* [1987] AC 625 (written representations only, and failure to offer an oral hearing, but none of the parties concerned asked for an oral hearing; note that the auditor in *Porter v Magill* [2001] UKHL 67, [2002] 2 AC 357, [2002] 1 All ER 465, offered, and held, oral hearings); *R v Secretary of State for Transport, ex p Pegasus Holidays (London) Ltd* [1989] 2 All ER 481, [1988] 1 WLR 990 (when a provisional decision is made in an emergency, less may be required as to the content of a hearing); *R v Secretary of State for Transport, ex p Richmond-upon-Thames London Borough Council (No 4)* [1996] 4 All ER 903, [1996] 1 WLR 1460, CA.

(iv) Natural Justice

A. IN GENERAL

629. Natural justice and fairness. There are two basic rules of natural justice. First, that no man is to be a judge in his own cause (*nemo judex in causa sua*).

Second, that no man is to be condemned unheard (*audi alteram partem*)[1]. These rules govern the way in which a decision is taken; they are not concerned with its correctness[2].

The rules of natural justice must be observed by courts, tribunals, arbitrators[3] and all those having the duty to act judicially[4], save where their application is excluded expressly[5] or by necessary implication[6], or by reason of other special circumstances[7]. However, this obligation is not confined to those acting in overtly judicial or quasi-judicial capacities[8]. The presumption is that when any administrative decision is taken, it is to be taken fairly. The distinction which was formerly drawn between the determination of rights (where the obligation applied) and the determination of privileges (where it did not) is defunct[9]. The courts now tend to speak in terms of procedural fairness or of a general duty to act fairly[10]. The erosion of these distinctions means that in some circumstances it is difficult to determine when the duty to act fairly applies, and the content of that duty. Indeed, whether a decision is 'administrative' or 'quasi-judicial', or whether the subject matter of the decision may be regarded as a 'right' or a 'privilege' may well be relevant in order to determine what fairness requires in any particular situation[11]. The duty to act fairly is highly flexible[12]. Although these two basic rules must normally, though not invariably[13], be observed, the precise procedure to be followed in a given situation depends on the subject matter of the decision or adjudication and on all the circumstances of the case[14].

Further, it is now clear that a person may complain of a breach of natural justice even though it is not the decision-making body itself which is at fault[15], although the court will not intervene where the fault is that of the person himself[16].

1 There is some authority to the effect that excessive delay in taking proceedings against a person amounts to a breach of natural justice: see *Bell v DPP* [1985] AC 937, [1985] 2 All ER 585, PC (criminal proceedings; common law jurisdiction to prevent a trial which is oppressive due to undue delay); *Collector of Land Revenue, South West District Penang v Kam Gin Paik* [1986] 1 WLR 412, PC (delay in holding inquiry to assess compensation after publication of decision compulsorily to acquire land). In *Porter v Magill* [2001] UKHL 67 at [106]–[115], [2002] 2 AC 357 at [106]–[115], [2002] 1 All ER 465 at [106]–[115] Lord Hope assumed that the common law and Convention produced the same result, namely that a person is entitled to a determination of his civil rights, or of a criminal charge, within a reasonable time; it is not necessary to show that any delay has caused prejudice. See also *Simpsons Motor Sales (London) Ltd v Hendon Corpn* [1963] Ch 57, [1962] 3 All ER 75, CA (affd [1964] AC 1088, [1963] 2 All ER 484, HL); *Abbott v A-G of Trinidad and Tobago* [1979] 1 WLR 1342, PC; *Re Preston* [1985] AC 835 at 869–871, [1985] 2 All ER 327 at 343–344, HL, per Lord Templeman; cf also *Engineers' and Managers' Association v Advisory, Conciliation and Arbitration Service and United Kingdom Association of Professional Engineers* [1980] 1 All ER 896, [1980] 1 WLR 302, HL; *Royal Society for the Prevention of Cruelty to Animals v Cruden* [1986] ICR 205, EAT (dismissal unfair because of six-month delay in starting disciplinary procedure); cf *Virdi v Law Society* [2009] EWHC 918 (Admin), [2009] All ER (D) 106 (Nov). But the courts ought not to create artificial limitation periods in criminal proceedings (*R v Grays Justices, ex p Graham* [1982] QB 1239, [1982] 3 All ER 653, DC); and a person cannot complain about delay caused by, for example, his own exercise of a right to appeal (*De Freitas v Benny* [1976] AC 239, [1975] 3 WLR 388, PC; *Abbott v A-G of Trinidad and Tobago*; *Grant v DPP* [1982] AC 190, [1981] 3 WLR 352, PC). See also *R v Brentford Justices, ex p Wong* [1981] QB 445, [1981] 1 All ER 884, DC; *R v Oxford City Justices, ex p Smith* [1982] RTR 201, DC; *R v Derby Crown Court, ex p Brooks* (1984) 80 Cr App Rep 164; *R v Chief Constable of the Merseyside Police, ex p Calveley* [1986] QB 424, [1986] 1 All ER 257, CA; *R v Governor of Pentonville Prison, ex p Parekh* (1988) Times, 19 May, DC.

As to adjourning civil proceedings or domestic disciplinary proceedings which might prejudice a forthcoming criminal trial see *Jefferson Ltd v Bhetcha* [1979] 2 All ER 1108, [1979] 1 WLR 898, CA; *R v British Broadcasting Corpn, ex p Lavelle* [1983] 1 All ER 241, [1983] 1 WLR 23; *R v Exeter Juvenile Court, ex p DLH* [1988] FCR 474, [1988] 2 FLR 214, considered in *Re W (children)* [2009] EWCA Civ 644, [2009] 3 FCR 1. Cf for concurrent sets of civil proceedings, *R v Institute of Chartered Accountants in England and Wales, ex p Brindle* [1994] BCC 297, CA; *R (on the application of Arthurworry) v Haringey London Borough Council* [2001] EWHC Admin 698, [2002] ICR 279; *R (on the application of Ranson) v Institute of Actuaries* [2004] EWHC 3087 (Admin), [2004] All ER (D) 411 (Oct). As to the rule *audi alteram partem* see PARA 639.

2   *Chief Constable of North Wales Police v Evans* [1982] 3 All ER 141, [1982] 1 WLR 1155, HL.

3   See eg *Re Brook, Delcomyn and Badart* (1864) 16 CBNS 403; *Modern Engineering (Bristol) Ltd v C Miskin & Son Ltd* [1981] 1 Lloyd's Rep 135, CA; *Fox v PG Wellfair Ltd* [1981] 2 Lloyd's Rep 514, CA. The particular nature of an arbitrator's functions may, however (depending on the terms of his appointment), be inconsistent with a duty to observe natural justice: *Hounslow London Borough Council v Twickenham Garden Developments Ltd* [1971] Ch 233 at 260, [1970] 3 All ER 326 at 348 per Megarry J.

4   See *Re Pollard* (1868) LR 2 PC 106; *Fisher v Keane* (1878) 11 ChD 353; *Labouchere v Earl of Wharncliffe* (1879) 13 ChD 346; *Dawkins v Antrobus* (1881) 17 ChD 615 at 630, CA, per James LJ; *Baird v Wells* (1890) 44 ChD 661 at 670, CA, per Stirling J; *Hope v I'Anson and Weatherby* (1901) 18 TLR 201 at 205, CA, per Stirling LJ; *Abbott v Sullivan* [1952] 1 KB 189 at 195, [1952] 1 All ER 226 at 230, CA, per Sir Raymond Evershed MR; *R v Hull Prison Board of Visitors, ex p St Germain (No 2)* [1979] 3 All ER 545 at 551–552, [1979] 1 WLR 1401 at 1408, DC, per Geoffrey Lane LJ. See further PARA 630.

5   But clear words will be necessary for this to be achieved: see PARA 641 note 8.

6   Eg where an exhaustive procedural code has been prescribed by statute: *Wiseman v Borneman* [1971] AC 297, [1969] 3 All ER 275, HL; *R v Secretary of State for the Environment, ex p Hammersmith and Fulham London Borough Council* [1991] 1 AC 521 at 599, [1990] 3 All ER 589 at 637, HL, per Lord Donaldson of Lymington MR; *R v Huntingdon District Council, ex p Cowan* [1984] 1 All ER 58, [1984] 1 WLR 501; *R v Chichester Justices, ex p Collins* [1982] 1 All ER 1000, [1982] 1 WLR 334, DC (clear words necessary to require a second hearing; overruled by *Re Wilson* [1985] AC 750, sub nom *Wilson v Colchester Justices* [1985] 2 All ER 97, HL (power capable of being exercised from time to time)); but cf *R v Secretary of State for the Home Department, ex p Fayed* [1997] 1 All ER 228, [1998] 1 WLR 763 (where rules of natural justice were added to an unparticularised statutory scheme); *R v Birmingham City Council, ex p Ferrero* [1993] 1 All ER 530. In principle, willingness or otherwise to add to statutory schemes will depend on the extent to which the scheme appears to be comprehensive, the nature of the requirement it is said should be implied, and the overall requirements of the duty of fairness in the circumstances of the situation.

In some situations disclosure of relevant information to an interested party would be contrary to the public interest: see *Collymore v A-G* [1970] AC 538, [1969] 2 All ER 1207, PC. And see, for the effect of the Convention for the Protection of Human Rights and Fundamental Freedoms (Rome, 4 November 1950; TS 71 (1953) Cmd 8969) art 6, the many cases about non-derogating control orders: eg *Secretary of State for the Home Department v AF* [2009] UKHL 28, [2009] 3 All ER 643; *Secretary of State for the Home Department v MB* [2007] UKHL 46, [2008] 1 AC 440, [2008] 1 All ER 657. See further PARA 639.

7   Eg necessity, urgency or national security: see PARA 639.

8   See eg *Furnell v Whangerei High Schools Board* [1973] AC 660 at 679, [1973] 1 All ER 400 at 411–412, PC; *R v Commission for Racial Equality, ex p Cottrell and Rothon* [1980] 3 All ER 265 at 270–271, [1980] 1 WLR 1580 at 1587, DC, per Lord Lane CJ; *Rea v Minister of Transport* (1984) 48 P & CR 239, [1984] RVR 180, CA. The first two decisions can perhaps be explained on the basis that they concerned preliminary investigations; cf *R (on the application of Clegg) v Secretary of State for Trade and Industry* [2002] EWCA Civ 519, [2002] All ER (D) 114 (Apr); and see the tri-partite analysis in *Norwest Holst Ltd v Secretary of State for Trade* [1978] Ch 201 at 228, [1978] 3 All ER 280 at 296, CA, per Geoffrey Lane LJ.

9   See *R v Gaming Board for Great Britain, ex p Benaim and Khaida* [1970] 2 QB 417 at 430, [1970] 2 All ER 528 at 533, CA, per Lord Denning MR.

10 See eg *Re HK* [1967] 2 QB 617, [1967] 1 All ER 226, DC; *Re Pergamon Press Ltd* [1971] Ch 388, [1970] 3 All ER 535, CA; *Breen v Amalgamated Engineering Union* [1971] 2 QB 175, [1971] 1 All ER 1148, CA; *Pearlberg v Varty (Inspector of Taxes)* [1972] 2 All ER 6, [1972] 1 WLR 534, HL; *Furnell v Whangerei High Schools Board* [1973] AC 660 at 679, [1973] 1 All ER 400 at 411–412, PC; *McInnes v Onslow Fane* [1978] 3 All ER 211 at 218, [1978] 1 WLR 1520 at 1530 per Megarry V-C; *R v Commission for Racial Equality, ex p Cottrell and Rothon* [1980] 3 All ER 265 at 270–271, [1980] 1 WLR 1580 at 1586, DC, per Lord Lane CJ; *O'Reilly v Mackman* [1983] 2 AC 237 at 275, [1982] 3 All ER 1124 at 1126–1127, HL, per Lord Diplock; *Council of Civil Service Unions v Minister for the Civil Service* [1985] AC 374 at 411, [1984] 3 All ER 935 at 951, HL, per Lord Diplock; *R v Panel on Take-overs and Mergers, ex p Datafin plc* [1987] QB 815 at 842, [1987] 1 All ER 564 at 579–580, CA, per Sir John

Donaldson MR; *Gray v Marlborough College* [2006] EWCA Civ 1262, [2006] ELR 516; *R (on the application of Smith) v Parole Board* [2005] UKHL 1, [2005] 1 All ER 755; cf *R (on the application of X) v Chief Constable of the West Midlands Police* [2004] EWCA Civ 1068, [2005] 1 All ER 610, [2005] 1 WLR 65; *R (on the application of Brooks) v Parole Board* [2004] EWCA Civ 80, [2004] All ER (D) 142 (Feb).

11 See eg *Wiseman v Borneman* [1971] AC 297, [1969] 3 All ER 275; *McInnes v Onslow-Fane* [1978] 3 All ER 211, [1978] 1 WLR 1520; *Lloyd v McMahon* [1987] AC 625 at 702, [1987] 1 All ER 1118 at 1160–1161, HL, per Lord Bridge of Harwich; *R v Secretary of State for the Home Department, ex p Doody* [1994] 1 AC 531, sub nom *Doody v Secretary of State for the Home Department* [1993] 3 All ER 92, HL; *Rea v Minister of Transport* (1982) 47 P & CR 207, CA; *Abbey Mine Ltd v Coal Authority* [2008] EWCA Civ 353, [2008] All ER (D) 228 (Apr); cf *R v Barnsley Metropolitan District Council, ex p Hook* [1976] 3 All ER 452, [1976] 1 WLR 1052, CA. In general, when determining what the content of the obligation should be in any particular case, the courts have had regard both to the individual interest at stake, and the effect of the obligation on the decision-making process.

12 See eg *Wiseman v Borneman* [1971] AC 297, [1969] 3 All ER 275, HL; *Furnell v Whangerei High Schools Board* [1973] AC 660 at 679, [1973] 1 All ER 400 at 411–412, PC; *Payne v Lord Harris of Greenwich* [1981] 2 All ER 842 at 844–845, [1981] 1 WLR 754 at 757, CA, per Lord Denning MR (note that *Payne v Lord Harris of Greenwich* has been overruled by *R v Secretary of State for the Home Department, ex p Doody* [1994] 1 AC 531, sub nom *Doody v Secretary of State for the Home Department* [1993] 3 All ER 92, HL, but this general dictum is unaffected); *R v Monopolies and Mergers Commission, ex p Matthew Brown plc* [1987] 1 All ER 463 at 467–468, [1987] 1 WLR 1235 at 1240 per Macpherson J; *R v Secretary of State for Transport, ex p Pegasus Holidays (London) Ltd* [1989] 2 All ER 481 at 489–490, [1988] 1 WLR 990 at 1000 per Schiemann J (comparatively little may be required in the case of a provisional decision made in an emergency).

13 If one of the rules of natural justice applies then normally both will apply, but this is not always the case: see eg *McInnes v Onslow-Fane* [1978] 3 All ER 211, [1978] 1 WLR 1520; *R v Aston University, ex p Roffey* [1969] 2 QB 538 at 552 per Donaldson J; *Hounslow London Borough Council v Twickenham Garden Developments* [1971] Ch 233 at 259 per Megarry J; *Leary v National Union of Vehicle Builders* [1971] Ch 34 at 52 per Megarry J (right to unbiased tribunal, but not to a hearing); *R v Secretary of State for Trade, ex p Perestrello* [1981] QB 19, [1980] 3 All ER 28 (rule against bias yielded to necessity when legislation envisaged that inspectors would be both prosecutor and judge, although consider now the application of the Convention for the Protection of Human Rights and Fundamental Freedoms (Rome, 4 November 1950; TS 71 (1953) Cmd 8969) art 6 (right to a fair trial) (see PARAS 652–654)); and see *R (on the application of Haase) v Independent Adjudicator* [2008] EWCA Civ 1089, [2009] 2 WLR 1004, for whether the Convention for the Protection of Human Rights and Fundamental Freedoms art 6 requires an independent prosecutor. As to the rule against bias see PARA 631 et seq. As to necessity see PARA 636. See also *Norwest Holst Ltd v Secretary of State for Trade* [1978] Ch 201 at 228, [1978] 3 All ER 280 at 296, CA, per Geoffrey Lane LJ.

14 See eg *Russell v Duke of Norfolk* [1949] 1 All ER 109; *Furnell v Whangerei High Schools Board* [1973] AC 660 at 679, [1973] 1 All ER 400 at 411–412, PC; *Bushell v Secretary of State for the Environment* [1981] AC 75 at 95, [1980] 2 All ER 608 at 612–613, HL, per Lord Diplock; *R (on the application of Edwards) v Environment Agency* [2008] UKHL 22, [2009] 1 All ER 57. In the case of a less formal tribunal or of an administrative body with a discretion to regulate its own procedure, the courts have on occasion taken the view that they should intervene only if the procedure adopted is so unfair that no reasonable tribunal or body could have adopted it: see eg *R v Monopolies and Mergers Commission, ex p Matthew Brown plc* [1987] 1 All ER 463 at 469, [1987] 1 WLR 1235 at 1242 per Macpherson J (doubted in *R v Monopolies and Mergers Commission, ex p Stagecoach* (1996) Times, 23 July, per Collins J); *R v Bedfordshire County Council, ex p C* (1986) 85 LGR 218 at 223 per Ewbank J. See also *R v Boundary Commission for England, ex p Foot* [1983] QB 600 at 633, [1983] 1 All ER 1099 at 1115–1116, CA, per Sir John Donaldson MR; *R v Secretary of State for the Environment, ex p Fielder Estates (Canvey) Ltd* (1988) 57 P & CR 424; cf *R v Panel on Take-overs and Mergers, ex p Guinness plc* [1990] 1 QB 146 at 183–184, 188–189, [1989] 1 All ER 509 at 531, 535–534, CA, per Lloyd LJ and at 193–194 and 538–539 per Woolf LJ; cf *R v South West London Supplementary Benefits Appeal Tribunal, ex p Bullen* (1976) 120 Sol Jo 437, DC; applied in *R v Birmingham City Council, ex p Quietlynn Ltd* (1985) 83 LGR 461 at 493 per Forbes J; on appeal sub nom *R v Peterborough City Council, ex p Quietlynn Ltd* (1986) 85 LGR 249, CA.

Other tests have also been suggested: did the complainant have 'a fair crack of the whip'? (*Fairmount Investments Ltd v Secretary of State for the Environment* [1976] 2 All ER 865 at

874, [1976] 1 WLR 1255 at 1266, HL, per Lord Russell of Killowen); would the complainant have gone away feeling 'I've not had a fair deal'? (*Performance Cars Ltd v Secretary of State for the Environment* (1977) 34 P & CR 92 at 97, CA, per Lord Denning MR); and would a reasonable person viewing the matter objectively and knowing all the facts consider that there was a risk that injustice or unfairness had resulted? (*Lake District Special Planning Board v Secretary of State for the Environment* [1975] JPL 220; applied in *Nicholson v Secretary of State for Energy* (1977) 76 LGR 693 at 700 per Sir Douglas Frank QC, pointing out that the views of a reasonable person as to what is required of a particular procedure will vary according to the changing climate of public opinion; in this case cross examination of witnesses should have been permitted).

Ultimately, however, the above formulations all amount to the same thing. Regardless of the formulation applied, it is the court which should decide for itself whether or not the requirements of procedural fairness have been satisfied, rather than apply a *Wednesbury* approach: *R v Panel on Take-overs and Mergers, ex p Guinness plc* [1990] 1 QB 146, [1989] 1 All ER 509; *R v Monopolies and Mergers Commission, ex p Stagecoach* (1996) Times, 23 July (although the decision-maker's own view as to what was fair would be a relevant consideration for the court to take into account when forming its own view). As to the *Wednesbury* approach see PARA 617.

15 Although in the following cases the actual decision-maker was not at fault, fault did lie with others intimately connected with the decision-making process (usually a prosecutor or quasi-prosecutor). Note also that many of the cases which follow arose in a criminal context: *R v Leyland Justices, ex p Hawthorn* [1979] QB 283, [1979] 1 All ER 209, DC; *R v Bolton Justices, ex p Scally* [1991] 1 QB 537, [1991] 2 All ER 619 (prosecution failure to disclose existence of witnesses, documents or evidence); *R v Blundeston Prison Board of Visitors, ex p Fox-Taylor* [1982] 1 All ER 646 (proceedings before prison visitors; prison authorities at fault); *R v Crown Court at Knightsbridge, ex p Goonatilleke* [1986] QB 1, [1985] 2 All ER 498, DC (court misled by prosecution witness effectively acting as prosecutor); *Bagga Khan v Secretary of State for the Home Department* [1987] Imm AR 543, CA. See also *R v Immigration Appeal Tribunal, ex p Enwia* [1983] 2 All ER 1045 at 1052–1053, [1984] 1 WLR 117 at 130, CA, per Stephenson LJ (though it is open to doubt whether this reasoning survives *R v Secretary of State for the Home Department, ex p Al-Mehdawi* [1990] 1 AC 876, [1989] 3 All ER 843, HL); *R v Crown Court at Liverpool, ex p Roberts* [1986] Crim LR 622, DC; and cf *R v Wells Street Justices, ex p Collett* [1981] RTR 272 (unclear if prosecution at fault: quashing order refused). See, however, *Dennis v UKCCN* (1993) 13 BMLR 146 (decision-maker not required to make applicant's case for him). As to quashing orders see PARA 693 et seq.

16 *R v Secretary of State for the Home Department, ex p Al-Mehdawi* [1990] 1 AC 876, [1989] 3 All ER 843, HL (negligence of own solicitors); distinguished, sed quaere, in *FP (Iran) v Secretary of State for the Home Department* [2007] EWCA Civ 13, [2007] Imm AR 450. Previous decisions had left open the possibility that relief could be granted: *R v Immigration Appeal Tribunal, ex p Enwia* [1983] 2 All ER 1045 at 1052–1053, [1984] 1 WLR 117 at 130, CA, per Stephenson LJ; *R v Diggines, ex p Rahmani* [1985] QB 1109, [1985] 1 All ER 1073, CA (affd on other grounds sub nom *Rahmani v Diggines* [1986] AC 475, [1986] 1 All ER 921, HL), but it was made clear that rarely if ever would the court's discretion be exercised in the applicant's favour. So if the claimant (or his agent) is at fault, he will not be entitled to any remedy, unless there is also material fault by the decision-maker or someone closely associated with him. For cases where the effect of fault by the claimant has been considered see *Cinnamond v British Airports Authority* [1980] 2 All ER 368, [1980] 1 WLR 582, CA; *Lovelock v Secretary of State for Transport* (1979) 39 P & CR 468 at 473, CA, per Lord Denning MR, and at 476 per Roskill LJ; *R v Clerkenwell Green Metropolitan Stipendiary Magistrate, ex p Ibrahim* (1983) Times, 7 December; *R v Macclesfield Justices, ex p Jones* [1983] RTR 143, DC; *Bagga Khan v Home Secretary* [1987] Imm AR 543, CA; *Sherry v R* [1989] 1 WLR 341 at 349, PC; *Hassan Jemel v Immigration Appeal Adjudicator* [1989] Imm AR 496, CA; and cf *R v Secretary of State for Transport, ex p Birmingham City Council* (1984) 83 LGR 79.

In some cases a failure to take an opportunity to object to a particular procedure at the time when it is adopted may bar a later complaint that it was unfair: cf *Sheringham Development Co Ltd v Browne* [1977] ICR 20, EAT; and similarly concerning a failure to object timeously to a procedural error in the service of a notice: *George v Secretary of State for the Environment* (1979) 38 P & CR 609, CA (no such thing as a technical breach of natural justice); but cf *Collector of Land Revenue, South West District Penang v Kam Gin Paik* [1986] 1 WLR 412 at 417, PC (failure to object ab ante to an illegal proceeding cannot convert it into a legal one). See also PARA 636.

630. Application and scope of the duty to act fairly. The situations in which a duty to act fairly or in accordance with natural justice will arise cannot be exhaustively listed and have tended to expand as the case law has developed[1]. In order to establish that a duty to act fairly applies to the performance of a particular function, it is no longer necessary to show that the function is analytically of a judicial character or that it involves the determination of a *lis inter partes*[2], or the determination of a personal right[3].

It may now be presumed that the duty will apply to the administrative decision-making process, absent any express provision to the contrary, unless the interest affected is insignificant or remote[4]. In most instances the real issue concerns the content of the duty to act fairly rather than whether or not it applies at all[5].

The content of the duty will be assessed by reference to a wide range of factors including the nature of the individual's interest and the impact of the decision on it, the type of decision being made, whether the decision is preliminary or final, the subject matter of the decision, and the terms of any relevant statutory provisions. Thus a presumption that natural justice must be observed will arise more readily where there is an express duty to decide only after conducting a hearing or inquiry[6], or where the decision is one entailing the determination of disputed questions of law and fact[7]. A duty to act in accordance with natural justice will arise when a decision directly affects any proprietary or personal right or interest. For example, decisions which affect a person's livelihood[8], legal status where that status is not merely terminable at pleasure[9], family or personal life[10], which deprive a person of liberty[11], or property rights[12], or another legitimate interest or expectation[13], or which impose a penalty on him[14]. By contrast, the conferring of a wide discretionary power exercisable in the public interest may be indicative of the absence of an obligation so to act[15].

Where a discretionary power to encroach on individual rights is exercised, factors to be taken into account in deciding what fairness requires in the exercise of the power include the nature of the interests to be affected, the circumstances in which the power falls to be exercised, and the nature of the sanctions, if any, involved[16]. The content of the duty to act fairly will normally be very limited where the authority is in the course of exercising a function not culminating in a binding decision[17], but that may not be the case if the words conferring the power, or the context, indicate that a fair hearing ought to be extended to persons likely to be prejudicially affected by an investigation or recommendation[18].

Specific case law has evolved in relation to committees of clubs[19], political parties[20], trade unions[21], other voluntary organisations[22], professional[23] and ecclesiastical bodies[24] and academic institutions[25] exercising functions of a disciplinary or similar nature[26] involving the imposition of a substantial sanction[27], even though their own rules do not oblige them to function in the same way as courts or tribunals[28]. However, the types of body to which the duty will apply have not been definitively established; nor have the requirements of the duty in each context. The application and scope of the duty must be determined having regard to all material circumstances[29].

1 The leading cases include *Ridge v Baldwin* [1964] AC 40, [1963] 2 All ER 66, HL; *R v Panel on Take-overs and Mergers, ex p Datafin plc* [1987] QB 815, [1987] 1 All ER 564, CA; *Leech v Deputy Governor of Parkhurst Prison* [1988] AC 533, [1988] 1 All ER 485, HL.

2 Earlier dicta to the effect that a duty to act in accordance with natural justice arises only in the performance of functions of a judicial nature must now be regarded as incorrect, although the outcome of particular cases may still be supportable on the basis that the standards of fairness

are highly flexible. See now *Ridge v Baldwin* [1964] AC 40, [1963] 2 All ER 66, HL; *Schmidt v Secretary of State for Home Affairs* [1969] 2 Ch 149, [1969] 1 All ER 904, CA (note the substantial changes in the legislative framework since the decision in this case); *R v Gaming Board for Great Britain, ex p Benaim and Khaida* [1970] 2 QB 417, [1970] 2 All ER 528, CA; *Durayappah v Fernando* [1967] 2 AC 337, [1967] 2 All ER 152, PC; *R v Board of Visitors of Hull Prison, ex p St Germain* [1979] QB 425, [1979] 1 All ER 701, CA; *Payne v Lord Harris of Greenwich* [1981] 2 All ER 842, [1981] 1 WLR 754, CA (the decision in this case was overruled by *R v Secretary of State for the Home Department, ex p Doody* [1994] 1 AC 531, sub nom *Doody v Secretary of State for the Home Department* [1993] 3 All ER 92, HL); *Bushell v Secretary of State for the Environment* [1981] AC 75, [1980] 2 All ER 608, HL. But the standards of fairness may be different where the proceedings take an inquisitorial form: *R v National Insurance Comr, ex p Viscusi* [1974] 2 All ER 724, [1974] 1 WLR 646, CA; *R v Panel on Take-overs and Mergers, ex p Guinness plc* [1990] 1 QB 146, [1989] 1 All ER 509, CA; cf *R v Monopolies and Mergers Commission, ex p Elders IXL Ltd* [1987] 1 All ER 451, [1987] 1 WLR 1221; *R v Monopolies and Mergers Commission, ex p Matthew Brown plc* [1987] 1 All ER 463, [1987] 1 WLR 1235.

3   See *R v Gaming Board for Great Britain, ex p Benaim and Khadia* [1970] 2 QB 417 at 430, [1970] 2 All ER 528 at 533, CA, per Lord Denning MR.

4   See *Cheall v Association of Professional Executive Clerical and Computer Staff* [1983] 2 AC 180, [1983] 1 All ER 1130, HL; *R v International Stock Exchange of the United Kingdom and the Republic of Ireland Ltd, ex p Else (1982) Ltd* [1993] QB 534, [1993] 1 All ER 420, CA; *R v Life Assurance Unit Trust Regulatory Organisation Ltd, ex p Ross* [1993] QB 17, [1993] 1 All ER 545, CA; although cf *R v Life Assurance Unit Trust Regulatory Organisation Ltd, ex p Tee* (1994) 7 Admin LR 289, CA; and *R v Liverpool Corpn, ex p Liverpool Taxi Fleet Operators Association* [1972] 2 QB 299, where legitimate expectations had arisen.

5   As to the flexibility of the concept of fairness see *R v Secretary of State for the Home Department, ex p Doody* [1994] 1 AC 531 at 560, sub nom *Doody v Secretary of State for the Home Department* [1993] 3 All ER 92 at 106, HL, per Lord Mustill (requirements of fairness in any particular situation an exercise in 'intuitive judgment'; an important component is knowledge of the gist of the case the claimant has to answer); and PARA 629.

6   As in *Ealing Borough Council v Minister of Housing and Local Government* [1952] Ch 856, [1952] 2 All ER 639; *General Medical Council v Spackman* [1943] AC 627, [1943] 2 All ER 337, HL; *R v Secretary of State for Transport, ex p Philippine Airlines Inc* (1984) Times, 17 October, CA ('after due inquiry').

7   See eg *R v Kent Police Authority, ex p Godden* [1971] 2 QB 662, sub nom *Re Godden* [1971] 3 All ER 20, CA (whether police officer permanently disabled and therefore subject to compulsory premature retirement); *Hoggard v Worsbrough UDC* [1962] 2 QB 93, [1962] 1 All ER 468 (decision of local authority on the question to whom to make payments in respect of well-maintained house subject to clearance order); *Board of Education v Rice* [1911] AC 179, HL.

8   See eg *R v Barnsley Metropolitan District Council, ex p Hook* [1976] 3 All ER 452, [1976] 1 WLR 1052, CA; *McInnes v Onslow Fane* [1978] 3 All ER 211, [1978] 1 WLR 1520; *R v Wear Valley District Council, ex p Binks* [1985] 2 All ER 699; *Re Lo-Line Electric Motors Ltd* [1988] Ch 477, [1988] 2 All ER 692 (disqualification as director); *R v Enfield London Borough Council, ex p TF Unwin (Roydon) Ltd* (1989) 46 BLR 1 (removal from council's list of contractors); *R v Secretary of State for Health, ex p United States Tobacco International Inc* [1992] QB 353, [1992] 1 All ER 212, DC (business interests); *R v Chief Constable for the West Midlands Police, ex p Carroll* (1995) 7 Admin LR 45, CA (person suspected of misconduct; unfair not to afford a disciplinary hearing); *R v Life Assurance Unit Trust Regulatory Organisation Ltd, ex p Ross* [1993] QB 17, [1993] 1 All ER 545, CA; *R v Broxtowe Borough Council, ex p Bradford* [2000] LGR 386, CA (applicant for employment with council entitled to hearing to rebut allegations of previous sexual abuse). See also *R v Secretary of State for the Environment, ex p Brent London Borough Council* [1982] QB 593 at 643, [1983] 3 All ER 321 at 355, DC, per Ackner LJ, referring to licensing cases, which include *R v Gaming Board for Great Britain, ex p Benaim and Khaida* [1970] 2 QB 417, [1970] 2 All ER 528, CA, although note in these situations that the exact content of the duty may depend on whether it is an initial application, a failure to renew, or a decision to revoke the licence. See also the cases cited in notes 19, 28.

9   *Ridge v Baldwin* [1964] AC 40, [1963] 2 All ER 66, HL (chief constable); *R v Aston University Senate, ex p Roffey* [1969] 2 QB 538, [1969] 2 All ER 964, DC; *Stevenson v United Road Transport Union* [1977] ICR 893 at 902–903, CA, per Buckley LJ; *R v Brent London Borough Council, ex p Assegai* (1987) 151 LG Rev 891, DC (removal from school governorship); *Wandsworth London Borough Council v A* [2000] 1 WLR 1246, (2001) 3 LGLR 3 (termination

of licence to parent of pupil to enter school premises). Cf *R v Governors of Darlington Free Grammar School* (1844) 6 QB 682; *Pillai v Singapore City Council* [1968] 1 WLR 1278, PC; and see *Vidyodaya University of Ceylon v Silva* [1964] 3 All ER 865, [1965] 1 WLR 77, PC (dismissal of university teacher); *Blanchard v Dunlop* [1917] 1 Ch 165, CA (dismissal of school teacher; dicta at 170–171 per Pickford LJ and at 173 per Warrington LJ indicated that a duty to act judicially might arise if there were a charge of misconduct). See, however, *Malloch v Aberdeen Corpn* [1971] 2 All ER 1278, [1971] 1 WLR 1578, HL (schoolteacher, though dismissible at pleasure, entitled to be heard on own behalf because of the statutory flavour of his terms of employment). See also *Fullbrook v Berkshire Magistrates' Courts Committee* (1970) 69 LGR 75 (clerk entitled to opportunity to be heard before forfeiture of pension for misconduct); *A-G v Ryan* [1980] AC 718, [1980] 2 WLR 143, PC (grant or refusal of citizenship); *R v Immigration Tribunal, ex p Mahmud Khan* [1983] QB 790, [1983] 2 All ER 420, CA; *R v Secretary of State for the Home Department, ex p Dannenberg* [1984] QB 766, [1984] 2 All ER 481, CA; but cf *R v Secretary of State for the Home Department, ex p Cheblak* [1991] 2 All ER 319, [1991] 1 WLR 890, CA (deportation on grounds of national security; statement to that effect sufficient; no reasons had to be given; note however that there is now a statutory right of appeal against such a decision).

10 *R v Birmingham Juvenile Court, ex p Birmingham City Council* [1988] 1 All ER 683, [1988] 1 WLR 337, CA (making an interim care order); *R v Wandsworth London Borough Council, ex p P* (1989) 87 LGR 370, [1989] 1 FLR 387 (removal from council list of foster parents); *R v Hampshire County Council, ex p K* [1990] 2 QB 71, [1990] 2 All ER 129, DC (application for care order); *R v Fernhill Manor School, ex p Brown* (1993) 5 Admin LR 159 (exclusion from a private school; no right to judicial review); *Wandsworth London Borough Council v A* [2000] 1 WLR 1246, [2000] LGR 81, CA (decision of headteacher to exclude parent from school premises subject to duty to act fairly); but cf *R v Wokingham District Council, ex p SJ* [1999] 2 FLR 1136, [1999] COD 336 (no duty to allow representations from mother prior to recommendation to adopt by reason of statutory context).

11 See eg *R v Board of Visitors of Hull Prison, ex p St Germain* [1979] QB 425, [1979] 1 All ER 701, CA; *Leech v Deputy Governor of Parkhurst Prison* [1988] AC 533, [1988] 1 All ER 485, HL; *R v Parole Board, ex p Wilson* [1992] QB 740, [1992] 2 All ER 576, CA (duty to give reasons for refusal to release on licence); *R v Secretary of State for the Home Department, ex p Doody* [1994] 1 AC 531, sub nom *Doody v Secretary of State for the Home Department* [1993] 3 All ER 92, HL (mandatory life prisoners to be able to make representations before tariff fixed); *R v Secretary of State for the Home Department, ex p McCartney* (1994) 6 Admin LR 629 (similar right for discretionary life prisoners), followed in *R (on the application of Nejad) Secretary of State for the Home Department* [2004] EWCA Civ 33, 148 Sol Jo LB 181; *R v Secretary of State for the Home Department, ex p Venables* [1998] AC 407, [1997] 3 All ER 97, HL (tariff setting); *R v Secretary of State for the Home Department, ex p Duggan* [1994] 3 All ER 277 (review of security classification).

This presumption is, however, displaced in time of serious emergency, and was displaced in the purely discretionary regulation of aliens and the regulation of Commonwealth immigrants: see *Schmidt v Secretary of State for Home Affairs* [1969] 2 Ch 149, [1969] 1 All ER 904, CA; but cf *R v Secretary of State for the Home Office, ex p Awuku* (1987) Times, 3 October (refusing refugees leave to enter); *R v Home Secretary, ex p Gaima* (1988) Independent, 7 December, CA. But note that the legislative context is now wholly different. See further BRITISH NATIONALITY, IMMIGRATION AND ASYLUM vol 4(2) (2002 Reissue) PARA 83 et seq; and WAR AND ARMED CONFLICT vol 49(1) (2005 Reissue) PARA 573 et seq.

12 See *Cooper v Wandsworth Board of Works* (1863) 14 CBNS 180; *Smith v R* (1878) 3 App Cas 614, PC; *Brutton v St George's, Hanover Square Vestry* (1871) LR 13 Eq 339; *Masters v Pontypool Local Government Board* (1878) 9 ChD 677; *Hopkins v Smethwick Local Board of Health* (1890) 24 QBD 712, CA; *Hall v Manchester Corpn* (1915) 84 LJ Ch 732, HL; *Urban Housing Co Ltd v Oxford City Council* [1940] Ch 70, [1939] 4 All ER 211, CA; *Maradana Mosque Board of Trustees v Mahmud* [1967] 1 AC 13, [1966] 1 All ER 545, PC; *R v Amber Valley District Council, ex p Jackson* [1984] 3 All ER 501, [1985] 1 WLR 298; cf *Cannock Chase District Council v Kelly* [1978] 1 WLR 1, (1978) 36 P & CR 219; *Sevenoaks District Council v Emmott* (1979) 78 LGR 346, (1980) 39 P & CR 404, [1980] JPL 517 (the tenants in both those cases would now have greater security of tenure); *R v Wear Valley District Council, ex p Binks* [1985] 2 All ER 699; *R v Ealing Magistrates' Court, ex p Fanneran* (1995) 160 JP 409, (1996) 8 Admin LR 351; [1996] COD 185 (destruction of a dog).

13 Eg that a permit or licence would be renewed or would not be revoked: see *Schmidt v Secretary of State for Home Affairs* [1969] 2 Ch 149 at 170–171, [1969] 1 All ER 904 at 909, CA, obiter per Lord Denning MR, and at 173 and 911 obiter per Widgery LJ. See also *Breen v Amalgamated Engineering Union* [1971] 2 QB 175 at 191, [1971] 1 All ER 1148 at

1154–1155, CA, per Lord Denning MR, dissenting. In *McInnes v Onslow Fane* [1978] 3 All ER 211, [1978] 1 WLR 1520 Sir Robert Megarry V-C distinguished, in the context of a licensing function, between a mere application, an application for renewal (of which there might be a legitimate expectation) and revocation or forfeiture, and suggested that the mere applicant would probably be entitled to relatively little by way of a hearing (at least in that context). This method of reaching a view about what fairness requires in a particular situation has been applied in eg *R v Secretary of State for the Environment, ex p Brent London Borough Council* [1982] QB 593, [1983] 3 All ER 321, DC; *R v Bristol City Council, ex p Pearce* (1984) 83 LGR 711 (hearing not necessary in a case where written representations considered).

This analysis is a helpful starting point, but is not exhaustive. Some applications will merit a hearing, or an opportunity to make written representations: eg *R v Secretary of State for Foreign and Commonwealth Affairs, ex p Everett* [1989] QB 811, [1989] 1 All ER 655, CA (issue of a passport; opportunity to make written representations to persuade a decision-maker to depart from a general policy necessary); *R v Secretary of State for the Home Department, ex p Fayed* [1997] 1 All ER 228, [1998] 1 WLR 763 (application for citizenship, but possible adverse inference as to character if application refused, notice of grounds of objection necessary); *R v Secretary of State for the Home Department, ex p Moon* [1997] INLR 165, (1996) 8 Admin LR 477; *R v Independent Television Commission, ex p TSW Broadcasting Ltd* [1996] EMLR 291, HL (failure to renew television franchise after open application process). See also *R v Huntingdon District Council, ex p Cowan* [1984] 1 All ER 58, [1984] 1 WLR 501 (applicant for licence entitled to be told of all information on which the decision was to be founded and given an opportunity to make representations orally or in writing). Further, some decisions where a fair hearing is required fall outside any of the three categories: eg *R v Great Yarmouth Borough Council, ex p Botton Bros Arcades Ltd* (1987) 56 P & CR 99 (neighbour objecting to development of land). In all cases the content of the duty must be determined by reference to all material circumstances.

14 Including other forms of financial detriment (eg loss of pension): *Lapointe v l'Association de Bienfaisance et de Retraité de la Police de Montréal* [1906] AC 535, PC; *Fullbrook v Berkshire Magistrates' Courts Committee* (1970) 69 LGR 75; *Asher v Secretary of State for the Environment* [1974] Ch 208, [1974] 2 All ER 156, CA. See also *Lloyd v McMahon* [1987] AC 625, [1987] 1 All ER 1118, HL.

15 Note that the circumstances in which the principles enunciated in all but the last case in this note will be applied are likely to be limited: see *R v Leman Street Police Station Inspector, ex p Venicoff* [1920] 3 KB 72, DC; *R v Governor of Brixton Prison, ex p Soblen* [1963] 2 QB 243, [1962] 3 All ER 641, CA (note that the powers considered in these cases have since been repealed); and the Immigration Act 1971 ss 3(5), 15 (repealed) (see BRITISH NATIONALITY, IMMIGRATION AND ASYLUM vol 4(2) (2002 Reissue) PARA 160). See also *Murray v Epsom Local Board* [1897] 1 Ch 35; *Irving v Patterson* [1943] Ch 180, [1943] 1 All ER 652; *Howell v Addison* [1943] 1 All ER 29, CA; *Marquis of Abergavenny v Bishop of Llandaff* (1888) 20 QBD 460; *Russell v Russell* (1880) 14 ChD 471; *Cassel v Inglis* [1916] 2 Ch 211; *Hutton v A-G* [1927] 1 Ch 427; *Laffer v Gillen* [1927] AC 886, PC; *Russell v Duke of Norfolk* [1949] 1 All ER 109, CA; *Schmidt v Secretary of State for Home Affairs* [1969] 2 Ch 149, [1969] 1 All ER 904, CA; *Essex County Council v Ministry of Housing and Local Government* (1967) 18 P & CR 531, (1967) 66 LGR 23; *R v Secretary of State for the Home Department, ex p Harrison* [1988] 3 All ER 86; *R (on the application of Tucker) v Director General of the National Crime Squad* [2003] EWCA Civ 57, [2003] ICR 599, [2003] IRLR 439; and cf *R v Wandsworth London Borough Council, ex p P* (1989) 87 LGR 370.

16 *Durayappah v Fernando* [1967] 2 AC 337 at 351–352, [1967] 2 All ER 152 at 156, PC; *Leech v Deputy Governor of Parkhurst Prison* [1988] AC 533, [1988] 1 All ER 485, HL. See also *R v Ethical Committee of St Mary's Hospital (Manchester), ex p H (or Harriott)* [1988] 1 FLR 512, [1998] Fam Law 165 (refusal of in vitro fertilisation). In *R v Secretary of State for the Environment, ex p Norwich City Council* [1982] QB 808 at 824, sub nom *Norwich City Council v Secretary of State for the Environment* [1982] 1 All ER 737 at 745, CA, Lord Denning MR applied the rules of natural justice to the exercise of a default power by a minister because of the constitutional importance of local self-government.

17 See PARA 639.

18 See PARA 639.

19 *Innes v Wylie* (1844) 1 Car & Kir 257; *Dawkins v Antrobus* (1881) 17 ChD 615, CA; *Fisher v Keane* (1878) 11 ChD 353; *Young v Ladies' Imperial Club* [1920] 2 KB 523, CA (per Scrutton LJ); *Nagle v Feilden* [1966] 2 QB 633, [1966] 1 All ER 689; *Jones v Welsh Rugby Football Union* (1997) Times, 6 March; *Flaherty v National Greyhound Racing Club Ltd* [2005] EWCA Civ 1117, [2005] All ER (D) 70 (Sep); and see CLUBS vol 13 (2009) PARA 238.

20 *Walsh v McLuskie* (1982) Times, 16 December; *John v Rees* [1970] Ch 345, [1969] 2 All ER 274; *Lewis v Heffer* [1978] 3 All ER 354, [1978] 1 WLR 1061, CA; *Choudhry v Triesman* [2003] EWHC 1203 (Ch), [2003] 22 LS Gaz R 29; *Watt (formerly Carter) v Ahsan* [2007] UKHL 51, [2008] 1 AC 696, sub nom *Ahsan v Watt (formerly Carter)* [2008] 1 All ER 869.

21 *Annamunthodo v Oilfield Workers' Trade Union* [1961] AC 945, [1961] 3 All ER 621, PC; *Lawlor v Union of Post Office Workers* [1965] Ch 712, [1965] 1 All ER 353; *Taylor v National Union of Seamen* [1967] 1 All ER 767, [1967] 1 WLR 532; *Leigh v National Union of Railwaymen* [1970] Ch 326, [1969] 3 All ER 1249; *Roebuck v National Union of Mineworkers (Yorkshire Area)* [1977] ICR 573; *Stevenson v United Road Transport Union*, [1977] 2 All ER 941, [1977] ICR 893; *Breen v Amalgamated Engineering Union* [1971] 2 QB 175 at 190–191 per Lord Denning MR; *Leary v National Union of Vehicle Builders* [1971] Ch 34, [1970] 2 All ER 713; *Edwards v SOGAT* [1971] Ch 354, [1970] 1 All ER 905. As to statutory controls on the exclusion, expulsion and disciplining of trade union members see EMPLOYMENT vol 40 (2009) PARA 977 et seq.

22 *Wood v Woad* (1874) LR 9 Exch 190 (expulsion from insurance society); *Byrne v Kinematograph Renters Society Ltd* [1958] 2 All ER 579, [1958] 1 WLR 762 (withholding of supplies by trade association); *John v Rees* [1970] Ch 345, [1969] 2 All ER 274 (suspension of constituency political party by national executive); but c f *Gaiman v National Association for Mental Health* [1971] Ch 317, [1970] 2 All ER 362 (exclusion from membership of company limited by guarantee did not attract duty to observe natural justice); and *Royal Society for the Prevention of Cruelty to Animals v A-G* [2001] 3 All ER 530, [2002] 1 WLR 448. The court should not encourage review of the bona fide decisions of bodies controlling sporting and other voluntary activities: *McInnes v Onslow Fane* [1978] 3 All ER 211 at 218, [1978] 1 WLR 1520 at 1535 per Megarry V-C.

23 *General Medical Council v Spackman* [1943] AC 627, [1943] 2 All ER 337, HL; *Lau Liat Meng v Disciplinary Committee* [1968] AC 391, [1967] 3 WLR 877, PC; *Gee v General Medical Council* [1987] 2 All ER 193, [1987] 1 WLR 564, HL; *Crompton v General Medical Council* [1982] 1 All ER 35, [1981] 1 WLR 1435, PC; *Hefferen v Central Council for Nursing, Midwifery and Health Visitors* (1988) Times, 21 March, DC; *R (on the application of Thompson) v Law Society* [2004] EWCA Civ 167, [2004] 2 All ER 113, [2004] 1 WLR 2522. Note that since these cases were decided there has been considerable legislative reform in relation to many medical professions (see generally MEDICAL PROFESSIONS) and the solicitor's profession (see generally LEGAL PROFESSIONS).

24 *Capel v Child* (1832) 2 Cr & J 558; *Bonaker v Evans* (1850) 16 QB 162. See also *R v North, ex p Oakey* [1927] 1 KB 491, CA; but c f *Marquess of Abergavenny v Bishop of Llandaff* (1888) 20 QBD 460; and *R v Archbishop of Canterbury, ex p Morant* [1944] KB 282, [1944] 1 All ER 179, CA.

25 *Glynn v Keele University* [1971] 2 All ER 89, [1971] 1 WLR 487 (suspension of student without hearing him; discretionary relief refused on the merits). See also *R v Aston University Senate, ex p Roffey* [1969] 2 QB 538, [1969] 2 All ER 964, DC (sending down for examination failure; duty to act fairly, but discretionary relief refused because of delay); *Ceylon University v Fernando* [1960] 1 All ER 631, [1960] 1 WLR 223, PC (suspension from university examinations for alleged cheating); and *Ex p Bolchover* (1970) Times, 7 October, DC (hearing before Oxford proctors for disciplinary offence). Cf *Ex p Death* (1852) 18 QB 647. See also *Ward v Bradford Corpn* (1971) 70 LGR 27, CA (expulsion of student teacher for misconduct; college acted fairly although rules changed specially and disciplinary reference instituted by the deciding body); *Herring v Templeman* [1973] 3 All ER 569, CA; *R v Fernhill Manor School, ex p Brown* (1993) 5 Admin LR 159 (expulsion from a private school; judicial review not available); *Gray v Marlborough College* [2006] EWCA Civ 1262, [2006] ELR 516 (expulsion from private school; question is has the parent had a fair deal of the kind he had bargained for); *R v Governors of London Oratory School, ex p Regis* [1989] Fam Law 67. The visitor, rather than the court, may have jurisdiction over internal questions in some academic foundations (a point which may have been overlooked in some of the cases). The visitor may himself be subject to judicial review: see e g *R v Judicial Committee of the Privy Council, ex p Vijayatunga* [1988] QB 322, [1987] 3 All ER 204, DC; affd sub nom *R v HM The Queen in Council, ex p Vijayatunga* [1990] 2 QB 444, [1989] 3 WLR 13, CA. The jurisdiction of the visitor is now subject to specific statutory exclusions under the Higher Education Act 2004 Pt 2 (ss 11–21), Pt 5 (ss 46–54): see EDUCATION vol 15(2) (2006 Reissue) PARAS 657, 1039 et seq. The office of the independent adjudicator for higher education (which replaces the visitor in some cases) is also amenable to judicial review: *R (on the application of Siborurema) v Office of the Independent Adjudicator* [2007] EWCA Civ 1365; [2008] ELR 209. See also *R v Governors of London Oratory School, ex p Regis* [1989] Fam Law 67 (expulsion from school).

26 See eg *R v Leicestershire Fire Authority, ex p Thompson* (1979) 77 LGR 373, DC; *R v Secretary of State for the Home Department, ex p Benwell* [1985] QB 554, [1984] 3 All ER 854 (not followed on one point in *R v Secretary of State for the Home Department, ex p Broom* [1986] QB 198, [1985] 3 WLR 778); *Leech v Deputy Governor of Parkhurst Prison* [1988] AC 533, [1988] 1 All ER 485, HL. Note that the mere fact that a person is employed by a public body does not entitle him to a public law remedy where a breach of natural justice is complained of; it is necessary to show some public law underpinning of his contractual position: *R v East Berkshire Health Authority, ex p Walsh* [1985] QB 152, [1984] 3 All ER 425, CA; and see *Ridge v Baldwin* [1964] AC 40, [1963] 2 All ER 66, HL; *Malloch v Aberdeen Corpn* [1971] 2 All ER 1278, [1971] 1 WLR 1578, HL; *R v Trent Regional Health Authority, ex p Jones* (1986) Times, 19 June. See also the cases cited in note 9.

27 As to the materiality of the nature of the sanction to be imposed see *Durayappah v Fernando* [1967] 2 AC 337 at 351–352, [1967] 2 All ER 152 at 156, PC. Proceedings casting a serious slur on a person's reputation or exposing him to a legal hazard may also call for the observance of minimum standards of natural justice even if they do not terminate in a binding decision: *Re Pergamon Press Ltd* [1971] Ch 388 at 402–403, [1970] 3 All ER 535 at 541–542, CA, per Sachs LJ; and see eg *R v Bedfordshire County Council, ex p C* (1986) 85 LGR 218 (local authority deciding not to rehabilitate child with parent); *R v Norfolk County Council, ex p M* [1989] QB 619, [1989] 2 All ER 359 (placing name on former register of suspected child abusers).

28 Semble such rules cannot directly exclude the operation of the rules of natural justice in cases of expulsion from membership: see *Edwards v Society of Graphical and Allied Trades* [1971] Ch 354, [1970] 3 All ER 689, CA; *Lawlor v Union of Post Office Workers* [1965] Ch 712, [1965] 1 All ER 353; *Hiles v Amalgamated Society of Woodworkers* [1968] Ch 440, [1967] 3 All ER 70; and see *Faramus v Film Artistes' Association* [1964] AC 925 at 941, [1964] 1 All ER 25 at 28, HL, per Lord Evershed, and at 947 and 33 per Lord Pearce; *St Johnstone Football Club Ltd v Scottish Football Association Ltd* 1965 SLT 171 at 175, Ct of Sess per Lord Kilbrandon (imposition of fine). Rules purporting to confer an absolute discretion to expel or to revoke an occupational licence have been held to be incompatible with a duty to observe natural justice: see *Maclean v Workers' Union* [1929] 1 Ch 602; *Russell v Duke of Norfolk* [1949] 1 All ER 109, CA. See also *Gaiman v National Association for Mental Health* [1971] Ch 317 at 336–337, [1970] 2 All ER 362 at 378–379 per Megarry J. The present authority of such decisions, however, is doubtful. The fact that the rules of the organisation, which represent the contract between its members, must be respected where the duty to observe natural justice is being implied into them so as to give the court the means of granting redress was stressed in *Herring v Templeman* [1973] 3 All ER 569, CA; and *Hamlet v General Municipal Boilermakers and Allied Trades Union* [1987] 1 All ER 631, [1987] 1 WLR 449. If no charge of discreditable conduct is involved and the effect of a decision is not to deprive a person of legal status or livelihood, a duty to observe natural justice will not readily be implied: see *Breen v Amalgamated Engineering Union* [1971] 2 QB 175, [1971] 1 All ER 1148, CA (refusal to endorse election of shop steward); *Flaherty v National Greyhound Racing Club Ltd* [2005] EWCA Civ 1117, [2005] All ER (D) 70 (Sep); *Colgan v Kennel Club* [2001] All ER (D) 403 (Oct); *Modahl v British Athletics Federation* [2001] EWCA Civ 1447, [2002] 1 WLR 1192. Express procedural protections contained in the contract have been enforced by the court in eg *R v British Broadcasting Corpn, ex p Lavelle* [1983] 1 All ER 241, [1983] 1 WLR 23; and see *Taylor v National Union of Mineworkers (Derbyshire Area)* [1984] IRLR 440. Note that there has been extensive legislative intervention in the relations between trades unions and their members: see the Trade Unions and Labour Relations (Consolidation) Act 1992; and EMPLOYMENT vol 40 (2009) PARA 977 et seq.

29 The circumstances will also determine where exceptions to the duty to act fairly will exist where the duty would otherwise apply: see PARA 639.

B. THE RULE AGAINST BIAS

631. Direct personal interest and apparent bias. It is a fundamental rule, often expressed in the maxim *nemo judex in causa sua*, that, in the absence of statutory authority, agreement or necessity, no man may be a judge in his own cause[1].

At common law this rule is applied in two broad classes of case. First, where an adjudicator has either a direct pecuniary or proprietary interest in the outcome of the matter, or can otherwise by reason of a direct personal interest be regarded as being a party to the action; second, where either by reason of a different form of interest or by reason of his conduct or behaviour there is a 'real possibility' of bias[2] on his part. In the former case there is an automatic, and irrebuttable, presumption of bias[3]. In the latter case the test for apparent bias is satisfied. Even if the disqualifying effect of a pecuniary interest has been removed by statute, it is still material to consider whether the nature of that interest gives rise to a real possibility of bias. Such statutory exceptions to the common law rule are construed narrowly[4].

If a case falls within either of the above classes, the decision is unlawful. So, where persons having a direct interest in the subject matter of an inquiry before an inferior tribunal[5] take part in adjudicating on it, the tribunal is improperly constituted and the court will grant a prohibiting order to prevent it from adjudicating, or a quashing order in respect of the decision which has been made[6], or such other remedy, for instance, an injunction or a declaration[7], as may be appropriate. The principle extends not only to courts and tribunals[8], but also to other bodies[9], including public authorities[10], determining questions affecting the civil rights of individuals[11]. The stringency with which the principle is applied may depend upon the importance of the right at stake or the decision to be taken[12].

1 As to the circumstances in which exemptions from prima facie disqualification will have effect see PARA 638. As to statutory disqualifications of magistrates see MAGISTRATES vol 29(2) (Reissue) PARA 506 et seq. As to necessity and statutory authority see PARA 636.

2 See *Porter v Magill* [2001] UKHL 67, [2002] 2 AC 357, [2002] 1 All ER 465, overruling *R v Gough* [1993] AC 646; and PARA 634. The test now requires the court to inform itself about all the circumstances which relate to the suggestion that the decision-maker is biased. It must then ask whether those would lead a fair-minded and informed observer to conclude that there was a real possibility that the decision-maker was biased. The test has been applied to judicial, and non-judicial decision-makers: *Helow v Secretary of State for the Home Department* [2008] UKHL 62, [2008] 2 All ER 1031, [2008] 1 WLR 2416; *R v Abdroikov* [2007] UKHL 37, [2008] 1 All ER 315, [2007] 1 WLR 2679; *Gillies v Secretary of State for Work and Pensions* [2006] UKHL 2, [2006] 1 All ER 731, [2006] 1 WLR 781; *Lawal v Northern Spirit Ltd* [2003] UKHL 35, [2004] 1 All ER 187, [2003] ICR 856 (judicial); *Re Duffy* [2008] UKHL 4, [2008] NI 152; *R (on the application of Al-Hasan) v Secretary of State for the Home Department* [2005] UKHL 13, [2005] 1 All ER 927 (non-judicial). Bias has been described as a departure from that standard of even-handed justice which the law requires from those who occupy judicial office or those who are commonly regarded as holding a quasi-judicial office: *Franklin v Minister of Town and Country Planning* [1948] AC 87 at 103, [1947] 2 All ER 289 at 296, HL, per Lord Thankerton. In the local government context, the courts have distinguished between a predisposition in favour of particular outcome, which is legitimate, and apparent pre-determination, which is unlawful: see eg *Condron v National Assembly for Wales* [2006] EWCA Civ 1573, [2007] LGR 87, [2007] 2 P & CR 38.

3 See *R v Bow Street Metropolitan Stipendiary Magistrate, ex p Pinochet Ugarte (No 2)* [2000] 1 AC 119, [1999] 1 All ER 577 (this principle held to be equally applicable to a case where decision of the judge lead to the promotion of a cause in which the judge was involved together with one of the parties); and *Locabail (UK) Ltd v Bayfield Properties Ltd* [2000] QB 451, [2000] 1 All ER 65, CA. *R v Bow Street Metropolitan Stipendiary Magistrate, ex p Pinochet Ugarte (No 2)* was distinguished on the facts in *Meerabux v A-G of Belize* [2005] UKPC 12, [2005] 2 AC 513, and *Smith v Kvaerner Cementation Foundations Ltd* [2006] EWCA Civ 242, [2006] 3 All ER 593, [2007] 1 WLR 370.

4 The test to be applied is now as stated in *Porter v Magill* [2001] UKHL 67, [2002] 2 AC 357, [2002] 1 All ER 465. For examples of such an approach see *R v Hain Licensing Justices* (1896) 12 TLR 323, DC; *R v Tempest* (1902) 86 LT 585; *R v Barnsley County Borough Licensing Justices, ex p Barnsley and District Licensed Victuallers' Association* [1960] 2 QB 167, [1960] 2 All ER 703, CA; *Jeffs v New Zealand Dairy Production and Marketing Board* [1967] 1 AC 551, [1966] 3 All ER 863, PC; and PARA 638.

5   The principle also applies to proceedings before the superior courts: *Dimes v Grand Junction Canal Proprietors* (1852) 3 HL Cas 759. As to superior courts see COURTS vol 10 (Reissue) PARA 309.

6   As to the scope of quashing and prohibiting orders see generally PARA 695.

7   Injunctions and declarations are the appropriate remedies where the tribunal is non-statutory and is not discharging functions of a public nature: see PARA 716 et seq. Where an injunction is sought, the court will consider whether the apprehended bias is irremediable: *Ellis v Inner London Education Authority* (1976) 75 LGR 382. An action for damages will lie if the tainted decision involves a breach of contract: see eg *Baird v Wells* (1890) 44 ChD 661, CA (in an ordinarily constituted club, an injunction is available, but if the club is a proprietary club, damages are the only remedy). Where a tribunal's jurisdiction is contractual and a right of appeal exists, a party's entitlement is to a fair result that has been reached overall, and apparent bias at one stage of the procedure will not breach the rule: see eg *Calvin v Carr* [1980] AC 574, [1979] 2 All ER 440, PC, applied by *Flaherty v National Greyhound Racing Club Ltd* [2005] EWCA Civ 1117, [2005] All ER (D) 70 (Sep).

8   See *Taylor v Lawrence* [2002] EWCA Civ 90, [2003] QB 528, [2002] 2 All ER 353. It extends to arbitrators and referees appointed by agreement: *Earl v Stocker* (1691) 2 Vern 251; *Scott v Liverpool Corpn* (1858) 1 Giff 216; on appeal 3 De G & J 334; *Hutchinson v Hayward* (1866) 15 LT 291. See also, in relation to a consultant appointed to advise a decision-maker, *SmithKline Beecham plc v Advertising Standards Authority* [2001] EWHC Admin 6, [2001] EMLR 598.

9   Eg committees of trade unions and clubs exercising disciplinary functions (see *Taylor v National Union of Seamen* [1967] 1 All ER 767, [1967] 1 WLR 532); a doctor certifying whether a police officer is permanently incapacitated for the purpose of compulsory retirement (*R v Kent Police Authority, ex p Godden* [1971] 2 QB 662, sub nom *Re Godden* [1971] 3 All ER 20, CA); a board of prison visitors exercising disciplinary functions (*O'Reilly v Mackman* [1983] 2 AC 237, [1982] 3 All ER 1124, HL); and police and fire service disciplinary tribunals (*R v Chief Constable of South Wales, ex p Thornhill* [1987] IRLR 313, CA; *R v Leicestershire Fire Authority, ex p Thompson* (1979) 77 LGR 373, DC). The courts will readily imply the principle into the terms of a contract between members of a private organisation such as a trade union, or into a document such as the Prison Rules: see PRISONS vol 36(2) (Reissue) PARA 502.

10   Eg local authorities: see *R v Hendon RDC, ex p Chorley* [1933] 2 KB 696, DC (grant of interim development permission in face of objections); *R (on the application of Richardson) v North Yorkshire County Council* [2003] EWCA Civ 1860, [2004] 2 All ER 31, [2004] 1 WLR 1920. See also *Hannam v Bradford City Council* [1970] 2 All ER 690, [1970] 1 WLR 937, CA (local education authority's sub-committee consenting to dismissal of teacher). Cf *Murray v Epsom Local Board* [1897] 1 Ch 35 (no duty cast on local authority to act judicially in deciding to remove obstructions from public footpath).

11   See PARA 630.

12   Eg *R v Chief Constable of South Wales, ex p Thornhill* [1987] IRLR 313, CA; *R v Barnsley Metropolitan District Council, ex p Hook* [1976] 3 All ER 452 at 459–460, [1976] 1 WLR 1052 at 1061–1062, CA, per Scarman LJ (revocation of street trader's licence leading to loss of livelihood). See also *Steeples v Derbyshire County Council* [1984] 3 All ER 468, [1985] 1 WLR 256 (council granting planning permission to itself). An allegation of bias was rejected in relation to a mere preliminary inquiry in *Moran v Lloyd's* [1981] 1 Lloyd's Rep 423, CA.

632.   Disqualification by reason of a direct personal interest. The rule that a man may not be judge in his own cause is not confined to situations where the judge is actually a party to the proceedings. It applies equally to any cause in which the judge has a direct personal interest. The most obvious form of direct personal interest is a financial interest. There is a presumption that any direct[1] financial interest, however small[2], in the matter in dispute disqualifies a person from adjudicating[3]. Membership of a company, association or other organisation which is financially interested may operate as a bar to adjudicating[4], as may a bare liability to costs where the decision itself will involve no pecuniary loss[5]. A fiduciary interest does not in itself disqualify[6]. However, financial interests are merely one form of direct personal interest. The rule also applies if the adjudicator's decision will lead to the promotion of a cause in which he is involved together with one of the parties[7].

1 See *Dimes v Grand Junction Canal Proprietors* (1852) 3 HL Cas 759; *Jeffs v New Zealand Dairy Production and Marketing Board* [1967] 1 AC 551, [1966] 3 All ER 863 (a strong case where the Board was authorised by statute to be judge in its own cause; an additional interest invalidated a zoning decision); although c f *Ex p Pettitmangin* (1864) 28 JP 87; *R v Manchester, Sheffield and Lincolnshire Rly Co* (1867) LR 2 QB 336; *R v McKenzie* [1892] 2 QB 519, DC; *R v Burton, ex p Young* [1897] 2 QB 468, DC; and *R v Mulvihill* [1990] 1 All ER 436, [1990] 1 WLR 438 (interests too remote and/or contingent). For a remote (and therefore irrelevant) interest in the case of a contractual arbitration see *AT & T Corpn v Saudi Cable Co* [2000] 2 All ER (Comm) 625, [2000] 2 Lloyd's Rep 127.

2 See *Re Hopkins* (1858) EB & E 100; *R v Hammond* (1863) 3 New Rep 140 (magistrates who were shareholders in railway company disqualified from hearing charges against persons charged with travelling on railway without tickets); *R v Holyhead General Comrs, ex p Roberts* (1982) 56 TC 127. See also *Bostock v Kay* (1989) 87 LGR 583, CA, followed in *R v Governors of Small Heath School, ex p Birmingham City Council* [1990] 2 Admin LR 154, CA. Although c f *Auckland Casino Ltd v Casino Control Authority* [1995] 1 NZLR 142, where the court accepted that a de minimis rule could apply here.

3 See *R v Cheltenham Comrs* (1841) 1 QB 467; *R v Hertfordshire Justices* (1845) 6 QB 753; *Grand Junction Canal v Dimes* (1852) 3 HL Cas 759; *R v Cambridge Recorder* (1857) 8 E & B 637; *R v Aberdare Canal Co* (1850) 14 QB 854; *R v London and North Western Rly Co* (1863) 3 New Rep 140; *R v Cumberland Justices, ex p Midland Rly Co* (1888) 58 LT 491, DC; *Blanchard v Sun Fire Office* (1890) 6 TLR 365; *R v Hain Licensing Justices* (1896) 12 TLR 323, DC; *R v Gee* (1901) 17 TLR 374, DC. See also *R v Hendon RDC, ex p Chorley* [1933] 2 KB 696, DC (interest of councillor as estate agent acting for party in transaction which was the subject of an application for interim development permission). Magistrates were formerly subject to disqualification in relation to rating appeals in their capacity as ratepayers: see *Great Charte Parish and Kennington Parish* (1742) 2 Stra 1173; *R v Yarpole Inhabitants* (1790) 4 Term Rep 71; *R v Rishton* (1813) 1 QB 480; *R v Suffolk Justices* (1852) 18 QB 416; *R v Brecknockshire Justices* (1873) 37 JP Jo 404; *R v Gudridge* (1826) 5 B & C 459; *R v Cambridge Recorder* (1857) 8 E & B 637; *R v Gaisford* [1892] 1 QB 381, DC. As to the statutory powers of magistrates and judges to act in cases relating to rates see the Senior Courts Act 1981 s 14; and COURTS vol 10 (Reissue) PARA 520. See also the Public Health Act 1875 s 258; the Public Health Act 1936 ss 304, 346; and PROTECTION OF ENVIRONMENT AND PUBLIC HEALTH vol 38 (2006 Reissue) PARA 112; LOCAL GOVERNMENT vol 69 (2009) PARA 569. As to the Senior Courts Act 1981 see PARA 602 note 4.

Where a statute or statutory instrument imposes a disqualification from voting on those members of a decision-making body with a potential interest in the result, public confidence in the integrity of the process requires strict compliance with the relevant provisions: see *Noble v Inner London Education Authority* (1983) 82 LGR 291, CA. A breach of the provisions will invalidate any resulting transaction, such as an appointment.

There may be cases involving decisions of a local authority where the authority itself rather than the individual members has a financial interest in the outcome, e g because it stands to gain from a development agreement if it grants itself planning permission. In these situations the test in *Porter v Magill* [2001] UKHL 67, [2002] 2 AC 357, [2002] 1 All ER 465 is the relevant standard (see PARA 634), rather than the presumption of disqualification: see e g *Steeples v Derbyshire County Council* [1984] 3 All ER 468, [1985] 1 WLR 256; *R v St Edmundsbury Borough Council, ex p Investors in Industry Commercial Properties Ltd* [1985] 3 All ER 234, [1985] 1 WLR 1168 (although in these cases a different, earlier, test is used).

4 See note 3. As to the effect of shareholdings see *Dimes v Grand Junction Canal Proprietors* (1852) 3 HL Cas 759; *Wakefield Local Board of Health v West Riding and Grimsby Rly Co* (1865) LR 1 QB 84; c f *R v Storks* (1857) 29 LTOS 107; *R v McKenzie* [1892] 2 QB 519, DC (obiter, three justices shareholders in ships insured with an association which was a member of the Federation of which the informant was a superintendent; no bias or likelihood of bias). See also *Ex p Chamberlain, R v Norfolk Justices* (1870) 34 JP Jo 773. The financial interest may consist in competition between the company to which the adjudicator belongs and a party to the proceedings: *R v Holyhead General Comrs, ex p Roberts* (1982) 56 TC 127.

5 *R v Rand* (1866) LR 1 QB 230 at 232 obiter per Blackburn J. See also *R v Surrey Justices* (1855) 26 LTOS 89; and c f *R v Burton, ex p Young* [1897] 2 QB 468, DC (speculative chance of such a liability insufficient).

6 *R v Rand* (1866) LR 1 QB 230; *R v Middlesex Justices, ex p Hendon Union Assessment Committee* (1908) 72 JP 251, DC; but there may be circumstances in which such an interest gives rise to a real possibility of bias.

7 See *R v Bow Street Metropolitan Stipendiary Magistrate, ex p Pinochet Ugarte (No 2)* [2000] 1 AC 119, [1999] 1 All ER 577, HL, where the 'striking and unusual' facts of the case led the

House of Lords to set aside a decision which it had previously made. In *R v Henley* [1892] 1 QB 504, DC, a justice who voted for the resolution to prosecute the defendant was held disqualified from sitting on the hearing of the summons, which was quashed. See also *R v Allan* (1864) 4 B & S 915. But a justice who though present at such a meeting, did not vote, was not disqualified: *R v Pwllheli Justices, ex p Soane* [1948] 2 All ER 815, DC. That case was distinguished in *R v Caernarvon Licensing Justices, ex p Benson* (1948) 113 JP 23, DC, in which a justice's presence at a meeting of local people who voted to oppose the granting of a licence disqualified him, even though he did not vote at the meeting.

633.   Apparent bias. It is generally unnecessary to establish the presence of actual bias[1], although the courts are not precluded from entertaining such an allegation[2]. It is enough to establish the appearance of bias. It is now established that a uniform test applies which requires the court to inform itself about all the circumstances which relate to the suggestion that the decision-maker is biased. It must then ask whether those circumstances would lead a fair-minded and informed observer to conclude that there was a real possibility that the decision-maker was biased[3]. In previous cases a variety of linguistic formulations were used, including a real danger, or a real likelihood, that in the circumstances of the case an adjudicator will be biased[4], or that a reasonable person acquainted with the outward appearance of the situation would have reasonable grounds for suspecting bias[5], or a more exacting test based on whether or not justice had been manifestly seen to be done[6]. Although these different formulations are no longer apposite, the decisions themselves still provide examples of the general principle in action.

1   There have been older cases outside the field of strictly judicial proceedings where a less stringent test has been applied: see *Ward v Bradford Corpn* (1971) 70 LGR 27 at 35, CA, per Lord Denning MR (the decisions of disciplinary bodies should be supported so long as they act fairly and justly); *Ellis v Inner London Education Authority* (1976) 75 LGR 382 (in dealing with disciplinary bodies as opposed to courts, there must be a serious want of natural justice, not just a technical breach of procedure); *Haddow v Inner London Education Authority* [1979] ICR 202, EAT; *R v Sevenoaks District Council, ex p Terry* [1985] 3 All ER 226 (in administrative matters such as the grant of planning permission, the sole question is whether there was a genuine and impartial exercise of discretion); *R v St Edmundsbury Borough Council, ex p Investors in Industry Commercial Properties Ltd* [1985] 3 All ER 234, [1985] 1 WLR 1168; *R v Chief Constable of South Wales, ex p Thornhill* [1987] IRLR 313, CA; and see *R v Camborne Justices, ex p Pearce* [1955] 1 QB 41 at 52, [1954] 2 All ER 850 at 855, DC, per Slade J (erroneous to give the impression 'that it is more important that justice should appear to be done than that it should in fact be done'). The better view is that a person or body of persons having legal authority to determine the rights of citizens has a duty to act judicially, and is bound by the same rules as judicial officers: see e g *R v North Worcestershire Assessment Committee, ex p Hadley* [1929] 2 KB 397 at 408 per Lord Hewart CJ. More recent cases take this position: see e g *Condron v National Assembly for Wales* [2006] EWCA Civ 1573, [2007] LGR 87. But the distinction between legitimate predisposition and unlawful predetermination, made in that case and in *R (on the application of Lewis) v Redcar and Cleveland Borough Council* [2009] EWCA Civ 3, [2009] 4 All ER 1232, [2009] 1 WLR 1461, makes allowances for the reality that councillors making decisions in areas such as planning will bring greater background knowledge to their decisions than judicial or quasi-judicial officers.
2   *R v Tempest* (1902) 86 LT 585 at 587, DC, obiter per Lord Alverstone CJ; and see the cases where persons instigating a prosecution have adjudicated on it: *R v Milledge* (1879) 4 QBD 332, explained in *R v Handsley* (1881) 8 QBD 383, DC ('substantially interested in the proceeding adjudicated upon so as to be likely to have a real bias in the matter'); *R v Lee* (1882) 9 QBD 394, DC; *R v Henley* [1892] 1 QB 504, DC; and *R v Burton, ex p Young* [1897] 2 QB 468 at 471, DC, per Lawrance J (allegation of disqualifying interest failed).
3   *Porter v Magill* [2001] UKHL 67, [2002] 2 AC 357, [2002] 1 All ER 465, overruling *R v Gough* [1993] AC 646 at 670, HL, per Lord Goff of Chieveley. For further applications of this test see PARA 631 note 2.
4   See *R v Rand* (1866) LR 1 QB 230 at 232–233 per Blackburn J; *R v Meyer* (1875) 1 QBD 173; *R v Sunderland Justices* [1901] 2 KB 357, CA; *Frome United Breweries Co Ltd v Bath Justices* [1926] AC 586, HL; *R (Donoghue) v Cork County Justices* [1910] 2 IR 271 at 275 per

Lord O'Brien LCJ; *R (De Vesci) v Queen's County Justices* [1908] 2 IR 285 at 294 per Lord O'Brien LCJ ('a real likelihood of an operative prejudice, whether conscious or unconscious'; 'the mere vague suspicions of whimsical, capricious or unreasonable people' not sufficient); *R v Salford Assessment Committee, ex p Ogden* [1937] 2 KB 1, [1937] 2 All ER 98, CA; *R v Camborne Justices, ex p Pearce* [1955] 1 QB 41, [1954] 2 All ER 850, DC; *R v Barnsley Licensing Justices, ex p Barnsley and District Licensed Victuallers' Association* [1960] 2 QB 167 at 187, [1960] 2 All ER 703 at 714–715, CA, per Devlin LJ; cf *Eckersley v Mersey Docks and Harbour Board* [1894] 2 QB 667 at 671, CA, per Lord Esher MR; *R (Taverner) v Tyrone County Justices* [1909] 2 IR 763; *R v Dean and Chapter of Rochester Cathedral* (1851) 17 QB 1; *R v Hendon RDC, ex p Chorley* [1933] 2 KB 696; *Roebuck v National Union of Mineworkers (Yorkshire Area) (No 2)* [1978] ICR 676; *Steeples v Derbyshire County Council* [1984] 3 All ER 468, [1985] 1 WLR 256; but cf *R v St Edmundsbury Borough Council, ex p Investors in Industry Commercial Properties Ltd* [1985] 3 All ER 234, [1985] 1 WLR 1168. Where the interest of the adjudicator is remote, there will often be no likelihood of bias: see *Leeds Corpn v Ryder* [1907] AC 420, HL; *R v Stockport Justices* (1896) 60 JP 552, DC; but see *R v Sunderland Justices*; *R v Tempest* (1902) 66 JP 472, DC.

5   In *Metropolitan Properties Co (FGC) Ltd v Lannon* [1969] 1 QB 577 at 606, [1968] 3 All ER 304 at 314, CA, Edmund Davies LJ held that disqualification was incurred even in the absence of a real likelihood of bias if a reasonable man would reasonably suspect bias. See also *Hannam v Bradford City Council* [1970] 2 All ER 690 at 700, [1970] 1 WLR 937 at 949, CA, per Cross LJ (equating the two tests); *R v Liverpool City Justices, ex p Topping* [1983] 1 All ER 490 at 494, [1983] 1 WLR 119 at 123, DC, per Ackner LJ ('would a reasonable and fair-minded person sitting in court and knowing all the relevant facts have a reasonable suspicion that a fair trial for the applicant was not possible?'); and *Cook International Inc v BV Handelmaatschappij; Jean Delvaux and Braat, Scott and Meadows* [1985] 2 Lloyd's Rep 225 (both tests applied to umpire and arbitrator). In *Steeples v Derbyshire County Council* [1984] 3 All ER 468, [1985] 1 WLR 256 it was suggested that the 'real likelihood' test might be applied to administrative decisions and the 'reasonable suspicion' test to judicial tribunals; this suggested distinction is no longer good law. But it has been said that the two tests will not generally lead to different results: *Hannam v Bradford City Council*; *R v Liverpool City Justices, ex p Topping*. See also *R v Buckinghamshire Justices* (1922) Times, 16 December, 86 JP Jo 636; *R v Spurgeon* (1920) Times, 21 October; *Cottle v Cottle* [1939] 2 All ER 535, DC.

In the older cases the reasonable man was to be taken to know all the relevant facts: *Metropolitan Properties Co (FGC) Ltd v Lannon*; *R v Liverpool City Justices, ex p Topping*. It was held in *Steeples v Derbyshire County Council* that this included all the material in evidence at trial, whether or not it had in fact been publicly known or available, but did not include the fact that in reality the decision had been fairly made; nor was the reasonable man to be assumed to have attended the relevant committee meeting. But in *R v St Edmundsbury Borough Council, ex p Investors in Industry Commercial Properties Ltd* it was said that the reasonable man would know all the facts leading to the conclusion that there was no actual bias. In *R v Chief Constable of South Wales, ex p Thornhill* [1987] IRLR 313, CA (where the chief officer who brought charge entered chief constable's room while he was considering decision and the applicant's representative asked who he was) it was held that a reasonable observer would not have recognised the chief officer or known his role, while the representative, if he had inquired further, would have discovered that there was in fact no injustice. It would appear that account may be taken of the personal characteristics of the particular complainant: see *British Muslims Association v Secretary of State for the Environment* (1987) 55 P & CR 205 at 212 per Stuart-Smith J.

Since the decision in *Porter v Magill* [2001] UKHL 67, [2002] 2 AC 357, [2002] 1 All ER 465, the Court of Appeal has held in *Condron v National Assembly for Wales* [2006] EWCA Civ 1573, [2007] LGR 87, [2007] 2 P & CR 38 that in applying the test the court must look at all the circumstances as they appear from the material before it, not just at the facts known to the objectors or to the hypothetical observer at the time of the decision. For the approach and knowledge to be attributed to the fair-minded and informed observer see also *Brunei Darussalam v Prince Jefri Bolkiah* [2007] UKPC 62 at [14]–[16], [2008] 2 LRC 196 at [14]–[16]; *Helow v Secretary of State for the Home Department* [2008] UKHL 62 at [26]–[27], [2009] 2 All ER 1031 at [26]–[27] per Lord Walker of Gestingthorpe and at [28]–[31] per Lord Cullen of Whitekirk.

Unreasonable suspicion of bias ought to be disregarded: *R v Taylor, ex p Vogwill* (1898) 14 TLR 185, DC; *R (De Vesci) v Queen's County Justices* [1908] 2 IR 285 at 294 per Lord O'Brien LCJ. It is wrong for a tribunal to refuse to continue to hear a case merely because a party alleges bias: *Automobile Proprietary Ltd v Healy* [1979] ICR 809, EAT. The fair-minded and informed observer is 'neither complacent nor unduly sensitive or suspicious': *Johnson v*

Johnson (2000) 174 ALR 655 at [53], (2000) 201 CLR 488 at [53] per Kirby J, cited with approval, for example, in *Helow v Secretary of State for the Home Department* at [2] per Lord Hope of Craighead. See also *Gillies v Secretary of State for Work and Pensions* [2006] UKHL 2 at [17], [2006] 1 All ER 731 at [17], [2006] 1 WLR 781 at [17] per Lord Hope of Craighead and [39] per Baroness Hale of Richmond.

6   *R v Sussex Justices, ex p McCarthy* [1924] 1 KB 256 at 259, DC, per Lord Hewart CJ (it is 'of fundamental importance that justice should not only be done, but should manifestly and undoubtedly be seen to be done'). This test is close to, if not identical in effect to, the test in *Porter v Magill* [2001] UKHL 67, [2002] 2 AC 357, [2002] 1 All ER 465. Cf *R v Essex Justices, ex p Perkins* [1927] 2 KB 475 at 488, DC, per Avory J, suggesting that 'be seen' should have read 'seem' (although it is unclear with what authority); and see *R v Byles, ex p Hollidge* (1912) 108 LT 270, DC. See, however, the cases cited in note 1. What will appear to be just is a question of degree: see *R v London Justices, ex p South Metropolitan Gas Co* (1908) 72 JP 137 at 139, CA, per Vaughan Williams LJ; *Jones v Jones* (1941) 105 JP 353, DC. A manifestly perverse decision by justices may be reversed on appeal by way of case stated: see *Afford v Pettit* (1949) 113 JP 433, DC (where it was also said that justices should not have tried an indictable case involving a councillor of the same borough). See also *Hill v Tothill* [1936] WN 126 (information given to justices in private concerning previous convictions); *R v Bodmin Justices, ex p McEwen* [1947] KB 321, DC (interviewing of witness in private by justices); and *Wilcox v HGS* [1976] ICR 306, CA.

Such a test has been applied in cases where a clerk to a tribunal has retired with the tribunal, and given the impression of participating in its decision, even though the clerk had no direct or indirect professional interest in the outcome of the proceedings giving rise to a suspicion of bias: see *R v Sussex Justices, ex p McCarthy* [1924] 1 KB 256, DC; *R v Essex Justices, ex p Perkins* [1927] 2 KB 475, DC; *R v Brakenridge* (1884) 48 JP 293, DC; cf *Ellis v Inner London Education Authority* (1976) 75 LGR 382; and for tribunals generally see *R v Leicestershire Fire Authority, ex p Thompson* (1979) 77 LGR 373, DC; but cf *R v Chief Constable of South Wales, ex p Thornhill* [1987] IRLR 313, CA. Decisions of magistrates and tribunals have been quashed where the clerk or some other person retired with the tribunal while it was considering its decision or otherwise appeared to participate in the decision. If justices, when retiring, wish their clerk to accompany them to give advice on the law, their request should be made clearly and in open court: *R v Eccles Justices, ex p Fitzpatrick* [1989] NLJR 435, DC; cf *Virdi v Law Society* [2009] EWHC 918 (Admin), [2009] All ER (D) 106 (Nov).

As to the principles applied, see generally *R v East Kerrier Justices, ex p Mundy* [1952] 2 QB 719, [1952] 2 All ER 144, DC; *R v Welshpool Justices, ex p Holley* [1953] 2 QB 403, [1953] 2 All ER 807, DC; *R v Barry (Glamorgan) Justices, ex p Kashim* [1953] 2 All ER 1005, [1953] 1 WLR 1320, DC; *Ex p How* [1953] 2 All ER 1562, [1953] 1 WLR 1480, DC; *Practice Direction* [1953] 2 All ER 1306n, [1953] 1 WLR 1416; *Practice Direction* [1954] 1 All ER 230, sub nom *Practice Note* [1954] 1 WLR 213. See further *R v Stafford Justices, ex p Ross* [1962] 1 All ER 540, [1962] 1 WLR 456, DC; *Hobby v Hobby* [1954] 2 All ER 395, [1954] 1 WLR 1020, DC; *R v Consett Justices, ex p Postal Bingo Ltd* [1967] 2 QB 9, [1967] 1 All ER 605, DC; *Simms v Moore* [1970] 2 QB 327, [1970] 3 All ER 1, DC; *Re B* [1975] Fam 127 at 136–137, [1975] 2 All ER 449 at 456, DC, per Sir George Baker.

As to tribunals generally see *R v Surrey Assessment Committee, North-Eastern Assessment Area, ex p FW Woolworth & Co Ltd* [1933] 1 KB 776, DC, as qualified by *Middlesex County Valuation Committee v West Middlesex Assessment Committee* [1937] Ch 361, [1937] 1 All ER 403, CA; *R v Salford Assessment Committee, ex p Ogden* [1937] 2 KB 1, [1937] 2 All ER 98, CA; *Re Lawson* (1941) 57 TLR 315, DC; *R v Architects' Registration Tribunal, ex p Jaggar* [1945] 2 All ER 131, DC; *R v Liverpool Dock Labour Board Appeal Tribunal, ex p Brandon* [1954] 2 Lloyd's Rep 186, DC; *R v Minister of Agriculture and Fisheries, ex p Graham, R v Agricultural Land Tribunal (South Western Province), ex p Benney* [1955] 2 QB 140, [1955] 2 All ER 129, CA. Where a person who is not a member of an adjudicating body does in fact take part in the adjudication, that body will be acting without jurisdiction inasmuch as it is improperly constituted: see *Lane v Norman* (1891) 66 LT 83; *Leary v National Union of Vehicle Builders* [1971] Ch 34 at 54–55, [1970] 2 All ER 713 at 724–725 per Megarry J; *Ward v Bradford Corpn* (1971) 70 LGR 27 at 33, CA, per Lord Denning MR, and at 37–38 per Phillimore LJ. A similar approach may be taken where the adjudicator is seen to have a conversation with one party out of the earshot of the other: *Furmston v Secretary of State for the Environment* [1983] JPL 49, DC; *Simmons v Secretary of State for the Environment* [1985] JPL 253; *British Muslims Association v Secretary of State for the Environment* (1987) 55 P & CR 205 at 212 per Stuart-Smith J (a mere casual exchange on a site visit would not normally lead to an inference of impropriety); cf *Cotterell v Secretary of State for the*

Environment [1991] 2 PLR 37 and *Barlow v Secretary of State for Local Government and the Regions* [2002] EWHC 2631 (Admin), [2002] All ER (D) 206 (Nov), where applications failed.

634. Interests which may give rise to the appearance of bias. In a wide range of other situations the test for apparent bias may be satisfied. A person ought not to participate or appear to participate in an appeal against his own decision[1], or act or appear to act as both prosecutor and judge[2]; the general rule is that in such circumstances the decision will be set aside[3]. Normally it will also be inappropriate for a member of the tribunal to act as witness[4]. Apparent bias may also arise because an adjudicator has already indicated partisanship by expressing opinions antagonistic or favourable to the parties before him[5], or has made known his views about the merits of the very issue or issues of a similar nature in such a way as to suggest prejudgment[6], or because he is so actively associated with the institution or conduct of proceedings before him, either in his personal capacity or by virtue of his membership of an interested organisation, as to make himself in substance, both judge and party[7], or because of his personal relationship with a party[8] or for other reasons[9]. It is not enough to show that the person adjudicating holds strong views on the general subject matter in respect of which he is adjudicating[10], or that he is a member of a trade union to which one of the parties belongs where the matter is not one in which a trade dispute is involved[11].

In an administrative, as opposed to a judicial context, the fact that the decision-maker may incline towards deciding an issue before him one way rather than another, in the light of implementing a policy for which he is responsible, will not affect the validity of his decision, provided that he acts fairly and with a mind not closed to argument[12]; and similar standards may be applied to other persons whose prior connection with the parties or the issues is liable to preclude them from acting with total detachment[13]. It seems that it is not necessarily fatal for the adjudicator to be aware of information extraneous to the adjudication, for example, facts gleaned from earlier proceedings, which might show a party in an unfavourable light[14], but there may be cases where such awareness gives rise to a real danger of bias[15].

1 *R v Lancashire Justices* (1906) 75 LJKB 198, DC. In *Hamlet v General Municipal Boilermakers and Allied Trades Union* [1987] 1 All ER 631, [1987] 1 WLR 449 it was held that there was no rule of natural justice that a member of a first instance tribunal was disabled from sitting on appeal, but it appears that not all the relevant authorities were cited, and the decision can be sustained on other grounds (ie that the procedure followed was required by the union's rules). See also *R v Keighley County Court, ex p Home Insulation Ltd* [1989] COD 174 (county court judge should not hear application to set aside his own arbitration award), considered in *R (on the application of Mahon) v Taunton County Court* [2001] EWHC Admin 1078, [2002] ACD 30, and in *R (on the application of Sivasubramaniam) v Wandsworth County Court* [2002] EWCA Civ 1738, [2003] 2 All ER 160, [2003] 1 WLR 475; *Jeyaretnam v Law Society of Singapore* [1989] AC 608, [1989] 2 All ER 193 at 203, [1989] 2 WLR 207 at 218, PC; *R v South Worcestershire Justices, ex p Lilley* [1995] 4 All ER 186, [1995] 1 WLR 1595; *R v Parole Board, ex p Watson* [1996] 2 All ER 641, [1996] 1 WLR 906, CA; cf *R (on the application of DPP) v Acton Youth Court* [2002] EWHC Admin 402, [2001] 1 WLR 1828.

Disqualification may be imposed by statute: see eg the Senior Courts Act 1981 s 56 (see COURTS vol 10 (Reissue) PARA 635); and the Crown Court Rules 1982, SI 1982/1109, r 5 (see COURTS vol 10 (Reissue) PARA 623). As to the Senior Courts Act 1981 see PARA 602 note 4. Yet it seems that in the absence of such provision a superior judge may participate in an appeal against his own decision: *R v Lovegrove* [1951] 1 All ER 804 (former Court of Criminal Appeal). However, this approach may properly be understood as one which was peculiar to the Court of Criminal Appeal, and derived either from necessity, or from a former practice: see *R v Bennett* (1914) 9 Cr App Rep 146; *R v Sharman* (1914) 9 Cr App Rep 130 (both Court of Criminal Appeal). It is suggested that it is unlikely to be applied nowadays, when benches are much larger (despite the decision in *R (on the application of Holmes) v General Medical Council*

[2002] EWCA Civ 1104, [2002] All ER (D) 524 (Jul). In administrative law the common law position appears to be as stated in the text: *R v Brixton Income Tax Comrs* (1913) 29 TLR 712, DC; *Cooper v Wilson* [1937] 2 KB 309, [1937] 2 All ER 726, CA; *Barrs v British Wool Marketing Board* 1957 SC 72, Ct of Sess; *Hannam v Bradford City Council* [1970] 2 All ER 690, [1970] 1 WLR 937, CA. See also *R v Surrey Assessment Committee, North-Eastern Assessment Area, ex p FW Woolworth & Co Ltd* [1933] 1 KB 776, DC (cf *Middlesex County Valuation Committee v West Middlesex Assessment Committee* [1937] Ch 361, [1937] 1 All ER 403, CA, where the officer was absent while the committee was taking its decision); and *R v Salford Assessment Committee, ex p Ogden* [1937] 2 KB 1, [1937] 2 All ER 98, CA (same person could not act as clerk to body making original decision and body reviewing it). Contrast *Roebuck v National Union of Mineworkers (Yorkshire Area) (No 2)* [1978] ICR 676 at 682 per Templeman J obiter (penalties imposed by union's disciplinary committee upheld by its council; held that some overlap of membership between bodies of this kind was inevitable in a domestic tribunal); *R v Secretary of State for the Environment, ex p Norwich City Council* [1982] QB 808, sub nom *Norwich City Council v Secretary of State for the Environment* [1982] 1 All ER 737, CA (not improper in the particular circumstances to use district valuer's staff for initial valuation of properties to be sold to council tenants, even though statute gave him final decision; objection taken by local housing authority, not tenants); cf *R (on the application of Primary Health Investment Properties Ltd) v Secretary of State for Health* [2009] EWHC 519 (Admin), [2009] All ER (D) 292 (Mar). Private discussion between the person hearing an internal appeal and the original decision-maker may make a dismissal unfair: *Campion v Hamworthy Engineering Ltd* [1987] ICR 966, CA.

2   *R v Meyer* (1875) 1 QBD 173; *Leeson v General Council of Medical Education and Registration* (1889) 43 ChD 366, CA; *Taylor v National Union of Seamen* [1967] 1 All ER 767, [1967] 1 WLR 532; *R v Barnsley Metropolitan District Council, ex p Hook* [1976] 3 All ER 452, [1976] 1 WLR 1052, CA; *Roebuck v National Union of Mineworkers (Yorkshire Area)* [1977] ICR 573; *Roebuck v National Union of Mineworkers (Yorkshire Area) (No 2)* [1978] ICR 676.

3   This is subject to the qualifications interposed by decisions cited in note 8. Whether it is proper for counsel for one party to adjudicate on the issue after having been elevated to the bench was discussed by the judges in *Thellusson v Lord Rendlesham* (1859) 7 HL Cas 429. It was there suggested that it would be proper. But this may have been a case of necessity, given the size of the nineteenth-century Bench. It is doubtful if it would be considered proper, or fair, in modern conditions.

4   *Roebuck v National Union of Mineworkers (Yorkshire Area)* [1977] ICR 573; *Roebuck v National Union of Mineworkers (Yorkshire Area) (No 2)* [1978] ICR 676. Such a course may not always be improper (see *R v Tooke* (1884) 48 JP 661; and *R v Farrant* (1887) 20 QBD 58, where a subpoena had been issued and the court declined to lay down a general rule that the issue of a subpoena prevented a judge from sitting), but giving evidence for one party may be indicative of partisanship. In *Jolliffe v Jolliffe* [1965] P 6 at 12–15, [1963] 3 All ER 295 at 301–302, DC, per Scarman J, it was observed that a magistrates' clerk ought not to officiate in a case in which he has given evidence. Different considerations apply when a judge is making a wasted costs order; *Re P (a barrister)* [2002] 1 Cr App Rep 19.

5   Personal friendship towards a party may constitute a disqualification: cf *Cottle v Cottle* [1939] 2 All ER 535, DC. The proposition that personal animosity may disqualify is supported by Irish decisions: see *R (Donoghue) v Cork County Justices* [1910] 2 IR 271; *R (Kingston) v Cork Justices* [1910] 2 IR 658; *R (Harrington) v Clare County Justices* [1918] 2 IR 116. See also *R v Abingdon Justices, ex p Cousins* (1964) 108 Sol Jo 840, DC (where a conviction was set aside because the accused had been an unsatisfactory pupil of the chairman of the bench; a reasonable person would have considered there was a real likelihood of bias); *R v Inner West London Coroner, ex p Dallaglio* [1994] 4 All ER 139, CA (language used by coroner about relatives of the deceased indicated a real possibility of subconscious bias); followed in *R v Highgate Justices, ex p Riley* [1996] RTR 150, [1996] COD 12, DC, a case in which an intervention from the bench suggested a general readiness to accept police evidence where there was a conflict; and see notes 14–15.

Partiality is a ground for setting aside an independent arbitrator's award: *Parker v Burroughs* (1702) Colles 257; *Catalina (Owners) v Norma (Owners)* (1938) 61 Ll L Rep 360. In disciplinary proceedings before a domestic tribunal it may be impracticable to insist that the decision can be taken only by persons holding no preconceptions (see *Maclean v Workers' Union* [1929] 1 Ch 602 at 625 per Maugham J; *White v Kuzych* [1951] AC 585, [1951] 2 All ER 435, PC; *R v Liverpool Dock Labour Board Appeal Tribunal, ex p Brandon* [1954] 2 Lloyd's Rep 186, DC), but strong personal hostility may preclude those who decide from complying with their duty to act fairly (see *Taylor v National Union of Seamen* [1967] 1 All ER

767, [1967] 1 WLR 532; *Breen v Amalgamated Engineering Union* [1971] 2 QB 175, [1971] 1 All ER 1148, CA; *Roebuck v National Union of Mineworkers (Yorkshire Area)* [1977] ICR 573; *Roebuck v National Union of Mineworkers (Yorkshire Area) (No 2)* [1978] ICR 676). It seems that in the case of such a tribunal a fair appeal will cure any unfairness below: *Modahl v British Athletics Federation* [2001] EWCA Civ 1447, [2002] 1 WLR 1192.

6   See *R v Kent Police Authority, ex p Godden* [1971] 2 QB 662, sub nom Re Godden [1971] 3 All ER 20, CA (doctor, having already formed unfavourable opinion of police officer's mental condition, was disqualified from determining whether officer was permanently disabled for the purpose of compulsory retirement); *R v Halifax Justices, ex p Robinson* (1912) 76 JP 233, CA (magistrate implacably opposed to granting liquor licence); *Ellis v Ministry of Defence* [1985] ICR 257, EAT (tribunal appearing to express concluded view half-way through hearing); *D v D* (1988) Times, 12 October, DC (judge suggesting order in advance of hearing); *R v Crown Court at Leeds, ex p Barlow* [1989] RTR 246 (judge interrupting and cross-examining witnesses, including the appellant, so as to appear to reject his case in the course of the evidence); c f *R (on the application of Bottomley) v General Commissioners of Income Tax, Pontefract Division* [2009] EWHC 1708 (Admin), [2009] All ER (D) 237 (Jul); *R v Bath Licensing Justices, ex p Cooper* [1989] 2 All ER 897, [1989] 1 WLR 878, DC (justice had recently adjudicated between same parties on the same point); contrast *R (on the application of Holmes) v General Medical Council* [2002] EWCA Civ 1104, [2002] All ER (D) 524 (Jul)), and *Ex p Wilder* (1902) 66 JP 761, DC (generalised hostility to motorists no disqualification). See also *R (Findlater) v Dublin Recorder and Justices* [1904] 2 IR 75 (note, however, that the correctness of this decision was doubted by Atkin LJ (dissenting) in *R v Bath Compensation Authority* [1925] 1 KB 685, and the decision of the majority was reversed in *Frome United Breweries Co v Bath Justices* [1926] AC 586, HL); *Goodall v Bilsland* 1909 SC 1152, HL; c f *McGeehan v Knox* 1913 SC 688 (membership of or subscription to body supporting changes in the law to suppress alcohol not a disqualification for adjudicating in licensing cases; active steps in that direction would disqualify; sed quaere); and compare the cases considered in *Locabail (UK) Ltd v Bayfield Properties Ltd* [2000] QB 451, [2000] 1 All ER 65, CA; *Taylor v Lawrence* [2002] EWCA Civ 90, [2003] QB 528, [2002] 2 All ER 353; *Helow v Secretary of State for the Home Department* [2008] UKHL 62, [2008] 2 All ER 1031, [2008] 1 WLR 2416.

7   See eg *R v Allan* (1864) 4 B & S 915; *R v Spedding, etc Justices* (1885) 2 TLR 163, DC; *R v Meyer* (1875) 1 QBD 173; *R v Milledge* (1879) 4 QBD 332, DC; *R v Winchester Justices* (1882) 46 JP Jo 724, DC; *R v Lee* (1882) 9 QBD 394, DC; *R v Ferguson* (1890) 54 JP Jo 101, DC; *R v Gaisford* [1892] 1 QB 381, DC; *R v LCC, ex p Akkersdyk, ex p Fermenia* [1892] 1 QB 190, DC; *R v Henley* [1892] 1 QB 504, DC; *R v Fraser* (1893) 9 TLR 613, DC; *Frome United Breweries Co Ltd v Bath Justices* [1926] AC 586, HL; *R v Sheffield Confirming Authority, ex p Truswell's Brewery Co Ltd* [1937] 4 All ER 114, DC; *R v Caernarvon Licensing Justices, ex p Benson* (1948) 113 JP 23, DC; *Hannam v Bradford Corpn* [1970] 2 All ER 690, [1970] 1 WLR 937, CA. See also *Law v Chartered Institute of Patent Agents* [1919] 2 Ch 276 (institute expelled member after having attempted to procure erasure from register by Board of Trade; expulsion invalid).

Inactive membership of a body instituting or participating in the proceedings does not necessarily disqualify: see *R v Deal Corpn and Justices, ex p Curling* (1881) 45 LT 439, DC (membership of RSPCA); *R v Handsley* (1881) 8 QBD 383 (members of local authority); *R v Burton, ex p Young* [1897] 2 QB 468, DC (membership of law society); *Leeson v General Council of Medical Education and Registration* (1889) 43 ChD 366, CA; *Allinson v General Council of Medical Education and Registration* [1894] 1 QB 750, CA (membership of union initiating proceedings for professional misconduct); *Hanson v Church Comrs for England* [1978] QB 823 at 831, [1977] 3 All ER 404 at 408, CA, per Lord Denning MR (Church Commissioners landlords in rent dispute; Master of Rolls and Lord Chief Justice not disqualified by ex officio, inactive membership); *Re S (a barrister)* [1981] QB 683, [1981] 2 All ER 952 (visitors to Inner Temple; disciplinary proceedings brought by committee of Bar Council forming part of Senate; given that offence did not involve opposition to Senate or Inns, it was permissible for members of Senate to form majority of tribunal); c f *Re P (a barrister)* [2005] 1 WLR 3019 (lay member of professional conduct committee disqualified from sitting on appeal to Visitors).

See also *R v Pwllheli Justices, ex p Soane* [1948] 2 All ER 815, DC (chairman of magistrates was member of fishery board which decided to prosecute; held not disqualified for, though present at the relevant meeting of the board, he took no part in the decision); *R v Barnsley County Borough Licensing Justices, ex p Barnsley and District Licensed Victuallers Association* [1960] 2 QB 167, [1960] 2 All ER 703, CA (licensing justices not disqualified although members of co-operative society applying for licence). Licensing justices have been allowed to show a degree of active partisanship in relation to forthcoming applications before them: see *R v Taylor, ex p Vogwill* (1898) 62 JP 67; *R v Nailsworth Licensing Justices, ex p Bird* [1953]

2 All ER 652, [1953] 1 WLR 1046, DC (although it is doubtful that such latitude would now be permitted). Licensing justices have been replaced by licensing authorities: see LICENSING AND GAMBLING vol 67 (2008) PARA 26 et seq. See also *R v Altrincham Justices, ex p Pennington* [1975] QB 549, [1975] 2 All ER 78, DC (prosecution for sale of goods to schools at short weight; magistrate belonging to education committee which concluded contract disqualified); *R v Bow Street Metropolitan Stipendiary Magistrate, ex p Pinochet Ugarte (No 2)* [2000] 1 AC 119, [1999] 1 All ER 577.

8   As to family relationship as a disqualification see *R v Rand* (1866) LR 1 QB 230 at 232–233 per Blackburn J; though cf *R (Murray and Wortley) v Armagh County Justices* (1915) 49 ILT 56; *Becquet v Lampriere* (1830) 1 Knapp 376, PC; though cf *Brookes v Earl of Rivers* (1668) Hard 503. See also *Metropolitan Properties Co (FGC) Ltd v Lannon* [1969] 1 QB 577, [1968] 3 All ER 304, CA (chairman of rent assessment committee lived with father who was tenant of landlord's associate company and had advised father in rent dispute); *University College of Swansea v Cornelius* [1988] ICR 735, EAT; *R v Wilson and Sprason* (1995) 8 Admin LR 1, CA; *R v Salt* (1996) 8 Admin LR 429. As to professional and business relationship as a disqualification see *Veritas Shipping Co v Anglo-Canadian Cement Ltd* [1966] 1 Lloyd's Rep 76; *R v Huggins* [1895] 1 QB 563, DC; *R v Sussex Justices, ex p McCarthy* [1924] 1 KB 256, DC; *R v Essex Justices, ex p Perkins* [1927] 2 KB 475, DC; *R v Legal Aid Board, ex p Donn & Co* [1996] 3 All ER 1; cf *R v Lower Munslow Justices, ex p Pudge* [1950] 2 All ER 756, DC; *R v Abdroikov* [2007] UKHL 37, [2008] 1 All ER 315, [2007] 1 WLR 2679; *Smith v Kvaerner Cementation Foundations Ltd* [2006] EWCA Civ 242, [2006] 3 All ER 593, [2007] 1 WLR 370; *Taylor v Lawrence* [2002] EWCA Civ 90, [2003] QB 528, [2002] 2 All ER 353; *Jones v DAS Legal Expenses Insurance Co Ltd* [2003] EWCA Civ 1071, [2004] IRLR 218. Members of the same barristers' chambers do not have control or undue influence over each other such as to disqualify one from chairing disciplinary proceedings brought after an inquiry chaired by another: *Ellis v Inner London Education Authority* (1976) 75 LGR 382; but cf *Smith v Kvaerner Cementation Foundations Ltd* (more modern arrangements for sharing expenses might make a difference). A solicitor should carry out a conflicts search before sitting: *Locabail (UK) Ltd v Bayfield Properties Ltd* [2000] QB 451, [2000] 1 All ER 65, CA. Nor can it be said that members of a professional governing body are necessarily incapable of hearing impartially a complaint against a member of the profession: *Re S (a barrister)* [1981] QB 683, [1981] 2 All ER 952 (visitors to Inner Temple); cf *Re P (a barrister)* [2005] 1 WLR 3019. Nor is shared representation of tribunal and one party in judicial review proceedings necessarily evidence of bias: *R v Vincent and the Department of Transport, ex p Turner* [1987] JPL 511; though cf *R (on the application of Alconbury Developments Ltd) v Secretary of State for the Environment, Transport and the Regions* [2001] UKHL 23, [2003] 2 AC 295, [2001] 2 All ER 929 for the greater importance now attributed to the visible independence of planning inspectors. An arbitrator who was involved in instructing counsel in relation to other proceedings between the parties to the arbitration could be removed: *Tracomin SA v Gibbs Nathaniel (Canada) Ltd* [1985] 1 Lloyd's Rep 586. It is inappropriate for advocates who regularly appear in front of a specialist tribunal to sit on it: *Lawal v Northern Spirit Ltd* [2003] UKHL 35, [2004] 1 All ER 187, [2003] ICR 856.

9   Eg hope of personal advancement: *R v Barnsley Borough Licensing Justices, ex p Barnsley and District Licensed Victuallers' Association* [1960] 2 QB 167 at 180–181, [1960] 2 All ER 703 at 710–711, CA, obiter per Lord Evershed MR, at 183–184 and 712 per Ormerod LJ, and at 186–188 and 714 per Devlin LJ; *Re Medicaments and Related Classes of Goods (No 2)* [2001] 1 WLR 700, [2001] ICR 564, CA. Although indebtedness to a party is not necessarily a disqualifying factor (*Morgan v Morgan* (1832) 1 Dowl 611), it may give rise to a likelihood of bias.
     A solicitor should not prosecute an accused whom he has earlier advised on his defence: *R v Dunstable Justices, ex p Cox* [1986] NLJ Rep 310, DC.

10   See eg *Ex p Wilder* (1902) 66 JP 761, DC; but cf *Locabail (UK) Ltd v Bayfield Properties Ltd* [2000] QB 451 at [25], [88]–[89], [2000] 1 All ER 65, CA, at [25], [88]–[89].

11   *Stevens v Stevens* (1929) 93 JP 120, DC; cf *R v Huggins* [1895] 1 QB 563 (magistrate disqualified from hearing proceedings brought for protection of small group to which he belonged).

12   *R v Chesterfield Borough Council, ex p Darker Enterprises Ltd* [1992] COD 466; *Franklin v Minister of Town and Country Planning* [1948] AC 87 at 103, [1947] 2 All ER 289 at 296, HL, per Lord Thankerton; *R v Amber Valley District Council, ex p Jackson* [1984] 3 All ER 501, [1985] 1 WLR 298 (majority political group on council adopted policy in favour of planning application before matter came to council; no evidence that objections would not be considered on merits); *R (on the application of Lewis) v Persimmon Homes Teeside Ltd* [2008] EWCA Civ 746, [2008] LGR 781, sub nom *R (on the application of Lewis) v Redcar and Cleveland*

Borough Council [2009] 1 WLR 83. See also *Steeples v Derbyshire County Council* [1984] 3 All ER 468, [1985] 1 WLR 256; *R v St Edmundsbury Borough Council, ex p Investors in Industry Commercial Properties Ltd* [1985] 3 All ER 234, [1985] 1 WLR 1168; *R v Carlisle City Council, ex p Cumbrian Co-operative Society Ltd* [1986] JPL 206, [1985] 2 EGLR 193; *R v Waltham Forest London Borough Council, ex p Baxter* [1988] QB 419, [1987] 3 All ER 671, CA (local councillor entitled to have regard to party whip when voting, but could not vote purely on that basis); *R v Buckinghamshire County Council, ex p Milton Keynes Borough Council* (1997) 9 Admin LR 158; cf the facts of *Porter v Magill* [2001] UKHL 67, [2002] 2 AC 357, [2002] 1 All ER 465. Where a body with a policing role exercises statutory powers of investigation it is wholly unrealistic to suggest that investigating officers, being potential prosecutors and acting necessarily on suspicions, should be unbiased; their duty was to exercise their powers fairly: *R v Secretary of State for Trade, ex p Perestrello* [1981] QB 19, [1980] 3 All ER 28. See also *R v Holderness Borough Council, ex p James Roberts Developments* (1992) 66 P & CR 46, 157 LG Rev 643, CA (builders were not prevented from acting as members of a planning committee on the basis that the applicant was a commercial rival).

13 As where an arbitrator or arbiter is employed by one of the parties to the dispute. See *Panamena Europea Navigacion Compania Limitada v Frederick Leyland & Co (J Russell & Co)* [1947] AC 428, HL (for the position where a contract provides that this should be so; the person in question is thus not in the position of an independent arbitrator); *Jackson v Barry Rly Co* [1893] 1 Ch 238, CA; and see *Hounslow London Borough Council v Twickenham Garden Developments Ltd* [1971] Ch 233, [1970] 3 All ER 326. As to arbitration generally see ARBITRATION vol 2 (2008) PARA 1201 et seq.

14 *Re B (TA) (an infant)* [1971] Ch 270 at 277–278, [1970] 3 All ER 705 at 711 per Megarry J; *R v Frankland Prison Board of Visitors, ex p Lewis* [1986] 1 All ER 272, [1986] 1 WLR 130; *R v Weston-super-Mare Justices, ex p Shaw* [1987] QB 640, [1987] 1 All ER 255 (magistrates aware of other outstanding charges); but cf *R v Liverpool City Justices, ex p Topping* [1983] 1 All ER 490, [1983] 1 WLR 119, DC (conviction quashed because magistrates did not consider whether they should have sat or not). See also *R v Colchester Stipendiary Magistrate, ex p Beck* [1979] QB 674, [1979] 2 All ER 1035, DC; *R v Secretary of State for Trade, ex p Perestrello* [1981] QB 19, [1980] 3 All ER 28; *R v Board of Visitors of Walton Prison, ex p Weldon* [1985] Crim LR 514; and *R v Oxford Regional Mental Health Review Tribunal, ex p Mackman* (1986) Times, 2 June; *R (on the application of M) v Mental Health Review Tribunal* [2005] EWHC 2791 (Admin), 90 BMLR 65.

15 *R v Gough* [1993] AC 646; *R v Grimsby Borough Quarter Sessions, ex p Fuller* [1956] 1 QB 36, [1955] 3 All ER 300, DC; *R v Liverpool City Justices, ex p Topping* [1983] 1 All ER 490, [1983] 1 WLR 119, DC; *R v Birmingham Magistrates' Court, ex p Robinson* (1985) 150 JP 1, DC; *R v Downham Market Magistrates' Court, ex p Nudd* [1989] RTR 169, DC, both considered in *R v Hereford Magistrates' Court, ex p Rowlands* [1998] QB 110, [1997] 2 WLR 854. See also *Wilcox v HGS* [1976] ICR 306, [1976] IRLR 222, CA (prospective witness wrote letter to tribunal at interlocutory stage containing comments on matter to be in issue).

635. Waiver and acquiescence. The right to challenge proceedings conducted in breach of the rule against bias may be lost by waiver, either express or implied[1]. There is no waiver or acquiescence unless the party entitled to object to an adjudicator's participation was made fully aware, or knew, of the nature of the disqualification and of his right to object[2] and had an adequate opportunity of objecting[3]. However, once these conditions are met a party will be considered to have acquiesced in the participation of a disqualified adjudicator unless he has objected at the earliest practicable opportunity[4]. The same principles apply where an adjudicator is subject to a statutory disqualification if that disqualification is merely declaratory of an existing common law disqualification[5]. In the case of a new statutory disqualification, there appears to be a presumption that regularity cannot be conferred by waiver or acquiescence[6], but a party who, being aware of the disqualification, fails to take objection to it at the hearing may be refused relief if he seeks a discretionary remedy when subsequently impugning the proceedings[7].

1 *Ex p Ilchester Parish* (1861) 25 JP 56; *R (Giant's Causeway etc Tramway Co) v Antrim County Justices* [1895] 2 IR 603.

2   Waiver cannot occur without full knowledge of rights: *Vyvyan v Vyvyan* (1861) 30 Beav 65 at 74 per Sir John Romilly MR (and see further note 3). In *R v Holyhead General Comrs, ex p Roberts* (1982) 56 TC 127, it was held that there could be no waiver without knowledge of the right to object; *R v Cumberland Justices, ex p Midland Rly Co* (1888) 58 LT 491, DC; *R v Essex Justices, ex p Perkins* [1927] 2 KB 475, DC; *R v Barnsley Metropolitan District Council, ex p Hook* [1976] 3 All ER 452, [1976] 1 WLR 1052, CA (indeed, the full material giving rise to the right to object may not emerge until the defendant, complying with its duty of candour, files its evidence). An advocate is not obliged to put 'fishing' questions in order to extract evidence of a disqualification which he suspects, and a failure to do so will not amount to waiver: *R v Barnsley Licensing Justices, ex p Barnsley and District Licensed Victuallers' Association* [1959] 2 QB 276 at 284, [1959] 2 All ER 635 at 640, DC, per Lord Parker CJ; on appeal [1960] 2 QB 167, [1960] 2 All ER 703, CA; *Smith v Kvaerner Cementation Foundations Ltd* [2006] EWCA Civ 242, [2006] 3 All ER 593, [2007] 1 WLR 370.

3   *R (Harrington) v Clare County Court Judge and County Justices* [1918] 2 IR 116; cf *R v Cambridgeshire Justices, ex p Steeple Morden Overseers* (1855) 25 LTOS 128. Where a party is unrepresented before a tribunal, the tribunal may be under a duty to point out to him that he is entitled to object on the ground of bias: see *Wilcox v HGS* [1976] ICR 306, [1976] IRLR 222, CA. Further, tribunal members should make full disclosure of potential disqualifying factors in all cases: *Locabail (UK) Ltd v Bayfield Properties Ltd* [2000] QB 451, [2000] 1 All ER 65, CA. See also *Fox v Secretary of State for the Environment* [1993] JPL 448; *Cotterell v Secretary of State for the Environment* [1991] JPL 1155; *Halifax Building Society v Secretary of State for the Environment* [1983] JPL 816.

4   *Auckland Casino Ltd v Casino Control Authority* [1995] 1 NZLR 142; *R v Byles, ex p Hollidge* (1912) 108 LT 270, DC; *Wakefield Local Board of Health v West Riding and Grimsby Rly Co* (1865) LR 1 QB 84; *R v Cheltenham Comrs* (1841) 1 QB 467. It seems that an applicant for a quashing order should specify in his witness statements or affidavits that neither he nor his advocate knew of the objection at the time of the hearing: *R v Richmond, Surrey Justices* (1860) 2 LT 373; *R v Kent Justices* (1880) 44 JP 298, DC; *R v Williams, ex p Phillips* [1914] 1 KB 608, DC. See also *Ex p Ilchester Parish* (1861) 25 JP 56. As to quashing orders see PARA 693 et seq.

5   *Wakefield Local Board of Health v West Riding and Grimsby Rly Co* (1865) LR 1 QB 84.

6   Inasmuch as the proceedings are to be treated as void: see *R v Williams, ex p Phillips* [1914] 1 KB 608, DC; and PARA 637. See also *R (Giant's Causeway & Tramway Co) v Antrim County Justices* [1895] 2 IR 603 at 636 per Sir O'Brien CJ.

7   *R v Williams, ex p Phillips* [1914] 1 KB 608, DC. See also *R v Inner London Quarter Sessions, ex p D'Souza* [1970] 1 All ER 481, [1970] 1 WLR 376, DC; *R v Simpson* [1914] 1 KB 66, DC.

636.   Necessity and statutory authority. If all members of the only tribunal competent to determine a matter are subject to disqualification, they may be authorised and obliged to hear and determine that matter by virtue of the operation of the common law doctrine of necessity. The rationale for the application of this doctrine is to prevent a failure of justice. The doctrine will, however, be applied only in clear and compelling circumstances[1].

Adjudicators subject to a common law disqualification may be authorised by statute to officiate[2]; or it may be provided by statute that the validity of proceedings is not to be affected by the participation of an adjudicator subject to specified disqualifications[3]. In such circumstances, the scope of an exemption from disqualification will be strictly construed[4], and adjudicators authorised to sit notwithstanding their interest in the matter may be held subject to disqualification for a different form of interest or likelihood of bias[5].

1   *Judges v A-G for Saskatchewan* (1937) 53 TLR 464, PC; *Great Charte Parish and Kennington Parish* (1742) 2 Stra 1173; *R v Essex Justices* (1816) 5 M & S 513; *Grand Junction Canal Co v Dimes* (1849) 12 Beav 63; revsd on the facts on this question sub nom *Dimes v Proprietors of the Grand Junction Canal* (1852) 3 HL Cas 759. Normally the appropriate course of action where members of a tribunal are all disqualified will be to commit the issue to the determination of a different tribunal having jurisdiction, if one can be lawfully constituted; cf *R v Barnsley Licensing Justices, ex p Barnsley and District Licensed Victuallers' Association* [1960] 2 QB 167, [1960] 2 All ER 703, CA; and see *Rose v Humbles* [1970] 2 All ER 519, [1970] 1 WLR 1061; on appeal [1972] 1 All ER 314, [1972] 1 WLR 33, CA (where it was possible to remit the

question to a differently constituted tribunal). If no such tribunal exists, it seems that the issue ought not to be determined at all unless inaction would be unfair or otherwise contrary to public policy.

In *R v Chief Constable of South Wales, ex p Thornhill* [1987] IRLR 313, CA (police disciplinary hearing; officer who decided to bring charge entered chief constable's room while the latter was deliberating on decision, in order to discuss urgent matter), weight was attached to the need for the normal functions of the police to continue without disruption. In other cases the context in which the decision must be taken may mean that there will inevitably be some appearance of bias: see eg *R v Board of Visitors of Frankland Prison, ex p Lewis* [1986] 1 All ER 272, [1986] 1 WLR 130; and *R v Crown Court at Bristol, ex p Cooper* [1990] 2 All ER 193, [1990] 1 WLR 1031, CA; cf *R (Chief Constable of the Lancashire Constabulary) v Crown Court at Preston* [2001] EWHC Admin 928, [2002] 1 WLR 1332. Compare also *Lower Hutt City Council v Bank* [1974] 1 NZLR 545; and *Laytons Wines Ltd v Wellington South Licensing Trust (No 2)* [1977] 1 NZLR 570. Cf also *Kingsley v United Kingdom* (2002) 35 EHRR 177 (a case under the Convention for the Protection of Human Rights and Fundamental Freedoms (Rome, 4 November 1950; TS 71 (1953) Cmd 8969) art 6 (see CONSTITUTIONAL LAW AND HUMAN RIGHTS vol 8(2) (Reissue) PARA 134 et seq): necessity does not prevent a breach of article 6 of the Convention).

2   See eg the Licensing Act 1964 s 130 (repealed). There is no doubt that Parliament can make a man judge in his own cause: *Lee v Bude and Torrington Junction Rly Co* (1871) LR 6 CP 576 at 582; *Wilkinson v Barking Corpn* [1948] 1 KB 721, [1948] 1 All ER 564, CA. Such provisions may well be incompatible with the Convention for the Protection of Human Rights and Fundamental Freedoms, however: see PARA 651. Further, in such cases the adjudicator must be especially scrupulous that his decision is seen to be fair: *Steeples v Derbyshire County Council* [1984] 3 All ER 468, [1985] 1 WLR 256 (local authority empowered to grant self planning permission). Similarly, the rules of a body such as a trade union (ie the contract between the members) may allow or require the person in question to adjudicate: eg *Herring v Templeman* [1973] 3 All ER 569, CA; *Hamlet v General Muncipal Boilermakers and Allied Trades Union* [1987] 1 All ER 631, [1987] 1 WLR 449. But clear words are necessary to exclude the normal principle in this way: *Roebuck v National Union of Mineworkers (Yorkshire Area)* [1977] ICR 573.

3   See eg the Justices of the Peace Act 1997 ss 6, 66 (repealed); and the Licensing Act 1964 s 193(6) (repealed).

4   As in *R v Henley* [1892] 1 QB 504, DC; *Mersey Docks Trustees v Gibbs* (1866) LR 1 HL 93 at 110 per Blackburn J. Further, a statutory provision which appears to require a person who would otherwise be disqualified to officiate will probably be construed as directory and not mandatory: *Jeyaretnam v Law Society of Singapore* [1989] 2 All ER 193 at 203, [1989] 2 WLR 207 at 218, PC. See also PARA 632.

5   See eg *R v Handsley* (1881) 8 QBD 383, DC, disapproving *R v Gibbon* (1880) 6 QBD 168, DC; *R v Barnsley Licensing Justices, ex p Barnsley and District Licensed Victuallers' Association* [1960] 2 QB 167, [1960] 2 All ER 703, CA; *Jeffs v New Zealand Dairy Production and Marketing Board* [1967] 1 AC 551, [1966] 3 All ER 863, PC; *Steeples v Derbyshire County Council* [1984] 3 All ER 468, [1985] 1 WLR 256; and see PARA 631 note 12.

637.   Effect of breach of the rule. If one of the adjudicators has a direct personal interest in the issue, the proceedings will be set aside even though none of his fellow adjudicators was thus disqualified[1]; and it appears that the same principle applies where one adjudicator is subject to disqualification for likelihood of bias[2]. In such cases the court will not consider whether the disqualified person did in fact influence the decision[3].

Where a person subject to disqualification leaves the impression that he is participating in the proceedings, the general rule is that the proceedings may be set aside even though he has not in fact taken an actual part in them[4]. If he is present during the proceedings, they will not be immune from challenge unless he has made it clear that he is not present as a participant[5].

1   *R v Bow Street Metropolitan Stipendiary Magistrate, ex p Pinochet Ugarte (No 2)* [2000] 1 AC 119, [1999] 1 All ER 577, HL; *R v Cheltenham Comrs* (1841) 1 QB 467 at 480 per Williams J; *R v Hertfordshire Justices* (1845) 6 QB 753 (in this case Patteson J departed from the more lenient view he had expressed in *R v Cheltenham Comrs*); *R v Hendon RDC, ex p Chorley* [1933] 2 KB 696, DC.

2   *R v Meyer* (1875) 1 QBD 173; *R v Huggins* [1895] 1 QB 563, DC; *R v Lancashire Justices*
    (1906) 75 LJKB 198, DC; *R v LCC, ex p Akkersdyk, ex p Fermenia* [1892] 1 QB 190, DC; *R v
    Barnsley Licensing Justices, ex p Barnsley and District Licensed Victuallers' Association* [1960]
    2 QB 167 at 181, [1960] 2 All ER 703 at 710–711, CA, per Lord Evershed MR, and at 186 and
    714 per Devlin LJ; *Roebuck v National Union of Mineworkers (Yorkshire Area)* [1977] ICR
    573; *Roebuck v National Union of Mineworkers (Yorkshire Area) (No 2)* [1978] ICR 676.

3   See the cases cited in note 2. This proposition is, however, subject to the possible qualification
    that it may exceptionally be right to overlook a likelihood of bias among a small number of
    members of a large administrative body exercising functions analogous to the judicial, if there
    was no supposition that they influenced the result: see *R v LCC, Re Empire Theatre* (1894) 71
    LT 638 at 640, DC, per Charles J; *R v Huggins* [1895] 1 QB 563 at 565–567, DC, per Wright J.
    In *R v LCC, ex p Akkersdyk, ex p Fermenia* [1892] 1 QB 190, DC, however, where a small
    group of councillors showed active partisanship in opposition to an application for renewal of a
    music and dancing licence, instructing counsel to represent them at the hearing before the
    council, as well as participating in the discussion, the council's decision not to renew the licence
    was held to be invalid although taken by a large majority and although the biased councillors
    abstained from voting; cf *R v Secretary of State for Trade, ex p Anderson Strathclyde plc* [1983]
    2 All ER 233 at 237, DC, per Dunn LJ.

4   *R v Chesterfield Borough Council, ex p Darker Enterprises Ltd* [1992] COD 466; *R v
    Hertfordshire Justices* (1845) 6 QB 753; *R v Suffolk Justices* (1852) 18 QB 416; *R v Surrey
    Justices* (1855) 26 LTOS 89; *R v Meyer* (1875) 1 QBD 173; *R v Lancashire Justices* (1906) 75
    LJKB 198, DC; *R v Hendon RDC, ex p Chorley* [1933] 2 KB 696, DC; *R (Uprichard) v Armagh
    County Justices* (1913) 47 ILT 84; *R v Barnsley Metropolitan Borough Council, ex p Hook*
    [1976] 3 All ER 452, [1976] 1 WLR 1052, CA. A similar principle applies to magistrates' clerks
    having a professional interest in the outcome of the proceedings: see *R v Sussex Justices,
    ex p McCarthy* [1924] 1 KB 256, DC; and PARA 634 note 8. See also *R v Great Yarmouth
    Justices* (1882) 8 QBD 525, DC (participation as appellant by chairman of bench who had
    presided over identical proceedings immediately beforehand).

5   *R v London Justices* (1852) 18 QB 421; *R v Budden etc, Kent Justices* (1896) 60 JP 166, DC;
    R v London Justices, ex p Kerfoot (1896) 60 JP 726, DC; *R v Byles, ex p Hollidge* (1912) 108
    LT 270, DC. In some circumstances even such an announcement at the time may not be
    sufficient: see *R v Leicestershire Fire Authority, ex p Thompson* (1979) 77 LGR 373 (fireman on
    disciplinary charge alleged victimisation by chief officer; chief officer retired with tribunal to
    advise on implications of available penalties).

638.   Whether proceedings void or voidable. There is authority for the
proposition that prima facie the participation of a disqualified person renders
proceedings voidable but not void[1], and this has been taken to mean that the
proceedings are to be treated as valid until set aside by a competent tribunal, and
until then are not open to collateral attack[2]. It may be, however, that these
propositions, if now acceptable at all, should be confined to the proceedings of
courts in a strict sense; for there are a number of dicta indicating that, where
other proceedings are tainted with this defect, they are not merely voidable but
void[3], and are to be assimilated to proceedings before an improperly constituted
tribunal[4]. Interest and likelihood of bias, like other defects going to jurisdiction,
are established by witness statement or affidavit[5]. Formulae purporting to
deprive the courts of supervisory jurisdiction are ineffective to bar review, not
only for jurisdictional defects in the narrow sense but also for breach of the rules
of natural justice[6]. A decision given in breach of the rule against interest and bias
may be declared void[7], and one such decision has been successfully impeached by
an order of mandamus[8]. In general, appeal is an inappropriate means of
attacking a decision vitiated by interest or likelihood of bias[9]; in this sense the
decision is to be treated as void[10]. Nevertheless, such a decision is not necessarily
to be regarded as a nullity for all purposes, and it may be considered to be valid
at least against third parties, until it is successfully impeached by a person

aggrieved[11]. Moreover, if the decision were absolutely null and void in relation to the person aggrieved, he would not be precluded from impugning it as the result of waiver or acquiescence[12].

1 *Dimes v Grand Junction Canal Proprietors* (1852) 3 HL Cas 759 at 786 per Mr Baron Parke; *Wildes v Russell* (1866) LR 1 CP 722; *Phillips v Eyre* (1870) LR 6 QB 1 at 22 per Willes J; *R (Hastings) v Galway Justices* [1906] 2 IR 499.

2 *Wildes v Russell* (1866) LR 1 CP 722 at 741–743 per Willes J; *R v Kent Justices* (1880) 44 JP 298; cf note 8.

3 See eg *Allinson v General Council of Medical Education and Registration* [1894] 1 QB 750 at 757, CA, per Lord Esher MR; *Thompson v British Medical Association (New South Wales Branch)* [1924] AC 764 at 780, PC; *Oscroft v Benabo* [1967] 2 All ER 548 at 557, [1967] 1 WLR 1087 at 1100, CA, per Diplock LJ. In *Anisminic Ltd v Foreign Compensation Commission* [1969] 2 AC 147, [1969] 1 All ER 208, HL, this point was made explicitly or by implication in dicta by Lord Reid at 171 and 213, by Lord Morris of Borth-y-Gest at 181 and 221, by Lord Pearce at 195 and 233, and by Lord Wilberforce at 207 and 244. No distinction was drawn between the effect of breach of the rule *nemo judex in causa sua* and the rule *audi alteram partem* (see PARA 629). A similar assumption was made in *O'Reilly v Mackman* [1983] 2 AC 237 at 276, [1982] 3 All ER 1124 at 1127, HL, per Lord Diplock; though cf *Durayappah v Fernando* [1967] 2 AC 337, [1967] 2 All ER 152, PC, where Lord Upjohn, giving reasons for the Privy Council's report, and referring to *Ridge v Baldwin* [1964] AC 40, [1963] 2 All ER 66, HL, held that the dissolution of the council in that case, carried out in breach of the *audi alteram partem* rule, was not a nullity, but voidable at the instance of the council only. The utility of the distinction between void and voidable acts has been questioned: see ADMINISTRATIVE LAW vol 1(1) (2001 Reissue) PARA 26. See also PARA 645.

4 See PARA 611.

5 *R v Nat Bell Liquors Ltd* [1922] 2 AC 128 at 160, PC; *R v Aberdare Canal Co* (1850) 14 QB 854.

6 See note 3; and ADMINISTRATIVE LAW vol 1(1) (2001 Reissue) PARA 21. However, in some cases it has been assumed that it is for the inferior tribunal itself expressly to consider whether it should hear the case, and that the court should not intervene unless it has, for example, applied the wrong test or reached a perverse conclusion: see *R v Sandwich Justices, ex p Berry* (1981) 74 Cr App Rep 132; *R v Liverpool City Council, ex p Topping* [1983] 1 All ER 490, [1983] 1 WLR 119; *R v Frankland Prison Board of Visitors, ex p Lewis* [1986] 1 All ER 272, [1986] 1 WLR 130; *R v Weston-super-Mare Justices, ex p Shaw* [1987] QB 640, [1987] 1 All ER 255. These were all cases in which the procedure adopted by decision-makers might have given rise to an appearance of bias because of their background knowledge of the case, and show that in such cases decision-makers must consider, applying the right test, whether it is right for them to hear the case. They are not cases involving disqualifying interests.

7 See *Cooper v Wilson* [1937] 2 KB 309, [1937] 2 All ER 726, CA; *Hannam v Bradford City Council* [1970] 2 All ER 690, [1970] 1 WLR 937, CA.

8 *R v LCC, ex p Akkersdyk, ex p Fermenia* [1892] 1 QB 190, DC; approved on broader grounds in *Frome United Breweries Ltd v Bath Justices* [1926] AC 586, HL; but cf *R v Kent Justices* (1880) 44 JP 298, DC. Orders of mandamus are now known as mandatory orders: see PARA 687 note 1. As to mandatory orders see PARA 703 et seq. The universal assumption that the courts have jurisdiction to declare void a decision reached in breach of the rule appears to imply the legitimacy of impeaching such a decision collaterally by a mandatory order which requires the matter to be heard according to law.

9 See *Metropolitan Properties Co (FGC) Ltd v Lannon* [1969] 1 QB 577, [1968] 3 All ER 304, CA. Appeal to a domestic body was held to be a necessary preliminary to recourse to the courts in *White v Kuzych* [1951] AC 585, [1951] 2 All ER 435, PC, despite allegations that the 'decision' challenged was vitiated by bias; but this reasoning depends on the interpretation of that body's rules. See *Lawlor v Union of Post Office Workers* [1965] Ch 712, [1965] 1 All ER 353; *Hiles v Amalgamated Society of Woodworkers* [1968] Ch 440, [1967] 3 All ER 70. Bias was not cured on appeal in *R v Metropolitan Police Comr and Home Secretary, ex p Warren* (10 May 1988, unreported), QBD; and see *R (on the application of AM (Cameroon)) v Asylum and Immigration Tribunal* [2008] EWCA Civ 100, [2008] 4 All ER 1159, [2008] 1 WLR 2062.

10 See ADMINISTRATIVE LAW vol 1(1) (2001 Reissue) PARA 26. The point is well illustrated by decisions on the effect of breach of the *audi alteram partem* rule: see eg *Annamunthodo v Oilfield Workers Trade Union* [1961] AC 945, [1961] 3 All ER 621, PC; *Ridge v Baldwin* [1964] AC 40, [1963] 2 All ER 66, HL; and PARA 645.

11 As to the possible implications of invalidity see further PARA 645; and ADMINISTRATIVE LAW vol 1(1) (2001 Reissue) PARA 26. As to persons aggrieved see PARA 664.

12 See PARA 636. The decisions in question were not all based upon the discretionary nature of the relief sought.

C. RIGHT TO NOTICE AND OPPORTUNITY TO BE HEARD

639. The right to be heard. The rule that no person is to be condemned unless that person has been given prior notice of the allegations against him and a fair opportunity to be heard (the *audi alteram partem* rule) is a fundamental principle of justice[1]. This rule has been refined and adapted to govern the proceedings of bodies other than judicial tribunals; and a duty to act in conformity with the rule has been imposed by the common law on administrative bodies not required by statute or contract to conduct themselves in a manner analogous to a court[2]. Moreover, even in the absence of any charge, the severity of the impact of an administrative decision on the interests of an individual may suffice in itself to attract a duty to comply with this rule[3]. Common law and statutory obligations of procedural fairness now also have to be read in the light of the right under the Convention for the Protection of Human Rights and Fundamental Freedoms to a fair trial[4] which will be engaged in cases involving the determination of civil rights or obligations or any criminal charge[5].

The rule generally applies, at least with full force, only to conduct leading directly to a final act or decision, and not to the making of a preliminary decision or to an investigation designed to obtain information for the purpose of a report or a recommendation on which a subsequent decision may be founded[6]. However, the nature of an inquiry or a provisional decision may be such as to give rise to a reasonable expectation that persons prejudicially affected should be afforded an opportunity to put their case at that stage; and it may be unfair not to require the inquiry to be conducted in a judicial spirit if its outcome is likely to expose a person to a legal hazard or other substantial prejudice[7].

The circumstances in which the rule will apply cannot be exhaustively defined, but they embrace a wide range of situations in which acts or decisions have civil consequences for individuals by directly affecting their interests or legitimate expectations[8]. In a particular context, the presumption in favour of the rule may be partly or wholly displaced where compliance with it would be inconsistent with a paramount need for taking urgent preventive or remedial action[9]; or with the interests of national security[10]; or where disclosure of confidential but relevant information to an interested party would be materially prejudicial to the public interest[11] or the interests of other persons[12]; or where it is impracticable to give prior notice or an opportunity to be heard[13]; or where an adequate substitute for a prior hearing is available[14]; or where a hearing would clearly serve no useful purpose[15]; or, in some cases, where Parliament has evinced an intention to exclude the operation of the rule either by conferring on the competent authority unfettered discretionary power[16], or by expressly providing for notice and opportunity to be heard for one purpose but omitting to make any such provision for another purpose[17]. Where, however, a general duty to act judicially is cast on the competent authority, only clear language will be interpreted as conferring a power to exclude the operation of the rule, and even in the absence of express procedural requirements fairness may still dictate that prior notice and an opportunity to be heard should be afforded[18].

The rule applies to all judicial proceedings[19]. It does not extend to the dismissal of an ordinary employee unless a procedure indicative of a duty to comply with the rule has been expressly prescribed, but it does apply prima facie where dismissal entails deprivation of legal status or forfeiture of a public office not held purely at pleasure[20]. However, it will often be applicable to the conduct of disciplinary proceedings[21], and to decisions whether to grant or withdraw a privilege such as a licence[22].

Whether, and if so the extent to which, the rule is to be applied in such situations will depend on the consideration and balancing of a variety of factors. These will include the impact of any procedure expressly prescribed for making the decision, the range of considerations that the decision-maker is entitled to take into account, the nature of the sanction, if any, to be imposed, whether the decision impacts upon any direct personal or proprietary interest, and if so, the extent of the potential impact, and the effect of the application of the rule on the decision-making process[23].

1   See *R v Chancellor of Cambridge University* (1723) 1 Stra 557 at 567 per Fortescue J; *Bonaker v Evans* (1850) 16 QB 162 at 171 per Parke B; *Painter v Liverpool Oil Gas Light Co* (1836) 3 Ad & El 433; *R v Dyer* (1703) 1 Salk 181; *R v Benn and Church* (1795) 6 Term Rep 198; *Harper v Carr* (1797) 7 Term Rep 270; *Gibbs v Stead* (1828) 8 B & C 528; *R v Totnes Union Guardians* (1845) 7 QB 690; *R v Cheshire Lines Committee* (1873) LR 8 QB 344; *Spackman v Plumstead Board of Works* (1885) 10 App Cas 229 at 240, HL, per Earl of Selborne LC; *Re Hamilton* [1981] AC 1038, [1981] 2 All ER 711, HL. As to the obligation of the European Commission to observe the principle see (Case 85/76) *Hoffmann-La Roche & Co AG v Commission of the European Communities* [1979] ECR 461, [1979] 3 CMLR 211, ECJ.
2   See PARAS 629–630.
3   See PARA 629. But where no charge or accusation is involved, the standards of procedural fairness may be less stringent: see e g *Maxwell v Department of Trade and Industry* [1974] QB 523, [1974] 2 All ER 122, CA. See also *R v HM Coroner at Hammersmith, ex p Peach (No 2)* [1980] QB 211 at 219–220, [1980] 2 WLR 496 at 503–504, DC, per Griffiths J (no obligation on coroner to disclose documents to deceased's brother, because the brother was in no danger of being attacked or criticised); *R v Secretary of State for the Environment, ex p Southwark London Borough Council* (1987) 54 P & CR 226, DC; *Public Disclosure Commission v Isaacs* [1989] 1 All ER 137, [1988] 1 WLR 1043, PC; *R (on the application of Seahawk Marine Foods Ltd) v Southampton Port Health Authority* [2002] EWCA Civ 54, [2002] EHLR 15; *R (on the application of L) v Secretary of State for the Home Department* [2003] EWCA Civ 25, [2003] 1 All ER 1062, [2003] 1 WLR 1230; and cf *R v North Yorkshire County Council, ex p M* [1989] QB 411, [1989] 1 All ER 143, [1988] 3 WLR 1344. The Parole Board in considering the revocation of a prisoner's licence is under a common law duty to act fairly: *R (on the application of West) v Parole Board* [2005] UKHL 1, [2005] 1 All ER 755, [2005] 1 WLR 350. A prison governor considering a prisoner's categorisation is, however, not obliged to hear representations: *R (on the application of Palmer) v Secretary of State for the Home Department* [2004] EWHC 1817 (Admin), (2004) Times, 13 September, [2004] All ER (D) 327 (Jul); *R v Secretary of State for the Home Department, ex p Allen* (2000) Times, 21 March, CA.
4   Ie the Convention for the Protection of Human Rights and Fundamental Freedoms (Rome, 4 November 1950; TS 71 (1953) Cmd 8969) art 6: see CONSTITUTIONAL LAW AND HUMAN RIGHTS vol 8(2) (Reissue) PARA 134 et seq.
5   Since the enactment of the Human Rights Act 1998 it is unlawful for a public authority to act incompatibly with a right under the Convention for the Protection of Human Rights and Fundamental Freedoms (1950). Those rights include the right under art 6(1) to a fair trial: 'In the determination of his civil rights and obligations or of any criminal charge against him, everyone is entitled to a fair and public hearing within a reasonable time by an independent and impartial tribunal established by law. Judgment shall be pronounced publicly but the press and public may be excluded from all or part of the trial in the interests of morals, public order or national security in a democratic society, where the interests of juveniles or the protection of the private life of the parties so require, or to the extent strictly necessary in the opinion of the court in special circumstances where publicity would prejudice the interests of justice'. See generally PARAS 650–654; and CONSTITUTIONAL LAW AND HUMAN RIGHTS vol 8(2) (Reissue) PARA 134 et seq.
6   The reason for this is that whether or not there has been compliance with the duty to act fairly will not in all cases depend on an individual analysis of each stage of the decision-making process. Depending on the circumstances it may be sufficient for the process, looked at overall, to have afforded the individual a full opportunity to make proper representations prior to the decision being made. See *Fredman v Minister of Health* (1935) 154 LT 240; *Wiseman v Borneman* [1971] AC 297, [1969] 3 All ER 275, HL (no right to be heard prior to decision

whether or not to prosecute); *Re Pergamon Press* [1971] Ch 388, [1970] 3 All ER 535, CA (content of duty to act fairly reduced by preliminary nature of the process); *Pearlberg v Varty (Inspector of Taxes)* [1972] 2 All ER 6, [1972] 1 WLR 534, HL; *Herring v Templeman* [1973] 3 All ER 569, CA; *Maxwell v Department of Trade and Industry* [1974] QB 523 at 534 per Lord Denning MR (right to cross-examination of witnesses not required); *Howard v Borneman (No 2)* [1975] Ch 201, [1974] 3 All ER 862, CA (affd on another point [1976] AC 301, [1975] 2 All ER 418, HL); *Norwest Holst Ltd v Secretary of State for Trade* [1978] Ch 201, [1978] 3 All ER 280, CA (no duty to receive representations before deciding whether or not to commence inquiry); *Moran v Lloyd's* [1981] 1 Lloyd's Rep 423, [1981] Com LR 46, CA (inquiry leading to recommendation as to whether or not to discipline not subject to natural justice); *Fayed v United Kingdom* (1994) 18 EHRR 393, ECtHR (functions of Companies Act inspectors are investigative rather than adjudicatory for the purposes of the Convention for the Protection of Human Rights and Fundamental Freedoms (1950) art 6; possibility of judicial review sufficient safeguard); *Furnell v Whangerei High Schools Board* [1973] AC 660, [1973] 1 All ER 400, PC (natural justice not applicable to decision to suspend without pay, although this outcome turned on the particular statutory context); *Giles v Law Society* (1995) 8 Admin LR 105, CA (natural justice not applicable to notice of intervention, on grounds of suspected dishonesty, by Law Society). But cf now *Brentnall v Free Presbyterian Church of Scotland* 1986 SLT 471, Ct of Sess (natural justice applied at time of decision to suspend); *Rees v Crane* [1994] 2 AC 173, [1994] 1 All ER 833, PC (temporary suspension did attract duty to act fairly because of significance of act in the circumstances); *Lewis v Heffer* [1978] 3 All ER 354 at 363–364, [1978] 1 WLR 1061 at 1072–1073, CA, per Lord Denning MR (natural justice applicable to decisions to suspend where the suspension is by way of punishment, rather than pending further investigation); *R v Haringey London Borough Council Leader's Investigative Panel, ex p Edwards* (1983) Times, 22 March. See also *R v Secretary of State for Trade, ex p Perestrello* [1981] QB 19, [1980] 3 All ER 28; *R v Secretary of State for the Environment, ex p Southwark London Borough Council* (1987) 54 P & CR 226, DC; *R v Secretary of State for Transport, ex p Pegasus Holidays (London) Ltd* [1989] 2 All ER 481, [1988] 1 WLR 990; *R (on the application of Haase) v Independent Adjudicator* [2008] EWCA Civ 1089, [2009] QB 550 (the Convention for the Protection of Human Rights and Fundamental Freedoms (1950) art 6 does not impose a general requirement for prosecutorial independence although there might be a violation of art 6 if lack of impartiality was shown on the particular facts to cause unfairness).

7 See *Selvarajan v Race Relations Board* [1976] 1 All ER 12, sub nom *R v Race Relations Board, ex p Selvarajan* [1975] 1 WLR 1686, CA, especially at 18–19 and 1693–1694 per Lord Denning MR: 'The fundamental rule is that, if a person may be subjected to pains or penalties, or be exposed to prosecution or proceedings, or deprived of remedies or redress, or in some such way adversely affected by the investigation and report, then he should be told the case made against him and be afforded a fair opportunity of answering it'. See also *Public Disclosure Commission v Isaacs* [1989] 1 All ER 137, [1988] 1 WLR 1043, PC; *R v Gaming Board for Great Britain, ex p Benaim and Khaida* [1970] 2 QB 417, [1970] 2 All ER 528, CA; *Wiseman v Borneman* [1971] AC 297, [1969] 3 All ER 275, HL; *Re Pergamon Press Ltd* [1971] Ch 388, [1970] 3 All ER 535, CA (obligation to put substance of allegations to person prior to publication of damaging report); *Saunders v United Kingdom* (1996) 23 EHRR 313, ECtHR; *R v Parole Board, ex p Wilson* [1992] QB 740, [1992] 2 All ER 576 (parole board subject to duty to act fairly, in limited form, even though its function was (at that time, but no longer following changes to the legislative framework) to make recommendation to the Home Secretary); *R (on the application of Wandsworth London Borough Council) v Secretary of State for Transport* [2005] EWHC 20 (Admin), [2006] 1 EGLR 91.

 Not every possible hardship will suffice to bring the rule into operation: see *Furnell v Whangerei High Schools Board* [1973] AC 660, [1973] 1 All ER 400, PC; but cf *Brentnall v Free Presbyterian Church of Scotland* 1986 SLT 471, Ct of Sess; *Rees v Crane* [1994] 2 AC 173, [1994] 1 All ER 833, PC (temporary suspension of judge sufficiently significant that duty to act fairly applied); *John v Rees* [1970] Ch 345, [1969] 2 All ER 274 (suspension by way of penalty did attract operation of duty to act fairly). In *R (on the application of Wright) v Secretary of State for Health* [2009] UKHL 3, [2009] 1 AC 739, [2009] 2 All ER 129, the House of Lords held that the provisional listing of a care worker under the Care Standards Act 2000 s 82(4)(b) (repealed: see CHILDREN AND YOUNG PERSONS vol 5(3) (2008 Reissue) PARA 654) as a person unsuitable to work with vulnerable adults was a determination of a civil right engaging the Convention for the Protection of Human Rights and Fundamental Freedoms (1950) art 6(1) and the lack of opportunity to answer the allegations was procedurally unfair and a breach of art 6(1). In *R (on the application of L) v Metropolitan Police Comr* [2009] UKSC 3, [2009] 3 WLR 1056, the Supreme Court held that a person applying for an enhanced criminal record certificate ought to be given the opportunity to make representations before sensitive material engaging the applicant's rights under the Convention for the Protection of Human Rights and Fundamental Freedoms (1950) art 8 was disclosed to third parties (*R (on the application of X) v Chief Constable of the West Midlands Police* [2004] EWCA Civ 80, [2005] 1 All ER 610, [2005] 1 WLR 65, disapproved).

Sometimes there may be statutory provision for representations to be made at a preliminary stage: see e g the Race Relations Act 1976 s 49(4) (repealed: see now the similar provisions in force under the Equality Act 2006 Sch 2 paras 6, 7); and DISCRIMINATION vol 13 (2007 Reissue) PARA 323. Where representations are required or permitted in the course of a preliminary investigation, this should not become the occasion for the adducing of detailed evidence or a prolonged exchange of argument: *Howard v Borneman (No 2)* [1973] 3 All ER 641, [1974] 1 WLR 15 (on appeal [1975] Ch 201, [1974] 3 All ER 862, CA; affd [1976] AC 301, [1975] 2 All ER 418, HL); *Hillingdon London Borough Council v Commission for Racial Equality* [1982] AC 779, [1982] 3 WLR 159, HL. See also *R v Commission for Racial Equality, ex p Cottrell and Rothon* [1980] 3 All ER 265, [1980] 1 WLR 1580, DC; *Re Prestige Group plc* [1984] 1 WLR 335, [1974] ICR 473, HL. It is sufficient to put the outline or substance of the case to the person concerned: *Selvarajan v Race Relations Board* [1976] 1 All ER 12, sub nom *R v Race Relations Board, ex p Selvarajan* [1975] 1 WLR 1686, CA; *Maxwell v Department of Trade and Industry* [1974] QB 523, [1974] 2 All ER 122, CA.

8 See generally PARA 630. As to legitimate expectations see PARA 649.

9 The right to act without notice or without regard to the full content of the duty to act fairly may be provided for expressly or by implication in the relevant statutory scheme. See *De Verteuil v Knaggs* [1918] AC 557 at 560–561, PC. See also *Earl of Lonsdale v Nelson* (1823) 2 B & C 302 at 311–312 per Best J; *Jones v Williams* (1843) 11 M & W 176 at 181–182 per Parke B (both instances of abatement of dangerous nuisances); *White v Redfern* (1879) 5 QBD 15, DC; *R v Davey* [1899] 2 QB 301 at 305–306, DC, per Channell J (summary action in interests of public health); *R v North London Metropolitan Magistrate, ex p Haywood* [1973] 3 All ER 50, [1973] 1 WLR 965, DC (binding-over because of conduct in the face of the court); *Re Davey* [1980] 3 All ER 342, [1981] 1 WLR 164 (court order directing execution of will by seriously ill person); *Wright v Jess* [1987] 2 All ER 1067, [1987] 1 WLR 1076, CA (committing for breach of court order without notice in exceptional circumstances); *R v Birmingham City Council, ex p Ferrero* (1991) 155 JP 721, CA (issue of suspension notice under consumer protection legislation); *R v Secretary of State for Transport, ex p Pegasus Holdings* [1989] 2 All ER 481, [1988] 1 WLR 990 (suspension of permit to operate charter aircraft); *R v Life Assurance Unit Trust Regulatory Organisation Ltd, ex p Ross* [1993] QB 17, [1993] 1 All ER 545, CA (suspension of insurance company without notice); *R v Powys County Council, ex p Horner* (1988) Times, 28 May (interests of the child); *R v Secretary of State for the Home Department, ex p Gallagher* [1995] ECR I-4253, [1996] 1 CMLR 557; *R v Secretary of State for the Environment, ex p Greater London Council* [1985] JPL 543; *R (on the application of Kent Pharmaceuticals Ltd) v Director of the Serious Fraud Office* [2004] EWCA Civ 1494, [2005] 1 All ER 449, [2005] 1 WLR 1302 (not always appropriate to give opportunity to owner of documents to make representations before they are disclosed to other government departments); *Lewis v Heffer* [1978] 3 All ER 354, [1978] 1 WLR 1061, CA; *Gaiman v National Association for Mental Health* [1971] Ch 317, [1970] 2 All ER 362.

However, regard must now be had to the Convention for the Protection of Human Rights and Fundamental Freedoms (1950) art 6 (see note 5) where the decision is one which concerns the determination of a civil right or obligation. The express derogation in art 6 refers only to the public nature of the hearing and the determination rather than the timing of the determination. Mere administrative inconvenience will not suffice: *R v Havering Justices, ex p Smith* [1974] 3 All ER 484. Self-induced urgency does not remove the need for a hearing: *R v Secretary of State for the Home Department, ex p Moon* (1995) 8 Admin LR 477.

10 The court will not question the opinion of the executive as to whether the requirements of national security outweigh those of fairness in a particular case, but it will require evidence that the decision to depart from a fair procedure was indeed due to national security considerations, and will intervene if the decision was one which no reasonable minister could have reached: *Council of Civil Service Unions v Minister for the Civil Service* [1985] AC 374, [1984] 3 All ER 935, HL. As to cases considering the impact of the Convention for the Protection of Human Rights and Fundamental Freedoms (1950) on the court's ability to balance the interests of national security against convention rights prior to the enactment of the Human Rights Act 1998 see also *R v Secretary of State for the Home Department, ex p Hosenball* [1977] 3 All ER 452, [1977] 1 WLR 766, CA; *R v Secretary of State for the Home Department, ex p Ruddock* [1987] 2 All ER 518, [1987] 1 WLR 1482; *R v Director of Government Communications Headquarters, ex p Hodges* [1988] COD 123, (1988) Times, 26 July, DC; *R v*

Secretary of State for the Home Department, ex p Cheblak [1991] 1 WLR 890 at 902, 907–908, CA, per Lord Donaldson of Lymington MR; *Balfour v Foreign and Commonwealth Office* [1994] 1 WLR 681 at 688, CA, per Russell LJ; *R v Secretary of State, ex p Chahal* [1995] 1 All ER 658, [1995] 1 WLR 526, CA; *R v Secretary of State for the Home Department, ex p Stitt* (1987) Times, 3 February; but cf *Johnston v Constable of the Royal Ulster Constabulary* [1986] 3 CMLR 240 at 262; *Chahal v United Kingdom* (1996) 23 EHRR 413, ECtHR.

11 *Local Government Board v Arlidge* [1915] AC 120, HL (inspector's report on local inquiry); *Hutton v A-G* [1927] 1 Ch 427 at 439 per Tomlin J (information about defence policy); *R v Gaming Board for Great Britain, ex p Benaim and Khaida* [1970] 2 QB 417, [1970] 2 All ER 528, CA; *Collymore v A-G of Trindad and Tobago* [1970] AC 538, [1969] 2 All ER 1207, PC (sources of information about personal character and possible breaches of the law). Evidence obtained in confidence from disinterested third parties may also be withheld where the court is exercising a quasi-paternal jurisdiction rather than resolving rights between parties: *Midland Cold Storage Ltd v Turner* [1972] ICR 230 at 234–235, NIRC, obiter per Sir John Donaldson (but cf *R v Chief Constable of West Midlands Police, ex p Wiley* [1995] 1 AC 274, [1994] 3 All ER 420, HL (in relation to classes of documents)). Even then disclosure is at the discretion of the judge and reports should only remain concealed from the parties in, say, wardship proceedings in the exceptional case where disclosure might be harmful to the young person involved: *B v W* [1979] 3 All ER 83, [1979] 1 WLR 1041, HL; and see the cases cited in note 12.

12 *R v Archbishop of Canterbury, ex p Morant* [1944] KB 282, [1944] 1 All ER 179, CA; *Official Solicitor v K* [1965] AC 201, [1963] 3 All ER 191, HL. See also *Re D (infants)* [1970] 1 All ER 1088, [1970] 1 WLR 599, CA; *Re PA (an infant)* [1971] 3 All ER 522, [1971] 1 WLR 1530, CA (no duty to disclose confidential reports, where disclosure would tend to injure others); but contrast *R v Enfield London Borough Council, ex p TF Unwin (Roydon) Ltd* (1989) 153 LG Rev 890, DC. Cf *Re WLW* [1972] Ch 456, [1972] 2 All ER 433 (Court of Protection); *R v Norfolk County Council, ex p M* [1989] QB 619, [1989] 2 All ER 359 (application for judicial review of entry on child abuse register reviewable despite confidential nature of the information); *R v Harrow Justices, ex p DPP* [1991] 3 All ER 873, [1991] 1 WLR 395; and see the cases cited in note 11.

In *R v Monopolies and Mergers Commission, ex p Elders IXL Ltd* [1987] 1 All ER 451, [1987] 1 WLR 1221 the court accepted the force of the argument that the duty to be fair to one party could not be interpreted so as to involve disproportionate unfairness to another through the enforced disclosure of commercially confidential material, but held that the Commission was entitled to make such disclosure because only by obtaining the first party's views on that material could it properly carry out its investigation in the public interest. See also *R v Oxfordshire Local Valuation Panel, ex p Oxford City Council* (1981) 79 LGR 432.

13 For example, because the number of persons affected is too great, or because the individual concerned impedes or evades service of notice: see *De Verteuil v Knaggs* [1918] AC 557 at 560–561, PC; *James v Institute of Chartered Accountants* (1907) 98 LT 225, CA. See also *R v Aston University, ex p Roffey* [1969] 2 QB 538, [1969] 2 All ER 964 (university could not be expected to interview all applicants for places, although compare *CCETSW v Edwards* (1978) Times, 5 May where the course was regarded as vital for the student's career); *R v Birmingham City Council, ex p Quietlynn Ltd* (1985) 83 LGR 461 at 483 per Forbes J (practical difficulties and risk of disruption if objectors to licensing application heard); on appeal sub nom *R v Peterborough City Council, ex p Quietlynn Ltd* (1987) 85 LGR 249, CA; *R v Monopolies and Mergers Commission, ex p Argyll Group* [1986] 2 All ER 257, [1986] 1 WLR 763, CA (remedy refused on account of need for finality); *R v Birmingham City Council, ex p Kaur* [1991] COD 21, DC (administratively impossible to provide translator). But mere administrative inconvenience is not enough: *Bradbury v Enfield London Borough Council* [1967] 3 All ER 434, [1967] 1 WLR 1311, CA. As to the effects of breach of the rule see further PARA 645.

14 For example, where there has already been a full hearing before another body or in relation to another question, as in *R v Secretary of State for the Home Department, ex p Santillo* [1981] QB 778, [1981] 2 All ER 897, CA (Secretary of State deciding to deport on recommendation of court); *R v Woking Justices, ex p Gossage* [1973] QB 448, [1973] 2 All ER 621, DC (binding-over acquitted defendant).

In some situations an opportunity for making informal representations before a decision became effective (see *A-G v Hooper* [1893] 3 Ch 483; *Robinson v Sunderland Corpn* [1899] 1 QB 751 at 757–758, DC, per Channell J) or an opportunity for full review or appeal ex post facto (*St James and St John, Clerkenwell Vestry v Feary* (1890) 24 QBD 703, DC; *De Verteuil v Knaggs* [1918] AC 557, PC) have been held to be adequate substitutes for the giving of prior notice and the opportunity to be heard, but they will seldom be held to remedy a complete failure to afford a full hearing initially: see PARA 645. Less stringent standards may apply to the rehearing of a matter: *R v St Marylebone General Comrs, ex p Hay* (1986) 57 TC 59, CA.

15 As a matter of principle, whether or not a hearing would have made a difference is irrelevant when considering if there has been a breach of the duty to act fairly: see *John v Rees* [1970] Ch 345, [1969] 2 All ER 274; *R v Hull Prison Board of Visitors, ex p St Germain (No 2)* [1979] 3 All ER 545, [1979] 1 WLR 1401; *Chief Constable of North Wales Police, ex p Evans* [1982] 3 All ER 141, [1982] 1 WLR 1155, HL; *R v Secretary of State for the Environment, ex p Brent London Borough Council* [1982] QB 593, [1983] 3 All ER 321; *R v Secretary of State for Education, ex p Prior* [1994] ICR 877; *Save Britain's Heritage v Secretary of State for the Environment* [1991] 2 All ER 10 sub nom *Save Britain's Heritage v Number One Poultry Ltd* [1991] 1 WLR 153; *R v Ealing Magistrates' Court, ex p Fanneran* (1995) 8 Admin LR 351, DC; and cf *Polkey v AE Dayton Services Ltd* [1988] AC 344 at 355, [1987] 3 All ER 974 at 977, HL, per Lord Mackay of Clashfern LC, and at 364 and 983–984 per Lord Bridge of Harwich ('no difference' question relevant in relation to whether acted fairly). Despite this, the courts have declined to accept any general proposition that a claim will succeed even if a hearing would have made no difference: see *Malloch v Aberdeen Corpn* [1971] 2 All ER 1278 at 1282, [1971] 1 WLR 1578 at 1582, HL, per Lord Reid, and at 1294 and 1595 per Lord Wilberforce; *Cheall v Association of Professional Executive Clerical and Computer Staff* [1982] 3 All ER 855 at 871, [1982] 3 WLR 685 per Bingham J (holding a hearing 'would have been a cruel deception') (affd [1983] 2 AC 180, [1983] 1 All ER 1130, HL); *R v Wareham Magistrates' Court, ex p Seldon* [1988] 1 All ER 746, [1988] 1 WLR 825 (no need for hearing on transferring the case to another court where both parties resident in that area); *R v Camden London Borough Council, ex p Paddock* [1995] COD 130; *R v Islington London Borough Council, ex p Degnan* (1997) 30 WLR 723, [1998] COD 46, CA.

Further, in some of the decisions no clear line has been drawn between the issue as to whether or not there has been a failure to act fairly, and the issue as to whether or not a discretionary remedy should be granted: see e g *Ward v Bradford Corpn* (1971) 70 LGR 27, CA. However, for practical purposes the distinction is immaterial.

16 See the cases cited in PARA 630; and *Musson v Rodriguez* [1953] AC 530, [1953] 3 WLR 212, PC. Where there is such a general discretion, for example to refuse a licence, the refusal does not necessarily carry any adverse imputation on the applicant's character, and therefore there may be less need for a hearing: *McInnes v Onslow Fane* [1978] 3 All ER 211, [1978] 1 WLR 1520. See also *Breen v Amalgamated Engineering Union* [1971] 2 QB 175, [1971] 1 All ER 1148, CA.

17 See PARA 641.

18 See PARAS 630, 641.

19 *Re Hamilton* [1981] AC 1038, [1981] 2 All ER 711, HL (committal for non-payment of fines or recognisance). See also, for example, *Sheldon v Bromfield Justices* [1964] 2 QB 573, [1964] 2 All ER 131 (binding-over witness); and see *R v Hendon Justices, ex p Gorchein* [1974] 1 All ER 168, [1973] 1 WLR 1502, DC); *R v Smith* [1975] QB 531, [1974] 1 All ER 651, CA (solicitors ordered to pay costs); *R v Poole Justices, ex p Fleet* [1983] 2 All ER 897, [1983] 1 WLR 974 (committing for non-payment where evidence required whether payments in fact made); *R v Uxbridge Justices, ex p Heward-Mills* [1983] 1 All ER 530, [1983] 1 WLR 56 (hearing surety before recognisance forfeited); *Peter Simper & Co Ltd v Cooke* [1984] ICR 6, EAT (ordering rehearing because of alleged bias); *R v Central Criminal Court, ex p Boulding* [1984] QB 813, [1984] 1 All ER 766, DC (imposing large recognisance on binding-over convicted accused); *R v Horsham Justices, ex p Richards* [1985] 2 All ER 1114, [1985] 1 WLR 986, DC (making compensation order in criminal proceedings); *R v Wareham Magistrates' Court, ex p Seldon* [1988] 1 All ER 746, [1988] 1 WLR 825 (ordering transfer of case to another court); and *R v Birmingham City Juvenile Court, ex p Birmingham City Council* [1988] 1 All ER 683, [1988] 1 WLR 337, CA (interim care order). Cf *R v Woking Justices, ex p Gossage* [1973] QB 448, [1973] 2 All ER 621, DC (binding-over acquitted accused); *R v Raymond* [1981] QB 910, [1981] 2 All ER 246, CA (seeking leave to prefer bill of indictment normally without notice); *R v Chichester Justices, ex p Collins* [1982] 1 All ER 1000, [1982] 1 WLR 334, DC (committing for non-payment of fine where only determining whether payments made to court and no power to grant relief); *Finegan v General Medical Council* [1987] 1 WLR 121, PC (no need for court or disciplinary tribunal to discuss specific possible penalties with counsel).

20 See PARA 630 note 16.

21 See PARA 630 note 20.

22 See PARA 630 note 19.

23 See PARA 630 note 15. See also, for example, *R v Central Criminal Court, ex p Boulding* [1984] QB 813, [1984] 1 All ER 766, DC (necessary to hear convicted accused before binding him over if proposing to impose relatively large recognisance); *R v Great Yarmouth Borough Council,*

ex p Botton Bros Arcades Ltd (1987) 56 P & CR 99 (number of factors combining to require hearing where none would normally be necessary).

640. Prior notice. The *audi alteram partem* rule requires that those who are likely to be directly affected by the outcome should be given prior notification of the action proposed to be taken, of the time and place of any hearing that is to be conducted, and of the charge or case they will be called upon to meet[1]. Similar notice ought to be given of a change in the original date and time, or of an adjourned hearing[2]. All who are likely to be so affected must be notified[3]; but there may be an express or implied dispensation from the normal duty to serve actual notice on each individual[4], and in the case of administrative proposals and procedures it is not uncommon for legislation to discriminate between a general duty to give public notice and a specific duty to serve personal notice on those who are particularly affected[5], and to define with precision the methods by which such notice may lawfully be given[6].

The particulars set out in the notice should be sufficiently explicit to enable the interested parties to understand the case they have to meet and to prepare their answer and their own cases[7]. This duty is not always imposed rigorously on domestic tribunals which conduct their proceedings informally[8], and a want of detailed specification may exceptionally be held to be immaterial if the person claiming to be aggrieved was, in fact, aware of the nature of the case against him[9], or if the deficiency in the notice did not cause him any substantial prejudice[10]. For example, when determining an appeal against an enforcement notice in town and country planning law, the Secretary of State may correct a defect in a notice if satisfied that it is immaterial, and may disregard the fact of non-service altogether if the omission has not substantially prejudiced the appellant or the person who should have been served[11]. Where charges are laid against a person, it is necessary to consider the particular procedure to be followed in order to determine whether the rule against duplicity applies[12].

Where national security or other matters render the disclosure of material to a party against the public interest, legislation may provide expressly or impliedly for the appointment of a special advocate to represent the excluded party's interests in closed sessions before a court, tribunal or decision-maker[13].

Notification of the proceedings or the proposed decision must also be given early enough to afford the persons concerned a reasonable opportunity to prepare representations or put their own case[14]. Otherwise the only proper course will be to postpone or adjourn the matter[15].

1 As to the *audi alteram partem* rule see PARA 639. In a large majority of the numerous cases where the rule has been broken, no notice at all of the relevant charge, allegation or proposed act or decision had been given to the party aggrieved: see eg *Bagg's Case* (1615) 11 Co Rep 93b; *R v Arkwright* (1848) 12 QB 960; *Cooper v Wandsworth Board of Works* (1863) 14 CBNS 180; *R v North, ex p Oakey* [1927] 1 KB 491, CA; *The Seistan* [1960] 1 All ER 32, [1960] 1 WLR 186, DC; *Annamunthodo v Oilfield Workers' Trade Union* [1961] AC 945, [1961] 3 All ER 621, PC; *Appuhamy v R* [1963] AC 474, [1963] 1 All ER 762, PC; *Abraham v Jutsun* [1963] 2 All ER 402, [1963] 1 WLR 658, CA; *Ridge v Baldwin* [1964] AC 40, [1963] 2 All ER 66, HL; *S v S* [1964] 3 All ER 915, [1965] 1 WLR 21, CA; *R v Industrial Tribunal, ex p George Green and Thomson Ltd* (1967) 2 KIR 259, DC; *Lau Liat Meng v Disciplinary Committee* [1968] AC 391, [1967] 3 WLR 877, PC; *Glynn v Keele University* [1971] 2 All ER 89, [1971] 1 WLR 487; *R v South Molton Justices, ex p Ankerson* [1988] 3 All ER 989, [1989] 1 WLR 40, DC. See also *Bradbury v Enfield London Borough Council* [1967] 3 All ER 434, [1967] 1 WLR 1311, CA; *Kanda v Government of the Federation of Malaya* [1962] AC 322, [1962] 2 WLR 1153, PC; *Re M* [1973] QB 108, [1972] 3 All ER 321, CA; *Chief Constable of the North Wales Police v Evans* [1982] 3 All ER 141, [1982] 1 WLR 1155, HL; *R (on the application of Banks) v Secretary of State for Environment, Food and Rural Affairs* [2004]

EWHC 416 (Admin), (2004) Times, 19 April; *Lewis v A-G of Jamaica* [2001] 2 AC 50, [2000] 3 WLR 1785, PC; *R (on the application of Q) v Secretary of State for the Home Department* [2003] EWCA Civ 364, [2004] QB 36, [2003] 2 All ER 905. See also *R v Secretary of State for Health, ex p United States Tobacco International Inc* [1992] QB 353, [1992] 1 All ER 212, DC.

The person charged may also be entitled to request further information regarding the allegations: see e g *R v General Medical Council, ex p Gee* [1987] 1 All ER 1204, [1986] 1 WLR 226; affd [1987] 1 All ER 1204, [1986] 1 WLR 1247, CA; affd on another point sub nom *Gee v General Medical Council* [1987] 2 All ER 193, [1987] 1 WLR 564, HL. Notice should be given of a fundamental change in the nature of the allegations to be pursued: *Re Lo-Line Electric Motors Ltd* [1988] Ch 477, [1988] 2 All ER 692.

2 *R v Devon and Cornwall Rent Tribunal, ex p West* (1974) 29 P & CR 316, DC; *Chiltern District Council v Keane* [1985] 2 All ER 118, [1985] 1 WLR 619, CA.

3 *Smyth v Darley* (1849) 2 HL Cas 789; *Young v Ladies' Imperial Club Ltd* [1920] 2 KB 523, CA; *John v Rees* [1970] Ch 345, [1969] 2 All ER 274; *Re Wykeham Terrace, Brighton, Sussex, ex p Territorial Auxilliary and Volunteer Reserve Association for the South East* [1971] Ch 204, [1970] 3 WLR 649. An express right to attend the meetings of a particular body carries with it the implied right to be notified of the time and date of such meetings and to be sent the agenda: *R v Manchester City Council, ex p Fulford* (1982) 81 LGR 292, DC.

4 The requirement to give notice usually entails the requirement that the notice must also be received (see *Re Wykeham Terrace, Brighton, Sussex, ex p Territorial Auxilliary and Volunteer Reserve Association for the South East* [1971] Ch 204, [1970] 3 WLR 649); but this is not always the position (see *R v Kensington and Chelsea Rent Tribunal, ex p MacFarlane* [1974] 3 All ER 390, [1974] 1 WLR 1486; *Baker v Birmingham City Council* [1999] LGR 184; *Goodall v Peak District National Park Authority* [2008] EWHC 734 (Admin), [2008] 1 WLR 2705, DC). Under CPR 55.3 (see LANDLORD AND TENANT vol 27(1) (2006 Reissue) PARA 660) summary proceedings for the possession of land can be instituted even though the identity of the unlawful occupiers is not ascertainable; cf *Re Wykeham Terrace, Brighton, Sussex*. In proceedings before bodies other than courts, where procedural rules governing service of notices have been laid down, a party may be disentitled from complaining of non-receipt if he has negligently failed to notify a change of address (*James v Institute of Chartered Accountants* (1907) 98 LT 225, CA; *Al-Mehdawi v Secretary of State for the Home Department* [1990] 1 AC 876, [1989] 3 All ER 843 (negligence on part of solicitors); *R (on the application of Mathialagan) v Southwark London Borough Council* [2004] EWCA Civ 1689, [2005] RA 43); or has obstructed service (*De Verteuil v Knaggs* [1918] AC 557 at 560–561, PC). In *R v Liverpool City Justices, ex p Greaves* (1979) 77 LGR 440, DC, it was held that, where a rating authority had followed the statutory procedure for giving written notice, the ratepayer could not complain of a breach of natural justice merely because by mischance the notice never reached him.

5 See e g the Town and Country Planning (Inquiries Procedure) (England) Rules 2000, SI 2000/1624, r 10; the Town and Country Planning (Major Infrastructure Project Inquiries Procedure) (England) Rules 2005, SI 2005/2115, r 14; and the Town and Country Planning (Inquiries Procedure) (Wales) Rules 2003, SI 2003/1266, r 10 (date and notification of inquiry) (see TOWN AND COUNTRY PLANNING vol 46(2) (Reissue) PARAS 667, 685).

6 See e g the Town and Country Planning Act 1990 s 329; and TOWN AND COUNTRY PLANNING vol 46(1) (Reissue) PARA 31. In the absence of such precise definition, there may be several different permissible ways of giving public notice, but the less extensive the method of publication adopted, the more important it becomes that the contents of the notice should be clear and unambiguous: *Wilson v Secretary of State for the Environment* [1974] 1 All ER 428, [1973] 1 WLR 1083. The notice must be in terms such as are fairly and reasonably necessary to enable an educated member of the public familiar (in an appropriate case) with the relevant area to appreciate that he is interested and to make representations, and the heading of a newspaper advertisement may be especially important in determining whether it is reasonable to expect such a person to go on and read the remainder: *Wilson v Secretary of State for the Environment.*

7 *Ex p Hopkins* (1891) 61 LJQB 240, DC; *Kanda v Government of Malaya* [1962] AC 322 at 337, PC, per Lord Denning; *R v Aylesbury Justices, ex p Wisbey* [1965] 1 All ER 602, [1965] 1 WLR 339, DC; *M'Donald v Lanarkshire Fire Brigade Joint Committee* 1959 SC 141; *Alpine Shipping Co v Vinbee (Manchester) Ltd, The Dusan* [1980] 1 Lloyd's Rep 400 (written arbitration); *Hillingdon London Borough Council v Commission for Racial Equality* [1982] AC 779, [1982] 3 WLR 159, HL; *Chief Constable of North Wales v Evans* [1982] 3 All ER 141, [1982] 1 WLR 1155, HL; *Chiltern District Council v Keane* [1985] 2 All ER 118, [1985] 1 WLR 619, CA; *R v Wandsworth London Borough Council, ex p P* (1989) 87 LGR 370; *R v Enfield London Borough Council, ex p TF Unwin (Roydon) Ltd* (1989) 46 BLR 1 (nature of allegations to be disclosed despite advice from police that it would hamper their inquiries); *R v*

Hampshire County Council, ex p K [1990] 2 QB 71, [1990] 2 All ER 129 (refusal to disclose to parents evidence in support of allegation of sexual abuse); *R v Huntingdon District Council, ex p Cowan* [1984] 1 All ER 58, [1984] 1 WLR 501 (applicant for licence entitled to know substance of allegations and to respond in writing); *R v Deputy Controller of HMP Buckley Hall, ex p Thomas* [2000] COD 491 (more rigorous duty of disclosure applied when fundamental right in play; in this case the right not to be unlawfully imprisoned); and cf *R (on the application of Gleaves) v Secretary of State for the Home Department* [2004] EWHC 2522 (Admin), (2004) Times, 15 November.

The whole case must be disclosed, but for the degree of particularity required see *Lloyd v McMahon* [1987] AC 625 at 707, [1987] 1 All ER 1118 at 1164–1165, HL, per Lord Bridge of Harwich; *Bushell v Secretary of State for the Environment* [1981] AC 75, [1980] 2 All ER 608, HL; *Hadmor Productions Ltd v Hamilton* [1983] 1 AC 191 at 233 per Lord Diplock; *R v Governors of St Gregory's RC Aided High School and Appeals Committee, ex p M* [1995] ELR 290 (no need to hear direct evidence from witnesses at exclusion hearing when pupil knew nature of the case); *Fairmount Investments v Secretary of State for the Environment* [1976] 1 WLR 1255 at 1260 per Viscount Dilhorne and at 1265–1266 per Lord Russell of Killowen; *Mahon v Air New Zealand* [1984] AC 808, [1984] 3 All ER 201, PC; *R v Secretary of State for the Home Department, ex p Abdi* (1994) Times, 10 March (high duty of fairness in asylum cases required disclosure of favourable as well as unfavourable information); *R v Kensington and Chelsea, ex p Campbell* (1995) 28 HLR 160 (disclosure of fact that decision-maker had doubts as to applicant's credibility; see also on this point *R v Secretary of State for the Home Department, ex p Fayed* [1997] 1 All ER 228, [1998] 1 WLR 763, CA); *R v Secretary of State for the Home Department, ex p Duggan* [1994] 3 All ER 277 (prisoner entitled to notice of matters relevant to decision on security classification); *R v Secretary of State for the Home Department, ex p McAvoy* [1998] 1 WLR 790, [1998] COD 148, CA (gist of report sufficient in relation to categorisation decision); *R v Norfolk County Council, ex p M* [1989] QB 619, [1989] 2 All ER 359 (full disclosure required because of 'exceptional' circumstances); *R v Harrow London Borough Council, ex p D* [1990] Fam 133, [1990] 3 All ER 12, CA (limited disclosure on account of interests of the child); *R v Secretary of State for the Home Department, ex p Mughal* [1974] QB 313, [1973] 3 All ER 796, CA (immigration officers); *R v Monopolies and Mergers Commission, ex p Matthew Brown plc* [1987] 1 All ER 463, [1987] 1 WLR 1235; *R v Monopolies and Mergers Commission, ex p Elders IXL Ltd* [1987] 1 All ER 451, [1987] 1 WLR 1221; *Re Pergamon Press* [1971] Ch 388, [1970] 3 All ER 535, CA (Companies Act inspectors); *R v Secretary of State for the Home Department, ex p Venables* [1998] AC 407, [1997] 1 All ER 327, CA (failure to disclose all material taken into account); *Robert Hitchens v Secretary of State for the Environment* [1995] EGCS 101 (undisclosed letters looked at objectively caused no unfairness; cf *R v Secretary of State for the Environment, ex p Slot* [1998] COD 118, CA); *R v Department of Health, ex p Gandhi* [1991] 4 All ER 547, [1991] 1 WLR 1053, DC; *R v Governors of Dunraven School, ex p B* [2000] LGR 494 (full disclosure required prior to school exclusion hearing; governors could not rely on information not disclosed).

Note also that the usual exceptions apply: see eg *R v Gaming Board, ex p Benaim and Khaida* [1970] 2 QB 417, [1970] 2 All ER 528, CA; *R v Secretary of State for the Home Department, ex p Hickey* [1995] QB 43, [1995] 1 All ER 479, CA; *R v Secretary of State for the Home Department, ex p Hickey (No 2)* [1995] 1 All ER 490, [1995] 1 WLR 734; *R v Army Board, ex p Anderson* [1992] QB 169, [1991] 3 All ER 375, DC; and PARA 639.

8   Cf *Norman and Moran v National Dock Labour Board* [1957] 1 Lloyd's Rep 455, CA. But the normal rule has been applied in, for example, *Stevenson v United Road Transport Union* [1977] 2 All ER 941, [1977] ICR 893, CA. In *Dean v Polytechnic of North London* [1973] ICR 490, NIRC, it was said that, precisely because of the relative informality of industrial tribunal proceedings, an adjournment should readily be granted at the request of a party taken by surprise.

9   *Russell v Duke of Norfolk* [1949] 1 All ER 109 at 117–118, CA, per Tucker LJ. See also *Abbott v Sullivan* [1952] 1 KB 189 at 195, [1952] 1 All ER 226 at 229–230, CA, per Sir Raymond Evershed MR; *Davis v Carew-Pole* [1956] 2 All ER 524 at 527, [1956] 1 WLR 833 at 840 per Pilcher J; *Stevenson v United Road Transport Union* [1977] ICR 893 at 905, CA, per Buckley LJ; *Alpine Shipping Co v Vinbee (Manchester) Ltd, The Dusan* [1980] 1 Lloyd's Rep 400; *Payne v Lord Harris of Greenwich* [1981] 2 All ER 842 at 844–845, [1981] 1 WLR 754 at 758, CA, per Lord Denning MR.

10 See *Sloan v General Medical Council* [1970] 2 All ER 686, [1970] 1 WLR 1130n, PC (charge framed in terms so general that on the facts there could be no defence; proceedings criticised but not held to constitute failure to hold due inquiry). See also PARA 645.

11 See the Town and Country Planning Act 1990 s 176; and TOWN AND COUNTRY PLANNING vol 46(2) (Reissue) PARA 609. See generally on this point *John v Rees* [1970] Ch 345 at 402 per Megarry J; *Rees v Crane* [1994] 2 AC 173, [1994] 1 All ER 833, PC; and PARA 639 note 15.

12 A count is duplicitous if it contains particulars of more than one offence, and this is objectionable if, for example, it prevents the person charged from making a submission of no case to answer, or from making an effective plea in mitigation. The rule will apply if the tribunal can only determine that the charge is proved or not proved, but not if it must specify exactly which facts it has found proved and give the person charged the opportunity to make representations or adduce evidence as to the consequences of those findings: *Gee v General Medical Council* [1987] 2 All ER 193 at 202–203, [1987] 1 WLR 564 at 575, HL, per Lord Mackay of Clashfern. See also *Peatfield v General Medical Council* [1987] 1 All ER 1197, [1986] 1 WLR 243, PC; *Harmsworth v Harmsworth* [1987] 3 All ER 816 at 823–824, [1987] 1 WLR 1676 at 1686, CA, per Woolf LJ; and cf *Chiltern District Council v Keane* [1985] 2 All ER 118, [1985] 1 WLR 619, CA (judge hearing application to commit for contempt must specify which of several allegations he finds proven); *Interbrew SA v Competition Commission* [2001] EWHC Admin 367, [2001] All ER (D) 305 (May).

13 There is an obvious conflict between the public interest in the maintenance of the confidentiality of certain highly sensitive material and a party's right to fair trial. The Prevention of Terrorism Act 2005 s 11, Schedule para 7 provides for the appointment of an advocate or solicitor by the Attorney General, Advocate General for Scotland or Advocate General for Northern Ireland to represent the interests of a party in proceedings in relation to control orders made under that Act from which he and his representatives are excluded. The special advocate has access to the closed material but may not communicate this to the party he represents. See further CRIMINAL LAW, EVIDENCE AND PROCEDURE vol 11(1) (2006 Reissue) PARA 464. In *Secretary of State for the Home Department v MB* [2007] UKHL 46, [2008] 1 AC 440, [2008] 1 All ER 657, the House of Lords held that only such measures restricting the controlled person's rights as were strictly necessary were permissible and such difficulties were to be sufficiently counterbalanced by procedures adopted by the judicial authorities (including the appointment of a special advocate). The court had to consider whether the process as a whole caused a significant injustice to the restricted party. In *Secretary of State for the Home Department v AF (No 3)* [2009] UKHL 28, [2009] 3 All ER 643, [2009] 3 WLR 74, the House of Lords held (applying *A v United Kingdom*, (Application 3455/05), (2009) 49 EHRR 625, (2009) Times, 20 February, ECtHR) that a party had to have disclosed to him sufficient of the case against him to allow him to give effective instructions to his special advocate and that the fair trial requirement under the Convention for the Protection of Human Rights and Fundamental Freedoms (Rome, 4 November 1950; TS 71 (1953) Cmd 8969) art 6 could not be satisfied where the case rested solely or to a decisive extent on undisclosed material. See PARA 639.

The special advocate procedure was held in *R (on the application of Roberts) v Parole Board* [2005] UKHL 45, [2005] 2 AC 738, sub nom *Roberts v Parole Board* [2006] 1 All ER 39, to be available to mitigate the disadvantages to a prisoner of the non-disclosure of information being considered by the Parole Board in relation to his possible release. See also on the use of special advocates in criminal proceedings *R v H* [2004] UKHL 3, [2004] 2 AC 134, [2004] 1 All ER 1269. In deportation cases the use of closed hearings is not restricted to cases where the closed material relates to national security: see *RB (Algeria) v Secretary of State for the Home Department* [2009] UKHL 10, [2009] 4 All ER 1045, [2009] 2 WLR 512.

A special advocate need not always be appointed where there is closed material but one should be appointed where it is just to do so having regard to the fact that the proceedings must be fair to both parties: *AHK v Secretary of State for the Home Department* [2009] EWCA Civ 287, [2009] 1 WLR 2049n.

14 *Lee v Department of Education and Science* (1967) 66 LGR 211; *R v Thames Magistrates' Court, ex p Polemis* [1974] 2 All ER 1219, [1974] 1 WLR 1371, DC; cf *Co-operative Retail Services Ltd v Secretary of State for the Environment* [1980] 1 All ER 449, [1980] 1 WLR 271, CA (in the case of a public inquiry, the length of notice required must be assessed having regard to the possibility of applying for adjournments during the inquiry in order for particular matters to be dealt with). The general rule is that material which is going to be available at a certain stage for the court should be made available as early as possible to the parties concerned with the case: *R v Epsom Juvenile Court, ex p G* [1988] 1 All ER 329 at 331–332, [1988] 1 WLR 145 at 149 per Ewbank J; *Lewis v A-G of Jamaica* [2001] 2 AC 50, [2000] 3 WLR 1785, PC (applying the principle to the proceedings of a committee considering the exercise of the prerogative of mercy in a death penalty case).

15 *M(J) v M(K)* [1968] 3 All ER 878, [1968] 1 WLR 1897, DC (where notice had been served but the tribunal proceeded although one party was known to be unable to attend); *Stevenson v United Road Transport Union* [1977] 2 All ER 941, [1977] ICR 893, CA. The same applies

where a party is misled into thinking that the hearing will not go ahead at the notified time: *Hanson v Church Comrs for England* [1978] QB 823, [1977] 3 All ER 404, CA. Sometimes an adjournment may be necessary because a party cannot attend or be represented on the date proposed, but this is less likely in the case of an administrative inquiry arranged well in advance and to which there are many parties; in such a case the appropriate course may be to hear the person concerned on a later day: *Ostreicher v Secretary of State for the Environment* [1978] 3 All ER 82, [1978] 1 WLR 810, CA. See also *R v Afan Justices, ex p Chaplin* [1983] RTR 168 at 171, DC, obiter per Webster J (refusal to adjourn for third time at request of applicant unable to attend was not a breach of natural justice). See also PARA 642.

641. Opportunity to be heard. A person or body determining a dispute between parties must give each party a fair opportunity to put his own case and to correct or contradict any relevant statement to the contrary[1]. A corresponding duty may rest upon an authority notwithstanding that its inquiry or decision relates to the affairs of one party only[2], or that the issue arises only between itself and a single party[3]. Whether a right to an oral hearing, as opposed to a right to make written representations, arises will depend on the circumstances of the case[4]. In some situations fairness will require a deciding body to take the initiative in inviting the interested parties to submit representations to it[5].

Where a particular procedure is prescribed by statute[6] and has been followed, but it is alleged that there has nonetheless been unfairness, the court must decide whether the statute is to be treated as a comprehensive code[7], or whether it is necessary to supplement the prescribed procedure[8].

In departmental decisions taken in the name of the minister or department, a party has no common law right to be heard in person before the officer who in fact made the decision or to know the identity of that officer; and a hearing may be conducted by one officer and the decision taken by another[9]. Other administrative bodies may be entitled to assign to a committee the function of hearing oral evidence and submissions[10], but the committee's report to the parent body must be full enough to enable that body to 'hear' as well as decide[11].

A party must not be precluded from putting his case adequately through being misled as to the basis on which the tribunal will found its decision[12]. Members of tribunals may be entitled to draw on their specialised or local knowledge of the type of issue before them in order to supplement as well as evaluate evidence[13], to find facts by inquisitorial methods[14] and inspections[15], and to obtain information from other persons[16]; but it will generally be a denial of justice to fail to disclose to a party specific material relevant to the decision if he is thereby deprived of any opportunity to comment on it[17]. Only in exceptional circumstances is it permissible for any tribunal to make use of private knowledge of a party which is undisclosed to all parties[18], and in any event such knowledge may give rise to a likelihood of bias[19]. Similarly, if the tribunal after the close of the hearing comes into possession of further evidence, the parties should be invited to comment upon it[20].

The general principles that evidential material obtained from an outside source must be disclosed for comment[21], and that in the absence of express authority a tribunal must not receive or appear to receive evidence without notice and fail to disclose it to an interested party[22] are well settled. However, on grounds of public policy in limited circumstances it will be legitimate to withhold certain types of relevant material, or the details or sources of such material, provided that the party concerned is not thereby denied a fair hearing[23].

1   *Board of Education v Rice* [1911] AC 179 at 182, HL, per Lord Loreburn LC. The like opportunity may still have to be given even though the matter is being determined on the basis of written representations rather than an oral hearing: *R v Housing Appeal Tribunal* [1920]

3 KB 334, DC; *Stafford v Minister of Health* [1946] KB 621. If written material is submitted the decision-maker must take this into account: *R v Manchester University, ex p Nolan* [1994] ELR 380. In certain circumstances the failure to request an oral hearing might amount to a waiver of the right to such an opportunity: see *R v Deputy Industrial Injuries Comr, ex p Moore* [1965] 1 QB 456 at 476, [1965] 1 All ER 81 at 87, CA, per Willmer LJ and at 490 and 95 per Diplock LJ; but cf *Hanson v Church Comrs* [1978] QB 823, [1977] 3 All ER 404, CA (not always open to applicant to waive right to a hearing). Sometimes it may be necessary to explain how and when representations are to be made: *Beacard Property Management and Construction Co Ltd v Day* [1984] ICR 837, EAT. But see also *Dennis v UK Central Council of Nursing, Midwifery and Health Visiting* (1993) 13 BMLR 146 (decision-maker not required to make applicant's case for him, although there may be a duty to explain the law so that representations can be made effectively).

It is a question of degree in any particular case whether a party is sufficiently informed of what is said against him by having the allegations summarised in writing, by being present to hear them made, or by having the allegations specifically put to him for his comments (*Bentley Engineering Co Ltd v Mistry* [1979] ICR 47, [1978] IRLR 436, EAT), and as to what degree of particularity is required (*R v Director of Government Communications Headquarters, ex p Hodges* [1988] COD 123, (1988) Times, 26 July, DC); and see the cases cited in PARA 639 note 7. See eg *Mahon v Air New Zealand Ltd* [1984] AC 808, [1984] 3 All ER 201, PC, for criticism of a failure to put allegations in cross-examination or in questions from the tribunal. If a person is being invited to supplement previous answers, he ought to be reminded of those answers, especially if a long time has elapsed since they were given: *Secretary of State for the Home Department v Thirukumar* [1989] Imm AR 402, CA; *Tudor v Ellesmere and Neston Port Borough Council* (1987) Times, 8 May (assertion that applicant was not fit and proper person to hold licence made for the first time in closing submissions); *R v Joint Higher Committee on Surgical Training, ex p Milner* (1994) 21 BMLR 11 (opinions, as opposed to facts, contained in references need not be put to person applying for approval of a professional body); *Maradana Mosque v Mahmud* [1967] 1 AC 13, [1966] 1 All ER 545, PC (if there is more than one charge, the person concerned must have the opportunity to respond to all of them); *R v Governors of Dunraven School, ex p B* [2000] LGR 494, [2000] ELR 156, CA (school exclusion hearing unfair where use of anonymous evidence meant pupil could not know case against him); *R (on the application of SP) v Secretary of State for the Home Department* [2004] EWCA Civ 1750, (2005) Times, 21 January (remand prisoner entitled to make representations as to making of segregation order).

There is nothing contrary to natural justice in a rule which prevents fresh evidence being adduced on an appeal: *Brown v Amalgamated Union of Engineering Workers* [1976] ICR 147.

2   As in *R v Registrar of Building Societies, ex p A Building Society* [1960] 2 All ER 549, [1960] 1 WLR 669, CA. More difficult questions may arise in relation to parties not directly affected by the decision but nonetheless having an interest in it: see eg *R v HM Coroner at Hammersmith, ex p Peach (No 2)* [1980] QB 211, [1980] 2 All ER 7, CA (brother of deceased not entitled to copies of witness statements supplied to coroner by police); *R v Birmingham City Council, ex p Quietlynn Ltd* (1986) 83 LGR 461 (local authority not normally obliged to hear objectors to application for sex shop licence) (on appeal sub nom *R v Peterborough City Council, ex p Quietlynn Ltd* (1987) 85 LGR 249, CA); *R v Bristol Justices, ex p Broome* [1987] 1 All ER 676, [1987] 1 WLR 352 (police to be given notice of and heard upon child's application for release after being detained by police under the Children and Young Persons Act 1969 s 28(2) (now repealed)); *R v Great Yarmouth Borough Council, ex p Botton Bros Arcades Ltd* (1987) 56 P & CR 99 (not usually necessary to hear objectors before determining application for planning permission, but may be required in exceptional case); *R v Secretary of State for the Environment, ex p Kent* [1988] JPL 706 (affd [1990] JPL 124, CA); cf *R v Bromley Licensing Justices, ex p Bromley Licensed Victuallers' Association* [1984] 1 All ER 794, [1984] 1 WLR 585; and see *Mahon v Air New Zealand Ltd* [1984] AC 808 at 821, [1984] 3 All ER 201 at 210, PC (every person represented at inquiry who would be adversely affected by a particular finding to know of risk of it being made and opportunity to adduce relevant evidence). See further note 3.

3   As in *Ridge v Baldwin* [1964] AC 40, [1963] 2 All ER 66, HL; *Durayappah v Fernando* [1967] 2 AC 337, [1967] 2 All ER 152, PC. Where the matter is properly regarded as a *lis* between two parties, or between one party and the decision-maker, other parties are not entitled to be heard: see eg *Brown v Amalgamated Union of Engineering Workers* [1976] ICR 147 (successful candidate in re-held election not entitled to make representations on complaint by previously successful candidate that original result should have been allowed to stand); *Cheall v Association of Professional Executive Clerical and Computer Staff* [1983] 2 AC 180, [1983]

1 All ER 1130, HL (individual trade union member not entitled to be heard by committee resolving dispute between unions as to which he was entitled to join).

4   See generally PARAS 629–630, 642.

5   See *Hoggard v Worsbrough UDC* [1962] 2 QB 93, [1962] 1 All ER 468; *R (on the application of Haringey Consortium of Disabled People and Carers Association) v Haringey London Borough Council* (2000) 58 BMLR 160, [2000] All ER (D) 1583; and PARA 623.

6   The court may be more willing to supplement a procedural code contained in an instrument other than an Act of Parliament, but the same issues of principle arise. An assumption that the prescribed procedure is a fair one may more readily be made where the instrument has the force of law, or is the product of agreement between, for example, employers' and trade union representatives: see eg *R (on the application of Edwards) v Environment Agency* [2008] UKHL 22, [2009] 1 All ER 57, [2008] 1 WLR 1587; *Furnell v Whangerei High Schools Board* [1973] AC 660, [1973] 1 All ER 400, PC; *Maynard v Osmond* [1977] QB 240, [1977] 1 All ER 64, CA; *Khanum v Mid Glamorgan Area Health Authority* [1979] ICR 40 at 46, EAT, per Bristow J. See also *R v Harrow London Borough Council, ex p D* [1990] Fam 133, [1989] FCR 407.

7   In *R v Dudley Magistrates' Court, ex p Payne* [1979] 2 All ER 1089, [1979] 1 WLR 891, DC, the court approached the question on the basis that nothing should be added to or taken away from the statute unless there were adequate grounds to justify the inference that Parliament had intended something which it had omitted to express, and that words should not therefore be read into the Act in the absence of clear necessity (overruled by *Re Hamilton* [1981] AC 1038, [1981] 2 All ER 711, HL); and see *Thompson v Goold & Co* [1910] AC 409 at 420, HL, per Lord Mersey. See also *Furnell v Whangerei High Schools Board* [1973] AC 660 at 679, [1973] 1 All ER 400 at 411–412, PC, approving dicta in *Brettingham-Moore v Municipality of St Leonards* (1969) 121 CLR 509 at 524 per Barwick CJ ('it is not for the court to amend the statute by engrafting upon it some provision which the court might think more consonant with a complete opportunity for an aggrieved person to present his views and to support them by evidentiary material'). See also *Pearlberg v Varty (Inspector of Taxes)* [1972] 2 All ER 6, [1972] 1 WLR 534, HL; *R (on the application of McNally) v Secretary of State for Education and Employment* [2001] EWCA Civ 332 at [38], [2002] LGR 584 at [38], [2002] ICR 15 at [38] per Dyson LJ; *R (on the application of B) v Leeds School Organisation Committee* [2002] EWHC 1927 (Admin), [2003] ELR 67.

The more detailed the procedural provisions in the statute, the more willing will be the court to assume that they were intended to be comprehensive: see eg *R v Dudley Magistrates' Court, ex p Payne*; *R v Secretary of State for the Environment, ex p Southwark London Borough Council* (1987) 54 P & CR 226, DC; *R v Ukpabio* [2007] EWCA Crim 2108, [2008] 1 WLR 728, [2008] 1 Cr App Rep 101; *R (on the application of BAPIO Action Ltd) v Secretary of State for the Home Department* [2007] EWCA Civ 1139 at [47], [2008] ACD 7 at [47] per Sedley LJ (affd but on different grounds [2008] UKHL 27, [2008] 1 AC 1003, [2009] 1 All ER 93). Similarly, if the particular procedural step which it is alleged should be added to the express provisions has in fact been provided for in other circumstances, it will readily be inferred that its omission in the situation in question was deliberate: see eg *Furnell v Whangerei High Schools Board* at 681 and 413 per Lord Morris of Borth-y-Gest; *Maynard v Osmond* [1977] QB 240 at 253, [1977] 1 All ER 64 at 80, CA, per Lord Denning MR. But if no sensible reason can be perceived for distinguishing the procedure to be followed in the two cases, the omission will be rectified: (*R v Wareham Magistrates' Court, ex p Seldon* [1988] 1 All ER 746, [1988] 1 WLR 825); and it will not always be correct to take account of the procedure laid down in one part of a statute when considering what procedure should apply to another (*R v Huntingdon District Council, ex p Cowan* [1984] 1 All ER 58, [1984] 1 WLR 501).

Even where the prescribed procedure is not treated as a comprehensive code, compliance with it may be evidence of fairness: *R v Secretary of State for the Home Department, ex p Hosenball* [1977] 3 All ER 452 at 459, [1977] 1 WLR 766 at 781, CA, per Lord Denning MR and at 463–464 and 786 per Geoffrey Lane LJ. See also PARA 629.

8   'When a statute has conferred on any body the power to make decisions affecting individuals, the courts will not only require the procedure prescribed by the statute to be followed, but will readily imply so much and no more to be introduced by way of additional procedural safeguards as will ensure the attainment of fairness': *Lloyd v McMahon* [1987] AC 625 at 703, [1987] 1 All ER 1118 at 1161, HL, obiter per Lord Bridge of Harwich. Parliament is presumed to have intended that the rules of natural justice should be observed by a tribunal it has created unless it has made express provision to the contrary: *O'Reilly v Mackman* [1983] 2 AC 237 at 276, [1982] 3 All ER 1124 at 1127, HL, per Lord Diplock. See also *Bonaker v Evans* (1850) 16 QB 162; *Cooper v Wandsworth Board of Works* (1863) 14 CBNS 180; *Fairmount Investments Ltd v Secretary of State for the Environment* [1976] 2 All ER 865 at 871–872, [1976] 1 WLR 1255

at 1263, HL, per Lord Russell of Killowen; *George v Secretary of State for the Environment* (1979) 38 P & CR 609, CA; *R v Preston Borough Council, ex p Quietlynn Ltd* (1985) 83 LGR 308, CA; *R v Birmingham City Council, ex p Quietlynn Ltd* (1985) 83 LGR 461 at 481 per Forbes J (on appeal sub nom *R v Peterborough City Council, ex p Quietlynn Ltd* (1987) 85 LGR 249, CA); *Reading Borough Council v Secretary of State for the Environment and Commercial Union Properties (Investments) Ltd* (1985) 52 P & CR 385; *Raji v General Medical Council* [2003] UKPC 24, [2003] 1 WLR 1052.

Similarly, express statutory derogations from the principle of *audi alteram partem* (see PARA 639) will be narrowly construed (see eg *Re Hamilton* [1981] AC 1038, [1981] 2 All ER 711, HL); and the fact that one right is expressly conferred may lead to the conclusion that another should be implied as being fairly ancillary to it (see *R v Milton Keynes Justices, ex p R* [1979] 1 WLR 1062, DC). But the courts ought not to fly in the face of a clearly evinced parliamentary intention to exclude the operation of the rule: *R v Raymond* [1981] QB 910 at 920, [1981] 2 All ER 246 at 254, CA, per Watkins LJ. See also *R v Secretary of State for Social Services, ex p Connolly* [1986] 1 All ER 998, [1986] 1 WLR 421, CA.

There is no especially heavy burden of proof upon a party alleging that there has been a breach of natural justice despite compliance with the statute: *Reading Borough Council v Secretary of State for the Environment*; but cf *R v Secretary of State for the Environment, ex p Southwark London Borough Council* (1987) 54 P & CR 226 at 235, DC, per Lloyd LJ. The statutory procedure will not be supplemented to confer extra rights on persons who are not directly affected by the decision in question: *R v Birmingham City Council, ex p Quietlynn Ltd* (objectors to applications for sex shop licences; statutory procedure supplemented only for benefit of applicants). In *R v Huntingdon District Council, ex p Cowan* [1984] 1 All ER 58, [1984] 1 WLR 501, the court took account of the universal practice of allowing a hearing before refusing an application for an entertainments licence which existed when the relevant Act was passed, on the basis that Parliament must be presumed to have been aware of it and to have intended that it should continue. A similar argument, however, was not regarded as persuasive in *Lloyd v McMahon*. See also PARA 629.

9 *Local Government Board v Arlidge* [1915] AC 120, HL; *Carltona Ltd v Works Comrs* [1943] 2 All ER 560, CA.

10 *Osgood v Nelson* (1872) LR 5 HL 636; *Selvarajan v Race Relations Board* [1976] 1 All ER 12 at 20–21, 22, sub nom *R v Race Relations Board, ex p Selvarajan* [1975] 1 WLR 1686 at 1696, 1698, CA, per Lord Denning MR; *Winder v Cambridgeshire County Council* (1978) 76 LGR 549, CA; *R v Commission for Racial Equality, ex p Cottrell and Rothon* [1980] 3 All ER 265, [1980] 1 WLR 1580, DC.

11 *Vine v National Dock Labour Board* [1957] AC 488, [1956] 3 All ER 939, HL; *Barnard v National Dock Labour Board* [1953] 2 QB 18, [1953] 1 All ER 1113, CA; *Jeffs v New Zealand Dairy Production and Marketing Board* [1967] 1 AC 551, [1966] 3 All ER 863, PC (on facts, permissible for decision to be made on the basis of a full report on the evidence and submissions); *R v Admiralty Board of the Defence Council, ex p Coupland* [1999] COD 27 (guidelines as to extent to which decision-maker can rely on summary of evidence obtained in course of investigation); *Chief Constable of the North Wales Police v Evans* [1982] 3 All ER 141 at 144, [1982] 1 WLR 1155 at 1161, HL, per Lord Hailsham of St Marylebone and at 147 and 1165 per Lord Bridge of Harwich (breach of duty to act fairly when applicant not allowed to comment on final version of report in breach of conditions in the statutory scheme); *R v Birmingham City Council, ex p Quietlynn Ltd* (1985) 83 LGR 461 at 491–492 per Forbes J (on appeal sub nom *R v Peterborough City Council, ex p Quietlynn Ltd* (1986) 85 LGR 249, CA) (report inadequate and challenge succeeded); cf *Osgood v Nelson* (1872) LR 5 HL 636. See also *R v Minister of Agriculture and Fisheries, ex p Graham* [1955] 2 QB 140, [1955] 2 All ER 129, CA. But the reporting body is entitled to be selective so long as the substantial and salient points are reported, and the court will only intervene if there has been a clear failure to refer to something which was on any view relevant or if the report is so inadequate as to distort the submissions which were made: *R v Birmingham City Council, ex p Quietlynn Ltd* at 492 and 502 per Forbes J. Also on this point see *R v Independent Television Commission, ex p TSW Broadcasting Ltd* [1996] EMLR 291, HL (any inadequacy in the report must be material and must have been relied upon in making the decision).

Where a decision-maker is required by statute to obtain a report from some other person or body before reaching its decision, that report ought to contain not merely a bare recommendation, but also some statement of the underlying reasoning: *R v Kirklees Metropolitan Borough Council, ex p Molloy* (1987) 86 LGR 115, CA; cf *R v Secretary of State for Education and Science, ex p Threapleton* [1988] COD 102, (1988) Times, 2 June, DC; *Nicol v Gateshead Metropolitan Borough Council* (1988) 87 LGR 435, sub nom *R v Gateshead Metropolitan Borough Council, ex p Nichol* [1988] COD 97, CA.

12 *Shareef v Registration of Indian and Pakistani Residents Comr* [1966] AC 47, [1965] 3 WLR
    704, PC (misleading impression created at the hearing as to importance attached by the tribunal
    to a particular issue); *Fairmount Investments Ltd v Secretary of State for the Environment*
    [1976] 2 All ER 865 at 869, [1976] 1 WLR 1255 at 1260, HL, per Viscount Dilhorne
    (decision-maker not to rely on own private inquiries without first disclosing the outcome of
    them); *TLG Building Materials v Secretary of State for the Environment* (1980) 41 P & CR
    243, DC (Secretary of State taking different view from inspector of what constituted planning
    unit); *R v Vaccine Damage Tribunal, ex p Loveday* (1984) Times, 10 November (not accepting
    agreed statement of facts); *R v Mental Health Review Tribunal, ex p Clatworthy* [1985]
    3 All ER 699 at 704 per Mann J (if decision to be made on basis of point not raised by either
    party, tribunal should inform the parties and give opportunity for evidence and argument on the
    point); *R v Monmouth Borough Council, ex p Jones* (1985) 53 P & CR 108 (plans not put
    before planning committee in same form as when inspected by objectors); *Swinbank v Secretary
    of State for the Environment* (1987) 55 P & CR 371 (inspector raising new issue not canvassed
    by enforcement notice); *R v Secretary of State for the Environment, ex p Lamb's Ltd* (1987)
    56 P & CR 404; *Garbutt & Sons Ltd v Secretary of State for the Environment and
    Loughborough Borough Council* (1987) 57 P & CR 284. In each situation, the key issue is
    whether or not the information in question properly gives rise to issues on which the applicant
    should have an opportunity to comment further: see eg *Crompton v General Medical Council*
    [1982] 1 All ER 35, [1981] 1 WLR 1435, PC; *R v Secretary of State for Health, ex p United
    States Tobacco International Inc* [1992] QB 353, [1992] 1 All ER 212, DC; and cf *Rea v
    Minister of Transport* (1984) 48 P & CR 239; *R v Assistant Metropolitan Police Comr,
    ex p Howell* [1985] RTR 181; *R v Bristol City Council, ex p Pearce* (1984) 83 LGR 711 (licence
    refused on basis of general policy as to number which should be granted).

        Non-disclosure to the parties of points of law on which the tribunal intends to rest its
    decision is arguably also contrary to natural justice: see *PJ Drakard & Sons Ltd v Wilton* [1977]
    ICR 642, EAT; *R v Immigration Appeal Tibunal, ex p Patel* (1984) Times, 15 February; cf *Re
    Chien Sing-Shou* [1967] 2 All ER 1228, [1967] 1 WLR 1155, PC. Where a tribunal has made a
    finding but proposes to reconsider it, it should alert the parties to the point which is troubling it
    and give them the opportunity to make submissions: *Lamont v Fry's Metals Ltd* [1983] ICR
    778, [1983] IRLR 434, EAT.

        If a point is raised at the hearing, a party will only be able to claim that he was not
    sufficiently alerted to it if the reference was so trifling and minimal that anybody could be
    excused for overlooking it: *R v Secretary of State for the Environment, ex p Melton Borough
    Council* (1985) 52 P & CR 318 at 327 per Forbes J, distinguishing *H Sabey & Co Ltd v
    Secretary of State for the Environment* [1978] 1 All ER 586. Nor need a tribunal or inquiry
    proposing to disbelieve or criticise a party warn him specifically of that possibility, provided that
    the evidence upon which its conclusion is founded has been properly put to him: *Maxwell v
    Department of Trade and Industry* [1974] QB 523, [1974] 2 All ER 122, CA. See also *R v
    Monopolies and Mergers Commission, ex p Matthew Brown plc* [1987] 1 All ER 463, [1987]
    1 WLR 1235.

        However, there is no obligation to make a 'preliminary decision' in order to allow parties
    affected to make further representations: see *Hoffmann-La Roche v Secretary of State for Trade
    and Industry* [1975] AC 295 at 369 per Lord Diplock; *Finegan v General Medical Council*
    [1987] 1 WLR 121, PC (no duty to discuss every possible type of penalty which could be
    imposed).

13 As to the limits to such a power see *Moxon v Minister of Pensions* [1945] KB 490, [1945]
    2 All ER 124, CA. See also *Reynolds v Llanelly Associated Tinplate Co* [1948] 1 All ER
    140, CA; *Crofton Investment Trust Ltd v Greater London Rent Assessment Committee* [1967]
    2 QB 955, [1967] 2 All ER 1103, DC; *Wetherall v Harrison* [1976] QB 773, [1976] 1 All ER
    241, DC; *Fairmount Investments Ltd v Secretary of State for the Environment* [1976] 2 All ER
    865, [1976] 1 WLR 1255, HL; *Kent v Stamps* [1982] RTR 273, DC; *Owen v Jones* [1988] RTR
    102, DC; *Mullen v Hackney London Borough Council* [1997] 2 All ER 906, [1997] 1 WLR
    1103, CA. Where the tribunal places reliance upon matters derived from the specialist
    knowledge of one of its members, it should bring to the parties' attention not only the fact that
    the tribunal member has that expertise but also the particular matters relied upon: *Dugdale v
    Kraft Foods Ltd* [1977] ICR 48 at 54–55, EAT, per Phillips J; *Hammington v Berker
    Sportcraft Ltd* [1980] ICR 248, EAT; cf *FR Waring (UK) Ltd v Administraçao Geral do Acucar
    e do Alcool EP* [1983] 1 Lloyd's Rep 45.

14 The degree of latitude permitted to particular tribunals varies; the conduct of proceedings is
    usually regulated by procedural rules, but informality is almost always greater than in judicial
    proceedings in the strict sense.

15 See eg *R v Brighton and Area Rent Tribunal, ex p Marine Parade Estates (1936) Ltd* [1950] 2 KB 410, [1950] 1 All ER 946, DC. As to the circumstances in which material gleaned from a physical inspection not made in the presence of the parties or their representatives may and may not be used by a judicial tribunal see *Goold v Evans* [1951] 2 TLR 1189, CA; *Salsbury v Woodland* [1970] 1 QB 324, [1969] 3 All ER 863, CA; *Hibernian Property Co Ltd v Secretary of State for the Environment* (1973) 27 P & CR 197; *Fairmount Investments Ltd v Secretary of State for the Environment* [1976] 2 All ER 865 at 873–874, [1976] 1 WLR 1255 at 1265–1266, HL, per Lord Russell of Killowen (merely because a party may be aware of a physical feature on the site does not necessarily mean that he should anticipate what inference the inspector may draw from it); *Winchester City Council v Secretary of State for the Environment* (1979) 39 P & CR 1, CA; *Parry v Boyle* [1987] RTR 282, DC. Jury experiments must be in open court: *R v Higgins* (1989) Times, 16 February, CA; *R v Stewart* (1989) Times, 23 March, CA.

16 See *R v Deputy Industrial Injuries Comr, ex p Moore* [1965] 1 QB 456, [1965] 1 All ER 81, CA; *Kiely v Minister for Social Welfare* [1971] IR 21 (medical reports). Again, much will depend on the characteristics of the particular tribunal. In departmental adjudication there is a presumption that recourse to the opinions of officials and experts within the civil service is permissible: see *Bushell v Secretary of State for the Environment* [1981] AC 75, [1980] 2 All ER 608, HL (minister's own department); *Kent County Council v Secretary of State for the Environment* (1976) 33 P & CR 70 (another department).

17 *Reynolds v Llanelly Associated Tinplate Co* [1948] 1 All ER 140, CA; *R v Deputy Industrial Injuries Comr, ex p Jones* [1962] 2 QB 677, [1962] 2 All ER 430, DC; *R v Paddington and St Marylebone Rent Tribunal, ex p Bell London and Provincial Properties Ltd* [1949] 1 KB 666, [1949] 1 All ER 720, DC; *B v W* [1979] 3 All ER 83, [1979] 1 WLR 1041, HL; *Crompton v General Medical Council* [1982] 1 All ER 35, [1981] 1 WLR 1435, PC; *R v Bedfordshire County Council, ex p C* (1986) 85 LGR 218; *R v Secretary of State for the Home Department, ex p Gaima* (1988) Independent, 7 December, CA (material going to applicant's credibility); *R (on the application of Rashid) v Secretary of State for the Home Department* [2005] EWCA Civ 744, [2004] Imm AR 608, [2005] INLR 550 (Secretary of State applying policy unknown even to his own officials). As to a decision-maker's duty to reveal legal considerations he is proposing to take into account see *Amec Capital Projects Ltd v Whitefriars City Estates Ltd* [2004] EWCA Civ 1418, [2005] 1 All ER 723 (no automatic right for parties to make submissions on legal advice sought by arbitrator as to his jurisdiction); but cf *Albion Hotel (Freshwater) Ltd v Silva* [2002] IRLR 200, [2001] All ER (D) 265 (Nov), EAT (employment tribunal should have brought to attention of parties authorities it considered important). See further notes 20–21.

18 *R (Giant's Causeway & Tramway Co) v Antrim County Justices* [1895] 2 IR 603 at 649 per Sir O'Brien CJ. As to the circumstances in which use may be made of knowledge of a party derived from earlier proceedings in which he has been involved see *Munday v Munday* [1954] 2 All ER 667, [1954] 1 WLR 1078, DC; *Thomas v Thomas* [1961] 1 All ER 19, [1961] 1 WLR 1, DC; *Brinkley v Brinkley* [1965] P 75, [1963] 1 All ER 493, DC; *Bowman v DPP* [1991] RTR 263; *Norbrook Laboratories (GB) Ltd v Health and Safety Executive* (1998) Times, 23 February (local knowledge relied on to be disclosed to parties and opportunity to comment given).

19 See PARA 633.

20 When the minister is considering the inspector's report following the close of a public inquiry, he should neither receive representations from one party without informing the others, nor receive evidence from other sources adverse to one party's case without giving that party an opportunity to answer it: see *Bushell v Secretary of State for the Environment* [1981] AC 75 at 101–102, [1980] 2 All ER 608 at 617–618, HL, per Lord Diplock. See also *Hibernian Property Co Ltd v Secretary of State for the Environment* (1973) 27 P & CR 197; *R v Secretary of State for the Home Department, ex p Santillo* [1981] QB 778 at 796, [1981] 2 All ER 897 at 920–921, CA, per Shaw LJ (where deportation recommendation by court followed by long prison sentence; Secretary of State should consider any representations as to changes in the circumstances); *Mahon v Air New Zealand Ltd* [1984] AC 808 at 828, [1984] 3 All ER 201 at 215–216, PC; *Prest v Secretary of State for Wales* (1982) 81 LGR 193, CA; cf *Winchester City Council v Secretary of State for the Environment* (1979) 39 P & CR 1, CA (points noted on inspection after close of inquiry not genuinely new material, but merely gave new force to previous evidence); *Rea v Minister of Transport* (1982) 47 P & CR 207 (not necessary to make new material available to objectors after close of inquiry, because it neither changed the whole basis of the proposal nor showed that any material consideration had not been taken into account at the inquiry). The rule does not apply to departmental advice obtained by a minister: *Kent County Council v Secretary of State for the Environment and Burmah Total Refineries Trust*

(1976) 33 P & CR 70; *Bushell v Secretary of State for the Environment*. Where there are representations by one party after an inquiry followed by the other party commenting on those representations, the decision-maker is entitled to say that at some point there must be finality: *Reading Borough Council v Secretary of State for the Environment and Commercial Union Properties (Investments) Ltd* (1985) 52 P & CR 385.

21 *Board of Education v Rice* [1911] AC 179 at 182, HL, per Lord Loreburn LC; *R v Milk Marketing Board, ex p North* (1934) 50 TLR 559, DC; *R v City of Westminster Assessment Committee, ex p Grosvenor House (Park Lane) Ltd* [1941] 1 KB 53, [1940] 4 All ER 132, CA; *R v Architects' Registration Tribunal, ex p Jaggar* [1945] 2 All ER 131, DC; *Kanda v Government of the Federation of Malaya* [1962] AC 322, [1962] 2 WLR 1153, PC; *Wilcox v HGS* [1976] ICR 306, [1976] IRLR 222, EAT; *R v Huntingdon District Council, ex p Cowan* [1984] 1 All ER 58, [1984] 1 WLR 501; *R v Birmingham City Council, ex p Quietlynn Ltd* (1985) 83 LGR 461 at 522 per Forbes J (on appeal sub nom *R v Peterborough City Council, ex p Quietlynn Ltd* (1986) 85 LGR 249, CA); *R v Assistant Metropolitan Police Comr, ex p Howell* [1986] RTR 52, CA. See also *United Kingdom Association of Professional Engineers v Advisory, Conciliation and Arbitration Service* [1979] 2 All ER 478, [1979] 1 WLR 570, CA (revsd [1981] AC 424, [1980] 1 All ER 612, HL); and see the cases cited in note 17; cf *R v Secretary of State for the Home Department, ex p Mughal* [1974] QB 313, [1973] 3 All ER 796, CA. However, it will not always be necessary to reveal every detail of the material or the identity of the source: *Re Pergamon Press Ltd* [1971] Ch 388, [1970] 3 All ER 535, CA; *Herring v Templeman* [1973] 3 All ER 569, CA; *R v Huntingdon District Council, ex p Cowan*. Nor is it always necessary for points raised by third parties to be disclosed in advance of a hearing, especially if they are matters with which the party making representations should expect to have to deal (*Quietlynn Ltd v Plymouth City Council* [1988] QB 114 at 133–134, [1987] 2 All ER 1040 at 1047–1048, DC, per Webster J; *R v Birmingham City Council, ex p Quietlynn Ltd* at 484, 496, 522 per Forbes J); or if any reasonable application for an adjournment is considered (*R v Criminal Injuries Compensation Board, ex p Brady* (1987) Times, 11 March; but cf *R v Epsom Juvenile Court, ex p G* [1988] 1 All ER 329, [1988] 1 WLR 145).

22 *Errington v Minister of Health* [1935] 1 KB 249, CA; *R v Newmarket Assessment Committee, ex p Allen Newport Ltd* [1945] 2 All ER 371, DC; *R v Bodmin Justices, ex p McEwen* [1947] KB 321, [1947] 1 All ER 109, DC; *R v Deputy Industrial Injuries Comr, ex p Jones* [1962] 2 QB 677, [1962] 2 All ER 430, DC; *Barrs v British Wool Marketing Board* 1957 SC 72, Ct of Sess; *Fowler v Fowler and Sine* [1963] P 311, [1963] 1 All ER 119, CA; *R v Birmingham City Justice, ex p Chris Foreign Foods (Wholesalers) Ltd* [1970] 3 All ER 945, [1970] 1 WLR 1428, DC; *Midland Cold Storage Ltd v Turner* [1972] 3 All ER 773, [1972] ICR 230, NIRC; *WEA Records Ltd v Visions Channel 4 Ltd* [1983] 2 All ER 589 at 591, [1983] 1 WLR 721 at 724, CA, per Sir John Donaldson MR. But where the material is in substance only an attempt to present clearly publicly available information, or is argument rather than evidence, and it is clear to all concerned that the tribunal is concerned with the matters with which the material deals, then disclosure to other parties will not always be required: see *R v Monopolies and Mergers Commission, ex p Matthew Brown plc* [1987] 1 All ER 463, [1987] 1 WLR 1235.

23 See PARA 639. See in particular *Local Government Board v Arlidge* [1915] AC 120, HL; *R v Gaming Board for Great Britain, ex p Benaim and Khaida* [1970] 2 QB 417, [1970] 2 All ER 528, CA; *Collymore v A-G of Trinidad and Tobago* [1970] AC 538, [1969] 2 All ER 1207, PC; *Ali v Southwark London Borough Council* [1988] ICR 567, [1988] IRLR 100.

642.   Conduct of the hearing. A tribunal enjoys a discretion to regulate its own method of proceeding[1]. If there is some statutory or other express procedure which applies to the decision or inquiry, that procedure must, obviously, be complied with[2]. However, in certain circumstances the courts will be willing to supplement an express procedure with implied obligations required by fairness[3].

The existence of an express or implied obligation to conduct a hearing of some kind does not necessarily imply that there must be an oral hearing[4]. If there is an oral hearing, the parties will normally be entitled to make submissions and call evidence on all relevant issues[5]. Natural justice does not impose on administrative and domestic tribunals a duty to observe all the technical rules of evidence applicable to proceedings before courts of law[6]. In judicial proceedings, the parties will usually also be entitled to cross-examine the witnesses of other parties[7], but this is not necessarily the case in other types of hearing[8]. It may also be contrary to natural justice to refuse an adjournment requested by a party who needs further time to prepare his case or to produce evidence[9].

A party to proceedings in a court of law will be entitled to be legally represented[10]. However, in proceedings before a domestic tribunal natural justice does not necessarily imply the right to be thus represented[11]. The tribunal is not normally under any obligation to assist an unrepresented party with the presentation of his case[12], although in some cases it may be necessary to make him aware of his rights[13].

Although at common law delay by a decision-maker in making a determination does not, in itself, render a decision unfair, the position is different where the decision involves the determination of civil rights or obligations or any criminal charge engaging the Convention for the Protection of Human Rights and Fundamental Freedoms (1950)[14]. There will be a breach of the Convention if a hearing is not held within a reasonable time[15].

1 See e g *Selvarajan v Race Relations Board* [1976] 1 All ER 12 at 19, sub nom *R v Race Relations Board, ex p Selvarajan* [1975] 1 WLR 1686 at 1694, CA, per Lord Denning MR; *Bushell v Secretary of State for the Environment* [1981] AC 75, [1980] 2 All ER 608, HL; *R v Milton Keynes Justices, ex p R* [1979] 1 WLR 1062; *R v Sunderland Juvenile Court, ex p G* [1988] FCR 17, [1988] 2 FLR 40 (affd [1988] 2 All ER 34, [1988] 1 WLR 398, CA); cf *R v Boundary Commission for England, ex p Foot* [1983] QB 600 at 632–633, [1983] 1 All ER 1099 at 1114–1116, CA, per Sir John Donaldson MR; *R v Willesden Juvenile Court, ex p Brent London Borough Council* (1988) 86 LGR 197, DC. However, even in tribunals where a relatively informal procedure is expected, it is important that certain rules should be consistently observed, so that parties are not surprised by a sudden deviation from the norm: *Aberdeen Steak Houses Group plc v Ibrahim* [1988] ICR 550, [1988] IRLR 420, EAT. As to the discretion as to where and when to sit see *R v Avon Magistrates' Courts Committee, ex p Broome* [1988] 1 WLR 1246, 152 JP 529, DC. For a discussion of the principles to be applied in determining when a court should interfere with procedural decisions of a tribunal see *R v Panel on Take-overs and Mergers, ex p Guinness plc* [1990] 1 QB 146, [1989] 1 All ER 509, CA. See also *Re Pergamon Press* [1971] Ch 388, [1970] 3 All ER 535, CA; *R v Lord Saville of Newdigate, ex p A* [1999] 4 All ER 860, [1999] COD 436, CA (tribunal under a duty to achieve procedures which would ensure procedural fairness).

2 Although not all procedural requirements are mandatory ones: see PARA 626.

3 See PARAS 629, 641.

4 See e g *R v Judge Amphlett* [1915] 2 KB 223, DC; *R v Central Tribunal, ex p Parton* (1916) 32 TLR 476, DC; *Stuart v Haughley Parochial Church Council* [1935] Ch 452; (affd [1936] Ch 32, CA); *Kavanagh v Chief Constable of Devon and Cornwall* [1974] QB 624; *McInnes v Onslow Fane* [1978] 3 All ER 211 at 224, [1978] 1 WLR 1520 at 1536 per Megarry V-C; *R v Hull Prison Board of Visitors, ex p St Germain (No 2)* [1979] 3 All ER 545, [1979] 1 WLR 1401, DC; *Zainal bin Hashim v Government of Malaysia* [1980] AC 734, [1979] 3 All ER 241, PC; *Bushell v Secretary of State for the Environment* [1981] AC 75, [1980] 2 All ER 608, HL (if dispute on material questions of fact, oral hearing normally required); *R v Huntingdon District Council, ex p Cowan* [1984] 1 All ER 58, [1984] 1 WLR 501; *R v Bristol City Council, ex p Pearce* (1984) 83 LGR 711; *R v Immigration Appeal Tribunal, ex p Jones* [1988] 2 All ER 65, [1988] 1 WLR 477, CA; *Lonrho plc v Secretary of State for Trade and Industry* [1989] 2 All ER 609 at 616–617, sub nom *R v Secretary of State for Trade and Industry, ex p Lonrho plc* [1989] 1 WLR 525 at 535, HL, per Lord Keith of Kinkel; *R v Army Board of the Defence Council, ex p Anderson* [1992] QB 169, [1991] 3 All ER 375; *R (on the application of West) v Parole Board* [2005] UKHL 1, [2005] 1 All ER 755, [2005] 1 WLR 350 (oral hearing by Parole Board considering licence revocation not required in every case but would be where facts in issue or might otherwise contribute to a just decision); but cf *R (on the application of Smith) v Secretary of State for the Home Department* [2005] UKHL 51, [2006] 1 AC 159, [2006] 1 All ER 407 (review of tariff of young person detained at Her Majesty's pleasure can properly be done in writing as oral hearings would introduce delay); *R (on the application of G) v Immigration Appeal Tribunal* [2004] EWCA Civ 1731, [2005] 2 All ER 165, [2005] 1 WLR 1445 (statutory review process on the papers adequate protection).

Legislation sometimes provides for the determination of claims by administrative bodies on the basis of written representations. An express right to legal representation is not inconsistent with a decision to permit only written representations: *R v Immigration Appeal Tribunal, ex p Jones.*

In *Lloyd v McMahon* [1987] AC 625, [1987] 1 All ER 1118, HL, it was held that there was no breach of natural justice where the district auditor considered only written representations from councillors before certifying that loss had been caused by their wilful misconduct. However, the House of Lords indicated that, if an oral hearing had been requested, which it was not, it should probably have been granted. The question in every case is whether the matter can be disposed of fairly without an oral hearing, which is less likely to be possible if there is a dispute about whether a party is telling the truth: *Re Smith & Fawcett Ltd* [1942] Ch 304, [1942] 1 All ER 542, CA; *Lloyd v McMahon* (see especially at 695 and 696 per Lord Keith of Kinkel). Other factors include the seriousness of the matter, and whether the party is being deprived of an existing right or merely applying for a privilege: *McInnes v Onslow Fane.*

If the deciding body has created the impression that it will hold an oral hearing, but then elects, in its discretion, to determine the matter without such a hearing, a party who has been misled into submitting written representations in outline only will be entitled to have the decision set aside: *R v Secretary of State for Wales, ex p Green* (1969) 67 LGR 560, DC. See also *R v Crown Court at Croydon, ex p Smith* (1983) 77 Cr App Rep 277, DC; and PARA 649.

Delay in convening a hearing can form the basis of a challenge if the delay is such that justice cannot be achieved: *R v Chief Constable of Merseyside, ex p Calveley* [1986] QB 424, CA; *R v United Kingdom Central Council for Nursing, Midwifery and Health Visiting, ex p Thompson* [1991] COD 275. Where there is an oral hearing, all possible steps should be taken to ensure that it takes place over consecutive days, but the unavoidable failure to achieve this is not a ground for challenging the decision: *Barnes v BPC (Business Forms) Ltd* [1976] 1 All ER 237, [1975] 1 WLR 1565. See also *R v Trafford Magistrates' Court, ex p Stott* (1988) 152 JP 633, DC; *R v Portsmouth City Council, ex p Gregory* (1990) 89 LGR 478 (proceedings should not go on for too long each day).

5   *General Medical Council v Spackman* [1943] AC 627, [1943] 2 All ER 337, HL; *Hodgkins v Hodgkins* [1965] 3 All ER 164, [1965] 1 WLR 1448, CA; *Disher v Disher* [1965] P 31, [1963] 3 All ER 933, DC; *R v Gravesend Justices, ex p Sheldon* [1968] 3 All ER 466n, [1968] 1 WLR 1699, DC; *Vye v Vye* [1969] 2 All ER 29, [1969] 1 WLR 588, DC; *Mayes v Mayes* [1971] 2 All ER 397, [1971] 1 WLR 679, DC; *R v Hull Prison Board of Visitors, ex p St Germain (No 2)* [1979] 3 All ER 545, [1979] 1 WLR 1401, DC; *Tomlinson v Tomlinson* [1980] 1 All ER 593, [1980] 1 WLR 322, DC; *R v Birmingham City Juvenile Court, ex p Birmingham City Council* [1988] 1 All ER 683, [1988] 1 WLR 337, CA. Within the rules of court and of procedure, a party or his representatives are entitled to conduct the proceedings as they see fit and call witnesses in what order they wish: *Barnes v BPC (Business Forms) Ltd* [1976] 1 All ER 237, [1975] 1 WLR 1565. But the tactical presentation of evidence in a way not normally allowed and which might embarrass another party ought to be prevented: *Aberdeen Steak Houses Group plc v Ibrahim* [1988] ICR 550, [1988] IRLR 420, EAT. Further, it is legitimate to direct that expert evidence must await the conclusion of all factual evidence: *Bayer v Clarkson Puckle Overseas Ltd* [1989] NLJR 256. It was not contrary to natural justice to stop counsel at a local inquiry making a speech about matters in regard to which he was not going to call evidence: *Re London (Hammersmith) Housing Order, Application of Land Development Ltd* [1936] 2 All ER 1063.

The tribunal is also entitled to prevent the abuse of the right, for example by refusing requests to call witnesses which are calculated to render adjudication impossible, or which go far beyond what is necessary to establish the point: *R v Hull Prison Board of Visitors, ex p St Germain (No 2)*. The rights to examine witnesses and to make a closing address are conditional upon their being used for the purposes for which they are given, but the power to curtail their exercise must be used only very sparingly and in obvious cases: *R v Morley* [1988] QB 601, [1988] 2 All ER 396, CA. See also *Bradman v Radio Taxicabs Ltd* (1984) 134 NLJ 1018 (discretion to refuse adjournment to call further witnesses properly exercised where applicant had been told in advance of right to call witnesses). Hearsay evidence may also be taken into account: *McCool v Rushcliffe Borough Council* [1998] 3 All ER 889, [1999] LGR 365.

6   See eg *General Medical Council v Spackman* [1943] AC 627, [1943] 2 All ER 337, HL; *Ceylon University v Fernando* [1960] 1 All ER 631, [1960] 1 WLR 223, PC; *R v Deputy Industrial Injuries Comr, ex p Moore* [1965] 1 QB 456, [1965] 1 All ER 81, CA; *Kavanagh v Chief Constable of Devon and Cornwall* [1974] QB 624, [1974] 2 All ER 697, CA; *R v Hull Prison Board of Visitors, ex p St Germain (No 2)* [1979] 3 All ER 545, [1979] 1 WLR 1401, DC; *Gee v General Medical Council* [1987] 2 All ER 193, [1987] 1 WLR 564, HL; and PARA 629.

7   *Blaise v Blaise* [1969] P 54, [1969] 2 All ER 1032, CA; *R v Edmonton Justices, ex p Brooks*
    [1960] 2 All ER 475, [1960] 1 WLR 697, DC; *R v Birmingham City Juvenile Court,*
    ex p Birmingham City Council [1988] 1 All ER 683, [1988] 1 WLR 337, CA.
    Cross-examination ought to be allowed where it is fairly ancillary to the right to meet an
    allegation by calling or giving evidence: *R v Milton Keynes Justices, ex p R* [1979] 1 WLR
    1062, DC. At a public inquiry, a person considering that he will be injuriously affected by the
    proposal ought to be allowed to cross-examine any witness who gives evidence contrary to his
    case, even if that witness has not been called by the party making the proposal: *Nicholson v*
    Secretary of State for Energy (1977) 76 LGR 693. See also *Re Stern (a bankrupt)* [1982]
    2 All ER 600, [1982] 1 WLR 860. But in the absence of a definite issue of fact
    cross-examination motivated solely by the hope that something discreditable will emerge may
    well be oppressive: *Re a Debtor, ex p Taylor* [1980] Ch 565, [1980] 1 All ER 129, DC. Nor may
    cross-examination be a 'fishing expedition' designed in effect to use an opposing witness to give
    evidence in chief: *Nicholson v Secretary of State for Energy.*
        Abuse of the right to cross-examine may be controlled: see *Nicholson v Secretary of State for*
    Energy; *Automobile Proprietary Ltd v Healy* [1979] ICR 809, EAT; *R v Morley* [1988] QB 601,
    [1988] 2 All ER 396, CA.

8   Whether or not it is necessary will depend on whether, having regard to all the circumstances, it
    is required in order to provide a hearing which satisfies the duty to act fairly. See *Khanum v*
    Mid-Glamorgan Area Health Authority [1979] ICR 40, [1978] IRLR 215, EAT; *R v*
    Commission for Racial Equality, ex p Cottrell and Rothon [1980] 3 All ER 265, [1980] 1 WLR
    1580, DC; *Bushell v Secretary of State for the Environment* [1981] AC 75, [1980] 2 All ER
    608, HL; *R (on the application of B) v Head Teacher of Alperton Community School* [2001]
    EWHC Admin 229, [2002] LGR 132, [2001] ELR 359 (cross-examination of witnesses not
    required in all school exclusion cases); *R v London Regional Passenger Committee, ex p Brent*
    London Borough Council (1985) Times, 23 May (affd (1985) Financial Times,
    29 November, CA) (no necessary obligation to allow each witness to be cross-examined by every
    party); cf *Nicholson v Secretary of State for Energy* (1977) 76 LGR 693; *Graham v Teesdale*
    (1981) 81 LGR 117. Where fairness requires an opportunity for cross-examination but it is
    impractical for the relevant witness to attend, his hearsay evidence may have to be excluded: *R v*
    Hull Prison Board of Visitors, ex p St Germain (No 2) [1979] 3 All ER 545, [1979] 1 WLR
    1401, DC; *Khanum v Mid Glamorgan Area Health Authority*; cf *R v Crown Court at*
    Aylesbury, ex p Farrer (1988) Times, 9 March, CA; *R (on the application of Brooks) v Parole*
    Board [2004] EWCA Civ 80, 148 Sol Jo LB 233. The inspector at a public local inquiry may
    disallow a line of cross-examination which would serve no useful purpose: *Bushell v Secretary of*
    State for the Environment.
        There may be exceptional occasions where witnesses may give evidence anonymously. Whilst
    witness anonymity does not necessarily breach the right to a fair hearing at common law or
    under the Convention for the Protection of Human Rights and Fundamental Freedoms (Rome,
    4 November 1950; TS 71 (1953) Cmd 8969) art 6, it was held to do so in a murder trial where
    the defendant was unable effectively to challenge decisive evidence against him: *R v Davis*
    [2008] UKHL 36, [2008] 1 AC 1128, [2008] 3 All ER 461. In considering an application for
    anonymity for a witness, the common law duty of fairness includes consideration of risk to life
    and subjective fears even if not well founded: *Re Officer L* [2007] UKHL 36, [2007] NI 277,
    [2007] 4 All ER 965.

9   A wrongful refusal to adjourn may lead to an unfair hearing: *Priddle v Fisher* [1968] 3 All ER
    506, [1968] 1 WLR 1478, DC; *Ottley v Morris* [1979] 1 All ER 65. The courts are prepared to
    substitute their own views for those of the decision-maker as to what a fair procedure requires.
    However, it is only likely that a court would intervene in such a case if there was a real risk of
    serious prejudice: see *R v Panel on Take-overs and Mergers, ex p Fayed* [1992] BCLC 938,
    [1992] BCC 524, CA; *R v Institute of Chartered Accountants in England and Wales,*
    ex p Brindle [1994] BCC 297, CA; *R v Criminal Injuries Compensation Board, ex p Cobb*
    [1995] COD 126; *Thorne v Sevenoaks General Comrs* [1989] STC 560; *R v Hereford*
    Magistrates' Court, ex p Rowlands [1998] QB 110, [1997] 2 WLR 854; *Albon (t/a NA*
    Carriage Co) v Naza Motor Trading Sdn Bhd (No 5) [2007] EWHC 2613 (Ch), [2008] 1 All ER
    995, [2008] 1 WLR 2380; *R (on the application of Mahfouz) v Professional Conduct*
    Committee of the General Medical Council [2004] EWCA Civ 233, 80 BMLR 113
    (adjournment of disciplinary proceedings to allow time for High Court challenge to composition
    of panel); *R (on the application of Land) v Executive Council of the Accountants' Joint*
    Disciplinary Scheme [2002] EWHC 2086 (Admin), [2002] All ER (D) 201 (Oct) (stay of
    regulatory proceedings pending civil proceedings refused); *R v Ealing Justices, ex p Avondale*
    [1999] COD 291 (general guidance as to circumstances relevant to decision whether to grant an
    adjournment).

Typically, a party may be entitled to an adjournment if he is taken by surprise at the hearing by new allegations or new evidence which ought to have been disclosed in advance: see *Dean v Polytechnic of North London* [1973] ICR 490, NIRC; *Performance Cars Ltd v Secretary of State for the Environment* (1977) 34 P & CR 92, CA. See also *R v Thames Magistrates' Court, ex p Polemis* [1974] 2 All ER 1219, [1974] 1 WLR 1371, DC; *R v Birmingham Justices, ex p Lamb* [1983] 3 All ER 23, [1983] 1 WLR 339, DC; *R v Enfield Magistrates' Court, ex p DPP* (1988) 153 JP 415, DC; and the cases cited in PARA 640 note 15. However, a party who is himself at fault in not having witnesses or counsel available at the hearing is not necessarily entitled to an adjournment (*Chettiar v Chettiar* [1962] AC 294 at 300, [1962] 1 All ER 494 at 496, PC, obiter; *Government of Australia v Harrod* [1975] 2 All ER 1, [1975] 1 WLR 745, HL), and will normally have to pay the other party's costs if one is granted. See also *R v Dudley Justices, ex p Southall* (1985) Times, 14 February, DC (justices should take account of possible appeal against refusal of legal aid). Where an adjournment is sought on the ground of a witness's absence, the court should inquire into the nature of his evidence: *R v Bracknell Justices, ex p Hughes* (1989) 154 JP 98, DC. An adjournment is less likely to be allowed in the case of a public inquiry where there are many parties to the proceedings, although the absent objector should be heard on another day if possible: *Ostreicher v Secretary of State for the Environment* [1978] 3 All ER 82, [1978] 1 WLR 810, CA (religious beliefs preventing attendance or being represented on day of inquiry; but this case largely turned upon the party's failure to ask for an adjournment); cf *R v Secretary of State for the Environment, ex p Mistral Investments Ltd* (1984) Times, 14 March. Where a party is ill, there is no purpose in an adjournment if there is no prospect of his recovering sufficiently to attend, but the mere fact that medical evidence does not indicate a reasonable prospect of his attending at a future date is only one factor to be considered: *Dick v Piller* [1943] KB 497, [1943] 1 All ER 627, CA; *Rose v Humbles (Inspector of Taxes), Aldersgate Textiles Ltd v IRC* [1972] 1 All ER 314, [1972] 1 WLR 33, CA; *Thorne v Sevenoaks General Comrs and IRC* [1989] STC 560. See also *R v South West London Supplementary Benefit Appeal Tribunal, ex p Bullen* (1976) 120 Sol Jo 437, DC; *R v Birmingham City Council, ex p Quietlynn Ltd* (1985) 83 LGR 461 at 493–495, 506–507 per Forbes J (on appeal sub nom *R v Peterborough City Council, ex p Quietlynn Ltd* (1986) 85 LGR 249, CA); *R v Panel on Take-overs and Mergers, ex p Guinness plc* [1990] 1 QB 146, [1989] 1 All ER 509, CA.

10 The possible choice of representative will depend upon the regulations and practice of the court as to rights of audience: see *Engineers' and Managers' Association v Advisory, Conciliation and Arbitration Service* [1979] 3 All ER 223, [1979] 1 WLR 1113, CA (revsd on another point [1980] 1 All ER 896, [1980] 1 WLR 302, HL); *Abse v Smith* [1986] QB 536, [1986] 1 All ER 350, CA; and LEGAL PROFESSIONS vol 66 (2009) PARA 1109 et seq.

A right to be legally represented is not an absolute right in the sense that proceedings cannot in any circumstances continue if a party is in fact unrepresented: cf *Robinson v R* [1985] AC 956, [1985] 2 All ER 594, PC (criticised by the United Nations Human Rights Commission as contrary to the International Covenant on Civil and Political Rights (16 December 1966; UN TS vol 999, p 171) art 14). However, there may be cases where the court ought not to proceed without making sure that a party is aware of the possibility of obtaining legal advice, and financial assistance if applicable: see *Re M (an infant)* [1973] QB 108, [1972] 3 All ER 321, CA. A court in civil proceedings has no power to instruct the Legal Services Commission to grant funding for legal representation but may only express its view as to whether representation is necessary for a fair hearing: *Perotti v Collyer-Bristow (a firm)* [2003] EWCA Civ 1521, [2004] 2 All ER 189. If a party is present but not legally represented and proceedings take a course not necessarily anticipated at the outset, an adjournment may be necessary to give that party the opportunity of being heard through the mouth of a trained and experienced person: see *Somerset County Council v Brice* [1973] 3 All ER 438 at 445–446, [1973] 1 WLR 1169 at 1178, DC, per Lord Widgery CJ (magistrates proposing to make compensation order against local authority as guardian of child accused); *R v Ilminster Justices, ex p Hamilton* (1983) Times, 23 June, DC; cf *R v Newbury Justices, ex p du Pont* (1983) 78 Cr App Rep 255, DC. See also *R v Crown Court at Guildford, ex p Siderfin* [1990] 2 QB 683, [1989] 3 All ER 7, DC (application to be excused jury service).

There is also a right for any person to attend as a friend and to take notes and make suggestions, although not to act as an advocate if he or she has no right of audience: *Collier v Hicks* (1831) 2 B & Ad 663; *McKenzie v McKenzie* [1971] P 33, [1970] 3 All ER 1034, CA (such persons are sometimes known as a 'McKenzie friend'). The Convention for the Protection of Human Rights and Fundamental Freedoms (Rome, 4 November 1950; TS 71 (1953) Cmd 8969) is engaged where a litigant in person applies to be assisted by a litigation friend and there is a very strong presumption in favour of granting such an application: *Re O (children)* [2005] EWCA Civ 759, [2006] Fam 1, [2005] 3 WLR 1191. A McKenzie friend may only address the court as an indulgence of the court but it may be in the interests of justice to let them do so: *Izzo v Philip Ross & Co* [2001] 35 LS Gaz R 37, (2001) Times, 9 August. See also *R v Southwark Juvenile Court, ex p J* [1973] 3 All ER 383, [1973] 1 WLR 1300, DC; *R v Leicester Justices, ex p Barrow* [1991] 2 QB 260. But a person being examined has no right to have an adviser at his elbow to consult upon matters of relevancy and privilege before answering questions: *R v Rathbone, ex p Dikko* [1985] QB 630, [1985] 2 WLR 375.

A person may be entitled to make use of an interpreter: cf *R v Kingston-upon-Thames Magistrates' Court, ex p Davey* (1985) 149 JPN 744, DC. In *R (on the application of Dirshe) v Secretary of State for the Home Department* [2005] EWCA Civ 421, [2005] 1 WLR 2685, the refusal to allow an asylum seeker's solicitor to tape record an interview with immigration officers was held to be procedurally unfair.

11   It appears that there will not normally be an absolute right to legal representation, but that the tribunal has a discretion to permit it as part of its general discretion to regulate its own procedure: see *R v Board of Visitors of the Maze Prison, ex p Hone* [1988] AC 379, sub nom *Hone v Maze Prison Board of Visitors* [1988] 1 All ER 321, HL; *Fraser v Mudge* [1975] 3 All ER 78, [1975] 1 WLR 1132, CA; *Maynard v Osmond* [1977] QB 240, [1977] 1 All ER 64, CA; *R v Secretary of State for the Home Department, ex p Tarrant* [1985] QB 251, [1984] 1 All ER 799, DC; *R v Secretary of State for the Home Department, ex p Cheblak* [1991] 2 All ER 319, [1991] 1 WLR 890, CA. Factors which ought to be taken into account in exercising the discretion include the seriousness of any allegations made or any potential penalty, whether any points of law are likely to arise, the capacity of the particular individual to present his or her own case, whether it will be necessary to cross-examine witnesses whose evidence has not been disclosed in advance, any potential delay, and the need for fairness as between all persons who may appear before the tribunal: *R v Board of Visitors of the Maze Prison, ex p Hone*; *R v Secretary of State for the Home Department, ex p Tarrant*; *R v Board of Visitors of HM Remand Centre Risley, ex p Draper* (1988) Times, 24 May, CA. See also *R v Board of Visitors of Long Lartin Prison, ex p Cunningham* (17 May 1988, unreported), QBD; *R v Board of Visitors of Parkhurst, ex p Norney* [1990] COD 133, DC.

However the Convention for the Protection of Human Rights and Fundamental Freedoms (Rome, 4 November 1950; TS 71 (1953) Cmd 8969) means that the authorities cited above have to be treated with a degree of caution. In *Ezeh v United Kingdom* [2004] Crim LR 472, (2004) 35 EHRR 1, ECtHR, there was held to be a breach of the Convention for the Protection of Human Rights and Fundamental Freedoms (1950) art 6(3)(c) where there was a denial of legal assistance in internal prison disciplinary proceedings that potentially resulted in additional days being added to a prisoner's sentence.

There may in some circumstances be a requirement under the Convention for the Protection of Human Rights and Fundamental Freedoms (1950) art 6 to allow legal representation in internal disciplinary proceedings in the employment field. In *R (on the application of G) v Governors of X School* [2009] EWHC 504 (Admin), [2009] LGR 799, [2009] IRLR 434 denial of legal representation was held to be in breach of the Convention for the Protection of Human Rights and Fundamental Freedoms (1950) art 6(1) where dismissal for misconduct would lead to a referral to the Secretary of State as a person unsuitable to work with children; but see also *R (on the application of Fleurose) v Securities and Futures Authority Ltd* [2001] EWHC Admin 292, [2001] 2 All ER (Comm) 481, [2001] IRLR 764 (no requirement for legal representation in disciplinary proceedings against a trader) (affd [2001] EWCA Civ 2015, [2002] IRLR 297).

To draw distinctions between adversarial and inquisitorial proceedings is unhelpful: *R v Secretary of State for the Home Department, ex p Tarrant* at 299 and 826–827 per Kerr LJ. It may be sufficient if representation by some suitable person is permitted, albeit not a lawyer: see *Maynard v Osmond* (representation by a senior officer in police disciplinary proceedings). Mere administrative inconvenience and the fact that some people will be unable to afford legal assistance are not of themselves sufficient grounds for refusing representation: *R v Secretary of State for the Home Department, ex p Tarrant*. See also *R v Assessment Committee of St Mary Abbotts, Kensington* [1891] 1 QB 378, CA; *Pett v Greyhound Racing Association Ltd* [1969] 1 QB 125, [1968] 2 All ER 545, CA; *Pett v Greyhound Racing Association Ltd (No 2)* [1970] 1 QB 46, [1969] 2 All ER 221 (settled on appeal [1970] 1 QB 67n, [1970] 1 All ER 243, CA); *Enderby Town Football Club Ltd v Football Association Ltd* [1971] Ch 591, [1971] 1 All ER 215, CA.

It was held in *R v Secretary of State for the Home Department, ex p Tarrant*, that there was also a discretion, but not an obligation, to allow assistance by a 'McKenzie friend' (as to which see note 10).

The right to legal representation may extend beyond the hearing: see *R v Secretary of State for the Home Department, ex p Leech (No 2)* [1994] QB 198, [1993] 4 All ER 539, CA (prison rules authorising opening of all correspondence held ultra vires); but cf *R v Governor of*

Whitemoor Prison, ex p Main [1997] COD 400, DC. It may also apply to decision-making processes which cannot be regarded as 'hearings' in any traditional sense: see *R v Cornwall County Council, ex p L-H* [2000] LGR 180.

12 *Snow v Secretary of State for the Environment* (1976) 33 P & CR 81 (inspector at planning inquiry under no duty to formulate cross-examination for objector); *Dennis v United Kingdom Central Council for Nursing, Midwifery and Health Visiting* (1993) 13 BMLR 146 (decision-maker not required to re-formulate party's case).

13 *Re M (an infant)* [1973] QB 108, [1972] 3 All ER 321, CA (mother resisting adoption proceedings should have been advised of her rights); *Holland v Cyprane Ltd* [1977] ICR 355, EAT (applicant who informed industrial tribunal of inability to attend due to illness should have been told of right to apply for adjournment); *Tomlinson v Tomlinson* [1980] 1 All ER 593, [1980] 1 WLR 322, DC (in suitable case, justices should suggest applying to exclude prospective witnesses); see also *Cannock Chase District Council v Kelly* (1978) 36 P & CR 219 at 228 per Lawton LJ; *R v Willesden Juvenile Court, ex p Brent London Borough Council* (1988) 86 LGR 197; cf *R v Board of Visitors of Swansea Prison, ex p McGrath* (1986) Times, 17 February.

14 Ie the Convention for the Protection of Human Rights and Fundamental Freedoms (1950) art 6. See CONSTITUTIONAL LAW AND HUMAN RIGHTS vol 8(2) (Reissue) PARA 134 et seq.

15 See eg *Porter v Magill* [2001] UKHL 67, [2002] 2 AC 357, [2002] 1 All ER 465; *Dyer (Procurator Fiscal, Linlithgow) v Watson* [2002] UKPC D1, [2004] 1 AC 379, [2002] 4 All ER 1; *Spiers (Procurator Fiscal) v Ruddy* [2007] UKPC D2, [2008] 1 AC 873, [2008] 2 WLR 608; *Burns v HM Advocate* [2008] UKPC 63, [2009] 1 AC 720, [2009] 2 WLR 935; *R (on the application of Minshall) v Marylebone Magistrates' Court* [2008] EWHC 2800 (Admin), [2009] 2 All ER 806.

643. Openness of judicial proceedings. The general public are entitled to see for themselves that justice is done. Therefore, whilst the court has an inherent power to sit in private[1], it may only do so if, in wholly exceptional circumstances, the party applying for the hearing to be in private shows that the objective of doing justice in accordance with the law is likely to be defeated by the public being present. Nor may any exercise of the court's inherent power to control the proceedings depart from the general rule of open justice to any greater extent than is necessary to serve the ends of justice[2]. However, unruly persons, including objectors at an inquiry, may be ejected[3], and it may also be proper to exclude witnesses from the court until the time comes for them to give evidence[4].

1 *R v Governor of Lewes Prison, ex p Doyle* [1917] 2 KB 254, DC; *R v Ealing Justices, ex p Weafer* (1981) 74 Cr App Rep 204, DC; *R v Reigate Justices, ex p Argus Newspapers Ltd* [1983] Crim LR 564, DC; *R v Malvern Justices, ex p Evans* [1988] QB 540, [1988] 1 All ER 371, DC. Similarly, information may be received in a documentary form and not be made publicly available: *R v Beckett* (1967) 51 Cr App Rep 180, CA; *R v Evesham Justices, ex p McDonagh* [1988] QB 553, [1988] 1 All ER 371 at 379 et seq, DC, per Watkins LJ. See also the statutory powers conferred by the Contempt of Court Act 1981 ss 4(2), 11 (see CONTEMPT OF COURT vol 9(1) (Reissue) PARAS 428, 432). It has been held that applications that the court should sit in private may have to be heard in private so as not to defeat their purpose: *R v Tower Bridge Magistrates' Court, ex p Osborne* (1987) 152 JP 310, (1989) 88 Cr App Rep 28, DC. As to the principles applied in wardship cases see *Re C (A Minor) (No 2)* [1990] Fam 39, [1989] 2 All ER 791, CA. Decisions to sit in private may be challenged under the Criminal Justice Act 1988 s 159: see CONTEMPT OF COURT vol 9(1) (Reissue) PARA 428.

   A requirement to sit in public does not mean that a venue must be chosen which allows everyone who so wishes to attend: *R v Inner North London Coroner, ex p Chambers* (1983) 127 Sol Jo 445.

   After a hearing in chambers, the decision whether to give judgment in open court is expressly for the judge's discretion: *British and Commonwealth Holdings plc v Quadrex Holdings Inc (No 2)* (1988) Times, 8 December (avoiding creation of false market in shares).

   See also the Convention for the Protection of Human Rights and Fundamental Freedoms (Rome, 4 November 1950; TS 71 (1953) Cmd 8969) art 6(1) which permits the exclusion of the press and public where the interests of juveniles or the protection of the private life of the parties so require: see PARA 639 note 5.

2 *Scott v Scott* [1913] AC 417, HL; *A-G v Leveller Magazine Ltd* [1979] AC 440, [1979] 1 All ER 745, HL; *R v Chief Registrar of Friendly Societies, ex p New Cross Building Society* [1984] QB

227, [1984] 2 All ER 27, CA; *R (on the application of Malik) v Central Criminal Court* [2006] EWHC 1539 (Admin), [2006] 4 All ER 1141, [2007] 1 WLR 2455; *R v Felixstowe Justices, ex p Leigh* [1987] QB 582, [1987] 1 All ER 551, DC (bona fide inquirer entitled to know names of justices); *R v Malvern Justices, ex p Evans* [1988] QB 540, [1988] 1 All ER 371, DC (defendant's embarrassment not a valid reason to sit in private); *R v Evesham Justices, ex p McDonagh* [1988] QB 553, [1988] 1 All ER 371 at 379 et seq, DC, per Watkins LJ (defendant's address not to be concealed to avoid harassment by ex-wife); *Chan U Seek v Alvis Vehicles Ltd (Guardian Newspapers Ltd intervening)* [2004] EWHC 3092 (Ch), [2005] 3 All ER 155, [2005] 1 WLR 2965 (non-party entitled to inspect pleadings and witness statements affirmed in open court). See also *R v Central Criminal Court, ex p Crook* (1984) Times, 8 November, DC; cf the different approach to an administrative function taken in *R v Farmer, ex p Hargrave* (1981) 79 LGR 676, DC (district auditor could sit in private to deal with ratepayer's objections to spending, to avoid prejudicing negotiations between local authority and third party); *R (on the application of Pelling) v Bow County Court* [2001] EWCA Civ 122, [2001] UKHRR 165. Specific provision may be made for such matters in the rules governing particular statutory inquiries and procedures. See also *R v London (North) Industrial Tribunal, ex p Associated Newspapers* [1998] ICR 1212, sub nom *Associated Newspapers Ltd v London (North) Industrial Tribunal* [1998] IRLR 569, EAT (scope of power of Employment Tribunals to make restricted reporting orders to conceal the identity of parties prior to promulgation of decision); *X v Metropolitan Police Comr* [2003] ICR 1031, [2003] IRLR 411, EAT; *Chief Constable of West Yorkshire Police v A* [2002] ICR 552, [2002] IRLR 103, EAT; *Fariad v Tradition Securities and Futures SA* [2009] IRLR 354, [2008] All ER (D) 90 (Dec), EAT. As to Employment Tribunals see EMPLOYMENT vol 41 (2009) PARA 1363 et seq.

3 *Lovelock v Minister of Transport* (1979) 39 P & CR 468, CA (also held that upon lifting the order there was no duty to search out the persons concerned). See also *R v Morley* [1988] QB 601, [1988] 2 All ER 396, CA.

4 A prospective witness need not leave the courtroom unless there has been an order excluding him: *Tomlinson v Tomlinson* [1980] 1 All ER 593, [1980] 1 WLR 322, DC. If an application is made for such an order, it ought to be granted unless the court is satisfied that it would be inappropriate to do so, and factors relevant to the exercise of the discretion include whether it is likely that the witness's evidence would be improperly affected, and whether his or her earlier presence would assist one of the parties or save time or duplication of evidence: *Tomlinson v Tomlinson*; *R v Willesden Juvenile Court, ex p Brent London Borough Council* (1988) 86 LGR 197. The parties themselves, their solicitors and expert witnesses should only be ordered to leave in exceptional circumstances: *R v Willesden Juvenile Court, ex p Brent London Borough Council*; *Ward v Police Service of Northern Ireland* [2007] UKHL 50, [2008] NI 138, [2008] 1 All ER 517 (exclusion of suspect and his solicitor from hearing of police application to extend detention). See also *Moore v Lambeth County Court Registrar* [1969] 1 All ER 782, [1969] 1 WLR 141, CA. The mere fact that police witnesses had conferred in the production of their witness statements for an inquiry into a fatal shooting by police did not in itself mean that there was not an effective inquiry for the purposes of the Convention for the Protection of Human Rights and Fundamental Freedoms (Rome, 4 November 1950; TS 71 (1953) Cmd 8969) art 2: *R (on the application of Saunders) v Independent Police Complaints Commission* [2008] EWHC 2372 (Admin), [2009] 1 All ER 379. See CONSTITUTIONAL LAW AND HUMAN RIGHTS vol 8(2) (Reissue) PARA 123.

644. The decision. A member of a tribunal who has not heard all the evidence must not participate or appear to participate in the tribunal's decision[1]. In some cases there is a statutory duty upon a decision-maker to give reasons[2]. In such cases, the reasons given must be adequate and intelligible and deal with the substantial points at issue[3]. However, it is not necessary to set out the full reasoning of the decision-maker[4], nor to record all the evidence given or submissions made[5]. Where there is no statutory duty to give reasons, the courts are becoming more willing to conclude that decision-makers are required to as a matter of natural justice[6], although a more stringent approach may be taken to judicial tribunals from which there is a right of appeal only on a question of law[7]. Where reasons are given and findings made, there must be evidence having some probative value, in the sense that it tends logically to show the existence of facts consistent with the findings and the reasons must not be logically self-contradictory[8].

The standard of proof to be applied in criminal and civil courts is well established[9]. Before domestic tribunals, even when dealing with disciplinary offences, the flexibility of the civil standard is normally to be preferred[10].

1　This is the rule governing proceedings of courts: see *Ng v R* [1987] 1 WLR 1356, PC; *R v Huntingdon Confirming Authority* [1929] 1 KB 698 at 714, CA, per Lord Hanworth MR and at 717 per Romer J; *Munday v Munday* [1954] 2 All ER 667, [1954] 1 WLR 1078, DC; *R v Manchester Justices, ex p Burke* (1961) 125 JP 387, DC; *Tameshwar v R* [1957] AC 476, [1957] 2 All ER 683, PC; *The Forest Lake* [1968] P 270, [1966] 3 All ER 833. It is not sufficient for the member who did not hear the evidence to have read a transcript of the proceedings: *Ng v R*. See also *R v Boycott, ex p Keasley* [1939] 2 KB 651, [1939] 2 All ER 626, DC (certificate of uneducability quashed because not signed by the doctor who had conducted the medical examination). Cf *Olympia Press Ltd v Hollis* [1974] 1 All ER 108, [1973] 1 WLR 1520, DC (large number of allegedly obscene books provided to justices in advance of hearing; acceptable for each book to have been read by only two or three out of six justices, provided that all six then discussed the totality of the material). See also *R v Croydon Metropolitan Stipendiary Magistrate, ex p Richman* (1985) Times, 8 March, DC.

　　There is no need for the members of the tribunal to consult with each other where they are unanimous as to their decision, but it is advisable to do so in the event of disagreement: *Howard v Borneman (No 2)* [1976] AC 301, [1975] 2 All ER 418, HL (holding also that there was no requirement for all the persons appointed to membership of a statutory tribunal to sit as the tribunal hearing a particular case). Similarly, only those who are making the decisions should attend and take part in the deliberations: see *R v Secretary of State for Education and Employment, ex p McNalty* (2001) Times, 23 March (person who acted as prosecutor not entitled to attend deliberations of decision-makers).

2　See PARA 646. Where there is a statutory requirement that one authority should obtain the opinion of another before taking a particular decision, then the latter ought to give the reasons for its view: *R v Secretary of State for the Home Department, ex p Dannenberg* [1984] QB 766 at 777, [1984] 2 All ER 481 at 488, CA, per Dunn LJ.

3　*South Bucks District Council v Porter (No 2)* [2004] UKHL 33, [2004] 4 All ER 775, [2004] 1 WLR 1953; *Flannery v Halifax Estate Agencies Ltd* [2000] 1 All ER 373, [2000] 1 WLR 377, CA; *R (on the application of the Asha Foundation) v Millennium Commission* [2003] EWCA Civ 88, [2003] ACD 50; *Dunster Properties Ltd v First Secretary of State* [2007] EWCA Civ 236, [2007] 2 P & CR 515; *R (on the application of Hirst) v Secretary of State for the Home Department* [2005] EWHC 1480 (Admin), (2005) Times, 4 July; *Re Poyser and Mills' Arbitration* [1964] 2 QB 467 at 478, [1963] 1 All ER 612 at 616 per Megaw J; *Earl of Iveagh v Minister of Housing and Local Government* [1962] 2 QB 147 at 160, [1961] 3 All ER 98 at 107 per Megaw J (affd [1964] 1 QB 395, [1963] 3 All ER 817, CA); *Givaudan & Co Ltd v Minister of Housing and Local Government* [1966] 3 All ER 696, [1967] 1 WLR 250; *Westminster Bank Ltd v Beverley Borough Council* [1969] 1 QB 499 at 508, [1968] 2 All ER 104 at 111 per Donaldson J; *Re Allen and Matthews' Arbitration* [1971] 2 QB 518, [1971] 2 All ER 259; *Niarchos (London) Ltd v Secretary of State for the Environment* (1977) 35 P & CR 259; *Westminster City Council v Great Portland Street Estates plc* [1985] AC 661 at 673, sub nom *Great Portland Street Estates plc v Westminster City Council* [1984] 3 All ER 744 at 752, HL, per Lord Scarman; *Barnham v Secretary of State for the Environment* (1985) 52 P & CR 10; *London Residuary Body v Secretary of State for the Environment* (1988) 58 P & CR 256 (assume a careful, unpedantic and well-tutored reader, but deep analysis should not be necessary); *R v Tower Hamlets London Borough Council, ex p Monaf* (1988) 86 LGR 709, CA. In cases of appeals from the refusal of planning permission, the Secretary of State or his inspector should normally give reasons for departing from the provisions of a local plan or structure plan: *Reading Borough Council v Secretary of State for the Environment* (1985) 52 P & CR 385 at 403–404 per David Widdicombe QC; *Wigan Metropolitan Borough Council v Secretary of State for the Environment* (1987) 54 P & CR 369 at 377 per David Widdicombe QC.

　　The duty to give reasons does not necessarily become more stringent merely because, for example, the matter is an important one or the Secretary of State is disagreeing with an inspector's recommendation: *GLC v Secretary of State for the Environment and London Docklands Development Corpn and Cablecross Projects Ltd* (1985) 52 P & CR 158, CA.

4 *Elliott v Southwark London Borough Council* [1976] 2 All ER 781, (1976) 74 LGR 265, CA; *Ellis v Secretary of State for the Environment* (1974) 31 P & CR 130, DC; *Edwin H Bradley & Sons Ltd v Secretary of State for the Environment* (1982) 47 P & CR 374; *Westminster City Council v Great Portland Street Estates plc* [1985] AC 661 at 673, sub nom *Great Portland Estates plc v Westminster City Council* [1984] 3 All ER 744 at 752, HL, per Lord Scarman; *R v Secretary of State for the Home Department, ex p Swati* [1986] 1 All ER 717, [1986] 1 WLR 477, CA. Where the question is in reality one of the judgment of the decision-maker, he cannot be expected to go beyond an explanation of the issues and a statement of what his judgment is: *GLC v Secretary of State for the Environment and London Docklands Development Corpn and Cablecross Projects Ltd* (1985) 52 P & CR 158, CA.

In *R v Birmingham City Council, ex p Quietlynn Ltd* (1985) 83 LGR 461 (on appeal sub nom *R v Peterborough City Council v Quietlynn Ltd* (1986) 85 LGR 249, CA) it was suggested that a distinction was to be drawn between proceedings analogous to a *lis inter partes*, where the equivalent of a reasoned judgment was to be expected, and matters such as the refusal of a licence or of planning permission. However, even in the latter category of case, where the applicant might be assisted in any future application, he must be informed intelligibly why he had been refused, and the giving of reasons could not be equated with a mere statement of the grounds for the decision; c f *R v Secretary of State for the Home Department, ex p Swati*. The duty to give reasons cannot be discharged by the use of vague general words not sufficient to bring to the mind of the recipient a clear understanding of why his request has been refused: *Elliott v Southwark London Borough Council*.

5 *Elliott v Southwark London Borough Council* [1976] 2 All ER 781, (1976) 74 LGR 265, CA; *Walters v Secretary of State for Wales* (1978) 77 LGR 529; *Gupta v General Medical Council* [2001] UKPC 61, [2002] 1 WLR 1691, [2002] ICR 785. However, the reasons given will often not be intelligible without a sufficient statement of the facts, and if distinct relevant issues of important fact have been canvassed at a hearing, the reasons must deal with them: *Hope v Secretary of State for the Environment* (1975) 31 P & CR 120. In *JA Pye (Oxford) Estates Ltd v West Oxfordshire District Council* (1982) 47 P & CR 125, it was held to be a breach of the duty to give reasons, though not a fatal one on the facts, where an inspector's report failed to mention an important policy contained in a departmental circular. Reasons need not necessarily be in writing or in any particular form: *R v Secretary of State for the Home Department, ex p Gunnell* [1984] Crim LR 170, DC (but see criticism of this decision in *Weeks v United Kingdom* (1987) 10 EHRR 293, ECtHR). For a good general statement of the standard of reasoning required of statutory tribunals see *Meek v Birmingham City Council* [1987] IRLR 250, CA. The reasoning of an expert tribunal should not be subjected to unduly critical analysis: see *AH (Sudan) v Secretary of State for the Home Department* [2007] UKHL 49, [2008] 1 AC 678, [2008] 4 All ER 190; *H v East Sussex County Council* [2009] EWCA Civ 249, [2009] ELR 161.

6 See PARA 647. This area of the law is currently subject to significant development and reconsideration. In earlier cases an extremely restricted approach was taken as to when the duty to act fairly would require the giving of reasons: see especially *McInnes v Onslow Fane* [1978] 3 All ER 211, [1978] 1 WLR 1520; *Payne v Lord Harris of Greenwich* [1981] 2 All ER 842, [1981] 1 WLR 754, CA. See also *Secretary of State for Employment v Associated Society of Locomotive Engineers and Firemen* [1972] ICR 19 at 63, CA, per Buckley LJ and at 75 per Roskill LJ; *Cannock Chase District Council v Kelly* (1978) 36 P & CR 219 at 226, CA, per Megaw LJ; *R v Boundary Commission for England, ex p Foot* [1983] QB 600 at 623, [1983] 1 All ER 1099 at 1108, CA, per Sir John Donaldson MR; *R v Secretary of State for the Home Department, ex p Dannenberg* [1984] QB 766 at 777, [1984] 2 All ER 481 at 488, CA, per Dunn LJ; *Peatfield v General Medical Council* [1987] 1 All ER 1197, [1986] 1 WLR 243, PC; *R v Secretary of State for the Home Department, ex p Harrison* [1988] 3 All ER 86, DC; *Lonrho plc v Secretary of State for Trade and Industry* [1989] 2 All ER 609, sub nom *R v Secretary of State for Trade and Industry, ex p Lonrho plc* [1989] 1 WLR 525, HL; but c f *R v Secretary of State for Foreign and Commonwealth Affairs, ex p Everett* [1989] 1 All ER 655, [1989] 2 WLR 224, CA; *Anheuser Busch Inc v Controller of Patents, Designs and Trade Marks* [1988] FSR 23.

However, the extent to which the same decisions would now be reached on similar facts must now be in doubt. Although it is still correct to say that there is no general duty to provide reasons, it is now the case that the courts are more willing to see a requirement to give reasons as a necessary feature of the duty to act fairly if the circumstances of the case require: see eg *Flannery v Halifax Estate Agencies Ltd* [2000] 1 All ER 373, [2000] 1 WLR 377, CA; *English v Emery Reimbold and Strick Ltd* [2002] EWCA Civ 605, [2002] 3 All ER 385, [2002] 1 WLR 2409; *R (on the application of Wooder) v Feggetter* [2002] EWCA Civ 554, [2003] QB 219, [2002] 3 WLR 591 (common law implied a duty to give reasons where personal liberty at stake). A duty to give reasons may also be implied in the light of rights under the Convention for the Protection of Human Rights and Fundamental Freedoms (Rome, 4 November 1950; TS 71 (1953) Cmd 8969): see eg *R v DPP, ex p Manning* [2001] QB 330, [2000] 3 WLR 463 (duty to give reasons for decision not to prosecute following inquest verdict of unlawful killing against identifiable individual); *Madan v General Medical Council* [2001] EWHC Admin 322, [2002] ACD 3, DC (reasons for an interim suspension order depriving doctor of his right to exercise his profession inadequate).

Where the decision-maker is expressly exempted from the requirement to give reasons contained in the Tribunals and Inquiries Act 1992 (see note 2; and PARA 646), the court will not create a category of 'special cases' where reasons ought to be given: *R v Secretary of State for Social Services, ex p Connolly* [1986] 1 All ER 998, [1986] 1 WLR 421, CA.

In *R v Secretary of State for the Environment, ex p Halton Borough Council* (1983) 82 LGR 662 at 668 per Taylor J, it was held that, although the Secretary of State was under no obligation to give reasons for directing a local authority to proceed with a gipsy site, his failure to do so could lead to the inference that he had merely applied a blanket policy and had not exercised his discretion. However, in *Lonrho plc v Secretary of State for Trade and Industry*, it was held that the absence of reasons for a decision where there is no duty to give them cannot itself support the contention that the decision is irrational, although an inference of irrationality may be drawn if all the known facts and circumstances are overwhelmingly in favour of a different decision.

7   In such cases the parties are entitled to the information which they need in order to know whether there is an appealable error of law: *Alexander Machinery (Dudley) Ltd v Crabtree* [1974] ICR 120, [1974] IRLR 56, NIRC. A detailed analysis of fact or law is not required, but the parties should be told in broad terms why they have won or lost: *Union of Construction, Allied Trades and Technicians v Brain* [1981] ICR 542 at 551, CA, per Donaldson LJ; *Varndell v Kearney & Trecker Marwin Ltd* [1983] ICR 683, CA. It must be apparent, whether directly or by necessary inference, both that the tribunal has considered the points at issue, and what evidence has caused it to reach its conclusions: *R v Immigration Appeal Tribunal, ex p Khan* [1983] QB 790, [1983] 2 All ER 420, CA. See also *R v Surrey County Council Education Committee, ex p H* (1984) 83 LGR 219, CA; *W v Greenwich London Borough Council* [1989] FLR 397. Reasons ought also to be given where a change of circumstances might, in the light of those reasons, lead to a renewed application to the court: *Hoey v Hoey* [1984] 1 All ER 177n, [1984] 1 WLR 464n, CA (application for care and control of children and ouster injunction).

But cf *R v Worthing Justices, ex p Norvell* [1981] 1 WLR 413, DC (no need for magistrate or clerk refusing to issue summons to give reasons; same would be true of a without notice application for leave to seek judicial review, or justices finding case not proved); *R v Crown Court at Croydon, ex p Smith* (1983) 77 Cr App Rep 277, DC; *R v Secretary of State for the Home Department, ex p Dannenberg* [1984] QB 766 at 777, [1984] 2 All ER 481 at 488, CA, per Dunn LJ (decision in that case not to be taken as encouraging justices to give reasons in normal cases); *Antaios Compania Naviera SA v Salen Rederierna AB, The Antaios* [1985] AC 191, [1984] 3 All ER 229, HL (judge need not give reasons for a decision whether to grant leave to appeal from arbitral award); *Mousaka Inc v Golden Seagull Maritime Inc* [2002] 1 All ER 726, [2002] 1 WLR 395, [2001] 2 All ER (Comm) 794 (applying *The Antaios*) (but for a decision to contrary effect, see *North Range Shipping Ltd v Seatrans Shipping Corpn, The Western Triumph* [2002] EWCA Civ 405, [2002] 4 All ER 390, [2002] 1 WLR 2397); *Peatfield v General Medical Council* [1987] 1 All ER 1197, [1986] 1 WLR 243, PC.

8   *R v Deputy Industrial Injuries Comr, ex p Moore* [1965] 1 QB 456, [1965] 1 All ER 81, CA; *Mahon v Air New Zealand Ltd* [1984] AC 808, [1984] 3 All ER 201, PC; *South Bucks District Council v Coates* [2004] EWCA Civ 1378, [2005] LGR 626; *E v Secretary of State for the Home Department* [2004] EWCA Civ 49, [2004] QB 1044, [2004] 2 WLR 1351. See also *R v Secretary of State for the Home Department, ex p Awuku* (1987) Times, 3 October. But obviously silly mistakes, miscalculations and clerical errors do not vitiate the reasons, because they do not prevent the parties from seeing whether the decision has been reached according to law: *Elmbridge Borough Council v Secretary of State for the Environment* (1980) 78 LGR 637. Where reasons have not been given and good grounds for the decision were in fact available, the party challenging the decision bears the burden of showing that those were not in fact the grounds upon which it was taken: *R v Secretary of State for Social Services, ex p Connolly* [1986] 1 All ER 998, [1986] 1 WLR 421, CA.

9   As to the standard of proof see CIVIL PROCEDURE vol 11 (2009) PARA 775; CRIMINAL LAW, EVIDENCE AND PROCEDURE vol 11(3) (2006 Reissue) PARA 1368 et seq.

10   *R v Hampshire County Council, ex p Ellerton* [1985] 1 All ER 599, [1985] 1 WLR 749, CA (this conclusion was reached despite the use of words such as 'offence' and 'accused' in the Fire Services (Discipline) Regulations 1948). See also *Saeed v Inner London Education Authority*

[1985] ICR 637, [1986] IRLR 23. Cf *R v Police Complaints Board, ex p Madden* [1983] 2 All ER 353, [1983] 1 WLR 447; *R v Secretary of State for the Home Department, ex p Tarrant* [1985] QB 251 at 285, [1984] 1 All ER 799 at 816, DC, per Webster J; *Khawaja v Secretary of State for the Home Department* [1984] AC 74, [1983] 1 All ER 765, HL. There is, however, only one civil standard of proof, namely 'the simple balance of probabilities': see *Re B (children) (sexual abuse: standard of proof)* [2008] UKHL 35, [2009] AC 11, [2008] 4 All ER 1 at [70] per Baroness Hale of Richmond.

The concept of the burden of proof is not appropriate to a procedure such as a planning appeal: *JA Pye (Oxford) Estates Ltd v West Oxfordshire District Council* (1982) 47 P & CR 125. Judges and tribunals of fact should only fall back upon the burden of proof where they cannot as a matter of practicality and their conscientious duty make findings of fact on the matters in dispute: *Morris v London Iron and Steel Co Ltd* [1988] QB 493, [1987] 2 All ER 496, CA. Where tied voting or other factors will make the original hearing ineffective or inconclusive, there is an inherent power to refer the matter to a newly constituted tribunal: *Fussell v Somerset Justices Licensing Committee* [1947] KB 276, [1947] 1 All ER 44, DC; *R v Industrial Tribunal, ex p Cotswold Collotype Co Ltd* [1979] ICR 190, DC; but in criminal proceedings justices must acquit if not satisfied by the prosecution: *R v Bromley Justices, ex p Haymill (Contractors) Ltd* [1984] Crim LR 235, DC. See also *R v Trafford Magistrates' Court, ex p Smith* (1988) Times, 8 July, DC.

645. Effect of breach of the rule and appeals. An act or a decision consequential upon contravention of the *audi alteram partem* rule[1] may be restrained by a prohibiting order[2] or an injunction[3], or set aside by a quashing order[4] or a statutory application to quash[5]. Moreover, a declaration may be granted that the decision is null and void[6]. In an appropriate case, a mandatory order unaccompanied by other relief may be made[7]. If the act has involved an encroachment on private rights, a person aggrieved by it may be entitled to recover damages for trespass[8] or another civil wrong[9]. The liability of such an act or a decision to collateral impeachment appears to presuppose that it is void and not merely voidable[10]. That the effect of breach of the rule is to render an act or a decision void is supported by a number of decisions[11], and by other consequences which tend to assimilate breach of the rule to an excess of jurisdiction[12]. However, the fact that the act or decision is void does not prevent it remaining in existence at least for certain purposes until set aside by a court or other competent body[13].

Breach is established by evidence by way of witness statement[14]. Formulae purporting to exclude the supervisory jurisdiction of the courts are ineffective to protect an act or a decision tainted by breach of the rule[15]. Recourse to extra-judicial appellate machinery prior to resorting to the courts for relief for breach of the rule may be unnecessary[16] or inappropriate[17]; if recourse is had to such machinery, the person aggrieved is not deemed to have waived his right to object in the courts[18], and it has been said that a fundamental breach of the rule cannot be waived[19]. If, however, the person aggrieved seeks a discretionary remedy in the courts, he may still be denied relief because of undue delay in instituting the proceedings or the presence of other grounds for refusing discretionary relief[20].

It has been held that there is no such thing as a technical breach of natural justice[21]; that is, non-compliance with the rule is immaterial if the party claiming to be aggrieved has not sustained any significant detriment[22]. But a mere risk that there has been actual prejudice will usually suffice[23], and the courts will not readily conclude that a fair hearing would have made no difference to the outcome[24].

The effect of failure to accord an adequate hearing or opportunity to be heard prior to a decision may be repaired by rescission or suspension of the original decision followed by a full and fair hearing or rehearing[25]. If this subsequent hearing is conducted by an appellate body, the correct approach will often be to ask whether, looking at the process as a whole, there has in the end been a fair result arrived at by fair methods[26], although in some cases an examination of the hearing structure in its context may lead to the conclusion that the person aggrieved has been denied a right to be treated fairly both at an original hearing and then at an appellate hearing[27].

1   As to the *audi alteram partem* rule see PARA 639.

2   *R v North, ex p Oakey* [1927] 1 KB 491, CA. As to prohibiting orders see PARA 693 et seq.

3   *Andrews v Mitchell* [1905] AC 78, HL. As to injunctions see PARA 716 et seq.

4   For example, *R v Kingston-upon-Hull Rent Tribunal, ex p Black* [1949] 1 All ER 260, DC. As to quashing orders see PARA 693.

5   *Errington v Minister of Health* [1935] 1 KB 249, CA.

6   As in *Ridge v Baldwin* [1964] AC 40, [1963] 2 All ER 66, HL. As to declaratory orders see PARA 716 et seq.

7   *Bagg's Case* (1615) 11 Co Rep 93b. This form of relief is appropriate to restore a person to a public office of which he has been unlawfully deprived. As to mandatory orders see PARA 703 et seq.

8   *Cooper v Wandsworth Board of Works* (1863) 14 CBNS 180.

9   For example, breach of contract where a contractual nexus is present: see *R v Lord Chancellor's Department, ex p Nangle* [1991] ICR 743, 752.

10 See ADMINISTRATIVE LAW vol 1(1) (2001 Reissue) PARA 26.

11 See *Wood v Woad* (1874) LR 9 Exch 190; *Andrews v Mitchell* [1905] AC 78, HL; *Ridge v Baldwin* [1964] AC 40, [1963] 2 All ER 66, HL; *Disher v Disher* [1965] P 31, [1963] 3 All ER 933, DC; *Annamunthodo v Oilfield Workers' Trade Union* [1961] AC 945, [1961] 3 All ER 621, PC; *Kanda v Government of the Federation of Malaya* [1962] AC 322, [1962] 2 WLR 1153, PC; *Anisminic Ltd v Foreign Compensation Commission* [1969] 2 AC 147, [1969] 1 All ER 208, HL (see dicta cited in PARA 638 note 3); *Hounslow London Borough Council v Twickenham Garden Developments Ltd* [1971] Ch 233 at 258–259, [1970] 3 All ER 326 at 347 per Megarry J; *Mayes v Mayes* [1971] 2 All ER 397, [1971] 1 WLR 679, DC; *Denton v Auckland City* [1969] NZLR 256, NZCA; *Hibernian Property Co Ltd v Secretary of State for the Environment* (1973) 27 P & CR 197; *Fairmount Investments Ltd v Secretary of State for the Environment* [1976] 2 All ER 865 at 871–872, [1976] 1 WLR 1255 at 1263, HL, per Lord Russell of Killowen; *Calvin v Carr* [1980] AC 574, [1979] 2 All ER 440, PC; *Dunlop v Woollahra Municipal Council* [1982] AC 158, [1981] 1 All ER 1202, PC. See also *Chief Constable of the North Wales Police v Evans* [1982] 3 All ER 141, [1982] 1 WLR 1155, HL; cf *R v Secretary of State for the Environment, ex p Ostler* [1977] QB 122, [1976] 3 All ER 90, CA.

12 See ADMINISTRATIVE LAW vol 1(1) (2001 Reissue) PARA 26; and *Hoffman-La Roche & Co AG v Secretary of State for Trade and Industry* [1975] AC 295, [1974] 2 All ER 1128, HL.

13 So that, for example, an appeal may lie from the nullified decision: see *Crane v DPP* [1921] 2 AC 299, HL; *Annamunthodo v Oilfield Workers' Trade Union* [1961] AC 945, [1961] 3 All ER 621, PC; *Calvin v Carr* [1980] AC 574 at 589–591, [1979] 2 All ER 440 at 445–447, PC; *Lovelock v Minister of Transport* (1980) 78 LGR 576 at 582, CA, per Lord Denning MR; *Lloyd v McMahon* [1987] AC 625 at 653, [1987] 1 All ER 1118 at 1135, CA, per Dillon LJ (affd on other grounds [1987] AC 625, [1987] 1 All ER 1118, HL); cf *Stevenson v United Road Transport Union* [1977] ICR 893 at 905–906, CA, per Buckley LJ.

14 *R v Wandsworth Justices, ex p Read* [1942] 1 KB 281, [1942] 1 All ER 56, DC (referring to evidence by way of affidavit, which was at that time the only form of written evidence).

15 See *Ridge v Baldwin* [1964] AC 40, [1963] 2 All ER 66, HL; *Anisminic Ltd v Foreign Compensation Commission* [1969] 2 AC 147, [1969] 1 All ER 208, HL; and ADMINISTRATIVE LAW vol 1(1) (2001 Reissue) PARA 21. Whether or not the existence of an appellate procedure will be regarded as an appropriate alternative remedy, and therefore should be pursued prior to any application for judicial review, will depend on the circumstances in which the decision arose. Consideration will therefore be afforded to: the statutory context, if any; the scope of any appeal rights and whether or not they would be appropriate to remedy the breach which has occurred; and the significance of the decision for the individual: see e g *R v Ministry of Defence Police, ex p Sweeney* [1999] COD 122; *R v General Court Martial at RAF Uxbridge, ex p Wright* (1999) 11 Admin LR 747 (existence of statutory right of appeal was a suitable alternative remedy and should have been pursued). See also the comments on appeals in note 26.

16 *Annamunthodo v Oilfield Workers' Trade Union* [1961] AC 945, [1961] 3 All ER 621, PC; *Lawlor v Union of Post Office Workers* [1965] Ch 712, [1965] 1 All ER 353; *Ridge v Baldwin* [1964] AC 40, [1963] 2 All ER 66, HL; and see note 15.

17 But see the cases cited in note 13.

18 See *Annamunthodo v Oilfield Workers' Trade Union* [1961] AC 945, [1961] 3 All ER 621, PC; *Ridge v Baldwin* [1964] AC 40, [1963] 2 All ER 66, HL.

19 *Mayes v Mayes* [1971] 2 All ER 397 at 400–401, [1971] 1 WLR 679 at 684, DC, per Sir Jocelyn Simon P. For a decision to the contrary effect see *R v British Broadcasting Corpn, ex p Lavelle* [1983] 1 All ER 241, [1983] 1 WLR 23. Cf the cases cited in note 21.

20 For example, *Ex p Fry* [1954] 2 All ER 118 at 120, [1954] 1 WLR 730 at 734, CA, per Hallett J; *R v Aston University Senate, ex p Roffey* [1969] 2 QB 538, [1969] 2 All ER 964, DC; *Fullbrook v Berkshire Magistrates' Courts Committee* (1970) 69 LGR 75; *Cinnamond v British Airports Authority* [1980] 2 All ER 368, [1980] 1 WLR 582, CA. See also *Hanlon v Traffic Comr* 1988 SLT 802 (failure to act amounted to tacit acquiescence); and see the cases cited in PARA 629 note 11.

21 *Lake District Special Planning Board v Secretary of State for the Environment* [1975] JPL 220; *George v Secretary of State for the Environment* (1979) 38 P & CR 609, CA. See also *Bushell v Secretary of State for the Environment* [1981] AC 75 at 100, [1980] 2 All ER 608 at 616, HL, per Lord Diplock ('when one is considering natural justice it is the result that matters').

22 *Lake District Special Planning Board v Secretary of State for the Environment* [1975] JPL 220; *George v Secretary of State for the Environment* (1979) 38 P & CR 609, CA; *Lovelock v Minister of Transport* (1980) 78 LGR 576 at 583, CA, per Lord Denning MR; *Cinnamond v British Airports Authority* [1980] 2 All ER 368 at 376–377, [1980] 1 WLR 582 at 593, CA, per Brandon LJ; *R v Secretary of State for the Home Department, ex p Santillo* [1981] QB 778 at 798, [1981] 2 All ER 897 at 922, CA, per Templeman LJ; *Reading Borough Council v Secretary of State for the Environment* (1985) 52 P & CR 385; *R v Secretary of State for the Environment, ex p Southwark London Borough Council* (1987) 54 P & CR 226 at 236, DC, per Lloyd LJ; *Swinbank v Secretary of State for the Environment* (1987) 55 P & CR 371 at 376 per David Widdicombe QC; *R v Deputy Chief Constable of Thames Valley Police, ex p Cotton* [1989] COD 318 (doubting *R v Chief Constable of Thames Valley Police, ex p Stevenson* (1987) Times, 22 April); *Mayes v Secretary of State for Wales* [1989] JPL 848; and see *R v Haringey London Borough Council Leader's Investigative Panel, ex p Edwards* (1983) Times, 22 March. See also *Glynn v Keele University* [1971] 2 All ER 89, [1971] 1 WLR 487; *Davis v Carew-Pole* [1956] 2 All ER 524 at 527, [1956] 1 WLR 833 at 840 per Pilcher J; *Byrne v Kinematograph Renters' Society* [1958] 2 All ER 579, [1958] 1 WLR 762 at 785 per Harman J. Cf the emphasis placed in *R v Thames Magistrates' Court, ex p Polemis* [1974] 2 All ER 1219, [1974] 1 WLR 1371, DC and *R v Hull Prison Board of Visitors, ex p St Germain (No 2)* [1979] 3 All ER 545, [1979] 1 WLR 1401, DC, on justice being seen to be done and the importance of the general rule transcending that of the particular case. For a restrictive view of the *Polemis* approach see *R v Panel on Take-overs and Mergers, ex p Guinness plc* [1989] 1 All ER 509 at 543–544, [1989] 2 WLR 863 at 906–907, CA, per Woolf LJ. In *R v Bristol City Council, ex p Pearce* (1984) 83 LGR 711, the presence or absence of prejudice seems to have been treated as a matter going to discretion.

23 *Kanda v Government of the Federation of Malaya* [1962] AC 322, [1962] 2 WLR 1153, PC; *Hibernian Property Co Ltd v Secretary of State for the Environment* (1973) 27 P & CR 197; *Performance Cars Ltd v Secretary of State for the Environment* (1977) 34 P & CR 92, CA. See also *R v Secretary of State for the Home Department, ex p Tarrant* [1985] QB 251, [1984] 1 All ER 799, DC.

24 *John v Rees* [1970] Ch 345 at 402, [1969] 2 All ER 274 at 309 per Megarry J (approved in *R (on the application of Amin) v Secretary of State for the Home Department* [2003] UKHL 51, [2004] 1 AC 653, [2003] 4 All ER 1264 at [52] per Lord Steyn); *R v Manchester City Council, ex p Fulford* (1982) 81 LGR 292, DC; *R v Secretary of State for the Environment, ex p Brent London Borough Council* [1982] QB 593, [1983] 3 All ER 321, DC; *R v British Coal Corpn, ex p Union of Democratic Mineworkers* [1988] ICR 36 at 44–45, CA, per Russell LJ; cf *Barnes v BPC (Business Forms) Ltd* [1976] 1 All ER 237, [1975] 1 WLR 1565; *R v Secretary of State for Foreign and Commonwealth Affairs, ex p Everett* [1989] QB 811, [1989] 1 All ER 655, CA; *R v Chief Constable of Thames Valley Police, ex p Cotton* [1990] IRLR 344; and see the cases referred to in PARA 639 note 13.

25 See *Calvin v Carr* [1980] AC 574, [1979] 2 All ER 440, PC; *De Verteuil v Knaggs* [1918] AC 557; *Ridge v Baldwin* [1964] AC 40 at 79, HL, per Lord Reid; *R v Uxbridge Justices, ex p Heward-Mills* [1983] 1 All ER 530 at 535–536, [1983] 1 WLR 56 at 63–64 per McCullough J.

26 *Calvin v Carr* [1980] AC 574, [1979] 2 All ER 440, PC (but note, this was a contractual process; the willingness to permit an appeal to cure an earlier defect may be greater in this context than when considering the decision made in a statutory context); *Modahl v British Athletics Federation* [2001] EWCA Civ 1447, [2002] 1 WLR 1192; *Lloyd v McMahon* [1987] AC 625, [1987] 1 All ER 1118, HL. The approach of considering fairness by reference to the procedure taken as a whole was applied to the case of an inquiry followed by the minister considering the inspector's report in *R v Secretary of State for Transport, ex p Gwent County Council* [1988] QB 429, [1987] 1 All ER 161, CA. See also *R v Secretary of State for Wales, ex p South Glamorgan County Council* [1988] COD 104; cf *Rees v Crane* [1994] 2 AC 173 at 192, PC (courts not to be bound by rigid rules on this point). The approach has also been applied in relation to the role of an Independent Appeal Panel considering a pupil's permanent exclusion from school in *R (on the application of DR) v Head Teacher of St George's Catholic School* [2002] EWCA Civ 1822, [2003] LGR 371, [2003] ELR 104. Again the court will have regard to all material circumstances when determining whether or not a re-hearing has 'cured' the earlier defect. These will include the nature of the original defect; whether it is practicable to assume that the defect did not itself taint the appeal process; how important the decision was to the individual; and the nature of the appeal process itself, for example was it a rehearing or merely a review; what is the extent of the powers of the appellate body to vary or revoke the original decision. The denial of a fair hearing at first instance in breach of the Convention for the Protection of Human Rights and Fundamental Freedoms (Rome, 4 November 1950; TS 71 (1953) Cmd 8969) art 6(1) may be a paramount consideration requiring an appellate body to extend time for appealing where the appeal is brought out of time: *Smith v Kvaerner Cementation Foundations Ltd* [2006] EWCA Civ 242, [2006] 3 All ER 593, [2007] 1 WLR 370, CA.

27 *Calvin v Carr* [1980] AC 574, [1979] 2 All ER 440, PC; *Leary v National Union of Vehicle Builders* [1971] Ch 34, [1970] 2 All ER 713.

D. THE DUTY TO GIVE REASONS

646. Statutory obligations. A duty to give reasons can arise under statute[1]. Such a duty may be either express or implied[2]. For example, if requested to do so, on or before the giving or notification of a decision, it is the duty of a statutory tribunal[3] or minister[4], after the holding by him or on his behalf of a statutory inquiry[5], to furnish a written or oral statement of the reasons for the decision[6]. The statement may be refused, or the specification of reasons restricted, on grounds of national security[7]. The tribunal or minister may refuse to furnish the statement to a person not primarily concerned with the decision if of the opinion that to furnish it would be contrary to the interests of any person primarily concerned[8]. The statement of reasons for the decision[9] is to be taken to form part of the decision and to be incorporated in the record[10]. A duty to give reasons may arise under European Union law as national authorities may need to give reasons for their decisions refusing to recognise rights said to be derived from European Union law in order to ensure that individuals are able to challenge such decisions and obtain an effective remedy[11]. While there is no general common law duty to give reasons, there may be such a duty in particular cases[12].

The reasons given in pursuance of any such obligation must be adequate and intelligible and must set out the conclusions on the principal important controversial points at issue indicating how any issue of fact and law was resolved[13]. Parties to the proceedings and the courts should be able to see what matters have been taken into consideration and what view has been formed by the tribunal or minister on the points of fact and law which arise. Reasons need not be lengthy and may, in appropriate circumstances be stated briefly, the precise degree of particularity depending on the circumstances[14]. A duty to give reasons may be enforced by mandatory order[15]. Furthermore, where adequate reasons are required but are not given, a court may regard that as an error which vitiates the decision and may grant a quashing order and remit the matter for a fresh decision[16].

Where it appears to them that the subject matter of decisions of a tribunal or minister, or the circumstances in which they are made, make the giving of reasons unnecessary or impracticable, the Lord Chancellor and the Secretary of State, after consultation with the Administrative Justice and Tribunals Council[17], may by order[18] direct that in such cases reasons need not be given[19].

1   See eg the Tribunals and Inquiries Act 1992 s 10 (see the text and notes 3–19). For examples of decisions where reasons have been required see eg *R v Minister of Housing and Local Government, ex p Chichester RDC* [1960] 2 All ER 407, [1960] 1 WLR 587; *Givaudan v Minister of Housing and Local Government* [1966] 3 All ER 696, [1967] 1 WLR 250; *Brayhead v Berkshire County Council* [1964] 2 QB 303, [1964] 1 All ER 149; *French Kier v Secretary of State for the Environment* [1977] 1 All ER 296; *R v Secretary of State for the Home Department, ex p Dannenberg* [1984] QB 766, [1984] 2 All ER 481; *Bone v MHRT* [1985] 3 All ER 330; *R v Mental Health Review Tribunal, ex p Pickering* [1986] 1 All ER 99; *Westminster City Council v Great Portland Estates* [1985] AC 661, sub nom *Great Portland Street Estates plc v Westminster City Council* [1984] 3 All ER 744, HL.

2   *Stefan v General Medical Council* [1999] 1 WLR 1293, 49 BMLR 161; *R v Secretary of State for the Home Department, ex p Doody* [1994] 1 AC 531, sub nom *Doody v Secretary of State for the Home Department* [1993] 3 All ER 92, HL; but cf *R v Secretary of State for the Home Department, ex p Stitt* (1987) Times, 3 February (properly construed, the statutory scheme was a complete code and, therefore, no room to imply additional right to reasons); *R v Secretary of State for the Home Department, ex p Owalabi* [1995] Imm AR 400 (no reasons required for refusal to exercise discretion not arising from statute). See also *Ynystawe, Ynyforgan and Glais Gipsy Site Action Group v Secretary of State for Wales* [1981] JPL 874; *R v Islington London Borough Council, ex p Rixon* [1997] ELR 66 (duty implied in both cases when decision departed from normal practice).

3   Ie those listed in the Tribunal and Inquiries Act 1992 Sch 1: see ADMINISTRATIVE LAW vol 1(1) (2001 Reissue) PARA 57.

4   'Minister' includes the Welsh Ministers and any Board presided over by a minister: Tribunal and Inquiries Act 1992 s 16(1) (definition amended by the Government of Wales Act 1998 s 125, Sch 12 para 33; and the Government of Wales Act 2006 s 160(1), Sch 10 para 38).

5   The provision applies also to a decision taken by a minister in a case in which a person concerned could, whether by objecting or otherwise, have required the holding of such a statutory inquiry: Tribunals and Inquiries Act 1992 s 10(1)(b)(ii). 'Statutory inquiry' means: (1) an inquiry or hearing held or to be held in pursuance of a duty imposed by any statutory provision; or (2) an inquiry or hearing, or an inquiry or hearing of a class, designated for these purposes by order; and 'statutory provision' means a provision contained in, or having effect under, any enactment: s 16(1). See also ADMINISTRATIVE LAW vol 1(1) (2001 Reissue) PARA 15. Section 10(1) does not apply to any decision taken after any inquiry or hearing which is a statutory inquiry by virtue of an order by the Lord Chancellor and the Secretary of State made under s 16(2) (see TOWN AND COUNTRY PLANNING vol 46(2) (Reissue) PARA 653) unless the order contains a direction that s 10 is to apply: s 10(4). In any enactment, 'Secretary of State' means one of Her Majesty's Principal Secretaries of State: see the Interpretation Act 1978 s 5, Sch 1; and STATUTES vol 44(1) (Reissue) PARA 1382. As to the office of Secretary of State see CONSTITUTIONAL LAW AND HUMAN RIGHTS vol 8(2) (Reissue) PARA 355.

6   See the Tribunals and Inquiries Act 1992 s 10(1). This does not apply to decisions in respect of which any other statutory provision has effect as to the giving of reasons, or to decisions of a minister in connection with the preparation, making, approval, confirmation or concurrence in regulations, rules, or byelaws, or orders or schemes of a legislative and not executive character: s 10(5). References to a decision in the Tribunals and Inquiries Act 1992 do not include references to decisions given in the exercise of executive functions by certain tribunals: see s 14(1); and for the tribunals concerned see ADMINISTRATIVE LAW vol 1(1) (2001 Reissue) PARA 57.

7   Tribunals and Inquiries Act 1992 s 10(2).

8   Tribunals and Inquiries Act 1992 s 10(3).

9   Ie whether given under this provision or under any other statutory provision: see the Tribunals and Inquiries Act 1992 s 10(6).

10 Tribunals and Inquiries Act 1992 s 10(6). The effect of this provision is that the statement of reasons forms part of the record for the purpose of any legal proceedings alleging error of law on the face of the record. See further PARA 616. See also *Earl of Iveagh v Minister of Housing and Local Government* [1962] 2 QB 147 at 160, [1961] 3 All ER 98 at 107 per Megaw J; affd [1964] 1 QB 395, [1963] 3 All ER 817, CA. For other statutory obligations to give reasons see e g the Immigration (Notices) Regulations 2003, SI 2003/658, reg 5(1)(a) (see BRITISH NATIONALITY, IMMIGRATION AND ASYLUM vol 4(2) (2002 Reissue) PARA 187); the Town and Country Planning (Inquiries Procedure) (England) Rules 2000, SI 2000/1624, r 18; the Town and Country Planning (Major Infrastructure Project Inquiries Procedure) (England) Rules 2005, SI 2005/2115, r 22; and the Town and Country Planning (Inquiries Procedure) (Wales) Rules 2003, SI 2003/1266, r 18 (see TOWN AND COUNTRY PLANNING vol 46(2) (Reissue) PARAS 667, 685).

11 See e g *Wachauf v Germany* [1989] ECR 2609, [1991] 1 CMLR 328; *Unectef v Heylens* [1987] ECR 4097, para [15]. There is also an obligation to provide the reasons for regulations, directives and decisions adopted by the relevant European institutions: see the Treaty on the Functioning of the European Union art 296 (formerly art 253 of the Treaty Establishing the European Community (Rome, 25 March 1957; TS 1 (1973); Cmnd 5179), which was renamed and renumbered by the Treaty of Lisbon Amending the Treaty on European Union and the Treaty Establishing the European Community (Lisbon, 13 December 2007; ECS 13 (2007); Cm 7294) (OJ C306, 17.12.2007, p 1); see the consolidated text of the EU Treaties (OJ C115, 9.5.2008, p 194).

12 See PARA 644. For examples see *R v Civil Service Board, ex p Cunningham* [1991] 4 All ER 310, [1992] ICR 816, CA; *Flannery v Halifax Estate Agencies Ltd* [2000] 1 All ER 373, [2000] 1 WLR 377, CA; *English v Emery Reimbold and Strick Ltd* [2002] EWCA Civ 605, [2002] 3 All ER 385, [2002] 1 WLR 2409.

13 *South Buckinghamshire District Council v Secretary of State for Transport, Local Government and the Regions* [2004] UKHL 33, [2004] 4 All ER 775, sub nom *South Buckinghamshire District Council v Porter (No 2)* [2004] 1 WLR 1953 at [36] per Lord Brown of Eaton-under-Heywood; *Re Poyser and Mills' Arbitration* [1964] 2 QB 467 at 478, [1963] 1 All ER 612 at 616 per Megaw J. See also *Givaudan & Co Ltd v Minister of Housing and Local Government* [1966] 3 All ER 696, [1967] 1 WLR 250; *Re Allen and Matthews' Arbitration* [1971] 2 QB 518, [1971] 2 All ER 1259; *Westminster City Council v Great Portland Street Estates plc* [1985] AC 661 at 673, sub nom *Great Portland Street Estates plc v Westminster City Council* [1984] 3 All ER 744 at 752, HL, per Lord Scarman; *Save Britain's Heritage v Number One Poultry Ltd* [1991] 1 WLR 153, HL. Reasons may be brief if that is sufficient to set out the substance of the decision: *R v Civil Service Appeal Board, ex p Cunningham* [1991] 4 All ER 310, [1992] ICR 816, CA; and see PARA 644.

14 There is no uniform standard of reasoning which is required. Questions of sufficiency will turn on the issues and circumstances involved in each case. See *South Buckinghamshire District Council v Secretary of State for Transport, Local Government and the Regions* [2004] UKHL 33, [2004] 4 All ER 775, sub nom *South Buckinghamshire District Council v Porter (No 2)* [2004] 1 WLR 1953; *Stefan v General Medical Council* [1999] 1 WLR 1293, 49 BMLR 161; *Earl of Iveagh v Minister of Housing and Local Government* [1962] 2 QB 147 at 160, [1961] 3 All ER 98 at 107 per Megaw J (affd [1964] 1 QB 395 at 410, 412, [1963] 3 All ER 817 at 820, 822, CA, per Lord Denning MR); *London Residuary Body v Secretary of State for the Environment* [1988] JPL 637; *R v Secretary of State for the Home Department, ex p Swati* [1986] 1 All ER 717, [1986] 1 WLR 477, CA; *Meek v Birmingham City Council* [1987] IRLR 250, CA; *R v Mental Health Review Tribunal, ex p Clatworthy* [1985] 3 All ER 699; cf *Seddon Properties v Secretary of State for the Environment* (1978) 42 P & CR 26n; *Flannery v Halifax Estate Agencies Ltd* [2000] 1 All ER 373, [2000] 1 WLR 377, CA (reasons should be given by court when determining a conflict of reasoned expert opinion; not sufficient simply to state that one expert's view is preferred over that of the other); *Elmbridge Borough Council v Secretary of State for the Environment* (1980) 39 P & CR 543; *R v Mendip District Council, ex p Fabre* [2000] COD 372 (decisions not to be scrutinised as if they were statutes; fair and sensible reading to be applied, taking into account the audience to whom the decision is addressed); *R v Birmingham City Council, ex p B* [1999] ELR 305 (standard form reasons not sufficient save in a 'run-of-the-mill' case); *McKerry v Teesdale and Wear Valley Justices* [2000] COD 199, DC; *R v Higher Education Funding Council, ex p Institute of Dental Surgery* [1994] 1 WLR 242 at 263 per Sedley J (standard required will be assessed in light of the importance of the issues at stake); *R v East Hertfordshire District Council, ex p Beckham* [1998] JPL 55 at 59 per Lightman J (clear and unambiguous reasons required when decision contrary to current policy).

15 *Parrish v Minister of Housing and Local Government* (1961) 59 LGR 411 at 418 per Megaw J; *Brayhead (Ascot) Ltd v Berkshire County Council* [1964] 2 QB 303 at 313–314, [1964]

1 All ER 149 at 154, DC, per Winn J; *Ex p Dorrington Investment Trust Ltd* (1966) 197 Estates Gazette 259, DC; *R v Higher Education Funding Council, ex p Institute of Dental Surgery* [1994] 1 All ER 651, [1994] 1 WLR 242.

16 See eg *R v Westminster City Council, ex p Ermakov* [1996] 2 All ER 302, 95 LGR 119, CA. The precise circumstances where quashing is required, rather than requiring the decision-maker to provide adequate reasons, have not been the subject of definitive resolution by the courts: see eg *Flannery v Halifax Estate Agencies Ltd* [2000] 1 All ER 373, [2000] 1 WLR 377, CA; *English v Emery Reimbold and Strick Ltd* [2002] EWCA Civ 605, [2002] 3 All ER 385, [2002] 1 WLR 2409. Where there is a statutory duty to give reasons, the courts are reluctant to allow the original reasons to be supplemented or added to although they may be elucidated and confirmed: see *R v Westminster City Council, ex p Ermakov*; *R (on the application of Leung) v Imperial College of Science, Technology and Medicine* [2002] EWHC 1358 (Admin), [2002] ELR 653.

17 Ie the Administrative Justice and Tribunals Council established under the Tribunals, Courts and Enforcement Act 2007 s 44: see ADMINISTRATIVE LAW.

18 Ie by statutory instrument subject to annulment by resolution of either House of Parliament: Tribunals and Inquiries Act 1992 s 15. An order may be revoked or varied by a subsequent order: s 10(8) (amended by virtue of SI 1999/678).

19 See the Tribunals and Inquiries Act 1992 s 10(7) (amended by virtue of SI 1999/678). The order may be made in respect of decisions of any particular tribunal or any description of such decisions, or any description of decisions of a minister: Tribunals and Inquiries Act 1992 s 10(7) (as so amended).

647. Towards a general duty to give reasons. Although it is still correct to say that there is no general duty, arising from requirements of procedural fairness, to give reasons for an administrative decision[1], in a substantial number of cases a duty to provide reasons has been found to exist on the particular facts of the case[2]. In these cases the conclusion was that having regard to the nature of the interest concerned and the impact of the decision on that interest, and all other relevant considerations, a reasoned decision was required[3]. Reasons may also be required if a decision appears to be aberrant and requires explanation[4].

1 *R v Gaming Board for Great Britain, ex p Benaim and Khaida* [1970] 2 QB 417 at 431, [1970] 2 All ER 528 at 534–535, CA, per Lord Denning MR; *McInnes v Onslow Fane* [1978] 1 WLR 1520 at 1532 per Megarry V-C; *R v Secretary of State for the Home Department, ex p Doody* [1994] 1 AC 531 at 564, sub nom *Doody v Secretary of State for the Home Department* [1993] 3 All ER 92 at 109, HL, per Lord Mustill; *Stefan v General Medical Council* [1999] 1 WLR 1293, 49 BMLR 161 (argument that duty to give reasons was exceptional was rejected).

2 *R v Secretary of State for the Home Department, ex p Doody* [1994] 1 AC 531, sub nom *Doody v Secretary of State for the Home Department* [1993] 3 All ER 92, HL; *R v Civil Service Appeal Board, ex p Cunningham* [1991] 4 All ER 310, [1992] ICR 816, CA; *Flannery v Halifax Estate Agencies Ltd* [2000] 1 All ER 373, [2000] 1 WLR 377, CA; *English v Emery Reimbold and Strick Ltd* [2002] EWCA Civ 605, [2002] 3 All ER 385, [2002] 1 WLR 2409; *R v Parole Board, ex p Wilson* [1992] QB 740, [1992] 2 All ER 576; *R v Criminal Injuries Compensation Board, ex p Cobb* [1995] COD 126; *R v Secretary of State for the Home Department, ex p Pegg* [1995] COD 84; *R v Secretary of State for the Home Department, ex p Hickey (No 2)* [1995] COD 164; *R v City of London Corpn, ex p Matson* [1997] 1 WLR 765; *R v Secretary of State for the Home Department, ex p Follen* [1996] COD 169; *R v Secretary of State for the Home Department, ex p Murphy* [1997] COD 478; *R v Secretary of State for the Home Department, ex p McAvoy* [1998] COD 148, CA; *R v Secretary of State for the Home Department, ex p Fayed* [1997] 1 All ER 228, [1998] 1 WLR 763, CA; *Ex p Bailey* [1995] COD 478; *R v Kensington and Chelsea Royal Borough Council, ex p Grillo* (1995) 28 HLR 94, CA (voluntary appeal procedure did not require provision of reasons); *R v Criminal Injuries Compensation Board, ex p Cook* [1996] 2 All ER 144, [1996] 1 WLR 1037, CA; *R v Criminal Injuries Compensation Board, ex p Moore* [1999] COD 241, CA.

3 Although the decisions referred to in notes 1–2 could be seen as a series of single instance determinations, a single rationale can be derived from them. The obligation to provide a reasoned decision will exist when general considerations of procedural fairness require it. On this basis it is relevant to consider factors such as the need for reasons to give substance to a right of appeal; to explain an otherwise aberrant outcome; to demonstrate that issues had been properly addressed; the nature of the interest affected by the decision and the extent to which

the interest is affected by the decision; the need to promote transparency in the decision-making process; whether the duty would impose an undue burden on the decision-maker or otherwise frustrate the purpose to be achieved by the decision-maker; and the extent to which the judgments made were capable of being reasoned, or whether they were simply matters of academic or other evaluation. This list is not exhaustive. What is relevant will depend on the particular context concerned. The outcome of the application of this principle will differ from case to case depending on the circumstances; this simply reflects the fact that the weight to be attached to similar considerations will vary from context to context. As to the standard of reasoning required see PARA 646.

4   See *R v Higher Education Funding Council, ex p Institute of Dental Surgery* [1994] 1 All ER 651, [1994] 1 WLR 242.

(4) LEGITIMATE EXPECTATION

648. Fairness. The court will intervene to ensure that public bodies do not act so unfairly that their conduct amounts to an abuse of power[1]. The circumstances in which the court will hold conduct to be unfair in this sense are exceptional[2]. Conduct which is equivalent to a breach of contract or representation[3], and the exercise of a discretion in a manner which is inconsistent as between affected persons[4], have been held to be sufficiently unfair to warrant intervention by the court. The categories of unfairness are not closed[5].

1   See *Re Preston* [1985] AC 835, [1985] 2 All ER 327, HL; *R v North and East Devon Health Authority, ex p Coughlan* [2001] QB 213, [2000] 3 All ER 850, CA. The principle is wider than the principle that a public body must act in a procedurally fair manner (see PARA 625 et seq) and extends to the requirement of fairness in the substance of a body's decisions. See further *HTV Ltd v Price Commission* [1976] ICR 170 at 185, CA, per Lord Denning MR, at 192 per Scarman LJ, and at 195 per Goff LJ; *Laker Airways Ltd v Department of Trade* [1977] QB 643 at 707, [1977] 2 All ER 182 at 194, CA, per Lord Denning MR (authority misuses its powers if it exercises them in circumstances which work injustice or unfairness to the individual without any countervailing benefit for the public); *IRC v National Federation of Self-Employed and Small Businesses Ltd* [1982] AC 617 at 650, [1981] 2 All ER 93 at 111, HL, per Lord Scarman (cf at 637 and 101–102 per Lord Diplock); *Re Findlay* [1985] AC 318, sub nom *Findlay v Secretary of State for the Home Department* [1984] 3 All ER 801, HL; *R v Secretary of State for the Home Department, ex p Khan* [1985] 1 All ER 40 at 52, [1984] 1 WLR 1337 at 1352, CA, per Dunn LJ (an unfair action can seldom be a reasonable one); *Wheeler v Leicester City Council* [1985] AC 1054 at 1078, [1985] 2 All ER 1106 at 1111, HL, per Lord Roskill; *R v Independent Television Commission, ex p Television South West Broadcasting* (1992) Times, 7 February, Independent, 6 February, CA; *R v IRC, ex p Matrix-Securities Ltd* [1993] STC 774 at 793, 137 Sol Jo LB 255, CA, per Dillon LJ; *R v Ministry of Agricuture, Fisheries and Food, ex p Hamble (Offshore) Fisheries Ltd* [1995] 2 All ER 714 at 724, [1995] COD 114 at 115 per Sedley J (the real question is one of fairness in public administration); *R v IRC, ex p Unilever plc* [1996] STC 681, 68 TC 205, CA (Revenue's conduct in enforcing time limit so unfair as to amount to abuse of power); *R v Secretary of State for Education and Employment, ex p Begbie* [2000] 1 WLR 1115, [2000] ELR 445, CA (departure by Secretary of State from policy on assisted places legitimate). See also *R v Secretary of State for the Home Department, ex p Pierson* [1998] AC 539 at 591, [1997] 3 All ER 577 at 607, HL, per Lord Steyn (rule of law enforces minimum standards of substantive and procedural fairness). As to challenge on the grounds of procedural unfairness see PARA 625 et seq.

2   *Re Preston* [1985] AC 835 at 864, sub nom *Preston v IRC* [1985] 2 All ER 327 at 339, HL, per Lord Templeman; *R v IRC, ex p Matrix Securities Ltd* [1993] STC 774 at 779, 137 Sol Jo LB 255, CA, per Laws J; *R v IRC, ex p Unilever plc* [1996] STC 681 at 695, 68 TC 205, CA, per Simon Brown LJ. See also *R v Secretary of State for the Home Department, ex p Pierson* [1998] AC 539 at 575, [1997] 3 All ER 577 at 592, HL, per Lord Browne-Wilkinson (no general principle yet established that the courts may quash on the simple ground that a decision is unfair).

3   *Re Preston* [1985] AC 835, sub nom *Preston v IRC* [1985] 2 All ER 327, HL. Ordinarily the court will only quash a decision which amounts to a breach of a representation where the applicant can show that the representation was clear and unambiguous, that it was made to him as an individual or as a member of a limited class of persons, and that he relied on it to his detriment, although the case law is inconsistent on whether these requirements are essential. The

principle is closely linked to the doctrine of legitimate expectation. As to legitimate expectation see PARA 649. See generally *R v North and East Devon Health Authority, ex p Coughlan* [2000] 3 All ER 850 at 870, [2000] 2 WLR 622 at 644, CA, per Lord Woolf MR giving the judgment of the court; and see also *R v Secretary of State for the Home Department, ex p Ruddock* [1987] 2 All ER 518, [1987] 1 WLR 1482 (doctrine of legitimate expectation not confined to procedural expectation); *R v IRC, ex p MFK Underwriting Agents Ltd* [1990] 1 WLR 1545 at 1569–1570, [1989] STC 873 at 892, DC, per Bingham LJ (doctrine of legitimate expectation is rooted in fairness); *R v Secretary of State for the Home Department, ex p Golam Mowla* [1992] 1 WLR 70, CA (representations concerning leave to remain created no substantive legitimate expectation); *R v Jockey Club, ex p RAM Racecourses Ltd* [1993] 2 All ER 225 at 236–237, [1990] COD 346 at 346, DC, per Stuart-Smith LJ; *R v IRC, ex p SG Warburg & Co Ltd* [1994] STC 518, 68 TC 300 (in the absence of reliance, Inland Revenue could not be bound in future to follow previous practice); *R v IRC, ex p Matrix Securities Ltd* [1994] 1 WLR 334, HL; *R v Ministry of Agriculture, Fisheries and Food, ex p Hamble (Offshore) Fisheries Ltd* [1995] 2 All ER 714, [1995] COD 114; *R v Devon County Council, ex p Baker* [1995] 1 All ER 73 at 88–89, (1992) 11 BMLR 141 at 156–157, CA, per Simon Brown LJ (requirement for clear and unambiguous representation); *R v IRC, ex p Unilever plc* [1996] STC 681, 68 TC 205, CA (no clear and unambiguous representation but long-standing practice of non-enforcement of time limits and reliance on practice by company; subsequent enforcement of time limits without warning so unfair as to be an abuse of power); *R v Secretary of State for Education and Employment, ex p Begbie* [2000] 1 WLR 1115 at 1123–1124, [2000] ELR 445 at [46], CA, per Peter Gibson LJ (unambiguous and unqualified representation sufficient but not necessary; detrimental reliance ordinarily required). Compare *R v Secretary of State for the Home Department, ex p Pierson* [1998] AC 539 at 590–591, [1997] 3 All ER 577, HL, per Lord Steyn (doctrine of substantive legitimate expectation controversial, but must be presumed that statutory powers may not be exercised contrary to the rule of law which enforces minimum standards of both substantive and procedural unfairness); *R v Barking and Dagenham London Borough Council, ex p Lloyd* (15 November 2000, unreported) (no legitimate expectation because no reliance on representation).

There is a conflict in the authorities as to the test the court should apply to determine whether a failure to fulfil a legitimate expectation of a substantive benefit is so unfair as to be an abuse of power: see *R v North and East Devon Health Authority, ex p Coughlan* at 872 and 645, per Lord Woolf MR, giving the judgment of the court, applying the approach adopted in *R v Ministry of Agriculture, Fisheries and Food, ex p Hamble (Offshore) Fisheries Ltd* at 731 per Sedley J (departure from representation made to applicant must be justified by sufficient overriding interest; court will determine whether interest is sufficient); and see *R v Secretary of State for the Home Department, ex p Khan* [1985] 1 All ER 40 at 46, [1984] 1 WLR 1337 at 1344, CA, per Parker LJ (Secretary of State cannot resile from conditions on which he had stated he would afford entry to the United Kingdom without affording interested persons a hearing and then only if overriding public interest demands it); cf *R v Secretary of State for the Home Department, ex p Hargreaves* [1997] 1 All ER 397 at 412, [1997] 1 WLR 906 at 921, CA, per Hirst LJ (authority may depart from representation or policy so long as it acts reasonably in the *Wednesbury* sense; the approach in *R v Ministry of Agriculture, Fisheries and Food, ex p Hamble (Offshore) Fisheries Ltd* was considered 'heresy'), and 416 per Pill LJ (approach in *R v Ministry of Agriculture, Fisheries and Foods, ex p Hamble Fisheries (Offshore) Ltd* is 'wrong in principle'); *R v Secretary of State for Transport, ex p Richmond-upon-Thames London Borough Council* [1994] 1 All ER 577 at 597, [1994] 1 WLR 74 at 94 per Laws J; see also *R v Walsall Metropolitan Borough Council, ex p Yapp* [1994] ICR 528, (1993) 92 LGR 110, CA (legitimate expectation only that council would depart from resolution on rational grounds and after due consultation with those affected).

Unfairness to third parties may amount to misuse of a power where fairness to such third parties is a relevant consideration in the exercise of that power: *R v Port Talbot Borough Council, ex p Jones* [1988] 2 All ER 207 at 214 per Nolan J.

4   *IRC v National Federation of Self-Employed and Small Businesses Ltd* [1982] AC 617 at 651, [1981] 2 All ER 93 at 112, HL, per Lord Scarman (duty to use powers so that discrimination between one group of taxpayers and another does not arise); *Kruse v Johnson* [1898] 2 QB 91, DC (byelaws must not be manifestly unjust or partial); *R v IRC, ex p Kaye and Kaye* [1992] STC 581 at 586, 5 Admin LR 369 at 373 per Macpherson J; *R v Tower Hamlets London Borough Council, ex p Khalique* [1994] 2 FCR 1074, 26 HLR 517; *R v Ministry of Agriculture, Fisheries and Food, ex p Hamble (Offshore) Fisheries Ltd* [1995] 2 All ER 714 at 722, [1995] COD 114 at 116 per Sedley J; *R v Ministry of Agriculture Fisheries and Food, ex p First City Trading Ltd* [1997] 1 CMLR 250 at 278, (1996) Times, 20 December per Laws J (treatment of identical cases differently would be prima facie irrational); *R v IRC, ex p Unilever plc* [1996]

STC 681 at 692, 68 TC 205 at 230, CA, per Simon Brown LJ; *R v Secretary of State for Social Security, ex p Joint Council for the Welfare of Immigrants* [1996] 4 All ER 385, [1997] 1 WLR 275, CA (disparate treatment of immigrants not unlawful); *R v North and East Devon Health Authority, ex p Coughlan* [2000] 3 All ER 850 at 876, [2000] 2 WLR 622 at 650, CA; *R v Secretary of State for Education and Employment, ex p Begbie* [2000] 1 WLR 1115 at 1132, [2000] ELR 445 at [87]–[93], CA, per Sedley LJ and at 1125 and [49]–[50] per Peter Gibson LJ; *R v National Lottery Commission, ex p Camelot Group plc* (2000) Times, 12 October, [2001] EMLR 43 (opportunity given to one bidder but not another so unfair as to be abuse of power).

5 *R v Secretary of State for Education, ex p Begbie* [2000] 1 WLR 1115 at 1123–1124, [2000] ELR 445, CA, per Peter Gibson LJ; see also *R v Independent Television Commission, ex p Television South West* (1992) Times, 7 February, CA (test in public law is fairness, not an adaptation of the law of contract or estoppel); *R v IRC, ex p Unilever plc* [1996] STC 681 at 695, CA, per Simon Brown LJ (unfairness amounting to an abuse of power not unlawful because would offend private law principles of misrepresentation, waiver, acquiescence or estoppel, or legitimate expectation, but because it is illogical or immoral or both for a public authority to act with conspicuous unfairness); *R v North and East Devon Health Authority, ex p Coughlan* [2000] 3 All ER 850 at 872, [2000] 2 WLR 622 at 645, CA, per Lord Woolf MR (legitimate expectation generally is a 'developing field of law').

649. Legitimate expectations. A person may have a legitimate expectation of being treated in a certain way by an administrative authority even though there is no other legal basis upon which he could claim such treatment[1]. The expectation may arise either from a representation or promise made by the authority[2], including an implied representation[3], or from consistent past practice[4]. In all instances the expectation arises by reason of the conduct of the decision-maker[5], and is protected by the courts on the basis that principles of fairness, predictability and certainty should not be disregarded[6].

The existence of a legitimate expectation may have a number of different consequences; it may give standing to seek permission to apply for judicial review[7], it may mean that the authority ought not to act so as to defeat the consequence of the expectation without some overriding reason of public policy to justify its doing so[8], or it may mean that, if the authority proposes to act contrary to the legitimate expectation, it must afford the person either an opportunity to make representations on the matter, or the benefit of some other requirement of procedural fairness[9]. A legitimate expectation may cease to exist either because its significance has come to a natural end or because of action on the part of the decision-maker[10].

In appropriate circumstances the existence of a legitimate expectation may require a public body to confer a substantive, as opposed to a procedural, benefit[11]. In such cases the courts will not permit the public body to resile from the representation if to do so would amount to an abuse of power[12].

1 *O'Reilly v Mackman* [1983] 2 AC 237 at 275, [1982] 3 All ER 1124 at 1126–1127, HL, per Lord Diplock; *A-G of Hong Kong v Ng Yuen Shiu* [1983] 2 AC 629, [1983] 2 All ER 346, PC; *Council of Civil Service Unions v Minister for the Civil Service* [1985] AC 374 at 408–409, [1984] 3 All ER 935 at 949, HL, per Lord Diplock. Four categories of legitimate expectations were identified in *R v Devon County Council, ex p Baker* [1995] 1 All ER 73 at 88–89, (1994) 6 Admin LR 113 at 130–132, CA, per Simon Brown LJ (a legitimate expectation of a substantive right, an interest in a benefit which the claimant hopes to retain, a fair procedure, and that a procedure which is not required by law will be held). The expectation must plainly be a reasonable one: *A-G of Hong Kong v Ng Yuen Shiu*. It seems that a person's own conduct may deprive any expectations he may have of the necessary quality of legitimacy: *Cinnamond v British Airports Authority* [1980] 2 All ER 368, [1980] 1 WLR 582, CA.

2 *R v Liverpool Corpn, ex p Liverpool Taxi Fleet Operators' Association* [1972] 2 QB 299, [1972] 2 All ER 589, CA; *A-G of Hong Kong v Ng Yuen Shiu* [1983] 2 AC 629, [1983] 2 All ER 346, PC (representation made to a class of persons rather than to specific individual, although cf *R v IRC, ex p Camacq Corpn* [1990] 1 All ER 173, [1990] 1 WLR 191, CA, representation only operative to the specific class rather than generally; and see generally *Lloyd*

v McMahon [1987] AC 625 at 696, [1987] 1 All ER 1118 at 1156, HL, per Lord Keith of Kinkel, and at 714 per Lord Templeman); *Council of Civil Service Unions v Minister for the Civil Service* [1985] AC 374, [1984] 3 All ER 935, HL; *Oloniluyi v Secretary of State for the Home Department* [1989] Imm AR 135, CA; *R v Brent London Borough Council, ex p MacDonagh* [1990] COD 3, 21 HLR 494; *New Zealand Maori Council v A-G for New Zealand* [1994] 1 AC 466, [1994] 1 All ER 623, PC (assurance that proposal made in the course of litigation would be honoured); *R v Funding Agency for Schools, ex p Bromley London Borough Council* [1996] COD 375, CA (on facts, no clear and unqualified representation); *Dey v Secretary of State for the Home Department* [1996] Imm AR 521, CA (return of passport did not give rise to legitimate expectation to remain). The representation must be made by a person having actual or ostensible authority to do so: *Matrix-Securities Ltd v IRC* [1994] 1 All ER 769, [1994] 1 WLR 334, HL; *R v DPP, ex p Kebeline* [2000] 2 AC 326, sub nom *R v DPP, ex p Kebeline* [1999] 4 All ER 801, DC (statement by minister not binding on Director of Public Prosecutions).

Although there is an obvious analogy between the doctrines of legitimate expectation and of estoppel, the two are distinct and detrimental reliance upon the representation has not always been regarded as a necessary ingredient of a legitimate expectation: see *R v Secretary of State for the Home Department, ex p Khan* [1985] 1 All ER 40 at 48, [1984] 1 WLR 1337 at 1347, CA, per Parker LJ, and at 52 and 1352 per Dunn LJ; cf *R v Jockey Club, ex p RAM Racecourses* [1993] 2 All ER 225 at 236–237, [1990] COD 346 at 346–347, DC, per Stuart-Smith LJ; and see ADMINISTRATIVE LAW vol 1(1) (2001 Reissue) PARA 23. In principle, the better view is that detrimental reliance is not an absolute requirement but is a relevant issue to consider: see *R v IRC, ex p MFK Underwriting Agents Ltd* [1990] 1 WLR 1545. In relation to Inland Revenue extra-statutory concessions and assurances see *R v A-G, ex p ICI plc* (1986) 60 TC 1; *R v HM Inspector of Taxes, Hull, ex p Brunfield* (1988) Times, 25 November; *R v IRC, ex p MFK Underwriting Agencies Ltd* (the representation must be clear, unambiguous and unqualified, and the person seeking to rely upon it must have made full disclosure on all relevant matters); *R v Ministry of Defence, ex p Walker* [2000] COD 153, HL. See also *R v IRC, ex p Unilver plc* [1996] STC 681, CA; cf *Re Preston* [1985] AC 835, [1984] 2 All ER 327, HL.

3   *R v Secretary of State for the Home Department, ex p Khan* [1985] 1 All ER 40, [1984] 1 WLR 1337, CA (setting out criteria for exercise of discretion in guidance letter given to prospective adoptive parents of children requiring entry clearance led to legitimate expectation that clearance would be granted where those criteria were satisfied). See also *R v Powys County Council, ex p Horner* [1989] Fam Law 320; *R v Brent London Borough Council, ex p MacDonagh* [1990] COD 3, 21 HLR 494. In *R v Brent London Borough Council, ex p Gunning* (1985) 84 LGR 168 the court appears to have relied in part on what were in effect express or implied representations by the Secretary of State, contained in departmental circulars, that there would be consultation, although the duty to consult was being imposed upon the local authority. See also *R v British Coal Corpn, ex p Vardy* [1993] ICR 720 (legitimate expectation of consultation prior to decision to close collieries).

4   *O'Reilly v Mackman* [1983] 2 AC 237 at 275, [1982] 3 All ER 1124 at 1126–1127, HL, per Lord Diplock; *Council of Civil Service Unions v Minister for the Civil Service* [1985] AC 374, [1984] 3 All ER 935, HL; *R v Brent London Borough Council, ex p Gunning* (1985) 84 LGR 168; *R v Secretary of State for the Home Department, ex p Ruddock* [1987] 2 All ER 518, [1987] 1 WLR 1482.

It is not clear to what extent a legitimate expectation may arise other than by way of a representation or of past practice; neither factor would seem to have been present in *R v Secretary of State for Transport, ex p GLC* [1986] QB 556, [1985] 3 All ER 300. See also note 8. Procedural duties imposed as a result of looking at all the surrounding circumstances, rather than the conduct of the decision-maker, will normally be treated as illustrations of the general duty to act fairly in all the circumstances (see PARA 629) rather than of a legitimate expectation. Cf *R v Great Yarmouth Borough Council, ex p Botton Bros Arcades Ltd* (1987) 56 P & CR 99 at 109 per Otton J; and see *Re Westminster City Council* [1986] AC 668 at 692–693, [1986] 2 All ER 278 at 288–289, HL, per Lord Bridge of Harwich, dissenting on another point.

Not all past practice will justify an expectation as to future conduct: *R v Secretary of State for the Environment, ex p Kent* [1988] JPL 706 (affd [1990] JPL 124, CA); *R v Secretary of State for the Home Department, ex p Islam* [1990] Imm AR 220.

5   See *R v Great Yarmouth Borough Council, ex p Botton Bros Arcades Ltd* (1987) 56 P & CR 99; *R v Secretary of State for Health, ex p United States Tobacco International Inc* [1992] QB 353, [1992] 1 All ER 212, DC. Thus the basis of rights which arise on the basis of legitimate expectation differs from the basis of rights which arise because the decision to be made impinges upon an individual's rights or interests. An expectation can arise even if the decision-maker did not intend it to: see *R v Jockey Club, ex p RAM Racecourses* [1993] 2 All ER 225.

6   Although in some circumstances an expectation may be defeated if based on a clear but incorrect representation: *R v Secretary of State for the Home Department, ex p Silva* (1994) Times, 1 April, CA.

7   *O'Reilly v Mackman* [1983] 2 AC 237 at 275, [1982] 3 All ER 1124 at 1126–1127, HL, per Lord Diplock; *Council of Civil Service Unions v Minister for the Civil Service* [1985] AC 374 at 408, [1984] 3 All ER 935 at 949, HL, per Lord Diplock; *Re Findlay* [1985] AC 318 at 338, [1984] 3 All ER 801 at 830, HL, per Lord Scarman. As to applications to seek permission to apply for judicial review see PARA 664.

8   *R v Liverpool Corpn, ex p Liverpool Taxi Fleet Operators' Association* [1972] 2 QB 299, [1972] 2 All ER 589, CA; *R v Secretary of State for the Home Department, ex p Khan* [1985] 1 All ER 40 at 46, [1984] 1 WLR 1337 at 1344, CA, per Parker LJ; *R v Secretary of State for the Home Department, ex p Ruddock* [1987] 2 All ER 518, [1987] 1 WLR 1482; and cf *HTV Ltd v Price Commission* [1976] ICR 170, CA. Where the expectation arises out of an administrative authority's existing policy, it can be argued that the extent of the expectation is only that the policy, for the time being in existence, will be fairly applied. However, if the policy is subsequently changed there is the possibility of tension between the no fettering rule and the desire to protect the legitimate expectation. Although a public body is free to alter its policy (see *Re Findlay* [1985] AC 318 at 338, [1984] 3 All ER 801 at 830, HL, per Lord Scarman; *R v Secretary of State for the Environment, ex p Barratt (Guildford) Ltd* (1988) Times, 3 April; and see *R v Secretary of State for the Home Department, ex p Ruddock*) it will not in all cases also be free to disregard the legitimate expectation: see *R v North and East Devon Health Authority, ex p Coughlan* [2001] QB 213, [2000] 3 All ER 850, CA; *R v Minister of Agriculture, Fisheries and Food, ex p Hamble (Offshore) Fisheries Ltd* [1995] 2 All ER 714.

9   *A-G of Hong Kong v Ng Yuen Shiu* [1983] 2 AC 629, [1983] 2 All ER 346, PC; *Council of Civil Service Unions v Minister for the Civil Service* [1985] AC 374, [1984] 3 All ER 935, HL; *R v Secretary of State for the Home Department, ex p Khan* [1985] 1 All ER 40, [1984] 1 WLR 1337, CA. Sometimes the expectation will itself be of consultation or the opportunity to be heard: *R v Liverpool Corpn, ex p Liverpool Taxi Fleet Operators' Association* [1972] 2 QB 299, [1972] 2 All ER 589, CA; *A-G of Hong Kong v Ng Yuen Shiu; Council of Civil Service Unions v Minister for the Civil Service*; and see *Lloyd v McMahon* [1987] AC 625 at 715, [1987] 1 All ER 1118 at 1170–1171, HL, per Lord Templeman (legitimate expectation is just a manifestation of the duty to act fairly). But the scope of the doctrine goes beyond the right to be heard: *R v Secretary of State for the Home Department, ex p Ruddock* [1987] 2 All ER 518, [1987] 1 WLR 1482. See also *R v Barnet London Borough Council, ex p Pardes House School Ltd* [1989] COD 512; *R v Powys County Council, ex p Horner* [1989] Fam Law 320; *R v Secretary of State for the Home Department, ex p Duggan* [1994] 3 All ER 277. There is, however, a legitimate expectation of re-appointment to a public body: *R v North East Thames Regional Health Authority, ex p de Groot* (1988) Times, 16 April.

10   See *Re Findlay* [1985] AC 318; *R v Secretary of State for Health, ex p United States Tobacco International Inc* [1992] QB 353, [1992] 1 All ER 212, DC; *R v Secretary of State for the Home Department, ex p Hargreaves* [1997] 1 All ER 397, [1997] 1 WLR 906, CA; *R v Council of Legal Education, ex p Eddis* (1995) 7 Admin LR 357, DC; *R v Torbay Borough Council, ex p Cleasby* [1991] COD 142, CA. If, however, the expectation is sufficiently long-established it might be necessary to provide an opportunity to make representations before any change in policy: *R v British Coal Corpn, ex p Vardy* [1993] ICR 720. An implied representation may be overtaken by events: *R v Secretary of State for the Home Department, ex p Malhi* [1991] 1 QB 194, [1990] 2 All ER 357, CA. In each case it will be a question of fact and degree.

11   *R v Secretary of State for the Home Department, ex p Khan* [1985] 1 All ER 40, [1984] 1 WLR 1337, CA; *R v Secretary of State for the Home Department, ex p Ruddock* [1987] 1 WLR 1482; *R v Preston* [1985] AC 835 at 868–869 per Lord Templeman; *R v IRC, ex p MFK Underwriting* [1990] 1 WLR 1545; *R v IRC, ex p Unilever plc* [1996] STC 681, CA. But cf *R v Panel on Take-overs and Mergers, ex p Fayed* [1992] BCLC 938; and *R v Shropshire County Council, ex p Jones* (1996) 9 Admin LR 625 (a 'very good chance' of getting a grant does not found a legitimate expectation of receiving one).

12   The leading cases on this point are *R v North and East Devon Health Authority, ex p Coughlan* [2001] QB 213, [2000] 3 All ER 850, CA; and *R v Secretary of State for Education and Employment, ex p Begbie* [2000] 1 WLR 1115, [2000] ELR 445, CA. The court is to determine for itself whether or not there would be an abuse of power. See also *R v Minister of Agriculture, Fisheries and Food, ex p Hamble (Offshore) Fisheries Ltd* [1995] 2 All ER 714; *R v Westminster City Council, ex p Union of Managerial and Professional Officers* [2000] LGR 611; and cf *R v Secretary of State for the Home Department, ex p Hargreaves* [1997] 1 All ER 397, [1997] 1 WLR 906 which preferred the less intrusive approach of the application of a *Wednesbury* test (see PARA 617), but was distinguished in *R v North and East Devon Health Authority, ex p*

Coughlan. See also *R v Secretary of State for Education and Employment, ex p Begbie* (courts would not give effect to a legitimate expectation if to do so would require a public authority to act in breach of the terms of a statute).

(5) HUMAN RIGHTS

650. Judicial review and human rights. In addition to seeking review of an administrative act on the traditional grounds of illegality, procedural impropriety and irrationality[1], a claimant in a judicial review matter may also seek to challenge the act of a public authority[2] on the grounds that the act is incompatible with the Convention for the Protection of Human Rights and Fundamental Freedoms[3]. It is unlawful for a public authority to act in a way which is incompatible with Convention rights[4], that is to say, with the provisions of that Convention which have effect for the purposes of the Human Rights Act 1998[5].

1 Ie the grounds formulated by Lord Diplock in *Council of Civil Service Unions v Minister for the Civil Service* [1985] AC 374 at 410, [1984] 3 All ER 935 at 950–951, HL: see PARA 602.
2 As to the meaning of 'public authority' see PARA 651 note 2. Cf PARA 604.
3 Ie the Convention for the Protection of Human Rights and Fundamental Freedoms (Rome, 4 November 1950; TS 71 (1953) Cmd 8969). The Human Rights Act 1998 incorporates certain of the provisions of the Convention into English law: see PARA 651; and CONSTITUTIONAL LAW AND HUMAN RIGHTS vol 8(2) (Reissue) PARA 101 et seq.
4 See the Human Rights Act 1998 s 6(1); and PARA 651. As to the meaning of 'Convention rights' see PARA 651 note 1.
5 See the Human Rights Act 1998 s 1; and CONSTITUTIONAL LAW AND HUMAN RIGHTS. See further PARA 651.

651. Human rights. Primary and secondary legislation must, so far as it is possible to do so, be read and given effect in a way which is compatible with rights protected by the Convention for the Protection of Human Rights and Fundamental Freedoms[1]. It is unlawful for a public authority[2] to act in a way which is incompatible[3] with a Convention right[4] but this does not apply to an act[5] if: (1) as a result of one or more provisions of primary legislation, the authority could not have acted differently[6]; or (2) in the case of one or more provisions of, or made under, primary legislation which cannot be read or given effect in a way which is compatible with the Convention rights, the authority was acting so as to give effect to or enforce those provisions[7].

A person who claims that a public authority has acted (or proposes to act) in a way which is unlawful[8] may (a) bring proceedings against that authority in the appropriate court or tribunal[9]; or (b) rely on his Convention rights in any legal proceedings[10], but only if he is (or would be) a victim of the unlawful act[11]. Proceedings under head (a) above must be brought before the end of (i) the period of one year beginning with the date on which the act complained of took place[12]; or (ii) such longer period as the court or tribunal considers equitable having regard to all the circumstances[13], but that is subject to any rule imposing a stricter time limit in relation to the procedure in question[14].

The court has to make a primary judgment (rather than performing a secondary review) as to whether the challenged decision is unlawful[15]. This will often involve the application of the doctrine of proportionality. Most Convention rights are not absolute[16] and allow the state to justify a prima facie breach that is prescribed by, or in accordance with, the law[17] and is necessary in a democratic society for the advancement of one or more specified objectives[18]. In deciding whether this test is met, the court will give weight to the considered opinion of the elected body or person whose act or decision is said to be incompatible with the Convention for the Protection of Human Rights and Fundamental Freedoms[19]. The court will take into account the constitutional status of the decision-maker[20]. The court will be more ready to defer to the judgment of the elected body or decision-maker in cases involving questions of politics, social or economic policy[21] and less ready to defer in cases where the right of the individual is of high constitutional importance[22] or of a kind which the court is especially well placed to assess the need for protection[23]. Whilst the application of the proportionality principle is wider than *Wednesbury* unreasonableness, it does not involve the court substituting its own decision for that of the legislature or public authority[24].

Where on an application for judicial review a person claims that his Convention rights have been infringed by a public authority, or that primary legislation is incompatible with a Convention right, the court will quash the act or decision of the public authority as unlawful[25], or will make a declaration that primary legislation is incompatible with the Convention for the Protection of Human Rights and Fundamental Freedoms[26]. It may, in an appropriate case, also award damages[27].

1   Human Rights Act 1998 s 3(1). The Human Rights Act 1998 incorporates certain provisions of the Convention for the Protection of Human Rights and Fundamental Freedoms (Rome, 4 November 1950; TS 71 (1953) Cmd 8969) into domestic law: see CONSTITUTIONAL LAW AND HUMAN RIGHTS. The Human Rights Act 1998 s 3(1) applies to 'Convention rights', which are defined to include only the Convention for the Protection of Human Rights and Fundamental Freedoms (1950) arts 2–12, 14, First Protocol arts 1–3, and the Thirteenth Protocol art 1: see the Human Rights Act 1998 s 1(1); and CONSTITUTIONAL LAW AND HUMAN RIGHTS. However, the Convention rights under the Human Rights Act 1998 are distinct legal obligations in the domestic legal systems of the United Kingdom and the Human Rights Act 1998 does not incorporate the international obligations as such: *R (on the application of Al-Jedda) v Secretary of State for Defence* [2007] UKHL 58, [2008] 1 AC 332, [2008] 3 All ER 28; but see also *R (on the application of Quark Fishing Ltd) v Secretary of State for Foreign and Commonwealth Affairs* [2005] UKHL 57, [2006] 1 AC 529, [2006] 3 All ER 111. As to the differences between the Convention rights and the rights under the Human Rights Act 1998 see *Re McKerr* [2004] UKHL 12, [2004] 2 All ER 409.

   Legislation may be compatible with the Convention rights if it provides greater protection than those rights: *R v Broadcasting Standards Commission, ex p British Broadcasting Corpn* [2001] QB 885, [2000] 3 All ER 989, CA.

   Prior to the coming into force of the Human Rights Act 1998 on 2 October 2000, the court applied a principle of statutory construction that Parliament did not intend statutory provisions which conferred a power to act or legislate in general terms to permit breaches of fundamental civil liberties (the 'principle of legality'): see *R v Secretary of State for the Home Department, ex p Pierson* [1998] AC 539, [1997] 3 All ER 577, HL; *R v Secretary of State for the Home Department, ex p Simms* [2000] 2 AC 115, [1999] 3 All ER 400, HL. See also *R v Secretary of State for the Home Department, ex p Leech* [1994] QB 198, [1993] 4 All ER 539 CA; *R v Lord Chancellor, ex p Witham* [1998] QB 575, [1997] 2 All ER 779, DC; *R v Lord Chancellor, ex p Lightfoot* [2000] QB 597, [1999] 4 All ER 583, CA.

2   'Public authority' bears its ordinary meaning (ie what are known as core public authorities) and is also defined to include: (1) a court or tribunal; and (2) any person certain of whose functions are functions of a public nature (known as hybrid public authorities), but does not include either House of Parliament or a person exercising functions in connection with proceedings in Parliament: Human Rights Act 1988 s 6(3). In relation to a particular act, a person is not a public authority by virtue only of head (2) if the nature of the act is private: s 6(5).

   A core public authority is a body whose nature is governmental, taking into account factors such as the possession of special powers, democratic accountability, public funding in whole or in part, an obligation to act in the public interest and a statutory constitution: *Aston Cantlow and Wilmcote with Billesley Parochial Church Council v Wallbank* [2003] UKHL 37, [2004] 1 AC 546, [2003] 3 All ER 1213. A core public authority must comply with Convention rights in respect of all activities.

In contrast, a hybrid public authority is only required to comply with Convention rights in respect of an act which is not private and which is pursuant to a function which is public in nature: *YL v Birmingham City Council* [2007] UKHL 27, [2008] 1 AC 95, [2007] 3 All ER 957. See also the earlier decisions of *Poplar Housing and Regeneration Community Association Ltd v Donoghue* [2001] EWCA Civ 595, [2002] QB 48, [2001] 4 All ER 604; *R (on the application of Heather) v Leonard Cheshire Foundation* [2002] EWCA Civ 366, [2002] 2 All ER 936; *R (on the application of West) v Lloyd's of London* [2004] EWCA Civ 506, [2004] 3 All ER 251; *James v London Electricity plc* [2004] EWHC 3226 (QB); *R (Mullins) v The Appeal Board of the Jockey Club* [2005] EWHC 2197 (Admin), [2006] LLR 151; *Cameron v Network Rail Infrastructure Ltd* [2006] EWHC 1133 (QB), [2007] 3 All ER 241, [2007] 1 WLR 163.

The Human Rights Act 1998 contains no definition of a function of a public nature. Following *YL v Birmingham City Council*, the courts will consider whether the task in question has been delegated by a core public authority which was under a duty to perform it, whether the task is part of public administration, whether the body has any special statutory powers and whether it is supported or subsidised by public funds. The decision in *YL v Birmingham City Council* was applied in *R (on the application of Weaver) v London and Quadrant Housing Trust* [2009] EWCA Civ 587, [2009] 4 All ER 865, [2009] 25 EG 137 (CS) (a registered social landlord was a hybrid public authority on the facts and its act of terminating a tenancy was not a private act). See also *Aston Cantlow and Wilmcote with Billesley Parochial Church Council v Wallbank*.

3   Incompatible means inconsistent: *A-G's Reference (No 2 of 2001)* [2003] UKHL 68, [2004] 2 AC 72, [2004] 1 All ER 1049.

4   Human Rights Act 1998 s 6(1). As to the meaning of 'Convention rights' see note 1.

5   An 'act' includes a failure to act but does not include a failure to: (1) introduce in, or lay before, Parliament a proposal for legislation; or (2) make any primary legislation or remedial order: Human Rights Act 1998 s 6(6).

6   Human Rights Act 1998 s 6(2)(a).

7   Human Rights Act 1998 s 6(2)(b). This applies where a public authority could have lawfully exercised the power, but it would have been inconsistent with the statutory scheme to have done so: *R (on the application of Hooper) v Secretary of State for Work and Pensions* [2005] UKHL 29, [2006] 1 All ER 487, [2005] 1 WLR 1681. For examples of the application of the Human Rights Act 1998 s 6(2)(b) see *R (on the application of Anderson) v Secretary of State for the Home Department* [2002] UKHL 46, [2003] 1 AC 837, [2002] 4 All ER 1089; *Aston Cantlow and Wilmcote with Billesley Parochial Church Council v Wallbank* [2003] UKHL 37, [2004] 1 AC 546, [2003] 3 All ER 1213; *R (on the application of Morris) v Westminster City Council* [2005] EWCA Civ 1184, [2006] 1 WLR 505; *Doherty v Birmingham City Council* [2008] UKHL 57, [2009] 1 AC 367, [2009] 1 All ER 653. Nothing in the Human Rights Act 1998 creates a criminal offence: s 7(8).

8   Ie unlawful by virtue of the Human Rights Act 1998 s 6: see the text and notes 2–7.

9   Human Rights Act 1998 s 7(1)(a). In s 7(1)(a), 'appropriate court or tribunal' means such court or tribunal as may be determined in accordance with rules; and proceedings against an authority include a counterclaim or similar proceeding: s 7(2). 'Rules' means: (1) in relation to proceedings before a court or tribunal outside Scotland, rules made by the Lord Chancellor or the Secretary of State for the purposes of s 7 or rules of court; (2) in relation to proceedings before a court or tribunal in Scotland, rules made by the Secretary of State for those purposes; (3) in relation to proceedings before a tribunal in Northern Ireland (a) which deals with transferred matters, and (b) for which no rules made under head (1) are in force, rules made by a Northern Ireland department for those purposes; and includes provision made by order under the Courts and Legal Services Act 1990 s 1 (see COURTS vol 10 (Reissue) PARA 579): Human Rights Act 1998 s 7(9). See the Proscribed Organisations Appeal Commission (Human Rights Act 1998 Proceedings) Rules 2006, SI 2006/2290. As to the Secretary of State see PARA 646 note 5.

In making rules, regard must be had to the Human Rights Act 1998 s 9: s 7(10). The minister who has power to make rules in relation to a particular tribunal may, to the extent he considers it necessary to ensure that the tribunal can provide an appropriate remedy in relation to an act (or proposed act) of a public authority which is (or would be) unlawful as a result of s 6(1) (see the text and note 4), by order add to: (i) the relief or remedies which the tribunal may grant; or (ii) the grounds on which it may grant any of them: s 7(11). An order made under s 7(11) may contain such incidental, supplemental, consequential or transitional provision as the minister making it considers appropriate: s 7(12). 'Minister' includes the Northern Ireland department concerned: s 7(13).

Proceedings under s 7(1)(a) in respect of a judicial act may be brought only by exercising a right of appeal or in such other forum as may be prescribed by rules: s 9(1). That does not affect any rule of law which prevents a court from being the subject of judicial review: s 9(2). 'Judicial act' means a judicial act of a court and includes an act done on the instructions, or on behalf, of a judge; 'judge' includes a member of a tribunal, a justice of the peace and a clerk or other officer entitled to exercise the jurisdiction of a court; and 'court' includes a tribunal: s 9(5). In proceedings under the Human Rights Act 1998 in respect of a judicial act done in good faith, damages may not be awarded otherwise than to compensate a person to the extent required by the Convention for the Protection of Human Rights and Fundamental Freedoms (1950) art 5(5) (see CONSTITUTIONAL LAW AND HUMAN RIGHTS vol 8(2) (Reissue) PARA 127): Human Rights Act 1998 s 9(3). An award of damages permitted by s 9(3) is to be made against the Crown; but no award may be made unless the minister responsible for the court concerned, or a person or government department nominated by him, if not a party to the proceedings, is joined: s 9(4), (5).

10   Human Rights Act 1998 s 7(1)(b).

11   For the purposes of the Human Rights Act 1998 s 7, a person is a victim of an unlawful act only if he would be a victim for the purposes of the Convention for the Protection of Human Rights and Fundamental Freedoms (1950) art 34 (see CONSTITUTIONAL LAW AND HUMAN RIGHTS vol 8(2) (Reissue) PARA 178) if proceedings were brought in the European Court of Human Rights in respect of that act: Human Rights Act 1998 s 7(7).

12   Human Rights Act 1998 s 7(5)(a).

13   Human Rights Act 1998 s 7(5)(b). The burden is on the claimant to persuade the court to exercise its discretion: *Cameron v Network Rail Infrastructure Ltd* [2006] EWHC 1133 (QB), [2007] 3 All ER 241, [2007] 1 WLR 163.

14   Human Rights Act 1998 s 7(5). For example judicial review proceedings.

15   *Huang v Secretary of State for the Home Department* [2007] UKHL 11, [2007] 2 AC 167, [2007] 4 All ER 15.

16   Absolute rights which permit of no restriction by national authorities include the Convention for the Protection of Human Rights and Fundamental Freedoms (1950) art 3 (prohibition of torture) and art 4 (prohibition of slavery and forced labour) (see CONSTITUTIONAL LAW AND HUMAN RIGHTS vol 8(2) (Reissue) PARAS 124–125). Rights which may be restricted in expressly prescribed circumstances include art 8 (right to respect for private and family life), art 9 (freedom of thought, conscience and religion), art 10 (freedom of expression) and art 11 (freedom of assembly and association) (see CONSTITUTIONAL LAW AND HUMAN RIGHTS vol 8(2) (Reissue) PARAS 109, 117). Rights which the courts have held by implication are not absolute include certain fair trial rights under art 6 (see CONSTITUTIONAL LAW AND HUMAN RIGHTS vol 8(2) (Reissue) PARA 134 et seq), including the right of access to the court and the right not to incriminate oneself: see e g *Brown v Stott* [2003] 1 AC 681, [2001] 2 All ER 97, PC; and PARA 618.

In assessing whether interference with a Convention right is lawful, the court must take into account, inter alia, the case law of the European Court of Human Rights so far as in the opinion of the court it is relevant: see the Human Rights Act 1998 s 2(1); and CONSTITUTIONAL LAW AND HUMAN RIGHTS. In the absence of special circumstances, domestic courts should follow any clear and constant jurisprudence of the European Court of Human Rights: *R (on the application of Alconbury Developments Ltd) v Secretary of State for the Environment, Transport and the Regions* [2001] UKHL 23, [2003] 2 AC 295, [2001] 2 All ER 929; *R (on the application of Ullah) v Special Adjudicator* [2004] UKHL 26, [2004] 2 AC 323, [2004] 3 All ER 785; *Kay v Lambeth London Borough Council* [2006] UKHL 10, [2006] 2 AC 465, [2006] 4 All ER 128; *R (on the application of Begum) v Headteacher and Governors of Denbigh High School* [2006] UKHL 15, [2007] 1 AC 100, [2006] 2 All ER 487; *R (on the application of Al-Skeini) v Secretary of State for Defence* [2007] UKHL 26, [2008] 1 AC 153, [2007] 3 All ER 685. However, such case law is not formally binding on domestic courts: *R (on the application of Holub) v Secretary of State for the Home Department* [2001] 1 WLR 1359, [2001] ELR 401, CA; *Huang v Secretary of State for the Home Department* [2007] UKHL 11, [2007] 2 AC 167; *R (on the application of Animal Defenders International) v Secretary of State for Culture, Media and Sport* [2008] UKHL 15, [2008] 1 AC 1312, [2008] 3 All ER 193; *Re G (Adoption: Unmarried Couple)* [2008] UKHL 38, [2009] 1 AC 173. A decision need not be followed, for example, if it is based on an imperfect understanding of domestic law or procedure: *Doherty v Birmingham City Council* [2008] UKHL 57, [2009] 1 AC 367, [2009] 1 All ER 653.

17   The state's conduct must have some basis in domestic law and that law must be clear and publicly accessible, rather than arbitrary: *R (on the application of Gillan) v Metropolitan Police Comr* [2006] UKHL 12, [2006] 2 AC 307, [2006] 4 All ER 1041; *R (on the application of Rottman) v Metropolitan Police Comr* [2002] UKHL 20, [2002] 2 AC 692, [2002] 2 All ER 865; *R v Shayler* [2002] UKHL 11, [2003] 1 AC 247, [2002] 2 All ER 477; *R (on the application of Munjaz) v Mersey Care NHS Trust* [2005] UKHL 58, [2006] 2 AC 148, [2006]

4 All ER 736. An ultra vires act is not prescribed by law: *R (on the application of Laporte) v Chief Constable of Gloucestershire Constabulary* [2006] UKHL 55, [2007] 2 AC 105, [2007] 2 All ER 529 (the Chief Constable's decision exceeded his common law powers); *Pascoe v First Secretary of State* [2006] EWHC 2356 (Admin), [2006] 4 All ER 1240 (Secretary of State had misdirected himself).

18 There are four distinct but inter-related issues: (1) the legislative objective must be sufficiently important to justify limiting a fundamental right; (2) the measure must be rationally connected to the objective (and not arbitrary, unfair or based on irrational considerations); (3) the means used to limit the right must be no more than is necessary to meet the legitimate objective; and (4) the interference must strike a fair balance between the rights of the individual and the interests of the community: *R v A* [2001] UKHL 25, [2002] 1 AC 45, [2001] 3 All ER 1; *R (on the application of Daly) v Secretary of State for the Home Department* [2001] UKHL 26, [2001] 2 AC 532, [2001] 3 All ER 433. As to sufficient importance see *Wilson v First County Trust Ltd* [2003] UKHL 40, [2004] 1 AC 816, [2003] 4 All ER 97 (the court may need to look outside the statute to see the complete picture); *R (on the application of the Countryside Alliance) v A-G* [2007] UKHL 52, [2008] 1 AC 719, [2008] 2 All ER 95. On rational connections see *A v Secretary of State for the Home Department* [2004] UKHL 56, [2005] 2 AC 68, [2005] 3 All ER 169. As to the minimal nature of the means see *De Freitas v Permanent Secretary of Ministry of Agriculture, Fisheries, Lands and Housing* [1999] 1 AC 69, [1998] 3 WLR 675, PC; *A v Secretary of State for the Home Department.* As to the balancing exercise as a distinct issue see *Huang v Secretary of State for the Home Department* [2007] UKHL 11, [2007] 2 AC 167, [2007] 4 All ER 15.

The test is different in relation to Article 1 of the First Protocol: *R (on the application of Clays Lanes Housing Co-operative Ltd) v Housing Corpn* [2004] EWCA Civ 1658, [2005] 1 WLR 2229.

19 This principle has been described as judicial deference or the 'margin of discretion' afforded to the legislature and executive by the courts: see *R v DPP, ex p Kebeline* [2000] 2 AC 326, [1999] 4 All ER 801, HL; *Brown v Stott* [2003] 1 AC 681, [2001] 2 All ER 97; *R (on the application of Isiko) v Secretary of State for the Home Department* [2001] 1 FCR 633, [2001] 1 FLR 930, CA; *R (on the application of Daly) v Secretary of State for the Home Department* [2001] UKHL 26, [2001] 2 AC 532, [2001] 3 All ER 433; *R (on the application of ProLife Alliance) v British Broadcasting Corpn* [2003] UKHL 23, [2004] 1 AC 185, [2003] 2 All ER 977. This is the ordinary judicial task of weighing up the competing considerations on each side and according appropriate weight to the judgment of the person with responsibility for a given subject matter and access to special sources of knowledge and advice: *Huang v Secretary of State for the Home Department* [2007] UKHL 11, [2007] 2 AC 167, [2007] 4 All ER 15.

20 The courts will allow a more extensive discretionary area of judgment to Parliament than to a minister or official: *R (on the application of Animal Defenders International) v Secretary of State for Culture, Media and Sport* [2008] UKHL 15, [2008] 1 AC 1312, [2008] 3 All ER 193.

21 *R v DPP, ex p Kebeline* [2000] 2 AC 326, [1999] 4 All ER 801, HL; *R (on the application of Isiko) v Secretary of State for the Home Department* [2001] 1 FCR 633, [2001] 1 FLR 930, CA (area of judgment to which court will defer in relation to immigration policies and the right to family life); *R (on the application of Saadi) v Secretary of State for the Home Department* [2002] UKHL 41, [2002] 4 All ER 785, [2002] 1 WLR 3131 (broad discretionary area of judgment in the context of immigration decisions because of rights under international law); *R (on the application of Samaroo) v Secretary of State for the Home Department* [2001] EWCA Civ 1139, [2001] 34 LS Gaz R 40; *R (on the application of Farrakhan) v Secretary of State for the Home Department* [2002] EWCA Civ 606, [2002] QB 1391, [2002] 4 All ER 289 (public order); *R v Secretary of State for the Environment, Transport and the Regions, ex p Spath Holme Ltd* [2001] 2 AC 349, [2001] 1 All ER 195, HL (allocation of public resources); *R (on the application of Carson) v Secretary of State for Work and Pensions* [2002] EWHC 978 (Admin), [2002] 3 All ER 994 (foreign relations). There is a greater degree of defence in matters of national security (*Secretary of State for the Home Department v Rehman* [2001] UKHL 47, [2003] 1 AC 153, [2002] 1 All ER 122), however, due deference does not mean abasement before the state's views and the ordinary principles must still be applied (*A v Secretary of State for the Home Department* [2004] UKHL 56, [2005] 2 AC 68, [2005] 3 All ER 169).

22 See *R v DPP, ex p Kebeline* [2000] 2 AC 326, [1999] 4 All ER 801, HL. This analysis includes consideration of the hierarchy of individual rights under the Human Rights Act 1998: *R v East Sussex County Council, ex p Reprotech (Pebsham) Ltd* [2002] UKHL 8, [2002] 4 All ER 58, [2003] 1 WLR 348.

23 For example criminal justice: *R v DPP, ex p Kebeline* [2000] 2 AC 326, [1999] 4 All ER 801, HL. See *R v Secretary of State for the Home Department, ex p Turgut* [2001] 1 All ER 719, [2000] Imm AR 306, CA (area of discretionary judgment in cases concerning the Convention for

the Protection of Human Rights and Fundamental Freedoms (1950) art 3 is narrow). The question is whether the court is especially well placed to assess whether an interference is necessary and proportionate: *R (on the application of the Countryside Alliance) v A-G* [2007] UKHL 52, [2008] 1 AC 719, [2008] 2 All ER 95.

24　See *R (on the application of Daly) v Secretary of State for the Home Department* [2001] UKHL 26, [2001] 2 AC 532, [2001] 3 All ER 433; *R (on the application of Begum) v Headteacher and Governors of Denbigh High School* [2006] UKHL 15, [2007] 1 AC 100, [2006] 2 All ER 487; *Miss Behavin' Ltd v Belfast City Council* [2007] UKHL 19, [2007] NI 89, [2007] 3 All ER 1007.

25　See the Human Rights Act 1998 s 8(1); and PARA 721.

26　Ie under the Human Rights Act 1998 s 4 (see CONSTITUTIONAL LAW AND HUMAN RIGHTS).

27　See the Human Rights Act 1998 s 8; and PARA 721. The court may not award damages in respect of a judicial act done in good faith except where compensation must be paid in respect of unlawful arrest or detention under the Convention for the Protection of Human Rights and Fundamental Freedoms (1950) art 5(5) (see CONSTITUTIONAL LAW AND HUMAN RIGHTS vol 8(2) (Reissue) PARA 127): see the Human Rights Act 1998 s 9(3); and note 9. See *Somerville v Scottish Ministers* [2007] UKHL 44, [2007] 1 WLR 2734 (the Human Rights Act 1998 s 8 does not exist to cap other remedies but to give the court power to grant further relief by way of damages if necessary to afford just satisfaction); *R (on the application of Greenfield) v Secretary of State for the Home Department* [2005] UKHL 14, [2005] 2 All ER 240, [2005] 1 WLR 673 (the question of compensation will usually be of secondary, if any, importance compared to bringing the infringement to an end).

652.　The right to a fair hearing. The Convention for the Protection of Human Rights and Fundamental Freedoms[1] is now largely incorporated into English law[2]. Primary and secondary legislation must, so far as is possible, be interpreted and applied in a way which is compatible with a Convention right[3]. In situations where no such interpretation is possible, the court may make a declaration of incompatibility[4]. It is unlawful for any public authority to act in a way which is incompatible with a Convention right unless the authority was required to act in that way by primary legislation[5].

In relation to issues of procedural fairness in public law the right to a fair hearing contained in the Convention for the Protection of Human Rights and Fundamental Freedoms is particularly relevant[6]. This provides for the right, in the determination of civil rights and obligations[7] or any criminal charge[8], to a fair[9] and public[10] hearing within a reasonable time[11] by an independent and impartial tribunal[12] established by law[13]. Following its incorporation into English law, this provision provides a further source of procedural standards. These are to be regarded as part of the duty to act fairly.

1　Ie the Convention for the Protection of Human Rights and Fundamental Freedoms (Rome, 4 November 1950; TS 71 (1953) Cmd 8969). As to the Convention see CONSTITUTIONAL LAW AND HUMAN RIGHTS vol 8(2) (Reissue) PARA 122 et seq.

2　See the Human Rights Act 1998 s 1 (see PARA 651). The Convention for the Protection of Human Rights and Fundamental Freedoms (1950) arts 1, 13 have not been incorporated: see the Human Rights Act 1998 s 1. As to the articles of the Convention for the Protection of Human Rights and Fundamental Freedoms (1950) which have been incorporated into English law see the Human Rights Act 1998 s 1(3), Sch 1. Similarly, the Protocols which have yet to be ratified by the United Kingdom government are not incorporated. The case law of the European Court of Human Rights is not formally binding on the English courts but, pursuant to s 2, must be taken into account by them. Prior to incorporation the courts nevertheless used the Convention as an aid to construction. Where a statute was ambiguous, a construction which was consistent with the Convention was normally preferred: see eg *R v Secretary of State for the Home Department, ex p Brind* [1991] 1 AC 696, sub nom *Brind v Secretary of State for the Home Department* [1991] 1 All ER 720, HL. See further CONSTITUTIONAL LAW AND HUMAN RIGHTS.

3　See the Human Rights Act 1998 s 3; and CONSTITUTIONAL LAW AND HUMAN RIGHTS. As to the meaning of 'Convention right' see PARA 651 note 1.

4　See the Human Rights Act 1998 s 4; and CONSTITUTIONAL LAW AND HUMAN RIGHTS. See eg *A v Secretary of State for the Home Department* [2004] UKHL 56, [2005] 2 AC 68, [2005] 3 All ER 169.

5   See the Human Rights Act 1998 s 6; and PARA 651. 'Public authority' is defined as including any court or tribunal, or any person certain of whose functions include functions of a public nature: see s 6(3); and PARA 651. However, a person is not a public authority by virtue only of being a person certain of whose functions include functions of a public nature if the nature of the act is private: see s 6(5); and PARA 651. However, the fact that courts and tribunals are themselves public authorities leaves open the possibility for the courts to develop the 'horizontal' effect of Convention rights, ie as between citizens, rather than merely the 'vertical' effect, ie as between citizens and public bodies. See further CONSTITUTIONAL LAW AND HUMAN RIGHTS.

6   In relation to criminal law and habeas corpus see also the Convention for the Protection of Human Rights and Fundamental Freedoms (1950) art 5 (the right to liberty and security of the person): see CONSTITUTIONAL LAW AND HUMAN RIGHTS vol 8(2) (Reissue) PARA 127. As to habeas corpus see ADMINISTRATIVE LAW.

7   This does not extend to administrative matters: see CONSTITUTIONAL LAW AND HUMAN RIGHTS vol 8(2) (Reissue) PARA 135.

8   This does not generally extend to disciplinary matters: see CONSTITUTIONAL LAW AND HUMAN RIGHTS vol 8(2) (Reissue) PARA 136. The Convention for the Protection of Human Rights and Fundamental Freedoms (1950) art 6(3) confers a number of further specific rights upon defendants in criminal cases: see CONSTITUTIONAL LAW AND HUMAN RIGHTS vol 8(2) (Reissue) PARA 134.

9   This entails principles similar to the English law concept of *audi alteram partem*, and also matters such as access to legal advice. As in English law, an oral hearing is not held to be necessary in all cases: see CONSTITUTIONAL LAW AND HUMAN RIGHTS vol 8(2) (Reissue) PARA 137. As to the English law concept of *audi alteram partem* see PARA 639.

10 See CONSTITUTIONAL LAW AND HUMAN RIGHTS vol 8(2) (Reissue) PARA 138.

11 See CONSTITUTIONAL LAW AND HUMAN RIGHTS vol 8(2) (Reissue) PARA 139.

12 Where an appeal is possible the tribunal will normally have to give reasons for its decision: see CONSTITUTIONAL LAW AND HUMAN RIGHTS vol 8(2) (Reissue) PARA 140.

13 See the Convention for the Protection of Human Rights and Fundamental Freedoms (1950) art 6(1); and CONSTITUTIONAL LAW AND HUMAN RIGHTS vol 8(2) (Reissue) PARA 13 et seq.

653.   The application of the right to a fair hearing to civil proceedings.   In relation to civil proceedings, the right to a fair hearing contained in the Convention for the Protection of Human Rights and Fundamental Freedoms[1] applies if the civil rights and obligations of the applicant are in issue, there is a dispute as to those civil rights and obligations, and the proceedings in question are determinative of those civil rights and obligations.

Civil rights and obligations are rights and obligations which arise in private law, rather than in public law. Thus administrative decisions which affect private law rights[2] fall within the scope of the Convention's protection. However, the distinction in English law between public law rights and private law rights is not determinative as to whether or not a civil right or obligation is in issue for the purposes of the Convention[3]. The dispute in question must relate to the existence of the right, or its scope, or the manner of its exercise, and the decision must have a direct effect on the rights and obligations in issue[4]. The proceedings must either determine the civil rights and obligations, or such determination must be an inevitable consequence of the proceedings[5].

1   Ie the Convention for the Protection of Human Rights and Fundamental Freedoms (Rome, 4 November 1950; TS 71 (1953) Cmd 8969) art 6: see PARA 652; and CONSTITUTIONAL LAW AND HUMAN RIGHTS vol 8(2) (Reissue) PARA 134 et seq.

2   For example property rights (see *Bryan v United Kingdom* (1995) 21 EHRR 342). See *R (on the application of Alconbury Developments Ltd) v Secretary of State for the Environment, Transport and the Regions* [2001] UKHL 23, [2003] 2 AC 295, [2001] 2 All ER 929; *Begum v Tower Hamlets London Borough Council* [2003] UKHL 5, [2003] 2 AC 430, [2003] 1 All ER 731 (entitlement to state benefits). Permanent exclusion from school is the determination of a civil right, but temporary exclusion is not: *R (on the application of B) v Head Teacher of Alperton Community School* [2001] EWHC Admin 229, [2002] LGR 132; *R (on the application of S) v Brent London Borough Council* [2002] EWCA Civ 693, [2002] ELR 556. The termination of an introductory or demoted tenancy is the determination of civil right: *R (on the*

application of McLellan) v Bracknell Forest Borough Council [2001] EWCA Civ 1510, [2002] QB 1129, [2002] 1 All ER 899; *R (on the application of Gilboy) v Liverpool City Council* [2008] EWCA Civ 751, [2008] 4 All ER 127, [2009] 3 WLR 300. However, accommodation rights under the Children Act 1989 s 20 (see CHILDREN AND YOUNG PERSONS vol 5(4) (2008 Reissue) PARA 863) involve evaluative judgments and therefore the Convention for the Protection of Human Rights and Fundamental Freedoms (1950) art 6 does not apply: *R (on the application of M) v Lambeth London Borough Council* [2008] EWCA Civ 1445, [2009] LGR 24, [2009] 1 FCR 317.

3   There are various decisions of the European Court of Human Rights to the effect that the categorisation of rights in national law as either public or private is not determinative for the purposes of the Convention: see e g *Ringeisen v Austria* (1971) 1 EHRR 455, ECtHR; *Anca v Belgium* (1984) 40 D & R 170 (decisions of the state affecting property rights within scope of the article); *Pudas v Sweden* (1987) 10 EHRR 380, ECtHR (licensing decision within scope of the article); *W v United Kingdom* (1987) 10 EHRR 29, ECtHR (decision relating to custody of and access to children within scope of the article); *Simpson v United Kingdom* (1989) 64 D & R 188 (decision relating to parental preference rights as to state education outside scope of the article). See also on this point *R v Richmond-upon-Thames London Borough Council, ex p JC* [2000] ELR 565, CA. In general, in order to decide whether a civil right or obligation is in issue the court will balance the public and private features of the obligation. The factors which will be relevant to this exercise will include those which relate to the importance of the interest at stake and the impact of the decision on the individual which the English courts presently take into account when determining the scope and content of the duty to act fairly: see PARAS 629–630.

4   *Van Marle v Netherlands* (1986) 8 EHRR 483, ECtHR. Note that there will be no dispute when the right claimed is not recognised under national law: *H v Belgium* (1987) 10 EHRR 339, ECtHR; *Powell and Rayner v United Kingdom* (1990) 12 EHRR 355. See *Vilho Eskelinen v Finland* (2007) 45 EHRR 985, ECtHR. The dispute must be at least arguably recognised under domestic law: *R v Lord Chancellor, ex p Lightfoot* [2000] QB 597, [1999] 4 All ER 583, CA. The dispute must be genuine and serious: *Begum v Tower Hamlets London Borough Council* [2003] UKHL 5, [2003] 2 AC 430, [2003] 1 All ER 731. The Convention for the Protection of Human Rights and Fundamental Freedoms (1950) art 6 does not impose any obligation on a state to create additional civil rights: *Matthews v Ministry of Defence* [2003] UKHL 4, [2003] 1 AC 1163, [2003] 1 All ER 689.

5   See e g *Ringeisen v Austria* (1971) 1 EHRR 455, ECtHR; *Fayed v United Kingdom* (1994) 18 EHRR 393 at 427–428, ECtHR. For examples in the domestic courts see *Southwark London Borough Council v St Brice* [2001] EWCA Civ 1138, [2002] 1 WLR 1537, [2002] LGR 117; *R (on the application of Thompson) v Law Society* [2004] EWCA Civ 167, [2004] 2 All ER 113, [2004] 1 WLR 2522; *R (on the application of M) Secretary of State for Constitutional Affairs and Lord Chancellor* [2004] EWCA Civ 312, [2004] 2 All ER 531, [2004] 1 WLR 2298; *R (on the application of Wright) v Secretary of State for Health* [2009] UKHL 3, [2009] 1 AC 739, [2009] 2 All ER 129 (provisional listing amounted to the determination of a civil right, even though the listed person would eventually have the opportunity of taking the case before the Care Standards Tribunal). Applications for interim relief fall outside the scope of the Convention for the Protection of Human Rights and Fundamental Freedoms (1950) art 6 (see CONSTITUTIONAL LAW AND HUMAN RIGHTS vol 8(2) (Reissue) PARA 134 et seq): *X v United Kingdom* (1981) 24 D & R 57.

654.   The requirements of the right to a fair hearing.   The Convention for the Protection of Human Rights and Fundamental Freedoms provides a right to a hearing which is fair, held in public, takes place within a reasonable time, and is conducted by an independent and impartial tribunal established by law[1].

With regard to the right to a hearing in the context of the administrative decision-making process, one key issue which arises is whether the fact that an administrative decision may be subject to judicial review satisfies the requirement of effective access to a court. The sufficiency of judicial review will depend on the subject matter of the decision, the content of the dispute (including the grounds of appeal) and whether the Administrative Court could cure any defects[2].

The concept of what amounts to a fair hearing is a flexible one[3]. In this respect, the requirements of the provision in a civil context reflect the requirements of the common law duty to act fairly[4]. The right to a public hearing is subject to the express derogations contained within the Convention[5]. Any decision to hold a hearing in private must be necessary to achieve one of these purposes and must also be a proportionate action in all the circumstances of the case[6]. The hearing must also take place within a reasonable time[7].

Whether or not a tribunal is independent will depend on a consideration of all material circumstances. These will include the manner of appointment of the tribunal[8], the duration of the term of office[9], the presence of guarantees, if any, against outside interference[10], the extent to which the judicial role is combined with other rules[11], and whether the tribunal has the appearance of independence[12]. The requirement of impartiality is in substance the same as the common law rule against bias[13].

1   See the Convention for the Protection of Human Rights and Fundamental Freedoms (Rome, 4 November 1950; TS 71 (1953) Cmd 8969) art 6; and CONSTITUTIONAL LAW AND HUMAN RIGHTS vol 8(2) (Reissue) PARA 134 et seq.

2   In *Begum v Tower Hamlets London Borough Council* [2003] UKHL 5, [2003] 2 AC 430, [2003] 1 All ER 731, the House of Lords held that whilst a local housing review officer taking decisions under the Housing Act 1996 Pt VII (ss 175–218) (see HOUSING vol 22 (2006 Reissue) PARA 275 et seq) was not an independent and impartial tribunal, the right of appeal to the County Court on issues of law was sufficient to ensure compliance with the Convention for the Protection of Human Rights and Fundamental Freedoms (1950) art 6(1). Similarly, see the Court of Appeal decision in *R (on the application of McLellan) v Bracknell Forest Borough Council* [2001] EWCA Civ 1510, [2002] QB 1129, [2002] 1 All ER 899. Contrast *Tsfayo v United Kingdon* (2006) 48 EHRR 457, [2007] LGR 1, where it was found that there was non-compliance with the Convention for the Protection of Human Rights and Fundamental Freedoms (1950) art 6 where the Housing Benefit Review Board was not independent and the central issue, namely the credibility of the applicant, could not be determined on appeal. The Court of Appeal followed *Begum v Tower Hamlets London Borough Council* and *R (on the application of McLellan) v Bracknell Forest Borough Council* in *R (on the application of Gilboy) v Liverpool City Council* [2008] EWCA Civ 751, [2008] 4 All ER 127, [2009] 3 WLR 300 (finding compliance with the Convention for the Protection of Human Rights and Fundamental Freedoms (1950) art 6 for extremely similar statutory language to that in *R (on the application of McLellan) v Bracknell Forest Borough Council*). For other domestic cases considering the impact of the Convention for the Protection of Human Rights and Fundamental Freedoms (1950) art 6 see also *R (on the application of Alconbury Developments Ltd) v Secretary of State for the Environment, Transport and the Regions* [2001] UKHL 23, [2003] 2 AC 295, [2001] 2 All ER 929; *Tehrani v United Kingdom Central Council for Nursing, Midwifery and Health Visiting* [2001] IRLR 208, 2001 SLT 879, Ct of Sess; *R (on the application of A) v Croydon London Borough Council* [2009] UKSC 8, [2009] 1 WLR 2557; *R (on the application of Thompson) v Law Society* [2004] EWCA Civ 167, [2004] 2 All ER 113, [2004] 1 WLR 2522; *R (Wright) v Secretary for Health* [2009] UKHL 3, [2009] 1 AC 739. See also *Ali v Birmingham City Council* [2008] EWCA Civ 1228, [2009] 2 All ER 510, [2009] LGR 1; *R (on the application of M) v Lambeth London Borough Council* [2008] EWCA Civ 1445, [2009] LGR 24, [2009] 1 FCR 317.

3   See for example *Golder v United Kingdom* (1975) 1 EHRR 524, ECtHR. In general the European Court of Human Rights has tended to look at the process as a whole and determine whether the irregularity alleged has had a material impact on the fairness of the proceedings: see eg *CG v United Kingdom* (2001) 34 EHRR 31, ECtHR. However, the right to an independent tribunal is absolute and therefore if the tribunal is not independent it is irrelevant whether the proceedings overall were fair: *Millar v Dickson (Procurator Fiscal, Elgin)* [2001] UKPC D4, [2002] 3 All ER 1041, [2002] 1 WLR 1615.

4   As to the common law duty to act fairly see PARA 629 et seq.

5   Namely in the interests of morals, public order, national security, where the interests of juveniles or the protection of the private lives of the parties require, or where publicity would prejudice the interests of justice: see the Convention for the Protection of Human Rights and Fundamental Freedoms (1950) art 6(1); and CONSTITUTIONAL LAW AND HUMAN RIGHTS vol 8(2) (Reissue) PARA 134.

6 *Campbell and Fell v United Kingdom* (1984) 7 EHRR 165, ECtHR (disciplinary proceedings before prison board of visitors); *Monnell and Morris v United Kingdom* (1987) 10 EHRR 205 (it is necessary to look at the procedure as a whole to determine whether this requirement is satisfied).

7 Breaches of this requirement are usually measured in years rather than months: see eg *Darnell v United Kingdom* (1993) 18 EHRR 205, ECtHR; *Mitchell v United Kingdom* (2003) 36 EHRR 951, (2002) 14 BHRC 431, ECtHR. However, the quantity of delay is not the determining factor. The court will also look at the impact of the delay on the individual and on the quality of the decision. No legitimate complaint should arise when the delay is caused by the applicant's own conduct, although any delay that is indirectly attributable to the state may amount to non-compliance: *Pafitis v Greece* (1998) 27 EHRR 566.

8 Appointment by the executive is normal, and does not of itself raise an inference of dependency: see eg *Starrs v Ruxton* 2000 JC 208, 2000 SLT 42.

9 See eg *Campbell and Fell v United Kingdom* (1984) 7 EHRR 165, ECtHR (three year term of office warranted for unpaid post); *R v Spear* [2002] UKHL 31, [2003] 1 AC 734, [2002] 3 All ER 1074 (four year appointment did not lead to inference of a lack of independence); but cf *Starrs v Ruxton* 2000 JC 208, 2000 SLT 42 (temporary appointment which could be terminated other than for cause fatal; thus temporary sheriffs did not meet the requirements of the Convention for the Protection of Human Rights and Fundamental Freedoms (1950) art 6).

10 See *Bryan v United Kingdom* (1995) 21 EHRR 342, ECtHR (power of Secretary of State to terminate appointment of inspector at will important indication of lack of independence). In fact, any power to remove save for misconduct or other exceptional reason may lead to a conclusion that the decision-maker is not independent. But the court will also look to the position in practice as well as what could technically happen: see *R v Spear* [2002] UKHL 31, [2003] 1 AC 734, [2002] 3 All ER 1074. In that case the court also assessed the general circumstances surrounding the appointment and conduct of courts martial in order to determine whether the requirement of independence was satisfied. This was applied in *R (on the application of D) v West Midlands and North West Mental Health Review Tribunal* [2003] EWHC 2469 (Admin), [2003] 48 LS Gaz R 17, [2003] All ER (D) 408 (Oct).

11 The combination in Sark of the judicial with the other functions of the Seneschal was inconsistent with the requirement of the Convention for the Protection of Human Rights and Fundamental Freedoms (1950) art 6 to establish by law an independent and impartial tribunal: *R (on the application of Barclay) v Secretary of State for Justice and the Lord Chancellor* [2008] EWCA Civ 1319, [2009] 2 WLR 1205, [2008] All ER (D) 32 (Dec). This point was not challenged on appeal to the Supreme Court: see *R (on the application of Barclay) v Secretary of State for Justice and the Lord Chancellor* [2009] UKSC 9, [2009] 3 WLR 1270, [2009] All ER (D) 15 (Dec).

12 See *Findlay v United Kingdom* (1997) 24 EHRR 221, ECtHR; *Coyne v United Kingdom* [1998] EHRLR 91. As to courts martial see *R v Spear* [2002] UKHL 31, [2003] 1 AC 734, [2002] 3 All ER 1074 (proceedings were now compliant with the Convention for the Protection of Human Rights and Fundamental Freedoms (1950) art 6).

13 See *R v Cambridge University, ex p Begg* (1999) 11 Admin LR 505, [1999] ELR 404; cf *Holm v Sweden* (1993) 18 EHRR 79, ECtHR. As to the common law rule against bias see PARAS 631–638.

3. BARRIERS TO JUDICIAL REVIEW

655. Exclusion of judicial control. Sometimes Parliament enacts formulae which are designed to protect administrative orders and determinations against judicial review by describing them as final, or by providing that no appeal or review will lie against them. These exclusions are construed restrictively so as not to deprive the courts of their supervisory jurisdiction. The courts remain entitled to review a decision on the traditional grounds on which an application for judicial review may be made. If the purported decision is ultra vires because the decision-maker did not have jurisdiction to make a decision, or because he misconstrued his powers, or because he acted in bad faith or contrary to the requirements of natural justice, or because he took into account irrelevant matters or failed to consider relevant matters, then there is no 'decision' to which the statutory exclusion can apply[1]. If a statute provides that the decision of a tribunal is to be final, the general rule is that no appeal to a court will lie against any such decision[2]. However, there is a presumption against ousting the jurisdiction of the courts to determine the ambit of civil rights and obligations[3], so that statutory language is seldom interpreted so as to exclude or attenuate the supervisory jurisdiction of the courts[4]. The fact that the evidence of a state of affairs on which the jurisdiction of a tribunal depends is expressed to be determinable by reference to the satisfaction or opinion of that tribunal does not bar a superior court from determining that very question[5].

On the other hand, the original jurisdiction of the superior courts may be indirectly ousted if the law regards some other body as having exclusive jurisdiction to resolve particular disputes[6], or where a statute creates a new legal right or obligation and prescribes a specific method for its enforcement, whether this method is by way of proceedings before an inferior court or tribunal[7] or by way of complaint or appeal to an administrative authority[8]. If recourse to the prescribed procedure is held to be mandatory[9], a superior court will not permit a party to raise the relevant issues before it in declaratory or other proceedings instead of before the designated body[10]. Modern examples are rare. Whether the court will regard its original jurisdiction as having been excluded[11] is primarily a question of statutory construction[12]. Where there is an alternative remedy, and jurisdiction has not been ousted expressly or by implication, the court has a discretion whether or not to grant judicial review. Its exercise depends on a number of factors: whether there has been misfeasance[13]; whether the act in question is ultra vires[14]; whether the statute is one which encroaches on existing legal rights[15]; whether there is an issue as to whether the circumstances fall outside the ambit of the prescribed procedure[16]; whether the prescribed alternative remedy is inadequate[17]; and whether there is any other reason why the interests of justice call for the intervention of the court[18]. If the body vested with exclusive original jurisdiction has purported to determine the matter, the validity of its decision can thereafter be impugned before a superior court exercising its supervisory jurisdiction in an appropriate form of proceedings[19]; and if the court declares that decision to be invalid, it may be prepared to declare what was the correct decision, if such a decision is implicit in the finding of invalidity[20]. The courts cannot, however, redetermine a question already validly determined by the designated body, save where that determination is not res judicata[21], or possibly where the consequence of a new determination would render the original erroneous determination unenforceable or where that body has power to rescind its own decision[22], for such an assertion of jurisdiction will be akin to an arrogation of appellate jurisdiction where none has been conferred[23].

1 For examples of a narrow construction see *R v Medical Appeal Tribunal, ex p Gilmore* [1957] 1 QB 574, [1957] 1 All ER 796, CA; *Anisminic Ltd v Foreign Compensation Commission* [1969] 2 AC 147, [1969] 1 All ER 208, HL; *R v Secretary of State for the Environment, ex p Stewart* (1978) 37 P & CR 279, DC; *A-G v Ryan* [1980] AC 718, [1980] 2 WLR 143, PC; *Islington London Borough Council v Secretary of State for the Environment* (1980) 43 P & CR 300 at 304; *Ex p Waldron* [1986] QB 824, sub nom *R v Hallstrom, ex p W* [1985] 3 All ER 775, CA; *R v Secretary of State for the Home Department, ex p Fayed* [1997] 1 All ER 228 at 235–237, [1998] 1 WLR 763 at 771–773, CA, per Lord Woolf MR; and see *HTV Ltd v Price Commission* [1976] ICR 170 at 188, CA, per Scarman LJ; cf *Spackman v Plumstead District Board of Works* (1885) 10 App Cas 229; *R v Smith* (1984) 48 P & CR 392, CA; *Farley v Child Support Agency* [2006] UKHL 31, [2006] 2 FCR 713, sub nom *Farley v Secretary of State for Work and Pensions* [2006] 3 All ER 935. As to the grounds on which an application for judicial review may be made see PARA 602.

2 *Westminster Corpn v Gordon Hotels Ltd* [1908] AC 142, HL; *Kydd v Liverpool Watch Committee* [1908] AC 327, HL; *Piper v St Marylebone Licensing Justices* [1928] 2 KB 221, DC; *Hall v Arnold* [1950] 2 KB 543, [1950] 1 All ER 993, DC (inferior tribunals); cf *R (on the application of AM (Cameroon)) v Asylum and Immigration Tribunal* [2008] EWCA Civ 100, [2008] 4 All ER 1159, [2008] 1 WLR 2062; and see ADMINISTRATIVE LAW vol 1(1) (2001 Reissue) PARA 21. See also *Re Racal Communications Ltd* [1981] AC 374, [1980] 2 All ER 634 (where a statutory provision makes the decision of a court of law final there is no appeal, either in respect of errors of fact or of law).

3 See eg *R (on the application of Sivasubramaniam) v Wandsworth County Court* [2002] EWCA Civ 1738, [2003] 2 All ER 160, [2003] 1 WLR 475; *R (on the application of G) v Immigration Appeal Tribunal* [2004] EWCA Civ 1731, [2005] 2 All ER 165, [2005] 1 WLR 1445; *R (on the application of Cart) v Upper Tribunal* [2009] EWHC 3052 (Admin). See ADMINISTRATIVE LAW vol 1(1) (2001 Reissue) PARA 21; STATUTES vol 44(1) (Reissue) PARA 1349.

4 As to the scope of supervisory jurisdiction see generally PARA 601.

5 See ADMINISTRATIVE LAW vol 1(1) (2001 Reissue) PARA 21.

6 Eg university visitors have exclusive jurisdiction to determine matters which, in accordance with the relevant regulating documents, they are empowered to determine (subject to the Higher Education Act 2004 Pt 2 (ss 11–21), Pt 5 (ss 46–54)): see further PARA 630 note 25; and EDUCATION vol 15(2) (2006 Reissue) PARAS 656 et seq, 1040 et seq. Accordingly judicial review will not lie in respect of any matter which falls within the exclusive jurisdiction of the visitor; it will lie only on the grounds that the visitor has taken action which he was not empowered to take, has abused his powers, or that he has acted in breach of the rules of natural justice: see *Thomas v University of Bradford* [1987] AC 795, [1987] 1 All ER 834, HL; *R v Lord President of the Privy Council, ex p Page* [1993] AC 682, sub nom *Page v Hull University Visitor* [1993] 1 All ER 97, HL; *R v Visitors to the Inns of Court, ex p Calder* [1994] QB 1, [1993] 2 All ER 876, CA.

7 Eg as in eg *Barraclough v Brown* [1897] AC 615, HL; *Wilkes v Gee* [1973] 2 All ER 1214, [1973] 1 WLR 742, CA; *Argosam Finance Co Ltd v Oxby (Inspector of Taxes)* [1965] Ch 390, [1964] 3 All ER 561, CA; *Autologic Holdings plc v IRC* [2005] UKHL 54, [2006] 1 AC 118, [2005] 4 All ER 1141.

8 *Wolverhampton New Waterworks Co v Hawkesford* (1859) 6 CBNS 336 at 356 per Willes J (an analogous situation); *Doe d Bishop of Rochester v Bridges* (1831) 1 B & Ad 847 at 859 per Lord Tenterden LCJ. See also *Robinson v Workington Corpn* [1897] 1 QB 619, CA; *Pasmore v Oswaldtwistle UDC* [1898] AC 387, HL; *Watt v Kesteven County Council* [1955] 1 QB 408, [1955] 1 All ER 473, CA; *Wood v Ealing London Borough Council* [1967] Ch 364, [1966] 3 All ER 514; *Cumings v Birkenhead Corpn* [1972] Ch 12, [1971] 2 All ER 881, CA; *Southwark London Borough Council v Williams* [1971] Ch 734, [1971] 2 All ER 175, CA; *Wyatt v Hillingdon London Borough Council* (1978) 76 LGR 727, DC; *Cowl v Plymouth City Council* [2001] EWCA Civ 1935, [2002] 1 WLR 803; *Marcic v Thames Water Utilities Ltd* [2003] UKHL 66, [2004] 2 AC 42, [2004] 1 All ER 135. Conversely, the absence of any such remedy is an argument in favour of the decision being susceptible to judicial review: *R v Local Comr for Administration for the South, the West, the West Midlands, Leicestershire, Lincolnshire and Cambridgeshire, ex p Eastleigh Borough Council* [1988] QB 855, [1988] 3 All ER 151, CA.

9 Recourse to the appointed tribunal may be obligatory although the working of the statute may be ex facie permissive: see *Crisp v Bunbury* (1832) 8 Bing 394; *Barraclough v Brown* [1897] AC

615, HL; though cf *Pyx Granite Co Ltd v Ministry of Housing and Local Government* [1960] AC 260, [1959] 3 All ER 1, HL (the distinction in those cases is between a new statutory right with a statutory mode of enforcement and an existing common law right which has not been expressly removed by a new statutory remedy); *A-G (Duchy of Lancaster) v Simcock* [1966] Ch 1, [1965] 2 All ER 32.

10 Leading cases include: *R v Hillingdon London Borough Council, ex p Royco Homes Ltd* [1974] QB 720 at 728–729, [1974] 2 All ER 643 at 648–649, DC (certiorari (now a quashing order: see PARAS 687 note 1, 688) will only go where there is no other equally effective and convenient remedy); *R v Epping and Harlow General Comrs, ex p Goldstraw* [1983] 3 All ER 257 at 262, CA (where other remedies are available and not used, the residual discretion to grant judicial review is only to be exercised in the most exceptional circumstances); *Re Preston* [1985] AC 835 at 852, [1985] 2 All ER 327 at 330, HL, per Lord Scarman, and at 862 and 337 per Lord Templeman; *R v Chief Constable of the Merseyside Police, ex p Calveley* [1986] QB 424, [1986] 1 All ER 257, CA. See also *Barraclough v Brown* [1897] AC 615, HL; *Wilkinson v Barking Corpn* [1948] 1 KB 721, [1948] 1 All ER 564, CA (distinguished in *Fullbrook v Berkshire Magistrates' Courts Committee* (1970) 69 LGR 75); *Gillingham Corpn v Kent County Council* [1953] Ch 37, [1952] 2 All ER 1107; *Argosam Finance Co Ltd v Oxby (Inspector of Taxes)* [1965] Ch 390 at 416, [1964] 3 All ER 561, CA; *A-G (Duchy of Lancaster) v Simcock* [1966] Ch 1, [1965] 2 All ER 32 (where *Jones v Gates* [1954] 1 All ER 158, [1954] 1 WLR 222, CA, was distinguished); *Jones v Pembrokeshire County Council* [1967] 1 QB 181, [1966] 1 All ER 1027; *Harrison v Croydon London Borough Council* [1968] Ch 479, [1967] 2 All ER 589; *Re Al-Fin Corpn's Patent* [1970] Ch 160, [1969] 3 All ER 396; *Vandervell Trustees Ltd v White* [1971] AC 912, [1970] 3 All ER 16, HL; *Department of Health and Social Security v Walker Dean Walker Ltd* [1970] 2 QB 74, [1970] 1 All ER 757. See also *Crisp v Bunbury* (1832) 8 Bing 394; *Joseph Crosfield & Sons Ltd v Manchester Ship Canal Co* [1904] 2 Ch 123, CA (affd on this point [1905] AC 421, HL); *Pasmore v Oswaldtwistle UDC* [1898] AC 387, HL; *Hanson v Church Comrs for England* [1978] QB 823, [1977] 3 All ER 404, CA; *R v IRC, ex p Opman International UK* [1986] 1 All ER 328 at 330, [1986] 1 WLR 568 at 571 per Woolf J; *R v Panel on Take-overs and Mergers, ex p Guinness plc* [1990] 1 QB 146 at 177, [1989] 1 All ER 509 at 526, CA, per Lord Donaldson MR, at 183–184 and 530–531 per Lloyd LJ, and at 201 and 544 per Woolf LJ; *R v London VAT Tribunal, ex p Theodorou* [1989] STC 292.

11 The existence of the alternative remedy goes to discretion rather than to jurisdiction, but it may be a ground for refusing leave to apply for judicial review: *R v Board of Visitors of Hull Prison, ex p St Germain* [1979] QB 425 at 455–456, [1979] 1 All ER 701 at 717, CA, per Shaw LJ, and at 465 and 724–725 per Waller LJ; *R v Secretary of State for the Environment, ex p Ward* [1984] 2 All ER 556 at 565–566, [1984] 1 WLR 834 at 844–845 per Woolf J, distinguishing *Kensington and Chelsea London Borough Council v Wells* (1973) 72 LGR 289, CA; *Leech v Deputy Governor of Parkhurst Prison* [1988] AC 533 at 561, [1988] 1 All ER 485 at 486, HL, per Lord Bridge of Harwich, and at 580–581 and 510–511 per Lord Oliver of Aylmerton; *R (on the application of Sivasubramaniam) v Wandsworth County Court* [2002] EWCA Civ 1738, [2003] 2 All ER 160, [2003] 1 WLR 475; *R (on the application of RK (Nepal)) v Secretary of State for the Home Department* [2009] EWCA Civ 359, [2009] All ER (D) 226 (Apr); and see further PARA 657 note 1.

12 See e g *R v Secretary of State for the Environment, ex p Ostler* [1977] QB 122, [1976] 3 All ER 90, CA; *R v Cornwall County Council, ex p Huntington* [1994] 1 All ER 694, CA; and see also *R (on the application of Richards) v Pembrokeshire County Council* [2004] EWCA Civ 1000, [2005] LGR 105.

13 See *Bradbury v Enfield London Borough Council* [1967] 3 All ER 434 at 442, [1967] 1 WLR 1311 at 1326, CA, per Diplock LJ (court remedy available in cases of malfeasance but not in cases of nonfeasance); *Wilkes v Gee* [1973] 2 All ER 1214, [1973] 1 WLR 742, CA ('wholly lacking in bona fides'); *Meade v Haringey London Borough Council* [1979] 2 All ER 1016 at 1031–1032, [1979] 1 WLR 637 at 655, CA, per Sir Stanley Rees. In *R v Chief Constable of the Merseyside Police, ex p Calveley* [1986] QB 424, [1986] 1 All ER 257, CA, the seriousness of the departure from proper procedure (significant delay amounting to an abuse of process) was treated as a ground for allowing judicial review despite failure to resort to an internal appeal provided for by disciplinary regulations. See also *R v Ealing London Borough Council, ex p Times Newspapers Ltd* (1986) 85 LGR 316, DC.

14 See *R v Hillingdon London Borough Council, ex p Royco Homes Ltd* [1974] QB 720, [1974] 2 All ER 643, DC; cf *Roberts v Dorset County Council* (1976) 75 LGR 462; *Meade v Haringey London Borough Council* [1979] 2 All ER 1016 at 1024–1025, [1979] 1 WLR 637 at 646–647, CA, per Lord Denning MR; *Re Preston* [1985] AC 835 at 862, [1985] 2 All ER 327 at 337–338, HL, per Lord Templeman (assuming that the appeal procedure there laid down

could not operate because the initial action was unlawful). See also *Calvin v Carr* [1980] AC 574, [1979] 2 All ER 440, PC (but this case concerned a hearing and appeal governed by contract); *R v Chief Constable of the Merseyside Police, ex p Calveley* [1986] QB 424 at 437, [1986] 1 All ER 257 at 265, CA, per May LJ. This approach may only be correct if a narrow, pre-*Anisminic Ltd v Foreign Compensation Commission* [1969] 2 AC 147, [1969] 1 All ER 208, HL (see note 1) approach to errors going to jurisdiction is taken: cf *R (on the application of Sivasubramaniam) v Wandsworth County Court* [2002] EWCA Civ 1738 at [56], [2003] 2 All ER 160 at [56] per Lord Phillips of Worth Matravers MR (a case where judicial review was not ousted); and see *R v Secretary of State for the Environment, ex p Ward* [1984] 2 All ER 556 at 565, [1984] 1 WLR 834 at 844 per Woolf J (the existence of an alternative remedy may be a restriction on the right of access to the court where it is sought to vindicate public law, rather than private law rights). See also the cases cited in note 16.

15 *Pyx Granite Co Ltd v Ministry of Housing and Local Government* [1960] AC 260, [1959] 3 All ER 1, HL (planning restrictions on rights of property owner); *Trafford v Ashby* (1969) 21 P & CR 293 (commons registration).

16 *Pyx Granite Co Ltd v Ministry of Housing and Local Government* [1960] AC 260, [1959] 3 All ER 1, HL (question whether planning permission required); *Stevens v Bromley London Borough Council* [1972] Ch 400, [1972] 1 All ER 712, CA (whether enforcement notice valid at all); cf *Winner Investments Ltd v Hammersmith London Borough Council* (1966) 64 LGR 447; *Ealing London Borough v Race Relations Board* [1972] AC 342, [1972] 1 All ER 105, HL (plaintiff claiming declaration that the case was not covered by the relevant Act); *Thorne v British Broadcasting Corpn* [1967] 2 All ER 1225, [1967] 1 WLR 1104, CA; *Meade v Haringey London Borough Council* [1979] 2 All ER 1016 at 1028, [1979] 1 WLR 637 at 651, CA, per Eveleigh LJ (minister's default powers directed to simple or single failure rather than deliberate decision by authority not to carry out statutory duty). See also *Booker v James* (1968) 19 P & CR 525; *Trafford v Ashby* (1969) 21 P & CR 293; *Thorne RDC v Bunting* [1972] Ch 470, [1972] 1 All ER 439 (court had jurisdiction to declare claims as to rights of common inasmuch as the statutory machinery for determining them had not yet been brought into operation); cf *Wilkes v Gee* [1973] 2 All ER 1214, [1973] 1 WLR 742, CA (for the position once statutory machinery is operational).

17 The court should ask itself which is the more effective and convenient remedy in all the circumstances, not merely for the applicant, but also in the public interest: *R v Huntingdon District Council, ex p Cowan* [1984] 1 All ER 58, [1984] 1 WLR 501; and see also *R v Paddington Valuation Officer, ex p Peachey Property Corpn Ltd* [1966] 1 QB 380 at 400, [1965] 2 All ER 836 at 840, CA, per Lord Denning MR (judicial review available where statutory remedy 'nowhere near so convenient, beneficial and effectual', but refused on the facts); cf *R v Chief Constable of the Merseyside Police, ex p Calveley* [1986] QB 424 at 436, [1986] 1 All ER 257 at 264, CA, per May LJ (the mere fact that judicial review is somewhat more efficient or convenient is not enough; judicial review granted on the facts). Where a statute provides a remedy for the normal case, an applicant seeking to bypass it will have to show that there is something special about his case: *Wilkes v Gee* [1973] 2 All ER 1214, [1973] 1 WLR 742, CA; *R v Secretary of State for the Home Department, ex p Swati* [1986] 1 All ER 717, [1986] 1 WLR 477, CA. It may also be sufficient that there is a mere discretion to review as opposed to a formal appeal procedure which can be invoked as of right (*R v Board of Visitors of Hull Prison, ex p St Germain* [1979] QB 425 at 448–449, [1979] 1 All ER 701 at 711–712, CA, per Megaw LJ, and at 465 and 725 per Waller LJ), or that the alternative remedy could not provide rectification of the record (*Leech v Deputy Governor of Parkhurst Prison* [1988] AC 533 at 567, [1988] 1 All ER 485 at 500, HL, per Lord Bridge of Harwich, and at 582 and 512 per Lord Oliver of Aylmerton). Other factors to be taken into account include whether the statutory remedy will be quicker or slower, whether it involves technical matters within the particular competence of the statutory appeal body, and whether it will be a means of resolving all outstanding issues together: *Ex p Waldron* [1986] QB 824 at 852, sub nom *R v Hallstrom, ex p W* [1985] 3 All ER 775 at 789–790, CA, obiter per Glidewell LJ; and see *Re Preston* [1985] AC 835 at 862, [1985] 2 All ER 327 at 337, HL, per Lord Templeman. See also *Sivyer v Amies* [1940] 3 All ER 285; *A-G (ex rel McWhirter) v Independent Broadcasting Authority* [1973] QB 629, [1973] 1 All ER 689, CA. See also the authorities on civil liability for breach of statutory duty set out in ADMINISTRATIVE LAW vol 1(1) (2001 Reissue) PARAS 182–190.

18 See e g *Enderby Town Football Club Ltd v Football Association Ltd* [1971] Ch 591 at 604–605, 607, [1971] 1 All ER 215 at 217, 220, CA, per Lord Denning MR, and at 608–609 and 221 obiter per Fenton Atkinson LJ (a case involving proceedings of a domestic tribunal; jurisdiction to declare true construction of rules of voluntary association either before or after determination by domestic tribunal). See also *Argyle Motors (Birkenhead) Ltd v Birkenhead Corpn* (1971) 22 P & CR 829 (concurrent jurisdiction of High Court and Lands Tribunal); *R v Camden*

London Borough Council, ex p Comyn Ching & Co (London) Ltd (1983) 47 P & CR 417 (essential for court to intervene because it was not clear that the alternative inquiry procedure was in fact going to be triggered); *R v Clerkenwell Metropolitan Stipendiary Magistrate, ex p DPP* [1984] QB 821 at 835, [1984] 2 All ER 193 at 201, DC, per Goff LJ (parties misled by earlier authority into thinking that alternative remedy not available); *R v Secretary of State for the Environment, ex p Ward* [1984] 2 All ER 556 at 565–566, [1984] 1 WLR 834 at 845 obiter per Woolf J (person not to be compelled to have resort to minister if complaint is of failure by him); *Re Preston* [1985] AC 835 at 852, [1985] 2 All ER 327 at 330, HL, per Lord Scarman (party not to be confined to appeal against decision where injustice lies in proceedings being started against him at all); *R (on the application of AM (Cameroon)) v Asylum and Immigration Tribunal* [2008] EWCA Civ 100, [2008] 4 All ER 1159 (unjust conduct of first instance hearing).

19 Eg on an application for a quashing order to quash the decision, or an action for a declaration that the decision is invalid: see e g *Barnard v National Dock Labour Board* [1953] 2 QB 18, [1953] 1 All ER 1113, CA; and PARA 687.

20 As in *Cooper v Wilson* [1937] 2 KB 309, [1937] 2 All ER 726, CA (purported dismissal of police officer after he had resigned held invalid; held he was entitled to refund of deductions from pay in respect of his contribution to pension fund to which he would have had a statutory right on resignation); and *Anisminic Ltd v Foreign Compensation Commission* [1969] 2 AC 147, [1969] 1 All ER 208, HL (decision that company not entitled to claim share of compensation fund declared void; company held to be so entitled).

21 *Bennett and White (Calgary) Ltd v Municipal District of Sugar City, No 5* [1951] AC 786, PC; contrast *Re Birkenhead Corpn's Resolutions, Quigley v Birkenhead Corpn* [1952] Ch 359, [1952] 1 All ER 262, where the issue was held to be res judicata.

22 *Punton v Ministry of Pensions and National Insurance (No 2)* [1964] 1 All ER 448 at 453, 455, [1964] 1 WLR 226 at 234, 236, CA, obiter per Sellers LJ.

23 *Punton v Ministry of Pensions and National Insurance (No 2)* [1964] 1 All ER 448, [1964] 1 WLR 226; *Healey v Minister of Health* [1955] 1 QB 221, [1954] 3 All ER 449, CA; *Tithe Redemption Commission v Wynne* [1943] KB 756, [1943] 2 All ER 370, CA; *Blencowe v Northamptonshire County Council* [1907] 1 Ch 504; *East Midlands Gas Board v Doncaster Corpn* [1953] 1 All ER 54, [1953] 1 WLR 54; *Memudu Lagunju v Olubadan-in-Council* [1952] AC 387, PC; *Re Al-Fin Corpn's Patent* [1970] Ch 160, [1969] 3 All ER 396.

656. Sufficient interest to apply for permission. A claimant must show that he has a sufficient interest (also referred to as standing, or locus standi) in the matter to which the application relates, in order to bring proceedings for judicial review[1]. The question of sufficient interest may arise at two stages.

At the permission stage it is only in obvious cases that the court may decide that the claimant lacks sufficient interest[2]. A person who has a genuine interest in seeking a remedy will not generally be refused permission on grounds of lack of standing even if the particular ground of challenge relied upon is not one in which he has a personal interest[3].

In most cases, however, the question of standing is determined on the substantive application for judicial review. Save in simple or clear cases the question whether the claimant has a sufficient interest will not be determined at the threshold stage as a preliminary issue independent of a full consideration of the merits of the complaint[4].

'Sufficient interest' is not defined, but it is in practice a broad, flexible concept. What is a 'sufficient interest' is a mixed question of fact and law. The determination of any issue as to whether the claimant has a sufficient interest to bring the challenge in question will depend on consideration of the relationship between the claimant and the matter to which the claim relates, having regard to all the circumstances of the case[5]. In appropriate cases, the court may also have regard to broader concerns, including the merits of the challenge, the importance of enforcing the law, the importance of the issue raised, the presence or absence of any other person with sufficient interest, the nature of the unlawful conduct alleged and the role of the claimant in relation to the issues under consideration[6].

In recent years, the rules on standing in judicial review claims have been considerably relaxed[7]. Individuals have been recognised as having standing not only where their rights or interests are affected but in a broad range of situations where in some way they are affected by a decision[8]. A public spirited citizen raising a serious issue of public importance may be recognised as possessing standing[9]. The courts have increasingly recognised that a wide range of pressure groups have standing to bring challenges in matter which concern their areas of interest or expertise[10].

1   See the Senior Courts Act 1981 s 31(3). The Senior Courts Act 1981 was previously known as the Supreme Court Act 1981 and was renamed by the Constitutional Reform Act 2005 s 59(5), Sch 11 Pt 1 as from 1 October 2009: see the Constitutional Reform Act 2005 (Commencement No 11) Order 2009, SI 2009/1604; and COURTS.

2   The concept underlying the requirement for the claimant to have a sufficient interest to apply for permission is to safeguard public authorities from being exposed to frivolous, vexatious or untenable applications for judicial review. This requirement is an essential protection against the abuse of legal process, eg by 'busybodies', 'cranks or other mischief-makers' or 'trivial complaints of administrative errors': see *IRC v National Federation of Self-Employed and Small Businesses Ltd* [1982] AC 617 at 642–643, [1981] 2 All ER 93 at 105, HL, per Lord Diplock, and at 653 and 113 per Lord Scarman. However, the courts have accepted that in some situations a public-spirited individual may be allowed permission where there is a serious issue of public importance to be determined: see *R v Secretary of State for Foreign and Commonwealth Affairs, ex p Rees-Mogg* [1994] QB 552, [1994] 1 All ER 457, DC; and compare *R v GLC, ex p Blackburn* [1976] 3 All ER 184, [1976] 1 WLR 550, CA; and see the text and note 9.

3   *R (on the application of Kides) v South Cambridgeshire District Council* [2002] EWCA Civ 1370, [2003] 1 P & CR 298 (resident challenging grant of planning permission even though she had no personal interest in the ground of challenge which related to the alleged failure to provide sufficient affordable housing). But see *R (on the application of Chandler) v Secretary of State for Children, Schools and Families* [2009] EWCA Civ 1011, [2009] All ER (D) 115 (Oct) (a parent who had no interest in the public procurement regulations had no standing to challenge a decision to approve an expression of interest in establishing an academy on the grounds that there had been a failure to comply with the procurement regulations as the regulations were not enacted for that purpose).

4   *IRC v National Federation of Self-Employed and Small Businesses Ltd* [1982] AC 617 at 630, [1981] 2 All ER 93 at 96–97, HL, per Lord Wilberforce: 'There may be simple cases in which it can be seen at the earliest stage that the person applying for judicial review has no interest at all, or no sufficient interest to support the application: then it would be quite correct at the threshold to refuse him leave to apply ... But in other cases this will not be so. In these it will be necessary to consider the powers or the duties in law of those against whom the relief is asked, the position of the applicant in relation to those powers or duties, and to the breach of those said to have been committed. In other words, the question of sufficient interest cannot, in such cases, be considered in the abstract, or as an isolated point: it must be taken together with the legal and factual context'. See also at 656 and 115 per Lord Roskill.

5   *IRC v National Federation of Self-Employed and Small Businesses Ltd* [1982] AC 617 at 630, [1981] 2 All ER 93 at 96–97, HL, per Lord Wilberforce. The same test of sufficient interest applies in relation to all the prerogative remedies, and declarations and injunctions when sought by way of a claim for judicial review. The concept of standing is, however, sufficiently flexible so that it is possible that a particular claimant may have a sufficient interest to apply for some remedies, but not others, albeit that the claims arise from the same circumstances: see *IRC v National Federation of Self-Employed and Small Businesses Ltd* at 631 and 97 per Lord Wilberforce.

6   *R v Secretary of State for Foreign Affairs, ex p World Development Movement Ltd* [1995] 1 All ER 611, [1995] 1 WLR 386, DC. Such factors are most likely to be relevant where the claimant is an interest group (or acting in a similar capacity): see eg *R v Hammersmith and Fulham London Borough Council, ex p People Before Profit Ltd* [1981] JPL 869, 80 LGR 322 (pressure group had sufficient interest).

7   *R v Secretary of State for Foreign Affairs, ex p World Development Movement Ltd* [1995] 1 All ER 611, [1995] 1 WLR 386, DC. See also *R v A-G, ex p ICI plc* (1985) 60 TC 1 at 30 per Woolf J ('it would be regrettable if a Court had to come to the conclusion that in a situation where the need for the intervention of the Court has been established this intervention was prevented by rules as to standing').

8   Examples of the practical application of this concept include *Arsenal Football Club Ltd v Smith (Valuation Officer)* [1979] AC 1, [1977] 2 All ER 267, HL (a ratepayer may have such an interest as regards the rates paid by other ratepayers); *R v Horsham Justices, ex p Farquharson* [1982] QB 762, [1982] 2 All ER 269, CA (both a journalist and the National Union of Journalists have a sufficient interest to apply for judicial review to quash the order of a magistrates' court prohibiting the reporting of proceedings before it until the trial); *R v Liverpool City Corpn, ex p Ferguson and Ferguson* [1985] IRLR 501 (a divisional official of a union had sufficient interest to apply for judicial review of a decision that only affected members of the union in that division); *R v Independent Broadcasting Authority, ex p Whitehouse* (1984) Times, 14 April (television viewer as a licence holder had sufficient interest to challenge decision of Independent Broadcasting Authority); *R v Secretary of State for the Environment, ex p Ward* [1984] 2 All ER 556, [1984] 1 WLR 834 (gipsy entitled to judicial review of council's decision to stop providing accommodation); *R v Kirklees Metropolitan Borough Council, ex p Molloy* (1987) 86 LGR 115, CA (parent challenging decision on school re-organisation); *R (on the application of Kides) v South Cambridgeshire District Council* [2002] EWCA Civ 1370, [2003] 1 P & CR 298 (resident challenging grant of planning permission); *R v St Edmundsbury Borough Council, ex p Investors in Industry Commercial Properties Ltd* [1985] 3 All ER 234, [1985] 1 WLR 1168 (unsuccessful applicant for planning permission able to challenge grant of planning permission to a rival); *R v A-G, ex p ICI plc* (1986) 60 TC 1, CA (one taxpayer allowed to challenge the method of valuation of a rival company's profits); *R v Monopolies and Mergers Commission, ex p Argyll Group plc* [1986] 2 All ER 257, [1986] 1 WLR 763, CA (one bidder for a company had sufficient interest to challenge a regulator's decision in respect of rival bids).

9   *R v HM Treasury, ex p Smedley* [1985] QB 657, [1985] 1 All ER 589, CA; *R v Secretary of State for Foreign and Commonwealth Affairs, ex p Rees-Mogg* [1994] QB 552, [1994] 1 All ER 457, DC.

10 *R v Hammersmith and Fulham London Borough Council, ex p People Before Profit Ltd* (1981) 80 LGR 322, (1981) 45 P & CR 364; *Covent Garden Community Association v GLC* [1981] JPL 183; *R v Secretary of State for Social Services, ex p Child Poverty Action Group* (1985) Times, 8 August; *Main v Swansea City Council* (1984) 49 P & CR 26; *R v Secretary of State for Foreign Affairs, ex p World Development Movement Ltd* [1995] 1 All ER 611, [1995] 1 WLR 386, DC; *R v Secretary of State for Trade and Industry, ex p Unison* [1996] ICR 1003; *R (on the application of Association of British Civilian Internees: Far East Region) v Secretary of State for Defence* [2003] EWCA Civ 473, [2003] QB 1397; *R (on the application of Corner House Research) v Director of Serious Fraud Office* [2008] UKHL 60, [2009] 1 AC 756, [2008] 4 All ER 927.

657.   Exhaustion of alternative remedies.   The courts in their discretion will not normally make the remedy of judicial review available where there is an alternative remedy by way of appeal[1] or internal complaints procedure or where some other body has exclusive jurisdiction in respect of the dispute[2]. However, judicial review may be granted where the alternative statutory remedy is 'nowhere near so convenient, beneficial and effectual'[3] or 'where there is no other equally effective and convenient remedy'[4]. This is particularly so where the decision in question is liable to be upset as a matter of law because it is clearly made without jurisdiction or in consequence of an error of law[5]. Factors to be taken into account by a court when deciding whether to grant relief by judicial review when an alternative remedy is available are whether the alternative statutory remedy will resolve the question at issue fully and directly; whether the statutory procedure would be quicker, or slower, than the procedure by way of judicial review[6]; and whether the matter depends on some particular or technical knowledge which is more readily available to the alternative appellate body[7]. Further, a court should bear in mind the purpose of judicial review and the essential difference between appeal and review[8].

1   *R v Chief Constable of the Merseyside Police, ex p Calveley* [1986] QB 424 at 433, [1986] 1 All ER 257 at 261–262, CA, per Sir John Donaldson MR, at 435 and 263 per May LJ, and at 440 and 267 per Glidewell LJ (in this case the delay in bringing disciplinary charges against a police officer was such a serious breach of the relevant regulations as to justify the grant of

judicial review without requiring an appeal to the Police Appeal Tribunal to be heard first). Cf *R v Secretary of State for the Home Department, ex p Swati* [1986] 1 All ER 717, [1986] 1 WLR 477, CA (application for judicial review dismissed where immigration officer's decision not first challenged by appeal to adjudicator and Immigration Appeal Tribunal). See also *R v Mid-Worcestershire Justices, ex p Hart* (1988) Times, 17 December (judicial review refused while appeal pending); *R v Civil Service Appeal Board, ex p Bruce* [1988] 3 All ER 686, [1988] ICR 649, DC (judicial review refused as the appropriate forum for resolution of a dispute about dismissal of an employee is an industrial tribunal); *R v Secretary of State for Employment, ex p Equal Opportunities Commission* [1995] 1 AC 1, sub nom *Equal Opportunities Commission v Secretary of State for Employment* [1994] 1 All ER 910, HL (an individual's claim for redundancy pay which involved allegations that restrictions on her entitlement to claim were indirectly discriminatory should have been brought before an industrial tribunal); *R v Secretary of State for the Home Department, ex p Attiror* (1987) Independent, 23 October, CA (where leave to apply for judicial review had been granted and the Secretary of State showed that the applicant had invoked an alternative appeal procedure but had on legal advice abandoned that appeal and pursued another application for leave to remain, the principle stated in *R v Secretary of State for the Home Department, ex p Swati* was applicable and the court would only in exceptional circumstances quash a decision in respect of which the applicant had a right of appeal which he had chosen not to pursue). In *Harley Development Inc v IRC* [1996] 1 WLR 727, [1996] STC 440, PC, it was held that judicial review was not the appropriate means to challenge an assessment to tax alleged to be a nullity because statute laid down a comprehensive appeals procedure. There are references in *R v Chief Constable of the Merseyside Police, ex p Calveley*, in *R v Secretary of State for the Home Department, ex p Swati*, and in *Harley Development Inc v IRC* to the need for 'exceptional circumstances' before the jurisdiction of judicial review will be exercised where there is an alternative remedy by way of appeal. See *R v Chief Constable of the Merseyside Police, ex p Calveley* at 440 and 267 per Glidewell LJ; *R v Secretary of State for the Home Department, ex p Swati* at 485 and 724 per Sir John Donaldson MR ('By definition, exceptional circumstances defy definition, but where Parliament provides an appeal procedure, judicial review will have no place, unless the applicant can distinguish his case from the type of case for which the appeal procedure was provided'), and at 490 and 728 per Parker LJ. In *R v Chief Constable of the Merseyside Police, ex p Calveley*, Sir John Donaldson MR said that judicial review is 'very rarely' available when there is an alternative remedy by way of appeal (at 433 and 261–262); and May LJ said that 'the normal rule' in cases such as this is that an applicant for judicial review should first exhaust whatever other rights he has by way of appeal (at 435 and 263). In *Harley Development Inc v IRC* at 736 and 449 Lord Jauncey of Tullichettle suggested that 'exceptional circumstances' would typically involve an allegation of abuse of power. See also *R v Panel on Take-overs and Mergers, ex p Guinness plc* [1990] 1 QB 146 at 177–178, [1989] 1 All ER 509 at 526, CA, per Lord Donaldson of Lymington MR, at 184–185 and 531 per Lloyd LJ, and at 201 and 544 per Woolf LJ. Despite this language the courts have in practice granted judicial review and not required alternative remedies to be exhausted where there has been illegality (see *Re Preston* [1985] AC 835, [1985] 2 All ER 327, HL; *R v Chief Immigration Officer, Gatwick Airport, ex p Kharrazi* [1980] 3 All ER 373, [1980] 1 WLR 1396, CA (note, however, that on the facts, the right of appeal exercisable from abroad would have been nugatory, per Lord Denning MR at 380 and 1403–1404); cf *R (on the application of RK (Nepal)) v Secretary of State for the Home Department* [2009] EWCA Civ 359, [2009] All ER (D) 226 (Apr); and see *R v Hillingdon London Borough Council, ex p Royco Homes Ltd* [1974] QB 720, [1974] 2 All ER 643). See also *R v Secretary of State for the Home Department, ex p Frieda Hindjou* [1989] Imm AR 24, where judicial review was granted of a decision of an immigration officer who misapplied the criteria for granting leave to enter. However, the normal rule is that, in the absence of exceptional circumstances, the right of appeal should be exercised from abroad and judicial review will not lie: see eg *Grazales v Secretary of State for the Home Department* [1990] Imm AR 505, CA. For cases where judicial review was not granted see eg *R (on the application of Sivasubramaniam) v Wandsworth County Court* [2002] EWCA Civ 1738, [2003] 2 All ER 160, [2003] 1 WLR 475; *R (on the application of Strickson) v Preston County Court* [2007] EWCA Civ 1132, [2008] All ER (D) 269 (Feb); *R (on the application of G) v Immigration Appeal Tribunal* [2004] EWCA Civ 1731, [2005] 2 All ER 165, [2005] 1 WLR 1445; *R (on the application of Sinclair Gardens Investments (Kensington) Ltd) v Lands Tribunal* [2005] EWCA Civ 1305, [2006] 3 All ER 650; *F (Mongolia) v Secretary of State for the Home Department* [2007] EWCA Civ 769, [2007] 1 WLR 2523, [2007] All ER (D) 384 (Jul); *R (on the application of JRP Holdings Ltd) v Spelthorne Borough Council* [2007] EWCA Civ 1122 (stop notices). For an immigration case where judicial review was granted see eg *R (on the application of AM (Cameroon)) v Asylum and Immigration Tribunal* [2008] EWCA Civ 100, [2008] 4 All ER

1159, [2008] 1 WLR 2062 (unjust conduct of first instance hearing). For judicial review of revenue decisions see eg *Autologic Holdings plc v IRC* [2005] UKHL 54, [2006] 1 AC 118, [2005] 4 All ER 1141; cf *Re Preston* [1985] AC 835, [1985] 2 All ER 327, HL.

2   Eg the jurisdiction of the Visitors of the Inns of Court in relation to disciplinary matters: see *Joseph v Council of Legal Education* [1994] ELR 407, 137 Sol Jo LB 1749; *R v Visitors to the Inns of Court, ex p Calder* [1994] QB 1, [1993] 2 All ER 876, CA. Judicial review does not lie in respect of any matter which falls within the exclusive jurisdiction of the visitor; it will lie only on the grounds that the visitor has acted outside, or abused, his powers or acted in breach of the rules of natural justice: see *Thomas v University of Bradford* [1987] AC 795, [1987] 1 All ER 834, HL; *R v Lord President of the Privy Council, ex p Page* [1993] AC 682, sub nom *Page v Hull University Visitor* [1993] 1 All ER 97, HL.

3   *R v Paddington Valuation Officer, ex p Peachey Property Corpn Ltd* [1966] 1 QB 380 at 400, [1965] 2 All ER 836 at 840, CA, per Lord Denning MR (because of the nature of the dispute in that case). See also *Connor v Law Society of British Columbia* (1980) 4 WWR 1038, BC SC. It is highly desirable in a specialised field where Parliament has provided machinery to deal with appeals from decisions under its legislation in that field, that the Divisional Court should be chary of bypassing such machinery: *R v Chief Adjudication Officer, ex p Bland* (1985) Times, 6 February; *R v Secretary of State for Social Services, ex p Connolly* [1986] 1 All ER 998 at 1010, [1986] 1 WLR 421 at 436, CA, per Slade LJ (social security statutory appeals procedure), applied in *R (on the application of Hook) v Secretary of State for Social Security* [2007] EWHC 1705 (Admin), [2007] All ER (D) 34 (Jul). See also *R v Epping and Harlow General Comrs, ex p Goldstraw* [1983] 3 All ER 257, [1983] STC 693, CA; *R v Brentford General Comrs, ex p Chan* [1986] STC 65; *R v Comr for the Special Purposes of the Income Tax Acts, ex p Napier* [1988] 3 All ER 166, sub nom *R v Special Comr, ex p Napier* [1988] STC 573, CA; *R v London VAT Tribunal, ex p Theodorou* [1989] STC 292 (approved in *R v Customs and Excise Comrs and London Value Added Tax Tribunal, ex p Menzies* [1990] STC 263 (judicial review does not lie to compel a statutory tribunal to hear an appeal where a condition precedent to the exercise of that right has not been met)); *R v IRC, ex p Emery* [1980] STC 549 (where judicial review was refused because of the existence of well-established statutory appeal procedures provided by the relevant taxation legislation); and see *Autologic Holdings plc v IRC* [2005] UKHL 54, [2006] 1 AC 118, [2005] 4 All ER 1141. In *R v IRC, ex p Opman International UK* [1986] 1 All ER 328 at 330, [1986] 1 WLR 568 at 571, Woolf J said the fact that there is an alternative procedure available in revenue matters does not mean that an application for judicial review should never be made; however, particularly in such matters, applicants should bear in mind that 'an application for judicial review is the procedure, so to speak, of last resort. It is a residual procedure which is available in those cases where the alternative procedure does not satisfactorily achieve a just resolution of the applicant's claim'; for such a case see *R (on the application of Smith) v North Eastern Derbyshire Primary Care Trust* [2006] EWCA Civ 1291, [2006] 1 WLR 3315, [2006] All ER (D) 108 (Aug). In *R v Battle Justices, ex p Shepherd* (1983) 147 JP 372, the Divisional Court would not exercise its discretion to entertain an application for judicial review to quash a compensation order made by a magistrates' court on conviction because the statutory framework which existed for the hearing of appeals against sentence from magistrates' courts to the Crown Court had not been exhausted. See also *R (on the application of Sivasubramaniam) v Wandsworth County Court* [2002] EWCA Civ 1738, [2003] 2 All ER 160, [2003] 1 WLR 475; *R (on the application of Strickson) v Preston County Court* [2007] EWCA Civ 1132, [2008] All ER (D) 269 (Feb); *R (on the application of G) v Immigration Appeal Tribunal* [2004] EWCA Civ 1731, [2005] 2 All ER 165, [2005] 1 WLR 1445; *R (on the application of Sinclair Gardens Investments (Kensington) Ltd) v Lands Tribunal* [2005] EWCA Civ 1305, [2006] 3 All ER 650; *F (Mongolia) v Secretary of State for the Home Department* [2007] EWCA Civ 769, [2007] 1 WLR 2523, [2007] All ER (D) 384 (Jul); cf *R (on the application of AM (Cameroon)) v Asylum and Immigration Tribunal* [2008] EWCA Civ 100, [2008] 4 All ER 1159, [2008] 1 WLR 2062.

4   *R v Hillingdon London Borough Council, ex p Royco Homes Ltd* [1974] QB 720 at 728, [1974] 2 All ER 643 at 648 per Lord Widgery LCJ. It would be wrong to conclude from this dictum that in every case where there is an alternative remedy, but one which is not as effective or as convenient as judicial review, this alone is enough to enable the court to put the alternative remedy on one side and to grant judicial review: *R v Chief Constable of the Merseyside Police, ex p Calveley* [1986] QB 424 at 436–437, [1986] 1 All ER 257 at 264, CA, per May LJ. In *R v Huntingdon District Council, ex p Cowan* [1984] 1 All ER 58 at 63, [1984] 1 WLR 501 at 507, Glidewell J said that 'a major factor to be taken into account' is whether judicial review or the alternative remedy available by way of appeal is the most effective and convenient in all the circumstances, not merely for the applicant, but in the public interest.

5   *R v Hillingdon London Borough Council, ex p Royco Homes Ltd* [1974] QB 720 at 729, [1974] 2 All ER 643 at 649 per Lord Widgery LCJ; *R v Paddington Valuation Officer, ex p Peachey Property Corpn Ltd* [1966] 1 QB 380 at 400, [1965] 2 All ER 836 at 840, CA, per Lord Denning MR; *R v Chief Constable of the Merseyside Police, ex p Calveley* [1986] QB 424 at 436–437, [1986] 1 All ER 257 at 264–265, CA. See also *R v Chief Immigration Officer, Gatwick Airport, ex p Kharrazi* [1980] 3 All ER 373, [1980] 1 WLR 1396 (decision of immigration officer who misdirected himself on point of law quashed; right of appeal nugatory on the facts), where Lord Denning MR said (at 380 and 1403) 'If there is a convenient remedy by way of appeal to an adjudicator, then certiorari may be refused; and the applicant left to his own remedy by way of appeal. But it has been held on countless occasions that the availability of appeal does not debar the court from quashing an order by prerogative writs, either of habeas corpus ... or certiorari'. See eg *Cooper v Wilson* [1937] 2 KB 309, [1937] 2 All ER 726; *R v Hillingdon London Borough Council, ex p Royco Homes Ltd*. See also *Ellis & Sons Fourth Amalgamated Properties Ltd v Southern Rent Assessment Panel* (1984) 14 HLR 48, (1984) 270 Estates Gazette 39 (Mann J noted, in a statutory appeal, the advantages of proceeding by way of judicial review rather than by appeal in the particular context of challenges by landlords to decisions of rent assessment committees); *R v Slough Justices, ex p B* [1985] FLR 384 per Wood J; *R v Ealing London Borough Council, ex p Times Newspapers Ltd* (1986) 85 LGR 316, [1987] IRLR 129; *R v Lambeth London Borough Council, ex p Stirling (Ahisah)* [1986] RVR 27, CA (order of commitment arising out of non-payment of rate arrears, considerable delay). As to the remedies formerly available by prerogative writs see PARA 687 et seq. Certiorari is now known as a quashing order: see PARAS 687 note 1, 688. As to habeas corpus see ADMINISTRATIVE LAW vol 1(1) (2001 Reissue) PARA 207 et seq.

6   When an appeal (or other equivalent process) is already in progress, judicial review may be refused: see *R v Civil Service Appeal Board, ex p Bruce* [1988] 3 All ER 686, [1988] ICR 649, DC; affd [1989] 2 All ER 907, [1989] ICR 171, CA. Judicial review will not usually be permitted of decisions taken in the course of a hearing: *R v Association of Futures Brokers and Dealers Ltd, ex p Mordens Ltd* (1990) 3 Admin LR 254; but cf *R (on the application of AM (Cameroon)) v Asylum and Immigration Tribunal* [2008] EWCA Civ 100, [2008] 4 All ER 1159, [2008] 1 WLR 2062.

7   *Ex p Waldron* [1986] QB 824 at 852, sub nom *R v Hallstrom, ex p W* [1985] 3 All ER 775 at 789–790, CA, per Glidewell LJ; *R v Chief Constable of the Merseyside Police, ex p Calveley* [1986] QB 424 at 440, [1986] 1 All ER 257 at 267, CA, per Glidewell LJ. See also *Re Preston* [1985] AC 835 at 862, [1985] 2 All ER 327 at 337, HL, per Lord Templeman, and at 852 and 330 per Lord Scarman. In *Ex p Watson* (1987) Times, 18 March, application for leave to apply for judicial review of a decision of Croydon County Court on the basis of the judge's misconduct in the conduct of the hearing was refused where the applicant was entitled to appeal against the judge's decision to the Divisional Court of the Chancery Division in Bankruptcy, which, if it allowed the appeal, would be able to grant the relief which the applicant had originally sought.

8   See *R v Chief Constable of the Merseyside Police, ex p Calveley* [1986] QB 424 at 437–439, [1986] 1 All ER 257 at 265–267, CA, per May LJ; *Chief Constable of the North Wales Police v Evans* [1982] 3 All ER 141 at 143–144, [1982] 1 WLR 1155 at 1160–1161, HL, per Lord Hailsham of St Marylebone LC, and at 153 and 1173 per Lord Brightman. As to the nature of judicial review see PARA 602.

658. Time limits and delay in commencing proceedings. A claim for judicial review must be commenced promptly, and in any event not later than three months after the grounds for bringing the claim first arose[1]. Where the claim is for a quashing order in respect of a judgment, order or conviction, the date when the grounds for making the claim first arose is the date of that judgment, order or conviction[2]; and where the challenge is to a decision, the time-limit normally runs from the date of the decision. There may be instances where the decision-making process has two or more stages, as is the case, for example, with grants of planning permission. The time-limit in such cases will generally run from the date of the measure which actually creates legal rights and obligations[3]. The time-limit runs from the date when the decision was made, not the date that the person learned of the decision or the grounds of challenge, although knowledge, together with other material facts, may be relevant to the question of whether there is a good reason to extend time[4]. Difficult questions arise when a claimant is seeking to enforce a statutory duty, including the question whether the statute contemplates a specific process whereby a duty is determined to be owed, in which case the time-limit may run from that determination, or the time when the duty was first owed, or whether the duty is a continuing duty, in which case the time-limit will not run whilst the duty is still owed[5].

The fact that a claim for judicial review has been made within three months from the date when the grounds for the application first arose does not necessarily mean that it has been made promptly[6]. Thus there may well be cases where a court may have to consider whether or not to extend the time for making an application, even within the three month period.

Wherever there is a failure to act promptly or within three months there is 'undue delay'[7]. Where there has been undue delay in making an application for judicial review, the court may refuse permission for the application to be brought or may refuse a remedy at the substantive hearing, if it considers that granting the remedy sought would be likely to cause substantial hardship to, or substantially prejudice the rights of, any person or would be detrimental to good administration[8].

The court may grant an extension of time for the bringing of a claim[9].

A decision at the permission stage that a claim has been brought promptly is normally final and cannot be re-opened at the substantive stage[10]. On occasions, if delay is in issue, a court may decide not to grant permission on the papers but order an oral hearing, or a rolled-up hearing where permission is dealt with first and the substantive hearing will follow immediately if permission is given. This enables the question of delay to be fully canvassed.

1 See CPR 54.5(1). The time limit in this rule may not be extended by agreement between the parties: CPR 54.5(2). CPR 54.5 does not apply when any other enactment specifies a shorter time limit for making the claim for judicial review: CPR 54.5(3).

2 See *Practice Direction—Judicial Review* (2000) PD 54A para 4.1.

3 See *R (on the application of Burkett) v Hammersmith and Fulham London Borough Council* [2002] UKHL 23, [2002] 3 All ER 97, [2002] 1 WLR 1593 (time ran from date of the grant of planning permission not the earlier resolution of the planning authority to grant it).

4 *R v Department of Transport, ex p Presvac Engineering Ltd* (1991) 4 Admin LR 121, (1991) Times, 10 July, CA. A claimant will be expected to act promptly once he has learned of the decision.

5 See eg *R v Hertfordshire County Council, ex p Cheung* (1986) Times, 4 April, CA (duty to pay a grant under the Education Act 1962 was not a continuing duty); *R v Dairy Produce Quota Tribunal for England and Wales, ex p Hood* [1990] COD 184 (duty to give reasons not a continuing duty).

6 The requirement for promptness will not necessarily be satisfied simply because the claim has been made within three months: see eg *R v ITC, ex p TVNI Ltd* (1991) Times, 30 December, CA; *R v Cotswold Parish Council, ex p Barrington Parish Council* [1997] EGCS 66, 75 P & CR 515; *Hardy v Pembrokeshire County Council* [2006] EWCA Civ 240, [2006] Env LR 659. In some areas promptness may be of particular importance: see eg *R v Education Committee of Blackpool Borough Council, ex p Taylor* [1999] ELR 237 (school admissions case; five month delay; explanation of delay on basis of exploration of alternative routes unsatisfactory since none of the routes explored had power to set aside decision under challenge; in cases concerning education of children particular duty to act promptly).

7 See *Caswell v Dairy Produce Quota Tribunal for England and Wales* [1990] 2 AC 738, [1990] 2 All ER 434, HL. This case dealt with the relationship between the Supreme Court Act 1981 (now known as the Senior Courts Act 1981: see note 8) s 31, and the previous procedural rule RSC Ord 53 (which is substantially the same as CPR Pt 54).

8 See the Senior Courts Act 1981 s 31(6). The Senior Courts Act 1981 was previously known as the Supreme Court Act 1981 and was renamed by the Constitutional Reform Act 2005 s 59(5), Sch 11 Pt 1 as from 1 October 2009: see the Constitutional Reform Act 2005 (Commencement No 11) Order 2009, SI 2009/1604; and COURTS.

The Senior Courts Act 1981 s 31(6) is without prejudice to any enactment or rule of court which has the effect of limiting the time within which an application for judicial review may be made: s 31(7). See e g *R v Brent London Borough Council, ex p O'Malley* (1997) 10 Admin LR 265 at 293–294, 30 HLR 328 at 380, CA, per Judge LJ; *Nichol v Gateshead Metropolitan Borough Council* (1988) 87 LGR 435, sub nom *R v Gateshead Metropolitan Borough Council, ex p Nichol*, [1988] COD 97, CA.

9   CPR 3.1(2)(a). This provision is without prejudice to any statutory provision which has the effect of limiting the time within which an application for judicial review may be made: see CPR 54.5(3). The predecessor to CPR Pt 54, RSC Ord 53, required that 'good reason' had to be shown in order for any extension of time to be granted. It is submitted that in practice this requirement will continue to exist. With regard to the exercise of this discretion, the courts will always have regard to the particular need for certainty (and hence short periods of limitation) in many administrative contexts: see e g *R v Institute of Chartered Accountants in England and Wales, ex p Andreou* (1996) 8 Admin LR 557, [1996] COD 489, CA. However, the existence of a 'good reason' for the delay is not, of itself, determinative in favour of an extension of time. Also relevant will be the reason for any delay, and whether or not any extension of time would cause prejudice or hardship or would otherwise be detrimental to good administration. Specific examples of the exercise of this discretion include *R v Crown Court at Lincoln, ex p Jones* [1990] COD 15; *R v Secretary of State for Health, ex p Furneaux* [1994] 2 All ER 652, 17 BMLR 49, CA (delay due to fault of lawyers not a good reason to extend time; also, where challenge affected third party rights 'promptly' meant 'with the utmost promptitude'; see further on third party rights *R v HM Coroner for North Northumberland, ex p Armstrong and Armstrong* (1987) 151 JP 773 at 776, DC); *R v Secretary of State for the Home Department, ex p Ruddock* [1987] 2 All ER 518, [1987] 1 WLR 1482 (applicant initially unaware of decision, but once aware had acted quickly; claim said to raise issue of general public importance); *R v Secretary of State for Foreign Affairs, ex p World Development Movement Ltd* [1995] 1 All ER 611 at 627, [1995] 1 WLR 386 at 402, DC, per Rose LJ; *R v Licensing Authority, ex p Novartis Pharmaceutical Ltd* [2000] COD 232; *R v Collins, ex p MS* [1998] COD 52; *R v Secretary of State for Trade and Industry, ex p Greenpeace Ltd (No 2)* [2000] 2 CMLR 94, [2000] COD 141; *R v Exeter City Council, ex p JL Thomas & Co* [1991] 1 QB 471, [1990] 1 All ER 413 (effect of delay may be mitigated by fact that claimant has put defendant on notice as to claim from an early stage); *R v Department of Transport, ex p Presvac Engineering Ltd* (1991) 4 Admin LR 121, (1991) Times, 10 July, CA (delay caused by applicant gathering evidence was not excusable); *R v Comr for Local Administration, ex p Croydon London Borough Council* [1989] 1 All ER 1033, DC (neither defendant nor intervenor able to demonstrate prejudice by reason of the delay); *R v IRC, ex p Sims* [1987] STC 211 at 214 per Schiemann J; *R v Stratford-upon-Avon District Council, ex p Jackson* [1985] 3 All ER 769, [1985] 1 WLR 1319, CA (delay caused by factors outside control of applicant excusable; in this case delay in decision as to grant of legal aid); *R v Greenwich London Borough Council, ex p Cedar Transport Ltd* [1983] RA 173; *R v Secretary of State for the Home Department, ex p Khan* [1987] Imm AR 173. As to applications for permission see PARA 664; and as to acknowledgment of service see PARA 665.

10 See *R v Criminal Injuries Compensation Board, ex p A* [1999] 2 AC 330, [1999] 2 WLR 974, HL. The question may, however, be considered at the substantive hearing if the judge granting permission so indicates, if new and relevant material is introduced, if the issues as they emerge at the substantive hearing put a different aspect on the question of promptness or if the judge granting permission has overlooked a relevant matter or reached a decision per incuriam: see *R v Lichfield Borough Council, ex p Lichfield Securities Ltd* [2001] EWCA Civ 304, 81 P & CR 213, *R (on the application of Litchfield Securities Ltd) v Lichfield District Council)* [2001] 3 PLR 33. The limited opportunity for dealing with delay at the substantive hearing underlines the need for any defendant who is seeking to raise a delay issue to address the point in the acknowledgement of service, and to put forward any evidence in support of the assertion, at the permission stage.

4. PRACTICE AND PROCEDURE

(1) INTRODUCTION

659. History of the procedure. In 1977 the former Order 53 of the Rules of the Supreme Court was replaced by a substituted Order 53[1] which introduced a new form of procedure known as an 'application for judicial review'. The principal effect of this fundamental reform was to enable a person seeking to challenge an administrative act or omission to apply to the High Court either for one of the prerogative orders of mandamus, certiorari or prohibition or for a declaration, an injunction or damages, or for any combination of these forms of relief, in the same proceedings[2]. The Rules were amended in 1980[3], and in the following year the Supreme Court Act 1981[4] gave statutory endorsement to some but not all of the provisions of the new Order 53. As from 2 October 2000, the provisions of Order 53 have been replaced by Part 54 of the Civil Procedure Rules, which in turn modifies the procedure under Part 8 of those Rules[5]. In addition as from 4 March 2002, judicial review cases have been the subject of a specific pre-action protocol[6]. The result of the changes introduced by the amendments to Order 53 has been the creation of a unified and simplified procedure for the exercise by the High Court of its supervisory jurisdiction over the proceedings and decisions of inferior courts, tribunals or other bodies of persons charged with the performance of public acts and duties[7].

1 It was substituted with effect from 11 January 1978 by the Rules of the Supreme Court (Amendment No 3) 1977, SI 1977/1955, rr 5, 13. The new order was based on the recommendations of the Law Commission made in their Report on Remedies in Administrative Law (Law Com No 73: Cmnd 6407 (1976)). The recommendations were similar to earlier procedural reforms introduced in Ontario by the Judicial Review Procedure Act 1971 and in New Zealand by the Judicature Amendment Act 1972. See now also the Administrative Decisions (Judicial Review) Act 1977 of Australia. RSC Ord 53 has itself now been replaced by CPR Pt 54: see PARA 660.

2 RSC Ord 53 rr 1, 2, 7. Before this change, Order 53 had been restricted to an application for certiorari, prohibition and mandamus. It was not possible to seek a prerogative order in the same proceedings as other remedies such as a declaration or an injunction or damages. Moreover, each separate remedy had its own separate origins and history and developed its own special procedural rules: see PARA 688. The prerogative orders of certiorari, prohibition and mandamus are now known as quashing orders, prohibiting orders and mandatory orders respectively: see PARA 687. As to declarations and injunctions see PARA 716 et seq.

3 See the Rules of the Supreme Court (Amendment No 4) 1980, SI 1980/2000, which came into effect on 12 January 1981.

4 Ie the Supreme Court Act 1981 s 31: see PARA 602. The Supreme Court Act 1981 has been renamed the Senior Courts Act 1981: see PARA 602 note 4.

5 See CPR Pt 54 and especially CPR 54.1(e). See PARA 660.

6 See *Pre-Action Protocol for Judicial Review*; and PARA 663.

7 *Cocks v Thanet District Council* [1983] 2 AC 286 at 295, [1982] 3 All ER 1135 at 1139, HL, per Lord Bridge of Harwich. The effect of the 1980 amendments was that as from 12 January 1981 most civil judicial review cases would be heard by a single judge of the Queen's Bench Division with expertise in administrative law. In July 1981 a special panel of judges was set up to hear applications for judicial review (listed for hearing in the Crown Office List) and other cases with an administrative law element: see *Practice Direction (Trials in London)* [1981] 3 All ER 61, [1981] 1 WLR 1296. The Crown Office List has, since 2 October 2000, been known as the Administrative Court, following a recommendation that it be re-named made to the Lord Chancellor by Sir Jeffrey Bowman in his Review of the Crown Office List (21 March 2000). There remains a list of judges nominated to hear cases in the Administrative Court. A lead nominated judge is appointed with responsibility for the speed, efficiency and economy with which the work of the Administrative Court is conducted: see *Practice Direction (Administrative Court: Establishment)* [2000] 4 All ER 1071, [2000] 1 WLR 1654. Since 21 April 2009, the Administrative Court has operated from a number of regional venues,

including Cardiff, Birmingham, Leeds and Manchester, as well as from the Royal Courts of Justice in London: see PD 54D *Practice Direction—Administrative Court (Venue).*

660. The procedure for judicial review. The court's permission to proceed is required in a claim for judicial review[1]. However, the effect of the Civil Procedure Rules is that, apart from the requirement to obtain the permission of the court to proceed, the claim proceeds as a Part 8 claim, but with the substantial modifications made by the provisions of the Civil Procedure Rules relating to judicial review[2]. Hence procedures relevant to private law claims (such as applications for disclosure[3] and orders for further information[4]) are applicable to claims for judicial review. The court has important powers in relation to, inter alia, reliance on additional grounds[5] and disclosure of documents[6]. Where permission is granted, the court may proceed to give directions, which may include a stay of the proceedings to which the claim relates[7]. The court may also grant interim remedies such as an interlocutory injunction or interim declaration[8].

The court may order a claim to continue as if it had not been started under the judicial review procedure and give directions for the future management of the claim, including provision for the transfer of the proceedings[9]. Certain applications for judicial review or for permission to apply for judicial review[10] must be transferred to the Upper Tribunal[11].

1   See the Supreme Court Act 1981 s 31(3); CPR 54.4; and PARA 664.
2   Ie CPR Pt 54: see PARA 661 et seq. As to Part 8 claims see CIVIL PROCEDURE vol 11 (2009) PARA 127 et seq.
3   Ie under CPR Pt 31: see CIVIL PROCEDURE vol 11 (2009) PARA 538 et seq. But see also PARA 670.
4   Ie under CPR Pt 18: see CIVIL PROCEDURE vol 11 (2009) PARAS 611–612. Formerly the procedures of discovery and interrogatories were not available when prerogative orders were sought: see *Barnard v National Dock Labour Board* [1953] 2 QB 18, [1953] 1 All ER 1113, CA, per Denning LJ. See also PARA 674.
5   See CPR 54.15; and PARA 670.
6   See CPR 54.16; *Practice Direction—Judicial Review* PD 54A para 12.1; and PARA 673.
7   See CPR 54.10; and PARA 664.
8   Ie under CPR Pt 25: see CIVIL PROCEDURE vol 11 (2009) PARA 315 et seq.
9   See CPR 54.20; and PARA 662. See *Trustees of the Dennis Rye Pension Fund v Sheffield City Council* [1997] 4 All ER 747 at 755–756, [1998] 1 WLR 840 at 848–849, CA, per Lord Woolf MR. The power under the CPR to treat cases as if they had not been begun using the judicial review procedure is far wider than the equivalent power under RSC Ord 53. The power under Ord 53 was to order proceedings to continue as if begun by writ only in cases where the relief sought was a declaration, an injunction or damages, such relief being derivative or ancillary, ie to cases which are in the field of public law only: see *R v Secretary of State for the Home Department, ex p Dew* [1987] 2 All ER 1049 at 1066, [1987] 1 WLR 881 at 901 per McNeill J. There was no such converse power to permit an action begun by writ to continue as if it were an application for judicial review: *O'Reilly v Mackman* [1983] 2 AC 237 at 284, [1982] 3 All ER 1124 at 1133, HL, per Lord Diplock; *Davy v Spelthorne Borough Council* [1984] AC 262 at 274, [1983] 3 All ER 278 at 284, HL, per Lord Fraser of Tullybelton. However, there is power to transfer the matter to the Administrative Court: see *Trustees of the Dennis Rye Pension Fund v Sheffield City Council.*
10   If the application: (1) only seeks a mandatory, prohibiting or quashing order of a declaration or injunction (ie relief under the Senior Courts Act 1981 s 31(1)(a), (b) (see PARA 691)), an award of damages (ie under s 31(4) (see PARA 722)), interests and costs; (2) does not call into question anything done by the Crown Court; (3) falls within a class specified under the Tribunals, Courts and Enforcement Act 2007 s 18(6) (see ADMINISTRATIVE LAW); and (4) does not call into question any decision made under the Immigration Acts, the British Nationality Act 1981, any instrument having effect under such an enactment, or any other provision of law for the time being in force which determines British citizenship, British overseas territories citizenship, the status of a British National (Overseas) or British Overseas citizenship, the High Court must by order transfer the application to the Upper Tribunal: Senior Courts Act 1981 s 31A(2), (4)–(7) (s 31A added by the Tribunals, Courts and Enforcement Act 2007 s 19(1)). As to the Senior

Courts Act 1981 see PARA 602 note 4. As to the Upper Tribunal see ADMINISTRATIVE LAW. If the application satisfies heads (1), (2) and (4) but does not fall within a class specified under the Tribunals, Courts and Enforcement Act 2007 s 18(6), the High Court may by order transfer the application to the Upper Tribunal if it appears to the High Court to be just and convenient to do so: Senior Courts Act 1981 s 31A(3) (as so added).

As from a day to be appointed, where an application is made which satisfies heads (1)–(3) and which calls into question a decision of the Secretary of State not to treat submissions as an asylum claim or a human rights claim within the meaning of the Nationality, Immigration and Asylum Act 2002 Pt 5 (see BRITISH NATIONALITY, IMMIGRATION AND ASYLUM) wholly or partly on the basis that they are not significantly different from material that has previously been considered (whether or not it calls into question any other decision), the High Court must by order transfer the application to the Upper Tribunal: Senior Courts Act 1981 s 31A(2A), (8) (added, as from a day to be appointed, by the Borders, Citizenship and Immigration Act 2009 s 53(1)). At the date at which this volume states the law no such day had been appointed. As to the Secretary of State see PARA 646 note 5

11 Senior Courts Act 1981 s 31A(1).

661. Procedural exclusivity. In an application for judicial review a claimant may apply in the same proceedings for any one or more of the prerogative orders (that is to say a quashing order, a prohibiting order or a mandatory order)[1] or, in appropriate circumstances, a declaration or an injunction[2] or damages[3]. An application for a quashing order, a prohibiting order or a mandatory order must be made using the judicial review procedure[4]. A declaration, injunction[5] or damages[6] may be obtained using the judicial review procedure[7] or by ordinary inter partes proceedings. However, if the proceedings are directed to challenging the lawfulness of an enactment or a decision or action or failure to act in relation to the exercise of a public function, a claimant will probably be required to use the judicial review procedure[8].

1 See CPR 54.2. CPR Pt 54 replaced the provisions of RSC Ord 53: see PARA 659. As to the prerogative orders see PARA 687 et seq.

2 See CPR 54.3(1); the Senior Courts Act 1981 s 31(2); and PARA 662. As to declarations and injunctions see PARA 716 et seq. As to the Senior Courts Act 1981 see PARA 602 note 4.

3 See CPR 54.3(2); the Senior Courts Act 1981 s 31(4); and PARA 662. As to damages see PARAS 662, 722. 'So Order 53 since 1977 has provided a procedure by which every type of remedy for infringement of the rights of individuals that are entitled to protection in public law can be obtained in one and the same proceedings by way of an application for judicial review, and whichever remedy is found to be the most appropriate in the light of what has emerged upon the hearing of the application, can be granted to him': *O'Reilly v Mackman* [1983] 2 AC 237 at 283, [1982] 3 All ER 1124 at 1133, HL, per Lord Diplock.

4 See the Senior Courts Act 1981 s 31(1); and CPR 54.2. As to the meaning of 'the judicial review procedure' see PARA 662 note 7. On its face, this provision is highly prescriptive, but see CPR 3.10 under which the court has a general power to rectify any error in procedure, and which specifically provides that an error of procedure such as a failure to comply with a rule does not invalidate any steps taken unless the court declares that to be the case: see CIVIL PROCEDURE vol 11 (2009) PARA 257.

Case law under RSC Ord 53 strongly suggests that in relation to applications for judicial review the courts will have little sympathy for technical arguments rooted only in procedural formalism: see *Trustees of the Dennis Rye Pension Fund v Sheffield City Council* [1997] 4 All ER 747, [1998] 1 WLR 840, CA; *British Steel plc v Customs and Excise Comrs* [1997] 2 All ER 366 at 379, CA, per Saville LJ; *Clark v University of Lincolnshire and Humberside* [2000] 3 All ER 752, [2000] 1 WLR 1988, CA; *Phonographic Performance Ltd v Department of Trade and Industry* [2004] EWHC 1795 (Ch), [2005] 1 All ER 369, [2004] 1 WLR 2893. Thus if a claim for judicial review is commenced other than under CPR Pt 54 the court should not strike out the claim on that basis alone. Rather, when considering such a point, the court will have regard to whether or not as a matter of substance the claim could be regarded as an abuse of process (for example, an attempt to circumvent a time limit which would have applied if Pt 54 had been used). Note also that this rule does not affect the use of public law arguments by way of defence in proceedings brought outside CPR Pt 54: see e g *Wandsworth London Borough Council v Winder* [1985] AC 461, [1984] 3 All ER 976, HL. As to judicial review proceedings as an abuse of process see further *Land Securities PLC v Fladgate Fielder (a firm)* [2009] EWCA Civ 1402, [2009] All ER (D) 187 (Dec).

5 An application for an injunction under the Senior Courts Act 1981 s 30 restraining a person from acting in an office in which he is not entitled to act must be brought by an application for judicial review: see CPR 54.2(d); and PARA 662.

6 See the Senior Courts Act 1981 s 31(4); CPR 54.3(2); and PARA 662.

7 See CPR 54.3; and PARA 662. The Senior Courts Act 1981 s 31 provides that an application for a declaration or an injunction 'shall' be made by an application for judicial review 'in any case where an application for judicial review, seeking that relief, has been made': see s 31(1), (2).

8 *O'Reilly v Mackman* [1983] 2 AC 237, [1982] 3 All ER 1124, HL, decided under RSC Ord 53. Recent examples of claims which were held to be an abuse of process because they were not brought under CPR Pt 54 include *Carter Commercial Developments Ltd v Bedford Borough Council* [2001] EWHC Admin 669, [2001] 34 EG 99 (CS); *Jones v Powys Local Health Board* [2008] EWHC 2562 (Admin), [2008] All ER (D) 234 (Nov). With regard to the circumstances in which either a declaration or an injunction should be sought by way of application under CPR Pt 54 rather than, for example, CPR Pt 7 see note 4. The court will have regard to the extent to which the claim for the relief sought turns on public law issues rather than private law ones: see *Roy v Kensington, Chelsea and Westminster Family Practitioner Committee* [1992] 1 AC 624, [1992] 1 All ER 705, HL; *Clark v University of Lincolnshire and Humberside* [2000] 3 All ER 752, [2000] 1 WLR 1988, CA. In practice the only substantial differences between the requirements of CPR Pt 54 and CPR Pt 7 concern the requirement for permission to bring a claim for judicial review and the time limit for an application for judicial review. Therefore if any argument arises as to whether or not CPR Pt 54 should have been used, the main considerations will be whether, having regard to the nature of the decision which is subject to challenge, it is appropriate to afford the decision-maker the protection of these procedural safeguards. If a claim is commenced under CPR Pt 54 when it would be more appropriate to have used another part of the CPR, the court may order that it proceed pursuant to that other procedure and give directions about the future management of the claim: see CPR 54.20. CPR Pt 30 (transfer: see CIVIL PROCEDURE vol 11 (2009) PARA 66 et seq) applies to transfers to and from the Administrative Court: CPR 54.20. In deciding whether a claim is suitable for transfer to the Administrative Court, a court will consider whether it raises issues of public law to which CPR Pt 54 should apply: *Practice Direction—Judicial Review* PD 54A para 14.2. Attention is drawn to CPR 30.5: *Practice Direction—Judicial Review* PD 54A para 14.1.

662. Overview. Applications for judicial review fall within the jurisdiction of the Administrative Court[1]. The procedural rules applicable to applications for judicial review are contained in the Civil Procedure Rules[2]. In this area, as in all others, the intention of the Civil Procedure Rules is that all applications will be dealt with justly in accordance with the overriding objective[3]. Although many of the new rules are in similar terms to those previously set out in the Rules of the Supreme Court[4], it should not be assumed that they will necessarily be construed or applied in the same way[5]. The progress of applications will also be shaped by the court's powers of case management, which may be exercised on its own initiative[6].

The judicial review procedure[7] must[8] be used in a claim for judicial review[9] where the claimant is seeking: (1) a mandatory order[10]; (2) a prohibiting order[11]; (3) a quashing order[12]; or (4) an injunction restraining a person from acting in any office in which he is not entitled to act[13]. The judicial review procedure may be used in a claim for judicial review where the claimant is seeking either an injunction or a declaration[14]. A claim for judicial review[15] may include a claim for damages or restitution but may not seek damages alone[16].

1 *Practice Direction—Judicial Review* PD 54A para 2.1; and see *Practice Direction—Administrative Court (Venue)* PD 54D. In general, the claim form in proceedings in the Administrative Court may be issued at the Administrative Court Office of the High Court at the Royal Courts of Justice in London or at the District Registry of the High Court at Birmingham, Cardiff, Leeds or Manchester: *Practice Direction—Administrative Court (Venue)* PD 54D para 2.1. Any claim started in Birmingham will normally be determined at a court in the Midland region; in Cardiff in Wales; in Leeds in the North-Eastern Region; in London at the

Royal Courts of Justice; and in Manchester, in the North-Western Region: *Practice Direction—Administrative Court (Venue)* PD 54D para 2.2. Certain categories of claim may only be heard in London. These categories comprise proceedings to which CPR Pt 76 or Pt 79 apply (see CIVIL PROCEDURE vol 12 (2009) PARA 1533), including proceedings relating to control orders, financial restrictions proceedings, proceedings relating to terrorism or alleged terrorists (where that is a relevant feature of the claim) and proceedings in which a special advocate is to be instructed; proceedings to which RSC Ord 115 applies; proceedings under the Proceeds of Crime Act 2002; appeals to the Administrative Court under the Extradition Act 2003; proceedings which must be heard by a Divisional Court; and proceedings relating to the discipline of solicitors: *Practice Direction—Administrative Court (Venue)* PD 54D paras 2.1, 3.1.

2 Ie CPR Pt 8 and Pt 54. Part 54 is known as the 'judicial review procedure'. See also *Practice Direction—Judicial Review* PD 54A; and the *Pre-Action Protocol—Judicial Review*. These rules apply to all applications for judicial review commenced after 1 October 2000, and applications commenced prior to that date remain subject to the RSC Ord 53 procedure: Civil Procedure (Amendment No 4) Rules 2000, SI 2000/2092, r 30.

3 As to the overriding objective see CPR 1.1; and CIVIL PROCEDURE vol 11 (2009) PARA 33.

4 Ie in RSC Ord 53.

5 Thus, case law in relation to the provisions of RSC Ord 53 will be regarded as persuasive rather than binding as to the construction and effect of CPR Pt 54.

6 See CPR Pt 3; and CIVIL PROCEDURE vol 11 (2009) PARA 36 et seq.

7 'Judicial review procedure' means the CPR Pt 8 procedure as modified by CPR Pt 54: CPR 54.1(e).

8 See CPR 54.2; and PARA 661.

9 A 'claim for judicial review' means a claim to review the lawfulness of: (1) an enactment; or (2) a decision, action or failure to act in relation to the exercise of a public function: CPR 54.1(2).

10 CPR 54.2(a). As to mandatory orders see PARA 703 et seq.

11 CPR 54.2(b). As to prohibiting orders see PARA 693 et seq.

12 CPR 54.2(c). As to quashing orders see PARA 693 et seq.

13 CPR 54.2(d). Such an injunction is brought under the Senior Courts Act 1981 s 30: see PARA 718. As to the Senior Courts Act 1981 see PARA 602 note 4.

14 CPR 54.3. As to the circumstances in which the court may grant a declaration or injunction in a claim for judicial review see the Senior Courts Act 1981 s 31(2); and PARA 716. Where the claimant is seeking a declaration or injunction in addition to one of the remedies listed in CPR 54.2 (see heads (1)–(4) in the text), the judicial review procedure must be used: CPR 54.3(1).

15 Ie made under CPR Pt 54.

16 CPR 54.3. If a claim under CPR Pt 54 does only seek damages the court will transfer it pursuant to CPR 54.20: see PARA 660. As to the circumstances in which the court may award damages on a claim for judicial review see the Senior Courts Act 1981 s 31(4); and PARA 691.

(2) PRE-HEARING

(i) Application for Permission

663. Pre-action protocol. Claimants should generally[1] follow the steps specified in the judicial review pre-action protocol, which sets out a code of good practice[2], before making a claim for judicial review[3]. The claimant should send a letter to the defendant to identify the issues in dispute and establish whether litigation can be avoided[4]. The defendant should normally respond[5] within 14 days[6]. If the claim is being conceded in full, the reply should say so in clear and unambiguous terms[7]. If the claim is being conceded in part or not being conceded at all, the reply should similarly say so in clear and unambiguous terms[8] and should provide further details of the defendant's position[9]. Parties should also consider whether some form of alternative dispute resolution procedure would be more suitable than litigation and, if so, endeavour to agree which form to adopt[10]. The pre-action protocol does not affect the time limit[11] which applies and requires that any claim form in an application for judicial review be filed promptly and in any event not later than three months after the grounds to make the claim first arose[12].

1 See the *Pre-Action Protocol for Judicial Review* which applies in England and Wales only: see *Pre-Action Protocol for Judicial Review* introduction. All claimants will need to satisfy themselves whether they should follow the protocol, depending upon the circumstances of his or her case: *Pre-Action Protocol for Judicial Review* para 7. The protocol will not be appropriate where the defendant does not have the legal power to change the decision being challenged, for example decisions issued by tribunals such as the Asylum and Immigration Tribunal: *Pre-Action Protocol for Judicial Review* para 6. Nor will it be appropriate in urgent cases, for example, when directions have been set, or are in force, for the claimant's removal from the United Kingdom, or where there is an urgent need for an interim order to compel a public body to act where it has unlawfully refused to do so (for example, the failure of a local housing authority to secure interim accommodation for a homeless claimant). In these cases, a claim should be made immediately: *Pre-Action Protocol for Judicial Review* para 6. However, even in emergency cases it is good practice to fax to the defendant the draft claim form which the claimant intends to issue: *Pre-Action Protocol for Judicial Review* para 7. A claimant is also normally required to notify a defendant when an interim mandatory order is being sought: *Pre-Action Protocol for Judicial Review* para 7. As to pre-action protocols see generally CIVIL PROCEDURE vol 11 (2009) PARA 107 et seq. As to interim relief see PARA 669. As to mandatory orders see PARA 703 et seq.

2 *Pre-Action Protocol for Judicial Review* para 5.

3 Where the use of the protocol is appropriate, the court will normally expect all parties to have complied with it and will take into account compliance or non-compliance (including the requirement to consider alternative dispute resolution) when giving directions for case management or making orders for costs: *Pre-Action Protocol for Judicial Review* para 7. See also *R (on the application of Mount Cook Land Ltd) v Westminster City Council* [2003] EWCA Civ 1346, [2004] 2 P & CR 405. As to costs in judicial review proceedings see PARAS 681–686.

4 *Pre-Action Protocol for Judicial Review* para 8. Claimants should normally use the suggested standard format for the letter outlined at Annex A to the Protocol: *Pre-Action Protocol for Judicial Review* para 9. The letter should contain: (1) the date and details of the decision, act or omission being challenged; (2) a clear summary of the facts on which the claim is based; (3) the details of any relevant information that the claimant is seeking and an explanation of why this is considered relevant; and (4) the details of any interested parties known to the claimant (who should be sent a copy of the letter before claim for information): *Pre-Action Protocol for Judicial Review* paras 10, 11. As to interested persons see PARA 664.

A claim should not normally be made until the proposed reply date given in the letter before claim has passed, unless the circumstances of the case require more immediate action to be taken: *Pre-Action Protocol for Judicial Review* para 12.

The protocol does not impose a greater obligation on a public body to disclose documents or give reasons for its decision than that already provided for in statute or common law. However, where the court considers that a public body should have provided relevant documents or information, particularly where this failure is a breach of a statutory or common law requirement, it may impose sanctions: *Pre-Action Protocol for Judicial Review* para 6.

5 The response should be sent to all interested parties identified by the claimant and should contain details of any other parties who the defendant considers also have an interest: *Pre-Action Protocol for Judicial Review* para 17.

6 *Pre-Action Protocol for Judicial Review* para 13. Defendants should normally respond using the standard format at Annex B to the *Protocol: Pre-Action Protocol for Judicial Review* para 13. Failure to do so will be taken into account by the court and sanctions may be imposed unless there are good reasons: *Pre-Action Protocol for Judicial Review* para 13. Where it is not possible to reply within the proposed time limit the defendant should send an interim reply and propose a reasonable extension. Where an extension is sought, reasons should be given and, where required, additional information requested. This will not affect the time limit for making a claim for judicial review. Nor will it bind the claimant where he or she considers this to be unreasonable. However, where the court considers that a subsequent claim is made prematurely it may impose sanctions: *Pre-Action Protocol for Judicial Review* para 14.

7 *Pre-Action Protocol for Judicial Review* para 15.

8 *Pre-Action Protocol for Judicial Review* para 16.

9 If the claim is being conceded in part or not being conceded at all, the reply should: (1) where appropriate, contain a new decision, clearly identifying what aspects of the claim are being conceded and what are not, or give a clear timescale within which the new decision will be

issued; (2) provide a fuller explanation for the decision, if considered appropriate to do so; (3) address any points of dispute, or explain why they cannot be addressed; (4) enclose any relevant documentation requested by the claimant, or explain why the documents are not being enclosed; and (5) where appropriate, confirm whether or not they will oppose any application for an interim remedy: *Pre-Action Protocol for Judicial Review* para 16.

10 *Pre-Action Protocol for Judicial Review* para 3.1 and see also *Cowl v Plymouth City Council* [2001] EWCA Civ 1935, [2002] 1 WLR 803. Options include discussion and negotiation, recourse to Ombudsmen, early neutral evaluation by an independent third party, and mediation: *Pre-Action Protocol for Judicial Review* para 3.2. The court may require the parties to provide evidence that alternative means of resolving their dispute were considered: *Pre-Action Protocol for Judicial Review* para 3.1. As to the relevance of alternative dispute resolution when determining costs, see *Pre-Action Protocol for Judicial Review* para 3.1; and PARA 681. However, no party can or should be forced to mediate or enter into any form of alternative dispute resolution: *Pre-Action Protocol for Judicial Review* para 3.4.

11 Ie the time limit specified in CPR 54.5(1): see PARA 658.

12 *Pre-Action Protocol for Judicial Review* introduction. The court does have discretion to permit a late claim: CPR 3.1(2)(a). However, compliance with the protocol alone is unlikely to be sufficient to persuade the court to allow a late claim: *Pre-Action Protocol for Judicial Review* introduction, note.

664. Application for permission. The court's permission to proceed is required in a claim for judicial review[1]. To obtain permission the claimant must file a claim form[2] in the Administrative Court Office[3]. The claim form must be served on the defendant and, unless the court otherwise directs, on any other person the claimant considers to be an interested party, within seven days after the date of filing[4]. An interested party is any person (other than the claimant and defendant) who is directly affected by the claim[5].

1 CPR 54.4. This requirement applies regardless of whether the claim has been commenced under CPR Pt 54 or whether the claim has been commenced pursuant to another provision of the CPR and has subsequently been transferred to the Administrative Court: CPR 54.4. There is a specific procedure to be followed in relation to urgent applications for permission: see *Practice Statement (Administrative Court: Listing and Urgent Cases)* [2002] 1 All ER 633, [2002] 1 WLR 810. Failure to comply with that guidance, leading to a manifestly inappropriate application, may lead to a wasted costs order: *Practice Statement (Administrative Court: Listing and Urgent Cases)*. As to the meaning of 'claim for judicial review' see PARA 662 note 9.

2 In addition to the matters set out in CPR 8.2 (contents of the claim form: see CIVIL PROCEDURE vol 11 (2009) PARA 128) the claimant must also state: (1) the name and address of any person he considers to be an interested party; (2) that he is requesting permission to proceed with a claim for judicial review; and (3) any remedy (including any interim remedy) he is claiming: CPR 54.6(1). As to the claim form see Form N461—*Judicial Review claim form*.

   The claim form must include or be accompanied by a detailed statement of the claimant's grounds for bringing the claim for judicial review, a statement of the facts relied on, any application to extend the time limit for filing the claim form, and any application for directions: CPR 54.6(2); *Practice Direction—Judicial Review* PD 54A para 5.6. The claimant should also provide any relevant information relating to alternative remedy. The claim form must confirm that the pre-action protocol has been complied with or give the reasons for any non-compliance: *Practice Statement (Administrative Court: Listing and Urgent Cases)* [2002] 1 All ER 633, [2002] 1 WLR 810. See also Form N461—*Judicial Review claim form*.

   Where the claimant is seeking to raise any issue under the Human Rights Act 1998, or seeks a remedy available under that Act, the claim form must include the information required by *Practice Direction—Statements of Case* PD 16 (see CIVIL PROCEDURE vol 11 (2009) PARA 584 et seq): *Practice Direction—Judicial Review* PD 54A para 5.3. Where the claimant intends to raise a devolution issue the claim form must comply with *Practice Direction—Judicial Review* PD 54A paras 5.4, 5.5.

   Although an application for permission is no longer strictly speaking a without notice application (since the defendant is now required to file an acknowledgment of service pursuant to CPR 54.8 (see PARA 665)), it should still be assumed that the claimant is under a duty on any application to make full and frank disclosure of all material facts: see *R (on the application of Derwent Holdings Ltd) v Trafford Borough Council* [2009] EWHC 1337 (Admin); *R (on the application of Burkett) v Hammersmith and Fulham London Borough Council* [2002] UKHL

23, [2002] 3 All ER 97, [2002] 1 WLR 1593 at [50] per Lord Steyn; *R v Lloyd's of London, ex p Briggs* [1993] 1 Lloyd's Rep 176, [1993] COD 66, DC; *R v Jockey Club Licensing Committee, ex p Wright* [1991] COD 306.

The claim form must be accompanied by: (a) any written evidence in support of the claim or application to extend time; (b) a copy of any order that the claimant seeks to have quashed; (c) where the claim relates to a decision of a court or tribunal, an approved copy of the reasons for reaching that decision; (d) copies of any documents on which the claimant proposes to rely; (e) copies of any relevant statutory material; and (f) a list of essential documents for advance reading by the court (with page references to the passages relied on): *Practice Direction—Judicial Review* PD 54A para 5.7. Where it is not possible to file all these documents, the claimant must indicate which documents have not been filed and the reasons why they are not currently available: *Practice Direction—Judicial Review* PD 54A para 5.8. Two copies of a paginated and indexed bundle containing all the above documents must also be filed: *Practice Direction—Judicial Review* PD 54A para 5.9. Regard should be had to CPR 8.5(1), (7) (see CIVIL PROCEDURE vol 11 (2009) PARA 132): *Practice Direction—Judicial Review* PD 54A para 5.10.

3   As to the time limits which apply see PARA 658. See *Practice Direction—Judicial Review* PD 54A para 2.1. Since the opening of regional Administrative Court centres in April 2009, *Practice Direction—Administrative Court (Venue)* PD 54D now determines the place in which a claim before the Administrative Court should be started and administered and the venue at which it will be determined: see PARA 659 note 7.

4   See CPR 54.7. Except as required by CPR 54.11 or 54.12(2), the Administrative Court will not serve documents and service must be effected by the parties: *Practice Direction—Judicial Review* PD 54A para 6.1.

5   CPR 54.1(2)(f). A person is 'directly affected' by the claim if he will be affected without the intervention of any intermediate agency; it will not suffice that he will suffer indirect financial consequences: see *R v Rent Officer Service, ex p Muldoon* [1996] 3 All ER 498, [1996] 1 WLR 1103, HL (decided under RSC Ord 53 r 5(3), which was in similar terms). See also *Re Williams* [2004] EWHC 163 (Admin), [2004] All ER (D) 271 (Jan); *R v MMC, ex p Milk Marque Ltd* [2000] COD 329 (the fact that the outcome of a decision is of 'the utmost significance and importance' does not necessarily mean that the person was directly affected; but in that case the Dairy Trade Federation was allowed to make representations under RSC Ord 53 r 9, which is now substantially repeated in CPR 54.17 (see PARA 671)); *R v Legal Aid Board, ex p Megarry* [1994] COD 468.

Where the claim for judicial review relates to proceedings in a court or tribunal, any other parties to those proceedings must be named in the claim form as interested parties under CPR 54.6(1) and therefore served with the claim form under CPR 54.7: *Practice Direction—Judicial Review* PD 54A para 5.1. For example, in a claim by a defendant for judicial review of a decision in a criminal case in the Magistrates' or Crown Court, the prosecution must always be named as an interested party: *Practice Direction—Judicial Review* PD 54A para 5.2.

(ii) Acknowledgment of Service

665. Acknowledgment of service. Any person served with a claim form who wishes to take part in the judicial review must file an acknowledgment of service in the relevant practice form[1]. Any acknowledgment of service must be filed not more than 21 days after service of the claim form[2]. It must be served on the claimant and any other person named in the claim form[3], as soon as practicable and, in any event, not later than seven days after it is filed[4]. These time limits cannot be extended by agreement between the parties[5].

Where the person filing the acknowledgment of service intends to contest the claim, the acknowledgment of service must set out a summary of his grounds for doing so[6], and must state the name and address of any person he considers to be an interested party[7]. It may include or be accompanied by an application for directions[8].

Where a person served with the claim form has failed to file an acknowledgment of service he may not take part in a hearing to decide whether permission should be given unless the court allows him to do so[9]. However, provided he complies with the requirements as to response[10] or any other direction of the court regarding the filing and service of detailed grounds for contesting the claim or supporting it on additional grounds and any written evidence, he may take part in the hearing of the judicial review[11].

1   CPR 54.8(1). This will include any interested party who has been served with the claim form: see PARA 664 note 5. Attention is drawn to CPR 8.3(2) and the relevant practice direction (see CIVIL PROCEDURE vol 11 (2009) PARA 130) and to CPR 10.5 (see CIVIL PROCEDURE vol 11 (2009) PARA 184): *Practice Direction—Judicial Review* PD 54A para 7.1. As to the relevant practice form see Form N462 *Judicial Review—Acknowledgment of service*.
2   CPR 54.8(2)(a). However, the acknowledgment of service should be filed as soon as possible and in urgent cases, it is good practice for the defendant and any interested party to make earlier contact with the Administrative Court office.
3   This is subject to any direction under CPR 54.7(b) that the claim form not be served on an interested party.
4   CPR 54.8(2)(b).
5   CPR 54.8(3). The provisions of CPR 10.3(2) (see CIVIL PROCEDURE vol 11 (2009) PARA 186) do not apply: CPR 54.8(5).
6   CPR 54.8(4)(a)(i). The summary of grounds required by CPR 54.8(4)(a)(i) is to be contrasted with the detailed grounds for contesting the claim and the supporting written evidence which are required following the grant of permission by CPR 54.14. As to the nature of the summary which should be included in the acknowledgment of service see *Ewing v Office of the Deputy Prime Minister* [2005] EWCA Civ 1583, [2006] 1 WLR 1260 at [43] per Carnwath LJ. The acknowledgment of service should specifically deal with any argument to be advanced on grounds of delay since this is an issue which should be determined at the permission stage: see *R v Criminal Injuries Compensation Board, ex p A* [1999] 2 AC 330, [1999] 2 WLR 974, HL; *R (on the application of Lichfield Securities) v Lichfield District Council* [2001] EWCA Civ 304, 81 P& CR 213, [2001] 3 PLR 33.
      Where a party wishes to claim the costs of serving an acknowledgment of service under the principles in *R (on the application of Mount Cook Land Ltd) v Westminster City Council* [2003] EWCA Civ 1346, [2004] 2 P & CR 405, the acknowledgment of service should include such a claim and a schedule of costs: see *Ewing v Office of the Deputy Prime Minister*; and PARA 682. Similarly, where a party wishes to contest the making of a protective costs order or to apply for his own costs liability to be capped, he should make this clear in the acknowledgment of service: see *R (on the application of Corner House Research) v Secretary of State for Trade and Industry* [2005] EWCA Civ 192, [2005] 4 All ER 1, [2005] 1 WLR 2600; and PARA 686.
7   CPR 54.8(4)(a)(ii). Although there is no requirement for the defendant to file or serve evidence at this stage, there is no reason why this could not be done in an appropriate case (although c f *Ewing v Office of the Deputy Prime Minister* [2005] EWCA Civ 1583 at [43], [2006] 1 WLR 1260 at [43] per Carnwath LJ). Note that the acknowledgment of service must be supported by a statement of truth, and so its contents are regarded as evidence on this basis: see Form N462 *Judicial Review—Acknowledgment of service*.
8   CPR 54.8(4)(b). As to whether it is possible for a defendant to seek summary judgment under CPR Pt 24 see *R (on the application of the Kurdistan Workers' Party) v Secretary of State for the Home Department* [2002] EWHC 644 (Admin) at [99], (2002) All ER (D) 99 (Apr) at [99] per Richards J.
9   CPR 54.9(1)(a).
10 Ie the requirements of CPR 54.14: see PARA 673.
11 CPR 54.9(1)(b). However, where that person takes part in the hearing of the judicial review, the court may take his failure to file an acknowledgment of service into account when deciding what order to make about costs: CPR 54.9(2). The provisions of CPR 8.4 (consequences of not filing an acknowledgment of service) (see CIVIL PROCEDURE vol 11 (2009) PARA 131) do not apply to judicial review: CPR 54.9(3).

(iii) Test for Permission

666. The test for the grant of permission. Permission should be granted if on the material then available the court considers, without going into the matter in depth, that there is an arguable case[1] for granting the relief sought by the claimant[2]. The grant of permission is nevertheless a matter within the discretion of the court. For example, when considering whether to grant permission to apply for judicial review, the court must take account of any alternative remedies available to the applicant, since where any alternative remedy has not been exhausted judicial review will not normally lie[3]. It is open to the court to grant permission in relation to some only of the matters of complaint raised in the claim form, or certain of the decisions under challenge[4]. If permission is granted neither the defendant nor any other person who was served with the claim form may apply to set the permission aside[5].

Applications for judicial review may be made with assistance from the Community Legal Service ('CLS') Fund[6].

1   An arguable case is one that has a realistic prospect of success: *Antoine v Sharma* [2006] UKPC 57 at [14], [2007] 1 WLR 780 at [14]; *R v Secretary of State for the Home Department, ex p Swati* [1986] 1 All ER 717, [1986] 1 WLR 477, CA. But cf *Mass Energy Ltd v Birmingham City Council* [1994] Env LR 298, CA (inter partes hearing at permission stage, detailed arguments advanced; more onerous test of 'likely to succeed' applied on decision whether or not to grant permission); and *R (on the application of Grierson) v Office of Communications* [2005] EWHC 1899 (Admin), [2005] 35 LS Gaz R 41.

2   *IRC v National Federation of Self-Employed and Small Businesses Ltd* [1982] AC 617 at 642–644, [1981] 2 All ER 93 at 106, HL, per Lord Diplock. See also *R v Secretary of State for the Home Department, ex p Swati* [1986] 1 All ER 717, [1986] 1 WLR 477, CA; cf *Puhlhofer v Hillingdon London Borough Council* [1986] AC 484, [1986] 1 All ER 467, HL; *R v Secretary of State for the Home Department, ex p Begum* [1990] COD 107, CA; *R v Legal Aid Board, ex p Hughes* (1992) 5 Admin LR 623, CA. Under RSC Ord 53 it was open to the court in a case where it was unclear whether or not permission should be granted to invite the defendant to attend a hearing to make representations on the point. It is submitted that this practice should continue under CPR Pt 54.

3   Permission to apply for judicial review will not normally be granted where there is a suitable alternative remedy, save in exceptional circumstances: see PARA 657. The parties should also consider alternative dispute resolution: *Cowl v Plymouth City Council* [2001] EWCA Civ 1935, [2002] 1 WLR 803; *Practice Statement (Administrative Court: Listing and Urgent Cases)* [2002] 1 All ER 633, [2002] 1 WLR 810 at para 5; and see PARA 664. However, no party can be forced to mediate or enter into any form of alternative dispute resolution: see *Pre-Action Protocol for Judicial Review* para 3.4; and PARA 663.

4   See *R v Staffordshire County Council Education Appeals Committee, ex p Ashworth* (1996) 9 Admin LR 373; *R v ASA, ex p City Trading* [1997] COD 202; *R v Radio Authority, ex p Wildman* [1999] COD 255, CA. This power is implicit in CPR 54.12 which allows for reconsideration of a decision to grant limited permission at an oral hearing.

5   CPR 54.13. The court has an inherent jurisdiction to set aside orders, including orders to grant permission to apply for judicial review: see *R v Secretary of State for the Home Department, ex p Chinoy* (1991) 4 Admin LR 457, [1991] COD 381, DC; *R (on the application of Wilkinson) v Chief Constable of West Yorkshire* [2002] EWHC 2353 (Admin), [2002] All ER (D) 310 (Oct). However, in light of the provisions of CPR 54.13 it is likely that applications to set aside permission will only rarely be available. Even when such an application is not excluded by CPR 54.13 it is clear that the jurisdiction will only be exercised in a very plain case: see *R v Secretary of State for the Home Department, ex p Chinoy*; *Re Ballyedmond Castle Farms Ltd's Application* [2000] NI 174, NI QB; *R v Environment Agency, ex p Gibson* [1998] All ER (D) 200; *R v Secretary of State for the Home Department, ex p Herbage (No 2)* [1987] QB 1077, [1987] 1 All ER 324, CA; *WEA Records Ltd v Visions Channel 4 Ltd* [1983] 2 All ER 589, [1983] 1 WLR 721, CA. Where appropriate circumstances arise, the correct procedure normally would be to apply to the judge who made the original order granting permission, with a view to inviting him to recall that decision and order: see *R (on the application of Wilkinson) v Chief Constable of West Yorkshire* at [40]–[43] per Davis J.

6   See LEGAL AID vol 65 (2008) PARAS 43, 45.

667. Consideration of the application for permission. The court will generally, in the first instance, consider the question of permission without a hearing[1]. Following this consideration the court will serve an order giving or refusing permission and any directions on the claimant and defendant and any other party who filed an acknowledgment of service[2]. The order must set out or be accompanied by the court's reasons for coming to its decision[3]. The order may also contain any directions which have been made for the future conduct of the proceedings[4]. The court has power to order a claim to continue as if it had not been started under the judicial review procedure and, where it does so, give directions about the future management of the claim[5].

A claimant whose application for permission has been refused on the papers has the right to request that the refusal be reconsidered at a hearing[6]. Such a request must be filed within seven days of service by the court of its reasons for making its decision[7]. Neither the defendant nor any other interested party need attend a hearing on the question of permission unless the court directs otherwise[8].

1 *Practice Direction—Judicial Review* PD 54A para 8.4. A specific procedure applies in cases of urgent judicial review: *Practice Statement (Administrative Court: Listing and Urgent Cases)* [2002] 1 All ER 633, [2002] 1 WLR 810. The court may, on occasion, direct that the question of permission and the substantive merits of the application be considered in a single 'rolled up' hearing: see eg *R (on the application of Westminster City Council) v Mayor of London* [2002] EWHC 2440 (Admin), [2003] LGR 611.

2 CPR 54.11. The grant of permission may be subject to conditions as to costs. As to orders for security for costs see CPR Pt 25; and PARA 681. As to the making of such orders in judicial review proceedings see *R v Westminster City Council, ex p Residents' Association of Mayfair* [1991] COD 182.

3 CPR 54.12(2); *Practice Direction—Judicial Review* PD 54A para 9.1.

4 CPR 54.10, 54.11; *Practice Direction—Judicial Review* PD 54A paras 8.1, 8.2. Note that CPR 3.7 provides a sanction for the non-payment of the fee payable when permission to proceed has been given (see CIVIL PROCEDURE vol 11 (2009) PARA 253): CPR 54.10(2).

5 CPR 54.20. CPR Pt 30 (transfer) (see CIVIL PROCEDURE vol 11 (2009) PARA 66) applies to transfers to and from the Administrative Court: CPR 54.20. See also *R (on the application of West) v Lloyd's of London* [2004] EWCA Civ 506 at [41], [2004] 3 All ER 251 at [41] per Brooke LJ (proceedings not transferred to the Chancery Division as the applicant would have to entirely reshape his case to identify the private law causes of action relied upon). The court may use this power to transfer any claim for damages out of the Administrative Court: see *R (on the application of the Kurdistan Workers' Party) v Secretary of State for the Home Department* [2002] EWHC 644 (Admin) at [87], (2002) All ER (D) 99 (Apr) at [87] per Richards J; *R v Chief Constable of Lancashire, ex p Parker* [1993] QB 577 at 588, [1993] 2 All ER 56 at 64 per Nolan LJ giving the judgment of the court.

6 CPR 54.12(3).

7 CPR 54.12(4). The claimant, defendant and any other person who has filed an acknowledgment of service will be given at least two days' notice of the hearing date: CPR 54.12(5). See also *Practice Statement (Administrative Court: Listing and Urgent Cases)* [2002] 1 All ER 633, [2002] 1 WLR 810.

8 *Practice Direction—Judicial Review* PD 54A para 8.5. Where the defendant or any party does attend a hearing, the court will not generally make an order for costs against the claimant: *Practice Direction—Judicial Review* PD 54A para 8.6; and see PARA 682. Clearly, the exception implicit in this provision is most likely to apply when the defendant has been directed to attend.

(iv) Directions and Interim Relief

668. Directions. On granting permission to apply for judicial review, the court may give any directions which are appropriate for the future conduct of the claim[1]. For example:

(1) it is open to the court to direct a stay of the proceedings for any purpose[2];

(2) the court may impose such terms as to costs and as to giving security as it thinks fit[3];

(3) the court may give directions on any other matter which is within its normal powers[4];

(4) the court may direct that the hearing of the claim be expedited[5];

(5)   the court may give directions as to whether the claim should be determined by a judge of another division of the High Court[6]; or

(6)   the court may consider any application to amend the claim (including any amendment as to the relief sought)[7].

Any directions which are sought at the permission stage should be set out in the claim form or acknowledgment of service, as appropriate. Any evidence in support of any such application should be provided at the same time[8].

1   See CPR 54.10; and PARA 664. Case management directions under CPR 54.10(1) may include directions about serving the claim form and any evidence on other persons: *Practice Direction—Judicial Review* PD 54A para 8.1. Where a claim is made under the Human Rights Act 1998 (see PARAS 650–654; and CONSTITUTIONAL LAW AND HUMAN RIGHTS), a direction may be made for giving notice to the Crown or joining the Crown as a party: *Practice Direction—Judicial Review* PD 54A para 8.2. See also CPR 19.4A; *Practice Direction—Addition and Substitution of Parties* PD 19 para 6 (see CIVIL PROCEDURE vol 11 (2009) PARA 596): *Practice Direction—Judicial Review* PD 54A para 8.2.

2   See CPR 54.10(1), (2). See *R v General Medical Council, ex p Popat* [1991] COD 245; and *R v CLA, ex p Abernethy* [2000] COD 56 (subsequent to the issue of the claim the defendant agreed to reconsider the decision subject to challenge; decision to stay proceedings with liberty to apply (note that it would generally be more in accordance with the CPR to limit the liberty to apply to a specific period following the reconsideration and provide that in the absence of any application within that time the proceedings would be dismissed)).

For the purposes of an application for a stay, 'proceedings' include the decision itself: see *R v Secretary of State for Education and Science, ex p Avon County Council* [1991] 1 QB 558, [1991] 1 All ER 282, CA; *R (on the application of Ashworth Hospital Authority) v Mental Health Review Tribunal for West Midlands and Northwest Region* [2002] EWCA Civ 923, [2003] 1 WLR 127, 70 BMLR 40; cf *Minister of Foreign Affairs, Trade and Industry v Vehicles and Supplies Ltd* [1991] 4 All ER 65, [1991] 1 WLR 550. It is likely that the matters considered by the court in determining an application for a stay will be comparable to those relevant to determination of an application for an interim injunction: see *R v Advertising Standards Authority Ltd, ex p Vernons Organisation Ltd* [1993] 2 All ER 202, [1992] 1 WLR 1289 (on the facts of that case, application for a stay was in truth an application for an injunction).

As to whether a stay may be granted to prevent the implementation of a decision made by a minister in the exercise of statutory powers see *R v Secretary of State for Education and Science, ex p Avon County Council* (stay may be granted against any defendant, including the Crown); cf *Minister of Foreign Affairs, Trade and Industry v Vehicles and Supplies Ltd* (stay cannot be granted to prevent the implementation of a decision made by a minister in the exercise of statutory powers; but the decision in *R v Secretary of State for Education and Science, ex p Avon County Council* was not cited or referred to). The relationship between these two decisions remains uncertain: see *R v Secretary of State for the Home Department, ex p Muboyayi* [1992] QB 244, [1991] 4 All ER 72, CA; *R v Department of Health and Social Security and Norgine Ltd, ex p Scotia Pharmaceuticals Ltd* [1993] COD 408, 19 BMLR 82.

Stays are not appropriate if the effect is to compel, rather than restrain, a public body from acting: see *R v Licensing Authority, ex p Smith Kline & French Laboratories Ltd (No 2)* [1990] 1 QB 574, [1989] 2 All ER 113; *R v HM Treasury, ex p British Telecommunications plc* [1994] 1 CMLR 621, CA. A stay is likely to be the appropriate form of interim relief where there is a challenge to a decision by a court or other body, or the process of arriving at such a decision, whereas an injunction is likely to be the appropriate form where it is sought to restrain another party or person concerned in the proceedings from some action: *R v Darlington Borough Council, ex p Association of Darlington Taxi Owners* [1994] COD 424. In principle the same criteria should apply to the grant of both a stay and an injunction, but in practice the relationship between the two interim remedies has yet to be worked out. As to interim injunctions see PARA 669. Note that particular considerations apply in mental health proceedings: *R (on the application of Ashworth Hospital Authority) v Mental Health Review Tribunal for West Midlands and Northwest Region* [2002] EWCA Civ 923, [2003] 1 WLR 127, 70 BMLR 40; *R (on the application of Care Principles Ltd) v Mental Health Review Tribunal* [2006] EWHC 3194 (Admin), 94 BMLR 145. The court will also consider the effect of any stay on third parties: see *R v Inspectorate of Pollution, ex p Greenpeace Ltd* [1994] 4 All ER 321, [1994] 1 WLR 570, CA; *R v Secretary of State for the Environment, ex p Royal Society for the Protection of Birds* (1995) 7 Admin LR 434, 139 Sol Jo LB 86, HL.

3 As to costs see PARA 681 et seq. As to protective costs orders and costs capping orders see *R (on the application of Corner House Research) v Secretary of State for Trade and Industry* [2005] EWCA Civ 192, [2005] 4 All ER 1, [2005] 1 WLR 2600; and PARA 686. As to the basis upon which security for costs may be ordered see CPR Pt 25; PARA 681; and CIVIL PROCEDURE vol 11 (2009) PARA 745 et seq.

4 For example, disclosure, further information, service of evidence, including abridgement of time for the service of evidence etc. As to disclosure see further PARA 673. For examples of other directions see the Children and Young Persons Act 1933 s 39 (reporting restrictions in cases involving young people: see CHILDREN AND YOUNG PERSONS vol 5(4) (2008 Reissue) PARA 1271). The High Court has the power in judicial review proceedings to make ancillary orders temporarily releasing an applicant from detention, in an exercise of original jurisdiction (as does the Court of Appeal on an appeal in such proceedings): *R (on the application of Sezek) v Secretary of State for the Home Department* [2001] EWCA Civ 795, [2002] 1 WLR 348, [2001] Imm AR 657. See also *R v Secretary of State for the Home Department, ex p Turkoglu* [1988] QB 398, [1987] 2 All ER 823, CA; *R v Secretary of State for the Home Department, ex p Swati* [1986] 1 All ER 717, [1986] 1 WLR 477, CA.

5 As to the court's case management powers see CPR Pt 3; and CIVIL PROCEDURE vol 11 (2009) PARA 246 et seq.

6 For example, in cases raising issues of family law, it may be appropriate for the claim to be assigned to a judge of the Family Division: see *R v Dover Magistrates' Court, ex p Kidner* [1983] 1 All ER 475.

7 See PARA 670.

8 See PARAS 664–665.

669. Interim relief. Applications for interim relief will also be considered at the permission stage. In most if not all cases this will take place at a hearing where all affected parties are present. Any applications for interim relief should be set out clearly in the claim form[1] and the special procedure for urgent cases should be followed in all appropriate cases[2]. The fact that permission has been granted does not mean that interim relief should be granted as a matter of course[3].

The most common application made at this stage is for an interim injunction[4]. The grant or refusal of an interim injunction in judicial review proceedings will normally depend on the application of the general principles which apply pursuant to the general procedural rules governing interim remedies[5], modified to take account of specific public law considerations[6]. Other interim applications which may be made in judicial review proceedings are for an interim declaration[7] or for a stay of the decision which is subject to challenge[8].

1 See CPR 54.6(1)(c); and PARA 664.

2 See *Practice Statement (Administrative Court: Listing and Urgent Cases)* [2002] 1 All ER 633, [2002] 1 WLR 810. See PARA 664 note 1.

3 See *R v Secretary of State for the Home Department, ex p Doorga* [1990] COD 109, [1990] Imm AR 98, CA.

4 See CPR 25.1(1)(a); and the Supreme Court Act 1981 s 31. An injunction is available against ministers of the Crown: *Re M* [1994] 1 AC 377, sub nom *M v Home Office* [1993] 3 All ER 537, HL. In some cases an injunction may be obtained prior to the issue of proceedings: see *M v Home Office* at 423 and 565 per Lord Woolf; and see generally CPR Pt 25; and CIVIL PROCEDURE vol 11 (2009) PARA 315 et seq.

5 The general procedural rules governing interim remedies are contained in CPR Pt 25: see CIVIL PROCEDURE vol 11 (2009) PARA 315 et seq. See eg the principles set out in *American Cyanamid Co v Ethicon Ltd* [1975] AC 396, [1975] 1 All ER 504, HL; *Films Rover International Ltd v Cannon Film Sales Ltd* [1986] 3 All ER 772, [1987] 1 WLR 670; *Lansing Linde Ltd v Kerr* [1991] 1 All ER 418, [1991] 1 WLR 251, CA; and see further PARA 718. The court will consider whether there is a serious issue to be tried, and if so determine whether the balance of convenience requires an injunction in the terms sought. When the injunction sought is in effect a mandatory order, different considerations apply: see *Nottingham Building Society v Eurodynamics Systems plc* [1993] FSR 468 at 474 per Chadwick LJ (unusually strong and clear case required a high degree of assurance that applicant would succeed following the final hearing; clearly any order which requires defendant to take a positive step at the interim stage

carries a high risk of injustice if it turns out to have been wrongly granted); *R v Kensington and Chelsea Royal London Borough Council, ex p Hammell* [1989] QB 518, [1989] 1 All ER 1202, CA; *R v Westminster City Council, ex p Augustin* [1993] 1 WLR 730, 91 LGR 89, CA; *R v Cardiff City Council, ex p Barry* (1990) 22 HLR 261; but cf *R v Servite Houses, ex p Goldsmith (interim relief)* (2000) 3 CCL Rep 354, CA. As to mandatory orders see PARA 703 et seq.

6 See *Belize Alliance of Conservative Non-Governmental Organisation v Department of the Environment* [2003] UKPC 63 at [35]–[39], [2003] 1 WLR 2839 at [35]–[39], [2004] 2 P & CR 13 at [35]–[39]; and see generally the approach to interim relief in public law cases in *R v Secretary of State for Transport, ex p Factortame Ltd (No 2)* [1991] 1 AC 603, sub nom *Factortame Ltd v Secretary of State for Transport (No 2)* [1991] 1 All ER 70, HL. For example, in public law cases, determining where the balance of convenience lies will require consideration to be given to any wider public interest which is relevant and material: see *Smith v Inner London Education Authority* [1978] 1 All ER 411, 142 JP 136, CA; *Sierbein v Westminster City Council* (1987) 86 LGR 431, CA; *R v Secretary of State for the National Heritage, ex p Continental Television BV* [1993] 2 CMLR 333 at 348, DC, per Leggatt LJ. See further *R v HM Treasury, ex p British Telecommunications plc* [1994] 1 CMLR 621, CA; and *R v Secretary of State for Health, ex p Imperial Tobacco Ltd* [1999] All ER (D) 1185; cf the approach in *R v Secretary of State for Health, ex p Imperial Tobacco Ltd* [2002] QB 161 at 185, [2000] 2 WLR 834 at 858, CA, per Laws LJ ('the stronger the case, the lower the damage hurdle').

Where the claim is that United Kingdom legislation is inconsistent with European Union law the test to apply is that set out in Case C-213/89 *R v Secretary of State for Transport, ex p Factortame Ltd (No 2)* [1991] 1 AC 603, sub nom *Factortame Ltd v Secretary of State for Transport (No 2)* [1991] 1 All ER 70, ECJ. See also *R v Secretary of State for Trade and Industry, ex p Trades Union Congress* [2000] IRLR 565; *R (on the application of Mayer Parry Recycling Ltd) v Environment Agency and Secretary of State for the Environment* [2001] Env LR 35. Interim relief may be granted in appropriate cases to suspend domestic legislation based on an invalid European Union Regulation: see Case C-143/88 *Zuckerfabrik Süderdithmarschen AG v Hauptzollamt Itzehoe* [1991] ECR I–415, [1993] 3 CMLR 1, ECJ; Case C-465/93 *Atlanta Fruchthandelsgesellschaft mbH v Bundesamt fur Ernahrung und Forstwirtschaft* [1995] ECR I-3761, [1996] 1 CMLR 575, ECJ; Case C-213/01 P *T Port GmbH & Co KG v European Commission* [2003] ECR I-2319 (see the opinion of Advocate General Leger); *R v Secretary of State for Health, ex p Imperial Tobacco Ltd* [2000] 1 All ER 572, [2001] 1 WLR 127, HL; *R (on the application of ABNA Ltd) v Secretary of State for Health* [2003] EWHC 2420 (Admin), [2004] 2 CMLR 934.

A cross-undertaking in damages is usually required, but this is a rule of practice rather than a rule of law: *R v Coventry City Council, ex p Finnie* (1996) 29 HLR 658. In most cases the court will be reluctant to grant injunctive relief if there is no cross-undertaking: see *R v Secretary of State for the Environment, ex p Rose Theatre Trust Co (No 1)* [1990] COD 47, (1989) Times, 18 July; *R v Her Majesty's Inspectorate of Pollution, ex p Greenpeace* [1994] 4 All ER 321 at 327–328, [1994] 1 WLR 570 at 577, CA, per Scott LJ; *R v Darlington Borough Council, ex p Association of Darlington Taxi Owners* [1994] COD 424; *R v Secretary of State for the Environment, ex p Royal Society for the Protection of Birds* (1995) 7 Admin LR 434, 139 Sol Jo LB 86, HL; *Rochdale Borough Council v Anders* [1988] 3 All ER 490. However, a cross-undertaking will not always be required: see eg *R v Lambeth London Borough Council, ex p Walter* (2 February 1989, unreported) CA; *R v Secretary of State for Transport, ex p Factortame Ltd (No 2)* (no undertaking required when judicial review was the only means by which a duty arising in public law could be enforced; see also on this point *Hoffman La-Roche & Co AG v Secretary of State for Trade and Industry* [1975] AC 295, [1974] 2 All ER 1128, HL; *Kirklees Metropolitan Borough Council v Wickes Building Supplies Ltd* [1993] AC 227, [1992] 3 All ER 717, HL; and *R v Hammersmith and Fulham London Borough Council, ex p People Before Profit Ltd* [1981] JPL 869 at 874, 80 LGR 322 at 336 per Comyn J (cross-undertaking would not have been required, but interim relief refused on other grounds)).

7 See CPR 25.1(1)(b); and the Supreme Court Act 1981 s 31. See also *R v Secretary of State for Trade and Industry, ex p Trades Union Congress* [2000] IRLR 565; *R (on the application of Mayer Parry Recycling Ltd) v Environment Agency and Secretary of State for the Environment* [2001] Env LR 35.

8 See PARA 668.

670. Interlocutory orders. On a claim for judicial review the court has the same interlocutory powers as when dealing with any other claim under the Civil Procedure Rules. However, given the nature of judicial review proceedings, two specific areas merit further consideration, namely the exercise of powers in relation to disclosure and applications to amend.

Although the disclosure provisions of the Civil Procedure Rules[1] apply with full effect to claims for judicial review, the nature of judicial review claims means that general disclosure orders will not be made as a matter of course[2]. Orders for disclosure are generally limited to specific documents or categories of document required fairly to dispose of the issues before the court[3]. Disclosure will not be ordered simply to make good defects in the claimant's evidence[4].

If, following the grant of permission, a claimant wishes to rely on additional grounds in support of his claim, the permission of the court must be obtained[5].

1   Ie CPR Pt 31: see CIVIL PROCEDURE vol 11 (2009) PARA 538 et seq.
2   See *Practice Direction—Judicial Review* PD 54A para 12.1; and *Tweed v Parades Commission for Northern Ireland* [2006] UKHL 53, [2007] 1 AC 650, [2007] NI 66. Disclosure is ordered in relatively few judicial review cases, and is generally restricted to specific documents or categories of document. As to the obligations of candour attaching to both claimant and defendant to a judicial review application see PARAS 664, 673. As to the statutory right of access to information held by public authorities see CONFIDENCE AND DATA PROTECTION vol 8(1) (2003 Reissue) PARA 583 et seq.
3   See *Tweed v Parades Commission for Northern Ireland* [2006] UKHL 53, [2007] 1 AC 650, [2007] NI 66. As claims for judicial review often involve matters relating to the operations of government, the question of public interest immunity may sometimes arise: see *IRC v Rossminster Ltd* [1980] AC 952 at 1013, [1980] 1 All ER 80 at 94, HL, per Lord Diplock. See also *Conway v Rimmer* [1968] AC 910, [1968] 1 All ER 874, HL; *Burmah Oil Co Ltd v Bank of England* [1980] AC 1090, [1979] 3 All ER 700, HL; *Air Canada v Secretary of State for Trade (No 2)* [1983] 2 AC 394, [1983] 1 All ER 910, HL; and CIVIL PROCEDURE vol 11 (2009) PARAS 574–579. As to the circumstances in which a special advocate may be appointed to consider material which attracts public interest immunity see *AHK v Secretary of State for the Home Department* [2009] EWCA Civ 287, [2009] 1 WLR 2049.
4   See *Tweed v Parades Commission for Northern Ireland* [2006] UKHL 53, [2007] 1 AC 650, [2007] NI 66; and see further *R v IRC, ex p Federation of Self-Employed and Small Businesses Ltd* [1982] AC 617, [1981] 2 All ER 93, HL; *R v IRC, ex p Taylor* [1988] COD 61; *R v Secretary of State for Education, ex p J* [1993] COD 146.
5   CPR 54.15; *Practice Direction—Judicial Review* PD 54A para 11.1. See also *R (on the application of Smith) v Parole Board* [2003] EWCA Civ 1014, [2003] 1 WLR 2548 (substantial justification required before a claimant will be allowed to advance an argument for which permission had been refused at a contested oral permission hearing). Where the claimant intends to apply to rely on additional grounds at the hearing of the claim for judicial review, he must give notice to the court and to any other person served with the claim form no later than seven clear days before the hearing (or the warned date where appropriate): *Practice Direction—Judicial Review* PD 54A para 11.1. As to whether or not permission to amend will be granted, normal principles apply: see CPR Pt 17; and CIVIL PROCEDURE vol 11 (2009) PARA 607 et seq.

(v) Parties and Intervenors

671.   Parties and intervenors.   The parties[1] to a claim for judicial review will normally be the claimant[2], the defendant and any interested parties[3]. If any dispute arises as to whether additional parties should be joined, the court is under a duty to take into account how best to resolve the claim in the interests of justice in accordance with the overriding objective of the Civil Procedure Rules[4]. This will include, for example, considerations as to the speed and economy of the proceedings. The court will not allow judicial review to be used simply as a method of punishing the defendant to the claim whether in costs or in any other way[5].

The court may not make a declaration of incompatibility or an award of damages under the Human Rights Act 1998[6], unless 21 days' notice, or such other period of notice as the court directs, has been given to the Crown[7]. Where such notice has been given, a minister, or other person permitted by the Human Rights Act 1998, is entitled to be joined as a party on giving notice to the court[8].

Any person who has not been joined as a party to the claim may apply for permission to file evidence, or to make representations[9] at the hearing of the judicial review[10]. Such an application may be made regardless of whether or not the person concerned falls within the definition of 'interested party'[11]. Persons intervening in a claim for judicial review are not entitled as of right to be heard on any appeal[12]. Again, the issue is one within the discretion of the court. The court may also, exceptionally, ask the Attorney General to appoint an amicus curiae to assist the court[13].

1   See CPR 54.1, 54.6, 54.7; *Practice Direction—Judicial Review* PD54A paras 5.1, 5.2; and *Pre-Action Protocol for Judicial Review* paras 11, 17.

2   As to the test in determining whether a claimant has sufficient interest in the matter to which the claim relates to have standing to bring an application for judicial review see the Supreme Court Act 1981 s 31(3); and PARA 664. As to the test for determining whether a claimant is a victim for the purposes of a claim under the Human Rights Act 1998 s 6 see the Convention for the Protection of Human Rights and Fundamental Freedoms (Rome, 4 November 1950; TS 71 (1953) Cmd 8969) art 34; the Human Rights Act 1998 s 7; and PARA 651.

3   See CPR 54.1(2)(f); and PARA 664.

4   As to the overriding objective see CPR 1.1; and CIVIL PROCEDURE vol 11 (2009) PARA 33. Where the court gives permission for joinder of an additional party, it may do so on conditions, such as to costs: see *R v Secretary of State for the Environment, Transport and the Regions, ex p O'Byrne* (1999) Times, 12 November.

5   See *R v Waltham Forest London Borough Council, ex p Baxter* [1988] QB 419, [1987] 3 All ER 671, CA.

6   Ie in accordance with the Human Rights Act 1998 s 4 or s 9: see PARA 651; and CONSTITUTIONAL LAW AND HUMAN RIGHTS.

7   CPR 19.4A(1). See CIVIL PROCEDURE vol 11 (2009) PARA 596.

8   See the Human Rights Act 1998 s 5(1), (2); CPR 19.4A; and *Practice Direction—Addition and Substitution of Parties* PD19 para 6. Notice under the Human Rights Act 1998 s 5(2) may be given at any time during the proceedings: s 5(3). Where a claim is made under the Human Rights Act 1998 s 9 for damages in respect of a judicial act, that claim must be set out in the statement of case or the appeal notice and notice must be given to the Crown: CPR 19.4A(3); and *Practice Direction—Addition and Substitution of Parties* PD19 para 6.6. In such circumstances, where the appropriate person has not applied to be joined as a party within 21 days, or such other period as the court directs, after the notice is served, the court may join the appropriate person as a party: CPR 19.4A(4). Note that a person who has been made a party to criminal proceedings (including all proceedings before the Courts-Martial Appeal Court) (other than in Scotland) as the result of a notice under the Human Rights Act 1998 s 5(2) may appeal to the Supreme Court against any declaration of incompatibility made in the proceedings, with leave granted by the court making the declaration of incompatibility or by the Supreme Court: Human Rights Act 1998 s 5(4), (5) (amended by the Constitutional Reform Act 2005 s 40(4), Sch 9 para 66(1), (3)).

9   Ie either in opposition to or in support of the application for judicial review: see CPR 54.17(1) (in contrast to the position under Ord 53 r 9, under which only interventions in opposition to the application were permissible).

10 CPR 54.17(1). Any such application must be made promptly: CPR 54.17(2). See also *Practice Direction—Judicial Review* PD 54A para 13.5 ('at the earliest reasonable opportunity'). Where all the parties consent, the court may deal with an application under CPR 54.17 without a hearing: *Practice Direction—Judicial Review* PD 54A para 13.1. An application for permission should be made by letter to the Administrative Court office, identifying the claim, explaining who the applicant is and indicating why and in what form the applicant wants to participate in the hearing: *Practice Direction—Judicial Review* PD 54A para 13.3. If the applicant is seeking a prospective order as to costs, the letter should say what kind of order and on what grounds: *Practice Direction—Judicial Review* PD 54A para 13.4. Where the court gives permission for a person to file evidence or make representations at the hearing of the claim for judicial review, it may do so on conditions and may give case management directions: *Practice Direction—Judicial Review* PD 54A para 13.2.

The Commission for Equality and Human Rights has capacity to institute or intervene in judicial review proceedings if it appears to the Commission that the proceedings are relevant to a matter in connection with which the Commission has a function: Equality Act 2006 s 30(1). This is subject to any limitation or restriction imposed by virtue of an enactment or in accordance with the practice of a court: s 30(4)(b). However, in so instituting proceedings or intervening, the Commission may rely on the Human Rights Act 1998 s 7(1)(b): see the Equality Act 2006 s 30(3). See DISCRIMINATION vol 13 (2007 Reissue) PARA 335.

11 See *R v MMC, ex p Milk Marque* [2000] COD 329. Clearly, those who do fall within the definition (but were not, for some reason served with the claim form) have a stronger claim that the discretion of the court be exercised in their favour. With regard to some general considerations which may apply to the exercise of the discretion see: *R v Department of Health, ex p Source Informatics Ltd* [2001] QB 424, [2000] COD 114, CA (intervenors allowed to appear at hearing of appeal against refusal of permission even though they had had no involvement prior to that stage). See also *R v Bournewood Community and Mental Health NHS Trust, ex p L* [1999] 1 AC 458, [1998] 3 All ER 289, HL; *R (on the application of the Howard League for Penal Reform) v Secretary of State for the Home Department* [2001] EWHC 1750 Admin (Association of Directors of Social Services, Local Government Association and the Department of Health to be invited to apply under CPR r 54.17).

12 *R v Licensing Authority, ex p Smith Kline and French Laboratories Ltd* [1988] COD 62, CA.

13 See *Islington London Borough Council v Camp* [2004] LGR 58 at 66 per Richards J.

(vi) Appeals against Refusal to Grant Permission

672. Appeals against refusal to grant permission. In a civil case, a person who has been refused permission to apply for judicial review at a hearing in the High Court may apply to the Court of Appeal for permission to appeal[1]. Any such application must be made within seven days of the decision to refuse permission to apply for judicial review[2]. On an application for permission to appeal, the Court of Appeal may give permission to apply for judicial review[3], rather than giving permission to appeal[4]. Where it does so, the case will proceed in the High Court unless the Court of Appeal orders otherwise[5]. There is no appeal to the Supreme Court if the Court of Appeal refuses permission to appeal[6].

There is no right of appeal to the Court of Appeal[7] against the refusal of permission to apply for judicial review in a criminal case[8].

Neither the defendant nor any other person served with the claim form may apply to set aside an order giving permission to proceed[9].

1 See CPR 52.15(1); the Senior Courts Act 1981 ss 16, 18; and CIVIL PROCEDURE vol 12 (2009) PARA 1701 et seq. As to the Senior Courts Act 1981 see PARA 602 note 4. See also *R v Secretary of State for Trade and Industry, ex p Eastaway* [2001] 1 All ER 27, [2000] 1 WLR 2222, HL. This rule applies both to a decision to refuse permission on any grounds and a decision to grant permission on some grounds but not others or subject to conditions: *R (on the application of Opoku) v Principal of Southwark College* [2002] EWHC 2092 (Admin), [2003] 1 All ER 272, [2003] 1 WLR 234. An appellant or respondent requires permission to appeal from the decision of a High Court judge, except where the appeal is against: (1) a committal order; (2) a refusal to grant habeas corpus; (3) a secure accommodation order made under the Children Act 1989 s 25 (see CHILDREN AND YOUNG PERSONS vol 5(4) (2008 Reissue) PARA 1037); or (4) as provided by *Practice Direction—Appeals* PD 52 (see CIVIL PROCEDURE vol 12 (2009) PARA 1660): see CPR 52.3(1). Where the Court of Appeal refuses permission to appeal without an oral hearing, the person seeking permission may request that the decision be reconsidered at a hearing save where the Court of Appeal has ordered otherwise: see CPR 52.3(4), (4A); and *Practice Direction—Appeals* PD 52 paras 4.11–4.16.

2 CPR 52.15(2). This is a strict time limit. The principles on which an extension of time should be granted are those set out in CPR 3.9 (see CIVIL PROCEDURE vol 11 (2009) PARA 256) and *Sayers v Clarke Walker* [2002] EWCA Civ 645, [2002] 3 All ER 490, [2002] 1 WLR 3095, although the way in which those principles are applied may differ in a public law appeal: see *R (on the application of Awan) v Immigration Appeal Tribunal* [2004] EWCA Civ 922, (2004) Times, 24 June (the seven day rule is to be taken 'very seriously' and, at least in an asylum context, time will only be extended in exceptional circumstances). Note that there are strict rules as to the documents which an appellant must file with his appellant's notice: see *Practice Direction—Appeals* PD 52; and CIVIL PROCEDURE vol 12 (2009) PARA 1663.

3 CPR 52.15(3).

4   Permission to appeal may be given only where: (1) the court considers that the appeal would
     have a real prospect of success; or (2) there is some other compelling reason why the appeal
     should be heard: CPR 52.3(6). See further *R (on the application of Werner) v IRC* [2002]
     EWCA Civ 979, [2002] STC 1213 (applying the test as to whether there is a real, as opposed to
     'fanciful', prospect of success set out in *Swain v Hillman* [2001] 1 All ER 91, [2000] PIQR P51;
     procedure where the Court of Appeal considers that there is a real prospect of the appellant
     being able to show at a contested appeal hearing that the application is fit for consideration at a
     substantive judicial review hearing but it wishes to hear the respondent on the matter). An order
     giving permission may: (a) limit the issues to be heard; and (b) be made subject to conditions: see
     CPR 52.3(7).

5   CPR 52.15(4). For examples of cases in which the Court of Appeal chose to retain the case and
     hear the claim itself see: *R v Panel on Take-overs and Mergers, ex p Datafin plc* [1987] QB 815,
     [1987] 1 All ER 564, CA; *R (on the application of Abbasi v Secretary of State for Foreign and
     Commonwealth Affairs* [2002] EWCA Civ 1598, [2003] 3 LRC 297 (the case raised important
     jurisdictional issues); and *R (on the application of Smith) v Parole Board* [2003] EWCA Civ
     1014, [2003] 1 WLR 2548 (final disposal of the arguments was only likely to be achieved by a
     decision of the Court of Appeal).

6   See *R v Secretary of State for Trade and Industry, ex p Eastaway* [2001] 1 All ER 27, [2000]
     1 WLR 2222, HL; *R (on the application of Burkett) v Hammersmith and Fulham London
     Borough Council* [2002] UKHL 23, [2002] 3 All ER 97, [2002] 1 WLR 1593. In contrast, the
     Supreme Court does have jurisdiction to hear an appeal where the Court of Appeal heard and
     dismissed a full appeal, rather than merely refusing permission to appeal: see *R (on the
     application of Burkett) v Hammersmith and Fulham London Borough Council* (House of
     Lords).

7   Note that, for this reason, the Administrative Court may wish to grant permission to apply for
     judicial review but dismiss the substantive application: see *R v DPP, ex p Camelot Group plc*
     (1998) 10 Admin LR 93.

8   See the Senior Courts Act 1981 s 18(1)(a); and CIVIL PROCEDURE vol 12 (2009) PARA 1705. As
     to the meaning of 'criminal case' see PARA 679 note 5. Note that matters relating to indictment
     are not amenable to judicial review: see s 29(3); and PARA 602.

9   CPR 54.13. However, the court retains its inherent jurisdiction to set aside an order granting
     permission where it would be in the interests of justice to do so: *R (on the application of Webb)
     v Bristol City Council* [2001] EWHC Admin 696; *R (on the application of Enfield Borough
     Council) v Secretary of State for Health* [2009] EWHC 743 (Admin), [2009] All ER (D) 100
     (Apr). See further *R (on the application of Karkut) v Lewisham London Borough Council*
     [2005] EWHC 354 (Admin); *R v Secretary of State for the Home Department, ex p Chinoy*
     (1991) 4 Admin LR 457, [1991] COD 381, DC; *Re Ballyedmond Castle Farms Ltd's
     Application* [2000] NI 174; *R v Environment Agency, ex p Gibson* [1998] All ER (D) 200.
        The question whether and in what circumstances a court would grant summary judgment
     under CPR Pt 24 (see CIVIL PROCEDURE vol 11 (2009) PARA 524) on an application for judicial
     review, so as to enable a defendant to challenge the judgment in the Court of Appeal remains
     unresolved: see *R (on the application of the Kurdistan Workers' Party) v Secretary of State for
     the Home Department* [2002] EWHC 644 (Admin) at [99], [2002] All ER (D) 99 (Apr) at [99]
     per Richards J.

(vii) Defendant's Response and Filing of Evidence

673.   Defendant's response and filing of evidence.   Following the grant of
permission, the defendant and any other person who has been served with the
claim form must file and serve: (1) detailed grounds for contesting the claim or
supporting it on additional grounds; and (2) any written evidence[1]. These
detailed grounds should contain all the factual material upon which the
defendant intends to rely at the hearing of the claim. Unless directions have been
given to the contrary, the response must be filed and served within 35 clear days
after service of the order giving permission[2]. No written evidence may be relied
on unless it has been served in accordance with the rules of procedure governing
judicial review[3] or any direction of the court or the court gives permission[4].
When preparing the detailed response the defendant must provide a full and fair
explanation of the reasons and facts underlying a decision and should provide

sufficient information to enable the court to determine whether it has acted lawfully or unlawfully[5]. On receipt of the evidence in response the claimant is obliged to reconsider whether or not to continue with the claim[6]. Any party may seek the permission of the court to serve further evidence, for example, where it is necessary to deal with new matters arising out of an affidavit of any other party to the application[7].

1 CPR 54.14(1). Where the party filing the detailed grounds intends to rely on documents not already filed, he must file a paginated bundle of those documents when he files the detailed grounds: *Practice Direction—Judicial Review* PD 54A para 10.1. The rules in CPR 8.5(3), (4) (defendant to file and serve written evidence at the same time as acknowledgment of service) and CPR 8.5(5), (6) (claimant to file and serve any reply within 14 days) (see CIVIL PROCEDURE vol 11 (2009) PARA 132) do not apply in these circumstances: CPR 54.14(2).

2 CPR 2.8, 54.14(1).

3 Ie in accordance with CPR Pt 54.

4 CPR 54.16(2). The rule in CPR 8.6 (evidence: see CIVIL PROCEDURE vol 11 (2009) PARA 133) does not apply: CPR 54.16(1). Disclosure is not required unless the Court orders otherwise: *Practice Direction—Judicial Review* PD 54A para 12.1. As to disclosure see further PARA 670.

5 See *Tweed v Parades Commission for Northern Ireland* [2006] UKHL 53, [2007] 1 AC 650, [2007] NI 66; *R v Lancashire County Council, ex p Huddleston* [1986] 2 All ER 941 at 945, [1986] NLJ Rep 562, CA, per Sir John Donaldson MR (a duty 'to make full and fair disclosure'); *R (on the application of Quark Fishing Ltd) v Secretary of State for Foreign and Commonwealth Affairs* [2002] EWCA Civ 1409, [2002] All ER (D) 450 (Oct) (a 'very high duty ... to assist the court with full and accurate explanations of all the facts relevant to the issue the court must decide'); *Belize Alliance of Conservation Non-Governmental Organisations v Department for the Environment* [2003] UKPC 63, [2003] 1 WLR 2839 (see the dissenting judgment of Lord Walker).

6 See *R (on the application of Bateman) v Legal Services Commission* [2001] EWHC Admin 797, [2001] All ER (D) 293 (Oct) at [21] per Munby J (failure in this regard may be visited with adverse costs orders); *R v Horsham District Council, ex p Wenman* [1994] 4 All ER 681, [1995] 1 WLR 680 (failure to review at this stage could lead to a wasted costs order). See further *R (on the application of B) v Lambeth London Borough Council* [2006] EWHC 639 (Admin), [2007] 1 FLR 2091 (party who fails to make necessary amendments to the grounds of claim could find his case summarily dismissed; lawyers could face an application for a wasted costs order); *R (on the application of W) v Essex County Council* [2004] EWHC 2027 (Admin), [2004] All ER (D) 103 (Aug) at [35]–[40] per Munby J; *R (on the application of Tshikangu) v Newham London Borough Council* [2001] EWHC Admin 118, (2001) Times, 27 April; *R (on the application of Done Brothers (Cash Betting)) v Crown Court at Cardiff* [2003] EWHC 3516 (Admin) (a claimant owes a continuing duty of candour); *R v Liverpool City Justices, ex p Price* [1998] COD 453, 162 JP 766, DC; *R v IRC, ex p Continental Shipping Ltd SA* [1996] STC 813, 68 TC 665; *R v Secretary of State for the Home Department, ex p Brown* (1984) Times, 6 February.

7 See CPR 54.16.

674. Evidence. In claims for judicial review[1] evidence is normally given by way of witness statement[2]. However, the court may, on the application of any party, order the attendance for cross-examination of the maker of a statement[3]. If such an order is made, but the person in question does not attend, the witness statement may not be used as evidence without the leave of the court[4]. However, in practice permission to cross-examine is only rarely granted[5]. Such an order will only be made where required in the interests of justice[6]. The mere fact that a conflict of evidence arises on the face of the witness statements does not require that cross-examination be permitted. Where there is a conflict of evidence on the witness statements but the probabilities can be shown to point to one account rather than another, the court can act on that factual footing.

The usual rules of evidence apply to judicial review claims as to any other type of claim[7]. Thus the only general rule is that all relevant evidence is admissible, subject to exceptions[8]. In the application of this rule particular regard must be had to the proper scope of the judicial review process. The court does not act as a court of appeal from the decision-maker. Thus, usually the court will not entertain fresh evidence which could only be relevant if the proceedings were an appeal[9]. However, this is not to say that in some cases the courts do not have to determine issues of fact. For example, there may be instances where the determination of an issue of fact is material to deciding the scope of the jurisdiction of the decision-maker. In such a case evidence as to that point is relevant, and therefore admissible[10] as the court is not acting as a court of appeal but is in fact exercising a *de novo* jurisdiction[11]. Similarly, where the challenge is on the basis of a failure to consider a relevant matter, the court will need to consider all material circumstances in order to assess the significance of the failure alleged; and where the challenge alleges misconduct (for example, bias) on the part of the decision-maker, evidence is admissible to prove the allegation[12]. Evidence is also admissible in order to demonstrate the nature of the material before the original decision-maker[13].

With specific regard to judicial review claims within the scope of the Civil Procedure Rules[14] the following points should be noted:

(1) As a general rule, the courts will not permit a decision-maker to put forward evidence which seeks to demonstrate that the basis of the decision was in fact different from that expressed in the original decision[15]. However, if there is genuine confusion as to the basis upon which the decision was taken, evidence is admissible to clarify or supplement the original decision[16].

(2) Where a quashing order[17] is sought on the ground of a jurisdictional error (an error of law on the face of the record), the court will not admit any extraneous evidence: the error must be apparent from the record itself[18].

(3) Where a quashing order is sought on the ground of absence or excess of jurisdiction, bias by interest, fraud or breach of natural justice, extraneous evidence of these matters will be admissible, and indeed necessary, if they are not apparent on the face of the record. However, it should be noted that the tendency of more recent decisions has been to broaden the concept of what constitutes 'the record'[19].

(4) Where mandatory or prohibiting orders[20] are sought, evidence will be necessary to demonstrate the facts constituting the ground of the claim[21].

(5) Where a mandatory order is sought in relation to the decision of an inferior tribunal, evidence will be admissible to show that the tribunal has refused to exercise jurisdiction, or has been influenced by irrelevant considerations or has failed to consider relevant matters[22].

(6) On an application for a mandatory order in relation to an inferior tribunal on the ground of refusal of jurisdiction, if the tribunal has given a decision and expressed it in language from which the court can ascertain what the decision was, the court will not accept affidavit evidence to say that the tribunal meant something different from what is said in its judgment; if there is an ambiguity, the court can send it back to clear up the ambiguity and ascertain exactly what the tribunal meant[23].

(7) Where error on the face of the proceedings is alleged, and a copy of the order or determination complained of cannot be obtained and verified by affidavit or witness statement, the claimant must provide evidence of the alleged defects according to the best of his information and belief[24].

(8) Where bias is alleged on the basis that a member of the tribunal had a pecuniary or personal interest in the outcome of the claim, the claimant ought to provide evidence that at the time of the hearing before the inferior tribunal he was unaware of the interest[25].

(9) Parliamentary materials, primarily Hansard, may be admitted in certain circumstances as an aid to statutory construction[26]. If a party wishes to rely on material from Hansard notice must be served[27].

1 Ie claims falling within CPR Pt 54. As to the meaning of 'claim for judicial review' see PARA 662 note 9.

2 No written evidence may be relied on unless it has been served in accordance with CPR Pt 54, or a direction of the court or the court gives permission: see CPR 54.16.

3 See CPR 8.6(3), 32.1, 54.16; and CIVIL PROCEDURE vol 11 (2009) PARA 133. See further *R (on the application of PG) v Ealing London Borough Council* [2002] EWHC 250 (Admin), [2002] All ER (D) 61 (Mar); *R (on the application of Wilkinson) v Responsible Medical Officer Broadmoor Hospital* [2001] EWCA Civ 1545, [2002] 1 WLR 419, 65 BMLR 15; *R (AN) v Secretary of State for Justice* [2008] EWHC 3110 (Admin).

4 If, however, the person does attend, his witness statement may be referred to prior to his cross-examination: see *Lewis v James* (1886) 32 ChD 326, CA.

5 This remains the case despite the comments in *O'Reilly v Mackman* [1983] 2 AC 237 at 282–283, [1982] 3 All ER 1124 at 1132, HL, per Lord Diplock. See further *R (on the application of PG) v Ealing London Borough Council* [2002] EWHC 250 (Admin), [2002] All ER (D) 61 (Mar); *R (AN) v Secretary of State for Justice* [2008] EWHC 3110 (Admin).

  Examples of where cross-examination was not permitted are far more frequent than those where it was: see *R v Radio Authority, ex p Wildman* [1999] COD 255, CA (Court of Appeal reluctant generally to interfere with the exercise of discretion of the first instance judge on this point); *R v Arts Council of England, ex p Women's Playhouse Trust* [1998] COD 175, (1997) Times, 20 August; *R v Westminster City Council, ex p Moozary-Oraky* (1993) 26 HLR 213; *R v Reigate Justices, ex p Curl* [1991] COD 66, DC; *R v Secretary of State for the Home Department, ex p Patel* [1986] Imm AR 208; *Khawaja v Secretary of State for the Home Department* [1984] AC 74, [1983] 1 All ER 765, HL; *IRC v Rossminster Ltd* [1980] AC 952, [1980] 1 All ER 80, HL; *George v Secretary of State for the Environment* (1979) 77 LGR 689, 38 P & CR 609, CA.

6 As to cross-examination in claims alleging breaches of the Convention for the Protection of Human Rights and Fundamental Freedoms (Rome, 4 November 1950; TS 71 (1953) Cmd 8969) see *R (on the application of Wilkinson) v Responsible Medical Officer Broadmoor Hospital* [2001] EWCA Civ 1545, [2002] 1 WLR 419, 65 BMLR 15; *R (AN) v Secretary of State for Justice* [2008] EWHC 3110 (Admin). As to human rights claims see PARAS 650–654.

  More generally, for examples of cases where cross-examination was allowed see: *R v Secretary of State for the Home Department, ex p Manuel* (1984) Times, 21 March (relevant that Manuel's counsel had earlier tendered him for cross-examination). See also *Jones v Secretary of State for Wales* [1995] 2 PLR 26, 70 P & CR 211, CA (comments made in context of statutory appeal under the Town and Country Planning Act 1990 s 228 (see TOWN AND COUNTRY PLANNING vol 46(2) (Reissue) PARA 939); cross-examination of inspector allowed on allegation of bias); *R v Horseferry Road Magistrates' Court, ex p Bennett (No 3)* [1994] COD 321, (1994) Times, 14 January (cross examination by video link); *R v Derbyshire County Council, ex p Times Supplements Ltd* (1990) 3 Admin LR 241, (1990) Times, 19 July (cross examination of councillors on whether influenced by particular consideration); *R v Mental Health Act Commission, ex p Mark Witham* (26 May 1988, unreported) (cross-examination of expert evidence permitted); *R v Waltham Forest London Borough Council, ex p Baxter* [1988] QB 419, [1987] 3 All ER 671, CA (cross-examination of councillors); *R v IRC, ex p J Rothschild Holdings plc* [1986] STC 410 (cross-examination of inland revenue witness on departmental practice); and *R v Stokesley (Yorks) Justices, ex p Bartram* [1956] 1 All ER 563n, [1956] 1 WLR 254, DC.

7 As to evidence see CPR Pt 32; and CIVIL PROCEDURE vol 11 (2009) PARA 749.

8 For general guidance as to how this 'rule' applies in practice to claims for judicial review see *Al-Mehdawi v Secretary of State for the Home Department* [1990] 1 AC 876, [1989] 3 All ER 843, HL; *R v Secretary of State for the Environment, ex p Powis* [1981] 1 All ER 788, [1981] 1 WLR 584, CA; *R v West Sussex Quarter Sessions, ex p Albert and Maud Johnson Trust Ltd*

[1974] QB 24 at 39, [1973] 3 All ER 289 at 298, CA, per Orr LJ, and at 42 and 301 per Lawton LJ; *Ashbridge Investments Ltd v Minister for Housing and Local Government* [1965] 3 All ER 371, [1965] 1 WLR 1320, CA.

However, note the developing doctrine of mistake of fact: see *R v Criminal Injuries Compensation Board, ex p A* [1999] 2 AC 330, [1999] 2 WLR 974, HL; *Patel v Secretary of State for Transport, Local Government and the Regions* [2002] EWHC 1963 (Admin), [2003] 2 P & CR 251; *E v Secretary of State for the Home Department* [2004] EWCA Civ 49, [2004] QB 1044, [2004] 2 WLR 1351.

9 See *R v Immigration Appeal Tribunal, ex p Ali* [1990] Imm AR 531; *Al-Mehdawi v Secretary of State for the Home Department* [1990] 1 AC 876 at 898–900, [1989] 3 All ER 843 at 849–851, HL, per Lord Bridge of Harwich; *R v Wycombe District Council, ex p Mahsood* (1988) 20 HLR 683; *R v Secretary of State for the Environment, ex p Powis* [1981] 1 All ER 788, [1981] 1 WLR 584, CA; *R v West Sussex Quarter Sessions, ex p Albert and Maud Johnson Trust Ltd* [1974] QB 24, [1973] 3 All ER 289, CA.

10 An example of this is the decision in *R v Boycott, ex p Keasley* [1939] 2 KB 651, [1939] 2 All ER 626, DC (whether or not a child was 'ineducable' was an issue going to the jurisdiction of the decision-maker; evidence admitted as to whether or not the child fell within the definition). See further *R (on the application of A) v Croydon London Borough Council* [2009] UKSC 8, [2009] 1 WLR 2557 (child's age is an objective question of fact).

11 See *Re Ripon (Highfield) Housing Confirmation Order 1938, White and Collins v Minister of Health* [1939] 2 KB 838, [1939] 1 All ER 508.

12 See eg *R v Secretary of State for the Environment, ex p Powis* [1981] 1 All ER 788, [1981] 1 WLR 584, CA.

13 *R v Secretary of State for the Environment, ex p Powis* [1981] 1 All ER 788, [1981] 1 WLR 584, CA; *Ashbridge Investments Ltd v Minister for Housing and Local Government* [1965] 3 All ER 371 at 374, [1965] 1 WLR 1320 at 1327, CA, per Lord Denning MR.

14 Ie within the scope of CPR Pt 54.

15 See, by way of example, *R (on the application of Richards) v Pembrokeshire County Council* [2004] EWCA Civ 1000, [2005] LGR 105; *R (on the application of O) v West London Mental Health NHS Trust* [2005] EWHC 604 (Admin), [2005] All ER (D) 275 (Mar); *R (on the application of Leung) v Imperial College of Science, Technology and Medicine* [2002] EWHC 1358 (Admin), [2002] ELR 653; *R (on the application of Nash) v Chelsea College of Art and Design* [2001] EWHC Admin 538, [2001] All ER (D) 133 (Jul); *R v Westminster City Council, ex p Ermakov* [1996] 2 All ER 302, 95 LGR 119, CA; *Breen v Amalgamated Engineering Union* [1971] 2 QB 175 at 192–193, [1971] 1 All ER 1148 at 1155–1156, CA, per Lord Denning MR; *R v Licensing Authority for Goods Vehicles for the Metropolitan Traffic Area, ex p BE Barrett Ltd* [1949] 2 KB 17 at 22, [1949] 1 All ER 656 at 658, DC, per Lord Goddard CJ.

16 See note 15; and see further *R v Governors of Bishop Challoner Roman Catholic Comprehensive School, ex p C and P* [1992] 2 AC 182, [1993] Fam Law 23, HL; *R v Hackney London Borough Council, ex p T* [1991] COD 454.

17 As to quashing orders see PARA 693 et seq.

18 The distinction between errors of law on the face of the record and other errors of law has now generally been rendered obsolete: see PARA 616.

It is clear that the 'record' includes any document embodying the reasons for the conclusions of the original decision-maker, even a transcript of reasons which have been given orally. With regard to the extension of what constitutes the 'record' see in particular *R v Preston Supplementary Benefits Appeal Tribunal, ex p Moore* [1975] 2 All ER 807 at 810, [1975] 1 WLR 624 at 628, CA, per Lord Denning MR (the record should be interpreted as including all the documents in the case); *R v Southampton Justices, ex p Green* [1976] QB 11, [1975] 2 All ER 1073, CA (affidavits to be treated as part of the record; quaere whether this applies to witness statements following the enactment of the CPR); cf *R v Southampton Justices, ex p Corker* (1976) 120 Sol Jo 214, DC; *R v Crown Court at Knightsbridge, ex p International Sporting Club (London) Ltd* [1982] QB 304, [1981] 3 All ER 417, DC (record includes transcript of oral judgment).

See also *R v Bolton* (1841) 1 QB 66; *Re Penny and South Eastern Rly Co* (1857) 7 E & B 660; *R (Reynolds) v Cork County Justices* (1882) 10 LR Ir 1; *R (Carl) v Tyrone Justices* [1917] 2 IR 437; *R v Nat Bell Liquors Ltd* [1922] 2 AC 128 at 155–156, PC; *R v Northumberland Compensation Appeal Tribunal, ex p Shaw* [1952] 1 KB 338 at 342–343, [1952] 1 All ER 122 at 126, CA, per Singleton LJ; *R v Agricultural Land Tribunal for South Eastern Area, ex p Bracey* [1960] 2 All ER 518, [1960] 1 WLR 911, DC. In the cases of *General Medical Council v Spackman* [1943] AC 627, [1943] 2 All ER 337, HL, and *R v West Riding of*

Yorkshire Justices, ex p Broadbent [1910] 2 KB 192, DC, where affidavit evidence was admitted, the ground of the application for certiorari (now known as a quashing order) was that there had been a breach of natural justice.

In *R v Northumberland Compensation Appeal Tribunal, ex p Shaw* at 353 and 131 per Denning LJ it was suggested that if both parties to the proceedings before the inferior tribunal desired a ruling of the High Court on a point of law which had been decided by the tribunal but which had not been entered on the record, the parties could agree that the question should be argued and determined as if it were expressed in the order, and might supplement the record by affidavits disclosing the points of law that had been decided by the tribunal.

19 See note 18.

20 As to mandatory orders see PARA 703 et seq; and as to prohibiting orders see PARA 693 et seq.

21 See *R v West Riding of Yorkshire Justices* (1845) 3 Dow & L 152; *Anon* (1682) 2 Mod Rep 316; *R v High Steward of Malmesbury* (1840) 4 Jur 222; *R v Simms* (1835) 4 Dowl 294. See also *Local Government Lands and Settlement Comr v Kaderbhai* [1931] AC 652, PC.

22 See e g *R v Cotham* [1898] 1 QB 802, DC. Where a quashing order is sought on the ground that the tribunal has taken into consideration irrelevant matters, the court may act on extraneous evidence to this effect, if it is not apparent from the record: *R v Fulham, Hammersmith and Kensington Rent Tribunal, ex p Hierowski* [1953] 2 QB 147, [1953] 2 All ER 4, DC. However this latter decision was not followed in *R v Agricultural Tribunal for South Eastern Area, ex p Bracey* [1960] 2 All ER 518, [1960] 1 WLR 911, DC.

23 *R v Licensing Authority for Goods Vehicles for the Metropolitan Traffic Area, ex p BE Barrett Ltd* as reported in [1949] 2 KB 17 at 22 per Lord Goddard CJ.

24 *R v Manchester and Leeds Rly Co* (1838) 8 Ad & El 413.

25 *R v Richmond, Surrey Justices* (1860) 2 LT 373; *R v Kent Justices* (1880) 44 JP 298; *R v Williams, ex p Phillips* [1914] 1 KB 608, DC; and see PARA 636.

26 See *Pepper v Hart* [1993] AC 593, [1993] 1 All ER 42, HL; *R v Secretary of State for the Environment, Transport and the Regions, ex p Spath Holme Ltd* [2001] 2 AC 349, [2001] 1 All ER 195, HL. However, note that in reaching the decision in *Pepper v Hart*, the House of Lords was at pains to point out that reference to Hansard would only be required in limited instances. See also *Melluish v BMI (No 3) Ltd* [1996] AC 454, [1995] 4 All ER 453, HL (House of Lords critical of attempt to use statements made by a minister in relation to one statutory provision as an aid to construction of a different provision; misuse of Hansard could be sanctioned by wasted costs order).

27 A party intending to refer to any extract from Hansard must, unless the judge directs otherwise, serve upon all other parties and the court copies of any such extract together with a brief summary of the argument intended to be based upon such extract, not less than five clear working days before the first day of the hearing: see *Practice Note* [1995] 1 All ER 234, sub nom *Practice Direction (Hansard Citation)* [1995] 1 WLR 192.

(viii) Other Steps prior to the Hearing

675. Other preparatory steps. The judicial review practice direction[1] sets out various other preparatory steps to be taken in advance of the hearing of any claim for judicial review. These include the preparation and lodging of skeleton arguments[2], and the preparation and lodging of bundles of documents[3]. Failure to comply with these requirements may result in an adverse costs order[4] or in the striking out of an application for judicial review or a defence[5].

The current practice for listing claims for judicial review is contained in a practice statement issued in 2002[6].

1 Ie *Practice Direction—Judicial Review* PD 54A.

2 See *Practice Direction—Judicial Review* PD 54A para 15. Skeleton arguments must also comply with the requirements as to citation of authorities in the *Practice Direction (Citation of Authorities)* [2001] 1 WLR 1001: see *R (on the application of Prokopp) v London Underground Ltd* [2003] EWCA Civ 961, [2004] 1 P & CR 479.

3 See *Practice Direction—Judicial Review* PD 54A para 16.

4 See *Haggis v DPP* [2003] EWHC 2481 (Admin), [2004] 2 All ER 382 (late service of skeleton arguments may lead to 'disagreeable orders as to costs').

5 See CPR 3.4(2)(c); *Practice Direction—Striking out a Statement of Case* PD 3A; and CIVIL PROCEDURE vol 11 (2009) PARA 520.

6   See *Practice Statement (Administrative Court: Listing and Urgent Cases)* Annex C [2002]
    1 All ER 633, [2002] 1 WLR 810.

(3) THE HEARING

676.   Appearance of persons served with the claim form.   It is not necessary
for every person served with the claim form or the order granting permission to
appear at the hearing. The court will both discourage and penalise any needless
duplication of interest representation[1]. If more than one interested party does
appear, and such duplication is unnecessary, the usual sanction will be in costs[2].

Where the decision challenged is one made by justices or other inferior courts
or tribunals it is not usually appropriate for the justices to appear at the hearing.
Usually justices may make and file a witness statement setting out the grounds of
the decision in issue, and any facts which have a material bearing on the issues in
the claim[3]. Where, however, the claim raises allegations concerning the bona
fides or character of the justices, the normal practice is for the justices to be
represented at the hearing[4]. An order will not be made compelling a justice who
has filed a witness statement to attend for cross-examination except in very
special circumstances[5].

1   For example, where both a defendant tribunal and some other defendant body intend to support
    the tribunal's decision, and there is no conflict of interest, they should agree amongst themselves
    who is to appear and instruct counsel: see *R v Industrial Disputes Tribunal, ex p American
    Express Co Inc* [1954] 2 All ER 764n, [1954] 1 WLR 1118, DC.

2   *R v Industrial Disputes Tribunal, ex p American Express Co Inc* [1954] 2 All ER 764n, [1954]
    1 WLR 1118, DC. As to costs see PARAS 681–686.

3   See the Review of Justices' Decisions Act 1872 s 2 (amended by the Statute Law Revision (No 2)
    Act 1893; and the Finance Act 1949 s 52(10), Sch 11 Pt V) which provides that a justice whose
    decision is called in question in a superior court may file an affidavit showing the grounds of his
    decision and setting out any material facts, without being required to pay a fee. See further *R v
    Newcastle-under-Lyme Justices, ex p Massey* [1995] 1 All ER 120, [1994] 1 WLR 1684, DC;
    R v Gloucester Crown Court, ex p Chester [1998] COD 365; *R v Feltham Justices, ex p Haid*
    [1998] COD 440. The witness statement must be made by the justice himself: see *R v Sperling
    Justices* (1873) 21 WR 461 (where an affidavit by the person on whose evidence the justices'
    decision was founded was rejected). If the decision in question has been reached by a majority of
    justices, the affidavit must be sworn by one of the majority, and no dissenting justice has the
    right to make an affidavit since no decision of his is being questioned: *R v Waddingham,
    Gloucestershire Justices and Tustin* (1896) 60 JP Jo 372, DC.
        Evidence filed by a justice must be considered by the court before it makes any order against
    the justice or justices, or otherwise determines the matter so as to overrule or set aside the acts
    or decisions to which the application relates, even though no counsel appears on behalf of the
    justices: Review of Justices' Decisions Act 1872 s 3. 'All that was intended by the statute was
    that, instead of the justices being put to the expense of instructing counsel, or being brought up
    in person, they might make affidavits themselves, and send them by to one of the masters of the
    court': *R v Sperling Justices* at 462 per Cockburn CJ.
        Where justices, or another inferior court or tribunal, do appear unnecessarily the sanction is
    by way of costs: see *R (on the application of Davies) v Birmingham Deputy Coroner* [2004]
    EWCA Civ 207, [2004] 3 All ER 543, [2004] 1 WLR 2739 (and the review of earlier case law
    therein); and see PARA 681.

4   See *R (on the application of Davies) v Birmingham Deputy Coroner* [2004] EWCA Civ 207,
    [2004] 3 All ER 543, [2004] 1 WLR 2739. See also *R v Newcastle-under-Lyme Justices,
    ex p Massey* [1995] 1 All ER 120, [1994] 1 WLR 1684, DC; *R v Camborne Justices,
    ex p Pearce*, as reported in [1954] 2 All ER 850 at 856, DC, per Lord Goddard CJ; *R v
    Thornton etc Justices, ex p Lacon & Co* (1898) 67 LJQB 249, CA (revsd on another point sub
    nom *Laceby v Lacon & Co* [1899] AC 222, HL); *R v Field Justices, ex p White* (1895) 11 TLR
    240, DC.

5   *R v Kent Justices, ex p Smith* [1928] WN 137, DC; and see *R v Stokesly (Yorkshire) Justices,*
    ex p Bartram [1956] 1 All ER 563n, [1956] 1 WLR 254, DC; although see now *O'Reilly v*
    Mackman [1983] 2 AC 237 at 283, [1982] 3 All ER 1124 at 1132, HL, per Lord Diplock; and
    PARA 674.

677.   Hearing of a claim for judicial review.   The hearing of a claim for judicial
review is normally before a single judge[1] in open court[2]. The hearing usually
consists of legal argument based upon the documentary evidence and the witness
statements. The claimant is entitled to act in person[3]. If parties are represented,
the practice is to hear only one counsel on each side. The claimant will have an
opportunity to reply to the defendant's submissions[4]. The court may also hear
representations from other interested parties or by those permitted to intervene[5].

The costs are in the discretion of the court[6].

Although the court has an inherent discretion in the interests of finality not to
allow a particular issue which has already been litigated to be re-opened, the
doctrine of issue estoppel does not apply strictly to claims for judicial review[7].

When determining any claim, the court is bound by the relevant principle of
stare decisis so that it will, although not bound to do so, follow a court of equal
jurisdiction unless the decision appears to be clearly wrong[8]. It is unlikely,
however, that a single judge would depart from a decision of a Divisional Court[9].

1   As to the procedural requirements for hearings see generally CPR Pt 39; and CIVIL PROCEDURE
    vol 12 (2009) PARA 1117 et seq. Applications in civil matters will normally be listed for hearing
    by a single judge. Applications in criminal causes or matters will normally be listed before a
    Divisional Court consisting of two judges. Similarly if the High Court has directed that a civil
    matter should be heard by a Divisional Court, the application will be listed before a two-judge
    Divisional Court. The court does have power to arrange for the sitting of a Divisional Court
    consisting of three judges but it is up to the parties to apply for such a court. Such an application
    should be made at an early stage, well in advance of the hearing, to allow for a third judge to be
    added. By analogy with the Court of Appeal procedure, it seems that a three-judge court will
    only be appropriate in complex cases or cases of general public importance: *Practice Note*
    [1982] 3 All ER 376 at 383–384, [1982] 1 WLR 1312 at 1318. See also *Wandsworth London*
    Borough Council v Winder [1985] AC 461 at 492–493, [1984] 3 All ER 83 at 106, CA, per
    Ackner LJ.

2   The court also has power to hold a hearing in private, to permit witnesses to give evidence in
    closed session or impose other conditions as to confidentiality, subject to the requirements of the
    Human Rights Act 1998 s 6 and the Convention for the Protection of Human Rights and
    Fundamental Freedoms (Rome, 4 November 1950; TS 71 (1953) Cmd 8969) art 6: see CIVIL
    PROCEDURE vol 11 (2009) PARA 6. See further *Re S (a child) (identification: restriction on*
    publication) [2004] UKHL 47, [2005] 1 AC 593, [2004] 4 All ER 683; the Children and Young
    Persons Act 1933 s 39 (see CHILDREN AND YOUNG PERSONS vol 5(4) (2008 Reissue) PARA 1271);
    and see *R (on the application of A) v Lord Saville of Newdigate (No 2)* [2001] EWCA Civ 2048,
    [2002] 1 WLR 1249. As to the appointment of a special advocate see *R (on the application of*
    Roberts) v Parole Board [2005] UKHL 45, [2005] 2 AC 738, sub nom *Roberts v Parole Board*
    [2006] 1 All ER 39; *R v Shayler* [2002] UKHL 11, [2003] 1 AC 247, [2002] 2 All ER 477.
    Specific provisions apply in relation to control order proceedings (see CPR Pt 76; and CIVIL
    PROCEDURE vol 11 (2009) PARA 45; CRIMINAL LAW, EVIDENCE AND PROCEDURE vol 11(1) (2006
    Reissue) PARA 454 et seq) and financial restrictions proceedings (see CPR Pt 79; and CRIMINAL
    LAW, EVIDENCE AND PROCEDURE vol 11(1) (2006 Reissue) PARA 466 et seq).

3   *Practice Note* [1947] WN 218, DC; *R v Staff Sub-Committee of LCC's Education Committee,*
    ex p Schonfeld [1956] 1 All ER 753n, [1956] 1 WLR 430, CA. See, however, the requirements
    of CPR 39.6 if the person is a company or other corporation (see CIVIL PROCEDURE vol 11
    (2009) PARA 223). As to the circumstances in which the court may give permission for a litigant
    in person to be assisted by a McKenzie friend see *McKenzie v McKenzie* [1971] P 33, [1970]
    3 All ER 1034; *Re O (children)* [2005] EWCA Civ 759, [2006] Fam 1, [2005] 3 WLR 1191 (the
    presumption in favour of a litigant in person being allowed the assistance of a McKenzie friend
    is a strong one, at least in the Family Division); but see also the restrictions expressed in *Paragon*
    Finance Ltd v Noueiri [2001] EWCA Civ 1402, [2001] 1 WLR 2357; *R v Bow County Court,*

ex p Pelling [1999] 4 All ER 751, [1999] 1 WLR 1807, CA; *Re N (a child) (McKenzie friends: rights of audience)* [2008] EWHC 2042 (Fam), [2008] 1 WLR 2743. See further CIVIL PROCEDURE vol 12 (2009) PARA 1126.

4 *R v Dunne, ex p Sinnatt* [1943] KB 516, [1943] 2 All ER 222, DC.

5 As to the meaning of 'interested party' see PARA 664. As to the court's discretion to permit persons to intervene see CPR 54.17; and PARA 671. See also *R v Central Criminal Court, ex p Francis and Francis* [1989] AC 346, sub nom *Francis and Francis (a firm) v Central Criminal Court* [1988] 3 All ER 775, HL.

6 See the Senior Courts Act 1981 s 51(1); and PARA 681. As to the Senior Courts Act 1981 see PARA 602 note 4.

7 See CIVIL PROCEDURE vol 12 (2009) PARA 1164 et seq. Strictly speaking there is no lis inter partes on a claim for judicial review. Historically, it was also argued that in the absence of formal pleadings (under RSC Ord 53) it could be difficult to determine the actual dispute resolved in any particular case. This objection is likely to have been removed by the requirement under CPR Pt 54 for formal claim forms and acknowledgments of service (see PARAS 664–665). See also *R (Ryan) v Swansea Crown Court* [2005] EWCA Civ 425; *R (on the application of Sheikh) v Secretary of State for the Home Department* [2001] Imm AR 219, [2000] All ER (D) 2164; *R v Secretary of State for the Environment, ex p Hackney London Borough Council* [1984] 1 All ER 956, [1984] 1 WLR 592, CA; and *Re Tarling* [1979] 1 All ER 981, sub nom *R v Governor of Pentonville Prison, ex p Tarling* [1979] 1 WLR 1417. However, the principle of finality of litigation is important: see further *Ali v Secretary of State for the Home Department* [1984] 1 All ER 1009 at 1014, sub nom *R v Secretary of State for the Home Department, ex p Momin Ali* [1984] 1 WLR 663 at 669–670, CA, per Sir John Donaldson MR. Issue estoppel in its strict sense is merely one servant of the general policy of promotion of finality and the avoidance of unnecessary litigation.

8 *R v Greater Manchester Coroner, ex p Tal* [1985] QB 67, [1984] 3 All ER 240, DC. See also *R (on the application of Kadhim) v Brent London Borough Council Housing Benefit Review Board* [2001] QB 955, [2001] 2 WLR 1674; *R v Simpson* [2003] EWCA Crim 1499, [2004] QB 118, [2003] 3 All ER 531 (rules of precedent not so rigid that they could not develop to meet contemporary needs); and *R (on the application of Amin) v Secretary of State for the Home Department* [2009] EWHC 1085 (Admin), [2009] All ER (D) 200 (May).

9 *R v Greater Manchester Coroner, ex p Tal* [1985] QB 67 at 81, [1984] 3 All ER 240 at 248, DC, per Goff LJ. In such a case a direction can be made by the single judge that the relevant application should be made before the Divisional Court: *R v Greater Manchester Coroner, ex p Tal*.

678. Uncontested proceedings. The court may decide a claim for judicial review[1] without a hearing where all the parties agree[2]. If the parties agree about the final order to be made in a claim for judicial review, they must file at the court a document (with two copies) signed by all the parties setting out the terms of the proposed agreed order together with a short statement of the matters relied on as justifying the proposed agreed order and copies of any authorities or statutory provisions relied on[3]. The court will consider the documents and will make the order if satisfied that the order should be made[4]. If the court is not satisfied that the order should be made, a hearing date will be set[5]. Where the agreement relates to an order for costs only, the parties need only file a document signed by all the parties setting out the terms of the proposed order[6].

It does not follow that an application for a mandatory order[7] or similar relief should be withdrawn merely because the defendant admits its breach and purports to fulfil its duty. The court may still grant the relief sought if the claimant is left in a position of doubt[8].

Where parties agree that the application should be dismissed, they may apply for such an order by consent[9]. Where leave of the court is not necessary for proceedings to be withdrawn and no order as to costs is sought, the claimant must inform the Administrative Court Office in writing, confirming that all other parties to the proceedings had been notified[10].

1 As to the meaning of 'claim for judicial review' see PARA 662 note 9.

2 CPR 54.18. This provision could include both situations where the application is uncontested and those where, although a dispute remains, the parties consent to determination of that dispute on the papers.

3 *Practice Direction—Judicial Review* PD 54A para 17.1; *Practice Statement (Administrative Court: uncontested proceedings)* [2009] 1 All ER 651, [2008] 1 WLR 1377 para 1. Note that the *Practice Statement (Administrative Court: uncontested proceedings)* indicates that this is the responsibility of both parties and that only one copy is required, whereas the *Practice Direction—Judicial Review* PD 54A para 17.1 states that it is the responsibility of the claimant and that two copies are required. In relation to criminal matters see also *Practice Note* [1983] 2 All ER 1020, [1983] 1 WLR 925, which continues to apply in so far as it is not superseded by *Practice Note* [1997] 2 All ER 799, sub nom *Practice Direction (Crown Office List: Consent Orders)* [1997] 1 WLR 825 or by *Practice Statement (Administrative Court: uncontested proceedings)*.

4 *Practice Direction—Judicial Review* PD 54A para 17.2; *Practice Statement (Administrative Court: uncontested proceedings)* [2009] 1 All ER 651, [2008] 1 WLR 1377 para 1. If the court is satisfied that the order should be made, parties or their representatives will not need to attend and the order will be publicised on the Court Service website: *Practice Statement (Administrative Court: uncontested proceedings)* para 1.

5 *Practice Direction—Judicial Review* PD 54A para 17.3; *Practice Statement (Administrative Court: uncontested proceedings)* [2009] 1 All ER 651, [2008] 1 WLR 1377 para 1. A hearing might be required in other circumstances even though the parties are in agreement. For example, note the longstanding practice in private law actions to the effect that declarations will not be made unless there has been a hearing: see *Wallersteiner v Moir* [1974] 3 All ER 217 at 251, [1974] 1 WLR 991 at 1029, CA, per Buckley LJ. This is a rule of practice rather than law: see *Patten v Burke Publishing Co Ltd* [1991] 2 All ER 821 at 823, [1991] 1 WLR 541 at 544 per Millett J. Nevertheless it is conspicuously applicable when the declaration might affect the rights of third parties who are not parties to the proceedings. This could well be the case in some claims for judicial review.

6 *Practice Direction—Judicial Review* PD 54A para 17.4.

7 As to mandatory orders see PARA 703 et seq.

8 *Parr v Wyre Borough Council* (1982) 2 HLR 71, CA.

9 See *Practice Direction—Judicial Review* PD 54A para 17; and *Practice Statement (Administrative Court: uncontested proceedings)* [2009] 1 All ER 651, [2008] 1 WLR 1377 para 3. The procedure to be followed in such circumstances is described in *Practice Statement (Administrative Court: uncontested proceedings)*. As to discontinuance of any claim see also CPR Pt 38; PARA 683; and CIVIL PROCEDURE vol 11 (2009) PARA 723 et seq.

10 See *Practice Statement (Administrative Court: uncontested proceedings)* [2009] 1 All ER 651, [2008] 1 WLR 1377 para 3. The court file would then be closed. A claimant who files a notice of discontinuance of a claim under CPR Pt 38 must serve a copy of the notice on every other party to the proceedings. Unless the court orders otherwise, a claimant who discontinues is liable for the costs which a defendant against whom he discontinues incurred on or before the date on which notice of discontinuance was served on him. On receipt of a notice of discontinuance the court file is closed: *Practice Statement (Administrative Court: uncontested proceedings)* para 3.

(4) APPEALS

679. Appeals. In civil cases, an appeal lies in the first instance to the Court of Appeal. Permission to appeal is required in almost all cases[1]. This should be sought initially from the first instance judge. If the permission is refused the application for permission should then be made to the Court of Appeal[2]. A further appeal lies to the Supreme Court if permission is obtained either from the Court of Appeal or from the Supreme Court[3]. An appeal does not operate as a stay of any order or decision of the lower court unless there is an order to that effect or the appeal is from the Asylum and Immigration Tribunal[4].

In criminal cases[5], there is no appeal to the Court of Appeal[6]. The only appeal available is to the Supreme Court[7]. Permission must be granted either by the first instance court or by the Supreme Court; however, permission will only be granted if the first instance court has certified that a point of law of general public importance is involved[8].

1   Permission is always required to appeal from the decision of a High Court judge except where the appeal is against a committal order (and is made by the alleged contemnor), a refusal to grant habeas corpus or a secure accommodation order made under the Children Act 1989 s 25 (see CHILDREN AND YOUNG PERSONS vol 5(4) (2008 Reissue) PARA 1037): see CPR 52.3; and *Poole Borough Council v Hambridge* [2007] EWCA Civ 990, [2008] CP Rep 1.

2   See the Senior Courts Act 1981 s 16(1) (amended by the Constitutional Reform Act 2005 s 40(4), Sch 9 para 36 (1), (3); and SI 2000/1071); and CPR 52.3. As to the Senior Courts Act 1981 see PARA 602 note 4. The application for permission may be made either to the first instance judge or to the Court of Appeal: see CPR 52.3(2). However, the general practice is to seek the permission of the first instance judge prior to any application to the Court of Appeal. The usual time limit for any application for permission to the Court of Appeal is 21 days: see CPR 52.4. As to the procedural requirements for appeals generally see CPR Pt 52; and CIVIL PROCEDURE vol 12 (2009) PARA 1657 et seq.

3   As to the procedural requirements relevant to applications and appeals to the Supreme Court see the *Supreme Court Practice Directions* (which at the date at which this volume states the law are available online at http://www.supremecourt.gov.uk/procedures/practice-directions.html).

4   See CPR 52.7; and *Leicester Circuits Ltd v Coates Brothers plc* [2002] EWCA Civ 474. As to the Asylum and Immigration Tribunal see BRITISH NATIONALITY, IMMIGRATION AND ASYLUM.

5   As to what is a 'criminal cause or matter' for the purposes of the Senior Courts Act 1981 s 18(1)(a) see *Amand v Home Secretary and Minister of Defence of Royal Netherlands Government* [1943] AC 147, [1942] 2 All ER 381, HL (decided under the Supreme Court of Judicature (Consolidation) Act 1925 s 31(1)(a)); *United States Government v Montgomery* [2001] UKHL 3, [2001] 1 All ER 815, [2001] 1 WLR 196; *R (on the application of McCann) v Manchester Crown Court* [2001] EWCA Civ 281, [2001] 4 All ER 264, [2001] 1 WLR 1084.

6   See the Senior Courts Act 1981 s 18(1)(a); and CIVIL PROCEDURE vol 12 (2009) PARA 1705.

7   Administration of Justice Act 1960 s 1(1) (amended by the Criminal Appeal Act 1968 s 54, Sch 7; the Access to Justice Act 1999 s 63(1); and the Constitutional Reform Act 2005 Sch 9 para 13(1), (2)(a)).

8   See the Administration of Justice Act 1960 s 1(2) (as amended: see note 7); and the *Supreme Court Practice Directions* (see note 3).

680. Fresh evidence on appeal. On an appeal the court has a discretion to consider further evidence which was not before the first instance court[1]. However, the basis upon which this discretion is exercised is limited. In most cases this means that fresh evidence will only be admissible at this stage if it would have been admissible at first instance, and either:

(1)   the evidence is as to matters occurring after the date of trial[2]; or

(2)   the evidence is as to matters occurring before trial which[3]:

(a)   could not have been obtained with reasonable diligence for use at trial;

(b)   is such that, if given, would probably have had an important influence on the result of the case, though it need not be decisive; and

(c)   is such that it is apparently credible though not necessarily incontrovertible,

subject always to the discretion of the court to depart from the above principles where the wider interests of justice so require[4].

1   See CPR 52.11(2); and CIVIL PROCEDURE vol 12 (2009) PARA 1672.

2   Note that CPR 52.11(2) applies as much to evidence of matters arising after the date of trial as to other fresh evidence: see further *R (Iran) v Secretary of State for the Home Department* [2005] EWCA Civ 982, [2005] All ER (D) 384 (Jul); *Mulholland v Mitchell* [1971] AC 666 at 679–680, [1971] 1 All ER 307 at 313, HL, per Lord Wilberforce (whether such evidence will be admitted is a question of discretion and degree).

3   See CPR 52.11(2); and *Riyad Bank v Ahli United Bank (UK) plc* [2005] EWCA Civ 1419, [2005] All ER (D) 299 (Nov); *E v Secretary of State for the Home Department* [2004] EWCA Civ 49, [2004] QB 1044, [2004] 2 WLR 1351 (the court has discretion to depart from these principles in exceptional circumstances); *Hamilton v Al Fayed (Joined Party)* [2000] 2 All ER 224, [2001] EMLR 15; *Hertfordshire Investments Ltd v Bubb* [2000] 1 WLR 2318, [2000] All ER (D) 1052. For cases heard prior to the coming into force of CPR 52.11(2) see *Ali v Secretary of State for the Home Department* [1984] 1 All ER 1009, sub nom *R v Secretary of State for the Home Department, ex p Momin Ali* [1984] 1 WLR 663, CA, applying a similar, but wider, test to that in *Ladd v Marshall* [1954] 3 All ER 745, [1954] 1 WLR 1489, CA. In relation to habeas corpus applications see also *Re Tarling* [1979] 1 All ER 981 at 987, sub nom *R v Governor of Pentonville Prison, ex p Tarling* [1979] 1 WLR 1417 at 1422–1423, DC, per Gibson J.

4   Note also the possibility that an application to adduce new evidence might amount to an abuse of process: compare *R v Lloyd's of London, ex p Briggs* [1993] 1 Lloyds Rep 176, (1992) 5 Admin LR 698, DC; and *R v Chief Constable of Sussex, ex p International Trader's Ferry Ltd* [1998] QB 477, [1997] 2 All ER 65 at 76, CA, per Kennedy LJ.

(5) COSTS

681.   Costs generally.   All courts have a discretion in regard to costs generally[1] which must be exercised judicially. The only immutable rule in relation to the exercise of the discretion on costs is that there are no immutable rules[2]. There are, however, particular considerations in relation to claims for judicial review and the courts have shown some willingness to depart from ordinary costs principles in cases raising issues of general public interest[3]. It is not possible to attempt to anticipate every situation where a less orthodox approach will be considered. Suffice it to say that the courts will act pragmatically to achieve practical justice in relation to costs on a case by case basis[4].

The court may make a wasted costs order against legal representatives if they have caused costs to be incurred by an improper, unreasonable or negligent act or omission[5]. This applies to judicial review proceedings as to all other proceedings[6]. To date, at least in the context of judicial review claims, the courts have applied this jurisdiction pragmatically and with caution[7].

As a general rule, the court will not order costs to be paid by a person who is not party to the proceedings. In principle, however, the jurisdiction to make such an order does exist[8], and in appropriate cases it has been exercised[9].

1   See the Senior Courts Act 1981 s 51 (substituted by the Courts and Legal Services Act 1990 s 4); CPR Pts 44, 48; and CIVIL PROCEDURE vol 12 (2009) PARA 1732. As to the Senior Courts Act 1981 see PARA 602 note 4. See also *R v Woodhouse* [1906] 2 KB 501. As to the width of the court's discretion on issues of costs see *Aiden Shipping Co Ltd v Interbulk Ltd* [1986] AC 965, [1986] 2 All ER 409, HL; *Taylor v Pace Developments Ltd* [1991] BCC 406 at 408, CA, per Lloyd LJ; *Roach v Home Office* [2009] EWHC 312 (QB), [2009] 3 All ER 510.

2   See *Taylor v Pace Developments Ltd* [1991] BCC 406 at 408, CA, per Lloyd LJ; and see also *R (on the application of the Ministry of Defence) v Wiltshire and Swindon Coroner* [2005] EWHC 889 (Admin), [2005] 4 All ER 40, [2006] 1 WLR 134.

3   If a court grants permission to apply for judicial review it may impose such terms as to costs and as to giving security as it thinks fit: see CPR Pt 25 (in relation to security for costs); and CIVIL PROCEDURE vol 11 (2009) PARA 745 et seq.

    The provisions of the CPR relating to the award of costs remain effective in environmental cases, and the principles of the Convention on Access to Information, Public Participation in Decision-making and Access to Justice in Environmental Matters (signed at the Fourth Ministerial Conference 'Environment for Europe' in June 1998; TS 24 (2005); Cm 6586) (the 'Aarhus Convention') including the requirement that judicial procedures allowing members of the public to challenge acts of public authorities which contravene laws relating to the environment should not be 'prohibitively expensive' are at most a matter to which the court may have regard in exercising its discretion (save, possibly, in cases concerning directly effective EC Directives which have incorporated principles of the Aarhus Convention): *Morgan v Hinton Organics (Wessex) Ltd* [2009] EWCA Civ 107, [2009] 2 P & CR 30, [2009] Env LR 30.

4 See, for example, in a non-judicial review context *Davies v Eli Lily & Co* [1987] 3 All ER 94, [1987] 1 WLR 1136, CA; *Chrzanowska v Glaxo Laboratories Ltd* [1990] 1 Med LR 385, DC. In a judicial review context see *Belize Alliance of Conservation Non-Governmental Organisations v Department for the Environment* [2003] UKPC 63, [2003] 1 WLR 2839; *R (on the application of Smeaton) v Secretary of State for Health (No 2)* [2002] EWHC 886 (Admin), [2002] 2 FLR 146; *R v Lord Chancellor, ex p Child Poverty Action Group*; *R v DPP, ex p Bull* [1998] 2 All ER 755, [1999] 1 WLR 347; *New Zealand Maori Council v A-G for New Zealand* [1994] 1 AC 466, [1994] 1 All ER 623, PC; *Re Interest Rate Swap Litigation* (1991) Times, 19 December.

5 See the Senior Courts Act 1981 s 51 (as substituted: see note 1); CPR 48.7–48.10; and CIVIL PROCEDURE vol 12 (2009) PARA 1811. As to the procedure to be adopted on the consideration of any such application see *Ridehalgh v Horsefield* [1994] Ch 205, [1994] 3 All ER 848, CA; applied in the context of judicial review in *R v Horsham District Council, ex p Wenman* [1994] 4 All ER 681, [1995] 1 WLR 680 (which contains a general review of the case law on this point).

6 *R v Horsham District Council, ex p Wenman* [1994] 4 All ER 681, [1995] 1 WLR 680. There is the possible exception of the determination of costs at the permission stage: see *R v Highbury Corner Magistrates' Court, ex p Ewing* [1991] 3 All ER 192, sub nom *Ex p Ewing* [1991] 1 WLR 388, CA (no jurisdiction to make a wasted costs order at the permission stage); cf *R v Immigration Appeal Tribunal, ex p Gulbamer Gulsen* [1997] COD 430 (where the court decided that the power did exist by virtue of the court's inherent jurisdiction).

7 See eg *R v Hackney London Borough Council, ex p Rowe* [1996] COD 155 (distinction drawn between unreasonable behaviour and the over-zealous actions of legal representatives). For an instance where a wasted costs order was made see *R v Secretary of State for the Home Department, ex p Mahmood* [1999] COD 119 (order made against both solicitors and counsel).

8 See *Aiden Shipping Co Ltd v Interbulk Ltd* [1986] AC 965, [1986] 2 All ER 409, HL, applying the Senior Courts Act 1981 s 51(3) (see CIVIL PROCEDURE vol 12 (2009) PARA 1732). See, however, *Aiden Shipping Co Ltd v Interbulk Ltd* at 980 and 416 per Lord Goff commenting that in the vast majority of cases it would be unjust to make such an order.

9 See *Ewing v Office of the Deputy Prime Minister* [2005] EWCA Civ 1583, [2006] 1 WLR 1260 (costs award may be made against a non-party who not only funds the proceedings but also substantially controls or is to benefit from them); *R v Secretary of State for the Home Department, ex p Osman* [1993] COD 204, DC (jurisdiction to be used sparingly; order made requiring the plaintiff's solicitors to disclose the identity of the third party who had funded the plaintiff, and directed that there should be a hearing to show cause why such an order should not be made against him). The general principles to be applied when considering such an application are set out in *Symphony Group plc v Hodgson* [1994] QB 179, [1993] 4 All ER 143, CA; and see *R v Darlington Borough Council, ex p Association of Darlington Taxi Owners (No 2)* [1995] COD 128 (principles in *Symphony Group v Hodgson* applied to determine whether order should be made against members of the plaintiff unincorporated association who were not personally parties to the action).

682. Costs at the permission stage. A grant of permission to pursue a claim for judicial review, whether made on the papers or after oral argument, is deemed to contain an order that costs be costs in the case. Any different order made by a judge must be reflected in the court order granting permission[1]. The court's general discretion applies to any order for costs at this stage[2].

As to costs when permission is refused, in a case in which the judicial review pre-action protocol[3] applies and where a defendant or other interested party has complied with it, a successful defendant or other party[4] at the permission stage who has filed an acknowledgment of service[5] should generally recover the costs of doing so from the claimant, whether or not he attends any permission hearing[6]. Where permission is refused without a hearing, the claimant will usually bear his own costs[7]. Where an application for permission is refused following an oral hearing, the general rule is that, save in exceptional circumstances, a claimant will not be ordered to pay the costs of a defendant or any other party who attends[8]. The court has a broad discretion as to whether, on the facts of each case, there are exceptional circumstances justifying the award of costs against an unsuccessful claimant[9].

1   See *Practice Note (Administrative Court)* [2004] 2 All ER 994, sub nom *Practice Statement (judicial review: costs)* [2004] 1 WLR 1760.
2   See the Senior Courts Act 1981 s 51; and PARA 681 text and note 1. See also *R (on the application of Mount Cook Land Ltd) v Westminster City Council* [2003] EWCA Civ 1346 at [67], [2004] 2 P & CR 405 at [67] per Auld LJ. As to the Senior Courts Act 1981 see PARA 602 note 4. As to protective costs orders see PARA 686.
3   Ie the *Pre-Action Protocol for Judicial Review*: see PARA 663.
4   Note that the suggestion in *R (on the application of Mount Cook Land Ltd) v Westminster City Council* [2003] EWCA Civ 1346, [2004] 2 P & CR 405 that an interested party should generally recover the costs of filing an acknowledgment of service pursuant to CPR 54.8 was obiter on the facts of that case.
5   Ie pursuant to CPR 54.8: see PARA 665.
6   *R (on the application of Mount Cook Land Ltd) v Westminster City Council* [2003] EWCA Civ 1346 at [76], [2004] 2 P & CR 405 at [76] per Auld LJ; *R (Leach) v Commissioner for Local Administration* [2001] EWHC Admin 445. See also *Ewing v Office of the Deputy Prime Minister* [2005] EWCA Civ 1583, [2006] 1 WLR 1260 (as to the procedure for claiming such costs: (1) where a proposed defendant or interested party wishes to seek costs at the permission stage, the acknowledgment of service should include an application for costs and should be accompanied by a schedule setting out the amount claimed; (2) the judge refusing permission should include in the refusal a decision whether to award costs in principle and, if so, an indication of the amount which he proposes to assess summarily; (3) the claimant should be given 14 days to respond in writing and should serve a copy on the defendant; (4) the defendant will have seven days to reply in writing to any such response, and to the amount proposed by the judge; and (5) the judge will then decide and make an award on the papers).
7   However, this may not necessarily be the position where the reason permission is refused is that, subsequent to the application for permission, the defendant has effectively consented to it by undertaking the actions sought by way of relief: see, by way of analogy, *R v Kensington and Chelsea Royal London Borough Council, ex p Ghebregiogis* [1994] COD 502, 27 HLR 602; cf *R v Hackney London Borough Council, ex p Rowe* [1996] COD 155.
8   See *Practice Direction—Judicial Review* PD 54A paras 8.5, 8.6; and *R (on the application of Mount Cook Land Ltd) v Westminster City Council* [2003] EWCA Civ 1346 at [72], [76], [2004] 2 P & CR 405 at [72], [76] per Auld LJ.
9   See *R (on the application of Mount Cook Land Ltd) v Westminster City Council* [2003] EWCA Civ 1346 at [76], [2004] 2 P & CR 405 at [76] per Auld LJ ('the Court of Appeal should be slow to interfere with the broad discretion of the court below in its identification of factors constituting exceptional circumstances and in the exercise of its discretion whether to award costs against an unsuccessful claimant'). As to whether a court should order an unsuccessful party to pay the costs of more than one other party see *Bolton Metropolitan District Council v Secretary of State for the Environment* [1996] 1 All ER 184, [1995] 1 WLR 1176. As to costs orders against publicly funded parties see *R (on the application of Gunn) v Secretary of State for the Home Department* [2001] EWCA Civ 891, [2001] 3 All ER 481, [2001] 1 WLR 1634.

683.   Costs of discontinuance.   Where a very clear case is discontinued due to the defendant performing the act for which an order is sought, the court may make an award of costs against the defendant, either before permission is granted[1], or after the grant of permission but prior to a substantive hearing[2]. In other circumstances, if the claimant discontinues his claim following the grant of permission (most commonly after receipt of the defendant's detailed response) the usual rules on discontinuance apply[3].

1   See *Boxall v Waltham Forest London Borough Council* [2000] All ER (D) 2445. See also *R v Kensington and Chelsea Royal London Borough Council, ex p Ghebregiogis* [1994] COD 502, 27 HLR 602; *R v Bassetlaw District Council, ex p Aldergate Estates* (17 April 2000, unreported); *R v London Borough of Hackney, ex p S* (13 October 2000, unreported); cf *R v Hackney London Borough Council, ex p Rowe* [1996] COD 155.
2   *R v Liverpool City Council, ex p Newman* [1993] COD 65, (1992) 5 Admin LR 669; *Boxall v Waltham Forest London Borough Council* [2000] All ER (D) 2445 (as to the relevant principles: (1) the court has power to make a costs order when the substantive proceedings have been resolved without a trial but the parties have not agreed about costs; (2) it will ordinarily be irrelevant that the claimant is legally aided; (3) the overriding objective is to do justice between the parties without incurring unnecessary court time and consequently additional cost; (4) at

each end of the spectrum there will be cases where it is obvious which side would have won had the substantive issues been fought to a conclusion; in between, the position will, in differing degrees, be less clear; how far the court will be prepared to look into the previously unresolved substantive issues will depend on the circumstances of the particular case, not least the amount of costs at stake and the conduct of the parties; (5) in the absence of a good reason to make any other order the fall back is to make no order as to costs; (6) the court should take care to ensure that it does not discourage parties from settling judicial review proceedings for example by a local authority making a concession at an early stage). See also *R (on the application of Scott) v Hackney London Borough Council* [2009] EWCA Civ 217, [2009] All ER (D) 124 (Jan); *DB v Worcestershire County Council* [2006] EWHC 2613 (Admin); *Sengoz v Secretary of State for the Home Department* [2001] EWCA Civ 1135, (2001) Times, 13 August; *R v ITC, ex p Church of Scientology* [1996] COD 443; *R v Holderness Borough Council, ex p James Robert Developments Ltd* [1993] 1 PLR 108, 66 P & CR 46, CA; *R v Islington London Borough Council, ex p Hooper* [1995] COD 76; *R v Calderdale Metropolitan Borough Council, ex p Houghton* (21 June 2000, unreported); *R v Horsham District Council, ex p Bayley* (26 June 2000, unreported); *R v Islington London Borough Council, ex p Hooper* [1995] COD 76; *R v Barnet London Borough Council, ex p Field* [1989] 1 PLR 30.

3 See CPR Pts 38, 44. See also *Barretts & Baird v Institution of Professional Civil Servants* [1987] IRLR 3; *R v Liverpool City Council, ex p Newman* [1993] COD 65, 5 Admin LR 669. If discontinuance is appropriate it is important that the claimant acts promptly: see *R v Warley Justices, ex p Callis* [1994] COD 240 (costs awarded against applicant who had not sought to withdraw claim until three days before the hearing).

684. Costs at the substantive hearing. Following the substantive hearing, the general rule is that costs will follow the event[1]. However, the discretion of the court is paramount, and when determining any application for costs the court will have regard to all material circumstances which prevail[2]. Circumstances that may justify departure from the usual rule that costs follow the event are too varied to list exhaustively. A factor which may tip the balance on one set of circumstances may be insufficient in a different situation. That said, the court will generally have regard to the conduct of the parties in the course of the litigation[3], whether or not (and if so, the extent to which) the need for the proceedings arose out of the default of either party[4], and whether or not the proceedings have served any substantive purpose[5]. An order for costs may be made against an unsuccessful party who is publicly funded[6].

Special rules have evolved in relation to the position of inferior courts and tribunals when one of their decisions is subject to judicial review[7]. In criminal cases the court has the power to order that all or part of the costs of any party to the proceedings be paid out of central funds[8].

The court will not generally order an unsuccessful party to pay more than one set of costs[9]. Thus, normally, an unsuccessful claimant will only be required to meet the costs of the defendant. However, orders in relation to more than one set of costs may be made if an interested party (or intervenor) dealt with a separate issue not dealt with by the defendant, or where each had distinct interests which justified separate representation[10].

1 See CPR Pt 44, and in particular (as to the factors to be taken into account in deciding the amount of costs) CPR 44.5 (see CIVIL PROCEDURE vol 12 (2009) PARA 1748). See also *Davey v Aylesbury District Council* [2007] EWCA Civ 1166, [2008] 2 All ER 178, [2008] 1 WLR 878 at [29] per Sir Anthony Clarke MR; *R v Lord Chancellor, ex p Child Poverty Action Group* [1998] 2 All ER 755 at 764, [1999] 1 WLR 347 at 355–356 per Dyson J.
2 See the Senior Courts Act 1981 s 51; CPR Pt 44; and PARA 681 text and note 1. As to the Senior Courts Act 1981 see PARA 602 note 4. In *Davey v Aylesbury District Council* [2007] EWCA Civ 1166, [2008] 2 All ER 178, [2008] 1 WLR 878 at [21] per Sedley LJ and at [33] per Sir Anthony Clarke MR, the Court of Appeal gave the following guidance: (1) on the conclusion of full judicial review proceedings in a defendant's favour, the nature and purpose of the particular claim is relevant to the exercise of the judge's discretion as to costs; in contrast to a claim brought wholly or mainly for commercial or proprietary reasons, a claim brought partly or

wholly in the public interest, albeit unsuccessful, may properly result in a restricted or no order for costs; (2) if awarding costs against the claimant, the judge should consider whether they are to include preparation costs in addition to acknowledgment costs; it will be for the defendant to justify these; there may be no sufficient reason why such costs, if incurred, should be recoverable; (3) it is highly desirable that these questions should be dealt with by the trial judge and left to the costs judge only in relation to the reasonableness of individual items; (4) if at the conclusion of such proceedings the judge makes an undifferentiated order for costs in a defendant's favour (a) the order has to be regarded as including any reasonably incurred preparation costs; but (b) *Practice Note (Administrative Court)* [2004] 2 All ER 994, sub nom *Practice Statement (Judicial Review: Costs)* [2004] 1 WLR 1760 should be read to as to exclude any costs of opposing the grant of permission in open court, which should be dealt with on the principles set out in *R (on the application of Mount Cook Land Ltd) v Westminster City Council* [2003] EWCA Civ 1346, [2004] 2 P & CR 405; and (5) a defendant who incurs more cost at the permission stage than was contemplated by Carnwath LJ in *Ewing v Office of the Deputy Prime Minister* [2005] EWCA Civ 1583, [2006] 1 WLR 1260 will not be awarded such costs if the application is unsuccessful.

As to the relevance of a refusal to participate in alternative dispute resolution see *Cowl v Plymouth City Council* [2001] EWCA Civ 1935, [2002] 1 WLR 803; and *Royal Bank of Canada v Secretary of State for Defence* [2003] EWHC 1841 (Ch) (relevant to consider pledge by Lord Chancellor that all government departments would participate in ADR); cf *R (A) v East Sussex County Council* [2005] EWHC 585 (Admin) (parties who reject an unreasonable or unrealistic proposal for mediation may still recover their costs).

3   For example, the extent to which the parties have complied with the requirements of CPR Pt 54, and the likelihood that costs have been unnecessarily incurred by reason of any such default.

4   This could be sufficient to deprive a successful party of his costs. In this regard the court will also have regard to the conduct of the parties prior to the commencement of the claim: see CPR 44.5. For an example of such a situation see *R v IRC, ex p Opman International UK* [1986] 1 All ER 328, [1986] 1 WLR 568.

5   This does not mean that a claimant will necessarily be refused his costs simply because the court has decided in the exercise of its discretion to grant no remedy. Rather, the court will have regard to whether it was necessary to commence proceedings in the first place and whether it remained necessary to pursue the matter at a substantive hearing.

6   See LEGAL AID vol 65 (2008) PARA 109. Note that it is in principle possible for a public authority to satisfy the 'severe hardship' requirement: *R v Greenwich London Borough Council, ex p Lovelace (No 2)* [1992] QB 155, [1992] 1 All ER 679. See also *R (on the application of Gunn) v Secretary of State for the Home Department* [2001] EWCA Civ 891, [2001] 3 All ER 481, [2001] 1 WLR 1634; *Re Wyatt (a child) (medical treatment: continuation of order) (costs)* [2006] EWCA Civ 529, [2006] 20 EG 293 (CS).

7   See the review of authorities in *R (on the application of Davies) v Birmingham Deputy Coroner* [2004] EWCA Civ 207, [2004] 3 All ER 543, [2004] 1 WLR 2739 (the established practice of the courts is to make no order for costs against an inferior court or tribunal which did not appear before it except where there was a flagrant instance of improper behaviour or when the inferior court or tribunal unreasonably declined or neglected to sign a consent order disposing of the proceedings; an inferior court or tribunal which resisted an application actively by way of argument so that it made itself an active party to the litigation would be treated as such a party for costs purposes; traditionally, if an inferior court or tribunal appeared in the proceedings in order to assist the court neutrally on questions of jurisdiction, procedure, specialist case law and such like, the established practice of the courts was to treat it as a neutral party, so that it would not make an order for costs in its favour or against it, however, the courts might exercise their discretion in such cases differently today where a successful applicant has to finance his own litigation without funding in a case where an inferior tribunal has gone wrong in law and there is no other very obvious candidate available to pay his costs). See the later cases of *R (on the application of Varma) v Redbridge Magistrates' Court* [2009] EWHC 836 (Admin) (costs shared equally between the Crown Prosecution Service and the Magistrates' Court where the CPS should not have contested the appeal and the Magistrates' Court unreasonably failed to sign a consent order); *T v Cardiff City and County Council* [2007] EWHC 2568 (Admin), [2007] All ER (D) 150 (Nov); *R (on the application of Tull) v Camberwell Green Magistrates' Court* [2004] EWHC 2780 (Admin), [2005] RA 31.

8   See the Prosecution of Offences Act 1985 ss 16, 17; and CRIMINAL LAW, EVIDENCE AND PROCEDURE vol 11(4) (2006 Reissue) PARAS 2059, 2062.

9   See *Bolton Metropolitan District Council v Secretary of State for the Environment* [1996] 1 All ER 184, [1995] 1 WLR 1176, HL. Thus normally costs will not be granted to the other party to a dispute as well as to the court or tribunal whose proceedings are in question: *R v*

Industrial Disputes Tribunal, ex p American Express Co Inc [1954] 2 All ER 764n, [1954] 1 WLR 1118. Cf *R (on the application of Mount Cook Land Ltd) v Westminster City Council* [2003] EWCA Civ 1346, [2004] 2 P & CR 405 (obiter suggestion that in a case in which the *Pre-Action Protocol for Judicial Review* applies and where an interested party has complied with it and filed an acknowledgment of service, and is then successful at the permission stage, he should generally recover the costs of doing so from the claimant, whether or not he attends any permission hearing). See PARA 663.

10   See *Bolton Metropolitan District Council v Secretary of State for the Environment* [1996] 1 All ER 184, [1995] 1 WLR 1176, HL. See also *Austin v Secretary of State for Communities and Local Government* [2008] EWHC 3200 (Admin), [2008] All ER (D) 25 (Dec) (separate representation justified on the facts of the case); *R (on the application of Bennett) v Secretary of State for Communities and Local Government* [2007] EWHC 737 (Admin), [2007] All ER (D) 15 (Mar); *R (on the application of A, B, X and Y) v East Sussex County Council* [2005] EWHC 585 (Admin), [2005] All ER (D) 70 (Apr) (fair, just and appropriate to depart from the ordinary rule); *R v Panel on Take-overs and Mergers, ex p Datafin plc* [1987] QB 815, [1987] 1 All ER 564, CA (where issues were complex and required separate representation).

685. Appeals against decisions on costs. A party can appeal against an order for costs but, in order to appeal, that party must first obtain permission to bring the appeal[1]. In practice, if the only issue on the appeal is costs the Court of Appeal will be reluctant to entertain the point unless it raises a matter of general importance[2]. Since a decision on costs is an exercise of discretion, for an appeal to succeed it must be demonstrated that the court erred in law, or effectively failed to exercise the discretion at all[3].

1   See the Senior Courts Act 1981 s 18; and CIVIL PROCEDURE vol 12 (2009) PARA 1705. As to the Senior Courts Act 1981 see PARA 602 note 4.

2   See *R v Holderness Borough Council, ex p James Robert Developments Ltd* (1993) 5 Admin LR 470, 66 P & CR 46, CA. In this case the three members of the Court of Appeal expressed different views. Butler-Sloss LJ concluded that there was no discretion and the court had to hear the appeal; Simon Brown LJ thought that there was a general discretion and the case would only be heard if there was a point of general importance; Dillon LJ agreed with Simon Brown LJ to the extent that a discretion existed but said that it would only be exercised to prevent the hearing of an appeal if the amount at stake was very small.

3   An example of this might be where the court took into account some wholly extraneous factor. For examples of such appeals see *Jones v McKie* [1964] 2 All ER 842, [1964] 1 WLR 960, CA; *R v Holderness Borough Council, ex p James Robert Developments Ltd* [1993] 1 PLR 108, 66 P & CR 46, CA; *Ainsbury v Millington* [1987] 1 All ER 929, [1987] 1 WLR 379n, HL (case law on this point reviewed).

686. Protective costs orders. The court has jurisdiction to make a protective costs order protecting a party[1] to judicial review proceedings[2] against the risk of a substantial costs order should he be unsuccessful or limiting the amount of costs which might be ordered[3]. The Court of Appeal has given guidance[4] to the effect that a court may make such an order at any stage of proceedings[5], on such conditions as it thinks fit, provided that it is satisfied that[6]: (1) the issues raised are of general public importance[7]; (2) the public interest requires that those issues be resolved; (3) possibly, that the applicant has no private interest in the outcome of the case[8]; (4) having regard to the financial resources of the applicant and the respondent and to the amount of costs that are likely to be involved, it is fair and just to make the order[9]; (5) if the order is not made the applicant will probably discontinue the proceedings and will be acting reasonably in doing so. An order capping the claimant's costs is likely to be required in all cases, except where the claimant's lawyers are acting pro bono and the effect of the protective costs order is to prescribe in advance that there should be no order as to costs in the substantive proceedings whatever the outcome[10].

1   A protective costs order may be made in an appropriate case to protect the position of a
    defendant, although such a case is likely to be rare: *R (on the application of the Ministry of
    Defence) v Wiltshire and Swindon Coroner* [2005] EWHC 889 (Admin), [2005] 4 All ER 40,
    [2006] 1 WLR 134. See further CIVIL PROCEDURE vol 12 (2009) PARA 1744.
2   In *Campaign Against Arms Trade v BAE Systems plc* [2007] EWHC 330 (QB), [2007] All ER
    (D) 324 (Feb), King J gave an obiter indication that the court had jurisdiction to make a
    protective costs order in a Norwich Pharmacal application which was ancillary to an intended
    set of public law proceedings, although it might not exercise its discretion to do so.
3   See the Senior Courts Act 1981 s 51; and CIVIL PROCEDURE vol 12 (2009) PARA 1732. As to the
    Senior Courts Act 1981 see PARA 602 note 4. See also *R (on the application of Corner House
    Research) v Secretary of State for Trade and Industry* [2005] EWCA Civ 192, [2005] 4 All ER 1,
    [2005] 1 WLR 2600; *R (on the application of the Campaign for Nuclear Disarmament) v Prime
    Minister* [2002] EWHC 2777 (Admin), [2003] 3 LRC 335; *R v Lord Chancellor, ex p Child
    Poverty Action Group*; *R v DPP, ex p Bull* [1998] 2 All ER 755, [1999] 1 WLR 347. As to the
    procedure for seeking such a protective costs order see the detailed guidance given by the Court
    of Appeal in *R (on the application of Corner House Research) v Secretary of State for Trade and
    Industry*; and CIVIL PROCEDURE vol 12 (2009) PARA 1744.
4   The guidance given in *R (on the application of Corner House Research) v Secretary of State for
    Trade and Industry* [2005] EWCA Civ 192, [2005] 4 All ER 1, [2005] 1 WLR 2600 is not to be
    treated as laying down hard and fast rules: see *R (on the application of Compton) v Wiltshire
    Primary Care Trust* [2008] EWCA Civ 749 at [23], [2009] 1 All ER 978 at [23], [2009] 1 WLR
    1436 at [23] per Waller LJ and [76] per Smith LJ; *Morgan v Hinton Organics (Wessex) Ltd*
    [2009] EWCA Civ 107, [2009] 2 P & CR 30; *R (on the application of Buglife, The Invertebrate
    Conservation Trust) v Thurrock Thames Gateway Development Corpn* [2008] EWCA Civ
    1209, [2008] 45 EG 101 (CS); *R (on the application of Goodson) v Bedfordshire and Luton
    Coroner* [2005] EWCA Civ 1172, [2005] All ER (D) 122 (Oct). There is no additional
    requirement that the applicant must show that his is an exceptional case: *R (British Union for
    the Abolition of Vivisection) v Secretary of State for the Home Department)* [2006] EWHC 250
    (Admin).
5   The same considerations apply in relation to an application for a protective costs order on
    appeal as at first instance, although the fact that the issue arises at the appellate stage may affect
    the exercise of the court's discretion: see *R (on the application of Goodson) v Bedfordshire and
    Luton Coroner* [2005] EWCA Civ 1172, [2005] All ER (D) 122 (Oct).
6   See *R (on the application of Corner House Research) v Secretary of State for Trade and Industry*
    [2005] EWCA Civ 192, [2005] 4 All ER 1, [2005] 1 WLR 2600.
7   Where someone is bringing an action to obtain resolution of issues which affect a wide
    community, and where that community has a real interest in the issues that arise being resolved,
    it is open to a judge to hold that there is a public interest in resolution of the issues and that the
    issues are ones of general public importance: see *R (on the application of Compton) v Wiltshire
    Primary Care Trust* [2008] EWCA Civ 749, [2009] 1 All ER 978, [2009] 1 WLR 1436.
8   See *R (on the application of Corner House Research) v Secretary of State for Trade and Industry*
    [2005] EWCA Civ 192, [2005] 4 All ER 1, [2005] 1 WLR 2600; *R (on the application of
    Goodson) v Bedfordshire and Luton Coroner* [2005] EWCA Civ 1172, [2005] All ER (D) 122
    (Oct); and *R (A) (Disputed Children) v Secretary of State for the Home Department* [2007]
    EWHC 2494 (Admin), [2007] All ER (D) 20 (Nov). But cf the serious doubts as to the
    correctness of this aspect of the guidance expressed in *Morgan v Hinton Organics (Wessex) Ltd*
    [2009] EWCA Civ 107, [2009] 2 P & CR 30 (impossible to ignore the criticisms of a narrow
    approach); *Re Kings Cross Railway Lands Group* (22 March 2007, unreported); *R (on the
    application of Eley) v Secretary of State for Communities and Local Government* (1 July 2008,
    unreported); *Wilkinson v Kitsinger* [2006] EWHC 835 (Fam), [2006] 2 FCR 537, [2006] 2 FLR
    397; *R (on the application of England) v Tower Hamlets London Borough Council* [2006]
    EWCA Civ 1742, [2006] All ER (D) 314 (Dec).
9   See *R (Corner House Research) v Secretary of State for Trade and Industry* [2005] EWCA Civ
    192, [2005] 1 WLR 2600 (the fact that the applicant's lawyers are acting pro bono will likely
    enhance the merits of the application for a protective costs order). However, it is not clear
    whether this will remain a significant factor since the enactment of the Legal Services Act 2007
    s 194, by which the court has power to order a person to make payments in respect of pro bono
    representation (see LEGAL PROFESSIONS vol 66 (2009) PARA 934).
10 See the detailed guidance on cost-capping given by the Court of Appeal in *R (Corner House
    Research) v Secretary of State for Trade and Industry* [2005] EWCA Civ 192, [2005] 1 WLR
    2600; *King v Telegraph Group Ltd* [2004] EWCA Civ 613 at [101]–[102], [2005] 1 WLR 2282
    at [101]–[102] per Brooke LJ; and see also *R (on the application of Buglife, The Invertebrate
    Conservation Trust) v Thurrock Thames Gateway Development Corpn* [2008] EWCA Civ

1209, [2008] 45 EG 101 (CS). There should be no assumption that it is appropriate where the claimant's liability for costs is capped, that the defendant's liability for costs should be capped in the same amount. Where a defendant wishes to seek an order capping its liability for costs, it should do so in the acknowledgment of service: see *R (on the application of Buglife, The Invertebrate Conservation Trust) v Thurrock Thames Gateway Development Corpn.*

5. JUDICIAL REMEDIES

(1) INTRODUCTION

687. Remedies in general. The principal non-statutory remedies available on an application for judicial review are quashing orders[1], prohibiting orders[2], mandatory orders[3], injunctions[4] and declaratory orders[5]. The court also has power in defined circumstances to make an award of damages or to order restitution or recovery of a sum due[6]. The principal statutory remedies in administrative law are appeals[7] and applications to quash certain orders such as compulsory purchase orders and certain planning decisions[8].

1   A quashing order was formerly known as an order of certiorari (see PARA 688) but was renamed by the Civil Procedure (Modification of Supreme Court Act 1981) Order 2004, SI 2004/1033, which amended the Supreme Court Act 1981. As to quashing orders see PARA 693 et seq. As to the CPR see PARA 659; and CIVIL PROCEDURE vol 11 (2009) PARA 30 et seq.
2   A prohibiting order was formerly known as an order of prohibition (see PARA 688) but was renamed by the Civil Procedure (Modification of Supreme Court Act 1981) Order 2004, SI 2004/1033, which amended the Supreme Court Act 1981. As to prohibiting orders see PARA 693 et seq.
3   A mandatory order was formerly known as an order of mandamus (see PARA 688) but was renamed by the Civil Procedure (Modification of Supreme Court Act 1981) Order 2004, SI 2004/1033, which amended the Supreme Court Act 1981. As to mandatory orders see PARA 703 et seq.
4   As to injunctions see PARA 716 et seq; and CIVIL PROCEDURE vol 11 (2009) PARA 331 et seq.
5   As to declaratory orders see PARAS 716, 719.
6   See CPR 54.3(2); and PARAS 722–723.
7   As to appeals see PARA 660.
8   See eg the Town and Country Planning Act 1990 ss 284, 287–288; and TOWN AND COUNTRY PLANNING vol 46(1) (Reissue) PARAS 43, 46–47.

688. Historical development of the prerogative remedies of certiorari, prohibition and mandamus. Historically, prohibition was a writ whereby the royal courts of common law prohibited other courts from entertaining matters falling within the exclusive jurisdiction of the common law courts; certiorari was issued to bring the record of an inferior court into the King's Bench for review or to remove indictments for trial in that court; and mandamus was directed to inferior courts and tribunals, and to public officers and bodies, to order the performance of a public duty[1]. All three were called prerogative writs[2]; since 1938 they have been designated as orders[3]. During the seventeenth century certiorari evolved as a general remedy to quash the proceedings of inferior tribunals and was used largely to supervise the justices of the peace in the performance of their criminal and administrative functions under various statutes. In 1700 it was held that the Court of King's Bench would examine the proceedings of all jurisdictions erected by Act of Parliament, and that, if under the pretence of such an act the inferior tribunals proceeded to arrogate jurisdiction to themselves greater than the act warranted, the court would send a certiorari to them to have their proceedings returned to the court, so that the court might restrain them from exceeding that jurisdiction[4]. If bodies exercising such jurisdiction did not perform their duty, the King's Bench would grant a mandamus[5]. Prohibition would issue if anything remained to prohibit[6]. The ambit of certiorari and prohibition was not limited to the supervision of functions that would ordinarily be regarded as strictly judicial[7], and in the nineteenth century the writs came to be used to control the exercise of certain administrative functions by local and central government authorities which did not necessarily act under judicial forms[8].

1 Prohibition, certiorari and mandamus have been respectively renamed as prohibiting, quashing and mandatory orders: see PARA 687 notes 1–3. As to prohibiting and quashing orders see PARA 693 et seq. As to mandatory orders see PARA 703 et seq.

2 As to the first collective description in a reported case of the three writs as 'prerogative' see *R v Cowle* (1759) 2 Burr 834 at 855–856 per Lord Mansfield CJ. As to the writ of habeas corpus see ADMINISTRATIVE LAW vol 1(1) (2001 Reissue) PARA 207 et seq. Another prerogative writ is the writ of ne exeat regno: see *Al Nahkel for Contracting and Trading Ltd v Lowe* [1986] QB 235, [1986] 1 All ER 729, DC; *Felton v Callis* [1969] 1 QB 200, [1968] 3 All ER 673, DC; *Parsons v Burk* [1971] NZLR 244, NZ SC. As to the obsolete writ of scire facias see ADMINISTRATIVE LAW vol 1(1) (2001 Reissue) PARA 264. For a recent review of the history of the prerogative remedies see *R (on the application of Cart) v Upper Tribunal* [2009] EWHC 3052 (Admin).

3 See the Administration of Justice (Miscellaneous Provisions) Act 1938 (repealed); the Senior Courts Act 1981 s 29; and PARA 602 note 4. The Senior Courts Act 1981 was previously known as the Supreme Court Act 1981 and was renamed by the Constitutional Reform Act 2005 s 59(5), Sch 11 Pt 1 as from 1 October 2009: see the Constitutional Reform Act 2005 (Commencement No 11) Order 2009, SI 2009/1604; and COURTS.

4 *R v Glamorganshire Inhabitants* (1700) 1 Ld Raym 580; *Groenvelt v Burwell* (1700) 1 Ld Raym 454.

5 *Groenvelt v Burwell* (1700) 1 Ld Raym 454.

6 As to the earliest time for applying for a prohibiting order see PARA 700.

7 Thus certiorari would issue to quash justices' orders fixing rates for the repair of bridges (*R v Glamorganshire Inhabitants* (1700) 1 Ld Raym 580) and for producing poor rate books (*Warwick Borough Case* (1734) 2 Stra 991), and prohibition would issue in respect of an order forbidding the clerk of the peace to take certain fees (*R v Coles* (1845) 8 QB 75). As to the limited circumstances in which the Upper Tribunal is amenable to judicial review see *R (on the application of Cart) v Upper Tribunal* [2009] EWHC 3052 (Admin).

8 See generally *R v Local Government Board* (1882) 10 QBD 309 at 321, CA, per Brett LJ. See also *R v Arkwright* (1848) 12 QB 960 (order to church building commissioners to quash order stopping up paths); *R v Aberdare Canal Co* (1850) 14 QB 854 (certiorari to quash sanction by ad hoc commissioners to build a bridge).

689. General scope of the prerogative orders. A quashing order[1] is an order of the High Court which lies to quash decisions of an inferior court or tribunal, public authority or other body which is susceptible to judicial review[2]. Such an order may be made where the decision-maker has acted in breach of one of the principles of public law; for example, where there has been a breach of the rules of natural justice or procedural fairness[3], or where there has been a breach of a legitimate expectation in the absence of overriding public need[4], or where the decision-maker has made an error of law[5].

A prohibiting order[6] is an order issuing out of the High Court and directed at an inferior court or tribunal, public authority or other body susceptible to judicial review which forbids that body to act in excess of its jurisdiction[7] or in breach of the principles of public law governing the exercise of its functions.

A mandatory order[8] is, in form, a command issuing from the High Court, directed to any person, corporation or inferior tribunal requiring him, or them, to do some particular thing specified in the command which appertains to his or their office and is in the nature of a public duty[9]. The breach of duty may be a failure to exercise a discretion, or a failure to exercise it according to proper legal principles[10].

The prerogative orders are available to control powers and duties derived from statute[11], or the royal prerogative[12] but the orders are also available to control the exercise of jurisdiction by non-statutory bodies performing functions of a public, as distinct from a private, nature[13]. The approach of the courts now is to consider whether the decision is taken in the exercise of a power or the performance of a duty which involves a public element, which may take a variety of forms, and the exclusion of functions that are not seen as public or where the body concerned acquires jurisdiction over individuals by virtue of contract[14].

1 A quashing order was formerly known as an order of certiorari: see PARAS 687 note 1, 688. As to quashing orders see PARA 693 et seq.

2 As to when a body is susceptible to judicial review see PARA 604.

3 As to natural justice and fairness see PARA 629.

4 As to legitimate expectation see PARA 649.

5 See PARAS 612, 616. At one time it was thought that before certiorari or prohibition could issue, a body had to have a duty to act judicially: see *R v Electricity Comrs, ex p London Electricity Joint Committee (1920) Ltd* [1924] 1 KB 171 at 205, CA, per Atkin LJ. However, this limitation no longer represents the law and cannot now be supported: see *Ridge v Baldwin* [1964] AC 40, [1963] 2 All ER 66, HL; *O'Reilly v Mackman* [1983] 2 AC 237, [1982] 3 All ER 1124, HL, per Lord Diplock.

6 A prohibiting order was formerly known as an order of prohibition: see PARAS 687 note 2, 688. As to prohibiting orders see PARA 693 et seq.

7 As to when a court has exceeded its jurisdiction see PARA 699.

8 A mandatory order was formerly known as an order of mandamus: see PARAS 687 note 3, 688. As to mandatory orders see PARA 703 et seq. The prerogative order of mandamus is to be distinguished from the action of mandamus by which a plaintiff could formerly claim a mandamus demanding the defendant to fulfil a duty in which the plaintiff was personally interested: see *R v Lambourn Valley Rly Co* (1888) 22 QBD 463 at 469, DC, per Manisty J; *Baxter v LCC* (1890) 63 LT 767 at 771 per Day J. As to the action of mandamus generally see *Bush v Beavan* (1862) 32 LJ Ex 54; *Baxter v LCC* (1890) 63 LT 767; *Smith v Chorley RDC* [1897] 1 QB 678, CA. The order is also to be distinguished from the mandatory order which may be granted under the Senior Courts Act 1981 s 29(3) (see PARA 602). See also *R v Chief Constable of Devon and Cornwall, ex p Central Electricity Generating Board* [1982] QB 458, [1981] 3 All ER 826, CA. The Senior Courts Act 1981 was previously known as the Supreme Court Act 1981 and was renamed by the Constitutional Reform Act 2005 s 59(5), Sch 11 Pt 1 as from 1 October 2009: see the Constitutional Reform Act 2005 (Commencement No 11) Order 2009, SI 2009/1604; and COURTS.

9 See e g *Padfield v Minister of Agriculture, Fisheries and Food* [1968] AC 997, [1968] 1 All ER 694, HL.

10 See PARAS 610 et seq, 703 et seq.

11 Thus it has been held that neither certiorari nor prohibition will issue to a private arbitral body which derives its jurisdiction from contract, or which has a voluntary, but not mandatory, jurisdiction conferred by statute: *R v National Joint Council for Craft of Dental Technicians Disputes Committee, ex p Neate* [1953] 1 QB 704, [1953] 1 All ER 327, DC; *Law v National Greyhound Racing Club* [1983] 3 All ER 300, 1983] 1 WLR 1302; *R v Disciplinary Committee of the Jockey Club, ex p Aga Khan* [1993] 2 All ER 853, [1993] 1 WLR 909; *R v Lloyd's of London, ex p Briggs* [1993] 1 Lloyd's Rep 176; *R (on the application of West) v Lloyd's of London* [2004] EWCA Civ 506, [2004] 3 All ER 251.

12 Hence certiorari was granted against the Criminal Injuries Compensation Board, which was a non-statutory tribunal established by administrative action under the prerogative and not exercising a statutory jurisdiction but awarding ex gratia payments out of money provided by Parliament: see *R v Criminal Injuries Compensation Board, ex p Lain* [1967] 2 QB 864, [1967] 2 All ER 770, DC. As to the Criminal Injuries Compensation Authority, which has replaced the Criminal Injuries Compensation Board, and as to the Criminal Injuries Compensation Scheme generally, see CRIMINAL LAW, EVIDENCE AND PROCEDURE vol 11(4) (2006 Reissue) PARA 2033 et seq. See also *Council of Civil Service Unions v Minister for the Civil Service* [1985] AC 374, [1984] 3 All ER 935, HL; *R (on the application of Bancoult) v Secretary of State for Foreign and Commonwealth Affairs* [2008] UKHL 61, [2009] 1 AC 453, [2008] 4 All ER 1055, confirming that powers derived from the prerogative are amenable to judicial review provided that the subject matter of the particular exercise of power gives rise to justiciable issues. As to non-statutory tribunals see PARA 606.

13 See *R v Panel on Take-overs and Mergers, ex p Datafin* [1987] QB 815, [1987] 1 All ER 564. Hence a private company established by a local authority, discharging functions previously discharged by the authority and funded by it, was held to be exercising public functions ands its decisions were amenable to judicial review: see *R (on the application of Beer) v Hampshire Farmers Market Ltd* [2003] EWCA Civ 1056, [2004] 1 WLR 233. By contrast, the provision of

services under contractual arrangements between a public authority and a private company may not involve the performance by the private company of public functions: see *R v Servite Houses, ex p Goldsmith* [2001] LGR 55, 33 HLR 369 (and for discussion of the analogous issue of when such situations involve the performance of public functions for the purposes of the Human Rights Act 1998 s 6 see *YL v Birmingham City Council* [2007] UKHL 27, [2008] 1 AC 95, [2007] 3 All ER 957; *R (on the application of Weaver) v London and Quadrant Housing Trust* [2009] EWCA Civ 587, [2009] 4 All ER 865, [2009] All ER (D) 179 (Jun)).

14 *R v Panel on Take-overs and Mergers, ex p Datafin* [1987] QB 815 at 838, [1987] 1 All ER 564 at 577 per Sir John Donaldson MR.

690. The ordinary remedies of injunction and declaration. An injunction is a discretionary equitable remedy awarded by a court to restrain the imminent threat or the commission or continuance of unlawful acts, in which case the injunction is prohibitory; or to compel the taking of steps to repair an unlawful omission or to restore the damage inflicted by an unlawful act, in which case the injunction will be mandatory[1]. A declaratory judgment is a judicial decision which involves the declaration of the law in relation to a particular matter, such as that a decision of a public body is ultra vires, or a declaration of the rights of a party without any reference to their enforcement[2].

1 As to injunctions see PARA 716 et seq; and CIVIL PROCEDURE vol 11 (2009) PARA 331 et seq.
2 See PARA 719.

691. Concurrent availability of non-statutory remedies. An application for a quashing order[1], a prohibiting order[2] or a mandatory order[3] must be made by way of an application for judicial review[4]. In appropriate cases a declaration or injunction may also be applied for by way of an application for judicial review[5]. As all remedies for infringements of rights protected by public law can thus be obtained on an application for judicial review, it may be held to be an abuse of the process of the court to proceed by way of an ordinary claim instead of using the judicial review procedure provided by the Civil Procedure Rules[6].

1 A quashing order was formerly known as an order of certiorari: see PARAS 687 note 1, 688. As to quashing orders see PARA 693 et seq.
2 A prohibiting order was formerly known as an order of prohibition: see PARAS 687 note 2, 688. As to prohibiting orders see PARA 693 et seq.
3 A mandatory order was formerly known as an order of mandamus: see PARAS 687 note 3, 688. As to mandatory orders see PARA 703 et seq.
4 See the Senior Courts Act 1981 s 31(1) (amended by SI 2004/1033); and CPR 54.2. The Senior Courts Act 1981 was previously known as the Supreme Court Act 1981 and was renamed by the Constitutional Reform Act 2005 s 59(5), Sch 11 Pt 1 as from 1 October 2009: see the Constitutional Reform Act 2005 (Commencement No 11) Order 2009, SI 2009/1604; and COURTS. As to the CPR see PARA 659; and CIVIL PROCEDURE vol 11 (2009) PARA 30 et seq. As to applications for judicial review see PARA 659 et seq.
5 See the Senior Courts Act 1981 s 31(2) (amended by SI 2004/1033); and CPR 54.3. In addition, on an application for judicial review the court may in appropriate cases award damages to the applicant: see the Senior Courts Act 1981 s 31(4) (substituted by SI 2004/1033); CPR 54.3(2); and PARA 602.
6 See *O'Reilly v Mackman* [1983] 2 AC 237 at 284–285, [1982] 3 All ER 1124 at 1133–1134, HL, per Lord Diplock; but see generally PARA 661. The text refers to the procedure provided by CPR Pt 54: see PARA 660 et seq.

692. Discretion. Quashing orders[1], prohibiting orders[2], mandatory orders[3], declaratory orders[4] and injunctions[5] are all discretionary[6]. The court has a discretion whether to grant a remedy at all and, if so, what form of remedy to grant.

In deciding whether to grant a remedy the court will take account of the conduct of the party applying, and consider whether it has been such as to disentitle him to relief. Undue delay[7], unreasonable[8] or unmeritorious[9] conduct, acquiescence in the irregularity complained of[10] or waiver of the right to object[11] may all result in the court declining to grant relief. Another consideration in deciding whether or not to grant relief is the effect of doing so[12]. Factors which may be relevant include whether the grant of the remedy is unnecessary[13] or futile[14], whether practical problems[15], including administrative chaos and public inconvenience[16], would result, the effect on third parties[17], and whether the form of the order would require close supervision by the court or be incapable of practical fulfilment[18]. A remedy may be refused when an alternative remedy to a claim for judicial review, such as an appeal or an internal complaints procedure, is or was available but was not used[19].

The court has an ultimate discretion whether to set aside decisions and may decline to do so in the public interest, notwithstanding that it holds and declares the decision to have been made unlawfully[20]. The demands of good public administration may lead to a refusal of relief[21]. However, there is a public interest in establishing that action taken by a public body is invalid and there needs to be good reason for not granting an appropriate remedy; thus, in some instances, the courts may refuse to quash a decision where is good reason to do so but may grant a declaration that there has been a breach of the relevant principles of public law[22]. Similarly where public bodies are involved the court may allow 'contemporary decisions to take their course, considering the complaint and intervening, if at all, later and in retrospect by declaratory orders'[23]. Declaratory relief was awarded to a probationer constable who was wrongly induced to resign[24], although an order of mandamus directing his reinstatement was the only satisfactory remedy so far as the applicant was concerned. In the absence of some basis for refusing relief as a matter of discretion, however, the courts will generally quash an unlawful decision to dismiss or declare it to be invalid[25].

1   A quashing order was formerly known as an order of certiorari: see PARAS 687 note 1, 688. As to quashing orders see PARA 693 et seq.
2   A prohibiting order was formerly known as an order of prohibition: see PARAS 687 note 2, 688. As to prohibiting orders see PARA 693 et seq.
3   A mandatory order was formerly known as an order of mandamus: see PARAS 687 note 3, 688. As to mandatory orders see PARA 703 et seq.
4   As to declaratory orders see PARAS 716, 719.
5   As to injunctions see PARA 717; and CIVIL PROCEDURE vol 11 (2009) PARA 331 et seq.
6   *R (on the application of Edwards) v Environment Agency* [2008] UKHL 22, [2009] 1 All ER 57, [2008] 1 WLR 1587 at [63] per Lord Hoffmann.
7   Claims for judicial review must be brought promptly and in any event within three months of the date when the grounds for review first arose: see CPR 54.5(1). Even if a court grants an extension of time for bringing a claim, there remains undue delay and a remedy may be refused: see *Caswell v Dairy Produce Quota Tribunal for England and Wales* [1990] 2 AC 738, [1990] 2 All ER 434, HL. As to the time limit for bringing an application for judicial review see PARA 658.
8   *R v Crown Court at Knightsbridge, ex p Marcrest Ltd* [1983] 1 All ER 1148, [1983] 1 WLR 300, CA; *Fullbrook v Berkshire Magistrates' Court Committee* (1970) 69 LGR 75; *Ex p Fry* [1954] 2 All ER 118 at 120, [1954] 1 WLR 730 at 734, CA, per Hallett J.
9   See *R v Chief National Insurance Comr, ex p Connor* [1981] QB 758, [1981] 1 All ER 769, DC; *Goordin v Secretary of State for the Home Department* (1981) 125 Sol Jo 624, (1981) Times, 11 August, CA. The impropriety of applying for a judicial remedy 'when political capital is sought to be made ... out of judicial review' has been emphasised: *R v GLC, ex p Royal Borough of Kensington and Chelsea* (1982) Times, 7 April (precept issued by the Greater London Council).
10 *R v Secretary of State for Education and Science, ex p Birmingham City Council* (1984) 83 LGR 79.
11 *Whelan v R* [1921] 2 IR 310; *R v Williams, ex p Phillips* [1914] 1 KB 608. See also PARA 626.

12 *R v Brent Health Authority, ex p Francis* [1985] QB 869, [1985] 1 All ER 74, DC; *R v Hillingdon Health Authority, ex p Goodwin* [1984] ICR 800. The court should not grant relief the effect of which will be to facilitate unlawful activity, eg trespass on the highway: see *R v Hereford and Worcester County Council, ex p Smith (Tommy)* [1994] COD 129, CA.

13 *R v GLC, ex p Blackburn* [1976] 3 All ER 184, [1976] 1 WLR 550, CA. See also *R v Boundary Commission for England, ex p Foot* [1983] QB 600, [1983] 1 All ER 1099, CA; *Clarke v Chadburn* [1985] 1 All ER 211, [1985] 1 WLR 78.

14 *R v Commonwealth Public Services Commission, ex p Killeen* (1914) 18 CLR 586 (Aust). See also *R v Secretary of State for Social Services, ex p Association of Metropolitan Authorities* [1986] 1 All ER 164, [1986] 1 WLR 1 (certiorari refused, but declaration granted; the regulations had been acted upon by local authorities and had since been consolidated into new regulations which were not challenged); *R v Ministry of Agriculture Fisheries and Food, ex p Live Sheep Traders Ltd* [1995] COD 297, DC (no declaration that legislation repealed prior to the making of the application was unlawful; it is no part of the court's function to make academic declarations). Cf *R v Northavon District Council, ex p Palmer* (1993) 25 HLR 674, 6 Admin LR 195, where Sedley J granted permission to apply for judicial review although the declaration sought was academic because there was no other means by which the applicant could bring a claim for damages (this approach was 'procedurally debatable' but to do otherwise would be 'a denial of justice': see at 679 and 200 per Sedley J).

15 *Chief Constable of the North Wales Police v Evans* [1982] 3 All ER 141, [1982] 1 WLR 1155, HL (despite the fact that the order of mandamus was the only satisfactory remedy from the respondent's point of view 'with some reluctance and hesitation' Lord Brightman felt that he would have to content himself with the less satisfactory remedy of declaration: see at 156 and 1176). More recently, the Privy Council has accepted that, in the absence of some good reason, the usual remedy in relation to an unlawful decision to dismiss a person from public office would be a quashing order or a declaration that the decision is invalid: see *McLaughlin v Governor of the Cayman Islands* [2007] UKPC 50, [2007] 1 WLR 2839. See also *Re Guyer's Application* [1980] 2 All ER 520 at 527, sub nom *R v Lancashire County Council, ex p Guyer* [1980] 1 WLR 1024 at 1033–1034, CA, where, finding no breach of duty by the council as highway authority under the Highways Act 1959 s 116(1) (repealed: see now the Highways Act 1980 s 130(1); and HIGHWAYS, STREETS AND BRIDGES vol 21 (2004 Reissue) PARA 340), Stephenson LJ said (at 527 and 1033–1034) 'if there were a breach and it was necessary to decide whether mandamus should go, the submission of counsel for [the applicant] that the court's direction should be almost as imprecise as Nelson's Trafalgar signal and direct the council to do its statutory duty would, in my opinion, be likely to prove fatal to the exercise of the court's discretion in the applicant's favour'. See also *R v National Dock Labour Board, ex p National Amalgamated Stevedores and Dockers* [1964] 2 Lloyd's Rep 420 at 428–429 per Lord Parker CJ.

16 *R v Paddington Valuation Officer, ex p Peachey Property Corpn Ltd* [1964] 3 All ER 200 at 208, [1964] 1 WLR 1186 at 1195, DC, per Widgery J; affd [1966] 1 QB 380, [1965] 2 All ER 836, CA. But see *R v Kerrier District Council, ex p Guppys (Bridport) Ltd* (1976) 32 P & CR 411 at 418, CA, per Orr LJ (the prospect of a vast number of applications resulting from the construction of certain words in a statute was considered an improper reason for refusing a mandamus); *R v Rochdale Metropolitan Borough Council, ex p Schemet* [1994] ELR 89, (1992) 91 LGR 425 (Roch J refused to quash an unlawful policy because to do so would affect two years' education budget for the local authority; instead a declaration was granted, giving rise to the possibility of a further challenge in the future if the authority persisted with the unlawful policy); *R v South Tyneside Metropolitan Borough Council and the Governors of Hebburn Comprehensive School, ex p Cram* (1997) 10 Admin LR 477 (no order of mandamus to compel a school to take back a pupil where there was a risk of widespread disruption to education and industrial action). See also *Secretary of State for Education and Science v Tameside Metropolitan Borough Council* [1977] AC 1014, [1976] 3 All ER 665, HL.

17 *R v Panel on Take-overs and Mergers, ex p Datafin plc* [1987] QB 815 at 842, [1987] 1 All ER 564 at 579–580, CA, per Sir John Donaldson MR, speaking of the panel on take-overs and mergers: 'I wish to make it clear beyond a peradventure that in the light of the special nature of the panel, its functions, the market in which it is operating, the time scales which are inherent in that market and the need to safeguard the position of third parties, who may be numbered in thousands, all of whom are entitled to continue to trade on an assumption of the validity of the panel's rules and decisions, unless and until they are quashed by the court, I should expect the relationship between the panel and the court to be historic rather than contemporaneous. I should expect the court to allow contemporary decisions to take their course, considering the complaint and intervening, if at all, later and in retrospect by declaratory orders which would enable the panel not to repeat any error and would relieve individuals of the disciplinary

consequences of any erroneous finding of breach of the rules' (commented on in *R v Panel on Take-overs and Mergers, ex p Guinness plc* [1990] 1 QB 146 at 157–158, [1989] 1 All ER 509 at 511–512, CA, per Lord Donaldson of Lymington MR).

18 'The court does not in its discretion allow mandamus to go if the form of the order may require day to day supervision and the detailed examination of circumstances which these two orders might involve': *R v Peak Park Joint Planning Board* (1976) 74 LGR 376 at 380, DC, per Lord Widgery CJ. See also *R v South Tyneside Metropolitan Borough Council and the Governors of Hebburn Comprehensive School, ex p Cram* (1997) 10 Admin LR 477 (no order of mandamus to compel a school to take back a pupil where incapable of practical fulfilment).

19 See eg *R (on the application of Sivasubramaniam) v Wandsworth County Court* [2002] EWCA Civ 1738, [2003] 2 All ER 160; *R (on the application of G) v Immigration Tribunal* [2004] EWCA Civ 1731, [2005] 2 All ER 165; *F (Mongolia) v Secretary of State for the Home Department* [2007] EWCA Civ 769, [2007] All ER (D) 384 (Jul); *R (on the application of Sinclair Gardens (Kensington) Ltd) v Lands Tribunal* [2005] EWCA Civ 1305, [2006] 3 All ER 650.

20 See eg *R v Monopolies and Mergers Commission, ex p Argyll Group plc* [1986] 2 All ER 257, [1986] 1 WLR 763, CA; *R v Secretary of State for Social Services, ex p Association of Metropolitan Authorities* (1992) 5 Admin LR 6 (Tucker J declined to quash regulations held to have been made unlawfully by reason of a failure to consult on the ground that to do so would be disruptive and lead to uncertainty and delay; a declaration was granted instead); but see also *R (on the application of C) v Secretary of State for Justice* [2008] EWCA Civ 882, [2009] QB 657, [2009] 2 WLR 1039 (delegated legislation had no special protected status and, in the absence of pressing reasons, relief would be granted if unlawfulness were established).

21 Good public administration is concerned with substance rather than form, and speed of decision, particularly in the financial field. Further, it requires a proper consideration of the public interest and a proper consideration of the legitimate interests of individual citizens as well as the applicant. In judging the relevance of an interest, however legitimate, regard has to be had to the purpose of the administrative process concerned and considerations such as decisiveness and finality: *R v Monopolies and Mergers Commission, ex p Argyll Group plc* [1986] 2 All ER 257 at 266, [1986] 1 WLR 763 at 774, CA, per Sir John Donaldson MR. See also *Nichol v Gateshead Metropolitan Borough Council* (1988) 87 LGR 435, CA; *R v Brent London Borough Council, ex p O'Malley* (1997) 10 Admin LR 265, 30 HLR 328, CA.

22 See eg *R (on the application of Gavin) v London Borough of Haringey* [2003] EWHC 2591 (Admin), [2004] 2 P & CR 209, [2003] All ER (D) 57 (Nov) (court refused to quash planning permission because of the hardship that would cause to the developer but granted a declaration that there had been a failure to comply with procedural requirements); *R v Lincolnshire County Council and Wealden District Council, ex p Atkinson* [1995] EGCS 145, 8 Admin LR 529 (court refused to quash a removal direction but granted a declaration).

23 *R v Panel on Take-overs and Mergers, ex p Datafin plc* [1987] QB 815 at 842, [1987] 1 All ER 564 at 580, CA, per Sir John Donaldson MR. See further the remarks of Sir John Donaldson MR at 842 and 579–580, quoted in note 16. See also *R v Panel on Take-overs and Mergers, ex p Guinness plc* [1990] 1 QB 146 at 157–158, [1989] 1 All ER 509 at 511–512, CA, per Lord Donaldson of Lymington MR.

24 *Chief Constable of the North Wales Police v Evans* [1982] 3 All ER 141, [1982] 1 WLR 1155, HL. See also *R v Cambridge Health Authority, ex p B* [1995] 2 All ER 129, [1995] 1 WLR 898, CA (jurisdiction to review the way in which a health authority in the exercise of its public duties allocated its resources should be used sparingly).

25 *McLaughlin v Governor of the Cayman Islands* [2007] UKPC 50, [2007] 1 WLR 2839.

(2) QUASHING ORDERS AND PROHIBITING ORDERS

(i) The Nature of Quashing and Prohibiting Orders

693. The nature of quashing orders and prohibiting orders. A quashing order[1] is an order of the High Court by which decisions of an inferior court[2], tribunal, public authority[3] or any other body of persons who are susceptible to judicial review[4] may be quashed. The effect of a quashing order is that the unlawful decision or order is set aside and deprived of all legal effect since its inception[5]. If the decision is quashed, the court may remit the matter to the decision-maker for him to reconsider the matter[6]. The decision-maker may, as long as the error of law[7] is not repeated and no other error committed, reach the same decision.

A prohibiting order[8] is an order issuing out of the High Court[9] and directed to an inferior court[10] or tribunal or public authority[11] or body which is susceptible to judicial review which forbids that court or tribunal or authority or body to act in excess of its jurisdiction or contrary to law[12].

Both quashing orders and prohibiting orders are employed for the control of inferior courts, tribunals and public authorities. They are remedies which have much in common so that they can be considered together[13]. Whereas quashing orders are concerned with decisions already taken, prohibiting orders are concerned with future actions or decisions[14].

1   A quashing order was formerly known as an order of certiorari: see PARAS 687 note 1, 688. As to the procedure to be followed on applications for quashing orders see PARA 693 et seq.

2   As to inferior courts see COURTS.

3   See *R v Electricity Comrs, ex p London Electricity Joint Committee Co (1920) Ltd* [1924] 1 KB 171 at 205, CA, per Atkin LJ.

4   As to when a body is susceptible to judicial review see PARA 604.

5   *McLaughlin v Governor of the Cayman Islands* [2007] UKPC 50, [2007] 1 WLR 2839; *Hoffman-La Roche & Co AG v Secretary of State for Trade and Industry* [1975] AC 295, [1974] 2 All ER 1128, HL.

6   Where the court quashes a decision it has power to remit the matter to the court, tribunal or authority concerned with a direction to reconsider it and to reach a decision in accordance with the judgment given by the court in judicial review proceedings: see the Senior Courts Act 1981 s 31(5)(a) (substituted by the Tribunals, Courts and Enforcement Act 2007 s 141); and CPR 54.19(2)(a). The judicial review court may substitute its own decision for that of a court or tribunal where the decision in question was quashed on the ground that there had been an error of law and, without the error, there would have been only one lawful decision that the court or tribunal could have reached: see the Senior Courts Act 1981 s 31(5A) (added by the Tribunals, Courts and Enforcement Act 2007 s 141); and CPR 54.19(2)(b). As to the CPR see PARA 660; and CIVIL PROCEDURE vol 11 (2009) PARA 30 et seq. The Senior Courts Act 1981 was previously known as the Supreme Court Act 1981 and was renamed by the Constitutional Reform Act 2005 s 59(5), Sch 11 Pt 1 as from 1 October 2009: see the Constitutional Reform Act 2005 (Commencement No 11) Order 2009, SI 2009/1604; and COURTS.

7   As to an error of law see PARA 612.

8   A prohibiting order was formerly known as an order of prohibition: see PARAS 687 note 2, 688. See Com Dig Prohibition; Bac Abr Prohibition; 3 BC Com; and *Mackonochie v Lord Penzance* (1881) 6 App Cas 424, HL.

9   The writ of prohibition (for which the order of prohibition was substituted by the Administration of Justice (Miscellaneous Provisions) Act 1938 (repealed)) was issued originally out of the King's Bench, as it was the King's prerogative writ. The history of the writ of prohibition was discussed in *R v Chancellor of St Edmundsbury and Ipswich Diocese, ex p White* [1948] 1 KB 195, [1947] 2 All ER 170, CA.

10   It has been held that prohibition will lie to an ecclesiastical court, whereas certiorari will not: *R v Chancellor of St Edmundsbury and Ipswich Diocese, ex p White* [1948] 1 KB 195, [1947] 2 All ER 170, CA. As to ecclesiastical courts see COURTS vol 10 (Reissue) PARA 805 et seq; ECCLESIASTICAL LAW vol 14 PARA 1259 et seq.

11   It has been held that a prohibition 'is available to prohibit administrative authorities from exceeding their powers or misusing them. In particular, it can prohibit a licensing authority from making rules or granting licences which permit conduct which is contrary to law': *R v GLC, ex p Blackburn* [1976] 3 All ER 184 at 192, [1976] 1 WLR 550 at 559, CA, per Lord Denning MR.

12   As to when the court has exceeded its jurisdiction see PARA 699.

13   In *R v Electricity Comrs, ex p London Electricity Joint Committee Co (1920) Ltd* [1924] 1 KB 171 at 206, CA, Atkin LJ said: 'I can see no difference in principle between certiorari and prohibition, except that the latter may be invoked at an earlier stage. If the proceedings establish that the body complained of is exceeding its jurisdiction by entertaining matters which would result in its final decision being subject to being brought up and quashed on certiorari, I think

that prohibition will lie to restrain it from so exceeding its jurisdiction'. As to the earliest time for applying for a prohibiting order see PARA 700.

14 Quashing orders and prohibiting orders are frequently sought together, eg where a quashing order is sought to quash the decision and the prohibiting order to restrain its execution. But either remedy may be sought by itself: see eg PARA 695. See *Wheeler v Leicester City Council* [1985] AC 1054 at 1079, [1985] 2 All ER 1106 at 1111–1112, HL, per Lord Roskill, where a council's decision not to allow a club to use their football ground was quashed but the need for further relief was contemplated. Other forms of certiorari, such as certiorari to remove an indictment or other proceedings for trial, are now obsolescent or obsolete and are not of practical importance in administrative law: see ADMINISTRATIVE LAW vol 1(1) (2001 Reissue) PARA 267.

694. Conditional orders. A prohibiting order[1] may also be granted conditionally[2], that is, it may be a conditional order in that it will prohibit a body or inferior court[3] from acting until it alters an earlier unlawful decision or complies with a relevant public law obligation or principle. Thus, for example, a local authority has been prohibited from exercising its licensing powers without first hearing representations on behalf of interested parties[4].

1 A prohibiting order was formerly known as an order of prohibition: see PARAS 687 note 2, 688. As to the nature of prohibiting orders see PARA 693.
2 This was previously referred to as an order quousque. See *Anon* (1704) 6 Mod Rep 308; *London Corpn v Cox* (1867) LR 2 HL 239 at 276 per Willes J. See also *White v Steele* (1862) 12 CBNS 383 at 411–412 per Willes J; *R v Australian Stevedoring Industry Board, ex p Melbourne Stevedoring Co Pty Ltd* (1953) 88 CLR 100 at 117, [1953] ALR 461 at 467, Aust HC.
3 As to inferior courts see COURTS.
4 *R v Liverpool Corpn, ex p Liverpool Taxi Fleet Operators' Association* [1972] 2 QB 299, [1972] 2 All ER 589, CA.

(ii) Scope of Quashing Orders and Prohibiting Orders

695. Examples of the grant of quashing orders and prohibiting orders. Quashing orders (formerly known as orders of certiorari)[1] are frequently made when applications for judicial review are successful. By way of example, orders of certiorari have been made against a department of state[2], an individual minister who made an invalid clearance order[3] or an order to take over a school for wrong reasons or in breach of natural justice[4] or an order wrongly not to hold a public inquiry[5], a local authority that wrongfully granted a licence[6] or planning permission[7], licensing justices[8], a valuation officer who made a rating list on wrong principles[9], an immigration officer who refused leave to enter on wrong grounds[10], the Gaming Board for refusal of a certificate of consent for a gaming club without a fair hearing[11], the Police Complaints Board[12], an election court[13], a local legal aid committee[14], rent tribunals[15], a rent assessment committee[16], a medical appeal tribunal[17], a vaccine damage tribunal[18], a dairy produce quotas tribunal[19], the Milk Marketing Board[20], the Health and Safety Commission[21], a prison board of visitors[22], a prison governor in respect of a disciplinary award[23], the Commission for Racial Equality[24], the Registrar of Companies in respect of the registration of a charge[25], and mental health commissioners[26].

Prohibiting orders (formerly known as orders of prohibition)[27] are also frequently made on applications for judicial review. By way of example, orders of prohibition have been made against Electricity Commissioners to prevent them from holding an inquiry with a view to bringing into force an ultra vires scheme for the supply of electricity[28], magistrates to prevent them from exceeding their jurisdiction[29], a prison board of visitors to prevent them from hearing a charge which they are not entitled to deal with[30], a local authority to prohibit it from acting on a resolution with regard to the number of taxi licences to be issued without first hearing representations on behalf of interested parties[31], or licensing indecent films[32], a minister making an invalid clearance order[33], a rent tribunal to prevent it from proceeding with a case outside its jurisdiction[34], a housing authority to prevent it from requiring the demolition of a house which was improperly condemned[35], Income Tax Commissioners[36], the Comptroller-General of Patents, Designs and Trade Marks[37], and a chief medical officer who was likely to be biased[38].

Declaratory orders rather than the prerogative orders[39] are generally regarded as more appropriate for declaring that delegated legislation is unlawful[40] although quashing orders have been granted quashing such subordinate legislation[41].

1 A quashing order was formerly known as an order of certiorari: see PARAS 687 note 1, 688. As to the nature of quashing orders see PARA 693.

2 See eg *Board of Education v Rice* [1911] AC 179, HL; *R v Local Government Board* (1882) 10 QBD 309, CA.

3 *R v Minister for Health, ex p Yaffe* [1930] 2 KB 98 (revsd on other grounds [1931] AC 494, HL). See also *R v Secretary of State for the Environment, ex p Brent London Borough Council* [1982] QB 593, [1983] 3 All ER 321, DC; *R v Immigration Appeal Tribunal, ex p Bastiampillai* [1983] 2 All ER 844 (decision of Secretary of State concerning removal of time limit on limited right of stay quashed when he failed to take into account change of circumstances); *R v Secretary of State for the Home Department, ex p Kirklees Borough Council* (1987) Times, 24 January (Home Secretary's refusal to issue television broadcast receiving licences at a concessionary rate quashed); *R v Secretary of State for the Home Department, ex p Dannenberg* [1984] QB 766, [1984] 2 All ER 481, CA (order for deportation of EEC citizen quashed for failure to give reasons).

4 *Maradana Mosque Board of Trustees v Mahmud* [1967] 1 AC 13, [1966] 1 All ER 545, PC. See also *Afful v Secretary of State for the Home Department* [1983] Imm AR 23 (decision to deport quashed because the applicant had not been given an opportunity to state her case); *R v Secretary of State for Transport, ex p Philippine Airlines Inc* (1984) Times, 17 October, CA (Secretary of State's decision permanently to vary the airline's operating permit vitiated by the absence of due inquiry required by the Air Navigation Order 1980, SI 1980/1965, art 59(1) (now revoked)). As to natural justice see PARA 629.

5 *R v Secretary of State for the Environment, ex p Binney* (1983) Times, 8 October (decision of Secretary of State for the Environment and Secretary of State for Transport not to hold a public inquiry into a proposed alteration of the A34 trunk road between Winchester and Newbury quashed).

6 *R v LCC, ex p Entertainments Protection Association* [1931] 2 KB 215, CA (cinematograph licences). See also *R v GLC, ex p Blackburn* [1976] 3 All ER 184, [1976] 1 WLR 550, CA.

7 *R v Hendon RDC, ex p Chorley* [1933] 2 KB 696; *R v Hillingdon London Borough Council, ex p Royco Homes Ltd* [1974] QB 720, [1974] 2 All ER 643, DC. See also *R v Sheffield City Council, ex p Mansfield* (1978) 37 P & CR 1 at 6, DC, per Lord Widgery CJ (application by ratepayers for certiorari to quash grant of planning permission refused on the merits). As to planning permission see TOWN AND COUNTRY PLANNING.

8 *R v Woodhouse* [1906] 2 KB 501, CA; *R v Dudley Justices, ex p Curlett* [1974] 2 All ER 38, [1974] 1 WLR 457, DC (liquor licence); *R v Barnsley Metropolitan Borough Council, ex p Hook* [1976] 3 All ER 452, [1976] 1 WLR 1052, CA (street trader's licence). Licensing functions are now carried out by licensing authorities under the Licensing Act 2003, and not by licensing justices: see LICENSING AND GAMBLING vol 67 (2008) PARA 26.

9 *R v Paddington Valuation Officer, ex p Peachey Property Corpn Ltd* [1966] 1 QB 380, [1965] 2 All ER 836, CA. As to valuation officers see RATING AND COUNCIL TAX vol 39(1B) (Reissue) PARAS 6, 129 note 1.

10 *R v Chief Immigration Officer, Lympne Airport, ex p Amrik Singh* [1969] 1 QB 333, [1968] 3 All ER 163, DC. See also *R v Chief Immigration Officer, Gatwick Airport, ex p Kharrazi* [1980] 3 All ER 373, [1980] 1 WLR 1396, CA; *R v Secretary of State for the Home Office, ex p Awuku* (1987) Times, 3 October (refusal by immigration officer and Home Secretary of permission to enter to three applicants who were formerly sergeants in military intelligence unit in Ghana who sought asylum in the United Kingdom quashed as they were given no opportunity

to comment on the grounds upon which they were refused entry). As to immigration officers see BRITISH NATIONALITY, IMMIGRATION AND ASYLUM vol 4(2) (2002 Reissue) PARA 140 et seq.

11 *R v Gaming Board for Great Britain, ex p Benaim and Khaida* [1970] 2 QB 417, [1970] 2 All ER 528, CA (relief refused on the facts). The functions of the Gaming Board are now carried out by the Gambling Commission: see LICENSING AND GAMBLING vol 67 (2008) PARA 5.

12 *R v Police Complaints Board, ex p Madden* [1983] 2 All ER 353, [1983] 1 WLR 447. The Police Complaints Board was replaced by the Police Complaints Authority, but complaints against the police are now dealt with by the Independent Police Complaints Commission: see POLICE vol 36(1) (2007 Reissue) PARA 316 et seq.

13 *R v Cripps, ex p Muldoon* [1984] QB 68, [1983] 3 All ER 72, DC; affd [1984] QB 686, [1984] 2 All ER 705, CA. As to the election court see ELECTIONS AND REFERENDUMS vol 15(4) (2007 Reissue) PARA 767 et seq.

14 *R v Manchester Legal Aid Committee, ex p Brand & Co Ltd* [1952] 2 QB 413, [1952] 1 All ER 480, DC. As to legal aid generally see LEGAL AID.

15 *R v Fulham, Hammersmith and Kensington Rent Tribunal, ex p Zerek* [1951] 2 KB 1, [1951] 1 All ER 482, DC. As to rent tribunals and rent assessment committees see LANDLORD AND TENANT vol 27(2) (2006 Reissue) PARAS 910, 988 et seq.

16 *Ellis and Sons Fourth Amalgamated Properties Ltd v Southern Rent Assessment Panel* (1984) 14 HLR 48, 270 Estates Gazette 39.

17 *R v Medical Appeal Tribunal, ex p Gilmore* [1957] 1 QB 574, sub nom *Re Gilmore;s Application* [1957] 1 All ER 796, CA. The functions of medical appeal tribunals were transferred to appeal tribunals under the Social Security Act 1998, but have now been transferred to the First-Tier Tribunal: see the Transfer of Tribunal Functions Order 2008, SI 2008/2833, Sch 1.

18 *R v Vaccine Damage Tribunal, ex p Loveday* (1984) Times, 10 November. The functions of vaccine damage tribunals have now been transferred to the First-Tier Tribunal.

19 *R v Dairy Produce Quotas Tribunal, ex p S Dimelow Farms* (1988) Times, 7 November. As to the abolition of Dairy Produce Quota Tribunals see AGRICULTURAL PRODUCTION AND MARKETING vol 1 (2008) PARA 740 note 5.

20 *R v Milk Marketing Board, ex p North* (1934) 50 TLR 559. The Milk Marketing Board has now been abolished: see the Milk Marketing Board (Dissolution) Order 2002, SI 2002/128. As to the marketing of agricultural produce generally see AGRICULTURAL PRODUCTION AND MARKETING vol 1 (2008) PARAS 701 et seq, 1080 et seq.

21 *R v Health and Safety Commission, ex p Spelthorne Borough Council* (1983) Times, 18 July. The Health and Safety Commission has been abolished: see the Legislative Reform (Health and Safety Executive) Order 2008, SI 2008/960, art 2. As to the newly-established Health and Safety Executive see the Health and Safety at Work etc Act 1974 ss 10, 11, Sch 2; the Legislative Reform (Health and Safety Executive) Order 2008, SI 2008/960; and HEALTH AND SAFETY AT WORK vol 52 (2009) PARA 361 et seq.

22 *R v Board of Visitors of Hull Prison, ex p St Germain* [1978] QB 678, [1978] 2 All ER 198, DC (revsd on appeal [1979] QB 425, [1979] 1 All ER 701, CA); *R v Blundeston Prison Board of Visitors, ex p Fox-Taylor* [1982] 1 All ER 646. As to Boards of Visitors, now known as Independent Monitoring Boards, see PRISONS vol 36(2) (Reissue) PARA 511 et seq.

23 *Leech v Deputy Governor of Parkhurst Prison* [1988] AC 533, [1988] 1 All ER 485, HL. See also *R v Secretary of State for the Home Department, ex p Herbage (No 2)* [1987] QB 1077, [1987] 1 All ER 324, CA (leave to apply for mandamus granted where allegation of 'cruel and unusual punishment' contrary to Bill of Rights (1688)). As to prison governors see PRISONS vol 36(2) (Reissue) PARA 522.

24 *R v Commission for Racial Equality, ex p Hillingdon London Borough Council* [1982] QB 276, CA; affd sub nom *Hillingdon London Borough Council v Commission for Racial Equality* [1982] AC 779, HL. The Commission for Racial Equality has been replaced by the Commission for Equality and Human Rights: see DISCRIMINATION vol 13 (2007 Reissue) PARA 305 et seq.

25 Ie pursuant to the Companies Act 1948 s 95(1) (repealed: see now the Companies Act 2006 s 860; and COMPANIES vol 15 (2009) PARA 1277). See *R v Registrar of Companies, ex p Esal (Commodities) Ltd (In liquidation)* [1986] QB 1114, [1985] 2 All ER 79; on appeal [1986] QB 1114, [1986] 1 All ER 105, CA. As to the Registrar of Companies see COMPANIES vol 14 (2009) PARA 131 et seq.

26 *R v Mental Health Commission, ex p W* (1988) Times, 27 May. The Care Quality Commission is now responsible for regulating health, mental health and adult social care: see SOCIAL SERVICES AND COMMUNITY CARE. As to mental health generally see MENTAL HEALTH.

27 A prohibiting order was formerly known as an order of prohibition: see PARAS 687 note 2, 688. As to prohibiting orders see PARA 693 et seq.

28 *R v Electricity Comrs, ex p London Electricity Joint Committee Co (1920) Ltd* [1924] 1 KB 171, CA. As to the dissolution of the Electricity Commissioners see FUEL AND ENERGY vol 19(2) (2007 Reissue) PARA 1033.

29 *R v Horseferry Road Justices, ex p Independent Broadcasting Authority* [1987] QB 54, [1986] 2 All ER 666, DC. As to when a court has exceeded its jurisdiction see PARA 699. See further MAGISTRATES.

30 *R v Board of Visitors of Dartmoor Prison, ex p Smith* [1987] QB 106, [1986] 2 All ER 651, CA.

31 *R v Liverpool Corpn, ex p Liverpool Taxi Fleet Operators' Association* [1972] 2 QB 299, [1972] 2 All ER 589, CA. See further LOCAL GOVERNMENT.

32 *R v GLC, ex p Blackburn* [1976] 3 All ER 184, [1976] 1 WLR 550, CA.

33 *R v Minister of Health, ex p Davis* [1929] 1 KB 619, CA.

34 *R v Tottenham and District Rent Tribunal, ex p Northfield (Highgate) Ltd* [1957] 1 QB 103, [1956] 2 All ER 863, DC.

35 *Estate and Trust Agencies (1927) Ltd v Singapore Improvement Trust* [1937] AC 898, [1937] 3 All ER 324, PC. As to housing authorities see HOUSING.

36 *Kensington Income Tax Comrs v Armayo* [1916] 1 AC 215, HL; *R v Aldrington, Houghton and Hove Income Tax Comrs, ex p Singer* (1916) 85 LJKB 1753, DC. In *R v Clerkenwell General Comrs of Taxes* [1901] 2 KB 879, CA, and *R v Bloomsbury Income Tax Comrs* [1915] 3 KB 768, DC, writs of prohibition were refused on the ground that, as the commissioners had not gone wrong on the finding of the necessary questions of fact to give themselves jurisdiction, the applicant's remedy was by way of appeal under the Income Tax Acts. The Income Tax Commissioners are now known as the Commissioners for Her Majesty's Revenue and Customs: see CUSTOMS AND EXCISE vol 12(3) (2007 Reissue) PARA 900 et seq; INCOME TAXATION.

37 *Re Hall* (1888) 21 QBD 137. Cf *Re Wingate's Patent* [1931] 2 Ch 272 (where it was held that prohibition would not lie against the comptroller for acts or decisions on matters arising in the administration of the provisions of the Patents and Designs Act 1907 (now repealed), which acts or decisions were either subject to appeal to the law officer, or done under the direction of the law officer, or against the law officer himself). See also *R v Comptroller-General of Patents, ex p Parke, Davis & Co* [1953] 1 All ER 862, [1953] 2 WLR 760, DC; affd [1953] 2 QB 48, [1953] 2 All ER 137, CA; affd sub nom *Parke, Davis & Co v Comptroller-General of Patents, Designs and Trade Marks* [1954] AC 321, [1954] 1 All ER 671, HL. As to the Comptroller-General of Patents, Designs and Trade Marks see PATENTS AND REGISTERED DESIGNS vol 79 (2008) PARA 577.

38 *R v Kent Police Authority, ex p Godden* [1971] 2 QB 662, [1971] 3 All ER 20, CA (prohibition to restrain a chief medical officer from examining a police officer in order to decide whether he was permanently disabled for the purpose of empowering the local police authority to exercise its power to retire him compulsorily; the doctor was likely to be biased, having examined the applicant officer recently for another purpose).

39 As to the prerogative orders see PARAS 688–689.

40 See e g *Brownsea Haven Properties Ltd v Poole Corpn* [1958] Ch 574, [1958] 1 All ER 205, CA. There is jurisdiction to declare such delegated legislation unlawful: see *R (on the application of Javed) v Secretary of State for the Home Department* [2001] EWCA Civ 789, [2002] QB 129.

41 *R (on the application of C) v Secretary of State for Justice* [2008] EWCA Civ 882, [2009] QB 657, [2009] 2 WLR 1039.

696. Superior courts. The prerogative orders[1], including quashing orders[2] and prohibiting orders[3], are not available in respect of the superior courts[4]. These include the High Court, the Court of Appeal and the Supreme Court[5]. There is an exception in relation to the Crown Court, where the court has jurisdiction to grant quashing orders, prohibiting orders and mandatory orders[6] against the Crown Court save in matters relating to trials on indictment[7].

1 As to the prerogative orders see PARAS 688–689.

2 A quashing order was formerly known as an order of certiorari: see PARAS 687 note 1, 688. As to the nature of quashing orders see PARA 693.

3 A prohibiting order was formerly known as an order of prohibition: see PARAS 687 note 2, 688. As to the nature of prohibiting orders see PARA 693.

4 *R v Oxenden* (1691) 1 Show KB 217; *Suratt v A-G of Trinidad and Tobago* [2007] UKPC 55 at [49], [2008] 1 AC 655 at [49].

5 See COURTS.

6 A mandatory order was formerly known as an order of mandamus: see PARAS 687 note 3, 688. As to mandatory orders see PARA 703 et seq.

7   See the Senior Courts Act 1981 s 29(3) (amended by SI 2004/1033). The Senior Courts Act 1981
    was previously known as the Supreme Court Act 1981 and was renamed by the Constitutional
    Reform Act 2005 s 59(5), Sch 11 Pt 1 as from 1 October 2009: see the Constitutional Reform
    Act 2005 (Commencement No 11) Order 2009, SI 2009/1604; and COURTS. As to the meaning
    of 'relating to trial by indictment' see *Re Smalley* [1985] AC 622, [1985] 1 All ER 769, HL; *R v
    DPP, ex p Kebiline* [2000] 2 AC 326, [1999] 4 All ER 801, HL; *R v Manchester Crown Court,
    ex p DPP* [1993] 1 WLR 1524, HL; *R v Maidstone Crown Court, ex p Harrow London
    Borough Council* [2000] QB 719, [1999] 3 All ER 542.

(iii) Special Rules relating to Quashing Orders

697.   Where matter is not within the jurisdiction of the High Court. Quashing
orders[1] can only be issued in respect of matters which are within the jurisdiction
of the High Court of Justice, for proceedings will not be removed into the
superior court unless they are capable of being determined there[2]. Such an order
will not, therefore, be directed to an ecclesiastical court[3] or to a court which is
not one of civil jurisdiction, for example a court-martial[4], unless it is shown that
civil rights have been affected[5].

1   A quashing order was formerly known as an order of certiorari: see PARAS 687 note 1, 688. As
    to the nature of quashing orders see PARA 693.
2   *Longbottom v Longbottom* (1852) 8 Exch 203 at 208 per Pollock CB; *Scott v Bye* (1824) 9
    Moore CP 649 at 660; *Bates v Turner* (1825) 10 Moore CP 32 at 34; *Tingle v Roston* (1825) 2
    Bing 463; *Bruce v Wait* (1837) 3 M & W 15 at 23. See also 1 Lilly's Abridgement 363 et seq. As
    to the jurisdiction of the High Court see COURTS.
3   *R v Chancellor of St Edmundsbury and Ipswich Diocese, ex p White* [1948] 1 KB 195, [1947]
    2 All ER 170, CA. As to ecclesiastical courts see COURTS vol 10 (Reissue) PARA 805 et seq;
    ECCLESIASTICAL LAW vol 14 PARA 1259 et seq.
4   *Re Mansergh* (1861) 1 B & S 400; *R v Army Council, ex p Ravenscroft* [1917] 2 KB 504, DC;
    R v Secretary of State for War, ex p Martyn [1949] 1 All ER 242, DC; *Re Clifford and
    O'Sullivan* [1921] 2 AC 570, HL (prohibition refused). More recently, the courts appeared
    prepared to consider claims for judicial review of refusal of petitions against decisions of
    court-martials: see eg *R v Admiralty Board of the Defence Council, ex p Coupland* [1996] COD
    147. However, there is now a statutory appeal under the Courts Martial (Appeals) Act 1968 s 8
    (see ARMED FORCES vol 2(2) (Reissue) PARA 530) against a decision of a court-martial and
    challenges would be expected to proceed via the statutory appeal route.
5   Eg where rights of life, liberty, or property are involved: *Re Mansergh* (1861) 1 B & S 400 at
    406 per Cockburn CJ. See also *R v Murphy* [1921] 2 IR 190 (where it was held that, if a
    court-martial acts without or in excess of jurisdiction, the court can exercise its controlling
    authority against the tribunal by writ of certiorari). The court will interfere by certiorari if the
    court-martial purports to deal with someone who is not subject to military law: see eg *R v
    Secretary of State for War, ex p Price* [1949] 1 KB 1, DC (where the order was refused on the
    merits); *R v Governor of Wormwood Scrubs Prison, ex p Boydell* [1948] 2 KB 193, [1948]
    1 All ER 438, DC (certiorari and habeas corpus issued).

698.   Statutory conditions for grant. In certain proceedings the legislature may
expressly provide that the remedy of a quashing order[1] is to be open to aggrieved
parties for the purpose of quashing the proceedings[2]. Where a quashing order is
expressly made available by statute, the order can only be granted subject to the
restrictions, if any, imposed by the statute, and upon the grounds, if any,
specified in it. The terms of the statute may permit the court to quash the
decision, not only on the usual grounds of want of jurisdiction or error on the
face of the record or breach of natural justice, but also on the merits as though
by way of appeal[3].

In modern statutes prescribing a procedure for challenging administrative acts
and decisions, it is not the practice to provide for review by a quashing order.

1   A quashing order was formerly known as an order of certiorari: see PARAS 687 note 1, 688. As
    to the nature of quashing orders see PARA 693.

2   See e g the Inclosure Act 1845 ss 39, 44 (both repealed).
3   *Re Dent Tithe Commutation* (1845) 8 QB 43.

(iv) Special Rules relating to Prohibiting Orders

699. When court has exceeded jurisdiction. A prohibiting order[1] may be used to ensure that inferior courts and tribunals do not exceed their jurisdiction[2]. A prohibiting order may be made as soon as the inferior court or tribunal proceeds to apply a wrong principle of law when deciding a fact on which its jurisdiction depends[3]. Where proceedings are pending before an inferior court[4], part of which is within, and part outside, its jurisdiction, no prohibiting order will be made until the inferior court has actually gone beyond its competence and jurisdiction[5]. In any event, where the jurisdiction of the inferior court depends on the judicial determination of facts the order does not lie until the inferior court has wrongfully on these facts purported to give itself jurisdiction[6].

1   A prohibiting order was formerly known as an order of prohibition: see PARAS 687 note 2, 688. As to the nature of prohibiting orders see PARA 693.
2   A prohibiting order may also be granted to restrain a public body from acting unlawfully: see e g *R v Kent Police Authority, ex p Godden* [1971] 2 QB 662, sub nom *Re Godden* [1971] 3 All ER 20, CA (where a chief medical officer was prohibited from deciding if a police inspector was disabled as the medical officer appointed to carry out the determination had previously been involved in the case, and so there was the appearance of bias); *R v Liverpool Corpn, ex p Liverpool Taxi Fleet Operators' Association* [1972] 2 QB 299, [1972] 2 All ER 589, CA (where a local authority was prohibited from granting taxi licences without first consulting interested parties).
3   *R v Kent Justices* (1889) 24 QBD 181, DC; *R v Longe, etc Justices and Cooke* (1897) 66 LJQB 278, DC. Cf *Ex p Burns* (1916) 86 LJKB 158, DC.
4   As to inferior courts see COURTS.
5   *Hallack v Cambridge University* (1841) 1 QB 593; *R v Twiss* (1869) LR 4 QB 407.
6   See *Re Skipton Industrial Co-operative Society Ltd v Prince* (1864) 33 LJQB 323; and PARA 624.

700. Earliest time for applying for a prohibiting order. An application for judicial review seeking a prohibiting order[1] to prevent an inferior court or tribunal exceeding its jurisdiction may be made as soon as the complete absence of jurisdiction is apparent on the record of the proceedings of the inferior court[2], without the question of jurisdiction being raised in that court[3].

Even though the jurisdictional defect is not patent, an applicant will not be required first to take objection before the tribunal whose proceedings he seeks to impugn when the question is one of law, not dependent on disputed issues of fact[4], or when he is contending that the tribunal is improperly constituted because of the likelihood of bias[5].

In any event it appears that a prohibiting order may be made once steps have been or are about to be taken involving a usurpation of jurisdiction[6].

1   A prohibiting order was formerly known as an order of prohibition: see PARAS 687 note 2, 688. As to the nature of prohibiting orders see PARA 693.
2   *London Corpn v Cox* (1867) LR 2 HL 239 (where the want of jurisdiction appeared on the declaration). 'Where ... it is apparent on the record that the [court] never had jurisdiction, ... the case is ripe for decision without waiting for any farther pleading' (*London Corpn v Cox* at 293 per Lord Cranworth); 'Where want of jurisdiction is apparent on the proceedings prohibition goes at any time after service of the process, and even before articles' (*London Corpn v Cox* at 281 per Willes J). See also *Francis v Steward* (1844) 5 QB 984 (where prohibition was granted after a citation 'because it is better for the party to apply for prohibition in the first stage than after expense is incurred'); *Wadsworth v Queen of Spain, De Haber v Queen of Portugal* (1851) 17 QB 171 (where no notice was taken of the proceedings by way of appearance or otherwise, except to apply for prohibition); *Buggin v Bennett* (1767) 4

Burr 2035 at 2037 per Lord Mansfield; *R v Electricity Comrs, ex p London Electricity Joint Committee Co (1920) Ltd* [1924] 1 KB 171 at 190, CA, per Bankes LJ. As to when a court has exceeded its jurisdiction see PARA 699. As to inferior courts see COURTS.

3 See *London Corpn v Cox* (1867) LR 2 HL 239 at 291, where Willes J stated that this had been the settled practice since 1 Will 4 c 21 (1830) (repealed).

4 *R v Tottenham and District Rent Tribunal, ex p Northfield (Highgate) Ltd* [1957] 1 QB 103, [1956] 2 All ER 863, DC.

5 *R v Kent Police Authority, ex p Godden* [1971] 2 QB 662, sub nom *Re Godden* [1971] 3 All ER 20, CA. The former practice is examined in *London Corpn v Cox* (1867) LR 2 HL 239 at 276–277 per Willes J.

6 *Byerley v Windus* (1826) 5 B & C 1 at 21 per Bayley J; *Zohrab v Smith* (1847) 17 LJQB 174 at 176; *London Corpn v Cox* (1867) LR 2 HL 239 at 276 per Willes J. See also *R v Minister of Health, ex p Davis* [1929] 1 KB 619, CA; *R v Minister of Health, ex p Villiers* [1936] 2 KB 29, [1936] 1 All ER 817, DC; and the cases cited in notes 4–5. See also *R v Local Comr for Administration for the North and East Area of England, ex p Bradford Metropolitan City Council* [1979] QB 287, [1979] 2 All ER 881, CA, where, on an application to prohibit a local commissioner from investigating certain matters, a declaration was granted that the commissioner should not investigate complaints that did not prima facie amount to allegations of maladministration. As to declaratory orders see PARAS 716, 719.

701. Statutory restrictions. It appears that where a statute provides that a person aggrieved by an act done or decision made in the purported exercise of powers conferred by that statute may challenge the validity of that act or decision on specified grounds within a limited time, by applying to the High Court for an interim order suspending its operation or for an order to quash it[1], and that, subject to this, such an act or decision is not to be questioned in any legal proceedings whatsoever, it is not open to a person claiming to be aggrieved to apply for a prohibiting order[2] in respect of that act[3].

1 A quashing order was formerly known as an order of certiorari: see PARAS 687 note 1, 688. As to the nature of quashing orders see PARA 693.

2 A prohibiting order was formerly known as an order of prohibition: see PARAS 687 note 2, 688. As to the nature of prohibiting orders see PARA 693.

3 See e g Town and Country Planning Act 1990 ss 284, 287–288 (see TOWN AND COUNTRY PLANNING vol 46(1) (Reissue) PARAS 43, 46–47); *Smith v East Elloe RDC* [1956] AC 736, [1956] 1 All ER 855, HL, a decision which, it is thought, is not undermined in this context by *Anisminic Ltd v Foreign Compensation Commission* [1969] 2 AC 147, [1969] 1 All ER 208, HL, although there is no reported authority on the effect of such a statutory formula on the availability of a prohibiting order. See *O'Reilly v Mackman* [1983] 2 AC 237 at 278–280, [1982] 3 All ER 1124 at 1129–1130, HL, per Lord Diplock. It would seem that the Tribunals and Inquiries Act 1992 s 12 (see PARA 616) does not affect the possibility of obtaining a prohibiting order in an appropriate case. See also ADMINISTRATIVE LAW vol 1(1) (2001 Reissue) PARA 21 note 12. See also *R v Secretary of State for the Environment, ex p Ostler* [1977] QB 122, [1976] 3 All ER 90, CA; *Terry Adams Ltd v Bolton Metropolitan Borough Council* (1996) 73 P & CR 446.

702. Claim by Crown. The Crown may claim a prohibiting order[1] at any stage of judicial proceedings[2].

1 A prohibiting order was formerly known as an order of prohibition: see PARAS 687 note 2, 688. As to the nature of prohibiting orders see PARA 693.

2 *Broad v Perkins* (1888) 21 QBD 533 at 535, CA, per Lord Esher MR. In Bac Abr Prohibition, it is said that the Sovereign may sue for a prohibition, though the plea be between two common persons, because the suit is in derogation of his crown and dignity.

(3) MANDATORY ORDERS

(i) Nature of the Order

703. Nature of the mandatory order. A mandatory order[1] is, in form, a command issuing from the High Court of Justice, directed to any person, corporation or inferior tribunal, requiring him or it to do some particular thing specified in the order which appertains to his or its office and is in the nature of a public duty[2]. Whereas the older authorities were concerned with restoration, admission and election to offices[3] and delivery up and production and inspection of documents, in modern times the purpose of a mandatory order is to compel the performance of a public duty, whether of an inferior court or tribunal to exercise its jurisdiction, or that of an administrative body to fulfil its public law obligations[4]. It is a discretionary remedy.

An applicant for judicial review may seek all or any of the prerogative orders[5] either in the alternative or cumulatively[6] with each other, as well as with any other remedies available on an application for judicial review. It is common practice to apply for a quashing order and a mandatory order together[7].

Disobedience to a mandatory order is a contempt of court[8], punishable by fine or imprisonment[9].

1   A mandatory order was formerly known as an order of mandamus: see PARAS 687 note 3, 688. An application for a mandatory order must be made by way of an application for judicial review: see CPR 54.2. As to the CPR see PARA 659; and CIVIL PROCEDURE vol 11 (2009) PARA 30 et seq.

      The mandatory order is to be distinguished from a mandatory injunction, an equitable remedy, which is in origin a private law remedy but may be sought to prevent unlawful public action (see *Glossop v Heston and Isleworth Local Board* (1878) 12 ChD 102; *Legg v Inner London Education Authority* [1972] 3 All ER 177, [1972] 1 WLR 1245 (injunction sought by parents to restrain defendants from ceasing to maintain a school); *Meade v Haringey London Borough Council* [1979] 2 All ER 1016, [1979] 1 WLR 637, CA; *R v Chief Constable of Devon and Cornwall, ex p Central Electricity Generating Board* [1982] QB 458, [1981] 3 All ER 826, CA), and from the action of mandamus by which a person could claim a judgment commanding the defendant to fulfil a duty in which the defendant was personally interested (the action is obsolete, except in some of the jurisdictions of the Commonwealth: see *Mudge v A-G* [1960] VR 43).

2   Mandamus was a common law remedy, based on royal authority. Mandatory orders are now available only in public law proceedings brought by way of judicial review.

3   An order of mandamus would lie to compel the restoration of a person to an office or franchise, whether spiritual or temporal, of which he has been wrongfully dispossessed, provided the office or franchise is of a public nature (3 Bl Com 110; *R v Blooer* (1760) 2 Burr 1043), eg to the office of mayor, alderman, recorder, town clerk or other municipal position (Com Dig Mandamus A; *R v London Corpn* (1733) 2 Term Rep 182n), to academic degrees, to a fellowship of a college where there is no visitor (Com Dig Mandamus A; 3 Bl Com 110), or to the offices of parish clerk and sexton (*R v Warren* (1776) 1 Cowp 370; *Neale v Bowles* (1835) 1 Har & W 584; *R v Smith* (1844) 5 QB 614; *R v Vicar and Churchwardens of Dymock* [1915] 1 KB 147, DC).

      A mandamus would also lie to admit to such an office or franchise a person who has a right to it but has never had possession (3 Bl Com 110; Com Dig Mandamus A). Mandamus has accordingly been issued to admit to the office of alderman of the City of London a candidate duly elected at a court of wardmote (*R v London Corpn* (1829) 4 Man & Ry KB 36; and see also *R v Peak Park Joint Planning Board* (1976) 74 LGR 376); to admit to the office of registrar of a corporation the candidate who had obtained the majority of legal votes (*R v Bedford Level Corpn* (1805) 6 East 356); to admit to the directorship of a registered company the candidate elected by a show of hands (*R v Government Stock Investment Co* (1878) 3 QBD 442); and to admit to the office of churchwarden a duly elected churchwarden (*R v Archdeacon of Lichfield and Coventry* (1835) 5 Nev & MKB 42; *R v Sowter* [1901] 1 KB 396, CA; *R v Bishop of Sarum* [1916] 1 KB 466, DC). When, however, the office in question was neither a corporate office nor a permanent one, but one which merely depended upon the will of a fluctuating body, no mandamus would lie to restore or admit to it: *Evans v Hearts of Oak Benefit Society* (1866) 12 Jur NS 163; *R v Vicar, etc of St Stephen's Coleman St* (1844) 14 LJQB 34. See also *R v Churchwardens of Croydon* (1794) 5 Term Rep 713; and *R v St Nicholas, Rochester, Guardians* (1815) 4 M & S 324 at 326.

A mandamus would lie to command an election to offices of a public nature in accordance with the rule that whenever it is the duty of a person or corporation to do an act, the court will order it to be done (*R v Fowey Corpn* (1824) 2 B & C 584 at 590 per Abbott CJ), eg to fill up a vacancy among the canons residentiary in a cathedral (*Bishop of Chichester v Harward and Webber* (1787) 1 Term Rep 650 at 652), or to elect churchwardens (*R v Wix Inhabitants* (1831) 2 B & Ad 197; *Re Barlow (Rector of Ewhurst)* (1861) 30 LJQB 271). As to elections to local government office see the Representation of the People Act 1983 ss 36, 39; and ELECTIONS AND REFERENDUMS. See also LOCAL GOVERNMENT.

A mandamus to restore, admit or elect to an office would not be granted unless the office was vacant (see *R v Chester Corpn* (1855) 25 LJQB 61; *R v Cambridge Corpn* (1767) 4 Burr 2008; *R v Bedford Corpn* (1800) 1 East 79; *R v Pembroke Corpn* (1840) 8 Dowl 302; *R v Government Stock Investment Co* (1878) 3 QBD 442; *R v Minister and Churchwardens of Stoke Damerel* (1836) 5 Ad & El 584; *R v Cork County Justices* (1910) 44 ILT 120; *Re Barnes Corpn, ex p Hutter* [1933] 1 KB 668, DC; *R v Mayor of Truro* (1816) 2 Chit 257).

The above authorities have not been invalidated, but in recent years applications for such orders have been virtually non-existent.

4 The mandatory order is one of the remedies available on an application for judicial review and it is in the context of judicial review that the order is now of primary relevance.

5 As to the prerogative orders see PARAS 688–689.

6 See the Senior Court Act 1981 s 31(1); CPR 54.2; and PARA 691. The Senior Courts Act 1981 was previously known as the Supreme Court Act 1981 and was renamed by the Constitutional Reform Act 2005 s 59(5), Sch 11 Pt 1 as from 1 October 2009: see the Constitutional Reform Act 2005 (Commencement No 11) Order 2009, SI 2009/1604; and COURTS.

7 Ie to quash a decision of a body and to require that body to go through the decision-making process again: see *R v Panel on Take-overs and Mergers, ex p Datafin plc* [1987] QB 815, [1987] 1 All ER 564, CA; *R v Epsom Justices, ex p Gibbons* [1984] QB 574, [1983] 3 All ER 523, DC; *R v Poole Justices, ex p Fleet* [1983] 2 All ER 897, [1983] 1 WLR 974, DC; *Board of Education v Rice* [1911] AC 179, HL.

8 As to contempt of court generally see CONTEMPT OF COURT.

9 See *R v Poplar Metropolitan Borough Council, ex p Metropolitan Asylums Board (No 2)* [1922] 1 KB 95, CA; *Re M* [1994] 1 AC 377, sub nom *M v Home Office* [1993] 3 All ER 537, HL.

704.   Enforcement of statutory duties.   A mandatory order (formerly known as an order of mandamus)[1] may be granted to require compliance with a statutory duty[2]. The nature and range of statutory duties is wide. Where statute imposes an unqualified duty on a public authority, a mandatory order is available to secure compliance with the duty. Even here, a court may be prepared to allow a public authority a reasonable time to comply with the duty before granting a mandatory order[3]. A statutory duty must, however, be performed without unreasonable delay and this may be enforced by a mandatory order. Thus an order of mandamus was granted against the Home Secretary requiring him to determine the application for an entry certificate of a would-be immigrant who was legally entitled to enter the country without let or hindrance[4]. Where a statute gives a body a discretion, an order may be granted requiring the body to consider the exercise of the discretion when the occasion arises. However, the court will not order that the discretion be exercised in a particular way[5]. Furthermore, modern statutes may impose general duties (often referred to as 'target duties'), particularly in the field of service provision; and such duties, properly interpreted, may leave the public body concerned with a broad discretion as to what steps should reasonably be taken to meet the general duty[6]. The courts may be reluctant to grant a mandatory order compelling a public body to do specific acts in such circumstances, preferring instead to declare what the public body's general duty is and leaving it to the public body to determine how to fulfil that duty.

1   A mandatory order was formerly known as an order of mandamus: see PARAS 687 note 3, 688. As to the nature of mandatory orders see PARA 703.

2   Com Dig Mandamus A ('mandamus is granted ... for the execution of the common law or of a statute'); *Ex p Robins* (1839) 7 Dowl 566; *Ex p Nash* (1850) 15 QB 92 at 96 per Lord Campbell CJ ('I cannot give countenance to the practice of trying in this form questions whether an act professedly done in pursuance of a statute was really justified by the statute'). In order that a mandatory order may issue to compel something to be done under a statute, it must be shown that the statute imposes a legal duty. See *Re Smyth, R v Treasury Lords Comrs* (1836) 4 Ad & El 976 at 981 per Lord Denman CJ; *Ex p Ricketts* (1836) 4 Ad & El 999 at 1001 per Lord Denman CJ; *York and North Midland Rly Co v Milner* (1846) 15 LJQB 379 at 380, Ex Ch; *R v Southampton Port Comrs* (1870) LR 4 HL 449 at 465 per Cleasby B; *Ex p Edmunds* (1871) 25 LT 705; *R v Postmaster-General* (1873) 28 LT 337; *Dartford RDC v Bexley Heath Rly Co* [1898] AC 210, HL; *R v Glamorgan County Council, ex p Miller* [1899] 2 QB 536, CA. Words that are prima facie permissive may exceptionally be construed as imposing a duty: see *R v Derby Justices, ex p Kooner* [1971] 1 QB 147, [1970] 3 All ER 399, DC (power of magistrates to grant legal aid, including representation by counsel, in committal proceedings where person accused of murder, construed as duty to grant such aid). Further, where a local authority has wrongfully declined to determine a question properly submitted to it, as by rejecting an application for a permit or licence without considering the merits of the individual case, it has been held that an order of mandamus would lie: see *R v Hounslow London Borough Council, ex p Pizzey* [1977] 1 All ER 305, [1977] 1 WLR 58, DC.

3   See eg *R v Newham London Borough Council, ex p Begum* [2000] 2 All ER 72, 32 HLR 808 (court would be unlikely to grant a mandatory order to enforce a duty to re-house persons displaced from accommodation in certain circumstances if the authority were seeking to enforce the duty and were not unreasonably delaying in doing so). Alternatively, the courts may interpret the statutory duties in question as giving some latitude to the public authority in question as to the manner and extent of their performance and the courts may only intervene when reasonable efforts to perform have not been made: see eg *R v Bristol Corpn, ex p Hendy* [1974] 1 All ER 1047, [1974] 1 WLR 498, CA.

4   *R v Secretary of State for the Home Department, ex p Phansopkar* [1976] QB 606, [1975] 3 All ER 497, DC. See also *R v Bolton Metropolitan Borough, ex p B* [1985] FLR 343 (order of mandamus made, directing a local authority to decide within 14 days whether to terminate access arrangements by a parent to a child in the authority's care and, if appropriate, to issue a notice of termination); and see also *R v Newham London Borough Council, ex p Begum* [2000] 2 All ER 72, 32 HLR 808 (duty to provide interim accommodation without unreasonable delay).

5   See eg *R v Port of London Authority, ex p Kynoch Ltd* [1919] 1 KB 176, CA; *Padfield v Minister of Agriculture, Fisheries and Food* [1968] AC 997, [1968] 1 All ER 694, HL; and PARA 621 et seq. The courts cannot order the competent authority to exercise its discretion in the applicant's favour: see *Lonrho plc v Secretary of State for Trade and Industry* [1989] 2 All ER 609, sub nom *R v Secretary of State for Trade and Industry, ex p Lonrho plc* [1989] 1 WLR 525, HL; *R v Kingston Justices, ex p Davey* (1902) 86 LT 589; but see *R v Derby Justices, ex p Kooner* [1971] 1 QB 147, [1970] 3 All ER 399, DC; *R v A Wreck Comr, ex p Knight* [1976] 3 All ER 8. If a local authority has exercised a discretion on the basis of principles that are inadmissible in law, it has been held that an order of mandamus would lie: see eg *R v Tower Hamlets London Borough Council, ex p Chetnik Developments Ltd* [1988] AC 858, HL; *R v Flintshire County Council County Licensing (Stage Plays) Committee, ex p Barrett* [1957] 1 QB 350, [1957] 1 All ER 112, CA.

6   See eg *R v Inner Education Authority, ex p Ali* (1990) 2 Admin LR 822 (duty to provide sufficient primary schools was a target duty; it was for local education authorities to determine what was sufficient and what steps it was reasonable to take to comply with the duty).

705. Enforcement of non-statutory duties. Occasionally, mandatory orders[1] may be sought to enforce a non-statutory duty, such as the duty of the police to prosecute offenders who break the law[2], or the duty of a local authority to produce documents which a councillor reasonably needs for the proper performance of his duties as such[3], or the decision of a regulatory trade body such as the Panel on Take-overs and Mergers[4].

1   A mandatory order was formerly known as an order of mandamus: see PARAS 687 note 3, 688. As to the nature of mandatory orders see PARA 703.

2 *R v Metropolitan Police Comr, ex p Blackburn* [1968] 2 QB 118 at 138–139, [1968] 1 All ER
   763 at 771, CA, per Salmon LJ (' ... the police owe the public a clear legal duty to enforce the
   law ... if, as is quite unthinkable, the chief police officer in any district were to issue an
   instruction that as a matter of policy the police would take no steps to prosecute any
   housebreaker, I have little doubt but that any householder in that district would be able to
   obtain an order of mandamus for the instruction to be withdrawn'). See also *R v DPP,
   ex p Manning* [2001] QB 330, [2000] All ER (D) 674, DC; *R v Metropolitan Police Comr,
   ex p Blackburn (No 3)* [1973] QB 241, [1973] 1 All ER 324, CA (the court refused to interfere,
   although Lord Denning MR said (at 254 and 331) that in 'extreme cases' where the police were
   not carrying out their duty, the court would interfere). See also *R v GLC, ex p Blackburn* [1976]
   3 All ER 184, [1976] 1 WLR 550, CA; *R v Oxford, ex p Levey* (1986) Times, 1 November (the
   court will not review the choice of methods adopted by a chief constable, provided he does not
   exceed the limits of his discretion). Other bodies with statutory responsibilities for the
   enforcement of the law would appear to be in the same position: *R v Lancashire County
   Council, ex p Guyer* (1977) 76 LGR 290, DC; cf *Stafford Borough Council v Elkenford Ltd*
   [1977] 2 All ER 519 at 528, [1977] 1 WLR 324 at 329, CA, per Lord Denning MR; *Vestey v
   IRC (No 2)* [1979] Ch 198 at 203–204, [1979] 2 All ER 225 at 233–234 per Walton J.

3 *R v Barnes Borough Council, ex p Conlon* [1938] 3 All ER 226, DC. However, if a councillor is
   inspired by an indirect motive to assist a person who is in litigation with the council, it has been
   held that an order for mandamus would not lie: *R v Hampstead Borough Council,
   ex p Woodward* (1917) 116 LT 213, DC. See also *R v Hackney London Borough Council,
   ex p Gamper* [1985] 3 All ER 275, [1985] 1 WLR 1229.

4 *R v Panel on Take-overs and Mergers, ex p Datafin plc* [1987] QB 815, [1987] 1 All ER
   564, CA (orders of certiorari (now known as quashing orders: see PARAS 687 note 1, 688, 693
   et seq) and mandamus refused). See also PARA 692 note 17. As to the Panel on Take-overs and
   Mergers see COMPANIES vol 15 (2009) PARA 1480 et seq.

706. Public duties by government officials. If public officials or public bodies
fail to perform any public duty with which they have been charged, a mandatory
order[1] may be made to compel them to carry out the duty[2].

1 A mandatory order was formerly known as an order of mandamus: see PARAS 687 note 3, 688.
   As to the nature of mandatory orders see PARA 703.

2 *Glossop v Heston and Isleworth Local Board* (1878) 12 ChD 102 at 115, CA, per James LJ; *R v
   Income Tax Special Purposes Comrs* (1888) 21 QBD 313 at 317, CA, per Lord Esher MR; *R v
   Stepney Corpn* [1902] 1 KB 317 at 321, DC, per Lord Alverstone CJ; *R v Wilts and Berks
   Canal Co* [1912] 3 KB 623, DC. See also *R v Metropolitan Police Comr, ex p Blackburn* [1968]
   2 QB 118, [1968] 1 All ER 763, CA; and PARA 705. See further *R v Metropolitan Police Comr,
   ex p Blackburn (No 3)* [1973] QB 241, [1973] 1 All ER 324, CA; *R v London Transport
   Executive, ex p GLC* [1983] QB 484, [1983] 2 All ER 262, DC.

707. Miscellaneous examples of public duties enforced by mandatory orders.
Orders of mandamus (now known as mandatory orders)[1] have been made to
compel the performance of other public duties, for example to a local authority
to obey a ministerial order relating to public health[2]; and to a local education
authority to obey an order of the Board of Education[3].

1 Orders of mandamus are now known as mandatory orders: see PARAS 687 note 3, 688. As to the
   nature of mandatory orders see PARA 703.

2 See *R v Staines Union* (1893) 62 LJQB 540, DC; and the Public Health Act 1875 s 299
   (repealed). See now the Public Health Act 1936 s 322; the Public Health (Control of Disease)
   Act 1984 s 71; and PROTECTION OF ENVIRONMENT AND PUBLIC HEALTH vol 38 (2006 Reissue)
   PARA 48.

3 See *A-G v West Riding of Yorkshire County Council* [1907] AC 29, HL; and the Education
   Act 1921 s 150 (repealed). As to the transfer of functions from the Board of Education to the
   Secretary of State see EDUCATION vol 15(1) (2006 Reissue) PARA 52.

708. Inferior tribunals. A mandatory order[1] may be made to require tribunals
exercising an inferior jurisdiction, to hear and determine according to the law[2].
Both statutory and in certain cases non-statutory tribunals[3] may be subjected to
mandatory orders.

A refusal to exercise jurisdiction may be conveyed in one of two ways: there may be an absolute refusal in terms[4] or there may be conduct amounting to a refusal. In the latter case a tribunal will be held to have refused to hear and determine only when it has been guilty of such delay as to amount to refusal[5], or when it has in substance shut its ears to the application which was made to it and has determined upon an application which was not made to it[6]. A tribunal does not decline jurisdiction where in the honest exercise of its discretion it has adopted a policy, and, without refusing to hear an applicant, intimates to him what its policy is and that after hearing him it will decide against him in accordance with that policy unless there is something exceptional in his case[7].

If on the hearing of a preliminary objection an inferior tribunal comes, on the evidence before it, to a conclusion of fact which justifies the objection, and in consequence dismisses a matter brought before it, the High Court will interfere only on very strong grounds[8]. The court will readily reconsider the inferior tribunal's decision where the preliminary objection turns on a question of law[9].

1   A mandatory order was formerly known as an order of mandamus: see PARAS 687 note 3, 688. As to the nature of mandatory orders see PARA 703.

2   See 3 Bl Com 110; *R v Kingston Justices, ex p Davey* (1902) 86 LT 589 at 590, DC, per Lord Alverstone CJ; *R v Registrar of Companies* [1912] 3 KB 23, DC; *R v Hudson* [1915] 1 KB 838, CA (mandamus to 'competent and impartial person' appointed under the National Insurance Act 1911 s 113 (repealed), to hear and determine an inquiry with regard to a draft order); *R v LCC, ex p Corrie* [1918] 1 KB 68, DC (mandamus to London County Council to hear and determine application for its consent under byelaw to sale of pamphlets in public parks).
    A distinction must be drawn between the position where there is a duty to hear and determine, but discretion as to the correct determination, and where there is a discretion not to act in the matter at all: see the Parliamentary Commissioner Act 1967 s 5(1) (under which the Parliamentary Commissioner for Administration has a discretion as to whether to institute any investigation (see ADMINISTRATIVE LAW vol 1(1) (2001 Reissue) PARA 41), and mandamus will not therefore issue to order him to entertain a complaint); *Re Fletcher's Application* [1970] 2 All ER 527n, CA; *Environmental Defence Society Inc v Agricultural Chemicals Board* [1973] 2 NZLR 758, NZ SC. But see *R v Local Comr for Administration for the North and East Area of England, ex p Bradford Metropolitan City Council* [1979] QB 287, [1979] 2 All ER 881, CA (prohibition granted).

3   *R v Criminal Injuries Compensation Board, ex p Lain* [1967] 2 QB 864, [1967] 2 All ER 770, DC; *R v Criminal Injuries Compensation Board, ex p A* [1999] 2 AC 330, HL; *R v Panel on Take-overs and Mergers, ex p Datafin plc* [1987] QB 815, [1987] 1 All ER 564, CA.

4   Eg where the inferior tribunal mistakenly believed it had no jurisdiction to hear a case: *R v West Norfolk Valuation Panel, ex p H Prins Ltd* (1975) 73 LGR 206. See also *R v Paddington South Rent Tribunal, ex p Millard* [1955] 1 All ER 691, [1955] 1 WLR 348. In *R v Immigration Appeal Tribunal, ex p SGH Khan* [1975] Imm AR 26, mandamus was issued when the Immigration Appeal Tribunal wrongly refused leave to appeal.

5   In *R v Central Professional Committee for Opticians, ex p Brown* [1949] 2 All ER 519, DC, mandamus was refused on the ground that the committee had not been guilty of such delay as to amount to refusal to consider and determine the application made to it.

6   *R v Port of London Authority, ex p Kynoch Ltd* [1919] 1 KB 176 at 183, CA, per Bankes LJ. See *R v Licensing Authority for Goods Vehicles for the Metropolitan Traffic Area, ex p BE Barrett Ltd* [1949] 2 KB 17, [1949] 1 All ER 656, DC.

7   *R v Port of London Authority, ex p Kynoch Ltd* [1919] 1 KB 176 at 184, CA, where Bankes LJ pointed out that there is a wide distinction to be drawn between this class of case and cases like *R v Sylvester* (1862) 31 LJMC 93, and *R v LCC, ex p Corrie* [1918] 1 KB 68, DC, where a tribunal has passed a rule, or come to a determination, not to hear any application of a particular character by whomsoever made.

8   *R v Fulham, Hammersmith and Kensington Rent Tribunal, ex p Zerek* [1951] 2 KB 1, [1951] 1 All ER 482, DC.

9   *R v Kesteven Justices* (1844) 3 QB 810.

709. The Crown Court. The Crown Court, established under the Courts Act 1971, is a superior court[1]. It supersedes courts of assize and quarter sessions[2]. The High Court has jurisdiction to award a mandatory order (formerly known as an order of mandamus)[3] to this court, as if it were an inferior court[4]; but a mandatory order will not issue to the Crown Court in respect of its jurisdiction in matters relating to trials on indictment[5]. Certain of the cases decided in relation to the issue of mandamus to quarter sessions are, therefore, relevant to the position of the Crown Court. The order would lie to courts of quarter sessions to hear and determine an appeal in which they had declined jurisdiction[6]. They were considered to have declined jurisdiction when they had wrongly allowed a preliminary objection on a point of law or practice and consequently refused to hear the case upon the merits[7], as when they had acted upon a supposed rule which was no rule[8], or under the mistaken belief that there was no jurisdiction, erroneously thinking, for example, that they were precluded from deciding what were the 'next practicable sessions'[9] or when, having heard one side, they refused to hear the other[10]. An order of mandamus has been made to require the Crown Court to grant an applicant leave to appeal out of time against conviction[11].

Where sessions made a false entry in their records, as where it was an entry which they had no power to make, mandamus would lie to compel its erasure[12].

A mandatory order lies to the Crown Court if it refuses to state a case, on the application of a person wishing to question a decision on the grounds of error of law or excess of jurisdiction, for the opinion of the High Court[13].

1   Courts Act 1971 ss 4(1), 51(1) (repealed). See now the Senior Courts Act 1981 s 45(1)–(3); and COURTS. The Senior Courts Act 1981 was previously known as the Supreme Court Act 1981 and was renamed by the Constitutional Reform Act 2005 s 59(5), Sch 11 Pt 1 as from 1 October 2009: see the Constitutional Reform Act 2005 (Commencement No 11) Order 2009, SI 2009/1604; and COURTS.

2   See the Senior Courts Act 1981 s 45(2), (3); and COURTS.

3   A mandatory order was formerly known as an order of mandamus: see PARAS 687 note 3, 688. As to the nature of mandatory orders see PARA 703.

4   *Weight v MacKay* [1984] 2 All ER 673, sub nom *R v Crown Court at Bournemouth, ex p Weight* [1984] 1 WLR 980, HL (Divisional Court had power to make orders of certiorari (now known as quashing orders: see PARAS 687 note 1, 688, 693 et seq) to quash Crown Court's decision to allow appeals against conviction on the ground of breach of natural justice, and of mandamus requiring a Crown Court rehearing of the appeals). As to inferior courts see COURTS.

5   See the Senior Courts Act 1981 s 29(3) (amended by SI 2004/1033).
    The text refers to the Crown Court's jurisdiction in matters relating to trials on indictment under the Senior Courts Act 1981 s 46 (see COURTS). The meaning of the phrase 'matters relating to trial on indictment' has been considered in a number of cases: see *Re Smalley* [1985] AC 622, sub nom *Smalley v Warwick Crown Court* [1985] 1 All ER 769, HL; *DPP v Crown Court at Manchester* [1993] 4 All ER 928, [1993] 1 WLR 1524, HL; *Re Ashton, R v Crown Court at Manchester, ex p DPP* [1994] AC 9, [1993] 2 All ER 663, HL; *R v Crown Court at Leeds, ex p Hussain* [1995] 3 All ER 527, [1995] 1 WLR 1329, DC; *R v DPP, ex p Kebilene* [2000] 2 AC 326, [1999] 4 All ER 801, HL; *R v Crown Court at Maidstone, ex p Harrow London Borough Council* [2000] QB 719, [1999] 3 All ER 542, DC; *R (on the application of Snelgrove) v Crown Court at Woolwich* [2004] EWHC 2172 (Admin), [2005] 1 WLR 3223, [2004] All ER (D) 177 (Sep).
    The policy of the Senior Courts Act 1981 s 29(3) is that criminal trials should not be delayed by collateral challenges and that, in general, courts would refuse to entertain applications for judicial review where the matter could be raised in the course of the trial: *R v DPP, ex p Kebilene* [2000] 2 AC 326, [1999] 4 All ER 801, HL. If a decision is made which the judge had no power to make, and if there was no alternative remedy, that may influence a court to find that judicial review is available in respect of that matter: *R v Crown Court at Maidstone, ex p Harrow London Borough Council* [2000] QB 719, [1999] 3 All ER 542, DC; *R (on the application of Kenneally) v Crown Court at Snaresbrook* [2001] EWHC Admin 968, [2002] QB 1169.

6　*R v Monmouthshire Justices* (1825) 4 B & C 844 at 849; *R v Oxfordshire Justices* (1843) 4 QB 177; *R v Denbighshire Justices* (1841) 9 Dowl 509; *R v Devon Justices, ex p DPP* [1924] 1 KB 503, DC. See further PARA 615; and CRIMINAL LAW, EVIDENCE AND PROCEDURE vol 11(4) (2006 Reissue) PARA 2014.

7　*R v Kesteven Justices* (1844) 3 QB 810, where it was held that the question of the sufficiency of the statement of the grounds of appeal against an order of removal was a question of fact and therefore a matter for sessions to decide (overruling *R v Carnarvonshire Justices* (1841) 2 QB 325; *R v West Riding of Yorkshire Justices* (1841) 2 QB 331).

8　*R v Kesteven Justices* (1844) 3 QB 810 at 819 per Lord Denman CJ.

9　*R v Derbyshire Justices* (1871) 25 LT 161 (appeal against order of removal).

10　*R v Carnarvon Justices* (1820) 4 B & Ald 86 at 88 per Holroyd J.

11　*R v Crown Court at Croydon, ex p Smith* (1983) 77 Cr App Rep 277, DC. See also *Re Raymond Worth's Application* (1979) 1 FLR 159, 10 Fam Law 54, CA.

12　*R v West Riding of Yorkshire Justices* (1843) 5 QB 1; cf *Ex p Ackworth Overseers* (1843) 3 QB 397.

13　See the Senior Courts Act 1981 s 28 (amended by the Local Government (Miscellaneous) Provisions Act 1982 s 2, Sch 3 para 27(6); the Access to Justice Act 1999 Sch 4 paras 21, 22; the Licensing Act 2003 Sch 7; and the Gambling Act 2005 Sch 17); and the Senior Courts Act 1981 s 29(1), (1A) (s 29(1) substituted, and s 29(1A) added, by SI 2004/1033). Judgments and other decisions relating to trials on indictment, and certain other classes of decision, are excluded from this form of appellate procedure: see the Senior Courts Act 1981 s 28(2) (as so amended).

710.　Magistrates.　An order of mandamus (now known as a mandatory order)[1] has been granted against magistrates to compel them to adjudicate in matters within their province in accordance with their obligation to do so[2]. They will be considered to have declined jurisdiction when they have dismissed an information on a point relating to their jurisdiction only, such as that it was necessary to bring all joint owners before them instead of simply the one against whom the information had been laid[3]; or when they have refused to issue summonses in consequence of having acted upon considerations which were extraneous and extra-judicial and which they ought not to have taken into account[4]; or when they have dismissed information without allowing the prosecution to present its case on the evidence available[5]; or when they have rejected evidence which was tendered to them, which rejection amounted to a refusal to enter upon an inquiry imposed upon them by statute[6]; or when they have refused to withdraw a warrant for the arrest of a person by whom, on the admitted facts, no criminal offence has been committed[7]; or when they have failed to pass sentence and thus have not disposed of a case[8]; or when they have drawn up a consent order in terms that did not reflect the agreement between the parties[9].

Where justices refuse to state a case the High Court may, on the application of the person who applied for the case to be stated, make a mandatory order requiring the justices to state a case[10]. The High Court has, of course, a discretion[11] and may refuse the order if the application is frivolous in the sense that it is futile, misconceived or academic[12].

1　A mandatory order was formerly known as an order of mandamus: see PARAS 687 note 3, 688. As to the nature of mandatory orders see PARA 703.

2　*R v Brown* (1857) 26 LJMC 183 at 184 per Coleridge J ('This may perhaps be a test: if the objection be such, that whatever the merits of the case, whether the defendant be guilty or not guilty, the justices hold that they cannot decide on the merits owing to the objection, for instance, either of want of parties or of notice, such holding is a declining of jurisdiction and not an adjudication'); *R v Pearce, ex p Raynes* [1918] WN 291, DC; *R v Holsworthy Justices, ex p Edwards* [1952] 1 All ER 411, DC; *R v Ogden, ex p Long Ashton RDC* [1963] 1 All ER 574, [1963] 1 WLR 274, DC (refusal to adjudicate in erroneous belief that jurisdiction ousted by claim of right or title); *R v Newham Justices, ex p Hunt* [1976] 1 All ER 839, [1976] 1 WLR 420, DC (wrongful refusal to adjudicate concerning an application to justices under the Public Health Act 1936 s 99 (now repealed) for a nuisance order to be made against a local authority as landlord); *Re Harrington* [1984] AC 473, sub nom *Harrington v Roots* [1984] 2 All ER 474, HL (dismissal of case without allowing prosecution to present its evidence; on the facts of the case no order made). On the use of mandamus to impugn the conduct of committal proceedings before their completion see *R v Wells St Stipendiary Magistrate, ex p Seillon* [1978] 3 All ER 257, [1978] 1 WLR 1002, DC; *Gleaves v Deakin* [1980] AC 477, [1979] 2 All ER 497, HL. See also *R v St Helens Magistrates' Court, ex p Critchley* (1987) 152 JP 102; *R v Inner London Crown Court, ex p Sloper* (1978) 69 Cr App Rep 1, DC (order of mandamus directed not to stipendiary magistrate who declined to accept not guilty plea, but to justices ordering them to hear and determine the case). As to committal proceedings see CRIMINAL LAW, EVIDENCE AND PROCEDURE.

3   *R v Brown* (1857) 26 LJMC 183.

4   *R v Adamson* (1875) 1 QBD 201 (where the application for a mandamus arose out of the refusal of magistrates to grant summonses against certain persons to answer a charge of conspiracy to breach the peace and do grievous bodily harm to certain persons at a public meeting, and Cockburn CJ, in making the rule absolute, said (at 205) that probably the magistrates 'were influenced by their distaste for the views and doctrines promulgated at the meeting, and thought that the sooner the matter was buried in oblivion the better; but these were considerations which ought not to have influenced them at all, and under the circumstances I think they must be taken to have declined jurisdiction'); *R v Evans* (1890) 62 LT 570, DC (where the magistrate adjourned a summons for libel for a long period in view of the fact that civil proceedings arising out of the same matter, but for a different libel, were pending between other parties; but cf PARA 623); *R v Bennett and Bond, ex p Bennet* (1908) 72 JP 362, DC (where the circumstance improperly taken into consideration was the prosecutor's previous conduct); *R v Byrde and Pontypool Gas Co* (1890) 63 LT 645, DC (where the ground on which the justices refused the summons was that a summons for an offence of the same nature, taken out by the same prosecutor 11 years before, had been dismissed on the ground that the offence alleged had been completed more than six months before the date of the summons and that there was, therefore, no jurisdiction to go again into the matter, in view of the fact that the Summary Jurisdiction Act 1848 s 11 (repealed: see now the Magistrates' Courts Act 1980 s 127; and MAGISTRATES vol 29(2) (Reissue) PARA 589) imposed such a limitation as to the time within which a complaint was to be made or such information laid). See also PARA 623.

5   *Re Harrington* [1984] AC 743, sub nom *Harrington v Roots* [1984] 2 All ER 474, HL (on the facts of the case no order made).

6   *R v Marsham* [1892] 1 QB 371, CA (where the magistrate had declined to determine a matter arising under a statute, namely whether certain expenses were paving expenses, and whether they were actually incurred. It was pointed out by Lord Esher MR (at 378), that 'the magistrate does not say that the evidence tendered would not prove the fact that the claim of the board included matters outside the statute; he has refused to hear the evidence, even though it would prove that fact; he has, therefore, declined jurisdiction').

7   *R v Crossman, ex p Chetwynd* (1908) 98 LT 760, DC.

8   See *R v Norfolk Justices, ex p DPP* [1950] 2 KB 558, DC (where the justices, having convicted the accused, purported to commit him to quarter sessions for sentence under the Criminal Justice Act 1948 s 29(1) (now repealed), although the case was not one to which the provision applied).

9   *R v Chester Justices, ex p Holland* [1984] FLR 725.

10 See the Magistrates' Courts Act 1980 s 111(6); and MAGISTRATES vol 29(2) (Reissue) PARA 887. See also *R v Daejan Properties Ltd, ex p Merton London Borough Council* [1978] RA 85, (1978) Times, 25 April.

11 *R v Davey* [1899] 2 QB 301, DC; *R (Murphy) v Cork Justices* [1914] 2 IR 249; *R v Shiel* (1900) 82 LT 587, CA.

12 *R v North West Suffolk (Mildenhall) Magistrates' Court, ex p Forest Heath District Council* (1997) 161 JP 401, (1997) Times, 16 May.

711. County courts. Any party requiring any act to be done by a judge or officer of a county court relating to the duties of his office may apply to the High Court by way of an application for judicial review for a mandatory order (formerly known as an order of mandamus)[1], and that court may make an order accordingly[2]. A county court judge who mistakenly declined to hear an action for possession by mortgagees on the ground that the court had no jurisdiction was ordered to hear and determine the case[3]. Similarly, an order of mandamus was made when a county court judge refused to investigate the correctness of jurisdictional facts on which the validity of a rent tribunal's decision depended, and which were properly disputed before him[4]. An order of mandamus was also granted to direct a county court judge to hear an appeal from a registrar's refusal to grant a certificate under the Matrimonial Causes Rules 1977[5] that the petitioner was entitled to a decree nisi of divorce[6].

1 A mandatory order was formerly known as an order of mandamus: see PARAS 687 note 3, 688. As to the nature of mandatory orders see PARA 703.

2 See the Senior Courts Act 1981 s 29(4) (amended by SI 2004/1033); and the Senior Courts Act 1981 s 31 (amended by the Tribunals, Courts and Enforcement Act 2007 s 141; and by SI 2004/1033). See also *R v Judge Dutton Briant, ex p Abbey National Building Society* [1957] 2 QB 497, [1957] 2 All ER 625, DC; and *R v Judge Pugh, ex p Graham* [1951] 2 KB 623, [1951] 2 All ER 307, DC. The Senior Courts Act 1981 was previously known as the Supreme Court Act 1981 and was renamed by the Constitutional Reform Act 2005 s 59(5), Sch 11 Pt 1 as from 1 October 2009: see the Constitutional Reform Act 2005 (Commencement No 11) Order 2009, SI 2009/1604; and COURTS.

3 *R v Judge Dutton Briant, ex p Abbey National Building Society* [1957] 2 QB 497, [1957] 2 All ER 625, DC.

4 *R v Judge Pugh, ex p Graham* [1951] 2 KB 623, [1951] 2 All ER 307, DC. As to rent tribunals see LANDLORD AND TENANT vol 27(2) (2006 Reissue) PARAS 910, 988 et seq.

5 Ie under the Matrimonial Causes Rules 1977, SI 1977/344, r 48 (revoked).

6 *R v Nottingham County Court, ex p Byers* [1985] 1 All ER 735, [1985] 1 WLR 403.

712. Ecclesiastical courts. If an ecclesiastical court[1] declines to exercise jurisdiction vested in it[2], the temporal court may by a mandatory order[3] compel the ecclesiastical court to take the case into consideration[4].

1 As to ecclesiastical courts see COURTS vol 10 (Reissue) PARA 805 et seq; ECCLESIASTICAL LAW vol 14 PARA 1259 et seq.

2 As to the scope of ecclesiastical jurisdiction see ECCLESIASTICAL LAW.

3 A mandatory order was formerly known as an order of mandamus: see PARAS 687 note 3, 688. As to the nature of mandatory orders see PARA 703.

4 *R v Archbishop of Canterbury* (1856) 6 E & B 546; *A-G v Dean and Chapter of Ripon Cathedral* [1945] Ch 239 at 246, [1945] 1 All ER 479 at 484, DC; but see PARA 689. See also PARA 715 note 7; and ECCLESIASTICAL LAW vol 14 PARAS 1267, 1269.

713. Coroners. The High Court may grant a mandatory order[1] by way of judicial review ordering a coroner to exercise his jurisdiction[2] lawfully and, in addition, the High Court has power by statute[3] on an application by or under the authority of the Attorney-General, to order an inquest to be held touching a death in respect of which a coroner refuses or neglects to hold an inquest[4], or in respect of which it is necessary or desirable in the interests of justice that another inquest should be held, by reason of fraud, rejection of evidence, irregularity of proceedings, insufficiency of inquiry or otherwise[5].

1 A mandatory order was formerly known as an order of mandamus: see PARAS 687 note 3, 688. As to the nature of mandatory orders see PARA 703.

2 As to coroners and their jurisdiction see CORONERS.

3 Ie under the Coroners Act 1988 s 13: see CORONERS vol 9(2) (2006 Reissue) PARA 1073.

4 As to inquests see CORONERS vol 9(2) (2006 Reissue) PARA 949 et seq.

5 See CORONERS vol 9(2) (2006 Reissue) PARA 1073. See also *R v HM Coroner for North Northumberland, ex p Armstrong* (1987) 151 JP 773 at 785 per Woolf LJ; *R v HM Coroner at Hammersmith, ex p Peach (Nos 1 and 2)* [1980] QB 211, [1980] 2 All ER 7, CA; *R v Inner London North District Coroner, ex p Linnane* [1989] 2 All ER 254, [1989] 1 WLR 395, DC (mandamus issued directing coroner to summon a jury); *R v Inner South London Coroner, ex p Kendall* [1989] 1 All ER 72, [1988] 1 WLR 1186, DC (mandamus issued requiring a new coroner to enter such verdict as he considered proper in the light of judgment of court).

(ii) Public Offices and Duties in respect of which a Mandatory Order will not Lie

714. Mandatory orders against the Crown and Crown servants. As no court can compel the Sovereign to perform any duty, no mandatory order[1] will be made against the Crown personally[2]. Where it is sought to establish a right against the Crown the appropriate procedure is by way of proceedings brought in accordance with the Crown Proceedings Act 1947[3].

In the past, the courts held that certain duties were owed by ministers to the Crown and not the public and so were not enforceable by way of mandatory orders[4]. This, however, is not the usual approach in modern times, and duties imposed on ministers are now generally regarded as owed to the public and enforceable by way of mandatory orders[5]. Thus where government officials are responsible for carrying out particular duties in relation to subjects, whether by royal charter, statute, or common law, they are under a legal obligation towards those subjects and a mandatory order can be made for the enforcement of those duties[6]. If, therefore, an act requires 'the minister' to do something, a mandatory order can be made to compel the minister to act.

1   A mandatory order was formerly known as an order of mandamus: see PARAS 687 note 3, 688. As to the nature of mandatory orders see PARA 703.

2   *R v Powell* (1841) 1 QB 352 at 361 per Lord Denman CJ ('that there can be no mandamus to the Sovereign, there can be no doubt, both because there would be an incongruity in the Queen commanding herself to do an act, and also because disobedience to the writ of mandamus is to be enforced by attachment'). See also *R v Treasury Lords Comrs* (1872) LR 7 QB 387 at 394 per Cockburn CJ. It has, however, been suggested by the Privy Council that mandamus could be awarded against cabinet ministers, requiring them to advise the Crown to perform its duty (*Teh Cheng Poh v Public Prosecutor, Malaysia* [1980] AC 458 at 473, [1979] 2 WLR 623 at 633, PC (the context was the proclamation of a security area in Malaysia which the Crown had a duty to revoke in certain circumstances)).

3   See further ADMINISTRATIVE LAW vol 1(1) (2001 Reissue) PARAS 182–185; CROWN PROCEEDINGS AND CROWN PRACTICE vol 12(1) (Reissue) PARA 110 et seq.

4   See *R v Secretary of State for War* [1891] 2 QB 326, CA (Secretary of State carrying out the provisions of a royal warrant owed a duty to the Crown and was under no legal duty to the public, and a mandatory order did not lie in respect of that duty). See also *R v Customs Comrs* (1836) 5 Ad & El 380 at 383 per Littledale J (where it was sought to obtain a mandamus commanding the delivery up of certain tobacco; but 'the goods are in the hands of the officers of the Crown: a mandamus to them in this case would be like a mandamus to the Crown, which we cannot grant'). See also *R v Lindsay and Customs Board* (1888) 4 TLR 464 at 465, DC (where Lord Coleridge CJ said that it was a very serious question whether a mandamus could be issued to the Board of Customs (now the Commissioners for Her Majesty's Revenue and Customs: see CUSTOMS AND EXCISE vol 12(3) (2007 Reissue) PARA 900 et seq; INCOME TAXATION)); *Ex p Reeve* (1837) 5 Dowl 668 (where a rule for a mandamus to compel the Woods and Forests Commissioners (now the Crown Estates Commissioners: see CROWN PROPERTY vol 12(1) (Reissue) PARA 278 et seq) to pay a certain poor rate was refused, as they held the lands in question on behalf of the King); *Re Baron de Bode* (1838) 6 Dowl 776 at 792 per Coleridge J (where a rule for a mandamus to the Lords of the Treasury to pay over certain money was refused, it being held by the court that the money was held by the Lords of the Treasury as 'the mere servants of the Crown', and 'against the servants of the Crown, as such, and merely to enforce the satisfaction of claims upon the Crown, it is an established rule that a mandamus will not lie'); *R v Treasury Lords Comrs* (1872) LR 7 QB 387 (where it was held that money voted as a supply to the Crown, appropriated to a specific purpose by the annual Appropriation Act, and paid to the Treasury under warrants or orders under the sign manual, was paid to the latter as a servant of the Crown, and that no mandamus would lie to it to pay over such money to a particular person). See contra *R v Treasury Lords Comrs* (1835) 4 Ad & El 286 (which was referred to in *R v Treasury Lords Comrs* (1872) LR 7 QB 387 at 395 per Cockburn CJ as 'a case of very doubtful authority'; and was expressly disapproved in *R v IRC, Re Nathan* (1884) 12 QBD 461, CA). In view of these expressions of disapproval the case can no longer be regarded as law: *Leen v President of Executive Council* [1938] IR 408, CA. Cf *R v*

Treasury Lords Comrs [1909] 2 KB 183 at 191 per Lord Alverstone CJ ('If this had been an application for a mandamus to order the Treasury to pay over part of a constable's pension, I do not think that it would lie. But ... I think that a mandamus will lie in order to set in motion the procedure whereby alone the respective liabilities to pay can be determined'). See also *Kariapper v Wijesinha* [1968] AC 717 at 745, [1967] 3 All ER 485 at 496, PC (where it was observed that even if the clerks of the House of Representatives in Ceylon had a legal duty to 'recognise' and make payments to members, it was a duty owed only to the House or to their employer, the Crown, and was not enforceable by mandamus at the suit of a member); and PARA 706.

5   *Re M* [1994] 1 AC 377, sub nom *M v Home Office* [1993] 3 All ER 537, HL ('After the introduction of judicial review in 1977 it was therefore not necessary to draw any distinction between an officer of the Crown 'acting as such' and an officer acting in some other capacity in public law proceedings': at 417 and 560 per Lord Woolf).

6   *M v Home Office* [1994] 1 AC 377, [1993] 3 All ER 537, HL. See also *R v Customs and Excise Comrs, ex p Cooke and Stevenson* [1970] 1 All ER 1068 at 1072–1073, [1970] 1 WLR 450 at 455, DC, per Lord Parker CJ; *Padfield v Minister of Agriculture, Fisheries and Food* [1968] AC 997, [1968] 1 All ER 694, HL; *R v Secretary of State for the Home Department, ex p Phansopkar* [1976] QB 606, [1975] 3 All ER 497, DC (order of mandamus made to compel the Secretary of State to hear and determine an application for a certificate of partiality); *R v Minister of Health, ex p Rush* [1922] 2 KB 28; *R v Secretary of State for the Environment, ex p Percy Bilton Industrial Properties Ltd* (1975) 31 P & CR 154.

715.   The superior courts.   A mandatory order[1] will not issue to any of the superior courts[2] other than the Crown Court[3]. Accordingly, no mandatory order will go to the Supreme Court, the Court of Appeal, or any of the Divisions which make up the High Court of Justice[4].

The court will also, it seems, refuse to issue a mandatory order to the Judicial Committee of the Privy Council[5], except, it would seem, when it is sitting as a court of appeal in ecclesiastical matters[6]. The order will not issue for the purposes of interfering with the internal affairs of Convocation of the Church of England[7].

1   A mandatory order was formerly known as an order of mandamus: see PARAS 687 note 3, 688. As to the nature of mandatory orders see PARA 703.

2   *The Rioters' Case* (1683) 1 Vern 175; *R v Oxenden* (1691) 1 Show 217; and see *Suratt v A-G of Trinidad and Tobago* [2007] UKPC 55 at [49], [2008] 1 AC 655 at [49].

3   See the Courts Act 1971 s 10(5) (repealed); the Senior Courts Act 1981 s 29(3) (amended by SI 2004/1033); and PARA 142. The Senior Courts Act 1981 was previously known as the Supreme Court Act 1981 and was renamed by the Constitutional Reform Act 2005 s 59(5), Sch 11 Pt 1 as from 1 October 2009: see the Constitutional Reform Act 2005 (Commencement No 11) Order 2009, SI 2009/1604; and COURTS.

4   Bac Abr Courts D. The order of mandamus would not issue to a court of assize (*Ex p Fernandez* (1861) 10 CBNS 3 at 49 per Willes J) or to the Central Criminal Court (*R v Central Criminal Court Justices* (1883) 11 QBD 479, DC; and see *R v Central Criminal Court Justices, ex p LCC* [1925] 2 KB 43, DC (certiorari to quash would not issue to that court)) as they were superior courts. Orders of certiorari are now known as quashing orders: see PARAS 687 note 1, 688. As to quashing orders see PARA 693 et seq. By the Interpretation Act 1889 s 13(4) (repealed) references to courts of assize included the Central Criminal Court. As to the supersession of assize courts by the Crown Court and the jurisdiction of the High Court to issue a mandatory order to that court see PARA 709. As to superior and inferior courts see COURTS.

When the Crown Court sits in the City of London it is known as the Central Criminal Court: see the Senior Courts Act 1981 s 8(3); and COURTS vol 10 (Reissue) PARA 624.

5   *Ex p Smyth* (1835) 3 Ad & El 719 (where the real object of the motion was to compel the rehearing of an appeal by the Judicial Committee of the Privy Council; Patteson J said (at 722): 'I never heard that we could compel any court to rehear a case already decided'. Littledale J said (at 722) that although the Court of Delegates, which was superseded by the Judicial Committee, might have granted a commission of review, 'I have no notion that this court can now accomplish the object of such a commission by a mandamus'). As to the Judicial Committee of the Privy Council see COURTS vol 10 (Reissue) PARA 401 et seq.

6   See ECCLESIASTICAL LAW vol 14 PARA 1288.

7   *R v Archbishop of York* (1888) 20 QBD 740 (where a mandamus to the Archbishop, as president of Convocation, directing him to admit a certain proctor into Convocation, was

refused; Lord Coleridge CJ said (at 748): 'What we are asked to do is to interfere in the internal affairs of an ancient body as old as Parliament and as independent ... Such an interference would not only be without a shadow of precedent, but would be inconsistent with the character and constitution of the body with which we are asked to interfere'). As to Convocations see ECCLESIASTICAL LAW vol 14 PARA 442 et seq.

(4) DECLARATIONS AND INJUNCTIONS

(i) Introduction

716. Claims for declaration or injunction. An application for a declaration or an injunction[1] may be made by way of an application for judicial review[2]. On such an application the court may grant the declaration or injunction claimed if it considers that it would be just and convenient for the declaration or injunction to be granted[3], having regard to:

(1) the nature of the matters in respect of which relief may be granted by way of a mandatory order, a prohibiting order or a quashing order[4];

(2) the nature of the persons and bodies against whom relief may be granted by such orders[5]; and

(3) all the circumstances of the case[6].

The availability of declaratory or injunctive relief on an application for judicial review is at least co-extensive with that of the prerogative remedies[7]. The jurisdiction to grant declaratory or injunctive relief on an application for judicial review is not limited to cases in which relief by way of one of the prerogative orders could have been available. Rather such relief may be granted in respect of a public law issue whenever it is just and convenient to do so[8].

The jurisdiction to grant a declaration or injunction on an application for judicial review is concurrent with the jurisdiction to grant such forms of remedy or relief in private law claims[9]. However, a person seeking to establish that a decision of a public authority infringes rights which he is entitled to have protected under public law must as a general rule proceed by way of an application for judicial review rather than by way of an ordinary claim[10].

1   This does not include an injunction under the Senior Courts Act 1981 s 30 to restrain a person from acting in an office in which he is not entitled to act, which must be made by way of an application for judicial review: see CPR 54.2; and PARA 718. The Senior Courts Act 1981 was previously known as the Supreme Court Act 1981 and was renamed by the Constitutional Reform Act 2005 s 59(5), Sch 11 Pt 1 as from 1 October 2009: see the Constitutional Reform Act 2005 (Commencement No 11) Order 2009, SI 2009/1604; and COURTS. As to the CPR see PARA 659; and CIVIL PROCEDURE vol 11 (2009) PARA 30 et seq.

2   See the Senior Courts Act 1981 s 31(1)(b), (2); and CPR 54.3. As to the procedure for seeking judicial review see PARA 660 et seq.

3   See the Senior Courts Act 1981 s 31(2).

4   Senior Courts Act 1981 s 31(2)(a) (amended by SI 2004/1033). As to prohibiting orders and quashing orders see PARA 693 et seq; and as to mandatory orders see PARA 703 et seq.

5   Senior Courts Act 1981 s 31(2)(b).

6   Senior Courts Act 1981 s 31(2)(c).

7   *IRC v National Federation of Self-Employed and Small Businesses Ltd* [1982] AC 617 at 639, [1981] 2 All ER 93 at 103, HL, per Lord Diplock; *Law v National Greyhound Racing Club Ltd* [1983] 3 All ER 300 at 306, [1983] 1 WLR 1302 at 1310, CA, per Fox LJ, and at 308 and 1313 per Slade LJ. Cf *R v Secretary of State for the Environment, ex p Ward* [1984] 2 All ER 556 at 565, [1984] 1 WLR 834 at 844, where Woolf J suggested that declarations and injunctions could only be obtained on an application for judicial review if the applicant could establish the infringement of a private right; this seems to be contrary to authority. Whilst an injunction or declaration will normally be used as an alternative to, or to supplement, one of the prerogative remedies, there may be cases where such relief is more appropriate than one of the prerogative remedies: see eg *R v Tower Bridge Magistrates' Court, ex p Osborne* (1987) 88 Cr App Rep

28, DC (certiorari (now known as a quashing order: see PARAS 687 note 1, 688) would have had no practical effect so a permanent injunction was granted as an alternative); *R v HM Treasury, ex p Smedley* [1985] QB 657, [1985] 1 All ER 589, CA (declaration appropriate where the legality of an Order in Council was questioned prior to its approval by both Houses of Parliament); *R v Panel on Take-overs and Mergers, ex p Datafin plc* [1987] QB 815 at 842, [1987] 1 All ER 564 at 579–580, CA, per Sir John Donaldson MR (because of the special nature of the respondents, the relationship between them and the court should be historic rather than contemporaneous, so that the court should allow contemporary decisions to take their course, considering the complaint and intervening, if at all, later and in retrospect by declaratory orders); *R v Secretary of State for the Home Department, ex p Ruddock* [1987] 2 All ER 518, [1987] 1 WLR 1482 (declaration sought where the decision questioned in the proceedings, namely the authorisation of phone tapping, was incapable of remedy because the event itself had already taken place). For a narrow interpretation of the availability of the remedies of declaration and injunction in judicial review proceedings see *R v Secretary of State for the Home Department, ex p Dew* [1987] 2 All ER 1049 at 1066, [1987] 1 WLR 881 at 901 per McNeill J.

As a matter of practice in judicial review proceedings the declaration is the usual form of relief granted against the Crown. In ordinary civil proceedings the court has power to make all such orders as it has power to make in proceedings between subjects: see the Crown Proceedings Act 1947 s 21(1); and CROWN PROCEEDINGS AND CROWN PRACTICE vol 12(1) (Reissue) PARA 134. That power is subject to the provisions of the Crown Proceedings Act 1947 which contain a number of exceptions to the general rule, the most notable, for present purposes, being the restriction on the grant of an injunction against the Crown or officers of the Crown, with a power in lieu to grant declaratory relief: see s 21(1)(a); and CROWN PROCEEDINGS AND CROWN PRACTICE vol 12(1) (Reissue) PARA 134. The Crown Proceedings Act 1947 does not apply to judicial review proceedings since these are proceedings on the Crown side of the Queen's Bench Division and are accordingly not included in the definition of 'civil proceedings' given in the Act: see s 38(2); *R v Secretary of State for Transport, ex p Factortame Ltd* [1990] 2 AC 85 at 146–147, sub nom *Factortame Ltd v Secretary of State for Transport* [1989] 2 All ER 692 at 706, HL, per Lord Bridge of Harwich; and CROWN PROCEEDINGS AND CROWN PRACTICE vol 12(1) (Reissue) PARA 103. There is no jurisdiction to grant injunctive relief (whether interim or final) against the Crown in judicial review proceedings: see *R v Secretary of State for Transport, ex p Factortame Ltd* [1990] 2 AC 85, sub nom *Factortame Ltd v Secretary of State for Transport* [1989] 2 All ER 692, HL. However, an injunction may be granted against an officer of the Crown: *Re M* [1994] 1 AC 377, sub nom *M v Home Office* [1993] 3 All ER 537, HL.

As to the prerogative remedies see PARA 688 et seq.

8   See *R v Secretary of State for Employment, ex p Equal Opportunities Commission* [1995] 1 AC 1, sub nom *Equal Opportunities Commission v Secretary of State for Employment* [1994] 1 All ER 910, HL, in which the House of Lords granted a declaration (that an Act of Parliament was incompatible with the Treaty Establishing the European Community (Rome, 25 March 1957; TS 1 (1973); Cmnd 5179) art 119) in circumstances where no prerogative order could have been granted. See also *R v Secretary of State for the Environment, ex p GLC* (1985) Times, 30 December; *R v Bromley London Borough Council, ex p Lambeth London Borough Council* (1984) Times, 16 June; *R v Secretary of State for the Environment, ex p Nottinghamshire County Council* (1986) Independent, 13 November. The basis of these cases seems to be that the decision in *IRC v National Federation of Self-Employed and Small Businesses Ltd* [1982] AC 617 at 631, [1981] 2 All ER 93 at 97, HL, per Lord Wilberforce, at 639 and 103 per Lord Diplock, at 647 and 109 per Lord Scarman, and at 657 and 116 per Lord Roskill, in so far as it suggested that RSC Ord 53 (now revoked) did not alter the substantive law but merely effected a procedural reform, must now be taken to be superseded by the enactment of the Senior Courts Act 1981 s 31 (see the text and notes 1–6): see *R v Bromley London Borough Council, ex p Lambeth London Borough Council* (1984) Times, 16 June.

9   See eg *Gillick v West Norfolk and Wisbech Area Health Authority* [1986] AC 112, [1985] 3 All ER 402, HL.

10   *O'Reilly v Mackman* [1983] 2 AC 237, [1982] 3 All ER 1124, HL. For a more detailed consideration of the effect of this case and the exceptions to it see PARA 661.

(ii) Injunctions

717. The injunction in public law. An injunction[1] is a discretionary equitable remedy awarded by a superior court or judge or, under restrictive conditions, by a county court judge[2], to restrain the imminent threat or the commission or continuance of unlawful acts, in which case the injunction is prohibitory; or to compel the taking of steps to repair an unlawful omission or to restore the damage inflicted by an unlawful act, in which case the injunction will be mandatory[3]. Save in very exceptional circumstances, an injunction will not issue to secure the provision of services or works that a court cannot effectively superintend[4]. An injunction will not be awarded where damages are an appropriate and adequate remedy[5].

An injunction cannot be awarded in ordinary civil proceedings against the Crown, nor in judicial review proceedings. However, an injunction, including an interim injunction, may be granted against an officer of the Crown, such as a minister, exercising statutory powers conferred on him and he may be held in contempt if he acts in breach of the injunction[6]. The courts have jurisdiction to award injunctions against other public bodies and officers, notwithstanding that compliance may give rise to practical difficulties[7].

An injunction will not issue to restrain proceedings in Parliament[8], but it seems that it may issue to restrain a body from unlawfully spending public funds for the purpose of introducing or opposing a private Bill[9], and there appears to be jurisdiction to restrain unlawful proceedings before subordinate legislatures[10]. The courts do have jurisdiction to grant an injunction in relation to a statutory instrument even where that instrument has been laid before and approved by both Houses of Parliament[11] although, in practice, the appropriate remedy in respect of subordinate legislation found to be unlawful will be a declaration of invalidity or, possibly, a quashing order[12]. All of the injunctions mentioned above should normally be sought by way of an application for judicial review unless the circumstances fall within one of the exceptions to the general rule[13].

1   For a more detailed consideration of the law relating to injunctions see CIVIL PROCEDURE vol 11 (2009) PARA 331 et seq.
2   As to the county court's jurisdiction see COURTS vol 10 (Reissue) PARA 710 et seq.
3   As to the general principles governing the award of mandatory injunctions see *Redland Bricks Ltd v Morris* [1970] AC 652, [1969] 2 All ER 576, HL. Mandatory injunctions are not as common as prohibitory injunctions and have played little part as a means of enforcing public law rights because of the existence of the prerogative mandatory order, which is and was the usual means of securing the enforcement of a public duty: see PARA 703 et seq. However, mandatory injunctions are available against a public authority and are a suitable remedy in a private law claim where the duty of the public authority in question is analogous to that of a private person: see *Parker v Camden London Borough Council* [1986] Ch 162, [1985] 2 All ER 141, CA. Mandatory injunctions are occasionally awarded at the interlocutory stage on an application for judicial review: see *R v Kensington and Chelsea Royal London Borough Council, ex p Hammell* [1989] QB 518, [1989] 1 All ER 1202, CA.
4   As to the general rule see *A-G v Colchester Corpn* [1955] 2 QB 207, [1955] 2 All ER 124 (no mandatory injunction to order continuance of ferry service); *Dowty Boulton Paul Ltd v Wolverhampton Corpn* [1971] 2 All ER 277, [1971] 1 WLR 204 (no injunction to require maintenance of airfield); cf, however, *Warwickshire County Council v British Railways Board* [1969] 3 All ER 631, [1969] 1 WLR 1117, CA (prohibitory injunction to restrain invalid closure of railway line).
5   In some instances an injunction may be awarded although no actionable wrong has been committed.
6   *Re M* [1994] 1 AC 377, sub nom *M v Home Office* [1993] 3 All ER 537, HL. The discretion to grant an injunction should only be exercised in the most limited circumstances: *Re M* [1994] 1 AC 377, sub nom *M v Home Office* [1993] 3 All ER 537, HL, at 422 and 564 per Lord Woolf; cf *R v Secretary of State for Transport, ex p Factortame* [1990] 2 AC 85, sub nom *Factortame Ltd v Secretary of State for Transport* [1989] 2 All ER 692, HL.
7   See eg *Pride of Derby and Derbyshire Angling Association Ltd v British Celanese Ltd* [1953] Ch 149, [1953] 1 All ER 179, CA, and the authorities there considered. See also *Bradbury v Enfield London Borough Council* [1967] 3 All ER 434 at 441, [1969] 1 WLR 1311 at 1324, CA, per Lord Denning MR ('even if chaos should result, still the law must be obeyed').

The test for the award of interlocutory injunctions against a public body in judicial review proceedings appears to be the same as the test in an ordinary private law claim (ie as laid down in *American Cyanamid Co v Ethicon Ltd* [1975] AC 396, [1975] 1 All ER 504, HL: see CIVIL PROCEDURE vol 11 (2009) PARA 383 et seq). The test must be applied in the context of the public law questions to which the judicial review proceedings give rise: see *R v Minister of Agriculture Fisheries and Food, ex p Monsanto plc* [1999] QB 1161, [1998] 4 All ER 321, DC. See also *R v Westminster City Council, ex p Costi* (1987) Independent, 12 March; *R v GLC, ex p Westminster City Council* (1985) Times, 22 January. See further *R v Kensington and Chelsea Royal London Borough Council, ex p Hammell* [1989] QB 518, [1989] 1 All ER 1202, CA.

8 See the Bill of Rights (1688) s 1, art 9; and PARLIAMENT vol 78 (2010) PARA 1082.

9 *A-G v London and Home Counties Joint Electricity Authority* [1929] 1 Ch 513. Quaere whether an injunction would be awarded directly to restrain promotion of, or opposition to, a Bill: see *Bilston Corpn v Wolverhampton Corpn* [1942] Ch 391, [1942] 2 All ER 447.

10 *Rediffusion (Hong Kong) Ltd v A-G of Hong Kong* [1970] AC 1136, [1970] 2 WLR 1264, PC (discretionary relief refused as premature on the facts of the case). It would seem that the jurisdiction referred to in the text will not be exercisable by United Kingdom courts but by courts overseas and, on appeal from them, by the Judicial Committee of the Privy Council.

11 *Hoffman-La Roche & Co AG v Secretary of State for Trade and Industry* [1975] AC 295, [1974] 2 All ER 1128, HL.

12 See eg *R (on the application of Javed) v Secretary of State for the Home Department* [2001] EWCA Civ 789, [2002] QB 129; *R (on the application of C) v Secretary of State for Justice* [2008] EWCA Civ 882, [2009] QB 657, [2008] All ER (D) 316 (Oct). The court also has jurisdiction to rule on the lawfulness of draft subordinate legislation: see *R v HM Treasury, ex p Smedley* [1985] QB 657, [1985] 1 All ER 589, CA (court has jurisdiction to review the legality of a draft Order in Council before it has been approved by both Houses of Parliament but appropriate remedy would normally be a declaration). As to quashing orders see PARA 693 et seq.

13 See PARA 661.

718. Injunctions to restrain persons from acting in an office. Where a person not entitled to do so acts in any of certain offices[1], the High Court may grant an injunction restraining him from so acting[2], and, if the case so requires, declare the office to be vacant[3]. An application for such an injunction must be made by way of an application for judicial review[4]. The order does not issue as a matter of course, and the applicant's conduct and motives may be inquired into[5].

1 Ie any substantive office of a public nature and permanent character which is held under the Crown or which has been created by any statutory provision or royal charter: Senior Courts Act 1981 s 30(2). The Senior Courts Act 1981 was previously known as the Supreme Court Act 1981 and was renamed by the Constitutional Reform Act 2005 s 59(5), Sch 11 Pt 1 as from 1 October 2009: see the Constitutional Reform Act 2005 (Commencement No 11) Order 2009, SI 2009/1604; and COURTS.

2 Senior Courts Act 1981 s 30(1)(a). This provision replaces the Administration of Justice (Miscellaneous Provisions) Act 1938 s 9 (repealed), which abolished the obsolete information of quo warranto: see further ADMINISTRATIVE LAW vol 1(1) (2001 Reissue) PARA 251 et seq.

3 Senior Courts Act 1981 s 30(1)(b).

4 See the Senior Courts Act 1981 s 31(1)(c); and CPR 54.2(d). As to the procedure for applying for judicial review see PARA 660 et seq. As to the CPR see PARA 659; and CIVIL PROCEDURE vol 11 (2009) PARA 30 et seq.

5 See *Everett v Griffiths* [1924] 1 KB 941 at 958 per McCardie J. For examples of cases decided under the old law that may be relevant to an application under the Senior Courts Act 1981 s 30 (see the text and notes 1–3) see ADMINISTRATIVE LAW vol 1(1) (2001 Reissue) PARA 251 et seq.

(iii) Declarations

719. Declarations in judicial review proceedings. A declaration may be granted even where no other prerogative remedy is available[1]. Declarations are regarded as a useful discretionary remedy[2] which permit the court to adopt a flexible and pragmatic approach[3]. By way of example, declarations have been granted in judicial review proceedings in respect of the applicant's right to hold an office or as to the power of a statutory disciplinary tribunal[4]. Declarations have also been used to resolve disputes between two public authorities[5], for deciding whether advice contained in circulars issued by the government was correct in law[6] and to consider the lawfulness of an Order in Council prior to the approval of both Houses of Parliament[7]. Declarations are frequently granted against Ministers of the Crown and government departments in preference to prerogative orders as such persons invariably observe the decisions of the court and comply with declaratory judgments[8]. The remedy is frequently granted by the court in the exercise of its discretion in preference to one of the prerogative remedies where, for example, the grant of the prerogative remedy would cause substantial hardship to third parties or would be unduly detrimental to good administration[9]. The grant of a declaratory remedy may serve the purpose of vindicating the rule of law and confirming that there has been a breach of the relevant principles of law[10].

Declarations will not generally be granted if they relate to hypothetical or academic issues[11]. Thus, for example, the courts have refused to grant a declaration in relation to the compatibility of legislation with European Union law where that legislation had already been repealed[12]. The courts will not generally grant purely advisory declarations as to what the law is where there is no live issue to be resolved between the parties[13]. Declarations will not be granted in relation to proceedings in Parliament[14]. In addition, the general principles governing the refusal of relief in relation to claims for the prerogative remedies in judicial review apply to the grant of declarations when sought in public law matters[15].

It is now possible for the court to grant an interim declaration[16]. Such an order might be granted in preference to an interim injunction[17].

Disregard of a declaratory judgment by the party affected by the order is not a contempt of court, although if the party affected does refuse to comply with the order the other party can go back to the court and seek an injunction to enforce it[18].

1   See *R v Secretary of State for Employment, ex p Equal Opportunities Commission* [1995] 1 AC 1, sub nom *Equal Opportunities Commission v Secretary of State for Employment* [1994] 1 All ER 910, HL. As to the prerogative remedies see PARA 688 et seq.

2   See *Gouriet v Union of Post Office Workers* [1978] AC 435 at 501, [1977] 3 All ER 70 at 99–100, HL, per Lord Diplock.

3   *R v Minister of Agriculture, Fisheries and Food, ex p Dairy Trade Federation Ltd* [1995] COD 3.

4   See eg *Chief Constable of the North Wales Police v Evans* [1982] 3 All ER 141, [1982] 1 WLR 1155, HL; *R v Secretary of State for the Home Department, ex p Benwell* [1985] QB 554, [1984] 3 All ER 854; *R v Committee of Lloyd's, ex p Postgate* (1983) Times, 12 January, DC.

5   Eg *R v London Transport Executive, ex p GLC* [1983] QB 484, [1983] 2 All ER 262.

6   *Royal College of Nursing of the United Kingdom v Department of Health and Social Security* [1981] AC 800, [1981] 1 All ER 545, HL; *Gillick v West Norfolk and Wisbech Area Health Authority* [1986] AC 112, [1985] 3 All ER 402, HL.

7   *R v HM Treasury, ex p Smedley* [1985] QB 657, [1985] 1 All ER 589, CA.

8   *Re M* [1994] 1 AC 377 at 397, sub nom *M v Home Office* [1993] 3 All ER 537 at 543, HL, per Lord Woolf.

9   See eg *R (on the application of Gavin) v Haringey London Borough Council* [2003] EWHC 2591 (Admin), [2004] 2 P & CR 209, [2003] All ER (D) 57 (Nov).

10 See eg *R v Lincolnshire County Council, ex p Atkinson* (1995) 8 Admin LR 529.

11 See eg *R v Secretary of State for the Home Department, ex p Wynne* [1993] 1 All ER 574, [1993] 1 WLR 115, HL; *R v Inland Revenue Commissioners, ex p Bishopp, R v Inland Revenue Commissioners, ex p Allan* [1999] STC 531, [1999] All ER (D) 419. The courts may, in public law cases, grant declarations where the case raises discrete questions of law, not dependent on

the facts of a particular case, and where a large number of similar claims are likely to arise in future: *R v Secretary of State for the Home Department, ex p Salem* [1999] AC 450, [1999] 2 All ER 42.

12 *R v Ministry of Agriculture Fisheries and Food, ex p Live Sheep Traders Ltd* [1995] COD 297, DC.

13 *R (on the application of Rusbridger) v A-G* [2003] UKHL 38, [2004] 1 AC 357 (court would not entertain claim that provisions of the Treasons Act 1848 were incompatible with the Convention for the Protection of Human Rights and Fundamental Freedoms (Rome, 4 November 1950; TS 71 (1953) Cmd 8969) (see CONSTITUTIONAL LAW AND HUMAN RIGHTS) as there was no prospect of any proceedings being brought); *R (on the application of Burke) v General Medical Council* [2005] EWCA Civ 1003, [2006] QB 273.

14 *Bradlaugh v Gossett* (1884) 12 QBD 271; and see also *R (on the application of Wheeler) v Office of the Prime Minister* [2008] EWHC 1409 (Admin), [2008] All ER (D) 333 (Jun).

15 See PARA 692.

16 CPR 25.1(1)(b). Such an order was previously unknown to the law: *F v Riverside Mental Health NHS Trust* [1994] 2 FCR 577, sub nom *Riverside Mental Health NHS Trust v Fox* [1994] 1 FLR 614, CA. See also *Meade v Haringey London Borough Council* [1979] 2 All ER 1016, [1979] 1 WLR 637, CA; *IRC v Rossminster Ltd* [1980] AC 952, [1980] 1 All ER 80, HL. As to the CPR see PARA 659; and CIVIL PROCEDURE vol 11 (2009) PARA 30 et seq.

17 *Re M* [1994] 1 AC 377 at 423, sub nom *M v Home Office* [1993] 3 All ER 537 at 565, HL, per Lord Woolf.

18 *Webster v Southwark London Borough Council* [1983] QB 698 at 706, 708 per Forbes J. As to contempt of court see CONTEMPT OF COURT.

(5) INTERIM REMEDIES

720.   Interim remedies.   The court has jurisdiction to grant interim relief on an application for judicial review[1]. When granting permission to apply for judicial review, a court may grant a stay of the proceedings to which the application relates; and this empowers the court to stay the proceedings of an inferior court or tribunal[2]. The power extends to imposing a stay on the decision-making process of a public body if it has not reached a final decision[3] or even a stay preventing the implementation of a decision already taken[4].

The courts also have power to grant interim relief, including interim injunctions, at any stage in judicial review proceedings[5]. In cases of extreme urgency, interim relief may also be granted before permission to apply for judicial review[6]. Interim injunctions may be granted against any public body, including ministers of the Crown[7]. Interim declarations may also be granted[8].

1 As to interim remedies see CPR Pt 25; and CIVIL PROCEDURE vol 11 (2009) PARA 315 et seq.

2 See CPR 54.10.

3 *R v Secretary of State for Education, ex p Avon County Council* [1991] 1 QB 558, [1991] 1 All ER 282. The Privy Council has taken a different view and considers that a stay is an order which puts a stop before proceedings before a tribunal or inferior court: see *Minister of Foreign Affairs, Trade and Industry v Vehicles and Supplies Ltd* [1991] 4 All ER 65, [1991] 1 WLR 550, PC.

4 *R (on the application of H) v Ashworth Hospital Authority* [2002] EWCA Civ 923, [2003] 1 WLR 127, [2002] All ER (D) 252 (Jun).

5 See CPR 25.2(1).

6 *Re M* [1994] 1 AC 377, sub nom *M v Home Office* [1993] 3 All ER 537, HL.

7 *Re M* [1994] 1 AC 377, sub nom *M v Home Office* [1993] 3 All ER 537, HL.

8 See CPR 25.1(1)(b); and PARA 719.

(6) OTHER REMEDIES

721.   Judicial remedies under the Human Rights Act 1998.   A court[1] may grant such relief or remedy, or make such order, within its powers as it considers just and appropriate in relation to any act (or proposed act) of a public authority which the court finds is (or would be) unlawful in that it would involve action incompatible with a Convention right[2]. Where a claim is brought by way of judicial review, the court has the power to grant any of the prerogative remedies[3], or an injunction or declaration (including interim remedies)[4].

The court on an application for judicial review has jurisdiction to award damages in respect of an act of a public authority which is unlawful in that it contravenes a Convention right[5]. However, no award of damages is to be made unless, taking account of all the circumstances of the case, including: (1) any other relief or remedy granted, or order made, in relation to the act in question (by that or any other court); and (2) the consequences of any decision (of that or any other court) in respect of that act, the court is satisfied that the award is necessary to afford just satisfaction to the person in whose favour it is made[6].

1 'Court' includes a tribunal: Human Rights Act 1998 s 8(6).
2 See the Human Rights Act 1998 ss 6(1), 8(1); and CONSTITUTIONAL LAW AND HUMAN RIGHTS. The text refers to a Convention right as defined by the Human Rights Act 1998 s 1: see CONSTITUTIONAL LAW AND HUMAN RIGHTS. As to unlawful acts of public authorities under the Human Rights Act 1998 see PARA 651.
3 As to the prerogative remedies see PARA 688 et seq.
4 As to injunctions see PARA 716 et seq; and CIVIL PROCEDURE vol 11 (2009) PARA 331 et seq. As to declaratory orders see PARAS 716, 719.
5 Damages may only be awarded by a court which has power to award damages, or to order the payment of compensation in civil proceedings: see the Human Rights Act 1998 s 8(2); and CONSTITUTIONAL LAW AND HUMAN RIGHTS. The High Court hearing an application for judicial review is such a court: see PARA 659 et seq. As to damages generally see PARA 722; and DAMAGES.
6 See the Human Rights Act 1998 s 8(3); and CONSTITUTIONAL LAW AND HUMAN RIGHTS. In determining (1) whether to award damages; or (2) the amount of an award, the court must take into account the principles applied by the European Court of Human Rights in relation to the award of compensation under the Convention for the Protection of Human Rights and Fundamental Freedoms (Rome, 4 November 1950; TS 71 (1953) Cmd 8969) art 41 (see CONSTITUTIONAL LAW AND HUMAN RIGHTS): Human Rights Act 1998 s 8(4). See generally *R (on the application of Greenfield) v Secretary of State for the Home Department* [2005] UKHL 14, [2005] 2 All ER 240, [2005] 1 WLR 673.

722. Damages. On an application for judicial review, the court may award damages providing that a claim for damages was included in the application and, if the matter had been brought by an ordinary claim, damages would be available[1]. This provision does not create any new substantive right to damages. Rather, it enables a claim for damages to be sought in an application for judicial review where a private law cause of action, such as negligence or false imprisonment, is made out against the public body. A claim for damages cannot be sought alone on an application for judicial review but must be combined with a claim for another remedy such as one of the prerogative remedies[2] or an injunction or declaration[3].

1 See the Senior Courts Act 1981 s 31(4) (substituted by SI 2004/1033); and CPR 54.3(2). The Senior Courts Act 1981 was previously known as the Supreme Court Act 1981 and was renamed by the Constitutional Reform Act 2005 s 59(5), Sch 11 Pt 1 as from 1 October 2009: see the Constitutional Reform Act 2005 (Commencement No 11) Order 2009, SI 2009/1604; and COURTS. As to damages generally see DAMAGES.
2 As to the prerogative remedies see PARA 688 et seq.
3 CPR 54.3(2). As to injunctions see PARA 716 et seq; and CIVIL PROCEDURE vol 11 (2009) PARA 331 et seq. As to declaratory orders see PARAS 716, 719.

723–800. Restitution and recovery of sums due. The court may award restitution or the recovery of a sum due on an application for judicial review[1]. By way of example, money paid to a public body pursuant to an ultra vires demand[2] or an agreement which is ultra vires the powers of the body[3] may be recovered on a claim for restitution. The claim for restitution or recovery cannot be sought alone on an application for judicial review but must be combined with a claim for another remedy such as one of the prerogative remedies[4] or an injunction or declaration[5].

1   See the Senior Courts Act 1981 s 31(4) (substituted by SI 2004/1033); and CPR 54.3(2). The Senior Courts Act 1981 was previously known as the Supreme Court Act 1981 and was renamed by the Constitutional Reform Act 2005 s 59(5), Sch 11 Pt 1 as from 1 October 2009: see the Constitutional Reform Act 2005 (Commencement No 11) Order 2009, SI 2009/1604; and COURTS.

2   *Woolwich Equitable Building Society v IRC (No 2)* [1993] AC 70, [1992] 3 All ER 737, HL.

3   *Kleinwort Benson Ltd v Lincoln City Council* [1999] 2 AC 349, [1998] 4 All ER 513, HL.

4   As to the prerogative remedies see PARA 688 et seq.

5   CPR 54.3(2). As to injunctions see PARA 716 et seq; and CIVIL PROCEDURE vol 11 (2009) PARA 331 et seq. As to declaratory orders see PARAS 716, 719.

JURIES

1. CONSTITUTION AND DUTIES OF JURIES

801.   Meaning of 'jury'. Juries are bodies of persons convened by process of law to represent the public at a trial or inquest[1] and to discharge upon oath or affirmation[2] defined public duties. Juries must be duly empanelled and returned[3].

The law concerning juries is consolidated in the Juries Act 1974, which repealed all but a small part of previous Acts and re-enacted those parts still viable[4]. It extends to England and Wales only[5] and revolutionised jury service there[6].

1   Trial by jury is also spoken of as trial per patriam or per pais, as distinguished from trial by ordeal (long since disused), trial by battle (abolished by 59 Geo 3 c 46 (Appeal of Murder, etc) (1819) (repealed)), and trial by wager of law (abolished by the Civil Procedure Act 1833 s 13 (repealed)). As to inquests see further CORONERS vol 9(2) (2006 Reissue) PARA 949 et seq.

2   The word 'jury' (Latin, jurata) denotes a 'sworn body', but a juror who objects to taking the oath may make a solemn affirmation in all places and for all purposes where an oath is required by law, and such an affirmation has the same force and effect as an oath: Oaths Act 1978 s 5.

3   Bill of Rights (1688 or 1689) s 1 (amended by the Juries Act 1825 s 62; and the Statute Law Revision Act 1950). As to the empanelling of juries see PARA 816 et seq.

4   See the Juries Act 1974. The Act was based on the recommendations of the *Report of the Departmental Committee on Jury Service* (Cmnd 2627) (1965) under the chairmanship of Lord Morris of Borth-y-Gest.

     The Juries Act 1974 enables the Lord Chancellor by order to make such amendments or repeals of any provisions of any local Acts as appear to him necessary or expedient in consequence of the Juries Act 1974 (see s 21(1)), and such transitional provisions as appear to him necessary or expedient (see s 21(2)). The power to make such an order is exercisable by statutory instrument subject to annulment by resolution of either House of Parliament, and includes power to vary or revoke any order previously made in the exercise of the power: s 21(3). At the date at which this volume states the law, no such order had been made. The Lord Chancellor's functions under s 21 are protected functions for the purposes of the Constitutional Reform Act 2005 s 19: see s 19(5), Sch 7 para 4; and CONSTITUTIONAL LAW AND HUMAN RIGHTS. As to the Lord Chancellor see CONSTITUTIONAL LAW AND HUMAN RIGHTS vol 8(2) (Reissue) PARA 477 et seq.

5   Juries Act 1974 s 23(4). As to the meanings of 'England' and 'Wales' see PARA 804 note 5.

6   Subject to the Juries Act 1974, all enactments and rules of law relating to trial by jury, juries and jurors continue in force and, in criminal cases, continue to apply to Crown Court proceedings: s 21(5).

802.   Duties of juries. The jury's duty is to return verdicts upon issues joined in courts of civil and criminal jurisdiction[1]. At an inquest the jury's duty, until a day to be appointed, is to return a verdict on matters of fact and, as from a day to be appointed, is to make a determination as to specified matters of fact[2].

1   As to the giving of verdicts see PARA 847 et seq. As to the functions of the judge and jury see also CIVIL PROCEDURE vol 11 (2009) PARA 795 et seq. As to the meaning of 'court' for the purposes of the Juries Act 1974 see PARA 804 note 1. As to juries in criminal courts see CRIMINAL LAW, EVIDENCE AND PROCEDURE vol 11(3) (2006 Reissue) PARA 1283 et seq. As to jury trial in civil cases see CIVIL PROCEDURE vol 12 (2009) PARA 1132.

2   At the date at which this volume states the law, no day had been appointed for the commencement of the relevant provisions of the Coroners and Justice Act 2009. As to juries at inquests see CORONERS vol 9(2) (2006 Reissue) PARAS 978–987.

803.   Number of a jury. The tradition that a jury consists of 12 persons is ancient and well established[1], but is no longer always carried out in practice[2]. A county court jury must consist of eight persons[3] and a jury at an inquest must consist of not less than seven nor more than 11 persons[4]. In the High Court and the Crown Court juries may consist of any number of persons, not above 12[5], provided (in the case of the Crown Court) there are at least nine[6].

1   See 3 Bl Com (14th Edn) 379; 4 Bl Com (14th Edn) 350. The tradition became statutory before
    1729: see 3 Geo 2 c 25 (Juries) (1729) s 11.
2   The Juries Act 1825 s 26, which laid down that a jury must consist of 12 men, was repealed by
    the Criminal Justice Act 1972 Sch 6 Pt I. The tradition of 12 jurors has also been broken in
    other parts of Her Majesty's dominions: see eg *Macnaghten v Paterson* [1907] AC 483 at 491,
    PC (Australia); *Gill v Westlake* [1910] AC 197, PC (Isle of Man).
3   County Courts Act 1984 s 67.
4   See the Coroners Act 1988 s 8(2)(a) (prospectively repealed by the Coroners and Justice
    Act 2009 Sch 23 Pt 1); the Coroners and Justice Act 2009 s 8(1) (not yet in force); and
    CORONERS vol 9(2) (2006 Reissue) PARA 980.
5   The presence of 13 persons improperly in the box, if not discovered until after the verdict, is a
    ground for a new trial: *Muirhead v Evans* (1851) 6 Exch 447 at 449 per Pollock CB.
6   See the Juries Act 1974 s 16(1); and PARA 837. As to majority verdicts see PARA 850.

2. QUALIFICATION, EXEMPTION AND EXCUSAL OF JURORS

804. Qualification and exemption. Every person is qualified to serve as a juror in the Crown Court, the High Court and county courts[1], and is liable accordingly to attend for service when summoned, if:

(1)   he is for the time being registered as a parliamentary or local government elector[2] and is not less than 18 nor more than 70 years of age[3];

(2)   he has been ordinarily resident[4] in the United Kingdom, the Channel Islands or the Isle of Man for any period of at least five years since attaining the age of 13[5];

(3)   he is not a mentally disordered person[6]; and

(4)   he is not disqualified for jury service[7].

These conditions also apply to juries at inquests[8].

A person summoned for service may be excused in certain circumstances[9] or his attendance for service may be deferred[10]. There are also provisions on disqualification[11].

1   For the purposes of the Juries Act 1974, 'court' means the Crown Court, the High Court or a county court: s 23(2). See generally COURTS.

2   As to registration of electors see ELECTIONS AND REFERENDUMS vol 15(3) (2007 Reissue) PARA 127 et seq. See also PARA 812.

3   Juries Act 1974 s 1(1)(a) (s 1 substituted by the Criminal Justice Act 2003 Sch 33 paras 1, 2). As to the exemption of aliens from jury service see BRITISH NATIONALITY, IMMIGRATION AND ASYLUM vol 4(2) (2002 Reissue) PARA 13.

4   As to the meaning of 'ordinarily resident' see BRITISH NATIONALITY, IMMIGRATION AND ASYLUM vol 4(2) (2002 Reissue) PARA 134; CONFLICT OF LAWS vol 8(3) (Reissue) PARA 58. See also INCOME TAXATION vol 23(2) (Reissue) PARA 1260.

5   Juries Act 1974 s 1(1)(b) (as substituted: see note 3).

    'United Kingdom' means Great Britain and Northern Ireland: Interpretation Act 1978 Sch 1. 'Great Britain' means England, Scotland and Wales: Union with Scotland Act 1706, preamble art I; Interpretation Act 1978 Sch 2 para 5(a). Neither the Channel Islands nor the Isle of Man are within the United Kingdom. See further CONSTITUTIONAL LAW AND HUMAN RIGHTS vol 8(2) (Reissue) PARA 3. 'England' means, subject to any alteration of the boundaries of local government areas, the areas consisting of the counties established by the Local Government Act 1972 s 1 (see LOCAL GOVERNMENT vol 69 (2009) PARAS 5, 24), and Greater London and the Isles of Scilly: see the Interpretation Act 1978 Sch 1. As to local government areas in England see LOCAL GOVERNMENT vol 69 (2009) PARAS 5, 22 et seq; and as to boundary changes see LOCAL GOVERNMENT vol 69 (2009) PARA 56 et seq. As to Greater London see LONDON GOVERNMENT vol 29(2) (Reissue) PARA 29. 'Wales' means the combined areas of the counties created by the Local Government Act 1972 s 20 (as originally enacted) (see LOCAL GOVERNMENT vol 69 (2009) PARA 5), but subject to any alteration made under s 73 (consequential alteration of boundary following alteration of watercourse: see LOCAL GOVERNMENT vol 69 (2009) PARA 90): see the Interpretation Act 1978 Sch 1 (definition substituted by the Local Government (Wales) Act 1994 Sch 2 para 9).

6   Juries Act 1974 s 1(1)(c) (as substituted: see note 3). For these purposes, 'mentally disordered person' means any person listed in Sch 1 Pt 1: s 1(2) (as so substituted). Those persons are: (1) a person who suffers or has suffered from mental disorder within the meaning of the Mental Health Act 1983 (see MENTAL HEALTH vol 30(2) (Reissue) PARA 402) and on account of that condition either is resident in hospital or a similar institution or regularly attends for treatment by a medical practitioner (Juries Act 1974 Sch 1 Pt 1 para 1 (Sch 1 substituted by the Criminal Justice Act 2003 Sch 33 paras 1, 15; and the Juries Act 1974 Sch 1 Pt 1 para 1 amended by the Mental Health Act 2007 Sch 1 para 18(1), (2))); (2) a person for the time being under guardianship under the Mental Health Act 1983 s 7 (see MENTAL HEALTH vol 30(2) (Reissue) PARA 469 et seq) or subject to a community treatment order under s 17A (see MENTAL HEALTH) (Juries Act 1974 Sch 1 Pt 1 para 2 (as so substituted; and amended by the Mental Health Act 2007 Sch 4 para 4)); and (3) a person who lacks capacity within the meaning of the Mental

Capacity Act 2005 (see MENTAL HEALTH vol 30(2) (Reissue) PARA 641) to serve as a juror (Juries Act 1974 Sch 1 Pt 1 para 3 (Sch 1 as so substituted; and Sch 1 Pt 1 para 3 substituted by the Mental Capacity Act 2005 Sch 6 para 20)).

7 Juries Act 1974 s 1(1)(d) (as substituted: see note 3). As to persons disqualified for jury service see Sch 1 Pt 2; and PARA 805. As to the eligibility of members of the criminal justice system to serve as jurors see *R v Abdroikov, R v Green, R v Williamson* [2007] UKHL 37, [2008] 1 All ER 315, [2007] 1 Cr App Rep 280; *R v Khan* [2008] EWCA Crim 531, [2008] 3 All ER 502; *R v Yemoh* [2009] EWCA Crim 930, [2009] Crim LR 888; *R v T* [2009] EWCA Crim 1638, [2009] All ER (D) 327 (Jul).

8 See the Coroners Act 1988 s 9(1) (prospectively repealed by the Coroners and Justice Act 2009 Sch 23 Pt 1); the Coroners and Justice Act 2009 s 8(4) (not yet in force); and CORONERS vol 9(2) (2006 Reissue) PARA 982.

9 See PARAS 806, 808.

10 See PARA 807.

11 See PARA 805.

805. Disqualified persons. The following are disqualified from jury service:

(1) a person who has at any time been sentenced in the United Kingdom[1], the Channel Islands or the Isle of Man: (a) to imprisonment for life, detention for life, custody for life; (b) to detention during Her Majesty's pleasure or during the pleasure of the Secretary of State[2]; (c) to imprisonment for public protection or detention for public protection; (d) to an extended sentence under the relevant provisions of the Criminal Justice Act 2003 or the Criminal Procedure (Scotland) Act 1995[3]; or (e) to a term of imprisonment of five years or more or a term of detention of five years or more[4];

(2) a person who at any time in the last ten years has: (a) in the United Kingdom, the Channel Islands or the Isle of Man, served any part of a sentence of imprisonment or a sentence of detention, or had passed on him a suspended sentence of imprisonment or had made in respect of him a suspended order for detention; (b) in England and Wales[5], had made in respect of him a community order[6]; or (c) had made in respect of him any corresponding order under the law of Scotland, Northern Ireland, the Isle of Man or any of the Channel Islands or a service community order or overseas community order under the Armed Forces Act 2006[7];

(3) a person who is on bail in criminal proceedings[8].

1 A sentence passed anywhere in respect of a service offence within the meaning of the Armed Forces Act 2006 (see ARMED FORCES) is to be treated as having been passed in the United Kingdom: Juries Act 1974 Sch 1 Pt 2 para 8(a) (Sch 1 substituted by the Criminal Justice Act 2003 Sch 33 paras 1, 15; and the Juries Act 1974 Sch 1 Pt 2 para 8(a) amended by the Armed Forces Act 2006 Sch 16 para 62(b)). As to the meaning of 'United Kingdom' see PARA 804 note 5. The reference to a service offence includes an SDA offence: Armed Forces Act 2006 (Transitional Provisions etc) Order 2009, SI 2009/1059, Sch 1 para 13. 'SDA offence' means: (1) any offence under the Army Act 1955 Pt 2 (ss 24–143) or the Air Force Act 1955 Pt 2 (ss 24–143); (2) any offence under the Naval Discipline Act 1957 Pt 1 (ss 1–43B) or s 47K; (3) an offence under the Army Act 1955 Sch 5A para 4(6) or s 18 or s 20 or the Air Force Act 1955 Sch 5A para 4(6) or the Naval Discipline Act 1957 Sch 4A or any of the Reserve Forces Act 1996 ss 95–97 committed before commencement; (4) an offence under the Reserve Forces Act 1996 Sch 1 para 5(1) committed before commencement by a person who: (a) after committing the offence and before commencement became a member of a reserve force and remained such a member until commencement, or immediately before commencement was subject to military law, air force law or the Naval Discipline Act 1957; or (b) after commencement becomes a member of the reserve forces: Armed Forces Act 2006 (Transitional Provisions etc) Order 2009, SI 2009/1059, art 2(4), (5). A person is sentenced to a term of detention, but only if:

    (i) a court passes on him, or makes in respect of him on conviction, any sentence or order which requires him to be detained in custody for any period; and

(ii)   the sentence or order is available only in respect of offenders below a certain age,
and any reference to serving a sentence of detention is to be construed accordingly: Juries
Act 1974 Sch 1 Pt 2 para 8(b) (Sch 1 as so substituted).

2   In any enactment, 'Secretary of State' means one of Her Majesty's principal Secretaries of State:
see the Interpretation Act 1978 Sch 1. The office of Secretary of State is a unified office, and in
law each Secretary of State is generally capable of performing the functions of all or any of
them: see CONSTITUTIONAL LAW AND HUMAN RIGHTS vol 8(2) (Reissue) PARA 355.

3   Ie an extended sentence under the Criminal Justice Act 2003 s 227 (extended sentence for
certain violent or sexual offences where the offender is aged 18 years or over) or s 228 (extended
sentence for certain violent or sexual offences where the offender is under 18): see SENTENCING
AND DISPOSITION OF OFFENDERS vol 92 (2010) PARA 75.

4   Juries Act 1974 Sch 1 Pt 2 para 6 (as substituted: see note 1).

5   As to the meanings of 'England' and 'Wales' see PARA 804 note 5.

6   Ie a community order under the Criminal Justice Act 2003 s 177, or any of the following orders
(which are no longer available): a community rehabilitation order, a community punishment
order, a community punishment and rehabilitation order, a drug treatment and testing order or
a drug abstinence order. As to community orders see SENTENCING AND DISPOSITION OF
OFFENDERS vol 92 (2010) PARAS 163, 168 et seq.

7   Juries Act 1974 Sch 1 Pt 2 para 7 (as substituted: see note 1). As to service community orders
and overseas community orders see ARMED FORCES.

8   Juries Act 1974 Sch 1 Pt 2 para 5 (as substituted: see note 1). As to the meaning of 'bail in
criminal proceedings' see the Bail Act 1976 s 1; and CRIMINAL LAW, EVIDENCE AND PROCEDURE
vol 11(3) (2006 Reissue) PARA 1166.

806.   Discretion to excuse persons from jury service. If a person summoned
under the Juries Act 1974[1] shows to the satisfaction of the appropriate officer[2]
that there is good reason why he should be excused from attending in pursuance
of the summons, the officer may[3] excuse him from so attending[4]. Without
prejudice to this[5], the appropriate officer must in certain circumstances excuse a
full-time serving member of the armed forces[6]. If the appropriate officer refuses[7],
there is a right of appeal to the court[8], or one of the courts, to which the person
is summoned[9]. Any court before which a person is summoned to attend under
the Juries Act 1974 may excuse him[10].

Where it appears to the appropriate officer that on account of insufficient
understanding of English there is doubt as to the capacity of a person attending
in pursuance of a summons for jury service to act effectively as a juror, the
person may be brought before the judge, who must determine whether or not he
should act as a juror and, if not, must discharge the summons[11].

Where it appears to the appropriate officer that on account of physical
disability there is doubt as to the capacity of a person attending in pursuance of
a summons to act effectively as a juror, the person may be brought before the
judge[12]. The judge must determine whether or not the person should act as a
juror, but he must affirm the summons unless he is of the opinion that the person
will not, on account of his disability, be capable of acting effectively as a juror, in
which case he must discharge the summons[13].

If a person summoned for jury service shows to the satisfaction of the
appropriate officer or the court, or any of the courts, to which he is summoned:

(1)   that he has served, or attended to serve, on a jury[14] within two years
        ending with the service of the summons on him[15]; or

(2)   that the Crown Court or any other court has excused him from service
        for a period which has not terminated[16],

the officer or court must excuse him from attending, or further attending, in
pursuance of the summons[17].

Similar provisions apply to service on a jury at an inquest[18].

1   Ie under the Juries Act 1974 s 2 (see PARA 813) or s 6 (see PARA 817).

2 'Appropriate officer' means such officer as may be designated for the purpose in question in accordance with arrangements made by the Lord Chancellor: Juries Act 1974 s 23(2). The Lord Chancellor's function under s 23(2) is a protected function for the purposes of the Constitutional Reform Act 2005 s 19: see s 19(5), Sch 7 para 4; and CONSTITUTIONAL LAW AND HUMAN RIGHTS. As to the Lord Chancellor see CONSTITUTIONAL LAW AND HUMAN RIGHTS vol 8(2) (Reissue) PARA 477 et seq.

3 Ie subject to the Juries Act 1974 s 9A(1A): see PARA 808.

4 Juries Act 1974 s 9(2) (amended by the Criminal Justice Act 2003 Sch 33 paras 1, 4, Sch 37 Pt 10). Those employed by prosecuting authorities become another category of persons who, as a result of their occupation, qualify for excusal: *R v Abdroikov, R v Green, R v Williamson* [2007] UKHL 37, [2008] 1 All ER 315, [2007] 1 Cr App Rep 280. As to excusal from a particular case, rather than jury service generally, see PARA 824. See also note 16.

5 Ie without prejudice to the Juries Act 1974 s 9(2) (see the text and notes 1–4).

6 See the Juries Act 1974 s 9(2A) (added by the Criminal Justice Act 2003 Sch 33 paras 1–5); and PARA 808.

7 Ie under the Juries Act 1974 s 9(2) or s 9(2A) (see the text and notes 1–6).

8 As to the meaning of 'court' see PARA 804 note 1.

9 See the Juries Act 1974 s 9(3) (amended by the Courts Act 2003 Sch 8 para 172(a), Sch 33 paras 1, 6); and PARA 810.

10 Juries Act 1974 s 9(4). As to excusal by the court see also note 16. As to the deferral of jury service see s 9A; and PARA 807.

11 Juries Act 1974 s 10 (amended by the Criminal Justice and Public Order Act 1994 Sch 11).

12 Juries Act 1974 s 9B(1) (s 9B added by the Criminal Justice and Public Order Act 1994 s 41). For these purposes, 'judge' means any judge of the High Court, or any circuit judge or recorder: Juries Act 1974 s 9B(3) (as so added). As from a day to be appointed, s 9B(3) is substituted so as to define 'judge' for the purposes of s 9B and s 10 as a judge of the High Court, a circuit judge, a District Judge (Magistrates' Courts), or a recorder: s 9B(3) (as so added; and prospectively substituted by the Courts Act 2003 Sch 4 para 3). At the date at which this volume states the law, no such day had been appointed.

13 Juries Act 1974 s 9B(2) (as added: see note 12). See *Re Osman* [1995] 1 WLR 1327, [1996] 1 Cr App Rep 126 (profoundly deaf juror discharged).

14 'Served on a jury' means service on a jury in any court, including any court abolished by the Courts Act 1971 but excluding a coroner's court: Juries Act 1974 s 8(5).

15 Juries Act 1974 s 8(1)(a), (2). The period of two years may be extended by the Lord Chancellor by order made by statutory instrument, subject to annulment in pursuance of a resolution of either House of Parliament; and the order may be varied or revoked by subsequent order: s 8(2). At the date at which this volume states the law, no such order had been made.

16 Juries Act 1974 s 8(1)(b). It is a practice among judges to direct that jurors who have served before them in cases which have occupied an exceptional length of time are excused from further service for a stated period, and even for life (eg exemptions for life were granted by Bigham J in *Tootal, Broadhurst, Lee & Co v London and Lancashire Fire Insurance Co* (1908) Times, 21 May, PC; and by Devlin J in *R v Adams* (1957) Times, 10 April), and to order certificates of exemption to be delivered to them by the officer of the court. In *R v Jameson* (1896) 12 TLR 551 at 580, Lord Russell of Killowen CJ considered that he had the power to do this, but he referred to no authority and rather assumed that there was precedent. The practice is said to have grown up since the Tichborne trials of 1871–1874.

17 Juries Act 1974 s 8(1).

18 See the Coroners Rules 1984, SI 1984/552, rr 49, 51, 52; and CORONERS vol 9(2) (2006 Reissue) PARAS 983–985. There is, however, no equivalent provision concerning the right to appeal against a refusal to excuse from jury service.

807. Deferral of jury service. If a person summoned under the Juries Act 1974[1] shows to the satisfaction of the appropriate officer[2] that there is good reason why his attendance in pursuance of the summons should be deferred, the officer may[3] defer his attendance[4]. If the officer refuses, there is a right of appeal to the court[5], or one of the courts, to which the person is summoned[6]. Any court before which a person is summoned may defer his attendance[7].

The attendance of a person in pursuance of a summons must not, however, be deferred by the appropriate officer under the above statutory power[8] where a deferral of such attendance has previously been made or refused[9] or where the special provisions made with regard to full-time serving members of Her Majesty's naval, military or air forces[10] apply[11].

1   Ie under the Juries Act 1974 s 2 (see PARA 813) or s 6 (see PARA 817).
2   As to the meaning of 'appropriate officer' see PARA 806 note 2.
3   Ie subject to the Juries Act 1974 s 9A(2) (see the text and notes 8–11).
4   Juries Act 1974 s 9A(1) (s 9A added by the Criminal Justice Act 1988 s 120; and the Juries Act 1974 s 9A(1) amended by the Criminal Justice Act 2003 Sch 33 paras 1, 7).
5   As to the meaning of 'court' see PARA 804 note 1.
6   See the Juries Act 1974 s 9A(3) (as added: see note 4); CrimPR 39.2; and PARA 810.
7   Juries Act 1974 s 9A(4) (as added: see note 4). See also *Practice Direction (Criminal Proceedings: Consolidation)* [2002] 3 All ER 904, [2002] 2 Cr App Rep 533 at IV.42.1, CA; *Amendment to the Consolidated Criminal Practice Direction (Jury service)* [2005] 3 All ER 89, sub nom *Practice Direction (Crown Court: Jury Service)* [2005] 1 WLR 1361, CA.
8   Ie under the Juries Act 1974 s 9A(1) (see the text and notes 1–4) or under s 9A(1A) (deferral of attendance of full-time serving member of armed forces: see PARA 808).
9   Ie under the Juries Act 1974 s 9A(1) (see the text and notes 1–4).
10 See the Juries Act 1974 s 9A(1A), (2A), (2B); and PARA 808.
11 Juries Act 1974 s 9A(2), (2A) (s 9A as added (see note 4); s 9A(2) substituted by the Criminal Justice Act 2003 Sch 33 paras 1, 9; and the Juries Act 1974 s 9A(2A) added by the Criminal Justice Act 2003 Sch 33 paras 1, 10). See also PARA 808.

808.   Special provisions for excusal and deferment for full-time serving members of the armed forces. Without prejudice to the general discretionary power of excusal[1], the appropriate officer[2] must excuse a full-time serving member of Her Majesty's naval, military or air forces from attending in pursuance of a summons for jury service if:

(1)   that member's commanding officer certifies to the appropriate officer that it would be prejudicial to the efficiency of the service if that member were to be required to be absent from duty[3]; and

(2)   either: (a) a deferral of his attendance has previously been made or refused under the general discretionary power to defer attendance[4], or made under the provisions described below[5]; or (b) the commanding officer additionally certifies that the position described in head (1) above is likely to remain so for the specified period[6].

If the appropriate officer fails to excuse the member as so required, there is a right of appeal to the court[7], or one of the courts, to which the person is summoned[8].

Without prejudice to the general discretionary power to defer attendance[9], the appropriate officer must:

(i)   defer[10] the attendance of a full-time serving member of Her Majesty's naval, military or air forces in pursuance of a summons if that member's commanding officer certifies to the appropriate officer that it would be prejudicial to the efficiency of the service if that member were to be required to be absent from duty[11]; and

(ii)   for this purpose vary the dates upon which that member is summoned to attend and the summons is to have effect accordingly[12].

If the appropriate officer fails to defer the member's attendance as so required, there is a right of appeal to the court, or one of the courts, to which the person is summoned[13].

1   Ie without prejudice to the Juries Act 1974 s 9(2) (see PARA 806).
2   As to the meaning of 'appropriate officer' see PARA 806 note 2.
3   Juries Act 1974 s 9(2A)(a) (s 9(2A), (2B) added by the Criminal Justice Act 2003 Sch 33 paras 1, 5).
4   Ie under the Juries Act 1974 s 9A(1) (see PARA 807).

5 Ie under the Juries Act 1974 s 9A(1A) (see the text and notes 9–12).

6 Juries Act 1974 s 9(2A)(b) (as added: see note 3); and see s 9A(2A), (2B) (s 9A added by the Criminal Justice Act 1988 s 120; and the Juries Act 1974 s 9A(2A), (2B) added by the Criminal Justice Act 2003 Sch 33 paras 1, 10). The Juries Act 1974 s 9(2A) does not affect the application of s 9(2) (see PARA 806) to a full-time serving member of Her Majesty's naval, military or air forces in a case where he is not entitled to be excused under s 9(2A): s 9(2B) (as added: see note 3).

The period referred to in the text is any period specified for these purposes in guidance issued by the Lord Chancellor under s 9AA (see PARA 809). As to the Lord Chancellor see CONSTITUTIONAL LAW AND HUMAN RIGHTS vol 8(2) (Reissue) PARA 477 et seq.

7 As to the meaning of 'court' see PARA 804 note 1.

8 See the Juries Act 1974 s 9(3); and PARA 810.

9 Ie without prejudice to the Juries Act 1974 s 9A(1) (see PARA 807).

10 The obligation to defer under the Juries Act 1974 s 9A(1A) is displaced if s 9A(2A) or (2B) (see head (2) in the text) applies: s 9A(2) (s 9A as added (see note 6); and s 9A(2) substituted by the Criminal Justice Act 2003 Sch 33 paras 1, 9).

11 Juries Act 1974 s 9A(1A)(a), (1B) (s 9A as added (see note 6); and s 9A(1A)–(1C) added by the Criminal Justice Act 2003 Sch 33 paras 1, 8).

12 Juries Act 1974 s 9A(1A)(b) (as added: see notes 6, 11). Nothing in s 9A(1A), (1B) affects the application of s 9A(1) (see PARA 807) to a full-time serving member of Her Majesty's naval, military or air forces in a case where s 9A(1B) does not apply: s 9A(1C) (as so added).

13 See the Juries Act 1974 s 9A(3); and PARA 810.

809. Requirement to issue guidance relating to excusal and deferment.

The Lord Chancellor[1], after consulting the Lord Chief Justice[2], must issue guidance as to the manner in which the functions of the appropriate officer[3] under the statutory provisions relating to excusal and deferment of jury service[4] are to be exercised[5].

The Lord Chancellor must lay the guidance, and any revised guidance, so issued before each House of Parliament[6] and must arrange for the guidance, or revised guidance, to be published in a manner which he considers appropriate[7].

1 As to the Lord Chancellor see CONSTITUTIONAL LAW AND HUMAN RIGHTS vol 8(2) (Reissue) PARA 477 et seq.

2 The Lord Chief Justice may nominate a judicial office holder (as defined in the Constitutional Reform Act 2005 s 109(4): see CONSTITUTIONAL LAW AND HUMAN RIGHTS) to exercise his functions under the Juries Act 1974 s 9AA: s 9AA(3) (s 9AA added by the Criminal Justice Act 2003 Sch 33 paras 1, 12; and the Juries Act 1974 s 9AA(3) added by the Constitutional Reform Act 2005 Sch 4 paras 77, 79(1), (3)).

3 As to the meaning of 'appropriate officer' see PARA 806 note 2.

4 Ie under the Juries Act 1974 ss 9, 9A: see PARAS 806–808.

5 Juries Act 1974 s 9AA(1) (as added (see note 2); and amended by the Constitutional Reform Act 2005 Sch 4 paras 77, 79(1), (2)). See *Guidance for summoning officers when considering deferral and excusal applications* issued by Her Majesty's Courts Service (June, 2009).

6 Juries Act 1974 s 9AA(2)(a) (as added: see note 2).

7 Juries Act 1974 s 9AA(2)(b) (as added: see note 2).

810. Appeals against refusal to excuse jury service or to defer attendance.

A person summoned for jury service[1] may appeal[2] against any refusal of the appropriate officer[3] to excuse him or to defer his attendance[4]. The appeal must be heard by the Crown Court[5] unless: (1) the appellant is summoned before the High Court in Greater London, in which case the appeal must be heard by a judge of the High Court; or (2) the appellant is summoned before the High Court outside Greater London or before a county court and the appeal has not been decided by the Crown Court before the day on which the appellant is required to attend, in which case it must be heard by the court before which he is summoned to attend[6]. The appeal must be commenced by written notice to the appropriate officer of the Crown Court or of the High Court in Greater London, as the case may be, specifying the matters upon which the appellant relies as providing good reason why he should be excused from attendance in pursuance of the summons or why his attendance should be deferred[7]; and the appeal may not be dismissed unless the appellant has been given an opportunity to make representations[8]. If the appeal is decided in the appellant's absence the appropriate officer must notify him of the decision without delay[9].

There is no right to legal representation on such an appeal; however, the judge has discretion to allow representation[10].

1   Ie under the Juries Act 1974 s 2 (see PARA 813) or s 6 (see PARA 817): see s 9(2) (amended by the Criminal Justice Act 2003 Sch 33 paras 1, 4, Sch 37 Pt 10); and the Juries Act 1974 s 9A(1) (s 9A added by the Criminal Justice Act 1988 s 120; and the Juries Act 1974 s 9A(1) amended by the Criminal Justice Act 2003 Sch 33 paras 1, 7).
2   Juries Act 1974 s 9(3) (amended by the Criminal Justice Act 2003 Sch 33 paras 1, 6); Juries Act 1974 s 9A(3) (as added (see note 1); and amended by the Criminal Justice Act 2003 Sch 33 paras 1, 11); CrimPR 39.1.
3   As to the meaning of 'appropriate officer' see PARA 806 note 2.
4   As to excusal see the Juries Act 1974 s 9(2), (2A); and PARA 806. As to deferral see s 9A(1), (1A); and PARA 807.
5   Crim PR 39.2(2). The appeal may be heard in chambers by a single judge: see Crim PR 16.11(2)(c).
6   Crim PR 39.2(3).
7   Crim PR 39.2(4).
8   Crim PR 39.2(5).
9   Crim PR 39.2(6).
10 *R v Crown Court at Guildford, ex p Siderfin* [1990] 2 QB 683, [1989] 3 All ER 7, DC. Where a conscientious objection to jury service forms the basis of the appeal, the discretion to allow representation should be exercised carefully and sympathetically: *R v Crown Court at Guildford, ex p Siderfin*.

811.   Offences. It is an offence: (1) for a person summoned for jury service[1] to make, or cause or permit to be made on his behalf, any false representation[2] to the appropriate officer[3] with the intention of evading service[4]; (2) for a person to make, or cause to be made, on behalf of another person who has been so summoned any false representation to that officer with the intention of enabling the other person to evade service[5]; (3) when any question is put by that officer to establish qualification[6], for a person to refuse without reasonable cause to answer, or to give an answer knowing it to be false in a material particular[7], or recklessly[8] to give an answer which is false in a material particular[9]; or (4) for a person to serve on a jury knowing that he is disqualified[10]. These offences are punishable on summary conviction[11].

Similar provisions apply to service as a juror at an inquest[12].

1   Ie under the Juries Act 1974 s 2 (see PARA 813) or s 6 (see PARA 817).
2   A statement, although literally true, may be false by reason of what it omits: see *R v Lord Kylsant* [1932] 1 KB 442, CCA; *R v Bishirgian* [1936] 1 All ER 586, CCA.
3   As to the meaning of 'appropriate officer' see PARA 806 note 2.
4   Juries Act 1974 s 20(5)(a).
5   Juries Act 1974 s 20(5)(b).
6   Ie in pursuance of the Juries Act 1974 s 2(5) (see PARA 813).
7   A particular may be material on the mere ground that it renders more credible something else: *R v Tyson* (1867) LR 1 CCR 107.
8   As to the meaning of 'recklessly' see in particular *R v G* [2003] UKHL 50, [2004] 1 AC 1034, [2003] 4 All ER 765 (meaning of recklessness in the criminal law). See further CRIMINAL LAW, EVIDENCE AND PROCEDURE vol 11(1) (2006 Reissue) PARA 11; MISREPRESENTATION AND FRAUD.
9   Juries Act 1974 s 20(5)(c).
10 Juries Act 1974 s 20(5)(d) (substituted by the Criminal Justice Act 2003 Sch 33 paras 1, 14). As to disqualification see PARA 805.

11 The maximum penalty for serving on a jury where disqualified is a fine of not more than level 5 on the standard scale and, in respect of any other offence mentioned in the text, a fine of not more than level 3 on the standard scale: Juries Act 1974 s 20(5) (amended by virtue of the Criminal Justice Act 1982 ss 38, 46). As to the standard scale see SENTENCING AND DISPOSITION OF OFFENDERS vol 92 (2010) PARA 142.

12 See the Coroners Act 1988 s 9(5), (6) (prospectively repealed by the Coroners and Justice Act 2009 Sch 23 Pt 1); the Coroners and Justice Act 2009 Sch 6 Pt 1 (not yet in force); and CORONERS vol 9(2) (2006 Reissue) PARA 982.

3. SUMMONING OF JURORS

812. Selection based on electoral register. As soon as practicable after the publication of any register of electors[1], the electoral registration officer for the area[2] must deliver to such officer as the Lord Chancellor[3] may designate such number of copies of the register as the designated officer may require for the purpose of summoning jurors[4], and on each copy there must be indicated those persons on the register whom the registration officer has ascertained to be, or to have been on a date indicated on the copy, less than 18 or more than 70 years of age[5].

1   This does not include a ward list within the meaning of the City of London (Various Powers) Act 1957 s 4(1) (see LONDON GOVERNMENT vol 29(2) (Reissue) PARA 41): Juries Act 1974 s 3(2). As to the register of electors see ELECTIONS AND REFERENDUMS vol 15(3) (2007 Reissue) PARA 160 et seq.

2   Ie under the Representation of the People Act 1983 (see ELECTIONS AND REFERENDUMS vol 15(3) (2007 Reissue) PARA 154).

3   The Lord Chancellor's function under the Juries Act 1974 s 3(1) is a protected function for the purposes of the Constitutional Reform Act 2005 s 19: see s 19(5), Sch 7 para 4; and CONSTITUTIONAL LAW AND HUMAN RIGHTS. As to the Lord Chancellor see CONSTITUTIONAL LAW AND HUMAN RIGHTS vol 8(2) (Reissue) PARA 477 et seq.

4   As to the summoning of jurors see PARA 813. The designated officer will often be the same as the appropriate officer (see PARA 806 note 2).

5   Juries Act 1974 s 3(1) (amended by the Criminal Justice Act 1988 Sch 15 para 44; and the Representation of the People Act 1983 Sch 8 para 17). See also PARA 804 head (1). If a register to be delivered under the Juries Act 1974 s 3(1) includes any anonymous entries (within the meaning of the Representation of the People Act 1983: see ELECTIONS AND REFERENDUMS vol 15(3) (2007 Reissue) PARA 154) the registration officer must, at the same time as he delivers the register, also deliver to the designated officer any record prepared in pursuance of provision made as mentioned in Sch 2 para 8A (see ELECTIONS AND REFERENDUMS vol 15(3) (2007 Reissue) PARA 127) which relates to such anonymous entries: Juries Act 1974 s 3(1A) (added by the Electoral Administration Act 2006 Sch 1 para 1).

813. Summoning procedure. The Lord Chancellor[1] is responsible for the summoning of jurors to attend for service in the Crown Court, the High Court and county courts[2] and for determining the occasions on which they are to attend when so summoned, and the number to be summoned[3].

Jurors must be summoned by written notice sent by post or delivered by hand[4], accompanied by a notice informing the potential juror of the effect of the statutory provisions[5] relating to qualification for jury service and related matters[6]. When a person is summoned[7] the appropriate officer may at any time put or cause to be put to him such questions as the officer thinks fit in order to establish whether or not the person is qualified for jury service[8].

A certificate signed by the appropriate officer and stating that a written summons, properly addressed and pre-paid, was posted by him is admissible as evidence in any proceedings, without proof of his signature or official character[9].

Records of persons summoned and included in panels[10] must be kept as directed by the Lord Chancellor, who may allow inspection of the records by the public in such circumstances and under such conditions as he may prescribe[11]. A person duly attending in compliance with a summons is entitled to a certificate recording that he has so attended[12].

1   The Lord Chancellor generally acts for these purposes through officers of the court, but also has power to contract out certain functions. The Lord Chancellor may authorise another person, or that person's employees, to perform the Lord Chancellor's functions under the Juries Act 1974 s 2, in so far as they involve the production and posting of jury summonses: see the Contracting Out (Jury Summoning Functions) Order 1999, SI 1999/2128. The Lord Chancellor's functions

under the Juries Act 1974 s 2 are protected functions for the purposes of the Constitutional Reform Act 2005 s 19: see s 19(5), Sch 7 para 4; and CONSTITUTIONAL LAW AND HUMAN RIGHTS. As to the Lord Chancellor see CONSTITUTIONAL LAW AND HUMAN RIGHTS vol 8(2) (Reissue) PARA 477 et seq. The discretion to summon jurors currently rests with the Jury Central Summoning Bureau. As to the power of the High Court, the Crown Court or a county court to summon jurors in exceptional circumstances see PARA 817.

2   As to the summoning of jurors for service on a jury at an inquest see the Coroners Act 1988 s 8 (prospectively repealed by the Coroners and Justice Act 2009 Sch 23 Pt 1); the Coroners and Justice Act 2009 s 8 (not yet in force); the Coroners Rules 1984, SI 1984/552, rr 44–46; and CORONERS vol 9(2) (2006 Reissue) PARA 980.

3   Juries Act 1974 s 2(1). In making arrangements to discharge this duty, the Lord Chancellor must have regard to the convenience of the persons summoned and their respective places of residence, and in particular to the desirability of selecting jurors within reasonable daily travelling distance of the place where they are to attend: s 2(2). Subject to this provision, there is no restriction on the places in England and Wales at which a person may be required to attend or serve on a jury: s 2(3). See further PARA 817. As to the meanings of 'England' and 'Wales' see PARA 804 note 5.

4   Juries Act 1974 s 2(4). For the purposes of the Interpretation Act 1978 s 7 (presumption as to receipt of letter properly addressed and sent by post: see STATUTES vol 44(1) (Reissue) PARA 1388), the notice is regarded as properly addressed if the address is that shown in the electoral register; and a notice so addressed, and delivered by hand to that address, is deemed to have been delivered personally to the person to whom it is addressed unless the contrary is proved: Juries Act 1974 s 2(4) (amended by virtue of the Interpretation Act 1978 s 17(2)(a)). See further CIVIL PROCEDURE vol 11 (2009) PARA 946. As to the offence of failing to attend in compliance with a summons see PARA 818.

5   The relevant statutory provisions are the Juries Act 1974 s 1 (see PARA 804), s 10 (see PARA 806) and s 20(5) (see PARA 811): see s 2(5)(a) (amended by the Criminal Justice Act 2003 Sch 37 Pt 10).

6   Juries Act 1974 s 2(5)(a) (as amended: see note 5). The potential juror must be informed that he may make representations to the appropriate officer (see PARA 806 note 2) with a view to obtaining the withdrawal of the summons, if for any reason he is not qualified for jury service, or wishes or is entitled to be excused: s 2(5)(b). Excusal from jury service must be ordered under s 8 (on grounds relating to previous jury service: see PARA 806) or s 9 (obligatory excusal of service personnel: see PARA 808), and may be ordered under s 9 (discretionary excusal: see PARA 806). In specified circumstances deferral of jury service for service personnel is obligatory under s 9A (see PARA 808), and a juror may be able to obtain a discretionary deferral of jury service under s 9A (see PARA 807) or a discharge of the summons under s 9B (disabled persons: see PARA 806) or s 10 (doubt as to capacity to act effectively as juror: see PARA 806).

7   Ie a summons under the Juries Act 1974 s 2(4) (see the text and note 4) or s 6 (see PARA 817).

8   Juries Act 1974 s 2(5) (amended by the Administration of Justice Act 1982 s 61).

9   Juries Act 1974 s 2(6). The Lord Chancellor may authorise another person, or that person's employees, to sign certificates of posting: see the Contracting Out (Jury Summoning Functions) Order 1999, SI 1999/2128.

10 As to panels see PARA 816.

11 Juries Act 1974 s 8(3).

12 Juries Act 1974 s 8(4). Similar provisions apply to service on a jury at an inquest: see the Coroners Rules 1984, SI 1984/552, r 50; and CORONERS vol 9(2) (2006 Reissue) PARA 986.

814. Withdrawal or alteration of summonses.

If it appears to the appropriate officer[1], at any time before the day on which any person summoned for jury service[2] is first to attend, that his attendance is unnecessary or can be dispensed with on any particular day or days, the officer may withdraw or alter the summons by notice served in the same way as a notice of summons[3].

1   As to the meaning of 'appropriate officer' see PARA 806 note 2.
2   Ie under the Juries Act 1974 s 2 (see PARA 813).
3   Juries Act 1974 s 4. As to service see PARA 813 text and note 4. Similar provisions apply to service on a jury at an inquest: see the Coroners Rules 1984, SI 1984/552, r 47; and CORONERS vol 9(2) (2006 Reissue) PARA 980.

815.   Attendance and service.   A person summoned for jury service[1] must attend for so many days as may be directed by the summons or by the appropriate officer[2], and is liable to serve on any jury in the Crown Court, the High Court or any county court at the place to which he is summoned, or in the vicinity[3].

1   Ie under the Juries Act 1974 s 2 (see PARA 813) or s 6 (see PARA 817).

2   As to the meaning of 'appropriate officer' see PARA 806 note 2.

3   Juries Act 1974 s 7. This is expressed to be subject to the provisions of the Juries Act 1974. As to the offence of failure to attend in compliance with a summons see PARA 818.

816.   Panels.   The arrangements to be made by the Lord Chancellor[1] include the preparation of lists (known as 'panels') of persons summoned as jurors[2]. The information to be included in panels, the court[3] sittings for which they are prepared, their division into parts or sets[4], their enlargement or amendment and all other matters relating to the contents and form of the panels are to be such as the Lord Chancellor may from time to time direct[5].

A party to proceedings in which jurors are or may be called on to try an issue, and any person acting on his behalf, is entitled to reasonable facilities for inspecting the panel from which the jurors are or will be drawn[6]. If it thinks fit, the court may also at any time afford to any person facilities for inspecting the panel[7].

1   Ie under the Juries Act 1974. As to the Lord Chancellor's duties under the Juries Act 1974 see s 2(1)–(2); and PARA 813. The Lord Chancellor's function under s 5(1) is a protected function for the purposes of the Constitutional Reform Act 2005 s 19: see s 19(5), Sch 7 para 4; and CONSTITUTIONAL LAW AND HUMAN RIGHTS. As to the Lord Chancellor see CONSTITUTIONAL LAW AND HUMAN RIGHTS vol 8(2) (Reissue) PARA 477 et seq.

2   Juries Act 1974 s 5(1). As to summoning see s 2 (see PARA 813) and s 6 (see PARA 817).

A trial judge has no power to interfere with the composition of a jury panel in order to secure a jury of a particular ethnic origin or from a particular section of the community: *R v Ford* [1989] QB 868, [1989] 3 All ER 445, CA. Nor has the judge power to order a jury to be summoned from outside the normal catchment area: *R v Tarrant* [1998] Crim LR 342, CA. In *R v Smith (Lance Percival)* [2003] EWCA Crim 283, [2003] 1 WLR 2229, it was held that the random process of jury selection under the Juries Act 1974 was not incompatible with the defendant's right to a fair hearing by an independent and impartial court under the Convention for the Protection of Human Rights and Fundamental Freedoms (Rome, 4 November 1950; TS 71 (1953); Cmd 8969) art 6 (see CONSTITUTIONAL LAW AND HUMAN RIGHTS vol 8(2) (Reissue) PARA 134 et seq). Contrast *Rojas v Berllaque (A-G for Gibraltar Intervening)* [2003] UKPC 76, [2004] 1 WLR 201 (where an all-male jury compiled in accordance with a Gibraltar ordinance, under which service was compulsory for males and voluntary for females, was held not to satisfy the constitutional requirement of a fair trial by an independent and impartial court because it was discriminatory between males and females). The Convention is commonly referred to as the European Convention on Human Rights and is enshrined in the Human Rights Act 1998 Sch 1: see CONSTITUTIONAL LAW AND HUMAN RIGHTS vol 8(2) (Reissue) PARA 122 et seq.

3   As to the meaning of 'court' see PARA 804 note 1.

4   Ie whether according to the day of first attendance or otherwise.

5   Juries Act 1974 s 5(1). The Lord Chancellor must consult the Lord Chief Justice before giving any such direction: s 5(5) (s 5(5), (6) added by the Constitutional Reform Act 2005 Sch 4 paras 77, 78). The Lord Chief Justice may nominate a judicial office holder (as defined in the Constitutional Reform Act 2005 s 109(4): see CONSTITUTIONAL LAW AND HUMAN RIGHTS) to exercise his functions under the Juries Act 1974 s 5: s 5(6) (as so added). At the outset of the trial the judge should warn the members of the jury: (1) that they must try the case on the evidence that they hear in court and on nothing else; (2) that they must not discuss the case with others outside court, such as members of their family; and (3) that they should not conduct their own private research, eg using the internet: *R v Marshall* [2007] EWCA Crim 35, [2007] All ER (D) 76 (Jan).

6   Juries Act 1974 s 5(2). The right is not exercisable after the close of the trial by jury or after the
    time when it is no longer possible for there to be a trial by jury: s 5(3).
7   Juries Act 1974 s 5(4).

817. Summoning in exceptional circumstances. If it appears to the court[1] that a jury to try an issue before it will be, or probably will be, incomplete[2], the court may, if it thinks fit, require any persons who are in, or in the vicinity of, the court to be summoned without written notice[3] for jury service up to the number needed[4] to make up a full jury[5]. Their names must be added to the panel and the court must proceed as if they had been included in the panel in the first instance[6].

1   As to the meaning of 'court' see PARA 804 note 1.
2   At common law it was not permissible to constitute a jury entirely of 'talesmen' (as jurors
    summoned under the procedure described in this paragraph were known) in the absence of
    jurors duly empanelled (*R v Solomon* [1958] 1 QB 203, [1957] 3 All ER 497, CCA). The word
    'incomplete' in the Juries Act 1974 s 6(1) suggests that a jury containing 'talesman' must include
    at least one juror who has been summoned in the usual way.
3   As to the need for notice generally see PARA 813 text and note 4.
4   Ie after allowing for any who may not be qualified under the Juries Act 1974 s 1 (see PARA 804),
    and for excusals (see PARAS 806, 808) and challenges (see PARA 825 et seq).
5   Juries Act 1974 s 6(1) (amended by the Criminal Justice Act 1988 Sch 15 para 45). As to the
    number of persons required for a jury see PARA 803. This procedure may be exercised before or
    after balloting has begun: see the Juries Act 1974 s 11(2); and PARA 823. Similar provisions
    apply to service on a jury at an inquest: see the Coroners Rules 1984, SI 1984/552, r 48; and
    CORONERS vol 9(2) (2006 Reissue) PARA 981.
6   Juries Act 1974 s 6(2).

818. Non-attendance by juror. A person who:

(1)   is duly summoned for jury service[1] and fails to attend on any day on which he is required to attend by the summons or by the appropriate officer[2] in compliance with the summons[3]; or

(2)   after attending in pursuance of a summons, is not available when called on to serve as a juror, or is unfit for service by reason of drink or drugs[4],

is liable to a fine[5]. Such an offence is punishable either on summary conviction or as if it were criminal contempt of court committed in the face of the court[6].

A person is not liable to be punished for such an offence if he shows some reasonable cause for his failure to comply with the summons or for not being available when called on to serve[7].

1   Ie under the Juries Act 1974 s 2 (see PARA 813) or s 6 (see PARA 817).
2   As to the meaning of 'appropriate officer' see PARA 806 note 2.
3   Juries Act 1974 s 20(1)(a). This does not apply to a person summoned, otherwise than under s 6
    (see PARA 817), unless the summons was duly served on him on a date not later than 14 days
    before the date fixed by the summons for his first attendance: s 20(3).
4   Juries Act 1974 s 20(1)(b).
5   Juries Act 1974 s 20(1) (amended by virtue of the Criminal Justice Act 1982 ss 38, 46). Such a
    fine must not exceed level 3 on the standard scale: Juries Act 1974 s 20(1). As to the standard
    scale see SENTENCING AND DISPOSITION OF OFFENDERS vol 92 (2010) PARA 142. These
    provisions have effect subject to the provisions of the Juries Act 1974 as to the withdrawal or
    alteration of a summons (see PARA 814) and as to the granting of any excusal (see PARAS 806,
    808) or deferral (see PARA 807): s 20(4) (amended by the Criminal Justice Act 1988 Sch 15
    para 46). As to offences in connection with failure to attend to serve on a jury at an inquest see
    the Coroners Act 1988 s 10 (prospectively repealed by the Coroners and Justice Act 2009 Sch 23
    Pt 1); the Coroners and Justice Act 2009 Sch 6 Pt 1 (not yet in force); and CORONERS vol 9(2)
    (2006 Reissue) PARA 987.
6   Juries Act 1974 s 20(2). As to the minimum requirements for a fair trial where a judge decides to
    deal with the case as if it were a contempt of court in the face of the court see *R v Dodds* [2002]
    EWCA Crim 1328, [2003] 1 Cr App Rep 60. As to criminal contempt of court see CONTEMPT
    OF COURT vol 9(1) (Reissue) PARA 404 et seq.

7 See the Juries Act 1974 s 20(4) (as amended: see note 5). See *R v Tullet* [2008] EWCA Crim 2394, [2008] All ER (D) 238 (Oct), sub nom *R v DA* [2009] Crim LR 289 (where a juror gives explanation for non-attendance which is capable of being 'reasonable cause' (in this case, verbal abuse by other jurors), the judge or magistrates must address the explanation in determining whether an offence has been committed under the Juries Act 1974 s 20(1)).

4. PROCEEDINGS BEFORE JURIES

(1) NEED FOR JURY

819. Trial juries and juries of inquiry. Trial juries are only used in the Crown Court, High Court or a county court[1]. Juries of inquiry are only used at an inquest[2].

1   As to trial by jury see PARA 801 note 1. As to the meaning of 'court' for the purposes of the Juries Act 1974 see PARA 804 note 1.
2   See the Coroners Act 1988 s 8(2) (prospectively repealed by the Coroners and Justice Act 2009 Sch 23 Pt 1); the Coroners and Justice Act 2009 s 8(3) (not yet in force); and CORONERS vol 9(2) (2006 Reissue) PARAS 978–987.

820. When juries are required. Juries are or are not required according to the circumstances.

Generally, in causes in which issue is joined between the Crown and a person charged upon indictment, a jury is sworn to try the issues[1]. However, certain trials on indictment may now take place without a jury[2]. Where a defendant in the Crown Court advances a special plea of autrefois acquit or autrefois convict it was formerly for a jury to try that issue, but the issue is now decided by the judge sitting without a jury[3]. Where a court has determined that a defendant in the Crown Court is unfit to stand trial, the question of whether the defendant did the act or made the omission charged is determined by a jury[4].

In the Queen's Bench Division there is a right to a jury if:

(1)   a charge of fraud[5] is made against the party applying for a jury; or
(2)   a claim in respect of libel, slander, malicious prosecution or false imprisonment is in issue; or
(3)   any question or issue of a kind prescribed[6] is raised,

unless the court or a judge is of the opinion that the trial requires a prolonged examination of documents or accounts or any scientific or local investigation which cannot conveniently be made with a jury[7]. In all other cases in the Queen's Bench Division it is in the discretion of the court or a judge to order trial with a jury[8], but in practice such an order is seldom made.

In the Chancery Division a jury is never required[9], nor used. The same is true in the Family Division.

Trial by jury in a county court is not permitted in respect of specified proceedings[10]. In all other proceedings in a county court the trial must be without a jury unless the court otherwise orders on an application by a party[11]. Where, on any such application, the court is satisfied that there is in issue:

(a)   a charge of fraud[12] against the party applying for a jury; or
(b)   a claim in respect of libel, slander, malicious prosecution or false imprisonment; or
(c)   any question or issue of a kind prescribed[13],

the action must be tried with a jury, unless the court or a judge is of the opinion that the trial requires a prolonged examination of documents or accounts or any scientific or local investigation which cannot conveniently be made with a jury[14]. Trial by jury is now rare in county courts.

In certain circumstances a jury is required at an inquest[15].

1   For the procedure for the indictment of offenders see CRIMINAL LAW, EVIDENCE AND PROCEDURE vol 11(3) (2006 Reissue) PARA 1202 et seq.

2 See the Criminal Justice Act 2003 Pt 7 (ss 43–50); and PARA 821. As to the commencement of Pt 7 see PARA 821 note 1.

3 See the Criminal Justice Act 1988 s 122. As to pleas of autrefois acquit or autrefois convict see CRIMINAL LAW, EVIDENCE AND PROCEDURE vol 11(3) (2006 Reissue) PARAS 1273–1275.

4 See the Criminal Procedure (Insanity) Act 1964 ss 4, 4A; and CRIMINAL LAW, EVIDENCE AND PROCEDURE vol 11(3) (2006 Reissue) PARA 1265. If an issue arises as to whether a defendant is mute of malice or by visitation of God, that issue must be determined by a jury: see *R v Schleter* (1866) 10 Cox CC 409; *R v Sharp* [1960] 1 QB 357n, [1958] 1 All ER 62n; and CRIMINAL LAW, EVIDENCE AND PROCEDURE vol 11(3) (2006 Reissue) PARA 1264.

5 An allegation of robbery is not a charge of fraud: *Barclays Bank Ltd v Cole* [1967] 2 QB 738, [1966] 3 All ER 948, CA. See also *Stafford Winfield Cook & Partners Ltd v Winfield* [1980] 3 All ER 759, [1981] 1 WLR 458 (for a case to come within the Senior Courts Act 1981 s 69(1) (see the text and note 7) fraud has to be an issue between the parties in the sense of being a question which has to be decided in order to determine the rights of the parties). As to applications by the prosecution for dispensing with a jury in trials on indictment for serious or complex fraud see the Criminal Justice Act 2003 s 43 (not yet in force); and PARA 821.

6 Ie prescribed under the Senior Courts Act 1981 s 69(1): see the text and note 7. At the date at which this volume states the law, no question or issue had been prescribed for these purposes.

7 Senior Courts Act 1981 s 69(1). The Senior Courts Act 1981 was previously known as the Supreme Court Act 1981 and was renamed by the Constitutional Reform Act 2005 s 59(5), Sch 11 Pt 1 as from 1 October 2009: see the Constitutional Reform Act 2005 (Commencement No 11) Order 2009, SI 2009/1604; and COURTS.

See *Racz v Home Office* [1994] 2 AC 45, [1994] 1 All ER 97, HL (there is no logical similarity between the torts enumerated in the Senior Courts Act 1981 s 69(1), therefore the similarity of some other tort to any of those torts is not a factor which has to be taken into account by the court in determining whether it is appropriate to rebut the presumption against jury trial created by s 69(3) (see the text and note 8)).

As to when a libel claim is suitable for jury trial see *Rothermere v Times Newspapers Ltd* [1973] 1 All ER 1013, [1973] 1 WLR 448, CA; *Goldsmith v Pressdram Ltd* [1987] 3 All ER 485, [1988] 1 WLR 64n, CA; *Viscount De L'Isle v Times Newspapers Ltd* [1987] 3 All ER 499, [1988] 1 WLR 49, CA; *Beta Construction Ltd v Channel Four Television Co Ltd* [1990] 2 All ER 1012, [1990] 1 WLR 1042, CA. The fact that a case involves issues of integrity and honour, not merely credibility, might be a weighty consideration in ordering trial by jury at the instance of the party whose integrity and honour were impugned, but is not a sufficient ground for ordering a jury trial against his wishes at the instance of the other party: *Williams v Beesley* [1973] 3 All ER 144, [1973] 1 WLR 1295, HL.

As to when the right to a jury arises in a case concerning allegations of malicious prosecution, misfeasance in public office and conspiracy see *Taylor v Anderton (Police Complaints Authority intervening)* [1995] 2 All ER 420, [1995] 1 WLR 447, CA. It has been held that in determining whether a case was suitable for jury trial three issues had to be identified: (1) whether there would be a prolonged examination of documents; (2) if so, whether it could be conveniently made with a jury; and (3) if not, whether the court should nevertheless exercise its discretion to order trial with a jury: see *Phillips v Metropolitan Police Comr* [2003] EWCA Civ 382, [2003] 21 LS Gaz R 30 (allegations included false imprisonment and malicious prosecution; the necessity for a prolonged examination of the documents in the case was the decisive factor which made it unsuitable for jury trial).

As to the appropriateness of a jury at preliminary hearing see *Armstrong v Times Newspapers Ltd* [2006] EWCA Civ 519, [2006] 1 WLR 2462, (2006) Times, 7 July.

8 See the Senior Courts Act 1981 s 69(3). When a judge exercises his discretion and takes all the relevant considerations into account, the burden is on the party contesting the exercise of that discretion to show that the judge was wrong: *Hodges v Harland and Wolff Ltd* [1965] 1 All ER 1086, [1965] 1 WLR 523, CA. See also CIVIL PROCEDURE vol 12 (2009) PARA 1132.

A jury will not be ordered in claims for personal injury unless there are exceptional circumstances: *Ward v James* [1966] 1 QB 273, [1965] 1 All ER 563, CA. Trial by jury is normally inappropriate for any personal injury claim in so far as the jury would be required to assess compensatory damages, because the jury would be unlikely to achieve compatibility with the conventional scale of awards: *H v Ministry of Defence* [1991] 2 QB 103, [1991] 2 All ER 834, CA.

For further examples as to the way in which the discretion has been exercised see *Hodges v Harland and Wolff Ltd* [1965] 1 All ER 1086, [1965] 1 WLR 523, CA; *Singh v London Underground* (1990) Independent, 25 April.

9 See *Stafford Winfield Cook & Partners v Winfield* [1980] 3 All ER 759, [1981] 1 WLR 458.

10 See the County Courts Act 1984 s 66(1); and CIVIL PROCEDURE vol 12 (2009) PARA 1132.

11 See the County Courts Act 1984 s 66(2); and CIVIL PROCEDURE vol 12 (2009) PARA 1132.

12 See note 5.

13 Ie prescribed under the County Courts Act 1984 s 66(3): see the text and note 14. At the date at which this volume states the law, no question or issue had been prescribed for these purposes.

14 See the County Courts Act 1984 s 66(3); and CIVIL PROCEDURE vol 12 (2009) PARA 1132.

15 See the Coroners Act 1988 s 8(3) (prospectively repealed by the Coroners and Justice Act 2009 Sch 23 Pt 1); the Coroners and Justice Act 2009 s 7(2) (not yet in force); and CORONERS vol 9(2) (2006 Reissue) PARA 978 et seq.

821. Trials on indictment without a jury. Provision is made[1] so that certain kinds of criminal trials that previously[2] took place on indictment in the Crown Court before a judge and jury may be conducted (or continued) by a judge sitting alone[3].

As from a day to be appointed, the prosecution may apply to a judge of the Crown Court for the trial to be conducted without a jury where one or more defendants is or are to be tried on indictment for one or more offences, and notice that the evidence reveals a case of serious or complex fraud has been given[4] in respect of that offence or those offences[5]. If such an application is made and the judge is satisfied that the complexity of the trial or the length of the trial (or both) is likely to make the trial so burdensome to the members of a jury hearing the trial that the interests of justice require that serious consideration should be given to the question of whether the trial should be conducted without a jury, then he may make an order that the trial is to be conducted without a jury; but if he is not so satisfied he must refuse the application[6].

Applications may now be made for a trial to be conducted by a judge sitting alone where there is evidence of jury tampering. The prosecution may apply to a judge of the Crown Court for the trial to be conducted without a jury where one or more defendants is or are to be tried on indictment for one or more offences[7]. If such an application is made and the judge is satisfied that:

(1)   there is evidence of a real and present danger that jury tampering would take place[8]; and

(2)   notwithstanding any steps (including the provision of police protection) which might reasonably be taken to prevent jury tampering, the likelihood that it would take place would be so substantial as to make it necessary in the interests of justice for the trial to be conducted without a jury[9],

he must make an order that the trial is to be conducted without a jury; but if he is not so satisfied he must refuse the application[10].

The judge also has power to discharge a jury during a trial because of jury tampering[11]. Before taking any steps to discharge the jury, a judge who is minded during a trial on indictment to discharge the jury because jury tampering appears to have taken place must inform the parties that he is minded to discharge the jury, inform the parties of the grounds on which he is so minded, and allow the parties an opportunity to make representations[12]. Where the judge, after considering any such representations, discharges the jury, he may make an order that the trial is to continue without a jury if, but only if, he is satisfied that jury tampering has taken place and that to continue the trial without a jury would be fair to the defendant or defendants[13]. However, if he considers that it is necessary in the interests of justice for the trial to be terminated, the judge must terminate the trial[14]. Where the judge so terminates the trial, he may make an order that any new trial which is to take place must be conducted without a jury if he is satisfied in respect of the new trial that the conditions in heads (1) and (2) are both likely to be fulfilled[15]. Appeals from such orders[16] lie to the Court of Appeal[17].

The effect of an order under these provisions[18] is that the trial to which the order relates is to be conducted or continued without a jury[19]. Where a trial is conducted or continued without a jury, the court is to have all the powers, authorities and jurisdiction which the court would have had if the trial had been conducted or continued with a jury (including power to determine any question and to make any finding which would be required to be determined or made by a jury)[20]. Where a trial is conducted or continued without a jury and the court convicts a defendant, the court must give a judgment which states the reasons for the conviction at, or as soon as reasonably practicable after, the time of the conviction[21].

Rules of court may make such provision as appears to the authority making them to be necessary or expedient for these purposes[22].

1   Ie by the Criminal Justice Act 2003 Pt 7 (ss 43–50). Part 7 is to be brought into force by order made under s 336(3). At the date at which this volume states the law, only ss 44–49 had been brought into force: see the Criminal Justice Act 2003 (Commencement No 2 and Saving Provisions) Order 2004, SI 2004/81, art 4; and the Criminal Justice Act 2003 (Commencement No 13 and Transitional Provision) Order 2006, SI 2006/1835.

2   See PARA 820.

3   See the Criminal Justice Act 2003 Pt 7; and the text and notes 4–22. Nothing in Pt 7 affects the requirement under the Criminal Procedure (Insanity) Act 1964 s 4A (see CRIMINAL LAW, EVIDENCE AND PROCEDURE vol 11(3) (2006 Reissue) PARA 1265) that any question, finding or verdict mentioned in that provision be determined, made or returned by a jury: Criminal Justice Act 2003 s 48(6) (amended by the Domestic Violence, Crime and Victims Act 2004 Sch 10 para 60).

4   Ie under the Crime and Disorder Act 1998 s 51B: see CRIMINAL LAW, EVIDENCE AND PROCEDURE vol 11(3) (2006 Reissue) PARA 1134.

5   Criminal Justice Act 2003 s 43(1), (2) (not yet in force). At the date at which this volume states the law, no day had been appointed for the commencement of s 43. See note 1.
    In the case of an application under s 43, the application must be determined at a preparatory hearing (within the meaning of the Criminal Justice Act 1987: see CRIMINAL LAW, EVIDENCE AND PROCEDURE vol 11(3) (2006 Reissue) PARA 1250): Criminal Justice Act 2003 s 45(1)(a), (2). The parties to a preparatory hearing at which such an application is to be determined must be given an opportunity to make representations with respect to the application: s 45(3). As to procedure and appeals see further CRIMINAL LAW, EVIDENCE AND PROCEDURE vol 11(3) (2006 Reissue) PARA 1247 et seq.

6   Criminal Justice Act 2003 s 43(3), (5) (not yet in force). In deciding whether or not he is satisfied that the condition is fulfilled, the judge must have regard to any steps which might reasonably be taken to reduce the complexity or length of the trial, but a step is not to be regarded as reasonable if it would significantly disadvantage the prosecution: s 43(6), (7) (not yet in force). The judge must not make an order under s 43 for trial without a jury without the approval of the Lord Chief Justice or a judge nominated by him: s 43(4) (not yet in force).

7   Criminal Justice Act 2003 s 44(1), (2). In the case of an application under s 44, the application must be determined at a preparatory hearing (within the meaning of the Criminal Procedure and Investigations Act 1996 Pt 3 (ss 28–38): see CRIMINAL LAW, EVIDENCE AND PROCEDURE vol 11(3) (2006 Reissue) PARA 1250): Criminal Justice Act 2003 s 45(1)(b), (2). The parties to a preparatory hearing at which such an application is to be determined must be given an opportunity to make representations with respect to the application: s 45(3). As to procedure and appeals see further CRIMINAL LAW, EVIDENCE AND PROCEDURE vol 11(3) (2006 Reissue) PARA 1247.

8   Criminal Justice Act 2003 s 44(4). The following are examples of cases where there may be evidence of a real and present danger that jury tampering would take place: (1) a case where the trial is a retrial and the jury in the previous trial was discharged because jury tampering had taken place; (2) a case where jury tampering has taken place in previous criminal proceedings involving the defendant or any of the defendants; (3) a case where there has been intimidation, or attempted intimidation, of any person who is likely to be a witness in the trial: s 44(6). The list in s 44(6) is not exhaustive or exclusive; just because particular facts fall within s 44(6) does

not conclusively establish the condition in s 44(4), nor does it create a presumption in favour of trial without a jury; the examples in s 44(6) indicate that the evidence which may demonstrate the statutory danger is not to be confined to evidence which would be admissible at the defendant's trial: see *R v T* [2009] EWCA Crim 1035, [2009] 3 All ER 1002, sub nom *R v Twomey* [2009] 2 Cr App Rep 412 (where it was held that the trial should be conducted without a jury because of the danger of jury tampering). The standard of proof for the purposes of the Criminal Justice Act 2003 s 44(4), (5) is the criminal standard: see *R v T* [2009] EWCA Crim 1035, [2009] 3 All ER 1002, sub nom *R v Twomey* [2009] 2 Cr App Rep 412.

9　　Criminal Justice Act 2003 s 44(5). As to the standard of proof see note 8. Section 44(5) requires that, after making due allowance for any reasonable steps which might address or minimise the danger of jury tampering, the judge should be sure that there would be a sufficiently high likelihood of jury tampering to make a judge-alone trial necessary; relevant matters for consideration are the feasibility of the measures, the cost of providing them, the logistical difficulties that they might give rise to, and the anticipated duration of any necessary precautions: *R v T* [2009] EWCA Crim 1035, [2009] 3 All ER 1002, sub nom *R v Twomey* [2009] 2 Cr App Rep 412.

10　Criminal Justice Act 2003 s 44(3).

11　See the Criminal Justice Act 2003 s 46; and see also *R v T* [2009] EWCA Crim 1035, [2009] 3 All ER 1002, sub nom *R v Twomey* [2009] 2 Cr App Rep 412.

12　Criminal Justice Act 2003 s 46(1), (2).

13　Criminal Justice Act 2003 s 46(3). Save in exceptional circumstances, the judge should order that the trial continue without a jury; the fact that the judge has been invited to consider material covered by public interest immunity principles should not normally lead to self-disqualification: *R v T* [2009] EWCA Crim 1035, [2009] 3 All ER 1002, sub nom *R v Twomey* [2009] 2 Cr App Rep 412.

14　Criminal Justice Act 2003 s 46(4).

15　Criminal Justice Act 2003 s 46(5). This provision is without prejudice to any other power that the judge may have on terminating the trial: s 46(6). Subject to s 46(5), nothing in s 46 affects the application of s 43 (see the text and notes 4–6) or s 44 (see the text and notes 7–10) in relation to any new trial which takes place following the termination of the trial: s 46(7).

16　Ie orders under the Criminal Justice Act 2003 s 46(3) (see the text and note 13) or s 46(5) (see the text and note 15).

17　Criminal Justice Act 2003 s 47(1). Such an appeal may be brought only with the leave of the judge or the Court of Appeal: s 47(2). An order from which an appeal under s 47 lies is not to take effect: (1) before the expiration of the period for bringing an appeal under s 47; or (2) if such an appeal is brought, before the appeal is finally disposed of or abandoned: s 47(3). On the termination of the hearing of an appeal under s 47, the Court of Appeal may confirm or revoke the order: s 47(4). Subject to rules of court made under the Senior Courts Act 1981 s 53(1) (power by rules to distribute business of Court of Appeal between its civil and criminal divisions: see COURTS vol 10 (Reissue) PARAS 639–640), the jurisdiction of the Court of Appeal under the Criminal Justice Act 2003 s 47 is to be exercised by the criminal division of that court, and references in s 47 to the Court of Appeal are to be construed as references to that division: s 47(5) (amended by the Constitutional Reform Act 2005 Sch 11 para 1(2)). The Senior Courts Act 1981 was previously known as the Supreme Court Act 1981 and was renamed by the Constitutional Reform Act 2005 s 59(5), Sch 11 Pt 1 as from 1 October 2009: see the Constitutional Reform Act 2005 (Commencement No 11) Order 2009, SI 2009/1604; and COURTS.

18　Ie the Criminal Justice Act 2003 Pt 7.

19　Criminal Justice Act 2003 s 48(1), (2).

20　Criminal Justice Act 2003 s 48(3). Except where the context otherwise requires, any reference in an enactment to a jury, the verdict of a jury or the finding of a jury is to be read, in relation to a trial conducted or continued without a jury, as a reference to the court, the verdict of the court or the finding of the court: s 48(4).

21　Criminal Justice Act 2003 s 48(5)(a).

22　Criminal Justice Act 2003 s 49(1). Without limiting s 49(1), rules of court may in particular make provision for time limits within which applications under Pt 7 must be made or within which other things in connection with Pt 7 must be done: s 49(2). Nothing in s 49 is to be taken as affecting the generality of any enactment conferring powers to make rules of court: s 49(3). At the date at which this volume states the law, no rules had been made under s 49.

822. Trial by jury of sample counts only. The prosecution may apply to a judge of the Crown Court for a trial on indictment to take place on the basis that the trial of some but not all of the counts included in the indictment may be conducted without a jury[1]. The judge may make an order, if satisfied that certain conditions are met, for the counts included in the indictment to be conducted without a jury[2]. The effect of such an order is that where a defendant is found guilty by a jury on a count which can be regarded as a sample of other counts to be tried in those proceedings, those other counts may be tried without a jury in those proceedings[3]. Where the trial of a count is conducted without a jury, and the court convicts the defendant, the court must give a judgment which states the reasons for the conviction as soon as reasonably practicable[4].

1   See the Domestic Violence, Crime and Victims Act 2004 s 17; and CRIMINAL LAW, EVIDENCE AND PROCEDURE vol 11(3) (2006 Reissue) PARA 1285.
2   See the Domestic Violence, Crime and Victims Act 2004 s 17; and CRIMINAL LAW, EVIDENCE AND PROCEDURE vol 11(3) (2006 Reissue) PARA 1285.
3   See the Domestic Violence, Crime and Victims Act 2004 s 19; and CRIMINAL LAW, EVIDENCE AND PROCEDURE vol 11(3) (2006 Reissue) PARA 1285.
4   See the Domestic Violence, Crime and Victims Act 2004 s 18; and CRIMINAL LAW, EVIDENCE AND PROCEDURE vol 11(3) (2006 Reissue) PARA 1285.

(2) SELECTION OF JURY

823. The ballot. The jury to try an issue before a court is selected by ballot in open court from the panel[1], or part of the panel, of jurors summoned[2] to attend at the time and place in question[3].

The jury selected by any one ballot must generally try only one issue[4], but it may try two or more issues if the trial of the second or last issue begins within 24 hours from the time when the jury is constituted[5]. On the trial of the second or any subsequent issue the court may, instead of proceeding with the same jury in its entirety, order any juror to withdraw if the court considers he could be justly challenged or excused or if the parties to the proceedings consent; and the juror to replace him must be selected by ballot in open court[6].

1   As to panels see PARA 816.
      Formerly, it was the invariable practice of the courts for the names of the jurors selected by ballot to be read out in open court. Where names are read out, it is not necessary that the names should be called in the order in which they stand in the panel: *Mansell v R* (1857) Dears & B 375, Ex Ch. If the clerk of the court calls into the jury box AB, whose name is in the panel, and YZ, whose name is also in the panel, goes into the jury box by mistake and is sworn in the name of AB and sits with the other jurors at the trial of a defendant, and the defendant is convicted, the mistake is not a ground for quashing the conviction (*R v Mellor* (1858) Dears & B 468, CCR) where it is not shown that, but for the misnomer, the defendant would have successfully challenged the juror (*R v Bottomley* (1922) 16 Cr App Rep 184, 127 LT 847, CCA). Where, however, a person not called as a juror personates a juror and sits in his place, the trial is a nullity and a venire de novo (see CRIMINAL LAW, EVIDENCE AND PROCEDURE vol 11(4) (2006 Reissue) PARA 1895) will be ordered: *R v Wakefield* [1918] 1 KB 216, 13 Cr App Rep 56, CCA.
      Now, however, where there is a risk of juror interference then jurors may be assigned numbers which are called out: *R v Comerford* [1998] 1 All ER 823, [1998] 1 WLR 191, CA.
2   As to summoning of jurors see PARA 813.
3   Juries Act 1974 s 11(1). The power of summoning jurors under s 6 (see PARA 817) may be exercised after balloting has begun, as well as earlier; if exercised after balloting has begun, the court may dispense with balloting for persons summoned under s 6: s 11(2).

4   Juries Act 1974 s 11(4). However, any juror is liable to be selected on more than one ballot: s 11(4). See *R v B* [2008] EWCA Crim 1997, [2009] 1 WLR 1545, [2009] 1 Cr App Rep 261 (the Juries Act 1974 s 11(4) does not prevent a jury from determining whether one defendant was guilty of a charge in an indictment at the same time as determining whether a co-defendant who has been determined to be unfit to stand trial did the act charged against him on the same indictment).

5 Juries Act 1974 s 11(5)(a). In a criminal case beginning with a special plea (ie a plea to the jurisdiction or a plea of pardon), the same jury may try the special plea as well as the general issue (see CRIMINAL LAW, EVIDENCE AND PROCEDURE vol 11(3) (2006 Reissue) PARA 1269 et seq): Juries Act 1974 s 11(5)(c).

6 Juries Act 1974 s 11(6) (amended by the Domestic Violence, Crime and Victims Act 2004 Sch 10 para 8(1), (3), Sch 11). This provision is subject to the Juries Act 1974 s 11(2) (see note 3): see s 11(6) (as so amended).

824. Composition of jury. Traditionally, a jury consists of 12 persons, but this is no longer always the case[1].

It may be appropriate for a judge to excuse a juror from a particular case if he is personally concerned in the facts of the particular case, or closely connected with a party to the proceedings or with a prospective witness[2].

An unqualified juror[3], although he is not challenged[4] by either party, may object to serve and, if the court finds that he is not qualified, he will be ordered to stand down[5].

The court has power to refuse to allow to be sworn any juror who from physical or mental infirmity, temporary or permanent, is incapable of duly attending to the evidence[6].

A judge may not order a jury to be composed of persons from a particular ethnic group or from a particular section of the community[7]; and there is no requirement in law that there should be a black member of a jury or of a jury panel[8].

1 See PARA 803.

2 *Practice Direction (Criminal Proceedings: Consolidation)* [2002] 3 All ER 904, [2002] 2 Cr App Rep 533 at IV.42.2, CA; *Amendment to the Consolidated Criminal Practice Direction (Jury service)* [2005] 3 All ER 89, sub nom *Practice Direction (Crown Court: Jury Service)* [2005] 1 WLR 1361 at IV.42.2, CA. As to the discretion to excuse a person from jury service generally, rather than from a particular case, see PARA 806. Where a juror with professional and public service commitments applies to the court to be excused, the application must be considered with common sense and according to the interests of justice; an explanation should be required for an application being much later than necessary: *Practice Direction (Criminal Proceedings: Consolidation)* [2002] 3 All ER 904, [2002] 2 Cr App Rep 533 at IV.42.1, CA; *Amendment to the Consolidated Criminal Practice Direction (Jury service)* [2005] 3 All ER 89, sub nom *Practice Direction (Crown Court: Jury Service)* [2005] 1 WLR 1361 at IV.42.1, CA. As to the situation where a juror unexpectedly finds himself in difficult professional or personal circumstances during the course of the trial see *Practice Direction (Criminal Proceedings: Consolidation)* [2002] 3 All ER 904, [2002] 2 Cr App Rep 533 at IV.42.3, CA; *Amendment to the Consolidated Criminal Practice Direction (Jury service)* [2005] 3 All ER 89, sub nom *Practice Direction (Crown Court: Jury Service)* [2005] 1 WLR 1361 at IV.42.3, CA.

3 As to qualification and disqualification as a juror see PARAS 804–805.

4 As to challenges see PARA 825 et seq. That a juror is not qualified to serve is a ground for challenge for cause: see PARA 831.

5 *R v Lord Grey* (1682) 9 State Tr 127; *R v Cook* (1696) 13 State Tr 311 at 313, 318.

6 *Mansell v R* (1857) 8 E & B 54 at 81, 109, Ex Ch; and see *R v Chandler (No 2)* [1964] 2 QB 322, 48 Cr App Rep 143, CCA. As to the power of the judge to discharge a person summoned for jury service on account of physical disability see PARA 833.

7 See *R v Ford* [1989] QB 868, 89 Cr App Rep 278, CA. See further PARA 816 note 2.

8 See *R v Danvers* [1982] Crim LR 680, CA; *R v Ford* [1989] QB 868, 89 Cr App Rep 278, CA; and PARA 826 text and note 5.

(3) CHALLENGES

(i) In general

825. Right to challenge. The right to challenge refers to the right to object to a person or persons called to serve on a jury. It arises upon a full body of jurors being assembled in the jury box[1]. Challenge is of two kinds: (1) challenge to the array (that is, to the whole number of persons in the panel)[2]; and (2) challenge to the polls (that is, to individual jurors)[3]. The right to challenge may be exercised by any party, which includes the Crown[4]. The challenge must be for cause (that is, for a definite reason assigned and proved)[5].

In criminal cases, the defendant is informed of his right to challenge by the clerk of the court[6]. Because the right to challenge postulates that the trial has already begun[7] there is no right to challenge jurors empanelled to try collateral issues before a criminal trial commences[8].

Any party to county court proceedings to be tried by a jury has the same right of challenge to all or any of the jurors as he would have in the High Court[9].

No challenge may be made of jurors at an inquest[10].

A challenge to the array must be made before any juror is sworn[11]; a challenge to the polls must be made after the juror's name has been drawn (unless the court has dispensed with balloting for him[12]) and before he is sworn[13]. The function of the defendant's right of challenge is not to provide a jury which is in a positive sense acceptable to him, but one which is free from elements which he may regard as objectionable[14].

If a juror is unchallenged and is sworn, he cannot afterwards be challenged on the ground of partiality[15].

1 *Vicars v Langham* (1618) Hob 235, Ex Ch; *R v Edmonds* (1821) 4 B & Ald 471 at 473; *Barrett v Long* (1851) 3 HL Cas 395 at 410.
2 As to challenge to the array see PARAS 826–828.
3 As to challenge to the polls see PARA 829 et seq.
4 As to the exercise of the right of challenge by the Crown see PARA 830.
5 The defendant's peremptory challenge, which was the right to challenge jurors without cause in criminal trials, has been abolished: Criminal Justice Act 1988 s 118(1); and see eg *R v Cornwall* [2009] EWCA Crim 2458, [2009] All ER (D) 290 (Nov). There is no right to make peremptory challenges in a civil case: *Creed v Fisher* (1854) 9 Exch 472. As to the Crown's power to ask that a juror stand by for the Crown see PARA 830.
6 However, failure to inform the defendant of his right to challenge does not necessarily amount to a denial of his right: see *R v Berkeley* [1969] 2 QB 446, [1969] 3 All ER 6, CA; and PARA 834 note 2.
7 See the Juries Act 1974 s 12.
8 See *R v Ratcliffe* (1746) 18 State Tr 429 (jury trying issue whether defendant was person previously convicted who had escaped). Thus there is no right of challenge under the Juries Act 1974 s 12 where a jury is empanelled to determine whether the defendant is mute of malice (see CRIMINAL LAW, EVIDENCE AND PROCEDURE vol 11(3) (2006 Reissue) PARA 1264) or by visitation of God or whether a special plea to the jurisdiction or of pardon is established: *R v Paling* (1978) 67 Cr App Rep 299, CA.
9 Juries Act 1974 s 12(2). As to the right to make a challenge to the array in the High Court see PARAS 826–828; and as to the right to make a challenge to the polls in the High Court see PARA 829 et seq.
10 *R v Ingham* (1864) 5 B & S 257 at 276 per Blackburn J.
11 See *R v Frost* (1839) 9 C & P 129 at 122.
12 Ie under the Juries Act 1974 s 11(2): see PARA 823.
13 See the Juries Act 1974 s 12(3). The practice is to permit challenges, as a matter of discretion, to be taken up until the juror has completed the oath or affirmation: see *R v Harrington, R v Hanlon* (1976) 64 Cr App Rep 1, CA.
14 See also *Mansell v R* (1857) 8 E & B 54 at 79, Ex Ch (until given in charge, when he must be tried by that jury, a defendant has no right to be tried by any particular jurors).
15 *R v Wardle* (1842) Car & M 647. In an appropriate case, however, the trial judge may discharge a juror, or the whole jury: see eg PARA 845.

(ii) Challenge to the Array

826. Challenge to the array. Challenge to the array is the taking of exception to the whole panel; it is a right of challenge on the ground that the person responsible for summoning the panel of jurors in question is biased or has acted improperly[1]. It is commonly divided into the following two classes:

(1) principal challenge, where the summoning officer is in a position inconsistent with impartiality[2], as by being party to the claim[3], related to one of the parties, having empanelled certain persons at the request of one of the parties or having a claim pending against him by either party; and

(2) challenge for favour, where the position of the summoning officer is not necessarily inconsistent with impartiality, but may be suspected[4].

The racial composition of a jury is not a ground for challenging the array[5]. Nor can the fact that the Attorney General has vetted the panel, in accordance with his guidelines, afford grounds for a challenge to the array[6].

Challenges to the array are very rare.

1 See the Juries Act 1974 s 12(6). This right is not affected by the transfer of responsibility for summoning jurors to officers appointed by the Lord Chancellor (ie under the Courts Act 1971 s 31 (repealed): see now the Juries Act 1974 s 2(1); and PARA 813): s 12(6). As to the Lord Chancellor see CONSTITUTIONAL LAW AND HUMAN RIGHTS vol 8(2) (Reissue) PARA 477 et seq. However, the vesting of that responsibility in the Lord Chancellor has made the possibility of a challenge to the array extremely remote.

2 *O'Connell v R* (1844) 11 Cl & Fin 155, HL.

3 *R v Sheppard* (1773) 1 Leach 101; and see *Baylis v Lucas* (1779) 1 Cowp 112; *Mason v Vickery* (1804) 1 Smith KB 304, where the summoning officer was attorney for a party to the cause.

4 Eg it is a principal challenge if the officer is of kin or affinity to one of the parties, but a challenge for favour if there is affinity between his son and a party's daughter: Co Litt 156a.

5 *R v Danvers* [1982] Crim LR 680, CA; *R v Ford* [1989] QB 868, [1989] 3 All ER 445, CA. In so far as *R v Thomas* (1989) 88 Cr App Rep 370 suggests there is a discretion it ought not to be followed: *R v Ford*.

6 *R v McCann* (1991) 92 Cr App Rep 239, [1991] Crim LR 136, CA. As to the Attorney General's guidelines see PARA 830.

827. Procedure. A challenge to the array must be in writing and the other party may respond in writing[1].

If both parties challenge the array or the matters constituting cause of challenge are admitted, it is the court's duty to quash the array[2]. The court must order the summoning officer (or, if a similar challenge prevails against his jury, two elisors or electors nominated by the jury) to return a new panel[3]. No challenge to the array can be taken against the panel returned by the elisors[4].

If the facts alleged are controverted, the court nominates two 'triers', who may be persons summoned as jurors, to ascertain them upon oath[5], and, if they do not constitute cause of principal challenge, to try further whether the array be impartial or favourable[6]. On the challenge being on either ground upheld, the judge must quash the array and a new panel must be ordered[7]. If there is a challenge to the fresh array, and that array is quashed, the jury nominates two elisors or electors to return a panel; and to this array no challenge is allowed[8].

1 *Carmarthen Corpn v Evans* (1842) 10 M & W 274. See also *R v Edmonds* (1821) 4 B & Ald 471 at 474; and see *R v Hughes* (1843) 1 Car & Kir 235. For the form of a challenge to the array see *R v Smith O'Brien* (1849) 7 State Tr NS 1; *R v O'Connell* (1844) 5 State Tr NS 1, 69, HL.

2 Co Litt 156a; Duncombe's Trials per Pais (8th Edn) 174.

3 *R v Dolby* (1823) 2 B & C 104; Co Litt 158a; 3 Bl Com (14th Edn) 354.

4 Co Litt 158a; 3 Bl Com (14th Edn) 354. However, a challenge to the polls can be taken: see PARA 829.

5 The person challenging the array, as also the challenger of a poll, must give prima facie evidence of cause: *R v Savage* (1824) 1 Mood CC 51; *R v Hughes* (1843) 1 Car & Kir 235.

6 *R v Dolby* (1823) 2 B & C 104; *R v Swain* (1838) 2 Lew CC 116.

7   Co Litt 156a. The quashing of an array upon a successful challenge is a matter of right, and not of the court's discretion: *R v Edmonds* (1821) 4 B & Ald 471 at 473.
8   Co Litt 158a.

828.   Time for challenge.   A challenge to the array must be made promptly[1] and must contain every cause of objection[2]. Every cause of challenge, whether to the array or to the polls, ought to be propounded in such a way that the opposite party may have an opportunity of controverting the facts alleged[3] and of appealing from a decision of the court[4].

1   It should be made if possible before the jury is sworn: *Brunskill v Giles* (1832) 9 Bing 13. For the principle that the court will not order a new trial on grounds which would have supported a challenge to the array see PARA 835.
2   Once a challenge to the array has been tried there cannot be challenge for another cause. For a form of challenge to the array see *R v Dolby* (1821) 1 Car & Kir 238.
3   In *O'Brien v R* (1849) 2 HL Cas 465 at 469, a challenge to the array was followed by a plea, a replication and a rejoinder (an Irish criminal case).
4   *R v Edmonds* (1821) 4 B & Ald 471 at 474.

(iii) Individual Jurors: Challenge to the Polls

829.   Challenge to the polls, procedure.   Challenge to the polls is exception taken for cause to individual members of a jury before they are sworn; and, in proceedings for the trial of any person for an offence on indictment, he[1] or the prosecution may challenge all or any of the jurors for cause.

The right to challenge to the polls is unlimited[2]. The challenge ought not to be made before the full jury has been called to the jury box[3]. The challenge should be made before the juror is sworn[4]. Strictly this means before the swearing of the juror begins (that is, before the book is given into the hands of the juror and the reading of the oath begins)[5], but there is a discretion to permit a challenge after the commencement but before the conclusion of the reading of the oath[6].

The defendant must conclude his challenges before the Crown can be required to justify its challenges[7]. In civil causes, whichever party first challenges must justify every challenge before the other party can be required to do so[8].

The challenge is tried by the trial judge[9]. A judge sitting in the Crown Court may order that a challenge for cause is to be heard in court in private or in chambers[10]. Failure to exercise a challenge through ignorance of a fact may afford a ground of appeal in a criminal case[11].

Every cause of challenge to the polls ought to be propounded in such a way that the opposite party may have an opportunity of controverting the facts alleged and of appealing from a decision of the court[12].

If the challenge for cause is allowed, the juror is ordered to stand down and a fresh juror is called[13].

1   Where several defendants are tried together, the practice is for each to assert his rights of challenge as if he were being separately tried; and if it seems that the total challenges to the polls may exhaust the panel of jurors, the judge may direct a separate trial of one or some of the defendants while a complete jury remains available. It is, however, no longer the practice to sever the trial if the defendants do not join in their challenges: see *R v Ram and Ram* (1893) 17 Cox CC 609; Fost 106; 2 Hale PC 268. In *R v Fisher* (1848) 3 Cox CC 68, Platt B said that it was an 'ill practice to allow the challenges to be severed' for the purposes of giving each defendant a separate trial.
2   See the Juries Act 1974 s 12(1)(a) (amended by the Criminal Justice Act 1988 Sch 16); and see also *R v Geach* (1840) 9 C & P 499.
3   See *R v Edmonds* (1821) 4 B & Ald 471; and PARA 825.
4   See the Juries Act 1974 s 12(3); and PARA 825.

5   *R v Brandeth* (1817) 32 State Tr 755; *R v Frost* (1839) 9 C & P 129 at 137; *R v Giorgetti* (1865) 4 F & F 546.

6   *R v Harrington* (1976) 64 Cr App Rep 1, CA.

7   Hawk PC (8th Edn) 569. As to challenges by the Crown see PARA 830.

8   See Duncombe's Trials per Pais (8th Edn) 189–190, where the time to challenge is exhaustively dealt with. There is the same right to challenge in a county court as in the High Court: see the Juries Act 1974 s 12(2); and PARA 825 note 8.

9   Juries Act 1974 s 12(1)(b). The juror is called into the box and examined as to cause, but in the exceptional circumstances in *R v Kray* (1969) 53 Cr App Rep 412, the trial judge allowed the defendant's counsel to indicate the cause on which he was relying and gave his ruling before any juror came into court. There must be a foundation of fact creating a prima facie case of probability of prejudice before the prospective juror may be cross-examined: *R v Kray* (1969) 53 Cr App Rep 412; *R v Chandler* [1964] 2 QB 322, 48 Cr App Rep 143, CCA.

10 See the Criminal Justice Act 1988 s 118(2).

11 *R v Pennington* (1985) 149 JP 615, 81 Cr App Rep 217, CA, in which the appeal was dismissed. It is thought that fresh material of bias would need to be compelling before the Court of Appeal would intervene: see *R v Bliss* (1987) 84 Cr App Rep 1, [1986] Crim LR 467, CA.

12 *R v Edmonds* (1821) 4 B & Ald 471 at 474. As to the principal causes of challenge to the polls see PARA 831.

13 If the panel is exhausted, the court may exercise its powers to order people in its vicinity to be summoned: see PARA 817.

830. Position of the Crown. In addition to its power to challenge a juror or jurors for cause[1], the Crown[2] may also direct any person whose name is called to stand by[3] until the panel has been called over and exhausted[4], and will not be put to assign cause[5] until it appears that there will not be a full jury without recourse to that person[6].

The Crown should assert its right to stand by only on the basis of clearly defined and restrictive criteria[7]. The circumstances in which it would be proper for the Crown to exercise that right are:

(1)   where a jury check authorised in accordance with the Attorney General's guidelines on jury checks[8] reveals information justifying the exercise of that right and its exercise is personally authorised by the Attorney General; or

(2)   where a person is about to be sworn as a juror who is manifestly unsuitable and the defence agrees that accordingly the exercise by the Crown of the right to stand by is appropriate[9].

An example of the exceptional circumstances which might justify the exercise of the right is where it becomes apparent that a juror selected for service to try a complex case is in fact illiterate[10].

Searches of criminal records for the purpose of ascertaining whether or not a jury panel includes any disqualified person may be carried out by the police[11]. In cases involving national security where part of the evidence is likely to be heard in private, and in terrorist cases, further investigations may be made, but only with the personal authority of the Attorney General on the application of the Director of Public Prosecutions[12]. No right of stand by should be exercised by the Crown on the basis of information obtained as a result of such authorised checks save with the personal authority of the Attorney General and unless the information is such as to afford strong reason for believing that a particular juror might be a security risk, be susceptible to improper approaches or be influenced in arriving at a verdict[13].

1   Juries Act 1825 s 29 (amended by the Statute Law Revision (No 2) Act 1988; the Courts Act 1971 Sch 4 para 3(2); and the Criminal Justice Act 1948 Sch 10 Pt I); Juries Act 1974 s 12(5). The Crown's right to peremptory challenge was abolished by 33 Edw 1 c 2 (Ordinatio

de Inquisicionibus) (1305) (repealed). See also *R v Frost* (1839) 9 C & P 129; *Mansell v R* (1857) 8 E & B 54 at 70–71, Ex Ch, per Lord Campbell CJ.

2   The defendant has no such right: *R v Chandler* [1964] 2 QB 322, 48 Cr App Rep 143, CCA.

3   2 Hale PC 271; 2 Hawk PC (8th Edn) 569; *R v Frost* (1839) 9 C & P 129; *R v Geach* (1840) 9 C & P 499. So, too, may an individual who prosecutes in the name of the Crown: *R v M'Gowan* (1858) unreported, but cited in *R v M'Cartie* (1859) 11 ICLR 188 at 206–207.

4   It seems that this will not be until every proper attempt has been made to secure the presence of those on the panel whose duty it is to attend: *Mansell v R* (1857) 8 E & B 54 at 104, Ex Ch, per Cockburn CJ. Thus if 12 jurors whose names are on the panel are discharged in another case, and become available, the Crown may require their names to be called before recourse is again had to those who have been ordered to stand by: *Mansell v R*.

5   Ie to make a challenge to the polls: see PARA 829.

6   *Mansell v R* (1857) 8 E & B 54, Ex Ch; followed in *R v Mason* [1981] QB 881, [1980] 3 All ER 777, CA.

7   *Practice Note* [1988] 3 All ER 1086, 88 Cr App Rep 123 (Attorney General's guidelines on the exercise by the Crown of its right of stand by).

8   See *Practice Note* [1988] 3 All ER 1086 at 1087, 88 Cr App Rep 123 at 124. Jury checks in accordance with the guidelines, and the exercise by the Attorney General of his right to stand by, are not unconstitutional: *R v McCann* (1990) 92 Cr App Rep 239, [1991] Crim LR 136, CA.

9   *Practice Note* [1988] 3 All ER 1086, 88 Cr App Rep 123.

10 *Practice Note* [1988] 3 All ER 1086, 88 Cr App Rep 123.

11 *Practice Note* [1988] 3 All ER 1086 at 1087, 88 Cr App Rep 123 at 124 (Attorney General's guidelines on jury checks); and see the recommendations of the Association of Chief Police Officers in respect of checks on criminal records, annexed to this practice note.

12 *Practice Note* [1988] 3 All ER 1086 at 1087, 88 Cr App Rep 123 at 124.

13 *Practice Note* [1988] 3 All ER 1086 at 1087, 88 Cr App Rep 123 at 124.

831. Causes of challenge. The principal causes of challenge to the polls are two in number[1]:

(1)   where the person called does not possess the necessary qualifications[2]; and

(2)   where there is actual or presumed bias on the part of an individual member of the jury[3].

1   Co Litt 156b. The Juries Act 1974 does not affect the law relating to challenge of jurors, except as mentioned in s 12(4) (see the text and note 2): s 12(4).

2   Juries Act 1974 s 12(4). As to the qualifications see Sch 1; and PARAS 804–805. A disqualification not discovered until after the verdict would not be ground for a new trial: *Peermain v Mackay* (1845) 9 Jur 491.

3   Some prima facie evidence of bias must be given before the person challenged can be examined on the voire dire: *R v Dowling* (1848) 3 Cox CC 509; *R v Chandler (No 2)* [1964] 2 QB 322, [1964] 1 All ER 761, CCA. As to examination upon the voire dire see PARA 832. It is now unusual for a challenge for cause on grounds of bias to be made; actual or presumed bias is normally dealt with under the judge's power to stand jurors down (see PARA 842). The mere fact that there has been a previous trial resulting in a verdict adverse to the defendant and that this has been widely reported in the press with comments on the evidence does not ordinarily provide a case of probable bias or prejudice in jurors empanelled on a later trial. It may be otherwise where newspapers, knowing that there is to be a subsequent trial, have widely publicised discreditable allegations whether of fact or fiction: *R v Kray* (1969) 53 Cr App Rep 412.

    In *R v Wilson* [1995] Crim LR 952, CA, a retrial was ordered after a challenge in respect of a juror married to a prison officer serving a prison where the appellants were on remand was refused.

    The questioning of potential jurors by the use of a questionnaire to establish whether they are biased ought to be avoided save in most exceptional circumstances: *R v Andrews (Tracey)* [1999] Crim LR 156, (1998) 142 Sol Jo LB 268, CA.

    As to challenge to the array where a jury has been empanelled by a partial person see PARA 826. As to the discharge of a juror on the grounds of bias see PARA 842.

832. Examination upon the voire dire. A person challenged may be examined upon oath[1], which is called examination upon the voire dire, as to the matters alleged concerning him[2], except as to whether he has expressed an opinion unfavourable to one of the parties[3] or if the cause of challenge touches his dishonour or discredit[4].

1 The special form of oath is: 'I swear by Almighty God that I will true answer make to all such questions as the court shall demand of me'. In the case of an affirmation the wording could be: 'I do solemnly, sincerely and truly declare and affirm that I will true answer make to all such questions as the court shall demand of me'.
2 *R v Cook* (1696) 13 State Tr 311. There must be a foundation of fact creating a prima facie case of probability of prejudice before the prospective juror can be cross-examined: *R v Chandler (No 2)* [1964] 2 QB 322, [1964] 1 All ER 761, CCA; *R v Kray* (1969) 53 Cr App Rep 412. The mere fact that a previous trial ending in a verdict adverse to the defendant has been reported at length in the press, with comments on the evidence, should not ordinarily provide a case of probable bias in jurors on a later trial of the defendant, but where newspapers had revived discreditable allegations from the defendant's past, which might be either fact or fiction and which had been publicised over a wide area, a prima facie case of probability of prejudice has been established and defending counsel is entitled to apply to be allowed to examine the jurors as they enter the box to be sworn: *R v Kray*.
3 *R v Edmonds* (1821) 4 B & Ald 471 at 490.
4 Co Litt 158b; *R v Cook* (1696) 13 State Tr 311 at 334; *R v Martin* (1848) 6 State Tr NS 925. The court has refused to let a juror be asked whether he belonged to an association for prosecuting frauds upon tradesmen: *R v Stewart* (1845) 1 Cox CC 174.

(iv) Incompetent Persons; Defects in Challenges

833. Incompetent persons. On the trial of a criminal issue, without challenge by the Crown or on the defendant's behalf, the judge may refuse to allow to be sworn any juror who from physical or mental infirmity, temporary or permanent, is incapable of duly attending to the evidence[1]. This common law power has been supplemented by statute[2].

1 *Mansell v R* (1857) 8 E & B 54 at 81, 109, Ex Ch.
2 See the Juries Act 1974 ss 9B, 10; and PARA 806.

834. Effect of improper disallowance of challenge. The improper disallowance of a challenge renders the subsequent proceedings before the jury absolutely void, and is ground for a new trial being ordered on appeal, by a writ of venire de novo in the case of criminal proceedings[1]. Therefore, it is not within the province of the appellate court to consider whether the person complaining has been prejudiced and to exercise a discretion as to granting a new trial[2].

1 Where a trial has been a nullity, the Court of Appeal may order a venire de novo: see CRIMINAL LAW, EVIDENCE AND PROCEDURE vol 11(4) (2006 Reissue) PARA 1895. The writ or order of venire de novo must be in such form as the court issuing it considers appropriate: Juries Act 1974 s 21(4). However, if the trial is not rendered a nullity, a mistrial will result in the conviction being quashed: see *R v Taylor* [1950] NI 57, CCA; *R v Gash* [1967] 1 All ER 811, [1967] 1 WLR 454, CA.
2 *R v Edmonds* (1821) 4 B & Ald 471 at 473 per Abbott CJ; *R v Williams* (1925) 19 Cr App Rep 67, CCA; *R v Wilson* [1995] Crim LR 952, CA (see PARA 831); but see *R v Berkeley* [1969] 2 QB 446, [1969] 3 All ER 6, CA (where the defendant was represented in court, and no objection was taken when his right of challenge was not explained to him; it was held that this was not a case of denial to a man of his right to challenge, but was merely a failure to follow what has been a long-continued practice of informing a defendant of the existence of that right).

835. Effect of omission to challenge. The court will only order a new trial on an application based on fact which would have constituted a ground for a challenge to the array at the original trial if it is shown that the facts were unknown at the time of the trial to the person making the application[1]. If facts relating to the qualification of a juror which would have constituted grounds for a challenge for cause become known to a party only after the trial, the court will normally only make an order of venire de novo[2] where there has been a personation of a juror or a mistake as to identity[3].

1   *Brunskill v Giles* (1832) 9 Bing 13. The fact that the attorney for the defendant was under-sheriff and had summoned the jury has been held to be no ground for new trial after a verdict for the defendant: *Mason v Vickery* (1804) 1 Smith KB 304; and see *Briggs v Sowton* (1840) 4 Jur 1014. Cf *Baylis v Lucas* (1779) 1 Cowp 112, where a writ of inquiry was set aside because the jury were returned by the plaintiff's attorney. As to challenge to the array see PARA 826.

2   See PARA 834.

3   *R v Sutton* (1828) 8 B & C 417, where an unqualified alien had served as a juror; *R v Kelly* [1950] 2 KB 164 at 173–174, [1950] 1 All ER 806 at 810–811, CCA, where a juryman was alleged to have been disqualified on grounds of criminal conviction (see PARA 805), distinguishing *Ras Behari Lal v R* (1933) 102 LJPC 144. A new trial was granted where in an action against a local authority a member had served as a juryman: *Atkins v Fulham London Borough Council* (1915) 31 TLR 564, DC. For the position where there has been personation or a mistake of identity see PARA 853.

(4) SWEARING AND GIVING IN CHARGE

836. Swearing the jury. On the conclusion of the challenges[1], the full jury in the box or, if there have been no challenges, the jurors called into the box are sworn[2] to try the issues joined between the parties[3]. A juror who objects to being sworn may make a solemn affirmation instead of taking an oath[4].

Once the jurors have been sworn the defendant is formally given into their charge[5]. Until then there is no necessity or right that he should be tried by the jurors already sworn[6].

1   As to challenges see PARAS 825–835.

2   The oath is administered by an officer of the court deputed for that purpose. Each juror must be sworn separately: Juries Act 1974 s 11(3). The form of the oath in criminal trials is: 'I swear by almighty God that I will faithfully try the defendant and give a true verdict according to the evidence': *Practice Direction (Criminal Proceedings: Consolidation)* [2002] 3 All ER 904, [2002] 2 Cr App Rep 533 at IV.42.4, CA. As to the taking of oaths in general see the Oaths Act 1978; and CIVIL PROCEDURE vol 11 (2009) PARA 1021 et seq. In the case of a person who is neither a Christian nor a Jew, the oath must be administered in any lawful manner: s 1(3). As to the swearing of the jury at an inquest see the Coroners Act 1988 s 8(2)(b) (prospectively repealed by the Coroners and Justice Act 2009 Sch 23 Pt 1); the Coroners and Justice Act 2009 s 8(3) (not yet in force); and CORONERS vol 9(2) (2006 Reissue) PARA 993. As to swearing in, taking the oath etc in Welsh, and as to the use of Welsh in legal proceedings, see CIVIL PROCEDURE vol 12 (2009) PARAS 1118, 1132.

3   After the jurors have been sworn, the cards with their names are kept apart until they have given a verdict or been discharged. From the names left in the box or remaining on the panel further juries are called in the same way if occasion requires. As to the provisions on the summoning, empanelling and selecting of jurors see PARA 812 et seq.

4   See the Oaths Act 1978 s 5(1), (4). In cases where it is not practicable without inconvenience or delay to administer an oath in the manner appropriate to a person's religious beliefs, he may (or may be required to) make an affirmation under s 5: see s 5(2), (3). The following words are used for the affirmation: 'I do solemnly, sincerely and truly declare and affirm that I will faithfully try the defendant and give a true verdict according to the evidence': *Practice Direction (Criminal Proceedings: Consolidation)* [2002] 3 All ER 904, [2002] 2 Cr App Rep 533 at IV.42.4, CA. As to the making of affirmations in general see the Oaths Act 1978 ss 5(1), 6(1); and CIVIL PROCEDURE vol 11 (2009) PARA 1023.

5   See CRIMINAL LAW, EVIDENCE AND PROCEDURE vol 11(3) (2006 Reissue) PARA 1298.

6   See *Mansell v R* (1857) 8 E & B 54 at 79, Ex Ch (on a trial for murder a juror who, after being sworn but before the defendant had been given in charge, stated that he had conscientious scruples against capital punishment, was discharged).

(5) CONDUCT DURING THE HEARING

837. Death or discharge of a juror in a criminal trial. If, in the course of a criminal trial of any person for an offence on indictment, any member of the jury dies or is discharged by the court[1] whether as being through illness incapable of continuing to act or for any other reason[2], the jury is nevertheless to be considered as remaining for all the purposes of that trial properly constituted so long as the number of its members is not less than nine, and the trial proceeds and a verdict may be given accordingly[3].

Notwithstanding these provisions, on the death or discharge of a member of the jury in the course of a trial of any person for an offence on indictment the court may discharge the jury in any case where the court sees fit to do so[4].

1   As to the meaning of 'court' see PARA 804 note 1. As to discharge of a jury during trial see further CRIMINAL LAW, EVIDENCE AND PROCEDURE vol 11(3) (2006 Reissue) PARAS 1328–1330.
2   Ie including misconduct or bias. As to misconduct see PARA 841; and see also CRIMINAL LAW, EVIDENCE AND PROCEDURE vol 11(3) (2006 Reissue) PARA 1329. As to bias see PARA 842.
3   Juries Act 1974 s 16(1). Section 16(1) does not expressly confer upon a judge power to discharge a juror; it provides that, if a juror is discharged, the jury is considered as remaining for all purposes of the trial: *R v Hambery* [1977] QB 924, 65 Cr App Rep 233, CA. No formality is required for the purposes of the discharge of a juror: *R v Browne* [1962] 2 All ER 621, [1962] 1 WLR 759, CCA. The discharge need not take place in open court but normally will do so: see *R v Richardson* [1979] 3 All ER 247, [1979] 1 WLR 1316, CA. Where a juror is discharged not through illness or bereavement, the trial judge is not required to consult counsel: *R v Richardson* [1979] 3 All ER 247, [1979] 1 WLR 1316, CA. The Juries Act 1974 provides that, in the case of a trial for any offence punishable with death, written assent to the application of s 16(1) must be given by the prosecution and the defendant: see s 16(2) (amended by the Criminal Justice Act 1988 Sch 16); and see also *R v Browne* [1962] 2 All ER 621, [1962] 1 WLR 759, CCA (where counsel signs a certificate on behalf of the defendant, the court is entitled to presume that the defendant has consented, and a defendant who, realising what is occurring, does not object at the time cannot subsequently maintain objection). Note that the sentence of death can no longer be imposed.
4   Juries Act 1974 s 16(3).

838. Adjournment and separation of jury. The court has power to adjourn a hearing, and the jury may be permitted to separate during such an adjournment[1].

In criminal cases jurors are permitted to separate prior to considering their verdict. Previously no separation was permitted after the jury retired; however, a trial judge now has a discretion to permit a jury to separate at any time, either before or after retirement[2]. On the first occasion when a jury separates the judge should warn jurors not to talk about the case to anyone outside their number[3]. The Court of Appeal has given guidance on the appropriate directions to be given to a jury permitted to separate after retirement to consider verdict[4].

In civil cases the separation of a jury after the summing-up does not invalidate the verdict, but should be permitted only in rare instances and when special circumstances demand it[5].

After having been sworn, jurors may, at the court's[6] discretion, be allowed reasonable refreshment at their own expense[7].

1   As to adjournment and separation of the jury in a criminal trial see CRIMINAL LAW, EVIDENCE AND PROCEDURE vol 11(3) (2006 Reissue) PARA 1327.
2   Juries Act 1974 s 13 (substituted by the Criminal Justice and Public Order Act 1994 s 43(1)).
3   *R v Prime* (1973) 57 Cr App Rep 632, CA.
4   *R v Oliver* [1996] 2 Cr App Rep 514, [1996] 01 LS Gaz R 21, CA.
5   *Fanshaw v Knowles* [1916] 2 KB 538, CA. It is misconduct if the jury separate without leave of the court: see PARA 841.
6   As to the meaning of 'court' see PARA 804 note 1.

7 Juries Act 1974 s 15. As to the subsistence allowance payable to jurors see PARA 855. It is misconduct for any juror to eat or drink at the expense of one of the parties before the verdict: see PARA 841.

839. Submissions and evidence in absence of jury. It is for the judge to decide whether or not a submission made during a criminal trial is to be heard in the absence of the jury[1], but only in exceptional circumstances may evidence be given in the absence of the jury[2].

1 See *R v Hendry* (1988) 88 Cr App Rep 187, CA; and CRIMINAL LAW, EVIDENCE AND PROCEDURE vol 11(3) (2006 Reissue) PARA 1324.
2 See CRIMINAL LAW, EVIDENCE AND PROCEDURE vol 11(3) (2006 Reissue) PARA 1325.

840. Views. In appropriate cases the judge may permit the jury to view the place in question at any time during the trial[1].

Criminal Procedure Rules and Civil Procedure Rules may make provision as respects views by jurors, and the places which a juror may be called on to go to view cannot be restricted to any particular county or area[2].

1 In the case of a criminal trial see further CRIMINAL LAW, EVIDENCE AND PROCEDURE vol 11(3) (2006 Reissue) PARA 1326. As to the position in coroners' courts see CORONERS vol 9(2) (2006 Reissue) PARA 998.
2 Juries Act 1974 s 14 (amended by the Courts Act 2003 Sch 8 para 173). At the date at which this volume states the law, no rules had been made under the Juries Act 1974 s 14.

841. Misconduct of jurors. A jury may be discharged or a new trial ordered if, after being sworn, any juror is guilty of misconduct[1], and, in particular, if the jurors separate without the leave of the court[2], eat or drink before the verdict at the expense of one of the parties[3], hold communication with any person or receive evidence, oral or documentary, out of court[4], determine their verdict by lot[5] or, being unable to agree, have 'split the difference'[6] or if a stranger was with them for a substantial time[7]. Such conduct will be more strictly scrutinised when it occurs after the summing-up and during the consideration of the verdict[8].

Misconduct or impropriety by a juror may be sufficient to result in that juror or the entire jury being discharged[9]. The factual situations that arise are many, and include drunkenness[10], alleged racism[11], improper pressure on other jurors[12], consulting an ouija board in the course of deliberations[13], declining to take part in the deliberations of the jury[14], making telephone calls after retirement[15], and lunching with a barrister not concerned with the proceedings[16].

The Court of Appeal has jurisdiction to hear an appeal against the discharge of a jury in a civil case[17] but not in a criminal case[18]. A decision to discharge a juror is an important step, and a capricious decision to discharge a juror may result in a conviction being overturned in a criminal case[19].

In a criminal case any communication between the jury after its retirement and the judge must be read out in open court[20], provided it relates to a matter in dispute which may result in conviction or acquittal[21]; if he considers it useful, the judge should seek the assistance of counsel[22]. Where it relates to a matter which cannot affect the merits of the case, the question whether to read the communication out in court is one for the discretion of the judge[23].

In a civil case such a communication should be read publicly in court or, if this is undesirable, it should be seen by counsel or, where a litigant is appearing in person, by him personally[24]. The terms of such a communication should be put on the record[25].

Generally no investigation into a jury's deliberations is permitted after the verdict is entered[26].

1 See CIVIL PROCEDURE vol 12 (2009) PARA 1714; CRIMINAL LAW, EVIDENCE AND PROCEDURE vol 11(3) (2006 Reissue) PARA 1329.

Trial judges should ensure that the jury is alerted to the need to bring any concerns about the behaviour of fellow jurors or of others affecting the jurors at the time and not to wait until the case is concluded: *Practice Direction (Criminal Proceedings: Consolidation)* [2002] 3 All ER 904, [2002] 2 Cr App Rep 533 at IV.42.6, CA; *Practice Direction (Crown Court: Guidance to Jurors)* [2004] 1 WLR 665, [2004] 2 Cr App Rep 3 at IV.42.6, CA. If there is an indication of an irregularity caused by extraneous influences (eg contact with other persons who may have passed on information which should not have been before the jury) which raises a reasonable suspicion, the judge must investigate the matter: see *R v Blackwell, R v Farley, R v Adams* [1995] 2 Cr App Rep 625, CA; *R v Oke* [1997] Crim LR 898, CA.

Where it is apparent that there is friction between members of a jury, so that the inference could be drawn that certain members of the jury might not be able to perform their duty, the whole jury should be questioned in open court as to their capacity, as a body, to continue: *R v Orgles* [1993] 4 All ER 533, 98 Cr App Rep 185, CA. Circumstances that give rise to such a situation would be internal to the jury and are to be distinguished from external circumstances that might make it appropriate to question an individual juror: *R v Orgles*. The Contempt of Court Act 1981 s 8(1) (see CONTEMPT OF COURT vol 9(1) (Reissue) PARA 451) does not preclude the judge from conducting an investigation into matters such as bias or irregularity in the jury room (*R v Connor, R v Mirza* [2004] UKHL 2, [2004] 1 AC 1118, [2004] 1 All ER 925), but as a general rule it is contrary to common law for the judge to ask the jury questions, or receive evidence, about anything said in the course of the jury's deliberations while it is considering its verdict (*R v Smith, R v Mercieca* [2005] UKHL 12, [2005] 2 All ER 29, [2005] 1 WLR 704). An exception to this rule may exist if an allegation is made which tends to show that the jury as a whole declined to deliberate at all, but decided the case by other means such as drawing lots or tossing a coin. Such conduct would be a negation of the function of a jury and a trial whose result was determined in such a manner would not be a trial at all: see *R v Connor, R v Mirza* at [123] per Lord Hope of Craighead. Where an investigation is impermissible, the judge has the choice of either discharging the jury or giving it a further direction. However, it is incumbent on the judge to ensure that the further direction is apposite, clear, and as emphatic as the situation requires: *R v Smith, R v Mercieca*.

2 *Hughes v Budd* (1840) 8 Dowl 315 (where a juror left the court during a hearing, returning with cigars, and he had been seen talking to the plaintiff's attorney in an adjoining public house); *R v Ward* (1867) 17 LT 220, CCR (where a juror left the court-house without leave after being sworn); *R v Ketteridge* [1915] 1 KB 467, CCA (where a conviction was quashed because, on the jury retiring, one of them left the precincts of the court for a quarter of an hour before joining the jury in its retiring room); *R v Alexander* [1974] 1 All ER 539, [1974] 1 WLR 422, CA (where a juror returned to the courtroom to collect an exhibit; no application was made for discharge of the jury and the conviction was upheld); *R v Goodson* [1975] 1 All ER 760, [1975] 1 WLR 549, CA (where a conviction was quashed as a juror had left the jury room to make a telephone call after the jury had retired). See also *R v Chandler* [1993] Crim LR 394, CA (the separation of one juror after retirement without permission was an irregularity but, on the particular facts, the integrity of the process of deliberation by the jury was not threatened). Jurors may now separate after retirement with the leave of the court (see PARA 838) and the authorities should be read in the light of the fact that the long-standing rule against separation after retirement has been relaxed. As to the meaning of 'court' see PARA 804 note 1.

3 Jurors are now at the court's discretion allowed reasonable refreshment at their own expense (see PARA 838).

4 Co Litt 227b; 2 Roll Abr 686; *R v Willmont* (1914) 78 JP 352, CCA (where the conviction was quashed because the clerk of assize had entered the jury's retiring room and answered questions put to him by them and a discussion took place); *Goby v Wetherill* [1915] 2 KB 674 (where the verdict was invalidated by a stranger's presence in the jury room for a substantial time); *R v Shepherd* (1910) 74 JP Jo 605 (where the jury was discharged because a woman had spoken to a juror during the adjournment); *R v Twiss* [1918] 2 KB 853, CCA; *R v Brandon* (1969) 53 Cr App Rep 466, CA (where the conviction was quashed because of prejudicial remarks of a jury bailiff when escorting jurors to the lavatory); *R v McNeil* [1967] Crim LR 540, CA (jury bailiffs retired with jury; conviction quashed); *R v Panayis* [1999] Crim LR 84, CA (juror had conversation with defendant's solicitor's clerk; co-defendant absconded; juror not discharged and conviction upheld); *R v Karakaya* [2005] 2 Cr App Rep 77, CA; *R v Thakrar* [2008] EWCA Crim 2359, [2009] Crim LR 357; *R v Marshall* [2007] EWCA Crim 35, [2007] All ER (D) 76

(Jan); *R v Hawkins* [2005] EWCA Crim 2842 (in each of these last four cases, jurors downloaded material from the internet; appeals allowed in first two cases because of risk that jury would have been influenced adversely to defendant by material downloaded; appeals not allowed in latter two cases because no such risk). See also *R v Thorpe, R v Nicholls, R v Burke, R v Boyd* [1996] 1 Cr App Rep 269, CA (where jurors rejected improper attempts to influence them and reported incidents promptly to judge, assuring him their deliberations would not thereby be influenced, no real risk of injustice; judge entitled to refuse to discharge jury).

5   *Hale v Cove* (1735) 1 Stra 642; *Harvey v Hewitt* (1840) 8 Dowl 598. Where the court was satisfied with the verdict, albeit arrived at by lot, a new trial was not ordered: *Prior v Powers* (1664) 1 Keb 811. See the Contempt of Court Act 1981 s 8; and note 1.

6   *Hall v Poyser* (1845) 13 M & W 600. See the Contempt of Court Act 1981 s 8; and note 1.

7   *Goby v Wetherill* [1915] 2 KB 674; *R v McNeil* [1967] Crim LR 540, CA.

8   A distinction has been drawn between the conduct of jurors when at the bar and when they have left it: 1 Chitty's Criminal Law (2nd Edn) 527. The court will have regard to all the circumstances before it puts the parties to the expense of a new trial: *R v Kinnear* (1819) 2 B & Ald 462; *Morris v Vivian* (1842) 10 M & W 137; *Sabey v Stephens* (1862) 7 LT 274, where the court refused to disturb a verdict when, the day after it was given, the foreman wrote to the successful party on behalf of himself and his fellow jurors asking for a remittance. See further CRIMINAL LAW, EVIDENCE AND PROCEDURE vol 11(3) (2006 Reissue) PARA 1329. For the power of the Court of Appeal to award a venire de novo see PARA 834.

As to the effect of discharge of the jury during the trial see CRIMINAL LAW, EVIDENCE AND PROCEDURE vol 11(3) (2006 Reissue) PARA 1329.

9   Whether an individual juror or the entire jury is discharged is in the discretion of the judge: *R v Hambery* [1977] QB 924, [1977] 3 All ER 561, CA. The Court of Appeal will not lightly review and overturn the decision of a judge to discharge or retain a juror: *R v Hambery*.

10   *R v Knott* (1992) Times, 6 February, CA (where a juror became drunk, it was not necessary to discharge the whole jury; the proper course would be to ask the individual juror to stand down).

11   Application 22299/93 *Gregory v United Kingdom* (1997) 25 EHRR 577, ECtHR.

12   *R v Lucas* [1991] Crim LR 844, CA.

13   *R v Young (Stephen)* [1995] QB 324, [1995] 2 Cr App Rep 379, CA (conviction quashed).

14   *R v Schot, R v Barclay* [1997] 2 Cr App Rep 383, [1997] Crim LR 827, CA (judge ought not to have discharged entire jury).

15   *R v McCluskey* [1993] Crim LR 976, CA (no material irregularity as juror had made only one call on his mobile phone, the call being related to his business).

16   *R v Devall* (1992) 13 Cr App Rep (S) 598, [1992] Crim LR 664, CA (in declining to discharge the entire jury, the judge had been wrongly influenced by the fact that the proceedings in question were a retrial; appeal allowed and retrial ordered).

17   Ie under the Senior Courts Act 1981 s 16(1) (see COURTS vol 10 (Reissue) PARA 639): *Gladding v Channel 4 Television Corpn* [1999] EMLR 475, CA. The Senior Courts Act 1981 was previously known as the Supreme Court Act 1981 and was renamed by the Constitutional Reform Act 2005 s 59(5), Sch 11 Pt 1 as from 1 October 2009: see the Constitutional Reform Act 2005 (Commencement No 11) Order 2009, SI 2009/1604; and COURTS.

18   *Winsor v R* (1866) LR 1 QB 390; *R v Lewis* [1908–10] All ER Rep 654, CCA.

19   See *R v Hambery* [1977] QB 924, [1977] 3 All ER 561, CA.

20   *R v Green* [1950] 1 All ER 38, CCA; *R v Gorman* [1987] 2 All ER 435, [1987] 1 WLR 545, CA (judge should state in open court the nature and content of the communication and, if he thinks it helpful, seek the assistance of counsel, before the jury returns to court); *R v Green* [1992] Crim LR 292, CA; cf *R v Furlong* [1950] 1 All ER 636, CCA (where a communication was read out in court after discharge of the jury, and the conviction was upheld). See also *R v Dempsey* (1991) Times, 9 January, CA (communication between judge and jury prior to retirement of the jury). See further CRIMINAL LAW, EVIDENCE AND PROCEDURE vol 11(3) (2006 Reissue) PARA 1333.

21   *R v Ion* (1950) 34 Cr App Rep 152, CCA; *R v Gorman* [1987] 2 All ER 435, [1987] 1 WLR 545, CA.

22   *R v Gorman* [1987] 2 All ER 435, [1987] 1 WLR 545, CA.

23   *R v Ion* (1950) 34 Cr App Rep 152, CCA; *R v Gorman* [1987] 2 All ER 435, [1987] 1 WLR 545, CA (the communication can be dealt with without any reference to counsel and without bringing the jury back into court).

24   *Fromhold v Fromhold* [1952] 1 TLR 1522, CA. As to communications made during the course of the trial see PARA 843.

25   *Naismith v London Film Productions Ltd* [1939] 1 All ER 794 at 798, CA.

26   See *R v Qureshi* [2001] EWCA Crim 1807, [2002] 1 WLR 518. As to the likelihood of injustice being caused by misconduct in jury deliberations, and as to the confidentiality of such

deliberations, see *A-G v Scotcher* [2005] UKHL 36, [2005] 3 All ER 1, [2005] 1 WLR 1867 (where an application for contempt of court under the Contempt of Court Act 1981 s 8(1) (see PARA 858; and CONTEMPT OF COURT vol 9(1) (Reissue) PARA 451) was allowed against a juror who had anonymously written to the mother of the defendant saying that there had been a miscarriage of justice and revealing details of what had occurred when the jury retired); and see also *A-G v Seckerson* [2009] EWHC 1023 (Admin), [2009] EMLR 371, [2009] All ER (D) 106 (May).

842. Bias. Actual or apparent bias in a juror gives grounds for discharge[1]. The appearance of bias is equally important as actual bias. Where actual bias is not established, the test the court should apply is whether, having regard to the relevant circumstances, as ascertained by the court, a fair-minded and informed observer would conclude that there was a real danger that a juror was or would be biased in the sense that he might unfairly regard with favour or disfavour the case of a party to the issue under consideration by him[2]. An affirmative answer to that question will necessitate the discharge of that juror and, depending on the facts of the case, the entire jury[3]. Bias may encompass deliberate hostility[4], inadvertent knowledge of the defendant's bad character[5], alleged racism[6], acquaintance with prosecution witnesses[7] or a close nexus with the case in some way[8].

1   As to bias providing a ground for challenge for cause see PARA 831.

2   *R v Gough* [1993] AC 646, [1993] 2 All ER 724, HL, as adjusted by the decision in *Re Medicaments and Related Classes of Goods (No 2)* [2001] 1 WLR 700, CA, so as to make the test in *R v Gough* compatible with the case law of the European Court of Human Rights. The correctness of the principle in *Re Medicaments and Related Classes of Goods (No 2)* was confirmed in *Porter v Magill, Weeks v Magill* [2001] UKHL 67, [2002] 2 AC 357, [2002] 1 All ER 465; applied in *Mitcham v R* [2009] UKPC 7, [2009] All ER (D) 145 (Apr). See also *R v Hawkins* [2005] EWCA Crim 2842 (there was no apparent bias where jurors notified judge of internet research by one their number and sought further direction); *R v Azam* [2006] EWCA Crim 161, [2006] Crim LR 776, (2006) Times, 16 March; *R v S* [2009] EWCA Crim 104, [2009] All ER (D) 75 (Jan). Where a dispute on evidence arises between a defendant and a witness who is employed in the administration of justice, such as a police officer or a solicitor employed by the Crown Prosecution Service, a fair minded and informed observer could conclude that, where one of the jurors is a colleague of the witness who is employed in the administration of justice, there is a real possibility that such a juror could be biased: *R v Abdroikov, R v Green, R v Williamson* [2007] UKHL 37, [2008] 1 All ER 315, [2007] 1 Cr App Rep 280; applied in *R v Khan* [2008] EWCA Crim 531, [2008] 3 All ER 502 (Crown Prosecution Service lawyer ought not to be a juror where Crown Prosecution Service is prosecuting authority; police officers are not by reason of their occupation to be considered to be biased in favour of prosecution); *R v C* [2008] EWCA Crim 1033, [2008] All ER (D) 370 (Apr) (fact that a juror is a police officer does not by itself create an appearance of bias, but one situation in which such an appearance may arise is where a police officer juror shares a connection (e g by service) with a police officer witness whose evidence is going to be disputed); *R v Yemoh* [2009] EWCA Crim 930, [2009] All ER (D) 07 (Jun) (defendant's abusive statement about police should not have led to discharge of juror who was a police officer); *R v T* [2009] EWCA Crim 1638, [2009] All ER (D) 327 (Jul) (it could not be assumed that a juror who was a police officer was biased where the defendant alleged police misconduct). See further *R v Thakrar* [2008] EWCA Crim 2359, [2009] Crim LR 357 (there was a real possibility of bias where one of the jurors had researched the defendants on the internet and disclosed a previous conviction to the other jurors); and see also *R v Cornwall* [2009] EWCA Crim 2458, [2009] All ER (D) 290 (Nov) (foreman of jury discovered to be newspaper columnist; defendant contended that juror was an outspoken polemicist who held strong and well-published views on crime, law and order; held that the juror had not demonstrated actual bias nor did his articles give rise to the possibility or risk of bias). Where a matter that could prejudice the jurors was mentioned before them and subsequently not referred to, it was for the judge to determine whether to discharge the jury or not: *Mitcham v R* [2009] UKPC 7, [2009] All ER (D) 145 (Apr).

3   See PARA 841. In *R v Appiah* [1998] Crim LR 134, CA, a juror who felt threatened by the sight of the defendant out of court was discharged and the trial continued with the remaining jurors not thereby prejudiced.

4   *R v O'Coigly* (1798) 26 State Tr 1191. Contrast *R v Wright* [1995] 2 Cr App Rep 134, [1995] Crim LR 251, CA (Court of Appeal upheld trial judge's refusal to discharge a juror who was said to show signs of hostility to a defendant during the defendant's cross-examination).

5   *R v Box* [1964] 1 QB 430, [1963] 3 All ER 240, CCA. See also *R v Lambert* [2006] EWCA Crim 827, [2006] 2 Cr App Rep (S) 699; *R v Lawson* [2005] EWCA Crim 84, [2007] 1 Cr App Rep 277; *R v Russell* [2006] EWCA Crim 470, [2006] All ER (D) 151 (Mar).

6   See Application 22299/93 *Gregory v United Kingdom* (1997) 25 EHRR 577, ECtHR.

7   *R v K (Jury: Appearance of Bias)* (1995) 16 Cr App Rep (S) 966, CA. See also *R v I* [2007] EWCA Crim 2999, [2007] All ER (D) 398 (Oct) (potential juror was police officer familiar with prosecution witnesses); *R v I* [2007] EWCA Crim 2999, [2007] All ER (D) 398 (Oct) (judge erred in not discharging the jury when a juror informed him that he thought he had worked with the defendant); *R v Hambleton* [2009] EWCA Crim 13, [2009] All ER (D) 67 (Jan) (juror who had stood down who knew the defendant informed another juror that the defendant was 'a bad lot'); *R v Ali* [2009] EWCA Crim 1763, [2009] All ER (D) 214 (Jul) (challenge to presence of police officer as member of jury); *R v Pintori* [2007] EWCA Crim 1700, [2007] Crim LR 997.

8   See *R v Wilson* [1995] Crim LR 952, CA (retrial ordered after a challenge in respect of a juror married to a prison officer serving a prison where the appellants were on remand was refused).

843. Expression of opinion before verdict. The mere expression of an opinion by a jury at an early stage of a case is not in itself such misconduct as would justify any person in refusing to submit his case to that tribunal, but if the members of the jury do not honestly and judicially approach the question before them, a new trial may be ordered[1].

1   *Campbell v Hackney Furnishing Co Ltd* (1906) 22 TLR 318. Alternatively, the judge may himself discharge the jury and begin the trial afresh: *R v Kirke* (1909) 43 ILT 130. There must be some positive and irregular expression of opinion: *Ramadge v Ryan* (1832) 9 Bing 333; *Allum v Boultbee* (1854) 9 Exch 738; and see *Ural Caspian Oil Corpn Ltd v Hume-Schweder* (1913) Times, 31 July, HL. On this principle the court will order a new trial if the sum awarded for damages has evidently resulted from compromise: *Hall v Poyser* (1845) 13 M & W 600; *Kelly v Sherlock* (1866) LR 1 QB 686 at 693; *Burrows v London General Omnibus Co* (1894) 10 TLR 298, CA.

      Notes indicating the extent of division between jurors are never disclosed; such a disclosure is said to be contrary to public policy and in breach of the confidentiality rule in the Contempt of Court Act 1981 (see PARA 858; and CONTEMPT OF COURT vol 9(1) (Reissue) PARa 451). See also *A-G v Scotcher* [2005] UKHL 36, [2005] 3 All ER 1, [2005] 1 WLR 1867; and PARA 841 note 26.

844. Premature verdict. In a civil trial where a jury, before hearing all the evidence of one party, finds a verdict for the other[1], or misleads counsel by an intimation that it does not wish to hear more evidence for his client and then finds a verdict for the other party[2], it is within the trial judge's discretion to decide whether he should discharge the jury and order a new trial or continue with the same jury[3]. In the second case he must direct the jury to hear the whole of the party's case against whom it proposes to find, and, after it has done so, he must direct it as to the issues[4]. If, in a claim for defamation, the claimant has failed to give evidence during the presentation of his own case but has undertaken, subject to the court's permission being granted, to give evidence in rebuttal of the evidence in support of the defendant's plea of justification, the jury, if it desires to give its verdict before the conclusion of the evidence on the defendant's behalf, must be directed to either ignore the evidence given on behalf of the defendant or wait until a ruling as to the claimant's right to give evidence in rebuttal has been obtained[5]. Any question of a jury stopping a case is a matter between the judge and the jury and not a matter which should be introduced to the jury by counsel on his own initiative[6].

In a criminal case the jury may acquit the defendant at any time after the close of the prosecution case[7].

1   *De Freville v Dill* (1927) 43 TLR 431, CA; *Hobbs v CT Tinling & Co Ltd* [1929] 2 KB 1, CA.
    Cf *Beevis v Dawson* [1956] 2 QB 165 at 173, [1956] 2 All ER 371 at 373 (revsd on appeal
    [1957] 1 QB 195 at 202, [1956] 3 All ER 837 at 840, CA), where the defendant was not entitled
    to object on the ground that the jury had found a verdict for the plaintiff before evidence on
    behalf of the defendant was concluded, since the defendant's counsel had invited it to do this,
    but a new trial was ordered on other grounds: see the text and note 5.
2   *Biggs v Evans* (1912) 106 LT 796, DC.
3   *De Freville v Dill* (1927) 43 TLR 431, CA; and see also *Biggs v Evans* (1912) 106 LT 796, DC;
    Hobbs v CT Tinling & Co Ltd [1929] 2 KB 1 at 24, CA; *Beevis v Dawson* [1956] 2 QB 165 at
    178–179, [1956] 2 All ER 371 at 376–377 (revsd on appeal [1957] 1 QB 195, [1956] 3 All ER
    837, CA).
4   *Hobbs v CT Tinling & Co Ltd* [1929] 2 KB 1 at 26, 33, 46, CA.
5   *Beevis v Dawson* [1957] 1 QB 195 at 218, [1956] 3 All ER 837 at 850, CA, per Parker LJ,
    where the defendant's counsel had, before the evidence for the defence was concluded, invited
    the jury to return a verdict for the plaintiff with contemptuous damages; the verdict was set
    aside and a new trial ordered in view of: (1) the absence of any ruling as to the plaintiff's right
    to give evidence in rebuttal; (2) misstatements as to the burden of proof of justification; and (3)
    the invitation to the jury to stop the case and the absence of any direction as to the possibility of
    evidence being given in rebuttal.
6   *Beevis v Dawson* [1957] 1 QB 195 at 208, 214, [1956] 3 All ER 837 at 844, 848, CA. As to
    counsel's duties see generally LEGAL PROFESSIONS.
7   See *R v Kemp* [1995] 1 Cr App Rep 151, CA; *R v Collins* [2007] EWCA Crim 854, [2007] All
    ER (D) 161 (Apr); and CRIMINAL LAW, EVIDENCE AND PROCEDURE vol 11(3) (2006 Reissue)
    PARA 1313.

845.   Discharge before verdict.   On the trial of any issue[1], civil or criminal, a
juror may be withdrawn by consent of the parties[2], and the court may in its
absolute discretion discharge the jury at any time before the verdict is given[3].
However, a jury ought not to be discharged at the instance of the prosecution for
the purpose of enabling the prosecution to put forward a stronger case[4].

1   If there are several distinct issues to be tried in one claim, the judge may, even without consent,
    accept the verdict on any issue on which the jury can agree, and discharge it upon the others,
    leaving the parties to take the undecided issues down to a new trial: *Marsh v Isaacs* (1876) 45
    LJQB 505. He may also discharge the jury on any issue which he deems immaterial: *R v Johnson*
    (1839) Macl & Rob 1, HL; *Powell v Sonnett* (1827) 1 Bli NS 545.
2   *R v Kinloch* (1746) Fost 16 at 22, 27. When a jury has been discharged it will be assumed that
    the discharge was by consent unless it appears to the contrary on the record: *Scott v Bennett*
    (1871) LR 5 HL 234. A civil claim does not thereby come to an end, and on breach of the terms
    on which the juror has been withdrawn the court may proceed to the trial thereof with the same
    or a fresh jury: *Norburn v Hilliam* (1870) LR 5 CP 129; *Thomas v Exeter Flying Post Co* (1887)
    18 QBD 822.
3   As to the power to discharge a jury in a criminal trial see CRIMINAL LAW, EVIDENCE AND
    PROCEDURE vol 11(3) (2006 Reissue) PARA 1328; as to the reasons for discharge during a
    criminal trial see CRIMINAL LAW, EVIDENCE AND PROCEDURE vol 11(3) (2006 Reissue) PARA
    1329; and as to the effect of discharge during trial see CRIMINAL LAW, EVIDENCE AND
    PROCEDURE vol 11(3) (2006 Reissue) PARA 1330. As to discharge in civil cases see *Morris v
    Davies* (1828) 3 C & P 427. As to the death or discharge of an individual juror see PARA 837.
    The court generally discharges the jury when satisfied that the jurors will not agree on a verdict:
    see further CRIMINAL LAW, EVIDENCE AND PROCEDURE vol 11(3) (2006 Reissue) PARA 1346. The
    discharge of a jury unable to agree was the subject of further consideration in *Winsor v R* (1866)
    LR 1 QB 289 at 309 (affd on appeal LR 1 QB 390, Ex Ch), where it was laid down that the
    judge's discretion in ordering the discharge was not open to review. It seems that the defendant
    need not be present when the jury is discharged: *R v Richardson* [1913] 1 KB 395, CCA. As to
    the discharge of a jury in a libel trial see *Gladding v Channel 4 Television Corpn Ltd* [1999]
    EMLR 475, CA.
4   See *R v Charlesworth* (1861) 1 B & S 460.

846.   Juror's own knowledge of facts.   A juror's personal knowledge of the
case or the defendant may be sufficient to found a challenge or render a
conviction unsafe[1]. A jury may act upon its general knowledge and look at

documents[2] of a public character, although they are not exhibits in the proceedings, when they are sent to it by or with the approval of the court[3], and in proper cases may have a view of the place in question[4].

1 See *R v Hood* [1968] 2 All ER 56, [1968] 1 WLR 773, CCA (juror was known to defendant's wife). As to unsafe convictions generally see the Criminal Appeal Act 1995; and CRIMINAL LAW, EVIDENCE AND PROCEDURE vol 11(4) (2006 Reissue) PARA 1878.
2 As to the functions of judge and jury with respect to the interpretation of documents see DEEDS AND OTHER INSTRUMENTS vol 13 (2007 Reissue) PARA 167.
3 *Vicary v Farthing* (1595) Cro Eliz 411; *Graves v Short* (1598) Cro Eliz 616; *Cole v De Trafford (No 2)* [1918] 2 KB 523, CA.
4 As to views see PARA 840; and CIVIL PROCEDURE vol 11 (2009) PARA 1108; CRIMINAL LAW, EVIDENCE AND PROCEDURE vol 11(3) (2006 Reissue) PARA 1326. It is undesirable for the jury to take newspaper reports of the proceedings into the jury room: *Salter v Beaverbrook Newspapers Ltd* (1964) 108 Sol Jo 941.

(6) GIVING OF VERDICT AND DISCHARGE

847. Types of verdict. Juries in both civil and criminal matters may find general or special verdicts[1]. General verdicts in criminal matters are findings of guilty or not guilty[2], and in civil causes are statements as to the party for which the juries find, with the amount of damages assessed, if such finding is for the claimant, or the sum awarded if the issue is one of assessment solely[3]. Special verdicts are findings of specific facts[4] on which, in criminal cases, the court must direct the jury to return the general verdict warranted by its special findings[5]. Special verdicts in criminal cases should be found only in the most exceptional circumstances[6].

1 As to the form of verdict in coroners' courts see CORONERS vol 9(2) (2006 Reissue) PARA 1030. As from a day to be appointed, a jury at an inquest will no longer return a verdict but will instead make a determination or finding: see the Coroners and Justice Act 2009 s 10 (not yet in force); and CORONERS. At the date at which this volume states the law, no such day had been appointed.
2 As to permissible verdicts see CRIMINAL LAW, EVIDENCE AND PROCEDURE vol 11(3) (2006 Reissue) PARA 1334.
3 Where there is more than one issue (eg (1) libel; (2) slander), the jury must apportion the damages, otherwise there is in effect no verdict: *Weber v Birkett* [1925] 2 KB 152, CA. As to a review of damages on appeal see DAMAGES vol 12(1) (Reissue) PARA 1162.
4 A special verdict must not consist of a mere statement of evidence: *Hubbard v Johnstone* (1810) 3 Taunt 177 at 209, Ex Ch; *Fryer v Roe* (1852) 12 CB 437. It must contain express findings of fact on which, and on which alone, judgment can be founded: *Tancred v Christy* (1843) 12 M & W 316. The whole findings must appear upon the record: *R v Aire and Calder Navigation (Undertakers)* (1778) 2 Term Rep 660 at 666. The jury may not attach a condition to its verdict: *Fanshaw v Knowles* [1916] 2 KB 538, CA. For an example of a special verdict given in pursuance of a nineteenth century local Act see *Harris Simon & Co Ltd v Manchester City Council* [1975] 1 All ER 412, [1975] 1 WLR 100, DC.
5 See *R v Dudley and Stephens* (1884) 14 QBD 273 at 280 per Lord Coleridge CJ. In *R v Jameson* [1896] 2 QB 425, Lord Russell of Killowen CJ put a series of questions in writing to the jury, which it answered, and then directed that the answers amounted to a verdict of guilty, whereupon the jury returned a general verdict of guilty. See further CRIMINAL LAW, EVIDENCE AND PROCEDURE vol 11(3) (2006 Reissue) PARA 1339. Note that, by way of exception, it is the jury which returns the special verdict of not guilty by reason of insanity; and, in an insanity case, a general verdict is not returned: see the Trial of Lunatics Act 1883 s 2; and CRIMINAL LAW, EVIDENCE AND PROCEDURE vol 11(1) (2006 Reissue) PARA 31; MENTAL HEALTH vol 30(2) (Reissue) PARA 499.
6 *R v Bourne* (1952) 36 Cr App Rep 125, CCA.

848. Special verdict a privilege. The finding of a special verdict is a privilege and not an obligation of a jury[1], and if it refuses to find one, or to accept the direction of the judge as to what the general verdict founded on it should be, it seems that the general verdict as delivered must stand[2].

1   *Devizes Corpn v Clark* (1835) 3 Ad & El 506; *R v Allday* (1837) 8 C & P 136.

2   If the jury returns a verdict of not guilty in spite of the judge's direction upon matters specially found by it, a defendant must be discharged: *R v Allday* (1837) 8 C & P 136; *R v Jameson* (1896) 12 TLR 551 at 593–594.

849. Where and how verdicts are given. A jury's verdict on the issue must be given in open court[1] in the presence of all the jurors[2], and preferably in the presence of the defendant[3]. If a jury gives a reason or adds to a direct verdict uncertain or contradictory matter, it is mere surplusage[4].

A judge will decline to hear the reasons upon which a jury has based its verdict and it must not be asked for them[5]. Where a jury has given a general verdict the judge is not entitled to ask the jury any further question for the purpose of ascertaining whether the ground of its verdict was one which there was evidence to support[6].

However, in cases of unlawful killing, where there is more than one possible ground for a verdict of guilty of manslaughter, one of which is diminished responsibility, the judge may invite the jury to give the ground for its verdict or to say whether it was based on both grounds[7]. However, the jury is under no obligation to respond to the invitation[8].

The verdict is forthwith entered on the record by the officer of the court. The jury is then discharged[9].

1   *Ellis v Deheer* [1922] 2 KB 113, CA. It is the judge's duty to stay to assist the jury so long as it is deliberating on its verdict: *Fanshaw v Knowles* [1916] 2 KB 538, CA; *Banbury v Bank of Montreal* [1917] 1 KB 409 at 442, CA, per Scrutton LJ; *Hawksley v Fewtrell* [1954] 1 QB 228 at 237, 242, 246, [1953] 2 All ER 1486 at 1490, 1494, 1496, CA. A verdict in a civil case given in court to the associate in the absence of the judge is a public verdict and although it is undesirable that a verdict should be given in the judge's absence, his absence does not of itself render it a nullity, even though the jury may have been discharged after giving the verdict and not called upon to appear again to return a verdict before the judge: *Hawksley v Fewtrell*. It is a question upon which the court will exercise its discretion as to granting a new trial, whether the associate (in the absence of the judge) rightly interpreted the meaning of the jury when he entered the verdict: *Doe d Lewis v Baster* (1836) 5 Ad & El 129; *Bentley v Fleming* (1845) 1 CB 479. An affidavit by a juror as to what took place in court upon the entering of the verdict will not be excluded by the rule excluding evidence of jurors as to the jury's deliberations (see PARA 852): *Roberts v Hughes* (1841) 7 M & W 399. It is the duty of the parties' solicitors to be in court to hear the verdict: *Dauntley v Hyde* (1841) 6 Jur 133. As to delivery of the verdict see further CRIMINAL LAW, EVIDENCE AND PROCEDURE vol 11(3) (2006 Reissue) PARA 1341.

2   This is in order that they may all hear if it is rightly delivered by the foreman, for if it is delivered in the presence of them all their assent will be presumed: *Raphael v Governor & Co of the Bank of England* (1855) 17 CB 161, where the court refused to admit an affidavit by jurors, who had heard what the foreman said and had not objected, to the effect that they had not understood his answers. Where three jurors were out of court and did not assent to what the foreman said a new trial was ordered: *R v Wooller* (1817) 2 Stark 111. Where three jurors could not hear what the foreman said, affidavits by them to show that the verdict was not unanimous were held admissible, even though objection was not raised until after the discharge of the jury, and a new trial was ordered: *Ellis v Deheer* [1922] 2 KB 113, CA. See contra *Nanan v The State* [1986] AC 860, [1986] 3 All ER 248, PC, in which juror affidavits challenging apparent unanimity were held to be inadmissible.

3   The giving of the verdict in the presence of the defendant is not necessary but usual (*R v Woodfall* (1770) 5 Burr 2661), except in the case of treason where it is compulsory (see CRIMINAL LAW, EVIDENCE AND PROCEDURE vol 11(3) (2006 Reissue) PARA 1356).

4   *Eve v Wright* (1627) Cro Car 75; *Plunket v Lord Kingsland* (1749) 7 Bro Parl Cas 404, HL; *Clark v Stevenson* (1772) 2 Wm Bl 803; *Brown v Bristol and Exeter Rly Co* (1861) 4 LT 830; *R v Warner* [1967] 3 All ER 93, [1967] 1 WLR 1209, CA (affd sub nom *Warner v Metropolitan Police Comr* [1969] 2 AC 256, [1968] 2 All ER 356, HL).

5   Such questions would breach the rule governing the confidentiality of jury deliberations: see the Contempt of Court Act 1981 s 8(1); PARA 858; and CONTEMPT OF COURT vol 9(1) (Reissue) PARA 451.
6   *Arnold v Jeffreys* [1914] 1 KB 512; *Horner v Watson* (1834) 6 C & P 680; *Barnes v Hill* [1967] 1 QB 579, [1967] 1 All ER 347, CA. Such a course of action would also amount to a breach of the rule protecting juror confidentiality: see the Contempt of Court Act 1981 s 8(1); PARA 858; and CONTEMPT OF COURT vol 9(1) (Reissue) PARA 451.
7   *R v Matheson* [1958] 2 All ER 87, 42 Cr App Rep 145, CCA. Contrast *R v Larkin* [1943] KB 174, 29 Cr App Rep 18, CCA (two possible defences to murder on facts: 'provocation' and 'no intent to injure'; judge should not seek to ascertain basis of manslaughter decision); *R v Byrne (Paul)* [2002] EWCA Crim 1975, [2003] 1 Cr App Rep (S) 338 (defence based on lack of intent; judge left provocation to jury; judge declined to ask jury for basis of manslaughter decision; held judge had discretion so to decline). If the jury is to be asked for the basis of a manslaughter verdict it should be warned to this effect in the summing up: *R v Jones (Douglas)* [1999] All ER (D) 118, (1999) Times, 17 February, CA.
8   *R v Jones (Douglas)* [1999] All ER (D) 118, (1999) Times, 17 February, CA.
9   After discharge, the court will not allow judgment to be entered for a larger sum than was originally declared, even though the jury joins in an affidavit stating that it was its intention to have given a larger sum: *Jackson v Williamson* (1788) 2 Term Rep 281; *Kilmore v Abdoolah* (1858) 27 LJ Ex 307.

850.   Majority verdicts. The verdict of a jury in proceedings in the Crown Court or the High Court need not be unanimous[1] if: (1) where there are not less than 11 jurors, ten of them agree; or (2) where there are ten jurors, nine of them agree[2]. The verdict of a complete jury of eight in a county court need not be unanimous if seven agree[3]. At an inquest held with a jury, if the minority consists of not more than two persons, a majority verdict (until a day to be appointed) or a majority determination (as from a day to be appointed) may be accepted[4].

No court[5] may accept a majority verdict unless it appears that the jury has had such period of time for deliberation as seems to the court reasonable having regard to the nature and complexity of the case in any event, and the Crown Court may not accept such a verdict unless it appears to the court that the jury has had at least two hours for deliberation[6]. Nor may the Crown Court accept a verdict of guilty by a majority unless the foreman has stated in open court the number who respectively agreed and dissented[7].

These provisions do not affect any practice in civil proceedings by which a court may accept a majority verdict by consent of the parties or by which the parties may agree to proceed with an incomplete jury[8].

A judge may urge a jury to avoid disagreement if it can do so without violating its convictions and may in civil trials point out the inconvenience and expense which would result if a new trial became necessary, but if he were to tell the jury that it was the duty of the minority to give up its independent judgment to that of the majority and to reach agreement even if it had not changed its own convictions, this would amount to a misdirection[9].

1   As to majority verdicts in criminal cases see further CRIMINAL LAW, EVIDENCE AND PROCEDURE vol 11(3) (2006 Reissue) PARAS 1340, 1342.
2   Juries Act 1974 s 17(1)(a), (b). These provisions are subject to s 17(3), (4) (see the text and notes 5–7): s 17(1).
3   Juries Act 1974 s 17(2). This is subject to s 17(4) (see the text and notes 5–6): s 17(2).
4   See the Coroners Act 1988 s 12(2) (prospectively repealed by the Coroners and Justice Act 2009 Sch 23 Pt 1); the Coroners and Justice Act 2009 s 9(2) (not yet in force); and CORONERS vol 9(2) (2006 Reissue) PARA 1029. As from a day to be appointed, juries at inquests will no longer return verdicts but will instead make a determination or finding: see ss 9, 10 (not yet in force); and CORONERS. At the date at which this volume states the law, no such day had been appointed. A majority determination can only be accepted if the jury has deliberated for a period of time that the senior coroner thinks reasonable in view of the nature and complexity of the case: see s 9(2) (not yet in force); and CORONERS.

5 As to the meaning of 'court' see PARA 804 note 1. Note that, in view of this definition, the Juries Act 1974 s 17 does not apply in coroners' courts.

6 Juries Act 1974 s 17(4). In a complicated criminal case much more than two hours should be allowed to elapse before a majority verdict is accepted: *R v Bateson* [1969] 3 All ER 1372, CA. Two hours and ten minutes should elapse from the time when the last juror leaves the jury box until the time when the jury is asked to deliver its verdict: *Practice Direction (Criminal Proceedings: Consolidation)* [2002] 3 All ER 904, [2002] 2 Cr App Rep 533 at IV.46.3, CA. See also *R v Black* [2008] EWCA Crim 344, [2008] All ER (D) 388 (Apr) (until the jury had had at least two hours for deliberation, a majority verdict was prohibited).

7 Juries Act 1974 s 17(3). Compliance with s 17(3) is mandatory; however, all that is necessary is that it is made clear how the jury is divided: *R v Pigg* [1983] 1 All ER 56, [1983] 1 WLR 6, HL (conviction allowed to stand where the foreman of the jury delivering a majority verdict stated only that ten jurors agreed with the verdict). See also PARA 851 note 2.

8 Juries Act 1974 s 17(5).

9 *Re Wright, Lambert v Woodham* [1936] 1 All ER 877 at 879, CA. Slightly different considerations apply in criminal trials, where the trial judge may give the direction set out in *R v Watson* [1988] QB 690, [1988] 1 All ER 897, CA, as follows: 'Each of you has taken an oath to return a true verdict according to the evidence. No one must be false to that oath, but you have a duty not only as individuals but collectively. That is the strength of the jury system. Each of you takes into the jury box with you your individual experience and wisdom. Your task is to pool that experience and wisdom. You do that by giving your views and listening to the views of others. There must necessarily be discussion, argument and give and take within the scope of your oath. That is the way in which agreement is reached. If, unhappily, ten of you cannot reach agreement you should say so'. The direction should be given after a jury has had time to consider a majority direction or as part of the summing up. Trial judges should not depart from the precise wording of the direction: *R v Buono* (1992) 95 Cr App Rep 338, CA. See also *Morrison v Chief Constable of West Midlands Police* [2003] All ER (D) 220 (Feb), CA (simply reminding the jury of the general expense of trials by jury did not automatically constitute misdirection by the judge).

851. Jury once discharged. Once a jury has been discharged after giving a verdict in a civil case upon which judgment has been entered, it cannot usually be recalled to rectify the verdict and there must be a new trial if the court considers that injustice has been done[1]. In a criminal trial, a jury once discharged is functus officio and accordingly any subsequent proceedings involving the jury are a nullity[2].

1 *Loveday's Case* (1608) 8 Co Rep 65b; *Doe d Lewis v Baster* (1836) 5 Ad & El 129. In *Cogan v Ebden* (1757) 1 Burr 383, it was suggested by Lord Mansfield, on a motion for a new trial on the ground that the jury had not returned the verdict it intended, that the record might be amended, and he referred to cases where this had been done. However, it now seems that the only remedy would be a new trial where the jury has left the court before the mistake is discovered. Affidavits of all 12 jurors stating that they had intended their answer to a question to be 'yes' instead of 'no' are not admissible: *Boston v WS Bagshaw & Sons* [1967] 2 All ER 87n, [1966] 1 WLR 1135n, CA; *Diven v Belfast Corpn* [1969] NI 34, CA. However, recent authority suggests that, where the interests of justice in the particular case so require, the judge does have the discretion to set aside a discharge of a jury and allow the jurors to deliberate further: *Igwemma v Chief Constable of Greater Manchester Police* [2001] EWCA Civ 953, [2002] QB 1012, [2001] 4 All ER 751 (where the very real possibility of a misunderstanding by the jurors of the answer to a question addressed to the judge and the very short time since the original answer were said to be key factors in the exercise of the discretion in favour of further deliberation).

2 *R v Russell* (1984) 148 JP 765, [1984] Crim LR 425, CA. See, however, *R v Aylott* [1996] 2 Cr App Rep 169, [1996] Crim LR 429, CA (jury which had reached a verdict but was then discharged by the trial judge acting under the belief that a verdict could not be reached was reconvened and verdict obtained); *R v Maloney* [1996] 2 Cr App Rep 303, 140 Sol Jo LB 85, CA (a failure to record the number of jurors who agreed and dissented can be rectified if the court reconvenes immediately the error is realised; discharge or dispersal of the jury is not a bar to rectification of the verdict); *R v S* [2005] EWCA Crim 1987, [2006] Crim LR 247, [2005] All ER (D) 394 (Jul) (the conviction was not unsafe where the judge had discharged the jury when counsel intervened and the judge promptly changed his mind and prompt effect was given to it).

Cf the correction of a jury's verdict in criminal proceedings: see CRIMINAL EVIDENCE, LAW AND PROCEDURE vol 11(3) (2006 Reissue) PARA 1334.

852.   Evidence by or about jurors.   Statements or affidavits by any member of a jury as to its deliberations or intentions on the matter to be adjudicated on are never receivable[1]. The deliberations of juries are confidential[2]. However, the affidavits of jurors or bystanders may be received as to what passed in open court on the bringing in of a verdict[3], the circumstances under which a juror went into the box[4], and his state of sobriety when in the jury box or jury room[5]; and a juror is entitled to be heard in his own defence[6]. Following a verdict, no statement should be taken from a juror without leave of the Court of Appeal[7].

1   *Palmer v Crowle* (1738) Andr 382; *R v Woodfall* (1770) 5 Burr 2661 at 2667; *R v Almon* (1770) 5 Burr 2686; *Vaise v Delaval* (1785) 1 Term Rep 11; *Jackson v Williamson* (1788) 2 Term Rep 281 (as to the amount of damages intended to be awarded); *Owen v Warburton* (1805) 1 Bos & PNR 326; *R v Wooller* (1817) 2 Stark 111; *Coster v Merest* (1822) 3 Brod & Bing 272; *Straker v Graham* (1839) 4 M & W 721 at 724; *Bentley v Fleming* (1845) 1 CB 479; *Raphael v Governor & Co of the Bank of England* (1855) 17 CB 161; *Nesbitt v Parrett* (1902) 18 TLR 510, CA; *R v Willmont* (1914) 78 JP 352, CCA; *R v Armstrong* [1922] 2 KB 555, CCA; *R v Thompson* [1962] 1 All ER 65, CCA; *Boston v WS Bagshaw & Sons* [1967] 2 All ER 87n, [1966] 1 WLR 1135n, CA. A juror cannot later give evidence of lack of unanimity where the verdict was returned in his presence and hearing: *R v Roads* [1967] 2 QB 108, [1967] 2 All ER 84, CA; *R v Connor, R v Mirza* [2004] UKHL 2, [2004] 1 AC 1118, [2004] 1 All ER 925. But see *Ellis v Deheer* [1922] 2 KB 113, CA; and PARA 849. This principle also applies where the statement or affidavit is not that of a juror, but of someone to whom the juror has made a communication: *Aylett v Jewel* (1779) 2 Wm Bl 1299; *Straker v Graham* (1839) 4 M & W 721; *Burgess v Langley* (1843) 5 Man & G 722. In *R v Thomas* [1933] 2 KB 489, CCA, the court refused to admit affidavits from two jurors that they did not understand English well enough to follow the proceedings; but in *Ras Behari Lal v R* (1933) 102 LJPC 144, the court admitted evidence to show that some members of the jury knew little or no English. As to whether a judge is obliged to question members of a jury before deciding to give further direction or to discharge the jury see *R v Smith* [2005] UKHL 12, [2005] 2 All ER 29, [2005] 1 WLR 704. See also *R v Adams* [2007] EWCA Crim 1, [2007] All ER (D) 25 (Jan).

2   It is a contempt of court to obtain, disclose or solicit any particulars of statements made, opinions expressed, arguments advanced or votes cast by members of a jury in the course of their deliberations in any legal proceedings: see the Contempt of Court Act 1981 s 8(1); PARA 858; and CONTEMPT OF COURT vol 9(1) (Reissue) PARAS 434, 451. See *R v Young (Stephen)* [1995] QB 324, [1995] 2 Cr App Rep 379, CA (jury's overnight stay at a hotel did not come within the meaning of deliberations; accordingly, the court was able to investigate events which had taken place at the hotel). It is not appropriate to conduct an investigation into the deliberations of a criminal jury on the basis that a juror has subsequently alleged that the verdict was not unanimous if the verdict was unambiguous, free from procedural defect and not dissented from when given: *R v Lewis* [2001] EWCA Crim 3048, [2001] All ER (D) 413 (Dec), (2001) Times, 26 April. See also *R v Connor, R v Mirza* [2004] UKHL 2, [2004] 1 AC 1118, [2004] 1 All ER 925 (the principle of the confidentiality of jury deliberations underpins the independence and impartiality of a jury as a whole; the Contempt of Court Act 1981 s 8 is addressed to third parties who can be punished for contempt, and not to the court which has the responsibility of ensuring that the defendant receives a fair trial).

3   *Cogan v Ebden* (1757) 1 Burr 383 (where the jury was asked to give a general verdict when it ought to have been asked to give a separate verdict on each of the two issues in the case); *R v Woodfall* (1770) 5 Burr 2661 at 2667; *R v Almon* (1770) 5 Burr 2686; *Harvey v Hewitt* (1840) 8 Dowl 598; *Roberts v Hughes* (1841) 7 M & W 399. See also PARA 849 note 1.

4   *Bailey v Macaulay* (1849) 13 QB 815 at 829.

5   *Ex p Morris* (1907) 72 JP 5, DC.

6   *Standewick v Hopkins* (1844) 2 Dow & L 502; *Jones v Powell* (1856) 4 WR 252.

7   *R v Mickleburgh* [1995] 1 Cr App Rep 297, CA.

853.   Stay or reversal of judgments after verdict.   A judgment after the verdict in a trial by jury in any court[1] cannot be stayed or reversed by reason that: (1) the statutory provisions about the summoning or empanelling of jurors, or the selection of jurors by ballot, have not been complied with[2]; (2) a juror was not qualified in accordance with the statutory provisions[3]; (3) any juror was misnamed or misdescribed[4]; or (4) any juror was unfit to serve[5].

This provision does not preclude an appeal in a criminal case on the ground that the conviction was rendered unsafe in such circumstances[6].

Nor does this provision apply to any objection to a verdict on the ground of personation[7].

1 As to the meaning of 'court' see PARA 804 note 1.

2 Juries Act 1974 s 18(1)(a). This does not apply to any irregularity if objection is taken at, or as soon as practicable after, the time it occurs, and the irregularity is not corrected: s 18(2). See *R v Jalil* [2008] EWCA Crim 2910, [2009] 2 Cr App Rep (S) 276, [2008] All ER (D) 51 (Dec) (a ballot was still valid where the defence objected to two jurors who were balloted and stood by). As to the provisions on the summoning, empanelling and selecting of jurors see PARA 812 et seq. If a juror is unchallenged and is sworn, he cannot afterwards be challenged on the ground of partiality: see PARA 825.

3 Juries Act 1974 s 18(1)(b). As to qualification of jurors see PARA 804. The mere fact of a juror's disqualification does not by itself make a conviction unsafe: *R v Richardson* [2004] EWCA Crim 2997, [2004] All ER (D) 318 (Dec). See also *R v Bliss* [1986] Crim LR 467, CA (verdict of jury should not be stayed or reversed by reason only of disqualified juror being part of it); *R v Raviraj* (1986) 85 Cr App Rep 93, CA (presence on jury of former police officer who was disqualified did not in the circumstances render the verdict unsafe and unsatisfactory).

4 Juries Act 1974 s 18(1)(c).

5 Juries Act 1974 s 18(1)(d). This includes physical infirmity: *R v Chapman* (1976) 63 Cr App Rep 75, CA (presence on jury of deaf person who could have been discharged did not render verdict unsafe or unsatisfactory); *R v Osmanioglu* [2002] EWCA Crim 930.

6 *R v Chapman* (1976) 63 Cr App Rep 75, [1976] Crim LR 581, CCA; *R v Bliss* (1987) 84 Cr App Rep 1, [1986] Crim LR 467, CA; *R v Raviraj* (1987) 85 Cr App Rep 93, CA; *R v Salt* [1996] Crim LR 517, CA.

7 Juries Act 1974 s 18(3). A venire de novo will be ordered in a criminal case if, by reason of personation, a person whose name is not on the panel serves as a juror and the personation is not discovered until after verdict and judgment: *R v Tremearne* (1826) 5 B & C 254; *R v Wakefield* [1918] 1 KB 216, CCA; and see *R v Kelly* [1950] 2 KB 164 at 173–174, [1950] 1 All ER 806 at 810–811, CCA. As to venire de novo see CRIMINAL LAW, EVIDENCE AND PROCEDURE vol 11(4) (2006 Reissue) PARA 1895. As to personation of a juror see PARA 858; and CRIMINAL LAW, EVIDENCE AND PROCEDURE vol 11(2) (2006 Reissue) PARA 730. Where a person whose name was on the panel answered to the name of another member of the panel by mistake when it was called and was sworn and served in that person's name, the court was divided on the question whether there had been a mistake: *R v Mellor* (1858) Dears & B 468, CCR. In a civil case, if a person not on the panel has served, there is a discretion whether or not to grant a new trial; a new trial will not be granted unless substantial injustice has been done by a wrong juror having served: *Wells v Cooper* (1874) 30 LT 721; *Hill v Yates* (1810) 12 East 228; and see *Earl of Falmouth v Roberts* (1842) 9 M & W 469, where the fact that the wrong person was serving as a juror was known to the defendant's attorney's clerk at the time of trial. In all these cases a new trial was refused. For an instance where a new trial was granted see *Norman v Beamont* (1744) Willes 484.

5. PAYMENT OF JURORS

854. Payment generally. A person who serves as a juror[1] is entitled, in respect of his attendance at court[2] for the purpose of jury service, to receive payments[3] at rates determined by the Lord Chancellor with the consent of the Minister for the Civil Service[4] and subject to any prescribed[5] conditions, by way of allowance:

(1) for travelling and subsistence[6]; and

(2) for financial loss, where in consequence of his attendance he has incurred any expenditure, other than on travelling and subsistence, to which he would not otherwise be subject or he has suffered any loss of earnings, or of benefit under the enactments relating to social security, which he would otherwise have made or received[7].

The determination of the amounts payable to persons under these provisions, and the manner of making them, must be in accordance with arrangements made by the Lord Chancellor, and all such payments are made out of money provided by Parliament[8].

Similar provision is made in respect of jurors at inquests[9].

1 A person who attends for jury service in obedience to a summons to serve is deemed to serve as a juror notwithstanding that he is not subsequently sworn: Juries Act 1974 s 19(4). Section 19 does not apply to service on a jury summoned for the purposes of a trial of the pyx under the Coinage Act 1971 s 8: Juries Act 1974 s 19(6). As to the trial of the pyx see FINANCIAL SERVICES AND INSTITUTIONS vol 49 (2008) PARA 1287 et seq.

2 As to the meaning of 'court' see PARA 804 note 1.

3 Save as provided by the Juries Act 1974 and the Coroners Act 1988, no person is entitled under any Act, rule of law, custom or agreement to payment for his services as a juror: Juries Act 1974 s 19(5) (amended by the Coroners Act 1988 Sch 3 para 16). As from a day to be appointed, this provision is amended so as to refer to the Coroners and Justice Act 2009 Sch 7 instead of the Coroners Act 1988 (see note 9): see the Juries Act 1974 s 19(5) (as so amended; and prospectively amended by the Coroners and Justice Act 2009 Sch 21 para 24). At the date at which this volume states the law, no such day had been appointed. See note 1.

4 The Lord Chancellor's functions under the Juries Act 1974 s 19 are protected functions for the purposes of the Constitutional Reform Act 2005 s 19: see s 19(5), Sch 7 para 4; and CONSTITUTIONAL LAW AND HUMAN RIGHTS. As to the Lord Chancellor see CONSTITUTIONAL LAW AND HUMAN RIGHTS vol 8(2) (Reissue) PARA 477 et seq. As to the Minister for the Civil Service see CONSTITUTIONAL LAW AND HUMAN RIGHTS vol 8(2) (Reissue) PARA 427.

5 'Prescribed' means prescribed by regulations made by statutory instrument by the Lord Chancellor with the consent of the Minister for the Civil Service: Juries Act 1974 s 19(4). As to the regulations made see the Jurors' Allowances Regulations 1978, SI 1978/1579; and PARAS 855–856.

6 Juries Act 1974 s 19(1)(a) (amended by the Administration of Justice Act 1977 Sch 2 para 7). The reference in head (1) in the text to payments by way of allowance for subsistence includes a reference to vouchers and other benefits which may be used to pay for subsistence, whether or not their use is subject to any limitations: Juries Act 1974 s 19(1A) (added by the Criminal Justice Act 2003 Sch 33 paras 1, 13). See note 1. As to travelling allowance and subsistence allowance see PARA 855.

7 Juries Act 1974 s 19(1)(b) (amended by the Administration of Justice Act 1977 Sch 2 para 7; and the Social Security (Consequential Provisions) Act 1975 Sch 1 Pt I). See note 1. As to compensation see PARA 856.

8 Juries Act 1974 s 19(3). See note 1.

9 See the Coroners Act 1988 s 25 (prospectively repealed by the Coroners and Justice Act 2009 Sch 23 Pt 1); the Coroners and Justice Act 2009 Sch 7 Pt 1 (not yet in force); and CORONERS vol 9(2) (2006 Reissue) PARA 1063.

855. Travelling allowance; subsistence allowance. Where a juror[1] travels to or from court by railway or other public conveyance, the fare actually paid may be allowed, provided that only the amount of the second class fare is allowed for travel by railway, unless for any special reason the court otherwise directs[2].

Where a juror travels to or from court by hired vehicle, there may be allowed, in the case of urgency or where no public service is reasonably available, the amount of the fare and any reasonable gratuity paid, and in any other case, the amount of the fare for travel by the appropriate public services[3]. Where a juror travels to or from court by private conveyance there may be allowed a sum not exceeding the relevant amount[4].

The subsistence allowance to which a juror is entitled[5] is the relevant amount[6].

Similar provision is made in respect of a juror at an inquest[7].

1   For these purposes, a reference to 'juror' includes a reference to a person who, in obedience to a summons to serve on a jury, attends for service as a juror notwithstanding that he is not subsequently sworn and any reference to service as a juror is to be construed accordingly: Jurors' Allowances Regulations 1978, SI 1978/1579, reg 2(1).
2   Jurors' Allowances Regulations 1978, SI 1978/1579, reg 3.
3   Jurors' Allowances Regulations 1978, SI 1978/1579, reg 4.
4   Jurors' Allowances Regulations 1978, SI 1978/1579, reg 5. The 'relevant amount' means an amount calculated in accordance with rates or scales for the time being determined for the relevant allowance by the Lord Chancellor, with the consent of the Minister for the Civil Service: reg 2(2). As to the Lord Chancellor see CONSTITUTIONAL LAW AND HUMAN RIGHTS vol 8(2) (Reissue) PARA 477 et seq. As to the Minister for the Civil Service see CONSTITUTIONAL LAW AND HUMAN RIGHTS vol 8(2) (Reissue) PARA 427.
5   Ie under the Juries Act 1974 s 19 (see PARA 854): Jurors' Allowances Regulations 1978, SI 1978/1579, reg 6.
6   Jurors' Allowances Regulations 1978, SI 1978/1579, reg 6. See note 4.
7   See the Jurors' (Coroners' Courts) Allowances Regulations 1975, SI 1975/1091; and CORONERS vol 9(2) (2006 Reissue) PARA 1063.

856.   Compensation for loss of earnings and additional expenses.   Where in consequence of his attendance a juror[1] has incurred any expenditure (other than travelling or subsistence) to which he would not otherwise be subject, or any loss of earnings or benefit under the enactments relating to national insurance which he would otherwise have received, the financial loss allowance to which he is entitled[2] is the amount of the expenditure or loss, provided it does not exceed the relevant amount[3].

Similar provision is made in respect of a juror at an inquest[4].

1   As to the meaning of 'juror' see PARA 855 note 1.
2   Ie under the Juries Act 1974 s 19 (see PARA 854): Jurors' Allowances Regulations 1978, SI 1978/1579, reg 7.
3   Jurors' Allowances Regulations 1978, SI 1978/1579, reg 7. As to the meaning of 'relevant amount' see PARA 855 note 4.
4   See the Jurors' (Coroners' Courts) Allowances Regulations 1975, SI 1975/1091; and CORONERS vol 9(2) (2006 Reissue) PARA 1063.

6. LIABILITY

857. Immunity of jurors exercising office. No juror, properly empanelled[1], is punishable for, nor will any claim lie against him in respect of, anything said or done by him in the discharge of his office[2].

1 The privilege would not extend to a person not summoned for jury service who by confederacy with the clerk of the court procured himself to be called and sworn on a jury with intent to serve some malicious purpose: *Scarlet's Case* (1612) 12 Co Rep 98. As to the empanelling of jurors see PARA 812 et seq.

2 The immunity of jurors in claims brought by persons injured by a wrongful verdict was established in *Floyd v Barker* (1607) 12 Co Rep 23, where it was held that a writ for conspiracy would not lie against a member of a grand jury on the part of a person indicted by it, but afterwards acquitted. The immunity of jurors from punishment for wrongful verdicts was established in *Bushell's Case* (1670) 6 State Tr 999, where on writ of habeas corpus the return was made that the defendants were committed for returning a verdict 'against the plain and manifest weight of evidence, and against the direction of the court on a point of law' and it was held by Vaughan CJ that a jury could not be punished in a criminal case for such a finding. See further 3 Hallam's Constitutional History 9–12; 1 Holdsworth's History of English Law (7th Edn) 343–346. A juror cannot be indicted for breaking his oath as juror: Hawk PC (8th Edn) 432. The immunity of jurors falls under the general principle that no prosecution or claim will lie for words written or spoken in the course of any judicial proceeding: see *R v Skinner* (1774) Lofft 54 at 56 per Lord Mansfield CJ; *Henderson v Broomhead* (1859) 4 H & N 569 at 579, Ex Ch, per Crompton J. As to absolute privilege in relation to the administration of justice see LIBEL AND SLANDER vol 28 (Reissue) PARAS 97–101.

858–900. Miscellaneous offences by or against jurors. It is contempt of court to use or threaten violence, or even to use threatening or abusive language, in or near the courts to a juror, and such an offence can be dealt with summarily upon complaint made[1].

Under the common law any person who attempts to corrupt or influence a jury is guilty of the offence of embracery, and any juror who wilfully or corruptly consents to embracery is guilty of an offence[2]. The offence of embracery is now all but obsolete and the better course may be to charge the persons concerned with perverting the course of justice[3]. There is also now a statutory offence of intimidation of a juror or potential juror[4].

It is an indictable offence at common law to personate a juror[5].

It is a contempt of court to obtain, disclose or solicit any particulars of statements made, opinions expressed, arguments advanced or votes cast by members of a jury in the course of their deliberations in any legal proceedings[6].

Jurors who determine their verdict capriciously, for example by lot or by tossing a coin, are in contempt of court[7].

Various statutory offences may be committed by persons summoned for jury service and by jurors who fail to attend for service[8].

1 Hawk PC (8th Edn) 62; 1 Duncombe's Trials per Pais (8th Edn) 269. See further CONTEMPT OF COURT vol 9(1) (Reissue) PARA 434. As to jury tampering see further PARA 821.

2 *Jepps v Tunbridge and Wiseman* (1611) Moore KB 815; and see CRIMINAL LAW, EVIDENCE AND PROCEDURE vol 11(2) (2006 Reissue) PARA 729. See also note 1.

3 See eg *R v Lalani* [1999] 1 Cr App Rep 481, [1999] Crim LR 992, (1999) Times, 28 January, CA (prosecution must prove intention to pervert the course of justice). As to perverting the course of justice see CRIMINAL LAW, EVIDENCE AND PROCEDURE vol 11(2) (2006 Reissue) PARA 731. See also note 1.

4 See the Criminal Justice and Public Order Act 1994 s 51; and CRIMINAL LAW, EVIDENCE AND PROCEDURE vol 11(2) (2006 Reissue) PARA 726. This offence is in addition to and not in derogation of offences subsisting at common law: s 51(11). As to the quashing of acquittals tainted by the intimidation of or interference with a juror see the Criminal Procedure and

Investigations Act 1996 Pt VII (ss 54–57); and CRIMINAL LAW, EVIDENCE AND PROCEDURE vol 11(3) (2006 Reissue) PARA 1276. See also note 1.

5 *R v Wakefield* [1918] 1 KB 216, 13 Cr App Rep 56, CCA. It is not necessary to prove any corrupt motive or an intention to deceive: *R v Clark* (1918) 82 JP 295, (1918) 26 Cox CC 138. As to personation of a juror see further CRIMINAL LAW, EVIDENCE AND PROCEDURE vol 11(2) (2006 Reissue) PARA 730. Personation is also contempt of court: *R v Levy* (1916) 32 TLR 238; and see CONTEMPT OF COURT vol 9(1) (Reissue) PARA 434.

6 Contempt of Court Act 1981 s 8(1). See also CONTEMPT OF COURT vol 9(1) (Reissue) PARAS 434, 451.

7 *Langdell v Sutton* (1737) Barnes 32; *Foster v Hawden* (1677) 2 Lev 205. Such an offence is almost impossible to prove given the provisions of the Contempt of Court Act 1981 s 8(1): see the text and note 6.

8 See PARAS 811, 818.

LANDFILL TAX

1. THE CHARGE TO LANDFILL TAX

(1) INTRODUCTION

901. Landfill tax. A tax, known as landfill tax, is charged in accordance with Part III of the Finance Act 1996[1]. The tax is under the care and management of the Commissioners for Her Majesty's Revenue and Customs[2].

1 Finance Act 1996 s 39(1). In Pt III (ss 39–71), 'tax' means landfill tax: s 70(1). Sections 64–70 apply for the purposes of Pt III: s 70(4). A reference to Pt III includes a reference to any order or regulations made under it and a reference to a provision of Pt III includes a reference to any order or regulations made under the provision, unless otherwise required by the context of any order or regulations: s 70(3).

2 Finance Act 1996 s 39(2). In Pt III, 'Commissioners' means the Commissioners for Her Majesty's Revenue and Customs: s 70(1) (amended by virtue of the Commissioners for Revenue and Customs Act 2005 s 50(1), (7)).

The Commissioners for Her Majesty's Revenue and Customs are appointed under the Commissioners for Revenue and Customs Act 2005 s 1 and have taken over the functions of the former Inland Revenue and Her Majesty's Customs and Excise: see CUSTOMS AND EXCISE; INCOME TAXATION. See also VALUE ADDED TAX vol 49(1) (2005 Reissue) PARA 13. References in any enactment, instrument or other document to the Commissioners of Customs and Excise or to customs and excise must now be taken to be references to the Commissioners for Her Majesty's Revenue and Customs, and references to a customs officer or an officer as defined by the Customs and Management Act 1979 s 1(1) must now be taken to be references to an officer of Revenue and Customs: see the Commissioners for Revenue and Customs Act 2005 s 50(1), (2), (7).

(2) CHARGE TO TAX

902. Charge to tax. Landfill tax[1] is charged on a taxable disposal[2]. A disposal is a taxable disposal if:

(1) it is a disposal of material as waste[3];

(2) it is made by way of landfill[4];

(3) it is made at a landfill site[5]; and

(4) it is made on or after 1 October 1996[6].

For this purpose a disposal is made at a landfill site if the land on or under which it is made constitutes or falls within land which is a landfill site at the time of the disposal[7].

1 As to the meaning of 'landfill tax' see PARA 901.

2 Finance Act 1996 s 40(1).

See generally *FL Gamble & Sons Ltd v Customs and Excise Comrs* [1998] V & DR 481, L0004 (disposal of waste 'by way of landfill'). See also *Customs and Excise Comrs v Parkwood Landfill Ltd* [2002] EWCA Civ 1707, [2003] 1 All ER 579, [2002] STC 1536 (material disposed of for recycling not liable to landfill tax); *Customs and Excise Comrs v Ebbcliff Ltd* [2004] EWCA Civ 1071, [2004] STC 1496 (exemptions and restoration). See also PARA 903 for prescribed landfill site activities treated as disposals.

3 Finance Act 1996 s 40(2)(a). In order for there to be a taxable disposal, all four conditions must be met at the same time, which is the time of disposal: *Customs and Excise Comrs v Parkwood Landfill Ltd* [2002] EWCA Civ 1707, [2003] 1 All ER 579, [2002] STC 1536.

A disposal of material is a disposal of it as waste if the person making the disposal does so with the intention of discarding the material: Finance Act 1996 s 64(1). See *Waste Recycling Group Ltd v Revenue and Customs Comrs* [2008] EWCA Civ 849, [2008] All ER (D) 300 (Jul), [2009] STC 200 in which the relevant intention was not that of the original producer of the material, but that of the landfill site operator which had acquired title to the material. The fact that the person making the disposal or any other person could benefit from or make use of the material is irrelevant: Finance Act 1996 s 64(2). Where a person makes a disposal on behalf of another person, for the purposes of s 64(1), (2) the person on whose behalf the disposal is made is treated as making the disposal: s 64(3). The reference in s 64(3) to a disposal on behalf of another person includes references to a disposal: (1) at the request of another person (s 64(4)(a)); and (2) in pursuance of a contract with another person (s 64(4)(b)).

'Material' means material of all kinds, including objects, substances and products of all kinds: s 70(1). As to consideration in cases decided under the Control of Pollution Act 1974 and the Environmental Protection Act 1990 of the meaning of 'a disposal of material as waste' see *ICI Chemicals and Polymers Ltd v Customs and Excise Comrs* [1998] V & DR 310, L00002; *NSR Ltd v Customs and Excise Comrs* L00007. As to the meaning of 'waste' under the Control of Pollution Act 1974 Pt I (ss 11–30) and the Environmental Protection Act 1990 Pt II (ss 29–78) see PROTECTION OF ENVIRONMENT AND PUBLIC HEALTH vol 38 (2006 Reissue) PARA 236.

4   Finance Act 1996 s 40(2)(b). See also note 3.
     A 'landfill disposal' is a disposal of material as waste (s 70(2)(a)), and made by way of landfill (s 70(2)(b)).
     There is a disposal of material by way of landfill if it is deposited on the surface of land or on a structure set into the surface (s 65(1)(a)), or if it is deposited under the surface of land (s 65(1)(b)). 'Land' includes land covered by water where the land is above the low water mark of ordinary spring tides: s 65(7). Section 65(1) applies whether or not the material is placed in a container before it is deposited: s 65(2). Section 65(1)(b) applies whether the material is covered with earth after it is deposited (s 65(3)(a)) or is deposited in a cavity (such as a cavern or mine) (s 65(3)(b)). 'Earth' includes similar matter (such as sand or rocks): s 65(8). If material is deposited on the surface of land (or on a structure set into the surface) with a view to it being covered with earth the disposal must be treated as made when the material is deposited and not when it is covered: s 65(4). An order may provide that the meaning of the disposal of material by way of landfill (as it applies for the time being) is to be varied: s 65(5). At the date at which this volume states the law no such order had been made under s 65(5). An order under s 65(5) may make provision in such way as the Treasury thinks fit, whether by amending any of the provisions of s 65(1)–(4) or otherwise: s 65(6). In *FL Gamble & Sons Ltd v Customs and Excise Comrs* [1998] V & DR 481, L00004, material to be converted into 'manufactured soil' was held to be waste at the time it was brought onto the site for conversion and to have been disposed of by way of landfill because: (1) it was disposed of; and (2) all of the ingredients of the Finance Act 1996 s 40 were present at the time of disposal. As to the Treasury see CONSTITUTIONAL LAW AND HUMAN RIGHTS vol 8(2) (Reissue) PARAS 512–517.

5   Finance Act 1996 s 40(2)(c). See also note 3.
     Land is a landfill site at a given time if at that time:
     (1)   a licence which is a site licence for the purposes of the Environmental Protection Act 1990 Pt II (ss 29–78) (waste on land: see PROTECTION OF ENVIRONMENT AND PUBLIC HEALTH vol 38 (2006 Reissue) PARA 234 et seq) is in force in relation to the land and authorises disposals in or on the land (Finance Act 1996 s 66(a));
     (2)   a resolution under the Environmental Protection Act 1990 s 54 (land occupied by waste disposal authorities in Scotland) is in force in relation to the land and authorises deposits or disposals in or on the land (Finance Act 1996 s 66(b));
     (3)   a permit under regulations under the Pollution Prevention and Control Act 1999 s 2 (see PROTECTION OF ENVIRONMENT AND PUBLIC HEALTH vol 38 (2006 Reissue) PARAS 170–172) is in force in relation to the land and authorises deposits or disposals in or on the land (Finance Act 1996 s 66(ba) (added by the Pollution Prevention and Control Act 1999 s 6(1), Sch 2 para 19));
     (4)   a disposal licence issued under the Pollution Control and Local Government (Northern Ireland) Order 1978, SI 1978/1049 (NI 19), Pt II (arts 3–36) (waste on land) is in force in relation to the land and authorises deposits on the land (Finance Act 1996 s 66(c));
     (5)   a resolution passed under the Pollution Control and Local Government (Northern Ireland) Order 1978, SI 1978/1049 (NI 19), art 13 (land occupied by district councils in Northern Ireland) is in force in relation to the land and relates to deposits on the land (Finance Act 1996 s 66(d)); or
     (6)   a licence under any provision for the time being having effect in Northern Ireland and corresponding to the Environmental Protection Act 1990 s 35 (waste management licences) (see PROTECTION OF ENVIRONMENT AND PUBLIC HEALTH vol 38 (2006 Reissue) PARA 273) is in force in relation to the land and authorises disposals in or on the land (Finance Act 1996 s 66(e)).

The Environmental Protection Act 1990 s 35, which defines a site licence for the purposes of the Environmental Protection Act 1990 Pt II (ss 29–78) (see head (1)), is repealed for England and Wales by the Environmental Permitting (England and Wales) Regulations 2007, SI 2007/3538, art 1, Sch 21 Pt 1. As from a day to be appointed the Environmental Protection Act 1990 s 54

(see head (2)) is repealed by the Environment Act 1995 s 120, Sch 24. At the date at which this
volume states the law no such day had been appointed.

Breach of the conditions of a licence which is a site licence for the purposes of the
Environmental Protection Act 1990 Pt II (ss 29–78) does not invalidate the licence; the licence
remains a valid site licence for the purposes of the Finance Act 1996 s 66 until it is suspended,
and therefore disposals made at the landfill site may be taxable disposals within s 40: see *R v
Harris* (2000) Times, 2 May, CA.

In respect of the Finance Act 1996 s 66(a) (see head (1)) see *Lancashire Waste Services Ltd v
Customs and Excise Comrs* [1999] V & DR 490, L00008.

6   Finance Act 1996 s 40(2)(d). See also note 3.
7   Finance Act 1996 s 40(3).

903. Prescribed landfill site activities treated as disposals. If a prescribed
landfill site activity[1] is carried out at a landfill site, the activity is to be treated:

(1)   as a disposal at the landfill site of the material[2] involved in the activity[3];
(2)   as a disposal of that material as waste[4]; and
(3)   as a disposal of that material made by way of landfill[5].

The following landfill site activities have been prescribed[6]:

(a)   the use of material to cover the disposal area[7] during a short term
       cessation in landfill disposal activity[8];
(b)   the use of material to create or maintain a temporary haul road[9];
(c)   the use of material to create or maintain temporary hard standing[10];
(d)   the use of material to create or maintain a cell bund[11];
(e)   the use of material to create or maintain a temporary screening bund[12]
       except where the material so used is naturally occurring material
       extracted from the landfill site in which the temporary screening bund is
       located[13];
(f)   the temporary storage of ashes (including pulverised fuel ash and
       furnace bottom ash)[14];
(g)   the use of material placed against the drainage layer or liner of the
       disposal area to prevent damage to that layer or liner[15]; and
(h)   any other landfill site activity if in relation to that activity there is a
       requirement[16] for a person to notify or give information or a
       requirement[17] for a person to designate a part of a landfill site as an
       information area[18], give information or maintain a record in respect of
       the area, and that requirement is not complied with[19].

A landfill site activity is excluded from the above if, or to the extent that, it
involves material that is or has been otherwise chargeable to landfill tax[20] or
exempted from landfill tax[21].

1   'Prescribed landfill site activity' means a landfill site activity prescribed in an order for the
    purposes of the Finance Act 1996 s 65A: s 65A(1) (s 65A added by the Finance Act 2009 s 119,
    Sch 60 para 2). Provision by such an order may be made in such way as the Treasury thinks fit:
    Finance Act 1996 s 65A(4) (as so added). An order may prescribe a landfill site activity by
    reference to conditions, which may, in particular relate to either or both of (1) whether the
    activity is carried out in a designated area of a landfill site; and (2) whether there has been
    compliance with a requirement to give information relating to the activity or the material
    involved in the activity, including information relating to whether the activity is carried out in a
    designated area: s 65A(5), (6) (as so added). An order may amend or otherwise modify Pt III
    (ss 39–71) (as amended: see PARA 901 note 1) or any other enactment relating to landfill tax, but
    may not alter any rate at which landfill tax is charged: s 65A(7) (as so added).
    Section 65A(5)–(7) does not limit the generality of s 65A(4): s 65A(8) (as so added). A
    'designated area' means an area of a landfill site designated in accordance with an order under
    s 65A(1) or regulations under Sch 5 Pt 1 (see PARA 970 et seq): s 65A(9) (as so added). As to the
    meaning of 'landfill tax' see PARA 901. As to the Treasury see CONSTITUTIONAL LAW AND
    HUMAN RIGHTS vol 8(2) (Reissue) PARAS 512–517.

Provision which appears to the Treasury to be necessary or expedient in connection with provision made by order under s 65A(1) may also be made by order: s 65A(3) (as so added).

A 'landfill site activity' means any of the following descriptions of activity, or an activity that falls within any of the following descriptions: (a) using or otherwise dealing with material at a landfill site; and (b) storing or otherwise having material at a landfill site: s 65A(9) (as so added). As to the meaning of 'landfill site' see PARA 902 note 5.

2 As to the meaning of 'material' see PARA 902 note 3.

3 Finance Act 1996 s 65A(2)(a) (as added: see note 1). The effect of heads (1)–(3) in the text is to treat the activity as a taxable disposal. As to the meaning of 'taxable disposal' see PARA 902.

4 Finance Act 1996 s 65A(2)(b) (as added: see note 1). As to the meaning of 'disposal of material as waste' see PARA 902 note 3.

5 Finance Act 1996 s 65A(2)(c) (as added: see note 1). As to the meaning of 'disposal of material by way of landfill' see PARA 902 note 4.

6 Ie for the purposes of the Finance Act 1996 s 65A.

7 'Disposal area' means any area of a landfill site where any landfill disposal takes place: Landfill Tax (Prescribed Landfill Site Activities) Order 2009, SI 2009/1929, art 2.

8 Landfill Tax (Prescribed Landfill Site Activities) Order 2009, SI 2009/1929, art 3(1)(a).

9 Landfill Tax (Prescribed Landfill Site Activities) Order 2009, SI 2009/1929, art 3(1)(b). A 'haul road' means any road within a landfill site which gives access to a disposal area: art 2.

10 Landfill Tax (Prescribed Landfill Site Activities) Order 2009, SI 2009/1929, art 3(1)(c). 'Hard standing' means a base within a landfill site on which any landfill site activity such as sorting, treatment, processing, storage or recycling is carried out: art 2.

11 Landfill Tax (Prescribed Landfill Site Activities) Order 2009, SI 2009/1929, art 3(1)(d). 'Cell bund' means a structure within a disposal area which separates units of waste: art 2.

12 'Screening bund' means any structure on a landfill site (whether below or above ground) put in place to protect or conceal any landfill site activity or to reduce nuisance from noise: Landfill Tax (Prescribed Landfill Site Activities) Order 2009, SI 2009/1929, art 2.

13 Landfill Tax (Prescribed Landfill Site Activities) Order 2009, SI 2009/1929, art 3(1)(e).

14 Landfill Tax (Prescribed Landfill Site Activities) Order 2009, SI 2009/1929, art 3(1)(f).

15 Landfill Tax (Prescribed Landfill Site Activities) Order 2009, SI 2009/1929, art 3(1)(g).

16 Ie under the Finance Act 1996 s 60, Sch 5 para 1B: see PARA 973.

17 Ie under the Landfill Tax Regulations 1996, SI 1996/1527, reg 16A: see PARA 972.

18 As to the meaning of 'information area' see PARA 972.

19 Landfill Tax (Prescribed Landfill Site Activities) Order 2009, SI 2009/1929, art 3(1)(h).

20 As to the meaning of 'landfill tax' see PARA 901.

21 Landfill Tax (Prescribed Landfill Site Activities) Order 2009, SI 2009/1929, art 3(2).

904. Special provisions relating to the time of taxable disposals. Where (1) a taxable disposal[1] is in fact made on a particular day; (2) within the period of 14 days beginning with that day the person liable to pay landfill tax[2] in respect of the disposal issues a landfill invoice[3] in respect of the disposal; and (3) he has not notified the Commissioners for Her Majesty's Revenue and Customs[4] in writing that he elects not to avail himself of this provision, then for the purposes of the landfill tax provisions[5] the disposal is to be treated as made at the time the invoice is issued[6].

The Commissioners may at the request of a person direct that the above provision applies:

(a) in relation to disposals in respect of which he is liable to pay tax; or

(b) in relation to such of them as may be specified in the direction,

as if for the period of 14 days there were substituted such longer period as may be specified in the direction[7].

1 As to the meaning of 'taxable disposal' see PARA 902.

2 As to the meaning of 'landfill tax' see PARA 901.

3 The reference to a landfill invoice is a reference to a document containing such particulars as regulations may prescribe for the purposes of the Finance Act 1996 s 61(1): s 61(2). 'Prescribed' means prescribed by an order or regulations under Pt III (ss 39–71): s 70(1). See the Landfill Tax Regulations 1996, SI 1996/1527, reg 37; and PARA 933 note 8.

4 As to the Commissioners for Her Majesty's Revenue and Customs see PARA 901 note 2.

5 Ie the Finance Act 1996 Pt III: see PARA 901 note 1.

6   Finance Act 1996 s 61(1).
7   Finance Act 1996 s 61(3).

(3) RATES OF TAX

905.   Amount of tax. The amount of landfill tax[1] charged on a taxable disposal[2] is found by taking:
(1)   the relevant amount[3] for each whole tonne disposed of and a proportionately reduced sum for any additional part of a tonne[4]; or
(2)   a proportionately reduced sum if less than a tonne is disposed of[5].

Where the material[6] disposed of consists entirely of qualifying material[7] this provision applies as if the reference to the relevant amount were a reference to a lower amount[8]. The Treasury must have regard to the object of securing that material is listed if it is of a kind commonly described as inactive or inert[9].

The Commissioners for Her Majesty's Revenue and Customs[10] may direct that where material is disposed of it must be treated as qualifying material if it would in fact be such material but for a small quantity of non-qualifying material; and whether a quantity of non-qualifying material is small must be determined in accordance with the terms of the direction[11]. The Commissioners may at the request of a person direct that where there is a disposal in respect of which he is liable to pay tax the material disposed of must be treated as qualifying material if it would in fact be such material but for a small quantity of non-qualifying material, and:
(a)   a direction may apply to all disposals in respect of which a person is liable to pay tax or to such of them as are identified in the direction[12];
(b)   whether a quantity of non-qualifying material is small must be determined in accordance with the terms of the direction[13].

An order may provide that material must not be treated as qualifying material unless prescribed[14] conditions are met[15]. A condition may relate to any matter the Treasury thinks fit (such as the production of a document which includes a statement of the nature of the material)[16].

1   As to the meaning of 'landfill tax' see PARA 901.
2   As to the meaning of 'taxable disposal' see PARA 902.
3   At the date at which this volume states the law the relevant amount is £40 and has effect in relation to taxable disposals made or treated as made, on or after 1 April 2009 and before 1 April 2010: see the Finance Act 2008 s 18. For such disposals from 1 April 2008 to 31 March 2009 the amount was £32, and for disposals from 1 April 2007 to 31 March 2008 the amount was £24. For such disposals from 1 April 2010 the amount is to be £48: see the Finance Act 2009 s 18.
4   Finance Act 1996 s 42(1)(a) (amended by the Finance Act 2009 s 18(1)).
5   Finance Act 1996 s 42(1)(b).
6   As to the meaning of 'material' see PARA 902 note 3.
7   As to the meaning of 'qualifying material' see PARA 906.
8   Finance Act 1996 s 42(2) (amended by the Finance Act 2007 s 15(4)). At the date at which this volume states the law the lower amount is £2.50 and has effect in relation to taxable disposals made, or treated as made, on or after 1 April 2008: see the Finance Act 2007 s 15(4), (5). For such disposals before 1 April 2008 the lower amount was £2.
9   Finance Act 1996 s 42(4). As to the Treasury see CONSTITUTIONAL LAW AND HUMAN RIGHTS vol 8(2) (Reissue) PARAS 512–517.
10 See PARA 901 note 2.
11 See the Finance Act 1996 s 63(1), (2).
12 Finance Act 1996 s 63(3)(a).
13 Finance Act 1996 s 63(3)(b). If a direction under s 63(3) applies to a disposal any direction under s 63(2) does not apply to it: s 63(4).

14 'Prescribed' means prescribed by an order or regulations under the Finance Act 1996 Pt III (ss 39–71): s 70(1).
15 Finance Act 1996 s 63(5). See the Landfill Tax (Qualifying Material) Order 1996, SI 1996/1528; and PARA 906.
16 Finance Act 1996 s 63(6).

906. Qualifying material. The material which is qualifying material[1] is divided into groups[2].

Group 1 consists of rocks and soils[3], but only if they are naturally occurring[4]. This group includes clay, sand, gravel, sandstone, limestone, crushed stone, china clay, construction stone, stone from the demolition of buildings or structures, slate, topsoil, peat, silt and dredgings[5].

Group 2 consists of ceramic or concrete materials[6]. This group comprises only glass[7], ceramics[8] and concrete[9].

Group 3 consists of minerals[10], but only if they are processed or prepared, not used[11]. This group comprises only moulding sands[12], clays[13], mineral absorbents, man-made mineral fibres[14], silica, mica, mineral abrasives[15] and used foundry sand[16].

Group 4 consists of furnace slags[17]. This group includes vitrified wastes and residues from thermal processing of minerals where, in either case, the residue is both fused and insoluble; and slag from waste incineration[18].

Group 5 consists of ash[19]. This group comprises only bottom ash and fly ash from wood, coal or waste combustion; and excludes fly ash from municipal, clinical and hazardous waste incinerators and sewage sludge incinerators[20].

Group 6 consists of low activity inorganic compounds[21]. This group comprises only titanium dioxide, calcium carbonate, magnesium carbonate, magnesium oxide, magnesium hydroxide, iron oxide, ferric hydroxide, aluminium oxide, aluminium hydroxide and zirconium dioxide[22].

Group 7 consists of calcium sulphate[23], but only if it is disposed of either at a site not licensed to take putrescible waste or in a containment cell which takes only calcium sulphate[24]. This group includes gypsum and calcium sulphate based plasters, but excludes plasterboard[25].

Group 8 consists of calcium hydroxide and brine[26], but only if it is deposited in a brine cavity[27].

Group 9 consists of water[28], but only water containing other qualifying material in suspension[29].

1 Ie for the purposes of the Finance Act 1996 s 42: see PARA 905. 'Qualifying material' is material for the time being listed for the purposes of s 42 in an order: s 42(3). As to the meaning of 'material' see PARA 902 note 3. As to the order that has been made see the Landfill Tax (Qualifying Material) Order 1996, SI 1996/1528, which came into force on 1 October 1996: see art 1.
 Where the owner of the material immediately prior to the disposal and the operator of the landfill site at which the disposal is made are not the same person, material must not be treated as qualifying material unless it satisfies the condition that a transfer note includes a proper description of the material in relation to each type of material of which the disposal consists: see arts 5–7. As to the meaning of 'landfill site operator' see PARA 929 note 4; and as to the meaning of 'landfill site' see PARA 902 note 5. 'Transfer note' has the same meaning as in the Environmental Protection (Duty of Care) Regulations 1991, SI 1991/2839, reg 2; definition applied by virtue of the Landfill Tax (Qualifying Material) Order 1996, SI 1996/1528, art 8. As to the Environmental Protection (Duty of Care) Regulations 1991, SI 1991/2839, see PROTECTION OF ENVIRONMENT AND PUBLIC HEALTH vol 38 (2006 Reissue) PARA 256.
2 See the Landfill Tax (Qualifying Material) Order 1996, SI 1996/1528, arts 2–4, Schedule.
3 See the Landfill Tax (Qualifying Material) Order 1996, SI 1996/1528, Schedule cols 1, 2.
4 See the Landfill Tax (Qualifying Material) Order 1996, SI 1996/1528, Schedule col 3.
5 See the Landfill Tax (Qualifying Material) Order 1996, SI 1996/1528, Schedule note 1.

6 See the Landfill Tax (Qualifying Material) Order 1996, SI 1996/1528, Schedule cols 1, 2.
7 See the Landfill Tax (Qualifying Material) Order 1996, SI 1996/1528, Schedule note 2(a).
   'Glass' includes fritted enamel, but excludes glass fibre and glass-reinforced plastic: Schedule
   note 3(a).
8 See the Landfill Tax (Qualifying Material) Order 1996, SI 1996/1528, Schedule note 2(b).
   'Ceramics' includes bricks, bricks and mortar, tiles, clay ware, pottery, china and refractories:
   Schedule note 3(b).
9 See the Landfill Tax (Qualifying Material) Order 1996, SI 1996/1528, Schedule note 2(c).
   'Concrete' includes reinforced concrete, concrete blocks, breeze blocks and aircrete blocks, but
   excludes concrete plant washings: Schedule note 3(c).
10 See the Landfill Tax (Qualifying Material) Order 1996, SI 1996/1528, Schedule cols 1, 2.
11 See the Landfill Tax (Qualifying Material) Order 1996, SI 1996/1528, Schedule col 3.
12 'Moulding sands' excludes sands containing organic binders: Landfill Tax (Qualifying Material)
   Order 1996, SI 1996/1528, Schedule note 5(a).
13 'Clays' includes moulding clays and clay absorbents, including Fuller's earth and bentonite:
   Landfill Tax (Qualifying Material) Order 1996, SI 1996/1528, Schedule note 5(b).
14 'Man-made mineral fibres' includes glass fibres, but excludes glass-reinforced plastic and
   asbestos: Landfill Tax (Qualifying Material) Order 1996, SI 1996/1528, Schedule note 5(c).
15 See the Landfill Tax (Qualifying Material) Order 1996, SI 1996/1528, Schedule note 4.
16 See HMRC VAT Notice 48 'Extra Statutory Concessions', ESC 5.1.
17 See the Landfill Tax (Qualifying Material) Order 1996, SI 1996/1528, Schedule cols 1, 2.
18 See the Landfill Tax (Qualifying Material) Order 1996, SI 1996/1528, Schedule note 6.
19 See the Landfill Tax (Qualifying Material) Order 1996, SI 1996/1528, Schedule cols 1, 2.
20 See the Landfill Tax (Qualifying Material) Order 1996, SI 1996/1528, Schedule note 7.
21 See the Landfill Tax (Qualifying Material) Order 1996, SI 1996/1528, Schedule cols 1, 2.
22 See the Landfill Tax (Qualifying Material) Order 1996, SI 1996/1528, Schedule note 8.
23 See the Landfill Tax (Qualifying Material) Order 1996, SI 1996/1528, Schedule cols 1, 2.
24 See the Landfill Tax (Qualifying Material) Order 1996, SI 1996/1528, Schedule col 3.
25 See the Landfill Tax (Qualifying Material) Order 1996, SI 1996/1528, Schedule note 9.
26 See the Landfill Tax (Qualifying Material) Order 1996, SI 1996/1528, Schedule cols 1, 2.
27 See the Landfill Tax (Qualifying Material) Order 1996, SI 1996/1528, Schedule col 3.
28 See the Landfill Tax (Qualifying Material) Order 1996, SI 1996/1528, Schedule cols 1, 2.
29 See the Landfill Tax (Qualifying Material) Order 1996, SI 1996/1528, Schedule col 3.

(4) DETERMINING THE WEIGHT OF MATERIAL

907. Regulations prescribing rules for determining weight. The weight of the
material[1] disposed of on a taxable disposal[2] is determined in accordance with
regulations[3]. The regulations may:

(1) prescribe rules for determining the weight[4];
(2) authorise rules for determining the weight to be specified by the
     Commissioners for Her Majesty's Revenue and Customs[5] in a
     prescribed[6] manner[7];
(3) authorise rules for determining the weight to be agreed by the person
     liable to pay the landfill tax[8] and an authorised person[9].

The regulations may in particular prescribe, or authorise the specification or
agreement of, rules about:

(a) the method by which the weight is to be determined[10];
(b) the time by reference to which the weight is to be determined[11];
(c) the discounting of constituents (such as water)[12].

The regulations may include provision that a specification authorised under
head (2) above may provide:

(i)   that it is to have effect only in relation to disposals of such descriptions
      as may be set out in the specification[13];
(ii) that it is not to have effect in relation to particular disposals unless the
      Commissioners are satisfied that such conditions as may be set out in
      the specification are met in relation to the disposals[14].

The conditions may be framed by reference to such factors as the Commissioners think fit (such as the consent of an authorised person to the specification having effect in relation to disposals)[15].

The regulations may include provision that where rules are agreed as mentioned in head (3) above, and the Commissioners believe that they should no longer be applied because they do not give an accurate indication of the weight or they are not being fully observed or for some other reason, the Commissioners may direct that the agreed rules are no longer to have effect[16]. The regulations must be so framed that where in relation to a given disposal no specification of the Commissioners has effect, and no agreed rules have effect, the weight is to be determined in accordance with rules prescribed in the regulations[17].

The regulations made under the above powers are contained in Part X of the Landfill Tax Regulations 1996[18].

1   As to the meaning of 'material' see PARA 902 note 3.
2   As to the meaning of 'taxable disposal' see PARA 902.
3   Finance Act 1996 s 68(1). As to the regulations made see the text to note 18; and PARAS 908–910.
4   Finance Act 1996 s 68(2)(a).
5   As to the Commissioners for Her Majesty's Revenue and Customs see PARA 901 note 2.
6   'Prescribed' means prescribed by an order or regulations under the Finance Act 1996 Pt III (ss 39–71): s 70(1).
7   Finance Act 1996 s 68(2)(b).
8   As to the meaning of 'landfill tax' see PARA 901.
9   Finance Act 1996 s 68(2)(c). An 'authorised person' means any person acting under the authority of the Commissioners for Her Majesty's Revenue and Customs: s 70(1).
10 Finance Act 1996 s 68(3)(a).
11 Finance Act 1996 s 68(3)(b).
12 Finance Act 1996 s 68(3)(c).
13 Finance Act 1996 s 68(4)(a).
14 Finance Act 1996 s 68(4)(b).
15 Finance Act 1996 s 68(4).
16 Finance Act 1996 s 68(5).
17 Finance Act 1996 s 68(6).
18 Ie the Landfill Tax Regulations 1996, SI 1996/1527, Pt X (regs 41–44): see PARAS 908–910. References in the Landfill Tax Regulations 1996, SI 1996/1527, Pt X to 'weight' must be construed as references to the weight of material comprised in a disposal: see reg 41. 'Disposal' means a landfill disposal made on or after 1 October 1996; and 'disposed of' must be construed accordingly: reg 2(1). As to the meaning of 'landfill disposal' see PARA 902 note 4.

908. Basic method. A registrable person[1] must determine weight[2] by weighing the material[3] concerned[4]. The weighing of the material must be carried out at the time of the disposal[5].

1   As to the meaning of 'registrable person' see PARA 958 note 1; definition applied by virtue of the Landfill Tax Regulations 1996, SI 1996/1527, reg 2(1).
2   As to the meaning of 'weight' see PARA 907 note 18.
3   As to the meaning of 'material' see PARA 902 note 3.
4   Landfill Tax Regulations 1996, SI 1996/1527, reg 42(1), which does not apply where reg 43 or reg 44 (see PARAS 909–910) applies and is subject to reg 42(2) (see the text to note 5): see reg 42(1).
5   Landfill Tax Regulations 1996, SI 1996/1527, reg 42(2). For this purpose any time at which the Finance Act 1996 s 61 (see PARA 904) requires the disposal to be treated as made must be disregarded: see reg 42(2) (amended by SI 2009/1930). 'Disposal' means a landfill disposal made on or after 1 October 1996; and 'disposed of' must be construed accordingly: Landfill Tax Regulations 1996, SI 1996/1527, reg 2(1). As to the meaning of 'landfill disposal' see PARA 902 note 4.

909.   Specification by Commissioners for Revenue and Customs. Except where a method for determining weight has been agreed[1], the following provisions apply where the Commissioners for Her Majesty's Revenue and Customs[2] have specified rules for determining weight[3] in a notice published by them and not withdrawn by a further notice[4]. Such a specification made by the Commissioners may make provision for:

(1)   the method by which weight is to be determined[5];

(2)   the time by reference to which weight is to be determined[6].

The specification may provide:

(a)   that it is to have effect only in relation to disposals[7] of such descriptions as may be set out in the specification[8];

(b)   that it is not to have effect in relation to particular disposals unless the Commissioners are satisfied that such conditions as may be set out in the specification are met in relation to the disposals[9].

Where such a specification has been made, the registrable person[10] must determine weight in accordance with the rules in the specification (and not under the basic method)[11].

1   Ie under the Landfill Tax Regulations 1996, SI 1996/1527, reg 44: see PARA 910.
2   As to the Commissioners for Her Majesty's Revenue and Customs see PARA 901 note 2.
3   As to the meaning of 'weight' see PARA 907 note 18.
4   Landfill Tax Regulations 1996, SI 1996/1527, reg 43(1).
5   Landfill Tax Regulations 1996, SI 1996/1527, reg 43(2)(a).
6   Landfill Tax Regulations 1996, SI 1996/1527, reg 43(2)(b).
7   As to the meaning of 'disposal' see PARA 908 note 5.
8   Landfill Tax Regulations 1996, SI 1996/1527, reg 43(3)(a).
9   Landfill Tax Regulations 1996, SI 1996/1527, reg 43(3)(b).
10   As to the meaning of 'registrable person' see PARA 958 note 1.
11   Landfill Tax Regulations 1996, SI 1996/1527, reg 43(4). As to the basic method see PARA 908.

910.   Agreed rules. The registrable person[1] and an authorised person[2] may agree in writing that weight[3] is to be determined in accordance with agreed rules[4]. Rules may be agreed as regards:

(1)   the method by which weight is to be determined[5];

(2)   the time by reference to which weight is to be determined[6];

(3)   the discounting of water[7] forming a constituent of material disposed of[8].

Where these provisions apply, the registrable person must determine weight in accordance with the rules agreed[9].

Where such rules have been agreed and the Commissioners for Her Majesty's Revenue and Customs[10] believe that they should no longer be applied because they do not give an accurate indication of the weight or they are not being fully observed or for some other reason they may direct that the agreed rules are no longer to have effect[11].

1   As to the meaning of 'registrable person' see PARA 958 note 1.
2   As to the meaning of 'authorised person' see PARA 907 note 9.
3   As to the meaning of 'weight' see PARA 907 note 18.
4   Landfill Tax Regulations 1996, SI 1996/1527, reg 44(1)(a). The rules referred to are rules other than those described in reg 42 (see PARA 908) or specified under reg 43 (see PARA 909): see reg 44(1)(a). Regulation 44 does not apply where a direction under reg 44(3) (see the text to note 10) has been given: reg 44(1)(b).
5   Landfill Tax Regulations 1996, SI 1996/1527, reg 44(2)(a).
6   Landfill Tax Regulations 1996, SI 1996/1527, reg 44(2)(b).
7   Subject to the Landfill Tax Regulations 1996, SI 1996/1527, reg 44(6)–(8), rules may be agreed regarding the discounting of water if, and only if:
    (1)   no water is present in the material naturally and the water is present because:

(a)   it has been added for the purpose of enabling the material to be transported for disposal (reg 44(5)(a)(i));

(b)   it has been used for the purpose of extracting any mineral (reg 44(5)(a)(ii)); or

(c)   it has arisen, or has been added, in the course of an industrial process (reg 44(5)(a)(iii)); or

(2)   the material is the residue from the treatment of effluent or sewage by a water treatment works (reg 44(5)(b)).

As to the meaning of 'material' see PARA 902 note 3. As to the meaning of 'disposal' see PARA 908 note 5.

Rules may not be agreed under reg 44(5) where any of the material is capable of escaping from the landfill site concerned by leaching unless: (i) it is likely to do so in the form of water only (reg 44(6)(a)); or (ii) the leachate is to be collected on the site concerned and treated in order to eliminate any potential it has to cause harm (reg 44(6)(b)). As to the meaning of 'landfill site' see PARA 902 note 5; definition applied by virtue of reg 2(1).

Where the material falls within reg 44(5)(a) (see head (1)), rules may not be agreed under reg 44(5) unless the total water which has been added, or (in a case falling within reg 44(5)(a)(iii)) has arisen or has been added or both, constitutes 25% or more of the weight at the time of the disposal: reg 44(7).

Where the material falls within reg 44(5)(b) (see head (2)), rules may not be agreed under reg 44(5) except for the discounting of water which has been added prior to disposal (and not of water which is present in the material naturally): reg 44(8). For the purposes of reg 44(8), any water which has been extracted prior to disposal must be deemed to be water that has been added, except that where the water extracted exceeds the quantity of water added that excess must be deemed to have been present naturally: reg 44(9).

8   Landfill Tax Regulations 1996, SI 1996/1527, reg 44(2)(c). As to the meaning of 'disposed of' see PARA 908 note 5.

9   Landfill Tax Regulations 1996, SI 1996/1527, reg 44(4). Ie the determination is not made in accordance with reg 42 (see PARA 908) or reg 43 (see PARA 909).

10 As to the Commissioners for Her Majesty's Revenue and Customs see PARA 901 note 2.

11 Landfill Tax Regulations 1996, SI 1996/1527, reg 44(3).

2. EXEMPTIONS

911. Material removed from water. A disposal is not a taxable disposal[1] for the purposes of the landfill tax provisions[2] if it is shown to the satisfaction of the Commissioners for Her Majesty's Revenue and Customs[3] that the disposal is of material[4]:

(1) all of which:
- (a) has been removed (by dredging or otherwise) from a river, canal or watercourse (whether natural or artificial) or a dock or harbour (whether natural or artificial)[5]; and
- (b) formed part of or projected from the bed of the water concerned before its removal[6];

(2) all of which:
- (a) has been removed (by dredging or otherwise) from water falling within the approaches to a harbour (whether natural or artificial)[7];
- (b) has been removed in the interests of navigation[8]; and
- (c) formed part of or projected from the bed of the water concerned before its removal[9];

(3) all of which:
- (a) consists of naturally occurring mineral material[10]; and
- (b) has been removed (by dredging or otherwise) from the sea in the course of commercial operations carried out to obtain substances such as sand or gravel from the seabed[11]; or

(4) all of which comprises material within head (1) or (2) above and other material which has been added to that material for the purpose of securing that it is not liquid waste[12].

1 As to the meaning of 'taxable disposal' see PARA 902.
2 Ie the Finance Act 1996 Pt III (ss 39–71): see PARA 901 note 1.
3 As to the Commissioners for Her Majesty's Revenue and Customs see PARA 901 note 2.
4 As to the meaning of 'material' see PARA 902 note 3.
5 Finance Act 1996 s 43(1)(a), (2).
6 Finance Act 1996 s 43(1)(b).
7 Finance Act 1996 s 43(3)(a).
8 Finance Act 1996 s 43(3)(b).
9 Finance Act 1996 s 43(3)(c).
10 Finance Act 1996 s 43(4)(a).
11 Finance Act 1996 s 43(4)(b).
12 Finance Act 1996 s 43(5) (added by SI 2007/2909).

912. Contaminated land. A disposal is not a taxable disposal[1] for the purposes of the landfill tax provisions[2] if:

(1) it is of material all of which has been removed from land in relation to which a reclamation of contaminated land certificate[3] was in force at the time of the removal[4];

(2) none of that material has been removed from a part of the land in relation to which, as at the time of the removal, the qualifying period has expired[5];

(3) it is a disposal in relation to which any conditions to which the certificate was made subject are satisfied[6]; and

(4) it is not a disposal of material the removal of which is required by statutory notice[7], except where the removal has been carried out by or on behalf of:

(a)		a local authority[8];
(b)		a development corporation[9];
(c)		the Environment Agency[10]; or
(d)		the Scottish Environment Protection Agency[11].

1	As to the meaning of 'taxable disposal' see PARA 902.
2	Ie the Finance Act 1996 Pt III (ss 39–71): see PARA 901 note 1.
3	Ie a certificate issued under the Finance Act 1996 s 43B: see PARA 913. See generally *Taylor Woodrow Construction Northern Ltd v Customs and Excise Comrs* L00003 (pollutants removed from development site were entitled to contaminated land certificate).
4	Finance Act 1996 s 43A(1), (2)(a) (s 43A added by SI 1996/1529). As to the meaning of 'material' see PARA 902 note 3. The removal of material includes its removal from one part of the land for disposal on another part of the same land: Finance Act 1996 s 43A(7)(a) (as so added). 'Land' includes land covered by water: s 43A(6) (as so added).
	As from 1 April 2012 Finance Act 1996 s 43A is repealed by the Landfill Tax (Material from Contaminated Land) (Phasing out of Exemption) Order 2008, SI 2008/2669, art 4(a).
5	Finance Act 1996 s 43A(2)(b) (as added: see note 4). The qualifying period expires, in relation to the part of the land in question:
	(1)	in the case of a reclamation which qualified under s 43B(7)(a) (see PARA 913), where the object involves the construction of a building or a civil engineering work, when the construction commences (s 43A(3)(a) (as so added));
	(2)	in any other case of a reclamation which qualified under s 43B(7)(a) (see PARA 913), when pollutants have been cleared to the extent that they no longer prevent the object from being fulfilled (s 43A(3)(b) (as so added)); or
	(3)	in the case of a reclamation which qualified under s 43B(7)(b) (see PARA 913), when pollutants have been cleared to the extent that the potential for harm has been removed (s 43A(3)(c) (as so added)).
	The clearing of pollutants includes their being cleared from one part of the land for disposal on another part of the same land: s 43A(7)(b) (as so added).
6	Finance Act 1996 s 43A(2)(c) (as added: see note 4).
7	Finance Act 1996 s 43A(2)(d) (as added: see note 4). Section 43A(2)(d) refers to a disposal not falling within s 43A(4) (as added and amended). A disposal is within s 43A(4) if it is of material the removal of any of which is required in order to comply with:
	(1)	a works notice served under the Control of Pollution Act 1974 s 46A (repealed) (Finance Act 1996 s 43A(4)(a) (as so added));
	(2)	an enforcement notice served under the Environmental Protection Act 1990 s 13 (see PROTECTION OF ENVIRONMENT AND PUBLIC HEALTH vol 38 (2006 Reissue) PARA 158) (Finance Act 1996 s 43A(4)(b) (as so added));
	(3)	a prohibition notice served under the Environmental Protection Act 1990 s 14 (see PROTECTION OF ENVIRONMENT AND PUBLIC HEALTH vol 38 (2006 Reissue) PARA 159) (Finance Act 1996 s 43A(4)(c) (as so added));
	(4)	an order under the Environmental Protection Act 1990 s 26 (see PROTECTION OF ENVIRONMENT AND PUBLIC HEALTH vol 38 (2006 Reissue) PARA 168) (Finance Act 1996 s 43A(4)(d) (as so added));
	(5)	a remediation notice served under the Environmental Protection Act 1990 s 78E (as added and amended) (see PROTECTION OF ENVIRONMENT AND PUBLIC HEALTH vol 38 (2006 Reissue) PARA 362) (Finance Act 1996 s 43A(4)(e) (as so added));
	(6)	an enforcement notice served under the Water Resources Act 1991 s 90B (see WATER vol 49(3) (2004 Reissue) PARA 708) (Finance Act 1996 s 43A(4)(f) (as so added));
	(7)	a works notice served under the Water Resources Act 1991 s 161A (as added and amended) (see WATER vol 49(3) (2004 Reissue) PARA 722 et seq) (Finance Act 1996 s 43A(4)(g) (as so added));
	(8)	an enforcement notice served under the Environmental Permitting (England and Wales) Regulations 2007, SI 2007/3538, reg 36 (Finance Act 1996 s 43A(4)(h) (s 43A(4)(h), (j), (k) added by SI 2000/1973; and substituted by SI 2007/3538);
	(9)	a suspension notice served under the Environmental Permitting (England and Wales) Regulations 2007, SI 2007/3538, reg 37 (Finance Act 1996 s 43A(4)(j) (as so added and substituted)); or
	(10)	an order under the Environmental Permitting (England and Wales) Regulations 2007, SI 2007/3538, reg 44 (Finance Act 1996 s 43A(4)(k) (as so added and substituted)).
	As from a day to be appointed, the provisions of the Finance Act 1996 s 43A(4)(b)–(d) are repealed by the Pollution Prevention and Control Act 1999 s 6(2), Sch 3. At the date at which this volume states the law no such day had been appointed.

8 Finance Act 1996 s 43A(5)(a) (s 43 as added (see note 4); and s 43A(5) amended by the Housing and Regeneration Act 2008 ss 56, 321(1), Sch 8 para 64, Sch 16). For the purposes of the Finance Act 1996, 'local authority' means: (1) the council of a county, county borough, district, London borough, parish or group of parishes (or, in Wales, community or group of communities); (2) the Common Council of the City of London and, as respects the Temples, the Sub-Treasurer of the Inner Temple and the Under-Treasurer of the Middle Temple respectively; (3) the council of the Isles of Scilly; and (4) any joint committee or joint board established by two or more of the foregoing: see s 70(2A) (added by SI 1996/1529).

9 Finance Act 1996 s 43A(5)(b) (as added: see note 4). 'Development corporation' means a corporation established under the Local Government, Planning and Land Act 1980 s 135 (see TOWN AND COUNTRY PLANNING vol 46(3) (Reissue) PARA 1428): Finance Act 1996 s 43A(6) (as so added).

10 Finance Act 1996 s 43A(5)(c) (as added: see note 4). 'Environment Agency' means the body established by the Environment Act 1995 s 1 (see PROTECTION OF ENVIRONMENT AND PUBLIC HEALTH vol 38 (2006 Reissue) PARA 52): Finance Act 1996 s 70(1) (definition added by SI 1996/1529). As to the Environment Agency see PROTECTION OF ENVIRONMENT AND PUBLIC HEALTH vol 38 (2006 Reissue) PARA 52 et seq.

11 Finance Act 1996 s 43A(5)(d) (as added: see note 4). 'Scottish Environment Protection Agency' means the body established by the Environment Act 1995 s 20: Finance Act 1996 s 70(1) (definition added by SI 1996/1529).

913. Reclamation of contaminated land certificates. The Commissioners for Her Majesty's Revenue and Customs[1] must issue a certificate in relation to any land[2] where:

(1) an application in writing is made before 1 December 2008[3] by a person carrying out, or intending to carry out, a reclamation of that land (the 'applicant')[4];

(2) the applicant provides to them such information as they may direct, whether generally or as regards that particular case, within such time as they may direct[5];

(3) the application is made not less than 30 days before the date from which the certificate is to take effect[6]; and

(4) the reclamation qualifies[7].

The Commissioners may not refuse an application for a certificate in a case where the conditions specified in heads (1) to (4) above are satisfied unless it appears to them:

(a) necessary to do so for the protection of the revenue[8]; or

(b) except where the applicant is one of certain specified bodies[9], that all or part of the reclamation of land to which the application relates is required in order to comply with any of certain statutory notices or orders[10].

The Commissioners may make a certificate subject to such conditions set out in the certificate as they think fit, including (but not restricted to) conditions:

(i) that the certificate is to be in force only in relation to a particular quantity of material[11];

(ii) that the certificate is to be in force only in relation to disposals made at a particular landfill site[12] or sites[13];

(iii) that the certificate is to be in force in relation to part only of the land to which the application relates[14].

A certificate so issued has effect from the date it is issued to the applicant or such later date as the Commissioners may specify in the certificate[15]; and ceases to have effect on such date as the Commissioners may set out in the certificate, but in any event no later than the day on which the person to whom the certificate was issued ceases to have the intention to carry out any activity involving reclamation of the land in relation to which the certificate was issued[16].

Where a certificate has been issued to a person, the Commissioners may vary it by issuing a further certificate to that person[17], or may withdraw it by giving notice in writing to that person[18]. However, the Commissioners may not withdraw a certificate unless it appears to them:

(A)   necessary to do so for the protection of the revenue[19];

(B)   that the reclamation did not in fact qualify[20] or no longer qualifies[21];

(C)   that there will not be any or any more disposals of material from the land to which the certificate relates[22]; or

(D)   except where the person to whom the certificate was issued is one of certain bodies[23], that the removal of material from the land to which the certificate relates is required in order to comply with any of certain statutory notices or orders[24].

1   As to the Commissioners for Her Majesty's Revenue and Customs see PARA 901 note 2.

2   As to the meaning of 'land' see PARA 912 note 4; definition applied by virtue of the Finance Act 1996 s 43B(12) (s 43B added by SI 1996/1529). See also note 3.

3   The Finance Act 1996 s 43B(1)–(3) is repealed as from 1 December 2008 by the Landfill Tax (Material from Contaminated Land) (Phasing out of Exemption) Order 2008, SI 2008/2669, art 3. The repeal does not have effect until 1 April 2012 in relation to applications made before 1 December 2008: art 3(2).

     The Finance Act 1996 s 43B(4)–(12) is repealed as from 1 April 2012 by the Landfill Tax (Material from Contaminated Land) (Phasing out of Exemption) Order 2008, SI 2008/2669, art 4.

4   Finance Act 1996 s 43B(1)(a) (as added: see note 2). See also note 3.

5   Finance Act 1996 s 43B(1)(b) (s 43B as added (see note 2); s 43B(1)(b) amended by SI 2008/2669). See also note 3.

6   Finance Act 1996 s 43B(1)(c) (as added: see note 2). See also note 3. This rule was varied by an extra-statutory class concession of 5 June 1997 (see *Business Brief 12/97*) for certificates issued prior to 30 June 1997 in relation to claims for remission of tax subject to the following conditions:

(1)   the waste must clearly have qualified for exemption;

(2)   such waste was charged to tax on disposal;

(3)   such waste must have come from reclamations which have at least some of their waste certified to ensure that the claim would have been subject to verification by a local officer of the Commissioners; and

(4)   the claim for remission was received by the Commissioners by 30 September 1997.

In *Zenith Builders v Customs and Excise Comrs* (1998) L00001, the tribunal considered an appeal against the Commissioners' refusal to exercise the concession where the material was not available to be subject to verification; on the Commissioners' application to strike out the appeal (there being no jurisdiction for the tribunal to consider the refusal of the concession) the matter was treated as a preliminary issue and it was clear that the circumstances meant that the appeal failed.

7   Finance Act 1996 s 43B(1)(d) (as added: see note 2). See also note 3. A reclamation qualifies for this purpose if:

(1)   it is, or is to be, carried out with the object of facilitating (in the sense of 'making easier' (see *Taylor Woodrow Construction Northern Ltd v Customs and Excise Comrs* (1998) L00003) development, conservation, the provision of a public park or other amenity, or the use of the land for agriculture or forestry (Finance Act 1996 s 43B(7)(a) (as so added)); or

(2)   in a case other than one within head (1), it is, or is to be, carried out with the object of reducing or removing the potential of pollutants to cause harm (s 43B(7)(b) (as so added)),

and, in either case, the following conditions are satisfied:

(a)   the reclamation constitutes or includes clearing the land of pollutants which are causing harm or have the potential for causing harm (s 43B(8)(a) (as so added));

(b)   in a case within s 43B(7)(a) (see head (1)), those pollutants would (unless cleared) prevent the object concerned being fulfilled (s 43B(8)(b) (as so added)); and

(c)   all relevant activities have ceased or have ceased to give rise to any pollutants in relation to that land (s 43B(8)(c) (as so added)).

For these purposes, the clearing of pollutants need not be such that all pollutants are removed (s 43B(9)(a) (as so added)), need not be such that pollutants are removed from every part of the land in which they are present (s 43B(9)(b) (as so added)), and may involve their being cleared from one part of the land and disposed of on another part of the same land (s 43B(9)(c) (as so added)).

An activity is relevant if:

(i)   it has at any time resulted in the presence of pollutants in, on or under the land in question otherwise than: (A) without the consent of the person who was the occupier of the land at the time; or (B) by allowing pollutants to be carried onto the land by air or water (s 43B(10)(a) (as so added)); and

(ii)   at that time it was carried out: (A) by the applicant or a person connected with him; or (B) by any person on the land in question (s 43B(10)(b) (as so added)).

Any question whether a person is connected with another is to be determined in accordance with the Income and Corporation Taxes Act 1988 s 839 (see INCOME TAXATION vol 23(2) (Reissue) PARA 1258): Finance Act 1996 s 43B(11)(a) (as so added). The occupier of land that is not in fact occupied is the person entitled to occupy it: s 43B(11)(b) (as so added).

As to the application of s 47B(7), (8) see *Taylor Woodrow Construction Northern Ltd v Customs and Excise Comrs* (1998) L00003; *Baldwin* L00022; *Augean plc v Revenue and Customs Comrs* [2008] EWHC 2026 (Ch), [2008] All ER (D) 100 (Aug), [2008] STC 2894.

8   Finance Act 1996 s 43B(2)(a) (as added: see note 2). See also note 3. As to the Commissioners' powers to withdraw certificates see *Taylor Woodrow Construction Northern Ltd v Customs and Excise Comrs* (1998) L00003.

9   Ie one of the bodies mentioned in the Finance Act 1996 s 43A(5) (as added and amended): see PARA 912.

10   Finance Act 1996 s 43B(2)(b) (as added: see note 2). See also note 3. The statutory notices and orders referred to in the text are those mentioned in s 43A(4) (as added and amended): see PARA 912 note 7.

11   Finance Act 1996 s 43B(3)(a) (as added: see note 2). See also note 3. As to the meaning of 'material' see PARA 902 note 3.

12   As to the meaning of 'landfill site' see PARA 902 note 5.

13   Finance Act 1996 s 43B(3)(b) (as added: see note 2). See also note 3.

14   Finance Act 1996 s 43B(3)(c) (as added: see note 2). See also note 3.

15   Finance Act 1996 s 43B(4)(a) (as added: see note 2). See also note 3.

16   Finance Act 1996 s 43B(4)(b) (as added: see note 2). See also note 3.

17   Finance Act 1996 s 43B(5)(a) (as added: see note 2). See also note 3.

18   Ie subject to Finance Act 1996 s 43B(6): s 43B(5)(b) (as added: see note 2). See also note 3.

19   Finance Act 1996 s 43B(6)(a) (as added: see note 2). See also note 3.

20   Ie under the Finance Act 1996 s 43B(7): see note 7.

21   Finance Act 1996 s 43B(6)(b) (as added: see note 2). See also note 3.

22   Finance Act 1996 s 43B(6)(c) (as added: see note 2). See also note 3.

23   See note 9.

24   Finance Act 1996 s 43B(6)(d) (as added: see note 2). See also note 3. The statutory notices and orders referred to in the text are those mentioned in s 43A(4) (as added and amended): see PARA 912 note 7.

914. Mining and quarrying. A disposal is not a taxable disposal[1] for the purposes of the landfill tax provisions[2] if it is shown to the satisfaction of the Commissioners for Her Majesty's Revenue and Customs[3] that the disposal is of material[4] all of which fulfils each of the following conditions[5]: (1) the material must result from commercial mining operations (whether the mining is deep or open-cast) or from commercial quarrying operations[6]; (2) the material must be naturally occurring material extracted from the earth in the course of the operations[7]; and (3) the material must not have been subjected to, or result from, a non-qualifying process[8] carried out at any stage between the extraction and the disposal[9].

1   As to the meaning of 'taxable disposal' see PARA 902.

2   Ie the Finance Act 1996 Pt III (ss 39–71): see PARA 901 note 1.

3   As to the Commissioners for Her Majesty's Revenue and Customs see PARA 901 note 2.

4   As to the meaning of 'material' see PARA 902 note 3.

5   Finance Act 1996 s 44(1).

6 Finance Act 1996 s 44(2). As to mining and quarrying see MINES, MINERALS AND QUARRIES.
7 Finance Act 1996 s 44(3).
8 A non-qualifying process is: (1) a process separate from the mining or quarrying operations (Finance Act 1996 s 44(5)(a)); or (2) a process forming part of those operations and permanently altering the material's chemical composition (s 44(5)(b)).
9 Finance Act 1996 s 44(4).

915.   Quarries.   A disposal is not a taxable disposal[1] for the purposes of the landfill tax provisions[2] if it is:

(1)   of material all of which is treated as qualifying material[3];

(2)   made at a quarry which is a qualifying landfill site[4]; and

(3)   made, or treated as made, on or after 1 October 1999[5].

1 As to the meaning of 'taxable disposal' see PARA 902.
2 Ie the Finance Act 1996 Pt III (ss 39–71): see PARA 901 note 1.
3 Finance Act 1996 s 44A(1)(a) (s 44A added by the Landfill Tax (Site Restoration and Quarries) Order 1999, SI 1999/2075, art 1). As to the meaning of 'qualifying material' see PARA 906.
4 Finance Act 1996 s 44A(1)(b) (as added: see note 3). A landfill site is a 'qualifying landfill site' for the purposes of s 44A (as added and amended) if at the time of the disposal:
    (1)   the landfill site is or was a quarry (s 44A(2)(a) (as so added));
    (2)   it is a requirement of planning consent in respect of the land in which the quarry or former quarry is situated that it be wholly or partially refilled (s 44A(2)(b) (as so added)), unless the quarry was in existence before 1 October 1999 and quarrying operations ceased before that date in which case the requirement must have been imposed on or before that date (s 44A(3) (as so added)); and
    (3)   the licence, permit or resolution authorising disposals on or in the land permits only the disposal of material which is qualifying material (s 44A(2)(c) (as so added; and amended by SI 2005/725)).
    Where a licence or permit does not meet the requirements of head (3) above and an application has been made to vary the licence or permit in order to meet them, it is deemed to meet them for the period before: (a) the application is disposed of; or (b) the second anniversary of the making of the application if it occurs before the application is disposed of: Finance Act 1996 s 44A(4) (as so added; and amended by SI 2005/725). An application is disposed of if: (i) it is granted; (ii) it is withdrawn; (iii) it is refused and there is no right of appeal against the refusal; (iv) a time limit for appeal against refusal expires without an appeal having been commenced; or (v) an appeal against refusal is dismissed or withdrawn and there is no further right of appeal: Finance Act 1996 s 44A(5) (as so added). As to mines and quarries see MINES, MINERALS AND QUARRIES.
5 Finance Act 1996 s 44A(1)(c) (as added: see note 3).

916.   Pet cemeteries.   A disposal is not a taxable disposal[1] for the purposes of the landfill tax provisions[2] if:

(1)   the disposal is of material[3] consisting entirely of the remains of dead domestic pets[4]; and

(2)   the landfill site[5] at which the disposal is made fulfils the test set out below[6].

The test is that during the relevant period[7]: (a) no landfill disposal[8] was made at the site[9]; or (b) the only landfill disposals made at the site were of material consisting entirely of the remains of dead domestic pets[10].

1 As to the meaning of 'taxable disposal' see PARA 902.
2 Ie the Finance Act 1996 Pt III (ss 39–71): see PARA 901 note 1.
3 As to the meaning of 'material' see PARA 902 note 3.
4 Finance Act 1996 s 45(1)(a).
5 As to the meaning of 'landfill site' see PARA 902 note 5.
6 Finance Act 1996 s 45(1)(b).
7 For the purposes of the Finance Act 1996 s 45(2), the relevant period begins with 1 October 1996 or (if later) with the coming into force in relation to the site of the licence, resolution or permit mentioned in s 66 (see PARA 902), and ends immediately before the disposal mentioned in s 45(1): s 45(3) (amended by SI 2005/725).
8 As to the meaning of 'landfill disposal' see PARA 902 note 4.

9   Finance Act 1996 s 45(2)(a).
10 Finance Act 1996 s 45(2)(b).

917.   Power to exempt or include by order.   Provision may be made by order
to produce the result that:

(1)   a disposal which would otherwise be a taxable disposal[1] (by virtue of
        the landfill tax provisions[2] as they apply for the time being) is not a
        taxable disposal[3];

(2)   a disposal which would otherwise not be a taxable disposal (by virtue of
        the landfill tax provisions as they apply for the time being) is a taxable
        disposal[4].

Without prejudice to the generality of the above provisions, such an order may:

(a)   confer   exemption   by   reference   to   certificates   issued   by   the
        Commissioners for Her Majesty's Revenue and Customs[5] and to
        conditions set out in certificates[6];

(b)   allow the Commissioners to direct requirements to be met before
        certificates can be issued[7];

(c)   provide for the reviews and appeals relating to decisions about
        certificates[8].

Such provision may be made in such way as the Treasury thinks fit (whether by
amending the legislation or otherwise)[9].

1   As to the meaning of 'taxable disposal' see PARA 902.
2   Ie the Finance Act 1996 Pt III (ss 39–71): see PARA 901 note 1.
3   Finance Act 1996 s 46(1)(a).
4   Finance Act 1996 s 46(1)(b).
5   As to the Commissioners for Her Majesty's Revenue and Customs see PARA 901 note 2.
6   Finance Act 1996 s 46(2)(a).
7   Finance Act 1996 s 46(2)(b).
8   Finance Act 1996 s 46(2)(c) (substituted by SI 2009/56).
9   Finance Act 1996 s 46(3). As to the Treasury see CONSTITUTIONAL LAW AND HUMAN RIGHTS
    vol 8(2) (Reissue) PARAS 512–517. For examples of orders made under s 46 see the Landfill Tax
    (Contaminated Land) Order 1996, SI 1996/1529; the Landfill Tax (Site Restoration and
    Quarries) Order 1999, SI 1999/2075; and the Landfill Tax (Site Restoration, Quarries and Pet
    Cemeteries) Order 2005, SI 2005/725.

3. DEEMED AMOUNTS OF TAX

918. Adjustment of contracts. In a case where:

(1) material[1] undergoes a landfill disposal[2];

(2) a payment falls to be made under a disposal contract relating to the material[3]; and

(3) after the making of the contract there is a change in the landfill tax chargeable[4] on the landfill disposal[5],

the amount of any payment mentioned in head (2) above must be adjusted, unless the disposal contract otherwise provides, so as to reflect the tax chargeable on the landfill disposal[6].

In a case where:

(a) work is carried out under a construction contract[7];

(b) as a result of the work, material undergoes a landfill disposal[8];

(c) the contract makes no provision as to the disposal of such material[9]; and

(d) the contract was made on or before 29 November 1994 (when the proposal to create landfill tax was announced)[10],

the amount of any payment which falls to be made: (i) under the construction contract; and (ii) in respect of the work, must be adjusted, unless the contract otherwise provides, so as to reflect the tax (if any) chargeable on the disposal[11].

1 As to the meaning of 'material' see PARA 902 note 3.

2 Finance Act 1996 s 60, Sch 5 para 45(1)(a). As to the meaning of 'landfill disposal' see PARA 902 note 4.

3 Finance Act 1996 Sch 5 para 45(1)(b).
   For the purposes of Sch 5 para 45, a disposal contract relating to material is a contract providing for the disposal of the material, and it is immaterial: (1) when the contract was made (Sch 5 para 45(3)(a)); (2) whether the contract also provides for other matters (Sch 5 para 45(3)(b)); (3) whether the contract provides for a method of disposal and (if it does) what method it provides for (Sch 5 para 45(3)(c)).

4 The reference in the Finance Act 1996 Sch 5 para 45(1) to a change in the landfill tax chargeable is a reference to a change: (1) to or from no tax being chargeable (Sch 5 para 45(4)(a)); or (2) in the amount of tax chargeable (Sch 5 para 45(4)(b)).

5 Finance Act 1996 Sch 5 para 45(1)(c).

6 Finance Act 1996 Sch 5 para 45(2).

7 Finance Act 1996 Sch 5 para 46(1)(a).
   For the purposes of Sch 5 para 46, a construction contract is a contract under which all or any of the following work is to be carried out: (1) the preparation of a site (Sch 5 para 46(3)(a)); (2) demolition (Sch 5 para 46(3)(b)); (3) building (Sch 5 para 46(3)(c)); (4) civil engineering (Sch 5 para 46(3)(d)).

8 Finance Act 1996 Sch 5 para 46(1)(b).

9 Finance Act 1996 Sch 5 para 46(1)(c).

10 Finance Act 1996 Sch 5 para 46(1)(d).

11 Finance Act 1996 Sch 5 para 46(2).

919. Adjustment of rent etc. In a case where:

(1) an agreement with regard to any sum payable in respect of the use of land (whether the sum is called rent or royalty or otherwise) provides that the amount of the sum is to be calculated by reference to the turnover of a business[1];

(2) the agreement was made on or before 29 November 1994 (when the proposal to create landfill tax[2] was announced)[3]; and

(3) the circumstances are such that (had the agreement been made after that date) it can reasonably be expected that it would have provided that tax be ignored in calculating the turnover[4],

the agreement must be taken to provide that tax be ignored in calculating the turnover[5].

1   Finance Act 1996 s 60, Sch 5 para 47(1)(a).
2   As to the meaning of 'landfill tax' see PARA 901.
3   Finance Act 1996 Sch 5 para 47(1)(b).
4   Finance Act 1996 Sch 5 para 47(1)(c).
5   Finance Act 1996 Sch 5 para 47(2).

4. REGISTRATION AND INFORMATION

(1) REGISTRATION FOR LANDFILL TAX

920. Registration. A person who carries out taxable activities[1], and is not registered, is liable to be registered[2]. Where a person at any time forms the intention of carrying out taxable activities, and he is not registered, he must notify the Commissioners for Her Majesty's Revenue and Customs[3] of his intention[4]. A person who at any time ceases to have the intention of carrying out taxable activities must notify the Commissioners of that fact[5]. Where a person is liable to be so registered the Commissioners must register him with effect from the time when he begins to carry out taxable activities[6].

Where the Commissioners are satisfied that a person has ceased to carry out taxable activities, they may cancel his registration with effect from the earliest practicable time after he so ceased[7].

Where:

(1)   a person notifies[8] the Commissioners of his intention to cease to carry out taxable activities;

(2)   they are satisfied that he will not carry out taxable activities;

(3)   they are satisfied that no tax which he is liable to pay is unpaid; and

(4)   they are satisfied that no credit to which he is entitled under regulations[9] is outstanding,

the Commissioners must cancel his registration with effect from the earliest practicable time after he ceases to carry out taxable activities[10].

Where:

(a)   a person notifies[11] the Commissioners of his ceasing to have the intention of carrying out taxable activities; and

(b)   they are satisfied that he has not carried out, and will not carry out, taxable activities,

the Commissioners must cancel his registration with effect from the time when he ceased to have the intention to carry out taxable activities[12].

For these purposes regulations may make provision:

(i)   as to the time within which a notification is to be made[13];

(ii)   as to the form and manner in which any notification is to be made and as to the information to be contained in or provided with it[14];

(iii) requiring a person who has made a notification to notify the Commissioners if any information contained in or provided in connection with it is or becomes inaccurate[15];

(iv)   as to the correction of entries in the register[16].

The register kept under these provisions may contain such information as the Commissioners think is required for the purposes of the care and management of the landfill tax[17].

1   A person carries out a taxable activity if: (1) he makes a taxable disposal in respect of which he is liable to pay tax (Finance Act 1996 s 69(1)(a)); or (2) he permits another person to make a taxable disposal in respect of which the first-mentioned person is liable to pay tax (s 69(1)(b)). As to the meaning of 'taxable disposal' see PARA 902. Where (a) a taxable disposal is made; and (b) it is made without the knowledge of the person who is liable to pay tax in respect of it, then that person must for the purposes of s 69 be taken to permit the disposal: s 69(2).

2   Finance Act 1996 s 47(2).

3   As to the Commissioners for Her Majesty's Revenue and Customs see PARA 901 note 2.

4   Finance Act 1996 s 47(3). Notification must be made on the prescribed form: Landfill Tax Regulations 1996, SI 1996/1527, reg 4(1). For the prescribed form see Schedule Form 1. Any

reference to a form prescribed in the Schedule to the Landfill Tax Regulations 1996, SI 1996/1527, includes a reference to a form which the Commissioners are satisfied is a form to the like effect: reg 2(4). Where the notification is made by a person who operates or intends to operate more than one landfill site, it must include the particulars set out on the prescribed form: reg 4(2), Schedule Form 2. Where the notification is made by a partnership, it must include the particulars set out on the prescribed form: reg 4(3), Schedule Form 3. The notification must be made within 30 days of the earliest date after 1 August 1996 on which the person either forms or continues to have the intention to carry out taxable activities: reg 4(4).

A person who fails to comply with the Finance Act 1996 s 47(3) is liable to a penalty equal to 5% of the relevant tax or, if it is greater or the circumstances are such that there is no relevant tax, to a penalty of £250: s 60, Sch 5 para 21(1). 'Relevant tax' means the tax (if any) for which the person concerned is liable for the period which:

(1)   begins on the date with effect from which he is, in accordance with s 47, required to be registered (Sch 5 para 21(2)(a)); and

(2)   ends on the date on which the Commissioners received notification of, or otherwise became aware of, his liability to be registered (Sch 5 para 21(2)(b)).

However, where, by reason of conduct falling within Sch 5 para 21(1):

(a)   a person is convicted of an offence (whether under Pt III (ss 39–71) or otherwise); or

(b)   a person is assessed to a penalty under Sch 5 para 18 (evasion: see PARA 987),

that conduct does not also give rise to liability to a penalty under Sch 5 para 21: Sch 5 para 21(4).

For obligations to comply with s 47(3) arising on or after 1 April 2010, Sch 5 para 21(1), (2) and (4) are repealed by the Finance Act 2008 s 123, Sch 41 para 25(h)(ii); Finance Act 2008, Schedule 41 (Appointed Day and Transitional Provisions) Order 2009, SI 2009/511, arts 2, 3. As to the penalty for failure to comply with the Finance Act 1996 s 47(2) or (3) where the obligation arises on or after 1 April 2010 see the Finance Act 2008, Sch 41 para 1; and INCOME TAXATION.

5   Finance Act 1996 s 47(4). A person who fails to comply with s 47(4) is liable to a penalty of £250: Sch 5 para 21(3).

6   Finance Act 1996 s 47(5). Section 47(5) applies whether or not he notifies the Commissioners under s 47(3) (see the text to note 4): see s 47(5).

7   Finance Act 1996 s 47(6). Section 47(6) applies whether or not he notifies the Commissioners under s 47(4) (see the text to note 5): see s 47(6).

8   Ie under the Finance Act 1996 s 47(4): see the text to note 5.

9   Ie regulations made under the Finance Act 1996 s 51: see PARA 938 et seq.

10   Finance Act 1996 s 47(7), which only applies where s 47(8) does not apply: see the text to note 12.

11   Ie under the Finance Act 1996 s 47(4): see the text to note 5.

12   Finance Act 1996 s 47(8).

13   Finance Act 1996 s 47(9)(a).

14   Finance Act 1996 s 47(9)(b).

15   Finance Act 1996 s 47(9)(c).

16   Finance Act 1996 s 47(9)(d). See also the Landfill Tax Regulations 1996, SI 1996/1527.

17   Finance Act 1996 s 47(1). As to the meaning of 'landfill tax' see PARA 901.

(2) REQUIREMENT TO PROVIDE INFORMATION

921. Information required to keep register up to date. Regulations[1] may make provision requiring a registrable person[2] to notify the Commissioners for Her Majesty's Revenue and Customs[3] of particulars which:

(1)   are of changes in circumstances relating to the registrable person or any business carried on by him[4];

(2)   appear to the Commissioners to be required for the purpose of keeping the register[5] up to date[6]; and

(3)   are of a prescribed[7] description[8].

Regulations may also make provision:

(a)   as to the time within which a notification is to be made[9];

(b)   as to the form and manner in which a notification is to be made[10];

(c)   requiring a person who has made a notification to notify the Commissioners if any information contained in it is inaccurate[11].

1   See the Landfill Tax Regulations 1996, SI 1996/1527, Pt II (regs 4–9); and PARAS 920, 970 et seq.
2   As to the meaning of 'registrable person' see PARA 958 note 1.
3   As to the Commissioners for Her Majesty's Revenue and Customs see PARA 901 note 2.
4   Finance Act 1996 s 48(1)(a).
5   Ie the register kept under the Finance Act 1996 s 47: see PARA 920.
6   Finance Act 1996 s 48(1)(b).
7   'Prescribed' means prescribed by an order or regulations under the Finance Act 1996 Pt III (ss 39–71): s 70(1).
8   Finance Act 1996 s 48(1)(c).
9   Finance Act 1996 s 48(2)(a).
10 Finance Act 1996 s 48(2)(b).
11 Finance Act 1996 s 48(2)(c).

922. Changes in particulars. A person who has made a notification of liability to be registered under the landfill tax regulations[1], must, within 30 days of discovering any inaccuracy in, or any change occurring which causes to become inaccurate, any of the information which was contained in or provided with the notification, notify the Commissioners for Her Majesty's Revenue and Customs[2] in writing and furnish them with full particulars[3].

Without prejudice to the above, a registrable person[4] must, within 30 days of any change occurring in any of certain circumstances[5], notify the Commissioners in writing and furnish them with particulars of the change[6] and the date on which the change occurred[7]. A registrable person who discovers that any information contained in or provided with such a notification was inaccurate must, within 30 days of his discovering the inaccuracy, notify the Commissioners in writing and furnish them with particulars of:

(1)   the inaccuracy[8];
(2)   the date on which the inaccuracy was discovered[9];
(3)   how the information was inaccurate[10]; and
(4)   the correct information[11].

Any person failing to comply with a requirement imposed in any of the above provisions is liable to a penalty[12]. Where in relation to a registered person[13] the Commissioners are satisfied that any of the information recorded in the register[14] is or has become inaccurate they may correct the register accordingly[15].

1   Ie a notification under the Landfill Tax Regulations 1996, SI 1996/1527, reg 4, whether or not it was made in accordance with reg 4(4): see PARA 920.
2   As to the Commissioners for Her Majesty's Revenue and Customs see PARA 901 note 2.
3   Landfill Tax Regulations 1996, SI 1996/1527, reg 5(1).
4   As to the meaning of 'registrable person' see PARA 958 note 1; definition applied by virtue of the Landfill Tax Regulations 1996, SI 1996/1527, reg 2(1).
5   Ie the following circumstances relating to the registrable person or any taxable business carried on by him:
        (1)   his name, his trading name (if different), his address and the landfill sites he operates (Landfill Tax Regulations 1996, SI 1996/1527, reg 5(4)(a));
        (2)   his status, namely whether he carries on business as a sole proprietor, body corporate, partnership or other unincorporated body (reg 5(4)(b));
        (3)   in the case of a partnership, the name and address of any partner (reg 5(4)(c)).
    'Taxable business' means a business or part of a business in the course of which taxable activities are carried out: reg 2(1). As to the meaning of 'taxable activity' see PARA 920 note 1. As to the meaning of 'landfill site' see PARA 902 note 5; definition applied by virtue of reg 2(1).
6   Landfill Tax Regulations 1996, SI 1996/1527, reg 5(2)(a).
7   Landfill Tax Regulations 1996, SI 1996/1527, reg 5(2)(b).
8   Landfill Tax Regulations 1996, SI 1996/1527, reg 5(3)(a).

9   Landfill Tax Regulations 1996, SI 1996/1527, reg 5(3)(b).
10   Landfill Tax Regulations 1996, SI 1996/1527, reg 5(3)(c).
11   Landfill Tax Regulations 1996, SI 1996/1527, reg 5(3)(d).
12   Landfill Tax Regulations 1996, SI 1996/1527, reg 5(5). The penalty is £250: see reg 5(5).
13   'Registered person' means a person who is registered under the Finance Act 1996 s 47 (see PARA 920); and 'register' and 'registration' must be construed accordingly: Landfill Tax Regulations 1996, SI 1996/1527, reg 2(1).
14   See note 13.
15   Landfill Tax Regulations 1996, SI 1996/1527, reg 5(6). For the purposes of reg 5(6), it is immaterial whether or not the registered person has notified the Commissioners of any change which has occurred in accordance with reg 5(1)–(3): reg 5(7).

923. Notification of cessation of taxable activities. A person who is required[1] to notify the Commissioners for Her Majesty's Revenue and Customs[2] of his having ceased to have the intention to carry out taxable activities[3] must, within 30 days of his so having ceased, notify the Commissioners in writing and thereby inform them of:

(1)   the date on which he ceased to have the intention of carrying out taxable activities[4]; and

(2)   if different, the date on which he ceased to carry out taxable activities[5].

1   Ie by the Finance Act 1996 s 47(4): see PARA 920.
2   As to the Commissioners for Her Majesty's Revenue and Customs see PARA 901 note 2.
3   As to the meaning of 'taxable activity' see PARA 920 note 1.
4   Landfill Tax Regulations 1996, SI 1996/1527, reg 6(a).
5   Landfill Tax Regulations 1996, SI 1996/1527, reg 6(b).

(3) SPECIAL CASES

924. Companies and partnerships. The registration under the landfill tax provisions[1] of a body corporate carrying on a business in several divisions may, if the body corporate so requests and the Commissioners for Her Majesty's Revenue and Customs[2] see fit, be in the names of those divisions[3].

Where anything is required to be done by or under the landfill tax provisions[4] by or on behalf of a partnership, it is the joint and several responsibility of every partner; but, if it is done by one partner, that is sufficient compliance with any such requirement[5].

1   Ie the Finance Act 1996 Pt III (ss 39–71): see PARA 901 note 1.
2   As to the Commissioners for Her Majesty's Revenue and Customs see PARA 901 note 2.
3   Finance Act 1996 s 58(3).
4   Ie whether by the Landfill Tax Regulations 1996, SI 1996/1527, or otherwise: see the Finance Act 1996 s 58(1).
5   See the Finance Act 1996 s 58(1); and the Landfill Tax Regulations 1996, SI 1996/1527, reg 8(3).

925. Groups of companies. Where any bodies corporate are treated as members of a group[1], then for the purposes of the landfill tax provisions[2]:

(1)   any liability of a member of the group to pay landfill tax is taken to be a liability of the representative member[3];

(2)   the representative member is taken to carry out any taxable activities[4] which a member of the group would carry out[5];

(3)   all members of the group are jointly and severally liable for any tax due from the representative member[6].

Where an application to that effect is made to the Commissioners for Her Majesty's Revenue and Customs[7] with respect to two or more bodies corporate eligible to be treated as members of a group, then:

(a) from the beginning of an accounting period[8] they are so treated; and

(b) one of them is the representative member,

unless the Commissioners refuse the application[9]. The Commissioners may not refuse the application unless it appears to them necessary to do so for the protection of the revenue[10].

Where any bodies corporate are treated as members of a group and an application to that effect is made to the Commissioners, then, from the beginning of an accounting period:

(i) a further body eligible to be so treated is to be included among the bodies so treated[11];

(ii) a body corporate is to be excluded from the bodies so treated[12];

(iii) another member of the group is to be substituted as the representative member[13]; or

(iv) the bodies corporate are no longer to be treated as members of a group[14],

unless the application is to the effect mentioned in head (i) or head (iii) above and the Commissioners refuse the application[15]. The Commissioners may refuse an application under head (i) or head (iii) above only if it appears to them necessary to do so for the protection of the revenue[16].

Such an application, with respect to any bodies corporate, must be made by one of those bodies or by the person controlling them and must be made not less than 90 days before the date from which it is to take effect, or at such later time as the Commissioners may allow[17]. Where a body corporate is treated as a member of a group as being controlled by any person and it appears to the Commissioners that it has ceased to be so controlled, they must, by notice given to that person, terminate that treatment from such date as may be specified in the notice[18].

1 Two or more bodies corporate are eligible to be treated as members of a group if: (1) one of them controls each of the others; (2) one person (whether a body corporate or an individual) controls all of them; or (3) two or more individuals carrying on a business in partnership control all of them, and the prospective representative member has an established place of business in the United Kingdom: Finance Act 1996 s 59(2), (3). For these purposes, a body corporate is taken to control another body corporate if it is empowered by statute to control that body's activities or if it is that body's holding company within the meaning of the Companies Act 2006 s 1159, Sch 6 (see COMPANIES vol 14 (2009) PARA 25); and an individual or individuals are taken to control a body corporate if he or they, were he or they a company, would be that body's holding company within the meaning of s 1159, Sch 6: Finance Act 1996 s 59(9) (amended by SI 2009/1890). 'United Kingdom' means Great Britain and Northern Ireland: Interpretation Act 1978 s 5, Sch 1. 'Great Britain' means England, Scotland and Wales: Union with Scotland Act 1706, preamble art I; Interpretation Act 1978 s 22(1), Sch 2 para 5(a). Neither the Isle of Man nor the Channel Islands are within the United Kingdom. See further CONSTITUTIONAL LAW AND HUMAN RIGHTS vol 8(2) (Reissue) PARA 3.

2 Ie the Finance Act 1996 Pt III (ss 39–71): see PARA 901 note 1.

3 Finance Act 1996 s 59(1)(a).

4 As to the meaning of 'taxable activity' see PARA 920 note 1.

5 Finance Act 1996 s 59(1)(b). The reference in the text is a reference to any taxable activities which the member would carry out (apart from s 59) by virtue of s 69 (see PARA 920 note 1).

6 Finance Act 1996 s 59(1)(c).

7 As to the Commissioners for Her Majesty's Revenue and Customs see PARA 901 note 2.

8 As to the meaning of 'accounting period' see PARA 928 note 17.

9 Finance Act 1996 s 59(4).

10 Finance Act 1996 s 59(4). As to the meaning of 'the protection of the revenue' in a similar provision relating to value added tax see *National Westminster Bank plc v Customs and Excise Comrs* VTD 15514. See also HM Customs and Excise Business Brief 15/99, 12 July 1999.

11 Finance Act 1996 s 59(5)(a).

12 Finance Act 1996 s 59(5)(b).

13 Finance Act 1996 s 59(5)(c).

14 Finance Act 1996 s 59(5)(d).

15 Finance Act 1996 s 59(5).

16 Finance Act 1996 s 59(6). See note 10.

17 Finance Act 1996 s 59(8).

18 Finance Act 1996 s 59(7). In relation to a similar provision for value added tax, it has been held that a company which ceases to be eligible to be part of a group remains part of the group until notice has been given under that provision: see *Customs and Excise Comrs v Barclays Bank plc* [2001] EWCA Civ 1513, [2001] STC 1558.

926. Unincorporated bodies. The registration under the landfill tax provisions[1] of an unincorporated body other than a partnership may be in the name of the body concerned; and in determining whether taxable activities[2] are carried out by such a body no account may be taken of any change in its members[3].

Where anything is required to be done by or under the landfill tax provisions[4] by or on behalf of an unincorporated body other than a partnership, it is to be the joint and several responsibility of:

(1)   every member holding office as president, chairman, treasurer, secretary or any similar office[5]; or

(2)   if there is no such office, every member holding office as a member of a committee by which the affairs of the body are managed[6]; or

(3)   if there is no such office or committee, every member[7].

If it is done by any of the persons referred to above, that is sufficient compliance with any such requirement[8]. However, where an unincorporated body other than a partnership is required to make a notification in relation to registration[9], it is not sufficient compliance unless the notification is made by a person upon whom a responsibility for making it is so imposed[10].

1 Ie the Finance Act 1996 Pt III (ss 39–71): see PARA 901 note 1.

2 As to the meaning of 'taxable activity' see PARA 920 note 1.

3 Finance Act 1996 s 58(2).

4 Ie whether by the Landfill Tax Regulations 1996, SI 1996/1527, or otherwise: see reg 8(1).

5 Landfill Tax Regulations 1996, SI 1996/1527, reg 8(1)(a).

6 Landfill Tax Regulations 1996, SI 1996/1527, reg 8(1)(b).

7 Landfill Tax Regulations 1996, SI 1996/1527, reg 8(1)(c).

8 Landfill Tax Regulations 1996, SI 1996/1527, reg 8(1). See also PARA 924.

9 Ie such a notification as is referred to in the Landfill Tax Regulations 1996, SI 1996/1527, regs 4–6: see PARAS 920, 922–923.

10 Landfill Tax Regulations 1996, SI 1996/1527, reg 8(2). See also PARA 924 note 5.

927. Businesses of insolvent persons. If a registrable person[1] becomes bankrupt or incapacitated[2], the Commissioners for Her Majesty's Revenue and Customs[3] may, from the date on which he became bankrupt or incapacitated, as the case may be, treat as a registrable person any person carrying on any taxable business[4] of his; and any legislation relating to landfill tax[5] applies to any person so treated as though he were a registered person[6]. Any person carrying on such business as aforesaid must, within 30 days of commencing to do so, inform the Commissioners in writing of that fact and the date of the bankruptcy order or of the nature of the incapacity and the date on which it began[7]. Where the

Commissioners have so treated a person carrying on a business as a registrable person, they must cease so to treat him if:

(1)   the registration[8] of the registrable person is cancelled, whether or not any other person is registered with the registration number[9] previously allocated to him[10];

(2)   the bankruptcy is discharged or the incapacity ceases[11]; or

(3)   he ceases carrying on the business of the registrable person[12].

1   As to the meaning of 'registrable person' see PARA 958 note 1; definition applied by virtue of the Landfill Tax Regulations 1996, SI 1996/1527, reg 2(1).

2   In relation to a registrable person which is a company, the references in the Landfill Tax Regulations 1996, SI 1996/1527, reg 9 to the registrable person becoming incapacitated are to be construed as references to its going into liquidation or receivership or entering administration; and references to the incapacity ceasing must be construed accordingly: reg 9(4) (amended by SI 2003/2096).

3   As to the Commissioners for Her Majesty's Revenue and Customs see PARA 901 note 2.

4   As to the meaning of 'taxable business' see PARA 922 note 5.

5   As to the meaning of 'landfill tax' see PARA 901.

6   See the Finance Act 1996 s 58(4) (amended by SI 2003/2096); and the Landfill Tax Regulations 1996, SI 1996/1527, reg 9(1). As to the meaning of 'registered person' see PARA 922 note 13.

7   Landfill Tax Regulations 1996, SI 1996/1527, reg 9(2).

8   As to the meaning of 'registration' see PARA 922 note 13.

9   As to the meaning of 'registration number' see PARA 928 note 9.

10   Landfill Tax Regulations 1996, SI 1996/1527, reg 9(3)(a).

11   Landfill Tax Regulations 1996, SI 1996/1527, reg 9(3)(b).

12   Landfill Tax Regulations 1996, SI 1996/1527, reg 9(3)(c).

928. Transfer of a going concern. Where:

(1)   a taxable business[1] is transferred as a going concern[2];

(2)   the registration[3] of the transferor has not already been cancelled[4];

(3)   as a result of the transfer of the business the registration of the transferor is to be cancelled and the transferee has become liable to be registered[5]; and

(4)   an application is made on the prescribed form[6] by both the transferor and the transferee[7],

the Commissioners for Her Majesty's Revenue and Customs[8] may with effect from the date of the transfer cancel the registration of the transferor and register the transferee with the registration number[9] previously allocated to the transferor[10].

Where the transferee of a business has been so registered with the registration number previously allocated to the transferor:

(a)   any liability of the transferor existing at the date of the transfer to make a return[11] or account for or pay any landfill tax[12] becomes the liability of the transferee[13];

(b)   any entitlement of the transferor, whether or not existing at the date of the transfer, to credit[14] or payment[15] becomes the entitlement of the transferee[16].

In addition, where the transferee of a business has been so registered with the registration number previously allocated to the transferor during an accounting period[17] subsequent to that in which the transfer took place (but with effect from the date of the transfer) and any:

(i)   return has been made[18];

(ii)   tax has been accounted for[19]; or

(iii)   entitlement to credit has been claimed[20],

by either the transferor or the transferee, it must be treated as having been done by the transferee[21].

Where:

(A)   a taxable business[22] is transferred as a going concern[23];

(B)   the transferee removes[24] material[25]; and

(C)   the transferor has paid tax on the disposal concerned[26],

then, whether or not the transferee has been so registered with the registration number previously allocated to the transferor, any entitlement to credit arising[27] becomes the entitlement of the transferee[28].

1   As to the meaning of 'taxable business' see PARA 922 note 5.
2   Landfill Tax Regulations 1996, SI 1996/1527, reg 7(1)(a). There is no statutory definition of 'going concern' but it is likely that the Commissioners for Her Majesty's Revenue and Customs will take the same approach as they do to the meaning of 'going concern' in value added tax cases. See VALUE ADDED TAX vol 49(1) (2005 Reissue) PARA 210.
3   As to the meaning of 'registration' see PARA 922 note 13.
4   Landfill Tax Regulations 1996, SI 1996/1527, reg 7(1)(b).
5   Landfill Tax Regulations 1996, SI 1996/1527, reg 7(1)(c).
6   See the Landfill Tax Regulations 1996, SI 1996/1527, reg 7(1)(d), Schedule Form 4. See also PARA 920 note 4.
7   Landfill Tax Regulations 1996, SI 1996/1527, reg 7(1)(d).
8   As to the Commissioners for Her Majesty's Revenue and Customs see PARA 901 note 2.
9   'Registration number' means the identifying number allocated to a registered person and notified to him by the Commissioners: Landfill Tax Regulations 1996, SI 1996/1527, reg 2(1). As to the meaning of 'registered person' see PARA 922 note 13.
10   See the Finance Act 1996 s 58(5), (6); and the Landfill Tax Regulations 1996, SI 1996/1527, reg 7(1). An application under reg 7(1) must be treated as the notification referred to in reg 6 (see PARA 923): reg 7(2).
11   As to the meaning of 'return' see PARA 935 note 4.
12   Ie under the Landfill Tax Regulations 1996, SI 1996/1527, Pt III (regs 10–16).
13   Landfill Tax Regulations 1996, SI 1996/1527, reg 7(3)(a).
14   'Credit', except where the context otherwise requires, means credit which a person is entitled to claim under the Landfill Tax Regulations 1996, SI 1996/1527, Pt IV (regs 17–20) (see PARA 938 et seq): see reg 7(3)(b).
15   Ie under the Landfill Tax Regulations 1996, SI 1996/1527, Pt IV.
16   Landfill Tax Regulations 1996, SI 1996/1527, reg 7(3)(b).
17   'Accounting period' means: (1) in the case of a registered person, each period of three months ending on the dates notified to him by the Commissioners, whether by means of a registration certificate issued by them or otherwise; (2) in the case of a registrable person who is not registered, each quarter; or (3) in the case of any registrable person, such other period in relation to which he is required by or under the Landfill Tax Regulations 1996, SI 1996/1527, reg 11 (see PARA 935) to make a return, and, in every case, the first accounting period of a registrable person begins on the effective date of registration: reg 2(1).
    As to the meaning of 'registrable person' see PARA 958 note 1; definition applied by virtue of reg 2(1). 'Quarter' means a period of three months ending at the end of March, June, September or December: reg 2(1). 'Effective date of registration' means the date determined in accordance with the Finance Act 1996 s 47 (see PARA 920) upon which the person was or should have been registered: Landfill Tax Regulations 1996, SI 1996/1527, reg 2(1).
18   Landfill Tax Regulations 1996, SI 1996/1527, reg 7(4)(a).
19   Landfill Tax Regulations 1996, SI 1996/1527, reg 7(4)(b).
20   Landfill Tax Regulations 1996, SI 1996/1527, reg 7(4)(c).
21   Landfill Tax Regulations 1996, SI 1996/1527, reg 7(4).
22   As to the meaning of 'taxable business' see PARA 922 note 5.
23   Landfill Tax Regulations 1996, SI 1996/1527, reg 7(5)(a).
24   Ie as described in the Landfill Tax Regulations 1996, SI 1996/1527, reg 21(2) or reg 21(4): see PARA 941.
25   Landfill Tax Regulations 1996, SI 1996/1527, reg 7(5)(b). As to the meaning of 'material' see PARA 902 note 3.
26   Landfill Tax Regulations 1996, SI 1996/1527, reg 7(5)(c). As to the meaning of 'disposal' see PARA 908 note 5.

27 Ie arising under the Landfill Tax Regulations 1996, SI 1996/1527, Pt V (reg 21): see PARA 941.
28 Landfill Tax Regulations 1996, SI 1996/1527, reg 7(5).

5. ACCOUNTING AND PAYMENT

(1) LIABILITY FOR TAX

929. Persons liable. The person liable to pay landfill tax[1] charged on a taxable disposal[2] is the landfill site[3] operator[4]. This reference to the landfill site operator is a reference to the person who is at the time of the disposal the operator of the landfill site which constitutes or contains the land on or under which the disposal is made[5].

1   As to the meaning of 'landfill tax' see PARA 901.
2   As to the meaning of 'taxable disposal' see PARA 902.
3   As to the meaning of 'landfill site' see PARA 902 note 5.
4   Finance Act 1996 s 41(1). The operator of a landfill site at a given time is:
    (1)   the person who is at the time concerned the holder of the licence, where s 66(a) (see PARA 902 note 5) applies (s 67(a));
    (2)   the waste disposal authority which at the time concerned occupies the landfill site, where s 66(b) (see PARA 902 note 5) applies (s 67(b));
    (3)   the person who is at the time concerned the holder of the permit, where s 66(ba) (see PARA 902 note 5) applies (s 67(ba) (added by SI 2000/1973));
    (4)   the person who is at the time concerned the holder of the licence, where the Finance Act 1996 s 66(c) (see PARA 902 note 5) applies (s 67(c));
    (5)   the district council which passed the resolution, where s 66(d) (see PARA 902 note 5) applies (s 67(d));
    (6)   the person who is at the time concerned the holder of the licence, where s 66(e) (see PARA 902 note 5) applies (s 67(e)).
    As to the secondary liability of the controller of a landfill site to pay landfill tax see Sch 5 Pt VIII paras 48–61; and PARA 930.
5   Finance Act 1996 s 41(2).

930. Secondary liability of controllers of landfill sites. Where (1) a taxable disposal is made at a landfill site[1]; (2) at the time when that disposal is made a person is the operator of the landfill site[2]; and (3) at that time a different person is the controller of the whole or part of the landfill site[3], the controller is liable to pay to the Commissioners for Her Majesty's Revenue and Customs[4] an amount of the landfill tax chargeable on the disposal[5].

The amount so chargeable (the 'relevant amount') is payable to the Commissioners only if a notice containing specified information[6] is served on the controller, or other reasonable steps are taken with a view to bringing the required information to his attention, before the end of two years beginning with the day immediately following the relevant accounting day[7].

Where an amount of landfill tax is assessed[8] and notified to a licensed operator[9], the Commissioners may also determine that a controller of the whole or part of any landfill site operated by that operator is liable to pay so much of the amount assessed as they consider just and equitable[10]. Amounts paid under these provisions are deemed to be an amount of tax due from the controller and are recoverable accordingly[11].

1   As to the meaning of 'landfill site' see PARA 902 note 5.
2   Ie by virtue of the Finance Act 1996 s 67(a), (c) or (e): see PARA 929.
3   A person is the controller of the whole, or a part, of a landfill site at a given time if he determines, or is entitled to determine, what disposals of material, if any, may be made at every part of the site at that time, or at that part of the site at that time, as the case may be; but a person who, because he is the employee or agent of another, has such power of, or such entitlement to, determination is not such a controller: Finance Act 1996 s 60 (amended by the Finance Act 2000 s 142(1), (2)); Finance Act 1996 Sch 5 para 48 (Sch 5 Pt VIII paras 48–61 added by the Finance Act 2000 s 142(3), Sch 37).

Where a person becomes, or ceases to be, a controller of the whole or part of a landfill site, the controller and the operator of that site must notify the Commissioners for Her Majesty's Revenue and Customs (see note 4), within 30 days beginning with the day immediately following the date of the change: (1) that a person has become or has ceased to be a controller; (2) of the identity of that person; and (3) of the date of the commencement or cessation: Finance Act 1996 Sch 5 para 60(1)–(3) (as so added). Amounts paid under these provisions are deemed to be an amount of tax due from him and are recoverable accordingly: Sch 5 para 55 (as so added). Failure to comply is visited with a penalty of £250, and results in the extension of the two-year time limit for the giving of notice of liability (or of the taking of reasonable steps to do so) to 20 years: Sch 5 paras 60(4), 61(2) (as so added).

4 As to the Commissioners for Her Majesty's Revenue and Customs see PARA 901 note 2.

5 Finance Act 1996 Sch 5 para 49(1) (as added: see note 3). For the purposes of heads (2) and (3) in the text, s 61 (see PARA 904) and any regulations made under s 62 (repealed) do not apply for determining the time when the disposal in question is made: Sch 5 para 49(8) (as so added).

The controller of the whole of the site is liable to pay the whole of the tax; the controller of part of the site is liable to pay the amount which would have been chargeable had a separate taxable disposal consisting of a specified amount of material been made at the time of the disposal mentioned in head (1) in the text: Sch 5 para 49(2)–(5) (as so added). The specified amount is the amount by weight of the material comprised in that disposal which was disposed of on the part of the site under his control (and if this amount is nil, the controller's liability is also nil): Sch 5 para 49(6), (7) (as so added). Where: (1) the operator of a landfill site is liable to pay landfill tax on a taxable disposal by reference to a particular accounting period; (2) a controller of the whole or a part of that site is otherwise liable to pay an amount of that tax under Sch 5 para 49; and (3) for the accounting period in question the operator is entitled to credit under regulations made under s 51 (see PARA 938 et seq), the amount of the tax which the controller is otherwise liable to pay is reduced by a specified formula: see Sch 5 para 50(1)–(4) (as so added). If the amount of the reduction is greater than the amount chargeable, the liability is nil: Sch 5 para 50(5) (as so added).

6 The specified information is the relevant amount and, if that amount has been reduced (see note 5): (1) the amount of the controller's unreduced liability; (2) the amount of credit to which he is entitled; and (3) the operator's gross tax liability: Finance Act 1996 Sch 5 para 51(6) (as added: see note 3).

7 Finance Act 1996 Sch 5 para 51(1), (2) (as added: see note 3). The relevant accounting day is the last day of the accounting period by reference to which the landfill site operator liable to pay the landfill tax in question is required to account for that tax: Sch 5 para 51(3) (as so added). If the controller is required under Sch 5 para 51 to pay the relevant amount, payment must be made before the end of the period of 30 days beginning with the day immediately following the day on which the notice is served (or the day on which the last of the 'other reasonable steps' is taken) (the 'notification day'): Sch 5 para 51(4), (5) (as so added).

8 Ie under the Finance Act 1996 s 50: see PARA 959.

9 Ie a person who is the operator of a landfill site by virtue of the Finance Act 1996 s 67(a), (c) or (e): see PARA 929.

10 Finance Act 1996 Sch 5 para 52(1), (6) (as added: see note 3). Payment is to be made as set out in the text to notes 6, 7: see Sch 5 para 52(2)–(5) (as so added). Where the relevant assessment is withdrawn or reduced, the Commissioners may determine that the controller's liability is cancelled, or reduced to such an amount as they consider to be just and equitable: Sch 5 para 53(1)–(3) (as so added). If notice has already been given to the controller of the liability which is so cancelled or reduced (or reasonable steps have been taken to do so), the Commissioners must notify him (or take reasonable steps to do so) within the period of 30 days beginning with the day immediately following that on which they make the determination that the liability is cancelled or reduced: Sch 5 para 53(4)(a), (6), (7) (as so added). Any amount so reduced is then payable (or treated as having been payable) on or before the day on which the original, unreduced amount was so payable: Sch 5 para 53(4)(b) (as so added). However, where notice of an amount which has been reduced has not been given (or reasonable steps taken to do so), the controller is only liable to pay if notice of the reduced amount is given (or reasonable steps taken) before the expiry of the period of two years beginning with the day immediately following that on which the Commissioners make their determination: Sch 5 para 53(5) (as so added).

Where the liability of a licensed operator is adjusted otherwise than by his being entitled to credit, by assessment, or by the withdrawal or reduction of an assessment, the Commissioners may determine that a controller of the whole or any part of a landfill site operated by him is liable to pay (or is entitled to an allowance of) such an amount as they consider just and equitable: Sch 5 para 54(1), (2) (as so added). Notification and payment are as set out in the text to notes 6, 7: Sch 5 para 54(3)–(8) (as so added).

Where:

(1)   (a) the operator of a landfill site is liable under s 41 (see PARA 929) for landfill tax; and (b) a controller is liable under Sch 5 para 49 (see note 5) to pay an amount of that tax (whether nor not reduced under Sch 5 para 50 (see note 5));

(2)   (a) the operator of a landfill site is notified of an amount of an assessment under s 50 (see PARA 959); and (b) in consequence of a determination made by the Commissioners under Sch 5 para 52 a controller is liable to pay an amount (whether or not reduced under Sch 5 para 53); or

(3)   (a) the liability of the operator of a landfill site to pay landfill tax is adjusted so that Sch 5 para 54 applies; and (b) in consequence of a determination made by the Commissioners under Sch 5 para 54(2)(a) in connection with the adjustment a controller is liable to pay an amount,

then the controller and the operator are jointly and severally liable for the principal liability (ie the amount payable under heads (1)(a), (2)(a) and (3)(a)) but the amount recoverable from the controller must not exceed the amount of the secondary liability (ie the amount payable under heads (1)(b), (2)(b) and (3)(b)): Sch 5 para 57 (as so added). Similarly, the operator of a landfill site and the controller of the whole or a part of that site are jointly and severally liable for any interest payable on the amount due, but the amount recoverable from the latter must not exceed the amount calculated in accordance with the specified formula: Sch 5 para 58(1)–(3) (as so added). The controller is liable for an amount of interest only if notice is served on him in accordance with the text to notes 6, 7, and payment is to be made accordingly. The provisions of Sch 5 para 28 (see PARA 999) apply for these purposes as they apply for those of Sch 5 para 27 (see PARA 998): Sch 5 para 58 (as so added).

11   Finance Act 1996 Sch 5 para 55 (as added: see note 3). The controller is not, however, to be treated for the purposes of the Finance Act 1996 as carrying out a taxable activity by reason only of any liability under Sch 5 Pt VIII: Sch 5 para 56 (as so added).

(2) RECORDS

931. Power to require records to be kept by registrable persons. Regulations may require registrable persons[1] to make records[2]. Such regulations may be framed by reference to such records as may be stipulated in any notice published by the Commissioners for Her Majesty's Revenue and Customs[3] in pursuance of the regulations and not withdrawn by a further notice[4]. Regulations may:

(1)   require registrable persons to preserve records of a prescribed[5] description (whether or not the records are required to be made in pursuance of regulations) for such period not exceeding six years as may be specified in the regulations[6];

(2)   authorise the Commissioners to direct that any such records need only be preserved for a shorter period than that specified in the regulations[7];

(3)   authorise a direction to be made so as to apply generally or in such cases as the Commissioners may stipulate[8].

Any duty under regulations to preserve records may be discharged by the preservation of the information contained in them by such means as the Commissioners may approve; and, where that information is so preserved, a copy of any document forming part of the records is admissible in evidence in any proceedings, whether civil or criminal, to the same extent as the records themselves[9]. The Commissioners may, as a condition of so approving any means of preserving information contained in any records, impose such reasonable requirements as appear to them necessary for securing that the information will be as readily available to them as if the records themselves had been preserved[10].

1   As to the meaning of 'registrable person' see PARA 958 note 1.

2   Finance Act 1996 s 60, Sch 5 para 2(1). As to the regulations made under Sch 5 para 2 see the Landfill Tax Regulations 1996, SI 1996/1527, reg 16; and PARA 933.

3   As to the Commissioners for Her Majesty's Revenue and Customs see PARA 901 note 2.
4   Finance Act 1996 Sch 5 para 2(2).
5   'Prescribed' means prescribed by an order or regulations under the Finance Act 1996 Pt III
    (ss 39–71): s 70(1).
6   Finance Act 1996 Sch 5 para 2(3)(a).
7   Finance Act 1996 Sch 5 para 2(3)(b).
8   Finance Act 1996 Sch 5 para 2(3)(c).
9   Finance Act 1996 Sch 5 para 2(4), which is expressed to be subject to Sch 5 para 2(5)–(7).
    Provisions as to admissibility in evidence are contained in Sch 5 para 2(6), most of which
    (except for Sch 5 para 2(6)(b), (c), in regard to proceedings in Scotland) is repealed. The Finance
    Act 1996 provides that, in the case of civil proceedings in England and Wales to which the Civil
    Evidence Act 1968 ss 5, 6 apply, a statement contained in a document produced by a computer
    is not admissible in evidence by virtue of the Finance Act 1996 Sch 5 para 2(4) except in
    accordance with the Civil Evidence Act 1968 ss 5, 6: see the Finance Act 1996 Sch 5 para 2(7).
    However, the Civil Evidence Act 1968 ss 5, 6 have been repealed. As to proof of statements and
    records of business see the Civil Evidence Act 1995 ss 8, 9; and CIVIL PROCEDURE vol 11 (2009)
    PARAS 816–817.
        As from a day to be appointed the Finance Act 1996 Sch 5 para 2(4) is to be substituted by
    the Finance Act 2009 s 98, Sch 50 para 21 so that a duty under regulations to preserve records
    may be discharged by preserving them, or the information contained in them, in any form and
    by any means, subject to any conditions or exceptions specified in writing by the
    Commissioners. As from the same date the Finance Act 1996 Sch 5 para 2(5)–(7) is to be
    repealed. At the date at which this volume states the law no such day had been appointed.
10 Finance Act 1996 Sch 5 para 2(5).

932.   Landfill tax account.   Every registrable person[1] must make and maintain
an account to be known as the 'landfill tax account'[2]. The landfill tax account
must be in such form and contain such particulars as may be stipulated in a
notice published by the Commissioners for Her Majesty's Revenue and Customs[3]
and not withdrawn by a further notice[4].

1   As to the meaning of 'registrable person' see PARA 958 note 1; definition applied by virtue of the
    Landfill Tax Regulations 1996, SI 1996/1527, reg 2(1).
2   Landfill Tax Regulations 1996, SI 1996/1527, reg 12(1).
3   As to the Commissioners for Her Majesty's Revenue and Customs see PARA 901 note 2.
4   Landfill Tax Regulations 1996, SI 1996/1527, reg 12(2). See Notice LFT1.

933.   Records required to be kept by registrable persons.   Every registrable
person[1] must, for the purpose of accounting for landfill tax[2], preserve the
following:
  (1)   his business and accounting records[3];
  (2)   his landfill tax account[4];
  (3)   transfer notes[5] and any other original or copy records in relation to
        material[6] brought onto or removed from the landfill site[7];
  (4)   all invoices (including landfill invoices[8]) and similar documents issued to
        him and copies of such invoices and similar documents issued by him[9];
  (5)   all credit or debit notes or other documents received by him which
        evidence an increase or decrease in the amount of any consideration for
        a relevant transaction, and copies of such documents that are issued by
        him[10];
  (6)   such other records as the Commissioners for Her Majesty's Revenue and
        Customs[11] may specify in a notice published by them and not
        withdrawn by a further notice[12].
In general, every registrable person must preserve the records specified in
heads (1) to (6) above for a period of six years[13]. However, a registrable person
who has made a landfill tax bad debt account[14] is to preserve that account for a
period of five years from the date of the claim made under the regulations[15]. The

Commissioners have power to direct that registrable persons must preserve the records specified in heads (1) to (6) above for a shorter period than that specified; and such direction may be made so as to apply generally or in such cases as the Commissioners may stipulate[16].

1   As to the meaning of 'registrable person' see PARA 958 note 1.
2   As to the meaning of 'landfill tax' see PARA 901.
3   Landfill Tax Regulations 1996, SI 1996/1527, reg 16(1)(a).
4   Landfill Tax Regulations 1996, SI 1996/1527, reg 16(1)(b). As to the meaning of 'landfill tax account' see PARA 932.
5   As to the meaning of 'transfer note' see the Environmental Protection (Duty of Care) Regulations 1991, SI 1991/2839, reg 2; definition applied by virtue of the Landfill Tax Regulations 1996, SI 1996/1527, reg 2(1) (as substituted by SI 2004/769). As to the Environmental Protection (Duty of Care) Regulations 1991, SI 1991/2839. see PROTECTION OF ENVIRONMENT AND PUBLIC HEALTH vol 38 (2006 Reissue) PARA 256.
6   As to the meaning of 'material' see PARA 902 note 3.
7   Landfill Tax Regulations 1996, SI 1996/1527, reg 16(1)(c) (amended by SI 2009/1930). This includes any record made on or before 31 August 2009 for the purpose of the Landfill Tax Regulations 1996, SI 1996/1527, Pt IX (regs 38–40) (revoked) before that Part was revoked with effect from 1 September 2009 and any record made for the purpose of reg 16A (information areas: see PARA 972): reg 16(1)(c) (as so amended). As to the meaning of 'landfill site' see PARA 902 note 5; definition applied by virtue of reg 2(1). The reference to material being brought onto a landfill site is a reference to material that is brought onto the site for the purpose of a relevant transaction: reg 16(5)(a). The reference to material being removed from a landfill site is a reference to material being removed that has at some previous time fallen wholly or partly within reg 16(5)(a): reg 16(5)(b). 'Relevant transaction' means a disposal or anything that would be a disposal but for the fact that the material is not disposed of as waste: reg 16(6). As to the meaning of 'disposal' see PARA 908 note 5. As to the meaning of 'disposal of material as waste material' see PARA 902 note 3.
8   An invoice is a landfill invoice if it contains the following information:
    (1)   an identifying number (Landfill Tax Regulations 1996, SI 1996/1527, reg 37(1)(a));
    (2)   the date of its issue (reg 37(1)(b));
    (3)   the date of the disposal or disposals in respect of which it is issued or, where a series of disposals is made for the same person, the dates between which the disposals were made (reg 37(1)(c));
    (4)   the name, address and registration number of the person issuing it (reg 37(1)(d));
    (5)   the name and address of the person to whom it is issued (reg 37(1)(e));
    (6)   the weight of the material disposed of (reg 37(1)(f));
    (7)   a description of the material disposed of (reg 37(1)(g));
    (8)   the rate of tax chargeable in relation to the disposal or, if the invoice relates to more than one disposal and the rate of tax for each of them is not the same, the rate of tax chargeable for each disposal (reg 37(1)(h));
    (9)   the total amount payable for which the invoice is issued (reg 37(1)(i)); and
    (10) where the amount of tax is shown separately, a statement confirming that that tax may not be treated as the input tax of any person (reg 37(1)(j)).
    As to the meaning of 'registration number' see PARA 928 note 9. As to the determination of the weight of the material disposed of see PARA 907.
    As to the meaning of 'input tax' see the Value Added Tax Act 1994 s 24(1); and VALUE ADDED TAX vol 49(1) (2005 Reissue) PARA 4 (definition applied by virtue of the Landfill Tax Regulations 1996, SI 1996/1527, reg 37(2)).
9   Landfill Tax Regulations 1996, SI 1996/1527, reg 16(1)(d).
10 Landfill Tax Regulations 1996, SI 1996/1527, reg 16(1)(e).
11 As to the Commissioners for Her Majesty's Revenue and Customs see PARA 901 note 2.
12 Landfill Tax Regulations 1996, SI 1996/1527, reg 16(1)(f).
13 Landfill Tax Regulations 1996, SI 1996/1527, reg 16(2).
14 As to the meaning of 'landfill tax bad debt account' see PARA 945.
15 Landfill Tax Regulations 1996, SI 1996/1527, reg 16(3).
16 Landfill Tax Regulations 1996, SI 1996/1527, reg 16(4). As to the penalty for failure to comply with this regulation see PARA 991.

934. Power to require records relating to material at landfill sites to be kept. Regulations may require a person to make records relating to material[1] at a landfill site[2] or a part of a landfill site[3]. Such regulations may make provisions about records relating to what is done with material[4].

1 As to the meaning of 'material' see PARA 902 note 3.
2 As to the meaning of 'landfill site' see PARA 902 note 5.
3 Finance Act 1996 s 60, Sch 5 para 2A(1) (Sch 5 para 2A added by the Finance Act 2009 s 119, Sch 60 para 9). The Finance Act 1996 Sch 5 para 2(2)–(7) (see PARA 931) applies in relation to regulations under Sch 5 para 2A as it applies in relation to regulations under Sch 5 para 2: Sch 5 para 2A(3) (as so added). In the application of Sch 5 para 2(3)(a) in relation to regulations under Sch 5 para 2A, the reference to registrable persons has effect as a reference to persons: Sch 5 para 2A(4) (as so added).
4 Finance Act 1996 Sch 5 para 2A(2) (as added: see note 3). As to the penalty for failure to comply with this requirement see PARA 991.

(3) RETURNS

935. Making of returns. Subject as mentioned below and save as the Commissioners for Her Majesty's Revenue and Customs[1] may otherwise allow, a registrable person[2] must, in respect of each accounting period[3], make a return to the Controller, Central Collection Unit (LT) in a form determined by the Commissioners in a public notice[4]. Subject as mentioned below, a registrable person must make each return not later than the last working day[5] of the month next following the end of the period to which it relates[6]. Where the Commissioners consider it necessary in the circumstances of any particular case, they may:

(1) vary the length of any accounting period or the date on which it begins or ends or by which any return must be made[7];

(2) allow or direct the registrable person to make a return in accordance with head (1) above[8];

(3) allow or direct a registrable person to make returns to a specified address[9].

Any person to whom the Commissioners give any such direction must comply with it[10].

1 As to the Commissioners for Her Majesty's Revenue and Customs see PARA 901 note 2.
2 As to the meaning of 'registrable person' see PARA 958 note 1; definition applied by virtue of the Landfill Tax Regulations 1996, SI 1996/1527, reg 2(1).
3 As to the meaning of 'accounting period' see PARA 928 note 17; definition applied by virtue of the Landfill Tax Regulations 1996, SI 1996/1527, reg 10.
4 See the Finance Act 1996 s 49; and the Landfill Tax Regulations 1996, SI 1996/1527, reg 11(1) (amended by SI 2009/1930). 'Return' means a return which is required to be made in accordance with the Landfill Tax Regulations 1996, SI 1996/1527, reg 11: reg 2(1). The form is LT100 and is contained in HMRC Notice LFT1, Section 20.
5 'Working day' means any day of the week except Saturday and Sunday and a bank holiday or public holiday, in either case, for England: Landfill Tax Regulations 1996, SI 1996/1527, reg 2(1).
6 Landfill Tax Regulations 1996, SI 1996/1527, reg 11(2).
7 Landfill Tax Regulations 1996, SI 1996/1527, reg 11(3)(a).
8 Landfill Tax Regulations 1996, SI 1996/1527, reg 11(3)(b).
9 Landfill Tax Regulations 1996, SI 1996/1527, reg 11(3)(c).
10 Landfill Tax Regulations 1996, SI 1996/1527, reg 11(3).

936. Correction of errors. The following provisions apply where a registrable person[1] has made a return[2] which was inaccurate as the result of an overdeclaration[3] or underdeclaration[4].

Where in any accounting period:

(1)   a registrable person discovers one or more overdeclarations or underdeclarations[5]; and

(2)   having treated the amount of those overdeclarations or underdeclarations as reduced by the amount respectively of any underdeclarations or overdeclarations for the same accounting periods, the total of those overdeclarations or underdeclarations does not exceed £50,000 or a specified alternative amount[6],

he may enter the overdeclarations or underdeclarations in his return for the accounting period in which they were discovered by including their amount in the boxes for overdeclarations and underdeclarations as appropriate[7]. Where a registrable person so enters an amount in a return he must calculate the landfill tax payable by him or the payment to which he is entitled accordingly[8].

Where an amount has been so entered in a return which has been made:

(a)   the return is to be regarded as correcting any earlier return to which that amount relates[9]; and

(b)   the registrable person is to be taken to have furnished information with respect to the inaccuracy in the prescribed[10] form and manner[11].

No amount must be entered in a return in respect of any overdeclaration or underdeclaration except in accordance with this provision[12].

1   As to the meaning of 'registrable person' see PARA 958 note 1; definition applied by virtue of the Landfill Tax Regulations 1996, SI 1996/1527, reg 2(1).
2   As to the meaning of 'return' see PARA 935 note 4.
3   'Overdeclaration' means, in relation to any return, the amount (if any) which was wrongly treated as landfill tax due for the accounting period concerned and which caused the amount of tax which was payable to be overstated, or the entitlement to a payment under the Landfill Tax Regulations 1996, SI 1996/1527, reg 20 (see PARA 940) to be understated (or both) or would have caused such an overstatement or understatement were it not for the existence of an underdeclaration in relation to that return: reg 13(1). As to the meaning of 'landfill tax' see PARA 901. As to the meaning of 'accounting period' see PARA 928 note 17; definition applied by virtue of reg 10.
        'Underdeclaration' means, in relation to any return, the aggregate of: (1) the amount (if any) of tax due for the accounting period concerned which was not taken into account; and (2) the amount (if any) which was wrongly deducted as credit, and which caused the amount of tax which was payable to be understated, or the entitlement to a payment under reg 20 to be overstated (or both), or would have caused such an understatement or overstatement were it not for the existence of an overdeclaration in relation to that return: reg 13(1).
        As to the meaning of 'credit' see PARA 928 note 14.
4   Landfill Tax Regulations 1996, SI 1996/1527, reg 13(2).
5   Landfill Tax Regulations 1996, SI 1996/1527, reg 13(4)(a) (reg 13(4) amended by SI 2008/1482; SI 2008/2693; SI 2009/1930).
6   Landfill Tax Regulations 1996, SI 1996/1527, reg 13(4)(b) (as amended: see note 5). If the registrable person's VAT turnover is small, the total mentioned in head (2) in the text must not exceed 1% of that turnover unless the total is £10,000 or less; if that person is not registered for VAT, the total must not exceed £10,000; and VAT turnover is 'small' only if Box 6 (total value of sales and all other outputs excluding any value added tax) of that person's value added tax return for the prescribed accounting period in which the discovery is made contains a total less than £5,000,000: reg 13(4) (as so amended). As to registration for VAT and value added tax returns for prescribed accounting periods see VALUE ADDED TAX vol 49(1) (2005 Reissue) PARAS 64 et seq, 247.
7   Landfill Tax Regulations 1996, SI 1996/1527, reg 13(4) (as amended: see note 5).
8   Landfill Tax Regulations 1996, SI 1996/1527, reg 13(5) (amended by SI 2008/1482).
9   Landfill Tax Regulations 1996, SI 1996/1527, reg 13(6)(a).
10   Ie for the purposes of the Finance Act 1996 s 60, Sch 5 para 20 (repealed).
11   Landfill Tax Regulations 1996, SI 1996/1527, reg 13(6)(b).
12   See the Landfill Tax Regulations 1996, SI 1996/1527, reg 13(7). As regards any underdeclaration that cannot be corrected under reg 13(4), a person is not to be taken to have

furnished information with respect to an inaccuracy in the prescribed form and manner for the purposes of the Finance Act 1996 Sch 5 para 20 (repealed) unless he provides such information to the Commissioners in writing: Landfill Tax Regulations 1996, SI 1996/1527, reg 13(7).

(4) PAYMENT OF TAX

937. Requirement to pay tax. Save as the Commissioners for Her Majesty's Revenue and Customs[1] may otherwise allow or direct, any person required to make a return[2] must pay to the Controller, Central Collection Unit (LT), such amount of landfill tax[3] as is payable by him in respect of the accounting period[4] to which the return relates no later than the last day on which he was required to make the return[5].

1   As to the Commissioners for Her Majesty's Revenue and Customs see PARA 901 note 2.
2   As to the meaning of 'return' see PARA 935 note 4.
3   As to the meaning of 'landfill tax' see PARA 901.
4   As to the meaning of 'accounting period' see PARA 928 note 17; definition applied by virtue of the Landfill Tax Regulations 1996, SI 1996/1527, reg 10.
5   Landfill Tax Regulations 1996, SI 1996/1527, reg 15.

6. CREDIT FOR TAX

(1) CLAIMING OF CREDIT

938. Relevant provisions. Part IV of the Landfill Tax Regulations 1996[1] applies to entitlements to credit arising under Part V[2], Part VI[3] or Part VII[4] of the Landfill Tax Regulations 1996[5]. No credit arising under any provision of the Landfill Tax Regulations 1996 may be claimed except in accordance with Part IV[6].

1   Ie the Landfill Tax Regulations 1996, SI 1996/1527, Pt IV (regs 17–20) (see PARAS 939–940): see reg 18(1). Any reference in the Landfill Tax Regulations 1996 to 'this Part' is a reference to the Part of the Regulations in which that reference is made: reg 2(3). The power to make regulations as to entitlements to credit is contained in the Finance Act 1996 s 51 (general: see PARA 938 et seq), s 52 (bad debts: see PARA 942 et seq), s 53 (bodies concerned with the environment: see PARA 949 et seq).

2   Ie the Landfill Tax Regulations 1996, SI 1996/1527, reg 21: see PARA 941.

3   Ie the Landfill Tax Regulations 1996, SI 1996/1527, regs 22–29: see PARA 942 et seq.

4   Ie the Landfill Tax Regulations 1996, SI 1996/1527, regs 30–36: see PARA 949 et seq.

5   Landfill Tax Regulations 1996, SI 1996/1527, reg 18(1).

6   Landfill Tax Regulations 1996, SI 1996/1527, reg 18(2).

939. Method of claiming credit. A person entitled to credit[1] may claim it by deducting its amount from any landfill tax[2] due from him for the relevant accounting period[3] or any subsequent accounting period and, where he does so, he must make his return[4] for that accounting period accordingly[5].

The Commissioners for Her Majesty's Revenue and Customs[6] may make directions generally or with regard to particular cases prescribing rules in accordance with which credit may or must be held over to be credited in an accounting period subsequent to the relevant accounting period[7]. Where such a direction has been made that credit, subject to any subsequent such direction varying or withdrawing the rules, may only be claimed in accordance with those rules[8].

1   As to the meaning of 'credit' see PARA 938.

2   As to the meaning of 'landfill tax' see PARA 901.

3   'Relevant accounting period' means: (1) in the case of an entitlement to credit arising under the Landfill Tax Regulations 1996, SI 1996/1527, Pt V (reg 21) (see PARA 941), the accounting period in which the re-use condition or, as the case may be, the enforced removal condition was satisfied; (2) in the case of an entitlement to credit arising under Pt VI (regs 22–29) (see PARA 942 et seq), the accounting period in which the period of one year from the date of the issue of the landfill invoice expired; (3) in the case of an entitlement arising under Pt VII (regs 30–36) (see PARA 949 et seq), the accounting period in which the qualifying contribution was made: reg 17. As to the meaning of 'accounting period' see PARA 928 note 17. As to the meaning of 'landfill invoice' see PARA 933 note 8.

4   As to the meaning of 'return' see PARA 935 note 4.

5   Landfill Tax Regulations 1996, SI 1996/1527, reg 19(1). Where the entitlement to credit arises under Pt VII (see PARA 949 et seq), reg 19(1) applies as if, instead of any subsequent accounting period, it referred to any subsequent accounting period in the same contribution year as determined in relation to that person under reg 31 (see PARA 950): reg 19(2).

6   As to the Commissioners for Her Majesty's Revenue and Customs see PARA 901 note 2.

7   Landfill Tax Regulations 1996, SI 1996/1527, reg 19(2).

8   Landfill Tax Regulations 1996, SI 1996/1527, reg 19(2).

940. Payments in respect of credit. Where the total credit[1] claimed by a registrable person[2] exceeds the total of the landfill tax[3] due from him for the accounting period[4], the Commissioners for Her Majesty's Revenue and Customs[5] must pay to him an amount equal to the excess[6].

Where the Commissioners have cancelled the registration of a person[7], and he is not a registrable person, he must make any claim in respect of credit by making an application in writing[8]. A person making such an application must furnish to the Commissioners full particulars in relation to the credit claimed, including (but not restricted to):

(1)   except in the case of an entitlement to credit for payments to bodies concerned with the environment arising under Part VII of the Landfill Tax Regulations 1996[9], the return in which the relevant tax[10] was accounted for[11];

(2)   except in the case of an entitlement to credit concerned with the environment arising under Part VII, the amount of the tax and the date and manner of its payment[12];

(3)   the events by virtue of which the entitlement to credit arose[13].

Where the Commissioners are satisfied that a person who has made such a claim is entitled to credit, and that he has not previously had the benefit of that credit, they must pay to him an amount equal to the credit[14].

The Commissioners are not liable to make any payment under the above provisions unless and until the person has made all the returns which he was required to make[15].

1   As to the meaning of 'credit' see PARA 938.
2   As to the meaning of 'registrable person' see PARA 958 note 1; definition applied by virtue of the Landfill Tax Regulations 1996, SI 1996/1527, reg 2(1).
3   As to the meaning of 'landfill tax' see PARA 901.
4   As to the meaning of 'accounting period' see PARA 928 note 17.
5   As to the Commissioners for Her Majesty's Revenue and Customs see PARA 901 note 2.
6   Landfill Tax Regulations 1996, SI 1996/1527, reg 20(1). This is subject to reg 20(5) (due making of returns: see the text to note 15): reg 20(1).
7   Ie in accordance with the Finance Act 1996 s 47(6): see PARA 920.
8   Landfill Tax Regulations 1996, SI 1996/1527, reg 20(2).
9   Ie the Landfill Tax Regulations 1996, SI 1996/1527, Pt VII (regs 30–36): see PARA 949 et seq.
10   'Relevant tax' means the tax, if any, that was required to have been paid as a condition of the entitlement to credit: Landfill Tax Regulations 1996, SI 1996/1527, reg 17.
11   Landfill Tax Regulations 1996, SI 1996/1527, reg 20(3)(a).
12   Landfill Tax Regulations 1996, SI 1996/1527, reg 20(3)(b).
13   Landfill Tax Regulations 1996, SI 1996/1527, reg 20(3)(c).
14   Landfill Tax Regulations 1996, SI 1996/1527, reg 20(4).
15   Landfill Tax Regulations 1996, SI 1996/1527, reg 20(5).

(2) CREDIT FOR RECYCLING, INCINERATION AND PERMANENT REMOVALS

941. Entitlement to credit. An entitlement to credit[1] arises[2] where:

(1)   a registered person[3] has accounted for an amount of landfill tax[4] and, except where the removal by virtue of which head (2) below is satisfied takes place in the accounting period[5] in which credit for recycling, incineration or permanent removal arising under Part V of the Landfill Tax Regulations 1996[6] is claimed in accordance with Part IV of the Landfill Tax Regulations 1996[7], he has paid that tax[8]; and

(2)   in relation to the disposal[9] on which that tax was charged, either the re-use condition has been satisfied[10] or the enforced removal condition has been satisfied[11].

The re-use condition is satisfied where:

(a)   the disposal has been made with the intention that the material[12] comprised in it

     (i)   would be recycled or incinerated[13]; or

     (ii)   removed for use (other than by way of a further disposal) at a place other than a relevant site[14]; or

     (iii)   removed for use in restoration of a relevant site and the material involved has previously been used to create or maintain temporary hard standing[15], to create or maintain a temporary screening bund[16] or to create or maintain a temporary haul road[17];

(b)   that material, or some of it, has been recycled, incinerated or permanently removed from the landfill site, as the case may be, in accordance with that intention[18];

(c)   that recycling, incineration or removal has taken place no later than one year after the date of the disposal[19], or where water had been added to the material in order to facilitate its disposal, has taken place no later than five years after the date of the disposal[20]; and

(d)   the registered person has, before the disposal, notified the Commissioners for Her Majesty's Revenue and Customs[21] in writing that he intends to make one or more removals of material in relation to which heads (a) to (c) above will be satisfied[22].

The enforced removal condition is satisfied where:

(A)   the disposal is in breach of the terms of the licence, resolution or permit, as the case may be, by virtue of which the land constitutes a landfill site[23];

(B)   the registered person has been directed to remove the material comprised in the disposal, or some of it, by a relevant authority[24] and he has removed it, or some of it[25]; and

(C)   a further taxable disposal[26] of the material has been made and, except where the registered person is the person liable for the tax chargeable on that further disposal, he has paid to the site operator[27] an amount representing that tax[28].

The amount of the credit for recycling, incineration or permanent removal arising under Part V of the Landfill Tax Regulations 1996 must be equal to the tax that was charged on the disposal; except that where only some of the material comprised in that disposal is removed, the amount of the credit must be such proportion of that tax as the material removed forms of the total of the material[29].

1   As to the meaning of 'credit' see PARA 938.

2   Ie under the Landfill Tax Regulations 1996, SI 1996/1527, Pt V (reg 21): see reg 21(1); and PARA 938 note 2.

3   As to the meaning of 'registered person' see PARA 922 note 13.

4   As to the meaning of 'landfill tax' see PARA 901.

5   As to the meaning of 'accounting period' see PARA 928 note 17.

6   Ie the Landfill Tax Regulations 1996, SI 1996/1527, Pt V (reg 21).

7   Ie the Landfill Tax Regulations 1996, SI 1996/1527, Pt IV (regs 17–20) (see PARAS 938–940): see reg 21(1).

8   Landfill Tax Regulations 1996, SI 1996/1527, reg 21(1)(a).

9   As to the meaning of 'disposal' see PARA 908 note 5.

10   Landfill Tax Regulations 1996, SI 1996/1527, reg 21(1)(b)(i).

11   Landfill Tax Regulations 1996, SI 1996/1527, reg 21(1)(b)(ii).

12   As to the meaning of 'material' see PARA 902 note 3.

13   Landfill Tax Regulations 1996, SI 1996/1527, reg 21(2)(a)(i).

14 Landfill Tax Regulations 1996, SI 1996/1527, reg 21(2)(a)(ii). A 'relevant site' is the landfill site at which the disposal was made or any other landfill site: reg 21(3). As to the meaning of 'landfill site' see PARA 902 note 5; definition applied by virtue of reg 2(1).

15 'Hard standing' means a base within a landfill site on which any landfill site activity such as sorting, treatment, processing, storage or recycling is carried out: Landfill Tax Regulations 1996, SI 1996/1527, reg 21(7) (added by SI 2009/1930). As to the meaning of 'landfill site activity' see PARA 903 note 1.

16 'Screening bund' means any structure on a landfill site (whether below or above ground) put in place to protect or conceal any landfill site activity or to reduce nuisance from noise: Landfill Tax Regulations 1996, SI 1996/1527, reg 21(7) (as added: see note 15).

17 Landfill Tax Regulations 1996, SI 1996/1527, reg 21(2)(a)(iii) (added by SI 2009/1930). 'Haul road' means any road within the landfill site which give access to a disposal area. A 'disposal area' means any area of a landfill site where any disposal takes place: Landfill Tax Regulations 1996, SI 1996/1527, reg 21(7) (as added: see note 15).

18 Landfill Tax Regulations 1996, SI 1996/1527, reg 21(2)(b).

19 Landfill Tax Regulations 1996, SI 1996/1527, reg 21(2)(c)(i).

20 Landfill Tax Regulations 1996, SI 1996/1527, reg 21(2)(c)(ii).

21 As to the Commissioners for Her Majesty's Revenue and Customs see PARA 901 note 2.

22 Landfill Tax Regulations 1996, SI 1996/1527, reg 21(2)(d).

23 Landfill Tax Regulations 1996, SI 1996/1527, reg 21(4)(a) (amended by SI 2005/759).

24 The following are relevant authorities:
    (1)   the Environment Agency (Landfill Tax Regulations 1996, SI 1996/1527, reg 21(5)(a));
    (2)   the Scottish Environment Protection Agency (reg 21(5)(b));
    (3)   the Department of the Environment for Northern Ireland (reg 21(5)(c));
    (4)   a district council in Northern Ireland (reg 21(5)(d)).
As to the meaning of 'Environment Agency' see PARA 912 note 10. As to the Environment Agency see PROTECTION OF ENVIRONMENT AND PUBLIC HEALTH vol 38 (2006 Reissue) PARA 52 et seq. As to the meaning of 'Scottish Environment Protection Agency' see PARA 912 note 11.

25 Landfill Tax Regulations 1996, SI 1996/1527, reg 21(4)(b).

26 As to the meaning of 'taxable disposal' see PARA 902.

27 As to the meaning of 'landfill site operator' see PARA 929 note 4.

28 Landfill Tax Regulations 1996, SI 1996/1527, reg 21(4)(c).

29 Landfill Tax Regulations 1996, SI 1996/1527, reg 21(6).

(3) CREDIT FOR BAD DEBTS

942. Entitlement to credit. An entitlement to credit[1] arises[2] where:

(1)   a registered person[3] has carried out a taxable activity[4] for a consideration in money for a customer[5] with whom he is not connected[6];

(2)   he has accounted for and paid landfill tax[7] on the disposal[8] concerned[9];

(3)   the whole or any part of the consideration for the disposal has been written off in his accounts as a bad debt[10];

(4)   he has issued a landfill invoice[11] in respect of the disposal which shows the amount of tax chargeable[12];

(5)   that invoice was issued:
    (a)   within 14 days of the date of the disposal[13]; or
    (b)   within such other period as may have been specified in a direction of the Commissioners for Her Majesty's Revenue and Customs[14];

(6)   a period of one year (beginning with the date of the issue of that invoice) has elapsed[15]; and

(7)   the provisions of Part VI of the Landfill Tax Regulations 1996[16] have been complied with[17].

1 As to the meaning of 'credit' see PARA 938.

2 Ie under the Landfill Tax Regulations 1996, SI 1996/1527, Pt VI (regs 22–29): see reg 23; and PARA 938 note 1.

3 As to the meaning of 'registered person' see PARA 922 note 13.

4 As to the meaning of 'taxable activity' see PARA 920 note 1.

5 'Customer' means a person for whom a taxable activity is carried out by the claimant: Landfill Tax Regulations 1996, SI 1996/1527, reg 22. 'Claim' means a claim in accordance with Pt IV (regs 17–20) for an amount of credit arising under Pt VI (see PARA 942 et seq); and 'claimant' must be construed accordingly: reg 22.

6 Landfill Tax Regulations 1996, SI 1996/1527, reg 23(a). Any question whether a person is connected with another is determined in accordance with the Income and Corporation Taxes Act 1988 s 839 (see INCOME TAXATION vol 23(2) (Reissue) PARA 1258): Landfill Tax Regulations 1996, SI 1996/1527, reg 2(2).

7 As to the meaning of 'landfill tax' see PARA 901.

8 As to the meaning of 'disposal' see PARA 908 note 5.

9 Landfill Tax Regulations 1996, SI 1996/1527, reg 23(b).

10 Landfill Tax Regulations 1996, SI 1996/1527, reg 23(c). See PARA 948.

11 As to the meaning of 'landfill invoice' see PARA 933 note 8.

12 Landfill Tax Regulations 1996, SI 1996/1527, reg 23(d).

13 Landfill Tax Regulations 1996, SI 1996/1527, reg 23(e)(i).

14 Ie made under the Finance Act 1996 s 61(3) (see PARA 904): see the Landfill Tax Regulations 1996, SI 1996/1527, reg 23(e)(ii). As to the Commissioners for Her Majesty's Revenue and Customs see PARA 901 note 2.

15 Landfill Tax Regulations 1996, SI 1996/1527, reg 23(f).

16 Ie the Landfill Tax Regulations 1996, SI 1996/1527, Pt VI (see PARA 942 et seq): see reg 23(g); and PARA 938 note 1.

17 Landfill Tax Regulations 1996, SI 1996/1527, reg 23(g).

943.   Amount of credit. The credit[1] arising in cases of bad debt[2] is to be of an amount equal to such proportion of the landfill tax[3] charged on the relevant disposal[4] as the outstanding amount forms of the total consideration[5].

'Outstanding amount' means, in relation to any claim: (1) if at the time of the claim the claimant has received no payment in respect of the amount written off in his accounts, the amount so written off; or (2) if at that time he has received a payment, the amount by which the amount written off exceeds the payment (or the aggregate of the payments)[6].

1 As to the meaning of 'credit' see PARA 928 note 14.

2 Ie arising under the Landfill Tax Regulations 1996, SI 1996/1527, Pt VI (regs 22–29) (see PARAS 942–948): see reg 24; and PARA 938 note 1.

3 As to the meaning of 'landfill tax' see PARA 901.

4 'Relevant disposal' means any taxable disposal upon which a claim is based: Landfill Tax Regulations 1996, SI 1996/1527, reg 22. As to the meaning of 'taxable disposal' see PARA 902. As to the meaning of 'claim' see PARA 942 note 5.

5 Landfill Tax Regulations 1996, SI 1996/1527, reg 24.

6 Landfill Tax Regulations 1996, SI 1996/1527, reg 22. As to the meaning of 'claimant' see PARA 942 note 5.

944.   Evidence required in support of claim. The claimant[1], before he makes a claim[2], must hold in respect of each relevant disposal[3]:

  (1)   a copy of the landfill invoice[4] issued by him[5];

  (2)   records or any other documents showing that he has accounted for and paid landfill tax[6] on the disposal[7]; and

  (3)   records or any other documents showing that the consideration has been written off in his accounts as a bad debt[8].

1 As to the meaning of 'claimant' see PARA 942 note 5.

2 As to the meaning of 'claim' see PARA 942 note 5.

3 As to the meaning of 'relevant disposal' see PARA 943 note 4.

4 As to the meaning of 'landfill invoice' see PARA 933 note 8.

5 Landfill Tax Regulations 1996, SI 1996/1527, reg 25(a).

6 As to the meaning of 'landfill tax' see PARA 901.

7 Landfill Tax Regulations 1996, SI 1996/1527, reg 25(b). As to the meaning of 'disposal' see PARA 908 note 5.
8 Landfill Tax Regulations 1996, SI 1996/1527, reg 25(c).

945. Records required to be kept: the landfill tax bad debt account. Any person who makes a claim[1] must make a record of that claim[2]. Such a record must contain the following information in respect of each claim made:

(1) in respect of each relevant disposal[3]:
    (a) the amount of landfill tax[4] charged[5];
    (b) the return[6] in which that tax was accounted for and when it was paid[7];
    (c) the date and identifying number of the landfill invoice[8] that was issued[9];
    (d) any consideration that has been received (whether before the claim was made or subsequently)[10];
    (e) the details of any transfer note[11];
(2) the outstanding amount[12];
(3) the amount of the claim[13];
(4) the return in which the claim was made[14].

Any records made in pursuance of this provision must be kept in a single account known as the 'landfill tax bad debt account'[15].

1 As to the meaning of 'claim' see PARA 942 note 5.
2 Landfill Tax Regulations 1996, SI 1996/1527, reg 26(1).
3 As to the meaning of 'relevant disposal' see PARA 943 note 4.
4 As to the meaning of 'landfill tax' see PARA 901.
5 Landfill Tax Regulations 1996, SI 1996/1527, reg 26(2)(a)(i).
6 As to the meaning of 'return' see PARA 935 note 4.
7 Landfill Tax Regulations 1996, SI 1996/1527, reg 26(2)(a)(ii).
8 As to the meaning of 'landfill invoice' see PARA 933 note 8.
9 Landfill Tax Regulations 1996, SI 1996/1527, reg 26(2)(a)(iii).
10 Landfill Tax Regulations 1996, SI 1996/1527, reg 26(2)(a)(iv).
11 Landfill Tax Regulations 1996, SI 1996/1527, reg 26(2)(a)(v). As to the meaning of 'transfer note' see the Environmental Protection (Duty of Care) Regulations 1991, SI 1991/2839, reg 2 (see PROTECTION OF ENVIRONMENT AND PUBLIC HEALTH vol 38 (2006 Reissue) PARA 256); definition applied by virtue of the Landfill Tax Regulations 1996, SI 1996/1527, reg 2(1).
12 Landfill Tax Regulations 1996, SI 1996/1527, reg 26(2)(b).
13 Landfill Tax Regulations 1996, SI 1996/1527, reg 26(2)(c).
14 Landfill Tax Regulations 1996, SI 1996/1527, reg 26(2)(d).
15 Landfill Tax Regulations 1996, SI 1996/1527, reg 26(3).

946. Attribution of payments. Where:
(1) the claimant[1] has carried out a taxable activity[2] for a customer[3];
(2) there exist one or more other matters in respect of which the claimant is entitled to a debt owed by the customer (whether they involve a taxable disposal[4] or not and whether they are connected with waste or not); and
(3) a payment has been received by the claimant from the customer,
the payment must be attributed to the taxable activity and the other matters in accordance with the rule set out below[5]. The debts arising in respect of the taxable activity and the other matters are collectively referred to as debts[6].

The payment must be attributed to the debt which arose earliest and, if not wholly attributed to that debt, thereafter to debts in the order of the dates on which they arose, except that attribution under this provision may not be made if the payment was allocated to a debt by the customer at the time of payment and the debt was paid in full[7]. Where:

(a)   the earliest debt and the other debts to which the whole of the payment could be attributed arose on the same day; or

(b)   the debts to which the balance of the payment could be attributed in accordance with the above provision arose on the same day,

the payment must be attributed to those debts by multiplying, for each such debt, the payment made by a fraction of which the numerator is the amount remaining unpaid in respect of that debt and the denominator is the amount remaining unpaid in respect of all those debts[8].

1   As to the meaning of 'claimant' see PARA 942 note 5.
2   As to the meaning of 'taxable activity' see PARA 920 note 1.
3   As to the meaning of 'customer' see PARA 942 note 5.
4   As to the meaning of 'taxable disposal' see PARA 902.
5   Landfill Tax Regulations 1996, SI 1996/1527, reg 27(1).
6   Landfill Tax Regulations 1996, SI 1996/1527, reg 27(1).
7   Landfill Tax Regulations 1996, SI 1996/1527, reg 27(2).
8   Landfill Tax Regulations 1996, SI 1996/1527, reg 27(3).

947.   Repayment of credit. Where a claimant[1]:

(1)   has benefited from an amount of credit[2] to which he was entitled in respect of bad debt[3]; and

(2)   either (a) a payment for the relevant disposal[4] is subsequently received; or (b) a payment is treated[5] as attributed to the relevant disposal,

he must repay to the Commissioners for Her Majesty's Revenue and Customs[6] such amount as equals the amount of the credit, or the balance thereof, multiplied by a fraction of which the numerator is the amount so received or attributed, and the denominator is the amount of the outstanding consideration[7].

Where the claimant fails to comply with specified record-keeping and production of documents requirements[8], he must repay to the Commissioners the amount of the claim[9] to which the failure to comply relates[10].

1   As to the meaning of 'claimant' see PARA 942 note 5.
2   As to the meaning of 'credit' see PARA 938.
3   Ie the under Landfill Tax Regulations 1996, SI 1996/1527, Pt VI (regs 22–29): see reg 28(1)(a); and PARA 938 note 1.
4   As to the meaning of 'relevant disposal' see PARA 943 note 4.
5   Ie by virtue of the Landfill Tax Regulations 1996, SI 1996/1527, reg 27: see PARA 946.
6   As to the Commissioners for Her Majesty's Revenue and Customs see PARA 901 note 2.
7   Landfill Tax Regulations 1996, SI 1996/1527, reg 28(1).
8   The specified requirements are those of the Landfill Tax Regulations 1996, SI 1996/1527, reg 26 (see PARA 945) or, in relation to the documents mentioned in reg 26, either reg 16 (duty to keep records: see PARA 933) or any obligation arising under the Finance Act 1996 s 60, Sch 5 para 3 (see PARA 978): Landfill Tax Regulations 1996, SI 1996/1527, reg 28(2).
9   As to the meaning of 'claim' see PARA 942 note 5.
10   Landfill Tax Regulations 1996, SI 1996/1527, regs 2(1), 28(2).

948.   Writing off debts. This provision applies for the purpose of determining whether, and to what extent, the consideration is to be taken to have been written off as a bad debt[1]. The whole or any part of the consideration for a taxable activity[2] is to be taken to have been written off as a bad debt where:

(1)   the claimant[3] has written it off in his accounts as a bad debt[4]; and

(2)   he has made an entry in relation to that activity in the landfill tax bad debt account[5] (and this applies regardless of whether a claim[6] can be made in relation to that activity at that time)[7].

Where the claimant owes an amount of money to the customer[8] which can be set off, the consideration written off in the landfill tax bad debt account must be reduced by the amount so owed[9]. Where the claimant holds in relation to the customer an enforceable security[10], the consideration written off in the landfill tax bad debt account must be reduced by the value of the security[11].

1   Landfill Tax Regulations 1996, SI 1996/1527, reg 29(1).
2   As to the meaning of 'taxable activity' see PARA 920 note 1.
3   As to the meaning of 'claimant' see PARA 942 note 5.
4   Landfill Tax Regulations 1996, SI 1996/1527, reg 29(2)(a). See PARA 945.
5   Ie in accordance with the Landfill Tax Regulations 1996, SI 1996/1527, reg 26 (see PARA 945): see reg 29(2)(b). As to the meaning of 'landfill tax bad debt account' see PARA 945.
6   As to the meaning of 'claim' see PARA 942 note 5.
7   Landfill Tax Regulations 1996, SI 1996/1527, reg 29(2)(b).
8   As to the meaning of 'customer' see PARA 942 note 5.
9   Landfill Tax Regulations 1996, SI 1996/1527, reg 29(3).
10 'Security' means in relation to England, Wales and Northern Ireland, any mortgage, charge, lien or other security: Landfill Tax Regulations 1996, SI 1996/1527, reg 22.
11 Landfill Tax Regulations 1996, SI 1996/1527, reg 29(4).

(4) CREDIT FOR PAYMENTS TO BODIES CONCERNED WITH THE ENVIRONMENT: THE LANDFILL TAX COMMUNITIES FUND

949. Qualifying contributions. An entitlement to credit[1] arises[2] in respect of qualifying contributions made by registered persons[3]. A payment is a 'qualifying contribution' if:

(1)   it is made by a registered person to an approved body[4];

(2)   it is made subject to a condition that the body must spend the sum paid or any income[5] derived from it or both only in the course or furtherance of its approved objects[6];

(3)   the statutory requirements[7] have been complied with in relation to that payment[8]; and

(4)   it is not repaid to him, or a contributing third party, in the same accounting period as that in which it was made[9].

'Contributing third party' means a person who has made or agreed to make (whether or not under a legally binding agreement) a payment to a registered person to secure the making by him of a qualifying contribution or to reimburse him, in whole or in part, for any such contribution he has made[10].

A body is only taken to spend a qualifying contribution in the course or furtherance of its approved objects:

(a)   in a case where the contribution is made subject to a condition that it may only be invested for the purpose of generating income, where the body so spends all of that income[11];

(b)   in a case not falling within head (a) above, where the body becomes entitled to income, where it so spends both the whole of the qualifying contribution and all of that income[12];

(c)   in a case not falling within either of heads (a) and (b) above, where the body so spends the whole of the qualifying contribution[13]; or

(d)   where: (i) it transfers any qualifying contribution or income derived from it to another approved body; and (ii) that transfer is subject to a condition that the sum transferred is to be spent only in the course or furtherance of that other body's approved objects[14].

Where any qualifying contribution or income derived from it is transferred to a body as described in head (d):

(A)   the body to whom the sum is transferred is treated as having received qualifying contributions of the amount concerned[15]; and

(B)   that body is treated as having received those qualifying contributions from the registered person or persons who originally paid them (but this does not give rise to any further entitlement to credit in respect of those contributions)[16].

1   As to the meaning of 'credit' see PARA 938.
2   Ie under the Landfill Tax Regulations 1996, SI 1996/1527, Pt VII (regs 30–36).
3   Landfill Tax Regulations 1996, SI 1996/1527, reg 31(1). As to the meaning of 'registered person' see PARA 922 note 13.
4   Landfill Tax Regulations 1996, SI 1996/1527, reg 32(1)(a). As to approved bodies see PARA 952.
5   'Income' includes interest: reg 30(1).
6   Landfill Tax Regulations 1996, SI 1996/1527, reg 32(1)(b). As to the meaning of 'approved object' see PARA 952.
7   Ie the requirements of the Landfill Tax Regulations 1996, SI 1996/1527, reg 32(2)–(2B): see PARA 955.
8   Landfill Tax Regulations 1996, SI 1996/1527, reg 32(1)(c) (amended by SI 1999/3270).
9   Landfill Tax Regulations 1996, SI 1996/1527, reg 32(1)(d) (amended by SI 1999/3270).
10 Landfill Tax Regulations 1996, SI 1996/1527, reg 30(1) (definition amended by SI 1999/3270).
11 Landfill Tax Regulations 1996, SI 1996/1527, reg 30(2)(a).
12 Landfill Tax Regulations 1996, SI 1996/1527, reg 30(2)(b).
13 Landfill Tax Regulations 1996, SI 1996/1527, reg 30(2)(c).
14 Landfill Tax Regulations 1996, SI 1996/1527, reg 30(2)(d).
15 Landfill Tax Regulations 1996, SI 1996/1527, reg 32(3)(a) (reg 32(3) substituted by SI 1999/3270).
16 Landfill Tax Regulations 1996, SI 1996/1527, reg 32(3)(b) (as substituted: see note 15).

950. Calculation of amount of credit. In general, a person is entitled to credit in respect of 90 per cent of the amount of each qualifying contribution[1] made by him in any accounting period[2]. For this purpose, a qualifying contribution made:

(1)   in one accounting period[3];

(2)   before the return[4] for the previous accounting period has been made[5]; and

(3)   before the period within which that return is required to be made has expired[6],

must be treated as having been made in the accounting period mentioned in head (2) above (and not in the accounting period in which it was in fact made)[7].

In respect of the qualifying contributions made in each contribution year[8], a person is not entitled to credit of an amount greater than 6.0 per cent of his relevant tax liability[9]. The relevant tax liability of a person is the aggregate of:

(a)   the landfill tax payable by him, if any, in respect of the accounting period in relation to which that liability falls to be determined; and

(b)   the tax payable by him, if any, in respect of any earlier accounting period or periods which fall within the same contribution year as that accounting period,

and where in respect of any accounting period he is entitled to a payment in respect of credit[10] the aggregate of the tax payable by him in respect of the accounting periods mentioned in heads (a) to (b) above is reduced by the amount of that payment[11].

Where one contribution year ends and another begins in an accounting period, the amount of any qualifying contribution which[12] is treated as made in that period must be apportioned between those contribution years[13]. The apportionment must be on the basis of either: (i) the number of days of the accounting period that fall before 1 April and the number of days that fall on and after that day[14]; or (ii) the amount of tax charged on taxable disposals made in the accounting period before 1 April and the amount of tax charged on taxable disposals[15] made in that period on and after that day[16], whichever the registered person may choose[17].

1 As to the meaning of 'qualifying contribution' see PARA 949.
2 Landfill Tax Regulations 1996, SI 1996/1527, reg 31(2). As to the meaning of 'accounting period' see PARA 928 note 17.
3 Landfill Tax Regulations 1996, SI 1996/1527, reg 31(2)(a) (substituted by SI 1999/3270).
4 As to the meaning of 'return' see PARA 935 note 4.
5 Landfill Tax Regulations 1996, SI 1996/1527, reg 31(2)(b).
6 Landfill Tax Regulations 1996, SI 1996/1527, reg 31(2)(c).
7 Landfill Tax Regulations 1996, SI 1996/1527, reg 31(2).
8 For the purposes of the Landfill Tax Regulations 1996, SI 1996/1527, reg 31(2), (3), the contribution year of a person is his first contribution year and then each period of 12 months beginning on 1 April: reg 31(4) (reg 31(4), (5) substituted by SI 2003/605). The reference to the first contribution year of a person is a reference to the period beginning with the effective date of registration and ending on the day immediately preceding the first day of the next contribution year: Landfill Tax Regulations 1996, SI 1996/1527, reg 31(5) (as so substituted).
9 Landfill Tax Regulations 1996, SI 1996/1527, reg 31(3) (amended by SI 2005/759; SI 2006/865; SI 2007/965; SI 2008/770).
10 Ie a payment under the Landfill Tax Regulations 1996, SI 1996/1527, reg 20 (see PARA 940).
11 Landfill Tax Regulations 1996, SI 1996/1527, reg 31(7) (amended by SI 1999/3270). For the purposes of the Landfill Tax Regulations 1996, SI 1996/1527, reg 31(7), any entitlement to credit is to be disregarded in determining the tax payable by a person in respect of any period: reg 31(10) (amended by SI 1999/3270).
12 Ie by virtue of the Landfill Tax Regulations 1996, SI 1996/1527, reg 31(2).
13 Landfill Tax Regulations 1996, SI 1996/1527, reg 31(6) (substituted by SI 2003/605).
14 Landfill Tax Regulations 1996, SI 1996/1527, reg 31(6A)(a) (reg 31(6A) added by SI 2003/605).
15 Landfill Tax Regulations 1996, SI 1996/1527, reg 31(6A)(b) (as added: see note 14).
16 As to the meaning of 'taxable disposal' see PARA 902.
17 Landfill Tax Regulations 1996, SI 1996/1527, reg 31(6A) (as added: see note 14).

951. Approved bodies. A body is eligible to be approved if:
 (1) it is a body corporate, or a trust, partnership or other unincorporated body[1];
 (2) its objects are or include any of the approved objects[2];
 (3) it is precluded from distributing and does not distribute any profit it makes or other income it receives[3];
 (4) it applies any profit or other income to the furtherance of its objects (whether or not approved objects)[4];
 (5) it is precluded from applying any of its funds for the benefit of any of the persons: (a) who have made qualifying contributions[5] to it; or (b) who were a contributing third party[6] in relation to such contributions, except that such persons may benefit where they belong to a class of persons that benefits generally[7];
 (6) it is not controlled[8] by one or more of certain persons and bodies[9];
 (7) none of certain persons or bodies[10] is concerned in its management[11]; and
 (8) it pays to the regulatory body[12] an application fee[13].

Any approval, or revocation of such approval, by the Commissioners for Her Majesty's Revenue and Customs or the regulatory body must be given by notice in writing to the body affected and takes effect from the date the notice is given or such later date as the Commissioners or, as the case may be, the regulatory body may specify in it[14].

1 Landfill Tax Regulations 1996, SI 1996/1527, reg 33(1)(a) (amended by SI 1999/3270).

2   Landfill Tax Regulations 1996, SI 1996/1527, reg 33(1)(b). As to the approved objects see PARA
     952.
3   Landfill Tax Regulations 1996, SI 1996/1527, reg 33(1)(c). 'Income' includes interest: reg 30(1).
4   Landfill Tax Regulations 1996, SI 1996/1527, reg 33(1)(d).
5   As to qualifying contributions see PARA 949.
6   As to the meaning of 'contributing third party' see PARA 949.
7   Landfill Tax Regulations 1996, SI 1996/1527, reg 33(1)(e) (substituted by SI 1999/3270).
8   For these purposes, a body or person (in either case, 'the person') is taken to control a body
     where:
     (1)   in the case of a body which is a body corporate, the person is empowered by statute to
            control that body's activities or if he is that body's holding company within the meaning
            of the Companies Act 2006 s 1159, Sch 6 (see COMPANIES vol 14 (2009) PARA 25); and
            an individual is taken to control a body corporate if he, were he a company, would be
            that body's holding company within the meaning of that Act (Landfill Tax
            Regulations 1996, SI 1996/1527, reg 33(9)(a) (amended by SI 1999/3270; and
            SI 2009/1890));
     (2)   in the case of a body which is a trust or a partnership, where: (a) the person, taken
            together with any nominee of his; or (b) any nominee of the person, taken together with
            any nominee of that nominee or any other nominee of the person, forms a majority of
            the total number of trustees or partners, as the case may be (Landfill Tax
            Regulations 1996, SI 1996/1527, reg 33(9)(b));
     (3)   in the case of any other body, where the person, whether directly or through any
            nominee, has the power to appoint or remove any officer of the body, to determine the
            objects of the body, or to determine how any of the body's funds may be applied
            (reg 33(9)(c)).
9   Landfill Tax Regulations 1996, SI 1996/1527, reg 33(1)(f) (substituted by SI 1999/3270). These
     persons and bodies are specified in the Landfill Tax Regulations 1996, SI 1996/1527,
     reg 33(1A), (1B) (added by SI 1999/3270).
         The persons and bodies specified in the Landfill Tax Regulations 1996, SI 1996/1527,
     reg 33(1A) are: (1) a local authority; (2) a body corporate controlled by one or more local
     authorities; (3) a registered person; (4) a person connected with any of the persons or bodies
     mentioned in heads (1)–(3).
         The persons and bodies specified in reg 33(1B) are: (a) a person who controlled or was
     concerned in the management of a body the approval of which was revoked otherwise than
     under reg 34(1)(ee) (see PARA 954); (b) a person who has been convicted of an indictable
     offence; (c) a person who is disqualified for being a charity trustee or a trustee for a charity by
     virtue of the Charities Act 1993 s 72 (see CHARITIES vol 8 (2010) PARA 273); (d) a person
     connected with any of the persons or bodies mentioned in heads (a)–(c); (e) a person who is
     incapable by reason of mental disorder. For the purposes of head (e), a person is treated as
     incapable by reason of mental disorder where, in England and Wales, the person lacks capacity
     within the meaning of the Mental Capacity Act 2005 to administer and manage his property
     and affairs (see MENTAL HEALTH vol 30(2) (Reissue) PARA 641 et seq), (or in Northern Ireland,
     the court has exercised any of its powers under the Mental Health (Northern Ireland)
     Order 1986, SI 1986/595 (NI 4), Pt VIII (arts 97–109)), but ceases to be so treated where the
     judge has made a finding that he is not or is no longer incapable of managing and administering
     his property and affairs: Landfill Tax Regulations 1996, SI 1996/1527, reg 33(1C) (added by
     SI 1999/3270; and amended by SI 2007/1898).
10   Ie the persons and bodies listed in note 9 heads (a)–(e).
11   Landfill Tax Regulations 1996, SI 1996/1527, reg 33(1)(g) (added by SI 1999/3270).
12   'Regulatory body' means such body, if any, as in relation to which an approval of the
     Commissioners for Her Majesty's Revenue and Customs under the Landfill Tax
     Regulations 1996, SI 1996/1527, reg 35 (see PARA 954) has effect for the time being: reg 30(1).
     As to the Commissioners for Her Majesty's Revenue and Customs see PARA 901 note 2.
13   Landfill Tax Regulations 1996, SI 1996/1527, reg 33(1)(h) (added by SI 1999/3270). The
     application fee is to be £100 or such lesser sum as the regulatory body may require: Landfill Tax
     Regulations 1996, SI 1996/1527, reg 33(1)(h) (as so added).
14   Landfill Tax Regulations 1996, SI 1996/1527, reg 30(3).

952. Approved objects. The objects of a body are approved objects in so far
as they are any of the following objects[1]:
     (1)   in relation to any land the use of which for any economic, social or
            environmental purpose has been prevented or restricted because of the

carrying on of an activity on the land which has ceased: (a) reclamation, remediation or restoration; or (b) any other operation intended to facilitate economic, social or environmental use[2];

(2)   in relation to any land the condition of which, by reason of the carrying on of an activity on the land which has ceased, is such that pollution (whether of that land or not) is being or may be caused: (a) any operation intended to prevent or reduce any potential for pollution; or (b) any operation intended to remedy or mitigate the effects of any pollution that has been caused[3];

(3)   where it is for the protection of the environment, the provision, maintenance or improvement of: (a) a public park; or (b) another public amenity, in the vicinity of a landfill site, provided certain conditions are satisfied[4];

(4)   where it is for the protection of the environment and[5] the conservation or promotion of biological diversity[6] through: (a) the provision, conservation, restoration or enhancement of a natural habitat; or (b) the maintenance or recovery of a species in its natural habitat, on land or in water situated in the vicinity of a landfill site[7];

(5)   where it is for the protection of the environment, the maintenance, repair or restoration of a building or other structure which: (a) is a place of religious worship or of historic or architectural interest; (b) is open to the public; and (c) is situated in the vicinity of a landfill site, provided certain conditions are satisfied[8];

(6)   the provision of financial, administration and other similar services to bodies which are within these provisions and only such bodies[9].

Where the objects of a body are or include any of the objects set out above, the following must also be regarded as approved objects:

(i)   the use of qualifying contributions[10] in paying the running costs of the body[11];

(ii)   the use of qualifying contributions in paying a contribution to the running costs of the regulatory body[12].

1   See the Landfill Tax Regulations 1996, SI 1996/1527, regs 30(1), 33; and the text to notes 2–12.

2   Landfill Tax Regulations 1996, SI 1996/1527, reg 33(2)(a). An object is not, or is no longer, regarded as falling within reg 33(2)(a) or reg 33(2)(b) if the reclamation, remediation, restoration or other operation: (1) is such that any benefit from it will accrue to any person who has carried out or knowingly permitted the activity which has ceased; (2) involves works which are required to be carried out by certain statutory notices or orders; or (3) is wholly or partly required to be carried out by a relevant condition: reg 33(3).

The notices and orders referred to are: (a) a works notice served under the Control of Pollution Act 1974 s 46A (repealed); (b) an enforcement notice served under the Environmental Protection Act 1990 s 13 (see PROTECTION OF ENVIRONMENT AND PUBLIC HEALTH vol 38 (2006 Reissue) PARA 158); (c) a prohibition notice served under s 14 (see PROTECTION OF ENVIRONMENT AND PUBLIC HEALTH vol 38 (2006 Reissue) PARA 159); (d) an order under s 26 (see PROTECTION OF ENVIRONMENT AND PUBLIC HEALTH vol 38 (2006 Reissue) PARA 168); (e) a remediation notice served under s 78E (as added and amended) (see PROTECTION OF ENVIRONMENT AND PUBLIC HEALTH vol 38 (2006 Reissue) PARA 362); (f) an enforcement notice served under the Water Resources Act 1991 s 90B (see WATER vol 49(3) (2004 Reissue) PARA 708); (g) a works notice served under the Water Resources Act 1991 s 161A (see WATER vol 49(3) (2004 Reissue) PARA 722 et seq); (h) an enforcement notice served under the Environmental Permitting (England and Wales) Regulations 2007, SI 2007/3538, reg 36; (i) a suspension notice served under reg 37; (j) an order under reg 44; (k) an enforcement notice under the Pollution Prevention and Control Regulations (Northern Ireland) 2003, SR 2003/46, reg 24; (l) a suspension notice served under reg 25; (m) an order under reg 36: see the Landfill Tax Regulations 1996, SI 1996/1527, reg 33(4) (heads (h)–(j) added by SI 2000/1973; substituted by SI 2007/3538; heads (k)–(m) added by the Pollution Prevention and Control

Regulations (Northern Ireland) 2003, SR 2003/46, reg 41, Sch 11 para 6). As to the prospective repeal and replacement of the Environmental Protection Act 1990 Pt I (ss 1–28) see PROTECTION OF ENVIRONMENT AND PUBLIC HEALTH vol 38 (2006 Reissue) PARA 143 note 2.

For the purposes of the Landfill Tax Regulations 1996, SI 1996/1527, reg 33(3), reg 33(3A) (see note 7), and reg 33(6) (see notes 4, 8), a condition is relevant if it is a condition of any planning permission or other statutory consent or approval granted on the application of any person making a qualifying contribution to the body, or a term of an agreement made under the Town and Country Planning Act 1990 s 106 (see TOWN AND COUNTRY PLANNING vol 46(1) (Reissue) PARA 244 et seq) or the Planning (Northern Ireland) Order 1991, SI 1991/1220 (NI 11), art 40 to which such a person is a party: Landfill Tax Regulations 1996, SI 1996/1527, reg 33(10) (amended by SI 1999/3270; SI 2003/2313).

3 Landfill Tax Regulations 1996, SI 1996/1527, reg 33(2)(b).
4 Landfill Tax Regulations 1996, SI 1996/1527, reg 33(2)(d). The conditions are that: (1) the provision of the park or amenity is not required by a relevant condition (see note 2); and (2) the park, amenity, building or structure (as the case may be) is not to be operated with a view to profit: reg 33(6)(a), (b). See also note 2.
5 Ie subject to the Landfill Tax Regulations 1996, SI 1996/1527, reg 3(3A): see note 7.
6 For these purposes, 'biological diversity' has the same meaning as in the United Nations Environmental Programme Convention on Biological Diversity of 1992: Landfill Tax Regulations 1996, SI 1996/1527, reg 33(2A) (added by SI 2003/2313).
7 Landfill Tax Regulations 1996, SI 1996/1527, reg 33(2)(da) (added by SI 2003/2313). However, an object is not, or is no longer, regarded as falling within the Landfill Tax Regulations 1996, SI 1996/1527, reg 33(2)(da) if it involves works which: (1) are required to be carried out by a notice or order within reg 33(4) (see note 2); (2) are required to be carried out in accordance with an agreement made under the National Parks and Access to the Countryside Act 1949 s 16 (see OPEN SPACES AND COUNTRYSIDE vol 78 (2010) PARAS 664, 671); (3) are required to be carried out in accordance with an agreement made under the Countryside Act 1968 s 15 (see OPEN SPACES AND COUNTRYSIDE vol 78 (2010) PARA 687); (4) give effect to any provision of a management scheme under the Wildlife and Countryside Act 1981 s 28J or are required to be carried out by a notice served under s 28K (see OPEN SPACES AND COUNTRYSIDE vol 78 (2010) PARAS 686, 688); (5) are wholly or partly required to be carried out by a relevant condition; or (6) are carried out with a view to profit: Landfill Tax Regulations 1996, SI 1996/1527, reg 33(3A) (added by SI 2003/2313). See also note 2.
8 Landfill Tax Regulations 1996, SI 1996/1527, reg 33(2)(e). The conditions are that the park, amenity, building or structure (as the case may be) is not to be operated with a view to profit: reg 33(6)(b). See also note 2.
9 Landfill Tax Regulations 1996, SI 1996/1527, reg 33(2)(f).
10 As to the meaning of 'qualifying contribution' see PARA 949.
11 Landfill Tax Regulations 1996, SI 1996/1527, reg 33(7)(a). The use of qualifying contributions in paying the running costs of the body must only be regarded as an approved object if the body determines so to use no more than such proportion of the total of qualifying contributions, together with any income derived from them (or, in the case of a contribution within reg 30(2)(a) (see PARA 949), only that income) as the proportion of that total forms of the total funds at its disposal and does not in fact use a greater amount: reg 33(8). 'Running costs' includes any cost incurred in connection with the management and administration of a body or its assets: reg 30(1).
12 Landfill Tax Regulations 1996, SI 1996/1527, reg 33(7)(b) (amended by SI 1999/3270).

953. Obligations of approved bodies. An approved body[1] must:
(1) continue to meet all the statutory requirements as to eligibility[2];
(2) comply with such conditions as the regulatory body[3] may impose from time to time, including any conditions varied by the regulatory body[4];
(3) apply qualifying contributions[5] and any income[6] derived there from only to approved objects[7];
(4) not apply any of its funds for the benefit of any of the persons who have made qualifying contributions to it or who were contributing third parties[8] in relation to such contributions (except to the extent that they benefit by virtue of belonging to a class of persons that benefits generally)[9];
(5) make and retain records of the following:

(a) the name, address and registration number of each registered person[10] making a qualifying contribution to the body[11];

(b) the name and address of any contributing third party in relation to a qualifying contribution received by the body[12];

(c) the amount and date of receipt of each qualifying contribution and the amount and date of receipt of any income derived from it[13];

(d) in the case of a transfer of the whole or part of any qualifying contribution or income derived from it to or from the body, the date of the transfer, the amount transferred, the name and enrolment number of the body from or, as the case may require, to which it was transferred, the name, address and registration number of the person who made the qualifying contribution and the name and address of any contributing third party in relation to the qualifying contribution[14];

(e) in respect of each qualifying contribution and any income derived from it, including any such amount transferred to the body by another approved body, the date of and all other details relating to its expenditure[15];

(6) provide the following information to the regulatory body or, if they are performing the functions of the regulatory body, to the Commissioners for Her Majesty's Revenue and Customs[16] within seven days of the receipt by it of any qualifying contribution:

(a) the amount of the contribution[17];

(b) the date it was received[18];

(c) the name and registration number of the person making the contribution[19];

(d) the name and address of any contributing third party in relation to the contribution notified[20] to it[21];

(7) notify the regulatory body within seven days of any transfer by it of qualifying contributions or of income derived therefrom of:

(a) the date of the transfer[22];

(b) the enrolment number of the approved body by which the transfer was made[23];

(c) the amount transferred[24];

(d) the name and registration number of the person who made the qualifying contribution[25];

(e) the name and address of any contributing third party in relation to the contribution[26]; and

(f) the approved objects to which the transferred funds are to be applied[27];

(8) provide the regulatory body or, if they are performing the functions of the regulatory body, the Commissioners with information from or access to the records referred to in head (5) above within 14 days (or such longer period as the regulatory body or, as the case may require, the Commissioners may allow) of a request being made for such information or access[28];

(9) submit to the regulatory body or, if they are performing the functions of the regulatory body, to the Commissioners within 28 days of the end of the relevant period[29] details of:

(a)   qualifying contributions and any other income or profit whatsoever received by it[30];

(b)   any expenditure made by it during the period[31]; and

(c)   any balances held by it at the end of the period[32];

(10)   submit to the regulatory body at its request, not later than 28 days after the request, so many of the following details as it requires at any time during the relevant period:

(a)   qualifying contributions and any other income or profit whatsoever received by it during the period[33];

(b)   any expenditure made by it during the period[34]; and

(c)   any balances held during the period[35];

(11)   if the Commissioners are performing the functions of the regulatory body, submit, at their request, not later than 28 days after the request, so many of the following details as they may require at any time during the relevant period:

(a)   qualifying contributions and any other income or profit whatsoever received by it during the period[36];

(b)   any expenditure made by it during the period[37]; and

(c)   any balances held during the period[38];

(12)   submit to the regulatory body at its request, not later than the fourteenth day following the day on which the request is made, independently audited financial accounts for the approved body's last financial year[39]; and

(13)   pay to the regulatory body an amount equal to 5 per cent of each qualifying contribution it receives, or such lesser amount as the regulatory body may require, towards its running costs within 14 days of receipt of a demand for payment[40].

1   As to approved bodies see PARA 951.
2   Landfill Tax Regulations 1996, SI 1996/1527, reg 33A(1)(a) (reg 33A added by SI 1999/3270). As to the statutory requirements see PARA 952.
3   As to the regulatory body see PARA 954.
4   Landfill Tax Regulations 1996, SI 1996/1527, reg 33A(1)(aa) (reg 33A(1)(aa), (ha), (hb), (3), (4) added by SI 2007/965). As to the imposition and variation of conditions by the regulatory body see PARA 954.
5   As to the meaning of 'qualifying contribution' see PARA 949.
6   As to the meaning of 'income' see PARA 951 note 3. See also *Re Groundwork Community Forests North East Developments Limited* [2009] EWHC 2173 (Ch), [2010] STC 37 (sale proceeds of landfill site not income derived from qualifying contributions).
7   Landfill Tax Regulations 1996, SI 1996/1527, reg 33A(1)(b) (as added: see note 2). As to approved objects see PARA 952.
8   As to the meaning of 'contributing third party' see PARA 949.
9   Landfill Tax Regulations 1996, SI 1996/1527, reg 33A(1)(c) (as added: see note 2).
10   As to the meaning of 'registered person' see PARA 922 note 13.
11   Landfill Tax Regulations 1996, SI 1996/1527, reg 33A(1)(d)(i) (as added: see note 2).
12   Landfill Tax Regulations 1996, SI 1996/1527, reg 33A(1)(d)(ii) (as added: see note 2).
13   Landfill Tax Regulations 1996, SI 1996/1527, reg 33A(1)(d)(iii) (as added: see note 2).
14   Landfill Tax Regulations 1996, SI 1996/1527, reg 33A(1)(d)(iv) (as added: see note 2).
15   Landfill Tax Regulations 1996, SI 1996/1527, reg 33A(1)(d)(v) (as added: see note 2).
16   As to the Commissioners for Her Majesty's Revenue and Customs see PARA 901 note 2.
17   Landfill Tax Regulations 1996, SI 1996/1527, reg 33A(1)(e)(i) (as added: see note 2).
18   Landfill Tax Regulations 1996, SI 1996/1527, reg 33A(1)(e)(ii) (as added: see note 2).
19   Landfill Tax Regulations 1996, SI 1996/1527, reg 33A(1)(e)(iii) (as added: see note 2).
20   Ie by virtue of the Landfill Tax Regulations 1996, SI 1996/1527, reg 32(2B): see PARA 955.
21   Landfill Tax Regulations 1996, SI 1996/1527, reg 33A(1)(e)(iv) (as added: see note 2).
22   Landfill Tax Regulations 1996, SI 1996/1527, reg 33A(1)(f)(i) (as added (see note 2); reg 33A(1)(f) amended by SI 2007/965).

23 Landfill Tax Regulations 1996, SI 1996/1527, reg 33A(1)(f)(ii) (as added (see note 2); and amended (see note 22)).
24 Landfill Tax Regulations 1996, SI 1996/1527, reg 33A(1)(f)(iii) (as added: see note 2).
25 Landfill Tax Regulations 1996, SI 1996/1527, reg 33A(1)(f)(iv) (as added: see note 2).
26 Landfill Tax Regulations 1996, SI 1996/1527, reg 33A(1)(f)(v) (as added: see note 2).
27 Landfill Tax Regulations 1996, SI 1996/1527, reg 33A(1)(f)(vi) (as added: see note 2).
28 Landfill Tax Regulations 1996, SI 1996/1527, reg 33A(1)(g) (as added (see note 2); and amended by SI 2002/1).
29 The relevant period in respect of an approved body is, in the case of the first such period, the period commencing with the date on which the body was approved and ending on the following 31 March: Landfill Tax Regulations 1996, SI 1996/1527, reg 33A(2)(a) (as added (see note 2); and substituted by SI 2007/965). In the case of subsequent periods, the relevant period in respect of an approved body is the period of 12 months commencing with the day after the end of the first or, as the case may require, a subsequent period: Landfill Tax Regulations 1996, SI 1996/1527, reg 33A(2)(b) (as so added and substituted).
30 Landfill Tax Regulations 1996, SI 1996/1527, reg 33A(1)(h)(i) (as added (see note 2); and amended by SI 2008/770). Where an approved body submits details in accordance with a request made under the Landfill Tax Regulations 1996, SI 1996/1527, reg 33A(1)(ha) or (hb) (as added: see note 4) (see heads (10), (11) in the text), the requirement in reg 33A(1)(h) does not apply in respect of those details: reg 33A(4) (as so added).
31 Landfill Tax Regulations 1996, SI 1996/1527, reg 33A(1)(h)(ii) (as added: see note 2).
32 Landfill Tax Regulations 1996, SI 1996/1527, reg 33A(1)(h)(iii) (as added: see note 2).
33 Landfill Tax Regulations 1996, SI 1996/1527, reg 33A(1)(ha)(i) (as added: see note 4).
34 Landfill Tax Regulations 1996, SI 1996/1527, reg 33A(1)(ha)(ii) (as added: see note 4).
35 Landfill Tax Regulations 1996, SI 1996/1527, reg 33A(1)(ha)(iii) (as added: see note 4).
36 Landfill Tax Regulations 1996, SI 1996/1527, reg 33A(1)(hb)(i) (as added: see note 4).
37 Landfill Tax Regulations 1996, SI 1996/1527, reg 33A(1)(hb)(ii) (as added: see note 4).
38 Landfill Tax Regulations 1996, SI 1996/1527, reg 33A(1)(hb)(iii) (as added: see note 4).
39 Landfill Tax Regulations 1996, SI 1996/1527, reg 33A(1)(i) (as added (see note 2); substituted by SI 2007/965; and amended by SI 2008/770). A request may not be made earlier than ten months following the end of the financial year concerned: Landfill Tax Regulations 1996, SI 1996/1527, reg 33A(1)(i) (as so added, substituted and amended).
40 Landfill Tax Regulations 1996, SI 1996/1527, reg 33A(1)(j) (as added: see note 2).

954. The regulatory body. The Commissioners for Her Majesty's Revenue and Customs[1] may approve a body to carry out the functions of the regulatory body[2] and may revoke the approval[3]. Without prejudice to the generality of this provision, the Commissioners may revoke their approval of the regulatory body where it appears to them necessary to do so for the proper operation of the credit scheme established by the regulations[4].

At the time the body is approved, or subsequently by notice delivered to that body, the Commissioners may impose such conditions as they see fit[5] and may, by such notice, vary or revoke any such condition[6]. The Commissioners may not approve a body without first revoking the approval for any other body with effect from a time earlier than that for which the new approval is to take effect[7].

Where:

(1)   the Commissioners revoke their approval of the regulatory body without approving another body with effect from the day after the revocation takes effect; and

(2)   they have not given notice in writing to each body which has been enrolled (and which has not been removed from the roll), no later than the date such revocation takes effect, that they will be performing any of the functions of regulatory bodies,

the approval of all such bodies is deemed to have been revoked on the day the Commissioners revoked their approval[8].

The regulatory body:

(a)   must, on application being made to it by a body which is eligible to be approved[9], approve that body[10];

(b)   may, at the time a body is approved, or subsequently by notice delivered to that body, impose such conditions as it sees fit[11];

(c)   may, by notice delivered to a body, vary or revoke any condition of the approval[12];

(d)   must revoke the approval of any body which applies for its approval to be revoked[13];

(e)   must maintain a roll of bodies which it has approved[14];

(f)   must allocate an identifying number (the enrolment number) to each such body[15];

(g)   must remove from the roll any body whose approval has been revoked[16];

(h)   must satisfy itself, by reference to such records or other documents or information it thinks fit, that the qualifying contributions[17] received by the body have been spent by it only in the course or furtherance of its approved objects[18];

(i)   must publish information regarding which bodies it has approved and which approvals have been revoked[19];

(j)   must, when notified by an approved body of the transfer to or by it of the whole or part of a qualifying contribution or of income derived from it, notify the registered person who made the qualifying contribution, and any contributing third party[20] in relation to it, of:
       (i)   the date of the transfer[21];
       (ii)   the name and enrolment number of the body by or, as the case may require, to whom the transfer was made[22];
       (iii)   the amount transferred[23]; and
       (iv)   the approved objects to which the transferred funds are to be applied[24]; and

(k)   must comply with such conditions as the Commissioners may impose from time to time, including any conditions which have been varied[25].

1   As to the Commissioners for Her Majesty's Revenue and Customs see PARA 901 note 2.
2   Landfill Tax Regulations 1996, SI 1996/1527, reg 35(1)(a) (substituted by SI 1999/3270). The approved body is ENTRUST. For any time as regards which no approval has effect, the Commissioners may perform any of the functions of the regulatory body: Landfill Tax Regulations 1996, SI 1996/1527, reg 35(1)(e). The Commissioners may disclose to the regulatory body information which relates to the tax affairs of registered persons and which is relevant to the credit scheme established by the regulations: reg 35(1)(f) (amended by SI 1999/3270). Having regard to any information received from the regulatory body, the Commissioners may serve repayment of credit notices (see PARA 956): Landfill Tax Regulations 1996, SI 1996/1527, reg 35(1)(g) (amended by SI 1999/3270; SI 2008/770).
3   Landfill Tax Regulations 1996, SI 1996/1527, reg 35(1)(c).
4   Landfill Tax Regulations 1996, SI 1996/1527, reg 35(2) (substituted by SI 1999/3270).
5   Landfill Tax Regulations 1996, SI 1996/1527, reg 35(1)(aa) (added by SI 2007/965).
6   Landfill Tax Regulations 1996, SI 1996/1527, reg 35(1)(ab) (added by SI 2007/965).
7   Landfill Tax Regulations 1996, SI 1996/1527, reg 35(1)(d).
8   Landfill Tax Regulations 1996, SI 1996/1527, reg 34(2) (amended by SI 1999/3270).
9   Ie under the Landfill Tax Regulations 1996, SI 1996/1527, reg 33: see PARA 951.
10   Landfill Tax Regulations 1996, SI 1996/1527, reg 34(1)(a) (substituted by SI 1999/3270). The Commissioners may revoke the approval if the approved body fails to comply with any of the relevant requirements: Landfill Tax Regulations 1996, SI 1996/1527, reg 35(1)(h) (added by SI 2008/770). The requirements referred to are those of the Landfill Tax Regulations 1996, SI 1996/1527, reg 33A(1): see PARA 953.
11   Landfill Tax Regulations 1996, SI 1996/1527, reg 34(1)(aa) (added by SI 2007/965).
12   Landfill Tax Regulations 1996, SI 1996/1527, reg 34(1)(ab) (added by SI 2007/965).

13 Landfill Tax Regulations 1996, SI 1996/1527, reg 34(1)(ee) (added by SI 1999/3270).
14 Landfill Tax Regulations 1996, SI 1996/1527, reg 34(1)(f).
15 Landfill Tax Regulations 1996, SI 1996/1527, reg 34(1)(g).
16 Landfill Tax Regulations 1996, SI 1996/1527, reg 34(1)(h) (amended by SI 2008/770). As to the revocation of approval see head (d) in the text and note 10.
17 As to the meaning of 'qualifying contribution' see PARA 949.
18 Landfill Tax Regulations 1996, SI 1996/1527, reg 34(1)(i).
19 Landfill Tax Regulations 1996, SI 1996/1527, reg 34(1)(j) (amended by SI 2008/770). As to the revocation of approval see head (d) in the text and note 10.
20 As to the meaning of 'contributing third party' see PARA 949.
21 Landfill Tax Regulations 1996, SI 1996/1527, reg 34(1)(k)(i) (reg 34(1)(k) added by SI 1999/3270).
22 Landfill Tax Regulations 1996, SI 1996/1527, reg 34(1)(k)(ii) (as added: see note 21).
23 Landfill Tax Regulations 1996, SI 1996/1527, reg 34(1)(k)(iii) (as added: see note 21).
24 Landfill Tax Regulations 1996, SI 1996/1527, reg 34(1)(k)(iv) (as added: see note 21).
25 Landfill Tax Regulations 1996, SI 1996/1527, reg 34(1)(l) (added by SI 2007/965).

955. Records and information. A person claiming credit in respect of contributions to bodies concerned with the environment[1] must make a record containing the following information:

(1) the amount and date of each payment he has made to an approved body[2];

(2) the name and enrolment number of that body[3];

(3) the name and address of any contributing third party[4];

(4) the amount of the payment made or to be made by the contributing third party and the date, or as the case may require, dates on which payment of the whole or any part of that amount: (a) was received; or (b) is expected to be received[5].

A person claiming credit for a contribution in relation to which there is a contributing third party must have provided to the regulatory body[6] or, if they are performing the functions of a regulatory body, to the Commissioners for Her Majesty's Revenue and Customs the following information:

(i) the name and address of the contributing third party[7];

(ii) the amount of the payment made or to be made by the contributing third party and the date, or as the case may require, dates on which payment of the whole or any part of that amount: (A) was received; or (B) is expected to be received[8];

(iii) the enrolment number of the approved body to whom the contribution was made[9].

A person claiming credit for a contribution in relation to which there is a contributing third party must have informed the approved body to which the contribution is made of the name and address of the contributing third party[10].

1 Ie credit arising under the Landfill Tax Regulations 1996, SI 1996/1527, Pt VII (regs 30–36): see PARA 949 et seq.
2 Landfill Tax Regulations 1996, SI 1996/1527, reg 32(2)(a). As to approved bodies see PARA 952.
3 Landfill Tax Regulations 1996, SI 1996/1527, reg 32(2)(b).
4 Landfill Tax Regulations 1996, SI 1996/1527, reg 32(2)(c) (added by SI 1999/3270). As to the meaning of 'contributing third party' see PARA 949.
5 Landfill Tax Regulations 1996, SI 1996/1527, reg 32(2)(d) (added by SI 1999/3270).
6 As to the regulatory body see PARA 954.
7 Landfill Tax Regulations 1996, SI 1996/1527, reg 32(2A)(a) (reg 32(2A) added by SI 1999/3270).
8 Landfill Tax Regulations 1996, SI 1996/1527, reg 32(2A)(b) (as added: see note 7).
9 Landfill Tax Regulations 1996, SI 1996/1527, reg 32(2A)(c) (as added: see note 7).
10 Landfill Tax Regulations 1996, SI 1996/1527, reg 32(2B) (added by SI 1999/3270).

956.   Repayment of credit.   Where a person has benefited from an amount of credit to which he was entitled in respect of contributions to bodies concerned with the environment[1], and the Commissioners for Her Majesty's Revenue and Customs[2] serve upon him a notice in relation to a qualifying contribution[3] paid to an approved body[4] specifying: (1) that they are not satisfied that the contribution has been spent by the body only in the course or furtherance of its approved objects[5] or that they are not satisfied that any income[6] derived from the contribution has been so spent by the body; (2) a breach of a condition to which the approval of the body was made subject and which occurred before the contribution was spent by the body; or (3) that the approval of the body has been revoked and that the contribution had not been spent by the body before that revocation took effect, he must repay to the Commissioners the credit claimed in respect of the qualifying contribution[7].

Where a person has benefited from an amount of credit to which he was entitled, and the whole or a part of the qualifying contribution in respect of which the entitlement to credit arose has been repaid to him or to a person who was a contributing third party[8] in relation to the qualifying contribution, he must pay to the Commissioners an amount equal to 90 per cent of the amount repaid to him[9].

Where a person has benefited from an amount of credit to which he was entitled, and he is entitled to a payment[10] in respect of a later accounting period in the same contribution year as the accounting period in respect of which that credit was claimed, the person must pay to the Commissioners an amount equal to the difference between:

(a)   the aggregate of the amount of the credit from which he has benefited, and any other amounts of credit arising which he is or was entitled to claim, in respect of that contribution year[11]; and

(b)   the amount of credit which he would have been entitled to claim if he had in fact claimed the aggregate amount mentioned in head (a) above in the return for the accounting period in respect of which he was entitled to the payment[12].

Where a person has benefited from an amount of credit to which he was entitled, and he acquires an asset[13] from a body to which he has made a qualifying contribution for no consideration, or a consideration which is less than the open market value of the asset[14], he must pay to the Commissioners an amount equal to 90 per cent of the amount by which the open market value exceeds the consideration[15]. A person required to pay such an amount is not required to pay more than the total amount of relevant credit[16], but is not entitled to claim any further amounts of credit in respect of qualifying contributions made by him to the body in question on or after the date on which he acquired the asset[17].

1   Ie credit arising under the Landfill Tax Regulations 1996, SI 1996/1527, Pt VII (regs 30–36): see PARA 949.

2   As to the Commissioners for Her Majesty's Revenue and Customs see PARA 901 note 2.

3   As to the meaning of 'qualifying contribution' see PARA 949.

4   As to approved bodies see PARA 951.

5   As to approved objects see PARA 952.

6   As to the meaning of 'income' see PARA 951 note 3.

7   Landfill Tax Regulations 1996, SI 1996/1527, reg 36(1). For the purpose of reg 36(1), where: (1) repayment is required in relation to credit that has been claimed in respect of more than one qualifying contribution in an accounting period; and (2) the provisions of reg 31(3) (see PARA 950) applied so that the amount of credit was restricted, the person is deemed to have claimed

credit in respect of such proportion of each contribution made in that accounting period as the total credit claimed forms of the total of the contributions made: reg 36(2). As to the meaning of 'accounting period' see PARA 928 note 17.

8   As to the meaning of 'contributing third party' see PARA 949.
9   Landfill Tax Regulations 1996, SI 1996/1527, reg 36(3) (substituted by SI 1999/3270).
10 Ie by the Commissioners under the Landfill Tax Regulations 1996, SI 1996/1527, reg 20: see PARA 940.
11 Landfill Tax Regulations 1996, SI 1996/1527, reg 36(4), (5)(a).
12 Landfill Tax Regulations 1996, SI 1996/1527, reg 36(4), (5)(b).
13 'Asset' includes land, goods or services and any interest in any of these: Landfill Tax Regulations 1996, SI 1996/1527, reg 36(8)(a).
14 The open market value of an asset is the amount of the consideration in money that would be payable for the asset by a person standing in no such relationship with any person as would affect that consideration: Landfill Tax Regulations 1996, SI 1996/1527, reg 36(8)(b).
15 Landfill Tax Regulations 1996, SI 1996/1527, reg 36(6).
16 Landfill Tax Regulations 1996, SI 1996/1527, reg 36(7)(a). 'Relevant credit' means credit arising under Pt VII from which a person has benefited, and which has arisen in respect of qualifying contributions made by him to the body in question or treated by virtue of reg 32(3) (see PARA 949 note 15) as having been received by that body from him: reg 36(8)(c).
17 Landfill Tax Regulations 1996, SI 1996/1527, reg 36(7)(b).

7. RECOVERY OF TAX DUE

(1) RECOVERY

957.   Power to recover tax. Landfill tax[1] due from any person is recoverable as a debt due to the Crown[2].

1   As to the meaning of 'landfill tax' see PARA 901.
2   Finance Act 1996 s 60, Sch 5 para 11.

958.   Amounts shown as tax on invoices. Where (1) a registrable person[1] issues an invoice[2] showing an amount as landfill tax[3] chargeable on an event; and (2) no tax is in fact chargeable on the event, an amount equal to the amount shown as tax is recoverable from the person as a debt due to the Crown[4].

Where (a) a registrable person issues an invoice showing an amount as tax chargeable on a taxable disposal[5]; and (b) the amount shown as tax exceeds the amount of tax in fact chargeable on the disposal, an amount equal to the excess is recoverable from the person as a debt due to the Crown[6].

1   References in the Finance Act 1996 Pt III (ss 39–71) to a 'registrable person' are references to a person who: (1) is registered under s 47 (see PARA 920); or (2) is liable to be so registered: s 47(10).
2   References to an invoice are references to any invoice, whether or not it is a landfill invoice within the meaning of the Finance Act 1996 s 61 (see PARA 904): s 60, Sch 5 para 44(3).
3   As to the meaning of 'landfill tax' see PARA 901.
4   Finance Act 1996 Sch 5 para 44(1).
5   As to the meaning of 'taxable disposal' see PARA 902.
6   Finance Act 1996 Sch 5 para 44(2).

(2) ASSESSMENTS

959.   Power to assess. Where:
(1)   a person has failed to make any returns required to be made under the landfill tax provisions[1];
(2)   a person has failed to keep any documents necessary to verify returns required to be made under those provisions[2];
(3)   a person has failed to afford the facilities necessary to verify returns[3]; or
(4)   it appears to the Commissioners for Her Majesty's Revenue and Customs[4] that returns required to be made by a person are incomplete or incorrect[5],

the Commissioners may assess the amount of landfill tax due from the person concerned to the best of their judgment and notify it to him[6]. Where a person has for an accounting period[7] been paid an amount to which he purports to be entitled under the regulations as to tax credits[8], then, to the extent that the amount ought not to have been paid or would not have been paid had the facts been known or been as they later turn out to be, the Commissioners may assess the amount as being tax due from him for that period and notify it to him accordingly[9]. Where a person is so assessed in respect of the same accounting period the assessments may be combined and notified to him as one assessment[10].

Where:
(a)   as a result of a person's failure to make a return in relation to an accounting period the Commissioners have made an assessment[11] for that period[12];

(b)   the tax assessed has been paid but no proper return has been made in relation to the period to which the assessment related[13]; and

(c)   as a result of a failure to make a return in relation to a later accounting period, being a failure by the person referred to in head (a) above or a person acting in a representative capacity in relation to him[14], the Commissioners find it necessary to make another assessment[15],

then, if the Commissioners think fit, having regard to the failure referred to in head (a) above, they may specify in the assessment referred to in head (c) above an amount of tax greater than that which they would otherwise have considered to be appropriate[16].

Where an amount has been assessed and notified to any person[17], it is deemed to be an amount of tax due from him and may be recovered accordingly unless, or except to the extent that, the assessment has subsequently been withdrawn or reduced[18].

1   Finance Act 1996 s 50(1)(a). The provisions referred to in the text are those of Pt III (ss 39–71): see PARA 901 note 1.
2   Finance Act 1996 s 50(1)(b).
3   Finance Act 1996 s 50(1)(c).
4   As to the Commissioners for Her Majesty's Revenue and Customs see PARA 901 note 2.
5   Finance Act 1996 s 50(1)(d).
6   Finance Act 1996 s 50(1). Where the person failing to make a return, or making a return which appears to the Commissioners to be incomplete or incorrect, was required to make the return as a personal representative, trustee in bankruptcy, receiver, liquidator or person otherwise acting in a representative capacity in relation to another person, s 50(1) applies as if the reference to tax due from him included a reference to tax due from that other person: s 50(4). For the purposes of s 50, notification to: (1) a personal representative, trustee in bankruptcy, receiver or liquidator; or (2) a person otherwise acting in a representative capacity in relation to another person, is treated as notification to the person acted for: s 50(8). As to the Commissioners' discretion in making an assessment see *Easter Hatton Environmental (Waste Away) Ltd* L00026.
7   As to the meaning of 'accounting period' see PARA 928 note 17.
8   Ie regulations made under the Finance Act 1996 s 51: see PARA 938 et seq.
9   Finance Act 1996 s 50(2).
10   Finance Act 1996 s 50(3).
11   Ie under the Finance Act 1996 s 50(1): see the text and notes 1–6.
12   Finance Act 1996 s 50(6)(a).
13   Finance Act 1996 s 50(6)(b).
14   Ie as mentioned in the Finance Act 1996 s 50(4): see note 6.
15   Finance Act 1996 s 50(6)(c). The reference is to an assessment under s 50(1): see the text and notes 1–6.
16   Finance Act 1996 s 50(6).
17   Ie under the Finance Act 1996 s 50(1) or s 50(2): see the text and notes 1–9.
18   Finance Act 1996 s 50(7).

960. Time limits for assessments. An assessment of an amount of tax due for an accounting period may not be made after the later of the following:

(1)   two years after the end of the accounting period[1];

(2)   one year after evidence of facts, sufficient in the Commissioners' opinion to justify the making of the assessment, comes to their knowledge[2].

However, where further such evidence comes to their knowledge after the making of such an assessment, another assessment may be made in addition to any earlier assessment[3].

In general, an assessment of the amount of landfill tax due from any person[4] may not be made more than three years after the end of the accounting period[5] concerned[6].

Where after a person's death the Commissioners for Her Majesty's Revenue and Customs[7] propose to assess an amount as due by reason of some conduct[8] of the deceased, the assessment must not be made more than three years after the death[9].

1 Finance Act 1996 s 50(5)(a).

2 Finance Act 1996 s 50(5)(b).

3 Finance Act 1996 s 50(5). Section 50(5) has effect subject to s 60, Sch 5 para 33(1)(a) (time limits) (see the text to note 3): s 50(9).

4 Ie an assessment under any provision of the Finance Act 1996 s 50: see PARA 959 and the text to notes (1)–(3). As to assessments of amounts due by way of penalty or interest see PARA 994.

5 As to the meaning of 'accounting period' see PARA 928 note 17.

6 Finance Act 1996 s 60, Sch 5 para 33(1)(a) (Sch 5 para 33(1), (4) amended by the Finance Act 1997 s 50(1), Sch 5 Pt II para 6(2)(c)). Subject to the Finance Act 1996 Sch 5 para 33(5) (assessment after death: see the text to notes 7–9), if tax has been lost: (1) as a result of conduct falling within Sch 5 para 18(1) (dishonest evasion: see PARA 987) or for which a person has been convicted of fraud; or (2) in circumstances giving rise to liability to a penalty under Sch 5 para 21 (failure to register: see PARA 920 note 4), an assessment may be made as if, in Sch 5 para 33(1), each reference to three years were a reference to 20 years: Sch 5 para 33(4) (as so amended).

As from 1 April 2010, Sch 5 para 33(1) is to be amended by, and Sch 5 para 33(1A) added by, the Finance Act 2009 s 99, Sch 51 para 40(2), (3) so that an assessment may not in general be made more than four years after the end of the accounting period concerned. As from 1 April 2010, Sch 5 para 33(4) is to be substituted by, and Sch 5 para 33(4A) added by, the Finance Act 2009 Sch 51 para 40(5) so that an assessment of an amount due from a person in a case involving a loss of tax brought about deliberately by that person (or by another person acting on his behalf) or attributable to a failure by the person to comply with an obligation under the Finance Act 1996 s 47(2), (3) (registration: see PARA 920) may be made at any time not more than 20 years after the end of the accounting period concerned. The reference to a loss brought about deliberately by the person includes a loss brought about as a result of a deliberate inaccuracy in a document given to Her Majesty's Revenue and Customs by or on behalf of that person: Sch 5 para 33(4A) (as so added).

7 As to the Commissioners for Her Majesty's Revenue and Customs see PARA 901 note 2.

8 As to the meaning of 'conduct' see PARA 987 note 3.

9 Finance Act 1996 Sch 5 para 33(5)(a). If the circumstances are as set out in Sch 5 para 33(4) (see note 3), the modification of Sch 5 para 33(1) contained in Sch 5 para 33(4) (see note 6) does not apply but any assessment which (from the point of view of time limits) could have been made immediately after the death may be made at any time within three years after it: Sch 5 para 33(5)(b).

As from 1 April 2010 Sch 5 para 33(5) is to be amended by the Finance Act 2009 Sch 51 para 40(6) so that an assessment must not be made more than four years after the death, and the Finance Act 1996 Sch 5 para 33(5)(b) is repealed.

961. Supplementary assessments. If, otherwise than in certain circumstances[1], it appears to the Commissioners for Her Majesty's Revenue and Customs[2] that the amount which ought to have been assessed in an assessment[3] exceeds the amount which was so assessed, then:

(1) under the like provision as that assessment was made; and

(2) on or before the last day on which that assessment could have been made,

the Commissioners may make a supplementary assessment of the amount of the excess and must notify the person concerned accordingly[4].

1 Ie circumstances falling within the Finance Act 1996 s 50(5)(b): see PARA 960.

2 As to the Commissioners for Her Majesty's Revenue and Customs see PARA 901 note 2.

3 Ie under any provision of the Finance Act 1996 s 50 (see PARA 959) or under s 60, Sch 5 para 32 (see PARA 994).

4 Finance Act 1996 Sch 5 para 34.

(3) SET-OFF

962. Power to make regulations as to set-off. Regulations may make provision in relation to any case where:

(1)   a person is under a duty to pay to the Commissioners for Her Majesty's Revenue and Customs[1] at any time an amount or amounts in respect of landfill tax[2]; and

(2)   the Commissioners are under a duty to pay to that person at the same time an amount or amounts in respect of any tax[3] (or taxes) under their care and management[4].

The regulations may provide that if the total of the amount or amounts mentioned in head (1) above exceeds the total of the amount or amounts mentioned in head (2) above, the latter must be set off against the former[5]; and, conversely, that if the total of the amount or amounts mentioned in head (2) above exceeds the total of the amount or amounts mentioned in head (1) above, the Commissioners may set off the latter in paying the former[6]. If the total of the amount or amounts mentioned in head (1) above is the same as the total of the amount or amounts mentioned in head (2) above, the regulations may provide that no payment need be made in respect of the former or the latter[7]. The regulations may provide for any limitation on the time within which the Commissioners are entitled to take steps for recovering any amount due to them in respect of landfill tax to be disregarded, in such cases as may be described in the regulations, in determining whether any person is under a duty to pay as is mentioned in head (1) above[8]. The regulations may include provision treating any duty to pay mentioned in heads (1) and (2) above as discharged accordingly[9].

Regulations may also make provision in relation to any case where:

(a)   a person is under a duty to pay to the Commissioners at any time an amount or amounts in respect of any tax[10] (or taxes) under their care and management[11]; and

(b)   the Commissioners are under a duty to pay to that person at the same time an amount or amounts in respect of landfill tax[12].

The regulations may provide that if the total of the amount or amounts mentioned in head (a) above exceeds the total of the amount or amounts mentioned in head (b) above, the latter must be set off against the former[13], and, conversely, that if the total of the amount or amounts mentioned in head (b) above exceeds the total of the amount or amounts mentioned in head (a) above, the Commissioners may set off the latter in paying the former[14]. If the total of the amount or amounts mentioned in head (a) above is the same as the total of the amount or amounts mentioned in head (b) above, the regulations may provide that no payment need be made in respect of the former or the latter[15]. The regulations may provide for any limitation on the time within which the Commissioners are entitled to take steps for recovering any amount due to them in respect of any of the taxes under their care and management to be disregarded, in such cases as may be described in the regulations, in determining whether any person is under a duty to pay as is mentioned in head (a) above[16]. The regulations may include provision treating any duty to pay mentioned in heads (a) and (b) above as discharged accordingly[17].

1   As to the Commissioners for Her Majesty's Revenue and Customs see PARA 901 note 2.
2   Finance Act 1996 s 60, Sch 5 para 42(1)(a). As to the meaning of 'landfill tax' see PARA 901.

3   References in the Finance Act 1996 Sch 5 para 42(1) to an amount in respect of a particular tax include references not only to an amount of tax itself but also to other amounts such as interest and penalty: Sch 5 para 42(6). For these purposes, 'tax' includes 'duty': Sch 5 para 42(7).
4   Finance Act 1996 Sch 5 para 42(1)(b). As to the regulations made under Sch 5 para 42 and Sch 5 para 43 (see the text to notes 10–17) see the Landfill Tax Regulations 1996, SI 1996/1527, regs 45–47; and PARAS 963–965.
5   Finance Act 1996 Sch 5 para 42(2). As to set-off generally see CIVIL PROCEDURE vol 11 (2009) PARAS 634–722.
6   Finance Act 1996 Sch 5 para 42(3).
7   Finance Act 1996 Sch 5 para 42(4).
8   Finance Act 1996 Sch 5 para 42(4A) (added by the Finance Act 1997 s 50(1), Sch 5 Pt II para 6(2)(c)).
9   Finance Act 1996 Sch 5 para 42(5).
10 References in the Finance Act 1996 Sch 5 para 43(1) to an amount in respect of a particular tax include references not only to an amount of tax itself but also to other amounts such as interest and penalty: Sch 5 para 43(6). For these purposes, 'tax' includes 'duty': Sch 5 para 43(7).
11 Finance Act 1996 Sch 5 para 43(1)(a).
12 Finance Act 1996 Sch 5 para 43(1)(b). As to the regulations made see note 4.
13 Finance Act 1996 Sch 5 para 43(2).
14 Finance Act 1996 Sch 5 para 43(3).
15 Finance Act 1996 Sch 5 para 43(4).
16 Finance Act 1996 Sch 5 para 43(4A) (added by the Finance Act 1997 Sch 5 Pt II para 6(2)(c)).
17 Finance Act 1996 Sch 5 para 43(5).

963.   Landfill tax amount owed to Commissioners for Revenue and Customs.
Where:

(1)   a person is under a duty to pay to the Commissioners for Her Majesty's Revenue and Customs[1] at any time an amount or amounts in respect of landfill tax[2]; and

(2)   the Commissioners are under a duty to pay to that person at the same time an amount or amounts in respect of any tax or taxes under their care and management[3],

and the total of the amount or amounts mentioned in head (1) above exceeds the total of the amount or amounts mentioned in head (2) above, the latter must be set off against the former[4]. Conversely, where the total of the amount or amounts mentioned in head (2) above exceeds the total of the amount or amounts mentioned in head (1) above, the Commissioners may set off the latter in paying the former[5]. Where the total of the amount or amounts mentioned in head (1) above is the same as the total of the amount or amounts mentioned in head (2) above, no payment need be made in respect of either[6]. Where an amount has been set off in accordance with any of the above provisions, the duty of both the person and the Commissioners to pay the amount or amounts concerned must be treated as having been discharged accordingly[7].

1   As to the Commissioners for Her Majesty's Revenue and Customs see PARA 901 note 2.
2   Landfill Tax Regulations 1996, SI 1996/1527, reg 45(1)(a). As to the meaning of 'landfill tax' see PARA 901. References in reg 45(1) to an amount in respect of a particular tax include references not only to an amount of tax itself but also to amounts of penalty, surcharge or interest: reg 45(6). For these purposes, 'tax' includes 'duty': reg 45(7).
3   Landfill Tax Regulations 1996, SI 1996/1527, reg 45(1)(b). See note 2.
4   Landfill Tax Regulations 1996, SI 1996/1527, reg 45(2). Regulation 45 is subject to reg 47 (insolvency procedure: see PARA 965): reg 45(1). As to set-off generally see CIVIL PROCEDURE vol 11 (2009) PARAS 634–722.
5   Landfill Tax Regulations 1996, SI 1996/1527, reg 45(3).
6   Landfill Tax Regulations 1996, SI 1996/1527, reg 45(4).
7   Landfill Tax Regulations 1996, SI 1996/1527, reg 45(5).

964.   Landfill tax amount owed by Commissioners for Revenue and Customs.
Where:

(1)   a person is under a duty to pay to the Commissioners for Her Majesty's
       Revenue and Customs[1] at any time an amount or amounts in respect of
       any tax[2] or taxes under their care and management[3]; and

(2)   the Commissioners are under a duty to pay to that person at the same
       time an amount or amounts in respect of landfill tax[4],

and the total of the amount or amounts mentioned in head (1) above exceeds the
total of the amount or amounts mentioned in head (2) above, the latter must be
set off against the former[5]. Conversely, where the total of the amount or amounts
mentioned in head (2) above exceeds the total of the amount or amounts
mentioned in head (1) above, the Commissioners may set off the latter in paying
the former[6]. Where the total of the amount or amounts mentioned in head (1)
above is the same as the total of the amount or amounts mentioned in head (2)
above, no payment need be made in respect of either[7]. Where an amount has
been set off in accordance with any of the above provisions, the duty of both the
person and the Commissioners to pay the amount or amounts concerned shall be
treated as having been discharged accordingly[8].

1   As to the Commissioners for Her Majesty's Revenue and Customs see PARA 901 note 2.
2   As to the meanings of 'an amount in respect of a particular tax' and 'tax' see PARA 963 note 2;
    definitions applied by virtue of the Landfill Tax Regulations 1996, SI 1996/1527, reg 46(6).
3   Landfill Tax Regulations 1996, SI 1996/1527, reg 46(1)(a).
4   Landfill Tax Regulations 1996, SI 1996/1527, reg 46(1)(b). As to the meaning of 'landfill tax'
    see PARA 901.
5   Landfill Tax Regulations 1996, SI 1996/1527, reg 46(2). Regulation 46 is subject to reg 47
    (insolvency procedure: see PARA 965): reg 46(1). As to set-off generally see CIVIL PROCEDURE
    vol 11 (2009) PARAS 634–722.
6   Landfill Tax Regulations 1996, SI 1996/1527, reg 46(3).
7   Landfill Tax Regulations 1996, SI 1996/1527, reg 46(4).
8   Landfill Tax Regulations 1996, SI 1996/1527, reg 46(5).

965.   No set-off where insolvency procedure applied.   The provisions relating
to set-off[1] do not require the credit[2] to be set against the debit[3] in any case
where:

(1)   an insolvency procedure[4] has been applied[5] to the person entitled to the
       credit[6];

(2)   the credit became due after that procedure was so applied[7];

(3)   the liability to pay the debit either arose before that procedure was so
       applied or (having risen afterwards) relates to, or to matters occurring
       in the course of: (a) the carrying on of any business; or (b) in the case of
       a specified sum[8], the carrying out of taxable activities[9], at times before
       the procedure was so applied[10].

1   Ie the Landfill Tax Regulations 1996, SI 1996/1527, regs 45, 46: see PARAS 963–964. As to
    set-off generally see CIVIL PROCEDURE vol 11 (2009) PARAS 634–722.
2   Ie any such amount as is mentioned in the Landfill Tax Regulations 1996, SI 1996/1527,
    reg 45(1)(b) (see PARA 963) or reg 46(1)(b) (see PARA 964).
3   Ie any such sum as is mentioned in the Landfill Tax Regulations 1996, SI 1996/1527,
    reg 45(1)(a) (see PARA 963) or reg 46(1)(a) (see PARA 964).
4   Subject to the Landfill Tax Regulations 1996, SI 1996/1527, reg 47(3) (see note 5), the following
    are the times when an insolvency procedure is to be taken, for the purposes of reg 47, to have
    been applied to any person, that is to say:
    (1)   when a bankruptcy order, winding-up order, administration order or award of
           sequestration is made in relation to that person or that person enters administration
           (reg 47(2)(a) (amended by SI 2003/2096));

   (2)   when that person is put into administrative receivership (Landfill Tax Regulations 1996, SI 1996/1527, reg 47(2)(b));

   (3)   when that person, being a corporation, passes a resolution for voluntary winding-up (reg 47(2)(c));

   (4)   when any voluntary arrangement approved in accordance with the Insolvency Act 1986 Pt I (ss 1–7) or Pt VIII (ss 252–263G) (see BANKRUPTCY AND INDIVIDUAL INSOLVENCY) or the Insolvency (Northern Ireland) Order 1989, SI 1989/2405, Pt 1 (arts 1–13) or Pt VIII Ch II (arts 226–237) comes into force in relation to that person (Landfill Tax Regulations 1996, SI 1996/1527, reg 47(2)(d));

   (5)   when a deed of arrangement registered in accordance with the Deeds of Arrangement Act 1914 (see BANKRUPTCY AND INDIVIDUAL INSOLVENCY) takes effect in relation to that person (Landfill Tax Regulations 1996, SI 1996/1527, reg 47(2)(e));

   (6)   when that person's estate becomes vested in any other person as that person's trustee under a trust deed (reg 47(2)(f)).

5   References in the Landfill Tax Regulations 1996, SI 1996/1527, reg 47, in relation to any person, to the application of an insolvency procedure to that person do not include:

   (1)   the making of a bankruptcy order, winding-up order, or award of sequestration or that person entering administration at a time when any such arrangements or deed as is mentioned in reg 47(2)(d)–(f) (see note 4 heads (4)–(6)) is in force in relation to that person (reg 47(3)(a) (amended by SI 2003/2096));

   (2)   the making of a winding-up order at any of the following times:

      (a)   immediately upon the appointment of the administrator ceasing to have effect (Landfill Tax Regulations 1996, SI 1996/1527, reg 47(3)(b)(i) (amended by SI 2003/2096));

      (b)   when that person is being wound-up voluntarily (Landfill Tax Regulations 1996, SI 1996/1527, reg 47(3)(b)(ii));

      (c)   when that person is in administrative receivership (reg 47(3)(b)(iii)); or

   (3)   the making of an administration order in relation to that person at any time when that person is in administrative receivership (reg 47(3)(c)).

   For the purposes of reg 47, a person is regarded as being in administrative receivership throughout any continuous period for which (disregarding any temporary vacancy in the office of receiver) there is an administrative receiver of that person, and the reference in reg 47(2) to a person being put into administrative receivership must be construed accordingly: reg 47(4).

6   Landfill Tax Regulations 1996, SI 1996/1527, reg 47(1)(a).

7   Landfill Tax Regulations 1996, SI 1996/1527, reg 47(1)(b).

8   Ie such as is mentioned in the Landfill Tax Regulations 1996, SI 1996/1527, reg 46(1)(b): see PARA 964.

9   As to the meaning of 'taxable activity' see PARA 920 note 1.

10 Landfill Tax Regulations 1996, SI 1996/1527, reg 47(1)(c).

8. RECOVERY OF OVERPAID TAX

966. Repayment of tax overpaid. Where a person has paid an amount to the Commissioners for Her Majesty's Revenue and Customs[1] by way of tax which was not tax due to them, they are liable to repay the amount to him[2]. The Commissioners are only liable to repay an amount under this provision on a claim being made for the purpose[3]. It is a defence, in relation to such a claim, that repayment of an amount would unjustly enrich the claimant[4]. The Commissioners are not liable, on such a claim, to repay any amount paid to them more than three years before the making of the claim[5]. Such a claim must be made in such form and manner and must be supported by such documentary evidence as may be prescribed[6] by regulations[7]. Except as provided by this provision, the Commissioners are not liable to repay an amount paid to them by way of tax by virtue of the fact that it was not tax due to them[8].

1   As to the Commissioners for Her Majesty's Revenue and Customs see PARA 901 note 2.
2   Finance Act 1996 Sch 5 para 14(1).
3   Finance Act 1996 Sch 5 para 14(2).
4   Finance Act 1996 Sch 5 para 14(3).
5   Finance Act 1996 Sch 5 para 14(4) (substituted by the Finance Act 1997 s 50(1), Sch 5 Pt II para 5(3)). As from 1 April 2010 the Finance Act 1996 Sch 5 para 14(4) is to be amended by the Finance Act 2009 s 99, Sch 51 para 38 so that the Commissioners are not liable to repay any amount paid to them more than four years before the making of the claim.
6   'Prescribed' means prescribed by an order or regulations under the Finance Act 1996 Pt III (ss 39–71): s 70(1). See note 7.
7   Finance Act 1996 Sch 5 para 14(5). Except where the amount to which the claim relates has been entered in a return in accordance with the Landfill Tax Regulations 1996, SI 1996/1527, reg 13 (correction of errors: see PARA 936), or is included in an amount so entered, any claim under the Finance Act 1996 Sch 5 para 14 must be made in writing to the Commissioners and must, by reference to such documentary evidence as is in the possession of the claimant, state the amount of the claim and the method by which that amount was calculated: Landfill Tax Regulations 1996, SI 1996/1527, reg 14.
8   Finance Act 1996 Sch 5 para 14(6).

967. Reimbursement arrangements. The following applies without prejudice to reimbursement arrangements made before 11 February 1998[1]. 'Reimbursement arrangements' means any arrangements (whether made before, on or after 30 January 1998) for the purposes of a claim[2] which: (1) are made by a claimant for the purpose of securing that he is not unjustly enriched by the repayment of any amount in pursuance of the claim; and (2) provide for the reimbursement of persons ('consumers') who have, for practical purposes, borne the whole or any part of the cost of the original payment of that amount to the Commissioners for Her Majesty's Revenue and Customs[3].

For the purpose of the defence by the Commissioners for Her Majesty's Revenue and Customs that repayment by them of an amount claimed would unjustly enrich the claimant[4], reimbursement arrangements made by a claimant are to be disregarded except where they include specified provisions[5] and are supported by specified undertakings[6].

The specified provisions are provisions providing that:

(a)   reimbursement for which the arrangements provide will be completed by no later than 90 days after the repayment to which it relates[7];

(b)   no deduction will be made from the relevant amount[8] by way of fee or charge, howsoever expressed or effected[9];

(c)   reimbursement will be made only in cash or by cheque[10];

(d)   any part of the relevant amount that is not reimbursed by the time mentioned in head (a) will be repaid by the claimant to the Commissioners[11];

(e)   any interest paid by the Commissioners on any relevant amount repaid by them will also be treated by the claimant in the same way as the relevant amount falls to be treated under heads (a), (b)[12]; and

(f)   the required records[13] will be kept by the claimant and produced[14] by him to the Commissioners, or to an officer of theirs as required by notice[15].

The undertakings supporting the arrangements must be given to the Commissioners by the claimant no later than the time at which he makes the claim for which the reimbursement arrangements have been made[16]. The undertakings must be in writing, must be signed and dated by the claimant, and must be to the effect that:

(i)   at the date of the undertakings he is able to identify the names and addresses of those consumers whom he has reimbursed or whom he intends to reimburse[17];

(ii)   he will apply the whole of the relevant amount repaid to him, without any deduction by way of fee or charge or otherwise, to the reimbursement in cash or by cheque, of such consumers by no later than 90 days after his receipt of that amount (except in so far as he has already so reimbursed them)[18];

(iii)   he will apply any interest paid to him on the relevant amount repaid to him wholly to the reimbursement of such consumers by no later than 90 days after his receipt of that interest[19];

(iv)   he will repay to the Commissioners without demand the whole or such part of the relevant amount repaid to him or of any interest paid to him as he fails to apply in accordance with the undertakings mentioned in heads (ii) and (iii)[20];

(v)   he will keep the required records[21];

(vi)   he will comply with any notice[22] given to him concerning the production of such records[23].

1   Ie without prejudice to the Landfill Tax Regulations 1996, SI 1996/1527, reg 14H: see note 6.
2   'Claim' means a claim made (irrespective of when it was made) under the Finance Act 1996 s 60, Sch 5 para 14 (see PARA 966) for repayment of an amount paid to the Commissioners for Her Majesty's Revenue and Customs by way of tax which was not tax due to them; and 'claimed' and 'claimant' must be construed accordingly: Landfill Tax Regulations 1996, SI 1996/1527, regs 2(1), 14A (reg 14A added by SI 1998/61). As to the meaning of 'landfill tax' see PARA 901. As to the Commissioners for Her Majesty's Revenue and Customs see PARA 901 note 2.
3   Landfill Tax Regulations 1996, SI 1996/1527, reg 14A (as added: see note 2).
4   Ie for the purpose of the Finance Act 1996 Sch 5 para 14(3): see PARA 966.
5   Landfill Tax Regulations 1996, SI 1996/1527, reg 14B(a) (reg 14B added by SI 1998/61). The Landfill Tax Regulations 1996, SI 1996/1527, reg 14B is without prejudice to reg 14H (see note 6): reg 14B (as so added).
6   Landfill Tax Regulations 1996, SI 1996/1527, reg 14B(b) (as added: see note 5).
     Reimbursement arrangements made by a claimant before 11 February 1998 must not be disregarded for the purposes of the Finance Act 1996 Sch 5 para 14(3) (see PARA 966) if, not later than 11 March 1998:
    (1)   he includes in those arrangements (if they are not already included) the provisions described in the Landfill Tax Regulations 1996, SI 1996/1527, reg 14C (see the text to notes 7–15) (reg 14H(a) (reg 14H added by SI 1998/61)); and
    (2)   he gives the undertakings described in the Landfill Tax Regulations 1996, SI 1996/1527, reg 14G (see the text to notes 16–23) (reg 14H(b) (as so added)).
7   Landfill Tax Regulations 1996, SI 1996/1527, reg 14C(a) (reg 14C added by SI 1998/61).

8 'Relevant amount' means that part (which may be the whole) of the amount of a claim which the claimant has reimbursed or intends to reimburse to consumers: Landfill Tax Regulations 1996, SI 1996/1527, reg 14A (as added: see note 2). The claimant must, without prior demand, make any repayment to the Commissioners that he is required to make by virtue of reg 14C(d), (e) within 14 days of the expiration of the period of 90 days referred to in reg 14C(a): reg 14D (added by SI 1998/61).
9 Landfill Tax Regulations 1996, SI 1996/1527, reg 14C(b) (as added: see note 7).
10 Landfill Tax Regulations 1996, SI 1996/1527, reg 14C(c) (as added: see note 7).
11 Landfill Tax Regulations 1996, SI 1996/1527, reg 14C(d) (as added: see note 7).
12 Landfill Tax Regulations 1996, SI 1996/1527, reg 14C(e) (as added: see note 7).
13 Ie the records described in the Landfill Tax Regulations 1996, SI 1996/1527, reg 14E (see PARA 968).
14 Ie in accordance with the Landfill Tax Regulations 1996, SI 1996/1527, reg 14F (see PARA 969).
15 Landfill Tax Regulations 1996, SI 1996/1527, reg 14C(f) (as added: see note 7).
16 Landfill Tax Regulations 1996, SI 1996/1527, reg 14G(1) (reg 14G added by SI 1998/61).
17 Landfill Tax Regulations 1996, SI 1996/1527, reg 14G(2)(a) (as added: see note 16).
18 Landfill Tax Regulations 1996, SI 1996/1527, reg 14G(2)(b) (as added: see note 16).
19 Landfill Tax Regulations 1996, SI 1996/1527, reg 14G(2)(c) (as added: see note 16).
20 Landfill Tax Regulations 1996, SI 1996/1527, reg 14G(2)(d) (as added: see note 16).
21 Landfill Tax Regulations 1996, SI 1996/1527, reg 14G(2)(e) (as added: see note 16). As to the required records see PARA 968.
22 Ie a notice given in accordance with the Landfill Tax Regulations 1996, SI 1996/1527, reg 14F (see PARA 969).
23 Landfill Tax Regulations 1996, SI 1996/1527, reg 14G(2)(f) (as added: see note 16).

968. Records. A claimant for repayment of tax[1] must keep records of the following matters:

(1) the names and addresses of those consumers[2] whom he has reimbursed or whom he intends to reimburse[3];

(2) the total amount reimbursed to each such consumer[4];

(3) the amount of interest included in each total amount reimbursed to each consumer[5];

(4) the date that each reimbursement is made[6].

1 See PARA 967 note 2.
2 See PARA 967.
3 Landfill Tax Regulations 1996, SI 1996/1527, reg 14E(a) (reg 14E added by SI 1998/61).
4 Landfill Tax Regulations 1996, SI 1996/1527, reg 14E(b) (as added: see note 3).
5 Landfill Tax Regulations 1996, SI 1996/1527, reg 14E(c) (as added: see note 3).
6 Landfill Tax Regulations 1996, SI 1996/1527, reg 14E(d) (as added: see note 3).

969. Production of records. Where a claimant for repayment of tax[1] is given notice to that effect, he must, in accordance with such notice produce to the Commissioners for Her Majesty's Revenue and Customs[2], or to an officer of theirs, the records that he is required to keep[3]. A notice so given must:

(1) be in writing[4];

(2) state the place and time at which, and the date on which, the records are to be produced[5]; and

(3) be signed and dated by the Commissioners, or by an officer of theirs[6],

and may be given before or after, or both before and after the Commissioners have paid the relevant amount[7] to the claimant[8].

1 See PARA 967 note 2.
2 As to the Commissioners for Her Majesty's Revenue and Customs see PARA 901 note 2.
3 Landfill Tax Regulations 1996, SI 1996/1527, reg 14F(1) (reg 14F added by SI 1998/61). As to the records which must be kept see the Landfill Tax Regulations 1996, SI 1996/1527, reg 14E; and PARA 968.
4 Landfill Tax Regulations 1996, SI 1996/1527, reg 14F(2)(a) (as added: see note 3).
5 Landfill Tax Regulations 1996, SI 1996/1527, reg 14F(2)(b) (as added: see note 3).

6   Landfill Tax Regulations 1996, SI 1996/1527, reg 14F(2)(c) (as added: see note 3).
7   As to the meaning of 'relevant amount' see PARA 967 note 8.
8   Landfill Tax Regulations 1996, SI 1996/1527, reg 14F(2) (as added: see note 3).

9. PROVISION OF INFORMATION AND INFORMATION AREAS

(1) PROVISION OF INFORMATION

970. Duty to give information. Every person who is concerned (in whatever capacity) with any landfill disposal[1] must furnish to the Commissioners for Her Majesty's Revenue and Customs[2] such information relating to the disposal as they may reasonably require[3]. Such information must be furnished within such time and in such form as the Commissioners may reasonably require[4].

1   As to the meaning of 'landfill disposal' see PARA 902 note 4.
2   As to the Commissioners see PARA 901 note 2.
3   Finance Act 1996 s 60, Sch 5 para 1(1).
4   Finance Act 1996 Sch 5 para 1(2). As to the penalty for failure to provide information as required see PARA 990. As from 1 April 2010, the Finance Act 1996 Sch 5 para 1 is repealed: Finance Act 2009, Section 96 and Schedule 48 (Appointed Day, Savings and Consequential Amendments) Order 2009, SI 2009/3054, art 3, Schedule para 7(a). See PARA 985 for the replacement cross-tax information powers under the Finance Act 2008 s 113, Sch 36.

971. Power to make regulations relating to material at landfill sites. Regulations may make provision about giving the Commissioners for Her Majesty's Revenue and Customs[1] information relating to material[2] at a landfill site[3] or a part of a landfill site[4]. Such regulations may require a person to give information[5]. They may require a person, or authorise an officer of Revenue and Customs to require a person, to designate a part of a landfill site (an 'information area') and may require material, or prescribed descriptions of material, to be deposited in an information area[6]. Such regulations may make provision about information relating to what is done with material[7].

1   As to the Commissioners see PARA 901 note 2.
2   As to the meaning of 'material' see PARA 902 note 3.
3   As to the meaning of 'landfill site' see PARA 902 note 5.
4   Finance Act 1996 s 60, Sch 5 para 1A(1) (Sch 5 para 1A added by the Finance Act 2009 s 119, Sch 60 para 7). The Finance Act 1996 Sch 5 para 1A(2)–(4) (see the text to notes 5 to 7) does not prejudice the generality of Sch 5 para 1A(1): Sch 5 para 1A(5) (as so added). As to the regulations made under Sch 5 para 1A see the Landfill Tax Regulations 1996, SI 1996/1527, reg 16A; and PARA 972.
5   Finance Act 1996 Sch 5 para 1A(2) (as added: see note 4).
6   Finance Act 1996 Sch 5 para 1A(3) (as added: see note 4).
7   Finance Act 1996 Sch 5 para 1A(4) (as added: see note 4). As to the penalty for failure to comply with regulations see PARA 991.

(2) INFORMATION AREAS

972. Designation of, and duty to deposit material in, information areas. An officer of Revenue and Customs is authorised to require a person to designate a part of a landfill site[1] (an 'information area'), and a person must designate an information area if so required[2].

Where material[3] at a landfill site is not going to be disposed of as waste[4] and the Commissioners for Her Majesty's Revenue and Customs[5] consider, or an officer of theirs considers, there to be a risk to the revenue, the material must be deposited in an information area[6]. In such a case, a registrable person[7] must maintain a record in relation to the information of the following information, and give this information to the Commissioners, or an officer, if requested:

(1)   the weight and description of all material deposited there:
(2)   the intended destination or use of all such material and, where any material has been removed or used, the actual destination or use of that material; and
(3)   the weight and description of any such material sorted or removed[8].

A designation ceases to have effect if a notice in writing to that effect is given to a registrable person by the Commissioners or by an officer of Revenue and Customs[9].

1   As to the meaning of 'landfill site' see PARA 902 note 5; definition applied by virtue of the Landfill Tax Regulations 1996, SI 1996/1527, reg 2(1).
2   Landfill Tax Regulations 1996, SI 1996/1527, reg 16A(1) (added by SI 2009/1930).
3   As to the meaning of 'material' see PARA 902 note 3.
4   As to the disposal of material as waste see PARA 902 note 3.
5   As to the Commissioners see PARA 901 note 2.
6   Landfill Tax Regulations 1996, SI 1996/1527, reg 16A(2)(a) (as added: see note 2).
7   As to the meaning of 'registrable person' see PARA 958 note 1; definition applied by virtue of the Landfill Tax Regulations 1996, SI 1996/1527, reg 2(1).
8   Landfill Tax Regulations 1996, SI 1996/1527, reg 16A(2)(b), (4) (as added: see note 2).
9   Landfill Tax Regulations 1996, SI 1996/1527, reg 16A(3) (as added: see note 2).

(3) SITE RESTORATION

973.   Information relating to site restoration.   Before commencing restoration of all or part of a landfill site[1], the operator of the site must notify the Commissioners for Her Majesty's Revenue and Customs[2] in writing that the restoration[3] is to commence and provide such other written information as the Commissioners may require generally or in the particular case[4].

1   As to the meaning of 'landfill site' see PARA 902 note 5.
2   As to the Commissioners see PARA 901 note 2.
3   'Restoration' means work, other than capping waste, which is required by a relevant instrument to be carried out to restore a landfill site to use on completion of waste disposal operations: Finance Act 1996 s 60, Sch 5 para 1B(2) (Sch 5 para 1B added by the Finance Act 2009 s 119, Sch 60 para 11). The following are 'relevant instruments': a planning consent; a waste management licence; and a permit authorising the disposal of waste on or in land: Landfill Tax Regulations 1996, SI 1996/1527, Sch 5 para 1B(3) (as so added). As to planning consents generally see TOWN AND COUNTRY PLANNING; and as to waste management licences see PROTECTION OF ENVIRONMENT AND PUBLIC HEALTH vol 38 (2006 Reissue) PARA 273 et seq.
4   Finance Act 1996 Sch 5 para 1B(1) (as added: see note 3).

(4) PUBLICATION AND DISCLOSURE OF INFORMATION

974.   Disclosure of information.   Notwithstanding any obligation not to disclose information that would otherwise apply, the Commissioners for Her Majesty's Revenue and Customs[1] may disclose information to:
(1)   the Secretary of State[2];
(2)   the Environment Agency[3];
(3)   the Scottish Environment Protection Agency[4];
(4)   the Department of the Environment for Northern Ireland[5];
(5)   a district council in Northern Ireland[6]; or
(6)   an authorised officer[7] of any person (a 'principal') mentioned in heads (1) to (5) above[8],
for the purpose of assisting the principal concerned in the performance of the principal's duties[9]; and any person mentioned in heads (1) to (6) above may disclose information to the Commissioners or to an authorised officer of the

Commissioners for the purpose of assisting the Commissioners in the performance of duties in relation to landfill tax[10]. Information that has been disclosed to a person by virtue of this provision must not be disclosed by him except:

(a) to another person to whom (instead of him) disclosure could by virtue of this provision have been made[11]; or

(b) for the purpose of any proceedings connected with the operation of any provision of, or made under, any enactment in relation to the environment or to tax[12].

No charge may be made for a disclosure made by virtue of these provisions[13].

1 As to the Commissioners for Her Majesty's Revenue and Customs see PARA 901 note 2.
2 Finance Act 1996 s 60, Sch 5 para 35(1)(a). In any enactment, 'Secretary of State' means one of Her Majesty's principal Secretaries of State: see the Interpretation Act 1978 s 5, Sch 1. The office of Secretary of State is a unified office, and in law each Secretary of State is generally capable of performing the functions of all or any of them: see CONSTITUTIONAL LAW AND HUMAN RIGHTS vol 8(2) (Reissue) PARA 355.
3 Finance Act 1996 Sch 5 para 35(1)(b). As to the meaning of 'Environment Agency' see PARA 912 note 10. As to the Environment Agency see PROTECTION OF ENVIRONMENT AND PUBLIC HEALTH vol 38 (2006 Reissue) PARA 52 et seq.
4 Finance Act 1996 Sch 5 para 35(1)(c). As to the meaning of 'Scottish Environment Protection Agency' see PARA 912 note 11.
5 Finance Act 1996 Sch 5 para 35(1)(d).
6 Finance Act 1996 Sch 5 para 35(1)(e).
7 References in the Finance Act 1996 Sch 5 para 35(1)–(3) to an authorised officer of any person (the 'principal') are references to any person who has been designated by the principal as a person to and by whom information may be disclosed by virtue of Sch 5 para 35: Sch 5 para 35(4). The Secretary of State must notify the Commissioners in writing of the name of any person designated by the Secretary of State under Sch 5 para 35(4): Sch 5 para 35(5).
8 Finance Act 1996 Sch 5 para 35(1)(f).
9 Finance Act 1996 Sch 5 para 35(1).
10 Finance Act 1996 Sch 5 para 35(2).
11 Finance Act 1996 Sch 5 para 35(3)(a).
12 Finance Act 1996 Sch 5 para 35(3)(b).
13 Finance Act 1996 Sch 5 para 35(6).

975. Publication of information. The Commissioners for Her Majesty's Revenue and Customs[1] may publish, by such means as they think fit, information which: (1) is derived from the landfill tax register[2]; and (2) falls within any of the descriptions set out below[3], namely:

(a) the names of registered persons[4];

(b) the addresses of any sites or other premises at which they carry on business[5];

(c) the registration numbers assigned to them in the register[6];

(d) the fact (where it is the case) that the registered person is a body corporate which is treated[7] as a member of a group[8];

(e) the names of the other bodies corporate so treated as members of the group[9];

(f) the addresses of any sites or other premises at which those other bodies carry on business[10].

Information may be published in accordance with this provision notwithstanding any obligation not to disclose the information that would otherwise apply[11].

1 As to the Commissioners for Her Majesty's Revenue and Customs see PARA 901 note 2.
2 Finance Act 1996 s 60, Sch 5 para 36(1)(a).
3 Finance Act 1996 Sch 5 para 36(1)(b).

4 Finance Act 1996 Sch 5 para 36(2)(a). As to the meaning of 'registered person' see PARA 922 note 13.
5 Finance Act 1996 Sch 5 para 36(2)(b).
6 Finance Act 1996 Sch 5 para 36(2)(c).
7 Ie under the Finance Act 1996 s 59: see PARA 925.
8 Finance Act 1996 Sch 5 para 36(2)(d).
9 Finance Act 1996 Sch 5 para 36(2)(e).
10 Finance Act 1996 Sch 5 para 36(2)(f).
11 Finance Act 1996 Sch 5 para 36(3).

976. Evidence by certificate etc. A certificate of the Commissioners for Her Majesty's Revenue and Customs[1]:

(1)   that a person was or was not at any time registered[2]; or
(2)   that any return required by regulations[3] has not been made or had not been made at any time[4];

is sufficient evidence of that fact until the contrary is proved[5].

A photograph of any document furnished to the Commissioners for the purposes of the landfill tax provisions[6] and certified by them to be such a photograph is admissible in any proceedings, whether civil or criminal, to the same extent as the document itself[7]. Any document purporting to be such a certificate is be taken to be such a certificate until the contrary is proved[8].

1   As to the Commissioners for Her Majesty's Revenue and Customs see PARA 901 note 2.
2   Finance Act 1996 s 60, Sch 5 para 37(1)(a). The reference to registration in the text is a reference to registration under s 47: see PARA 920.
3   Ie regulations made under the Finance Act 1996 s 49: see PARA 935.
4   Finance Act 1996 Sch 5 para 37(1)(b).
5   Finance Act 1996 Sch 5 para 37(1) (amended by the Finance Act 2008 s 138(2), Sch 44 para 7). As to certificates of debt see the Commissioners for Revenue and Customs Act 2005 s 25A; and INCOME TAXATION.
6   Ie the Finance Act 1996 Pt III (ss 39–71): see PARA 901 note 1.
7   Finance Act 1996 Sch 5 para 37(2).
8   Finance Act 1996 Sch 5 para 37(3).

10. OTHER REVENUE AND CUSTOMS POWERS

977. Power to make orders and regulations. The power to make an order under the statutory provisions relating to landfill tax provisions[1] is generally exercisable by the Treasury[2]. Any power to make regulations under the landfill tax provisions is exercisable by the Commissioners for Her Majesty's Revenue and Customs[3]. Any such power to make an order or regulations is exercisable by statutory instrument[4].

Certain orders must be laid before the House of Commons; and unless such an order is approved by that House before the expiration of a period of 28 days beginning with the date on which it was made it ceases to have effect on the expiration of that period, but without prejudice to anything previously done under the order or to the making of a new order[5]. A statutory instrument containing any other order or regulations is subject to annulment in pursuance of a resolution of the House of Commons[6].

Any power to make an order or regulations under the landfill tax provisions may be exercised as regards prescribed[7] cases or descriptions of case[8], and may be exercised differently in relation to different cases or descriptions of case[9].

An order or regulations may include such supplementary, incidental, consequential or transitional provisions as appear to the Treasury or the Commissioners (as the case may be) to be necessary or expedient[10].

Though not part of the law relating to landfill tax, the Commissioners have published information notes for the guidance of landfill site operators[11].

1 Ie the Finance Act 1996 Pt III (ss 39–71): see PARA 901 note 1.
2 See the Finance Act 1996 s 71(1). As to the Treasury see CONSTITUTIONAL LAW AND HUMAN RIGHTS vol 8(2) (Reissue) PARAS 512–517.
3 Finance Act 1996 s 71(2). As to the Commissioners for Her Majesty's Revenue and Customs see PARA 901 note 2.
4 Finance Act 1996 s 71(3).
5 Finance Act 1996 s 71(4). In reckoning any such period no account may be taken of any time during which Parliament is dissolved or prorogued or during which the House of Commons is adjourned for more than four days: s 71(5).
    Section 71(4) applies to:
    (1) an order under s 42(3) (see PARA 906) providing for material which would otherwise be qualifying material not to be qualifying material (s 71(7)(a));
    (2) an order under s 46 (see PARA 917) which produces the result that a disposal which would otherwise not be a taxable disposal is a taxable disposal (s 71(7)(b));
    (3) an order under s 63(5) (see PARA 905) other than one which provides only that an earlier order under s 63(5) is not to apply to material (s 71(7)(c));
    (4) an order under s 65A (see PARA 903) which produces the result that a landfill site activity which would not otherwise be prescribed for the purposes of s 65A is so prescribed (s 71(7)(ca) (added by the Finance Act 2009 s 119, Sch 60 para 3));
    (5) an order under the Finance Act 1996 s 65A (see PARA 903) which amends Pt III or any enactment contained in an Act (s 71(7)(cb) (added by the Finance Act 2009 Sch 60 para 3));
    (6) an order under the Finance Act 1996 s 65(5) (see PARA 902) providing for anything which would otherwise not be a disposal of material by way of landfill to be such a disposal (s 71(7)(d)).
    As to the meaning of 'material' see PARA 902 note 3. As to the meaning of 'qualifying material' see PARA 906. As to the meaning of 'taxable disposal' see PARA 902. As to the meaning of 'disposal by way of landfill' see PARA 902 note 4.
6 Finance Act 1996 s 71(6).
7 'Prescribed' means prescribed by an order or regulations under the Finance Act 1996 Pt III: s 70(1).
8 Finance Act 1996 s 71(8)(a).
9 Finance Act 1996 s 71(8)(b).

10   Finance Act 1996 s 71(9). No specific provision of Pt III about an order or regulations is to prejudice the generality of s 71(8), (9): s 71(10).

11   The information notes were originally announced in *Business Brief* 18/96, 27 August 1996. See now Notice LFT1 *A General Guide to Landfill Tax* and Notice LFT2 *Reclamation of Contaminated Land*.

978. Documents. Every person who is concerned (in whatever capacity) with any landfill disposal[1] must upon demand made by an authorised person[2] produce or cause to be produced for inspection by that person any documents relating to the disposal[3]. Where an authorised person has power so to require the production of any documents from any person, he has the like power to require production of the documents concerned from any other person who appears to the authorised person to be in possession of them; but where any such other person claims a lien on any document produced by him, the production is without prejudice to the lien[4]. Such documents are to be produced at such time and place as the authorised person may reasonably require[5].

An authorised person may take copies of, or make extracts from, any document so produced[6]. If it appears to him to be necessary to do so, an authorised person may, at a reasonable time and for a reasonable period, remove any document so produced and must, on request, provide a receipt for it; and where a lien is claimed on a document the removal of the document is not to be regarded as breaking the lien[7]. Where a document so removed by an authorised person is reasonably required for any purpose he must, as soon as practicable, provide a copy of the document, free of charge, to the person by whom it was produced or caused to be produced[8].

Where any documents removed under the above powers are lost or damaged the Commissioners for Her Majesty's Revenue and Customs are liable to compensate their owner for any expenses reasonably incurred by him in replacing or repairing the documents[9].

1   As to the meaning of 'landfill disposal' see PARA 902 note 4.
2   As to the meaning of 'authorised person' see PARA 907 note 9.
3   Finance Act 1996 s 60, Sch 5 para 3(1). As from 1 April 2010, the Finance Act 1996 Sch 5 para 3 is repealed: Finance Act 2009, Section 96 and Schedule 48 (Appointed Day, Savings and Consequential Amendments) Order 2009, SI 2009/3054, art 3, Schedule para 7(a). See PARA 985 for the replacement cross-tax information powers under the Finance Act 2008 s 113, Sch 36.
4   Finance Act 1996 Sch 5 para 3(2). As to lien generally see LIEN.
5   Finance Act 1996 Sch 5 para 3(3).
6   Finance Act 1996 Sch 5 para 3(4).
7   Finance Act 1996 Sch 5 para 3(5).
8   Finance Act 1996 Sch 5 para 3(6).
9   Finance Act 1996 Sch 5 para 3(7).

979. Powers of entry and inspection. For the purpose of exercising any powers under the landfill tax provisions[1] an authorised person[2] may at any reasonable time enter and inspect premises used in connection with the carrying on of a business[3].

1   Ie the Finance Act 1996 Pt III (ss 39–71): see PARA 901 note 1.
2   As to the meaning of 'authorised person' see PARA 907 note 9.
3   Finance Act 1996 s 60, Sch 5 para 4. As from 1 April 2010, the Finance Act 1996 Sch 5 para 4 is repealed: Finance Act 2009, Section 96 and Schedule 48 (Appointed Day, Savings and Consequential Amendments) Order 2009, SI 2009/3054, art 3, Schedule para 7(a). See PARA 985 for the replacement cross-tax inspection powers under the Finance Act 2008 s 113, Sch 36.

980. Order for access to recorded information. Where, on an application by an authorised person[1], a justice of the peace is satisfied that there are reasonable grounds for believing[2]:

(1) that an offence in connection with landfill tax[3] is being, has been or is about to be committed[4]; and

(2) that any recorded information (including any document of any nature whatsoever) which may be required as evidence for the purpose of any proceedings in respect of such an offence is in the possession of any person[5],

he may make an order for access[6].

Such an access order is an order that the person who appears to the justice to be in possession of the recorded information to which the application relates must[7]:

(a) give an authorised person access to it[8]; and

(b) permit an authorised person to remove and take away any of it which he reasonably considers necessary[9],

not later than the end of the period of seven days beginning with the date of the order or the end of such longer period as the order may specify[10].

Where the recorded information consists of information stored in electronic format, such an order has effect as an order to produce the information in a form in which it is visible and legible or from which it can readily be produced in a visible and legible form and, if the authorised person wishes to remove it, in a form in which it can be removed[11].

1 As to the meaning of 'authorised person' see PARA 907 note 9.
2 Finance Act 1996 s 60, Sch 5 para 7(1).
3 As to the meaning of 'landfill tax' see PARA 901.
4 Finance Act 1996 Sch 5 para 7(1)(a).
5 Finance Act 1996 Sch 5 para 7(1)(b).
6 Finance Act 1996 Sch 5 para 7(1). Schedule 5 para 7 is without prejudice to Sch 5 paras 3, 4 (production of documents and powers of entry: see PARAS 978–979) or Sch 5 para 5 (repealed): Sch 5 para 7(5).
7 Finance Act 1996 Sch 5 para 7(2).
8 Finance Act 1996 Sch 5 para 7(2)(a). The reference to giving an authorised person access to the recorded information to which the application relates includes a reference to permitting the authorised person to take copies of it or to make extracts from it: Sch 5 para 7(3).
9 Finance Act 1996 Sch 5 para 7(2)(b).
10 Finance Act 1996 Sch 5 para 7(2).
11 Finance Act 1996 Sch 5 para 7(4) (amended by the Criminal Justice and Police Act 2001 s 70, Sch 2 Pt 2 para 13(1)(a), (b), (2)(h)).

981. Removal of documents etc. An authorised person[1] who removes anything in the exercise of a power of entry or an order for access[2] must, if so requested by a person showing himself: (1) to be the occupier of premises from which it was removed; or (2) to have had custody or control of it immediately before the removal, provide that person with a record of what he removed[3]. The authorised person must provide the record within a reasonable time from the making of the request for it[4].

If a request for permission to be allowed access to anything which: (a) has been removed by an authorised person; and (b) is retained by the Commissioners for Her Majesty's Revenue and Customs[5] for the purposes of investigating an offence, is made to the officer in overall charge[6] of the investigation by a person who had custody or control of the thing immediately before it was so removed or by someone acting on behalf of such a person, the officer must allow the person who made the request access to it under the supervision of an authorised person[7].

If a request for a photograph or copy of any such thing is made to the officer in overall charge of the investigation by a person who had custody or control of the thing immediately before it was so removed, or by someone acting on behalf of such a person, the officer must:

(i)   allow the person who made the request access to it under the supervision of an authorised person for the purpose of photographing it or copying it[8]; or

(ii)   photograph or copy it, or cause it to be photographed or copied[9].

Where anything is photographed or copied under head (ii) above the officer must supply the photograph or copy, or cause it to be supplied, to the person who made the request[10]. The photograph or copy must be supplied within a reasonable time of the request[11].

There is no duty under these provisions to allow access to, or to supply a photograph or copy of, anything if the officer in overall charge of the investigation for the purposes of which it was removed has reasonable grounds for believing that to do so would prejudice:

(A)   that investigation[12];

(B)   the investigation of an offence other than the offence for the purposes of the investigation of which the thing was removed[13]; or

(C)   any criminal proceedings which may be brought as a result of the investigation of which he is in charge or any such investigation as is mentioned in head (B) above[14].

Where, on an application[15], the appropriate judicial authority[16] is satisfied that a person has failed to comply with such imposed requirements, the authority may order that person to comply with the requirement within such time and in such manner as may be specified in the order[17].

1   As to the meaning of 'authorised person' see PARA 907 note 9.
2   Ie by or under the Finance Act 1996 s 60, Sch 5 para 5 (repealed) or Sch 5 para 7 (see PARA 980).
3   Finance Act 1996 Sch 5 para 8(1).
4   Finance Act 1996 Sch 5 para 8(2).
5   As to the Commissioners for Her Majesty's Revenue and Customs see PARA 901 note 2.
6   Any reference in the Finance Act 1996 Sch 5 para 8 to the officer in overall charge of the investigation is a reference to the person whose name and address are indorsed on the warrant concerned as being the officer so in charge: Sch 5 para 8(8).
7   Finance Act 1996 Sch 5 para 8(3).
8   Finance Act 1996 Sch 5 para 8(4)(a).
9   Finance Act 1996 Sch 5 para 8(4)(b).
10   Finance Act 1996 Sch 5 para 8(5).
11   Finance Act 1996 Sch 5 para 8(6).
12   Finance Act 1996 Sch 5 para 8(7)(a).
13   Finance Act 1996 Sch 5 para 8(7)(b).
14   Finance Act 1996 Sch 5 para 8(7)(c).
15   Such an application is to be made:
        (1)   in the case of a failure to comply with any of the requirements imposed by Sch 5 para 8(1), (2) (see the text and notes 1–4), by the occupier of the premises from which the thing in question was removed or by the person who had custody or control of it immediately before it was so removed (Sch 5 para 9(2)(a)); and
        (2)   in any other case, by the person who had such custody or control (Sch 5 para 9(2)(b)).
16   'Appropriate judicial authority' means a magistrates' court: Finance Act 1996 Sch 5 para 9(3)(a).
17   Finance Act 1996 Sch 5 para 9(1). An application for an order under Sch 5 para 9 is made by way of complaint: Sch 5 para 9(4). See MAGISTRATES vol 29(2) (Reissue) PARAS 681–686.

982. Power to take samples. If it appears to him necessary for the protection of the revenue against mistake or fraud, an authorised person[1] may at any time take, from material[2] which he has reasonable cause to believe is intended to be, is being, or has been disposed of as waste by way of landfill[3], such samples as he may require with a view to determining how the material ought to be or to have been treated for the purposes of landfill tax[4]. Any such sample taken must be disposed of in such manner as the Commissioners for Her Majesty's Revenue and Customs[5] may direct[6].

1 As to the meaning of 'authorised person' see PARA 907 note 9.
2 As to the meaning of 'material' see PARA 902 note 3.
3 As to the meaning of 'a disposal of material by way of landfill' see PARA 902 note 4.
4 Finance Act 1996 s 60, Sch 5 para 10(1). As to the meaning of 'landfill tax' see PARA 901.
5 As to the Commissioners for Her Majesty's Revenue and Customs see PARA 901 note 2.
6 Finance Act 1996 Sch 5 para 10(2).

983. Designation, direction or approval. Any designation, direction or approval by the Commissioners for Her Majesty's Revenue and Customs[1] under or for the purposes of the Landfill Tax Regulations 1996[2] is to be made or given by a notice in writing[3].

1 As to the Commissioners for Her Majesty's Revenue and Customs see PARA 901 note 2.
2 Ie the Landfill Tax Regulations 1996, SI 1996/1527.
3 Landfill Tax Regulations 1996, SI 1996/1527, reg 3.

984. Service of notices etc. Any notice, notification or requirement to be served on, given to or made of any person for the purposes of the landfill tax provisions[1] may be served, given or made by sending it by post in a letter addressed to that person at his last or usual residence or place of business[2].

The following provisions apply to directions, specifications and conditions which the Commissioners for Her Majesty's Revenue and Customs[3] or an authorised person[4] may give or impose[5]. A direction, specification or condition given or imposed by the Commissioners may be withdrawn or varied by them[6]. A direction, specification or condition given or imposed by an authorised person may be withdrawn or varied by him or by another authorised person[7]. No direction, specification or condition has effect as regards any person it is intended to affect unless a notice containing it is served on him[8], or other reasonable steps are taken with a view to bringing it to his attention[9].

No withdrawal or variation of a direction, specification or condition has effect as regards any person the withdrawal or variation is intended to affect unless a notice containing the withdrawal or variation is served on him[10], or other reasonable steps are taken with a view to bringing the withdrawal or variation to his attention[11].

1 Ie the Finance Act 1996 Pt III (ss 39–71): see PARA 901 note 1.
2 Finance Act 1996 s 60, Sch 5 para 38.
3 As to the Commissioners for Her Majesty's Revenue and Customs see PARA 901 note 2.
4 As to the meaning of 'authorised person' see PARA 907 note 9.
5 Ie under any provision of the Finance Act 1996 Sch 5 Pt VII paras 31–47: Sch 5 para 39(1).
6 Finance Act 1996 Sch 5 para 39(2).
7 Finance Act 1996 Sch 5 para 39(3).
8 Finance Act 1996 Sch 5 para 39(4)(a).
9 Finance Act 1996 Sch 5 para 39(4)(b).
10 Finance Act 1996 Sch 5 para 39(5)(a).
11 Finance Act 1996 Sch 5 para 39(5)(b).

985. Other powers. The application of provisions of the Police and Criminal Evidence Act 1984 to investigations conducted by officers of Revenue and Customs is discussed elsewhere in this work[1].

Her Majesty's Revenue and Customs' cross-tax powers to obtain information and to inspect premises are also discussed elsewhere in this work[2].

1   See CRIMINAL LAW, EVIDENCE AND PROCEDURE vol 11(2) (2006 Reissue) PARA 856.
2   See the Finance Act 2008 s 113, Sch 36; and INCOME TAXATION. The powers are extended to apply to landfill tax as from 1 April 2010: see the Finance Act 2009 s 96, Sch 48; and the Finance Act 2009, Section 96 and Schedule 48 (Appointed Day, Savings and Consequential Amendments) Order 2009, SI 2009/3054.

11. OFFENCES AND PENALTIES

(1) CRIMINAL OFFENCES AND PENALTIES

986. Criminal offences. A person is guilty of an offence if:

(1) being a registrable person[1], he is knowingly concerned in, or in the taking of steps with a view to, the fraudulent evasion of landfill tax[2] by him or another registrable person[3]; or

(2) not being a registrable person, he is knowingly concerned in, or in the taking of steps with a view to, the fraudulent evasion of tax by a registrable person[4].

A person guilty of such an offence[5] is liable on summary conviction to a penalty of the statutory maximum or of three times the amount of the tax, whichever is the greater, or to imprisonment for a term not exceeding six months or to both[6], and on conviction on indictment to a penalty of any amount or to imprisonment for a term not exceeding seven years or to both[7].

A person is guilty of an offence if with the requisite intent:

(a) he produces, furnishes or sends, or causes to be produced, furnished or sent, for the purposes of the landfill tax provisions[8] any document which is false in a material particular[9]; or

(b) he otherwise makes use for those purposes of such a document[10].

The requisite intent is intent to deceive or to secure that a machine will respond to the document as if it were a true document[11].

A person is guilty of an offence if in furnishing any information he makes a statement which he knows to be false in a material particular or recklessly makes a statement which is false in a material particular[12].

A person guilty of an offence under either of the above provisions[13] is liable on summary conviction to a penalty of the statutory maximum (or, in certain cases[14], to the alternative penalty there specified if it is greater) or to imprisonment for a term not exceeding six months or to both[15], and on conviction on indictment to a penalty of any amount or to imprisonment for a term not exceeding seven years or to both[16]. Where the document concerned is a return or the information concerned is contained in or otherwise relevant to a return, the alternative penalty is a penalty equal to three times the aggregate of the amount (if any) falsely claimed by way of credit and the amount (if any) by which the gross amount of tax was understated[17].

A person is guilty of an offence if his conduct during any specified period must have involved the commission by him of one or more offences under the preceding provisions; and the preceding provisions apply whether or not the particulars of that offence or those offences are known[18]. A person guilty of an offence under this provision is liable on summary conviction to a penalty of the statutory maximum (or, if greater, three times the amount of any tax that was or was intended to be evaded by his conduct) or to imprisonment for a term not exceeding six months or to both, and on conviction on indictment to a penalty of any amount or to imprisonment for a term not exceeding seven years or to both[19].

A person is guilty of an offence if he enters into a taxable landfill contract[20], or he makes arrangements for other persons to enter into such a contract, with reason to believe that tax in respect of the disposal concerned will be evaded[21]. A person guilty of an offence under this provision is liable on summary conviction to a penalty of level 5 on the standard scale or three times the amount of the tax, whichever is the greater[22].

A person is guilty of an offence if he carries out taxable activities[23] without giving security (or further security) he has been required[24] to give[25]. A person guilty of an offence under this provision is liable on summary conviction to a penalty of level 5 on the standard scale[26].

1　As to the meaning of 'registrable person' see PARA 958 note 1.
2　As to the meaning of 'landfill tax' see PARA 901. Any reference in the Finance Act 1996 s 60, Sch 5 para 15(1) to the evasion of landfill tax includes a reference to the obtaining of a payment under the provisions as to credits (see PARA 938 et seq): see Sch 5 para 15(2).
3　Finance Act 1996 Sch 5 para 15(1)(a).
4　Finance Act 1996 Sch 5 para 15(1)(b).
5　Ie an offence under the Finance Act 1996 Sch 5 para 15(1).
6　Finance Act 1996 Sch 5 para 16(1)(a). The reference in Sch 5 para 16(1) to the amount of the tax is to be construed, in relation to tax itself or a payment falling within Sch 5 para 15(2), as a reference to the aggregate of: (1) the amount (if any) falsely claimed by way of credit (Sch 5 para 16(2)(a)); and (2) the amount (if any) by which the gross amount of tax was falsely understated (Sch 5 para 16(2)(b)). 'Credit' means credit for which provision is made by regulations under s 51 (see PARA 938): Sch 5 para 16(8)(a). 'Gross amount of tax' means the total amount of tax due before taking into account any deduction for which provision is made by the credit regulations (see PARA 938 et seq): Sch 5 para 16(8)(b). As to the statutory maximum see SENTENCING AND DISPOSITION OF OFFENDERS vol 92 (2010) PARA 140.
7　Finance Act 1996 Sch 5 para 16(1)(b).
8　Finance Act 1996 Sch 5 para 15(3)(a).
9　Ie the Finance Act 1996 Pt III (ss 39–71): see PARA 901 note 1.
10　Finance Act 1996 Sch 5 para 15(3)(b).
11　Finance Act 1996 Sch 5 para 15(3).
12　Finance Act 1996 Sch 5 para 15(4).
13　Ie the Finance Act 1996 Sch 5 para 15(3) or Sch 5 para 15(4).
14　Ie where the Finance Act 1996 Sch 5 para 16(4) applies. See the text to note 17.
15　Finance Act 1996 Sch 5 para 16(3)(a).
16　Finance Act 1996 Sch 5 para 16(3)(b).
17　Finance Act 1996 Sch 5 para 16(4).
18　Finance Act 1996 Sch 5 para 15(5).
19　Finance Act 1996 Sch 5 para 16(5). Schedule 5 paras 15(2), 16(2) apply for the purposes of Sch 5 para 16(5) as they apply respectively for the purposes of Sch 5 paras 15(1), 16(1): Sch 5 para 16(5).
20　A 'taxable landfill contract' is a contract under which there is to be a taxable disposal: Finance Act 1996 Sch 5 para 15(8). As to the meaning of 'taxable disposal' see PARA 902.
21　Finance Act 1996 Sch 5 para 15(6).
22　Finance Act 1996 Sch 5 para 16(6). As to the standard scale see SENTENCING AND DISPOSITION OF OFFENDERS vol 92 (2010) PARA 142.
23　As to the meaning of 'taxable activity' see PARA 920 note 1.
24　Ie under the Finance Act 1996 Sch 5 para 31: see PARA 1002.
25　Finance Act 1996 Sch 5 para 15(7).
26　Finance Act 1996 Sch 5 para 16(7). The Customs and Excise Management Act 1979 ss 145–155 (proceedings for offences, mitigation of penalties and certain other matters) apply in relation to offences under the Finance Act 1996 Sch 5 para 15 and penalties imposed under Sch 5 para 16 as they apply in relation to offences and penalties under the Customs and Excise Acts as defined in the Customs and Excise Management Act 1979 (see CUSTOMS AND EXCISE vol 12(3) (2007 Reissue) PARA 1188 et seq): Finance Act 1996 Sch 5 para 17.

(2) CIVIL EVASION PENALTIES

987. Conduct involving dishonesty. Where for the purpose of evading landfill tax[1], a registrable person[2] does any act or omits to take any action and his conduct[3] involves dishonesty (whether or not it is such as to give rise to criminal liability), he is liable to a penalty equal to the amount of tax evaded, or (as the case may be) sought to be evaded[4], by his conduct[5]. Where, by reason of conduct falling within this provision, a person is convicted of an offence[6] that conduct does not also give rise to liability to a penalty under this provision[7].

Statements made or documents produced by or on behalf of a person are not inadmissible in criminal proceedings in respect of any tax offence, or in any proceedings for the recovery of tax[8], by reason only that it has been drawn to his attention:

(1)   that, in relation to tax, the Commissioners for Her Majesty's Revenue and Customs[9] may assess an amount due by way of a civil penalty instead of instituting criminal proceedings and, though no undertaking can be given as to whether the Commissioners will make such an assessment in the case of any person, it is their practice to be influenced by the fact that a person has made a full confession of any dishonest conduct to which he has been a party and has given full facilities for investigation[10]; and

(2)   that the Commissioners or, on appeal, an appeal tribunal[11] have power[12] to reduce a penalty under this provision[13],

and that he was or may have been induced thereby to make the statements or produce the documents[14].

1   As to the meaning of 'landfill tax' see PARA 901. The reference in the Finance Act 1996 s 60, Sch 5 para 18(1)(a) to evading tax includes a reference to obtaining a payment under regulations as to credits (see PARA 938 et seq) in circumstances where the person concerned is not entitled to the sum: Sch 5 para 18(2).
2   As to the meaning of 'registrable person' see PARA 958 note 1.
3   'Conduct' includes any act, omission or statement: Finance Act 1996 s 70(1).
4   The reference in the Finance Act 1996 Sch 5 para 18(1) to the amount of tax evaded or sought to be evaded is a reference to the aggregate of: (1) the amount (if any) falsely claimed by way of credit (Sch 5 para 18(3)(a)); and (2) the amount (if any) by which the gross amount of tax was falsely understated (Sch 5 para 18(3)(b)).
        'Credit' means credit for which provision is made by regulations under s 51 (see PARA 938 et seq): Sch 5 para 18(4)(a). 'Gross amount of tax' means the total amount of tax due before taking into account any deduction for which provision is made by regulations (see PARA 939): Sch 5 para 18(4)(b).
5   Finance Act 1996 Sch 5 para 18(1). The provisions of Sch 5 para 18 are repealed by the Finance Act 2008 s 122, Sch 40 para 21 as from 1 April 2009 in so far as they relate to conduct involving dishonesty which relates to an inaccuracy in a document or a failure to notify Her Majesty's Revenue and Customs ('HMRC') of an under-assessment by HMRC: Finance Act 2008, Schedule 40 (Appointed Day, Transitional Provisions and Consequential Amendments) Order 2009, SI 2009/571, art 6. As to the penalty for an inaccuracy in a document or a failure to notify HMRC of an under-assessment by HMRC see the Finance Act 2007 s 97, Sch 24; and PARA 989.
6   Whether under the Finance Act 1996 Pt III (ss 39–71) or otherwise.
7   Finance Act 1996 Sch 5 para 18(7).
8   Finance Act 1996 Sch 5 para 18(6).
9   As to the Commissioners for Her Majesty's Revenue and Customs see PARA 901 note 2.
10   Finance Act 1996 Sch 5 para 18(5)(a).
11   As to the meaning of 'appeal tribunal' see PARA 1003 note 1.
12   Ie under the Finance Act 1996 Sch 5 para 25: see PARA 996.
13   Finance Act 1996 Sch 5 para 18(5)(b).
14   Finance Act 1996 Sch 5 para 18(5).

988.   Liability of named officer. Where it appears to the Commissioners for Her Majesty's Revenue and Customs[1] that a body corporate is liable to a penalty for tax evasion[2], and that the conduct giving rise to that penalty is, in whole or in part, attributable to the dishonesty of a person who is, or at the material time was, a director or managing officer[3] of the body corporate (a 'named officer'), the Commissioners may serve a notice on the body corporate and on the named officer[4]. The notice must state the amount of the basic penalty[5], and that the Commissioners propose to recover from the named officer such portion (which may be the whole) of the basic penalty as is specified in the notice[6]. Where such a notice is served, the portion of the basic penalty specified in the notice is recoverable from the named officer as if he were personally liable[7] to a penalty which corresponds to that portion; and the amount of that penalty may be assessed and notified to him accordingly[8].

Where such a notice is served, the amount which may be assessed[9] as the amount due by way of penalty from the body corporate is to be only so much (if any) of the basic penalty as is not assessed on and notified to a named officer, and the body corporate is treated as discharged from liability for so much of the basic penalty as is so assessed and notified[10].

No appeal lies against such a notice as such but:

(1) where a body corporate is so assessed[11], the body corporate may appeal against the Commissioners' decision as to its liability to a penalty and as to the amount of the basic penalty as if it were specified in the assessment[12];

(2) where an assessment is made on a named officer[13], the named officer may appeal against the Commissioners' decision that the conduct of the body corporate is, in whole or in part, attributable to his dishonesty and of their decision as to the portion of the penalty which the Commissioners propose to recover from him[14].

1 As to the Commissioners for Her Majesty's Revenue and Customs see PARA 901 note 2.

2 Ie a penalty under the Finance Act 1996 s 60, Sch 5 para 18: see PARA 987.

3 'Managing officer', in relation to a body corporate, means any manager, secretary or other similar officer of the body corporate or any person purporting to act in any such capacity or as a director: Finance Act 1996 Sch 5 para 19(6). Where the affairs of a body corporate are managed by its members, Sch 5 para 19 applies in relation to the conduct of a member in connection with his functions of management as if he were a director of the body corporate: Sch 5 para 19(6).

4 Finance Act 1996 Sch 5 para 19(1).
   The provisions of Sch 5 para 19 are repealed by the Finance Act 2008 s 122, Sch 40 para 21 as from 1 April 2009 in so far as they relate to conduct involving dishonesty which relates to an inaccuracy in a document or a failure to notify Her Majesty's Revenue and Customs ('HMRC') of an under-assessment by HMRC: Finance Act 2008, Schedule 40 (Appointed Day, Transitional Provisions and Consequential Amendments) Order 2009, SI 2009/571, art 6. As to the penalty for an inaccuracy in a document or a failure to notify HMRC of an under-assessment by HMRC see the Finance Act 2007 s 97, Sch 24; and PARA 989.

5 Finance Act 1996 Sch 5 para 19(2)(a).

6 Finance Act 1996 Sch 5 para 19(2)(b).

7 Ie under the Finance Act 1996 Sch 5 para 18: see PARA 987.

8 Finance Act 1996 Sch 5 para 19(3).

9 Ie under the Finance Act 1996 Sch 5 para 32: see PARA 994.

10 Finance Act 1996 Sch 5 para 19(4).

11 Ie assessed as mentioned in Sch 5 para 19(4)(a).

12 Finance Act 1996 Sch 5 para 19(5)(a) (Sch 5 para 19(5) amended by SI 2009/56). The provisions of the Finance Act 1996 ss 54–56 (see PARAS 1003–1010) apply accordingly: Sch 5 para 19(5)(c) (as so amended).

13 Ie by virtue of the Finance Act 1996 Sch 5 para 19(3).

14 Finance Act 1996 Sch 5 para 19(5)(b) (as amended: see note 12). The provisions of the Finance Act 1996 ss 54–56 (see PARAS 1003–1010) apply accordingly: Sch 5 para 19(5)(c) (as so amended).

(3) OTHER CIVIL PENALTIES

989. Errors in documents and assessments. The cross-tax penalty for inaccuracies in documents and failure to notify Her Majesty's Revenue and Customs[1] of an under-assessment applies in relation to landfill tax and is discussed elsewhere in this work[2].

1   As to the Commissioners for Her Majesty's Revenue and Customs see PARA 901 note 2.
2   See the Finance Act 2007 s 97, Sch 24; and INCOME TAXATION.

990. Failure to provide information or make records. If a person:

(1)   fails to comply with any provision with regard to the furnishing of information[1], or the production of documents[2]; or

(2)   fails to make records as required by any provision of regulations[3],

he is liable to a penalty[4].

Where a penalty (an 'initial penalty') is so imposed on a person and the failure which led to the initial penalty continues after its imposition, he is liable to a further penalty for each day during which (or any part of which) the failure continues after the day on which the initial penalty was imposed[5].

A person who fails to preserve records in compliance with any provision of regulations[6] is liable to a penalty[7].

1   Ie any provision of the Finance Act 1996 s 60, Sch 5 para 1: see PARA 970.
2   Ie any provision of the Finance Act 1996 Sch 5 para 3: see PARA 978.
3   Ie made under the Finance Act 1996 Sch 5 paras 2, 2A: see PARAS 931, 934.
4   Finance Act 1996 Sch 5 para 22(1). The penalty is a sum of £250: see Sch 5 para 22(1).
    Where by reason of a failure falling within Sch 5 para 22(1) or Sch 5 para 22(3) (see the text and note 7): (1) a person is convicted of an offence (whether under Pt III (ss 39–71) or otherwise); or (2) a person is assessed to a penalty under Sch 5 para 18 (see PARA 987) or a penalty for a deliberate inaccuracy under the Finance Act 2007 Sch 24 (see PARA 989), that failure does not also give rise to liability to a penalty under the Finance Act 1996 Sch 5 para 22: Sch 5 para 22(4) (amended by SI 2009/571).
    As from 1 April 2010, the Finance Act 1996 Sch 5 para 22(1)(a) (see head (1) in the text) is repealed: Finance Act 2009, Section 96 and Schedule 48 (Appointed Day, Savings and Consequential Amendments) Order 2009, SI 2009/3054, art 3, Schedule para 7(b). Despite the repeal, the Finance Act 1996 Sch 5 para 22(1)(a) continues to have effect on and after 1 April 2010 where Her Majesty's Revenue and Customs requested information or documents before that day: Finance Act 2009, Section 96 and Schedule 48 (Appointed Day, Savings and Consequential Amendments) Order 2009, SI 2009/3054, art 6.
5   Finance Act 1996 Sch 5 para 22(2). The further penalty is a sum of £20 for each such day: see Sch 5 para 22(2).
6   Ie made under the Finance Act 1996 Sch 5 para 2 (see PARA 931), read with Sch 5 para 2 and any direction given under the regulations.
7   Finance Act 1996 Sch 5 para 22(3). The penalty is a sum of £250: see Sch 5 para 22(3). See also note 4.

991. Breach of regulations. Where regulations made under the landfill tax provisions[1] impose a requirement on any person, they may provide that if the person fails to comply with the requirement he is liable to a penalty[2].

1   Ie the Finance Act 1996 Pt III (ss 39–71): see PARA 901 note 1.
2   Finance Act 1996 s 60, Sch 5 para 23(1). The penalty is a sum of £250: see Sch 5 para 23(1).
    Where, by reason of any conduct: (1) a person is convicted of an offence (whether under the Finance Act 1996 Pt III or otherwise); or (2) a person is assessed to a penalty under Sch 5 para 18 (see PARA 987) or a penalty for a deliberate inaccuracy under the Finance Act 2007 Sch 24 (see PARA 989), that conduct does not also give rise to liability to a penalty under the regulations: Finance Act 1996 Sch 5 para 23(2) (amended by SI 2009/571). As to the meaning of 'conduct' see PARA 987 note 3.

The Finance Act 1996 Sch 5 para 23(1) does not apply to any failure mentioned in Sch 5 para 22 (see PARA 990): Sch 5 para 23(3).

992. Breach of a controlled goods agreements. As from a day to be appointed[1] the following provisions apply where an enforcement agent[2] has entered into a controlled goods agreement[3] with the person in default[4].

If the person in default removes or disposes of goods (or permits their removal or disposal) in breach of the agreement, he is liable to a penalty equal to half of the tax or other amount recoverable[5].

The person in default is not liable to a penalty if he satisfies the Commissioners for Her Majesty's Revenue and Customs[6] or, on appeal, an appeal tribunal[7], that there is a reasonable excuse for the breach in question[8].

1   The Finance Act 1996 Sch 5 para 23A (added by the Tribunals, Courts and Enforcement Act 2007 s 62(3), Sch 13 para 123) is to be brought into force by order made under s 148(5) as from a day to be appointed. At the date at which this volume states the law no such day had been appointed.
    As from a day to be appointed, the Finance Act 1996 Sch 5 para 23A (as so added) is to be repealed by the Finance Act 2008 s 129, Sch 43 para 5. At the date at which this volume states the law no such day had been appointed.
2   Ie an enforcement agent acting under the power conferred by the Finance Act 1997 s 51(A1) (not yet in force): Finance Act 1996 s 60, Sch 5 para 23A(1) (as added: see note 1). As to the Finance Act 1997 s 51 (enforcement by distress) see DISTRESS vol 13 (2007 Reissue) PARA 1127.
    As from a day to be appointed, s 51(A1) is to be repealed by the Finance Act 2008 s 129, Sch 43 para 6. At the date at which this volume states the law no such day had been appointed. As to the power, in force as from a day to be appointed, of the Commissioners for Her Majesty's Revenue and Customs to use the procedure in the Tribunals, Courts and Enforcement Act 2007 Sch 12 to take control of goods where a person does not pay a sum payable to the Commissioners see the Finance Act 2008 ss 127, 129; and INCOME TAXATION. As to the Commissioners for Her Majesty's Revenue and Customs see PARA 901 note 2.
3   A 'controlled goods agreement' has the meaning conferred by the Tribunals, Courts and Enforcement Act 2007 Sch 12 para 13(4): see CIVIL PROCEDURE vol 12 (2009) PARA 1393.
4   Finance Act 1996 Sch 5 para 23A(1) (as added: see note 1). The 'person in default' means the person against whom the power conferred by the Finance Act 1997 s 51(A1) (not yet in force) (see note 2) is exercisable: Finance Act 1996 Sch 5 para 23A(1) (as so added).
5   Finance Act 1996 Sch 5 para 23A(3) (as added: see note 1).
6   See note 2.
7   As to the meaning of 'appeal tribunal' see PARA 1003 note 1.
8   Finance Act 1996 Sch 5 para 23A(4) (as added: see note 1).

993. Breach of a walking possession agreement. The following provisions apply where:

(1)   in accordance with regulations[1] a distress is authorised to be levied on the goods and chattels of a person (a 'person in default') who has refused or neglected to pay any landfill tax[2] due from him or any amount recoverable as if it were tax due from him[3]; and

(2)   the person levying the distress and the person in default have entered into a walking possession agreement[4].

If the person in default is in breach of the undertaking contained in a walking possession agreement, he is liable to a penalty equal to half of the tax or other amount referred to in head (1) above[5].

A walking possession agreement is an agreement under which, in consideration of the property distrained upon being allowed to remain in the custody of the person in default and of the delaying of its sale, the person in default:

(1)   acknowledges that the property specified in the agreement is under distraint and held in walking possession[6]; and

(2)   undertakes that, except with the consent of the Commissioners for Her Majesty's Revenue and Customs and subject to such conditions as they may impose, he will not remove or allow the removal of any of the specified property from the premises named in the agreement[7].

1   Ie regulations under the Finance Act 1997 s 51 (enforcement by distress: see DISTRESS vol 13 (2007 Reissue) PARA 1127): see the Finance Act 1996 s 60, Sch 5 para 24(1)(a). As to distress generally see DISTRESS.
2   As to the meaning of 'landfill tax' see PARA 901.
3   Finance Act 1996 Sch 5 para 24(1)(a) (amended by the Finance Act 1997 s 53(8)). As from a day to be appointed, the Finance Act 1996 Sch 5 para 24(4) is substituted by the Tribunals, Courts and Enforcement Act 2007 s 62(3), Sch 13 para 124 so that the Finance Act 1996 Sch 5 para 24 extends only to Northern Ireland. At the date at which this volume states the law no such day had been appointed.
4   Finance Act 1996 Sch 5 para 24(1)(b).
5   Finance Act 1996 Sch 5 para 24(3).
6   Finance Act 1996 Sch 5 para 24(2)(a).
7   Finance Act 1996 Sch 5 para 24(2)(b). As to the Commissioners for Her Majesty's Revenue and Customs see PARA 901 note 2.

(4) ASSESSMENT OF PENALTIES AND MITIGATION

994. Assessments of penalties or interest. Where a person is liable to a penalty[1], or for interest[2], the Commissioners for Her Majesty's Revenue and Customs[3] may, subject to the following provision, assess the amount due by way of penalty or interest (as the case may be) and notify it to him accordingly; and the fact that any conduct[4] giving rise to a penalty may have ceased before an assessment is so made does not affect the power of the Commissioners to make such an assessment[5]. In the case of the penalties and interest referred to in heads (1) to (4) below, the assessment is to be of an amount due in respect of the accounting period[6] which in the head concerned is referred to as the relevant period:

(1)   in the case of a penalty relating to the evasion of landfill tax[7], and in the case of interest[8] on an amount due by way of such a penalty, the relevant period is the accounting period for which the tax evaded was due[9];

(2)   in the case of a penalty relating to the obtaining of a payment of credit under regulations[10], and in the case of interest on an amount due by way of such a penalty, the relevant period is the accounting period in respect of which the payment was obtained[11];

(3)   in the case of interest on underdeclared tax[12], and in the case of interest on an amount due by way of interest[13], the relevant period is the accounting period in respect of which the tax was due[14];

(4)   in the case of interest on an amount of unpaid tax[15], the relevant period is the accounting period in respect of which the tax was due[16].

Where a person is assessed under these provisions to an amount due by way of any penalty or interest falling within heads (1) to (4) above and is also assessed to tax[17] for the accounting period which is the relevant period, the assessments may be combined and notified to him as one assessment, but the amount of the penalty or interest must be separately identified in the notice[18].

In a case where the amount of any penalty or interest falls to be calculated by reference to tax which was not paid at the time it should have been and that tax cannot be readily attributed to any one or more accounting periods, it is treated as tax due for such period or periods as the Commissioners may determine to the best of their judgment and notify to the person liable for the tax and penalty or interest[19].

In the case of an amount due by way of interest on unpaid tax[20]:

(a)   a notice of assessment must specify a date, being not later than the date of the notice, to which the amount of interest which is assessed is calculated[21]; and

(b)   if the interest continues to accrue after that date, a further assessment or further assessments may be made in respect of amounts which so accrue[22].

Where an amount has been assessed and notified to any person under these provisions, it is recoverable as if it were tax due from him unless, or except to the extent that, the assessment has subsequently been withdrawn or reduced[23].

1   Ie under the Finance Act 1996 s 60, Sch 5 Pt V paras 18–25: see PARA 987 et seq.
2   Ie under the Finance Act 1996 Sch 5 para 26 (see PARA 997) or Sch 5 para 27 (see PARA 998).
3   As to the Commissioners for Her Majesty's Revenue and Customs see PARA 901 note 2.
4   As to the meaning of 'conduct' see PARA 987 note 3.
5   Finance Act 1996 Sch 5 para 32(1). Section 50(8) (power to assess: see PARA 959) applies for the purposes of Sch 5 para 32 as it applies for the purposes of s 50 (see PARA 959): Sch 5 para 32(9).
6   As to the meaning of 'accounting period' see PARA 928 note 17.
7   Ie a penalty under the Finance Act 1996 Sch 5 para 18: see PARA 987.
8   Ie under the Finance Act 1996 Sch 5 para 27: see PARA 998.
9   Finance Act 1996 Sch 5 para 32(2)(a).
10   Ie a penalty under the Finance Act 1996 Sch 5 para 18: see PARA 987.
11   Finance Act 1996 Sch 5 para 32(2)(b).
12   Ie under the Finance Act 1996 Sch 5 para 26: see PARA 997.
13   Ie under the Finance Act 1996 Sch 5 para 27: see PARA 998.
14   Finance Act 1996 Sch 5 para 32(2)(c).
15   Ie under the Finance Act 1996 Sch 5 para 27 (see PARA 998): see Sch 5 para 32(2)(d).
16   Finance Act 1996 Sch 5 para 32(2)(d).
17   Ie the Finance Act 1996 s 50(1) or s 50(2) (see PARA 959).
18   Finance Act 1996 Sch 5 para 32(4).
19   Finance Act 1996 Sch 5 para 32(3).
20   Ie under the Finance Act 1996 Sch 5 para 27: see PARA 998.
21   Finance Act 1996 Sch 5 para 32(5), (6)(a). If, within such period as may be notified by the Commissioners to the person liable for the interest under Sch 5 para 27 (see PARA 998), the amount referred to in Sch 5 para 27(2), (4), (6), (8) or (10) (as the case may be) is paid, it is treated for the purposes of Sch 5 para 27 as paid on the date specified as mentioned in Sch 5 para 32(6)(a): Sch 5 para 32(7).
22   Finance Act 1996 Sch 5 para 32(5), (6)(b).
23   Finance Act 1996 Sch 5 para 32(8).

995.   Time limits for assessments of penalty.   In general, an assessment of an amount due by way of penalty or interest[1] may not be made more than six years after the end of the accounting period concerned[2].

In the case of an assessment of an amount due by way of a penalty which is not one of certain specified penalties[3], the assessment may not be made more than three years after the event giving rise to the penalty[4]. If tax has been lost: (1) as a result of conduct involving dishonesty[5] or for which a person has been convicted of fraud; or (2) in circumstances giving rise to liability to a penalty for failure to register[6], an assessment may be made as if, the reference to three years were a reference to 20 years[7].

An assessment of: (a) an amount due by way of one of certain specified penalties[8]; or (b) an amount due by way of interest, may be made at any time before the expiry of the period of two years beginning with the time when the amount of landfill tax due for the accounting period concerned[9] has been finally determined[10].

Where after a person's death the Commissioners for Her Majesty's Revenue and Customs[11] propose to assess an amount as due by reason of some conduct[12] of the deceased, the assessment must not be made more than three years after the death[13].

1   Ie an assessment under the Finance Act 1996 s 60, Sch 5 para 32: see PARA 994.
2   Finance Act 1996 Sch 5 para 33(1)(b) (Sch 5 para 33(1), (4) amended by the Finance Act 1997 s 50(1), Sch 5 Pt II para 6(2)(c)).
     As from 1 April 2010, Sch 5 para 33(1), (3) is to be amended by, and Sch 5 para 33(1A) added by, the Finance Act 2009 s 99, Sch 51 para 40(2)–(4) so that an assessment may not in general be made more than four years after the end of the accounting period concerned or four years after the event giving rise to the penalty. As from 1 April 2010, the Finance Act 1996 Sch 5 para 33(4) is to be substituted by, and Sch 5 para 33(4A) added by, the Finance Act 2009 Sch 51 para 40(5) so that an assessment of an amount due from a person in a case involving a loss of tax brought about deliberately by that person (or by another person acting on his behalf) or attributable to a failure by the person to comply with an obligation under the Finance Act 1996 s 47(2), (3) (registration: see PARA 920) may be made at any time not more than 20 years after the end of the accounting period concerned or 20 years after the event giving rise to the penalty. The reference to a loss brought about deliberately by the person includes a loss brought about as a result of a deliberate inaccuracy in a document given to Her Majesty's Revenue and Customs by or on behalf of that person: Sch 5 para 33(4A) (as so added).
3   The specified penalties are those referred to in the Finance Act 1996 Sch 5 para 32(2) (see PARA 994 heads (1)–(4)).
4   Finance Act 1996 Sch 5 para 33(1) (as amended: see note 2)
5   Ie conduct falling within the Finance Act 1996 Sch 5 para 18(1) (dishonest evasion: see PARA 987).
6   Ie a penalty under the Finance Act 1996 Sch 5 para 21 (failure to register: see PARA 920 note 4).
7   Finance Act 1996 Sch 5 para 33(4) (as amended: see note 2). Sch 5 para 33(4) is stated to be subject to Sch 5 para 33(5) (assessment after death: see the text to notes 11–13): Sch 5 para 33(4) (as so amended).
8   Ie any penalty referred to in the Finance Act 1996 Sch 5 para 32(2).
9   In relation to an assessment under the Finance Act 1996 Sch 5 para 32, any reference in Sch 5 para 33(1) or Sch 5 para 33(2) to the accounting period concerned is a reference to that period which, in the case of the penalty or interest concerned, is the relevant period referred to in Sch 5 para 32(2): Sch 5 para 33(3).
10   Finance Act 1996 Sch 5 para 33(2). Sch 5 para 33(2) is stated to be subject to Sch 5 para 33(5) (assessment after death: see the text to notes 11–13): Sch 5 para 33(2).
11   As to the Commissioners for Her Majesty's Revenue and Customs see PARA 901 note 2.
12   As to the meaning of 'conduct' see PARA 987 note 3.
13   Finance Act 1996 Sch 5 para 33(5)(a). If the circumstances are as set out in Sch 5 para 33(4) (see the text to note 7), the modification of Sch 5 para 33(1) contained in Sch 5 para 33(4) (see the text to note 7) does not apply but any assessment which (from the point of view of time limits) could have been made immediately after the death may be made at any time within three years after it: Sch 5 para 33(5)(b).
     As from 1 April 2010 Sch 5 para 33(5) is to be amended by the Finance Act 2009 Sch 51 para 40(6) so that an assessment must not be made more than four years after the death, and the Finance Act 1996 Sch 5 para 33(5)(b) is repealed.

996.   Appeals against penalties.   Where a person is liable to a penalty[1] the Commissioners for Her Majesty's Revenue and Customs[2] or, on appeal, an appeal tribunal[3] may reduce the penalty to such amount (including nil) as they think proper[4]. Where the person concerned satisfies the Commissioners or, on appeal, an appeal tribunal that there is a reasonable excuse for any breach, failure or other conduct[5], that is a factor which (among other things) may be taken into account[6]. In the case of a penalty so reduced by the Commissioners, on an appeal relating to the penalty the appeal tribunal may cancel the whole or any part of the reduction made by the Commissioners[7].

1   Ie under the Finance Act 1996 s 60, Sch 5 Pt V paras 18–25.
2   As to the Commissioners for Her Majesty's Revenue and Customs see PARA 901 note 2.
3   As to the meaning of 'appeal tribunal' see PARA 1003 note 1.
4   Finance Act 1996 Sch 5 para 25(1).
5   As to the meaning of 'conduct' see PARA 987 note 3.
6   Finance Act 1996 Sch 5 para 25(2).
7   Finance Act 1996 Sch 5 para 25(3).

12. INTEREST

(1) INTEREST PAID BY THE TAXPAYER

997.   Interest on underdeclared tax. Where:

(1)   the Commissioners for Her Majesty's Revenue and Customs[1] assess[2] an amount of landfill tax[3] due from a registrable person[4] for an accounting period[5] and notify it to him[6]; and

(2)   the assessment is made on the basis that the amount (the 'additional amount') is due from him in addition to any amount shown in a return made in relation to the accounting period[7],

then the additional amount is to carry interest for the period which:

(a)   begins with the day after that on which the person is required[8] to pay tax due from him for the accounting period[9]; and

(b)   ends with the day before the relevant day[10]. The 'relevant day' is the earlier of the day on which the assessment is notified to the person and the day on which the additional amount is paid[11].

Where the Commissioners assess[12] an amount, which has been paid as a credit which is not due, as being tax due from a registrable person for an accounting period and notify it to him[13], the amount must carry interest for the period which:

(i)   begins with the day after that on which the person is required[14] to pay tax due from him for the accounting period[15]; and

(ii)   ends with the day before the relevant day[16]. The 'relevant day' is the earlier of the day on which the assessment is notified to the person and the day on which the amount is paid[17].

Interest under the above provisions is payable at the applicable rate[18] and must be paid without any deduction of income tax[19].

Where an amount would normally carry interest under the above provisions[20], and all or part of the amount turns out not to be due[21], then:

(A)   the amount or part (as the case may be) does not carry interest under this provision and is treated as never having done so[22]; and

(B)   all such adjustments as are reasonable are to be made, including adjustments by way of repayment by the Commissioners where appropriate[23].

1   As to the Commissioners for Her Majesty's Revenue and Customs see PARA 901 note 2.
2   Ie under the Finance Act 1996 s 50(1): see PARA 959.
3   As to the meaning of 'landfill tax' see PARA 901.
4   As to the meaning of 'registrable person' see PARA 958 note 1.
5   As to the meaning of 'accounting period' see PARA 928 note 17.
6   Finance Act 1996 s 60, Sch 5 para 26(1)(a).
7   Finance Act 1996 Sch 5 para 26(1)(b).
8   Ie by provision made under the Finance Act 1996 s 49: see PARA 935.
9   Finance Act 1996 Sch 5 para 26(2)(a).
10 Finance Act 1996 Sch 5 para 26(2)(b).
11 Finance Act 1996 Sch 5 para 26(3).
12 Ie under the Finance Act 1996 s 50(2): see PARA 959.
13 Finance Act 1996 Sch 5 para 26(4).
14 Ie by provision made under the Finance Act 1996 s 49: see PARA 935.
15 Finance Act 1996 Sch 5 para 26(5)(a).
16 Finance Act 1996 Sch 5 para 26(5)(b).
17 Finance Act 1996 Sch 5 para 26(6).

18 Finance Act 1996 Sch 5 para 26(7). The applicable rate is the rate provided for by regulations made by the Treasury under s 197: see PARA 1001 note 3. As to the Treasury see CONSTITUTIONAL LAW AND HUMAN RIGHTS vol 8(2) (Reissue) PARAS 512–517.
19 Finance Act 1996 Sch 5 para 26(8).
20 Finance Act 1996 Sch 5 para 26(9)(a).
21 Finance Act 1996 Sch 5 para 26(9)(b).
22 Finance Act 1996 Sch 5 para 26(10)(a).
23 Finance Act 1996 Sch 5 para 26(10)(b).

998. Interest on unpaid tax and assessments. Where a registrable person[1] makes a return[2] (whether or not he makes it at the time required)[3], and the return shows that an amount of landfill tax[4] is due from him for the accounting period[5] in relation to which the return is made[6], then the amount carries interest for the period which begins with the day after that on which the person is required[7] to pay tax due from him for the accounting period[8], and ends with the day before that on which the amount is paid[9].

Where the Commissioners for Her Majesty's Revenue and Customs[10] assess an amount of tax due from a registrable person for an accounting period in respect of failure to make or verify returns[11] and notify it to him[12], and the assessment is made on the basis that no return has been made by the person in relation to the accounting period[13], then the amount carries interest for the period which begins with the day after that on which the person is required to pay tax due from him for the accounting period[14], and ends with the day before that on which the amount is paid[15].

Where the Commissioners assess an amount of tax due from a registrable person for an accounting period in respect of failure to make or verify returns[16] and notify it to him[17], and the assessment (the 'supplementary assessment') is made on the basis that the amount (the 'additional amount') is due from him in addition to any amount shown in a return, or in any previous assessment, made in relation to the accounting period[18], then the additional amount carries interest for the period which begins with the day on which the supplementary assessment is notified to the person[19], and ends with the day before that on which the additional amount is paid[20].

Where the Commissioners assess an amount as being tax due from a registrable person for an accounting period in respect of credit to which he was not entitled[21] and notify it to him[22], the amount carries interest for the period which begins with the day on which the assessment is notified to the person[23], and ends with the day before that on which the amount is paid[24].

Where the Commissioners assess an amount due from a person by way of penalty[25] and notify it to him[26], or assess an amount due from a person by way of interest[27] and notify it to him[28], the amount carries interest for the period which begins with the day on which the assessment is notified to the person[29], and ends with the day before that on which the amount is paid[30].

Interest under the above provisions is to be compound interest calculated at the penalty rate[31] and with monthly rests[32] and is paid without any deduction of income tax[33]. The penalty rate is the rate found by taking the rate at which interest is payable[34] and adding ten percentage points to that rate[35].

Where an amount would normally carry interest under the above provisions, and all or part of the amount turns out not to be due, then that amount or part (as the case may be) does not carry interest under this provision and is treated as never having done so[36], and all such adjustments as are reasonable must be made, including adjustments by way of repayment by the Commissioners where appropriate[37].

1   As to the meaning of 'registrable person' see PARA 958 note 1.
2   Ie under provision made under the Finance Act 1996 s 49: see PARA 935.
3   Finance Act 1996 s 60, Sch 5 para 27(1)(a).
4   As to the meaning of 'landfill tax' see PARA 901.
5   As to the meaning of 'accounting period' see PARA 928 note 17.
6   Finance Act 1996 Sch 5 para 27(1)(b).
7   See note 2.
8   Finance Act 1996 Sch 5 para 27(2)(a). As to the suspension of interest under Sch 5 para 27(2) during the currency of an agreement for deferred payment see the Finance Act 2009 s 108; and INCOME TAXATION.
9   Finance Act 1996 Sch 5 para 27(2)(b).
10 As to the Commissioners for Her Majesty's Revenue and Customs see PARA 901 note 2.
11 Ie an assessment under the Finance Act 1996 s 50(1): see PARA 959.
12 Finance Act 1996 Sch 5 para 27(3)(a).
13 Finance Act 1996 Sch 5 para 27(3)(b).
14 Finance Act 1996 Sch 5 para 27(4)(a).
15 Finance Act 1996 Sch 5 para 27(4)(b).
16 Ie an assessment under the Finance Act 1996 s 50(1): see PARA 959.
17 Finance Act 1996 Sch 5 para 27(5)(a).
18 Finance Act 1996 Sch 5 para 27(5)(b).
19 Finance Act 1996 Sch 5 para 27(6)(a).
20 Finance Act 1996 Sch 5 para 27(6)(b). Where: (1) the Commissioners assess and notify an amount as mentioned in Sch 5 para 27(5)(a) or Sch 5 para 27(7) or Sch 5 para 27(9)(a) or (b); (2) they also specify a date for this purpose; and (3) the amount concerned is paid on or before that date, then the amount does not carry interest by virtue of Sch 5 para 27(6), (8) or (10) (as the case may be): Sch 5 para 27(13).
21 Ie an assessment under the Finance Act 1996 s 50(2): see PARA 959.
22 Finance Act 1996 Sch 5 para 27(7). See also note 20.
23 Finance Act 1996 Sch 5 para 27(8)(a).
24 Finance Act 1996 Sch 5 para 27(8)(b).
25 Ie under the Finance Act 1996 Sch 5 para 32: see PARA 994.
26 Finance Act 1996 Sch 5 para 27(9)(a). See also note 20.
27 Ie under the Finance Act 1996 Sch 5 para 26: see PARA 997.
28 Finance Act 1996 Sch 5 para 27(9)(b). See also note 20.
29 Finance Act 1996 Sch 5 para 27(10)(a).
30 Finance Act 1996 Sch 5 para 27(10)(b).
31 Finance Act 1996 Sch 5 para 27(11)(a).
32 Finance Act 1996 Sch 5 para 27(11)(b).
33 Finance Act 1996 Sch 5 para 27(12).
34 Ie under the Finance Act 1996 Sch 5 para 26 (see PARA 997).
35 Finance Act 1996 Sch 5 para 27(11).
36 Finance Act 1996 Sch 5 para 27(14), (15)(a).
37 Finance Act 1996 Sch 5 para 27(14), (15)(b).

999. Appeal against interest. Where a person is liable to pay interest[1] the Commissioners for Her Majesty's Revenue and Customs[2] or, on appeal, an appeal tribunal[3] may reduce the amount payable to such amount (including nil) as they think proper[4]. Where the person concerned satisfies the Commissioners or, on appeal, an appeal tribunal that there is a reasonable excuse for the conduct giving rise to the liability to pay interest, that is a factor which (among other things) may be taken into account[5].

In the case of interest reduced by the Commissioners[6], on an appeal relating to the interest, the appeal tribunal may cancel the whole or any part of the reduction made by the Commissioners[7].

1   Ie interest on unpaid tax or assessments: see PARA 998.
2   As to the Commissioners for Her Majesty's Revenue and Customs see PARA 901 note 2.
3   As to the meaning of 'appeal tribunal' see PARA 1003 note 1.
4   Finance Act 1996 s 60, Sch 5 para 28(1).

5   Finance Act 1996 Sch 5 para 28(2). See *Caird Environmental v Customs and Excise Comrs*
    (29 April 1999, unreported) (where the tribunal found on the balance of probabilities that the
    taxpayer's cheque had not been submitted with its landfill tax return; it did not therefore have a
    reasonable excuse).
6   Ie under the Finance Act 1996 Sch 5 para 27(1): see PARA 998.
7   Finance Act 1996 Sch 5 para 28(3).

(2) INTEREST PAYABLE BY COMMISSIONERS FOR REVENUE AND CUSTOMS

1000.   Interest payable due to error by Commissioners for Revenue and Customs.   Where, due to an error on the part of the Commissioners for Her Majesty's Revenue and Customs[1], a person:

(1)   has paid to them by way of landfill tax[2] an amount which was not tax due and which they are in consequence liable to repay to him[3];

(2)   has failed to claim payment of an amount of credit to the payment of which he was entitled[4]; or

(3)   has suffered delay in receiving payment of an amount[5] due to him from them in connection with tax[6],

then, if and to the extent that they would not be liable to do so apart from these provisions, they must pay interest to him on that amount for the applicable period[7] at the applicable rate[8].

The applicable period, in a case falling within head (1) above, is the period beginning with the date on which the payment is received by the Commissioners, and ending with the date on which they authorise payment of the amount on which the interest is payable[9]. The applicable period, in a case falling within head (2) or head (3) above, is the period beginning with the date on which, apart from the error, the Commissioners might reasonably have been expected to authorise payment of the amount on which the interest is payable, and ending with the date on which they in fact authorise payment of that amount[10]. In determining the applicable period there must be left out of account any period by which the Commissioners' authorisation of the payment of interest is delayed by the conduct[11] of the person claiming interest[12].

This reference to a period by which the Commissioners' authorisation of the payment of interest is delayed by the conduct of the person who claims it includes, in particular, any period which is referable to:

(a)   any unreasonable delay in the making of the claim or in the making of any claim for the payment or repayment of the amount on which interest is claimed[13];

(b)   any failure by that person or a person acting on his behalf or under his influence to provide the Commissioners, at or before the time of making the claim or subsequently in response to a request for information by the Commissioners with all the information required by them to enable the existence and amount of the claimant's entitlement to payment or repayment, to be determined[14]; and

(c)   the making, as part of or in association with either the claim for interest or any claim for the payment or repayment of the amount on which interest is claimed, of a claim to anything to which the claimant was not entitled[15].

In determining for these purposes whether any period of delay is referable to a failure by any person to provide information in response to a request by the

Commissioners, there is taken to be so referable, except so far as may be provided by regulations, any period which:

(i)   begins with the date on which the Commissioners require that person to provide information which they reasonably consider relevant to the matter to be determined[16]; and

(ii)   ends with the earliest date on which it would be reasonable for the Commissioners to conclude:

    (A)   that they have received a complete answer to their request for information[17];

    (B)   that they have received all that they need in answer to that request[18];

    (C)   that it is unnecessary for them to be provided with any information in answer to that request[19].

The Commissioners are only liable to pay interest under these provisions on a claim made in writing for that purpose[20]. Such a claim must not be made more than three years after the end of the applicable period to which it relates[21].

Where interest is payable by the Commissioners to a person entitled to credit under the relevant regulations[22], the interest is treated as an amount to which he is entitled by way of credit[23].

1   As to the Commissioners for Her Majesty's Revenue and Customs see PARA 901 note 2.
2   As to the meaning of 'landfill tax' see PARA 901.
3   Finance Act 1996 s 60, Sch 5 para 29(1)(a). This reference to an amount which the Commissioners are liable to repay in consequence of the making of a payment that was not due is a reference to only so much of that amount as is the subject of a claim that the Commissioners are required to satisfy or have satisfied: Sch 5 para 29(1A)(a) (Sch 5 para 29(1A) added by the Finance Act 1997 s 50, Sch 5 Pt III para 11).
    References in the Finance Act 1996 Sch 5 para 29 to receiving payment of any amount from the Commissioners, or the authorisation by the Commissioners of the payment of any amount, include references to the discharge by way of set-off (whether in accordance with regulations (see PARAS 963–964) or otherwise) of the Commissioners' liability to pay that amount: Sch 5 para 29(9) (substituted by the Finance Act 1997 Sch 5 Pt III para 11).
4   Finance Act 1996 Sch 5 para 29(1)(b). As to payments of credit see the regulations made under s 51; and PARA 938 et seq.
5   This does not include any amount of interest payable under the Finance Act 1996 Sch 5 para 29: Sch 5 para 29(1A)(b) (as added: see note 3).
6   Finance Act 1996 Sch 5 para 29(1)(c).
7   Finance Act 1996 Sch 5 para 29(1).
8   Finance Act 1996 Sch 5 para 29(10). The applicable rate is the rate provided for by regulations made by the Treasury under s 197: see PARA 1001 note 3. As to the Treasury see CONSTITUTIONAL LAW AND HUMAN RIGHTS vol 8(2) (Reissue) PARAS 512–517.
9   Finance Act 1996 Sch 5 para 29(2).
10 Finance Act 1996 Sch 5 para 29(3).
11 As to the meaning of 'conduct' see PARA note 3.
12 Finance Act 1996 Sch 5 para 29(4) (substituted by the Finance Act 1997 Sch 5 Pt III para 12).
13 Finance Act 1996 Sch 5 para 29(4A)(a) (Sch 5 para 29(4A) added by the Finance Act 1997 Sch 5 Pt III para 12).
14 Finance Act 1996 Sch 5 para 29(4A)(b) (as added: see note 13).
15 Finance Act 1996 Sch 5 para 29(4A)(c) (as added: see note 13).
16 Finance Act 1996 Sch 5 para 29(5)(a) (Sch 5 para 29(5) substituted by the Finance Act 1997 Sch 5 Pt III para 12). At the date at which this volume states the law no regulations had been made under the Finance Act 1996 Sch 5 para 29(5).
17 Finance Act 1996 Sch 5 para 29(5)(b)(i) (as substituted: see note 16).
18 Finance Act 1996 Sch 5 para 29(5)(b)(ii) (as substituted: see note 16).
19 Finance Act 1996 Sch 5 para 29(5)(b)(iii) (as substituted: see note 16).
20 Finance Act 1996 Sch 5 para 29(7).
21 Finance Act 1996 Sch 5 para 29(8) (substituted by the Finance Act 1997 Sch 5 Pt III para 11). As from 1 April 2010 the Finance Act 1996 Sch 5 para 29(8) is to be amended by the Finance

Act 2009 s 99, Sch 51 para 39 so that a claim must not be made more than four years after the end of the applicable period to which it relates.
22   See PARA 938 et seq.
23   Finance Act 1996 Sch 5 para 30(1). Schedule 5 para 30(1) is disregarded for the purpose of determining a person's entitlement to interest or the amount of interest to which he is entitled: Sch 5 para 30(2).

(3) RATES OF INTEREST

1001.   Rate of interest payable to or by Commissioners for Revenue and Customs. The rate of interest applicable for the purposes of the provisions as to interest payable to or by the Commissioners for Her Majesty's Revenue and Customs[1] in connection with landfill tax[2] is the rate provided for by regulations[3] made by the Treasury[4].

1   As to the Commissioners for Her Majesty's Revenue and Customs see PARA 901 note 2.
2   Ie the Finance Act 1996 s 60, Sch 5 paras 26, 29: see PARAS 997, 1000. As to the meaning of 'landfill tax' see PARA 901.
3   Regulations may:
   (1)   make different provision for different enactments or for different purposes of the same enactment (Finance Act 1996 s 197(3)(a));
   (2)   either themselves specify a rate of interest for the purposes of an enactment or make provision for any such rate to be determined, and to change from time to time, by reference to such rate or the average of such rates as may be referred to in the regulations (s 197(3)(b));
   (3)   provide for rates to be reduced below, or increased above, what they otherwise would be by specified amounts or by reference to specified formulae (s 197(3)(c));
   (4)   provide for rates arrived at by reference to averages or formulae to be rounded up or down (s 197(3)(d));
   (5)   provide for circumstances in which changes of rates of interest are or are not to take place (s 197(3)(e)); and
   (6)   provide that changes of rates are to have effect for periods beginning on or after a day determined in accordance with the regulations in relation to interest running from before that day, as well as in relation to interest running from, or from after, that day (s 197(3)(f)).
   The power to make regulations under this provision is exercisable by statutory instrument subject to annulment in pursuance of a resolution of the House of Commons: s 197(4).
4   Finance Act 1996 s 197(1). The following rates are prescribed under s 197(1):
   (1)   8.5% in respect of interest on undeclared tax under Sch 5 para 26 (see PARA 997) and of interest on unpaid tax found on appeal to be due under s 56(5) (see PARA 1005) (see the Air Passenger Duty and Other Indirect Taxes (Interest Rate) Regulations 1998, SI 1998/1461, reg 4(1) (substituted by SI 2000/631; and amended by SI 2001/3337; and SI 2009/56));
   (2)   5% in respect of interest payable by the Commissioners under the Finance Act 1996 Sch 5 para 29 (see PARA 1000); interest on tax found on appeal not to be payable under s 56(3) (see PARA 1005) and interest on an amount due to an appellant found on appeal not to have been paid under s 56(4) (see PARA 1005) (see the Air Passenger Duty and Other Indirect Taxes (Interest Rate) Regulations 1998, SI 1998/1461, reg 5(1) (substituted by SI 2000/631; and amended by SI 2001/3337; and SI 2009/56)).
   The regulations make provision for changes in the applicable interest rate and for the formula to be used in calculating the new rate: see the Air Passenger Duty and Other Indirect Taxes (Interest Rate) Regulations 1997, SI 1998/1461, regs 4(2), (3), 5(2), (3) (substituted by SI 2000/631). As to the Treasury see CONSTITUTIONAL LAW AND HUMAN RIGHTS vol 8(2) (Reissue) PARAS 512–517.

13. SECURITY FOR TAX

1002. Security for tax. Where it appears to the Commissioners for Her Majesty's Revenue and Customs[1] requisite to do so for the protection of the revenue they may require a registrable person[2], as a condition of his carrying out taxable activities[3], to give security (or further security) of such amount and in such manner as they may determine for the payment of any landfill tax[4] which is or may become due from him[5].

1   As to the Commissioners for Her Majesty's Revenue and Customs see PARA 901 note 2.
2   As to the meaning of 'registrable person' see PARA 958 note 1.
3   As to the meaning of 'taxable activity' see PARA 920 note 1.
4   As to the meaning of 'landfill tax' see PARA 901.
5   Finance Act 1996 s 60, Sch 5 para 31.

14. APPEALS AND REVIEWS

(1) APPEALS

1003. Appeals in general. An appeal lies to an appeal tribunal[1] from any person who is or will be affected by any of the following decisions:

(1)   a decision as to the registration or cancellation of registration of any person under the landfill tax provisions[2];

(2)   a decision as to whether tax is chargeable in respect of a disposal or as to how much tax is chargeable[3];

(3)   a decision to refuse an application for a reclamation certificate[4] made before 1 December 2008, or to withdraw such a certificate[5];

(4)   a decision to make such a certificate subject to a condition that it is to be in force in relation to part only of the land to which the application for the certificate related[6];

(5)   a decision as to whether a person is entitled to credit[7] or as to how much credit a person is entitled to or as to the manner in which he is to benefit from credit[8];

(6)   a decision to withdraw approval of an environmental body under the provisions on credits for payments to bodies concerned with the environment[9];

(7)   a decision as to an assessment[10] or as to the amount of an assessment[11];

(8)   a decision to refuse a request[12] by a body corporate for registration of its divisions[13];

(9)   a decision to refuse an application[14] by bodies corporate to be treated as members of a group[15];

(10)   a decision as to whether conditions set out in a specification by the Commissioners for Her Majesty's Revenue and Customs[16] as weight of material disposed of[17] are met in relation to a disposal[18];

(11)   a decision to give a direction[19] that agreed rules as to determining weight are no longer to have effect[20];

(12)   a decision as to a claim[21] for the repayment of overpaid tax[22];

(13)   a decision as to liability to a penalty[23] or as to the amount of such a penalty[24];

(14)   a decision as to liability of a body corporate to a penalty[25] for tax evasion[26];

(15)   a decision as to any liability to pay interest on underdeclared or unpaid tax[27] or as to the amount of the interest payable[28];

(16)   a decision as to any liability of the Commissioners to pay interest[29] or as to the amount of the interest payable[30];

(17)   a decision to require any security[31] or as to its amount[32];

(18)   a decision as to the amount of any penalty or interest specified[33] in an assessment[34];

(19)   a decision of the Commissioners under the provisions on secondary liability of controllers of landfill sites[35].

1 'Appeal tribunal' means the First-tier Tribunal or, where determined by or under Tribunal Procedure Rules, the Upper Tribunal: Finance Act 1996 s 70(1) (amended by SI 2009/56). As to the First-tier and Upper Tribunals see ADMINISTRATIVE LAW. As to Tribunal Procedure Rules see ADMINISTRATIVE LAW.
2 Finance Act 1996 s 54(1)(a).
3 Finance Act 1996 s 54(1)(b).

4   Ie a certificate under the Finance Act 1996 s 43B: see PARA 913.
5   Finance Act 1996 s 54(1)(ba) (s 54(1)(ba), (bb) added by SI 1996/1529). The Finance Act 1996
    s 54(1)(ba) is to be repealed with effect from 1 April 2012: Landfill Tax (Material from
    Contaminated Land) (Phasing out of Exemption) Order 2008, SI 2008/2669, arts 3, 4.
6   Finance Act 1996 s 54(1)(bb) (as added: see note 5). Section 54(1)(bb) applies only in relation to
    applications made before 1 December 2008 and is to be repealed with effect from 1 April 2012:
    Landfill Tax (Material from Contaminated Land) (Phasing out of Exemption) Order 2008,
    SI 2008/2669, art 3.
7   As to credit see PARA 938 et seq.
8   Finance Act 1996 s 54(1)(c).
9   Finance Act 1996 s 54(1)(ca) (s 54(1)(ca) added by the Finance Act 2008 s 151(1)(3)). As to
    credits for payments to bodies concerned with the environment see PARA 949 et seq.
10 Ie an assessment under the Finance Act 1996 s 50 (see PARA 959) in respect of an accounting
    period in relation to which a return required to be made by virtue of regulations under s 49 (see
    PARA 935) has been made: s 54(2). As to the meaning of 'accounting period' see PARA 928 note
    17.
11 Finance Act 1996 s 54(1)(d).
12 Ie under the Finance Act 1996 s 58(3): see PARA 924.
13 Finance Act 1996 s 54(1)(e).
14 Ie under the Finance Act 1996 s 59: see PARA 925.
15 Finance Act 1996 s 54(1)(f).
16 As to the Commissioners for Her Majesty's Revenue and Customs see PARA 901 note 2.
17 Ie under the Landfill Tax Regulations 1996, SI 1996/1527, reg 43(3): see PARA 909.
18 Finance Act 1996 s 54(1)(g).
19 Ie under the Landfill Tax Regulations 1996, SI 1996/1527, reg 44(3): see PARA 910.
20 Finance Act 1996 s 54(1)(h).
21 Ie under the Finance Act 1996 s 60, Sch 5 para 14: see PARA 966.
22 Finance Act 1996 s 54(1)(i).
23 Ie under the Finance Act 1996 Sch 5 Pt V paras 18–25: see PARA 987 et seq.
24 Finance Act 1996 s 54(1)(j).
25 Ie under the Finance Act 1996 Sch 5 para 19 (as mentioned in Sch 5 para 19(5)): see PARA 988.
26 Finance Act 1996 s 54(1)(k).
27 Ie under the Finance Act 1996 Sch 5 para 26 or Sch 5 para 27: see PARAS 997–998.
28 Finance Act 1996 s 54(1)(l).
29 Ie under the Finance Act 1996 Sch 5 para 29: see PARA 1000.
30 Finance Act 1996 s 54(1)(m).
31 Ie under the Finance Act 1996 Sch 5 para 31 (see PARA 1002): see s 54(1)(n).
32 Finance Act 1996 s 54(1)(n).
33 Ie under the Finance Act 1996 Sch 5 para 32: see PARA 994.
34 Finance Act 1996 s 54(1)(o).
35 The provisions are those under the Finance Act 1996 Sch 5 Pt VIII paras 48–61: see PARA 930.
    Section 54 applies to a decision of the Commissioners under Sch 5 Pt VIII: (1) that a person is a
    controller; (2) that a person is liable under Sch 5 Pt VIII to pay any amount (including a penalty
    under Sch 5 para 60 (see PARA 930)); (3) that a person is not entitled under Sch 5 Pt VIII to an
    allowance; or (4) as to the amount of any liability or any allowance under Sch 5 Pt VIII as it
    applies to the other decisions of the Commissioners specified in s 54(1): Sch 5 para 59 (added by
    the Finance Act 2000 s 142, Sch 37).

1004. Bringing of appeals. An appeal[1] must be made to the appeal tribunal[2]
before the later of the end of the relevant period[3] or the end of the period of 30
days beginning with:

(1)   in a case where the person (P) to whom the decision has been notified is
      the appellant, the date of the document notifying the decision to which
      the appeal relates; or

(2)   in a case where a person other than P is the appellant, the date that
      person becomes aware of the decision[4].

In a case where Her Majesty's Revenue and Customs ('HMRC') are required
to undertake a review[5], an appeal may not be made until the conclusion date[6]
and any appeal must be made within the period of 30 days beginning with the
conclusion date[7].

In a case where HMRC are requested to undertake a review[8], an appeal may not be made unless HMRC have decided whether or not to undertake a review, and, if they decide to undertake a review, until the conclusion date[9]. Any appeal must be made within the period of thirty days beginning with the conclusion date or the date on which HMRC decide not to undertake a review[10].

In a case where HMRC are required to undertake a review but do not give notice of the conclusions within the specified time period[11], an appeal may be made at any time from the end of the specified time period to the date 30 days after the conclusion date[12].

An appeal may be made after the end of any of the above periods only if the appeal tribunal gives permission to do so[13].

1   Ie under the Finance Act 1996 s 54: see PARA 1003.
2   As to the appeal tribunal see PARA 1003 note 1.
3   As to the meaning of 'relevant period' see PARA 1008 note 3.
4   Finance Act 1996 s 54G(1) (s 54G added by SI 2009/56).
5   Ie under the Finance Act 1996 s 54C: see PARA 1007.
6   The 'conclusion date' is the date of the document notifying the conclusions of the review: Finance Act 1996 s 54G(7) (as added: see note 4). See PARA 1010.
7   Finance Act 1996 s 54G(3) (as added: see note 4).
8   Ie under the Finance Act 1996 s 54E: see PARA 1009.
9   Finance Act 1996 s 54G(4)(a) (as added: see note 4).
10 Finance Act 1996 s 54G(4)(b) (as added: see note 4).
11 Ie the time period specified in the Finance Act 1996 s 54F(6): see PARA 1010.
12 Finance Act 1996 s 54G(5) (as added: see note 4).
13 Finance Act 1996 s 54G(6) (as added: see note 4).

1005. Further provisions relating to appeals. Where an appeal is made with respect to a decision as to tax chargeable or an assessment[1] the appeal is not to be entertained unless the amount which Her Majesty's Revenue and Customs ('HMRC') have determined to be payable as tax has been paid or deposited with them[2].

Where the amount determined has not been paid or deposited an appeal may nevertheless be entertained if HMRC are satisfied (on the application of the appellant) or the appeal tribunal[3] decides (HMRC not being so satisfied and on the application of the appellant) that the requirement to pay or deposit the amount determined would cause the appellant to suffer hardship[4].

Where on an appeal[5]:

(1)   it is found that the amount specified in the assessment is less than it ought to have been[6]; and

(2)   the appeal tribunal gives a direction specifying the correct amount[7],

the assessment has effect as an assessment of the amount specified in the direction and that amount is deemed to have been notified to the appellant[8].

Where on an appeal[9] it is found that the whole or part of any amount paid or deposited[10] is not due, so much of that amount as is found not to be due must be repaid with interest at the applicable rate[11]. Where on an appeal it is found that the whole or part of any amount due to the appellant as credit[12] has not been paid, so much of that amount as is found not to have been paid must be paid with interest at the applicable rate[13].

Where an appeal has been entertained notwithstanding that an amount determined by the Commissioners to be payable as tax has not been paid or deposited and it is found on the appeal that that amount is due, it is to be paid with interest at the applicable rate[14]. Interest is paid without any deduction of income tax[15].

1 Ie a decision falling within the Finance Act 1996 s 54(1)(b) or s 54(1)(d): see PARA 1003.
2 Finance Act 1996 s 55(3) (substituted by SI 2009/56). Without prejudice to the Finance
   Act 1996 s 60, Sch 5 para 25 (see PARA 996), nothing in s 55 is to be taken to confer on a
   tribunal any power to vary an amount assessed by way of penalty except in so far as it is
   necessary to reduce it to the amount which is appropriate under Sch 5 paras 18–24 (see PARA
   987 et seq): s 56(6). Without prejudice to Sch 5 para 28 (see PARA 999), nothing in s 55 is taken
   to confer on a tribunal any power to vary an amount assessed by way of interest except in so far
   as it is necessary to reduce it to the amount which is appropriate under Sch 5 para 26 or Sch 5
   para 27 (see PARAS 997, 998): s 56(7).
      On an appeal under s 55 against an assessment to a penalty for evasion under Sch 5 para 18
   (see PARA 987), the burden of proof as to the matters specified in Sch 5 para 18(1)(a), (b) lies
   upon the Commissioners: s 55(4).
3 As to the meaning of 'appeal tribunal' see PARA 1003 note 1.
4 Finance Act 1996 s 55(3A) (s 55(3A), (3B) added by SI 2009/56). The decision of the tribunal as
   to the issue of hardship is final, notwithstanding the provisions of the Tribunals, Courts and
   Enforcement Act 2007 s 11 and s 13 (see ADMINISTRATIVE LAW) (right of appeal to the Upper
   Tribunal and to the Court of Appeal etc): Finance Act 1996 s 55(3B) (as so added).
5 Ie under the Finance Act 1996 s 54: see PARA 1003.
6 Finance Act 1996 s 56(2)(a) (s 56(2) amended by SI 2009/56).
7 Finance Act 1996 s 56(2)(b) (as amended: see note 6).
8 Finance Act 1996 s 56(2) (as amended: see note 6).
9 Ie under the Finance Act 1996 s 55: see the text and notes 2, 3.
10 Ie in pursuance of the Finance Act 1996 s 55(3): see the text and note 2.
11 Finance Act 1996 s 56(3) (amended by SI 2009/56). The applicable rate is the rate applicable
   under the Finance Act 1996 s 197: see PARA 1001.
12 As to credit see PARA 938 et seq.
13 Finance Act 1996 s 56(4) (amended by SI 2009/56). As to the applicable rate see note 12.
14 Finance Act 1996 s 56(5) (amended by SI 2009/56). As to the applicable rate see note 11. The
   Value Added Tax Act 1994 ss 85, 85B (settling of appeals by agreement and payment of tax
   where there is a further appeal: see VALUE ADDED TAX vol 49(1) (2005 Reissue) PARAS 348, 369)
   have effect as if: (1) the references to s 83 included references to the Finance Act 1996 s 54
   (s 56(8)(a) (s 56(8) substituted by SI 2009/56)); and (2) the references to value added tax
   included references to landfill tax (Finance Act 1996 s 56(8)(b) (as so substituted)).
15 Finance Act 1996 s 56(5A) (added by SI 2009/56).

(2) REVIEWS

1006. Offer of and right to require review. Her Majesty's Revenue and
Customs ('HMRC') must offer a person (P) a review[1] of a decision that has been
notified to a person if an appeal[2] lies in respect of the decision[3]. The offer must
be made by notice given to P at the same time as the decision is notified to P[4].

Any person other than P who has the right of appeal[5] against a decision may
require HMRC to review that decision if that person has not appealed[6] to the
appeal tribunal[7]. A notification that such a person requires a review must be
made within 30 days of that person becoming aware of the decision[8].

1 As to the nature of a review see PARA 1010.
2 Ie under the Finance Act 1996 s 54: see PARA 1003.
3 Finance Act 1996 s 54A(1) (s 54A added by SI 2009/56). The Finance Act 1996 s 54A does not
   apply to the notification of the conclusions of a review (see PARA 1010): s 54A(3) (as so added).
4 Finance Act 1996 s 54A(2) (as added: see note 3).
5 Ie under the Finance Act 1996 s 54: see PARA 1003.
6 Ie under the Finance Act 1996 s 54G: see PARA 1004.
7 Finance Act 1996 s 54B(1) (s 54B added by SI 2009/56). As to the meaning of 'appeal tribunal'
   see PARA 1003 note 1.
8 Finance Act 1996 s 54B(2) (as added: see note 7).

1007. Review by Her Majesty's Revenue and Customs. Her Majesty's
Revenue and Customs ('HMRC') must review a decision[1] if they have offered a
review of the decision[2] and P[3] notifies them accepting the offer within 30 days

from the date of the document containing the notification of the offer[4]. P may not notify acceptance of the offer if P has already appealed[5] to the appeal tribunal[6].

HMRC must also review a decision if a person other than P notifies them[7] requiring a review[8].

HMRC are not required to review a decision if P or another person has appealed[9] to the appeal tribunal in respect of the decision[10].

1 As to the nature of a review see PARA 1010.
2 Ie under the Finance Act 1996 s 54A: see PARA 1006.
3 See PARA 1006.
4 Finance Act 1996 s 54C(1) (s 54C added by SI 2009/56).
5 Ie under the Finance Act 1996 s 54G: see PARA 1004.
6 Finance Act 1996 s 54C(2) (as added: see note 4). As to the meaning of 'appeal tribunal' see PARA 1003 note 1.
7 Ie under the Finance Act 1996 s 54B: see PARA 1006.
8 Finance Act 1996 s 54C(3) (as added: see note 4).
9 Ie under the Finance Act 1996 s 54G: see PARA 1004.
10 Finance Act 1996 s 54C(4) (as added: see note 4).

1008. Extensions of time. If Her Majesty's Revenue and Customs ('HMRC') have offered P[1] a review of a decision[2], they may within the relevant period[3] notify P that the relevant period is extended[4]. If another person may require[5] HMRC to review a matter, they may within the relevant period notify that person that the relevant period is extended[6].

If notice is given the relevant period is extended to the end of 30 days from the date of the notice or any other date set out in the notice or a further notice[7].

1 See PARA 1006.
2 Ie under the Finance Act 1996 s 54A: see PARA 1006. As to the nature of a review see PARA 1010.
3 The 'relevant period' means (1) the period of 30 days referred to in the Finance Act 1996 s 54C(1) (see PARA 1007) or, in a case within s 54D(2) (see the text and note 6), in s 54B(2) (see PARA 1006); or (2) if notice under these provisions has previously been given, the period in head (1) as extended (or most recently extended) in accordance with s 54D(3) (see the text and note 7): s 54D(4) (s 54D added by SI 2009/56).
4 Finance Act 1996 s 54D(1) (as added: see note 3).
5 Ie under the Finance Act 1996 s 54B: see PARA 1006.
6 Finance Act 1996 s 54D(2) (as added: see note 3).
7 Finance Act 1996 s 54D(3) (as added: see note 3).

1009. Review out of time. If Her Majesty's Revenue and Customs ('HMRC') have offered a review of a decision[1] and P[2] does not accept the offer within the time allowed[3] or a person who requires a review[4] does not notify HMRC within the time allowed[5], HMRC must review the decision[6] if:

(1) after the time allowed, P or the other person notifies HMRC in writing requesting a review out of time;

(2) HMRC are satisfied that P or the other person had a reasonable excuse for not accepting the offer or requiring the review within the time allowed; and

(3) HMRC are satisfied that P or the other person made the request in head (1) without unreasonable delay after the excuse had ceased to apply[7].

HMRC are not required to review a decision if P or another person has appealed[8] to the appeal tribunal[9] in respect of the decision[10].

1 Ie under the Finance Act 1996 s 54A: see PARA 1006. As to the nature of a review see PARA 1010.

2   See PARA 1006.
3   Ie under the Finance Act 1996 s 54C(1) (as added: see PARA 1007) or s 54D(3) (as added: see PARA 1008).
4   Ie under the Finance Act 1996 s 54B: see PARA 1006.
5   Ie under the Finance Act 1996 s 54B (as added: see PARA 1006) or s 54D(3) (as added: see PARA 1008).
6   Ie under the Finance Act 1996 s 54C: see PARA 1007.
7   Finance Act 1996 s 54E(1)(2) (s 54E added by SI 2009/56).
8   Ie under the Finance Act 1996 s 54G: see PARA 1004.
9   As to the meaning of 'appeal tribunal' see PARA 4003 note 1.
10 Finance Act 1996 s 54E(3) (as added: see note 7).

1010.   Nature of a review. The following applies if Her Majesty's Revenue and Customs ('HMRC') are required to undertake a review[1].

The nature and extent of a review are to be such as appear appropriate to HMRC in the circumstances[2]. The review must take account of any representations made by P[3] or the other person[4] at a stage which gives HMRC a reasonable opportunity to consider them[5].

The review may conclude that the decision is to be upheld, varied or cancelled[6]. HMRC must give P or the other person notice of the conclusions of the review and their reasoning within a period of 45 days beginning with the relevant date[7] or such other period as HMRC and P or the other person may agree[8]. Where HMRC are required to undertake a review but do not give notice of the conclusions within the specified time period, the conclusion of the review is deemed to be that the decision is upheld[9]. HMRC must notify the appellant of the deemed conclusion[10].

1   Finance Act 1996 s 54F(1) (s 54F added by SI 2009/56). As to the requirement for HMRC to undertake a review see the Finance Act 1996 ss 54C, 54E; and PARAS 1007, 1009.
2   Finance Act 1996 s 54F(2) (as added: see note 1). For this purpose, HMRC must, in particular, have regard to steps taken before the beginning of the review by HMRC in reaching the decision and by any person in seeking to resolve disagreement about the decision: s 54F(3) (as so added).
3   See PARA 1006.
4   See PARAS 1006, 1008.
5   Finance Act 1996 s 54F(4) (as added: see note 1).
6   Finance Act 1996 s 54F(5) (as added: see note 1).
7   The 'relevant date' means (1) in a case falling within the Finance Act 1996 s 54A (see PARA 1006), the date HMRC received P's notification accepting the offer of a review; (2) in a case falling within s 54B (see PARA 1006), the date HMRC received notification from another person requiring a review; or (3) in a case falling within s 54E (see PARA 1009), the date on which HMRC decided to undertake the review: s 54F(7) (as added: see note 1).
8   Finance Act 1996 s 54F(6) (as added: see note 1).
9   Finance Act 1996 s 54F(8) (as added: see note 1).
10 Finance Act 1996 s 54F(9) (as added: see note 1).

INDEX

International Relations Law

References are to paragraph numbers; superior figures refer to notes

References are to paragraph numbers; superior figures refer to notes

GOVERNMENTS—*continued*
  recognition of—*continued*
    United Kingdom domestic law, in, 39
    where required, 44
  succession, effect on treaty rights and
    obligations, 70

HEAD OF STATE
  privileges and immunities, 263

HIGH SEAS
  meaning, 147
  arrest of ship on, 162
  broadcasting from, 196
  contiguous zones—
    control over, 153
    removal of objects on seabed, 153
  continental shelf. *See* CONTINENTAL
    SHELF
  deep sea bed—
    development, legal regime for, 173
    exploration, regime for, 173
    Food and Environment Protection
      Act, disapplied provisions, 189
    mining—
      breach of statutory duty, civil
        liability for, 188
      exploration and exploitation
        licences—
        grant of, 176
        reciprocating countries, granted
          by, 177
        variation and revocation, 180
      foreign discriminatory action, 181
      fund, 183
      information, disclosure of, 186
      inspectors, 184
      legislation and agreements, 174
      levy, 182
      licensed operations, prevention of
        interference with, 178
      marine environment, protection of,
        179
      offences, 187
      regulations and orders, 185
      unlicensed, prohibition, 175
    sovereign rights, no claim of, 173
    submarine cables and pipelines on,
      169
  drug trafficking, suppression of, 195
  exclusive economic zones—
    establishment of, 154
    rights and duties as to, 154
    states with opposite or adjacent
      coasts, delimitation between, 154
  exclusive fishery zones, establishment
    of, 154
  fishing, right of, 190

HIGH SEAS—*continued*
  freedom of, 147
  hot pursuit—
    commencement, 161
    constructive presence, and, 162
    exercise of, 161
    lawful, conditions for, 161
  living resources, conservation and
    management of—
    European Community, competence
      of, 192
    fishing, right of, 190
    international fisheries agreements,
      192
    marine environment, protection and
      preservation of, 193
    marine scientific research, 194
    states, duties of, 191
    whaling, 192
  marine scientific research, 194
  navigation, freedom of, 148
  obligations of states, 152
  piracy. *See* PIRACY
  ships—
    foreign, jurisdiction over, 148
    penal jurisdiction over, 150
    status of, 149
    warships, jurisdiction over, 151

HUMAN RIGHTS
  treaties, succession to right and
    obligations, 61

INTERNAL WATERS
  meaning, 121
  bay as part of, 131
  hot pursuit, commencement of, 161
  jurisdiction, 122
  right to enter, 121

INTERNATIONAL ATOMIC ENERGY
  AUTHORITY
  constitution, 533n[19]
  status of, 533

INTERNATIONAL CENTRE FOR
  SETTLEMENT OF INVESTMENT
  DISPUTES (ICSID)
  Convention, 481
  establishment of, 496
  jurisdiction, 496
  role of, 488
  settlement of investment disputes—
    common forms of arbitration, 489
    ICSID Convention, under, 488, 496

INTERNATIONAL COURT OF JUSTICE
  access to, 502
  admissibility of claims, 507
  advisory opinions, 512
  applicable law, 509

INTERNATIONAL CRIMINAL
TRIBUNAL FOR
RWANDA—*continued*
Statute, 436n[11]
INTERNATIONAL CRIMINAL
TRIBUNAL FOR THE FORMER
YUGOSLAVIA
co-operation with, 436
Statute, 436n[11]
INTERNATIONAL DEVELOPMENT
BANKS
agreements establishing, 459
INTERNATIONAL DISPUTE
settlement. *See* SETTLEMENT OF
INTERNATIONAL DISPUTES
INTERNATIONAL LAW
Act of State—
foreign states, 23
justiciability—
foreign state, of, 25
United Kingdom government, of,
24
use of term, 22
acts of foreign states, justiciability of,
25
acts of UK government, justiciability
of, 24
administrative powers—
legislation implementing international
obligations, exercise under, 20
legitimate expectations, reliance on,
21
constitutional context, 13
customary—
English law, relationship with, 16
remedy on basis of, 16
source of law, as, 4
source of public international law,
as, 4
domestic law, relationship with, 13
English courts, proof in, 14
facts of State, 15
hierarchy in—
international community, obligations
owed to, 11
peremptory norms, 11
UN Charter, primacy of, 10
national legal systems, distinct from, 12
obligations erga omnes, 11
peremptory norms, 11
persons in violation of, seizure of, 233
recognition of states and governments
in, 41
scope of, 1
sources of—
customary law, 4

INTERNATIONAL LAW—*continued*
sources of—*continued*
general principles of law, 5
International Court of Justice, applied
by, 2
international organisations, decisions
of, 9
judicial decisions, 6
Statute of International Court of
Justice, listed in—
customary law, 4
general principles of law, 5
judicial decisions, 6
treaties, 3
writings, 7
treaties, 3
unilateral declarations, 8
writings, 7
subjects of—
individuals, 37
international organisations, 36
international persons, 38
states. *See* STATE
subsidiary means for determination of,
13
INTERNATIONAL LAW COMMISSION
diplomatic protection, work on, 328
international responsibility, work on,
328
status of, 328n[1]
INTERNATIONAL LEGAL
PERSONALITY
individuals, of, 37
international organisations, of, 36
international persons, of, 38
notion of, 32
states. *See* STATE
INTERNATIONAL ORGANISATION
body corporate, as—
European Union Treaty, bodies
established under, 316
legal capacities, 312
status of, 311
decisions of as sources of international
law, 9
economic, 459
European, 518
financial, 459
headquarters agreements, 308
intergovernmental, 517
international, 518
international responsibility. *See*
INTERNATIONAL RESPONSIBILITY
judicial, 314
law of, 517

References are to paragraph numbers; superior figures refer to notes

MINING—*continued*
  deep sea—*continued*
    exploration and exploitation
      licences—
      grant of, 176
      reciprocating countries, granted
        by, 177
      variation and revocation, 180
      foreign discriminatory action, 181
      fund, 183
      information, disclosure of, 186
      inspectors, 184
      legislation and agreements, 174
      levy, 182
      licensed operations, prevention of
        interference with, 178
      marine environment, protection of,
        179
      offences, 187
      regulations and orders, 185
      unlicensed, prohibition, 175
MISTAKE
  treaty, invalidity of, 102
NATIONALITY
  aircraft, of, 397
  citizenship, and, 393
  corporations, of, 394
  diplomatic protection, requirements for.
    See DIPLOMATIC PROTECTION
  individuals, of, 392
  law governing, 392
  multiple, 393
  ships, of—
    change of flag, 396
    rules for, 395
    two or more flags, sailing under, 396
  state succession, effect of, 69
  treaty provisions, 392
OUTER SPACE
  astronauts, assistance to, 216
  claims against government, indemnity
    for, 215
  demilitarisation, 209
  international law, in, 207
  licensing of activities in, 212
  non-governmental entities, activities of,
    210
  offences, 213
  Outer Space Treaty, 208
  space objects—
    jurisdiction over, 217
    register of, 214
  state responsibility for activities in, 210
  treaties, 207
  United Kingdom, enforcement of
    international obligations of, 211

OUTER SPACE—*continued*
  unlicensed activities, 213
PARLIAMENT
  international relations, conduct of, 27
  treaty-making by, 27
PARLIAMENTARY SOVEREIGNTY
  overriding principle of, 13
PERMANENT COURT OF
  ARBITRATION
  establishment of, 495
PIPELINES
  bed of high seas, on, 169
  continental shelf, on, 168
PIRACY
  meaning, 156
  acts of, 156
  English courts, jurisdiction of, 159
  international law, crime against, 422n[1]
  international law, in, 155
  pirate ships and aircraft, nationality of,
    158
  punishment, 160
  repression, rights and obligations of
    states, 157
  universal jurisdiction, 155
RESERVATIONS. *See* TREATY
SCIENTIFIC RESEARCH
  marine, 194
SECRETARY OF STATE
  meaning, 29
  international relations, conduct of, 29
SETTLEMENT OF INTERNATIONAL
  DISPUTES
  arbitration—
    meaning, 492
    ad hoc, 493
    administered, 494
    institutional, 494
    model rules, 493
    optional rules, 493
    Permanent Court, 495
    UN Convention on the Law of the
      Sea, under, 497
  conciliation, 491
  European Court of Human Rights, 513
  good offices, 491
  inquiry, by, 491
  International Court of Justice. *See*
    INTERNATIONAL COURT OF JUSTICE
  International Tribunal for the Law of
    the Sea, 514
  investment disputes—
    common forms of arbitration, 489
    ICSID Convention, arbitration
      under, 488
  mediation, 491

References are to paragraph numbers; superior figures refer to notes

TERRITORIAL SEA—*continued*
  passage through—*continued*
    warships, 140
  rocks, 127
  UNCLOS, provisions of, 123
  warships, passage of, 140
TERRITORY
  meaning, 111
  acquisition of—
    accretion, by, 116
    cession, by, 117
    effective control, 119
    government, by, 113
    new states, by creation of, 120
    occupation, by, 115
    prescription, by, 118
  cession, treaties of, 28
  disposal, means of, 113
  effective control of, 119
  state, of, 222
  title to—
    disputes, 114
    nature and extent of, 111
    perfecting, 115
  United Kingdom, of, 112
TORTURE
  defence to, 433
  international crime, as, 433
TRADE LAWS
  extraterritorial application, 229
TRADING INTERESTS
  overseas measures affecting, 235
  protection of—
    multiple damages, recovery of awards
      for, 239
    overseas courts and authorities,
      documents and information
      required by, 236
    overseas judgments, restriction on
      enforcement of, 238
    requests for evidence in other
      jurisdictions, order giving effect
      to, 237
    scope of, 234
    statutory provisions, 234
TREATY
  meaning, 71
  acceptance, 79
  accession to, 80
  adoption and authentication of text, 75
  amendment, 100
  application in time, 93
  approval, 79
  breach of, 107
  capacity to conclude, 72
  cession, of, 28

TREATY—*continued*
  coercion, consent procured by, 103
  consent to be bound, expressing, 76
  corruption, effect of, 102
  Crown, made by, 27
  depositaries, 104
  domestic law, incorporation in, 18
  English law, effect in, 13
  entering into—
    acceptance, 79
    accession to, 80
    adoption and authentication of text,
      75
    approval, 79
    capacity to conclude, 72
    consent to be bound, expressing, 76
    exchange of instruments, 78
    full powers—
      meaning, 73n^2
      absence of requirement, 74
      representation of state, for, 73
    object and purpose, obligation not to
      defeat prior to entry into
      force, 82
    ratification, 79
    representation of state for purposes
      of, 73
    reservations—
      meaning, 83
      formulation of, 84
    signature, 77
    traditional methods, variations on, 81
  entry into force, 89
  error in, 102
  exchange of instruments, 78
  fraud, effect of, 102
  interpretation—
    courts, approach of, 18n^8
    general rule, 95
    good faith, in, 95
    matters taken into account, 96
    ordinary meaning of words, 95
    preparatory work, recourse to, 97
    supplementary means, 97
    two or more languages, text in, 98
  invalidity—
    coercion, consent procured by, 103
    corruption, due to, 102
    error, in case of, 102
    fraud, due to, 102
    lack of competence to conclude, for,
      101
    peremptory norm, conflict with, 103
    procedure, 109
    threat or use of force, consent
      procured by, 103

References are to paragraph numbers; superior figures refer to notes

Judicial Review

References are to paragraph numbers; superior figures refer to notes

Juries

References are to paragraph numbers; superior figures refer to notes

Landfill Tax

References are to paragraph numbers; superior figures refer to notes

References are to paragraph numbers; superior figures refer to notes

Words and Phrases

Words in parentheses indicate the context in which the word or phrase is used